LEARNING LEGAL RESEARCH

A How-To Manual

CHARLES P. NEMETH, JD., PH. D., LL. M.

Professor/Director of Graduate Legal Studies CRJ
California University of Pennsylvania
Member of New York, Pennsylvania, and North Carolina Bar.

HOPE I. HAYWOOD, M.B.A.

Graduate Legal Studies/Criminal Justice California University of Pennsylvania

Upper Saddle River, New Jersey

Library of Congress Cataloging-in-Publication Data

Nemeth, Charles P., 1951-
Learning legal research : a how-to manual / Charles P. Nemeth, Hope Haywood.—1st ed.
p. cm.
Includes bibliographical references and index.
ISBN 0-13-045034-0
1. Legal research—United States. I. Haywood, Hope. II. Title.

KF240.N458 2005
340'.072'073—dc22

2004014510

Director of Production and Manufacturing: Bruce Johnson
Executive Editor: Elizabeth Sugg
Consulting Editor: Athena Groups, Inc.
Editorial Assistant: Cyrenne Bolt de Freitas
Marketing Manager: Leigh Ann Sims
Managing Editor—Production: Mary Carnis
Manufacturing Buyer: Ilene Sanford
Production Liaison: Denise Brown
Production Editor: Melissa Scott/Carlisle Publishers Services
Composition: Carlisle Communications, Ltd.
Director, Image Resource Center: Melinda Reo
Manager, Rights and Permissions: Zina Arabia
Manager, Visual Research: Beth Brenzel
Manager, Cover Visual Research and Permissions: Karen Sanatar
Image Permission Coordinator: Cynthia Vincenti
Design Director: Cheryl Asherman
Senior Design Coordinator: Christopher Weigand
Cover Image: Getty Image
Cover Design: Kevin Kall
Cover Printer: Coral Graphics
Printer/Binder: Courier Westford

Pearson Education LTD.
Pearson Education Singapore, Pte. Ltd
Pearson Education, Canada, Ltd
Pearson Education–Japan
Pearson Education Australia PTY, Limited
Pearson Education North Asia Ltd
Pearson Educación de Mexico, S.A. de C.V.
Pearson Education Malaysia, Pte. Ltd

10 9 8 7 6 5 4 3 2
ISBN 0-13-045034-0

CONTENTS

5

FINAL CONSIDERATIONS 381

To Michael Augustine; my youngest of seven children: No greater gift could he be—always optimistic and filled with charity

To St. Thomas Aquinas; Certitude of knowledge varies in various natures, according to the various conditions of each nature. Because man forms a sure judgment about a truth by the discursive process of his reason: and so human knowledge is acquired by means of demonstrative reasoning. On the other hand, in God, there is a sure judgment of truth, without any discursive process, by simple intuition.

Summa Theorlogica II-II at Question 9.

PREFACE

Learning Legal Research is a textbook for those in need of a journey into the world of legal research. It is a journey that will be new for some, and a refresher for others. At its heart, the text introduces the reader to the fundamentals of legal research; exposes the reader to the primary and secondary materials and affords a convenient way of entrance and excursion through the halls of a law library without ever setting foot in the building. Of course, students are free to roam the environs of any law library, but in the absence of that forum, this textbook brings the law library to the reader. When done, the skill level of the reader will be sufficient to tackle any significant task of legal research. Hence, this journey opens doors to not only a refined and esoteric skill, but a world of concepts and subject matter that complicates life and befuddles the average person. When done, the confidence to conduct research in a legal setting will be internally obvious, and a new world of opportunity will emerge for those who become captivated by the subject matter.

Chapter 1 lays out the elementary concepts that define our legal system by examining the structure and forms of law in the American experience, from statutory to common law designations. Additionally, the chapter surveys the structural makeup of judicial process and legal advocacy by scrutinizing the makeup of court systems, reviewing the diverse powers in a democracy, and providing a general context for conducting legal research.

Chapter 2 poses the methodology of legal research and analysis and delivers specific examples of how legal research is conducted. A systematic approach to legal research is essential to success and the methods assessed, namely, TAPP, the West Key System, the Cartwheel tactic are analyzed in depth. More specifically, the chapter lays out special techniques and strategies for conducting legal research including topical and key word approaches, the role and value of precedential authority, jurisdictional differences, and the principles of legal authority and other tactics.

Chapter 3 delivers an overview of the Citation Method, unique to legal research. Citation, whether in text or brief, scholarly material or legal memoranda, is the preferential system for all legal research. Citation formats for cases, statutory, legislative, administrative, and journals and other scholarly materials are fully provided.

Chapter 4 covers the role and use of an index and indices in legal research. For most researchers, the use of an index can only be described as indispensable. Types and format of indices will also be covered and includes subject matter, words and phrases, descriptive, plaintiff/defendant and other means to finds legal authority.

Chapter 5 portrays the critical role that digests play in the legal research process. Digests are fundamentally a shortcut to case law. How digest systems operate, what types of digests exist and are utilized, and how to update and cross-check digest results are included in the chapter.

Chapter 6 introduces the diverse and eclectic skills associated with Computer-Assisted Legal Research (CALR). The influence of technology has seriously and most productively impacted the many processes of legal research. It is now common place for computer-assisted research to take a front position in the conduct of legal research. Trips to law libraries have been replaced by the access and ease of CALR. The chapter thoroughly reviews search engines, specific legal databases, Lexis/Nexis and the Westlaw systems, as well as the most common search engines on the Web.

Chapter 7 commences the examination of secondary legal source materials with a review of law books, texts, services and periodicals. Special emphasis is given to periodical literature since its content often serves as the backbone for legal appeals. Law reviews and other peer assessed materials receive significant scrutiny. How to utilize the various indices associated with scholarly materials will be examined.

Chapter 8 evaluates other sources of secondary legal authority—legal encyclopedias and dictionaries. Both sources are commonly employed by researchers, often as a starting point in the assessment of a legal question. The two primary encyclopedic systems, namely *Corpus Juris Secundum* and *American Jurisprudence* anchor the content of the chapter.

Chapter 9 delivers an overview of the ALR Series—*The American Law Reports.* ALR reports are a unique style of legal analysis with a topical starting point that many lawyers find useful and very common. ALRs examine typical legal problems in question form and then deliver a learned and highly authoritative examination of the problem posed. ALRs are excellent issue framers and afford numerous citations for the advanced researcher.

Chapter 10 zeroes in on material that the entire legal system comes to depend upon in the assessment and analyses of cases—CASE Law. Starting with a look at how cases are published, in the Reporter system, the chapter then treats case law jurisdictionally and geographically, from state to federal, from subject matter to appeals, from special courts to those of general jurisdiction. Analyzing cases, finding suitable and contrary precedent, and becoming adept at updating case law and history are offered up to the reader.

Chapter 11 reviews the nature and essence of Statutes and Legislative Resources. The chapter hones in on the many techniques for reviewing and updating statutory authority, addresses the diverse types of statutory materials and gives helpful suggestions on how to find, evaluate, and verify the current dependability of statute and other codification. The chapter provides further suggestions on how to scrutinize legislative histories and to assess the political steps from bill to enactment.

Chapter 12 scans the diverse approaches to researching administrative law. Commencing with an overview of the administrative process, the chapter evaluates the usual means to conduct administrative research including a close look at the Code of Federal Regulations, the nature of notice and rulemaking and the challenge to the legitimacy of administrative rule and regulation.

Chapter 13 reviews the unique and unquestionably effective means of update—the Shepard's System. Steps and strategies to Shepardizing and keen suggestions on how to update specialized legal materials are all provided. A bevy of exercises assures competency in this critical step in the legal research process.

Chapter 14 covers the extraordinary nature of government materials, publications, and compilations. Legal research has become increasingly dependent on the use of government source materials from many quarters including the Department of Justice and its branches of operations. The role and use of Government Printing Offices and Government Libraries and Depositories, THOMAS, and the crucial mission of the National Criminal Justice Reference Service that compiles and readily makes available justice materials to the professional community is equally important. The skills and attributes of the solid legal researcher soon come to depend on these useful materials.

Chapter 15 delivers insight on writing and legal method. Legal research often culminates in the authorship and the draft of a legal document. The more common version of legal writings will include investigative formats, reports, legal memoranda, evidentiary writings, motions, pleadings and complaints, legal briefs and appellate documentation. The chapter will also review scholarly materials that are crucial to the production of scholarly works such as book reviews, essays, term papers, and periodical literature.

Visit www.prenhall.com/legal_studies for online access to course support or for information about additional material available from Pearson Prentice Hall.

- **Instructor's Manual Web Site**—Classroom support free to instructors.
- **Versus Law® Online Legal Research Access**—One-semester subscription access code cards (0-13-118514-4) are free packaged with any Pearson Legal Series title. Student access allows them to work from anywhere there is an Internet connection.
- **LexiBrief™ and the Lexiverse Dictionary**—Both on one CD-ROM (0-13-112310-6) that can be packaged for free with any Pearson Legal Series textbook, these tools help students develop skills for a successful career in any legal industry.
- **Paralegal Videos**—Select at least one free video for your classroom from the range on videos offered through the Kapio'lani Community College program and Pearson Prentice Hall. Contact your Pearson Prentice Hall representative or visit www.prenhall.com/legal_studies for details.

ACKNOWLEDGMENT

The editors and authors wish to thank these valuable experts for their input to this edition: Enika Schulze, Athena Group; William Covington, Esq., Edmonds Community College; Adam Epstein, Esq., Central Michigan University; Sait R. Tarhan, Esq., Cincinnati State and Technical College.

This text would never have come to fruition without the help and assistance of so many. My co-author, Hope Haywood, possesses the type of tenacity and determination to move through the minutia and to conquer the many administrative requirements that my personality often is repelled by. I am also thankful to Prentice Hall for resurrecting my very early work, whose intent has always been to bring the law library to the masses. Thanks to Elizabeth Sugg, Judy Casillo, and especially Enika Schulze. While she is still young, we surely go back a long, long way.

Student assistants have also been undeniably part of this project and provided immeasurable assistance. Gratitude is extended to Nikole Bashforth and Sarah Tobin whose performance is most appreciated.

Finally, as is my custom, all praise and glory are extended to my family, my partner for life, Jean Marie, and the seven children we have been so fortunate to rear together, Eleanor, Stephen, Anne Marie, John, Joseph, Mary Clare and Michael Augustine.

Charles P. Nemeth

First and foremost, my thanks are extended to my co-author Charles P. Nemeth. Ever the mentor, colleague and friend, he devises and creates projects where my talents can flourish and compliment his genius. Thanks are also extended to the exemplary staff of Prentice Hall, specifically Elizabeth Sugg, Judy Casillo, and Enika Schulze. Without them, the renewal of this "old" text couldn't have been possible.

None of my accomplishments in this short life could have been possible without the support and encouragement of my parents, Val & Dale Coddington. They gave me a foundation to build on. Thank you.

Lastly, my undying love and heartfelt gratitude are extended to my husband, Rick, and our three beautiful children, Derek, Andrew and Rachel. They graciously endured many long days and nights to bring this project to life, and are the reason behind any venture of worth.

Hope I. Haywood

LEGAL RESEARCH—PRELIMINARY CONSIDERATIONS

SECTION I

CHAPTER

1

INTRODUCTION TO LEGAL RESEARCH

Before undertaking any in-depth discussion regarding legal research, some preliminary background study is in order. Legal research concerns the laws of the United States and the processes and actions that those laws regulate. Because of this, it is necessary to review the branches of government, what types of law they make, and the court structure in state and federal governments. If a researcher does not understand the different types of law, who promulgates them, and the structure of the courts in which litigation occurs, research will not be as meaningful, effective, or efficient.

I. THE STRUCTURE AND FORM OF LAW IN THE AMERICAN EXPERIENCE

In civics class, one learns from an early age the dual nature of our legal system: both federal and state in design. A national system of government coexists with independent state governments. Each system, whether national or state, has three branches: the **executive** (the president/governor and the cabinet), the **legislative** (elected by the people to represent the citizenry in matters of state), and the **judiciary** (elected or appointed officials who rule on cases before the bar). The powers and activities of the federal government are regulated by the **United States Constitution**, and the state governments are regulated by the state constitutions. Constitutions are generally the supreme rule of government, though the United States Constitution ultimately is the rule of last resort in most significant national legal matters.

Some political theorists have called the **administrative agency** and its corresponding rules the fourth branch of government. The administrative agency can be either **executive**, located in the executive branch of the government, or **independent**, standing completely outside the three-tiered government structure. At the federal level, these agencies are created by statute, which is why they are sometimes called *statutory agencies.* These agencies are responsible for creating rules and regulations pertaining specifically to that department's purpose. The Department of Education, for example, makes regulations regarding educational matters that are applicable throughout the country. The Department of Defense deals with matters of military and national security.

Administrative regulations are enforced through administrative hearings, though these decisions and the regulations of each agency are subject to review by appellate courts. High-ranking officers of the executive agencies are appointed by the president, with congressional approval, and can be removed from office at any time. Examples of executive agencies are the Department of Labor, the Department of Justice, and the Department of Education. The appointment of directors of independent agencies follows a similar pattern: The main difference is that the officials are appointed for a fixed term and can be removed from office only under certain conditions, with congressional approval. This is done to insulate the agencies from shifting political pressure. Examples of some independent agencies are the Federal Emergency Management Agency (FEMA), the Securities and Exchange Commission (SEC), and the Nuclear Regulatory Commission (NRC). See Figure 1.1 for a graphic representation of the structure of the federal government and its branches and agencies.

The organization of administrative agencies is similar at the state level. The first difference is that some officials are elected rather than appointed. For example, in Pennsylvania the state treasurer is an elected position, whereas at the federal level it is appointed. The second difference is that some state-level agencies are created

FIGURE 1.1

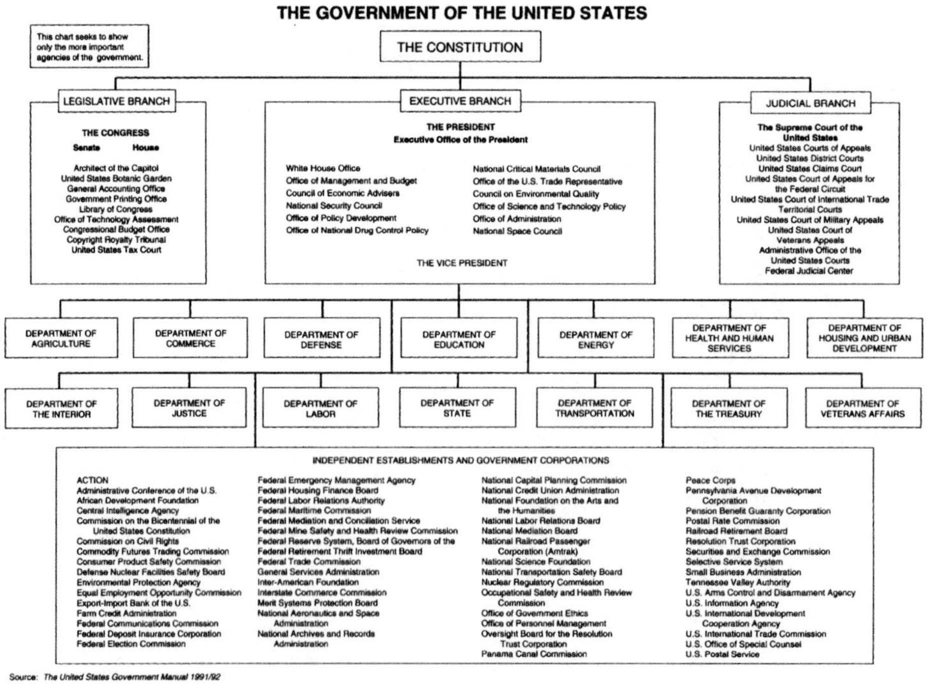

Source: *The United States Government Manual 1991/92*

by the state constitution, instead of being statutorily created as are federal agencies. Every other aspect of state regulatory procedure is similar to the federal government structure and process.

For the researcher, the statement that "the legislature makes laws, the judiciary interprets the law, and the executive enforces the law" is only partially helpful and requires further refinement. The executive branch lacks the authority and power to enact or promulgate statutes, though it is quite influential in the political processes related to lawmaking. Administrative agencies, however, regardless of executive control, have extraordinary powers to create rules and regulations that have the force of law. For those undertaking legal research, investigation of administrative law and agencies often constitutes the bulk of the task, as so much of governmental function has been delegated to these agencies by legislative decisionmaking. Neither Congress nor the president has the time or resources to deal with the myriad of governmental affairs that these agencies conduct and oversee. Hence, the legal researcher will often start and end the analysis with this fourth branch of government.

Why is an understanding of governmental structure important? In the final analysis, legal research can be effective only if the researcher understands the territory. Each branch of government has unique and compelling subject matter. Each branch makes a different type of law. The legislature creates statutory and codified law; agencies create administrative law; the judiciary issues case opinions and interpretations of both common and statutory law; and the executive branch issues decrees by orders, executive fiat, and other specialized authority.

A. Statutory Law

Statutory law comes into being by the action of state and federal legislatures that pass bills in a House, Senate, or other chamber. Once legislated, the bill becomes law only after being signed by a higher authority, usually the president or governor. Statutes are organized either chronologically or topically. **Session laws** are chronological compendiums of statutes. At the federal level, they appear in a series called Statutes at Large. Session laws are reported, from the earliest to the latest, by the date of enactment.

Codes organize statutes by subject matter (that is, topically). When laws are organized this way, they are said to be codified. The United States Code, United States Code Service, and United States Code Annotated are all codifications of federal statutes. Dates are not used when organizing codified laws; rather, they are grouped by subject. All laws that deal with the same topic will be grouped together under the same title, with each major subject having a different title number. For example, at the federal level, bankruptcy statutes appear in Title 13 of the United States Code and criminal laws are organized in Title 18. Statutes are also generally codified this way at the state level, though there are differences in the manner of organization. Local governments also pass statutes called **ordinances**, which regulate local concerns such as zoning, local speed limits, and building permits. These are also usually organized topically.

B. Administrative Law

Administrative rules and regulations are created by administrative agencies that are empowered by congressional or executive delegation. The creation of these rules differs from the creation of statutes. First, an agency can create a rule only if it publishes the rule and allows a period of public comment. Second, hearings are held to afford a public airing of the proposed rule and allow for certain types of challenges and comments. Once approved, the rule is published in its final form.

All federal administrative rules and regulations are organized chronologically and topically, regardless of which agency created them. All rules are published chronologically in the *Federal Register* and topically in the Code of Federal Regulations. It can be very easy to confuse administrative rules with statutes because of the similar citation formats. Care must be taken to verify the correctness of a statute or rule identification.

Many states do not publish administrative rules in bound volumes for the general public, so it is necessary to contact the appropriate agency to obtain this information. Given the availability of the World Wide Web today, this is much easier than it used to be. A visit to an agency's Web site will provide a wealth of information, though the organization of the rules in agency databases may be haphazard and confusing.

C. Common Law

The judiciary issues opinions on cases brought to trial, either criminal or civil in nature. These court decisions, called **common** or **case law**, are published chronologically in **case reporters**. Small summaries of cases also appear topically in **case digests**, finding tools that will be discussed later. A multitude of case reporters exist for both the federal and state systems, with both official and commercially published volumes covering each level of the systems. These reporters are covered in depth in the section on court structure and in Chapter 10 on case law.

D. Constitutions

Constitutions, either at the state or federal level, are probably the most important legal documents governing the jurisdiction. Governmental powers, organization, and functions are comprehensively outlined in a constitution. Like statutes, constitutions regulate and set forth uniform standards for government and citizens, but the standards are much more fundamental and universal, and tend to be bedrock principles that do not change dramatically over time. Whereas statutes deal with specific problems and occurrences in particular legal subject matter (such as the law of crimes, tax, or immigration), constitutional frameworks deal with more abstract concepts like freedom, rights, and guarantees for the citizenry. Constitutions are foundational documents that serve as the basis of public redress in a civilized society. The federal Constitution reigns supreme in areas where it explicitly grants the citizen rights. The United States Constitution applies to both state and federal governments; a state constitution applies only to the enacting state.

Figure 1.2 summarizes the branches of government and the types of law they make.

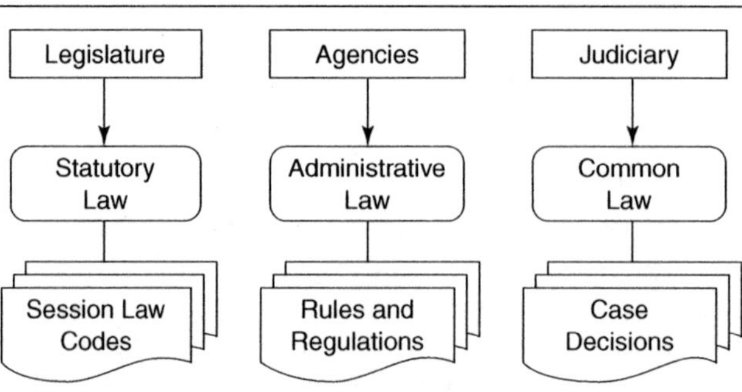

FIGURE 1.2 Branches of government and the types of law they create.

II. STATE AND FEDERAL COURT STRUCTURE

Most court systems have a three-tiered structure that includes a trial court, an appellate court, and a court of last resort, usually called a supreme court (Figure 1.3). Trial courts determine the facts of a case and apply the laws of the jurisdiction to those facts to reach a decision. Appellate courts review the decisions of the courts below them to ensure that the law was correctly applied. Normally they do not reevaluate the facts in a case except under extreme circumstances.

Some jurisdictions use a four-tiered structure and include a second court of appeals, called an *intermediate appellate court,* which reviews the decisions of the appellate court before they reach the supreme court. The purpose of the intermediate appellate court is to take some of the load off the jurisdiction's highest court: The number of appeals has escalated rapidly since the 1970s, making the workload of trial courts and upper-division appellate courts critically burdensome and slowing the judicial process significantly.

At the federal level, the trial courts are called *United States District Courts.* Each state has at least one district court within its borders; the actual number of courts is determined by population and the geographical size of the state. Pennsylvania, as an illustration, has three district courts: the United States District Court for the Western District of Pennsylvania, the United States District Court for the Middle District of Pennsylvania, and the United States District Court for the Eastern District of Pennsylvania. Alaska has only one, the United States District Court for the District of Alaska.

Appellate courts in the federal system are called **United States Courts of Appeal** or **circuit courts**. The circuit courts review the decisions of the district courts as to correct application of the law. There are 11 numbered circuits, a federal circuit, and a Circuit for the District of Columbia. The numbered circuits and the D.C. Circuit hear appeals from the district courts in their respective territories. The Federal Circuit Court of Appeal reviews cases from the United States Court of Customs and Patent Appeals, the United States Court of Federal Claims, the United States Court of International Trade, the Merit Services Protection Board, the Board of Contract Appeals, and certain administrative decisions of the Secretaries of Agriculture and Commerce.

After a request for review, or an *appeal,* is filed and all procedural requirements are met, the request may be either approved or rejected by the circuit court. The courts are not bound to review every case requested, only those that the circuit court believes have merit. Decisions made within the circuit court's jurisdiction are binding on the lower courts within that circuit only. For instance, a decision reached by the 1st Circuit will be binding on the states of Maine, New Hampshire, Massachusetts, Rhode Island, and Puerto Rico, but will not be applicable to Florida, which is in the 11th Circuit. Figure 1.4 maps the United States Courts of Appeals.

The court of last resort in the federal system is the United States Supreme Court, which hears appeals from decisions of the United States Courts of Appeal,

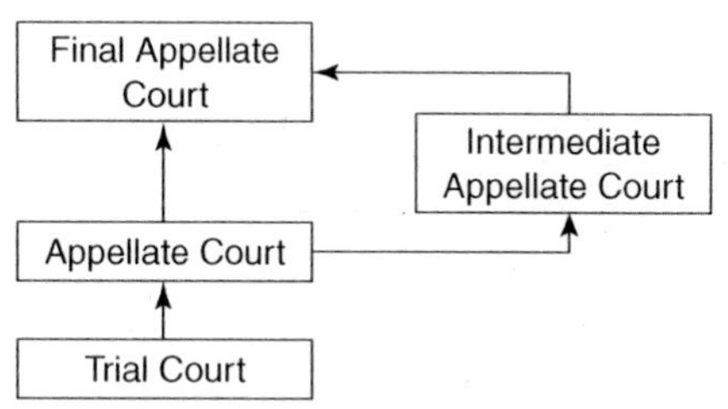

FIGURE 1.3
Court structure.

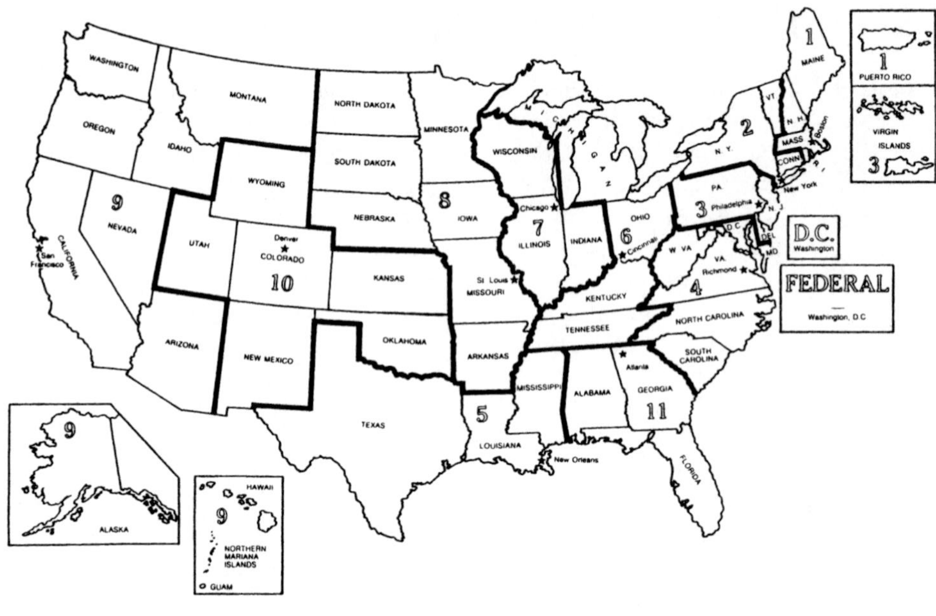

FIGURE 1.4 The 13 federal judicial circuits.

See 28 U.S.C.A. § 41

emergency cases, and cases of original jurisdiction. There are two paths to Supreme Court jurisdiction. The first is by a **writ of certiorari**, which is a discretionary grant to hear a case from a lower court. Whether the Court exercises this type of jurisdiction depends on various factors, including timeliness, ripeness, urgency, and conflict and contradiction in the lower federal courts. On very rare occasions the Supreme Court will accept a case directly from a district court. The second way to procure Supreme Court review is through an appeal of right, known as **original jurisdiction**. Examples of this mandatory form of review include disputes between two states or a state and the federal government, and cases involving international treaties or foreign dignitaries or citizens.

State court systems are organized in much the same way as the federal system, each having trial, appellate (sometimes called superior), specialty, and supreme courts. Two major differences appear across the 50 states, the first being the existence of intermediate appellate courts in many state systems. The second is the abundance of limited- or specialty-jurisdiction courts (e.g., small claims and municipal courts) that enforce local ordinances and have jurisdiction in only one district or township. Specialty courts, such as domestic or family courts, drug courts, and probate courts, serve a much larger geographic jurisdiction but over a narrow content. Figure 1.5 shows a flowchart outlining the progress of a case through the state and federal systems.

III. PRELIMINARY INSIGHTS INTO THE PROCESS OF LEGAL RESEARCH

Legal research, like any other form of research, requires diligence, organization, and persistence, but above all it requires a method. The paths taken to secure results are varied and often reflect the individual style of the researcher. Knowledge of the diverse methods and tools of legal research cannot be overemphasized.

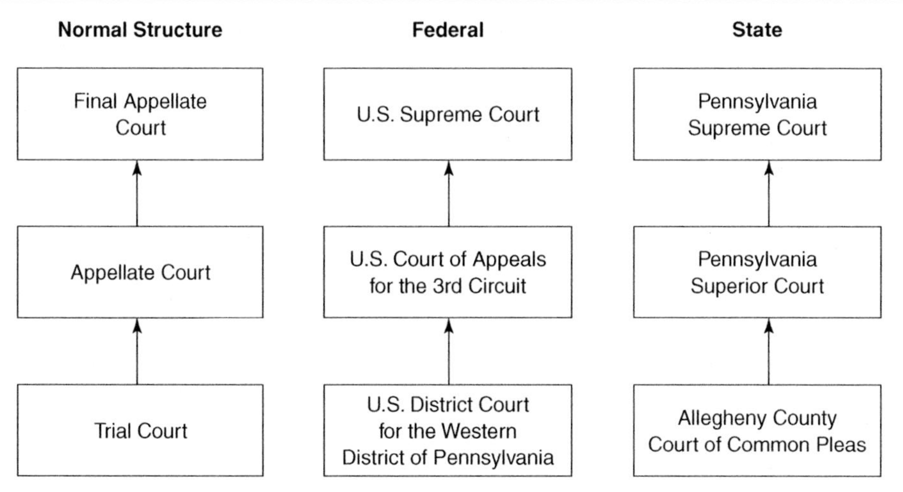

FIGURE 1.5 Case advancement through the court structure.

Do not confuse legal research with legal analysis. Although both depend on method, **legal research** is the process, the means and approach used to gain information on a particular topic. In contrast, **legal analysis** is the method used to dissect facts to determine the topic of research, as well as the method used to analyze, scrutinize, and employ the results of the research effort. Research and analysis can be daunting tasks, but both are equally critical to success. In fact, the more adept the researcher becomes with the methods and tools of research, the quicker and more efficiently the analysis can be done. In this sense, research methods and analysis are forever dependent on one another. Time and experience will yield insight to those who adopt a method for legal analysis and then use the appropriate research method for the case at hand.

The same types of library resources used in other fields are used in the legal research field: books, computers, search engines, databases, indexes, resource rooms, government document centers, and other familiar references. Not surprisingly, law libraries have alphabetized catalogues, periodical rooms, and newspaper reading rooms—the familiar trappings of any general library.

Just as knowledge of chemistry is critical to perform research in that field, legal research requires familiarity with basic legal concepts and issues. Completion of several courses in political science, paralegal studies, criminal justice, or in a law and justice program more than adequately prepares a student to research a variety of legal topics. Do not be overwhelmed or inordinately in awe of the field. Like other knowledge bases, exposure builds confidence. Do not hesitate to learn about the subject matter, even if you are self-taught.

Remember that legal topics are indexed by broad subjects, such as estate law, commercial law, corporate law, and criminal law, just like topics in a college library (such as history, science, mathematics, and literature). In essence, the law library is no more than a reflection of legal study as a whole, with each section of the library dedicated to a specific topical area.

Although topics are easy to find in legal research, particular ideas, citations, cases, statutes, or other secondary or supporting materials are not always easy to locate. Success in legal research, more than anything else, requires deductive, inferential, and focused thinking. Always begin with the broadest topic, like criminal law, and then start the focusing process. Ask questions such as "What is the specific topic am I dealing with?" "What particular issues are essential to the research question posed?" Start big and refine your focus to smaller concepts. Refinement of ideas and problems characterizes the legal research process. Commence globally and achieve the result in a narrow construct.

For example, to examine a criminal law question involving murder or homicide and the correct charge in light of the facts, you would take the following steps. The journey from the broad to the specific in criminal law follows the same track as other legal problems. First, find the state resources, and then locate the state code. Using a codified version, locate the criminal law title and then the chapter on murder. Next, consult sections regarding definitions, degrees, and grades of the offenses. In short order you will be able to discern the basic elements necessary for a murder or manslaughter charge. (This process can also be followed using the index for the appropriate code title). After this process of refinement, you would continue by examining the various statutory criteria that set out and differentiate the diverse homicide charges. The research results, in an outline format, would look like this.

- I. State Resources
  - A. State Code
    - 1. Criminal Code
      - a. definitions of offenses
        - 1) homicide/murder
          - definition of
          - degrees of
          - grading/classification

No matter what the issue, legal research demands conceptual refinement, focused thought, and precise attention to the issues. View research as a journey, a safari into the inner sanctum of the library. Within legal texts, whether on shelves or in computer databases, you will eventually discover the answers you seek.

This text delivers a basic overview of the steps that will ensure success in the law library. It touches on all major research sources, from case reporters to law reviews. Attention is also given to the tactics of discovery relevant to research, including the use of indexes, shepardizing, and cross-referencing, as well as to the various rules governing citations and access to governmental material.

Before you embark on the research journey, be patient with yourself and the process and realize that the skills of legal research are never fully mastered. Research is like a habit, be it good or bad. The more research activity is engaged in, the easier the process becomes. Experience and repetition instruct just as effectively as tutors and yield insights, reveal shortcuts in research methods, and nurture a second sense about where to go and what to look for. Though there is much to learn, have confidence that mastery is right around the corner.

CHAPTER

2

Analysis and Research Methods: The Most Important Tasks

Many ask, "Aren't legal analysis and legal research the same thing?" As stated in Chapter 1, **legal analysis** is the art of extracting concrete legal topics and issues out of given facts and ordering them in a hierarchy of importance. Legal analysis is the starting point for legal research, and thus is the most important step of the journey. Legal research, in contrast, is the way the researcher actually finds relevant information. The method used is determined by the results of legal analysis. The results may be keywords, topics, phrases, authorities, and so on, and each result calls for a different research method. Remember, ineffective and incomplete research can lead to incorrect conclusions.

Legal analysis is also conducted after research is complete; the information garnered during the research phase is applied to the case at hand either to support or to refute specific positions, or to resolve a problem or issue. One of the most prominent methods of legal analysis, and a highly recommended method of briefing a case, is called *IRAC* (*I*ssue, *R*ule, *A*pplication, *C*onclusion), and is discussed in Chapter 15. The methods of analysis discussed in this chapter are not for use in writing legal memoranda or briefs, but are specifically geared toward extracting relevant issues from given facts to facilitate legal research.

This chapter discusses various methods of legal analysis and legal research. Suggestions to keep in mind while conducting research are also given here.

I. METHODS OF LEGAL ANALYSIS WHEN CONSIDERING A RESEARCH QUESTION

Questions such as "Where do I start?" "What's the most important issue?" and "How do I make sense of all this information?" are commonly heard as the research process commences. This chapter delivers concrete suggestions on how to begin. Legal analysis and legal research processes can be compared to a set of stairs, one building on another, rising level by level until the destination is reached.

Initially the process originates with factual analysis. Weigh and assess the facts completely and efficiently. Once you have mastered the facts, the focus shifts to the formulation of legal issues that bear on the facts in question. Once you have identified the facts and legal issues, formulate a precise legal question that must be resolved. After these preliminary steps, you can begin legal research. Figure 2.1 describes the research and analysis process.

Legal analysis for forming a research question is completed by following these four basic steps.

1. *Gather the facts* All pertinent facts must be obtained about what happened and to whom. When gathering your facts, ask: Who did it? Who was it done to? What was done? When did it occur? Where did the act take place? Why did it happen? How did it happen?
2. *Analyze the facts* Use one of the many available systems of analysis (discussed later) to determine which facts are important.

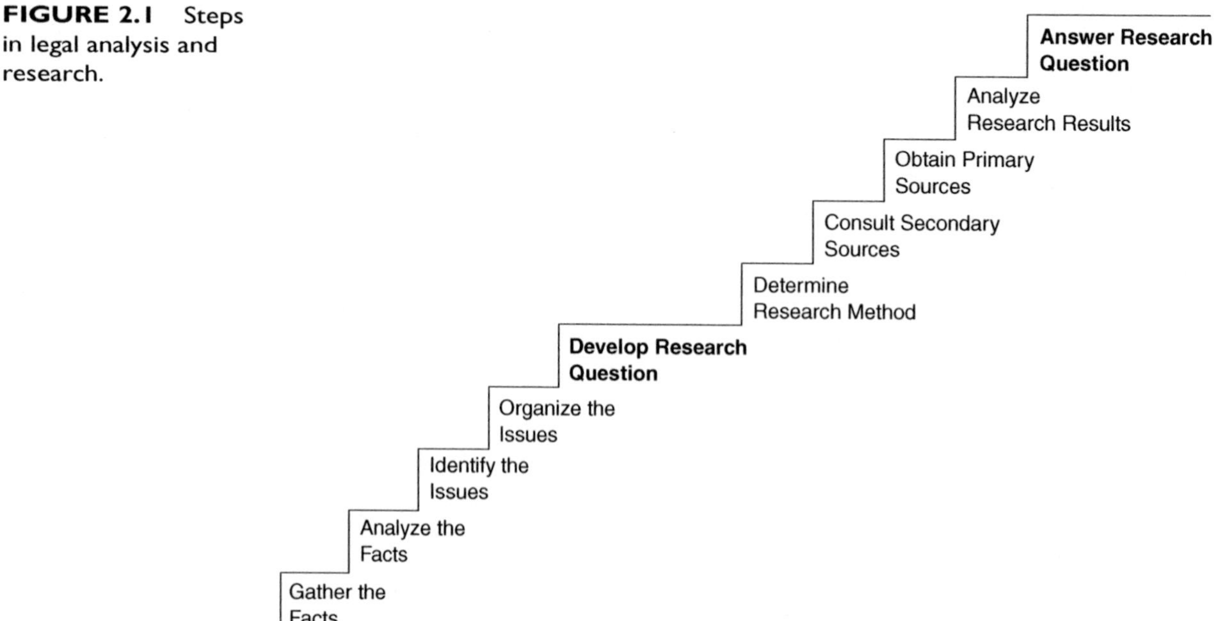

FIGURE 2.1 Steps in legal analysis and research.

3. *Identify legal issues* From the determinations made in step 2, draw conclusions about what the legal issues may be. For example, if you have determined that there is a victim, a perpetrator, a gun, and a death, at least one of the legal issues to be explored will probably be murder. Be sure to identify all possible issues.
4. *Organize legal issues* After you have identified all the issues, organize them in a continuum of importance. What is the most important topic? Using the preceding example, murder would top the list, but other possible topics include self-defense, crimes of passion, accidental death, defenses to crimes of passion, and so on. You must explore all angles and examine both sides of the case. In criminal cases, the defense should anticipate the prosecution and vice versa.

There are many legal analysis strategies; three are reviewed here. The first system is one advocated by Lawyer's Cooperative Publishing, called the TAPP (*T*hings, *A*cts, *P*ersons, and *P*laces) system. Second, an analysis system advocated by West Publishing Company is explained. Last, a system devised by Professor William P. Statsky, known as the Cartwheel, is discussed. The same set of facts will be used for explaining these three methods of legal analysis. To begin, familiarize yourself with the fact pattern in Figure 2.2.

A. TAPP

The TAPP system may be the least involved method of analyzing facts, but it can provide cogent results. As with any method, be sure to match the method to the case at hand. In this system, the researcher needs to address four different categories when dissecting the facts:

Things involved

Acts involved

Persons involved

Places where the action took place

I. Gather the Facts. Throughout this section, the facts in Figure 2.2 are used for analysis, so this step will be omitted from subsequent discussions. In this step the researcher gathers the facts of the case and sorts and organizes them in an easily understandable manner. Information may be obtained from the parties in the case, investigating agencies, witness interviews, and pertinent law enforcement/court documents.

John Smith and Jane Doe, who are Maine residents, are engaged and they desire a prenuptial agreement. Jane Doe has received a substantial sum of money due to an inheritance and she wants to ensure that John will not receive any if they divorce in the future. Jane has two children from a previous marriage and John wants to make sure that he does not have to provide for them in the event of a divorce. John also has one child whom Jane does not want to support if they are divorced. Neither Jane nor John is currently receiving support from their ex-spouses.

FIGURE 2.2 Fact pattern.

II. Analyze the Facts. After all the facts are gathered, the next step is to make a list using the TAPP categories. Using the facts in Figure 2.2, the list would likely look something like this.

Things—nuptial agreement, child support, inheritance, prenuptial agreement

Acts—engagement, marriage, divorce

Persons—bride, groom, children

Places—applicable jurisdiction, family court

III. Identify the Legal Issues. This step can be intimidating if the researcher is unfamiliar with the legal topic. Reviewing some journal or law review articles or information from legal encyclopedias or treatises will help you gain a basic understanding of the topic. Using the words identified in step 2, identify concrete legal ideas that can be addressed. Take words from several categories and form them into a question applicable to the case at hand. Examples are:

What provisions can be made regarding child support in a prenuptial agreement?

What are the basic, contractual provisions included in a prenuptial agreement written in Maine?

What standard clauses should be included regarding the event of divorce?

What effect will the agreement have on inheritance rights?

IV. Organize the Issues. After shaping research questions, determine which directs itself most precisely to the legal problem at hand. Of all the questions posed, which relates most specifically to the topic? Once you have determined this, the question of where to start your research has been answered. From then on, the research builds issue by issue. Thus, as with building blocks, the first question serves as the foundation for subsequent queries. In this particular case, the question is: "What contractual provisions must be included in an enforceable prenuptial agreement in the state of Maine?" After this question is resolved, proceed to the next question. Ask the most efficient and productive questions, the types that lead to multiple lines of inquiry and response. If you find too much information, narrow the search by crafting a more specific question.

What topics should be searched? What are the most important words in the question? *Maine* clearly would be one, as it shapes the issue of jurisdiction. Other keywords to consider are *agreement* or *prenuptial agreement* and *marital contract provisions.* A word of caution: Be mindful of the multiple meanings inherent in language. Check for synonyms and contrary meanings, and remember that words and terms can be listed simultaneously under various headings and indexes. Therefore, *prenuptial* may be listed, as well as a related term or topic such as *marital agreement.*

B. West Publishing Company Method

The method of analysis suggested by West is a bit more involved than the TAPP system, but often delivers better results. The outcome will depend on the case and the specific questions surrounding it. Remember to choose the method that works best for the researcher and the case. It may even be appropriate to employ multiple approaches while conducting research.

The West system addresses five basic issues:

1. *Parties involved in the case* Who are the people involved?
2. *Places, objects, and things involved* Where did the action occur? Were any objects or things, either tangible or intangible, involved?
3. *Basis of the case, or issues involved* What are the "action" words? What acts took place?
4. *Defenses* Could any defenses, like self-defense or entrapment, be used? Could any affirmative defenses come into play?
5. *Relief sought* What does each party want? How could the case be resolved?

The inclusion of defenses and relief sought is a unique feature of the West model and affords a far-reaching perspective in simple research tasks. Refer to the fact pattern in Figure 2.2, remembering that step 1, "Gather the facts," has been omitted.

I. Analyze the Facts. Using the West system, the factual list would cover these issues:

Parties—bride, groom, children

Places, objects, things—jurisdiction is Maine, family court; inheritance, agreement, support

Basis of case—prenuptial agreement, marriage, engagement, protection of inheritance

Defense—incompetence, faulty execution of agreement, invalid agreement

Relief sought—Creation of prenuptial agreement, exclusion of support for children and spouse

II. Identifying the Legal Issues. As in the TAPP system, examine and scrutinize the results. By so doing, the researcher will find that concrete questions and issues emerge. The results using the West method will be similar, though it would not be surprising to see additional questions on defense and relief issues.

III. Organize the Legal Issues. Organize these issues in much the same way as with the TAPP method. A question regarding defenses may be the most important in this case. Pay close attention to any defense information that might affect the case, especially technical defenses such as statute of limitations and other issues that involve automatic exclusion of premarital property from a divorce settlement.

C. The Cartwheel: Using the Index and Table of Contents of Law Books

The **Cartwheel** method takes a somewhat different approach to legal analysis, in that it blends analysis and research. Essentially, this method has the researcher consult indexes and tables of contents in select legal materials to find appropriate information. Again using the prenuptial agreement fact pattern, outline the process.

The first step in using the index and table of contents in any law text or series is to look up the word *prenuptial* in that index and table of contents. If not successful with this word (either because the word is not in the index or contents, or because the page or section references in the index or table or contents do not lead you to relevant material in the body of the book), the next step is to think of as many different phrasings and contexts as possible relating to the word *prenuptial*. Here the Cartwheel earns its keep.

1. Identify all the major words or ideas in the facts of the client's problem. Place each word or idea in the center of a Cartwheel (see Figure 2.3). In the index and table of contents, look up all these words.
2. Identify the broader categories of these major words. In the index and table of contents, look up all these broader categories.
3. Identify the narrower categories of these words. In the index and table of contents, look up all these narrower categories.
4. Identify potential synonyms of these words. In the index and table of contents, look up all these synonyms.
5. Identify all the antonyms of these words. In the index and table of contents, look up these antonyms.
6. Identify all closely related words. In the index and table of contents, look up all these closely related words.
7. Identify all procedural terms related to these words. In the index and table of contents, look up all these procedural terms.
8. Identify all agencies, if any, that might have some connection to these words. In the index and table of contents, look up all these agencies.
9. Identify all long shots. In the index and table of contents, look up all these long shots.

Note: The preceding categories are suggestions; any given case may require use of other or additional categories.

If we were to apply these nine steps of the Cartwheel to the term *prenuptial agreement,* and check the resulting words and phrases in the index and table of contents of a family law book, the results might be as follows:

Broader words contract, agreement, provisions for children

Narrower words legality of contract, rights of children

Synonyms antenuptial, nuptial, child support, heirs

Antonyms recission, breach, release

Closely related words estate, heirs, property

Procedural terms enforcement, execution, registration

Agencies clerk of courts

Long shots incompetence, previous marriage

FIGURE 2.3

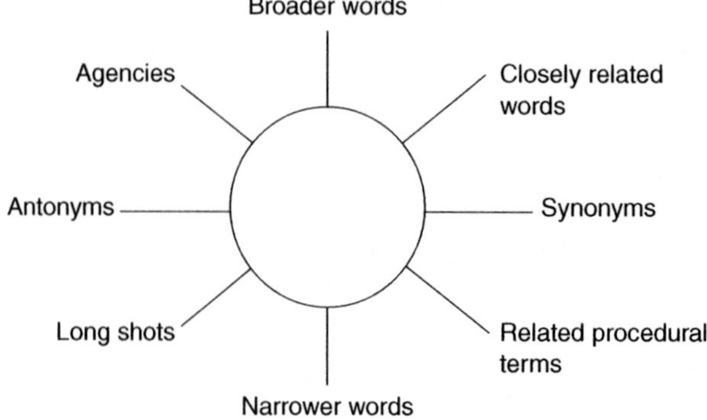

As indicated in the chart, there may be some overlap among categories; they are not mutually exclusive. Also, it is *not* significant whether you place a word in one category or another as long as you research that word when you comb through the index and table of contents. The Cartwheel is, in effect, a word association tool that should become second nature with practice. Perhaps you think some of the word selections in the sample categories shown are farfetched. However, it is difficult to know for sure whether a word will be fruitful until it is tried. Be imaginative and take some risks.

II. LEGAL RESEARCH METHODS

Now that you have formulated and organized research questions, you can begin formal research. As in all other aspects of the research process, starting points are tough to detect. Three basic methods are used in the research process, and each depends on the amount of information the researcher has and the thoroughness of the initial analysis. This section addresses the research method; that is, how the research is actually conducted.

A. Known Authority Approach

Unfortunately, this is the method the researcher may use the least when looking for case law. The known authority method is exactly what it suggests: The researcher has in his or her possession either a good, relevant case or a statute that is still in full force. A citation to an applicable case or statute will open a research spigot; usually, one good case leads to other cases that may be applicable to the problem. In some instances, the case triggers an avalanche of other relevant cases. Within the cases will be a wealth of referential material, such as citations to statutes, scholarly materials, and other legal authority. The first case can lead to the gold mine.

The process with this method is simple. First, "pull" the known case using a commercially produced reporter. At the beginning of the case, headnotes outline various points of law involved in the case. The key numbers or universal topic numbers found in the headnotes can be cross-referenced to other resources from that publisher (see Figure 2.4).

An applicable topic number in a case reporter will send you to that same topic number in a digest or a legal encyclopedia that reports parallel case references. Commercial reporters also include references to other publications by the same publisher, such as encyclopedias, practice aids, form books, and ALR citations. For example, extra bits of information called "Research References" are set off after the headnotes (Figure 2.5).

Many annotated statutes and codes also contain information on key cases and references to digest or encyclopedia sections. See Figure 2.6 for an example.

Another way to trace the progress and influence of a case is through *Shepard's Citations,* which lists case histories. With this tool you can trace the path a case has taken. This resource gives you the complete history of any case, as well as how other cases have treated, applied, or referenced that case. Chapter 13 fully covers the process of shepardizing. West's KeyCite system produces similar results. In short, one good case goes a long way in the world of legal research.

B. Known Topic Approach

This approach can be used when the researcher is sure of the topic involved. Most often used by experienced researchers, it can provide cogent results more quickly.

FIGURE 2.4

Nadja Linette PANZARDI–SANTIAGO et al Plaintiffs

v.

UNIVERSITY OF PUERTO RICO et al Defendants

No. CIV. 95–2316(CCC/ADC).

United States District Court, D. Puerto Rico.

March 19, 2002.

Disabled prospective student sued Commonwealth and University of Puerto Rico, alleging that she had been prevented from enrolling at university by physical barriers to her getting around campus in wheelchair in violation of Americans with Disabilities Act (ADA). On defendants' motion to dismiss, or for summary judgment, the District Court, Delgado-Colon, United States Magistrate Judge, held that: (1) university did not waive its Eleventh Amendment immunity; (2) abrogation of Eleventh Amendment immunity under Title II of ADA exceeded Congress' authority; (3) student was not excluded from programs and activities at university; (4) fact questions precluded summary judgment on issue of whether public pathway was accessible to student; (5) student was not entitled to jury on ADA claim; and (6) student was entitled to jury on Rehabilitation Act claim.

Ordered accordingly.

1. Federal Courts ⚷265

Commonwealth of Puerto Rico is state for purposes of Eleventh Amendment. U.S.C.A. Const.Amend. 11.

2. Federal Courts ⚷269

University of Puerto Rico is arm of state entitled to Eleventh Amendment immunity in federal courts. U.S.C.A. Const. Amend. 11.

3. Federal Courts ⚷266.1

State may waive its Eleventh Amendment immunity by voluntarily invoking jurisdiction of federal court, or by making clear declaration that it intends to submit itself to federal court's jurisdiction. U.S.C.A. Const.Amend. 11.

4. United States ⚷82(2)

Congress may, in exercise of its spending power, condition its grant of funds to states on their taking certain actions that Congress could not require them to take, and acceptance of funds entails states' agreement to actions. U.S.C.A. Const. Art. 1, § 8, cl. 1.

5. Federal Courts ⚷266.1

State university's participation in programs funded under ADA could not be presumed to constitute waiver of its Eleventh Amendment immunity from suit in federal court by disabled prospective student, alleging that she had been prevented from enrolling by physical barriers to her getting around campus in wheelchair in violation of ADA; nothing in ADA manifested clear intent to condition participation in programs on state's consent to waive its immunity. U.S.C.A. Const. Amend. 11.

6. Constitutional Law ⚷243.2

Federal Courts ⚷265

Abrogation of states' Eleventh Amendment immunity from suit for damages under Title II of ADA exceeded Congress' authority to enact "appropriate legislation" to enforce Fourteenth Amendment; there was lack of evidence in Congressional record that states had engaged in widespread pattern of unconstitutional discrimination against disabled people when providing accommodations to public services. U.S.C.A. Const.Amends. 11, 14;

FIGURE 2.5

U.S. SUPREME COURT REPORTS 146 L Ed 2d

venue statutes are deemed to be restrictive, but that analysis of special venue provisions must be specific to the statute.

RESEARCH REFERENCES

4 Am Jur 2d, Alternative Dispute Resolution §§ 251, 252

9 USCS §§ 9-11

L Ed Digest, Arbitration § 11; Courts § 459

L Ed Index, Arbitration and Award

Annotations:

What kind of contracts containing arbitration agreements are subject to stay and enforcement provisions of §§ 1-4 and 8 of Federal Arbitration Act (FAA) (9 USCS §§ 1-4 and 8, and similar predecessor provisions)—Supreme Court cases. 130 L Ed 2d 1189.

Validity, under Federal Constitution, of arbitration statutes—Supreme Court cases. 87 L Ed 2d 787.

SHEPARD'S® Citations Service. For further research of authorities referenced here, use SHEPARD'S to be sure your case or statute is still good law and to find additional authorities that support your position. SHEPARD'S is available exclusively from LexisNexis™.

Remember to check the table of contents for each relevant topic. In digests, statutes, and encyclopedia volumes, at the beginning of each major topic heading, there is a table of contents for the topic. Scan through the table of contents to find the relevant section. See Figures 2.7 and 2.8 for examples.

Also included in the initial volume of many digests is a complete listing of all the topics included in the digest series. It is advisable to check this listing for any other leads you may have overlooked.

C. Keyword Approach

Sometimes, even though you have analyzed the facts as well as possible, you will still have difficulty formulating a research question. Also, if you use the Cartwheel approach, you will have only a list of keywords. In this instance, a keyword approach is in order. The amount of knowledge you possess on the subject matter will determine your starting point. No matter which reference you use, the process is the same. Find the series general index and look up the first keyword. Scan the entries under the keyword and then look up a promising entry in the corresponding volume. If you are searching for case law, consult the appropriate digest and look up the keyword in the index. From the host of subtopics available, choose a relevant topic; consult that volume, scan the entries, and look for relevant case summaries. Similarly, if you are searching for a statute, look up the keyword in the index and scan through subheadings to arrive at the pertinent section number. See Figure 2.9 for an example from the Purdon's Pennsylvania Consolidated Statutes index.

FIGURE 2.6

1959, April 29, P.L. 58, § 722
(75 P.S.§ 722).
1953, April 24, P.L. 188, § 1.
1941, July 18, P.L. 409, § 1.
1937, June 29, P.L. 2329, § 9.
1929, May 1, P.L. 905, Art. VII, § 717.1
(75 P.S. § 306.1).

Cross References

Inspection of vehicles, see 75 Pa.C.S.A. § 4701 et seq.

Library References

Automobiles ⚷ 5(2), 115.
WESTLAW Topic No. 48A.
C.J.S. Motor Vehicles §§ 26, 44, 56.

§ 1959. Messenger service

(a) Annual registration.—The annual fee for registration of a messenger service as provided for in Chapter 75 (relating to messenger service)[1] shall be $50.

(b) Additional places of business.—The annual fee for registration of additional place of business or branch office which a messenger service may transact business shall be $25.

(c) Transfer of location.—The fee for the transfer of location of a registered place of business or branch office of a messenger service during a period of registration shall be $5.

1976, June 17, P.L. 162, No. 81, § 1, effective July 1, 1977.

[1]75 Pa.C.S.A. § 7501 et seq.

Historical and Statutory Notes

Prior Laws:
1959, April 29, P.L. 58, No. 32, § 1308, added 1974, Dec. 10, P.L. 907, No. 299, § 1 (75 P.S. § 1308).

Library References

Automobiles ⚷ 98, 102.
WESTLAW Topic No. 48A.
C.J.S. Motor Vehicles §§ 137, 142.

§ 1960. Reinstatement of operating privilege or vehicle registration

The department shall charge a fee of $25 or, if section 1786(d) (relating to required financial responsibility) applies, a fee of $50 to restore a person's operating privilege or the registration of a vehicle following a suspension or revocation.

1980, June 18, P.L. 229, No. 68, § 3, effective in 60 days. Amended 1990, Feb. 7, P.L. 11, No. 6, § 21, effective July 1, 1990.

FIGURE 2.7

PURDON'S
PENNSYLVANIA CONSOLIDATED
STATUTES ANNOTATED

TITLE 75

VEHICLES

Sections 1701 to 3755 appear in this volume

PART I.—PRELIMINARY PROVISIONS

Secondary resources, such as encyclopedias and the American Law Reports (ALR) series, may also be consulted in the same manner. All these resources will lead the researcher to relevant legal authorities, and the annotated references therein will provide a bevy of leads.

III. IMPORTANT ADVICE FOR THE NOVICE RESEARCHER

A. Realize the Importance of Precedent

In a system that relies on proof and evidence, in which schools, colleges, universities, and training programs endlessly stress the value of real evidence and firsthand information, is it any wonder that jurists rely so heavily on precedent? Critics of precedent decry what they perceive as an almost unquestioning reliance on previous judicial reasoning; others argue that overreliance on precedent thwarts legal creativity and slows needed change in the legal system. These detractors claim that the system gives longer life to bad law than would be so without the nervousness about precedence. In a less cynical light, precedent should be viewed as a sign of common thought and common reasoning. Precedent manifests a certain respect for the thoughts of legal predecessors and attempts to further the goal of consistency and predictability in legal matters—treating like cases alike. Precedent demonstrates that a line of reasoning or decisions has been capable of withstanding a generally critical audience, that of lawyers and judges. This does not mean that once a

FIGURE 2.8

EXECUTIONS, ETC. 30 Am Jur 2d

II. EXECUTION AND LEVY, GENERALLY [§§ 43–455]
- A. In General [§§ 43–49]
- B. Judgment as Basis of Execution [§§ 50–57]
- C. Writ of Execution [§§ 58–112]
- D. Property Subject to Execution [§§ 113–204]
- E. Authority and Duty of Execution Officer [§§ 205–212]
- F. Levy of Execution [§§ 213–260]
- G. Custody of Property [§§ 261–289]
- H. Inventory and Appraisement [§§ 290–294]
- I. Return of Execution [§§ 295–333]
- J. Satisfaction of and by Execution [§§ 334–345]
- K. Relief from Execution and Levy [§§ 346–433]
- L. Redemption [§§ 434–455]

III. EXECUTION SALES [§§ 456–603]
- A. In General [§§ 456–556]
- B. Title, Rights, Remedies, and Obligations of Purchaser [§§ 557–594]
- C. Proceeds of Execution Sales [§§ 595–603]

IV. ACTIONS FOR WRONGFUL EXECUTION [§§ 604–625]
- A. In General [§§ 604–609]
- B. Grounds [§§ 610–612]
- C. Damages; Attorneys' Fees [§§ 613–620]
- D. Practice and Procedure [§§ 621–625]

V. EXECUTION AGAINST THE PERSON [§§ 626–642]
- A. In General [§§ 626–631]
- B. Practice and Procedure [§§ 632–642]

VI. POSTJUDGMENT GARNISHMENT AND OTHER SUPPLEMENTARY PROCEEDINGS AND REMEDIES [§§ 643–763]
- A. In General [§§ 643–650]
- B. Property Subject to Proceedings [§§ 651–668]
- C. Prerequisites to Initiation of Proceedings [§§ 669–677]
- D. Procedural Matters [§§ 678–713]
- E. Remedies Available [§§ 714–763]

VII. ENFORCEMENT OF JUDGMENTS REQUIRING SPECIFIC ACTS [§§ 764–772]

precedent has been set, the law is incapable of modification, but only that there would be scant support for a system that changes too often.

B. Frustration and Legal Research, A Natural State of Affairs

Those who claim that research will not be frustrating, and even aggravating at times, have little exposure to the practice. Deductive, inferential, and contrarian analysis calls for hard and sometimes very tedious thinking. Legal research is a form-disciplined mental inquisition, a forced, disciplined method directed toward a fo-

FIGURE 2.8
continued

30 Am Jur 2d EXECUTIONS, ETC.

I. INTRODUCTION

A. Enforcement of Judgments, In General

1. General Considerations

§ 1. Generally
§ 2. Governing law
§ 3. Judicial powers and duties
§ 4. Legislative power
§ 5. Necessity of validity, certainty, and definiteness of judgment
§ 6. Time of enforcement
§ 7. —After term
§ 8. Persons entitled to enforce judgments
§ 9. Persons against whom judgments may be enforced
§ 10. —Enforcement against persons not originally parties; joint debtors

2. Methods of Enforcement

§ 11. Generally; enforcement at law, generally
§ 12. Enforcement in equity, generally
§ 13. —Prerequisites to granting relief; proof
§ 14. Enforcement by writ of fieri facias
§ 15. Enforcement by writ of scire facias

B. Stay of Proceedings to Enforce Judgment

1. In General

a. Basic Principles

§ 16. Generally
§ 17. Necessity of application for stay

cused subject matter. During some exercises, the end sought will be elusive and almost impossible to find. Persistence and tenacity of purpose, as well as continued practice, will certainly minimize the predictable frustration that often arises in legal research.

C. Type of Law Equates to Type of Research

Legal practitioners frequently charge into the research exercise forgetting about the most basic concept: namely, exactly what type of law will govern the question and thus the research. Choosing the wrong form of law has both short- and long-term

FIGURE 2.9 **MUNICIPALITIES**

FIGURE 2.10

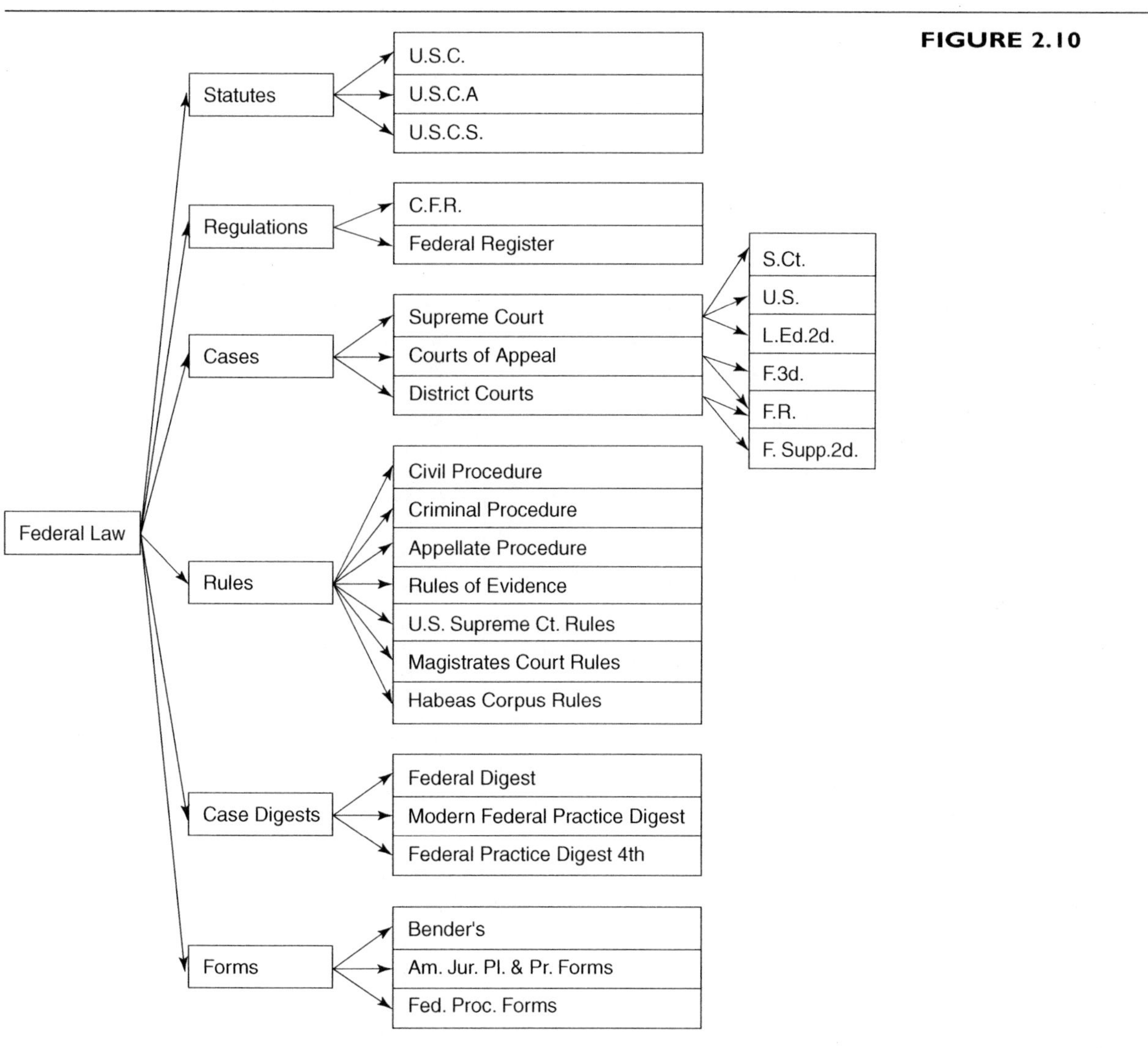

consequences. How an area of law is perceived and interpreted is inevitably tied to the context in which the law is researched. For example, damages awards are not properly within the criminal law sphere, because verdicts of guilt and innocence do not result in damage awards. O. J. Simpson was found innocent in the criminal court, but held liable for $34 million in damages in the civil court.

The distinction may appear minor, but it is not. Looking in the wrong books for the right law or in the right books for inapplicable law cannot bear meaningful research fruit. The researcher must ask, at the outset, what kind of law is under consideration. Has the correct legal topic been chosen? Have the correct terms and definitions been selected? Are terms and definitions being misapplied in the research exercise? Be sure the research matches the end sought. Law books have exacting and specific topical coverage, so you must choose the texts that match your problem and facts. Figure 2.10 outlines federal law sources. Figure 2.11 provides more suggestions on appropriate avenues of research.

FIGURE 2.11

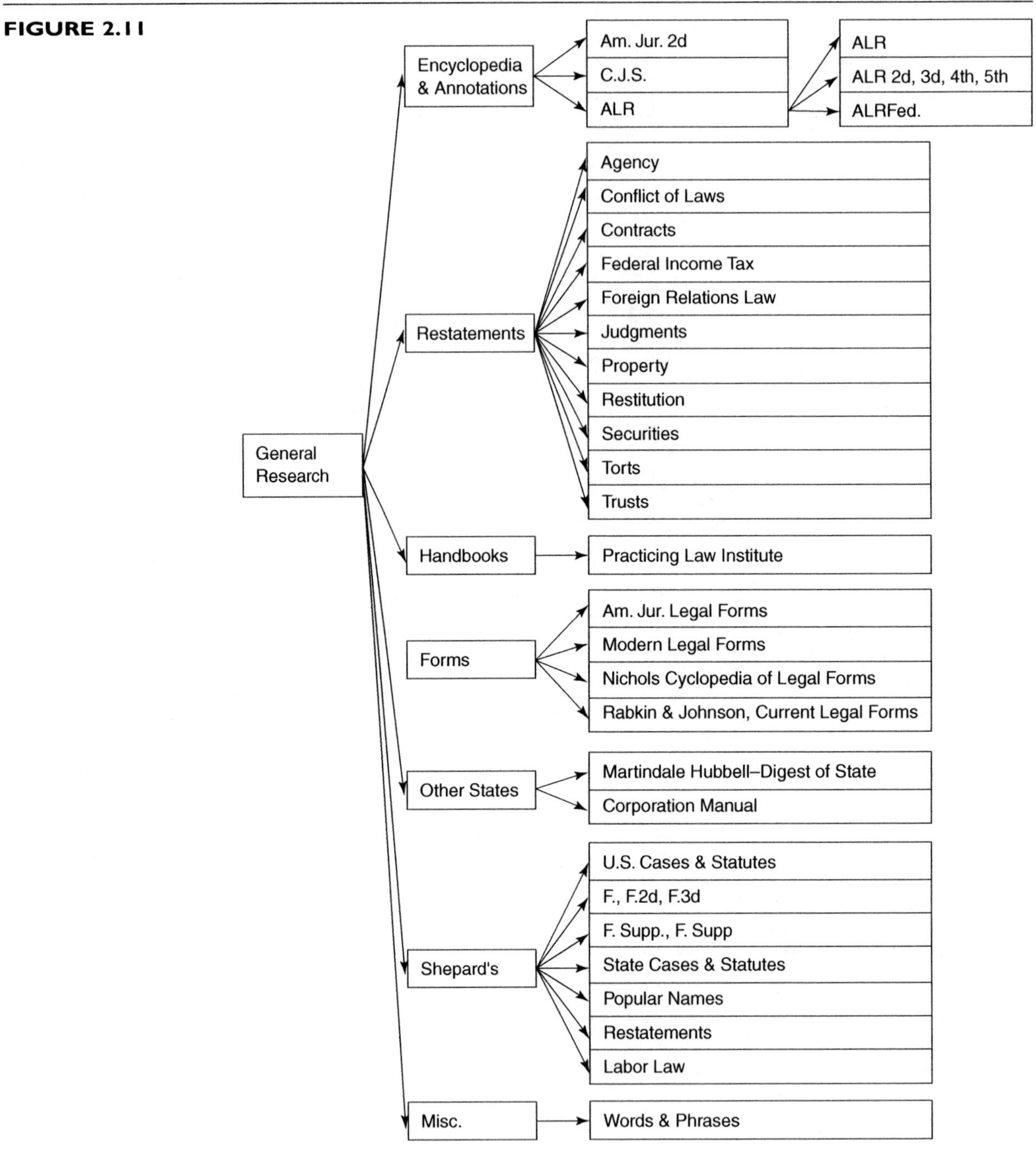

Directed, focused topical analysis provides a researcher with the appropriate target. Choose the right law and the right texts and other source materials to match. Within the chosen legal materials, locate the pertinent volume, chapter, and provision. Focused topical analysis distinguishes among broad topics such as those shown in Figure 2.12.

FIGURE 2.12

1. Administrative law
2. Appellate decisions
3. Business and Professional law
4. Civil Rights law
5. Constitutional law
6. Consumer law
7. Contracts law
8. Copyright, Trademark, and Patent law
9. Corporation law
10. Correctional law
11. Criminal law
12. Divorce law
13. Domestic relations law
14. Education law
15. Employment law
16. Energy law
17. Environmental law
18. Estate Planning law
19. Evidence law
20. Family law
21. Guardianship and Adoption law
22. Health law
23. Housing law
24. International law
25. Insurance law
26. Juvenile law
27. Labor law
28. Landlord/Tenant law
29. Maritime law
30. Military law
31. Motor Vehicle law
32. Municipal law
33. Penal law
34. Prison law
35. Public Utilities law
36. Social Security law
37. Tax law
38. Torts
39. Trusts
40. Unemployment insurance
41. Veteran's law
42. Welfare law, social welfare law
43. Wills
44. Worker's Compensation law
45. Zoning law

D. Know the Legal Subject Generally and the Particulars Will Come Easily

Just as any reporter thoroughly investigates a story before compiling a first draft, so does the legal researcher. To arrive at the conceptual heart of a legal problem requires a lot of hard work and sometimes an exhausting amount of research. However, a general knowledge of two basic things will go a long way toward making research less arduous. First, master the definitions and terms relevant to the research. No researcher can solve a legal dilemma without understanding the terminology. Pull out *Black's Law Dictionary* or another practical resource and look up terms that you do not understand completely. Once the facts and definitions are in place, you can broadly assess the problem in a legal context. Legal encyclopedias such as *Corpus Juris Secundum* and *American Jurisprudence* will greatly assist the researcher in gaining a broad, general understanding of law in the pertinent area. Textbooks, hornbooks, and Restatements of Law, which provide thorough yet nationalized discussions of applicable law, are also strongly recommended. These resources are covered in depth in later chapters.

E. Focus on the Legal Problem

Now that you understand the general principles bearing on the problem, you must determine how they relate to the client's case. What facts in the case involve these general principles? Has a similar case been presented before? Are there defenses that make a victory impossible? How does the client's case really fit the general scenario?

The best suggestion for achieving a focused outlook on a case at this stage is to review the volumes in the American Law Reports system (thoroughly discussed in Chapter 9). The ALR series does a splendid job in educating researchers about issues, dilemmas, and problems that emerge regularly. ALR focuses on individual case issues and gives the researcher a significant supply of citations and commentary.

The second best suggestion for issue resolution is to use the various indexes discussed in Chapter 4. In particular, the *Index to Legal Periodicals* will provide the researcher with incisive food for thought, stimulating academic challenges, and a multitude of references and citations.

F. Collect Cases, Statutes, and Other Primary Support

After the problem is concretely and squarely identified and the researcher's thinking is crystal clear, it is time to gather supporting data. As we will shortly see, cases can be found in many sources:

- Reports at the state level
- Reporters in the national system
- Specialized reporter systems
- Digests
- Annotations provided by the ALR series
- Annotations provided through the Shepard's network
- United States Code Annotated (U.S.C.A.)
- United States Code Service (U.S.C.S.)
- State annotated services
- Other regulatory publications

Also helpful is the checklist of various books shown in Figure 2.13.

The key to success in research lies in the initial issue identification. Intellectual support for a proposed resolution or remedy plainly is not possible unless the researcher knows exactly what he or she is looking for.

G. Let the Law Speak for Itself

The multiplicity of lawsuits, causes of action, and criminal cases makes it extremely likely that something similar to your client's particular case has already been litigated in some forum. Search for precedent in the particular facts of your case. Consult the most recent resources. What is precedent now may not have been a short time ago! Law is constantly changing and evolving. This does not mean that there isn't a first time for a particular case, but chances are that precedent exists.

If the research shows that the client has little hope of a favorable decision, do not automatically assume that you can overturn precedent. The end result of legal research, if done correctly and competently, is usually an accurate, truthful reflection of the law.

H. Choose and Confirm Jurisdiction

Jurisdiction errors are one of the most common mistakes by novice researchers. Be sure of the forum. If researching a state-level case regarding the validity of an oral contract, review the statutory and case law from that state first. After that, consult any federal court decisions applicable to that jurisdiction only. Avoid the law of jurisdictions with contrary views.

FIGURE 2.13 Kinds of law books.

KINDS OF LAW BOOKS

Kind of Law	Sets of Books That Contain the Full Text of This Kind of Law	Sets of Books That Can Be Used to Locate This Kind of Law	Sets of Books That Can Be Used to Help Explain This Kind of Law	Sets of Books That Can Be Used to Help Determine the Current Validity of This Kind of Law
Opinions	Reports Reporters ALR Series Legal Newspapers Loose-Leaf Services Slip Opinions Advance Sheets	Digests ALR Annotations Shepard's Legal periodicals Encyclopedias Treatises Loose-Leaf Services Words and Phrases	Legal Periodicals Encyclopedias Treatises ALR Annotations Loose-Leaf Services	Shepard's
Statutes	Statutory Code Statutes at Large Session Laws Laws Compilations Consolidated Laws Slip Law Acts & Resolves	Index volumes of statutory code Loose-Leaf Services	Legal Periodicals Encyclopedias Treatises ALR Annotations Loose-Leaf Services	Shepard's
Constitutions	Statutory Code Separate volumes containing the Constitution	Index volumes of statutory code Loose-Leaf Services	Legal Periodicals Encyclopedias Treatises ALR Annotations Loose-Leaf Services	Shepard's
Administrative Regulations	Administrative Codes Separate volumes containing the regulations of certain agencies Loose-Leaf Services	Index volumes of administrative code Loose-Leaf Services	Legal Periodicals Encyclopedias Treatises ALR Annotations Loose-Leaf Services	Shepard's
Administrative Decisions	Separate volumes containing the decisions of certain agencies Loose-Leaf Services	Index or digest volumes to the decisions Loose-Leaf Services	Legal Periodicals Treatises ALR Annotations Loose-Leaf Services	Shepard's
Ordinances	Municipal Code Office Journal Legal Newspaper	Index volumes of municipal code	Legal Periodicals Treatises ALR Annotations	Shepard's
Charters	Separate volume containing charter Municipal Code Official Journal Legal Newspaper	Index volumes of the charter or the municipal code	Legal Periodicals Treatises ALR Annotations	Shepard's
Rules of Court	Separate Rules Volumes Statutory Code Practice Manuals	Index to rules volumes Index to statutory code Index to practice manuals	Encyclopedias Treatises ALR Annotations Loose-Leaf Services Practice Manuals	Shepard's

Adapted from *Legal Research Writing and Analysis, Second Edition*, p. 12–13, by William P. Statsky, Copyright © 1982 by West Publishing Co.

I. Types of Authority

In the end, legal research is nothing more than a search for authority—a search for something that will cause a court to decide in your favor or lead the opposing party to settle out of court. Many times the researcher can feel overwhelmed by the sheer volume of resources unearthed. If the researcher keeps the various types of authorities in mind, and remembers the basic aim of research, though, the task will prove less onerous and cumbersome.

There are five basic types of authority, grouped into two categories:

1. Primary, secondary, or tertiary
2. Persuasive or mandatory

Primary authority may be the simplest to understand, because it is nothing more than the law itself. **Primary authority** consists of constitutions, statutes, administrative rules, executive orders, and the like; these are legally binding directives issued by governmental bodies. **Secondary authority** consists of court decisions (interpreting primary authority), attorney general opinions, administrative rulings, and so on; these are legally binding, but are interpretations or applications of primary law. **Tertiary authority** includes commentary on, descriptions of, or analysis of primary and/or secondary authority, such as is found in treatises, texts, law reviews, Restatements, and the like. Tertiary authority is not legally binding, but often carries a great deal of persuasive weight.

Mandatory authority refers to a legal authority that a court must abide by; it is binding in all situations within that jurisdiction. For example, a Texas Supreme Court decision is mandatory authority for all lower courts in Texas, but is not mandatory authority for a court in California. **Persuasive authority** is authority that a court may follow if it believes the legal reasoning is correct and it is persuaded to do so. A Texas Supreme Court decision is not mandatory authority in California, but it may possibly be considered persuasive authority. If the facts of the California case are similar to those in the Texas case, and the legal issues coincide, and the statutes involved are essentially the same, the Texas decision may be regarded as persuasive. Primary and secondary authority are either persuasive or mandatory, depending on jurisdiction, legal issues, and so on. Tertiary authority may or may not be legally persuasive.

IV. SUMMARY

The key to any effective legal research endeavor is the method or system of analysis and research. Once the researcher gains control of the method, any fear of the law can be overcome. The basic agenda for the legal researcher is to *start big* and *end small:* Attack the legal problem from its broadest terms and work down to a small, but more clearly focused, issue.

The effective legal researcher must dig for more than just the statistical facts; he or she must search for and understand the personal aspects of the legal issue as well. As facts are amassed, start the process of *issue identification:*

1. Begin to focus the issue in broad but reasonable terms.
2. Use precedents to help focus and clarify the legal issue.
3. Know and understand the legal terms.
4. Learn to divide the law into categories and topics.

5. Above all, do not get frustrated! Legal research is hard work and demands patience and patient analysis. Learn how to divide the law up and break it down.

V. LEGAL RESEARCH ASSIGNMENTS

Using each of the following fact patterns, develop research questions. These fact patterns will be used throughout this book to explain the use of each resource. Become familiar with the content.

A. Fact Pattern 1

John Smith, a bartender by trade, consumes seven 1½-ounce shots of vodka. Smith begins having difficulty completing his job and several witnesses say they saw him breaking glasses. On his way home from work, Smith strikes a pedestrian, Jack Jones, from behind. Jones's head hits the windshield of Smith's auto. Jones is thrown through the air and lands 30 feet away from the impact site. Jones is dead when the paramedics arrive. Smith leaves the scene, but returns to the area when he hears sirens. He is arrested and a blood alcohol test is performed. The results show his blood alcohol level to be .268. Smith is charged with driving under the influence/driving while intoxicated and vehicular homicide.

B. Fact Pattern 2

ABC Company enters into an agreement of sale with the Small Town Bank and Trust, in which ABC agrees to purchase a piece of unimproved real estate. The agreement of sale, which originally was comprised of several documents, is subsequently orally modified. The original packet consists of (1) an offer letter from ABC company; (2) an undated and unsigned agreement of sale; (3) a copy of a check made payable to Small Town Bank and Trust, drawn on ABC Company's account, which was cashed by Small Town Bank and Trust; and (4) a dated draft agreement of sale signed by ABC Company and Small Town Bank and Trust. ABC Company requests that the agreement of sale be enforced. Small Town Bank and Trust states that there never was a signed, valid agreement.

CHAPTER

3

CITATION METHOD

Understanding legal citations does not require a secret decoder ring, only a knowledge of the formulas used. Once a citation format is thoroughly understood, all citations can easily be deciphered by applying the same technique.

Being able to read and understand legal citations is paramount for the researcher because research is a citation-intensive exercise. If you cannot make heads nor tails of a citation, you will be unable to locate the authority and research will stop. Legal citations are abbreviated references to cases, statutes, books, and periodicals. Citations tell researchers where to find what they are looking for. Researchers must be able to identify each element in a citation to pull out the information contained therein and use it to locate the cited item.

Throughout this chapter, citations are explained using the seventeenth edition of *The Bluebook: A Uniform System of Citation,* published by the Harvard Law Review Association. Only basic citation methods will be covered, because a discussion of all forms of *Bluebook* references would take an entire work in itself. The *Bluebook* is the industry standard for format and is employed in all legal reference materials, be it case reporters, statutory compilations, law reviews, or digests and encyclopedias. That said, be aware that almost all publishers (even those that purport to follow *Bluebook*) have their own usages or proprietary styles that vary in some respects from the standard. The variations may be as small as spacing or typeface differences or as large as a reordering of the elements. *Shepard's Citations* in particular uses space-saving symbols that differ from *Bluebook* forms. Also, the court rules of some states mandate the use of variant citation forms, especially for cases and statutory codes. Nevertheless, if you understand the *Bluebook* style and format, you will have no trouble deciphering these variant citation formats.

Two special citation types should be mentioned here: pinpoint and parallel citations. A *pinpoint citation,* sometimes called a *jump cite,* is exactly what it suggests: a reference to a specific place in a case opinion, law review article, or other source.

When an actual quotation from an opinion is included in a law review article, for example, the author must state exactly where the quote came from, and thus will include a pinpoint citation in a reference. It will look like this:

People v. Armor, 590 N.W.2d 61, 65 (Mich. 1999)

The number "61" is the first page of the opinion, and the number "65" is the reference to the page where the quoted material appears.

The second type of format is the parallel citation. Parallel citations refer to the same case or law but give different location information. Many primary materials are published in two or three different sources, and it is customary to include references to all the various locations as a courtesy or convenience to a researcher who may not have access to some sources. Parallel citations are not to different opinions, but are references to the same opinion appearing in different sources. Most common are references to decisions of the United States Supreme Court, which appear in three different reporters: the *United States Reports* (U.S.), the *Supreme Court Reporter* (S. Ct.) and the *United States Supreme Court Reports, Lawyers' Edition* (L. Ed. and 2d). The U.S. citation is always placed first because it is the official reporter of the U.S. Supreme Court. A parallel citation looks like this:

Slimy v. United States, 825 U.S. 4, 19 S. Ct. 1099, 29 L. Ed. 306 (1984)

I. BASIC CITATION FORM: CASES

The following diagrams dissect citations for a case or opinion from a court. (See also the *Bluebook* explanations at pages 5–9.)

A. State Court Decisions

People v. Armour, 590 N.W.2d 61, 65 (Mich. 1999)

The case name comes first. Depending on where it is cited, it may or may not be italicized. *Bluebook* has many rules about format and abbreviations, but the case name always indicates the party or parties involved.

Notice the reporter in which the case is published: the North Western Reporter, Second Series, volume 590, beginning at page 61. Regional reporters are preferred in citations because these reporters are distributed to most law libraries nationwide; it cannot be assumed that the *Michigan Reporter,* the official court reporter for the state of Michigan, will be as well stocked. Although law libraries in states other than Michigan may have the *Michigan Reporter,* other agencies, courts, or governmental bodies very well may not. This void is filled by the North Western Reporter series, which publishes cases from Iowa, Michigan, Minnesota, Nebraska, North Dakota, South Dakota, and Wisconsin. It is necessary to cite to at least one reporter, and the regional reporters are preferred.

Note also the parenthetical information at the end of the citation, which identifies the state where the case was decided. After the state abbreviation, the court abbreviation may be listed. In this instance, because the case is a decision of the highest state court, no court is specified, just the year of the decision. If this case had been cited to a state reporter (the *Michigan Reporter*) instead of the regional reporter, the state abbreviation in the parenthetical would be omitted as redundant.

If the case has not yet been published, the docket number may be substituted for the volume, reporter name, and page number. If a specific page in an unpublished decision is being cited, the docket number is listed, the pinpoint cite is introduced with "slip op.", and then the page number(s) being referred to are listed. For example:

Charlesworth v. Mack, No.90-345, slip op. at 6 (D. Mass. Dec. 4, 1990)

This docket format is used for the large number of cases that have not been published when cited.

B. U.S. Court Decisions

I. U.S. District Courts.

Charlesworth v. Mack, 727 F. Supp. 1407 (D. Mass. 1990)

See how the basic components of the case citation do not change? The fundamental format is always similar, namely:

Parties, volume number Reporter and series abbreviation page (jurisdiction: court, state, district, etc. and date/year)

The only changes are the reporters cited, the court designations, and state or district abbreviations. When citing a U.S. District Court case, the reporter most frequently used is the *Federal Supplement* (F. Supp.) or the *Federal Supplement, Second Series* (F. Supp. 2d). Some specialty district court decisions are reported in the *Bankruptcy Reporter* or the *Federal Rules Service.* The most difficult part of citing a U.S. District Court case is citing the correct district: here it is the District (D.) of Massachusetts (Mass.). Chapter 1 noted that some states have one district and some have two, three, or four. These are the districts that are identified within the parentheses. A case decided in the District Court for the Middle District of Pennsylvania would have the abbreviation "M.D. Pa." in the parenthetical;"S.D.N.Y." stands for the Southern District of New York. Figure 3.1 lists the standard abbreviations for states, courts, and districts.

II. U.S. Court of Appeals.

Kubrick v. United States, 581 F.2d 1092 (3d Cir. 1978)

U.S. Appellate Court decisions will always be cited to the *Federal Reporter* unless the decision has not yet been published. A circuit number must also be noted in the parentheses, because it is not clear from the name of the reporter which court decided the case.

III. U.S. Supreme Court Decisions. The same basic rules of citation hold for Supreme Court decisions, except that it is normal (though not necessary) practice for a U.S. Supreme Court decision to be cited to all three reporters covering the Supreme Court. When citing to all three reporters, the citation would appear as follows:

Slimy v. United States, 825 U.S. 4, 19 S. Ct. 1099, 29 L. Ed. 2d 306 (1984)

A court designation is not included in the parenthetical information at the end of the citation because it is clear from the reporter name that the case cited is a U.S. Supreme Court case. The only time a U.S. Supreme Court reference is included in the parentheses is when the decision has not yet been published in any of the three reporters and it is necessary to cite using a docket number:

Charlesworth v. Mack, No. 92-212 (U.S. Feb. 4, 1992)

Courts / Districts		FIGURE 3.1
Appeals/Appellate Court	App. Ct.	
Bankruptcy	Bankr.	
Central District	C.D.	
Circuit Court (state)	Cir. Ct.	
Circuit Court of Appeals (federal)	Cir.	
Circuit Court of Appeals (state)	Cir. Ct. App.	
Common Pleas	C.P.	
Commonwealth Court	Commw. Ct.	
Court	Ct.	
Court of Appeals (federal)	Cir.	
Court of Appeals (state)	Ct. App.	
District	D.	
District Court (federal)	D.	
District Court (state)	Dist. Ct.	
District Court of Appeals	Distr. Ct. App.	
Division	Div.	
Eastern District	E.D.	
Family Court	Fam. Ct.	
Middle Court	M.D.	
Municipal Court	[name] Mun. Ct.	
Northern District	N.D.	
Probate Court	Prob. Ct.	
Public Utilities Commission	P.U.C.	
Southern District	S.D.	
Superior Court	Super. Ct.	
Supreme Court (federal)	U.S.	
Supreme Court (other)	Sup. Ct.	
Supreme Court Appellate Division	App. Div.	
Western District	W.D.	

States			
Alabama	Ala.	District of Columbia	D.C.
Alaska	Alaska	Florida	Fla.
Arizona	Ariz.	Georgia	Ga.
Arkansas	Ark.	Hawaii	Haw.
California	Cal.	Idaho	Idaho
Colorado	Colo.	Illinois	Ill.
Connecticut	Conn.	Indiana	Ind.
Delaware	Del.	Iowa	Iowa

continued

FIGURE 3.1
continued

States (continued)			
Kansas	Kan.	North Carolina	N.C.
Kentucky	Ky.	North Dakota	N.D.
Louisiana	La.	Ohio	Ohio
Maine	Me.	Oklahoma	Okla.
Maryland	Md.	Oregon	OR
Massachusetts	Mass.	Pennsylvania	Pa.
Michigan	Mich.	Rhode Island	R.I.
Minnesota	Minn.	South Carolina	S.C.
Mississippi	Miss.	South Dakota	S.D.
Missouri	Mo.	Tennessee	Tenn.
Montana	Mont.	Utah	Utah
Nebraska	Neb.	Vermont	Vt.
Nevada	Nev.	Virginia	Va.
New Hampshire	N.H.	Washington	Wash.
New Jersey	N.J.	West Virginia	W.Va.
New Mexico	N.M.	Wisconsin	Wis.
New York	N.Y.	Wyoming	Wyo.

Reporters	
US Supreme Court	
United States Reports	U.S.
Supreme Court Reporter	S. Ct.
United States Supreme Court Reports, Lawyers, Edition	L.Ed.2d

U.S. Court of Appeals	
Federal Reporter	F., F.2d, F.3d

U.S. District Courts	
Federal Supplement	F.Supp., F.Supp.2d

Regional Reporters	
Atlantic Reporter	A., A.2d
North Eastern Reporter	N.E., N.E.2d
North Western Reporter	N.W., N.W.2d
Pacific Reporter	P., P.2d, P.3d
South Eastern Reporter	S.E., S.E.2d
South Western Reporter	S.W., S.W.2d
Southern Reporter	So., So.2d

II. STATUTORY COMPILATIONS

A. Constitutions

References to constitutional provisions are common in appellate briefs and other written legal arguments. The format is straightforward.

U.S. CONST. art. II, § 12, cl. 3

Dates are not included when citing constitutional provisions that are currently in force. If the provision cited has been repealed, amended, or superseded, indicate parenthetically what action was taken and the year it was taken.

U.S. CONST. amend. XVIII (repealed 1933)

B. Federal Statutes

Citations to federal statutes are generally uniform, though caution must be expressed concerning official or nonofficial state codifications with annotations. Consult the appropriate reference for the abbreviations it uses. The following is the standard pattern:

21 U.S.C. § 841 (1970) [title number, code name, section number (year)]

If citing a "popular name" or official name of a statute, the formula is as follows:

National Environmental Policy Act of 1969, § 102, 42 U.S.C. § 4332 (1994)

When citing to unofficial codes—either the *United States Code Annotated* (U.S.C.A.) or the *United States Code Service* (U.S.C.S.)—the following formats are used:

12 U.S.C.A. § 1426 (West Supp. 1991)

12 U.S.C.S. § 1710 (Law. Co-op. 1978 & Supp. 1990)

These add the publisher identification to the parenthetical material.

C. State Statutes

Because of variations in the organization of state statutes, proper citation of state codes and statutes can be a confusing endeavor. The major confusion arises from the varied organization of titles, chapters, and sections. These are two basic formats for citing state statutes. The first is identical to the federal format.

5 Ill. Comp. Stat. 70/4 (2003)
or
5 Ill. Comp. Stat. Ann. 70/4 (West 2003)

The second, and more popular, format places the official name of the code first.

Neb. Rev. Stat. § 33–114 (1989)
Vt. Stat. Ann. tit.12, § 3087 (1973 & Supp. 1990)

In the Nebraska Revised Statutes example, *33* indicates the chapter number and *114* is the section number. The Vermont example contains the same information as the Illinois examples, but the information is given in a different order. As always, if you cite an unofficial version, you must note that fact parenthetically, as well as published supplements applicable to the cited section. See Figure 3.2 for a representative citation from each state. (*Note:* Strict *Bluebook* form often requires identification of the code publisher in the parenthetical material, though this is often omitted in practice. Many states have "official" code compilations [though these are usually produced and printed under contract by private publishing companies]; some have competing unofficial versions that are privately produced and published. The latter very often include many additional features that are not technically part of the code, but may be extremely useful to the researcher. Regardless of the version, the statutory texts and numbering will be identical.)

III. LAW REVIEWS/PERIODICALS

Those familiar with traditional academic citation styles for periodicals must be thoroughly reeducated in legal citation. Other than citation format, a second difference emerges: consecutive and nonconsecutively paginated journals. Although it sounds quite confusing, the distinction is rather simple.

A. Consecutively Paginated Journals

Consecutively paginated journals are those that start at page 1 and continue using consecutive page numbers until the next volume is begun. Normally, scholarly law journals annually publish four issues. For example, volume 10, issue 1, begins with page 1 and ends at page 258. Volume 10, issue 2, which is published three months later, starts at page 259 and ends with page 514. Consecutive pagination simply means that pages are consecutively numbered throughout the entire volume, regardless of the published issue.

Consider this example of a periodical citation:

John Gibeaut,[1] *Getting Tough on Substance Abusers*[2], 83[3] A.B.A.J.[4] 62[5], 65[6] (1997)[7]

1. Author
2. Name of article, usually in italics
3. Volume number of journal
4. Journal or review name, abbreviated (*Note:* Strict *Bluebook* style mandates the use of large and small capitals for this item. Again, this prescription is largely ignored in practice.)
5. Page number
6. Pinpoint page number
7. Year of publication

The first major difference between this method of citation and other methods is the manner in which the author's name is cited. The order is always "first name last name," contrary to the reversed order used by most citation methods. The second difference is the way the journal information is cited. Volume number always precedes the abbreviation of the journal name, followed by the first page of the article, and then by the pinpoint page number (if any).

FIGURE 3.2
Sample state code citations.

State	Citation
Alabama	Ala. Code § x-x-x (year). Ala. Code § 21-3A-6 (1975).
Alaska	Alaska Stat. § x.x.x (year). Alaska Stat. § 04.06.010 (2001).
Arizona	Ariz. Rev. Stat. § x-x (year). Ariz. Rev. Stat. § 17-101 (2001).
Arkansas	Ark. Code Ann. § x-x-x (year). Ark. Code Ann. § 26-51-201 (2001).
California	Cal. [subject] Code § x (West year). Cal. Bus. & Prof. Code § 2050 (West 2001).
Colorado	Colo. Rev. Stat. § x-x-x (year). Colo. Rev. Stat. § 4-4-107 (2001).
Connecticut	Conn. Gen. Stat. § x-x (year). Conn. Gen. Stat. § 52-190 (2001).
Delaware	Del. Code Ann. tit. x, § x (year). Del. Code Ann. tit. 13, § 904 (2001).
District of Columbia	D.C. Code Ann. § x-x (year). D.C. Code Ann. § 13-302 (2001).
Florida	Fla. Stat. ch. x.x (year). Fla. Stat. ch.112.312 (2002).
Georgia	Ga. Code Ann. § x-x-x (year). Ga. Code Ann. § 30-3-5 (2001).
Hawaii	Haw. Rev. Stat. § x-x (year). Haw. Rev. Stat. § 350C-5 (2001).
Idaho	Idaho Code § x-x (year). Idaho Code § 11-206 (2001).
Illinois	x Ill. Comp. Stat. x/x (year). 425 Ill. Comp. Stat. 50/5 (2001).
Indiana	Ind. Code § x-x-x-x (year). Ind. Code § 10-7-5-1 (2001).
Iowa	Iowa Code § x.x (year). Iowa Code § 709.3 (2001).
Kansas	Kan. Stat. Ann. § x-x (year). Kan. Stat. Ann. § 20-302 (2001).
Kentucky	Ky. Rev. Stat. Ann. § x.x (year). Ky. Rev. Stat. Ann. § 23A.050 (2001).
Louisiana	La. Rev. Stat. Ann. § x:x (year). La. Rev. Stat. Ann. § 2:2.1 (2001).
Maine	Me. Rev. Stat. Ann. tit. x, § x (year). Me. Rev. Stat. Ann. tit. 4, § 559 (2001).

continued

FIGURE 3.2
continued

Maryland	Md. Code Ann., [subject] § x-x (year). Md. Code Ann., Bus. Reg. § 1-202 (2001).
Massachusetts	Mass. Gen. Laws ch. X, § x (year). Mass. Gen. Laws ch. 267, § 5 (2001).
Michigan	Mich. Comp. Laws § x.x (year). Mich. Comp. Laws § 3.111 (2001).
Minnesota	Minn. Stat. § x.x (year). Minn. Stat. § 84.0274 (2001).
Mississippi	Miss. Code Ann. § x-x-x (year). Miss. Code Ann. § 47-5-545 (2001).
Missouri	Mo. Rev. Stat. § x.x (year). Mo. Rev. Stat. § 313.280 (2001).
Montana	Mont. Code Ann. § x-x-x (2001). Mont. Code Ann. § 16-2-201 (2001).
Nebraska	Neb. Rev. Stat. § x-x (year). Neb. Rev. Stat. § 12-606 (2002).
Nevada	Nev. Rev. Stat. § x.x (year). Nev. Rev. Stat. § 199.220 (2001).
New Hampshire	N.H. Rev. Stat. Ann. § x-x:x (year). N.H. Rev. Stat. Ann. § 188-E:1 (2002).
New Jersey	N.J. Stat. Ann. § x:x-x (year). N.J. Stat. Ann. § 36:2-10 (2002).
New Mexico	N.M. Stat. Ann. § x-x-x (year). N.M. Stat. Ann. § 29-3-8 (2001).
New York	N.Y. [subject] Law § x (year). N.Y. Educ. Law § 6805 (2002).
North Carolina	N.C. Gen. Stat. § x-x (year). N.C. Gen. Stat. § 67-29 (2001).
North Dakota	N.D. Cent. Code § x-x-x (year). N.D. Cent. Code § 28-05-08 (2002).
Ohio	Ohio Rev. Code Ann. § x.x (Anderson year). Ohio Rev. Code Ann. § 2309.59 (Anderson 2002).
Oklahoma	Okla. Stat. tit. x, § x (year). Okla. Stat. tit. 10, § 76.1 (2002).
Oregon	Or. Rev. Stat. § x.x (year). Or. Rev. Stat. § 163.245 (2001).
Pennsylvania	X Pa Cons. Stat. § x (year). 42 Pa. Cons. Stat. § 4523 (2002).
Rhode Island	R.I. Gen. Laws § x-x-x (year). R.I. Gen. Laws § 15-9-2 (2001).

FIGURE 3.2 *continued*

South Carolina	S.C. Code Ann. § x-x-x (year). S.C. Code Ann. § 19-5990 (2001).
South Dakota	S.D. Codified Laws § x-x-x (year). S.D. Codified Laws § 27A-3-1.1 (year).
Tennessee	Tenn. Code Ann. § x-x-x (year). Tenn. Code Ann. § 23-1-103 (2001).
Texas	Tex. [subject] Code Ann. § x.x (year). Tex. Penal Code Ann. § 33.02 (2002).
Utah	Utah Code Ann. § x-x-x (year). Utah Code Ann. § 39-4-6 (2002).
Vermont	Vt. Stat. Ann. tit. x, § x (year). Vt. Stat. Ann. tit. 13, § 4944 (2001).
Virginia	Va. Code Ann. § x-x (year). Va. Code Ann. § 4.1-507 (2002).
Washington	Wash. Rev. Code § x.x.x (year). Wash. Rev. Code § 4.12.030 (2002).
West Virginia	W.Va. Code § x-x-x. W.Va. Code § 15-2B-6.
Wisconsin	Wis. Stat. § x.x (year). Wis. Stat. § 40.62 (2001).
Wyoming	Wyo. Stat. Ann. § x-x-x (year). Wyo. Stat. Ann. § 5-4-202 (2002).

B. Nonconsecutively Paginated Journals

In nonconsecutive journals, pagination restarts with each issue of the publication. These types of publications are generally produced monthly or bimonthly. Most monthly magazines are included in this category and are cited differently than consecutively paginated journals.

Robert J. Samuelson, *A Slow Fix for the Banks,* NEWSWEEK, Feb. 18, 1991, at 55, 56

Newspaper articles are cited in the same basic manner:

Seth Mydans, *Los Angeles Police Chief Removed for 60 Days in Inquiry on Beating,* N.Y. TIMES, Apr. 5, 1991, at A1

IV. LAW TEXTBOOKS

Citation of a law book is a far cry from most academic footnote or reference methods. In most instances the publishing company is omitted, and the first and last name of the author are not reversed and separated by a comma. For law reviews, textbooks, and similar publications, *Bluebook* mandates that the author's name and title of the book be set in large and small capital letters:

JOHN C. KLOTTER, CRIMINAL LAW, 6th ed. (2001)

Many publishers do not follow this typographic convention, however.

V. SPECIAL CITATION FORMATS

A. Encyclopedias and Treatises

Many treatises and encyclopedias have set citation formats (see the following examples). The *Bluebook* or the introductory materials of the book itself will yield citation and abbreviation information.

88 C.J.S. *Trial* § 192 (1955)
WILLIAM PROSSER, TORTS 14 (3d ed. 1964)
2 WILLIAM BLACKSTONE, COMMENTARIES * 152
21 AM. JUR. 2D *Attorney and Client* § 38 (1968)

B. Dictionaries

When referencing dictionary pages, be sure to include the edition used. Here are two sample citations to popular legal dictionaries:

BALLENTINE'S LAW DICTIONARY 1190 (3d ed. 1969)
BLACK'S LAW DICTIONARY 712 (7th ed. 1999)

C. Internet Sources

When creating Internet citations, clearly indicate the source of the information. When citing cases, statutes, and other sources that appear online, and can also be found in print, follow the previous citation rules, and then include the URL (Uniform Resource Locator, the Web address) at the end of the citation.

Minnesota v. McArthur, No. C4-99-502 (Minn. Ct. App. Sept. 28, 1999), **http://www.courts.state.mn.us/library/archive/ctapun/9909/502.htm**

If no print version of the information is available, use "at":

J.T. Westermeler, *Ethical Issues for Lawyers on the Internet and World Wide Web,* 6 RICH. J.L. & TECH. 5, ¶ 7 (1999), at **http://www.richard.edu/jolt/v6i1/westerm eler.html**

When citing dated information, use either (1) the date on which the Web location was last modified, using the wording provided in the site; or (2) the date the Web location was last visited.

Randall R. Smith, *Jones on the Internet: Confusion and Confabulation,* CITATION FORUM, at **http://www.citations.org** (last visited Jan. 20, 2000)

Some Internet sources can be difficult to cite. Web sites that contain informational pages should be cited following the standard for books or periodicals. Always give as much information as possible, being sure to include the title of the Web site and the referenced page; any authors noted for the referenced page, if other than the Web site owner; the URL; and the date of the article, the date the site was last modified, or the date visited.

FBI, Community Outreach Program, *About the COP,* at **http://www.fbi.gov/hq/ood/opca/outreach/aboutcop.htm** (last visited Aug. 18, 2002)

MADD, *Victim Services and Information Page,* at **http://www.madd.org/victims** (last visited Aug. 18, 2002)

VI. SUMMARY

An essential key to unlocking the sometimes perplexing system of legal references is the citation method. Case citations use the fundamental format of Parties—Volume—Reporter & Series—Page—Date. There are slightly different formats for constitutions, federal and state statutes, law reviews, periodicals, and law textbooks. Review each of the citation diagrams given in this chapter, and refer often to the citation standard, the *Bluebook.* Once you gain a proper understanding of citation methods and formats, you will know how to find and cite invaluable reference sources.

VII. LEGAL RESEARCH ASSIGNMENTS

These assignments must be done using *The Bluebook: Uniform System of Citation,* 17th ed., published and distributed by the Harvard Law Review Association, Gannett House, Cambridge, MA 02138 (available at a minimal price at most law school bookstores or via the Web). If you have any trouble finding out where to get a copy, contact your local law librarian, your instructor, or any large bookstore specializing in research, law, or other related fields.

A. Exercise 3.1: Citation Formats

1. There is optional use of large and small capitals in law review footnotes.
   a. True
   b. False
2. To italicize means to put in capital letters.
   a. True
   b. False
3. Book titles, particularly those not in a series, are cited in all capital letters.
   a. True
   b. False
4. Constitutions are cited in all capital letters.
   a. True
   b. False
5. Newspapers do not have a basic citation form.
   a. True
   b. False

6. Various introductory signals in the text are used as a sort of code to highlight the case.
   a. True
   b. False
7. Abbreviations are frowned upon in legal research writing.
   a. True
   b. False
8. *Id.* *is* a short citation form.
   a. True
   b. False
9. Which of the titles are appropriate for a justice?
   a. Mr. Justice
   b. Mme. Justice
   c. Justice
   d. All of the above
10. *Hereinafter* means that the writer has decided not to use the material cited again.
    a. True
    b. False
11. The signal *accord* means that the authority cited is contradictory.
    a. True
    b. False
12. The signal *cf.* means that the authority cited is different but analogous.
    a. True
    b. False
13. The signal *see also* means that the authority cited provides background to a question analogous to that examined in the text.
    a. True
    b. False
14. The proper order for citing statutes according to jurisdiction is (1) state, (2) U.S., (3) foreign.
    a. True
    b. False
15. Which is the correct abbreviation for amendment?
    a. amd.
    b. amend.
16. Which is the correct abbreviation for chapter?
    a. ch.
    b. chap.
17. Which is the correct abbreviation for section?
    a. sec.
    b. §
    c. All of the above
18. Which is the correct abbreviation for volume?
    a. V.
    b. vol.
19. Which is the correct abbreviation for decision?
    a. dec.
    b. ds.

20. Which is the correct abbreviation for appendix?
    a. apdx.
    b. app.
21. As a general rule, the volume number of a series is put first in the citation.
    a. True
    b. False
22. In a case citation, the page number usually follows the reporter name or other identifier.
    a. True
    b. False
23. Groups of authorities and textual materials that are cross-referenced within an article or other work should be referred to as "id.," using quotation marks.
    a. True
    b. False
24. When an authority has been fully cited previously in the text (not the footnotes), the use of *supra* is proper.
    a. True
    b. False
25. Which is the correct citation form for a case that has been filed but not decided?
    a. *Floyd v. Floyd,* No. 39-8180 (E.D. Mich. filed Sept. 18, 1984)
    b. *Floyd v. Floyd,* 226 F.2d 191.
26. Select the correct citation form for a case disposed of on appeal.
    a. *Rooney v. Rooney,* 310 F. Supp. 110 (D. Mass. 1975), 1012 F.2d 1811.
    b. *Rooney v. Rooney,* 310 F. Supp. 110 (D. Mass. 1975), *aff'd,* 1012 F.2d 1811 (9th Cir. 1984).
27. The use of "Ex rel." in a case citation generally means
    a. For the use of
    b. On behalf of
    c. Exit
    d. Both a and b
28. Abbreviations are commonly used in case citations.
    a. True
    b. False
29. What is the correct abbreviation for National?
    a. Nat'l
    b. Nat.
30. What is the correct abbreviation for Public?
    a. P.
    b. Pub.
31. What is the correct abbreviation for Association?
    a. Assoc.
    b. Ass'n
32. What is the correct abbreviation for Civil Court of Record?
    a. Cir. Ct.
    b. Civ. Ct. Rec.
33. What is the correct abbreviation for Court of Claims?
    a. Ct. Cl.
    b. Cust. Ct.

34. What is the correct abbreviation for Board of Tax Appeals?
    a. BTA
    b. B.T.A.
35. What is the correct abbreviation for Magistrate's Court?
    a. M.C.
    b. Magis. Ct.
36. What is the correct abbreviation for Superior Court?
    a. Super. Ct.
    b. S. Ct.
37. What is the correct abbreviation for a state supreme court?
    a. S. Ct.
    b. Sup. Ct.
38. As a general rule, the year in a case citation is usually put in parentheses.
    a. True
    b. False
39. An example of a citation of codified law is
    a. 28 U.S.C.A. § 1981 (West Supp. 1933)
    b. N.Y. Trade Law § 1380 (McKinney 1931)
    c. 13 N.J. Stat. Ann. § 95 (West Supp. 1985)
    d. All of the above
40. When citing statutes, cite statutes of the official code first in order of preference.
    a. True
    b. False

B. Exercise 3.2: Citation Forms

Review the following citations and decide whether the style is correct or incorrect.

1. Uniform Commercial Code: U.C.C. § 9-108 (1972 version).
   a. Correct
   b. Incorrect
2. Internal Revenue Code: Int. Rev. Code of 1954, ch. 9 § 119d.
   a. Correct
   b. Incorrect
3. Federal Rules of Civil Procedure: Fed. R. Civ. P.
   a. Correct
   b. Incorrect
4. Congressional bill: S 4998, 87th Cong., 4th
   a. Correct
   b. Incorrect
5. What is the appropriate abbreviation for the Code of Federal Regulations?
   a. Code of F. Reg.
   b. C.F.R.
6. What is the appropriate abbreviation for an opinion delivered by the Attorney General?
   a. Att'y Gen.
   b. Op. Att'y Gen.

7. The abbreviation for annotated is
   a. ann.
   b. ant.
8. The abbreviation for editor is
   a. ed.
   b. edt.
9. Which is the correct citation for a restatement?
   a. RESTATEMENT (SECOND) OF AGENCY
   b. RESTATEMENT OF TORTS
10. In periodical citations, the volume number is last.
   a. True
   b. False
11. Periodical: Ronco, *Strict Liability and the Smokeless Phone,* 39 COLUM. L. REV. 9999 (1934)
   a. Correct
   b. Incorrect
12. Statute: ARK. STAT. ANN § 3941
   a. Correct
   b. Incorrect
13. How would a book be properly cited?
   a. By author, name of book, page, and year
   b. By name and page only
   c. By author, name, page, year, and publishing company
   d. By normal footnoting style
14. Which of the following would not use large and small capital letters in the citation?
   a. Foreign statutory code
   b. Treaties
   c. Books
   d. ABA Canons of Ethics
15. What is the proper citation to the American Law Reports?
   a. ALR
   b. Am. L. Rep.
   c. A.L.R.
   d. RAL
16. J. CRIM. L.C.E.P.S. is a correct abbreviation for the *Journal of Criminal Litigation, Criminal Theory and Public Sociology.*
   a. True
   b. False
17. REF. J. stands for the *Journal of National Conference of Referees in Bankruptcy.*
   a. True
   b. False
18. The abbreviation for sociology is
   a. Soc.
   b. Soc'y
19. Duke Law School cannot be abbreviated.
   a. True
   b. False

20. Syracuse Law School cannot be abbreviated.
    a. True
    b. False
21. Loose-leaf publications generally must be capitalized.
    a. True
    b. False
22. The *Bankruptcy Law Reporter* is cited as BNKR. L. REP. (CCH).
    a. True
    b. False
23. The *Federal Estate and Gift Tax Reporter* is cited as F. EST. E G. TX. REP. (CCH).
    a. True
    b. False
24. The *United States Law Week* is cited as USLAWW.
    a. True
    b. False
25. *Wills, Estates, Trusts* is cited as WILLS, EST, TR. (CCH).
    a. True
    b. False
26. The citation for the U.S. Supreme Ct. is U.S.L.W.
    a. True
    b. False
27. The citation abbreviation for *West's California Reporter* is Cal. Rptr.
    a. True
    b. False
28. The Colorado Court of Appeals 1912–1915 is Colo. App.
    a. True
    b. False
29. The Connecticut Circuit Court Reports is *C.C.R.C.*
    a. True
    b. False
30. The Illinois Appellate Reports from 1877 on is Ill. App. 3d.
    a. True
    b. False
31. The Indiana Statutes Annotated is IND. CODE ANN.
    a. True
    b. False
32. The Annotated Code of Maryland (1957) is MD. A. C.
    a. True
    b. False
33. The Massachusetts Reports 1861–1867 is, for example, *10 Mass (I Alien).*
    a. True
    b. False
34. The Massachusetts District Appellate Courts is Mass. A.D.
    a. True
    b. False

35. The New Jersey Reporter is N.J.L.
    a. True
    b. False
36. The New Jersey Statutes Annotated is N.J. REV. STAT.
    a. True
    b. False
37. The New York Supplement is N.Y.S. or N.Y.S.2d.
    a. True
    b. False
38. The New York Court of Chancery from 1845–1848 is Barb.Ch.
    a. True
    b. False
39. Many cases in New York prior to 1888 were reported in Abb. Pr.
    a. True
    b. False
40. The New York City Criminal Court Act (29a) is C. CRIM. CT. ACT.
    a. True
    b. False
41. The Ohio Court of Appeals is cited as Ohio St. 2d.
    a. True
    b. False
42. The citation D & C in Pennsylvania stands for the Superior Court.
    a. True
    b. False
43. Purdon's refers to the Pennsylvania Consolidated Statutes Annotated.
    a. True
    b. False
44. R.I. stands for Rhode Island.
    a. True
    b. False
45. Most eastern-state cases are published in the Atlantic Reporter, Second Series.
    a. True
    b. False
46. Tennessee cases, at the appellate level, are also published in the South Western Reporter series.
    a. True
    b. False
47. The citation for the Tennessee Code is TENN. CODE ANNOT.
    a. True
    b. False
48. Texas has numerous statutory compilations.
    a. True
    b. False
49. TEX. CODE ANN. includes art. X on Criminal Procedure.
    a. True
    b. False

50. V.I. stands for Virginia.
    a. True
    b. False
51. Supreme Court cases in Wisconsin from 1839–1852 are symbolized by the term PIN.
    a. True
    b. False
52. The State Court of Appeals abbreviation is County J.
    a. True
    b. False
53. North Dakota publishes administrative reports.
    a. True
    b. False
54. Oklahoma cases are also published in the Pacific Reporter system.
    a. True
    b. False
55. A full, proper citation requires a state case citation, a regional reporter citation, and the date.
    a. True
    b. False
56. A.S. CODE stands for *Alaska Statutes Annotated.*
    a. True
    b. False
57. Cal. App. Supp. refers to the California Supreme Court.
    a. True
    b. False
58. C. P. refers to Courts of Common Pleas.
    a. True
    b. False
59. Del. Cos. refers to *Delaware Chancery Reports.*
    a. True
    b. False
60. App. D.C. refers to appellate decisions of California.
    a. True
    b. False

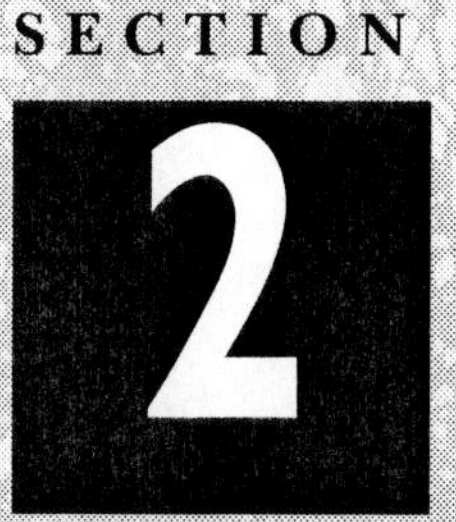

FINDING TOOLS

CHAPTER

4

The Index: The Most Powerful Tool in Legal Research

Finding tools are nothing more than the books, indexes, search engines, and digests that researchers use to find the primary and secondary resources they need. Effective use of these tools, especially indexes, will enable the researcher to find necessary information as efficiently as possible.

The index is the lifeblood of research, whether for making a cursory review of the legal encyclopedia *Corpus Juris Secundum,* or for collecting law review articles in a major research project. Simply put, the researcher cannot function productively without the index. Whether based on keywords or cases, statute or code, digest or legal compendium, the tactics of legal research inevitably include the index at some stage.

Most books have indexes, and law books are no exception. If anything, law books have highly sophisticated indexing systems, which provide the researcher with a variety of different approaches to any given problem. Indexes are the keys to the doors of knowledge. They focus ideas, topics, concepts, and themes, though they are far from self-directing. As a rule, indexes require the researcher to think conceptually and to focus on the issue by labeling or targeting the issue to be reviewed (e.g., *search and seizure, gag orders, insurance, impeachment,* and so on). The researcher's first conceptual identification is usually too broad, so it requires refinement and cognitive honing. Hence, *search and seizure* may be further reduced to *warrants—lack of; probable cause—lack of,* or *reasonable suspicion.* As noted earlier, the research process predictably begins with too large a horizon, and if successful sets its sights on the smaller picture. The index is the point of departure for the research journey.

Indexes serve and are designed for varying purposes and can be organized into the following categories:

1. Alphabetical topics
2. Descriptive words
3. Words and phrases
4. Names of plaintiffs or defendants
5. Case tables

Each of these major categories has an express purpose and direction.

I. MAJOR TYPES OF INDEXES

A. Subject/General Index

All law textbooks, hornbooks, treatises, Restatements, and so on provide a basic subject index. Even this text will deliver this useful tool to the researcher. Often a forgotten component of a work, readers shortchange their analyses by bypassing this remarkable tool. At its best, the index is a window to the content of the work. Never allow the research process to skip a review of the index.

Subject indexes usually provide just a topical overview of the book's content and presentation. The more complete, thorough, and exhaustive the index is, the better it will be for topical and subject-oriented research. In some resources, usually large multiple-volume series, a general index is included at the end of each subject volume. See Figure 4.1 for an example of a general index.

FIGURE 4.1

NEC

NECESSARIES—Cont'd
Wills, support and maintenance legacies, nature and extent, **Wills** § 1136

NECESSARY AND PROPER PARTIES
Worker's Compensation (this index)

NECESSARY DAMAGES
Definition. **Damag § 2**

NECESSARY HEIRS
Descent and distribution. **Des&Dist § 30**

NECESSARY PARTIES
Parties (this index)
Property tax refunds, **Tax § 949**
Venue, **Venue § 121**

NECK
Injury
damages, **Damag § 261**
whiplash injuries, **Damag § 272**

NECKLACES
Customs duties, **Cust Dut § 33, 45(4)**
Obscenity, admissibility of evidence, **Obscen § 25**

NE EXEAT—Cont'd
Discharge (this index)
Estates, executory interests in personal property. **Estates § 153-158**
Evidence. **Ne Ext § 14**
Federal Courts (this index)
Form, **Ne Ext § 17**
Husband and Wife (this index)
Intended departure, necessity of, **Ne Ext § 7**
Issuance, **Ne Ext § 11-17**
Judgments and decrees, **Ne Ext § 16**
Jurisdiction, **Ne Ext § 12**
Jurisdiction (this index)
Nonresidents (this index)
Orders of court, **Ne Ext § 16**
Other remedies distinguished, **Ne Ext § 4**
Persons against whom writ issued, **Ne Ext § 10**
Persons entitled to writ, **Ne Ext § 9**
Probable Cause (this index)
Purpose, **Ne Ext § 2**
Representatives (this index)
Requisites, **Ne Ext § 17**
Return of writ, **Ne Ext § 20**
Service of writ, **Ne Ext§ 18**
Statutory provisions, **Ne Ext § 5**

B. Topical Index

Topical indexes are provided in many texts and series. Examples of this type of indexing are most often seen in encyclopedias and digests, and are found at the beginning of each major subject. Frequently, a series with a large number of volumes will have both a general index and a topical index. Figure 4.2 shows an excerpt from the topical index from West's *Federal Practice Digest 4th*.

C. Descriptive Index

Another method of indexing is the descriptive method. Descriptive indexes provide insight into the typical places, objects, and things relevant to the party's action, as well as acts, defenses, and types of relief sought. These indexes are very similar to general indexes, but provide extra commentary on exactly what is included under that heading. The example in Figure 4.3 is from the *Federal Practice Digest 4th* series. Notice how phrases are included with the entries.

D. Words and Phrases Index

An example of the words and phrases index type is shown in Figure 4.4. This is an excellent resource for additional information on a given topic. These indexes are organized alphabetically and are exactly what they say—definitions, explanations, and analyses of legal subjects, objects, and actions. Each explanation references the court case that either legally defined a word or phrase or analyzed its content and legal applicability.

FIGURE 4.2

98 F P D 4th—497 **NOTARIES**

References are to Digest Topics and Key Numbers

NOMINATION—Cont'd
PRIMARY meeting, nomination by primary meeting. Elections 125
PROCESS in nomination contests. Elections 154(9¼)
PUBLICATION of lists of nominees. Elections 157
QUESTIONS for jury in nomination contests. Elections 154(11)
SUMMARY proceedings for review of acts of public officers in respect to nominations. Elections 154(4)
TEACHERS by district board. Schools 133.2
VACANCIES, nomination to fill. Elections 147
VENUE of nomination contests. Elections 154(8)
VOTES for persons not nominated. Elections 159
WITHDRAWAL of nominee. Elections 146

NON COMPOS FACTUM
MENTAL health, generally, see this index Mental Health

NON EST FACTUM
PLEA of, in action on—
Bills or notes. Bills & N 475
Evidence admissible under plea. Bills & N 489(4)

NON OBSTANTE VEREDICTO
See generally, this index Judgment Notwithstanding Verdict

NONRESIDENCE
See this index Domicile or Residence

NONSUIT
See this index Dismissal and Nonsuit

NONSUPPORT
See this index Support of Persons

NONUSER
CHARITABLE gift. Char 29
DEDICATED property. Dedi 63
EASEMENTS. Ease 30
FRANCHISE—
Corporate franchise as ground for dissolution. Corp 596
HIGHWAYS. High 79(2, 5)
PROPERTY acquired under power of eminent domain. Em Dom 323
STATUTE. Statut 173
STREETS. Mun Corp 657(3)
WATERS. Waters 48

NOON HOUR
WORKERS' compensation for injuries to servant. Work Comp 768

FIGURE 4.3

97 F P D 4th—415 **DEAD**

References Are to Digest Topics and Key Numbers

E. Plaintiff/Defendant/Case Table

Case tables (see Figure 4.5) can be invaluable when using a digest or encyclopedia, though to use them the researcher needs to know the parties' names and, in some instances, additional information. Listing cases covered in the volumes by plaintiff and defendant, plaintiff/defendant case tables reference volume or topic numbers, and even, depending on the series utilized, deliver explanatory information or case synopses. As noted in the Chapter 2 discussion of the known authority research method, this type of index helps lead the researcher from case to case.

F. Other Related Indexes

Solid legal researchers know that true knowledge has no bounds or, as they say, "The more you learn, the less you know." Do not disregard many of these superb indexing systems:

114 F P D 4th—441 **VEHICLES** **FIGURE 4.4**

VAUGHN *INDEXING*

N.D.Cal. 1991. "*Vaughn* indexing" is a procedure whereby agencies claiming that requested documents are exempt from release under the Freedom of Information Act (FOIA) must itemize and index for the court the documents and portions of documents which they seek to withhold, in order for the court to assess the applicability of each claimed exemption. 5 U.S.C.A. § 552.—Rosenfeld v. U.S. Dept. of Justice, 761 F.Supp. 1440, affirmed in part, reversed in part 57 F.3d 803, certiorari dismissed 116 S.Ct. 833, 516 U.S. 1103, 133 L.Ed.2d 832.—Records 62.

VAULT

D.Kan. 1996. In context of patent for vehicle mounted surveillance and videotaping system, term "vault" in claim disclosing "a vault for housing said video recorder" meant durable box-type steel container, that could be locked, and that was of a size capable of housing video recorder and being placed in the trunk of automobile.—P.A.T., Co. v. Ultrak, Inc., 948 F.Supp. 1506.—Pat 101(2).

VECTOR

D.Mass. 1996. "Vector," as referenced in patents for methods of inducing production of human proteins in nonhuman "host" cells through use of recombinant deoxyribonucleic acid (DNA), was DNA molecule capable of reproducing itself in host cell.—Biogen, Inc. v. Amgen, Inc., 913 F.Supp. 35.—Pat 14.

Abuse Prevention and Control Act of 1970, § 511(a)(4), 21 U.S.C.A. § 881(a)(4).—U.S. v. One 1989 Stratford Fairmont, 986 F.2d 177, rehearing denied.—Drugs & N 191.

C.A.5 (Tex.) 1994. Term "vehicle" was not ambiguous, as used in petition in personal injury action against insured by its employee and, therefore, did not give rise to such potential coverage under general business liability policy containing automobile exclusion as would oblige insurer, under Texas law, to defend insured; although insured claimed that "vehicle" could be interpreted to mean horse-drawn carriage, which was not excluded from coverage, allegations in employee's petition clearly indicated that the vehicle he was driving was an automobile.—Gulf States Ins. Co. v. Alamo Carriage Service, 22 F.3d 88, rehearing granted, on rehearing 22 F.3d 1095.—Insurance 2278(13).

D.Del. 1989. Trailers fall within definition of "vehicle" under Delaware law, and thus constitute "conveyances" subject to innocent owner defense to forfeiture. Comprehensive Drug Abuse Prevention and Control Act of 1970, § 511(a)(4)(C), 21 U.S.C.A. § 881(a)(4)(C); 21 Del.C. § 101(45, 48).—U.S. v. A Single Story Double Wide Trailer, 727 F.Supp. 149.—Forfeit 4.

D.Kan. 1996. For purposes of patent for vehicle mounted surveillance and videotaping system term "vehicle" would be interpreted to mean conveyance or transport including any type of public or private transportation; term would be given its ordinary and accustomed meaning, and was not limited to

Public Affairs Information Service

American Statistics Index

Legal Contents

Infotrac: Computer Based Legal Index

Index to Foreign Legal Periodicals

Ebsco Host (First Search) to Legal Articles

WEBSPIRS: Computerized Database for Criminal Justice

II. SUMMARY

Indexes provide an excellent starting point for the legal researcher to focus the legal issue more precisely as he or she works from big to small. A variety of indexes are available to the researcher: (1) subject indexes give the researcher a topical overview of the book's content and presentation; (2) topical indexes break down and index the law according to topic; (3) descriptive indexes break the law down even more minutely, providing relevant information on names and places, objects,

FIGURE 4.5

SINCLAIR 103C F P D 4th—38

See Guidelines for Arrangement at the beginning of this Volume

396 US 869, 24 Led2d 123, appeal after remand General Steel Products, Inc. v N L R B, 445 F2d 1350.—Labor 199, 201, 367, 384, 394, 557, 574, 615, 677.1

Sinclair-Ganos, In re, BkrtcyWDMich, 133 BR 382.—Bankr 2023, 3351.1.

Sinclair Global Brokerage Corp.; Hanline v., WDMo, 652 FSupp 1457, cause dism 815 F2d 713.—Const Law 305(5); Fed Cts 94, 96; RICO 44, 73.

Sinclair Intern.; Maxfield v., CA3 (Pa), 766 F2d 788, cert den 106 SCt 796, 474 US 1057, 88 L.Ed2d 773.—Civil R 170, 380, 388, 406.1, 407; Fed Civ Proc 2395.

Sinclair Oil Co.; U.S. v., DMont, 767 FSupp 200.—Fed Civ Proc 2543; Nav Wat 38.

Sinclair Oil Corp., Application of, DWyo, 881 FSupp 535.—Fed Civ Proc 1293; Stip 13, 14(1).

Sinclair Oil Corp. v. Amoco Production Co., CA10 (Utah), 982 F2d 437.—Deel Judgm 5.1; Fed Cts 573.

Sinclair Oil Corp. v. Atlantic Richfield Co., DUtah, 720 FSupp 894.—Lim of Act 58(1), 104(1), 104(2), 126.5; War 152.

Sinclair Oil Corp. v. County of Santa Barbara, CA9 (Cal), 96 F3d 401, cert den 118 SCt 1386, 523 US 1059, 140 LEd2d 646.—Const Law 278.2(1); Decl Judgm 319; Em Dom 2(1), 2(1.2), 69, 277, 293(1); Fed Cts 43, 46, 47.1, 65, 776; Zoning 30, 562.

Sinclair Oil Corp.; Dow Chemical Co. v., DWyo, 3 FSupp2d 1252.—Interest 39(2.20).

Sinclair Oil Corp. v. Dymon, Inc., DKan, 988 FSupp 1394.—Contrib 7; Fed Civ Proc 2737.5; Health & E 25 5(5.5)

S Industries, Inc. v. Diamond Multimedia Systems, Inc., NDI11, 17 FSupp2d 775.—Cons Prot 42; Trade Reg 61, 331, 408, 729.

S Industries, Inc. v. Diamond Multimedia Systems, Inc., NDI11, 991 FSupp 1012.—Trade Reg 61, 66.1, 67, 212, 254.1, 332, 363.1, 364, 366, 462, 543, 544, 729, 870(2).

S Industries, Inc. v. Hobbico, Inc., NDI11, 940 FSupp 210.—Monop 12(5); Trade Reg 261, 563.

S Industries, Inc. v. JL Audio, Inc., NDI11, 29 FSupp2d 878.—Trade Reg 10, 65, 254.1, 333, 334.1, 340.1, 350.1, 466, 578, 584.1, 596, 736.

S Industries, Inc. v. Stone Age Equipment, Inc., NDI11, 12 FSupp2d 796.—Trade Reg 27, 61, 64, 65, 66.1, 131, 251, 254.1, 331, 332, 334.1, 337, 340.1, 345.1, 361, 461, 464.1, 586, 704, 722, 729, 736.

Sine v. Local No. 992 Intern. Broth. of Teamsters, CA4 (Md), 882 F2d 913.—Fed Cts 893; Judges 49(1), 51(2), 51(3), 51(4).

Sine v. Local No. 992, Intern. Broth. of Teamsters, CA4 (Md), 790 F2d 1095, appeal after remand 882 F2d 913.—Fed Cts 668, 681.

Sine v. Local No. 992, Intern. Broth. of Teamsters, CA4 (Md), 730 F2d 964, on remand 603 FSupp 1264, vac 790 F2d 1095, appeal after remand 882 F2d 913.—Judgm 585(3), 715(1); Labor 751, 758.1, 760.

Sine v. Local No. 992 Intern. Broth. of Teamsters, CA4 (Md), 644 F2d 997, cert den 102 SCt 507, 454 US 965, 70 LEd2d 381, cert den Eastern Conference of Teamsters v. Sine, 102 SCt 507, 454 US 965, 70 LEd2d 381, appeal after remand 730 F2d 964, on remand 603 FSupp 1264,

and things; (4) words and phrases indexes define specific words and phrases and give appropriate case citations.

Although an index can be an excellent source of related issues and reference material, the researcher needs to focus on the "guts" of the legal issue. Resource tools are only as good as the thought you put into using them.

III. LEGAL RESEARCH ASSIGNMENTS

Remember that all legal research texts and materials have some type of indexing system, whether organized by words and phrases, topic, subject, or other descriptive format. Indexes are the key to each and every legal problem, so it makes no sense to attack any legal text without first mastering what is in its index. The following assignments give ample opportunity to review and analyze indexes.

A. Exercise 4.1: *Corpus Juris Secundum* General Index

1. Which section of the encyclopedia discusses the definition of impeachment?
   a. Volume 42
   b. Witn § 474
   c. Crim. L. § 917
   d. Volume 161
2. State impeachment can be found in which section(s) of the encyclopedia?
   a. States § 88
   b. States § 54
   c. States § 129
   d. All of the above
3. What type of person is not covered under the impeachment category?
   a. Ministers, rabbis, or priests
   b. Judges
   c. Guardians
   d. Witnesses
4. What other volumes or sections should be cross-referenced in the analysis of impeachment?
   a. Indem. § 14
   b. Gas § 42
   c. Marriage § 36
   d. Witn § 474
5. To study a case involving the requirements for process and proof of service, see
   a. Refer § 49
   b. Proc § 87
   c. Impediment 1072
   d. U.S. § 29
6. Which topic is not discussed in the section on states?
   a. journals
   b. state officers
   c. governor
   d. liability
7. Federal courts are indexed in the title index to federal civil procedure.
   a. True
   b. False
8. Impl&CC stands for *Impleader and Criminal Complaint.*
   a. True
   b. False
9. Broker is indexed in the title index to brokers.
   a. True
   b. False

EXERCISE 4.1

B. Exercise 4.2: *American Jurisprudence* General Index

1. Length of jury deliberation is found in Trials § 1648 only.
   a. True
   b. False
2. States § 38 stands for selection of officers.
   a. True
   b. False
3. States § 59 discusses the enactment of taxes at special legislative sessions.
   a. True
   b. False
4. To research a case involving the lending of money, look under
   a. Lead
   b. Bailments
   c. Insurance
   d. Loans
5. Federal tax enforcement can be found in the same index division as in question 4.
   a. True
   b. False

C. Exercise 4.3: Statutory Index: Pennsylvania Worker's Compensation

1. Which section covers the limit on physicians' and surgeons' fees?
   a. 77 P.S. § 2613
   b. 77 P.S. § 3604
   c. 77 P.S. § 999
   d. 77 P.S. § 832
2. A severe burn may qualify for a worker's compensation award.
   a. True
   b. False
3. Which section governs claims brought to the compensation board by the employee or his or her dependents?
   a. 77 P.S. § 751
   b. 77 P.S. § 2623
   c. both a and b
   d. neither a nor b
4. You would look at 77 P.S. § 565 to determine if professional athletes are covered by worker's compensation.
   a. True
   b. False
5. No provisions are made for appeal of cases.
   a. True
   b. False

EXERCISE 4.2

 For assistance using this index, call 1-800-328-4880

continued

GENERAL INDEX

continued

D. Exercise 4.4: U.S.C.A. General Index

1. Which title covers the crime of forgery?
   a. 53
   b. 18
   c. 30
   d. 50
2. Dismissal of a frivolous action is guided by Title 28 § 1919.
   a. True
   b. False
3. Forgery covers all but which of the following topics?
   a. Coins
   b. Revenue stamps
   c. Bank notes
   d. Artworks
4. *Forma pauperis* proceedings in the U.S. Supreme Court guidelines can be found in Title 28 § 672.
   a. True
   b. False

E. Exercise 4.5: Decennial Digest Descriptive Word Index

1. Using children to sell marijuana would be covered under what digest section(s)?
   a. Drugs & N 61
   b. Drugs & N 78
   c. Drugs & N 68.1
   d. None of the above
2. The topic of drug tests is digested at Search 7(7).
   a. True
   b. False
3. At Prisons 17.5, a digest case elaborates on the effects of an illegal search and seizure on a parolee.
   a. True
   b. False
4. Sentencing and punishment as they relate to restitution are discussed at Crim. Law 1208.4(2).
   a. True
   b. False
5. The sale of prescription drugs as an unlawful practice of medicine is discussed at.
   a. Drugs & N 30
   b. Drugs & N 61
   c. Phys 6(7)
   d. Drugs & N 29

EXERCISE 4.5

DREDGING

continued

DRUGS

continued

EXERCISE 4.5 *continued*

CHAPTER

5

THE DIGEST: A REMARKABLE FINDING TOOL

I. THE NATURE OF A DIGEST

A digest is a synthesizer, a vehicle in which very broad concepts are reduced to smaller, working parts. To digest is to get rid of the extraneous and zero in on the essential. How do digests serve the researcher?

Digests provide the researcher with a capsulation or summary of a case or decision. Whereas case reporters publish the whole text of a judicial opinion, the digest, by comparison, delivers an abbreviated perspective in the form of a **headnote**, or summary, of a specific point, fact, or related legal issue. Figure 5.1 shows a sample digest page.

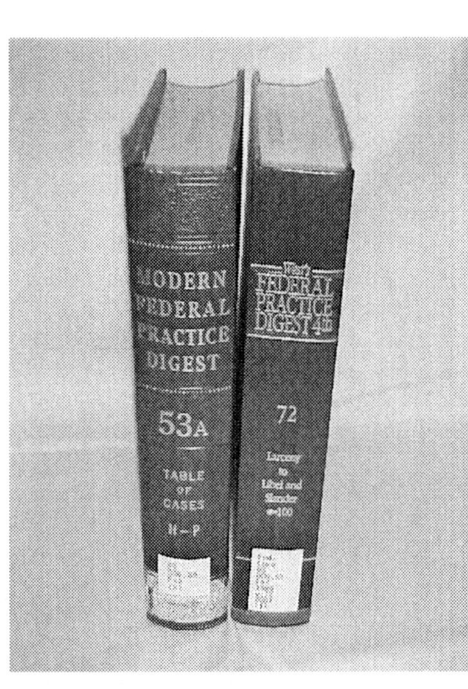

Each of the paragraphs listed at the beginning of the annotated version of a case is a headnote. Look at one of the paragraphs. First is the abbreviation of the court. On this page, C.A. stands for U.S. Court of Appeals (a circuit

FIGURE 5.1

77B F P D 4th—197 **NEGLIGENCE ⚿ 1076**

For references to other topics, see Descriptive-Word Index

express or implied invitation; his entry is connected with owner's business or with activity owner conducts or permits to be conducted on his land; and there is mutuality of benefit or benefit to owner.

Figueroa v. Evangelical Covenant Church, 879 F.2d 1427, rehearing denied.

C.A.7 (Ind.) 1993. Under Indiana negligence law, landowner owes duty to business invitee to exercise reasonable care to discover possibly dangerous conditions and to take reasonable precautions to protect the invitee.

Bafia v. Northern Indiana Public Service Co., 993 F.2d 1306.

C.A.7 (Ind.) 1990. Under Indiana law, business invitee is not entitled to higher standard of care than stranger; point of classification, rather, is that invitees are entitled to same standard of care as strangers, and hence to higher standard than social guests, other licensees and trespassers under Indiana law.

Justice v. CSX Transp., Inc., 908 F.2d 119, rehearing denied.

on its property, if store would anticipate hazards might cause injury.

Gearin v. Wal-Mart Stores, Inc., 53 F.3d 216.

C.A.5 (Miss.) 1998. Mississippi imposes on business owners the duty to maintain premises in reasonably secure or safe condition for business patrons or invitees; this duty includes protection of patrons from wrongful acts of third parties on the premises.

Whitehead v. Food Max of Mississippi, Inc., 163 F.3d 265.

Foreseeability of injury sustained is touchstone for liability of premises owner, under Mississippi law, for failure to maintain premises in reasonably secure or safe conditions for business patrons or invitees.

Whitehead v. Food Max of Mississippi, Inc., 163 F.3d 265.

C.A.5 (Miss.) 1994. Under Mississippi law, operator of business premises owes duty to invitee to exercise reasonable care to keep premises in reasonably safe condition, but operator is not insurer against all injuries that occur

court). Next is the state or district, then the year of the decision. The information following is a synopsis of the court's decision regarding one specific point of law. Last is the full citation of the case. Figure 5.2 demonstrates how key numbers in the West Key Number System correspond to specific subjects across West publications.

Digests have strong advantages in that a large database of case law can be screened for relevancy, assessed for historical influences on any given point of law, evaluated regarding the relative strengths or weaknesses of a legal argument or theory, and cross-referenced to other resources using the key or section number. Digests are one of the most often used finding tools for researchers in appellate practice because of their efficiency.

Digests build foundations for precedent or arguments of first instance. With so many cases available, arranged by pertinent topic, cross-referenced to other relevant topics, and showing historical and chronological information, one can discern why these texts are a favorite of skilled legal researchers.

II. ORGANIZATION OF THE DIGEST

The variety of digest series relates directly to the level of case-law reporting across the state and federal systems. Digests summarize one point of law of the case in question, in one sentence. Just as there are multiple reporting mechanisms, so too are there diverse digest tools. Hence, there is a digest series for each series of reporter, as well as specialty digests at the federal level. Figure 5.3 outlines the West Key Number Digests.

FIGURE 5.2

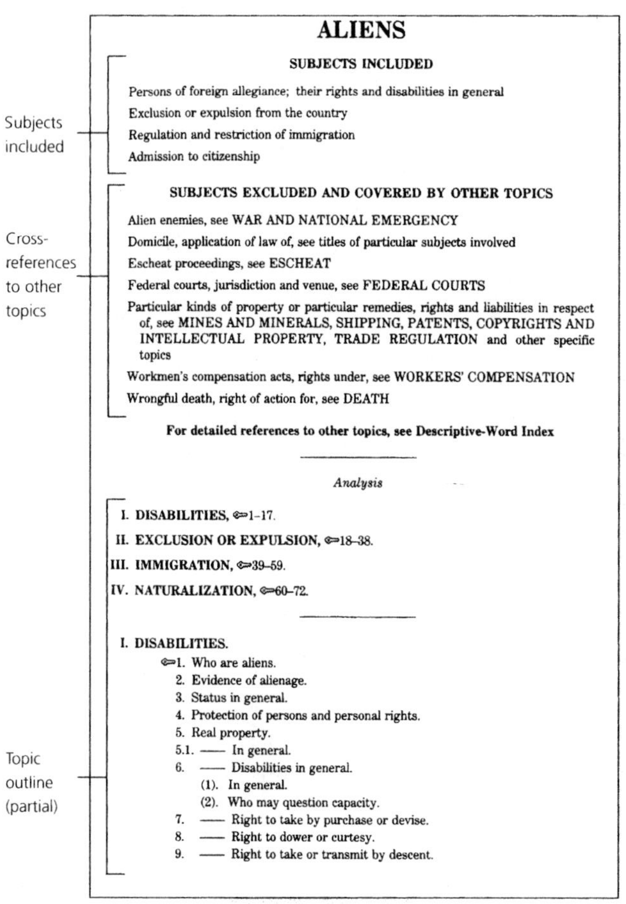

ALIENS

SUBJECTS INCLUDED

Persons of foreign allegiance; their rights and disabilities in general
Exclusion or expulsion from the country
Regulation and restriction of immigration
Admission to citizenship

SUBJECTS EXCLUDED AND COVERED BY OTHER TOPICS

Alien enemies, see WAR AND NATIONAL EMERGENCY
Domicile, application of law of, see titles of particular subjects involved
Escheat proceedings, see ESCHEAT
Federal courts, jurisdiction and venue, see FEDERAL COURTS
Particular kinds of property or particular remedies, rights and liabilities in respect of, see MINES AND MINERALS, SHIPPING, PATENTS, COPYRIGHTS AND INTELLECTUAL PROPERTY, TRADE REGULATION and other specific topics
Workmen's compensation acts, rights under, see WORKERS' COMPENSATION
Wrongful death, right of action for, see DEATH

For detailed references to other topics, see Descriptive-Word Index

Analysis

I. **DISABILITIES**, ⚿1–17.
II. **EXCLUSION OR EXPULSION**, ⚿18–38.
III. **IMMIGRATION**, ⚿39–59.
IV. **NATURALIZATION**, ⚿60–72.

I. **DISABILITIES.**
⚿1. Who are aliens.
2. Evidence of alienage.
3. Status in general.
4. Protection of persons and personal rights.
5. Real property.
5.1. —— In general.
6. —— Disabilities in general.
(1). In general.
(2). Who may question capacity.
7. —— Right to take by purchase or devise.
8. —— Right to dower or curtesy.
9. —— Right to take or transmit by descent.

Excerpt from *West's® Federal Practice Digest® 4th*

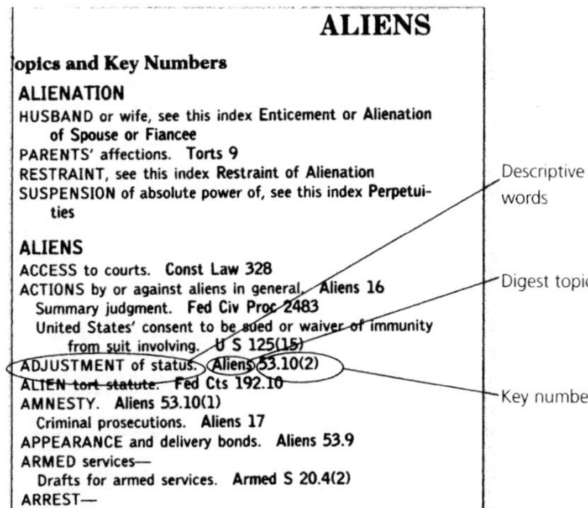

ALIENS

opics and Key Numbers

ALIENATION
HUSBAND or wife, see this index **Enticement or Alienation of Spouse or Fiancee**
PARENTS' affections. **Torts 9**
RESTRAINT, see this index **Restraint of Alienation**
SUSPENSION of absolute power of, see this index **Perpetuities**

ALIENS
ACCESS to courts. **Const Law 328**
ACTIONS by or against aliens in general. **Aliens 16**
Summary judgment. **Fed Civ Proc 2483**
United States' consent to be sued or waiver of immunity from suit involving. **U S 125(15)**
ADJUSTMENT of status. **Aliens 53.10(2)**
ALIEN tort statute. **Fed Cts 192.10**
AMNESTY. **Aliens 53.10(1)**
Criminal prosecutions. **Aliens 17**
APPEARANCE and delivery bonds. **Aliens 53.9**
ARMED services—
Drafts for armed services. **Armed S 20.4(2)**
ARREST—

Excerpt from Descriptive-Word Index to *West's Federal Practice Digest 4th*

continued

FIGURE 5.2
continued

Using West digest to find relevant case law

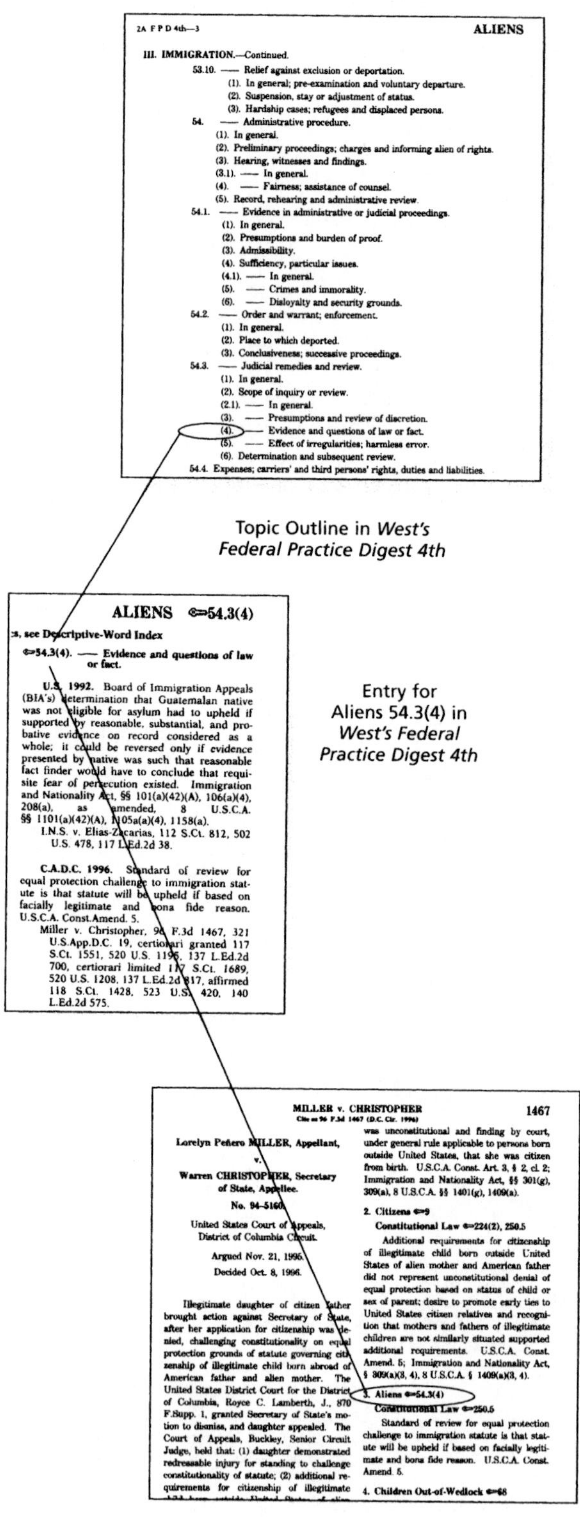

2A F P D 4th—3 **ALIENS**

III. IMMIGRATION.—Continued.

53.10. —— Relief against exclusion or deportation.
(1). In general; pre-examination and voluntary departure.
(2). Suspension, stay or adjustment of status.
(3). Hardship cases; refugees and displaced persons.
54. —— Administrative procedure.
(1). In general.
(2). Preliminary proceedings; charges and informing alien of rights.
(3). Hearing, witnesses and findings.
(3.1). —— In general.
(4). —— Fairness; assistance of counsel.
(5). Record, rehearing and administrative review.
54.1. —— Evidence in administrative or judicial proceedings.
(1). In general.
(2). Presumptions and burden of proof.
(3). Admissibility.
(4). Sufficiency, particular issues.
(4.1). —— In general.
(5). —— Crimes and immorality.
(6). —— Disloyalty and security grounds.
54.2. —— Order and warrant; enforcement.
(1). In general.
(2). Place to which deported.
(3). Conclusiveness; successive proceedings.
54.3. —— Judicial remedies and review.
(1). In general.
(2). Scope of inquiry or review.
(2.1). —— In general.
(3). —— Presumptions and review of discretion.
(4). —— Evidence and questions of law or fact.
(5). —— Effect of irregularities; harmless error.
(6). Determination and subsequent review.
54.4. Expenses; carriers' and third persons' rights, duties and liabilities.

Topic Outline in *West's Federal Practice Digest 4th*

ALIENS ⟹54.3(4)

s, see Descriptive-Word Index

⟹54.3(4). —— Evidence and questions of law or fact.

U.S. 1992. Board of Immigration Appeals (BIA's) determination that Guatemalan native was not eligible for asylum had to upheld if supported by reasonable, substantial, and probative evidence on record considered as a whole; it could be reversed only if evidence presented by native was such that reasonable fact finder would have to conclude that requisite fear of persecution existed. Immigration and Nationality Act, §§ 101(a)(42)(A), 106(a)(4), 208(a), as amended, 8 U.S.C.A. §§ 1101(a)(42)(A), 1105a(a)(4), 1158(a).
I.N.S. v. Elias-Zacarias, 112 S.Ct. 812, 502 U.S. 478, 117 L.Ed.2d 38.

C.A.D.C. 1996. Standard of review for equal protection challenge to immigration statute is that statute will be upheld if based on facially legitimate and bona fide reason. U.S.C.A. Const.Amend. 5.
Miller v. Christopher, 96 F.3d 1467, 321 U.S.App.D.C. 19, certiorari granted 117 S.Ct. 1551, 520 U.S. 1195, 137 L.Ed.2d 700, certiorari limited 117 S.Ct. 1689, 520 U.S. 1208, 137 L.Ed.2d 817, affirmed 118 S.Ct. 1428, 523 U.S. 420, 140 L.Ed.2d 575.

Entry for Aliens 54.3(4) in *West's Federal Practice Digest 4th*

MILLER v. CHRISTOPHER 1467
Cite as 96 F.3d 1467 (D.C. Cir. 1996)

Lorelyn Peñero MILLER, Appellant,
v.
Warren CHRISTOPHER, Secretary of State, Appellee.
No. 94-5160.
United States Court of Appeals, District of Columbia Circuit.
Argued Nov. 21, 1995.
Decided Oct. 8, 1996.

Illegitimate daughter of citizen father brought action against Secretary of State, after her application for citizenship was denied, challenging constitutionality on equal protection grounds of statute governing citizenship of illegitimate child born abroad of American father and alien mother. The United States District Court for the District of Columbia, Royce C. Lamberth, J., 870 F.Supp. 1, granted Secretary of State's motion to dismiss, and daughter appealed. The Court of Appeals, Buckley, Senior Circuit Judge, held that: (1) daughter demonstrated redressable injury for standing to challenge constitutionality of statute; (2) additional requirements for citizenship of illegitimate

was unconstitutional and finding by court, under general rule applicable to persons born outside United States, that she was citizen from birth. U.S.C.A. Const. Art. 3, § 2, cl. 2; Immigration and Nationality Act, §§ 301(g), 309(a), 8 U.S.C.A. §§ 1401(g), 1409(a).

2. Citizens ⟹9

Constitutional Law ⟹224(2), 250.5

Additional requirements for citizenship of illegitimate child born outside United States of alien mother and American father did not represent unconstitutional denial of equal protection based on status of child or sex of parent; desire to promote early ties to United States citizen relatives and recognition that mothers and fathers of illegitimate children are not similarly situated supported additional requirements. U.S.C.A. Const. Amend. 5; Immigration and Nationality Act, § 309(a)(3, 4), 8 U.S.C.A. § 1409(a)(3, 4).

3. Aliens ⟹54.3(4)

Constitutional Law ⟹250.5

Standard of review for equal protection challenge to immigration statute is that statute will be upheld if based on facially legitimate and bona fide reason. U.S.C.A. Const. Amend. 5.

4. Children Out-of-Wedlock ⟹68

Miller v. Christopher, 96 F.3d 1467 (D.C. Cir. 1996) in *West's Federal Reporter® 3d*

FIGURE 5.3

The West Key Number Digests

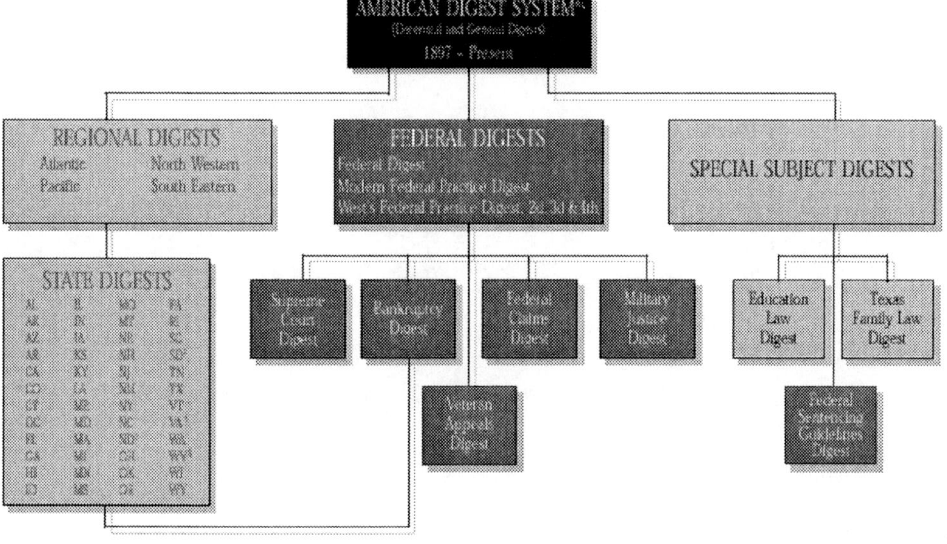

[1] The American Digest System also includes the *Century Digest*, which indexes cases from 1658–1896. The *Century Digest* does not contain key numbers.
[2] North and South Dakota are combined into one set called *Dakota Digest*.
[3] Virginia and West Virginia are combined into one set called *Virginia and West Virginia Digest*.

The broadest jurisdictional coverage available in the digest system comes from the American Digest Series, which includes the Century, Decennial, and General Digests. The Century Digest abstracts decisions from 1658 to 1896. The First Decennial Digest picks up from there, with a new series every 10 years (hence the name). Currently, Decennial Digests are published every five years, broken into Part 1 and Part 2, due to the large volume of cases going through the system today. Until cases are included in a Decennial Digest, new cases are digested in the General Digest. Multiple federal and state court decisions are summarized during certain chronological periods, as well as for specific geographical regions. The following list highlights this extensive coverage.

The American Digest Series *Case headnotes are provided for all reported decisions in the federal and state courts.*

1858–1896: Centennial Digest

1897–1905: 1st Decennial Digest

1905–1915: 2d Decennial Digest

1916–1925: 3d Decennial Digest

1926–1935: 4th Decennial Digest

1936–1945: 5th Decennial Digest

1946–1955: 6th Decennial Digest

1956–1965: 7th Decennial Digest

1966–1975: 8th Decennial Digest

1976–1981: 9th Decennial Digest, Part 1

1981–1986: 9th Decennial Digest, Part 2

1986–1991: 10th Decennial Digest, Part 1

1991–1996: 10th Decennial Digest, Part 2

Specific Courts *Case headnotes are provided for all reported decisions from each specific court only.*

U.S. Supreme Court Digest

Federal Digest

Modern Federal Practice Digest

West's Bankruptcy Digest

West's Federal Practice Digest, 4th

West's Military Justice Digest

U.S. Court of Claims Digest

Reporter Digests *Case headnotes are provided for all reported decisions in that reporter's coverage area.*

Atlantic

North Western

Pacific

South Eastern . . .

State Digests *Case headnotes are provided for all reported decisions in that state court system.*

Alabama Digest

Alaska Digest

Arizona Digest

Arkansas Digest

California Digest

Colorado Digest

Connecticut Digest

Dakota Digest

District of Columbia Digest

Florida Digest

Georgia Digest

Hawaii Digest

Idaho Digest

Illinois Digest

Indiana Digest

Iowa Digest . . .

The digest volumes themselves are like any legal series, organized topically by volume and then within each volume by section or key number. In the West system, topics are broken down into 414 key numbers. These key numbers (or section numbers in non-West publications) will lead to other cases, both at the state and federal level, that deal with the same point of law. For example, key number 82(3), First Amendment Guarantees, will always direct you to cases dealing with that subject.

Several additional helpful features included in the West system are a descriptive word index for topic searches, a chart of commonly used abbreviations of courts and publications, a table of cases with references to case history and corresponding topics and key numbers, a defendant-plaintiff table, an outline of the organization of the series according to the seven main divisions of law, and an alphabetical listing of all digest topics. In addition, each topic has its own descriptive word index, table of cases, defendant-plaintiff index, and words and phrases section. Digests also refer to specific sections of other resources. Commonly seen are references to legal encyclopedias, law review articles, desk books, and other practice aids. Digests also contain pocket parts, which should always be checked for up-to-date information.

Periodically, it is necessary for West to update the Key Number System. When this occurs, check the *Consolidated Table of Key Numbers* in the General Digest to confirm the key number. To convert the section numbers for cases listed in the Century Digest, you must consult the Table of Concordance located in volume 21 of the First Decennial. To convert Decennial section numbers to Century numbers, use the cross-references in the First and Second Decennial Digests. Figure 5.4 lists the topics in the West Key Number System.

FIGURE 5.4

Westlaw® Quick Reference Guide

The West Key Number System®

ALPHABETICAL LIST OF DIGEST TOPICS

Westlaw is available on the Web at www.westlaw.com.

For technical assistance, call West Customer Technical Support at 1-800-WESTLAW (1-800-937-8529).

For search assistance, call the West Reference Attorneys at 1-800-REF-ATTY (1-800-733-2889).

If you are a law student, call 1-800-850-WEST (1-800-850-9378) for assistance.

Westlaw.

continued

FIGURE 5.4
continued

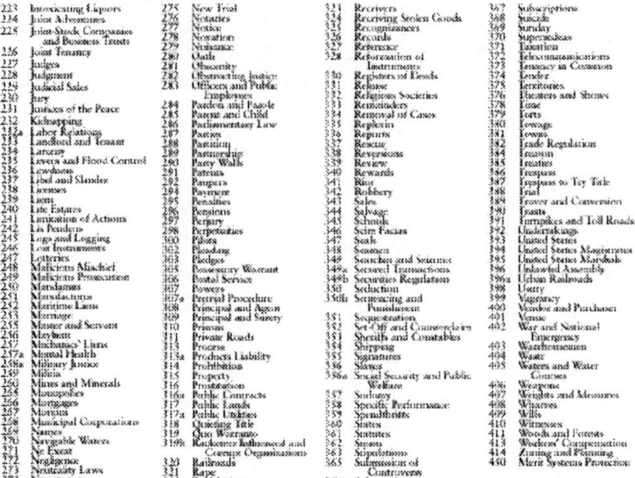

223 Intoxicating Liquors
224 Joint Adventures
225 Joint-Stock Companies and Business Trusts
226 Joint Tenancy
227 Judges
228 Judgment
229 Judicial Sales
230 Jury
231 Justices of the Peace
232 Kidnapping
232a Labor Relations
233 Landlord and Tenant
234 Larceny
235 Levees and Flood Control
236 Lewdness
237 Libel and Slander
238 Licenses
239 Liens
240 Life Estates
241 Limitation of Actions
242 Lis Pendens
245 Logs and Logging
246 Lost Instruments
247 Lotteries
248 Malicious Mischief
249 Malicious Prosecution
250 Mandamus
251 Manufactures
252 Maritime Liens
253 Marriage
255 Master and Servant
256 Mayhem
257 Mechanics' Liens
257a Mental Health
258a Military Justice
259 Militia
260 Mines and Minerals
265 Monopolies
266 Mortgages
267 Motions
268 Municipal Corporations
269 Names
270 Navigable Waters
271 Ne Exeat
272 Negligence
273 Neutrality Laws
274 Newspapers
275 New Trial
276 Notaries
277 Notice
278 Novation
279 Nuisance
280 Oath
281 Obscenity
282 Obstructing Justice
283 Officers and Public Employees
284 Pardon and Parole
285 Parent and Child
286 Parliamentary Law
287 Parties
288 Partition
289 Partnership
290 Party Walls
291 Patents
292 Paupers
294 Payment
295 Penalties
296 Pensions
297 Perjury
298 Perpetuities
300 Pilots
302 Pleading
303 Pledges
305 Possessory Warrant
306 Postal Service
307 Powers
307a Pretrial Procedure
308 Principal and Agent
309 Principal and Surety
310 Prisons
311 Private Roads
313 Process
313a Products Liability
314 Prohibition
315 Property
316 Prostitution
316a Public Contracts
317 Public Lands
317a Public Utilities
318 Quieting Title
319 Quo Warranto
319h Racketeer Influenced and Corrupt Organizations
320 Railroads
321 Rape
322 Real Actions
323 Receivers
324 Receiving Stolen Goods
325 Recognizances
326 Records
327 Reference
328 Reformation of Instruments
330 Registers of Deeds
331 Release
332 Religious Societies
333 Remainders
334 Removal of Cases
335 Replevin
336 Reports
337 Rescue
338 Reversions
339 Review
340 Rewards
341 Riot
342 Robbery
343 Sales
344 Salvage
345 Schools
346 Scire Facias
347 Seals
348 Seamen
349 Searches and Seizures
349a Secured Transactions
349b Securities Regulation
350 Seduction
350h Sentencing and Punishment
351 Sequestration
352 Set-Off and Counterclaim
353 Sheriffs and Constables
354 Shipping
355 Signatures
356 Slaves
356a Social Security and Public Welfare
357 Sodomy
358 Specific Performance
359 Spendthrifts
360 States
361 Statutes
362 Steam
363 Stipulations
365 Submission of Controversy
366 Subrogation
367 Subscriptions
368 Suicide
369 Sunday
370 Supersedeas
371 Taxation
372 Telecommunications
373 Tenancy in Common
374 Tender
375 Territories
376 Theaters and Shows
378 Time
379 Torts
380 Towage
381 Towns
382 Trade Regulation
384 Treason
385 Treaties
386 Trespass
387 Trespass to Try Title
388 Trial
389 Trover and Conversion
390 Trusts
391 Turnpikes and Toll Roads
392 Undertakings
393 United States
394 United States Magistrates
395 United States Marshals
396 Unlawful Assembly
396a Urban Railroads
398 Usury
399 Vagrancy
400 Vendor and Purchaser
401 Venue
402 War and National Emergency
403 Warehousemen
404 Waste
405 Waters and Water Courses
406 Weapons
407 Weights and Measures
408 Wharves
409 Wills
410 Witnesses
411 Woods and Forests
413 Workers' Compensation
414 Zoning and Planning
450 Merit Systems Protection

Topic field searching

On Westlaw, you can retrieve cases with headnotes classified under a specific West digest topic by using a topic field (to) restriction. In addition to the topic name and number, the topic field contains the hierarchical classification information, key number, and text of the related key line.

For example, to retrieve cases with headnotes classified under topic 409 (Wills), type to(409) or to(wills). The broader search is to(wills) because it retrieves cases in which the term *wills* is mentioned in the key line or other levels of the hierarchy, even if the headnotes are not classified under topic 409. To focus your search even more, you can add descriptive terms; for example, type to(409) /p "condition subsequent".

Topic and key number searching

When you use a topic and key number search, you do not need to use a field restriction. Simply type the topic number, the letter *k*, and the key number. For example, to retrieve cases with headnotes classified under topic 162 and key number 315.6(1), type 162k315.6(1). The elements of the search are as follows:

162 = West digest topic number for Executors and Administrators
k = West key number symbol
315.6(1) = West digest key number for Order or decree for distribution; Conclusiveness; In general.

To narrow your search, add search terms. For example, the query 343k255 /p privity retrieves cases with headnotes classified under topic 343 (Sales) and key number 255 (Parties) that also contain the term *privity* in the same digest paragraph.

To broaden your search, use a number from an upper level of the digest classification hierarchy. For example, the query 409vi retrieves all cases containing headnotes classified under 409VI, which includes lower levels such as 409VI(D) and 409k438. The digest classification hierarchy is displayed on Westlaw above each headnote.

You can also use the Custom Digest and KeySearch® to find topic and key numbers to use in a search. The Custom Digest contains the complete, current West topic and key number outline. To access the Custom Digest, choose **Key Numbers & Digest** from the *More* drop-down list. KeySearch is a tool powered by the West Key Number System that identifies key numbers and terms related to your legal issue and creates a query for you. KeySearch retrieves documents that contain key numbers, such as cases with West headnotes, as well as documents that don't contain key numbers, such as law reviews and cases without West headnotes. To access KeySearch, click **KeySearch** on the toolbar. Browse the list of topics and subtopics in the right frame by clicking the **Browse** icons. You can also scan the list of topics and subtopics for specific terms by typing the terms in the text box in the left frame and clicking GO.

III. USING A DIGEST

The digest system literally covers every topic in law across federal and state jurisdictions. Figure 5.5 shows a very small sample to illustrate the range of topics analyzed.

Because these categories are essentially major index headings, the researcher will have to engage in the usual deductive and inferential reasoning to refine the subject matter. There are times when a search of your state or regional digest will yield no results—but that only means there are no cases dealing with that topic of law in your jurisdiction. In this event, first check the pocket part to be sure there are no new cases, then check the Decennial Digest or a digest of a broader jurisdiction under the appropriate topic and key number.

Three methods of digest research are commonly used.

A. Case Name

Digest series have tables of cases, which alphabetically list cases decided in that jurisdiction, with references to topics and key numbers. If the researcher already knows of an applicable case, the table of cases is an efficient finding tool. First find the case name in the table of cases to locate the correct topic and key number for

FIGURE 5.5

FIGURE 5.6

SPANG 77 Pa D 2d—342

See Guidelines for Arrangement at the beginning of this Volume

Spang and Co.; Grecco v., WDPa, 566 FSupp 413, aff 787 F2d 582.—Civil R 381, 407.

Spang & Co.; Grecco v., WDPa, 530 FSupp 782.—Civil R 388; Fed Civ Proc 2142, 2497.1; Witn 275(2).

Spang and Co.; Grecco v., WDPa, 527 FSupp 987, opinion am 530 FSupp 782, aff 779, F2d 42, cert den 106 SCt 1246, 475 US 1036, 89 LEd2d 354, aff Appeal of Spang & Co, 779 F2d 44, cert den 106 SCt 1246, 475 US 1036, 89 LEd2d 354.—Civil R 375, 377.1, 378, 388, 389.

Spang & Co.; Marshall v., WDPa, 321 FSupp 1310.—Corp 214; Fed Civ Proc 2732.1.

Spang & Co. v. Reed, Smith, Shaw & McClay, PaComPl, 37 D & C4th 452.—Lim of Act 55(3).

Spang & Co. v. U.S. Steel Corp., Pa, 545 A2d 861, 519 Pa 14, appeal after remand 599 A2d 978, 410 PaSuper 254, appeal den 611 A2d 712, 531 Pa 640.—App & E 977(3); Contracts 348; Damag 189; New Tr 6, 75(3).

Spang & Co., v. U.S. Steel Corp., PaSuper, 518 A2d 273, 358 PaSuper 543, appeal gr 532 A2d 1137, 516 Pa 630, rev 545 A2d 861, 519 Pa 14, appeal after remand 599 A2d 978, 410 PaSuper 254, appeal den 611 A2d 712, 531 Pa 640.—New Tr 7.

Spang & Co. v. USX Corp., PaSuper, 599 A2d 978, 410 PaSuper 254, appeal den 611 A2d 712, 531 Pa 640.—App & E 110, 854(6), 867(2), 1096(3), 1097(1), 1195(1); Damag 189; Interest 39(2.30), 60.

Spang Crest Home v. Com., Dept. of Public Welfare, PaCmwlth, 538 A2d 87, 113 PaCmwlth 563.—Admin Law 413; Social S 241.91.

Spangenberg; Com., Dept. of Transp., Bureau of Traffic Safety v., PaCmwlth, 519 A2d 1118, 103 PaCmwlth 223.—Schools 159.5(6).

Spangler v. Danko, Pa, 49 A2d 378, 355 Pa 199.—New Tr 68.4(6).

Spangler v. Fiss, PaComPl, 49 D & C 366, 54 Dauph 288.—Const Law 52, 58, 70.1(1), 72, 77, 79; Mand 28; States 30.

Spangler v. Helm's Motor Exp., PaComPl, 7 Lebanon 111, rev 153 A2d 490, 396 Pa 482.—App & E 1004(5); Death 86(1).

Spangler v. Helm's New York-Pittsburgh Motor Exp., Pa, 153, A2d 490, 396 Pa 482.—App & E 977(3); Damag 6, 15, 127; Death 77, 87, 88, 95(1), 99(4); New Tr 13.

Spangler v. Kramer, PaComPl, 84 York 154.—Covenants 53, 111.

Spangler v. Latrobe Road Const., Inc., PaComPl, 22 Cambria CR 49.—Neglig 1513(1); Plead 243.

Spangler v. McCleary, PaComPl, 8 Adams LJ 96.—Judgm 135, 139, 143(10), 153(1), 163.

Spangler; Real Resources, Inc. v., PaComPl, 62 D & C2d 630, 86 York 192, 87 York 71.—Zoning 358, 581.

Spangler; Showers v., CA3 (Pa), 182 F3d 165.—Civil R 214(2), 214(6); Game 10; Searches 24, 79.

Spangler; Showers v., MDPa, 957 FSupp 584, aff in part, rev in part 182 F3d 165.—Admin Law 390.1; Civil R 132.1, 214(1), 214(2), 214(3), 214(6); Fed Civ Proc 2491.5, 2554; Fish 16; Game 10; Searches 12, 26, 79.

Spangler v. Spangler, PaComPl, 12 D & C3d 290.—Divorce 85, 172.

Spangler; Spangler v., PaComPl, 12 D & C3d 290.—Divorce 85, 172.

Spangler; U.S. v., CA3 (Pa), 838 F2d 85, cert den Mairone v. US, 108 SCt 2018, 486 US 1033, 100 LEd2d 605, cert den 108 SCt 2884, 487 US 1224. 101 LEd2d 918.—Crim

the subject matter. Then locate the corresponding digest volume; you can find the known case, as well as other cases dealing with the topic, in the digest volumes using the applicable key number. Cases with similar legal issues will be included in the same section. This is the purpose of key numbers: they are assigned to cases with similar issues for ease of organization, identification, and location. Look at Figure 5.6, an example of a case name index/table that gives not only the case citation but also the appropriate reference numbers within the digest system. Pay close attention to the topical abbreviation, as these can sometimes be confusing. If you are unsure what volumes the abbreviations point to, find the abbreviation in the table located in the beginning of each digest volume. For example, to find the correct digest volume and section for a reference to "Judgm 253(1)," first find the volume labeled "Judgments." Then locate section 253(1).

FIGURE 5.7

INTERVENING cause—
Injuries from operation or use of highways. **Autos 201(9)**
Questions for jury as to proximate cause of injury. **Autos 245(65)**
INTOXICATING liquors, see this index **Intoxicating Liquors**
INVITEES, ability of private owner or operator for injuries to. **Autos 181(2)**
JAYWALKING. **Autos 160(4)**
JOINT adventures, see this index **Joint Adventures**
JOINT and several liability, see this index **Joint and Several Liabilities**
JOINT enterprise—
University and religious organization—
Reimbursement for cost of van. **Autos 197(1)**
JOINT owners, see this index **Joint Owners or Ownership**
JUDGMENT—
Injuries from—
Defects of obstructions in highway. **Autos 311**
Operation, or use of highway. **Autos 248**
Notwithstanding verdict, evidence. **Judgm 199(3.17)**
Prosecution for offenses. **Autos 359**
State court judgment, persons concluded by in Federal courts. **Judgm 828(3.27)**
JURISDICTION—
Injuries from—
Defects or obstructions in highway. **Autos 295**
Operation or use of highways. **Autos 232**
Offenses. **Autos 350**
JUSTIFICATION of homicide in operation. **Autos 346**
KEY in ignition, precaution against starting. **Autos 173(8)**
KNOWLEDGE—
Contributory negligence of one having knowledge of danger or peril. **Autos 205, 227(4), 285**
Element of offense. **Autos 319**
Evidence of knowledge of defects in vehicles. **Autos 243(6)**

Concurrent and conflicting regulations. **Autos 134**
Constitutional and statutory provisions. **Autos 13**
Construction and effect. **Autos 142**
Control and regulation. **Autos 130**
Due process in suspension or revocation. **Const Law 287**
Fees, licenses. **Autos 141**
Financial responsibility requirements, suspension or revocation of license. **Autos 144.1(4)**
Incompetency affecting liability of owner for injuries. **Autos 193(13)**
Local regulations. **Autos 133**
New license. **Autos 144.3**
Proceedings to procure. **Autos 139**
Reinstatement or new license. **Autos 144.3**
Revocation or suspension—
Administrative procedure. **Autos 144.2(1)**
Discipline. **Autos 144.2(8)**
Discretion. **Autos 144.2(3)**
Financial responsibility requirements, procedure under. **Autos 144.2(7)**
Hardship and mitigating circumstances. **Autos 144.2(8)**
Procedure arising out of criminal prosecutions. **Autos 144.2(5)**
Trial de novo. **Autos 144.2(4)**
Suspension or revocation of license—
Intoxication as ground. **Autos 144.1(1.10)**
Transfer of rights. **Autos 143**
Unlicensed or unregistered operators, rights and liabilities. **Autos 145**
Due process of law. **Const Law 287.3**
Eligibility. **Autos 37**
Equal protection. **Const Law 230.5**
Evidence—
Injuries from operation, or use of highway. **Autos 243(11)**

B. Descriptive Word Index

The descriptive word index (Figure 5.7) is similar to other indexes discussed thus far. The researcher attempts to focus conceptually on his or her topic and refine the concept as far as possible. Murder is too broad a topic, but a survey of the descriptive word index leads to *premeditation*, *self-defense*, and *defenses*. Peruse the index very aggressively! Main topics are broken down into multiple headings and subdivisions, like most other indexes. When you find the appropriate topic, it will be associated with a key number. As before, find the appropriate volume and then turn to the key number given in the index. Cases that deal with the corresponding subject matter will be listed under that key number. Again, pay special attention to topical abbreviations when locating the correct volume.

C. Topical Outline

The third way to use a digest is by consulting the topical outline or table of contents at the beginning of the appropriate topic. Seasoned practitioners and researchers who are knowledgeable about the subject matter may choose to use this method. The detailed topical outline contains a multitude of divisions and subdivisions listing the topics covered in all the volumes of the digest. An outline is located at the beginning of each of the subtopics in the digest system. Scan the outline included at the beginning of each topic to locate the appropriate key number, then turn to that section in the correct volume(s). Figure 5.8 is an example of a topical outline.

FIGURE 5.8

V. INJURIES FROM OPERATION, OR USE OF HIGHWAY.—Continued.

(A) NATURE AND GROUNDS OF LIABILITY.—Continued.

182. Rights of person injured.
183. Persons liable.
184. —— In general.
185. —— Statutory and local regulations.
186. —— Owners in general.
187. —— Government; immunity and waiver thereof.
 (1). In general.
 (2). Municipal corporations; districts.
 (3). Counties.
 (4). States.
 (5). United States.
188. —— Infants.
189. —— Insane persons.
190. —— Husband and wife.
191. —— Parent and child.
192. —— Owner's liability for acts of third person in general.
 (1). In general.
 (2). Defects in vehicles.
 (3). Lights and equipment.
 (4). Co-owners.
 (5). Community liability for acts of husband or wife.
 (6). Borrower or hirer.
 (7). Prospective purchasers or sales agents.
 (8). Buyer under conditional sale.
 (9). Servants of others.
 (10). Persons employed by or assisting operator.
 (11). Permitting operation by incompetent person.
 (12). Presence of owner in vehicle.
193. —— Owner's liability for acts of servant or agent.
 (1). In general.
 (2). Statutory or local regulations.
 (3). Relation of parties.
 (3.1). —— In general.
 (4). —— Persons employed by or assisting servants.
 (5). —— Servants employed by or under control of third persons.
 (6). —— Termination of relation.
 (7). Nature of agency.
 (8). Scope of employment.
 (8.1). —— In general.
 (9). —— Acts unnecessary to performance of duty.
 (10). —— Acts of servant in behalf of himself or of third person.
 (11). —— Acts permitted by servant.
 (12). —— Selection of route.
 (13). Incompetency of servant.
 (14). Deviation from instructions.
 (15). Willful and malicious acts of servant.
 (16). Criminal acts of servant.
 (17). Ratification or repudiation of acts of servant.

FIGURE 5.9

INTERSECTIONAL collisions,
Generally, **Autos 🔑 171, 244(11)**
Boulevard rule, **Autos 🔑 171(5)**
Defects in road design, liability for, **Autos 🔑 259**
Defects in signs and signals, liability for, **Autos 🔑 279**
Duty to stop, **Autos 🔑 171(11)**
Left turns, **Autos 🔑 171(12), 244(11)**
Lookout, **Autos 🔑 171(9, 12)**
Right of way,
Determination of, **Autos 🔑 171(4)**
Failure to yield, **Autos 🔑 171, 244(11)**
Right to assume care by others, **Autos 🔑 171(13)**
INTERVENING cause, **Autos 🔑 201(9)**
INTOXICATION,
Generally, **Autos 🔑 157, 244(31)**

AUTOMOBILE ACCIDENTS—Cont'd
INTOXICATION—Cont'd
Admissibility of evidence, **Autos 🔑 243(1, 3)**
Dram shop liability. See heading **DRAM SHOP ACT,** generally.
Negligent entrustment. See subheading NEGLIGENT entrustment under this heading.
Social host liability. See heading **INTOXICATING LIQUORS,** CIVIL actions against seller or provider.
JUDGMENT. See heading **JUDGMENT,** generally.
JURISDICTION over lawsuit, **Autos 🔑 232, 295**
See also heading **JURISDICTION,** generally

Fact Pattern 1. Using volume 97, the Descriptive Word Index, A–CI, look up the keyword *Automobile Accidents.* Look for the subheading "Intoxication." Under that subheading, you find "Generally, **Autos 157, 244(31).**" See Fact Pattern Figure 5.9.

Next, find the "Automobile" volume with the appropriate section number. Browse through the pages and read the summaries to find appropriate cases. See Fact Pattern Figure 5.10.

Fact Pattern 2. Using volume 97A, the Descriptive Word Index, CJ–DQ, look up the keyword *Contracts.* Look for the subheading "Execution of Contracts." Under that subheading, you find "Execution of contract, **Contracts 34.**" See Fact Pattern Figure 5.11.

Next, find the "Contracts" volume with the appropriate section number. Nothing looks promising, but the next section, 35, is "Signatures." Browse through the pages and read the summaries to find appropriate cases. See Fact Pattern Figure 5.12.

IV. SUMMARY

In the researcher's never-ending quest to go from big issues to small issues, digests are a crucial resource. Digests provide a short synopsis of a reported case or decision, arrange cases by topic, cross-reference them to other relevant cases, and allow the researcher to assess the strengths or weaknesses of any given case. Because their coverage is brief, digests cover virtually all topics of the law, all neatly indexed by topic or case name. Though the format is short, digests can provide the researcher with a valuable source of reference points and related materials.

FIGURE 5.10

For references to other topics, see Descriptive-Word Index

⚷155. Injuries to persons or property not on highway.

Library references

C.J.S. Motor Vehicles §§ 349(1) et seq., 424.

N.D.Miss. 1986. Motorist's failure to see pedestrian until she was at midpoint of his car directly in front of him, although he was allegedly looking in the direction toward which he was traveling, constituted a failure to maintain a reasonable lookout and was negligent, especially as motorist was driving through an employee parking lot and should have anticipated that employees would be crossing lot.

Coleman v. Lehman, 649 F.Supp. 363.

⚷156. Defects in vehicles.

Library references

C.J.S. Motor Vehicles §§ 260 et seq., 430.

C.A.6 (Ky.) 1991. Driver of truck leased to certified interstate motor carrier pursuant to trip lease was intended beneficiary of federal statute and regulations requiring lessee to assume control over vehicle and bear responsibility for defects in vehicle, and, thus, administratrix of driver's estate had private right of action against lessee carrier under federal and Kentucky law. 49 U.S.C.A. §§ 11107, 11107(a)(4), 117095, 11705(b)(2), (c)(1); KRS 446.070; Interstate Commerce Act, § 204(e), 49 U.S.C.(1976 Ed.) § 304(e); Motor Carrier Safety Act of 1984, §§ 202 et seq., 204(1), 49 U.S.C.A.App. §§ 2501 et seq., 2503(1).

Johnson v. S.O.S. Transport, Inc., 926 F.2d 516.

S.D.Ga. 1990. Under Georgia law, party may bring cause of action based in tort for negligent inspection of insured's vehicles by insurance companies.

Kennedy v. Georgia-Carolina Refuse and Waste Co., Inc., 739 F.Supp. 604.

Under Georgia law, guardian ad litem of passenger injured in collision with garbage truck failed to establish his claim against truck's insurer for negligent inspection, where passenger did not establish or even allege that he relied upon survey conducted by insurer, and insurance contract did not require any inspection by insurer.

Kennedy v. Georgia-Carolina Refuse and Waste Co., Inc., 739 F.Supp. 604.

Automobile accident victim's "expectancy" that garbage truck's insurer would have made sure through safety inspection that all state and federal standards were met did not constitute reliance sufficient to establish cause of action for tort of negligent inspection under Georgia law.

Kennedy v. Georgia-Carolina Refuse and Waste Co., Inc., 739 F.Supp. 604.

⚷157. Incompetency or inexperience of operator.

Library references

C.J.S. Motor Vehicles §§ 2654, 265, 273.

C.A.6 (Ky.) 1993. City was not liable to victim involved in automobile accident with driver who was suffering from epileptic seizure at time of accident, for failing to have reported previous accidents allegedly involving seizures suffered by same driver to state driver's license authorities; epileptic driver was not acting as agent of city, nor was there special relationship between city and epileptic driver or between city and accident victim, and while epileptic driver was definite danger behind wheel of motor vehicle, he was no more a danger to victim than to any other citizen on city's street. 42 U.S.C.A. § 1983.

Jones v. City of Carlisle, Ky., 3 F.3d 945, rehearing and suggestion for rehearing denied, certiorari denied 114 S.Ct. 1218, 510 U.S. 1177, 127 L.Ed. 2d 564.

M.D.Ala 1993. Under Alabama law, one who is driving under the influence of alcohol or who runs stop sign is generally considered to be negligent per se.

Borden v. CSX Transp., Inc., 843 F.Supp. 1410.

D.D.C. 1996. Under District of Columbia law, 16-year-old unlicensed motorist who struck and injured friend who was standing in roadway and attempting to wave motorist to a stop during game of "chicken" was negligent in driving without a license, in failing to avoid friend, and in operating at excessive speed in residential neighborhood.

Athridge v. Iglesias, 950 F.Supp. 1187, affirmed 1997 WL 404854.

E.D.N.C. 1989. It is negligence per se for person to operate motor vehicle with blood alcohol concentration of 0.10 or more. N.C.G.S. § 20–138.1(a)(2).

Hinkamp v. American Motor Corp., 735 F.Supp. 176, affirmed 900 F.2d 252.

E.D.Pa. 1991. It is negligence per se in North Carolina to operate motor vehicle with blood alcohol level in excess of .10.

Martin by Martin v. General Motors Corp., 759 F.Supp. 271, vacated 953 F.2d 1380.

E.D.Texc. 1995. Plea of guilty to involuntary manslaughter in connection with automobile accident constituted admission for purposes of civil liability trial and established negligence per see in the death of the victims.

Midrange v. Fontenot, 879 F.Supp. 679.

E.D.Wash. 1993. Motorist whose vehicle collided with National Guard truck that was entering highway from driveway violated statutory duty under Washington

For later cases see same Topic and Key Number in Pocket Part

law by driving under the influence of alcohol. West's RCWA 5.40.060.

Richardson v. U.S. 835 F.Supp. 1236.

Driving under the influence is negligence per se under Washington law. West's RCWA 5.40.060.

Richardson v. U.S., 835 F.Supp. 1236.

🔑158. Willful, wanton, or reckless acts of conduct.

Library references

C.J.S. Motor Vehicles § 258.

C.A.11 (Ala.) 1990. Reasonable jury could not have found wantonness in truck driver owner's conduct, in negligence action brought by highway worker who was injured when truck wheels disengaged from truck on basis that evidence of disrepair or neglect demonstrated awareness of condition, awareness demonstrated appreciation of danger, and appreciation of danger was accurate; probability of last or ultimate inference was too attenuated to demonstrate wantonness.

Salter v. Westra, 904 F.2d 1517.

E.D.Ark 1989. Police officer's pursuit of suspected thief who was driving a stolen car and his collision with another car would not be grossly negligent under Arkansas law; chase lasted about a minute in light traffic; and officer was on verge of breaking off pursuit when accident occurred.

Britt v. Little Rock Police Dept., 721 F.Supp. 189.

S.D.Ga. 1997. While motorist's initial act of speeding away from pursuing police officer may have been merely negligent, motorist's ensuing actions during high speed chase, including loss of control of vehicle, amounted to willful and wanton misconduct for purposes of willful and wanton misconduct exception to Georgia's Fireman's Rule.

McClelland v. Riffle, 970 F.Supp. 1053.

N.D.Ill. 1990. Under Illinois law, Government was not liable, under Federal Tort Claims Act (FTCA), for actions of officer with naval base police department with respect to his alleged negligence in engaging in high speed pursuit of automobile which allegedly caused automobile to get into accident and kill passenger in another automobile, on basis of willful and wanton negligent conduct; officer turned on his lights, used his siren, and pursued automobile to protect public from driver who had already displayed reckless behavior, at no time did officer's driving affect safety of others, and officer's failure to stop pursuit earlier did not evidence a "willful and wanton" disregard for safety of others. Ill.S.H.A. ch. 85, ¶ 1–101 et seq.; 28 U.S.C.A. §§ 1346(b), 2671–2680.

Estate of Warner v. U.S. 754 F.Supp. 1271.

🔑159. Acts of emergencies.

Library references

C.J.S. Motor Vehicles §§ 257, 368.

C.A.11 (Ala.) 1990. "Sudden emergency" or "mechanical defect or failure" doctrines usually refer to standard of care applicable to allegedly negligent conduct in operation of motor vehicle in face of unexpected circumstances.

Salter v. Westra, 904 F.2d 1517.

Even when claim centers on allegation of negligent conduct in handling of vehicle in face of either "mechanical failure" or nonmechanical "sudden emergency," defendant's right to have allegedly negligent conduct be judged in light of emergency circumstances turns on whether defect or emergency was foreseeable or arose without fault of driver under Alabama law.

Salter v. Westra, 904 F2d 1517.

C.A.8 (Iowa) 1984. Iowa's legal excuse doctrine is applicable if it is impossible to comply with a statute or ordinance, by forces beyond the driver's control a vehicle is placed in a position contrary to the provisions of the statute, the driver is confronted by an emergency not of his own making and compelled not to comply with provisions of the statute or a statute specifically provides for an excuse or exception.

Zimmer v. Miller Trucking Co., Inc., 743 F.2d 601.

C.A.1 (Mass.) 1990. District court properly concluded under Massachusetts law that navy captain motorist was not negligent in connection with accident which occurred when he encountered puddle after changing lanes; motorist's driving under posted limit at speed consistent with other driver could have been found to have been traveling at reasonable rate of speed, motorist confronted with other drivers braking in front of him chose reasonable alternative of changing lanes rather than braking in passing lane, puddle was not in line of motorist's vision until it was only 50 feet away, at which time he changed lanes, his actions to turn away from concrete wall were prudent to avoid immediate threat, and his actions in backing away from oncoming traffic in passing lane after spinning 180 degrees rather than attempting to turn vehicle around were reasonable.

Deguio v. U.S., 920 F.2d 103.

🔑160. Persons on foot in general.

Library references

C.J.S. Motor Vehicles § 382 et seq.

🔑160(1). In general.

C.A.D.C. 1994. Under District of Columbia law, rule that property owner is liable to trespasser prior to discovery of trespasser only for wilful or wanton negligence did

FIGURE 5.11

CONTRACTS

97A F P D 4th—176

References are to Digest Topics and Key Numbers

CONTRACTS—Cont'd
EXCUSES for nonperformance or defects—
Cont'd
- Building contacts, **Contracts 🔑 303(5)**
- Operation of law, **Contracts 🔑 303(2)**
- Other party preventing performance, **Contracts 🔑 303(4)**

EXECUTED contracts,
- Generally, **Contracts 🔑 6**
- Illegality, relief of parties to executed illegal contracts, **Contracts 🔑 138(2)**
- Mutuality of obligation, **Contracts 🔑 10(1)**

EXECUTION. See heading **EXECUTION IN JUDICIAL PROCEEDINGS,** generally.

EXECUTION of contract, **Contacts 🔑 34**

EXECUTION contracts, **Contracts 🔑 6**

EXEMPTIONS,
- Exemption from liability. See subheading DISCLAIMER of liability under this heading.
- Waiver of prospective exemptions, **Exemp 🔑 92**

EXISTENCE and condition of subject matter, **Contracts 🔑 8**

EXPRESS contracts, **Contracts 🔑 3**

EXPRESSIO unius est exclusio alterius, **Contracts 🔑 152**

EXTRA work,
- Authority to do extra work or furnish materials, **Contracts 🔑 232(3, 4)**
- Compensation for, **Contracts 🔑 232**
- Delay in performance caused by, **Contracts 🔑 300(2)**
- Instructions as to extra work, in action for breach of contract, **Contracts 🔑 353(11)**

EXTRINSIC circumstances, construction and operation of contracts, **Contracts 🔑 169**

EXTRINSIC evidence. See heading **PAROL AND EXTRINSIC EVIDENCE,** generally.

FAIR dealing,
- Implied covenant of good faith and fair dealing, **Contracts 🔑 168**
- Obligation of good faith and fair dealing, **Contracts 🔑 168, 169**

FALSE representations. See subheading FRAUD and misrepresentation under this heading.

CONTRACTS—Cont'd
FEDERAL courts,
- Appeal and error,
  - Questions of fact, verdicts and findings, **Fed Cts 🔑 859, 874**
- Jurisdiction,
  - Amount in controversy, **Fed Cts 🔑 341**
  - Claims, Court of Federal, **Fed Cts 🔑 1076, 1077**
  - District court, **Fed Cts 🔑 976**
  - Federal question, **Fed Cts 🔑 202, 223**
  - Venue and personal jurisdiction, 🔑 **Fed Cts 🔑 76.30, 89, 109**
- State laws as rules of decision, **Fed Cts 🔑 412.1, 413**

FEDERAL preemption, state laws and regulations, **States 🔑 18.15**

FILING or recording contracts, **Contracts 🔑 44**

FORFEITURES, **Contracts 🔑 318**

FORUM selection clauses,
- Construction and operation, **Contracts 🔑 206**
- Validity, **Contracts 🔑 127(4)**

FRANCHISE agreements,
- Construction and operation, **Contracts 🔑 202(1)**
- Statutory regulation, **Trade Reg 🔑 871**

FRAUD and misrepresentation
- See also heading **FRAUD, CONTRACTS.**
  - Generally, **Contracts 🔑 94**
- Burden of proof, **Contracts 🔑 99(1)**
- Certificate of architect, engineer, or others as to performance of contract, **Contracts 🔑 292**
- Concealment, **Contracts 🔑 94(8)**
- Contents of writing, Representations as to, **Contracts 🔑 94(4)**
- Defenses to actions, **Fraud 🔑 36**
- Duty to disclose, **Contracts 🔑 94(8)**
- Effect of invalidity, **Contracts 🔑 98**
- Election of remedies, **Fraud 🔑 31-32**
- Estoppel, **Contracts 🔑 97**
- Evidence,
  - Admissibility, **Contracts 🔑 99(2)**
  - Sufficiency, **Contracts 🔑 99(3)**
- Failure to disclose, **Contracts 🔑 94(8)**
- Fraud in execution, **Contracts 🔑 94**
- Fraud in factum, **Contracts 🔑 94**
- Fraud in inducement, **Contracts 🔑 94**
- Future events, representations as to, **Contracts 🔑 94(6)**
- Inducing fraud or breech of trust, legality of contracts, **Contracts 🔑 113**

FIGURE 5.12

For later cases see same Topic and Key Number in Pocket Part

tance of offer be manifested by conduct that indicates assent to proposed bargain.

Marks v. U.S., 15 Cl.Ct. 609.

⊂⊃ **35. Signature.**

Library references

C.J.S. Contracts § 62.

C.A.D.C. 1996. Under District of Columbia law, purchase order may stand as offer with performance of its terms constituting acceptance, even where purchase order is signed only by one party.

U.S. ex rel. Modern Elec., Inc. v. Ideal Electronic Sec. Co., Inc., 81 F.3d 240, 317 U.S.App.D.C. 145.

C.A.9 (Cal.) 1991. Alleged agreement between author's agent and film maker, subject to author's approval, was not enforceable contract where it was not signed by author and essential terms were missing.

Roth v. Garcia Marquez, 942 F.2d 617.

C.A. 7 (Ill.) 1988. Party may become bound to contract by accepting its benefits, even through he did not sign it.

Skelton v. General Motors Corp., 860 F.2d 250, rehearing denied, certiorari denied 110 S.Ct. 53, 493 U.S. 810, 107 L.Ed.2d 22.

C.A.8 (Minn.) 1993. Parties to agreement may agree that they will not be bound until agreement is signed.

International Travel Arrangers v. NWA, Inc., 991 F.2d 1389, rehearing denied, certiorari denied 114 S.Ct. 345, 510 U.S. 932, 126 L.Ed.2d 309.

C.A.8 (Neb.) 1985. In assessing whether particular contract provision is unconscionable, courts generally look for gross inequality in bargaining power and a misunderstanding or unawareness of the provisions in question: those factors are examined in the light of totality of the circumstances.

Langemeier v. National Oats Co., Inc., 775 F.2d 975.

C.A.2 (N.Y.) 1993. Under New York law, relevant writings creating contract may be signed by only one party and, in fact, need not be signed by either party.

Consarc Corp. v. Marine Midland Bank, N.A. 996 F.2d 568.

C.A.10 (Okl.) 1993. Under Oklahoma law, writing can be binding if only signed by one party and accepted by the other.

Oklahoma Radio Associates v. D.D.I.C., 987 F.2d 685, motion denied 3 F.3d 1436.

C.A.3 (Pa.) 1995. Developer consented to limitation of liability clause attached to architectural firm's proposal to conduct a feasibility study, under Pennsylvania law, though developer did not sign contract as requested in proposal, where developer authorized firm to proceed after reviewing each proposal containing such clause, and firm expressly invited developer to negotiate for higher limit of liability if developer found conditions unacceptable, the developer's only response was to fax letter to firm authorizing it to proceed.

Valhal Corp. v. Sullivan Associates, Inc., 44 F.3d 195, rehearing denied 48 F.3d 760.

Pennsylvania law does not condition enforcement of limitation of liability provision on any specific form of consent, and unsigned contract can include enforceable agreement to limit liability if both parties manifest their approval of the terms, and this is also true of exculpatory clause or indemnification clause.

Valhal Corp. v. Sullivan Associates, Inc., 44 F.3d 195, rehearing denied 48 F.3d 760.

C.A.3 (Pa.) 1987. Correspondence may constitute a contract and it is not necessary for both parties to sign the writing if the parties, acting pursuant to its terms, evidence their acceptance.

Hershey Foods Corp. v. Ralph Chapek, Inc., 828 F.2d 989.

C.A.5 (Tex.) 1996. If agreement has been reduced to writing, assent to writing must be manifested; manifestation of assent commonly consists of signing and delivery.

Scaife v. Associated Air Center Inc., 100 F.3d 406.

C.A.9 (Wash.) 1995. Although Russia law requires signatures of all parties for agreement to be binding, agreement signed in Washington state by representative of Russian partnership was enforceable under Washington law; there was no indication in agreement that it was to be governed by Russia law or that representative did not have full authority to bind Russian partnership. West's RCWA 19.36.010.

International Ambassador Programs, Inc. v. Archexpo, 68 F.3d 337, certiorari denied 116 S.Ct. 1567, 134 L.Ed.2d 666.

C.A.7 (Wis.) 1995. Under Wisconsin law, written agreement may be effective even if both parties have not signed, if parties otherwise demonstrate intent to have contract.

Zeige Distributing Co., Inc. v. All Kitchens, Inc., 63 F.3d 609.

D.Ariz. 1987. Validity of contract as between subcontractor and materialman was not affected by fact that general contactor, who was also listed as party to contract, never signed contract.

U.S. for Use and Benefit of Metal Mfg., Inc. v. Federal Ins. Co., 656 F.Supp. 1194.

For cited U.S.C.A. sections and legislative history, see United States Code Annotated

V. LEGAL RESEARCH ASSIGNMENTS

Digests can be used in a wide variety of situations. A myriad of topics, the majority of jurisdictions at the state and federal level, and cross-referencing to other legal series and materials make these tools indispensable for research. This section includes assignments that stress these varied techniques. Pay close attention to the appropriate headings and focus on the question asked.

A. Exercise 5.1: Pennsylvania Digest Criminal Law Section 622(2)

1. Which case held that a denial of severance is not error, when charges against the defendants are the same?
   a. *U.S. v. De Larosa*
   b. *U.S. v. Barrow*
   c. *U.S. v. Tomlin*
   d. Both a and b
2. Which procedural rules are cited at 622(2)?
   a. The 10th *Atlantic Reporter*
   b. The Federal Rules of Criminal Procedure
   c. Civil Rights Acts
   d. None of the above
3. The *Atlantic Reporter* is not referred to in the digest at 622(2).
   a. True
   b. False
4. Which case was initiated in the state court, and received some federal review, but was denied certiorari by the U.S. Supreme Court?
   a. *Com. v. Aiello*
   b. *Com. v. Horner*
   c. *Com. v. Kumitis*
   d. None of the above
5. Which case probably involved the trial of organized crime figures?
   a. *U.S. v. Torquato*
   b. *U.S. v. Forsythe*
   c. *U.S. v. Boscia*
   d. *U.S. v. Rosa*

B. Exercise 5.2: Pennsylvania Digest Sections 625.25–627.5(1)

1. The discretion of the trial judge in determining competency is guided by the provisions of
   a. 50 P.S. § 7402(a)
   b. 50 P.S. § 7403(a)
   c. Neither a nor b
   d. Both a and b
2. Under 627.2, what rule of criminal procedure is highlighted?
   a. 627.6
   b. 15(a)
   c. U.S.C.A.
   d. 621979

name, trial court properly denied defendant's motion for severance. 18 U.S.C.A. § 2113; Fed.Rules Crim.Proc. rule 13, 18 U.S.C.A.

U.S. v. Howell, 240 F.2d 149.

Confession, which codefendant allegedly made, did not constitute evidence against defendant, and, therefore, afforded no reason for a separate trial of defendant and codefendant in prosecution for bank robbery. 18 U.S.C.A. § 2113.

U.S. v. Howell, 240 F.2d 149.

Where, in prosecution of defendant and codefendant for bank robbery, defendant, on his motion for severance, did not urge alleged fact that codefendant was insane and was of weak character, and it was not shown that defendant was not accorded a fair trial by reason of refusal of trial court to sever the trial of codefendant, denial of motion of severance was not an abuse of discretion.

U.S. v. Howell, 240 F.2d 139.

D.C.Pa. 1983. Certain defendants in prosecution for conspiracy in unreasonable restraint of interstate trade and commerce were not entitled to severance from codefendants, although defendants contended they were unable to review "highly prejudicial" testimony of codefendants because they could not cross-examine codefendants, where defendants were given every opportunity to cross-examine codefendants and thus to place in record questions and answers so that trial court could evaluate prejudice to defendants arising from the codefendants' testimony and defendants did not request in camera hearing on cross-examination of codefendants. Sherman Anti-Trust Act, § 1, 15, U.S.C.A.§ 1.

U.S. v. H. & M, Inc., 562 F.Supp. 651.

D.C.Pa. 1983. Defendants convicted of collecting claimed extensions of credit by extortionate means and conspiracy to do so were not entitled to severance merely because evidence may have been more damaging against a codefendant and there was a danger of spillover, in that there was no showing as to why jury would not be able to compartmentalize evidence as it pertained to each defendant. Fed.Rules Cr.Proc.Rules 8, 8(a), 18 U.S.C.A.; 18 U.S.C.A. § 894(a).

U.S. v. DiPasquale, 561 F.Supp. 1338.

D.C.Pa. 1982. Defendant was not entitled to severance of trial from codefendant on ground that joint trial would deprive him of allegedly exculpatory testimony of codefendant, notwithstanding that codefendant had submitted affidavit indicating willingness to testify if called by defendant were severance to be granted, where exculpatory significance of codefendant's testimony and degree to which codefendant would be impeached were difficult to predict, both defendants had able counsel, and contradictory defenses did not seem likely to emerge. Fed.Rules Cr.Proc. Rule 14, 18 U.S.C.A.

U.S. v. Litman, 547 F.Supp. 645.

D.C.Pa. 1982. For purposes of determining defendant's motion to sever on basis that codefendant would be likely to testify at separate trial, it is proper to assume that codefendant would claim Fifth Amendment privilege against self-incrimination at second trial and thereby satisfy requirement that witness be unavailable for hearsay exception for statements which expose declarant to criminal liability. Fed. Rules Evid.Rule 804(a)(1), (b)(3), 28 U.S.C.A.; U.S.C.A.Const.Amend. 5.

U.S. v. Ditizio, 530 F.Supp. 175.

It was sufficiently likely that testimony codefendant regarding "off-the-record" statements could be introduced at separate trial of defendant for purpose of determining whether defendant was entitled to severance from his codefendant in prosecution for conspiracy to commit arson. Fed.Rules Evid.Rule 804(b)(3), 28 U.S.C.A.

U.S. v. Ditizio, 530, F.Supp. 175.

For purposes of determining whether defendant was entitled to severance from codefendant in prosecution for conspiracy to commit arson, it was sufficiently likely that testimony regarding "off-the-record" statements of codefendant could be admitted under hearsay exception for statements not specifically covered by other exceptions, but having equivalent circumstantial guarantees of trustworthiness Fed.Rules Evid.Rule 804(b)(5), 28 U.S. C.A.

U.S. v. Ditizio, 530 F.Supp. 175.

For purpose of determining whether defendant was entitled to severance from his codefendant in prosecution for conspiracy to commit arson, fact that Government could seek to persuade jury that statements of codefendant were not reliable was insufficient to deny severance for that testimony would tend to exculpate defendant.

U.S. v. Ditizio, 530 F.Supp. 175.

Defendant was entitled to severance from his codefendant in prosecution for conspiracy to commit arson where risk of unduly restricting defendant's defense by preventing him from introducing important exculpatory testimony in joint trial was sufficiently clear that considerations of judicial economy were outweighed.

U.S. v. Ditizio, 530 F.Supp. 175.

D.C.Pa. 1981. Mere allegation that defendant would suffer from collective culpability if not given a severance was insufficient to entitle him to the severance.

U.S. v. Lewis, 514 F.Supp. 169.

continued

For later cases see same Topic and Key Number in Pocket Part

heavy burden of demonstrating that his right to fair trial was prejudiced by trial court's refusal to sever his trial from that of codefendant, despite defendant's contention that codefendant had indicated willingness to testify on his behalf, but that he would not give up his right to refuse to testify in his own trial. 18 U.S.C.A. § 1951; Fed.Rules Crim.Proc. rule 14, 18 U.S.C.A.

U.S. v. Rosa, 560 F.2d 149, certiorari denied 98 S.Ct. 191.

C.A.Pa. 1972. Defendant failed to show error in failure of trial court to sever his trial from that of his codefendant indicted for violating statutes relating to bank robbery and aiding and abetting statute. 18 U.S.C.A. §§ 2, 2113.

U.S. v. Brown, 471 F.2d 297.

C.A.Pa. 1972. Where testimony by the spouse of one defendant is sought by a codefendant and defendant fears that his defense will be prejudiced, even unintentionally, by some testimony of his spouse or by the very fact that she testifies for a codefendant and not for him, proper procedure is to grant a severance and then permit the witness to testify for the defendant who is not his or her spouse.

U.S. v. Fields, 458 F.2d 1194, certiorari denied 93 S.Ct. 2755, 412 U.S. 927, 37 L.Ed.2d 154.

C.A.Pa. 1971. Although defendant made motion to sever on ground that unruly conduct of codefendant would be prejudicial to this case, motion was properly denied, where it became apparent that codefendant would conduct himself in an orderly manner in courtroom.

U.S. v. Archie, 452 F.2d 897, certiorari denied 92 S.Ct. 1521, 405 U.S. 1071, 31 L.Ed.2d 804.

C.A.Pa. 1971. A defendant is not entitled to severance merely because evidence against codefendant is more damaging than evidence against him, and, while such disparity in the proofs is sufficient in certain cases, primary consideration is whether jury can reasonably be expected to compartmentalize the evidence as it relates to separate defendants in view of its volume and limited admissibility.

U.S. v. De Larosa, 450 F.2d 1057, certiorari denied Baskin v. U.S., 92 S.Ct. 978, 405 U.S. 927, 30 L.Ed.2d 800, certiorari denied Noel v. U.S., 92 S.Ct. 1188, 405 U.S. 957, 31 L.Ed.2d 235, and Jones v. U.S., 92 S.Ct. 1189, 405 U.S. 957, 31 L.Ed.2d 236.

Where jury deliberated on essentially single criminal transaction in prosecution for bank robbery and assault in course of bank robbery, denial of three defendants' motions for severance from trial of fourth was not an abuse of discretion, although surgical gloves were found near fourth defendant at arrest and segment of one was found in bank, sole of his shoe matched imprint on cash-in slip in bank, fourth defendant wore clothes allegedly associated with black militants, one of his witnesses knew him by name allegedly associated with black militants, such witnesses were somewhat hostile and all had prior criminal records.

U.S. v. De Larosa, 450 F.2d 1057, certiorari denied Baskin v. U.S. 92 S.Ct. 978, 405 U.S. 927, 30 L.Ed.2d 800, certiorari denied Noel v. U.S., 92 S. Ct. 1188, 405 U.S. 957, 31 L.Ed.2d 235, and Jones v. U.S., 92 S. Ct. 1189, 405 U.S. 957, 31 L.Ed.2d 236.

Severance was not required by unfavorable impression which may have been created by one defendant's identification with unpopular social and political group.

U.S. v. De Larosa, 450 F.2d 1057, certiorari denied Baskin v. U.S. 92 S.Ct. 978, 405 U.S. 927, 30 L.Ed.2d 800, certiorari denied Noel v. U.S., 92 S. Ct. 1188, 405 U.S. 957, 31 L.Ed.2d 235, and Jones v. U.S., 92 S.Ct. 1189, 405 U.S. 957, 31 L.Ed.2d 236.

Trial court did not abuse discretion in denying defendant's motion for severance made after codefendant testified regarding prior imprisonment of defendant.

U.S. v. De Larosa, 450 F.2d 1057, certiorari denied Baskin v. U.S., 92 S.Ct. 978, 405 U.S. 927, 30 L.Ed.2d 800, certiorari denied Noel v. U.S., 92 S.Ct. 1188, 405 U.S. 957, 31 L.Ed.2d 235, and Jones v. U.S., 92 S.Ct. 1189, 405 U.S. 957 31 L.Ed.2d 236.

C.A.Pa. 1967. Denial of severance to defendant tried with co-defendant who was also charged with conspiracy to commit same substantive offense was within trial court's discretion.

U.S. v. Tomlin, 380 F.2d 373.

C.A.Pa. 1966. Denial of motions for severance and separate trials was not abuse of discretion in prosecution for conspiracy and substantive violations for antiracketeering statute. Fed.Rules Crim.Proc. rule 14, 18 U.S. C.A.; 18 U.S.C.A. §§ 371, 1952.

U.S. v. Barrow, 363 F.2d 62, certiorari denied 87 S.Ct. 703, 385 U.S. 1001, 17 L.Ed.2d 541.

C.A.Pa. 1957. Where defendant was jointly indicted with another for bank robbery, and defendant contended that his true name was not that stated in the indictment, and superseding indictment was returned against defendant in what he contended was his true

For legislative history of cited statutes

made to appear prejudiced as the decision is within the discretion of the trial judge.

Com. v. Breslin, 7 Lycoming 146, affirmed 165 A.2d 415, 194 Pa.Super. 83.

Pa.Quar.Sess. 1957. A motion to sever the trial of one defendant charged with assault and battery in resisting arrest and engaging in lottery from that of another charged with selling of pools, lottery and gambling is properly denied where evidence of the activities of both defendants indicates they were acting in concert.

Com. v. Aiello, 9 D. & C.2d 767, affirmed 136 A.2d 325, 184 Pa.Super. 553.

Pa.Quar.Sess. 1944. In all cases in which two or more persons are jointly indicted for any offense, it shall be in the discretion of the court to try them jointly or severally, except in cases of felonious homicide.

Com. v. Horner, 57 York 169.

Pa.O. & T. 1959. A defendant may properly be tried on a conspiracy count alone and separate from his coconspirators.

Com. v. Kumitis, 17 D. & C.2d 445, 8 Bucks 250, affirmed 151 A.2d 653, 190 Pa.Super. 133, certiorari denied 80 S.Ct. 165, 361 U.S. 890, 4 L.Ed.2d 124.

⚩ 622(2). Proceedings in which severance may be granted or grounds therefore.

C.A.Pa. 1982. Despite defendant's argument that severance was necessary because testimony of certain witness would implicate defendant in criminal matters unrelated to charges for which defendant was then being tried, district court did not abuse its discretion by denying severance, where severance would not have affected such testimony, since witness would presumably have been called upon by Government to testify against each defendant.

U.S. v. Frankenberry, 696 F.2d 239, certiorari denied 103 S.Ct. 3544.

C.A.Pa. 1979. In prosecution under the Hobbs Act, the trial court did not abuse discretion by denying defendant's motions for severance. 18 U.S.C.A. § 1951.

U.S. v. Torquato, 602 F.2d 564, certiorari denied 100 S.Ct. 295, 444 U.S. 941, 62 L.Ed.2d 307.

C.A.Pa. 1979. In prosecution for violation of the Racketeer Influenced and Corrupt Organizations Act, trial court did not err in denying defendant's motion for severance. 18 U.S.C.A. § 1962(d).

U.S. v. Forsythe, 594 F.2d 947.

C.A.Pa. 1978. Where defendant's contention of a "spill over" of incriminating evidence was countered by evidence of single conspiracy in which he played a part and by instructions specifically directing jury to evaluate each defendant's guilt or innocence individually, no unfairness resulted to defendant arising from his joinder with other defendants and thus denial of his motion to sever his case did not constitute abuse of discretion. Fed.Rules Crim.Proc. rule 14, 18 U.S.C.A.

U.S. v. Boyd, 595 F.2d 120.

C.A.Pa. 1978. Trial court did not abuse its discretion in denying motion for severance of defendants who were charged with making false statements in a loan application to a federally insured bank and aiding and abetting that offense. 18 U.S.C.A. §§ 2, 1014; Fed. Rules Crim.Proc. rule 8(a, b), 18 U.S.C.A.

U.S. v. Scalzitti, 578 F.2d 507.

C.A.Pa. 1978. Refusal to sever cases of several defendants charged with mail fraud was not abuse of discretion where defendants did not make a strong showing of likelihood that their codefendants would testify, showing as to exculpatory nature of the desired testimony was weak and consideration of judicial economy weighted heavily against separate trials. 18 U.S.C.A. §§ 371, 1341; Fed.Rules Crim.Proc. rule 14, 18 U.S.C.A.

U.S. v. Boscia, 573 F.2d 827, certiorari denied 98 S.Ct. 2248, 436 U.S. 911, 56 L.Ed.2d 411, DeSantis v. U.S., 98 S.Ct. 2248, 436 U.S. 911, 56 L.Ed.2d 411, Plusquellec v. U.S. 98 S.Ct. 2248, 436 U.S. 911, 56 L.Ed.2d 411 and Scolieri v. U.S., 98 S.Ct. 2248, 436 U.S. 911, 56 L.Ed.2d 411, rehearing denied 98 S.Ct. 3130, 438 U.S. 908, 57 L.Ed.2d 1152, certiorari denied Adams v. U.S., 99 S.Ct. 165, 439 U.S. 854, 58 L.Ed.2d 160.

Refusal to sever trial of one of several defendants charged with mail fraud in connection with filing of false insurance claims was not improper on ground that evidence against other defendants prejudiced movant's case where scheme was not so complex nor actors so numerous that the charges and evidence against each defendant could not be kept separate in the minds of the jurors. 18 U.S.C.A. §§ 371, 1341; Fed.Rules Crim.Proc. rule 14, 18 U.S.C.A.

U.S. v. Boscia, 573 F.2d 827, certiorari denied 98 S.Ct. 2248, 436 U.S. 911, 56 L.Ed.2d 411, DeSantis v. U.S., 98 S.Ct. 2248, 436 U.S. 911, 56 L.Ed.2d 411, Plusquellec v. U.S., 98 S.Ct. 2248, 436 U.S. 911, 56 L.Ed.2d 411 and Scolieri v. U.S., 98 S.Ct. 2248, 436 U.S. 911, 56 L.Ed.2d 411, rehearing denied 98 S.Ct. 3130, 438 U.S. 908, 57 L.Ed.2d 1152, certiorari denied Adams v. U.S., 99 S.Ct. 165, 439 U.S. 854, 58 L.Ed.2d 160.

C.A.Pa. 1977. Defendant in prosecution for attempted extortion failed to discharge

3. A deposition may be taken when the interests of justice so require.
   a. True
   b. False
4. Section 627.1(2) deals with grounds for disclosure and discovery.
   a. True
   b. False
5. Which case stands for the proposition that five days' notice before a trial commences is a reasonable notice period?
   a. *Com. v. Wilson*
   b. *Com. v. Vagnoni*
   c. *Com. v. Brown*
   d. *Com. v. Knight*
6. Federal Rule 15(a) is contained in 18 U.S.C.A.
   a. True
   b. False
7. Discovery of documents is covered in digest section 626.6(5).
   a. True
   b. False
8. A defendant's competency to stand trial is evaluated by his or her mental condition at the time of the crime charged.
   a. True
   b. False

C. Exercise 5.3: *Pennsylvania Digest* Section 641.13(6)

1. Trial counsel who fails to interview all prospective witnesses posed by the client will be automatically declared ineffective.
   a. True
   b. False
2. Which federal constitutional amendment is cited in these digest pages?
   a. Second
   b. Third
   c. Fourth
   d. Sixth
3. Which case cites a federal statute dealing with drugs and their control?
   a. *U.S. v Piccolo*
   b. *Com. v. Begley*
   c. *U.S. v. Williams*
   d. *Irrizari v. U.S.*
4. Defense counsel's strategic choices must be based on reasonable professional judgment.
   a. True
   b. False
5. Which case holds that a failure to photograph evidence does not automatically mean that defense counsel is ineffective?
   a. *Jacobs v. Horn*
   b. *Laird v. Horn*
   c. *Com. v. Begley*
   d. *Holland v. Horn*

For later cases, see same Topic and Key Number in Pocket Part

E.D.Pa. 1973. In a determination of competency to stand trial the judge is the fact finder and the decision is a factual one. 18 U.S.C.A. § 4244.

U.S. v. Horowitz, 360 F.Supp. 772.

M.D.Pa. 1966. Question of whether defendant is mentally competent to stand trial is a factual issue to be resolved by court. 18 U.S.C.A. § 4244.

Crawn v. U.S., 254 F.Supp. 669.

Pa. 1978. Trial court in murder prosecution did not err in ruling on afternoon of third day of trial that defendant was competent to stand trial.

Com. v. Brown, 393 A.2d 650, 482 Pa. 256.

Pa. 1956. Where a commission was appointed under the Mental Health Act to investigate the mental condition of a criminal defendant, evidence did not establish an abuse of discretion by the court with the respect to the hearing of additional testimony on defendant's mental condition. 50 P.S. §§ 1071-1622.

Com. v. Moon, 125 A.2d 594, 386 Pa. 205.

625.25. —— Retrospective or nunc pro tunc hearing.

For other cases see earlier editions of this digest, the Decennial Digests, and WESTLAW.

625.30. —— Determination; acquittal.

Pa. 1956. Where a commission was appointed under a Mental Health Act to investigate the mental condition of a defendant convicted of murder, the court would have rejected although not arbitrarily, the commission's findings and conclusions respecting the sanity of the defendant and could have independently determined from the evidence that defendant's capacity to use his customary self-control and discretion had not been so lessened that it was necessary for him to be under care. 50 P.S. §§ 1071-1622, 1225(d).

Com. v. Moon, 125 A.2d 594, 386 Pa. 205.

Where a commission is appointed under the Mental Health Act to investigate the mental condition of a criminal defendant, the report of the commission is advisory only. 50 P.S. §§ 1071–1622.

Com. c. Moon, 125 A.2d 594, 386 Pa. 205.

Pa.Super. 1982. Decision as to competency of defendant, appearing before the court for probation revocation hearing, was within discretion of the lower court, but court was bound to enter upon careful and complete inquiry and make decision based on evidence. 50 P.S.§§ 7101 et seq.; 7402(a).

Com. v. Edward, 450 A.2d 15, 303 Pa.Super. 454.

Pa.Super. 1980. Decision as to defendant's competency to stand trial rests within discretion of trial judge. 50 P.S. §§ 7402(a), 7403(a).

Com. v. Knight, 419 A.2d 492, 276 Pa.Super. 348.

Pa.Super. 1956. Where a commission under the Mental Health Act is appointed to investigate the mental condition of a criminal defendant; the report of the commission is advisory. 50 P.S. §§ 1071–1622.

Com. v. Robinette, 126 A.2d 495, 182 Pa.Super. 346.

625.35. —— Waiver or objection by defendant.

Pa. Super. 1996. After defendant objected to further examination concerning his competency to stand trial, failure to order further examination was not abuse of discretion, as prima facie case of incompetency had not been established; psychiatrist's report indicated that, although defendant at times became agitated regarding his case and was experiencing difficulties cooperating and communicating with his attorney in helping to formulate rational defense, defendant understood roles and functions of various courtroom personnel, was aware of various charges against him, and was also aware of potential consequences of being found guilty, and in court-conducted colloquy, defendant expressly indicated that he understood nature of charges against him and that he was not having difficulty communicating with his attorney. 50 P.S. § 7402(d).

Com. v. Mayer, 685 A.2d 571, 454 Pa.Super. 353.

626. Notice of trial.

Library references

C.J.S. Criminal Law § 1143.

Pa. Super. 2001. It is of paramount importance that notice of a written order, which reschedules a defendant's trial, be given in strict accordance with the notice rule. Rules Crim. Proc., Rule 9025 (1999).

Com. v. Parks, 768 A.2d 1168.

Pa.Super. 1982. Adequate and timely notice to accused of court proceedings is fundamental to constitutionally guaranteed right to fair trial.

Com. v. Hollerbush, 444 A.2d 1235, 298 Pa.Super. 397.

Pa.Super. 1979. Where defendant was represented by private counsel form time of preliminary hearing and pressed for enforcement of rule requiring trial within 180 days, five days' notice of trial was reasonable.

Com. v. Vagnoni, 416 A.2d 99, 272 Pa.Super. 396.

†This case was not selected for publication in the National Report System
For legislative history of cited statutes, see Purdon's Pennsylvania Statutes Annotated

continued

PaSuper. 1950. District attorney's failure to give notice by postal card to defendant's counsel was not ground for reversal where defendant did not give name of his counsel or anyone else to magistrate for that purpose and defendant's counsel was given notice by telephone though he never entered appearance. 19 P.S. § 30.

Com. v. Kaysier, 71 A.2d 846, 166 Pa.Super. 369.

⚿ 627. Service of copy of indictment, information, or minutes of evidence.

⚿ 627(1). In general.

Pa.Super. 1942. The statute requiring peace officers arresting violators of the Vehicle Code upon view to file with the magistrate before whom the arrested person is taken an information setting forth the offense and to furnish a copy thereof to the person arrested was intended to give defendant prompt notice of the charge on which he was arrested. 75 P.S. § 733(a).

Com. v. Wideman, 28 A.2d 801, 150 Pa.Super. 524.

Pa. O. & T. 1952. Defendant in a criminal proceeding is not entitled to a certified copy of the transcribed testimony taken by the district attorney of a preliminary hearing taken before a justice of the peace for his own information in connection with further proceedings, since such testimony does not constitute part of the record.

Com. ex rel. Botch v. Erie County Court, 80 D. & C. 605, 35 Erie 29.

⚿ 627(2). Necessity to serve.

Pa. 1958. Where the defendant had hearing before justice of the peace and had been arraigned, and information and indictment were read to him, he was given sufficient opportunity to examine charge prior to trial.

Com. ex rel. Haines v. Banmioller, 143 A.2d 661, 393 Pa. 439, certiorari denied 79 S.Ct. 101, 358 U.S. 868, 3 L.Ed.2d 100.

Pa.Quar.Sess. 1966. An information charging defendant with driving while under suspension, and his summary conviction thereof, will on petition be quashed, where defendant at the time of his arrest on view was not furnished with a copy of the information, as required by section 1204 of The Vehicle Code of April 29, 1959, P.L. 58 (75 P.S. § 1204).

Com. v. Ellenberger, 40 D. & C.2d 99, 48 West. 175.

Pa.Quar.Sess. 1940. Under The Vehicle Code of May 1, 1929, P.L. 905, art. XII, § 1202, 75 P.S. § 1202, where the defendant is criminally charged before a justice of the peace, a copy of the information must be furnished the defendant, but the copy need not be exact, and is sufficient if it notifies the defendant of the charge against him and of the time and place when he is alleged to have violated the law.

Com. v. Gerhard, 36 D. & C. 714, 55 Montg. 319.

⚿ 627(3)–627(4). ***For other cases see earlier editions of this digest, the Decennial Digests, and WESTLAW.***

⚿ 6275. Sufficiency of copy.

Pa.Com.Pl. 1971. The right of an accused to have his physician examine him pursuant to Section 524.1(g) of The Vehicle Code (75 P.S. § 624.1(g)) is subject to the following limitations: a. Such examination is only in addition to and not in lieu of the right of the police to have the accused examined. b. The accused has the burden of producing his physician. c. The production and the examination by the accused's physician must be promptly made.

Case of McGinnis Auto. License, 21 Bucks 320.

Pa.Quar.Sess. 1940. Under the Vehicle Code of May 1, 1929, P.L. 905, art. XII, § 1202, 75 P.S. § 1202, where the defendant is criminally charged before a justice of the peace, a copy of the information must be furnished the defendant, but the copy need not be exact, and is sufficient if it notifies the defendant of the charge against him and of the time and place when he is alleged to have violated the law.

Com. v. Gerhard, 36 D. & Co. 714, 55 Montg. 319.

The same exactitude and nicety in the preparation of papers required in a court of record are not required from the minor judiciary, not trained in the law.

Com. v. Gerhard, 36 D. & C. 714, 55 Montg. 319.

⚿ 627(6). Requisites of service.

Pa.Com.Pl. 1972. Where notations of police officer was not taken verbatim as a statement it was error to deny them to defense and where remark made by District Attorney was brought on by statement of defense counsel no mistrial would be granted.

Com. v. Hunt, 59 Del.Co. 565, affirmed 302 A.2d 840, 224 Pa.Super. 177.

⚿ 627(7). Objections for failure to serve, and waiver thereof.

Pa.Super. 1942. Where accused, arrested upon view on a charge of operating a motor vehicle while he was intoxicated, following a hearing before the magistrate, his being held for court, and finding of a true bill based upon the magistrate's transcript which gave accused full information of the offense with which he was charged, entered

†This case was not selected for publication in the National Reporter System
For legislative history of cited statutes, see Purdon's Pennsylvania Statutes Annotated

For later cases, see same Topic and Key Number in Pocket Part

bail for his appearance in court to answer the indictment, entry of bail was a "waiver" of arresting officer's failure to file information and to furnish accused a copy thereof. 75 P.S. § 733(a).

Com. v. Wideman, 28 A.2d 801, 150 Pa.Super. 524.

⊂⊃627.1. Lie detector, polygraph, drug or truth serum tests.

Library references

C.J.S. Criminal Law §§ 500, 501.

⊂⊃627.2. Depositions.

Library references

C.J.S. Criminal Law § 468.

C.A.3 (Pa.) 1989. Rule of criminal procedure dealing with notice of taking of deposition did not require that defendant subject to pretrial detention be present for depositions of witnesses in foreign country where defendant's attorney was physically present during depositions and where defendant was able to both hear witnesses and consult with attorney during depositions by means of telephone hookup. Fed. Rules Cr.Proc.Rule 15(b), 18 U.S.C.A.

U.S. v. Gifford, 892 F.2d 263, rehearing denied, certiorari denied 110 S.Ct. 3243, 497 U.S. 1006, 111 L.Ed.2d 754.

Pretrial detainee's due process rights were not violated as result of Government's deposing witnesses in foreign country, outside detainee's physical presence; detainee's attorney was present at depositions, and detainee was both able to her witnesses' testimony and consult with attorney during depositions by means of telephone hook-up. U.S.C.A. Const.Amends. 5, 14.

U.S. v. Gifford, 892 F.2d 263, rehearing denied, certiorari denied 110 S.Ct. 3243, 497 U.S. 1006, 111 L.Ed.2d 754.

C.A. 3 (Pa.) 1979. Although, in exceptional circumstances, the court may, upon motion, order that a deposition of a prospective witness be taken when it is in the interest of justice to do so, attendance of witnesses at trial is the favored method of presenting testimony; depositions are not favored in criminal cases. Fed. Rules Crim.Proc. rule 15(a), 18 U.S.C.A.

U.S. v. Wilson, 601 F.2d 95.

Where, at the time that petition for deposition of witness was presented, the witness was in a country which refused to extradite him and it was doubtful that he would return to the United States for trial and where his affidavit established that his testimony was relevant and, if believed, would be exculpatory to some extent, sufficient showing had been made to justify the taking of a deposition. Fed.Rules. Crim. Proc. rule 15(a), 18 U.S.C.A.

U.S. v. Wilson, 601 F.2d 95.

Fact that the person whose deposition defendants sought to take and introduce at trial was a fugitive did not provide a basis for denying the motion. Fed.Rules Crim.Proc. rule 15(a), 18 U.S.C.A.

U.S. v. Wilson, 601 F.2d 95.

E.D.Pa. 1988. Government made reasonable good-faith efforts to produce Belgian witnesses for trial, and hence, witnesses, who were unwilling to come to United States to testify, were unavailable, so as to allow admission of their videotaped depositions; witnesses were advised that Government would pay for their transportation, lodging and food while they were in the United States, and would pay them standard witness fee, and, notwithstanding Government's offer, witnesses refused to come to United States to testify at trial. Fed.Rules Evid. Rule 804(a), 28 U.S.C.A.; Fed.Rules Cr. Proc. Rule 15(e), 18 U.S.C.A.

U.S. v. Gifford, 684 F.Supp. 125, affirmed U.S. v. Kelly, 892 F.2d 255, hearing denied, certiorari denied 110 S.Ct. 3243, 497 U.S. 1006, 111 L.Ed.2d 754, affirmed in part, vacated in part 892 F.2d 263, rehearing denied, certiorari denied, 110 S.Ct. 3243, 497 U.S. 1006, 111 L.Ed.2d 754.

Depositions of custodians of foreign records were admissible, where their testimony by deposition permitted cross-examination by defendants' counsel, an opportunity which would have been foreclosed by permissible alternative of introducing records through foreign certification, and Government represented that witnessed were unwilling to come to United States for trial. 18 U.S.C.A. § 3505.

U.S. v. Gifford, 684 F.Supp. 125, affirmed U.S. v. Kelly, 892 F.2d 255, rehearing denied, certiorari denied, 110 S.Ct. 3243, 497 U.S. 1006, 111 L.Ed.2d 754, affirmed in part, vacated in part 892 F.2d 263, rehearing denied, certiorari denied 110 S.Ct. 3243, 497 U.S. 1006, 111 L.Ed.2d 754.

E.D.Pa. 1985. United States court cannot order that deposition of foreign national be taken.

U.S. v. Strong 608 F.Supp. 188.

Federal district court has power to issue request for judicial assistance or letters rogatory to foreign judiciary in criminal case.

U.S. v. Strong, 608 F.Supp. 188.

E.D.Pa. 1963. All of deposition of internal revenue agent, who had been discharged from internal revenue service, was not admissible, in prosecution for attempted tax evasion, as dying declaration, where it appeared that,

For references to other topics, see Descriptive-Word Index

although deponent was ill, there was no indication his case was hopeless or that he had given up all hope of survival.

U.S. v. Schwartz, 213 F.Supp. 306, reversed 325 F.2d 355.

Court has discretion to exclude parts of deposition bearing no probative value in case.

U.S. v. Schwartz, 213 F.Supp. 306, reversed 325 F.2d 355.

Any or all of deposition, so long as it is admissible under rules of evidence, may be used at trial. Fed.Rules Civ.Proc. rule 26(d), 28 U.S.C.A.

U.S. v. Schwartz, 213 F.Supp. 306, reversed 325 F.2d 355.

Objectionable evidence in depositions ought to be ruled out at trial. Fed.Rules Civ.Proc. rule 26(d), 28 U.S.C.A.

U.S. v. Schwartz, 213 F.Supp. 306, reversed 325 F.2d 355.

W.D.Pa. 1971. Testimony of defendant's doctor, a specialist in internal medicine and diabetes, as to defendant's medical condition would not have been admissible in income tax evasion prosecution had doctor taken stand, where doctor had never seen defendant in insulin shock and did not conclude that defendant lacked capacity to conform his conduct to requirements of law, and testimony was not admissible on deposition. Fed.Rules Crim.Proc. rule 15, 18 U.S.C.A.; 26 U.S.C.A. (I.R.C.1954) § 7201.

U.S. v. Mathews, 335 F.Supp. 157, appeal dismissed 462 F.2d 182, certiorari denied 93 S.Ct. 123, 409 U.S. 896, 34 L.Ed.2d 153.

Pa. 1999. Witnesses who had previously testified before grand jury against drug defendant, but said that they would not testify at trial, were not "unavailable" within meaning of rule allowing court to order the preservation of testimony. Rules Crim.Proc., Rule 9015, 42 Pa. C.S.A.

Com. V. Rizzo, 726 A.2d 378, 556 Pa. 10.

Rule allowing trial court to order the preservation of testimony should be used only when it is anticipated that a witness will be unable to be present at trial. Rules Crim.Proc., Rule 9015, 42 Pa. C.S.A.

Com. V. Rizzo, 726 A.2d 378, 556 Pa. 10.

Pa. 1993. Admission of deposition transcript of unavailable witness whose testimony exculpated codefendant and implicated defendant as "shooter" in homicide was reversible error, where jury's conclusion that defendant was guilty of third-degree murder while codefendant was only guilty of voluntary manslaughter could only have been due to jury disbelieving codefendant and at same time using witness' testimony against defendant in spite of trial court's instructions not to do so.

Com. v. LaRosa, 626 A.2d 103, 533 Pa. 479.

Pa. 1977. In order for common-law rule which gives state right to take and use depositions of unavailable witnesses to be applicable, the declarant's inability to give live testimony must in no way be the fault of the state.

Com. v. Stasko, 370 A.2d 350, 471 Pa. 373.

Under common-law rule which gives state right to take and use depositions of "unavailable" witnesses, witness is not "unavailable" unless prosecutorial authorities have made a good-faith effort to obtain his presence at trial. Fed.Rules Crim.Proc. rule 15, 18, U.S.C.A.; 18 U.S.C.A. § 3503.

Com. v. Stasko, 370 A.2d 350, 471 Pa. 373.

Trial court correctly permitted prosecution to take and use at trial a videotape deposition of an eyewitness to alleged murder where, inter alia, defendant was present at the deposition and his counsel extensively cross-examined the witness, deposition was conducted by judge who presided at trial, jury had opportunity through videotape to observe the witness' demeanor and judge her credibility and where witness' inability to give live testimony was due to illness which, in the opinion of her attending physician, would have been greatly aggravated by emotional strain of appearing at trial. P.S.Const. art. 1, § 9; U.S.C.A.Const. Amends. 6, 14; Fed.Rules Crim.Proc. rule 15, 18 U.S.C.A.; 18 U.S.C.A. § 3503.

Com. v. Stasko, 370 A.2d 350, 471 Pa. 373.

Pa. 1968. The court will not issue a commission or letters rogatory merely because it is in the best interests of petitioner; the interest of justice in general must require that the commission or letters rogatory be issued.

In re Mackarus' Estate, 246 A.2d 661, 431 Pa. 585.

Pa.Super. 1996. Pretrial hearing held pursuant to rule entitled preservation of testimony after institution of criminal proceedings was de facto a hearing regarding the validity of grant of immunity to witnesses, who were reluctant to testify against drug defendant, where prosecution requested and obtained orders of immunity after learning that witnesses would not testify at defendant's trial, and witnesses invoked their Fifth Amendment rights against self-incrimination, which made them unavailable. U.S.C.A. Const.Amend. 5; Rules Crim.Proc., Rule 9015, 42 Pa.C.S.A.

Com. v. Rizzo, 688 A.2d 185, 455 Pa.Super. 311, reargument denied, appeal granted 698 A.2d 593, 548 Pa. 668, reversed 726 A.2d 378, 556 Pa. 10.

†This case was not selected for publication in the National Reporter System
For legislative history of cited statutes, see Purdon's Pennsylvania Statutes Annotated

For later cases, see same Topic and Key Number in Pocket Part

⊂⇒ **627.5. Discovery prior to and incident to trial.**

Library references

C.J.S. Criminal Law §§ 486, 1210.

⊂⇒ **627.5(1). In general; examination of victim or witness.**

Examination to determine competency of witness, see WITNESSES.

C.A.3 (Pa.) 1975. Determination by district court of reasonableness of discovery request requires balancing the interests favoring and opposing discovery and whether scales are tipped for or against discovery depends upon where lies the most compelling need. Fed. Rules Crim.Proc. rule 16(b), 18 U.S.C.A.

U.S. v. Liebert, 519 F.2d 542, certiorari denied 96 S.Ct. 392, 423 U.S. 985, 46 L.Ed.2d 301.

Even when evidence sought in pretrial discovery is material for defense of criminal prosecution, discovery order should not have effect of lifting mantle of privacy of person having no connection with case if there are reasonable alternative means for securing information requested. Fed.Rules Crim.Proc. rule 16(b), 18 U.S.C.A.

U.S. v. Liebert, 519 F.2d 542, certiorari denied 96 S.Ct. 392, 423 U.S. 985, 46 L.Ed.2d 301.

C.A.3 (Pa.) 1972. Limiting of pretrial discovery in criminal cases is not constitutionally impermissible.

U.S. v. Randolph, 456 F.2d 132, certiorari denied Waller v. U.S., 92 S.Ct. 2507, 408 U.S. 926, 33 L.Ed.2d 337.

E.D.Pa. 2001. State prisoner convicted of rape had due process right of access to genetic material taken from rape victims, which was held by district attorney's office, for the limited purpose of conducting DNA testing; although prisoner's detailed and voluntary confession to the rapes was powerful inculpatory evidence, any DNA testing that would exclude prisoner as source of genetic material would be powerful exculpatory evidence. U.S.C.A. Const.Amend. 14.

Godschalk v. Montgomery County Dist. Attorney's Office, 177 F.Supp.2d 366.

E.D.Pa. 1993. Under Pennsylvania law, defendant has no independent right to his own copy of discoverable documents in state court criminal proceeding when represented by counsel and when documents are provided to defense counsel. Rules Crim.Proc., Rule 305, 42 Pa.C.S.A.

Williams v. Dark, 844 F.Supp. 210, affirmed 19 F.3d 645.

E.D.Pa. 1980. Fishing expeditions into government's files and records are not cognizable under *Brady* and its progeny, especially at the pretrial stage.

U.S. v. Deerfield Specialty Papers, Inc., 501 F.Supp. 796.

E.D.Pa. 1980. Defendant is entitled neither to wholesale discovery of Government's evidence nor to list of Government's prospective witnesses, and, ultimately, granting of motion for bill of particulars remains discretionary matter with trial court.

U.S. v. Holman, 490 F.Supp. 755.

E.D.Pa. 1979. Defendant was entitled to evidentiary hearing if he could make initial showing that there was a "colorable basis" for his selective prosecution claim, and to do this, defendant had to adduce some credible evidence tending to show existence of essential elements of this defense and that testimony would indeed be probative thereof, that is, defendant had to show existence of facts sufficient to raise reasonable doubt about prosecutor's purpose, and to take questions past frivolous stage.

U.S. v. Shober, 489 F.Supp. 393.

E.D.Pa. 1979. Criminal defendant is not entitled, in advance, to complete preview of government's evidence in case or to "wholesale discovery" of prosecutor's file. Fed.Rules Crim.Proc. rule 7(a), 18 U.S.C.A.

U.S. v. Pfeifer, 474 F.Supp. 498, affirmed 615 F.2d 1354, certiorari denied 100 S.Ct. 2162, 446 U.S. 940, 64 L.Ed.2d 794.

E.D.Pa. 1979. In prosecution for, among other things, participation in affairs of police department through a pattern of racketeering activity, indictment was drawn in sufficient detail to advise defendant of charges against him and to protect him from second prosecution for same offense and Government produced all discovery required by rule and, thus, court did not err in denial of motion for bill of particulars and for discovery. 18 U.S.C.A. § 1962(c, d); 26 U.S.C.A. (I.R.C. 1954) § 7206(1).

U.S. v. Nacrelli, 468 F.Supp. 241, affirmed 614 F.2d 771.

E.D.Pa. 1977. Purpose of Jencks Act is to restrict judicial power to order discovery against Government in criminal cases; although courts may advise, urge and request Government to turn over Jencks Act material at pretrial stage, they may not compel its production. 18 U.S.C.A. § 3500.

U.S. v. Bloom, 78 F.R.D. 591.

E.D.Pa. 1972. United States Supreme Court decision holding that suppression by prosecution of evidence favorable to accused on request violates due process when evidence is material either to guilt or to punishment, irrespective of good faith or bad faith of prosecution,

†This case was not selected for publication in the National Reporter System
For legislative history of cited statutes, see Purdon's Pennsylvania Statutes Annotated

effective assistance of counsel because trial counsel failed to question inference that petitioner possesses weapon found under front armrest of car he drove, where *Wisor* decision, under which it could have been argued that it was not proper to infer that petitioner knew of presence of weapon, was decided after petitioner's trial was concluded, and moreover counsel did argue, in nature of demurrer, that Commonwealth had not proven that petitioner exercised control over weapon and argued the "equal access" question to jury. 18 Pa.C.S.A. §§ 901 et seq., 906, 6106.—Com. v. Lowry, 394 A.2d 1015, 260 Pa.Super. 454.

Pa.Cmwlth.2001. Counsel can never be deemed ineffective for failing to raise a claim that has not merit. U.S.C.A. Const.Amend. 6.—Com. v. Bailey, 775 A.2d 881.

⊂⊃ 641.13(3).—Indigent's or incompetent's counsel and public defenders.

Library references

ABA Standards for Criminal Justice

The Defense Function 3.9 1st Ed.

⊂⊃ 641.13(5).—Pretrial proceedings; sanity hearing.

C.A.3 (Pa.) 2001. In assessing prejudice due to allegedly deficient performance of counsel in the context of a determination regarding a defendant's competency, the question is whether there was a reasonable probability that he would have been found incompetent to stand trial. U.S.C.A. Const. Amend. 6.—Jermyn v. Horn, 266 F.3d 257.

Failure on part of counsel to request that trial court to order to hearing or evaluation on the issue of the defendant's competency may violate the defendant's right to effective assistance of counsel, provided there are sufficient indicia of incompetence to give objectively reasonable counsel reason to doubt the defendant's competency, and there is a reasonable probability that the defendant would have been found incompetent to stand trial had the issue been raised and fully considered. U.S.C.A. Const.Amend. 6.—Id.

An attorney renders ineffective assistance of counsel if he or she fails to inquire into a defendant's competency and fails to request a competency hearing, despite indicia of incompetence that would provide reasonable counsel reason to doubt the defendant's ability to understand the proceedings, communicate with counsel, and assist in his own defense. U.S.C.A. Const.Amend. 6.—Id.

Capital murderer defendant failed to show that his counsel was ineffective in failing to seek competency hearing or evaluation prior to or during trial, even though counsel had been unable to have normal, orderly conversations with defendant regarding his representation, where counsel had obtained a competency evaluation of defendant from mental health expert, but there was no indication in record as to what expert's conclusions were. U.S.C.A. Const.Amend. 6.—Id.

E.D.Pa. 2001. Defendant knowingly waived his right to challenge sentencing guideline calculations to which he had stipulated, even if defense counsel failed to inform him of his right to counsel on appeal, where government's counsel advised defendant during guilty plea colloquy that he was giving up his right to appeal sentence imposed and right to challenge sentence subsequent to appeal in any collateral attack, defendant acknowledged that statement by government's counsel accurately reflected his agreement, court informed defendant that he was entitled to appointed counsel at every step in proceedings, and defendant failed to identify any potentially meritorious basis on which appeal would have been successful.—U.S. v. Maldonado, 166 F.Supp.2d 1049.

E.D.Pa. 2001. Defendant charged with drug conspiracy was not denied effective assistance of counsel on ground that he decided to enter plea of guilty based upon counsel's advice of likely sentence far less than what he received, and he would not have pled guilty if counsel had given him correct advice about consequences of guilty plea, absent evidence of prejudice; judge informed defendant during his change of plea hearing that he faced life imprisonment and that, regardless of any statements by his attorney concerning length of his sentence, court would decide sentence and could sentence him to life in prison, and sentence imposed was less that statutory maximum. U.S.C.A. Const.Amend. 6; Comprehensive Drug Abuse Prevention and Control Act of 1970, § 401(b), 21 U.S.C.A. § 841(b).—Irrizari v. U.S., 153 F.Supp.2d 722.

E.D.Pa. 2001. Attorney's failure to provide defendant advice concerning an entrapment defense did not constitute ineffective assistance of counsel, although defendant allegedly entered guilty plea to gain two-point sentence reduction for acceptance of responsibility even though he could have gotten reduction if he had gone to trial and argued entrapment defense, where reduction was essentially meaningless in view of statutory minimum sentence, and defendant was willing and eager to consummate drug transaction that led to his conviction, he was not lured into committing criminal act, and his will was not overpowered by federal agent. U.S.C.A. Const.Amend. 6.—U.S. v. Piccolo, 132 F.Supp.2d 326.

M.D.Pa. 2000. Failure to warn a client of the deportation consequence of a plea does not constitute ineffective assistance of counsel. U.S.C.A. Const.Amend. 6.—Taveras-Lopez v. Reno, 127 F.Supp.2d 598.

Pa. 1980. Failure of trial counsel to have a large group of black males present at preliminary hearing so it would be more difficult for the victim to make an identification of defendant did not amount to ineffective assistance of counsel.—Com. v. Arthur, 412 A.2d 498, 488 Pa. 262, certiorari denied Arthur v. Pennsylvania, 101 S.Ct. 166, 449 U.S. 862, 66 L.Ed.2d 79.

Pa. Super. 2001. Generally, counsel has a duty to communicate plea bargains to his client, as well as to explain the advantages and disadvantages of the offer, and failure to do so may be considered ineffectiveness of counsel if the defendant is sentenced to a longer prison term than the term he would have accepted under the plea bargain. U.S.C.A. Const.Amend. 6.—Com. v. Marinez, 777 A.2d 1121.

Pa.Super. 2001. Defendant was not prejudiced by trial counsel's failure to file defendant's motion to withdraw his plea of nolo contendere in a timely manner, and thus defendant could not prevail on his claim that counsel was ineffective, as the trial court nonetheless considered the motion on the merits.—Com. v. Jefferson, 777 A.2d 1104.

⊂⊃ 641.13(6).—Evidence; procurement, presentation and objections.

C.A.3 (Pa.) 2001. Right to assistance of counsel does not require that a criminal defense attorney leave no stone unturned and no witness unpursued, but it does require a reasoned judgment as to the amount of investigation the particular circumstances of a given case require. U.S.C.A. Const. Amend. 6.—Jermyn v. Horn, 266 F.3d 257.

Strategic choices made by counsel after less than complete investigation are reasonable precisely to the extent that reasonable professional judgments support the limitations in investigation. U.S.C.A. Const.Amend. 6.—Id.

C.A.3 (Pa.) 2001. Defendant was not prejudiced, so as to establish ineffective assistance of counsel, by trial counsel's failure to object to testimony that would have been admitted over objection. U.S.C.A. Const.Amend. 6.—Keller v. Larkins, 251 F.3d 408, certiorari denied 122 S.Ct. 396.

E.D.Pa. 2001. Defense counsel's alleged failure to investigate and interview witness who purportedly could provide evidence of collusion among government witness was not ineffective assistance of counsel in prosecution for armed bank robbery and conspiracy to commit such offense; defendant did not define what such evidence was. U.S.C.A. Const.Amend. 6; 18 U.S.C.A. §§ 371, 2113(d).—U.S. v. Williams, 166 F.Supp.2d 286.

For a failure to investigate to constitute ineffective assistance, a defendant must show what exculpatory evidence would have been uncovered by further investigation. U.S.C.A. Const.Amend. 6.—Id.

Even if an attorney is deficient in the decision not to conduct pretrial investigation, a defendant asserting ineffective assistance of counsel must show a reasonable likelihood that, but for the deficiency, the result of the proceeding would have been different. U.S.C.A. Const.Amend. 6.—Id.

A defendant alleging that failure to investigate was ineffective assistance of counsel must show a reasonable likelihood that the investigation would have produced useful information not already known to counsel. U.S.C.A. Const.Amend. 6.—Id.

Defense counsel's failure to obtain "scribes and diaries" taken from a government witness was not ineffective assistance of counsel in prosecution for armed bank robbery; defendant made absolutely no showing as to what type of evidence would have been revealed by this discovery. U.S.C.A. Const. Amend. 6; 18 U.S.C.A. § 2113(d).—Id.

E.D.Pa. 2001. Failure to conduct any pretrial investigation generally constitutes a clear instance of ineffectiveness of counsel. U.S.C.A. Const. Amend. 6.—Holloway v. Horn, 161 F.Supp.2d 452.

There can be no strategic or tactical reason for counsel to fail to request that a mental health expert be appointed to assist the defense when mental health issues could be a significant factor at either the guilt or penalty phase, because such an expert is necessary to effectively develop and present such evidence, as well as to assist counsel and his client in deciding whether such evidence should be presented at trial. U.S.C.A. Const.Amend. 6.—Id.

E.D.Pa. 2001. Under *Strickland,* counsel's failure to assert a particular defense can not be characterized as a "strategy" unless counsel has investigated and consciously rejected a particular defense. U.S.C.A. Const.Amend. 6.—Laird v. Horn, 159 F.Supp.2d 58.

E.D.Pa. 2001. Defendant's trial counsel was not constitutionally ineffective for presenting allegedly harmful arguments and evidence at trial; thus, no cause or prejudice existed by which to excuse defendant's state procedural default of ineffective assistance of counsel subclaims, and therefore they were not reviewable by federal habeas court. U.S.C.A. Const.Amend. 6; 28 U.S.C.A. § 2254(b, c)—Holland v. Horn, 150 F.Supp.2d 706.

E.D.Pa. 2001. Defense counsel was not ineffective because he failed to interview and call certain potential witnesses; witnesses who were not called were not helpful to the planned defense and defendant never told counsel about certain witnesses who were not interviewed. U.S.C.A. Const.Amend. 6.—Levan v. U.S., 128 F.Supp.2d 270.

Determining which witnesses to call at trial is intrinsically strategic and therefore left to the discretion of counsel. U.S.C.A. Const.Amend. 6.—Id.

E.D.Pa. 1983. McNeil v. Cuyler, 576 F.Supp. 1343, vacated, on subsequent appeal 782 F.2d 443, certiorari denied 107 S.Ct. 654, 479 U.S. 1010, 93 L.Ed.2d 709.

M.D.Pa. 2001. Trial counsel's performance was not deficient for failing to adequately investigate and present evidence supporting the diminished capacity defense in capital murder trial; no evidence was presented that counsel had any indicia of a disorder on defendant's part that would have triggered his duty to investigate for purposes of the guilt phase of the trial. U.S.C.A. Const.Amend. 6.—Jacobs v. Horn, 129 F.Supp.2d 390.

Trial counsel's performance was not deficient for not properly investigating and impeaching the testimony of defendant's mother concerning admissions that he made to her; because the trial testimony of the defendant's mother was consistent with defendant's own testimony, it was important that her current version and recollection of her conversations with the defendant be viewed as accurate by the jury, and, therefore, counsel's actions were sound trial strategy and not ineffective assistance of counsel. U.S.C.A. Const.Amend. 6.—Id.

Trial counsel was not ineffective for not objecting to lay opinion testimony from a police officer and appeal counsel was not ineffective for not raising the issue on appeal; officer was merely commenting on the appearance of cuts that he personally observed, and any error was harmless. U.S.C.A. Const.Amend. 6.—Id.

Pa. 2001. Defense counsel's failing to object to the admission of several photographs depicting the gravesite as it appeared both prior to and during the police excavation, none of which included a close-up view of victim's body, was not ineffective assistance; photographs gave jury greater insight into the actual condition of the gravesite at the time that the police arrived at the scene, corroborated testimony regarding partial excavation, of grave by witnesses who discovered it, and documented ongoing grid excavation of gravesite that police employed to preserve integrity of evidence discovered there. U.S.C.A. Const.Amend. 6.—Com. v. Begley, 780 A.2d 605.

Defense counsel's alleged ineffective assistance in failing to call defendant's friend to testify did not prejudice defendant; proposed testimony that defendant once declined offer to borrow rifle for deer hunting would not have established defendant would never borrow a firearm, proposed testimony that defendant once cleaned a gun for friend in a "meticulous" fashion did contradict testimony that shotgun had been cleaned up a little bit, when defendant returned it, and proposed testimony that friend once saw defendant cut a piece of duct tape and fold end of roll did not prove defendant would have done so when using tape to gag young woman before murdering her. U.S.C.A. Const.Amend. 6.—Id.

For a defendant to establish that he is entitled to relief based on a claim of ineffective assistance of counsel for failing to present a witness, he must prove that: (1) the witness existed; (2) counsel was either aware of or should have been aware of the witness's availability; (3) the witness was willing and able to cooperate on behalf of the defendant; and (4) the proposed testimony was necessary to avoid prejudice to the defendant. U.S.C.A. Const. Amend. 6.—Id.

Defense counsel's failing to present testimony to establish that murder victim was in an abusive relationship, that she had a falling out with her boyfriend prior to her disappearance, and that boyfriend was not seen in a restaurant that he frequented for a couple of days around the time of victim's disappearance was a reasonable tactical decision, rather than ineffective assistance; counsel opted against pointing a finger of suspicion at boyfriend based on belief that it would only offend the jury to do so absent any direct or circumstantial evidence linking boyfriend to the murder. U.S.C.A. Const.Amend 6.—Id.

D. Exercise 5.4: Illinois Digest Section 9(3)

1. A case in which words impeached the creditworthiness of a merchant, by imputing bankruptcy, would possibly be actionable as a libel case.
   a. True
   b. False
2. Only oral statements or assertions can be the subject matter of an actionable libel suit.
   a. True
   b. False
3. All of the decisions cited in this section are appellate.
   a. True
   b. False
4. Statements that impugn the business or professional reputation of a person are actionable.
   a. True
   b. False
5. Teachers cannot bring an action for libel.
   a. True
   b. False

E. Exercise 5.5: West's Federal Practice Digest, 4th (Topical Outline to Contracts)

1. To determine if a minor is capable of entering into a contract, which section should be consulted?
   a. 1
   b. 11
   c. 14
   d. 15
2. The possibility of a case resulting from a contract is not evident in this outline.
   a. True
   b. False
3. Some of the formal requirements of a contract are
   a. Signature
   b. Attestation
   c. Both a and b
   d. Neither a nor b
4. This outline implies that consideration can take the form of things other than money.
   a. True
   b. False

termination of distributor did not imply commission of criminal offense, so as to be actionable per se by implying that distributor lacked integrity and was dishonest.—Darovec Marketing Group, Inc. v. Bio-Genics, Inc., 42 F.Supp.2d 810.

Ill.App. 1 Dist. 2000. In order to constitute defamation per se for inputing commission of a criminal offense, crime must be indictable one, involving moral turpitude and punishable by death.—Gardner v. Senior Living Systems, Inc., 246 Ill.Dec. 822, 731 N.E.2d 350, 314 Ill.App.3d 114.

Ill.App. 1 Dist. 1999. Four categories of statements are considered "defamatory per se": words that impute commission of crime; words that impute infection with loathsome communicable disease; words that impute inability to perform or want of integrity in discharge of duties of office or employment; and words that prejudice party, or impute lack of ability, in his or her trade, profession or business.—Dubinsky v. United Airlines Master Executive Council, 236 Ill.Dec. 855, 708 N.E.2d 441, 303 Ill.App.3d 317, appeal denied 239 Ill.Dec. 607, 714 N.E.2d 526, 184 Ill.2d 555.

⚡7(6). Assault, burglary, robbery and homicide.

Ill.App. 1 Dist. 1998. Van Horne v. Muller, 229 Ill.Dec. 138, 691 N.E.2d 74, 294 Ill.App.3d 649, appeal allowed 232 Ill.Dec. 853, 699 N.E.2d 1038, 178 Ill.2d 597, affirmed in part, reversed in part 235 Ill.Dec. 715, 705 N.E.2d 898, 185 Ill.2d 299, rehearing denied, certiorari denied 120 S.Ct. 43, 528 U.S. 811, 145 L.Ed.2d 39.

⚡7(16). Want of chastity or sexual crimes in general.

Ill.App. 1 Dist. 2000. Statements that fall into the category of defamatory per se include those that: (1) impute the commission of a criminal offense, (2) impute infection with a loathsome communicable disease, (3) impute inability to perform or lack of integrity in the discharge of duties of office or employment, (4) prejudice a party or impute lack of ability in her trade, profession or business, and (5) those that impute adultery or fornication.—Gardner v. Senior Living Systems, Inc., 246 Ill.Dec. 822, 731 N.E.2d 350, 314 Ill. App.3d 114.

⚡8. Words imputing contagious or venereal disease.

Ill.App. 1 Dist. 2000. Four categories of statements are considered defamatory per se: (1) words that impute the commission of a criminal offense, (2) words that impute infection with a loathsome communicable disease, (3) words that impute an inability to perform or want of integrity in the discharge of duties of office of employment, and (4) words that prejudice a party, or impute a lack of ability, in his or her trade, profession, or business.—Wynne v. Loyola Univ. of Chicago, 251 Ill.Dec. 782, 741 N.E.2d 669, 318 Ill.App.3d 443.

Ill.App. 1 Dist. 2000. The four recognized categories of per se defamatory statements are words that impute: (1) the commission of a crime; (2) infection with a communicable disease; (3) inability to perform or want of integrity to discharge duties of office or employment and prejudice to a party; or (4) lack of ability in a person's trade, profession or business.—Moriarty v. Greene, 247 Ill.Dec. 675, 732 N.E.2d 730, 315 Ill.App.3d 225, rehearing denied, appeal denied 253 Ill.Dec. 3, 744 N.E.2d 285, 193 Ill.2d 589.

Ill.App. 1 Dist. 2000. Statements that fall into the category of defamatory per se include those that: (1) impute the commission of a criminal offense, (2) impute infection with a loathsome communicable disease, (3) impute inability to perform or lack of integrity in the discharge of duties of office or employment, (4) prejudice a party or impute lack of ability in her trade, profession or business, and (5) those that impute adultery or fornication.—Gardner v. Senior Living Systems, Inc., 246 Ill.Dec. 822, 731 N.E.2d 350, 314 Ill. App.3d 114.

Ill.App. 1 Dist. 1999. Four categories of statements are considered "defamatory per se": words that impute commission of crime; words that impute infection with loathsome communicable disease; words that impute inability to perform or want of integrity in discharge of duties of office or employment; and words that prejudice party, or impute lack of ability, in his or her trade, profession or business.—Dubinsky v. United Airlines Master Executive Council, 236 Ill.Dec. 855, 708 N.E.2d 441, 303 Ill.App.3d 317, appeal denied 239 Ill.Dec. 607, 714 N.E.2d 526, 184 Ill.2d 555.

⚡9(1). In general.

C.A.7 (Ill.) 2001. An author's opinion about business ethics isn't defamatory under Illinois law.—Wilkow v. Forbes, Inc., 241 F.3d 552, rehearing and rehearing denied.

While capitalism does not depend on sharp practices, an allegation of sharp dealing is not anything more than an uncharitable opinion, which is not defamatory under Illinois law.—Id.

N.D.Ill. 2001. In evaluating claim of defamation per se under Illinois law, innocent construction rule requires that court should, if context permits, limit statements about plaintiff to particular setting or single instance, so that statements do not generally impugn plaintiff's fitness for his or her chosen occupation.—Skolnick v. Correctional Medical Services, Inc., 312 F.Supp.2d 1116.

Under Illinois law, statement is actionable as defamatory per se if, when taken in context, it generally impugns person's fitness for his or her profession, even if statement is limited to particular setting or single instance.—Id.

N.D.Ill. 1999. Under Illinois law, memorandum sent by manufacturer to other representatives upon termination of distributor did not imply lack of ability in distributor's business, so as to be actionable per se, by speaking in terms of distributor's character.—Darovec Marketing Group, Inc. v. BioGenics, Inc., 42 F.Supp.2d 810.

Under Illinois law, memorandum sent by manufacturer to other representatives upon distributor's termination imputed want of business integrity to distributor's principals, so as to be defamatory per se, by referring to manufacturer's commitment to honesty and integrity and indicating that distributor's termination stemmed in part from policy violations and "blatant" disregard for other distributors.—Id.

Under Illinois law, statement in official memorandum sent by manufacturer to its other distributors, which announced that former distributor had blatantly disregarded welfare of their other distributors and therefore lacked integrity, was reasonably interpreted as stating actual facts, rather than nonactionable opinion. U.S.C.A. Const.Amend. 1.—Id.

Ill.App. 1 Dist. 2000. Four categories of statements are considered defamatory per se: (1) words that impute the commission of a criminal offense, (2) words that impute infection with a loathsome communicable disease, (3) words that impute an inability to perform or want of integrity in the discharge of duties of office of employment, and (4) words that prejudice a party, or impute a lack of ability, in his or her trade, profession, or business.—Wynne v. Loyola Univ. of Chicago, 251 Ill.Dec. 782, 741 N.E.2d 669, 318 Ill.App.3d 443.

Ill.App. 1 Dist. 2000. Newspaper columnist's statement that psychologist chosen by biological father to help child adjust to new custody arrangement after child was removed from adoptive parents' home has readily admitted that she sees her job as doing whatever the natural parents instruct her to do was "defamatory per se"; on its face, it stated psychologist's inability to perform, or

continued

want of integrity to discharge, duties of employment, and it stated psychologist's lack of ability in her profession.—Moriarty v. Greene, 247 Ill.Dec. 675, 732 N.E.2d 730, 315 Ill.App.3d 225, rehearing denied, appeal denied 253 Ill.Dec. 3, 744 N.E.2d 285, 193 Ill.2d 589.

The four recognized categories of per se defamatory statements are words that impute: (1) the commission of a crime; (2) infection with a communicable disease; (3) inability to perform or want of integrity to discharge duties of office or employment and prejudice to a party; or (4) lack of ability in a person's trade, profession or business.—Id.

A defamatory meaning that psychologist would ignore her professional obligations, rather than an innocent construction, was more probable as to newspaper columnist's statement that the psychologist, who was chosen by biological father to help child adjust to new custody arrangement after child was removed from adoptive parents' home, "has readily admitted that she sees her job as doing whatever the natural parents instruct her to do," where the overriding point of the column was that the psychologist was aiding and abetting the desires of the biological father, who allegedly was not acting in his child's best interest.—Id.

Newspaper columnist's statement that psychologist chosen by biological father to help child adjust to new custody arrangement after child was removed from adoptive parents' home 'has readily admitted that she sees her job as doing whatever the natural parents instruct her to do' was not an "opinion" that was entitled to First Amendment protection in the psychologist's defamation action. U.S.C.A. Const. Amend. 1.—Id.

Newspaper column merely expressed columnist's "opinion," which was protected by the First Amendment as to psychologist's defamation action, that it would be unprofessional for the psychologist, who was chosen by biological father to help child adjust to new custody arrangement after child was removed from adoptive parents' home, to write a book about the child, where the column quoted the psychologist's affirmative statement that she was no longer considering writing a book about the child. U.S.C.A. Const. Amend. 1.—Id.

Newspaper columnist's suggestion that a professional psychologist would not participate in or condone the abrupt removal of a child from an adoptive home where he had lived for four years was a nonactionable "opinion."—Id.

Newspaper columnist's suggestion that a reputable psychologist would not take a vacation while a client was in crisis was a nonactionable "opinion."—Id.

Newspaper columnist's suggestion that a reputable psychologist would not counsel a complete separation of a child from his adoptive family and siblings in the particular circumstances cited in the column, and the resulting reasonable inference that plaintiff was a bad psychologist, was a nonactionable "opinion."—Id.

Statement by newspaper columnist that the plaintiff psychologist was 'the woman who came up with the plan to take [the child] from his adoptive home suddenly with no transition period' was a nonactionable "opinion."—Id.

Newspaper columnist's statement that the plaintiff psychologist was 'the person selected by the natural parents to treat [the child,] and she does not feel the brothers who loved each other need to see or speak with each other,' was a nonactionable "opinion" regarding psychologist chosen by biological father to help child adjust to new custody arrangement after child was removed from adoptive parents' home.—Id.

Statement by newspaper columnist that psychologist, chosen by biological father to help child adjust to new custody arrangement after child was removed from adoptive parents' home, had a 'sudden removal plan' was nonactionable "opinion."—Id.

Statement by newspaper columnist that psychologist had said it would be a 'wonderful feather in my professional hat' to prove that her plan for the child had worked was a nonactionable "opinion" in defamation action against columnist, brought by psychologist chosen by biological father to help child adjust to new custody arrangement after child was removed from adoptive parents' home.—Id.

Ill.App. 1 Dist. 2000. Statements that fall into the category of defamatory per se includes those that: (1) impute the commission of a criminal offense, (2) impute infection with a loathsome communicable disease, (3) impute inability to perform or lack of integrity in the discharge of duties of office or employment, (4) prejudice a party or impute lack of ability in her trade, profession or business, and (5) those that impute adultery or fornication.—Gardner v. Senior Living Systems, Inc., 246 Ill.Dec. 822, 731 N.E.2d 350, 314 Ill. App.3d 114.

Ill.App. 1 Dist. 1999. Four categories of statements are considered "defamatory per se": words that impute commission of crime; words that impute infection with loathsome communicable disease; words that impute inability to perform or want of integrity in discharge of duties of office or employment; and words that prejudice party, or impute lack of ability, in his or her trade, profession or business.—Dubinsky v. United Airlines Master Executive Council, 236 Ill.Dec. 855, 708 N.E.2d 441, 303 Ill.App.3d 317, appeal denied 239 Ill.Dec. 607, 714 N.E.2d 526, 184 Ill.2d 555.

⊂⊃ 9(5). Teachers.

N.D.Ill. 2001. Fellow-teachers' statements, that first grade teacher's behavior around female students was "unprofessional," was actionable as defamation under Illinois law, when accompanied by allegations of specific conduct on part of teacher, capable of verification.—Bogosian v. Board of Educ. of Community Unit School Dist. 200, 134 F.Supp.2d 952.

Fellow teachers gave opinions regarding first grade teacher, not actionable as defamation under Illinois law, when they stated that teacher had "need" to touch female students, and that his conduct "wasn't right," when statements were not accompanied by any factual allegations capable of verification.—Id.

Ill.App. 1 Dist. 2000. Statements regarding professor in memorandum authored by university employee did not constitute actionable defamation, where none of the phrases used by employee were capable of verification, and employee was merely expressing her opinions regarding professor.—Wynne v. Loyola Univ. of Chicago, 251 Ill.Dec. 782, 741 N.E.2d 669, 318 Ill.App.3d 443.

⊂⊃ 9(8). Authors and newspapers.

N.D.Ill. 2001. Under Illinois law, letter from attorney for health care provider for correctional institutions to newspaper stating that reporter employed objectionable newsgathering tactics and was deliberately deceptive, dishonest, and fraudulent by failing to tell provider that he was writing article for newspaper was not defamatory per se, where reporter admitted he did not name newspaper, and context of letter demonstrated that strong language therein was more rhetoric and hyperbole.—Skolnick v. Correctional Medical Services, Inc., 132 F.Supp.2d 1116.

Under Illinois law, statement in letter from chief medical officer for health care provider for correctional institutions to medical journal that one of its reporters employed "questionable reporting tactics" was limited to single instance and did not

I. REQUISITES AND VALIDITY.

(A) NATURE AND ESSENTIALS IN GENERAL.

⚷ 1. Nature and grounds of contractual obligation.
2. What law governs.
3. Express contract.
6. Executed contract.
7. Nature of subject-matter.
8. Existence and condition of subject-matter.
9. Certainty as to subject-matter.
  (1). In general.
  (2). Services and compensation therefor.
  (3). Place and time.
10. Mutuality of obligation.
  (1). In general.
  (2). Building, manufacturers, and services.
  (3). Contracts of carriage.
  (4). Sales in general.
  (5). Sales and conveyances of land.
  (6). Loans and advances.
  (7). Slot machine contract.

(B) PARTIES, PROPOSALS, AND ACCEPTANCE.

⚷ 11. Capacity to contract in general.
12. Contract in particular capacity.
13. Number of parties.
14. Intent of parties.
15. Necessity of assent.
16. Offer and acceptance in general.
17. Request or advertisement for proposals.
18. Making and communication of offer.
19. Revocation or withdrawal of offer.
20. Lapse of offer.
21. Rejection of offer.
22. Acceptance of offer and communication thereof.
  (1). In general.
  (2). Acceptance shown by signature.
  (3). Necessity of communicating acceptance.
23. Qualified or conditional acceptance of offer.
24. Acceptance varying from offer.
25. Agreement to make contract in future.
26. Contracts by correspondence.
27. Implied agreements.
28. Evidence of agreement.
  (.5). In general.
  (1). Presumptions and burden of proof.
  (2). Admissibility.
  (3). Weight and sufficiency.
29. Questions for jury.

(C) FORMAL REQUISITES.

⚷ 30. Form as element of contract.

continued

25 F P D 4th—247 **CONTRACTS**

I. REQUISITES AND VALIDITY.—Continued.

(C) FORMAL REQUISITES.—Continued.

31. Necessity of writing in general.
32. Agreements to be reduced to writing.
33. Form and contents of instrument.
34. Execution.
35. Signature.
36. Seal.
37. Attestation.
38. Affixing revenue stamps.
39. Incomplete instruments.
40. Several instruments.
41. Confirmation or ratification of defective instrument.
42. Delivery.
43. Acceptance.
44. Filing or recording.
45. Evidence.
46. Questions for jury.

(D) CONSIDERATION.

🔑 47. Necessity in general.
48. Contracts under seal.
49. Nature and elements.
50. —— In general.
51. —— Benefit to promisor.
52. —— Detriment to promisee.
53. Adequacy.
54. Sufficiency in general.
    (1). In general.
    (2). Withholding competition.
    (3). Surrender or payment of doubtful or disputed claim.
55. Mutual promises.
56. —— In general.
57. —— Mutuality.
58. —— Contingent or conditional promises.
59. —— Options and refusals.
60. Personal rights and relations.
61. Services.
62. Property and rights therein in general.
    (1). In general.
    (2). Rights in public lands.
    (3). Property and rights therein of married women.
63. Money, investments, and securities.
64. Loans and advances.
65. Rights under contracts.
    (1). In general.
    (2). Consideration for subsidiary provision of contract.
    (3). Release or transfer of interest in contract or claim.
    (4). Repayment of amount received on contract.
66. Assumption of liability.

CHAPTER

6

COMPUTER-ASSISTED LEGAL RESEARCH

In the 1980s, with the increased use of computers, databases of legal information were created to assist the researcher. These early forays into the realms of computer-assisted legal research (CALR), involving statutes and case law, were long, complicated journeys. In the late 1980s to early 1990s, CDs were created that could hold 70 times the amount of information a floppy disk could. Statutes, formbooks, and various other resources that contained great amounts of information were published on these small, portable disks. Over the last 15 years, with the advance of technology and the advent and abundant usage of the Internet, legal research has gone in another direction: online searchable databases with instantaneous results. Legal resources have never been more available! Free online resources such as FindLaw, the Legal Information Institute of Cornell University Law School, congressional and senate law libraries, the Government Printing Office, and most state Web sites make our nation's law available to anyone with a computer and access to the World Wide Web.

Two groundbreakers in the field of CALR are LexisNexis and Westlaw. Always the first with new innovations, both have taken computer-assisted research to new dimensions, constantly improving and expanding services to meet the needs of their ever-growing customer base. This chapter gives the researcher a basic overview of the art of CALR and introduces some of the many search engines available today. The exercises provided throughout this text will help develop the necessary skills for this unique form of research. It is also suggested that the fact patterns previously presented in this work be used to hone the researcher's skills using any available method of CALR.

I. TERMINOLOGY OF THE SEARCH ENGINES

What is a **Boolean** search? In a Boolean search, only the words searched for will appear in the results. Words such as "and," "or," and "not" are used either to connect words or to exclude certain undesirable terms that might otherwise appear in search results. For example, if the topic of research is sexual assault statistics among adults, resources concerning children would appear in the search results if only the words "sexual assault statistics" were searched. By including the terms "AND" and "NOT" in the query and using the following sequence, resources that include references to children should be excluded:

(sexual assault) AND statistics AND adult NOT children

Another type of search, called a **concept search**, requires the researcher to enter key terms that can be identified as a concrete idea. This type of search will also look for related concepts. For example, if the researcher needs information regarding varying forms of homicide and the evidence needed to prove guilt, the following words may be entered in a concept search:

homicide evidence proof guilt

The search engine will also identify "murder," "manslaughter," and "elements of crime" as valid hits. A **pattern search** will look for words with patterns similar to the inserted search words. This is a handy feature when the spelling of a term or a person's name varies, or if the researcher is uncertain about the spelling.

Wildcard searching is used when the same root word is desired with different endings. For examples, if the word *evidence* is applicable and *evidentiary* is as well, the following could be entered in the search field:

eviden*
or eviden!

Whether an asterisk or an exclamation point is used depends on the search engine. These characters are often called **expanders**. When they are used in a search, the engine will search for words beginning with "eviden" and return results with various endings.

Limiters do exactly as the name indicates: limit the placement of words in relation to other words. The most common form for the usage of limiters on the Internet is as follows:

word1 word2 within N

This means that word 1 must appear within N number of words of word 2. For example, if the case at hand concerns rape *and* burglary, but searches are only returning separate results for each term, limiters may narrow the search results if the following terms are entered:

rape burglary within 10

These are only a few of the different types of searches that are possible today on the Web. Special guidance appears in most search engines regarding limiters, Boolean operators, and advanced searches. If the results are not as expected, make sure to check the site's instructions for guidance.

II. LEGAL DATABASES FOR THE GENERAL PUBLIC

Several excellent Web sites for legal research are available free of charge for anyone in need of them. These sites feature easy-to-use search engines and return results in a variety of ways.

A. FindLaw

Perhaps the most-used free legal research Web site in existence is **FindLaw**, at **http://www.findlaw.com**. Owned and operated by Westlaw, FindLaw features user-friendly search engines and easy-to-navigate tables of contents in its legal references section. See FindLaw's home page in Figure 6.1. Sections for legal professionals, law students, businesses, and the general public are included on this site, which includes an enormous number of references.

FindLaw's "Cases and Codes" section contains many state and federal resources commonly needed. Federally, its database includes the U.S. Constitution, the U.S. Code, the Code of Federal Regulations, the *Federal Register*, and links to the U.S. Supreme Court, U.S. Courts of Appeal, and various U.S. trial court decisions. Many of the resources are onsite, although some require redirection to other Web sites. Figure 6.2 shows the FindLaw search page for the U.S. Code.

The search page for the U.S. Code, and the similar page for the C.F.R., are simple to use and give the option to search by title and section number or by keyword. United States Supreme Court opinions since 1893 are available onsite in both searchable and browsable formats. The search screen is reproduced in Figure 6.3.

FIGURE 6.1

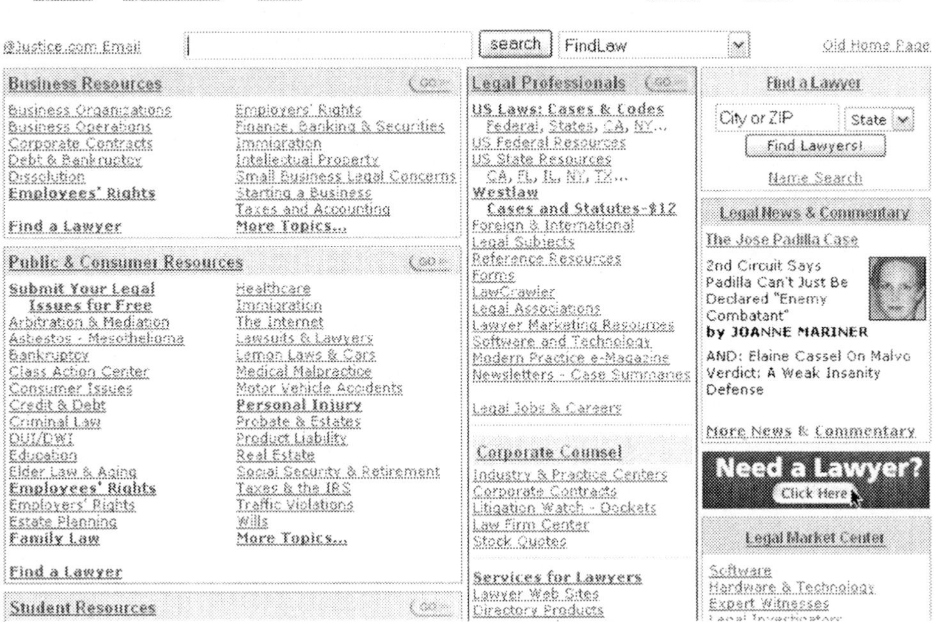

FIGURE 6.2

FindLaw
for Legal Professionals
We Have Your Expert.
Cases & Codes | Forms | Legal Subjects | Federal | State | Library | Boards
Law Firm FirmSites | Legal Jobs | CLE
Lawyer Search City or ZIP State Select a Practice Area Find Lawyers!
Search! FindLaw
Client Development Tools For Your Practice Area
Intellectual Property
FindLaw : Cases and Codes : Federal and State Codes : US Code

U.S. Code (Laws made by the U.S. Congress)

Search the U.S. Code by Title and Section :
If you already know which Title and Section of the U.S. Code you want to retrieve, fill in the following boxes. (Example: If you are looking for 42 USC 1395, fill in Title 42, Section 1395)

Title: Section: Search

Search the U.S. Code by keyword:
Search

Browse the U.S. Code by Title Name or by Popular Name (e.g.,Family and Medical Leave Act)

Other U.S. Code links:

- US Code Home Page (U.S. House Of Representatives)

FindLaw

Opinions are searchable by citation, party name, or full text (keyword); Boolean operators and wildcards are enabled. Supreme Court opinions are browsable by volume or year, with recent decisions being highlighted (Figure 6.4).

On the state level, FindLaw includes codes, state regulations, and some state-level case law. On each state page, links to the appropriate U.S. Court of Appeals also appear, for ease in searching. See the Indiana resource page shown in Figure 6.5.

State statutory references link to offsite resources, normally those provided by that state's government, so search engines and availability of resources differ. See Figure 6.6 for the Indiana General Assembly's page for the Indiana Code.

Many other resources of interest to the researcher are also available on FindLaw, such as:

Legal dictionaries

Forms

Information by subject matter

Continuing legal education references

Links to law school journals

Bar exam information

Law school course information by subject

B. Cornell Law School's Legal Information Institute

Cornell Law School sponsors the **Legal Information Institute** (LII) through its Web site at **http://www.law.cornell.edu**. The LII offers excellent resources for state and

FIGURE 6.3

Cases & Codes | Forms | Legal Subjects | Federal | State | Library | Boards Law Firm FirmSites | Legal Jobs | CLE

Lawyer Search City or ZIP State Select a Practice Area Find Lawyers!

Search! FindLaw

FindLaw : Cases and Codes : Supreme Court Opinions

Public Beta

Selected Cases

- THE AMISTAD, 40 U.S. 518 (1841)

Browsing

U.S. Supreme Court Decisions: by volume, by year
Recent Decisions
2003 Decisions
2002 Decisions
2001 Decisions
2000 Decisions
1999 Decisions

Opinion Summaries Archive: September 2000 - Present

Citation Search

U.S. get it e.g. 410 U.S. 113

Client Development Tools For Your Practice Area

And More!!

west.thomson.com

THOMSON WEST

FindLaw Newsletters

Top Legal News Headlines

Legal Grounds

FIGURE 6.4

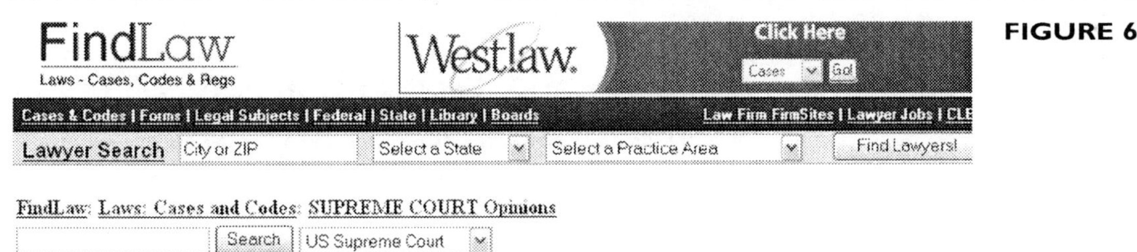

FindLaw

Laws - Cases, Codes & Regs

Westlaw. Click Here Cases Go!

Cases & Codes | Forms | Legal Subjects | Federal | State | Library | Boards Law Firm FirmSites | Lawyer Jobs | CLE

Lawyer Search City or ZIP Select a State Select a Practice Area Find Lawyers!

FindLaw: Laws: Cases and Codes: SUPREME COURT Opinions

Search US Supreme Court

U.S. SUPREME COURT Opinions

Volumes:

150 151 152 153 154 155 156 157 158 159 160 161 162 163 164 165 166 167 168 169
170 171 172 173 174 175 176 177 178 179 180 181 182 183 184 185 186 187 188 189
190 191 192 193 194 195 196 197 198 199 200 201 202 203 204 205 206 207 208 209
210 211 212 213 214 215 216 217 218 219 220 221 222 223 224 225 226 227 228 229
230 231 232 233 234 235 236 237 238 239 240 241 242 243 244 245 246 247 248 249
250 251 252 253 254 255 256 257 258 259 260 261 262 263 264 265 266 267 268 269
270 271 272 273 274 275 276 277 278 279 280 281 282 283 284 285 286 287 288 289
290 291 292 293 294 295 296 297 298 299 300 301 302 303 304 305 306 307 308 309
310 311 312 313 314 315 316 317 318 319 320 321 322 323 324 325 326 327 328 329
330 331 332 333 334 335 336 337 338 339 340 341 342 343 344 345 346 347 348 349
350 351 352 353 354 355 356 357 358 359 360 361 362 363 364 365 366 367 368 369
370 371 372 373 374 375 376 377 378 379 380 381 382 383 384 385 386 387 388 389

FIGURE 6.5

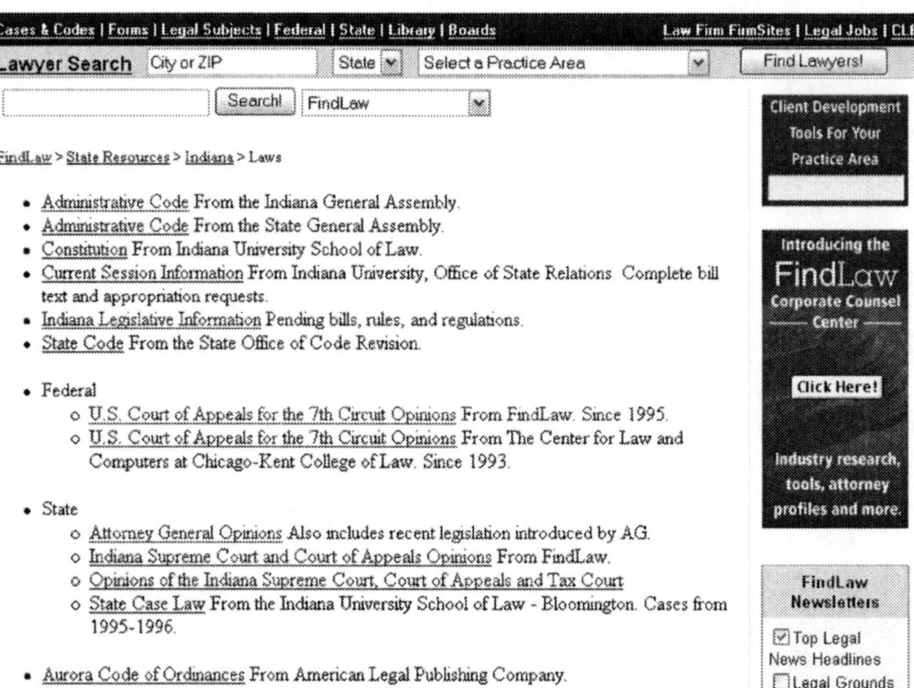

FIGURE 6.6

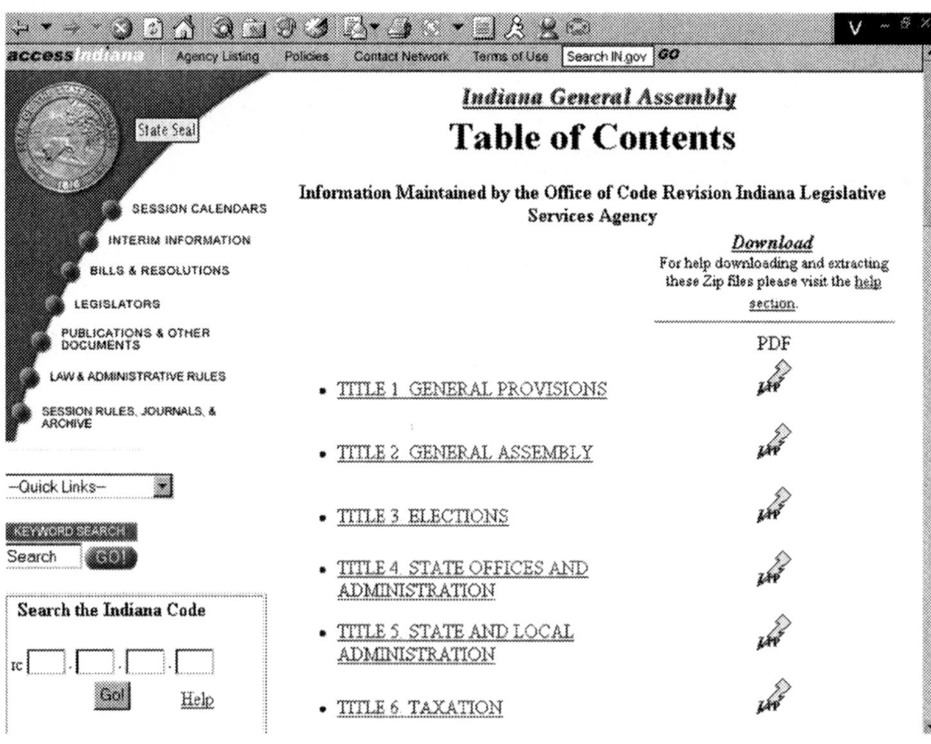

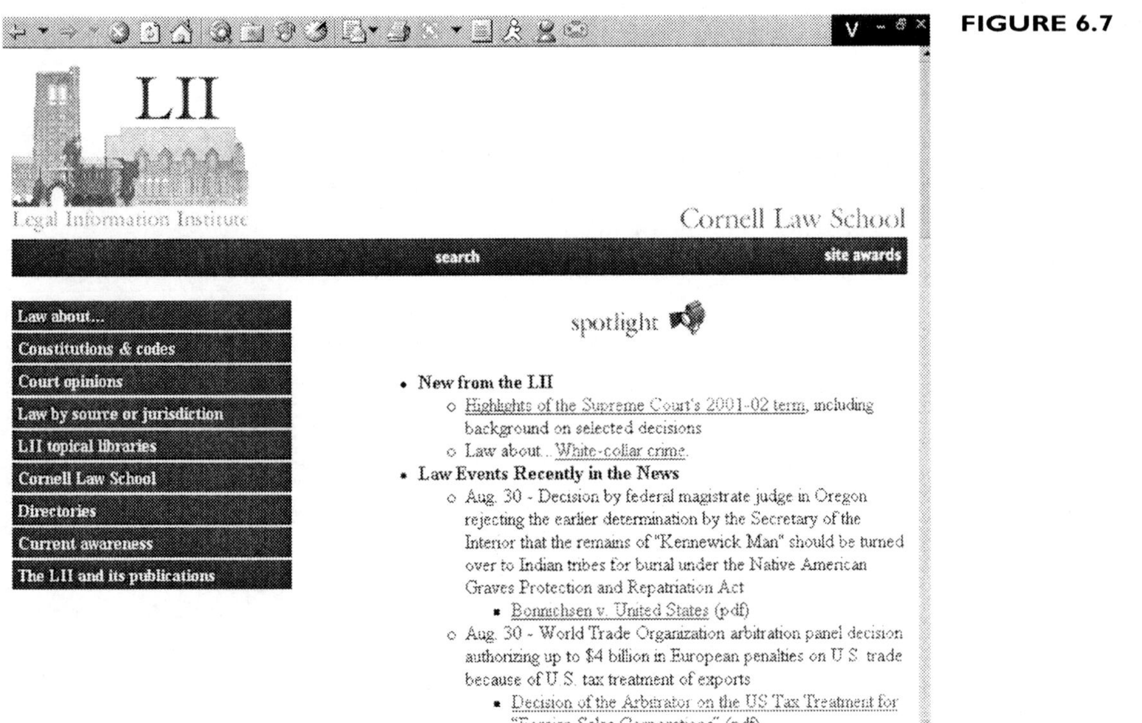

FIGURE 6.7

federal legal materials. Although more limited in scope than FindLaw, LII is a top-notch reference. See the LII's home page shown in Figure 6.7.

Court opinions are offered onsite and through links to other sites on the state and federal level. United States Supreme Court cases since 1990 are available on the LII site, along with selected historical decisions. The LII archive is searchable by topic of law, author, or party name. Figure 6.8 shows the Supreme Court Decision main page.

LII posts current Supreme Court decisions, orders, and case updates on the site to help increase public awareness of the activities of the Court. Also included on this site are links to other federal resources, such as the Code of Federal Regulations, the *Federal Register,* and the U.S. Code, and links to various branches of the government, departments, and agencies. Figure 6.9 shows a page of such links.

The state materials on LII are listed by jurisdiction or by topic of law. The Legal Information Institute's main State Page is shown in Figure 6.10. Almost all of the links in the state section redirect the researcher to user-friendly offsite search engines. Colorado's page on the Legal Information Institute site is reproduced in Figure 6.11. Note that under "Judicial Opinions" alternate sites are given to introduce the researcher to even more online references.

If you are a law student, be aware that most American law schools have designated research locations for the law library; the depth and breadth of services will vary by institution.

C. The Internet Law Library

Pritchard Law Webs owns and operates the **Internet Law Library (ILL)** at **http://www.priweb.com/internetlawlib**, another wonderful free resource for the researcher.

FIGURE 6.8

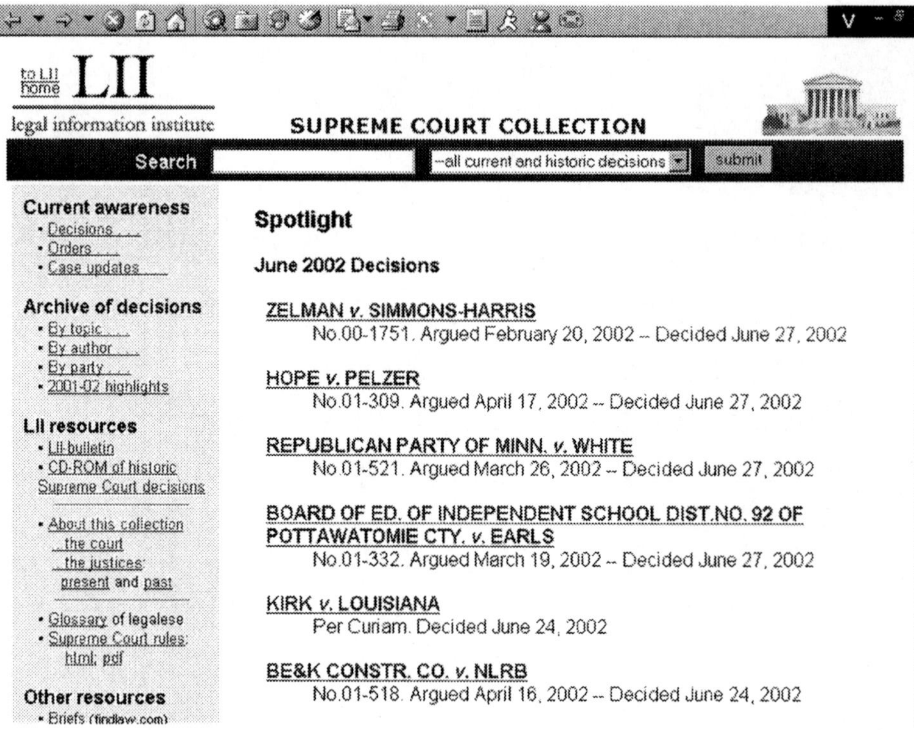

FIGURE 6.9

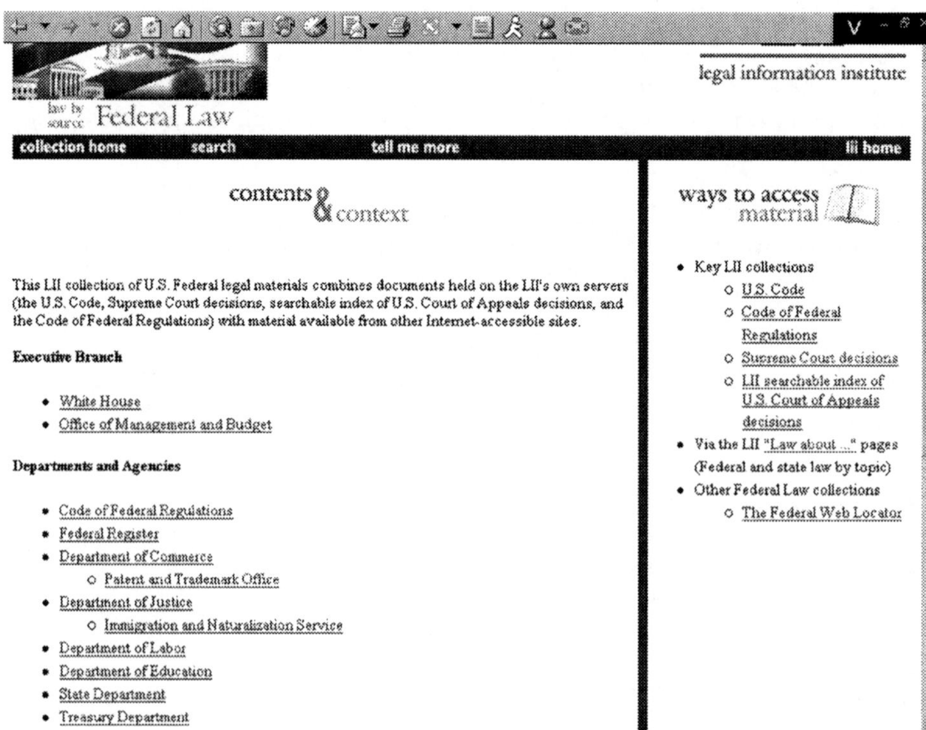

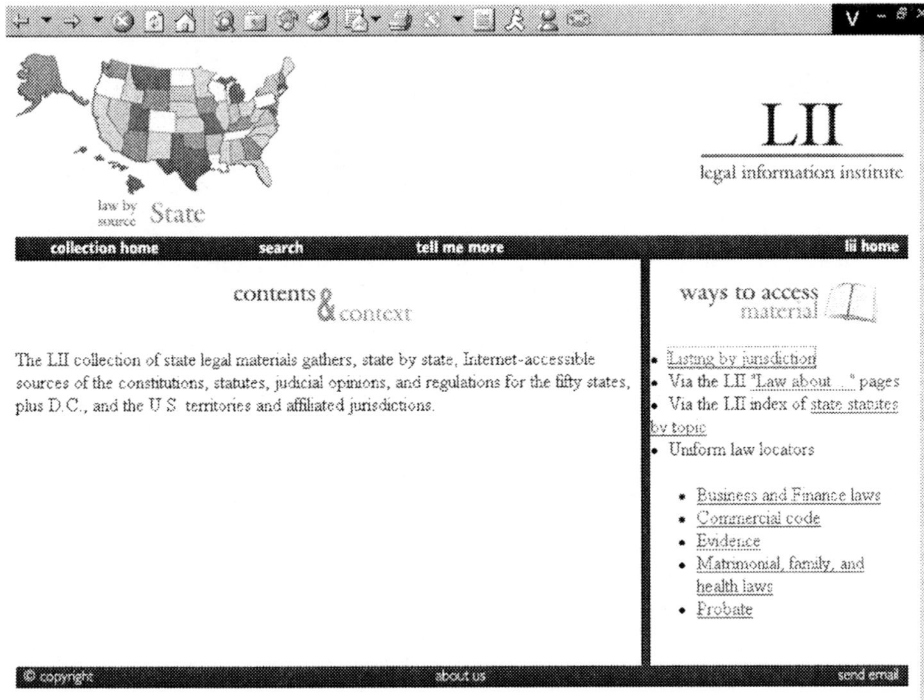

FIGURE 6.10

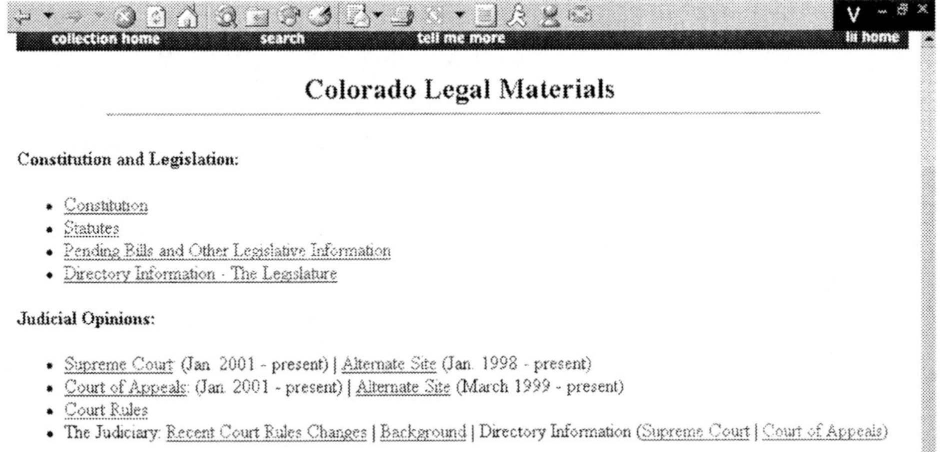

FIGURE 6.11

FIGURE 6.12

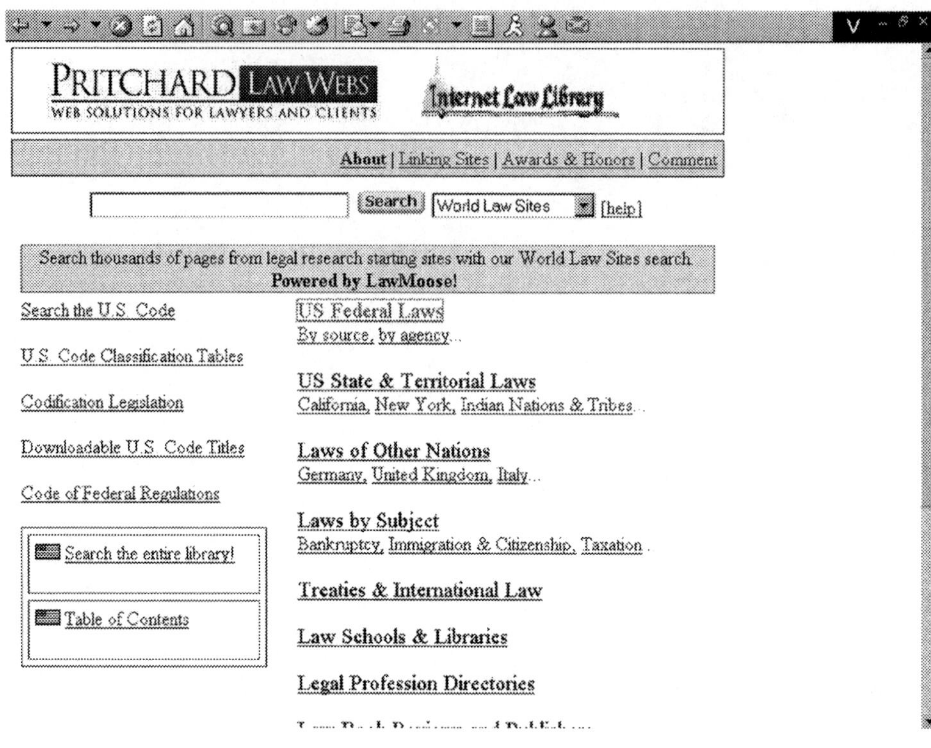

Organized similarly to FindLaw and LII, the ILL includes many state and federal resources, and also has many other references to aid the legal researcher or practitioner. The Internet Law Library's home page is shown in Figure 6.12.

Most links on the Internet Law Library direct the researcher to offsite collections at federal or state government sites. See the ILL Federal Laws page shown in Figure 6.13.

The wealth of U.S. Supreme Court resources on the ILL is astounding! Seven different sources of Supreme Court decisions are listed on the site, along with various links to the U.S. Courts of Appeal and U.S. District Courts. Figure 6.14 shows the Internet Law Library's Federal Court Decisions and Rules Page. Similarly, six references for the U.S. Code are provided on the site's federal statute page.

III. LEXISNEXIS TOTAL RESEARCH SYSTEM

LexisNexis (**www.lexis.com**), a division of Reed Elsevier, is one of the premier fee-based online legal research sites, and has been a major innovator in the field since its inception. Various subscriptions are available, depending on the needs of the researcher; the company also operates another site, called LexisOne, specifically for the solo practitioner. An academic version of Lexis is also available for colleges and universities. The LexisNexis home page is shown in Figure 6.15.

A. A Brief Overview

LexisNexis offers many services to subscribers other than in-depth legal research abilities. The news, business, and public records resources include a person locator

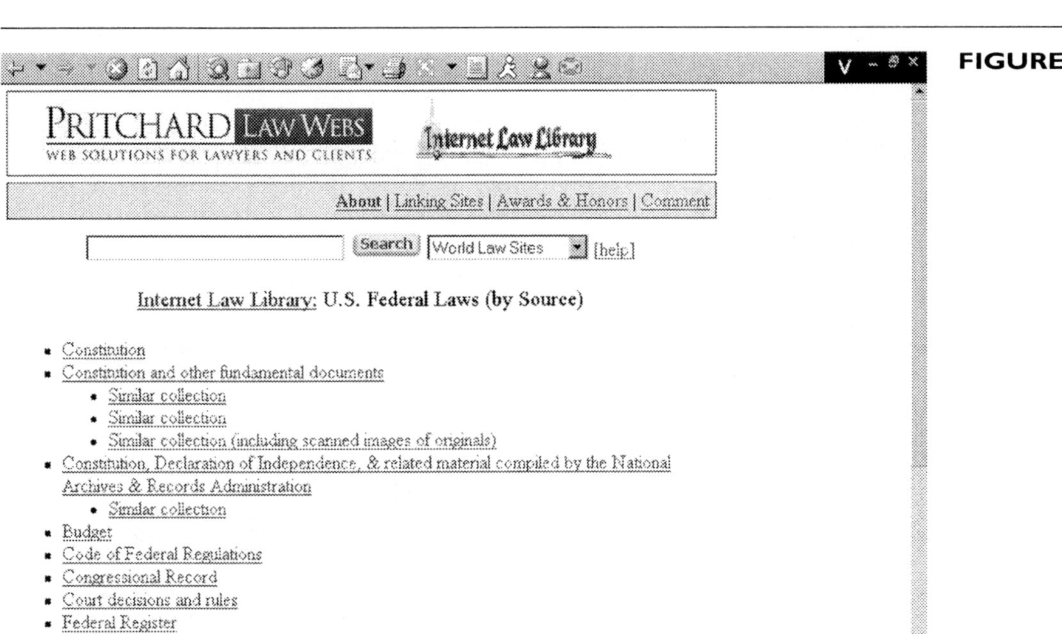
PRITCHARD LAW WEBS
WEB SOLUTIONS FOR LAWYERS AND CLIENTS
Internet Law Library
About | Linking Sites | Awards & Honors | Comment
Search
World Law Sites
[help]
Internet Law Library: U.S. Federal Laws (by Source)
Constitution
Constitution and other fundamental documents
Similar collection
Similar collection
Similar collection (including scanned images of originals)
Constitution, Declaration of Independence, & related material compiled by the National Archives & Records Administration
Similar collection
Budget
Code of Federal Regulations
Congressional Record
Court decisions and rules
Federal Register
Federalist Papers, Declaration of Independence, and other early writings of the Republic
GAO Reports
Hearings of Congressional committees
House and Senate Documents
Legislation
Presidential documents

FIGURE 6.13

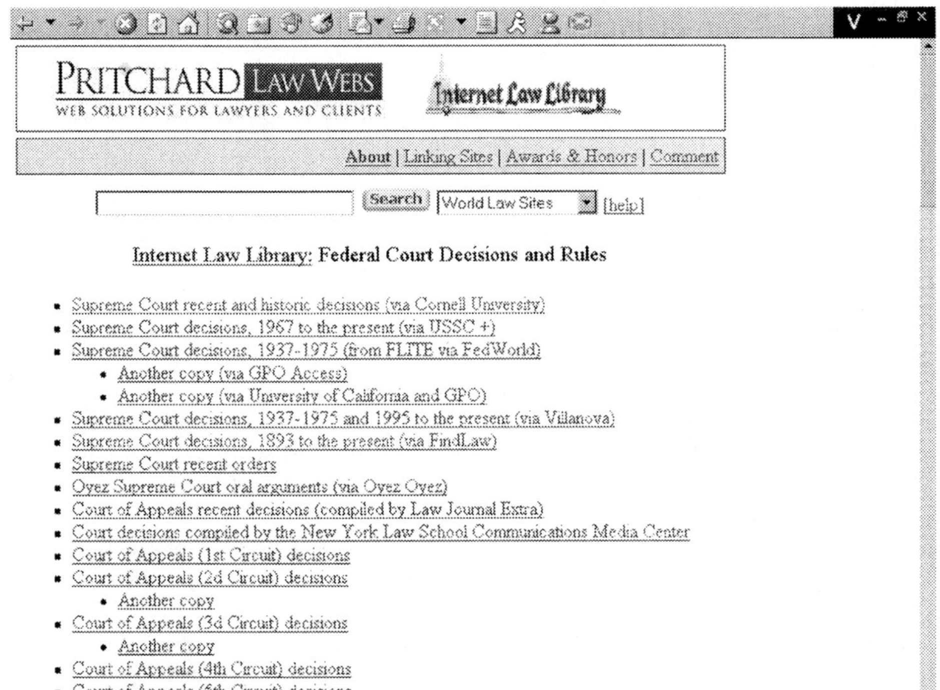
PRITCHARD LAW WEBS
WEB SOLUTIONS FOR LAWYERS AND CLIENTS
Internet Law Library
About | Linking Sites | Awards & Honors | Comment
Search
World Law Sites
[help]
Internet Law Library: Federal Court Decisions and Rules
Supreme Court recent and historic decisions (via Cornell University)
Supreme Court decisions, 1967 to the present (via USSC +)
Supreme Court decisions, 1937-1975 (from FLITE via FedWorld)
Another copy (via GPO Access)
Another copy (via University of California and GPO)
Supreme Court decisions, 1937-1975 and 1995 to the present (via Villanova)
Supreme Court decisions, 1893 to the present (via FindLaw)
Supreme Court recent orders
Oyez Supreme Court oral arguments (via Oyez Oyez)
Court of Appeals recent decisions (compiled by Law Journal Extra)
Court decisions compiled by the New York Law School Communications Media Center
Court of Appeals (1st Circuit) decisions
Court of Appeals (2d Circuit) decisions
Another copy
Court of Appeals (3d Circuit) decisions
Another copy
Court of Appeals (4th Circuit) decisions
Court of Appeals (5th Circuit) decisions
Court of Appeals (6th Circuit) decisions

FIGURE 6.14

FIGURE 6.15

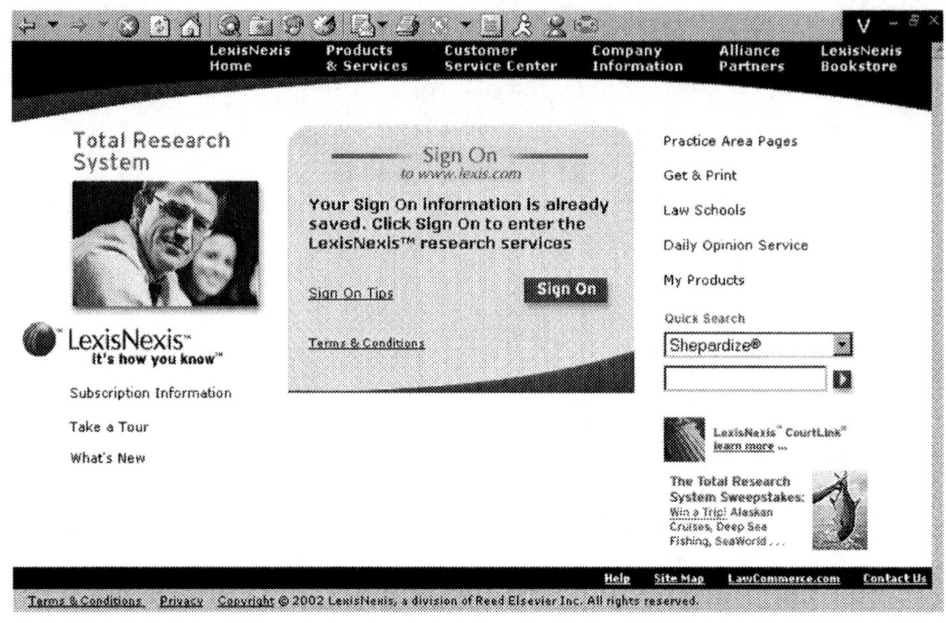

that searches 392 million records, including previous names and addresses. Also included in this service are professional license information, deed transfers, tax assessment records, state judgments and liens, and bankruptcy information. Magazines, newspapers, news transcripts, and wire services are available through the news section. Figure 6.16 shows information regarding these services.

Legal resources included on LexisNexis are comparable to those that researchers would find in their favorite law libraries. Some of the available resources are detailed on the Legal Source page shown in Figure 6.17.

Guided search forms are available for federal and state law, cases, codes, by area of law, law reviews, and many other categories. Guided search forms allow the researcher to specify which resources will be searched. If only federal court decisions and the ALR are required, you can specify them in the search criteria and have information from other sources eliminated from the search. See the guided search for federal materials shown in Figure 6.18.

Information can also be accessed by using the LexisNexis Search Advisor, which is a finding tool for legal material based on legal topics. This is a great advantage when the researcher is unsure of the exact legal topic. It helps target the correct issues, look for alternatives, identify needed sources, and formulate queries. For example, you know that a particular case deals with imported products, but you are unsure of exactly what to search first. You would initially consult the Search Advisor legal topic page (Figure 6.19).

You would probably then select international trade law, based on the main issue of the case. You then keep selecting topics—going from big to small—until the most relevant topic is displayed, a jurisdiction is selected, and additional search terms are chosen. See Figures 6.20 and 6.21.

Documents can also be retrieved, by citation, from any publication on the site. An alphabetical listing of all retrievable publications is provided to ensure that searchers use the correct format. Even if only part of the resource name is known, the document can still be retrieved (Figure 6.22).

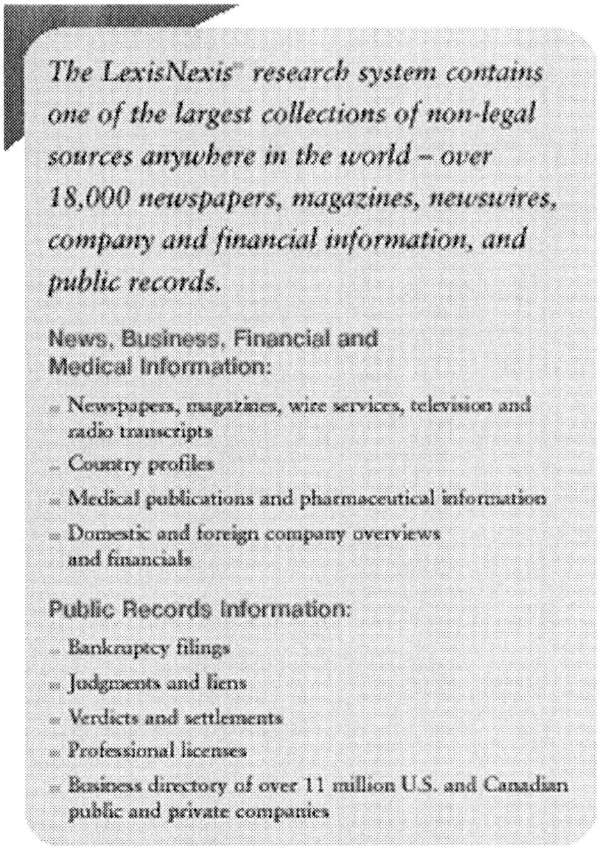

FIGURE 6.16

The LexisNexis® research system contains one of the largest collections of non-legal sources anywhere in the world – over 18,000 newspapers, magazines, newswires, company and financial information, and public records.

News, Business, Financial and Medical Information:

- Newspapers, magazines, wire services, television and radio transcripts
- Country profiles
- Medical publications and pharmaceutical information
- Domestic and foreign company overviews and financials

Public Records Information:

- Bankruptcy filings
- Judgments and liens
- Verdicts and settlements
- Professional licenses
- Business directory of over 11 million U.S. and Canadian public and private companies

FIGURE 6.17

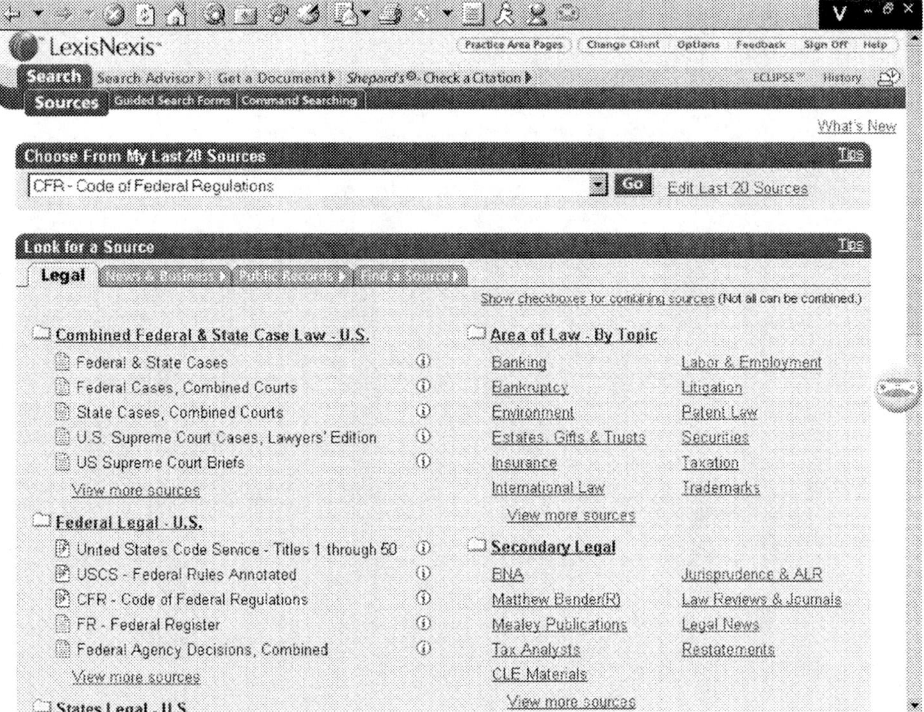

FIGURE 6.18

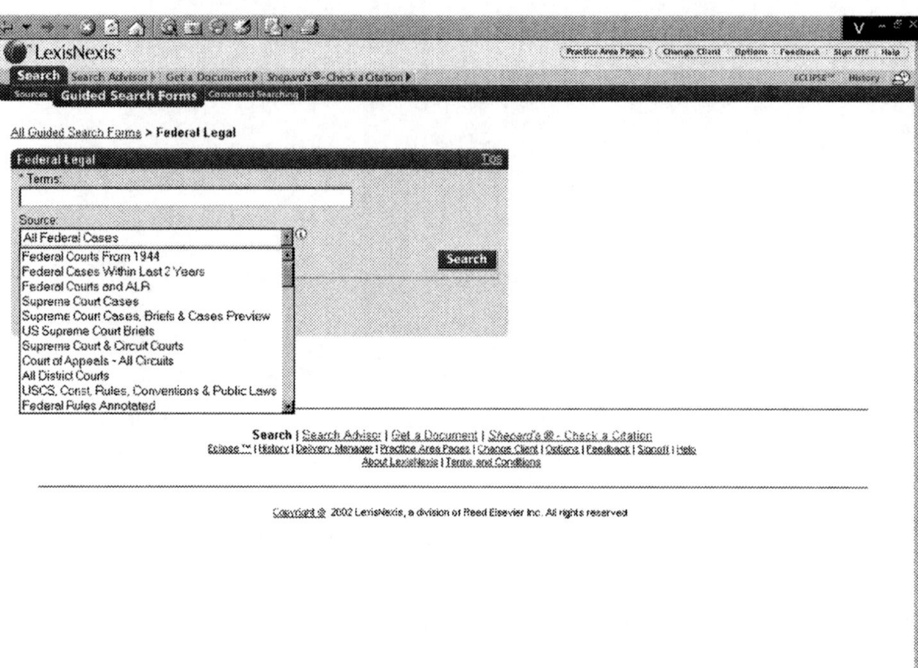

FIGURE 6.19

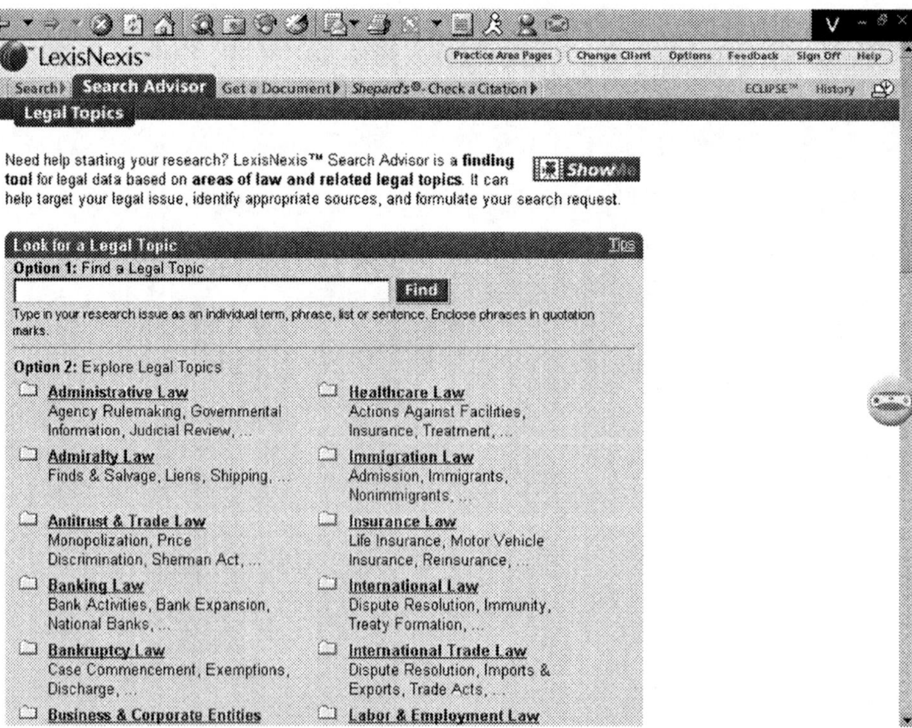

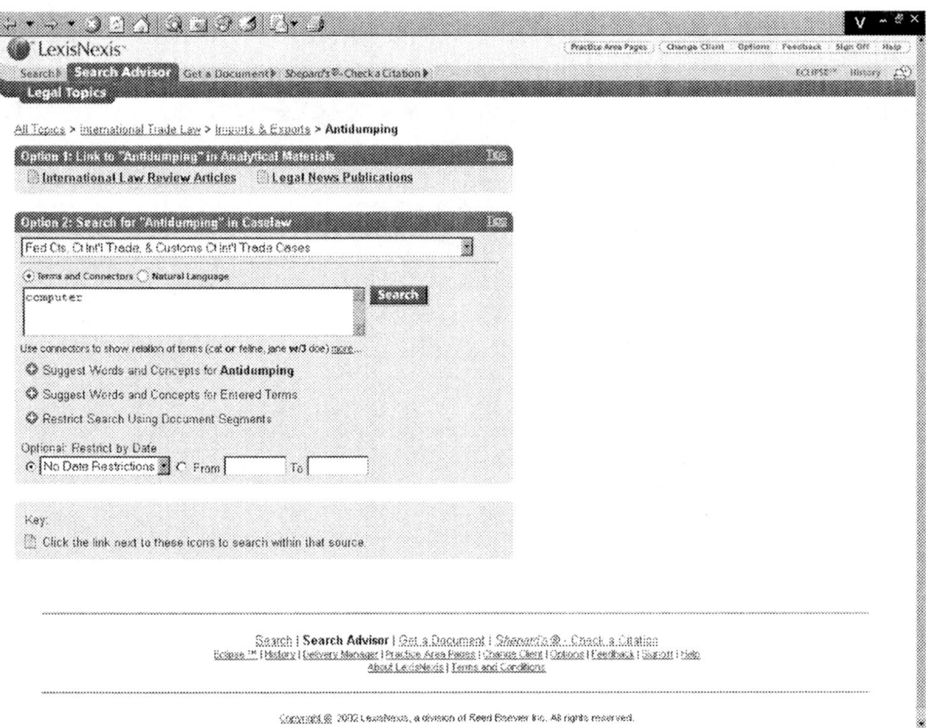

FIGURE 6.20

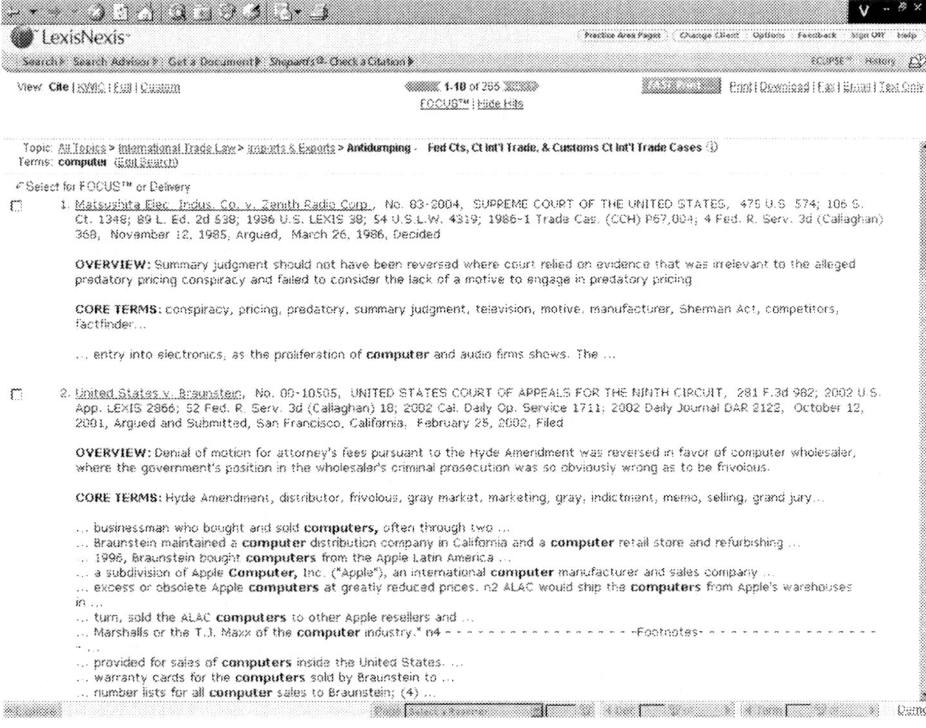

FIGURE 6.21

FIGURE 6.22

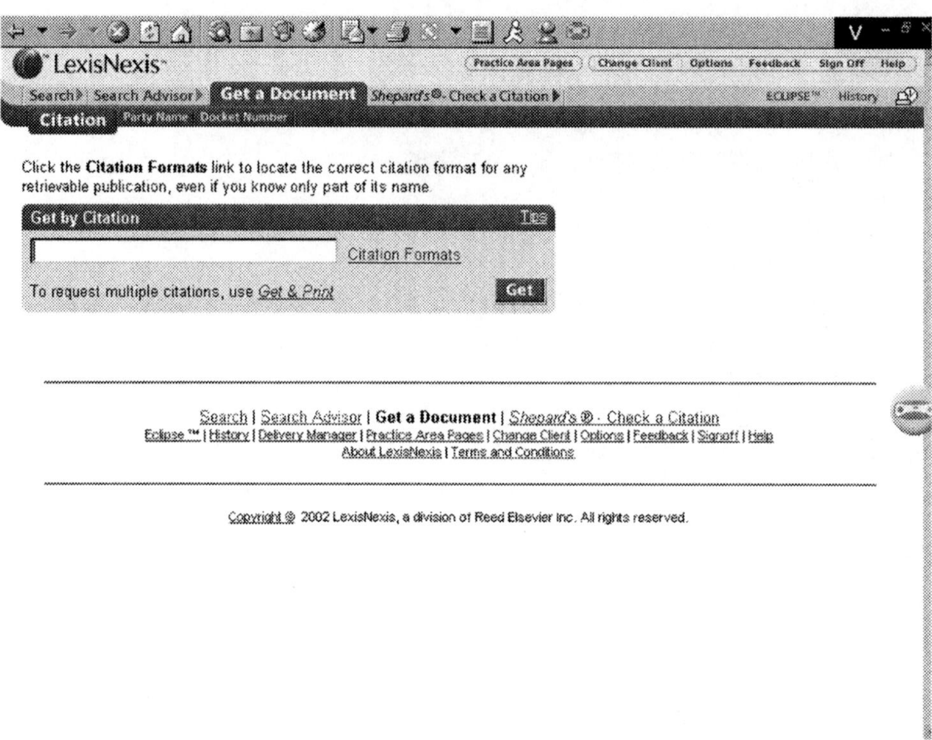

Shepard's Citations, one of the most important updating and researching tools in legal research, is included on the site as well. Statutes and case law can be searched for "Validation" or "Research" purposes simply by entering the citation and clicking the appropriate button. Results are returned with appropriate histories, and include direct links to the citations provided.

LexisNexis also permits the use of certain connectors to make searches more efficient. Section I of this chapter covered the usage of AND, OR, and NOT. LexisNexis also allows numerical limiters to be set, but in a different format. Instead of typing the whole word "within," the researcher uses "w/" followed by either a specific number or another abbreviation representing paragraph, segment, sentence, and so on. The abbreviations are as follows:

w/n	within "n" number of words
w/p	within the same paragraph
w/s	within the same sentence
w/seg	within the same segment (title, section, etc.)

This has been only a very brief overview of the vast and wonderful resources available on LexisNexis. The next two sections will walk you through searches performed on LexisNexis based on the information contained in Fact Pattern 1. (No exercises are provided at the end of this chapter, but it is suggested that you use Fact Pattern 2 to conduct research using any available online legal research engine at your disposal.) Formulation of good search queries and keywords that return usable results is a learned art that, as with other forms of research, takes practice.

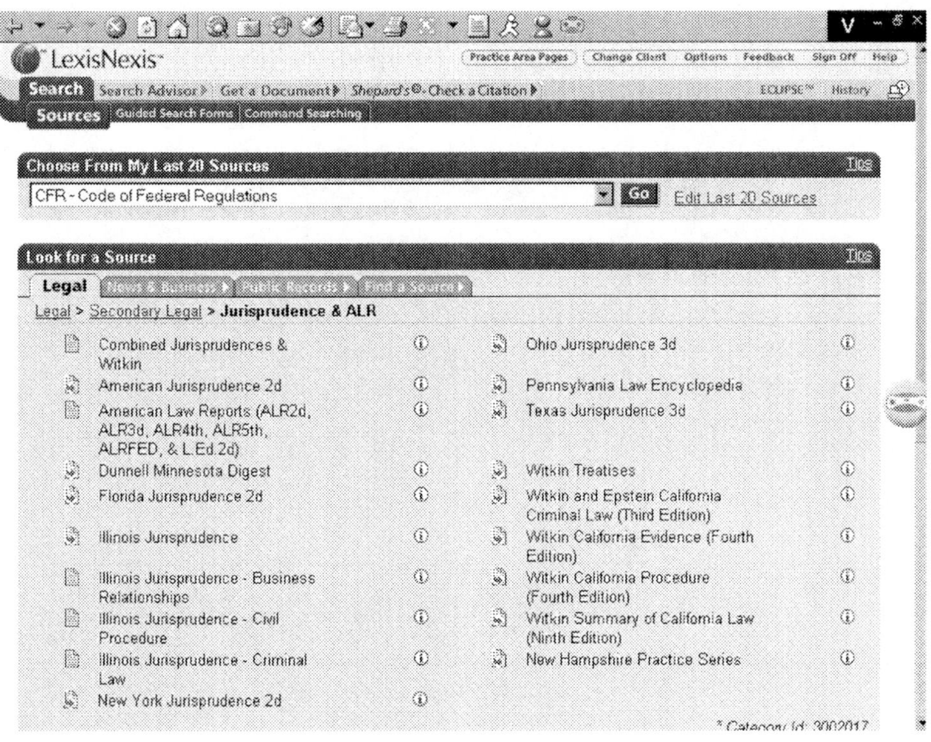

FIGURE 6.23

B. Fact Pattern I

Initially, you (the researcher) decide that secondary resources are needed to provide more background information dealing with homicides related to driving under the influence. A scan of *American Jurisprudence, 2d* will be the first step. First, the secondary legal resources are located on the legal source page of LexisNexis (Figure 6.23) and *American Jurisprudence, 2d* is selected.

You are then given the option of proceeding to the table of contents of Am. Jur. 2d or searching; "continue with your search" is selected. "Driving under the influence w/p homicide" is entered in the search field, the "Terms and Connectors" button is selected, and the search button is clicked. See the search screen shown in Figure 6.24.

Various results from Am. Jur. 2d will be returned, similar to those shown in Figures 6.25 and 6.26.

The *American Jurisprudence* articles on LexisNexis include active links in the text and footnotes to statutes, cases, other American Jurisprudence articles, and ALR annotations, as well as other references found in the print edition of the series. See Figure 6.27.

You can then link directly to the ALR article at 64 A.L.R. 4th 166. See Figure 6.28.

Now that you have a few secondary materials at your disposal, it is time to collect primary resources. Going back to the Legal Sources page, "Pennsylvania Criminal Cases" is selected after navigating through the selections. See Figure 6.29.

Court cases are retrievable and searchable only. You decide to use the same terms used when searching for the secondary resources, but to include the additional element of leaving the scene of the crime. You believe that using a wildcard

FIGURE 6.24

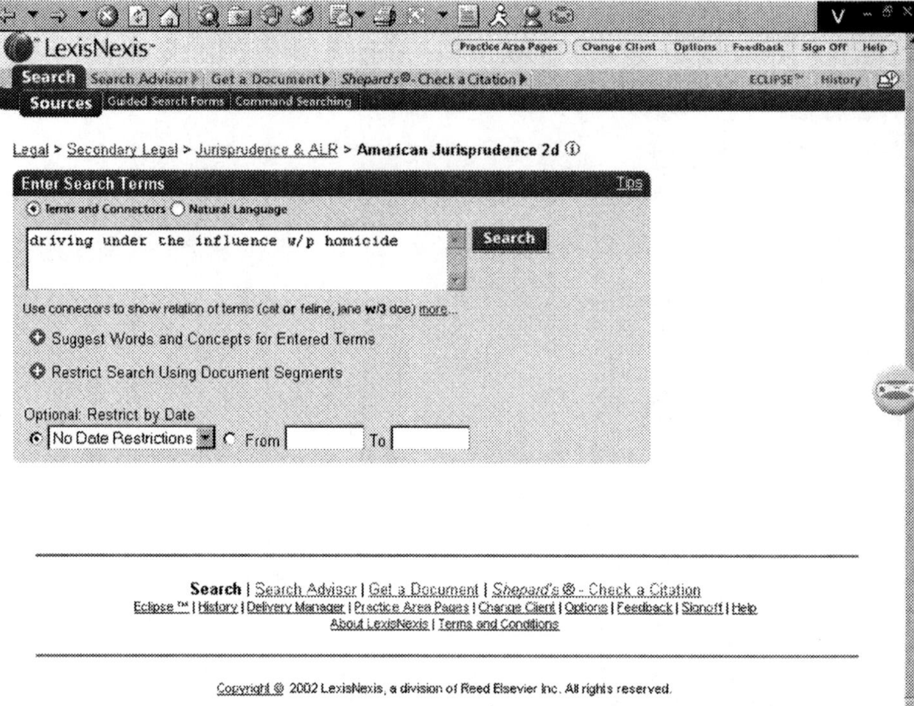

FIGURE 6.25

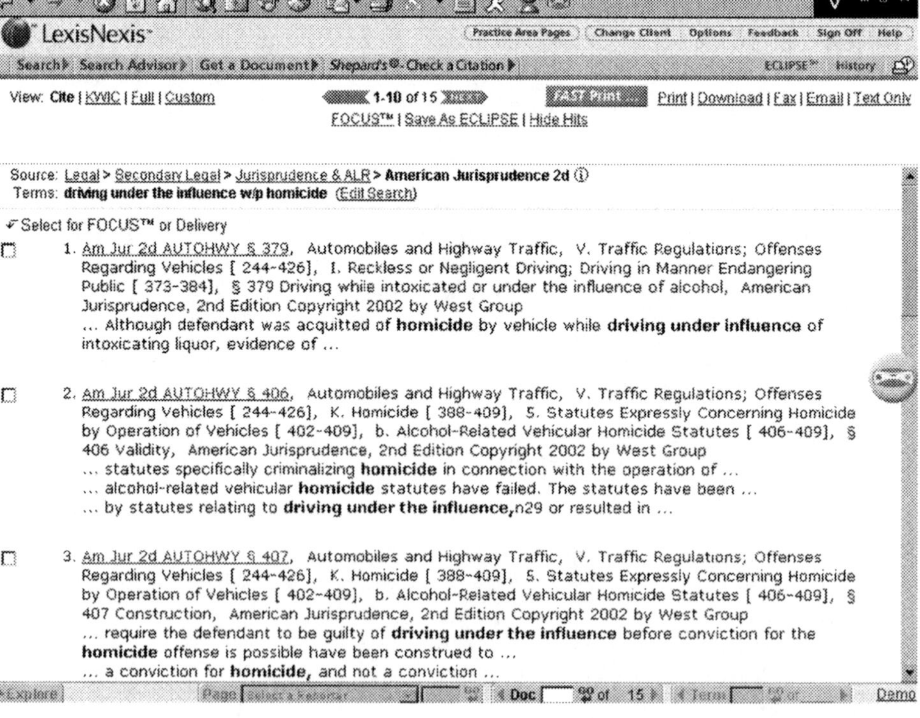

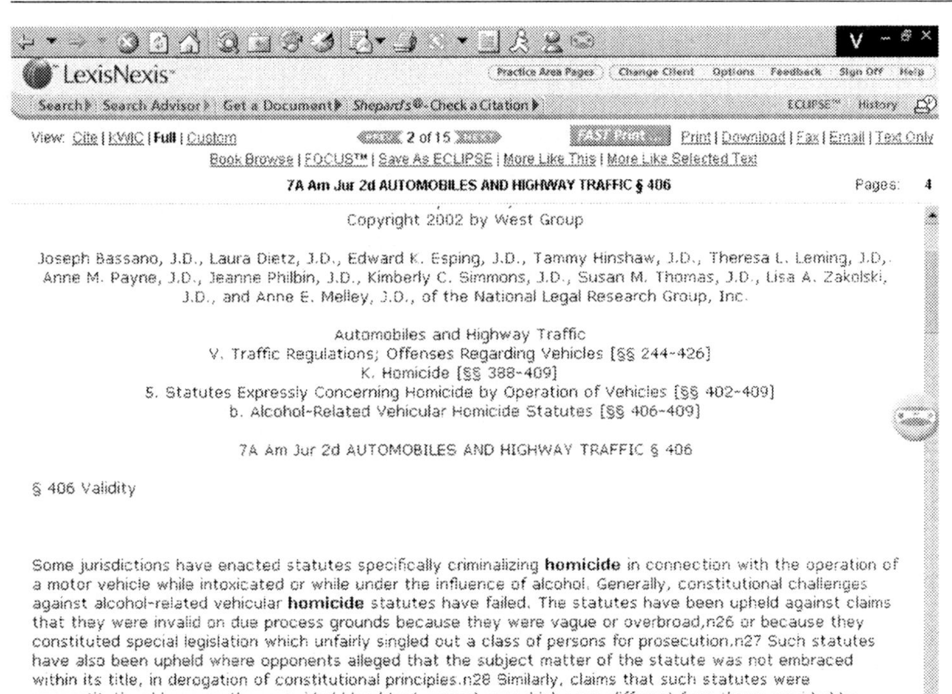

LexisNexis

Search | Search Advisor | Get a Document | Shepard's®-Check a Citation | ECLIPSE™ | History

View: Cite | KWIC | Full | Custom   2 of 15   FAST Print   Print | Download | Fax | Email | Text Only

Book Browse | FOCUS™ | Save As ECLIPSE | More Like This | More Like Selected Text

7A Am Jur 2d AUTOMOBILES AND HIGHWAY TRAFFIC § 406   Pages: 4

Copyright 2002 by West Group

Joseph Bassano, J.D., Laura Dietz, J.D., Edward K. Esping, J.D., Tammy Hinshaw, J.D., Theresa L. Leming, J.D., Anne M. Payne, J.D., Jeanne Philbin, J.D., Kimberly C. Simmons, J.D., Susan M. Thomas, J.D., Lisa A. Zakolski, J.D., and Anne E. Melley, J.D., of the National Legal Research Group, Inc.

Automobiles and Highway Traffic
V. Traffic Regulations; Offenses Regarding Vehicles [§§ 244-426]
K. Homicide [§§ 388-409]
5. Statutes Expressly Concerning Homicide by Operation of Vehicles [§§ 402-409]
b. Alcohol-Related Vehicular Homicide Statutes [§§ 406-409]

7A Am Jur 2d AUTOMOBILES AND HIGHWAY TRAFFIC § 406

§ 406 Validity

Some jurisdictions have enacted statutes specifically criminalizing **homicide** in connection with the operation of a motor vehicle while intoxicated or while under the influence of alcohol. Generally, constitutional challenges against alcohol-related vehicular **homicide** statutes have failed. The statutes have been upheld against claims that they were invalid on due process grounds because they were vague or overbroad,n26 or because they constituted special legislation which unfairly singled out a class of persons for prosecution.n27 Such statutes have also been upheld where opponents alleged that the subject matter of the statute was not embraced within its title, in derogation of constitutional principles.n28 Similarly, claims that such statutes were unconstitutional because they provided blood test procedures which were different from those provided by statutes relating to **driving under the influence**.n29 or resulted in different penalties than those resulting from

Explore   Doc 2 of 15   Term of 3   Demo

FIGURE 6.26

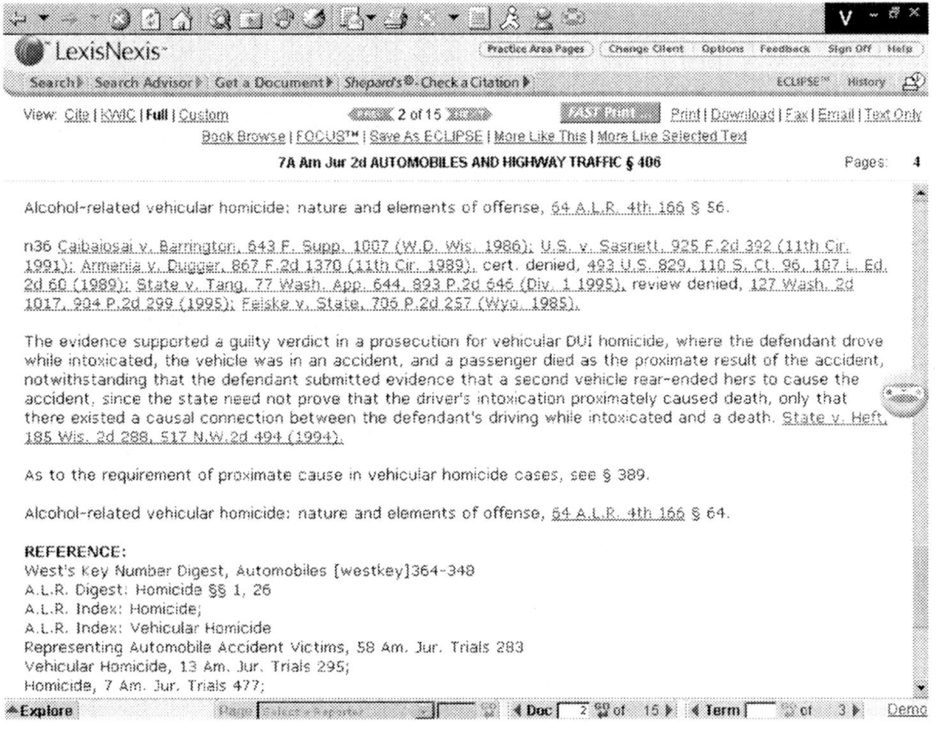

LexisNexis

Search | Search Advisor | Get a Document | Shepard's®-Check a Citation | ECLIPSE™ | History

View: Cite | KWIC | Full | Custom   2 of 15   FAST Print   Print | Download | Fax | Email | Text Only

Book Browse | FOCUS™ | Save As ECLIPSE | More Like This | More Like Selected Text

7A Am Jur 2d AUTOMOBILES AND HIGHWAY TRAFFIC § 406   Pages: 4

Alcohol-related vehicular homicide: nature and elements of offense, 64 A.L.R. 4th 166 § 56.

n36 Caibaiosai v. Barrington, 643 F. Supp. 1007 (W.D. Wis. 1986); U.S. v. Sasnett, 925 F.2d 392 (11th Cir. 1991); Armenia v. Dugger, 867 F.2d 1370 (11th Cir. 1989), cert. denied, 493 U.S. 829, 110 S. Ct. 96, 107 L. Ed. 2d 60 (1989); State v. Tang, 77 Wash. App. 644, 893 P.2d 646 (Div. 1 1995), review denied, 127 Wash. 2d 1017, 904 P.2d 299 (1995); Feiske v. State, 705 P.2d 257 (Wyo. 1985).

The evidence supported a guilty verdict in a prosecution for vehicular DUI homicide, where the defendant drove while intoxicated, the vehicle was in an accident, and a passenger died as the proximate result of the accident, notwithstanding that the defendant submitted evidence that a second vehicle rear-ended hers to cause the accident, since the state need not prove that the driver's intoxication proximately caused death, only that there existed a causal connection between the defendant's driving while intoxicated and a death. State v. Heft, 185 Wis. 2d 288, 517 N.W.2d 494 (1994).

As to the requirement of proximate cause in vehicular homicide cases, see § 389.

Alcohol-related vehicular homicide: nature and elements of offense, 64 A.L.R. 4th 166 § 64.

REFERENCE:
West's Key Number Digest, Automobiles [westkey]364-348
A.L.R. Digest: Homicide §§ 1, 26
A.L.R. Index: Homicide;
A.L.R. Index: Vehicular Homicide
Representing Automobile Accident Victims, 58 Am. Jur. Trials 283
Vehicular Homicide, 13 Am. Jur. Trials 295;
Homicide, 7 Am. Jur. Trials 477;

Explore   Doc 2 of 15   Term of 3   Demo

FIGURE 6.27

FIGURE 6.28

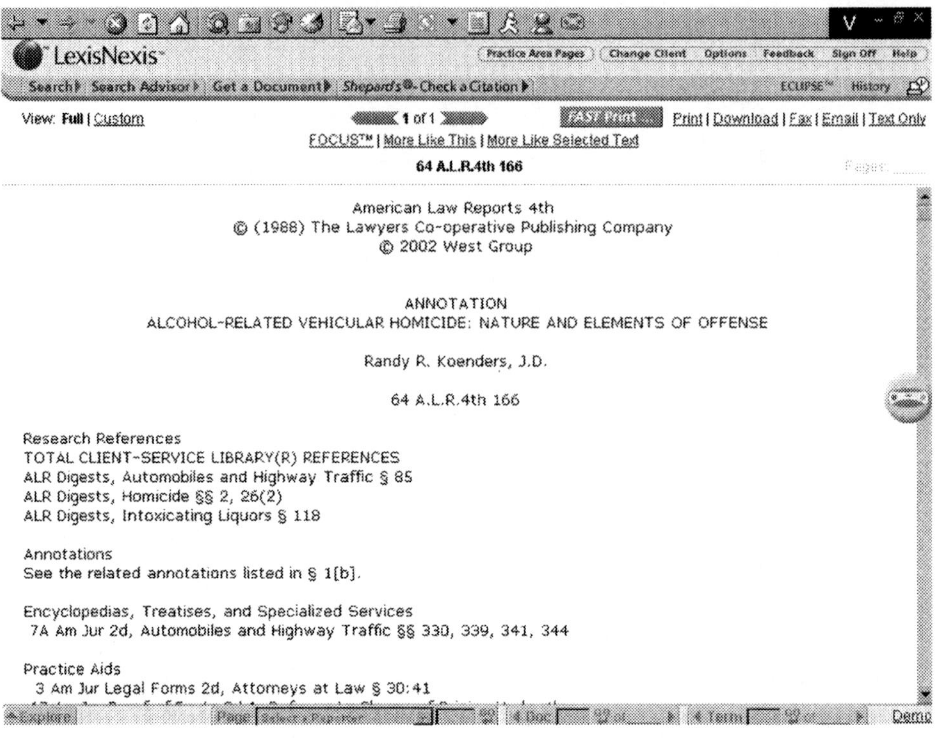

American Law Reports 4th
© (1988) The Lawyers Co-operative Publishing Company
© 2002 West Group

ANNOTATION
ALCOHOL-RELATED VEHICULAR HOMICIDE: NATURE AND ELEMENTS OF OFFENSE

Randy R. Koenders, J.D.

64 A.L.R.4th 166

Research References
TOTAL CLIENT-SERVICE LIBRARY(R) REFERENCES
ALR Digests, Automobiles and Highway Traffic § 85
ALR Digests, Homicide §§ 2, 26(2)
ALR Digests, Intoxicating Liquors § 118

Annotations
See the related annotations listed in § 1[b].

Encyclopedias, Treatises, and Specialized Services
7A Am Jur 2d, Automobiles and Highway Traffic §§ 330, 339, 341, 344

Practice Aids
3 Am Jur Legal Forms 2d, Attorneys at Law § 30:41

FIGURE 6.29

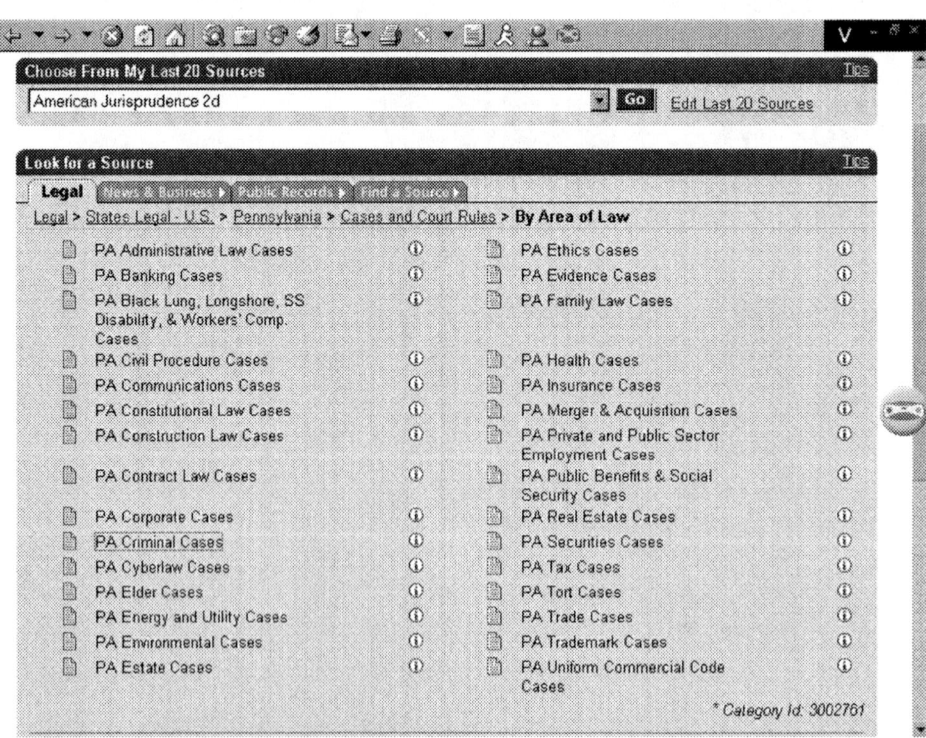

PA Administrative Law Cases
PA Banking Cases
PA Black Lung, Longshore, SS Disability, & Workers' Comp. Cases
PA Civil Procedure Cases
PA Communications Cases
PA Constitutional Law Cases
PA Construction Law Cases
PA Contract Law Cases
PA Corporate Cases
PA Criminal Cases
PA Cyberlaw Cases
PA Elder Cases
PA Energy and Utility Cases
PA Environmental Cases
PA Estate Cases
PA Ethics Cases
PA Evidence Cases
PA Family Law Cases
PA Health Cases
PA Insurance Cases
PA Merger & Acquisition Cases
PA Private and Public Sector Employment Cases
PA Public Benefits & Social Security Cases
PA Real Estate Cases
PA Securities Cases
PA Tax Cases
PA Tort Cases
PA Trade Cases
PA Trademark Cases
PA Uniform Commercial Code Cases

* Category Id: 3002761

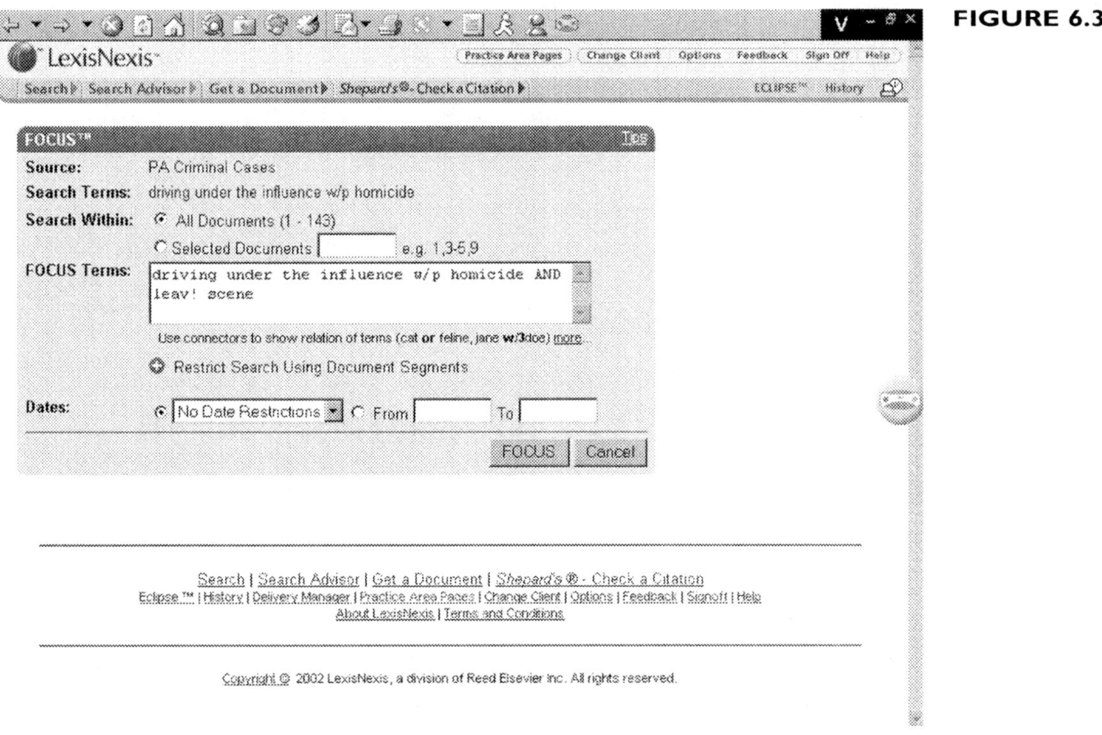

FIGURE 6.30

in this instance will yield the best results, so you add "AND leav! scene" to the query. (LexisNexis uses an exclamation point instead of an asterisk for wildcards.) See Figure 6.30 for the search screen and Figure 6.31 for the search results.

A similar process is followed when searching for statutory materials: by selecting the appropriate jurisdiction, then the correct resource from the Legal Source page, a researcher arrives at the search screen. In our example, the query "homicide AND vehicle AND driving under influence" is entered and searched. See the results at Figures 6.32 and 6.33.

Law reviews and journals are searched in a similar manner. See the search screen at Figure 6.34.

Recently many enhancements have been made to LexisNexis. In June 2002, Lexis announced that new Mealey's content enhancements were added to the service to provide full-text court documents, summaries of cases, news articles, and commentaries, with instant e-mail delivery of Mealey's content also available. Also in June came the addition of Dun & Bradstreet Reports and a "Sounds Like" search feature for public records data. The available Dun & Bradstreet Reports include Business Information Report, Payment Analysis Report, Supplier Evaluation Report, Comprehensive Report, Government Activity Report, Business Background Report, and Dun's Financial Profile. Lexis offers many other services that cannot be covered in this work. For information on the full range of services, visit its Web site at **www.lexis.com**. See Figure 6.35 for an excellent reference material called LexisNexis At A Glance.

FIGURE 6.31

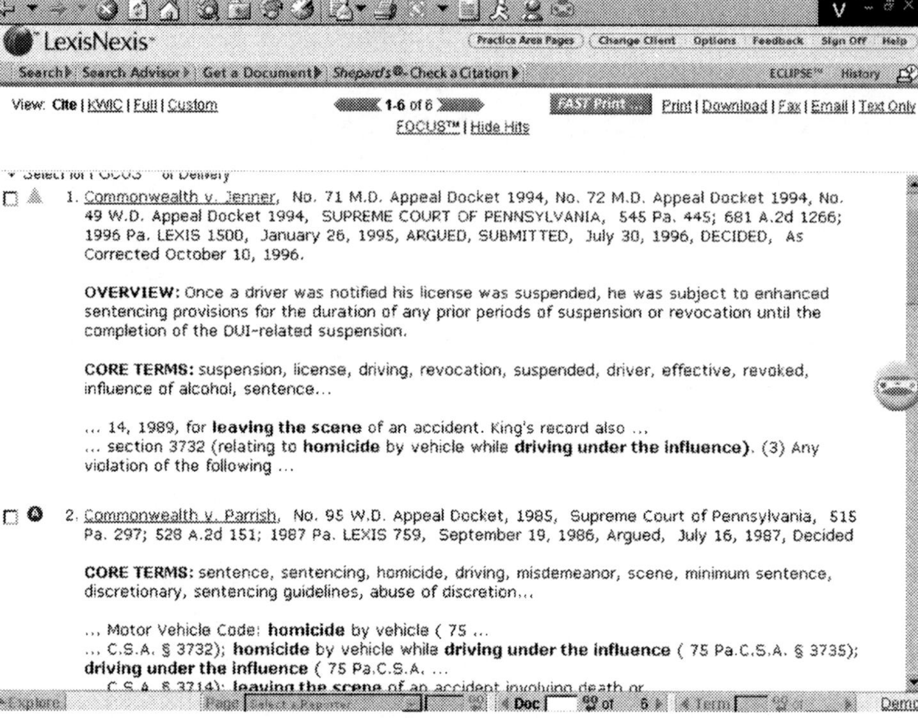

LexisNexis

Practice Area Pages | Change Client | Options | Feedback | Sign Off | Help

Search | Search Advisor | Get a Document | Shepard's®-Check a Citation | ECLIPSE™ | History

View: Cite | KWIC | Full | Custom   1-6 of 6   FAST Print   Print | Download | Fax | Email | Text Only

FOCUS™ | Hide Hits

1. Commonwealth v. Jenner, No. 71 M.D. Appeal Docket 1994, No. 72 M.D. Appeal Docket 1994, No. 49 W.D. Appeal Docket 1994, SUPREME COURT OF PENNSYLVANIA, 545 Pa. 445; 681 A.2d 1266; 1996 Pa. LEXIS 1500, January 26, 1995, ARGUED, SUBMITTED, July 30, 1996, DECIDED, As Corrected October 10, 1996.

OVERVIEW: Once a driver was notified his license was suspended, he was subject to enhanced sentencing provisions for the duration of any prior periods of suspension or revocation until the completion of the DUI-related suspension.

CORE TERMS: suspension, license, driving, revocation, suspended, driver, effective, revoked, influence of alcohol, sentence...

... 14, 1989, for **leaving the scene** of an accident. King's record also ...
... section 3732 (relating to **homicide** by vehicle while **driving under the influence**). (3) Any violation of the following ...

2. Commonwealth v. Parrish, No. 95 W.D. Appeal Docket, 1985, Supreme Court of Pennsylvania, 515 Pa. 297; 528 A.2d 151; 1987 Pa. LEXIS 759, September 19, 1986, Argued, July 16, 1987, Decided

CORE TERMS: sentence, sentencing, homicide, driving, misdemeanor, scene, minimum sentence, discretionary, sentencing guidelines, abuse of discretion...

... Motor Vehicle Code: **homicide** by vehicle (75 ...
... C.S.A. § 3732); **homicide** by vehicle while **driving under the influence** (75 Pa.C.S.A. § 3735); **driving under the influence** (75 Pa.C.S.A. ...

Explore | Page | Doc | of 6 | Term | Demo

FIGURE 6.32

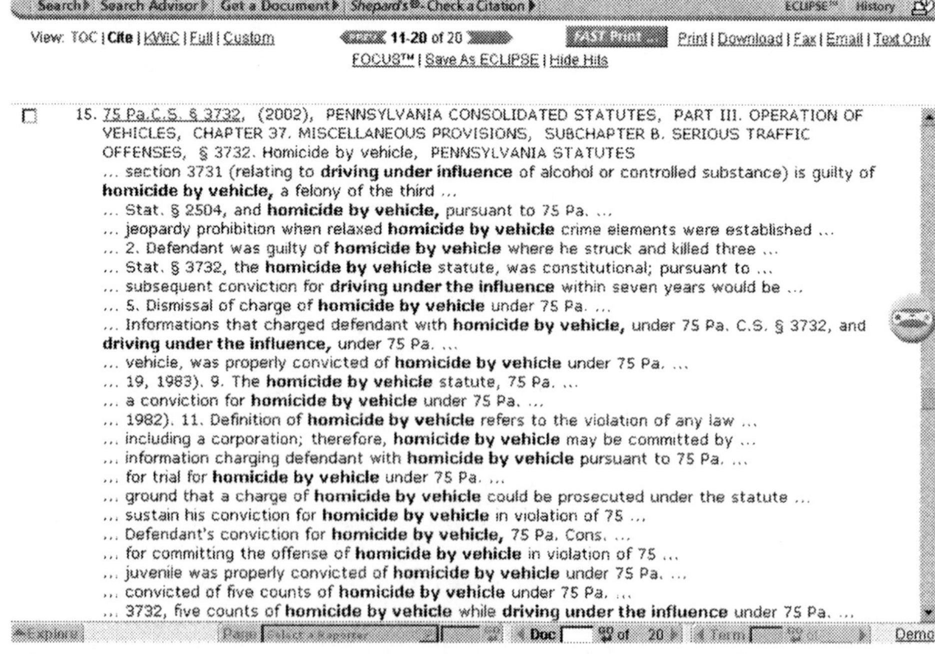

LexisNexis

Practice Area Pages | Change Client | Options | Feedback | Sign Off | Help

Search | Search Advisor | Get a Document | Shepard's®-Check a Citation | ECLIPSE™ | History

View: TOC | Cite | KWIC | Full | Custom   11-20 of 20   FAST Print   Print | Download | Fax | Email | Text Only

FOCUS™ | Save As ECLIPSE | Hide Hits

15. 75 Pa.C.S. § 3732, (2002), PENNSYLVANIA CONSOLIDATED STATUTES, PART III. OPERATION OF VEHICLES, CHAPTER 37. MISCELLANEOUS PROVISIONS, SUBCHAPTER B. SERIOUS TRAFFIC OFFENSES, § 3732. Homicide by vehicle, PENNSYLVANIA STATUTES
... section 3731 (relating to **driving under influence** of alcohol or controlled substance) is guilty of **homicide by vehicle,** a felony of the third ...
... Stat. § 2504, and **homicide by vehicle,** pursuant to 75 Pa. ...
... jeopardy prohibition when relaxed **homicide by vehicle** crime elements were established ...
... 2. Defendant was guilty of **homicide by vehicle** where he struck and killed three ...
... Stat. § 3732, the **homicide by vehicle** statute, was constitutional; pursuant to ...
... subsequent conviction for **driving under the influence** within seven years would be ...
... 5. Dismissal of charge of **homicide by vehicle** under 75 Pa. ...
... Informations that charged defendant with **homicide by vehicle,** under 75 Pa. C.S. § 3732, and **driving under the influence,** under 75 Pa. ...
... vehicle, was properly convicted of **homicide by vehicle** under 75 Pa. ...
... 19, 1983). 9. The **homicide by vehicle** statute, 75 Pa. ...
... a conviction for **homicide by vehicle** under 75 Pa. ...
... 1982). 11. Definition of **homicide by vehicle** refers to the violation of any law ...
... including a corporation; therefore, **homicide by vehicle** may be committed by ...
... information charging defendant with **homicide by vehicle** pursuant to 75 Pa. ...
... for trial for **homicide by vehicle** under 75 Pa. ...
... ground that a charge of **homicide by vehicle** could be prosecuted under the statute ...
... sustain his conviction for **homicide by vehicle** in violation of 75 ...
... Defendant's conviction for **homicide by vehicle,** 75 Pa. Cons. ...
... for committing the offense of **homicide by vehicle** in violation of 75 ...
... juvenile was properly convicted of **homicide by vehicle** under 75 Pa. ...
... convicted of five counts of **homicide by vehicle** under 75 Pa. ...
... 3732, five counts of **homicide by vehicle** while **driving under the influence** under 75 Pa. ...

Explore | Page | Doc | of 20 | Term | Demo

FIGURE 6.33

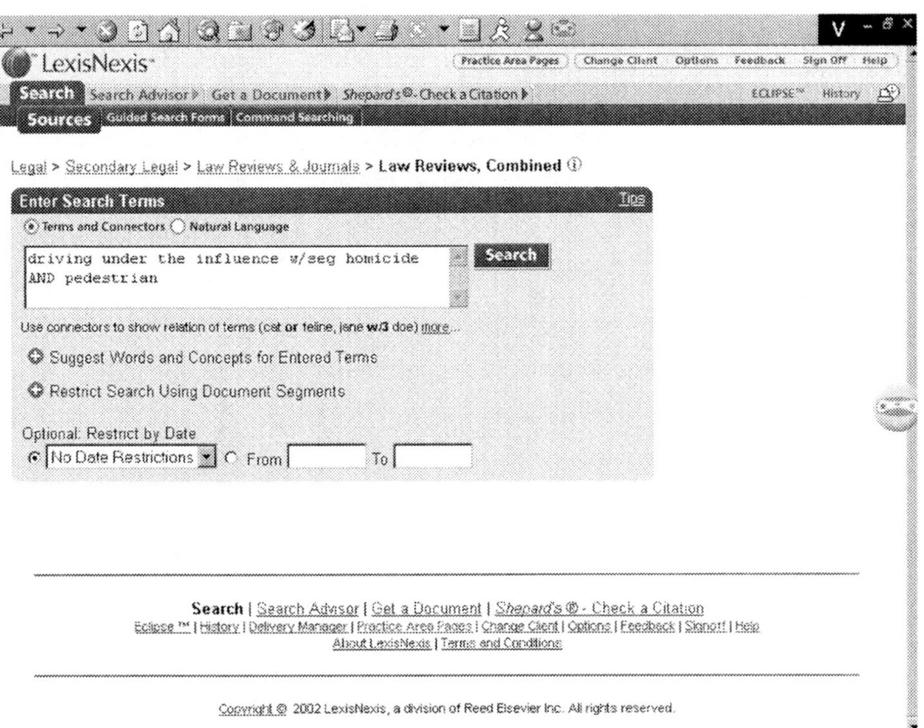

FIGURE 6.34

FIGURE 6.35

At A Glance

Sign On

1. Establish an Internet connection and go to *www.lexisnexis.com/lawschool*
2. Click the red **Sign On** button.
3. Type your **LexisNexis™ ID** in the open field of the Sign On template.
4. Click **Sign On**.

Customize Your Law School ID

To change your LexisNexis ID to something easy to remember:

1. Click the **Create a Custom ID** link on the Sign On template.
2. Complete the requested information.
3. Click **Finish** to submit.

For a lost or forgotten ID or for research assistance, call LexisNexis Customer Support at 1-800-455-3947.

Get a Document

By Citation — Full text of a case, law review article, or a statute

1. Click **Get a Document by Citation** tab.
2. Type **citation** in open field.
3. Make sure the **Full Text** radio button is selected.
4. Click **Get**.

Click Citation Formats to verify correct citation format.

By Party Name — Full text of a case

1. Click **Get a Document** tab, then **Party** tab.
2. Type **party name(s)** in open field(s); e.g., *Griggs v. Duke*.
3. Choose **jurisdiction**. If not known, accept default setting.
4. Click **Search**.

Brief Cases with LexisNexis™ Case Brief

LexisNexis Case Brief offers an accurate, succinct snapshot of a case, published or unpublished opinions, with an easy-to-read format that includes a LexisNexis™ Case Summary, LexisNexis™ Headnotes, and the *Shepard's* Signal™ indicator.

To get a LexisNexis Case Brief:

1. Click **Get a Document by Citation** tab.
2. Type **citation** in open field.
3. Make sure the **Case Brief** radio button is selected.
4. Click **Get**.

Formulating a Natural Language Search

1. Choose source at **Search-Sources** screen.
2. Type **words or phrases** in the open field, separating words with a comma. Click on **Natural Language** radio button.
3. Click **Suggest Words and Concepts** to see list of words that can be included in search (if available). Click on listed words to select.
4. Click **Search**.

Getting the Main Points of Law with LexisNexis™ Headnotes

Easily review the main points of law in the court's own language and quickly locate the language throughout the case with LexisNexis Headnotes.

With LexisNexis Headnotes you get:

- **Relevance and accuracy** with language used by the courts and written by LexisNexis attorney editors.
- **Easily expanded research** by linking to Lexis® Search Advisor for additional cases, analytical materials, or legal news related to the headnote.
- **No wasted time** because LexisNexis Headnotes are numbered and linked to easily find the headnote language in the body of a case.
- **Up-to-date information** because LexisNexis Headnotes are normally available within 24 hours of a judge's decision.
- **Comprehensive coverage** because LexisNexis is the only publisher to provide summaries for both published and unpublished opinions.
- **Easy-to-use headnote numbers** that appear in both the online and the printed case and make it easy to find the language of the headnotes in the body of a case.

Validate Research and Find More Documents with *Shepard's®* Citations Service

The *Shepard's* Citations Service provides full treatment and history analysis to verify status of a case as well as a complete and timely listing of authorities that have cited your case.

Shepard's covers:

- Federal/state case law and statutory materials
- Regulations, including the CFR
- U.S. and state constitutional provisions
- Court rules, including Federal Rules
- Law review articles
- Individual U.S. patents
- Canadian case law

To verify that a case is still good law or to find more relevant documents:

1. Click *Shepard's* Signal™ indicator while viewing a case OR click *Shepard's* tab.

   If you click the *Shepard's* tab, type citation in open field, click on *Shepard's* for Research (Full) button, click Check.
2. View *Shepard's* report and click Custom to narrow results to specifically listed jurisdictions, analyses, headnotes, and dates.
3. Click underlined case name to view text of a case.
4. Click FOCUS™ to further narrow results, finding issues or fact patterns. Type terms* in FOCUS template's field and click FOCUS.

*Use Terms and Connectors for FOCUS search.

Search Tips

- ***Shepard's* Summary** provides references at a glance and holds editorial treatment that generated the *Shepard's* Signal.
- Use the **Navigation Bar** to move easily among the references.
- Click on the **Legend** link for a list of all *Shepard's* Signals and definitions.

Shepard's Signal Indicators

- **Warning** — Negative treatment indicated — e.g., *overruled or reversed.*
- **Caution** — Possible negative treatment indicated — e.g., *limited or criticized.*
- **Positive treatment indicated** — History or treatment of case has positive impact on your case — e.g., *affirmed or followed.*
- **Cited and neutral analysis indicated** — Neither negative nor positive.
- **Citation information available** — Citing references available for your case but do not have history or treatment analysis.

FIGURE 6.35 *continued*

Develop Topical Search with Lexis® Search Advisor

What is Lexis Search Advisor?

- A finding tool for legal materials based on areas of law and related legal topics.
- When unsure where to begin legal research, Lexis Search Advisor helps to target legal issues, look for alternative research paths, identify appropriate sources, and formulate search requests.

Three ways to use Lexis Search Advisor

- **Choose from My Last 20 Legal Topics** allows you to select from topics previously used for research.
- **Option 1: Find a Legal Topic** is used when you have a legal issue or keywords and you want to find all of the possible areas of law in which it could be included.
- **Option 2: Explore Legal Topics** is used when you know the area of law. Allows you to drill down through topical hierarchy and examine possible issues and alternative research paths.

Using Lexis Search Advisor when you don't know the area of law (Option 1)

1. Click on **Search Advisor** tab.
2. Type **key words** in open field under Option 1: Find a Legal Topic. Click **Find**.
3. Click on **topic that is closest match**.
4. Click on arrow beside **Select Jurisdiction** to select jurisdiction, or click to select **Law Reviews or Analytical Materials**.
5. Click **Natural Language** radio button.
6. Type **key words** and/or click on **Suggested Words and Concepts** (optional) to select terms and phrases.
7. Click **Search**.

Using Lexis Search Advisor when you know the area of law (Option 2)

1. Click on **Search Advisor** tab.
2. Click on topics until you reach the **topic that is most relevant** and select a topic. Click on ⓘ to learn more about the topic.
3. Click on arrow beside **Select Jurisdiction** to select jurisdiction, or click to select **Law Reviews or Analytical Materials**.
4. Click **Natural Language** radio button.
5. Type **key words** and/or click on **Suggested Words and Concepts** (optional) to select terms and phrases.
6. Click **Search**.

Lexis Search Advisor Tips

- Click **In-Depth Discussion** at top of page to view the 15 cases that have the most in-depth discussion of your topic.
- Use **Retrieve All from the Headnote** to quickly and easily expand your research to retrieve all the headnotes and additional cases on a specific topic.

Choose a Source

A source is the data you choose to search; e.g., a single source is U.S. Supreme Court Cases, a combined source is Federal Cases, Combined Courts. Choose a source from:

- **Look for a Source** — Click Search category tab (e.g., Legal), then click through logical source path to choose; e.g., Legal > Cases - U.S. > Federal Cases, Combined Courts.
- **Look for A Source with Find a Source** — Click Find a Source tab, type source name in open field, click Match terms in long names radio button, click Find.
- **Choose from My Last 20 Sources** — Click down arrow to display list of 20 previously selected sources, highlight source in list, click Go.
- **Guided Search Forms** — Click tab, select from list of topic categories, complete template's required fields, click Search.

Construct a Search with Terms and Connectors

What is a term or a word?

- Any series of letters or numbers preceded or followed by a space (e.g., *contract or $1,234*).
- Singular, possessive and plural forms are automatically found if regular (e.g., *endings with s, 's, es, ies*).
- Some common equivalents are found (e.g., *cal finds Calif. and California*).
- Common noise words are **not** found (e.g., *the, and, is, at, of*).

Tips for finding specific words

- **Exclamation Point**: replaces any ending to a word. To use, add an exclamation point after root of the word where you want other endings to apply (e.g., *litigat! finds litigation, litigate, litigating, litigated, litigates, litigator*).
- **Asterisk**: replaces a single letter within word or at end of word (e.g., *wom*n finds woman or women*). Cannot start word with an asterisk.
- **ATLEAST**: finds documents with multiple occurrences of specific word(s). Specify from 1 to 255 occurrences of word or phrase. To use, e.g., type ***atleast5(bankruptcy)*** and connect to rest of search request with **AND** connector.
- **Plural**: finds only words in plural form. To use, e.g., type ***plural(aids)*** and connect to rest of search request with **AND** connector.
- **Singular**: finds only words in singular form. To use, e.g., type ***singular(aid)*** and connect to rest of search request with **AND** connector.
- **ALLCAPS**: finds only words that are completely capitalized. To use, e.g., type ***allcaps(aids)*** and connect to rest of search request with **AND** connector.

Connectors

Connectors establish a logical connection between search terms in search requests. Connectors are read left to right in order of the following priority:

CONNECTOR	EXAMPLE	EXPLANATION
1. ***or***	*environmental protection agency* ***or*** *EPA*	Finds any listed search word
2. ***/n***	*market* ***/5*** *share*	Finds two search words in same document within *n* words of each other
3. ***pre/n***	*cable* ***pre/2*** *television*	Finds two words in same document with first word preceding second word by *n* words
4. ***not/n***	*rico* ***not/5*** *puerto*	Finds two words in same document but second word cannot be within *n* words of first word
5. ***/s***	*circumstances* ***/s*** *mitigating*	Finds words in same sentence
6. ***/p***	*rule* ***/p*** *sanction*	Finds words in same paragraph
7. ***and***	*bank!* ***and*** *deregulat!*	Finds words that must appear somewhere in same document
8. ***and not***	*trust* ***and not*** *charitable*	Excludes any words that follow *and not* in search request

NOTE: *n* = any number from 1–255.

IV. WESTLAW

Westlaw (**www.westlaw.com**), a division of West Group, is another popular fee-based research system. It includes thousands of databases found in print in all large law libraries, powerful research tools, and the West editorial enhancements found in the company's print publications. West's Key Number System is utilized throughout the millions of documents available in this library to make the transition between print and electronic information easier. The KeySearch, Wizards, databases, and KeyCite features of Westlaw are discussed in this section, but this introduction by no means supplies complete coverage of this excellent resource.

To use the KeySearch feature in Westlaw, navigate through the topics and subtopics until the appropriate legal topic is displayed. Then click the "**search all of**" link at the top of the page or the open folder icon next to it. Alternatively, you can scan the list of KeySearch topics and subtopics, type keywords in the search box, and then click "Go" (Figure 6.36).

KeySearch can also construct a search query after the appropriate topics have been selected. Additional terms are typed in a text box and KeySearch then creates a query based on the supplied information (Figure 6.37).

FIGURE 6.36

Beginning Your Research with KeySearch®

KeySearch is a tool powered by the West Key Number System® that identifies key numbers and terms related to your legal issue and runs a query created by a West attorney-editor for you. KeySearch retrieves documents that contain key numbers, such as cases with West headnotes, as well as documents that don't contain key numbers, such as law reviews and cases without West headnotes. For a complete discussion of KeySearch, refer to *Using KeySearch in westlaw.com*, Material #40197436.

1. To access KeySearch, click **KeySearch** on the toolbar.
2. Browse the list of topics and subtopics in the right frame by clicking the Browse icons. When you see a topic or subtopic related to your issue, select it by clicking the **Search all of ...** link at the top of the page or by clicking the Search icon next to it.

   You can also scan the list of KeySearch topics and subtopics for specific terms by typing the terms in the text box in the left frame and clicking GO.

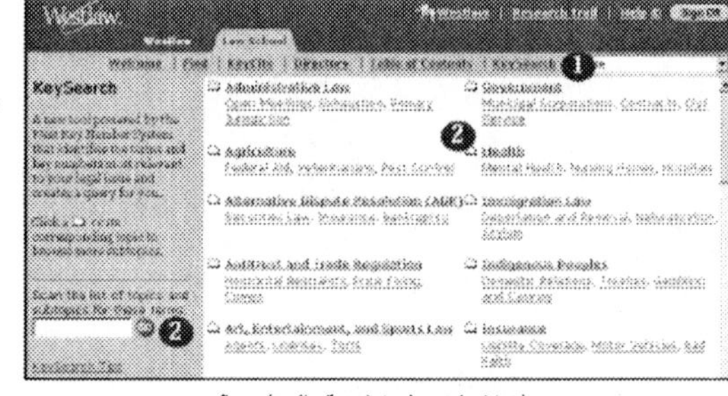

Browsing KeySearch topics and subtopics

FIGURE 6.37

3. Once you've selected a topic or subtopic to search, choose the source from which you want to retrieve documents, including cases, encyclopedias and treatises, and law reviews.
4. Type additional search terms (optional) in the *Add search terms* text box. KeySearch constructs a query for you based on the topic or subtopic and source you selected and on any search terms you entered in the *Add search terms* text box.
5. Click Search to run the KeySearch query.

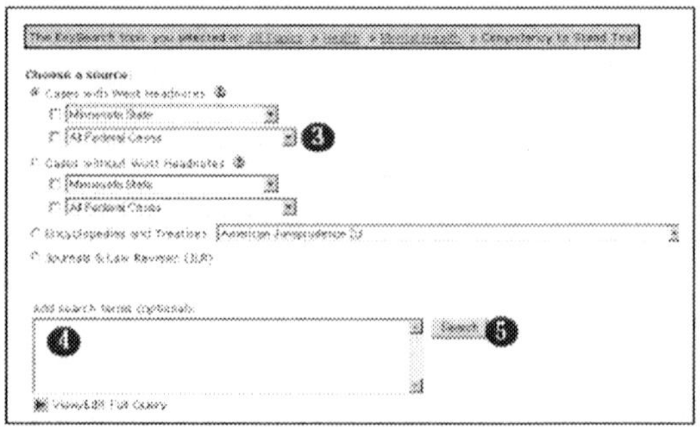

USING A WIZARD FOR YOUR COMMON RESEARCH TASKS

FIGURE 6.38

The easiest way to find a database for your Westlaw research and to create a KeyCite Alert entry is to use a wizard.

IDENTIFYING RELEVANT DATABASES FOR YOUR RESEARCH WITH THE FIND WIZARDS

Click **Find** on the toolbar. At the Find a Document page, click **Find a Person**, **Find a Company**, or **Find a Database** in the left frame, depending on the type of information you want to retrieve. Click **Next** to move through the wizard. Click **Finish** to run a search in the database you select.

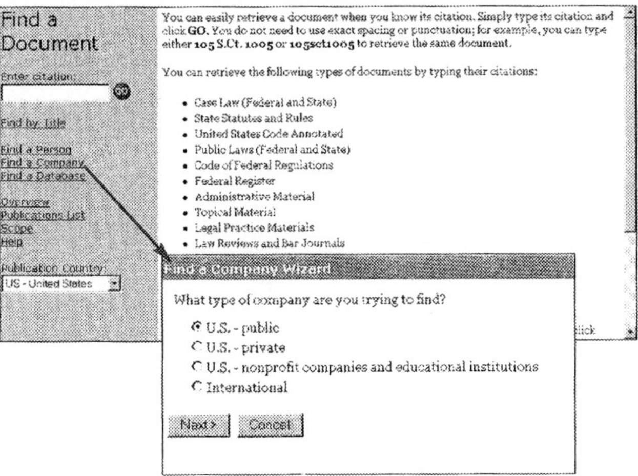

FIGURE 6.39

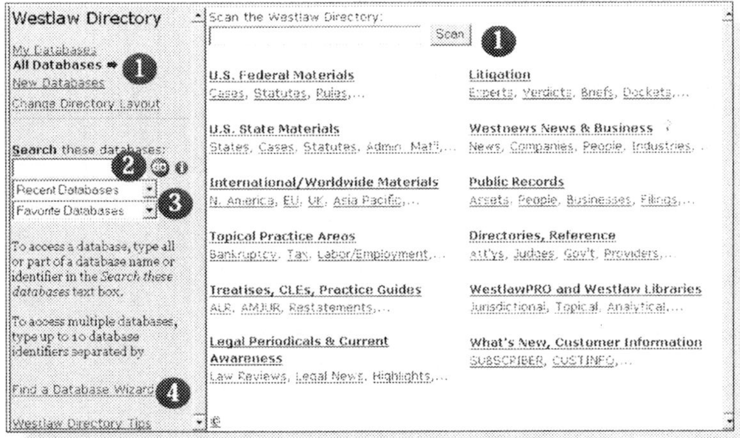

Accessing databases in the Westlaw Directory

The appropriate databases for a search can be identified using the Find Wizards included in Westlaw. Click on the "**Find**" toolbar and at the next page select "**Find a Person,**" "**Find a Company**" or "**Find a Database.**" Navigate through the Wizard selecting the appropriate information, then search (Figure 6.38).

You can view a list of all searchable databases in Westlaw by clicking on "**Directory**" in the toolbar. You then select the database by browsing through the di-

FIGURE 6.40

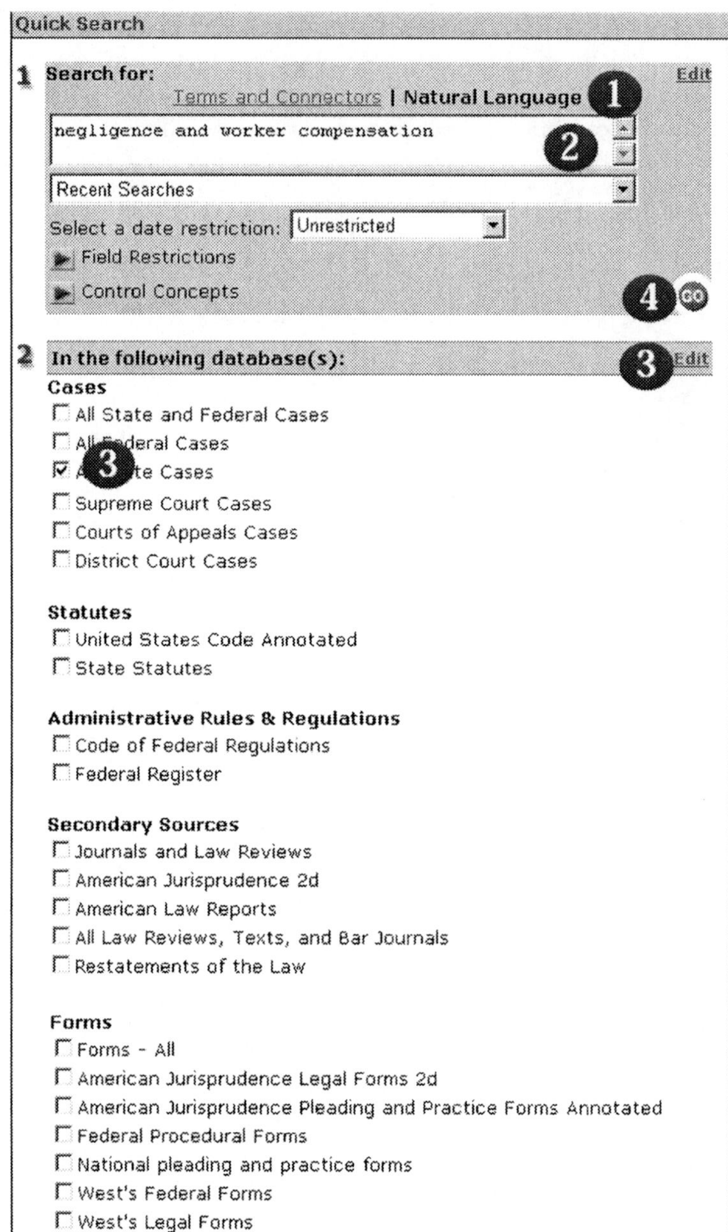

Searching Westlaw

rectory using the plus (+) or minus (−) symbols, by typing the name of the directory or its identifier, or by accessing recently used or favorite databases (Figure 6.39).

Westlaw offers natural-language or terms-and-connectors searches of its databases. The natural-language method allows the researcher to use plain English to search for and retrieve needed documents (Figure 6.40).

FIGURE 6.41

Connector	Type	Westlaw retrieves documents	For example
AND	&	containing both search terms	narcotics & warrant
OR	a space	containing either search term or both terms	car automobile
Grammatical Connectors	/p	containing search terms in the same paragraph	hearsay /p utterance
	/s	containing search terms in the same sentence	design /s defect
	+s	containing the first term preceding the second in the same sentence	attorney +s fee
Numerical Connectors	/n	containing search terms within *n* terms of each other (where *n* is a number from 1 to 255)	personal /3 jurisdiction
	+n	containing the first term preceding the second by *n* terms (where *n* is a number from 1 to 255)	42 +7 1942
Phrase	" "	containing search terms appearing in the same order as in the quotation marks	"attractive nuisance"
BUT NOT	%	not containing the term or terms following the percent symbol	r.i.c.o. % "puerto rico"

The more common terms-and-connectors method is also available. Reference lists, field restrictions, and other useful information are readily available on the "Terms and Connectors" search screen (Figure 6.41).

Search results in Westlaw are also easy to navigate. Key numbers and links to additional documents are provided, as well as KeyCite flags that tell the researcher the type of treatment given in the document (Figure 6.42). These help the researcher decide whether the information may be favorable, neutral, or unfavorable to the case at hand.

KeyCite, which is Westlaw's equivalent of Shepard's Citations, helps the researcher validate and update research. All the cases in West's National Reporter System, as well as more than 1 million unpublished cases, select administrative decisions, the U.S.C.S., the C.F.R., and state statutes, are covered by KeyCite. Figure 6.43 gives an overview of this feature.

V. SUMMARY

Electronic media, CD compilations, and the Internet have advanced the field of legal research tremendously over the years. With the prevalence of electronic and online databases, available in real time, 24 hours a day, the researcher's job has been made easier and faster. Legal research can be performed anywhere an Internet connection is available, making it possible for many to work from home on a regular basis. Students of all disciplines now have at their disposal court decisions, statutes, rules, and regulations that affect their specific field of study. Free online resources available to the public at large have added to the nonlegal, common person's ability to access information that was unavailable in the past. The future of computer-assisted legal research is definitely bright and the vast resources available will only improve in the future.

FIGURE 6.42

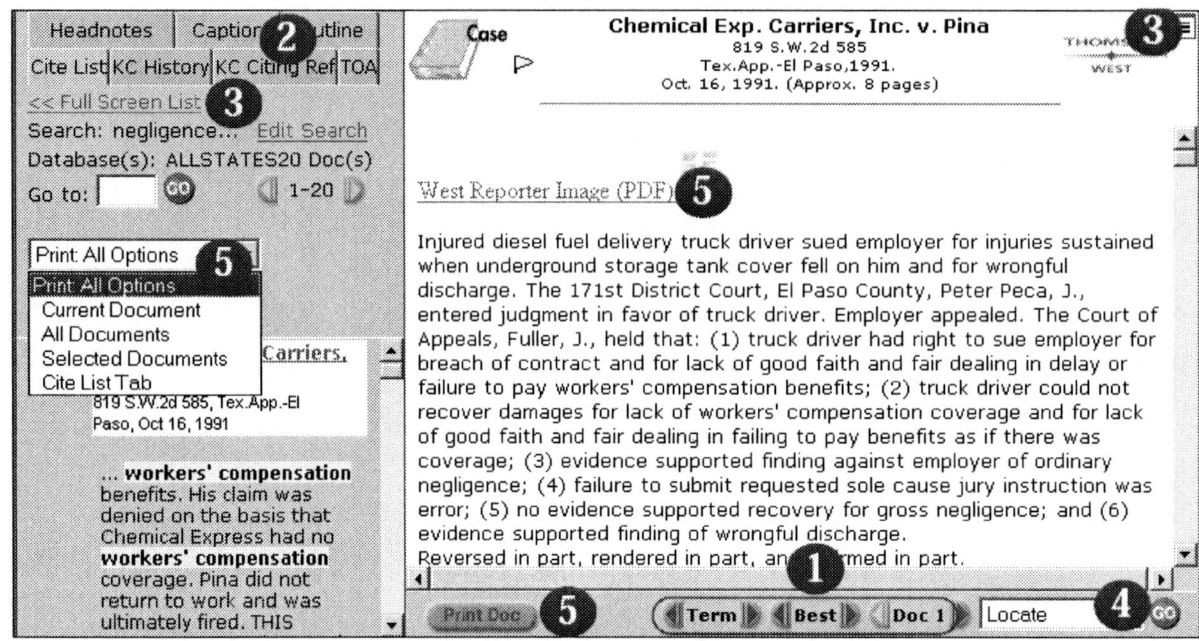

Browsing a search result

FIGURE 6.43

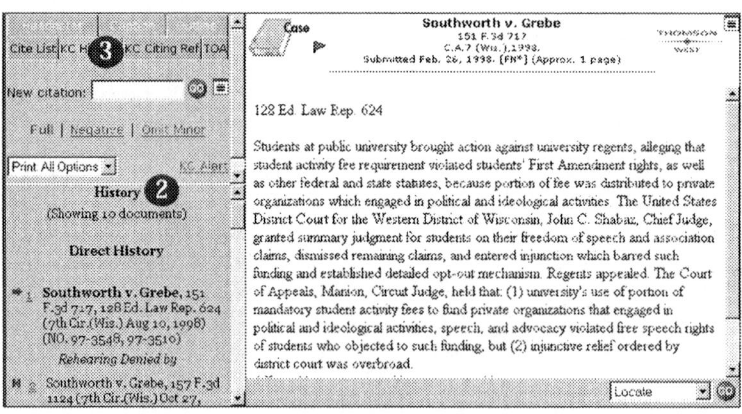

Viewing KeyCite history

TERTIARY RESOURCES

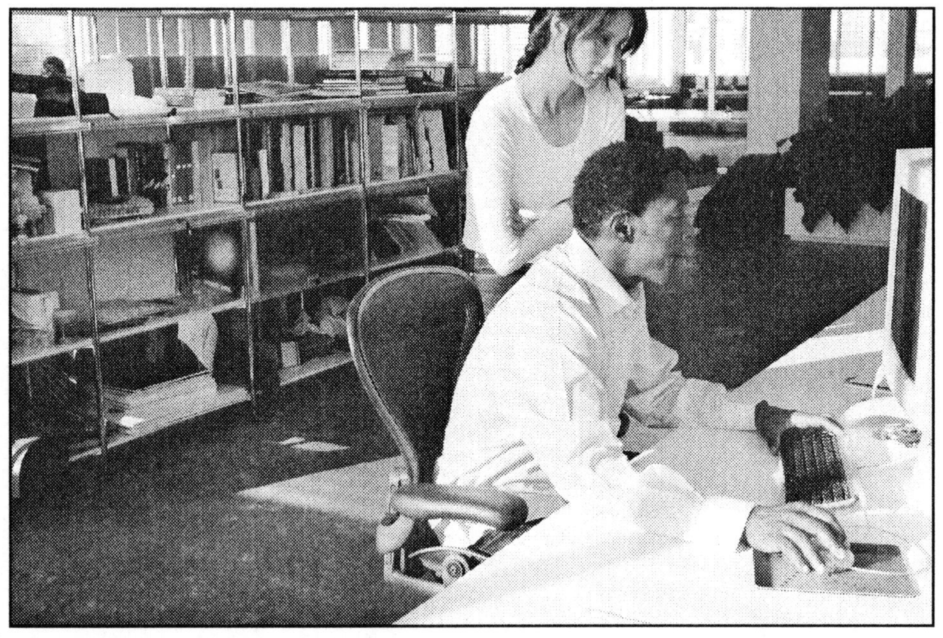

CHAPTER

7

Law Books, Texts, Services, and Periodicals

A **tertiary resource** is a reference or work that explains, interprets, or discusses statutes, case law, and administrative law. Common law decisions are analyzed, statutory meaning is defined and explained, and administrative rules and regulations are thoroughly enunciated in a myriad of different works. Resources such as encyclopedias, periodicals, journal articles, treatises, and textbooks are all classified as tertiary resources because they are not themselves law, but rather explanations, comparisons, and definitions of the law, detailing and commenting on the law's applicability and enforcement in given situations.

Books of the legal genre are distinctive. Physically, they are often thick, heavy, imposing, and bound in eye-catching colors of leather-look material. Although the packaging appears aimed to impress, the design is largely driven by functionality due to constant handling and regular use. They must possess workhorse qualities to survive vigorous usage, repeated reference, and regular copying. Volumes are most often found in a series, system, or group with other books. It is not uncommon for a tertiary resource like a law review, reporter, or digest to be part of a series of 300 to 600 other books.

Law books are not intended for general reading. Instead, such texts serve as compilations, compendiums, collections, and depositories of legal thought and theory, containing explanations of rules, regulations, statutes, codes, and, in certain volumes, legal analysis, court cases, or syntheses of court decisions. No effort is made here to categorize all law books, but the researcher must understand initially that law books serve entirely different ends than most other books.

I. LAW TEXTBOOKS

Students of law, from paralegals and criminal justice majors to law students, rely on text materials in class instruction. Law textbooks, or **casebooks**, play a very large part in a legal education and cover broad areas of the law. College, university, and law school textbooks are primarily geared to teach or explain general principles of law and uniform issues in the resolution of legal problems. The textbooks generally contain some references to various state or federal statutes; provide cases, problems, and assignments; and deliver the fundamental aspects of a particular area of law. Casebooks used in the law school setting are just that: books of case reprints. Legal principles involved in those cases are taught using the Socratic method, so these books are very different from traditional textbooks.

Textbooks and casebooks are a very effective way to gain a general understanding of a certain type of law. Find a copy of a criminal and a real estate law textbook or casebook. Review the table of contents and the index from each book and search for keywords, using the examples with our ongoing fact patterns. What are your results?

Fact Pattern 1

Keywords:

DUI/DWI

Blood alcohol content

Vehicular homicide

Negligent manslaughter

Accident—vehicular-leaving scene

Fact Pattern 2

Keywords:

Agreement of sale—execution of agreement

Earnest money or Hand money or deposit

Oral agreement—enforceability of

Specific performance

II. HORNBOOKS (TREATISES)

Hornbooks, or **treatises**, can appropriately be described as highly sophisticated textbooks. The authors of these texts attempt to provide an exhaustive scholarly analysis of a specific law topic. This in-depth analysis is usually extremely thorough and generally includes federal and state references, and a large number of footnotes that cite both primary and secondary law, as well as other tertiary sources. To achieve treatise status, the text has to be well accepted by the legal community and withstand critical review. The list in Figure 7.1 includes some of the preeminent hornbooks.

Again referring to Fact Patterns 1 and 2, examples from the indexes of two hornbooks are provided using the same keywords as above. Note that these books' general indexes have far greater detail and more subheadings than the typical textbook.

FIGURE 7.1

Administrative Law—Davis
Agency—Seavy
Agency and Partnership—Reuschlein & Gregory
Antitrust—Sullivan
Common Law Pleading—Koffler & Reppy
Common Law Pleading—Shipman
Conflict of Laws—Scoles & Hay
Constitutional Law—Nowak, Rotunda & Young
Contracts—Calamari & Perillo
Contracts—Simpson
Corporate Taxation—Kahn
Corporations—Henn & Alexander
Criminal Law—LaFave & Scott
Damages—McCormick
Domestic Relations—Clark
Environmental Law—Rogers
Estate & Gift Taxes—Lowndes, Kramer & McCord
Evidence—McCormick
Evidence, Introduction—Lilly
Federal Courts—Wright
Future Interests—Simes
Income Taxation of Individuals—Posin
Insurance—Keeton
Labor Law—German
Law Problems—Ballantine
Legal Writing—Weihofen
Local Government Law—Reynolds
New York Practice—Sieged
Oil & Gas—Hemingway
Poor, Law of the—LaFrance, Schroeder, Bennett & Boyd
Property, Law of—Cunningham, Whitman & Stoebuck
Property, Survey—Boyer
Real Estate Finance Law—Osborne, Nelson & Whitman
Real Property Introduction—Moynihan
Remedies—Dobbs
Sales—Nordstrum
Secured Transactions Under UCC—Henson
Torts—Prosser & Keeton
Trusts—Bogert
UCC—White & Summers
Urban Planning & Land Development Control—Hagman
Wills—Atkinson
Black's Law Dictionary

Fact Pattern 1. See the index and corresponding pages from Clark & Marshall's *Treatise on the Law of Crimes* in Fact Pattern Figure 7.2.

Fact Pattern 2. See the excerpts from Williston's *Treatise on the Law of Contracts* in Fact Pattern Figure 7.3.

FIGURE 7.2

1067

Of course, judges and jurors have not observed the behavior of an accused person leading to the charge for which he is being tried. The acts of the defendant are uninspected save in an historical sense, and exclusive of some cases of criminal contempt. More frequently juries are the fact finders, though a jury can be waived and in such a situation finding the facts is then a judicial function. In any event, the operative facts are arrived at in criminal cases by drawing inferences from the evidence received during such trials. Parenthetically it should be noted that the substantial evidence rule and, indeed, the rules of evidence play a significant part in these trials. The former by precluding, at least theoretically, verdicts based upon conjecture and speculation; while the latter serves to delimit the problem and avoidance of bias and prejudice.

Reaching a verdict in criminal cases is a species of problem solving bringing into play the preconceived notions, analogy, fixedness, intuition and personal predilections of persons engaged in the process. Putting these important aspects to one side, however, it is theoretically significant to notice that juries are expected to decide a homicide case, for example, within certain frames of reference. Jurors acquire knowledge, it is hoped, of the applicable law through instructions given them by the trial judge. Jurors then are directed to apply the law, thus given them, to the facts they find from the evidence—they determine whether the facts fit the defining properties of the offenses and doctrines explained by the trial judge. Fact finders then determine what in the evidence exhibits and fits the defining attributes of the offense of which the defendant stands accused. Shortly stated, jury instructions approximate cues for categorizing human behavior taken cognizance of by criminal law. (See § 1.01.)

In Figure 4, based on common law, the whole diagram represents the class of human behavior denoted as homicide. Boxes I, II, III and IV depict the four common law concepts of murder, manslaughter, excusable and justifiable homicides. These four sub-classes of homicide fall into two major

continued

FIGURE 7.2 *continued*

631

I. MURDER	II. MANSLAUGHTER
§ 10.00 Unlawful Killing of a Human Being with Malice Aforethought Express or Implied 1. Express Malice—Actual intent to cause death of: (a) The person killed, (b) Any other person. 2. Malice is usually implied when homicide results if: (a) There is intent to inflict great bodily harm (b) An act is wilfully performed or omitted and the natural tendency of such behavior is to cause death or great bodily harm (c) Resisting lawful arrest, or in obstructing an officer attempting to suppress affray or riot (d) In an attempt to commit, or during commission of some other dangerous felony	**§ 10.11 Voluntary—Intentional Homicide Without Malice Aforethought in Heat of Blood Produced by Reasonable Provocation** **§ 10.12 Involuntary—Unintentional Homicides During:** 1. Commission of a criminal act not amounting to a felony, nor naturally tending to cause death or grievous bodily harm 2. Omission to perform a legal duty, under circumstances evidencing criminal-culpable negligence 3. Performing lawful act with criminal-culpable negligence
III. EXCUSABLE	**IV. JUSTIFIABLE**
§ 7.02 Misadventure (Per Infortunium) **§ 7.03 Self-defense Upon a Sudden Affray (Se Defendendo)**	**§ 7.01 Homicides Through:** 1. Executions pursuant to lawful court orders imposing death penalty 2. Preventing felony 3. Suppressing riot 4. Effecting arrest or preventing escape **§ 7.03 Self-defense**

Figure 4—Some classes of Homicide.

III. RESTATEMENTS OF THE LAW

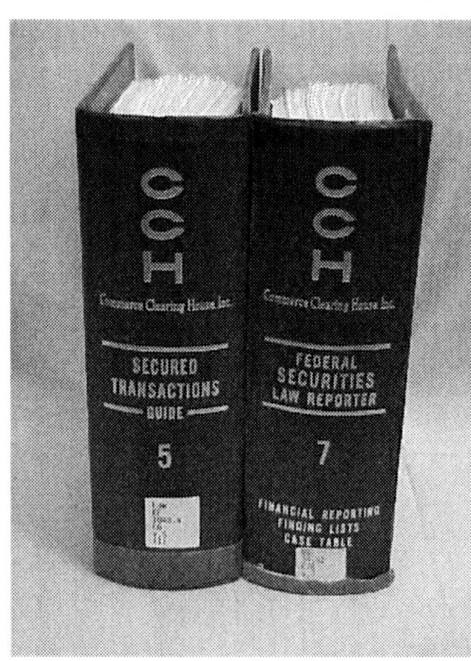

The **American Law Institute (ALI)**, located in Philadelphia, consists of learned scholars, practitioners, and judges whose task is to rewrite or state the law as presently understood and to make recommendations or suggestions regarding the future direction of legislation. Judges at all levels place heavy reliance on the authority of the restatements. A complete list of the ALI Restatements series is provided at Figure 7.4.

A single topical series of any restatement usually comprises many volumes and a very efficient index. In most multivolume sets, an index is included in the back of each volume, covering information in that volume only (although it may provide cross-references to other volumes). If the set consists of a large number of volumes, a general index (in its own volume or volumes) will accompany the series.

IV. LOOSELEAF SERVICES

Because textbooks, hornbooks, and restatements are in printed and bound form, immediate updating and revision are not possible. Even in the most conservative framework, the law regularly

 Pub 11/2001

continued

the property, and should therefore go to the purchaser if he or she desires it.

§ 50:44. Assignment or Subcontract by Purchaser

One who has contracted to purchase land may assign the right[35] or may contract that he or she will acquire title and then transfer it. In both cases, an interest in the land that is to be transferred passes.[36] The assignment operates as a conveyance of the purchaser's equitable title.[37]

One who is deceived by the common phrase that a vendor

was allowed to recover part of the price when land was condemned).

NY: Clarke v. Long Island Realty Co., 126 A.D. 282, 110 N.Y.S. 697 (2d Dep't 1908).

Ohio: In re Appropriation of Easement for Highway Purposes (Director of Highways v. Bennett), 118 Ohio App. 207, 25 Ohio Op. 2d 57, 193 N.E.2d 702 (6th Dist. Lucas County 1962).

Ore: Blondell v. Beam, 243 Or. 293, 413 P.2d 397 (1966).

RI: Salvatore v. Fuscellaro, 53 R.I. 271, 166 A. 26 (1933).

Annotations: Rights and liabilities of parties to executory contract for sale of land taken by eminent domain, 27 A.L.R.3d 572.

35. **Cal:** Johnston v. Landucci, 21 Cal. 2d 63, 130 P.2d 405, 148 A.L.R. 1355 (1942).

Conn: Gavin v. Johnson, 131 Conn. 489, 41 A.2d 113, 156 A.L.R. 1130 (1945).

Ga: Pawn World, Inc. v. Estate of Sam Farkas, Inc., 218 Ga. App. 334, 461 S.E.2d 295 (1995).

Ill: Lewis v. McCreedy, 378 Ill. 264, 38 N.E.2d 170, 138 A.L.R. 198 (1941).

Mich: Ross Properties v. Sheng, 151 Mich. App. 729, 391 N.W.2d 464 (1986).

Mo: Lewis v. Gray, 356 Mo. 115, 201 S.W.2d 148 (1947).

NY: Cochran v. Taylor, 273 N.Y. 172, 7 N.E.2d 89 (1937) (the interest of one who has contracted to purchase can be assigned, but so can that of the holder of an option).

SD: Orr v. Allen, 73 S.D. 547, 45 N.W.2d 737 (1951) (an assignee of a purchaser of real property takes subject to all the rights of the vendor under the original contract of sale, including all defenses available to the vendor).

Wis: Milbrandt v. Huber, 149 Wis. 2d 275, 440 N.W.2d 807 (Ct. App. 1989).

36. **Ala:** Chapman v. Glassell, 13 Ala. 50, 1848 WL 293 (1848).

Mich: People's Sav. Bank v. Geistert, 253 Mich. 694, 235 N.W. 888 (1931).

NJ: Grunauer v. Westchester Fire Ins. Co., 72 N.J.L. 289, 62 A. 418 (N.J. Ct. Err. & App. 1905).

37. **Ala:** Chapman v. Glassell, 13 Ala. 50, 1848 WL 293 (1848).

Mich: People's Sav. Bank v. Geistert, 253 Mich. 694, 235 N.W. 888 (1931).

Barnard v. Huff, 252 Mich. 258, 233 N.W. 213, 77 A.L.R. 259 (1930) (overruled in part on other grounds by, People's Sav. Bank v. Geistert, 253 Mich. 694, 235 N.W. 888 (1931)).

FIGURE 7.4

Restatement of the Law of Security © 1941
Restatement of the Law, Second: Agency © 1958
Conflict of Laws © 1989
Contracts © 1981
Property (Donative Transfers) © 1983, 86, 88, 92
Judgments © 1982
Property (Landlord and Tenant) © 1997
Property © 1936, 1940, 1944
Torts © 1965
Trusts © 1959
Restatement, Third Foreign Relations Law © 1986
Law Governing Layers © 2000
Property (Mortgages) © 1997
Torts: Product Liability © 1998
Property (Servitudes) © 2000
Property (Wills and Other Donative Transfers) © 1999
Suretyship and Guaranty © 1996
Trusts © 1992
Unfair Competition © 1995

changes; examples are quite evident in tax, labor, and consumer law. Numerous areas of law that are prone to change can be more readily reported by **looseleaf services**. Looseleaf products are packaged in ring binders, into which single *looseleaf* pages are inserted. As updates are needed, the binder is opened and new pages are inserted to replace the old. Some services in rapidly changing areas of law are updated as often as weekly.

Four major publishing houses dominate the looseleaf market:

Bureau of National Affairs (BNA)

Environmental Reporter, Occupational Safety and Health Reporter, Product Safety and Health Reporter, Fair Employment Practice Service, Labor Relations Reporter, Housing and Development Reporter, Criminal Law Reporter, Family Law Reporter, United States Law Week

Callaghan and Company

Federal Tax Services, Criminal Practice, and Legal Checklists

Commerce Clearing House (CCH)

Labor Law Reports, Employment Safety and Health Guide, Unemployment Insurance—Social Security, Workmen's Compensation Law Reports, Medicare—Medicaid Guide, Poverty Law Reports, Urban Affairs Reports, Consumer Product Safety Guide, Consumer Credit Guide, Bankruptcy Law Reports, Federal Tax Reports, State Tax Reports

Prentice-Hall

Social Security and Unemployment Compensation, Wage and Hour, Labor Relations, State Labor Laws, Corporation Federal Taxes, State and Local Tax Service

V. CONTINUING EDUCATION MATERIALS

A thriving proliferation of materials, dedicated to both practical and theoretical aspects of law, is a welcome boon for the modern practitioner. Some of the more notable publishers of continuing legal education (and other) materials include:

ALI-ABA Committee on Continuing Professional Education

California Continuing Education of the Bar

New Jersey Institute for Continuing Legal Education

Pennsylvania Bar Institute

Practicing Law Institute

Check with your local jurisdiction or state bar to see if a similar group or publisher exists in your area. Without question, these types of publications are extremely useful to the practitioner. They are written, constructed, and designed for utility only, emphasizing nuts-and-bolts issues. The researcher will find the authors of these publications attuned to the step-by-step issues and processes so crucial to the productive practice of law. Materials of this sort can be exceptionally useful to the researcher, for example, in narrowing and framing real-world, concrete legal questions that relate to practical issues and specific facts.

VI. LEGAL PERIODICALS

A. Law Reviews

Every law school publishes its own **law review**, which is a collection of articles, reviews, or commentaries on various issues of law. The typical law review article is scholarly in approach, and written with extensive footnotes and citations to legal authority. For example, the University of Baltimore School of Law publishes a law review in the fall and spring of each academic year. Whatever topic is selected is handled within an academic framework and substantially analyzed.

To the researcher, such intellectual dissection is generally helpful, though busy practitioners sometimes seem indifferent to these high-level forms of discourse. Law review articles provide the researcher with a multitude of other relevant sources, particularly the case law so necessary in the establishment of proof, the testing of a legal argument or principle, or the making of a prima facie case. Comparative statutory analysis is also common, giving the researcher a flavor of national trends in law. Courts, as well, increasingly rely on law reviews for support in the reasoning and justification of decisions.

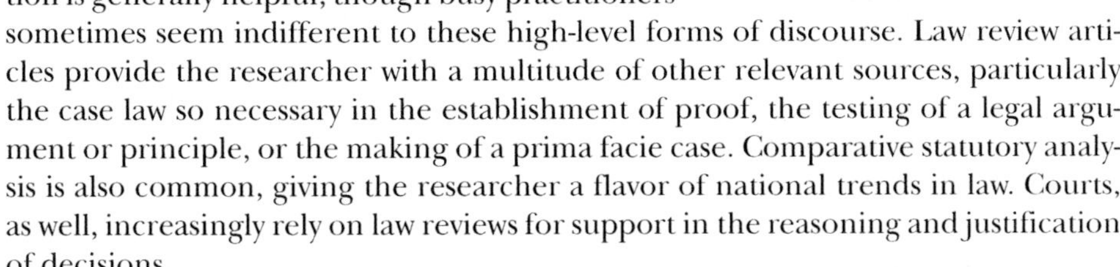

B. Commercial Journal Publications

Although academic institutions play the primary role in law review publication, private and commercial publishing houses have entered the production arena as well. Some perceive this as undermining the academic quality and integrity of the law review. For others, the content promulgated by the for-profit businesses fills a void that the law reviews have failed to fill. Critics of nonacademic publications note that commercialism, rather than the search for truth, dictates policy in the analysis of a problem. What these detractors apparently fail to realize is that commercial journals tend to fill needs heretofore unmet by the academic sector, covering topics so specialized or so practice-oriented that academic thinkers are unlikely to be exposed to or have an interest in the topic. Hence, commercial journals are playing an ever-increasing role in the dissemination of legal information. Some examples of commercial journals are:

Food, Drug, Cosmetic Law Journal
Insurance Law Journal
Journal of Real Estate Investments
Labor Law Journal

C. Bar Association Periodicals

State and county bar associations frequently publish institutional periodicals. At the county level, the information can be crucial, particularly as it frequently relates to procedural changes, legal notices, and practice pointers. Of course, the American Bar Association publishes its renowned *ABA Journal,* which is read widely throughout the world. Divisions of the ABA, like the Individual Rights and Responsibilities Section, also publish well-respected periodicals, such as *Human Rights* and other works.

D. Professional Association Periodicals

An expansive list of highly useful periodicals could easily be compiled from the publications of professional associations and groups. Associations such as the National College for Criminal Defense, the National Association of Criminal Defense, and the *National Council of Juvenile Court Judges* all publish journals that examine specific areas of practice and theoretical expertise. A partial listing is provided in Figure 7.5 for illustrative purposes.

The researcher is also well advised to access *Legal and Law Enforcement Periodicals,* compiled by Oxbridge Communication, for "Facts on File," a comprehensive and up-to-date directory to more than 3,000 publications covering law and justice in the United States.

E. Legal Newspapers

Since the founding of the *Legal Intelligencer,* a publication for members of the Philadelphia legal community, in 1843, legal newspapers have served a major role in the dissemination of law to the masses. Newspapers, like looseleaf services, often provide the researcher with the most current information on a given topic, whether it be legal notices, important case synopses, or other general legal news. The practitioner should consult all legal newspapers in his or her particular locality, as well as the emerging national legal newspapers, for up-to-date information. Some of the most prominent legal newspapers are:

The National Law Journal
The Legal Times
The American Lawyer

FIGURE 7.5

AELE Law Enforcement Legal Defense Manual. Americans for Effective Law Enforcement, 841 W. Touhy Ave., Park Ridge, IL 60068-3351

American Academy of Matrimonial Lawyers Newsletter. A.A.M.L., 150 N. Michigan Ave., Suite 2040, Chicago, IL 60601.

American Bar Association Journal. America Bar Association, 750 N. Lake Shore Dr. FL 7, Chicago, IL 60606

American Criminal Law Review. Section on Criminal Law, American Bar Association, 740 15th Street NW, 10th Floor, Washington, DC 20005-1009

American Criminologist. American Association of Criminology, 1314 Kinnear Rd., Columbus, OH 43212-1156

APLA Bulletin. American Patent Law Association, 4565 Ruffner St., Suite 2000, San Diego, CA 92111

Association of Trial Lawyers of America Law Journal. Association of Trial Lawyers of America, The Leonard M. Ring Law Center, 1050 31st St., NW, Washington, DC 20007

Barrister. American Bar Association Young Lawyers' Section, 321 S. Plymouth Ct., Chicago, IL 60604-3997

Briefcase. National Legal Aid and Defense Association, 1625 K St. NW, Suite 800, Washington, DC 20006-1604

Civil Liberties. American Civil Liberties Union, 125 Broad St., New York, NY 10004

Commercial Law Journal. Commercial Law League of America, 150 N. Michigan Ave., Suite 600, Chicago, IL 60601

Council on Legal Education for Professional Responsibility Newsletter. Center for Professional Responsibility, American Bar Association, 541 North Fairbanks Ct., Chicago, IL 60611-3314

First Amendment Lawyers Association Bulletin. First Amendment Lawyers Association, 200 S. Wacker Dr., Suite 3100, Chicago, IL 60606

Guild Practitioner. National Lawyers Guild, 126 University Pl., Fifth Floor, New York, NY 10003

Human Rights Bulletin. International League for Human Rights, 823 UN Plaza Suite 717, New York, NY 10017

Industrial Health Foundation, Legal Series Bulletin. Industrial Health Foundation Inc., 34 Penn Cir., West Pittsburgh, PA 15206

Judicature. American Judicature Society, 180 N. Michigan Ave., Suite 600, Chicago, IL 60601

Legal Aid Digest. National Legal Aid and Defense Association, 1625 K St. NW, Suite 800, Washington, DC 20006-1604

Municipal Law Court Decisions. International Municipal Lawyers Association (IMLA), 1110 Vermont Ave., NW, Suite 200, Washington, DC 20005

National Tax Journal. National Tax Association, 725 15th St NW #600, Washington, DC 20005-2109

Prosecutor. National District Attorneys Association, 99 Canal Center Plaza, Suite 510 Alexandria, VA 22314

Quarterly. Christian Legal Society, 4208 Evergreen Lane, Suite 222, Annandale, VA 22003-3264

The Criminologist Newsletter. American Society of Criminology, 1314 Kinnea Rd., Columbus, OH 43212-1156

Trial. Association of Trial Lawyers of America, The Leonard M. Ring Law Center, 1050 31st St. NW, Washington, DC 20007

Women Lawyers Journal. National Association of Women Lawyers, American Bar Center, 750 North Lake Shore Drive, Chicago, IL 60611

F. How to Find Periodical Articles

A vital research tool for the researcher, the *Index to Legal Periodicals* has been published since 1908. Another resource, *The Current Law Index,* which debuted in the legal indexing field in 1980, is just as valuable. Several other indexes are available that may prove fruitful: *Criminology Index, Criminal Justice Abstract, WEBSPIRS, Infotrac,* and *Index to Foreign Legal Periodicals* are representative examples.

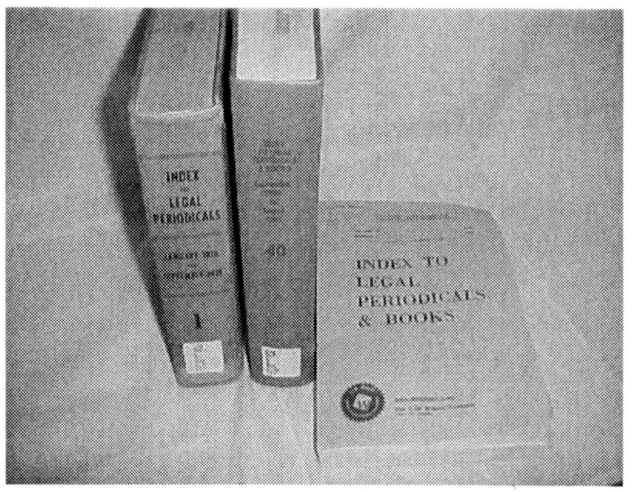

These indexes are user-friendly, with primary topics found in a subject-author section. If you have a focused topic, like *rape* and *character,* or *evidence,* or the article author's exact name and year of general publication, it should be no trouble to create a well-developed bibliography of respected authorities. Indexes point the researcher to the very best in legal writing and analysis and lead the researcher to a variety of other citations as well, including cases, statutes, and practice material. Many also include book reviews and a table of statutes.

Fact Pattern 1. See Fact Pattern Figure 7.6 for pages from the *Index to Legal Periodicals* under the heading of "Driving Under the Influence." Which periodicals would you consult for basic information?

Fact Pattern 2. The pages from the *Current Law Index* reproduced in Fact Pattern Figure 7.7 shows the heading of "Contracts." Peruse this page and determine which articles would be useful.

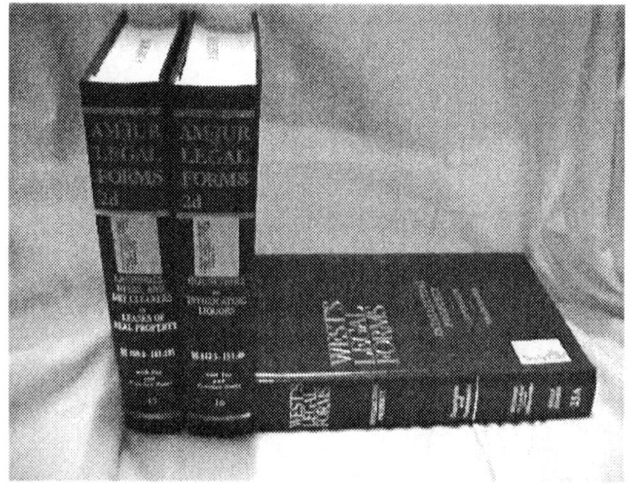

VII. FORMBOOKS AND PRACTICE MATERIALS

In an ideal world, practitioners would draft and design each new contract, will, trust, or other document individually to reflect the case at hand. However, this is neither humanly nor technically possible in the life of busy practitioners. The complexity of legal and justice practice in the 20th and 21st centuries has spawned numerous publications that compile forms, model clauses, and provisionary exhibits and checklists. These forms are provided for both illustrative and practical purposes. Most practitioners rely on standardized forms as a starting point in the creation of legal documents. Given the variations in jurisdictional requirements and the multitude of construction and drafting methods, formbooks aid both the novice and the seasoned advocate. Using a "skeleton" pleading, will, trust, contract, or other legal document, the drafter can incorporate material responsive to individual client needs and desires into the generic form. Figure 7.8 is an example of a model will.

Figure 7.9 is a cross-examination sequence from *American Jurisprudence—Trials.* Figure 7.10 is an example of a motion for stay from the *U.S. Supreme Court Rules.*

At first blush, it might seem that generic forms, formbooks, and similar practice materials would be of only marginal use to the researcher. Upon closer examination, however, you will realize that they reveal an enormous amount about the

FIGURE 7.6

Draft, Military *See* Military service
Drahozal, Christopher R.
Enforcing vacated international arbitration awards: an economic approach. 11 no4 *Am. Rev. Int'l Arb.* 451-79 2000
Drainage
See also
Water and watercourses
North Dakota
Burlington Northern, et al v. Benson County—the North Dakota Supreme Court dammed water district from extending reasonable use to diffused surface waters in natural drainways. J. M. Kelley, student author. 6 no2 *Great Plains Nat. Resources J.* 162-9 Spr/Summ 2002
Dram shop acts *See* Dram shop liability
Dram shop liability
Missouri
Reinventing the "legislative intent, or rather the legislative mandate" on dram shop liability in Missouri: a look at Kilmer v. Mun. M. L. Young, student author. 45 no2 *St. Louis U. L.J.* 625-65 Spr 2001
Dramshop acts *See* Dram shop liability
Drapeau, Daniel S.
First steps in the millennium: trade-mark jurisprudence of the Federal Court of Canada. 15 no3 *Intell. Prop. J.* 319-475 F 2002
Draper, Matthew
Justice as a building block of democracy in transitional societies: the case of Indonesia. 40 no2 *Colum. J. Transnat'l L.* 391-418 2002
Draper, Wickliffe Preston, d. 1972
about
"The American breed": Nazi eugenics and the origins of the Pioneer Fund. P. A. Lombardo. 65 no3 *Alb. L. Rev.* 743-830 2002
Draskovich, Dena
The Minnesota taconite production tax: an alternative index; by P. Kalela, H. Haas, D. Draskovich. 16 no1 *J. Nat. Resources & Envtl. L.* 43-58 2001/2002
Drauz, Götz
Unbundling GE/Honeywell: the assessment of conglomerate mergers under EC competition law. 25 no4 *Fordham Int'l L.J.* 885-908 Ap 2002
Drazin, Brian D.
Screening potential cases involving mass torts or class actions: the connection between causation and damages. no 215 *N.J. Law.* 22-6, 29 Je 2002
Drebes, Ralph
Notification obligations in connection with the purchase of shares in a German stock corporation. 13 no4 *Int'l Company & Com. L. Rev.* 163-73 Ap 2002
Dreifact, Kenneth M.
Postcards from the edge: surveying the digital divide; by A. C. Celli, K. M. Dreifach. 20 no1 *Cardozo Arts & Ent. L.J.* 53-71 2002
Dreyfuss, Rochelle Cooper
Coming of age with TRIPS: a comment on J. H. Reichman, The TRIPS Agreement comes of age: conflict or cooperation with the developing countries? 33 no2 *Case w. Res. J. Int'l L.* 179-85 Spr 2001
Driggs, Ken
Regulating the five steps to death: a study of death penalty direct appeals in the Florida Supreme Court, 1991-2000. 14 no4 *St. Thomas L. Rev.* 759-823 Summ 2002
Dripps, Donald A.
On the costs of uniformity and the prospects of dualism in constitutional criminal procedure. 45 no2 *St. Louis U. L.J.* 433-44 Spr 2001
Driver, J. Christopher
African AIDS crisis: implications from the rise of managed care in South Africa. 30 no 2 *Ga. J. Int'l & Comp. L.* 305-30 2002
Driving under the influence *See* Driving while intoxicated
Driving while intoxicated
See also
Blood tests
Dram shop liability
Drug testing
Narcotics
DUI as a crime of violence under 18 U.S.C. § 16(b); does a drunk driver risk "using" force. MN. G. Salemi, student author. 33 no3 *Loy. U. Chi. L.J.* 691-747 Spr 2002
The removal of aliens who drink and drive: felony DWI as a crime of violence under 18 U.S.C. § 16(b). J. A. Rah, student author. 70 no5 *Fordham L. Rev.* 2109-48 Ap 2002
Australia
Imprisonment for driving while disqualified: disproportionate punishment or sound public policy? R. Edney, M. Bagaric. 25 no1 *Crim. L.J.* 7-18 F 2001
Illinois
Every lawyer's guide to DUI. D. J. Ramsell. 90 no6 *Ill B.J.* 311-12, 316 Je 2002
Representing DUI revoked or suspended drivers before the Secretary of State. L. A. Davis. 90 no6 *Ill. B.J.* 292-9 Je 2002
New York (State)
New York allows drunk driver's widow to sue automaker. C. Magnuson. 38 no5 *Trial* 80-2 My 2002
New Zealand
Innocent in fact—guilty at law. R. Mahoney. 2002 *N.Z. L.J.* 97 Ap 2002
Ohio
State v. Homan [732 N.E.2d 952 (Ohio 2000)] B. Neill, student author. 28 no1 *Ohio N.U. L. Rev.* 149-69 2001
Victoria (Australia)
Drink-driving in the year 2000. W. Walsh-Buckley. 74 no11 *Law Inst. J.* 52-5 D 2000
Drug-driving: the new offences. W. Walsh-Buckley, J. Marquis. 75 no2 *Law Inst. J.* 79-82 Mr 2001
The rise and fall and rise of drink-driving offences in Victoria. W. Walsh-Buckley, 25 no5 *Crim. L.J.* 276-84 O 2001
Drown, Chad
Dishonoring oral option to buy securities gives rise to securities claims; by D. G. Keyko, C. Drown, 4 no4 *Can. Int'l Law.* 230-2 D 2001
Druff, Jack
State court sovereign immunity: just when is the emperor armor-clad? 24 no2 *U. Ark. Little Rock L. Rev.* 255-75 Wint 2002
Drug abuse *See* Substance abuse
Drug courts
The difficult role of the defense lawyer in a post-adjudication drug treatment court: accommodating therapeutic jurisprudence and due process. M. Reisig. 38 no2 *Crim L. Bull.* 216-24 Mr/Ap 2002
The drug court model as a response to "broken windows" criminal justice for the homeless mentally ill. J. Hodulik, student author. 91 no 4 *J. Crim. L. & Criminology* 1073-100 Summ 2001
Alaska
Therapeutic justice in Alaska's courts. T. W. Carns, M. G. Hotchkin, E. M. Andrews. 19 no1 *Alaska L. Rev.* 1-55 Je 2002
New South Wales (Australia)
Design and implementation of Australia's first drug court. R. Lawrence, K. Freeman. 35 no1 *Austl. & N.Z. J. Criminology* 63-78 Ap 2002
Victoria (Australia)
An important initiative. R. Stary. 76 no4 *Law Inst. J.* 30 My 2002
Victoria's new drug court. R. Hulls. 76 no4 *Law Inst. J.* 29-30 My 2002
Drug labeling
Drug safety, testing, and availability for children. R. E. Kauffman. 18 no2 *Children's Legal Rts. J.* 27-34 Spr 1998
Is the FDA's nose growing?: The FDA does not "exaggerate its overall place in the universe" when regulating speech incident to "off-label" prescription drug labeling and advertising. N. Endejann, student author. 35 no3/4 *Akron L. Rev.* 491-529 2001/2002
Canada
Medical pornography or fair warning: should the United States adopt Canada's gruesome new tobacco labels? J. P. Strouss, III, student author. 27 no2 *J. Corp. L.* 315-31 Wint 2002
Regulation of natural health products in Canada. G. S. Jepson. 57 no1 *Food & Drug L.J.* 59-71 2002
United States
Medical pornography or fair warning: should the United States adopt Canada's gruesome new tobacco labels? J. P. Strouss, III, student author. 27 no2 *J. Corp. L.* 315-31 Wint 2002
Drug testing
See also
Blood tests
Driving while intoxicated
A decision without a solution: Ferguson v. City of Charleston. J. E. Rhodes, student author. 53 no3 *S.C. L. Rev.* 717-36 Spr 2002
Is mama a criminal?—An analysis of potential criminal liability of HIV-infected pregnant women in the context of mandated drug therapy. L. Ayers, student author. 50 no2 *Drake L. Rev.* 293-314 2002
New developments on the urinalysis front: a Green light in naked urinalysis prosecutions? M. R. Stahlman. 2002. *Army Law.* 14-19 Ap 2002

FIGURE 7.7

SUBJECT INDEX — **CONTRACTS**

CONTRACT research *see*
Industrial research

CONTRACT services *see*
Outsourcing

CONTRACTING for services *see*
Outsourcing

CONTRACTING out *see*
Contracts
Outsourcing

CONTRACTORS

Singapore Court of Appeal: two recent decisions. (construction arbitration in Hiap Hong 2d Co. v. Hong Huat Development Co. and Management Corp. Strata Title Plan 1933 v. Liang Huat Aluminium Ltd.) by Ian N. Duncan Wallace
17 Construction Law Journal 479-485 Nov-Dec, 2001

The contractor's perspective: the contractor's place in TMDL litigation.(Can TMDLs Ensure a Clean and Healthful Environment?)(total maximum daily loads) by Michael Kakuk
22 Public Land & Resources Law Review 31-38 Annual, 2001

see also
Government contractors
Outsourcing

CONTRACTORS, Independent *see*
Independent contractors

CONTRACTS *see also*
Agency (Law)
Bailments
Breach of contract
Buy-sell agreements
Compromise and settlement
Consideration (Law)
Contracts. Agricultural
Contracts. Unconscionable
Debtor and creditor
Deeds
Delivery of goods (Law)
Discharge of contracts
Disclosure (Conveyancing)
Export sales contracts
Extinguishment of debts
Impossibility of performance
Installment contracts
Insurance policies
Labor contracts
Leases
Liability (Law)
Liberty of contract
Licensing agreements
Lost profits damages
Maritime contracts
Negotiable instruments
Non-competition agreements
Offer and acceptance
Options (Finance)
Performance (Law)
Pledges (Law)
Priorities of claims and liens
Privity
Public contracts
Repurchase agreements
Rescission (Law)
Retention of title
Third parties (Law)
Undue influence
Unjust enrichment

-Cases

Evidence of Arkansas' hazy choice of law rules and the need for a modern solution.(Case Note) Heating & Air Specialists, Inc. v. Jones by Helen Graves Woodyard
54 Arkansas Law Review 915-947 Fall, 2001

-Innovations

Another New York innovation.(written letters of engagement by attorneys)
69 Defense Counsel Journal 136(2) April, 2002

-Interpretation and construction

Challenging the practices of the recording industry.(18th Annual Entertainment Law Issue) by A. Barry Cappello and Troy A. Thielemann
25 Los Angeles Lawyer 14(5) May, 2002

Indemnification clauses in commercial contracts.
18 Corporate Counsel's Quarterly 14-21 April, 2002

Access agreement.(groundwater sampling of neighboring properties) by Michael Hickok
18 Corporate Counsel's Quarterly 114-116 April, 2002

Associated Alloys Pty Ltd v ACN 001 452 106 Pty Ltd: A Commentary and Analysis. Associated Alloys Pty. v. ACN 001 452 106 Pty. by Tyrone M. Carlin
30 Australian Business Law Review 106(12) April, 2002

Nit-picking or significant contract choices?(part 1) by K.K. DuVivier
31 Colorado Lawyer 43(2) March, 2002

"Best efforts".(the use of the phrase "best efforts" in commercial contracts) by Lars Gorton
Journal of Business Law 143-162 March, 2002

Seller beware: no safe harbor in selling as is.(commercial real estate contracts)(Arizona) by Andrew D. Schorr
38 Arizona Attorney 34(2) Feb, 2002

Negotiating international power contracts - the major issues. by Nick Henchie
19 The International Construction Law Review 97-114 Jan, 2002

Contractual assent and enforceability in cyberspace. by Ryan J. Casamiquela
17 Berkeley Technology Law Journal 475(21) Wntr, 2002

Construction in Puerto Rico: navigating the legal quagmire. by Stuart A. Weinstein-Bacal and Dennis B. Parces-Enriquez
71 Revista Juridica de la Universidad de Puerto Rico 29-109 Wntr, 2002

A comment on language and norms in complex business contracting.(Symposium: Theory Informs Business Practice) by Claire A. Hill
77 Chicago-Kent Law Review 29-57 Winter, 2001

The written contract as safe harbor for dishonest conduct.(Symposium: Theory Informs Business Practice) by Lawrence M. Solan
77 Chicago-Kent Law Review 87-120 Winter, 2001

Why contracts are written in "legalese".(Symposium: Theory Informs Business Practice) by Claire A. Hill
77 Chicago-Kent Law Review 59-85 Winter, 2001

Drafting and risk allocation in the new Hong Kong standard form of building contract. by Denis Levett
18 The International Construction Law Review 716-723 Oct, 2001

Les clauses abusives dans les contrats d'adhesion.(Actes du Forum international des juristes francophones) by Marc Lemieux
42 Cahiers de Droit 841-872 Sept, 2001

A comment on Fuller and Perdue, the Reliance Interest in Contract Damages. by Daniel Friedman
Issues in Legal Scholarship NA August 23, 2001

The principle contra proferentem in standard form contracts: in particular, the Spanish case. by Pablo Salvador Coderch and Juan A. Ruiz Garcia
1 Global Jurist Topics NA July 17, 2001

An introduction to interpretation of express contractual indemnity provisions in construction contract under California and Nevada law. by Richard D. Brown and Mara E. Fortin
32 McGeorge Law Review 1019-1029 Summer, 2001

A primer on drafting contractual provisions to cure environmental impairments.(California) by Jennifer T. Taggart
19 California Real Property Journal 21(28) Summer-Fall, 2001

The scope and effect of an exclusive jurisdiction clause: Donohue v. Armco Inc.(United Kingdom) Donohue v. Armco, Inc. by Adrian Briggs
71 British Yearbook of International Law 459-465 Annual, 2000

-Laws, regulations, etc.

Contractual limitations of liability (a/k/a "LOLs," or why the other party is laughing out loud).(software) by Marc T. Shivers and Andre J. Brunel
19 The Computer & Internet Lawyer 6(11) May, 2002

Offset contracts in Poland. by Piotr Kochanski
9 Corporate Counsel A13(2) April, 2002

The family agreement: legal good sense or social bad taste for the aged?(Australia) by Brian Herd
27 Alternative Law Journal 72(6) April, 2002

The legal recognition of same-sex couples - the French perspective. by Claudina Richards
51 International and Comparative Law Quarterly 305-324 April, 2002

Relationship debt and the aged: welfare v. commerce in the law of guarantees.(Law and Older People)(Australia) by Juliet Lucy Cummins
27 Alternative Law Journal 63(67) April, 2002

Employment agreements and tender offers: reforming the problematic treatment of severance plans under Rule 14d-10. by Ben Walther
102 Columbia Law Review 774-811 April, 2002

Contract law - mergers and acquisitions - Delaware Chancery Court addresses default interpretation of broadly written material adverse effect clauses. IBP, Inc. Shareholders Litigation v. Tyson Foods, Inc.
115 Harvard Law Review 1737-1744 April, 2002

The contractual nexus: is reliance essential?(United Kingdom) by Paul Mitchell and John Phillips
22 Oxford Journal of Legal Studies 115-134 Spring, 2002

The euro, and U.S. creditors. by Nancy L. Williams and Marguerita Young-Jones
119 Banking Law Journal 211-213 March, 2002

Application of the UCC to construction projects: suppliers beware.(Uniform Commercial Code)(Virginia) by Fred R. Kozak
28 VBA News Journal 14(3) March, 2002

Recent developments on commencement of laytime. by Paul Todd
Journal of Business Law 217-234 March, 2002

A multimodal mix-up.(contracts for delivery of goods that call for combined methods of carriage) Quantaum v. Plane Trucking by Malcolm Clarke
Journal of Business Law 210-217 March, 2002

Privity of contract in the Supreme Court of Canada: fare thee well or welcome back? by M.H. Ogilvie
Journal of Business Law 163-176 March, 2002

71

FIGURE 7.8

Last Will and Testament

-of-

Name

I, (name), residing at (address), being of sound mind and disposing memory, and well knowing the true extent of my worldly possessions, and the natural objects of my bounty, do hereby make, publish and declare this instrument to be my Last Will and Testament, hereby revoking any and all other Wills and Codicils at any time heretofore made by me.

FIRST:

I direct my Executor to pay my just debts, funeral expenses, and the expenses of my last illness as soon after my demise as practicable.

SECOND:

I hereby give, devise and bequeath the following bequests:

A, To my beloved son (name), my jewelry consisting of my rings, watches, gold bracelets, and religious artifacts, for his use, now and forevermore.

THIRD:

I give, devise, and bequeath all the rest, residue, and remainder of my estate, real, personal, and mixed, of whatsoever kind of nature, and wheresoever situate, of which I may die seized or possessed, or to which I may be in any way entitled to have an interest, including all property over which I have the power to appoint (hereafter referred to as my residuary estate), to my beloved husband, (name), for his own use absolutely and forever.

FOURTH:

In the event my beloved husband (name) predeceases me, I give, devise, and bequeath to my beloved son (name), per stirpes, all the rest, residue, and remainder of my estate, real, personal, and mixed, of whatsoever kind or nature, and wheresoever situate, of which I may die seized or possessed, or to which I may be in any way entitled to have an interest, including all property over which I have the power to appoint (hereafter referred to as my residuary estate) for his own use absolutely and forever.

FIFTH:

A. I hereby nominate, constitute, and appoint as Executor under this my Last Will and Testament, my beloved husband, (name). In the event that he shall predecease me, fail to qualify, or become unable to serve for any reason, then I nominate, constitute, and appoint as alternate Executor my son, (name).

B. I direct that my Executor (including my Alternate) be permitted to qualify and serve without furnishing a bond or other security for the faithful performance of his duties, in this or any jurisdiction, any laws of any state to the contrary notwithstanding.

SIXTH:

A. In the event that any Beneficiary or Beneficiaries under this Will and I should die in a common accident or disaster, or under such circumstances that it cannot be established by proof who died first, then all provisions of this Will shall take effect in like manner as if such beneficiary or beneficiaries had predeceased me as the case may be.

continued

FIGURE 7.8 *continued*

B. In the event that my beloved husband, (name), and I die in a common accident or disaster or under such circumstances that there is not sufficient evidence to determine who predeceased the other, I herby declare it to be my will and intent that it shall be presumed that my husband shall have predeceased me and that this Last Will and Testament and any and all of its provisions, shall be construed on the assumption and basis that he shall have predeceased me as the case may be.

SEVENTH:

As used in this Will, wherever necessary or appropriate, the masculine gender shall be deemed to include the feminine and neuter genders and vice versa, and the singular shall be deemed to include the plural and vice versa.

IN WITNESS WHEREOF, I have hereunto set my hand and affixed my seal this _______ day of (specify).

____

Name

The foregoing instrument, consisting of three (3) pages including this one, each identified by the initials of the Testatrix, (name), was signed, sealed, published, and declared by the above-named Testatrix as and for her Last Will and Testament, in the presence of us, who in her presence, at her request, and in the presence of each other, have hereunto subscribed our names as witnesses this ______ day of (specify), this attestation clause having first been read aloud.

__________________________ residing at __________________________

__________________________ residing at __________________________

__________________________ residing at __________________________

STATE OF __________________________)

COUNTY OF __________________________):

being severally sworn, depose and say that they witnessed the execution of the attached Will of (name), the within named Testatrix on the ______ day of month, year; that the said Testatrix in their presence subscribed said Will at the end thereof and at the time of making such subscription declared the instrument so subscribed by her to be her Last Will and Testament; that they at the request of the Testatrix and in her sight and presence and in the sight and presence of each other witnessed the execution of said Will and subscribed their names as such, and each, after observing the Testatrix herein, observed her and in their opinion believe her to be of sound mind, memory and understanding, not under any restraint or in respect incompetent to make a Will; that the attached Will was so executed at (address) and that they are making this affidavit at the request of the Testatrix.

Severally subscribed and sworn to me
this ______ day of (specify).

____

Notary Public

_______________, the night of the shooting that is the basis of this lawsuit?

A. Yes, sir. I was.

Q. Did you make a call to _______________ *[address]* in this city on that particular night?

A. Yes.

Q. How did you get that call?

A. Well, I got a radio dispatch saying that there had been a shooting at such and such an address.

Q. When did you arrive at the scene?

A. About two or three minutes after the emergency ambulance arrived.

Q. Did you see the victim at all?

A. Only briefly.

Q. Did you say anything to him?

A. No, I didn't. He was rushed into the ambulance and taken to the hospital before I had a chance to talk to him.

Q. Are you required to interview all participants regarding shootings?

A. We're supposed to investigate thoroughly.

Q. Did you interview Mr. _______________, the defendant in this cause?

A. I did.

Q. What did he tell you happened?

A. Well, he was a little shook up, but basically he indicated to me that the plaintiff had shot himself.

Q. Do you recall what he said and did you fill out a report to that effect.

A. Yes. I talked to him, and he said that a pistol was being handled and went off, and the bullet hit Mr. _______________, the plaintiff.

Q. Do you recall the words the defendant used to describe the shooting?

A. Well, I don't recall the exact words but the impression he left clearly with me was that _______________ *[victim]* had accidentally shot himself and that the defendant did not know very much about it.

continued

Q. Did you fill out a report to that effect?
A. Yes, sir. I did.
Q. Did you get the defendant to sign a statement?
A. I had it typed up and brought it out to him to sign, but he wouldn't sign it.

§ 136. Cross-Examination of Police Officer

The following is an illustrative cross-examination of the investigating police officer by defense counsel:

Q. Officer, after you prepared a statement based on the interview you had with him, you asked him to sign it, is that correct?
A. Yes.
Q. Mr. .... *[defendant]* refused to sign the statement that you prepared, is that correct?
A. Yes, he did not want to sign it.
Q. Officer, basically what you are saying is that the defendant refused to sign what was an erroneous report, isn't that correct?
A. Yes, I guess you could say it that way.
Q. Now the truth of the matter is that the defendant was very frightened that night too, wasn't he?
A. Yes.
Q. Now you had given him his constitutional warnings saying he had a right to get a lawyer and right to a court appointed lawyer and all that sort of thing too, didn't you?
A. Yes.
Q. And that frightened him even worse, didn't it?
A. I don't know whether it did or not, you would have to ask him.
Q. Did Mr. .... , *[defendant]* say to you that a pistol was being handled or words to that effect?
A. I don't remember exactly, but that might have been the way it was.
Q. Did the defendant say that the gun had gone off accidentally?
A. Yes.

Form No. 23:3

Motion for Stay in Connection with Petition for Certiorari to State Court[1]

SUPREME COURT RULES, RULE 23

No. . . . .

IN THE SUPREME COURT OF THE UNITED STATES

October Term, ...

. . . ., (*Name of Party*)
. . . . (*Petitioner, Appellant, or Plaintiff*)
v.
. . . ., (*Name of Party*)
. . . . (*Respondent, Appellee, or Defendant*)

. . . . from the United States Court of Appeals for the . . . . Circuit

---

(*Motion for Stay*)

---

[1] *See* Comment to Rule 23, *supra. See also* Rule 38, *infra*, (fees). For format requirements, see Rules 22, 33, and 34.

Form adapted from papers used in connection with *Ocala Star–Banner Co. v. Damron*, 401 U.S. 295, 91 S.Ct. 628, 28 L.Ed.2d 57 (1971), furnished courtesy of Loftin and Wahl of Jacksonville, Florida. The Court held that a charge of criminal conduct against an official or a candidate, no matter how remote in time or place, is always relevant to his fitness for office for purposes of applying the *New York Times* rule of knowing falsehood or reckless disregard of the truth.

continued

FIGURE 7.10
continued

Name of Counsel of Record
Post Office Address
Telephone Number

Now come the Petitioners and respectfully represent unto the Court under 28 U.S.C. 2101(f) and Supreme Court Rules 23 and 38 as follows:

1. Petitioners have filed or a filing with the Clerk of this Court their Petition for Certiorari to the . . . . District Court of Appeal, ... District (decision reported at . . . . So. 2d . ., and clearly contrary to the *New York Times* rule), together with certified record.

2. The Petitioners and Respondent filed Stipulation in the Supreme Court of . . . . as follows:

> It is further stipulated that the present $25,000 supersedeas bond is sufficient at least until such time as the Supreme Court of the United States has either granted or denied certiorari, provided petition for certiorari be timely filed.

3. The Supreme Court of . . . . (which denied review of the District Court of Appeal decision) on . . . ., entered its Order as follows:

> Appellants' motion for stay is hereby granted and proceedings in this Court, the District Court of Appeal, First District, and in the Circuit Court of the Fifth Judicial Circuit in and for . . . . County, ..., are hereby stayed to and including . . . .
> ,. ., to enable appellants to seek review in the Supreme Court of the United States and obtain any further stay from that court.

WHEREFORE, Petitioners pray that the Supreme Court of the United States will stay all proceedings from . . . .,. ., until this Court has finally acted upon the Petition for Certiorari and proceedings have been completed in this Court.

areas of law to which they pertain. Their utility will, of course, depend on the subject (and objective) of your research, but through a formbook or model form you may easily discover the answer to such questions as:

- What clauses or provisions must be included in a document of this type?
- What elements are necessary to make this document valid?
- Does your jurisdiction mandate particular language for this provision?
- How do practitioners usually handle this problem? Why did they do it that way?
- Does this form reveal issues or facets of the research question that you have not yet considered?

Some formbooks even contain citations to statutes or cases that bear directly on the clause or language of interest—yet another source for further research!

Other forms packages are available from local bar associations, clerks of court, and private publishers. Forms are often included in the rules of court for a jurisdiction, and many are now available in CD or disk format.

VIII. SUMMARY

Law books provide the legal researcher with a vast array of source materials that compile, cite, and explicate the statutes, rules, and cases of our judicial system. Some of the more prominent law books to keep in mind include: (1) *law textbooks,* which cover broad areas of the law and aid the researcher in learning the fundamental principles and aspects of the law; (2) *hornbooks,* highly sophisticated texts dealing with specific legal topics and interpretations of the law by learned members of the legal profession; (3) *looseleaf services,* which provide time-sensitive materials and quick updates of legal areas; (4) *law reviews,* which, like hornbooks, provide in-depth analyses of a specific legal issue; (5) *periodicals,* which are journals and newspapers produced by academic, professional, private, and federal sources; and (6) *formbooks,* which allow the practitioner to tailor legal documents to individual needs by using generic legal forms. Above all, do not be intimidated by these huge collections of reference materials. Master the use of these sources and integrate them into the solution of the problem under consideration.

IX. LEGAL RESEARCH ASSIGNMENTS

The following assignments are provided to complement the previous discussion. A variety of sample materials are included for your use. Keep in mind that these are only sample pages from complete texts, and are being used here to highlight the sources discussed.

A. Exercise 7.1: Law Reviews

1. Which of the articles by the following authors would be most appropriate when examining the moral aspects of abortion?
   a. S. Buchanan
   b. J. A. Van Detta

c. J. B. Raskin & C. L. LeBlanc
d. P. A. Topper

2. For articles regarding accessories to crime, which heading is suggested?
   a. Accomplices
   b. Abettors
3. Books are never given as references in the index to legal periodicals.
   a. True
   b. False
4. For articles regarding damages stemming from vehicular homicide, the index suggests
   a. Accident compensation
   b. Damages
   c. Traffic accidents
   d. All of the above
5. The case *Apprendi v. New Jersey* is the subject in the *Criminal Law Bulletin* only.
   a. True
   b. False
6. An article citing *Kolstad v. American Dental Association* appears in
   a. 2001 BYU Law Review
   b. 33 Columbia Human Rights Law Review
   c. 34 Suffolk University Law Review
   d. None of the above
7. Which of the following articles would yield the most recent information regarding *A&M Records v. Napster, Inc.*?
   a. *39 American Business Law Journal*
   b. 24 European Intellectual Property Review
   c. 18 Georgia State University Law Review
   d. 59 University of Chicago Law Review
8. Sections of the Americans with Disabilities Act can be found where in the United States Code?
   a. 104 U.S.C. § 327
   b. 42 U.S.C. § 12101
   c. 47 U.S.C. § 12101
   d. 42 U.S.C. § 611
9. For an article regarding failure to pay child support under 18 U.S.C. § 228, see
   a. 51 Catholic University Law Review
   b. 55 Vanderbilt Law Review
   c. 78 University of Detroit Mercy Law Review
   d. *29 Fordham Urban Law Journal*
10. An article regarding campus crime statistics reporting under 20 U.S.C. § 1092(f) appears in
    a. *Fordham Urban Law Journal*
    b. *77 Indiana Law Journal*
    c. Both a and b
    d. Neither a nor b

INDEX TO LEGAL PERIODICALS & BOOKS

APRIL 2002

401(k) plan
Prop. regs. issued on age 50 "catch-up" deferrals for Sec. 401(k), 403(b) and other plans. S. Tievsky. 33 no1 *Tax Adviser* 10-12 Ja 2002

A

ABA *See* American Bar Association
ABA model code of judicial conduct. 1998 ed American Bar Association 1998 vii, 44p
ISBN 1-570-73524-7 LC 97-223707
Abatement and revival *See* Remedies
Abduction *See* Kidnapping
Abdy, J. T. (John Thomas)
See/See also the following book(s):
Kent's commentary on international law; edited by J.T. Abdy. 2d ed, rev and brought down to the present time W.S. Hein & Co 2001 xvi, 525p
ISBN 1-575-88671-5 ((alk. paper)) LC 2001-16729
Abella, Rosalie S.
Judging in the 21st century. 25 no2 *Advoc. Q.* 131-40 Ja 2002
Abettors *See* Accomplices
Abolins, J. D.
The challenges of responding to Internet vandalism. no213 *N.J. Law.* 33-6 F 2002
Aborigines, Australian *See* Australian aborigines
Abortion
See also
Partial-birth abortion
The abortion issue: an agonizing clash of values. S. Buchanan. 38 no5 *Hous. L. Rev.* 1481-8 Spr 2002
Constitutionalizing Roe [Roe v. Wade, 93 S. Ct. 705 (1973)], Casey [Planned Parenthood of Southeastern Pennsylvania v. Casey, 112 S. Ct. 2791 (1992)] and Carhart [Stenberg v. Carhart, 120 S. Ct. 2597 (2000)]: a legislative due-process anti-discrimination principle that gives constitutional content to the "undue burden" standard of review applied to abortion control legislation. J. A. Van Detta. 10 no2 *S. Cal. Rev. L. & Women's Stud.* 211-92 Spr 2001
Defining a person under the Fourteenth Amendment: a constitutionally and scientifically based analysis. K. J. Hollowell. 14 no1 *Regent Univ. L. Rev.* 67-95 2001/2002
Storming the gates of a massive cultural investment: reconsidering Roe [Roe v. Wade, 93 S. Ct. 705 (1973)] in light of its flawed foundation and undesirable consequences. H. Baker. 14 no1 *Regent Univ. L. Rev.* 35-65 2001/2002
Civil disobedience
Disfavored speech about favored rights: Hill v. Colorado [120 S. Ct. 2480 (2000)], the vanishing public forum and the need for an objective speech discrimination test. J. B. Raskin, C. L. LeBlanc. 51 no2 *Am. U. L. Rev.* 179-228 D 2001
Hill v. Colorado [120 S. Ct. 2480 (2000)]: the Supreme Court's deviation from traditional First Amendment jurisprudence to silence the message of abortion protestors. M. Villanueva, student author. 51 no1 *Cath. U. L. Rev.* 371-404 Fall 2001
The threatening Internet: Planned Parenthood v. ACLA [244 F.3d 1007 (9th Cir. 2001)] and a context-based appraoch to Internet threats. P. A. Topper, student author. 33 no1 *Colum. Hum. Rts. L. Rev.* 189-240 Fall 2001
Parental notification
Inconceivable? H. Silverstein. 20 no1 *Law & Ineq.* 141-55 Wint 2002
Preserving the right to choose: a minor's right to confidential reproductive health care. J. Bertuglia, student author. 23 no1 *Women's Rts. L. Rep.* 63-77 Summ/Fall 2001
Abramovsky, Abraham
The post-Sheinbein Israeli extradition law: has it solved the extradition problems between Israel and the United States or has it merely shifted the battleground? by A. Abramovsky, J. I. Edelstein. 35 no1 *Vand. J. Transnat'l L.* 1-72 Ja 2002
Abrams, Edward S.
In memoriam: John M. Brumbaugh. 61 no1 *Md. L. Rev.* 8-10 2002
Abrams, Kathryn
The legal subject in exile. 51 no1 *Duke L.J.* 27-74 O 2001
Abrams, Stanley D.
See/See also the following book(s):
Land use practice and forms; handling the land use case; John J. Delaney, Stanley D. Abrams, Frank Schnidman. 2nd ed Clark Boardman Callaghan 1998 2 v (loose-leaf)p
ISBN 0-8366-1088-1 ((alk. paper)) LC 96-38796
Absolute liability *See* Strict liability
Abstracts of title *See* Title to land
Abuse of process
Ontario
Extending "abuse of process": Canam Enterprises Inc. v. Coles [[2000] 194 D.L.R.4th 648] M. Teplitsky. 25 no2 *Advoc. Q.* 250-6 Ja 2002
Abused wives *See* Battered women
Abusive litigation *See* Frivolous litigation
Access to justice
Anastasoff v. United States [223 F.3d 898 (8th Cir. 2000)]: uncertainty in the Eighth Circuit—is there a constitutional right to cite unpublished opinions? D. R. Quitschau, student author. 54 no4 *Ark. L. Rev.* 847-78 2002
The malleability of constitutional doctrine and its ironic impact on prisoners' rights. C. E. Smith. 11 no1 *B.U. Pub. Int. L.J.* 73-96 Fall 2001
Canada
Expensive justice is justice denied. T. Matlow. 25 no2 *Advoc. Q.* 129-30 Ja 2002
Colorado
The role of lawyers and judges in providing access: the Access to Justice Conference. J. A. V. Salazar. 31 no2 *Colo. Law.* 35-6 F 2002
Georgia
Lawyers foundation awards challenge grants. S. I. Bartleson. 7 no4 *Ga. B.J.* 48-9 F 2002
Michigan
Assisting people with cognitive or psychological disabilities. K. Harris. 81 no2 *Mich. B.J.* 54-5 F 2002
Access to Justice Act 1999; the Funding Code. Stationery Office 2000 v, 59p
ISBN 0-11-702489-9 LC 00-361437
Accessories *See* Accomplices
Accident compensation
U.S. gears up September 11 Victim Compensation Fund. 69 no1 *Def. Couns. J.* 15-16 Ja 2002
Accident compensation schemes *See* Accident compensation
Accidents
See also
Accident compensation
Damages
Negligence
Personal injuries
Traffic accidents
Criminalization of negligent acts by employees of U.S. and foreign corporations. R. M. Dunn, D. Hazouri, J. Rannik. 69 no1 *Def. Couns. J.* 17-26 Ja 2002
Wisconsin
Reflections on the accident at Miller Park and the prosecution of work-related fatalities in Wisconsin. E. A. Fallone. 12 no1 *Marq. Sports L. Rev.* 105-26 Fall 2001
Accomplices
Casting light on the gray area: an analysis of the use of neutral pronouns in non-testifying codefendant redacted confessions under Bruton [Bruton v. United States, 88 S. Ct. 1620 (1968)], Richardson [Richardson v. Marsh, 107 S. Ct. 1702 (1987)], and Gray [Gray v. Maryland, 118 S. Ct. 1151 (1998)] B. M. Richardson, student author. 55 no4 *U. Miami L. Rev.* 826-66 Jl 2001
The exception that swallows the rule: the disparate treatment of Federal Rule of Evidence 804(b)(3) as interpreted in United States v. Williamson [114 S. Ct. 2431 (1994)] R. T. Sahuc, student author. 55 no4 *U. Miami L. Rev.* 867-89 Jl 2001
The future implications of Lilly v. Virginia [119 S. Ct. 1887 (1999)] J. Christianson, student author. 55 no4 *U. Miami L. Rev.* 891-928 Jl 2001

TABLE OF CASES

2 Broadway LLC v. Credit Suisse First Boston Mtg. Capital, LLC, 2001 WL 410074 (S.D.N.Y.)
119 no2 *Banking L.J.* 206-9 F 2002
203 N. LaSalle St. P'ship; Bank of Am. Nat'l Trust & Sav. Ass'n v., 119 S. Ct. 1411 (1999)
31 no3 *Colo. Law.* 45-8 Mr 2002

A

A. v. United Kingdom, [1999] 27 E.H.R.R. 611
2002 *Crim. L. Rev.* 98-113 F 2002
A.I. Trade Fin., Inc. v. Bulgarian Foreign Trade Bank, Case No. T 1881-99 (S. Ct. of Sweden. Oct. 27, 2000)
19 no1 *J. Int'l Arb.* 1-31 F 2002
A.Z. v. B.Z., 725 N.E.2d 1051 (Mass. 2000)
81 no5 *B.U. L. Rev.* 1093-118 D 2001
A&G Imports Ltd.; Davidoff SA v., Cases C-414/99, C-415/99, C-416-99 (E.C.J., Apr. 5, 2001)
24 no2 *Eur. Intell. Prop. Rev.* 93-6 F 2002
A&M Records, Inc. v. Napster, Inc., 239 F.3d 1004 (9th Cir. 2001)
39 no1 *Am. Bus. L.J.* 57-98 Fall 2001
24 no2 *Eur. Intell. Prop. Rev.* 65-73 F 2002
18 no2 *Ga. St. U. L. Rev.* 507-62 Wint 2001
69 no1 *U. Chi. L. Rev.* 263-324 Wint 2002
Adams; Circuit City Stores, Inc. v., 121 S. Ct. 1302 (2001)
24 no1 *Campbell L. Rev.* 93-113 Fall 2001
27 no4 *Empl. Rel. L.J.* 69-99 Spr 2002
Agard; Portuondo v., 120 S. Ct. 1119 (2000)
78 no1 *Denv. U. L. Rev.* 173-91 2000
Ajax; Ansul v., (S. Ct., Neth., Jan. 26, 2001)
no144 *Trademark World* 8 F 2002
Allwright; Smith v., 64 S. Ct. 757 (1944)
29 no1 *Fla. St. U. L. Rev.* 55-107 Fall 2001
ALS Scan, Inc. v. RemarQ Cmtys., Inc., 239 F.3d 619 (4th Cir. 2001)
11 no2 *DePaul LCA J. Art & Ent. L.* 479-93 Fall 2001
Am. Coalition of Life Activists (Planned Parenthood IV); Planned Parenthood v., 244 F.3d 1007 (9th Cir. 2001)
33 no1 *Colum. Hum. Rts. L. Rev.* 189-240 Fall 2001
Am. Dental Ass'n; Kolstad v., 119 S. Ct. 2118 (1999)
34 no1 *Suffolk U. L. Rev.* 219-26 2000
Am. Home Prods. Corp.; Kohl v., 78 F. Supp. 2d 885 (W.D. Ark. 1999)
2001 no3 *B.Y.U. L. Rev.* 1349-81 2001
Am. Maize-Prods. Co.; Grain Processing Corp. v., 185 F.3d 1341 (Fed. Cir. 1999)
38 no5 *Hous. L. Rev.* 1489-519 Spr 2002
Am. Trucking Ass'ns, Inc.; Whitman v., 121 S. Ct. 903 (2001)
87 no2 *Cornell L. Rev.* 452-85 Ja 2002
18 no2 *Ga. St. U. L. Rev.* 627-70 Wint 2001
Amchem Prods., Inc. v. Windsor, 117 S. Ct. 2231 (1997)
13 no1 *Prac. Litig.* 33-8 Ja 2002
Analog Devices, Inc.; Sextant Avionique, S.A. v., 172 F.3d 817 (Fed. Cir. 1999)
32 no1 *Seton Hall L. Rev.* 266-98 2001
Anastasoff v. United States, 223 F.3d 898 (8th Cir. 2000)
54 no4 *Ark. L. Rev.* 847-78 2002
50 no1 *Drake L. Rev.* 181-206 2001
Ansul v. Ajax, (S. Ct., Neth., Jan. 26, 2001)
no144 *Trademark World* 8 F 2002
Apprendi v. New Jersey, 120 S. Ct. 2348 (2000)
37 no6 *Crim. L. Bull.* 627-59 N/D 2001
37 no6 *Crim. L. Bull.* 602-26 N/D 2001
37 no6 *Crim. L. Bull.* 575-601 N/D 2001
37 no6 *Crim. L. Bull.* 553-74 N/D 2001
37 no6 *Crim. L. Bull.* 552-659 N/D 2001
90 no2 *Geo. L.J.* 387-459 Ja 2002
Arcadia Mach. & Tool; James v., No. ESX-L-6059-99 (N.J. 2001)
38 no2 *Trial* 88-91 F 2002
Armendariz v. Penman, 75 F.3d 1311 (9th Cir. 1996)
37 no4 *Willamette L. Rev.* 661-89 Aut 2001
AT&T Corp. v. City of Portland, 216 F.3d 871 (9th Cir. 2000)
37 no4 *Willamette L. Rev.* 717-56 Aut 2001
Atl. Richfield Co.; Union Oil Co. v., 208 F.3d 989 (Fed. Cir. 2000)
38 no5 *Hous. L. Rev.* 1557-84 Spr 2002
Attorney Gen. of Can.; Hillier v., [2001] F.C.A. 197
49 no5 *Can. Tax J.* 1248-52 2001
Attorney-Gen.'s Reference No. 3 of 2000, In re, [2001] Crim L.R. 645
6 no1 *Int'l J. Evidence & Proof* 38-61 2002
Atwater v. City of Lago Vista, 121 S. Ct. 1536 (2001)
38 no1 *Crim. L. Bull.* 160-75 Ja/F 2002
38 no1 *Willamette L. Rev.* 137-85 Wint 2002
2 no1 *Wyoming L. Rev.* 127-67 2002
Aust'l Bank Ltd.; Idoport Pty. Ltd. v., [2001] N.S.W.S.C. 838
11 no3 *J. Jud. Admin.* 116-22 F 2002
Australian Indus. Relations Comm'n; Constr., Forestry, Mining & Energy Union v., [2001] 75 A.L.J.R. 670
24 no1 *U.N.S.W. L.J.* 228-36 2001
Austria; Comm'n v., [2000] E.C.R. I-7367
2002 *J. Bus. L.* 195-209 Mr 2002
Azzopardi; R. v., [2001] H.C.A. 25
6 no1 *Int'l J. Evidence & Proof* 62-8 2002

B

B.C. Auto. Ass'n v. Office & Prof'l Employees Int'l Union, [2001] 10 C.P.R.4th 423
13 no3 *C. de Prop. Intell.* 793-802 My 2001
46 *Intell. Prop. F.* 57-9 S 2001
B.C. Ferry Corp. v. The Queen, [2001] G.T.C. 3541
49 no5 *Can. Tax J.* 1233-41 2001
B.J.F.; Florida Star v., 109 S. Ct. 2603 (1989)
50 no1 *Drake L. Rev.* 93-158 2001
B.Z.; A.Z. v., 725 N.E.2d 1051 (Mass. 2000)
81 no5 *B.U. L. Rev.* 1093-118 D 2001
Baker v. General Motors Corp., 118 S. Ct. 657 (1998)
58 no1 *Wash. & Lee L. Rev.* 47-108 Wint 2001
Baltimore Orioles, Inc. v. Major League Baseball Players Ass'n, 805 F.2d 663 (7th Cir. 1986)
25 no2 *Seton Hall Legis. J.* 469-98 2001
Bank of Am. Nat'l Trust & Sav. Ass'n v. 203 N. LaSalle St. P'ship, 119 S. Ct. 1411 (1999)
31 no3 *Colo. Law.* 45-8 Mr 2002
Bank of Eng.; Three Rivers Dist. Council v., [2000] 2 W.L.R. 1220
17 no2 *J. Int'l Banking L.* 41-4 F 2002
Bank of Jam.; Dextra Bank & Trust Co. Ltd. v., [2001] U.K.P.C. 50
2001 *N.Z. L.J.* 468 D 2001
Barerra; Phil. Indem. Ins. Co. v., 21 P.3d 395 (Ariz. 2001)
43 no4 *Ariz. L. Rev.* 1001-6 Wint 2001
Bassett v. Mashantucket Pequot Tribe, 204 F.3d 343 (2d Cir. 2000)
11 no2 *DePaul LCA J. Art & Ent. L.* 361-95 Fall 2001
Bates v. State Bar, 97 S. Ct. 2691 (1977)
9 no1 *UCLA Ent. L. Rev.* 89-112 Fall 2001
Batson v. Kentucky, 106 S. Ct. 1712 (1986)
53 no1 *Ala. L. Rev.* 273-94 Fall 2001
Bd. of Trs. of Univ. of Ala. v. Garrett, 121 S. Ct. 955 (2001)
11 no1 *B.U. Pub. Int. L.J.* 1-33 Fall 2001
Bell Atlantic Md., Inc. v. Prince George's County, 212 F.3d 863 (4th Cir. 2000)
51 no1 *Cath. U. L. Rev.* 191-214 Fall 2001
Beretta, U.S.A. Corp.; Camden County Bd. of Chosen Freeholders v. 273 F.3d 536 (3d Cir. 2001)
38 no2 *Trial* 88-91 F 2002
Berg v. Hudesman, 801 P.2d 222 (Wash. 1990)
56 no2 *Wash. St. B. News* 32-9 F 2002
Bestfoods; United States v., 118 S. Ct. 1876 (1998)
27 no1 *J. Corp. L.* 29-62 Fall 2001
Boggs v. Boggs, 117 S. Ct. 1754 (1997)
35 no3 *Fam. L.Q.* 425-50 Fall 2001
Boggs; Boggs v., 117 S. Ct. 1754 (1997)
35 no3 *Fam. L.Q.* 425-50 Fall 2001

TABLE OF STATUTES

UNITED STATES

Federal

Abandoned Shipwreck Act of 1987. Pub. L. 100-298, Apr. 28, 1988, 102 Stat. 432; 43 U.S.C. §§ 2101, 2101 note, 2102 to 2106
10 no2 *Int'l J. Cultural Prop.* 276-314 2001

American Competitiveness in the Twenty-first Century Act of 2000. Pub. L. 106-313, Title I, Oct. 17, 2000, 114 Stat. 1251; codified in scattered sections of 8, 29, and 42 U.S.C.
58 no11 *Bench & B. Minn.* 21-3 D 2001

Americans with Disabilities Act of 1990. Pub. L. 101-336, July 26, 1990, 104 Stat. 327; 42 U.S.C. § 12101 et seq.; 47 U.S.C. §§ 152, 221, 225, 611
43 no4 *Ariz. L. Rev.* 965-1000 Wint 2001

Antiterrorism and Effective Death Penalty Act of 1996. Pub. L. 104-132, Apr. 24, 1996, 110 Stat. 1214; codified in scattered sections of 8 and 28 U.S.C.
02 no1 *Immigr. Brief.* 1-20 Ja 2002

Arbitration. General Provisions. Validity, irrevocability and enforcement of agreements to arbitrate. 9 U.S.C. § 2
51 no1 *Duke L.J.* 521-60 O 2001

Bankruptcy. Case Administration. Administrative Powers. Executory contracts and unexpired leases. 11 U.S.C. § 365
11 no1 *J. Bankr. L. & Prac.* 83-95 N/D 2001

Bribery, Graft, and Conflicts of Interest. Bribery of public officials and witnesses. 18 U.S.C. § 201(c)
49 no1 *Fed. Law.* 21-3 Ja 2002

Brownfields Revitalization and Environmental Restoration Act of 2001.
88 *A.B.A. J.* 24 Mr 2002

Child Online Protection Act of 1998. 47 U.S.C. § 231
51 no1 *Cath. U. L. Rev.* 245-99 Fall 2001

Coastal Zone Management Improvement Act of 1980. Pub. L. 96-464, Oct. 17, 1980, 94 Stat. 2060; 16 U.S.C. §§ 1451 to 1464
48 *Naval L. Rev.* 84-131 2001

Commerce and Trade. Electronic Signatures in Global and National Commerce. Pub. L. 106-229, June 30, 2000, 114 Stat. 464; 15 U.S.C. §§ 7001 to 7006, 7021, 7031; 47 U.S.C. § 231 note
19 no2 *J. Marshall J. Computer & Info. L.* 401-34 Wint 2001
35 no4 *U. Rich. L. Rev.* 943-1006 Ja 2002

Commerce and Trade. Trademarks. False designation of origin, false descriptions, and dilution forbidden. Cyberpiracy prevention. Pub. L. 106-113, Nov. 29, 1999, 113 Stat. 1501; 15 U.S.C. § 1125(d)
5 no8 *J. Internet L.* 1-20 F 2002
42 no1 *Santa Clara L. Rev.* 63-104 2001
150 no2 *U. Pa. L. Rev.* 719-60 D 2001

Commodity Futures Modernization Act of 2000. Pub. L. 106-554, Dec. 21, 2000, 114 Stat. 2763; 7 U.S.C. §§ 1 to 25
21 no3 *Nw. J. Int'l L. & Bus.* 573-87 Spr 2001

Copyrights—Term extension and music licensing exemption. Pub. L. 105-298, Title I, Oct. 27, 1998, 112 Stat. 2827; 17 U.S.C. §§ 101 nt, 108, 203, 301 to 304
8 no2 *J. Intell. Prop. L.* 223-43 Spr 2001

Crimes and Criminal Procedure. Military Extraterritorial Jurisdiction. Pub. L. 106-523, Nov. 22, 2000, 114 Stat. 2488; 18 U.S.C. §§ 3261 to 3267
51 no1 *Cath. U. L. Rev.* 55-134 Fall 2001
105 no3 *Dick. L. Rev.* 419-40 Spr 2001

Crimes. Child Support. Failure to pay legal child support obligations. Pub. L. 102-521, Oct. 25, 1992, 106 Stat. 3403; 18 U.S.C. § 228, 42 U.S.C. §§ 3793, 3796 to 3797, 12301 note
78 no4 *U. Det. Mercy L. Rev.* 699-721 Summ 2001

Crimes. General Provisions. Special maritime and territorial jurisdiction of the United States defined. 18 U.S.C. § 7
105 no3 *Dick. L. Rev.* 419-40 Spr 2001

Digital Millennium Copyright Act. Pub. L. 105-304, Oct. 28, 1998, 112 Stat. 2860; codified in scattered sections of 5, 17, 28, and 35 U.S.C.
24 no2 *Eur. Intell. Prop. Rev.* 65-73 F 2002
12 no1 *Fordham Intell. Prop. Media & Ent. L.J.* 157-94 Aut 2001
8 no2 *J. Intell. Prop. L.* 275-301 Spr 2001
42 no1 *Santa Clara L. Rev.* 247-76 2001

Drug Price Competition and Patent Term Restoration Act of 1984. Pub. L. 98-417, Sept. 24, 1984, 98 Stat. 1585; codified in scattered sections of 15, 21, 28 and 35 U.S.C.
34 no4 *J. Health L.* 657-71 Fall 2001

Economic Growth and Tax Relief Reconciliation Act of 2001. Pub. L. 107-16, June 7, 2001, 115 Stat. 38; codified in scattered sections of 26 U.S.C.
2001 *Army Law.* 21-8 D 2001
14 no1 *DePaul Bus. L.J.* 1-19 Fall 2001
90 no2 *Ill. B.J.* 80-7 F 2002

Education. Education of Individuals with Disabilities. Assistance for Education of All Children with Disabilities. Procedural safeguards. Placement in alternative educational setting. Authority of school personnel. 20 U.S.C. § 1415(k)(1)
29 no2 *Fordham Urb. L.J.* 513-38 D 2001

Education. General Provisions Concerning Education. General Requirements and Conditions Concerning Operation and Administration of Education Programs; General Authority of Secretary. Records; Privacy. Family educational and privacy rights. Pub. L. 93-380, Title V, § 513, Aug. 21, 1974, 88 Stat. 571; 20 U.S.C. § 1232g
77 no1 *Ind. L.J.* 143-66 Wint 2002

Education. General Provisions Relating to Student Assistance Programs. Institutional and financial assistance information for students. Disclosure of campus security policy and campus crime statistics. 20 U.S.C. § 1092(f)
77 no1 *Ind. L.J.* 143-66 Wint 2002

Emergency Planning and Community Right-to-Know Act of 1986. Pub. L. 99-499, Oct. 17, 1986, 100 Stat. 1613; 42 U.S.C. §§ 11001 to 11005, 11021 to 11023, 11041 to 11050
16 no3 *Nat. Resources & Env't* 172-6, 208 Wint 2002

Employee Retirement Income Security Act of 1974. 29 U.S.C. § 1144
42 no1 *Santa Clara L. Rev.* 105-83 2001

Endangered Species Act of 1973. Pub. L. 93-205, Dec. 28, 1973, 87 Stat. 884; 16 U.S.C. §§ 1531-1544
31 no2 *Colo. Law.* 61-6 F 2002

Fair Housing Amendments Act of 1988. Pub. L. 100-430, Sept. 13, 1988, 102 Stat. 1619; 42 U.S.C. §§ 3601 to 3631
34 no1 *Suffolk U. L. Rev.* 97-124 2000

Fairness in Music Licensing Act of 1998. Pub. L. 105-298, Oct. 27, 1998, 112 Stat. 2830; 17 U.S.C. §§ 101, 110, 504, 512
11 no2 *DePaul LCA J. Art & Ent. L.* 397-424 Fall 2001

Family and Medical Leave Act of 1993. Pub. L. 103-03, Feb. 5, 1993, 107 Stat. 6; codified in scattered sections of 2, 5, and 29 U.S.C.
55 no1 *Vand. L. Rev.* 261-308 Ja 2002

Federally Supported Health Centers Assistance Act of 1992. Pub. L. 102-501, Oct. 24, 1992, 106 Stat. 3268; 42 U.S.C. §§ 201 note, 233, 233 notes
18 no2 *Ga. St. U. L. Rev.* 415-47 Wint 2001

Health Care Quality Improvement Act of 1986. Pub. L. 99-660, Nov. 14, 1986, 100 Stat. 3743; 42 U.S.C. §§ 11101, 11111 to 11115, 11131 to 11137, 11151 to 11152
49 no1 *Fed. Law.* 32-6 Ja 2002

Illegal Immigration Reform and Immigrant Responsibility Act of 1996. Pub. L. 104-208, Sept. 30, 1996, 110 Stat. 3009; codified in scattered sections of U.S.C.
02 no1 *Immigr. Brief.* 1-20 Ja 2002

Indian Child Welfare Act of 1978. Pub. L. 95-608, Nov. 8, 1978, 92 Stat. 3069; 25 U.S.C. § 1901 et seq.
46 no1 *St. Louis U. L.J.* 213-45 Wint 2002

Indian Gaming Regulatory Act. Pub. L. 100-497, Oct. 17, 1988, 102 Stat. 2467; 18 U.S.C. §§ 1166 to 1168; 25 U.S.C. §§ 2701 to 2721
37 no2 *Willamette L. Rev.* 399-432 Spr 2001

Individuals with Disabilities Education Act Amendments of 1994. Pub. L. 103-218, Mar. 9, 1994, 108 Stat. 95; codified at 20 U.S.C. §§ 1400 to 1491
29 no2 *Fordham Urb. L.J.* 759-90 D 2001

Internal Revenue Code. Estate and Gift Taxes. Estate Tax. Estate tax will be repealed after 2009. 26 U.S.C. § 2210(a)
25 no2 *Seton Hall Legis. J.* 525-48 2001

Internal Revenue Code. Income Taxes. Normal Taxes and Surtaxes. Exempt Organizations. Political Organizations. 26 U.S.C. § 527(j)
77 no1 *Ind. L.J.* 167-87 Wint 2002

B. Exercise 7.2: *American Jurisprudence*, Pleading and Practice Forms

1. Sample complaints include all of the information needed to file; no changes or additions are necessary.
   a. True
   b. False
2. References to other secondary sources are included to provide the researcher with additional information.
   a. True
   b. False
3. If a landlord wanted to recover unpaid rent from a tenant from the time the tenant abandoned the property to the time the property was re-rented, which form would be used?
   a. § 50
   b. § 51
   c. § 48
   d. None of the above
4. For more information regarding the right to recover attorney fees in an action to recover rent, which of the following would you consult?
   a. 49 Am. Jur. 2d, Landlord & Tenant § 790, 792
   b. 77 ALR2d 735
   c. both a and b
   d. neither a nor b
5. If a landlord has terminated a lease and is denying the lessee access to the property, and the lessee wishes to recover damages, which of the following forms would be appropriate?
   a. § 51
   b. § 52
   c. § 53
   d. None of the above

defendant of the covenant to pay rent; to hold defendant liable for rents then accrued; to relet the premises after notice to defendant; to hold defendant liable for any deficiency in the rent resulting from a reletting; and to hold defendant liable for the rent for the full term of the lease if plaintiff is unable, with the exercise of reasonable diligence, to relet the premises during the lease term.

6. On defendant's failure to pay the $_______ rent due on _______ *[date]*, plaintiff notified defendant in writing, as required by the lease, of the intent to reenter and resume possession of the leased premises on _______ *[date]*, in the event of defendant's failure to pay the rent then due.

7. Thereafter, defendant failed to pay the rent due, and plaintiff, pursuant to the notice to defendant, reentered the leased premises and resumed possession on _______ *[date]*.

8. On _______ *[date]*, plaintiff notified defendant of plaintiff's intention to relet the premises and to hold defendant liable for any deficiency in rent resulting from the reletting or, in the event of plaintiff's inability, despite the exercise of reasonable diligence, to relet the premises, to hold defendant liable for the rent for the full term of the lease.

9. Thereafter, plaintiff exercised due diligence in the attempt to relet the leased premises, but was unable to rent the premises during the lease term.

10. Plaintiff has demanded payment from defendant of the rents accruing under the lease on _______ *[specify due dates]*, but defendant has failed to pay the accrued rents and still refuses to do so. There is now due and owing plaintiff from defendant and unpaid $_______ in accrued rents for the lease term.

11. _______ *[Allege generally plaintiff's performance of any other conditions precedent to defendant's payment.]*

WHEREFORE, plaintiff requests:

1. Judgment against defendant in the amount of $_______, as the rent to be paid by defendant to plaintiff for the period plaintiff was unable to relet the premises on defendant's failure to pay rent, and on plaintiff's reentry;
2. Costs of this action; and
3. Such other and further relief as the court deems just.

Dated: _______.

[Signature]

NOTES TO FORM

Research References

Text References

Tenant's liability under lease provision for the payment of rent after forfeiture. 49 Am Jur 2d, Landlord and Tenant §§ 321 et seq.

§ 48 Complaint, petition, or declaration—To recover rent—Rent of marketing stall—Expenses of advertising and refrigeration services—Costs and reasonable attorney fees

[Caption, see § 10]

COMPLAINT

Plaintiff, _______, alleges:

1. Plaintiff resides at _______ *[address]*, _______ *[city]*, _______ County, _______ *[state]*.

2. Defendant resides at _______ *[address]*, _______ *[city]*, _______ County, _______ *[state]*.

3. By a lease agreement dated and executed on _______ *[date]*, plaintiff leased to defendant and defendant leased from plaintiff for _______ *[number]* _______ *[months or years]*, commencing on _______ *[date]*, a marketing stall, No. _______, covering _______ square feet, in the _______ Market, located at _______ *[address]*, _______ *[city]*, _______ County, _______ *[state]*. The lease provided for a total rent of $_______, payable in equal installments of $_______ each, in advance, on the _______ day of each month. A copy of the lease is attached as Exhibit _______, and made a part of this pleading.

4. During the times mentioned, plaintiff provided refrigeration service at $_______ per month and advertising services at $_______ per month for tenants of the market desiring those services.

5. On or about _______ *[date]*, defendant took possession of the leased premises pursuant to the lease agreement with plaintiff and continued in possession under the lease until _______ *[date]*.

6. At defendant's request, plaintiff furnished to defendant refrigeration services for the period of _______ *[date]* to _______ *[date]*; and defendant agreed to pay to plaintiff for those services $_______ per month.

7. At defendant's request, plaintiff also furnished defendant with advertising services for the period of _______ *[date]* to _______ *[date]*; and defendant agreed to pay to plaintiff $_______ per month for those services.

8. Defendant failed to pay to plaintiff the monthly rent of $_______ due on _______ *[specify due dates]* and there is now due and owing to plaintiff from defendant a total rent of $_______, no part of which has been paid.

9. Defendant failed to pay to plaintiff the $_______ monthly charge for advertising services as well as the $_______ monthly charge for refrigeration service due on _______ *[specify due dates]*, and there is now due and owing to plaintiff from defendant for those services $_______, no part of which has been paid.

10. Pursuant to Paragraph _______ of the lease, defendant agreed to pay and discharge all reasonable costs, attorney fees, and expenses reasonably incurred by plaintiff to enforce the covenants, terms, and conditions of the lease in the event of defendant's default in performance; and by reason of defendant's default in payments, it has become necessary for plaintiff to employ an attorney to enforce such payment; $_______ are reasonable attorney fees for the bringing and prosecution of this action, and defendant has not paid any part of that fee or of the costs and expenses in connection with this proceeding.

11. _______ *[Allege generally plaintiff's performance of conditions precedent to defendant's payment.]*

12. Plaintiff has notified defendant in writing of defendant's default in payment for rents, for refrigeration services, and for advertising services, and has demanded payment from defendant, but defendant neglects and refuses to make the payments so accrued.

WHEREFORE, plaintiff requests:

1. Judgment against defendant in the total amount of $_______, as the rent to be paid by defendant to plaintiff, the charges for refrigeration services

furnished defendant, and the charges for advertising services furnished defendant;

2. Costs of this action, including reasonable attorney fees; and
3. Such other and further relief as the court deems just.

Dated: ______.

[Signature]

NOTES TO FORM

Research References

Text References

Requirement that all rent installments due be included in action for rent; right to attorney fees under lease provisions. 49 Am Jur 2d, Landlord and Tenant §§ 790, 792

ALR Annotations

Construction and effect of lease provision relating to attorneys' fees. 77 ALR2d 735

§ 49 Complaint, petition, or declaration—To recover rent—By landlord who relet abandoned premises

[Caption, see § 10]

COMPLAINT

Plaintiff, ______, alleges:

1. Plaintiff resides at ______ *[address]*, ______ *[city]*, ______ County, ______ *[state]*.

2. Defendant resides at ______ *[address]*, ______ *[city]*, ______ County, ______ *[state]*.

3. Plaintiff, as lessor, and defendant, as lessee, entered into a lease agreement dated and executed on ______ *[date]*, by the terms of which the parties agreed for the lease of the premises at ______ *[address]*, ______ *[city]*, ______ County, ______ *[state]*, for the term commencing on ______ *[date]* and ending on ______ *[date]*, for a total rent of $______, payable as follows: ______ *[set forth amount and intervals of rental payments]*. A copy of the lease is attached as Exhibit ______, and made a part of this pleading.

4. Defendant took possession of the leased premises pursuant to the terms and conditions of the lease on or about ______ *[date]*, and paid the lease rents accruing on the following dates: ______ *[set forth due dates of accrued rents paid]*.

5. Thereafter, on ______ *[date]*, defendant offered to surrender the leased premises to plaintiff, abandoned the leased premises in violation of defendant's covenant under Paragraph ______ of the lease, and refused to pay and still refuses to pay the rents accruing on ______ *[date]*, and thereafter.

6. Plaintiff refused to accept defendant's surrender of the leased premises and notified defendant in writing on ______ *[date]* of the intent to relet the premises for the most rent obtainable and to seek recovery from defendant of the difference between the rent reserved in the lease and the rent received, if less, from any tenant plaintiff might obtain.

7. Thereafter, plaintiff at all times diligently attempted to rent the leased premises; but, despite such attempts, the premises remained vacant from the

time of defendant's abandonment until _______ *[date]*, at which time a total of $_______ in rents had accrued under the lease and were due and payable by defendant to plaintiff.

8. On _______ *[date]*, plaintiff rented the leased premises to _______, on a month-to-month basis, at an agreed rent of $_______ per month, and received from the new tenant the rent monthly for the remainder of the term of defendant's lease, for a total of $_______.

9. _______ *[Allege generally plaintiff's performance of conditions precedent to defendant's payment of rent.]*

10. Plaintiff has demanded payment from defendant of $_______ for the monthly rents of $_______ that accrued on _______ *[due dates for unpaid rents prior to the reletting]* and $_______, for the difference between the lesser rent paid during the reletting and the rent due under the lease, or a total of $_______; but defendant has neglected and refused to pay this amount and still refuses to do so.

WHEREFORE, plaintiff requests:

1. Judgment against defendant in the amount of $_______, as the rent to be paid by defendant to plaintiff for the period plaintiff was unable to relet the premises on defendant's failure to pay rent;

2. Costs of this action; and

3. Such other and further relief as the court deems just.

Dated: _______.

[Signature]

NOTES TO FORM

Research References

Text References

Landlord's right to recover difference between rent reserved in lease and rent received from reletting after refusing to accept tenant's surrender and giving notice to tenant of intent to relet. 49 Am Jur 2d, Landlord and Tenant §§ 783 et seq.

§ 50 Complaint, petition, or declaration—To recover rent—By landlord who relet abandoned premises—Subject to tenant's reentry

[Caption, see § 10]

COMPLAINT

Plaintiff, _______, alleges:

1. Plaintiff resides at _______ *[address]*, _______ *[city]*, _______ County, _______ *[state]*.

2. Defendant resides at _______ *[address]*, _______ *[city]*, _______ County, _______ *[state]*.

3. Plaintiff leased to defendant a building located at _______ *[address]*, _______ *[city]*, _______ County, _______ *[state]*, for _______ *[number]* _______ *[months or years]*, commencing on _______ *[date]*, for $_______, payable as follows: _______ *[specify amount and intervals of rental payments]*. A copy of the lease is attached as Exhibit _______, and made a part of this pleading.

4. On or about _______ *[date]*, defendant took possession of the leased premises and continued in possession until _______ *[date]*, when defendant abandoned the leased premises without legal right or just cause and refused and failed to pay the rent accruing on _______ *[date]*, and thereafter.

5. On _______ *[date]*, plaintiff notified defendant in writing that defendant was being held liable for the rents under the lease, that if defendant did not reoccupy the leased building within a reasonable time plaintiff would relet it for defendant, subject to defendant's reentry at any time during the lease term, and that defendant would be credited with the amounts received from any such reletting.

6. Defendant failed to reoccupy the leased building; and on _______ *[date]*, plaintiff relet the building, subject to defendant's reentry, to _______ for $_______ per month.

7. The new tenant occupied the leased building from _______ *[date]* until _______ *[date]*, and paid to plaintiff $_______, for the use and occupancy of the premises. At no time during occupancy did defendant reenter the leased building or offer to pay or pay any rent.

8. Between _______ *[date]*, the date of defendant's abandonment of the leased building, and the termination of the lease pursuant to its term on _______ *[date]*, $_______ in rents accrued under the lease.

9. Plaintiff notified defendant of a credit of $_______ against accrued rents for the amounts paid by the new tenant, and demanded payment from defendant of the remaining $_______ due under the terms of the lease; but defendant refused and neglected to pay the same and still refuses to do so.

WHEREFORE, plaintiff requests:

1. Judgment against defendant in the amount of $_______, as the rent to be paid by defendant to plaintiff for the period defendant was obligated to pay rent pursuant to the lease agreement, after deducting those rents paid by the new tenant found by plaintiff;

2. Costs of this action; and

3. Such other and further relief as the court deems just.

Dated: _______.

[Signature]

NOTES TO FORM

Research References

Text References

Landlord's right to recover difference between rent reserved in lease and rent received from reletting. 49 Am Jur 2d, Landlord and Tenant §§ 783 et seq.

§ 51 Complaint, petition, or declaration—To recover rent—After tenant's abandonment of premises

[Caption, see § 10]

COMPLAINT

Plaintiff, _______, alleges:

1. Plaintiff resides at _______ *[address]*, _______ *[city]*, _______ County, _______ *[state]*.

continued

2. Defendant resides at _______ *[address]*, _______ *[city]*, _______ County, _______ *[state]*.

3. By a written lease dated _______, defendant leased from plaintiff, for _______ *[number]* _______ *[months or years]* commencing on _______ *[date]*, the premises at _______ *[address]*, _______ *[city]*, _______ County, _______ *[state]*, for $_______, payable as follows: _______ *[amount and intervals of rental payments]*. A copy of the lease is attached as Exhibit _______, and made a part of this pleading.

4. Paragraph _______ of the lease provides for an award of reasonable attorney fees to the prevailing party in any litigation involving the lease.

5. On _______ *[date]*, defendant entered into possession of the described premises pursuant to the lease between plaintiff and defendant.

6. In accordance with the lease defendant paid plaintiff rent as it fell due through _______ *[date]*, but, in breach of the lease, defendant failed to pay either in whole or in part the rent that became due on _______ *[date]*, or the rent that became due on any subsequent date.

7. On or about _______ *[date]*, defendant vacated and abandoned the premises, without the knowledge or consent of plaintiff, and the lease was terminated on _______ *[date]*.

8. Paragraph _______ of the lease provides that if the lessee abandons the premises before the lease term expires, the damages plaintiff may recover include the worth at the time of judgment of the amount by which the unpaid rent for the balance of the lease term after the date of judgment exceeds the amount of the rental loss for the same period that the tenant proves could be reasonably avoided, and that the worth at the time of judgment is to be computed by discounting the amount at the discount rate of the Federal Reserve Bank of _______ *[city]* at the time of the award plus _______%.

9. On _______ *[date]*, plaintiff, in a good-faith effort to mitigate the damages, by a written lease relet the property to _______, at a monthly rental of $_______, for a term commencing on _______ *[date]*, terminating on _______ *[date]*. A copy of the lease is attached as Exhibit _______, and incorporated by reference.

10. On _______ *[date]*, the date defendant's lease was terminated as alleged above, and rent was due, owing, and unpaid in the sum of $_______. As a proximate result of defendant's failure to pay this rent or any part of it on the date it was due, or since, plaintiff has been damaged in the sum of $_______, together with interest on that sum at the rate of _______% per annum, as provided in the lease.

11. As a further proximate result of defendant's breach of the lease and abandonment of the premises, and the consequent termination of the lease, as alleged in this complaint, plaintiff has been further damaged in the sum of $_______ per month from _______ *[date]* until the date judgment is entered in this case, together with interest at the rate of _______% per annum, less the sums received by plaintiff during this period as rent from the reletting of the premises.

12. As a further proximate result of defendant's breach of the lease and abandonment of the premises, and the consequent termination of the lease, as alleged in this complaint, plaintiff has been further damaged in the sum of $_______ per month for the period after the date of the judgment and until the judgment is paid, less any sums received by plaintiff during that period.

13. As a further proximate result of defendant's breach of the lease and abandonment of the premises as alleged in this complaint, plaintiff sustained additional damages and expenses in seeking to relet the premises, in the sum of $_______.

WHEREFORE, plaintiff requests judgment against defendant for:

1. Damages in the amount of $_______;
2. Reasonable attorney fees in the amount of $_______;
3. Costs of suit; and
4. Such other and further relief as the court deems just and proper.

Dated: _______.

[Signature]

NOTES TO FORM

Research References

Text References

Landlord's right to recover difference between rent reserved in lease and rent received from reletting. 49 Am Jur 2d, Landlord and Tenant §§ 783 et seq.

§ 52 Complaint, petition, or declaration—For declaratory judgment, injunction, and accounting—Regarding termination of lease

[Caption, see § 10]

COMPLAINT

Plaintiff, _______, alleges:

1. Plaintiff is a resident of _______ *[city]*, _______ County, _______ *[state]*. Plaintiff is the owner of _______ *[business]*, located at _______ *[address]*, _______ *[city]*, _______ County, _______ *[state]*.

2. Defendant, _______, is a corporation duly organized and existing under the laws of _______ *[state]*. Defendant is the owner of real estate situated at _______ *[address of defendant's business]*.

3. On or about _______ *[date]*, plaintiff and defendant entered into a lease agreement pursuant to which plaintiff became the tenant of the premises located at _______ *[address of plaintiff's business]*. A copy of that lease is attached as Exhibit _______, and made a part of this pleading.

4. Pursuant to the lease, plaintiff is entitled to occupy the premises at _______ *[address of plaintiff's business]* for a term of _______ years for the purpose of operating a _______ *[business]*.

5. On or about _______ *[date]*, defendant sent plaintiff a letter signed by _______, as vice president of defendant, a copy of which is attached as Exhibit _______, and made a part of this pleading. In this letter, defendant stated that "We are exercising our termination option and notify you of our intention to terminate this Lease on _______ *[date]*."

FIRST CAUSE OF ACTION

6. Plaintiff repeats and realleges the allegations of Paragraphs 1-5 of this complaint as if again set forth in their entirety.

continued

7. The letter dated on or about _______ is defective and of no legal force and effect because it was not mailed within _______ days of the default alleged in that letter as required by Paragraph _______ of the lease in order to effect a valid termination of the lease.

8. The default alleged in the letter dated on or about _______ does not exist because _______ *[specify reasons]*.

9. Defendant breached its obligation under Paragraph _______ of the lease by failing to pay real estate taxes due on the leased premises and failing to provide plaintiff an accounting of the disposition of monies received for the tax escrow account on the premises.

10. The threat by defendant to terminate plaintiff's lease constitutes a breach of that lease.

11. Any noncompliance by plaintiff with _______ *[his or her]* obligations under the lease were waived by defendant, in that _______ *[specify]*.

WHEREFORE, plaintiff requests entry of a declaratory judgment specifying the rights of the parties, including, but not limited to, a declaration that the termination allegedly made by defendant's letter is void, has no legal force and effect, and is in violation of the lease, together with all costs and disbursements on this action and such other and further relief as to this court seems just and warranted.

SECOND CAUSE OF ACTION

12. Plaintiff repeats and realleges the allegations of Paragraphs 1-5 of this complaint as if again set forth in their entirety.

13. The termination of the lease as threatened by defendant would cause irreparable injury to plaintiff by _______ *[specify injury, such as "would force plaintiff to close its business which is dependent on customers living in the vicinity of plaintiff's premises and which could not be effectively continued at another site"]*.

14. Plaintiff has no adequate remedy of law, in that _______ *[specify]*.

WHEREFORE, plaintiff requests a preliminary and permanent injunction enjoining defendant, and any party, known or unknown, acting on behalf of defendant, from terminating the lease, reentering the leasehold premises, or otherwise interfering with plaintiff's rights under the lease, together with all costs and disbursements on this action and such other and further relief as to this court seems just and warranted.

THIRD CAUSE OF ACTION

15. Plaintiff repeats and realleges the allegations of Paragraphs 1-5 of this complaint as if again set forth in their entirety.

16. By reason of the above, plaintiff requests an accounting as to the disposition of all tax escrow payments made by plaintiff to defendant and all transactions concerning the tax escrow account from _______ *[date]* to the present, together with all costs and disbursements of this action and such other and further relief as to this court seems just and warranted.

Dated: _______.

[Signature]

NOTES TO FORM

Research References

Text References

Equitable relief from forfeiture of lease. 49 Am Jur 2d, Landlord and Tenant §§ 339 et seq.

§ 53 Complaint, petition, or declaration—For damages for wrongful termination of lease

[Caption, see § 10]

COMPLAINT

Plaintiff, _______, alleges:

1. Plaintiff is, and at all times relevant was, a citizen and resident of _______ *[city]*, _______ County, _______ *[state]*.

2. _______, defendant, is, and at all times relevant was, a citizen and resident of _______ *[city]*, _______ County, _______ *[state]*.

3. On _______ *[date]*, plaintiff, as lessee, and defendant, as lessor, entered into a written lease agreement for the lease of a structure located at _______ *[address]*, _______ *[city]*, _______ County, _______ *[state]*, for a term _______ *[specify]* on the terms and conditions set forth in that lease. A copy of the lease is attached as Exhibit _______, and made a part of this pleading.

4. At all times mentioned, plaintiff used the leased premises for a _______ *[specify]* business.

5. On or about _______ *[date]*, defendant unlawfully and without any justification terminated the lease between the parties and denied plaintiff access to and use of the leased premises and continues to deny plaintiff access to and use of the leased premises to the present time.

6. At all times mentioned, plaintiff fulfilled all _______ *[his or her]* duties and obligations required pursuant to the above-described lease between the parties.

7. As a result of plaintiff's inability to gain access to and use of the leased premises, plaintiff has been deprived of various items of equipment, machinery, supplies, and inventory which are located on the leased premises and has been unable to conduct _______ *[his or her]* business from _______ *[date]* to the present, damaging plaintiff in the sum of $_______.

WHEREFORE, plaintiff requests judgment against defendant in the sum of $_______, together with the costs and disbursements of this action.

Dated: _______.

[Signature]

NOTES TO FORM

Research References

Text References

Damages for wrongful eviction. 49 Am Jur 2d, Landlord and Tenant §§ 668 et seq.

ALR Annotations

Application to commercial lease of rule that lease may be cancelled only for material breach. 54 ALR4th 595

CHAPTER

8

LEGAL ENCYCLOPEDIAS AND DICTIONARIES

I. LEGAL ENCYCLOPEDIAS

Legal encyclopedias, no matter what their area of topical coverage, provide readers with broad legal concepts. Comprehensive coverage is not the goal of the encyclopedia; rather, it is intended to give an overview of legal ideas and principles. Encyclopedias deliver a skeletal framework from which to operate, and thus serve as an incomparable starting point for any research. These multivolume sets are sources of background information and points of departure for further analysis. As the illustration in Figure 8.1 clearly demonstrates, a wealth of footnotes and annotations accompany the text.

The two major legal encyclopedias are *Corpus Juris Secundum* (C.J.S.), by West Publishing Company, and *American Jurisprudence* (Am. Jur., Am. Jur. 2d), by Lawyer's Cooperative Company in Rochester, New York; both are now owned by the Thomson Corporation. Both encyclopedias are national in scope, but are not averse to select state references. West also publishes state-specific encyclopedias for larger states such as California and New York. Figure 8.2 shows an encyclopedia accessed through Westlaw.

FIGURE 8.1

beyond that common to his or her trade, he or she is held to that higher standard of care.

§ 126 Consequences and danger

The care to be exercised in a particular case is proportionate to the seriousness of the consequences which are reasonably to be anticipated as a result of the conduct in question, and commensurate with the danger which is known or reasonably to be anticipated.

Research References

West's Key Number Digest, Negligence ⚿ 231 to 233

The care to be exercised in a particular case must always be proportionate to the seriousness of the consequences which are reasonable to be anticipated as a result of the conduct in question.[1] So, in determining what is reasonable or ordinary care under the circumstances, the degree or extent of the injury which may be inflicted by lack of proper care is a matter proper for consideration.[2] Where the consequence of negligence will probably be serious injury to others, and where the means of avoiding the infliction of injury upon others are completely within the party's power, ordinary care requires almost the utmost degree of human vigilance and foresight.[3] Due care does not require special precautions against something which is only remotely possible,[4] or which circumstances, as known, do not suggest as likely to happen.[5]

The dangers involved in an act are to be taken into account in determining what constitutes due care or the exercise thereof.[6] The duty of care is commensurate with the danger present in a situation or incident to an opera-

---

than is required of a reasonable person in the same or similar circumstances.

Wyo.—Ely v. Kirk, 707 P.2d 706 (Wyo. 1985)

[6]Iowa—Hartig v. Francois, 562 N.W.2d 427 (Iowa 1997).

[Section 126]

[1]U.S.—Urie v. Thompson, 337 U.S. 163, 60 S. Ct. 1018, 93 L. Ed. 1282, A.L.R.2d 252 (1949).

Conn.—Trasacco v. New York, N. H. & H. R. Co., 113 Conn. 355, 155 A. 493 (1931).

Mo.—Bronson v. Kansas City, 323 S.W.2d 526 (Mo. Ct. App. 1959).

Duty to anticipate consequences, see § 49.

Foresight as determining factor

Whether due care was being exercised is to be determined by foresight and not by hindsight.

Me.—Feely v. Morton, 149 Me. 119, 99 A.2d 285 (1953); Melanson v. Reed Bros., 146 Me. 16, 76 A.2d 853 (1950).

Repairman

Repairman called to perform a job on premises owes a duty to exercise ordinary care to protect members of public and invitees of operator using the equipment from being injured by dangerous condition, if any, created by his work.

Cal.—Alvarado v. Anderson, 175 Cal. App. 2d 166, 346 P.2d 73 (4th Dist. 1959).

[2]La.—Levi v. Southwest Louisiana Elec. Membership Co-op. (SLEMCO), 542 So. 2d 1081 (La. 1989), reh'g dismissed, (May 26, 1989).

Or.—Suko v. Northwestern Ice & Cold Storage Co., 166 Or. 557, 113 P.2d 209 (1941).

[3]Md.—Philadelphia, W. & B.R. Co. v. Kerr, 25 Md. 521, 1866 WL 2035 (1866).

[4]Mass.—Geary v. H. P. Hood & Sons, Inc., 336 Mass. 369, 145 N.E.2d 716 (1957).

Miss.—Burnside v. Gulf Refining Co., 166 Miss. 460, 148 So. 219 (1933).

Extraordinary peril

"Ordinary care " does not involve forethought of extraordinary peril.

Minn.—Despatch Oven Co. v. Rauenhorst, 229 Minn. 436, 40 N.W.2d 73 (1949).

[5]Fla.—Sprick v. North Shore Hospital, Inc., 121 S. 2d 682 (Fla. Dist. Ct. App. 3d Dist. 1960).

S.D.—Ford Robinson, 76 S.D. 457, 80 N.W.2d 471 (1957).

Behavior of reasonable man

The reasonable man, whose ideal behavior is looked to as standard of duty, will neither neglect what he can forecast as probable, nor waste his anxiety on events that are barely possible, but will order his precaution by measure of what appears likely in the known course of things.

Ill.—Hays v. Place, 350 Ill. App.l 504, 113 N.E.2d 178 (4th Dist. 1953).

Likelihood and gravity of injury

Degree of care required depends on both likelihood of injury and gravity thereof.

U.S.—In re Spencer Kellogg & Sons, 52 F.2d 129 (C. C.A. 2d Cir. 1931), cert. granted, 284 U.S. 610, 52 S. Ct. 126, 76 L. Ed. 522 (1931) and rev'd on other grounds, 285 U.S. 502, 52 S. Ct. 450, 76 L. Ed. 903 (1932).

[6]U.S.—Holland v. Yellowstone Pipe Line Co., 306 F.2d 621 (9th Cir. 1962).

N.J.—Smith v. Okerson, 8 N.J. Super. 560, 73 A.2d 857 (Ch. Div. 1950).

Ohio—Witherspon v. Haft, 157 Ohio St. 474, 47 Ohio Op. 350, 106 N.E.2d 296 (1952).

FIGURE 8.2

WRONGFUL DISCHARGE

Laura Hunter Dietz, J.D.

Scope

This article discusses wrongful discharge, generally, with specific discussion as to: the employment-at-will doctrine; general bases and theories of liability for wrongful discharge actions, and exceptions from the employment-at-will rule; particular types of employees who may bring wrongful discharge actions; the impropriety of discharges from employment based on particular reasons or particular types of employee conduct, and actions based thereon; traditional tort claims as elements of or alternatives to actions for wrongful discharge; defenses to wrongful discharge claims; and various matters of practice and procedure, as well as remedies and relief available in wrongful discharge actions.

Federal Aspects

Federal constitutional provisions and statutes are covered in this article as they pertain to employment discrimination, bases of wrongful discharge liability, and whistleblower protection for employees. For U.S.C.A. citations, see "Statutory References," below.

Treated Elsewhere

Adverse employment actions as constituting prohibited retaliation under federal law, generally, see 45A Am. Jur. 2d, Job Discrimination § 234

Age, race, color, religion, sex, or national origin, rights of employees discharged or disciplined because of, generally, see 45B Am. Jur. 2d, Job Discrimination §§ 1055 et seq.

Americans with Disabilities Act, prohibition of discrimination against individual because of opposition to act or practice made unlawful under, generally, see Am. Jur. 2d New Topic Service, Americans with Disabilities Act § 670

Arbitrability of contract disputes pertaining to discharges, see 48, 48A Am. Jur. 2d, Labor and Labor Relations §§ 484, 485, 518, 3378, 3379, 3409

Church officers, removal of, generally, see 66 Am. Jur. 2d, Religious Societies

Civil servants: federal statutory prohibition against specific personnel practices against federal, generally, see 15A Am. Jur. 2d, Civil Service § 41; power to remove, generally, see 15A Am. Jur. 2d, Civil Service § 50; compulsory retirement of, see 15A Am. Jur. 2d, Civil Service § 56; grounds for removal of, see 15A Am. Jur. 2d, Civil Service §§ 63 et seq.; abolition of position or reduction of working force, see 15A Am. Jur. 2d, Civil Service §§ 78 et seq.

Title outline

FIGURE 8.2
continued

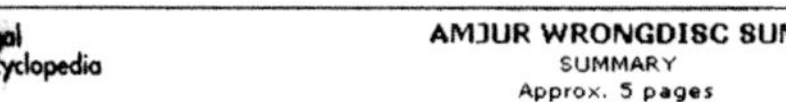

AMJUR WRONGDISC SUM
SUMMARY
Approx. 5 pages

THOMSON WEST

82 Am Jur 2d Wrongful Discharge Summary

American Jurisprudence, Second Edition
Database updated January 2003

Wrongful Discharge
Laura Hunter Dietz, J D

Topic Contents, Parallel References, List of Topics, Index

SUMMARY

Scope of Topic:

This article discusses wrongful discharge, generally, with specific discussion as to: the employment-at-will doctrine; general bases and theories of liability for wrongful discharge actions, and exceptions from the employment-at-will rule; particular types of employees who may bring wrongful discharge actions; the impropriety of discharges from employment based on particular reasons or particular types of employee conduct, and actions based thereon; traditional tort claims as elements of or alternatives to actions for wrongful discharge; defenses to wrongful discharge claims; and various matters of practice and procedure, as well as remedies and relief available in wrongful discharge actions.

• • •

Statutes, Rules, Etc.

U.S.C.A. Const.Amends. 1, 4, 5
2 U.S.C.A. §§ 1302, 1314, 1317 (Congressional Accountability Act)
3 U.S.C.A. § 417
5 U.S.C.A. §§ 1101 et seq. (Civil Service Reform Act)
5 U.S.C.A. § 2302
10 U.S.C.A. § 2409
11 U.S.C.A. § 525 (Bankruptcy Code)
12 U.S.C.A. §§ 21 et seq. (National Bank Act)
12 U.S.C.A. §§ 1421 et seq. (Federal Home Loan Bank Act)
12 U.S.C.A. §§ 1790b, 1831
12 U.S.C.A. §§ 2001 et seq. (Farm Credit Act)
15 U.S.C.A. §§ 1 et seq. (Sherman Act)
15 U.S.C.A. §§ 2601 et seq. (Toxic Substances Control Act)
20 U.S.C.A. §§ 3608, 4018

Wrongful discharge topic summary

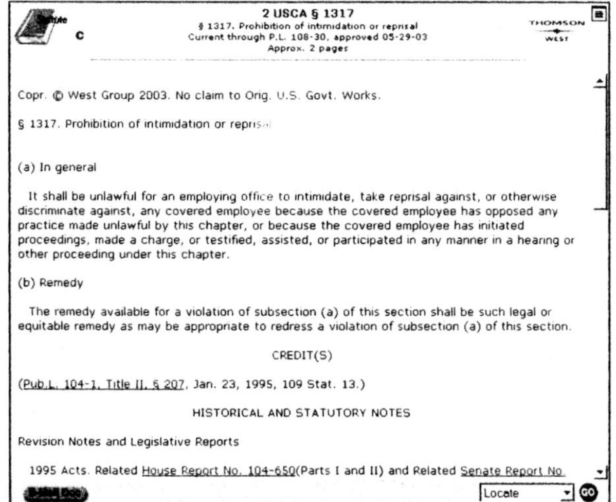

2 USCA § 1317
§ 1317. Prohibition of intimidation or reprisal
Current through P.L. 108-30, approved 05-29-03
Approx. 2 pages

THOMSON WEST

Copr. © West Group 2003. No claim to Orig. U.S. Govt. Works.

§ 1317. Prohibition of intimidation or reprisal

(a) In general

It shall be unlawful for an employing office to intimidate, take reprisal against, or otherwise discriminate against, any covered employee because the covered employee has opposed any practice made unlawful by this chapter, or because the covered employee has initiated proceedings, made a charge, or testified, assisted, or participated in any manner in a hearing or other proceeding under this chapter.

(b) Remedy

The remedy available for a violation of subsection (a) of this section shall be such legal or equitable remedy as may be appropriate to redress a violation of subsection (a) of this section.

CREDIT(S)

(Pub.L. 104-1, Title II, § 207, Jan. 23, 1995, 109 Stat. 13.)

HISTORICAL AND STATUTORY NOTES

Revision Notes and Legislative Reports

1995 Acts. Related House Report No. 104-650(Parts I and II) and Related Senate Report No.

Locate

A. Organization of an Encyclopedia

Common to all encyclopedias are the following features:

- Comprehensive general index, alphabetized by fact or descriptive word
- Topical, narrative analysis
- Extensive footnotes and annotations
- Emphasis on the prevailing rule of law

Differences in presentation appear when one compares *Corpus Juris Secundum* and *American Jurisprudence;* the main variances are:

- Footnotes in C.J.S. try to cite all reported federal and state cases, whereas Am. Jur. 3d only footnotes selected federal cases.
- C.J.S. uses the Key Number System common to all West publications.
- Am. Jur. 3d cross-references to articles in *American Law Reports, Restatements of the Law,* legal periodicals, and other practice books published by Lawyer's Co-op.

Because encyclopedias are so general, it is best to use them as a starting or preliminary source. Encyclopedias are not primary legal materials, but are appropriately used as sources of leads to secondary and even other tertiary material. Recognizing this limitation will steer the research in a productive direction. Much of an article's content may not apply to the particular legal dilemma under consideration. Many points of law may be covered under a single heading or section, which may be applicable to any given problem. Double-check and verify case and other legal citations before relying on them.

B. Using Encyclopedias

Despite the enormous amount of information included in an encyclopedia, the imposing design, and meticulous presentation, these works remain the backbone of any sensible legal research strategy. The paths to effective usage are relatively simple.

I. Keyword. After analyzing facts applicable to the research question, the researcher develops keywords. A **keyword** is usually a legal term, definition, concept, or principle, such as *negligence, defamation,* or a similar term. Encyclopedias are arranged by keywords, especially within the index and table of contents. Keywords lead to specific topics and sections by designated key numbers.

II. Topical Approach. There are two ways to use a topical approach. With the first, you determine the topic and section key numbers. Then find the encyclopedia from the correct publisher and correlate the key numbers with the correct volume.

The second method works when you know and can identify the correct topic even though you lack a section or key number. Find the appropriate volume and scan the table of contents or topical outline in the beginning of the section. The front matter of an encyclopedia usually consists of a table of contents that lists major topics and subheadings with the corresponding numbers. Next, use the index in the back of the appropriate volume to find specific corresponding citations. Accurate topic identification will often achieve better results than the Key Number System because it pinpoints the desired coverage. The chief point the encyclopedia researcher needs to remember is that there are diverse avenues to the same information.

Fact Pattern 1. First, find the General Index, M–Q. Next look up the keyword *motor vehicles*. Scan through the listings to find the topic "homicide," and, under that, "negligent vehicular homicide, **MotorVeh § 657**" (Fact Pattern Figure 8.3).

Find the "Motor Vehicle" volume on the shelf and turn to the appropriate section. At § 657(2), the difference between murder and manslaughter in a vehicular case is discussed (Fact Pattern Figure 8.4).

Fact Pattern 2. First, using *American Jurisprudence*, 2d, find the General Index, R–S. Next, look up the topic "sale or transfer of real property." Scan through the listings to find topic "remedies of purchaser," and, under that, "specific performance, **Vendor § 604, 605**" (Fact Pattern Figure 8.5).

Find the "Vendor and Purchaser" volume on the shelf and turn to the appropriate section (Fact Pattern Figure 8.6).

II. LEGAL DICTIONARIES

Precision of thought and language is a paramount ingredient of success for any legal researcher. Law depends on rigorous definition for proper interpretation and application, and so should avoid use of vague, sloppy, or undisciplined jargon. In short, law must define its terms rigidly. Dictionaries serve the legal community by alleviating conceptual confusion, ambiguities in language, and imprecision in the written word. Dictionaries serve as a common ground for resolving disputes in terminology and as a repository for the millions of terms, words, and phrases in law that no one person could ever remember. When in doubt about what a term means, turn to the dictionary.

The information in Figure 8.7 is taken from *Black's Law Dictionary*, the premier compilation of legal terms and definitions. Another popular dictionary, *Ballantine's Law Dictionary*, provides similar information in an abbreviated format, citing references to court case and legal treatises where necessary.

Fact Pattern 1. Using Fact Pattern 1 and any legal dictionary, locate keywords and phrases. What are your results?

Fact Pattern 2. Using Fact Pattern 2 and any legal dictionary, locate keywords and phrases. What are your results? Chapter summarizes frequently used secondary sources that are essential to successful legal research from the encyclopedia to the dictionary, these sources provide the starting point as well as general backdrop for each legal problem to be analyzed.

FIGURE 8.3

Consult Correlation Tables in text volumes for references to materials published after this index.

FIGURE 8.4

the act have jurisdiction over the offense, even though the deceased died in another state.[16.20]

New trial Where basic and fundamental error is involved, the fact that only a general exception, and not specific exceptions, was taken thereto does not justify the overruling of a motion for a new trial.[17]

§ 657(2). —— Particular Offenses

a. Murder
b. Manslaughter

a. Murder

In general, an intentional killing of a human being through the agency or operation of a motor vehicle may constitute murder.

Library References

Automobiles ⚷ 343, 344.

Under or apart from statute, an intentional killing of a human being by means of the operation or driving of a motor vehicle constitutes murder.[18] Accordingly, in the absence of any circumstances of justification or excuse, a driver of a motor vehicle may be adjudged guilty of murder where he knowingly operates his vehicle toward and against another person with intent to run him down,[19] or with reckless disregard for his life,[20] or where he intentionally runs into an obstruction causing a passenger to be thrown from the car,[21] and thereby causes his death. Also, a homicide resulting from the operation of a motor vehicle in violation of law may be adjudged murder where the unlawful manner of operation is such as naturally tends to destroy human life,[22] and, under some statutes, in order to make a case of murder against a motorist driving in an unlawful and negligent manner, it must appear that such conduct was directly perilous to human life or that human life would probably be endangered thereby.[23]

Under statutes making a homicide murder when committed by acts greatly dangerous to others and evincing depravity of mind, a driver is guilty of the crime when he operates his motor vehicle at high speed or otherwise negligently or unlawfully, without regard to the presence or lives of other persons, and kills a human being,[24] although he had no preconceived purpose to kill anyone.[25] A driver of a motor vehicle may be adjudged guilty of murder where the homicide is committed in the perpetration of a felony.[25.5]

b. Manslaughter

Generally one who unintentionally causes the death of a human being by means of the operation of a motor vehicle may be guilty of manslaughter, or of some grade or degree thereof.

In accordance with the rule that an unintentional homicide occasioned by the careless handling of a deadly weapon may be manslaughter, as discussed in Homicide § 62, and since a motor vehicle may be considered a dangerous instrumentality or deadly weapon,[25.50] one who through the agency, or in the operation, of a motor vehicle causes the death of a human being under circumstances such as to impose criminal liability therefor is guilty of manslaughter, or some grade or degree thereof, where the act or conduct casing the death is not such as to make the offense murder or some other specific grade of criminal homicide.[26] The question

16.20 Pa.—Commonwealth v. Burns 85 Pa.Dist. & Co. 325, 2 Bucks Co. 267.

17. Pa.—Commonwealth v. Kurtz, 33 Pa.Dist. & Co. 661.

18. Minn.—State v. Bolsinger, 21 N. W.2d 480, 221 Minn. 154.

Statute not repealed

Amendment to manslaughter statute did not repeal by implication any application of murder statute when death is caused by operation of motor vehicle with malice aforethought.

Ariz.—State v. Chalmers, 411 P.2d 448, 100 Ariz. 70.

19. Cal.—People v. Brown, 200 P. 727, 53 C.A. 664.

Ohio.—State v. Butler, 227 N.E.2d 627, 11 Ohio St.2d 23.

Degrees of murder see Homicide §§ 29–36.

Justifiable or excusable homicide generally see Homicide §§ 97–138.

Dangerous instrumentality

An automobile driven with a deliberate intention to run over another is a dangerous instrumentality.

Md.—Faulcon v. State, 126 A.2d 858, 211 Md. 249.

20. Ala.—Hammell v. State, 111 So. 191, 21 Ala.App. 633.

Ga.—Herrington v. State, 120 S.E. 554, 31 Ga.App. 167.

21. W.Va.—State v. Weisengoff, 101 S.E. 450, 85 W.Va. 271.

42 C.J. p 1354 note 33.

22. Ga.—Geter v. State, 132 S.E.2d 30, 219 Ga. 125—Powell v. State, 18 S.E.2d 678, 193 Ga. 398.

23. Tenn.—Shorter v. State, 247 S.W. 985, 147 Tenn. 355.

42 C.J. p 1354 note 38.

24. Wis.—Montgomery v. State, 190 N.W. 105, 178 Wis. 461.

42 C.J. p 1354 note 36.

25. Ala.—Berness v. State, 83 So.2d 607, 38 Ala.App. 1, affirmed 83 So. 2d 613, 263 Ala. 641—State v. Massey, 100 So. 625, 20 Ala.App. 56.

25.5 Cal.—People v. Pulley, 37 Cal. Rptr. 376, 225 C.A.2d 366.

Colo.—Whitman v. People, 420 P.2d 416.

25.50 S.C.—State v. Caldwell, 98 S.E.2d 259, 231 S.C. 184—State v. Phillips, 84 S.E.2d 855, 226 S.C. 297—State v. Staggs, 195 S.E. 130, 186 S.E. 531, 181 S.C. 1.

26. Neb.—Hoffman v. State, 77 N.W.2d 592, 162 Neb. 806—Benton v. State, 247 N.W. 21, 124 Neb. 485.

N.C.—State v. Lindsey, 142 S.E.2d 355, 264 N.C. 588—State v. Duncan, 141 S.E.2d 23, 264 N.C. 123.

Ohio.—State v. Yudick, App., 99 N.E. 2d 4, reversed on other grounds 98 N.E.2d 415, 155 Ohio St. 269.

FIGURE 8.5

 FIGURE 8.6

signed and delivered by the aggrieved party.[39] However, a waiver or renunciation, regardless of whether for consideration, or a claim or right arising out of an alleged breach of contract, by which a party agrees to forego rights given by the Uniform Land Transactions Act or by a contract, is invalid if the court finds as a matter of law that the waiver or renunciation is unconscionable or that it was secured in an unconscionable manner; the competence of the aggrieved party, any material misrepresentation, failure to disclose, or overreaching by the other party, and the value of any consideration for the waiver or renunciation are relevant to the issue or unconscionability.[40]

§ 604. Specific performance

A purchaser may be entitled to specific performance of a contract for the sale of real estate if special and peculiar reasons exist which make it impossible for the injured party to obtain relief by way of damages in any action at law.[41] However, in an action to enforce specific performance of a contract for the sale of an interest in land, money damages ordinarily do not constitute an adequate remedy for the breach of such contract; the courts thus often assume jurisdiction without the necessity of an actual showing of the inadequacy of legal remedies.[42]

A purchaser who defaults by committing a material breach of his or her contractual obligations is not entitled to this equitable remedy.[43] A prospective purchaser therefore must show that he or she is ready, willing, and able to perform in order to obtain specific performance of the contract.[44] Thus, in an action by the purchasers for specific performance of a real-estate contract, it is not error to deny the relief sought where the purchasers have failed to satisfy a contractual contingency of obtaining a loan by the closing date and, thus, have failed to prove substantial compliance with their part of the agreement.[45]

A vendee is not entitled to specific performance where he or she knows at the time of execution of the contract of purchase that the vendor doe snot have title to the property.[46] Yet, even though the vendor may not be able to convey the full title or the full amount of property which he contracted to convey, the vendee may compel the vendor to execute the contract so

39. Uniform Land Transactions Act § 1-305(a).

40. Uniform Land Transactions Act § 1-305(b).

41. Stacy v. Lin, 34 Ark App 97, 806 SW2d 15.

42. 71 Am Jur 2d, Specific Performance § 112.

43. Youngblut v Wilson (Iowa) 294 NW2d 813; Flath v Bauman (Mo App) 722 SW2d 125; Scott v Vandor (Tex App Houston (1st Dist)) 671 SW2d 79, writ ref n r e (Sep 12, 1984) and rehg of writ of error overr (Oct 17, 1984).

In an action by a prospective purchaser for specific performance of a contract for real property, the sellers were equitably barred from defending on the basis of a standard time-of-the-essence clause in the contract, where the parties had extended the time for closing three times and executed the third extension 2 days after the date for closing set in the second extension. Quirk v Schenk, 34 Mass App 931, 612 NE2d 1194, review den 415 Mass 1106, 616 NE2d 809, 21 MLW 3036.

44. C. Robert Nattress & Associates v CIDCO(4th Dist) 184 Cal App 3d 55, 229 Cal Rptr 33; Smith v Johnson, 245 Mont 137, 798 P2d 106; Sunrise Assoc. v Pilot Realty Co. (1st Dept) 170 pp Div 2d 214, 565 NYS2d 108.
Forms: Notice—Purchaser's tender of performance for specific performance of purchase agreement. 24 Am Jr Pl & Pr Forms (Rev), Vendor and Purchaser, Form 50.1.

45. Covington v Countryside Inv. Co., 263 Ga 125, 428 SE2d 562, 93 Fulton County D R 1677.

46. Bellamah v Schmider, 68 NM 247, 360 P2d 656.

Under Alabama law, equity will not decree specific performance of conveyance of land where the vendor has no title. Health Science Prods. v Taylor (In re Hearlth Science Prods.)

continued

far as he is able, with an abatement of the purchase price sufficient to compensate for the defect in title or the deficiency in quantity.[47]

> **IIII** *Observation:* The equitable remedy f specific performance and the remedy of injunctive relief against breach of contract have much in common; the power of the court in either case is intended to bring about full performance of the contract.[48]

A contractual provision may prevent an award of specific performance in favor of the purchaser; for example, a city is entitled to cancel its proposed sale of real estate and obtain dismissal of the buyer's causes of action for specific performance and damages, even though the buyer has fulfilled conditions precedent to the planned building of a motel on the lot to be sold, where the terms of sale give the city the option to cancel the sale prior to closing and limit the city's liability to the return of payments made, plus costs of the title search and survey.[49] On the other hand, the vendor cannot force the purchaser to resort to a specific performance remedy provided by contract by the filing of a consent to have the parties' original contract enforced, as well as by agreeing to such enforcement in its amended answer and counterclaim; in the absence of any contractual language making the remedy exclusive, the vendor's consent to specific performance does not preclude the purchaser from seeking any other form of additional relief.[50]

§ 605.—Under Uniform Land Transactions Act

Under the Uniform Land Transactions Act, specific performance may be decreed against a seller and, if the seller is unable to convey the full interest he or she contracted to convey because of a defect in title or otherwise, the seller may be compelled, except as otherwise provided in the Act, to convey the interest he or she has and to pay damages to the buyer.[51] If a seller is able to convey so small a part of that which he or she contacted to convey, in quantity, quality, or interest, as to make it inequitable specifically to enforce the contract and award damages for breach, the court may refuse specific performance or grant specific performance upon terms the court deems equitable.[52]

land where the vendor has no title. Health Science Prods. v Taylor (In re Health Science Prods.) (BC ND Ala) 183 BR 903 (also holding that, until the date specified by contract for legal title to be transferred, the vendee is not entitled to specific performance).

47. 71 Am Jur 2d, Specific Performance § 116.

48. 42 Am Jur 2d, Injunctions § 288.

As to injunctive relief as a remedy available to a purchaser of real estate, generally, see § 599.

49. L.J.B. Corp. v New York (1st Dept) 182 App Div 2d 485, 581 NYS2d 798, app den 80 NY2d 755, 588 NYS2d 823, 602 NE2d 231 (holding that the buyer's disappointment was not enough to surmount the language of the sales contract, or to negate the openly functional purpose of the cancellation option).

50. King v Lindley (Tex App Corpus Christi) 697 SW2d 749, writ ref n r e (Jan 15, 1986) (stating that the purchaser has the right to elect whether it wishes to attempt to obtain specific performance of the contract, rather than having the vendor choose its remedy for it).

Forms: Failure of performance by seller—Election of purchaser's rights. 15B am Jur Legal Forms 2d, Real Estate ales § 219:858.

51. Uniform Land Transactions Act § 2-511(a).

52. Uniform Land Transactions Act § 2-511(b).

FIGURE 8.7

BENEVOLENT SOCIETY. Benevolent association. Spring Park Ass'n v. Rosedale Park Amusement Co., 216 Ala. 549, 114 So. 43, 44. In English law, "benevolent societies" are societies established and registered under the Friendly Societies Act, 1875, for any charitable or benevolent purposes.

BENEVOLENTIA REGIS HABENDA. The form in ancient fines and submissions to purchase the king's pardon and favor in order to be restored to place, title or estate. Paroch.Antiq. 172.

BENHURST. In Berkshire, a remedy for the inhabitants thereof to levy money recovered against them on the statute of hue and cry. 39 Eliz. c. 25.

BENIGNE FACIENDÆ SUNT INTERPRETATIONES CHARTARUM, UT RES MAGIS VALEAT QUAM PEREAT; ET QUÆ LIBET CONCESSIO FORTISSIME CONTRA DONATOREM INTERPRETANDA EST. Liberal interpretations are to be made of deeds, so that the purpose may rather stand than fall; and every grant is to be taken most strongly against the grantor. Hayes v. Kershow, 1 Sandf.Ch. (N.Y.) 258, 268.

BEGIGNE FACIENDÆ SUNT INTERPRETATIONES, PROPTER SIMPLICITATEM LAICORUM, UT RES MAGIS VALEAT QUAM PEREAT; ET VERBA INTENTIONI, NON E CONTRA, DEBENT INSERVIRE. Constructions [of written instruments] are to be made liberally, on account of the simplicity of the laity, [or common people,] in order that the thing [or subject-matter] may rather have effect than perish, [or become void]; and words must be subject to the intention, not the intention to the words. 2 Bla.Com. 379; 1 Bulstr. 175; Krider v. Lafferty, 1 Whart. (Pa.) 315.

BENIGNIOR SENTENTIA IN VERBIS GENERALIBUS SEU DUBIIS, EST PRÆFERENDA. The more favorable construction is to be placed on general or doubtful expressions. 2 Kent 557.

BENIGNIUS LEGES INTERPRETANDÆ SUNT QUO VOLUNTAS EARUM CONSERVETUR. Laws are to be more liberally interpreted, in order that their intent may be preserved. Dig. 1, 3, 18.

BENZINE. A crude petroleum distillate. George K. Hale Mfg. Co. v. Hafleigh & Co., C.C.A.Pa., 52 F.2d 714, 718.

BEQUEATH. To give personal property by will to another. Fielding v. Alkire, 124 Kan. 592, 261 P. 597, 599. It therefore is distinguishable from "devise," which is properly used of realty Stubbs v. Abel, 114 Or. 610, 233 P. 852, 857; Fleck v. Harmstad, 155 A. 875, 876, 309 Pa. 302, 77 A.L.R. 874.

But if the context clearly shows the intention of the testator to use the word "bequeath" as synonymous with "devise," it may be held to pass real property. Stubbs v. Abel, 114 Or. 610, 233 ZP. 852, 859.

BEQUEST. A gift by will of personal property; a legacy. In re Fratt's Estate, 60 Mont. 526, 199 P. 711, 714; In re Wood's Estate 6 N.W.2d 846, 848, 232 Iowa 1004; Disposition of realty in will is termed "devise." Grand Island Trust Co. v. Snell 249 N.W. 293, 125 Neb. 148.

The term does not mean a "gift" in the narrow sense of a voluntary act of charity or good will, but ordinarily means a testamentary disposition of the testator's personalty. First Presbyterian Church of Mt. Vernon v. Dennis. 178 Iowa, 1352, 161 N.W. 183, 185, L.R.A.1917C, 1005. It is not necessarily limited to a gratuity, and may include a recompense. U.S. v. Merriam, 4 S.Ct. 69, 70, 263 U.S. 179, 68 L.Ed. 240, 29 A.L.R. 1547.

"Bequest" and "devise" are often used synonymously. In re McGovern's Estate, 77 Mont. 182, 250 P. 812, 817.

Conditional Bequest

One the taking effect or continuing of which depends upon the happening or non-occurrence of a particular event. Merrill V. College, 74 Wis. 415, 43 N.W. 104.

Executory Bequest

The bequest of a future, deferred, or contingent interest in personalty.

Residuary Bequest

A gift of all the remainder of the testator's personal estate, after payment of debts and legacies, etc.

Specific Bequest

One whereby the testator gives to the legatee all his property of a certain class or kind; as all his pure personalty.

BERAT. Also *barat.* A warrant or patent of dignity or privilege given by an Oriental monarch. Cent. Dict.

BERBIAGE. A rent paid for the pasturing of sheep. Wharton.

BERCARIA. In old English law, a sheepfold; also a place where the bark of trees was laid to tan.

BERCAURUS, or BERCATOR A shepherd.

BERWEICHA, or BEREWICA. In old English law. A term used in Domesday for a village or hamlet belonging to some town or manor.

BERG. A rock (Cent. Dict.); a hill (Wharton); in South Africa, a mountain (Webster).

BERGHMAYSTER. An officer having charge of a mine. A bailiff or chief officer among the Derbyshire miners, who, in addition to his other duties, executes the office of coroner among them. Blount; Cowell.

BERGHMOTH, or BERGHMOTE. The ancient name of the court now called "barmote," *(q. v.).*

BERIA, BERIE, or BERRY. A plain; a large open field. Wharton. See Berr.

BERM BANK. A ledge at the bottom of a cutting or bank, as of a creek, to catch earth that may roll down the slope, or to strengthen the bank. Miller v. State, 149 N.Y.S. 788, 789, 164 App.Div. 522.

III. LEGAL RESEARCH ASSIGNMENTS

A. Exercise 8.1: *Corpus Juris Secundum*

1. Which volume of the *Corpus Juris Secundum* is this?
   a. 464
   b. 51
   c. 51A
   d. 452
2. An arbitrator should be qualified for the position and should have a fundamental understanding of the dispute.
   a. True b. False
3. Which case holds that substitution of an arbitrator does not render a grievance incapable of arbitration?
   a. *Boston Mutual Life Ins. Co. v. Insurance Agents Int. Union*
   b. *Arnold v. United Air Lines*
   c. *D'Elia v. New York*
   d. *Flores v. Barnem*
4. The dispute concerning arbitration arose from the interpretation of a union contract.
   a. True b. False
5. Members of adjustment or system boards are considered naturally neutral.
   a. True b. False
6. If the collective bargaining agreement has no language or provisions relating to an arbitrator making an award or decision, the authority of any arbitrator can be questioned.
   a. True b. False
7. Which case holds that arbitrators are partial when they make their views known in advance of the formal decision?
   a. *W.V. Tel. Co. v. Selly*
   b. *Simons v. N. Syndicate*
   c. *Publishers v. N.Y. Typographical Union No. 6*
   d. None of the above
8. Hearings on grievances in the railway system shall be held first before an officer of the carrier.
   a. True b. False
9. From which jurisdiction do most of these decisions come?
   a. Illinois
   b. New York
   c. Connecticut
   d. District of Columbia
10. Encyclopedia citations lack which essential part?
    a. Dates
    b. Page numbers
    c. Reporter cites
    d. None of the above

provided for in the arbitration agreement[5] except to the extent it may be authorized by statute to appoint an arbitrator.[6]

Under a permissive statute, the parties to a collective bargaining contract may authorize a labor board to appoint the arbitrators,[7] but until mediation occurs, the obligation to select an arbitrator may not be triggered by the statute.[8] Where, however, the statute provides for the appointment of a conciliator by a state board where the collective bargaining process reaches a stalemate, a hearing and evidence are not preconditions to such an appointment.[9]

Collective bargaining agreements frequently provide for a tripartite arbitration board; one made up of members selected by management, an equal number selected by labor and one or more neutrals.[10] Unlike ordinary arbitration, where the arbitrators are expected to be neutral and disinterested, it is anticipated that the labor and management members will be somewhat partisan,[11] but the board should not be dominated by one member.[12] Persons who participated in arbitration without objection may not object that the arbitrators were not impartial in that one had been selected by union and one by the employer and that only the third was impartial.[13]

Ordinarily, the parties will not be permitted to attack the qualification as arbitrator or impartial chairman whom they selected.[14] Thus, a contention that an arbitrator is not impartial is immaterial where the arbitrator is selected in the manner provided for by the contract.[15] If one of the parties agrees that the award should be made by certain designated persons, he or she thereby waives objection to any apparent bias.[16] However, where an impartial or neutral arbitrator is selected without disclosure by him or her that he or she is in fact interested or had had business relations with one of the parties, he or she is disqualified.[17] Where during the course of the proceeding an event occurs which affects the qualifications of the arbitrator, he or she may become disqualified to act further on the objection of a party.[18] A charge of partiality is not sustained by showing that the arbitrator erred on the law and facts or made known his or her views in advance of the formal decision,[19] and an employer's filing of an intentional interference with contract suit against an arbitrator hearing the employment dispute will not give the arbitrator an interest in the outcome of arbitration, thereby automatically disqualifying him or her.[20] Likewise, evidence that an arbitrator hearing a dispute between an employer and the trustees of union pension and welfare funds has been retained

proceeding concerning labor arbitration, 59 A.L.R. Fed. 733.

[5]Nev.—United Ass'n of Journeymen and Apprentices of Plumbing and Pipe Fitting Industry of U.S. and Canada, Local Union No. 525, Las Vegas v. Eighth Judicial Dist. Court In and For Clark County, 82 Nev. 103, 412 P.2d 352 (1966).

[6]N.Y.—Application of William Faehndrich Inc., 15 Misc. 2d 370, 181 N.Y.S.2d 918 (Sup. 1959).

[7]Wis.—Dunphy Boat Corp. v. Wisconsin Employment Relations Bd., 267 Wis. 316, 64 N.W.2d 866 (1954).

[8]Pa.—Lancaster County v. Pennsylvania Labor Relations Bd., 761 A.2d 1250 (Pa. Commw. Ct. 2000), appeal granted, 565 Pa. 678, 775 A.2d 810 (2001).

[9]Wis.—Wisconsin Telephone Co. v. Wisconsin Employment Relations Bd., 253 Wis. 584, 34 N.W.2d 844 (1948).

[10]Nev.—United Ass'n of Journeymen and Apprentices of Plumbing and Pipe Fitting Industry of U.S. and Cando, Local Union N. 525, Las Vegas v. Eighth Judicial Dist. Court In and For Clark County, 82 Nev. 103, 412 P.2d 352 (1966).

[11]Nev.—United Ass'n of Journeymen and Apprentices of Plumbing and Pipe Fitting Industry of U.S. and Canada, Local Union No. 525, Las Vegas v. Eighth Judicial Dist. Court In and For Clark County, 82 Nev. 103, 412 P.2d 352 (1966).

[12]Wash.—Gord v. F. S. Harmon & Co., 188 Wash. 134, 61 P.2d 1294 (1936).

[13]La.—Johnson v. Jahncke Service, Inc., 147 So. 2d 247 (La. Ct. App. 4th Cir. 1962).

[14]N.Y.—Suffridge v. Metropolitan Package Store Ass'n, 87 N.Y.S.2d 75 (Sup 1949), judgment aff'd, 275 A.D. 801, 88 N.Y.S.2d 913 (1st Dep't 1949).

[15]U.S.—Jenni, Inc. v. Illinois District Council No. 1 of Intern. Union of Bricklayers and Allied Craftworkers, AFL-CIO, 170 L.R.R.M. (BNA) 3217, 2002 WL 1968565 (N.D. Ill. 2002).

[16]Or.—Rueda v. Union Pac. R. Co., 180 Or. 133, 175 P.2d 78 (1946).

Annotation References: Setting aside arbitration award on ground of interest or bias of arbitrator—labor disputes, 66 A.L.R. 5th 611.

[17]N.Y.—Application of Siegal, 153 N.Y.S.2d 673 (Sup 1956).

[18]N.Y.—Application of Steuen, 97 N.Y.S.2d 613 (Sup 1950).

continued

as a "permanent arbitrator" to preside over contribution delinquency hearings does not show that the arbitrator is biased or lacks neutrality.[21]

An arbitrator appointed by the court to adjust and settle a controversy, arising out of a labor dispute, such as a strike, must have the proper qualifications and ability for the performance of such duties,[22] and the removal of an arbitrator, so appointed, is within the discretion of the court.[23] It is not sufficient to justify his or her appointment that he or she possesses honesty and integrity, if he or she has evinced a course of conduct showing an ardor of advocacy for the cause of labor, and, where such fact is established, the court which appointed the arbitrator may declare the office of arbitrator, on the emotion of the employer.[24] Where, there is a constitutional provision prohibiting the delegation of legislative power to an arbitrator empowered to make binding decisions on a public collective bargaining agreement, however, any arbitrator appointed must be politically accountable to an elected official.[25]

§ 552 Members of railroad boards

Members of adjustment or system boards are not in fact or legal contemplation supposed to be neutral.

Research References

West's Key Number Digest, Labor Relations ⚷ 453

Members of adjustment or systems boards under the Railway Labor Act are not in fact or in legal contemplation supposed to be neutral; they are carrier and labor organization representatives.[1] Such a board is bipartisan rather than impartial and disinterested.[2] However, provision is made for the appointment of a neutral person known as a referee in the event of a deadlock.[3]

The member of a special board of adjustment created pursuant to an arbitration award need not be impartial, disinterested, and without bias.[4]

Under the Railway Labor Act, it is contemplated that the hearings of a grievance will be before an officer of the carrier, and it is only when the case reaches the adjustment board that the employee is entitled to a hearing before an impartial hearing officer.[5]

4. Authority of Arbitrators

§ 553 Generally

The arbitrators of labor disputes have such power and authority as are conferred on them by the collective bargaining contract or submission under which they act.

Research References

West's Key Number Digest, Labor Relations ⚷ 454

Arbitrators are part of a system of self-government created by and confined to the

---

Objection prior to hearing

U.S.—Black v. National Football League Players Ass'n, 87 F. Supp. 2d 1 (D.D.C. 2000).

[19]N.Y.—Publishers Ass'n of New York City v. New York City Typographical Union No. 6, 168 misc. 267, 5 N.Y.S.2d 847 (Sup 1938).

[20]U.S.—National Football League Players Ass'n v. Office and Professional Employees Intern. Union Local 2, 947 F. Supp. 540 (D.D.C. 1996), aff'd, 1997 WL 362761 (D.C. Cir. 1997).

[21]U.S.—Teamsters-Employer Local No. 945 Pension Fund v. Acme Sanitation Corp. 963 F. Supp. 340 (D.N.J. 1997).

[22]N.Y.—W.U. Tel. Co. v. Selly, 60 N.Y.S.2d 411 (Sup 1946), order aff'd, 270 A.D. 938, 61 N.Y.S.2d 911 (1st Dep't 1946), appeal granted, 270 A.D. 894, 62 N.Y.S.2d 604 (1st Dep't 1946) and order aff'd, 295 N.Y. 395, 68 N.E.2d 183 (1946).

[23]N.Y.—W. U. Tel. Co. v Selly, 295 N.Y. 395, 68 N.E.2d 183 (1946).

[24]N.Y.—W.U. Tel. Co. v. Selly, 60 N.Y.S.2d 411 (Sup 1946), order aff'd, 270 A.D. 839, 61 N.Y.S.2d 911 (1st Dep't 1946), appeal granted, 270 A.D. 894, 62 N.Y.S.2d 604 (1st Dep't 1946) and order aff'd, 295 N.Y. 395, 68 N.E.2d 183 (1946).

[25]Colo.—Fraternal Order of Police, Colorado Lodge #519 b. City of Commerce City, 996 P.2d 133 (Colo. 2000), as modified on denial of reh'g, (Apr. 10, 2000).

[Section 552]

[1]U.S.—Arnold v. United Air Lines, Inc., 296 F.2d 191 (7th Cir. 1961).

[2]U.S.—Arnold v. United Air Lines, Inc., 296 F.2d 191 (7th Cir. 1961).

[3]U.S.—Arnold v. United Air Lines, Inc., 296 F.2d 191 (7th Cir. 1961).

[4]U.S.—Brotherhood of R. R. Trainmen v. Chicago, M., St. P. & P. R. Co. (Lines East), 237 F. Supp. 404 (D. D.C. 1964).

Annotation References: Setting aside arbitration award on ground of interest or bias or arbitrator—labor disputes, 66 A.L.R. 5th 611.

[5]U.S.—D'Elia v. New York, N. H. & N. R. R., 338 F.2d 701 (2d Cir. 1964).

B. Exercise 8.2: *American Jurisprudence, 2d*

1. Compensation statutes normally state that the worker injured or disabled due to employment must pay for medical care until it is determined that the injuries are compensable.
   a. True
   b. False
2. Which of the following cases states that one can be simultaneously incapacitated and disfigured?
   a. *Aetna Life Ins. Co. v. Moses*
   b. *Dayton Power and Light v. Westinghouse*
   c. *Scalora v. Dattco, Inc.*
   d. *State v. Vinther*
3. A worker cannot change his or her physician under any circumstances.
   a. True
   b. False
4. Where is a form for an employer's agreement with a physician found?
   a. 20 Am Jur Legal Forms 2d, Workmen's Compensation § 267:51
   b. 25 Am Jur Pl & Pr Forms (Rev), Workmen's Compensation, Form 72
   c. 7 Am Jur POF3d 143
   d. All of the above
5. Which section in the encyclopedia would be consulted regarding compensation for artificial limbs?
   a. 435-442
   b. 80
   c. 393
   d. None of the above

C. Exercise 8.3: *American Jurisprudence, 2d,* Topical Outline

1. For more information on a charge of vagrancy for an intoxicated individual, consult 45 Am Jur 2d, Intoxicating Liquors § 36.
   a. True
   b. False
2. Which constitutional amendments would be relevant to the issue of vagrancy?
   a. 4
   b. 1
   c. 8
   d. All of the above
3. Vagrancy and loitering appear to be the same offense.
   a. True
   b. False
4. In the ALR index, the following keywords are suggested.
   a. Begging
   b. Due process
   c. Police power
   d. All of the above
5. Loitering is never connected with illegal drug activity.
   a. True
   b. False

§ 432. Duration of awards for death

The duration of workers' compensation awards to dependents for the death of a worker are generally fixed by statute, as, for example, where the statute provides that death benefits paid to a surviving dependent parent are to continue as long as the parent is not independently self-supporting.[98] Alternatively, the statute may provide that a parent who is dependent upon a deceased worker at the time of the worker's death may receive benefits for life notwithstanding any subsequent improvement in his or her economic circumstances.[99] Death benefits to a surviving spouse are often payable for life or until remarriage,[1] or for a specified maximum length of time.[2] The remarriage of a surviving spouse may entitle him or her to a lump sum payment, after which no more benefits are payable to him or her.[3]

> ▮▮▮▮ *Observation:* The statute may also permit termination of death benefits where the surviving spouse enters into a meretricious relationship.[4]

Death benefits to children are generally payable until the child has attained the age specified by statute at which he or she is no longer conclusively presumed to be dependent.[5] Once the child has attained this age, the statute may direct that benefits cease, or may permit continued payment of benefits upon proof of actual dependency.[6]

§ 433. Waiting time

Workers' compensation acts generally provide that an injured worker must have been disabled or have missed work for a certain number of days following an injury in order to be eligible for benefits based on disability.[7] It has been held under such a provision that a 7-day waiting period for eligibility for benefits referred to working days rather than calendar days.[8] In some jurisdictions the waiting period applies only to benefits for temporary total, as distinguished from temporary partial, disability.[9] Some statutes provide that benefits will be paid for the waiting period if the worker is ultimately disabled for a certain period of time.[10]

§ 434. Awards for separate injuries as concurrent or consecutive

As to whether awards for separate compensable injuries run concurrently or consecutively, several cases have held that payments, or periods of payment,

98. Goodwin v R. E. H. Corp. (3d Dept) 69 App Div 2d 973, 416 NYS2d 91.

99. Deguffroy & Associates, Inc. v Workmen's Compensation Appeal Board (Bianchetti), 94 Pa Cmwlth 566, 503 A2d 994.

1. Martin v Rollins Services Inc. (La App 4th Cir) 424 So 2d 429.

2. Employers National Ins. Co. v Winters (App) 101 NM 315, 681 P2d 741 (600 weeks).

3. Lackey v D & M Trucking, 9 Kan App 2d 679, 687 P2d 23; Employers National Ins. Co. v Winters (App) 101 NM 315, 681 P2d 741.

4. Nevius v Workmen's Compensation Appeal Board, 52 Pa Cmwlth 418, 416 A2d 1134.

5. § 579.

6. § 579.

7. Pinkston v General Tire & Rubber Co., 30 Ark App 46, 782 SW2d 375; Wright v Rhode Island Superior Court (RI) 535 A2d 318 (3 days).

8. Western Surety Co. v Mydland, 85 SD 172, 179 NW2d 3.

9. Volan v Keller (Jefferson Co) 20 Ohio App 2d 204, 49 Ohio Ops 2d 286, 253 NE2d 309.

10. Commonwealth, Dept. of Transp. v Workmen's Compensation Appeal Bd. (Hockenberry), 106 Pa Cmwlth 511, 527 A2d 197 (statute providing for 7-day waiting period also provided that if disability extends for more than 14 days, compensation is paid for entire period of disability, including the first 7 days).

should not be made or computed concurrently, but consecutively.[11] In some cases this rule has been justified by the need to avoid allowing the aggregate of the awards for separate injuries to exceed the maximum weekly allowance prescribed by the act.[12] In other cases, however, it has been held that payments, or periods of payment, run concurrently.[13] The payment of benefits for disfigurement concurrently with disability benefits arising from the same accident has also been approved.[14]

E. Medical, Surgical, Nursing, Hospital, and Burial Services [§§ 435–445]

Research References

ALR Digests: Workers' Compensation §§ 75(1), 75(2)
Index to Annotations: Workers' Compensation
25 Am Jur Pl & Pr Forms (Rev), Workmen's Compensation, Form 72
20 Am Jur Legal Forms 2d, Workmen's Compensation § 267:51
7 Am Jur POF3d 143, Workers' Compensation for Attendant Care Services by Family Members

---

1. In General [§§ 435–442]

§ 435. Generally

The compensation statutes usually provide that a worker injured or disabled in the course of employment shall be furnished with proper medical or surgical care and treatment, including nursing and hospitalization, at the expense of the employer, insurer, or compensation fund.[15] Compensable medical benefits may include psychiatric treatment necessitated by a physical

11. Dunn v Eaton, 233 Ky 699, 26 SW2d 513; Limron v Blair, 181 Mich 76, 147 NW 546; Hamilton & Hartman v Badgett, 164 Okla 31, 22 P2d 350; Leos v State Employees Workers' Compensation Div. (Tex) 734 SW2d 341 (worker who lost the use of both feet for 5 years was entitled to compensation for 250 weeks rather than 125 weeks).

12. State ex rel. Minneapolis Office & School Furniture Co. v District Court of Hennepin County, 136 Minn 447, 162 NW 527.

13. Nelson v Service Oil Co., 121 Neb 762, 238 NW 525; Erickson v Preuss, 223 NY 365, 119 NE 555; Barlock v Orient Coal & Coke Co., 319 Pa 119, 178 A 840, 99 ALR 893.

14. Scalora v Dattco, Inc., 39 Conn Supp 449, 466 A2d 334 (distinguishing prior consecutive awards for total and partial disability, based on concurrent separate injuries, on the basis of statutory language and the fact that while one cannot at the same time be totally and partly incapacitated, one can be simultaneously incapacitated and disfigured).

15. Olson v AIC/Martin J. V. (Alaska) 818 P2d 669; J. T. Thorp, Inc. v Workers' Compensation Appeals Board (3d Dist) 153 Cal App 3d 327, 200 Cal Rptr 219; Pokorny v Getta's Garage, 219 Conn 439, 594 A2d 446; Davis v South Carolina Dept. of Corrections, 289 SC 123, 345 SE2d 245.

For discussion of an employer liability for failing to furnish medical treatment to an employee under a special contract obligating the employer to furnish such treatment, see § 80.

As to the liability of an employer for the negligence of a physician treating a worker, see § 441.

For discussion of the liability of an employer as affected by his having gratuitously furnished medical, surgical, or nursing services, see § 240.

For discussion of the effect on the right to compensation of a worker's failure to submit to medical treatment of an injury, see § 389.

Forms: Employer's agreement with physician—Medical services to be furnished to employees. 20 Am Jur Legal Forms 2d, Workmen's Compensation § 267:51.

injury,[16] and the furnishing of therapeutic devices or appliances.[17] A worker's entitlement to such medical benefits generally lasts as long as treatment is necessary.[18]

Entitlement to medical benefits is not necessarily coextensive with a period of disability resulting from a compensable injury.[19] Medical benefits may be paid before entitlement to disability benefits has been established,[20] and after such benefits stop.[21] Under some statutes, however, entitlement to remedial medical care ceases following maximum medical improvement of the worker's condition.[22]

> **IIII** *Observation:* The rule that the cessation of worker's compensation payments based on disability does not affect the worker's entitlement to medical benefits has been followed in cases where the employer's liability for disability payments was settled by payment of a lump sum.[23]

§ 436. Choice of physician rendering services

Under some workers' compensation statutes, an injured employee may choose his or her physician subject to administrative approval,[24] while under others the employer is entitled to designate the physician.[25] Under a third approach, the worker is permitted to choose a physician from a list approved by the employer[26] or by the state agency charged with administration of the workers' compensation statute.[27]

16. Peeples v Home Indem. Co. (Tex Civ App San Antonio) 617 SW2d 274 (jury's finding that medical care by psychiatrist was not reasonably required for worker as result of leg injury was against the great weight and preponderance of the evidence in view of psychiatrist's testimony as to treatment's natural relationship with the worker's loss of the use of his leg, and testimony of orthopedic surgeon that he had referred worker to psychiatrist).

17. Miami v Harris (Fla App D1) 452 So 2d 115 (self-insured employer would be required to reimburse injured worker for funds worker expended purchasing therapeutic hospital bed, where bed was prescribed by authorized, treating physician and was reasonable and necessary medical expense); State ex rel. General Motors Corp., Assembly Div. v Industrial Com. of Ohio (Franklin Co) 30 Ohio App 3d 57, 30 Ohio BR 112, 506 NE2d 269 (approving benefits for purchase of whirlpool bath pursuant to physician's prescription).

For medical benefits as including the furnishing of artificial limbs, see § 393.

18. Miller v Weyerhaeuser Co., 77 Or App 402, 713 P2d 643; Mountain States Casing Services v McKean (Utah) 706 P2d 601.

19. Brown v Georgia Casualty & Surety Co. (La App 2d Cir) 490 So 2d 639 (superseded by statute on other grounds as stated in Frazier v Conagra, Inc. (La App 2d Cir) 552 So 2d 536, cert den (La) 559 So 2d 124).

20. J. T. Thorp, Inc. v Workers' Comp. Appeals Bd. (3rd Dist) 153 Cal App 3d 327, 200 Cal Rptr 219 (noting that medical benefits are payable for any injury or disease arising from employment regardless of whether disability results).

21. Mad Butcher, Inc. v Parker, 4 Ark App 124, 628 SW2d 582 (superseded by statute on other grounds as stated in Wright Contracting Co. v Randall, 12 Ark App 358, 676 SW2d 750); Glover v Industrial Com. of Illinois (3d Dist) 140 Ill App 3d 361, 92 Ill Dec 794, 485 NE2d 605.

22. Gainesville v Helton (Fla App D1) 458 So 2d 1195, 9 FLW 2378, later proceeding (Fla App D1) 543 So 2d 820, 14 FLW 1159.

23. Brooks v Arkansas-Best Freight System, Inc., 247 Ark 61, 444 SW2d 246; Depue v Barsh Truck Lines (Okla) 493 P2d 80.

24. Burrgess v Industrial Com. (1st Dist) 169 Ill App 3d 670, 120 Ill Dec 118, 523 NE2d 1029; Schofield v Great Atlantic & Pacific Tea Co., 299 NC 582, 264 SE2d 56; Reynaga v Northwest Farm Bureau, 300 Or 255, 709 P2d 1071 (statute permitting worker to choose physician within state).

25. Electro-Air v Villines, 16 Ark App 102, 697 SW2d 932.

26. Home Ins. Co. v Dickey (Tex Civ App Amarillo) 552 SW2d 552.

27. Medical Associates of Capitol Hill v District of Columbia Dept. of Employment Services (Dist Col App) 565 A2d 86.

A worker who receives and pays for medical care from a physician other than the one rightfully designated by the employer or the agency will not be reimbursed for the expenses of such care.[28] However, if an authorized treating physician, in the exercise of medical judgment, refers the worker to another physician, the bills of the second physician are compensable even though he or she is not on the list of approved physicians from which the worker could have made an initial choice.[29]

If an employer required to do so by statute refuses to designate a list of physicians to an employee in need of compensable medical care, the employee may secure such care from a licensed physician of his own choice and receive compensation accordingly.[30]

> **IIII** *Caution:* An employer whose choice of treating physician is unreasonable under the circumstances may be required to pay medical expenses incurred by a worker in consulting a physician of the worker's own choice.[31]

§ 437. Worker's right to change of physician

A worker dissatisfied with the care provided for a compensable injury by his or her present physician may petition the agency administering the workers' compensation statute for permission to consult and receive treatment from another physician.[32] Although some jurisdictions will permit such a change in the absence of a determination by the agency that it is not in the worker's best interest,[33] under other statutes a stronger showing is required, as, for example, where the statute requires proof that the medical care currently being provided is injurious to the health of the worker.[34]

A worker who fails to receive the required authorization before effecting a change of physician is not entitled to reimbursement of the costs incurred in consulting the new physician.[35] This rule applies even where the worker, under

28. Manatee Memorial Hospital v Love (Fla App D1) 382 So 2d 751.

29. Genpak Corp. v Gibson (Ala App) 534 So 2d 312; Green v Chromalloy-Turbocumbustor (Fla App D1) 540 So 2d 874, 14 FLW 597.

30. Roadway Express, Inc. v Workmen's Compensation Appeal Bd. (Ostir), 104 Pa Cmwlth 7, 520 A2d 1261.

31. Commercial Carrier Corp. v Fox (Fla App D1) 400 So 2d 154, holding that an employer was required to pay for medical treatment provided an employee by his home-town physician, from whom the employee had received both emergency and remedial treatment without authorization, where the employer had insisted on referring the employee to physicians located approximately 50 miles from his home, despite the fact that the employee had a painful back which would be aggravated by riding long distances, and where the employer subsequently referred the employee to a local physician whose practice was limited to obstetrics and gynecology and who was unsuited to treat the employee for a severe arthritic condition.

32. Sterling Stores v Deen, 16 Ark App 36, 696 SW2d 784.

33. Ellerbee v Concorde Roofing Co. (Fla App) 487 So 2d 388, 11 FLW 961.

34. Kennecott Copper Corp. v Industrial Com. of Arizona (App) 115 Ariz 184, 564 P2d 407.

35. Kennecott Copper Corp. v Industrial Com. of Arizona (App) 115 Ariz 184, 564 P2d 407.

Where a workers' compensation claimant had reached maximum medical improvement and had been released by her treating physician at the time she expressed dissatisfaction with the physician's services and requested a change of physicians, she was required to obtain an order from the deputy commissioner requiring the compensation carrier to furnish additional medical treatment, and where the claimant enlisted the aid of a second physician without such an order, the deputy properly found that the carrier could not be held responsible for payment of the second doctor's charges. Oak Crest Enterprises, Inc. v Ford (Fla App D1)

EXERCISE 8.3

VAGRANCY AND RELATED OFFENSES

by

Tracy A. Bateman, J. D.

Scope of Topic: This article discusses the criminal offense of vagrancy, as defined by common law or statute, and other related offenses such as loitering and begging, which have been widely prohibited by statutes that have generally replaced traditional vagrancy laws. It includes discussions concerning acts generally constituting vagrancy, loitering, and related offenses, and the validity of statutes and ordinances governing such offenses.

Federal Aspects: This article discusses challenges to laws criminalizing vagrancy, loitering, begging, and related offenses based on various provisions of the United States Constitution.

Treated Elsewhere:

Crimes of status, mode of life, or reputation, generally, see 21 Am Jur 2d, Criminal Law § 32

Curfew, imposition of as violation of right to travel, see 16A Am Jur 2d, Constitutional Law § 610

Curfew ordinances, see 42 Am Jur 2d, Infants § 19; 56 Am Jur 2d, Municipal Corporations, Counties, and Other Political Subdivisions § 486

Disorderly conduct, see 12 Am Jur 2d, Breach of Peace and Disorderly Conduct

Exclusion from United States of alien who is a professional beggar or vagrant, see 3A Am Jur 2d, Aliens and Citizens § 807

Gambling, see 38 Am Jur 2d, Gambling

Habitual criminals, see 39 Am Jur 2d, Habitual Criminals and Subsequent Offenders

Impeachment of witness by showing that he or she has been convicted of vagrancy, see 81 Am Jur 2d, Witnesses § 191

Income obtained from begging as bearing on question of earnings of person seeking workers' compensation benefits, see 82 Am Jur 2d, Workers' Compensation § 426

Keeping houses of prostitution or ill fame, see 24 Am Jur 2d, Disorderly Houses

Loitering for the purposes of prostitution, statutes prohibiting, see 63C Am Jur 2d, Prostitution § 12

Prostitution, generally, see 63C Am Jur 2d, Prostitution

Public drunkenness, see 45 Am Jur 2d, Intoxicating Liquors § 36

Trespass, see 75 Am Jur 2d, Trespass

Research References

Text References:

McQuillin, Municipal Corporations (3rd ed.) §§ 24.108-24.110

Torcia, Wharton's Criminal Law (14th ed) §§ 535-537

Annotation References:

ALR Digest: Highways and Streets; Municipal Corporations; Vagrancy

ALR Index: Begging; Constitutional Law; Due Process; Equal Protection of Law;

75

Freedom of Association; Freedom of Speech and Press; Municipal Corporations; Overbreadth; Police Power; Vagrancy and Loitering

Practice References:

8 Am Jur Pl & Pr Forms (Rev), Criminal Procedure

13 Am Jur POF2d 609, Discriminatory Enforcement of Criminal Law

Federal Legislation:

US Const, Amends 1, 4, 8, 14

Insta-Cite®: Cases referred to herein can be further researched through the **Insta-Cite®** computer-assisted research service. Use Insta-Cite to check citations for form, parallel references, and prior and later history.

Table of Parallel References

To convert General Index references to section references in this volume, or to ascertain the disposition (or current equivalent) of sections of articles in the prior edition of this publication, see the Table of Parallel References beginning at p xi.

Outline

I. STATUTES AND ORDINANCES DEFINING PARTICULAR PERSONS AS VAGRANTS

§ 1. In general
§ 2. Validity of vagrancy laws

II. STATUTES AND ORDINANCES PROHIBITING LOITERING

§ 3. Validity
§ 4. —Statute based on Model Penal Code provisions
§ 5. Elements; generally
§ 6. —In statutes or ordinances based on Model Penal Code
§ 7. Loitering connected with illegal drug activity
§ 8. In specific locations; schools

continued

III. STATUTES AND ORDINANCES PROHIBITING OTHER ACTIVITIES

I. STATUTES AND ORDINANCES DEFINING PARTICULAR PERSONS AS VAGRANTS [§§ 1, 2]

Research References

ALR Digest: Vagrancy § 1

ALR Index: Constitutional Law; Municipal Corporations; Vagrancy and Loitering

McQuillin, Municipal Corporations (3rd ed) §§ 24.108-24.110

Torcia, Wharton's Criminal Law (14th ed) § 535

---

§ 1. In general

Vagrancy statutes have their origins in feudal laws aimed against runaway serfs, and in the English poor laws.[1] Vagrancy was defined at common law as wandering or going about from place to place by an idle person who has no lawful visible means of support, and who subsists on charity and does not work for a living although he is able so to do.[2] Vagrancy laws have been said to rest upon the economic principle that industry is necessary for the preservation of society, and that he who is able to work, but who deliberately plans to exist by the labor of others, is an enemy to society and to the Commonwealth.[3] It has been stated that a vagrant is a probable criminal, and that the purpose of vagrancy statutes is to prevent crime which may likely flow form his mode of living.[4] Statutory enactments on the subject are generally looked upon as regulatory measures to prevent crime rather than as ordinary criminal laws, which prohibits and punish certain acts as crimes.[5]

1. Fenster v Leary, 20 NY2d 309, 282 NYS2d 739, 229 NE2d 426, 25 ALR3d 784.

2. Parsall v State, 62 Rex Crim 177, 138 SW 759; Huntington v Salyer, 135 W Va 397, 63 SE2d 575.

3. State v Hogan, 63 Ohio St 202, 58 NE 572.

At common law, one of the aims of making a crime of vagrancy was to force the idle to work. Fonte v State, 213 Tenn 204, 373 SW2d 445.

In England, vagrancy was criminalized on the theory that persons not visibly employed were more likely to commit crimes. City of Akron v Rowland, 67 Ohio St 3d 374, 618 NE2d 138.

4. Alegata v Commonwealth, 353 Mass 287, 231 NE2d 201.

In order to prevent the emergence of a class of able-bodied vagrants who would support themselves by preying upon society, and who would threaten the public peace and security, it was determined that individuals were to be compelled to engage in some legitimate and gainful occupation by which they might maintain themselves; thus, the temptation to led a life of crime or to become a public charge was removed. Fenster v Leary, 20 NY2d 309, 282 NYS2d 739, 229 NE2d 426, 25 ALR3d 784.

5. Fenster v Leary, 20 NY2d 309, 282 NYS2d

D. Exercise 8.4: *Barron's Law Dictionary*

1. A sight draft is defined as a draft payable on demand, as is discussed by
   a. 276 p. 262
   b. U.C.C. § 3-108
   c. 405 P.2d 488
   d. All of the above
2. A draft is also defined as a draw.
   a. True
   b. False
3. For more information regarding the liability of a tavern owner for the death of a third party caused by an intoxicated customer of that tavern, see
   a. 158 NE 2d 7
   b. 143 P.2d 952
   c. 45 Am. Jur. 2d 612
   d. 73 Nev. 2d 135
4. Due care is defined as "care which is reasonably commensurate with a known danger and the seriousness of the consequences which are liable to follow its omission" by
   a. *Barron's Law Dictionary*
   b. 438 P.2d 477, 482
   c. 153 S.E.2d 356, 359
   d. 198 S.E.2d 526, 529
5. Which court case formally established the notion that due process of law adjusts with changing jurisprudential values?
   a. 302 U.S. 319
   b. 397 U.S. 254
   c. 341 U.S. 123
   d. Both a and c

E. Exercise 8.5: *Black's Law Dictionary,* 4th Edition

1. Which case did not define as that which a reasonably prudent person would not do?
   a. *Ottenheimer v. Molohan*
   b. *Behen v. Philadelphia*
   c. *Donahue v. R.A. Sherman's Sons Co.*
   d. *Clayton v. Philadelphia*
2. The decision of *Chicago, R.I. & P.R. Co. v. Rogers* stated that "assumption of risk" and "contributory negligence" are synonymous.
   a. True
   b. False
3. Gross negligence is defined as "the failure to exercise slight care" by:
   a. *Jones v. Atchison*
   b. *Burton Construction Co. v. Metcalfe*
   c. Both a and b
   d. Neither a nor b
4. Negligence and incompetence are synonymous.
   a. True
   b. False

Dower rights have been abrogated in many jurisdictions or limited to interests which the husband holds at his death. American Law of Property §§5.31-5.32. Where they still exist, a wife can join in a conveyance and thereby give up her dower rights. ID. at §18.95

DOWRY money and personalty which the wife brings to the husband to support the expenses of marriage; a donation to the maintenance and support of the marriage. See 22 Mo.206, 254.

DRAFT an order in writing directing a person other than the **maker** to pay a specified sum of money to a named person; automobiles are often purchased by used car dealers through 'dealer's drafts," i.e., by a document setting forth a bank's promise to pay on the dealer's behalf for the automobile once it has been properly **indorsed** by the dealer. Drafts may or may not be **negotiable instruments** depending upon whether the elements of negotiability are satisfied. See U.C.C. §3-104(3). Draft is synonymous with BILL OF EXCHANGE although "draft" is the preferred term. See id. at §3-104(2)(a).

SIGHT DRAFT a draft payable on demand. 276 P. 262; U.C.C. §3-108. A bill of exchange for immediate collection. 405 P. 488, 490.

TIME DRAFT a draft which is not payable until a specified future time. For instance, a post-dated check is a time draft. U.C.C. §3-109.

In a military context, the term connotes the compulsory conscription of citizens into the military service.

More generally, it refers to the preliminary form of a legal document (e.g., the draft of a contract—often called "rough draft"). It also refers to the process of preparing or DRAWING a legal document (e.g., drafting a will) or piece of proposed legislation.

DRAM SHOP ACT is a legislative enactment imposing strict liability upon the seller of intoxicating beverages when the sale results in harm to a third party's person, property, or means of support. Under common law, no cause of action existed against the person dispensing intoxicating beverages for the resulting damages that might be inflicted by the intoxicated person. The common law theorized that the **proximate cause** of the injury was not the furnishing of liquor but rather the act of the purchaser in drinking the liquor. 143 P. 2d 952. In many jurisdictions, the legislature has enacted CIVIL DAMAGE ACTS or "dram shop acts" creating a statutory remedy against the seller of intoxicating beverages, provided that the resulting intoxication causes the injury. Under such acts, the plaintiff has a cause of action against the vendor when, by reason of the intoxication of another, he sustains personal injury, property damage, or loss of support. Under this theory, some jurisdictions have held that a wife may recover "for injuries to means of support" when her husband dies as a result of intoxication, either his own or another's. 158 N.E. 2d 7. Since the statute involves strict liability, the plaintiff need not show negligence on the part of the seller. The law is unsettled though, as to the seller's rights of indemnity from the intoxicated person who proximately caused the injury. 45 Am. Jur. 2d 612.

DRAW see draft.

DRAWEE one to whom a **bill of exchange** or a **check** directs a request to pay a certain sum of money specified therein. In the typical checking account situation, the bank is the drawee, the person writing the check is the maker of drawer, and the person to whom the check is written is the **payee.**

DRAWER person who draws a check or bill of exchange.

DRIVING WHILE INTOXICATED [D.W.I.] the offense of operating a motor vehicle while under the influence of alcohol or drugs. State law controls both the definition of "operating," such as whether it includes the actual driving of the car or merely sitting in the car, and the level of intoxication needed in order to be found in violation of the law. Some statutes refer to DRIVING UNDER THE INFLUENCE [D.U.I.] or DRIVING WHILE IMPAIRED and it is possible to do so without being intoxicated. 73 N.W. 2d. 135.

DROIT (*drwäh*)—Fr: a right; law; the whole body of the law.

DRUG ABUSE the repeated or uncontrolled use of controlled substances. While possession or use of controlled substances may be a crime, addiction to drugs is a disease which cannot be made a crime under the **due process** clause of the Constitution. 370 U.S. 660. Drug abuse or addiction is a ground for divorce in some states.

DRUG LAW see **generic** [GENERIC DRUG LAW].

DRUGS see **controlled substances; driving while intoxicated**

DUAL CITIZENSHIP "where two different sovereigns within their respective territorial confines claim citizenship of the same person and he of them." 76 F. Supp. 664, 666. A person having dual citizenship can lose his United States citizenship after attaining the age of twenty-two unless he resides in the United States or takes an oath of allegiance to the United States. 8 U.S.C. §1482.

DUCES TECUM see **subpoena** (SUBPOENA DUCES TECUM).

DUE CARE a concept used in **tort** law to indicate the standard of care or the **legal duty** one owes to others. Negligence, in the context of due care, is the failure to use that degree of care which a person of ordinary prudence and reason [the **reasonable man**] would exercise under the same circumstances. See 198 S.E. 2d 526, 529. Also, the "[F]ailure to exercise due care is the failure to perform some specific duty required by law." 153 S.E. 2d 356, 359. It "means care which is reasonably commensurate with a known danger and the seriousness of the consequences which are liable to follow its ommission. . . . Due care may be either ordinary care or a high degree of care, according to the circumstances of the particular case." 438 P. 2d 477, 482.

DUE COURSE see **payment in due course.**

DUE DATE time fixed for payment of debt, tax, etc.

DUE PROCESS OF LAW a phrase which was first expressly introduced into American jurisprudence in the Fifth Amendment to the Constitution which provides that "nor [shall any person] be deprived of life, liberty, or property, without due process of law;" This provision is applicable only to the actions of the federal government. 7 Pet. 243 (1833). The phrase was made applicable to the states with the adoption of the Fourteenth Amendment. Section 1, which states that "Nor shall any State deprive any person of life, liberty or property, without due process of law"; The phrase does not have a fixed meaning but expands with jurisprudential attitudes of fundamental fairness, 302 U.S. 319. The legal substance of the phrase is divided into the areas of substantive due process, and procedural due process. The constitutional safe-guard of SUBSTANTIVE DUE PROCESS requires that all legislation be in furtherance of a legitimate governmental objective. Since the late 1930s, the Supreme Court has generally limited judicial review on the basis of "substantive due process" to determine whether the law is rationally related to a legitimate goal. Only where legisla-

§4.01(1), now used by a number of jurisdictions, 471 F. 2d 969, 971. See **insanity defense.**

DUTY obligatory conduct owed by a person to another person. In **tort** law, duty is a legally sanctioned obligation the **breach** of which results in the **liability** of the actor. See 247 F. Supp. 188, 191. Thus, under the law of **negligence,** if an individual owed to others a DUTY OF CARE, he must conduct himself so as to avoid negligent injury to them. See **breach** [BREACH OF DUTY]; **due care.**

In tax law, a duty is a levy [tax] on **imports** and **exports.** See 119 F. Supp. 352, 354.

See **delegable duty.**

DUTY, LEGAL see **legal duty.**

DUTY ON PRODUCING EVIDENCE see **burden of proof.**

DUTY TO MITIGATE DAMAGES see **mitigation of damages.**

DWELLING HOUSE one's residence or abode; a structure or apartment used as a home for a family unit. As used in **restrictive covenant** the term PRIVATE DWELLING may be limited to single-family occupation even though two-family use does not change the outward character of the house. 198 N.Y.S. 311, 312. In the law of real property, it "includes everything pertinent and accessory to the main building and may consist of a cluster of buildings." 121 Ga. App. 240.

In criminal law, a house in which the occupier and his family usually reside, temporary absence being insufficient to destroy the status of the structure as a dwelling. 4 Bl. Comm. *225. For the purpose of the crime of **burglary** the dwelling house includes mobile homes, 46 A. 2d 35, 36; apartment units, 26 N.Y. 200; even a hotel room if one is living therein and thus is not a mere transient. Compare 99 N.E. 357, 359 with 86 N.Y. 360. See generally, Perkins and Boyce. Criminal Law 255059 (3rd ed. 1982).

D.W.I. see **driving while intoxicated.**

DYING DECLARATIONS see **hearsay rule.**

EARNEST at **civil law,** something of value given by one party to another to bind a **contract,** usually a sales agreement. Derived from Roman law and the Napoleonic Code, the earnest serves both as party payment or performance and as a method of predetermining liquidated damages for breach of contract. On breach by buyer, seller retains the earnest, while in seller's breach, buyer is entitled to twice the value of the earnest. Justinian, Institutes, III, 23; Code Napoleon, Art. 1590 (1804); La. Rev. Stat. Art. 2463 (1978).

At common law, earnest is often used to denote a down payment but, unlike a down payment, earnest is by definition forfeited on breach of contract. 255 N.W. 2d 827, 829. The earnest was originally used as a device to render a contract enforceable despite the **Statute of Frauds** requirement of a writing. 255 N.W. 134. Unlike **escrow,** in which a neutral third party holds the goods or money pending distribution to a proper party, an earnest is transferred directly to the other contracting party.

An earnest differs from an **option** to purchase in that the earnest serves to bind the actual contract of sale, while money given for an option results in the buyer acquiring only a right to purchase, without the obligation to do so. 65 S. 2d 185.

EXERCISE 8.5

NEGGILDARE. To claim kindred. Jac. L. Dict.

NEGLECT. May mean to omit, fail, or forbear to do a thing that can be done, or that is required to be done, but it may also import an absence of care or attention in the doing or omission of a given act. State v. Sheldon, 135 Okl. 278, 276 P. 468, 472; Same v. Butterfield, 138 Okl. 112, 276 P. 473.

And it may mean a designed refusal or unwillingness to perform one's duty. In re Perkins, 234 Mo.App. 716, 117 S.W.2d 686, 692.

The term is used in the law of bailment as synonymous with "negligence." But the latter word is the close translation of the Latin *"negligentia."*

Failure to pay money which the party is bound to pay without demand. Kimball v. Rowland, 6 Gray, Mass., 224. An omission to do or perform some work, duty, or act. Esposito v. St. George Swimming Club, 143 Misc. 15, 255 N.Y.S. 794, 801. Failure to perform or discharge a duty, covering positive official misdoing or official misconduct as well as negligence. Commonwealth ex rel. and to Use of Allegheny County v. De Luca, 131 Pa.Super. 451, 200 A. 712, 714.

Culpable Neglect. In this phrase, the word "culpable" means not only criminal, but censurable. As he has merely lost a right of action which he might voluntarily relinquish, and has wronged nobody but himself, culpable neglect to preserve rights conveys the idea of neglect which exists where the loss can fairly be ascribed to the party's own carelessness, improvidence, or folly. State ex rel. Fulton v. Coburn, 133 Ohio St. 192, 12 N.E.2d 471, 477.

Willful Neglect. The neglect of the husband to provide for his wife the common necessaries of life, he having the ability to do so; or it is the failure to do so by reason of idleness, profligacy, or dissipation. Civil Code Cal. st 105.

NEGLECTED MINOR. One suffering from neglect and in state of want. People v. De Pue, 217 N.Y.S. 205, 206, 217 App.Div. 321.

NEGLIGENCE. The omission to do something which a reasonable man, guided by those ordinary considerations which ordinarily regulate human affairs, would do, or the doing of something which a reasonable and prudent man would not do. Schneeweisz v. Illinois Cent. R. Co., 196 Ill.App. 248, 253; Schneider v. C. H. Little Co., 1984 Mich. 315, 151 N.W. 587, 588; Hulley v. Moosbrugger, 88 N.J.L. 161, 95 A. 1007, 1010, L.R.A. 1916C, 1203.

The term refers only to that legal delinquency which results whenever a man fails to exhibit the care which he ought to exhibit; whether it be slight, ordinary, or great. Hazzard v. Chase Nat. Bank of New York, 159 Misc. 57, 287 N.Y.S. 541, 552. It is characterized chiefly by inadvertence, thoughtlessness, inattention, and the like, while "wantonness" or "recklessness" is characterized by willfulness. People v. Orr, 243 Mich. 300, 220 N.W. 777, 779. The law of "negligence" is founded on reasonable conduct or reasonable care under all circumstances of particular case. Charbonneau v. MacRury, 84 N.Y. 501, 153 A. 457, 462, 73 A.L.R. 1266. Doctrine of negligence restson duty of every person to exercise due care in his conduct toward others from which injury may result. Johnson v. Grand Trunk Western R. Co., 246 Mich. 52, 224 N.W. 448, 449. "Negligence" is not intentional conduct. Gunther v. Morey Larue Laundry Co., 129 N.J.L. 345, 29 A.2d 713, 714. Inaction as well as action may be "negligence". Public Service Co. of New Hampshire v. Elliott, C.C.A.N.H., 123 F.2d 2, 5. It is not act itself, but fact which defines character of act and makes it legal wrong. Metzger v. Gambill, Tex.Civ. App., 37 S.W.2d 1077, 1078. It is immaterial to the question of "negligence" whether violated standard of conduct is established by statute or by the common law, Armit v. Loveland, C.C.A.Pa. 115 F.2d 308, 311, 312. It is the failure to do hat which a person of ordinary prudence, Ottenheimer v. Molohan, 146 Md. 175, 126 A. 97, 100; an ordinarily prudent person, Wichita Valley Ry. Co. v. Meyers, Tex.Civ.App., 248 S.W. 444, 447; a reasonable and prudent person. Chickasha Cotton Oil Co. v. Brown, 39 Okl. 245, 134 P. 850; Baltimore & P. R. Co. v. Jones, 96 U.S. 441, 24 L.Ed. 506; a person of ordinary care. Citizens' Nat. Bank of Jasper v. Ratcliff & Lanier, Tex.Civ.App., 238 S.W. 362, 365; a reasonable, prudent person, Boswell v. Whitehead Hosiery Mills, 191 N.C. 549, 132 S.E. 598, 602; a person of ordinary prudence and care, Illinois Cent. R. Co. v. Nelson, C.C.A.Iowa, 203 F. 956, 959; an ordinarily reasonable, careful, and prudent person, Johnson c. Omaha & Council Bluffs Street Ry. Co., 194 Iowa 1233, 190 N.W. 977, 978: or a reasonably prudent person, guided by those considerations which ordinarily regulate conduct of human affairs would do, or doing something which such a person would not do, under like or similar circumstances. McKee v. Iowa Ry. & Light Co., 204 Iowa 44, 214 N.W. 564, 565; Bowers b. J. D. Halstead Lumber Co., 28 Ariz. 122, 236 f. 124, 125.

The failure to use ordinary care, Curtis V. Mauger, 186 Ind. 118, 114, N.E. 408, 409; reasonable care, Crowley v. Chicago, B. & Q. R. Co., 204 Iowa 1385, 213 N.W. 403, 407, 53 A.L.R. 964; or ordinary or reasonable care under the circumstances, Thrasher v. St. Louis & S. F. Ry. Co. 826 Okl. 88, 206 P. 212, 214.

The failure to exercise that degree of care which a prudent person, Getsinger v. Corbell, 188 N.C. 553, 125 S.E. 180, 181; an ordinarily prudent person, Faulk v. Kansas City Rys. Co., Mo.App., 247 S.W. 253; a reasonably prudent person, Moir v. Hart, 189 Ill.App. 566, 567; City of Decatur v. Eady, 186 Ind. 205, 115 N.E. 577, 579, L.R.A. 1917E, 242; a reasonable and prudent person, Heller v. New York, N. H. & H. R. Co., C.C.A.N.Y., 265 F. 192, 198, 17 A.L.R. 823; a reasonably careful person, Behen v. Philadelphia, B. & W. R. Co., 93 A. 903, 904, 5 Boyce, Del., 389; an ordinary prudent person. Donahue v. R. A. Sherman's Sons Co., R.I. 373, 98 A. 109, 114, L.R.A.1917A., 76; a reasonably prudent, careful person, Gray v. Pennsylvania R. Co., 3 W.W.Harr., Del., 450, 138 A. 66, 75; a reasonably prudent and careful person, Lemmon v. Broadwater, 108 A. 273. 274, 7 Boyce, Del., 472; or an ordinarily prudent and careful person would exercise under like circumstances. Clayton v. Philadelphia, B. & W. R. Co., 106 A. 577, 579, 7 Boyce, Del., 343.

The failure to exercise ordinary care. Anderson v. Atlantic Coast Line R. Co., 161 N.C. 462, 77 S.E. 402, 404. Ordinary or reasonable care being that care which ordinarily prudent persons, Travis v. Louisville & N. R. Co., 183 Ala. 415, 62 So. 851, 854; reasonably prudent persons, Burns v. Polar Wave Ice & Fuel Co., MoApp., 197 S.W. 145, 148; persons of ordinary prudence, Shirley Hill Coal Co. v. Moore, 181 Ind. 513, 103 N.E. 802, 804; ordinary careful, prudent persons. Yellow Pine Paper Mill Co. v. Wright, Tex., 154 S.W. 1168, 1171; or ordinarily careful or prudent persons, would exercise under like or similar circumstances. Loverage v. Carmichael, 164 Minn. 76, 204 N.W. 921, 922.

The breach of a legal duty. Taylor v. Neuse Lumber Co., 173 N.C. 112, 91 S.E. 719, 920: Jones v. Atchison, T. & S. F. Ry. Co., 98 Kan. 133, 157 P. 399, 400: Pickett v. Waldorf System, 241 Mass. 569, 136 N.E. 64, 65, 23 A.L.P., 1014; Schell v. Du Bois, 94 Ohio St. 93, 113 N.E. 661, 668, L.R.A. 1917A, 710.

Negligence usually consists in the "involuntary and casual"—that is, "accidental"—doing or omission to do something which results in an injury, Root v. Topeka Rv. Co., 96 Kan. 6984, 153 P. 550; and is synonymous with heedlessness, carelessness, thoughtlessness, disregard, inattention, inadvertance, remissness and oversight, Payne v. Vance, 103 Ohio St. 59, 133 N.E. 85, 87.

"Negligence" in official conduct is ordinarily the failure to use such reasonable care and caution as would be expected of a prudent man. Hamrick v. McCutcheon, 101 W. Va. 485, 133 S.E. 127, 129.

Negligence is any culpable omission of a positive duty. It differs from heedlessness, in that heedlessness is the doing of an act in violation of a negative duty, without adverting to its possible consequences. In both cases there is inadvertence, and thee is breach of duty. Aust. Jr. § 630.

Negligence or carelessness signifies want of care, caution, attention, diligence, or discretion in one having no positive intention to

continued

NEGLIGENCE

injure the person complaining thereof. The words "reckless," "indifferent,"careless," and "wanton" are never understood to signify positive will or intention, unless when joined with other words which show that they are to receive an artificial or unusual, if not an unnatural, interpretation. Lexington v. Lewis, 10 Bush, Ky., 677.

"Negligence" is not synonymous with "incompetency," since the competent may be negligent. Alabama City G. & A. Ry. Co. v. Bessiere, 190 Ala. 59, 66 So. 805, 806; Barclay v. Wetmore & Morse Granite Co., 92 Vt. 195, 1092 A. 493, 495.

See Care.

Actionable Negligence. See Actionable Negligence.

Collateral Negligence. In the law relating to the responsibility of an employer or principal for the negligent acts or omissions of his employee, the term "collateral" negligence is sometimes used to describe negligence attributable to a contractor employed by the principal and for which the latter is not responsible, though he would be responsible for the same thing if done by his servant. Weber v. Railway Co., 200 App.Div. 292, 47 N.Y.S. 11.

Comparative Negligence. See Comparative Negligence.

Concurrent Negligence. Arises where the injury is approximately caused by the concurrent wrongful acts or omissions of two or more persons acting independently. Carr v. St. Louis Auto Supply Co., 293 Mo. 562, 238 S.W. 827, 828.

Contributory Negligence. The act or omission amounting to want of ordinary care on part of complaining party, which, concurring with defendant's negligence, is proximate cause of injury. Honaker v. Crutchfield, 247 Ky. 495, 57 S.W.2d 502.

Any want of ordinary care on the part of the person injured, (or on the part of another whose negligence is imputable to him,) which combined and concurred with the defendant's negligence, and contributed to the injury as a proximate cause thereof, and as an element without which the injury would not have occurred. Railroad Co. v. Young, 153 Ind. 163, 54 N.E. 7981; Barton v. Railroad Co., 52 Mo. 253, 14 Am.Rep. 418; McLaughlin v. Electric Light Co., 100 Ky. 173, 37 S.W. 851, 34 L.R.A. 812; 25 C.J. S. Damages; Townsend v. Missouri Pac. R. Co., 163 La. 872, 113 So. 130, 132, 54 A.L.R. 538.

The negligent act of plaintiff which, concurring and cooperating with negligent act of defendant, becomes real, efficient, and proximate cause of injury, or cause without which the injury would not have occurred. Elder v. Plaza Ry., 194 N.C. 617, 140 S.E. 298, 299; James V. Delaware, L. & W. R. Co., 92 N.J.L. 149, 104 A. 328, 333.

"Assumption of risk" and "contributory negligence" are not synonymous. Chicago, R. I. & P. R. Co. v. Rogers, 60 Okl. 249, 159 P. 1132, 1136.

Concurrent Contributory Negligence. Knowledge of specific danger and negligent failure to avoid it. Sprinkle v. St. Louis & S. F. R. Co., 215 Ala. 191, 110 So. 137, 140.

Mutual Contributory Negligence. Exists when injury would not have happened but for negligence of both parties. Alexander v. Missouri, K. & T. R. Co. of Texas, Tex.Civ.App., 287 S.W. 153, 155.

Criminal Negligence. Criminal negligence which will render killing a person manslaughter is the omission on the part of the person to do some act which an ordinarily careful and prudent man would do under like circumstances, or the doing of some act which an ordinarily careful, prudent man under like circumstances would not do by reason of which another person is endangered in life or bodily safety; the word "ordinary" being synonymous with "reasonable" in this connection. State v. Coulter, Mo.Sup., 204 S.W. 5.

Negligence of such a character, or occurring under such circumstances, as to be punishable as a crime by statute; or (at common law) such a flagrant and reckless disregard of the safety or others, or willful indifference to the injury liable to follow, as to convert an act otherwise lawful into a crime when it results in personal injury or death. 4 Bl. Comm. 1982, note: Cook v. Railroad Co., 72 Ga. 48; Rankin v. Transportation Co., 73 Ga. 229, 54 Am.Rep. 874; Railroad Co. v. Chollette, 33 Neb. 143, 49 N.W. 1114.

Culpable Negligence. Failure to exercise that degree of care rendered appropriate by the particular circumstances, and which a man of ordinary prudence in the same situation and with equal experience would not have omitted. Carter v. Lumber Co., 129 N.C. 203, 39 S.E., 828; Woodman v. Nottingham, 49 N.H. 387, 6 Am.Rep. 526; Kimball v. Palmer, C.C.A. Va., 25 C.C.A. 394, 80 F. 240.

Degrees of Negligence. There are degrees of care, and failure to exercise power degree of care is "negligence," but there are no degrees of negligence. Murray v. De Luxe Motor Stages of Illinois, Mo.App. 133, S.W.2d 1074, 1078.

Classification of "negligence" as "gross," "ordinary," and "slight" indicates only that under special circumstances great care and caution, or ordinary care, or slight care are required, but failure to exercise care demanded is "negligence." 38 Del.Laws, c. 26. Gallegher v. Davis, 7 .W.Harr. 370, 183 A. 620.

Gross Negligence. The intentional failure to perform a manifest duty in reckless disregard of the consequences as affecting the life or property of another; such a gross want of care and regard for the rights of others as to justify the presumption of willfulness and wantonness. Seelig v. First Nat. Bank, D.C.Ill., 20 F.Supp. 61, 68.

The failure to exercise slight care. Jones v. Atchison, T. & S. F. Ry. Co., 98 Kan. 133, 157 P. 399, 400; Burton Const. Co. v. Metcalfe, 162 Ky. 366, 172 S.W. 698,701.

The want of slight diligence. The want of that care which every man of common sense, how inattentive soever, takes of his own property. The omission of that care which even inattentive and thoughtless men never fail to take of their own property. Litchfield v. White, 7 N.Y. 442, 57 Am.Dec. 534; Sybil v. National Currency Bank, 54 N.Y. 299, 13 Am.Rep. 583; Briggs v. Spaulding, 41 U.S. 132, 11 Sect. 925, 35 Led. 662; The want of ordinary diligence and care which usually prudent man takes of his own property of like description. Dalton v. Hamilton Hotel Operating Co., 242 N.Y. 481, 152 N.E. 268, 270. In the law of torts (and especially with reference to personal injury cases), the term means such negligence as evidences a reckless disregard of human life, or of the safety of persons exposed to its dangerous effects, or that entire want of care which would raise the presumption of a conscious indifference to the rights of others which is equivalent to an intentional violation of them. McDonald v. Railroad Co., Ted.Civ.App., 21 S.W. 775; Railroad Co., v. Western Union Tel. Co., 130 Cal. 657, 63 P. 83, 53 L.R.A. 678; Bremer v. Lake Erie & W. R. Co., 318 Ill., 11, 148 N. E. 862, 866, 41 A.L.R. 1345.

Indifference to present legal duty and utter forgetfulness of legal obligations, so far as other persons may be affected, and a manifestly smaller amount of watchfulness and circumspection than the circumstances require a person of ordinary prudence. Burke v. Cook, 246 Mass. 518, 141 N.E. 585, 586. Negligence bordering on recklessness. People v. Adams, 289 Ill. 339, 124 N.E. 575, 577.

"Gross negligence," is substantially higher in magnitude than simple inadvertence, but falls short of intentional wrong. Young v. City of Worcester, 253 Mass. 481,

5. "Failure to exercise that degree of care rendered appropriate by the particular circumstances, and which a man of ordinary prudence in the same situation and with equal experience would not have omitted" is which type of negligence?
   a. Contributory
   b. Gross
   c. Culpable
   d. Criminal

CHAPTER

9

The American Law Reports Series

I. WHAT IS THE A.L.R.?

The **American Law Reports** (A.L.R.) system is an incisive and scholarly review of relevant case law by specified subject matter. In contrast to the national reporter system, the main thrust of which is to provide as many cases as possible within a given geographical area and court level, the A.L.R. system is more selective. The A.L.R. attempts to provide the practitioner with only those cases that are legally significant for daily practice. Cases that are mundane, repetitive, or easily resolved are relegated to the footnotes; no effort is made to reproduce the body of these opinions. Instead, the A.L.R. system selects a valuable and important case upon which it builds significant annotations, references, and practice pointers.

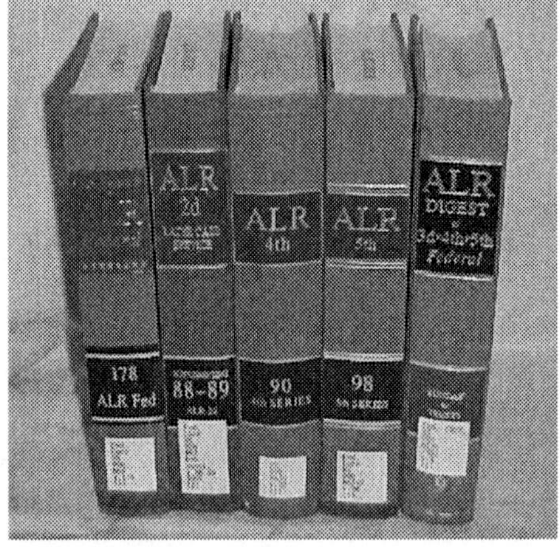

II. ORGANIZATION OF THE A.L.R. SYSTEM

In brief, the system operates like this:

1. A reported case of legal interest is found and thought worthy of publication.
2. The subject or issue of the case is clearly identified.

3. A brief synopsis of the case is written.
4. Headnotes are drafted to summarize the court's holding.
5. The text of the opinion is published.
6. An annotation, which may be extensive, is written. It follows the opinion, along with
   - References to other tertiary material
   - Practice pointers
   - Jurisdictional table
   - References to appropriate statutes
   - Summary of basic legal principles
   - Analysis of all relevant cases
   - Other case citations

As you might guess, the bulk of the work in producing the A.L.R. system takes place at step 6. To achieve a high level of understanding through the A.L.R. system, the researcher must clearly identify the problem before he or she opens the books. Ample indexes, including a words-and-phrases index, are provided, as well as a table of cases by name for annotation purposes. The cross-referencing capacity is excellent, too.

The entire A.L.R. system is a system of monographs or exercises in high-level research, which is why some practitioners prefer it to any other case law service. A.L.R. has simply done a good deal of the homework already.

Due to the extensive scope of A.L.R.'s content, the system is now in its fifth series, organized as follows:

A.L.R. 1st (1919–1948)—state and federal cases

A.L.R. 2d (1948–1965)—state and federal cases

A.L.R. 3d (1965–1980)—state and federal

A.L.R. 4th (1980–1991)—state cases

A.L.R. 5th (1969–)—state cases

A.L.R. Fed. (1969–)—federal decisions

A.L.R. Digest

After compilation of the A.L.R. 3d, federal cases were broken out into the A.L.R. Federal series. This choice reflects both an increase in the number of jurisdictions and a growing expansion of the subject-matter scope of jurisdictions. Because of the large number of state courts, continuing to include the federal cases with the state became impractical. Also, the scope of the subject matter in federal jurisdictions is much narrower than in the state counterparts, so there are fewer cases on the federal level. Continuing to include both state and federal cases in one series would have made the A.L.R. series highly cumbersome.

III. USING THE A.L.R.

Despite the size of this resource, the A.L.R. is surprisingly easy to use. The first step is to locate the A.L.R. Quick Index for the appropriate series. If using the third through the fifth series, because your question is state-oriented, select the index shown in Figure 9.1.

FIGURE 9.1

COVERING

ALR 3d
ALR 4th
ALR 5th, Vols. 1–99

INDEX
A–Z

JULY 2002 EDITION

Look up the keyword or topic in the index to locate an A.L.R. article. Next, find the appropriate volume on the shelf and read the article. See Figure 9.2 for advice from West Publishing Company on using the A.L.R. series.

Fact Pattern 1. In the index, look up "driving while intoxicated." Several annotations look promising. See Fact Pattern Figure 9.3. "Homicide, alcohol-related vehicular homicide, nature and elements of offense" seems to be the best choice. Next, locate the fourth series of A.L.R., take volume 46 off the shelf, and turn to page 166. There you will find the needed article (Figure 9.4).

FIGURE 9.2

EMPLOYER'S LIABILITY FOR ASSAULT, THEFT, OR SIMILAR INTENTIONAL WRONG COMMITTED BY EMPLOYEE AT HOME OR BUSINESS OF CUSTOMER

by Phoebe Carter, J.D.

An employee who enters a customer's home or business while representing his or her employer generally does so with the trust of the customer, who assumes that a reputable employer would not hire or give authority to a disreputable employee. However, this trust may be violated by an unscrupulous or intemperate employee who assaults the customer, steals items from the customer's premises, or commits some other intentional act, such as setting a fire on the customer's premises. The issue then is whether the employer should be held liable for its employee's acts. In the case of Smith v Orkin Exterminating Co. (1989, La App 1st Cir) 540 So 2d 363, 13 ALR5th 962, for example, a homeowner trusted a pest control company's employee to come upon her premises and perform a legitimate service, and was rewarded by the employee's sexual

C. CONVERSION, THEFT, ROBBERY, AND THE LIKE

§ 14. Respondeat superior

§ 15. Negligent hiring

[a] Theory established or supportable

[b] Theory not established

Article outline

Index

Texts

4E Matthew Bender, Personal Injury: Actions, Defenses, Damages §§ 2.01[3], 2.03[5]

Callaghan, Negligence Compensation Cases Annotated (4th), vol 55, Employer Liability for Negligent Hiring 1-122

Encyclopedias

3 Am Jur 2d, Agency §§ 267, 280

6 Am Jur 2d, Assault and Battery §§ 131-145

19 Amjur 2d, Corporations §§ 1427 et seq.

Research references

§§ 15. Negligent hiring

[a] Theory established or supportable

In the following cases where employees committed thefts from the business premises they were assigned by their employers to protect, the courts held that the evidence established or supported the employers' liability under a theory of negligent hiring because the employers failed to exercise due care in screening their employees.

Where an employee, who was assigned to patrol the premises of the security system company's customer, stole a blank check, forged the name of an official of the tenant company, and made the check payable to himself in the amount of $11,000, the court in C.K. Secur. Systems, Inc. v Hartford Acci. & Indem. Co. (1976) 137 Ga App 159, 223 SE2d 453, held that the evidence adduced for purposes of the defendant's motion for summary judgment was not

Substantive text

continued

FIGURE 9.2
continued

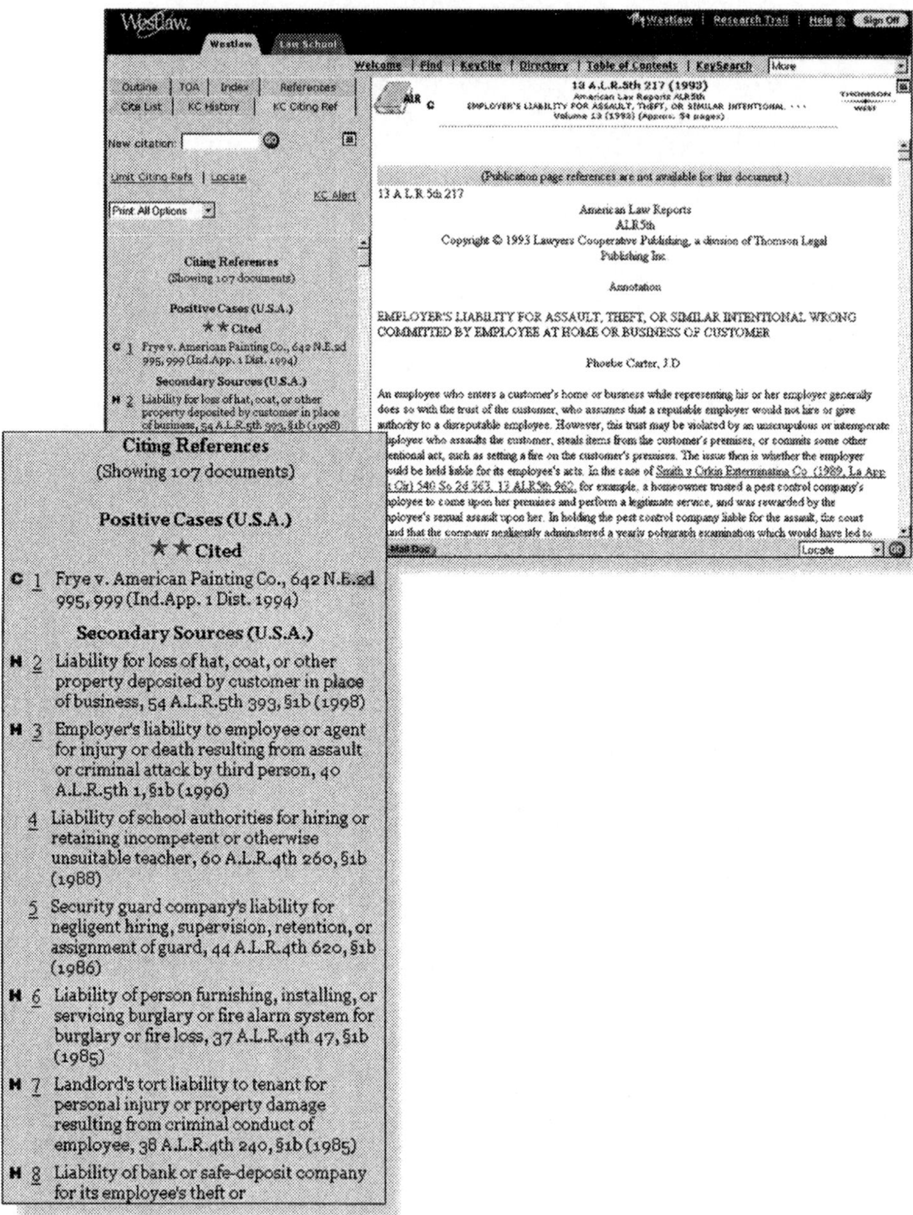

KeyCite citing references

FIGURE 9.3

ALR QUICK INDEX

For assistance using this Index, call 1-800-328-4880

FIGURE 9.4

Alcohol-related vehicular homicide: nature and elements of offense

INDEX

continued

Homicide by automobile as murder. 21 ALR3d 116.

What amounts to negligence within meaning of statutes penalizing negligent homicide by operation of motor vehicle. 20 ALR3d 473.

Automobiles: driving under the influence, or when addicted to the use, of drugs as criminal offense. 17 ALR3d 815.

Criminal responsibility for injury or death in operation of mechanically defective motor vehicle. 88 ALR2d 1165.

Motor vehicle operator's criminal responsibility for homicide where he and deceased were racing, though accused's care was not otherwise involved in the collision or incident. 82 ALR2d 463.

Criminal responsibility of motor vehicle operator for accident arising from physical defect, illness, drowsiness, or falling asleep. 63 ALR2d 983.

What amounts to reckless diving of motor vehicle within statute making such a criminal offense. 52 ALR2d 1337.

Bates, Murder Convictions for Homicides Committed in the Course of Driving While Intoxicated, 8 Cumberland L Rev 476 (1977-78)

§ 2. Summary and comment

[a] Generally

Alcohol-related vehicular homicide statutes are the product of a comparatively recent reaction to the frequency of human tragedies caused by drunken drivers and the difficulty of obtaining convictions of these drivers under the general statutes on homicide because of the reluctance of juries to attach the onus of "manslaughter" to those who have caused the death of others through operation of motor vehicles.[3] However, such statutes have not gone untested. As a result of challenges posed by drivers subject to prosecution under alcohol-related vehicular homicide statutes, the courts have considered the constitutionality of the statutes defining the offense, the relationship of the offense to other crimes, and the meaning and effect of various provisions included in such statutes.

Generally, constitutional challenges against alcohol-related vehicular homicide statutes have failed. The statutes have been upheld against claims that, viewed as a whole, they were vague or overbroad (§ 3) or constituted special legislation which unfairly singled out a class of persons for prosecution (§ 4). They have also been upheld where opponents alleged that the subject matter of the statute was not embraced within its title, in derogation of constitutional proscriptions (§ 5). Similarly, claims that such statutes were invalid on constitutional grounds because they provided blood test procedures which were different than those provided by statutes relating to driving under the influence (§ 20), or resulted in different penalties than those resulting from similar offenses (§ 21), and thus violated equal protection limitations, have been unsuccessful.

3. 7A Am Jur 2d, Automobiles and Highway Traffic § 340.

FIGURE 9.4 *continued*

I. Overview

§ 1. Introduction

[a] Scope

This annotation collects and analyzes the state and federal cases in which the courts have discussed the nature and elements of a statutory offense specifically dealing with vehicular homicide by a driver who is under the influence of alcohol, intoxicated by alcohol,[1] or operating a vehicle with a specified blood-alcohol content.[2]

Beyond the scope of this annotation are cases in which the courts have discussed vehicular homicide under statutes which lack any provisions specifically related to alcohol but which involve misconduct which could be proven by evidence of a driver's intoxication.

A number of jurisdictions have rules, regulations, constitutional provisions, or legislative enactments bearing upon this subject. Since these are discussed herein only to the extent that they are reflected in the reported cases within the scope of this annotation, the reader is advised to consult the appropriate statutory or regulatory compilations.

[b] Related matters

Validity, construction, and application of statutes directly proscribing driving with blood-alcohol level in excess of established percentage. 54 ALR4th 149.

Statute prohibiting reckless driving: definiteness and certainty. 52 ALR4th 1161.

Lesser-related state offense instructions: modern status. 50 ALR4th 1081.

Failure to restrain drunk driver as ground of liability of state or local government unit or officer. 48 ALR4th 320.

Drunk driving: motorist's right to private sobriety test. 45 ALR4th 11.

Admissibility in criminal case of evidence that accused refused to take test of intoxication. 26 ALR4th 1112.

Reckless driving as lesser included offense of driving while intoxicated or similar charge. 10 ALR4th 1252.

What constitutes driving, operating, or being in control of motor vehicle for purposes of driving while intoxicated statutes. 93 ALR3d 7.

1. This annotation excludes discussion of "DWI" statutes, or statutes relating to driving while intoxicated, except to the extent that they specifically refer to homicide or death.

2. For purposes of this annotation, a statute is considered to specifically deal with alcohol-related vehicular homicide if the statute refers to homicide caused by the driver's use of an "intoxicant" but does not state whether this term refers to alcoholic or nonalcoholic substances.

With regard to those statutes in which other offenses, in addition to the offense pertaining to alcohol-related vehicular homicide, have been defined, only those cases which have discussed the intoxication offense in such statutes have been included in this annotation.

IV. LEGAL RESEARCH ASSIGNMENTS

A. Exercise 9.1: A.L.R. Annotation

1. Which annotation section outlines or analyzes a ruling or decision from the 10th Federal Circuit?
   a. 3,4[a]
   b. 4[a]
   c. 4[b]
   d. 4[c]
2. This annotation relates only to federal decisions.
   a. True
   b. False
3. Which rule of federal civil procedure is analyzed in this annotation?
   a. 52
   b. 34(a)
   c. Fed 104
   d. 50(c)(l)
4. This annotation tries to provide the researcher with information about standards governing when a case should proceed to the initial trial phase.
   a. True
   b. False
5. If you want to research the appeal of an order denying motion for a direct verdict, go to 69 A.L.R. 2d 449.
   a. True
   b. False
6. The text to Rule 50(c)(l) is reproduced for the researcher's review.
   a. True
   b. False
7. Which of the following is not in the "Total Client-Service Library"?
   a. A.L.R. Quick Index on Appeal and Error
   b. *American Jurisprudence*
   c. A.L.R. digests
   d. U.S.C.A.
8. Generally, new trials will not be granted unless the appellate court finds some abuse of discretion at the lower court level.
   a. True
   b. False
9. Which section of this annotation analyzes the grant of a new trial when legal error is noted?
   a. 1
   b. 5
   c. 6
   d. 10
10. What should be consulted for later cases and statutory changes?
    a. Pocket part
    b. Quick index
    c. Rule 50(c)(l)
    d. Related annotations

ANNOTATION

WHAT STANDARDS GOVERN APPELLATE REVIEW OF TRIAL COURT'S CONDITIONAL RULING, PURSUANT TO RULE 50(c)(1) OF FEDERAL RULES OF CIVIL PROCEDURE ON PARTY'S MOTION FOR NEW TRIAL

by

Michelle Migdal Gee, J.D.

TOTAL CLIENT-SERVICE LIBRARY® REFERENCES

5 Am Jur 2d, Appeal and Error §§ 850–852, 887; 58 Am Jur 2d, New Trial §§ 212, 213, 218, 223

1 Federal Procedural Forms L Ed, Actions in District Court §§ 1:1661–1:1663

2 Am Jur Pl & Pr Forms (Rev), Appeal and Error, Forms 1581–1596; 18 Am Jur Pl & Pr Forms (Rev), New Trial, Form 23

USCS, Court Rules, Federal Rules of Civil Procedure, Rule 50 (c)

US L Ed Digest, Appeal and Error §§ 1417–1420; Court Rules, Rules of Civil Procedure, Rule 50 (c)

ALR Digests,

L Ed Index to Annos, Appeal and Error; Federal Rules of Civil Procedure; Motions; New Trial

ALR Quick Index, Appeal and Error; Conditions; Motions; New Trial; Rules of Civil Procedure

Federal Quick Index, Appeal and Error; Covenants and Conditions; Evidence; Motions; New Trial

Consult POCKET PART in this volume for later cases and statutory changes

continued

TABLE OF COURTS AND CIRCUITS

Consult POCKET PART in this volume for later cases and statutory changes

First Cir: §§ 3, 4[a]
Second Cir: § 6
Third Cir: §§ 3, 4[a, b], 5
Fifth Cir: §§ 3, 4[a], 6, 7
Sixth Cir: § 4[a]
Seventh Cir: §§ 4[a, b]
Eighth Cir: §§ 3, 4[a, b], 5
Ninth Cir: § 4[a]
Tenth Cir: § 4[b]
Dist Col Cir: §§ 3, 4[a]

§ 1. Introduction

[a] Scope

This annotation collects and analyzes the federal cases in which the courts have discussed the scrutiny with which appellate courts will review a conditional decision as to a new trial pursuant to Rule 50(c)(1) of the Federal Rules of Civil Procedure. Treated are cases in which a party's motion for judgment notwithstanding the verdict has been granted, and the trial judge has also conditionally ruled on a joint or alternative motion for new trial in the event the judgment is thereafter vacated or reversed. Cases are within the scope of this annotation if they were decided after 1963, the effective date of Rule 50(1)(c), whether or not specific reference is made to the Rule.

[b] Related matters

Motions for new trial: time limitations under Rule 59(b) of Federal Rules of Civil Procedure. 45 ALR Fed 104.

Practice and procedure with respect to motions for judgment notwithstanding or in default of verdict under Federal Civil Procedure Rule 50(b) or like state provisions. 69 ALR2d 449.

Participation in, acceptance of, or submission to new trial as precluding appellate review of order granting it or of issue determined in first trial. 67 ALR2d 191.

Appealability of order denying motion for directed verdict or for judgment notwithstanding the verdict where movant has been granted a new trial. 57 ALR2d 1198.

[c] Text of Rule 50(c)(1)

Rule 50(c)(1) of the Federal Rules of Civil Procedure provides as follows:

(c) Same: Conditional Rulings on Grant of Motion.

(1) If the motion for judgment notwithstanding the verdict, provided for in subdivision (b) of this rule, is granted, the court shall also rule on the motion for a new trial, if any, by determining whether it should be granted if the judgment is thereafter vacated or reversed, and shall

B. Exercise 9.2: A.L.R. Quick Index

1. Which of the following is a main topic headline in this index?
   a. Fraudulent Conveyances
   b. Statute of Frauds
   c. Title to real estate
   d. Community Property
2. The requirement for a stepparent to support a child after divorce is discussed at 44 ALR4th 520.
   a. True
   b. False
3. The Uniform Commercial Code includes a statute of frauds.
   a. True
   b. False
4. Which of these issues may be applicable to a real estate sale?
   a. Oil and gas royalty
   b. Lottery winnings
   c. Conspiracy to defraud
   d. Signatures
5. Which A.L.R. annotation discusses the enforceability of an employment contract when an employee relies on the validity of such contract, even though it violates the statute of frauds?
   a. 4 A.L.R.3d 383
   b. 71 A.L.R.3d 1000
   c. 54 A.L.R.3d 715
   d. 45 A.L.R.3d 1181

C. Exercise 9.3: A.L.R. Quick Index

1. Which A.L.R. article would contain information regarding court review of a bar examiner's decision on an application examination?
   a. 88 A.L.R.3d 192
   b. 39 A.L.R.3d 719
   c. Both a and b
   d. Neither a or b
2. If an attorney wanted to charge someone with defamation for criticizing his or her abilities, which A.L.R. article would most likely be consulted?
   a. 2 A.L.R.3d 861
   b. 46 A.L.R.4th 326
   c. 2 A.L.R.4th 27
   d. 12 A.L.R.5th 909
3. For information regarding attorney-client privilege, another section of this index must be consulted.
   a. True
   b. False
4. The major heading not included in these page selections is
   a. Attorney-Client Privilege.
   b. Attorney General.
   c. Arbitration and Award.
   d. Attorney or Assistance of Attorney.

EXERCISE 9.2

ALR QUICK INDEX

For assistance using this Index, call 1-800-328-4880

EXERCISE 9.3

ALR QUICK INDEX

For assistance using this Index, call 1-800-328-4880

continued

EXERCISE 9.3 *continued*

ALR QUICK INDEX

For assistance using this Index, call 1-800-328-4880

5. There are no articles relating to the attorney's work product doctrine.
   a. True
   b. False

D. Exercise 9.4: A.L.R. Federal

1. An A.L.R. annotation includes which of the following elements?
   a. Research references
   b. Text of the statute
   c. Tables of cases
   d. All of the above
2. The Research References include which of the following types of works?
   a. Formbooks
   b. Digests
   c. Electronic resources
   d. All of the above
3. This article deals with
   a. anticybersquatting.
   b. jurisdictional questions.
   c. personal liability.
   d. None of the above.
4. Each A.L.R. annotation has its own index.
   a. True
   b. False

E. Exercise 9.5: A.L.R. Digest

1. Which of the following is not a major heading?
   a. Generally
   b. Defenses
   c. Attempts
   d. Solicitation
2. Delirium tremens is a subtopic covered under Intoxication.
   a. True
   b. False
3. Homicide is the only violent crime discussed in this digest excerpt.
   a. True
   b. False
4. Which resource would lead you to practice aids relating to mental disorders and incapacity?
   a. 5 Am Jur Proof of Facts 2d 189
   b. 4 Am Jur Proof of Facts 549
   c. 6 Am Jur Proof of Facts 469
   d. 8 Am Jur Proof of Facts 13
5. 46 A.L.R.3d 544 contains an article discussing the fact that amnesia can affect one's capacity to commit a crime or stand trial.
   a. True
   b. False

177 ALR Fed 1

VALIDITY, CONSTRUCTION, AND APPLICATION OF ANTICYBERSQUATTING CONSUMER PROTECTION ACT, 15 U.S.C.A. § 1125(d)

by
Elizabeth D. Lauzon J.D M.L.S.

The Anticybersquatting Consumer Protection Act (ACPA), 15 U.S.C.A. § 1125(d) amended the Lanham Act to provide trademark owners with stronger remedies against cybersquatters, who register domain names of well-known trademarks and then try to profit from the marks. Under the ACPA, a trademark owner is entitled to relief, including transfer, forfeiture, or cancellation of the domain name and/or recovery of up to $100,000 for each domain name, if the trademark owner shows: (1) that it owns a distinctive or famous mark; (2) that the defendant registers, uses, or traffics in a domain name that is identical to or confusingly similar to the distinctive or famous mark; and (3) that the defendant had a "bad faith intent to profit" from the mark. The court in Ford Motor Co. v. Greatdomains.Com, Inc., 177 F. Supp. 2d 635, 177 A.L.R. Fed. 637 (E.D. Mich. 2001), held that the trademarks owner stated a claim against the domain name registrants under the ACPA, the auction website owner did not "traffic in" domain names in violation of the ACPA, and the auction website owner was not subject to contributory liability under the ACPA to the trademarks owner. This annotation collects and analyzes cases discussing the validity, construction and application of the Anticybersquatting Consumer Protection Act (ACPA), 15 U.S.C.A. § 1125(d).

Ford Motor Co. v. Greatdomains.Com, Inc. is fully reported at page 637, infra.

TABLE OF CONTENTS

ARTICLE OUTLINE

continued

Research References

TOTAL CLIENT-SERVICE LIBRARY® REFERENCES

The following references may be of related or collateral interest to a user of this annotation.

Annotations

See the related annotations listed in the body of the annotation.

Encyclopedias and Texts

74 Am Jur 2d, Trademarks and Tradenames §§ 84–178

32 Federal Procedure, L Ed, Lanham Trade-Mark Act Litigation §§ 75:478–75:505

Practice Aids

16 Federal Procedural Forms, L Ed, Trade Regulation and Unfair Trade Practices § 65:338

17 Am Jur Proof of Facts 3d 609, Monetary Recovery for Trademark Infringement23A Am Jur Pl & Pr Forms (Rev), Trademarks and Tradenames, Internet, Domain Name, Complaint for Infringement by § 67.2

47 Am Jur Proof of Facts 2d 643, Wrongful Use of Another's Trademark or Tradename

8 Am Jur Trials 359, Trademark Infringement and Unfair Competition Litigation

Federal Statutes

15 U.S.C.A. §§ 1117, 1125(d)

Digests and Indexes

ALR Digest, Trademarks, Tradenames and Unfair Trade Practices § 31

ALR Index, Internet; Trademarks, Tradenames and Unfair Trade Practices

KeyCite®

Cases and other legal materials listed in KeyCite® Scope can be researched through West Group's KeyCite service on WESTLAW®. Use KeyCite to check citations for form, parallel references, prior and later history, and comprehensive citator information, including citations to other decisions and secondary materials.

RESEARCH SOURCES

The following are the research sources that were found to be helpful in compiling this annotation.

4

continued

Encyclopedias

74 Am Jur 2d, Trademarks and Tradenames §§ 84–178

87 CJS, Trade-Marks, Trade-Names and Unfair Competition §§ 227–339

Texts

2B West's Federal Forms, Infringement and Unfair Competition, Complaints, District Court §§ 1757 et seq.

4 West's Federal Forms, Infringement and Unfair Competition, District Court § 4309

4A West's Federal Forms, Preliminary Injunction, Infringement and Unfair Competition, District Court § 5334

Brookman, Trademark Law, Protection, Enforcement and Licensing Ch 7

Gilson, Trademark Protection and Practice § 2:7A.06

McCarthy, McCarthy on Trademarks and Unfair Competition § 7:17.1

Law Review Articles

Steven R. Borgman, The New Federal Cybersquatting Laws, 8 Tex. Intell. Prop. L.J. 265 (2000)

John M. Carson et al., Claim Jumping on the Newest Frontier: Trademarks, Cybersquatting, and the Judicial Interpretation of Bad Faith, 8 UCLA Ent. L. Rev. 27 (2000)

Matthew E. Searing, "What's in a Domain Name?" A Critical Analysis of the National and International Impact on Domain-Name Cybersquatting, 40 Washburn L.J. 110 (2000)

Electronic Search Query

WESTLAW® Search Query: (cybersquatting anticybersquatting ACPA) (15 /s 1125(d))

West Digest Key Numbers

Trade Regulation 331–333, 334.1, 335, 340.1, 350.1, 362, 366, 373, 374

INDEX

Consult other ALR Digests for earlier cases

VII. RECORD, § 224

continued

§ 88 —For other particular causes
§ 89 Acquittal as bar to prosecution for perjury

(B) IDENTITY OF OFFENSES

§ 90 Generally
§ 90.3 Identity of acts or transaction as test
§ 90.5 Identity of time, place, and circumstances as test
§ 90.7 Identity of evidence as test
§ 91 Continuing or separate offenses
§ 91.5 —Period covered by prosecution
§ 92 Offenses of different degrees
§ 93 Different offenses in same act or transaction
§ 94 Assault and other offenses
§ 95 Larceny, embezzlement, robbery, or burglary, and other offenses
§ 96 Offenses involving intoxication or intoxicating liquors, and other offenses
§ 97 Forgery and other offenses
§ 98 Sexual crimes and other offenses
§ 98.3 Conspiracy and other offenses
§ 98.5 Miscellaneous particular offenses
§ 99 Offenses against different sovereignties
§ 99.5 Offenses against different persons

(C) WAIVER OF OBJECTIONS

§ 100 Generally

III. CONVICTION OR ACQUITTAL OF PERSON JOINTLY INDICTED

§ 100.5 Generally

IV. PROCEDURE

(A) IN GENERAL

§ 101 Generally
§ 101.3 Trial by, or province of, court or jury
§ 101.5 Election between crimes growing out of same transaction
§ 102 Preliminary complaint
§ 103 Preliminary examination
§ 104 —Evidence to justify commitment
§ 105 Leave to file information
§ 105.5 Time for trial, or setting cases for trial
§ 106 Person or official instituting or conducting prosecution
§ 106.5 Defendant's conduct of defense
§ 107 Second or subsequent indictment
§ 108 Consolidation of indictments; joint trial of several charges
§ 108.5 Separate trial of defendants
§ 108.7 —Grounds for separate trial
§ 109 Nolle prosequi
§ 109.3 Dismissal
§ 109.5 —Upon motion of complainant, prosecuting attorney, or attorney general
§ 109.7 —Upon motion of defendant
§ 109.9 Abatement

(B) PROTECTION AND RIGHTS OF ACCUSED GENERALLY

§ 110 Generally
§ 110.3 Right to psychiatric examination
§ 111 Representation by, assistance of, and consultation with, counsel
§ 111.1 —Advice as to rights
§ 111.2 —Communication with counsel; interrogation of accused
§ 111.3 —Preliminary hearing and preparations for trial
§ 111.5 —New trial or appeal, and preparations therefor
§ 111.7 —Attorneys designated
§ 111.8 —Effectiveness of counsel
§ 112 Inspection of indictment or minutes of evidence before grand jury
§ 112.5 Fair and impartial trial
§ 113 Public trial
§ 114 Speedy trial; effect of delay
§ 115 —Delay in retrial, or trial de novo upon appeal
§ 116 —Delay caused by accused
§ 117 —Computation of elapsed time
§ 118 Presence of accused
§ 118.5 —At view of premises
§ 119 —On return of verdict
§ 119.5 Interrogation or admonition of accused; allocation
§ 120 Right to confront witnesses
§ 121 —Use of documentary evidence; depositions
§ 121.5 —Former testimony
§ 122 Compulsory process for witnesses
§ 123 Crimination of self [See Witnesses]
§ 125 Fettering; retention of custody of accused
§ 126 Photographing, measuring, and fingerprinting
§ 127 Waiver or loss of rights
§ 128 —Jurisdiction
§ 128.5 —Preliminary examination
§ 128.7 —Representation by, assistance of, and consultation with, counsel
§ 129 —To public and speedy trial
§ 130 —To be present at trial generally
§ 131 —To be present at view of premises

(C) WARRANT; COMMITMENT

§ 132 Generally
§ 133 Sufficiency of warrant
§ 134 —Oath or affirmation to support

(D) MODE OF PROSECUTION; NECESSITY OF INDICTMENT, PRESENTMENT, OR INFORMATION

§ 135 Generally
§ 136 Necessity of presentment or indictment
§ 137 —Effect of kind or nature of crime
§ 137.3 —Effect of nature of punishment
§ 137.5 —Effect of amendment or consolidation
§ 137.7 —Information instead of indictment
§ 138 Necessity of information

(E) ARRAIGNMENT; PLEADING; MOTIONS; DEMURRER

§ 138.5 Generally
§ 139 Necessity of arraignment
§ 140 Pleas
§ 141 —Necessity of
§ 142 —Verification of
§ 143 —What must be pleaded

termine whether he was competent to stand trial and whether he could be held criminally responsible for the crime charged; although the trial judge granted the motion for examinations, he clearly indicated that at no time did he believe that the defendant was incompetent and that he ordered the examinations in an attempt to fully satisfy the defendant of his constitutional rights; the psychiatrist and a psychologist who examined the defendant found no evidence to indicate that he was incompetent; although the final psychiatric report was received 10 days before trial, no motion for a competency hearing was filed until the morning of trial; the defendant's main purpose in requesting a hearing was to obtain evidence of his mental condition at the time of the offense, but a state statute did not require a pretrial hearing on the issue of criminal responsibility; and the defendant introduced no psychiatric evidence of incompetency at trial, apparently because the reports would have been counterproductive to the defense in the trial. *State v Audia (1983, W Va) 301 SE2d 199, 52 ALR4th 943, cert den 464 US 934, 78 L Ed 2d 307, 104 S Ct 338.*

§ 22 —Delirium tremens or insanity resulting from intoxication

Text References:

21 Am Jur 2d, Criminal Law §§ 45, 47-49, 54, 55, 155-157; 40 Am Jur 2d, Homicide §§ 133, 517

Practice References:

8 Am Jur Pl & Pr Forms (Rev), Criminal Procedure, Forms 163, 191

4 Am Jur Proof of Facts 549, Drugs, Supp., Proof 2; 6 Am Jur Proof of Facts 469, 483, Intoxication; 8 Am Jur Proof of Facts 13, 38, Mental Disorder and Incapacity; 5 Am Jur Proof of Facts 2d 189, Lack of Capacity to Form Specific Intent—Voluntary Intoxication

7 Am Jur Trials 477

L Ed Digest, Criminal Law §§ 18, 76, 78; Drugs, Narcotics & Poisons § 6

Annotations:

When intoxication deemed involuntary so as to constitute a defense to criminal charge, 73 ALR3d 195

Effect of voluntary drug intoxication upon criminal responsibility, 73 ALR3d 98

Drug addiction or related mental state as defense to criminal charge, 73 ALR3d 16

Amnesia as affecting capacity to commit crime or stand trial, 46 ALR3d 544

Comment Note.—on mental or emotional condition as diminishing responsibility for crime, 22 ALR3d 1228

Modern status of rules as to burden and sufficiency of proof of mental irresponsibility in criminal case, 17 ALR3d 146

Appealability of orders or rulings, prior to final judgment in criminal case, as to accused's mental competency, 16 ALR3d 714

Modern status of the rules as to voluntary intoxication as defense to criminal charge, 8 ALR3d 1236

Test of insanity in federal criminal trial, 1 ALR Fed 965

In keeping with the legislative policy that voluntary intoxication is no defense to a crime except insofar as the jury may take it into account in determining purpose, motive, or intent, a state of mind created by voluntary intoxication, which is the immediate result of a particular alcoholic bout, is not a major mental disorder or disease or mental derangement which amounts to legal insanity, whereas an alcoholic psychosis, such as delirium tremens, resulting from long-continued habits of excessive drinking, may amount to legal insanity. *McIntyre v State (1963, Alaska) 379 P2d 615, 8 ALR3d 1231 (ovrld Evans v State (Alaska) 645 P2d 155).*

[Annotated]

§ 23 Infancy

Text References:

21 Am Jur 2d, Criminal Law §§ 38, 76, 77; 29 Am Jur 2d, Evidence § 154; 65 Am Jur 2d, Rape §§ 1 et seq.

Practice References:

1 Am Jur Proof of Facts 315, Age

14 Am Jur Trials 619, Juvenile Court Proceedings

Annotations:

Defense of infancy in juvenile delinquency proceedings, 83 ALR4th 1135

Burden of proof of defendant's age, in prosecution where attainment of particular age is statutory requisite of guilt, 49 ALR3d 526

Mens rea or guilty intent as necessary element of offense of contributing to delinquency or dependency of minor, 31 ALR3d 848

Criminal liability of contributing to delinquency of minor as affected by the fact that minor has not become a delinquent, 18 ALR3d 824

Mistake or lack of information as to victim's age as defense to statutory rape, 8 ALR3d 1100

Although subject to exceptions and qualifications, a minor in certain cases may be liable for his torts and responsible for his crimes and yet not be bound by his contracts. *Porter v Wilson (1965) 106 NH 270, 209 A2d 730, 13 ALR3d 1247.*

(C) ATTEMPTS

§ 24 Generally

Text References:

7A Am Jur 2d, Automobiles and Highway Traffic § 348; 16 Am Jur 2d, Conspiracy § 18; 21 Am Jur 2d, Criminal Law §§ 158-161, 227-231; 32 Am Jur 2d, False Pretenses §§ 4, 12 et

PRIMARY RESOURCES

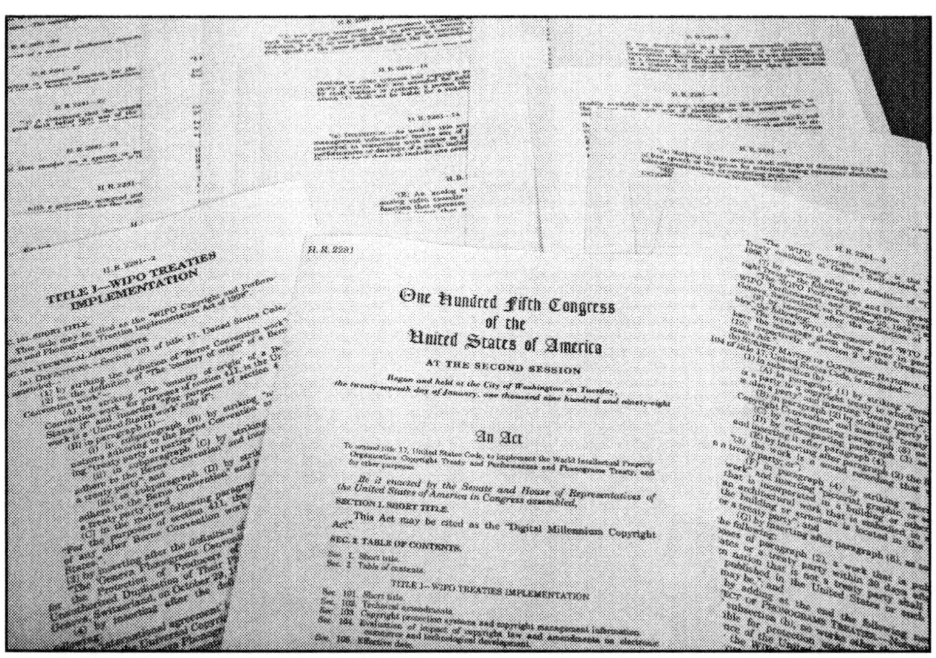

CHAPTER

10

CASE LAW ANALYSIS

I. THE REPORTER SYSTEM

Earlier, this text stressed the indispensability of the reporter system in the publication of case law and decisions. Case law is primary resource material for the analysis of legal problems. Cases contain judicial determinations and interpretations of statutes and legal questions, and hence are mandatory sources for every problem that requires legal research. Because the legal system relies heavily upon precedent and adheres to the doctrine of **stare decisis** (preference for the maintenance of precedent), case law will always remain central to the resolution of legal research problems.

The message of the citation chapter is worth remembering. The typical case citation looks like this:

Jones v. Mary, 18 Pa. Super. 14, 198 A.2d 1845 (1951)

Cases such as *Jones* represent a particular jurisdiction's interpretation of existing law. Here the case, decided in 1951, comes from the Commonwealth of Pennsylvania. In addition, the case is appellate, as it emanates from the state's superior court. Page numbers, volume numbers, and the opposing party are also listed. This short story is replayed in every American jurisdiction to some extent, and the volumes of published judicial opinions fill the shelves to the rafters in the typical law library.

Reporters are collections of cases from the states' highest courts and the courts in the federal realm. Cases are usually published if they go beyond the trial stage and involve some significant question of law or fact. See Figure 10.1 for detailed description of all the resources included in an annotated reporter from Westlaw.

FIGURE 10.1

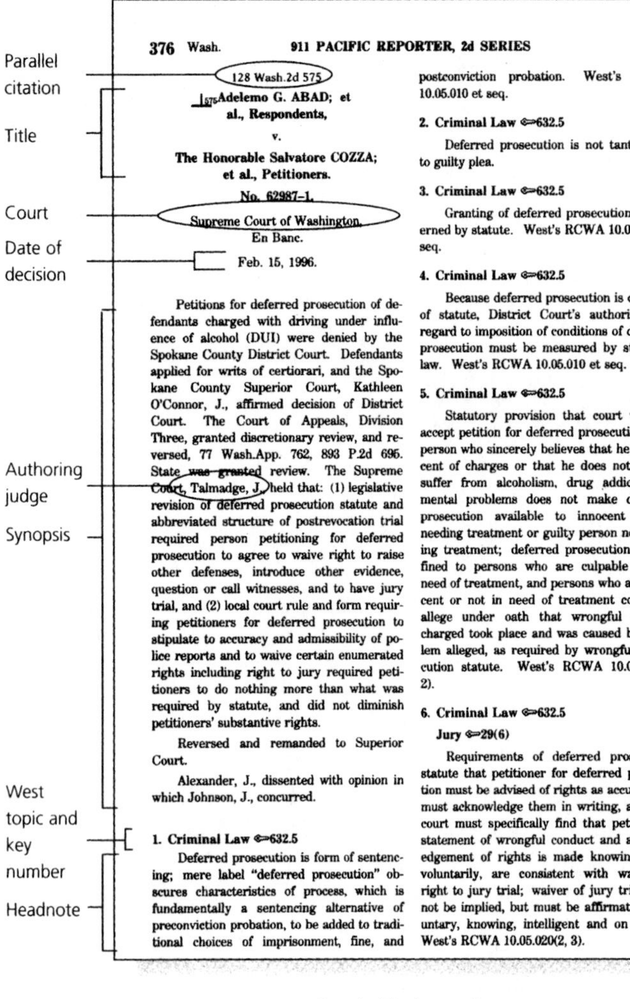

376 Wash. **911 PACIFIC REPORTER, 2d SERIES**

128 Wash.2d 575

575Adelemo G. ABAD; et al., Respondents,

v.

The Honorable Salvatore COZZA; et al., Petitioners.

No. 62987-1.

Supreme Court of Washington, En Banc.

Feb. 15, 1996.

Petitions for deferred prosecution of defendants charged with driving under influence of alcohol (DUI) were denied by the Spokane County District Court. Defendants applied for writs of certiorari, and the Spokane County Superior Court, Kathleen O'Connor, J., affirmed decision of District Court. The Court of Appeals, Division Three, granted discretionary review, and reversed, 77 Wash.App. 762, 893 P.2d 695. State was granted review. The Supreme Court, Talmadge, J., held that: (1) legislative revision of deferred prosecution statute and abbreviated structure of postrevocation trial required person petitioning for deferred prosecution to agree to waive right to raise other defenses, introduce other evidence, question or call witnesses, and to have jury trial, and (2) local court rule and form requiring petitioners for deferred prosecution to stipulate to accuracy and admissibility of police reports and to waive certain enumerated rights including right to jury required petitioners to do nothing more than what was required by statute, and did not diminish petitioners' substantive rights.

Reversed and remanded to Superior Court.

Alexander, J., dissented with opinion in which Johnson, J., concurred.

1. Criminal Law 🔑632.5

Deferred prosecution is form of sentencing; mere label "deferred prosecution" obscures characteristics of process, which is fundamentally a sentencing alternative of preconviction probation, to be added to traditional choices of imprisonment, fine, and postconviction probation. West's RCWA 10.05.010 et seq.

2. Criminal Law 🔑632.5

Deferred prosecution is not tantamount to guilty plea.

3. Criminal Law 🔑632.5

Granting of deferred prosecution is governed by statute. West's RCWA 10.05.010 et seq.

4. Criminal Law 🔑632.5

Because deferred prosecution is creature of statute, District Court's authority with regard to imposition of conditions of deferred prosecution must be measured by statutory law. West's RCWA 10.05.010 et seq.

5. Criminal Law 🔑632.5

Statutory provision that court will not accept petition for deferred prosecution from person who sincerely believes that he is innocent of charges or that he does not in fact suffer from alcoholism, drug addiction or mental problems does not make deferred prosecution available to innocent person needing treatment or guilty person not needing treatment; deferred prosecution is confined to persons who are culpable and in need of treatment, and persons who are innocent or not in need of treatment could not allege under oath that wrongful conduct charged took place and was caused by problem alleged, as required by wrongful prosecution statute. West's RCWA 10.05.020(1, 2).

6. Criminal Law 🔑632.5

Jury 🔑29(6)

Requirements of deferred prosecution statute that petitioner for deferred prosecution must be advised of rights as accused and must acknowledge them in writing, and that court must specifically find that petitioner's statement of wrongful conduct and acknowledgement of rights is made knowingly and voluntarily, are consistent with waiver of right to jury trial; waiver of jury trial must not be implied, but must be affirmative, voluntary, knowing, intelligent and on record. West's RCWA 10.05.020(2, 3).

Case in West reporter

ALIENS 🔑54.3(4)

:s, see Descriptive-Word Index

🔑54.3(4). —— Evidence and questions of law or fact.

U.S. 1992. Board of Immigration Appeals (BIA's) determination that Guatemalan native was not eligible for asylum had to upheld if supported by reasonable, substantial, and probative evidence on record considered as a whole; it could be reversed only if evidence presented by native was such that reasonable fact finder would have to conclude that requisite fear of persecution existed. Immigration and Nationality Act, §§ 101(a)(42)(A), 106(a)(4), 208(a), as amended, 8 U.S.C.A. §§ 1101(a)(42)(A), 1105a(a)(4), 1158(a).
I.N.S. v. Elias-Zacarias, 112 S.Ct. 812, 502 U.S. 478, 117 L.Ed.2d 38.

C.A.D.C. 1996. Standard of review for equal protection challenge to immigration statute is that statute will be upheld if based on facially legitimate and bona fide reason. U.S.C.A. Const.Amend. 5.
Miller v. Christopher, 96 F.3d 1467, 321 U.S.App.D.C. 19, certiorari granted 117 S.Ct. 1551, 520 U.S. 1195, 137 L.Ed.2d 700, certiorari limited 117 S.Ct. 1689, 520 U.S. 1208, 137 L.Ed.2d 817, affirmed 118 S.Ct. 1428, 523 U.S. 420, 140 L.Ed.2d 575.

West's Federal Practice Digest 4th (detail)

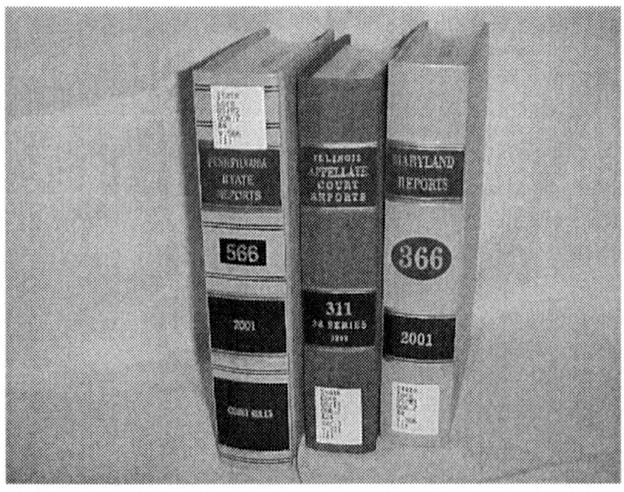

A. State Reporting Systems

Every state, from Maine to Alaska, has a system of reporters. Hardbound editions are kept current by **advance sheets**, which are weekly or monthly updates covering more recent decisions. Advance sheets are eventually redone in a bound volume when enough new decisions exist to fill one.

Some states, such as New York, publish a larger array of case law than their counterparts because of their size and reputation in legal affairs. New York participates in the national reporter system by and through its *New York Supplement Reporter.*

FIGURE 10.2

NATIONAL REPORTER SYSTEM		
Reporter	**Series Abbreviation**	**State Coverage**
Atlantic Reporter	A. and A.2d	Washington, D.C.; Connecticut; Delaware; Maine; Maryland; New Hampshire; New Jersey; Pennsylvania; Rhode Island; Vermont
Northeastern Reporter	N.E. and N.E.2d	New York (Ct. App. only), Illinois, Indiana, Massachusetts, Ohio
Northwestern Reporter	N.W. and N.W.2d	Iowa, Michigan, Minnesota, Nebraska, North Dakota, South Dakota, Wisconsin
Pacific Reporter	P. and P.2d	Alaska, Arizona, California, Colorado, Hawaii, Idaho, Kansas, Montana, Nevada, New Mexico, Oklahoma, Oregon, Utah, Washington, Wyoming
Southeastern Reporter	S.E. and S.E.2d	Georgia, North Carolina, South Carolina, Virginia, West Virginia
Southern Reporter	So. and So. 2d	Alabama, Florida, Louisiana, Mississippi
Southwestern Reporter	S.W. and S.W.2d	Arkansas, Kentucky, Missouri, Tennessee, Texas
New York Supplement	N.Y.S. and N.Y.S.2d	All New York appellate courts
California Reporter	Cal. Rptr.	All California appellate courts

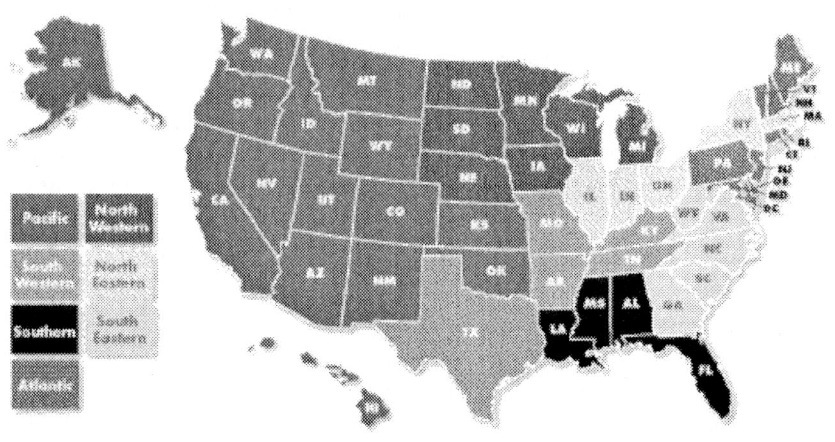

FIGURE 10.3

B. National/Regional Reporters

Decisions of adjoining states in particular geographic regions are compiled in **regional reporters**. Because of the expense of procuring reporters, regional reporters are preferred to their state counterparts. Figure 10.2 outlines the breakdown of West's National Reporter System.

At times, researchers forget the advantages of the regional reporter over the state reporter. In a world moving toward uniform legal application and an increasing reliance on local as well as national precedents, it is imperative to review the regionally reported cases. The table in Figure 10.3 illustrates how the 50 states and the District of Columbia fit into the National Reporter System.

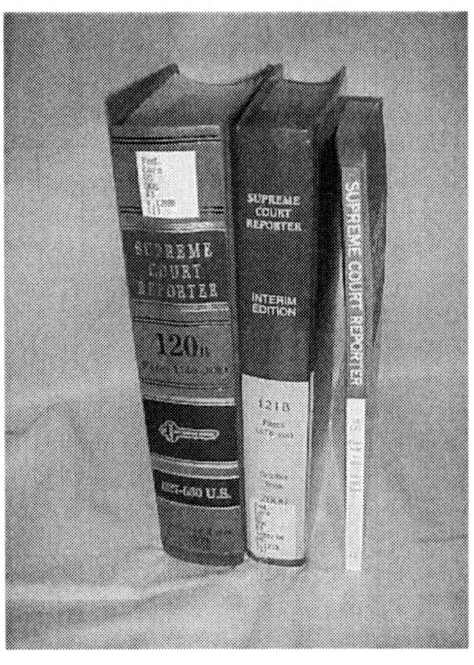

C. Supreme Court

Supreme Court decisions have been published in the reporter format since 1882. There are three different versions of Supreme Court reporters. The *United States Reports* (U.S.) is the official published compilation of decisions of the U.S. Supreme Court. The two unofficial (but well-respected and much-used) reporters are the *Supreme Court Reporter* (S. Ct.), published by West; and the *U.S. Supreme Court Reports, Lawyers Edition, 2d Series* (L. Ed. 2d), put out by Lawyers Cooperative. These unofficial reporters include headnotes and references to each company's other publications.

D. Federal Courts

With the existence of so many federal district courts, and the diverse appellate and specialized courts in the same court system, only a reporter could provide full and comprehensive coverage. United States Courts of Appeal cases are reported in the *Federal Reporter*, now in its third series (F.3d).

U. S. District Courts, including the U.S. Court of Claims, Court of International Trade, and some other now-defunct courts, have decisions reported nationally in the *Federal Supplement* (F. Supp.).

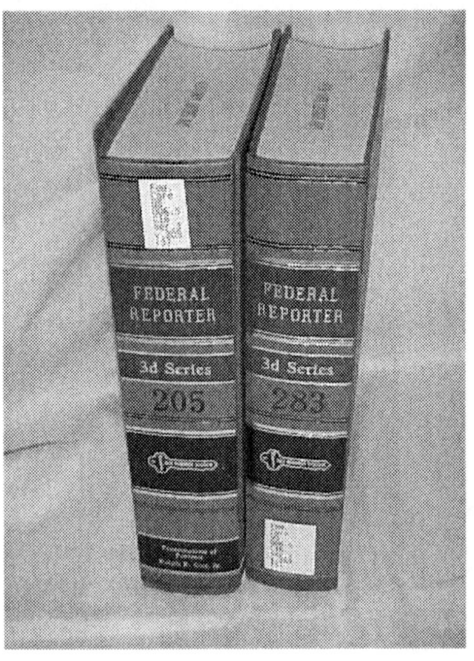

E. Other National Reporter Programs

The trend toward uniform legal application bodes well for the National Reporter System. Those involved in the judicial system also now regularly review and rely upon ancillary and aligned jurisdictions for legal reasoning and have come to depend on nationalized compendia of case law in various areas. For example, West Publishing Company produces four topical national reporters:

1. Military Justice Reporter
2. Bankruptcy Reporter
3. U.S. Claims Court Reporter
4. Federal Rules Decisions

Aside from a reproduction of the court's opinion in full, reporters also provide a syllabus of the case or a synopsis of the entire decision, as well as a set of **headnotes** with **key referencing**, which highlight important issues in the case. The reporter also allows the researcher to cross-reference statutes interpreted in the cases and to find all references within the reporter to the American Bar Association's **Standards in Criminal Justice** and the **Federal Rules of Evidence**, **Civil**, **Criminal**, and **Appellate Procedure**.

II. HOW TO ANALYZE CASE DECISIONS

When analyzing a case law decision, it is good practice to ask, "What words describe the parties concerned; the places or things involved; the basis of the action or issue;

the possible defense or defenses, and the relief sought?" Of course, these inquisitional skills and techniques are also applicable to statutes, rules, and other related legal materials. When evaluating facts, keep in mind the different methods of analyzing factual situations learned in Chapter 2.

Of all these analytical requirements, none is more compelling than **issue identification**. In fact, the identification and analysis of legal issues is the chief intellectual activity of the legal professional. It is not enough to know the facts; it is more essential to know and understand the basis for a legal position and argument. In short, why is the case before the tribunal? What is the dispute? What legal rules apply: statutes, code provisions, and constitutional amendments? It is here that the legal issues are clarified and the researcher earns his or her keep. Although facts and defenses to a case are still important, the most challenging task for the researcher remains issue identification and clarification. Be patient in the development of this skill. Realize that the capacity for issue resolution largely depends on practice, experience, and a substantive knowledge of the law being dealt with. Time and practice are allies.

III. FINDING CASE LAW

Digests are the primary finding tool for case law. Unlike other primary resources, reporters do not have their own indexes, so you must use a digest. Cases found using the digest pages, relating to the fact patterns in Chapter 5, are shown in the accompanying figures.

Fact Pattern 1: See Fact Pattern Figure 10.4.

Fact Pattern 2: See Fact Pattern Figure 10.5.

IV. SUMMARY

Precedent supports and buttresses any legal argument. Case decisions constitute a huge proportion of that precedent; they also reveal trends in legal thought, the strength of particular arguments, and possible lines of alternate arguments, as well as provide excellent cross-references and other leads for researching a legal issue. The reporter systems are collections of cases from the states' highest courts. Most states have their own reporting series, which are eventually compiled by private companies such as West Publishing Company and Lawyer's Cooperative. Supreme Court and other federal court cases are also published in their own case collections within the reporter system. Other decisions of federal courts and dependent courts are published in the *Federal Supplement*. Besides the text of decisions, the reporter systems deliver additional benefits in the form of syllabi of cases, reviews of decisions, and headnotes for easy cross-references. The A.L.R. series provides a review of relevant case law by subject matter, though it covers only significant cases. The legal researcher must first identify the legal problem and then begin researching the specific issue.

EEPA may be guided by principles of law under the ADEA, as well as under Title VII.

Like Title VII, the ADEA explicitly encompasses discriminatory hiring practices, as well as wrongful termination. At least one court has specifically held that the ADEA prohibits an employer form unjustifiably basing its hiring decision on a job applicant's age. *Reed v. Signode Corp.,* 652 F.Supp. 129 (D.Conn.1986). *See also Zinger v. Blanchette,* 549 F.2d 901 (C.A.Pa.1977), *cert. denied,* 434 U.S. 1008, 98 S.Ct. 717, 54 L.Ed.2d 750 (1977) (holding that the primary purpose of the ADEA is to prevent age discrimination in hiring and discharging workers). In addition, courts have consistently held that the ADEA is remedial and humanitarian in nature and should be literally interpreted to effectuate the congressional purpose of ending age discrimination. *Dartt v. Shell Oil Co.,* 539 F.2d 1256 (C.A.Okl.1976), *aff'd,* 434 U.S. 99, 98 S.Ct. 600, 54 L.Ed.2d 270 (1977), *rehearing denied,* 434 U.S. 1042, 98 S.Ct. 785, 54 L.Ed.2d 792 (1978). *See also Danner v. Phillips Petroleum Col.,* 447 F.2d 159, 161 (5th Cir.1971); *Holliday v. Ketchum, MacLeod & Grove, Inc.* 584 F.2d 1221 (C.A.Pa. 1978); *Vazquez v. Eastern Air Lines, Inc.,* 579 F.2d 107 (C.A.Puerto Rico 1978).

The federal law of age discrimination, then, certainly encompasses discrimination in the hiring context as well as in the termination context. Therefore, if we must look to principles of federal law for guidance in interpreting the EEPA, it is logical to extend the protection of the EEPA to discriminatory hiring practices. The language of the EEPA bolsters this argument. The legislative declaration of the EEPA states: "It is the public policy of this State to protect and safeguard the right and opportunity of all persons to *seek, obtain,* and hold employment without discrimination . . ." (emphasis added). The statute goes on to explain the reasons for such a policy:

> It is recognized that the practice of denying employment opportunity and discriminating in the terms of employment foments domestic strife and unrest, deprives the State of the fullest utilization of its capacities for advancement and development, and substantially and adversely affects the interests of employees, employers, and the public in general.

Allowing a cause of action for wrongfully refusing to hire an individual based on age discrimination will further this public policy at both the hiring and employment stages, and will contribute toward alleviating the concerns referred to in the statute. If it violates public policy for an employer to discriminate against an individual during employment or as a basis for termination, then it is equally abusive to discriminate against an individual seeking employment. Therefore, Plaintiff can maintain a cause of action for failure to hire in violation of the public policy articulated in N.C.G.S. § 143–422.1 *et seq.*

In his complaint, Plaintiff has alleged sufficient facts to state a claim of wrongful failure to hire in violation of the public policy stated in the EEPA. Accordingly, Defendant's motion to dismiss is DENIED.

SO ORDERED.

Cornell BRANTLEY, Plaintiff,

v.

Arthur A. VAUGHAN, and Anita L. Flippen, Defendants.

Civ. A. No. 9:93–1969–19.

United States District Court,
D. South Carolina,
Beaufort Division.

Oct. 14, 1993.

Pedestrian brought personal injury action in South Carolina state court against driver of vehicle which struck him and vehicle's owner. Driver removed action to federal district court. On pedestrian's motion to remand, the District Court, Shedd, J., held there: (1) where Rule 12(b)(6) motion to dismiss and claim of fraudulent joinder were both made, it would be improper to resolve Rule 12(b)(6) motion prior to resolving claim of fraudulent joinder, which was jurisdictional inquiry; (2) pedestrian demonstrated possibility of right of recovery in negligent entrustment action against owner, and thus did not fraudulently join owner in action.

Motion granted.

1. Removal of Cases ⚷ **82**

Absent certain exceptions, all defendants must join in petition for removal within 30 days from date they are served or case is not properly removed.

2. Removal of Cases ⚷ **82**

Petition for removal is considered defective if it fails to explain why all defendants have not joined therein.

3. Removal of Cases ⚷ **82**

In cases involving fraudulent joinder, consent of alleged fraudulently joined party is not required in order for case to be removed.

4. Removal of Cases ⚷ **107(7)**

Party seeking removal bears burden of establishing right to remove action, and any doubts concerning propriety of removal must be resolved in favor of state court jurisdiction.

5. Federal Civil Procedure ⚷ **1825**

Where Rule 12(b)(6) motion to dismiss and claim of fraudulent joinder are both made, it is improper to resolve Rule 12(b)(6) motion prior to resolving claim of fraudulent joinder, which is jurisdictional inquiry. Fed. Rules Civ.Proc.Rule 12(b)(6), 28 U.S.C.A.

6. Automobiles ⚷ **192(11)**

Under theory of negligent entrustment of an automobile, owner or one in control of vehicle and responsible for its use who is negligent in entrusting it to another can be held liable for such negligent entrustment.

7. Automobiles ⚷ **192(11)**

Where claim of negligent entrustment is based on driver's alleged impairment due to use of alcohol, elements of cause of action are: (1) knowledge of, or knowledge inputed to, owner of automobile that driver was either under influence of intoxicants, addicted to intoxicants, or had habit of drinking; (2) owner knew or had inputable knowledge that driver was likely to drive while intoxicated; and (3) under these circumstances, owner of vehicle entrusted it to driver.

8. Federal Courts ⚷ **303**

Pedestrian demonstrated possibility of recovery in negligent entrustment action against owner of automobile which struck him, and thus did not fraudulently join owner in action; although inference could be drawn that pedestrian joined owner for purpose of defeating diversity jurisdiction, pedestrian's motive was irrelevant so long as there was good faith basis for cause of action.

Mark D. Ball, Peters, Murdaugh, Parker, Eltzroth & Detrick, P.A., Hampton, SC, for plaintiff.

Dixie W. Cooper, Charleston, SC, for defendants.

ORDER

SHEDD, District Judge.

This personal injury action is before the Court on defendant Anita L. Flippen's motion to dismiss pursuant to Rule 12(b)(6) of the Federal Rules of Civil Procedure and plaintiff's motion to remand to state court pursuant to 28 U.S.C. § 1447(c). After carefully reviewing the record and the controlling legal principles, the Court concludes that the motion to remand should be granted for the reasons set forth below. As a consequence of this determination, the Court is without jurisdiction to resolve the motion to dismiss.

I

The relevant facts in the record are as follows. On December 11, 1991, plaintiff, a resident of South Carolina, filed a negligence action in the Court of Common Pleas for Jasper County, South Carolina, against Arthur A. Vaughan seeking to recover an unspecified amount of actual and punitive damages which allegedly were the result of his being struck by an automobile driven by

continued

Vaughan. Vaughan, who is a resident of New York, thereafter removed that action to this Court based on grounds of diversity of citizenship. In response, plaintiff filed a motion to remand because the amount in controversy did not exceed $50,000 or, in the alternative, to dismiss without prejudice.

By Order entered March 5, 1993, the Court denied the motion to remand and granted the motion to dismiss without prejudice on the condition that plaintiff reimburse Vaughan for the reasonable costs he incurred following removal of the case from state court. Although plaintiff initially indicated his unwillingness to reimburse Vaughan's costs, he eventually did so after the Court ordered that the action would be dismissed with prejudice if plaintiff refused to reimburse Vaughan. Thereafter, by Order entered April 7, the Court dismissed that action without prejudice.

Plaintiff filed this action in the Court of Common Pleas for Jasper County on July 2. In the Complaint, plaintiff again seeks an unspecified amount of actual and punitive damages against Vaughan based on his alleged negligence. Plaintiff also makes a claim against Flippen, who is a resident of South Carolina, under a theory of negligent entrustment because Flippen owned the automobile which Vaughan was driving at the time of the accident. Plaintiff contends that Vaughan was impaired in his ability to operate a motor vehicle at the time of the accident and that Flippen knew or should have known of his impairment.[1] Plaintiff served the Summons and Complaint on Vaughan on July 9. There is no evidence in the record as to when Flippen was served.

[1–3] On August 6, Vaughan filed in this Court a Notice of Removal based on grounds of diversity of citizenship and an answer to the Complaint; and Flippen filed an answer and a motion to dismiss pursuant to Rule 12(b)(6), in which she contends that the Complaint fails to state a claim against her upon which relief can be granted. In the Notice of Removal, Vaughan argues that Flippen was fraudulently joined in this action to destroy diversity of citizenship. Flippen has not filed a petition for removal and there is nothing in the Notice of Removal, or elsewhere in the record, which indicates that she joins in Vaughan's Notice of Removal.[2]

Plaintiff files his motion to remand this action pursuant to 28 U.S.C. § 1447(c) on September 7 and, on September 13, plaintiff filed an amended motion to remand to reflect the proper caption of this case. In both motions, the text of which are identical, plaintiff states without elaboration that diversity jurisdiction does not exist because the minimum amount in controversy is not present.[3] However, in a memorandum in support of the motion to remand which plaintiff filed on September 3,[4] plaintiff argues only that diversity of citizenship does not exist because both he and Flippen are residents of South Carolina.

II

[4] It is clear from the record that the sole potential basis for jurisdiction in this Court is diversity of citizenship between the parties. Vaughan, as the party seeking removal, bears the burden of establishing his right to remove this action—that is, diversity

1. There is no federal question or other basis for federal jurisdiction raised in the Complaint.

2. Absent certain exceptions, it is settled law that all defendants must join in a petition for removal within thirty days from the date they are served or the case is not properly removed. *Chicago, R.I. & P. Ry. Co. v. Martin,* 178 U.S. 245, 248, 20 S.Ct. 854, 855, 44 L.Ed. 1055 (1900). A petition for removal is considered defective if it fails to explain why all defendants have not joined therein. *Shaw v. Dow Brands, Inc.,* 994 F.2d 364, 368 (7th Cir.1993). However, in cases involving allegations of fraudulent joinder, consent of the alleged fraudulently joined party is not required. *Jernigan v. Ashland Oil Co.,* 989 F.2d 812, 815 (5th Cir.), *cert. denied,* — U.S. —, 114 S.Ct. 192, — L.Ed.2d — (Oct. 4, 1993).

3. In the motion to remand in the first action, plaintiff stipulated that his damages are less than $50,000. However, the Court found in that action that it did not appear to a legal certainty that the amount in controversy did not exceed $50,000. That ruling applies in this case notwithstanding plaintiff's prior stipulation.

4. There is nothing in the record to indicate why plaintiff filed his memorandum in support of the motion to remand 4 days *prior to* the date he filed the motion to remand.

jurisdiction is present—and any doubts concerning the propriety of removal must be resolved in favor of state court jurisdiction. *Able v. Upjohn Co.,* 829 F.2d 1330, 1332 (4th Cir.1987), *cert. denied,* 485 U.S. 963, 108 S.Ct. 1229, 99 L.Ed.2d 429 (1988); *Toyota of Florence, Inc. v. Lynch,* 713 F.Supp. 898, 900 (D.S.C.1989). Because the requisite amount in controversy is present and plaintiff and Flippen are both residents of South Carolina, the focus is on whether, as Vaughan contends, plaintiff fraudulently joined Flippen to destroy diversity. If plaintiff properly joined Flippen, then Vaughan improvidently removed this case and the Court must remand it to state court for lack of jurisdiction. Conversely, if plaintiff fraudulently joined Flippen, then the Court must dismiss Flippen and exercise jurisdiction over this case.

A.

[5] As noted, the parties have placed this issue before the Court by means of Flippen's 12(b)(6) motion to dismiss, and plaintiff's motion to remand coupled with Vaughan's assertion that Flippen was fraudulently joined. The Fourth Circuit has summarized the standard for reviewing a 12(b)(6) motion to dismiss as follows:

> A motion to dismiss under Rule 12(b)(6) tests the sufficiency of a complaint; importantly, it does not resolve contests surrounding the facts, the merits of a claim, or the applicability of defenses. Our inquiry then is limited to whether the allegations constitute " 'a short and plain statement of the claim showing that the pleader is entitled to relief.' " "[A] complaint should not be dismissed for failure to state a claim unless it appears beyond doubt that the plaintiff can prove no set of facts in support of his claim which would entitle him to relief." We must assume that the allegations of the complaint are true and construe them in the light most favorable to the plaintiff.

Republican Party of N.C. v. Martin, 980 F.2d 943, 952 (4th Cir.) (citations omitted and alterations in original), *cert. denied,* — U.S. —, 114 S.Ct. 93, 126 L.Ed.2d 60 (1993). In contrast, the Fourth Circuit has summarized the standard for reviewing a claim of fraudulent joinder as follows:

> In order to establish that a nondiverse defendant has been fraudulently joined, the removing party must establish either "[T]hat there is *no possibility* that the plaintiff would be able to establish a cause of action against the in-state defendant in state court; or [T]hat there has been outright fraud in the plaintiff's pleading of jurisdictional facts." The burden on the defendant claiming fraudulent joinder is heavy; the defendant must show that the plaintiff cannot establish a claim against the nondiverse defendant even after resolving all issues of fact and law in the plaintiff's favor. A claim need not ultimately succeed to defeat removal; only a possibility of a right to relief need be asserted.
>
> In order to determine whether an attempted joinder is fraudulent, the Court is not bound by the allegations of the pleadings, but may instead "consider the entire record, and determine the basis of joinder by any means available."

Marshall v. Manville Sales Corp., 6 F.3d 229 (4th Cir.1993) (emphasis and alterations in original); *AIDS Counseling & Testing Centers v. Group W Television, Inc.,* 903 F.2d 1000, 1003 (4th Cir.1990) (citation omitted).

In analyzing and resolving this issue, the Court is guided by the opinion in *Batoff v. State Farm Insurance Company,* 977 F.2d 848 (3d Cir.1992), in which the Third Circuit addressed the interplay between a 12(b)(6) motion to dismiss and a motion to remand where there is a claim of fraudulent joinder. The court in *Batoff* found that "the inquiry into the validity of a complaint triggered by a motion to dismiss under Rule 12(b)(6) is more searching than that permissible when a party makes a claim of fraudulent joinder" and, therefore, held that where, as here, a 12(b)(6) motion and a claim of fraudulent joinder are both made, it is improper to resolve the 12(b)(6) motion prior to resolving the claim of fraudulent joinder, which is a jurisdictional inquiry. 977 F.2d at 852. The court noted that "it is possible that a party is not fraudulently joined, but that the claim against that party ultimately is dismissed for

continued

failure to state a claim upon which relief may be granted." *Id.*

Although *Batoff* is not binding precedent, the Court finds the analysis set forth by the Third Circuit in *Batoff* to be proper in light of the above-noted standards articulated by the Fourth Circuit. Therefore, the Court will proceed to address plaintiff's motion to remand and Vaughan's claim that Flippen was fraudulently joined.

B.

[6 7] Plaintiff's purported claim against Flippen is for negligent entrustment of an automobile. Under the theory of negligent entrustment, " 'the owner or one in control of the vehicle and responsible for its use who is negligent in entrusting it to another can be held liable for such negligent entrustment.' " *American Mut. Fire Ins. Co. v. Passmore,* 275 S.C. 618, 274 S.E.2d 416, 418 (1981) (citation omitted). Where, as here, the claim of negligent entrustment is based on the driver's alleged impairment due to use of alcohol, the elements of the cause of action are: (1) knowledge of, or knowledge imputed to, the owner of the automobile that the driver was either under the influence of intoxicants, addicted to intoxicants, or had the habit of drinking, (2) the owner knew or had imputable knowledge that the driver was likely to drive while intoxicated, and (3) under these circumstances, the owner of the vehicle entrusted it to the driver. *See Jackson v. Price,* 288 S.C. 377, 342 S.E.2d 628, 631 (App.1986).

[8] In construing the entire record, the Court concludes that plaintiff has unquestionably demonstrated a possibility of a right of recovery against Flippen. For example, in the Complaint, plaintiff alleges that Vaughan, while driving an automobile owned by Flippen, crossed the center line and struck him as he was walking in the road. With respect to Flippen, plaintiff specifically alleges that "at the time of the accident, the defendant, Vaughan, was impaired in his ability to operate a motor vehicle; [and] that the defendant, Flippen, knew and should have known the defendant Vaughan was impaired." Plaintiff further alleges that his injuries were proximately caused by defendants' conduct in several particulars, including "knowingly allowing someone to operate a motor vehicle in an impaired state." Both Vaughan and Flippen admit in their answers that Vaughan was driving Flippen's car at the time of the accident. Moreover, plaintiff has submitted an affidavit of a deputy sheriff for Hampton County who was at the scene of an accident (purportedly between plaintiff and Vaughan) in which the deputy sheriff states that "it was apparent the driver had been consuming alcoholic beverages" and that in his opinion, "the driver was impaired in his abilities to operate the vehicle." *Affidavit of Scottie Smith,* ¶¶3–4.[5]

Vaughan's main argument in support of his claim of fraudulent joinder is that plaintiff knew of Flippen's existence and relation to the underlying accident when he filed the first lawsuit and his failure to include her in that suit, coupled with his effort to remain in state court, shows that Flippen was added solely to destroy diversity. There is no question that plaintiff does not want to litigate this case in federal court. Plaintiff filed both of these actions in state court and has fought Vaughan's effort to remove both cases to federal court. An inference could certainly be drawn from the record that plaintiff joined Flippen in this action for the purpose of defeating diversity jurisdiction. However, plaintiff's motive in joining Flippen is immaterial so long as there is a good faith basis for the cause of action he has asserted against her. *Mecom v. Fitzsimmons Drilling Co.,* 284 U.S. 183, 189–90, 52 S.Ct. 84, 87, 76 L.Ed. 233 (1931). Because the Court has found that plaintiff has alleged a claim against Flippen for which he has at least the possibility of recovery, the Court cannot conclude that he brought the claim against her in bad faith.[6]

5. There is no specific indication in the affidavit that this was the accident which is at issue in this case.

6. Because the case is to be remanded, the Court is without jurisdiction to resolve the motion to dismiss. The Court notes that nothing in this Order should be construed as an expression of whether plaintiff has actually stated a valid claim against Flippen. *See Batoff,* 977 F.2d at 854.

III

IT IS THEREFORE ORDERED on this the 14th day of October, 1993, at Columbia, South Carolina, that plaintiff's motion to remand be **GRANTED.** The Clerk of Court is **DIRECTED** to remand this action to the Court of Common Pleas for Jasper County.

Susan HARRIS, Plaintiff,

v.

PALMETTO TILE, INC., Henry Goldberg and Marque Collins, Defendants.

Civ. A. No. 3:92–3391–19.

United States District Court,
D. South Carolina,
Columbia Division.

Oct. 14, 1993.

Plaintiff brought Title VII action against her employer. Employer moved for summary judgment. The District Court, Shedd, J., held that plaintiff's employer and another entity were not a "single employer" for Title VII purposes.

Motion granted.

1. Federal Civil Procedure ⚷ 2461

Summary judgment is not a disfavored procedural shortcut, but rather an integral part of the federal rules as a whole which are designed to secure the just, speedy and inexpensive determination of every action. Fed. Rules Civ.Proc.Rule 56(c), 28 U.S.C.A.

2. Federal Civil Procedure ⚷ 2544

When movant properly supports its summary judgment motion with showing that it is entitled to judgment as a matter of law, party opposing motion must present affirmative evidence to establish genuine dispute of material fact which is necessary to defeat motion. Fed.Rules Civ.Proc.Rule 56(c), 28 U.S.C.A.

3. Federal Civil Procedure ⚷ 2543, 2544

In reviewing motion for summary judgment, district court is required to view any permissible inferences to be drawn from underlying facts in light most favorable to nonmovant and if, after so viewing the evidence, court finds that nonmovant has failed to make showing sufficient to establish existence of element essential to its case and on which it will bear burden of proof at trial, court must grant summary judgment against that party. Fed.Rules Civ.Proc.Rule 56(c), 28 U.S.C.A.

4. Civil Rights ⚷ 143

As jurisdictional prerequisite to maintenance of Title VII action, plaintiff must prove that defendant employer is person engaged in industry affecting commerce who has 15 or more employees for each working day in each of 20 or more calendar weeks in the current or preceding calendar year. Civil Rights Act of 1964, § 701 et seq., 42 U.S.C.A. § 2000e et seq.

5. Civil Rights ⚷ 143

Fact that plaintiff's employer and another company pooled their resources in the administration of their insurance and profit sharing plans did not indicate that participating employees were employees of both entities so as to satisfy Title VII's jurisdictional prerequisite of 15 employees. Civil Rights Act of 1964, § 701 et seq., 42 U.S.C.A. § 2000e et seq.

6. Civil Rights ⚷ 143

Even if evidence that plaintiff's employer and another company pooled their resources in the administration of their insurance and profit sharing plans supported inference that plaintiff was employed by both entities, that fact alone could not support conclusion that entities were a single employer for Title VII purposes. Civil Rights Act of 1964, § 701 et seq., 42 U.S.C.A. § 2000e et seq.

7. Civil Rights ⚷ 143

It is the relationship between the two entities, not fact that both entities happen to

C. *Other Issues*

It follows that Plaintiffs' state law claim for nuisance has no "common nucleus of operative fact" with any federal claim remaining against a party to this litigation, *see United Mine Workers of America v. Gibbs,* 383 U.S. 715, 86 S.Ct. 1130, 16 L.Ed.2d 218 (1966), and must therefore also be dismissed. Finally, Plaintiff's Motion to Compel Discovery of Defendant J & J Shapiro, Inc. a/k/a J & H Shapiro must be deemed moot.

IV.

Accordingly, it is ordered that:

(1) Defendants' Motion for Summary Judgment, filed August 14, 1992, is GRANTED.

(2) Plaintiff's Motion to Compel Discovery of Defendant J & H Shapiro, Inc. a/k/a J & H Shapiro, filed November 17, 1992, is DEEMED MOOT.

(3) Defendants' names are to be removed from the caption of this case.

The CITY AND COUNTY OF DENVER, et al., Plaintiffs,

v.

ADOLPH COORS COMPANY, et al., Defendants.

Civ. A. No. 91–F–2233.

United States District Court, D. Colorado.

Jan. 13, 1993.

Governmental entities brought environmental cleanup action, and defendant moved for summary judgment on ground that parties had previously entered into binding settlement agreement. The District Court, Sherman G. Finesilver, Chief Judge, held that: (1) governmental entities' alleged secret intent not to dismiss corporation as party unless partnership in which it held interest could be added as defendant did not prevent parties from entering into binding settlement agreement, and (2) government entities' failure to execute written settlement agreement did not preclude formation of binding settlement.

Motion granted.

1. Compromise and Settlement ⚷ 21

Trial court has inherent power to summarily enforce settlement agreements entered into by litigants in cases before court.

2. Compromise and Settlement ⚷ 2

Settlement agreements are favored by courts.

3. Compromise and Settlement ⚷ 21

Settlement agreement will be enforced only if terms of settlement are clear, unambiguous and capable of enforcement.

4. Compromise and Settlement ⚷ 11

Settlement agreements are construed in same way as contracts in determining whether and how they should be enforced.

5. Compromise and Settlement ⚷ 8(1)

Governmental entities' alleged secret intent not to dismiss corporation as party in environmental cleanup case unless partnership in which it held interest could be added as defendant did not prevent parties from entering into binding settlement agreement dismissing corporation as party, where settlement agreement did not mention this alleged condition precedent and governmental entities admitted that they never discussed their purported intentions with corporation.

6. Contracts ⚷ 14

Parties' mutual assent to contract is to be judged only by their overt acts and words, rather than by their hidden and secret intentions.

7. Contracts ⚷ 147(1)

When contested term is unambiguous, contract is formed, regardless of any unexpressed intention that one party may have had.

8. Contracts ⚷ 35

Signature is not always necessary to create binding contract; purpose of signature is to demonstrate mutuality of assent, which can as well be shown by conduct of parties.

9. Contracts ⚷ 32

Party is not bound by oral agreement if he does not intend to be bound until formal document is executed.

10. Contracts ⚷ 175(1)

Burden is on party arguing that it was parties' intent not to be bound until formal writing was executed to demonstrate either that both parties understood they were not to be bound until executed contract was delivered, or that other party should have known that disclaiming party did not intend to be bound before contract was signed.

11. Contracts ⚷ 32

In deciding whether execution of formal written agreement is prerequisite to contact formation, court should consider: whether parties have stated intention not to be bound absent executed writing; whether one party has performed partially and the other party has accepted such performance; whether issues remain to be negotiated, or whether signing of contract is merely ministerial; and whether contact concerns complex business matters such that written agreement would be the norm, not the exception.

12. Compromise and Settlement ⚷ 5(1)

Governmental entities' failure to sign written agreement which they had drafted, dismissing corporation as party in environmental cleanup case, did not preclude formation of binding settlement agreement, where governmental entities had agreed to settlement, represented as much to court, and forwarded written agreement to corporation with unqualified statement that it would be executed by governmental entities upon agreement's return.

13. Federal Civil Procedure ⚷ 1827.1

Governmental entities were not entitled to evidentiary hearing prior to dismissal of corporate defendant from case pursuant to settlement agreement, where trial court's determination that binding settlement had been reached was based on governmental entities' own representations and affidavits, and not on any allegations of corporation that could be fruitfully attacked on cross-examination.

14. Federal Civil Procedure ⚷ 2737.13

Defendant that had successfully sued to enforce settlement agreement dismissing it from case was entitled to its reasonable costs and attorney fees, pursuant to clause in agreement providing that prevailing party in any dispute over agreement would be awarded reasonable attorney fees and costs.

Daniel E. Muse, T. Shaun Sullivan, Steven J. Coon; Russell E. Yates, Carolyn L. Buchholz, James D. Ellman, Denver, CO; P.B. ("Lynn") Walker, Englewood, CO, and Robert S. Treece, and Daniel S. Maus, Denver, CO, for plaintiffs.

Linda Rockwood and James L. Harrison, Denver, CO, for Earth Sciences, Inc.

ORDER REGARDING ENFORCEMENT OF SETTLEMENT AND SUMMARY JUDGMENT:

1993–2

SHERMAN G. FINESILVER, Chief Judge.

This is a case involving environmental contamination at the Lowry Landfill site ("Lowry"), operated at various times by Plaintiffs City and County of Denver ("Denver"), Waste Management of Colorado, Inc. ("WMC"), and Chemical Waste Management, Inc. ("CWM"). This matter comes before the Court on Defendant Earth Sciences, Inc.'s ("ESI") Motion for Summary Judgment, to Dismiss With Prejudice, and to Enforce Settlement Agreement. Jurisdiction is based on 28 U.S.C.A. § 1331 (West 1992). The parties have fully briefed the issues. For the reasons stated below, the motion is GRANTED.

continued

I.

ESI and Plaintiffs dispute whether they have entered into a binding settlement agreement ("the Agreement").

ESI was initially identified by the EPA as having contributed to the environmental waste at Lowry two waste streams totaling over six million gallons. In June 1992, EPA revised ESI's share of the waste to a mere 3800 gallons, attributing the remaining six million gallons to Alumet Partnership ("Alumet"), a partnership in which ESI is a general partner. ESI subsequently wrote Plaintiffs requesting an offer of settlement as a *de minimis* party, in accordance with Plaintiffs' usual policy of allowing *de minimis* settlor status to contributors of under 300,000 gallons of waste. Plaintiffs' agreement to negotiate such a settlement was conditioned on an agreement between the parties that Plaintiffs would move to amend the First Amended Complaint to join Alumet as a defendant and that ESI would not oppose the joinder.

After considerable negotiations and correspondence back and forth, the parties achieved a final draft of the Agreement. Plaintiffs sent the Agreement to ESI for signing and instructed ESI to return the Agreement so that Plaintiffs could execute it. One of Plaintiffs' numerous counsel represented to the Court in a status conference on October 23, 1992, that the parties had reached a settlement. Before Plaintiffs executed the Agreement, however, the Court denied Plaintiffs' motion to add Alumet as a party defendant. Plaintiffs then refused to sign the Agreement.

ESI seeks summary judgment on all claims against it and enforcement of the Agreement to dismissing ESI with prejudice. ESI disputes that Plaintiffs ever made joinder of Alumet a condition of settlement. Nowhere in the Agreement is such a condition either stated or implied.

II. Summary Judgment Standard

Granting summary judgment is appropriate when there is no genuine issue of material fact and the moving party is entitled to judgment as a matter of law. Fed.R.Civ.P. 56(c); *Ash Creek Mining Co. v Lujan,* 934 F.2d 240, 242 (10th Cir.1991); *Metz v. United States,* 933 F.2d 802, 804 (10th Cir.1991), *cert. denied,* — U.S. —, 112 S.Ct. 416, 116 L.Ed.2d 436 (1991); *Continental Casualty Co. v P.D.C., Inc.,* 931 F.2d 1429, 1430 (10th Cir.1991). A genuine issue of material fact exists only where "there is sufficient evidence favoring the nonmoving party for a jury to return a verdict for that party." *Merrick v. Northern Natural Gas Co.,* 911 F.2d 426, 429 (10th Cir.1990). Only disputes over facts that might affect the outcome of the case will properly preclude the entry of summary judgment. *Anderson v. Liberty Lobby, Inc.,* 477 U.S. 242, 106 S.Ct. 2505, 91 L.Ed.2d 202 (1986); *Allen v. Dayco Prods., Inc.,* 758 F.Supp. 630, 631 (D.Colo.1990).

In reviewing a motion for summary judgment, the court must view the evidence in the light most favorable to the party opposing the motion. *Newport Steel Corp. v. Thompson,* 757 F.Supp. 1152, 1155 (D.Colo. 1990). All doubts must be resolved in favor of the existence of triable issues of fact. *Boren v. Southwestern Bell Tel. Co.,* 933 F.2d 891, 892 (10th Cir.1991); *Mountain Fuel Supply v. Reliance Ins. Co.,* 933 F.2d 882, 889 (10th Cir.1991).

In a motion for summary judgment, the moving party's initial burden is slight. In *Celotex Corp. v. Catrett,* 477 U.S. 317, 327, 106 S.Ct. 2548, 2555, 91 L.Ed.2d 265 (1986), the Supreme Court held that the language of rule 56(c) does not require the moving party to show an absence of issues of material fact in order to be awarded summary judgment. Rule 56 does not require the movant to negate the opponent's claim. *Id.* at 323, 106 S.Ct. at 2552–53. The moving party must allege an absence of evidence to support the opposing party's case and identify supporting portions of the record. *Id.*

Once the movant has made an initial showing, the burden of going forward shifts to the opposing party. The nonmovant must establish that there are issues of material fact to be determined. *Id.* at 322–23, 106 S.Ct. at 2552–53. The nonmovant must go beyond the pleadings and designate specific facts showing genuine issues for trial on every element challenged by the motion. *Tillett v. Lujan,* 931 F.2d 636,

639 (10th Cir.1991). Conclusory allegations will not establish issues of fact sufficient to defeat summary judgment. *McVay v. Western Plains Serv. Corp.*, 823 F.2d 1395, 1398 (10th Cir.1987).

In reviewing the evidence submitted, the court should grant summary judgment only when there is clearly no issue of material fact remaining. In *Anderson*, 477 U.S. at 249–50, 106 S.Ct. at 2510–11, the Court held that summary judgment should be granted if the pretrial evidence is merely colorable or is not significantly probative. In *Matsushita Elec. Indus. Co. v. Zenith Radio Corp.*, 475 U.S. 574, 106 S.Ct. 1348, 89 L.Ed.2d 538 (1986), the Court held that summary judgment is appropriate when the trial judge can conclude that no reasonable trier of fact could find for the nonmovant on the basis of evidence presented in the motion and the response. *Id.* at 587, 106 S.Ct. at 1356.

III.

[1–4] A trial court has the inherent power to summarily enforce settlement agreements entered into by the litigants in cases before the court. *United States v. Hardage*, 982 F.2d 1491, 1496 (10th Cir. 1993); *Dankese v. Defense Logistics Agency*, 693 F.2d 13, 16 (1st Cir.1983); *Bonser v. Safeway, Inc.*, 809 F.Supp. 799 (D.Colo. 1992). Settlement agreements are favored by the courts. *Autera v. Robinson*, 419 F.2d 1197, 1199 (D.C.Cir.1969). The terms of the settlement agreement must be clear, unambiguous, and capable of enforcement. *Bonser*, 809 F.Supp. at 803; *United Mine Workers of America District No. 5 v. Consolidation Coal Co.*, 666 F.2d 806, 810 (10th Cir.1981). Settlement agreements are construed in the same way as contracts in determining whether and how they should be enforced. *Republic Resources Corp. v. ISI Petroleum West Caddo Drilling Program 1981*, 836 F.2d 462, 465 (10th Cir.1987); *Mulvaney v. St. Louis Southwestern Railway Co.*, 1992 WL 223771 (D.Kan. Aug. 13, 1992). The question before the Court is whether the parties entered into an enforceable settlement agreement.

A. Intent of the Parties

[5] Plaintiffs argue, first, they did not and could not have intended to release ESI from its potential partnership liability for over six million gallons of Alumet's waste for the price of 3800 gallons,[1] and second, Plaintiffs' failure to execute the Agreement is fatal to its enforcement.

Nowhere does the Agreement mention either joinder of Alumet or the Alumet waste stream. Although Plaintiffs in their brief repeatedly refer to the joinder of Alumet as a "condition precedent," joinder was never expressly made a condition in either the negotiations or the Agreement itself. Plaintiffs can find no comfort in their euphemistic assertion that "[i]t has also been plaintiffs' practice not to *clutter* settlement agreements with conditions precedent that must occur before plaintiffs execute agreements." Plain. Opp. to ESI's Mot. for Summ.J., at 5 (emphasis added). Such 'clutter' is the stuff of which contracts are made. No contract would be safe if a party could keep its conditions precedent close to the vest.

Distinguishing between the waste streams of ESI and Alumet was also apparently not thought to be particularly important. When the Agreement refers to ESI and dismissal, its language is unqualified

1. Plaintiffs cite ESI's initial letter advising Plaintiffs that the EPA had revised ESI's waste stream liability to 3800 gallons and requesting *de minimis* settlement (presumably, Plaintiffs appear to suggest, for that 3800 gallons). Plaintiffs also cite ESI's responses to discovery, which distinguished between discovery for the 3800 gallons, which ESI said it would no longer respond to, and discovery for Alumet's share, which ESI did respond to. ESI claims it responded because Alumet's joinder had not yet been refused by the Court and ESI saw no reason that it would be; therefore, ESI claims, it answered discovery for the information it had on Alumet.

We note that one problem with Plaintiff's very persuasive argument—that it could not have intended to let 6 million gallons off the hook—is that with or without the Agreement, it would not be required to do so. Enforcement of the Agreement does not extinguish Plaintiff's right to recover from Alumet for the six million gallons in another action.

V. LEGAL RESEARCH ASSIGNMENTS

Clearly, a researcher must be skilled in the analysis of case law and decisions. Experience is the best teacher of case analysis. To gain some practice in dealing with case decisions, carefully read the following case decisions, summarize the key issues and events, and answer the related questions. Be as precise as possible.

A. Exercise 10.1: Case Law Analysis: Practice Questions and Exercises

1. What is the proper citation for the *Patty* case shown in Exercise 10.1?
   a. 603F.2d587
   b. No 78-3142
   c. 603 Federal Reporter, 2d Series
   d. 603 F.2d 587 (6th Cir. 1979).
2. From what state did this case emerge?
   a. Georgia
   b. Kentucky
   c. New York
   d. United States
3. Which court wrote this opinion?
   a. U.S. Supreme Court
   b. U.S. District Court for Western Kentucky
   c. U.S. Court of Appeals, Sixth Circuit
   d. U.S.C.A.
4. Which judge filed and drafted the opinion?
   a. Merritt
   b. Weick
   c. Yaros
   d. Peck
5. When was this case argued?
   a. June 21, 1979
   b. August 16,1974
   c. June 19, 1974
   d. Last week
6. What two constitutional amendments control the analysis in this case?
   a. 14th and 21st
   b. First and Fourth
   c. Fifth and Sixth
   d. 8th and 13th
7. Which of the following cases is not cited in this opinion?
   a. *Chapman v. California*
   b. *Griffin v. California*
   c. *Wigmore v. McNaughton*
   d. *Herring v. New York*
8. The opinion of the case revolves around a particular state statute. Which statute is it?
   a. Rule 9.5 of the Kentucky Rules of Criminal Procedure
   b. U.S.C.A. Amendment 4

c. VIII Wigmore, Evidence 2268
d. Kentucky Habitual Criminal Act, formerly Ky. Rev. Stat. 431.190

9. The best description of the issue in this case is:
   a. Were the defendant's rights under the Fifth and Sixth Amendments violated by direct examination of the defendant?
   b. Was the defendant ripped off?
   c. Is a habitual criminal statute a due process violation?
   d. Was the defendant's right to a bifurcated trial, and the grant of the writ of habeas corpus, a violation of the Eighth Amendment?
10. The court's decision relates to
    a. all of the defendant's other convictions.
    b. the unconstitutionality of habitual criminal statutes.
    c. the state's power to seek a retrial.
    d. the right of the defendant's counsel to make a closing or final argument to the jury.

B. Exercise 10.2: *United States v. Gross*

1. Which court had jurisdiction over this case?
   a. U.S. Court of Appeals, Ninth Circuit
   b. U.S. District Court
   c. Court of Southern California
   d. California Supreme Court
2. Which circuit judges heard arguments on this case?
   a. Trask and McNichols
   b. McNichols and Walsh
   c. Hufstedler, Trask, and McNichols
3. Which set of facts best describes the events in this case?
   a. A drug deal resulted in a conviction for the use of cocaine.
   b. There was a trial relating to an assault and battery of a federal officer who was attempting to affect an arrest. The assault was charged against the wife of the drug dealer.
   c. This case involves DEA agents who illegally searched and seized the defendant and his property.
   d. None of the above adequately describes the facts.
4. Which of the following is not a correct rule of law that comes from this opinion?
   a. Drug convictions are not technically crimes of falsehood *(crimen falsi)* and cannot always be used to impeach.
   b. The prosecution, upon request, must disclose evidence favorable to the accused.
   c. In this case, evidence of the defendant's drug convictions was considered by the court to be too prejudicial for admission.
   d. There are no circumstances in which disclosure of evidence favorable to the defendant is required *unless* the defense asks the prosecution.
5. Which federal rules of evidence are cited in this case?
   a. Rule 604
   b. Rule 6399
   c. III U.S.C. 18
   d. Rule 609

Chester PATTY, Petitioner-Appellant,

v.

Donald E. BORDENKIRCHER, Jr., Superintendent Kentucky State Penitentiary, Respondent-Appellee.

No. 78-3142.

United States Court of Appeals, Sixth Circuit.

Argued June 21, 1979.

Decided Aug. 16, 1979.

State prisoner filed petition for writ of habeas corpus. The United States District Court for the Western District of Kentucky, Charles M. Allen, Chief Judge, denied petition, and petitioner appealed. The Court of Appeals, Merritt, Circuit Judge, held that: (1) petitioner was deprived of his Fifth Amendment right not to be compelled to be a witness against himself when prosecutor, during hearing on habitual criminal charge against petitioners, called petitioner to witness stand in order to prove petitioner's prior criminal conviction, and (2) in habitual criminal portion of bifurcated state criminal trial, petitioner was deprived of his Sixth Amendment right to counsel as a result of trial court's refusal to permit petitioner's counsel to make a closing or final argument to the jury.

Reversed.

John W. Peck, Senior Circuit Judge, concurred specially and filed opinion.

1. Witnesses ⇐300

Petitioner was deprived of his Fifth Amendment right not to be compelled to be a witness against himself when prosecutor, during hearing on habitual criminal charge against petitioner, called petitioner to witness stand in order to prove petitioner's prior criminal conviction. U.S.C.A.Const. Amend. 5.

2. Criminal Law ⇐641.12(1)

In habitual criminal portion of bifurcated state criminal trial, petitioner was deprived of his Sixth Amendment right to counsel as a result of trial court's refusal to permit petitioner's counsel to make a closing or final argument to the jury. U.S.C.A. Const. Amend. 6.

Chester Patty, pro se.

G. David Yaros, [court-appointed CJA], Cincinnati, Ohio, for petitioner-appellant.

Robert F. Stephens, Atty. Gen., Frankfort, Ky., David Russell Marshall, for respondent-appellee.

Before WEICK and MERRITT, Circuit Judges and PECK, Senior Circuit Judge.

MERRITT, Circuit Judge.

Chester Patty, as petitioner for a writ of habeas corpus, collaterally attacks his forty year sentence in the Commonwealth of Kentucky imposed on June 19, 1974, under Kentucky's old Habitual Criminal Act. On June 19, 1974, Patty was convicted of burglary in the criminal court of Caldwell County at Princeton, Kentucky. Patty took the stand in his own defense at this trial. Two days later a second separate, so-called "bifurcated" trial was conducted on the habitual criminal charge.[1] In the habitual criminal proceeding, Patty was called to the witness stand by the prosecutor who elicited evidence of a prior criminal conviction, an element of the habitual criminal offense. Neither the Court nor the prosecutor advised Patty of his right under the fifth amendment not to "be compelled in any

1. Kentucky's former Habitual Criminal Act, Ky.Rev.Stat. § 431.190, repealed effective January 1, 1975, provided in part: "Any person convicted a second time of felony shall be confined in the penitentiary not less than double the time of such sentence under the first conviction . . . . Judgment in such cases shall not be given for the increased penalty unless the jury finds . . . the fact of former convictions for felony committed by the prisoner . . ." Petitioner's "first conviction" was for a Georgia burglary several years earlier where he was given a 20 year sentence. Petitioner does not attack the constitutionality of this provision of the old Habitual Criminal Act.

criminal case to be a witness against himself." His counsel did not object to the action of the prosecutor.

In addition, the Court did not permit Patty's counsel to make a closing or final argument to the jury in the habitual criminal trial. Under Rule 9.54(1) of the Kentucky Rules of Criminal Procedure, it is the "duty of the Court to instruct the jury in writing" as to the law of the case. These instructions are given by the Court "to the jury prior to the closing summations of counsel." The record of the habitual criminal trial shows that the trial judge, after instructing the jury, asked the sheriff if the jury room were "ready" and told the members of the jury to "accompany the sheriff to the jury room to deliberate upon the rest of your verdict." At that point Patty's counsel objected "to the failure of the court to allow final argument in the pending case," and the trial judge replied: "Let the record reflect that there was no request made by any counsel at this phase of the case to argue this phase of the case before the jury." The jury then retired to consider its verdict. If found petitioner guilty as a habitual criminal and gave him a forty year sentence.

On October 15, 1975, the Court of Appeals of Kentucky affirmed Patty's conviction and sentence without a discussion of the issues raised on appeal. He raised the claim that his right not to be a witness against himself had been violated when the prosecutor called him to the witness stand and further claimed that his right to counsel and a fair trial under the sixth amendment had been abridged when the trial court declined to allow his counsel the opportunity to make a closing argument.

On petition for a writ of habeas corpus, the District Court found that Patty had adequately exhausted his state court remedies. But the District Court concluded on the self-incrimination question that

> The petitioner was represented by counsel at the time of his trial below; yet no objection was made when the petitioner was called to the stand to testify about his prior conviction. Therefore any right against self incrimination that may have existed was waived. *See Cravens v. United States,* 62 F.2d 261, 273 (8th Cir.), *cert. denied,* 289 U.S. 733, 53 S.Ct. 594, 77 L.Ed. 1481 (1933); *cf. United States v. Doremus,* 414 F.2d 252 (6th Cir. 1969).

With respect to the sixth amendment question, the District Court held that "the trial court's refusal to allow petitioner a closing argument did violate his sixth and fourteenth amendment right to the effective assistance of counsel," citing *Herring v. New York,* 422 U.S. 853, 95 S.Ct. 2550, 45 L.Ed.2d 593 (1975). The District Court went on to hold, however, "since the jury's duty in sentencing under the habitual criminal statute, KRS 431.190, is mandatory, and no fact question was presented to them, that violation was harmless beyond a reasonable doubt." We reverse.

[1] 1. *Self-Incrimination.*—We do not remember or find any cases where the prosecutor has called a criminal defendant to the stand in order to prove an element of the crime. The general acquiescence of lawyers in a custom to the contrary suggests that Professor Wigmore's observations on this subject are correct:

> For the party-defendant in a criminal case, the privilege permits him to refuse answering any question whatever in the cause, on the general principle that it "tends to criminate" . . . .
>
> This being so, the prosecution could nevertheless on principle have a right at least to call him to be sworn, because, as with an ordinary witness, it could not be known beforehand whether he would exercise his privilege. But no Court seems ever to have sanctioned this application of the principle.
>
> This result may be rested on several considerations:
>
> (1) Historically, the privilege existed long before the abolition of the accused's disqualification; hence, until those statutory changes (in 1860–1900), the accused could not testify even if he were willing; thus, to call him would be useless, and the negative practice became fixed. (2) Under the modern statutory competency of

continued

the accused, if he should choose to testify when the time comes for putting in his case, the prosecution may on his cross-examination put the questions which it could have put on calling him earlier, and thus the prosecution's opportunity to find whether he will exercise his privilege is practically obtained. (3) Even though the prosecution might technically be entitled to that opportunity at the earlier stage, still the exercise of this technical right need hardly be conceded, since the procedure could only have, as its chief effect, the emphasizing of his refusal, should he refuse, and thus the indirect suggestion of that inference against him from which he is protected by another aspect of the principle . . . . (4) By the express tenor, in most jurisdictions, of the statute qualifying the accused, he is declared to be a competent witness "at his own request, but not otherwise" . . . . Whether this form of words was chosen with a view to its present bearing can only be surmised; but its evident effect is to forbid the calling of the accused by the prosecution. VIII Wigmore, Evidence § 2268 (McNaughton ed. 1940).

See also Griffin v. California, 380 U.S. 609, 85 S.Ct. 1229, 14 L.Ed.2d 106 (1965), in which the court held that a prosecutor's comment on defendant's failure to take the stand violates the privilege against self-incrimination. Nothing could more effectively emphasize and undermine a defendant's exercise of this right than to allow the prosecutor to call him to the stand and put him to the test in front of the jury.

[2] 2. *Final Argument.*—The Supreme Court has recently held in *Herring v. New York*, 422 U.S. 853, 858–59, 95 S.Ct. 2550, 2553–54 (1975), that "a total denial of the opportunity for final argument" abridges "the basic [sixth amendment] right of the accused to make his defense" and that this is true "no matter how strong the case for the prosecution may appear to the presiding judge." This is a *per se* rule. The Supreme Court has indicated that the strength of the prosecution's case is not a factor. The District Court erred, therefore, in applying the harmless error rule of *Chapman v. California*, 386 U.S. 18, 87 S.Ct. 824, 17 L.Ed.2d 705 (1967).

For these reasons we hold that the state abridged petitioner's fifth and sixth amendment rights in the conduct of the habitual criminal trial. We reverse and remand with instructions to the District Court to grant the petition for a writ of *habeas corpus ad subjiciendum* and set aside petitioner's conviction and sentence under the Kentucky Habitual Criminal Act, formerly Ky.Rev.Stat. § 431.190. Our decision only affects Patty's habitual criminal conviction, not any convictions for other crimes, and does not affect or decide any question regarding the state's power to seek retrial on the habitual criminal charge.

JOHN W. PECK, Senior Circuit Judge, concurring.

I concur in the result reached in the majority opinion, but because that result is clearly mandated by the refusal of the trial court to permit defense counsel to make an oral argument to the jury, I see no occasion to deal with the Fifth Amendment issue on the record presented by this case.

Like my brethren, I am surprised, not to say startled, by the fact that the prosecution established an essential element of its case by calling the defendant as its own witness. Unorthodox as this procedure may be, the further fact is that the defendant was represented by counsel, and strategy considerations for interposing no objection suggest themselves. For example, keeping in mind that the element involved was whether the defendant was the individual named in the Georgia record of conviction (a formal element easily established by other, albeit more cumbersome, evidence), counsel may very well have concluded that to require the government to go the long route to establish this point could antagonize the judge and jury, whereas cooperation might well result in favorable consideration.

Present counsel argues that the failure to object establishes his predecessor's incompetence, and suggests the possibility that that

590 603 FEDERAL REPORTER, 2d SERIES

EXERCISE 10.1
continued

predecessor did not advise the defendant of his Fifth Amendment rights. However, in the light of the entire record and particularly trial counsel's articulate objection upon being denied the right to present oral argument, thereby preserving that issue for our review, it seems more likely that he knew exactly what he was doing, and that as a competent lawyer he fully advised his client of his rights.

I see no occasion to reach this issue, since I have reservations concerning the advisability of establishing a per se rule in this area.

6. The court's decision was to
   a. reverse and require a new trial.
   b. affirm the defendant's conviction.
   c. reverse.
   d. dismiss all charges.
7. Which of the following cases relate to the standard of materiality?
   a. *State v. Cook*
   b. *Brady v. Maryland*
   c. *United States v. Hastings*
   d. *United States v. Ortega*
8. If you were compiling a group of precedent cases highlighting the materiality question, which would be the most recent?
   a. *United States v. Augurs*
   b. *United States v. Shelton*
   c. *Skinner v. Cardwell*
   d. *Brady v. Maryland*
9. Which topics are in the West Key Number System?
   a. Witnesses
   b. *Per curiam*
   c. 18 U.S.C. 111
   d. DEA
10. Were there any footnotes in this case?
    a. Yes
    b. No

C. Exercise 10.3: New Jersey Superior Court

1. Which key number is used to signify the synopsis?
   a. There is no key number reference
   b. 229(2.4)
   c. 349.1
   d. 171.1

UNITED STATES of America, Appellee,

v.

Jackie Yvonne GROSS, Appellant.

No. 78-2379.

United States Court of Appeals, Ninth Circuit.

Aug. 30, 1979.

Defendant was convicted in the United States District Court for the Southern District of California, Howard B. Turrentine, J., of assaulting a federal officer, and she appealed. The Court of Appeals held that: (1) evidence was sufficient to sustain defendant's conviction, but (2) it was prejudicial error to admit, over her objection, defendant's two prior narcotics convictions to impeach her.

Reversed.

1. Assault and Battery ⇐91

Evidence that defendant grabbed the hair of a federal agent who was in an argument with her husband involving alleged drug trafficking was sufficient to support her conviction for assaulting a federal officer. 18 U.S.C.A. § 111.

2. Criminal Law ⇐1170½(1)
Witnesses ⇐337(6)

In prosecution for assaulting a federal officer arising from incident in which defendant grabbed the hair of a federal officer who was in an argument with her husband concerning alleged drug trafficking, it was prejudicial error to admit, over her objection, defendant's two prior narcotics convictions to impeach her. Fed.Rules Evid. rules 609, 609(a), 28 U.S.C.A.

3. Criminal Law ⇐627.6(1)

Evidence favorable to an accused must be disclosed upon request where evidence is material to guilt or punishment; standard of materiality varies depending upon nature of information withheld and type of request made by defendant.

4. Criminal Law ⇐627.6(1), 700

If a general request or no request is made, disclosure of evidence is required only if omitted evidence creates reasonable doubt that did not otherwise exist; however, if a specific request for disclosure of evidence was made, standard of materiality is whether evidence might have affected the outcome of trial.

Robert L. Miller, Miller & Miller, Los Angeles, Cal., David P. Curnow, Amos & Curnow (argued), San Diego, Cal., for appellant.

John J. Robinson, Asst. U. S. Atty. (on the brief), Michael H. Walsh, U. S. Atty., John J. Robinson, Asst. U. S. Atty. (argued), San Diego, Cal., for appellee.

Appeal from the United States District Court for the Southern District of California.

Before HUFSTEDLER and TRASK, Circuit Judges, and McNICHOLS,* District Judge.

PER CURIAM:

Appellant was convicted for assaulting a federal officer in violation of 18 U.S.C. § 111. She complains that (1) the evidence was insufficient to support her conviction; (2) the district court prejudicially erred in admitting, over objection, two prior narcotics convictions to impeach her; (3) *Brady* material was improperly suppressed; and (4) the jury was improperly instructed.

On February 24, 1978, DEA Agent Hu, and a government informant, Bogan, tried to buy cocaine from Warren Gross, appellant's husband. Bogan was given $1,500 Government money with which to purchase the cocaine. Warren Gross and Bogan transacted their business outside Hu's presence. Thereafter, Bogan gave Hu a bag of white powder, which turned out to be either

* Honorable Ray McNichols, Chief Judge, United States District Court, District of Idaho, sitting by designation.

extremely poor cocaine or a substance that was not cocaine. Later on the same day a strip search of Bogan revealed $700 of the Government's money in one of his shoes.

After Bogan's "rip-off," DEA Agents Hu and McKinnon, among other agents, together with Bogan, went to visit Warren Gross, who was staying at the apartment of Norris. Hu, McKinnon, and Bogan reached the apartment about 11:00 p. m. When appellant's husband answered the door, a loud argument ensued. Appellant joined the group. Warren Gross refused the agents' request to go inside the apartment. Thereafter, a shoving match between Warren and McKinnon occurred. Agent Hu turned to help McKinnon, and appellant grabbed Agent Hu by the hair. Waiting agents joined the melee, and eventually appellant, her husband, and the other occupants of the apartment were subdued.

Appellant's defense at trial was that she was justifiably acting in defense of her husband. She claimed that she had heard nothing about any mention of drugs, that she had only heard references to "a package."

I

[1] The evidence was sufficient to support her conviction. The jury was not obliged to believe her version of the events. Nevertheless, her defense and her credibility with respect to that defense become important on the Rule 609 and *Brady* issues to which we now turn.

At the time this case was tried, neither the court nor counsel had the benefit of a number of cases, throughout the country, interpreting Rule 609(a) of the Federal Rules of Evidence. We held this case pending the *en banc* determination of *United States v. Cook,* (9th Cir., *en banc,* 1979) [Slip Op'n 2303].

Appellant's prior convictions for narcotics offenses are not technically within the concept of *crimen falsi,* and, therefore, were inadmissible unless the Government bore its burden of proving that the probative value of the prior convictions for impeachment purposes exceeded the prejudicial effect of their admission. (*E. g., United States v. Cook, supra; United States v. Ortega,* 561 F.2d 803 (9th Cir. 1977) (shoplifting); *United States v. Hayes,* 553 F.2d 824 (2d Cir. 1977) (importing cocaine); *United States v. Hastings,* 577 F.2d 38 (8th Cir. 1978) (narcotics).) The Government offered no theory explaining how the probative value of appellant's prior narcotics convictions could outweigh the prejudice. To the extent that this issue was discussed at the time of trial, the argument was presented by defense counsel, who pointed out "as soon as the jury hears that she has been convicted previously of either smuggling or using narcotics—heroin—they are going to just assume, because of that, that she was involved with whatever Warren was supposed to have done, and it is going to unduly prejudice the jury's mind against her because she is only charged with assault, not anything else." The court did not require that any kind of showing be made by the Government in response. The court's explanation in overruling the objection does not suggest that the court was weighing the prejudicial effect against the probative value, for the only purpose for which it could have been admissible, which was impeachment.[1]

When appellant testified, she did not represent herself as a person who had no knowledge of drugs or drug trafficking. Therefore, nothing developed between the time at which the court issued its preliminary ruling and the conclusion of her testimony, that lent any added strength to the probative value of the evidence for impeachment purposes. Under these circumstances, the Government did not carry its burden of proving that the probative value was greater than the prejudicial effect of the evidence.

1. The court said, "I will charge the jury that it isn't to be considered in arriving at her guilt or innocence. It only goes to her credibility. It is not evidence of the guilt of the crime. It just goes to the credibility. I will give the usual instruction and I think it will be more advantageous to the jury to understand this than it will be prejudicial to her. If she wishes to take the stand, I am afraid she will have to suffer the consequences . . . ."

[2] Of course, we cannot know what factors the jury weighed in deciding the credibility issues against appellant. But we would be entirely unrealistic if we failed to perceive that the very prejudice that defense counsel anticipated occurred when the Government impeached her with her prior narcotics convictions. At least a hint that the jury was thus influenced appears from the jury's acquittal of a third defendant, who lived in the apartment and who asserted a defense of property. The acquittal occurred even though that defendant was involved in an extended brawl with several agents that lasted long after appellant had ceased resisting. We conclude that the erroneous admission of the prior convictions was prejudicial.

II

Appellant moved for disclosure of "all internal affairs records, files, and reports relating to complaints filed against and discipline imposed upon Agents Raymond J. McKinnon and Ululaulani M. B. Hu for the use of excessive force or other aggressive behavior." The Government thereupon produced certain documents for an *in camera* inspection. The district court determined that the material was not subject to disclosure.

[3, 4] Evidence favorable to an accused must be disclosed upon request where the evidence is material to guilt or to punishment. (*Brady v. Maryland*, 373 U.S. 83, 83 S.Ct. 1194, 10 L.Ed.2d 215 (1963).) The standard of materiality varies depending on the nature of the information withheld and the type of request made by a defendant. (*United States v. Agurs*, 427 U.S. 97, 96 S.Ct. 2392, 49 L.Ed.2d 342 (1976); *Skinner v. Cardwell*, 564 F.2d 1381 (9th Cir. 1977).) If a general request or no request is made, disclosure is required only "if the omitted evidence creates a reasonable doubt that did not otherwise exist." (*United States v. Agurs, supra*, 427 U.S. at 112, 96 S.Ct. at 2402.) If a specific request is made, the standard of materiality is whether the evidence "might have affected the outcome of the trial." (*Id.* at 104, 96 S.Ct. at 2398.) Appellant's request was unquestionably specific; "[i]t gave the prosecutor notice of exactly what the defendant desired." (*Id.* at 106, 96 S.Ct. at 2399; *United States v. Shelton*, 588 F.2d 1242 (9th Cir. 1978).) Implicit in the district court's decision that the information need not be produced is the court's determination that the disclosure could not have affected the outcome of the trial.

We have concluded that it is unnecessary for us to decide whether the district court correctly determined the materiality of the documents produced by the Government for *in camera* inspection. Although we must reverse for Rule 609 error, Gross will not be retried. She has served her sentence while the case was pending on appeal. For the same reason, it is unnecessary specifically to address any of the remaining questions that she raises.

REVERSED.

2. In which county of New Jersey was this decision handed down?
   a. Orange
   b. Sussex
   c. Middlesex
   d. Gloucester
3. The issue of this case can be best described as:
   a. Can an insured party receive coverage without paying the premium?
   b. Can an insurance carrier cancel an insured's policy without justification?
   c. Can an insurance carrier cancel an insured when the insured fully pays the original policy premium, yet fails to pay a premium on a subsequent endorsement?
   d. Can an insured move to another residence and still be covered?
4. What is the proper citation for this case?
   a. 180 N.J. 416
   b. 185 N.J. 1981
   c. 180 N.J. Super. 400
   d. 180 N.J. Super. 416 (1981)
5. It could be said that, with the subsequent endorsement, these were really two different, divisible contracts.
   a. True
   b. False
6. Who was the attorney for the insurance company?
   a. Greenberg
   b. Sachs
   c. Keife
   d. Netto
7. Which case cited in the opinion holds that an insurance company is to be held to a fair reading of the policy, enabling the insured to obtain coverage?
   a. *Weathers v. Hartford Ins. Group*
   b. *Jersey Police v. MCI*
   c. *Hudson v. Knickerbocker*
   d. *Fenwick Machinery v. A. Tomal*
8. This case holds that the cancelled policy could be upheld only as it related to the 1971 Oldsmobile.
   a. True
   b. False
9. What was the name of the insurance company?
   a. Travelers
   b. Union Pacific
   c. Hartford
   d. Kemper
10. The original policy could be upheld because those payments were current.
    a. True
    b. False

EXERCISE 10.3

Service: **Get by LEXSEE®**
Citation: **1981 N.J. Super. LEXIS 677**

*180 N.J. Super. 416, *; 434 A.2d 1160, **;*
*1981 N.J. Super. LEXIS 677, ****

JOSEPH P. STUDZINSKI, PLAINTIFF, v. THE TRAVELERS INSURANCE CO., DEFENDANT AND THIRD-PARTY PLAINTIFF, v. MOTOR CAR INSURANCE CO., THIRD-PARTY DEFENDANT

L-50898-78

Superior Court of New Jersey, Law Division, Middlesex County

180 N.J. Super. 416; 434 A.2d 1160; 1981 N.J. Super. LEXIS 677

June 29, 1981, Decided

CASE SUMMARY

PROCEDURAL POSTURE: Plaintiff brought an action to recover under an automobile insurance policy for a vehicle that was stolen.

OVERVIEW: The original insurance policy covering a Dodge van was issued for a term of one year with the premium payable in installments. Plaintiff moved and did not notify defendant of the change of address. Plaintiff later requested an endorsement to the policy extending coverage to include a 1971 Oldsmobile and paid an additional premium toward the endorsement. Although plaintiff made no further payment in connection with the endorsement, plaintiff continued to make the original premium installments. The Dodge van was stolen and plaintiff sought compensation. The court found that payments made by plaintiff subsequent to the endorsement were clearly intended to apply to the original premium charge because he did not receive the endorsement notices. Likewise, defendant clearly indicated an intention to allocate premium payments to the initial premium rather than on account for both premiums.

OUTCOME: The court entered judgment in favor of plaintiff on the grounds that defendant did not have the right to cancel the entire policy where the breach went to a divisible part of the contract.

CORE TERMS: premium, endorsement, insured, cancellation, coverage, notice of cancellation, original policy, notice, partial payment, severable, divisible, insurance policy, right to cancel, installment, insurer, separately, assent, automobile liability policy, unearned premium, paid in full, fully paid, nonpayment, effective, allocate, notify

CORE CONCEPTS - ◆ Hide Concepts

Insurance Law : Motor Vehicle Insurance : Cancellation & Nonrenewal

See N.J. Stat. Ann. § 17:29C-10.

Insurance Law : Claims & Contracts : Policy Interpretation : Contract Interpretation Rules

An insurance company is to be held to a fair reading of the policy, enabling the insured to obtain the coverage he reasonably expected.

Insurance Law : Claims & Contracts : Policy Interpretation : Contract Interpretation Rules

Whether a contract is entire is a mixed question of fact and law. It depends on the intentions of the parties, to be ascertained from the circumstances surrounding the agreement and contract itself. A contract is entire when the promise of one party is conditioned on the entire performance of the contract by the other, and is divisible when the part to be performed by one party consists of several distinct and separate items respecting which the consideration is apportioned to each item or is left to be implied in law. The essential inquiry is whether there was a single assent to a whole transaction involving several kinds of property or a separate assent to each of several things involved.

Insurance Law : Claims & Contracts : Premiums

The New Jersey courts will not construe partial payment to create pro rata coverage of time or properties. A partial payment is no better than no payment.

COUNSEL: [*1]**

Aaron G. Greenberg for plaintiff.

Peter W. Sachs for defendant and third-party plaintiff (*Sachs & Sachs*, attorneys).

JUDGES: Keefe, J.S.C.

OPINIONBY: KEEFE

OPINION: [*418] [1161]** The issue to be decided is whether defendant insurance carrier had the right to cancel plaintiff's entire coverage when plaintiff had fully paid the premium on the original policy but had failed to complete premium payments due on a subsequent endorsement. The question has not been previously addressed by the courts of this State. The case was submitted on a stipulated set of facts upon which the court heard oral arguments.

The original insurance policy covering a 1977 Dodge van, was issued on November 29, 1977, for a term of one year. The premium was to be paid in installments. Application for this assigned risk automobile liability policy was through the third-party defendant, Motor Car Insurance Co. (hereinafter MCI), and assigned to Travelers Insurance Co. (hereinafter Travelers). It was served with process but has filed no answering pleadings. It is not a party to the stipulation and no relief is sought against it at this time.

Sometime after November 29, 1977, and before October **[***2]** 2, 1978, plaintiff moved and did not notify Travelers of the change of address. On January 9, 1978, plaintiff requested an endorsement to the policy extending coverage to include a 1971 Oldsmobile. At that time plaintiff paid an additional premium of $ 78 toward the endorsement. Although plaintiff made no further payment in connection with the endorsement, plaintiff continued to make payments on the original premium installments.

Sometime after the 1971 Oldsmobile was added to the insurance policy, plaintiff was sent a premium notice, showing an installment premium due in the amount of $ 112.80, and a due date of May 19, 1978. This premium notice was sent to plaintiff's original address. When this payment was not received by Travelers, a notice of cancellation of the policy was issued on June 9, 1978. The notice of cancellation was also addressed to **[*419]** plaintiff's original address, and provided for an effective date of cancellation of June 29, 1978. Plaintiff did not receive either the statement of the additional premium owed or the notice of cancellation.

On August 22, 1978, defendant issued a draft in the amount of $ 212.10 representing the unearned premium for **[***3]** the cancelled insurance policy. This draft was issued to the

continued

order of Motor Car Insurance Agency, and in due course was deposited by MCI.

On November 3, 1978 Studzinski reported to the Newark, New Jersey, Police Department that the Dodge Van was stolen. As of that time Studzinski believed that he was still insured by Travelers.

The premium for insurance coverage of the Dodge Van was $ 472 which was paid in full by plaintiff. The additional premium for the add-on Oldsmobile was not paid in full.

At the outset the court notes that Travelers met the procedural requirements for cancellation. Plaintiff had a duty under the policy to notify Travelers of his change of address. Absent notification, Travelers' notices to plaintiff were correct. Under *N.J.S.A.* 17:29C-10 "cancellation may be effective whether or not the insured has actually received the notice of cancellation since proof of mailing, not proof of receipt is the determinative factor." *Weathers v. Hartford Ins. Group*, 77 *N.J.* 228, 234 (1978).

An insurance company is to be held to a fair reading of the policy, enabling the insured to obtain the coverage he reasonably expected. *Fenwick Machinery, Inc.* **[***4]** *v. A. Tomae & Sons, Inc.*, 159 *N.J. Super.* 373 (App.Div.1978). Plaintiff's expectation of coverage here is reasonable only if the subsequent endorsement is severable from the original policy.

Whether a contract is entire is a mixed question of fact and law. It depends **[**1162]** on the intentions of the parties, to be ascertained from the circumstances surrounding the agreement and contract itself. A contract is entire when the promise of **[*420]** one party is conditioned on the entire performance of the contract by the other, and is divisible when the part to be performed by one party consists of several distinct and separate items respecting which the consideration is apportioned to each item or is left to be implied in law. *Rothman Realty Corp. v. Machain*, 16 *N.J. Super.* 280 (*Ch. 1951*), aff'd 21 *N.J. Super.* 172 App.Div. 1952); *Riddlestorffer v. Rahway*, 82 *N.J. Super.* 423 (Law Div. 1964). The essential inquiry is whether there was a single assent to a whole transaction involving several kinds of property or a separate assent to each of several things involved. *Dixon v. Smyth Sales Corp.*, 110 *N.J.L.* 459 (E. & A. 1933).

Although the **[***5]** question of divisibility in regard to an automobile liability policy has never been decided by our courts, a similar analysis arose in the context of a group insurance policy. In *Riddlestorffer v. Rahway, supra*, the court found that the parties intended the contract to be severable where consideration was separately apportioned among the insureds and each person was considered to be a distinct and separate risk.

Our neighboring courts in New York, however, have directly addressed the issue at bar. In *Nationwide Mut. Ins. Co. v. Mason*, 37 *A.D.*2d 15, 322 *N.Y.S.*2d 164 (App.Div. 1971), where the insured had fully paid on the original policy prior to adding the endorsement coverage of a second automobile, the court found that the breach of payment affected only the subsequent endorsement policy. In denying the insurance carrier's right to cancel the entire policy the court noted:

> Here, too, the premium for each risk, one for the Buick and the other for the Chevrolet, is "separately fixed" and therefore, since "the policy in suit is severable and divisible", Lumbermens could only cancel that part of the risk assumed by it for which the premium had not been paid, **[***6]** i.e., on the Chevrolet [at 168].

The facts in the instant action vary only slightly from the facts in the New York case. In this case the insured had not completed the installment payments due under the original policy prior to the requested endorsement, whereas the insured had completed payment before the endorsement in the New **[*421]** York case. However, payments made by plaintiff subsequent to the endorsement in this case were clearly intended to apply to the original premium charge as is evidenced by the checks that were issued to MCI.

Likewise, Travelers' conduct in this matter clearly indicates an intention to allocate premium payments to the initial premium rather than on account for both premiums. For example, the premium notice issued by Travelers showed the premium charged for the endorsement to be $ 212, with an allocation of credit for $ 78 paid on deposit and a balance of $ 134 due by May 19, 1978. In addition, on June 9, 1978 Travelers' cancellation notice stated that the reason for cancellation to be effective on June 29, 1978 was for nonpayment of the endorsement balance of $ 134. Thus, although plaintiff made several payments after he requested **[***7]** the endorsement in January 1978, Travelers did not apply those payments to reduce the total premium due on the policy, as it could have, but rather treated the endorsement as a separate undertaking both by the insured in terms of payment and by it in terms of identifying a separate risk.

The noted allocation of payment distinguishes this case from a situation where partial payment is made on a policy which, when issued, covered two separate automobiles. In that case cancellation for nonpayment of the balance due would properly be against the entire policy, absent an agreement to the contrary. Our courts will not construe partial payment to create *pro rata* coverage of time or properties. A partial payment is no better than no payment. *Hudson v. Knickerbocker Life Ins. Co. of New York*, 28 *N.J.Eq.* 167, 172 (Chancery 1877).

[1163]** In finding that Travelers did not have the right to cancel the entire policy where the breach went to a divisible part of the contract, this court notes that public policy supports a finding to the greatest extent possible in favor of coverage where two interpretations may be had in an ambiguous situation. *Concoran v. Hartford Fire* **[***8]** *Ins. Co.*, 132 *N.J. Super.* 234 (App. Div. 1975).

[*422] No unreasonable burden is being put on the insurer here to apportion premium payments or impose liability on the insurer solely upon an insured's subjective statement as to how he intended the premium payments to be allocated. The insured, not having received the bill for the added premium, could not have intended to make any payments other than on the original premium, while the defendant insurer chose to allocate premium payments to the original premium charge rather than to the total premium charge.

Judgment will be entered in favor of plaintiff. It was stipulated that the damages sustained by reason of plaintiff's loss was $ 7,178.29 less a $ 100 deductible, or $ 7,078.29. In addition, defendant is entitled to a credit for the unearned premium of $ 212.10 which was returned to plaintiff upon cancellation of the policy. Plaintiff will therefore submit an order of judgment in the amount of $ 6,866.19.

Service: **Get by LEXSEE®**
Citation: **1981 N.J. Super. LEXIS 677**
View: Full

D. Exercise 10.4: *State ex rel. Copeland v. Judges*

1. In which term of the Ohio Supreme Court was this case decided?
   a. July term of 1980
   b. January term of 1981
   c. Neither a nor b
2. Who were the attorneys representing the respondents?
   a. Weaner, Hutchinson, Zimmerman, and Bacon
   b. Arthur, O'Neil, and Robinson
   c. Celebrezze, Brown, and Locher
3. The equal protection clause of the U.S. Constitution comes from the
   a. 14th Amendment.
   b. Eighth Amendment.
   c. 13th Amendment.
   d. Fourth Amendment.
4. Which statement best summarizes the *issue* in this case?
   a. Is not an indigent defendant entitled to equal amounts of money spent on his or her defense, or made available to the defendant, as the wealthy defendant?
   b. Can the state provide some differential treatment for defendants depending on income?
   c. Is not the denial of a trial transcript to an indigent defendant a violation of the due process and equal protection clauses of the 14th Amendment?
   d. Is failure to provide counsel at the trial level a violation of the Fourth Amendment?
5. Aside from Ohio precedent and case authority, what other state authorities are cited in the opinion?
   a. Oklahoma
   b. Vermont
   c. New Hampshire
   d. Texas
6. The decision of the court can be best characterized as follows:
   a. A defendant, under any reasonable circumstances, can constitutionally demand a trial transcript for appellate review.
   b. The right to a trial transcript is not unqualified. Defendant should demonstrate a specific, colorable, or particularized need for its use at the appellate level.
   c. If a defendant is poor, he or she is entitled to fair and adequate representation, which includes a trial transcript.
   d. None of the above is correct.
7. What type of writ did the defendant (petitioner) file in this case?
   a. Writ of habeas corpus
   b. Writ of garnishment
   c. Writ of mandamus
   d. Writ of due process
8. What U.S. Supreme Court case is cited as influential?
   a. *State v. Williams*
   b. *Britt v. North Carolina*
   c. *State v. Shepard*
   d. *State v. Scott*

9. Which of these factors is considered critical in determining the right to a transcript?
   a. Public expense
   b. Age of defendant
   c. Sex of the defendant
   d. None of the above
10. Ohio law refers to the party seeking the transcript as the
    a. appellant.
    b. relator.
    c. defendant.
    d. All of the above.

E. Exercise 10.5: *Draper v. United States*

1. Which other court affirmed the conviction of the defendant proper?
   a. California, the Seventh Circuit
   b. U.S. Court of Appeals (248 F.2d 295)
   c. Federal District Court (146 F. Supp. 689)
2. Factually, which statement is most descriptive and accurate?
   a. A federal narcotics agent's arrest of a drug dealer was based on his eyewitness account of the defendant's drug activities.
   b. A federal narcotics agent's arrest was based on a simple hunch and guess.
   c. A federal narcotics agent's arrest and eventual search were based on the information supplied by an informant who could be considered reliable.
3. Which of the following principles guide probable cause determinations?
   a. Probable cause deals with probabilities, not absolute theory.
   b. Probable cause for an arrest must be demonstrated by evidence beyond a reasonable doubt.
   c. Probable cause cannot be based on the word of an informant.
   d. Probable cause is guided by the Fifth Amendment.
4. Federal law grants federal agents the right to arrest without warrants, under certain circumstances.
   a. True
   b. False
5. This Court is clearly satisfied that the information provided by Hereford was a sufficient basis for probable cause.
   a. True
   b. False
6. Rulings from federal courts have found the following principles true:
   a. The terms *probable cause* and *reasonable grounds* are generally synonymous.
   b. Police officers, agents, and other justice officers are not legal technicians, only prudent, reasonable persons.
   c. Both a and b
   d. Neither a nor b
7. What action did the Supreme Court take in regard to defendant's conviction?
   a. Reversed
   b. Remanded
   c. Affirmed
   d. Dismissed

EXERCISE 10.4

Service: **Get by LEXSEE®**
Citation: **1981 Ohio LEXIS 542**

*67 Ohio St. 2d 1, *; 424 N.E.2d 279, **;*
*1981 Ohio LEXIS 542, ***; 21 Ohio Op. 3d 1*

THE STATE, EX REL. COPELAND, v. JUDGES OF THE COURT OF APPEALS OF THE THIRD APPELLATE DISTRICT

No. 80-1369

Supreme Court of Ohio

67 Ohio St. 2d 1; 424 N.E.2d 279; 1981 Ohio LEXIS 542; 21 Ohio Op. 3d 1

July 1, 1981, Decided

PRIOR HISTORY: [*1]**

IN MANDAMUS.

Willie Copeland, relator, was charged in the Paulding County Court with aggravated menacing pursuant to R.C. 2903.21, and was found guilty of the charge on June 18, 1980. He was sentenced to imprisonment for a period of 60 days, less 59 days of which were suspended on the condition that he have no further violations for one year. He was also fined one dollar. Notice of appeal from that judgment was filed with the Court of Appeals for Paulding County on June 27, and a request for a complete transcript was also filed with that court on July 11. On August 1, relator filed a motion in the Court of Appeals for appointment of an attorney and the provision of a transcript at public expense. n1 The motion was overruled on August 26. On September 5, relator filed with the Court of Appeals a motion to certify the record to this court and also an application for reconsideration of the motion for appointment of counsel and provision of transcript. The motion to certify was overruled on September 15, and the application for reconsideration was denied on September 29.

n1 It is the trial court's responsibility to provide free transcripts. The Court of Appeals is responsible for the appointment of counsel. *State, ex rel. Heller, v.. Miller* (1980), 61 Ohio St. 2d 6, 14. **[***2]**

Relator filed a complaint for writ of mandamus with this court on September 29. Relator also filed a motion to stay respondents' order requiring him to file the record relative to his appeal by October 2. The motion was sustained by this court.

DISPOSITION: *Writ denied.*

CORE TERMS: indigent, Fourteenth Amendment, trial transcript, buy, effective, colorable, public expense, petty, convicted, constitutional guarantees, clear legal right, indigent criminal, writ of mandamus, free transcript, automatically, verbatim, equal protection, appointed counsel, appointed, perfect

HEADNOTES: *Criminal law -- Petty offense -- Indigent defendant -- Right to appointed counsel and trial transcript at public expense -- Need therefor not shown, when -- Mandamus relief denied.*

COUNSEL: *Rodney M. Arthur Co., L.P.A., Mr. Joseph W. O'Neil* and *Mr. Mark A. Robinson,* for relator.

Messrs. Weaner, Hutchinson, Zimmerman & Bacon and *Mr. Roger V. Bacon,* for respondents.

JUDGES: CELEBREZZE, C. J., W. BROWN, P. BROWN, SWEENEY, LOCHER, HOLMES and C. BROWN, JJ., concur.

OPINIONBY: PER CURIAM

OPINION:

[*2] [280]** The relator seeks to have this court compel the Court of Appeals to grant him a complete transcript of his trial without cost and to appoint counsel for his appeal. Relator asserts that the Equal Protection Clause of the Fourteenth Amendment to the United States Constitution requires that an indigent defendant, convicted of a misdemeanor punishable by incarceration and monetary fines, be provided **[***3]** a trial transcript and trial records at public expense and court-appointed counsel in order to perfect an effective appeal.

The rights to a transcript and appointed counsel can only exist under the constitutional guarantees of due process and equal protection found in the Fourteenth Amendment, and in Sections 1, 2, 16 and 19 of Article I of the Ohio Constitution. n2 **[*3]** Beginning with *Griffin* v.. *Illinois* (1956), 351 U.S. 12, the United States Supreme Court has delineated the limits of the constitutional guarantee to a transcript on appeal. In *Griffin,* the denial of a trial transcript to indigent petitioners, who sought to appeal convictions for armed robbery, was held to violate the Due Process and Equal Protection Clauses of the Fourteenth Amendment. n3 The court held, at page 17, that "[i]n criminal trials a State can no more discriminate on account of poverty than on account of religion, race, or color." Further, the court stated, at page 18, that "[t]here is no meaningful distinction between a rule which would deny the poor the right to defend themselves in a trial court and one which effectively denies the poor an adequate appellate review accorded to **[***4]** all who have money enough to pay the costs in advance."

- - - - - - - - - - - - - - - - - -Footnotes- - - - - - - - - - - - - - - - - -

n2 "The right to appointed counsel and a transcript can only exist under the constitutional guarantees of due process and equal protection of the law found in the Fourteenth Amendment to the United States Constitution, and in Sections 1, 2, 16 and 19 of Article I of the Ohio Constitution. We look to federal case law to delineate the right of relators under both the state and federal provisions." *State, ex rel. Heller, supra,* at page 8.

n3 In *Griffin,* the United States Supreme Court reviewed an Illinois statute which required a bill of exceptions to be prepared in order to obtain full appellate review of alleged errors.

- - - - - - - - - - - - - - - - -End Footnotes- - - - - - - - - - - - - - - - -

Although the court held, at page 19, in *Griffin* that "[d]estitute defendants must be afforded as adequate appellate review as defendants who have money enough to buy transcripts," that right is not unqualified. The court specifically pointed out that a state is not required to purchase a transcript in every case where **[***5]** an indigent criminal defendant cannot buy it, so long as a means of affording "adequate and effective" appellate review is provided to that defendant. *Id.,* at page 20.

continued

In *Douglas* v.. *California* (1963), 372 U.S. 353, 355, the reasoning of *Griffin* was extended to the right to counsel on appeal. n4 *Douglas,* however, did not set forth an absolute rule that counsel must be afforded an indigent criminal defendant in every appeal. The court, at page 356, held that "* * * a State can, consistently with the Fourteenth Amendment, provide for differences [in the **[**281]** appellate process] so long as the result **[*4]** does not amount to a denial of due process or an 'invidious discrimination' * * *."

- - - - - - - - - - - - - - - - - -Footnotes- - - - - - - - - - - - - - - - - -

n4 In *Douglas,* the United States Supreme Court examined a California court rule that appellate counsel would be appointed only after an initial review by a state appellate court which would determine whether the appointment would be of advantage to the defendant or helpful to the court. Such an initial determination forced the state appellate court to prejudge the merits of the case before counsel was appointed. That procedure was held to deny an indigent any real chance of showing that his appeal had "hidden merit." *Id.,* at page 356.

- - - - - - - - - - - - - - - - -End Footnotes- - - - - - - - - - - - - - - - - **[***6]**

In *Draper* v.. *Washington* (1963), 372 U.S. 487, the court, at page 495, reiterated its holding in *Griffin* that "a state need not purchase a stenographer's transcript in every case where a defendant cannot buy it." The court held that "[a]lternative methods of reporting trial proceedings are permissible if they place before the appellate court an equivalent report of the events at trial from which the appellant's contentions arise. * * * Moreover, part or all of the stenographic transcript * * * will not be germane to consideration of the appeal * * *," and the state will not be required to supply one in such circumstances. *Id.* n5

- - - - - - - - - - - - - - - - - -Footnotes- - - - - - - - - - - - - - - - - -

n5 "* * * If, for instance, the points urged relate only to the validity of the statute or the sufficiency of the indictment upon which conviction was predicated, the transcript is irrelevant and need not be provided. If the assignments of error go only to rulings on evidence or to its sufficiency, the transcript provided might well be limited to the portions relevant to such issues. Even as to this kind of issue, however, it is unnecessary to afford a record of the proceedings pertaining to an alleged failure of proof on a point which is irrelevant as a matter of law to the elements of the crime for which the defendant has been convicted." *Draper* v.. *Washington* (1963), 372 U.S. 487, 495-496.

- - - - - - - - - - - - - - - - -End Footnotes- - - - - - - - - - - - - - - - - **[***7]**

The United States Supreme Court in *Mayer* v.. *Chicago* (1971), 404 U.S. 189, extended the rationale of *Griffin* and *Draper* to non-felony n6 cases and, also, by implication, the *Douglas* rationale. n7 The court in *Mayer* stressed, however, that a record of sufficient completeness does not automatically translate into a complete verbatim transcript. *Id.,* at page 194. Although a full verbatim record is required where it is necessary to assure the indigent an appeal as effective as that available to the defendant with financial resources, a "colorable need" for a complete transcript must be demonstrated before the burden will be placed upon the state to show that only a portion of the transcript or an alternative device will suffice for an effective appeal. *Id.,* at page 195.

- - - - - - - - - - - - - - - - - -Footnotes- - - - - - - - - - - - - - - - - -

n6 The United States Supreme Court had earlier reversed a refusal by an Oklahoma Court of Criminal Appeals to pay for a transcript required by an indigent to perfect his appeal from a "petty" offense conviction in *Williams* v.. *Oklahoma City* (1969), 395 U.S. 458. "Petty offense" was defined by the Oklahoma court as a "violation of a city ordinance, quasi-criminal

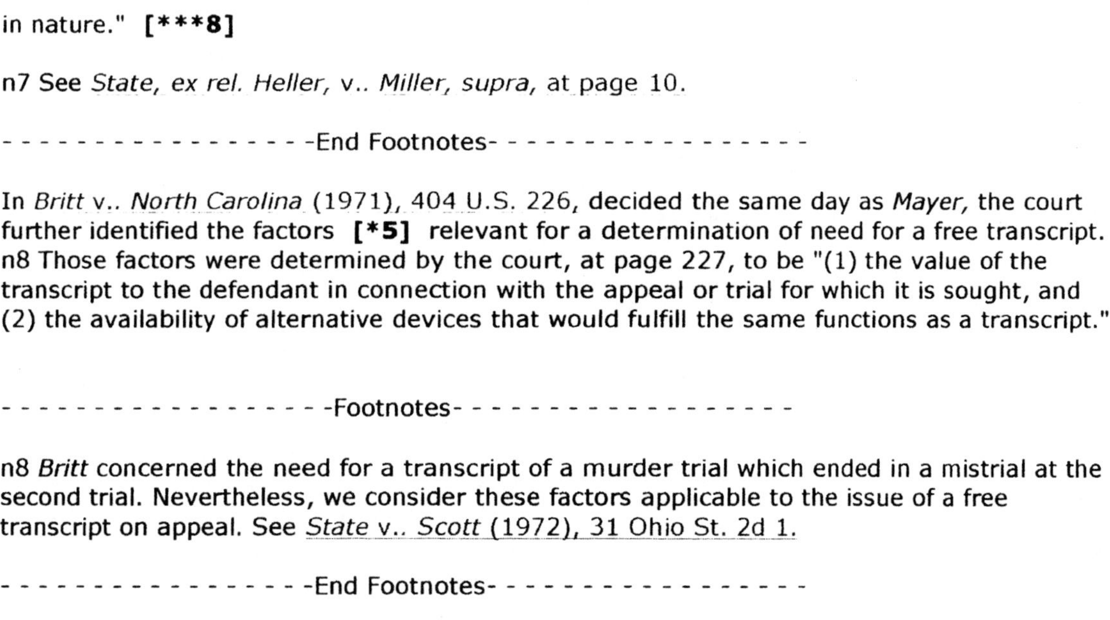

in nature." **[***8]**

n7 See *State, ex rel. Heller, v.. Miller, supra,* at page 10.

- - - - - - - - - - - - - - - - -End Footnotes- - - - - - - - - - - - - - - - -

In *Britt* v.. *North Carolina* (1971), 404 U.S. 226, decided the same day as *Mayer,* the court further identified the factors **[*5]** relevant for a determination of need for a free transcript. n8 Those factors were determined by the court, at page 227, to be "(1) the value of the transcript to the defendant in connection with the appeal or trial for which it is sought, and (2) the availability of alternative devices that would fulfill the same functions as a transcript."

- - - - - - - - - - - - - - - - - -Footnotes- - - - - - - - - - - - - - - - - -

n8 *Britt* concerned the need for a transcript of a murder trial which ended in a mistrial at the second trial. Nevertheless, we consider these factors applicable to the issue of a free transcript on appeal. See *State* v.. *Scott* (1972), 31 Ohio St. 2d 1.

- - - - - - - - - - - - - - - - -End Footnotes- - - - - - - - - - - - - - - - -

This court has consistently recognized that a defendant convicted of a felony has a constitutional right to counsel **[***9]** and to a trial transcript on an appeal as of right to the Court of Appeals from his judgment of conviction. *State* v.. *Catlino* (1967), 10 Ohio St. 2d 183; *State* v.. *Shepard* (1967), 10 Ohio St. 2d 264; *State* v.. *Talley* (1967), 11 Ohio St. 2d 190. However, such right does not extend automatically to cases where an alternative method to exemplify errors exists. *Toledo* v.. *Smith* (1965), 3 Ohio St. 2d 80. Rather, the necessity for a transcript, and, by implication, for counsel on appeal, is based upon an analysis of the request by use of the two *Britt* factors. *State* v.. *Scott* (1972), 31 Ohio St. 2d 1; **[**282]** *State* v.. *Arrington* (1975), 42 Ohio St. 2d 114; and *State, ex rel. Seigler,* v.. *Rone* (1975), 42 Ohio St. 2d 361.

In applying the *Britt* factors, this court has held that some claim must be made as to what specific value the transcript would have, "independent of the overworked concept that what the 'rich man' can buy must *always* be supplied to the 'indigent.'" *State* v.. *Scott, supra,* at page 11. Further, we have held that the *Britt* factors of need are independent of each other, and the existence of **[***10]** either would justify denial of a transcript. *State* v.. *Arrington, supra,* at page 116.

Mandamus is a proper remedy to compel appointment of counsel on appeal and the provision of a transcript. See *State, ex rel. Wright,* v.. *Cohen* (1962), 174 Ohio St. 47. An actual appeal must be pending, however, before a transcript will be provided. *State, ex rel. Partee,* v.. *McMahon* (1963), 175 Ohio St. 243; *State, ex rel. Catlino,* v.. *Clerk of Courts* (1967), 9 Ohio St. 2d 101; *State* v.. *Williams* (1967), 11 Ohio St. 2d 236. In order for a writ of mandamus to be granted in this cause, we must find that relator has a clear legal right to the relief prayed for, **[*6]** that respondents are under a clear legal duty to perform the requested act, and that relator has no plain and adequate remedy at law. *State, ex rel. Heller,* v.. *Miller* (1980), 61 Ohio St. 2d 6, paragraph one of the syllabus.

Relator in the case *sub judice* has not satisfied the requirement of *State, ex rel. Heller,* v.. *Miller, supra,* to show a clear legal right to a transcript and counsel on appeal. His complaint for writ of mandamus is bare of any showing of need for such **[***11]** extraordinary relief other than the fact of his indigency and that "[y]our Relator's [*sic*] will not be able to appeal his criminal conviction without representation and a transcript provided at public expense." The complaint fails to sufficiently demonstrate that the granting of the writ is necessary to a

continued

successful appeal. n9 "*Mayer* and *Britt* stand for the proposition that once an indigent defendant has made a colorable, as opposed to a particularized, showing that a complete or partial transcript of a prior proceeding is of value, the state must demonstrate that an available alternative device will provide substantially the same information, and serve substantially the same function, as a transcript." *State v.. Peterson* (1976), 46 Ohio St. 2d 425, at page 429. That "colorable showing" has not been made here with regard to the right to a transcript and counsel on appeal.

- - - - - - - - - - - - - - - - - -Footnotes- - - - - - - - - - - - - - - - - -

n9 We cannot discern from the face of the complaint whether the basis of appeal would be, *e.g.,* the constitutionality of the statute or some other theory which would not require a complete trial transcript.

- - - - - - - - - - - - - - - - -End Footnotes- - - - - - - - - - - - - - - - - **[***12]**

Accordingly, the writ is denied.

Writ denied.

Service: **Get by LEXSEE®**
Citation: **1981 Ohio LEXIS 542**
View: Full

8. Select the proper citation for this case:
   a. 3 L. Ed. 2d 327
   b. 79 S. Ct. 329
   c. 358 U.S. 307, 79 S. Ct. 329, 3 L. Ed. 2d 327 (1959)
   d. None of the above
9. Which judge delivered the opinion of the Court?
   a. Douglas
   b. Whittaker
   c. Warren
   d. Burger
10. Defendant (Petitioner) clearly argued incorrectly to the Supreme Court concerning
    a. requirements for a warrant.
    b. sufficiency of the evidence for a finding of guilt.
    c. the exclusionary rule.
    d. the use of hearsay evidence to effect an arrest.

***[358 US 307]**
*JAMES ALONZO DRAPER, Petitioner,

v

UNITED STATES OF AMERICA

358 US 307, 3 L ed 2d 327, 79 S Ct 329

[No. 136]

Argued December 11, 1958. Decided January 26, 1959.

SUMMARY

A federal narcotics agent was informed by a reliable paid informer that the defendant was peddling narcotics to several addicts in Denver and that he would return from Chicago to Denver, bringing back a quantity of heroin, on the morning of either September 8 or September 9, 1956. The informer gave the agent a detailed physical description of defendant and the agent arrested him, without a warrant, on his return by train. A search of the person of the defendant yielded a quantity of heroin and a syringe. Prior to his trial on charges of knowingly concealing and transporting narcotic drugs, the defendant moved to suppress the evidence so secured, and the Untied States District Court for the District of Colorado overruled the motion. (146 F Supp 689). At the subsequent trial, that evidence was received over defendant's renewed objection and he was convicted. The Court of Appeals for the Tenth Circuit affirmed the conviction. (248 F2d 295.)

On certiorari, the United States Supreme Court affirmed. In an opinion by WHITTAKER, J., expressing the views of six members of the Court, it was held that the arrest without warrant was lawful, since the arresting officer had "probable cause," within the meaning of the Fourth Amendment, providing that no warrant shall issue but upon probable cause, and "reasonable grounds" within the meaning of § 104(a) of the Narcotic Control Act of 1956, authorizing arrests without warrant where the arresting officer has reasonable grounds to believe that the person to be arrested has committed or is committing a violation of the federal narcotics laws.

DOUGLAS, J., dissented, on the ground that the arrest without warrant was unlawful, the arresting office having no evidence, apart from the mere word of an informer, that defendant was committing a crime.

WARREN, Ch. J., and FRANKFURTER, J., did not participate.

SUBJECT OF ANNOTATION

Beginning on page 1736, infra

What constitutes "probable cause" or "reasonable grounds" justifying arrest of narcotics suspect without warrant

HEADNOTES

Classified to U.S. Supreme Court Digest, Annotated

Arrest § 2 — without warrant — probable cause — narcotics.

1. The terms "probable cause," as used in the Fourth Amendment, providing that no warrant shall issue but upon probable cause, and "reasonable

continued

grounds," as used in § 140(a) of the Narcotic Control Act of 1956 (26 USC § 7607), authorizing arrests without warrant for violation of the narcotics laws where the arresting officer has reasonable grounds to believe that the person to be arrested is committing such a violation, are substantial equivalents of the same meaning.

[*See annotation p.* 1736, *infra*]

Arrest § 2 — without warrant — probable cause — narcotics.

2. In assessing whether a federal narcotics agent has "probable cause" within the meaning of the Fourth Amendment (which provides that no warrants shall issue but upon probable cause) and "reasonable grounds" within the meaning of § 104(a) of the Narcotics Control Act of 1956 (26 USC § 7607) (which authorizes arrests without warrant for violations of any narcotics laws where the arresting officer has reasonable grounds to believe that the person to be arrested has committed or is committing such a violation) to arrest a suspect without a warrant, evidence within the knowledge of the agent may be considered, even though the evidence is not legally competent evidence in a criminal trial, such as hearsay.

[*See annotation, p.* 1736, *infra*]

Evidence §§ 681, 881 — mode and quantum — of guilt — in proceeding to suppress evidence.

3. There is a large difference in the quanta and modes of proof required to establish guilt in a criminal trial and to substantiate the existence of probable cause in a pretrial proceeding to suppress evidence as having been secured through an unlawful search and seizure, since there is a like difference between the two things to be proved, as well as between the tribunals which determine them.

[*See annotation p.* 1736, *infra*]

Arrest § 2; Evidence § 681; Search and Seizure § 12 — without warrant — probable cause — narcotics.

4. Information given to a federal narcotics agent by a reliable paid informer that a certain person, named and described with accuracy by the informer, was peddling narcotics to several addicts in a specified city and would bring heroin to the city by train on a specified morning or on the morning following, justifies an arrest without warrant, since it shows "probable cause" within the meaning of the Fourth Amendment, providing that no warrants shall issue but upon probable cause, and "reasonable grounds" within the meaning of § 104(a) of the Narcotic Control Act of 1956 (26 USC § 7607), authorizing the appropriate federal officers to make arrests without warrant for violations of any federal narcotics laws where such officer has reasonable grounds to believe that the person to be arrested has committed or is committing a violation of these laws; consequently, a subsequent search of the suspect's person and the seizure of heroin so found are lawful, the denial of a motion to suppress the evidence is proper, and the seized heroin is competent evidence lawfully received at the trial.

[*See annotation reference and annotation, p.* 1736, *infra*]

Arrest § 2 — without warrant — probable cause.

5. The existence of "probable cause," justifying an arrest without a warrant, is determined by factual and practical considerations of everyday life on which reasonable and prudent men, not legal technicians, act.

Arrest § 2 — without warrant — probable cause.

6. Probable cause justifying an arrest without warrant exists where the facts and circumstances within the arresting officer's knowledge and of which he had reasonably trustworthy

ANNOTATION REFERENCE

Right of search and seizure incident to a lawful arrest, without a search warrant, 32 ALR 680, 51 ALR 424, 74 ALR 1387, 82 ALR 782. See 94 L ed 671 (search of premises as incident of arrest).

information are sufficient in themselves to warrant a man of reasonable caution in the belief that an offense has been or is being committed.

Search and Seizure § 12 — arrest.

7. A search and seizure made incident to a lawful arrest is lawful.

[*See annotation reference and annotation, p.* 1736, *infra*]

APPEARANCES OF COUNSEL

Osmond K. Fraenkel, of New York City, argued the cause for petitioner.

Leonard B. Sand, of Washington, D.C., argued the cause for respondent.

OPINION OF THE COURT

Mr. Justice **Whittaker** delivered the opinion of the Court.

Petitioner was convicted of knowingly concealing and transporting narcotic drugs in Denver, Colorado, in violation of 35 Stat 614, as amended, 21 USC § 174. His conviction was based in part on the use of evidence against him of two "envelopes containing [865 grains of] heroin" and a hypodermic syringe that had been taken from his person, following his arrest, by the arresting officer. Before the trial, he moved to suppress that evidence as having been secured through an unlawful search and seizure. After hearing, the District Court found that the arresting officer had probable cause to arrest petitioner without a warrant and that the subsequent search and seizure were therefore incident to a lawful arrest, and overruled the motion to suppress. 146 F Supp 689. At the subsequent trial, that evidence was offered and, over petitioner's renewed objection, was received in evidence, and the trial resulted, as we have said, in petitioner's conviction. The Court of Appeals affirmed the conviction, 248 F2d 295, and certiorari was sought on the sole ground that the search and seizure violated the Fourth Amendment[1] and therefore the use of the heroin in evidence vitiated the conviction. We granted the writ to determine that question. 357 US 935, 2 L ed 2d 1549, 78 S Ct 1386.

***[358 US 309]**

*The evidence offered at the hearing on the motion to suppress was not substantially disputed. It established that one Marsh, a federal narcotic agent with 29 years' experience, was stationed at Denver; that one Hereford had been engaged as a "special employee" of the Bureau of Narcotics at Denver for about six months, and from time to time gave information to Marsh regarding violations of the narcotic laws, for which Hereford was paid small sums of money, and that Marsh had always found the information given by Hereford to be accurate and reliable. On September 3, 1956, Hereford told Marsh that James Draper (petitioner) recently had taken up abode at a stated address in Denver and "was peddling narcotics to several addicts" in that city. Four days later, on September 7, Hereford told Marsh "that Draper had gone to Chicago the day before [September 6] by train [and] that he was going to bring back three ounces of heroin [and] that he would return to

1. The Fourth Amendment of the Constitution of the United States provides: "The right of the people to be secure in their persons, houses, papers, and effects, against unreasonable searches and seizures, shall not be violated, and no Warrants shall issue, but upon probable cause, supported by Oath or affirmation, and particularly describing the place to be searched, and the persons or things to be seized."

continued

Denver either on the morning of the 8th of September or the morning of the 9th of September also by train." Hereford also gave Marsh a detailed physical description of Draper and of the clothing he was wearing,[2] and said that he would be carrying "a tan zipper bag," and that he habitually "walked real fast."

On the morning of September 8, Marsh and a Denver police officer went to the Denver Union Station and kept watch over all incoming trains from Chicago, but they did not see anyone fitting the description that Hereford had given. Repeating the process on the morning of September 9, they saw a person, having the exact physical attributes and wearing the precise clothing described by Hereford, alight from an

***[358 US 310]**

incoming Chicago train and *start walking "fast" toward the exit. He was carrying a tan zipper bag in his right hand and the left was thrust in his raincoat pocket. Marsh, accompanied by the police officer, overtook, stopped and arrested him. They then searched him and found the two "envelopes containing heroin" clutched in his left hand in his raincoat pocket, and found the syringe in the tan zipper bag. Marsh then took him (petitioner) into custody. Hereford died four days after the arrest and therefore did not testify at the hearing on the motion.

26 USC (Supp V) § 7607, added by § 104(a) of the Narcotic Control Act of 1956, 70 Stat 570, provides, in pertinent part:

"The Commissioner . . . and agents, of the Bureau of Narcotics . . . may—

"(2) make arrests without warrant for violations of any law of the United States relating to narcotic drugs . . . where the violation is committed in the presence of the person making the arrest or where such person has reasonable grounds to believe that the person to be arrested has committed or is committing such violation."

The crucial question for us then is whether knowledge of the related facts and circumstances gave Marsh "probable cause" within the meaning of the Fourth Amendment, and "reasonable grounds" within the meaning of § 104(a), supra,[3] to believe that petitioner had committed or was committing a violation of the narcotic laws. If it did, the arrest, though without a warrant,

***[358 US 311]**

was lawful *and the subsequent search of petitioner's person and the seizure of the found heroin were validly made incident to a lawful arrest, and therefore the motion to suppress was properly overruled and the heroin was competently received in evidence at the trial. Weeks v United States, 232 US 383, 392, 58 L ed 652, 655, 34 S Ct 341, LRA 1915B 834, Ann Cas 1915C 1177; Carroll v United States, 267 US 132, 158, 69 L ed 543, 553, 45 S Ct 280, 39 ALR 790; Agnello v United States, 269 US 20, 30, 70 L ed 145, 148, 46 S Ct 4, 51 ALR 409; Giordenello v United States, 357 US 480, 483, 2 L ed 2d 1503, 1507, 78 S Ct 1245.

Petitioner does not dispute this

2. Hereford told Marsh that Draper was a Negro of light brown complexion, 27 years of age, 5 feet 8 inches tall, weighed about 160 pounds, and that he was wearing a light colored raincoat, brown slacks and black shoes.

3. The terms "probable cause" as used in the Fourth Amendment and "reasonable grounds" as used in § 104(a) of the Narcotic Control Act, 70 Stat 570, are substantial equivalents of the same meaning. United States v Walker, 246 F2d 519, 526 (CA7th Cir); cf United States v Bianco, 189 F2d 716, 720 (CA3d Cir).

Headnote 1

analysis of the question for decision. Rather, he contends (1) that the information given by Hereford to Marsh was "hearsay" and, because hearsay is not legally competent evidence in a criminal trial, could not legally have been considered, but should have been put out of mind, by Marsh in assessing whether he had "probable cause" and "reasonable grounds" to arrest petitioner without a warrant, and (2) that, even if hearsay could lawfully have been considered, Marsh's information should be held insufficient to show "probable cause" and "reasonable grounds" to believe that petitioner had violated or was violating the narcotic laws and to justify his arrest without a warrant.

Considering the first contention, we find petitioner entirely in error. Brinegar v United States, 338 US 160, 172, 173, 93

Headnote 2 L ed 1879, 1888, 1889, 69 S Ct 1302, has settled the question the other way. There, in a similar situation, the convict contended "that the factors relating to inadmissibility of the evidence [for] *purposes of proving guilt at the trial,* deprive[d] the evidence as a whole of sufficiency to show probable cause for the search ...." Id. 338 US at 172. (Emphasis added.) But this Court, rejecting that contention, said: "[T]he so-called distinction places a wholly unwarranted emphasis upon the criterion of admissibility in evidence, to prove the accused's guilt, of the facts relied upon to show probable cause. That emphasis, we think goes much too far in confusing and disregarding the difference between what is required to prove guilt in a

***[358 US 312]**

criminal case and what is *required to show probable cause for arrest or search. It approaches requiring (if it does not in practical effect require) proof sufficient to establish guilt in order to substantiate the existence of probable cause. There is a large differ-

Headnote 3 ence between the two things to be proved [guilt and probable cause], as well as between the tribunals which determine them, and therefore a like difference in the quanta and modes of proof required to establish them."[4] 338 US, at 172, 173.

Nor can we agree with petitioner's second contention that Marsh's information was insufficient to show probable

Headnote 4 cause and reasonable grounds to believe that petitioner

4. In United States v Heitner, 149 F2d 105, 106 (CA2d Cir), Judge Learned Hand said "It is well settled that an arrest may be made upon hearsay evidence; and indeed, the 'reasonable cause' necessary to support an arrest cannot demand the same strictness of proof as the accused's guilt upon a trial, unless the powers of peace officers are to be so cut down that they cannot possibly perform their duties."

Grau v United States, 287 US 124, 128, 77 L ed 212, 215, 53 S Ct 38, contains a dictum that "A search warrant may issue only upon evidence which would be competent in the trial of the offense before a jury (Giles v United States, 284 F 208: Wagner v United States, 8 F2d 581). . . ." But the principles underlying that proposition were thoroughly discredited and rejected in Brinegar v United States, supra (338 US at 172–174, and notes 12 and 13). There are several cases in the federal courts that followed the now discredited dictum in the Grau Case, Simmons v United States (CA8 Okla) 18 F2d 85, 88; Worthington v United States (CA6 Mich) 166 F2d 557, 564, 565; cf Reeve v Howe (DC Pa) 33 F Supp 619, 622; United States v Novero (DC Mo) 58 F Supp 275, 279, but the great weight of authority is the other way. See, e.g., Wrightson v United States, 98 App DC 377, 236 F2d 672; United States v Heitner, 149 F2d 105, supra (CA2d Cit); United States v Bianco, 189 F2d 716 (CA3rd Cir); Wisniewski v United States, 47 F2d 825 (CA6th Cir); United States v Walker, 246 F2d 519 (CA 7th Cir); Mueller v Powell, 203 F2d 797 (CA8th Cir). And see Note, 46 Harv L Rev 1307, 1310–1311, criticizing the Grau dictum.

continued

had violated or was violating the narcotic laws and to justify his arrest without a warrant. The information given to narcotic agent

***[358 US 313]**

Marsh by "special employee" *Hereford may have been hearsay to Marsh, but coming from one employed for that purpose and whose information had always been found accurate and reliable, it is clear that Marsh would have been derelict in his duties had he not pursued it. And when, in pursuing that information, he saw a man, having the exact physical attributes and wearing the precise clothing and carrying the tan zipper bag that Hereford had described, alight from one of the very trains from the very place stated by Hereford and start to walk at a "fast" pace toward the station exit, Marsh had personally verified every facet of the information given him by Hereford except whether petitioner had accomplished his mission and had the three ounces of heroin on his person or in his bag. And surely, with every other bit of Hereford's information being thus personally verified, Marsh had "reasonable grounds" to believe that the remaining unverified bit of Hereford's information—that Draper would have the heroin with him—was likewise true.

"In dealing with probable cause, . . . as the very name implies, we deal with probabilities. These are not technical; they are the factual and practical considerations of everyday life on which reasonable and prudent men, not legal technicians, act." Brinegar v United States, supra (338 US at 175). Probable cause exists where "the facts and circumstances within [the arresting officers"] knowledge and of which they had reasonably trustworthy information [are] sufficient in themselves to warrant a man of reasonable caution in the belief that" an offense has been or is being committed. Carroll v United States, 267 US 132, 162, 69 L ed 543, 555, 45 S Ct 280, 39 ALR 790.[5]

***[358 US 314]**

*We believe that, under the facts and circumstances here, Marsh had probable cause and reasonable grounds to believe that petitioner was committing a violation of the laws of the United States relating to narcotic drugs at the time he arrested him. The arrest was therefore lawful, and the subsequent search and seizure, having been made incident to that lawful arrest, were likewise valid.[6] It follows that petitioner's motion to suppress was properly denied and that the seized heroin was competent evidence lawfully received at the trial.

Affirmed.

The Chief Justice and Mr. Justice Frankfurter took no part in the consideration or decision of this case.

5. To the same effect are: Husty v United States, 282 US 694, 700, 701, 75 L ed 629, 632, 633, 51 S Ct 240, 74 ALR 1407; Dumbra v United States, 268 US 435, 441, 69 L ed 1032, 1036, 45 S Ct 546; Steele v United States, 267 US 498, 504, 505, 69 L ed 757, 760, 761, 45 S Ct 414; Stacey v Emery, 97 US 642, 645, 24 L ed 1035, 1036; Brinegar v United States, supra (338 US at 175, 176).

6. Weeks v United States, 232 US 383. 392, 58 L ed 652, 655, 34 S Ct 341, LRA 1915B 834, Ann Cas 1915C 1177; Carroll v United States, 267 US 132, 158, 69 L ed 543, 553, 45 S Ct 280, 39 ALR 790; Agnello v United States, 269 US 20, 30, 70 L ed 145, 148, 46 S Ct 4, 51 ALR, 409; Giordenello v United States, 357 US 480, 483, 2 L ed 2d 1503, 1507, 78 S Ct 1245.

SEPARATE OPINION

Mr. Justice **Douglas,** dissenting.

Decisions under the Fourth Amendment,[1] taken in the long view, have not given the protection to the citizen which the letter and spirit of the Amendment would seem to require. One reason, I think, is that wherever a culprit is caught red-handed, as in leading Fourth Amendment cases, it is difficult to adopt and enforce a rule that would turn him loose. A rule protective of law-abiding citizens is not apt to flourish where its advocates are usually criminals. Yet the rule we fashion is for the innocent and guilty alike. If the word of the

***[358 US 315]**

informer *on which the present arrest was made is sufficient to make the arrest legal, his word would also protect the police who, acting on it, hauled the innocent citizen off to jail.

Of course, the education we receive from mystery stories and television shows teaches that what happened in this case is efficient police work. The police are tipped off that a man carrying narcotics will step off the morning train. A man meeting the precise description does alight from the train. No warrant for his arrest has been—or, as I see it, could then be—obtained. Yet he is arrested; and narcotics are found in his pocket and a syringe in the bag he carried. This is the familiar pattern of crime detection which has been dinned into public consciousness as the correct and efficient one. It is, however, a distorted reflection of the constitutional system under which we are supposed to live.

With all due deference, the arrest made here on the mere word of an informer violated the spirit of the Fourth Amendment and the requirement of the law, 26 USC (Supp V) § 7607, governing arrests in narcotics cases. If an arrest is made without a warrant, the offense must be committed in the presence of the officer or the officer must have "reasonable grounds to believe that the person to be arrested has committed or is committing" a violation of the narcotics law. The arresting officers did not have a bit of evidence, known to them and as to which they could take on oath had they gone to a magistrate for warrant, that petitioner had committed any crime. The arresting officers did not know the grounds on which the informer based his conclusion; nor did they seek to find out what they were. They acted solely on the informer's word. In my view that was not enough.

The rule which permits arrest for felonies, as distinguished from misdemeanors, if there are reasonable grounds for believing a crime has been or is being committed (Carroll v United States, 267 US 132, 157, 69 L ed 543, 553, 45 S Ct 280, 39

***[358 US 316]**

ALR 790), *grew out of the need to protect the public safety by making prompt arrests. Id. Yet, apart from those cases where the crime is committed in the presence of the officer, arrests without warrants, like searches without warrants, are the exception, not the rule in our society. Lord Chief Justice Pratt in Wilkes v Wood, 19 How St Tr 1153, condemned not only the odious gen-

1. The Fourth Amendment provides:

"The right of the people *to be secure in their persons,* houses, papers, and effects, *against unreasonable* searches and *seizures,* shall not be violated and no Warrants shall issue, but *upon* probable *cause,* supported by Oath or affirmation, and particularly describing the place to be searched, and the persons or things to be seized." (Italics added.)

continued

eral warrant,[2] in which the name of the citizen to be arrested was left blank, but the whole scheme of seizures and searches[3] under "a discretionary power" of law officers to act "wherever their suspicions may chance to fall"—a practice which he denounced as "totally subversive of the liberty of the subject." Id. 19 St Tr at 1167. See III May, Constitutional History of England, ch XI. Wilkes had written in 1762, "To take any man into custody, and deprive him of his liberty, without having some seeming foundation at least, on which to justify such a step, is inconsistent with wisdom and sound policy." The Life and Political Writings of John Wilkes, p 372.

George III in 1777 pressed for a bill which would allow arrests on suspicion of treason committed in America. The words were "suspected of" treason and it was to these words that Wilkes addressed himself in Parliament. "There is not a syllable in the Bill of the degree of probability attending the *suspicion*. . . . Is it possible, Sir, to give more despotic powers to

***[358 US 317]**

a bashaw of the Turkish *empire? What security is left for the devoted objects of this Bill against the malice of a prejudiced individual, a wicked magistrate . . . ?" The Speeches of Mr. Wilkes, p 102.

These words and the complaints against which they were directed were well known on this side of the water. Hamilton wrote about "the practice of arbitrary imprisonments" which he denounced as "the favorite and most formidable instruments of tyranny." The Federalist No. 84. The writs of assistance, against which James Otis proclaimed,[4] were vicious in the same way as the general warrants, since they required no showing of "probable cause" before a magistrate, and since they allowed the police to search on suspicion and without "reasonable grounds" for believing that a crime has been or was being committed. Otis' protest was eloquent; but he lost the case. His speech, however, rallied public opinion. "Then and there," wrote John Adams, "the child Independence was born." 10 Life and Works of John Adams (1856), p 248.

The attitude of Americans to arrests and searches on suspicion was also greatly influenced by the lettres de cachet extensively used in France.[5] This was an order emanating from the King and countersigned by a minister directing the seizure of a person for purposes of immediate imprisonment or exile. The ministers issued the lettres in an arbitrary manner, often at the request of the head of a noble family to punish a deviant son or relative. See Mirabeau, A Victim of

2. The general warrant was declared illegal by the House of Commons in 1766. See 16 Hansard, Parl Hist Eng, 207.

3. The nameless general warrant was not the only vehicle for intruding on the privacy of the subjects without a valid basis for believing them guilty of offenses. In declaring illegal a warrant to search a plaintiff's house for evidence of libel, issued by the Secretary of State without any proof of the named accused was the author of the alleged libels, Lord Camden said, "we can safely say there is no law in this country to justify the defendants in what they have done; if there was, it would destroy all the comforts of society." Entick v Carrington, 2 Wils KB 275, 291.

4. See Quincy's Mass Rep, 1761–1772, Appx 1, p 469.

5. "Experience . . . has taught us that the power [to make arrests, searches and seizures] is one open to abuse. The most notable historical instance of it is that of lettres de cachet. Our Constitution was framed during the seethings of the French Revolution. The thought was to make lettres de cachet impossible with us." United States v Innelli (DC Pa) 286 F 731.

the Lettres de Cachet, 3 Am Hist Rev 19. One who was so arrested

***[358 US 318]**

*might remain incarcerated indefinitely, as no legal process was available by which he could seek release. "Since the action of the government was secret, his friends might not know whither he had vanished, and he might even be ignorant of the cause of his arrest." 8 The Camb Mod Hist 50. In the Eighteenth Century the practice arose of issuing the lettres in blank, the name to be filled in by the local mandatory. Thus the King could be told in 1770 "that no citizen of your realm is guaranteed against having his liberty sacrificed to revenge. For no one is great enough to be beyond the hate of some minister, nor small enough to be beyond the hate of some clerk." III Encyc Soc Sci 138. As Blackstone wrote, ". . . if once it were left in the power of any, the highest, magistrate to imprison arbitrarily whomever he or his officers thought proper, (as in France it is daily practiced by the crown,) there would soon be an end of all other rights and immunities." I Commentaries (4th ed Cooley), 135.

The Virginia Declaration of Rights, adopted June 12, 1776, included the forerunner of the Fourth Amendment:[6]

"That general warrants, whereby an officer or messenger may be commanded to search suspected places without evidence of a fact committed, or to seize any person or persons not named, or whose offence is not particularly described and *supported by evidence,* are grievous and oppressive, and ought not to be granted." (Italics added.)

The requirement that a warrant of arrest be "supported by evidence" was by then deeply rooted in history. And it is inconceivable that in those days, when the right of

***[358 US 319]**

*privacy was so greatly cherished, the mere word of an informer—such as we have in the present case—would be enough. For whispered charges and accusations, used in lieu of evidence of unlawful acts, were the main complaint of the age. Frisbie v Butler (Conn) Kirby 1785–1788, p. 213, decided in 1787, illustrates, I think, the mood of the day in the matter of arrests on suspicion. A warrant of arrest and search was issued by a justice of the peace on the oath of a citizen who had lost some pork from a cellar, the warrant stating, "said Butler suspects one Benjamin Frisbie, of Harwinton, to be the person that hath taken said pork." The court on appeal reversed the judgment of conviction, holding inter alia that the complaint "contained no direct charge of the theft, but only an averment that the defendant was suspected to be guilty." Id. Kirby at 215. Nothing but suspicion is shown in the instant case—suspicion of an informer, not that of the arresting officers. Nor did they seek to obtain from the informer any information on which he based his belief. The arresting officers did not have a bit of *evidence* that the petitioner had committed or was committing a crime before the arrest. The only *evidence* of guilt was provided by the arrest itself.

When the Constitution was up for adoption, objections were made that it contained no Bill of Rights. And Patrick Henry was one who complained in particular that it con-

6. See also Maryland Declaration of Rights (1776), Art XXIII; Massachusetts Constitution (1780), Part First, Art XIV; New Hampshire Constitution (1784), Part I, Art XIX; North Carolina Declaration of Rights (1776), Art XI; Pennsylvania Constitution (1776), Art X.

continued

tained no provision against arbitrary searches and seizures:

". . . general warrants, by which an officer may search suspected places, without evidence of the commission of a fact, or seize any person without evidence of his crime, ought to be prohibited. As these are admitted, any man may be seized, any property may be taken, in the most arbitrary manner, without any evidence or reason.

***[358 US 320]**

Every thing the most sacred *may be searched and ransacked by the strong hand of power. We have infinitely more reason to dread general warrants here than they have in England, because there, if a person be confined, liberty may be quickly obtained by the writ of habeas corpus. But here a man living many hundred miles from the judges may get in prison before he can get that writ." I Elliot's Debates, 588.

The determination that arrests and searches on mere suspicion would find no place in American law enforcement did not abate following the adoption of a Bill of Rights applicable to the Federal Government. In Conner v Commonwealth (Pa) 3 Binn 38, an arrest warrant issued by a magistrate stating his "strong reason to suspect" that the accused had committed a crime because of "common rumor and report" was held illegal under a constitutional provision identical in relevant part to the Fourth Amendment. "It is true, that by insisting on an oath, felons may sometimes escape. This must have been very well known to the framers of our constitution; but they thought it better that the guilty should sometimes escape, than that every individual should be subject to vexation and oppression." Id. 3 Binn at 43–44. In Grumon v Raymond, 1 Conn 40, the warrant stated that "several persons are suspected" of stealing some flour which is concealed in Hyatt's house or somewhere else, and ordered the constable to search Hyatt's house or other places and arrest the suspected persons if found with the flour. The court held the warrant void, stating it knew of "no such process as one to arrest all suspected persons, and bring them before a court for trial. It is an idea not to be endured for a moment," Id. 1 Conn at 44. See also Fisher v McGirr, 67 Mass (1 Gray) 1; 6 Am Dec 381; Lippman v People, 175 Ill 101, 51 NE 872; Somerville v Richards, 37 Mich 299; Commonwealth v Dana, 43 Mass (2 Met) 329, 335, 336.

***[358 US 321]**

*It was against this long background that Professors Hogan and Snee of Georgetown University recently wrote:

". . . it must be borne in mind that any arrest based on suspicion alone is illegal. This indisputable rule of law has grave implications for a number of traditional police investigative practices. The roundup or dragnet arrest, the arrest on suspicion, for questioning, for investigation or on an open charge all are prohibited by the law. It is undeniable that if those arrests were sanctioned by law, the police would be in a position to investigate a crime and to detect the real culprit much more easily, much more efficiently, much more economically, and with much more dispatch. It is equally true, however, that society cannot confer such power on the police without ripping away much of the fabric of a way of life which seeks to give the maximum of liberty to the individual citizen. The finger of suspicion is a long one. In an individual case it may point to all of a certain race, age group or locale. Commonly it extends to any who have committed similar crimes in the past. Arrest on mere suspicion collides violently with the basic human right of liberty. It can be tolerated only in a society which is willing to concede to its government powers which history and experience teach are the inevitable accoutrements of tyranny." 47 Geo LJ 1, 22.

Down to this day our decisions have closely heeded that warning. So far as I can ascertain the mere word of an informer, not bolstered

***[358 US 322]**

by some evidence[7] that a *crime had been or was being committed, has never been approved by this Court as "reasonable grounds" for making an arrest without a warrant. Whether the act complained of be seizure of goods, search of premises, or the arrest of the citizen, the judicial inquiry has been directed toward the reasonableness of inferences to be drawn from suspicious circumstances attending the action thought to be unlawful. Evidence required to prove guilt is not necessary. But the attendant circumstances must be sufficient to give rise in the mind of the arresting officer at least to inferences of guilt. Locke v United States (US) 7 Cranch 339, 3 L ed 364; The Thompson (The Isabella Thompson v United States) (US) 3 Wall 155, 18 L ed 55; Stacey v Emery, 97 US 642, 24 L ed 1035; Director General v Kastenbaum, 263 US 25, 68 L ed 146, 44 S Ct 52; Carroll v United States, 267 US 132, 159–162, 69 L ed 543, 554, 555, 45 S Ct 280, 39 ALR 790; United States v Di Re, 332 US 581, 591, 592, 92 L ed 210, 218, 219, 68 S Ct 222; Brinegar v United States, 338 US 160, 165–171, 93 L ed 1879, 1885–1888, 69 S Ct 1302.

The requirement that the arresting officer know some facts suggestive of guilt has been variously stated:

"If the facts and circumstances before the officer are such as to warrant a man of prudence and caution in believing that the offense has been committed, it is sufficient." Stacey v Emery, supra (97 US at 645).

". . . good faith is not enough to constitute probable cause. That faith must be grounded on facts within knowledge of the . . . agent, which in the judgment of the court would make his faith reasonable." Director General v Kastenbaum, supra (263 US at 28).

***[358 US 323]**

*Even when officers had information far more suggestive of guilt than the word of the informer used here, we have not sustained arrests without a warrant. In Johnson v United States, 333 US 10, 16, 92 L ed 436, 441, 68 S Ct 367, the arresting officer not only had an informer's tip but he actually smelled opium coming out of a room; and on breaking in found the accused. That arrest was held unlawful. Yet the smell of opium is far more tangible direct evidence than an unverified report that someone is going to commit a crime. And in United States v Di Re, 332 US 581, 92 L ed 210, 68 S Ct 222, supra, an arrest

7. Hale, who traced the evolution of arrests without warrants in The History of the Pleas of the Crown (1st Am ed 1847), states that while officers need at times to act on information from others, they must make that information, so far as they can, their own. He puts a case where A, suspecting B "on reasonable grounds" of being a felon, asks an officer to arrest B. The duty of the officer was stated as follows:

"He ought to inquire and examine the circumstances and causes of the suspicion of A which tho he cannot do it upon oath, yet such an information may carry over the suspicion even to the constable, whereby it may become his suspicion as well as the suspicion of A." Id., at 91.

continued

without a warrant of a man sitting in a car, where counterfeit coupons had been found passing between two men, was not justified in absence of any shred of evidence implicating the defendant, a third person. And see Giacona v State, 164 Tex Crim 325, 298 SW2d 587. Yet the evidence before those officers was more potent than the mere word of the informer involved in the present case.

The Court is quite correct in saying that proof of "reasonable grounds" for believing a crime was being committed need not be proof admissible at the trial. It could be inferences from suspicious acts, e.g., consort with known peddlers, the surreptitious passing of a package, an intercepted message suggesting criminal activities, or any number of such events coming to the knowledge of the officer. See People v Rios, 46 Cal2d 297, 294 P 2d 39. But, if he takes the law into his own hands and does not seek the protection of a warrant, he must act on some evidence known to him.[8]

***[358 US 324]**

The law goes far to protect *the citizen. Even suspicious acts observed by the officers may be as consistent with innocence as with guilt. That is not enough, for even the guilty may not be implicated on suspicion alone. Baumboy v United States (CA9 Cal) 24 F2d 512. The reason is, as I have said, that the standard set by the Constitution and by the statute is one that will protect both the officer and the citizen. For if the officer acts with "probable cause" or on "reasonable grounds," he is protected even though the citizen is innocent.[9] This important requirement should be strictly enforced, lest the whole process of arrest revert once more to whispered accusations by people. When we lower the guards as we do today, we risk making the role of the informer—odious in our history—once more supreme. I think the correct rule was stated in Poldo v United States (CA9 Cal) 55 F2d 866, 869. "Mere suspicion is not enough; there must be circumstances represented to the officers through the testimony of their senses sufficient to justify them in a good-faith belief that the defendant had violated the law."

Here the officers had no evidence—apart from the mere word of an informer—that petitioner was committing a crime. The fact that petitioner walked fast and carried a tan zipper bag was not evidence of any crime. The officers knew nothing except what they had been told by the informer. If they went to a magistrate to get a warrant of arrest and relied solely on the report of the informer, it is not conceivable to me that one would be granted. See Giordenello v United States, 357 US 480, 486, 2 L ed 2d 1503, 1510, 78 S Ct 1245. For they could not present to the magistrate any of the facts which the informer may have had.

8. United States v Heitner (CA2 NY) 149 F2d 105, 106, that says an arrest may be made "upon hearsay evidence" was a case where the arrest was made after the defendant on seeing the officers tried to get away. Our cases cited by that court in support of the use of hearsay were Carroll v United States, 267 US 132, 69 L ed 543, 45 S Ct 280, 39 ALR 790; Dumbra v United States, 268 US 435, 69 L ed 1032, 45 S Ct 546; and Husty v United States, 282 US 694, 75 L ed 629, 51 S Ct 240, 74 ALR 1407. But each of them was a case where the information on which the arrest was made, though perhaps not competent at the trial, was known to the arresting officer.

9. Maghan v Jerome, 67 App DC 9, 88 F2d 1001; Pritchett v Sullivan (CA8 Kan) 182 F 480. See Ravenscroft v Casey (CA2 NY) 139 F2d 776.

They could swear only to the fact that the informer had made the accusation. They could swear to no evidence that lay in their own knowl-

***[358 US 325]**

edge. They could *present, on information and belief, no facts which the informer disclosed. No magistrate could issue a warrant on the mere word of an officer, without more.[10] See Giordenello v United States, supra. We are not justified in lowering the standard when an arrest is made without a warrant and allowing the officers more leeway than we grant the magistrate.

With all deference I think we break with tradition when we sustain this arrest. We said in United States v Di Re, supra (332 US at 595), ". . . a search is not to be made legal by what it turns up. In law it is good or bad when it starts and does not change character from its success." In this case it was only after the arrest and search were made that there was a shred of evidence known to the officers that a crime was in the process of being committed.[11]

NOTE

An annotation on "What constitutes 'probable cause' or 'reasonable grounds' justifying arrest of narcotics suspect without warrant" appears p. 1736, infra.

10. See State v Gleason, 32 Kan 245, 4 P 363; State v Smith (Mo App) 262 SW 65, arising under state constitutions having provisions comparable to our Fourth Amendment.

11. The Supreme Court of South Carolina has said:

"Some things are to be more deplored than the unlawful transportation of whiskey; one is the loss of liberty. Common as the event may be, it is a serious thing to arrest a citizen, and it is a more serious thing to search his person; and he who accomplishes it, must do so in conformity to the laws of the land. There are two reasons for this: one to avoid bloodshed, and the other to preserve the liberty of the citizen. Obedience to law is the bond of society, and the officers set to enforce the law are not exempt from its mandates.

"In the instant case the possession of the liquor was the body of the offense; that fact was proven by a forcible and unlawful search of the defendant's person to secure the veritable key to the offense. It is fundamental that a citizen may not be arrested and have his person searched by force and without process in order to secure testimony against him. . . . It is better that the guilty shall escape, rather than another offense shall be committed in the proof of guilt." Blacksburg v Beam, 104 SC 146, 148, 88 SE 441, LRA 1916E 714.

F. Exercise 10.6: *United States v. Romero*

1. Precedent is very important in legal analysis. Review *Romero* and cite a few cases that were viewed with some authority or respect as precedent.
2. Using the same case, find the following and cite in the proper legal format. Please use the citation format suggested in Chapter 5.
   a. Statute
   b. Federal case
   c. Supreme Court case
3. What is the main statute, law, or legislation in dispute? What are its exact provisions?
4. When was this case decided?
5. When was it argued?
6. What circuit was the case in?
7. In what area of the country was this case heard?
8. Briefly describe these essential features of the *Romero* case:
   a. Facts of the case
   b. Issues of the case
   c. The court's finding or holding
   d. The court's reasoning for its decision

UNITED STATES of America, Plaintiff-Appellee,

v.

Craig Paul ROMERO, Defendant-Appellant.

No. 78–1779.

United States Court of Appeals, Seventh Circuit.

Argued Jan. 19, 1979.

Decided Aug. 2, 1979.

Defendant was convicted of possession of firearms after prior conviction of felony, and appealed from the United States District Court for the Eastern District of Illinois, East St. Louis Division, James L. Foreman, J. The Court of Appeals held that where trial was before bench, jury having been waived, it would be presumed that judge disregarded prejudicial effect of evidence of multiple prior convictions, and there was thus no prejudicial error in admitting evidence of multiple prior convictions, but thenceforth and under normal circumstances Government would not be permitted to prove more than one prior felony regardless of whether jury was waived.

Conviction affirmed.

Criminal Law ⟹260.11(2)
Weapons ⟹17(3)

Where trial of prosecution for possession of firearms by convicted felon was before bench, jury having been waived, it would be presumed that judge disregarded prejudicial effect of evidence of multiple prior convictions, and there was thus no prejudicial error in admitting evidence of multiple prior convictions, but thenceforth and under normal circumstances Government would not be permitted to prove more than one prior felony regardless of whether jury was waived. 18 U.S.C.A. App. § 1202(a)(1).

Timothy Paridon, Belleville, Ill., for defendant-appellant.

James R. Burgess, U. S. Atty., Robert L. Simpkins, Asst. U. S. Atty., East St. Louis, Ill., for plaintiff-appellee.

Before SWYGERT and CUMMINGS, Circuit Judges, and CROWLEY, District Judge.[1]

PER CURIAM.

The question in this appeal is whether the district court committed error by permitting the Government to prove that the defendant had been convicted of more than one prior felony under a charge that the defendant had possessed a firearm in violation of 18 App. U.S.C. § 1202(a)(1).[2] We hold that the district judge did commit error but that under the circumstances of this case, the error was harmless. *Chapman v. State of California,* 386 U.S. 18, 87 S.Ct. 824, 17 L.Ed. 705 (1967).

On November 8, 1977 Fred Donini, a special agent of the Illinois Division of Investigation, and an informant, Frank Crockett, drove to Cahokia, Illinois, and went to the trailer residence of defendant Craig Paul Romero, where they found Romero in his front yard. Donini and Crockett accompanied Romero inside the trailer.

The purpose of the visit to Romero's residence was to purchase a firearm. Crockett told Romero that he and Donini had just

1. The Honorable John Powers Crowley, United States District Judge for the Northern District of Illinois, sitting by designation.

2. 18 App. U.S.C. § 1202(a)(1) reads in pertinent part:

Any person who—

(1) has been convicted by a court of the United States or of a State or any political subdivision thereof of a felony,

* * * * * *

and who receives, possesses, or transports in commerce or affecting commerce, after the date of enactment of this Act, any firearm shall be fined not more than $10,000 or imprisoned for not more than two years, or both.

continued

come from California where they had engaged in various burglaries and armed robberies. Crockett told Romero that he wanted to purchase a weapon and asked Romero if he had any guns. Romero then asked if a nine-millimeter-weapon would suit their purpose. Romero opened a chest of drawers and pulled out a brown paper bag which contained a 32-caliber revolver. Romero handed the revolver to Crockett who unloaded the weapon and examined it. Crockett paid Romero $50.00 for the revolver. (The 32-caliber revolver which Crockett and Donini purchased from Romero had previously been shipped in interstate commerce from Florida to California, and from California to Cahokia, Illinois.)

The Government introduced evidence that Romero had been convicted of felony-burglary in 1967 in Illinois and that he had been convicted of a felony-theft in 1973. Over objection, the Government also was permitted to show that in 1973 Romero had been convicted of a felony in the Eastern District of Illinois for dealing in firearms without a license and for the transfer of a firearm to a resident of another state.

The Government contends that 18 U.S.C. App. § 1202(a)(1) permits proof of more than one prior felony conviction for jurisdictional purposes. We disagree. The statute speaks of "a" prior conviction, not one or more. The Government cites *United States v. Burkhart*, 545 F.2d 14 (6th Cir. 1976), and *United States v. Smith*, 520 F.2d 544 (8th Cir. 1975), to support its position. Both the Eighth and Sixth Circuits held in these cases that the Government was not limited to establishing only one prior conviction. In *United States v. Barfield*, 527 F.2d 858 (5th Cir. 1976), however, the court assumed arguendo that "the Government may prove only one [prior] conviction under normal circumstances," ultimately holding that a curative instruction erased the error.

With deference to the holdings of the Eighth and Sixth Circuits, we adopt a different view. In those opinions the courts offered no explanation why the Government needed to establish more than one prior conviction. We think there is no such need. In *Barfield*, the Government argued that if the conviction used as proof in the gun prosecution later was vacated, then the gun conviction also could be overturned on a habeas corpus attack. Not only is this eventuality remote, but the Fifth Circuit also correctly pointed out that when a defendant stipulates to "a prior conviction" the Government's gun conviction would not be based on any single prior conviction; thus the invalidation of a prior conviction would not invalidate the gun conviction so long as one valid, prior conviction remained. *Barfield, supra* at 861. There is, of course, the distinction to be drawn from the use of a prior conviction which is *void, United States v. Lufman*, 457 F.2d 165 (7th Cir., 1972) and one which is *voidable, United States v. Liles*, 432 F.2d 18 (7th Cir., 1970). The United States Attorney can easily avoid these problems by careful pre-trial preparation.

At oral argument in this case, Government counsel suggested that identity problems could arise: a defendant might deny that he was the person named in the prior conviction offered by the government. If, however, a defendant in a gun prosecution did not object immediately to a prior conviction offered by the government against him, it is unlikely that he would assert later that he was not the person identified in the prior conviction. If eventually he did make such an objection, its validity would be suspect and its persuasive impact on a court minimal. Thus, we can see no justification for offering more than a prior conviction into evidence; the introduction of multiple convictions can only encourage the conviction of a defendant because he was a "bad man". *Barfield, supra* at 861.

In the instant case the jury was waived and there was a bench trial. We are unable to say on the basis of this record that the trial judge was influenced by the improperly admitted evidence. It must be presumed that he disregarded the prejudicial effect of the multiple convictions in reaching his decision of guilty.

We hold, however, that henceforth and under normal circumstances the Government shall not be permitted to prove more than one prior felony conviction under the statute regardless of whether or not a jury is waived. The introduction into evidence of more than one prior felony conviction can only be prejudicial to the defendant and serves no jurisdictional purpose.

The evidence was sufficient to permit a finding of guilty beyond a reasonable doubt. The judgment of conviction is affirmed.

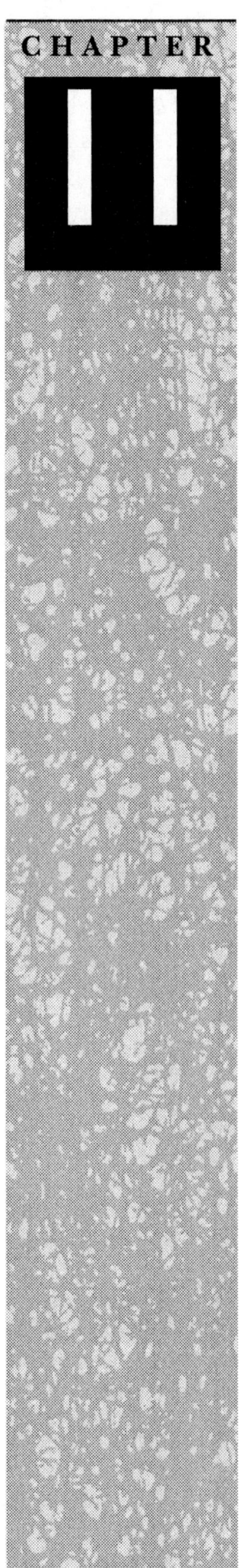

Statutes and Legislative Resources

I. TYPES OF STATUTORY LAW

Another primary resource in the researcher's arsenal is statutory law. The term **statutes** refers to the actual laws passed by state and federal authorities. Statutes and codes are the end result of the political process and the product of the legislative system in government. In the modern age of governmental activism, it is hardly surprising that there is no shortage of statutory authority. Examples such as these populate the legal landscape: Gambling Devices Act of 1962; Freedom of Information Act; Federal Tort Claims Act. The endless litany of legislative enactments manifests how active government is in the lives of its citizens, from defining criminal behavior to assuring fairness in housing.

A. Federal Statutory Law

The burgeoning number of federal programs, rights, and entitlements certainly has heightened legal research interest in federal statutes. Consider civil rights, fair housing, equal pay, environmental protection, and veterans' rights as representative examples of federal activism. Understanding the content of a federal statute is only one part of this complicated and vital process. The mechanical steps that lead to codification are just as important to the legal researcher.

When legislation is adopted at the federal level, it is generally published first as a **slip law**, which is nothing more than a pamphlet with the text of the law. The next destination for a federal law is publication in the *U.S. Statutes at Large* as a **session law**. A session law is simply a law that was passed by the current legislative session. Soon thereafter, the adopted law is published in the relevant title of the official *United States Code* (U.S.C.), with assigned chapter and section citation numbers. Last,

PHOTO 11.1

and most inevitably, because the U.S.C. provides no more than the legislation itself, the new law will be included in the two authoritative annotated code services:

> *United States Code Annotated* (U.S.C.A.) by West Publishing Company
>
> *United States Code Service* (U.S.C.S.) by Lawyer's Cooperative

Annotation consists of commentary on a wide range of legal subject matter (as in other annotated references, from citations to law reviews), covering legislative history to everything from judicial interpretation of the statute. Why this preference for annotation? Both the U.S.C.A. and the U.S.C.S. publish the exact language of the adopted legislation, of course, but the value-added features of these annotated services allow the researcher to perform these additional functions:

- Review historical issues and trends in the legislation published
- Assess the influence of case law on applicability of the statute
- Compile and compare case law
- Cross-reference with other services, including A.L.R. and the reporter system
- Refer to the *Code of Federal Regulations* (C.F.R.)
- Update information through pocket parts and supplements
- Consult advance sheets and services

Other features worth noting in the annotated services include the easy-to-use index systems, which cite laws by popular name, such as the "*Anti-Dumping Act of 1921*" or the "Anti-Beer Act," and correlate those names to the relevant statutes. Also helpful to the researcher at the federal level is the list of title and chapter headings provided. See Figure 11.1 for an outline of the resources included in the *United States Code* and Figure 11.2 for sample pages from the *United States Code Annotated*.

B. State Statutes

Little difference exists between the annotation methods employed at the state and federal levels. From slip laws to annotation, the state process is fundamentally the same. An example from the New York Penal Law § 130.80 appears in Figure 11.3.

FIGURE 11.1

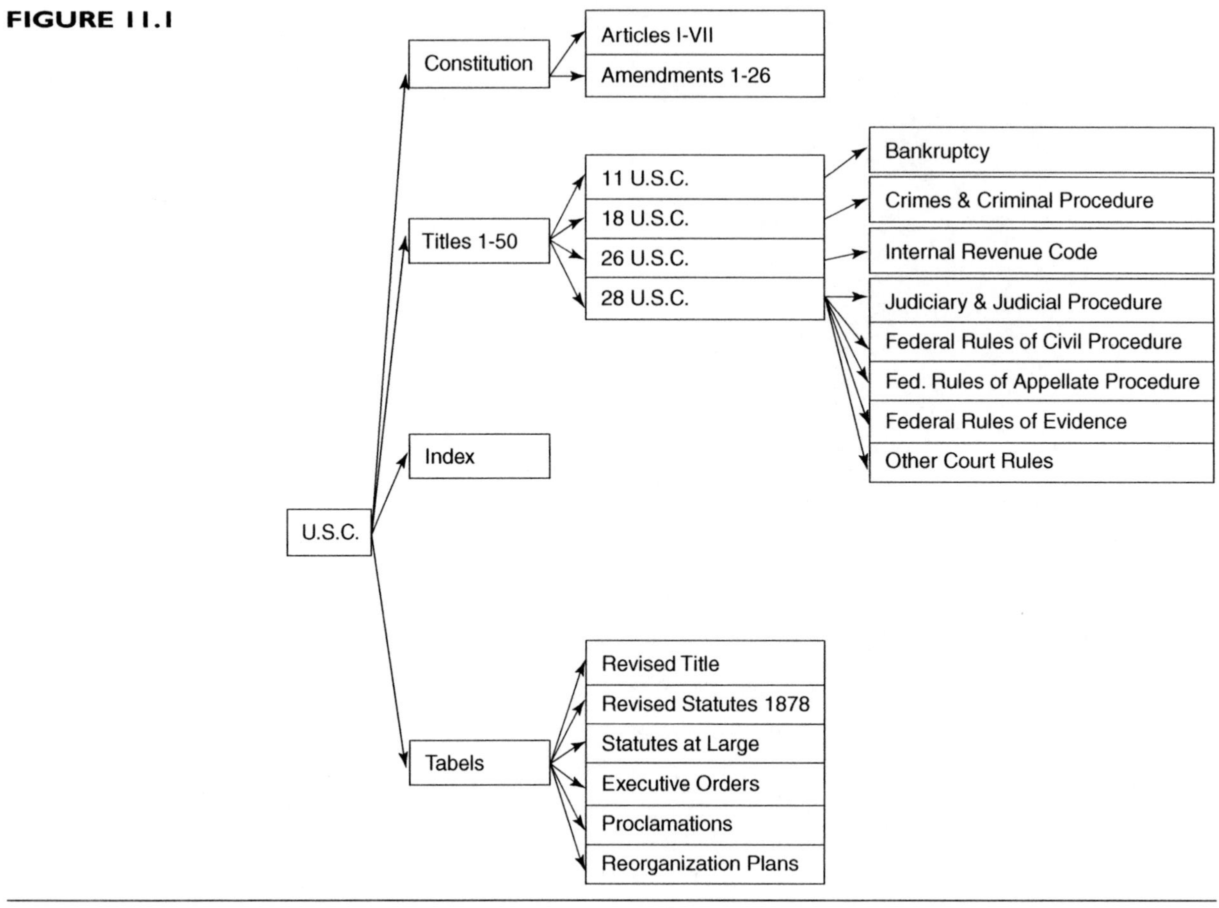

C. Rules of Court

Practitioners depend on the State Rules of Court series published by West Publishing Company. **Rules of court** (also called *court rules*) highlight the procedural requirements most pertinent to daily practice, as well as prescribe the process and procedures for various courts. They are packaged in a desk copy edition for quick and easy reference.

D. Constitutions

The researcher should never bypass the most fundamental enumerator of rights—the constitution. Constitutions are codified in codes and statutes. Although state constitutions generally emulate the federal model, striking differences can and do exist. The analysis of a legal problem should always include an assessment of constitutional implications. Failure to pose constitutional queries leads to incomplete analysis.

In the criminal context, constitutional law is absolutely indispensable. Research in constitutional law issues requires a multifaceted approach, including analysis of the *United States Code Annotated* or the *United States Code Service.* Other avenues of constitutional inquiry include review of the following sources:

- The Library of Congress edition of *The Constitution of the United States of America: Analysis and Interpretation*

FIGURE 11.2

CHAPTER 18—CONGRESSIONAL, CABINET, AND SUPREME COURT ASSASSINATION, KIDNAPPING, AND ASSAULT

Sec

351. Congressional, Cabinet, and Supreme Court assassination, kidnapping, and assault; penalties.

HISTORICAL AND STATUTORY NOTES

Amendments

1994 Amendments. Pub.L. 103–322, Title XXXIII, § 330021(1), Sept. 13, 1994, 108 Stat. 2150, substituted "kidnapping" for "kidnaping" wherever appearing.

1982 Amendments. Pub.L. 97–285, § 2(b), (c), Oct. 6, 1982, 96 Stat. 1219, substituted "Congressional, Cabinet, and Supreme Court assassination, kidnaping, and assault" for "Congressional assassination, kidnaping, and assault" as the chapter 18 heading and, in the analysis of sections in the chapter, substituted "Congressional, Cabinet, and Supreme Court assassination, kidnaping, and assault; penalties" for "Congressional assassination, kidnapping and assault; penalties" as item 351.

WESTLAW COMPUTER ASSISTED LEGAL RESEARCH

WESTLAW supplements your legal research in many ways. WESTLAW allows you to

- update your research with the most current information
- expand your library with additional resources
- retrieve current, comprehensive history citing references to a case with KeyCite

For more information on using WESTLAW to supplement your research, see the WESTLAW Electronic Research Guide, which follows the Explanation.

§ 351. Congressional, Cabinet, and Supreme Court assassination, kidnapping, and assault; penalties

(a) Whoever kills any individual who is a Member of Congress or a Member-of-Congress-elect, a member of the executive branch of the Government who is the head, or a person nominated to be head during the pendency of such nomination, of a department listed in section 101 of title 5 or the second ranking official in such department, the Director (or a person nominated to be Director during the pendency of such nomination) or Deputy Director of Central Intelligence, a major Presidential or Vice Presidential candidate (as defined in section 3056 of this title), or a Justice of the United States, as defined in section 451 of title 28, or a person nominated to be a Justice of the United States, during the pendency of such nomination, shall be punished or provided by sections 1111 and 1112 of this title.

29

continued

- Shepard's United States Citations (Federal Courts)
- Digests covering Supreme Court opinions

II. FINDING STATUTES

Statutory compilations have indexes, as do most other legal resources. A general index is provided at the end of each set, and each title includes a very detailed topical outline. There are two methods for finding information included in statutes, depending on the amount of information possessed from the outset. See Figure 11.4 from Westlaw explaining the different parts of annotated statutes.

FIGURE 11.2
continued

18 § 351 **CRIMES Part 1**

(b) Whoever kidnaps any individual designated in subsection (a) of this section shall be punished (1) by imprisonment for any term of years or for life, or (2) by death or imprisonment for any term of years or for life, if death results to such individual.

(c) Whoever attempts to kill or kidnap any individual designated in subsection (a) of this section shall be punished by imprisonment for any term of years or for life.

(d) If two or more persons conspire to kill or kidnap any individual designated in subsection (a) of this section and one or more of such persons do any act o effect the object of the conspiracy, each shall be punished (1) by imprisonment for any term of years or for life, or (2) by death or imprisonment for any term of years or for life, if death results to such individual.

(e) Whoever assaults any person designated in subsection (a) of this section shall be fined under this title, or imprisoned not more than one year or both; and if the assault involved the use of a dangerous weapon, or personal injury results, shall be fined under this title, or imprisoned not more than ten years, or both.

(f) If Federal investigative or prosecutive jurisdiction is asserted for a violation of this section, such assertion shall suspend the exercise of jurisdiction by a State or local authority, under any applicable State or local law, until Federal action is terminated.

(g) Violations of this section shall be investigated by the Federal Bureau of Investigation. Assistance may be requested from any Federal, State, or local agency, including the Army, Navy, and Air Force, any statute, rule, or regulation to the contrary notwithstanding.

(h) In a prosecution for an offense under this section the Government need not prove that the defendant knew that the victim of the offense was an individual protected by this section.

(i) There is extraterritorial jurisdiction over the conduct prohibited by this section.

(Added Pub.L. 91–644, Title IV, § 15, Jan. 2, 1971, 84 Stat. 1891, and amended Pub.L. 97–285, §§ 1, 2(a), Oct. 6, 1982, 96 Stat. 1219; Pub.L. 99–646, § 62, Nov. 10, 1986, 100 Stat. 3614; Pub.L. 100–690, Title VII, § 7074, Nov. 18, 1988, 102 Stat. 4405; Pub.L. 103–322, Title XXXII, § 320101(d), Title XXXIII, §§ 330016(1)(K), (L), 330021(1), Sept. 13, 1994, 108 Stat. 2108, 2147, 2150; Pub.L. 104–294, Title VI, § 604(b)(12)(C), (c)(2), Oct. 11, 1996, 110 Stat. 3507, 3509.)

A. Existing Authority

If you already know the citation to the statute, track the numbers to the appropriate volume. Find the relevant title number and go to the relevant section. Be sure you are looking in the correct set of statutes. Each state and the *United States Code* have different methods of organization. Title numbers will not be the same in each state.

B. Keywords

If you lack the citation, turn to the keyword method and consult the general index. A general index is organized alphabetically, with broad topics and much subdivision. See the following examples using Fact Patterns 1 and 2.

Fact Pattern 1. First locate the General Index, M to Z, of Purdon's *Pennsylvania Consolidated Statutes Annotated.* Look up the keyword "Driving Under the Influence," which then directs the researcher to look under the topic "Traffic Rules and Regulations." Under this section, you find "Driving under influence of alcohol or con-

HISTORICAL AND STATUTORY NOTES

Revision Notes and Legislative Reports

1971 Acts. Senate Report No. 91–1253 and Conference Report No. 91–1768, see 1970 U.S. Code Cong. and Adm. News, p. 5804.

1982 Acts. House Report No. 97–803, see 1982 U.S. Code Cong. and Adm. News, p. 2428.

1986 Acts. House Report No. 99–797, see 1896 U.S. Code Cong. and Adm. News, p. 6138.

1988 Acts. For Related Reports, see 1988 U.S. Code Cong. and Adm. News, p. 5937.

1994 Acts. House Reports Nos. 103–324 and 103–489, and House Conference Report No. 103–711, see 1994 U.S. Code Cong. and Adm. News, p. 1801.

1996 Acts. House Report No. 104–788, see 1996 U.S. Code Cong. and Adm. News, p. 4021.

Amendments

1996 Amendments. Subsec. (e). Pub.L. 104–294; § 604(b)(12)(C), repealed duplicative amendment by section 320101(d)(3) of Pub.L. 103–322, which required no change in text. See Repeals and Effective Date notes under this section.

Pub.L. 104–294, § 604(c)(2), substituted "involved the use of a dangerous weapon" for "involved in the use of a dangerous weapon".

1994 Amendments. Heading. Pub.L. 103–322, § 330021(1), substituted "kidnapping" for "kidnaping".

Subsec. (e). Pub.L. 103–322, § 320101(d)(1), substituted "fined under this title," for "fined not more than $5,000," preceding "or imprisoned not more than one year".

Pub.L. 103–322, § 330016(1)(K), directed that "under this title" be substituted for "not more than $5,000".

Pub.L. 103–322, § 320101(d)(2), inserted "the assault involved in the use of a dangerous weapon, or".

Pub.L. 103–322, § 320101(d)(3), (4), substituted "fined under this title, or imprisoned not more than ten years" for "fined not more than $10,000, or imprisoned for not more than ten years". See Repeals note set out under this section.

Pub.L. 103–322, § 330016(1)(L), directed that "under this title" be substituted for "not more than $10,000". Identical amendment was made pursuant to section 320101(d)(3) of Pub.L. 103–322.

1988 Amendments. Subsec. (a). Pub.L. 100–690 inserted "," after "section 3056 of this title)".

1986 Amendments. Subsec. (a). Pub.L.99–646, § 62(1), inserted "a major Presidential or Vice Presidential candidate (as defined in section 3056 of this title)" after "Central Intelligence,".

Subsec. (h). Pub.L. 99–646, § 62(2), substituted "individual" for "official".

1982 Amendments. Catchline. Pub.L. 97–285 § 2(a), substituted "Congressional, Cabinet, and Supreme Court assassination, kidnaping, and assault; penalties" for "Congressional assassination, kidnaping, and assault".

Subsec. (a). Pub.L. 97–285, § 1(a), expanded the coverage of the subsection to cover the killing of any individual who is a member of the executive branch of the Government and the head, or a person nominated to be head during the pendency of such nomination, of a department listed in section 101 of title 5 or the second ranking official in such department, the Director (or a person nominated to be Director during the pendency of such nomination) or Deputy Director of Central Intelligence, or a Justice of the United States, as defined in section 451 of title 28, or a person nominated to be a Justice of the United States, during the pendency of such nomination.

Subsecs. (h), (i). Pub.L. 97–285, § 1(b), added subsecs. (h) and (i).

Effective and Applicability Provisions

1996 Acts. Amendment by section 604 of Pub.L. 104–294 effective Sept. 13, 1994, see section 604(d) of Pub.L. 104–294, set out as a note under section 13 of this title.

Repeals

Pub.L. 103–322, Title XXXII, § 320101(d)(3), Sept. 13, 1994, 108 Stat. 2108, appearing in the credit of this section, was repealed by Pub.L. 104–294, Title VI, § 604(b)(12)(C), Oct. 11, 1996, 110 Stat. 3507.

FIGURE 11.2
continued

Report to Member of Congress on Investigation Conducted Subsequent to Threat on Member's Life

Pub.L. 95–624, § 19, Nov. 9, 1978, 92 Stat. 3466, provided that: "The Federal Bureau of Investigation shall provide a written report to a Member of Congress on any investigation conducted based on a threat on the Member's life under section 351 of title 18 of the United States Code [this section]."

CROSS REFERENCES

"Federal crime of terrorism" defined as in this section for purposes of acts of terrorism transcending national boundaries, see 18 USCA § 2332b.

Mitigating and aggravating factors to be considered in determining whether a sentence of death is justified and death during commission of another crime, see 18 USCA § 3592.

Providing material support for terrorists, see 18 USCA § 2339A.

Terrorism and extension of statute of limitations for certain offenses, see 18 USCA § 3286.

FEDERAL SENTENCING GUIDELINES

See Federal Sentencing Guidelines §§ 2A1.5, 2A2.1, 2A2.2, 2A2.3, 2A4.1, 18 USCA.

LIBRARY REFERENCES

American Digest System

Assault and Battery ⚷ 47 et seq.
Homicide ⚷ 7, 8.
Kidnapping ⚷ 1.

Encyclopedias

Assault and Battery, see C.J.S. § 62.
Homicide, see C.J.S. § 29 et seq.
Kidnapping, see C.J.S. §§ 1, 2.
Assault, 6 Am Jur 2d §§ 10–15.

Law Review and Journal Commentaries

Recent developments in the United States and internationally regarding capital punishment—An appraisal. Ved P. Nanda, 67 St.John's L.Rev. 523 (1993).

Texts and Treatises

Instruction on assault, see Devitt and Blackmar § 23.01 et seq.
Criminal Procedure, 8 Fed Proc L Ed §§ 22:41, 232.

WESTLAW ELECTRONIC RESEARCH

See WESTLAW guide following the Explanation pages of this volume.

Notes of Decisions

1. Constitutionality

This section gives adequate notice to persons of ordinary intelligence of prohibited conduct and does not include innocent or constitutionally protected conduct within its proscription. U.S. v. Guerrero, C.A.10 (Colo.) 1981, 667 F.2d 862, certiorari denied 102 S.Ct. 2044, 456 U.S. 964, 72 L.Ed.2d 490.

32

This section barring assault on congressmen did not deny equal protection and due process nor violate defendant's right to free speech under U.S.C.A. Const. Amend. 1, nor was it vague or overbroad. U.S. v. Calderon, C.A.10 (Colo.) 1981, 655 F.2d 1037.

2. Purpose

Congress in enacting this section intended not merely to protect peace and order of community but to single out congressmen for protection because of position they hold in constitutional government, their protection being important to integrity of national government and therefor serving important interest of government itself. U.S. v. Layton, N.D.Cal.1981, 509 F.Supp. 212, appeal dismissed 645 F.2d 681, certiorari denied 101 S.Ct. 3128, 452 U.S. 972, 69 L.Ed.2d 984.

3. Offenses within section

This section barring assault on a Congressman applied to defendant who threw raw eggs at congressman during 1980 Presidential Campaign. U.S. v. Calderon, C.A.10 (Colo.) 1981, 655 F.2d 1037.

4. Assault

Throwing of eggs at congressman while he was addressing political rally at time when he was candidate for President constituted "assault" within meaning of this section. U.S. v. Guerrero, C.A.10 (Colo.) 1981, 667 F.2d 862, certiorari denied 102 S.Ct. 2044, 456 U.S. 964, 72 L.Ed.2d 490.

5. Intent

Conviction of assaulting a member of Congress required proof that defendant willfully caused an offensive touching; it was not necessary to prove that defendant intended a more severe injury. U.S. v. Masel, C.A.7 (Wis.) 1977, 563 F.2d 322, certiorari denied 98 S.Ct. 1496, 435 U.S. 927, 55 L.Ed.2d 523.

6. Persons protected

Victim, who was serving term in Congress at time defendant threw two eggs at him while he was addressing political rally, was a "member of Congress" within protection of this section, and fact that he was running for President did not do away with protection provided. U.S. v. Guerrero, C.A.10 (Colo.) 1981, 667 F.2d 862, certiorari denied 102 S.Ct. 2044, 450 U.S. 964, 72 L.Ed.2d 490.

Congressman who traveled to Guyana as part of his duties as member of house committee on foreign affairs and as member of international operations subcommittee and who did so with express approval of chairman of that committee and who traveled to Guyana also to fulfill duties both as representative of his constituents and as representative of other American citizens who had expressed concern about conditions and events there was particularly within protection of this section. U.S. v. Layton, N.D.Cal. 1981, 509 F.Supp. 212, appeal dismissed 645 F.2d 681, certiorari denied 101 S.Ct. 3128, 452 U.S. 972, 69 L.Ed.2d 984.

7. Jurisdiction

District court had jurisdiction to try defendant on charges of conspiracy to kill member of Congress and aiding and abetting in killing of member of Congress, though conduct occurred outside United States; statute prohibited acts which obstruct governing process and thus, locus of conduct was not relevant to end sought by statute. U.S. v. Layton, C.A.9 (Cal.) 1988, 885 F.2d 1388, certiorari denied 109, S.Ct. 1178, 489 U.S. 1046, 103 L.Ed.2d 244.

Extraterritorial application could be inferred as to statute providing punishment for whoever kills member of Congress or member-of-Congress elect or conspires to kill or kidnap such individual, either on basis that statute represented effort by government to protect itself against obstructions and frauds or that vulnerability of United States outside its own territory to occurrence of prohibited conduct was sufficient because of the nature of offense to permit reasonable inference that Congress meant to reach those extraterritorial acts, and same was particularly true in light of particular congressman's citizenship and official nature of his trip to Guyana where he was killed. U.S. v. Layton, N.D.Cal.1981, 509 F.Supp. 212, appeal dismissed 645 F.2d 681, certiorari denied 101 S.Ct. 3128, 452 U.S. 972, 69 L.Ed.2d 984.

8. Venue

Under section 3238 of this title relating to offenses nor committed in any district, venue for both indictment and trial on charges arising from killing of Congressman at airport in Guyana and wounding of deputy chief of mission for the United States in the republic of Guyana was

continued

FIGURE 11.2
continued

18 § 351 **CRIMES Part 1**
Note 8

Northern District of California, which was defendant's last known residence, where indictment was returned before defendant was found in or brought in the United States, though, following defendant's subsequent arrest, he was initially brought into the United States via New York. U.S. v. Layton, N.D.Cal.1981, 519 F.Supp. 942, appeal dismissed 665 F.2d 274.

9. Evidence

In prosecution for assault on member of Congress based on throwing of two eggs at congressman while he was addressing a political rally, trial court, which viewed videotape before it was shown to jury and limited its impact by allowing only visual portion to be presented, did not abuse its discretion in admitting videotape depicting actual throwing of eggs; even if tape was improperly admitted, error was harmless where prosecution offered other substantial evidence to prove identification of defendant as egg thrower. U.S. v. Guerrero, C.A.10 (Colo.) 1981, 667 F.2d 862, certiorari denied 102 S.Ct. 2044, 456 U.S. 964, 72 L.Ed.2d 490.

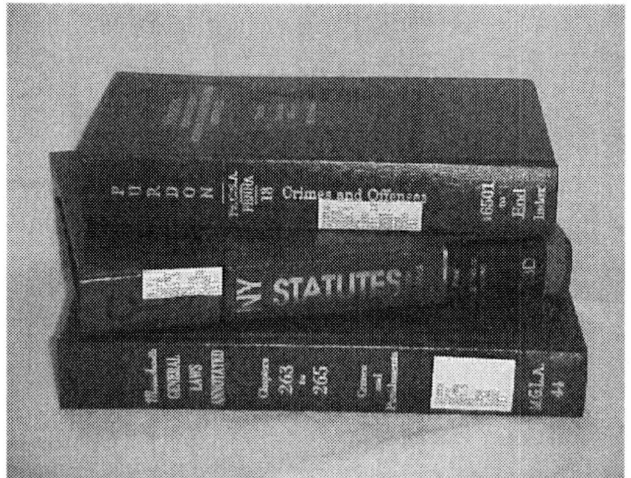

PHOTO 11.2

trolled substances" and a subentry for "Homicide," which directs the researcher to 75 Pa.C.S.A. § 3735. See Fact Pattern Figure 11.5.

Next locate Title 75, Vehicles, on the shelf; choose the volume that includes § 3735, and locate the section. See Fact Pattern Figure 11.6.

Fact Pattern 2. After much searching, using the keywords "agreement," "contract," and "real estate," you check the topic "sales." Under this heading you find "Buyers," with a subdivision for "Rights." See Fact Pattern Figure 11.7.

Under this "Specific performance or replevin" may be applicable. You then locate the title 13 volume and turn to § 2716. See Fact Pattern Figure 11.8.

C. Known Topic

If you know the subject matter of the applicable statute, you can bypass use of the general index. Locate the appropriate title and consult the table of contents at the

CASE NOTES

Defendant, who was charged with engaging in course of sexual conduct against female child under 11 years of age for more than 3 months, failed to meet his burden of proving that CLS Penal § 130.75 was unconstitutionally vague on its face, or as applied to him. CLS Penal § 130.75(a) which provides that jury must unanimously agree that at least 2 acts of sexual conduct occurred, without requiring agreement as to which 2, does not violate state constitutional right to unanimous jury verdict. CLS Penal § 130.75(a), which defines single crime based on repeated sexual assault of same child during specific period of time, does not violate defendant's right to specificity in indictment under CLS CPL § 200.50, which is derived from CLS NY Const Art I § 6 and (presumably) CLS US Const Amend 6. People v Calloway (1998, Co Ct) 176 Misc 2d 161, 672 NYS2d 638.

§ 130.80. Course of sexual conduct against a child in the second degree

(a) A person is guilty of course of sexual conduct against a child in the second degree when, over a period of time not less than three months in duration, he or she engages in two or more acts of sexual conduct with a child less than eleven years old.

(b) A person may not be subsequently prosecuted for any other sexual offense involving the same victim unless the other charged offense occurred outside the time period charged under this section.

Course of sexual conduct against a child in the second degree is a class D felony.

HISTORY:

Add, L 1996, ch 122, § 6, eff Aug 1, 1996 (see 1996 note below).

NOTES:

Editor's Notes:

Laws 1996, ch 122, § 7, eff Aug 1, 1996, provides as follows:

§ 7. This act shall take effect on the first day of August next succeeding the date on which it shall have become a law and shall apply only to offenses occurring on or after such date.

FEDERAL ASPECTS:

Protection of children from sexual predators act of 1998, P. L. 105-314.

RESEARCH REFERENCES AND PRACTICE AIDS:

65 Am Jur 2d, Rape §§ 15 et seq.
18 Am Jur Trials 341, Handling the Defense in a Rape Prosecution.
34 Am Jur Trials 1, Representing Sex Offenders and the "Chemical Castration Defense.".
6 Am Jur Proof of Facts 2d 63, Mistake as to Age of Statutory Rape Victim.
24 Am Jur Proof of Facts 2d 515, Defense to Charge of Sex Offense.

Texts:

8 New York Criminal Practice (Matthew Bender), Chapter 70, Sex Offenses and Offenses against Marriage.

Criminal Jury Instructions:

CJI (NY) 2d PL 130.80.

§ 130.85. Female genital mutilation

1. A person is guilty of female genital mutilation when:

(a) a person knowingly circumcises, excises, or infibulates the whole or any part of the labia majora or labia minora or clitoris of another person who has not reached eighteen years of age; or

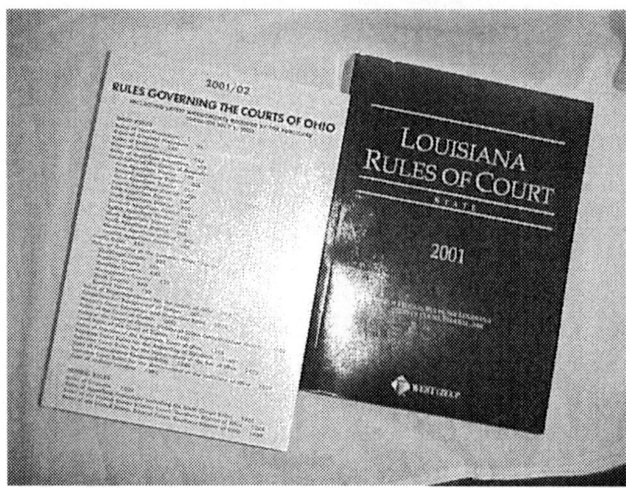

PHOTO 11.3

beginning of the title. The table of contents included in a statutory compilation, as with other legal resources, is very detailed and contains many references to subtopics. If you use this method, be very careful not to overlook topics that may seem inapplicable. Be sure to consult all titles that could possibly apply to the situation at hand. See Figure 11.9 for an example of a table of contents from the *United States Code Annotated.*

III. LEGAL RESEARCH ASSIGNMENTS

When completing assignments that deal with statutory materials and legislative analysis, be precise as possible. Case decisions depend largely on interpretation of statutes, and often hinge on a technical provision within a statute.

A. Exercise 11.1: Federal Rules of Criminal Procedure

1. Which section relates the factors involving issuance or probable cause?
   a. Rule 41
   b. Rule 41(c)(2)
   c. Rule 41(c)(2)(C)
   d. Rule 41(b)
2. Which section permits the issuance of a warrant without a written affidavit?
   a. Rule 41(c)(2)(A)
   b. Rule 41(a)(2)(A)
   c. Rule 41(c)(2)(G)
   d. None of the above
3. What two parties are given the right to issue warrants?
   a. Attorneys
   b. Police officers

FIGURE 11.4

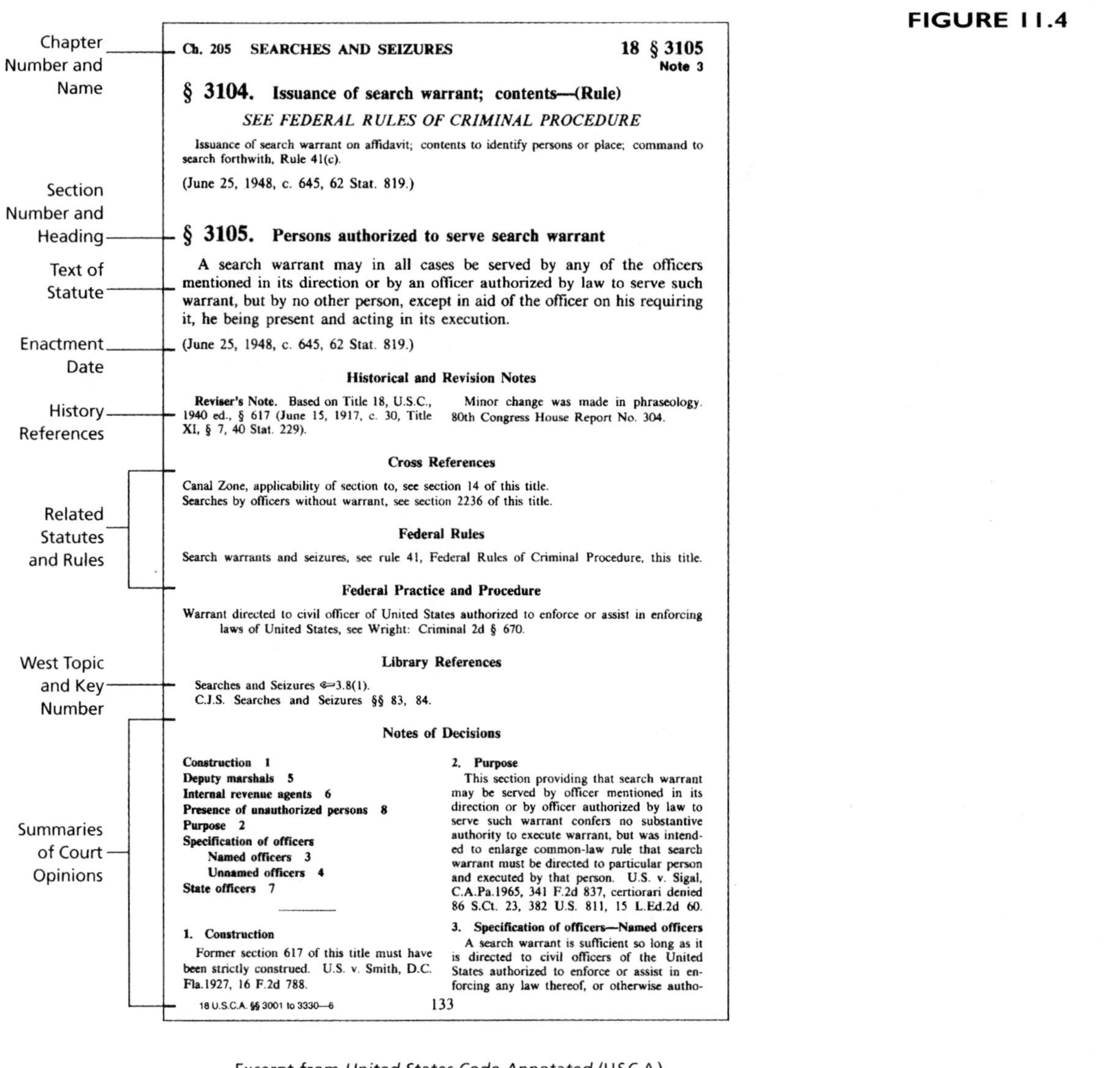

Ch. 205 SEARCHES AND SEIZURES 18 § 3105
Note 3

§ 3104. Issuance of search warrant; contents—(Rule)

SEE FEDERAL RULES OF CRIMINAL PROCEDURE

Issuance of search warrant on affidavit; contents to identify persons or place; command to search forthwith, Rule 41(c).

(June 25, 1948, c. 645, 62 Stat. 819.)

§ 3105. Persons authorized to serve search warrant

A search warrant may in all cases be served by any of the officers mentioned in its direction or by an officer authorized by law to serve such warrant, but by no other person, except in aid of the officer on his requiring it, he being present and acting in its execution.

(June 25, 1948, c. 645, 62 Stat. 819.)

Historical and Revision Notes

Reviser's Note. Based on Title 18, U.S.C., 1940 ed., § 617 (June 15, 1917, c. 30, Title XI, § 7, 40 Stat. 229).

Minor change was made in phraseology. 80th Congress House Report No. 304.

Cross References

Canal Zone, applicability of section to, see section 14 of this title.
Searches by officers without warrant, see section 2236 of this title.

Federal Rules

Search warrants and seizures, see rule 41, Federal Rules of Criminal Procedure, this title.

Federal Practice and Procedure

Warrant directed to civil officer of United States authorized to enforce or assist in enforcing laws of United States, see Wright: Criminal 2d § 670.

Library References

Searches and Seizures ⇐3.8(1).
C.J.S. Searches and Seizures §§ 83, 84.

Notes of Decisions

Construction 1
Deputy marshals 5
Internal revenue agents 6
Presence of unauthorized persons 8
Purpose 2
Specification of officers
Named officers 3
Unnamed officers 4
State officers 7

1. Construction

Former section 617 of this title must have been strictly construed. U.S. v. Smith, D.C. Fla.1927, 16 F.2d 788.

2. Purpose

This section providing that search warrant may be served by officer mentioned in its direction or by officer authorized by law to serve such warrant confers no substantive authority to execute warrant, but was intended to enlarge common-law rule that search warrant must be directed to particular person and executed by that person. U.S. v. Sigal, C.A.Pa.1965, 341 F.2d 837, certiorari denied 86 S.Ct. 23, 382 U.S. 811, 15 L.Ed.2d 60.

3. Specification of officers—Named officers

A search warrant is sufficient so long as it is directed to civil officers of the United States authorized to enforce or assist in enforcing any law thereof, or otherwise autho-

18 U.S.C.A. §§ 3001 to 3330—6 133

Excerpt from *United States Code Annotated* (U.S.C.A.)

continued

c. Federal magistrates
d. Judge of state court and federal magistrates

4. When does a warrant become stale or legally too old?
   a. In excess of 10 days
   b. 5 days or more
   c. 1 year
   d. 3 hours
5. A person requesting the warrant should be placed under oath.
   a. Yes
   b. No

FIGURE 11.4
continued

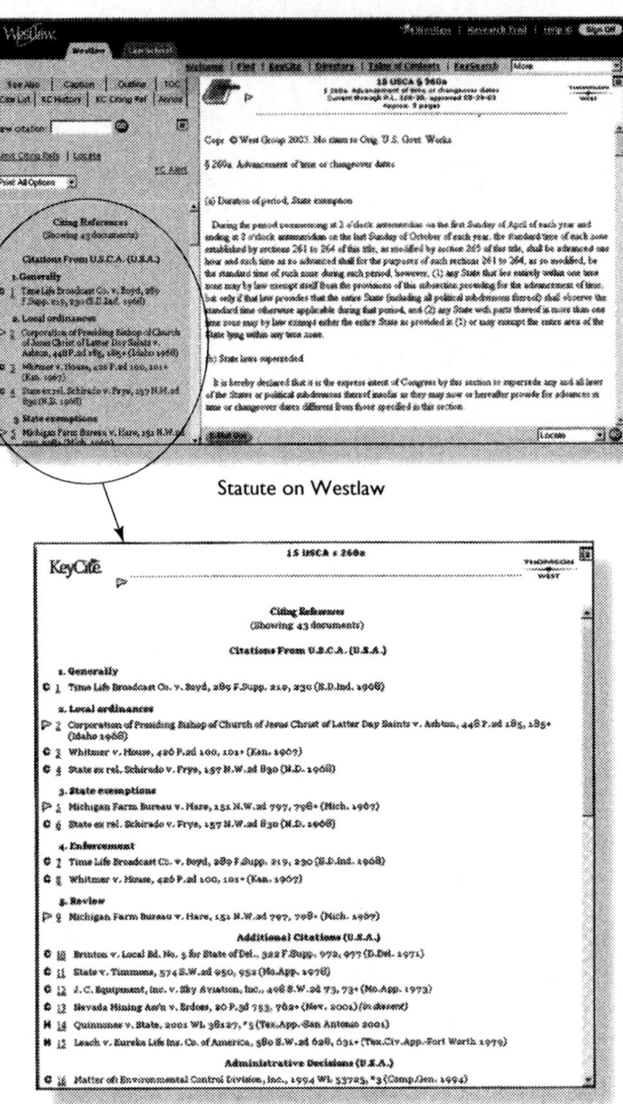

Statute on Westlaw

KeyCite citing references (detail)

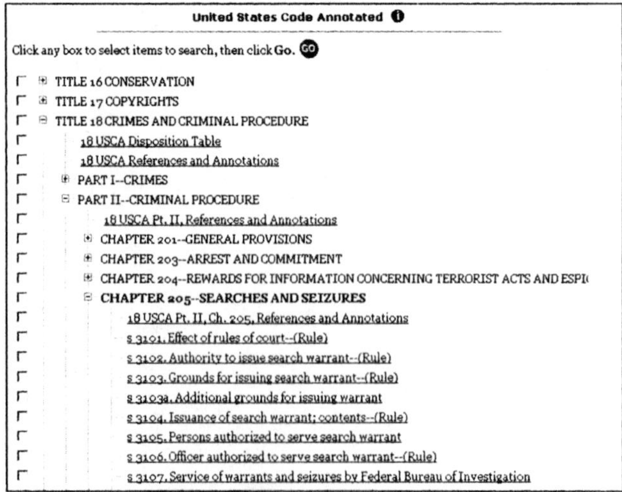

Table of Contents service

en together with a subsequent offense for driving while intoxicated, were properly used for categorizing motorist as an habitual offender by reason of "three convictions arising from separate acts of any one or more of the following offenses committed either singularly or in combination." Com., Dept. of Transp., Bureau of Traffic Safety v. McDevitt, 427 A.2d 280, 57 Pa.Cmwlth. 589, Cmwlth.1981, affirmed 458 A.2d 939, 500 Pa. 532.

3. Suspension of license

The suspension of a motor vehicle operator's license for violation of 75 P.S. § 1038 (repealed) was reversed on appeal where the court at a hearing de novo found that although appellant did turn off the lights of his vehicle, he did not do so for the purpose of avoiding identification or arrest. License of Buerk, 65 Pa. D. & C.2d 239 (1974).

§ 3735. Homicide by vehicle while driving under influence

(a) Offense defined.—Any person who unintentionally causes the death of another person as the result of a violation of section 3731 (relating to driving under influence of alcohol or controlled substance) and who is convicted of violating section 3731 is guilty of a felony of the second degree when the violation is the cause of death and the sentencing court shall order the person to serve a minimum term of imprisonment of not less than three years.

(b) Applicability of sentencing guidelines.—The sentencing guidelines promulgated by the Pennsylvania Commission on Sentencing shall not supersede the mandatory penalty of this section.

1982, Dec. 15, P.L. 1268, No. 289, § 11, effective in 30 days. Amended 1996, Feb. 23, P.L. 21, No. 8, § 1, effective in 60 days.

Historical and Statutory Notes

The 1996 amendment, in subsec. (a), preceding "result", deleted "direct", and changed the offense from a third degree felony to a second degree felony.

Cross References

Criminal laboratory user fee, see 42 Pa.C.S.A. § 1725.3.

Law Review Commentaries

Pennsylvania drunk driving law. 87 Dick.L.Rev. 805 (1983).

Warrantless arrest by police officers in Pennsylvania. Francis Barry McCarthy, 92 Dick.L.Rev. 105 (1987).

Notes of Decisions

708

burden of proving that his injury was proximately caused by failure of the weapon to conform to the manufacturer's representations. Klages v. General Ordnance Equipment Corp., 367 A.2d 304, 240 Pa.Super. 356, Super.1976.

20. Instructions

Objection to instruction as to damages "insofar as it applies to implied warranty in view of" contention "that implied warranty is not part of this case" was insufficient to meet requirements of rule for raising point that jury was instructed without reference to Uniform Commercial Code of Pennsylvania, and improperly instructed that particular damages need not have been contemplated or foreseeable by defendant. Boeing Airplane Co. v. O'Malley, C.A.8 (Minn.) 1964, 329 F.2d 585.

§ 2716. Right of buyer to specific performance or replevin

(a) Specific performance.—Specific performance may be decreed where the goods are unique or in other proper circumstances.

(b) Terms and conditions of decree.—The decree for specific performance may include such terms and conditions as to payment of the price, damages, or other relief as the court may deem just.

(c) Replevin.—The buyer has a right of replevin for goods identified to the contract if after reasonable effort he is unable to effect cover for such goods or the circumstances reasonably indicate that such effort will be unavailing, or if the goods have been shipped under reservation and satisfaction of the security interest in them has been made or tendered.

1979, Nov. 1, P.L. 255, No. 86, § 1, effective Jan. 1, 1980.

Uniform Commercial Code Comment

Prior Uniform Statutory Provision: Section 68, Uniform Sales Act.

For text of prior provision, see Appendix in end volume of Uniform Laws Annotated, U.C.C., Master Edition.

Changes: Rephrased.

Purposes of Changes: To make it clear that:

1. The present section continues in general prior policy as to specific performance and injunction against breach. However, without intending to impair in any way the exercise of the court's sound discretion in the matter, this Article seeks to further a more liberal attitude than some courts have shown in connection with the specific performance of contracts of sale.

2. In view of this Article's emphasis on the commercial feasibility of replacement, a new concept of what are "unique" goods is introduced under this section. Specific performance is no longer limited to goods which are already specific or ascertained at the time of contracting. The test of uniqueness under this section must be made in terms of the total situation which characterizes the contract. Output and requirements contracts involving a particular or peculiarly available source or market present today the typical commercial specific performance situation, as contrasted with contracts for the sale of heirlooms or priceless works of art which were usually involved in the older cases. However, uniqueness is not the sole basis of the remedy under this section for the relief may also be granted "in other proper circumstances" and inability to cover is strong evi-

CROSS REFERENCES

Changes in removal of alien terrorist pensions and restriction on disclosure, see 8 USCA § 1534.
Missing persons personnel files wrongful withholding, see 10 USCA § 1506.
Obscene or harassing use of telecommunications facilities under Communications Act of 1934, see 47 USCA § 223.
Pipeline carrier and general criminal penalty when specific penalty not provided, see 49 USCA § 16105.
Restrictions on discharging and obtaining contactor bid or proposal information or source selection information, see 41 USCA § 423.
Transportation—
Recordkeeping and reporting violations, see 49 USCA § 16102.

TITLE 18

CRIMES AND CRIMINAL PROCEDURE

[1]Appendix analysis editorially added.

HISTORICAL AND STATUTORY NOTES

1970 Amendments. Pub.L. 91–452, Title II, § 201(b), Oct. 15, 1970, 84 Stat. 928, added Part V.

PART I—CRIMES

Chapters 1 to 15 appear in this volume

9

continued

FIGURE 11.9
continued

CRIMES AND CRIMINAL PROCEDURE

10

[1]So in original. "Weapons" probably should not be capitalized.

[2]Heading of chapter 39 amended without amending Part I analysis to reflect the change.

[3]Chapter added without adding chapter heading to Part I analysis.

HISTORICAL AND STATUTORY NOTES

Codifications

Pub.L. 104–294, Title VI, § 601(j)(2)(A), Oct. 11, 1996, 110 Stat. 3501, which directed that item for chapter relating to torture be redesignated from 113B to 113C, was incapable of execution due to prior identical amendment by section 303(c)(2) of Pub.L. 104–132.

Amendment by section 40221(b) of Pub.L. 103–322, adding item for chapter 110A, was executed to chapter analysis despite directory language referring to "part analysis", as the probable intent of Congress.

Section 506(b) of Pub.L. 103–236, directing that the item relating to chapter 113B, Torture, be inserted after the item relating to chapter 113A, was executed instead by inserting the item relating to chapter 113B, Torture, after the item re-

B. Exercise 11.2: Federal Rules of Criminal Procedure

1. Under what title of the Federal Rules does the topic of venue arise?
   a. 14
   b. 6
   c. 3
   d. 5
2. Were any previous Rules of Criminal Procedure rescinded under this title?
   a. Rule 23
   b. Rule 21
   c. Rule 19
   d. None of the above
3. *Venue* can be roughly defined as
   a. the place of the arrest.
   b. the place of eventual incarceration.
   c. the place where the offense is committed and where trial and prosecution can occur.
   d. the place where witnesses can go.
4. It is not possible for defendant to ask for a transfer as it relates to venue.
   a. True
   b. False
5. What rationale(s) will a court employ in deciding whether to allow a transfer?
   a. Potential for very great prejudice against the defendant
   b. Convenience of the parties
   c. Both a and b
   d. None of the above

C. Exercise 11.3: Federal Rules of Civil Procedure

1. A party who makes a request to the court for a physicalor mental examination still has the right to assert the doctrine of privilege.
   a. True
   b. False
2. Which section outlines the basis for granting an order for examination?
   a. Rule 36
   b. Rule 37(c)(b)
   c. Rule 35(b)(3)
   d. Rule 35(a)
3. In what types of cases do you see such an order being requested?
   a. Paternity
   b. Civil commitment
   c. Mental or physical damages
   d. All of the above
4. To properly understand Rule 36, it is necessary to understand what other rule?
   a. Rule 25
   b. Rule 35
   c. Rule 26(g)
   d. None of the above

EXERCISE 11.1

Rule 41. Search and Seizure

(a) AUTHORITY TO ISSUE WARRANT.

Upon the request of a federal law enforcement officer or an attorney for the government, a search warrant authorized by this rule may be issued (1) by a federal magistrate judge, or a state court of record within the federal district, for a search of property or for a person within the district and (2) by a federal magistrate judge for a search of property or for a person either within or outside the district if the property or person is within the district when the warrant is sought but might move outside the district before the warrant is executed and (3) in an investigation of domestic terrorism or international terrorism (as defined in section 2331 of title 18, United States Code), by a Federal magistrate judge in any district in which activities related to the terrorism may have occurred, for a search of property or for a person within or outside the district.

(b) PROPERTY OR PERSONS WHICH MAY BE SEIZED WITH A WARRANT.

A warrant may be issued under this rule to search for and seize any (1) property that constitutes evidence of the commission of a criminal offense; or (2) contraband, the fruits of crime, or things otherwise criminally possessed; or (3) property designed or intended for use or which is or has been used as the means of committing a criminal offense; or (4) person for whose arrest there is probable cause, or who is unlawfully restrained.

(c) ISSUANCE AND CONTENTS.

(1) ***Warrant Upon Affidavit.***

A warrant other than a warrant upon oral testimony under paragraph (2) of this subdivision shall issue only on an affidavit or affidavits sworn to before the federal magistrate judge or state judge and establishing the grounds for issuing the warrant. If the federal magistrate judge or state judge is satisfied that grounds for the application exist or that there is probable cause to believe that they exist, that magistrate judge or state judge shall issue a warrant identifying the property or person to be seized and naming or describing the person or place to be searched. The finding of probable cause may be based upon hearsay evidence in whole or in part. Before ruling on a request for a warrant the federal magistrate judge or state judge may require the affiant to appear personally and may examine under oath the affiant and any witnesses the affiant may produce, provided that such proceeding shall be taken down by a court reporter or recording equipment and made part of the affidavit. The warrant shall be directed to a civil officer of the United States authorized to enforce or assist in enforcing any law thereof or to a person so authorized by the President of the United States. It shall command the officer to search, within a specified period of time not to exceed 10 days, the person or place named for the property or person specified. The warrant shall be served in the daytime, unless the issuing authority, by appropriate provision in the warrant, and for reasonable cause shown, authorizes its execution at times other than daytime. It shall designate a federal magistrate judge to whom it shall be returned.

(2) ***Warrant Upon Oral Testimony.***

(A) GENERAL RULE.

If the circumstances make it reasonable to dispense, in whole or in part, with a written affidavit, a Federal magistrate judge may issue a warrant based upon sworn testimony communicated by telephone or other appropriate means, including facsimile transmission.

(B) APPLICATION.

The person who is requesting the warrant shall prepare a document to be known as a duplicate original warrant and shall read such duplicate original warrant, verbatim, to the Federal magistrate judge. The Federal magistrate judge shall enter, verbatim, what is so read to such magistrate judge on a document to be known as the original warrant. The Federal magistrate judge may direct that the warrant be modified.

(C) ISSUANCE.

If the Federal magistrate judge is satisfied that the circumstances are such as to make it reasonable to dispense with a written affidavit and that grounds for the application exist or that there is probable cause to believe that they exist, the Federal magistrate judge shall order the issuance of a warrant by directing the person requesting the warrant to sign the Federal magistrate judge's name on the duplicate original warrant. The Federal magistrate judge shall immediately sign the original warrant and enter on the face of the original warrant the exact time when the warrant was ordered to be issued. The finding of probable cause for a warrant upon oral testimony may be based on the same kind of evidence as is sufficient for a warrant upon affidavit.

(D) RECORDING AND CERTIFICATION OF TESTIMONY.

When a caller informs the Federal magistrate judge that the purpose of the call is to request a warrant, the Federal magistrate judge shall immediately place under oath each person whose testimony forms a basis of the application and each person applying for that warrant. If a voice recording device is available, the Federal magistrate judge shall record by means of such device all of the call after the caller informs the Federal magistrate judge that the purpose of the call is to request a warrant. Otherwise a stenographic or longhand verbatim record shall be made. If a voice recording device is used or a stenographic record made, the Federal magistrate judge shall have the record transcribed, shall certify the accuracy of the transcription, and shall file a copy of the original record and the transcription with the court. If a longhand verbatim record is made, the Federal magistrate judge shall file a signed copy with the court.

(E) CONTENTS.

The contents of a warrant upon oral testimony shall be the same as the contents of a warrant upon affidavit.

(F) ADDITIONAL RULE FOR EXECUTION.

The person who executes the warrant shall enter the exact time of execution on the face of the duplicate original warrant.

(G) MOTION TO SUPPRESS PRECLUDED.

Absent a finding of bad faith, evidence obtained pursuant to a warrant issued under this paragraph is not subject to a motion to suppress on the ground that the circumstances were not such as to make it reasonable to dispense with a written affidavit.

(d) EXECUTION AND RETURN WITH INVENTORY.

The officer taking property under the warrant shall give to the person from whom or from whose premises the property was taken a copy of the warrant and a receipt for the property taken or shall leave the copy and receipt at the place from which the property was taken. The return shall be made promptly and shall be accompanied by a written inventory of any property taken. The inventory shall be made in the presence of the applicant for the warrant and the person from whose possession or premises the property was taken, if they are present, or in the presence of at least one credible person other than the applicant for the warrant or the person from whose possession or premises the property was taken, and shall be verified by the officer. The federal magistrate judge shall upon request deliver a copy of the inventory to the person from whom or from whose premises the property was taken and to the applicant for the warrant.

(As amended Dec. 27, 1948, eff. Oct. 20, 1949; Apr. 9, 1956, eff. July 8, 1956; Apr. 24, 1972, eff. Oct. 1, 1972; Mar. 18, 1974, eff. July 1, 1974; Apr. 26 and July 8, 1976, eff. Aug. 1, 1976; July 30, 1977, eff. Oct. 1, 1977; Apr. 30, 1979, eff. Aug. 1, 1979; Mar. 9, 1987, eff. Aug. 1, 1987; Apr. 25, 1989, eff. Dec. 1, 1989; May 1, 1990, eff. Dec. 1, 1990; Apr. 22, 1993, eff. Dec. 1, 1993; Oct. 26, 2001.)

EXERCISE 11.2

V. VENUE

Rule 18. Place of Prosecution and Trial. Except as otherwise permitted by statute or by these rules, the prosecution shall be had in a district in which the offense was committed. The court shall fix the place of trial within the district with due regard to the convenience of the defendant and the witnesses and the prompt administration of justice.
(As amended Feb. 28, 1966, eff. July 1, 1966; Apr. 30, 1979, eff. Aug. 1, 1979.)

[Rule 19. Transfer Within the District.] (Rescinded Feb. 28, 1966, eff. July 1, 1966.)

Rule 20. Transfer From the District for Plea and Sentence.

(a) INDICTMENT OR INFORMATION PENDING.

A defendant arrested, held, or present in a district other than that in which an indictment or information is pending against that defendant may state in writing a wish to plead guilty or nolo contendere, to waive trial in the district in which the indictment or information is pending, and to consent to disposition of the case in the district in which that defendant was arrested, held, or present, subject to the approval of the United States attorney for each district. Upon receipt of the defendant's statement and of the written approval of the United States attorneys, the clerk of the court in which the indictment or information is pending shall transmit the papers in the proceeding or certified copies thereof to the clerk of the court for the district in which the defendant is arrested, held, or present, and the prosecution shall continue in that district.

(b) INDICTMENT OR INFORMATION NOT PENDING.

A defendant arrested, held, or present, in a district other than the district in which a complaint is pending against that defendant may state in writing a wish to plead guilty or nolo contendere, to waive venue and trial in the district in which the warrant was issued, and to consent to disposition of the case in the district in which that defendant was arrested, held, or present, subject to the approval of the United States attorney for each district. Upon filing the written waiver of venue in the district in which the defendant is present, the prosecution may proceed as if venue were in such district.

(c) EFFECT OF NOT GUILTY PLEA.

If after the proceeding has been transferred pursuant to subdivision (a) or (b) of this rule the defendant pleads not guilty, the clerk shall return the papers to the court in which the prosecution was commenced, and the proceeding shall be restored to the docket of that court. The defendant's statement that the defendant wishes to plead guilty or nolo contendere shall not be used against that defendant.

(d) JUVENILES.

A juvenile (as defined in 18 U.S.C. Sec. 5031) who is arrested, held, or present in a district other than that in which the juvenile is alleged to have committed an act in violation of a law of the United States not punishable by death or life imprisonment may, after having been advised by counsel and with the approval of the court and the United States attorney for each district, consent to be proceeded against as a juvenile delinquent in the district in which the juvenile is arrested, held, or present. The consent shall be given in writing before the court but only after the court has apprised the juvenile of the juvenile's rights, including the right to be returned to the district in which the juvenile is alleged to have committed the act, and of the consequences of such consent.

(As amended Feb. 28, 1966, eff. July 1, 1966; Apr. 22, 1974, eff. Dec. 1, 1975; July 31, 1975, eff. Dec. 1, 1975; Apr. 28, 1982, eff. Aug. 1, 1982; Mar. 9, 1987, eff. Aug. 1, 1987.)

Rule 21. Transfer From the District for Trial.

(a) FOR PREJUDICE IN THE DISTRICT.

The court upon motion of the defendant shall transfer the proceeding as to that defendant to another district whether or not such district is specified in the defendant's motion if the court is satisfied that there exists in the district where the prosecution is pending so great a prejudice against the defendant that the defendant cannot obtain a fair and impartial trial at any place fixed by law for holding court in that district.

(b) TRANSFER IN OTHER CASES. For the convenience of parties and witnesses, and in the interest of justice, the court upon motion of the defendant may transfer the proceeding as to that defendant or any one or more of the counts thereof to another district.

(c) PROCEEDINGS ON TRANSFER. When a transfer is ordered the clerk shall transmit to the clerk of the court to which the proceeding is transferred all papers in the proceeding or duplicates thereof and any bail taken, and the prosecution shall continue in that district.
(As amended Feb. 28, 1966, eff. July 1, 1966; Mar. 9, 1987, eff. Aug. 1, 1987.)

Rule 22. Time of Motion To Transfer. A motion to transfer under these rules may be made at or before arraignment or at such other time as the court or these rules may prescribe.

5. A request for admission can be deemed admitted if not answered within 30 days after service.
   a. True
   b. False

D. Exercise 11.4: Civil Practice Law and Rules of New York

1. If Charles Smith and Monte Ronco were involved in a serious car crash in 1969, a defense of contributory negligence, if proven, may bar all recovery.
   a. True
   b. False
2. If that same accident occurred on August 31, 1975, there would be no bar to recovery.
   a. True
   b. False
3. A case arises in which a person suffers $1 million in physical and mental damages. What amount would be awarded to the party?
   a. $ 1 million minus interest
   b. $ 1 million minus damages attributable to claimant's behavior
   c. $ 1 million minus funeral expenses
   d. $ 1 million minus the burden of proof
4. Who has the burden of proving the reduction of damages?
   a. The victim
   b. The judge
   c. The defendant by affirmative defense
   d. The party who assumes the risk
5. By inference, what two defenses are discussed in §§ 1411 and 1412?
   a. Consent and duress
   b. Coercion and laches
   c. Assumption and risk
   d. Assumption of risk and contributory negligence

E. Exercise 11.5: Civil Practice Law and Rules of New York

1. What is the proper time for filing a set of written interrogatories?
   a. Before the injury ever takes place
   b. After commencement of any action
   c. Only after the opposition agrees
   d. By permission of the court
2. To properly *serve* those interrogatories, the rules require that
   a. any party may serve.
   b. only a deputy sheriff may serve.
   c. attorneys must serve each other.
   d. a private investigator must be hired.
3. Section 3130 does not allow a party to serve written interrogatories and demand a bill of particulars at the same time.
   a. True
   b. False

EXERCISE 11.3

Rule 35. Physical and Mental Examination of Persons

(a) Order for Examination. When the mental or physical condition (including the blood group) of a party or of a person in the custody or under the legal control of a party, is in controversy, the court in which the action is pending may order the party to submit to a physical or mental examination by a suitably licensed or certified examiner or to produce for examination the person in the party's custody or legal control. The order may be made only on motion for good cause shown and upon notice to the person to be examined and to all parties and shall specify the time, place, manner, conditions, and scope of the examination and the person or persons by whom it is to be made.

(b) Report of Examiner.

(1) If requested by the party against whom an order is made under Rule 35(a) or the person examined, the party causing the examination to be made shall deliver to the requesting party a copy of the detailed written report of the examiner setting out the examiner's findings, including results of all tests made, diagnoses and conclusions, together with like reports of all earlier examinations of the same condition. After delivery the party causing the examination shall be entitled upon request to receive from the party against whom the order is made a like report of any examination, previously or thereafter made, of the same condition, unless, in the case of a report of examination of a person not a party, the party shows that the party is unable to obtain it. The court on motion may make an order against a party requiring delivery of a report on such terms as are just, and if an examiner fails or refuses to make a report the court may exclude the examiner's testimony if offered at trial.

(2) By requesting and obtaining a report of the examination so ordered or by taking the deposition of the examiner, the party examined waives any privilege the party may have in that action or any other involving the same controversy, regarding the testimony of every other person who has examined or may thereafter examine the party in respect of the same mental or physical condition.

(3) This subdivision applies to examinations made by agreement of the parties, unless the agreement expressly provides otherwise. This subdivision does not preclude discovery of a report of an examiner or the taking of a deposition of the examiner in accordance with the provisions of any other rule.

Rule 36. Request for Admission

(a) Request for Admission. A party may serve upon any other party a written request for the admission, for purposes of the pending action only, of the truth of any matters within the scope of Rule 26(b)(1) set forth in the request that relate to statements or opinions of fact or of the application of law to fact, including the genuineness of any documents described in the request. Copies of documents shall be served with the request unless they have been or are otherwise furnished or made available for inspection and copying. Without leave of court or written stipulation, requests for admission may not be served before the time specified in Rule 26(d) .

Each matter of which an admission is requested shall be separately set forth. The matter is admitted unless, within 30 days after service of the request, or within such shorter or longer time as the court may allow or as the parties may agree to in writing, subject to Rule 29, the party to whom the request is directed serves upon the party requesting the admission a written answer or objection addressed to the matter, signed by the party or by the party's attorney. If objection is made, the reasons therefor shall be stated. The answer shall specifically deny the matter or set forth in detail the reasons why the answering party cannot truthfully admit or deny the matter. A denial shall fairly meet the substance of the requested admission, and when good faith requires that a party qualify an answer or deny only a part of the matter of which an admission is requested, the party shall specify so much of it as is true and qualify or deny the remainder. An answering party may not give lack of information or knowledge as a reason for failure to admit or deny unless the party states that the party has made reasonable inquiry and that the information known or readily obtainable by the party is insufficient to enable the party to admit or deny. A party who considers that a matter of which an admission has been requested presents a genuine issue for trial may not, on that ground alone, object to the request; the party may, subject to the provisions of Rule 37(c), deny the matter or set forth reasons why the party cannot admit or deny it.

The party who has requested the admissions may move to determine the sufficiency of the answers or objections. Unless the court determines that an objection is justified, it shall order that an answer be served. If the court determines that an answer does not comply with the requirements of this rule, it may order either that the matter is admitted or that an amended answer be served. The court may, in lieu of these orders, determine that final disposition of the request be made at a pre-trial conference or at a designated time prior to trial. The provisions of Rule 37(a)(4) apply to the award of expenses incurred in relation to the motion.

(b) Effect of Admission. Any matter admitted under this rule is conclusively established unless the court on motion permits withdrawal or amendment of the admission.

ARTICLE 14-A—DAMAGE ACTIONS: EFFECT OF CONTRIBUTORY NEGLIGENCE AND ASSUMPTION OF RISK

EXERCISE 11.4

§ 1411. Damages recoverable when contributory negligence or assumption of risk is established.
In any action to recover damages for personal injury, injury to property, or wrongful death, the culpable conduct attributable to the claimant or to the decedent, including contributory negligence or assumption of risk, shall not bar recovery, but the amount of damages otherwise recoverable shall be diminished in the proportion which the culpable conduct attributable to the claimant or decedent bears to the culpable conduct which caused the damages.

§ 1412. Burden of pleading; burden of proof.
Culpable conduct claimed in diminution of damages, in accordance with section fourteen hundred eleven, shall be an affirmative defense to be pleaded and proved by the party asserting the defense.

§ 1413. Applicability.
This article shall apply to all causes of action accruing on or after September first, nineteen hundred seventy-five.

4. Interrogatories should, by the information given in § 3131, be very narrow questions on matters not related to documents and photographs.
   a. True
   b. False
5. Which rule relates to discovery and disclosure?
   a. 3107
   b. 3041
   c. 3101
   d. 3132

F. Exercise 11.6: Title 2C, New Jersey Code of Criminal Justice

1. A person who smokes in any public place can be found guilty as a petty disorderly person.
   a. True
   b. False
2. Section 2C:33-13 grants municipalities the right to limit smoking in certain public places.
   a. True
   b. False

EXERCISE 11.5

§ 3130. Use of interrogatories.

1. Except as otherwise provided herein, after commencement of an action, any party may serve upon any other party written interrogatories. Except in a matrimonial action, a party may not serve written interrogatories on another party and also demand a bill of particulars of the same party pursuant to section 3041. In the case of an action to recover damages for personal injury, injury to property or wrongful death predicated solely on a cause or causes of action for negligence, a party shall not be permitted to serve interrogatories on and conduct a deposition of the same party pursuant to rule 3107 without leave of court.

2. After the commencement of a matrimonial action or proceeding, upon motion brought by either party, upon such notice to the other party and to the non-party from whom financial disclosure is sought, and given in such manner as the court shall direct, the court may order a non-party to respond under oath to written interrogatories limited to furnishing financial information concerning a party, and further provided such information is both reasonable and necessary in the prosecution or the defense of such matrimonial action or proceeding.

§ 3131. Scope of interrogatories.

Interrogatories may relate to any matters embraced in the disclosure requirement of section 3101 and the answers may be used to the same extent as the depositions of a party. Interrogatories may require copies of such papers, documents or photographs as are relevant to the answers required, unless opportunity for this examination and copying be afforded.

Rule 3132. Service of interrogatories.

After commencement of an action, any party may serve written interrogatories upon any other party. Interrogatories may not be served upon a defendant before that defendant's time for serving a responsive pleading has expired, except by leave of court granted with or without notice. A copy of the interrogatories and of any order made under this rule shall be served on each party.

Rule 3133. Service of answers or objections to interrogatories.

(a) Service of an answer or objection.
Within twenty days after service of interrogatories, the party upon whom they are served shall serve upon each of the parties a copy of the answer to each interrogatory, except one to which the party objects, in which event the reasons for the objection shall be stated with reasonable particularity.

(b) Form of answers and objections to interrogatories. Interrogatories shall be answered in writing under oath by the party served, if an individual, or, if the party served is a corporation, a partnership or a sole proprietorship, by an officer, director, member, agent or employee having the information. Each question shall be answered separately and fully, and each answer shall be preceded by the question to which it responds.

(c) Amended answers.
Except with respect to amendment or supplementation of responses pursuant to subdivision (h) of section 3101, answers to interrogatories may be amended or supplemented only by order of the court upon motion.

§ 3140. Disclosure of appraisals in proceedings for condemnation, appropriation or review of tax assessments.

Notwithstanding the provisions of subdivisions (c) and (d) of section 3101, the chief administrator of the courts shall adopt rules governing the exchange of appraisal reports intended for use at the trial in proceedings for condemnation, appropriation or review of tax assessments.

3. What remedy is available to the court if it finds the owner of a building guilty of maintaining a nuisance?
   a. It may force the owner to smoke in a public place.
   b. It may close his or her facility for a lifetime.
   c. It may burn the facility down.
   d. None of the above is available.

4. The difference between abating and maintaining a nuisance is best characterized as:
   a. In the case of abatement, the state has to decide what to do with property found within the nuisance.
   b. In the case of abatement, the state has to decide whether a defendant convicted of maintaining nuisance can have a will.
   c. Both a. and b
   d. Neither a nor b
5. Which of the following sections was most recently enacted?
   a. 2C:33-12-18
   b. RS 40:48-1
   c. 2C:43-3
   d. 2C:33-12 and-12.1

G. Exercise 11.7: Title 2C, New Jersey Code of Criminal Justice

1. The term *something of value* relates only to money.
   a. True
   b. False
2. The definition of *gambling* does not include playing pool.
   a. True
   b. False
3. A gambling resort must be on a tropical island.
   a. True
   b. False
4. The definitions of gambling and related activities will probably continue to expand due to the creative interpretations of these provisions.
   a. True
   b. False
5. What constitutes a lottery?
   a. An element of chance to win something of value
   b. A slot machine
   c. Something of value paid by players
   d. Both a and c

H. Exercise 11.8: Title 2C, New Jersey Code of Criminal Justice

1. A violation of 2C:39-5 is less serious than a violation of 2C:39-4.
   a. True
   b. False
2. Which of the following would be a good, solid defense to 2C:39-5?
   a. Machine guns are fun to have, so an owner has a right to carry it around.
   b. The suspect has a license to possess that particular weapon.
   c. The suspect met the requirements of 2C:58-3.
   d. Both b and c
3. Can a person be convicted of both 2C:39-4 and 2C:39-5 if she possesses a firearm?
   a. Yes
   b. No

EXERCISE 11.6

2C:33-7. Obstructing highways and other public passages

a. A person, who, having no legal privilege to do so, purposely or recklessly obstructs any highway or other public passage whether alone or with others, commits a petty disorderly persons offense. "Obstructs" means renders impassable without unreasonable inconvenience or hazard. No person shall be deemed guilty of recklessly obstructing in violation of this subsection solely because of a gathering of persons to hear him speak or otherwise communicate, or solely because of being a member of such a gathering.

b. A person in a gathering commits a petty disorderly persons offense if he refuses to obey a reasonable official request or order to move:

(1) To prevent obstruction of a highway or other public passage; or

(2) To maintain public safety by dispersing those gathered in dangerous proximity to a fire or other hazard.

An order to move, addressed to a person whose speech or other lawful behavior attracts an obstructing audience, shall not be deemed reasonable if the obstruction can be readily remedied by police control of the size or location of the gathering.

L.1978, c. 95, s. 2C:33-7, eff. Sept. 1, 1979.

2C:33-8. Disrupting meetings and processions

A person commits a disorderly persons offense if, with purpose to prevent or disrupt a lawful meeting, procession or gathering, he does an act tending to obstruct or interfere with it physically.

L.1978, c. 95, s. 2C:33-8, eff. Sept. 1, 1979.

2C:33-9. Desecration of venerated objects

A person commits a disorderly persons offense if he purposely desecrates any public monument, insignia, symbol, or structure, or place of worship or burial. "Desecrate" means defacing, damaging or polluting.

L.1978, c. 95, s. 2C:33-9, eff. Sept. 1, 1979.

2C:33-10. Causing fear of unlawful bodily violence, crime of third degree; act of graffiti, additional penalty

1. A person is guilty of a crime of the third degree if he purposely, knowingly or recklessly puts or attempts to put another in fear of bodily violence by placing on private property of another a symbol, an object, a characterization, an appellation or graffiti that exposes another to threats of violence. A person shall not be guilty of an attempt unless his actions cause a serious and imminent likelihood of causing fear of unlawful bodily violence.

A person convicted of an offense under this section that involves an act of graffiti may, in addition to any other penalty imposed by the court, be required either to pay to the owner of the damaged property monetary restitution in the amount of the pecuniary damage caused by the act of graffiti or to perform community service, which shall include removing the graffiti from the property, if appropriate. If community service is ordered, it shall be for either not less than 20 days nor less than the number of days necessary to remove the graffiti from the property.

L.1981,c.282,s.1; amended 1995,c.211,s.4; 1995,c.251,s.2

2C:33-11. Defacement of private property, crime of fourth degree; act of graffiti, additional penalty

2. A person is guilty of a crime of the fourth degree if he purposely defaces or damages, without authorization of the owner or tenant, any private premises or property primarily used for religious, educational, residential, memorial, charitable, or cemetery purposes, or for assembly by persons for purpose of exercising any right guaranteed by law or by the Constitution of this State or of the United States by placing thereon a symbol, an object, a characterization, an appellation, or graffiti that exposes another to threat of violence.

A person convicted of an offense under this section that involves an act of graffiti may, in addition to any other penalty imposed by the court, be required either to pay to the owner of the damaged property monetary restitution in the amount of pecuniary damage caused by the act of graffiti or to perform community service, which shall include removing the graffiti from the property, if appropriate. If community service is ordered, it shall be for either not less than 20 days or not less than the number of days necessary to remove the graffiti from the property.

L.1981,c.282,s.2; amended 1995,c.211,s.5; 1995,c.251,s.3.

2C:33-12. Maintaining a nuisance

A person is guilty of maintaining a nuisance when:

a. By conduct either unlawful in itself or unreasonable under all the circumstances, he knowingly or recklessly creates or maintains a condition which endangers the safety or health of a considerable number of persons;

b. He knowingly conducts or maintains any premises, place or resort where persons gather for purposes of engaging in unlawful conduct; or

c. He knowingly conducts or maintains any premises, place or resort as a house of prostitution or as a place where obscene material, as defined in N.J.S. 2C:34-2 and N.J.S. 2C:34-3, is sold, photographed, manufactured, exhibited or otherwise prepared or shown, in violation of N.J.S. 2C:34-2, N.J.S. 2C:34-3, and N.J.S. 2C:34-4.

A person is guilty of a disorderly persons offense if the person is convicted under subsection a. or b. of this section. A person is guilty of a crime of the fourth degree if the person is convicted under subsection c. of this section.

Upon conviction under this section, in addition to the sentence authorized by this code, the court may proceed as set forth in section 2C:33-12.1.

L.1978, c. 95, s. 2C:33-12, eff. Sept. 1, 1979. Amended by L.1979, c. 178, s. 64, eff. Sept. 1, 1979; L.1982, c. 233, s. 1, eff. Jan. 7, 1983; L.1983, c. 234, s. 1, eff. June 30, 1983.

2C:33-12.1. Abating nuisance

a. In addition to the penalty imposed in case of conviction under N.J.S.2C:33-12 or under section 2 of P.L.1995, c.167 (C.2C:33-12.2), the court may order the immediate abatement of the nuisance, and for that purpose may order the seizure and forfeiture or destruction of any chattels, liquors, obscene material or other personal property which may be found in such building or place, and which the court is satisfied from the evidence were possessed or used with a purpose of maintaining the nuisance. Any such forfeiture shall be in the name and to the use of the State of New Jersey, and the court shall direct the forfeited property to be sold at public sale, the proceeds to be paid to the treasurer of the county wherein conviction was had.

b. If the owner of any building or place is found guilty of maintaining a nuisance, the court may order that the building or place where the nuisance was maintained be closed and not used for a period not exceeding one year from the date of the conviction.

EXERCISE 11.6 *continued*

Amended 1982,c.233,s.2; 1983,c.234,s.2; 1995,c.167,s.1.

2C:33-12.2. Sexually oriented business, nuisance; crime
2.a. As used in this act:

(1) "Sexually oriented business" means:

(a) A commercial establishment which as one of its principal business purposes offers for sale, rental, or display any of the following:
Books, magazines, periodicals or other printed material, or photographs, films, motion pictures, video cassettes, slides or other visual representations which depict or describe a "specified sexual activity" or "specified anatomical area"; or still or motion picture machines, projectors or other image-producing devices which show images to one person per machine at any one time, and where the images so displayed are characterized by the depiction of a "specified sexual activity" or "specified anatomical area"; or instruments, devices, or paraphernalia which are designed for use in connection with a "specified sexual activity"; or

(b) A commercial establishment which regularly features live performances characterized by the exposure of a "specified anatomical area" or by a "specified sexual activity," or which regularly shows films, motion pictures, video cassettes, slides, or other photographic representations which depict or describe a "specified sexual activity" or "specified anatomical area";

(2) "Person" means an individual, proprietorship, partnership, corporation, association, or other legal entity.

(3) "Specified anatomical area" means:

(a) Less than completely and opaquely covered human genitals, pubic region, buttock or female breasts below a point immediately above the top of the areola; or

(b) Human male genitals in a discernibly turgid state, even if covered.

(4) "Specified sexual activity" means:

(a) The fondling or other erotic touching of covered or uncovered human genitals, pubic region, buttock or female breast; or

(b) Any actual or simulated act of human masturbation, sexual intercourse or deviate sexual intercourse.

b. In addition to any activities proscribed by the provisions of N.J.S.2C:33-12, a person is guilty of maintaining a nuisance when the person owns or operates a sexually oriented business which offers for public use booths, screens, enclosures or other devices which facilitate sexual activity by patrons.

c. Notwithstanding any other provision of law, a municipality shall have the power to determine restrictions, if any, on the hours of operation of sexually oriented businesses.

d. A person who violates this act is guilty of a crime of the fourth degree.

L.1995,c.167,s.2.

2C:33-13. Smoking in public
Smoking in Public.

a. Any person who smokes or carries lighted tobacco in or upon any bus or other public conveyance, except group charter buses, specially marked railroad smoking cars, limousines or livery services, and, when the driver is the only person in the vehicle, autocabs, is a petty disorderly person.

b. Any person who smokes or carries lighted tobacco in any public place, including but not limited to places of public accommodation, where such smoking is prohibited by municipal ordinance under authority of R.S. 40:48-1 and 40:48-2 or by the owner or person responsible for the operation of the public place, and when adequate notice of such prohibition has been conspicuously posted, is guilty of a petty disorderly persons offense. Notwithstanding the provisions of 2C:43-3, the maximum fine which can be imposed for violation of this section is $200.00.

c. The provisions of this section shall supersede any other statute and any rule or regulation adopted pursuant to law.

L. 1978, c. 95, s. 2C:33-13, eff. Sept. 1, 1979. Amended by L. 1979, c. 178, s. 66A, eff. Sept. 1, 1979; L. 1985, c. 187, s. 1.

4. Which of the following does not fall into the exemption category under these provisions?
   a. Jail warden
   b. State police
   c. National Guard officers on duty
   d. Drug dealer in fear of his life
5. Under what section could a New Jersey tax agent find a defense to a violation of 2C:39-5?
   a. 2C:39-6(8)
   b. 2C:39-6C(1)
   c. 2C:39-6C(4)
   d. 2C:39-6a(6)

I. Exercise 11.9: Title 2C, New Jersey Code of Criminal Justice

1. Under which chapter is suspension of sentence?
   a. 158
   b. 2C
   c. 45
   d. 1983

EXERCISE 11.7

2C:37-1. Definitions

The following definitions apply to this chapter and to chapter 64:

a. "Contest of chance" means any contest, game, pool, gaming scheme or gaming device in which the outcome depends in a material degree upon an element of chance, notwithstanding that skill of the contestants or some other persons may also be a factor therein.

b. "Gambling" means staking or risking something of value upon the outcome of a contest of chance or a future contingent event not under the actor's control or influence, upon an agreement or understanding that he will receive something of value in the event of a certain outcome.

c. "Player" means a person who engages in any form of gambling solely as a contestant or bettor, without receiving or becoming entitled to receive any profit therefrom other than personal gambling winnings, and without otherwise rendering any material assistance to the establishment, conduct or operation of the particular gambling activity. A person who gambles at a social game of chance on equal terms with the other participants therein does not thereby render material assistance to the establishment, conduct or operation of such game if he performs, without fee or remuneration, acts directed toward the arrangement or facilitation of the game, such as inviting persons to play, permitting the use of premises therefor or supplying cards or other equipment used therein. A person who engages in "bookmaking" as defined in this section is not a "player."

d. "Something of value" means any money or property, any token, object or article exchangeable for money or property, or any form of credit or promise directly or indirectly contemplating transfer of money or property or of any interest therein, or involving extension of a service, entertainment or a privilege of playing at a game or scheme without charge. This definition, however, does not include any form of promise involving extension of a privilege of playing at a game without charge on a mechanical or electronic amusement device, other than a slot machine as an award for the attainment of a certain score on that device.

e. "Gambling device" means any device, machine, paraphernalia or equipment which is used or usable in the playing phases of any gambling activity, whether such activity consists of gambling between persons or gambling by a person involving the playing of a machine. Notwithstanding the foregoing, lottery tickets, policy slips and other items used in the playing phases of lottery and policy schemes are not gambling devices.

f. "Slot machine" means any mechanical, electrical or other device, contrivance or machine which, upon insertion of a coin, token or similar object therein, or upon payment of any consideration whatsoever, is available to play or operate, the play or operation of which, whether by reason of the skill of the operator or application of the element of chance, or both, may deliver or entitle the person playing or operating the machine to receive cash or tokens to be exchanged for cash, whether the payoff is made automatically from the machine or in any other manner whatsoever. A device so constructed, or readily adaptable or convertible to such use, is no less a slot machine because it is not in working order or because some mechanical act of manipulation or repair is required to accomplish its adaptation, conversion or workability.

g. "Bookmaking" means advancing gambling activity by unlawfully accepting bets from members of the public upon the outcome of future contingent events as a business.

h. "Lottery" means an unlawful gambling scheme in which (a) the players pay or agree to pay something of value for chances, represented and differentiated by numbers or by combinations of numbers or by some other media, one or more of which chances are to be designated the winning ones; and (b) the winning chances are to be determined by a drawing or by some other method based upon the element of chance; and (c) the holders of the winning chances are to receive something of value.

i. "Policy" or "the numbers game" means a form of lottery in which the winning chances or plays are not determined upon the basis of a drawing or other act on the part of persons conducting or connected with the scheme, but upon the basis of the outcome or outcomes of a future contingent event or events otherwise unrelated to the particular scheme.

j. "Gambling resort" means a place to which persons may resort for engaging in gambling activity.

k. "Unlawful" means not specifically authorized by law.

L.1978, c. 95, s. 2C:37-1, eff. Sept. 1, 1979. Amended by L.1979, c. 176, s. 4, eff. Sept. 1, 1979; L.1982, c. 60, s. 1, eff. July 8, 1982.

2. How many days can a defendant who has been placed on probation serve in prison concurrently?
   a. 45 days
   b. No more than a year
   c. No more than 364 days
   d. 10 days

EXERCISE 11.8

2C:39-4. Possession of weapons for unlawful purposes

a. Firearms. Any person who has in his possession any firearm with a purpose to use it unlawfully against the person or property of another is guilty of a crime of the second degree.

b. Explosives. Any person who has in his possession or carries any explosive substance with a purpose to use it unlawfully against the person or property of another is guilty of a crime of the second degree.

c. Destructive devices. Any person who has in his possession any destructive device with a purpose to use it unlawfully against the person or property of another is guilty of a crime of the second degree.

d. Other weapons. Any person who has in his possession any weapon, except a firearm, with a purpose to use it unlawfully against the person or property of another is guilty of a crime of the third degree.

e. Imitation firearms. Any person who has in his possession an imitation firearm under circumstances that would lead an observer to reasonably believe that it is possessed for an unlawful purpose is guilty of a crime of the fourth degree.

Amended 1979, c.179, s.3; 1989,c.120,s.2.

2C:39-5. Unlawful possession of weapons

a. Machine guns. Any person who knowingly has in his possession a machine gun or any instrument or device adaptable for use as a machine gun, without being licensed to do so as provided in N.J.S.2C:58-5, is guilty of a crime of the third degree.

b. Handguns. Any person who knowingly has in his possession any handgun, including any antique handgun without first having obtained a permit to carry the same as provided in N.J.S.2C:58-4, is guilty of a crime of the third degree.

c. Rifles and shotguns.

(1) Any person who knowingly has in his possession any rifle or shotgun without having first obtained a firearms purchaser identification card in accordance with the provisions of N.J.S.2C:58-3, is guilty of a crime of the third degree.

(2) Unless otherwise permitted by law, any person who knowingly has in his possession any loaded rifle or shotgun is guilty of a crime of the third degree.

d. Other weapons. Any person who knowingly has in his possession any other weapon under circumstances not manifestly appropriate for such lawful uses as it may have is guilty of a crime of the fourth degree.

e. Firearms or other weapons in educational institutions.

(1) Any person who knowingly has in his possession any firearm in or upon any part of the buildings or grounds of any school, college, university or other educational institution, without the written authorization of the governing officer of the institution, is guilty of a crime of the third degree, irrespective of whether he possesses a valid permit to carry the firearm or a valid firearms purchaser identification card.

(2) Any person who knowingly possesses any weapon enumerated in paragraphs (3) and (4) of subsection r. of N.J.S.2C:39-1 or any components which can readily be assembled into a firearm or other weapon enumerated in subsection r. of N.J.S.2C:39-1 or any other weapon under circumstances not manifestly appropriate for such lawful use as it may have, while in or upon any part of the buildings or grounds of any school, college, university or other educational institution without the written authorization of the governing officer of the institution is guilty of a crime of the fourth degree.

(3) Any person who knowingly has in his possession any imitation firearm in or upon any part of the buildings or grounds of any school, college, university or other educational institution, without the written authorization of the governing officer of the institution, or while on any school bus is a disorderly person, irrespective of whether he possesses a valid permit to carry a firearm or a valid firearms purchaser identification card.

f. Assault firearms. Any person who knowingly has in his possession an assault firearm is guilty of a crime of the third degree except if the assault firearm is licensed pursuant to N.J.S.2C:58-5; registered pursuant to section 11 of P.L.1990, c.32 (C.2C:58-12) or rendered inoperable pursuant to section 12 of P.L.1990, c.32 (C.2C:58-13).

g. (1) The temporary possession of a handgun, rifle or shotgun by a person receiving, possessing, carrying or using the handgun, rifle, or shotgun under the provisions of section 1 of P.L.1992, c.74 (C.2C:58-3.1) shall not be considered unlawful possession under the provisions of subsection b. or c. of this section.

(2) The temporary possession of a firearm by a person receiving, possessing, carrying or using the firearm under the provisions of section 1 of P.L.1997, c.375 (C.2C:58-3.2) shall not be considered unlawful possession under the provisions of this section.

Amended 1979, c.179, s.4; 1990, c.32, s.2; 1992, c.74, s.2; 1992, c.94, s.1; 1995, c.389; 1997, c.375, s.2.

2C:39-6. Exemptions

2C:39-6. a. Provided a person complies with the requirements of subsection j. of this section, N.J.S.2C:39-5 does not apply to:

(1) Members of the Armed Forces of the United States or of the National Guard while actually on duty, or while traveling between places of duty and carrying authorized weapons in the manner prescribed by the appropriate military authorities;

(2) Federal law enforcement officers, and any other federal officers and employees required to carry firearms in the performance of their official duties;

(3) Members of the State Police and, under conditions prescribed by the superintendent, members of the Marine Law Enforcement Bureau of the Division of State Police;

(4) A sheriff, undersheriff, sheriff's officer, county prosecutor, assistant prosecutor, prosecutor's detective or investigator, deputy attorney general or State investigator employed by the Division of Criminal Justice of the Department of Law and Public Safety, investigator employed by the State Commission of Investigation, inspector of the Alcoholic Beverage Control Enforcement Bureau of the Division of State Police in the Department of Law and Public Safety authorized to carry such weapons by the Superintendent of State Police, State park ranger, or State conservation officer;

(5) A prison or jail warden of any penal institution in this State or his deputies, or an employee of the Department of Corrections engaged in the interstate transportation of convicted offenders, while in the performance of his duties, and when required to possess the weapon by his superior officer, or a cor-

continued

rection officer or keeper of a penal institution in this State at all times while in the State of New Jersey, provided he annually passes an examination approved by the superintendent testing his proficiency in the handling of firearms;

(6) A civilian employee of the United States Government under the supervision of the commanding officer of any post, camp, station, base or other military or naval installation located in this State who is required, in the performance of his official duties, to carry firearms, and who is authorized to carry such firearms by said commanding officer, while in the actual performance of his official duties;

(7)(a) A regularly employed member, including a detective, of the police department of any county or municipality, or of any State, interstate, municipal or county park police force or boulevard police force, at all times while in the State of New Jersey;

(b) A special law enforcement officer authorized to carry a weapon as provided in subsection b. of section 7 of P.L.1985, c.439 (C.40A:14-146.14);

(c) An airport security officer or a special law enforcement officer appointed by the governing body of any county or municipality, except as provided in subsection (b) of this section, or by the commission, board or other body having control of a county park or airport or boulevard police force, while engaged in the actual performance of his official duties and when specifically authorized by the governing body to carry weapons;

(8) A full-time, paid member of a paid or part-paid fire department or force of any municipality who is assigned full-time or part-time to an arson investigation unit created pursuant to section 1 of P.L.1981, c.409 (C.40A:14-7.1) or to the county arson investigation unit in the county prosecutor's office, while either engaged in the actual performance of arson investigation duties or while actually on call to perform arson investigation duties and when specifically authorized by the governing body or the county prosecutor, as the case may be, to carry weapons. Prior to being permitted to carry a firearm, such a member shall take and successfully complete a firearms training course administered by the Police Training Commission pursuant to P.L.1961, c.56 (C.52:17B-66 et seq.), and shall annually qualify in the use of a revolver or similar weapon prior to being permitted to carry a firearm;

(9) A juvenile corrections officer in the employment of the Juvenile Justice Commission established pursuant to section 2 of P.L.1995, c.284 (C.52:17B-170) subject to the regulations promulgated by the commission.

b. Subsections a., b. and c. of N.J.S.2C:39-5 do not apply to:

(1) A law enforcement officer employed by a governmental agency outside of the State of New Jersey while actually engaged in his official duties, provided, however, that he has first notified the superintendent or the chief law enforcement officer of the municipality or the prosecutor of the county in which he is engaged; or

(2) A licensed dealer in firearms and his registered employees during the course of their normal business while traveling to and from their place of business and other places for the purpose of demonstration, exhibition or delivery in connection with a sale, provided, however, that the weapon is carried in the manner specified in subsection g. of this section.

c. Provided a person complies with the requirements of subsection j. of this section, subsections b. and c. of N.J.S.2C:39-5 do not apply to:

(1) A special agent of the Division of Taxation who has passed an examination in an approved police training program testing proficiency in the handling of any firearm which he may be required to carry, while in the actual performance of his official duties and while going to or from his place of duty, or any other police officer, while in the actual performance of his official duties;

(2) A State deputy conservation officer or a full-time employee of the Division of Parks and Forestry having the power of arrest and authorized to carry weapons, while in the actual performance of his official duties;

(3) (Deleted by amendment, P.L.1986, c.150.)

(4) A court attendant serving as such under appointment by the sheriff of the county or by the judge of any municipal court or other court of this State, while in the actual performance of his official duties;

(5) A guard in the employ of any railway express company, banking or building and loan or savings and loan institution of this State, while in the actual performance of his official duties;

(6) A member of a legally recognized military organization while actually under orders or while going to or from the prescribed place of meeting and carrying the weapons prescribed for drill, exercise or parade;

(7) An officer of the Society for the Prevention of Cruelty to Animals, while in the actual performance of his duties;

(8) An employee of a public utilities corporation actually engaged in the transportation of explosives;

(9) A railway policeman, except a transit police officer of the New Jersey Transit Police Department, at all times while in the State of New Jersey, provided that he has passed an approved police academy training program consisting of at least 280 hours. The training program shall include, but need not be limited to, the handling of firearms, community relations, and juvenile relations;

(10) A campus police officer appointed under P.L.1970, c.211 (C.18A:6-4.2 et seq.) at all times. Prior to being permitted to carry a firearm, a campus police officer shall take and successfully complete a firearms training course administered by the Police Training Commission, pursuant to P.L.1961, c.56 (C.52:17B-66 et seq.), and shall annually qualify in the use of a revolver or similar weapon prior to being permitted to carry a firearm;

(11) A person who has not been convicted of a crime under the laws of this State or under the laws of another state or the United States, and who is employed as a full-time security guard for a nuclear power plant under the license of the Nuclear Regulatory Commission, while in the actual performance of his official duties;

(12) A transit police officer of the New Jersey Transit Police Department, at all times while in the State of New Jersey, provided the officer has satisfied the training requirements of the Police Training Commission, pursuant to subsection c. of section 2 of P.L.1989, c.291 (C.27:25-15.1);

(13) A parole officer employed by the State Parole Board at all times. Prior to being permitted to carry a firearm, a parole officer shall take and successfully complete a basic course for regular police officer training administered by the Police Training Commission, pursuant to P.L.1961, c.56 (C.52:17B-66 et seq.), and shall annually qualify in the use of a revolver or similar weapon prior to being permitted to carry a firearm;

(14) A Human Services police officer at all times while in the State of New Jersey, as authorized by the Commissioner of Human Services;

(15) A person or employee of any person who, pursuant to and as required by a contract with a governmental entity, supervises or transports persons charged with or convicted of an offense;

(16) A housing authority police officer appointed under P.L.1997, c.210 (C.40A:14-146.19 et al.) at all times while in the State of New Jersey; or

(17) A probation officer assigned to the "Probation Officer Community Safety Unit" created by section 2 of P.L.2001, c.362 (C.2B:10A-2) while in the actual performance of the probation officer's official duties. Prior to being permitted to carry a firearm, a probation officer shall take and successfully complete a basic course for regular police officer training administered by the Police Training Commission, pursuant to P.L.1961, c.56 (C.52:17B-66 et seq.), and shall annually qualify in the use of a revolver or similar weapon prior to being permitted to carry a firearm.

d. (1) Subsections c. and d. of N.J.S.2C:39-5 do not apply to antique firearms, provided that such antique firearms are unloaded or are being fired for the purposes of exhibition or demonstration at an authorized target range or in such other manner as has been approved in writing by the chief law enforcement officer of the municipality in which the exhibition or demonstration is held, or if not held on property under the control of a particular municipality, the superintendent.

(2) Subsection a. of N.J.S.2C:39-3 and subsection d. of N.J.S.2C:39-5 do not apply to an antique cannon that is capable of being fired but that is unloaded and immobile, provided that the antique cannon is possessed by (a) a scholastic institution, a museum, a municipality, a county or the State, or (b) a person who obtained a firearms purchaser identification card as specified in N.J.S.2C:58-3.

(3) Subsection a. of N.J.S.2C:39-3 and subsection d. of N.J.S.2C:39-5 do not apply to an unloaded antique cannon that is being transported by one eligible to possess it, in compliance with regulations the superintendent may promulgate, between its permanent location and place of purchase or repair.

(4) Subsection a. of N.J.S.2C:39-3 and subsection d. of N.J.S.2C:39-5 do not apply to antique cannons that are being loaded or fired by one eligible to possess an antique cannon, for purposes of exhibition or demonstration at an authorized target range or in the manner as has been approved in writing by the chief law enforcement officer of the municipality in which the exhibition or demonstration is held, or if not held on property under the control of a particular municipality, the superintendent, provided that performer has given at least 30 days' notice to the superintendent.

(5) Subsection a. of N.J.S.2C:39-3 and subsection d. of N.J.S.2C:39-5 do not apply to the transportation of unloaded antique cannons directly to or from exhibitions or demonstrations authorized under paragraph (4) of subsection d. of this section, provided that the transportation is in compliance with safety regulations the superintendent may promulgate. Nor do those subsections apply to transportation directly to or from exhibitions or demonstrations authorized under the law of another jurisdiction, provided that the superintendent has been given 30 days' notice and that the transportation is in compliance with safety regulations the superintendent may promulgate.

e. Nothing in subsections b., c. and d. of N.J.S.2C:39-5 shall be construed to prevent a person keeping or carrying about his place of business, residence, premises or other land owned or possessed by him, any firearm, or from carrying the same, in the manner specified in subsection g. of this section, from any place of purchase to his residence or place of business, between his dwelling and his place of business, between one place of business or residence and another when moving, or between his dwelling or place of business and place where such firearms are repaired, for the purpose of repair. For the purposes of this section, a place of business shall be deemed to be a fixed location.

f. Nothing in subsections b., c. and d. of N.J.S.2C:39-5 shall be construed to prevent:

(1) A member of any rifle or pistol club organized in accordance with the rules prescribed by the National Board for the Promotion of Rifle Practice, in going to or from a place of target practice, carrying such firearms as are necessary for said target practice, provided that the club has filed a copy of its charter with the superintendent and annually submits a list of its members to the superintendent and provided further that the firearms are carried in the manner specified in subsection g. of this section;

(2) A person carrying a firearm or knife in the woods or fields or upon the waters of this State for the purpose of hunting, target practice or fishing, provided that the firearm or knife is legal and appropriate for hunting or fishing purposes in this State and he has in his possession a valid hunting license, or, with respect to fresh water fishing, a valid fishing license;

(3) A person transporting any firearm or knife while traveling:

(a) Directly to or from any place for the purpose of hunting or fishing, provided the person has in his possession a valid hunting or fishing license; or

(b) Directly to or from any target range, or other authorized place for the purpose of practice, match, target, trap or skeet shooting exhibitions, provided in all cases that during the course of the travel all firearms are carried in the manner specified in subsection g. of this section and the person has complied with all the provisions and requirements of Title 23 of the Revised Statutes and any amendments thereto and all rules and regulations promulgated thereunder; or

(c) In the case of a firearm, directly to or from any exhibition or display of firearms which is sponsored by any law enforcement agency, any rifle or pistol club, or any firearms collectors club, for the purpose of displaying the firearms to the public or to the members of the organization or club, provided, however, that not less than 30 days prior to the exhibition or display, notice of the exhibition or display shall be given to the Superintendent of the State Police by the sponsoring organization or club, and the sponsor has complied with such reasonable safety regulations as the superintendent may promulgate. Any firearms transported pursuant to this section shall be transported in the manner specified in subsection g. of this section;

Amended 1979, c.179, s.5; 1979, c.332, s.8; 1981, c.108, s.1; 1981, c.219, s.1; 1981, c.294, s.1; 1981, c.409, s.2; 1981, c.480, s.1; 1981, c.511, s.4; 1982, c.154, s.1; 1982, c.173, s.1; 1983, c.479, s.3; 1983, c.552; 1985, c.76, s.8; 1985, c.150, s.1; 1985, c.324, s.1 (s.3 eff. date amended 1986, c.64); 1985, c.376, s.1; 1985, c.439, s.13,(s.15 eff. date amended 1986, c.2); 1986, c.150, ss.7,8; 1987, c.139; 1987, c.172; 1989, c.291, s.4; 1991, c.327, s.2; 1991, c.386, s.3; 1992, c.94, s.2; 1993, c.246, s.2; 1995, c.273, s.2; 1995, c.280, s.21; 1997, c.67, s.1; 1997, c.210, s.6; 1997, c.393; 2001, c.79, s.15; 2001, c.362, s.4.

3. If the court wanted to ensure that the probationer would support his or her family, what conditions would serve that purpose?
   a. 2C:45-1(b)(1) and (2)
   b. 2C:45-1(b)(1) and (8)
   c. 2C:45-1(b)(1)(2) and (4)
   d. 2C:45-1(b)(1)(2), (4), (9)
4. Which conditions assist the victim of crime?
   a. None of them
   b. (b)(8)
   c. (b)(9)
   d. (b)(3)
5. Who promulgates probationary conditions?
   a. Judge
   b. Jury
   c. Lawyers
   d. County probation departments

J. Exercise 11.10: General Laws of Rhode Island

1. Section 11-27-2 was previously enacted as Public Law 1935, ch. 2190.
   a. True
   b. False
2. Which case in the annotation stands for the proposition that regulation of the practice of law is not a usurpation of judicial power?
   a. *Lorraine v. Wilson*
   b. *Wilson v. Ambulance Chasers*
   c. *Creditors' Service Corp. v. Cummings*
   d. 151 A.L.R. 796
3. Which of the following action(s) would be characterized as the practice of law?
   a. The drafting of a will
   b. The giving of advice on matter of law
   c. The organization of a corporation
   d. All of the above
4. Soliciting claims for fine losses for a percentage fee can be considered a practice of law.
   a. True
   b. False
5. Which series or text is cross-referenced in this section?
   a. American Law Reports
   b. *Corpus Juris Secundum*
   c. *American Jurisprudence*
   d. *Rhode Island Digest*

K. Exercise 11.11: General Laws of Rhode Island

1. What is the most commonly cross-referenced legal series in this annotation at 11-6-2?
   a. Connecticut Gen. Statutes
   b. Mass. Ann. Laws
   c. American Law Reports

EXERCISE 11.9

2C:44-6 Procedure on sentence; pre-sentence investigation and report.

a. The court shall not impose sentence without first ordering a pre-sentence investigation of the defendant and according due consideration to a written report of such investigation when required by the Rules of Court. The court may order a pre-sentence investigation in any other case.

b. The pre-sentence investigation shall include an analysis of the circumstances attending the commission of the offense, the defendant's history of delinquency or criminality, family situation, financial resources, including whether or not the defendant is an enrollee or covered person under a health insurance contract, policy or plan, debts, including any amount owed for a fine, assessment or restitution ordered in accordance with the provisions of Title 2C, employment history, personal habits, the disposition of any charge made against any codefendants, the defendant's history of civil commitment, any disposition which arose out of charges suspended pursuant to N.J.S.2C:4-6 including the records of the disposition of those charges and any acquittal by reason of insanity pursuant to N.J.S.2C:4-1, and any other matters that the probation officer deems relevant or the court directs to be included. The defendant shall disclose any information concerning any history of civil commitment. The report shall also include a medical history of the defendant and a complete psychological evaluation of the defendant in any case in which the defendant is being sentenced for a first or second degree crime involving violence and:

(1) the defendant has a prior acquittal by reason of insanity pursuant to N.J.S.2C:4-1 or had charges suspended pursuant to N.J.S.2C:4-6; or

(2) the defendant has a prior conviction for murder pursuant to N.J.S.2C:11-3, aggravated sexual assault or sexual assault pursuant to N.J.S.2C:14-2, kidnapping pursuant to N.J.S.2C:13-1, endangering the welfare of a child which would constitute a crime of the second degree pursuant to N.J.S.2C:24-4, or stalking which would constitute a crime of the third degree pursuant to P.L.1992, c.209 (C.2C:12-10); or

(3) the defendant has a prior diagnosis of psychosis.

The court, in its discretion and considering all the appropriate circumstances, may waive the medical history and psychological examination in any case in which a term of imprisonment including a period of parole ineligibility is imposed. In any case involving a conviction of N.J.S.2C:24-4, endangering the welfare of a child; N.J.S.2C:18-3, criminal trespass, where the trespass was committed in a school building or on school property; section 1 of P.L.1993, c.291 (C.2C:13-6), attempting to lure or entice a child with purpose to commit a criminal offense; section 1 of P.L.1992, c.209 (C.2C:12-10), stalking; or N.J.S.2C:13-1, kidnapping, where the victim of the offense is a child under the age of 18, the investigation shall include a report on the defendant's mental condition.

The pre-sentence report shall also include a report on any compensation paid by the Victims of Crime Compensation Board as a result of the commission of the offense and, in any case where the victim chooses to provide one, a statement by the victim of the offense for which the defendant is being sentenced. The statement may include the nature and extent of any physical harm or psychological or emotional harm or trauma suffered by the victim, the extent of any loss to include loss of earnings or ability to work suffered by the victim and the effect of the crime upon the victim's family. The probation department shall notify the victim or nearest relative of a homicide victim of his right to make a statement for inclusion in the pre-sentence report if the victim or relative so desires. Any such statement shall be made within 20 days of notification by the probation department.

The pre-sentence report shall specifically include an assessment of the gravity and seriousness of harm inflicted on the victim, including whether or not the defendant knew or reasonably should have known that the victim of the offense was particularly vulnerable or incapable of resistance due to advanced age, disability, ill-health, or extreme youth, or was for any other reason substantially incapable of exercising normal physical or mental power of resistance.

c. If, after the pre-sentence investigation, the court desires additional information concerning an offender convicted of an offense before imposing sentence, it may order any additional psychological or medical testing of the defendant.

d. Disclosure of any pre-sentence investigation report or psychiatric examination report shall be in accordance with law and the Rules of Court, except that information concerning the defendant's financial resources shall be made available upon request to the Victims of Crime Compensation Board or to any officer authorized under the provisions of section 3 of P.L.1979, c.396 (C.2C:46-4) to collect payment on an assessment, restitution or fine and that information concerning the defendant's coverage under any health insurance contract, policy or plan shall be made available, as appropriate to the Commissioner of the Department of Corrections and to the chief administrative officer of a county jail in accordance with the provisions of P.L.1995, c.254 (C.30:7E-1 et al.).

e. The court shall not impose a sentence of imprisonment for an extended term unless the ground therefor has been established at a hearing after the conviction of the defendant and on written notice to him of the ground proposed. The defendant shall have the right to hear and controvert the evidence against him and to offer evidence upon the issue.

f. (Deleted by amendment, P.L.1986, c.85).

Amended 1981, c.481, s.1; 1983, c.317, s.2; 1986, c.85, s.1; 1991, c.329, s.7; 1994, c.92; 1995, c.254, s.7; 1996, c.39, s.2; 1997, c.216, s.2.

2C:44-7. Appellate review of actions of sentencing court

Any action taken by the court in imposing sentence shall be subject to review by an appellate court. The court shall specifically have the authority to review findings of fact by the sentencing court in support of its findings of aggravating and mitigating circumstances and to modify the defendant's sentence upon his application where such findings are not fairly supported on the record before the trial court.

L.1978, c. 95, s. 2C:44-7, eff. Sept. 1, 1979.

2C:45-1. Conditions of suspension or probation

a. When the court suspends the imposition of sentence on a person who has been convicted of an offense or sentences him to be placed on probation, it shall attach such reasonable conditions, authorized by this section, as it deems necessary to insure that he will lead a law-abiding life or is likely to assist him to do so. These conditions may be set forth in a set of standardized conditions promulgated by the county probation department and approved by the court.

continued

EXERCISE 11.9 *continued*

b. The court, as a condition of its order, may require the defendant:

(1) To support his dependents and meet his family responsibilities;
(2) To find and continue in gainful employment;
(3) To undergo available medical or psychiatric treatment and to enter and remain in a specified institution, when required for that purpose;
(4) To pursue a prescribed secular course of study or vocational training;
(5) To attend or reside in a facility established for the instruction, recreation or residence of persons on probation;
(6) To refrain from frequenting unlawful or disreputable places or consorting with disreputable persons;
(7) Not to have in his possession any firearm or other dangerous weapon unless granted written permission;
(8) (Deleted by amendment, P.L.1991, c.329);
(9) To remain within the jurisdiction of the court and to notify the court or the probation officer of any change in his address or his employment;
(10) To report as directed to the court or the probation officer, to permit the officer to visit his home, and to answer all reasonable inquiries by the probation officer;
(11) To pay a fine;
(12) To satisfy any other conditions reasonably related to the rehabilitation of the defendant and not unduly restrictive of his liberty or incompatible with his freedom of conscience;
(13) To require the performance of community-related service.

c. The court, as a condition of its order, shall require the defendant to pay any assessments required by section 2 of P.L.1979, c.396 (C.2C:43-3.1) and shall, consistent with the applicable provisions of N.J.S.2C:43-3, N.J.S.2C:43-4 and N.J.S.2C:44-2 or section 1 of P.L. 1983, c.411 (C.2C:43-2.1) require the defendant to make restitution.

L.1978, c. 95, s. 2C:45-3, eff. Sept. 1, 1979. Amended by L.1979, c. 178, s. 99, eff. Sept. 1, 1979; L.1979, c. 180, s. 3, eff. Sept. 1, 1979; L.1981, c. 290, s. 41, eff. Sept. 24, 1981.

2. What is the punishment for adultery?
   a. Only a term of imprisonment
   b. Only a fine
   c. Possibility of either a fine or imprisonment
   d. None of the above
3. Defense to bigamy includes which of the following?
   a. Venereal disease
   b. Dissolution of cohabitation
   c. Decree of annulment in first marriage
   d. Privilege
4. Adultery is only possible with two or more persons.
   a. True
   b. False
5. Of these offenses, which is the least severe?
   a. Bigamy
   b. Adultery

L. Exercise 11.12: General Statutes of Connecticut

1. What happened to Section 52-146a?
   a. It was demoted.
   b. It was transferred to Section 52-146d.
   c. It was repealed.
2. Communications between a psychologist and patient are not privileged if
   a. the patient asserts mental distress or damages in a civil case.
   b. the patient asserts the insanity defense in a criminal case.
   c. a judge finds that the confidentiality between the parties is not as important as the interests of justice that require disclosure.
   d. All of the above.

NOTES TO DECISIONS

ANALYSIS

1. Constitutionality.
2. Judicial power.

1. Constitutionality.

This chapter is not violative of due process clause of U.S. Const., amend. 14, § 1, but is valid exercise of police power. Creditors' Serv. Corp. v. Cummings, 57 R.I. 291, 190 A. 2 (1937).

This chapter is not an impairment of the obligation of contracts in violation of R.I. Const., art. 1, § 12, but is a valid exercise of the police power which can affect contracts of individuals. Creditors' Serv. Corp. v. Cummings, 57 R.I. 291, 190 A. 2 (1937).

2. Judicial Power.

The only way to acquire the right to practice law in this state is through the procedure prescribed by the supreme court. Rhode Island Bar Ass'n v. Automobile Serv. Ass'n, 55 R.I. 122, 179 A. 139 (1935).

This chapter is in aid of rather than derogation of the power of the supreme court. Rhode Island Bar Ass'n v. Automobile Serv. Ass'n, 55 R.I. 122, 179 A. 139 (1935).

That an act is not made punishable by this chapter does not prevent the court from finding such act to be unauthorized practice of law and prohibiting such act by its own power. Rhode Island Bar Ass'n v. Automobile Serv. Ass'n, 55 R.I. 122, 179 A. 139 (1935).

11-27-2. "Practice of law" defined. — As used in this chapter, "practice law" means the doing of any act for another person usually done by attorneys at law in the course of their profession, and, without limiting this generality, includes:

(1) The appearance or acting as the attorney, solicitor, or representative of another person before any court, referee, master, auditor, division, department, commission, board, judicial person, or body authorized or constituted by law to determine any question of law or fact or to exercise any judicial power, or the preparation of pleadings or other legal papers incident to any action or other proceeding of any kind before or to be brought before the court or other body;

(2) The giving or tendering to another person for a consideration, direct or indirect, of any advice or counsel pertaining to a law question or a court action or judicial proceeding brought or to be brought;

(3) The undertaking or acting as a representative or on behalf of another person to commence, settle, compromise, adjust, or dispose of any civil or criminal case or cause of action;

(4) The preparation or drafting for another person of a will, codicil, corporation organization, amendment, or qualification papers, or any instrument which requires legal knowledge and capacity and is usually prepared by attorneys at law.

History of Section.

G.L., ch. 401, § 45; P.L. 1935, ch. 2190, § 1; G.L. 1938, ch. 612, § 43; G.L. 1956, § 11-27-2.

NOTES TO DECISIONS

ANALYSIS

1. Constitutionality.
2. Judicial power.
3. Claim adjustment.
4. Effect of unauthorized practice.

1. Constitutionality.

This section, by defining all debt collection activities as the practice of law and limiting those activities to members of the Rhode Island bar, places an unconstitutional burden on interstate commerce because it bars out-

continued

of-staters from offering a commercial service within its borders and confers the right to provide that service and to reap the associated economic benefit upon a class largely composed of Rhode Island citizens. National Revenue Corp. v. Violet, 807 F.2d 285 (1st Cir. 1986).

2. Judicial Power.

The supreme court may regulate the practice of law outside the courtroom and not directly connected therewith. Rhode Island Bar Ass'n v. Automobile Serv. Ass'n, 55 R.I. 122, 179 A. 139 (1935).

3. Claim Adjustment.

Soliciting claims for fire losses and representing claimants in negotiations for settlements with insurance companies for a percentage fee amounted to practice of law as contemplated in this section, and such activities could be enjoined. Rhode Island Bar Ass'n v. Lesser, 68 R.I. 14, 26 A.2d 6 (1942).

4. Effect of Unauthorized Practice.

An appeal filed through the business agent of the union was substantial compliance with the requirements of the Workers' Compensation Act although insofar as the agent was personally concerned his action was contrary to the provisions of this chapter. Lorraine Mfg. Co. v. Wilson, 73 R.I. 313, 55 A.2d 861 (1947).

Collateral References. Ambulance chaser, acting as, as practice of law. 151 A.L.R. 796.

Authority of attorney to compromise action — modern cases. 90 A.L.R.4th 326.

Business of debt adjusting as practice of law. 95 A.L.R.2d 1355.

Drafting of will or other estate-planning activities as illegal practice of law. 22 A.L.R.3d 1112; 71 A.L.R.3d 1000.

Drafting, or filling in blanks in printed forms, of instruments relating to land by real-estate agents, brokers, or managers as constituting practice of law. 53 A.L.R.2d 788.

Handling, preparing, presenting, or trying workers' compensation claims or cases as practice of law. 58 A.L.R.5th 449.

Liability in tort for interference with attorney-client relationship. 90 A.L.R.4th 621.

Measure and elements of damages recoverable for attorney's negligence in preparing or conducting litigation—twentieth century cases. 90 A.L.R.4th 1033.

Operations of collection agency as unauthorized practice of law. 27 A.L.R.3d 1152.

Propriety and effect of corporation's appearance pro se, through agent who is not attorney. 8 A.L.R.5th 653.

Representation of another before state public utilities or service commission as involving practice of law. 13 A.L.R.3d 812.

Tax matters, services in connection with, as practice of law. 9 A.L.R.2d 797.

Title examination activities by lending institution, insurance company, or title and abstract company, as illegal practice of law. 85 A.L.R.2d 184.

Title or probate matters, services in, as practice of law. 111 A.L.R. 31; 125 A.L.R. 1173; 151 A.L.R. 781.

Trust company's acts as fiduciary as practice of law. 69 A.L.R.2d 404.

What activities of stock or security broker constitute unauthorized practice of law. 34 A.L.R.3d 1305.

What amounts to practice of law. 151 A.L.R. 781.

11-27-3. Receipt of fees as practice of law. — Any person, partnership, corporation, or association that receives any fee or any part of a fee for the services performed by an attorney at law shall be deemed to be practicing law contrary to the provisions of this chapter.

History of Section.

G.L. 1923, ch. 401, § 46; P.L. 1935, ch. 2190, § 1; G.L. 1938, ch. 612, § 44; G.L. 1956, § 11-27-3.

NOTES TO DECISIONS

1. In General.

This section does not come into play until such time as an assignee actually receives a portion of the attorney's fee. Pearlman v. Rowell, 401 A.2d 19 (R.I. 1979).

11-6-1. Bigamy. — Every person who has a former husband or wife living and who is convicted of being married to or of cohabiting with, another as husband and wife shall be fined not more than one thousand dollars ($1,000). This provision shall not extend to any person whose husband or wife remains outside of this state for seven (7) years, when the person only marries after that time in ignorance of whether that person s spouse is still living. This provision further does not apply to any person who is divorced at the time of a second marriage, nor to any person whose previous marriage was made when the man was less than fourteen (14) and the woman less than twelve (12) years of age.

History of Section.
G.L. 1896, ch. 281, § 1; G.L. 1909. ch. 347, § 1; G.L. 1923, ch. 399, § 1; G.L. 1938, ch. 610, § 1; G.L. 1956, § 11-6-1; P.L. 1989, ch. 214, § 1.

Cross References. Bigamous marriages void, § 15-1-5.

Knowingly performing bigamous marriage, § 15-3-11.

Comparative Legislation. Adultery:
Conn. Gen. Stat. § 53a-81.
Mass. Ann. Laws ch. 272, § 14.
Bigamy:
Conn. Gen. Stat. § 53a-190.
Mass. Ann. Laws ch. 272, § 15.
Fornication:
Mass. Ann. Laws ch. 272, § 18.
Incest:
Conn. Gen. Stat. § 53a-191.
Mass. Ann. Laws ch. 272, § 17.

NOTES TO DECISIONS

Analysis

1. Elements of offense.
2. Indictment.
3. Admissions.

1. Elements of Offense.

Second marriage is a necessary element of the offense. In re Watson, 19 R.I. 342, 33 A. 873 (1896).

2. Indictment.

Indictment under this section need not negative the proviso. State v. Gallagher, 20 R.I. 266, 38 A. 655 (1897).

3. Admissions.

Admissions by defendant as to first marriage are admissible in bigamy trial. State v. Gallagher, 20 R.I. 266, 38 A. 655 (1897).

Collateral References. Aiding and abetting, reduction by appellate court of punishment for. 29 A.L.R. 331; 89 A.L.R. 295.

Common law marriage, prosecution based on. 70 A.L.R. 1036.

Crimes against spouse within exception permitting testimony by one spouse against other in criminal prosecution — modern state cases. 74 A.L.R.4th 223.

Decree of annulment of marriage, admissibility in prosecution for bigamy and polygamy. 87 A.L.R. 1264.

Dissolution of former marriage, presumption as to, in prosecution for bigamy. 34 A.L.R. 482; 56 A.L.R. 1273; 77 A.L.R. 738; 14 A.L.R.2d 19.

Liability of church or religious society for sexual misconduct of clergy. 5 A.L.R.5th 530.

Marital privilege under Rule 501 of Federal Rules of Evidence. 46 A.L.R. Fed. 735.

Mistake as to validity or effect of divorce as defense to. 56 A.L.R.2d 915.

Mistaken belief in existence, validity, or effect of divorce or separation as mitigating punishment for bigamy or allied offense. 56 A.L.R.2d 938.

Presumption from lapse of time of death of former spouse, marriage in reliance on, while former spouse is still living and undivorced, as sustaining prosecution for bigamy. 144 A.L.R. 747.

Privileged communications and letters between husband and wife in prosecution for bigamy. 63 A.L.R. 107.

Religious belief as affecting crime of bigamy. 24 A.L.R. 1237.

Single person who marries one already married, criminal responsibility of. 5 A.L.R. 783; 74 A.L.R. 1110; 131 A.L.R. 1323.

Validation of marriage by death of former spouse. 95 A.L.R. 1292.

continued

11-6-2. Adultery. — (a) As used in this section, "adultery" means illicit sexual intercourse between any two (2) persons, where either of them is married to another person; this conduct constitutes adultery in each of the persons.

(b) Every person who commits adultery shall be fined not more than five hundred dollars ($500).

History of Section.
G.L. 1896, ch. 281, § 2; G.L. 1909, ch. 347, § 2; G.L. 1923, ch. 399, § 2; G.L. 1938, ch. 610, § 2; G.L. 1956, § 11-6-2; P.L. 1989, ch. 214, § 1.

Reenactments. The 2000 Reenactment redesignated the subsections.

Cross References. Adultery as ground for divorce, § 15-5-2.

Collateral References. Cohabitation under marriage contracted after divorce decree as adultery, where decree is later reversed or set aside. 63 A.L.R.2d 816.

Criminal charge of abandonment against husband, adultery of wife as affecting. 17 A.L.R. 999.

Discontinuance by injured spouse of prosecution for. 4 A.L.R. 1340; 61 A.L.R. 973.

Isolated acts of sexual intercourse as constituting criminal offense of adultery. 74 A.L.R. 1361.

Liability of church or religious society for sexual misconduct of clergy. 5 A.L.R.5th 530.

Mistaken belief in existence, validity, or effect of divorce or separation as defense to prosecution for adultery. 56 A.L.R.2d 915.

Mistaken belief in existence, validity, or effect of divorce or separation as mitigating punishment for bigamy or allied offense. 56 A.L.R.2d 938.

Reduction by appellate court of punishment imposed by trial court. 29 A.L.R. 313; 89 A.L.R. 300.

Validity of statute making adultery and fornication criminal offense. 41 A.L.R.3d 1338.

Venereal disease as evidence of. 5 A.L.R. 1020; 8 A.L.R. 1540.

Weight and sufficiency of blood grouping tests to establish adultery. 46 A.L.R.2d 1027; 43 A.L.R.4th 579.

Witnesses, adultery as a crime against other spouse within statute relating to competency of husband or wife as witness against the other. 11 A.L.R.2d 646; 74 A.L.R.4th 223; 46 A.L.R. Fed. 735.

11-6-3, 11-6-4. [Repealed.]

Repealed Sections. Sections 11-6-3 and 11-6-4 (G.L. 1896, ch. 281, §§ 8, 9; G.L. 1909, ch. 347, §§ 8, 9; P.L. 1915, ch. 1219, § 2; G.L. 1923, ch. 399, § 9; G.L. 1938, ch. 610, § 9; G.L. 1956, §§ 11-6-3, 11-6-4), concerning fornication and incest, respectively, were repealed by P.L. 1989, ch. 214, § 1, effective July 5, 1989.

CHAPTER 7

BRIBERY

3. Only the person making the communication can waive the privilege.
   a. True
   b. False
4. What legal cite supports your answer to the preceding question?
   a. 171 C. 586
   b. 1949 Rev. S. 7869
   c. 52-146-E
   d. 52-146
5. *Clergyman* is a broadly defined category.
   a. True
   b. False

M. Exercise 11.13: Uniform Commercial Code

1. A "Purchased" is defined at:
   a. Definitional Cross References
   b. Section 23, Uniform Negotiable Instruments Law
   c. Section 8-316
   d. Point 3
2. An unauthorized signature placed on a security instrument is not ineffective if done by an authenticating trustee.
   a. True
   b. False
3. Which case holds that insurers are responsible for signatures placed upon securities by parties claiming authorization to prepare such securities?
   a. *Dollar Savings v. Pittsburgh Plate Glass*
   b. *Healey v. Steele Center*
   c. *Jarvis v. Manhattan Beach Co.*
   d. *Hudson Trust v. American Linseed*
4. U.C.C. definitional cross-references are quite substantial. Which section cross-references "Issued"?
   a. 8-102
   b. 8-201
   c. 8-103
   d. 1-201
5. Which crime is mentioned in this annotation?
   a. Blackmail
   b. Forgery
   c. Theft
   d. Fraud

N. Exercise 11.14: Pennsylvania Statutes Annotated

1. What other provision of the Pennsylvania statutes is referred to in this section?
   a. 404
   b. 5327
   c. 7.40
   d. 11.51

EXERCISE 11.12

Sec. 52-144. Form of subpoena. The form of a subpoena may be as follows:

To A. B. and C. D. of . . . . :

By authority of the state of Connecticut, you are hereby commanded to appear before the . . . . court, to be held at . . . . on the . . . . day of . . . . or to such day thereafter and within sixty days hereof on which the action is legally to be tried, to testify what you know in a certain civil action pending in the court, between E. F. of H., plaintiff, and G. A. of M., defendant.

Hereof fail not, under penalty of the law.

To any proper officer or indifferent person to serve and return.

Dated at H., etc.

J. K., (title of officer authorized to sign subpoena).

(1949 Rev., S. 7867; 1955, S. 3151d; P.A. 79-6; P.A. 82-160, S. 60.)

History: P.A. 79-6 required appearance within sixty rather than thirty days after subpoena; P.A. 82-160 rephrased the section.

Cited. 12 CA 364, 371.

Sec. 52-145. Certain witnesses not disqualified. Credibility. (a) A person shall not be disqualified as a witness in any action because of, (1) his interest in the outcome of the action as a party or otherwise, (2) his disbelief in the existence of a supreme being, or (3) his conviction of crime.

(b) A person's interest in the outcome of the action or his conviction of crime may be shown for the purpose of affecting his credibility.

(1949 Rev., S. 7868; P.A. 82-160, S. 61.)
History: P.A. 82-160 rephrased the section and inserted Subsec. indicators.
Wife may testify for husband. 3 D. 57; 20 C. 354. The conviction must be of an infamous crime; a petty offense is not sufficient. 57 C. 432; 104 C. 124. Record of a judgment of conviction vacated by appeal is insufficient. 57 C. 432. Particular instances of untruthfulness inadmissible to affect credit of witness. 72 C. 204. Cited. 58 C. 64. Attorney trying case cannot ordinarily be witness therein; 72 C. 437; 80 C. 531; 81 C. 350; otherwise, if he is also a party; 68 C. 206; 85 C. 211; and he may be called by adverse party. 81 C. 344. Insolvent debtor may testify as to knowledge of insolvency when transfer was made. 75 C. 17. Incapacity to manage his affairs does not disqualify witness. 76 C. 406. Where accused becomes witness for himself, usual rules as to attacking credit apply. 67 C. 290; 76 C. 94; 87 C. 22; 89 C. 417. Evidence of arrest alone not sufficient. 76 C. 92; 86 C. 262. Party to action is ordinarily competent. 79 C. 478. Members of a commission may testify as to proceedings before it; 75 C. 248; 76 C. 567; so judge, as to claims of law made on trial. 82 C. 51. Evidence that witness has incurred expenses which he must pay if party producing him loses is admissible. 74 C. 555. Nature of crimes conviction of which may be shown. 95 C. 501; 104 C. 124; id., 264; 106 C. 350. When a child is competent. 100 C. 570. Improper reference to this statute held cured by instruction of judge. 108 C. 192. Statement of witness that he has scruples against taking oath must be taken as true; belief in supreme being does not destroy witness's right to take affirmation instead of oath. 109 C. 712. Purpose of statute to remove common law disqualification of witness because of conviction of crime. 121 C. 678. For purpose of affecting credibility conviction of crime may be shown by questions on cross- examination. 121 C. 678; 132 C. 574; Overruling 72 C. 205 and 97 C. 452. Owner is competent witness to location of bounds and occupancy of own land when within his personal knowledge. 125 C. 333. Where plaintiff administrator was questioned on direct as to decedent's health and financial standing, question on cross as to whether he expected to share in recovery in case was proper. 131 C. 515. Cited. 136 C. 106. Fact that conviction was ten years before went to weight not to admissibility. 137 C. 140. Conviction of section 53-246 "intoxication" is not infamous crime to attack credibility of a witness. 140 C. 39. Cited. 149 C. 125; 153 C. 208; 154 C. 68, 74. A plea of guilty by one of several persons charged with a crime can be no more than hearsay as to others so charged. Therefore, while the plea may be used to attack the credibility of the one so pleading if he testifies as a witness for or against the others, it is not admissible on the trial of the others to establish that the crime was committed. 150 C. 195. The conviction of a crime, whether or not denominated a felony by statute, is admissible in evidence to affect credibility under this section only if the maximum permissible penalty for the crime may be imprisonment for more than one year, and the presence or absence of moral turpitude is not a consideration affecting the admissibility. 152 C. 472. Where defendant chose to take stand on his own behalf, question on cross-examination as to prior conviction was properly asked of him in his capacity as a witness, but court does not consider whether defendant could raise his constitutional privilege against compulsory self-incrimination. 153 C. 30. In same case, use of defendant's answer, over his objection, in second part of information, brought under habitual criminal statute, was a violation of his constitutional privilege against compulsory self-incrimination. Id., 34, 35. Writ, summons and complaint in another action brought by plaintiff admissible to affect credibility insofar as testimony in present action is inconsistent with prior claim. On redirect plaintiff should be allowed to show extent of his knowledge of allegations in prior writ. 155 C. 197. Cited. 158 C. 156. Where statement of witness was offered to show bias against defendant, it was properly excluded where it related to criminal activity of witness for which he had not been convicted. 158 C. 536. Judge's discretion to exclude evidence as prejudicial. 160 C. 47. Court's instructions to jury as to historic common law background and purpose of statute does not raise any federal constitutional questions. 160 C. 171, 175. Cited. 160 C. 378. Impeachment of witness on the basis of misconduct accomplished only by proof of felony convictions. 164 C. 145. Specific acts of misconduct to show lack of veracity cannot be shown by extrinsic evidence. Id. Cited. 165 C. 559, 573. Cited. 165 C. 599, 606. Cited. 166 C. 226, 230. Cited re constitutional separation of powers (dissent). 166 C. 501. Credibility of a witness may be impeached by proof of convictions of crimes for which imprisonment may be more than one year. 167 C. 539. Cited. 182 C. 207, 217. Cited. 185 C. 372, 383. Cited. 186 C. 654, 670. Cited. 187 C. 513, 521. Cited. 188 C. 259, 267; Id., 515, 519. Cited. 189 C. 631, 642, 643. Cited. 190 C. 20, 23, 25. Prudent course where trial court faced with decision on admission as evidence of credibility prior convictions for crimes not directly reflecting on credibility is to allow prosecution to mention that defendant was convicted of unspecified crime or crimes carrying a penalty of more than one year. 194 C. 1, 6, 10, 12. Cited. Id., 297, 307. Where a prior charge resulted in a determination that defendant was a youthful offender and not in a criminal conviction, it was not admissible for impeachment purposes under the statute. 196 C. 122, 128. Cited. 198 C. 273, 277. Cited. 201 C. 74, 85, 86, 88, 89. Cited. 202 C.

224, 228. Cited. 210 C. 359, 395. Cited. 211 C. 555, 560. Cited. Id., 555, 561. Cited. 227 C. 417, 434. Cited. Id., 711, 735.
Cited. 3 CA 684, 686, 688. Cited. 7 CA 217, 219. Cited. 20 CA 6, 14. Cited. 22 CA 610, 620. Cited. 23 CA 479, 485. Cited. Id., 692, 700. Cited. 26 CA 157, 163. Cited. 38 CA 815, 821.
Credit of witness may not be attacked by showing his conviction of a crime which is not infamous, that is, for which maximum penalty cannot be more than six months in jail. 23 CS 294. Cited. 33 CS 586, 590. Cited. 36 CS 89, 90.
Conviction of crime of trespass inadmissible under this statute. 3 Conn. Cir. Ct. 391. Any question about previous arrests is improper because statute allows questions about convictions only in establishing credibility and reputation of witness. 6 Conn. Cir. Ct. 441.
Subsec. (a):
Cited. 198 C. 454, 474. Subdiv. (3) cited. 210 C. 359, 360, 394, 395. Cited. 211 C. 555, 560.
Cited. 7 CA 217, 219. Cited. Id., 601, 603. Cited. 34 CA 823, 828.
Subsec. (b):
Cited. 194 C. 297, 307. Cited. 196 C. 122, 127. Cited. 199 C. 255, 260. Cited. 202 C. 224, 228. Cited. 210 C. 359, 394. Cited. 211 C. 555, 561. Cited. 227 C. 389, 409. Cited. 228 C. 412, 430. Trial court abused discretion in barring evidence of victim's prior felony conviction for larceny since outcome of case depended upon relative credibility of victim and defendant, and state was allowed to impeach credibility of defendant with a prior felony conviction. 245 C. 351.
Cited. 3 CA 459, 460. Cited. 6 CA 189, 190. Cited. 7 CA 217, 219. Cited. Id., 377, 387. Cited. Id., 445, 451. Cited. 10 CA 71, 72. Cited. 16 CA 346, 348. Cited. 26 CA 758, 762. Cited. 27 CA 279, 289. Cited. 32 CA 773, 782. Cited. 37 CA 722, 731. Cited. 40 CA 151, 158. Cited. 42 CA 810. Cited. 44 CA 280. Cited. Id., 790. Cited. 45 CA 390. Cited. 46 CA 285.

Sec. 52-146. Wife as a witness against her husband. A wife may be compelled to testify in any action brought against her husband for necessaries furnished her while living apart from him.

(1949 Rev., S. 7869.)

Cited. 190 C. 813. Cited. 211 C. 555, 560.

Sec. 52-146a. Transferred to Sec. 52-146d.

Sec. 52-146b. Privileged communications made to clergymen. A clergyman, priest, minister, rabbi or practitioner of any religious denomination accredited by the religious body to which he belongs who is settled in the work of the ministry shall not disclose confidential communications made to him in his professional capacity in any civil or criminal case or proceedings preliminary thereto, or in any legislative or administrative proceeding, unless the person making the confidential communication waives such privilege herein provided.

(1967, P.A. 826.)
"Priest-penitent" privilege found waived where defendant testified as to what he told priest and conversation did not relate to religious or spiritual advise, aid or comfort. 171 C. 586, 592, 594. Cited. 211 C. 555, 560.

Sec. 52-146c. Privileged communications between psychologist and patient. (a) As used in this section:

(1) "Person" means an individual who consults a psychologist for purposes of diagnosis or treatment;

(2) "Psychologist" means an individual licensed to practice psychology pursuant to chapter 383;

(3) "Communications" means all oral and written communications and records thereof relating to the diagnosis and treatment of a person between such person and a psychologist or between a member of such person's family and a psychologist;

(4) "Consent" means consent given in writing by the person or his authorized representative;

(5) "Authorized representative" means (A) an individual empowered by a person to assert the confidentiality of communications which are privileged under this section, or (B) if a person is deceased, his personal representative or next of kin, or (C) if a person is incompetent to assert or waive his privileges hereunder, (i) a guardian or conservator who has been or is appointed to act for the person, or (ii) for the purpose of maintaining confidentiality until a guardian or conservator is appointed, the person's nearest relative.

(b) Except as provided in subsection (c) of this section, in civil and criminal actions, in juvenile, probate, commitment and arbitration proceedings, in proceedings preliminary to such actions or proceedings, and in legislative and administrative proceedings, all communications shall be privileged and a psychologist shall not disclose any such communications unless the person or his authorized representative consents to waive the privilege and allow such disclosure. The person or his authorized representative may withdraw any consent given under the provisions of this section at any time in a writing addressed to the individual with whom or the office in which the original consent was filed. The withdrawal of consent shall not affect communications disclosed prior to notice of the withdrawal.

(c) Consent of the person shall not be required for the disclosure of such person's communications:

(1) If a judge finds that any person after having been informed that the communications would not be privileged, has made the communications to a psychologist in the course of a psychological examination ordered by the court, provided the communications shall be admissible only on issues involving the person's psychological condition;

(2) If, in a civil proceeding, a person introduces his psychological condition as an element of his claim or defense or, after a person's death, his condition is introduced by a party claiming or defending through or as a beneficiary of the person, and the judge finds that it is more important to the interests of justice that the communications be disclosed than that the relationship between the person and psychologist be protected;

(3) If the psychologist believes in good faith that there is risk of imminent personal injury to the person or to other individuals or risk of imminent injury to the property of other individuals;

(4) If child abuse, abuse of an elderly individual or abuse of an individual who is disabled or incompetent is known or in good faith suspected;

(5) If a psychologist makes a claim for collection of fees for services rendered, the name and address of the person and the amount of the fees may be disclosed to individuals or agencies involved in such collection, provided notification that such disclosure will be made is sent, in writing, to the person not less than thirty days prior to such disclosure. In cases where a dispute arises over the fees or claims or where additional information is needed to substantiate the claim, the disclosure of further information shall be limited to the following: (A) That the person was in fact receiving psychological services, (B) the dates of such services, and (C) a general description of the types of services; or

continued

(6) If the communications are disclosed to a member of the immediate family or legal representative of the victim of a homicide committed by the person where such person has, on or after July 1, 1989, been found not guilty of such offense by reason of mental disease or defect pursuant to section 53a-13, provided such family member or legal representative requests the disclosure of such communications not later than six years after such finding, and provided further, such communications shall only be available during the pendency of, and for use in, a civil action relating to such person found not guilty pursuant to section 53a-13.

(1969, P.A. 597, S. 13; P.A. 82-160, S. 63; P.A. 89-154, S. 1; P.A. 92-225, S. 3, 5.)
History: P.A. 82-160 rephrased the section and inserted Subsec. indicators; P.A. 89-154 amended Subsec. (a) to redefine "person" and to add the definitions of "psychologist", "communications", "consent", and "authorized representative", amended Subsec. (b) to rephrase its provisions, to extend the prohibition on disclosure to "juvenile, probate, commitment and arbitration proceedings", and to add provisions re the manner and effect of a withdrawal of consent, and amended Subsec. (c) to replace the introductory provision that "Relevant communications under this section shall not be privileged" with "Consent of the person shall not be required for the disclosure of such person's communications", to delete reference to a "clinical" psychologist in Subdiv. (1), to add Subdiv. (3) re exception when there is risk of imminent injury to person or property, to add Subdiv. (4) re exception when abuse is known or suspected, and to add Subdiv. (5) re exception when claim is made for collection of fees for services rendered; P.A. 92-225 amended Subsec. (c) to add Subdiv. (6) re exception when communications are disclosed under limited circumstances to the immediate family or legal representative of certain homicide victims.
Cited. 191 C. 453, 456. Cited. 203 C. 641, 652, 658. Erroneous denial of psychiatrist-patient privilege does not infringe upon right of any person other than the one to whom the privilege is given. 208 C. 683, 686. Cited. 211 C. 555, 560.
Cited. 18 CA 273, 280. Cited. 23 CA 98, 105. Cited. Id., 330, 335–339, 341. Cited. 24 CA 287, 290. Court did not violate statute by ordering disclosure of substance abuse and psychiatric treatment records of parents in case involving termination of their parental rights. 48 CA 563.
Subsec. (c):
Cited. 23 CA 330, 339.

Sec. 52-146d. (Formerly Sec. 52-146a). Privileged communications between psychiatrist and patient. Definitions. As used in sections 52-146d to 52-146i, inclusive:

(1) "Authorized representative" means (A) a person empowered by a patient to assert the confidentiality of communications or records which are privileged under sections 52-146c to 52-146i, inclusive, or (B) if a patient is deceased, his personal representative or next of kin, or (C) if a patient is incompetent to assert or waive his privileges hereunder, (i) a guardian or conservator who has been or is appointed to act for the patient, or (ii) for the purpose of maintaining confidentiality until a guardian or conservator is appointed, the patient's nearest relative;

(2) "Communications and records" means all oral and written communications and records thereof relating to diagnosis or treatment of a patient's mental condition between the patient and a psychiatrist, or between a member of the patient's family and a psychiatrist, or between any of such persons and a person participating under the supervision of a psychiatrist in the accomplishment of the objectives of diagnosis and treatment, wherever made, including communications and records which occur in or are prepared at a mental health facility;

(3) "Consent" means consent given in writing by the patient or his authorized representative;

(4) "Identifiable" and "identify a patient" refer to communications and records which contain (A) names or other descriptive data from which a person acquainted with the patient might reasonably recognize the patient as the person referred to, or (B) codes or numbers which are in general use outside of the mental health facility which prepared the communications and records;

(5) "Mental health facility" includes any hospital, clinic, ward, psychiatrist's office or other facility, public or private, which provides inpatient or outpatient service, in whole or in part, relating to the diagnosis or treatment of a patient's mental condition;

(6) "Patient" means a person who communicates with or is treated by a psychiatrist in diagnosis or treatment;

(7) "Psychiatrist" means a person licensed to practice medicine who devotes a substantial portion of his time to the practice of psychiatry, or a person reasonably believed by the patient to be so qualified.

(1961, P.A. 529; 1969, P.A. 819, S. 1; P.A. 75-567, S. 36, 80; P.A. 82-160, S. 64; P.A. 89-154, S. 2.)
History: 1969 act deleted detailed provisions re privileged communications (but see Sec. 52-146e for replacement provisions) and added definitions of "consent", "communications and records", "mental health facility" and records which "identify" or are "identifiable"; Sec. 52-146a transferred to Sec. 52-146d in the 1969 Supplement to the General Statutes; P.A. 75-567 applied definitions to Secs. "52-146c to 52-146i" rather than to Secs. "52-146d to 52-146j"; P.A. 82-160 alphabetized the defined terms and inserted Subdiv. indicators; P.A. 89-154 applied definitions to Secs. "52-146d to 52-146i" rather than to Secs. "52-146c to 52-146i".
Case decided before effective date of statute. 150 C. 689. Cited. 152 C. 510, 512. Psychiatrist-patient privilege does not extend to records relative to drug-dependency treatment. 169 C. 223. Cited. Id., 223, 230, 234. Psychiatric-patient privilege not waived and testimony of psychiatrist hired by state, but not as a result of court order, held inadmissible. 178 C. 626, 629. Cited. 191 C. 453, 456. Cited. 199 C. 693, 706. Cited. 201 C. 211, 213, 218, 222. Cited. 203 C. 641, 658. Cited. 208 C. 365, 379. Cited. Id., 683, 684. Cited. 211 C. 555, 560. Cited. 212 C. 50, 55. Cited. 217C. 243, 256. Cited. 218 C. 85, 133. Cited. 225 C. 700, 703. Cited. Id., 450, 478. Cited. 228 C. 1, 3, 9, 10. Cited. 235 C. 185, 190, 192. Former Sec. 52-146a cited. Id., 185, 195. Cited. 236 C. 625, 635. Cited. 238 C. 313.
Cited. 1 CA 384, 393, 394. Secs. 52-146d–52-146j cited. 14 CA 552, 557. Cited. 19 CA 304, 318. Cited. 24 CA 287, 290. Cited. 25 CA 653, 655; judgment reversed, see 223 C. 52 et seq. Cited. 30 CA 839, 851. Cited. 33 CA 647, 654. Cited. 35 CA 94, 98; judgment reversed, see 235 C. 185 et seq.
Cited. 28 CS 57.
Subdiv. (2):
Cited. 190 C. 813, 818. Cited. 217 C. 243, 257. Cited. 218 C. 85, 133.
Cited. 1 CA 384, 389. Cited. 14 CA 552, 557. Cited. 24 CA 287, 292. Cited. 33 CA 253, 268. Cited. 35 CA 94, 98; judgment reversed, see 235 C. 185 et seq.
Subdiv. (3):
Cited. 201 C. 211, 223.

Subdiv. (4):
Cited. 223 C. 450, 456, 458. Subpara. (A) cited. Id., 450, 458, 459.
Subdiv. (5):
Cited. 24 CA 287, 292.
Subdiv. (6):
Purpose of the statutory privilege is to protect a therapeutic relationship, communications that bear no relationship to the purpose for which privilege was enacted are admissible subject to normal rules of evidence. 190 C. 813, 817.
Cited. 24 CA 287, 292.
Subdiv. (7):
Cited. 219 C. 314, 337.

Sec. 52-146e. Disclosure of communications. (a) All communications and records as defined in section 52-146d shall be confidential and shall be subject to the provisions of sections 52-146d to 52-146j, inclusive. Except as provided in sections 52-146f to 52-146i, inclusive, no person may disclose or transmit any communications and records or the substance or any part or any resume thereof which identify a patient to any person, corporation or governmental agency without the consent of the patient or his authorized representative.

(b) Any consent given to waive the confidentiality shall specify to what person or agency the information is to be disclosed and to what use it will be put. Each patient shall be informed that his refusal to grant consent will not jeopardize his right to obtain present or future treatment except where disclosure of the communications and records is necessary for the treatment.

(c) The patient or his authorized representative may withdraw any consent given under the provisions of this section at any time in a writing addressed to the person or office in which the original consent was filed. Withdrawal of consent shall not affect communications or records disclosed prior to notice of the withdrawal.

(1969, P.A. 819, S. 2, 3; P.A. 82-160, S. 65.)
History: P.A. 82-160 rephrased and reorganized section.
Cited. 169 C. 223, 230, 234. Psychiatrist-patient privilege not waived and testimony of psychiatrist hired by state, but not as a result of court order, held inadmissible. 178 C. 626, 629. Cited. 190 C. 813, 815. Cited. 191 C. 453, 456. Cited. 192 C. 166, 177. Cited. 197 C. 326, 328, 329. Cited. 199 C. 693, 708. Before privilege is applied court should conduct voir dire for purpose of determining existence of impeaching evidence in order to protect constitutional right of confrontation. 201 C. 211, 213, 218, 222, 223, 227, 228. Cited. Id., 244, 256. Cited. 205 C. 386, 402. Cited. 211 C. 555, 560. Cited. 212 C. 50, 55, 56. Cited. 218 C. 85, 133. Cited. 221 C. 447, 457. Cited. 223 C. 450, 451. Cited. 225 C. 450, 478. Cited. Id., 700, 703. Cited. 228 C. 1, 3, 4, 9, 10. Cited. 235 C. 185, 190, 192, 193, 195, 198–200. Cited. Id., 595, 606. Cited. 236 C. 514, 522. Cited. Id., 625, 635. Cited. 238 C. 313. Cited. 242 C. 666.
Psychiatric patient privilege and defendant's right to confrontation discussed. 1 CA 384, 389, 393, 394. Cited. 8 CA 216, 236, 237. Cited. 10 CA 103, 107, 110. Cited. 14 CA 552, 557, 558. Secs. 52-146d–52-146j also cited. Id. Cited. 15 CA 222, 241. Cited. 17 CA 174, 178. Cited. 18 CA 273, 276. Cited. 19 CA 304, 318. Cited. 20 CA 101, 110, 111. Cited. 24 CA 287, 290. Cited. 25 CA 653, 655; judgment reversed, see 223 C. 52 et seq. Cited. 30 CA 839, 851, 852. Cited. 33 CA 647, 654. Cited. 35 CA 94, 98; judgment reversed, see 235 C. 185 et seq. Need for information to institute claim creates compelling countervailing interest that requires disclosure of limited information. 50 CA 694. Cited. 52 CA 408.
Subsec. (a):
Cited. 217 C. 243, 256. Cited. 218 C. 85, 133. Cited. 223 C. 450, 456, 460. Cited. 230 C. 43, 58.
Psychiatrist-patient privilege cannot be overridden by provisions of Sec. 19a-14(a)(10). 14 CA 552, 553, 558. Cited. 33 CA 253, 268.
Subsec. (b):
Cited. 201 C. 211, 223.

Sec. 52-146f. Consent not required for disclosure, when. Consent of the patient shall not be required for the disclosure or transmission of communications or records of the patient in the following situations as specifically limited:

(1) Communications or records may be disclosed to other persons engaged in the diagnosis or treatment of the patient or may be transmitted to another mental health facility to which the patient is admitted for diagnosis or treatment if the psychiatrist in possession of the communications or records determines that the disclosure or transmission is needed to accomplish the objectives of diagnosis or treatment. The patient shall be informed that the communications or records will be so disclosed or transmitted. For purposes of this subsection, persons in professional training are to be considered as engaged in the diagnosis or treatment of the patients.

(2) Communications or records may be disclosed when the psychiatrist determines that there is substantial risk of imminent physical injury by the patient to himself or others or when a psychiatrist, in the course of diagnosis or treatment of the patient, finds it necessary to disclose the communications or records for the purpose of placing the patient in a mental health facility, by certification, commitment or otherwise, provided the provisions of sections 52-146d to 52-146j, inclusive, shall continue in effect after the patient is in the facility.

redemption or exchange must give rise to the question in a purchaser's mind as to why it has not been surrendered. After the lapse of a reasonable period of time a purchaser can no longer claim "no reason to know" of any defects or irregularities in its issue. Where funds are available for the redemption the security certificate is normally turned in more promptly and a shorter time is set as the "reasonable period" than is set where funds are not available.

Defaulted certificated securities may be traded on financial markets in the same manner as unmatured and undefaulted instruments and a purchaser might not be placed upon notice of irregularity by the mere fact of default. An issuer, however, should at some point be placed in a position to determine definitely its liability on an invalid or improper issue, and for this purpose a security under this section becomes "stale" two years after the default. A different rule applies when the question is notice not of issuer's defenses but of claims of ownership. Section 8–105 and Comment.

3. Nothing in this section is designed to extend the life of preferred stocks called for redemption as "shares of stock" beyond the redemption date. After such a call, the security represents only a right to the funds set aside for redemption.

Definitional Cross References:

"Certificated security". Section 8–102(a)(4).

"Notice". Section 1–201(25).

"Purchaser". Sections 1–201(33) & 8–116.

"Security". Section 8–102(a)(15).

"Security certificate". Section 8–102(a)(16).

"Uncertificated security". Section 8–102(a)(18).

§ 8–204. Effect of Issuer's Restriction on Transfer.

A restriction on transfer of a security imposed by the issuer, even if otherwise lawful, is ineffective against a person without knowledge of the restriction unless:

(1) the security is certificated and the restriction is noted conspicuously on the security certificate; or

(2) the security is uncertificated and the registered owner has been notified of the restriction.

Official Comment

1. Restrictions on transfer of securities are imposed by issuers in a variety of circumstances and for a variety of purposes, such as to retain control of a close corporation or to ensure compliance with federal securities laws. Other law determines whether such restrictions are permissible. This section deals only with the consequences of failure to note the restriction on a security certificate.

This section imposes no bar to enforcement of a restriction on transfer against a person who has actual knowledge of it.

2. A restriction on transfer of a certificated security is ineffective against a person without knowledge of the restriction unless the restriction is noted conspicuously on the certificate. The word "noted" is used to make clear that the restriction need not be set forth in full text. Refusal by an insurer to register a transfer on the basis of an unnoted restriction would be a violation of the issuer's duty to register under Section 8–401.

3. The policy of this section is the same as in Section 8–202. A purchaser who takes delivery of a certificated security is entitled to rely on the terms stated on the certificate. That policy obviously does not apply to uncertificated securities. For uncertificated securities, this section requires only that the registered owner has been notified of the restriction. Suppose, for example, that A is the registered owner of an uncertificated security, and that the issuer has notified A of a restriction on transfer. A agrees to sell the security to B, in violation of the restriction. A completes a written instruction directing the

issuer to register transfer to B, and B pays A for the security at the time A delivers the instruction to B. A does not inform B of the restriction, and B does not otherwise have notice or knowledge of it at the time B pays and receives the instruction. B presents the instruction to the issuer, but the issuer refuses to register the transfer on the grounds that it would violate the restriction. The issuer has complied with this section, because it did notify the registered owner A of the restriction. The issuer's refusal to register transfer is not wrongful. B has an action against A for breach of transfer warranty, see Section 8–108(b)(4)(iii). B's mistake was treating an uncertificated security transaction in the fashion appropriate only for a certificated security. The mechanism for transfer of uncertificated securities is registration of transfer on the books of the issuer; handing over an instruction only initiates the process. The purchaser should make arrangements to ensure that the price is not paid until it knows that the issuer has or will register transfer.

4. In the indirect holding system, investors neither take physical delivery of security certificates nor have uncertificated securities registered in their names. So long as the requirements of this section have been satisfied at the level of the relationship between the issuer and the securities intermediary that is a direct holder, this section does not preclude the issuer from enforcing a restriction on transfer. See Section 8–202(a) and Comment 2 thereto.

5. This section deals only with restrictions imposed by the issuer. Restrictions imposed by statute are not affected. See *Quiner v. Marblehead Social Co.,* 10 Mass. 476 (1813); *Madison Bank v. Price,* 79 Kan. 289, 100 P. 280 (1909); *Healey v. Steele Center Creamery Ass'n,* 115 Minn. 451, 133 N.W. 69 (1911). Nor does it deal with private agreements between stockholders containing restrictive covenants as to the sale of the security.

Definitional Cross References:

"Certificated security". Section 8–102(a)(4).
"Conspicuous". Section 1–201(10).
"Issuer". Section 8–201.
"Knowledge". Section 1–201(25).
"Notify". Section 1–201(25).
"Purchaser". Sections 1–201(33) & 8–116.
"Security". Section 8–102(a)(15).
"Security certificate". Section 8–102(a)(16).
"Uncertificated security". Section 8–102(a)(18).

§ 8–205. Effect of Unauthorized Signature on Security Certificate.

An unauthorized signature placed on a security certificate before or in the course of issue is ineffective, but the signature is effective in favor of a purchaser for value of the certificated security if the purchaser is without notice of the lack of authority and the signing has been done by:

(1) an authenticating trustee, registrar, transfer agent, or other person entrusted by the issuer with the signing of the security certificate or of similar security certificates, or the immediate preparation for signing of any of them; or

(2) an employee of the issuer, or of any of the persons listed in paragraph (1), entrusted with responsible handling of the security certificate.

Official Comment

1. The problem of forged or unauthorized signatures may arise where an employee of the issuer, transfer agent, or registrar has access to securities which the employee is required to prepare for issue by affixing the corporate seal or by adding a signature necessary for issue. This section is based upon the issuer's duty to avoid the negligent en

735

EXERCISE 11.13
continued

trusting of securities to such persons. Issuers have long been held responsible for signatures placed upon securities by parties whom they have held out to the public as authorized to prepare such securities. See *Fifth Avenue Bank of New York v. The Forty–Second & Grand Street Ferry Railroad Co.,* 137 N.Y. 231, 33 N.E. 378, 19 L.R.A. 331, 33 Am.St.Rep. 712 (1893); *Jarvis v. Manhattan Beach Co.,* 148 N.Y. 652, 43 N.E. 68, 31 L.R.A. 776, 51 Am.St.Rep. 727 (1896). The "apparent authority" concept of some of the case-law, however, is here extended and this section expressly rejects the technical distinction, made by courts reluctant to recognize forged signatures, between cases where forgers sign signatures they are authorized to sign under proper circumstances and those in which they sign signatures they are never authorized to sign. *Citizens' & Southern National Bank v. Trust Co. of Georgia,* 50 Ga.App. 681, 179 S.E. 278 (1935). Normally the purchaser is not in a position to determine which signature a forger, entrusted with the preparation of securities, has "apparent authority" to sign. The issuer, on the other hand, can protect itself against such fraud by the careful selection and bonding of agents and employees, or by action over against transfer agents and registrars who in turn may bond their personnel.

2. The issuer cannot be held liable for the honesty of employees not entrusted, directly or indirectly, with the signing, preparation, or responsible handling of similar securities and whose possible commission of forgery it has no reason to anticipate. The result in such cases as *Hudson Trust Co. v. American Linseed Co.,* 232 N.Y. 350, 134 N.E. 178 (1922), and *Dollar Savings Fund & Trust Co. v. Pittsburgh Plate Glass Co.,* 213 Pa. 307, 62 A. 916, 5 Ann.Cas. 248 (1906) is here adopted.

3. This section is not concerned with forged or unauthorized indorsements, but only with unauthorized signatures of issuers, transfer agents, etc., placed upon security certificates during the course of their issue. The protection here stated is available to all purchasers for value without notice and not merely to subsequent purchasers.

Definitional Cross References:

"Certificated security". Section 8–102(a)(4).

"Issuer". Section 8–201.

"Notice". Section 1–201(25).

"Purchaser". Sections 1–201(33) & 8–116.

"Security certificate". Section 8–102(a)(14).

"Unauthorized signature". Section 1–201(43).

§ 8-206. Completion of Alteration of Security Certificate.

(a) If a security certificate contains the signatures necessary to its issue or transfer but is incomplete in any other respect:

(1) any person may complete it by filling in the blanks as authorized; and

(2) even if the blanks are incorrectly filled in, the security certificate as completed is enforceable by a purchaser who took it for value and without notice of the incorrectness.

(b) A complete security certificate that has been improperly altered, even if fraudulently, remains enforceable, but only according to its original terms.

Official Comment

1. The problem of forged or unauthorized signatures necessary for the issue or transfer of a security is not involved here, and a person in possession of a blank certificate is not, by this section, given authority to fill in blanks with such signatures. Completion of blanks left in a transfer instruction is dealt with elsewhere (Section 8–305(a)).

2. Blanks left upon issue of a security certificate are the only ones dealt with here, and a purchaser for value without notice is protected. A purchaser is not in a good

2. It is never necessary, when service of process occurs by mail, to require a return receipt from the mail service to verify delivery of process.
   a. True
   b. False
3. For rules regarding service of process on individuals who live outside of Pennsylvania, see PA Rules of Civil Procedure
   a. Rule 2098.
   b. Rule 404.
   c. Rule 400.
   d. Rule 449.
4. Which case stated that service by newspaper publication may be substituted as effective service for process when, according to information possessed by plaintiffs, defendant maintains a residence and has relatives in the county in question?
   a. *Romeo v. Woks*
   b. *In re Arthur Treacher's*
   c. *National Expositions Inc. v. DeBois*
   d. None of the above
5. What work should one consult to gather additional information regarding depositions outside of Pennsylvania?
   a. 5 Pennsylvania Practice § 11.51
   b. 5 Pennsylvania Practice § 7.40
   c. 1 Pennsylvania Practice § 221
   d. All of the above

residents should not be treated differently for personal jurisdiction purposes merely because business is conducted over Internet computer network. Zippo Mfg. Co. v. Zippo Dot Com, Inc., W.D.Pa.1997, 952 F.Supp. 1119, 42 U.S.P.Q.2d 1062.

Online computer news service purposefully availed itself of doing business in Pennsylvania and thus could be subject to personal jurisdiction there, by operating Internet site to advertise and solicit customers for its service and by entering contracts with approximately 3000 individuals and seven Internet access providers in Pennsylvania for purpose of providing those individuals with its service; service's contacts with Pennsylvania residents were not "fortuitous," and allegedly small quantity of contacts was not dispositive. Zippo Mfg. Co. v. Zippo Dot Com, Inc., W.D.Pa.1997, 952 F.Supp. 1119, 42 U.S.P.Q.2d 1062.

Causes of action by manufacturer of "Zippo" tobacco lighters alleging trademark dilution, infringement, and false designation under Lanham Act against on computer news service that used Internet domain names "zippo.com," "zippo.net," and "zipponews.com" were sufficiently related to service's contacts in Pennsylvania and thus supported exercise of personal jurisdiction there; contacts consisted of service's contracts with Internet access providers and purchasers of service, which was delivered over Internet, alleged infringement and dilution occurred in Pennsylvania because purchasers received and viewed messages from service there, and manufacturer was Pennsylvania corporation and so would suffer injury there. Zippo Mfg. Co. v. Zippo Dog Com, Inc., W.D.Pa.1997, 952 F.Supp. 1119, 42 U.S.P.Q.2d 1062.

Exercise of personal jurisdiction over defendant computer news service would be reasonable in action by Pennsylvania manufacturer of "Zippo" tobacco lighters alleging trademark dilution, infringement, and false designation under Lanham Act based on service's use of Internet domain names "zippo.com," "zippo.net," and "zipponews.com"; Pennsylvania had strong interest in disputes invoking resident corporations' trademarks, manufacturer chose to seek relief in Pennsylvania, and service consciously chose to conduct business in Pennsylvania. Zippo Mfg. Co. v. Zippo Dot Com. Inc., W.D.Pa.1997, 952 F.Supp. 1119, 42 U.S.P.Q.2d 1062.

87. Trade secret misappropriation

Federal district court sitting in Pennsylvania had jurisdiction under state long-arm statute over British citizens alleged to have misappropriated complainant's trade secrets or confidential business information while testing complainant's proprietary medical technology in England; complainants had alleged that English citizens had committed tort in England resulting in injury in Pennsylvania and one defendant had accepted election as director of corporation in Pennsylvania. Supra Medical Corp. v. McGonigle, E.D.Pa. 1997, 955 F.Supp. 374.

88. Patent infringement

Mere feeling of effects of alleged patent infringement in Pennsylvania was not sufficient to subject nonresident to specific personal jurisdiction of court there, in absence of sufficient minumum contacts. Visual Sec. Concepts, Inc. v. KTV, Inc., E.D.Pa.2000, 102 F.Supp.2d 601.

89. Non-forum co-conspirator

Under Pennsylvania law, personal jurisdiction over a non-forum co-conspirator may be asserted only where a plaintiff demonstrates that substantial acts in furtherance of the conspiracy occurred in Pennsylvania and that the non-forum co-conspirator was aware or should have been aware of those acts. Santana Products, Inc. v. Bobrick Washroom Equipment, M.D.Pa.1998, 14 F.Supp.2d 710.

Personal jurisdiction over architectural representative for plaintiff's competitor under Pennsylvania long-arm statute could not be based on theory that co-conspirators committed acts within Pennsylvania which could be imputed to representative where no allegations or exhibits concerned activities that occurred within Pennsylvania, and there were no allegations that representative was aware or should have been aware of substantial acts in furtherance of alleged conspiracy occurring in Pennsylvania. Santana Products, Inc. v. Bobrick Washroom Equipment, M.D.Pa.1998, 14 F.Supp.2d 710.

§ 5323. Service of process on persons outside this Commonwealth

Rules of Civil Procedure

This section is not suspended or affected by the Rules of Civil Procedure, Rules 400 to 441, governing service of original process and other legal papers. See Rule 449.

Pa.R.C.P. 2098, 2148, 2173 and 2198, 42 Pa.C.S.A., referred to in the main volume italic note, were rescinded June 3, 1994, effective July 1, 1994.

Cross References

Service of process on corporations, etc., see Pa.R.C.P. Rule 424, 42 Pa.C.S.A.

Service outside the Commonwealth, see Pa.R.C.P. No. 404, 42 Pa.C.S.A.

Notes of Decisions

Tolling 17

1. In general

Nonresident defendant was not entitled to dismissal on basis of fact that service of process was made on him when he was present in state solely for purpose of giving testimony in another action where it appeared that he could have been served pursuant to state's long-arm statute. In re Arthur Treacher's Franchisee Litigation, E.D.Pa.1981, 92 F.R.D. 398.

Where a court ordered that service of process on a nonresident motorist-defendant whose whereabouts were unknown be made by serving both the Secretary of the Commonwealth and a Pennsylvania insurance adjuster retained by defendant's insurance carrier, the preliminary objections of the insurance adjuster alleging lack of jurisdiction and non-agency could be properly dismissed. Snyder v. Marion, 19 Pa. D. & C.3d 352 (1981).

5. Mailing process

Term, "any form of mail", in Pennsylvania statute governing service outside the Commonwealth encompasses private mail service and such service was proper in federal court action even if federal rules contemplate only public mail. Allen Organ Co. v. Elka S.p.A., E.D.Pa.1985, 615 F.Supp. 328, 227 U.S.P.Q. 973.

Service upon Japanese defendant by certified mail with return receipt was in compliance with applicable rules. Allen Organ Co. v. Kuwai Musical Instruments Mfg. Co., Ltd., E.D.Pa.1984, 593 F.Supp. 107, 224 U.S.P.Q. 907.

Service of process by mail was not proper under Pennsylvania law where plaintiff did not receive receipt of any kind from post office indicating that delivery had been accomplished or even attempted. Coil Co., Inc. v. Weather-Twin Corp., 1982, 539 F.Supp. 464.

Mere sending of registered mail addressed to nonresidents' last known addresses, whether received by them or not, would not constitute effective service of process under this section authorizing section by any form of mail addressed to person to be served and requiring signed receipt. National Expositions, Inc. v. DuBois, W.D.Pa.1983, 97 F.R.D. 400.

The Uniform Interstate and International Procedure Act, 42 Pa.C.S.A. § 5321 et seq., permitted service of a complaint by mail, and the provisions for such service had to be strictly followed; it did not matter that defendants ultimately received a copy if the statutory procedure had not been followed. Miller v. Stimpson, 20 Pa. D. & C.3d 31 (1981).

6. Substituted service

Federal diversity courts are bound by Pennsylvania court's construction of its own substitute service rules and statutes. National Expositions, Inc. v. DuBois, W.D.Pa.1983, 97 F.R.D. 400.

Before resort to substituted service may be had, plaintiff must have demonstrated good-faith effort to locate defendant through a more direct means and must comply with provisions of long-arm statute. Romeo v. Looks, 535 A.2d 1101, 369 Pa.Super. 608, Super. 1987, appeal denied 542 A.2d 1370, 518 Pa. 641, appeal denied 542 A.2d 1370, 518 Pa. 642.

Substituted service by newspaper of publication after sheriffs of two counties were unable to serve defendant in counties in which defendant had maintained a residence or had close relative who had maintained residence was reasonably calculated to provide defendant with actual notice of lawsuit based on information plaintiffs had in their possession at time of application. Romeo v. Looks, 535 A.2d 1101, 369 Pa.Super. 608, Super.1987, appeal denied 542 A.2d 1370, 518 Pa. 641, appeal denied 542 A.2d 1370, 518 Pa. 642.

For substituted service of process, service "reasonably calculated to give actual notice" is that which is reasonably certain to notify a defendant of litigation pending against him. Romeo v. Looks, 535 A.2d 1101, 369 Pa.Super. 608, Super.1987, appeal denied 542 A.2d 1370, 518 Pa. 641, appeal denied 542 A.2d 1370, 518 Pa. 642.

Substituted service upon defendant's motor vehicle insurer in action arising out of motor vehicle collision was proper under substituted service statute as it could be reasonably expected that notice of the action would be transmitted to defendant, and insurer did in fact make telephone contact with defendant, who was residing in Florida, after default judgment. Romeo v. Looks, 535 A.2d 1101, 369 Pa.Super. 608, Super.1987, appeal denied 542 A.2d 1370, 518 Pa. 641, appeal denied 542 A.2d 1370, 518 Pa. 642.

Substituted service on defendant through Pennsylvania Department of Motor Vehicles was rational where defendant owned motor vehicle while she was in Pennsylvania and mishap with her vehicle occurred in Pennsylvania. Romeo v. Looks, 535 A.2d 1101, 369 Pa.Super. 608, Super.1987, appeal denied 542 A.2d 1370, 518 Pa. 641, appeal denied 542 A.2d 1370, 518 Pa. 642.

8. Receipt of process

Service reasonably calculated to provide defendant with actual notice of suit was not rendered invalid by defendant's claimed inability to actually receive notice based on post hoc analysis of defendant's purported predicament of which she alone was aware at the time plaintiffs attempted various methods of service upon her. Romeo v. Looks, 535 A.2d 1101, 369 Pa.Super. 608, Super.1987, appeal denied 542 A.2d 1370, 518 Pa. 641, appeal denied 542 A.2d 1370, 518 Pa. 642.

Under the Uniform Interstate & International Procedure Act, 42 Pa.C.S. § 5323(a)(3), service of process is proper outside of the commonwealth by certified mail when addressed to the person to be served even though the return receipt is signed by the spouse of the person to be served. Engler v. City of Philadelphia, 34 Pa. D. & C.3d 30 (1984).

11. Defective service

Since plaintiffs in action alleging branch of oral personal service contract failed to conform to statutory requirements for service of process, there was no predicate

continued

for district court to exercise jurisdiction over a nonresident defendant, warranting dismissal. Bucks County Playhouse v. Bradshaw, E.D.Pa.1983, 577 F.Supp. 1203.

Where review of record revealed that plaintiffs had reasonable chance to ultimately serve nonresident defendants properly, insufficient service made as to such defendants would merely be quashed, rather than dismissing action as to them, and plaintiffs could again attempt to serve them with process. National Expositions, Inc. v. DuBois, W.D.Pa.1983, 97 F.R.D. 400.

Where record contained no fact which might support reasonable prospect of plaintiffs being able to serve nonresident defendants adequately with process, action would be dismissed as to such defendants for insufficiency of service. National Expositions, Inc. v. DuBois, W.D.Pa.1983, 97 F.R.D. 400.

Dismissal is not invariably required where service of process is found to be ineffective; rather, under such circumstances court has discretion either to dismiss or to quash service which has been made on defendants. National Expositions, Inc. v. DuBois, W.D.Pa.1983, 97 F.R.D. 400.

15. Due process

Due process, reduced to its most elemental component, requires notice, and the adequacy of notice as applied to substituted service of process, depends upon whether it is reasonably calculated to give the party actual notice of pending litigation. Romeo v. Looks, 535 A.2d 1101, 369 Pa.Super. 608, Super.1987, appeal denied 542 A.2d 1370, 518 Pa. 641, appeal denied 542 A.2d 1370, 518 Pa. 642.

17. Tolling

This section providing for basis of personal jurisdiction over persons outside Commonwealth precludes tooling of statute of limitations where plaintiff knows defendant's out-of-state address and can serve him there by certified mail. Bywaters v. Bywaters, E.D.Pa.1989, 721 F.Supp. 84, affirmed 902 F.2d 1559.

§ 5325. When and how a deposition may be taken outside this Commonwealth

Library References

Depositions, forms, motion for leave of court to take depositions, see Gibbons, 5 Pennsylvania Practice § 7.40.

Notes of Decisions

In general 1

1. In general

Trial court abused its discretion by allowing defendants' telephone deposition of witness on Friday before Monday trial; record did not indicate that notice was given to plaintiffs; trial court issued rule to show cause to plaintiffs three days before deposition; and defendants had at least four years after notice of lawsuit to depose witness. Wertz v. Kephart, 542 A.2d 1019, 374 Pa.Super. 274, Super.1988, appeal denied 554 A.2d 510, 520 Pa. 618, appeal denied 554 A.2d 511, 520 Pa. 619.

§ 5326. Assistance to tribunals and litigants outside this Commonwealth with respect to depositions

Library References

Foreign discovery, discovery in Pennsylvania for use in another state or country, discovery in Pennsylvania for use in proceedings pending in another state or country, in general, see Gibbons, 5 Pennsylvania Practice § 11.51.

Notes of Decisions

1. In general

Pursuant to this rule, a court may order a college to produce a student's records for use in a criminal proceeding in another jurisdiction. Com v. McPherson, 28 Pa. D. & C.3d 699 (1983).

§ 5327. Determination of foreign law

Library References

Judicial notice, judicial notice of law, see Packel & Poulin, 1 Pennsylvania Practice § 221.

105

CHAPTER

12

GOVERNMENT REGULATIONS/ ADMINISTRATIVE LAW

I. ORGANIZATION OF ADMINISTRATIVE LAW

Debate grows about the sheer volume of law and regulation in our society, particularly at the federal level. The tentacles of federal law seem to entwine every facet of life and community, from education to transportation, business and commerce to the environment. Federal law requires that any rules, and amendments thereto, be regularly published. After adoption, federal agency rules and regulations generally end up in the **Code of Federal Regulations** (C.F.R.), which can be found in any library listing itself as a government depository. See Figure 12.1 for sample C.F.R. pages.

PHOTO 12.1

§ 701.28 [Reserved]

§ 701.29 Designated counties.

The State committee in consultation with the State Forester, will designate the counties or parties of counties in which the program will be operated. The following will be considered in making the selections:

(a) The total acreage in the county devoted to desirable types of softwood and hardwood timber.

(b) The estimated area in the county that is under eligible ownership.

(c) The estimated acreage suitable for the production of forest products.

(d) The availability of funds.

(e) The enhancement of other forest resources.

§ 701.30 Eligible person, land, and ownerships.

(a) An eligible person is a private individual, group, Indian Tribe or other native group, association, corporation excluding corporations whose stocks are publicly traded, or other legal entity which owns eligible land. Firms principally engaged in the manufacture of wood products are not eligible. However, forest landowners who manufacture forest products on a part-time or irregular basis, are eligible.

(b) Eligible land is "nonindustrial" private forest land capable of producing at least 50 cubic feet of wood per acre per year.

(c) Eligible farms are those not exceeding a total of 1,000 acres of eligible private nonindustrial forest land in the United States or any commonwealth, territory or possession of the United States. The State Committee with the concurrence of the State Forester may approve cost-sharing with landowners owning more than 1,000 but not more than 5,000 acres of eligible forest land where it is deemed to be to the public's significant benefit.

(d) Significant public benefits are primarily those resulting from cost-effective timber production, with related benefits to aesthetics, recreation, other resource values, watershed protection and erosion reduction.

§ 701.31 Program funds.

(a) *State and counties.* Each designated State and county will receive a share of the funds provided nationally for the program. Funds will be distributed on the basis of the forest production opportunities in each State, considering the acreage of private nonindustrial forest lands, the number of eligible owners, the potential productivity of such lands and the need for reforestation, timber stand improvement, other forestry management needs, and the enhancement of other forest resources. The Director, Conservation and Environmental Protection Division, FSA, will allocate funds after consultation with representatives of the U.S. Forest Service and a committee of not less than five State foresters or equivalent State officials selected by a majority of the State foresters or equivalent State officials. The State committee will consult with the State forester when determining the allocation of such funds to the designated counties.

(b) A limitation on the amount of funds which may be obligated under long-term agreements shall be established by the State committee in accordance with guidelines provided by the Deputy Administrator, State and County Operations.

§ 701.32 Eligible practices and cost-share requirements.

(a) Cost-sharing may be available for the following National practices and authority:

(1) *Practice FP1.* Planting Trees.

(2) *Practice FP2.* Improving a Stand of Forest Trees.

(3) *Practice authority—SF Practice.* Special Forestry Practices. The Director, Conservation and Environmental Protection Division, FSA, after consultation with the Forest Service, may approve special forestry practices needed to solve a significant and unique local condition for which the National practices are not adequate. Such practices may be approved for inclusion in a county program after consultation with the program development group, and the recommendation of the county committee, the service forester, the State committee and the State forester.

(b) A forest management plan is required as a condition of cost-sharing.

The plan will be developed in consultation with the landowner,approved by the service forester, and will contain information for accurate evaluation of practice effectiveness. The participant will be required to perform those measures in the plan which are essential to the effectiveness of the practice for which costs are shared. In the development of the plan, consideration will be given to wildlife, watershed protection, recreation, erosion control, aesthetics, and other associated forest resources values as well as cost-effective timber production.

§ 701.33 The National program.

The National program is based on recommendations developed by the Director, Conservation and Environmental Protection Division, FSA, in consultation with representatives of the U.S. Forest Service and the committee of State foresters provided for in § 701.31.

§ 701.34 Development of State programs.

(a) A State program shall be developed in each State in accordance with the provisions contained in this part and in the National program and such modifications thereof as may thereafter be made. The program shall be developed by the State forestry committee as provided in § 701.2.

(b) The program for the State shall be that recommended by the State committee and State forester and approved by the Director, Conservation and Environmental Protection Division, FSA, after consulting the U.S. Forest Service.

§ 701.35 Development of county programs.

(a) A county program shall be developed in each designated county in accordance with the provisions of the State program and such modifications thereof as may be made. The county program shall be developed by the county conservation review group. The county conservation review group, working with the governing body of the conservation district, the State forestry agency representatives, the county supervisor of the Farmers Home Administration, and others with conservation and environmental interest, shall develop recommendations for the county program.

(b) The program for the county shall be that recommended by the county committee and service forester and approved by the State committee and State forester.

[45 FR 49522, July 25, 1980, as amended at 47 FR 46999, Oct. 22, 1982]

§ 701.36 Adaptation of practices.

(a) The practices included in the State program meet the conditions and requirements of the National program. National program provisions may be modified or deleted to make practices more restrictive where such changes meet the objectives of the program.

(b) The practices included in the county program must meet the conditions and requirements of the State program. State program provisions may be modified or deleted to make practices more restrictive where such changes will still result in the practices effectively meeting the objectives of the program.

§ 701.37 Levels and rates of cost-sharing.

(a) The maximum cost-share for each practice shall be the percentage of the actual cost of performing the practice considered necessary to obtain the needed performance of the practice, but which will be such that the participant will make a significant contribution to the cost of performing the practice.

(b) Levels of cost-sharing shall be approved by the State ASC committee and shall not be in excess of 65 percent of actual costs incurred by the landowners.

(c) For the purpose of establishing rates of cost-sharing, the average cost of performing a practice may be the average cost for a State, a county or a part of a county, as determined by the State committee.

(d) The rates of cost-sharing for practices included in the county program may be lower than the rates approved for general use in the State.

[45 FR 49222, July 25, 1980, as amended at 47 FR 20109, May 11, 1982]

Proposals for regulations, executive orders, and general bureaucratic news from the federal government are published in the **Federal Register**, which can be obtained as easily as the C.F.R. Because the C.F.R. is an annual publication, it is imperative that you consult the *Federal Register* in conjunction with any research concerning federal regulations. Both the C.F.R. and the *Federal Register* are fully available on the Web at (**http://www.gpoaccess.gov/fr/**).

At the state level, the researcher must ardently hope that there is a published set of regulations or rules of any particular agency. Some states regularly publish and freely distribute such information. A visit, a phone call, or an e-mail query to the agency itself, or a visit to its Web site (if there is one), will determine the strategy for acquiring state rules and regulations.

II. FINDING FEDERAL ADMINISTRATIVE LAW

The *Code of Federal Regulations* is organized and cited just like the *United States Code*, by title and section number. Consult the index if you do not have a specific citation; then locate the correct volumes containing the referenced title and section numbers. Federal regulations may not mirror the content of the *U.S. Code* in its entirety; that is, some *Code* sections do not have corresponding regulations. Therefore, be prepared for a lack of regulatory materials relevant to the research.

III. SUMMARY

The sheer size of government agencies, regulations, and laws tends to intimidate, but proficient legal researchers liberally use government resources. Federal regulations are compiled in the *Code of Federal Regulations* (C.F.R.). Any proposals for regulations, executive orders, and bureaucratic news will be found in the *Federal Register.* The researcher may have to try several avenues to discover pertinent state agency regulations.

IV. LEGAL RESEARCH ASSIGNMENTS

A. Exercise 12.1: *Code of Federal Regulations*

1. How many occupations can be classified by the broad occupational categories "light" or "sedentary"?
   a. 1,600–2,500
   b. 60
   c. 10,000
   d. 100
2. Transferability of skills is most easily demonstrated in the older worker, between the ages of 60–64.
   a. True
   b. False

3. A worker who claims a disability will generally have an easy time meeting the burden of proof if he or she is close to retirement, has little experience, and has minimal education.
   a. True
   b. False
4. Rule 202.07 will deny a finding of disability to a high school graduate with nontransferable skills.
   a. True
   b. False
5. Rule 202.09 makes it easier to declare an illiterate, unskilled person disabled.
   a. True
   b. False
6. Transferability of skills means that one's skills can be transferred *identically* from job to job.
   a. True
   b. False
7. Which of the following provisions guides the determination of disability?
   a. 42 U.S.C. 405
   b. 46 FR 29204
   c. 53 Stat. 1368, as amended
   d. All of the above
8. An individual with marginal education and long work experience, primarily unskilled, who has a severe impairment must retrain and retool for a new occupation.
   a. True
   b. False
9. Disability relates only to blindness.
   a. True
   b. False
10. "Medium" work requires some physical strength, more so than "sedentary".
   a. True
   b. False
11. The Social Security Administration has the right to order a claimant to consult with a physician or specialist for an independent review to determine disability.
   a. True
   b. False
12. What kind of impairment is required before a disability will be declared?
   a. Harsh
   b. Severe
   c. Terrible
   d. Frustrating
13. How long must the disability last for the person to receive benefits?
   a. 5 months
   b. 2 years
   c. 12 months
   d. None of the above

14. A person may have some physical impairment that will not interfere with basic work activities as described in 404.1520.
    a. True
    b. False
15. What is the content of the appendix referred to in 404.1520?
    a. Listing of impairments
    b. Residual functional capacity
    c. Evaluation of disability
    d. Severe mental distress

B. Exercise 12.2: *Code of Federal Regulations*

1. What title is the regulation included in?
    a. Regulations of the Department of Education
    b. *Code of Federal Regulations*
    c. State Grants Program
    d. Education
2. The *Federal Register* provision in volume 65, at 19606 and 19610, is the authority for enactment of this regulation.
    a. True
    b. False
3. The *United States Code* is not cross-referenced in the C.F.R.
    a. True
    b. False
4. The provision at 34 C.F.R. 611.11 is not applicable to postsecondary institutions.
    a. True
    b. False
5. In evaluating the quality of applications for state grants under the Teacher Quality Enhancements Program, the secretary uses which of the following categories for selection of funding recipients?
    a. Quality of project design
    b. Significance of the project
    c. Quality of the project resources
    d. Quality of the management plan
    e. All of the above

C. Exercise 12.3: *Code of Federal Regulations*

1. The Director of Security at NASA Headquarters is consulted prior to establishing any permanent security area in a NASA facility.
    a. True
    b. False
2. This regulation has not been changed since it was first created.
    a. True
    b. False

§ 404.1518 If you do not appear at a consultative examination.

(a) *General.* If you are applying for benefit and do not have a good reason for failing or refusing to take part in a consultative examination or test which we arrange for you to get information we need to determine your disability or blindness, we may find that you are not disabled or blind. If you are already receiving benefits and do not have a good reason for failing or refusing to take part in a consultative examination or test which we arranged for you, we may determine that your disability or blindness has stopped because of your failure or refusal. Therefore, if you have any reason why you cannot go for the scheduled appointment, you should tell us about this as soon as possible before the examination date. If you have a good reason, we will schedule another examination. We will consider your physical, mental, educational, and linguistic limitations (including any lack of facility with the English language) when determining if you have a good reason for failing to attend a consultative examination.

(b) *Examples of good reasons for failure to appear.* Some examples of what we consider good reasons for not going to a scheduled examination include—

(1) Illness on the date of the scheduled examination or test:

(2) Not receiving timely notice of the scheduled examination or test, or receiving no notice at all;

(3) Being furnished incorrect or incomplete information, or being given incorrect information about the physician involved or the time or place of the examination or test, or:

(4) Having had death or serious illness occur in your immediate family.

(c) *Objections by your physician.* If any of your treating physicians tell you that you should not take the examination or test, you should tell us at once. In many cases, we may be able to get the information we need in another way. Your physician may agree to another type of examination for the same purpose.

[45 FR 55584. Aug. 20, 1980, as amended at 59 FR 1635, Jan. 12, 1994]

STANDINGS TO BE USED IN DETERMINING WHEN A CONSULTATIVE EXAMINATION WILL BE OBTAINED IN CONNECTION WITH DISABILITY DETERMINATIONS

§ 404.1519 The consultative examination.

A consultative examination is a physical or mental examination or test purchased for you at our request and expense from a treating source or another medical source, including a pediatrician when appropriate. The decision to purchase a consultative examination will be made on an individual case basis in accordance with the provisions of §§ 404.1519a through 404.1519f. Selection of the source for the examination will be consistent with the provisions of § 404.1519j. The rules and procedures for requesting consultative examinations set forth in §§ 404.1519a and 404.1519b are applicable at the reconsideration and hearing levels of review, as well as the initial level of determination.

[56 FR 36956. Aug. 1, 1991, as amended at 65 FR 11875. Mar. 7, 2000]

§ 404.1519a When we will purchase a consultative examination and how we will use it.

(a)(1) *General.* The decision to purchase a consultative examination for you will be made after we have given full consideration to whether the additional information needed (e.g., clinical findings, laboratory tests, diagnosis, and prognosis) is readily available from the records of your medical sources. See § 404.1512 for the procedures we will follow to obtain evidence from your medical sources. Before purchasing a consultative examination, we will consider not only existing medical reports, but also the disability interview form containing your allegations as well as other pertinent evidence in your file.

(2) When we purchase a consultative examination, we will use the report from the consultative examination to try to resolve a conflict or ambiguity if one exists. We will

needed medical evidence the file does not contain such as clinical findings, laboratory tests, a diagnosis or prognosis necessary for decision.

(b) *Situations requiring a consultative examination.* A consultative examination may be purchased when the evidence as a whole, both medical and nonmedical, is not sufficient to support a decision on your claim. Other situations, including but not limited to the situations listed below, will normally require a consultative examination:

(1) The additional evidence needed is not contained in the records of your medical sources;

(2) The evidence that may have been available from your treating or other medical sources cannot be obtained for reasons beyond your control, such as death or noncooperation of a medical source;

(3) Highly technical or specialized medical evidence that we need is not available from your treating or other medical sources;

(4) A conflict, inconsistency, ambiguity or insufficiency in the evidence must be resolved, and we are unable to do so by recontacting your medical source; or

(5) There is an indication of a change in your condition that is likely to affect your ability to work, but the current severity of your impairment is not established.

[56 FR 36956. Aug. 1, 1991]

§ 404.1519b When we will not purchase a consultative examination.

We will not purchase a consultative examination in situations including, but not limited to, the following situations:

(a) In period of disability and disability insurance benefit claims, when you do not meet the insured status requirement in the calendar quarter you allege you became disabled or later and there is no possibility of establishing an earlier onset;

(b) In claims for widow's or widower's benefits based on disability, when your alleged month of disability is after the end of the 7-year period specified in §404335(c)(1) and there is no possibility of establishing an earlier onset date, or when the 7-year period expired in the past and there is no possibility of establishing an onset date prior to the date the 7-year period expired;

(c) In disability insurance benefit claims, when your insured status expired in the past and there is no possibility of establishing an onset date prior to the date your insured status expired;

(d) When any issues about your actual performance of substantial gainful activity or gainful activity have not been resolved;

(e) In claims for child's benefits based on disability, when it is determined that your alleged disability did not begin before the month you attained age 22, and there is no possibility of establishing an onset date earlier than the month in which your attained age 22;

(f) In claims for child's benefits based on disability that are filed concurrently with the insured individual's claim and entitlement cannot be established for the insured individual;

(g) In claims for child's benefits based on disability where entitlement is precluded based on other nondisability factors.

[56 FR 36956. Aug. 1, 1991]

STANDARDS FOR THE TYPE OF REFERRAL AND FOR REPORT CONTENT

§ 404.1519f Type of purchased examinations.

We will purchase only the specific examinations and tests we need to make a determination in your claim. For example, we will not authorize a comprehensive medical examination when the only evidence we need is a special test, such as an X-ray, blood studies, or an electrocardiogram.

[56 FR 36956, Aug. 1, 1991]

§ 404.1519g Who we will select to perform a consultative examination.

(a) We will purchase a consultative examination only from a qualified medical source. The medical source may be your own physician or psychologist, or another source. If you are a child, the medical source we choose may be a pediatrician. For a more complete list of medial sources, see § 404.1513.

(b) By "qualified," we mean that the medical source must be currently licensed in the State and have the training and experience to perform the type of examinations or test we will request; the medical source must not be barred from participation in our programs under the provisions of § 404.1503a. The medical source must also have the equipment required to provide an adequate assessment and record of the existence and level of severity of your alleged impairments.

(c) The medical source we choose may use support staff to help perform the consultative examination. Any such support staff (e.g, X-ray technician, nurse) must meet appropriate licensing or certification requirements of the State. See § 404.1503a.

[56 FR 36957. Aug. 1, 1991. as amended at 65 FR 11876. Mar. 7, 2000]

§ 404.1519h Your treating source.

When in our judgment your treating source is qualified, equipped, and willing to perform the additional examination or tests for the fee schedule payment, and generally furnishes complete and timely reports, your treating source will be the preferred source to do the purchased examination. Even if only a supplemental test is required, your treating source is ordinarily the preferred source.

[65 FR 11876. Mar. 7, 2000]

§ 404.1519i Other sources for consultative examinations.

We will use a medical source other than your treating source for a purchased examination or test in situations including, but not limited to, the following situations:

(a) Your treating source prefers not to perform such an examination or does not have the equipment to provide the specific data needed;

(b) There are conflicts or inconsistencies in your life that cannot be resolved by going back to your treating source;

(c) You prefer a source other than your treating source and have a good reason for your preference;

(d) We know from prior experience that your treating source may not be a productive source, *e.g.*, he or she has consistently failed to provide complete or timely reports.

[65 FR 11876. Mar. 7, 2000]

§ 404.1519j Objections to the medical source designated to perform the consultative examination.

You or your representative may object to your being examined by a medical source we have designated to perform a consultative examination. If there is a good reason for the objection, we will schedule the examination with another medical source. A good reason may be that the medical source we designated had previously represented an interest adverse to you. For example, the medical source may have represented your employer in a workers' compensation case or may have been involved in an insurance claim or legal action adverse to you. Other things we will consider include: The presence of a language barrier, the medical source's office location, (*e.g.*, 2nd floor, no elevator), travel restrictions, and whether the medical source had examined you in connection with a previous disability determination or decision that was unfavorable to you. If your objection is that a medical source allegedly "lacks objectivity" in general, but not in relation to you personally, we will review the allegations. See § 404.1519s. To avoid a delay in processing your claim, the consultative examination in your case will be changed to another medical source while a review is being conducted. We will handle any objection to use of the substitute medical source in the same manner. However, if we had previously conducted such a review and found that the reports of the medical source in question conformed to our guidelines, we will not change your examination.

[65 FR 11876, Mar. 7, 2000]

§ 404.1519k Purchase of medical examinations, laboratory tests, and other services.

We may purchase medical examinations, including psychiatric and psychological examinations, X-rays and laboratory tests (including specialized tests, such as pulmonary function studies, electrocardiograms, and stress tests) from a medical source.

continued

(a) The rate of payment to be used for purchasing medical or other services necessary to make determinations of disability may not exceed the highest rate paid by Federal or public agencies in the State for the same or similar types of services. See §§ 404.1624 and 404.1626.

(b) If a physician's bill or a request for payment for a physician's services includes a charge for a laboratory test for which payment may be made under this part, the amount payable with respect to the test shall be determined as follows:

(1) If the bill or request for payment indicates that the test was personally performed or supervised by the physician who submitted the bill (or for whose services the request for payment was made) or by another physician with whom that physician shares his or her practice, the payment will be based on the physician's usual and customary charge for the test or the rates of payment which the State uses for purchasing such services, whichever is the lesser amount.

(2) If the bill or request for payment indicates that the test was performed by an independent laboratory, the amount of reimbursement will not exceed the billed cost of the independent laboratory or the rate of payment which the State uses for purchasing such services, whichever is the lesser amount. A nominal payment may be made to the physician for collecting, handling and shipping a specimen to the laboratory if the physician bills for such a service. The total reimbursement may not exceed the rate of payment which the State uses for purchasing such services.

(c) The State will assure that it can support the rate of payment it uses. The State shall also be responsible for monitoring and overseeing the rate of payment it uses to ensure compliance with paragraphs (a) and (b) of this section.

[56 FR 36957. Aug. 1, 1991, as amended at 65 FR 11876. Mar. 7, 2000]

§ 404.1519m Diagnostic tests or procedures.

We will request the results of any diagnostic tests or procedures that have been performed as part of a workup by your treating source or other medical source and will use the results to help us evaluate impairment severity or prognosis. However, we will not order diagnostic tests or procedures that involve significant risk to you, such as myelograms, arteriograms, or cardiac catheterizations for the evaluation of disability under the Social Security program. Also, a State agency medial consultant must approve the ordering of any diagnostic test or procedure when there is a chance it may involve significant risk. The responsibility for deciding whether to perform the examination rests with the medical source designated to perform the consultative examination.

[56 FR 36957. Aug. 1, 1991, as amended at 65 FR 11876. Mar. 7, 2000]

§ 404.1519n Informing the medical source of examination scheduling, report content, and signature requirements.

The medical sources who perform consultative examinations will have a good understanding of our disability programs and their evidentiary requirements. They will be made fully aware of their responsibilities and obligations regarding confidentiality as described in § 401.105(e). We will fully inform medical sources who perform consultative examinations at the time we first contact them, and at subsequent appropriate intervals, of the following obligations:

(a) *Scheduling.* In scheduling full consultative examinations, sufficient time should be allowed to permit the medical source to take a case history and perform the examination, including any needed tests. The following minimum scheduling intervals (i.e., time set side for the individual, not the actual duration of the consultative examination) should be used.

(1) Comprehensive general medical examination—at least 30 minutes;

(2) Comprehensive musculoskeletal or neurological examination—at least 20 minutes;

(3) Comprehensive psychiatric examination—at least 40 minutes;

(4) Psychological examination—at least 60 minutes (Additional time may be required depending on types of psychological tests administered); and

(5) All others—at least 30 minutes, or in accordance with accepted medical practices.

We recognize that actual practice will dictate that some examinations may require longer scheduling intervals depending on the circumstances in a particular situation. We also recognize that these minimum intervals may have to be adjusted to allow for those claimants who do not attend their scheduled examination. The purpose of these minimum scheduling timeframes is to ensure that such examinations are complete and that sufficient time is made available to obtain the information needed to make an accurate determination in your case. State agencies will monitor the scheduling of examinations (through their normal consultative examination oversight activities) to ensure that any overscheduling is avoided, as overscheduling may lead to examinations that are not thorough.

(b) *Report content.* The reported results of your medical history, examination, requested laboratory findings, discussions and conclusions must conform to accepted professional standards and practices in the medical field for a complete and competent examination. The facts in a particular case and the information and findings already reported in the medical and other evidence of record will dictate the extent of detail needed in the consultative examination report for that case. Thus, the detail and format for reporting the results of a purchased examination will vary depending upon the type of examination or testing requested. The reporting of information will differ from one type of examination to another when the requested examination relates to the performance of tests such as ventilatory function tests, treadmill exercise tests, or audiological tests. The medical report must be complete enough to help us determine the nature, severity, and duration of the impairment, and residual functional capacity. The report should reflect your statement of your symptoms, not simply the medical source's statements or conclusions. The medical source's report of the consultative examination should include the objective medical facts as well as observations and opinions.

(c) *Elements of a complete consultative examination.* A complete consultative examination is one which involves all the elements of a standard examination in the applicable medical specialty. When the report of a complete consultative examination is involved, the report should include the following elements:

(1) Your major or chief complaint(s);

(2) A detailed description, within the area of specialty of the examination, of the history of your major complaint(s);

(3) A description, and disposition, of pertinent "positive" and "negative" detailed findings based on the history, examination and laboratory tests related to the major complaint(s), and any other abnormalities or lack thereof reported or found during examination or laboratory testing;

(4) The results of laboratory and other tests (e.g., X-rays) performed according to the requirements stated in the Listing of Impairments (see appendix 1 of this subpart P);

(5) The diagnosis and prognosis for your impairment(s);

(6) A statement about what you can still do despite your impairment(s), unless the claim is based on statutory blindness. This statement should describe the opinion of the medical source about your ability, despite your impairment(s), to do work-related activities, such as sitting, standing, walking, lifting, carrying, handling objects, hearing, speaking, and traveling; and, in cases of mental impairment(s), the opinion of the medical source about your ability to understand, to carry out and remember instructions, and to respond appropriately to supervision, coworkers and work pressures in a work setting. Although we will ordinarily request, as part of the consultative examination process, a medical source statement about what you can still do despite your impairment(s), the absence of such a statement in a consultative examination report will not make the report incomplete. See § 404.1527; and

(7) In addition, the medical source will consider, and provide some explanation or comment on, your major complaint(s) and

continued

any other abnormalities found during the history and examination or reported from the laboratory tests. The history, examination, evaluation of laboratory test results, and the conclusions will represent the information provided by the medical source who signs the report.

(d) *When a complete consultative examination is not required.* When the evidence we need does not require a complete consultative examination (for example, we need only a specific laboratory test result to complete the record), we may not require a report containing all of the elements in paragraph (c).

(e) *Signature requirements.* All consultative examination reports will be personally reviewed and signed by the medical source who actually performed the examination. This attests to the fact that the medical source doing the examination or testing is solely responsible for the report contents and for the conclusions, explanations or comments provided with respect to the history, examination and evaluation of laboratory test results. The signature of the medical source on a report annotated "not proofed" or "dictated but not read" is not acceptable. A rubber stamp signature of a medical source or the medical source's signature entered by any other person is not acceptable.

[56 FR 36958. Aug. 1, 1991, as amended at 65 FR 11876. May. 7, 2000]

§ 404.1519o When a properly signed consultative examination report has not been received.

If a consultative examination report is received unsigned or improperly signed we will take the following action.

(a) *When we will make determinations and decisions without a properly signed report.* We will make a determination or decision in the circumstances specified in paragraphs (a)(1) and (a)(2) of this section without waiting for a properly signed consultative examination report. After we have made the determination or decision, we will obtain a properly signed report and include it in the file unless the medical source who performed the original consultative examination has died:

(1) Continuous period of disability allowance with an onset date as alleged or earlier than alleged; or

(2) Continuance of disability.

(b) *When we will not make determinations and decisions without a properly signed report.* We will not use an unsigned or improperly signed consultative examination report to make the determinations or decisions specified in paragraphs (b)(1), (b)(2), (b)(3), and (b)(4) of this section. When we need a properly signed consultative examination report to make these determinations or decisions, we must obtain such a report. If the signature of the medical source who performed the original examination cannot be obtained because the medical source is out of the country for an extended period of time, or on an extended vacation, seriously ill, deceased, or for any other reason, the consultative examination will be rescheduled with another medical source:

(1) Denial; or

(2) Cessation; or

(3) Allowance of a period of disability which has ended; or

(4) Allowance with an onset date later than alleged.

[56 FR 36958. Aug. 1, 1991, as amended at 65 FR 11877, Mar. 7, 2000]

§ 404.1519p Reviewing reports of consultative examinations.

(a) We will review the report of the consultative examination to determine whether the specific information requested has been furnished. We will consider the following factors in reviewing the report:

(1) Whether the report provides evidence which serves as an adequate basis for decisionmaking in terms of the impairment it assesses;

(2) Whether the report is internally consistent; Whether all the diseases, impairments and complaints described in the history are adequately assessed and reported in the clinical findings; Whether the conclusions correlate the findings from your medical history, clinical examination and laboratory tests and explain all abnormalities;

(3) Whether the report is consistent with the other information available to us within the specialty of the examination requested; Whether the report fails to mention an

important or relevant complaint within that specialty that is noted in other evidence in the file (e.g., your blindness in one eye, amputations, pain, alcoholism, depression);

(4) Whether this is an adequate report of examination as compared to standards set out in the course of a medical education; and

(5) Whether the report is properly signed.

(b) If the report is inadequate or incomplete, we will contact the medical source who performed the consultative examination, give an explanation of our evidentiary needs, and ask that the medical source furnish the missing information or prepare a revised report.

(c) With your permission, or when the examination discloses new diagnostic information or test results that reveal a potentially life-threatening situation, we will refer the consultative examination report to your treating source. When we refer the consultative examination report to your treating source without your permission, we will notify you that we have done so.

(d) We will perform ongoing special management studies on the quality of consultative examinations purchased from major medical sources and the appropriateness of the examinations authorized.

(e) We will take steps to ensure that consultative examinations are scheduled only with medical sources who have access to the equipment required to provide an adequate assessment and record of the existence and level of severity of your alleged impairments.

[56 FR 36959. Aug. 1, 1991, as amended at 65 FR 11877, Mar. 7, 2000]

§ 404.1519q Conflict of interest.

All implications of possible conflict of interest between medical or psychological consultants and their medical or psychological practices will be avoided. Such consultants are not only those physicians and psychologists who work for us directly but are also those who do review and adjudication work in the State agencies. Physicians and psychologists who work for us directly as employees or under contract will not work concurrently for a State agency. Physicians and psychologists who do review work for us will not perform consultative examinations for us without our prior approval. In such situations, the physician or psychologist will disassociate himself or herself from further involvement in the case and will not participate in the evaluation, decision, or appeal actions. In addition, neither they, nor any member of their families, will acquire or maintain, either directly or indirectly, any financial interest in a medical partnership, corporation, or similar relationship in which consultative examinations are provided. Sometimes physicians and psychologists who do review work for us will have prior knowledge of a case; for example, when the claimant was a patient. Where this is so, the physician or psychologist will not participate in the review or determination of the case. This does not preclude the physician or psychologist from submitting medical evidence based on treatment or examination of the claimant.

[56 FR 36959. Aug. 1, 1991]

Authorizing and Monitoring the Referral Process

§ 404.1519s Authorizing and monitoring the consultative examination.

(a) Day-to-day responsibility for the consultative examination process rests with the State agencies that make disability determination for us.

(b) The State agency will maintain a good working relationship with the medical community in order to recruit sufficient numbers of physicians and other providers of medical services to ensure ready availability of consultative examination providers.

(c) Consistent with Federal and State laws, the State agency administrator will work to achieve appropriate rates of payment for purchased medical services.

(d) Each State agency will be responsible for comprehensive oversight management of its consultative examination program, with special emphasis on key providers.

(e) A key consultative examination provider is a provider that meets at least one of the following conditions:

(1) Any consultative examination provider with an estimated annual billing to the Social Security disability programs of at least $100,000; or

(2) Any consultative examination provider with a practice directed primarily towards evaluation examinations rather than the treatment of patients; or

(3) Any consultative examination provider that does not meet the above criteria, but is one of the top five consultative examination providers in the State by dollar volume, as evidenced by prior year data.

(f) State agencies have flexibility in managing their consultative examination programs, but at a minimum will provide:

(1) An ongoing active recruitment program for consultative examination providers;

(2) A process for orientation, training, and review of new consultative examination providers, with respect to SSA's program requirements involving consultative examination report content and not with respect to medical techniques;

(3) Procedures for control of scheduling consultative examinations;

(4) Procedures to ensure that close attention is given to specific evaluation issues involved in each case;

(5) Procedures to ensure that only required examinations and tests are authorized in accordance with the standards set forth in this subpart;

(6) Procedures for providing medical or supervisory approval for the authorization or purchase of consultative examinations and for additional tests or studies requested by consulting medical sources. This includes physician approval for the ordering of any diagnostic test or procedure where the question of significant risk to the claimant/beneficiary might be raised. See § 404.1519m.

(7) Procedures for the ongoing review of consultative examination results to ensure compliance with written guidelines;

(8) Procedures to encourage active participation by physicians in the consultative examination oversight program;

(9) Procedures for handling complaints;

(10) Procedures for evaluating claimant reactions to key providers; and

(11) A program of systematic, onsite reviews of key providers that will include annual onsite reviews of such providers when claimants are present for examinations. This provision does not contemplate that such reviews will involve participation in the actual examinations but, rather, offer an opportunity to talk with claimants at the provider's site before and after the examination and to review the provider's overall operation.

(g) The State agencies will cooperate with us when we conduct monitoring activities in connection with their oversight management of their consultative examination programs.

[56 FR 36959. Aug. 1, 1991, as amended at 65 FR 11877, Mar. 7, 2000]

Procedures to Monitor the Consultative Examination

§ 404.1519t Consultative examination oversight.

(a) We will ensure that referrals for consultative examinations and purchases of consultative examinations are made in accordance with our policies. We will also monitor both the referral processes and the product of the consultative examinations obtained. This monitoring may include reviews by independent medical specialists under direct contract with SSA.

(b) Through our regional offices, we will undertake periodic comprehensive reviews of each State agency to evaluate each State's management of the consultative examination process. The review will involve visits to key providers, with State staff participating, including a program physician when the visit will deal with medical techniques or judgment, or factors that go to the core of medical professionalism.

(c) We will also perform ongoing special management studies of the quality of consultative examinations purchased from key providers and other sources and the appropriateness of the examinations authorized.

[56 FR 36960, Aug. 1, 1991]

EVALUATION OF DISABILITY

§ 404.1520 Evaluation of disability in general.

(a) *Steps in evaluating disability.* We consider all evidence in your case record when we make a determination or decision whether you are disabled. When you file a claim for a period of disability and/or disability insurance benefits or for child's benefits based on disability, we use the following evaluation process. If you are doing substantial gainful activity, we will determine that you are not disabled. If you are not doing substantial gainful activity, we will first consider the effect of your physical or mental impairment; if you have more than one impairment, we will also consider the combined effect of your impairments. Your impairment(s) must be severe and meet the duration requirement before we can find you to be disabled. We follow a set order to determine whether you are disabled. We review any current work activity, the severity of your impairment(s), your residual functional capacity, your past work, and your age, education, and work experience. If we can find that you are disabled or not disabled at any point in the review, we do not review your claim further. Once you have been found entitled to disability benefits, we follow a somewhat different order of evaluation to determine whether your entitlement continues, as explained in § 404.1594(f).

(b) *If you are working.* If you are working and the work you are doing is substantial gainful activity, we will find that you are not disabled regardless of your medical condition or your age, education, and work experience.

(c) *You must have a severe impairment.* If you do not have any impairment or combination of impairments which significantly limits your physical or mental ability to do basic work activities, we will find that you do not have a severe impairment and are, therefore, not disabled. We will not consider your age, education, and work experience. However, it is possible for you to have a period of disability for a time in the past even through you do not now have a severe impairment.

(d) *When your impairment(s) meets or equals a listed impairment in appendix 1.* If you have an impairment(s) which meets the duration requirement and is listed in appendix 1 or is equal to a listed impairment(s), we will find you disabled without considering your age, education, and work experience.

(e) *Your impairment(s) must prevent you from doing past relevant work.* If we cannot make a decision based on your current work activity or on medical facts alone, and you have a severe impairment(s), we then review your residual functional capacity and the physical and mental demands of the work you have done in the past. If you can still do this kind of work, we will find that you are not disabled.

(f) *Your impairment(s) must prevent you from doing any other work.* (1) If you cannot do any work you have done in the past because you have a severe impairment(s), we will consider your residual functional capacity and your age, education, and past work experience to see if you can do other work. If you cannot, we will find you disabled.

(2) If you have only a marginal education, and long work experience (i.e., 35 years or more) where you only did arduous unskilled physical labor, and you can no longer do this kind of work, we use a different rule (see § 404.1562).

[50 FR 8727. Mar. 5, 1985; 50 FR 19164. May 7, 1985, as amended at 56 FR 36960. Aug. 1, 1991; 65 FR 80308. Dec. 21, 2000]

§ 404.1520a Evaluation of mental impairments.

(a) *General.* The steps outlined in § 404.1520 apply to the evaluation of physical and mental impairments. In addition, when we evaluate the severity of mental impairments for adults (persons age 18 and over) and in persons under age 18 when Part A of the Listing of Impairments is used, we must follow a special technique at each level in the administrative review process. We describe this special technique in paragraphs (b) through (e) of this section. Using the technique helps us:

(1) Identify the need for additional evidence to determine impairment severity;

(2) Consider and evaluate functional consequences of the mental disorder(s) relevant to your ability to work; and

continued

or

J. Diarrhea, lasting for 1 month or longer, resistant to treatment, and requiring hydration, intravenous alimentation, or tube feeding.

or

K. Cardiomyopathy, as described under the criteria in 104.00ff or 1.04.

or

L. Lymphoid interstitial pneumonia/pulmonary lymphoid hyperplasia (LIP/PLH complex), with respiratory symptoms that significantly interfere with age-appropriate activities, and that cannot be controlled by prescribed treatment.

or

M. Nephropathy, as described under the criteria in 106.00

or

N. One or more of the following infections (other than described in A–M, above), resistant to treatment or requiring hospitalization or intravenous treatment 3 or more times in 1 year (or evaluate sequelae under the criteria for the affected body system):

1. Sepsis:
2. Miningitis; or
3. Pneumonia; or
4. Septic arthritis; or
5. Endocarditis; or
6. Radiographically documented sinusitis, or

O. Any other manifestation(s) or HIV infection (including any listed in 114.08A–N, but without the requisite findings, e.g., oral candidiasis not meeting the criteria in 114.08F, diarrhea not meeting the criteria in 114.08J, or any other manifestation(s), e.g., oral hairy leukoplakia, hepatomegaly), resulting in one of the following:

1. For children from birth to attainment of age 1, at least one of the criteria in paragraphs A–E of 112.12; or
2. For children age 1 to attainment of age 3, at leastone of the appropriate age-group criteria in paragraph B1 of 112.02; or
3. For children age 3 to attainment of age 18, at least two of the appropriate age-group criteria in paragraph B2 of 112.02.

[50 FR 35066, Aug. 28, 1985]

EDITORIAL NOTE 1: FOR FEDERAL REGISTER citations affecting appendix 1 to subpart P of part 404, see the List of CFR Sections Affected, which appears in the Finding Aids section of the printed volume and on GPO Access.

APPENDIX 2 TO SUBPART P OF PART 404—MEDICAL-VOCATIONAL GUIDELINES

200.00 *Introduction.* (a) The following rules reflect the major functional and vocational patterns which are encountered in cases which cannot be evaluated on medical considerations alone, where an individual with a severe medically determinable physical or mental impairment(s) is not engaging in substantial gainful activity and the individual's impairment(s) prevents the performance of his or her vocationally relevant past work. They also reflect the analysis of the various vocational factors (i.e., age, education, and work experience) in combination with the individual's residual functional capacity (used to determine his or her maximum sustained work capability for sedentary, light, medium, heavy, or very heavy work) in evaluating the individual's ability to engage in substantial gainful activity in other than his or her vocationally relevant past work. Where the findings of fact made with respect to a particular individual's vocational factors and residual functional capacity coincided with all of the criteria of a particular rule, the rule directs a conclusion as to whether the individual is or is not disabled. However, each of these findings of fact is subject to rebuttal and the individual may present evidence to refute such findings. Where any one of the findings of fact does not coincide with the corresponding criterion of a rule, the rule does not apply in that particular case and, accordingly, does not direct a conclusion of disabled or not disabled. In any instance where a rule does not apply, full consideration must be given to all of the relevant facts of the case in accordance with the definitions and discussions of each factor in the appropriate sections of the regulations.

(b) The existence of jobs in the national economy is reflected in the "Decisions" shown in the rules: i.e., in promulgating the rules, administrative notice has been taken of the numbers of unskilled jobs that exist throughout the national economy at the various functional levels (sedentary, light, medium, heavy, and very heavy) as supported by the "Dictionary of Occupational Titles" and the "Occupational Outlook Handbook," published by the Department of Labor; the

"County Business Patterns" and "Census Surveys" published by the Bureau of the Census; and occupational surveys of light and sedentary jobs prepared for the Social Security Administration by various State employment agencies. Thurs, when all factors coincide with the criteria of a rule, the existence of such jobs is established. However, the existence of such jobs for individuals whose remaining functional capacity or other factors do not coincide with the criteria of a rule must be further considered in terms of what kinds of jobs or types of work may be either additionally indicated or precluded.

(c) In the application of the rules, the individual's residual functional capacity (i.e., the maximum degree to which the individual retains the capacity for sustained performance of the physical-mental requirements of jobs), age, education, and work experience must first be determined. When assessing the person's residual functional capacity, we consider his or her symptoms (such as pain), signs, and laboratory findings together with other evidence we obtain.

(d) The correct disability decision (i.e., on the issue of ability to engage in substantial gainful activity) is found by then locating the individual's specific vocational profile. If an individual's specific profile is not listed within this appendix 2, a conclusion of disabled or not disabled is not directed. Thus, for example, an individual's ability to engage in substantial gainful work where his or her residual functional capacity falls between the ranges of work indicated in the rules (e.g., the individual who can perform more than light but less than medium work), is decided on the basis of the principles and definitions in the regulations, giving consideration to the rules for specific case situations in this appendix 2. These rules represent various combinations of exertional capabilities, age, education and work experience and also provide an overall structure for evaluation of those cases in which the judgments as to each factor do not coincide with those of any specific rule. Thus, when the necessary judgments have been made as to each factor and it is found that no specific rule applies, the rules still provide guidance for decisionmaking, such as in cases involving combinations of impairments. For example, if strength limitations resulting from an individual's impairment(s) considered with the judgments made as to the individual's age, education and work experience correspond to (or closely approximate) the factors of a particular rule, the adjudicator then has a frame of reference for considering the jobs or types of work precluded by other, nonexertional impairments in terms of numbers of jobs remaining for a particular individual.

(e) Since the rules are predicated on an individual's having an impairment which manifests itself by limitation in meeting the strength requirements of jobs, they may not be fully applicable where the nature of an individual's impairment does not result in such limitations, e.g., certain mental, sensory, or skin impairments. In addition, some impairments my result solely in postural and manipulative limitations or environmental restrictions. Environmental restrictions are those restrictions which result in inability to tolerate some physical feature(s) of work settings that occur in certain industries or types of work, e.g., an inability to tolerate dust or fumes.

(1) In the evaluation of disability where the individual has solely a nonexertional type of impairment, determination as to whether disability exists shall be based on the principles in the appropriate sections of the regulations, giving consideration to the rules for specific case situations in this appendix 2. The rules do not direct factual conclusions of disabled or not disabled for individuals with solely nonexertional types of impairments.

(2) However, where an individual has an impairment or combination of impairments resulting in both strength limitations and nonexertional limitations, the rules in this subpart are considered in determining first whether a finding of disabled may be possible based on the strength limitations alone and, if not, the rule(s) reflecting the individual's maximum residual strength capabilities, age, education, and work experience provide a framework for consideration of how much the individual's work capability is further diminished in terms of any types of jobs that would be contraindicated by the nonexertional limitations. Also, in these combinations of nonexertional and exertional limitations which cannot be wholly determined under the rules in this appendix 2, full consideration must be given to all of the relevant facts in the case in accordance with the definitions and discussions of each factor in the appropriate sections of the regulations, which will provide insight into the adjudicative weight to be accorded each factor.

201.00 *Maximum sustained work capability limited to sedentary work as a result of severe medically determinable impairment(s).* (a) Most sedentary occupations fall within the skilled, semi-skilled, professional, administrative, technical, clerical, and benchwork classifications. Approximately 200 separate unskilled sedentary occupations can be identified, each representing numerous jobs in the national economy. Approximately 85 percent of these jobs are in the machine trades and benchwork occupational categories. These jobs (unskilled sedentary occupations) may be performed after a short demonstration or within 30 days.

(b) These unskilled sedentary occupations are standard within the industries in which they exist. While sedentary work represents a significantly restricted range of work, this range in itself is not so

continued

prohibitively restricted as to negate work capability for substantial gainful activity.

(c) Vocational adjustment to sedentary work may be expected where the individual has special skills or experience relevant to sedentary work or where age and basic educational competences provide sufficient occupational mobility to adapt to the major segment of unskilled sedentary work. Inability to engage in substantial gainful activity would be indicated where an individual who is restricted to sedentary work because of a severe medically determinable impairment lacks special skills or experience relevant to sedentary work, lacks educational qualifications relevant to most sedentary work (e.g., has a limited education or less) and the individual's age, though not necessarily advanced, is a factor which significantly limits vocational adaptability.

(d) The adversity of functional restrictions to sedentary work at advanced age (55 and over) for individuals with no relevant past work or who can no longer perform vocationally relevant past work and have no transferable skills, warrants a finding of disabled in the absence of the rare situation where the individual has recently completed education which provides a basis for direct entry into skilled sedentary work. Advanced age and a history of unskilled work or no work experience would ordinarily offset any vocational advantages that might accrue by reason of any remote past education, whether it is more or less than limited education.

(e) The presence of acquired skills that are readily transferable to a significant range of skilled work within an individual's residual functional capacity would ordinarily warrant a finding of ability to engage in substantial gainful activity regardless of the adversity of age, or whether the individual's formal education is commensurate with his or her demonstrated skill level. The acquisition of work skills demonstrates the ability to perform work at the level of complexity demonstrated by the skill level attained regardless of the individual's formal educational attainments.

(f) In order to find transferability of skills to skilled sedentary work for individuals who are of advanced age (55 and over), there must be very little, if any, vocational adjustment required in terms of tools, work processes, work settings, or the industry.

(g) Individuals approaching advanced age (age 50–54) may be significantly limited in vocational adaptability if they are restricted to sedentary work. When such individuals have no past work experience or can no longer perform vocationally relevant past work and have no transferable skills, a finding of disabled ordinarily obtains. However, recently completed education which provides for direct entry into sedentary work will preclude such a finding. For this age group, even a high school education or more (ordinarily completed in the remote past) would have little impact for effecting a vocational adjustment unless relevant work experience reflects use of such education.

(h) The term *younger individual* is used to denote an individual age 18 through 49. For those within this group who are age 45–49, age is a less positive factor than for those who are age 18–44. Accordingly, for such individuals: (1) who are restricted to sedentary work, (2) who are unskilled or have no transferable skills, (3) who have no relevant past work or who can no longer perform vocationally relevant past work, and (4) who are either illiterate or unable to communicate in the English language, a finding of disabled is warranted. On the other hand, age is a more positive factor for those who are under age 45 and is usually not a significant factor in limiting such an individual's ability to make a vocational adjustment, even an adjustment to unskilled sedentary work, and even where the individual is illiterate or unable to communicate in English. However, a finding of disabled is not precluded for those individuals under age 45 who do not meet all of the criteria of a specific rule and who do not have the ability to perform a full range of sedentary work. The following examples are illustrative: Example 1: An individual under age 45 with a high school education can no longer do past work and is restricted to unskilled sedentary jobs because of a severe medically determinable cardiovascular impairment (which does not meet or equal the listings in appendix 1). A permanent injury of the right hand limits the individual to sedentary jobs which do not require bilateral manual dexterity. None of the rules in appendix 2 are applicable to this particular set of facts, because this individual cannot perform the full range of work defined as sedentary. Since the inability to perform jobs requiring bilateral manual dexterity significantly compromises the only range of work for which the individual is otherwise qualified (i.e., sedentary), a finding of disabled would be appropriate. Example 2: An illiterate 41 year old individual with mild mental retardation (IQ of 78) is restricted to unskilled sedentary work and cannot perform vocationally relevant past work, which had consisted of unskilled agricultural field work: his or her particular characteristics do not specifically meet any of the rules in appendix 2, because this individual cannot perform the full range of work defined as sedentary. In light of the adverse factors which further narrow the range of sedentary work for which this individual is qualified, a finding of disabled is appropriate.

(i) While illiteracy or the inability to communicate in English may significantly limit an individual's vocational scope, the primary work functions in the bulk of unskilled work relate to working with things (rather than with data or people) and in these work functions at the unskilled level, literacy or ability to communicate in English has the least significance. Similarly, the lack of relevant work experience would have little significance since the bulk of unskilled jobs require no qualifying work experience. Thus, the functional capability for a full range of sedentary work represents sufficient numbers of jobs to indicate substantial vocational scope for those individuals age 18–44 even if they are illiterate or unable to communicate in English.

TABLE NO. 1—RESIDUAL FUNCTIONAL CAPACITY: MAXIMUM SUSTAINED WORK CAPABILITY LIMITED TO SEDENTARY WORK AS A RESULT OF SEVERE MEDICALLY DETERMINABLE IMPAIRMENT(S)

Rule	Age	Education	Previous work experience	Decision
201.01	Advanced age	Limited or less	Unskilled or none	Disabled
201.02	...do	...do	skilled or semiskilled—skills not transferable[1].	Do.
201.03	...do	...do	Skilled or semiskilled—skills transferable[1]	Not disabled
201.04	...do	High school graduate or more—does not provide for direct entry into skilled work.[2]	Unskilled or none	Disabled
201.05	...do	High school graduate or more—provides for direct entry into skilled work[2]	...do	Not disabled
201.06	...do	High school graduate or more—does not provide for direct entry into skilled work[2]	Skilled or semiskilled—skills not transferable[1].	Disabled
201.07	...do	...do	Skilled or semiskilled—skills transferable[1].	Not disabled
201.08	...do	High school graduate or more—provides for direct entry into skilled work[2]	Skilled or semiskilled—skills not transferable[1].	Do.
201.09	Closely approaching advanced age.	Limited or less	Unskilled or none	Disabled
201.10	...do	...do	Skilled or semiskilled—skills not transferable.	Do.
201.11	...do	...do	Skilled or semiskilled—skills transferable.	Not disabled
201.12	...do	High school graduate or more—does not provide for direct entry into skilled work[3]	Unskilled or none	Disabled
201.13	...do	High school graduate or more—provides for direct entry into skilled work[3]	...do	Not disabled
201.14	...do	High school graduate or more—does not provide for direct entry into skilled work[3]	Skilled or semiskilled—skills not transferable.	Disabled
201.15	...do	...do	Skilled or semiskilled—skills transferable.	Not disabled
201.16	...do	High school graduate or more—provides for direct entry into skilled work[3]	Skilled or semiskilled—skills not transferable.	Do.
201.17	Younger individual age 45–49.	Illiterate or unable to communicate in English.	Unskilled or none	Disabled
201.18	...do	Limited or less—at least literate and able to communicate in English.	...do	Not disabled
201.19	...do	Limited or less	Skilled or semiskilled—skills not transferable.	Do.
201.20	...do	...do	Skilled or semiskilled—skills transferable.	Do.
201.21	...do	High school graduate or more	Skilled or semiskilled—skills not transferable.	Do.
201.22	...do	...do	Skilled or semiskilled—skills transferable.	Do.
201.23	Younger individual age 18–44.	Illiterate or unable to communicate in English.	Unskilled or none	Do.[4]
201.24	...do	Limited or less—at least literate and able to communicate in English.	...do	Do.[4]
201.25	...do	Limited or less	Skilled or semiskilled—skills not transferable.	Do.[4]
201.26	...do	...do	Skilled or semiskilled—skills transferable.	Do.[4]
201.27	...do	High school graduate or more	Unskilled or none	Do.[4]
201.28	...do	...do	Skilled or semiskilled—skills not transferable	Do.[4]

continued

TABLE NO. 1—RESIDUAL FUNCTIONAL CAPACITY: MAXIMUM SUSTAINED WORK CAPABILITY LIMITED TO SEDENTARY WORK AS A RESULT OF SEVERE MEDICALLY DETERMINABLE IMPAIRMENT(S)—CONTINUED

Rule	Age	Education	Previous work experience	Decision
201.29 . . .	. . . do.	. . . do	Skilled or semiskilled—skills transferable.	Do.[4]

[1]See 201.00(f)
[2]See 201.00(d)
[3]See 201.00(g)
[4]See 201.00(h)

202.00 *Maximum sustained work capability limited to light work as a result of severe medically determinable impairment(s).* (a) The functional capacity to perform a full range of light work includes the functional capacity to perform sedentary as well as light work. Approximately 1,600 separate sedentary and light unskilled occupations can be identified in eight broad occupational categories each occupation representing numerous jobs in the national economy. These jobs can be performed after a short demonstration or within 30 days, and do not require special skills or experience.

(b) The functional capacity to perform a wide or full range of light work represents substantial work capability compatible with making a work adjustment to substantial numbers of unskilled jobs and, thus, generally provides sufficient occupational mobility even for severely impaired individuals who are not of advanced age and have sufficient educational competences for unskilled work.

(c) However, for individuals of advanced age who can no longer perform vocationally relevant past work and who have a history of unskilled work experience, or who have only skills that are not readily transferable to a significant range of semi-skilled or skilled work that is within the individual's functional capacity, or who have no work experience, the limitations in vocational adaptability represented by functional restriction to light work warrant a finding of disabled. Ordinarily, even a high school education or more which was completed in the remote past will have little positive impact on effecting a vocational adjustment unless relevant work experience reflects use of such education.

(d) Where the same factors in paragraph (c) of this section regarding education and work experience are present, but where age, though not advanced, is a factor which significantly limits vocational adaptability (i.e., closely approaching advanced age, 50–54) and an individual's vocational scope is further significantly limited by illiteracy or inability to communicate in English, a finding of disabled is warranted.

(e) The presence of acquired skills that are readily transferable to a significant range of semi-skilled or skilled work within an individual's residual functional capacity would ordinarily warrant a finding of not disabled regardless of the adversity of age, or whether the individual's formal education is commensurate with his or her demonstrated skill level. The acquisition of work skills demonstrates the ability to perform work at the level of complexity demonstrated by the skill level attained regardless of the individual's formal educational attainments.

(f) For a finding of transferability of skills to light work for individuals of advanced age who are closely approaching retirement age (age 60–64), there must be very little, if any, vocational adjustment required in terms of tools, work processes, work settings, or the industry.

(g) While illiteracy or the inability to communicate in English may significantly limit an individual's vocational scope, the primary work functions in the bulk of unskilled work relate to working with things (rather than with data or people) and in these work functions at the unskilled level, literacy or ability to communicate in English has the least significance. Similarly, the lack of relevant work experience would have little significance since the bulk of unskilled jobs require no qualifying work experience. The capability for light work, which includes the ability to do sedentary work, represents the capability for substantial numbers of such jobs. This, in turn, represents substantial vocational scope for younger individuals (age 18–49) even if illiterate or unable to communicate in English.

TABLE NO. 2—RESIDUAL FUNCTIONAL CAPACITY: MAXIMUM SUSTAINED WORK CAPABILITY LIMITED TO LIGHT WORK AS A RESULT OF SEVERE MEDICALLY DETERMINABLE INPAIRMENT(S)

Rule	Age	Education	Previous work experience	Decision
202.01 . . .	Advanced age	Limited or less	Unskilled or none	Disabled.

TABLE NO. 2—RESIDUAL FUNCTIONAL CAPACITY: MAXIMUM SUSTAINED WORK CAPABILITY LIMITED TO LIGHT WORK AS A RESULT OF SEVERE MEDICALLY DETERMINABLE INPAIRMENT(S)—CONTINUED

Rule	Age	Education	Previous work experience	Decision
202.02 . . .	. . . do.	. . . do	Skilled or semiskilled—skills not transferable.	Do.
202.03 . . .	. . . do.	. . . do	Skilled or semiskilled—skills transferable[1].	Not disabled.
202.04 . . .	. . . do.	High school gradate or more—does not provide for direct entry into skilled work.[2]	Unskilled or none.	Disabled.
202.05 . . .	. . . do.	High school graduate or more—provides for direct entry into skilled work[2].	. . .do	Not disabled.
202.06 . . .	. . . do.	High school graduate or more—does not provide for direct entry into skilled work.[2]	Skilled or semiskilled—skills not transferable.	Disabled.
202.07 . . .	. . . do.	. . . do	Skilled or semiskilled—skills transferble[2].	Not disabled.
202.08 . . .	. . . do.	High school graduate or more—provides for direct entry into skilled work[2].	Skilled or semiskilled—skills not transferable.	Do.
202.09 . . .	Closely approaching advanced age.	Illiterate or unable to communicate in English.	Unskilled or none.	Disabled.
202.10 . . .	. . . do.	Limited or less—at least literate and able to communicate in English.	. . .do	Not disabled.
202.11 . . .	. . . do.	Limited or less	Skilled or semiskilled—skills not transferable.	Do.
202.12 . . .	. . . do.	. . . do	Skilled or semiskilled—skills transferable.	Do.
202.13 . . .	. . . do.	High school graduate or more	Unskilled or none.	Do.
202.14 . . .	. . . do.	. . . do	Skilled or semiskilled—skills not transferable.	Do.
202.15 . . .	. . . do.	. . . do	Skilled or semiskilled—skills transferble.	Do.
202.16 . . .	Younger individual	Illiterate or unable to communicate in English.	Unskilled or none.	Do.
202.17 . . .	. . . do.	Limited or less—at least literate and able to communicate in English.	. . .do	Do.
202.18 . . .	. . . do.	Limited or less	Skilled or semiskilled—skills not transferable.	Do.
202.19 . . .	. . . do.	. . . do	Skilled or semiskilled—skills transferable.	Do.
202.20 . . .	. . . do.	High school graduate or more	Unskilled or none	Do.
202.21 . . .	. . . do.	. . . do	Skilled or semiskilled—skills not transferable.	Do.
202.22 . . .	. . . do.	. . . do	Skilled or semiskilled—skills transferable.	Do.

[1]See 202.00(f)
[2]See 201.00(c)

203.00 *Maximum sustained work capability limited to medium work as a result of severe medically determinable impairment(s).* (a) The functional capacity to perform medium work includes the functional capacity to perform sedentary, light, and medium work. Approximately 2,500 separate sedentary, light, and medium occupations can be identified, each occupation representing numerous jobs in the national economy which do not require skills or previous experience and which can be performed after a short demonstration or within 30 days.

(b) The functional capacity to perform medium work represents such substantial work capability at even the unskilled level that a finding of disabled is ordinarily not warranted in cases where a severely impaired individual retains the functional capacity to perform medium work. Even the adversity of advanced age (55 or over) and a work history of unskilled work may be offset by the substantial work capability to perform medium work. However, an individual with a marginal education and long work experience (i.e., 35 years or more) limited to the performance of arduous unskilled labor, who is not working and is no longer able to perform this labor because of a severe impairment(s), may still be found disabled

continued

even though the individual is able to do medium work.

(c) However, the absence of any relevant work experience becomes a more significant adversity for individuals of advanced age (55 and over). Accordingly, this factor, in combination with a limited education or less, militates against making a vocational adjustment to even this substantial range of work and a finding of disabled is appropriate. Further, for individuals closely approaching retirement age (60–64) with a work history of unskilled work and with marginal education or less, a finding of disabled is appropriate.

TABLE NO. 3—RESIDUAL FUNCTIONAL CAPACITY: MAXIMUM SUSTAINED WORK CAPABILITY LIMITED TO MEDIUM WORK AS A RESULT OF SEVERE MEDICALLY DETERMINABLE IMPAIRMENT(S)

Rule	Age	Education	Previous work experience	Decision
203.01 ...	Closely approaching retirement age.	Marginal or none	Unskilled or none	Disabled.
203.02 ...	...do	Limited or less....................	None	Do.
203.03 ...	...do	Limited	Unskilled...........	Not disabled.
203.04 ...	...do	Limited or less....................	Skilled or semiskilled—skills not transferable.	Do.
203.05 ...	...do	...do	Skilled or semiskilled—skills transferable.	Do.
203.06 ...	...do	High school graduate or more	Unskilled or none	Do.
203.07 ...	...do	High school graduate or more—does not provide for direct entry into skilled work.	Skilled or semiskilled—skills not transferable.	Do.
203.08 ...	...do	...do	Skilled or semiskilled—skills transferable.	Do.
203.09 ...	...do	High school graduate or more—provides for direct entry into skilled work.	Skilled or semiskilled—skills not transferable.	Do.
203.10 ...	Advanced age.......	Limited or less....................	None	Disabled.
203.11 ...	...do	...do	Unskilled...........	Not disabled.
203.12 ...	...do	...do	Skilled or semiskilled—skills not transferable.	Do.
203.13 ...	...do	...do	Skilled or semiskilled—skills transferable.	Do.
203.14 ...	...do	High school graduate or more	Unskilled or none	Do.
203.15 ...	...do	High school graduate or more—does not provide for direct entry into skilled work.	Skilled or semiskilled—skills not transferable.	Do.
203.16 ...	...do	...do	Skilled or semiskilled—skills transferable.	Do.
203.17 ...	...do	High school graduate or more—provides for direct entry into skilled work.	Skilled or semiskilled—skills not transferable.	Do.
203.18 ...	Closely approaching advanced age.	Limited or less....................	Unskilled or none	Do.
203.19 ...	...do	...do	Skilled or semiskilled—skills not transferable.	Do.
203.20 ...	...do	...do	Skilled or semiskilled—skills transferable.	Do.
203.21 ...	...do	High school graduate or more	Unskilled or none	Do.
203.22 ...	...do	High school graduate or more—does not provide for direct entry into skilled work.	Skilled or semiskilled—skills not transferable.	Do.
203.23	...do	...do	Skilled or semiskilled—skills transferable.	Do.
203.24	...do	High school graduate or more—provides for direct entry into skilled work.	Skilled or semiskilled—skills not transferable.	Do.
203.25	Younger individual	Limited or less....................	Unskilled or none	Do.
203.26	...do	...do	Skilled or semiskilled—skills not transferable.	Do.
203.27	...do	...do	Skilled or semiskilled—skills transferable.	Do.
203.28 ...	...do	High school graduate or more	Unskilled or none	Do.
203.29 ...	...do	High school graduate or more—does not provide for direct entry into skilled work.	Skilled or semiskilled—skills not transferable.	Do.
203.30 ...	...do	...do	Skilled or semiskilled—skills transferable.	Do.

TABLE NO. 3—RESIDUAL FUNCTIONAL CAPACITY: MAXIMUM SUSTAINED WORK CAPABILITY LIMITED TO MEDIUM WORK AS A RESULT OF SEVERE MEDICALLY DETERMINABLE IMPAIRMENT(S)—CONTINUED

Rule	Age	Education	Previous work experience	Decision
203.31 . . .	. . . do	High school graduate or more—provides for direct entry into skilled work.	Skilled or semiskilled—skills transferable.	Do.

204.00 *Maximum sustained work capability limited to heavy work (or very heavy work) as a result of severe medically determinable impairment(s).* The residual functional capacity to perform heavy work or very heavy work includes the functional capability for work at the lesser functional levels as well, and represents substantial work capability for jobs in the national economy at all skill and physical demand levels. Individuals who retain the functional capacity to perform heavy work (or very heavy work) ordinarily will not have a severe impairment or will be able to do their past work—either of which would have already provided a basis for a decision of "not disabled". Environmental restrictions ordinarily would not significantly affect the range of work existing in the national economy for individuals with the physical capability for heavy work (or very heavy work). Thus an impairment which does not preclude heavy work (or very heavy work) would not ordinarily be the primary reason for unemployment, and generally is sufficient for a finding of not disabled, even though age, education, and skill level of prior work experience may be considered adverse.

[45 FR 55584. Aug. 20, 1980, as amended at 56 FR 57944. Nov. 14, 1991]

Subpart Q—Determinations of Disability

AUTHORITY: Secs. 205(a), 221, and 702(a)(5) of the Social Security Act (42 U.S.C. 405(a), 421, and 902(a)(5)).

SOURCE: 46 FR 29204. May 29, 1981, unless otherwise noted.

GENERAL PROVISIONS

§ 404.1601 Purpose and scope.

This subpart described the standards of performance and administrative requirements and procedures for States making determinations of disability for the Commissioner under title II of the Act. It also establishes the Commissioner's responsibilities in carrying out the disability determination function.

(a) Sections 404.1601 through 404.1603 describe the purpose of the regulations and the meaning of terms frequently used in the regulations. They also briefly set forth the responsibilities of the Commissioner and the States covered in detail in other sections.

(b) Sections 404.1610 through 404.1618 describe the Commissioner's and the State's responsibilities in performing the disability determination function.

(c) Sections 404.1620 through 404.1633 describe the administrative responsibilities and requirements of the States. The corresponding role of the Commissioner is also set out.

(d) Sections 404.1640 through 404.1650 describe the performance accuracy and processing time standards for measuring State agency performance.

(e) Sections 404.1660 through 404.1661 describe when and what kind of assistance the Commissioner will provide State agencies to help them improve performance.

(f) Sections 404.1670 through 404.1675 describe the level of performance below which the Commissioner will consider a State agency to be substantially failing to make disability determinations consistent with the regulations and other written guidelines and the resulting action the Commissioner will take.

(g) Sections 404.1680 through 404.1683 describe the rules for resolving disputes concerning fiscal issues and providing hearings when we propose to find that a State is in substantial failure.

(h) Sections 404.1690 through 404.1694 describe when and what action the Commissioner will take and what action the State will be expected to take if the Commissioner assumes the disability determination function from a State agency.

[46 FR 29204, May 29, 1981, as amended at 62 FR 38451, July 18, 1997]

§ 404.1602 Definitions.

For purposes of this subpart:

Act means the Social Security Act, as amended.

Class or classes of cases means the categories into which disability claims are divided according to their characteristics.

Commissioner means the Commissioner of Social Security or his or her authorized designee.

Determination of disability or *disability determination* means one or more of the following decisions:

(a) Whether or not a person is under a disability;

(b) The date a person's disability began: or

(c) The date a person's disability ended.

Disability means *disability* or *blindness* as defined in sections 216(i) and 223 of the Act or as defined in title IV of the Federal Mine Safety and Health Act of 1977, as amended.

Disability determination function means making determinations as to disability and carrying out related administrative and other responsibilities.

Disability program means, as appropriate, the Federal programs for providing disability insurance benefits under title II of the Act and disability benefits under title IV of the Federal Mine Safety and Health Act of 1977, as amended.

Initial means the first level of disability adjudication.

Other written guidelines means written issuances such as Social Security Rulings and memoranda by the Commissioner of Social Security, the Deputy Commissioner for Programs and Policy, or the Associate Commissioner for Disability and the procedures, guides, and operating instructions in the Disability Insurance sections of the Program Operations Manual System, that are instructive, interpretive, clarifying, and/or administrative and not designated as advisory or discretionary. The purpose of including the foregoing material in the definition is to assure uniform national application of program standards and service delivery to the public.

Regulations means regulations in this subpart issued under sections 205(a), 221 and 1102 of the Act, unless otherwise indicated.

State means any of the 50 States of the United States, the Commonwealth of Puerto Rico, the District of Columbia, or Guam. It includes the State agency.

State agency means that agency of a State which has been designated by the State to carry out the disability determination function.

We, us, and *our* refers to the Social Security Administration (SSA).

[46 FR 29204. May 29, 1981, as amended at 56 FR 11018. Mar. 14, 1991: 62 FR 38452. July 18, 1997]

§ 404.1603 Basic responsibilities for us and the State.

(a) *General.* We will work with the State to provide and maintain an effective system for processing claims of those who apply for and who are receiving benefits under the disability program. We will provide program standards, leadership, and oversight. We do not intend to become involved in the State's ongoing management of the program except as is necessary and in accordance with these regulations. The State will comply with our regulations and other written guidelines.

(b) *Our responsibilities.* We will:

(1) Periodically review the regulations and other written guidelines to determine whether they insure effective and uniform administration of the disability program. To the extent feasible, we will consult with and take into consideration the experience of the States in issuing regulations and guidelines necessary to insure effective and uniform administration of the disability program:

(2) Provide training materials or in some instances conduct or specify training, see § 404.1622;

(3) Provide funds to the State agency for the necessary cost of performing the disability determination function, see § 404.1626;

(4) Monitor and evaluate the performance of the State agency under the established standards, see §§ 404.1644 and 404.1645; and

(5) Maintain liaison with the medical profession nationally and with national

one (or more) of the Nation's Empowerment Zones and Enterprise Communities.

(Approved by the Office of Management and Budget under control number 1840-0007)

(Authority: 20 U.S.C. 1021 *et seq.*)

[65 FR 19609, Apr. 11, 2000]

Subpart B—State Grants Program

SOURCE: 65 FR 19610, Apr. 11, 2000, unless otherwise noted.

§ 611.11 What are the program's general selection criteria?

In evaluating the quality of applications, the Secretary uses the following selection criteria.

(a) *Quality of project design.* (1) The Secretary considers the quality of the project design.

(2) In determining the quality of the project design, the Secretary considers the extent to which—

(i) The project design will result in systemic change in the way that all new teachers are prepared, and includes partners from all levels of the education system;

(ii) The Governor and other relevant executive and legislative branch officials, the K–16 education system or systems, and the business community are directly involved in and committed to supporting the proposed activities;

(iii) Project goals and performance objectives are clear, measurable outcomes are specified, and a feasible plan is presented for meeting them;

(iv) The project is likely to initiate or enhance and supplement systemic State reforms in one or more of the following areas: teacher recruitment, preparation, licensing, and certification;

(v) The applicant will ensure that a diversity of perspectives is incorporated into operation of the project, including those of parents, teachers, employers, academic and professional groups, and other appropriate entities; and

(vi) The project design is based on up-to-date knowledge from research and effective practice.

(b) *Significance.* (1) The Secretary considers the significance of the project.

(2) In determining the significance of the project, the Secretary considers the extent to which—

(i) The project involves the development or demonstration of promising new strategies or exceptional approaches in the way new teachers are recruited, prepared, certified, and licensed;

(ii) Project outcomes lead directly to improvements in teaching quality and student achievement as measured against rigorous academic standards;

(iii) The State is committed to institutionalize the project after federal funding ends; and

(iv) Project strategies, methods, and accomplishments are replicable, thereby permitting other States to benefit from them.

(c) *Quality of resources.* (1) The Secretary considers the quality of the project's resources.

(2) In determining the quality of the project resources, the Secretary considers the extent to which—

(i) Support available to the project, including personnel, equipment, supplies, and other resources, is sufficient to ensure a successful project;

(ii) Budgeted costs are reasonable and justified in relation to the design, outcomes, and potential significance of the project; and

(iii) The applicant's matching share of the budgeted costs demonstrates a significant commitment to successful completion of the project and to project continuation after federal funding ends.

(d) *Quality of management plan.* (1) The Secretary considers the quality of the project's management plan.

(2) In determining the quality of the management plan, the Secretary considers the following factors:

(i) The extent to which the management plan, including the workplan, is designed to achieve goals and objectives of the project, and includes clearly defined activities, responsibilities, timelines, milestones, and measurable outcomes for accomplishing project tasks.

(ii) The adequacy of procedures to ensure feedback and continuous improvements in the operation of the project.

continued

(iii) The qualifications, including training and experience, of key personnel charged with implementing the project successfully.

(Approved by the Office of Management and Budget under control number 1840-0007)

(Authority: 20 U.S.C. 1020 *et seq.*)

§ 611.12 What additional selection criteria are used for an application proposing teacher recruitment activities?

In reviewing applications that propose to undertake teacher recruitment activities, the Secretary also considers the following selection criteria:

(a) In addition to the elements contained in § 611.11(a) (Quality of project design), the Secretary considers the extent to which the project addresses—

(1) Systemic changes in the ways that new teachers are to be recruited, supported and prepared; and

(2) Systemic efforts to recruit, support, and prepare prospective teachers from disadvantaged and other underrepresented backgrounds.

(b) In addition to the elements contained in § 611.11(b) (Significance), the Secretary considers the applicant's commitment to continue recruitment activities, scholarship assistance, and preparation and support of additional cohorts of new teachers after funding under this part ends.

(c) In addition to the elements contained in § 611.11(c) (Quality of resources), the Secretary considers the impact of the project on high-need LEAs and high-need schools based upon—

(1) The amount of scholarship assistance the project will provide students from federal and non-federal funds;

(2) The number of students who will receive scholarships; and

(3) How those students receiving scholarships will benefit from high-quality teacher preparation and an effective support system during their first three years of teaching.

(Approved by the Office of Management and Budget under control number 1840-0007)

(Authority: 20 U.S.C. 1021 *et seq.*)

§ 611.13 What competitive preference does the Secretary provide?

The Secretary provides a competitive preference on the basis of how well the State's proposed articles in any one or more of the following statutory priorities are likely to yield successful and sustained results:

(a) Initiatives to reform State teacher licensure and certification requirements so that current and future teachers possess strong teaching skills and academic content knowledge in the subject areas in which they will be certified or licensed to teach.

(b) Innovative reforms to hold higher education institutions with teacher preparation programs accountable for preparing teachers who are highly competent in the academic content areas and have strong teaching skills.

(c) Innovative efforts to reduce the shortage (including the high turnover) of highly competent teachers in high-poverty urban and rural areas.

(Approved by the Office of Management and Budget under control number 1840-0007)

(Authority: 20 U.S.C. 1021 *et seq.*)

Subpart C—Partnership Grants Program

SOURCE: 65 FR 19611, Apr. 11, 2000, unless otherwise noted.

§ 611.21 What are the program's selection criteria for pre-applications?

In evaluating the quality of pre-applications, the Secretary uses the following selection criteria.

(a) *Project goals and objectives.* (1) The Secretary considers the goals and objectives of the project design.

(2) In determining the quality of the project goals and objectives, the Secretary considers the following factors:

(i) The extent to which the partnership's vision will produce significant and sustainable improvements in teacher education.

(ii) The needs the partnership will address.

(iii) How the partnership and its activities would be sustained once federal support ends.

3. Which of the following areas are most heavily secured?
   a. Restricted areas
   b. Limited areas
   c. Closed areas
   d. Security areas
4. If someone accidentally wanders into a closed security area, he or she will be criminally prosecuted under 18 U.S.C. §799.
   a. True
   b. False
5. Which of the following is a reason for revocation of a security area?
   a. The director does not like you
   b. The dress code was not adhered to
   c. Ties to a group of terrorists
   d. Lack of need for security services

D. Exercise 12.4: Code of Federal Regulations

1. 28 C.F.R. §0.55 has been modified 10 times.
   a. True
   b. False
2. 28 C.F.R. §0.55 is nothing more than a job description for the United States Assistant Attorney General of the Criminal Division.
   a. True
   b. False
3. Under 28 C.F.R. §0.56, the determination of whether the federal government possesses either exclusive or concurrent jurisdiction lies solely in the hands of the
   a. U.S. Supreme Court.
   b. U.S. Attorney General.
   c. U.S. Attorney General, Criminal Division.
   d. None of the above.
4. 28 C.F.R. §§ 0.55–0.57 refers to which of the following sections of the *United States Code*?
   a. 18 U.S.C. § 5031 *et seq.*
   b. 8 U.S.C. § 301
   c. 1 U.S.C. § 1182
   d. None of the above
5. In the "Notes" section, cross-references are made to other provisions in the C.F.R. that may be applicable to that regulation.
   a. True
   b. False

E. Exercise 12.5: *Federal Register*—Proposed Rules

1. How much time is given for comments on this proposed rule?
   a. 1 month
   b. 2 weeks
   c. 1 year
   d. None of the above

which will exceed 30 days from date of establishment.

§ 1203a.102 Establishment, maintenance, and revocation of security areas.

(a) *Establishment.* (1) Directors of NASA field and component installations, and the Director of Headquarters Administration for NASA Headquarters (including component installations) may establish, maintain, and protect such areas as restricted, limited, or closed depending upon the opportunity available to unauthorized persons either to:

(i) Obtain knowledge of classified information,

(ii) Damage or remove property, or to

(iii) Disrupt Government operations.

(2) The concurrence of the Director of Security NASA Headquarters, will be obtained prior to the establishment of a permanent security area.

(3)(i) As a minimum, the following information will be submitted to the Director of Security 15 workdays prior to establishment of each permanent security area:

(*a*) The name and specific location of the NASA field or component installation, facility, or property to be protected.

(*b*) A statement that the property is owned by, or leased to, the United States for use by NASA or is the property of a NASA contractor located on a NASA installation or component installation.

(*c*) Designation desired: i.e., restricted, limited, or closed.

(*d*) Specific purpose(s) for the establishment of a security area.

(ii) For those areas currently designated by the installation as "permanent security areas," the information set forth in paragraph (d)(3)(i) of this section will be furnished to the Security Division, NASA Headquarters, within 30 workdays of the effective date of this part.

(b) *Maintenance.* The security measures which may be utilized to protect such areas will be determined by the requirements of individual situations. As a minimum such security measures will:

(1) Provide for the posting of signs at entrances and at such intervals along the perimeter of the designated area as to provide reasonable notice to persons about to enter thereon. The Director of Security, NASA Headquarters, upon request, may approve the use of signs that are now being used pursuant to a State statute.

(2) Regulate authorized personnel entry and movement within the area.

(3) Deny entry of unauthorized persons or property.

(4) Prevent unauthorized removal of classified information and material or property from a NASA installation or component installation.

(c) *Revocation.* Once the need for an established permanent security area no longer exists, the area will be returned immediately to normal controls and procedures or as soon as practicable. The Director of Security will be informed of permanent security area revocations within 15 workdays.

§ 1203a.103 Access to security areas.

(a) Only those NASA employees, NASA contractor employees, and visitors who have a need for such access and who meet the following criteria may enter a security area:

(1) *Restricted area.* Be authorized to enter the area alone or be escorted by or under the supervision of a NASA employee or NASA contractor employee who is authorized to enter the area.

(2) *Limited area.* Possess a security clearance equal to the level of the classified information or material involved or be the recipient of a satisfactorily completed national agency check if classified material or information is not involved. Personnel who do not meet the requirements for unescorted access may be escorted by a NASA employee or NASA contractor employee who meets the access requirements and has been authorized to enter the area.

(3) *Closed area.* Possess a security clearance equal to the classified information or material involved.

(b) The directors of NASA field and component installations, and the Director of Headquarters Administration for NASA Headquarters (including component installations) may rescind previously granted authorizations to enter a security area when an individual's continued presence therein is no longer required, threatens the security of the property therein, or is disruptive of Government operations.

§ 1203a.104 Violation of security areas.

(a) *Removal of unauthorized persons.* The directors of NASA field and component installations (or their designees) and the Director of Headquarters Administration for NASA Headquarters (including component installations) or his designee may order the removal or eviction of any person whose presence in a designated security area is in violation of the provisions of this part or any regulation or order established pursuant to the provisions of this part.

(b) *Criminal penalties for violation.* Whoever willfully violates, attempts to violate, or conspires to violate any regulation or order establishing requirements or procedures for authorized entry into an area designated restricted, limited, or closed pursuant to the provisions of this part may be subject to prosecution under 18 U.S.C. 799 which provides penalties for a fine of not more than $5,000 or imprisonment for not more than 1 year, or both.

§ 1203a.105 Implementation by field and component installations.

If a Director of a NASA field or component installation finds it necessary to issue supplemental instructions to any provision of this part, the instructions must first be published in the FEDERAL REGISTER. Therefore, the proposed supplemental instructions will be sent to the Security Division (Code DHZ), NASA Headquarters, in accordance with NASA Management Instruction 1410.10 for processing.

PART 1203b—SECURITY PROGRAMS; ARREST AUTHORITY AND USE OF FORCE BY NASA SECURITY FORCE PERSONNEL

Sec.

AUTHORITY: Sec. 304(f) of the National Aeronautics and Space Act of 1958 (42 U.S.C. 2456a).

SOURCE: 57 FR 4926, Feb. 11, 1992, unless otherwise noted.

§ 1203b.100 Purpose.

This regulation implements section 304(f) of the National Aeronautics and Space Act of 1958, as amended (42 U.S.C. 2456a), by establishing guidelines for the exercise of arrest authority and for the exercise of physical force, including deadly force, in conjunction with such arrest authority.

§ 1203b.101 Scope.

This part applies to only those NASA and NASA contractor security force personnel who are authorized to exercise arrest authority in accordance with 42 U.S.C. 2456a and this regulation.

§ 1203b.102 Definitions.

Accredited Course of Training. A course of instruction offered by the Federal Law Enforcement Training Center, or an equivalent course of instruction offered by another Federal agency. See § 1203b.103(a)(1).

Arrest. An act, resulting in the restriction of a person's movement, other than a brief detention for purposes of questioning about a person's identity and requesting identification, accomplished by means of force or show of authority under circumstances that would lead a reasonable person to believe that he/she was not free to leave the presence of the officer.

Contractor. NASA contractors and subcontractors at all tiers.

§ 1203b.103 Arrest authority.

(a) NASA security force personnel may exercise arrest authority, provided that:

(1) They graduate from an accredited training course (see § 1203b.102(a)); and

(2) They have been certified in writing by the Associate Administrator for Management Systems and Facilities, or designee, as specifically authorized to exercise arrest authority.

EXERCISE 12.4

28 CFR
§ 0.55 General functions.

The following functions are assigned to and shall be conducted, handled, or supervised by, the Assistant Attorney General, Criminal Division:

(a) Prosecutions for Federal crimes not otherwise specifically assigned.

(b) Cases involving criminal frauds against the United States except cases assigned to the Antitrust Division by § 0.40(a) involving conspiracy to defraud the Federal Government by violation of the antitrust laws, and tax fraud cases assigned to the Tax Division by subpart N of this part.

(c) All criminal and civil litigation under the Controlled Substances Act, 84 Stat. 1242, and the Controlled Substances Import and Export Act, 84 Stat. 1285 (titles II and III of the Comprehensive Drug Abuse Prevention and Control Act of 1970).

(d) Civil or criminal forfeiture or civil penalty actions (including petitions for remission or mitigation of forfeitures and civil penalties, offers in compromise, and related proceedings) under the Federal Aviation Act of 1958, the Contraband Transportation Act, the Copyrights Act, the customs laws (except those assigned to the Civil Division which involve sections 592, 704(i)(2) or 734(i)(2) of the Tariff Act of 1930), the Export Control Act of 1949, the Federal Alcohol Administration Act, the Federal Seed Act, the Gold Reserve Act of 1934, the Hours of Service Act, the Animal Welfare Act, the Immigration and Nationality Act (except civil penalty actions and petitions and offers related thereto), the neutrality laws, laws relating to cigarettes, liquor, narcotics and dangerous drugs, other controlled substances, gambling, war materials, pre-Colombian artifacts, coinage, and firearms, locomotive inspection (45 U.S.C. 22, 23, 28-34), the Organized Crime Control Act of 1970, prison-made goods (18 U.S.C. 1761-1762), the Safety Appliance Act, standard barrels (15 U.S.C. 231-242), the Sugar Act of 1948, and the Twenty-Eight Hour Law.

(e) Subject to the provisions of subpart Y of this part, consideration, acceptance, or rejection of offers in compromise of criminal and tax liability under the laws relating to liquor, narcotics and dangerous drugs, gambling, and firearms, in cases in which the criminal liability remains unresolved.

(f) All criminal litigation and related investigations and inquiries pursuant to all the power and authority of the Attorney General to enforce the Immigration and Nationality Act and all other laws relating to the immigration and naturalization of aliens; all advice to the Attorney General with respect to the exercise of his parole authority under 8 U.S.C. 1182(d)(5) concerning aliens who are excludable under 8 U.S.C. 1182(a)(23), (28), (29), or (33); and all civil litigation with respect to the individuals identified in 8 U.S.C. 1182(a)(33), 1251(a)(19).

(g) Coordination of enforcement activities directed against organized crime and racketeering.

(h) Enforcement of the Act of January 2, 1951, 64 Stat. 1134, as amended by the Gambling Devices Act of 1962, 76 Stat. 1075, 15 U.S.C. 1171 et seq., including registration thereunder. (See also 28 CFR 3.2)

(i) All civil proceedings seeking exclusively equitable relief against Criminal Division activities including criminal investigations, prosecutions and other criminal justice activities (including without limitation, applications for writs of habeas corpus not challenging exclusion, deportation or detention under the immigration laws and coram nobis), except that any proceeding may be conducted, handled, or supervised by another division by agreement between the head of such division and the Assistant Attorney General in charge of the Criminal Division.

(j) International extradition proceedings.

(k) Relation of military to civil authority with respect to criminal matters affecting both.

(l) All criminal matters arising under the Labor-Management Reporting and Disclosure Act of 1959 (73 Stat. 519).

(m) Enforcement of the following-described provisions of the United States Code—

(1) Sections 591 through 593 and sections 595 through 612 of title 18, U.S. Code, relating to elections and political activities;

(2) Sections 241, 242, and 594 of title 18, and sections 1973i and 1973j of title 42, U.S. Code, insofar as they relate to voting and election matters not involving discrimination or intimidation on grounds of race or color, and section 245(b)(1) of title 18 U.S. Code, insofar as it relates to matters not involving discrimination or intimidation on grounds of race, color, religion, or national origin;

(3) Section 245(b)(3) of title 18, U.S. Code, pertaining to forcible interference with persons engaged in business during a riot or civil disorder; and

(4) Sections 241 through 256 of title 2, U.S. Code (Federal Corrupt Practices Act). (See § 0.50(a).)

(n) Civil actions arising under 39 U.S.C. 3010, 3011 (Postal Reorganization Act).

(o) Resolving questions that arise as to Federal prisoners held in custody by Federal officers or in Federal prisons, commitments of mentally defective defendants and juvenile delinquents, validity and construction of sentences, probation, and parole.

(p) Supervision of matters arising under the Escape and Rescue Act (18 U.S.C. 751, 752), the Fugitive Felon Act (18 U.S.C. 1072, 1073), and the Obstruction of Justice Statute (18 U.S.C. 1503).

(q) Supervision of matters arising under the Bail Reform Act of 1966 (28 U.S.C. 3041-3143, 3146-3152, 3568).

(r) Supervision of matters arising under the Narcotic Addict Rehabilitation Act of 1966 (18 U.S.C. 4251-4255; 28 U.S.C. 2901-2906; 42 U.S.C. 3411-3426, 3441, 3442).

(s) Civil proceedings in which the United States is the plaintiff filed under the Organized Crime Control Act of 1970, 18 U.S.C. 1963-1968.

(t) Upon request, certifications under 18 U.S.C. 245.

(u) Exercise of the authority vested in the Attorney General under 10 U.S.C. 374(b)(2)(E) to approve the use of military equipment by Department of Defense personnel to provide transportation and base of operations support in connection with a civilian law enforcement operation.

HISTORY:

[Order No. 423-69, 34 FR 20388, Dec. 31, 1969, as amended by Order No. 446-70, 35 FR 19666, Dec. 29, 1970; Order No. 458-71, 36 FR 10862, June 4, 1971; Order No. 481-72, 37 FR 9214, May 6, 1972; Order No. 511-73, 38 FR 8152, March 29, 1973; Order No. 960-81, 46 FR 52345, Oct. 27, 1981; Order No. 1002-83, 48 FR 9523, Mar. 7, 1983; Order No. 1034-83, 48 FR 50713, Nov. 3, 1983; Order No. 1364-89, 54 FR 36304, Sept. 1, 1989; Order No. 1540-91, 56 FR 55235, Oct. 25, 1991]

AUTHORITY:

AUTHORITY NOTE APPLICABLE TO ENTIRE PART:

5 U.S.C. 301; 28 U.S.C. 509, 510, 515-519.

NOTES:

NOTES APPLICABLE TO ENTIRE CHAPTER:

CROSS REFERENCES: Customs Service, Department of the Treasury: See Customs Duties, 19 CFR chapter I.

Internal Revenue Service, Department of the Treasury: See Internal Revenue Service, 26 CFR chapter I.

Employees' Benefits: See title 20.

Federal Trade Commission: See Commercial Practices, 16 CFR chapter I.

Other regulations issued by the Department of Justice appear in title 4; title 8; title 21; title 45; title 48.

§ 0.56 Exclusive or concurrent jurisdiction.

The Assistant Attorney General in charge of the Criminal Division is authorized to determine administratively whether the Federal Government has exclusive or concurrent jurisdiction over offenses committed upon lands acquired by the United States, and to consider problems arising therefrom.

HISTORY:

Order No. 423-69, 34 FR 20388, Dec. 31, 1969, as amended by Order 445-70, 35 FR 19397, Dec. 23, 1970.

AUTHORITY:

AUTHORITY NOTE APPLICABLE TO ENTIRE PART:

5 U.S.C. 301; 28 U.S.C. 509, 510, 515-519.

NOTES:

NOTES APPLICABLE TO ENTIRE CHAPTER:

CROSS REFERENCES: Customs Service, Department of the Treasury: See Customs Duties, 19 CFR chapter I.

Internal Revenue Service, Department of the Treasury: See Internal Revenue Service, 26 CFR chapter I.

Employees' Benefits: See title 20.

Federal Trade Commission: See Commercial Practices, 16 CFR chapter I.

Other regulations issued by the Department of Justice appear in title 4; title 8; title 21; title 45; title 48.

§ 0.57 Criminal prosecutions against juveniles.

The Assistant Attorney General in charge of the Criminal Division and his Deputy

continued

EXERCISE 12.4
continued

Assistant Attorneys General are each authorized to exercise the power and authority vested in the Attorney General by sections 5032 and 5036 of title 18, United States Code, relating to criminal proceedings against juveniles. The Assistant Attorney General in charge of the Criminal Division is authorized to redelegate any function delegated to him under this section to United States Attorneys and to the Chief of the Section within the Criminal Division which supervises the implementation of the Juvenile Justice and Delinquency Prevention Act (18 U.S.C. 5031 et seq.).

HISTORY:
[Order No. 579-74, 39 FR 37771, Oct. 24, 1974, as amended by Order No. 894-80, 45 FR 34269, May 22, 1980]

AUTHORITY:
AUTHORITY NOTE APPLICABLE TO ENTIRE PART:

5 U.S.C. 301; 28 U.S.C. 509, 510, 515-519.

NOTES:
NOTES APPLICABLE TO ENTIRE CHAPTER:

CROSS REFERENCES: Customs Service, Department of the Treasury: See Customs Duties, 19 CFR chapter I.

Internal Revenue Service, Department of the Treasury: See Internal Revenue Service, 26 CFR chapter I.

Employees' Benefits: See title 20.

Federal Trade Commission: See Commercial Practices, 16 CFR chapter I.

Other regulations issued by the Department of Justice appear in title 4; title 8; title 21; title 45; title 48.

2. The reasoning behind the change of regulations is not explained in the *Federal Register.*
   a. True
   b. False
3. The general intent behind the changes to the regulations governing contributions to a TSP is
   a. to make the procedure more complicated.
   b. to lower the amount of contributions that may be made.
   c. to clarify the regulations governing makeup contributions.
   d. to disallow makeup contributions due to military service.
4. The original citation to the *Federal Register* for each of the proposed regulations is not given.
   a. True
   b. False
5. Proposed amendments to the regulation are not included in the *Federal Register.*
   a. True
   b. False

F. Exercise 12.6: *Federal Register*—Notices

1. The notice at 67 FR 44606 concerns a
   a. proposed rule.
   b. proposed regulation.
   c. proposed consent agreement.
   d. proposed comment period.

Proposed Rules

Federal Register
Vol. 67, No. 96
Friday, May 17, 2002

This section of the FEDERAL REGISTER contains notices to the public of the proposed issuance of rules and regulations. The purpose of these notices is to give interested persons an opportunity to participate in the rule making prior to the adoption of the final rules.

FEDERAL RETIREMENT THRIFT INVESTMENT BOARD

5 CFR Parts 1605, 1620, 1651, and 1655

Correction of Administrative Errors; Expanded and Continuing Eligibility; Death Benefits; Loan Program

AGENCY: Federal Retirement Thrift Investment Board.

ACTION: Proposed rule with request for comments.

SUMMARY: The Executive Director of the Federal Retirement Thrift Investment Board (Board) proposes to revise the Board's Uniformed Services Employment and Reemployment Rights (USERRA) regulations regarding Thrift Savings Plan (TSP) contributions and loan payments, and to update the definitions used in those regulations. The Executive Director also proposes to amend the Board's death benefit regulations to allow the spouse of a deceased participant to transfer a TSP death benefit payment to an eligible retirement plan or to the spouse's existing TSP account. Finally, the Executive Director proposes to amend the Board's loan regulations to explain that the Soldier's and Sailors' Civil Relief Act of 1940 allows a participant returning to civilian service from active duty military service to reduce to 6 percent the interest rate owed on a TSP loan for the period of missed TSP loan payments due to military leave.

DATES: Comments must be received on or before June 17, 2002.

ADDRESSES: Comments may be sent to Patrick J. Forrest, Federal Retirement Thrift Investment Board, 1250 H Street, NW., Washington, DC 20005. The Board's Fax number is (202) 942–1676.

FOR FURTHER INFORMATION CONTACT: Patrick J. Forrest on (202) 942–1661.

SUPPLEMENTARY INFORMATION: The Board administers the TSP, which was established by the Federal Employees' Retirement System Act of 1986 (FERSA), Public Law 99–335, 100 Stat. 514. The TSP provisions of FERSA have been codified, as amended, largely at 5 U.S.C. 8351 and 8401–79. The TSP is a tax-deferred retirement savings plan for Federal civilian employees and members of the uniformed services which is similar to cash or deferred arrangements established under section 401(k) of the Internal Revenue Code (26 U.S.C. 401(k)).

Contributions

Section 4(a)(1) of the Uniformed Services Employment and Reemployment Rights Act of 1994 (USERRA), codified at 5 U.S.C. 8351(b)(8) and 8432b, describes the rights to TSP benefits afforded to civilian TSP participants who are reemployed in civilian service or restored from a nonpay status to pay status following a release from military service, discharge from hospitalization related to that service, or other similar event. On June 9, 1999, the Board published a final rule in the **Federal Register** (64 FR 31052) to explain how TSP participants can obtain the benefits of USERRA. The rule is codified at 5 CFR part 1620, subpart E; this proposed rule amends the final rule.

Current § 1620.42 explains that a participant can make up TSP contributions missed due to military service if he or she is reemployed or restored to pay status in the civilian service under USERRA. It provides that a participant can file a contribution election immediately when he or she returns to civilian service under USERRA, and does not have to wait for an Open Season to begin making current TSP contributions. Section 1620.42 does not place a time limit on making an immediate contribution election under USERRA. Under 5 CFR 1600.12(a)(1) and 1604.3(b), new civilian employees and service members can file a TSP contribution election any time within the first 60 days of their hiring or appointment, without waiting for a TSP Open Season. Experience has shown this to be an adequate time for making a contribution election. Therefore, the Executive Director proposes to amend § 1620.42 to adopt a 60-day time limit for the filing of contribution elections under USERRA.

The regulation at 5 CFR 1605.31, published by the Board in the **Federal Register** on August 22, 2001 (66 FR 44276), explains how to compute USERRA makeup contributions. It does not explain how a participant's right to make up contributions under USERRA is affected by contributions the participant made to a uniformed services TSP account under 5 U.S.C. 8440e during his or her period of military service. The Executive Director proposes to revise § 1605.31(c) to explain that the amount of employee makeup contributions must be reduced by the amount the participant contributed to his or her uniformed services TSP account. In addition, proposed § 1605.31(c) explains that a FERS participant who made contributions from basic pay to a uniformed services account during a period of military service will immediately upon return to civilian service or pay status receive agency matching makeup contributions to his or her civilian account for those uniformed services contributions. Finally, proposed § 1605.31(c) explains that a participant who makes up missed employee contributions will receive attributable agency matching contributions to the extent he or she did not receive matching contributions on employee contributions made to a uniformed services account.

Loans and Withdrawals

The repayment of a TSP loan is governed by FERSA, the Internal Revenue Code, and by the regulations issued by the Internal Revenue Service (IRS) and the Board. Section 414(u) of the Internal Revenue Code (26 U.S.C. 414(u)) establishes the Federal income tax rules relating to USERRA. Under section 414(u)(4) and the IRS regulations interpreting that provision (26 CFR 1.72(p)–1, Q&A–9), a retirement plan may suspend a participant's obligation to make loan payments during a period of military service.

Under the Board's current regulations, the TSP will declare a loan to be a taxable distribution if a participant separates from service without repaying the loan or is in nonpay status for more than one year. 5 CFR 1655.13(a)(1), (a)(2). A participant may be eligible to have the taxable distribution reversed if he or she is reemployed or restored to pay status under USERRA. 5 CFR 1620.45(b). If the participant is eligible to have the distribution reversed, the TSP will reinstate the loan so that the participant can resume loan payments, subject to limitations on the term of a

continued

TSP loan, or give the participant an opportunity to repay the loan in full. If reinstated, a general purpose TSP loan must be repaid within five years of disbursement; a residential TSP loan must be repaid within 18 years of disbursement.

The Executive Director proposes to amend § 1620.45 to provide for the suspension of loan payments for a participant who enters nonpay status to perform military service beyond one year, thereby avoiding a taxable distribution. Interest will accrue on the loan during the period that payments are suspended. When the participant returns to pay status, the loan payments will resume and the period of military service will be added to the loan repayment period. Therefore, the participant or the employing agency must notify the TSP record keeper of the beginning and ending dates of military service.

Under the proposed amendment, the TSP will continue to close a loan account and declare a taxable distribution if a participant separates from government employment and does not repay the loan, or if the participant is in nonpay status for more than one year and the TSP does not receive documentation that the nonpay status is due to military service. However, if the participant in fact separated or entered nonpay status to perform military service, he or she can later request that the loan be reinstated when the participant is reemployed or returns to pay status under USERRA.

Current § 1620.45(c) allows a participant who is reemployed pursuant to USERRA one year to decide whether to reinstate a loan or to return a mandatory withdrawal that was paid out when the participant separated from civilian service. In analogous situations, where participants are separated from Federal service and later reinstated, TSP regulations give participants 90 days to decide whether to reinstate a loan or return a withdrawal. *See* 5 CFR 1605.13(d) and (e). In the interest of conformity, the Executive Director proposes to amend § 1620.45 to provide a 90-day period for the same decisions by members of the uniformed services.

The Executive Director also proposes an amendment to the Board's loan regulations which is unrelated to USERRA. The TSP's loan regulations were first published in the **Federal Register** on January 10, 1990, and amended on November 18, 1996, and August 26, 1998 (55 FR 978, 61 FR 58754, 63 FR 45391, respectively). Those regulations are codified at 5 CFR part 1655. Current § 1655.7 states that the interest rate for a TSP loan is established at the time the loan is approved and remains constant for the life of the loan. However, under the Soldiers' and Sailors' Civil Relief Act of 1940, 50 U.S.C. app. 526, when a person enters active duty military service, no obligation or liability incurred before entry into active duty military service may continue to bear an interest rate in excess of 6 percent per annum. The Board interprets the term "obligation" to apply to a TSP loan because a participant is required by statute and regulation to repay a TSP loan with interest, even though the repayment is to his or her own account. Therefore, the Executive Director is proposing to amend § 1655.7 to provide that a participant who returns to civilian service from active duty military service may request that the interest rate on his or her TSP loan be reduced to 6 percent for the period the participant was in active duty military service. The proposed amendment also explains the process for requesting this benefit.

USERRA Definitions

The Executive Director also proposes to revise the definition section of the USERRA regulation, 5 CFR 1620.41. Specifically, the definitions "basic pay" and "leave without pay" are deleted because they are not used in the regulatory text. In addition, the definitions "current contributions" and "reemployed or reemployment" are simplified; the definition "separation or separated" is rewritten as "separate from civilian service" to conform to the usage in the proposed rule; and the definitions "retroactive period," "retroactive period beginning date," and "retroactive period ending date" are updated and condensed into one definition to reflect a recent amendment to FERSA allowing employees who are reemployed or returned to pay status immediately to begin making TSP contributions.

Death Benefits

FERSA provides that a deceased participant's TSP account will be paid to his or her beneficiary or beneficiaries. 5 U.S.C. 8433(e) and 8424(d). The Board's regulations governing the payment of a TSP death benefit were published in the **Federal Register** on June 13, 1997 (62 FR 32426) and are codified at 5 CFR part 1651.

Current § 1651.14(c) states that a deceased participant's spouse may transfer a TSP death benefit payment to an individual retirement account (IRA), but not to another eligible retirement plan. That provision is based on section 402(c)(9) of the Internal Revenue Code (26 U.S.C. 402(c)(9)), in effect before January 1, 2002. However, the Internal Revenue Code was amended effective January 1, 2002, to provide that a death benefit may be transferred to any eligible retirement plan described at 26 U.S.C. 402(c)(8). *See* The Economic Growth and Tax Relief Reconciliation Act (EGTRRA) of 2001, Public Law 107–16, sec. 641(d), 115 Stat. 38, at 120. The Executive Director is proposing to adopt this policy for the TSP by amending § 1651.14(c).

Since the TSP itself is an eligible retirement plan, the Executive Director also proposes to permit the spouse of a deceased TSP participant to transfer a TSP death benefit payment from the deceased participant's account to the spouse's TSP account (if he or she has one). Proposed § 1651.14(c) explains how such a transfer can be requested.

Finally, the proposed rule amends §§ 1651.2, 1651.5, and 1651.14 to substitute the word "spouse" for the words "widow" and "widower." This change conforms the terms used in the death benefit regulations to those used in TSP publications.

Regulatory Flexibility Act

I certify that these regulations will not have a significant economic impact on a substantial number of small entities. They will affect only employees of the Federal Government.

Paperwork Reduction Act

I certify that these regulations do not require additional reporting under the criteria of the Paperwork Reduction Act of 1980.

Unfunded Mandates Reform Act of 1995

Pursuant to the Unfunded Mandates Reform Act of 1995, 2 U.S.C. 602, 632, 653, 1501–1571, the effects of this regulation on state, local, and tribal governments and the private sector have been assessed. This regulation will not compel the expenditure in any one year of $100 million or more by state, local, and tribal governments, in the aggregate, or by the private sector. Therefore, a statement under § 1532 is not required.

List of Subjects

5 CFR Part 1605

Claims, Employment benefit plans, Government employees, Military personnel, Pensions, Retirement.

5 CFR Part 1620

District of Columbia, Employment benefit plans, Government employees, Military personnel, Pensions, Retirement.

5 CFR Part 1651

Employment benefit plans, Government employees, Pensions, Retirement.

5 CFR Part 1655

Employment benefit plans, Government employees, Military personnel, Pensions, Retirement.

Roger W. Mehle,

Executive Director, Federal Retirement Thrift Investment Board.

For the reasons set forth in the preamble, the Board proposes to amend 5 CFR chapter VI as follows:

PART 1605—CORRECTION OF ADMINISTRATIVE ERRORS

1. The authority citation for part 1605 is revised to read as follows:

Authority: 5 U.S.C. 8351, 8432a, and 8474(b)(5) and (c)(1).

Section 1605.14 also issued under Title II, Pub. L. 106–265, 114 Stat. 770.

Subpart D also issued under 5 U.S.C. 8432b(b)(4) and (i); Div. A, Title VI, sec. 661(b), Pub. L. 106–65, 114 Stat. 1654.

Subpart D—Miscellaneous Provisions

2. Section 1605.31 is revised to read as follows:

§ 1605.31 Contributions missed as a result of military service.

(a) *Applicability.* This section applies to employees who meet the conditions specified at 5 CFR 1620.40 and who are eligible to make up employee contributions or to receive employing agency contributions missed as a result of military service.

(b) *Missed employee contributions.* An employee who separates or enters nonpay status to perform military service may be eligible to make up TSP contributions when he or she is reemployed or restored to pay status in the civilian service. Eligibility for making up missed employee contributions will be determined in accordance with the rules specified at 5 CFR part 1620, subpart E. Missed employee contributions must be made up in accordance with the rules set out in § 1605.11(c) and the following procedures:

(1) The employing agency will use the contribution election on file for the employee at the time he or she separated or was placed in nonpay status. If an employee terminated TSP contributions within two months before entry into military service, he or she may make a retroactive election to resume contributions for the first open season following the termination. The employee may also make retroactive contribution elections for any open season that occurred during the period of military service, as described at 5 CFR 1620.42.

(2) The pay used to determine the amount of contributions eligible for makeup is the pay the employee would have earned had he or she remained continuously employed in the position held immediately before the separation or placement in nonpay status.

(3) If the employee contributed to a uniformed services TSP account during the period of military service, the amount of employee contributions available for makeup will be reduced by the total amount of employee contributions made to the uniformed services TSP account. (This includes contributions from basic pay, incentive pay, and special pay, including bonus pay.)

(c) *Missed agency contributions.* A FERS employee who separates or enters nonpay status to perform military service is eligible to receive agency makeup contributions when he or she is reemployed or restored to pay status in the civilian service, as follows:

(1) The employee is entitled to receive the agency automatic (1%) contributions that he or she would have received had the employee remained in civilian service or pay status. Within 60 days of the employee's reemployment or restoration to pay status, the employing agency must calculate the agency automatic (1%) makeup contributions and report those contributions to the record keeper. After the contribution has been reported, the agency must submit lost earnings records for the contribution.

(2) An employee who contributed to a uniformed services TSP account during the period of military service is also immediately entitled to receive agency matching makeup contributions to his or her civilian account for the employee contributions to the uniformed services account that were deducted from his or her basic pay, subject to any reduction in matching contributions required by paragraph (c)(4) of this section. However, an employee is not entitled to receive agency matching makeup contributions on contributions that were deducted from his or her incentive pay or special pay, including bonus pay, while performing military service.

(3) An employee who makes up missed contributions is entitled to receive attributable agency matching makeup contributions (unless the employee has already received the maximum amount of matching contributions, as described in paragraphs (c)(2) and (c)(4) of this section).

(4) If the employee received uniformed services matching contributions, the agency matching makeup contributions will be reduced by the amount of the uniformed services matching contributions.

(d) *Lost earnings.* The employing agency will submit lost earnings records pursuant to 5 CFR part 1606 for missed agency contributions received by the employee under paragraph (c) of this section. The employee will elect to have the lost earnings calculated using either the rates of return based on the contributions allocation(s) on file for the participant during the period of military service or using the rates of return for the G Fund; the participant must make this election at the same time his or her makeup schedule is established pursuant to § 1606.11(c).

PART 1620—EXPANDED AND CONTINUING ELIGIBILITY

3. The authority citation for part 1620 continues to read as follows:

Authority: 5 U.S.C. 8474(b)(5) and (c)(1).

Subpart C also issued under 5 U.S.C. 8440a(b)(7), 8440b(b)(8), and 8440c(b)(8).

Subpart D also issued under Pub. L. 104–106, sec. 1043(b), 110 Stat. 186, 434–5; and Pub. L. 101–508, sec. 7202(m)(2), 104 Stat. 1388.

Subpart E also issued under 5 U.S.C. 8432b(i) and Div. A, Title VI, sec. 661(b), Pub. L. 106–65, 114 Stat. 1654.

Subpart E—Uniformed Services Employment and Reemployment Rights Act (USERRA)—Covered Military Service

4. Section 1620.41 is revised to read as follows:

§ 1620.41 Definitions.

As used in this subpart:

Current contributions means contributions that must be made for the current pay date which is reported on the journal voucher that accompanies the payroll submission.

Nonpay status means an employer-approved temporary absence from duty.

Reemployed or returned to pay status means reemployed in or returned to a pay status, pursuant to 38 U.S.C. chapter 43, to a position that is subject to 5 U.S.C. 8351 or chapter 84.

Retroactive period means the period for which an employee can make up missed employee contributions and receive retroactive agency contributions. It begins the day after the employee separates or enters nonpay status to perform military service and ends when the employee is reemployed or returned to pay status.

2. The Federal Trade Commission placed the proposed consent order on the public record for 30 days to receive comments from
   a. all interested persons.
   b. the government.
   c. Biovail Corporation.
   d. Elan Corporation.
3. The company distributing the generic forms of Adalat were
   a. Elan.
   b. Biovail.
   c. Teva.
   d. Both b and c
4. Biovail and Elan entered the distribution agreement, with Teva Pharmaceuticals participating in the negotiations.
   a. True
   b. False
5. The proposed order states that
   a. Biovail can no longer sell its products in the United States.
   b. Elan can no longer sell its products in the United States.
   c. Teva can no longer sell products for either Biovail or Elan.
   d. None of the above.

44606 Federal Register / Vol. 67, No. 128 / Wednesday, July 3, 2002 / Notices

records management inspections and its role as Archivist.

h. Disclosure to contractors, grantees or volunteers performing or working on a contract, service, grant, cooperative agreement, or job for the Board.

Disclosure to consumer reporting agencies:
Not applicable.

Policies and practices for storing, retrieving, accessing, retaining, and disposing of records in the system:

Storage: Records are maintained in paper and electronic format.

Retrievability: Electronically–stored information may be retrieved based on name, social security number, passport or visa number, or date of birth.

Safeguards: Only authorized personnel will have access to this information. Access to information derived from law enforcement data bases will be extremely limited.

Retention and disposal: Information in this system of records will be destroyed two years after the date the individual is admitted to the Board's premises.

System manager(s) and address:
Billy Sauls, Chief of Uniform Security, Management Division, Board of Governors of the Federal Reserve System, 20th and Constitution Avenue, NW., Washington, DC 20551.

Notification procedure:
Inquiries should be sent to the Secretary of the Board, Board of Governors of the Federal Reserve System, 20th and Constitution Avenue, NW., Washington, DC 20551. The request should contain the individual's name, date of birth, Social Security or passport number, and approximate date of record.

Record access procedures:
Same as "Notification procedure" above.

Contesting record procedures:
Same as "Notification procedure" above.

Record source categories:
Information will be gathered primarily from the individual who wishes to enter the Board's premises. Additional information may be gathered from law enforcement data bases where appropriate.

Systems exempted from certain provisions of the act:
This system is exempt from 5 U.S.C. 552a(c)(3), (d), (e)(1), (e)(4)(G), (e)(4)(H), (e)(4)(I), and (f) of the Privacy Act pursuant to 5 U.S.C. 552a(k)(2).

By order of the Board of Governors of the Federal Reserve System, June 27, 2002.

Jennifer J. Johnson,

Secretary of the Board.

[FR Doc. 02–16724 Filed 7–2–02; 8:45 am]

BILLING CODE 6210–01–S

FEDERAL TRADE COMMISSION

[File No. 011 0132]

Biovail Corporation and Elan Corporation, plc; Analysis To Aid Public Comment

AGENCY: Federal Trade Commission.

ACTION: Proposed Consent Agreement.

SUMMARY: The consent agreement in this matter settles alleged violations of Federal law prohibiting unfair or deceptive acts or practices or unfair methods of competition. The attached Analysis to Aid Public Comment describes both the allegations in the draft complaint that accompanies the consent agreement and the terms of the consent order—embodied in the consent agreement—that would settle these allegations.

DATES: Comments must be received on or before July 29, 2002.

ADDRESSES: Comments filed in paper form should be directed to: FTC/Office of the Secretary, Room 159–H, 600 Pennsylvania Avenue, NW., Washington, DC 20580. Comments filed in electronic form should be directed to: *consentagreement@ftc.gov,* as prescribed below.

FOR FURTHER INFORMATION CONTACT: Joseph Simmons or Randall Marks, Bureau of Competition, 600 Pennsylvania Avenue, NW., Washington, DC 20580, (202) 326–3300 or 326–2571.

SUPPLEMENTARY INFORMATION: Pursuant to Section 6(f) of the Federal Trade Commission Act, 28 Stat. 721, 15 U.S.C. 46(f), and Section 2.34 of the Commission's Rules of Practice, 16 CFR 2.34, notice is hereby given that the above-captioned consent agreement containing a consent order to cease and desist, having been filed with and accepted, subject to final approval, by the Commission, has been placed on the public record for a period of thirty (30) days. The following Analysis to Aid Public Comment describes the terms of the consent agreement, and the allegations in the complaint. An electronic copy of the full text of the consent agreement package can be obtained from the FTC Home Page (for June 27, 2002), on the World Wide Web, at *http://www.ftc.gov/os/2002/06/index.htm.* A paper copy can be obtained from the FTC Public Reference Room, Room 130–H, 600 Pennsylvania Avenue, NW., Washington, DC 20580, either in person or by calling (202) 326–2222.

Public comments are invited, and may be filed with the Commission in either paper or electronic form. Comments filed in paper form should be directed to: FTC/Office of the Secretary, Room 159–H, 600 Pennsylvania Avenue, NW., Washington, DC 20580. If a comment contains nonpublic information, it must be filed in paper form, and the first page of the document must be clearly labeled "confidential." Comments that do not contain any nonpublic information may instead be filed in electronic form (in ASCII format, WordPerfect, or Microsoft Word) as part of or as an attachment to email messages directed to the following email box: *consentagreement@ftc.gov.* Such comments will be considered by the Commission and will be available for inspection and copying at its principal office in accordance with Section 4.9(b)(6)(ii) of the Commission's Rules of Practice, 16 CFR 4.9(b)(6)(ii)).

Analysis To Aid Public Comment

The Federal Trade Commission has accepted for public comment an agreement and proposed consent order with Biovail Corporation ("Biovail") and Elan Corporation, plc ("Elan"), settling charges that the two companies illegally agreed to restrain competition in the market for generic Adalat CC. The Commission has placed the proposed consent order on the public record for thirty days to receive comments by interested persons. The proposed consent order has been entered into for settlement purposes only and does not constitute an admission by either Biovail or Elan that it violated the law or that the facts alleged in the complaint, other than the jurisdictional facts, are true.

Background

Biovail is a Canadian manufacturer of branded and generic pharmaceutical products. Elan is an Irish manufacturer of branded and generic pharmaceutical products. Biovail and Elan are the only two sellers of generic forms of Adalat CC ("generic Adalat"), a once-a-day antihypertension medication. No other company has even sought Food and Drug Administration ("FDA") approval to sell a 30 mg or a 60 mg dosage form of generic Adalat. Bayer AG ("Bayer") manufactures branded Adalat CC. In 1999, before the entry of generic equivalents to Adalat CC, Bayer's United States sales of the 30 mg and 60 mg doses of Adalat CC were in excess of $270 million.

Biovail was the first to file an Abbreviated New Drug Application ("ANDA") for FDA approval on the 60 mg dosage, and Elan was the first to file an ANDA for FDA approval on the 30 mg dosage. Thus, Elan had 180 days of exclusivity for the 30 mg product upon receiving final FDA approval, and Biovail had the 180-day exclusivity on the 60 mg product upon receiving final FDA approval. Each was the second to file on the other dosage.

In October 1999, after both Biovail and Elan (hereinafter sometimes referred to as "Respondents") had filed for FDA approval of their 30 mg and 60 mg generic Adalat products, they entered into an agreement involving all

continued

four of their generic Adalat products. That agreement (the "Agreement"), and the Respondents' conduct arising out of that Agreement, are the subject of the Commission's complaint. The complaint alleges that, by entering the Agreement, Respondents illegally created market power in the United States market for sales of 30 mg and 60 mg dosages of generic Adalat. There is little prospect of new entry in the near future, because no other companies have applied for FDA approval of a 30 mg or a 60 mg generic Adalat product.

The Challenged Conduct

Under the Respondents' Agreement, Elan appointed Biovail as the exclusive distributor of Elan's 30 mg and 60 mg generic Adalat products. At the time of the Agreement, neither Elan nor Biovail distributed its own generic drugs in the United States. Teva Pharmaceuticals, Inc. ("Teva"), a distributor of some of Biovail's products, participated in the negotiations leading up to the Agreement. The Agreement provided that Biovail appoint Teva to sub-distribute Elan's 30 mg generic Adalat product in the United States. With respect to Elan's 60 mg product, the Agreement provided that, upon notice from Elan that Elan's 60 mg product was ready for commercial launch, Biovail would appoint either Teva or another company as a sub-distributor of that product. The Agreement has a minimum term of 15 years.

The FDA approval Elan's mg generic Adalat product in March 2000 and its 60 mg product in October 2001. It approved Biovail's 30 mg and 60 mg generic Adalat products in December 2000. Biovail began selling Elan's 30 mg product immediately after receiving final FDA approval. Biovail began selling its own 60 mg product through Teva immediately after the FDA gave final approval to that product. Neither Elan's 60 mg product nor Biovail's 30 mg product, however, has ever been launched commercially. Thus, although two 30 mg generic Adalat products and two 60 mg generic Adalat products have had FDA approval for many months, consumers can purchase only one product at each strength.

The complaint alleges that, in exchange for the right to distribute Elan's products and share in the profits of those products, Biovail agreed to make specified payments to Elan. To date, Biovail has paid Elan approximately $33 million in connection with its distribution of Elan's 30 mg generic Adalat product, and $12.75 million in connection with the right to distribute Elan's 60 mg generic Adalat product.

As the complaint alleges, the Agreement gave Biovail substantial incentives not to launch its own 30 mg product. Although Biovail has had final FDA approval to market its 30 mg product for over one year, and the Agreement purports to require Biovail to use "reasonable commercial endeavors" to launch that product "with reasonable dispatch," Biovail has not yet launched that product. Biovail's launch of its own 30 mg product could be expected to cause a significant reduction in the price of Elan's incumbent 30 mg product, and generate for Elan's product lower total profits, which Biovail shares with Elan. For the same reasons, the Agreement diminished Biovail's incentives to exercise maximum efforts at eliminating the technological obstacles, if any, that Biovail asserts have impeded its ability to launch a self-manufactured 30 mg product. Elan also does not have any incentive to enforce the Agreement's provision requiring that Biovail use reasonable efforts to launch its 30 mg product in competition with Elan's product.

Similarly, the complaint alleges that the Agreement gave Elan substantial incentives not to launch its 60 mg product. Under the Agreement, in exchange for receiving a large up-front payment, Elan, in effect, stood to receive no royalties upon launch of its 60 mg product, until that product generated certain profits for Biovail. It would take several years of sales before Elan's 60 mg product would generate such profits, and once that triggering event happened, Elan's royalty was to be only 6% of profits. Accordingly, the complain alleges that the Agreement compensated Elan for its 60 mg product up-front and pre-entry, while substantially diminishing that product's value to Elan thereafter. The Agreement also diminished Elan's incentives to exercise maximum efforts at eliminating any technological obstacles to launching its 60 mg product, if any, that Elan has asserted to exist. Moreover, neither Elan nor Biovail had any financial incentives to enforce the provision requiring launch of Elan's 60 mg product. As with the launch of Biovail's 30 mg product, Respondents knew that Elan's launch of its own 60 mg product could be expected to cause a reduction in the price of Biovail's incumbent 60 mg product by a significant amount and generate lower total profits for Biovail's product. It was in Bilvail's strategic interest, therefore, for Elan not to launch its 60 mg products.

The complaint further alleges that even its Bilvail had launched its 30 mg product and Elan had launched its 60 mg product, the Agreement allows Biovail to control or influence pricing and other competitive features of both its and Elan's 30 mg and 60 mg generic Adalat products. Biovail was thus in a position to profit by suppressing competition between its and Elan's products.

For the above reasons, the complaint alleges that Respondents' Agreement is an agreement not to compete between the only two producers of the 30 mg and 60 mg generic Adalat products. As a result, Teva, Biovail's distributor, is the only firm selling generic Adalat to consumers in the United States, and consumers have had access to only one of two approved generic Adalat products at each strength. Moreover, the Agreement is not justified by an countervailing efficiency.

The Proposed Order

The proposed order remedies the Respondents' anticompetitive conduct by requiring them to end their anticompetitive Agreement and barring them from engaging in similar conduct in the future. It maintains supply of the incumbent generic Adalat products while Respondents unwind their anticompetitive Agreement and eliminates the anticompetitive obstacles to entry of a second 30 mg and a second 60 mg generic Adalat product.

Paragraph I of the proposed order contains definitions, one of which defines the "Adalat CC Agreement" as the "License, Distribution & Supply Agreement" covering generic Adalat that Biovail and Elan executed on October 4, 1999, and all modifications and amendments thereto. We discuss other definitions below, as needed to explain the substantive provisions of the proposed order.

Paragraph II of the proposed order is a core provision, prohibiting Biovail or Elan from repeating the instant conduct by entering anticompetitive price, output, or distribution agreements with other generic drug companies. This provision targets agreements between either Respondent and other persons concerning a generic drug for which both parties to the agreement have filed for FDA approval of an ANDA referencing the same pioneer drug product. It aims to prohibit agreements between competing generic drug manufacturers that restrict the marketing of competing generic drugs.

Paragraph III of the proposed order requires Biovail and Elan to terminate their agreement on generic Adalat no later than the date on which the order becomes final. Paragraph 13 of the Agreement Containing Consent Order required them to start the termination process upon their execution of that document. The proviso to Paragraph III allows Biovail and Elan to resolve financial issues connected to the termination of their agreement on generic Adalat on mutually agreeable terms; however, they cannot resolve those financial issues by using sales, revenues, or profits generated by generic Adalat or any other drug product, or by transferring rights connected to any drug product. This limitation is intended to ensure that, in resolving the financial issues, Respondents do not perpetuate the anticompetitive effects of the Agreement by continuing the entanglements between them on generic Adalat or on other drug products.

Paragraph IV of the proposed order prohibits Elan from distributing its generic Adalat product through Teva. This prohibition is necessary because Biovail and Teva have a longstanding commercial relationship, whereby Teva distributes some of Biovail's product. Forbidding Elan from distributing this generic Adalat products through Teva will minimize the risk of inappropriate information exchange among Biovail, Elan, and Teva regarding generic Adalat, by eliminating any legitimate reason for all three companies to discuss their marketing of the products. Thus, it will help ensure that the termination of the Agreement fully restores the proper competitive incentives for each company.

The proviso to Paragraph IV requires Elan to supply Teva, through Biovail, with Elan's 30 mg product, until the earlier of Biovail's launch of its own 30 mg product or May 31, 2003 (the "Interim Supply Agreement"). This provision eliminates any disruption of supply of the 30 mg product to consumers while Elan makes alternate arrangements for the distribution of its products. Once Elan begins to distribute its own product through an independent distributor, the Interim Supply Agreement will assure that consumers have access to two generic 30 mg Adalat products. The Interim supply Agreement may continue for up to a year, to give consumers the continued benefit of two 30 mg generic Adalat products while Biovail solves its purported manufacturing difficulty. Biovail has assured the Commission that it expects to overcome any manufacturing problems it has and launch its 30 mg generic Adalat product within a year. (Paragraph V further addresses Biovail's launch of its own 30 mg product, as we discuss below.)

Paragraph IV prohibits Elan from charging Biovail more than Elan's "Cost" for the product. Paragraph I of the proposed order defines "Cost" to mean Elan's actual manufacturing cost. The cost definition is narrow, to minimize Elan's ability to profit from the Interim Supply Agreement through manipulation of the definition. Preventing Elan from profiting by supplying Biovail with the Elan 30 mg generic Adalat product gives Elan a strong incentive to launch its own 30 mg product through an indecent distributor as quickly as possible. Only through that launch will Elan begin to earn a profit on its 30 mg product. Because, under the Interim Supply Agreement, Biovail will receive Elan's 30 mg product at Elan's 30 mg product at Elan's manufacturing cost, Biovail will be in the same competitive position with respect to the cost of the 30 mg product as will Elan. In addition, Biovail will have to compete with Elan's new distributor to gain and maintain market share. Thus, the narrow cost definition will also give consumers the benefit of immediate price competition between the 30 mg product marketed by Teva and the 30 mg product marketed by Elan's independent distributor.

Paragraph V of the proposed order require Elan to use best efforts to launch its 30 mg and 60 mg generic Adalat products as promptly as possible through a distributor other than Teva. It also requires Biovail to use best efforts to manufacture and distribute its 30 mg Adalat product, and to use best efforts to continue to manufacture and distribute its 60 mg generic Adalat product through a distributor other than Elan's generic Adalat distributor. Paragraph V.C states that the purpose of these requirements is to restore competitive incentives in the market for generic Adalat, and to remedy the lessening of competition resulting from the anticompetitive practices alleged in the Commission's complaint. This provision covers all four generic Adalat products, to ensure that Biovail and generic market their 30 mg and 60 mg products through separate distributors. The proposed order defines "Launch" to require Biovail and Elan to deliver commercial quantities of their generic Adalat products to a viable pharmaceutical distributor pursuant to a commercially reasonable, multi-year contract. This definition will ensure that the launch of Elan's 60 mg product and of Biovail's 30 mg product is on a competitive scale.

The Commission will closely monitor Respondents' efforts to market their products. To facilitate this, the proposed order includes reporting requirements. Paragraph VIII requires Biovail and Elan to submit to the Commission verified written reports detailing each of their efforts to comply with the proposed order. Biovail and Elan must submit these reports every thirty days until they have complied with the proposed order.

Paragraph VI of the proposed order requires Biovail and Elan to give the Commission notice of two types of agreements with other pharmaceutical manufacturers. First, Paragraph VI.A requires Biovail and Elan to give notice of agreements where, at the time of the agreement, the parties to the agreement each own, control, or license another product that is in the same "Therapeutic Class" as the product covered by the agreement. (The proposed order defines "Therapeutic Class" as a class of drugs categorized by the Unified System of Classification contained in the most recent version of the IMS Health Incorporated publication Market Research Database: Product Directory.) Aa proviso excepts from the reporting requirement agreements that only transfer "Drug Delivery Technology" in exchange for a commercially reasonable cash royalty not to exceed drive per cent of revenue. The proposed order defines "Drug Delivery Technology" to mean technology that controls the release rate, or enhances the absorption or utilization of a pharmaceutical compound.)

Second, Paragraph VI.B requires Biovail and Elan to give notice of agreements involving a product for which one party to the agreement has an ANDA that references a New Drug Application ("DNA") that the other party owns, controls, or licenses. The notification provisions contained in Paragraph VI are necessary, because the core prohibition in Paragraph II only reaches agreements involving ANDAs that reference the same branded drug. Paragraph VI ensures that the Commission will receive notice of potentially anticompetitive agreements not covered by Paragraph II (*i.e.*, agreements involving potentially competitive branded products, and agreements regarding a brand product and its generic equivalent.)

Paragraphs VII, VIII, IX, and X of the proposed order contain reporting and other standard Commission order provisions designed to assist the Commission in monitoring compliance with the order. Paragraph XI provides that the order will expire in ten years.

Opportunity for Public Comment

The proposed order has been placed on the public record for thirty days in order to receive comments from interested persons. Comments received during this period will become part of the public record. After thirty days, the Commission will again review the proposed order and the comments received and will decide whether it should withdraw from the agreement

continued

Federal Register / Vol. 67, No. 128 / Wednesday, July 3, 2002 / Notices **44609**

containing the proposed order or make the proposed order final.

By accepting the proposed order subject to final approval, the Commission anticipates that the competitive issues alleged in the complaint will be resolved. The purpose of this analysis is to facilitate public comment on the agreement. It is not intended to constitute an official interpretation of the agreement, the complaint, or the proposed consent order, or to modify their terms in any way.

By direction of the Commission.

Donald S. Clark,

Secretary.

[FR Doc. 02–16711 Filed 7–2–02; 8:45 am]

BILLING CODE 6750–01–M

DEPARTMENT OF HEALTH AND HUMAN SERVICES

Centers for Disease Control and Prevention

[60Day–02–67]

Proposed Data Collections Submitted for Public Comment and Recommendations

In compliance with the requirement of section 3506(c)(2)(A) of the Paperwork Reduction Act of 1995 for opportunity for public comment on proposed data collection projects, the Centers for Disease Control and Prevention (CDC) will publish periodic summaries of proposed projects. To request more information on the proposed projects or to obtain a copy of the data collection plans and instruments, call the CDC Reports Clearance Officer on (404) 498–1210.

Comments are invited on: (a) Whether the proposed collection of information is necessary for the proper performance of the functions of the agency, including whether the information shall have practical utility; (b) the accuracy of the agency's estimate of the burden of the proposed collection of information; (c) ways to enhance the quality, utility, and clarity of the information to be collected; and (d) ways to minimize the burden of the collection of information on respondents, including through the use of automated collection techniques or other forms of information technology. Send comments to Seleda Perryman, CDC Assistant Reports Clearance Officer, 1600 Clifton Road, MS-D24, Atlanta, GA 30333. Written comments should be received within 60 days of this notice.

Proposed Project: Descriptive Epidemiology of Missed or Delayed Diagnosis for Conditions Detected by Newborn Screening—New—National Center for Environmental Health (NCEH), Centers for Disease Control and Prevention (CDC).

Background

Every state in the United States and Washington DC has a public health program to test newborn babies for congenital metabolic and other disorders through laboratory testing of dried blood spots. These programs screen between 4 and 30 different conditions including phenylketonuria (PKU) and congenital hypothroidism, with testing performed in both state laboratories and private laboratories contracted by state health departments. The screening process or system is broader than the state public health newborn screening program, which is composed only of the laboratory and follow-up personnel. It involves the collection of blood from a newborn, analysis of the sample in a screening laboratory, follow up of abnormal results, confirmatory testing and diagnostic work up.

Parents, hospitals, medical providers including primary care providers and specialists, state laboratory and follow-up personnel, advocates, as well as other partners such as local health departments, police, child protection workers and courts play important roles in this process. Most children born with metabolic disease are identified in a timely manner and within the parameters defined by the newborn screening system of each state. These children are referred for diagnosis and treatment. However, some cases are not detected at all or the detection comes too late to prevent harm. These "missed cases" often result in severe morbidity such as mental retardation or death.

In this project, we will update and expand a previous epidemiological study of missed cases of two disorders published in 1986. We will assess the number of cases of each disorder missed, the reasons for the miss and legal outcomes, if any. The reasons for the miss will be tabulated according to which step or steps of the screening process it occurred. Data will be collected by asking state public health laboratory directors, newborn screening laboratory managers, follow up coordinators, lawyers and parent groups with an interest in newborn screening for information regarding missed cases. An estimated 250 subjects will be requested to complete a short questionnaire that asks for information regarding the details of any missed cases of which they are aware. Follow-up telephone calls may be necessary to clarify responses. There is no cost to the respondents.

The survey will highlight procedures and actions taken by states and other participants in newborn screening systems to identify causes of missed cases and to modify policies and procedures to prevent or minimize recurrences. The information gleaned from this study may be used to help craft changes in the screening protocols that will make the process more organized and efficient and less likely to fail an affected child. Further, it is not clear that there is a systematic assessment of missed cases on a population basis; this project will seek to identify procedures for routine surveillance of missed cases.

Respondents	Number of respondents	Number of responses/respondents	Average burden/response (in hours)	Total burden (in hours)
Questionnaire	125	2	15/60	62
Telephone Follow-up	75	2	10/60	24
Total				86

FINAL CONSIDERATIONS

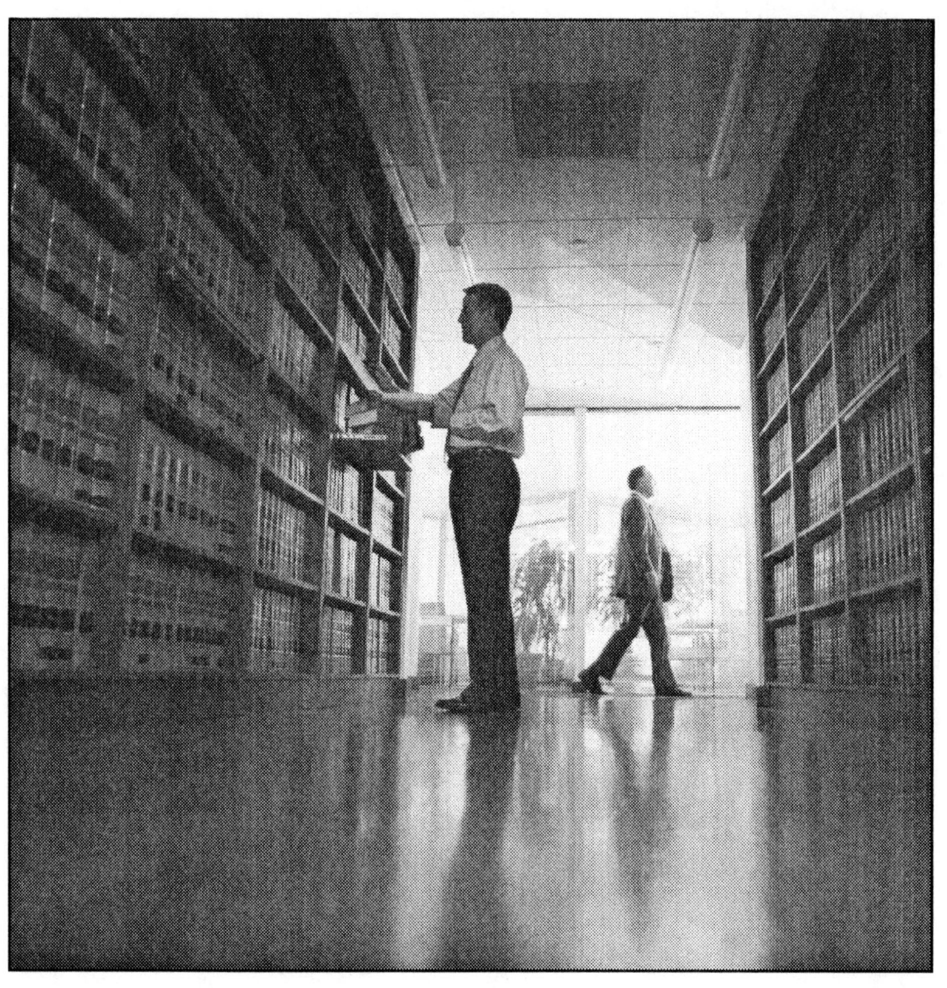

CHAPTER 13

UPDATING THE LAW

I. SHEPARD'S SYSTEM

Consider the following questions:

- Is there some way of continually tracing the history of a case? Is it possible to keep track of where a case goes in the national limelight?
- Can one do the same with statutes, law review materials, administrative rules and regulations, and Supreme Court rulings?
- Can I compare cases within my own region under the reporter system with actions in other states?
- Has a particular case been criticized? Compared? Affirmed? Disregarded? Distinguished? Cited?

The **Shepard's** system is capable of helping the researcher answer each of these questions. At first glance, the Shepard's system often unnerves the first-time user, but once conquered, there is no better way to track the history of case law.

The Shepard's operation is essentially grounded in the need for and use of legal precedent. Practitioners must be sure to have current information, and legal scholars and researchers must find primary-law support that legitimates their arguments. The collection and compilation of cases on similar issues, with either supporting or contrary perspectives, shows litigants just where they stand. If an appellate court has overruled previous rulings, the system will report the result. If a decision is capable of distinction and contrary opinion, the system lays this out as well. Shepard's reports the relative strengths and weaknesses of case law. The **shepardizing** process highlights case law that has been reversed, overruled, upheld, affirmed, or otherwise modified.

The hierarchy of legal decisions, especially the appellate structure of state and federal courts, makes the shepardizing process mandatory. Many decisions by the lower courts are eventually overturned, not only for misapplication of law but also for misinterpretation of law. Lower court decisions, though usually intelligently made, can sometimes be grossly wrong. The Shepard's system reveals the legitimacy of the ruling by comparison and case history. The authority and legitimacy of any case will largely depend on whether its holdings are explained, harmonized, followed, affirmed, or treated in some other positive fashion. Legal researchers should place little reliance on cases that lack history.

When you shepardize a case, you are essentially trying to find out who has referenced that case, where the reference appeared, and what they said about it. The Shepard's system is most useful for its collection, compilation, and chronological review of a given case, as well for its presentation of all subsequent cases (and other materials) that have cited the case in point. Court decisions are listed by volume and page in boldface type. Subsequent citations of the case are listed by volume and page, with an abbreviated judicial history or commentary on the case in point and its treatment by subsequent decisions.

A. Steps in Shepardizing a Court Case

1. Get a case citation.

   109 Wash. 2d 191 (1987)
2. Go to the Shepard's set of books applicable to the *Washington Reporter*, Second Series. Shepard's books are deep red, bound volumes, with accompanying paperback books and pocket parts, and often thin update pamphlets.
3. Look up the volume number of your case within the Shepard's book (in the example, "109"). The volume numbers are shown across the top of the page and the page numbers are shown within the columns (Figure 13.1).
4. Find the citation page number. Immediately following the page number is information regarding the cited case (Figure 13.2).
5. Read and note all the citations that follow (Figure 13.3). See Figures 13.4 and 13.5 for examples from LexisNexis, the owner of *Shepard's Citations* and the purveyor of the online version of Shepard's.

These following lines are all citations to other cases or materials that have somehow mentioned or are related to your case. These interrelationships are indicated by codes placed next to the citation, such as "a" (for affirmed), "d" (for dismissed), and other symbols.

B. Steps in Shepardizing a Statute

1. Find the correct citation for the jurisdiction. The statute in this example is Michigan Compiled Laws Annotated Section 208.23, so you will use Shepards' Michigan citations.
2. Use the headings at the top of the page to locate the correct title number or code section. Then look down the columns to find the appropriate code section (Figure 13.6).
3. Read the lines of citations that follow to find cases that reference the statute in question (Figure 13.7). See the examples from Lexis in Figures 13.8 and 13.9.

FIGURE 13.1

Vol. 109 — WASHINGTON REPORTS, 2d SERIES

55WAp[28]779
e 56WAp850
57WAp224
f 59WAp[1]16
f 59WAp[28]16
59WAp[29]119
59WAp286
f 61WAp[1]407
d 61WAp[24]417
64WAp[13]169
Cir. 1
901F2d203
Cir. 2
700FS[28]1282
Cir. 9
915F2d1327
693FS[8]900
693FS[8]903
d 709FS200
e 143FRD[6]699
28Goz39
63WsL769
65NYL1173
70TxL604
17PcL249
17PcL269
AE§ 1.13

—191—

Greer v Northwestern National Insurance Co. 1987

(743P2d1244)
s 36WAp330
j 109Wsh2d745
111Wsh2d[3]456
112Wsh2d[7]11
113Wsh2d[8]94
50WAp[3]572
54WAp[1]339
56WAp[1]585
57WAp[1]346
d 57WAp[4]351
61WAp109
64WAp[2]575
64WAp921
Cir. 9
f 927F2d[1]464
711FS[2]1044
718FS[2]843
720FS858
f 729FS[4]725
790FS1053
28Goz502
28Goz559
28Goz612
28Goz641
11InL273
LPIB§ 3.59

—207—

Washington v Dunaway 1987

(743P2d1237)
(749P2d160)
s 56WAp915
110Wsh2d82
110Wsh2d[1]262
110Wsh2d[7]507
j 110Wsh2d518
f 112Wsh2d[1]403
j 112Wsh2d412
e 114Wsh2d[1]16
f 114Wsh2d[7]66
114Wsh2d318
114Wsh2d[1]319
114Wsh2d[7]540
f 115Wsh2d[1]301
115Wsh2d303
115Wsh2d456
115Wsh2d[7]623
116Wsh2d186
f 116Wsh2d334
116Wsh2d[2]792
f 117Wsh2d[2]163
117Wsh2d[2]215
117Wsh2d[4]216
117Wsh2d[3]706
117Wsh2d[8]712
f 49WAp[1]899
f 49WAp[1]902
50WAp[7]541
50WAp[7]562
50WAp[5]758
51WAp284
51WAp[1]460
52WAp[7]24
52WAp[6]420
52WAp[7]463
52WAp[7]468
52WAp660
e 52WAp[1]661
52WAp[2]664
53WAp[5]226
53WAp312
53WAp[4]497
f 53WAp[1]853
53WAp925
f 54WAp[1]60
d 54WAp[4]326
54WAp[2]381
54WAp757
f 55WAp[1]68
55WAp587
55WAp[4]590
55WAp[8]752
f 55WAp[2]860
55WAp[8]866
55WAp881
55WAp[1]894
56WAp[8]118
f 56WAp[1]558
e 56WAp653
f 56WAp[1]810
d 57WAp105
57WAp[1]206
57WAp[1]764
57WAp[2]799
57WAp[4]800
58WAp[2]78
58WAp[1]451
58WAp[5]451
58WAp477
58WAp[2]625
58WAp[6]629
58WAp[7]817
59WAp[3]148
59WAp417
d 59WAp[1]451
f 59WAp[3]454
59WAp[1]465
e 59WAp[1]467
59WAp[2]518
f 59WAp[1]828
59WAp829
59WAp[1]847
f 59WAp[1]855
61WAp[1]233
61WAp561
61WAp[3]612
f 61WAp[1]815
61WAp[2]927
62WAp[2]31
62WAp777
63WAp[3]150
f 63WAp[1]307
64WAp[1]491
64WAp[6]531
64WAp[2]624
64WAp912
26Goz153
65WsL398

—222—

Washington v Thomas 1987

(743P2d816)
s 46WAp723
111Wsh2d[3]72
115Wsh2d[2]808
f 116Wsh2d[2]548
f 50WAp703
51WAp[2]553
f 51WAp[3]553
53WAp[3]766
55WAp652
f 55WAp[2]938
f 56WAp218
56WAp[2]224
j 56WAp226
e 56WAp[1]616
59WAp[2]374
60WAp[1]171
d 60WAp180
61WAp26
63WAp[2]649
64WAp[2]286
d 64WAp[1]289
2Æ27s

—235—

Lockwood v A C & S Inc. 1987

(744P2d605)
s 44WAp330
113Wsh2d[1]335
117Wsh2d[1]247
f 50WAp[3]366
f 50WAp[4]366
50WAp[8]368
52WAp170
52WAp[5]624
55WAp[10]60
f 57WAp[1]188
58WAp182
59WAp271
59WAp295
60WAp472
61WAp[8]429
62WAp[10]561
63WAp884
Cir. 2
971F2d[2]837
Cir. 3
914F2d380
928F2d[8]1375
Cir. 5
949F2d[2]172
Cir. 6
727FS[2]334
Cir. 9
960F2d817
f 960F2d818
977F2d1343
978F2d[2]477
699FS237
Cir. 10
e 861F2d1462
27Goz159

—270—

In the Matter of Personal Restraint of Montoya 1987

(744P2d340)
49WAp[3]849
50WAp[3]704
53WAp[3]907

—282—

Chelan County Sheriffs Assoc. v Chelan 1987

(745P2d1)
s 45WAp812
s 46WAp163
116Wsh2d731
54WAp228
55WAp95
59WAp[3]730

—303—

Washington v Aver 1987

(745P2d479)
111Wsh2d[2]6
j 111Wsh2d19
111Wsh2d[2]26
111Wsh2d[1]27
e 111Wsh2d34
111Wsh2d[1]540
111Wsh2d[2]545
111Wsh2d547
111Wsh2d916
111Wsh2d[2]917
113Wsh2d598
114Wsh2d[5]83
115Wsh2d[2]177
51WAp[5]265
f 53WAp[3]399
f 55WAp[3]40
c 55WAp[3]42
e 55WAp[3]43
f 62WAp[8]126
64WAp[2]122

—320—

Washington v Box 1987

(745P2d23)
s 45WAp1043
110Wsh2d590
111Wsh2d534
f 113Wsh2d638
53WAp622
58WAp[1]558
60WAp834

—336—

Washington v Black 1987

(745P2d12)
s 46WAp259
110Wsh2d[1]279
j 110Wsh2d842
50WAp[1]472
d 53WAp[1]764
d 55WAp[1]62
55WAp297
f 57WAp[1]29
e 58WAp[1]496
d 58WAp[1]645
d 59WAp[1]423
d 59WAp[2]423
d 59WAp[1]748
d 59WAp[2]748
f 60WAp[1]385
d 62WAp907
63WAp178
d 64WAp964
Cir. 4
688FS1075
688FS[1]1076
f 688FS[2]1077
Cir. 9
944F2d483
25Goz344
63WsL1063
52LCP(4)95
52LCP(4)134
73MnL67

—357—

Washington v Hensler 1987

(745P2d34)
56WAp820
57WAp685
31Æ565s

—363—

Weyerhaeuser Co. v Cowlitz County 1987

(745P2d488)
117Wsh2d[8]127

—377—

Skagit State Bank v Rasmussen 1987

(745P2d37)
s 43WAp178
111Wsh2d[1]83
56WAp[1]83
Cir. 9
839F2d1368
850F2d[1]1353
740FS[1]1487
740FS1489

—389—

Washington v Southerland 1987

(745P2d33)
s 45WAp885
51WAp[1]762
54WAp[1]155
77Æs1053n

192

FIGURE 13.2

Cited Case

Washington Reports, Second Series

Vol. 109 — Volume number in easy-to-find box

—191— — Page number in large bold print

Greer v Northwestern National Insurance Co. 1987 — Case name and date

(743P2d1244) — Pacific Reporter parallel

s36WAp330 — Complete history shown

FIGURE 13.3

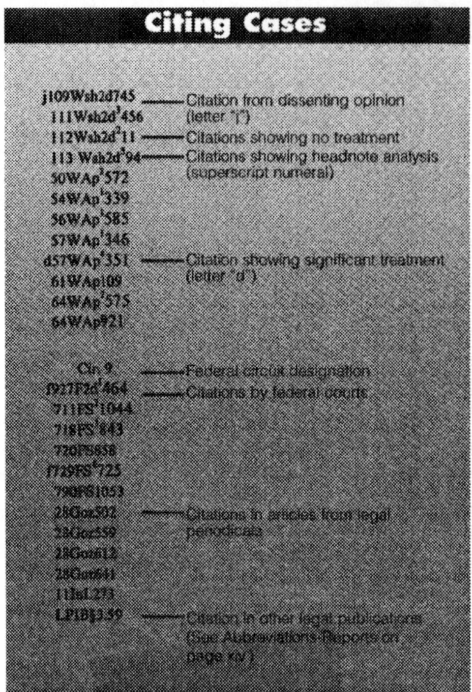

FIGURE 13.4

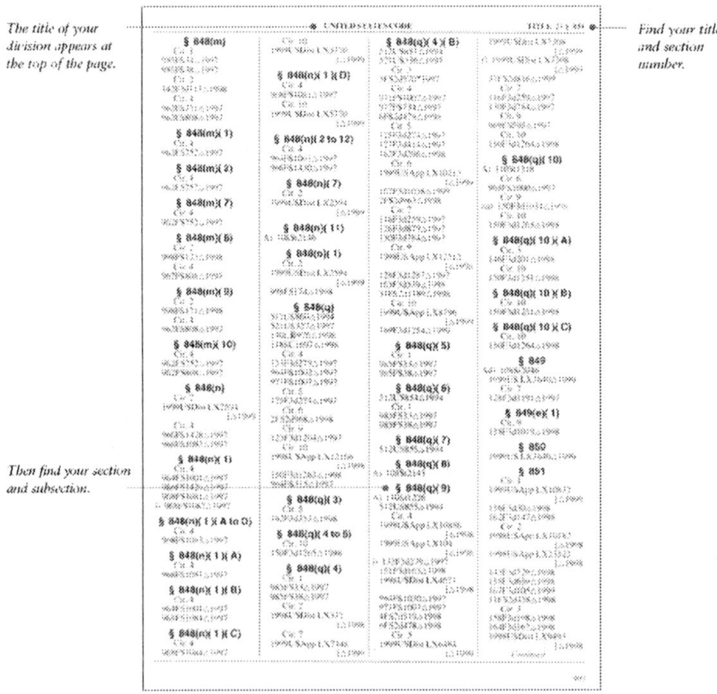

FIGURE 13.5 

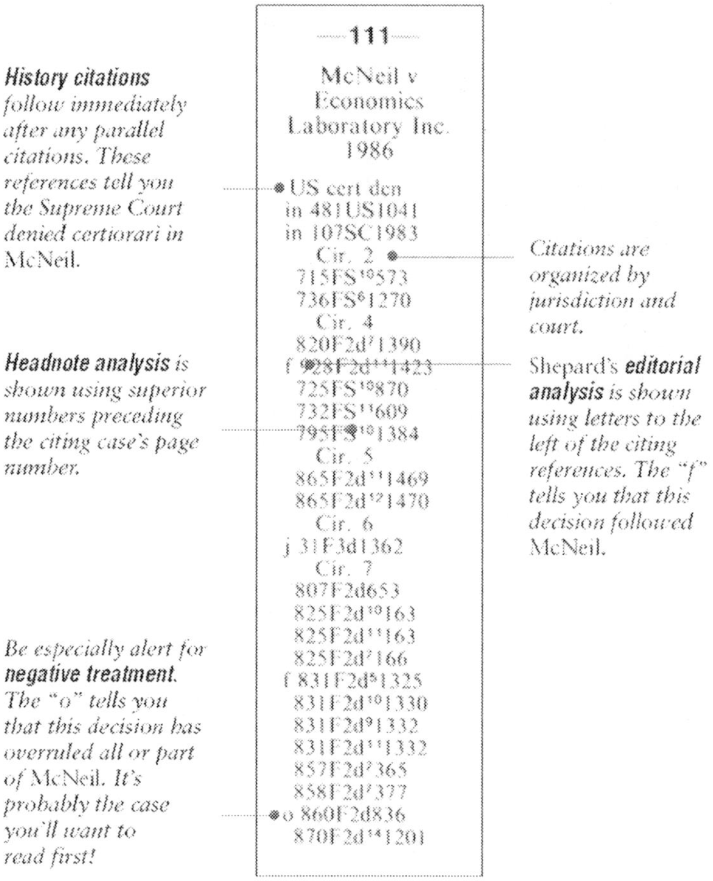

History citations *follow immediately after any parallel citations. These references tell you the Supreme Court denied certiorari in* McNeil.

Headnote analysis *is shown using superior numbers preceding the citing case's page number.*

Be especially alert for ***negative treatment****. The "o" tells you that this decision has overruled all or part of* McNeil*. It's probably the case you'll want to read first!*

—111—

McNeil v
Economics
Laboratory Inc.
1986

US cert den
in 481US1041
in 107SC1983
Cir. 2
715FS[10]573
736FS[6]1270
Cir. 4
820F2d[7]1390
f 928F2d[11]1423
725FS[10]870
732FS[11]609
795FS[10]1384
Cir. 5
865F2d[11]1469
865F2d[12]1470
Cir. 6
j 31F3d1362
Cir. 7
807F2d653
825F2d[10]163
825F2d[11]163
825F2d[7]166
f 831F2d[8]1325
831F2d[10]1330
831F2d[9]1332
831F2d[11]1332
857F2d[7]365
858F2d[7]377
o 860F2d836
870F2d[14]1201

Citations are organized by jurisdiction and court.

Shepard's ***editorial analysis*** *is shown using letters to the left of the citing references. The "f" tells you that this decision followed* McNeil.

FIGURE 13.6

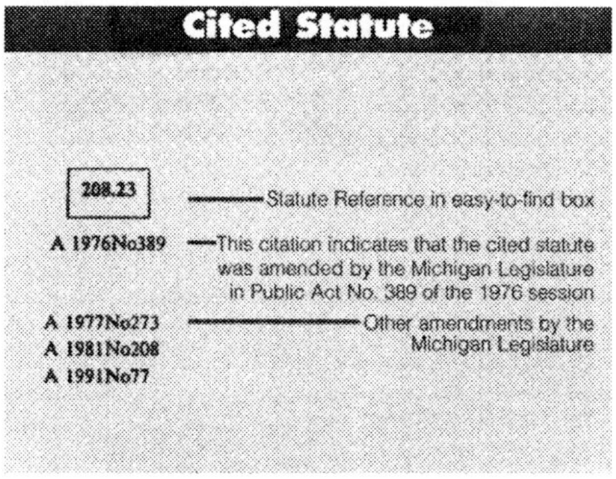

Cited Statute

208.23 — Statute Reference in easy-to-find box

A 1976No389 — This citation indicates that the cited statute was amended by the Michigan Legislature in Public Act No. 389 of the 1976 session

A 1977No273
A 1981No208
A 1991No77
— Other amendments by the Michigan Legislature

FIGURE 13.7

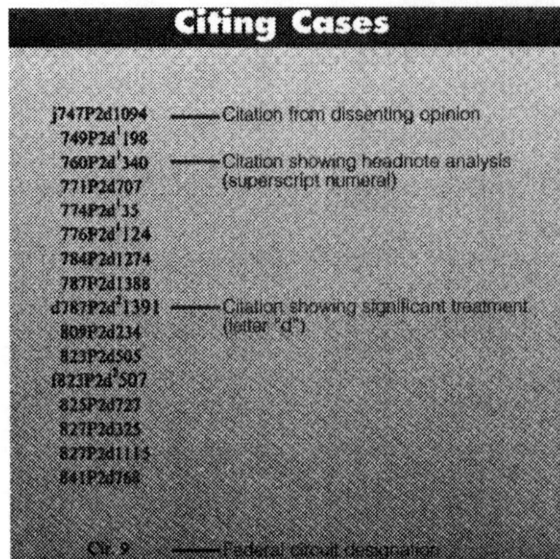

FIGURE 13.8

C. Code Interpretation

The Shepard's coding enables the researcher to perform many functions, especially in assessing the strengths and weaknesses of his or her case. Use the information in Figure 13.10 to interpret the citations you find.

EXAMPLE 1: WASHINGTON REPORTS, 2D.

d 57 WA p[4] 351

The letter "d" tells the researcher that the *Greer* opinion was distinguished by the opinion in volume 57 of the Washington Appellate Reports at page 351. The su-

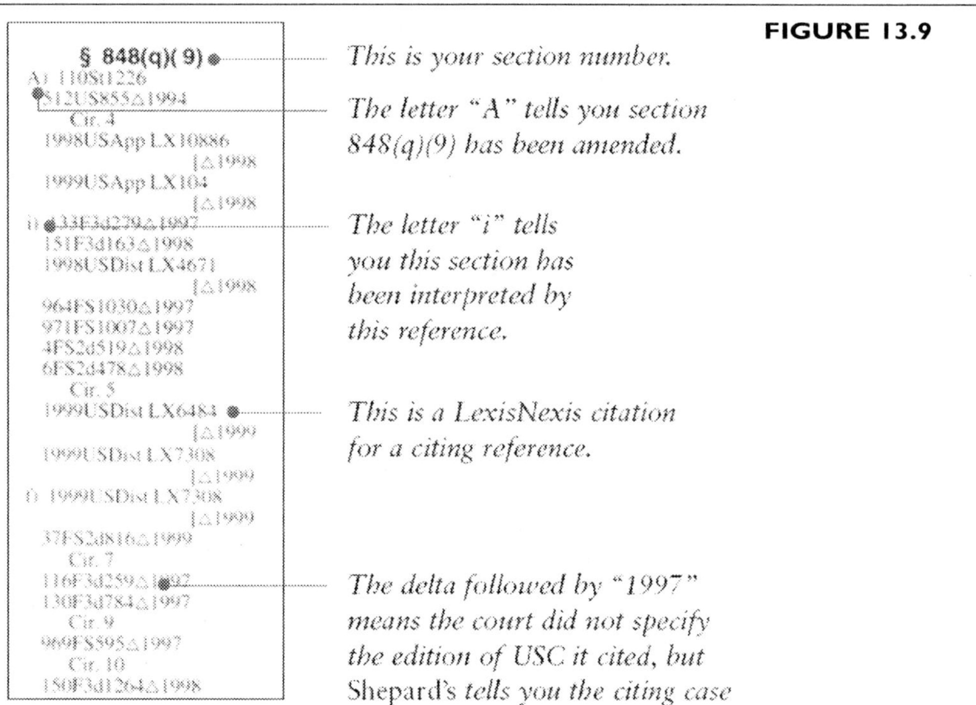

FIGURE 13.9

perscript 4 indicates that the point of law discussed in headnote 4 of *Greer* is discussed in this case.

EXAMPLE 2: WASH. REP. 2D.

f 927 F.2d[1] 464

The letter "f" in this citation informs the researcher that in the case at 927F2d464, the *Greer* opinion was followed and the superscript 1 indicates that the point of law in headnote 1 of the *Greer* decision is discussed.

EXAMPLE 3: MICH. COMP. L. ANN.

C 498 U.S. 358

The "C" in this citation means that the case reported at 498 US 358 found this statute constitutional.

EXAMPLE 4: MICH. COMP. L. ANN.

A 1976 No.389

This citation tells the researcher that Public Law No. 389 amended ("A") this statute in 1976.

EXAMPLE 5: MICH. COMP. L. ANN.

65 MBJ 322

This statute was discussed in an article in volume 65 of the *Michigan Bar Journal* at page 322.

A word of warning is in order about use of Shepard's Citations. Although the code letters assigned by Shepard's are extremely useful, they are in no sense official. Do not rely on them as a substitute for your own research, analysis, and interpretation of the citing case or other material. Shepard's will point you in the right direction,

FIGURE 13.10 **The Following Letters are used to Indicate the History of the Case**

a *(affirmed)* Same case affirmed on appeal.

cc *(connected case)* The case is related to your case in some way. Either it involves the same parties, or it arises out of the same subject matter. However, it is not the same action.

d *(dismissed)* Appeal from a lower court to a higher court is dismissed by that court.

De *(denied)* A petition for review or rehearing has been denied by a higher court.

Dp *(dismissed in part)* Appeal from the same case dismissed in part.

GP *(granted and citable)* Review granted and ordered published.

Gr *(granted)* A petition for review by a higher-level court, or a petition for rehearing by the same or higher-level court has been granted.

m *(modified)* The lower court's decision is changed in some way either during a rehearing or by action of a higher court.

Np *(not published) The Reporter of Decisions* has been directed not to publish the opinion.

Op *(original opinion)* Citation of original opinion.

r *(reversed)* The case you are shepardizing was reversed on appeal.

Re *(republished) The Reporter of Decisions* has been directed to publish opinion previously ordered not published.

s *(same case)* The case you are shepardizing involves the same litigation as the citing case, although at a different stage of the proceedings. "Same case" refers to many different situations, including motions and opinions that preceded your case. It is important to look up these cases if you need to know exactly what occurred.

S *(superseded)* A subsequent opinion has been substituted for your case.

v *(vacated)* The opinion has been vacated and is no longer good law.

US app pndg *(U.S. appeal pending)* An appeal to the United States Supreme Court has been filed.

US cert den *(U.S. certiorari denied)* Certiorari has been denied by the United States Supreme Court.

US cert dis *(U.S. certiorari dismissed)* Certiorari has been dismissed by the United States Supreme Court.

US reh den *(U.S. rehearing denied)* Rehearing denied by the United States Supreme Court.

US reh dis *(U.S. rehearing dismissed)* Rehearing dismissed by the United States Supreme Court.

NOTE: Not all letters are applied in all jurisdictions.

The Following Letters Relate to Treatment of Cases

c *(criticized)* The court disagrees with the soundness of the case being shepardized, although the court may not have the authority to materially affect its precedential value.

d *(distinguished)* The case is different from your case in a significant way. Generally, the case presents either a differing fact situation, or differs in its application of the law.

e *(explained)* The court interprets your case in a significant way.

f *(followed)* Your case is being relied upon as controlling authority.

h *(harmonized)* The cases differ in some way; however, the court finds a way to reconcile the differences.

j *(dissenting opinion)* Your case is cited in the dissent of the opinion.

FIGURE 13.10
continued

L *(limited)* The court restricts the application of your opinion. The court usually finds that the reasoning of your opinion applies only in very specific instances.

o *(overruled)* The court has determined that the reasoning in your case is no longer good law, either in part or in its entirety

p *(parallel)* The case is substantially similar to or on all fours with your case in its law or facts.

q *(questioned)* The soundness of your case is at issue. For example, your decision may have been legislatively overruled, or the court may recognize that an opposing line of authority overrules your case.

REMEMBER! The treatment letter may refer to your case as a whole, or to a single point made in the opinion.

The Following Letters Relate to Treatment of Statutes

C *(constitutional)* A court has upheld the statute as constitutional.

i *(interpreted)* The statute has been interpreted or construed by a court in a significant way.

rt *(retroactive')* Retroactive application of the statute is discussed.

U *(unconstitutional)* A court has found the statute to be unconstitutional.

Up *(unconstitutional in part)* A portion of the statute has been found unconstitutional by a court.

V *(void or invalid)* A statute is not good law because a court has found it conflicts with a law that takes priority.

Va *(valid)* A statute has been judged valid by a court.

Vp *(void or invalid in part)* Part of a statute conflicts with another law that takes priority.

The Following Letters Relate to Legislative Impact on Statutes

A *(amended)* Statute amended.

Ad *(added)* New section added.

E *(extended)* Provisions of an existing statute extended in their application to a later statute, or allowance of additional time for performance of duties required by a statute (within a limited time).

L *(limited)* Provisions of an existing statute declared not to be extended in their application to a later statute.

R *(repealed)* Abrogation of an existing statute.

Re-en *(re-enacted)* Statute re-enacted.

Rn *(renumbered)* Renumbering of existing sections.

Rp *(repealed in part)* Abrogation of part of an existing statute.

Rs *(repealed and superseded)* Abrogation of an existing statute and substitution of new legislation therefore.

Rv *(revised)* Statute revised.

S *(superseded)* Substitution of new legislation for an existing statute not expressly abrogated.

Sd *(suspended)* Statute suspended.

Sdp *(suspended in part)* Statute suspended in part.

Sg *(supplementing)* New matter added to an existing statute.

Sp *(superseded in part)* Substitution of new legislation for part of an existing statute not expressly abrogated.

but you are still responsible for going to the citing piece, reading it, and making your own analysis and evaluation of its holding and/or relationship to your material in hand (the cited case or statute).

D. Extent of Shepard's Coverage

The Shepard's system expands each year, much to the delight of research specialists. Mastery of these very basic techniques permits a researcher the joy of locating quickly and evaluating with confidence all relevant authorities. The Shepard's system provides access to all of the following material:

- Bankruptcy Citations
- Environmental Law Citations
- Federal Energy Law Citations
- United States Administrative Citations
- United States Patents and Trademarks Citations
- Federal Tax Law Citations
- Labor Law Citations
- Federal Occupational Safety and Health Citations
- Immigration and Naturalization Citations
- Labor Arbitration Citations
- Military Justice Citations
- Code of Federal Regulations Citations
- Federal Law in Selected Law Reviews
- Federal Circuit Table
- Federal Rules Citations
- Acts and Cases by Popular Name
- Citations for Annotations
- Law Review Citations
- Professional and Judicial Conduct Citations
- Restatement of the Law Citations
- Criminal Justice Citations
- Employment Law Citations
- Uniform Commercial Code Citations
- Uniform Commercial Code Case Citations

See the materials from LexisNexis on the *Shepards's Citation* service and Westlaw's KeyCite in Figures 13.11 and 13.12 for guidance on computerized updating.

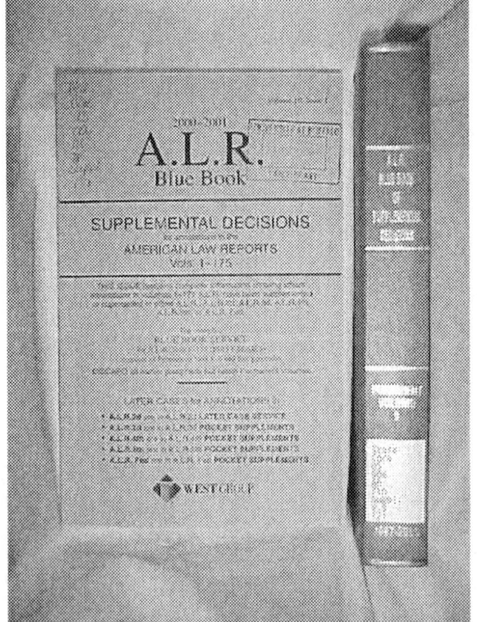

PHOTO 13.1

II. A.L.R. BLUE BOOKS

As in most solid legal series, continuity and conceptual follow-up are essential to long life and respectability. A.L.R. also provides its own means of update, the *Blue Book*. The *Blue Book* is easy to understand, as legal research builds from bottom to top, and each annotation is updated in this manner. Assume the citation is 1 A.L.R. 610. How would you trace the case: its history, growth, and spread of influence amongst various jurisdictions? Simply go to the *Blue Book*, find the citation, and read below it. This basic annotation may be further supplemented by another annotation

FIGURE 13.11

SHEPARD'S® CITATIONS SERVICE

LexisNexis™ At-A-Glance

Shepard's has been a cornerstone of the legal-research process for over 125 years. Today, *Shepard's* Citations Service, only available on LexisNexis, is the premier way to check cites to insure the highest degree of accuracy and confidence. The citation method of legal research starts with the simple premise that if a later decision cites your case, the later decision must be discussing some of the same issues. In our common law system, written judicial opinions or cases are an important source of primary legal authority. *Shepard's* Citations Service guides you to the decisions involving legal or factual issues similar to the case you select as your starting point for citation-based legal research.

In addition to case law, the *Shepard's* Citations Service covers a wide spectrum of primary and secondary sources:

- *United States Code*
- Regulations, including the *Code of Federal Regulations*
- Court rules, including the Federal Rules
- Law review articles
- Statutes from all 50 states
- U.S. and state constitutional provisions
- Annotations
- Individual U.S. patents

Shepard's is used in two important ways:

1. **As a finding tool**

Use *Shepard's* early in your research process – as soon as you've discovered an on-point case or statute – to find other relevant authorities.

2. **As a validation tool**

A court may find reasons to distinguish, criticize, limit or even overrule an earlier decision. A new statute or regulation can impact the continuing validity of a legal authority. Before you rely on a legal authority to support your argument, use *Shepard's* to be absolutely sure of its current precedential value.

Getting Started with *Shepard's* Citations Service

1. **Sign on** the LexisNexis research service.
2. Click the **Check a Citation** tab.
3. Click the ***Shepard's*** tab.
4. Type **your citation** in the open field.
5. Click the radio button for ***Shepard's* for Research** (Full) or ***Shepard's* for Validation** (KWIC™).
6. Click **Check** to process your request.

Ⓐ *Shepard's* Signal indicator tells you that negative treatment is indicated.

Ⓑ Click here to narrow research results, finding the issues or fact patterns that you specify within the full text of your citing references.

Ⓒ Show Signals displays graphical indicators that provide treatment and history status of each citing reference.

Ⓓ Custom Restrictions previews where and how your case has been cited. Custom Restrictions displays only those treatment codes, jurisdictions, and headnotes available in the list of citing references to the citation you have researched in *Shepard's*.

Ⓔ Click here to see the full text of this case.

Ⓕ Click here to Hide/Show Prior History citing references.

Ⓖ Click on an underlined case name to see the full text of that case.

Ⓗ Click here to Hide/Show Subsequent Appellate History citing references.

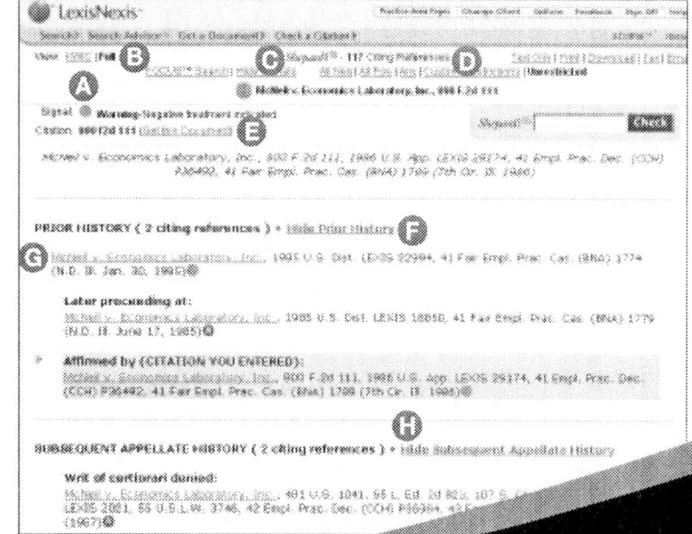

LexisNexis™

It's how you know™

continued

FIGURE 13.11 *continued*

SHEPARD'S® CITATIONS SERVICE

Editorial Analyses

The following list includes some of the most commonly used *Shepard's* editorial analysis codes. For complete lists, consult on-screen information or the tables of abbreviations in print.

Cases

Print	Electronic	Definition
a	◆ Affirmed	On appeal, reconsideration or rehearing, the citing case affirms or adheres to the case you are researching in *Shepard's*.
c	▲ Criticized	The citing case disagrees with the reasoning/result of the case you are researching in *Shepard's*, although the citing court may not have the authority to materially affect its precedential value.
d	▲ Distinguished	The citing case differs from the case you are researching in *Shepard's*, either involving dissimilar facts or requiring a different application of the law.
e	◆ Explained	The citing case interprets or clarifies the case you are researching in *Shepard's* in a significant way.
f	◆ Followed	The citing case relies on the case you are researching in *Shepard's* as a controlling or persuasive authority.
L	▲ Limited	The citing case restricts the application of the case you are researching in *Shepard's*, finding that its reasoning applies only in specific, limited circumstances.
m	▲ Modified	On appeal, reconsideration or rehearing, the citing case modifies or changes in some way, including affirmance in part and reversal in part, the case you are researching in *Shepard's*.
o	● Overruled	The citing case expressly overrules or disapproves all or part of the case you are researching in *Shepard's*.
q	● Questioned	The citing case questions the continuing validity or precedential value of the case you are researching in *Shepard's* because of intervening circumstances, including judicial or legislative overruling.
r	● Reversed	On appeal, reconsideration or rehearing, the citing case reverses the case you are researching in *Shepard's*.

Statutes and Regulations

Print	Electronic	Definition
A	Amended	The citing reference, typically a session law or other record of legislative action, or a record of administrative action, amends or alters the statute, regulation or order you are researching in *Shepard's*.
C	Constitutional	The citing case upholds the constitutionality of the statute, rule or regulation you are researching in *Shepard's*.
i	Interpreted or Construed	The citing opinion interprets the statute, rule or regulation you are researching in *Shepard's* in some significant way, often including a discussion of the statute's legislative history.
R	Repealed	The citing reference, typically a session law or other record of legislative action, repeals or abrogates the statute you are researching in *Shepard's*.
U	Unconstitutional	The citing case declares unconstitutional the statute, rule or regulation you are researching in *Shepard's*.
Va	Valid	The citing case upholds the validity of the statute, rule or regulation or order you are researching in *Shepard's*.
V	Void or Invalid	The citing case declares void or invalid the statute, rule, regulation or order you are researching in *Shepard's* because it conflicts with an authority that takes priority.

www.lexisnexis.com/lawschool

FIGURE 13.12

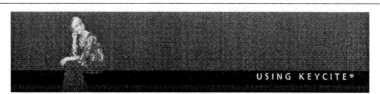

Is your case or statute good law?

Westlaw is available on the Web at **lawschool.westlaw.com**.

For assistance, call **1-800-850-WEST** (1-800-850-9378) or send an e-mail message to **west.student @thomson.com**.

Once you find a relevant case or statute, you need to determine whether it is good law. The fastest way to do so is to use KeyCite, West's citation research service. You can access KeyCite on Westlaw® via **lawschool.westlaw.com**

Why update your case or statute?

Your research does not end simply because you've found an appellate court case or a statute that appears to support your argument. Even a case directly on point may lose its authority if it is reversed or modified on appeal. Similarly, a statute may be rendered moot, amended, repealed by subsequent legislation, declared unconstitutional, or preempted.

It is therefore necessary to verify the validity of any case or statute you cite by checking its history and finding other sources that have cited it. Only after doing so can you be confident the case or statute supporting your argument is good law.

Accessing KeyCite

You can access KeyCite via lawschool.westlaw.com using one of the following methods:

- In the left frame of a tabbed page, type a citation in the *KeyCite this citation* text box and click **GO**.
- Click **KeyCite** on the toolbar to display the KeyCite page. In the left frame, type a citation in the *Enter citation* text box and click **GO**.
- You can also access KeyCite directly from a case or statute you are viewing by clicking the **KC History** tab or **KC Citing Ref** tab or by clicking the KeyCite status flag, when available.

KeyCite status flags for cases

- A red flag warns that a case is no longer good law for at least one of the points it contains.
- A yellow flag warns that the case has some negative history but hasn't been reversed or overruled.
- H A blue H indicates that the case has some history.
- C A green C indicates that the case has citing references but no direct or negative indirect history.

KeyCite status flags for statutes

- A red flag warns that the statute or has been amended by a recent session law, repealed, superseded, or held unconstitutional or preempted in whole or in part.
- A yellow flag warns that a statute has been renumbered or transferred by a recent session law; that an uncodified session law or pending legislation affecting the statute is available (statutes merely referenced, i.e., mentioned, are marked with a green C); that the statute was limited on constitutional or preemption grounds or its validity was otherwise called into doubt; or that a prior version of the statute received negative treatment from a court.

continued

or completely superseded. Cases are also commonly cited. Figure 13.7 shows a note stating that the article at 1 A.L.R. 610 is supplemented at 34 A.L.R. 597.

III. POCKET PARTS

Pocket parts are included in the back of all updatable, printed legal resources. Check the pocket parts for all legal reference materials, particularly encyclopedias, digests, statutes, and codifications. Only then can you be assured of the most timely information.

IV. SUMMARY

When you are trying to find related or updated legal material concerning a case or legal issue, the Shepard's system delivers an invaluable resource. Once you are in possession of a citation, you can use Shepard's to find lists of all citing cases, as well as code designations indicating the relationship to the case in question. With its wide coverage and variety of reference materials, Shepard's provides an easy, efficient way to find relevant, timely information on the legal issue.

FIGURE 13.12
continued

Viewing history of the case

When you retrieve a case on Westlaw and click the **KC History** tab, the case history is displayed in the left frame, and the full text or a portion of the case is displayed in the right frame. (See list of case history categories below.) You can customize the case history display by clicking **Full** to view the full history of a case, clicking **Negative** to view only negative history, or clicking **Omit Minor** to omit minor history such as minor procedural history and references to related litigation.

Case history categories

- **Direct History** traces the same case through the appellate process and includes both prior and subsequent history.
- **Negative Indirect History** lists cases outside the direct appellate line that may have a negative impact on the precedential value of your case.
- **Related References** lists cases that involve the same parties and facts as your case, whether or not the legal issues are the same.

KeyCite case history display

Viewing citing references to the case

Click the **KC Citing Ref** tab (or green C, if one is displayed) to view a list of cases and other materials that cite your case. The KC Citing Ref tab lists all published and unpublished cases on Westlaw—plus administrative materials and secondary sources—that cite your case. The first portion of the KC Citing Ref tab lists negative citing cases, followed by a list of other cases, administrative materials, and secondary sources citing your case. You can restrict the list of citing references by clicking **Limit Citing Refs** on the KC Citing Ref tab to display the KeyCite Limits page. Use the KeyCite Limits page to restrict citing references by headnote, Locate term, jurisdiction, date, document type, or depth of treatment.

Depth of Treatment Stars

KeyCite categorizes citing cases by the depth of treatment they give your case: citing cases that discuss your case in depth are listed on the KC Citing Ref tab above the cases that only briefly mention your case. The depth of treatment categories are as follows:

★★★★ **Examined**
The citing case contains an extended discussion of the cited case, usually more than a printed page of text.

★★★ **Discussed**
The citing case contains a substantial discussion of the cited case, usually more than a paragraph but less than a printed page.

★★ **Cited**
The citing case contains some discussion of the cited case, usually less than a paragraph.

★ **Mentioned**
The citing case contains a brief reference to the cited case, usually in a string citation.

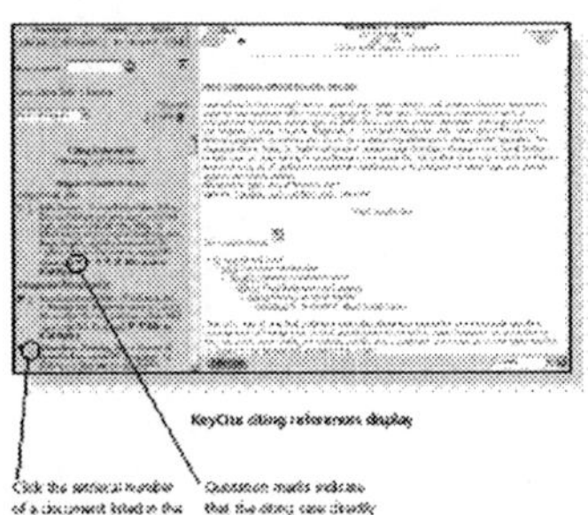

KeyCite citing references display

Click the sequential number of a document listed in the left frame to view its full text in the Link Viewer.

Quotation marks indicate that the citing case directly quotes the cited case.

V. LEGAL RESEARCH ASSIGNMENTS

A. Exercise 13.1: Volume 226, *Federal Supplement*

Use the abbreviations list cited in the chapter to answer many of the following questions.

1. The *Yale Law Journal* cites a case on what page of vol. 226 of the *Federal Supplement?*
   a. 19
   b. 59
   c. 118
   d. 140
2. Which reference series does *not* cite to the case on page 49?
   a. American Law Reports
   b. *Federal Supplement*
   c. *Federal Reporter, 2d Series*
   d. *Federal Rules Decisions*
3. Which decision cited is questioned for its reasoning?
   a. 226 FS 112
   b. 554 F2d 570
   c. 226 FS 115
   d. Cir. 4

FIGURE 13.12 *continued*

Viewing history of the statute

When you access KeyCite, the history of the statute is displayed in the left frame, and the full text or a portion of the statute is displayed in the right frame. Statute history includes legislation affecting the statute, as well as cases that have affected the validity of the statute, e.g., a case that held the statute unconstitutional.

KeyCite statute history display

Statute history categories

- **Updating Documents** lists citations to session laws that have amended or repealed the section.
- **Pending Legislation** lists citations to pending bills that reference a statute (available for federal, California, and New York statutes).
- **Credits** lists in chronological order citations to session laws that have enacted, amended, or renumbered the section.
- **Historical and Statutory Notes** describe the legislative changes affecting the section.

Viewing citing references to the statute

Click the **KC Citing Ref** tab to view a list of documents that cite your statute. The documents are listed in the following order: cases affecting the statute's validity, cases from *United States Code Annotated*® and annotated state statutes, cases on Westlaw that do not appear in notes of decisions, administrative materials, and secondary sources. You can restrict the list of citing references by clicking **Limit Citing Refs** on the KC Citing Ref tab to display the KeyCite Limits page, which allows you to restrict the citing references by notes of decisions, Locate term, jurisdiction, date, or document type.

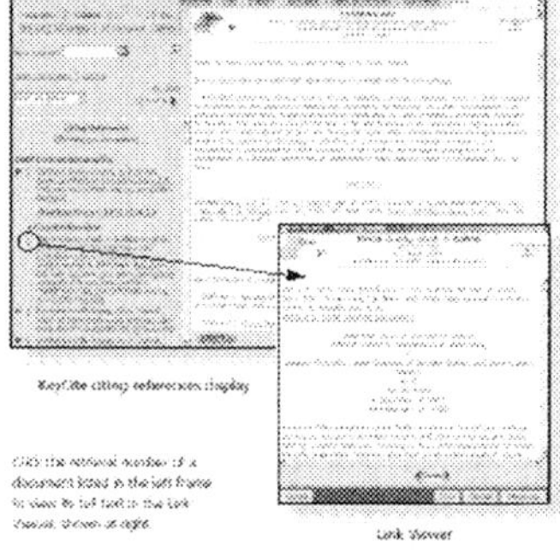

KeyCite citing references display

Click the retrieval number of a document listed in the left frame to view its full text in the Link Viewer, shown at right.

Link Viewer

continued

4. All the cases cited in the *Federal Supplement* are federal in nature and do not relate to state issues.
   a. True
   b. False
5. Which state is this citation from: 226 FS 19?
   a. Georgia
   b. Florida
   c. Maryland
   d. Pennsylvania
6. Which circuit court at the federal level heard the case cited as 299 FS 604?
   a. Circuit 5
   b. Circuit 6
   c. Circuit 7
   d. Circuit 8
7. Did any of these cases end up in the Tax Court of the United States?
   a. Yes
   b. No
8. Which reporter system is cross-referenced?
   a. Atlantic
   b. Southeastern
   c. California
   d. All of the above

FIGURE 13.12
continued

Using KeyCite Alert

KeyCite Alert automatically monitors the status of cases and statutes and sends you updates when their KeyCite information changes. When you create a KeyCite Alert entry, you specify how frequently your citation should be checked, for example, weekly, biweekly, or monthly. KeyCite Alert can deliver results to a printer or an e-mail address or download the results to disk. You can also save your result on Westlaw for 30 days and access the result in the Offline Print Directory.

Creating a KeyCite Alert entry

To create a KeyCite Alert entry, do one of the following:

- Choose **KeyCite Alert** from the More drop-down list on the toolbar to display the KeyCite Alert page. Then click **Create Entry** or **Entry Wizard**.
- Click **KC Alert** on the Cite List tab of a case or statute retrieved with Find or on the KC History or KC Citing Ref tab to add the citation of the case or statute displayed in the right frame to the KeyCite Alert wizard.

The KeyCite Alert wizard provides step-by-step guidance in creating a KeyCite Alert entry

Keeping track of your KeyCite Alert entries

The KeyCite Alert Directory lists your entries in the order you saved them, and they remain in the Directory until you delete them. (After you have created one or more KeyCite Alert entries, you can access the Directory by choosing **KeyCite Alert** from the More drop-down list on the toolbar.) You can use the KeyCite Alert Directory to view, edit, or delete entries. Click the number in front of the citation to modify an entry. To remove an entry from the Directory, click **Delete** next to that entry.

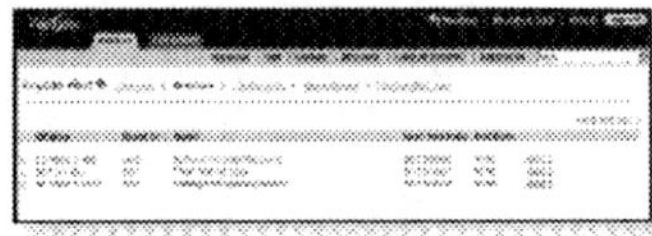

KeyCite Alert Directory

THOMSON
WEST

9. Frequent citations are given to *American Law Reports.*
   a. True
   b. False
10. Volume 225 ends with page 1015.
    a. True
    b. False

B. Exercise 13.2: Volume 393, *Federal Supplement*

1. Louisiana cases are reported in the *Atlantic Reporter.*
   a. True
   b. False
2. Which citation relates to the Antitrust Adviser?
   a. 393 F. Supp. 712
   b. 393 F. Supp. 741
   c. 393 F. Supp. 843
   d. None of the above
3. Massachusetts's cases are reported in the *Northeastern Reporter.*
   a. True
   b. False

4. Florida cases are reported in the *Southern Reporter.*
   a. True
   b. False
5. In which federal circuit was 791 F2d 308 decided?
   a. Circuit 2
   b. Circuit 4
   c. Circuit 5
   d. Circuit 12
6. Which decision is cited in a dissenting opinion?
   a. 913 F2d 77
   b. 490 US 59
   c. Neither a nor b
   d. Both a and b
7. Which decision is a connected case arising out of the same subject matter?
   a. 446 FS 1317
   b. 572 FS 1306
   c. 511 FS 1338
   d. 456 FS 85
8. Which decision from the 5th Federal Circuit distinguishes itself factually or legally from the case cited?
   a. 510 FS 84
   b. 562 F2d 351
   c. 576 F2d 604
   d. 422 FS 949
9. A3 stands for:
   a. *Aviation Annual*
   b. Atlantic
   c. *Atlantic Reporter, 3d*
   d. American Law Reports, Third Series
10. Most cases cited on these two pages have been reversed.
    a. True
    b. False

C. Exercise 13.3: Volume 464, *Federal Supplement*

1. Which decision was reversed?
   a. 614 F2d 495
   b. 464 FS 101
   c. 679 F2d 324
   d. None of the above
2. Which case was modified on appeal?
   a. 612 F2d 135
   b. 175 FS 464
   c. 464 FS 175
   d. All of the above
3. At least three cases from the District of Columbia are cited.
   a. True
   b. False

388FS[1]780
77Æ2641s

—1007—
Talco Capital Corp. v Canaveral International Corp. 1964
a 344F2d962
Cir. 8
380F2d[5]260
Cir. 11
920F2d831
920F2d[6]838
Fla
466 So2d1073
547 So2d215
Mich
144 McA717
376 NW394
Minn
308 NW714
N Y
26 NYAD178
271 NYS2d811
55Æ2481s
7ÆRF234n
7ÆRF275n

—1015—
W. E. Bassett Co. v H. C. Cook Co. 1963
s 302F2d268
s 156FS209
s 164FS278
s 201FS821

Vol. 226

—1—
Sangster v Celebrezze 1964
s 374F2d498
s 240FS638
Cir. 3
262FS[1]163
Cir. 8
f 233FS[4]248
f 233FS[1]249
77Æ2641s

—8—
Beechwood Music Corp. v Vee Jay Records Inc. 1964
a 328F2d728
Cir. 2
247FS[5]135
763FS1245

—15—
Wirtz v Miller 1964
Cir. 2
280FS380
Cir. 9
391F2d[5]3

—19—
Pennsylvania ex rel Prater v Myers 1964
s 377US1005
s 12LE1054
s 84SC1942
Cir. 2
325FS[2]445
325FS[3]445
Cir. 4
287FS[2]931
Cir. 5
416F2d[2]100

—20—
Copeland v Secretary of State 1964
v 378US588
v 12LE1041
v 84SC1931
s 376US967
s 12LE83
s 84SC1140
Cir. 5
391FS[2]849
W Va
173 WV603
319 SE371
14LE887n
58LE924n

—43—
In the Matter of Paddock of California 1964
Cir. 1
d 654F2d[1]253
24BRW611
Cir. 2
294FS[1]1165
11BRW[1]986
Cir. 3
235FS[1]773
Cir. 9
d 447F2d[1]396
Calif
99 CA3d466
160 CaR168

—49—
Richardson v United States 1964
Cir. 3
463FS[1]913
Cir. 4
518F2d[1]1141
605F2d[1]722
249FS[1]629
311FS[1]371
f 444FS[1]320
f 514FS[1]1322
542FS725
Cir. 6
416F2d[1]359
Cir. 7
230FS[1]765
d 244FS[1]765
Cir. 8
357F2d[1]229
643F2d493
j 643F2d498
Cir. 9
d 704F2d1440
601FS[1]99
6LE1422s
31ÆRF164n
31ÆRF219n
88ÆRF48n

—51—
United States v Steffes 1964
s 35FRD24
Cir. 5
266FS[3]620
Cir. 6
234FS[3]63
Cir. 9
229FS[2]86

—53—
Montgomery v K & K Oil Company Inc. 1963

—56—
Exchange and Savings Bank of Berlin v United States 1964
s 368F2d334
s 242FS838
Cir. 2
500F2d[2]1011
c 500F2d[3]1011
d 365FS386
417FS[2]79
759FS1079
Cir. 3
335F2d101
Cir. 6
d 322FS[3]980
d 395FS[3]175
ClCt
d 14ClC[3]803
CtCl
399F2d[3]211
185CCL191
219CCL584
223CCL790
76TCt1165
1988TCM#557
27ÆRF727n

—59—
Atlantic City Electric Co. v General Electric Co. 1964
s 312F2d236
s 337F2d844
s 207FS613
s 207FS620
s 217FS36
392US[3]492
20LE[3]1240
88SC[3]2231
Cir. 2
391F2d[1]827
440F2d[5]1088
651F2d[2]95
f 244FS[3]950
312FS[5]321
497FS[2]249
Cir. 3
377F2d[2]782
245FS[5]298
50FRD[3]21
50FRD[4]21
50FRD[5]21
Cir. 7
335F2d[1]204
594FS[2]889
59FRD592
67FRD[5]464
Cir. 8
299FS[1]600
299FS[2]604
299FS[4]605
299FS[7]605
299FS[5]607
308FS[7]964
f 308FS[4]965
308FS[1]966
Cir. 9
j 791F2d1378
230FS[3]745
Cir. 10
53FRD[5]633
53FRD[2]636
ML
j 375FS[3]1393
N Y
60 NYAD236
400 NYS2d81
46ChL626
77CR1001
78CR1425
85YLJ641
86YLJ826
1ÆRF508n
16ÆRF19n
16ÆRF24n
16ÆRF64n

—72—
A. C. Samford Inc. v United States 1963
Cir. 2
419FS[8]1277
Cir. 3
98FRD685
e 98FRD[1]686
e 98FRD[2]686
Cir. 4
263FS[4]868
e 756FS[8]945
75FRD[2]743
Cir. 5
300FS[4]758
315FS[3]831
315FS[6]831
498FS165
509FS250
Cir. 6
98FRD[2]511
125FRD[1]456
Cir. 7
20BRW762
Cir. 9
736F2d[1]1382
550FS[1]1255
Cir. 11
902F2d[1]900
570FS[6]284
672FS[4]1456
Ariz
14 AzA408
484 P2d20
N D
467 NW442
R I
103 RI162
235 A2d672
11LE1262n
10Æ2932s
1ÆRF51n
1ÆRF98n
1ÆRF203n
29ÆRF19n
29ÆRF26n
29ÆRF39n

—80—
Maryland Citizens Committee for Fair Congressional Redistricting Inc. v Tawes 1964
s 228FS956
Cir. 2
273FS[4]988
Cir. 6
228FS[3]827
228FS[4]827
j 228FS[5]833
Cir. 8
257FS[3]976
257FS[4]976
279FS[3]976
Cir. 10
229FS[1]273
Mo
528 SW436

—82—
Steele Wholesale Builders Supply Co. v United States 1963
4Æ21223s

—84—
Schwartz v United States 1964
Cir. DC
d 419F2d[1]710
D C
d 136 ADC[1]128
45LCP(3)96
1Æ2 222s
11Æ2 751s
36Æ3 450n
19Æ4 58n
37Æ4 247n
9ÆRF93n

—87—
Cox v Nash 1964
cc 352 SW665
Cir. 8
439F2d[3]1336
487F2d[1]1241
242FS[1]631
297FS[3]12
298FS[3]996
313FS[3]276
316FS[3]654
324FS[3]1264
326FS[3]1123
331FS[3]1197
332FS[3]153
333FS[1]98
351FS[2]911
360FS[1]365
362FS[3]1040
414FS[2]348

—89—
Baldridge v Celebrezze 1964
77Æ2 641s
22Æ3 448n

—91—
Velten v Daughtrey 1964
Cir. 9
381F2d[1]373
95Æ2 1033s
9ÆRF874n

—94—
Brinson v Metropolitan Life Insurance Co. 1963
Cir. 4
406FS[1]644
Cir. 8
504FS[1]1020
504FS[2]1020
d 504FS[4]1020
Tex
448 SW811

—96—
Hamel v Nelson 1963
Cir. 2
320FS[4]1184
Cir. 4
489F2d[3]498
Cir. 8
370F2d[2]533
Cir. 9
443F2d[3]456
243FS[3]116
267FS[3]823
305FS[2]729
4INT 140

—99—
Pennsylvania Insurance Co. v Allstate Insurance Co. 1964
Cir. 4
413FS[4]1103
Cir. 8
415F2d[3]815
Cir. 10
603F2d[2]823
La
198 So2d539

—103—
Clark Marine Corp. v Cargill Inc. 1964
US cert den
in 382US1011
a 345F2d79
Cir. 2
364FS874
Cir. 5
597F2d985

Cir. 6
609F2d[5]853
Cir. 10
e 367FS[5]349
53TxL1220

—112—
United States v Laughlin 1964
s 474F2d444
s 222FS264
s 223FS623
s 154 ADC196
cc 344F2d187
cc 385F2d287
cc 120 ADC93
cc 128 ADC27
Cir. 1
669F2d[10]26
Cir. 3
d 316FS[3]849
Cir. 4
q 479F2d[9]229
Cir. 5
255FS[3]440
Cir. 9
j 488F2d201
e 500F2d[3]905
e 500F2d[4]905
540F2d[3]994
Cir. DC
250FS736
Calif
125 CA3d204
178 CaR27
N Y
45 NYM576
257 NYS2d285
20LE1742n
13Æ2 1409s
9Æ3 442n
49Æ4 446n
3ÆRF70n
49ÆRF193n

—115—
Samples v United States 1963
Cir. 2
q 554F2d[1]570
64TCt 726
64TCt 739
77TCt 772

—116—
United States v Boonville Farms Cooperative Inc. 1964

—117—
Weber v Hydroponics Inc. 1962
Cir. 9
f 34FRD[1]517
19Æ3 153n

—118—
United States ex rel Montanez v Rundle 1964
cc 200 PaS424
cc 29 DC2d383
cc 189 A2d597
Cir. 3
292FS[1]832
316FS[1]1042
317FS[1]774

—120—
Max Factor & Co. v Factor 1963
Cir. 2
569F2d735
662FS[5]207
Cir. 3
d 425FS[1]710
490FS[6]826
Cir. 4
670FS[5]669
Cir. 5
243FS[2]228
Cir. 9
d 244FS[1]689
Cir. DC
899F2d[6]39
Okla
635 P2d329
44Æ2 1156s
38ÆRF391n
38ÆRF414n

—129—
Baker v United States 1964
a 343F2d222
Cir. 2
d 486F2d[7]37
Cir. 4
407F2d[7]824
244FS[6]134
244FS[7]134
280FS[5]151
280FS[6]151
295FS[1]451
Cir. 5
783F2d[3]1232
409FS1293
Cir. 8
599F2d258
423FS[7]753
497FS[7]191
557FS[1]1209
751FS152
751FS[7]153
Cir. 9
482FS[5]705
482FS[7]709
Cir. 10
727F2d904
Cir. DC
j 382F2d[4]167
d 419F2d[7]710
Del
539 A2d1074
Kan
234 Kan497
673 P2d97
Mo
416 SW128
Wash
71 Wsh2d423
429 P2d115
6LE1422s
1Æ2 222s
25Æ2 29s
70Æ2 347s
99Æ2 607n
9Æ3 1342n
9Æ3 1364n
19Æ4 43n
19Æ4 62n
9ÆRF36n
9ÆRF91n

—136—
Anderton v Sheridan 1964
Cir. 2
304FS[2]927
416FS[4]374
Cir. 3
384F2d[2]271
384F2d[1]273

330FS[1]501
330FS[2]502
Cir. 4
e 540F2d686
Cir. 9
263FS[4]919

—140—
New York Central Railroad Co. Texaco Inc 1964
Cir. 2
284FS[9]456
305FS[6]643

—152—
United States United State Steel Corp. 1964
Cir. 2
233FS[9]157
Cir. 9
548F2d857
5LE973s
86Æ2 1343s

—157—
Wojcinski v Foley 1963
a 327F2d665
Cir. 4
278FS[2]398
Ind
173 InA581
364 NE1031

—161—
Hiller v Liquor Salesmen's Union Local No. 2 1964
r 338F2d778
Cir. 2
282FS[1]428
24Æ2 752s
26Æ3 608n

—166—
First National Bank of Miami v United States 1963
a 341F2d737

680

EXERCISE 13.2

—661—
Sobus v Lumbermens Mutual Casualty Co. 1975
a 532F2d751
Cir. 1
716F2d[10]943
Cir. 4
d 558FS[10]432
d 558FS[11]432
Fla
483 So2d516
Md
334 Md394
96 MdA291
624 A2d1317
639 A2d658
40ALR2d168s
34ALR3d533s

—680—
Edwards v First Bank of Dundee 1975
s 534F2d1242
Cir. 5
497FS[4]509
497FS[2]510
La
397 So2d1070
55TxL863
17ARF33s
61ARF94n
62ARF353n
63ARF461n

—683—
United States v Gurney 1974
s 393FS688
Cir. 4
d 415FS[1]1039

—688—
United States v Gurney 1974
s 393FS683
Cir. 1
c 565F2d[1]1227
610FS[10]998
Cir. 5
d 510FS[15]701
Cir. 6
e 429FS[5]790
e 429FS[6]790
e 429FS[7]790
e 429FS[9]790
e 429FS[14]790
e 429FS797
Cir. 7
407FS[1]914
Cir. 8
623FS99
Cir. 11
659F2d[10]601
659F2d[11]608
Ariz
127 Az470
622 P2d29
38ALR2d225s
17ARF590s
36ARF386n
68ARF811n

—707—
United States v Adler 1975
Cir. 3
687F2d[4]753
Cir. 10
553FS[3]103
100ALR2d525s

—712—
Curran v Fireman's Fund Insurance Co. 1975
Cir. 9
d 664FS[2]1317
Conn
174 Ct335
39 CS94
387 A2d542
469 A2d1237
N H
120 NH725
422 A2d1317
N M
98 NM170
646 P2d1234
Okla
619 P2d596
23ALR4th18n
23ALR4th26n

—715—
New York State Association for Retarded Children Inc. v Carey 1975
s 711F2d1136
s 357FS752
s 466FS487
s 551FS1165
cc 596F2d27
cc 706F2d956
cc 438FS440
cc 456FS85
cc 466FS722
cc 492FS1099
cc 544FS330
Cir. 2
572FS1306
572FS[1]1343
574FS996
Cir. 3
532F2d[1]947
j 612F2d126
446FS1317
Cir. 6
82FRD262
Cir. 7
511FS[1]1338
619FS[1]378
N Y
61 NY2d161
92 NYAD2d128
89 NYM2d1005
131 NYM2d88
460 NE2d1340
392 NYS2d983
460 NYS2d75
472 NYS2d905
499 NYS2d592
Okla
609 P2d749
78CR741
93HLR28
93HLR493
72NwL463
126PaL588
126PaL718
31StnL566
31StnL615
31StnL657
31StnL682
31StnL726
31StnL764
34StnL1190
65VaL52
93YLJ497

—719—
Wisconsin Potowatomies of Hannahville Indian Community v Houston 1973
490US[16]35
490US[13]42
j 490US59
104LE2d[16]38
104LE2d[13]42
j 104LE2d53
109SC[16]1601
109SC[13]1605
j 109SC1614
Cir. 8
874F2d516
Alk
718 P2d155
722 P2d221
Ariz
115 Az88
115 Az89
563 P2d887
563 P2d888
Md
276 Md346
347 A2d236
Mich
202 McA496
509 NW2d824
Mont
189 Mt537
617 P2d128
N M
89 NM616
99 NM502
555 P2d916
660 P2d592
Okla
742 P2d1075
Ore
23 OrA677
543 P2d1080
S D
429 NW2d55
Utah
732 P2d969
Wash
87 Wsh2d658
555 P2d1340
36CLA1090

—735—
United States v Detrex Chemical Industries Inc. 1975
Cir. 3
d 913F2d[1]77
615FS1426
Cir. 4
791F2d[1]308
f 611FS[1]1554
Cir. 8
e 580FS[1]1045
Cir. 10
599F2d[2]375
Cir. 11
897F2d[1]1138
Calif
94 CA3d529
156 CaR546
Ohio
438 NE2d127
71ALR2d986s

—739—
Sanders v Federal National Mortgage Assoc. 1975
Cir. 1
420FS[3]1298
Cir. DC
c 403FS[3]1343
Mass
381 Mas184
409 NE2d172
63ALR3d50s

—741—
Caldwell v Genesco Employees Credit Assoc. 1975
63Cor221

—749—
Hulver v United States 1975
US reh den
in 436US923
in 98SC2275
s 562F2d1132
Cir. 2
528F2d[2]445
Cir. 3
427FS[8]344
427FS[9]344
Cir. 10
563F2d[10]424
465FS[2]1074
Alk
578 P2d600
6LE2d1422s
23ALR2d574s
80ALR2d368s
9ARF16s
29ARF489n

—755—
United States v Kelley 1975
Cir. 2
j 737F2d213
Cir. 5
562F2d[3]351
Cir. 7
623FS[3]1090
e 684FS[1]544
e 684FS[4]544
Cir. 10
431FS[3]66
431FS[3]69
526FS[2]693
Cir. DC
e 790FS[3]306
Fla
395 So2d529
402 So2d405
402 So2d407
N D
270 NW2d352
62VaL1046

—757—
Stokes v Hurdle 1975
(28ARF270)
a 535F2d1250
Cir. 1
437FS[4]313
Cir. 2
623FS[15]401
Cir. 3
500FS[6]35
500FS[8]35
Cir. 5
532F2d495

—763—
United States v Chadwick 1975
a 532F2d773
s 429US814
s 429US975
s 430US962
s 433US1
s 50LE2d74
s 50LE2d582
s 52LE2d354
s 53LE2d538
s 97SC54
s 97SC481
s 97SC1640
s 97SC2476
456US[16]810
72LE2d[16]585
102SC[16]2165
Cir. 1
979F2d[4]264
Cir. 2
442FS738
Cir. 3
488FS[3]452
Cir. 5
576F2d[16]604
Cir. 6
f 425FS[13]1335
Cir. 7
d 620F2d[1]639
d 620F2d[3]639
782F2d760

714FS[12]334
Cir. 8
582F2d[18]1169
582F2d[19]1169
Cir. DC
j655F2d1185
Fla
369 So2d374
4LE1999s

—778—

Provo v Bunker Hill Co. 1975

Cir. 3
522FS1075
Cir. 8
557FS[12]557
Cir. 9
417FS[4]944
Alk
601 P2d260
Del
441 A2d231
Idaho
100 Ida593
104 Ida334
603 P2d159
659 P2d88
Nev
97 Nev269
628 P2d1124
N M
92 NM747
594 P2d1203
N D
268 NW472
Ohio
15 OS3d106
49 OS3d177
472 NE1059
551 NE966
Tenn
586 SW833
23ALR1190n

—788—

Madison v Sielaff 1975

Cir. 5
542F2d[3]250
Cir. 6
607FS[1]1039
Cir. 10
f414FS[2]809

—790—

Burke v Mathiasen's Tanker Industries Inc. 1975

Cir. 2
613FS[13]593

—795—

Muntwyler v Ranger Insurance Co. 1975

s 387FS966
Cir. 7
721FS997
Ill
57 IlA871
373 NE496

—798—

In re Kirk Kabinets Inc. 1975

Cir. 1
45BRW41
Cir. 2
2BRW[1]308
Cir. 4
475FS[6]614
Cir. 5
422FS[6]949
424FS[6]861
Cir. 6
419FS[5]67
449FS[5]630
Cir. 10
44BRW[2]853
Cir. 11
654FS809

—804—

Celani v Weinberger 1975

Cir. 2
461FS[9]46
462FS[9]80
Cir. 4
438FS[10]932
438FS[12]932
452FS[7]214
d 570FS425
77ALR641s
22ALR440s

—812—

Stevenson v Board of Regents of University of Texas 1975

—819—

Mason v U. S. Army Corps of Engineers 1974

—823—

DeJulis v Alexander 1975

Cir. 3
71FRD[4]83
Cir. 4
460FS[4]336
Cir. 8
462FS[5]64
11ALR359s

—826—

Wall v Coleman 1975

Cir. 4
582FS[4]1322
Cir. 5
639F2d[2]273
767F2d[4]151
434FS525
608FS[4]213
866FS[2]1022
Cir. 8
418FS[1]503
d 537FS211
Cir. 9
f 639F2d[1]512
f 639F2d[4]512
410FS[1]601
Cir. 10
e 654F2d[4]1375
921F2d1104
921F2d[4]1105
Cir. 11
758F2d584
Ill
235 IlA1043
235 IlA1053
601 NE1299
601 NE1305
81LE902n
81LE906n
72ARF543n

110ARF499n

—831—

Miller v United States 1975

a 527F2d231

—838—

Lemmon Transport Company Inc. v United States 1975

Cir. 4
413FS[5]126
Cir. 5
576F2d[8]682
421FS[2]319
421FS[5]320
421FS[8]323
421FS[6]329
Cir. 6
536F2d[2]130
802F2d[2]845
Cir. DC
551F2d[8]1328
Nebr
197 Neb468
249 NW738
R I
118 RI607
376 A2d6

—843—

United States v 1971 Volvo 2-Door Sedan 1975

Cir. 2
490FS[5]732
Cir. 7
863FS816
Cir. 10
739FS560
Ala
340 So2d1126
Fla
423 So2d538
Mass
380 Mas421
403 NE941
Mich
71 McA750
249 NW166
59ARF774n
59ARF806n
59ARF813n

—847—

Baird v Bellotti 1975

US reh den
in 444US887
in 100SC185
v 428US132
v 49LE844
v 96SC2857
s 423US982
s 424US952
s 429US892
s 439US925
s 439US1000
s 439US1065
s 439US1112
s 439US1126
s 440US904
s 443US622
s 46LE301
s 47LE358
s 50LE175
s 58LE317
s 58LE675
s 59LE29
s 59LE70
s 59LE86
s 59LE451
s 61LE797
s 96SC390
s 96SC1425
s 97SC251
s 99SC307
s 99SC607
s 99SC827
s 99SC1013
s 99SC1041
s 99SC1208
s 99SC1209
s 99SC3035
s 428FS854
s 450FS997
cc 555FS579
35LE735s
Cir. 1
527F2d[9]584
Cir. 2
j 605F2d48
440FS[10]1202
440FS[8]1207
533FS[1]627
Cir. 3
401FS[15]566
405FS536
Cir. 5
517F2d[9]793
474FS1167
Cir. 6
446FS329
Cir. 7
582F2d[15]1382
d 448FS[2]1003
q 449FS[15]1313
Cir. 8
557F2d[2]174
416FS[15]718

483FS[12]683
483FS[5]1030
d 483FS[4]1031
Cir. 9
j 537F2d[1]1035
Mass
371 Mas743
7 MaA816
360 NE290
390 NE1135
23CLA725
66MnL472
62VaL303
35LE735s

—865—

Sipe v Local Union No. 191 United Brotherhood of Carpenters and Joiners of America 1975

Cir. 2
417FS[10]812
417FS[8]813
438FS[4]1247
438FS[7]1247
837FS565
Cir. 3
f 552F2d[14]560
419FS[2]273
426FS[14]1096
433FS[14]1232
443FS[2]487
536FS760
536FS[11]762
Cir. 5
535F2d917
Cir. 11
665FS[10]1582
5ALR1040s
40ARF307n
43ARF23n
75ARF642n

—874—

United States v Jarrett 1975

r 536F2d388
Cir. 6
d 411FS[1]308

4. What happened to the case cited at 464 F. Supp. 133?
   a. It was affirmed.
   b. It was denied review by the U.S. Supreme Court.
   c. It was overturned in Arkansas.
   d. None of the above
5. 464 F. Supp. 133 is also published in which of the following?
   a. 449 US 949
   b. 68 LE 402
   c. 101 SC 851
   d. All of the above

D. Exercise 13.4: *Federal Rules Decisions*

1. Which case, finding, or ruling was affirmed?
   a. 170 FRD 113
   b. 171 FRD 82
   c. 79 FRD 412
   d. None of the above
2. Is 78 FRD 108 the same as 895 FS 902?
   a. Yes
   b. No
3. 79 FRD 246 includes citations to California, Florida, and Pennsylvania decisions.
   a. True
   b. False
4. In the entry for 78 FRD 388, which case is cited as controlling?
   a. 79 FRD 499
   b. 918 FS 1541
   c. 79 FRD 567
   d. None of the above
5. What is the symbol abbreviation for the Federal American Law Reports?
   a. A.L.R.
   b. FAL
   c. ALRF
   d. ARF

E. Exercise 13.5: A.L.R. *Blue Book*

1. The citation 295 A.L.R.2d 1985 could not be found in this volume.
   a. True
   b. False
2. 1 A.L.R. 459-470 is supplemented in 46 A.L.R. 1192.
   a. True
   b. False
3. 1 A.L.R. 329-331 is supplemented and further analyzed in 36 A.L.R.2d 861.
   a. True
   b. False
4. 1 A.L.R. 449-450 has been superseded.
   a. True
   b. False

EXERCISE 13.3

Cir. 3
500FS121
738FS821
Cir. 4
549FS[1]484
Cir. 6
526FS326
526FS[2]327
Cir. 7
845FS1263
845FS[1]1264
Fla
365 So2d773

—1360—

Felix v Milliken 1978

Cir. 1
614F2d[2]1
Cir. 2
519FS[4]857
519FS[9]859
Cir. 5
539FS[7]823
539FS[8]824
Cir. 8
912F2d265
Alk
687 P2d339
Ariz
143 Az114
692 P2d293
Mass
378 Mas83
389 NE2d980
Mich
423 Mch703
377 NW2d817
99YLJ1503

—1389—

United States v 1975 Ford Ranger XLT 1979

59ALRF786n

Vol. 464

—1—

C. Douglas Wilson & Co. v Insurance Company of North America, Philadelphia, Pennsylvania 1977

US cert den
in 444US831
in 100SC59
a 590F2d1275
23ALR2d1243s

—19—

Calumet Industries Inc. v MacClure 1978

Cir. 3
549FS1071
e 549FS[4]1074
772FS[10]867
Cir. 4
706FS[10]1252
Cir. 7
633F2d[14]61
36BRW[10]690
Ind
427 NE2d730
N H
121 NH613
433 A2d1253
89McL538
43StnL897
12LE2d1235s
6ALRF906s
110ALRF791n

—35—

In the Matter of Bohack Corp. 1978

cc 607F2d258
Cir. 2
2BRW[1]64

—38—

McManama v Lukhard 1978

a 616F2d727
Cir. 2
f 711F2d[9]1154
Cir. 4
937F2d[5]930
477FS[2]512
477FS[1]513
618FS[3]1224
Me
464 A2d184
N Y
95 NYAD305
132 NYM529
466 NYS2d359
504 NYS2d391
43ALRF243s

—44—

Eric v Secretary of United States Department of Housing and Urban Development 1978

Cir. 1
507FS1063
Cir. 7
577FS807
Cir. 8
564FS[2]1411
e 564FS[7]1413
Cir. 9
474FS[7]846
Cir. 10
521FS[1]1141

—50—

Sorin v Board of Education of School District of Warrensville Heights 1978

Cir. 6
536FS[4]249
c 93FRD[8]381
24BRW[5]534
Cir. 7
487FS[1]1247
544FS[1]833
638FS[3]1495
Ohio
66 OA3d376
584 NE2d62
Vt
148 Vt444
535 A2d785
Wash
27 WAp269
616 P2d1262
9ALR2d228s
30ALR4th584n

—53—

Murphy v Fenton 1978

Cir. 3
489FS[4]1088
Cir. 10
526FS[7]881

—59—

McKinney v Rodney C. Hunt Co. 1978

Cir. 1
629FS[2]1202
629FS[2]1573
706FS[2]968
Cir. 2
515FS[4]459
651FS[7]1418
Cir. 4
543FS[2]446
543FS[3]446
543FS[4]446
e 713FS[3]188
748FS[2]436
812FS[4]616
812FS[2]617
Cir. 5
775F2d[1]1317
Cir. 6
744FS[2]168
744FS[3]168
Cir. 7
520FS[2]375
815FS243
Cir. 11
f 532FS[7]1037
f 532FS[8]1037
560FS[2]590
19ALR2d748s
58ALRF470n
58ALRF484n

—65—

International Pizza Hut Franchise Holders Association Inc. v Supreme Pizza Inc. 1978

Cir. 10
692F2d1313
462FS[5]1250
648FS1446
Kan
15 KA2d239
805 P2d1254
23ALR3d551s

—68—

Cervase v Rangel 1978

20LE2d1671s

—73—

Rediker v Geon Industries Inc. 1978

cc 531F2d39
cc 381FS1063
Cir. 2
j 629F2d722
495FS[8]32
561FS[6]162
621FS[2]496
Cir. 3
621FS[1]472
776FS869
80NwL1549
12LE2d1235s
12ALR2d695s
4ALRF1048s

—83—

H. S. Equities Inc. v Hartford Accident & Indemnity Co. 1978

a 609F2d669
Fla
380 So2d472
Ill
120 IlA1027
458 NE2d930

—88—

Corporacion de Mercadeo Agricola v Mellon Bank International 1978

a 608F2d43
Cir. 10
663FS[1]255

—94—

Abouchalache v Hilton International Co. 1978

a 628F2d1344
Cir. 2
789F2d[5]995
f 141FRD[1]9
141FRD[3]11
Cir. 4
528FS[4]818

—99—

United States v Paige 1978

Mich
429 Mch586
420 NW2d513
Ore
298 Ore350
692 P2d589
39ALRF570s

—101—

United States v WIYN Radio Inc. 1978

r 614F2d495
Cir. 3
679F2d324
33ALR2d1196s
62ALR4th408n
62ALR4th525n
56ALRF591n

—110—

Wenning v Jim Walter Homes Inc. 1978

a 606F2d784
Cir. 7
545FS542

—113—

Treho v United States 1978

Cir. 7
490FS1281
Cir. 8
769FS309
64LE2d877n

—117—

Holland v United States 1978

Cir. 4
514FS[9]758
Cir. 6
d 482FS[10]437
d 521FS[8]187
Cir. 10
610FS[4]89
12ALRF163s

Continued

continued

13ALRF762s
63ALRF420n

—125—

Chan v Bell
1978

Cir. 1
661FS1245
661FS[1]1249
Cir. 4
736FS1374
Cir. 6
779F2d[4]348
Cir. 9
h 607F2d[5]870
Cir. 11
546FS[7]694
86ALRF146n
86ALRF160n

—133—

Buczynski v General Motors Corp.
1978

US cert dis
in 448US911
in 101SC25
s 449US949
s 449US950
s 449US1074
s 450US906
s 451US504
s 66LE213
s 66LE797
s 67LE329
s 68LE402
s 101SC351
s 101SC352
s 101SC851
s 101SC852
s 101SC1340
s 101SC1341
s 101SC1895
s 456FS867
cc 616F2d1238
Cir. 3
643FS1341
Cir. 6
637F2d[3]1084
Cir. 7
472FS[5]1091
e 472FS[2]1092
Cir. 9
504FS[4]966
q 504FS[5]967

—138—

Rice v St. Louis
1978

a 607F2d791

Cir. 5
777F2d[6]213
674FS[6]210
65Cor40
73VaL1328
36ALRF9s

—143—

Environmental Study & Protection v PAC
1978

Cir. 9
f 598F2d[2]1170
17F3d1212
37ALRF320s
38ALRF578s

—149—

Thorp v Serraglio
1978

Cir. 2
612FS[2]1076
Cir. 3
609FS[3]1555
678FS[3]106
Cir. 7
529FS[1]497
Cir. 8
511FS[3]342
Cir. 9
618FS[3]213
Ill
149 IlA211
499 NE589

—152—

Becker v Blum
1978

s 439FS324
s 487FS873
Cir. 2
474FS1128
Cir. 3
f 609F2d[6]699
596FS[2]1024
Cir. 9
945F2d1473
700FS[7]472
Calif
213 CA3d921
261 CaR884

—158—

Medoff v United States Central Intelligence Agency
1978

47ALRF443n
55ALRF283n
55ALRF289n

—164—

In the Matter of Motion for Property at 2029 Hering Street, Bronx, New York
1979

Cir. 2
100FRD[6]703
Wyo
777 P2d73

—173—

Jordan v Wokle
1979

s 444FS599
s 450FS213
s 460FS1080
s 463FS641
s 75FRD696
Cir. 7
514FS[2]1380
43ALRF243s
106ALRF660n
118ALRF25n

—175—

Bradshaw v Rawlings
1979

m 612F2d135
Kan
237 Kan41
697 P2d854
Wash
39 WAp561
694 P2d669
63A21393s
69A2449s
75A2833s
97A3551n

—185—

Baldwin v Wrecking Corporation of America
1979

Cir. 4
f 791FS[2]605
Va
30 VCO105

—189—

United States v Cawley
1979

Cir. 1
647FS[3]1421
Cir. 4
31BRW[1]582
Cir. 7
e 489FS647
d 489FS[3]648
Cir. 10
652FS[4]779
3UCR2d 387
3UCR2d 401
3UCR2d 877
6UCR2d 711
14UCR2d 1287
Haw
65 Haw279
650 P2d581
Idaho
102 Ida498
632 P2d687
Wash
47 WAp26
51 WAp879
61 WAp14
733 P2d579
756 P2d750
809 P2d762
36CLA5
59A3369s
7A4359n
7A4458n
10A4424n

—196—

New York ex rel Larson v Holy Spirit Assoc. for World Unification
1979

Cir. 2
536FS[5]621
822FS1055

—199—

Panayotopulas v Chemical Bank
1979

Cir. 2
q 770F2d[1]312
518FS[7]595
582FS[3]498
f 582FS[1]499
f 582FS[4]499
669FS[10]1261
89FRD50
Cir. 3
468FS[11]1182
689FS[3]1396
Cir. 4
c 603F2d1090
Cir. 5
e 487FS[8]505
34ALRF542s

—205—

United States v Becklean
1979

US cert den
in 444US864
in 100SC135
a 598F2d1122
Cir. 7
601FS[3]505
Cir. 9
572FS113
9ALRF309s

—210—

Hamilton v United States
1979

Cir. 3
11F3d[2]1148
32ALRF914s

—214—

Reimann v Saturday Evening Post Co.
1979

Cir. 2
540FS[1]429
63A21337s

—223—

Jordan v Robinson
1979

Cir. 3
607FS257
Cir. 9
628FS[2]112

—227—

United States v Lefkowitz
1979

US cert den
in 449US824
in 101SC86
a 618F2d1313
Cir. 2
897F2d[3]649
897F2d[4]649
502FS[7]1045
502FS[9]1046
Cir. 7
565FS[3]362
Cir. 8
619F2d[2]1260
Cir. 10
846F2d[3]595
Cir. 11
706F2d1556
8MJ615
Ill
90 IlA1096
414 NE489
Iowa
309 NW424
Me
427 A2d945
14A2605s
78A2246s

—234—

Troupe v Fairview Apartments
1979

s 642F2d453

—236—

Westchester General Hospital Inc. v Department of Health, Education & Welfare
1979

cc 434FS435

182

EXERCISE 13.4

—440—
Elster v Alexander
1977
Cir. 6
168FRD[6]621

—452—
Wobb v Ford Motor Co.
1977
Fla
d) 694So2d66

—474—
Schreiber v Blankfort
1977
Cir. 2
896FS128

—559—
Magnaleasing Inc. v Staten Island Mall
1977
Cir. 2
d) 166FRD283
189BRW571
Cir. 4
169FRD74

—565—
Carter v Montgomery Ward and Co.
1976
Cir. 2
909FS215
918FS[11]803

—570—
In re Plywood Anti-Trust Litigation
1976
Cir. 2
167FRD[17]385
169FRD[10]514
Cir. 5
68F3d957

—624—
Weiner v Bache Halsey Stuart Inc.
1977
Cir. 10
161FRD[1]105

—644—
McNary v American Savings and Loan Assoc.
1977
Cir. 5
921FS[4]445

—656—
Liberty Mutual Insurance Co. v Pacific Indemnity Co.
1977
Cir. 3
72F3d[4]368
160FRD[6]69
160FRD[7]69
Cir. 6
171FRD[4]208

Vol. 77

—10—
SCM Corp. v Xerox Corp.
1977
Cir. 3
66F3d609
66F3d[1]610
Cir. 8
928FS[2]844

—16—
SCM Corp. v Xerox Corp.
1977
S D
f) 565NW77

—43—
Coburn v 4-R Corp.
1977
Cir. 5
90F3d983
162FRD526
Ind
693NE619
80Cor957

—54—
Nelson v United Credit Plan Inc.
1978
Cir. 7
161FRD[10]69

—359—
Lister v Plunk
1977
Cir. 1
911FS32

—361—
National Super Spuds Inc. v New York Mercantile Exchange
1977
Cir. 2
169FRD513
Conn
244Ct681

—378—
Founding Church of Scientology v Kelley
1977
135LE[4]110
116SC[4]1782
Cir. 5
174FRD384
Ala
674So2d532

—384—
Unilever Ltd. v M-T Stolt Boel
1977
129ARF283n

—391—
Sley v Jamaica Water and Utilities Inc.
1977
Cir. 3
931FS1194
Cir. 11
168FRD[4]326

—415—
Clark v Lutcher
1977
Cir. 2
985FS[8]425

—430—
Sun First National Bank of Orlando v Miller
1978
Cir. 2
941FS[6]1368

—455—
Perrignon v Bergen Brunswig Corp.
1978
Cir. 4
880FS451
895FS103
Cir. 5
161FRD[4]53
Cir. 9
161FRD[8]698
161FRD[10]698
Cir. 10
129F3d1369
f) 168FRD63

—488—
Health Corporation of America Inc. v New Jersey Dental Assoc.
1978
Cir. DC
956FS[2]24
128ARF129n

—492—
Johnston v Spriggs
1978
36A5 12n

—501—
Maldonado v St. Croix Discount Inc.
1978
Cir. 3
174FRD[2]585
174FRD[3]585

—507—
N J
292NJS598
679A2d668

—613—
Vt
165Vt329
683A2d1004

—662—
Stastny v Southern Bell Telephone and Telegraph Co.
1978
Tex
899SW404

—668—
Smith v Community Federal Savings & Loan Association of Tupelo
1977
N D
568NW926

—702—
R. S. E. Inc. v Pennsy Supply Inc.
1977
Cir. 3
936FS[3]309

—735—
Oldfield v Alston
1978
Cir. 2
964FS[8]796
93McL725

Vol. 78

—50—
Dunn v H. K. Porter Company Inc.
1978
Cir. 2
171FRD133

—108—
Krehl v Baskin-Robbins Ice Cream Co.
1978
Cir. 5
168FRD[2]189
Cir. 6
895FS902
172FRD253
d) 172FRD261

—130—
Greenspan v Brassler
1978
Cir. 2
165FRD364
172FRD[6]42
d) 172FRD47
Cir. 5
173FRD426
Cir. 11
168FRD[6]353

—150—
Saylor v Bastedo
1978
Cir. 10
64F3d1442
Nev
110Nev448

—218—
Wheeler v Shoemaker
1978
Cir. 9
162FRD636

—295—
Lewis v Capital Mortgage Investments
1977
Cir. 4
162FRD[29]101

—319—
Harasimowicz v McAllister
1978
Cir. 3
886FS1226
Pa
f) 541Pa486
f) 664A2d531

—325—
Del Noce v Delyar Corp.
1978
125ARF384n

—388—
Karan v Nabisco Inc.
1978
Pa
d) 671A2d1186

—413—
Institutionalized Juveniles in Pennsylvania Institutions for Mentally Ill and Mentally Retarded v Secretary of Public Welfare of Pennsylvania
1978
71NYL120

continued

—415—
Todd v Oppenheimer & Co. Inc.
1978
Cir. 2
874FS[5]584
f) 884FS[5]856
908FS[5]1238
Cir. 11
904FS[5]1365
Ind
693NE72

—427—
Allegaert v Perot
1978
Cir. 2
884FS[5]653

—433—
Wells v General Electric Co.
1978
Cir. 6
f) 168FRD[1]230

—445—
Phoenix Canada Oil Company Ltd. v Texaco Inc.
1978
Calif
40CA4th709
d) 58CA4th1037
46CaR2d893
d) 68CaR2d430
Fla
674So2d90
j) 699So2d718

—499—
Porcelli v Joseph Schlitz Brewing Co.
1978
Cir. 11
f) 918FS1541

—549—
I.M.A.G.E. v Bailar
1978
71NYL122

—575—
Cir. 4
73F3d531
Cir. 9
102F3d1532
j) 102F3d1543

80Cor928
93McL748

—622—
In re Bristol Bay Alaska Salmon Fishery Antitrust Litigation
1978
Cir. 2
165FRD[4]364
Cir. 11
168FRD364

—631—
Hubbard v Rubbermaid Inc.
1978
Cir. 1
d) 164FRD[4]128
Mass
423Mas338
667NE1142
145ARF533n

—663—
Mattocks v Daylin Inc.
1978
42CLA1045

—669—
Weisman v Darneille
1978
Cir. 11
168FRD[1]353
Tex
903SW152

—671—
Weisman v Darneille
1978
Cir. 2
172FRD[1]41

Vol. 79

—25—
Rea v An-Son Corp.
1978
Cir. 4
930FS[2]214

—55—
Charles Labs Inc. v Banner
1978
Cir. 2
d) 214BRW[3]117

—59—
Bernstein v Universal Pictures Inc.
1978
Cir. 9
910FS[2]1469

—72—
Mitsui & Co. Inc. v Puerto Rico Water Resources Authority
1978
Ohio
97OA3d311
646NE850

—85—
Germain v Semco Service Machine Co. Inc.
1978
Cir. 7
180BRW1023

—95—
Levine v Berg
1978
Cir. 2
d) 172FRD[3]47

—98—
Black Grievance Committee v Philadelphia Electric Co.
1978
Cir. 2
169FRD[4]288

—141—
Beacon v R. M. Jones Apartment Rentals
1978
Cir. 6
j) 137F3d918
163FRD[2]266

—173—
Wis
197Wis2d913
541NW228

—228—
Inmates of Lycoming County Prison v Strode
1978
Cir. 8
160FRD[2]116

—246—
Sullivan v Chase Investment Services of Boston Inc.
1978
Cir. 2
163FRD[11]423
Cir. 6
160FRD679
Cir. 9
51F3d[13]1465
NY
668NYS2d313
Tex
914SW610
80Cor1099
71NYL122
133ARF554n

—272—
Mulcahey v Petrofunds Inc.
1978
Cir. 3
962FS514

—283—
In re Gap Stores Securities Litigation
1978
Cir. 9
169FRD[10]128
Cir. 10
179BRW269
179BRW[5]272
71NYL122
71NYL437

—309—
Slade v Shearson Hammill & Co. Inc.
1978
Cir. 2
906FS150

—316—
Gill v Monroe County Department of Social Services
1978
Cir. 2
885FS560

—341—
Wellman v Dickinson
1978
Cir. 2
163FRD423
71NYL86

—363—
Fase v Seafarers Welfare and Pension Plan
1978
Cir. 2
911FS[2]688
918FS799

—392—
Cook v Moran Atlantic Towing Corp.
1978
56AL5 6n

—412—
United States v International Business Machines Corp.
1978
Cir. 2
170FRD[1]113
171FRD[1]82

—419—
Hernandez v United Fire Insurance Co.
1978
Cir. 1
d) 159FRD[18]342
Cir. 7
d) 886FS653
886FS[25]653
979FS[28]654
Cir. 10
167FRD176
167FRD184

—444—
Barkwell v Sturm Ruger Co. Inc.
1978
Cir. 10
166FRD[4]482

—531—
Spelbrink v Jacobs
1977
Cir. 3
901FS[1]897

—543—
Brandenberg v El Al Israel Airlines
1978
Cir. 2
163FRD[3]228
Cir. 3
169FRD71
Cir. 5
164FRD199
164FRD[4]202
Cir. 9
161FRD94
161FRD[3]96
NJ
281NJS608
310NJS502
658A2d1337
708A2d1248

—547—
J. D. Simmons Inc. v Alliance Corp.
1978
Okla
915P2d399

—552—
In re Independent Gasoline Antitrust Litigation
1978
Cir. 2
167FRD380
167FRD[9]381
Cir. 11
168FRD[13]356

—567—
Sarne v Fiesta Motel
1978
RI
f) 689A2d1050

5. When an A.L.R. annotation is superseded, parts or sections of that annotation remain for use or analysis.
   a. True
   b. False
6. The basic annotation can be supplemented more than once.
   a. True
   b. False
7. The A.L.R. *Blue Book* is really the same as a digest, as it provides capsulized analyses of case decisions.
   a. True
   b. False
8. *Vandeventer v. Vanderventer* is cited at 1 A.L.R. 394-400.
   a. True
   b. False
9. Which topical annotation seems to have received the most review and study by the courts?
   a. 1 A.L.R. 725-734
   b. 1 A.L.R. 394-400
   c. Neither a nor b
   d. Both a and b

F. Exercise 13.6: A.L.R. *Blue Book*

1. *Henderson v. City of Crystal Lake* is cited at 80 A.L.R. 1382-1398.
   a. True
   b. False
2. The article at 81 A.L.R. 349-355 was
   a. superseded.
   b. supplemented.
   c. not changed.
   d. annotated.
3. Which of the following is cited in 80 A.L.R. 862-865?
   a. *Weed v. County of Fillmore*
   b. *Allegheny Energy Supply v. County of Greene*
   c. Both a. and b.
   d. None of the above
4. Which article was supplemented by 87 A.L.R. 846?
   a. 80 A.L.R. 586-591
   b. 80 A.L.R. 941-950
   c. 81 A.L.R. 502-511
   d. None of the above

2000-2001 A.L.R. Blue Book

Supplementing Permanent Volumes 1–9 of the A.L.R. Blue Book of Supplemental Decisions

Volumes 1–175 A.L.R.

1 A.L.R. 143-145
Supplemented 38 A.L.R. 229 and 89 A.L.R. 966 ◆

1 A.L.R. 148-149
Superseded 74 A.L.R.2d 828 ◆

1 A.L.R. 156-162
Supplemented 99 A.L.R. 93 ◆◆

1 A.L.R. 203-218
Supplemented 2 A.L.R. 767 and 41 A.L.R. 405 ◆

1 A.L.R. 222-264
Supplemented 102 A.L.R. 174 and 116 A.L.R. 1064 ◆
Subdiv VIII superseded 71 A.L.R.2d 1140 ◆

1 A.L.R. 272-274
Supplemented 18 A.L.R. 87 ◆

1 A.L.R. 329-331
Superseded 36 A.L.R.2d 861 ◆

1 A.L.R. 336-338
Supplemented 20 A.L.R. 1535 and 73 A.L.R. 1494 ◆

1 A.L.R. 343-349
Superseded 51 A.L.R.2d 1404 ◆

1 A.L.R. 374-389
Supplemented 101 A.L.R. 1282 and 104 A.L.R. 1352 ◆

1 A.L.R. 383-392
Superseded 13 A.L.R.4th 1153 ◆

1 A.L.R. 394-400
Ind.—Meyer Waste Systems, Inc. v. Indiana Dept. of State Revenue, 741 N.E.2d 1 (Ind. Tax Ct. 2000).
Ohio.—Vandeventer v. Vandeventer, 132 Ohio App. 3d 762, 726 N.E.2d 534 (12th Dist. Butler County 1999).
Pa.—Lear Inc. v. Eddy, 2000 PA Super 97, 749 A.2d 971 (Pa. Super. Ct. 2000).
S.C.—Hadfield v. Gilchrist, 343 S.C. 88, 538 S.E.2d 268 (Ct. App. 2000).

1 A.L.R. 436-439
Supplemented 46 A.L.R. 1192 at p 1194 ◆

1 A.L.R. 449-450
Superseded 28 A.L.R.2d 662 ◆

1 A.L.R. 459-470
Supplemented 160 A.L.R. 295 ◆

1 A.L.R. 483-488
Supplemented 46 A.L.R. 814 ◆

1 A.L.R. 498-502
Supplemented 72 A.L.R. 278 ◆

1 A.L.R. 528-532
Superseded 87 A.L.R.4th 11 ◆

1 A.L.R. 546-547
Superseded 50 A.L.R.2d 1324 ◆

1 A.L.R. 564-568
Supplemented 8 A.L.R. 493 ◆

1 A.L.R. 610-617
Supplemented 34 A.L.R. 597 ◆

1 A.L.R. 664-668
Supplemented 24 A.L.R. 479, 48 A.L.R. 803 and 76 A.L.R. 794 ◆

1 A.L.R. 693-714
Supplemented 67 A.L.R. 970 ◆

1 A.L.R. 717-720
Supplemented 85 A.L.R. 357 and 102 A.L.R. 28 ◆

1 A.L.R. 725-734
Idaho—State v. Camp, 134 Idaho 662, 8 P.3d 657 (Ct. App. 2000).

1 A.L.R. 834
Superseded 91 A.L.R.2d 1344 ◆

1 A.L.R. 840-856
Supplemented 75 A.L.R. 559 ◆

1 A.L.R. 861-878
Superseded 41 A.L.R.2d 1213 ◆

1 A.L.R. 884-892
Supplemented 66 A.L.R. 1099 and 98 A.L.R. 1291 ◆
Superseded, as to private easements. 25 A.L.R.2d 1265 ◆

1 A.L.R. 900-913
Supplemented 175 A.L.R. 1162 ◆

1 A.L.R. 953-955
Supplemented 12 A.L.R. 1371, 31 A.L.R. 572 and 44 A.L.R. 162 ◆

◆ When Supplemented see later Note and Blue Book under caption of later Note

EXERCISE 13.6

80 A.L.R. 494-496
Superseded 52 A.L.R.2d 1403 ◆

80 A.L.R. 539-549
Supplemented 118 A.L.R. 1511 ◆

80 A.L.R. 553-561
Supplemented subdivs III and IV of annotation 104 A.L.R. 312 ◆
Supplemented 44 A.L.R.2d 238 ◆

80 A.L.R. 586-591
Superseded 52 A.L.R.2d 792 ◆

80 A.L.R. 624-637
Superseded 169 A.L.R. 798 ◆

80 A.L.R. 692-701
Superseded 35 A.L.R.3d 1177 ◆

80 A.L.R. 706-709
Superseded 70 A.L.R.2d 962 ◆

80 A.L.R. 725-735
This annotation has been substantially superseded in later annotations. See 51 A.L.R.2d 8, 51 A.L.R. 2d 120 and 52 A.L.R.2d 350 ◆

80 A.L.R. 862-865
Minn.—Weed v. County of Fillmore, 630 N.W.2d 419 (Minn. 2001).
N.J.—City of Atlantic City v. Boardwalk Regency Corp., 19 N.J. Tax 164, 2000 WL 33155622 (Super. Ct. App. Div. 2000).
Pa.—Allegheny Energy Supply Co. v. County of Greene, 788 A.2d 1085 (Pa. Commw. Ct. 2001).

80 A.L.R. 880-890
Supplemented 115 A.L.R. 1026 ◆

80 A.L.R. 919-935
Superseded 15 A.L.R.3d 13 ◆

80 A.L.R. 941-950
Superseded 30 A.L.R.3d 797 ◆

80 A.L.R. 957-968
Supplemented 111 A.L.R. 1420 and 169 A.L.R. 290 ◆

80 A.L.R. 970-983
Supplemented 116 A.L.R. 712 ◆

80 A.L.R. 1034-1037
Superseded 4 A.L.R.4th 1122 ◆

80 A.L.R. 1049-1052
Superseded 60 A.L.R.2d 917 ◆

80 A.L.R. 1064-1066
Superseded 59 A.L.R.2d 1173 ◆

80 A.L.R. 1145-1147
Superseded 18 A.L.R.2d 1287 ◆

80 A.L.R. 1151-1165
Supplemented 39 A.L.R.2d 782 ◆

80 A.L.R. 1170-1173
Superseded 41 A.L.R.2d 739 ◆

80 A.L.R. 1186-1198
Supplemented 114 A.L.R. 759 ◆

80 A.L.R. 1225-1229
Supplemented 101 A.L.R. 64, 110 A.L.R. 644, 119 A.L.R. 243 and 155 A.L.R. 1383 ◆

80 A.L.R. 1235-1286
Supplemented 115 A.L.R. 1510 ◆

80 A.L.R. 1290-1293
Supplemented 135 A.L.R. 1173 ◆

80 A.L.R. 1296-1302
Supplemented 143 A.L.R. 1381 ◆

80 A.L.R. 1306-1334
Supplemented 78 A.L.R.2d 1359 ◆

80 A.L.R. 1374-1376
Superseded 105 A.L.R. 640 ◆

80 A.L.R. 1382-1398
U.S.—Frontier Traylor Shea, LLC v. Metropolitan Airports Com'n, 132 F. Supp. 2d 1193 (D. Minn. 2000).
Cal.—Kajima/Ray Wilson v. Los Angeles County Metropolitan Transp. Authority, 23 Cal. 4th 305, 96 Cal. Rptr. 2d 747, 1 P.3d 63 (2000).
Ill.—Joseph J. Henderson and Son, Inc. v. City of Crystal Lake, 318 Ill. App. 3d 880, 252 Ill. Dec. 845, 743 N.E.2d 713 (2d Dist. 2001).
La.—J. Caldarera & Co., Inc. v. Louisiana Stadium & Exposition Dist., 750 So. 2d 284 (La. Ct. App. 5th Cir. 1999).
Wallace C. Drennan, Inc. v. Sewerage & Water Bd. of New Orleans, 798 So. 2d 1167 (La. Ct. App. 4th Cir. 2001).
D & O Contractors, Inc. v. St. Charles Parish, 778 So.2d 1285 (La. Ct. App. 5th Cir. 2001).
N.J.—Muirfield Const. Co., Inc. v. Essex County Improvement Authority, 336 N.J. Super. 126, 763 A.2d 1272 (App. Div. 2000).
In re Bid of Agate Const. Co., Inc., 335 N.J. Super. 161, 761 A.2d 1110 (App. Div. 2000).
Ohio—Lewis & Michael, Inc. v. Ohio Dept. of Adm. Serv., 103 Ohio Misc. 2d 29, 724 N.E.2d 885 (Ct. Cl. 1999).
BECDIR Constr. Co. v. Proctor, 144 Ohio App. 3d 389, 760 N.E.2d 437 (10th Dist. Franklin County 2001).
Smith & Johnson Constr. Co. v. Ohio Dept. of Transp., 134 Ohio App. 3d 521, 731 N.E.2d 720 (10th Dist. Franklin County 1998).
Pa.—Shaeffer v. City of Lancaster, 754 A.2d 719 (Pa. Commw. Ct. 2000).

80 A.L.R. 1434-1437
Superseded 142 A.L.R. 615 ◆

80 A.L.R. 1456-1480
Tex.—Frady v. May, 23 S.W.3d 558 (Tex. App. Fort Worth 2000).

80 A.L.R. 1487-1493
Supplemented 99 A.L.R. 1217 ◆

80 A.L.R. 1502-1520
Supplemented 174 A.L.R. 262 ◆

80 A.L.R. 1527-1530
Supplemented 130 A.L.R. 977 ◆

80 A.L.R. 10-69
Va.—Henrico County School Bd. v. Etter, 36 Va. App. 437, 552 S.E.2d 372 (2001).

81 A.L.R. 110-114
Superseded 92 A.L.R.2d 219 ◆

81 A.L.R. 185-195
For annotations covering various aspects of this subject, see the A.L.R. Digests, the A.L.R. Quick Index, and the A.L.R. Index.

81 A.L.R. 292-300
Supplemented 92 A.L.R. 173 ◆

81 A.L.R. 320-326
U.S.—Matthews v. Pickett County, TN, 136 F. Supp. 2d 861 (M.D. Tenn. 2000).
Ferris v. Pennsylvania Federation Broth. of Maintenance of Way Employees, 153 F. Supp. 2d 736, 168 L.R.R.M. (BNA) 2119, 144 Lab. Cas. (CCH) ¶11102 (E.D. Pa. 2001).
Tex.—Graco, Inc. v. CRC, Inc. of Texas, 47 S.W.3d 742 (Tex. App. Dallas 2001).
Wis.—Koffman v. Leichtfuss, 246 Wis. 2d 31, 2001 WI 111, 630 N.W.2d 201 (2001).

81 A.L.R. 332-342
Superseded 2 A.L.R.2d 943 ◆

80 A.L.R. 349-355
Supplemented 129 A.L.R. 763 ◆

80 A.L.R. 379-394
Supplemented 99 A.L.R. 1171 ◆

80 A.L.R. 423-472
U.S.—Rebolledo v. Herr-Voss Corp., 101 F. Supp. 2d 1034 (N.D. Ill. 2000).
N.Y.—Royal v. Booth Memorial Medical Center, 270 A.D.2d 243, 704 N.Y.S.2d 109 (2d Dep't 2000).
Lopez v. Kenmore-Tonawanda School Dist., 275 A.D.2d 894, 713 N.Y.S.2d 607 (4th Dep't 2000).

81 A.L.R. 502-511
Supplemental 87 A.L.R. 846 ◆

◆ **When Supplemented see later Note and Blue Book under caption of later Note**

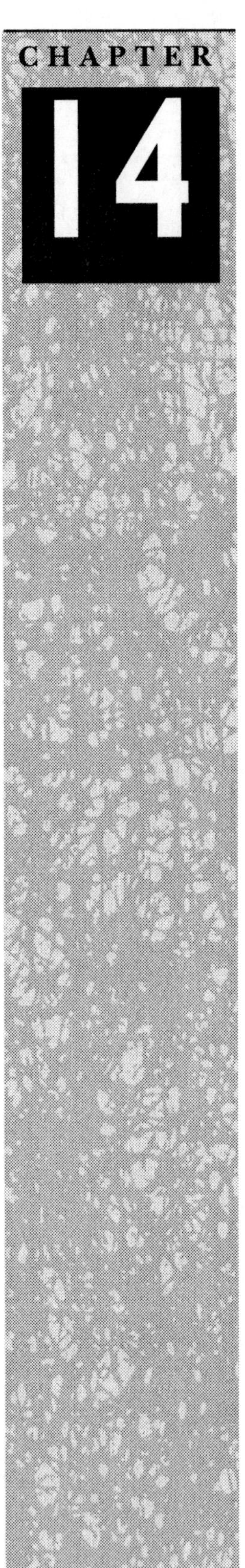

CHAPTER 14

GOVERNMENT MATERIALS, PUBLICATIONS, AND COMPILATIONS

I. GOVERNMENT AGENCY PUBLICATIONS

Government agencies provide many avenues for compiling and initiating research materials and designs. Law students and practitioners are particularly fortunate in that very large government agencies dedicate a good deal of their time to research-oriented tasks. A few of the agencies that provide a wealth of information to the law and justice community are:

- Department of Justice
- National Institute of Justice
- Bureau of Justice Statistics
- Office of Juvenile Justice and Delinquency Prevention
- Federal Bureau of Investigation

The published works generally are of high quality and written with a pragmatic orientation. Very often the material provided includes forms, checklists, and suggestions or hints on how to perform successfully in a given field. Many of these publications are produced by government experts, and are both the results and reports of in-depth research and analysis.

A. Department of Justice

The United States Department of Justice (DOJ) is the principal agency in charge of a great number of justice-centered government publications. Aside from its own publications, the DOJ is the provider of oversight and funding for numerous agencies under its very large umbrella. Through the Office of Justice Programs, support is provided to many other agencies, such as the Office for Victims of Crime, the Of-

FIGURE 14.1

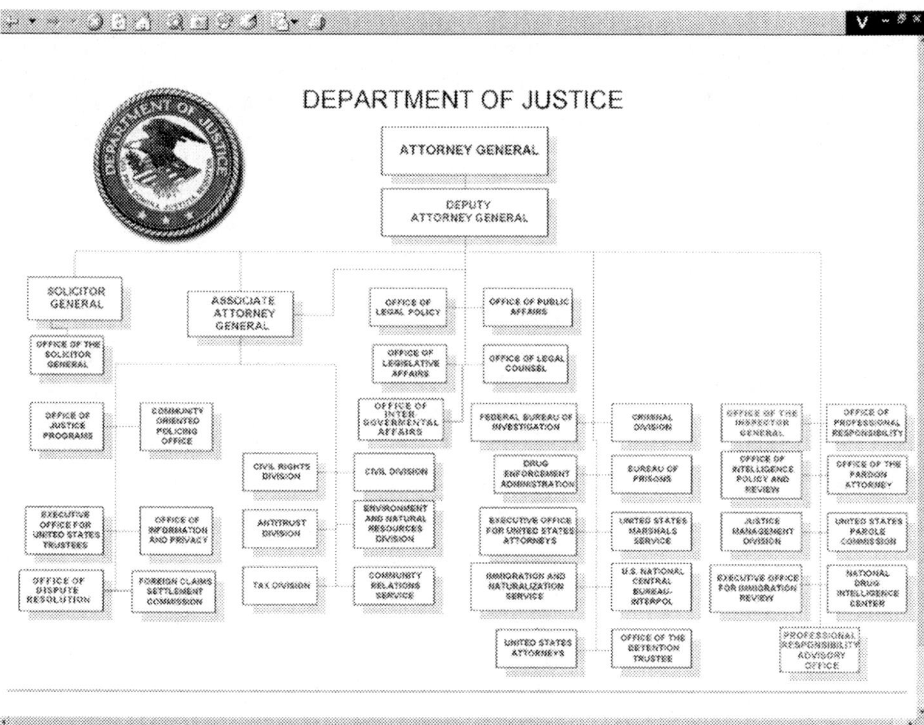

fice of Juvenile Justice and Delinquency Prevention, and the National Institute of Justice. Figure 14.1 shows the organization chart of the U.S. Department of Justice.

The Department of Justice's Web site, at **http://www.usdoj.gov**, offers the researcher many publications that are educational as well as useful. Numerous guides, checklists, reports, and fact sheets are available. An excerpt from the DOJ Web site is shown in Figure 14.2.

Most DOJ publications are normally available in many formats, including online for download or printing. Hardbound volumes and print materials are also available upon request; a nominal fee is required for some.

B. Bureau of Justice Statistics

The Bureau of Justice Statistics (BJS), funded by the Office of Justice Programs, is the primary statistical generator and reporter of the U.S. Department of Justice. The BJS collects, analyzes, and publishes information on all aspects of the justice system (Figure 14.3).

Annually, data is published on criminal victimization, correctional facility populations, and federal offenders. BJS data is distributed through its own Web site, at **http://www.ojp.usdoj.gov/bjs**, through the BJS Clearinghouse (a component of the National Criminal Justice Reference Service), the National Archive of Criminal Justice Data (NACJD), and many other resources. Figure 14.4 shows a Bureau of Justice Statistics Publications Web page.

Almost all of the BJS publications are available online in PDF, HTML, or ASCII format. Print publications can be ordered directly from the Bureau.

FIGURE 14.2

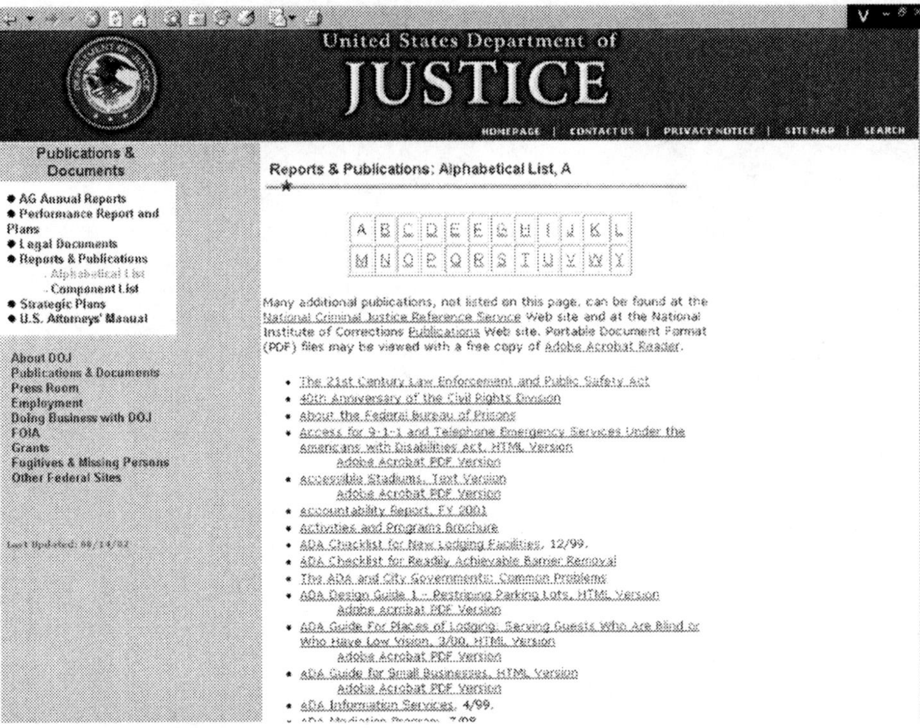

FIGURE 14.3

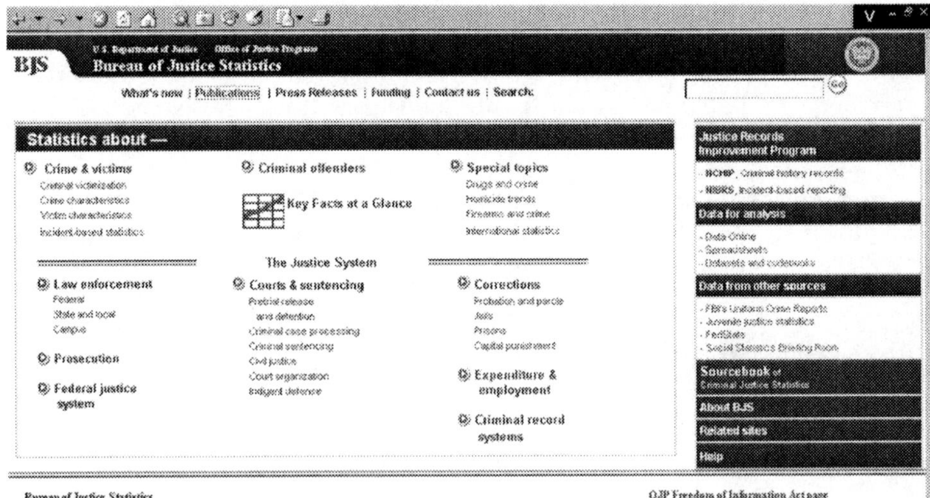

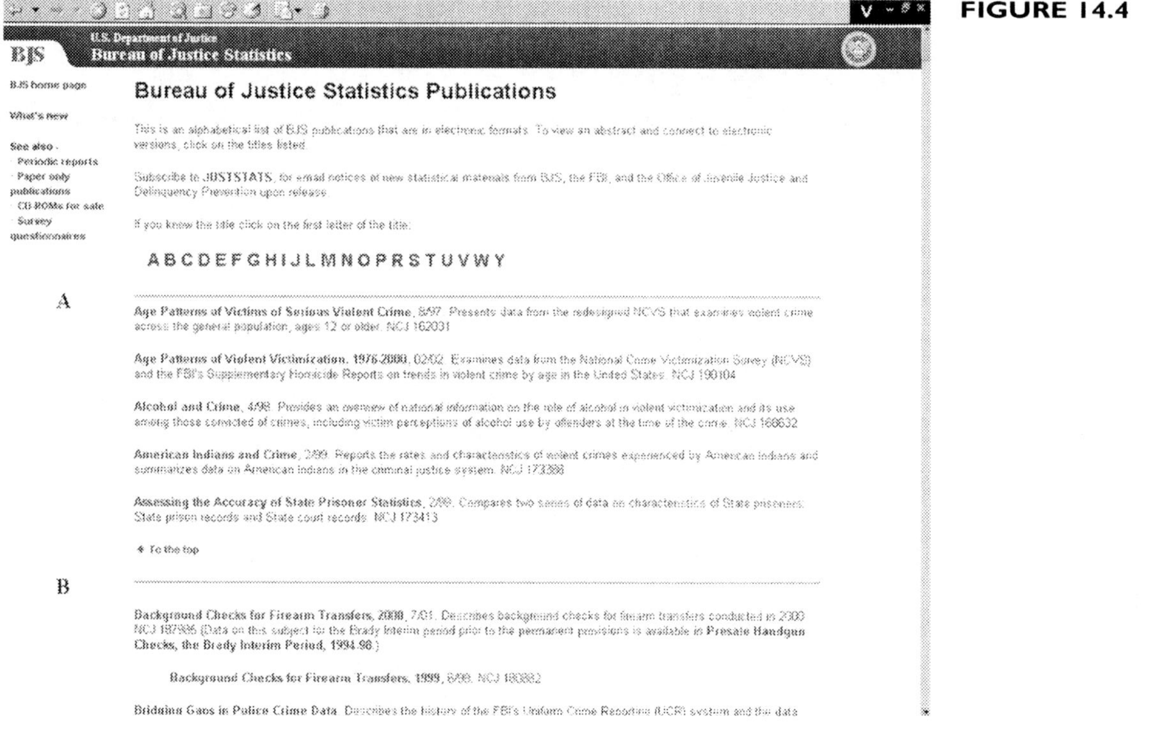

FIGURE 14.4

C. Bureau of Justice Assistance

Not to be confused with the BJS, the Bureau of Justice Assistance (BJA), also an arm of the Office of Justice Programs, provides support for local justice strategies to achieve safe communities. BJA programs stress coordination and cooperation among local, state, and federal law enforcement agencies. In keeping with and in furtherance of its mission, the BJA produces publications to help with community justice problems, provide solutions, and introduce new ideas and processes that may be effective for achieving safer communities (Figure 14.5).

BJA publications are available online or in print directly from the Bureau. Visit its Web site at **http://www.ojp.usdoj.gov/BJA**.

D. National Institute of Justice

The National Institute of Justice (NIJ) is the research and development arm of the federal Department of Justice, and is solely dedicated to research on the issues of crime control and justice. Its many publications are aimed at a state and local audience. NIJ's mission is to:

- research the nature and impact of crime and delinquency
- develop applied technologies, standards, and tools for criminal justice practitioners
- evaluate existing programs and responses to crime
- test innovative concepts and program models in the field

FIGURE 14.5

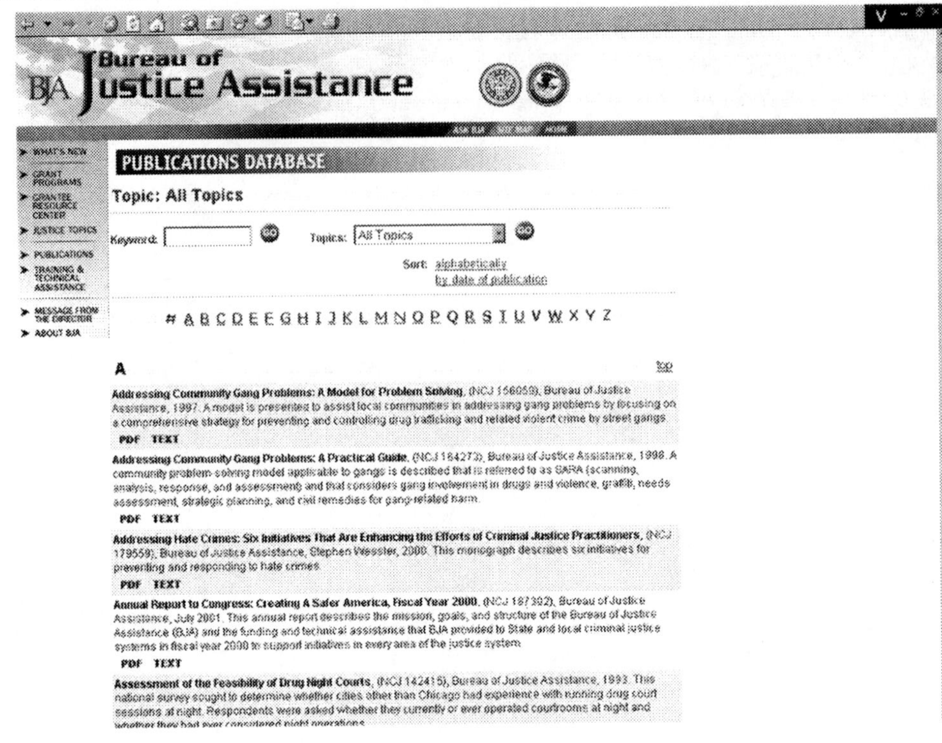

- assist policymakers, program partners, and justice agencies
- disseminate knowledge to many audiences (NIJ Web site, *About NIJ*, at **http://www.ojp.usdoj.gov/nij/about.htm**, visited 4 September 2002)

The NIJ Web site is an enormous clearinghouse of information on the topics of law enforcement, drugs and crime, courts, victims, corrections, crime prevention, science and technology, international justice, investigative sciences, and research and evaluation. Figure 14.6 reproduces the DIJ Publications page.

NIJ also provides a search engine capable of searching the National Institute of Justice publications, all of the Office of Justice Programs publications, the National Criminal Justice Reference Service, or all of the agencies concurrently. See Figure 14.7 for the NIJ's Collection Search screen.

As with the other agencies discussed thus far, publications are available online or in print form. Small fees may be applicable in certain cases.

E. Office for Victims of Crime

The mission of the Office for Victims of Crime (OVC) is to help those who assist the victims of crimes. It administers a crime victims fund, supports assistance services for victims and training for those who work with them, and publishes works that discuss effective treatment techniques for the victims of crime. The OVC's Resource Center is a clearinghouse of research, statistics, and other literature centered on victims issues. The Resource Center's publications can be found either on the OVC Web site or on NCJRS, in various formats. Visit the OVC Publications page at **http://www.ojp.usdoj.gov/ovc** (Figure 14.8).

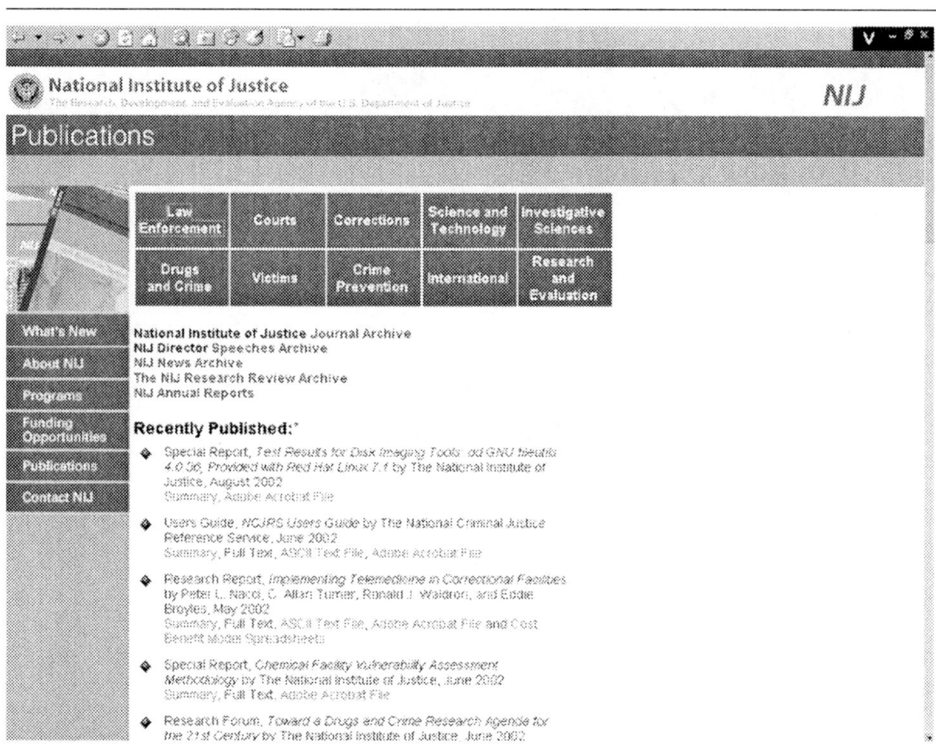

FIGURE 14.6

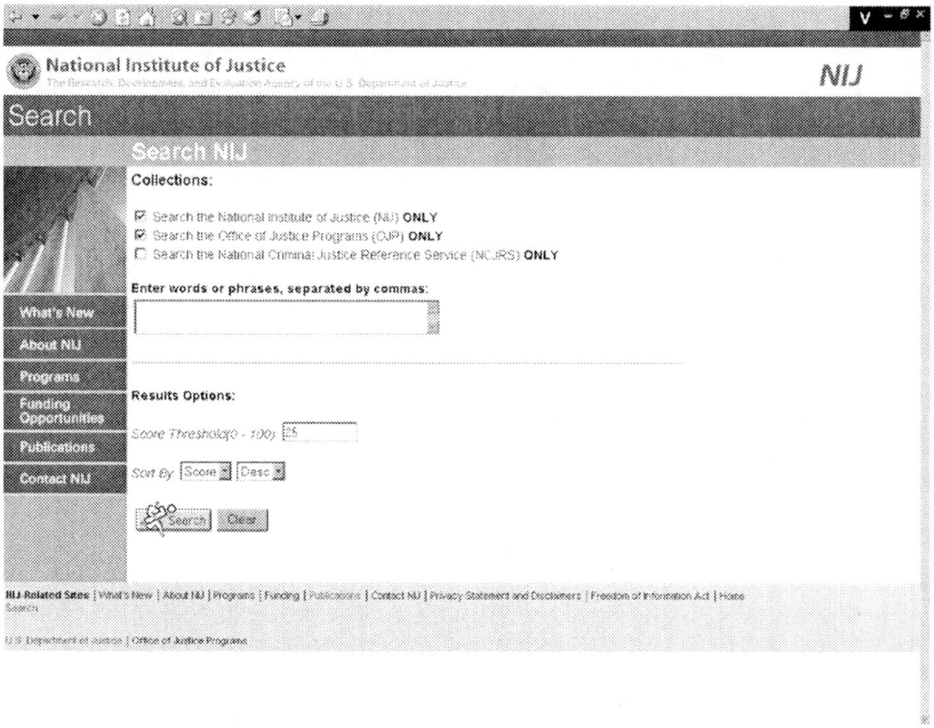

National Institute of Justice

NIJ

Search

Search NIJ

Collections:

☑ Search the National Institute of Justice (NIJ) **ONLY**

☑ Search the Office of Justice Programs (OJP) **ONLY**

☐ Search the National Criminal Justice Reference Service (NCJRS) **ONLY**

Enter words or phrases, separated by commas:

What's New | About NIJ | Programs | Funding Opportunities | Publications | Contact NIJ

Results Options:

Score Threshold(0 - 100): 25

Sort By Score Desc

Search Clear

NIJ-Related Sites | What's New | About NIJ | Programs | Funding | Publications | Contact NIJ | Privacy Statement and Disclaimers | Freedom of Information Act | Home

Search

U.S. Department of Justice | Office of Justice Programs

FIGURE 14.7

FIGURE 14.8

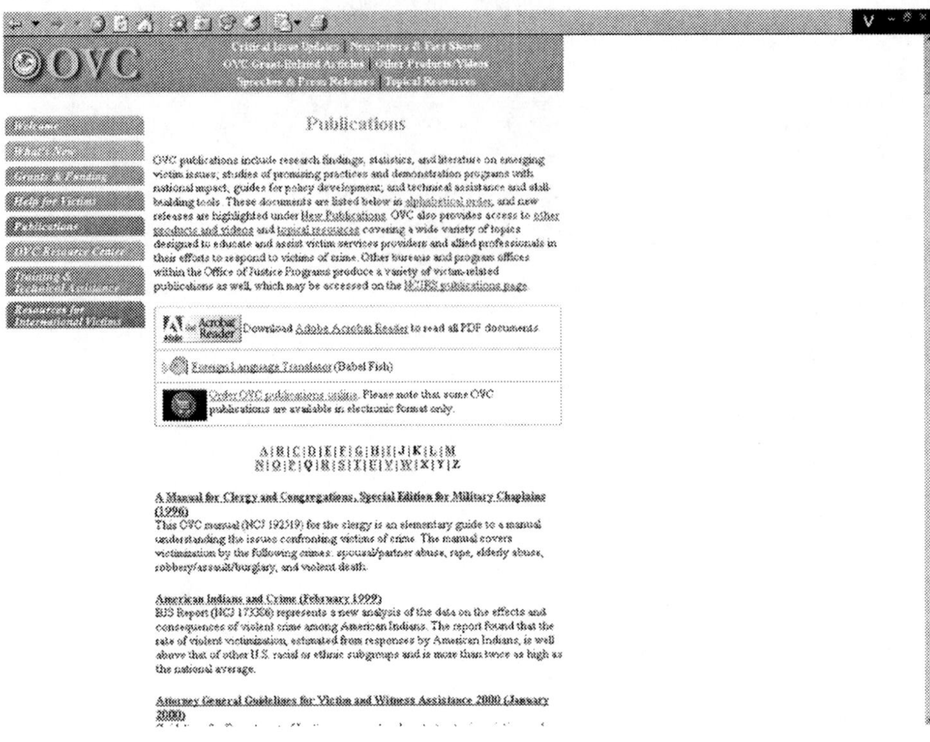

F. Office of Juvenile Justice and Delinquency Prevention

The Office of Juvenile Justice and Delinquency Prevention (OJJDP) exists

> to provide national leadership, coordination, and resources to prevent and respond to juvenile delinquency and victimization. OJJDP accomplishes this by supporting State and local communities in their efforts to develop and implement effective and coordinated prevention and intervention programs and improve the juvenile justice system so that it protects that public safety, holds offenders accountable, and provides treatment and rehabilitative services tailored to the needs of families and each individual juvenile. (OJJDP Web site, main page, at **http://www.ojjdp.ncjrs.org/index.html**, visited 4 September 2002)

The main page from the OJJDP Publications section appears in Figure 14.9. OJJDP publications are available onsite and through NCJRS in multiple formats.

G. Bureau of Alcohol, Tobacco, and Firearms

The Bureau of Alcohol, Tobacco, and Firearms (ATF), a division of the United States Treasury Department, also publishes many works in the (predictable) areas of alcohol and tobacco, firearms, explosives, arson and fire, and tax issues. In addition to these resources, quarterly ATF Bulletins, rulings, and procedural guidelines are also available. Figure 14.10 is from the Bureau's Publications page at **http://www.treas.atf.gov**.

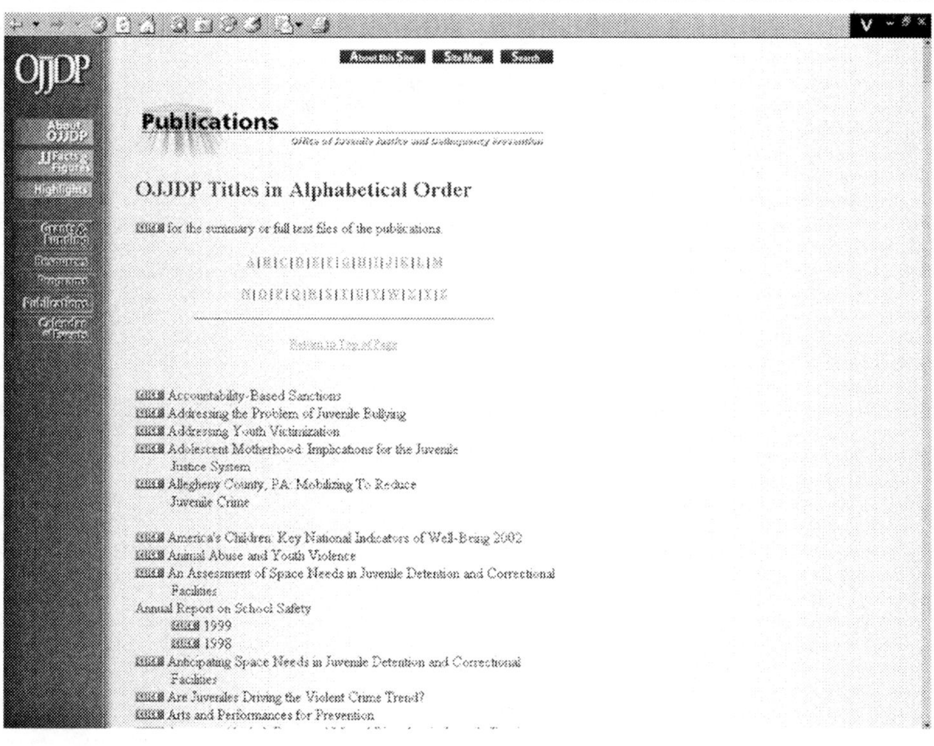

FIGURE 14.9

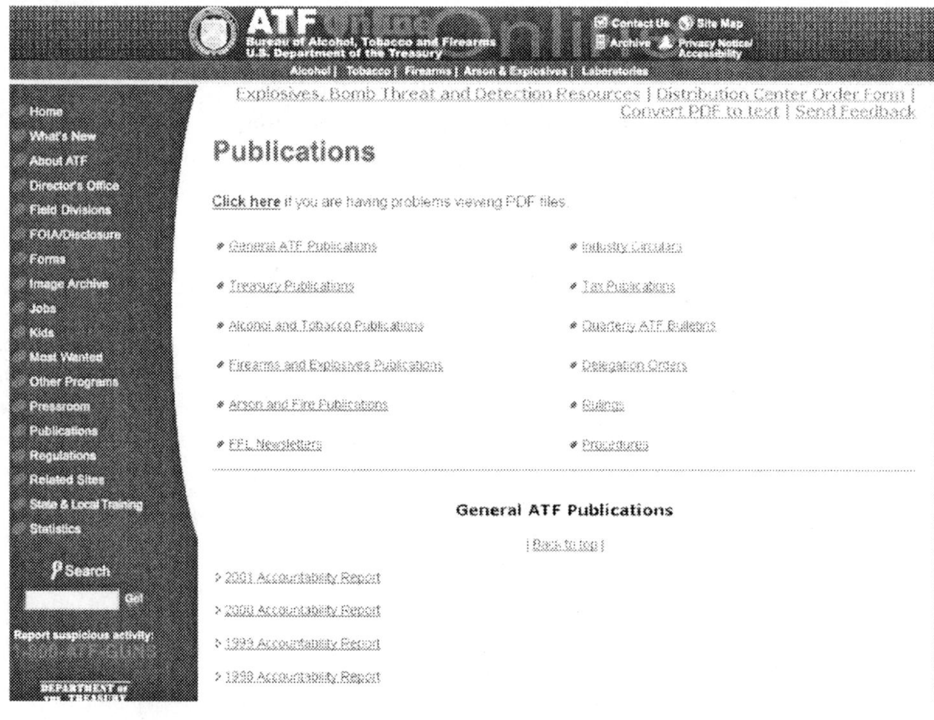

FIGURE 14.10

FIGURE 14.11

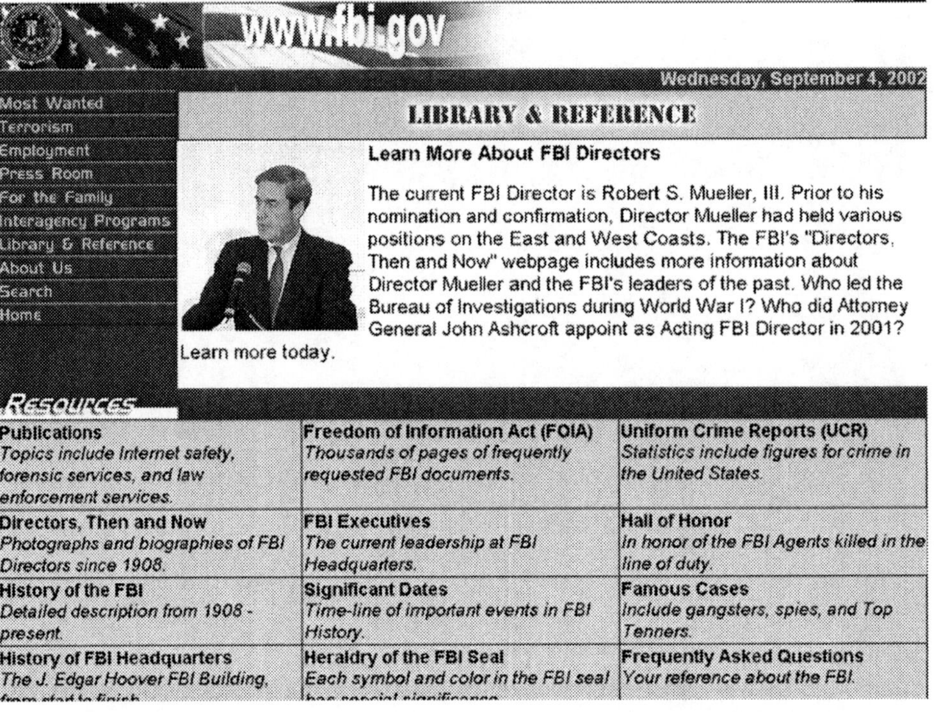

H. Federal Bureau of Investigation

The Federal Bureau of Investigation (FBI) is the agency that produces the country's Uniform Crime Reports (UCR), which include data on crimes from across the nation. It is freely available online at the FBI Web site at **http://www.fbi.gov**. The FBI Web site also includes publications regarding Internet safety, forensics, and law enforcement. See Figure 14.11 for the FBI's Library and Reference page.

II. NATIONAL CRIMINAL JUSTICE REFERENCE SERVICE

Another great aid in legal research is provided by the National Criminal Justice Reference Service (NCJRS), whose home page (**http://www.ncjrs.org**) is shown in Figure 14.12. Federally funded in the early 1970s, the NCJRS has been a major resource for all researchers in the justice sector. The NCJRS's primary purpose is to compile, disseminate, and generate research information, data, reports, studies, and other relevant material concerning justice and substance abuse among the many justice officials, academics, and practitioners.

A. NCJRS Sponsors

NCJRS offers publications from all of its sponsor agencies, which include:

U.S. Department of Justice

  Office of Justice Programs

    Office of the Assistant Attorney General

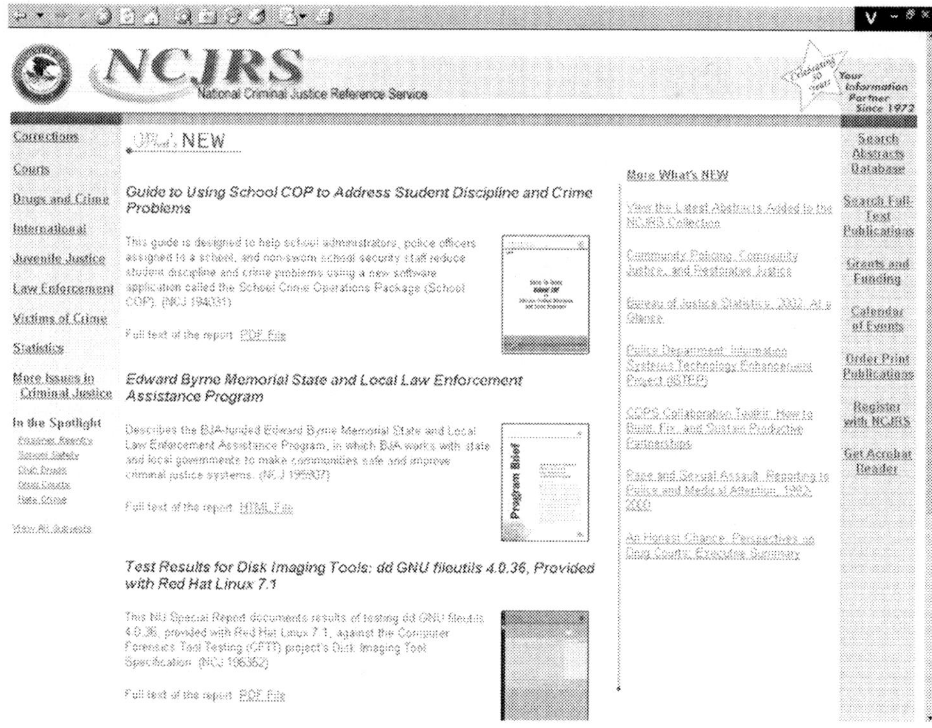

FIGURE 14.12

- Corrections Program Office
- Drug Courts Program Office
- Executive Officer for Weed and Seed
- Office for Domestic Preparedness
- Office of the Police Corps and Law Enforcement Education
- Violence Against Women Office
- Bureau of Justice Assistance
- Bureau of Justice Statistics
- National Institute of Justice
- Office for Victims of Crime
- Office of Juvenile Justice and Delinquency Prevention

National Institute of Corrections
Office of Community Oriented Policing Services
Executive Office of the President
Office of National Drug Control Policy

B. NCJRS Services

NCJRS's many services are freely available to anyone interested in the information it compiles. It also offers an extensive reference and referral service to answer questions about a myriad of topics. The staff will offer statistics, referrals, and publications; compile information packages; and search for extra resources tailored to the

FIGURE 14.13

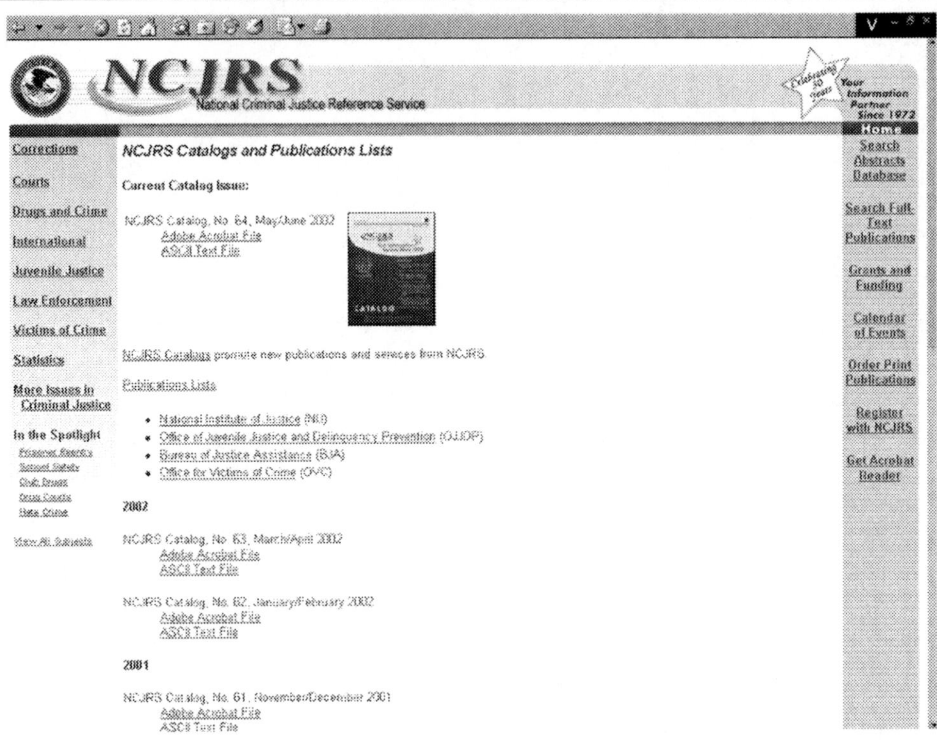

researcher's particular needs. NCJRS offers both an e-mail catalog and a print version, published periodically for registered users. Catalogs and publication lists from sponsoring agencies are available online and in printed format. Back issues of catalogs are fully available on the NCJRS Web site (Figure 14.13).

JUSTINFO is a biweekly electronic newsletter with links to wonderful full-text sources. Publications are summarized by topic and information regarding the type of resource. Notes on whether an item is an online resource, a publication available in printed format, a conference, or a funding opportunity is also provided. A sample of the biweekly newsletter is shown in Figure 14.14.

Registering online for any of the NCJRS services is simple. It takes only a few minutes to become a subscriber with firsthand knowledge of the newest publications in the field.

I. Abstracts Database. NCJRS's Abstracts Database is one of the largest criminal justice libraries in existence. The database includes holdings from the 1970s to the present and contains more than 170,000 publications, reports, articles, and audiovisual products. The resources include information such as statistical reports, research findings, program descriptions, and training materials. The search function in the Abstracts Database is capable of performing both keyword and index-term searches to easily retrieve relevant information. Figure 14.15 shows the Abstract Database search screen. The information from an abstract search contains all of the information necessary to obtain the publication, including a short summary of the item's contents. You may have to purchase some resources from a third party.

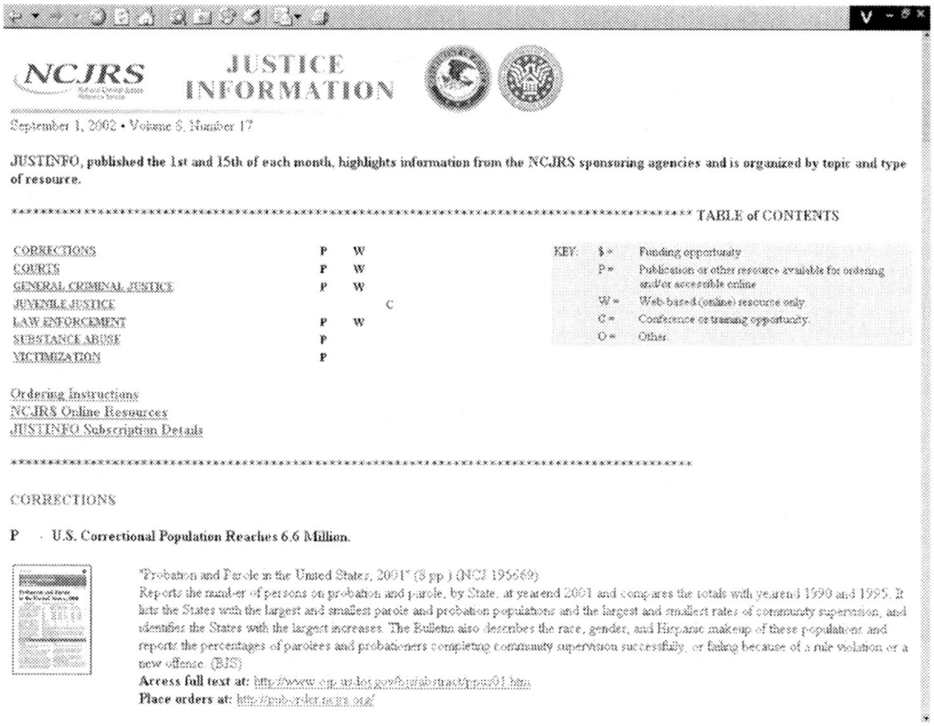

FIGURE 14.14

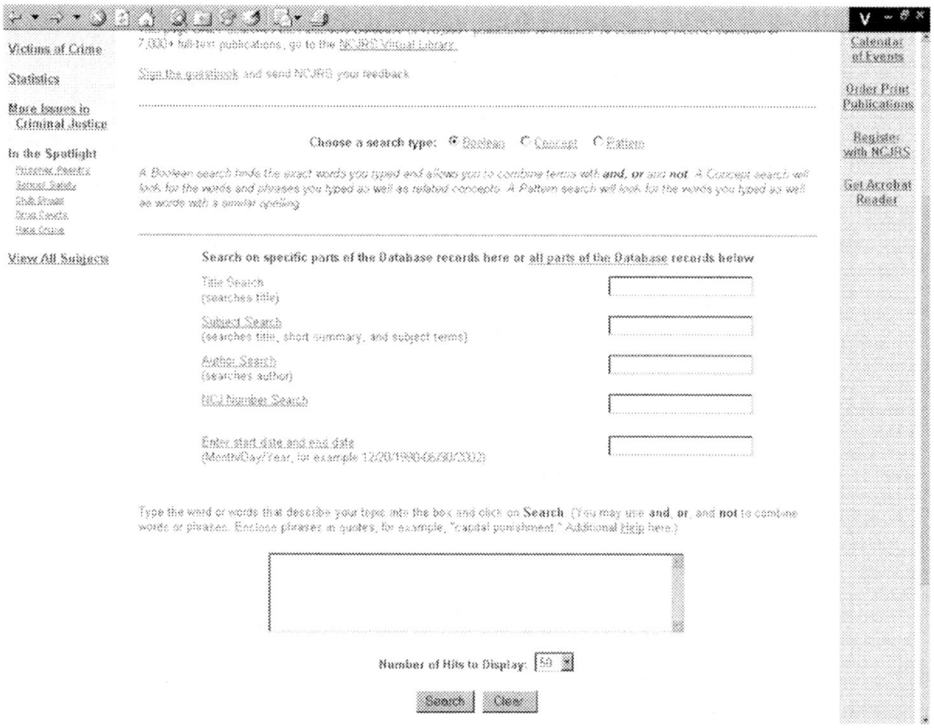

NCJRS — JUSTICE INFORMATION

September 1, 2002 • Volume 8, Number 17

JUSTINFO, published the 1st and 15th of each month, highlights information from the NCJRS sponsoring agencies and is organized by topic and type of resource.

******************** TABLE of CONTENTS

CORRECTIONS	P	W	
COURTS	P	W	
GENERAL CRIMINAL JUSTICE	P	W	
JUVENILE JUSTICE			C
LAW ENFORCEMENT	P	W	
SUBSTANCE ABUSE	P		
VICTIMIZATION	P		

KEY: \$ = Funding opportunity; P = Publication or other resource available for ordering and/or accessible online; W = Web-based (online) resource only; C = Conference or training opportunity; O = Other.

Ordering Instructions
NCJRS Online Resources
JUSTINFO Subscription Details

****

CORRECTIONS

P · U.S. Correctional Population Reaches 6.6 Million.

"Probation and Parole in the United States, 2001" (8 pp.) (NCJ 195669)
Reports the number of persons on probation and parole, by State, at yearend 2001 and compares the totals with yearend 1990 and 1995. It lists the States with the largest and smallest parole and probation populations and the largest and smallest rates of community supervision, and identifies the States with the largest increases. The Bulletin also describes the race, gender, and Hispanic makeup of these populations and reports the percentages of parolees and probationers completing community supervision successfully, or failing because of a rule violation or a new offense. (BJS)
Access full text at: http://www.ojp.usdoj.gov/bjs/abstract/ppus01.htm
Place orders at: http://puborder.ncjrs.org/

FIGURE 14.15

Victims of Crime
Statistics
More Issues in Criminal Justice
In the Spotlight
View All Subjects

7,000+ full-text publications, go to the NCJRS Virtual Library.

Sign the guestbook and send NCJRS your feedback

Choose a search type: Boolean · Concept · Pattern

A Boolean search finds the exact words you typed and allows you to combine terms with **and, or** *and* **not**. *A Concept search will look for the words and phrases you typed as well as related concepts. A Pattern search will look for the words you typed as well as words with a similar spelling.*

Search on specific parts of the Database records here or all parts of the Database records below

Title Search (searches title)
Subject Search (searches title, short summary, and subject terms)
Author Search (searches author)
NCJ Number Search
Enter start date and end date (Month/Day/Year, for example 12/20/1990-06/30/2002)

Type the word or words that describe your topic into the box and click on **Search**. (You may use **and**, **or**, and **not** to combine words or phrases. Enclose phrases in quotes, for example, "capital punishment." Additional Help here.)

Number of Hits to Display: 50

Search · Clear

Calendar of Events
Order Print Publications
Register with NCJRS
Get Acrobat Reader

FIGURE 14.16

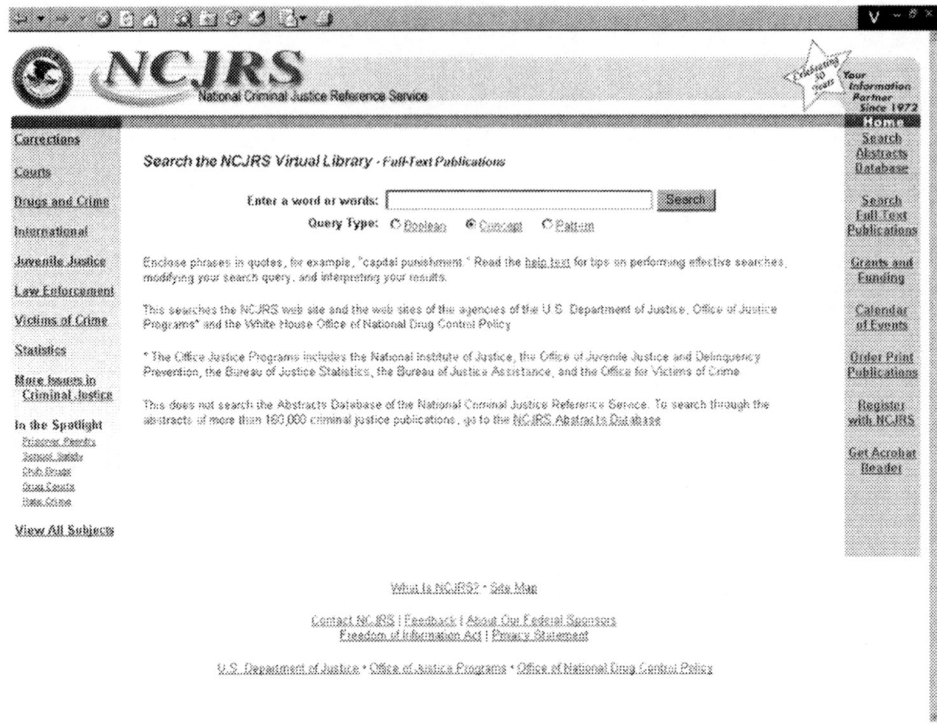

II. Full-Text Publications Search. In addition to the search function in the Abstracts Database, NCJRS provides a search engine to search all full-text publications in its virtual library. The full-text search is a completely separate entity from the Abstracts Database; both must be searched separately to obtain the full benefits of the great quantity of information provided by NCJRS. The search engine accepts Boolean, concept, and pattern searches to allow the researcher to tailor searches for the most accurate results. Results include direct links to the publications, which are available in various formats, including PDF, ASCII, or HTML. See the search screen shown in Figure 14.16.

NCJRS's publications can also be ordered online if you need a printed, bound format; there is a nominal fee for some publications. Items can be found either by a keyword search or by entering the appropriate NCJ identifying number for that publication (Figure 14.17).

III. Fact Pattern I Search. Using the keywords "vehicular homicide" and "driving under the influence," searches were performed in the Abstracts Database and the full-text search. The search in the Abstracts Database yielded 17 hits, the first of which is shown in Figure 14.18.

The survey, *Alcohol Use Among Drivers and Pedestrians Fatally Injured in Motor Vehicle Accidents: Canada 1993,* may not assist the U.S. researcher regarding substantive law. However, background information and trends can be identified from articles similar to this, and the information can be applied to the trends in the United States. The full-text search found 428 documents, with numerous possibilities for useful items. See Figure 14.19 for the search results.

FIGURE 14.17

ONLINE ORDERING SYSTEM

SEARCH | SHOPPING CART | CHECKOUT | YOUR ACCOUNT | CATALOG | HELP

Title/Keyword Search NCJ Number Search

What's Hot?
TOP 10 Publications
Search for the most frequently requested publications

What's New?
Browse recently added products
NCJRS constantly adds products to this online store

OJJDP News @ a Glance, May/June 2002 The bimonthly newsletter provides readers with current news about OJJDP activities, publications, funding opportunities, and events. This issue features a cover story on J. Robert Flores and his vision for OJJDP as its new Administrator. The issue also describes OJJDP's observance of National Missing Children's Day and the activities of the Coordinating Council on Juvenile Justice and Delinquency Prevention and highlights the upcoming OJJDP Report "A Law Enforcement Guide on International Parental Kidnapping."
Read More

Trafficking in Persons: A Guide for Non-governmental Organizations Brochure is intended for non-governmental organizations, such as service providers and other community-based organizations, to use as a reference guide to help trafficking victims.
Read More

Trafficking in Persons: A Guide for Non-governmental Organizations Brochure is intended for non-governmental organizations, such as service providers and other community-based organizations, to use as a reference guide to help trafficking victims.
Read More

BJA Publications The Bureau of Justice Assistance provides leadership and assistance to local governments and communities to reduce crime, violence, drug abuse and to strengthen the nation's criminal justice system. This catalog lists publications currently available that detail promising and proven programs.
Read More

FIGURE 14.18

Previous Document | Document 1 of 17 | Next Document

Back To Search Results

new
To download this abstract, check the box next to the NCJ number then click the "Back To Search Results" link. Click the "Download" button on the Search Results page.

NCJ Number: 157234

Title: Alcohol Use Among Drivers and Pedestrians Fatally Injured in Motor Vehicle Accidents: Canada, 1993

Author: D R Mayhew ; S W Brown ; H M Simpson

Corporate Author: Transport Canada
Canada

Sale: Transport Canada
Tower C, Place de Ville, 28th Fl
Ottawa, Ontario K1A 0N5,
Canada

Publication Date: 1995

Pages: 192

Type: Surveys

Origin: United States

Language: English

Note: U.S. Department of Justice, Bureau of Justice Statistics, International Crime Statistics Program

Annotation: Data from police and coroners formed the basis on alcohol use by persons fatally injured in traffic accidents on or off public highways in Canada in 1993, as well as trends over the past 21 years.

Abstract: The research focused mainly on fatally injured drivers, but also focused on alcohol in fatally injured pedestrians. Results revealed that 44.7 percent of the fatally injured drivers in 1993 had been drinking, and most of these had illegal blood alcohol levels. The average blood alcohol was more than twice the statutory limit. Alcohol was most frequently detected among drivers ages 26-35 and least frequently among drivers over age 55. In addition, 44 percent of the fatally injured pedestrians had been drinking; their average blood alcohol level was considerably higher than that for fatally injured drinking drivers. Alcohol was most frequently detected among pedestrians ages 20-35 and those ages 36-45. Both driver and pedestrian fatalities have gradually declined over the past 21 years; findings also suggest that progress has been occurred in addressing the alcohol-related traffic death problem. However, further gains have not occurred in the past few years. Tables, figures, data for each province, appended methodological information, and 18 references

Main Term: Drug related fatalities

Index Term: Driving under the influence ; Highway safety ; Pedestrians ; Alcohol-related crimes ; Drunk offenders ; Vehicular homicide ; Foreign crime statistics ; Canada

*A link to the full-text document is provided whenever possible. For documents not available on-line, a link to the publisher's Web site is provided.

FIGURE 14.19

NCJRS Virtual Library Search Results

Your Search for "vehicular homicide" "driving under the influence" found 428 Documents.
(How Documents are Found, Ranked, and Displayed)

1. [78] ***Use and Management of Criminal History Record Information: A Comprehensive Report***
   URL - http://www.ojp.usdoj.gov/bjs/pub/pdf/cchuse.pdf
2. [76] ***Survey of Criminal History Information Systems, 1993: With Supplementary Information on Presale Firearm Checks, 1994***
   URL - http://www.ojp.usdoj.gov/bjs/pub/pdf/schis93.pdf
3. [78] ***Use and Management of Criminal History Record Information: A Comprehensive Report, 2001 Update***
   URL - http://www.ojp.usdoj.gov/bjs/pub/pdf/umchri01.pdf
4. [60] ***National Resources for Information on Underage Drinking***
   URL - http://www.ncjrs.org/html/ojjdp/compendium/2001/natres.html
5. [59] ***PORTLAND'S ASSET FORFEITURE PROGRAM***
   URL - http://www.ncjrs.org/policing/por673.htm
6. [59] ***2001 National Victim Assistance Academy - June 2001***
   URL - http://www.ojp.usdoj.gov/ovc/assist/nvaa2001/chapter13.html
7. [59] ***2001 National Victim Assistance Academy - June 2001***
   URL - http://www.ojp.usdoj.gov/ovc/assist/nvaa2001/chapter1.html
8. [59] ***Chapter 12 - NVAA 1999***
   URL - http://www.ojp.usdoj.gov/ovc/assist/nvaa99/chap12.htm
9. [59] ***Chapter 13 - NVAA***
   URL - http://www.ojp.usdoj.gov/ovc/assist/nvaa2000/academy/chapter13.htm

III. GOVERNMENT DEPOSITORY LIBRARIES: AN OVERVIEW

To help fulfill its responsibility to inform the public of the policies and programs of the federal government, Congress established the **depository library program**. This program is based on three principles.

1. With certain specified exceptions, all government publications shall be made available to depository libraries.
2. Depository libraries shall be located in each state and congressional district in order to make governmental publications widely available.
3. These government publications shall be available for the free use of the general public.

Many commonly used publications can also be acquired by mail or online from the Government Printing Office (GPO) or through one of its authorized bookstores and distribution centers, listed in Figure 14.20. The GPO online bookstore includes an excellent search engine to help the researcher in the search for publications. See the bookstore search page shown in Figure 14.21.

The wealth of information included in government publications should not be overlooked. Most publications from the GPO are subject to a nominal fee. Accounting, census results, energy, personnel management, taxes, and worker's compensation are only a few of the myriad topics on which government publications are

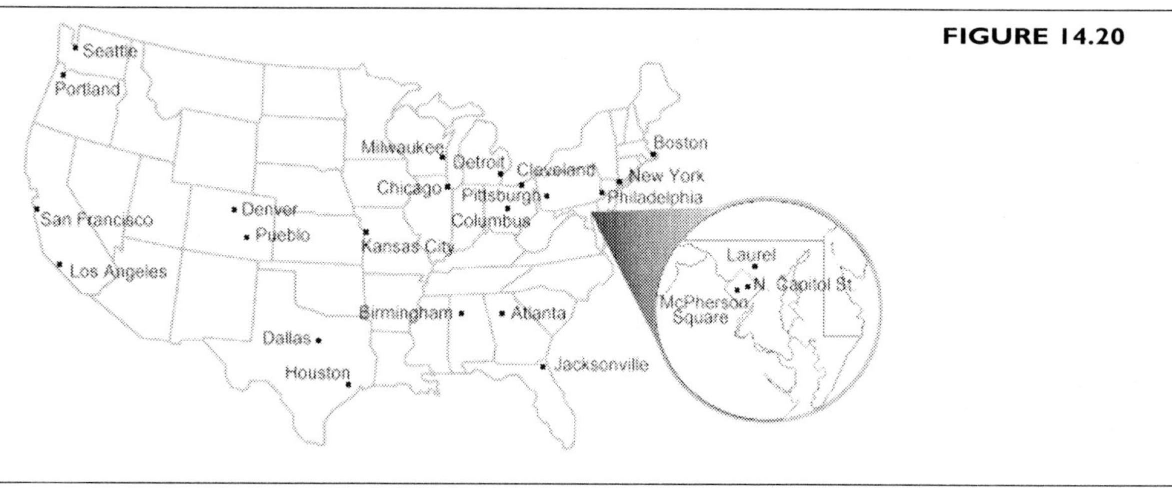

FIGURE 14.20

FIGURE 14.21

available. The GPO Web site also includes information on bookstore locations, distribution centers, and depository libraries. See search results corresponding to Fact Pattern 1, garnered using the Abstract Database, in Figure 14.22.

A. Types of Libraries Designated

The provisions of Title 44 of the U.S.C. authorize certain libraries to be designated as depositories. In several instances, there are three or more depository libraries in

FIGURE 14.22

For: "DRIVING UNDER INFLUENCE ALCOHOL"

[1]
Title: Alcohol and Health: Eighth Special Report to the United States Congress
Size: 2196 , Score: 1000 , TEXT , Add to Cart

[2]
Title: Alcohol and Tobacco: From Basic Science to Clinical Practice
Size: 2235 , Score: 944 , TEXT , Add to Cart

[3]
Title: United States Department of Transportation (DOT) Breath Alcohol Testing Form
Size: 1261 , Score: 842 , TEXT

[4]
Title: Tenth Special Report to the United States Congress on Alcohol and Health: Highlights From Current Research
Size: 1947 , Score: 821 , TEXT , Add to Cart

[5]
Title: Alcohol and the Cardiovascular System
Size: 1840 , Score: 665 , TEXT , Add to Cart

[6]
Title: Screening Test Technician (STT) Training: Instructor Training Curriculum
Size: 1388 , Score: 647 , TEXT , Add to Cart

[7]
Title: Setting and Improving Policies for Reducing Alcohol and Other Drug Problems on Campus: A Guide for Administrators
Size: 1505 , Score: 643 , TEXT

[8]
Title: Alcohol Research & Health
Size: 1793 , Score: 586 , TEXT , Add to Cart

[9]
Title: Clinical Research Guide for Therapists Treating Individuals With Alcohol Abuse and Dependence, V. 2: Motivational Enhancement Therapy Manual
Size: 2226 , Score: 564 , TEXT , Add to Cart

the same congressional district, all designated by representatives, due to redistricting after each decennial census. Currently, a total of 1,339 libraries are designated as depositories, with 53 being regional depositories. Figure 14.23 gives a breakdown of the types of depository libraries.

B. Regional Depositories

The 1962 amendments to the law provided for the designation of not more than two libraries in each state and the Commonwealth of Puerto Rico as **regional depositories**. Regional depositories assume the responsibility of retaining depository material permanently and of providing interlibrary loan and reference services in the region served. Regional depositories also provide assistance to selective depositories regarding the disposal of unwanted material; the regionals are encouraged to add the unwanted material to their own collections so citizens will have access to a copy of all federal publications in the libraries in their own region.

C. Government Publication Selection Procedures

Depository libraries are authorized to receive "Government publications except those determined by their issuing components to be required for official use only, or for strictly administrative or operational purposes which have no public interest or educational value and publications classified for reasons of national security." Section 1903 of Title 44 provides exemptions for "so-called cooperative publications

FIGURE 14.23

Categories of depository libraries

Academic (general) Libraries	50%
Public Libraries	20%
Academic Law Libraries	11%
Community College Libraries	5%
Federal Agency Libraries	3.5%
State Libraries	3%
State Court Libraries	2.7%
Special Libraries	1.7%
Federal Court Libraries	1.2%
Military Service Academy Libraries	0.4%

Depository libraries by size of collection

Up to 150,000 volumes	27%
150,000 to 600,000 volumes	47%
More than 600,000 volumes	26%

which must necessarily be sold in order to be self-sustaining." These are primarily certain publications of the Library of Congress and the National Technical Information Service.

A list of the series and groups of government publications available for distribution is furnished to all depositories. This list of classes is revised as new series are published by existing agencies, or as new agencies are established, to permit depositories to select from the new material. The annual appropriations act for the Government Printing Office, beginning with July 1, 1922, provides that no part of the sum appropriated shall be used to supply depository libraries with any publications not requested by such libraries, and that such requests must be made in advance of printing. A number is assigned to each library by the Superintendent of Documents at the Government Printing Office so that the correct library will receive the publications chosen. Publications are supplied to the libraries in paper, microform, and CD-ROM formats.

Contact any large local library or college or university in your area for the location of the closest U.S. depository library. Librarians and government officials will be more than happy to be of assistance in finding the closest source of information.

Government depository libraries allow the general public free access to and use of the vast amount of government resource materials. With the large number of depository libraries across the United States and its possessions, this system provides a great opportunity for law professionals to gain valuable research materials and information. Conquer the complexity of government by learning how to use its vast resources to your advantage.

IV. THOMAS: LEGISLATIVE INFORMATION ON THE INTERNET

Following orders from the 104th Congress to make federal legislative information available to the public on the Internet, the Library of Congress created the THOMAS World Wide Web System in 1995. In the beginning, THOMAS only included the text of proposed legislation, but it was rapidly expanded to include the *Congressional Record* and its index and the Constitution and other historical documents. Figure 14.24 shows the THOMAS homepage, at **http://www.thomas.loc.gov.**

Currently, THOMAS offers the following resources online:

House Floor This Week

Quick Search of Bill Text (Figure 14.25)

Legislative bill summaries and status

Bill texts

Public laws by law number

Votes

House and Senate roll call votes

Congressional Record (Figure 14.26)

Congressional Record index

Session calendars

Committee reports (Figure 14.27)

FIGURE 14.24

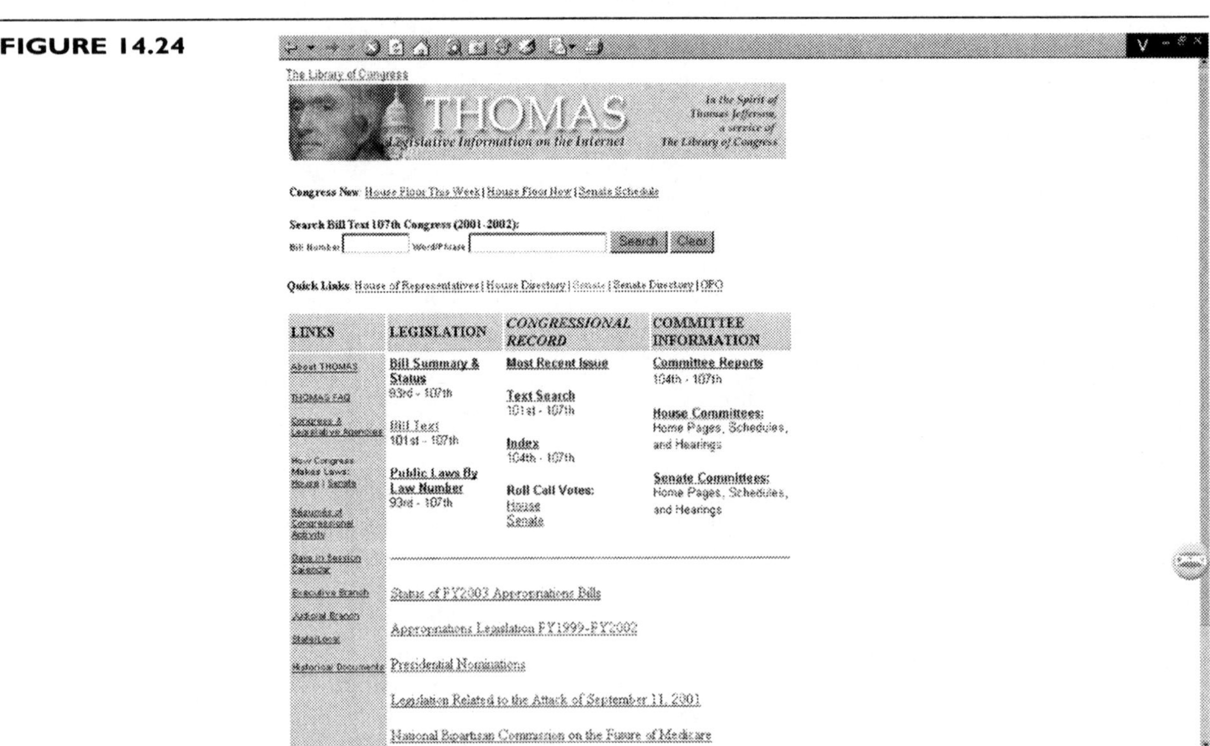

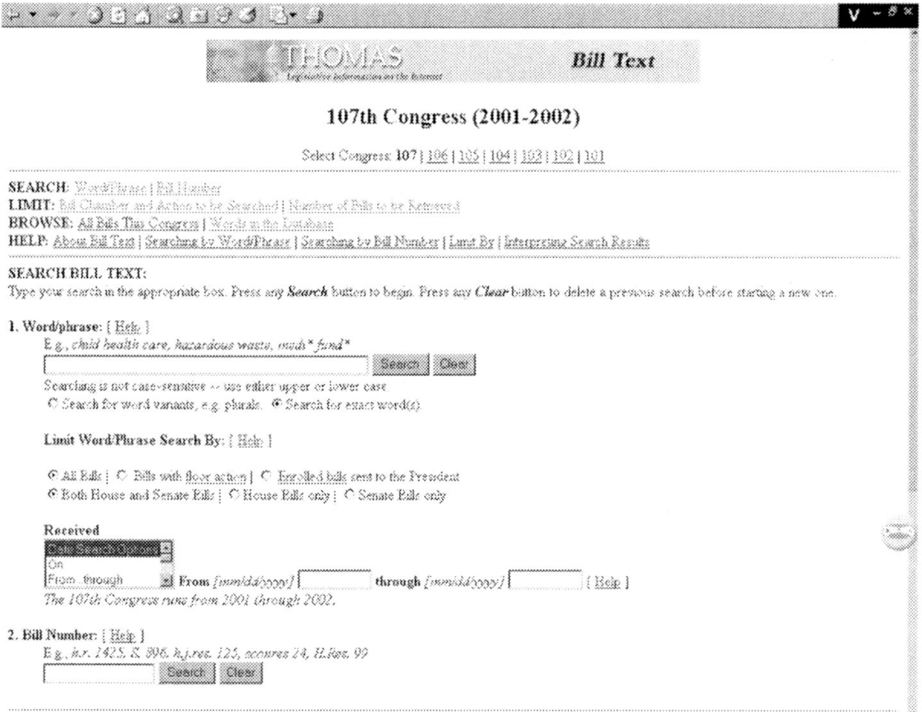

FIGURE 14.25

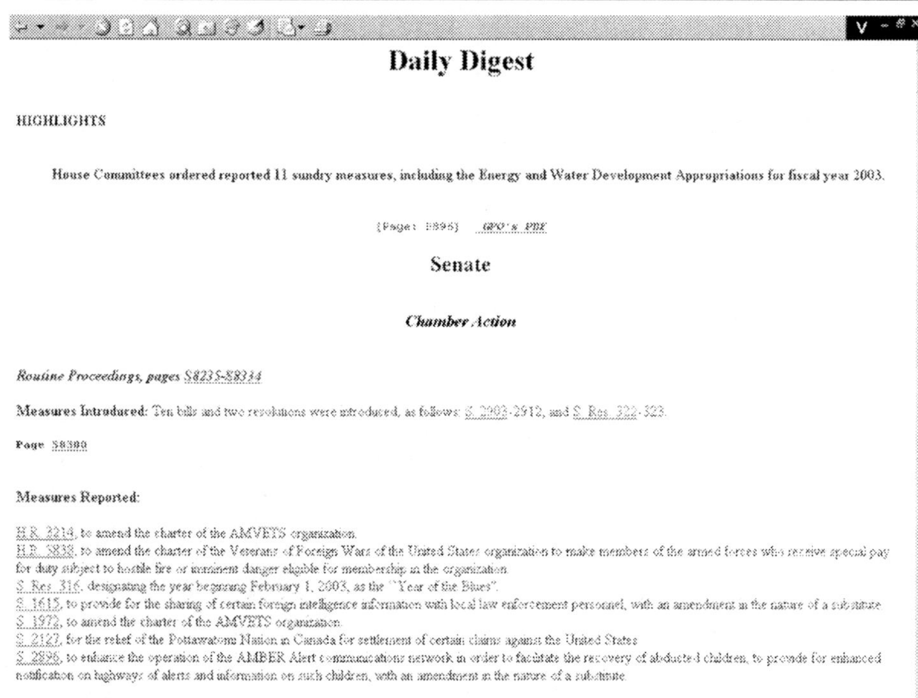

Daily Digest
HIGHLIGHTS
House Committees ordered reported 11 sundry measures, including the Energy and Water Development Appropriations for fiscal year 2003.
Senate
Chamber Action
Routine Proceedings, pages S8235-S8334
Measures Introduced:
Measures Reported:

FIGURE 14.26

FIGURE 14.27

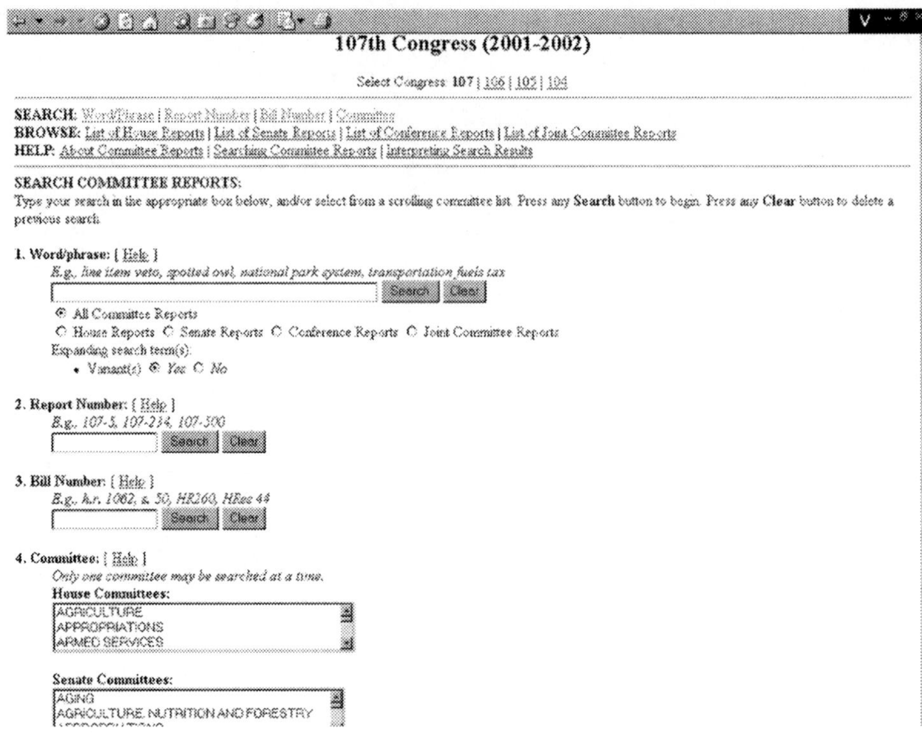

Committee home pages

House and Senate committees and directories

Historical documents (Figure 14.28)

Overview of the legislative process

A host of other information is also included on the site. THOMAS is continually updated so the most current information is available to the public.

V. STATE UNIFORM CRIME REPORT

The quantification of crime has enormous policy implications for the law enforcement, correctional, judicial, and legal systems. Year-end assessments of a state's criminal activity provide planners, policymakers, and politicians with the data to support a cause, lobby for increased fiscal support, or develop strategies in crime control. Although the judiciary is supposedly not a political branch of government—at least in its decision-making—its sentencing patterns and policies can be influenced by this information.

VI. SUMMARY

Government publications contain an enormous amount of high-quality information on a huge range of topics. Researchers can access this information through depository libraries, government agencies, and the Government Printing Office. Much government information is now available through agency Web sites, in a variety of

FIGURE 14.28

formats, as well as in traditional printed form. Many publications are free; others can be obtained for a nominal fee. Particularly fruitful research avenues are provided by the Department of Justice agencies: BJS, BJA, NIJ, OVC, OJJDP, ATF, and FBI. Other excellent sources include the National Criminal Justice Reference Service, THOMAS (the federal government's informational Web site), the State Uniform Crime Report, and the Internal Revenue Service Web site.

VII. LEGAL RESEARCH ASSIGNMENTS

A. Exercise 14.1: 2001 Crime Index

1. The most common method of committing an aggravated assault was with a gun.
   a. True
   b. False
2. Part 2 offenses were the most frequently committed type of crime in Pennsylvania in 2001.
   a. True
   b. False
3. In terms of frequency, what crime occurs more than any other?
   a. Robbery
   b. Auto theft

c. Larceny
d. Rape

4. The term *cleared* means solved or resolved in some manner acceptable to the system. Which crimes have a very low clearance ratio?
   a. Attempted burglary
   b. Murder
   c. Rape
   d. Aggravated assault

5. The overall clearance rate demonstrates that the majority of crimes are not solved or resolved.
   a. True
   b. False

B. Exercise 14.2: Murder Victims, 2001

1. In terms of race, more non-whites are victims of murder than whites.
   a. True
   b. False

2. More females are victims of murder than males.
   a. True
   b. False

EXERCISE 14.1

Offenses Reported in Pennsylvania
2001

TABLE 1

Offense Classification	Number of Offenses	Cleared Offenses	Offense Clearance Rate	Rate per 100,000 Population	Offense Percent Change From 2000	Offense Clearance Percent Change From 2000
Murder and Nonnegligent Manslaughter	648	475	73.5	5.3	12.0	6.5
Manslaughter by Negligence	43	41	95.3	.4	59.3	41.4
Rape by Force	2,699	1,582	58.6	22.0	2.2	2.3
Assault to Rape - Attempts	440	288	65.5	3.6	8.9	23.1
Total Forcible Rape	3,139	1,870	59.6	25.6	3.1	5.0
Robbery Firearm	6,804	1,857	27.3	55.4	-6.0	2.6
Robbery Knife or Cutting Instrument	1,172	420	35.8	9.5	.3	10.5
Robbery Other Dangerous Weapon	1,031	398	38.6	8.4	-7.0	13.1
Robbery Strong Arm(Hands, Feet, Etc.)	7,508	2,963	38.5	61.1	-5.8	-3.0
Total Robbery	16,515	5,638	34.1	134.5	-5.6	.7
Assault Firearm	5,315	2,728	51.3	43.3	-2.0	-2.0
Assault Knife or Cutting Instrument	3,760	2,679	71.3	30.6	-4.9	-5.7
Assault Other Dangerous Weapon	6,853	4,439	64.8	55.8	-4.9	1.2
Assault Hands, Fist, Feet, Etc.	9,409	7,387	78.5	76.6	-13.0	-10.8
Total Aggravated Assault	25,337	17,234	68.0	206.3	-7.5	-5.8
Burglary Forcible Entry	28,349	6,055	21.4	230.8	-3.9	-2.2
Burglary Unlawful Entry - No Force	15,559	2,986	19.2	126.7	-1.4	-7.3
Burglary Attempted Forcible Entry	4,532	643	14.2	36.9	-6.1	-1.2
Total Burglary	48,440	9,684	20.0	394.4	-3.3	-3.8
Larceny-Theft	191,543	44,938	23.5	1,559.7	-6.6	-4.6
Motor Vehicle Theft - Autos	28,536	6,364	22.3	232.4	-4.1	3.9
Motor Vehicle Theft - Trucks and Buses	1,695	379	22.4	13.8	-11.4	-12.3
Motor Vehicle Theft - Other Vehicles	2,524	521	20.6	20.6	-1.7	16.8
Total Motor Vehicle Theft	32,755	7,264	22.2	266.7	-4.3	3.7
Arson	2,382	582	24.6	19.2	-35.9	-22.6
Total Part 1	320,780	87,726	27.3	2,612.0	-6.1	-3.7
Other Assaults - Not Aggravated	87,389	55,534	63.5	711.6	2.9	2.7
Forgery and Counterfeiting	6,937	3,901	56.2	56.5	-8.0	-10.5
Fraud	29,912	14,792	49.5	243.6	10.5	-1.2
Embezzlement	850	453	53.3	6.9	-14.5	.4
Stolen Prop., Rec., Posses., Buying	4,285	2,906	67.8	34.9	-16.8	-10.4
Vandalism	124,234	20,981	16.9	1,011.6	-7.5	-12.3
Weapons, Carrying, Posses, Etc.	4,310	3,551	82.4	35.1	-.8	-.8
Prostitution and Commercialized Vice	2,954	2,874	97.3	24.1	16.1	19.5
Sex Offenses (Except 92 and 180)	7,696	4,395	57.1	62.7	-6.8	-2.9
Drug Sale/Mfg - Opium - Cocaine	12,090	9,902	81.9	98.4	-.8	-.8
Drug Sale/Mfg - Marijuana	4,465	3,542	79.3	36.4	2.8	-1.9
Drug Sale/Mfg - Synthetic	820	603	73.5	6.7	25.6	15.3
Drug Sale/Mfg - Other	598	477	79.8	4.9	-9.1	-2.2
Total Drug Sale or Manufacturing	17,973	14,524	80.8	146.3	.7	-.5
Drug Possession - Opium - Cocaine	6,576	6,059	92.1	53.5	2.8	1.8
Drug Possession - Marijuana	12,696	11,618	91.5	103.4	-2.2	-.9
Drug Possession - Synthetic	818	642	78.5	6.7	17.2	16.5
Drug Possession - Other	2,328	1,938	83.2	19.0	8.1	9.8
Total Drug Possession	22,418	20,257	90.4	182.5	.7	1.3
Total Drug Abuse Violations	40,391	34,781	86.1	328.9	.7	.6
Gambling - Book Making	42	6	14.3	.3	90.9	-53.8
Gambling - Numbers, Etc.	40	20	50.0	.3	-23.1	-53.5
Gambling - Other	429	301	70.2	3.5	32.4	52.0
Total Gambling	511	327	64.0	4.2	26.4	28.7

EXERCISE 14.1
continued

Offenses Reported in Pennsylvania
2001

TABLE 1

Offense Classification	Number of Offenses	Cleared Offenses	Offense Clearance Rate	Rate per 100,000 Population	Offense Percent Change From 2000	Offense Clearance Percent Change From 2000
Offenses Against Family & Children	4,946	2,858	57.8	40.3	-15.8	-11.0
Driving Under the Influence	39,698	38,641	97.3	323.2	-14.8	-2.2
Liquor Law	18,582	17,845	96.1	151.1	-6.9	-5.7
Drunkenness	19,629	18,786	95.7	159.8	-7.1	-5.9
Disorderly Conduct	79,889	56,981	71.3	650.5	-12.2	-10.6
Vagrancy	1,134	575	50.7	9.2	-21.9	-24.4
All Other Offenses (Except Traffic)	98,218	58,313	59.4	799.8	-19.8	-8.3
Total Part 2	571,544	338,504	59.2	4,653.8	-8.5	-5.0
TOTAL	892,324	425,230	47.8	7,265.8	-7.8	-4.7

EXERCISE 14.2

Murder Victims by Age, Sex, and Race, 2001

Table 5

Age Group	Percent	Total	Total Male	Total Female	White Total	White Male	White Female	Non-White Total	Non-White Male	Non-White Female
Infant	1.4	9	5	4	4	1	3	5	4	1
1-4	2.2	14	6	8	7	2	5	7	4	3
5-9	.8	5	4	1	3	2	1	2	2	0
10-14	.8	5	4	1	0	0	0	5	4	1
15-17	3.1	20	13	7	6	1	5	14	12	2
18-19	6.5	42	40	2	8	7	1	34	33	1
20-24	22.9	148	133	15	38	29	9	110	104	6
25-29	13.2	85	69	16	26	19	7	59	50	9
30-34	10.7	69	52	17	28	19	9	41	33	8
35-39	8.4	54	41	13	24	16	8	30	25	5
40-44	8.8	57	37	19	34	22	11	23	15	8
45-49	6.0	39	27	12	20	11	9	19	16	3
50-54	3.7	24	15	9	14	7	7	10	8	2
55-59	3.4	22	10	12	14	4	10	8	6	2
60-64	2.2	14	11	3	7	5	2	7	6	1
65-69	1.9	12	9	3	9	6	3	3	3	0
70+	4.2	27	16	11	19	10	9	8	6	2
Distribution		100.0	76.2	23.7	40.4	24.9	15.3	59.6	51.2	8.4
Total	100.0	646	492	153	261	161	99	385	331	54

3. From age 40 on, the number of murders continually decreases.
   a. True
   b. False
4. No murders of children under the age of one were recorded.
   a. True
   b. False
5. Which conclusion can be drawn from the data provided in this chart?
   a. Murder appears to be a major problem among females.
   b. The most likely candidates to be murder victims are people aged 35 or above.
   c. The most likely murder victim is a male aged 20–24.
   d. None of the above.

C. Exercise 14.3: Victims' Relationship to Offender

1. The data in Exercise 14.3 indicates that most rape victims know their attackers.
   a. True
   b. False

2. The most frequent relationship between the victim of the crime of robbery and its perpetrator is
   a. intimate.
   b. stranger.
   c. other relative.
   d. acquaintance.
3. This data reflects an inability to categorize at least 2 percent of relationships when violent crime was committed.
   a. True
   b. False
4. The most uncommon relationship between rapist and victim is
   a. acquaintance.
   b. intimate.
   c. stranger.
   d. other relative.

D. Exercise 14.4: Sexual Offender and Offense Characteristics

1. Where is the most common place for a sexual assault to take place?
   a. A friend's home
   b. The victim's home
   c. A parking lot
   d. On a street

EXERCISE 14.3

Table 4. Victim and offender relationship, 2000

Relationship with victim	Violent crime		Rape or sexual assault		Robbery		Aggravated assault		Simple assault	
	Number	Percent	Number	Percent	Number	Percent	Number	Percent	Number	Percent
All victims										
Total	6,322,730	100%	260,950	100%	731,780	100%	1,292,510	100%	4,037,500	100%
Nonstranger	3,376,520	53%	162,160	62%	203,630	28%	550,190	43%	2,460,530	61%
Intimate	655,350	10	45,100	17	38,000	5	66,350	5	505,900	13
Other relative	339,930	5	4,730	2*	20,650	3*	67,610	5	246,940	6
Friend/acquaintance	2,381,240	38	112,330	43	144,980	20	416,230	32	1,707,690	42
Stranger	2,829,840	45%	89,180	34%	507,170	69%	720,940	56%	1,512,540	38%
Relationship unknown	116,380	2%	9,600	4%*	20,970	3%*	21,380	2%*	64,420	2%
Male victims										
Total	3,612,390	100%	14,770	100%*	494,650	100%	915,970	100%	2,187,000	100%
Nonstranger	1,585,130	44%	9,260	63%*	113,430	23%	329,190	36%	1,133,250	52%
Intimate	98,850	3	0	0*	0	0*	18,380	2*	80,470	4
Other relative	107,970	3	0	0*	2,310	1*	36,930	4	68,730	3
Friend/acquaintance	1,378,310	38	9,260	63*	111,110	23	273,870	30	984,060	45
Stranger	1,945,980	54%	5,510	37%*	365,730	74%	565,410	62%	1,009,340	46%
Relationship unknown	81,280	2%	0	0%*	15,500	3%*	21,380	2%*	44,400	2%
Female victims										
Total	2,710,340	100%	246,180	100%	237,130	100%	376,540	100%	1,850,500	100%
Nonstranger	1,791,390	66%	152,900	62%	90,210	38%	221,010	59%	1,327,280	72%
Intimate	556,500	21	45,100	18	38,000	16	47,970	13	425,430	23
Other relative	231,960	9	4,730	2*	18,340	8*	30,680	8	178,220	10
Friend/acquaintance	1,002,930	37	103,070	42	33,870	14	142,360	38	723,630	38
Stranger	883,860	33%	83,680	34%	141,450	60%	155,530	41%	503,200	27%
Relationship unknown	35,090	1%	9,600	4%*	5,470	2%*	0	0%*	20,020	1%*

Note: Percentages may not total to 100% because of rounding. *Based on 10 or fewer sample cases.

2. Most convicted sex offenders are under the care, custody, or control of probation officers.
   a. True
   b. False
3. Since 1990, the rate of forcible rape reported to law enforcement officers has
   a. increased.
   b. decreased.
   c. stayed the same.
   d. impossible to say from the statistics.
4. The highest reported arrest rate for forcible rape occurred in which year?
   a. 1992
   b. 1991
   c. 1990
   d. 1989
5. Most sexual assault victims report the incident to the police.
   a. True
   b. False

EXERCISE 14.4

Revised 2/6/97

Data points and sources for the graphical figures

Cover figure. About 234,000 convicted sex offenders are under the care, custody, or control of corrections agencies on an average day. Nearly 60% are under conditional supervision in the community.

Total	233,636
Probation	106,710
Local jails	10,345
State and Federal prisons	88,975
Parole	27,606

Source: BJS, National Crime Victimization Survey.

Figure 1, page 2. Estimated number of rape/sexual assault victimizations among residents age 12 or older and the number reported to law enforcement authorities, 1993-95

Year	Number of victimizations	Reported to law enforcement
1993	485,000	140,000
1994	433,000	137,000
1995	355,000	113,000

Source: BJS, National Crime Victimization Survey.

Figure 3, page 3. Victim's reports of where rapes and sexual assaults took place, 1993

	Percent of rape/sexual assault victimizations
At victim's home	37.4%
At friend's, neighbor's, or relative's home	19.2
On street away from home	10.0
Parking lot/garage	7.3
All other locations	26.1

Source: BJS, National Crime Victimization Survey.

Figure 7, page 6. Rate of forcible rape recorded by law enforcement agencies, 1976-95

Year	Number of forcible rapes of female victims per 100,000 females in the population
1976	52
1977	57
1978	60
1979	67
1980	71
1981	69
1982	65
1983	66
1984	69
1985	71
1986	73
1987	73
1988	73
1989	75
1990	80
1991	83
1992	84
1993	79
1994	77
1995	72

Source: FBI, Uniform Crime Reports, 1995.

Figure 8, page 8. Estimated number of arrests for forcible rape and other sex offenses, 1980-95

Year	Forcible rape	Other sex offenses	Total U.S. population
1980	31,380	67,400	227,726,463
1981	31,710	72,000	229,966,237
1982	33,600	78,800	232,187,835
1983	34,080	87,000	234,307,207
1984	36,700	97,800	236,348,292
1985	36,970	100,600	238,466,283
1986	37,140	100,600	240,650,756
1987	36,310	100,100	242,803,533
1988	38,310	106,300	245,021,414
1989	39,110	104,800	247,341,697
1990	39,160	107,600	249,912,527
1991	40,120	106,000	252,649,535
1992	39,100	108,400	255,418,704
1993	38,420	104,100	258,137,251
1994	36,610	100,700	260,659,690
1995	34,650	94,500	263,033,968

Source: FBI, Uniform Crime Reports, 1995.

E. Exercise 14.5: NCJRS

1. Where can the researcher obtain publications from NCJRS?
   a. Online
   b. Direct purchase from the NCJRS
   c. Both a and b
   d. Neither a nor b
2. How large is the NCJRS library and abstract database?
   a. 60,000 +
   b. 1,000,000+
   c. 150,000 +
   d. 5,000,000+
3. Is it possible for the NCJRS to perform certain research tasks upon request?
   a. Yes
   b. No
4. Which of the following services are offered by NCJRS?
   a. JUSTINFO Electronic Newsletter
   b. Reference and Referral Services
   c. Fax on Demand
   d. All of the above
5. The only publications offered on the NCJRS Web site are those written by NCJRS.
   a. True
   b. False

F. Exercise 14.6: IRS Publication 504

Locate IRS Publication 504 on the Internal Revenue Service Web site at **http://www.irs.gov** and answer the following questions.

1. Publication 504 states that you are considered unmarried if
   a. a final decree of divorce was issued by the last day of the tax year.
   b. a decree of annulment was obtained.
   c. both a and b
   d. neither a nor b
2. You are considered married for a whole year if
   a. you obtained a decree of annulment.
   b. you are separated but have not obtained a final decree of divorce.
   c. you are separated under an interlocutory decree.
   d. Both b and c
3. Which of the following is *not a* correct statement of tax law?
   a. For a return to be considered joint, it must be signed by both parties.
   b. There are no exceptions in which only *one* spouse is responsible for taxes owed.
   c. Both parties may be responsible for taxes owed before divorce.
   d. Amended returns are necessary after an annulment.
4. What other publication would be helpful, ackording to the IRS?
   a. 555
   b. 504
   c. 502
   d. 515

EXERCISE 14.5

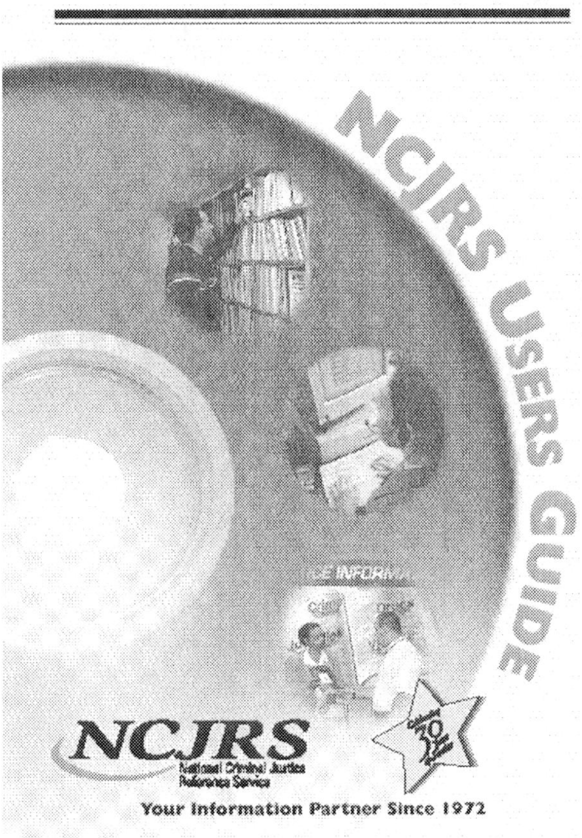

continued

G. Exercise 14.7: IRS Publication 590—IRAs

Locate IRS Publication 590 on the Internal Revenue Service Web site at **http://www.irs.gov** and answer the following questions.

1. *Compensation,* as defined in Publication 590, does not include
   a. pension income.
   b. annuity income.
   c. military retirement income.
   d. all of the above.
2. IRAs are not available to people in retirement plans.
   a. True
   b. False
3. Payments to an IRA account cannot be made by
   a. property (fair market value).
   b. cash.
   c. check.
   d. money order.

EXERCISE 14.5 *continued*

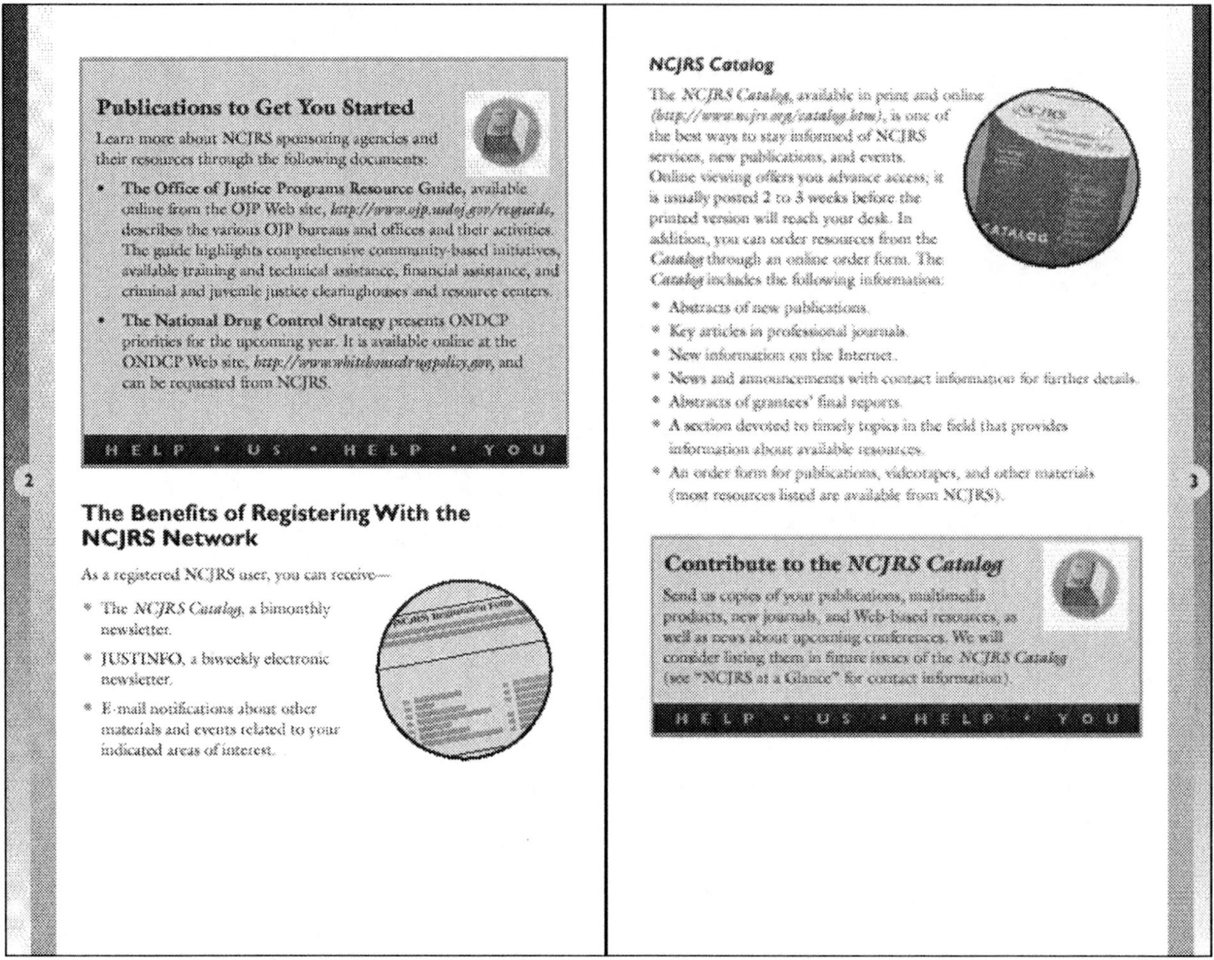

Publications to Get You Started

Learn more about NCJRS sponsoring agencies and their resources through the following documents:

- **The Office of Justice Programs Resource Guide,** available online from the OJP Web site, *http://www.ojp.usdoj.gov/reguide,* describes the various OJP bureaus and offices and their activities. The guide highlights comprehensive community-based initiatives, available training and technical assistance, financial assistance, and criminal and juvenile justice clearinghouses and resource centers.
- **The National Drug Control Strategy** presents ONDCP priorities for the upcoming year. It is available online at the ONDCP Web site, *http://www.whitehousedrugpolicy.gov,* and can be requested from NCJRS.

HELP • US • HELP • YOU

2

The Benefits of Registering With the NCJRS Network

As a registered NCJRS user, you can receive—

- The *NCJRS Catalog,* a bimonthly newsletter.
- JUSTINFO, a biweekly electronic newsletter.
- E-mail notifications about other materials and events related to your indicated areas of interest.

NCJRS Catalog

The *NCJRS Catalog,* available in print and online (*http://www.ncjrs.org/catalog.htm*), is one of the best ways to stay informed of NCJRS services, new publications, and events. Online viewing offers you advance access; it is usually posted 2 to 3 weeks before the printed version will reach your desk. In addition, you can order resources from the *Catalog* through an online order form. The *Catalog* includes the following information:

- Abstracts of new publications.
- Key articles in professional journals.
- New information on the Internet.
- News and announcements with contact information for further details.
- Abstracts of grantees' final reports.
- A section devoted to timely topics in the field that provides information about available resources.
- An order form for publications, videotapes, and other materials (most resources listed are available from NCJRS).

Contribute to the *NCJRS Catalog*

Send us copies of your publications, multimedia products, new journals, and Web-based resources, as well as news about upcoming conferences. We will consider listing them in future issues of the *NCJRS Catalog* (see "NCJRS at a Glance" for contact information).

HELP • US • HELP • YOU

3

4. There is no limit on how much an individual can contribute to a traditional IRA.
   a. True
   b. False
5. Which of the following is *not* a type of traditional IRA?
   a. Individual Retirement Annuity
   b. Employer and Employee Association Trust Account
   c. Simplified Employee Pension
   d. Savings Incentive Match Plan for Employees

H. Exercise 14.8: Congressional Record: Senate Bill Number 455

1. The exclusion relating to gain from certain small-business stock is being decreased from 75 percent to 50 percent.
   a. True
   b. False

EXERCISE 14.5 *continued*

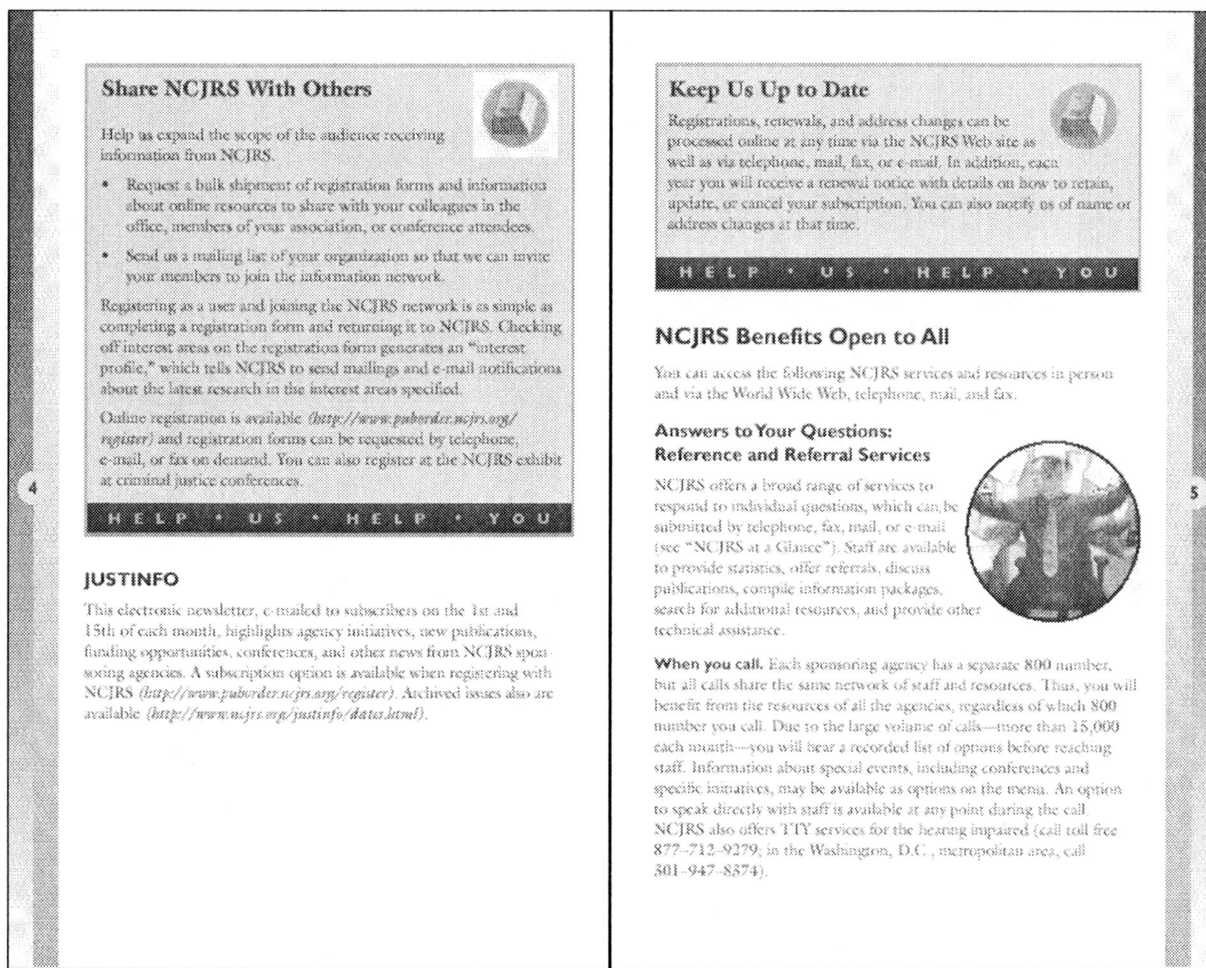

Share NCJRS With Others

Help us expand the scope of the audience receiving information from NCJRS.

- Request a bulk shipment of registration forms and information about online resources to share with your colleagues in the office, members of your association, or conference attendees.
- Send us a mailing list of your organization so that we can invite your members to join the information network.

Registering as a user and joining the NCJRS network is as simple as completing a registration form and returning it to NCJRS. Checking off interest areas on the registration form generates an "interest profile," which tells NCJRS to send mailings and e-mail notifications about the latest research in the interest areas specified.

Online registration is available *(http://www.puborder.ncjrs.org/register)* and registration forms can be requested by telephone, e-mail, or fax on demand. You can also register at the NCJRS exhibit at criminal justice conferences.

HELP • US • HELP • YOU

JUSTINFO

This electronic newsletter, e-mailed to subscribers on the 1st and 15th of each month, highlights agency initiatives, new publications, funding opportunities, conferences, and other news from NCJRS sponsoring agencies. A subscription option is available when registering with NCJRS *(http://www.puborder.ncjrs.org/register)*. Archived issues also are available *(http://www.ncjrs.org/justinfo/dates.html)*.

4

Keep Us Up to Date

Registrations, renewals, and address changes can be processed online at any time via the NCJRS Web site as well as via telephone, mail, fax, or e-mail. In addition, each year you will receive a renewal notice with details on how to retain, update, or cancel your subscription. You can also notify us of name or address changes at that time.

HELP • US • HELP • YOU

NCJRS Benefits Open to All

You can access the following NCJRS services and resources in person and via the World Wide Web, telephone, mail, and fax.

Answers to Your Questions: Reference and Referral Services

NCJRS offers a broad range of services to respond to individual questions, which can be submitted by telephone, fax, mail, or e-mail (see "NCJRS at a Glance"). Staff are available to provide statistics, offer referrals, discuss publications, compile information packages, search for additional resources, and provide other technical assistance.

When you call. Each sponsoring agency has a separate 800 number, but all calls share the same network of staff and resources. Thus, you will benefit from the resources of all the agencies, regardless of which 800 number you call. Due to the large volume of calls—more than 15,000 each month—you will hear a recorded list of options before reaching staff. Information about special events, including conferences and specific initiatives, may be available as options on the menu. An option to speak directly with staff is available at any point during the call. NCJRS also offers TTY services for the hearing impaired (call toll free 877-712-9279; in the Washington, D.C., metropolitan area, call 301-947-8374).

5

continued

2. The entire text of Section 1202 is included in this bill.
   a. True
   b. False
3. The amendments in subsections (a) and (d)(1) apply to stock issued
   a. after the bill is enacted.
   b. after the bill is published.
   c. after August 10, 1993.
   d. after March 5, 2001.
4. Which of the following information is listed at the beginning of the bill?
   a. Congressional session
   b. House bill number
   c. Legislators who introduced the bill
   d. All of the above

EXERCISE 14.5 *continued*

NCJRS staff will ask for your name and organizational affiliation to determine whether you are already a part of the NCJRS information network and to expedite your request. To ensure that your information needs are met, you may also be asked the following questions:

- What information are you looking for?
- How will it be used?
- What is your deadline?

When you send an e-mail, fax, or letter. Requests can be sent via mail, e-mail, or fax. Please be sure to include contact information (your name, shipping address, telephone and fax numbers, and e-mail address) and answers to the three questions noted above.

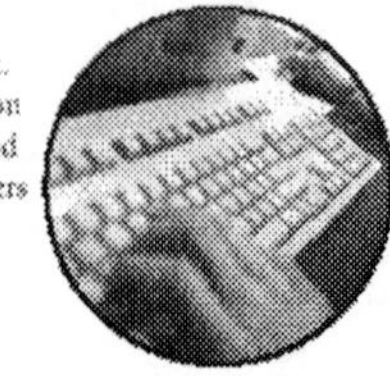

NCJRS Is a Two-Way Partnership

The NCJRS network is designed to meet your information needs and to influence research, policies, and local practices that keep people, their homes, and their communities safe.

NCJRS's success depends on you and your colleagues using its services and offering feedback and new resources to improve them.

6

NCJRS Online

The easiest way to access NCJRS is to visit its Web site at *http://www.ncjrs.org*, where "What's New" and "In the Spotlight" sections showcase recent publications and topical issues related to criminal justice, juvenile justice, and drug policy. In addition to links to the NCJRS Federal sponsors and other organizations and agencies, the site offers the following resources.

Full-text publications. The full text of more than 2,000 titles produced by the sponsoring agencies is available in a variety of formats for easy online viewing, downloading, and cutting and pasting into your own reports. These publications are organized by topic area and can also be sorted alphabetically and by date.

When you request assistance, we may refer you (for quick access) to the online version of one of these publications or guide you through the NCJRS online ordering system (see below) for a printed copy. Depending on the type and number of publications ordered, there may be a nominal charge to cover postage and handling; these fees also apply to requests from outside the United States. You are encouraged to photocopy NCJRS sponsoring agency publications to share with your colleagues and to reprint them in your newsletters or journals—unless otherwise stated in a copyright notice in the document. If you reprint one of these publications, please cite the appropriate agency and authors.

NCJRS library and Abstracts Database. A good way to learn from the experiences of others is to use the NCJRS library and Abstracts Database, both of which grow at the rate of about 500 publications per month. This database, available online at *http://abstractsdb.ncjrs.org/content/AbstractsDB_search.asp*, offers one of the world's largest collections of materials focusing on criminal justice and contains almost 170,000 publications, reports, articles, and audiovisual products. Materials date from the early 1970s through the present and come from the United States and around the world. The collection includes statistics, research findings, program descriptions, congressional hearing transcripts, and training materials.

7

I. Exercise 14.9: Congressional Record: Senate Bill Number 289

1. The short title of this bill is the
   a. College Savings Act.
   b. Act.
   c. Collegiate Learning and Student Savings Act.
   d. Student Savings Act.
2. The phase "qualified State tuition" is *not* being replaced by "qualified tuition" in which sections?
   a. 135(c)(2)(C)
   b. 4973
   c. 529
   d. 6693(a)(2)(C)

EXERCISE 14.5 *continued*

As each product is received, it is assigned an NCJ number and is abstracted for inclusion in the database. Each abstract includes the title, author, sponsoring agency, purchasing address, and journal citation, as well as a 100- to 200-word summary. Keyword searches of the database are easy. Abstracts are provided in English for all documents written in foreign languages.

The database is indexed using the National Criminal Justice Thesaurus, which contains more than 8,000 subject, geographic, and organizational index terms and 30,000 cross-references. Using the index terms listed in the thesaurus, you can quickly retrieve all the citations relevant to your question or interest area.

In addition to online availability, the database is accessible—

* **On DIALOG.** Ask your local librarian to search the database for you on DIALOG, an international electronic information retrieval service.
* **By contacting NCJRS.** Staff can help you refine your search strategies and create searches tailored to your specific needs.

No matter how you access the database, the purpose is the same: to find the information you need. The database abstracts will help you determine whether a specific resource is appropriate. There are several ways for you to obtain the full text of publications cited in the search:

* Abstracts in the online database include a link to the full text if it is available on the NCJRS Web site.
* If there are no copyright restrictions, NCJRS will make and send you a copy for a nominal fee.
* If a copyright applies, you can request a copy from the sponsoring agency or organization cited in the abstract or borrow a copy from NCJRS (see below).
* All publications in the database are available from the NCJRS library and can be borrowed through the American Library Association's interlibrary loan program.

If you have questions about the availability of a publication, contact NCJRS and provide the NCJ number found on the publication abstract.

If you are in the Washington, D.C., metropolitan area, you may want to schedule an appointment to visit the NCJRS library in Rockville, Maryland (see "NCJRS at a Glance").

8

Add Your Materials to the Library and Database

Send copies of publications, training curriculums, videotapes, and other information resources from your organization to NCJRS so they can be added to the NCJRS library and Abstracts Database. Other people can then find your resources when they search the database. NCJRS can lend the material through interlibrary loan or reproduce a document for a nominal fee (depending on copyright). If you provide an electronic version, a link from the abstract to the full text can be added.

HELP • US • HELP • YOU

Calendar of Events. The calendar available at *http://eventcalendar.ncjrs.org* highlights upcoming conferences, training sessions, workshops, and other events held around the world. Included are the location of the event, topics to be discussed, and contact information. Search the calendar to identify events that are in your area or that address subjects of interest to you. Promote your agency or organization's upcoming conference in the calendar by posting your information.

Online ordering. A new feature of the Web site at *http://puborder.ncjrs.org* allows you to browse and order publications, CD-ROMs, videotapes, and other products whenever you want, day or night. If you know exactly what you want to order, search for products by title, keyword, or publication number. The "What's New" section includes recently added products, and "What's Hot" features the most frequently requested titles.

Online registration. Staying informed about news and announcements from NCJRS and its sponsoring agencies is easy through online registration at *http://puborder.ncjrs.org/register.* You can sign up to stay informed through the *NCJRS Catalog*, JUSTINFO, and e-mail notifications (see page 2).

Funding opportunities. The "Grants and Funding" section highlights funding opportunities available from OJP and other Federal agencies. You can also link to other resources, such as *Federal Business Opportunities* and the *Federal Register*, to learn about future funding activities.

9

continued

3. What action has been taken so far on this bill?
   a. Read twice
   b. Reviewed by the Committee on Finance
   c. Unable to determine from the information provided
   d. Passed by both the House and Senate and signed into law
4. This bill only makes changes to Section 529 of the Internal Revenue Code of 1986.
   a. True
   b. False

The NCJRS Web site at *http://www.ncjrs.org* also has a keyword search function and an e-mail address for submitting questions to staff (*askncjrs@ncjrs.org*).

Fax on Demand

Several of the 800 numbers offer an option to have publications such as Fact Sheets, short Bulletins, and funding notices and applications faxed 24 hours a day, 7 days a week. You can request a list of available titles or, if you know the four-digit fax-on-demand number, you can enter it directly. You then will be prompted to enter your fax number. Depending on the request volume, you will receive your fax within a few minutes.

Conference Support and Attendance

In addition to promoting your upcoming events on *http://eventcalendar.ncjrs.org*, NCJRS participates in (as an exhibitor or presenter), or ships publications to, more than 500 national, State, and local conferences and workshops each year. The online Calendar of Events identifies the events NCJRS staff will attend.

10

Supporting Your Conferences

Contact NCJRS and ask for staff in the Conference/Networking Unit to discuss how NCJRS can support your upcoming conference, training session, or workshop.

HELP • US • HELP • YOU

Criminal Justice Editors' Group

Even though NCJRS reaches millions of people each year through mailings, Web sites, conferences, and other services, the community interested in the issues it addresses is much larger. To help reach this broader community, NCJRS coordinates the Criminal Justice Editors' Group (CJEG), a network of more than 100 editors of national, State, and local periodicals. NCJRS provides information, including copies of recently released publications from sponsoring agencies and CJEG members, to CJEG on a monthly basis. Editors can share these resources with their organizations' members by announcing them in their periodicals. NCJRS also provides artwork for announcements and articles on specific topics or NCJRS products and services. Members are invited to attend semiannual meetings with guest speakers on topics that range from timely criminal justice issues to those associated with publishing, marketing, and dissemination.

Calling All Editors

If your organization or agency produces a periodical—either for subscribers or as an internal resource for staff—and you are willing to share resources with and about NCJRS and its sponsoring agencies, contact NCJRS and ask for staff in the Conference/Networking Unit to discuss joining the Criminal Justice Editors' Group.

HELP • US • HELP • YOU

11

EXERCISE 14.6

II

107TH CONGRESS
1ST SESSION

S. 455

To amend the Internal Revenue Code of 1986 to increase and modify the exclusion relating to qualified small business stock and for other purposes.

IN THE SENATE OF THE UNITED STATES

MARCH 5, 2001

Ms. COLLINS (for herself, Mr. CLELAND, Mr. BREAUX, Mr. ALLARD, Mr. CRAPEO, Mr. LIEBERMAN, Ms. LANDRIEU, Mr. HATCH, and Mr. HUTCHINSON) introduced the following bill; which was read twice and referred to the Committee on Finance

---

A BILL

To amend the Internal Revenue Code of 1986 to increase and modify the exclusion relating to qualified small business stock and for other purposes.

Be it enacted by the Senate and House of Representatives of the United States of America in Congress assembled,

SECTION 1. SHORT TITLE.

This Act may be cited as the "Encouraging Investment in Small Business Act".

2

SEC. 2. INCREASED EXCLUSION AND OTHER MODIFICATIONS APPLICABLE TO QUALIFIED SMALL BUSINESS STOCK.

(a) INCREASED EXCLUSION.—Section 1202(a) of the Internal Revenue Code of 1986 (relating to partial exclusion for gain from certain small business stock) is amended by striking "50 percent" each place it appears and inserting "75 percent".

(b) REDUCTION IN HOLDING PERIOD.—

(1) IN GENERAL.—Section 1202(a) of the Internal Revenue Code of 1986 is amended by striking "5 years" and inserting "3 years"

(2) CONFORMING AMENDMENTS.—Subsections (g)(2)(A) and (j)(1)(A) of section 1202 of such Code are each amended by striking "5 years" and inserting "3 years".

(c) REPEAL OF MINIMUM TAX PREFERENCE.—

(1) IN GENERAL.—Section 57(a) of the Internal Revenue Code of 1986 (relating to items of tax preference) is amended by striking paragraph (7).

(2) TECHNICAL AMENDMENT.—Section 53(d)(1)(B)(ii)(II) of such Code is amended by striking ", (5), and (7)" and inserting "and (5)".

(d) OTHER MODIFICATIONS.—

(1) WORKING CAPITAL LIMITATION.—

•S 455 IS

continued

(A) IN GENERAL.—Section 1202(e)(6) of the Internal Revenue Code of 1986 (relating to working capital) is amended—

(i) in subparagraph (B), by striking "2 years" and inserting "5 years"; and

(ii) by striking "2 years" in the last sentence and inserting "5 years".

(B) LIMITATION ON ASSETS TREATED AS USED IN ACTIVE CONDUCT OF BUSINESS.—The second sentence of section 1202(e)(6) of such Code is amended by inserting "described in subparagraph (A)" after "of the corporation".

(2) EXCEPTION FROM REDEMPTION RULES WHERE BUSINESS PURPOSE.—Section 1202(c)(3) of such Code (relating to certain purchases by corporation of its own stock) is amended by adding at the end the following:

"(D) WAIVER WHERE BUSINESS PURPOSE.—A purchase of stock by the issuing corporation shall be disregarded for purposes of subparagraph (B) if the issuing corporation establishes that there was a business purpose for such purchase and one of the principal purposes of the purchase was not to avoid the limitations of this section."

(e) EXCLUDED QUALIFIED TRADE OR BUSINESS.—Section 1202(e)(3) of the Internal Revenue Code of 1986 (relating to qualified trade or business) is amended—

(1) by inserting ", and is anticipated to continue to be," before "the reputation" in subparagraph (A), and

(2) by inserting "but not including the business of raising fish or any business involving biotechnology applications" after "trees" in subparagraph (C).

(f) INCREASE IN CAP ON ELIGIBLE GAIN FOR JOINT RETURNS.—

(1) IN GENERAL.—Section 1202(b)(1)(A) of the Internal Revenue Code of 1986 (relating to per-issuer limitations on taxpayer's eligible gain) is amended by inserting "($20,000,000 in the case of a joint return)" after "$10,000,000".

(2) CONFORMING AMENDMENT.—Section 1202(b)(3) of such Code is amended by striking subparagraph (A) and redesignating subparagraphs (B) and (C) as subparagraphs (A) and (B), respectively.

(g) DECREASE IN CAPITAL GAINS RATE.—

(1) IN GENERAL.—Subparagraph (A) of section 1(h)(5) of the Internal Revenue Code of 1986 (relat-

EXERCISE 14.6 *continued*

5

ing to 28-percent gain) is amended to read as follows:

"(A) collectibles gain, over".

(2) CONFORMING AMENDMENTS.—

(A) Section 1(h) of such Code is amended by striking paragraph (8).

(B) Paragraph (9) of section 1(h) of such Code is amended by striking ", gain described in paragraph (7)(A)(i), and section 1202 gain" and inserting "and gain described in paragraph (7)(A)(i)".

(h) INCREASE IN ROLLOVER PERIOD FOR QUALIFIED SMALL BUSINESS STOCK.—Subsections (a)(1) and (b)(3) of section 1045 of the Internal Revenue Code of 1986 (relating to rollover of gain from qualified small business stock to another qualified small business stock) are each amended by striking "60-day" and inserting "180-day".

(i) EFFECTIVE DATES.—

(1) IN GENERAL.—Except as provided in paragraph (2), the amendments made by this section shall apply to stock issued after the date of the enactment of this Act.

•S 455 IS

6

(2) SPECIAL RULE.—The amendments made by subsections (a) and (d)(1) apply to stock issued after August 10, 1993.

•S 455 IS

EXERCISE 14.7

II

107TH CONGRESS
1ST SESSION

S. 289

To amend the Internal Revenue Code of 1986 to provide additional tax incentives for education.

IN THE SENATE OF THE UNITED STATES

FEBRUARY 8, 2001

Mr. SESSIONS (for himself and Mr. GRAHAM, Mr. BINGAMAN, Mr. FRIST, Mr. GRAMM, Mr. HUTCHINSON, Mr. MURKOWSKI, Mr. BREAUX, Mr. SHELBY, Ms. COLLINS, Mr. HELMS, Mr. INHOFE, Mr. ROBERTS, Mr. SANTORUM, Ms. LANDRIEU) introduced the following bill; which was read twice and referred to the Committee on Finance

---

A BILL

To amend the Internal Revenue Code of 1986 to provide additional tax incentives for education.

Be it enacted by the Senate and House of Representatives of the United States of America in Congress assembled,

SECTION 1. SHORT TITLE.

This Act may be cited as the "Collegiate Learning and Student Savings Act".

SEC. 2. ELIGIBLE EDUCATIONAL INSTITUTIONS PERMITTED TO MAINTAIN QUALIFIED TUITION PROGRAMS.

(a) IN GENERAL.—Section 529(b)(1) of the Internal Revenue Code of 1986 (defining qualified State tuition program) is amended by inserting "or by 1 or more eligible educational institutions or a consortium that consists solely of eligible educational institutions" after "maintained by a State or agency or instrumentality thereof".

(b) PRIVATE QUALIFIED TUITION PROGRAMS LIMITED TO BENEFIT PLANS.—Clause (ii) of section 529(b)(1)(A) of the Internal Revenue Code of 1986 is amended by inserting "in the case of a program established and maintained by a State or agency or instrumentality thereof" before "may make".

(c) CONFORMING AMENDMENTS.—

(1) The text and headings of each of the sections 72(e)(9), 135(c)(2(C), 135(d)(1)(D), 529, 530(b)(2)(B), 4973(e), and 6693(a)(2)(C) of the Internal Revenue Code of 1986 is amended by striking "qualified State tuition" each place it appears and inserting "qualified tuition".

(2)(A) The section heading of section 529 of such Code is amended to read as follows:

3

"SEC. 529. QUALIFIED TUITION PROGRAMS.".

(B) The item relating to section 529 in the table of sections for part VIII of subchapter F of chapter 1 of such Code is amended by striking "State".

(d) EFFECTIVE DATE.—The amendments made by this section shall apply to taxable years beginning after December 31, 2001.

SEC. 3. EXCLUSION FROM GROSS INCOME OF EDUCATION DISTRIBUTIONS FROM QUALIFIED TUITION PROGRAMS.

(a) IN GENERAL.—Section 529(c)(3)(B) of the Internal Revenue Code of 1986 (relating to distributions) is amended to read as follows:

"(B) DISTRIBUTIONS FOR QUALIFIED HIGHER EDUCATION EXPENSES.—

"(i) IN GENERAL.—If a distributee elects the application of this clause for any taxable year—

"(I) no amount shall be includible in gross income under subparagraph (A) by reason of a distribution which consists of providing a benefit to the distributee which, if paid for by the distributee, would constitute pay-

•S 280 IS

4

ment of a qualified higher education expense, and

"(II) the amount which (but for the election) would be includible in gross income under subparagraph (A) by reason of any other distribution shall not be so includible in an amount which bears the same ratio to the amount which would be so includible as such expenses bear to such aggregate distributions.

"(ii) IN-KIND DISTRIBUTIONS.—Any benefit furnished to a designated beneficiary under a qualified State tuition program shall be treated as a distribution to the beneficiary for purposes of this paragraph.

"(iii) DISALLOWANCE OF EXCLUDED AMOUNTS AS CREDIT OR DEDUCTION.—No deduction or credit shall be allowed to the taxpayer under any other section of this chapter for any qualified higher education expenses to the extent taken into account in determining the amount of the exclusion under this subparagraph.".

•S 280 IS

continued

EXERCISE 14.7 *continued*

(b) BENEFICIARY MAY CHANGE PROGRAM.—Section 529(c)(3)(C) of the Internal Revenue Code of 1986 (relating to change in beneficiaries) is amended—

(1) in clause (i), by inserting "to another qualified tuition program for the benefit of the designated beneficiary or" after "transferred", and

(2) in the heading, by inserting "OR PROGRAMS" after "BENEFICIARIES".

(c) ADDITIONAL TAX ON AMOUNTS NOT USED FOR HIGHER EDUCATION EXPENSES.—Section 529(c)(3) of the Internal Revenue Code of 1986 (relating to distributions) is amended by adding at the end the following:

"(E) ADDITIONAL TAX ON AMOUNTS NOT USED FOR HIGHER EDUCATION EXPENSES.—The tax imposed by section 530(d)(4) shall apply to payments and distributions from qualified tuition programs in the same manner as such tax applies to education individual retirement accounts.".

(d) COORDINATION WITH EDUCATION CREDITS.—Section 25A(e)(2) of the Internal Revenue Code of 1986 (relating to coordination with exclusions) is amended—

(1) by inserting "a qualified tuition program or" before "an education individual retirement account", and

(2) by striking "section 530(d)(2)" and inserting "section 529(c)(3)(B) or 530(d)(2)".

(e) EFFECTIVE DATES.—

(1) IN GENERAL.—Except as provided in paragraph (2), the amendments made by this section shall apply to distributions made after December 31, 2001, for education furnished in academic periods beginning after such date.

(2) PRIVATE PROGRAMS.—In the case of a qualified tuition program established and maintained by an entity other than a State or agency or instrumentality thereof, the amendments made by subsections (a), (c), and (d) shall apply to distributions made after December 31, 2005, for education furnished in academic periods beginning after such date.

SEC. 4. QUALIFIED TUITION PROGRAMS INCLUDED IN SECURITIES EXEMPTION.

(a) EXEMPTED SECURITIES.—Section 3(a)(4) of the Securities Act of 1933 (15 U.S.C. 77c(a)(4)) is amended by striking "individual;" and inserting "individual or any security issued by a prepaid tuition program described in section 529 of the Internal Revenue Code of 1986;".

(b) QUALIFIED TUITION PROGRAMS NOT INVESTMENT COMPANIES.—Section 3(c) of the Investment Com-

EXERCISE 14.7 *continued*

pany Act of 1940 (15 U.S.C. 80a–3(c)) is amended by adding at the end the following:

"(15) Any prepaid tuition program described in section 529 of the Internal Revenue Code of 1986.".

◇

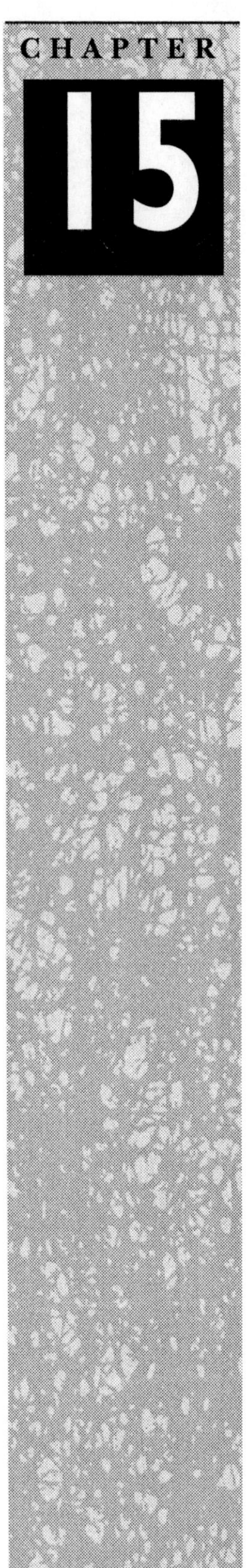

CHAPTER

15

WRITING APPLICATIONS IN THE LAW AND JUSTICE FIELD

Writing skills have always been of utmost importance to lawyers, paralegals, and criminal justice professionals. The ability to write accurate, detailed accounts, reports, statements, briefs, memoranda, and other assigned tasks cannot be overemphasized. The judicial, legal, and police systems, with their heavy emphasis on investigation and research, rely on the accuracy and validity of documentation. For example, police crime reports contain information that ultimately results in a prosecutor's judgment to charge or release a suspect in a criminal matter. Sloppy investigative procedures reflect poorly on the quality and character of a police agency, so its recordkeeping and documentation must be of the highest caliber. The purpose of the following exercises is to improve the quality of writing, to pinpoint chronic errors in communicative style, and to offer suggestions for improvement. In addition, the discipline of developing good, masterful writing skills will assist legal personnel in performing investigative procedures and processes. Thus, many of the following exercises are designed to sharpen the skills of proper usage, punctuation, sentence structure, and sequential style.

I. GENERAL WRITING STYLE

Although work in law-related fields demands a high level of insight, focused reasoning, and logic, the fundamental writing style is strict exposition. Creative thinking is of course desirable, but creative writing is not. **Expository writing** stresses the factual, explanatory, and the objectively analytical. Expository writing avoids emotion and opinion, giving priority instead to reason, observation, inquiry, study, and application. Effective legal writing requires the ability to sift through myriad facts, latching onto relevant information and discarding the immaterial. Therefore, competent legal writers maintain an expository style by adhering to these rules:

1. Conduct a proper inquiry—a thorough examination of relevant information—by taking complete and accurate notes.
2. Analyze and organize the findings of the inquiry.
3. Communicate all relevant findings in an adequate written report.

II. FIELD NOTES, REPORTS, LEGAL DESCRIPTIONS, AND EVIDENTIARY WRITINGS

Legal professionals commonly take **field notes**. Notes serve as a rough draft for future, more concisely drawn legal writings, such as investigative reports, accident reconstructions, and pleadings. Just as the student takes notes in the classroom, the police officer, lawyer, paralegal, and judge must take good notes to help focus the legal issue. The notes that the police officer jots down at the scene of the crime are used by the lawyers as evidence in a case. What all justice professionals have in common is a basic system of legal writing: Get the facts, organize the relevant information, and support the conclusions with evidence. The ability to take good notes and to write in a good legal fashion is a skill to be learned by every researcher. The following exercises will give you some practice in legal writing.

A. Objective and Accurate Notation

Assume that the page in Figure 15.1 is from the field notes of a police officer.

1. Is any significant information missing?
2. Should any part of the this material be excluded from a report? Why or why not?

FIGURE 15.1

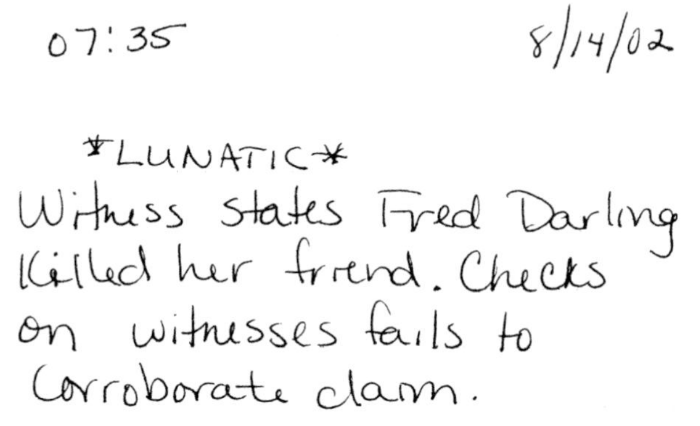

07:35 8/14/02

LUNATIC
Witness states Fred Darling
Killed her friend. Checks
on witnesses fails to
Corroborate claim.

FIGURE 15.2

04:03 9/1/02
193 Riverside Drive

The victim, John, (young male) resides on Riverside. Stated he locked door today. Around midnight, met his friend and went drinking at local bar.

B. Incomplete Field Notes

Assume that the page in Figure 15.2 is from the field notes of a police officer. Point out all the information that could be crucial to the case that is lacking in these notes.

C. Field Notes

1. Watch a television program dealing with a police investigation; if possible, watch a rerun of "Colombo," "Dragnet," or another well-known police drama. As the investigating officers gather evidence and information, write down your impressions as though you were one of them. Then analyze and organize your notes, checking them for accuracy, completeness, brevity, and fairness in content and form. Make certain that the notes are ready for use in writing a report on the investigation.
2. Write a short essay analyzing and commenting on the investigation.

D. Description of the Criminal Elements

Proof of any crime requires proof of the statutory elements of that crime. The writer must describe, in legally specific style, how the suspect has broken the law. For example, a charge of arson requires evidence of a burning, scorching, or charring of specific material. The officers', or district attorney/prosecutor's, crime report and indictment must reflect these statutory realities.

Review the following case summary. Analyze the facts and incorporate the elements of the statute into a formal complaint information or indictment.

1. *Burglary in the third degree* A person is guilty of burglary in the third degree when he or she knowingly enters or remains unlawfully in a building with intent to commit a crime therein.
2. *Summary of facts* On Friday, April 26, 2004, between the hours of 7:30 a.m. and 12:00 noon, the subject broke into the apartment of the victim, Ms. Mary Jane

Doe, W/F, age 25, residing at 1000 Oak St., Apt. #45, and stole the following items from the top of the dresser in the bedroom: one lady's gold Elgin wristwatch, valued at $90; one turquoise and silver lapel pin, valued at $50; two pairs of gold earrings, valued at $45 each. The victim stated that these items were on the dresser when she left the apartment at 7:30 a.m., same date, to go to work (professor of English at state university). When she returned to the apartment at 12:00 noon, she observed that items on the dresser had been disarranged and that the items of jewelry listed above were missing. The victim then called the police. A check of the front door (north) revealed scratch marks, suggesting that the lock had been picked. No instrument was found. A canvass of the neighborhood produced one witness, Mrs. Snow White, B/F, age 35, residing at 1001 Oak St. (across the street from the apartment). Witness White stated that at about 10:30 a.m., same date, she walked outside her residence to check the mail and observed a W/M, unknown to her, riding a bicycle down the drive from the apartment house. In the basket was a large grocery bag. The subject appeared to be about 20 years old, was about 6 ft. tall, and weighed about 175 lbs. He was wearing jeans and a black jacket.

Do these facts justify a charge of burglary? Why or why not?

Prepare a criminal complaint with the preceding information, using the format shown in Figure 15.3.

E. Description of Peculiarities

There is little question that all people exhibit peculiarities, idiosyncrasies, and obvious personal habits. The researcher must become an adept human observer, able to translate such qualities into specific words. Watch the local news tonight, paying close attention to portrayals of suspects in custody. In the form provided shown in Figure 15.4, make notations of any peculiar behavior exhibited by the suspect as he or she appears on camera, particularly as relates to appearance, speech, mannerisms, and clothing.

F. Description of Evidence

Assume that the pictures in Figures 15.5 through 15.8 contain items seized in a raid for stolen property. Effective report writing requires a clear description of the evidence seized. Write a precise description next to each item.

G. Composition of the Crime Report

Figure 15.9 is a form for a standard crime report. Using the facts in the burglary example from Exercise D, fill in the form. Remember to be exact and objective, and do not leave any blanks.

H. Sample Confession

The proper wording of a valid confession is a delicate legal and constitutional issue. Under federal law, a confession must be given voluntarily, without coercion or duress. Therefore, the wording of a signed confession must accurately reflect the defendant's state of mind. Statements as to guilt should not be emotional apologies, but businesslike statements of facts that support the finding of criminal culpability.

FIGURE 15.3

IN THE COURT OF COMMON PLEAS OF THE 17th JUDICIAL DISTRICT
UNION COUNTY BRANCH

Criminal Action No. __________, 19__

COMMONWEALTH OF PENNSYLVANIA

vs

____

____

____

Defendant(s)

THE DISTRICT ATTORNEY of Union County by this information charges that on or about the _______________ day of __________________________________, 19____,

____

______________________________________ the Defendant(s) above named, in the County aforesaid and within the jurisdiction of this Court, did

all of which is against the Acts of Assembly and the peace and dignity of the Commonwealth of Pennsylvania.

____
Attorney for the Commonwealth

____
Citation of Statute and Section

FIGURE 15.3 *continued*

I, ______________________________, Defendant named in the within information hereby enter a plea of ______________.

DATE ____________ ______________________________
(Defendant)

____
(Attorney For Defendant)

I, ______________________________, Defendant named in the within information hereby enter a plea of ______________.

DATE ____________ ______________________________
(Defendant)

____
(Attorney For Defendant)

WITNESSES:

______________ Pros.

CRIMINAL ACTION NO. ____________

COMMONWEALTH OF PENNSYLVANIA

vs

____

Defendant(s)

INFORMATION

AND NOW ______________, 19___,
the Defendant ______________,
being arraigned, pleads not guilty.

____
(Defendant)

____
(Counsel)

AND NOW ______________, 19___,
the Defendant ______________,
being arraigned, pleads not guilty.

____
(Defendant)

____
(Counsel)

AND NOW ______________, 19___,
the Defendant ______________,
being arraigned, pleads not guilty.

____
(Defendant)

____
(Counsel)

OFFICE OF THE DISTRICT ATTORNEY
Union County, Pennsylvania

FIGURE 15.4

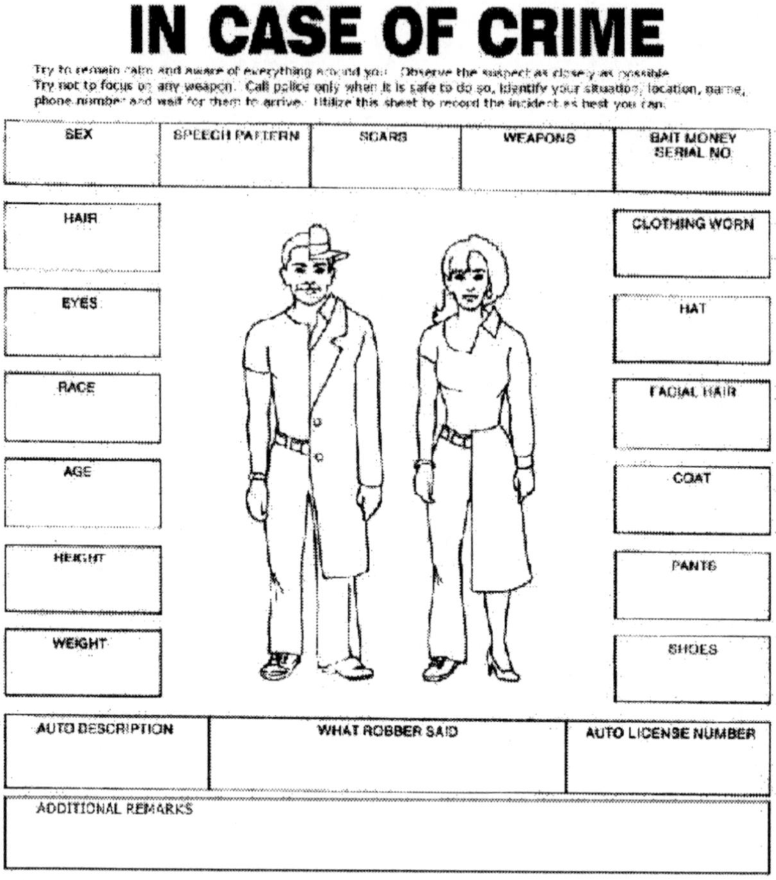

IN CASE OF CRIME

Try to remain calm and aware of everything around you. Observe the suspect as closely as possible. Try not to focus on any weapon. Call police only when it is safe to do so, identify your situation, location, name, phone number and wait for them to arrive. Utilize this sheet to record the incident as best you can.

SEX	SPEECH PATTERN	SCARS	WEAPONS	BAIT MONEY SERIAL NO.

HAIR

EYES

RACE

AGE

HEIGHT

WEIGHT

CLOTHING WORN

HAT

FACIAL HAIR

COAT

PANTS

SHOES

AUTO DESCRIPTION	WHAT ROBBER SAID	AUTO LICENSE NUMBER

ADDITIONAL REMARKS

Assess the following facts and use the form in Figure 15.10 to construct a sample confession.

John Smith admits to committing robbery, illegal possession of weapons, and assault. John's motive is clearly the result of rage and jealousy over certain circumstances.

III. THE LEGAL MEMORANDUM

A. Nature of the Memorandum

Drafting a memorandum of law is—or at least should be—a common task for the paralegal, investigator, lawyer, law clerk, or other party engaged in legal research. The memorandum is a tool that weighs and evaluates the state of the law as it applies to the facts at hand. In particular, the memorandum seeks to identify issues, pose questions, and cite relevant authorities. The memorandum apprises the private attorney, prosecutor, or administrative head on the current state of the law and the implications for the case currently being litigated. Therefore, a quality product depends on the skills of a competent legal researcher and requires a significant

STANTON **S-650**

New!

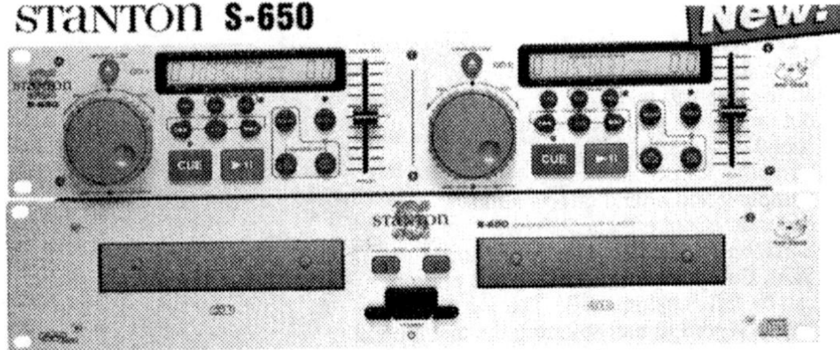

With the S-650 you never need to worry about your CD skipping again.
Features: • 40-Seconds of Anti-Shock/20 second per side • Real Seamless Looping • Buffer Memory • Digital Outputs • Relay Playback (Flip Flop) • Fader Start (cables included) • Instant Start • Up to +/- 16% Pitch Bend • Multi-purpose Jog Wheel • Auto Cue eliminates dead space• Pitch Display • 8x Over Sampling • 30 Programmable Play Tracks on each side • 6 Different Speed Scans • 8cm CD Singles Compatible • Real-time Cue • Instant Cue point recall • 60 Seconds transport protection (tray closes after 60 sec.) • Reads CD-R • Repeat one, Repeat All, Single, continue, sleep modes

$399.99

FIGURE 15.5

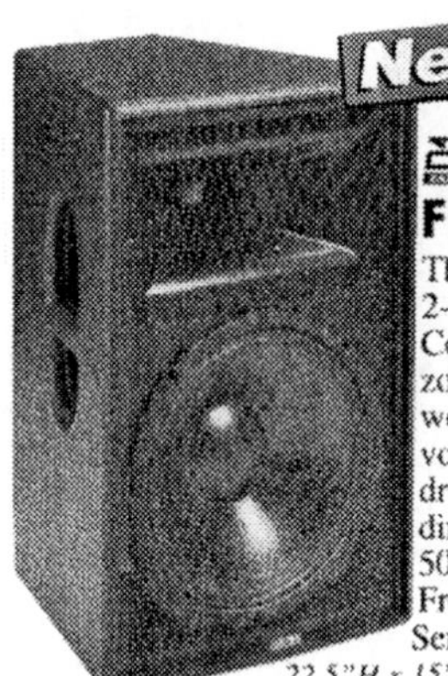

New!

EAW

FR-129Z

The FR-129Z Features:
2-Way full range system
Compact vented trapezoidal enclosure 12" woofer and a 1" 50mm voice coil compression driver on a 90x45 constant directivity horn
500 Watts @ 8 ohms
Freq Resp: 60Hz-18kHz
Sensitivity: 97 dB

22.5"H x 15"W x 14.75"D, 46 lbs.

$699.99

FIGURE 15.6

Technics RS-TR575

With the Technics RS-TR575 Double Auto-Reverse Dual Recording Cassette Deck, you get a quality brand name with loads of features. Features like: Dual linear electronic tape counters, Simultaneous parallel recording from the same source, Double auto-reverse w/3-hour series recording & 24-hour series playback, Dolby HX Pro & Dolby B-C NR Systems, High-speed editing w/synchro start/stop, 2-color FL peak-hold meters and it comes with a wireless remote. *16 15/16" x 5 5/16" x 11 7/32, 9.7 lbs.*

$249.99

FIGURE 15.7

FIGURE 15.8

PSR-282

The PSR-262 is Yamaha's first model with General MIDI Tone Generation for better sound. Features include: 61 Full-size touch sensitive keys, General MIDI In and Out, Yamaha Education Suite 2, Portable Grand "Stereo Piano Sample", DJ Button Accesses Special Dance Voices (256 Total voices), 2-Speaker stereo system w/bass ports, 8 banks of registration memories on 2 pads and 5 song, 6 track recorder. It also has Multi-fingering auto accompainment DSP Chorus and Reverb Effects, 10 Drum kits and a Large backlit LCD w/Icons & Characters. 100 built-in songs you can learn to play. 100 Song book and Music rest included.

37.3" (L) x 14.8" (W) x 5.2" (H), 12.5 lbs

$229.99

PA-3B AC Adaptor.....$19.99
Instructional Video for PSR-282/PSR-GX76....$19.99

FIGURE 15.9

BOROUGH OF GREEN TREE POLICE DEPARTMENT
OFFENSE REPORT
10 W Manilla Avenue * Pittsburgh Pennsylvania * 15220 * 412-921-8624

INCIDENT #__________________

CRIME/INCIDENT: __________________ WEATHER: UCR:
LOCATION: __________________
OCCURRED BETWEEN DAY:____ DATE: ____ TIME:____ DATE REPORTED:______
AND: DAY:____ DATE:____ TIME:____ TIME:____ DAY:_____
REPORTING OFFICER:_____ 2ND OFFICER:_____
REPORTING PERSON:__________________ RACE:____ SEX:____ DOB:______
ADDRESS: __________________ PHONE RES:____________
CITY/STATE/ZIP:__________________ PHONE BUS:____________

VICTIM:
Name:______________________________Race:_____Sex:_____DOB:______
Address:______________________________ Phone Res:______________
City/State/Zip:____________________________ Phone Bus:______________
Place of Employment:______________________

VEHICLE:
Make:____________Model:______________Year:______Reg State:________
Reg #:__________ Vin:_____________________________Color: __________

SUSPECT:
Name:___________Sex:___Race:___DOB:____Ht:____Wgt:____Hair:____ Eyes:____
Address:_________________________Clothes:______________________
♦
Name:___________Sex:___Race:___DOB:____Ht:____Wgt:____Hair:____ Eyes:____
Address:_________________________Clothes:______________________

PROPERTY: Lost ☐ Stolen ☐ Damage ☐ Other ☐

Qty	Description	Ser # and/or Model #	Value
_____	______________	______________	__________
_____	______________	______________	__________
_____	______________	______________	__________
_____	______________	______________	__________
_____	______________	______________	__________

Property Report #________

Begin narrative on reverse side

expenditure of time and energy in the collection of information and its eventual crafting into memo form. The structure of a memorandum adheres to this format:

- *Title* Identifies the particular matter with which the memorandum deals.
- *Question presented* Indicates exactly what issues or questions of law the memorandum proposes to answer. This portion informs the reader of the scope and content of the memorandum and facilitates the filing and indexing of a copy of the memorandum for future use.
- *Brief answer* Provides a summary of the conclusion, which usually serves as a timesaver for attorneys and judges who wish to know the answer immediately without referring to the conclusion or reading the entire memo.
- *Statement of facts* Includes the pertinent facts.
- *Discussion* Applies the principles of existing law to the issues raised.
- *Conclusion* Proposes a specific and clear resolution of the issues presented, together with a brief explanation of the reasoning upon which the answer is based. It is important to indicate whether the law on a given question is well established or in a state of flux. Some sample pages from a memorandum are reproduced in Figure 15.11.

B. Rules of Draftsmanship

Common errors in the design of legal memoranda include:

1. Failure to explain conclusions
2. Excessive reliance on judicial language
3. Failure to support contentions with appropriate authority
4. Excessive citation of precedents
5. Lack of objectivity in the analysis

Some rules of citation, usage, and construction to be kept in mind are:

Citation of law: All statements of law must be supported by cited authority, unless

a. the authority relied upon is already set forth in the text; or
b. the principle is so generally known and understood that it requires no citation.

Quotations:

a. All quotations must be the exact words of the entity being quoted (author, court, etc.). Ellipses should be used if part or parts of a quotation are omitted. Brackets must be used if explanatory material is inserted.
b. Quotations exceeding five or six lines must be indented; quotation marks should then be omitted.
c. Always cite the exact page of the source where the quotation appears, rather than merely the initial page of the opinion.

Personal opinion:

a. The writer should make it clear if he or she is expressing a personal opinion. Generally, personal opinion should be avoided.

Rod Borlase, JD, MLS, Head of Student Reference and Research Services in the O'Quinn Law Library at the University of Texas, suggests eight rules to follow when drafting any type of legal document:

<u>RULE 1:</u> Be simple and plain

<u>RULE 2:</u> Less is more

FIGURE 15.10

Borough of Green Tree

Police Department

VOLUNTARY STATEMENT

THE FOLLOWING IS THE VOLUNTARY STATEMENT OF ____________________

____________________, ____________________, AGE ________ YEARS,

OF ____

TAKEN AT ____

ON ____________________ 19____, AT ____________________.

INTERVIEWED BY: TYPEWRITTEN BY:

Q. When you were taken into custody, you were read a warning form, advising you of your constitutional rights. Did you fully understand this form?

A.

Q. ____________________, before going any further, at this time, I wish to advise you of your constitutional rights under which you have the right to remain silent, and in the event that you do make a statement, it can and will be used against you at the time of your trial in a court of law. Do you fully understand this?

A.

Q. ____________________, you are also entitled to talk to a lawyer of your own choosing and may have him present before making any statement. Do you fully understand this?

A.

Q. ____________________, if you cannot afford a lawyer, we have in Allegheny County a public defenders office who will furnish you with a lawyer, without any cost to you, if you so desire. Do you fully understand this?

A.

Q. ____________________, having been informed of your rights, and stating that you fully understand them, do you now wish to exercise any of these rights or are you now willing to go ahead and give us this statement?

A.

-1-

PAGE 2 OF THE VOLUNTARY STATEMENT OF ______________________

FIGURE 15.10
continued

Q. What is your full name?

A.

Q. What is your address?

A.

Q. Do you have a telephone, if so, what is the number?

A.

Q. What is the date of your birth?

A.

Q. Where were you born?

A.

Q. Where and how far did you go in school?

A.

Q. Are you married or single?

A.

Q. What is your wife's/husband's first name?

A.

Q. Do you have any children, and if so, what are their names and ages?

A.

Q. Are you employed, and if so, where and how long have you been employed?

A.

Q. Are you on any medication?

A.

Q. When did you take this medication and what was it?

A.

continued

FIGURE 15.10
continued

```
PAGE 3 OF THE VOLUNTARY STATEMENT OF ____________________________

Q.   How do you feel now?

A.

Q.   Have you drank any alcoholic beverages recently?

A.

Q.   What and how much have you had to drink?

A.

Q.   All right then ______________________, slowly and in your own
     words, tell us all that you know about
```

RULE 3: Use terms of art (technical terms) consistently

RULE 4: Get to the point

RULE 5: Legal authority trumps personal wisdom

RULE 6: Be accurate and precise

RULE 7: Make sense

RULE 8: Know your issue's "standard of review" (Rod Borlase, Borlase Legal Research Guides, *Drafting Legal Memoranda, Pleadings, Trial & Appellate Briefs*, **http://www.law.uh.edu/guides/appeals.html**, 1999)

C. Sample Office Memorandum

Figure 15.12 is a comprehensive office memorandum prepared to illustrate how the *Peters v. Simmons* case might have looked to a young associate in the office of the defendant's attorney. This memorandum has been prepared for educational purposes only.

D. A Word on IRAC

When writing a legal memorandum, you are in effect condensing the current applicable law to a few pages, with analysis regarding the applicability of this law to the case at hand. Knowledge of the IRAC (issues, rule, analysis, conclusion) method will definitely prove helpful when drafting memoranda, briefing cases, or answering examination questions. The first step in the IRAC method is to "*i*ssue spot." This is not necessarily the easiest task, given the complex nature of some cases. Sometimes words such as "question," "dilemma," and even "issue" will help you determine what the exact issue is. Also, be sure whether you are dealing with a question of law or a question of fact.

Determining the *r*ule is the second step in the IRAC method. This is nothing more than finding what the governing law is—bearing in mind that it could be either

PAGE ________ OF THE VOLUNTARY STATEMENT OF ____________________

FIGURE 15.10
continued

Q. ________________, how have you been treated since coming into custody of the Green Tree Police?

A.

Q. Have you been threatened or promised anything by the Green Tree Police Dept. for making this statement?

A.

Q. Is there anything that you wish to add or delete from this statement?

A.

Q. Do you read and write the English language?

A.

Q. I will then ask you to read the foregoing statement slowly, and carefully, and if after reading it you find it to be true and correct as you have stated, will you then sign it?

A.

I, ______________________________, having read the foregoing statement find it to be true and correct just as I have stated and therefore I will affix my signature to it.

Statement completed at ________________________, 19____

____
SIGNATURE

WITNESSES:

____

____

____

____

common law or statutory law. Determine what the elements of the law are, if there are any exceptions to the rule, and where the authority comes from. Always be sure to discuss why the particular rule is applicable to the issue at hand.

The third step in the IRAC method is *a*nalysis. In this step, use each fact and determine whether the rule applies to that fact. Discuss why each rule is applicable to each fact. If there are exceptions, discuss whether they are applicable to the situation at hand. The analysis is nothing more than a discussion of how the issues or facts relate to the rule.

FIGURE 15.11

STATEMENT OF THE QUESTIONS INVOLVED

1. WHETHER A UNITED STATES DEPARTMENT OF EDUCATION'S OFFICE OF STUDENT FINANCIAL ASSISTANCE FINAL AUDIT DETERMINATION OF RESPONDENT DISREGARDS EXISTING REGULATIONS, AT 34 C.F.R. § 668.2, *et seq.*, AND WHETHER SAID FINAL AUDIT DETERMINATION IS ARBITRARY AND CAPRICIOUS?

2. WHETHER RESPONDENT'S COURSE LENGTH IS SUFFICIENT IN LAW TO MEET FEDERAL FINANCIAL AID ELIGIBILITY CRITERIA FOR PELL GRANT PARTICIPATION, AS ENUNCIATED IN 34 C.F.R. § 668.8?

3. WHETHER THE OFFICE OF STUDENT FINANCIAL ASSISTANCE AUDIT DETERMINATION OF RESPONDENT'S NON-COMPLIANCE WITH ACCREDITOR CONVERSION REQUIREMENT FOR CLOCK HOUR TO CREDIT HOUR CHANGE, WAS SUFFICIENT IN LAW OR FACT?

STATEMENT OF RESPONDENT'S CASE

This is an appeal of a Final Audit Determination (F.A.D.) conducted by the U.S. Department of Education's Office of the Inspector General, Office of Audit, as permitted under 34 C.F.R. § 668.111-121. The period of the audit was January 1, 1991 to January 31, 1993.

The F.A.D. contends that Respondent owes refunds on Pell Grant distributions due to insufficient program length, and inadequate conversion credits from its clock hour formulation, in the sum of $828,463.00, though this figure has been internally modified on previous occasions. Respondent, Truck Driving Academy of Sacramento, California, disagrees with the F.A.D., proclaiming full adherence to course or curriculum length, meeting or exceeding both the regulatory and accreditation guidelines, and full compliance with the conversion practices that are approved by the Accreditor and the U.S. Department of Education. As a result, a formal appeal request before a qualified hearing office was filed on December 30, 1994.

The Brief within is filed on behalf of Respondent.

SUMMARY OF THE ARGUMENT

1. THAT RESPONDENT DID ADHERE TO PUBLISHED REGULATORY GUIDELINES ON COURSE LENGTH AND SUFFICIENCY WHEN PARTICIPATING IN THE TITLE IV PELL GRANT PROGRAM.
2. THAT RESPONDENT FULLY AND COMPREHENSIVELY MET EACH AND EVERY RULE, STANDARD OR GUIDELINE PROMULGATED BY ITS ACCREDITOR RELATIVE TO PROGRAM SUFFICIENCY AND THE CONVERSION OF CLOCK TO CREDIT HOUR MEASUREMENT.
3. THAT RESPONDENT HAS BEEN THE RECIPIENT OF ARBITRARY AND CAPRICIOUS DECISIONMAKING BY THE U.S. DEPARTMENT OF EDUCATION'S OFFICE OF THE INSPECTOR GENERAL, OFFICE OF AUDIT, SINCE THE STATUTES, RULES AND REGULATIONS GOVERNING PROGRAM LENGTH AND CONVERS WERE NOT THE BASIS FOR ADMINISTRATIVE ACTION.

ARGUMENT FOR RESPONDENT

1. **WHETHER A UNITED STATES DEPARTMENT OF EDUCATION'S OFFICE OF STUDENT FINANCIAL ASSISTANCE FINAL AUDIT DETERMINATION OF RESPONDENT DISREGARDS EXISTING REGULATIONS, AT 34 C.F.R. § 668.2, *et seq.*, AND WHETHER SAID FINAL AUDIT DETERMINATION IS ARBITRARY AND CAPRICIOUS?**

Respondent only pleads for enforcement of the existing regulatory framework guiding vocational and proprietary school operations and eligibility for federal aid participation.

The Final Audit Determination asserts that Respondent's course length and level of outside preparation is insufficient to justify a program length of 24 quarter credits.

> Despite the Accreditor's approval of the questioned academic program, at *Exhibit 1,* and the United States Department of Education's subsequent approval, at *Exhibit 2,* the Auditor creates a new standard—one not cited in any binding regulation or law governing proprietary or vocational schools. The rules are simple enough. Under either definition—the *Vocational School* or *Proprietary Institution*—Respondent's eligibility is quarter hours or units at a school using credit hours or units to measure the academic program.

(B) Three hundred clock hours of supervised training *Student* reviewer may set aside an agency determination if it is:

(A) arbitrary, capricious, an abuse of discretion, or otherwise not in accordance with law;
(B) contrary to constitutional right, power, privilege, or immunity;
(C) in excess of statutory jurisdiction, authority, or limitations, or short of statutory right;
(D) without observance of procedure required by law;
(E) unsupported by substantial evidence. (See: 5 USC § 706(2)).

Deference is not robotic approval. The principle of deference is not the rubber stamp, automatically approving every agency interpretation of statute, but a search and careful inquiry into facts of each case to determine that agency has acted within the scope of statutory authority is required. (See: *Ohio v. Ruckelshaus,* 776 F. 2d. 1333, 16 ELR 20013, *cert den* 476 US 1169, 90 L.Ed. 2d. 977, 106 S.Ct. 2889 (1985).)

> In making a decision, the agency must examine relevant data, explain evidence which is available, and offer a rational connection between the facts found and the choice made; if the agency performs these functions, its decision is not arbitrary or capricious; conversely, if the agency fails to consider an important aspect of the problem, its decision is arbitrary and capricious. (See: *RSR Corp. v. EPA,* 588 F. Supp. 1251. controlling weight unless it is plainly erroneous or inconsistent with the regulation." (at 26)

Respondent's case does not represent such honest differences of opinion. The Auditor avoids the regulations. The principle of deference finds no home in irrational or inconsistent decision-making. Weight to be accorded the Auditor depends on the thoroughness of his or her analysis, validity of the reasoning employed, consistency, and predictability of action. This is the very reason the regulations exists—to thwart a hodgepodge of qualitative and quantitative judgments. While any reviewer of agency action must respect the agency's expertise, it cannot and should not uphold erroneous interpretation. Those entrusted with judicial oversight cannot uphold agency interpretations if their application produces results inconsistent with the statute and regulations. Nor can the agency's action be upheld when it is a clear error of judgment. To uphold the agency audit will result in inconsistent and unpredictable agency practices. Whether avoiding the regulations, or relying upon non-legal authorities, the F.A.D. continually reaffirms its desire for outside classroom preparation, something not in the regulations, namely as a component of course sufficiency. The F.A.D. states:

When it assigned the credit hours, the Academy did not consider the outside study expected of students who would earn 24 credit hours. (at 4)

CONCLUSION

Each allegation of the F.A.D. is factually and legally erroneous.

First, the Auditor's contention that program content mandates a categorical, hourly period of outside preparation is legal fantasy. Neither the statutes or rules implemented to further its end, make any mention of the outside activities suggested in the F.A.D. The plain, unambiguous, lucid description of program sufficiency, fully set out in statute and rule, is what

continued

FIGURE 15.11
continued

guides the school operation, the bureaucrat, the auditor and the inspector. Given that the conversion plan was fully endorsed by the U.S. Department of Education, it is folly to retreat from the initial approval.

Second, the Respondent followed, to the letter, the Accreditor's requirements. The Auditor's continuous references to 1989 standards, moot and inapplicable to Respondent, are a form of factual delusion. The modified 1990 conversion formula, fully confirmed and corroborated by Respondent, is solely relevant. The conversion approval by both the Accreditor and the U.S. Department of Education further manifests the due diligence that overcomes any claim of chicanery or misrepresentation.

Third, since the Auditor refuses to abide by the regulatory definitions guiding institutional operations, and repetitively misrepresents the factual and legal nuances in Respondent's conversion from clock to credit hours, it is properly deduced that the auditor and agency act arbitrarily and capriciously.

Therefore, Respondent respectfully requests the quash of the reimbursement order, an elimination of all liability in approximately the sum of $828,463.00, plus interest and associated fines or penalties, and the award of Respondent's counsel fees and costs associated with the maintenance of this request for review.

Respectfully submitted,
Charles P. Nemeth, Esquire
1240 Lindale Avenue
Drexel Hill, PA 19026
(610) 446 - 4917

After the analysis, a *c*onclusion must be drawn. In light of the analysis, does the rule apply to your set of facts? Be sure you have a factual basis for your conclusion, and that you have supported and thoroughly analyzed the issue. Make sure that you take a position and support it.

IV. THE TERM PAPER

Nothing is more intimidating to many students than the term paper. How do you formulate a thesis? What is quantitative research, and how is it conducted? Can a topic be too broad? These concerns and many more can confuse and overwhelm even the best students. With ample preparation, thought, and guidelines, however, the research and construction of a paper can be an extremely rewarding learning experience. The first issue to address is the type of paper that will be written.

A. A Research Report

A research report normally reports findings from some type of quantitative research and involves scientific method. Scientific method consists of proving a theory through the testing of a hypothesis. A hypothesis is an educated guess, statements that should be true if the theory is correct. An example of a theory is:

The crime rate is affected by various economic factors.

FIGURE 15.12

TITLE: *Peters v. Simmons*—Attorney Malpractice—Statute of Limitations
REQUESTED BY: (Prepared for illustrative purposes only)
SUBMITTED BY: Glenna S. Hall
DATE SUBMITTED:

QUESTIONS PRESENTED

In a suit against an attorney for malpractice, does the applicable statute of limitations begin to run on the date of the alleged negligent action, and thus bar an action commenced more than three years after such date, or does it begin to run on the date of discovery of the negligent action and thus serve as a defense where the date of discovery falls outside the three-year period?

1. Do mandatory precedents require a lower court to apply the three-year limitation period for actions on contracts not in writing (RCW 4.16,080 (3) with the period beginning to run as of the time of the breach of duty?
2. Assuming that the answer to question 1 is affirmative, will our Supreme Court extend the date of discovery rule to an action against an attorney for malpractice?
   a. Do Washington precedents conclusively characterize an attorney malpractice action as an action on contract so that the three-year limitation period governing actions for negligence, RCW 4.16.080(2), with the period beginning to run from discovery, will be held to be inapplicable?
   b. When does an action against an attorney for malpractice "accrue" within the meaning of the general statute of limitations, RCW 4.16.010?

BRIEF ANSWER

Defendant should be successful, at least at the trial level, in asserting the statute of limitations defense. The Washington Supreme Court has stated that attorney malpractice actions are grounded in contract and that the statute of limitations begins to run on the date the allegedly negligent act *was* committed. Even though other jurisdictions have recently tended to abandon this doctrine, the Washington precedents are binding upon a trial court in this state, and a motion for summary judgment should be granted. The probability of a change in the doctrine at the Supreme Court level, however, should be anticipated. The Washington court has recently applied the date of discovery rule in malpractice actions against other types of professionals, and it is likely that it will decide to do so in regard to attorneys, especially now that courts of other jurisdictions have applied the discovery rule to attorney malpractice actions. The discovery rule could be so extended by the Washington court on the basis of any of the following rationales: That such actions sound in tort, or that a cause of action for broach of contractual duty does not arise until more than nominal harm occurs, or that public policy requires the application of the extension discovery rule.

STATEMENT OF FACTS

Our client, an attorney, is being sued for his alleged negligence in failing to obtain the signature of a corporate officer as a personal guarantor on a contract for purchase of plaintiff's business. This instrument was signed in May 1969, more than three years prior to the commencement of the action against our client on July 17, 1974. The complaint does not allege the date when plaintiffs discovered that the corporate officer was not bound by the contract, but the trial court dismissed with prejudice plaintiff's action against the corporate officer on June 19, 1974. You have asked me to determine whether the applicable statute of limitations can be successfully interposed as a defense against plaintiff's action against our client and, specifically, whether a motion for summary judgment against plaintiff based on this affirmative defense is likely to be granted.

continued

FIGURE 15.12
continued

APPLICABLE STATUTES

RCW 4.16.010 *Commencement of actions limited—Objections, how taken.* Actions can only be commenced within the periods herein prescribed after the cause of action shall have accrued, except when in special cases a different limitation that is prescribed by statute; but the objection that the action was not commenced with the time limited can only be taken by answer or demurrer.

RCW 4.16.080 *Actions limited to* three years. Within three years:

(1) ......
(2) An action for taking, detaining or injuring personal property including an action for the specific recovery thereof, or for any other injury to the person or rights of another not hereinafter enumerated.
(3) An action upon a contract or liability, express or implied, which is not in writing, and does not arise out or any written instrument.
(4) An action for relief upon the ground of fraud, the cause of action in such case not to be deemed to have accrued until discovery by the aggrieved party of the facts constituting the fraud.

The statements that are proven true or false—the hypothesis—will determine whether the theory is correct. Some hypotheses that may be tested are:

- When the unemployment rate increases, the rate of theft increases.
- When the per capita income in the United States decreases, the overall crime index increases.
- When the Gross National Product increases, the murder rate decreases.

Data is then collected and compared, statistically analyzed, and charted and graphed to determine whether any of the hypotheses are correct. If the hypotheses are correct, then the theory is proven true. Data may also be inconclusive and subject to further testing.

This is only a thumbnail overview of quantitative research, which is much more involved than described here, of course. This description is only given to explain the very basics of this type of research.

The format of the research report differs from other reports because of the types of data utilized and discussed. The major divisions of a research report are as follows.

I. Title Page. As with all reports, a title page is the first page, with the title of the report, the researcher's name, and other necessary information centered there on. Some information may be included in the bottom righthand corner of the page as well.

II. Abstract. An ***abstract*** is a short summary of the entire report and may include a brief overview of the theory, hypotheses, research methods, and findings. This short paragraph is normally about five or six sentences long, and generally no more than 175 words.

III. Introduction. The purpose of the paper is discussed in the introduction. A summary of the impact of the research, a discussion of any previous research on the topic, and a precise statement of aims of the paper or the hypotheses is included in this section.

IV. Method. In this section, the method by which the research was conducted is explained, in enough detail that another could conduct the study in the same manner. Normally included are sections on the subjects of the research, any apparatus or equipment that was used, and the procedures used for collecting data.

V. Results. The manner in which the collected data was analyzed, be it by statistical or other methods, is the concern of the "results" section. At times, graphs, tables, or charts are included to make the data more easily understandable. The results are not discussed in this section, only reported.

VI. Discussion. Whether the results of the research support the hypotheses and prove the theory is the major topic of the "discussion" section. Other items discussed include a comparison of the results with those of similar studies, the overall implications of the research, and any problems encountered or inconsistencies in the results.

VII. Appendices and References. At the end of paper, two sections are used to list information that is not appropriate for the body of the report. Appendices are included to discuss or report any information that is supplementary in nature. Such information commonly statistics used to create graphs and charts, data from other reports, and a complete list of other reports on the topic.

References to previous research, papers, or authors that are cited within the text of the report are included in the "references" section. All sources cited in the text must be included in the reference section. Various forms exist for the reporting of this information; the most common form for this type of paper is American Psychological Association (APA) style. Always double-check to ensure that you are using the correct citation format. Other popular styles include ASA, SCS, MLA, Harvard Bluebook, and the form set forth in the *Chicago Manual of Style.*

This is only a brief summary of the necessary elements of a research report, and is intended merely to shed a bit of light on the topic. Additional information can be found in the following resources:

Dean J. Champion. *Research Methods for Criminal Justice and Criminology,* 2d ed. (Prentice Hall, 2000).

Frank E. Hagan. *Research Methods in Criminal Justice and Criminology,* 5th ed. (Allyn & Bacon, 2000).

James R. Lasley. *Essentials of Criminal Justice and Criminology Research.* (Prentice Hall, 1999).

Jon L. Proctor & Dian M. Badzinski. *Introductory Statistics for Criminal Justice and Criminology* (Prentice Hall, 2002).

B. A Formal Essay

A formal essay can take many forms. Book reviews, policy analysis papers, reaction papers, and case studies are all examples of the formal essay. The major difference between an essay and a research report is that the essay lacks the scientific method present in a research report. Qualitative data is gathered instead of quantitative data.

Statistics may be reported, but they are used to support factual statements. For example, an essay states that "between the years of 1990 and 1995, the murder rate across the United States decreased." Something like a chart, diagram, or table from the Uniform Crime Report would have to be included or referenced to support this statement.

Written exposition, argument of a point of law, and discussion of various topics and trends are all in the province of the essay. Previously reported data may be compared to newer data, even when no new data is collected. The impact of a new government policy or regulation can be discussed; the impact may be analyzed using best-case and worst-case scenarios. As with research reports, formal essays are broken up into several discrete sections:

I. Title Page. As with the research report, a title page, carrying the title of the paper, the author, the date, and course section, is included. The title is normally centered on the page, with the author and other information included in the bottom right corner, although preferred formats vary by institution.

II. Introduction. An introduction can vary in length from a paragraph to two or three pages, depending on the overall length of the paper and the amount of background information that must be given. Previous reports can be discussed and the history of the subject matter can be given; almost always, a brief statement of the purpose and thesis of the paper and a preliminary mention of the conclusions are included in the introduction.

III. Body of the Essay. A logical, orderly discussion of the points presented is undertaken in the body of an essay. Materials that either support or refute the thesis are discussed and final statements are made regarding each issue. Positions must be taken and adequately defended using various authorities and arguments. This may be followed by a discussion of and arguments for the opposing point of view.

IV. Conclusion. After each issue is thoroughly discussed and final statements are made regarding each topic addressed, the conclusion is drafted. The conclusion is a wrap-up of the entire discussion that concisely reiterates the final positions taken on each issue and states whether they support or refute the thesis.

V. Endnotes, References, and Appendices. Various citation formats are used in essays. Endnotes require the inclusion of a short reference immediately following the text being supported. If footnotes are used, this step is not necessary. If in-text citation is used in conjunction with either footnotes or endnotes, the appropriate reference page is included after the endnotes, or, in the case of footnote usage, at the end of the text. Various appendices may also be included, to contain (among many other possibilities) informational diagrams, organizational charts, lists of agencies, addresses, or relevant court cases, statutes, or studies.

The following are some excellent resources that may be consulted for further assistance:

Barbara Fine Clouse, *The Student Writer,* 5th ed. (McGraw Hill, 2000).

Joseph Gibaldi, *MLA Handbook for Writers of Research Papers,* 5th ed. (Modern Language Association of America, 1999).

William A. Johnson, Jr. et al. *The Criminal Justice Student Writer's Manual* (Prentice Hall, 1999).

Marc Riedel, *Research Strategies for Secondary Data* (Sage Publications, 2000).

V. SUMMARY

The legal system is inundated with paperwork. Writing letters, forms, reports, descriptions, and memoranda is an essential part of the researcher's job. The rule of thumb for all legal writing is *exposition.* Keep legal writings short, factual, and to the point. Focus the issue as clearly as possible and disregard irrelevant information. Legal memoranda drive legal work and legal reasoning: get the facts, fashion the issue, and deliver the intellectual authority to support the argument.

INDEX

Page numbers in *italics* indicate figures.

Chpt 4, pg. 51: Michael Newman, PhotoEdit
Chpt 7, pg. 136: Photolibrary.com
Chpt 10, pg. 233; Tony Freeman, PhotoEdit
Chpt 13, pg. 381: Keith Brofsky, Getty Images, Inc.–Photodisc.

S0-AIT-603

The GALE ENCYCLOPEDIA *of* SCIENCE

SECOND EDITION

The GALE ENCYCLOPEDIA of SCIENCE

SECOND EDITION

VOLUME 5
Phosphorus-Spectrum

Kimberley A. McGrath, Senior Editor
Stacey Blachford, Assistant Editor

Detroit
New York
San Francisco
London
Boston
Woodbridge, CT

The GALE ENCYCLOPEDIA *of* SCIENCE

SECOND EDITION

GALE GROUP STAFF

Kimberley A. McGrath, *Senior Editor*
Stacey L. Blachford, *Assistant Editor*
Christine B. Jeryan, *Contributing Editor*

Deirdra S. Blanchfield, *Assistant Editor*
Melissa C. McDade, *Assistant Editor*
Ellen Thackery, *Associate Editor*

Andrea Lopeman, *Programmer Analyst*
Mark Springer, *Technical Training Specialist*

Barbara Yarrow, Manager, *Imaging and Multimedia Content*
Robyn Young, Senior Editor, *Imaging and Multimedia Content*
Randy Bassett, *Imaging Supervisor*
Robert Duncan, *Senior Imaging Specialist*
Pamela A. Reed, Coordinator, *Imaging and Multimedia Content*

Maria Franklin, *Permissions Manager*
Shalice Shah, *Permissions Associate*

Victoria B. Cariappa, *Research Manager*
Maureen Richards, *Research Specialist*

Mary Beth Trimper, *Manager, Composition and Electronic Prepress*
Evi Seoud, Assistant Manager, *Composition Purchasing and Electronic Prepress*
Dorothy Maki, *Manufacturing Manager*

Kenn Zorn, *Product Design Manager*
Michelle DiMercurio, *Senior Art Director*

Laurie Androit, *Indexing Specialist*
Lynne Maday, *Indexing Specialist*
Marco Di Vita, Graphix Group, *Typesetting*

Line art illustrations provided by:
Argosy, West Newton, Massachusetts
Electronic Illustrators Group, Morgan Hill, California

ISBN 0-7876-4370-X (set)
0-7876-4371-8 (Vol. 1)
0-7876-4372-6 (Vol. 2)
0-7876-4373-4 (Vol. 3)
0-7876-4374-2 (Vol. 4)
0-7876-4375-0 (Vol. 5)
0-7876-4376-9 (Vol. 6)

Library of Congress Card Number: 00-106824

Printed in Canada
10 9 8 7 6 5 4 3 2 1

CONTENTS

ORGANIZATION OF THE ENCYCLOPEDIA

The Gale Encyclopedia of Science, Second Edition has been designed with ease of use and ready reference in mind.

- Entries are **alphabetically arranged** in a single sequence, rather than by scientific field.
- Length of entries varies from **short definitions** of one or two paragraphs to longer, more **detailed entries** on complex subjects.
- Longer entries are arranged so that an **overview** of the subject appears first, followed by a detailed discussion conveniently arranged under subheadings.
- A list of **key terms** are provided where appropriate to define unfamiliar terms or concepts.
- **Bold-faced terms** direct reader to reated articles.
- Longer entries conclude with a **further reading** section, which points readers to other helpful sources.
- The **contributor's name** appears at the end of longer entries. His or her affiliation can be found in the "Contributors" section at the front of each volume.
- **"See-also" references** appear at the end of entries to point readers to related entries.
- **Cross-references** placed throughout the encyclopedia direct readers to where information on subjects without their own entries can be found.
- A comprehensive **general index** guides readers to all topics and persons mentioned in the book.

ADVISORY BOARD

A number of experts in the library and scientific communities provided invaluable assistance in the formulation of this encyclopedia. Our advisory board performed a myriad of duties, from defining the scope of coverage to reviewing individual entries for accuracy and accessibility. We would therefore like to express our appreciation to them:

CONTRIBUTORS

Nasrine Adibe
Professor Emeritus
Department of Education
Long Island University
Westbury, New York

Mary D. Albanese
Department of English
University of Alaska
Juneau, Alaska

Margaret Alic
Science Writer
Eastsound, Washington

James L. Anderson
Soil Science Department
University of Minnesota
St. Paul, Minnesota

Monica Anderson
Science Writer
Hoffman Estates, Illinois

Susan Andrew
Teaching Assistant
University of Maryland
Washington, D.C.

John Appel
Director
Fundación Museo de Ciencia y Tecnología
Popayán, Colombia

David Ball
Assistant Professor
Department of Chemistry
Cleveland State University
Cleveland, Ohio

Dana M. Barry
Editor and Technical Writer
Center for Advanced Materials Processing
Clarkston University
Potsdam, New York

Puja Batra
Department of Zoology
Michigan State University
East Lansing, Michigan

Donald Beaty
Professor Emeritus
College of San Mateo
San Mateo, California

Eugene C. Beckham
Department of Mathematics and Science
Northwood Institute
Midland, Michigan

Martin Beech
Research Associate
Department of Astronomy
University of Western Ontario
London, Ontario

Massimo D. Bezoari
Associate Professor
Department of Chemistry
Huntingdon College
Montgomery, Alabama

John M. Bishop III
Translator
New York, New York

T. Parker Bishop
Professor
Middle Grades and Secondary Education
Georgia Southern University
Statesboro, Georgia

Carolyn Black
Professor
Incarnate Word College
San Antonio, Texas

Larry Blaser
Science Writer
Lebanon, Tennessee

Jean F. Blashfield
Science Writer
Walworth, Wisconsin

Richard L. Branham Jr.
Director
Centro Rigional de Investigaciones Científicas y Tecnológicas
Mendoza, Argentina

Patricia Braus
Editor
American Demographics
Rochester, New York

David L. Brock
Biology Instructor
St. Louis, Missouri

Leona B. Bronstein
Chemistry Teacher (retired)
East Lansing High School
Okemos, Michigan

Brandon R. Brown
Graduate Research Assistant
Oregon State University
Corvallis, Oregon

Lenonard C. Bruno
Senior Science Specialist
Library of Congress
Chevy Chase, Maryland

Scott Christian Cahall
Researcher
World Precision Instruments, Inc.
Bradenton, Florida

G. Lynn Carlson
Senior Lecturer
School of Science and Technology
University of Wisconsin-Parkside
Kenosha, Wisconsin

James J. Carroll
Center for Quantum Mechanics
The University of Texas at Dallas
Dallas, Texas

Steven B. Carroll
Assistant Professor
Division of Biology
Northeast Missouri State University
Kirksville, Missouri

Rosalyn Carson-DeWitt
Physician and Medical Writer
Durham, North Carolina

Yvonne Carts-Powell
Editor
Laser Focus World
Belmont, Massachustts

Chris Cavette
Technical Writer
Fremont, California

Lata Cherath
Science Writer
Franklin Park, New York

Kenneth B. Chiacchia
Medical Editor
University of Pittsburgh Medical Center
Pittsburgh, Pennsylvania

M. L. Cohen
Science Writer
Chicago, Illinois

Robert Cohen
Reporter
KPFA Radio News
Berkeley, California

Sally Cole-Misch
Assistant Director
International Joint Commission
Detroit, Michigan

George W. Collins II
Professor Emeritus
Case Western Reserve
Chesterland, Ohio

Jeffrey R. Corney
Science Writer
Thermopolis, Wyoming

Tom Crawford
Assistant Director
Division of Publication and Development
University of Pittsburgh Medical Center
Pittsburgh, Pennsylvania

Pamela Crowe
Medical and Science Writer
Oxon, England

Clinton Crowley
On-site Geologist
Selman and Associates
Fort Worth, Texas

Edward Cruetz
Physicist
Rancho Santa Fe, California

Frederick Culp
Chairman
Department of Physics
Tennessee Technical
Cookeville, Tennessee

Neil Cumberlidge
Professor
Department of Biology
Northern Michigan University
Marquette, Michigan

Mary Ann Cunningham
Environmental Writer
St. Paul, Minnesota

Les C. Cwynar
Associate Professor
Department of Biology
University of New Brunswick
Fredericton, New Brunswick

Paul Cypher
Provisional Interpreter
Lake Erie Metropark
Trenton, Michigan

Stanley J. Czyzak
Professor Emeritus
Ohio State University
Columbus, Ohio

Rosi Dagit
Conservation Biologist
Topanga-Las Virgenes Resource Conservation District
Topanga, California

David Dalby
President
Bruce Tool Company, Inc.
Taylors, South Carolina

Lou D'Amore
Chemistry Teacher
Father Redmund High School
Toronto, Ontario

Douglas Darnowski
Postdoctoral Fellow
Department of Plant Biology
Cornell University
Ithaca, New York

Sreela Datta
Associate Writer
Aztec Publications
Northville, Michigan

Sarah K. Dean
Science Writer
Philadelphia, Pennsylvania

Sarah de Forest
Research Assistant
Theoretical Physical Chemistry Lab
University of Pittsburgh
Pittsburgh, Pennsylvania

Louise Dickerson
Medical and Science Writer
Greenbelt, Maryland

Marie Doorey
Editorial Assistant
Illinois Masonic Medical Center
Chicago, Illinois

Herndon G. Dowling
Professor Emeritus
Department of Biology
New York University
New York, New York

Marion Dresner
Natural Resources Educator
Berkeley, California

John Henry Dreyfuss
Science Writer
Brooklyn, New York

Roy Dubisch
Professor Emeritus
Department of Mathematics
New York University
New York, New York

Russel Dubisch
Department of Physics
Sienna College
Loudonville, New York

Carolyn Duckworth
Science Writer
Missoula, Montana

Peter A. Ensminger
Research Associate
Cornell University
Syracuse, New York

Bernice Essenfeld
Biology Writer
Warren, New Jersey

Mary Eubanks
Instructor of Biology
The North Carolina School of Science and Mathematics
Durham, North Carolina

Kathryn M. C. Evans
Science Writer
Madison, Wisconsin

William G. Fastie
Department of Astronomy and Physics
Bloomberg Center
Baltimore, Maryland

Barbara Finkelstein
Science Writer
Riverdale, New York

Mary Finley
Supervisor of Science Curriculum (retired)
Pittsburgh Secondary Schools
Clairton, Pennsylvania

Gaston Fischer
Institut de Géologie
Université de Neuchâtel
Peseux, Switzerland

Sara G. B. Fishman
Professor
Quinsigamond Community College
Worcester, Massachusetts

David Fontes
Senior Instructor
Lloyd Center for Environmental Studies
Westport, Maryland

Barry Wayne Fox
Extension Specialist, Marine/Aquatic Education
Virginia State University
Petersburg, Virginia

Ed Fox
Charlotte Latin School
Charlotte, North Carolina

Kenneth L. Frazier
Science Teacher (retired)
North Olmstead High School
North Olmstead, Ohio

Bill Freedman
Professor
Department of Biology and School for Resource and Environmental Studies
Dalhousie University
Halifax, Nova Scotia

T. A. Freeman
Consulting Archaeologist
Quail Valley, California

Elaine Friebele
Science Writer
Cheverly, Maryland

Randall Frost
Documentation Engineering
Pleasanton, California

Robert Gardner
Science Education Consultant
North Eastham, Massachusetts

Gretchen M. Gillis
Senior Geologist
Maxus Exploration
Dallas, Texas

Kathryn Glynn
Audiologist
Portland, Oregon

Natalie Goldstein
Educational Environmental Writing
Phoenicia, New York

David Gorish
TARDEC
U.S. Army
Warren, Michigan

Louis Gotlib
South Granville High School
Durham, North Carolina

Hans G. Graetzer
Professor
Department of Physics
South Dakota State University
Brookings, South Dakota

Jim Guinn
Assistant Professor
Department of Physics
Berea College
Berea, Kentucky

Steve Gutterman
Psychology Research Assistant
University of Michigan
Ann Arbor, Michigan

Johanna Haaxma-Jurek
Educator
Nataki Tabibah Schoolhouse of Detroit
Detroit, Michigan

Monica H. Halka
Research Associate
Department of Physics and Astronomy
University of Tennessee
Knoxville, Tennessee

Jeffrey C. Hall
Astronomer
Lowell Observatory
Flagstaff, Arizona

C. S. Hammen
Professor Emeritus
Department of Zoology
University of Rhode Island

Beth Hanson
Editor
The Amicus Journal
Brooklyn, New York

Clay Harris
Associate Professor
Department of Geography and Geology
Middle Tennessee State University
Murfreesboro, Tennessee

Clinton W. Hatchett
Director Science and Space Theater
Pensacola Junior College
Pensacola, Florida

Catherine Hinga Haustein
Associate Professor
Department of Chemistry
Central College
Pella, Iowa

Dean Allen Haycock
Science Writer
Salem, New York

Paul A. Heckert
Professor
Department of Chemistry and Physics
Western Carolina University
Cullowhee, North Carolina

Darrel B. Hoff
Department of Physics
Luther College
Calmar, Iowa

Dennis Holley
Science Educator
Shelton, Nebraska

Leonard Darr Holmes
Department of Physical Science
Pembroke State University
Pembroke, North Carolina

Rita Hoots
Instructor of Biology, Anatomy, Chemistry
Yuba College
Woodland, California

Selma Hughes
Department of Psychology and Special Education
East Texas State University
Mesquite, Texas

Mara W. Cohen Ioannides
Science Writer
Springfield, Missouri

Zafer Iqbal
Allied Signal Inc.
Morristown, New Jersey

Sophie Jakowska
Pathobiologist, Environmental Educator
Santo Domingo, Dominican Republic

Richard A. Jeryan
Senior Technical Specialist
Ford Motor Company
Dearborn, Michigan

Stephen R. Johnson
Biology Writer
Richmond, Virginia

Kathleen A. Jones
School of Medicine
Southern Illinois University
Carbondale, Illinois

Harold M. Kaplan
Professor
School of Medicine
Southern Illinois University
Carbondale, Illinois

Anthony Kelly
Science Writer
Pittsburgh, Pennsylvania

Amy Kenyon-Campbell
Ecology, Evolution and Organismal Biology Program
University of Michigan
Ann Arbor, Michigan

Eileen M. Korenic
Institute of Optics
University of Rochester
Rochester, New York

Jennifer Kramer
Science Writer
Kearny, New Jersey

Pang-Jen Kung
Los Alamos National Laboratory
Los Alamos, New Mexico

Marc Kusinitz
Assistant Director Media Relations
John Hopkins Medical Institution
Towsen, Maryland

Arthur M. Last
Head
Department of Chemistry
University College of the Fraser Valley
Abbotsford, British Columbia

Nathan Lavenda
Zoologist
Skokie, Illinios

Jennifer LeBlanc
Environmental Consultant
London, Ontario

Benedict A. Leerburger
Science Writer
Scarsdale, New York

Betsy A. Leonard
Education Facilitator
Reuben H. Fleet Space Theater and Science Center
San Diego, California

Scott Lewis
Science Writer
Chicago, Illinois

Frank Lewotsky
Aerospace Engineer (retired)
Nipomo, California

Karen Lewotsky
Director of Water Programs
Oregon Environmental Council
Portland, Oregon

Kristin Lewotsky
Editor
Laser Focus World
Nashua, New Hamphire

Stephen K. Lewotsky
Architect
Grants Pass, Oregon

Sarah Lee Lippincott
Professor Emeritus
Swarthmore College
Swarthmore, Pennsylvania

David Lunney
Research Scientist
Centre de Spectrométrie Nucléaire et de Spectrométrie de Masse
Orsay, France

Steven MacKenzie
Ecologist
Spring Lake, Michigan

J. R. Maddocks
Consulting Scientist
DeSoto, Texas

Gail B. C. Marsella
Technical Writer
Allentown, Pennsylvania

Karen Marshall
Research Associate
Council of State Governments and Centers for Environment and Safety
Lexington, Kentucky

Liz Marshall
Science Writer
Columbus, Ohio

James Marti
Research Scientist
Department of Mechanical Engineering
University of Minnesota
Minneapolis, Minnesota

Elaine L. Martin
Science Writer
Pensacola, Florida

Lilyan Mastrolla
Professor Emeritus
San Juan Unified School
Sacramento, California

Iain A. McIntyre
Manager
Electro-optic Department
Energy Compression Research Corporation
Vista, California

Jennifer L. McGrath
Chemistry Teacher
Northwood High School
Nappanee, Indiana

G. H. Miller
Director
Studies on Smoking
Edinboro, Pennsylvania

J. Gordon Miller
Botanist
Corvallis, Oregon

Christine Miner Minderovic
Nuclear Medicine Technologist
Franklin Medical Consulters
Ann Arbor, Michigan

David Mintzer
Professor Emeritus
Department of Mechanical Engineering
Northwestern University
Evanston, Illinois

Christine Molinari
Science Editor
University of Chicago Press
Chicago, Illinois

Frank Mooney
Professor Emeritus
Fingerlake Community College
Canandaigua, New York

Partick Moore
Department of English
University of Arkansas at Little Rock
Little Rock, Arkansas

Robbin Moran
Department of Systematic Botany
Institute of Biological Sciences
University of Aarhus
Risskou, Denmark

J. Paul Moulton
Department of Mathematics
Episcopal Academy
Glenside, Pennsylvania

Otto H. Muller
Geology Department
Alfred University
Alfred, New York

Angie Mullig
Publication and Development
University of Pittsburgh Medical Center
Trafford, Pennsylvania

David R. Murray
Senior Associate
Sydney University
Sydney, New South Wales
Australia

Sutharchana Murugan
Scientist
Three Boehringer Mannheim Corp.
Indianapolis, Indiana

Muthena Naseri
Moorpark College
Moorpark, California

David Newton
Science Writer and Educator
Ashland, Oregon

F. C. Nicholson
Science Writer
Lynn, Massachusetts

James O'Connell
Department of Physical Sciences
Frederick Community College
Gaithersburg, Maryland

Dónal P. O'Mathúna
Associate Professor
Mount Carmel College of Nursing
Columbus, Ohio

Marjorie Pannell
Managing Editor, Scientific Publications
Field Museum of Natural History
Chicago, Illinois

Gordon A. Parker
Lecturer
Department of Natural Sciences
University of Michigan-Dearborn
Dearborn, Michigan

David Petechuk
Science Writer
Ben Avon, Pennsylvania

John R. Phillips
Department of Chemistry
Purdue University, Calumet
Hammond, Indiana

Kay Marie Porterfield
Science Writer
Englewood, Colorado

Paul Poskozim
Chair
Department of Chemistry, Earth Science and Physics
Northeastern Illinois University
Chicago, Illinois

Andrew Poss
Senior Research Chemist
Allied Signal Inc.
Buffalo, New York

Satyam Priyadarshy
Department of Chemistry
University of Pittsburgh
Pittsburgh, Pennsylvania

Patricia V. Racenis
Science Writer
Livonia, Michigan

Cynthia Twohy Ragni
Atmospheric Scientist
National Center for Atmospheric Research
Westminster, Colorado

Jordan P. Richman
Science Writer
Phoenix, Arizona

Kitty Richman
Science Writer
Phoenix, Arizona

Vita Richman
Science Writer
Phoenix, Arizona

Michael G. Roepel
Researcher
Department of Chemistry
University of Pittsburgh
Pittsburgh, Pennsylvania

Perry Romanowski
Science Writer
Chicago, Illinois

Nancy Ross-Flanigan
Science Writer
Belleville, Michigan

Belinda Rowland
Science Writer
Voorheesville, New York

Gordon Rutter
Royal Botanic Gardens
Edinburgh, Great Britain

Elena V. Ryzhov
Polytechnic Institute
Troy, New York

David Sahnow
Associate Research Scientist
John Hopkins University
Baltimore, Maryland

Peter Salmansohn
Educational Consultant
New York State Parks
Cold Spring, New York

Peter K. Schoch
Instructor
Department of Physics and Computer Science
Sussex County Community College
Augusta, New Jersey

Patricia G. Schroeder
Instructor
Science, Healthcare, and Math Division
Johnson County Community College
Overland Park, Kansas

Randy Schueller
Science Writer
Chicago, Illinois

Kathleen Scogna
Science Writer
Baltimore, Maryland

William Shapbell Jr.
Launch and Flight Systems Manager
Kennedy Space Center, Florida

Kenneth Shepherd
Science Writer
Wyandotte, Michigan

Anwar Yuna Shiekh
International Centre for Theoretical Physics
Trieste, Italy

Raul A. Simon
Chile Departmento de Física
Universidad de Tarapacá
Arica, Chile

Michael G. Slaughter
Science Specialist
Ingham ISD
East Lansing, Michigan

Billy W. Sloope
Professor Emeritus

Department of Physics
Virginia Commonwealth University
Richmond, Virginia

Douglas Smith
Science Writer
Milton, Massachusetts

Lesley L. Smith
Department of Physics and Astronomy
University of Kansas
Lawrence, Kansas

Kathryn D. Snavely
U.S. General Accounting Office
Policy Analyst, Air Quality Issues
Raleigh, North Carolina

Charles H. Southwick
Professor
Environmental, Population, and Organismic Biology
University of Colorado at Boulder
Boulder, Colorado

John Spizzirri
Science Writer
Chicago, Illinois

Frieda A. Stahl
Professor Emeritus
Department of Physics
California State University, Los Angeles
Los Angeles, California

Robert L. Stearns
Department of Physics
Vassar College
Poughkeepsie, New York

Ilana Steinhorn
Science Writer
Boalsburg, Pennsylvania

David Stone
Conservation Advisory Services
Gai Soleil
Chemin Des Clyettes
Le Muids, Switzerland

Eric R. Swanson
Associate Professor
Department of Earth and Physical Sciences
University of Texas
San Antonio, Texas

Cheryl Taylor
Science Educator
Kailua, Hawaii

Nicholas C. Thomas
Department of Physical Sciences
Auburn University at Montgomery
Montgomery, Alabama

W. A. Thomasson
Science and Medical Writer
Oak Park, Illinois

Marie L. Thompson
Science Writer
Ben Avon, Pennsylvania

Laurie Toupin
Science Writer
Pepperell, Massachusetts

Melvin Tracy
Science Educator
Appleton, Wisconsin

Karen Trentelman
Research Associate
Archaeometric Laboratory
University of Toronto
Toronto, Ontario

Robert K. Tyson
Senior Scientist
W. J. Schafer Assoc.
Jupiter, Florida

James Van Allen
Professor Emeritus
Department of Physics and Astronomy
University of Iowa
Iowa City, Iowa

Julia M. Van Denack
Biology Instructor
Silver Lake College
Manitowoc, Wisconsin

Kurt Vandervoort
Department of Chemistry and Physics
West Carolina University
Cullowhee, North Carolina

Chester Vander Zee
Naturalist, Science Educator
Volga, South Dakota

Rashmi Venkateswaran
Undergraduate Lab Coordinator
Department of Chemistry
University of Ottawa
Ontario, Canada

R. A. Virkar
Chair
Department of Biological Sciences
Kean College
Iselin, New Jersey

Kurt C. Wagner
Instructor
South Carolina Governor's School for Science and Technology
Hartsville, South Carolina

Cynthia Washam
Science Writer
Jensen Beach, Florida

Terry Watkins
Science Writer
Indianapolis, Indiana

Joseph D. Wassersug
Physician
Boca Raton, Florida

Tom Watson
Environmental Writer
Seattle, Washington

Jeffrey Weld
Instructor, Science Department Chair
Pella High School
Pella, Iowa

Frederick R. West
Astronomer
Hanover, Pennsylvania

Glenn Whiteside
Science Writer
Wichita, Kansas

John C. Whitmer
Professor
Department of Chemistry
Western Washington University
Bellingham, Washington

Donald H. Williams
Department of Chemistry
Hope College
Holland, Michigan

Robert L. Wolke
Professor Emeritus
Department of Chemistry
University of Pittsburgh
Pittsburgh, Pennsylvania

Jim Zurasky
Optical Physicist
Nichols Research Corporation
Huntsville, Alabama

Phosphorus

Phosphorus is a chemical element with the **atomic number** 15 and **atomic weight** 30.9738. Phosphorus forms the basis of a large number of compounds, by far the most environmentally important of which are phosphates. All plants and animals need phosphates for growth and function, and in many natural waters the production of **algae** and higher plants is limited by the low natural levels of phosphorus. As the amount of available phosphorus in an aquatic environment increases, **plant** and algal growth can increase dramatically leading to **eutrophication**. In the past, one of the major contributors to phosphorus **pollution** was household detergents containing phosphates. These substances have now been banned from these products. Other contributors to phosphorus pollution are **sewage treatment** plants and runoff from cattle feedlots. (**Animal** feces contain significant amounts of phosphorus.) **Erosion** of farmland treated with phosphorus **fertilizers** or animal manure also contributes to eutrophication and **water pollution**.

See also Phosphoric acid; Phosphorus removal.

Phosphorus cycle

We live in a world that is constantly **recycling** materials. All life is composed of the very same **matter** that exists in the non-living, or abiotic, world. The elements that are found in living things, like **carbon**, **hydrogen**, and **calcium** are also found in abioic compounds of the environment, like **soil** or rock. Because the quantities of usable sources of materials and elements that compose the living things on our **planet** are limited, life on **earth** is dependent on recycling. The chemical constituents that make up a **plant**, for instance, might once have been the constituents of a former **animal** that died. The **water** we drink and is incorporated into our bodies, might once have been the same water that existed within dinosaurs, now long extinct. But matter is not simply recycled among living things. It is also recycled between the living and the non-living. The potassium in a **banana**, for instance, is recycled from potassium found in soil. This process of recycling, especially **nutrients**, between living and non-living components of the environment is called biogeochemical cycling. The **phosphorus** cycle is the biogeochemical cycling of phosphorus, a very important element of living things, between the living and non-living parts of our world. Human activity can have effects on phosphorus cycling, which in turn has profound effects on ecological systems.

Biogeochemical cycles

Life is a complex interplay of matter and **energy**. Nearly all life on Earth derives its energy from the **sun**. The center of our **solar system**, the sun is a **star** that bombards our planet with solar **radiation**. It is a nearly inexhaustible source of light energy for the living organisms that inhabit the earth. As abundant as this energy source is, however, there is a finite quantity of matter, or chemical elements, available to make up living things. Therefore, life on earth, since it depends both on energy and matter, must depend on the reclaiming of materials for use over and over again. Essential nutrient elements are recycled between living and abiotic components of ecosystems in biogeochemical cycles, or cycles involving living (bio-), geological (geo-), and chemical processes. When living things die, they return their chemical elements to the non-living components of ecosystems as they decompose. However, even while alive, organisms contribute to nutrient cycling as they consume matter and excrete waste products into the environment.

There are several major biogeochemical cycles rotating continuously within and among ecosystems. An **ecosystem** is an area including all of the living and non-living things found within it. The most important cycles of ecosystems are the **carbon cycle**, the **nitrogen** cycle, the phosphorus cycle, and the water cycle. These interacting biogeochemical cycles involve travel of carbon, nitrogen, phosphorus, and water through living things, air, water, soil, and rock. For instance, the carbon cycle involves the gas **carbon dioxide** found in air. Plants use carbon dioxide during **photosynthesis** to make plant material, like **cellulose**. Here, carbon moves from an inorganic gaseous form, to living, or organic, form. Then, as plants die, they decompose and release organic molecules into water, which then runs into oceans. The organic material settles to the bottom where, over very long time periods, is incorporated into rock. Thus, the carbon existed as a gas in air, living material in plants, dissolved matter in water, and as solid form in rock. In much the same way, phosphorus is recycled in the environment. Not every cycle, however, includes each of these stages.

Phosphorus functions and recycling

All living things require phosphorus. In the environment, phosphorus is often in the form of phosphate molecules, composed of one phosphorus atom and four **oxygen atoms**. One important function of phosphate groups of organic molecules within living organisms is energy storage. **Adenosine triphosphate**, or ATP, is an example. ATP, the "energy currency" of cells is used to transfer stored chemical energy from one **molecule** to another to perform work. The energy is stored in the phosphate

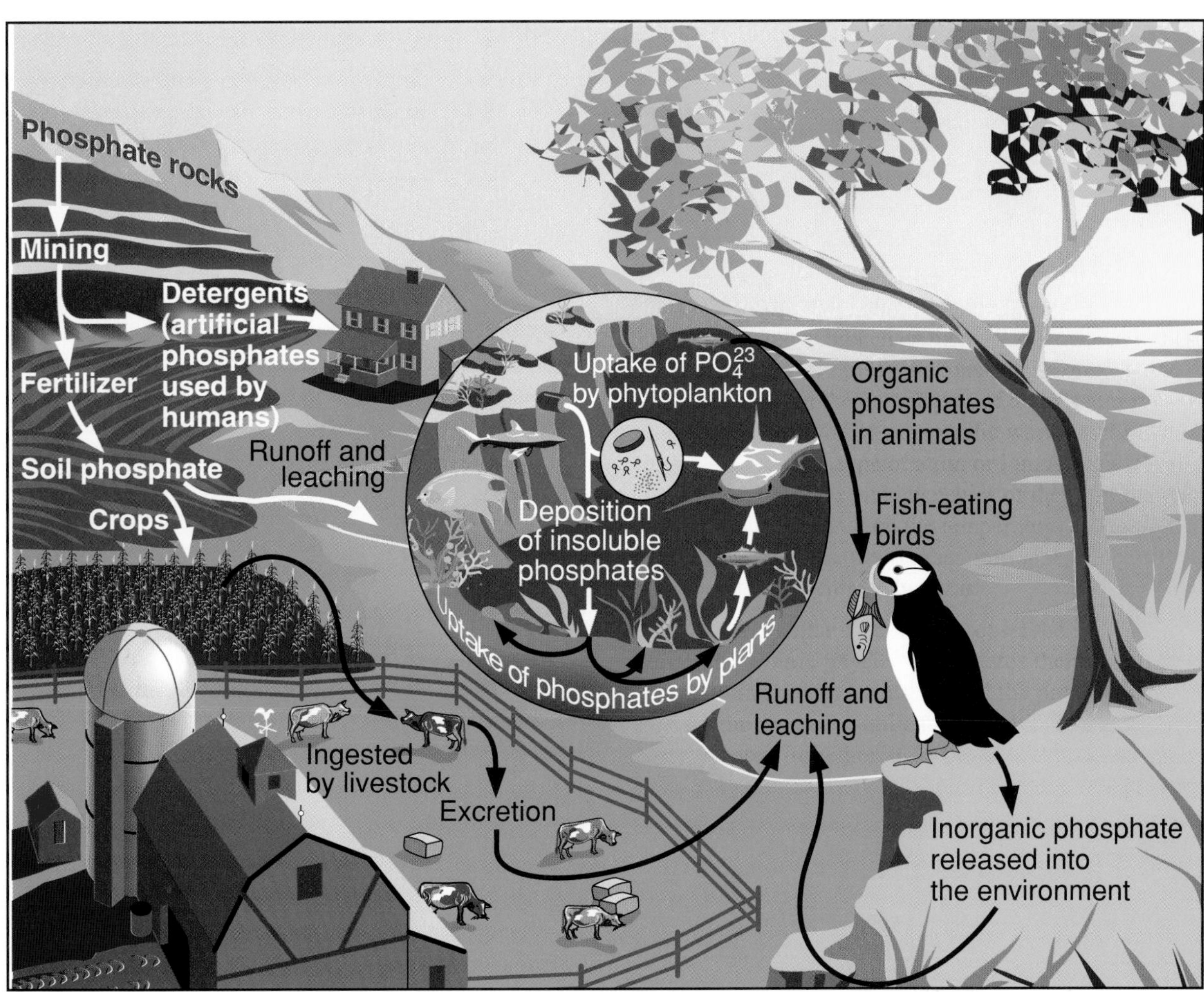

The phosphorus cycle. Geological uplift accounts for the presence of the phosphate rocks (upper left).

portion of the molecule. The energy we derive from food, for example, is stored in the form of ATP. Phosphorus is also required for the formation of phospholipids of cells. Phospholipids are the major component of **cell** membranes. Also, phosphate groups activate and deactivate enzymes within cells that catalyze major chemical reactions. Phosphate is a mineral **salt** component of bones and teeth in vertebrate animals. In addition, phosphate is an important structural component of DNA itself. So, recycling of limited phosphorus is vital.

Unlike the carbon cycle, the phosphorus cycle does not include transition of phosphorus through the atmosphere as a gas. Phosphorus-containing gases are not common. Also, phosphate has a limited number of inorganic forms outside of living organisms, making its recycling scheme relatively simple. **Weathering** of **rocks** containing phosphate **minerals** is accomplished by rain. The **erosion** moves inorganic phosphate into soil where it is rapidly absorbed by plants and incorporated into organic molecules (DNA, ATP, phospholipids). Plants containing phosphorus die or are consumed by animals. When consumed by animals, the phosphorus is incorporated into animal **mass**. When phosphorus containing animals die, along with plants, their **decomposition** returns phosphorus from their tissues back into soil for new use by plants (or by **fungi**).

Not all of the phosphate eroded from rock is incorporated into plant and animal **tissue** directly. A portion of the run-off from phosphorus deposits in rock either enters streams and **rivers** that flow to the **ocean**, or leaches into the water table, gradually draining into the sea. Phosphates in the ocean very gradually build-up in sediments. Also, phosphorus in decaying aquatic organisms falls to the bottom to accompany the phosphorus built-up in inorganic sediment. Over extremely long periods of time, phosphorus-containing sediment is transformed into rock, buried deep in the ocean floor. Here, the phosphorus remains, not participating in the rest of the cycle. Most of the phosphorus on earth is found here, at the bottom of

KEY TERMS

Abiotic—A term used to describe the portion of an ecosystem that is not living, such as water, or soil.

Artificial Eutrophication—A large increase in the primary productivity of a lake due to the actions of man, like fertilizer run-off from agricultural activities.

Biogeochemical cycle—The process of recycling nutrients necessary for life among living non-living components of an ecosystem. The recycling can include geological, chemical, and living components.

Biomass—The weight, excluding water, of living organisms such as plants.

Ecosystem—An area including all of the living organisms and non-living factors that interact.

Limiting Nutrient—A chemical nutrient, such as phosphorus, which is necessary for growth but is found in limited quantities in a given ecosystem. Limiting nutrients limit the growth of dependent organisms.

Primary productivity—The rate of conversion of sunlight energy into chemical energy within plants, called primary producers.

the ocean as a part of the earth's crust. Periodically, violent geological shifts raise the once buried deposits. Now on land, exposed to **wind** and rain, the phosphorus minerals are free to participate in the rest of the cycle.

Phosphorus as a limiting nutrient in ecosystems

The measure of how quickly and to what extent sunlight is converted into organic material by plants during photosynthesis is called primary productivity. Some ecosystems have high primary productivity, while others have very low productivity. For example, the ocean is the world's most productive ecosystem because of its huge area. Oceanic **algae** create new plant **biomass**, or weight of living material, on a vast scale. However, plant primary productivity is not simply dependent on the availability of sunlight alone. In addition to water, other vital inorganic nutrients are required for growth and optimum primary productivity. Phosphorus is one such nutrient.

In ecosystems, rarely will all required nutrients be used up at the same rate. When one nutrient is used before other nutrients, it is called a limiting nutrient. Limiting nutrients prevent growth with their absence. When returned to the lacking environment, limiting nutrients jump-start productivity, which continues until the limiting nutrient again is depleted. Phosphorus is a limiting nutrient in many terrestrial and aquatic ecosystems. The productivity of the primary producers in these areas is limited, held in check, by the amount of available phosphorus that is so vital for life. This fact is why phosphorus is a main component of agricultural and household plant foods and **fertilizers**. The addition of phosphorus that is normally in limited supply allows for maximal plant growth.

Normally, because phosphorus availability is limited in the phosphorus cycle, plant growth in lakes is also limited. A major problem with the use of phosphorus in fertilizers is the process of artificial **eutrophication**. Eutrophication is a large increase in the primary productivity of a **lake**. Eutrophication can be harmful to the natural balance of a lake and result in massive death of **fish** and other animals as dissolved oxygen levels are depleted from the water. As the growth of algae and aquatic plants goes unchecked, the lake slowly stagnates, becoming fouled. Artificial eutrophication can occur when run-off rain water from agricultural fertilizers that are used in excess reaches lakes. Another human cause of artificial eutrophication is run-off from mines. **Mining** in areas where rock is rich in phosphorus minerals can create dust that is blown by wind into nearby water systems. Similarly, rainwater can wash from mining areas to nearby lakes. A third cause of artificial eutrophication is the introduction of phosphorus into phosphorus-limited lakes by man-made laundry detergents. Many detergents in the past contained phosphorus. Effluent from households eventually made its way to lakes where massive plant overgrowth occurred, spoiling the natural balance present. Today, considerable progress has been made in producing phosphate-free detergents, which do not cause artificial eutrophication and preserve the normal cycling of phosphorus.

Further Reading

Cunningham, W.P. *Understanding Our Environment: An Introduction.* W.C.Brown, 1994.

Ricklefs, R.E. *The Economy of Nature, 3rd Ed.*W.H.Freeman. 1993.

Walker, D. *Energy, Plants, and Man.* University Science Books, 1992.

Terry Watkins

Phosphorus removal

Phosphorus (usually in the form of phosphate) is a normal part of the environment. It occurs in the form

of phosphate-containing **rocks** and as the excretory and decay products of plants and animals. Human contributions to the **phosphorus cycle** result primarily from the use of phosphorus-containing detergents and **fertilizers**.

The increased load of phosphorus in the environment as a result of human activities has been a **matter** of concern for more than four decades. The primary issue has been to what extent additional phosphorus has contributed to the **eutrophication** of lakes, ponds, and other bodies of **water**. Scientists have long recognized that increasing levels of phosphorus are associated with eutrophication. But the evidence for a direct cause and effect relationship is not entirely clear. Eutrophication is a complex process involving **nitrogen** and **carbon** as well as phosphorus. The role of each nutrient and the interaction among them is still not entirely clear.

In any case, environmental engineers have long explored methods for the removal of phosphorus from wastewater in order to reduce possible eutrophication effects. Primary and secondary treatment techniques are relatively inefficient in removing phosphorus with only about 10% extracted from raw wastewater in each step. Thus, special procedures during the tertiary treatment stage are needed to remove the remaining phosphorus.

Two methods are generally available: biological and chemical. **Bacteria** formed in the activated sludge produced during secondary treatment have an unusually high tendency to adsorb phosphorus. If these bacteria are used in a tertiary treatment stage, they are very efficient in removing phosphorus from wastewater. The sludge produced by this bacterial action is rich in phosphorus and can be separated from the wastewater leaving water with a **concentration** of phosphorus only about 5% of its original level.

The more popular method of phosphorus removal is chemical. A compound is selected that will react with phosphate in wastewater, forming an insoluble product that can then be filtered off. The two most common substances used for this process are alum, **aluminum** sulfate and lime, or **calcium** hydroxide. An alum treatment works in two different ways. Some aluminum sulfate reacts directly with phosphate in the wastewater to form insoluble aluminum phosphate. At the same time, the aluminum ion hydrolyzes in water to form a thick, gelatinous precipitate of **aluminum hydroxide** that carries phosphate with it as it settles out of solution.

The addition of lime to wastewater results in the formation of another insoluble product, calcium hydroxyapatite, which also settles out of solution.

By determining the concentration of phosphorus in wastewater, these chemical treatments can be used very precisely. Exactly enough alum or lime can be added to precipitate out the phosphate in the water. Such treatments are normally effective in removing about 95% of all phosphorus originally present in a **sample** of wastewater.

See also Waste management; Water pollution.

Further Reading

Phosphorus Management Strategies Task Force. *Phosphorus Management for the Great Lakes*. Windsor, Ont.: International Joint Commission, 1980.

Retrofitting POTWs for Phosphorus Removal in the Chesapeake Bay Drainage Basin: A Handbook. Cincinnati, Ohio: U. S. Environmental Protection Agency, 1987.

Symposium on the Economy and Chemistry of Phosphorus. *Phosphorus in the Environment: Its Chemistry and Biochemistry*. New York: Elsevier, 1978.

David E. Newton

Photic zone

The photic zone, also called the euphotic or limnetic zone, is the **volume** of **water** where the rate of **photosynthesis** is greater than the rate of **respiration** by **phytoplankton**. Phytoplankton are microscopic plants living suspended in the water column that have little or no means of motility. They are primary producers that use solar **energy** as a food source. The compensation point, where photosynthesis equals respiration, defines the lower limit of the photic zone. Above this point, the phytoplankton population grows rapidly because there is abundant sunlight to support fast rates of photosynthesis. Below the compensation point, the intensity of sunlight is too low and the rate of respiration is faster than the rate of photosynthesis, and therefore the phytoplankton cannot survive. The photic zones of the world's lakes and oceans are critically important because the phytoplankton, the primary producers upon which the rest of the food web depends, are concentrated in these zones.

Other layers in oceans and lakes

Below the photic zone, in both oceans and lakes, is the profundal zone. In the profundal zone there is still some light, but not enough to support photosynthesis. In oceans, the even deeper volume is called the abyssal zone. This volume has virtually no sunlight, and is usually deeper than 6,562 ft (2,000 m). The deepest layer of the **ocean**, below 19,686 ft (6,000 m), is called the hadal zone. All of these zones receive a constant rain of organic debris and

wastes from the photic zone which serves as a food source for the organisms living in the deeper volumes.

All of these are open-water zones, as compared with the shallow areas near the edges of oceans and lakes, called the coastal and littoral zones, respectively. Most of these smaller, shallow areas receive sufficient sunlight to allow **plant** productivity to occur right down to the **lake** or ocean bottom.

The importance of nutrients and light in photic zone

Primary production in the photic zone is influenced by three major factors—**nutrients** and **light**, which are essential for photosynthesis, and grazing pressure, which is the rate at which the plants are eaten by herbivores. Nutrients, especially phosphate and nitrate, are often scarce in the photic zone because they are used up quickly by plants during photosynthesis. External inputs of nutrients are received through rainfall, riverflow, the **weathering** of **rocks** and **soil** and from human activities, such as sewage dumping. Nutrient enrichments also occur through internal physical processes such as mixing and **upwelling** that resuspend nutrients from deeper volumes of the water.

As plants in the photic zone grow and reproduce, they are consumed by herbivores, which excrete their wastes into the water column. These wastes and other organic particles then rain down into the lower volumes and eventually settle into the sediment. During periods of resuspension, such as remixing and upwelling, some of these nutrient-rich wastes are brought back up to the photic zone. Remixing refers to processes whereby the water of a lake is thoroughly mixed from top to bottom, usually by the **force** of **wind**.

Upwellings can sometimes occur in cool lakes with warm underground springs, but they are much more important in oceans. An upwelling is an area in the ocean where the deeper, nutrient-rich waters are brought to the surface. Oceanic upwellings can be caused when the wind tends to blow in a consistent direction across the surface of the ocean. This causes the water to pile up at the lee end of the wind's reach and, through the sheer weight of the accumulation, pushes down on the deeper volumes of water at the thick end. This pushing causes the deeper, nutrient-rich water to rise to the surface back at the region where the winds began.

Upwellings can also be caused by deep ocean currents that are driven upwards because of differences in water temperatures. Such upwellings tend to be very extensive. Upwellings can also occur on a short-term basis when underwater uplands and sea mounts force deep currents to the surface. Regardless of the origin of the resuspension event, these cooler, nutrient-rich waters stimulate the productivity of phytoplankton in the photic zone. Photic zones that are replenished with nutrients by either upwellings and or remixing events tend have very high primary production.

Light is essential to photosynthesis. The depth to which light penetrates a water column can vary substantially in space and time. The depth of the photic zone can vary from a few centimeters to several hundred meters. Sunlight is scattered and absorbed by particles and dissolved organic **matter** in the water column, and its intensity in water decreases with depth. In some cases, when nutrient concentrations are high, the photic zone becomes shallower. This is because the nutrients stimulate the growth of phytoplankton, and these cells then absorb more of the sunlight entering the water column and shade the layers below. Other areas may have very deep photic zones because the nutrient **concentration** is very small and therefore, the growth of primary producers is limited.

The ideal convergence of sufficient nutrients and sunlight occurs in relatively few areas of our oceans and lakes. These areas are, however, extremely productive. For example, areas off the coasts of Peru, northern Chile, eastern Canada, and **Antarctica** are responsible for much of the **fish** production of the world.

Research in the photic zone

Research in the photic zone is focused on three main priorities: **eutrophication** of water bodies, fundamental food web research, and the understanding of nutrient movement and cycling. Eutrophication is the enrichment of water bodies through the addition of nutrients, often leading to excessive phytoplankton growth. Eutrophication is a well understood process, but it remains as a serious problem in much of the world.

Another important area is research into basic food webs. Many things are still to be discovered regarding the relative roles of species within aquatic food webs. The recent closure of the fisheries off eastern Canada exemplifies the importance of basic understanding of food webs in these productive photic zones.

A third area of research within the photic zone involves nutrient movements and cycling within water bodies. Especially in oceans the movements of particles and nutrients by water currents are not well understood. We are just beginning to understand the connections among wind, ocean currents, and global **weather** patterns. All life ultimately depends on the continued productivity of the photic zones of the world, and we need to work harder to understand the physical, chemical, and biological nature of these zones.

KEY TERMS

Abyssal Zone—Volume of water near the bottom of the ocean where there is no sunlight, usually below 6,562 ft (2,000 m).

Compensation Point—The point at which the rate of photosynthesis just equals the rate of respiration by phytoplankton. This is the lower limit of the photic zone.

Eutrophication—The enrichment of natural water bodies through the addition of nutrients, usually phosphate and/or nitrate, leading to an excessive growth of phytoplankton.

Hadal zone—The deepest layer of the ocean, below 19,686 ft (6,000 m).

Photosynthesis—The process of converting water and carbon dioxide into carbohydrates (sugars), using solar energy as an energy source. Oxygen is released during this process.

Phytoplankton—Microscopic plants having no or little ability to move themselves, and therefore are subject to dispersal by water movement.

Primary Production—The production of organic matter (biomass) by green plants through photosynthesis.

Profundal Zone—Zone below the photic zone where there is some light but not enough to support photosynthesis.

See also Ocean zones.

Further Reading

Barnes, R. S. K., and K. H. Mann, eds. *Fundamentals of Aquatic Ecology.* 2nd ed. Cambridge, MA: Blackwell Scientific Publications, 1991.

Begon, M., J. L. Harper, and C. R. Townsend. *Ecology: Individuals, Populations and Communities.* 2nd ed. Cambridge, MA: Blackwell Scientific Publications, 1990.

Cousteau, Jacques-Yves. *The Ocean World of Jacques Cousteau: Window in the Sea.* World Publishing Company, 1973.

Culliney, J. L. "The Fluid Forests." In *The Forests of the Sea: Life and Death on the Continental Shelf.* San Francisco, CA: Sierra Club Books, 1976.

Miller, G. Tyler, Jr. *Environmental Science: Sustaining the Earth.* 3rd ed. Belmont, CA: Wadsworth Publishing, 1986.

Jennifer LeBlanc

Photochemistry

Photochemistry is the study of light-induced chemical reactions and physical processes. A photochemical event involves the absorption of light to create an excited species that may subsequently undergo a number of different reactions. These include unimolecular reactions such as **dissociation**, ionization, and isomerization; bimolecular reactions, which involve a reaction with a second **molecule** or atom to form a new compound; and reactions producing an **emission** of light, or **luminescence**. A photochemical reaction differs notably from a thermally, or **heat**, induced reaction in that the rate of a photochemical reaction is frequently greatly accelerated, and the products of the photochemical reaction may be impossible to produce otherwise. With the advent of lasers, which are powerful, single-color light sources, the field of photochemistry has advanced tremendously over the past few decades. An increased understanding of photochemistry has great implications outside of the laboratory, as photochemical reactions are an extremely important aspect of everyday life, underlying the processes of **vision**, **photosynthesis**, **photography**, atmospheric **chemistry**, the production of **smog**, and the destruction of the **ozone** layer.

The absorption of light by **atoms** and molecules to create an excited species is studied in the field of **spectroscopy**. The study of the reactions of this excited species is the **domain** of photochemistry. However, the fields are closely related; spectroscopy is routinely used by photochemists as a tool for identifying reaction pathways and products and, recently, for following reactions as they occur in real time. Some lasers can produce a pulse of light that is only "on" for 1 femtosecond (10^{-15} seconds). A femtosecond **laser** can be used like an extremely high-speed strobe camera to spectroscopically "photograph" a photochemical reaction.

The basic laws of photochemistry

In the early 1800s Christian von Grotthus (1785-1822) and John Draper (1811-1882) formulated the first law of photochemistry, which states that only light that is absorbed by a molecule can produce a photochemical change in that molecule. This law relates photochemical activity to the fact that each chemical substance absorbs only certain wavelengths of light, the set of which is unique to that substance. Therefore, the presence of light alone is not sufficient to induce a photochemical reaction; the light must also be of the correct wavelength to be absorbed by the reactant species.

In the early 1900s the development of the quantum theory of light—that light is absorbed in discrete packets of **energy** called photons—led to the extension of the

laws of photochemistry. The second law of photochemistry, developed by Johannes Stark (1874-1957) and Albert Einstein (1879-1955), states that only one quantum, or one **photon**, of light is absorbed by each molecule undergoing a photochemical reaction. In other words, there is a **one-to-one correspondence** between the number of absorbed photons and the number of excited species. The ability to accurately determine the number of photons leading to a reaction enables the efficiency, or quantum yield, of the reaction to be calculated.

Photochemistry induced by visible and ultraviolet light

Light that can break molecular bonds is most effective at inducing photochemical reactions. The energy required to break a molecular bond ranges from approximately 150 kiloJoules per **mole** to nearly 1000 kJ/mol, depending on the bond. The bond dissociation energies for some diatomic and polyatomic molecules are listed in Table I. Visible light, having wavelengths ranging from 400-700 nanometers, corresponds to energies ranging from approximately 300-170 kJ/mol, respectively. Note that this is enough energy to dissociate relatively weak bonds such as the single **oxygen** (O-O) bond in **hydrogen** peroxide (HO-OH), which is why **hydrogen peroxide** must be stored in a light-proof bottle.

Ultraviolet light, having wavelengths ranging from 200-400 nm, corresponds to higher energies ranging from approximately 600-300 kJ/mol, respectively. Ultraviolet light can dissociate relatively strong bonds such as the double oxygen (O=O) bond in molecular oxygen (O_2) and the double C=O bond in **carbon** dioxide (CO_2); ultraviolet light can also remove **chlorine** atoms from compounds such as chloromethane (CH_3Cl). The ability of ultraviolet light to dissociate these molecules is an important aspect of the stability—and destruction—of ozone molecules in the upper atmosphere.

Reaction pathways

A photochemical process may be considered to consist of two steps: the absorption of a photon, followed by reaction. If the absorption of a photon causes an **electron** within an atom or molecule to increase its energy, the species is said to be electronically excited. The absorption and reaction steps for a molecule AB may be written as: $AB + h\nu \rightarrow AB^*$ $AB^* \rightarrow$ products where $h\nu$ represents the energy of a photon of **frequency** ν and the asterisk indicates that the species has become electronically excited. The excited species, AB^*, has the additional energy of the absorbed photon and will react in order to reduce its energy. Although the excited species generally does not live long, it is sometimes formally indicated when writing photochemical reactions to stress that the reactant is an electronically excited species. The possible reactions that an electronically excited species may undergo are illustrated below. Note: the symbols * and † denote different levels of electronic excitation.

$$AB + hv \rightarrow AB^*$$

Absorption of a photon (electronic excitation)

Followed by:

i)	$AB^* \rightarrow A + B$	Dissociation
ii)	$AB^* \rightarrow AB^+ + e^-$	Ionization
iii)	$AB^* \rightarrow BA$	Isomerization
iv)	$AB^* + C \rightarrow AC + B$ or ABC	Reaction
v)	$AB^* + DE \rightarrow AB + DE^*$	Energy Transfer (intermolecular)
vi)	$AB^* + M \rightarrow AB + M$	Physical Quenching
vii)	$AB^* \rightarrow AB^\dagger$	Energy Transfer (intramolecular)
viii)	$AB^* \rightarrow AB + h\upsilon$	Luminsecence

Dissociation

The energy of an absorbed photon may be sufficient to break molecular bonds (path i), creating two or more atomic or molecular fragments. An important example of photodissociation is found in the photochemistry of stratospheric ozone. Ozone (O_3) is produced in the stratosphere from molecular oxygen (O_2) through the following pair of reactions: $O_2 + h\nu \rightarrow O + O$ and $O + O_2 \rightarrow O_3$ where hn represents the energy of a photon of ultraviolet light with a wavelength less than 260 nm. Ozone is also dissociated by short-wavelength ultraviolet light (200-300 nm) through the reaction: $O_3 + h\nu \rightarrow O_2 + O$. The oxygen atom formed from this reaction may recombine with molecular oxygen to regenerate ozone, thereby completing the ozone cycle. The great importance of stratospheric ozone is that it absorbs harmful short-wavelength ultraviolet light before it reaches the Earth's surface, thus serving as a protective shield.

In recent years, the effect of chlorofluorocarbons, commonly known as Freons or CFCs, on the ozone cycle has become of great concern. CFCs rise into the stratosphere where they are dissociated by ultraviolet light, producing chlorine atoms (Cl) through the reaction: CFC + $h\nu \rightarrow$ Cl + CFC(minus one Cl). These chlorine atoms react with ozone to produce ClO and molecular oxygen: $Cl + O_3 \rightarrow ClO + O_2$. ClO reacts with the oxygen atoms produced from the photodissociation of ozone in reaction 5 to produce molecular oxygen and a chlorine atom: $ClO + O \rightarrow O_2 + Cl$. Therefore, the presence of CFCs in-

terrupts the natural ozone cycle by consuming the oxygen atoms that should combine with molecular oxygen to regenerate ozone. The net result is that ozone is removed from the stratosphere while the chlorine atoms are regenerated in a catalytic process to continue the destructive cycle.

Ionization

The separation of an electron from an atom or molecule, leaving a positively charged ion, is a special form of dissociation called ionization. Ionization following absorption of a photon (path ii) usually occurs with light of very short wavelengths (less than 100 nm) and therefore is usually not studied by photochemists, although it is of great importance in x-ray technology. X **rays** are also sometimes referred to as **ionizing radiation**.

Isomerization

An excited molecule may undergo a rearrangement of its bonds, forming a new molecule made up of the same atoms but connected in a different manner; this process is called isomerization (path iii). The first step in the vision process involves the light-induced isomerization of pigments in the retina that subsequently undergo a number of thermally and enzymatically driven reactions before ultimately producing a neural signal.

Reaction

An electronically excited species may react with a second species to produce a new product, or set of products (path iv). For example, the products of the ultraviolet dissociation of ozone (reaction 5) are themselves electronically excited: $O_3 + h\nu \rightarrow O_2^* + O^*$. These excited fragments may react with other atmospheric molecules such as **water**: $O^* + H_2O \rightarrow OH + OH$. Or they may react with ozone: $O_2^* + O_3 \rightarrow 2O_2 + O$. These reactions do not readily occur for the corresponding non-excited species, confirming the importance of electronic excitation in determining reactivity.

Energy transfer

In some cases the excited species may simply transfer its excess energy to a second species. This process is called intermolecular **energy transfer** (path v). Photosynthesis relies on intermolecular energy transfer to redistribute the light energy gathered by **chlorophyll** to a reaction center where the carbohydrates that nourish the **plant** are produced. Physical quenching (path vi) is a special case of intermolecular energy transfer in which the chemical **behavior** of the species to which the energy is transferred does not change. An example of a physical quencher is the walls of a container in which a reaction is confined. If the energy transfer occurs within the same molecule, for example, and if the excess electron energy is transferred into internal **motion** of the molecule, such as vibration, it is called intramolecular energy transfer (path vii).

Luminescence

Although it is not strictly a photochemical reaction, another pathway by which the excited species may reduce its energy is by emitting a photon of light. This process is called luminescence (path viii). Luminescence includes the processes of **fluorescence** (prompt emission of a photon) and phosphorescence (delayed emission of a photon). Optical brighteners in laundry detergents contain substances that absorb light of one wavelength, usually in the ultraviolet range, but emit light at a longer wavelength, usually in the visible range—thereby appearing to reflect extra visible light and making clothing appear whiter. This process is called fluorescence and only occurs while the substance is being illuminated. The related process, phosphorescence, persists after the excitation source has been removed and is used in "glow-in-the-dark" items.

See also Photosynthesis

KEY TERMS

Absorption—The acquisition of energy from a photon of light by an atomic or molecular species, often causing electronic excitation.

Electronic excitation—The state of an atom or molecule in which an electron has been given additional energy.

Emission—The generation of a photon of light from an electronically excited atomic or molecular species in order to reduce its total energy.

Photodissociation—The breaking of one or more molecular bonds resulting from the absorption of light energy.

Photon—A quantum, or discrete packet, of light energy.

Quantum yield—In a photochemical reaction, the number of product species divided by the number of photons that were absorbed by the reactant.

Wavelength—The distance between adjacent peaks or troughs on a wave. The wavelength of light is one way of specifying the "color," even for light that lies outside of the visible region.

Further Reading

Chang, Raymond. *Chemistry, Fourth Edition*. New York: McGraw-Hill, Inc., 1991.

Toon, Owen B. and Richard P. Turco. "Polar Stratospheric Clouds and Ozone Depletion." *Scientific American*. no. 264 (1991): pp. 68-74.

Wayne, Richard. *Principles and Applications of Photochemistry*. Oxford: Oxford Science Publications, 1988.

Williamson, Samuel J. and Herman Z. Cummins. *Light and Color in Nature and Art*. New York: John Wiley and Sons, 1983.

Zewail, Ahmed. "The Birth of Molecules." *Scientific American*. no. 263 (1990): pp. 76-82.

Karen Trentelman

Photocopying

Photocopying is the process by which light is used to make copies of book pages and other **paper** documents. Today the most widely used form of photocopying is xerography ("dry writing"), invented by New York patent attorney Chester Carlson in the 1930s. Indeed, the name of the company founded to develop Carlson's invention, Xerox Corporation, has become synonymous with the process of photocopying. However, a number of other forms of photocopying pre-dated the Carlson invention and are still used for special applications. Among these other forms of photocopying are thermography, diazo processes, and electrostatic copying.

Xerography

Many different models of xerographic copying machines are available today, but they all operate on some common principles. The core of such machines is a photoconducting surface to which is added a **negative** charge of about 600 volts. The surface could be a selenium-coated drum or an endless moving belt mounted on **rollers**, for example. The charged placed on the photoconducting surface is usually obtained from a corona bar, a thin wire that runs just above the surface of the photoconducting surface. When the wire is charged negatively, a strong electrical field is produced which causes ionization of air molecules in the vicinity of the wire. The negative ions thus produced are repelled by the negatively charged wire and attach themselves to the photoconducting surface.

In another part of the machine, the original document to be copied is exposed to light. The light reflected off that document is then reflected off a series of **mirrors** until it reaches the negatively-charged photoconducting surface. When light strikes the photoconducting surface, it erases the negative charges there.

Notice the way the image on the original document is transferred to the photoconducting surface. Dark regions on the original document (such as printed letters) do not reflect any light to the photoconducting surface. Therefore, those portions of the photoconducting surface retain their negative charge. Light regions on the original document (such as blank spaces) do reflect light to the photoconducting surface, causing the loss of negative charge in these regions. A letter "a" on the original document becomes an a-shaped region of negative electrical charge on the photoconducting surface. Similarly, areas of gray in the original document are also matched on the photoconducting surface because greater or lesser amounts of light are reflected off the document, causing greater or lesser loss of negative charge on the photoconducting surface.

Addition of toner and fusing

The next step in copying involves the addition of a toner to the photoconducting surface. A toner is a positively charged material that is added to the photoconducting surface. Since it carries an electrical charge opposite that of the negatively-charged photoconducting surface, the toner sticks to the surface. The photoconducting surface now carries toner on its surface that matches regions of negative electrical charge which, in turn, matches dark regions on the original document, such as the "a" mentioned above.

Finally, paper carrying a negative electrical charge is brought into contact with the photoconducting surface. The negative charge on the paper is made great enough to pull the positively-charge toner away from the photoconducting surface and onto itself. The letter "a" formed by toner on the photoconducting surface, for example, has now been transferred to the paper. The paper passes through a pair of rollers that fuses (squeezes) the toner into the paper, forming a positive image that exactly corresponds to the image on the original document.

As the final copy is delivered to a tray outside the machine, the photoconducting surface continues on its way. Any remaining electrical charge is removed and the surface is cleaned. It then passes on to the charger, where the whole cycle is ready to be repeated.

Many kinds of toners have been developed for use in this process. As an example, one kind of toner consists of a thermoplastic resin (one that melts when it is heated) mixed with finely divided **carbon**. When the copy paper is passed through the rollers at the end of the copying process, the resin melts and then forms a permanent mixture with the carbon when it re-cools. Another kind of

toner consists of finely divided carbon suspended in a petroleum-like liquid. The toner is sprayed on the photoconducting surface and, when the liquid evaporates, the carbon is left behind.

Color copying

The general principle in color copying is the same as it is for black-and-white copying. The main difference is that the light reflected off the original document must be passed through three filters - one green, one blue, and one red - before it is transmitted to the photoconducting surface. Then, toner particles of three distinct colors - yellow, magenta, and cyan - must be available to correspond to each of the three document colors. The toners are added separately in three separate and sequential operations. These operations must be overlaid very carefully (kept "in register") so that the three images correspond with each other exactly to give a copy that faithfully corresponds to the original document.

Electrostatic copying

A process somewhat similar to that used in xerography is electrostatic copying. The major difference between these two processes is that in electrostatic copying, the endless photoconducting surface is omitted from the machine and the copy paper is specially treated to pick up the toner.

The paper used in electrostatic copying is treated with a material consisting of zinc oxide combined with a thermoplastic resin. When that paper is fed into the copy machine, it is first passed through a corona charging bar, similar to the one used in xerography. Within the charging bar, the zinc oxide coating picks up a negative electrical charge.

In the next section of the copy machine, the original document is exposed to light, which reflects off the white portions of the document (as in a xerographic machine). Dark portions of the document, such as the letter "a" in the document, do not reflect light. Light reflected off the original document is then reflected by a series of mirrors to the treated copy paper which has been passed into this section of the machine. Light striking the copy paper removes negative charges placed by the charged bar, leaving charged sections that correspond to the absence of light, that is, the dark places on the original document. In this respect, the copying process is exactly like that which occurs in xerography.

Next, the exposed copy paper is passed through a toner bath, where positively-charged toner attaches itself to negatively-charged areas on the copy paper. When the paper is passed through a pair of rollers, the toner is pressed into the copy paper, forming a permanent positive image that corresponds to the image on the original document.

The electrostatic copy process became less popular when xerographic processes were improved. The main drawback of the electrostatic process was the special paper that was needed, a kind of paper that felt different from ordinary paper and was more expensive to produce and to mail.

Thermography

Thermography ("heat writing") is a method of copying that is based on the fact that dark regions of a document absorb **heat** more readily than do light spaces. If heat is applied to this page, for example, it will be absorbed more readily by the letters on the page than by the white spaces between the letters. As with electrostatic copying, themographic copying requires the use of specially treated paper. The paper used in thermography is coated with ferric [iron(III)] compounds in an acidic environment. When the paper is exposed to heat, a chemical reaction occurs that produces a dark image.

In use, a thermographic copy machine requires that the original document and the copy paper be placed into the machine in contact with each other. Some machines also use a "transfer sheet" placed in contact with the copy paper on the opposite side of the original document. A beam of infrared light is then shined through the document-copy paper (or document-copy paper-transfer sheet) combination. The infrared light heats dark spaces on the original document more strongly than light spaces. These heated areas - the places where text occurs on the document, for example - then cause darkening on the copy paper, producing a positive image copy of the original document.

Diazo copying

Diazo copying gets its name from the fact that it makes use of copy paper that has been treated with a type of chemical known as diazonium compounds. As with the thermographic process described above, diazonium compounds change color when exposed to heat. In diazo copying, the original document and the diazo-treated copy paper are placed in contact with each other in a light box and then exposed to a strong source of ultraviolet light. Dark regions on the original document become warm, causing corresponding areas on the diazo paper to darken. The color in these regions is brought about by exposing the copy paper to a developing agent such as **ammonia** gas. Blue-printing and brown-printing are specialized kinds of diazo copying.

Further Reading

Mort, J. *The Anatomy of Xerography: Its Invention and Evolution.* Jefferson, NC: McFarland, 1989.

"Photocopier" and "Xerography" in *Illustrated Encyclopedia of Science and Technology.* Westport, CT: H. S. Stuttman, 1982.

"Photocopying Processes," in *McGraw-Hill Encyclopedia of Science & Technology.* 7th edition. New York: McGraw-Hill Book Company, 1992.

The Way Things Work. New York: Simon and Schuster, 1967.

"Xerography" in ed., *The Encyclopedia of How It's Made.* Donald Clarke, ed. New York: A&W Publishers, Inc., 1978.

David E. Newton

KEY TERMS

Copy paper—Plain or treated paper on which the image of an original document is produced in a copy machine.

Corona bar—A device used to add an electrical charge to a surface, given that name because a pale blue light (a "corona") often surrounds the device.

Diazo copying—A copying process that makes use of changes in certain chemical compounds (diazonium compounds) when heat is added to them.

Electrostatic copying—A copying process similar to xerography, but somewhat simpler in its procedure and requiring a specially-treated copy paper.

Photoconducting surface—Any kind of surface on which a copy of a document can be made using light as the copying medium.

Thermography—A type of photocopying in which portions of specially treated copy paper darken as a result of being exposed to heat.

Toner—A material that carries an electrical charge opposite to that of a photoconducting surface that is added to that surface in a copy machine.

Xerography—A type of photocopying that makes use of an endless photocopying surface to record light and dark areas in an original document as charged or uncharged areas on a photoconducting surface.

Photoelectric cell

During the latter half of the nineteenth century many scientists and engineers were simultaneously observing a strange phenomenon: electrical devices constructed from certain metals seemed to conduct **electricity** more efficiently in the daytime than at night. This phenomenon, called the **photoelectric effect**, had been noted years earlier by the French physicist A. E. Becquerel (1820-1891), who had invented a very primitive device for measuring the intensity of light by measuring the elecrical current produced by photochemical reactions. It was becoming evident that one **metal** in particular—selenium—was far more reactive when exposed to light than any other substance. Using selenium as a base, several scientists set out to develop a practical device for measuring light intensity.

A number of them succeeded. In 1883 the American inventor Charles Fritts created a working photoelectric cell; that same year a German engineer, Paul Nipkow, used a photoelectric cell in his "Nipkow's disk"—a device which could take a picture by measuring the lighter and darker areas on an object and translate them into electrical impulses. The precursor to the modern photoelectric cell was invented by the German physicists Hans Geitel (1855-1923) and Julius Elster(1859-1920) by modifying a cathode-ray tube.

Strangely, the explanation for why selenium and other metals produced electrical current did not come until 1902, when Phillip Lenard showed that **radiation** within the visible **spectrum** caused these metals to release electrons. This was not particularly surprising, since it had been known that both longer **radio** waves and shorter x rays affected electrons. In 1905 Albert Einstein (1879-1955) applied the quantum theory to show that the current produced in photoelectric cells depended upon the intensity of light, not the wavelength; this proved the cell to be an ideal tool for measuring light.

The affordable Elster-Geitel photoelectric cell made it possible for many industries to develop photoelectrical technology. Probably the most important was the invention of transmittable pictures, or **television**. Employing a concept similar to that used in Nipkow's scanning disk, a television camera translates the light and dark areas within its view (and, later, the colors within) into a signal that can be sent and decoded into a picture.

Another interesting application of photoelectric cells was the invention of **motion** pictures. As a film is being shot, the sound is picked up by a microphone and converted into electrical impulses. These impulses are used to drive a lamp or neon light tube that causes a flash, and this flash is recorded on the side of the film as a sound track. Later, when the film is played back, a pho-

toelectric cell is used to measure the changes in intensity within the soundtrack and turn them back into electrical impulses that, when sent through a speaker, become sound. This method replaced the old practice of playing a gramophone recording of the actors' voices along with the film, which was very difficult to time to the action on the screen. Stored on the same film, a soundtrack is always perfectly synchronized with the action.

The photoelectric cell has since proven useful in many different applications. In factories items on a conveyor belt pass between a beam of light and a photoelectric cell; when each item passes it interrupts the beam and is recorded by a computer, so that the exact number of items leaving a factory can be known simply by adding up these interruptions. Small light meters are installed in streetlights to turn them on automatically when darkness falls, while more precise light meters are used daily by professional photographers. Alarm systems have been designed using photoelectric cells that are sensitive to ultraviolet light and are activated when movement passes a path of invisible light. Cousin to the photoelectric cell is the **photovoltaic cell** which, when exposed to light, can store electricity. Photovoltaic cells form the basis for solar batteries and other solar-powered machines.

Photoelectric effect

The process in which visible light, x rays or gamma rays incident on **matter** cause an **electron** to be ejected. The ejected electron is called a photoelectron.

History

The photoelectric effect was discovered by Heinrich Hertz in 1897 while performing experiments that led to the discovery of electromagnetic waves. Since this was just about the time that the electron itself was first identified the phenomenon was not really understood. It soon became clear in the next few years that the particles emitted in the photoelectric effect were indeed electrons. The number of electrons emitted depended on the intensity of the light but the **energy** of the photoelectrons did not. No matter how weak the light source was made the maximum kinetic energy of these electrons stayed the same. The energy however was found to be directly proportional to the **frequency** of the light. The other perplexing fact was that the photoelectrons seemed to be emitted instantaneously when the light was turned on. These facts were impossible to explain with the then current wave theory of light. If the light were bright enough it seemed reasonable, given enough time, that an electron in an atom might acquire enough energy to escape regardless of the frequency. The answer was finally provided in 1905 by Albert Einstein who suggested that light, at least sometimes, should be considered to be composed of small bundles of energy or particles called photons. This approach had been used a few years earlier by Max Planck in his successful explanation of black body **radiation**. In 1907 Einstein was awarded the Nobel Prize in **physics** for his explanation of the photoelectric effect.

The Einstein photoelectric theory

Einstein's explanation of the photoelectric effect was very simple. He assumed that the kinetic energy of the ejected electron was equal to the energy of the incident **photon** minus the energy required to remove the electron from the material, which is called the work function. Thus the photon hits a surface, gives nearly all its energy to an electron and the electron is ejected with that energy less whatever energy is required to get it out of the atom and away from the surface. The energy of a photon is given by $E = hg = hc/l$ where g is the frequency of the photon, l is the wavelength, and c is the **velocity** of light. This applies not only to light but also to **x rays** and gamma rays. Thus the shorter the wavelength the more energetic the photon.

Many of the properties of light such as **interference** and **diffraction** can be explained most naturally by a wave theory while others, like the photoelectric effect, can only be explained by a particle theory. This peculiar fact is often referred to as wave-particle duality and can only be understood using quantum theory which must be used to explain what happens on an atomic scale and which provides a unified description of both processes.

Applications

The photoelectric effect has many practical applications which include the photocell, photoconductive devices and solar cells. A photocell is usually a **vacuum** tube with two electrodes. One is a photosensitive **cathode** which emits electrons when exposed to light and the other is an **anode** which is maintained at a positive voltage with respect to the cathode. Thus when light shines on the cathode, electrons are attracted to the anode and an electron current flows in the tube from cathode to anode. The current can be used to operate a relay which might turn a motor on to open a door or ring a bell in an alarm system. The system can be made to be responsive to light, as described above, or sensitive to the removal of light as when a beam of light incident on the cathode is interrupted, causing the current to stop. Photocells are also useful as exposure meters for cameras in which case

KEY TERMS

Photocell—A vacuum tube in which electric current will flow when light strikes the photosensitive cathode.

Photoconductivity—The substantial increase in conductivity acquired by certain materials when exposed to light.

Photoelectric effect—The ejection of an electron from a material substance by electromagnetic radiation incident on that substance.

Photoelectron—Name given the electron ejected in the photoelectric effect.

Solar cell—A device constructed from specially prepared silicon which acquires a potential difference across its terminals when exposed to light.

Work function—The amount of energy required to just remove a photoelectron from a surface. This is different for different materials.

the current in the tube would be measured directly on a sensitive meter.

Closely related to the photoelectric effect is the photoconductive effect which is the increase in **electrical conductivity** of certain non metallic materials such as cadmium sulfide when exposed to light. This effect can be quite large so that a very small current in a device suddenly becomes quite large when exposed to light. Thus photoconductive devices have many of the same uses as photocells.

Solar cells, usually made from specially prepared silicon, act like a **battery** when exposed to light. Individual solar cells produce voltages of about 0.6 volts but higher voltages and large currents can be obtained by appropriately connecting many solar cells together. **Electricity** from solar cells is still quite expensive but they are very useful for providing small amounts of electricity in remote locations where other sources are not available. It is likely however that as the cost of producing solar cells is reduced they will begin to be used to produce large amounts of electricity for commercial use.

Further Reading

Chalmers, Bruce. "The Photovoltaic Generation of Electricity." *Scientific American*. Oct. 1976, Vol. 235, No. 4 pp. 34-43.

Richtmyer, Kennard and Cooper. *Introduction to Modern Physics*. 6th Ed. McGraw Hill, pp. 150-160.

Stone, Jack L. "Photovoltaics: Unlimited Electrical Energy From the Sun." *Physics Today*. Sept., 1993, pp. 22-29.

Zweibel, Ken. "Thin-Film Photovoltaic Cells." *American Scientist*. Vol. 81, No. 4, July-August, 1993.

Robert Stearns

Photography

Photography is the art and science of creating images using light. For most of its history, this has usually meant using silver compounds that darken when exposed to light. With the growth of computers, photography can also be done with **electronics** that measure light intensities and create images based on them.

The invention and perfection of photography has affected many areas of life. Of course, nearly every family now has albums full of snapshots, portraits, and wedding photographs. But photography is also an **integral** part of the modern printing, publishing, and advertising industries, and is used extensively for scientific purposes. Motion pictures consist of a series of photographs, taken at the rate of 24 per second.

The origins of photography

Photography has been called the art of fixing a shadow. The ancient Greeks knew that a clear (though upside down) image of the outside world will be projected if one makes a tiny hole in the wall of a dark room. But no one knew how to make this image permanent. Called a camera obscura, such rooms were chiefly used as aids to drawing, and understanding perspective. After the Renaissance, when perspective became important, camera obscuras become smaller and more sophisticated. By the late 18th century, devices had been created that used a series of telescoping boxes and a **lens** to focus an image. Some even used a mirror to reflect the image upwards onto a piece of **glass**, making tracing images easier. Gentlemen brought small, portable camera obscuras with them when they traveled, tracing the images onto a piece of **paper** as a way to record their journeys. In today's terms, by 1800 the camera had long since been invented, but no one had created film for it.

Many people were thinking about this problem, however. Some chemists had noticed that sunlight cased certain mixtures of silver nitrates to darken. By the early 19th century, inventors were trying to combine the camera with these chemical discoveries. The main problems included exposure times as long as eight hours, and how to make photographic images permanent. If light created photographic images, how could they be kept from further darkening once they were finished? This problem

was eventually solved by using hyposulfite of soda (now called **sodium** thiosulfite) to remove the undarkened silver particles.

Early photographic processes

During the 1830s two different photographic processes were invented. The Daguerrotype became more popular at first. It was created by Louis Jacques Mande Daguerre, who created illusions for French theater, with help from Joseph Niepce, an inventor. Their process created images on **copper** plates coated with a mixture of photosensitive silver compounds and iodine. Dagurre realized he could significantly shorten the exposure time by using mercury vapor to intensify, or develop, the image after a relatively short exposure. This made the process more practical, but also dangerous to the photographer since mercury is poisonous. Also, no copies could be make of Daguerroptypes, making it virtually useless for purposes of reproduction.

A rival process was created in England by Fox Talbot, a scientist and mathematician. He created images on paper sensitized with alternate layers of **salt** and silver nitrate. Talbot also used development to bring out his image, resulting in exposure times of 30 seconds on a bright sunny day. Talbot's process produced **negative** images, where light areas appear as dark, and dark areas as light. By waxing these negatives to make them clear, and putting another sheet of photographic paper under them, Talbot could make an unlimited number of positive images. This process was called a Calotype.

The Daguerrotype produced a positive image with extremely fine detail and was initially more popular. The **Industrial Revolution** had helped create a growing middle class with money to spend, and an interest in new and better ways of doing things. Soon the area around Paris filled on weekends with families out to take portraits and landscapes. These early processes were so slow, however, that views of cities turned into ghost towns since anything moving became blurred or invisible. Portraits were ordeals for the sitter, who had sit rigidly still, often aided by armatures behind them.

Other photography processes followed quickly. Some were quite different than the previous two methods. One method, invented by French civil servant Hippoyte Bayard in 1839, used light as a **bleach** that lightened a piece of paper darkened with silver chloride and potassium iodide. Papers employing **carbon** and **iron** rather than silver were also used. Platinum chloride, though expensive, proved popular with serious or wealthy photographers because it rendered a fuller range of gray tones than any other process.

Because Calotype negatives were pieces of paper, prints made from them picked up the texture of the paper fibers, making the image less clear. As a result, many artists and inventors experimented with making negatives on pieces of glass. A popular method bound silver compounds in collodion, a derivative of gun **cotton** that became transparent and sticky when dissolved in **alcohol**. Negatives made using this process required a shorter exposure than many previous methods, but had to be developed while still wet. As a result, landscape photographers had to bring portable darkrooms around them. These wet collodion negatives were usually printed on a paper treated with albumen. This produced a paper with a smooth surface that could be used in large quantities and reproduced rich photographic detail.

Dry plates using silver bromide in a **gelatin** ground appeared in 1878. They proved popular because they were easier than wet plates, and were soon produced by companies throughout the United States and **Europe**. In 1883, manufacturers began putting this **emulsion** on celluloid, a transparent mixture of **plant** fibers and plastic. Because celluloid was durable and flexible, its use lead to the commercial development of negative film on long rolls that could be loaded into cameras. By 1895, such film came with a paper backing so that it could be loaded outside of a darkroom. It was also far more sensitive to light than early photographic processes. These developments made photography more accessible to the average person, and lead to the widespread popularity photography has today.

Roll film also proved important to the motion picture industry because it allowed a series of photographs to be recorded sequentially on the same strip of film.

The evolution of cameras

A commercial camera based on Daguerre's patent, came out in France in 1839. New camera designs followed, mirroring the changing uses for and technologies used in photography. Large portrait cameras, small, foldable cameras for portable use, and twin-lensed cameras for stereoscope photos came out soon after the invention of photography. Bellows cameras allowed photographers to precisely control the focus and perspective of images by moving the front and back ends of a camera, and thus the focal planes.

The single lens reflex camera, which allowed for great control over focus and a fast exposure time, was an important advance that lead toward today's cameras. This camera used a mirror, usually set at a 45 degree **angle** to the lens, to allow photographers to look directly through the lens and see what the film would "see." When the shutter opened, the mirror moved out of the way, causing

the image to reach the film rather than the photographers **eye**. Single lens reflex cameras were in use by the 1860s, and used roll film by the 1890s. Because they were easy to use and allowed for a great degree of spontaneity, this type of camera proved popular with photojournalists, naturalists, and portrait photographers.

In early photography, exposures were made by simply taking off and replacing the lens cap. With the introduction of dry plates and film that were more sensitive to light, photographers required a more precise way of making fast exposures, and shutters became necessary. By 1900, shutters were sophisticated enough to all control of the aperture size and shutter speeds, which generally went from one second to 1/100th of a second. Lenses were improved to allow larger apertures without a loss of focus resolution. With exposure times becoming more precise, methods of precisely measuring light intensity became important. Initially, a strip of light-sensitive paper was used, then pieces of specially treated glass. The most accurate method used selenium, a light-sensitive element. Photoelectric meters based on selenium were introduced in 1932. They became smaller and less expensive, until by the 1940s, many cameras came with built-in light meters.

Cameras continued to become lighter and smaller throughout the 20th century. The 35 millimeter roll film camera so widely used today had it's origins in a 1913 Leitz camera designed to use leftover movie film. In 1925 Leitz introduced the Leica 35mm camera, the first to combine speed, versatility, and high image quality with lightness and ease of use. It revolutionized professional and artistic photography, while later models following its basic design did the same for amateur photography. In the years that followed, motor drives that automatically advanced film, and flashes that provided enough light in dark situations were perfected. The flash started in the mid-19th century as a device that burned a puff of **magnesium** powder. By 1925 it had become the flashbulb, using a magnesium wire. In the 1950s, the invention of the **transistor** and dry-cell batteries lead to smaller, lighter flashes, and smaller, lighter cameras as well. In all but the simplest cameras, photographic exposures are controlled by two factors: how long the shutter stays open, and the size of the hole in the lens is that admits light into the camera. This hole, called the aperture, is usually measured as a proportion of the **distance** from the aperture to the film divided by the actual diameter of the aperture.

Early uses of photography

Many artists were threatened by the invention of photography. Immediately after photography was first displayed to the public, the painter Paul Delaroche said, "From today, painting is dead." In fact, many portrait painters realized that photography would steal their livelihood, and began to learn it. Ironically, many early photographic portraits are overly stiff and formal. With exposure times that could easily be half a minute, subjects had to be in poses in which they could remain motionless. As the **chemistry** of photography improved, exposure times shortened. The public appetite for photographs grew quickly. By the 1860s, portraits on cards presented when visiting someone, and stereographic photos, which used two photographs to create an illusion of three-dimensional space, were churned out by machine in large batches.

The world's first photograph, taken by Joseph Nicephore Niepce in 1826, of the courtyard of his family's estate in France.

As with the camera obscura, one of the biggest initial uses of photography was to record travel and exotic scenery. Photographers lugged the cumbersome equipment used for wet collodion prints through Egypt, India, and the American West. At the time, Europeans were increasingly interested in exotic places (and were colonizing some of them), while most Americans got their first glimpses of a wilderness they would never see through photography. With more people living in cities and working in industrial settings, views of unspoiled nature were in demand.

England's Francis Frith became famous for his photographs of the Middle East in the 1850s. After the end of the Civil War in 1865, photographers like Edward Muybridge and Timothy O'Sullivan did the same in the American West, often emphasizing its desolate grandeur. (Muybridge's photographic studies of motion later helped lead to **motion pictures.**) The West was still an unexplored frontier, and often these photographers traveled as part of mapping expeditions. The pictures they took of geysers in 1871 and 1872 and brought William H. Jack-

son played an important role in the decision to create Yellowstone National Park, America's first national park. Some of these photographs sold thousands of copies and became part of how Americans saw their country.

Photography as an art form

For much of its early history, people argued about whether photography should be considered art. Some, including many artists (many of whom used photographs as guides for their own work), considered photography a purely mechanical process, produced by chemicals rather than human sensibility. Others said that photography was similar to other printmaking processes like etching and **lithography**, and no one argued that they were not art. Still, at large expositions, curators usually hung the photographs in the science and industry sections rather than with the paintings.

An 1893 showing of photographs in Hamburg, Germany's art museum still provoked controversy. But that was about to change. In 1902, American photographer Alfred Stieglitz formed the PhotoSecession in New York City. The group's shows and publications firmly advocated the view that photography was art. Their magazine, "Camera Works," which used high-quality engravings to reproduce photographs, proved extremely influential, showing that photography could be used for artistic purpose.

Artistic photography reflected many of the same trends as other branches of art. By the end of World War I in 1918, leading-edge photography had moved away from the soft-focus pictorialism of the 19th century. It became more geometric and abstract. Photographers began concentrating on choosing details that evoked situations and people. Lighter, more versatile cameras enabled photographers to take scenes of urban streets. Photography proved important in documenting the Great Depression. Many photographers concentrated on stark depictions of the downtrodden.

At the other end of the **spectrum**, this interest in spare but elegant depictions of everyday objects worked well with advertising, and many art photographers had careers in advertising or taking glamorous photographs for picture magazines.

Landscape photography also flourished. The best known 20th century landscape photographer, Ansel Adams, created a system for precisely controlling the exposure and development of film to manipulate the amount of contrast in negatives.

These developments helped give photography a separate and unique identity. The Museum of Modern Art in New York formed a department of photography in 1940, showing that the medium had been accepted as an art form. Since then, art photography has thrived, with many artists making important contributions in areas ranging from landscape to street photography to surrealist photomontage.

Reproducing photographs using ink

The history of photography is intimately linked to that of mass production. Publishing was growing quickly even as photography did, fueled by the growth of cities and newspapers and increased literacy. Before photography, newspapers, magazines, and illustrated books used **wood** engravings to illustrate their articles. These engravings could be printed in the same presses, using the same methods and papers as the movable type used to print text. The images and type could therefore be printed on the same piece of paper at the same time. For photography to become practical for publishing, a way of cheaply reproducing photos in large editions had to be found. Some were skeptical that photography would ever prove important as an illustrative method. Most illustrations for newspaper articles were created by artists who had not seen the events they were rendering. If the imagination was so important in illustration, what need was there for the immediacy and truthfulness of a photograph?

Finding a method for mechanically reproducing photographs in large numbers proved difficult. By the late 19th century, several methods had been perfected that created beautiful reproductions. But these methods were not compatible with type or with **mass production**. This limited their usefulness for editions larger than a couple of hundred copies. An early method that was compatible with type, developed by Frenchman Charles Gillot around 1875, produced **metal** relief plates that could reproduce only lines and areas of solid tone.

The method that finally worked, called photoengraving, broke the continuous tones of a photograph down into patterns of black dots that were small enough to look like varying shades of gray when seen from a slight distance. Such dot patterns, called screens, can easily be seen in a newspaper photograph, but a photograph in the finest magazine or art book uses essentially the same method, although it may require a magnifying glass to see the dots. Though Fox Talbot had conceived of using a screen to reproduce photographs as early as 1853, a practical screening method was first patented in 1881 by Frederick E. Ives.

A photoengraving is made by coating a printing plate with light-sensitive emulsion. A negative is then printed on the plate through a grid, called a screen, that breaks the image into dots. The dots are made acid resistant, then the plate is put into a bath of acid. This re-

moves areas around the dots, making the dots raised. The dots can then be inked with a roller, and printed on paper using a printing press.

By the 1890s these halftones (so called because they were composed of areas that were either black or white), were appearing in magazines and books, and some newspapers. With the edition of photographs, publications evolved, changing their layouts to emphasize the powerful realism of the new medium. Magazines began sending photographers to the scenes of wars and revolutions. The resulting photographs often did not appear until days or weeks later, but the images they brought back from conflicts like the Spanish-American war and World War I fascinated the public to a degree it is hard to imagine now that wars are broadcast live on **television**.

The **mass production** of photographic images affected more than publications. Original photographs were costly. But such images became affordable when printed by a printing press. We think nothing of getting a postcard with a photograph on it, but until the invention of photoengraving, such postcards were far more expensive. Nor did an image have to be a photograph to benefit from photoengraving. A drawing or painting, whether for an art book or an advertisement, could be photographed, then printed through a screen to create a mass-reproducible image.

Halftone reproductions quickly increased in quality, partly under pressure from magazine advertisers, who wanted their products to look good. By the time World War I began in 1914, magazine reproductions were sometimes as good as less expensive modern reproductions.

These developments expanded and changed the audience for photography. To appear in a mass-circulation magazine, a photograph had to have mass appeal. Many photographers had earned a living selling photographs and postcards or local sights. This became difficult to do once photographs of the most famous international sights and monuments became widely available.

Reproductions were not the only way large audiences could see photographs, however. Many photos were shown in the 19th century equivalent of the slide projector. Called the magic lantern, it was often used to illustrate lectures. Early documentary photography was often shot to accompany lectures on subjects like the condition of the poor in urban slums.

Color photography

From the invention of photography, most people considered its inability to render **color** to be an important defect. Many early photographs had color painted on by hand in an attempt to compensate. Those attempting to solve the problem of creating color photographs took their cues from researchers into human **vision**, who theorized that all colors in nature are made from combinations of red, green and blue. Thus early attempts to create color photographs centered on making three layers of transparent images, one in each of these colors, and sandwiching them together. Each layer was photographed using filters to block out other colors of light. This resulted in photographs that were foggy with poor color.

In 1904, the first practical method of creating color images, called the Autochrome, was invented by the Lumiere brothers of Lyon, France. Autochromes used a layer of **potato** starch particles, dyed red, green and blue, attached to a layer of silver bromide photographic emulsion, all on a plate of glass. They were expensive and required long exposures, but Autochromes had significantly better color and were easier to process than previous methods. By 1916, two other color methods competed with the autochrome. All were considered imperfect, however, because they were grainy, and their color was inaccurate and changed over time. Therefore, with the publishing industry and the public hungry for color photographs, attention turned to subtractive color methods.

The subtractive color starts with white light, a mixture of all wavelengths of light, and subtracts color from it. The process uses a three-layer emulsion of yellow, cyan (a greenish-blue) and magenta (a cool pink). When subtracted from white, these colors produce their opposites: red, green and blue. Kodak released a subtractive color film for motion pictures in 1935, and in 1938 a sheet film for photography, while the German Agfa Company released its own variation in 1936. Other companies followed. By the 1940s, color negative roll film for use in 35 millimeter cameras was available.

Two methods are currently used for creating color prints. In the chromogenic method the color dyes are created when the print is processed. In the dye-bleach or dye-destruction method, the color dyes are present before processing. The dyes not needed for the image are removed by bleaching.

Snapshots: popular photography

For the first 50 years of its existence, photography was so difficult it usually dissuaded amateurs. In 1888, the first Kodak camera, aimed at the amateur market, sold for $25. It used factory-loaded film of 100 exposures, and had to be returned to the factory for film development. In 1900, the first of the very popular Brownie cameras was released. The camera cost $1, the film was 15 cents a roll, and the camera was light and simple to operate. The Brownie, and the cameras that followed it, quickly made photography an part of American family life.

Instant photographs

Instant print film, which was introduced by Polaroid in 1948, delivers finished photographs within minutes. The film consists a packet that includes film and processing chemicals, and often photographic paper. After exposure, the packet is pulled from the camera. In the process it gets squeezed between **rollers** which break open the developing and fixing chemicals, spreading them evenly across the photographic surface. Although popular with amateurs for instant snapshots, instant photographs are often used by professional photographers as well because they can be used to test how lighting and compositions look to a camera before they shoot for later development.

The uses of photography in science

Photography has became an essential component of many areas of science. Ever since the U.S. Surgeon General's office compiled a six-volume record of Civil War wounds shortly after the war, it has played a crucial role in the study of **anatomy**. Photographs can provide an objective standard for defining the visual characteristics of a species of **animal** or a type of rock formation.

But photography can also depict things the human eye cannot see at all. Hours-long exposures taken through telescopes bring out astronomical details otherwise unseeable. Similar principals apply to some photos taken through microscopes. High-speed photography allows us to see a bullet in flight. In 1932, the existence of neutrons was proven using photographs, as was the existence of viruses in 1942. The **planet Pluto** was discovered through comparisons of photographic maps taken through telescopes.

"X rays" taken at hospitals are really photographs taken with x-ray light rather than visible light. Similarly, infra-red and ultra-violet photographs, which detect invisible wavelengths of light, can be used for numerous purposes including **astronomy** and medicine, and the detection of cracks in pipes or **heat** loss from buildings. In all these cases, evidence and experimental results can be easily exchanged between scientists using photographs.

Photography enters the computer age

Like many other things, photography has been deeply affected by computers. Photographs now can be taken by cameras that don't even use film. Instead they use electronic sensors to measure light intensities and translate them into digital code that can be read by a computer. The computer translates the digital code into a grid of points, each assigned a number that represents a color (or level of gray for black-and-white photos). The process is similar to the way in which music is translated into digital form when it is put on a **compact disc**.

Once digitized, images can be manipulated by computers in many of the same ways they can be changed while making prints in a darkroom. But because digital images are essentially a series of numbers, they can be manipulated in other ways as well. For publishing purposes, digital images can be converted to halftones by the computer, making the process easier and faster. As a result, many newspapers, magazines and advertising firms have switched to digital photography for increasing amounts of their work.

See also Photocopying; Scanners, digital.

KEY TERMS

Aperture—The size of the opening in a camera lens through which light comes.

Camera obscura—A dark room or box with a lightadmitting hole that projects an image of the scene outside.

Negative—Images with tonal values reversed, so that objects appear dark. Usually negatives are film from which positive prints are made.

Photoengraving—A process through which the continuous tones of a photograph are converted into black and white dots that can be reproduced on a printing press.

Single lens reflex camera—A camera that uses a single lens and a mirror to admit light for the film and for the photographer to use to focus on.

Further Reading

London, Barbara, and Upton, John: *Photography, Fifth Edition.* New York: Harper Collins College Publishers, 1994.

Rosenblum, Naomi, *A World History of Photography.* New York: Abbeville Press, 1984.

Szarkowski, John, *Photography Until Now.* The Museum of Modern Art, New York: 1989.

Turner, Peter, *History of Photography.* New York: Exeter Books, 1987.

Scott M. Lewis

Photography, electronic

Like all other forms of information, photographs and images have entered the electronic age. In 1981, the

Sony Corporation unveiled its filmless, electronic camera (termed a still video camera) the Mavica. Mavica is an acronym for *Ma*gnetic *Vi*deo *Ca*mera; it uses a still video system to record 50 analog images on a diskette. Although they are recorded on a diskette, they are not digital images. The images are played back on a monitor and can be printed out by standard black-and-white or **color** computer printers on regular **paper** or on photographic paper. Use of high-resolution equipment produces a printed photograph that is almost identical to a traditional photo print.

In 1986, Canon was the first company to introduce a professional electronic camera on a major, commercial scale. Two years later, in 1988, Sony released the ProMavica for use in professional and industrial applications. The ProMavica is compatible with a set of standards agreed on by 43 potential still video manufacturers also in 1988 called the Hi-band standard. This agreement established international guidelines for still video **photography** much like the VHS standards for video tape recordings. The Hi-band standard includes industry standards for resolution (400 horizontal lines per image) and image quality. By 1990, Nikon, Minolta, and a number of other makers had joined Sony and Canon in producing still video cameras for both professionals and amateurs.

The still video camera records the images it sees as analog electrical signals on the magnetic layer of a diskette. It scans the image one line at a time so a recognizable pattern is established for storing and reproducing the electronic signals. Resolution is carried by one signal, and two others carry color (much like hue and saturation on a **television** image). Liquid **crystal** display (**LCD**) screens may soon be added to still video cameras so the photographer can see the electronic image; but, by the late 1990s, electronic cameras used viewfinders much like film-based cameras. Diskettes are also a limitation and may be replaced by data storage on compact discs, which can already be used as a photographic storage method but not directly from the camera.

Advantages of the still video camera are that processing is not needed (and processing chemicals are eliminated), images can be viewed or printed instantly, diskettes are erasable and can be re-recorded, and captured images can be manipulated and transmitted via e-mail and other methods using **computer software** that is relatively inexpensive.

The digital still camera

Fuji's digital still camera (which debuted in 1988) converts analogs signals—the means by which an electronic camera "sees" an image—to digital signals and stores them on a slide-in card that has fewer complications of motors and drives than a diskette-based system. Resolution is better than the analog system, and, because the digital camera is typically connected to other digital devices for transfer or manipulation of its data, these transfers occur more quickly. The card also carries 50 images, and manufacturers are working on linking this technology to the digital audio tape (DAT) recording system to store 1,000 images on one tape in an electronic photo album; audio messages can also be recorded on this tape and played concurrently.

Applications

Uses for electronic still photography extend as far as the imagination. Some examples:

- In the styling/beauty salon, an operator can take an electronic photo of the customer and superimpose hundreds of hair styles and colors on the image, which is available from the camera immediately.
- Wholesale and retail buyers traveling long distances from main offices can photograph potential merchandise and have it reviewed and approved by management at home as quickly as the images can be transferred. Purchases can be negotiated on the same buying trip, saving travel time or communications time after the buyers return home.
- Journalism, including photojournalism, benefits by transferring photographic data over **telephone** lines via electronic mail (e-mail). Pictures from distant locations around the world are available for the next edition.
- Medical specialists can review photos of physical conditions or surgeries without the time and expense of moving either the patient or the specialist.
- Police departments and other crime investigation agencies can immediately transmit artists' renderings and photographs of suspects around the world. Still video is also critical to searches for missing children.
- Thanks to CCD technology, amateur stargazers can use still video cameras attached to their telescopes to photograph the skies. Standard CCDs have to modified to include a greater magnitude of resolution and a greater wavelength range, but, with these changes, sensitive images and even spectrogram, which are made with special optics that spread starlight into the **spectrum**, can be recorded through backyard telescopes with digital cameras attached.

Video cameras

Video cameras are common in hand-held versions for the home photographer, but many professional video cameras are used to take still photos for professional uses. They obtain high resolution especially through the super

VHS format and can be linked to modems for immediate transfer of video or still shots. Specialized cameras with digital-video-image storage systems were used to take the first photographs of the HMS *Titanic* when she was discovered in her underwater grave in the Atlantic Ocean in 1986. The cameras were attached to an undersea sled called the *Argo*, and the versatility of the **video recording** method allowed many scientists means of analyzing the photographic findings. Sophisticated video cameras are also used extensively in medicine, especially in operating rooms to permit several doctors to offer immediate comments on procedures and conditions.

Other methods for electronic photography

The specialized field known as "image processing" is growing out of electronic photography. An electronic photograph may be taken using a still video camera, a video camera (using a single frame for the still image), or by digitizing a photographic image by using a scanner. After the photographic data has been stored, it can be manipulated by computer software in any number of ways. Parts of the photo can be erased, colors can be changed, composites can be made from several photographs, and contrast, sharpness, overall size, and size changes by cropping can be accomplished by tweaking the data. By the late 1980s, the advertising industry especially had experimented extensively with this new technology and produced startling images by combining photographic images in unlikely combinations. By the 1990s, scanners had improved greatly in resolution as well as dropping in price and were becoming standard accessories for the home computer.

Scanners and other image input devices have been made possible largely because of charge-coupled devices or CCDs. A CCD is an **integrated circuit** that produces an electrical charge that is unique to light striking a sensor element in the circuit. They are used in cameras (still and video), scanners, high definition televisions (HDTVs), and many other image-makers. Their speed and sensitivity has improved dramatically since they were first introduced in the 1970s, and they have made imaging devices affordable for desktop use.

Scanners are available in a wide range of models that use different techniques. Desktop versions scan flat photographs in either black and white or color (color uses three scans to capture the basic image in black and white and then add color in two scans), and scanners for 35-millimeter slides are also in desktop sizes and are often used for professional work.

Part of the attraction of electronic photography is the fact that images can be compressed as digital files and stored in a number of ways. Magnetic diskettes, rewritable CD-ROMS that use optical **memory** and recover images with **laser** readers, and cards and chips offer storage options depending on uses and cost. They also make the "electronic darkroom" possible for retouching and altering images; techniques for modifying photographs form the bridge between photographic images and computer-generated ones.

Technologies that are affordable by the general public may still have some limitations in quality, especially in resolution (clearness of the image), shading and color ranges, and saturation. Systems used to make commercials and magazine ads, however, produce high-quality images.

Larish, John J. *Electronic Photography.* TAB Professional and Reference Books, Blue Ridge Summit, PA, 1990.

Glumac, Nick. "Building a fiber-optic spectrograph." *Sky & Telescope.* (Feb. 1999): p. 134+.

Shaefer, Bradley E. "Limiting magnitudes for CCDs." *Sky & Telescope.* (May 1998): p. 117+.

Gillian S. Holmes

Photon

The *photon* is the basic unit or "piece" of **light**. This is a simple statement, but at first it seems to make no sense at all. How can the light given off by a flashlight, or a lamp be made of pieces? Despite this strange idea, visible light really does behave this way, and so do other forms of "light" that are not visible to our eyes.

The visible light that we see, the x rays that dentists use, and the **radio** waves that carry music to our radios are all forms of *electromagnetic radiation*. Other forms include the microwaves which we use to cook food and gamma rays which are produced when radioactive elements disintegrate. Although they seem quite different, all types of electromagnetic **radiation** behave in similar ways. If you think about it, the shadows of our teeth that are produced by x rays and captured on special film are really not that different from our visible shadows cast by the **sun**. If **x rays** and light are essentially the same, why is one visible to our eyes and the other invisible?

We know that visible light comes in many different colors, like those we see in a rainbow. The colors can be understood by thinking of light as a vibration moving through **space**. Any vibration, or *oscillation*, repeats itself with a certain rhythm, or *frequency*. For light, every shade of every color corresponds to a different **frequency**, and the vibration of blue light, for example, has a higher frequency than that of red light. It turns out that our eyes can only detect electromagnetic radiation for a

relatively narrow range of frequencies, and so only those vibrations are "visible." However, other forms of electromagnetic radiation are all around us with frequencies our eyes cannot detect. If our eyes could detect very high frequencies, we could see the x rays which can pass through many solid objects just like visible light passes through tinted **glass**.

Originally, vibrations of light were thought to be somehow similar to **water** waves. The **energy** carried by that kind of vibration is related to the height of the wave, so a brighter source of light would seem to simply produce bigger waves. This idea provided a very effective way of understanding electromagnetic radiation until about 100 years ago. At that time several phenomena were found which could only be explained if light was considered to be made up of extremely small pieces or "wave packets," which still had some of the properties of waves. One of the most important phenomena was the *photoelectric effect*. It was discovered that when visible light shined on certain metals, electrons were ejected from the material. Those free electrons were called *photoelectrons*. It was also found that it took a certain minimum amount of energy to release electrons from the **metal**. The original vibration concept suggested that any color(frequency) of light would do this if a bright enough source (lamp) was used. This was because eventually the waves of light would become large enough to carry enough energy to free some electrons. However, this is not what happened! Instead it was found that, for example, even dim blue light could produce photoelectrons while the brightest red light could not. The original vibration theory of light could not explain this so another idea was needed.

In 1905 Albert Einstein suggested that this effect meant that the vibrations of light came in small pieces or "wave packets." He also explained that each packet contained a predetermined amount (or *quantum*) of energy which was equal to a constant multiplied by the frequency of the light (see the entry for *Quantum Mechanics* for a full discussion of this idea). This meant that a bright source of a particular colorof light just produced more packets than a dim source of the same color did. If the energy, and therefore the frequency, of a packet was large enough, an **electron** could be freed from the metal. More packets of that frequency would release more electrons. On the other hand when the energy of a packet was too small, it did not matter how many packets struck the metal, no electrons would be freed. This new idea explained all the newly-discovered phenomena and also agreed with effects which had been known for hundreds of years. Einstein's wave packets became known as photons, which are somehow like indivisible pieces (like small particles) and also like vibrations. The discovery of this split personality was one of the factors that led to the extremely important theory of **quantum mechanics**. Still it is difficult to visualize what an individual photon actually looks like and even experts can become confused trying to do so.

If the light from a lamp really consists of photons, why does the light we see appear to be reaching us continuously instead of in lumps? Well, this is actually easy to understand by performing an experiment with sand. First, we need to fill a plastic bucket with sand and hold it over a bathroom scale. Next, we make a small hole in the bottom of the bucket so that sand will slowly drain out and fall on the scale. As more and more sand collects on the scale, we will see that the weight increases in an apparently continuous manner. However, we know that sand is made up of particles and so the weight on the scale must really be increasing by jumps (whenever a new grain of sand lands on the scale). The trick is that the size of the grains is so small that the individual increments by which the weight changes are too small for us to detect. The same thing happens with light, only in a more exaggerated way. If we look into a lamp (not recommended) there may be more than 1,000,000,000,000,000,000,000,000,000 photons reaching our eyes in every second, with each photon carrying only a small amount of energy. If we dim the lamp, we can never notice the jumps as we decrease the number of photons to (1,000,000,000,000,000,000,000,000,000 -1), then to (1,000,000,000,000,000,000,000,000,000 -2), etc.

KEY TERMS

Electromagnetic radiation—A term used to describe all forms of light, whether visible to the human eye or not.

Quantum (plural is quanta)—An allowed amount of a measurable property, such as the energy carried by a photon.

Quantum mechanics—The theory used to provide an understanding of the behavior of extremely small objects such as electrons and atoms, and individual photons.

Further Reading

Albert, A.Z. *Quantum Mechanics and Experience*. Cambridge, MA: Harvard University Press, 1992.

Gregory, B. *Inventing Reality: Physics as Language*. New York: John Wiley & Sons, 1990.

Han, M.Y. *The Probable Universe*. Blue Ridge Summit, PA: TAB Books, 1993.

James J. Carroll

Photosynthesis

Photosynthesis is the biological conversion of **light energy** into chemical energy. It occurs in green plants and photosynthetic **bacteria** through a series of many biochemical reactions. In higher plants and **algae**, light absorption by **chlorophyll** catalyzes the synthesis of carbohydrate ($C_6H_{12}O_6$) and oxygen gas (O_2) from **carbon dioxide** gas (CO_2) and water (H_2O). Thus, the overall chemical equation for photosynthesis in higher plants is expressed as:

$$6CO_2 + 6H_2O \xrightarrow[\text{chlorophyll}]{\text{light}} C_6H_{12}O_6 + 6O_2$$

The overall equation in photosynthetic bacteria is similar, although not identical.

History of research

People have long been interested in how plants obtain the **nutrients** they use for growth. The early Greek philosophers believed that plants obtained all of their nutrients from the soil. This was a common belief for many centuries.

In the first half of the seventeenth century, Jan Baptista van Helmont (1579-1644), a Dutch physician, chemist, and alchemist, performed important experiments which disproved this early view of photosynthesis. He grew a willow **tree** weighing 5 lb (2.5 kg) in a clay pot which had 200 lb (91 kg) of **soil**. Five years later, after watering his willow tree as needed, it weighed about 169 lb (76.5 kg) even though the soil in the pot lost only 2 oz (56 g) in weight. Van Helmont concluded that the tree gained weight from the **water** he added to the soil, and not from the soil itself. Although van Helmont did not understand the role of sunlight and atmospheric gases in **plant** growth, his early experiment advanced our understanding of photosynthesis.

In 1771, the noted English chemist Joseph Priestley performed a series of important experiments which implicated atmospheric gases in plant growth. Priestley and his contemporaries believed a noxious substance, which they called *phlogiston*, was released into the air when a flame burned. When Priestley burned a candle within an enclosed container until the flame went out, he found that a mouse could not survive in the "phlogistated" air of the container. However, when he placed a sprig of mint in the container after the flame had gone out, he found that a mouse could survive. Priestley concluded that the sprig of mint chemically altered the air by removing the "phlogiston." Shortly after Priestly's experiments, Dutch physician Jan Ingenhousz (1730-1799) demonstrated that plants "dephlogistate" the air only in sunlight, and not in darkness. Further, Ingenhousz demonstrated that the green parts of plants are necessary for" dephlogistation" and that sunlight by itself is ineffective.

As Ingenhousz was performing his experiments, the celebrated French chemist Antoine Lavoisier (1743-1794) disproved the phlogiston theory. He conclusively demonstrated that candles and animals both consume a gas in the air which he named **oxygen**. This implied that the plants in Priestley's and Ingenhousz's experiments produced oxygen when illuminated by sunlight. Considered by many as the founder of modern **chemistry**, Lavoisier was condemned to death and beheaded during the French revolution.

Lavoisier's experiments stimulated Ingenhousz to reinterpret his earlier studies of "dephlogistation." Following Lavoisier, Ingenhousz hypothesized that plants use sunlight to split carbon dioxide (CO_2) and use its carbon (C) for growth while expelling its oxygen (O_2) as waste. This model of photosynthesis was an improvement over Priestley's, but was not entirely accurate.

Ingenhousz's hypothesis that photosynthesis produces oxygen by splitting carbon dioxide was refuted about 150 years later by the Dutch-born microbiologist Cornelius van Niel (1897-1985) in America. Van Niel studied photosynthesis in **anaerobic** bacteria, rather than in higher plants. Like higher plants, these bacteria make carbohydrates during photosynthesis. Unlike plants, they do not produce oxygen during photosynthesis and they use bacteriochlorophyll rather than chlorophyll as a photosynthetic pigment. Van Niel found that all species of photosynthetic bacteria which he studied required an oxidizable substrate. For example, the purple **sulfur** bacteria use **hydrogen** sulfide as an oxidizable substrate and the overall equation for photosynthesis in these bacteria is:

$$CO_2 + 2H_2S \xrightarrow[\text{bateriochlorophyll}]{\text{light}} (CH_2O) + H_2O + 2S$$

On the basis of his studies with photosynthetic bacteria, van Niel proposed that the oxygen which plants produce during photosynthesis is derived from water, not from carbon dioxide. In the following years, this hypothesis has proven true. Van Niel's brilliant insight was a major contribution to our modern understanding of photosynthesis.

The study of photosynthesis is currently a very active area of research in **biology**. Hartmut Michel and Johann Deisenhofer recently made a very important contribution to our understanding of photosynthesis. They made crystals of the photosynthetic reaction center from

Rhodopseudomonas viridis, an anaerobic photosynthetic bacterium, and then used x-ray crystallography to determine its three-dimensional structure. In 1988, they shared the Nobel Prize in Chemistry with Robert Huber for this ground-breaking research.

Modern plant physiologists commonly think of photosynthesis as consisting of two separate series of interconnected biochemical reactions, the light reactions and the dark reactions. The light reactions use the light energy absorbed by chlorophyll to synthesize labile high energy molecules. The dark reactions use these labile high energy molecules to synthesize carbohydrates, a stable form of chemical energy which can be stored by plants. Although the dark reactions do not require light, they often occur in the light because they are dependent upon the light reactions. In higher plants and algae, the light and dark reactions of photosynthesis occur in chloroplasts, specialized chlorophyll-containing intracellular structures which are enclosed by double membranes.

Light reactions

In the light reactions of photosynthesis, light energy excites photosynthetic pigments to higher energy levels and this energy is used to make two high energy compounds, ATP (adenosine triphosphate) and NADPH (nicotinamide adenine dinucleotide phosphate). ATP and NADPH do not appear in the overall equation for photosynthesis because they are consumed during the subsequent dark reactions in the synthesis of carbohydrates.

Location of light reactions

In higher plants and algae, the light reactions occur on the thylakoid membranes of the chloroplasts. The thylakoid membranes are inner membranes of the chloroplasts which are arranged like flattened sacs. The thylakoids are often stacked on top of one another, like a roll of coins. A stack of thylakoids is referred to as a granum.

The light reactions of higher plants require photosynthetic pigments, chlorophyll-a, chlorophyll-b, and various types of carotenoids. These pigments are associated with special proteins which are embedded in the thylakoid membranes. Chlorophyll-a and chlorophyll-b strongly absorb light in the red and blue regions of the **spectrum**. Most carotenoids strongly absorb blue light. Thus, plant leaves are green simply because their photosynthetic pigments absorb blue and red light but not green light.

Non-cyclic energy transfer

Once light is absorbed by pigments in the **chloroplast**, its energy is transferred to one of two types of reaction centers, Photosystem-II (PS-II) or Photosystem-I (PS-I).

In non-cyclic **energy transfer**, light absorbed by PS-II splits a water **molecule**, producing oxygen and exciting chlorophyll to a higher energy level. Then, the excitation energy passes through a series of special **electron** carriers. Each electron carrier in the series is slightly lower in energy than the previous one. During electron transfer, the excitation energy is harnessed to synthesize ATP. This part of photosynthesis is referred to as non-cyclic photophosphorylation, where "photo-" refers to the light requirement and "-phosphorylation" refers to addition of a phosphate to ADP (**adenosine diphosphate**) to make ATP.

Finally, one of the electron carriers of PS-II transfers electrons to PS-I. When chlorophyll transfers its excitation energy to PS-I, it is excited to higher energy levels. PS-I harnesses this excitation energy to make NADPH, analogous to the way PS-II harnessed excitation energy to make ATP.

In the 1950s, the botanist Robert Emerson (1903-1959) demonstrated that the rate of photosynthesis was much higher under simultaneous illumination by shorter wavelength red light (near 680 nm) and long wavelength red light (near 700 nm). We now know this is because PS-II absorbs shorter wavelength red light (680 nm) whereas PS-I absorbs long wavelength red light (700 nm) and both must be photoactivated to make the ATP and NADPH needed by the dark reactions.

Cyclic energy transfer

ATP can also be made by a special series of light reactions referred to as cyclic photophosphorylation. This also occurs in the thylakoid membranes of the chloroplast. In cyclic photophosphorylation, the excitation energy from PS-I is transferred to a special electron carrier and this energy is harnessed to make ATP.

The relative rates of cyclic and non-cyclic photophosphorylation determine the **ratio** of ATP and NADPH which become available for the dark reactions. Photosynthetic plant cells regulate cyclic and non-cyclic energy transfer by phosphorylating (adding a phosphate) to the pigment-protein complexes associated with PS-I and PS-II.

Dark reactions

The photosynthetic dark reactions consist of a series of many enzymatic reactions which make carbohydrates from carbon dioxide. The dark reactions do not require light directly, but they are dependent upon ATP and NADPH which are synthesized in the light reactions. Thus,

the dark reactions indirectly depend on light and usually occur in the light. The dark reactions occur in the aqueous region of the chloroplasts, referred to as the stroma.

Calvin cycle

The main part of the dark reactions is often referred to as the Calvin cycle, in honor of their discoverer, the chemist Melvin Calvin. The Calvin cycle consists of 13 different biochemical reactions, each catalyzed by a specific **enzyme**. The Calvin cycle can be summarized as consisting of carboxylation, reduction, and regeneration. Its final product is starch, a complex carbohydrate.

In carboxylation, a molecule of carbon dioxide (with one carbon atom) is combined with a molecule of RuBP (ribulose bisphosphate, with five carbon **atoms**) to make two molecules of PGA (phosphoglycerate), each with three carbon atoms. This reaction is catalyzed by the enzyme RuBISCO (Ribulose bisphosphate carboxylase). RuBISCO accounts for about 20% of the total amount of protein in a plant **leaf** and is by far the most abundant enzyme on **Earth**.

In reduction, ATP and NADPH (made by the light reactions) supply energy for synthesis of high energy carbohydrates from the PGA made during carboxylation. Plants often store their chemical energy as carbohydrates because these are very stable and easily transported throughout the **organism**.

In regeneration, the carbohydrates made during reduction pass through a series of enzymatic reactions so that RuBP, the initial reactant in carboxylation, is regenerated. The regeneration of RuBP is the reason these reactions are considered a cycle. Once the Calvin cycle has gone around six times, six molecules of carbon dioxide have been fixed, and a molecule of glucose, a six-carbon **carbohydrate**, is produced.

The series of dark reactions described above is often referred to as C-3 photosynthesis because the first reaction product of carbon dioxide fixation is a 3-carbon molecule, PGA (phosphoglycerate).

C-4 photosynthesis

In the early 1960s, plant physiologists discovered that **sugarcane** and several other plants did not produce the three-carbon molecule, PGA, as the first reaction product of their dark reactions. Instead, these other plants combined carbon dioxide with PEP (phosphoenol pyruvate), a three-carbon molecule, to make OAA (oxaloacetate), a four-carbon molecule. After a series of additional enzymatic reactions, carbon dioxide is introduced to the Calvin cycle, which functions more or less as described above.

This variant of photosynthesis is referred to as C-4 photosynthesis because carbon dioxide is first fixed into a four-carbon molecule, OAA. C-4 photosynthesis occurs in many species of tropical **grasses** and in many important agricultural plants such as corn, sugarcane, **rice**, and sorghum.

Plants which have C-4 photosynthesis partition their C-4 **metabolism** and their Calvin cycle metabolism into different cells within their leaves. Their C-4 metabolism occurs in mesophyll cells, which constitute the main body of the leaf. The Calvin cycle occurs in specialized cells referred to as bundle sheath cells. Bundle sheath cells surround the vascular tissue (veins) which penetrate the main body of the leaf.

In at least 11 different genera of plants, some species have C-3 metabolism whereas other species have C-4 metabolism. Thus, plant physiologists believe that C-4 photosynthesis evolved independently many times in many different species. Recently, plant physiologists have found that some plant species are C-3/C-4 intermediates, in that they perform C-3 photosynthesis in some environments and C-4 photosynthesis in other environments. Study of these intermediates may help elucidate the **evolution** and physiological significance of C-4 photosynthesis.

CAM photosynthesis

Another variant of photosynthesis was originally found in many plants of the Crassulaceae family. The photosynthetic leaves of these plants accumulate malic acid or isocitric acid at night and metabolize these acidic compounds during the day. This type of photosynthesis is referred to as Crassulacean Acid Metabolism or more simply, CAM photosynthesis.

During the night, the following reactions occur in plants with CAM photosynthesis: (a) they open up special pores in their leaves, referred to as stomata, and the leaves take in carbon dioxide from the atmosphere; (b) they metabolize some of their stored starch to PEP (phosphoenol pyruvate), a 3-carbon molecule; (c) they combine carbon dioxide with PEP to form malic acid or isocitric acid, 4-carbon molecules; (d) they accumulate large amounts of malic acid or isocitric acid in their leaves, so that they **taste** somewhat sour if sampled at night or early morning.

During the day, the following reactions occur in plants with CAM photosynthesis: (a) they close their stomata; (b) they release carbon dioxide from the accumulated malic acid or isocitric acid; (c) they combine this released carbon dioxide with RuBP and the Calvin cycle operates more or less as described above.

Most plants with CAM photosynthesis grow in deserts and other arid environments. In such environments, evaporative loss of water is lower in CAM plants because they close their stomata during the day.

Species from over 20 different plant families, including Cactaceae, Orchidaceae, Liliaceae, and Bromeliaceae have been identified as having CAM photosynthesis. Thus, plant physiologists believe that CAM photosynthesis evolved independently many times. Many CAM plants are succulents, plants with thick leaves and a high ratio of **volume** to surface area. Interestingly, while CAM photosynthesis is genetically determined, some plants can switch from C-3 photosynthesis to CAM photosynthesis when they are transferred to an arid environment.

Photorespiration

In the 1920s, the German biochemist Otto Warburg (1883-1970) discovered that plants consumed oxygen at a higher rate when they were illuminated. He also found that this increased rate of oxygen consumption inhibited photosynthesis. Stimulation of oxygen consumption by light is now referred to as photorespiration. Biochemical studies indicate that photorespiration consumes ATP and NADPH, the high energy molecules made by the light reactions. Thus, photorespiration is a wasteful process because it prevents plants from using their ATP and NADPH to synthesize carbohydrates.

RuBISCO, the enzyme which fixes carbon dioxide during the Calvin cycle, is also responsible for oxygen fixation during photorespiration. In particular, carbon dioxide and oxygen compete for access to RuBISCO. RuBISCO's affinity for carbon dioxide is much higher than its affinity for oxygen. Thus, fixation of carbon dioxide typically exceeds fixation of oxygen, even though atmospheric carbon dioxide levels are about 0.035% whereas oxygen is about 21%.

If photorespiration is so wasteful, why does it occur at all? Many plant physiologists believe that photorespiration is an artifact of the ancient evolutionary history of photosynthesis. In particular, RuBISCO originated in bacteria several billion years ago when there was very little atmospheric oxygen present. Thus, there was little selection **pressure** for the ancient RuBISCO to discriminate between carbon dioxide and oxygen and RuBISCO originated with a structure that reacts with both. Even though most modern plants are under great selection pressure to reduce photorespiration, evolution cannot easily alter RuBISCO's structure so that it fixes less oxygen yet still efficiently fixes carbon dioxide.

Interestingly, photorespiration has been observed in all C-3 plants which have been examined, but is virtually nonexistent in C-4 plants. This is because C-4 plants segregate their RuBISCO enzyme in bundle sheath cells deep within the leaf and the carbon dioxide concentration in these cells is maintained at very high levels. C-4 plants generally have higher growth rates than C-3 plants simply because they do not waste their ATP and NADPH in photorespiration.

Photosynthesis in lower organisms

Algae

There are many different groups of photosynthetic algae. Like higher plants, they all have chlorophyll-a as a photosynthetic pigment, two photosystems (PS-I and PS-II), and the same overall chemical reactions for photosynthesis (equation 1). They differ from higher plants in having different complements of additional chlorophylls. The Chlorophyta and Euglenophyta have chlorophyll-a and chlorophyll-b. The Chrysophyta, Pyrrophyta, and Phaeophyta have chlorophyll-a and chlorophyll-c. The Rhodophyta have chlorophyll-a and chlorophyll-d. The different chlorophylls and other photosynthetic pigments allow algae to utilize different regions of the solar spectrum to drive photosynthesis.

Cyanobacteria

This group was formerly called the blue-green algae and these organisms were once considered members of the plant kingdom. However, unlike the true algae, Cyanobacteria are prokaryotes, in that their DNA is not sequestered within a nucleus. Like higher plants, they have chlorophyll-a as a photosynthetic pigment, two photosystems (PS-I and PS-II), and the same overall equation for photosynthesis (equation 1). The Cyanobacteria differ from higher plants in that they have additional photosynthetic pigments, referred to as phycobilins. Phycobilins absorb different wavelengths of light than chlorophyll and thus increase the wavelength range which can drive photosynthesis. Phycobilins are also present in the Rhodophyte algae, suggesting a possible evolutionary relationship between these two groups.

Chloroxybacteria

This is a group of bacteria represented by a single genus, *Prochloron*. Like the Cyanobacteria, the Chloroxybacteria are prokaryotes. Like higher plants, *Prochloron* has chlorophyll-a, chlorophyll-b and carotenoids as photosynthetic pigments, two photosystems (PS-I and PS-II), and the same overall equation for photosynthesis (equation 1). In general, *Prochloron* is rather like a free-living chloroplast from a higher plant.

KEY TERMS

Calvin cycle—Dark reactions of photosynthesis which use the ATP and NADPH made by the light reactions to synthesize carbohydrates.

Chloroplast—Green organelle of higher plants and algae in which the light and dark reactions of photosynthesis occur.

Cyanobacteria—Prokaryotic organisms which use chlorophylla and phycobilins to drive oxygenic photosynthesis.

Enzyme—Biological molecule, usually a protein, which promotes a biochemical reaction but is not consumed by the reaction.

Eukaryote—Cell whose DNA occurs within a nucleus, considered more advanced than a prokaryote.

Organelle—Membrane enclosed structure within a eukaryotic cell which is specialized for specific cellular functions.

Prokaryote— Cell without a nucleus, considered more primitive than a eukaryote.

Stomata—Pores in plant leaves which function in exchange of carbon dioxide, oxygen, and water during photosynthesis.

Stroma—Aqueous region of the chloroplast in which the dark reactions occur.

Thylakoid—Inner membrane of the chloroplast in which the light reactions occur.

Anaerobic photosynthetic bacteria

This is a group of bacteria which do not produce oxygen during photosynthesis and only photosynthesize in environments which are anaerobic (lacking oxygen). All these bacteria use carbon dioxide and another oxidizable substrate, such as hydrogen sulfide, to make carbohydrates (see equation 2). These bacteria have bacteriochlorophylls and other photosynthetic pigments which are similar to the chlorophylls used by higher plants. Their photosynthesis is different from that of higher plants, algae and cyanobacteria in that they only have one photosystem. This photosystem is similar to PS-I. Most biologists believe that photosynthesis first evolved in anaerobic bacteria several billion years ago.

Halobacterium

There are two species in the genus *Halobacterium.* Most biologists now place this genus with methanogenic (methane-producing) bacteria in the Archaebacteria, a separate kingdom of organisms. Halobacteria thrive in very salty environments, such as the Dead Sea and the Great Salt Lake. In general, halobacteria prefer environments with NaCl **concentration** of about 5 Molar, and cannot tolerate environments with NaCl concentration below about 3 Molar.

Halobacteria are unique in that they perform photosynthesis without chlorophyll. Instead, their photosynthetic pigments are bacteriorhodopsin and halorhodopsin. These pigments are similar to sensory rhodopsin, the pigment which humans and other animals use for vision. Bacteriorhodopsin and halorhodopsin are embedded in the **cell** membranes of halobacteria and each pigment consists of retinal, a vitamin-A **derivative**, bound to a protein. Irradiation of these pigments causes a structural change in their retinal, referred to as photoisomerization. Retinal photoisomerization leads to the synthesis of ATP, the same high energy compound synthesized during the light reactions of higher plants. Interestingly, halobacteria also have two additional rhodopsins, sensory rhodopsin-I and sensory rhodopsin-II which regulate phototaxis, the directional movement in response to light. Bacteriorhodopsin and halorhodopsin seem to have an indirect role in phototaxis as well.

See also Plant pigment.

Further Reading

Attenborough, D. *The Private Life of Plants.* Princeton, NJ: Princeton University Press, 1995.

Corner, E. J. *The Life of Plants.* Chicago: University of Chicago Press, 1981.

Galston, A. W. *Life Processes of Plants: Mechanisms for Survival.* New York: W. H. Freeman Press, 1993.

Kaufman, P. B., et al. *Plants: Their Biology and Importance.* New York: HarperCollins, 1990.

Wilkins, M. *Plant Watching.* New York: Facts on File, 1988.

Peter A. Ensminger

Phototropism

Phototropism is the orientation of an **organism** in response to asymmetric illumination. Phototropism is commonly observed in the stems of higher plants, which grow bent toward a **light** source. Phototropism can be positive (bending toward a light source) or negative (bending away from a light source), depending on the organism and nature of the illumination. Phototropism and other tropisms are different from nastic movements, which are also common in plants. A tropism is the orientation of an organism in response to an external **stimulus**

Plants respond to the direction and amount of light they receive. The seedling at the right was grown in normal, all-around light. The one in the center received no light. The plant at the left grew toward the light that it received on only one side.

in which the stimulus determines the orientation of the movement. A nastic movement is a growth movement in which the stimulus does not determine the orientation of the movement.

History of phototropism research

Plant physiologists have investigated phototropism for over 100 years. The best known early research on phototropism was by Charles Darwin, who reported his experiments in a book published in 1880, *The Power of Movement in Plants*. Although Darwin was better known for his earlier books on **evolution** (*The Origin of Species* and *The Descent of Man*), this book was an important contribution to plant **physiology**.

Darwin studied phototropism in canary grass and oat coleoptiles. The coleoptile is a hollow sheath of **tissue** which surrounds the apical axis (stem) of these and other **grasses**. Darwin demonstrated that these coleoptiles are phototropic in that they bend toward a light source. When he covered the tips of the coleoptiles, they were not phototropic but when he covered the lower portions of the coleoptiles, they were phototropic. Darwin concluded from these and other experiments that (a) the tip of the coleoptile is the most photosensitive region; (b) the middle of the coleoptile is responsible for most of the bending; and (c) an influence which causes bending is transmitted from the top to the middle of the coleoptile.

The Dutch-American botanist Frits Went built upon Darwin's studies and began his own research on phototropism as a student in the 1920s. In particular, Went attempted to isolate the chemical influence which Darwin described. He took tips of oat coleoptiles and placed them on small blocks of agar, a special type of gel. Then, he placed these agar blocks on the sides of other coleoptiles whose tops he cut off. Each coleoptile bent away from the side which had the agar block. Went also performed important control experiments. He observed that plain agar blocks which were placed beneath the lower portions of coleoptiles had no effect on coleoptile bending. Went concluded that the coleoptile tips contained a chemical substance which diffused into the agar blocks and he named this substance auxin. The auxin which Went studied was subsequently identified by chemists as indole-3-acetic acid (IAA). IAA is one of many plant **hormones** which control a number of aspects of plant growth and development.

Cholodny-Went theory

These and other experiments by Went led to what has become known as the Cholodny-Went theory of tropic curvature. In terms of phototropism, the Cholodny-Went theory proposes that (a) auxin is synthesized in the coleoptile tip; (b) the coleoptile tip perceives the asymmetric illumination and this causes auxin to move into the un-irradiated side; (c) auxin moves down the coleoptile so that lower regions develop an auxin asymmetry; and

(d) the higher auxin **concentration** on the un-irradiated side causes the coleoptile to bend toward the light source.

There is currently vigorous debate among plant physiologists about the Cholodny-Went theory. Critics have noted that Went and other early researchers never actually measured the auxin concentrations but only relied on bioassays performed with agar blocks. Furthermore, the early studies relied on small **sample** sizes which were statistically unreliable, and the researchers may have wounded the coleoptiles during tip removal.

In addition, numerous recent experiments indicate that the coleoptile tip is not always necessary for tropic responses and that auxin gradients form in the tissue more slowly than the development of curvature.

Despite these criticisms, many plant physiologists maintain that the basic features of the Cholodny-Went theory have been upheld. The debate about the Cholodny-Went theory has stimulated much new research in phototropism and gravitropism. Many researchers currently are investigating tropic curvature using modern time-lapse **photography**. Others are examining the role of additional plant hormones in regulating phototropism and gravitropism.

The photoreceptor pigment

There has also been an active search for the identity of the photoreceptor pigment, an aspect of phototropism not covered by the Cholodny-Went theory. In the 1930s, many researchers believed the photoreceptor was a carotenoid, a class of mostly orange plant pigments. They argued that carotenoids strongly absorb blue light and phototropism is most effectively elicited by blue light. Furthermore, retinal, a carotenoid derivative, was identified as the photoreceptive pigment controlling **vision** in humans and other animals.

However, more recent experiments appear to rule out a carotenoid as the photoreceptor. In particular, when seedlings are treated with norflurazon, a chemical inhibitor of carotenoid synthesis, they still exhibit phototropism. In addition, mutants of plants and **fungi** which have greatly reduced amounts of carotenoids are unaffected in their phototropic responses.

A great variety of different experiments now indicate that a flavin (vitamin B-2) is the photoreceptor pigment. Like carotenoids, flavins strongly absorb blue light. However, unlike most carotenoids, they also strongly absorb **radiation** in the near-ultraviolet (370 nm) region. Radiation in the near-ultraviolet region of the **spectrum** is also highly effective in phototropism.

KEY TERMS

Agar—Carbohydrate derived from a red alga which biologists use in a gel form for culture media or other purposes.

Bioassay—Estimation of the amount of a substance, such as a hormone, based upon its effect on some easily measured response of an organism.

Coleoptile—Hollow sheath of tissue which surrounds the stem of young grass plants.

Gravitropism—Orientation of an organism in response to gravity.

Nastic movement—Growth movement controlled by external or endogenous factors in which the orientation of the movement is not determined by an external stimulus .

Tropism—Orientation of an organism in response to an external stimulus such as light, gravity, wind, or other stimuli, in which the stimulus determines the orientation of the movement.

Phototropism in other organisms

While phototropism has been most intensively studied in higher plants, many other organisms also exhibit phototropism. Phototropism occurs in the filaments and rhizoids of **algae**, germ tubes and protonemas of mosses, rhizoids and protonemas of **ferns**, spore-bearing stalks of certain fungi, and numerous other organisms.

Many phototropism experiments have been performed on *Phycomyces blakesleeanus*, a zygomycete fungus. *Phycomyces* has slender spore-bearing stalks, referred to as sporangiophores, which bend in response to light and other external stimuli. Incredibly, the sporangiophore of *Phycomyces* is about as photosensitive as the eyes of humans and about one thousand times more photosensitive than a grass coleoptile. Furthermore, the sporangiophore has the ability to adapt to a one hundred million fold change in ambient light intensity. These and other interesting characteristics of *Phycomyces* have made it an excellent model organism for investigation of phototropism.

Phototropism in nature

Laboratory studies of phototropism have a bearing upon the life of plants in nature. It is advantageous for a young seedling, such as a coleoptile, to bend toward the light so that its leaves can intercept more sunlight for **photosynthesis** and grow faster. Phototropism is also re-

lated to solar tracking, the orientation of a plant's leaves in response to the **Sun**. Unlike the response in coleoptiles, which is caused by differential stem growth, solar tracking responses in most species are caused by **pressure** changes in special cells at the **leaf** base. Depending on the species and other factors, the blades of a mature leaf may be oriented **perpendicular** to the Sun's **rays** to maximize photosynthesis or **parallel** to the Sun's rays to avoid over-heating and desiccation.

See also Geotropism.

Further Reading

Hart, J. W. *Plant Tropisms and Other Growth Movements*. London: Routledge, Chapman & Hall, 1990.

Peter A. Ensminger

Photovoltaic cell

A photovoltaic cell, often called a solar cell, converts the **energy** in **light** directly into electrical potential energy using a physical process called the photovoltaic effect. Photovoltaic cells are used to produce **electricity** in situations where they are more economical than other power generation methods. Occasionally, they are used as photodetectors.

The photovoltaic effect has been known since Edmund Becquerel observed light-induced currents in a dilute acid in 1839. Explanation of the effect depends on quantum theories of light and solids that were proposed by Planck in 1900 and Wilson in 1930.

The first solid-state photovoltaic cells were designed in 1954, after the development of solid-state diodes and transistors. Since then, the number of applications of photovoltaic cells has been increasing, the cost per watt of power generated has been declining, and efficiency has been increasing. Enough photovoltaic modules to provide 50 MW of power were made in 1991. The production rate appears to be increasing by about 20% each year.

Photovoltaic cells have been used since 1958 to power many satellites orbiting the **earth**. On earth, they are used in remote areas where the cost of transporting electricity to the site is costly. Their use is one of a variety of alternative energy methods being developed that do not depend on **fossil fuels**. They are also used for low-power mobile applications such as hand-held calculators and wrist watches.

How they work

Photovoltaic cells are made of semiconducting materials—usually silicon—with impurities added to certain regions to create either a surplus of electrons (*n*-type doping) or a scarcity of electrons (*p*-type doping, also called a surplus of holes). The extra electrons and holes carry electrical charges, allowing current to flow in the semiconducting material.

When a **photon** hits the top surface of a photovoltaic cell, it penetrates some **distance** into the semiconductor until it is absorbed. If the photon's energy is at least as large as the material's energy bandgap, the energy from the photon creates an electron-hole pair. Usually, the **electron** and the hole stay together and recombine. In the presence of an electric field, however, the negatively charged electron and the positively charged hole are pulled in opposite directions. This occurs for the same reason that one end of a magnet is attracted to another magnet while the other end is repelled.

Junctions in semiconductors create electrical fields. A junction can be formed at the border between *p*- and *n*-doped regions, or between different semiconducting materials (a heterojunction), or between a semiconductor and certain metals (forming a Schottky barrier).

The movement of the charges in the photovoltaic cell creates a voltage (electrical potential energy) between the top and bottom of the cell. Electrical contacts attached to the cell at the *p* and *n* sides (the top and bottom) complete the cell. Wires attached to these contacts make the voltage available to other devices.

The distance into the material that a photon goes before being absorbed depends on both how efficient the material is at absorbing light and the energy of the photon-high-energy photons penetrate further than low-energy photons. This is why **x rays** are used to image your bones, but most visible light stops at your skin.

Efficiency of a cell depends on the losses that occur at each stage of the photovoltaic process. Many of the sun's photons get absorbed or deflected in the atmosphere before reaching the earth's surface (this is described by a term called air **mass**). Some photons will reflect off or pass through the cell. Some electron-hole pairs recombine before carrying charges to the contacts on the ends of the cell. Some of the charges at the ends of the cells don't enter the contacts, and some energy is lost to resistance in the **metal** contacts and wires.

The efficiency of the cell can be increased by shining more light onto it using a concentrator (such as a focusing **lens**), by adding coatings (such as a mirror to the bottom of the cell to reflect unabsorbed light back into the cell), or by creating heterojunction cells with materials that have different bandgaps, and thus are efficient at absorbing a variety of wavelengths. One of the most efficient photovoltaic cells reported

A custom-designed solar powered desalination system in Jeddah, Saudi Arabia. It is composed of 210 photovoltaic modules that supply 8 kilowatts of power (peak) for conversion of highly saline water into fresh drinking water.

was two-junction cell made of gallium arsenide and gallium antimony, coupled with a concentrator that increased the intensity of the light 100 times: it worked with 33% efficiency in a laboratory. In practice, ground-based solar cells tend to have efficiencies in the teens or less.

Applications

For low-power portable **electronics**, like calculators or small fans, a photovoltaic array may be a reasonable energy source rather than a **battery**. Although using photovoltaics lowers the cost (over time) of the device to the user-who will never need to buy batteries-the cost of manufacturing devices with photovoltaic arrays is generally higher than the cost of manufacturing devices to which batteries must be added. Therefore, the initial cost of photovoltaic devices is often higher than battery-operated devices.

In other situations, such as solar battery chargers, watches, and flashlights, the photovoltaic array is used to generate electricity that is then stored in batteries for use later.

Solar-electric homes

Electricity for homes or other buildings farther than a couple football fields from the nearest electrical lines, may be cheaper if obtained from photovoltaic cells than by buying electricity from the local power utility, because of the cost of running an electrical line to the house. In most urban areas, however, buying electricity from a utility is much cheaper than using photovoltaics.

The cost of using photovoltaic technology depends not only on the photovoltaic cells themselves but also on the batteries and equipment needed to condition the electricity for household use. Modules made of groups of photovoltaic cells set side-by-side and connected in series generate direct current (DC) electricity at a relatively low voltage, but most household appliances use 120-V alternating current (AC). Inverters and power conditioners can transform DC to AC current at the correct voltage.

The types of appliances in the house are also a consideration for whether to use photovoltaic. Some devices - like televisions, air conditioners, blow-dryers, or **laser** printers require a lot of power, sometimes all at once. Because photovoltaic cells don't change the amount of voltage they can

supply, this sort of load can drain batteries rapidly. Many people with houses powered by photovoltaic cells buy energy-efficient lights and appliances and limit the number of unnecessary electrical devices in their homes.

In remote parts of the world, entire villages are powered by photovoltaic systems. A few utility companies in the United States and **Europe** run "solar farms" to produce electricity. Other industrial uses exist for photovoltaic cells, too. These are usually low-power applications in locations inconvenient for traditional electrical sources. Some emergency roadside phones have batteries that are kept charged by photovoltaic cells. Arrays of cells power cathodic protection: the practice of running current through metal structures to slow **corrosion**.

Materials

Many semiconductor materials can be used to make photovoltaic cells, but silicon is most popular-not because it is most efficient, but because it is inexpensive because a lot of silicon is produced for making microelectronics chips. Semiconductors such as gallium arsenide, cadmium sulphide, cadmium telluride, and **copper** indium diselenide are used in special-purpose high-efficiency cells, but are more expensive than silicon cells. The highest-efficiency photovoltaic cells are made of such materials.

Amorphous silicon

The least expensive type of solar cell is made of a disordered type of silicon mixed with **hydrogen**. This hydrogenated amorphous silicon is used in photovoltaic cells for calculators and wristwatches. Amorphous silicon is deposited on a substrate as a coating.

In 1974, David Carlson at RCA's David Sarnoff Laboratory first made an amorphous silicon photovoltaic cell. By 1988, amorphous cells with about 13% efficiency were made using a stacked-junction PIN device.

Because large areas can be coated, the cost-per-device is relatively low. Its bandgap is 1.7 eV, which means that it absorbs light at shorter wavelengths than the crystalline silicon and that it works well under fluorescent lights. Because it absorbs light efficiently, the cells can be made very thin, which uses less material and also helps make the cells less expensive. These devices, however, degrade in direct sunlight and have a shorter lifetime than crystalline cells.

Crystalline silicon

Cells made of single-crystal silicon, the same material used for microelectronics chips, supply more current than the other types of silicon. Unlike amorphous silicon, the voltage stays fairly constant when different loads are applied. Single-crystal silicon photovoltaic cells that are protected from oxidizing last about 20 years.

Polycrystalline silicon is not uniform enough to make electronic chips, but works well for photovoltaic cells. It can be grown with less stringent control than single-crystal silicon but works nearly as efficiently.

See also Alternative energy sources.

Further Reading

Catalano, A. Chap. 2 In *Amorphous & Microcrystalline semiconductor Devices: Optoelectronic Devices.* J. Kanicki, ed. Norwood, Mass.: Artech House, 1991.

Lasnier, F. and T. Gan Ang. *Photovoltaic Engineering Handbook.* Bristol, England: IOP Publishing, 1990.

Markvart, T., ed. *Solar Electricity.* Chichester, England: John Wiley, 1994.

Partain, L. D., ed. *Solar Cells and Their Applications.*Wiley Series in Microwave and Optical Engineering. New York: Wiley Interscience, 1995.

Roberts, S. *Solar Electricity.* New York: Prentice Hall, 1991.

Treble, F. C., ed. *Generating Electricity from the Sun.* Oxford, England: Pergamon Press, 1994.

Yvonne Carts-Powell

Phylogeny

Phylogeny is the inferred evolutionary history of a group of organisms. Paleontologists are interested in understanding life through time—not just at one time in the past or present, but over long periods of past time. Before they can attempt to reconstruct the forms, functions, and lives of once-living organisms, paleontologists have to place these organisms in context. The relationships of those organisms to each other are based on the ways they have branched out, or diverged, from a common ancestor. A phylogeny is usually represented as a phylogenetic tree or cladogram, which are like genealogies of species.

Phylogenetics, the science of phylogeny, is one part of the larger field of systematics, which also includes **taxonomy**. Taxonomy is the science of naming and classifying the diversity of organisms. Not only is phylogeny important for understanding **paleontology** (study of fossils), but paleontology in turn contributes to phylogeny. Many groups of organisms are now extinct, and without their fossils we would not have as clear a picture of how modern life is interrelated.

There is an amazing diversity of life, both living and extinct. For biologists to communicate with each other about these many organisms, there must also be a classi-

fication of these organisms into groups. Ideally, the classification should be based on the evolutionary history of life, such that it predicts properties of newly discovered or poorly known organisms.

Phylogenetic systematics is an attempt to understand the evolutionary interrelationships of living things, trying to interpret the way in which life has diversified and changed over time. While classification is primarily the creation of names for groups, systematics goes beyond this to elucidate new theories of the mechanisms of **evolution**.

Cladistics is a particular method of hypothesizing relationships among organisms. Like other methods, it has its own set of assumptions, procedures, and limitations. Cladistics is now accepted as the best method available for phylogenetic analysis, for it provides an explicit and testable hypothesis of organismal relationships.

The basic idea behind cladistics is that members of a group share a common evolutionary history, and are "closely related," more so to members of the same group than to other organisms. These groups are recognized by sharing unique features which were not present in distant ancestors. These shared derived characteristics are called synapomorphies. Synapomorphies are the basis for cladistics.

In a cladistic analysis, one attempts to identify which organisms belong together in groups, or clades, by examining specific derived features or characters that those organisms share. For example, if a genus of plants has both red flowered and white flowered **species**, then **flower** color might be a useful character for determining the evolutionary relationships of those plants. If it were known that the white flowered form arose from the previously existing red flowered form (i.e., through a **mutation** that prevents formation of the red pigment), then it could be inferred that all of the white colored species arose from a single red-colored ancestor. Characters that define a clade (e.g., white flower color in the example above) are called synapomorphies. Characters that do not unite a clade because they are primitive (e.g., red flower color) are called plesiomorphies.

In a cladistic analysis, it is important to know which character states are primitive and which are derived (that is, evolved from the primitive state). A technique called outgroup comparison is commonly used to make this determination. In outgroup comparison, the individuals of interest (the ingroup) are compared with a close relative. If some of the individuals of the ingroup possess the same character state as the outgroup, then that character state is assumed to be primitive. In the example discussed above, the outgroup has red flowers, so white is the derived state for flower color.

There are three basic assumptions in cladistics:

- 1. Any group of organisms are related by descent from a common ancestor.
- 2. There is a bifurcating pattern of cladogenesis.
- 3. Change in characteristics occurs in lineages over time.

The first assumption is a general assumption made for all evolutionary **biology**. It essentially means that life arose on **earth** only once, and therefore all organisms are related in one way or another. Because of this, we can take any collection of organisms and determine a meaningful pattern of relationships, provided we have the right kind of information.

The second assumption is that new kinds of organisms may arise when existing species or populations divide into exactly two groups. The final assumption, that characteristics of organisms change over time, is the most important assumption in cladistics. It is only when characteristics change that we are able to recognize different lineages or groups. The convention is to call the "original" state of the characteristic plesiomorphic and the "changed" state apomorphic. The terms *primitive* and *derived* have also been used for these states, but they are often avoided by cladists, since those terms have been abused in the past.

Cladistics is useful for creating systems of classification. It is now the most commonly used method to classify organisms because it recognizes and employs evolutionary theory. Cladistics predicts the properties of organisms. It produces hypotheses about the relationships of organisms in a way that makes it possible to predict properties of the organisms. This can be especially important in cases when particular genes or biological compounds are being sought. Such genes and compounds are being sought all the time by companies interested in improving crop yield or disease resistance, and in the search for medicines. Only an hypothesis based on evolutionary theory, such as cladistic hypotheses, can be used for these endeavors.

As an example, consider the **plant** species *Taxus brevifolia*. This species produces a compound, taxol, which is useful for treating **cancer**. Unfortunately, large quantities of **bark** from this rare tree are required to produce enough taxol for a single patient. Through cladistic analysis, a phylogeny for the genus *Taxus* has been produced that shows *Taxus cuspidata*, a common ornamental shrub, to be a very close relative of *T. brevifolia*. *Taxus cuspidata*, then, may also produce large enough quantities of taxol to be useful. Having a classification based on evolutionary descent will allow scientists to select the species most likely to produce taxol.

Cladistics helps to elucidate mechanisms of evolution. Unlike previous systems of analyzing relationships, cladistics is explicitly evolutionary. Because of this, it is possible to examine the way characters change within groups over time—the direction in which characters change, and the relative **frequency** with which they change. It is also possible to compare the descendants of a single ancestor and observe patterns of origin and **extinction** in these groups, or to look at relative size and diversity of the groups. Perhaps the most important feature of cladistics is its use in testing long-standing hypotheses about **adaptation**.

Physical therapy

Physical therapy is a medical specialty that provides treatment using various devices or the hands to strengthen muscles and supply flexibility to a part of the body that is subnormal. The need for physical therapy can be the result of a genetic condition, **disease**, **surgery**, or a trauma such as a **burn** or **automobile** accident. The goal of physical therapy is not necessarily to restore normality but to allow the patient to return to a comfortable and productive life even if the problem persists.

This exacting science has evolved from centuries of using natural therapeutic methods such as sunlight, warm springs, and warm mud to treat injuries. The modern form of physical therapy bloomed after World War I when wounded soldiers were in great need of such services. Further incentive was provided by World War II, and the **epidemic** of **poliomyelitis** in the mid-1950s again brought on great numbers of patients in need of therapy. The development of **antibiotics** and other modern therapeutic measures preserved the lives of those who earlier would have died. These wounded, limbless, or diseased individuals needed a means to regain their independence and ability to earn a living.

Modern physical therapists use **heat** and cold, **electricity**, massage, and various types of machines designed to assist flexibility or restore strength to a given body part. Efforts must go far beyond the simple exercising or heating of an injured limb, however. Most physical therapy is carried out by a team headed by a physiatrist, a physician who specializes in the application of various means of physical therapy. The physical therapist, a technician who is schooled in the muscles and joints and how to **exercise** them, carries out the exercise program with the patient. Devices that apply **pressure** in certain directions and on which resistance can be adjusted are employed in the exercise program, as is simpler methodology such as walking or running. An engineer can build special equipment as needed or alter existing machinery to better suit the patient's needs. The **rehabilitation** nurse provides basic medical care and tracks the patient's progress. If needed, a psychologist is brought in to help the patient adjust to a new, less-comfortable lifestyle. An occupational therapist can assess the patient's needs and provide instruction on how to move about his home, use prosthetic devices, and specially constructed assist devices such as doorknobs or fork handles that allow someone with a paralyzed hand to open doors or feed himself.

The modalities of physical therapy

Four basic modalities are employed in physical therapy, each applied where and when it will do the most good. Not all of the modalities are used in every case.

Cold therapy

Cold therapy or cryotherapy is an effective means of reducing **inflammation** following an accident or injury. Cold therapy is applied in the form of ice packs, sometimes combined with massage, cold **water** bath of the injured area, and other methods. The reduced **temperature** will quell the firing of the nerve-muscle units and reduce muscle spasms, and that along with the anesthetic effect of the cold temperature will ease **pain**. Also, the cold reduces **blood** flow into the injury and reduces any bleeding that may be present and reduces **oxygen** demands of the injured **tissue**, thus preserving the muscle cells. An ice pack often is applied with a compression wrap to reduce swelling, and with elevation of the injured extremity above **heart** level for maximal reduction in swelling.

Heat therapy

Heat or thermotherapy may be employed only after the active swelling of the injury has abated, 24-48 hours following the injury. Heat is conveyed into the injured area by the use of moist heat packs, hot paraffin, hot air or hot water as in a whirlpool bath, by infrared lamp, and by conversion. Conversion is the development of heat brought about by the passage of sound waves or **electric current** through tissue. Diathermy is an example of electrical waves directed into tissue and converted into heat. Ultrasound, very high-frequency sound waves, bring about the vibration of the tissues, which increases the temperature within them. A form of application of sound waves called phonophoresis consists of application of a medication to the injured area followed by ultrasound to drive the medication deep into the tissues.

Heat increases blood flow to an area, so should not be used when internal bleeding accompanies an injury. However, like cryotherapy, heat reduces muscle spasms by increasing the blood flow to an area, which helps to wash out metabolic waste products and increase the amount of oxygen reaching the tissues.

Electrical stimulation

Application of electrical stimulation can restore muscle tone by stimulating muscles to contract rhythmically. This method is used often when an injured person has been confined to bed for a long period of time. Over time, muscles will atrophy and the patient will require long, arduous periods of exercise once he is mobile. The use of electrical stimulation can prevent muscle atrophy and reduce the necessary physical therapy regimen required later. Electricity is also used to drive molecules of medication through the skin into the tissues. This is called iontophoresis. A special machine called a TENS machine (transcutaneous electrical nerve stimulation) beams electric current through the skin (transcutaneously) into the injured area specifically to stop pain. Why TENS has this ability to assuage pain remains open to question, but it is thought that it prevents pain **perception** by the sensory nerves in the injured area. That is, the nerves that normally would detect pain and carry the impulse to the spinal cord do not sense pain. The electrical signal from the TENS machine can be adjusted for **frequency** and strength to achieve its effect without patient discomfort. All electrical stimulation is delivered by placing pads on or around the injured area to conduct the electrical current.

Mechanical manipulation

The use of massage, manipulation of the injured limb, traction, and weight lifting are part of the mechanical form of physical therapy. Massage is the rubbing, tapping, or kneading of an injured area to increase blood circulation and relieve pain. Manipulation consists of putting an injured joint through its movements from one extreme to the other. This is designed to restore full range of **motion** to the joint and eliminate pain from movement. Traction is the application of weight to stretch muscles or to help increase the space between vertebrae and relieve nerve compression. Manipulation may be carried out by a trained technician or by using a machine especially constructed to exercise the injured joint. Resistance can be altered in the machine to make joint extension or flexing more difficult, thus helping to build the muscles that control the joint movement.

Many forms of physical therapy can be carried out at home, but the exercises must first be carefully explained by a trained therapist. Incorrect application of a physical therapy modality can be as harmful as any traumatic injury. Most modalities are applied two or three times daily over a period of time to help restore movement, flexibility, or strength to an injured area.

Physical Therapy and the Aging Adult

Aging is a normal process. Some age-related bodily changes may be misunderstood and unnecessarily limit daily activities. Normal aging need not result in pain and decrease in physical mobility. A physical therapist is a source of information to understand these changes and offer assistance for regaining lost abilities or develop new ones. A physical therapist working with older adults understands the anatomical and physiological changes that occur with normal aging. The physical therapist will evaluate and develop a specially designed therapeutic exercise program. Physical therapy intervention may prevent life long disability and restore the highest level of functioning.

Through the use of tests, evaluations, exercises, treatments with modalities, screening programs, as well as educational information, physical therapists:

- Increase, restore or maintain range of motion, physical strength, flexibility, coordination, balance and endurance.
- Recommend adaptations to make the home accessible and safe.
- Teach positioning, transfers, and walking skills to promote maximum function and independence within an individual's capability.
- Increase overall fitness through exercise programs.
- Prevent further decline in functional abilities through education, **energy conservation** techniques, joint protection, and use of assistive devices to promote independence.
- Improve sensation, joint proprioception and reduce pain.

Common Conditions

A vast number of conditions are treated effectively with physical therapy intervention. Examples of specific diseases and conditions that may be improved with physical therapy include:

- Arthritis
- Sports/Orthopedic Injuries
- Joint Replacements
- Cerebral Vascular Accident (Stroke)
- Coordination and Balance Disorders
- Alzheimer's Disease

See also Syndrome.

KEY TERMS

Cryo—A prefix meaning cold.

Modality—Any of the forms into which physical therapy is divided.

Thermo—A prefix meaning heat.

Transcutaneous—A term meaning through the skin.

Further Reading

Larson, David E. (Ed.). *Mayo Clinic Family Healthbook.* New York: William Morrow & Co. Inc., 1990.

Pisetsky, David S. and Trien, Susan F. *The Duke University Medical Center Book of Arthritis.* New York: Fawcett Columbine, 1992.

Larry Blaser

Physics

Physics is the science that deals with **matter** and **energy** and with the interaction between them. Physics is one of the oldest of the sciences, having originated to a large extent with the work of Galileo Galilei in the first half of the seventeenth century. Many of the principles as to how information about the natural world should be collected, were laid out by the great Italian scientist. For example, it is an axiom among physicists today, as Galileo taught, that the road to sure knowledge about the natural world is to carry out controlled observations (experiments) that will lead to measurable quantities. It is for this reason that experimental techniques, systems of measurements, and mathematical systems for expressing results lie at the core of research in physics.

Classical and modern physics

The field of physics is commonly sub-divided into two large categories: classical and modern physics. The dividing line between these two sub-divisions can be drawn in the early 1900s, when a number of revolutionary new concepts about the nature of matter were proposed. Included among these were Einstein's theories of general and special relativity, Planck's concept of the quantum, Heisenberg's principle of indeterminacy, and the concept of the equivalence of matter and energy.

In general, classical physics can be said to deal with topics on the macroscopic scale, that is on a scale that can be studied with the largely unaided five human senses. Modern physics, in contrast, concerns the nature and behavior of particles and energy at the sub-microscopic level. As it happens, the laws of classical physics are generally inapplicable or applicable only as approximations to the laws of modern physics.

The discoveries made during the first two decades of the twentieth century required a profound re-thinking of the nature of physics. Some broadly-accepted laws had to be completely re-formulated. For example, many classical laws of physics are entirely deterministic. That is, one can say that if A occurs, B is certain to follow. This cause-and-effect relationship was long regarded as one of the major pillars of physics.

The discoveries of modern physics have demanded that this relationship be re-evaluated. Physicists are now more inclined to say that if A occurs, there is an X percent chance that B will follow. Determinism in physics has been replaced by probability.

Divisions of physics

Like other fields of science, physics is commonly subdivided into a number of more specific fields of research. In classical physics, those fields include mechanics, **thermodynamics**, sound, **light** and optics, and **electricity** and **magnetism**. In modern physics, some major sub-divisions include atomic, nuclear, and particle physics.

Mechanics, the oldest field of physics, is concerned with the description of **motion** and its causes. Many of the basic concepts of mechanics were developed by the work of Sir Isaac Newton in about 1687. Thermodynamics grew out of efforts to develop an efficient **steam engine** in the early 1800s. The field deals with the nature of **heat** and its connection with work.

Sound, optics, electricity and magnetism are all divisions of physics in which the nature and propagation of waves are important. The study of sound is also related to practical applications that can be made of this form of energy, as in **radio** communication and human **speech**. Similarly, optics deals not only with the reflection, refraction, **diffraction**, **interference**, polarization, and other properties of light, but also the ways in which these principles have practical applications in the design of tools and instruments such as telescopes and microscopes.

The study of electricity and magnetism focuses not only on the properties of particles at rest, but also on the properties of those particles in motion. Thus, the field of static electricity examines the forces that exist between charged particles at rest, while current electricity deals with the movement of electrical particles.

In the area of modern physics, nuclear and atomic physics involve the study of the atomic nucleus and its

KEY TERMS

Determinism—The notion that a known effect can be attributed with certainty to a known cause.

Energy—The ability to do work.

Matter—Anything that has mass and takes up space.

Mechanics—The science that deals with energy and forces and their effects on bodies.

Sub-microscopic—Referring to levels of matter that can not be directly observed by the human senses, even with the best of instruments; the level of atoms and electrons.

parts, with special attention to changes that take place (such as nuclear decay) in the atom. Particle and high-energy physics, on the other hand, focus on the nature of the fundamental particles of which the natural world is made. In these two fields of research, very powerful, very expensive tools, such as linear **accelerators** and synchrotrons ("atom-smashers") are required to carry out the necessary research.

Interrelationship of physics to other sciences

One trend in all fields of science over the past century has been to explore ways in which the five basic sciences (physics, **chemistry**, **astronomy**, **biology**, and **earth** sciences) are related to each other. This has led to another group of specialized sciences in which the laws of physics are used to interpret phenomena in other fields. **Astrophysics**, for example, is a study of the composition of astronomical objects, such as stars, and the changes that they undergo. Physical chemistry and chemical physics, on the other hand, are fields of research that deal with the physical nature of chemical molecules. **Biophysics**, as another example, is concerned with the physical properties of molecules essential to living organisms.

Further Reading

Baez, Albert V. *The New College Physics: A Spiral Approach.* San Francisco: W. H. Freeman and Company, 1967.

Weber, Robert L., Kenneth V. Manning, Marsh W. White, and George A. Weygand. *College Physics.* 5th edition. New York: McGraw-Hill Book Company, 1974.

Wilson, Jerry D. *Physics: Concepts and Applications.* 2nd edition. Lexington, MA: D. C. Heath, 1981.

David E. Newton

Physiology

Physiology is the study of how various biological components work independently and together to enable organisms, from animals to microbes, to function. This scientific discipline covers a wide variety of functions from the cellular and subcellular level to the interaction of **organ** systems that keep more complex biological machines, like humans, running.

Physiological studies are aimed at answering many questions. For instance, physiologists investigate why plants grow or **bacteria** divide, how food is processed in various organisms, and how thought processes occur in the **brain** (a branch of this discipline known as neurophysiology). It is often physiology-related investigations that uncover the origins of diseases.

Human (or mammalian) physiology is the oldest branch of this science dating back to at least 420 B.C. and the time of Hippocrates, the father of medicine. Modern physiology first appeared in the 17th century when scientific methods of observation and experimentation were used to study **blood** movement, or circulation, in the body. In 1929, American physiologist W. B. Cannon coined the term **homeostasis** to describe one of the most basic concerns of physiology: how the varied components of living things adjust to maintain a constant internal environment conducive to optimal functioning.

With the steady advance of scientific technology-from the simple **microscope** to ultra high-tech computerized scanning devices-the field of physiology grew in scope. No longer confined to investigating the functioning components of life that could be observed with the naked **eye**, physiologists began to delve into the most basic life forms, like bacteria. They could also study organisms' basic molecular functions, like the electrical potentials in cells that help control the **heart** beat.

The branches of physiology are almost as varied as the countless life forms that inhabit the **earth**. Viral physiology, for example, focuses on how these minute life forms feed, grow, reproduce, and excrete by-products. However, the more complex an **organism**, the more avenues of research open to the physiologist. Human physiology, for instance, is concerned with the functioning of organs, like the heart and liver, and how the senses, like sight and **smell**, work.

Physiologists also observe and analyze how certain body systems, like the circulatory, respiratory, and nervous systems, work independently and in concert to maintain life. This branch of physiology is known as comparative physiology. Ecological physiology, on the other hand, studies how animals developed or evolved

specific biological mechanisms to cope with a particular environment. An example is dark skin, which provides protection against harmful rays of the **sun** for humans who live in tropical clients. Cellular physiology, or **cell biology**, focuses on the structures and functions of the cell. Like the term cell biology, many branches of physiology are better known by other names including **biochemistry**, **biophysics**, and endocrinology (the study of secreting tissues).

See also Circulatory system; Disease; Nervous system; Reproductive system.

Physiology, comparative

While **anatomy** is the study of the structures of an **organism**, **physiology** is the science dealing with the study of the function of an organism's component structures. However, it often is not enough to know what an **organ**, **tissue**, or other structure does. Physiologists want to know how something functions. For example, physiological questions might ask: What is the function of human lung tissue? How can a seal survive under **water** without breathing for over ten minutes? How do **camels** survive so long without water? How do **insects** see ultraviolet light? Physiology examines functional aspects at many levels of organization, from molecules, to cells, to tissues, to organs, to organ systems, to an entire organism. It is the branch of **biology** that investigates the operations and vital processes of living organisms that enable life to exist.

Comparative physiology, then, is the comparison of physiological adaptations among organisms to diverse and changing environments. Comparative physiology, like comparative anatomy, attempts to uncover evolutionary relationships between organisms or groups of organisms. Comparative physiology seeks to explain the **evolution** of biological functions by likening physiological characteristics between and among organisms (usually animals.) This branch of biology constructs phylogenetic relationships (or, more loosely, evolutionary connections) between and among groups of organisms. Comparative physiology, in conjunction with other comparative disciplines, enables us to trace the evolution of organisms and their unique structures and to view ourselves in a broader light. By comparing the physiology among living things, scientists can gain insights into how groups of organisms have solved the adaptive problems in their natural environments over time.

Comparative physiology compares basic physiological processes like **cellular respiration** and gas exchange, thermoregulation, circulation, water and ion balance, nerve impulse transmission, and muscle contraction. Because it focuses on function, comparative physiology can also be referred to as *functional anatomy*. The form of an organ, or other biological structure, is tied to its function much in the same way a tool is linked to its purpose. For example, the function of anenzyme (a protein **molecule** that speeds up a chemical reaction) depends heavily upon its three-dimensional shape. If the 3-D conformation of the **enzyme** molecule is altered (by **heat** or acid), the function of the enzyme will also be altered. If the shape of an enzyme is changed considerably, its biological activity will be lost.

A major theme dominating the topic of comparative physiology is the concept of **homeostasis**. The term is derived from two Greek words (*homeo*, meaning "same," and *stasis*, meaning "standing still") and literally means staying the same. Homeostasis thus refers to the ability of animals to maintain an internal environment that compensates for changes occurring in the external environment. Only the surface cells of the human body, for example, and the lining of the gastrointestinal and respiratory tracts come into direct contact with the outside surroundings (like the atmosphere). The vast majority of cells of the body are enclosed by neighboring cells and the extracellular fluid (fluid found outside of cells) that bathes them. So the body in essence exists in an internal environment that is protected from the wider range of conditions that are found in the external surroundings. Therefore, to maintain homeostasis, the body must have a system for monitoring and adjusting its internal environment when the external environment changes. Comparative physiologists observe physiological similarities and differences in adaptations between organisms in solving identical problems concerning homeostasis.

Some of the problems that animals face in maintaining physiological homeostasis involve basic life processes. **Energy** acquisition from food (digestion) and its expenditure, the maintenance of body **temperature** and metabolic rate, the use of **oxygen** or the ability to live in its absence, and the way body size affects **metabolism** and heat loss are examples of problems that require homeostatic systems. Comparative physiologists might, for example, compare the efficiency of the relative oxygen capturing abilities of mammalian hemoglobin (in red **blood** cells) and insect hemolymph. Both groups of animals must maintain homeostasis and regulate the amount of oxygen reaching their tissues, yet each group solves the problem differently.

Comparative physiology makes specific measurements to obtain biologically relevant information from which to make comparisons. The kinds of processes that physiologists measure from anatomical structures to gain insight into their function include: rates (how fast some-

thing occurs), changes in rates, gradients (increasing or decreasing concentrations of substances), pressures, rate of flow (of a fluid such as air or blood), **diffusion** (the act of a substance moving from an area of high **concentration** to one of low concentration), tension (material stress caused by a pull), **elasticity**, electrical current, and voltage. For example, a comparative physiologist might measure the rate of diffusion of sugar molecules across intestinal **cell** membranes, or the **pressure** exerted on the walls of blood vessels that are close to the **heart**. In each case, the comparative physiologist is trying to gain information that will help explain how a particular structure functions and how it compares with similar structures in other organisms in solving the same homeostatic problem. The conclusions derived, then, tell us all about our evolutionary history.

Phytoplankton

Phytoplankton are microscopic, photosynthetic organisms that float in the **water** of the oceans and bodies of **freshwater** (the word phytoplankton is derived from the Greek for "drifting plants"). The most abundant organisms occurring within the phytoplankton are **algae** and blue-green **bacteria**, but this group also includes certain kinds of protists (especially protozoans) that contain symbiotic algae or bacteria.

Phytoplankton are responsible for virtually all of the primary production occurring in the oceans. Marine phytoplankton range in size from extremely small blue-green bacteria, to larger (but still microscopic) unicellular and colonial algae. Oceanic phytoplankton are grazed by tiny animals known as **zooplankton** (most of which are crustaceans). These are eaten in turn by larger zooplankton and small **fish**, which are fed upon by larger fish and baleen whales. Large predators such as bluefin **tuna**, **sharks**, **squid**, and toothed whales are at the top of the marine food web. Marine phytoplankton are much more productive near the shores of continents, and particularly in zones where there are persistent upwellings of deeper water. These areas have a much better nutrient supply, and this stimulates a much greater productivity of phytoplankton than occurs in the open **ocean**. In turn, these relatively fertile regions support a higher productivity of animals. This is why the world's most important marine fisheries are supported by the continental shelves (such as the Grand Banks and other shallow waters of northeastern **North America**, near-shore waters of western North and **South America**, and the Gulf of Mexico) and regions with persistent upwellings (such as those off the coast of Peru and elsewhere off western South America, and extensive regions of the Antarctic Ocean).

Some inland waterbodies occur in inherently fertile watersheds, and are naturally eutrophic, meaning they have a high productivity and **biomass** of phytoplankton (in shallow waters, larger aquatic plants may also be highly productive). So-called cultural eutrophication is a kind of **pollution** caused by nutrient inputs associated with human activities, such as the dumping of sewage waste and the runoff of fertilizer from agricultural land. Both fresh and marine waters can become eutrophic through increases in their nutrient supply, although the problem is more usually severe in freshwaters. The most conspicuous symptom of **eutrophication** is a large increase in the biomass of phytoplankton, which in extreme cases is known as an algal "bloom."

Pi

Pi is one of the most fundamental constants in all of **mathematics**. It is normally first encountered in **geometry** where it is defined as the **ratio** of the circumference of a **circle** to the diameter: $\pi = C/d$ where C is the circumference and d is the diameter. This fact was known to the ancient Egyptians who used for π the number 22/7 which is accurate enough for many applications. A closer **approximation** in fractions is 355/113. Students often use a decimal approximation for π, such as 3.14 or 3.14159.

Actually, the number π is not even a **rational number**. That is, it is not exactly equal to a fraction, m/n where m and n are whole numbers or to any finite or repeating decimal. This fact was first established in the middle of the eighteenth century by the German mathematician, Johann Lambert. Even further, it is a transcendental number. That is, it is not the root of any polynomial equation with rational coefficients. This was first proved by another German mathematician, Ferdinand Lindeman, in the latter half of the nineteenth century.

There are many infinite series that can be used to calculate approximations to π. One of these is

$$\pi/4 = 1-1/3 + 1/5-1/7 + 1/9-1/11 + 1/13-...$$

where the denominators are the consecutive odd numbers.

Roy Dubisch

Pigeons and doves

Pigeons and doves include about 300 **species** of **birds** in the family Columbidae. Most species are found

in **forests** of various types, with fewer species occurring in more open habitats. By far the greatest richness of species of pigeons and doves occurs in moist tropical and sub-tropical forests. Many tropical oceanic islands have **endemic** species of pigeons and doves that evolved in isolation. Many of these local (or endemic) species have become endangered by **habitat** loss or predation by introduced **mammals** (such as **cats** and **rats**), and some are already extinct.

Larger birds in this family are usually called pigeons, while the smaller ones are called doves. Other than this vague criterion, there is no substantial difference between pigeons and doves.

Birds in this family are distinguished by their relatively small head, short neck, a soft but dense plumage, and a naked, fleshy **tissue** (known as a cere) at the top of the upper mandible. Pigeons typically have "cooing" calls, which are used in **courtship** and in some respects are equivalent to the songs of other birds. The plumage of many species of pigeons is a subdued grey, brown, and white, and is often tinged with iridescence. However, some tropical species have very bright and spectacularly colored plumage.

Biology of pigeons and doves

The smallest species of pigeon is the diamond dove (*Geopelia cuneata*), only 2 in (15 cm) long and weighing 1 oz (30 g). The largest species is the Victoria crowned pigeon (*Goura victoria*), 32 in (80 cm) long and 5 lbs (2.4 kg) in weight.

Most pigeons are strong fliers, and some species are capable of undertaking long-distance movements and migrations. Other pigeons, especially those living in moist tropical forest, are local birds that spend a great deal of time walking on the ground, foraging for their food of **fruits**. The pheasant pigeon (*Otidiphaps nobilis*) of New Guinea is almost entirely terrestrial, and rather fowl-like in its appearance and **behavior**.

Pigeons are almost entirely seed and fruit eaters. Pigeons have a large, muscular gizzard, which is useful in grinding hard fruits, for example **tree** "mast" such as acorns, hazelnuts, chestnuts, and other nutritious fruits that most birds are not capable of digesting.

Pigeons have the ability to suck **water** when drinking. This is rather distinctive, because almost all other birds can only swallow water by taking some into their mouth, and then tilting their head back to let the liquid run down their throat.

Pigeons are monogamous, laying one to two eggs on a rough platform nest, commonly built of twigs. Both sexes share the incubation of the eggs, the male during the day, and the female at night. Young pigeons are initially fed by a material known as "pigeon milk," which is a rich, nutritious secretion of the lining of the crop of the adult birds. This material is collected from the crop by the young birds, which must insert their head rather deeply into the adult's throat to do so. Older chicks are also fed regurgitated **seeds** and other **plant** foods.

A Victoria crowned pigeon (*Goura victoria*). Both sexes of this species possess the crest, but only the male performs the courtship display in which it is shown off.

Pigeons of North America

Seven native species of pigeons occur regularly in **North America**. The most widespread of these is the mourning dove (*Zenaidura macroura*), named after its loud, soulful cooings. This species occurs widely south of the boreal forest. The mourning dove is migratory in the northern parts of its range, although suburban birds can manage to survive the winter if they have access to dependable food at feeders.

All other native pigeons are relatively southern in their distribution. The band-tailed pigeon (*Columba fasciata*) and white-winged dove (*Zenaida asiatica*) are southwestern in distribution, while the ground dove (*Columbigallina passerina*) also occurs in the southeast. The white-crowned pigeon (*Columba leucocephala*) only occurs in the Florida Keys and a few places on the immediately adjacent mainland.

Wherever these native pigeons are abundant, they may be hunted for sport. One North American species, the passenger pigeon (*Ectopistes migratorius*), was driven into **extinction** as a result of overhunting for sale in urban markets.

The domestic pigeon

The natural range of the rock dove or feral pigeon (*Columba livia*) was probably regions of the Mediterranean **basin** with rocky cliffs where these birds can nest. However, this species has been domesticated by humans, and it has now been introduced to suitable habitats around the world, including North America. The rock dove may now be the world's most widely distributed bird.

The domestic pigeon is the cultivated variety of *Columba livia* that is raised for food. It is most commonly the young birds, which are known as squabs, that are eaten.

The domestic pigeon develops an intense affinity for the place where it nests and roosts at night. This bird is also very skillful at finding its way back to its home roost after it has been taken some **distance** away. Humans have exploited this characteristic by using "carrier pigeons" to transport messages over long distances. The invention of the **radio** and other methods of long-distance communication eventually replaced carrier pigeons, but competitions are still held to test the homing abilities of individual racing birds.

Domestic pigeons have also been bred into some very unusual varieties of color, feather displays, and body shape. People who find the aesthetics of unusual pigeons to be interesting form clubs, and they avidly compare, trade, and sell their varieties of domestic pigeons.

Feral pigeons are domestic pigeons that have escaped and are breeding in the wild. Feral pigeons usually live in cities and other built-up areas, although they sometimes breed in more natural habitats as well. These birds are often considered to be **pests**, because they can be a nuisance when abundant, soiling statues and buildings with their excrement, and sometimes fouling people walking along streets or in parks.

However, feral pigeons are among the few non-human creatures that can tolerate the environmental conditions of cities, and they contribute a positive aesthetic to urban areas. Many people enjoy hand-feeding urban pigeons in parks and other public places where these birds can be abundant and tame.

A few other species of pigeons are kept in captivity, usually as pets. Common ornamental pigeons include the collared dove (*Streptopelia decaocto*), spotted dove (*S. chinensis*), turtle dove (*S. turtur*), and ringed turtle dove (*S. risoria*). Some of these birds have escaped from captivity and established feral populations outside of their natural range, for example, in southern parts of the United States.

The passenger pigeon

One of the most famous examples of an extinction caused by humans involves the passenger pigeon. This species became extinct in the early twentieth century through gross overhunting coupled with the loss of most of its natural habitat of mature **angiosperm** forests, which was widely converted to agriculture.

The natural range of the passenger pigeon was southeastern North America. Prior to its overhunting, about 300 years ago, the passenger pigeon may have been the world's most abundant landbird. Its pre-impact population has been estimated at three to five billion individuals, which may have accounted for one quarter of the population of all birds in North America.

During its migrations, the passenger pigeon occurred in tremendous flocks that were described as obscuring the **sun** on an otherwise clear day, and could take hours to pass. In 1810, Alexander Wilson, an American naturalist, guessed that a single migratory flock, perhaps 0.3 mi (0.6 km) wide and 89 mi (144 km) long, contained two billion birds. Many other impressions written by naturalists of those times also suggest that the passenger pigeon was an extraordinarily abundant bird.

Because passenger pigeons tended to migrate and breed in large, dense groups, it was easy for commercial hunters to kill them in large numbers and then sell the carcasses in urban markets. The passenger pigeon was slaughtered in enormous numbers using guns, clubs, nets, and smoke. The size of some of the hunts is astonishing, for example, in 1869 an estimated one billion birds inhabited Michigan alone. This intensity of exploitation, occurring at the same time as the destruction of much of its breeding habitat, proved to be unsustainable, and the passenger pigeon quickly declined in abundance. The last known nesting attempt in the wild occurred in 1894, and the last passenger pigeon died in a zoo in 1914.

The extinction of the passenger pigeon has become a metaphor for the sorts of damages that uncontrolled ex-

ploitation by humans can cause to even enormously abundant ecological resources.

See also Critical habitat.

Further Reading

Baskett, T., ed. *Ecology and Management of the Mourning Dove.* Harrisburg, PA.: Stackpole Books, 1993.

Brooke, M. and T. Birkhead, eds. *The Cambridge Encyclopedia of Ornithology.* Cambridge, U.K.: Cambridge University Press, 1991.

Freedman, B. *Environmental Ecology,* 2nd ed. San Diego: Academic Press, 1994.

Harrison, C. J. O., ed. *Bird Families of the World.* New York: H.N. Abrams Pubs., 1978.

Skutch, A.F. *The Life of the Pigeon.* Ithaca, New York: Cornell University Press, 1991.

Bill Freedman

Pigs

Pigs, hogs, or swine consist of about eight species of **mammals** in the family Suidae, which is part of the order Artiodactyla, the cloven-hoofed **ungulates**. Pigs are closely related to the **peccaries** (family Tayassuidae) and **hippopotamuses** (family Hippopotamidae). The natural distribution of pigs includes **Africa**, **Europe**, and **Asia**, but one species, the domestic pig (*Sus scrofa*), is now found almost worldwide as a domestic and feral species.

Pigs have a relatively large head, with a long, cone-shaped snout, small eyes, long ears, a short neck, short legs, and a stout body. The skin of pigs is thick and tough, and it may be sparsely or thickly haired, depending on species. The largest pigs can weigh more than 660 lbs (300 kg).

Pigs have a flat-fronted, cartilaginous, malleable, almost hairless nose that is very tactile, and along with the extremely keen sense of **smell**, helps these animals to find and root out their food, which is often buried underground. Pigs also have an excellent sense of **hearing**, which is very useful in helping them to detect the activities of potential predators. However, pigs have poor **vision**, and they can only see effectively over short distances. The canine teeth of pigs grow continuously, and in male animals (or boars) these can be very large, and curl as tusks outside of the mouth. These sharp teeth can be used by mature pigs as slashing weapons, either in defence against a **predator**, or in combat between male pigs during the breeding season.

Pigs are omnivorous animals, eating a highly varied diet. Most of the foods consumed by pigs are **plant** tissues, especially underground roots, rhizomes, and tubers, which are excavated using the snout. Pigs also eat the foliage of many plants, as well as nuts, **seeds**, and **fruits** that may be found on the ground. Pigs are opportunistic predators, and will eagerly eat **birds** eggs and nestlings if these are discovered, as well as small **rodents**, **snakes**, and other **prey**. Pigs will also attack larger, disabled animals, and will eat carrion.

Pigs occur in a wide range of habitats, from alpine **tundra**, through most types of temperate and tropical **forests**, savannas, swamps, and the vicinity of human settlements. Wet places are a necessary component of all pig habitats, because mud bathing is important to the physical and mental health of these animals.

Most species of pigs are social, with the animals generally living in family groups consisting of at least a mature female (or sow) and her young. Mature boars are generally solitary, except during the mating season. Grunting and squeaking noises are important in the communications among pigs. Baby pigs are precocious, and can move about only a few hours after their **birth**. Broods of pigs can be quite large, and can exceed a dozen piglets. Young pigs often fall victim to predators, but mature animals can be ferocious in their self-defence, and are not an easy mark as prey. Pigs can live to be as old as 25 years.

Species of pigs

The true pigs include four species in the genus *Sus*. The wild boar (*Sus scrofa*) is the progenitor of the domestic pig. This species is native to the temperate regions of Europe, North Africa, and temperate and tropical Asia. The wild boar has been introduced far beyond its original range, and now occurs widely in parts of **North America**, New Guinea, **Australia**, New Zealand, and many other islands of the Pacific Ocean.

Wild boars can reach a weight of up to 770 lbs (350 kg). The curved, sharp tusks of large boars can reach a length of 9 in (23 cm). These formidable tusks are used as slashing weapons, and for cutting and digging up food. Wild boars live in social groups, commonly consisting of one or several mature females and their offspring, which can total as many as twelve in a single litter, although the usual number is smaller. Mature male animals tend to live by themselves, except during the breeding season.

Wild boars live in an extremely varied range of habitats, from dry prairies and savannahs to wet swamps, and from lowland near **sea level** to montane and alpine ecosystems as much as 13,120 ft (4,000 m) in elevation. In addition, wild boars will eat an amazingly wide range of foods. Wild boars are primarily vegetarian, feeding on fruits, nuts, seeds, tubers, and rhizomes, with the relative importance of these in the diet varying geographically and with seasonal

A warthog (*Phacochoerus aethiopicus*) in Kenya.

availability. However, wild boars will also opportunistically avail themselves of any **animal** foods that present themselves, including animals that are found dead as carrion, as well as those that can be easily predated, such as the eggs or nestlings of ground-nesting birds, or slow-moving rodents, **frogs**, or **reptiles**. Other than humans, wild boars may be more omnivorous than any other animal.

The bearded pig (*Sus barbatus*) occurs in tropical rainforests and mangrove forests of Malaysia and the Sunda Islands of Indonesia. This species can achieve a weight of up to 330 lbs (150 kg), and it develops a beard of long hairs on its cheeks. Bearded pigs live in family groups or larger herds, which roam through the jungle looking for fallen fruits and other foods. Bearded pigs are relatively sedentary in most parts of their range, but in northeastern Borneo they undertake seasonal migrations in large numbers. Because these movements involve routes that are traditionally used, and are known to human hunters, these bearded pigs can be easily killed in large numbers during their **migration**.

The Javan pig (*Sus verrucosus*) occurs in **grasslands**, forests, and swamps on the islands of Java and Sulawesi in Indonesia, and also in some of the Philippine islands. Javan pigs can weigh as much as 330 lbs (150 kg). The pygmy hog (*Sus salvanius*) occurs in forests of the southern Himalayas, particularly Nepal. This is a very rare species of pig, and can achieve a weight of about 440 lbs (200 kg).

The bush pigs (*Potamochoerus porcus*) occur in tropical-forest habitats throughout sub-Saharan Africa and on Madagascar. Boars of these species have well developed and sharp canine teeth. These animals generally forage in small groups at dusk or during the night.

The warthog (*Phacochoerus aethiopicus*) is a barrel-shaped animal of the extensive savannas and open forests of central and southern Africa. The warthog has a big head decorated with large skin warts, and huge, outcurving tusks, which can be as long as 26.8 in (68 cm), but are more usually about 11.8 in (30 cm). Warthogs feed most actively during the day.

The giant forest hog (*Hylochoerus meinertzhageni*) is a rare species that occurs in tropical rain-forests of central Africa. Although the giant forest hog is a large animal, weighing as much as 297 lbs (135 kg), it is shy and lives deep in relatively inaccessible habitats, and was not known to science until 1904.

The babirusa (*Babyrousa babyrussa*) is a strange-looking, almost hairless pig of swampy jungles and reedy thickets of Sulawesi and nearby islands in Indonesia. This species grows as large as 220 lbs (100 kg). Some old boars can grow enormous, curling, upper tusks as long as 16.9 in (43 cm), that can develop as a complete, 360-degree **circle**. The upper canines of babirusa boars actually curl and grow upwards, and penetrate right through the skin of the upper jaw, so the head is actually protected by four, curling tusks, two on each side.

The domestic pig

The many distinctive races of domestic pig are all derived from the wild boar, and are sometimes designated as their own subspecies, *Sus scrofa domesticus*. The domestic pig is mostly raised as food for humans, and today a population of about 0.85-billion pigs are being raised in agriculture around the world.

Pigs are an ancient domesticate, and they have been cultivated by people for many thousands of years. Today, pigs are raised using various systems of husbandry, which vary enormously in their intensity. The oldest and simplest systems depend on locally free-ranging pigs, which return to their designated domiciles in the village each evening. Whenever they are needed for food or to sell as a cash-crop, individual pigs are killed or taken to the market, while the breeding nucleus is still conserved. Raising pigs in this relatively simple way is common in many subsistence agricultural systems in poorer parts of the world. For example, in the highlands of New Guinea pigs have long been an important agricultural crop, as well as being very prominent in the culture of the indigenous peoples, who measure their wealth in terms of the numbers of pigs owned by a person or village.

Of course, modern industrial agriculture involves much more intensive management of pigs than is practiced in these sorts of subsistence systems. Pigs raised on factory farms may be bred with close attention to carefully designed breeding lineages, often using artificial insemination to control the stud line. Industrial piggeries keep their animals indoors, under quite crowded conditions, while feeding the pigs a carefully monitered diet that is designed to optimize the growth rates. Fecal materials and urine represent a substantial disposal problem on factory farms, which may be resolved by disposal onto fields or into a nearby **water** body, or if this is prohibited, by building a **sewage treatment** facility. Pigs grown under these types of rather unsanitary, crowded conditions are susceptible to diseases and infections. Therefore, close attention must be paid to the health of the animals, and regular inoculations and treatments with **antibiotics** may be required.

KEY TERMS

Feral—This refers to domesticated animals that have escaped to natural habitats beyond their natural range, and can maintain wild populations, as is the case of many introductions of wild boars.

Husbandry—The science of propagating and raising domestic animals, especially in agriculture.

Omnivore—An animal that eats a very wide range of foods, including plant materials, as well as animals. The animal foods may be either predated, or scavenged as carrion.

The intensively managed husbandry systems by which pigs and other **livestock** are raised in industrial agriculture are often criticized by environmentalists and ethicists. The environmentalists tend to focus on the ecological damages associated with various agricultural activities, for example, the disposal of sewage and other wastes. The ethicists complain about the morality of forcing intelligent animals such as pigs to live under highly unnatural conditions. The life of an industrial pig includes living under conditions lacking in many sensory stimuli, **exercise**, and numerous other elements of a happy life, eventually to be crowded into trucks and trains to be transported to a central abattoir, where the animal is slaughtered and processed under generally brutal conditions. The environmental and ethical dimensions of modern animal husbandry are becoming increasingly important considerations in the ongoing debate about the relationships of humans with other species, and to ecosystems more generally. These are important issues in terms of the sustainability of our resource-use systems.

Domestic pigs are sometimes used in southern France to hunt for truffles, which are extremely flavorful and valuable **mushrooms** that are prized by gourmet cooks. The truffles develop beneath the ground, but they can be easily detected by specially trained pigs, thanks to their relatively high intelligence and extremely sensitive sense of smell.

Sometimes, individuals of the smaller races of pigs are kept as housepets. Pigs are highly social animals, and if raised from a young age they will become highly affectionate and loyal to humans. Pigs are quite intelligent animals, similar in this respect to the domestic dog (*Canis familiaris*), and this characteristic also enhances their qualities as a pet. In addition, pigs can be rather easily toilet trained. One of the most favored races of pig as pets is the Vietnamese pot-bellied pig.

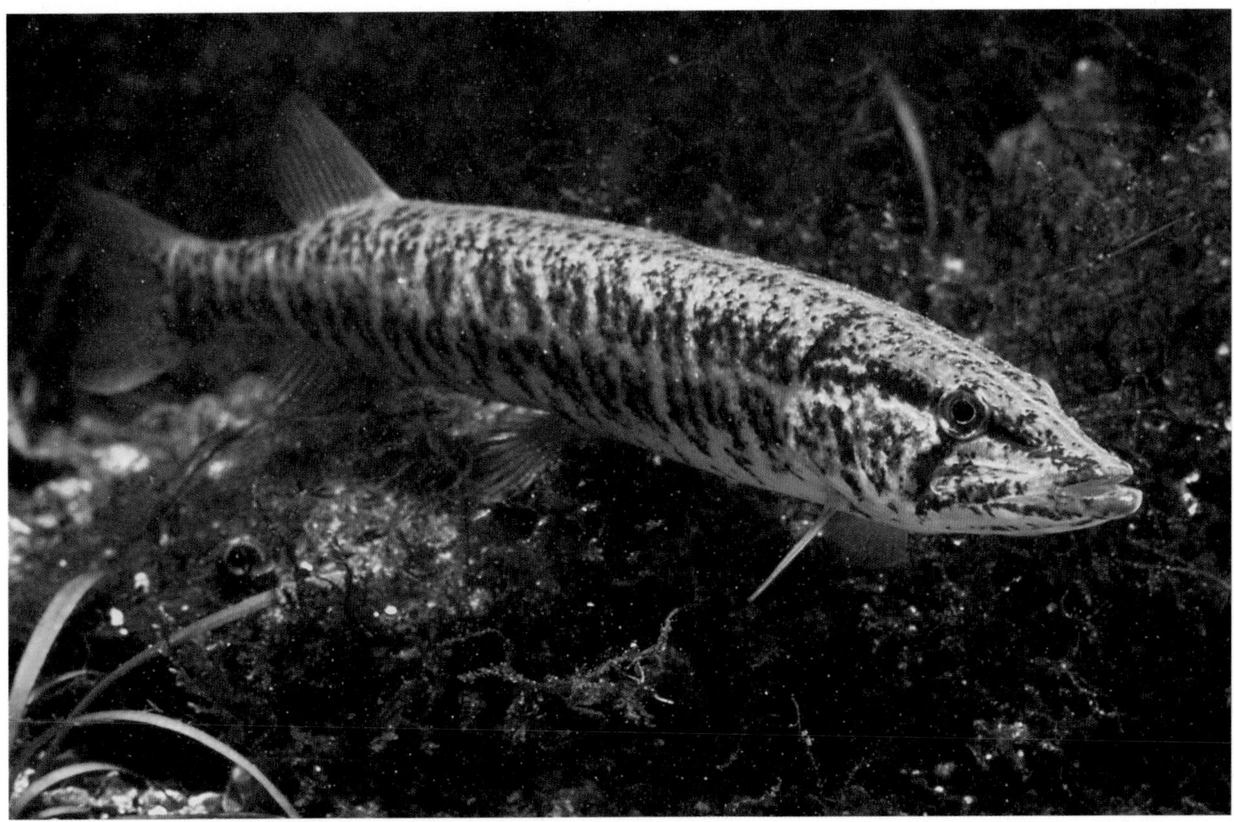

A redfin pickerel.

Further Reading

Grzimek, B. (ed.). *Grzimek's Encyclopedia of Mammals.* London: McGraw Hill, 1990.

Nowak, R. M. (ed.) *Walker's Mammals of the World.* 5th ed. Baltimore: Johns Hopkins University Press, 1991.

Porter, V. *Pigs: A Handbook to the Breeds of the World.* Pica Press, 1993.

Wilson, D.E. and D. Reeder (comp.). *Mammal Species of the World.* 2nd ed. Washington, D.C., Smithsonian Institution Press, 1993.

Bill Freedman

Pikas see **Lagomorphs**

Pike

Pike are large carnivorous species of **bony fish** in the genus *Esox* in the family Esocidae. Pike occur in static and slowly flowing fresh-water habitats, throughout most of **Europe**, northern **Asia**, and **North America**.

Pike have a relatively long, streamlined, fusiform body, adapted to swimming in rapid bursts to catch their **prey** of smaller **fish** (including other pike), **amphibians**, **crayfish**, small **mammals**, and even ducklings. The fins of pike are soft-rayed, and the dorsal and ventral fins are sited relatively far back on the body. Pike have large mouths, with the jaw joint extending relatively far back on the head, commonly to behind the **eye**. The mouth is armed with numerous, needle-like teeth. Pike normally hunt by ambush-lying quietly in beds of aquatic plants or other cover until prey comes close, when it is seized by a rapid strike.

The largest individuals of northern pike (*Esox lucius*) are enormous animals from eastern Siberia, that weigh from 77 to 154 lb (35 to 70 kg-as much as an average human). More typically, adults of this species can weigh up to 33 lb (15 kg), but most weigh considerably less. The largest individual pikes are females, which may exceed 60 years of age.

Pike spawn in the spring in shallow **water** habitats. The largest females are also the most fecund, and can lay more than one million eggs.

The northern pike or jackfish (*E. lucius*) is the most widespread species in this family, occurring both in northern Eurasia and North America. Other species in

KEY TERMS

Symbiotic relationship—A relationship between two organisms that is beneficial to both.

North America include the chain pickerel (*E. niger*) and pickerel (*E. americanus*) of the east, the grass pickerel (*E. verniculatus*) of the central and southern parts of the **continent**, and the muskellunge (*E. masquinongy*) of the Great Lakes and nearby lakes, which can achieve a weight of 110 lbs (50 kg). The Amur pike (*E. reicherti*) occurs in parts of central Siberia.

Pike of all species are considered to be valuable gamefish, and are avidly sought after by sport fishers. This is especially true of the larger species, particularly the northern pike and muskellunge.

Piltdown hoax

On December 18, 1912, Charles Dawson (1865–1916) announced to the Geological Society in London that he had discovered skull fragments and a partial jaw in a gravel formation in Piltdown Common, Fletching, near Lewes, Sussex, England. The skull fragments were accompanied by bones of relatively recent hippopotamus, **deer**, beaver, and horse, as well as ancient bones of extinct mastodon and **rhinoceros**. Collected over a period of years, the skull fragments had an unusually thick **brain** case but were otherwise considered to be human. The jaw remnant was clearly primitive. This spectacular announcement was considered evidence, found in Britain, that supported the Darwinian evolutionary theory and provided a true representational link to modern man. Named in honor of its discoverer, Dawn man (*Eoanthropus dawsoni*), would eventually be known as Piltdown man, the most deceptive scientific hoax of the twentieth century that would take 40 years to disprove.

Initially, there was skepticism and scientists proposed that the jaw and cranium fragments were from two creatures, rather than one. However, in 1915, a second Piltdown man was discovered two miles from the original site. The second set of fossil remains seemed to indicate that the possibility of a human cranium and an ape jaw coming together purely by chance was unlikely. Clearly, both jaw and cranium fragments were from one type of human ancestor that provided evidence of an intermediary stage between ape and human, however when compared to other authentic prehuman fossils, it was unclear where piltdown man fit in the evolutionary development of man.

Even with the lack of **continuity** between Piltdown man and other prehuman fossil remains, the authenticity of Piltdown man was not disproved until 1953, when **dating techniques** unequivocally proved it a fraud. Piltdown man was merely a hoax made up of an ancient human skull and a contemporary orangutan jaw. The dark color of the fragments that was representative of fossil find in the area was artificial. The teeth in the orangutan jaw had been mechanically ground down to resemble humanlike wear, rather than that of **apes**. In 1912, accurate dating techniques were unavailable and the fervor to provide evidence to support the cherished belief that humans had first developed a big brain, and then later developed other human characteristics was great.

Pineapple see **Bromeliad family**

Pinecone fish

A pinecone **fish** has a plump, deep body, measuring about 5 in (12.7 cm) long. The body is covered by heavy, platelike scales that overlap, giving the fish the appearance of a pinecone-hence its name. Under each pinecone fish's lower jaw, there are two phosphorescent organs, giving the impression that the fish itself produces light. The light is actually produced by luminous **bacteria** that have a symbiotic relationship with the fish.

Pinecone fish belong to the Order Beryciformes, which includes 15 families and 143 species of fish, all marine. This order is considered to be a primitive predecessor of perches. Characteristically deep sea fish, most families within the order are small, including fewer than 12 species. Some other forms of Beryciformes are whalefish, **squirrel fish**, laterneyes, and slimeheads. Pinecone fish belong to the family Monocentridae; there are two genera within the family, *Cleidopus* and *Monocentris*, with a total of four species.

Aside from having unusual scales and light producing organs, the fins of pinecone fish are a bit out of the ordinary. First of all, the fish has two dorsal fins located on its back. The first one consists of a series of 4–7 stout spines that point alternately to the left and to the right. The second dorsal fin has 9-12 soft **rays**. Its pelvic fin, the first fin located on the fish's underside, is composed of a very strong, large spine with 2–4 small, soft rays.

These fish inhabit the Indian and Pacific Oceans, as far south as South **Africa** and as far north as Japan. They move in schools at depths of between 98-820 ft (30-250 m). The Japanese pinecone fish form predatory schools near the bottom of deep waters. Another species is located off of the Australian coast.

Kathryn Snavely

Pines

The pines are species of trees in the genus *Pinus*, of the family Pinaceae and phylum Coniferophyta, the cone-bearing plants (conifers). Relatives of the pines include other conifers such as fir, Douglas fir, **spruce**, hemlock, cypress, and redwood. Pines and these other conifers are all considered gymnosperms, because they bear their **seeds** naked, rather than within an ovary as in the angiosperms (flowering plants). There are about 100 different species of pines in the world.

General characteristics

All of the pines are woody plants. The mugo pine (*Pinus mugo*), native to the Alps of **Europe**, is one of the smallest pines. At maturity, it is really more of a bush than a **tree**, and is often planted in gardens of Europe and **North America**. Many other pines which are native to North America are large trees which can grow 197-262 ft (60-80 m) or more in height.

The leaves of all pines are needle-like and arise from the stem in bundles, called fascicles. Each fascicle is often associated with a fascicle sheath, a special **tissue** at its base. Most species have two to five needles per fascicle, but some species have as few as one and others have as many as eight needles per fascicle. The needles of pines are arranged in a **spiral** about the stem. Each year, as the branch of a pine tree grows, it produces a whorl of new leaves, called a candle. The needles of pines last about two years and most species are evergreen, meaning they have some needles at all times. Since pines have needles throughout the year, they have the potential to photosynthesize whenever conditions are suitable.

The needles of pines, like those of other conifers, are well-adapted for growth in dry environments. In particular, the outer surface of pine needles has a thick waxy layer, called a cuticle, which reduces evaporative **water** loss. Like the leaves of all higher plants, pine needles have special microscopic pores on their surface, called stomata, which are important for exchange of water vapor, **carbon dioxide**, and **oxygen**. The stomata are usually arranged in rows on the underside of the needles, where they appear as white lines. At the microscopic level, the stomata are beneath the surface cells, so they are often called 'sunken stomata'. This stomatal **adaptation** reduces evaporative water loss.

The pines are vascular plants, in that their trunks and stems have specialized cells, xylem and phloem, for the transport of water and food. The xylem of pines consists mainly of tracheids, elongated cells with thick walls and tapered ends. The phloem of pines consists mainly of sieve cells, elongated cells with relatively unspecialized sieve areas at the ends. Sieve cells are characteristic of gymnosperms and free-sporing plants, whereas sieve tube elements are characteristic of the more evolutionarily advanced flowering plants.

Evolution and classification

The oldest known fossil of the pine family (Pinaceae) is a cone from the Lower Cretaceous period, about 130 million years ago. The structure of this fossilized pine cone is similar to that of modern cones of the *Pinus* genus.

Today, there are about 100 species of pines. Pines grow throughout the Northern Hemisphere, and only one species (*Pinus merkusii*) is native to the Southern Hemisphere. More than 70 species are native to Mexico and Central America, and this is their likely center of origin. Pines are distributed in North America from the subarctic of northern Canada and Alaska to the tropics. There are about 35 species of pines in the United States and Canada. Although only one species is native to the Southern Hemisphere, many pines have been introduced and cultivated there for timber or as ornamental plants.

There are two subgenera of pines, and botanists believe these are evolutionarily distinct groups. These subgenera are *Diploxylon,* commonly called the hard pines, and *Haploxylon,* commonly called the soft pines. As suggested by their names, the **wood** of soft pines tends to be soft, and the wood of hard pines tends to be hard.

The needles of hard pines have the following characteristics: (a) they usually arise in fascicles (bundles) of two or three; (b) they have a semicircular shape in cross-section; and (c) they have two main veins, as revealed by a cross-section. In addition, the fascicle sheaths of hard pines remain attached as the needles mature.

The needles of soft pines have the following characteristics: (a) they usually arise in fascicles (bundles) of five; (b) they have a triangular shape in cross-section; and (c) they have only one main vein, as revealed by a cross-section. In addition, the fascicle sheaths of soft pines wither away as the needles mature.

Life cycle

All species of pines are monoecious, in that male and female reproductive structures occur on the same **plant**. Once a pine tree reaches a certain stage of maturity, it forms male and female reproductive structures, termed strobili (singular: strobilus). The strobili of pines are unisexual, in that they contain either male or female reproductive organs, but not both. The male strobili are typically about 0.4-0.8 in (1-2 cm) in diameter and form on the lower part of the tree. The female strobili are much larger and form on the upper part of the tree.

The male strobilus is composed of many modified leaves, called microsporophylls, which are spirally arranged about a central axis. Each microsporophyll has two microsporangia attached. Microsporangia are organs which contain microsporocytes, immature pollen grains. The microsporocytes develop into pollen grains with four cells each. The four cells of the pollen grain are haploid, in that each contains one set of chromosomes. Thus, the pollen grain of pines is a multicellular haploid tissue, and is the male gametophyte. In the spring time, the male strobilus releases pollen into the **wind**, and then shrivels up and dies.

The female strobilus is larger than the male strobilus. It is composed of many scales (modified leaves) which are spirally arranged about a central axis. Each scale has a sterile bract and two ovules, egg-forming structures, attached to it. The ovule consists of two types of tissues, the nucellus and its surrounding integument. A special pore, called a micropyle, passes through the integument to the nucellus.

In **pollination**, a pollen grain lands on the female strobilus and sticks to a special fluid in the micropyle. As this fluid evaporates, the pollen grain is drawn into contact with the nucellus. This causes the pollen grain to germinate and form a pollen tube. Then, the female tissue produces four megaspores. The megaspores are haploid cells, in that each has one set of chromosomes. One of the megaspores develops into a megagametophyte, a multicellular haploid tissue, and the others degenerate. Then, more than one year after the pollen grain has landed on the female strobilus, the female megagametophyte forms archegonia, reproductive structures which contain egg cells.

In **fertilization**, the pollen tube arrives at the surface of the egg **cell** and releases two haploid sperm nuclei into it. One of these sperm nuclei degenerates and the other unites with the nucleus of the egg to form a cell with two sets of chromosomes. This is the zygote. The zygote develops into a seed, which contains an embryo. The entire process from pollination to formation of a mature seed typically takes two to three years. This is much slower than in the flowering plants (angiosperms).

A Scotch pine.

Wind or foraging animals generally disperse pine seeds into the environment. The seed germinates following stimulation by certain environmental signals, such as exposure to **light** or **temperature** changes. Most species of pines can live for a hundred or more years and some species, such as the bristlecone pine (see below), can live for thousands of years.

Economic importance

Pines are very important economically. The wood of many species is used as timber for construction and furniture. Pines are also used for the manufacture of turpentine, rosin, pulp, and **paper**.

One of the most economically important pines of the 1800s was the eastern white pine (*Pinus strobus*). This pine once dominated forested regions in Pennsylvania, New York, New Jersey, much of New England, and southeastern Canada. Most of these pines were several hundred years old and 197-230 ft (60-70 m) in height. During the 1800s, most of these pine **forests** were clearcut and the lumber was used for construction in North America, or was shipped to Europe where lumber was in short supply. More recently, the eastern white pine and the red pine (*Pinus resinosa*) have been used for reforestation in parts of eastern North America.

In modern times, several other species of pine are economically important. The ponderosa pine (*Pinus ponderosa*) of the western United States is currently the most economically important pine of North America. The southeastern United States also has economically important pines such as loblolly pine (*Pinus taeda*), shortleaf pine (*P. echinata*), slash pine (*P. elliottii*), and longleaf pine (*P. palustris*). Many of these southeastern pines are cultivated in plantations. Outside of North America, *Pinus pinaster* of the Mediterranean region and *Pinus longifolia* from India are major commercial species.

Bristlecone pine

The bristlecone pine (*Pinus aristata*) is an important species to scientists because it lives so long, and has tree rings can provide important clues about the climate of previous eras. This species grows in the arid mountainous regions of California, Nevada, Utah, and Colorado at an elevation of about 9,840 ft (3,000 m). Bristlecone pine grows very slowly, but can live for several thousand years. The oldest known specimen is nearly 5,000 years old. Bristlecone pines have been intensively studied by dendrochronologists, scientists who examine and interpret tree rings.

The tree rings of bristlecone pines and other trees appear as concentric rings, and are visible in a cross-section of a trunk or in a core **sample**. A new growth ring typically forms each year, as the tree trunk expands. Growth rings are relatively wide in years favorable for growth, and narrow in unfavorable years. Bristlecone pines grow so slowly that there can be more than a hundred rings in the space of only a few centimeters, so their tree rings must be examined with a **microscope**. The width and other features of these growth rings provide valuable clues to archaeologists about the prevailing local climate during the period when ancient native American cultures inhabited the western United States.

Pine cones

One of the most familiar feature of pines is their cones. Biologically, a pine cone is simply a fertilized female strobilus containing seeds within.

While their economic significance is not as great as that of pines, which are harvested for timber (see above), the pinyon pines (*Pinus cembroides, P. monophylla, P. quadrifolia, and P. edulis*) are prolific producers of edible pine "nuts," which are technically seeds. These seeds are often used in salads, sauces, desserts, and other foods. The pinyon pines are native to semi-arid regions of the western United States and Mexico.

The largest pine cones come from the sugar pine (*Pinus lambertiana*). This species grows in western North America and its pine cones are typically 15-18 in (38-46 cm) long and 4 in (10 cm) wide. The cones of the big cone pine (*Pinus coulteri*), a native of California, are somewhat smaller, but can weigh over 4.4 lb (2 kg), heavier than any other species.

One of the most interesting pine cone adaptations occurs in jack pine (*Pinus banksiana*), pitch pine (*P. rigida*), knobcone pine (*P. attenuata*) and several other species. The cones of these species are serotinous, meaning that they are "late opening." In particular, the pine cones remain closed long after the seeds have matured. They typically open up to disperse the seeds only after exposure to very high temperatures, such as occurs during a fire. At the biochemical level, the **heat** of a fire apparently softens the **resins** that hold together the scales of the cone. Pine trees with serotinous cones often grow in ecosystems that have a high **frequency** of fires. For example, the pitch pine grows in the New Jersey pine barrens, where natural or man-made fires have occurred for many centuries.

Endangered Species

The U. S. Fish and Wildlife Service's Division of Endangered Species List includes no pine species. However, this list does not cover non-U. S. species, and there are endangered pine species in Mexico and in **Asia**.

The rapid disappearance of the pine forests of Mexico and Central America have been largely due to disease, **insects** and human activity. Mexico's population increases by over a million people each year, and this places heavy demand on firewood and land for agricultural uses.

There are nine Mexican pines that are considered either endangered or rare; they are:

- *Pinus culminicola* (Potosi Pinyon)
- *P. maximartinezii* (Large Cone Martinez Pine)
- *P. rzedowskii* (Rzedowski Pine)
- *P. pinceana* (Weeping Pinyon)
- *P. johannis* (Johannis Pinyon)
- *P. radiata var. binata* (Monterey Pine)
- *P. lagunae (Laguna Pinyon)*
- *P. jaliscana (Jalisco Pine)*
- *P. nelsoni (Nelson Pine)*

Of these, the first four are considered very rare and very endangered. The next two, *P. johannis* and *P. radiata*, are classified as rare and endangered, and the last three are considered rare.

According to the World Conservation Union-IUCN, the following Asian pines are considered to be the most endangered:

- *P. dalatensis* (found in South Vietnam)
- *P. massoniana var. hainanensis*
- *P. wangii* (found in small area in Yunnan Province, China)

Other endangered species on the World Conservation Union's list are:

- *P. bungeana (in N. Central China)*
- *P. dabeshanensis (in the Dabie shan Mountains of E. Central China)*
- *P. culminicola*

KEY TERMS

Cuticle—Layer of wax covering the surface of leaves and other plant parts.

Dendrochronology—Scientific examination and interpretation of tree rings.

Diploid—Nucleus or cell containing two copies of each chromosome, generated by fusion of two haploid nuclei.

Fascicle—Bundle of leaves, in the pines often associated with a fascicle sheath, a special tissue at its base.

Fertilization—Union of male and female sex cells to form a diploid cell.

Haploid—Nucleus or cell containing one copy of each chromosome.

Pollination—Movement of pollen from the male reproductive organ to the female reproductive organ, usually followed by fertilization.

Strobilus—Reproductive organ consisting of modified leaves (sporophylls) spirally arranged about a central axis, colloquially referred to as a cone.

- *P. maximartinezii*
- *P. rzedowski*
- *P. torreyana subsp. Torreyana*
- *P. torreyana subsp. Insularis*
- *P. radiata var. bipinata*

Enlightened Forestry

Tree conservationists have learned that when forests are eliminated, the trees that grow back are seldom the same ones that were there before. The pine trees felled in Michigan in the late nineteenth century never grew back, and were replaced by **oaks** and aspens, which the gypsy moth is fond of. The hardwoods in the southern part of the country were cut to make room for pines that could be harvested 20-40 years later. There are now pine plantations from North Carolina to Arkansas, where the trees frequently do not grow as rapidly as had been planned.

Today, enlightened foresters practice sustainable **forestry**, a practice that places nature ahead of timber harvests, and removes tree from the forest at a rate that can be maintained indefinitely. Models for returning land to forest come from the old stands of unmanaged forest, which have sustained themselves for thousands of years.

See also Conifer; Gymnosperm.

Further Reading

Johnson, H. *Encyclopedia of Trees.* New York: Random House, 1990.

Lannenner, R. M. *The Pinon Pine: A Natural and Cultural History.* Reno: University of Nevada Press, 1981.

Margulis, L., and K. V. Schwartz. *Five Kingdoms.* San Francisco: W. H. Freeman and Company, 1988.

Pielou, E. C. *The World of Northern Evergreens.* Ithaca, NY: Comstock Publishing Associates, 1988.

Peter A. Ensminger
Randall Frost

Pion see **Subatomic particles**

Pipefish

Pipefish (family Syngnathidae) are slim, elongate **fish** with large heads and extended, tubular mouths. The extended snout frequently measures more than half of the total head length. The body is enclosed in a tough, segmented skin and the fins, with the exception of the dorsal fin, are greatly reduced in comparison to other fish. Pipefish are widely distributed in tropical and warm-temperate waters; most species are marine but some **freshwater** species are also known from the tropics. Most species live in shallow waters, usually less than 65 ft (20 m) in depth. Many are estuarine-dwellers. Pipefish are masters at concealing themselves from predators: those species that live in and around seaweed fronds or sea grass beds align themselves with the vegetation and drift with the current, appearing as additional floating fragments of vegetation.

Most pipefish are a dull green or olive color, but many are ringed with more striking colors. Some species can alter their background color to help blend in with their surroundings. Successful camouflage is also an advantage when stalking **prey**. Small fish, for example, are hunted visually: when the pipefish is within striking **distance**, they are snapped up with a rapid lunge, the open mouth and tubular snout being extended at the same time. A wide range of small crustaceans are also eaten.

Pipefish swim in a leisurely fashion, characteristically in an upright position, gliding slowly through the **water** by means of rapid wavelike movements of the dorsal fin. Should they need to move faster, they can propel themselves forward by bending the body over and moving forward in a series of jumplike movements.

Breeding may take place throughout the year in the tropics, but is limited to June through August in more

A pipefish (*Sygnathus* sp.) swimming through the water.

temperate waters. As with the closely related sea horses, parental responsibilities in pipefish belong to the male. Male fish incubate the developing eggs either in a shallow groove on the underside of the tail or in special folds of soft skin on the abdomen. Some species carry the eggs directly attached to the abdomen, the female having laid them there directly. The young fry, which may measure just 0.35 in (9 mm) in length, are free-living and free-swimming but remain close to the adult male for several days after hatching.

Pistachio see **Cashew family**

Pistil see **Flower**

Pitcher plant see **Carnivorous plants**

Placebo

In medicine, especially in clinical trials conducted for medical research, a placebo is a substance used as a control in a double-blind test. Half of a group of test subjects are given a medicinal substance being investigated, while the other half is administered an inert material, like a sugar pill, made to look indistinguishable from the medicine. In the optimal double-blind test, neither the research staff nor the test patients are allowed to know which is which until the study has been completed. By this process, psychological effects of the placebo are hopefully kept separate from the biological effects of the chemically active agent being tested.

The non-medical definition of the word placebo indicates the general phenomenon called the placebo effect. Any action, such as gift-giving, which is intended to soothe an agitated person without directly solving any problem is referred to as a placebo. As far back as the sixteenth century, the writer Montaigne commented that a patient's faith in a doctor had more bearing on the successful outcome of a therapy than any other **factor**.

The initial and often ongoing symptom being treated by a physician is **pain**, whether or not the cause of this pain is curable or even treatable. Sometimes treatment for an illness such as **cancer** leads to painful side effects, which must be tended. Only recent studies have begun to unlock the secrets of endorphins, analgesic or pain-reducing chemical agents produced by the human **brain**. They serve the same purpose as **morphine**, a **narcotic** first extracted from the poppy in the 1800s, and long used as an analgesic and anesthetic. There are still many questions as to what triggers an increase of endorphins in the body, how this contributes to the placebo effect, and how much endorphin production may be consciously controlled by a patient.

Other causes of pain are psychosomatic: stress-related, neurotic or phobic reactions with no detectable organic origin. Chronic discomforts describable as psychosomatic include allergies, **ulcers** and **hypertension**. These conditions not only respond positively to placebos, they can also arise in a patient after taking a placebo, as **negative** aftereffects. Attempts to isolate a typical "placebo personality" have yet to succeed in predicting if any one person might be more susceptible to the placebo effect than another.

Even **surgery** can be used as a placebo, by cutting open a patient under **anesthesia** without actually operating. Control groups among angina sufferers have reported a decrease in chest pains after such "dummy" surgery, which indicates that angina may be at least partially psychosomatic. The problem with extreme placebos is the ethical issue of leaving any one patient untreated for the sake of being a control. The Tuskeegee syphilis experiment conducted in Alabama during the late 1930s is one example of an extreme clinical trial, during which penicillin was deliberately withheld from certain patients without their knowledge. While a few of these untreated patients survived, others died painful and preventable deaths.

See also Double-blind study

Plaice see **Flatfish**

Planarians see **Flatworms**

Planck mass see **Cosmology**

Planck's constant see **Quantum mechanics**

Plane

Generally, the term plane, together with point, line, and solid, is considered an undefined term. Every definition in **mathematics** attempts to use simpler and better understood terms to define more complex ones. As the terms to be defined become ever simpler, this eventually becomes impossible. The simplest terms are so well understood that there is little sense in attempting a formal definition, since often times the term itself must be used in the definition. Notice that the definition attributed to Euclid relies on an intuitive understanding of the terms point, line, straight, and surface. A plane is infinite in extent, both in length and width, so that flat physical objects are represented mathematically by some portion of a plane. A plane has only width and length. It has no thickness. While a plane is strictly two dimensional, so is the curved surface of a solid such as a **sphere**. In order to distinguish between curved surfaces and planes, Euclid devised a definition for plane similar to the following: given two points on a surface, the surface is planar if every point on the straight line that connects these two points is also on the surface. Plane is a term used in mathematics (especially **geometry**) to express, in abstract form, the physical property of flatness. A point or line can be contained in a plane, a solid cannot. Instead, the intersection of a plane with a solid is a **cross section** of the solid consisting of a portion of the plane.

See also Line, equations of; Locus; Point.

Plane family

The Plane family is a family of trees and large shrubs known to botanists as the Platanaceae. This family has a single genus, *Platanus*, and 7-10 different species. The two most familiar species are the American sycamore (*Platanus occidentalis*), which is native to eastern and central United States, and the London plane, a **hybrid** tree species which is commonly planted as an ornamental in the United States and **Europe**. Both species have thick trunks at maturity which have very characteristic scaly **bark**. The Platanaceae is probably closely related to the Hamamelidaceae, a **plant** family which includes the witch hazels and sweet gums.

Botanical characteristics

The leaves of all plants in the plane family are simple, deciduous, palmate, and somewhat maple-like in appearance. The leaves are palmately veined and have three to nine lobes, depending on the species. The leaves arise from a long petiole (stalk) which is swollen at its base on the twig. The leaves arise alternately on the stem (rather than opposite one another) and the twigs have a characteristic zig-zag appearance.

The flowers of all species are unisexual in that they contain either male organs or female organs, but not both. All species are monoecious, in that male and female flowers arise from the same individual tree. The flowers are minute and arise in large spherical clusters.

The fruit is a characteristic spherical cluster of small, one-seeded, dry, indehiscent **fruits**, referred to as achenes. Depending on the species, one to several of these spherical fruit clusters arises from a single long peduncle (stem) which is attached to the twig. The small **seeds** are **wind** dispersed.

The best known tree of this family is the American sycamore. Its fruit balls are about 1 in (2.5 cm) in diameter and consist of several hundred seeds densely packed together. Naturalist and writer Henry Thoreau eloquently described the seeds of this species as "standing on their points like pins closely packed in a globular pin-cushion, surrounded at the base by a bristly down of a tawny color, which answers the purpose of a parachute."

Geographic distribution

Of the 7-10 species in the plane family, all but two are native to **North America**. Three species are native to the United States. The well-known American sycamore grows in moist alluvial soils in central and eastern North America. The two other American species are small trees of western United States. The Arizona sycamore (*Platanus wrightii*) grows along stream banks in Arizona and New Mexico. The California sycamore (*Platanus racemosa*) grows along stream banks in the Sierra Nevada region.

Two species in the Plane family are from Europe and **Asia**. The Oriental planetree (*Platanus orientalis*) is native to the Balkans and Himalayas, and *Platanus kerrii* is native to Indochina.

American sycamore

The American sycamore is also referred to as the American planetree or the buttonwood. These trees grow in moist areas, such as along stream banks, in eastern and central United States. They can live for 500 years or more. At maturity, these trees can be over 100 ft (30.5 m) in height and have trunks up to 8 ft (2.4 m) in diameter. The American sycamore is the most massive tree species in eastern North America.

The bark of the American sycamore has a very characteristic mottled or scaly appearance. Its palmate leaves

are 4-7 in (10.2-17.8 cm) in diameter and have three to five lobes each. The spherical fruit clusters are about 1 in (2.5 cm) in diameter and one fruit cluster arises from each stalk.

The **wood** of the American sycamore is very difficult to split. This property makes it ideal for construction of butcher's blocks. The wood has also been used as a veneer for furniture.

Oriental planetree

The Oriental planetree grows in alluvial soils in regions with a moderate climate in the Balkans (Greece, Turkey, elsewhere in the Mediterranean) and Himalayas of Asia. This species differs from the American sycamore in that it has several spherical clusters of fruits on each peduncle. This tree is often cultivated as an ornamental plant in the Mediterranean region of Europe.

London planetree

In the early to mid 1600s, botanists grew the American sycamore and Oriental planetree close to one another at the well-known Oxford Botanical Gardens in England. Apparently, these two species spontaneously hybridized in the late 1600s and produced a new hybrid species, the London planetree (*Platanus X hybrida*, but also given other Latin names). Although *Platanus occidentalis* and *Platanus orientalis* are believed to have been separate species for at least 50 million years, their hybrid was fertile and produced its own seeds.

The London planetree combines some of the characteristics of each of its parent species, as is typical of hybrid species. The leaves of the American sycamore have shallow lobes, the leaves of the Oriental planetree have deep lobes, and the leaves of the London planetree have lobes with intermediate depth. One fruit cluster is borne on each peduncle in the American sycamore, several fruit clusters are borne on each fruit cluster of the Oriental planetree, and two (or occasionally three) fruit clusters are borne on each peduncle of the London planetree.

Like the American sycamore, but unlike the Oriental planetree, the London planetree can endure cold climates. The London planetree can endure **pollution** and other environmental stresses better than either species. Thus, it is often cultivated as an ornamental tree and planted along streets in America and Britain. Moreover, the London planetree can grow up to 3 ft (0.9 m) per year, making it a very popular shade tree for homeowners.

In the 1920s, more than 60% of the trees planted along the streets of London were London planetrees. They are also well known in the Kensington Gardens of London.

KEY TERMS

Achene—Dry, indehiscent, one-seeded fruit, with the outer layer fused to the seed.

Hybrid—Offspring of the sexual union of two different species.

Peduncle—Stalk which bears a cluster of flowers.

Further Reading

Heywood, V. H. *Flowering Plants of the World.* Oxford: Oxford University Press, 1993.

Johnson, H. *Encyclopedia of Trees.* New York: Random House, 1990.

Peter A. Ensminger

Planet

A planet is a relatively cold body that orbits a **star**. Planets are thought to have formed from the same gas and dust that condensed to make the parent star. They can be seen by **eye** and **telescope** because of the light they reflect from their star. The planets themselves often have orbiting moons and dust rings.

The nine planets in our **solar system** that are in elliptical orbits near the *ecliptic plane* are divided into two classes: the inner and outer planets. The inner planets (Mercury, **Venus**, **Earth**, and **Mars**) are made of rocky material surrounding an iron-nickel metallic core. Earth and Venus have substantial cloud-forming atmospheres, and Mars has a thin atmosphere similar in composition to the of Venus.

The outer planets (**Jupiter**, **Saturn**, **Uranus**, **Neptune**, and **Pluto**) are, with the exception of Pluto, large masses of **hydrogen** in gaseous, liquid, and solid form surrounding Earth-size rock plus **metal** cores. Pluto, made of ice and rock, is probably an escaped **moon** of Neptune.

It is likely that other stars have planets orbiting them since the star- and planet-formation mechanisms are similar throughout the universe. When stars form the leftover gas and dust accumulate by mutual gravitational attraction into *planetesmals*. Observation of disk-shaped dust **clouds** around newly formed stars are an indication of planet formation in progress.

Planetary **astronomy** is a very active field, thanks to new **space** probes like the Galileo unmanned space-

craft. In 1995 scientists found evidence that Jupiter's moon Europa has a liquid **ocean** and, perhaps, the right conditions for life. The **Mars Pathfinder** mission landed a small roving vehicle on the planet in 1997, providing up-close pictures suggesting that liquid **water** had once scoured the surface. Pathfinder's roving vehicle Sojourner also performed **soil chemistry** analysis, and other probes like the Mars Polar Lander will continue to provide new information about planetary surfaces.

Astronomers have also found planets circling stars other than our own. The first was in 1995, when Michel Mayor and Didier Queloz found a planet around star 51 Pegasi, an almost perfect twin of the **Sun**. Since then nearly two dozen "extrasolar" planets had been discovered by 1999. These new planets are usually large, like Jupiter. They cannot be seen directly, but are inferred from the wobble seen on some stars, as observed from large telescopes on Earth. The wobble is caused by the gravitational pull of large planets near the star. Because these planets are big, gassy, and close to their star, they are not likely to contain any life, but their existence shows that there is nothing special about the fact that planets **circle** our Sun.

Other special arrangements have been found in the 1990s. The **Hubble Space Telescope** captured an image of a dust ring around the star HR 4796A, 220 light-years from Earth. The ring roughly resembles that of Saturn, but on a vastly larger scale. Some objects in the rings could be planets, or the slender shape of the ring may be influenced by nearby planets. The Hubble Space Telescope has also found possible evidence of "rogue planets" not much bigger then Earth, but which have broken free of their stars and are wandering.

One extrasolar planet has been found only 15 light-years from Earth, circling the star Gliese 876. This is much closer than other **extrasolar planets**, which mostly lie at a **distance** of 40 to 80 light-years. Gliese 876 is a small star, less than 1/3 the **mass** of the Sun, suggesting that extrasolar planets are anything but rare.

In 1999 astronomers announced the first-ever detection of an entire solar system around a star. Only 44 light-years from Earth, three large planets were found circling the star Upsilon Andromedae, a sun-like star visible to the naked eye on Earth. Again the presence of the planets was inferred from gravitational wobbling. Astronomers suspect the planets are similar to Jupiter and Saturn—huge spheres of gas without a solid surface. One of them completely circles its star in only 4.6 Earth days. Such discoveries show that planetary science will likely be a fruitful and surprising field for years to come.

KEY TERMS

Ecliptic plane—The plane of the Earth's orbit around the Sun. The other planets of the solar system also have their orbits near this plane and in the same direction of rotation as the Earth.

Planetesmals—Small clumps of matter held together by electromagnetic forces that, when gathered together, form the planets.

See also Mercury (planet); Minor planets (asteroids); Planetary atmospheres; Planetary nebulae; Planetary ring systems.

James O'Connell

Planet X

Is there another **planet** beyond **Pluto**? Prior to 1781 that question could have been asked in regard to **Saturn**. In that year, Sir William Herschel discovered **Uranus**, after detecting what he believed to be a comet. Calculations to determine the **orbit** of Uranus were made, and the planet was found to conform to the "law" of planetary distances suggested by Johann Elert Bode (1747-1826).

However, a problem later arose. After sixty years, it was noticed Uranus was not following its predicted orbit, evidence that suggested another planet, the gravity of which was perturbing Uranus, must exist beyond it. Calculations for the position of this planet were made by Jean Urbain Le Verrier (1811-1879) and John Couch Adams and, in 1846, **Neptune** was discovered by Johann Galle (1812-1910) and Heinrich d'Arrest (1822-1875). Neptune's gravitational pull accounted for most of the differences between the predicted and observed positions of Uranus, but there was still a discrepancy.

The search continued for yet another planet. Percival Lowell (1855-1916) expended a great deal of **energy** looking, but came up empty-handed. However, Lowell's calculations laid the groundwork for the discovery of Pluto, which was finally found by Clyde Tombaugh (1906-) in 1930. However, Pluto turned out to be such a small, low-mass object that it could not possibly account for the perturbations. Perhaps another planet, with a **mass** of three to five times that of the **Earth**, might be out there.

If there is a Planet X, it will be very difficult to find. Calculations show it would have a highly inclined

(tipped) orbit, and would take 1,000 years to complete a trip around the **Sun**. At that **distance** the amount of sunlight it would reflect would be very small, making it a very dim object. Worse yet, one calculation places it within the **constellation** of Scorpius, which has a dense **concentration** of stars. Finding a faint planet there would be comparable to identifying a particular grain of sand on a beach.

To make a bad situation worse, there is no agreement on where in the sky to look; some have suggested the constellations Gemini and **Cancer**. It has also been suggested that the gravitational tug of a Planet X could perturb material in the Oort cloud. This cloud, suggested by astronomer Jan Oort, could be the source of **comets**. Planet X could deflect some of this material, causing it to fall into the inner **solar system** and become new comets.

Some scientists claim there is no Planet X. Tombaugh's search for Pluto was very extensive; he found Pluto and nothing else, because there is nothing else, the argument goes. As far as the remaining perturbations, perhaps they are just errors in the imperfect calculations made in the nineteenth century.

Planetary atmospheres

The term planetary atmosphere refers to the envelope of gases that surrounds any of the planets in our **solar system**. A complete understanding of the properties of a planet's atmosphere involves a number of different areas including atmospheric temperatures, chemical composition of the atmosphere, atmospheric structure, and circulation patterns within the atmosphere.

The study of planetary atmospheres is often sub-divided into two large categories, separating the planets nearest the **sun** (the terrestrial planets) from the planets outside Earth's **orbit** (the giant planets). Included in the first group are Mercury, **Venus**, **Earth**, **Mars**, and, sometimes, the **Moon**. The second group includes **Jupiter**, **Saturn**, **Uranus**, and **Neptune**. On the basis of **distance** from the sun the ninth **planet**, **Pluto**, might be included in this second group but it is not a giant planet and little is now known about the planet and its atmosphere.

Until recently our knowledge of planetary atmospheres consisted almost entirely of telescopic observations and intelligent guesses based on what scientists already know about Earth's atmosphere. This situation began to change in the early 1960s when Soviet and American **space** scientists launched space probes designed to study the inner planets first and later the outer planets. The most successful of the early flights were the NASA's Mariner 2, which flew past Venus in December 1962; its Mariner 4, which flew past Mars in July 1965; and the Soviet Union's Venera 3 **space probe**, which landed on Venus on March 1, 1966.

Studies of the outer planets have been conducted under the auspices of the United States Pioneer and Voyager programs. On December 3, 1972, Pioneer 10 flew past Jupiter exactly nine months after its launch. Flybys of Jupiter and Saturn were accomplished with the Voyager I space probe on March 5, 1979 and November 13, 1980, while Uranus and Neptune were first visited by the Voyager 2 spacecraft on January 24, 1986 and August 25, 1989, respectively.

The 1990s saw advancement in the type of probes launched to explore planetary atmospheres. After a six-year journey, the Galileo Probe entered Jupiter's atmosphere on December 7, 1995. During its parachute descent it studied the atmosphere of Jupiter with seven different scientific experiments, with the results radioed back to Earth. Galileo may have entered Jupiter's atmosphere at a somewhat special point, but the results indicated that the upper atmosphere of Jupiter was much hotter and more dense than expected—about 305°F (152°C), with an **atmospheric pressure** of about 24 bars. Galileo also found that winds below Jupiter's **clouds** were about 700 km/hr (435 mi/hr), and that the atmosphere was surprisingly dry, containing very little **water** vapor.

On December 11, 1998 NASA launched a space probe to explore Mars, called the Mars Climate Orbiter. It is expected to reach Mars in September, 1999, when it will study Martian **weather** and climate. The Orbiter will generate weather maps and profile the thin but dusty Martian atmosphere over a full Martian year (687 days).

The Cassini mission, launched in September 1997, will arrive at Saturn in 2004. One of the largest, heaviest, and most complex interplanetary spacecraft ever built, Cassini will deploy a probe, called the Huygens probe, to Saturn's largest moon Titan. Titan is unique in the solar system, having a dense atmosphere consisting of **nitrogen**, and other chemicals in smaller proportions. The atmospheric **pressure** at Titan's surface is about twice that of Earth's.

One interesting proposal for future exploration of planetary or lunar atmospheres are "aerobots." Aerobots would be unmanned scientific exploration vehicles designed to float like balloons for up to several months in the atmospheres of planets, conducting scientific experiments and radioing results back to Earth. Aerobots are being studied by the Jet Propulsion Lab in Pasadena, California.

Origin and evolution

When the terrestrial planets formed 4.6 billion years ago, they did so within the solar nebula (a giant disk of gas and dust). The solar nebula's rocky solids, ice, and nebulan gas aggregated into larger solid bodies over time, eventually becoming the four terrestrial planets. They grew by the accretion (formation by sweeping up smaller bodies) of planetesimals (smaller, pre-planet bodies); their atmospheres formed by heating, outgassing (releasing), and reprocessing volatiles (volatiles are substances that readily vaporize at relatively low **temperature**). The terrestrial planets probably obtained equal amounts of volatiles, water, **carbon**, and nitrogen from planetesimals located in the solar system or the asteroid belt. The cratering process and a high ultraviolet flux from the early Sun probably drove large amounts of light atmospheric gases into space. Once formed, the atmospheres have changed in oxidation, total **mass**, and gaseous amount, as the Sun and its intensity has changed.

The giant planets' atmospheres may have similar starting points to the terrestrials', but they did not evolve in the same manner over time, nor is much known about this transformation. Jupiter and Saturn grew with the addition of icy solids and the collapse of nebular gas around them. Uranus and Neptune grew too late to capture nebular gas so the icy dominates. Because these planets have no solid surfaces and strong gravitational fields, their atmosphere only resembles the terrestrial planets by having a complex atmospheric **chemistry**.

For all planets, the escape of some gases and the retention of others due to temperature and surface gravity played an important role in how their atmosphere's evolved. Distance from the Sun affected what could be retained. The transient **heat** and pressure generated during planetisimals' impacts drove chemical reactions between the volatile elements and the rock-forming **minerals** that determined the chemical composition of the gases released. Released gases did not always remain—some were lost to space because of the initial impact and the Sun's ultraviolet **radiation**.

General principles

The structure and properties of a planet's atmosphere depend on a number of factors. One is proximity to the Sun. Those planets closest to the Sun are less likely to contain lighter gases that are driven off by the Sun's radiant **energy**. Mercury illustrates this principle. It is so close to the Sun that it has essentially no atmosphere. Its atmospheric pressure is only 10^{-12} millibars, one-quadrillionth that of Earth's atmospheric pressure. The major gases found in this planet's very thin atmosphere are helium and **sodium**, both of which are probably remnants of the Sun's **solar wind** rather than intrinsic parts of the planet's own structure. Some astronomers believe that contributions come from gases seeping out from the planet's interior.

Another property determining the nature of a planet's atmosphere is cloud cover or other comparable features. Cloud cover has a variety of sometimes contradictory effects on a planet's atmosphere. As sunlight reaches the planet clouds will reflect some portion of that sunlight back into space. The amount that is reflected depends partly on the composition of clouds, with whiter, brighter clouds reflecting more light than darker clouds. Some of the light that does pass through clouds is absorbed by gases in the planet's atmosphere, and the rest reaches the planet's surface. The distribution of solar radiation that is absorbed and reflected will depend on the gases present in the atmosphere. For example, **ozone** absorbs radiation in the ultraviolet region of the electromagnetic **spectrum**, protecting life on Earth from this harmful radiation.

Of the solar radiation that reaches a planet's surface, some will be absorbed, causing the surface to heat up. In response, the surface emits infrared radiation which consists of wavelengths significantly longer than that of the incoming radiation. Depending on the composition of the atmosphere, this infrared radiation may be absorbed, trapping heat energy in the atmosphere. **Carbon dioxide** in a planet's atmosphere will absorb radiation emitted from a planet's surface, although the gas is transparent to the original incoming solar radiation. This process is known as the **greenhouse effect** and is responsible for the warmer atmospheres on some planets than would be predicted based on their proximity to the Sun.

A planet's rotational patterns also influence its atmospheric properties. One can describe the way gases would flow in an idealized planet atmosphere. Since the equator of any planet is heated more strongly than the poles, gases near the equator would tend to rise upward, drift toward the poles, be cooled, return to the surface of the planet, and then flow back toward the equator along the planet's surface. This flow of atmospheric gases, driven by temperature differences, is called convection. The simplified flow pattern described is named the Hadley **cell**. In a planet like Venus, where **rotation** occurs very slowly, a single planet-wide Hadley cell may very well exist. In planets that rotate more rapidly, such as Earth, single Hadley cells cannot exist because the movement of gases is broken up into smaller cells and because Earth's oceans and continents create a complex pattern of temperature variations over the planet's surface.

The terrestrial planets

The primary gases present in the atmospheres of Venus, Earth, and Mars are nitrogen, carbon dioxide, **oxygen**, water, and argon. For Venus and Mars carbon dioxide is by far the most important of these, making up 96% and 95% of the two planets' atmospheres, respectively. The reason that Earth's carbon dioxide content (about 335 parts per million, or 0.0335%) is so different is that the compound is tied up in rocky materials such as limestone, chalk, and calcite, having been dissolved in seawater and deposited in carbonate **rocks** such as these. Nitrogen is the most abundant gas in Earth's atmosphere (77%), although it is also a major component of the Venusian (3.5%) and the Martian (2.7%) atmospheres.

The presence of oxygen in Earth's atmosphere is a consequence of the presence of living organisms on the planet. The widespread incorporation of carbon dioxide into rocky materials can also be explained on the same basis. Water is present in all three planets' atmospheres but in different ways. On Venus trace amounts of the compound occurs in the atmosphere in combination with oxides of **sulfur** in the form of **sulfuric acid** (most of the water that Venus once had has long since disappeared). On Earth most water has condensed to the liquid form and can be found in the massive oceans that cover the planet's surface. On Mars the relatively small amounts of water available on the planet have been frozen out of the atmosphere and have condensed in **polar ice caps**, although substantial quantities may also lie beneath the planet's surface, in the form of permafrost. Such ice may be detected with the Mars Polar Lander arrives on the Martian surface in December 1999.

On the basis of solar proximity alone one would expect the temperatures of the four terrestrial plants to decrease as a function of their distance from the Sun. That pattern tends to be roughly true for Mercury, Earth, and Mars, whose average surface temperatures range from 333°F (167°C) to 59°F (15°C) to -67°F (-55°C), respectively. But the surface temperature on Venus—855°F (457°C)—reflects the powerful influence of the planet's very thick atmosphere of carbon dioxide, **sulfur dioxide**, and sulfuric acid, all strong greenhouse gases.

Atmospheric circulation patterns

The gases that make up a planet's atmosphere are constantly in motion—convection and rotation are key to understanding circulation. The patterns characteristic of any given planetary atmosphere depend on a number of factors, such as the way the planet is heated by the Sun, the rate at which it rotates, and the presence or absence of surface features. As indicated above, solar heating is responsible for at least one general circulation pattern, known as a Hadley cell, and observed on all terrestrial planets except Mercury. In the case of Venus and Mars, one cell is observed for the whole atmosphere, while Earth's atmosphere appears to consist of three such cells but with a vast complexity introduced by temperature contrasts between oceans and continents.

The presence of extensive **mountain** ranges and broad expanses of water in the oceans on Earth are responsible for an atmospheric phenomenon known as stationary eddies. In most cases, these eddies involve the vertical transport of gases through the atmosphere, as when air is warmed over land adjacent to water and then pushed upward into the atmosphere. Eddies of this kind have also been observed in the Venusian and Martian atmospheres. The dynamics by which such eddies are formed are different from those on Earth, since neither planet has oceans comparable to Earth.

One interesting example of a circulation pattern is the famous Red Spot on Jupiter. It is a giant **storm** in Jupiter's atmosphere, similar to a hurricane, 40,000 km (25,000 mi) across. It has been continuously observed for more than 300 years, and while the Spot itself has never disappeared, the circulation patterns within the Spot are continuously changing.

The giant planets

Two critical ways in which the giant planets differ from the terrestrial planets are their distance from the Sun and their size. For example, Jupiter, the giant planet closest to Earth has an average **mean** distance of 778 million kilometers (483 million miles) from the Sun, more than five times that of Earth. Its mass is 1.9 x 10^{27} kilograms, about 300 times greater than that of Earth. These two factors mean that the chemical composition of the giant planet atmospheres is very different from that of the terrestrial planets. Lighter gases such as **hydrogen** and helium that were probably present at the formation of all planets have not had an opportunity to escape from the giant planets as they have from the terrestrial planets. Light gases never condensed in the inner solar nebula and so were absent from the terrestrial planets to begin with.

An indication of this fact is that these two gases make up almost 100% of the atmospheres of Jupiter, Saturn, Uranus, and Neptune. Other gases, such as water vapor, **ammonia**, methane, and hydrogen sulfide, also occur in their atmospheres but in very small concentrations. The atmosphere of Jupiter contains about 0.2% methane, 0.03% ammonia, and 0.0001% water vapor.

One of the intriguing features of the giant planets' atmospheres is the existence of extensive cloud systems. These cloud systems appear to be carried along by

rapidly moving winds that have velocities reaching a maximum of 1,640 ft (500 m) per second on Saturn to a maximum of about 300 ft (100 m) per second on Jupiter. The most rapid winds are found above the equators of the planets, with **wind** speeds dropping off to near **zero** near the poles.

The cloud systems tend to be confined to narrow latitudinal bands above the planets' surfaces. Their composition appears to be a function of height within the atmosphere. On Jupiter and Saturn the lowest clouds seem to be composed of water vapor, while those at the next higher level of an ammonia/hydrogen sulfide compound, and those at the highest level, of ammonia.

We know very little about the atmosphere of the most distant planet, Pluto. On June 9, 1988, a group of astronomers watched as Pluto occulted a **star** of the 12th magnitude. What they observed was that the star's light did not reappear suddenly after occultation but was restored gradually over a period of a few minutes. From this observation, astronomers concluded that Pluto must have some kind of atmosphere that would "smudge out" the star light that had been occulted. They have hypothesized that the major constituent of Pluto's atmosphere is probably methane, which exists in a solid state for much of the Pluto's very cold year. Depending upon the exact temperature, a certain amount of methane should form a tenuous atmosphere around Pluto. As the temperature changes, the atmosphere's pressure on Pluto's surface could vary up to 500 times as the methane evaporates and redeposits on the surface. Alternatively, based on the 1988 observations, a haze of photochemical **smog** might be suspended above the planet's surface. Others, like William Hubbard, theorize that it may contain **carbon monoxide** or nitrogen.

In 1995 the **Hubble Space Telescope** found that Jupiter's second moon, Europa (which is about the size of our Moon), has a very thin atmosphere that consists of molecular oxygen. While its surface pressure is only one-hundred billionth that of Earth's. Unlike Earth, though, Europa's oxygen atmosphere is produced purely by non-biological processes. Though Europa's surface is icy, its surface temperature is -230°F (-145°C), too cold to support life.

See also Atmosphere, composition and structure of; Atmospheric circulation; Atmospheric temperature.

KEY TERMS

Atmosphere—The envelope of gases that surrounds a planet.

Giant planets—Relatively large planets more distant from the Sun than the terrestrial planets. The giant planets are Jupiter, Saturn, Uranus, and Neptune.

Greenhouse effect—The phenomenon that occurs when gasses in a planet's atmosphere capture radiant energy radiated from a planet's surface thereby raising the temperature of the atmosphere and the planet it surrounds.

Hadley cell—A circulation of atmospheric gases that occurs when gases above a planet's equator are warmed and rise to higher levels of the atmosphere, transported outward toward the planet's poles, cooled and return to the planet's surface at the poles, and then transported back to the equator along the planet's surface.

Stationary eddy current—A movement of atmospheric gases caused by pronounced topographic features, such as mountain ranges and the proximity of large land masses to large water masses.

Terrestrial planets—Planets with Earth-like characteristics relatively close to the Sun. The terrestrial planets are Mercury, Venus, Earth, and Mars.

Further Reading

Atreya, S. K., J. B. Pollack, and M. S. Matthews, eds. *Origin and Evolution of Planetary and Satellite Atmospheres.* Tucson: University of Arizona Press, 1989.

Beatty, J. Kelly, and Andrew Chaikin, eds. *The New Solar System.* 3rd ed. Cambridge: Sky Publishing Corporation, 1990.

Ingersoll, A. P. "Uranus." *Scientific American.* 256 (January 1987): 38-45.

Kasting, J. F., O. B. Toon, and J. B. Pollack. "How Climate Evolved on the Terrestrial Planets." *Scientific American.* 258 (February 1988): 90-97.

Littman, M. "The Triumphant Grand Tour of Voyager 2." *Astronomy.* 16 (December 1988): 34-40.

Sheehan, William. *Worlds in the Sky: Planetary Discovery from Earliest Times through Voyager and Magellan.* Tucson: University of Arizona Press, 1992.

David E. Newton

Planetary motion see **Celestial mechanics**; **Orbit**

Planetary nebulae

High-density interstellar dust or **clouds** are referred to as nebulae. These nebulae, both dark and luminous,

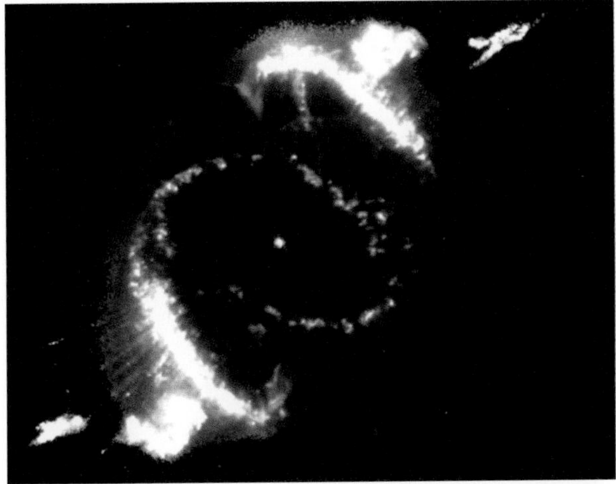

The Cat's Eye Nebula (NGC 6543) as seen from the Hubble Space Telescope. The shells of gas were expelled from a dying star (center) during its last stages of life. It has been suggested, in order to explain the intricate features seen in the shells, that another star is orbiting around the dying star. The knots and thin filaments seen along the periphery of the gas (bottom right and top left) might have been formed by a pair of high-speed jets ejected by the companion star interacting with the gas in the shells.

are equally important since the chemical analyses of these objects contribute significantly to the study of cosmic abundances. Bright or incandescent nebulae, just as dark nebulae, are not self-luminous.

It is the **star** or stars imbedded in these nebulae which produce the luminous objects and are responsible for the atomic processes that may take place. Nebulae may be divided into four groups: dark, reflection, diffuse, and planetary, with the latter three representing the luminous objects.

The study of bright-line spectra of gaseous nebulae, namely diffuse and planetary, is important because it contributes in no small way to the determination of cosmic abundances. It has been suggested that these objects can be studied with greater ease since all portions of a nebula are observable, and even though departures from thermodynamic equilibrium are significant, the processes seem to be well understood and can be treated theoretically.

A disadvantage in using gaseous nebulae is that many of them possess a filamentary structure that is due to non-uniform **density** and **temperature**, from point-to-point. In instances where stratification occurs, the temperature and excitation level will be different for the inner and outer parts of the nebula. Also, an element may be observed in one or two stages of ionization and yet may exist in several unobserved stages of ionization.

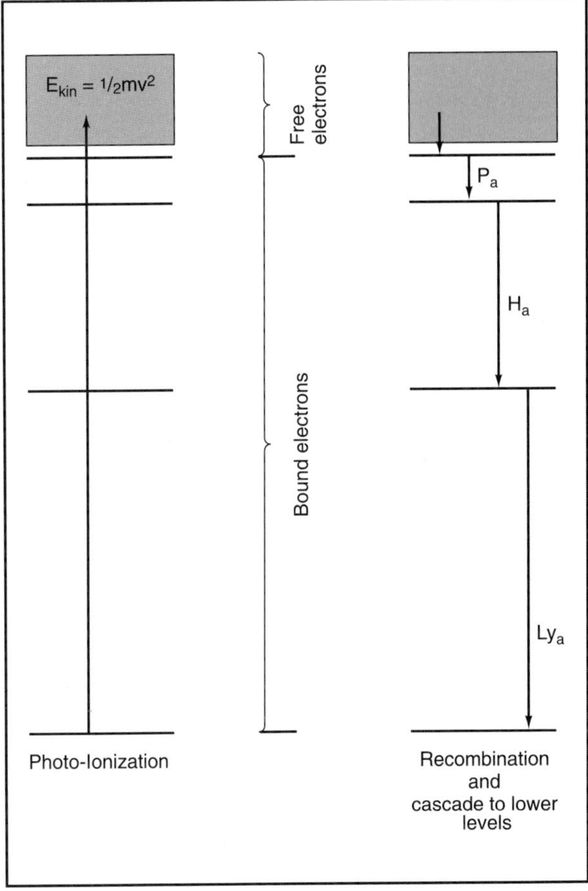

Figure 1.

In the study of nebulae there are four fundamental quantities that are needed at the outset: **distance**, **mass**, **electron** temperature, and density. Of these, the distance parameter is probably the most important one because without it the real dimensions of the nebula cannot be determined from the apparent ones. To determine the mass it is necessary to know the density, and this can be determined, in some cases, from forbidden line data.

For diffuse nebulae, the distances are found from the stars with which they are associated, and the most commonly used methods are statistical parallaxes and moving clusters. However, for planetary nebulae none of these methods apply because they are too far away for a direct trigonometric measurement; they are not members of moving clusters, and statistical parallaxes are inapplicable since they do not appear to move randomly. Instead, the approach is to obtain parallaxes of the individual objects, or by special methods in which the mass of the nebular shell is assumed constant, or the absolute magnitude of nebula is assumed constant.

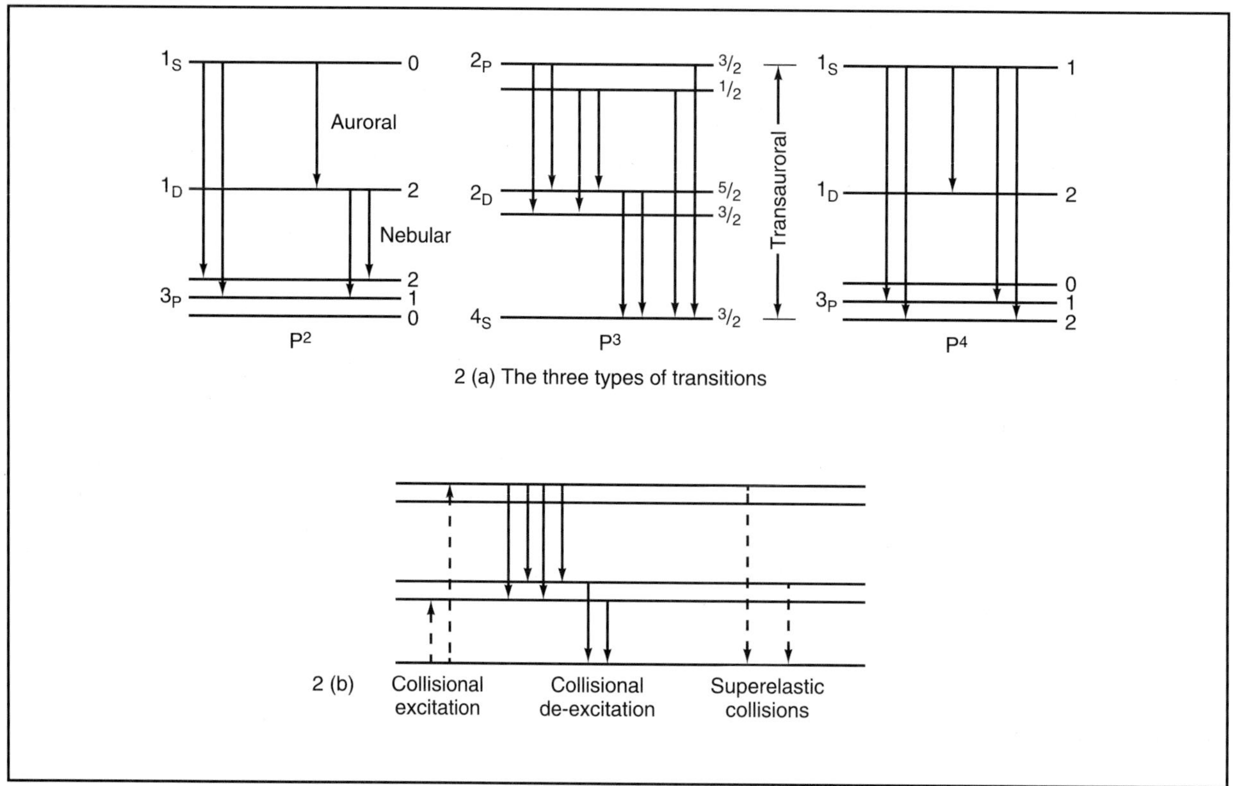

Figure 2.

From the bright-line spectra of gaseous nebulae the abundances of the elements and ions can be determined, the contribution to the elements and ions can be determined, and the contribution to the cosmic abundances can be assessed. The mechanism of excitation (ionization), and recombination that operate is well understood, so that from these spectra reliable results can be expected. Physically, the electron from the ionized atom, for example **hydrogen**, moves about freely for approximately 10 years, and during that period it will collide with other electrons, thereby altering its **energy**. Also, periodically it will excite ions to the metastable levels. Since the electron undergoes so many energy exchanges with other electrons, the **velocity** distribution turns out to be Maxwellian so that the gas kinetic temperature, and specifically the electron temperature, is of physical significance. It must be noted, also, that an atom in the nebula is subjected to dilute or attenuated temperature **radiation** from a star that subtends a very small **angle**. The energy distribution or quality of this radiation corresponds to temperatures ranging from 36,000–180,000°F (20,000–100,000°C). However, the density of this radiation is attenuated by a **factor** of 10^{14}.

The mechanisms that are operating in gaseous nebulae are as follows:

Primary mechanism

In general terms, an atom or ion may be ionized by very energetic photons, a process referred to as photoionization. Photons of the far ultraviolet region have sufficient energy to ionize an atom that is in the ground state. After being photo-ionized from the ground level, the ion recaptures an electron in any one of its various excited levels. After this recombination, as it is called, the electron cascades down to the lower levels, emitting photons of different frequencies. The origin of the permitted lines of hydrogen and helium are explained in this manner. This also applies to the ionic permitted lines of **carbon**, **nitrogen**, **oxygen**, and neon observed in the ordinary optical region. These lines are weaker, however, than those of H and He, and this is due to their much lower abundance in the nebula.

Collisional excitation mechanism

The excitation of **atoms** and ions to metastable levels by electron collision is followed by cascade to lower levels which, in the process, emit the so-called forbidden quanta. The transition probabilities of **spectral lines** are quite few by comparison to the allowed transition. The allowed transitions are electric **dipole** radiations, whereas

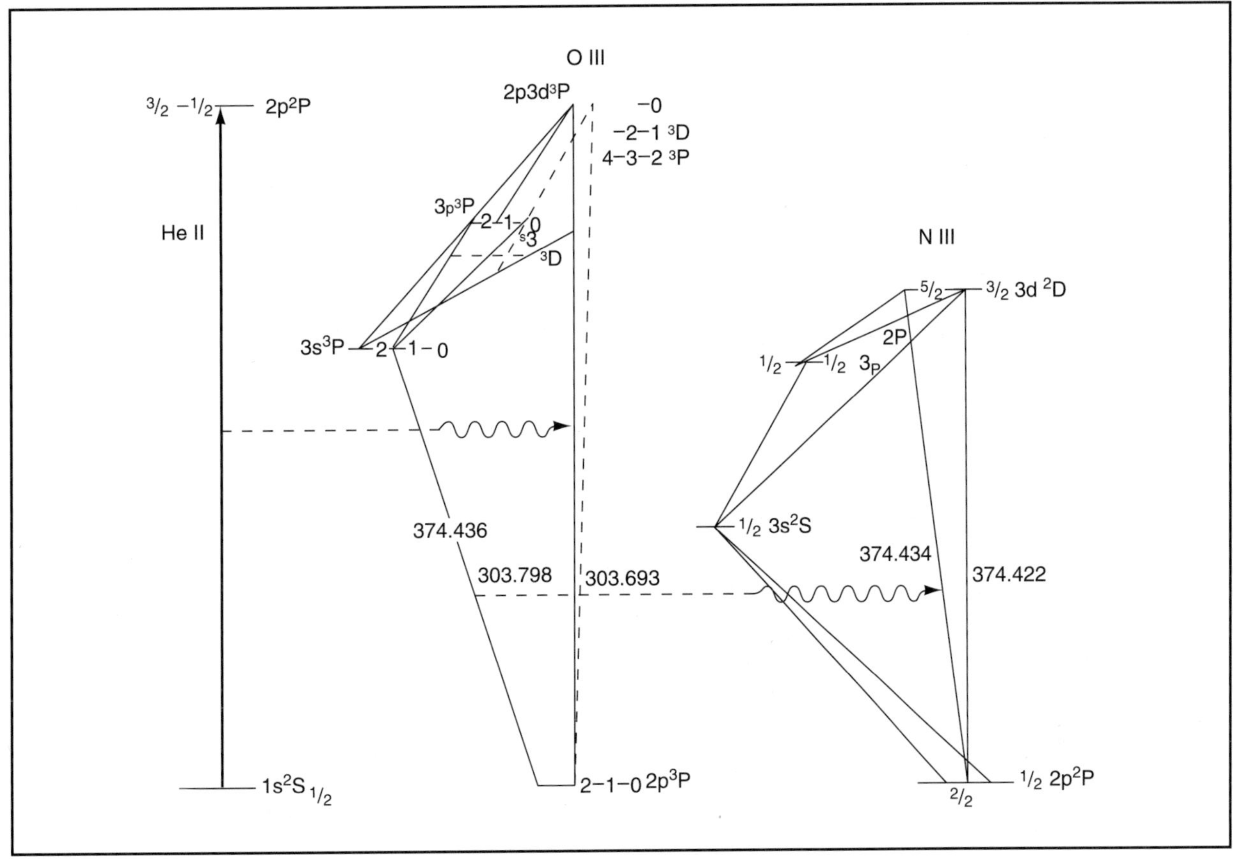

Figure 3.

forbidden transitions correspond to magnetic-dipole and/or electric-quadruple radiations. There are three types of transitions which are the result of collisional excitation: nebular, auroral, and transauroral. All the upward transitions are due to collisional excitation only; however, the downward transitions can be one of two types, i.e., superelastic collisions, or radiation of forbidden lines. The level density and atomic constants determine which of the latter transitions is likely to take place in depopulating the level. Also, the forbidden spectra are observed only for ions whose metastable levels lie a few electron volts above the ground state. Collisionally excited lines are observed in low lying levels of the spectra of CIII, CIV, NIII, NIV, NV, SIIII, etc., in the far ultraviolet.

The study of forbidden lines is one of the major areas of investigation in gaseous nebulae since they dominate the spectra of most gaseous nebulae.

Bowen's fluorescent mechanism

In the spectra of many high excitation planetary nebula, certain permitted lines of OIII and NIII appear, and these are sometimes quite intense. Bowen observed that the OIII lines could be produced by atoms cascading from the 2p3d $^3P_2$ level. Bowen noticed that there was a **frequency** coincidence between the resonant Ly transition of the HeII and the transition from the $2p^2\ 3P_2$ to the 2p3d $^3P_2$ level of OIII, i.e., 303.78Å Ly of HeII and the 3033.693Å and 303.799Å of OIII. Bowen further observed an equally surprising similarity, namely that the final transition of the OIII, i.e., 2p3s ^3PÅ-2p $^3P_2$emitting a **photon** of 374.436Å, coincides with the **resonance** line 374.442Å of the $2p^2P_{3/2}$-$3d^2D_{3/2}$ of NIII which also produces in this ion a similar fluorescent cycle. Detailed investigations and analyses showed that the Bowen fluorescent mechanism was fundamentally correct both qualitatively and quantitatively. It has applications to high excitation gaseous nebulae, quasars, and stellar envelopes.

Continuous spectra mechanism

In addition to emitting discrete line radiation, the bright-line spectra of a nebula emits a characteristic continuum. The physical mechanisms which are involved in the production of a nebular continuum are as follows: (a) Recombinations of electrons on discrete levels of hydro-

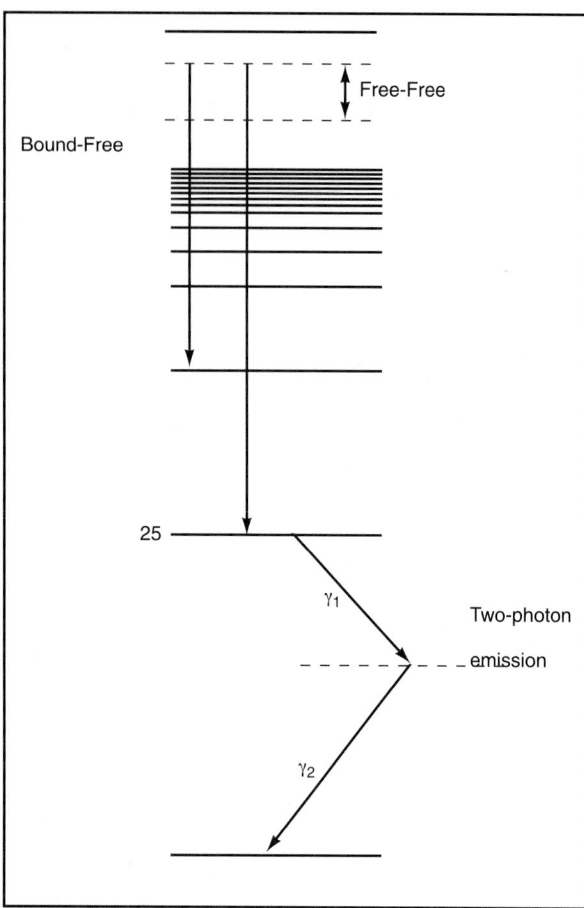

Figure 4.

gen and to a lesser degree of helium, i.e., because of its lower abundance helium gives only a minor contribution.

(b) Free-free transitions wherein kinetic energy is lost in the electrostatic field of the ions. The thermal radiation from these free-free transitions is observed particularly in the radio-frequency region since these transitions become more important at lower frequencies.

(c) The 2-photon **emission** is produced by hydrogen atoms cascading from the 2s level to the ground level. The two-photon emission in hydrogen can be expressed as $\nu_1+\nu_2=\nu_{Ly}$ between the series limits. The recombination spectra decrease as the rate of $e^{-h\nu/kT}$ (where h is Planck's constant, ν the light frequency, k is Boltzmann's constant, and T is the nebula temperature) and it has a maximum approximately halfway between the origin and the Ly. Besides the above, there are other possibilities for contributions to the nebular continuum, namely, electron scattering, **fluorescence**, and H- emissions. However, the contributions from these do not appear to be especially significant.

KEY TERMS

Absolute magnitude—Apparent magnitude a star would have at a distance of 10 parsecs.

Apparent magnitude or brightness—A measure of the observed brightness received from a star or other object at the Earth.

Balmer lines—Emission or absorption lines in the spectrum of hydrogen that arise from transitions between the second- (or first-excited) and higher-energy states of the hydrogen atom.

Dark nebula—A cloud of interstellar dust that obscures the light of more distant stars and appears as an opaque curtain—for example, the Horsehead nebula.

Diffuse nebula—A reflection or emission nebula produced by interstellar matter.

Excitation—The process of imparting to an atom or an ion an amount of energy greater than that it has in its normal state, raising an electron to a higher energy level.

Forbidden lines—Spectral lines that are not usually observed under laboratory conditions because they result from atomic transitions that are of low probability.

Free-free transition—An atomic transition in which the energy associated with an atom or ion and a passing electron changes during the encounter, but without capture of the electron by the atom or ion.

Ionization—The process by which an atom gains or loses electrons.

Nebula—A relatively dense dust cloud in interstellar space that is illuminated by imbedded starlight.

Planetary nebula—A shell of gas ejected from, and expanding about, a certain kind of extremely hot star that is nearing the end of its life.

Recombination—The reverse of excitation or ionization.

Statistical parallax—The mean parallax for a selection of stars, derived from the radial velocities of the stars and the components of their proper motions that cannot be affected by the solar motion.

Temperature (effective)—The temperature of a blackbody that would radiate the same total amount of energy that a star does.

The most important feature that is observed in the continuum is the jump, referred to as the Balmer Jump, at the **limit** of the Balmer series which is produced by the recombination of electron and ions in the n = 2 level of hydrogen. A smaller jump has also been observed at the Paschen limit. The spectral quantities, as well as angular diameter, surface brightness, relative brightness of the principal emission lines, and at times the brightness of the central star are, by and large, readily measurable. Due to this fact, significant contribution can be made to the cosmic abundances as well as to galactic structure.

Further Reading

Abell, G.O. *Exploration of the Universe.* Philadelphia: Sanders College Publishing Co., 1982.

Aller, L.H. *Atoms, Stars, and Nebulae.* Cambridge, Mass: Harvard University Press, 1971.

Physics of Thermal Gaseous Nebulae. Dorderecht, Holland: D. Reidel Publishing Co., 1984.

Harwit, M. *Astrophysical Concepts.* New York: John Wiley and Sons, 1973.

Smith, E., and K. Jacobs. *Introductory Astronomy and Astrophysics.* Philadelphia: W.P. Sanders Co., 1973.

Stanley J. Czyzak

Planetary ring systems

A peek at **Saturn** through a small **telescope** reveals the solar system's jewelry, a breathtaking system of rings. These rings consist of a large number of individual particles orbiting Saturn. The diameter of Saturn's ring system is about 167,670 mi (270,000 km), a little less than the **distance** between the **Earth** and the **Moon**. Yet the rings are only a few hundred meters thick. Saturn has the only ring system that we can see directly from the Earth. **Jupiter**, **Uranus**, and **Neptune**, do however all have ring systems. So rings do seem to be a common feature of giant gas planets.

History

Galileo almost discovered Saturn's rings in 1610. His new telescope revealed something on either side of the **planet**. Galileo's drawings almost look as if Saturn had grown a pair of giant ears. Galileo was seeing, but not quite resolving, Saturn's rings. In 1655 Christian Huygens correctly described Galileo's appendages as a flat system of coplanar rings that were not attached to Saturn. In 1675, Giovanni Cassini first noticed structure in the ring system, a gap now called Cassini's division. He also first suggested that the rings are composed not of a solid body but of individual particles orbiting Saturn. In the 19th century, James Clerk Maxwell proved mathematically that Cassini's suggestion must be correct. In 1895 James Keeler observed the orbital speed of different parts of Saturn's rings, finally proving that they are a large number of individual particles. In 1980 the Voyager spacecraft sent back amazing pictures of the rings, showing a wealth of detailed structure.

The rings around Uranus were discovered next. On March 10, 1977, four groups of astronomers observed Uranus pass in front of a **star** and occult it, in hopes of **learning** something about Uranus as the starlight dimmed. To their surprise, the star winked, several times, both before and after the occultation. Winking once would suggest a moon, but several symmetric winks before and after suggested rings. The group of astronomers from Cornell University, led by James Elliot, obtained the most complete data and discovered five rings. In 1978, four additional rings were found during another occultation. The *Voyager* flyby in 1986 confirmed the previously discovered rings and found two more for a total of 11. The rings of Uranus were later observed from the Earth, with infrared telescopes, which reveal the long wavelength **emission** from the icy ring particles. On August 14, 1994 the repaired **Hubble Space Telescope** photographed Uranus showing, but not fully resolving, the rings.

In 1979, the *Voyager 1* and *2* flybys discovered a very thin ring around the planet Jupiter that is not observable from Earth. By 1979 Saturn, Uranus, and Jupiter were known to have rings. What about Neptune? *Voyager 2* did not fly past Neptune until 1989. To avoid waiting 10 years to see if Neptune had rings, astronomers observed occultations of Neptune. Perhaps rings could be discovered indirectly from the Earth as for Uranus. Some observations seemed to show rings; others did not. The mixed results suggested partial rings. In 1989, the *Voyager* photographs finally revealed that Neptune does indeed have a ring system. However the rings vary in width. Narrower parts of the rings would be harder to detect from the Earth, so the occultations gave mixed results. It is not know why these rings vary in width.

Structure of the rings

Prior to the *Voyager* mission, astronomers thought that Saturn had at most six different rings, labeled A through F. *Voyager* photographs show an amazing amount of unexpected detail in Saturn's rings. There are hundreds of individual ringlets in the 43,470 mi (70,000 km) wide main rings. The smallest may be as small as the 1.2 mi (2 km) width that the *Voyager* camera was able to resolve. (An even finer structure was discovered by another *Voyager* instrument which monitored bright-

ness in a star that was occulted by the rings.) The very narrow F ring appeared braided to the *Voyager 1*, but the braids disappeared for the *Voyager 2* nine months later.

Most of the complex structure appears to be the result of the combined gravitational forces of Saturn's many moons. Astronomers think that Saturn's moons cause **resonance** effects that perturb ring particles out of positions where the particles would have orbital periods exactly equal to a simple fraction (e.g. one-half, one-third, etc.) of the period of one of the moons, thus creating gaps. Two small moons may also act together as shepherding moons to confine ring particles to a narrow ring. Shepherding moons have also been observed in the rings of Uranus. Some of the ringlets of Saturn are spiral-shaped, rather than circular, and are thought to be created by spinal **density** waves, again triggered by gravitational forces due to the moons.

In addition to the many ringlets, Saturn's rings also showed unexpected spokes, pointing away from the planet, that do not travel around Saturn at the orbital speed as ring particles do. These dark spokes appear to be small particles that are swept along by Saturn's magnetic field as the planet rotates.

Saturn's rings are highly reflective, reflecting roughly 60% of the incident light. Therefore, the individual ring particles are probably ice or ice coated. These chunks of ice average about 3.3 ft (1 m) in diameter, with a likely range of sizes from dust grains to about 33 ft (10 m). The total **mass** of the rings is about 10^{16} kg, roughly equivalent to an icy moon 6.2 mi (10 km) in diameter.

The ring systems of Uranus and Neptune are much less extensive. One of Uranus' 11 rings is 1,553 mi (2,500 km) wide, the rest are only several kilometers wide. The widest of Neptune's five rings is 3,726 mi (6,000 km). These rings are narrower and more widely separated than those of Saturn. The individual particles are much darker, reflecting only 5% of the incident light, so they are more likely dark rock than ice. Jupiter's ring is composed of tiny dark dust grains produced by **erosion** from the inner moons.

There is still much we don't know about planetary rings. What is their origin? Are they short lived or have they lasted the 5 billion year history of the **solar system**? What causes the structure in the ring systems? The *Voyager* mission represents a beginning to our study of planetary rings. Future **space** missions will help us better understand ring systems.

KEY TERMS

Occultation—When the moon or a planet passes in front of a star.

Rings—Systems of particles orbiting a planet.

Shepherding moons—Small moons thought to confine ring particles to a particular ring by their gravitational forces.

Voyager—A pair of spacecraft that flew by the outer planets returning data on the planets, their moons, and their rings.

Further Reading

Baugher, Joseph F. *The Space-Age Solar System*. New York:. Wiley, 1988.

Hartmann, William K. *Moons & Planets*. Belmont, CA: Wadsworth, 1993.

Morrison, David, and Owen, Tobias. *The Planetary System*. Reading, MA: Addison-Wesley, 1988.

Morrison, David, Sidney Wolff, and Andrew Fraknoi. *Abell's Exploration of the Universe*. 7th ed. Philadelphia: Saunders College Publishing, 1995.

Zeilik, Michael. *Astronomy: The Evolving Universe*. 7th ed. New York: Wiley, 1994.

Paul A. Heckert

Plankton

Plankton are organisms that live in the **water** column and drift with the currents. **Bacteria**, **fungi**, **algae**, protozoans, **invertebrates**, and some **vertebrates** are represented, some organisms spending only parts of their lives (e.g., larval stages) as members of the plankton. Plankton is a relative term, since many planktonic organisms possess some means by which they may control their horizontal and/or vertical positions. For example, organisms may possess paddlelike **flagella** for propulsion over short distances, or they may regulate their vertical distributions in the water column by producing oil droplets or gas bubbles. Plankton comprise a major item in aquatic food chains.

See also Phytoplankton; Zooplankton.

Plant

A plant is an **organism** in the kingdom Plantae. According to the five-kingdom classification system used by most biologists, plants have the following characteris-

tics: they are multicellular during part of their life; they are eukaryotic, in that their cells have nuclei; they reproduce sexually; they have chloroplasts with chlorophyll-a, chlorophyll-b and carotenoids as photosynthetic pigments; they have **cell** walls with **cellulose**, a complex **carbohydrate**; they have life cycles with an alternation of a sporophyte phase and a gametophyte phase; they develop organs which become specialized for **photosynthesis**, reproduction, or mineral uptake; and most live on land during their life cycle.

Biologists have identified about 500,000 species of plants, although there are many undiscovered species in the tropics.

Plant evolution and classification

From the time of Aristotle until the 1950s, most people classified all organisms into the **animal** kingdom or the plant kingdom. **Fungi** and plant-like, single-celled organisms were placed into the plant kingdom, in view of certain highly derived, but superficial characteristics of these organisms.

In 1959, Robert Whittaker advocated a five-kingdom classification system. According to a recent modification of that system, the five kingdoms are: Monera (single-celled, prokaryotic organisms, such as **bacteria**), Protoctista (various eukaryotic groups, such as **algae** and **water** molds), Fungi (spore-forming eukaryotes which lack **flagella**, such as **mushrooms** and various molds), Animalia (various multicellular eukaryotic groups, such as **jellyfish** and **vertebrates**), and Plantae, or plants.

Biologists now recognize an additional kingdom of prokaryotes, the **Archaebacteria** or ancient bacteria, which have unique characteristics that distinguish them from **Eubacteria**, or true bacteria in the kingdom Monera. The evolutionary relationships of Eukaryotes, Archaebacteria, and Eubacteria are uncertain at the present time. Undoubtedly, as our knowledge of **evolution** and biological diversity increases, Whittaker's five kingdom classification system will require further modification.

Evolution of plants

There was little life on land 500 million years ago, although the oceans abounded with diverse photosynthetic organisms, as well as species in the Monera, Protoctista, and Animalia kingdoms. Land plants appear to have evolved from photosynthetic, aquatic ancestors about 500 million years ago, probably from the Chlorophyta, or green algae. Both groups use chlorophyll-a and chlorophyll-b as photosynthetic pigments, store their **energy** reserves as starch, and have cellulose in their cell walls.

The evolution of the terrestrial habit required special adaptations of reproductive and vegetative tissues for protection against desiccation. The most significant **adaptation** of the reproductive tissues is enclosure of the sex cells (egg and sperm) within specialized tissues, and retention of the fertilized egg as it develops into a multicellular embryo. The most significant adaptation of the vegetative **tissue** is development of a parenchymatous cell organization, in which unspecialized cells (parenchyma) are embedded in a dense **matrix** of cells. This reduces water loss by reducing the overall surface area of the plant per cell, and also provides the plant with a body matrix for differentiation of specialized tissues .

The life cycle of all plants consists of an alternation of generations, in which a haploid gametophyte (tissue in which each cell has one copy of each **chromosome**) alternates with a diploid sporophyte (tissue in which each cell has two copies of each chromosome). A major trend in plant evolution has been the increasing dominance of the sporophyte. Chlorophyta (green algae), the ancestors of land plants, have a dominant gametophyte and greatly reduced sporophyte. Bryophyta, the most primitive land plants, have a more elaborate sporophyte than Chlorophyta, although their gametophyte is still dominant. Free-sporing vascular plants (Filicinophyta, Lycopodophyta, and Sphenophyta) have a somewhat more dominant sporophyte phase than gametophyte phase. However, seed plants, the most advanced of the land plants, have a greatly reduced gametophyte, and a dominant sporophyte.

Classification of plants

All species are classified hierarchically. Related species are grouped into a genus; related genera into a family; related families into an order; related orders into a class; related classes into a phylum; and related phyla into a kingdom. Below, the most significant characteristics of the nine phyla of the kingdom Plantae are briefly considered.

Bryophyta is a phylum with three classes, the largest of which is the mosses, with about 15,000 species. The gametophyte phase is dominant, and in mosses this is the familiar, small, green, leafy plant. Bryophytes do not have true leaves, stems, or roots, and they lack a vascular system for transporting food and water. They reproduce by making spores, and are mostly found in bogs or moist woodlands, so their sperm can swim through water to reach the eggs. Mosses are particularly prominent in the northern boreal forest and arctic and alpine **tundra**.

The Lycopodophyta is a phylum with about 1,000 species. The sporophyte phase is dominant, and is the familiar, low-growing, green plant in many species which

superficially resembles the branch of a pine. Their leaves are tiny structures, termed microphylls, and are arranged in whorls on the stem. The stems of lycopods and all subsequent phyla have vascular tissues for efficient transport of food and water. Like bryophytes, they reproduce by making spores, and are mostly found in wet areas so their sperm can swim to reach the eggs. Lycopods are most abundant in the tropics, although numerous species of *Lycopodium* (ground pine) grow in woodlands in the temperate zone.

The Sphenophyta has a single genus, *Equisetum*, with about 10 species. *Equisetum* is commonly called horsetail, because the dominant sporophyte phase of these plants superficially resembles a horse's tail. It is an erect stem, with whorls of microphylls, and a spore-producing, cone-like structure, termed a strobilus, on top. **Horsetails** are mostly found in moist woodlands of the temperate zone, since their sperm must swim to reach the eggs.

The Filicinophyta has about 11,000 species, which are known commonly as **ferns**. The sporophyte phase is dominant, and is the more familiar form of ferns that is commonly seen in temperate-zone woodlands. Like the leaves of all subsequent phyla, those of ferns have a complex system of branched veins, and are referred to as megaphylls. Ferns reproduce by making spores, and they are mostly restricted to moist environments so their sperm can swim to reach the eggs. Most species occur in tropical and subtropical ecosystems.

The Cycadophyta has about 200 species, which are known commonly as **cycads**. Like all subsequent phyla, cycads are seed-producing plants. They are considered gymnosperms, because they bear their **seeds** naked on specialized leaves called sporophylls. The sporophyte phase is dominant, and appears rather like a shrublike palm in many species, although cycads are only distantly related to **palms**. Cycads have flagellated sperm which swim to fertilize the eggs, a characteristic of evolutionarily primitive, free-sporing plants (all phyla above), but not of other seed plants (except for *Ginkgo,* see below). Cycads grow in tropical and subtropical regions of the world.

The Ginkgophyta consists of a single species, *Ginkgo biloba,* a **gymnosperm** which bears its seeds in green, fruit-like structures. The sporophyte phase of *Ginkgo* is dominant, and is a **tree** with fan-shaped leaves that arise from spurs on the branches. Like the cycads, **Ginkgo** has flagellated sperm that swim to fertilize the eggs. *Ginkgo* only exists in cultivation, and is widely planted as an ornamental tree throughout the United States and other temperate countries.

The Coniferophyta has about 600 species, and includes familiar evergreen trees such as **pines**, spruces, and **firs**. The **conifers** are the best known and most abundant of the gymnosperms. The sporophyte phase is dominant, and is the familiar cone-bearing tree. Male reproductive structures produce pollen grains, or male gametophytes, which travel by **wind** to the female reproductive structures. The pollen fertilizes the ovules to produce seeds, which then develop within characteristic cones. Conifers grow throughout the world, and are dominant trees in many northern **forests**. Many conifers are used for lumber, **paper**, and other important products.

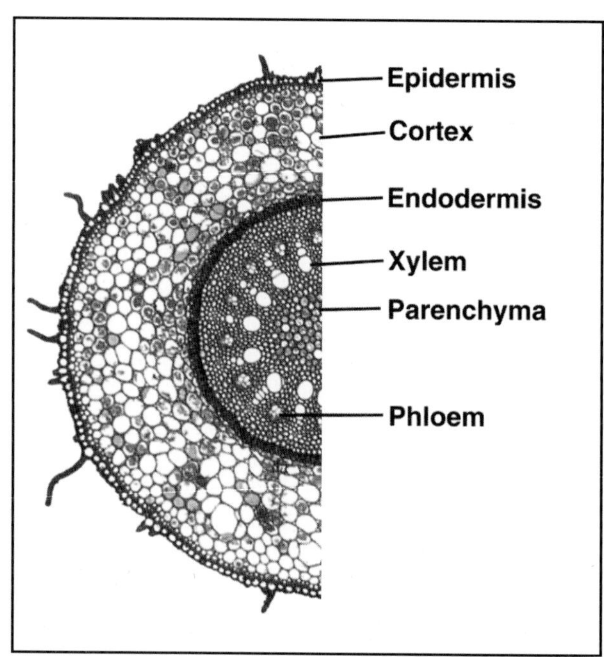

Some features common to the roots of monocots can be seen in this cross section of a *Smilax* root.

The Gnetophyta is a phylum of unusual gymnosperms, with about 70 species in three genera, *Gnetum, Ephedra,* and *Welwitschia*. These three genera differ significantly from one another in their vegetative and reproductive structures, although all are semi-desert plants. The mode of **fertilization** of species in the *Ephedra* genus resembles that of the Angiospermophyta (flowering plants), and many botanists consider them to be close relatives.

The Angiospermophyta is the largest and most important plant phylum, with at least 300,000 species. All species reproduce by making flowers, which develop into **fruits** with seeds upon fertilization. The **flower** originated about 130 million years ago, as a structure adapted to protect the ovules (immature seeds), which are born naked and unprotected in the more primitive gymnosperms. The highly specialized characteristics of many flowers evolved to facilitate **pollination**. There are two natural groups of angiosperms, the monocots, whose

seeds have one cotyledon (or seed-leaf), and the dicots, whose seeds have two cotyledons. Nearly all of the plant foods of humans and many drugs and other economically important products come from angiosperms.

A recent scientific effort has created new theories about the classification of plants. Many genetic experiments were performed by plant biologists around the world in an effort to answer questions of the evolution of plants as a single large group of organisms. Some startling, and controversial results were attained just before the turn of the new century. In 1999, the group of scientists concluded that the kingdom Plantae should, in fact, be split into at least three separate kingdoms because the group is so highly diverse and the genetic evidence gathered indicated sufficient divergence among members. Also, the studies uncovered that the three proposed kingdoms each formed from a single plant-like ancestor that colonized land, not directly from the sea as was previously thought, but from fresh water. These ideas have yet to be accepted by the majority of biologists, and remain a matter of debate.

Plant structure

The seed plants (gymnosperms and angiosperms) are the dominant and most studied group of plants, so their **anatomy** and development are considered here. The leaves and other aerial portions are all covered with a cuticle, a waxy layer that inhibits water loss. The leaves have stomata, microscopic pores which open in response to certain environmental cues for uptake of **carbon dioxide** and release of **oxygen** during photosynthesis. Leaves have veins, which connect them to the stem through a vascular system which is used for transport of water and **nutrients** throughout the plant.

There are two special types of cells in the vascular system, xylem and phloem. Xylem is mainly responsible for the movement of water and **minerals** from the roots to the aerial portions, the stems and leaves. Phloem is mainly responsible for the transport of food, principally carbohydrates produced by photosynthesis, from the leaves throughout the plant. The vascular system of plants differs from the **circulatory system** of animals in that water moves out of a plant's leaves by **transpiration**, whereas an animal's **blood** is recirculated throughout the body.

The roots of a plant take up water and minerals from the **soil**, and also anchor the plant. Most plants have a dense, fibrous network of roots, and this provides a large surface area for uptake of water and minerals. Mycorrhizae are symbioses between fungi and most plant roots and are important for water and mineral uptake in most plants. The fungal partner benefits by receiving carbohydrates from the plant, which benefits by being better able to absorb minerals and water from the soil. Mycorrhizae form on the roots of nearly all land plants, and many biologists believe they played a vital role in the evolution of the terrestrial habit.

Plant development

As a plant grows, it undergoes developmental changes, known as morphogenesis, which include the formation of specialized tissues and organs. Most plants continually produce new sets of organs, such as leaves, flowers, and fruits, as they grow. In contrast, animals typically develop their organs only once, and these organs merely increase in size as the animal grows. The meristematic tissues of plants (see below) have the capacity for **cell division** and development of new and complex tissues and organs, even in older plants. Most of the developmental changes of plants are mediated by hormonal and other chemical changes, which selectively alter the levels of expression of specific genes.

A plant begins its life as a seed, a quiescent stage in which the metabolic rate is greatly reduced. Various environmental cues such as light, **temperature** changes, or nutrient availability, signal a seed to germinate. During early **germination**, the young seedling depends upon nutrients stored within the seed itself for growth.

As the seedling grows, it begins to synthesize **chlorophyll** and turn green. Most plants become green only when exposed to sunlight, because chlorophyll synthesis is light-induced. As plants grow larger, new organs develop according to certain environmental cues and genetic programs of the individual.

In contrast to animals, whose bodies grow all over as they develop, plants generally grow in specific regions, referred to as meristems. A meristem is a special tissue containing undifferentiated, actively growing, and dividing cells. Apical meristems are at the tips of shoots and roots, and are responsible for elongation of a plant. Lateral meristems are parallel to the elongation axis of the shoots and roots, and are responsible for thickening of the plant. Differences in apical meristems give different species their unique **leaf** arrangements; differences in lateral meristems give different species their unique stems and **bark**.

Many of the morphogenetic changes of developing plants are mediated by hormones—chemical messengers that are active in very small concentrations. The major plant **hormones** are auxins, gibberellins, cytokinins, abscissic acid, and ethylene. Auxins control cell expansion, apical dominance, and fruit growth. Gibberellins control cell expansion, seed germination, and fruit development. Cytokinins promote cell division and **organ** development, but impede senescence. Abscissic acid can induce dormancy of seeds and buds, and accelerate plant senes-

cence. Ethylene accelerates senescence and fruit ripening, and inhibits stem growth.

Characteristics of plant cells

Like all other organisms, plants are made up of cells, which are semi-autonomous units consisting of protoplasts surrounded by a special layer of lipids and **proteins**, termed the **plasma membrane**. Plant cells are all eukaryotic, in that their genetic material (DNA) is sequestered within a nucleus inside the cell, although some DNA also occurs inside plastids and mitochondria (see below). Plant cells have rigid cell walls external to their plasma membrane.

In addition to nuclei, plant cells contain many other small structures, which are specialized for specific functions. Many of these structures are membrane-enclosed, and are referred to as organelles (small organs).

Cell structures and their functions

The cells of plants, fungi, and bacteria are surrounded by rigid cell walls. Plant cell walls are typically one to five micrometers thick, and their primary constituent is cellulose, a **molecule** consisting of many glucose units connected end-to-end. In plant cell walls, many cellulose molecules are bundled together into microfibrils (small fibers), like the fibers of a string. These microfibrils have great tensile strength, because the component strands of cellulose are interconnected by **hydrogen** bonds. The cellulose microfibrils are embedded in a dense, cell-wall matrix consisting of other complex molecules such as hemicellulose, pectic substances, and enzymes and other proteins. Some plant cells become specialized for transport of water or physical support, and these cells develop a secondary wall that is thick and impregnated with lignin, another complex carbohydrate.

All living cells are surrounded by a plasma membrane, a viscous lipid-and-protein matrix which is about 10 nm thick. The plasma membrane of plant cells lies just inside the cell wall, and encloses the rest of the cell, the cytoplasm and nucleus. The plasma membrane regulates transport of various molecules into and out of the cell, and also serves as a sort of two-dimensional scaffolding, upon which many biochemical reactions occur.

The nucleus is often considered to be the control center of a cell. It is typically about 10 micrometers in diameter, and is surrounded by a special double-membrane with numerous pores. The most important molecules in the nucleus are DNA (deoxyribonucleic acid), RNA (ribonucleic acid), and proteins. DNA is a very long molecule, and is physically associated with numerous proteins in plants and other eukaryotes. Specific segments of DNA make up genes, the functional units of heredity which encode specific characteristics of an organism. Genes are connected together into chromosomes, thread-like structures that occur in a characteristic number in each species. Special enzymes within the nucleus use DNA as a template to synthesize RNA. Then, the RNA moves out of the nucleus where it is used as a template for the synthesis of enzymes and other proteins.

Plastids are organelles only present in plants and algae. They have a double membrane on their outside, and are specilized for the storage of starch (amyloplasts), storage of lipids (elaioplasts), photosynthesis (chloroplasts), or other functions. Chloroplasts are the most important type of plastid, and are typically about 10 micrometers in diameter. Chloroplasts are specialized for photosynthesis, the biological conversion of light energy absorbed by chlorophylls, the green leaf pigments, into potential chemical energy such as carbohydrates. Some of the component reactions of photosynthesis occur on special, inner membranes of the chloroplasts, referred to as thylakoids; other reactions occur in the aqueous interior of the **chloroplast**, referred to as the stroma. Interestingly, plastids are about the size of bacteria and, like bacteria, they also contain a circular loop of DNA. These and many other similarities suggest that cells with chloroplasts originated several billion years ago by symbiogenesis, the union of formerly separate, prokaryotic cells.

Mitochondria are organelles which are present in nearly all living, eukaryotic cells. A mitochondrion has a double membrane on its outside, is typically ovoid or oblong in shape, and is about 0.5 micrometers wide and several micrometers long. Mitochondria are mainly responsible for the controlled oxidation (metabolic breakdown) of high-energy food molecules, such as fats and carbohydrates, and the consequent synthesis of ATP (**adenosine triphosphate**), the energy source for cells. Many of the mitochondrial enzymes that oxidize food molecules are embedded in special internal membranes of the mitochondria. Like plastids, mitochondria contain a circular loop of DNA, and are believed to have originated by symbiogenesis.

Golgi bodies are organelles present in most eukaryotic cells, and function as biochemical processing centers for many cellular molecules. They appear as a cluster of flattened vesicles, termed cisternae, and associated spherical vesicles. The Golgi bodies process carbohydrates, which are used to synthesize the cell wall, and lipids, which are used to make up the plasma membrane. They also modify many proteins by adding sugar molecules to them, a process referred to as glycosylation.

Vacuoles are fluid-filled vesicles which are separated from the cytoplasm by a special membrane, referred

to as a tonoplast. Vacuoles are present in many eukaryotic cells. The vacuoles of many plant cells are very large, and can constitute 90% or more of the total cell **volume**. The main constituent of vacuoles is water. Depending on the type of cell, vacuoles are specialized for storage of foods, ions, or water-soluble plant pigments.

The endoplasmic reticulum is a complex system of interconnected double membranes, which is distributed throughout most eukaryotic cells. The membranes of the endoplasmic reticulum are often continuous with the plasma membrane, the outer nuclear membrane, the tonoplast, and Golgi bodies. Thus, the endoplasmic reticulum functions as a conduit for chemical communication between different parts of the cell. The endoplasmic reticulum is also a region where many proteins, lipids, and carbohydrates are biochemically modified. Many regions of the endoplasmic reticulum have **ribosomes** associated with them. Ribosomes are subcellular particles made up of proteins and RNA, and are responsible for synthesis of proteins from information encoded in RNA.

Importance to humans

Plants provide food to humans and all other nonphotosynthetic organisms, either directly or indirectly. Agriculture began about 10,000 years ago in the fertile crescent of the Near East, where people first cultivated **wheat** and **barley**. Scientists believe that as people of the fertile crescent gathered wild seeds, they selected for certain genetically determined traits, which made the plants produced from those seeds more suited for cultivation and as foods. For example, most strains of wild wheat bear their seeds on stalks that break off to disperse the mature seeds. As people selected wild wheat plants for food, they unknowingly selected genetic variants in the wild population whose seed stalks did not break off. This trait made it easier to harvest and cultivate wheat, and is a feature of all of our modern varieties of wheat.

The development of agriculture led to enormous development of human cultures, as well as growth in the human population. This, in turn, spurred new technologies in agriculture. One of the most recent agricultural innovations is the "Green Revolution," the development of new genetic varieties of crop plants. In the past 20-30 years, many new plant varieties have been developed that are capable of very high yields, surely an advantage to an ever-growing human population.

Nevertheless, the Green Revolution has been criticized by some people. One criticism is that these new crop varieties often require large quantities of **fertilizers** and other chemicals to attain their high yields, making them unaffordable to the relatively poor farmers of the developing world. Another criticism is that the rush to use these new genetic varieties may hasten the **extinction** of native varieties of crop plants, which themselves have many valuable, genetically-determined characteristics.

Regardless of one's view of the Green Revolution, it is clear that high-tech agriculture cannot provide a simple solution to poverty and starvation. Improvements in our crop plants must surely be coupled to advances in politics and diplomacy to ensure that people of the developing nations are fed in the future.

See also Angiosperm; Bryophyte; Mycorrhiza; Plant pigment; Root system.

KEY TERMS

Diploid—A nucleus or cell containing two copies of each chromosome, generated by fusion of two haploid nuclei.

Eukaryote—A cell whose DNA occurs within a nucleus, considered more advanced than a prokaryote.

Gametophyte—The haploid, gamete-producing generation in a plant's life cycle.

Haploid—A nucleus or cell containing one copy of each chromosome.

Meristem—Special plant tissues which contain undifferentiated, actively growing and dividing cells.

Morphogenesis—Developmental changes that occur during growth of an organism, such as formation of specialized tissues and organs.

Prokaryote—A cell without a nucleus, considered more primitive than a eukaryote.

Sporophyte—The diploid spore-producing generation in a plant's life cycle.

Symbiosis—A close relationship of two or more organisms, which typically involves exchange of food or other resources.

Further Reading

Attenborough, D. *The Private Life of Plants.* Princeton: Princeton University Press, 1995.

Galston, A. W. *Life Processes of Plants: Mechanisms for Survival.* San Francisco: W. H. Freeman Press, 1993.

Kaufman, P. B., et al. *Plants: Their Biology and Importance.* New York: HarperCollins, 1990.

Margulis, L., and K. V. Schwartz. *Five Kingdoms*. San Francisco: W. H. Freeman and Company, 1988.
Wilkins, M. *Plant Watching*. New York: Facts on File, 1988.

Peter A. Ensminger

Plant breeding

Plant breeding began when early humans saved **seeds** and planted them. The cultural change from living as nomadic hunter-gatherers, to living in more settled communities, depended on the ability to cultivate plants for food. Present knowledge indicates that this transition occurred in several different parts of the world, about 10,000 years ago.

Today, there are literally thousands of different cultivated varieties (cultivars) of individual species of crop plants. As examples, there are more than 4,000 different peas (*Pisum sativum*), and more than 5,000 grape cultivars, adapted to a wide variety of soils and climates.

The methods by which this diversity of **crops** was achieved were little changed for many centuries, basically requiring observation, selection, and cultivation. However, for the past three centuries most new varieties have been generated by deliberate cross-pollination, followed by observation and further selection. The science of **genetics** has provided a great deal of information to guide breeding possibilities and directions. Most recently, the potential for plant breeding has advanced significantly, with the advent of methods for the incorporation of genes from other organisms into plants via recombinant DNA-techniques. This capacity is broadly termed "genetic engineering." These new techniques and their implications have given rise to commercial and ethical controversies about "ownership," which have not yet been resolved.

Early selection

The plants that were eaten habitually by hunter-gatherer communities were palatable and non-toxic. These characteristics had been determined by trial and **error**. Then, by saving the largest seeds from the healthiest plants, a form of selection was practiced that provided the initial foundation of plant domestication and breeding.

Among the fruit and seed characters favored by selection in prehistoric times were cereal stalks that did not fall into separate pieces at maturity, and pods that did not open as they dried out, dispersing seeds onto the ground. **Wheat** or **barley** heads that remained unified, and pea or lentil pods that remained closed allowed easier and more efficient collection of grain and seeds.

Seed dormancy

Another seed character whose selection was favored long ago was the ability to germinate soon after planting. In cases where seed dormancy was imposed by thick, impermeable seed-coats, a selected reduction in seed-coat thickness allowed more prompt **germination**. Wild or semi-domesticated peas, found as carbonized remains in **archeological sites** throughout the Middle East, possessed thick seed-coats with a characteristic, gritty surface texture. Similarly, the seed-coats of *Cicer reticulatum* from Turkey, the immediate progenitor of the chick pea, account for about one-quarter of the total material in the seed. However, modern cultivars of the chick pea (*Cicer arietinum*) commit only 4-9% of the seed weight to seed-coats. The seed-coats are thinner because there are fewer cells in the outermost sclereid layers. Cultivated chick peas also lack the brown and green pigments typical of wild-type seeds.

Seed dormancy imposed by natural growth regulators was also selected against in prehistoric times. For example, cultivated oats (*Avena sativa*) lack the dormancy mechanisms of wild oats (*Avena fatua*), and germinate soon after seasonal planting.

Quality

Among **fruits** and **vegetables**, flavor, size, shape, sweetness, texture and acidity have long been desirable characters. Trees or vines producing superior fruits were prized above those that did not. This is known from the writings of the Egyptians, Greeks, and Romans. Plant remains in the gardens of Pompeii, covered by the eruption of Mt Vesuvius in A.D. 79, confirm that almond, lemon, peach, pear, grape, cherry, plum, fig, and olive were cultivated at that time. The particular varieties of onion and cabbage grown around Pompeii were highly regarded, according to the Roman author Columella (A.D. 50).

Climatic adaptation

Cultivars adapted to different types of climatic conditions were also selected in ancient times. In **North America**, various Indian tribes developed and maintained lines of maize adapted to different **temperature** ranges. Colonel George Morgan of Princeton, New Jersey, collected so-called "Indian corns," which included the Tuscorora, King Philip, and Golden Sioux lines of field corn. An early sweet corn was also obtained from the tribes of The Six Nations (Iroquois) by U. S. General Sullivan in 1779. In July 1787 a visitor to Sullivan's garden noted: "he had Indian corn growing, in long rows, from different kinds of seed, collected from the different latitudes on this **continent**, as far north as the most northern parts of Canada, and south as far as the West Indies."

Pollination and hybridization

The genetic discoveries of Gregor Mendel with pea plants, first published in 1866, were revolutionary, although Mendel's work remained obscure until translated from German into English by William Bateson in 1903. Nevertheless, the relationship between pollen lodging on the stigma and subsequent fruit production was realized long before Mendel's work. The first **hybrid** produced by deliberate pollen transfer is credited to Thomas Fairchild, an eighteenth-century, English gardener. He crossed sweet william with the carnation in 1719, to produce a new horticultural plant.

Towards the end of that century, Thomas Andrew Knight, another Englishman, demonstrated the practical value of cross-pollination on an unprecedented scale. He produced hybrid fruit trees by cross-pollination, and then grafted shoots of their seedlings onto established, compatible root stalks. This had the effect of greatly shortening the time until fruit production, so that the horticultural success of the hybridization could be evaluated. After selecting the best fruit, the hybrid seeds could be planted, and the process of grafting the seedlings and selection could be continued. The best hybrids, which were not necessarily stable through **sexual reproduction**, could be propagated by grafting. Thomas Knight was also responsible for the first breeding of wrinkled-seeded peas, the kind that provided Mendel with one of his seven key characters (round being dominant, with one allele sufficient for expression; wrinkled being recessive, requiring two copies of the allele for expression).

The impact of hybridization on plant breeding in the United States

Most food plants brought from **Europe** to the United States in the seventeenth century failed to prosper widely. Some could not be grown successfully anywhere, because they could not adapt to the climate, or were susceptible to newly-encountered **pests** or diseases. At the beginning of the nineteenth century, the range of varieties available for any given plant was extremely limited. Apples, however, were an exception. This fruit crop had benefited from a number of chance varieties such as the Newtown Pippin (about 1700), the Baldwin (1742), and the Jonathan (1829). However, it was in the more typical context of low diversity that Thomas Jefferson said "the greatest service that can be rendered any country is to add a useful plant to its culture."

The Rural Visiter, a periodical published in Burlington, Vermont, in 1810, ran a series of extracts from Knight's "Treatise on the Culture of the Apple and Pear." Knight's grafting methods were further described by James Thatcher in his *American Orchardist* in 1822. In this way the principles behind Knight's work became understood in the United States.

The first variety of a fruit **tree** to be bred in the United States was a pear produced by William Prince, around 1806. He crossed St. Germain with White Doyenne (the pollen donor), and from the seed selected a variety known as Prince's St. Germain. Later, further improvements of the pear were made by the discovery of natural hybrids between the European pear (binomial) and the introduced Chinese sand-pear (binomial). The Kiefer, Le Conte, and Garber pears all arose in this fashion, and allowed pear cultivation to extend beyond California into the eastern and southern states.

The contribution of C. M. Hovey

C.M. Hovey produced new hybrid strawberries by 1838. The most important, Hovey's Seedling, became the leading strawberry for more than 30 years. Unfortunately this variety was finally lost, although some derivatives were maintained. Hovey was also successful with flowers. He crossed existing yellow calceolarias (binomial) with the purple *Calceolaria purpurea*, imported in 1827. Flowers ranging in color from pale yellow to deep orange, and from light red to deep scarlet, were subsequently produced.

Hovey was later involved in the development of hybrid **grapes**. In 1844 he advocated a breeding strategy that required crossing the Isabella and Catawba, two cultivars derived from native species, with European varieties such as Golden Chasselas as pollen donors. The Delaware, named about 1850, was a chance hybrid between native and European grapes. Although many useful grape hybrids were subsequently produced by American breeders in the latter part of the nineteenth century, the grafting of European cultivars onto American rootstocks proved to be more beneficial for this crop on a worldwide scale.

Luther Burbank

The concept of "diluting" hybrids by crossing them back to either parent also developed in the latter part of the nineteenth century. This strategy was introduced to ameliorate undesirable characters that were expressed too strongly. Luther Burbank, based in California, became a master of this art. He bred larger walnuts from hybrids involving *Juglans californica, J. regia*, and *J. nigra*. From the 1870s onwards, he was especially successful with plums bred by hybridization of native American plums with a Japanese species, (*Prunus triflora*). Burbank once found a Californian poppy (*Eschscholtzia*

californica) that displayed a crimson thread through one petal. By repeated selection he eventually developed an all-crimson poppy. His series of hybrids between blackberry and raspberry also produced some remarkable plants. The Primus blackberry (from western dewberry and Siberian raspberry) produced larger fruit that ripened many weeks in advance of either parent, while out-yielding both and maintaining flavor. By the turn of the century, Burbank was justly famous for having bred numerous superior cultivars of many different kinds of plants of horticultural and agricultural importance.

In genetic terms, there are two kinds of back-crossing. When one parent of a hybrid has many recessive characters, these are masked in the F_1 (first filial) hybrid generation by dominant alleles from the other parent. However, a cross of the F_1 hybrid with the recessive parent will allow the complete range of genetic variation to be expressed in the F_2 progeny. This is termed a test cross. A cross of the F_1 to the parent with more dominant characters is termed a back cross.

The goals of modern plant breeding

The broad aims of current plant breeding programs have changed little from those of the past. Improvements in yield, quality, plant hardiness, and pest resistance are actively being sought. In addition, the ability of plants to survive increasing intensities of ultraviolet **radiation**, due to damage in the **ozone** layer, and to respond favorably to elevated atmospheric concentrations of **carbon dioxide** are being assessed. To widen the available **gene** pools, collections of cultivars and wild relatives of major crop species have been organized at an international level. The United Nations' Food and Agriculture Organization (FAO) supported the formation of the International Board for Plant Genetic Resources in 1974. However, many cultivars popular in the nineteenth century have already fallen into disuse and been lost. The need to conserve remaining "heritage" varieties has been taken up by associations of enthusiasts in many countries, such as the Seed Savers' Exchange in the United States

Plant cloning and artificial hybridization

Genetically-identical plants, or clones, have been propagated from vegetative cuttings for thousands of years. Modern cloning techniques are used extensively to select for cultivars with particular characteristics, since there are limits to what can be achieved through direct hybridization. Some individual species or groups of cultivars cannot be genetically crossed. Sometimes this is because of natural polyploidy, when plant cells carry extra copies of some or all of the chromosomes, or because of inversions of DNA within chromosomes. In cases where cross-fertilization has occurred, "embryo rescue" may be used to remove hybrid embryos from the ovules and culture them on artificial media.

Pollen mother-cells in the anthers of some species have been treated with colchicine, to generate nuclei with double the haploid **chromosome** number, thus producing diploid plants that are genetically-identical to the haploid pollen. The use of colchicine to induce polyploidy in dividing vegetative cells first became popular in the 1940s, but tetraploids generated from diploids tend to mask recessive alleles. Generating diploids from haploids doubles all of the existing recessive alleles, and thereby guarantees the expression of the recessive characters of the pollen source.

Somatic hybridization

In other difficult cases, the barriers to sexual crossing can sometimes be overcome by preparing protoplasts from vegetative (somatic) tissues from two sources. This involves treatment with cell-wall degrading enzymes, after which the protoplasts are encouraged to fuse by incubation in an optimal **concentration** of polyethylene **glycol**. A successful fusion of protoplasts from the two donors produces a new protoplast that is a somatic hybrid. Using **tissue** cultures, such cells can, in some cases, be induced to develop into new plants.

Somatic fusion is of particular interest for characters related to the **chloroplast** or mitochondrion. These plastids contain some genetic information in their specific, non-nuclear DNA, which is responsible for the synthesis of a number of essential **proteins**. In about two-thirds of the higher plants, plastids with their DNA are inherited in a "maternal" fashion—the cytoplasm of the male **gamete** is discarded after fusion of the egg and sperm cells. In contrast, in the minority of plants with biparental inheritance of plastid DNA, or when fusion of somatic protoplasts occurs, there is a mixing of the plastids from both parents. In this way, there is a potential for new plastid-nucleus combinations.

For chloroplasts, one application of plastid fusion is in the breeding of resistance to the effects of triazine **herbicides**. For mitochondria, an application relevant to plant breeding is in the imposition of male sterility. This is a convenient character when certain plants are to be employed as female parents for a hybrid cross. The transfer of male-sterile cytoplasm in a single step can avoid the need for several years of backcrosses to attain the same condition. Somatic hybridization has been used successfully to transfer male sterility in **rice**, carrot, rapeseed (canola), sugar **beet**, and citrus. However, this character can be a disadvantage in maize, where male sterility simultaneously confers sensitivity to the blight

fungus, *Helminthosporium maydis*. This sensitivity can lead to serious losses of maize crops.

Somaclonal variation

Replicate plant cells or protoplasts that are placed under identical conditions of tissue culture do not always grow and differentiate to produce identical progeny (clones). Frequently, the genetic material becomes destabilized and reorganized, so that previously-concealed characters are expressed. In this way, the tissue-culture process has been used to develop varieties of sugar cane, maize, rapeseed, alfalfa, and tomato that are resistant to the toxins produced by a range of parasitic **fungi**. This process can be used repeatedly to generate plants with multiple disease resistance, combined with other desirable characters.

Genetic engineering

The identification of numerous mutations affecting plant morphology has allowed the construction of genetic linkage maps for all major cultivated species. These maps are constantly being refined. They serve as a guide to the physical location of individual genes on chromosomes.

DNA sequencing of plant genomes has shown that gene expression is controlled by distinct "promoter" regions of DNA. It is now possible to position genes under the control of a desired promoter, to ensure that the genes are expressed in the appropriate tissues. For example, the gene for a bacterial toxin (Bt) (from *Bacillus thuringiensis*) that kills insect larvae might be placed next to a leaf-development promoter sequence, so that the toxin will be synthesized in any developing **leaf**. Although the toxin might account for only a small proportion of the total protein produced in a leaf, it is capable of killing larvae that eat the genetically-modified leaves.

Vectors for gene transfer

Agrobacterium tumefaciens and *A. rhizogenes* are **soil bacteria** that infect plant roots, causing crown gall or "hairy roots" diseases. Advantage has been taken of the natural ability of *Agrobacterium* to transfer plasmid DNA into the nuclei of susceptible plant cells. *Agrobacterium* cells with a genetically-modified plasmid, containing a gene for the desired trait and a marker gene, usually conferring antibiotic resistancen, are incubated with protoplasts or small pieces of plant tissue. Plant cells that have been transformed by the plasmid can be selected on media containing the antibiotic, and then cultured to generate new, transgenic plants.

Many plant species have been transformed by this procedure, which is most useful for dicotyledonous plants. The gene encoding Bt, as well as genes conferring resistance to viral diseases, have been introduced into plants by this method.

Direct gene transfer

Two methods have been developed for direct gene transfer into plant cells - electroporation and biolistics. Electroporation involves the use of high-voltage electric pulses to induce pore formation in the membranes of plant protoplasts. Pieces of DNA may enter through these temporary pores, and sometimes protoplasts will be transformed as the new DNA is stably incorporated (i.e., able to be transmitted in mitotic **cell** divisions). New plants are then derived from cultured protoplasts. This method has proven valuable for maize, rice, and sugar cane, species that are outside the host range for vector transfer by *Agrobacterium*.

Biolistics refers to the bombardment of plant tissues with microprojectiles of tungsten coated with the DNA intended for transfer. Surprisingly, this works. The size of the particles and the entry **velocity** must be optimized for each tissue, but avoiding the need to isolate protoplasts increases the potential for regenerating transformed plants. Species that cannot yet be regenerated from protoplasts are clear candidates for transformation by this method.

Genetically-modified plants

In 1992, a tomato with delayed ripening became the first genetically-modified (GM) commercial food crop. More than 40 different GM crops are now being grown commercially. GM corn and **cotton** contain bacterial genes that kill **insects** and confer herbicide-resistance on the crops. GM squash contains viral genes that confer resistance to viruses. Potatoes carry the Bt gene to kill the Colorado **potato** beetle and a viral gene that protects the potato from a **virus** spread by **aphids**. Mauve-colored carnations carry a petunia gene required for making blue pigment. In many cases, GM crops result in increased yields and reduced use of **pesticides**. New research is focused on producing GM foods containing increased vitamins and human or **animal** vaccines.

GM crops are very controversial. There is concern that the widespread dissemination of the Bt gene will cause insects to become resistant. It has been reported that pollen from Bt corn is toxic to the caterpillars of monarch **butterflies**. It also is possible that GM crops will interbreed with wild plants, resulting in "superweeds" resistant to herbicides. There is also concern that the antibiotic-resistance genes, used as markers for gene transfer, may be passed from the plants to soil **microorganisms** or bacteria in humans who eat the food. Finally,

KEY TERMS

Alleles—Different versions of a gene. A dominant allele will be expressed if there is a single copy present; a recessive allele will be masked unless two copies are present, one on each of two homologous chromosomes.

Antibiotic—A compound produced by a microorganism that kills other microorganisms or retards their growth. Genes for antibiotic resistance are used as markers to indicate that successful gene transfer has occurred.

Biolistics—The bombardment of small pieces of plant tissue with tungsten microprojectiles coated with preparations of DNA.

Colchicine—An alkaloid compound derived from seeds and corms of the autumn crocus (*Colchicum autumnale*). Colchicine has the ability to disrupt the cell cycle, causing a doubling of chromosome numbers in some plant cells.

Cytoplasmic inheritance—The transmission of the genetic information contained in plastids (chloroplasts, mitochondria, and their precursors). In most flowering plants this proceeds through the egg cell alone, i.e. is maternal.

Cultivar—A cultivated variety of a crop plant, and generally identified by name, or a reference number.

Diploid—Possessing two complete sets of homologous chromosomes (double the haploid number n, and designated as 2n).

Dormancy—The inability to germinate (seeds) or grow (buds), even though environmental conditions are adequate to support growth.

Electroporation—The induction of transient pores in the plasmalemma by pulses of high voltage, in order to admit pieces of DNA.

Gametes—Specialized cells capable of fusion in the sexual cycle; female gametes are termed egg cells; male gametes may be zoospores or sperm cells.

Gene—A discrete unit of inheritance, represented by a portion of DNA located on a chromosome.

Haploid—The possession of a single complete set of chromosomes (designated n), as in the gametes of a plant that is diploid (2n).

Hybrid—A hybrid plant is derived by crossing two distinct parents, which may be different species of the same genus, or varieties of the same species. Many plant hybrids are infertile and must therefore be maintained by vegetative propagation.

Plasmid—A specific loop of bacterial DNA located outside the main circular chromosome in a bacterial cell.

Polyploidy—The condition where somatic cells have three or more sets of n chromosomes (where n is the haploid number). Functional ploidy is unusual in plants above the level of tetraploid (4n).

Transgenic plant—A plant that has successfully incorporated a transferred gene or constructed piece of DNA into its nuclear or plastid genomes.

Zygote—The cell resulting from the fusion of male and female gametes. Normally the zygote has double the chromosome number of either gamete, and gives rise to a new embryo.

the possibility of allergic reactions to the new compounds in food exists. Many countries have banned the production and importation of GM crops.

See also Gene; Genetic engineering; Graft; Mendelian laws of inheritance; Plant diseases.

Further Reading

Hartmann, H. T., et. al. *Plant Science-Growth, Development and Utilization of Cultivated Plants.* 2nd ed. Englewood Cliffs, NJ: Prentice-Hall, 1988.

Leonard, J. N. *The First Farmers.* New York: Time-Life Books, 1974.

Murray, David R., ed. *Advanced Methods in Plant Breeding and Biotechnology.* Oxford: C.A.B. International, 1991.

Simmonds, N. W., ed. *Evolution of Crop Plants.* London: Longman, 1979.

David R. Murray

Plant diseases

Like human beings and other animals, plants are subject to diseases. In order to maintain a sufficient food supply for the world's population, it is necessary for those involved in **plant** growth and management to find ways to combat plant diseases that are capable of destroying **crops**

on a large scale. There are many branches of science that participate in the control of plant diseases. Among them are **biochemistry**, **biotechnology**, **soil** science, **genetics** and **plant breeding**, meteorology, mycology (**fungi**), nematology (nematodes), virology (viruses), and weed science. **Chemistry**, **physics**, and **statistics** also play a role in the scientific maintenance of plant health. The study of plant diseases is called plant pathology.

The most common diseases of cultivated plants are bacterial wilt, **chestnut** blight, **potato** late blight, **rice** blast, coffee rust, stem rust, downy **mildew**, ergot, root knot, and tobacco mosaic. This is a small list of the more than 50,000 diseases that attack plants. Diseases can be categorized as annihilating, devastating, limiting, or debilitating. As the term suggests, annihilating diseases can totally wipe out a crop, whereas a devastating plant disease may be severe for a time and then subside. Debilitating diseases weaken crops when they attack them successively over time and limiting diseases reduce the viability of growing the target crop, thereby reducing its economic value. Plant diseases are identified by both common and scientific names. The scientific name identifies both the genus and the species of the disease-causing agent.

For the past 50 years, the ability to combat plant diseases through the use of modern farm management methods, **fertilization** of crops, **irrigation** techniques, and pest control have made it possible for the United States to produce enough food to feed its population and to have surpluses for export. However, the use of **pesticides**, fungicides, **herbicides**, **fertilizers** and other chemicals to control plant diseases and increase crop yields also poses significant environmental risks. Air, **water**, and soil can become saturated with chemicals that can be harmful to human and **ecosystem** health.

History of plant pathology

While early civilizations were well aware that plants were attacked by diseases, it was not until the invention of the first **microscope** that people began to understand the real causes of these diseases. There are references in the Bible to blights, blasts, and mildews. Aristotle wrote about plant diseases in 350 B.C. and Theophrastus (372-287 B.C.) theorized about cereal and other plant diseases. During the Middle Ages in **Europe**, ergot fungus infected grain and Shakespeare mentions **wheat** mildew in one of his plays.

After Anton von Leeuwenhoek constructed a microscope in 1683, he was able to view organisms, including **protozoa** and **bacteria**, not visible to the naked **eye**. In the eighteenth century, Duhumel de Monceau described a fungus disease and demonstrated that it could be passed from plant to plant, but his discovery was largely ignored. About this same time, nematodes were described by several English scientists and by 1755 the treatment of **seeds** to prevent a wheat disease was known.

In the nineteenth century, Ireland suffered a devastating potato famine due to a fungus that caused late blight of potatoes. At this time, scientists began to take a closer look at plant diseases. Heinrich Anton DeBary, known as the father of modern plant pathology, published a book identifying fungi as the cause of a variety of plant diseases. Until this time, it was commonly believed that plant diseases arose spontaneously from decay and that the fungi were caused by this spontaneously generated disease. DeBary supplanted this theory of spontaneously generated diseases with the **germ theory** of disease. Throughout the rest of the nineteenth century scientists working in many different countries, including Julian Gotthelf Kühn, Oscar Brefeld, Robert Hartig, Thomas J. Burrill, Robert Koch, Louis Pasteur, R. J. Petri, Pierre Millardet, Erwin F. Smith, Adolph Mayer, Dimitri Ivanovski, Martinus Beijerinck, and Hatsuzo Hashimoto, made important discoveries about specific diseases that attacked targeted crops.

During the twentieth century advances were made in the study of nematodes. In 1935 W. M. Stanley was awarded a Nobel Prize for his work with the tobacco mosaic **virus**. By 1939 virus particles could be seen under the new **electron** microscope. In the 1940s fungicides were developed and in the 1950s nematicides were produced. In the 1960s Japanese scientist Y. Doi discovered mycoplasmas, organisms that resemble bacteria but lack a rigid **cell** wall, and in 1971 T. O. Diener discovered viroids, organisms smaller than viruses.

Causes of plant disease

Plant diseases can be infectious (transmitted from plant to plant) or noninfectious. Noninfectious diseases are usually referred to as disorders. Common plant disorders are caused by deficiencies in plant **nutrients**, by waterlogged or polluted soil, and by polluted air. Too little (or too much) water or improper **nutrition** can cause plants to grow poorly. Plants can also be stressed by **weather** that is too hot or too cold, by too little or too much light, and by heavy winds. **Pollution** from automobiles and industry, and the excessive application of herbicides (for weed control) can also cause noninfectious plant disorders.

Infectious plant diseases are caused by pathogens, living **microorganisms** that infect a plant and deprive it of nutrients. Bacteria, fungi, nematodes, mycoplasmas, viruses and viroids are the living agents that cause plant

diseases. Nematodes are the largest of these agents, while viruses and viroids are the smallest. None of these pathogens are visible to the naked eye, but the diseases they cause can be detected by the symptoms of wilting, yellowing, stunting, and abnormal growth patterns.

Bacteria

Some plant diseases are caused by rod-shaped bacteria. The bacteria enter the plant through natural openings, like the stomata of the leaves, or through wounds in the plant **tissue**. Once inside, the bacteria plug up the plant's vascular system (the vessels that carry water and nutrients) and cause the plant to wilt. Other common symptoms of bacterial disease include rotting and swollen plant tissues. Bacteria can be spread by water, **insects**, infected soil, or contaminated tools. Bacterial wilt attacks many **vegetables** including corn and tomatoes, and flowers. Crown gall, another bacterial plant disease, weakens and stunts plants in the **rose family** and other flowers. Fireblight attacks apple, pear, and many other ornamental and shade trees.

Fungi

About 80% of plant diseases can be traced to fungi, which have a great capacity to reproduce themselves both sexually and asexually. Fungi can grow on living or dead plant tissue and can survive in a dormant stage until conditions become favorable for their proliferation. They can penetrate plant tissue or grow on the plant's surface. Fungal spores, which act like seeds, are spread by **wind**, water, soil, and animals to other plants. Warm, humid conditions promote fungal growth. While many fungi play useful roles in plant growth, especially by forming mycorrhizal associations with the plant's roots, others cause such common plant diseases as anthracnose, late blight, apple scab, club root, black spot, damping off, and powdery mildew. Many fungi can attack are variety of plants, but some are specific to particular plants.

The list of fungi and the plants they infect is a long one. Black spot attacks roses, while brown rot damages stone **fruits**. Damping off is harmful to seeds and young plants. Downy mildew attacks flowers, some fruits, and most vegetables. Gray **mold** begins on plant debris and then moves on to attack flowers, fruits, and vegetables. Oak root fungus and oak wilt are particularly damaging to **oaks** and fruit trees. Peach **leaf** curl targets peaches and nectarines. Powdery mildew, rust, sooty mold, and southern blight attack a wide variety of plants, including **grasses**. Texas root rot and water mold root rot can also infect many different plants. Verticillium wilt targets tomatoes, potatoes, and strawberries.

Viruses and viroids

The viruses and viroids that attack plants are the hardest pathogens to control. Destroying the infected plants is usually the best control method, since chemicals to inactivate plant viruses and viroids have not proven effective. While more than 300 plant viruses have been identified, new strains continually appear because these organisms are capable of mutating. The symptoms of viral **infection** include yellowing, stunted growth in some part of the plant, and plant malformations like leaf rolls and uncharacteristically narrow leaf growth. The mosaic viruses can infect many plants. Plants infected with this virus have mottled or streaked leaves; infected fruit trees produce poor fruit and a small yield.

Nematodes

Nematodes are tiny microscopic animals with wormlike bodies and long, needlelike structures called stylets that suck nutrients from plant cells. They lay eggs that hatch as larvae and go through four stages before becoming adults. Nematodes have a 30-day life cycle, but they can remain in a dormant state for more than 30 years. Nematicides are chemicals used to control nematode infestations. Marigolds are resistant to nematodes and are often planted to help eliminate them from infected soil.

Nematodes primarily attack plant roots, but they may also destroy other parts of the plant either internally or externally. They thrive in warm, sandy, moist soil and attack a variety of plants including corn, lettuce, potatoes, tomatoes, alfalfa, rye, and onions. However, all nematodes are not harmful to plants. Some are actually used to control other plant **pests** such as cutworms, armyworms, and beetle grubs.

Other causes of plant diseases

Mycoplasmas are single-celled organisms that lack rigid cell walls and are contained within layered cell membranes. They are responsible for the group of plant diseases called yellow diseases and are spread by insects such as the leafhopper.

Parasitic plants, such as **mistletoe**, cannot get their nutrients from the soil, but must attach themselves to other plants and use nutrients from the host plant to survive. They weaken the **wood** of their host trees and deform the branches.

Disease cycles

An equilateral disease triangle is often used to illustrate the conditions required for plant diseases to occur. The base of the triangle is the host and the two equal

sides represent the environment and the pathogen. When all three factors combine, then disease can occur. Pathogens need plants in order to grow because they cannot produce their own nutrients. When a plant is vulnerable to a pathogen and the environmental conditions are right, the pathogen can infect the plant causing it to become diseased.

Plant disease control is achieved by changing the host plant, by destroying the pathogen or by changing the plant's environment. The key to success in growing plants, whether in the home garden or commercially, is to change one or more of the three factors necessary to produce disease. Disease-resistant plants and enrichment of soil nutrients are two ways of altering the disease triangle.

Weather is one environmental **factor** in the plant disease triangle that is impossible to control. When weather conditions favor the pathogen and the plant is susceptible to the pathogen, disease can occur. **Weather forecasting** provides some help; satellites monitor weather patterns and provide farmers with some advance warning when conditions favorable to disease development are likely to occur. Battery-powered microcomputers and microenvironmental monitors are place in orchards or fields to monitor **temperature**, rainfall, light levels, wind, and humidity. These monitors provide farmers with information that helps them determine the measures they need to take to reduce crop loss due to disease.

Control

Control of plant disease begins with good soil management. The best soil for most plants is loamy, with good drainage and aeration. This minimizes diseases that attack the roots and allows the roots to feed nutrients from the soil to the rest of the plant. Organic methods, such as the addition of compost, can improve soil quality, and fertilizers can be added to the soil to enrich the nutrient base. Soil **pH** measures the degree of acidity or alkalinity of the soil. Gardeners and farmers must be aware of the pH needs of their plants, since the right pH balance can help reduce susceptibility to disease, especially root diseases like club root or black root rot.

Other important factors in the control of plant disease are the selection of disease-resistant plants (cultivars), proper watering, protection of plants from extreme weather conditions, and **rotation** of crops. Disposal of infected plants is important in the control of diseases, as is the careful maintenance of tools and equipment used in farming and gardening. Many plant diseases can easily be spread by hand and by contact with infected tools, as well as by wind, rain and soil **contamination**. Plant diseases can also be spread by seeds, and by transplants and cuttings; careful attention to the presence of disease in seeds, transplants, and cuttings can avoid the spread of pathogens.

Crop rotation is an important part of reducing plant diseases. Pathogens that favor a specific crop are deprived of their preferred host when crops are rotated. This reduces the virulence of the pathogen and is a natural way to reduce plant disease. Soil solarization is another natural method used by gardeners to reduce diseases.

Barriers or chemical applications to eliminate pests that may carry pathogens to plants are another method of disease control. The use of chemical pesticides has become standard practice among home gardeners and commercial growers alike. Among the organic chemicals used today are **copper**, lime-sulfur, Bordeaux mixture, fungicidal **soap**, and **sulfur**. After World War II, DDT, a synthetic insecticide, was used to destroy plant pests. Today, the use of this and a number of other pesticides has been banned or restricted because they were found to present hazards to the health of human, **wildlife**, and the environment.

See also Bacteria; DDT; Rusts and smuts.

KEY TERMS

Cultivar—A cultivated plant with distinct characteristics that can be reproduced.

Disease triangle—The presence of a host plant, favorable environment, and a pathogen that is capable of causing disease.

Infectious plant diseases—Disease caused by living agents (pathogens) that are able to spread to healthy plants.

Noninfectious plant diseases—Usually called plant disorders, these conditions are caused by nonliving agents, such as soil pH, pesticides, fertilizers, pollution, or soil contamination.

Pathogen—An organism able to cause disease in a host.

Plant pathology—The study of plant diseases.

Further Reading

Garden Pests and Diseases. Menlo Park, CA: Sunset Publishing, 1993.

Heitefuss, Rudolf. *Crop and Plant Protection.* Chichester, England: Ellis Horwood Ltd., 1989.

Lucas, G. B., C. L. Campbell, and L. T. Lucas. *Introduction to Plant Diseases.* Westport, CT: AVI Publishing, 1985.

Manners, J. G. *Principles of Plant Pathology.* 2nd ed. Cambridge: Cambridge University Press, 1993.

Michalak, Patricia S. *Controlling Pests and Diseases.* Emmaus, PA: Rodale Press, 1994.

Smith, Miranda, and Anna Carr. *Garden Insect, Disease, and Weed Identification Guide.* Emmaus, PA: Rodale Press, 1988.

Vita Richman

Plant pigment

A **plant** pigment is any type of colored substance produced by a plant. In general, any chemical compound which absorbs visible **radiation** between about 380 nm (violet) and 760 nm (ruby-red) is considered a pigment. There are many different plant pigments, and they are found in different classes of organic compounds. Plant pigments give color to leaves, flowers, and **fruits** and are also important in controlling **photosynthesis**, growth, and development.

Absorption of radiation

An absorption **spectrum** is a measure of the wavelengths of radiation that a pigment absorbs. The selective absorption of different wavelengths determines the color of a pigment. For example, the chlorophylls of higher plants absorb red and blue wavelengths, but not green wavelengths, and this gives leaves their characteristic green color.

The molecular structure of a pigment determines its absorption spectrum. When a pigment absorbs radiation, it is excited to a higher **energy** state. A pigment **molecule** absorbs some wavelengths and not others simply because its molecular structure restricts the energy states which it can enter.

Once a pigment has absorbed radiation and is excited to a higher energy state, the energy in the pigment has three possible fates: (a) it can be emitted as **heat**, (b) it can be emitted as radiation of lower energy (longer wavelength), or (c) it can engage in photochemical work, i.e. produce chemical changes. Flavonoids, carotenoids, and betalains are plant pigments which typically emit most of their absorbed light energy as heat. In contrast, **chlorophyll**, phytochrome, rhodopsin, and phycobilin are plant pigments which use much of their absorbed light energy to produce chemical changes within the plant.

Chlorophylls

The chlorophylls are used to drive photosynthesis and are the most important plant pigments. Chlorophylls occur in plants, **algae**, and photosynthetic **bacteria**. In plants and algae, they are located in the inner membranes of chloroplasts, organelles (**membrane** enclosed structures) within plant cells which perform photosynthesis. Photosynthesis uses the light energy absorbed by chlorophylls to synthesize carbohydrates. All organisms on **earth** depend upon photosynthesis for food, either directly or indirectly.

Chemists have identified more than 1,000 different, naturally occurring chlorophylls. All chlorophylls are classified as metallo-tetrapyrroles. A pyrrole is a molecule with four **carbon atoms** and one **nitrogen** atom arranged in a ring; a tetrapyrrole is simply four pyrroles joined together. In all chlorophylls, the four pyrrole rings are themselves joined into a ring. Thus, the chlorophyll molecule can be considered as a "ring of four pyrrole rings." A **metal** ion, such as **magnesium**, is in the center of the tetrapyrrole ring and a long **hydrocarbon** chain, termed a phytol tail, is attached to one of the pyrroles. The phytol tail anchors the chlorophyll molecule to an inner membrane within the **chloroplast**.

The different types of chlorophylls absorb different wavelengths of light. Most plants use several photosynthetic pigments with different absorption spectra, allowing use of a greater portion of the solar spectrum for photosynthesis. Chlorophyll-a is present in higher plants, algae, cyanobacteria, and chloroxybacteria.

Higher plants and some groups of algae also have chlorophyll-b. Other algae have chlorophyll-c or chlorophyll-d. There are also numerous types of bacteriochlorophylls found in the photosynthetic bacteria.

Carotenoids

Carotenoids are yellow, orange, or red pigments synthesized by many plants, **fungi**, and bacteria. In plants, carotenoids can occur in roots, stems, leaves, flowers, and fruits. Within a plant **cell**, carotenoids are found in the membranes of plastids, organelles surrounded by characteristic double membranes. Chloroplasts are the most important type of plastid and they synthesize and store carotenoids as well as perform photosynthesis. Two of the best known carotenoids are Beta-carotene and lycopene. Beta-carotene gives carrots, sweet potatoes, and other **vegetables** their orange color. Lycopene gives tomatoes their red color. When a human eats carrots or other foods containing carotenoids, the liver splits the carotenoid molecule in half to create two molecules of vitamin-A, an essential micro-nutrient.

Chemists have identified about 500 different, naturally occurring carotenoids. Each consists of a long hydrocarbon chain with a 6-carbon ionone ring at each end. All carotenoids consist of 40 carbon atoms and are syn-

thesized from eight 5-carbon isoprene subunits connected head-to-tail. There are two general classes of carotenoids: carotenes and xanthophylls. Carotenes consist only of carbon and **hydrogen** atoms; Beta-carotene is the most common carotene. Xanthophylls have one or more **oxygen** atoms; lutein is one of the most common xanthophylls.

Carotenoids have two important functions in plants. First, they can contribute to photosynthesis. They do this by transferring some of the light energy they absorb to chlorophylls, which then use this energy to drive photosynthesis. Second, they can protect plants which are over-exposed to sunlight. They do this by harmlessly dissipating excess light energy which they absorb as heat. In the absence of carotenoids, this excess light energy could destroy **proteins**, membranes, and other molecules. Some plant physiologists believe that carotenoids may have an additional function as regulators of certain developmental responses in plants.

Flavonoids

Flavonoids are widely distributed plant pigments. They are **water** soluble and commonly occur in vacuoles, membrane-enclosed structures within cells which also store water and **nutrients**.

Interestingly, light absorption by other photoreceptive plant pigments, such as phytochrome and flavins, induces synthesis of flavonoids in many species. Anthocyanins are the most common class of flavonoids and they are commonly orange, red, or blue in color. Anthocyanins are present in flowers, fruits, and vegetables. Roses, wine, apples, and cherries owe their red color to anthocyanins. In the autumn, the leaves of many temperate zone trees, such as red maple (*Acer rubrum*), change color due to synthesis of anthocyanins and destruction of chlorophylls.

Chemists have identified more than 3,000 naturally occurring flavonoids. Flavonoids are placed into 12 different classes, the best known of which are the anthocyanins, flavonols, and flavones. All flavonoids have 15 carbon atoms and consist of two 6-carbon rings connected to one another by a carbon ring which contains an oxygen atom. Most naturally occurring flavonoids are bound to one or more sugar molecules. Small changes in a flavonoid's structure can cause large changes in its color.

Flavonoids often occur in fruits, where they attract animals which eat the fruits and disperse the **seeds**. They also occur in flowers, where they attract insect pollinators. Many flavones and flavonols absorb radiation most strongly in the ultraviolet (UV) region and form special UV patterns on flowers which are visible to **bees** but not humans. Bees use these patterns, called **nectar** guides, to find the flower's nectar which they consume in recompense for pollinating the **flower**. UV-absorbing flavones and flavonols are also present in the leaves of many species, where they protect plants by screening out harmful ultraviolet radiation from the **Sun**.

Phytochrome

Phytochrome is a blue-green plant pigment which regulates plant development, including seed **germination**, stem growth, **leaf** expansion, pigment synthesis, and flowering. Phytochrome has been found in most of the organs of seed plants and free-sporing plants. It has also been found in green algae. Although phytochrome is an important plant pigment, it occurs in very low concentrations and is not visible unless chemically purified. In this respect, it is different from chlorophylls, carotenoids, and flavonoids.

Phytochrome is a protein attached to an open chain tetrapyrrole (four pyrrole rings). The phytochrome **gene** has been cloned and sequenced and many plants appear to have five or more different phytochrome genes. The phytochrome tetrapyrrole absorbs the visible radiation and gives phytochrome its characteristic blue-green color. Phytochrome exists in two inter-convertible forms. The red absorbing form (Pr) absorbs most strongly at about 665 nm and is blue in color. The far-red absorbing form (Pfr) absorbs most strongly at about 730 nm and is green in color. When Pr absorbs red light, the structure of the tetrapyrrole changes and Pfr is formed; when Pfr absorbs far-red light, the structure of the tetrapyrrole changes and Pr is formed. Natural sunlight is a mixture of many different wavelengths of light, so plants in nature typically have a mixture of Pr and Pfr within their cells which is constantly being converted back and forth.

There are three types of phytochrome reactions which control plant growth and development. The "very low fluence responses" require very little light, about one second of sunlight; the "low fluence responses" require an intermediate amount of light, about one sound of sunlight; and the "high irradiance responses" require prolonged irradiation, many minutes to many hours of sunlight.

The low fluence responses exhibit red/far-red reversibility and are the best characterized type of response. For example, in the seeds of many species, a brief flash of red light (which forms Pfr) promotes germination and a subsequent flash of far-red light (which forms Pr) inhibits germination. When seeds are given a series of red and far-red light flashes, the color of the final flash determines the response. If it is red, they germinate; if it is far-red, they remain dormant.

KEY TERMS

Chloroplast—Green organelle in higher plants and algae in which photosynthesis occurs.

Isoprene—Five-carbon molecule with the chemical formula $CH_2C(CH_3)CHCH_2$.

Organelle—Membrane-enclosed structure within a cell which has specific functions.

Photosynthesis—Biological conversion of light energy into chemical energy.

Plastid—Organelle surrounded by a double membrane which may be specialized for photosynthesis (chloroplast), storage of pigments (chromoplast) or other functions.

Vacuole—Membrane-enclosed structure within cells which store pigments, water, nutrients, and wastes.

Additional plant pigments

Phycobilins are water soluble photosynthetic pigments. They are not present in higher plants, but do occur in red algae and the cyanobacteria, a group of photosynthetic bacteria.

Betalains are red or yellow pigments which are synthesized by plants in ten different families. Interestingly, none of the species which have betalains also produce anthocyanins, even though these two pigments are unrelated.

Flavins are orange-yellow pigments often associated with proteins. Some flavins are specialized for control of **phototropism** and other developmental responses of plants. Like phytochrome, flavins occur in low concentrations and cannot be seen unless purified.

Rhodopsin is a pigment which controls light-regulated movements, such as phototaxis and photokinesis, in many species of algae. Interestingly, humans and many other animals also use rhodopsin for **vision**.

Further Reading

Corner, E. J. *The Life of Plants.* Chicago: University of Chicago Press, 1981.

Galston, A. W. *Life Processes of Plants: Mechanisms for Survival.* San Francisco: W. H. Freeman Press, 1993.

Kaufman, P. B., et al. *Plants: Their Biology and Importance.* New York: HarperCollins, 1990.

Wilkins, M. *Plant Watching.* New York: Facts on File, 1988.

Peter A. Ensminger

Plasma see **Phases of matter**

Plasma

Plasma is the liquid portion of **blood** which is about 90% **water** and transports **nutrients**, wastes, antibodies, ions, **hormones**, and other molecules throughout the body. Humans typically have about 1.3-1.5 gals (5-6 l) of blood, which is about 55% plasma and 45% cells-red blood cells, white blood cells, and platelets. The plasma of humans and other **vertebrates** is nearly colorless, since the red color of hemoglobin is sequestered inside red blood cells. In contrast, many **invertebrates** have hemoglobin or hemocyanin carried directly in their plasma, so that their plasma is red, green, or blue.

Proteins make up about 8% by weight of human plasma. Humans have over 60 different proteins in their plasma, but the major ones are albumins, globulins, and fibrinogen. Albumins constitute about half (by weight) of all plasma protein and are important as carriers of ions, **fatty acids**, and other organic molecules. The most important class of globulins is the immunoglobulins, which are the antibodies that defend the body against attack by foreign organisms. Fibrinogen is a plasma protein important in the formation of blood clots following damage to a blood vessel. In clotting, fibrinogen is converted into fibrin and the fibrin molecules form an insoluble **polymer**, a blood clot. Additional plasma proteins serve as carriers for lipids, hormones, vitamins and other molecules.

Ions make up only about 1% by weight of human plasma. However, they are the major contributors to plasma molarity, since their molecular weights are much less than those of proteins. Thus, ions are important in preventing blood cells from bursting by taking up excess water in **osmosis**. **Sodium chloride** (NaCl) constitutes more than 65% of the plasma ions. Bicarbonate, potassium, **calcium**, phosphate, sulfate, and **magnesium** are other plasma ions. The kidneys regulate the levels of plasma ion concentrations.

Plasma is also a transport medium for nutrients and wastes. The nutrients include amino acids (used to synthesize proteins), glucose (an **energy** source), and fatty acids (an energy source). The plasma transorts waste products such as **urea** and uricacid to the kidneys, where they are excreted.

Cholesterol and cholesterol esters are also present in plasma. Cholesterol is used as an energy source, as a metabolic precursor for the synthesis of steroid hormones, and is incorporated in **cell** membranes. Excess cholesterol and saturated fatty acids in the plasma can be

deposited in arteries and can lead to **arteriosclerosis** (hardening of the arteries) and to **heart** disease.

The plasma of vertebrates also contains dissolved gases. Most of the **oxygen** in blood is bound to hemoglobin inside the red blood cells but some oxygen is dissolved directly in the plasma. Additional plasma gases include **carbon dioxide** (which forms bicarbonate ions) and **nitrogen** (which is inert).

Plasma physics see **Physics**

Plastic surgery

Plastic surgery is the specialized branch of surgery concerned with repairing deformities, correcting functional deficits, and enhancing appearance. Unlike most surgical specialties, plastic surgery is not confined to one specific anatomical or functional area of the body. Often, plastic surgery is classified as either reconstructive or aesthetic surgery. All plastic surgery procedures seek to restore or improve patients' appearances, however, reconstructive surgery focuses on patients with physical problems or deformities while aesthetic (or cosmetic) surgery often focuses on patients who want to improve their appearance even though they have no serious physical defect.

History of plastic surgery

Long before the word plastic was first applied in 1818 to denote surgery largely concerned with the patient's appearance, physicians performed a number of reconstructive procedures on the noses and **ear** lobes of soldiers who were injured during battle. As far back as 25 B.C. to 50 A.D., physicians were taking **tissue** from one part of the body and using it to correct physical defects in other areas. Much of the ancient pioneering efforts in plastic surgery took place in the ancient Arab and Hindu schools of medicine.

During the early part of the sixteenth century, the Branca family in Sicily began practicing plastic surgery procedures, including using flaps or masses of tissue from patient's arms to repair mutilated ears and lips. However, Gaspare Tagliacozzi of Bologna, Italy, is generally credited with initiating the modern era of plastic surgery during the latter half of the sixteenth century.

After Tagliacozzi's death in 1599, the art of plastic surgery languished for nearly two centuries, partly because many surgeons tried unsuccessfully to use donor flaps and skin from slaves and others. The transplantation of tissue between two individuals would not be successfully achieved until the second half of the twentieth century, when scientists learned more about differences in **blood** types and immune systems and the role these differences played in hindering transplantation of tissues between two people.

A resurgence of interest in plastic surgery began in the nineteenth century with renewed interest in reconstruction of the nose, lips, and other areas of the human body. During this time, a number of surgeons throughout **Europe** refined techniques for performing a variety of procedures. One of the most beneficial was the development of skin grafting on humans in 1817 to repair burnt or scarred skin.

The next major advances in plastic surgery would not take place until well into the next century, when various new flap techniques were developed in the 1960s and 1970s. The first successful reattachment of a severed arm was accomplished in 1970. And, in 1972, the advancement of microsurgical techniques that enabled surgeons to reattach minute nerves and blood vessels further enhanced this surgical field. It was during this time that cosmetic plastic surgery also began to bloom, as new techniques were refined to enhance physical appearances, including breast implants and face lifts.

Reconstructive plastic surgery

The primary aim of reconstructive plastic surgery is to restore the normal appearance and functioning of disfigured and/or impaired areas of the human body. Craniofacial reconstructive surgery, for example, focuses on face and skull defects. These defects may be **congenital** (**birth**) or due to trauma (an injury or wound). Craniofacial surgeons also reconstruct parts of the face deformed by **cancer** and other diseases. The cleft palate, a split in the bony roof of the mouth that usually runs from the front of the mouth to the back, is one of the most common **birth defects** corrected by craniofacial plastic surgery.

Vascular, microvascular, and peripheral nerve surgery focuses on reestablishing the complex connections of nerve and blood vessels that may have been severed or otherwise damaged. Plastic surgeons also transplant muscles and tendons from one part of the body to another to restore common functions such as walking or other activities that incorporate these anatomical structures.

Skin grafting is a reconstructive surgical technique that transplants skin from one part of the body to another damaged area where the skin grows again. This technique is used to treat burned or otherwise damaged skin.

Flaps

In the realm of plastic surgery, flaps are large masses of tissue that may include **fat** and muscle. Flaps are

taken from one place on the body and then attached to another area. These operations are much more complex than skin grafts because they involve the need to reestablish various vascular, or blood, connections.

A pedicle flap **graft** involves connecting the tissue and/or muscle to the new site while keeping part of it attached to the original site. This technique maintains the old blood vessel connections until the flap naturally creates new connections (revascularization) at the transplanted site. For example, a **mass** of tissue on an undamaged finger can be partially peeled back and connected to an adjacent finger until revascularization takes place. Then the flap can be totally severed from its original site.

A free flap is when tissue or muscles are completely severed from the body and then transplanted to the new site where the blood vessels are then reconnected surgically. An advantage of the free flap procedure is that the transplanted tissue can be taken from anywhere on the body and does not have to be in an area close to (or can be placed close to) the new site.

The advancement of microsurgical techniques have greatly improved the success of free flap surgical procedures. Using a **microscope**, tiny needles, and nearly invisible thread, the surgeon can painstakingly reconstruct the vascular web that supplies nourishment in the form of blood to the transplanted tissues.

Aesthetic plastic surgery

Aesthetic plastic surgery procedures are as varied as the many areas of the body they seek to enhance. They range from reshaping the nose and enlarging women's breasts to hair transplants for balding men and liposuction to remove unwanted fat from the body. For many years aesthetic plastic surgery, popularly known as cosmetic surgery, was held in low esteem by many within the plastic surgery field. This disdain was largely because aesthetic surgery was generally not a necessary procedure based on medical need or gross deformity, but rather on the patient's vanity or desire to have his or her looks surgically enhanced.

Today, hundreds of thousands of aesthetic plastic surgery procedures are conducted each year. Many of the operations are outpatient procedures, meaning they require no hospitalization overnight. However, the complexity of the procedures vary. Breast enlargements, for example, are made with a simple incision in the breast in which a bag-like structure filled with either silicone or saline is inserted and sewn into place. Facelifts, on the other hand, involve cutting the skin from the hairline to the back of the ear. The loosened skin can then be stretched upward from the neck and stitched together for a tighter, wrinkle free appearance. Another aesthetic surgery for facial skin is called skin peeling, which is used primarily on patients with scarred faces due to **acne** or some other **disease**. A surgical skin peel involves removal of the skin's surface layers with mechanical devices that scrape off the skin or grind it down.

If a person desires a new nose, they can undergo a procedure that involves making incisions inside the nose to reduce scarring and then breaking and reshaping the nasal bone. Another facial cosmetic surgery is the eyelid tuck, which removes fleshy bags under the eyes.

In recent years, a cosmetic surgery called liposuction has rapidly grown in popularity. Developed in France, this procedure involves removing fat from specific areas of the body by vacuuming it out through a long **metal** probe that is connected to a pump.

Drawbacks to aesthetic surgery

Although there is nothing wrong with wanting to look good, there are some troubling ethical issues associated with aesthetic plastic surgery. First and foremost, they are not 100% percent safe. Almost all surgical procedures are associated with the risk of infections, which can lead to death if not identified early and treated properly. In rare cases, liposuction has resulted in too much fluid loss and the formation of blood clots, which can also lead to death. Despite the lack of concrete scientific

KEY TERMS

Aesthetic surgery—Surgery designed primarily to enhance or improve the looks of an individual who may not have a gross deformity or physical impairment. This type of surgery is often referred to as cosmetic surgery.

Craniofacial—Having to do with the face and skull.

Flap—A mass of tissue used for transplantation.

Graft—Bone, skin, or other tissue taken from one place on the body (or, in some cases, from another body), and then transplanted to another place where it begins to grow again.

Reconstructive surgery—Surgery designed to restore the normal appearance and functioning of disfigured and/or impaired areas of the human body.

Transplantation—The removal of body parts, organs, or tissues from one person and surgically placing them on or into the body of another person.

evidence, some concern has arisen over the possibility that silicone gel breast implants may cause a variety of diseases, including cancer. As a result, most implants are now filled with a saline solution similar to that naturally produced in the body.

Another important issue to consider is that not all aesthetic surgeries result in an improved appearance. Some surgeries, like facial reconstruction, have occasionally resulted in the patient being maimed and disfigured. Others, like the facelift, only last 3-10 years. Finally, some people may come to rely on these form of surgeries to improve their looks while ignoring the need to maintain the healthy lifestyles that not only promote looks but prolong life.

Further Reading

Becker, Daniel G. "A 3-Year Multi-institutional Experience With the Liposhaver." *The Journal of the American Medical Association,* Vol 282 (24 Nov 1999): 1902.

Camp, John. *Plastic Surgery: The Kindest Cut.* New York: Henry Holt and Company, 1989.

Fu, Freddie H., et. al. "Current Trends in Anterior Cruciate Ligament Reconstruction." *The American Journal of Sports Medicine,* Vol 28 (Jan 2000): p124.

"The Manly Mammary." *Discover,* (1 Jan 2000).

Neimark, Jill. "Change of Face...Change of Fate." *Psychology Today.* (May/June, 1994): 94.

Smith, James W. and Sherrel J. Aston, eds. *Grabb and Smith's Plastic Surgery.* Boston: Little, Brown, 1991.

Vreeland, Leslie N. "Cosmetic Surgery: Avoiding the Pitfalls." *American Health,* (July/August 1992): 47-53.

David Petechuk

Plastics

In the twentieth century, the term plastic has come to refer to a class of materials that, under suitable conditions, can be deformed by some kind of shaping or molding process to produce an end product that retains its shape. When used as an adjective, the term plastic (from Greek "plastikos" meaning to **mold** or form) describes a material that can be shaped or molded with or without the application of **heat**. With few exceptions, plastics do not flow freely like liquids, but retain their shapes like solids even when flowing.

When used in a chemical sense, the term plastic usually refers to a synthetic high **molecular weight** chain **molecule**, or **polymer**, that may have been combined with other ingredients to modify its physical properties. Most plastics are based on **carbon**, being derived from materials that have some relationship to living, or organic, materials, although, although some plastics, like acetal **resins** and silicones, contain **oxygen** or silicon **atoms** in their chains.

As plastics are heated to moderate temperatures, the polymer chains are able to flow past each other. Because of the organic nature of most plastics, they usually cannot withstand high temperatures and begin to decompose at temperatures around 392°F (200°C).

The oldest known examples of plastic materials are soft waxes, asphalts, and moist clays. These materials are capable of flowing like synthetic plastics, but because they are not polymeric, they are usually not referred to as plastics.

History

The history of synthetic plastics goes back over 100 years to the use of **cellulose** nitrate (celluloid) for billiard balls, men's collars, and shirt cuffs. Before plastics were commercialized, most household goods and industrial products were made of metals, **wood**, **glass**, **paper**, leather, and vulcanized (sulfurized) natural rubber.

The first truly synthetic polymer was Bakelite, a densely cross-linked material based on the reaction of phenol and formaldehyde. It has been used for many applications, including electrical appliances and **phonograph** records. Among the first plastics developed that could be reformed under heat (thermoplastics) were polyvinyl chloride, polystyrene, and nylon 66.

The first polymers used by man were actually natural products such as **cotton**, starch, **proteins**, or wool. Certain proteins that are in fact natural polymers once had commercial importance as industrial plastics, but they have played a diminishing role in the field of plastics production in recent years.

Chemistry

There are more than 100 different chemical atoms, known as elements. They are represented by the chemist by the use of simple symbols such as "H" for **hydrogen**, "O" for oxygen, "C" for carbon, "N" for **nitrogen**, "Cl" for **chlorine**, and so on; these atoms have atomic weights of 1, 16, 12, 14, and 17 atomic units, respectively.

A chemical reaction between two or more atoms forms a molecule. Each molecule is characterized by its elemental constitution and its molecular weight. For example, when carbon is burned in oxygen, one atom of carbon (C) reacts with two atoms of oxygen (O_2; equivalent to one molecule of molecular oxygen) to form **carbon dioxide** (CO_2). The chemist represents this reaction by a chemical equation, i.e.,

TABLE 1. CHANGE IN MOLECULAR PROPERTIES WITH MOLECULAR CHAIN LENGTH		
Number of CH_2 units in chain	***Appearance at room temperature***	***Uses***
1 to 4	simple gas	cooking gas
5 to 11	simple liquid	gasoline
9 to 16	medium viscosity liquid	kerosene
16 to 25	high viscosity liquid	oil and grease
25 to 50	simple solid	paraffin wax candles
1000 to 3000	tough plastic solid	polyethylene bottle and containers

$$C + O_2 = CO_2$$

Similarly, when four atoms of hydrogen ($2H_2$; equivalent to two molecules of molecular hydrogen) and two atoms of oxygen (O_2; equivalent to one molecule of oxygen) react to form two molecules of **water** ($2H_2O$), the chemist writes

$$2H_2 + O_2 = 2H_2O$$

Note that one molecule of oxygen combines with two molecules of hydrogen, and one atom of carbon combines with one molecule of hydrogen. This is because different elements have different combining capacities. Thus hydrogen forms one bond, oxygen two bonds, and carbon four bonds. These bonding capacities, or valences, are taken for granted when writing a chemical formula like H_2O.

In the case of methane, or CH_4, the carbon is bonded to four hydrogen atoms. But carbon can also form double bonds, as in ethylene (C_2H_4) where two CH_2molecules share a double bond. The chemist could also describe the ethylene molecule by the formula CH_2=CH_2, where the double bond is represented by an equal sign.

Plastic materials consist of many repeating groups of atoms or molecules (called monomers) in long chains, and hence are also known as polymers or macromolecules. Elements present in a polymer chain typically include oxygen, hydrogen, nitrogen, carbon, silicon, fluorine, chlorine, or **sulfur**. The way the polymer chains are linked together and the lengths of the chains determine the mechanical and physical properties of the plastic.

Molecular weight

Polymers exist on a continuum that extends from simple gases to molecules of very high molecular weights. A relatively simple polymer has the structure

$$H - (CH_2)_n\text{-}H$$

where the number (n) of monomers (CH_2 groups, in this case) in the chain may extend up to several thousand. Table 1 shows how the physical properties and uses of the polymer change with the number of repeating **monomer** units in the chain.

Polymerization

Most commercial plastics are synthesized from simpler molecules, or monomers. The simple chemicals from which monomers, and ultimately polymers, are derived are usually obtained from crude oil or **natural gas**, but may also come from **coal**, sand, **salt**, or air.

For example, the molecules used to form polystyrene, a widely used plastic, are **benzene** and ethylene. These two molecules are reacted to form ethyl benzene, which is further reacted to give a styrene monomer. With the aid of a catalyst, styrene monomers may form a chain of linked, bonded styrene units. This method of constructing a polymer molecule is known as addition polymerization, and characterizes the way most plastics—including polystyrenes, acrylics, vinyls, fluoroplastics—are formed.

When two different molecules are combined to form a chain in such a way that a small molecule such as water is produced as a by-product, the method of building the molecule is known as condensation polymerization. This

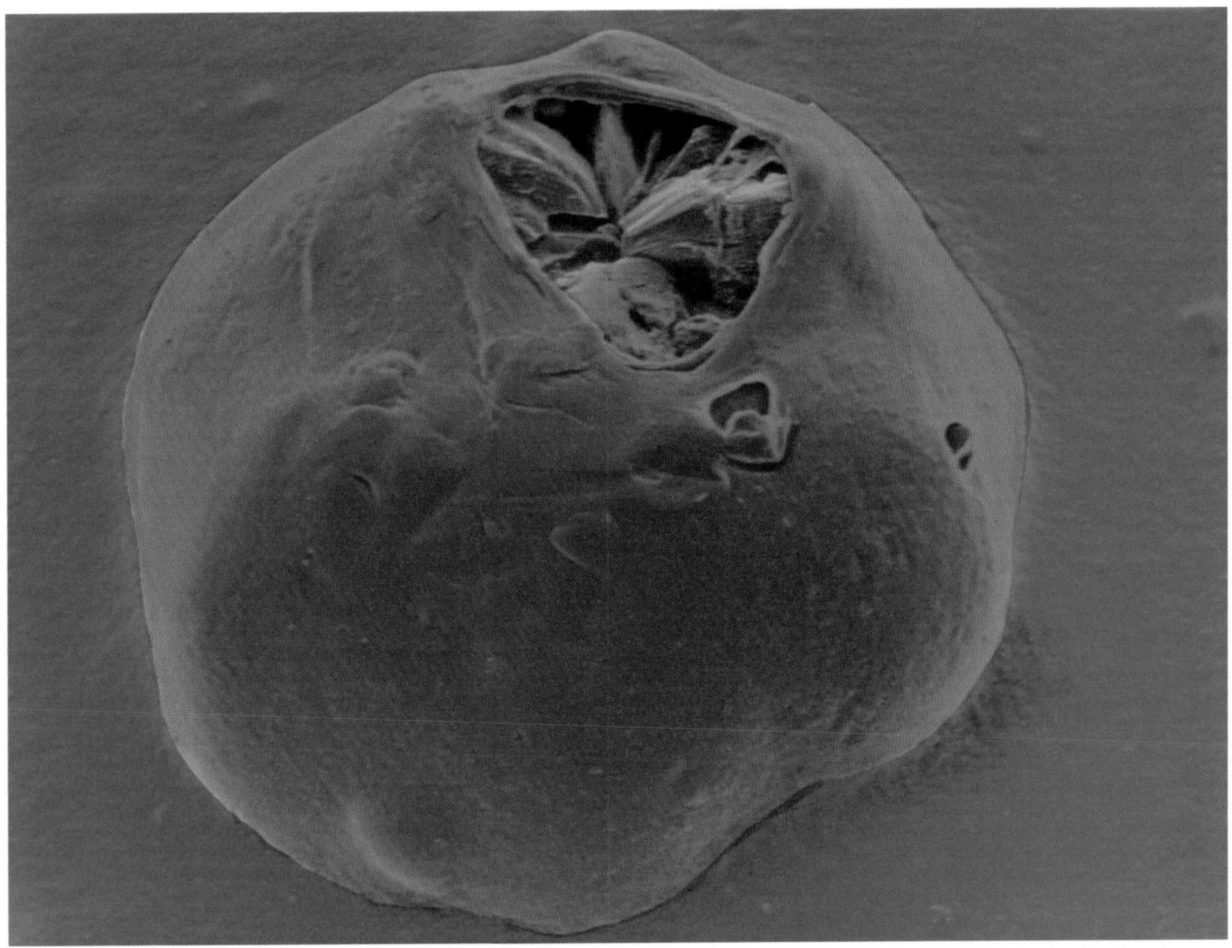

A scanning electron micrograph (SEM) of the surface of a sheet of biodegradable plastic. The spherical object that dominates the image is one of many granules of starch embedded in the surface of the plastic. When the plastic is buried in soil the starch grains take up water and expand. This breaks the material into small fragments, increasing the contact area with the soil bacteria that digest plastic.

type of polymerization characterizes a second class of plastics. Nylons are examples of condensation polymers.

Manufacture and processing

When polymers are produced, they are shipped in pelletized, granulated, powdered, or liquid form to plastics processors. When the polymer is still in its raw material form, it is referred to as a resin. This term antedates the understanding of the **chemistry** of polymer molecules and originally referred to the resemblance of polymer liquids to the pitch on trees.

Plastics can be formed or molded under **pressure** and heat, and many can be machined to high degrees of tolerance in their hardened states. Thermoplastics are plastics that can be heated and reshaped; thermosets are plastics that cannot.

Thermoplastics

Thermoplastics are plastics that become soft and malleable when heated, and then become hard and solid again when cooled. Examples of thermoplastics include acetal, acrylic, cellulose acetate, nylon, polyethylene, polystyrene, vinyl, and nylon. When thermoplastic materials are heated, the molecular chains are able to move past one another, allowing the mass to flow into new shapes. Cooling prevents further flow. Thermoplastic elastomers are flexible plastics that can be stretched up to twice their length at room **temperature** and then return to their original length when released.

The state of a thermoplastic depends on the temperature and the time allowed to measure its physical properties. At low enough temperatures, amorphous, or noncrystalline, thermoplastics are stiff and glassy. This is the glassy state, sometimes referred to as the vitreous

TABLE 2. THERMOPLASTICS		
Type	***Chemical basis***	***Uses***
ABS plastics	Derived from acrylonitrile, butadiene, and styrene	Electroplated plastic parts; automotive components; business and telecommunication applications such as personal computers, terminals, keyboards, and floppy disks; medical disposables; toys; recreational applications; cosmetics packaging; luggage; housewares
Acetals	Consist of repeating -CH_2-O-units in a polymer backbone	Rollers, bearings and other industrial products; also used in automotive, appliance, plumbing and electronics applications
Acrylics	Based on polymethyl methacrylate	Automobile lenses, fluorescent street lights, outdoor signs, and boat windshields; applications requiring high resistance to discoloration and good light transmission properties
Cellulosics	Derived from purified cotton or special grades of wood cellulose	Insulation, packaging, toothbrushes
Fluoroplastics	Consist of carbon, fluorine, and or hydrogen atoms in a repeating polymer backbone	Applications requiring optimal electrical and thermal properties, almost complete moisture resistance, chemical inertness; non-stick applications
Nylons	Derived from the reaction of diamines and dibasic acids; characterized by the number of carbon atoms in the repeating polymeric unit	Electrical and electronic components; industrial applications requiring excellent resistance to repeated impact; consumer products such as ski boots and bicycle wheels; appliances and power tool housings; food packaging; wire and cable jacketing; sheets, rods, and tubes; and filaments for brush bristles, fishing line, and sewing thread
Polyarylates	Aromatic polyesters	Automotive appliance, and electrical applications requiring low shrinkage, resistance to hydrolysis, and precision void-free molding

TABLE 2. THERMOPLASTICS (cont'd)		
Type	***Chemical basis***	***Uses***
Polyarylsulfones	Consist of phenyl and biphenyl groups linked by thermally stable ether and sulfone groups	Electrical and electronic applications requiring thermal stability including circuit boards, connectors, lamp housings, and motor parts
Polybutylenes	Polymers based on poly(1-butene)	Cold- and hot-water pipes; hot-metal adhesives and sealants
Polybutylene terephthalate (PBT)	Produced by reaction of dimethyl terephthalate with butanediol	Automotive applications such as exterior auto parts; electronic switches; and household applications such as parts for vacuum cleaners and coffee makers
Polycarbonates	Derived from the reaction of bisphenol A and phosgene	Applications requiring toughness, rigidity, and dimensional stability; high heat resistance; good electrical properties; transparency; exceptional impact strength. Used for molded products, solution-cast or extruded films, tubes and pipes, prosthetic devices, nonbreakable windows, street lights, household appliances; compact discs; optical memory disks; and for various applications in fields related to transportation, electronics sporting goods, medical equipment, and food processing
Polyesters	Produced by reacting dicarboxylic acids with dihydroxy alcohols	Reinforced plastics, automotive parts, foams, electrical encapsulation, structural applications, low-pressure laminates, magnetic tapes, pipes, bottles. Liquid crystal polyesters are used as replacements for metals in such applications chemical pumps, electronic components, medical components, and automotive components
Polyetherimides	Consist of repeating aromatic imide and ether units	Temperature sensors; electrical/electronic, medical (surgical instrument parts), industrial; appliance, packaging, and specialty applications

TABLE 2. THERMOPLASTICS (cont'd)		
Type	*Chemical basis*	*Uses*
Polyetherketones	Polymerized aromatic ketones	Fine monofilaments, films, engine parts, aerospace composites, and wire and cables, and other applications requiring chemical resistance; exceptional toughness, strength, and rigidity; good radiation resistance; and good fire-safety characteristics
Polyethersulfones	Consist of diaryl sulfone groups with ether linkages	Electrical applications including multipin connectors, integrated circuit sockets, edge and round multipin connectors, terminal blocks, printed circuit boards
Polyethylenes, polypropylenes, and polyallomers	Polyethylenes consist of chains of repeated ethylene units; polypropylenes consist of chains of repeated propylene units; polyallomers are copolymers of propylene and ethylene	Low density polyethylene is used for packaging films, liners for shipping containers, wire and cable coatings, toys, plastic bags, electrical insulation. High density polyethylene is used for blow-molded items, films and sheets, containers for petroleum products. Low molecular weight Polyethylenes are used as mold release agents, coatings, polishes, and textile finishing agents. Polypropylenes are used as packaging films, molded parts, bottles, artificial turf, surgical casts, nonwoven disposable filters. Polyallomers are used as vacuum-formed, injection molded, and extruded products, films, sheets, and wire cables
Polyethylene terephthalate	Prepared from ethylene glycol and either terephthalic acid or an ester of terephthalic acid	Food packaging including bottles, microwave/conventional oven-proof trays; x-ray and other photographic films; magnetic tape
Polyimides and polyamide-imides	Polyimides contain imide (-CONHCO-) groups in the polymer chain; polyamide-imides also contain amide (-CONH-) groups	Polyimides are used as high temperature coatings, laminates, and composites for the aerospace industry; ablative materials; oil sealants; adhesive; semiconductors; bearings; cable insulation; printed circuits; magnetic tapes; flame-resistant fibers. Polyamide-imides have been used as replacements for metal parts in the aerospace industry, and as mechanical parts for business machines

TABLE 2. THERMOPLASTICS (cont'd)		
Type	***Chemical basis***	***Uses***
Polymethylpentene	Polymerized 4-methylpentene-1	Laboratory ware (beakers, graduates, etc.); electronic and hospital equipment; food packaging; light reflectors
Polyphenylene ethers, modified	Consist of oxidatively coupled phenols and polystyrene	Automobile instrument panels, computer keyboard bases
Polyphenylene sulfides	Para-substituted benzene rings with sulfur links	Microwave oven components, precision molded assemblies for disk drives
Polystyrenes	Polymerized ethylene and styrene	Packaging, refrigerator doors, household wares, electrical equipment; toys, cabinets; also used as foams for thermal insulations, light construction, fillers in shipping containers, furniture construction
Polysulfones	Consist of complicated chains of phenylene units linked with isopropylidene, ether, and sulfone units	Power tool housings, electrical equipment, extruded pipes and sheets, automobile components, electronic parts, appliances, computer components; medical instrumentation and trays to hold instruments during sterilization; food processing equipment; chemical processing equipment; water purification devices
Vinyls	Polymerized vinyl monomers such as polyvinyl chloride and polyvinylidene chloride	Crystal-clear food packaging, water pipes, monolayer films

state. On warming up, thermoplastics soften in a characteristic temperature range known as the glass transition temperature region. In the case of amorphous thermoplastics, the glass transition temperature is the single-most important factor determining the physical properties of the plastic.

Crystalline and noncrystalline thermoplastics

Thermoplastics may be classified by the structure of the polymer chains that comprise them.

In the liquid state, polymer molecules undergo entanglements that prevent them from forming regularly arranged domains. This state of disorder is preserved in the amorphous state. Thus, amorphous plastics, which include polycarbonate, polystyrene, acrylonitrile-butadiene-styrene (ABS), and polyvinyl chloride, are made up of polymer chains that form randomly organized structures.

These polymer chains may themselves have attached side chains, and the side chains may also be quite long. When the side chains are particularly bulky, molecular branching prevents the molecules from forming ordered regions, and an amorphous plastic will almost certainly result.

Under suitable conditions, however, the entangled polymer chains can disentangle themselves and pack into orderly crystals in the solid state where the chains are symmetrically packed together; these materials are known as crystalline polymers.

TABLE 3. THERMOSETTING PLASTICS		
Type	***Chemical basis***	***Uses***
Alkyd polyesters	Polyesters derived from the reaction of acids with two acid groups, and alcohols with three alcoholic groups per molecule	Moldings, finishes; applications requiring high durability, excellent pigment dispersion, toughness, good adhesion, and good flowing properties
Allyls	Polyesters derived form the reaction of esters of allyl alcohol with dibasic acids	Electrical insulation, applications requiring high resistance to heat, humidity, and corrosive chemicals
Bismaleimides	Generally prepared by the reaction of a diamine with maleic anhydride	Printed wire boards; high performance structural composites
Epoxies	Derived from the reaction of epichlorohydrin with hydroxylcontaining compounds	Encapsulation, electrical insulations, laminates, glass-reinforced plastics, floorings, coatings adhesives
Melamines	Derived from the reaction of formaldehyde and amino compounds containing NH_2 groups	Molded plates, dishes, and other food containers
Phenolics	Derived from the reaction of phenols and formaldehydes	Cements, adhesives
Polybutadienes	Consist of polyethylene with a cross-link at every other carbon in the main chain	Moldings, laminating resins, coatings, cast-liquid and formed-sheet products; applications requiring outstanding electrical properties and thermal stability
Polyesters (thermosetting)	Derived from reactions of dicarboxylic acids with dihydroxy alcohols	Moldings, laminated or reinforced structures, surface gel coatings, liquid castings, furniture products, structures
Polyurethanes	Derived from reactions of polyisocyanates and polyols	Rigid, semi-flexible, and flexible foams; elastomers

Crystalline thermoplastics consist of molecular chains packed together in regular, organized domains that are joined by regions of disordered, amorphous chains. Examples of crystalline thermoplastics include acetals, nylons, polyethylenes, polypropylenes, and polyesters.

Liquid crystalline plastics are polymers that form highly ordered, rodlike structures. They have good mechanical properties and are chemically unreactive, and they have melting temperatures comparable to those of crystalline plastics. But unlike crystalline and amorphous plastics, liquid crystalline plastics retain molecular ordering even as liquids. Consequently, they exhibit the lowest shrinkage and warpage of any of the thermoplastics.

Thermosets

Thermosetting plastics, or thermosets, include amino, epoxy, phenolic and unsaturated polyesters.

TABLE 3. THERMOSETTING PLASTICS (cont'd)		
Type	*Chemical basis*	*Uses*
Silicones	Consist of alternating silicon and oxygen atoms in a polymer backbone, usually with organic side groups attached to the chain	Applications requiring uniform properties over a wide temperature range; low surface tension; high degree of lubricity; excellent release properties; extreme water repellency; excellent electrical properties over a wide range of temperature and frequency; inertness and compatibility; chemical inertness; or weather resistance
Ureas	Derived from the reaction of formaldehyde and amino compounds containing NH_2 groups	Dinnerware, interior plywood, foams, insulation

These materials undergo a chemical change during processing and become hard solids. Unlike the linear molecules in a thermoplastic, adjacent molecules in a thermosetting plastic become cross-linked during processing, resulting in the production of complex networks that restrain the movement of chains past each other at any temperature.

Typical thermosets are phenolics, urea-formaldehyde resins, epoxies, cross-linked polyesters, and most polyurethanes. Elastomers may also be thermosetting. Examples include both natural and synthetic rubbers.

Manufacturing methods

At some stage in their processing, both thermoplastics and thermosetting plastics are sufficiently fluid to be molded and formed. The manufacture of most plastics is determined by their final shape.

Many cylindrical plastic objects are made by a process called extrusion. The extrusion of thermoplastics consists of melting and compressing plastic granules by rotating them in a screw conveyor in a long barrel, to which heat may be applied if necessary. The screw forces the plastic to the end of the barrel where it is pushed through a screen on its way to the nozzle. The nozzle determines the final shape of the extruded form. Thermosets may also be extruded if the screw in the conventional extruder is replaced with a plunger-type hydraulic pump.

Plastic powders are directly converted into finished articles by molding. Two types of molding processes are compression molding and injection molding. In compression molding, which is used with thermosetting materials, steam is first circulated through the mold to raise it to the desired temperature; then a plastic powder or tablets are introduced into the mold; and the mold is closed under high pressure and the plastic is liquefied so that it flows throughout the mold. When the mold is reopened, the solid molded unit is ejected. Injection molding differs from compression molding in that plastic material is rendered fluid outside the mold, and is transferred by pressure into the cooled mold. Injection molding can be used with practically every plastic material, including rubbers.

Sheets, blocks, and rods may be made in a casting process that in effect involves in situ, or in-place, polymerization. In the case of acrylics, sheets are cast in glass cells by filling cells with a polymer solution. The polymer solution solidifies and the sheet is released by separating the glass plates after chilling the assembly in cold water. Blocks can be made in the same way using a demountable container; and rods can be made by polymerizing a polymer syrup under pressure in a cylindrical **metal** tube.

Plastic foams are produced by compounding a polymer resin with a foaming agent or by injecting air or a volatile fluid into the liquid polymer while it is being processed into a finished product. This results in a finished product with a network of gas spaces or cells that makes it less dense than the solid polymer. Such foams are light and strong, and the rigid type can be machined.

KEY TERMS

Amorphous—Noncrystalline, lacking a definite crystal structure and a well-defined melting point.

Casting—Formation of a product either by filling an open mold with liquid monomer and allowing it to polymerize in place, or by pouring the liquid onto a flat, moving surface.

Composite—A mixture or mechanical combination (on a macroscopic level) of materials that are solid in their finished state, that are mutually insoluble, and that have different chemistries.

Crystalline—Having a regular arrangement of atoms or molecules; the normal state of solid matter.

Extrusion—An operation in which material is forced through a metal forming die, followed by cooling or chemical hardening.

Glass—An amorphous, highly viscous liquid having all of the appearances of a solid.

Inorganic—Not containing compounds of carbon.

Molding—Forming a plastic or rubber article in a desired shape by applying heat and pressure.

Monomer—A substance composed of molecules that are capable of reacting together to form a polymer. Also known as a mer.

Organic—Containing carbon atoms, when used in the conventional chemical sense. Originally, the term was used to describe materials of living origin.

Plastic—Materials, usually organic, that under suitable application of heat and pressure, can be caused to flow and to assume a desired shape that is retained when the pressure and temperature conditions are withdrawn.

Polymer—A substance, usually organic, composed of very large molecular chains that consist of recurring structural units.

Synthetic—Referring to a substance that either reproduces a natural product or that is a unique material not found in nature, and which is produced by means of chemical reactions.

Thermoplastic—A high molecular weight polymer that softens when heated and that returns to its original condition when cooled to ordinary temperatures.

Thermoset— A high molecular weight polymer that solidifies irreversibly when heated.

Fillers and other modifications

Very few plastics are used in their commercially pure state. Additives currently used include the following: Finely divided rubbers added to more brittle plastics to add toughness; glass, carbon, boron, or metal fibers added to make **composite materials** with good stress-strain properties and high strength; carbon black or silica added to improve resistance to tearing and to improve stress-strain properties; plasticizers added to soften a plastic by lowering its glass transition temperature or reducing its degree of crystallinity; silanes or other bonding agents added to improve bonding between the plastic and other solid phases; and fillers such as fire retardants, heat or light stabilizers, lubricants, or colorants.

Filled or reinforced plastics are usually referred to as composites. However, some composites includes neither fillers nor reinforcement. Examples are laminates such as plastic sheets or films adhered to nonplastic products such as **aluminum** foil, cloth, paper or plywood for use in packaging and manufacturing. Plastics may also be metal plated.

Plastics, both glassy and rubbery, may be crosslinked to improve their elastic behavior and to control swelling. Polymers may also be combined to form blends or alloys.

Applications

Plastics have been important in many applications to be listed here. Table 2, "Thermoplastics," and Table 3, "Thermosetting Plastics," list hundreds of commercial applications that have been found for specific plastics.

Engineering plastics are tough plastics that can withstand high loads or stresses. They can be machined and remain dimensionally stable. They are typically used in the construction of machine parts and **automobile** components. Important examples of this class of plastics include nylons, acetals, polycarbonates, ABS resins, and polybutylene terephthalate. The structure of their giant chains makes these plastics highly resistant to shock, and gives them a characteristic toughness.

Plastics are almost always electrically insulating, and for this reason they have found use as essential com-

ponents of electrical and electronic equipment (including implants in the human body).

Major applications have been found for plastics in the aerospace, adhesives, coatings, construction, electrical, electronic, medical, packaging, textile, and automotive industries.

Further Reading

Brandrup, J. and E. H. Immergut, eds. *Polymer Handbook*. 3rd Edition. New York, NY: Wiley-Interscience, 1990.

Couzens, E. G. and V. E. Yarsley. *Plastics in the Modern World*. Baltimore, MD: Penguin, 1968.

Juran, Rosalind, ed. *Modern Plastics Encyclopedia*. Hightstown, NJ: McGraw-Hill, 1988.

Sperling, L. H. *Introduction to Physical Polymer Science*. New York, NY: John Wiley & Sons, 1992.

Randall Frost

Plate tectonics

Plate tectonics is the study of the large-scale features of Earth's surface and the processes that form them. These features define a series of major regions of Earth's crust known as plates. Plates move and shift their positions relative to one another. Movement of and contact between plates either directly or indirectly accounts for most of the major geologic features at Earth's surface.

Imagine for a moment that the **earth** is like a baseball—rough seams project up from the surface of the ball and completely surround it. Now imagine that the stuffing from inside the ball is constantly pushing its way out of the seams and forming a new cover. Older areas of the cover are descending back inside the ball elsewhere to again become part of the stuffing.

This is a lot like what happens to the covering, that is, the crust of the earth. At the" seams," known as mid-oceanic ridges, molten rock, or **magma**, constantly rises toward the surface to form new oceanic crust and pushes the existing sea floor out of its way. This process is known as sea floor spreading. Meanwhile, old crust constantly descends into deep depressions, or **ocean** trenches, where it is destroyed. This process, known as subduction, makes room for the new crust being formed by sea floor spreading.

Continental drift versus plate tectonics

Plate tectonics is a comparatively new idea. The theory of plate tectonics gained widespread acceptance only in the late 1960s to early 1970s. About 50 years earlier, Alfred Wegener, a climatologist, developed a related theory known as **continental drift**. Wegener contended that the positions of Earth's continents are not fixed. He believed instead that they are mobile, and over time drift about on Earth's surface; hence the name "continental drift."

Evidence

Wegener used several different types of evidence to support his theory. The most obvious evidence was the fact that several of the world's continents fit together like pieces in a jig-saw puzzle. Based on this, he proposed that the continents of the world were previously joined together in one large continental mass, a supercontinent, which Wegener called Pangaea (all land). He believed this supercontinent had subsequently broken up into the six continents we know today. His other evidence concerned the striking similarities among geologic features and fossils that are now found widely separated on different continents.

Shortcomings

What Wegener's continental drift theory lacked was a propelling mechanism. Other scientists wanted to know what was moving these continents around. Unfortunately, Wegener could not provide a convincing answer. Therefore, other scientists heavily disputed his theory and it fell into disrepute.

History of the development of the theory of plate tectonics

During and after World War II, geoscientists used newly developed technologies to explore the deep ocean basins in detail. For the first time, they mapped and sampled large regions of the sea bottom. This provided new information, much of which contradicted many existing theories on the nature of the ocean basins, and raised many new questions. Pondering these questions, a few geoscientists recognized compelling evidence for a new model, or paradigm, of how Earth's exterior forms and behaves. Many types of evidence were collected and interpreted before the theory of plate tectonics began to unfold in the early 1960s, and new ideas are considered every year as the theory is further refined.

The early evidence

Ocean topography: Nineteenth century surveys of the oceans indicated that rather than being flat featureless plains, as was previously thought, some ocean areas are mountainous while others plummet to great depths. Contemporary geologic thinking could not easily explain these topographic variations, or "oceanscapes." Surveys in the 1950s and 1960s provided an even more detailed

A section of the San Andreas Fault south of San Francisco is occupied by a reservoir.

picture of the ocean bottom. Long, continuous **mountain** chains appeared, as well as numerous ocean deeps shaped like troughs. Geoscientists later identified the mountainous features as the mid-oceanic ridges (MORs) where new plates form, and the deep ocean trenches as subduction zones where plates descend into the subsurface.

Paleomagnetism and magnetic reversals: In the late nineteenth century, scientists discovered that iron-rich **minerals** in **rocks** act like the needle in a compass; that is, during formation they align themselves according to the orientation of **Earth's magnetic field**. Therefore some minerals "point" toward magnetic north. By the early twentieth century, scientists had discovered that the orientation of Earth's magnetic field periodically reverses itself; consequently, the iron-rich minerals in rocks formed during these periods of reversed **magnetism** would be oriented toward the south pole rather than the north pole. Scientists based their conclusions on studies of ancient rocks with reversed magnetic fields.

In the late 1950s to early 1960s, marine geologists began doing magnetic surveys in the ocean. Magnetic surveys study the character of the ocean floor, the distribution of different types of rocks, and aid in discovering economically important mineral deposits. During magnetic surveys of the deep ocean basins, geologists found areas where numerous magnetic reversals occur in the ocean crust. These look like stripes, oriented roughly **parallel** to one another and to the MORs. When surveys were run on the other side of the MORs, they showed that the magnetic reversal patterns were remarkably similar on both sides of the MORs.

After much debate, scientists concluded that new ocean crust must form at the MORs, recording the current magnetic orientation. This new ocean crust pushes older crust out of the way, away from the MOR. When a magnetic reversal occurs, new ocean crust faithfully records it as a reversed magnetic "stripe" on both sides of the MOR. Older magnetic reversals were likewise recorded; these stripes are now located farther from the MOR.

Earthquake and **volcano** distribution: Earthquake experts recognized an interesting pattern of earthquake distribution. Most major earthquakes occur in belts rather than being randomly distributed around Earth. Most volcanoes exhibit a similar pattern. This pattern later served as evidence for the location of plate margins, that is, the zones of contact between different crustal plates. Eathquakes result from **friction** caused by one plate moving against another.

Ocean drilling: In the 1960s ocean research ships began drilling into the sediments and the solid rock below the sediment, called **bedrock**, in the deeper parts of the ocean. Perhaps the most striking discovery was the great age difference between the oldest continental bedrock and the oldest oceanic bedrock. Continental bedrock is over a billion years old in many areas of the continents, with a maximum age of 3.6 billion years. Nowhere is the ocean crust older than 180 million years.

Marine geologists discovered another curious relationship as well. The age of the oceanic bedrock and the sediments directly above it increase as you move from the deep ocean basins to the continental margins. That is, the ocean floor is oldest next to the continents and youngest near the center of ocean basins. In addition, ocean crust on opposing sides of MORs show the same pattern of increasing age away from the MORs.

We now know the great age of continental rocks results from their inability to be subducted (this will be discussed later). Once formed, continental crust becomes a permanent part of Earth's surface. We also know that the increase in age of ocean crust away from ocean basins results from creation of new sea floor at the MORs, with destruction of older sea floor at ocean trenches, which are often located near continental margins.

Hot spots: As you probably know, the Hawaiian Islands are of volcanic origin. The age of their rocks is easily determined using radiometric **dating techniques**. The Hawaiian Islands increase in age as you move north up the chain of islands. In addition, only the islands at the southern end of the chain are still volcanically active. At first appearance, these facts might be difficult to explain. However, picture a block of ocean crust moving north while riding on a conveyor belt, and a lava source remaining stationary below the belt. It is easy to see that above the lava source, a volcanic **island** will form. However, as the conveyor belt continues to move, this island moves off towards the north, and a new island begins to form over the stationary lava source.

This is similar to how the Hawaiian Islands formed. The Pacific plate is moving north over a stationary lava source in the mantle, known as a **hot spot**. Lava rises upwards from this hot spot to the surface and forms a volcano. After a few million years, that volcano becomes extinct as it moves north, away from the hot spot, and a new volcano begins to form to the south. A new volcano is forming today on the ocean floor south of the island of Hawaii.

Rates

Plates move at rates of about an inch (a few centimeters) per year. Scientists first estimated the rate of plate movement based on radiometric dating of ocean crust. By determining the age of a crustal **sample**, and knowing its **distance** from the MOR at which it formed, they estimate the rate of new ocean floor production and plate movement. Today, satellites capable of measurement of plate **motion** provide a more direct method. Results from these two methods agree fairly closely. The fastest plates move more than 4 in (10 cm) per year. The rate of motion of the North American plate averages 1.2 in (3 cm) per year.

Plate structure

Earth's tectonic plates are rigid slabs of rock. They consist of the crust and the uppermost part of the mantle, together known as the **lithosphere**. The plates of the lithosphere move about while "floating" upon the underlying **asthenosphere**, a layer of dense, solid but plastic (that is, soft) rock in the upper mantle.

The crust of the ocean is different from that of the continents in both composition and thickness. Oceanic crust is composed primarily of the igneous rock basalt, that is, it has a *mafic* composition. The rocks of the continental crust have a composition similar to that of the igneous rock granite (a *felsic* composition) and most of the continental crust is granite. Oceanic crust is thin, ranging 3-6 mi (5-10 km) in thickness; continental crust is thick, ranging 12.5-55 mi (20-90 km) thick. As a result, the lithosphere below the continents is likewise thicker—as much as 150 mi (250 km) thick, whereas below the deep oceans the lithosphere is no more than 60 mi (100 km) thick.

Scale and number of plates

Estimates of the number of plates differ, but most geologists recognize at least fifteen and some as many as twenty. These plates have many different shapes and sizes. Some, such as the Juan de Fuca plate off the west coast of Washington State, have surface areas of a few thousand square miles. The largest, the Pacific plate, underlies most of the Pacific Ocean and covers an area of hundreds of thousands of square miles. In the distant geologic past, Earth's lithosphere perhaps consisted of many more of these smaller plates, rather than the comparatively few, larger plates now present.

Plate interactions

Tectonic plates can interact in one of three ways. They can move toward one another, or converge; move away from one another, or diverge; or slide past one another, a movement known as transform motion. All plate margins along which plate movement is occurring have

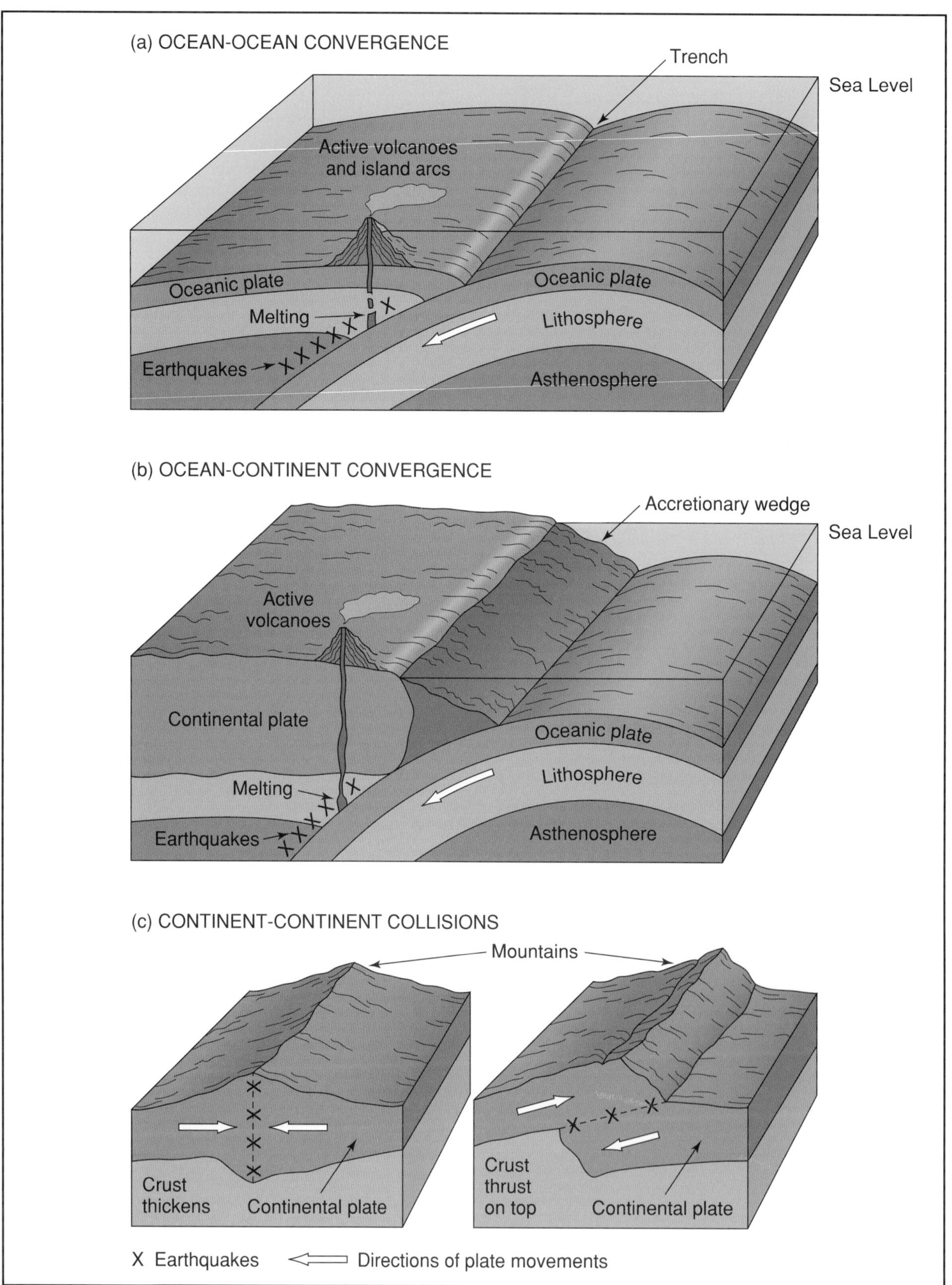

Types of plate convergence. (a) Oceanic-continental. (b) Oceanic-oceanic. (c) Continental-continental.

one thing in common—earthquakes. In fact, most earthquakes happen along plate margins. The other types of activity that occur when two plates interact is dependent on the nature of the plate interaction and of the margins. Plate margins (or boundaries) come in three varieties: oceanic-oceanic, continental-continental, and continental-oceanic.

Oceanic-oceanic plates

Recall that plates in continental areas are thicker and less dense than in oceanic areas. When two oceanic plates converge (an oceanic-oceanic convergent margin) one of the plates subducts into a trench. The subducted plate sinks downward into the mantle where it begins to melt. Molten rock from the melting plate rises toward the surface and forms a chain of volcanic islands, or a volcanic island **arc**, behind the ocean trench. Subduction of the Pacific plate below the North American plate along the coast of Alaska formed the Aleutian Trench and the Aleutian Islands, a volcanic island arc. At oceanic-oceanic divergent margins, sea floor spreading occurs and the ocean slowly grows wider. Today, **Europe** and **North America** move about 3 in (7.6 cm) farther apart every year as the Atlantic Ocean grows wider.

Continental-continental plates

Due to their lower **density** and greater thickness, continental-continental convergent plate margins act quite differently than oceanic-oceanic margins. Continental crust is too light to be carried downward into a trench. At continental-continental convergent margins neither plate subducts. The two plates converge, buckle, **fold**, and **fault** to form complex mountains ranges of great height. Continental-continental convergence produced the Himalayas when the Indian-Australian plate collided with the Eurasian plate.

Continental-continental divergence causes a **continent** to separate into two or more smaller continents when it is ripped apart along a series of fractures. The forces of divergence literally tear a continent apart as the two or more blocks of continental crust begin slowly moving apart and magma pushes into the rift formed between them. Eventually, if the process of continental rifting continues (it may fail, leaving the continent fractured but whole), a new sea is born between the two continents. In this way rifting between the Arabian and African plates formed the Red Sea.

Continental-oceanic plates

When continental and oceanic plates converge, the scenario is a predictable one. Due to its greater density, the oceanic plate easily subducts below the edge of the continental plate. Again subduction of the oceanic plate leads to volcano formation, but in this setting, the chain of volcanoes forms on the continental crust. This volcanic mountain chain, known as a volcanic arc, is usually several hundred miles inland from the plate margin. The Andes Mountains of **South America** and the Cascade Mountains of North America are examples of volcanic arcs formed by subduction along a continental-oceanic convergent margin. Continental-oceanic convergence may form a prominent trench, but not always. No continental-oceanic divergent margins exist today. As you can imagine, they are unlikely to form and would quickly become oceanic-oceanic divergent margins as sea floor spreading occurred.

Transform margins

In addition to convergence and divergence, transform motion may occur along plate margins. Transform margins, in many ways, are less spectacular than convergent and divergent ones, and the type of plates involved is really of no significance. Along transform margins, about all that occurs are faults and earthquakes. Plate movement produces the earthquakes, as the two rock slabs slide past one another. The best known example of a transform plate margin is the San Andreas fault in California, where the Pacific and North American plates are in contact.

Continent formation

If sea floor spreading only produces basaltic (oceanic) rock, where did the continents come from? Knowledge of the processes involved is somewhat limited, but formation of the early continents resulted from subduction at oceanic-oceanic convergent margins. When plates subduct, a process known as partial melting occurs. Partial melting of mafic rock results in the production of magma that is more felsic in composition; that is, it has a composition intermediate between basalt and granite. In addition, **weathering** of mafic rock at the earth's surface also produces sediments with a more felsic composition. When these sediments subduct, they yield magma of felsic composition via partial melting.

Repeated episodes of subduction and partial melting, followed by volcanic eruption, produced lavas of increasingly felsic composition. Finally, this cycle formed volcanic island arcs that were too buoyant to be subducted and became a permanent part of Earth's surface. When sea floor spreading pushes one of these buoyant volcanic island arcs toward a subduction zone, rather than subducting, it welds, or accretes, onto the side of the volcanic island arc forming on the other side of the trench. Over time, these microcontinents, through accretion, formed larger continental masses.

KEY TERMS

Accretion—The addition of sediment or rock to a plate's margin at a subduction zone. Material is scraped off the subducting plate and adheres to the edge of the overriding plate.

Basalt—A dense, dark colored igneous rock, with a composition rich in iron and magnesium (a mafic composition).

Convection cells—The circular movement of a fluid in response to alternating heating and cooling. Convection cells in the earth's interior involve molten rock that rises upwards below midoceanic ridges.

Convergence—The movement of two plate margins toward one another; usually associated with plate subduction or the collision of two continents.

Crust—The uppermost division of the solid earth; the bedrock above Earth's mantle.

Divergence—The separation of two plate margins as they move in opposing directions; usually associated with either sea floor spreading or continental rifting.

Granite—A light colored igneous rock that is less dense than basalt due to an abundance of lighter elements, such as silicon and oxygen (a felsic composition).

Hot spots—Areas in the mantle, associated with rising plumes of molten rock, which produce frequent, localized volcanic eruptions at Earth's surface.

Magnetic reversals—Periods during which the earth's magnetic poles flipflop; that is, the orientation of Earth's magnetic field reverses. During these periods of reversed magnetism, compass needles point toward the south pole.

Mantle—The thick, dense layer of rock that underlies Earth's crust.

Microcontinents—Volcanic islands of intermediate to felsic composition that were too buoyant to subduct, and therefore formed the first continental crust.

Mid-oceanic ridges—Continuous submarine mountain ranges, composed of basalt, where new sea floor is created.

Ocean trench—A deep depression in the sea floor, created by an oceanic plate being forced downward into the subsurface by another, overriding plate.

Plates—Large regions of the earth's surface, composed of the crust and uppermost mantle, which move about, forming many of Earth's major geologic surface features.

Sea floor spreading—Process in which new sea floor forms as molten rock from Earth's interior rises toward the surface, pushing the existing sea floor out of its way.

Subduction—Tectonic process that involves one plate being forced down into the mantle at an oceanic trench. The descending plate eventually undergoes partial melting.

Transform motion—Horizontal plate movement in which one plate margin slides past another.

Continents "float" on the plastic material making up the mantle like a block of **wood** floats on **water**. As **erosion** occurs, sediments are carried from mountains and higher elevations out to sea, where they accumulate on the **continental shelf**, forming wedges of sediment. Such accretionary wedges can extend far out to sea, depending on the size and shape of the continental shelf. As erosion moves sediments from the interior of the continent to the edges, the continent gets thinner but its surface area becomes larger. If conditions remain stable, accretionary wedges can go on accumulating for a very long time, reaching hundreds of miles out into the ocean. Sometimes, the wedge becomes so thick it rises above **sea level** to become dry land.

Continents have either passive or active margins. Passive margins are found where the continent's edge is on the same plate as the adjacent ocean, and it is along passive margins that accretionary wedges form. Active margins are found where the continent and the bordering oceanic crust are on separate plates. In these situations, a subduction zone is usually present. In general, the continents bordering the Atlantic Ocean have passive margins, while those surrounding the Pacific Ocean, which has a very active MOR, have active margins.

Driving mechanism

Most geologists believe convective cells in the **earth's interior** are the driving force for plate motion. If you have ever seen a rapidly boiling pot of water, then you know about convection cells. In the center of the pot, bubbles rise to the surface and push water to the sides.

Along the sides, the water cools and descends back down to the bottom of the pot to be heated again.

In a similar way, convection cells in the mantle bring molten rock to the surface along MORs where it forms new ocean crust. Below the crust, **pressure** is exerted on the bottom of the plates by the convection **cell**, helping to push the plates along, and causing divergence. At the trenches, the cells may also exert a downward force on the descending plates, helping to pull them down into the mantle.

Importance of plate tectonics

Plate tectonics revolutionized the way geologists view Earth. This new paradigm brings together nearly all the divisions of geologic study. Like the theory of **evolution** in **biology**, plate tectonics is the unifying concept of **geology**. Plate tectonics' initial appeal and rapid acceptance resulted from its ability to provide answers to many nagging questions about a variety of seemingly unrelated phenomena. Plate tectonics also revitalized the field of geology by providing a new perspective from which to interpret many old ideas. Finally, plate tectonics explains nearly all of Earth's major surface features and activities. These include faults and earthquakes, volcanoes and volcanism, mountains and mountain building, and even the origin of the continents and ocean basins.

Further research

Plate tectonics has raised almost as many questions as it answered. Among the more pressing questions are the following: Why and how do trenches, MORs, and continental rifts form? What is a hot spot and why do they exist? How long has plate tectonics been operative on Earth? Do any of the other inner planets show evidence of plate tectonic activity, if so, how is it different? How exactly do convection cells drive plate motion? As Earth's interior cools, at what rate will plate tectonic activity slow, and what will happen when plate motion eventually stops? What configurations of plates and continents existed in the past and will exist in the future? Answers to these questions will significantly advance our understanding of how plate tectonics works but will probably also pose even more questions.

See also Hydrothermal vents.

Further Reading

Bowler, P.J. "The Earth Sciences," In *The Norton History of the Environmental Sciences.* New York: W.W. Norton and Company, 1992.

Brown, G.C., C.J. Hawkesworth, and R.C.L. Wilson, eds. *Understanding the Earth—A New Synthesis.* Cambridge, U.K.: Cambridge University Press, 1992.

Dixon, D. *The Practical Geologist.* New York: Simon and Schuster, Inc., 1992.

Shurkin, J., and T. Yulsman. "Assembling Asia," In: *Earth: The Science of Our Planet.* vol. 4, no. 3 (June 1995): 52-59.

Clay Harris

Platinum see **Element, chemical; Precious metals**

Platonic solids

The term platonic solids refers to regular polyhedra. In **geometry**, a **polyhedron**, (the word is a Greek neologism meaning *many seats*) is a solid bounded by **plane** surfaces, which are called the *faces*; the intersection of three or more edges is called a *vertex* (plural: *vertices*). What distinguishes regular polyhedra from all others is the fact that all of their faces are congruent with one another. (In geometry, congruence means that the coincidence of two figures in **space** results in a one-to-one correspondence.) The five platonic solids, or regular polyhedra, are: the **tetrahedron** (consisting of four faces that are equilateral triangles), the hexahedron, also known as a cube (consisting of six **square** faces), the octahedron (consisting of eight faces that are equilateral triangles), the dodecahedron (12 pentagons), and the icosahedron (20 equilateral triangles).

Historical significance

The regular polyhedra have been known to mathematicians for over 2,000 years, and have played an important role in the development of Western philosophy and science. Drawing on the teaching of his predecessors Pythagoras (sixth century B.C.) and Empedocles (c. 490-c. 430 B.C.), and contributing many original insights, the Greek philosopher Plato (c. 427-347 B.C.) discusses the regular polyhedra, subsequently named after him, in *Timaeus*, his seminal cosmological work. Plato's narrator, the astronomer Timaeus of Locri, uses triangles-as fundamental figures—to create four of the five regular polyhedra (tetrahedron, hexahedron, octahedron, icosahedron). Timaeus's four polyhedra are further identified with the four basic elements—the hexahedron with **earth**, the tetrahedron with fire, the octahedron with air, and the icosahedron with **water**. Finally, in Plato's view, the regular polyhedra constitute the building-blocks not

merely of the inorganic world, but of the entire physical universe, including organic and inorganic **matter**. Plato's ideas greatly influenced subsequent cosmological thinking: for example, Kepler's fundamental discoveries in **astronomy** were directly inspired by Pythagorean-Platonic ideas about the cosmic significance of geometry. Platonic geometry also features prominently in the work of the noted American inventor and philosopher R. Buckminster Fuller (1895-1983).

See also Geodesic dome; Kepler's laws.

Further Reading

Coplestone, Frederick. *Greece and Rome*. Vol. 1 of *A History of Philosophy*. Garden City, NY: Doubleday, 1985.

Kline, Morris. *Mathematics in Western Culture*. London: Oxford University Press, 1964.

Koestler, Arthur. *The Sleepwalkers*. New York: Grosset & Dunlap, 1959.

Millington, T. Alaric, and William Millington. *Dictionary of Mathematics*. New York: Harper & Row, 1966.

Stewart, Ian, and Martin Golubitsky. *Fearful Symmetry: Is God a Geometer?*. London: Penguin Books, 1993.

Zoran Minderovic

Platypus

The platypus is an egg laying mammal that is well adapted to the **water**. Physically, it looks like a **mole** or otter, with a beaver's flattened tail and a duck's bill. It also has short, powerful legs and webbed feet. While the fur on its back is dense, bristly, and reddish or blackish brown, the fur on its underbelly is soft and gray. Its eyes are very small, and it does not have external ears. The platypus measures around 17.7 in (45 cm) in length, with its tail adding an additional 5.9 in (15 cm). Commonly referred to as the duck-billed platypus, it spends several hours each day in the creeks and **rivers** of eastern **Australia** and Tasmania. The rest of its time is spent in burrows, which it digs in the river banks.

The platypus is classified in the order Monotremata (meaning single hole), consisting of two families and three genera; the families are Tachyglossidae (spiny anteater family) and Ornithorhynchidae (platypus family). There is only one species of platypus, *Ornithorhynchus anatinus*, which is comprised of four subspecies. All three species in the order Monotremata are considered primitive, combining mammalian features with those of lower orders of **vertebrates** such as **reptiles**. For example, **monotremes** are the only egg-laying **mammals**. In other mammals, the young are conceived within the female's body and are born alive. In monotremes, the eggs are fertilized internally, but are incubated and hatched outside the body. Monotremes, like all reptiles, also have a cloaca, a single opening through which feces, urine, and sperm or eggs pass. In other mammals, the cloaca is divided into an anus and genitourinary passages. Like other mammals, monotremes have fur, nurse their young with milk, and are warm-blooded.

Physical characteristics

The platypus' flat tail, duck-bill, short legs, and webbed feet are all characteristics enabling it to hunt in aquatic environments. However, since it spends most of its time on land, it has a few physical traits that can be modified depending on its particular location. For instance, on its webbed feet, the five individual digits end in claws. When the platypus is in the water, the skin of its webbed forefeet extends beyond these claws, so that it can better use its forefeet to paddle. On land, however, this skin folds back, revealing the claws, thus enabling the **animal** to dig.

The platypus' eyes and ears have similar modifications. Both are surrounded by deep folds of skin. Underwater, the platypus can use this skin to close its eyes and ears tightly; on land, it is able to see and hear quite well. Interestingly, the platypus' nostrils, which are located at the end of its bill, can only function when its head is above water as well. Thus, when the platypus is submerged with its eyes and ears covered and its nose inoperable it relies heavily on its sense of **touch**. Fortunately for the platypus, its leathery bill is very sensitive and, therefore, is its primary tool in locating **prey** while underwater.

Like all male members in the order Monotremata, the male platypus has spurs on each ankle connected to poison **glands** in its thighs. Rather than using these poisonous spurs to attack prey, the platypus only uses them against other platypus or predators.

Feeding

The duck-billed platypus feeds on insect larvae, **snails**, worms, small **fish**, and crustaceans; it is most active at dawn and dusk. Typically, before feeding, the creature floats serenely on the surface of the water, resembling a log. When it decides to dive for food, it can do so quickly, with one swipe of its tail.

The platypus generally feeds near the bottom of **freshwater** creeks and rivers. It probes the muddy bottoms with its supersensitive bill to locate its prey. Until recently, it was thought that the platypus only located its prey by touch, but it now appears that the platypus' bill is also electroreceptive, allowing the animal to detect mus-

cle activity in prey animals. Sometimes, the platypus stores small prey temporarily in its cheek pouches. Commonly, it stays submerged for about one minute, but, if threatened, it can stay underwater for up to five minutes.

Burrows and breeding

Platypuses construct two kinds of burrows in the banks of rivers and streams. A very simple burrow provides shelter for both males and females outside the breeding season, and is retained by males during the breeding season. At this time, the female constructs a deeper, more elaborate nesting burrow. Commonly, this burrow opens about 1 ft (0.3 m) above the water level and goes back into the bank as far as 59 ft (18 m). The female usually softens a portion of the nest with folded wet leaves. Whenever the female leaves young in her nesting burrow, she plugs the exit with **soil**.

The female usually lays two eggs, although sometimes she lays one or three. Typically, the eggs are about 0.7 in (1.7 cm) in diameter, are a bit rounder than most bird eggs, and are soft and compressible with a pliant shell. After she lays her eggs, the female curls around them, incubating them for seven to ten days. During this time, she only leaves her nest to wet her fur and to defecate. Measuring about 1 in (2.5 cm) long, a newly hatched platypus is blind and nude. The female platypus has no teats, therefore, she feeds her young on milk secreted through skin pores on her abdomen. The milk flows into two milk grooves on the abdomen and the young lap up the pools of milk. When the young platypus is about four months old, it leaves the burrow.

When the first platypus was sent to England, scientists thought it was a fake. Years passed before the existence of the animal was proven. Although platypus populations were formerly reduced by hunting for the fur trade, effective government **conservation** efforts have resulted in a successful comeback. Under the Australian **Endangered Species** Act of 1992 guidelines, today the platypus is neither on the endangered list nor officially on the list of vulnerable species. However, serious concern is raised because the platypus range closely follows densely populated regions of Australia where human activity greatly affects waterways. The species **habitat** may be disrupted by **dams**, **irrigation** projects, or **pollution**.

See also Spiny anteaters

Further Reading

Grzimek, B., ed. *Grzimek's Animal Life Encyclopedia.* New York: Van Nostrand Reinhold Company, 1993.

Moffat, Averil, ed. *Handbook of Australian Animals.* London: Bay Books, 1985.

Nowak, Ronald M., ed. *Walker's Mammals of the World.* 5th ed. Baltimore: Johns Hopkins University Press, 1991.

Whitfield, Phillip, ed. *Macmillan Illustrated Animal Encyclopedia.* New York: Macmillan Publishing Company, 1984.

Kathryn Snavely

Plovers

Plovers are **shore birds** in the family Charadriidae, order Charadriiformes. Plovers have short, straight bills, with a small swelling towards the tip. Their wings are pointed at the tips, usually with a white wing-stripe on the underside, and the flight of these birds is fast and direct. Plovers and the closely related **sandpipers** (family Scolopacidae) are affectionately known as "peeps" by bird watchers, because of the soft, high-pitched vocalizations that these birds make.

Plovers are active feeders, constantly walking and running along the shores, mudflats, prairies, **tundra**, or fields in search of a meal of small **invertebrates**. Plovers typically feed by poking their bill into mud for invertebrates, or by picking **arthropods** from the surface of mud, **soil**, shore debris, or sometimes foliage.

Plovers nest on the ground in simple open scrapes that blend well with the surroundings and can be very difficult to locate. When a **predator** or other intruder, such as a human, is close to its nest, a plover will usually display a "broken-wing" charade. This remarkable **behavior** aims to lure away the potential nest predator, and during this routine the plover often comes dangerously close to the threatening **animal**. However, the plover is actually very alert and nimble, and stays just beyond reach while tenaciously leading the intruder away. Plover chicks are capable of leaving their nest within hours of their hatching, and they immediately move with their parents and feed themselves.

Plovers are monogamous, which means that each mating season the male and female pairs are faithful to each other, with both parents sharing in the incubation of eggs and care of their young. The only exception is the **mountain** plover (*Eupoda montana*) of southwestern **North America**; this species is polyandrous, meaning that a particular female will mate with one or more males, leaving at least one of them a clutch of eggs to incubate and care for while the female lays another clutch to incubate and care for by herself. This interesting breeding strategy is more common among species of sandpipers.

There are 63 species in the Charadriidae, which are found worldwide with the exception of **Antarctica**. Most species breed on marine or **freshwater** shores, but a few species breed in prairies, savannas, or deserts.

Plovers that breed in Arctic regions undertake long-distance migrations between their breeding and wintering ranges. For example, the semipalmated plover (*Charadrius semipalmatus*) and the black-bellied plover (*Pluvialis squatarola*) breed in the Arctic of North America, but may winter as far south as Tierra del Fuego at the southern tip of **South America**. Plovers are gregarious during their migrations, appearing in flocks of their own species, and often with other, similar-sized shore birds such as sandpipers. Tropical species of plovers are relatively sedentary, except for those species that breed in deserts; these may be widely nomadic or migratory.

Nine species of plover regularly breed in North America. The black-bellied plover, lesser golden plover (*Pluvialis dominica*), ringed plover (*Charadrius hiaticula*), and semipalmated plover all breed in the Arctic tundra, and are long-distance migrants. The mountain plover breeds in short-grass **prairie** and semi-desert of the western United States.

The piping plover (*C. melodus*), the snowy plover (*C. alexandrinus*), and Wilson's plover (*C. wilsonia*) breed on sandy beaches and mudflats in various areas. However, all of these plovers are rare and to various degrees endangered, mostly because of the loss of much of their natural **habitat** to urbanization and the recreational use of beaches.

The killdeer (*Charadrius vociferous*) breeds widely in temperate and southern regions of North America. This is the plover most frequently seen by North Americans, because the killdeer is an abundant species that commonly breeds in disturbed environments, usually in proximity to **water**. The killdeer was directly named after the loud call that it gives when alarmed, especially around the nest. Many species of birds have been named after their distinctive vocalizations, a practice known to etymologists as onomatopoeia.

During their migrations and on their wintering grounds, many species of plovers appear predictably in large flocks in particular places, often in association with large numbers of other shore birds. These particular natural habitats represent critical ecosystems for these species, and must be preserved in their natural condition if these birds are to survive.

Further Reading

Harrison, C. J. O., ed. *Bird Families of the World.* New York: H. N. Abrams, 1978.

Hayman, P., J. Marchant, and T. Prater. *Shore Birds: An Identification Guide to the Waders of the World.* London: Croom Helm, 1986.

Richards, A. *Birds of the Tideline: Shore Birds of the Northern Hemisphere.* Limpsfield, England: Dragon's World, 1988.

Bill Freedman

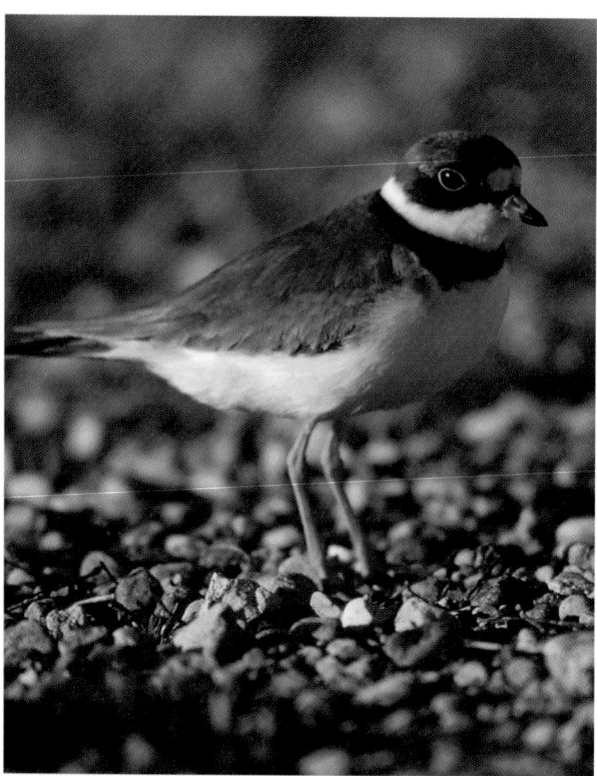

A semipalmated plover.

Plum see **Rose family**

Pluto

The ninth **planet** from the **Sun**, Pluto is one of the least well understood objects in the **solar system**. It is the smallest of the major planets, and has a most unusual **orbit**. Pluto's companion **moon**, Charon, is so large that the pair essentially form a binary system. How the Pluto-Charon system formed and how the system acquired its special 2-to-3 orbital **resonance** with **Neptune** are unanswered questions at the present time.

Basic properties

Pluto has the most eccentric (non-circular) orbit of all the planets in our solar system. While the planet's **mean distance** from the Sun is 39.44 Astronomical Units (AU), it can be as far as 49.19 AU from the Sun and as close as 29.58 AU. The time required for Pluto to complete one orbit about the Sun (its sidereal period) is 248.03 years, and the time for the planet to repeat alignments with respect to the **Earth** and the Sun (its synodic period) is 366.7 days.

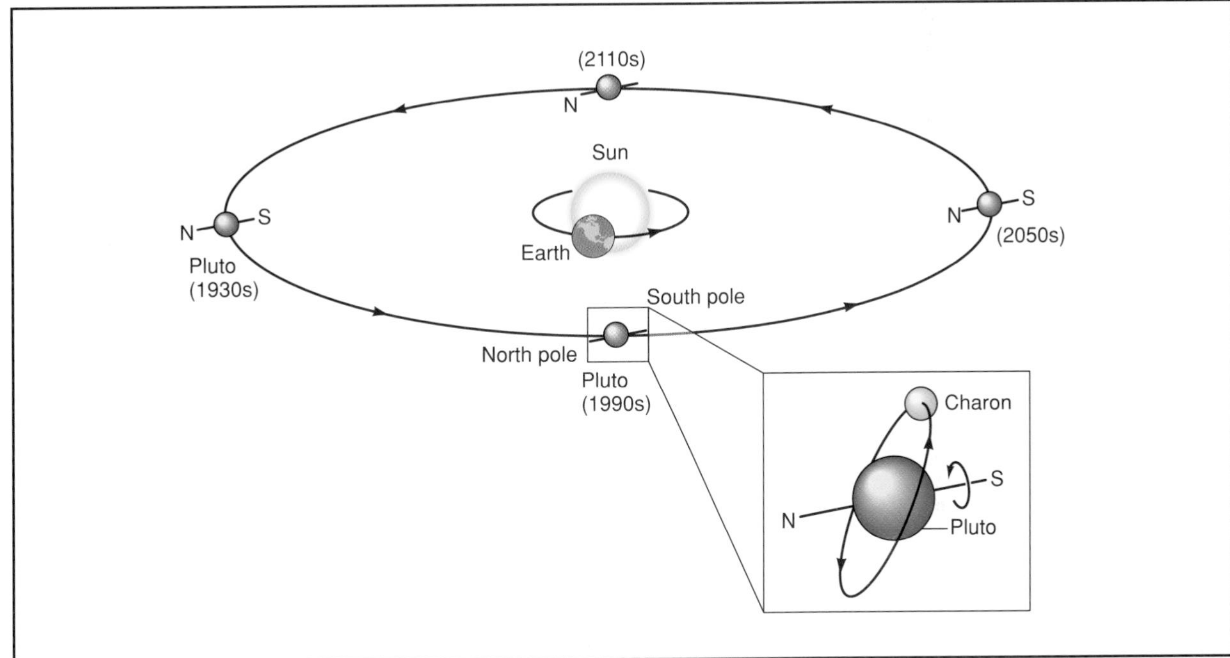

Figure 1. The Pluto-Charon system.

While commonly referred to as the ninth and outermost planet of our solar system, the large eccentricity of Pluto's orbit can bring the planet closer to the Sun than Neptune. Pluto, in fact, last edged closer to the Sun than Neptune in January of 1979, and remained the eighth most distant planet from the Sun until March of 1999. On September 5, 1989, Pluto reached perihelion, its closest point to the Sun, when it was at its brightest when viewed from Earth. Pluto is not a conspicuous night-sky object, and can only be viewed with telescopic aid. Under good viewing conditions, Pluto can be seen as a star-like point in any **telescope** having an objective diameter greater than 7.9 in (20 cm). Pluto moves only slowly through the constellations; due to the fact that the planet is both small and very distant.

At its closest approach to Earth, Pluto's planetary disk is smaller than 0.25 **arc** seconds (that is, 0.00007°) across. Periodic variations in the planet's brightness, however, have revealed that Pluto rotates once every 6.3827 days. Pluto's spin axis is inclined at 123° to the **plane** of its orbit about the Sun and consequently its **rotation** is retrograde. The extreme tilt of Pluto's spin-axis results in the Earth-based observer seeing different hemispheric projections as the planet moves around the Sun. In the early 1950s, for example, Pluto presented its south pole towards the Earth, today, we see its equatorial regions. In the year 2050 Pluto will present its north pole towards the Earth.

Careful long-term monitoring of the variations in Pluto's brightness indicate that the planet is brightest when seen pole-on. This observation suggests that the poles are covered by reflective ices, and that the planet has a dark patch (lower **albedo**) on, or near its equator. It is highly likely that Pluto's brightness variations undergo seasonal changes, but as yet, astronomers have only been able to monitor the planet during about 1/6 of one orbit about the Sun.

At its mean distance of about 40 AU from the Sun, Pluto receives 1/1600 the amount of sunlight received at Earth. Consequently Pluto is a very cold world, with a typical daytime surface **temperature** of about -351°F (-213°C). Spectroscopic observations indicate the presence of methane, **nitrogen** and **carbon monoxide** ices on Pluto's surface. Most surprisingly, however, and in spite of its small size and low escape **velocity** (0.68 mi/sec (1.1 km/sec), Pluto is able to support a very tenuous atmosphere.

That Pluto might have a thin methane atmosphere was first suggested, on the basis of spectroscopic observations, in the early 1980s. Conclusive evidence for the existence of a Plutonian atmosphere was finally obtained, however, on June 9, 1988, when Pluto passed in front of a faint **star** producing what astronomers call a stellar occultation. As Pluto moved between the star and the Earth, observers found that rather than simply vanishing from view, the star gradually dimmed. This observation indicates the presence of a Plutonian atmosphere. Indeed, Pluto's atmosphere appears to have a tenuous outer layer and a more opaque layer near its surface.

It has been suggested that Pluto only supports an atmosphere when it is near perihelion, and that as the planet moves further away from the Sun the atmosphere freezes out. This freezing and thawing of Pluto's atmosphere may explain why the planet has a relatively high surface albedo of about 40%. Essentially the periodic freezing and thawing of Pluto's atmosphere continually refreshes the methane ice at the planet's surface.

The discovery of Pluto

Speculations about the existence of a ninth planet arose soon after astronomers discovered that the planet Neptune (discovered in 1846) did not move in its orbit as predicted. The small differences between Neptune's predicted and actual position were taken as evidence that an unseen object was introducing slight gravitational perturbations in the planet's orbit. The first search for a trans-Neptunian planet appears to have been carried out by David Peck Todd, of the U.S. Naval Observatory, in 1877. Todd conducted a visual search during 30 clear nights between November 1887 and March 1888, but he found nothing that looked like a planet.

The first systematic survey for a trans-Neptunian planet, using photographic plates, was carried out by the American astronomer Percival Lowell, at the Flagstaff Observatory, in Arizona between 1905 and 1907. No new planet was found, however. A second survey was conducted at Flagstaff in 1914, but again, no new planet was discovered. On the basis of predictions made by W. H. Pickering in 1909, Milton Humason, at Mount Wilson Observatory, carried out yet another photographic survey for a trans-Neptunian planet, with **negative** results, in 1919.

A third photographic survey to look for objects beyond the orbit of Neptune was initiated at Flagstaff Observatory in 1929. Clyde Tombaugh was the young astronomer placed in charge of the program. The survey technique that Tombaugh used entailed the exposure of several photographic plates, of the same region of the sky, on a number of different nights. In this way, an object moving about the Sun will shift its position, with respect to the unmoving, background stars, when two plates of the same region of sky are compared. The object that we now know as the planet Pluto was discovered through its "shift" on two plates taken during the nights of January 23rd and 29th, 1930. The announcement that a new planet had been discovered was delayed until March 13, 1930, to coincide with the 149th anniversary of the discovery of **Uranus**, and to mark the 78th anniversary of Lowell's **birth**. Humason, it turns out in retrospect, was unlucky in his survey of 1919, in that a re-examination of his plates revealed that Pluto had, in fact, been recorded twice. Unfortunately for Humason, one image of Pluto fell on a flaw in the photographic plate, and the second image was obscured by a bright star.

An artist's view of Pluto and its only moon Charon.

After its discovery, it was immediately clear that the Pluto was much smaller and fainter than the theoreticians had suggested it should be. Indeed, a more refined analysis of Neptune's orbit has revealed that no "extra" planetary perturbations are required to explain its orbital **motion**.

Charon

Charon, Pluto's companion moon, was discovered by James Christy in June, 1978. Working at the U.S. Naval Observatory in Flagstaff, Arizona, Christy noted that what appeared to be "bumps" on several photographic images taken of Pluto reappeared on a periodic basis. With this information, Christy realized that what had previously been dismissed as image distortions were really composite images of Pluto and a companion moon. Christy suggested that the new moon be named

Charon, after the mythical boatman that ferried the souls of the dead across the river Styx to Hades, where Pluto, God of the underworld, sat in judgment.

Charon orbits Pluto once every 6.39 days, which is also the rate at which Pluto spins on its axis. Charon is therefore in synchronous orbit about Pluto. As seen from the satellite-facing hemisphere of Pluto, Charon hangs motionless in the sky, never setting, nor rising. The average Pluto-Charon separation is 12,196 mi (19,640 km), which is about 1/20 the distance between the Earth and the Moon.

Soon after Charon was discovered astronomers realized that a series of mutual **eclipses** between Pluto and its **satellite** would be seen from Earth every 124 years. During these eclipse **seasons**, which last about five years each, observes on Earth would witness a whole series of passages of Charon across the surface of Pluto. The last eclipse season ended in 1990, and the next series of eclipses will take place in 2114.

By making precise measurements of the brightness variations that accompany Charon's movement in front of and behind Pluto, astronomers have been able to construct detailed albedo (reflectivity) maps of the two bodies. They have also been able to derive accurate measurements of each components size; Pluto has a diameter of 1,413 mi (2,274 km), making the planet 1.5 times smaller than Earth's Moon, and 2 times smaller than Mercury. Charon has a diameter of 737 mi (1186 km).

Since Pluto has a satellite, Kepler's 3rd law of planetary motion can be used to determine its **mass**. A mass equivalent to about 1/500 that of the Earth, or about 1/5 that of the Moon has been derived for Pluto. Charon's mass is about 1/8 that of Pluto's. Given the high mass **ratio** of 8:1 and the small relative separation between Pluto and Charon, the center of mass about which the two bodies rotate actually falls outside of the main body of Pluto. This indicates that rather than being a planet-satellite system, Pluto and Charon really constitute a binary system, or, in other words, a double planet.

Pluto has a bulk **density** of about 2 g/cm^3, while Charon has a lower bulk density of about 1.2 g/cm^3. This difference in densities indicates that while Pluto is probably composed of a mixture of rock and ice, Charon is most probably an icy body. In general terms, Pluto can be likened in internal structure to one of Jupiter's Galilean moons, while Charon is more similar in structure to one of Saturn's moons. In fact, astronomers believe that Pluto's internal structure and surface appearance may be very similar to that of Triton, Neptune's largest moon.

Pluto is the only planet in the solar system that has not been visited by a space probe. Plans are being made, however, at the NASA Goddard Space Flight Center for a launch scheduled for 2004 of the Pluto Kuiper Express, designed to fly by and make studies of Pluto and Charon in 2012. The probe will then fly by Pluto into the Kuiper belt, a group of at least 70,000 objects beyon Neptune with diameters larger than 60 mi (100 km) between about 30 and 50 AU from the sun.

Pluto's strange orbit

The Pluto-Charon system has the strangest orbit of all the planets in the solar system. It has a large eccentricity and a high orbital inclination of 17.1° to the ecliptic. These extreme orbital characteristics suggest that since its formation the Pluto-Charon system may have undergone some considerable orbital **evolution**.

Shortly after Pluto was first discovered, astronomers realized that unless some special conditions prevailed, Pluto would occasionally undergo close encounters with Neptune, and consequently suffer rapid orbital evolution. In the mid-1960s, however, it was discovered that Pluto is in a special 2-to-3 resonance with Neptune. That is, for every three orbits that Neptune completes about the Sun, Pluto completes two. This resonance ensures that Neptune always overtakes Pluto in its orbit when Pluto is at aphelion, and that the two planets are never closer than about 17 AU. How this orbital arrangement evolved is presently unclear.

The close structural compatibility of Pluto and Triton (i.e., they have the same size, mass, and composition) has lead some astronomers to suggest that the two bodies may have formed in the same region of the solar nebula. Subsequently, it is argued, Triton was captured to become a moon of Neptune, while Pluto managed to settle into its present orbit about the Sun. Numerical calculations have shown that small, moon-sized objects that formed with low inclination, circular orbits beyond Neptune do evolve, within a few hundred million years, to orbits similar to that of Pluto's. This result suggests that Pluto is the lone survivor of a (small) population of moon-sized objects that formed beyond Neptune, its other companions being either captured as satellites around Uranus and Neptune, or being ejected from the Solar System. One important, and as yet unsolved snag with the orbital evolution scenario just outlined, is that Pluto and Charon have different internal structures, implying that they formed in different regions of the solar nebula. It is presently not at all clear how the Pluto-Charon system formed.

Using a specially designed computer, Gerald Sussman and Jack Wisdom of the Massachusetts Institute of Technology, have modeled the long-term orbital motion of Pluto. Sussman and Wisdom set the computer to follow

KEY TERMS

Objective diameter—The diameter of a telescope's main light-collecting lens, or mirror.

Occultation—The passing of one astronomical object (e.g., a planet or asteroid) in front of another.

Retrograde rotation—A planet, or satellite is said to show retrograde rotation if it spins in the opposite sense to that in which it moves in its orbit.

Solar nebula—The primordial cloud of gas and dust out of which our Solar System formed.

Pluto's orbital motion over a time span equivalent to 845 million years; interestingly they found that Pluto's orbit is chaotic on a time scale of several tens of millions of years.

Further Reading

Binzel, R. P. "Pluto." *Scientific American*. June 1990.

Levy, David. *Clyde Tombaugh: Discoverer of Planet Pluto*. The University of Arizona Press, Tucson, 1991.

Moore, Patrick. *The Guinness Book of Astronomy*. U.K.: Guinness Books, Enfield, 1988.

Whyte, Anthony. *The Planet Pluto*. London: Pergamon Press, 1980.

Martin Beech

Pluton see **Igneous rocks**

Plutonium see **Element, transuranium**

Pneumonia

Pneumonia is an **infection** of the lung, and can be caused by nearly any class of **organism** known to cause human infections, including **bacteria**, viruses, **fungi**, and **parasites**. In the United States, pneumonia is the sixth most common disease leading to death, and the most common fatal infection acquired by already hospitalized patients. In developing countries, pneumonia ties with diarrhea as the most common cause of death.

Anatomy of the lung

In order to better understand pneumonia, it is important to understand the basic anatomic features of the **respiratory system**. The human respiratory system begins at the nose and mouth, where air is breathed in (inspired), and out (expired). The air tube extending from the nose is called the nasopharynx; the tube carrying air breathed in through the mouth is called the oropharynx. The nasopharynx and the oropharynx merge into the larynx. Because the oropharynx also carries swallowed substances, including food, **water**, and salivary secretions, which must pass into the esophagus and then the stomach, the larynx is protected by a trap door called the epiglottis. The epiglottis prevents substances that have been swallowed, as well as substances that have been regurgitated (thrown up) from heading down into the larynx and toward the lungs.

A useful method of picturing the respiratory system is to imagine an upside-down tree. The larynx flows into the trachea, which is the tree trunk, and thus the broadest part of the respiratory tree. The trachea divides into two tree limbs, the right and left bronchi, each of which branches off into multiple smaller bronchi, which course through the **tissue** of the lung. Each bronchus divides into tubes of smaller and smaller diameter, finally ending in the terminal bronchioles. The air sacs of the lung, in which oxygen-carbon dioxide exchange actually takes place, are clustered at the ends of the bronchioles like the leaves of a tree, and are called alveoli.

The tissue of the lung which serves only a supportive role for the bronchi, bronchioles, and alveoli, is called the lung parenchyma.

Function of the respiratory system

The main function of the respiratory system is to provide **oxygen**, the most important **energy** source for the body's cells. Inspired air travels down the respiratory tree to the alveoli, where the oxygen moves out of the alveoli and is sent into circulation throughout the body as part of the red **blood** cells. The oxygen in the inspired air is exchanged within the alveoli for the body's waste product, **carbon dioxide**, which leaves the alveoli during expiration.

Respiratory system defenses

The normal, healthy human lung is sterile, meaning that there are no normally resident bacteria or viruses (unlike the upper respiratory system and parts of the gastrointestinal system, where bacteria dwell even in a healthy state). There are multiple safeguards along the path of the respiratory system which are designed to keep invading organisms from leading to infection.

The first line of defense includes the hair in the nostrils, which serves as a filter for larger particles. The epiglottis is a trap door of sorts, designed to prevent food and other swallowed substances from entering the larynx and then trachea. Sneezing and coughing, both provoked

by the presence of irritants within the respiratory system, help to clear such irritants from the respiratory tract.

Mucous, produced throughout the respiratory system, also serves to trap dust and infectious organisms. Tiny hair-like projections (cilia) from cells lining the respiratory tract beat constantly, moving debris, trapped by mucus, upwards and out of the respiratory tract. This mechanism of protection is referred to as the mucociliary escalator.

Cells lining the respiratory tract produce several types of immune substances which protect against various organisms. Other cells (called macrophages) along the respiratory tract actually ingest and kill invading organisms.

The organisms which cause pneumonia, then, are usually carefully kept from entering the lungs by virtue of these host defenses. However, when an individual encounters a large number of organisms at once, either by inhaling contaminated air droplets, or by aspiration of organisms inhabiting the upper airways, the usual defenses may be overwhelmed, and infection may occur.

Conditions predisposing to pneumonia

In addition to exposure to sufficient quantities of causative organisms, certain conditions may predispose an individual to pneumonia. Certainly, the lack of normal anatomical structure could result in an increased risk of pneumonia. For example, there are certain inherited defects of cilia which result in less effective protection. **Cigarette smoke**, inhaled directly by a smoker or second-hand by an innocent bystander, interferes significantly with ciliary function, as well as inhibiting macrophage function.

Stroke, seizures, **alcohol**, and various drugs interfere with the function of the epiglottis, leading to a leaky seal on the trap door, with possible **contamination** by swallowed substances and/or regurgitated stomach contents. Alcohol and drugs also interfere with the normal cough **reflex**, further decreasing the chance of clearing unwanted debris from the respiratory tract.

Viruses may interfere with ciliary function, allowing themselves or other microorganism invaders, such as bacteria, access to the lower respiratory tract. One of the most important viruses which in recent years has resulted in a huge increase in the incidence of pneumonia is HIV (Human Immunodeficiency Virus), the causative virus in **AIDS** (Acquired Immune Deficiency Syndrome). Because AIDS results in a general decreased effectiveness of many aspects of the host's **immune system**, a patient with AIDS is susceptible to all kinds of pneumonia, including some previously rare parasitic types which would be unable to cause illness in an individual possessing a normal immune system.

The elderly have a less effective mucociliary escalator, as well as changes in their immune system, all of which cause them to be more at risk for the development of pneumonia.

Various chronic conditions predispose to pneumonia, including **asthma**, **cystic fibrosis**, **neuromuscular diseases** which may interfere with the seal of the epiglottis, esophageal disorders which result in stomach contents passing upwards into the esophagus (increasing the risk of aspiration of those stomach contents with their resident bacteria), as well as diabetes, **sickle cell anemia**, lymphoma, leukemia, and **emphysema**.

Pneumonia is one of the most frequent infectious complications of all types of surgeries. Many drugs used during and after **surgery** may increase the risk of aspiration, impair the cough reflex, and cause a patient to underfill their lungs with air. **Pain** after surgery also discourages a patient from breathing deeply and coughing effectively.

Causative organisms

The list of organisms which can cause pneumonia is very large, and includes nearly every class of infecting organism: viruses, bacteria, bacteria-like organisms, fungi, and parasites (including certain worms). Different organisms are more frequently encountered by different age groups. Further, other characteristics of the host may place an individual at greater risk for infection by particular types of organisms.

Viruses, especially respiratory syncytial virus, parainfluenza and **influenza** viruses, and adenovirus, cause the majority of pneumonias in young children. Pneumonia in older children and young adults is often caused by the bacteria-like *Mycoplasma pneumoniae*. Adults are more frequently infected with bacteria (such as *Streptococcus pneumoniae,* Hemophilus inflenzae, and *Staphylococcus aureus*).

The parasite *Pneumocystis carinii* is an extremely important cause of pneumonia in patients with immune problems, such as patients being treated for **cancer** with chemotherapy, or patients with AIDS. People who have reason to come in contact with bird droppings, such as poultry workers, are at risk for pneumonia caused by the parasite *Chlamydia psittaci*. A very large, serious outbreak of pneumonia occurred in 1976, when many people attending an American Legion convention were infected by a previously unknown organism (subsequently named *Legionella pneumophila*) which was traced to air conditioning units in the convention hotel.

Signs and symptoms of pneumonia

Pneumonia is suspected in any patient who presents with fever, cough, chest pain, shortness of breath, and increased respirations (number of breaths per minute). Fever with a shaking chill is even more suspicious, and many patients cough up clumps of mucus (sputum) which may appear streaked with pus or blood. Severe pneumonia results in the signs of oxygen deprivation, including blue appearance of the nail beds (cyanosis).

Pathophysiology of pneumonia

The invading organism causes symptoms, in part, by provoking an overly exuberant immune response in the lungs. The small blood vessels in the lungs (capillaries) become leaky, and protein-rich fluid seeps into the alveoli. This results in less functional area for oxygen-carbon dioxide exchange. The patient becomes relatively oxygen deprived, while retaining potentially damaging carbon dioxide. The patient breathes faster and faster, in an effort to bring in more oxygen and blow off more carbon dioxide.

Mucus production is increased, and the leaky capillaries may tinge the mucus with blood. Mucus plugs actually further decrease the efficiency of gas exchange in the lung. The alveoli fill further with fluid and debris from the large number of white blood cells being produced to fight the infection.

Consolidation, a feature of bacterial pneumonias, occurs when the alveoli, which are normally hollow air spaces within the lung, instead become solid, due to quantities of fluid and debris.

Viral pneumonias, and mycoplasma pneumonias, do not result in consolidation. These types of pneumonia primarily infect the walls of the alveoli and the parenchyma of the lung.

Diagnosis

Diagnosis is for the most part based on the patient's report of symptoms, combined with examination of the chest. Listening with a stethoscope will reveal abnormal sounds, and tapping on the patient's back (which should yield a resonant sound due to air filling the alveoli) may instead yield a dull thump if the alveoli are filled with fluid and debris.

Laboratory diagnosis can be made of some bacterial pneumonias by staining sputum with special chemicals and looking at it under a **microscope**. Identification of the specific type of bacteria may require culturing the sputum (using the sputum **sample** to grow greater numbers of the bacteria in a lab dish).

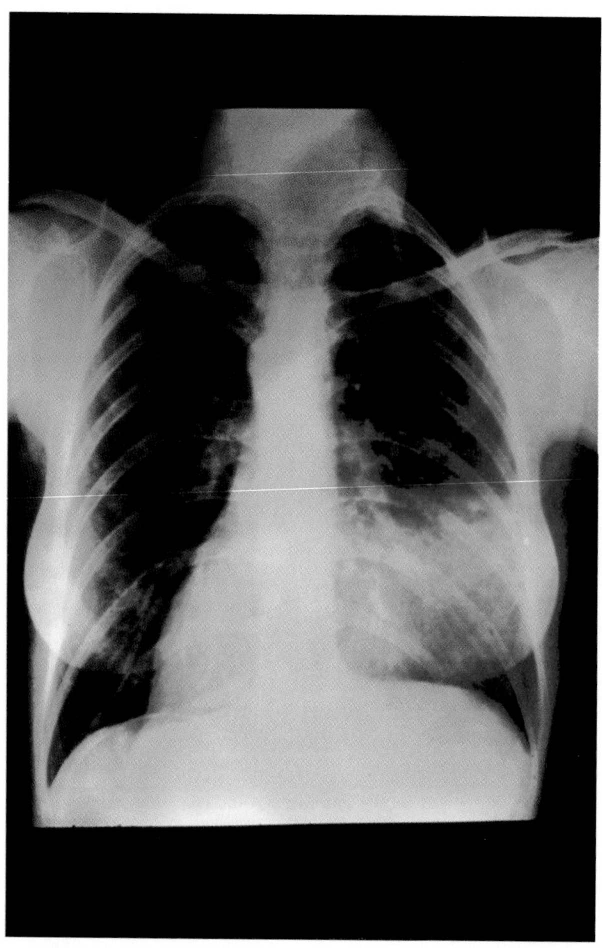

A chest x ray showing lobar pneumonia in the lower lobe of a patient's right lung. The alveoli (air sacs) of the lung become blocked with pus, which forces air out and causes the lung to become solidified.

X-ray examination of the chest may reveal certain abnormal changes associated with pneumonia. Localized shadows obscuring areas of the lung may indicate a bacterial pneumonia, while streaky or patchy appearing changes in the x-ray picture may indicate viral or mycoplasma pneumonia. These changes on x-ray, however, are known to lag in time behind the patient's actual symptoms.

Treatment

Bacterial pneumonia prior to the discovery of penicillin **antibiotics** was a virtual death sentence. Today, antibiotics, especially given early in the course of the disease, are very effective against bacterial causes of pneumonia. Erythromycin and tetracycline improve recovery time for symptoms of mycoplasma pneumonia, but do not eradicate the organisms. Amantadine and acyclovir may be helpful against certain viral pneumonias.

KEY TERMS

Alveoli (singular=alveolus)—The air sacs of the lung, in which oxygencarbon dioxide exchange occurs.

Bronchiole—The smallest diameter air tubes, branching off of the bronchi, and ending in the alveoli.

Bronchi (singular=bronchus)—The major, larger diameter air tubes running from the trachea to the bronchioles.

Cilia—Tiny, hair-like projections off of individual cells, which beat regularly, thus moving substances along.

Consolidation—One of the main symptoms of bacterial pneumonia, in which the alveoli become filled not with air, but with fluid and cellular debris, thereby decreasing the lung's ability to effectively exchange oxygen and carbon dioxide.

Epiglottis—The trap door in the larynx which prevents swallowed substances from heading down toward the lungs, instead directing them to flow appropriately into the esophagus and then stomach.

Esophagus—The tube down which swallowed substances must pass in order to reach the stomach.

Larynx—The air tube made by the merging of the nasopharynx and oropharynx. Air passes through the larynx and into the trachea.

Nasopharynx—The tube which carries air inspired or expired through the nose.

Oropharynx—The tube which carries air inspired or expired through the mouth.

Parenchyma—The tissue of the lung which is not involved with carrying air or oxygen-carbon dioxide exchange, but which provides support to other functional lung structures.

Sputum—Clumps of mucus which can be coughed up from the lungs and bronchi.

Trachea—The large diameter air tube which extends between the larynx and the main bronchus.

Prevention

Because many bacterial pneumonias occur in patients who are first infected with the influenza virus (the flu), yearly vaccination against influenza can decrease the risk of pneumonia for certain patients, particularly the elderly and people with chronic diseases (such as asthma, cystic fibrosis, other lung or **heart** diseases, sickle cell disease, diabetes, kidney disease, and forms of cancer).

A specific **vaccine** against *Streptococcus pneumoniae* is very protective, and should also be administered to patients with chronic illnesses. Patients who have decreased immune resistance (due to treatment with chemotherapy for various forms of cancer or due to infection with the AIDS virus), and therefore may be at risk for infection with *Pneumocystis carinii*, are frequently put on a regular drug regimen of Trimethoprim sulfa and/or inhaled pentamidine to avoid *Pneumocystis*pneumonia.

See also Legionnaire's disease.

Further Reading

Andreoli, Thomas E., et al. *Cecil Essentials of Medicine.* Philadelphia: W. B. Saunders Company, 1993.

Berkow, Robert, and Andrew J. Fletcher. *The Merck Manual of Diagnosis and Therapy.* Rahway, NJ: Merck Research Laboratories, 1992.

Isselbacher, Kurt J., et al. *Harrison's Principles of Internal Medicine.* New York:McGraw Hill, 1994.

Mandell, Douglas, et al. *Principles and Practice of Infectious Diseases.* New York: Churchill Livingstone Inc., 1995.

Sherris, John C., et al. *Medical Microbiology.* Norwalk, CT: Appleton & Lange, 1994.

Rosalyn Carson-DeWitt

Podiatry

Podiatry is a medical specialty that focuses on the **diagnosis** and treatment of foot disease and deformity. The term is from the Greek word for foot (*podos*) and means "to heal the foot." Until recent years this specialty was called chiropody, literally meaning "to heal the hand and foot." References to physicians who treated abnormalities or injuries in the foot are found in ancient Greek and Egyptian writings. The first modern text on chiropody was published by D. Low in England in 1774, and was titled *Chiropodologia.* Physicians who specialized in foot treatment appeared first in England in the late eighteenth century. Later, during the nineteenth century, so-called corn cutters roamed the rural areas of America. These often-untrained, unschooled therapists traveled through-

out the country offering help for those who had corns, bunions, blisters, and other discomforts of the foot.

To help establish professionalism and standards within the profession of chiropody, the National Association of Chiropodists (NAC) was founded in the U.S. in 1912. In 1917, M. J. Lewi coined the name podiatry as one more suitable to the profession of foot doctoring. Not until 1958, however, was the NAC renamed the American Podiatric Association to reflect the greater popularity of the new term.

Podiatrists must have at least two years of college to be accepted into a school of podiatry, where the student undertakes four years of medically-oriented study with a special emphasis on the foot and its diseases. The graduate is a Doctor of Podiatry.

Podiatrists can diagnose and treat common foot ailments and deformities. They can prescribe medications and perform minor surgeries, such as removal of corns and ingrown nails. A podiatrist can treat a patient with an abnormal walk, one leg shorter than the other, or a foot turned in or out by recommending braces, special shoes, or other devices. A wedge or lift placed appropriately in the shoe can turn a foot to face the proper direction or correct an abnormal walk. It is especially important that young children who have such abnormalities see a podiatrist; since children's bones are still developing, corrections started early can become permanent as the person grows.

See also Osteoporosis; Physical therapy; Surgery.

pOH see **pH**

Poinsettia see **Spurge family**

Point

A point is an undefined term in **geometry** that expresses the notion of an object with position but with no size. Unlike a three-dimensional figure, such as a box (whose dimensions are length, width, and height), a point has no length, no width, and no height. It is said to have dimension 0. Geometric figures such as lines, circles, planes, and spheres, can all be considered as sets of points.

Point source

A point source is a situation where large quantities of pollutants are emitted from a single, discrete source, such as a smokestack, a sewage or thermal outfall into a waterbody, or a **volcano**. If the emissions from a point source are large, the environment will be characterized by strong but continuous gradients of ecological stress, distributed more-or-less concentrically around the source, and diminishing exponentially with increasing **distance**. The stress results in damages to organisms, but because tolerance differs among species, the net result is a continuous gradient of change in the ecological community and in ecological processes, such as productivity and nutrient cycling.

This ecological phenomenon has been well studied around a number of point sources of ecological stress. For example, the structure of terrestrial vegetation has been examined along transects originating at a large smelter located at Sudbury, Ontario. This smelter is a point source of great emissions of toxic **sulfur dioxide** and metals. The immediate vicinity of the smelter is characterized by severe ecological degradation, because only a few species can tolerate the toxic stress. However, at increasing distances from the smelter the intensity of the toxic stresses decreases rapidly. Consequently, there is a progressive survival and/or invasion of sundry **plant** species at greater distances from the smelter, depending on their specific tolerances of the toxic environment at various distances. Farther than about 18.6 mi (30 km) from the smelter the toxicity associated with its point-source emissions no longer has a measurable influence on the vegetation, and there is a mature forest, characteristic of the regional unpolluted, landscape.

Often, species that are most tolerant of the toxic stresses close to a point source are uncommon or absent in the surrounding, non-polluted habitats. Usually, only a few tolerant species are present close to point sources of intense ecological stress, occurring as a sparse, low-growing community. At greater distances shrubs may dominate the plant community, and still further away relatively tolerant species of **tree** may maintain an open forest. Eventually, beyond the distance of measurable ecological responses to the toxic stress, a reference forest occurs. However, it is important to recognize that these ecological changes are continuous, as are the gradients of environmental stress associated with the point source. This **syndrome** of degradation of vegetation along transects from smelters and other large point sources has been characterized as a "peeling" of the vegetation.

In addition to changes in ecological communities along environmental gradients associated with point sources, there are also predictable changes in ecological functions, such as productivity, nutrient cycling, and litter **decomposition**.

See also Non-point source; Stress, ecological.

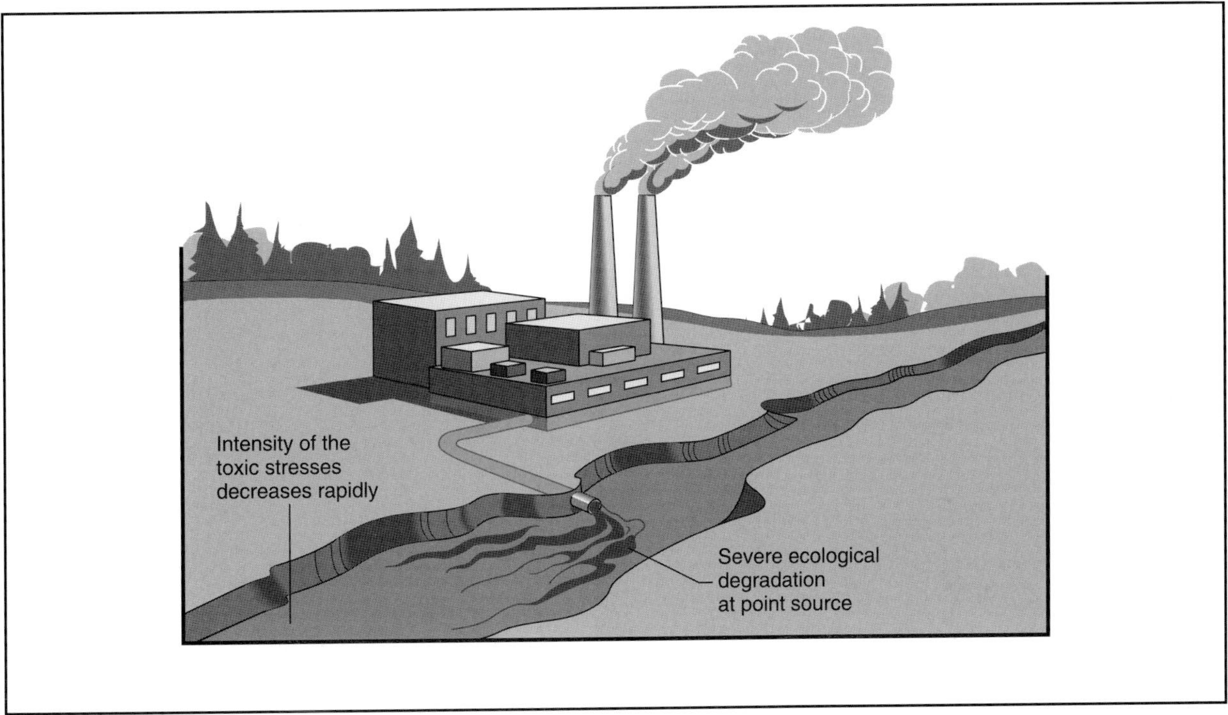

A point source.

Poison hemlock see **Carrot family**

Poison ivy see **Cashew family**

Poison oak see **Cashew family**

Poisons and toxins

A chemical is said to be a poison if it causes some degree of metabolic disfunction in organisms. Strictly speaking, a toxin is a poisonous chemical of biological origin, being produced by a microorganism, **plant**, or **animal**. In common usage, however, the words poison and toxin are often used interchangeably, and in this essay they are also treated as synonyms.

It is important to understand that potentially, all chemicals are toxic. All that is required for a chemical to cause toxicity, is a dose (or exposure) that is large enough to affect the **physiology** of an **organism**. This fact was first recognized by a Swiss physician and alchemist known as Paracelsus (1493-1541), who is commonly acknowledged as the parent of the modern science of **toxicology**. Paracelsus wrote that: "Dosage alone determines poisoning." In other words, if an exposure to a chemical is to cause poisoning, it must result in a dose that exceeds a threshold of physiological tolerance. Smaller exposures to the same chemical do not cause poisoning, at least not on the short term. (The differences between short-term and longer-term toxicities are discussed in the next section.) Species of plants, animals, and **microorganisms** differ enormously in their tolerance of exposures to potentially toxic chemicals. Even within populations of the same species, there can be substantial differences in sensitivity to chemical exposures. Some individuals, for example, may be extremely sensitive to poisoning by particular chemicals, a phenomenon known as hypersensitivity.

Because chemicals are present everywhere, all organisms are continuously exposed to potentially toxic substances. In particular, the environments of modern humans involve especially complex mixtures of chemicals, many of which are synthesized through manufacturing and are then deliberately or accidentally released into the environment. People are routinely exposed to potentially toxic chemicals through their food, medicine, **water**, and the atmosphere.

Toxicity

Toxicity can be expressed in many ways. Some measures of toxicity examine biochemical responses to exposures to chemicals. These responses may be detectable at doses that do not result in more directly observed effects, such as **tissue** damage, or death of the organism. This sort of small-dose, biochemical toxicity

might be referred to as a type of "hidden injury," because of the lack of overt, visible symptoms and damages. Other measures of toxicity may rely on the demonstration of a loss of productivity, or tissue damage, or ultimately, death of the organism. In extreme cases, it is possible to demonstrate toxicity to entire ecosystems.

The demonstration of obvious tissue damage, illness, or death after a short-term exposure to a large dose of some chemical is known as acute toxicity. There are many kinds of toxicological assessments of the acute toxicity of chemicals. These can be used to **bioassay** the relative toxicity of chemicals in the laboratory. They can also assess damages caused to people in their workplace, or to ecosystems in the vicinity of chemical **emission** sources ambient environment. One example of a commonly used index of acute toxicity is known as the LD_{50}, which is based on the dose of chemical that is required to kill one-half of a laboratory population of organisms during a short-term, controlled exposure. Consider, for example, the following LD_{50}'s for laboratory **rats** (measured in mg of chemical per kg of body weight): sucrose (table sugar) 30,000 mg/kg; **ethanol** (drinking **alcohol**) 13,700; glyphosate (a herbicide) 4,300; **sodium chloride** (table **salt**) 3,750; malathion (an insecticide) 2,000; **acetylsalicylic acid** (aspirin) 1,700; mirex (an insecticide) 740; 2,4-D (a herbicide) 370; DDT (an insecticide) 200; **caffeine** (a natural **alkaloid**) 200; **nicotine** (a natural alkaloid) 50; phosphamidon (an insecticide) 24; carbofuran (an insecticide) 10; saxitoxin (paralytic shellfish poison) 0.8; tetrodotoxin (globe-fish poison) 0.01; TCDD (a **dioxin isomer**) 0.01.

Clearly, chemicals vary enormously in their acute toxicity. Even routinely encountered chemicals can, however, be toxic, as is illustrated by the data for table sugar.

Toxic effects of chemicals may also develop after a longer period of exposure to smaller concentrations than are required to cause acute poisoning. These long-term effects are known as chronic toxicity. In humans and other animals, long-term, chronic toxicity can occur in the form of increased rates of **birth** defects, cancers, **organ** damages, and reproductive dysfunctions, such as spontaneous abortions. In plants, chronic toxicity is often assayed as decreased productivity, in comparison with plants that are not chronically exposed to the toxic chemicals in question. Because of their relatively indeterminate nature and long-term lags in development, chronic toxicities are much more difficult to demonstrate than acute toxicities.

It is important to understand that there appear to be thresholds of tolerance to exposures to most potentially toxic chemicals. These thresholds of tolerance must be exceeded by larger doses before poisoning is caused. Smaller, sub-toxic exposures to chemicals might be referred to as **contamination**, while larger exposures are considered to represent poisoning, or **pollution** in the ecological context.

The notion of contamination is supported by several physiological mechanisms that are capable of dealing with the effects of relatively small exposures to chemicals. For example, cells have some capability for repairing damages caused to DNA (deoxyribonucleic acid) and other nuclear materials. Minor damages caused by toxic chemicals might be mended, and therefore tolerated. Organisms also have mechanisms for detoxifying some types of poisonous chemicals. The mixed-function oxidases, for example, are enzymes that can detoxify certain chemicals, such as **chlorinated hydrocarbons**, by metabolizing them into simpler, less-toxic substances. Organisms can also partition certain chemicals into tissues that are less vulnerable to their poisonous influence. For example, chlorinated hydrocarbons are most often deposited in the fatty tissues of animals.

All of these physiological mechanisms of dealing with small exposures to potentially toxic chemicals can, however, be overwhelmed by exposures that exceed the limits of tolerance. These larger exposures cause poisoning of people and other organisms and ecological damages.

Some naturally occurring poisons

Many poisonous chemicals are present naturally in the environment. For example, all of metals and other elements are widespread in the environment, but under some circumstances they may occur naturally in concentrations that are large enough to be poisonous to at least some organisms.

Examples of natural "pollution" can involve surface exposure of **minerals** containing large concentrations of toxic elements, such as **copper**, lead, selenium, or arsenic. For example, soils influenced by a mineral known as serpentine can have large concentrations of toxic nickel and cobalt, and can be poisonous to most plants.

In other cases, certain plants may selectively take up elements from their environment, to the degree that their foliage becomes acutely toxic to herbivorous animals. For example, soils in semi-arid regions of the western United States often contain selenium. This element can be bioaccumulated by certain species of **legumes** known as locoweeds (*Astragalus* spp.), to the degree that the plants become extremely poisonous to cattle and to other large animals that might eat their toxic foliage.

In some circumstances, the local environment can become naturally polluted by gases at toxic concentrations, poisoning plants and animals. This can happen in the vicinity of volcanoes, where vents known as fumaroles frequently emit toxic **sulfur dioxide**, which can poison and kill nearby plants. The sulfur dioxide can also dry-deposit to the nearby ground and surface water, causing a severe acidification, which results in soluble **aluminum** ions becoming toxic.

Other naturally occurring toxins are biochemicals that are synthesized by plants and animals, often as a deterrent to herbivores and predators, respectively. In fact, some of the most toxic chemicals known to science are biochemicals synthesized by organisms. One such example is tetrodotoxin, synthesized by the Japanese globe **fish** (*Spheroides rubripes*), and extremely toxic even if ingested in tiny amounts. Only slightly less toxic is saxitoxin, synthesized by species of marine **phytoplankton**, but accumulated by shellfish. When people eat these shellfish, a deadly **syndrome** known as paralytic shellfish poisoning results. There are numerous other examples of deadly biochemicals, such as snake and bee venoms, toxins produced by pathogenic microorganisms, and mushroom poisons.

Poisons produced by human technology

Of course, in the modern world, humans are responsible for many of the toxic chemicals that are now being dispersed into the environment. In some cases, humans are causing toxic damages to organisms and ecosystems by emitting large quantities of chemicals that also occur naturally, such as sulfur dioxide, hydrocarbons, and metals. Pollution or poisoning by these chemicals represents an intensification of damages that may already be present naturally, although not to nearly the same degree or extent that results from additional human emissions.

Humans are also, however, synthesizing large quantities of novel chemicals that do not occur naturally, and these are also being dispersed widely into the environment. These synthetic chemicals include thousands of different pesticidal chemicals, medicines, and diverse types of industrial chemicals, all of them occurring in complex mixtures of various forms. Many of these chemicals are directly toxic to humans and to other organisms that are exposed to them, as is the case with many **pesticides**. Others result in toxicity indirectly, as may occur when **chlorofluorocarbons (CFCs)**, which are normally quite inert chemicals, find their way to the upper atmospheric layer called the stratosphere. There the CFCs degrade into simpler chemicals that consume **ozone**, resulting in less shielding of Earth's surface from the harmful effects of solar ultraviolet **radiation**, with subsequent toxic effects such as skin cancers, cataracts, and immune disorders.

As an example of toxicity caused to humans, consider the case of the accidental release in 1984 at Bhopal, India, of about 40 tonnes of poisonous methyl isocyanate vapor, an intermediate chemical in the manufacturing of an agricultural insecticide. This emission caused the death of almost 3,000 people and more than 20,000 others were seriously injured.

As an example of toxicity caused to other animals, consider the effects of the use of carbofuran, an insecticide used in agriculture in **North America**. Carbofuran exerts its toxic effect by poisoning a specific **enzyme**, known as **acetylcholine** esterase, which is essential for maintaining the functioning of the **nervous system**. This enzyme is critical to the healthy functioning of **insects**, but it also occurs in **vertebrates** such as **birds** and **mammals**. As a result, the normal use of carbofuran in

KEY TERMS

Acute toxicity—A poisonous effect produced by a single, short-term exposure to a toxic chemical, resulting in obvious tissue damage, and even death of the organism.

Bioassay—This is an estimate of the concentration or effect of a potentially toxic chemical, measured using a biological response under standardized conditions.

Chronic toxicity—This is a poisonous effect that is produced by a long period of exposure to a moderate, sub-acute dose of some toxic chemical. Chronic toxicity may result in anatomical damages or disease, but it is not generally the direct cause of death of the organism.

Exposure—In toxicology, exposure refers to the concentration of a chemical in the environment, or to the accumulated dose that an organism encounters.

Hidden injury—This refers to physiological damages, such as changes in enzyme or other biochemical functions, that occur after exposure to a dose of a poison that is not sufficient to cause acute injuries.

Response—In toxicology, response refers to effects on physiology or organisms that are caused by exposure to one or more poisons.

agriculture results in toxic exposures to numerous birds, mammals, and other animals that are not the intended targets of the insecticide application. Many of these non-target animals are killed by their exposure to carbofuran, a chemical that is well-known as causing substantial ecological damages during the course of its normal, legal usage in agriculture.

Synopsis

It is critical to understand that while any chemical can cause poisoning, a threshold of tolerable dose must be exceeded for this to actually happen. The great challenge of toxicology is to provide society with a clearer understanding of the exposures to potentially toxic chemicals that can be tolerated by humans, other species, and ecosystems before unacceptable damages are caused. Many naturally occurring and synthetic chemicals can be used for diverse, useful purposes, but it is important that we understand the potentially toxic consequences of increasing exposures to these substances.

See also Bioaccumulation.

Further Reading

Freedman, B. *Environmental Ecology.* 2nd ed. San Diego: Academic Press, 1995.

Klaassen, C., M. Amdur, and J. Doull. *Cassarett and Doull's Toxicology: The Basic Science of Poisons.* 4th ed. Boston: Little, Brown, 1991.

Smith, R. P. *A Primer of Environmental Toxicology.* Philadelphia: Lea & Febiger, 1992.

Bill Freedman

Polar coordinates

One of the several systems for addressing points in the **plane** is the polar-coordinate system. In this system a point P is identified with an ordered pair (r,θ) where r is a **distance** and θ an **angle**. The angle is measured counter-clockwise from a fixed ray OA called the "polar axis." The distance to P is measured from the end point O of the ray. This point is called the "pole." Thus each pair determines the location of a point precisely.

When a point P is given coordinates by this scheme, both r and θ will be positive. In working with polar coordinates, however, it occasionally happens that r, θ, or both take on **negative** values. To handle this one can either convert the negative values to positive ones by appropriate rules, or one can broaden the system to allow such possibilities. To do the latter, instead of a ray through O and P one can imagine a number line with θ the angle formed by OA and the positive end of the number line, as shown here. One can also say that an angle measured in a clockwise direction is negative. For example, the point (5, 30°) could also be represented by (-5, -150°).

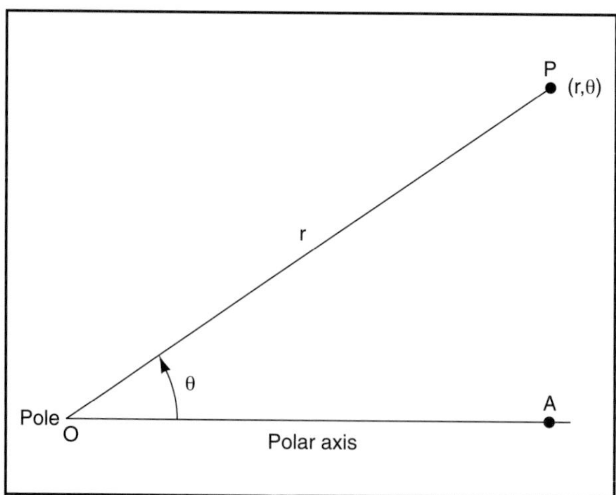

Figure 1.

To convert r and θ to positive values, one can use these rules:

$$\text{I}\ (-r, \theta) = (r, \theta \pm \pi) \text{ or } (r, \theta \pm 180°)$$
$$\text{II}\ (r, \theta) = (r, \theta \pm 2\pi) \text{ or } (r, \theta \pm 360°)$$

(Notice that θ can be measured in radians, degrees, or any other measure as long as one does it consistently.) Thus one can convert (-5, -150°) to (5, 30°) by rule I alone. To convert (-7, -200°) would require two steps. Rule I would take it to (7, -20°). Rule II would convert it to (7, 340°).

Rule II can also be used to reduce or increase θ by any multiple of 2π or 360°. The point (6.5, 600°) is the same as (6.5, 240°), (6.5, 960°), (6.5, -120°), or countless others.

It often happens that one wants to convert polar coordinates to rectangular coordinates, or vice versa. Here one assumes that the polar axis coincides with the positive x-axis and the same scale is used for both. The equations for doing this are

$$r = \sqrt{x^2 + y^2}$$
$$\theta = \arctan y/x$$
$$x = r \cos \theta$$
$$y = r \sin \theta$$

For example, the point (3, 3) in rectangular coordinates becomes (=++18, 45°) in polar coordinates. The polar point (7, 30°) becomes (6.0622, 3.5). Some scien-

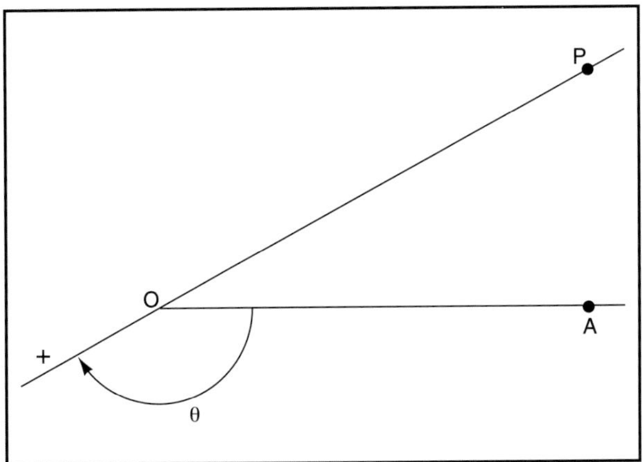

Figure 2.

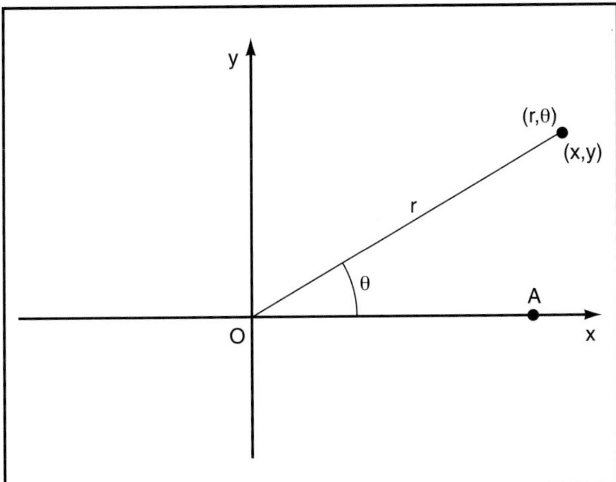

Figure 3.

tific calculators have built-in functions for making these conversions.

These formulas can also be used in converting equations from one form to the other. The equation $r = 10$ is the polar equation of a **circle** with it center at the origin and a radius of 10. Substituting for r and simplifying the result gives $x^2 + y^2 = 100$. Similarly, $3x - 2y = 7$ is the equation of a line in rectangular coordinates. Substituting and simplifying gives $r = 7/(3 \cos \theta - 2 \sin \theta)$ as its polar equation.

As these examples show, the two systems differ in the ease with which they describe various curves. The Archimedean **spiral** $r = k\theta$ is simply described in polar coordinates. In rectangular coordinates, it is a mess. The **parabola** $y = x^2$ is simple. In polar form it is $r = \sin \theta/(1 - \sin^2 \theta)$. (This comparison is a little unfair. The polar forms of the **conic sections** are more simple if one puts the focus at the pole.) One particularly interesting way in which polar coordinates are used is in the design of **radar** systems. In such systems, a rotating **antenna** sends out a pulsed **radio** beam. If that beam strikes a reflective object the antenna will pick up the reflection. By measuring the time it takes for the reflection to return, the system can compute how far away the reflective object is. The system, therefore, has the two pieces of information it needs in order determine the position of the object. It has the angular position, θ, of the antenna, and the distance r, which it has measured. It has the object's position (r, θ) in polar coordinates.

For coordinatizing points in **space** a system known as cylindrical coordinates can be used. In this system, the first two coordinates are polar and the third is rectangular, representing the point's distance above or below the polar plane. Another system, called a spherical coordinate system, uses a radius and two angles, analogous to the latitude and longitude of points on **earth**.

Polar coordinates were first used by Isaac Newton and Jacob (Jacques) Bernoulli in the seventeenth century, and have been used ever since. Although they are not as widely used as rectangular coordinates, they are important enough that nearly every book on **calculus** or **analytic geometry** will include sections on them and their use; and makers of professional quality graph **paper** will supply paper printed with polar-coordinate grids.

KEY TERMS

Coordinate system—A system of describing the position of points by means of combinations of numbers.

Polar coordinates—A coordinate system in which one number represents a distance and the other number an angle.

Rectangular coordinates—A coordinate system in which two or more numbers represent distances in mutually orthogonal directions.

Further Reading

Boyer, Carl B. *A History of Mathematics.* New York: John Wiley and Sons, 1968.

Finney, Ross L., et al. *Calculus: Graphical, Numerical, Algebraic, of a single variable..* Reading, Mass.: Addison Wesley Publishing Co., 1994.

J. Paul Moulton

Polar covalent bond see **Bond, chemical**

Polar ice caps

The polar ice caps cover the north and south poles and their surrounding territory, including the entire **continent** of **Antarctica** in the south, the Arctic Ocean, the northern part of Greenland, parts of northern Canadian, and bits of Siberia and Scandinavia also in the north. Polar ice caps are dome-shaped sheets of ice that feed ice to other glacial formations, such as ice sheets, ice fields, and ice islands. They remain frozen year-round, and they serve as sources for **glaciers** that feed ice into the polar seas in the form of **icebergs**. Because the polar ice caps are very cold (temperatures in Antarctica have been measured to -126.8 °F [-88°C]) and exist for a long time, the caps serve as deep-freezes for geologic information that can be studied by scientists. Ice cores drawn from these regions contain important data for both geologists and historians about paleoclimatology and give clues about the effects human activities currently having on the world.

Polar ice caps also serve as reservoirs for huge amounts of the earth's **water**. Geologists suggest that three-quarters of the world's fresh water is frozen at the north and south pole. Most of this **freshwater** ice is in the southern hemisphere. The Antarctic ice cap alone contains over 90% of the world's glacial ice, sometimes in huge sheets over 2.5 mi (4 km) deep and averaging 1.5 mi (2 km) deep across the continent. It has been estimated that enough water is locked up in Antarctica to raise sea levels around the globe over 20 ft (60 m), drowning most of the world's major cities, destroying much of the world's food-producing capacity, and ending civilization.

Polar ice caps and geologic history

Although the polar ice caps have been in existence for millions of years, scientists disagree over exactly how long they have survived in their present form. It is generally agreed that the polar cap north of the Arctic Circle, which covers the Arctic Ocean, has undergone contraction and expansion through some 26 different glaciations in just the past few million years. Parts of the Arctic have been covered by the polar ice cap for at least the last 5 million years, with estimates ranging up to 15 million. The Antarctic ice cap is more controversial; although many scientists believe extensive ice has existed there for 15 million years, others suggest that volcanic activity on the western half of the continent it covers causes the ice to decay, and the current south polar ice cap is therefore no more than about 3 million years old.

At least five times since the formation of the **earth**, because of changes in **global climate**, the polar ice has expanded north and south toward the equator and has stayed there for at least a million years The earliest of these known **ice ages** was some 2 billion years ago, during the Huronian epoch of the Precambrian era. The most recent ice age began about 1.7 million years in the Pleistocene epoch. It was characterized by a number of fluctuations in North polar ice, some of which expanded over much of modern **North America** and **Europe**, covered up to half of the existing continents, and measured as much as 1.8 mi (3 km) deep in some places. These glacial expansions locked up even more water, dropping sea levels worldwide by more than 30ft (100 m). **Animal** species that had adapted to cold **weather**, like the mammoth, thrived in the polar conditions of the Pleistocene glaciations, and their ranges stretched south into what is now the southern United States.

The glaciers completed their retreat and settled in their present positions about ten to twelve thousand years ago. There have been other fluctuations in global temperatures on a smaller scale, however, that have sometimes been known popularly as ice ages. The four hundred year period between the fourteenth and the eighteenth centuries is sometimes called the Little Ice Age. Contemporaries noted that the Baltic Sea froze over twice in the first decade of the 1300s. Temperatures in Europe fell enough to shorten the growing season, and the production of grain in Scandinavia dropped precipitously as a result. The Norse communities in Greenland could no longer be maintained and were abandoned by the end of the fifteenth century. Scientists believe that we are currently in an interglacial period, and that North polar ice will again move south some time in the next 23 thousand years.

Causes and effects of polar ice expansion

Scientists believe the growth of polar ice caps can be triggered by a combination of several global climactic factors. The major element is a small drop (perhaps no more than 15° F [-9°C]) in average world temperatures. The factors that cause this drop can be very complex. They include fluctuations in atmospheric and oceanic **carbon dioxide** levels, increased amounts of dust in the atmosphere, heightened winds—especially in equatorial areas—and changes in surface oceanic currents. The Milankovitch theory of glacial cycles also cites as factors small variations in the earth's orbital path around the **sun**, which in the long term could influence the expansion and contraction of the polar ice caps. Computer models based on the Milankovitch theory correlate fairly closely with observed behavior of glaciation over the past 600 million years.

Scientists use material preserved in the polar ice caps to chart these changes in global glaciation. By measuring

the relationship of different **oxygen** isotopes preserved in ice cores, they have determined both the **mean temperature** and the amount of dust in the atmosphere in these latitudes during the recent ice ages. Single events, such as volcanic eruptions and variations in solar activity and **sea level**, are also recorded in polar ice. These records are valuable not only for the information they provide about past glacial periods; they serve as a standard to compare against the records of more modern periods.

The process of **global warming**, which has been documented by scientific investigation, is also reflected in the ice caps. Should global warming continue unchecked, scientists warn, it could have a drastic effect on polar ice. Small variations over a short period of time could shrink the caps and raise world sea levels. Even a small rise in sea level could affect a large percentage of the world's population, and it could effectively destroy major cities like New York. Ironically, global warming could also delay or offset the effects of the coming ice age.

Further Reading

Covey, Curt."The Earth's Orbit and the Ice Ages"*Scientific American,* February, 1984.

Flint, Richard F. *Glacial and Quaternary Geology.* New York, NY: Wiley. 1971.

Kerr, R.A."Milankovitch Climate Cycles through the Ages."*Science.* 27 February 1987.

Monastersky, Richard."Sea Change in the Arctic." *Science News.* 13 February 1999, 104.

National Ice Core Laboratory. *"Why Study Ice Cores?"* http://&.nicl- smo.sr.unh.edu/NICL/nicl/whatis/intro.html

Spiessbach, Kathleen."One Very Cold Lake." *Discover.* 18 (January 1997): 26.

Kenneth R. Shepherd

Polarization see **Optics**

Polaroid photography see **Photography**

Poliomyelitis

There are three viruses responsible for the infectious disease now called poliomyelitis. It has been called infantile paralysis and is now commonly referred to as polio. While the disease usually afflicts young children, adults can succumb to it also.

A notable example of polio in an adult was the case of President Franklin Delano Roosevelt, the 32nd president of the United States. He contracted poliomyelitis at the age of 40. While he was able to return to health through an intense effort of **physical therapy**, he lost the use of his legs. As the President of the United States he used canes and orthotic devices to stand when he appeared before audiences in the 1930s and 40s. Although he was bound to a wheelchair, to most people he was able to convey the illusion that he was still able to walk.

Infection from poliomyelitis is spread through infectious contact with someone who already has the disease or as a result of poor sanitation where human waste products infect others. The mouth is the usual pathway of the **virus** which then enters the **blood** system. Paralysis mostly to the arms and legs occurs from lesions to the central **nervous system**. These lesions occur when the polio viruses begin to invade the central nervous system.

Clinical reactions to the polio viruses can range from none to symptoms that are mild ones which resemble the common cold (headache, sore throat, slight fever). These symptoms can vanish in a short period of time, anywhere from one to three days. A major illness of polio can be defined when the viruses attack the central nervous system, and even in these cases about 50% of the patients will fully recover. Of the remaining 50% about half of those will retain some mildly disabling after- effects, while the other one-half will show signs of permanent disability. Special devices may have to be used in these cases, such as an **iron** lung to assist in breathing when the **respiratory system** is impaired by the disease.

A form of the disease that can be fatal is the kind that leads to a paralysis of the muscles in the throat. This type of paralysis can lead to the regurgitation of the gastric juices into the respiratory system thus causing it to shut down. The large majority of these cases (80%) can still recover through proper treatment. This complication of the disease is known as bulbar poliomyelitis.

Because infants in underdeveloped parts of the world may have built up immunity from their mothers who had been exposed to the virus, there has been a belief that these children were less at risk of contracting polio than children in advanced countries with improved sanitation. Demographic **statistics** of incident rates, however, tend to raise questions about the effectiveness of natural, infant immunities developing in backward countries. Immunization programs against poliomyelitis as well as other common **childhood diseases** is still carried on by the World Health Organization as the only reliable way of eradicating the disease.

In the 1950s two types of vaccines were developed in the United States. One type, the Salk **vaccine**, named after its developer Jonas Salk, used dead polio viruses that were injected. The other type is called the Sabin vaccine, after Albert Sabin, and is an oral vaccine using a weaker strain of the polio viruses for immunity.

Since both vaccines are effective against all three strains of the polio viruses, there has been a virtual eradication of the disease in the United States and other countries that are able to employ a successful immunization program for their populations.

For those who contracted the disease before the vaccination programs became fully effective there have been reports of a disorder which is referred to as post-polio **syndrome**. This condition is characterized by fatigue, pains in the joints and muscles, problems with breathing, and a loss of muscle strength. Physical and occupational treatment therapies have been developed to deal with this problem.

Incubation and natural immunity

The term *infantile paralysis* for poliomyelitis was appropriate to the extent that the majority of cases, 70-90%, do occur in early childhood, below the age of three. In countries with temperate climates the infection rate rises seasonally during the **heat** and humidity of the summer months. The viruses are passed along either orally or through contact with infected feces or even through inhalation of moisture particles from infected individuals, such as by cough.

There may be some peaking of the disease in the tropics, but it is less evident. It takes from four to thirty-five days for the virus to incubate. Symptoms in most cases will begin to show after one to three weeks after contracting the virus.

The view is still current with some polio epidemiologists (physicians who study ways of preventing the spread of disease) that by the age of six, children in countries with poor sanitation have acquired a permanent immunity to polio, whereas children in countries with good sanitation are more apt to get the disease in their adult years since they were not exposed to it at an earlier period of life. Statistical analysis has left this assumption open to debate.

The iron lung

In the cases of polio that paralyzed the muscles necessary for breathing the so-called iron lung was developed in the mid-1900s. The iron lung is an artificial **respirator**. The patient's body is enclosed in a **metal** tank that uses air **pressure** changes to expand and contract the chest walls. In the 1920s a physiologist named Philip Drinker invented this innovative way of dealing with the respiratory problems of polio patients. The iron lung used a continuous power source which made it superior to existing respirators.

Drinker's original design was improved by physicians to increase the patient's care and comfort. The medical community depended on the iron lung in the treatment of patients with paralysis of the respiratory muscles. It was heavily used during the polio **epidemic** of 1931. Large, hospital-based respirator centers were developed to care for the many polio patients with respiratory paralysis. These centers were the predecessors of today's intensive care units.

World eradication of polio

The goal for the total eradication of polio, just as small pox has been eliminated, has annually been nearing a reality. About 600,000 cases of polio were reported each year before the introduction and full use of the polio vaccines. That number held firm from the mid-1950s to the early part of the next decade of the 1960s. By 1992 the number of reported cases throughout the world dropped to 15,406. Peru in 1991 was the only country in the western hemisphere to report one case of polio.

There are, however, areas in the world that still are at risk for the transmission of polio viruses. The World Health Organization recommends that immunization of children below the age of 5 be carried out and that oral polio vaccine be used instead of the Salk type. According to WHO, at least 5 doses of the oral vaccine should be given door to door on immunization designated days. Networks of clinics and reporting services should also be available to monitor the effective implementation of these immunization drives.

It was the World Health Organization that was responsible for the world eradication of **smallpox** by waging an 11-year campaign against the virus that caused it, the variola virus. WHO was able to bring countries together to use a vaccine that had been discovered 170 years ago. The polio viruses, however, are still active and there really may be ten times as much polio in the world than is actually officially reported.

Feasibility for eradication

One of the problems of testing for the eradication of polio infections is that the majority of cases do not show any clinical symptoms. They are asymptomatic. Less than 1% of polio infections lead to paralysis and most of the cases that go on to paralysis are caused by the type 1 poliovirus. Type 1 is also the one most responsible for outbreaks of epidemics. Along with type 3 it represents probably less than one case out of a thousand polio infections.

Another problem in tracking the polio virus is that there are other viruses (Enteroviruses) that create symptoms that are exactly like the ones created by the polio viruses. There are also some unusual types of symptoms in some polio infections that resemble a disorder known

as **Guillain-Barre syndrome**. Only a careful laboratory examination that includes isolating the viruses from the patient's stool can be considered for giving a correct **diagnosis** of the infection. The presence of such laboratory facilities, especially in backward areas, therefore, becomes an important factor in the program to eliminate infections from polio viruses.

Polio vaccines

In 1955 the Salk inactivated polio vaccine was introduced. It was followed by the Sabin live, attenuated oral vaccine in 1961. These two vaccines have made it possible to eliminate polio on a global level.

The Salk vaccine as it has been presently developed produces a high level of immunity after two or three injections with only minor side-effects. The major defense the Salk vaccine provides against polio viruses is to prevent them from spreading from the **digestive system** to the nervous system and respiratory system. But it cannot prevent the viruses from entering the intestinal tract. The Salk vaccine has been effective in certain countries, like those in Scandinavia and the Netherlands, where children received a minimum of six shots before reaching the age of 15. Those countries have good sanitation and the major form of spreading the viruses was through respiratory contagion.

In countries that do not have good sanitation, the Sabin vaccine is preferred because as an oral vaccination it is goes straight to the intestinal tract and builds up immunity there as well as in other parts of the body. Those who have received the vaccine may pass on vaccine viruses through the feces to non-vaccinated members of the population, and that spreads the good effects of immunization. There is, however, the rare adverse side-effect of 1 out of 2,500,000 doses of the Sabin vaccine producing a case of poliomyelitis.

The number of doses to achieve a high level of immunity for the Sabin oral vaccine in temperate, economically advanced countries may be two or three. In tropical countries the degree of immunization is not as high against all three types of polio viruses. The effectiveness of the Sabin oral vaccine in tropical countries is improved when it is administered in the cool and dry **seasons** and when it is given as part of mass campaign where there is a chance of vaccinated persons passing the vaccine virus on to non-vaccinated persons.

Toward the global eradication of polio, the World Health Organization recommends the Sabin oral vaccine for its better performance in creating overall polio immunity, its convenient form of administration, and for its lower cost.

Need for surveillance

For the total eradication of a disease it is necessary to have the mechanisms for determining the existence of even one solitary instance or case of the disease. That means in effect a quick system of reporting and collection of any suspected occurrence of the disease so that laboratory analysis may be made as soon as possible. Health care providers are given the criteria for determining the presence of the disease. In the case of polio the appearance of a certain type of paralysis called acute flaccid paralysis along with the Guillain-Barre syndrome for a child under 5 or any physician diagnosed case of polio at any age should receive immediate attention.

Within 24-48 hours two stool specimens are collected along with clinical information, other laboratory findings, and information on whether the person has recently traveled. A 60 day follow-up after the onset of the illness should be made to see if there are any paralytic after effects.

Importance of laboratories

Laboratory confirmation of polio viruses requires an efficient network of laboratories. Each WHO region develops a network of laboratories to support the various countries within that area. In these laboratories the staff is trained to isolate and identify the different types of polio viruses. Some countries send specimens to a regional laboratory in a neighboring country. Regional reference laboratories have been set up to tell the differences between vaccine poliovirus from wild poliovirus. A few of these laboratories produce the needed testing agents, do research, and develop training materials for health workers. These laboratories are coordinated with central libraries that contain genotypic information and samples to help in the identification process.

Cost of global eradication

In many of the countries where polio viruses still exist and are transmitted the cost of eradication cannot be afforded. WHO estimates that global polio eradication, with a 10-year effort, may cost as much as a billion dollars. It is argued that countries in the West and those with advancing economies that are free of polio will benefit by the global eradication of poliomyelitis. For example, the United States could save more than $105 million a year on polio vaccine. Money could also be saved by not having to administer the vaccine. The Netherlands suffered an outbreak of polio in 1991-92. It spent more than $10 million controlling this outbreak. More money will also have to be spent for the long-term care and **rehabilitation** for the survivors of the Netherlands' outbreak. According to the cost-analysis of leading polio

epidemiologists, the total cost of eradication could be recovered in savings within a few years of certification that the world is polio-free.

Treatment of post-polio syndrome

For older survivors of previous polio epidemics in the United States and elsewhere there have been a group of related symptoms known as post-polio syndrome.

The amount of **exercise** recommended for post-polio people has been an issue in question. While it was felt that this syndrome, characterized by muscle atrophy and fatigue, called for some restrictions on exercise because of the weakened condition of the muscles, a more recent view is calling for a reexamination of that position. The newer view is that exercise training of muscles is more important than avoidance of exercise even though it becomes more difficult in the aging process. It is important to maintain a high level of activity as well as the right kind and amount. Studies have shown that post-polio muscles that have lost strength can recover strength with the right kind of exercise.

It is also possible for these people to improve their endurance, but it is important for them not to have expectations that exceed their physical limitations. One criterion that can be followed for improving the strength of a limb is to determine how much function remains in the limb. The strength of the limb should at least remain the same with the exercise, but if it begins to decrease, then it is possible it is being overexerted. Experts in the field of physical rehabilitation maintain that the limb should have at least 15 percent of normal function before it can be further improved with exercise. If it is below that amount the exercise may not help to improve strength and endurance.

Use of drugs

Drug studies show that using high doses of prednisone, a drug used as an immunosuppressant did not produce added strength or endurance. Amantadine, used for **Parkinson's disease** and the fatigue of multiple sclerosis, also was not effective. Another drug, Mestinon, however, showed that post-polio people could benefit from its use. Physicians advise their patients to try it for a one month period starting with a small dose and then over a period of a month to build up the dosage. After the full dosage is reached the user should be able to determine whether or not it will help improve symptoms, especially in the area of strengthening weak muscles. It is particularly recommended to deal with fatigue in emergency situations, such as when driving a car when a low dose can carry the person through the activity safely.

KEY TERMS

Acute flaccid paralysis—An early symptom of poliomyelitis.

Guillain-Barre syndrome—A rare disorder of the peripheral nerves that causes weakness and paralysis, usually caused by an allergic reaction to a viral infection.

Iron lung—An artificial respirator developed in the twenties and widely used throughout the polio epidemics in the United States and other countries of the thirties and thereafter.

L-Carnitine—A health food substance being used by some postpolio people.

Post-polio syndrome—A group of symptoms experienced by survivors of the polio epidemics before the period of vaccination.

Sabin vaccine—The oral polio vaccine developed by Albert Sabin from weakened live polio viruses and introduced in 1961; the vaccine WHO recommends for immunization programs.

Salk vaccine—The polio vaccine introduced by Jonas Salk in the mid–1950s using dead polio viruses by injection.

Smallpox—A viral disease with a long history which in 1980 WHO announced was eradicated as a result of an effective worldwide immunization program.

Wild poliovirus—As opposed to vaccine polio viruses which are transmitted as a result of the Sabin vaccine, wild polio viruses are those naturally circulated from natural sources of contagion.

World Health Organization—A body of the United Nations formed in 1948 to deal with world health problems, such as epidemics.

Another medication post-polio people have found helpful and which is available at health food stores is L-Carnitine. This is a substance that is already present in the muscles and it has been used in Switzerland and **Australia**. It is now being tried in the United States to help build up strength and endurance for post-polio people.

Further Reading

Crofford, Emily and Michael, Steve. *Healing Warrior: A Story about Sister Elizabeth Kenny.* Minneapolis: Carolrhoda Books, 1989.

Markel, Howard. "The Genesis of the Iron Lung." *Archives of Pediatrics and Adolescent Medicine*. November, 1994, v. 146, n. 11:1174-1181.

Rogers, Naomi. *Dirt and Disease: Polio Before FDR*. New Brunswick, NJ: Rutgers University Press, 1992.

Smith, Jane S. *Patenting the Sun: Polio and the Salk Vaccine*. New York: William Morrow. 1990.

Jordan P. Richman

Pollen see **Flower**

Pollen analysis

Pollen analysis, or **palynology**, is the study of fossil pollen (and to a lesser degree, **plant** spores) preserved in **lake** sediments, bog peat, or other matrices. Usually, the goal of palynology is to reconstruct the probable character of local plant communities in the historical past, as inferred from the abundance of plant species in dated potions of the pollen record. Palynology is a very important tool for interpreting historical plant communities, and the speed and character of their response to changes in environmental conditions, especially climate change. Pollen analysis is also useful in archaeological and ecological reconstructions of the probable habitats of ancient humans and wild animals, and in determining what they might have eaten. Pollen analysis is also sometimes useful in exploration for resources of **fossil fuels** .

Pollen and spores

Pollen is a fine powdery substance, consisting of microscopic grains containing the male gametophyte of gymnosperms (conifers and their relatives) and angiosperms (monocotyledonous and dicotyledonous flowering plants). Pollen is designed for long-distance dispersal from the parent plant, so that **fertilization** can occur among individuals, in preference to self- fertilization. (However, many species of plants are indeed self-fertile, some of them exclusively so.) Plant spores are another type of reproductive grain intended for dissemination. Plant spores are capable of developing as a new individual, either directly or after fusion with another germinated **spore**. Among the vascular plants, these types of spores are produced by **ferns**, **horsetails**, and clubmosses. However, spores with somewhat simpler functions are also produced by mosses, liverworts, **algae**, **fungi**, and other less complex organisms.

Pollen of many plants can be microscopically identified to genus and often to species on the basis of the size, shape, and surface texturing of the grain. In general, spores can only be identified to higher taxonomic orders, such as family or order. This makes pollen, more so than spores, especially useful in typical palynological studies. The integrity of the outer **cell** wall of both pollen and spores is well maintained under conditions with little physical disturbance and poor in **oxygen**, and this is why these grains are so well preserved in lake sediment, bog peat, and even the drier deposits of archaeological sites. Fossil pollen has even been collected, and identified, from the teeth and viscera of extinct animals, such as mammoths found frozen in arctic permafrost.

Plant species are not represented in the record of fossil pollen of lake sediments and bog peat in a manner that directly reflects their abundance in the nearby vegetation. For example, plants that are pollinated by **insects** are rarely detected in the pollen record, because their relatively small production of pollen is not distributed into the environment in a diffuse manner. In contrast, wind-pollinated species are well represented, because these plants emit large quantities of pollen and disseminate it in a broadcast fashion. However, even among wind-pollinated plants, certain species are particularly copious producers of pollen, and these are disproportionately represented in the fossil record, as is the case of herbaceous species of ragweed (for example, *Ambrosia artemesiifolia*). Among temperate species of trees, **pines** are notably copious producers of pollen, and it is not unusual to find a distinct, pollen-containing, yellow froth along the edges of lakes and ponds in many areas during the pollen season of pines. Because of the large differences in pollen production among plant species, interpretation of the likely character of local vegetation based on observations of fossil pollen records requires an understanding of pollen production rates by the various species, as well as annual variations in this characteristic.

Dating palynological samples

Palynologists must understand the temporal context of their samples, which means that they must be dated. A number of methods are available to palynologists for dating their samples of mud or peat. Most commonly used in typical palynological studies is a method known as radiocarbon dating, which takes advantage of the fact that once an **organism** dies and is removed from the direct influence of the atmosphere, it no longer absorbs additional carbon-14, a rare, radioactive **isotope** of this element. Therefore, the amount of carbon-14 decreases progressively as a **sample** of dead **biomass** ages, and this fact can be used to estimated the age of organic samples on the basis of the remaining quantity of carbon-14, and its

ratio to stable carbon-12. The rate of **radioactive decay** of carbon-14 is determined by its **half-life**, which is about 5,700 years. Radiological dating using carbon-14 is useful for samples aged between about 150,000 and 40,000-50000 years. Younger samples can sometimes be dated on the basis of their content of lead-210, and older samples using other elemental isotopes having longer half-lives.

Some palynological studies have investigated sediment collected from an unusual type of lake, called meromictic, in which there is a permanent stratification of the **water** caused by a steep **density** gradient associated with a rapid changes in **temperature** or **salt concentration**. This circumstance prevents surface waters from mixing with deeper waters, which eventually become anoxic because the biological demand for oxygen exceeds its ability to diffuse into deeper waters. Because there is insufficient oxygen, animals cannot live in the sediment of meromictic lakes. Consequently, the seasonal **stratigraphy** of material deposition is not disturbed by benthic creatures, and meromictic lakes often have well-defined, annual sediment layers, called varves. These can be dated in carefully collected, frozen cores by directly counting backwards from the surface. Sometimes, a few radiocarbon dates are also measured in varved cores, to confirm the chronology, or to compensate for a poor collection of the youngest, surface layers. Although meromictic lakes are unusual and rare, palynologists seek them out enthusiastically, because of the great advantages that the varved cores have for dating and interpretation.

Sometimes, palynologists work in cooperation with archaeologists. In such cases, it may be possible to date sample locations through their physical association with cultural artifacts that have been dated by archaeologists, perhaps based on their known dates of occurrence elsewhere.

Sometimes it is not necessary to accurately know the absolute date of a sample-it may be enough to understand the relative age, that is, whether one sample is younger or older than another. Often, relative aging can be done on the basis of stratigraphic location, meaning that within any core of lake sediment or peat, older samples always occur deeper than younger samples.

Pollen analysis

Palynologists typically collect cores of sediment or peat, date layers occurring at various depths, and extract, identify, and enumerate samples of the fossil pollen grains that are contained in the layers. From the dated assemblages of fossil pollen, palynologists develop inferences about the nature of the **forests** and other plant communities that may have occurred in the local environment of the sampled lake or bog. These interpretations must be made carefully, because as noted above species do not occur in the pollen record in a fashion that directly reflects their abundance in the mature vegetation.

Most palynological investigations attempt to reconstruct the broad characteristics of the local vegetation at various times in the past. In the northern hemisphere, many palynological studies have been made of post-glacial changes in vegetation in places that now have a temperate climate. These vegetation changes have occurred since the continental-scale **glaciers** melted back, a process that began in some places 12,000-14,000 years ago. Although the particular, inferred dynamics of vegetation change vary among sites and regions, a commonly observed pattern is that the pollen record of samples representing recently deglaciated times contains species that are now typical of northern **tundra**, while the pollen of somewhat younger samples suggests a boreal forest of spruces, fir, and birch. The pollen assemblage of younger samples is generally dominated by species such as **oaks**, **maples**, **basswood**, **chestnut**, hickory, and other species of trees that presently have a relatively southern distribution.

However, within the post-glacial palynological record there are clear indications of occasional climatic reversals-for example, periods of distinct cooling that interrupt otherwise warm intervals. The most recent of these coolings was the so-called "Little Ice Age" that occurred between the 14th and 19th centuries.. However, palynology has detected much more severe climatic deteriorations, such as the Younger Dryas event that began about 11,000 years ago, and that caused the redevelopment of glaciers in many areas, and extensively reversed the broader patterns of post-glacial vegetation development.

Other interesting inferences from the palynological record have involved apparent declines of particular species of trees, occurring for reasons that are not known. For example, palynological records from various places in eastern **North America** have exhibited a large decline in the abundance of pollen of eastern hemlock (*Tsuga canadensis*), occurring over an approximately 50-year period about 4,800 years ago. It is unlikely that the hemlock decline was caused by climate change, because other **tree** species with similar ecological requirements did not decrease in abundance, and in fact, appear to have increased in abundance to compensate for the decline of hemlock. The hemlock decline may have been caused by an outbreak of an insect that specifically attacks that tree, by a disease, or by some other, undiscovered **factor**. Palynology has also found evidence for a similar phenomenon in **Europe** about 5,000 years ago, when there was a widespread decline of elms (*Ulmus* spp.). This decline could have been caused by wide-

KEY TERMS

Half-life—The time to disappearance of one-half of an initial quantity of material, for example, by radioactive decay of carbon–14.

Pollen analysis (palynology)—the inferred reconstruction of historical occurrences of local vegetation, as interpreted from the record of fossil pollen preserved in dated sediments of lakes or peat of bogs.

spread clearing of the forest by Neolithic humans, or by an unknown disease or insect.

Further Reading

Faegri, K. and J. Iversen. *Textbook of Pollen Analysis.* New York: Hafner Press, 1975.

Pielou, E.C. *After the Ice Age.* Chicago: University of Chicago Press, 1991.

Bill Freedman

Pollen dating see **Dating techiques**

Pollination

Pollination is the transfer of pollen from the male reproductive organs to the female reproductive organs of a **plant**, and it precedes **fertilization**, the fusion of the male and the female sex cells. Pollination occurs in seed-producing plants, but not in the more primitive spore-producing plants, such as **ferns** and mosses. In plants such as **pines**, **firs**, and spruces (the gymnosperms), pollen is transferred from the male cone to the female cone. In flowering plants (the angiosperms), pollen is transferred from the flower's stamen (male **organ**) to the pistil (female organ). Many species of angiosperms have evolved elaborate structures or mechanisms to facilitate pollination of their flowers.

History of pollination studies

The German physician and botanist Rudolf Jakob Camerarius (1665-1721) is credited with the first empirical demonstration that plants reproduce sexually. Camerarius discovered the roles of the different parts of a **flower** in seed production. While studying certain bisexual (with both male and female reproductive organs) species of flowers, he noted that a stamen (male pollen-producing organ) and a pistil (female ovule-producing organ) were both needed for seed production. The details of fertilization were discovered by scientists several decades after Camerarius's death.

A honeybee becomes coated in pollen while gathering nectar and transports the pollen as it goes from flower to flower.

Among the many other scientists who followed Camerarius's footsteps in the study of pollination, one of the most eminent was Charles Darwin. In 1862, Darwin published an important book on pollination: *The Various Contrivances by which Orchids Are Fertilized by Insects.* In part, Darwin wrote this book on orchids in support of his theory of **evolution** proposed in *The Origin of Species*, published in 1859.

Darwin demonstrated that many orchid flowers had evolved elaborate structures by **natural selection** in order to facilitate cross-pollination. He suggested that orchids and their insect pollinators evolved by interacting with one another over many generations, a process referred to as coevolution .

One particular example illustrates Darwin's powerful insight. He studied dried specimens of *Angraecum sesquipedale*, an orchid native to Madagascar. The white flower of this orchid has a foot-long (30 cm) tubular spur with a small drop of **nectar** at its base. Darwin claimed that this orchid had been pollinated by a moth with a foot-long tongue. He noted, however, that his statement "has been ridiculed by some entomologists." And indeed, around the turn of the century, a Madagascan moth with a one-foot-long tongue was discovered. Apparently,

the moth's tongue uncoils to sip the nectar of *A. sesquipedale* as it cross-pollinates the flowers.

Darwin continued his studies of pollination in subsequent years. In 1876, he wrote another important book on pollination **biology**, *The Effects of Cross and Self Fertilization in the Vegetable Kingdom.*

The Austrian monk and botanist Johann Gregor Mendel (1822-1884) also conducted important pollination studies in Brno (now in the Czech Republic) in the mid-1800s. He studied heredity by performing controlled cross-pollinations of pea plants thereby laying the foundation for the study of heredity and **genetics**.

Evolution of pollination

Botanists theorize that seed plants with morphologically distinct pollen (male) and ovules (female) evolved from ancestors with free-sporing heterospory, where the male and the female spores are also morphologically distinct.

The evolution of pollination coincided with the evolution of seed. Fossilized pollen grains of the **seed** ferns, an extinct group of seed-producing plants with fern-like leaves, have been dated to the late Carboniferous period (about 300 million years ago). These early seed plants relied upon **wind** to transport their pollen to the ovule. This was an advance over free-sporing plants, which were dependent upon **water**, as their sperm had to swim to reach the egg. The evolution of pollination therefore allowed seed plants to colonize terrestrial habitats.

It was once widely believed that insect pollination was the driving **force** in the evolutionary origin of angiosperms. However, paleobotanists have recently discovered pollen grains of early gymnosperms, which were too large to have been transported by wind. This and other evidence indicates that certain species of early gymnosperms were pollinated by **insects** millions of years before the angiosperms had originated.

Once the angiosperms had evolved, insect pollination became an important **factor** in their evolutionary diversification. By the late Cretaceous period (about 70 million years ago), the angiosperms had evolved flowers with complex and specific adaptations for pollination by insects and other animals. Furthermore, many flowers were clearly designed to ensure cross-pollination, exchange of pollen between different individuals. Cross-pollination is often beneficial because it produces offspring which have greater genetic heterogeneity, and are better able to endure environmental changes. This important point was also recognized by Darwin in his studies of pollination biology.

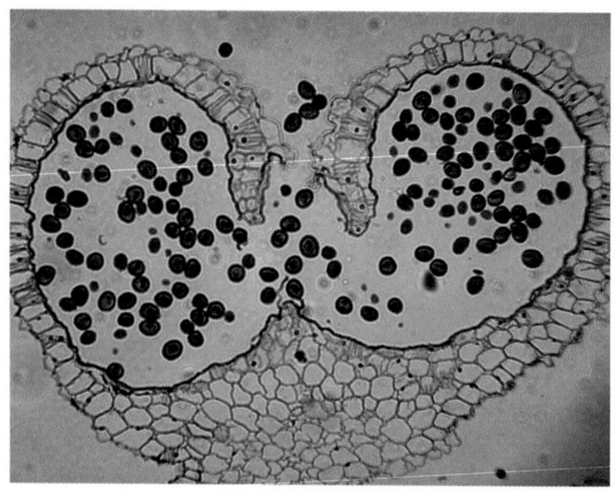

A cross section of the anther of a lily, showing open pollen sacs and the release of pollen grains.

Wind pollination

Most modern gymnosperms and many angiosperms are pollinated by wind. Wind-pollinated flowers, such as those of the **grasses**, usually have exposed stamens, so that the light pollen grains can be carried by the wind.

Wind pollination is a primitive condition, and large amounts of pollen are usually wasted, because it does not reach female reproductive organs. For this reason, most wind pollinated plants are found in temperate regions, where individuals of the same species often grow close together. Conversely, there are very few wind pollinated plants in the tropics, where plants of the same species tend to be farther apart.

Pollination by animals

In general, pollination by insects and other animals is more efficient than pollination by wind. Typically, pollination benefits the **animal** pollinator by providing it with nectar, and benefits the plant by providing a direct transfer of pollen from one plant to the pistil of another plant. **Angiosperm** flowers are often highly adapted for pollination by insect and other animals.

Each taxonomic group of pollinating animals is typically associated with flowers which have particular characteristics. Thus, one can often determine which animal pollinates a certain flower species by studying the morphology, color, and odor of the flower. For example, some flowers are pure red, or nearly pure red, and have very little odor. **Birds**, such as **hummingbirds**, serve as pollinators of most of these flowers, since birds have excellent **vision** in the red region of the **spectrum**, and a rather undeveloped sense of **smell**. Interestingly, **Europe** has no native pure red flowers and no bird pollinated flowers.

KEY TERMS

Angiosperm—A plant which produces seeds within the mature ovary of a flower, commonly referred as a flowering plant.

Coevolution— Evolution of two or more closely interacting species, such that the evolution of one species affects the evolution of the other(s).

Gametophyte—Haploid gamete-producing generation in a plant's life cycle.

Gymnosperm—Plant which produces its seed naked, rather than within a mature ovary.

Haploid—Nucleus or cell containing one copy of each chromosome.

Ovule—Female haploid gametophyte of seed plants, which develops into a seed upon fertilization by a pollen grain.

Pollen—Male haploid gametophyte of seed plants, which unites with the ovule to form a seed.

Some flowers have a very strong odor, but are very dark in color. These flowers are often pollinated by **bats**, which have very poor vision, are often active during the night, and have a very well developed sense of smell.

The flowers of many species of plants are marked with special ultraviolet absorbing pigments (flavonoids), which appear to direct the pollinator toward the pollen and nectar. These pigments are invisible to humans and most animals, but bees' eyes have special ultraviolet photoreceptors which enable the **bees** to detect patterns and so pollinate these flowers.

See also Gymnosperm; Sexual reproduction.

Further Reading

Gould, S. J. *The Panda's Thumb.* New York: W. W. Norton, 1980.

Meeuse, B., and S. Morris. *The Sex Life of Flowers.* New York: Facts on File, 1984.

Peter A. Ensminger

Pollution

The term pollution is derived from the Latin *pollutus*, which means to be made foul, unclean, or dirty. Anything that corrupts, degrades or makes something less valuable or desirable can be considered pollution. There is, however, a good deal of ambiguity and contention about what constitutes a pollutant. Many reserve the term for harmful physical changes in our environment caused by human actions. Others argue that any unpleasant or unwanted environmental changes whether natural or human-caused constitute pollution. This broad definition could include smoke from lightening-ignited forest fires, ash and toxic fumes from volcanoes, or bad-tasting **algae** growing naturally in a **lake**. Some people include social issues in their definition of pollution, such as noise from a **freeway**, visual blight from intrusive billboards, or cultural pollution when the worst aspects of modern society invade a traditional culture. As you can see, these definitions depend on the observer's perspective. What is considered unwanted change by one person might seem like a welcome progress to someone else. A chemical that is toxic to one **organism** can be an key nutrient for another.

The seven types of **air pollution** considered the greatest threat to human health in the United States, and the first regulated by the 1970 United States Clean Air Act, include **sulfur** dioxide, particulates (dust, smoke, etc.), **carbon monoxide**, volatile organic compounds, **nitrogen** oxides, **ozone**, and lead. In 1990, another 189 volatile chemical compounds from more than 250 sources were added to the list of regulated air pollutants in the United States. Air contaminants are divided into two broad categories: primary pollutants are those released directly into the air. Some examples include dust, smoke, and a variety of toxic chemicals such as lead, mercury, vinyl chloride, and carbon monoxide. In contrast, **secondary pollutants** are created or modified into a deleterious form after being released into the air.

A variety of chemical or photochemical reactions (catalyzed by light) produce a toxic mix of secondary pollutants in urban air. A prime example is the formation of ozone in urban **smog**. A complex series of chemical reactions involving volatile organic compounds, nitrogen oxides, sunlight, and molecular **oxygen** create highly reactive ozone molecules containing three oxygen **atoms**. Stratospheric ozone in the upper atmosphere provides an important shield against harmful ultraviolet **radiation** in sunlight. Stratospheric ozone depletion—destruction by **chlorofluorocarbons (CFCs)** and other anthropogenic (human-generated) chemicals—is of great concern because it exposes living organisms to dangerous ultraviolet radiation. Ozone in ambient air (that surrounding us), on the other hand, is highly damaging to both living organisms and building materials. Recent regulations that have reduced releases of smog-forming ozone in ambient air have significantly improved air quality in many American cities.

Among the most important types ofwater pollution are sediment, infectious agents, toxins, oxygen-demanding wastes, **plant nutrients**, and thermal changes. Sediment (dirt, **soil**, insoluble solids) and trash make up the largest **volume** and most visible type of **water** pollution in most **rivers** and lakes. Worldwide, **erosion** from croplands, **forests**, grazing lands, and construction sites is estimated to add some 75 billion tons of sediment each year to rivers and lakes. This sediment smothers gravel beds in which **fish** lay their eggs. It fills lakes and reservoirs, obstructs shipping channels, clogs hydroelectric turbines, and makes drinking water purification more costly. Piles of plastic waste, oil slicks, tar blobs, and other flotsam and jetsam of modern society now defile even the most remote **ocean** beaches.

Pollution control regulations usually distinguish between point and nonpoint sources. Factory smoke stacks, sewage outfalls, leaking underground mines, and burning dumps, for example, are point sources that release contaminants from individual, easily identifiable sources that are relatively easy to monitor and regulate. In contrast, nonpoint pollution sources are scattered or diffuse, having no specific location where they originate or discharge into our air or water. Some nonpoint sources include **automobile** exhaust, runoff from farm fields, urban streets, lawns, and construction sites. Whereas point sources often are fairly uniform and predictable, nonpoint runoff often is highly irregular. The first heavy rainfall after a dry period may flush high concentrations of oil, gasoline, rubber, and trash off city streets, for instance. The irregular timing of these events, as well as their multiple sources, **variable** location, and lack of specific ownership make them much more difficult to monitor, regulate, and treat than point sources.

In recent years, the United States and most of the more developed countries have made encouraging progress in air and **water pollution** control. While urban air and water quality anywhere in the world rarely matches that of pristine wilderness areas, pollution levels in most of the more prosperous regions of **North America**, Western **Europe**, Japan, **Australia**, and New Zealand have generally been dramatically reduced. In the United States, for example, the number of days on which urban air is considered hazardous in the largest cities has decreased 93% over the past 20 years. Of the 97 metropolitan areas that failed to meet clean air standards in the 1980s, nearly half had reached compliance by the early 1990s. Perhaps the most striking success in controlling air pollution is airborne lead. Banning of leaded gasoline in the United States in 1970 resulted in a 98% decrease in atmospheric concentrations of this toxic **metal**. Similarly, particulate materials have decreased in urban air nearly 80% since the passage of the U.S. Clean Air Act, while sulfur dioxides, carbon monoxide, and ozone are down by nearly one-third.

Pollution over the New Jersey turnpike.

Unfortunately, the situation often is not so encouraging in other countries. The major metropolitan areas of developing countries often have appalling levels of air pollution, which rapid population growth, unregulated industrialization, lack of enforcement, and corrupt national and local politics only make worse. Mexico City, for example, is notorious for bad air. Pollution levels exceed World Health Organization (WHO) standards 350 days per year. More than half of all children in the city have lead levels in their **blood** sufficient to lower intelligence and retard development. The 130,000 industries and 2.5 million motor vehicles spew out more than 5,500 metric tons of air pollutants every day, which are trapped by mountains ringing the city.

While we have not yet met our national goal in the United States of making all surface waters "fishable and swimmable," investments in **sewage treatment**, regulation of toxic waste disposal and factory effluents and other forms of pollution control have resulted in significant water quality increases in many areas. Nearly 90% of all the river miles and lake acres that are assessed for water quality in the United States fully or partly support their designed uses. Lake Erie, for instance, which was widely described in the 1970s as being "dead," now has much cleaner water and more healthy fish populations than would ever have been thought possible 25 years ago. Unfortunately, surface waters in some developing countries have not experienced similar progress in pollution control. In most developing countries, only a tiny fraction of human wastes are treated before being dumped into rivers, lakes, or the ocean. In consequence, water pollution levels often are appalling. In India, for example, two-thirds of all surface waters are considered dangerous to human health. Hopefully, as development occurs, these countries will be able to take advantage of

pollution control equipment and knowledge already available in already developed countries.

Pollution control

Pollution control is the process of reducing or eliminating the release of pollutants into the enviroment. It is regulated by various environmental agencies which establish pollutant discharge limits for air, **water**, and land.

Air pollution control strategies can be divided into two categories, the control of particulate **emission** and the control of gaseous emissions. There are many kinds of equipment which can be used to reduce particulate emissions. Physical separation of the particulate from the air using settling chambers, cyclone collectors, impingers, wet scrubbers, electrostatic precipitators, and **filtration** devices, are all processes that are typically employed.

Settling chambers use gravity separation to reduce particulate emissions. The air stream is directed through a settling chamber, which is relatively long and has a large **cross section**, causing the **velocity** of the air stream to be greatly decreased and allowing sufficient time for the settling of solid particles.

A cyclone collector is a cylindrical device with a conical bottom which is used to create a tornado-like air stream. A centrifugal **force** is thus imparted to the particles, causing them to cling to the wall and roll downward, while the cleaner air stream exits through the top of the device.

An impinger is a device which uses the inertia of the air stream to impinge mists and dry particles on a solid surface. Mists are collected on the impinger plate as liquid forms and then drips off, while dry particles tend to build up or reenter the air stream. It is for this reason that liquid sprays are used to wash the impinger surface as well, to improve the collection efficiency.

Wet scrubbers control particulate emissions by wetting the particles in order to enhance their removal from the air stream. Wet scrubbers typically operate against the current by a water spray contacting with the gas flow. The particulate matter becomes entrained in the water droplets, and it is then separated from the gas stream. Wet scrubbers such as packed bed, venturi, or plate scrubbers utilize initial impaction, and cyclone scrubbers use a centrifugal force.

Electrostatic precipitators are devices which use an electrostatic field to induce a charge on dust particles and collect them on grounded electrodes. Electrostatic precipitators are usually operated dry, but wet systems are also used, mainly by providing a water mist to aid in the process of cleaning the particles off the collection plate.

One of the oldest and most efficient methods of particulate control, however, is filtration. The most commonly-used filtration device is known as a baghouse and consists of fabric bags through which the air stream is directed. Particles become trapped in the fiber mesh on the fabric bags, as well as the filter cake which is subsequently formed.

Gaseous emissions are controlled by similar devices and typically can be used in conjunction with particulate control options. Such devices include scrubbers, absorption systems, condensers, flares, and incinerators.

Scrubbers utilize the phenomena of adsorption to remove gaseous pollutants from the air stream. There is a wide variety of scrubbers available for use, including spray towers, packed towers, and venturi scrubbers. A wide variety of solutions can be used in this process as absorbing agents. Lime, **magnesium** oxide, and **sodium** hydroxide are typically used.

Adsorption can also be used to control gaseous emissions. Activated **carbon** is commonly used as an adsorbent in configurations such as fixed bed and fluidized bed absorbers.

Condensers operate in a manner so as to condense vapors by either increasing the **pressure** or decreasing the **temperature** of the gas stream. Surface condensers are usually of the shell-and-tube type, and contact condensers provide physical contact between the vapors, coolant, and condensate inside the unit.

Flaring and **incineration** take advantage of the combustibility of a gaseous pollutant. In general, excess air is added to these processes to drive the **combustion** reaction to completion, forming **carbon dioxide** and water.

Another means of controlling both particulate and gaseous air pollutant emission can be accomplished by modifying the process which generates these pollutants. For example, modifications to process equipment or raw materials can provide effective source reduction. Also, employing fuel cleaning methods such as desulfurization and increasing fuel-burning efficiency can lessen air emissions.

Water pollution control methods can be subdivided into physical, chemical, and biological treatment systems. Most treatment systems use combinations of any of these three technologies. Additionally, water **conservation** is a beneficial means to reduce the volume of wastewater generated.

Physical treatment systems are processes which rely on physical forces to aid in the removal of pollutants. Physical processes which find frequent use in water pol-

lution control include screening, filtration, sedimentation, and flotation. Screening and filtration are similar methods which are used to separate coarse solids from water. Suspended particles are also removed from water with the use of sedimentation processes. Just as in air pollution control, sedimentation devices utilize gravity to remove the heavier particles from the water stream. The wide array of sedimentation basins in use slow down the water velocity in the unit to allow time for the particles to drop to the bottom. Likewise, flotation uses differences in particle densities, which in this case are lower than water, to effect removal. Fine gas bubbles are often introduced to assist this process; they attach to the particulate matter, causing them to rise to the top of the unit where they are mechanically removed.

Chemical treatment systems in water pollution control are those processes which utilize chemical reactions to remove water pollutants or to form other, less toxic, compounds. Typical chemical treatment processes are chemical **precipitation**, adsorption, and disinfection reactions. Chemical precipitation processes utilize the addition of chemicals to the water in order to bring about the precipitation of dissolved solids. The solid is then removed by a physical process such as sedimentation or filtration. Chemical precipitation processes are often used for the removal of heavy metals and **phosphorus** from water streams. Adsorption processes are used to separate soluble substances from the water stream. Like air pollution adsorption processes, activated carbon is the most widely used adsorbent. Water may be passed through beds of granulated activated carbon (GAC), or powdered activated carbon (PAC) may be added in order to facilitate the removal of dissolved pollutants. Disinfection processes selectively destroy disease-causing organisms such as **bacteria** and viruses. Typical disinfection agents include **chlorine**, **ozone**, and ultraviolet **radiation**.

Biological water pollution control methods are those which utilize biological activity to remove pollutants from water streams. These methods are used for the control of biodegradable organic chemicals, as well as nutrient s such as **nitrogen** and phosphorus. In these systems, **microorganisms** consisting mainly of bacteria convert carbonaceous matter as well as **cell tissue** into gas. There are two main groups of microorganisms which are used in biological treatment, **aerobic** and **anaerobic** microorganisms. Each requires unique environmental conditions to do its job. Aerobic processes occur in the absence of **oxygen**. Both processes may be utilized whether the microorganisms exist in a suspension or are attached to a surface. These processes are termed suspended growth and fixed film processes, respectively.

Solid pollution control methods which are typically used include landfilling, **composting**, and incineration.

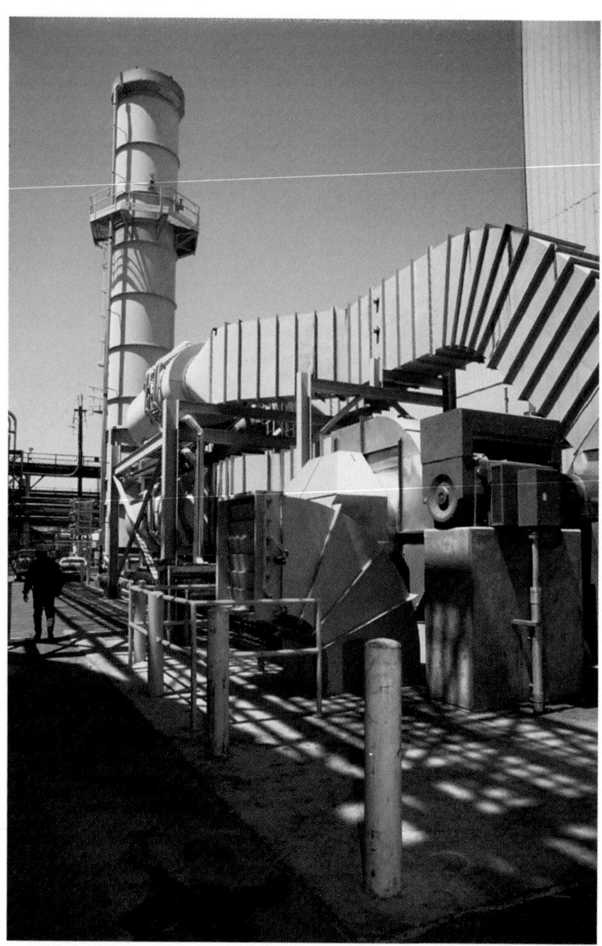

Equipment for the complete recovery and control of air, acids, and oxide emissions.

Sanitary **landfills** are operated by spreading the solid waste in compact layers which are separated by a thin layer of **soil**. Aerobic and anaerobic microorganisms help to break down the **biodegradable** substances in the landfill and produce carbon dioxide and methane gas which is typically vented to the surface. Landfills also generate a strong wastewater called leachate which must be collected and treated to avoid groundwater **contamination**.

Composting of solid wastes is the microbiological biodegradation of organic matter under either aerobic or anaerobic conditions. This process is most applicable for readily biodegradable solids such as sewage sludge, **paper**, food waste, and household garbage, including garden waste and organic matter. This process can be carried out in static pile, agitated beds, or a variety of reactors.

In an incineration process, solids are burned in large furnaces thereby reducing the volume of solid wastes which enter landfills, as well as reducing the possibility of groundwater contamination. Incineration residue can

also be used for **metal** reclamation. These systems are typically supplemented with air pollution control devices.

Further Reading

Advanced Emission Control for Power Plants. Paris: Organization for Economic Cooperation and Development, 1993.

Handbook of Air Pollution Technology. New York: Wiley, 1984.

Jorgensen, E. P., ed. *The Poisoned Well: New Strategies for Groundwater Protection.* Washington, DC: Island Press, 1989.

Kenworthy, L., and E. Schaeffer. *A Citizens Guide to Promoting Toxic Waste Reduction.* New York: INFORM, 1990.

Wentz, C. A. *Hazardous Waste Management.* New York: McGraw-Hill, 1989.

Polonium see **Element, chemical**

Polybrominated biphenyls (PBBs)

Polybrominated biphenyls (or PBBs) are chemicals used to make **plastics** flame retardant. In Michigan in the early 1970s one type of PBB was accidentally mixed into **livestock** feed and fed to farm animals, resulting in sickening and/or death of tens of thousands of animals. A large portion of Michigan's 9 million residents became ill as a result of eating contaminated meat or poultry.

Polybrominated biphenyls are made from a chemical known as **benzene** (sometimes referred to as " phenyl") which is derived from **coal** tar. Benzene contains 6 **carbon atoms** connected in a hexagonal ring formation with two **hydrogen** atoms attached to each carbon atom along the outside of the ring. Two benzene rings can be linked together to form a diphenyl **molecule**. When a bromine atom replaces one of the hydrogen atoms on the phenyl rings, the compound is said to be "brominated;" when more than one such replacement occurs the compound is "polybrominated." The term "polybrominated biphenyl" is somewhat imprecise since it does not specify how many bromine atoms are present or to which carbon atoms they are attached.

One specific type of PBB, hexabrominated biphenyl (which contains 6 bromine atoms), was developed for use as a flame retardant for plastics. This white crystalline solid is incorporated into the hard plastics used to make telephones, calculators, hair dryers, televisions, **automobile** fixtures, and similar other objects at risk of overheating. The advantage of using hexabrominated biphenyl in plastics is that when they are exposed to flame, the presence of the PBB allows the plastic to melt (rather than catch on fire) and therefore flow away from the ignition source. The primary disadvantage of this material is its high toxicity; in fact, similar compounds are used in **pesticides** and **herbicides** due to their ability to effectively kill **insects** and weeds at very low levels. Another **negative** side effect is its ability to persist in the environment for long periods of time.

In the early 1970s hexabrominated biphenyl was manufactured by a small chemical company in Michigan under the trade name Firemaster BP-6 (BP-6 stood for BiPhenyl,6 bromine atoms). BP-6 was sold to companies making various plastics and in 1973 alone, over 3 million pounds of this material were sold. The same company also manufactured **magnesium** oxide, another white crystalline solid material, which is used as an additive in cattle feed to improve digestion. Due to poor labeling procedures it is believed that thousands of pounds of Firemaster were mistakenly identified as magnesium oxide and shipped to companies which manufactured **animal** feed. As a result, tons of livestock feed were contaminated with hexabrominated biphenyl. When this feed was given to cattle and poultry they also became contaminated with PBBs.

Many of the animals developed minor symptoms such as disorientation. Others become severely ill, with internal hemorrhaging or skin lesions, while many others died. (Controlled animal feeding studies later showed that PBBs can cause gastrointestinal hemorrhages, liver damage, as well as well as **birth defects** like exencephaly, a deformation of the skull.) When their cattle began sickening and dying the farmers were understandably upset, but since they didn't know the cause of the problem, they didn't realize the tainted meat from these animals posed a health risk. Therefore, meat from some of the sick animals was incorporated into animal feed which in turn contaminated other animals. Worse still, meat from the healthier cows which were slaughtered was sold for human consumption. Also, poultry which consumed the contaminated feed laid eggs containing high levels of PBBs. A tremendous number of people in Michigan and beyond (estimated at greater than 9 million individuals), unwittingly ingested health-threatening quantities of PBBs.

The symptoms of PBB ingestion in humans depend upon the **concentration** and varies with the individual but stomach aches, abnormal bleeding, loss of balance, skin lesions, joint pains, and loss of resistance to disease are common. Hundreds of farm families developed extended illnesses as a result of PBB **contamination**. All told, long-term contamination for many Michigan residents occurred and because the long term effects of PBBs are still not fully understood, it may be decades before the true impact of this crisis is known.

Polychlorinated biphenyls (PCBs)

Polychlorinated biphenyls are a mixture of compounds having from one to ten **chlorine** atoms attached to a biphenyl ring structure. There are 209 possible structures theoretically; the manufacturing process results in approximately 120 different structures. PCBs resist biological and **heat** degradation and were once used in numerous applications, including dielectric fluids in capacitors and transformers, **heat transfer** fluids, hydraulic fluids, plasticizers, dedusting agents, adhesives, dye carriers in carbonless copy **paper**, and pesticide extenders. The United States manufactured PCBs from 1929 until 1977, when they were banned due to adverse environmental effects and ubiquitous occurrence. They bioaccumulate in organisms and can cause skin disorders, liver dysfunction, reproductive disorders, and **tumor** formation. They are one of the most abundant organochlorine contaminants found throughout the world.

Polycyclic aromatic hydrocarbons

Polycyclic aromatic hydrocarbons, or polynuclear aromatic hydrocarbons, are a family of hydrocarbons containing two or more closed aromatic ring structures, each based on the structure of **benzene**. The simplest of these chemicals is naphthalene, consisting of two fused benzene rings. Sometimes there is limited substitution of **halogens** for the **hydrogen** of polycyclic aromatic hydrocarbons, in which case the larger category of chemicals is known as polycyclic aromatic compounds. Some of the better known polycyclic aromatic compounds in environmental **chemistry** include anthracene, benzopyrene, benzofluoranthene, benzanthracene, dibenzanthracene, phenanthrene, pyrene, and perylene.

Benzopyrene, for example, is an organic chemical with the general formula $C_{20}H_{12}$, containing a five-ring structure. Benzopyrene is extremely insoluble in **water** but very soluble in certain organic solvents such as benzene. There are various isomers, or structural variants of benzopyrene which differ greatly in their toxicological properties. The most poisonous form is benzo(a)pyrene, which is believed to be highly carcinogenic. In contrast, benzo(e)pyrene is not known to be carcinogenic. Similarly, benzo(b)fluoranthene demonstrates carcinogenicity in laboratory assays, but benzo(k)fluoranthene does not.

Benzo(a)pyrene and other polycyclic aromatic compounds are among the diverse products of the incomplete oxidation of organic fuels, such as **coal**, oil, **wood**, and organic wastes. Consequently, polycyclic aromatic compounds can be found in the waste gases of coal- and oil-fired generating stations, steam plants, **petroleum** refineries, incinerators, and coking ovens. Polycyclic aromatic compounds are also present in the exhaust gases emitted from diesel and internal **combustion** engines of vehicles, in fumes from barbecues, in smoke from wood stoves and fireplaces, and in cigarette, cigar, and pipe smoke. Residues of polycyclic aromatic compounds are also found in burnt toast, barbecued meat, smoked **fish**, and other foods prepared by charring. Forest fires are an important natural source of **emission** of polycyclic aromatic compounds to the atmospheric environment.

Many human cancers, probably more than half, are believed to result from some environmental influence. Because some polycyclic aromatic compounds are strongly suspected as being carcinogens, and are commonly encountered in the environment, they are considered to be an important problem in terms of toxicity potentially caused to humans. The most important human exposures to polycyclic aromatic compounds are voluntary and are associated, for example, with cigarette smoking and eating barbecued foods. However, there is also a more pervasive **contamination** of the atmospheric environment with polycyclic aromatic compounds, resulting from emissions from power plants, refineries, automobiles, and other sources. This chronic contamination largely occurs in the form of tiny particulates that are within the size range that is retained by the lungs upon inhalation (that is, smaller than about 3 æm in diameter).

Both voluntary and non-voluntary exposures to polycyclic aromatic compounds are considered to be important environmental problems. However, the most intense exposures are caused by cigarette smoking. These are also among the most easily prevented sources of emission of these (and other) toxic chemicals.

See also Carcinogen; Hydrocarbon.

Further Reading

Harvey, R.G. *Polycyclic Aromatic Hydrocarbons*. VCH Publications, 1997.

Polyester see **Artificial fibers**; **Polymer**

Polyethylene see **Polymer**

Polygons

Polygons are closed **plane** figures bounded by three or more line segments. In the world of **geometry**, poly-

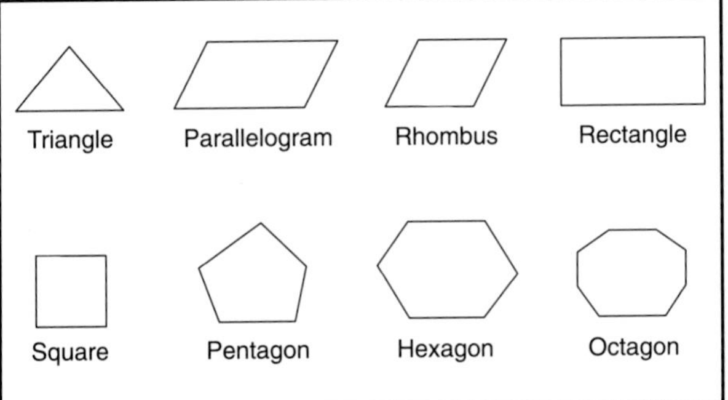

Figure 1.

gons abound. The term refers to a multisided geometric form in the plane. The number of angles in a polygon always equals the number of sides.

Polygons are named to indicate the number of their sides or number of noncollinear points present in the polygon.

A **square** is a special type of polygon, as are triangles, parallelograms, and octagons. The prefix of the term, *poly* comes from the Greek word for many, and the root word *Gon* comes from the Greek word for **angle**.

Classification

A regular polygon is one whose whose sides and interior angles are congruent. Regular polygons can be inscribed by a **circle** such that the circle is tangent to the sides at the centers, and circumscribed by a circle such that the sides form chords of the circle. Regular polygons are named to indicate the number of their sides or number of vertices present in the figure. Thus, a hexagon has six sides, while a decagon has ten sides. Examples of regular polygons also include the familiar square and octagon.

Not all polygons are regular or symmetric. Polygons for which all interior angles are less than 180° are called convex. Polygons with one or more interior angles greater than 180° are called concave.

The most common image of a polygon is of a multisided perimeter enclosing a single, uninterrupted area. In reality, the sides of a polygon can intersect to form multiple, distinct areas. Such a polygon is classified as reflex.

Angles

In a polygon, the line running between non-adjacent points is known as a diagonal. The diagonals drawn from a single vertex to the remaining vertices in an n-sided polygon will divide the figure into n-2 triangles. The sum of the interior angles of a convex polygon is then just (n-2)* 180.

KEY TERMS

Angle—a figure formed by two lines Diagonal: the line which links-connects any two non adjacent vertices

Concave—A polygon whose at least one angle is larger than the straight angle (180°)

Convex—A polygon whose all angles are less than the straight angle (180°)

Equiangular—A polygon is equiangular if all of its angles are identical

Equilateral—A polygon is equilateral if all the sides are equal in length

Parallelogram—a rectangle with both pair of sides parallel

Perimeter—the sum of the length of all sides

Rectangle—a parallelogram in which all angles are right angles

Reflex polygon—a polygon in which two non-adjacent sides intersect

Regular polygon—an equilateral, equiangular polygon

Rhombus—a parallelogram whose adjacent sides are equal

Square—a rectangle whose sides are equal

Vertex—a point where any two of the straight lines connect

If the side of a polygon is extended past the intersecting adjacent side, it defines the *exterior* angle of the vertex. Each vertex of a convex polygon has two possible exterior angles, defined by the continuation of each of the sides. These two angles are congruent, however, so the exterior angle of a polygon is defined as one of the two angles. The sum of the exterior angles of any convex polygon is equal to 360 degrees.

Kristin Lewotsky

Polyhedron

A polyhedron is a three-dimensional closed surface or solid, bounded by **plane** figures called **polygons**.

The word polyhedron comes from the Greek prefix *poly-* , which means "many," and the root word *hedron*

TABLE 1 . POLYGONS		
Name of the polygon	*Number of sides in polygon*	*Number of vertices of polygon*
Triangle	3	3
Rectangle	4	4
Pentagon	5	5
Hexagon	6	6
Heptagon	7	7
Octagon	8	8
Nonagon	9	9
Decagon	10	10
n-gon	n	n

which refers to "surface." A polyhedron is a solid whose boundaries consist of planes. Many common objects in the world around us are in the shape of polyhedrons. The cube is seen in everything from dice to clock-radios; CD cases, sticks of butter, or the World Trade Center towers are in the shape of polyhedrons called parallelpipeds. The pyramids are a type of polyhedron, as are **geodesic** domes. Most shapes formed in nature are irregular. In an interesting exception, however, crystals grow in mathematically perfect, and frequently complex, polyhedrons.

The bounding polygons of a polyhedron are called the faces. The line segments along which the faces meet are called the edges. The points at which the ends of edges intersect (think of the corner of a cereal box) are the vertices. Vertices are connected through the body of the polyhedron by an imaginary line called a diagonal.

A polyhedron is classified as convex if a diagonal contains only points inside of the polyhedron. Convex polyhedrons are also known as Euler polyhedrons, and can be defined by the equation $E=v+f-e=2$, where v is the number of vertices, f is the number of faces, and e is the number of edges. The intersection of a plane and a polyhedron is called the **cross section** of the polyhedron. The cross-sections of a convex polyhedron are all convex polygons.

Types of polyhedrons

Polyhedrons are classified and named according to the number and type of faces. A polyhedron with four sides is a **tetrahedron**, but is also called a **pyramid**. The six-sided cube is also called a hexahedron. A polyhedron with six rectangles as sides also has many names—a rectangular parallelepided, rectangular **prism**, or box.

A polyhedron whose faces are all regular polygons congruent to each other, whose polyhedral angels are all equal, and which has the same number of faces meet at each vertex is called a regular polyhedron. Only five regular polyhedrons exist: the tetrahedron (four triangular faces), the cube (six square faces), the octahedron (eight triangular faces—think of two pyramids placed bottom to bottom), the dodecahedron (twelve pentagonal faces), and the icosahedron (twenty triangular faces).

Other common polyhedrons are best described as the same as one of previously named that has part of it cut off, or truncated, by a plane. Imagine cutting off the corners of a cube to obtain a polyhedron formed of triangles and squares, for example.

Kristin Lewotsky

Polymer

Polymers are made up of extremely large, chain-like molecules consisting of numerous, smaller, repeating units called monomers. Polymer chains, which could be compared to paper clips linked together to make a long strand, appear in varying lengths. They can have branches, become intertwined, and can have cross-links. In addition, polymers can be composed of one or more types of **monomer** units, they can be joined by various kinds of chemical bonds, and they can be oriented in different ways. Monomers can be joined together by addition, in which all the **atoms** in the monomer are present in the polymer, or by condensation, in which a small **molecule** byproduct is also formed. Addition polymers include polyethylene, polypropylene, Teflon, Lucite, and rubber. etc. Condensation polymers include nylon, Dacron, and Formica.

The importance of polymers is evident as they occur widely both in the natural world in such materials as wool, hair, silk and sand, and in the world of synthetic materials in nylon, rubber, **plastics**, Styrofoam, and many other materials. The usefulness of polymers depends on their specific properties. Some of the sought-after properties of the synthetic polymers over natural ones include greater strength, non-reactivity with other substances, non-stickiness, and light weight. Modern lifestyles rely heavily on qualities of the readily available synthetic polymers.

History

Although the 1920s became known as the "plastic age" and the plastic industry did not really boom until World War II, chemists actually began modifying very large, natural macromolecules, such as **cellulose**, in 1861. In the strict sense, plastic means materials that can be softened and molded by **heat** and **pressure** but the term is also sometimes used to describe other macromolecular (large-molecule) materials, whether they be structural materials, films, or fibers. The first plastic material, prepared by Alexander Parkes when he mixed nitrocellulose with **wood** naphtha, was patented as "Parkesine" but this material found few commercial uses. The product was improved by Daniel Spill and marketed as "Xylonite" which found a market in combs and shirt collars. In 1884, it was adopted by the Sheffield cutlery industry for producing cheaper knife handles than the traditional bone.

In 1870, in response to a contest offering $10,000 to find a substitute for the costly ivory used to make billiard balls, John Wesley Hyatt again improved on the easily deformed and flammable "Parkesine." The new product "Celluloid," though still flammable, could be molded into smooth, hard balls and proved to be not only a substitute for ivory billiard balls, but also replaced the expensive tortoise-shell used for mirror backings and hair or tooth brushes. It became the material of choice for George Eastman in 1889 in the development of roll film for snapshots and movies, and as such, brought in large profits.

With the success of these products, chemists began experimenting with other natural products. By the turn of the century a Bavarian chemist, Adolf Spitteler, added formaldehyde to milk and produced an ivory-like substance called "Galalith" that was used in button-making. At this time, scientists also began working with small molecules to produce large ones rather than just trying to modify large, natural molecules. Around 1910 in a reaction between phenol and formaldehyde, the Belgian photographic chemist Leo H. Baekeland produced a black, hard plastic he called Bakelite that proved to be a good insulator and a pleasing substance for use in making telephones and household appliances. It wasn't until the 1920s that plastics were produced that could be mixed with pigments to produce color.

It was about 1930 when scientists first began to understand and accept the evidence that polymers were giant, chain-like molecules that were flexible. American chemists were more receptive to these new ideas than were their European counterparts. In 1928 Du Pont chemical company, whose major research interest prior to this point had been gunpowder manufacture, hired Wallace H. Carothers, a chemist who chose polymer formation as his basis for research. He was able to show how the individual units of the polymer chain joined together chemically and resulted in chain growth. He soon developed a new fiber which was marketed by Du Pont in 1938 as Nylon. It turned out to be Du Pont's greatest money-maker and was extremely important for use in parachutes in World War II. At about the same time two other chemists, Gibson and Fawcett, who were working in England, discovered polyethylene which had an important role in World War II as **radar** insulators. Clearly, the "Age of Plastics" was in full swing.

Polymers and plastics

Polymers are extremely large molecules composed of long chains, much like paper clips that are linked together to make a long strand. The individual subunits, which can range from as few as 50 to more than 20,000, are called monomers (from the Greek *mono* meaning one and *meros* meaning part). Because of their large size, polymers (from the Greek *poly* meaning many) are referred to as macromolecules.

Like strands of paper clips, polymer chains can be of varying lengths, they can have branches and they can

become intertwined. Polymers can be made of one or more kinds of monomer units, they can be joined by different kinds of chemical bonds and they can be oriented differently. Each of these variations either produces a different polymer or gives the existing polymer different properties. All of these possibilities provide numerous opportunities for research and there are more chemists employed in the polymer industry than in any other branch of **chemistry**. Their job is to modify existing polymers so that they have more desirable properties and to synthesize new ones.

Although polymers are often associated only with man-made materials, there are many polymers that occur in nature such as wood, silk, **cotton**, DNA, RNA, starch, and even sand and **asbestos**. They can make the material soft as in goose down, strong and delicate as in a spider web, or smooth and lustrous as in silk. Examples of man-made polymers include plastics such as polyethylene, styrofoam, Saran wrap, etc.; fibers such as nylon, Dacron, rayon, Herculon, etc.; and other materials such as Formica, Teflon, PVC piping, etc. In all of these synthetic compounds, man is trying to make substitutes for materials that are in short supply or too expensive, or is trying to improve the properties of the material to make it more useful.

Most synthetic polymers are made from the non-renewable resource, **petroleum**, and as such, the "age of plastics" is limited unless other ways are found to make them. Since most polymers have **carbon** atoms as the basis of their structure, in theory at least, there are numerous materials that could be used as starting points. But the research and development process is long and costly and replacement polymers, if they ever become available, are a long way in the future. Disposing of plastics is also a serious problem, both because they contribute to the growing mounds of garbage accumulating everyday and because most are not biodegradable. Researchers are busy trying to find ways to speed-up the **decomposition** time which, if left to occur naturally, can take decades.

Recycling is obviously a more economical and practical solution to both the **conservation** and disposal of this valuable resource. Only about 1% of plastics are currently recycled and the rest goes into municipal waste, making up about 30% by **volume**. Because different plastics have different chemical compositions, recycling them together yields a cheap, low-grade product called "plastic lumber." These plastics are usually ground up and the chips are bonded together for use in such things as landscaping timbers or park benches. For a higher grade material, the plastics must be separated into like kinds. To facilitate this process, many plastics today are stamped with a recycling code number between one and six that identifies the most common types. Then, depending on the kind, the plastic can be melted or ground and reprocessed. New ways of reprocessing and using this recycled plastic are constantly being sought.

Addition polymers

In order for monomers to chemically combine with each other and form long chains, there must be a mechanism by which the individual units can join or bond to each other. One method by which this happens is called addition because no atoms are gained or lost in the process. The monomers simply "add" together and the polymer is called an addition polymer.

The simplest chemical structure by which this can happen involves monomers that contain double bonds (sharing two pairs of electrons). When the double bond breaks and changes into a single bond, each of the other two electrons are free and available to join with another monomer that has a free **electron**. This process can continue on and on. Polyethylene is an example of an addition polymer. The polymerization process can be started by using heat and pressure or ultraviolet light or by using another more reactive chemical such as a peroxide. Under these conditions the double bond breaks leaving extremely reactive unpaired electrons called free radicals. These free radicals react readily with other free radicals or with double bonds and the polymer chain starts to form.

Different catalysts yield polymers with different properties because the size of the molecule may vary and the chains may be linear, branched, or cross-linked. Long linear chains of 10,000 or more monomers can pack very close together and form a hard, rigid, tough plastic known as high-density polyethylene or HDPE. Bottles for milk, **water**, **bleach**, **soap**, etc. are usually made of HDPE. It can be recognized by the recycling code number 2 that is marked on the bottom of the bottles.

Shorter, branched chains of about 500 monomers of ethylene cannot pack as closely together and this kind of polymer is known as low-density polyethylene or LDPE. It is used for plastic food or garment bags, spray bottles, plastic lids, etc. and has a recycling code number 4. Polyethylene belongs to a group of plastics called thermoplastic polymers because it can be softened by heating and then remolded.

The ethylene monomer has two **hydrogen** atoms bonded to each carbon for a total of four hydrogen atoms that are not involved in the formation of the polymer. Many other polymers can be formed when one or more of these hydrogen atoms are replaced by some other atom or group of atoms. Polyvinyl chloride (PVC), with a recycling code number 3, is formed if one of the hydro-

gen atoms is replaced by a **chlorine** atom. Polypropylene (P/P), with a recycling code number 5, is formed if one hydrogen atom is replaced by a methyl (CH_3) group. Polystyrene (PS) with a recycling code number 6 is formed if one hydrogen atom is replaced by a phenyl (C_6H_5) group. Other polymers that are derivatives of ethylene include polyacrylonitrile (known by the trade name Orlon or Acrilan), when one hydrogen is replaced by a cyanide (CN) group; polymethyl methacrylate (trade name Plexiglas or Lucite), when one hydrogen is replaced by a methyl (CH_3) group and another is replaced by a CO_2CH_3 group; and polytetrafluoroethylene (Teflon), when all four hydrogen atoms are replaced by fluorine atoms.

Natural and synthetic rubbers are both addition polymers. Natural rubber is obtained from the sap that oozes from rubber trees. It was named by Joseph Priestley who used it to rub out pencil marks, hence, its name, a rubber. Natural rubber can be decomposed to yield monomers of isoprene. It was used by the early American Indians to make balls for playing games as well as for water-proofing footwear and other garments. But, useful as it was, it also had undesirable properties. It was sticky and smelly when it got too hot and it got hard and brittle in cold **weather**. These undesirable properties were eliminated when, in 1839, Charles Goodyear accidentally spilled a mixture of rubber and **sulfur** onto a hot stove and found that it did not melt but rather formed a much stronger but still elastic product. The process, called **vulcanization**, led to a more stable rubber product that withstood heat (without getting sticky) and cold (without getting hard) as well as being able to recover its original shape after being stretched. The sulfur makes cross-links in the long polymer chain and helps give it strength and resiliency, that is, if stretched, it will spring back to its original shape when the stress is released.

Because the supply of natural rubber was limited and because it had still other undesirable properties, chemists began experimenting to find synthetic products that would be even better than natural rubber. Today there are many monomers and mixtures of two or three different monomers, called copolymers, that can polymerize to form rubberlike substances. Neoprene, produced from 2-chlorobutadiene, was one of the first synthetic rubbers. The biggest commercial product in the United States is the copolymer, styrene-butadiene or SBR, which is composed of one styrene monomer for every three butadiene monomers.

Condensation polymers

A second method by which monomers bond together to form polymers is called condensation. The formation of condensation polymers is more complex that the formation of addition polymers. Unlike addition polymers, in which all the atoms of the monomers are present in the polymer, two products result from the formation of condensation polymers, the polymer itself and another small molecule which is often, but not always, water. These polymers can form from a single kind of monomer, or, copolymers can form if two or more different monomers are involved. Most of the natural polymers are formed by condensation.

One of the simplest of the condensation polymers is a type of nylon called nylon 6. It is formed from an **amino acid**, 6-aminohexanoic acid that has six carbon atoms in it, hence the name nylon 6. All amino acids molecules have an amine group (NH_2) at one end and a carboxylic acid (COOH) group at the other end. A polymer forms when a hydrogen atom from the amine end of one molecule and an oxygen-hydrogen group (OH) from the carboxylic acid end of a second molecule split off and form a water molecule. The monomers join together as a new **chemical bond** forms between the **nitrogen** and carbon atoms. This new bond is called an amide linkage. Polymers formed by this kind of condensation reaction are referred to as polyamides. The new molecule, just like each of the monomers from which it formed, also has an amine group at one end (that can add to the carboxylic acid group of another monomer) and it has a carboxylic acid group at the other end (that can add to the amine end of another monomer). The chain can continue to grow and form very large polymers. Each time a monomer is added to the chain, a small molecule by-product of water is also formed.

All of the various types of nylons are polyamides because the condensation reaction occurs between an amine group and an acid group. The most important type of nylon is a copolymer called nylon 66, so-named because each of the monomers from which it forms has six carbon atoms. Nylon 66 is formed from adipic acid and hexamethylenediamine. Adipic acid has a carboxylic acid group at both ends of the molecule and the hexamethylenediamine molecule has an amine group at both ends of the molecule. The polymer is formed as alternating monomers of adipic acid and hexamethylenediamine bond together in a condensation reaction and a water molecule splits away.

Nylon became a commercial product for Du Pont when their research scientists were able to draw it into long, thin, symmetrical filaments. As these polymer chains line up side-by-side, weak chemical bonds called hydrogen bonds form between adjacent chains. This makes the filaments very strong. Nylon was first introduced to the public as nylon stockings (replacing the weaker natural fiber, silk) in October, 1939 in Delaware.

Four thousand pairs sold in no time. A few months later, four million pairs sold in New York City in just one day. But the new found treasure was short-lived since, when the United States entered World War II in December, 1941, all the nylon went into making war materials. Women again had to rely on silk, rayon, cotton and some even went to painting their legs. Nylon hosiery did not become available again until 1946.

Another similar polymer of the polyamide type is the extremely light-weight but strong material known as Kevlar. It is used in bullet-proof vests, **aircraft**, and in recreational uses such as canoes. Like nylon, one of the monomers from which it is made is terephthalic acid. The other one is phenylenediamine.

Polyesters are another type of condensation polymer, so-called because the linkages formed when the monomers join together are called esters. Probably the best known polyester is known by its trade name, Dacron. It is a copolymer of terephthalic acid (which has a carboxylic acid at both ends) and **ethylene glycol** (which has an **alcohol**, OH group), at both ends. A molecule of water forms when the OH group from the acid molecule splits away and bonds with a hydrogen atom from the alcohol group. The new polymer is called polyethylene terephthalate or PET and can be recognized by its recycling code number 1.

Dacron is used primarily in fabrics and clear beverage bottles. Films of Dacron can be coated with metallic oxides, rolled into very thin sheets (only about one-thirtieth the thickness of a human hair), magnetized and used to make audio and video tapes. When used in this way, it is extremely strong and goes by the trade name Mylar. Because it is not chemically reactive, and is not toxic, allergenic or flammable, and because it does not promote blood-clotting, it can be used to replace human **blood** vessels when they are severely blocked and damaged or to replace the skin of **burn** victims.

There are other important condensation polymers that are formed by more complex reactions. These include the formaldehyde **resins** the first of which was Bakelite. These plastics are thermosetting plastics; that is, once they are molded and formed, they become permanently hard and they cannot be softened and remolded. Today their major use is in plywood adhesives, Melmac for dinnerware, Formica for table and counter tops, and other molding compounds.

Polycarbonate polymers are known for their unusual toughness, yet they are so clear that they are used for "bullet-proof" windows and in visors for space helmets. The tough, baked-on finishes of automobiles and major appliances are cross-linked polymers formed from an alcohol, such as **glycerol**, and an acid, such as phthalic acid, and are called alkyds. Silicone oils and rubbers are condensation polymers that have silicon rather than carbon as part of their structural form. These compounds are generally more stable at high temperatures and more fluid at low temperatures than the carbon compounds. They are often used for parts in space ships and jet planes.

KEY TERMS

Addition polymer—Polymers formed when the individual units are joined together without the gain or loss of any atoms.

Condensation polymer—Polymers formed when the individual units are joined together with the splitting off of a small molecule by-product.

Copolymer—Polymers formed from two or more different monomers.

Macromolecule—A giant molecule.

Monomers—Small, individual subunits which join together to form polymers.

Plastics—A group of natural or synthetic polymers that are capable of being softened and molded by heat and pressure; also sometimes used to include other structural materials, films and fibers.

Polyamide—A polymer, such as nylon, in which the monomers are joined together by amide linkages.

Polyester—A polymer, such as Dacron, in which the monomers are joined together by ester linkages.

Polymer—Extremely large molecules made of numerous, small, repeating units.

Recycling code—Numbers between one and six that are stamped on many plastics and used for recycling purposes which identify the various kinds of polymers.

See also Artificial fibers.

Further Reading

Ball, Philip. *Designing the Molecular World: Chemistry at the Frontier.* Princeton: Princeton University Press, 1994.

Brock, William H. *The Norton History of Chemistry.* New York: W. W. Norton & Company, 1993.

Gordon, J.E. *The New Science of Strong Materials.* Princeton: Princeton University Press, 1976.

Newhouse, Elizabeth L. et al, eds, *Inventors and Discovers: Changing Our World.* Washington, D. C.: National Geographic Society, 1988.

Rodriguez, F. *Principles of Polymer Systems.* New York: McGraw-Hill Book Co, 1982.

Treloar, L.R.G. *Introduction to the Polymer Science.* London: Taylor and Francis Ltd.: 1982.

Leona B. Bronstein

Polymerization see **Polymer**

Polynomials

Polynomials are among the most common expressions in **algebra**. Each is just the sum of one or more powers of x, with each power multiplied by various numbers. In formal language, a polynomial in one **variable**, x, is the sum of terms ax^k where k is a non-negative integer and a is a constant. Polynomials are to algebra about what **integers** or whole numbers are to **arithmetic**. They can be added, subtracted, multiplied, and factored. Division of one polynomial by another may leave a remainder.

There are various words that are used in conjunction with polynomials. The degree of a polynomial is the **exponent** of the highest power of x. Thus the degree of

$$2x^3 + 5x^2 - x + 2$$

is 3. The leading **coefficient** is the coefficient of the highest power of x. Thus the leading coefficient of the above equation is 2. The constant term is the term that is the coefficent of x^0 (=1). Thus the constant term of the above equation is 2 whereas the constant term of $x^3 + 5x^2 + x$ is 0.

The most general form for a polynomial in one variable is

$$a_nx^n + a_n\text{-}1x^{n-1} +. .. + a_1x + a_0$$

where a_n, a_{n-1},. . ., a_1, a_0 are **real numbers**. They can be classified according to degree. Thus a first degree polynomial, $a_1x + a_2$, is, is linear; a second degree polynomial $a_1x^2 + a_2x + a_3$ is quadratic; a third degree polynomial, $a_3x^3 + a_2x^2 + a_1x+a_0$ is a cubic and so on. An irreducible or prime polynomial is one that has no factors of lower degree than a constant. For example, $2x^2 + 6$ is an irreducible polynomial although 2 is a factors. Also $x^2 + 1$ is irreducible even though it has the factors x + i and x - i that involve **complex numbers**. Any polynomial is the product of of irreducible polynomials just as every integer is the product of **prime numbers**.

A polynomial in two variables, x and y, is the sum of terms, ax^ky^m where a is a real number and k and m are non-negative integers. For example,

$$x^3y + 3x^2y^2 + 3\ xy -4x + 5y -12$$

is a polynomial in x and y. The degree of such a polynomial is the greatest of the degrees of its terms. Thus the degree of the above equation is 4 - both from x^3y (3 + 1 = 4) and from x^2y^2 (2 + 2 = 4).

Similar definitions apply to polynomials in 3, 4, 5 ellipsevariables but the term "polynomial" without qualification usually refers to a polynomial in one variable.

A polynomial equation is of the form P = 0 where P is a polynomial. A polynomial function is one whose values are given by polynomial.

Further Reading

Roland E Larson and Richard P Hosteler, *Algebra and Trigonometry,* D.C. Health and Company, 1993.

Murray Gechtman, *Precalculus,* Wm. C. Brown Companies, 1992.

Roy Dubisch

Polypeptide see **Protein**

Polysaccharide see **Carbohydrate**

Polystyrene see **Polymer**

Polyunsaturated fat see **Fat**

Polyvinyl chloride see **Polymer**

Pomegranate see **Myrtle family**

Popcorn see **Grasses**

Poplar see **Willow family**

Poppies

Poppies belong to a small family of flowering plants called the Papaveraceae. Poppies are annual, biennial, or perennial herbs, although three New World genera (*Bocconia*, *Dendromecon*, and *Romneya*) are woody shrubs or small trees. The leaves are alternate, lack stipules, and are often lobed or deeply dissected. The flowers are usually solitary, bisexual, showy, and crumpled in the bud. The fruit is a many-seeded capsule which opens by a ring of pores or by valves. One of the most characteristic features of the family is that when cut, the stems or leaves ooze a milky, yellow, orange, or occasionally clear latex from special secretory canals.

The family consists of 23 genera and about 250 species that are primarily distributed throughout northern temperate and arctic regions. The true poppies, which be-

long to the genus *Papaver*, are found mostly in **Europe**, much of **Asia**, the Arctic, and Japan. Only one true poppy occurs naturally in the United States. The only true poppy in the Southern Hemisphere is *P. aculeatum*, which occurs in South **Africa** and **Australia**. In **North America**, members of the poppy family are most common in the Arctic and in the west. Only two members of the poppy family are native to eastern North America. Bloodroot (*Sanguinaria canadensis*) is a common spring **flower** of cool **forests**. When the underground stem (**rhizome**) or roots of bloodroot are broken, they exude a red juice. The celandine poppy (*Stylophorum diphyllum*) is the other native poppy of eastern North America, occurring in rich woods.

In North America it is the west, especially California and adjacent states, that has the highest diversity of poppies. Ten genera of poppies occur in western North America. Perhaps the most interesting of these are the Californian **tree** poppies in the genus *Romneya*. These spectacular plants have attractive gray leaves and large (3.9-5.1 in/10-13 cm across), fragrant, white flowers with an inner ring of bright yellow stamens. *R. coulteri* grows among sun-baked **rocks** and in gullies of parts of southern California and is most abundant in the mountains southeast of Los Angeles; its fleshy stems can reach heights of 9.8 ft (3 m)-more the size of a shrub than a tree. The other, less well known, genus of tree poppy in California is *Dendromecon*, which is one of the few truly woody shrubs of the poppy family. *D. harfordii* is an erect, evergreen shrub that reaches 9.8 ft (3 m) and is found only on the islands of Santa Cruz and Santa Rosa off the coast of California. The tree celandines (*Bocconia*) of Central America truly reach tree size, growing to a maximum height of 23 ft (7 m). Californian poppies, which belong to the genus *Eschscholzia*, are restricted to western North America where they are generally found in arid regions in and around California. Many of the Californian poppies are widely cultivated. Prickly poppies (*Agremone*) are common in western North America.

Many poppies are highly prized as garden ornamentals. Poppies are admired for their delicate yet boldly colored flowers, which may be white, yellow, orange, or red. The blue poppies of the genus *Meconopsis* are special favorites of gardeners because no other genus of poppies contains species with blue flowers, making them something of a beautiful oddity among poppy fanciers. Among the more widely cultivated species are the Iceland poppy (*P. nudicaule*), whose natural distribution is circumboreal, the California poppy (*Eschscholzia californica*) which is the state flower of California, the common poppy (*P. dubium*) of Europe, the oriental poppy (*P. orientale*) from Armenia and Iran, the corn poppy (*P. rhoeas*) of Europe, and many others, including many of those previously discussed from western North America.

Arctic poppies (*Papaver radicatum*).

The most famous and economically important member of the poppy family is the opium poppy (*P. somniferum*). The opium poppy has been cultivated for thousands of years and naturalized in many places. Its origin is uncertain, but it is believed to have come from Asia Minor. Crude opium contains the addictive drugs **morphine** (11%) as well as **codeine** (1%). Morphine is an important pain-killer and heroin is made from morphine. Controlled, commercial supplies for medicinal use are produced mostly in the Near East. The Balkans, the Near East, Southeast Asia, Japan, and China all produce opium and have long histories of its use.

The opium poppy is an annual **plant** and so must be sown each year. Opium is collected once the plant has flowered and reached the fruiting stage. The urn-shaped seed capsules are slit by hand, generally late in the evening. The milky latex oozes out during the night, coagulates, and is then scraped from the capsule in the morning. The coagulated latex is dried and kneaded into balls of crude opium which is then refined. Because the cutting of individual capsules is labor-intensive, opium production is generally restricted to areas with inexpensive labor.

Poppies have a number of lesser uses. The **seeds** of opium poppy are commonly used in baking; the seeds do not contain opium. The corn poppy is cultivated in Europe for the oil in its seeds which compares favorably with olive oil. In Turkey and Armenia the heads of oriental poppies are considered a great delicacy when eaten green. The **taste** has been described as acrid and hot.

The poppy was immortalized as a symbol of remembrance of the supreme sacrifice paid by those who fought in the First World War by Colonel John McCrae in the poem entitled In Flanders Fields, which begins with the lines:" In Flanders fields the poppies blow/Between the crosses, row on row." A red poppy now symbolizes the sacrifice of those who died in the two World Wars and is

KEY TERMS

Latex—A milky, usually white fluid produced by secretory cells of certain flowering plants.

worn on Remembrance Day, November 11, which commemorates the end of World War I.

Further Reading

Bateman, G., ed. *Flowering Plants of the World.* Oxford: Oxford University Press, 1978.

Grey-Wilson, C. *Poppies: A Guide to the Poppy Family in the Wild and in Cultivation.* Portland, OR: Timber Press, 1993.

Les C. Cwynar

Population growth see **Population ecology; Populations, human**

Population growth and control (human)

The numbers of humans on **Earth** have increased enormously during the past several millennia, but especially during the past two centuries. By the end of the twentieth century, the global population of humans was 6.0 billion. That figure is twice the population of 1960, a mere 30 years earlier. Moreover, the human population is growing at about 1.5% annually, equivalent to an additional 89 million people per year. The United Nations Population Fund estimates that there will likely be about nine billion people alive in the year 2050.

In addition, the numbers of animals that live in a domestic **mutualism** with humans have also risen. These companion species must be supported by the **biosphere** along with their human patrons, and can be considered an important component of the environmental impact of the human enterprise. The large domestic animals include about 1.7 billion **sheep** and **goats**, 1.3 billion cows, and 0.3 billion **horses**, **camels**, and **water** buffalo. Humans are also accompanied by a huge population of smaller animals, including 10-11 billion chickens and other fowl.

The biological history of *Homo sapiens* extends more than one million years. For almost all of that history, a relatively small population was engaged in a subsistence lifestyle, involving the hunting of wild animals and the gathering of edible plants. The global population during those times was about a million people. However, the discoveries of crude tools, weapons, and hunting and gathering techniques allowed prehistoric humans to become increasingly more effective in exploiting their environment, which allowed increases in population to occur. About ten thousand years ago, people discovered primitive agriculture through the domestication of a few **plant** and **animal** species, and ways of cultivating them to achieve greater yields of food. These early agricultural technologies and their associated socio-cultural systems allowed an increase in the **carrying capacity** of the environment for humans and their domesticated species. This resulted in steady population growth because primitive agricultural systems could support more people than a hunting and gathering lifestyle.

Further increases in Earth's carrying capacity for the human population were achieved through additional technological discoveries that improved capabilities for controlling and exploiting the environment. These included the discovery of the properties of metals and their alloys, which allowed the manufacturing of superior tools and weapons, and the inventions of the wheel and ships, which permitted the transportation of large amounts of goods. At the same time, further increases in agricultural yields were achieved by advances in the domestication and genetic modification of useful plants and animals, and the discovery of improved methods of cultivation. Due to innovations, the growth of the human population grew from about 300 million people in the year 1 A.D. to 500 million in 1650 A.D.

Around that time, the rate of population growth increased significantly, and continues into the present. The relatively recent and rapid growth of the human population occurred for several reasons. The discovery of better technologies for sanitation and medicine has been especially important, because of the resulting decreases in death rates. This allowed populations to increase rapidly, because of continuing high **birth** rates. There have also been great advances in technologies for the extraction of resources, manufacturing of goods, agricultural production, transportation, and communications, all of which have increased the carrying capacity of the environment for people. Consequently, the number of humans increased to 1 billion in 1850, 2 billion in 1930, 4 billion in 1975, 5 billion in 1987, and 6 billion in 1999. This rapid increase in the population has been labeled the "population explosion." While there are clear signs that the rate of population increase is slowing, estimates show the number of humans on the **planet** to be nine billion in 2050.

Because the populations of humans and large domestic animals have become so big, some predict severe environmental damage caused by **pollution** and overly

intense use of natural resources. If this were to happen, the carrying capacity for the human population would decrease, and famines could occur. A controversial movement in the latter years of the twentieth century for "zero population growth" advocates the widespread use of birth control, in order to maintain the birth rate at equal numbers to the death rate.

Population, human

The number of humans on **Earth** has increased enormously during the past several millennia, but especially rapidly during the last two centuries. Moreover, there is every indication that the already large human population will continue to increase rapidly into the future.

The impact of the human population in some region, or on the **biosphere** as a whole, is a function of two interacting factors: (1) the actual number of humans, and (2) their per-capita environmental impact, which largely depends on the degree of industrialization of the society and on the lifestyles of individuals.

The remarkable growth of the human population has resulted in intense damage to the biosphere, representing a global environmental crisis. The degradation has occurred on a scale and intensity that is comparable to the enormous effects of such geological processes as glaciation.

The size of the human population

Homo sapiens is by far the most abundant large **animal** on Earth. The total population of humans in 1999 was more than 6.0 billion individuals. That enormous population was growing at about 1.5% annually, equivalent to an additional 80 million people per year. If this rate of growth is maintained, the size of the human population would double in only about 47 years, at which time there would be about 12 billion people on Earth.

No other large animal is known to have ever achieved such an enormous abundance. Prior to its overhunting during the nineteenth century the American **bison** (*Bison bison*) numbered about 60-80 million animals and may have been the world's most populous wild large animal. The most abundant large animals in the wild now are the white-tailed **deer** (*Odocoileus virginianus*) of the Americas with 40-60 million individuals, and the crabeater seal (*Lobodon carcinophagus*) of **Antarctica** with 15-30 million. These species have populations less than 1% of that of humans in 1999.

Some other large animals that live in a domestic **mutualism** with humans have also become enormously abundant. These companion species must be supported by the biosphere in concert with their human patrons. Therefore, they can be considered an important component of the environmental impact of the human enterprise. The larger domestic animals include about 1.7 billion **sheep** and **goats**, 1.3 billion cows, and 0.3 billion **horses**, **camels**, and **water** buffalo. Humans are also accompanied by an enormous population of smaller domesticated animals, including 10-11 billion chickens and other fowl.

Carrying capacity and growth of the human population

Populations of organisms change in response to the balance of the rates at which new individuals are added by births and immigration and the rates at which they are lost by deaths and emigration. **Zero** population growth occurs when the growth and loss parameters are in equilibrium. So-called intrinsic population change is only influenced by the balance of births and deaths. These demographic relationships hold for all species, including humans.

The history of *Homo sapiens* extends to somewhat more than one million years. For almost all of that time relatively small populations of humans were engaged in subsistence lifestyles that involved predation upon wild animals and the gathering of edible plants. The global population of humans during those times may have been as large as a million or so individuals. However, occasional discoveries of crude tools, weapons, and improved techniques allowed prehistoric humans to become increasingly more effective in gathering wild foods and hunting animals. This enhanced the ability of humans to exploit ecological resources, allowing increases in population to occur.

About 10,000 years ago, the first significant developments of primitive agriculture began to occur. These included the initial domestication of a few **plant** and animal species and the discoveries of ways of cultivating them to achieve greater yields of food for humans. The development of these early agricultural technologies and their associated socio-cultural systems allowed enormous increases to be achieved in environmental **carrying capacity** for humans and their domesticated species, so that steady population growth could occur. Even primitive agricultural systems could support many more people than could a subsistence lifestyle based on the hunting and gathering of wild animals and plants.

Further enhancements of Earth's carrying capacity for the human enterprise were achieved through other technological discoveries that improved the capability for controlling and exploiting the environment. For example, the discoveries of the properties of metals and

their alloys allowed the development of superior tools and weapons. Similarly, the inventions of the wheel and ships allowed the easy transportation of large quantities of valuable commodities from regions of surplus to those of deficit. At the same time, greatly increased yields in agriculture were achieved through a series of advances in the domestication and genetic modification of useful plants and animals, along with the discovery of better methods of managing the environment to foster the productivity of these species.

Clearly, the **evolution** of human socio-cultural systems has involved a long series of discoveries and innovations that increased the effective carrying capacity of the environment, permitting growth of the population. As a result of this process, there were about 300 million people alive in 0 A.D., and 500 million in 1650.

At about that time the rate of population growth increased significantly, a trend that has been maintained to the present. The recent, unprecedentedly rapid growth of the human population has resulted because of a number of factors. Especially important has been the discovery of increasingly effective technologies for medicine and sanitation, which have greatly decreased death rates in human populations. There have also been enormous advances in the technologies that allow effective extraction of resources, manufacturing, agriculture, transportation, and communications, all of which have achieved further increases in the carrying capacity of the environment for humans.

As a result of these relatively recent developments of the past several centuries, the global abundance of humans increased rapidly to one billion in 1850, two billion in 1930, four billion in 1975, and five billion in 1987. In 1999, the human population surpassed six billion individuals.

More locally, there have been even greater increases in the rate of growth of some human populations. In recent decades some countries have achieved population growth rates of 4% per year, which if maintained would double the population in only 18 years.

These sorts of population growth rates place enormous **pressure** on the ecosystems that must sustain the additional humans and their agricultural and/or industrial activities. For example, the human population of central Sudan was 2.9 million in 1917, but it was 18.4 million in 1977, an increase of 6.4 times. During that same period the population of domestic cattle increased by a **factor** of 20 (to 16 million), camels by 16 times (to 3.7 million), sheep by 12.5 times (to 16 million), and goats by 8.5 times (to 10.4 million). Substantial degradation of the carrying capacity of drylands in that region of **Africa** has been caused by these sorts of increases in the populations of humans and their large-mammal symbionts, and there have been many other ecological damages as well.

Another example of this commonly occurring phenomenon of rapid population growth is the numbers of people in the province of Rondonia in Amazonian Brazil. This population increased 12-fold between 1970 and 1988, mostly through immigration, while the population of cattle increased by 30 times. These population increases were accompanied by intense ecological damage, as the natural **rain forests** were "developed" to sustain humans and their activities.

Future human populations

The growth rate of the global human population achieved a maximum during the late 1960s when it was 2.1% per year. If sustained, this rate was capable of doubling the population in only 33 years. This rate of increase slowed somewhat to 1.5% per year in the 1999, equivalent to a doubling time of 47 years. However, even at that somewhat slowed growth rate, the human population increases by about 80 million people each year.

Reasonable predictions can be made of future increases of the human population. The predictions are based on assumptions about the factors influencing changes in the size of populations, for example in the rates of fecundity, mortality, and other demographic variables. Of course, it is not possible to accurately predict these dynamics because unanticipated changes, or "surprises," may occur. For example, a global war could have an enormous influence on human demographics, as could the emergence of new diseases. AIDS is an example of the latter effect, because this lethal viral disease was unknown prior to the early 1980s.

As a result of these uncertainties, it is not possible to accurately forecast the future abundance of humans. However, reasonable assumptions about demographic parameters can be based on recent trends in birth and death rates. Similarly, changes in the carrying capacity of Earth's regions for the human economy can be estimated from recent or anticipated advances in technology and on predictions of environmental changes that may be caused by human activities. These types of information can be used to model future populations of humans.

A typical prediction of recent population models is that the global abundance of humans could reach about 6.1 billion by the year 2000, and 8.9 billion by 2050. The models tend to predict that the human population could stabilize at about 10-12 billion when zero population growth is achieved.

In summary, it is probable that the global abundance of humans will approximately double from its population

around 1999 before it stabilizes. This prediction is likely to be fulfilled unless there is an unpredicted, intervening catastrophe such as a collapse of the carrying capacity of the environment for the human enterprise, an unprecedented and deadly pandemic, or a holocaust of warfare.

The structure of human populations

Population structure refers to the relative abundance of males and females, and of individuals in various age classes. The latter type of structure is significantly different between growing and stable populations and has important implications for future changes in population size.

Populations that have not been increasing or decreasing for some time have similar proportions in various age classes. In other words, there are comparable numbers of people aged five to 15 years old as those 35-45 years old. The distribution of people is equitable among age classes except for the very young and the very old, for whom there are disproportionately high risks of mortality.

In contrast, populations that are growing rapidly have relatively more young individuals than they do older people. Therefore, the age-class structure of growing populations is triangular, or much wider at the bottom than at the top. For example, more than one-half of the people in a rapidly growing human population can be less than 20 years old. This type of population structure implies an enormous inertia for further growth because of the increasingly larger numbers of people that are continually coming of reproductive age.

Human populations that are growing rapidly for intrinsic reasons have a much higher birth rate than death rate and a markedly triangular age-class structure. The so-called demographic transition refers to the intermediate stage during which birth rates decrease to match death rates. Once this occurs, the age-class structure eventually becomes more equitable in distribution until zero population growth is achieved.

Environmental effects of human populations

The huge increases in size of the human population have resulted in a substantial degradation of environmental conditions. The changes have largely been characterized by **deforestation**, unsustainable harvesting of potentially renewable resources (such as wild animals and plants that are of economic importance), rapid **mining** of non-renewable resources (such as metals and **fossil fuels**), **pollution**, and other ecological damages.

At the same time that human populations have been increasing, there has also been a great intensification of per-capita environmental impacts. This has occurred through the direct and indirect consequences of increased resource use to sustain individual humans and their social and technological infrastructure.

This trend can be illustrated by differences in the intensity of **energy** use among human societies, which also reflect the changes occurring during the history of the evolution of socio-cultural systems. The average per-capita consumption of energy in a hunting society is about 20 megajoules per day (MJ/d), while it is 48 MJ/d in a primitive agricultural society, 104 MJ/d in advanced agriculture, 308 MJ/d for an industrializing society, and 1025 MJ/d for an advanced industrial society. The increases of per-capita energy usage, and of per-capita environmental impact, have been especially rapid during the past century of vigorous technological discoveries and economic growth.

In fact, global per-capita economic productivity and energy consumption have both increased more rapidly during the 20th century than has the human population. This pattern has been most significant in industrialized countries. In 1980, the average citizen of an industrialized country utilized 199 gigajoules of energy, compared with only 17 GJ/yr in less-developed countries. Although industrialized countries only had 25% of the human population, they accounted for 80% of the energy use by humans in 1980. Another illuminating comparison is that

KEY TERMS

Carrying capacity—The maximum population of a species that can be sustained within degrading the quality of the habitat.

Cultural evolution (or socio-cultural evolution)—The process by which human societies adaptively accumulate knowledge and technological capabilities and develop social systems, allowing an increasingly more effective exploitation of environmental resources.

Demography—The science of population statistics.

Demographic transition—This occurs when a rapidly growing population changes from a condition of a high birth rate and a low death rate, to one with a low birth rate that is in balance with the death rate, so that the population stops increasing in size.

Doubling time—The time required for an initial population to double in size.

the world's richest 20% of people consume 86% of the goods and services delivered by the global economy, while the poorest 20% consumes just 1.3%. Therefore, if energy use and economic consumption are used as simple indicators of environmental impacts, the relatively small numbers of people living the resource-intense lifestyles of richer countries are responsible for more of the biosphere's environmental damages than are the more numerous but poorer people that live in less-developed countries.

This observation underscores that fact that population impacts are not only related to raw numbers of people. In this sense, overpopulation does not only involve hordes of poor people. It also involves the smaller numbers of wealthier people who are engaged in environmentally destructive lifestyles.

Further Reading

Ehrlich, P. R., and A. H. Ehrlich. *The Population Explosion.* New York: Simon & Schuster, 1990.

Freedman, B. *Environmental Ecology.* 2nd ed. San Diego: Academic Press, 1994.

Goldemberg, J. *Energy, Technology, Development.* Ambio, 1992.

Polunin, N. (ed.). *Population and Global Security.* Cambridge University Press, 1998.

Shah, A. *Ecology and the Crisis of Overpopulation: Future Prospects for Global Sustainability.* Edward Algar Pub., 1998 .

Bill Freedman

Porcupines

Two families of **rodents** are called porcupines. They all have at least some hair modified into quills. The Old World porcupines belong to family Hystricidae of **Europe**, **Asia**, and **Africa**. The New World porcupines are 10 species of forest dwellers of the family Erethizontidae. The most common of these is the North American porcupine (Erthizon dorsatum). The name *porcupine* means "quill pig," though these rodents are not **pigs**.

Porcupines have one of the most unusual kinds of fur in the **animal** kingdom. Hidden beneath its shaggy brown, yellowish, or black coat of guard hairs is a **mass** of long sharp quills. Quills are actually specialized hairs, solid toward the skin and hollow toward the dark end. They lie flat when the animal is relaxed and rise alarmingly if the animal is startled. When the animal tenses its muscles the quills rise out of the guard hairs, providing a protective shield that keeps enemies away.

They do give warning, however. Either the quills themselves make a rattling sound when shaken or the animal's tail makes a warning sound. The animal also stamps its feet and hisses. If the warnings go unheeded, the animal turns its back and moves quickly backward or sideways toward the approaching **predator**, giving it little time to realize its own danger.

Myth holds that a porcupine can actively shoot its quills into a predator. This is not true. However, if an enemy attacks, the quills stick into its flesh and are easily pulled out of the porcupine's skin. Quills have small barbs on the end that prevent the quill from being pulled out. Instead, they have to be carefully removed, rather like a fishhook. In the wild, quills gradually work their way into the predator's body, harming organs, or into the throat, preventing the animal from eating until it starves to death. The porcupine grows new quills to replace the lost ones within a few weeks.

American porcupines

The North American porcupine has a head-and-body length that averages about 30 in (76 cm), with an upward-angled tail 9 to 10 in (23-25 cm) long. A male porcupine weighs about 14 lbs (6.4 kg), with the female several pounds less. An adult porcupine possesses about 100 quills per square inch (about per 6 sq cm) from its cheeks, on the top of its head, down its back and onto its tail. There are no quills on its undersides or on the hairless bottom of its feet.

Porcupines are primarily woodland and forest animals of all parts of Canada except the Arctic islands and the United States except the **prairie** states and Southeast. Nocturnal animals, they readily climb trees, gripping with powerful, curved claws, and may even stay up in the branches for several days at time. They have typical rodent front teeth. These long incisors are orange in color and they grow continuously. Like **beavers**, porcupines munch **bark** off trees, although they prefer **vegetables** and **fruits**. In spring, however, they go after new buds and leaves. They often swim in order to reach **water** plants. They are made buoyant by their hollow quills.

One of the few animals that willingly takes on a porcupine is the weasel called a fisher. It teases the animal until it is worn out and easily turned over, where its unquilled underparts can be attacked. Some areas of the country that are being overrun by porcupines have introduced fishers to help eliminate them.

In winter, a porcupine develops a thick, woolly coat under its guard hairs and quills. It will spend much of its time in a den, which is usually a hollow **tree**, **cave**, or burrow dug by another animal. It does not hibernate or

A porcupine (*Hystrix africaeaustralis*) with its quills erect.

even **sleep** more than usual. It goes out regularly in the winter to feed.

Adult porcupines are solitary creatures except when mating, after which the male disappears and is not seen again. After a gestation of 29 to 30 weeks, usually a single well-developed baby, sometimes called a porcupette, is born in an underground burrow. The quills of a newborn are few and soft, but they harden within a few hours. The young stay with the mother for about six months before going off on their own. They become sexually mature at about 18 months and live to be about 10 years old if they can avoid cars on highways.

The Brazilian thin-spined porcupine (Chaetomys subspinosus) has quills only on its head. Another species, the prehensile-tailed porcupine (Coendou prehensilis) has a tail almost as long as its body, which can be wrapped around a tree branch to support the animal.

Old World porcupines

Old World porcupines of Africa and Asia are often smaller than New World ones and are more apt to have more than one offspring at time. Their tails are structured so that they make a rattling sound when moved, giving warning to an approaching predator.

The brush-tailed porcupines (Atherurus) have thin tails that end in a brush of white hair. They have more bristles-thick, coarse hair-than quills, which are located only on the back. They climb trees, especially when going after fruit. The long-tailed porcupine (Trichys fasciculata) of Malaysia lacks the rotund body of most porcupines and looks more like a rat. Its few quills cannot be rattled.

The crested porcupine (Hystrix cristata) of Africa has quills that may be as much as 12 in (30 cm) long. The hair on its head and shoulders stands up like a crest which is so coarse as to look like more quills. Crested

KEY TERMS

Incisors—The front cutting teeth of a mammal. In rodents, they grow continuously.

Prehensile—Capable of grasping.

porcupines are more versatile in their habitats than most animals. They can live in **desert**, damp forest, open **grasslands**, and even rocky terrain. Old World Porcupines are regarded as good eating by native people.

Further Reading

Caras, Roger A. *North American Mammals: Fur-bearing Animals of the United States and Canada.* New York: Meredith Press, 1967.

Green, Carl R., and Sanford, William R. *The Porcupine.* Wildlife Habits and Habitat series. Mankato, MN: Crestwood House, 1985.

Jean F. Blashfield

Porpoises see **Cetaceans**

Portuguese man-of-war see **Jellyfish**

Positive number

Positive numbers are commonly defined as numbers greater than **zero**, the numbers to the right of zero on the number line. Zero is not a positive number. The opposite, or additive inverse, of a positive number is a **negative** number. Negative numbers are always preceded by a negative sign (-), while positive numbers are only preceded by a positive sign (+) when it is required to avoid confusion. Thus 15 and +15 are the same positive number.

Positive numbers are used to identify quantities, such as the length of a line, the area of a **circle**, or the **volume** of a glass jar. They are used to identify the magnitude of physical quantities, as well. For example, positive numbers are used to indicate the amount of electric power it takes to light a light bulb, the magnitude of the **force** required to launch a **space** shuttle, the speed required to reach a destination in a fixed time, the amount of **pressure** required pump **water** uphill, and so on.

Very often physical quantities also have a direction associated with them (they are represented by one-dimensional vectors). Positive numbers are used in conjunction with these quantities to indicate the direction. We may arbitrarily choose a certain direction as being positive and call the **velocity**, for instance, positive in that direction. Then a negative velocity corresponds to a velocity in the opposite direction. For instance, if north is chosen as the positive direction, a car traveling due north at a speed of 50 miles per hour has a velocity of 50 mi/hr, and a car traveling due south at 50 miles per hour has a velocity of -50 mi/hr. In other instances, we may say a car has positive velocity when traveling in drive and negative velocity when traveling in reverse.

Force is also a directed quantity. Gravity exerts a force down on all massive bodies. To launch a **space shuttle** requires a force larger than that of gravity, and oppositely directed. If we choose down as positive, then the force of gravity is positive, and the force required for launch will be negative. There must be a net negative force on the shuttle, which really means a positive force larger than gravity applied in the negative direction.

This discussion gives meaning to positive as being greater than zero, or, in a geometric sense, as having a particular direction or location relative to zero. A more fundamental definition of positive numbers is based on the definition of positive **integers** or **natural numbers** such as the ones given by the German mathematician F. L. G. Frege or the Italian Giuseppe Peano. Frege based his ideas on the notion of **one-to-one correspondence** from **set theory**. One-to-one correspondence means that each element of the first set can be matched with one element from the second set, and vice versa, with no elements from either set being left out or used more than once. Pick a set with a given number of elements, say the toes on a human foot. Then, form the collection of all sets with the same number of elements in one-to-one correspondence with the initial set, in this case the collection of every conceivable set with five elements. Finally, define the **cardinal number** 5 as consisting of this collection. Peano defined the natural numbers in terms of 1 and the successors of 1, essentially the same method as counting. Using either the Frege or Peano definitions produces a set of natural numbers that are essentially the same as the positive integers. Ratios of these are the positive rational numbers, from which positive **real numbers** can be derived. In this case, there is no need to consider "greater than 0" as a criterion at all - but this concept can then be derived.

Note that **complex numbers** are not considered to be positive or negative. Real numbers, however, are always positive, negative, or zero.

Further Reading

Boyer, Carl B. *A History of Mathematics.* 2nd ed. Revised by Uta C. Merzbach. New York: John Wiley and Sons, 1991.

Hamilton, A. G. *A First Course in Linear Algebra*. New York: Cambridge University Press, 1987.

Pascoe, L. C. *Teach Yourself Mathematics*. Lincolnwood, Ill: NTC Publishing Group, 1992.

Paulos, John Allen. *Beyond Numeracy, Ruminations of a Numbers Man*. New York: Alfred A Knopf, 1991.

J. R. Maddocks

Positron emission tomography (PET)

Positron emission tomography (PET) is a scanning technique used in conjunction with small amounts of radiolabeled compounds to visualize **brain anatomy** and function.

PET was the first scanning method to provide information on brain function as well as anatomy. This information includes data on **blood** flow, **oxygen** consumption, glucose **metabolism**, and concentrations of various molecules in brain **tissue**.

PET has been used to study brain activity in various neurological diseases and disorders, including **stroke**; **epilepsy**; **Alzheimer's disease**, **Parkinson's disease**, and **Huntington's disease**; and in some psychiatric disorders, such as **schizophrenia**, **depression**, obsessive-compulsive disorder, attention-deficit/hyperactivity disorder, and Tourette **syndrome**. PET studies have helped to identify the brain mechanisms that operate in drug **addiction**, and to shed light on the mechanisms by which individual drugs work. PET is also proving to be more accurate than other methods in the **diagnosis** of many types of **cancer**. In the treatment of cancer, PET can be used to determine more quickly than conventional tests whether a given therapy is working. PET scans also give accurate and detailed information on **heart** disease, particularly in women, in whom breast tissue can interfere with other types of tests.

Description

A very small amount of a radiolabeled compound is inhaled by or injected into the patient. The injected or inhaled compound accumulates in the tissue to be studied. As the radioactive **atoms** in the compound decay, they release smaller particles called positrons, which are positively charged. When a positron collides with an **electron** (negatively charged), they are both annihilated, and two photons (light particles) are emitted. The photons move in opposite directions and are picked up by the detector ring of the PET scanner. A computer uses this information to generate three-dimensional, cross-sectional images that represent the biological activity where the radiolabeled compound has accumulated.

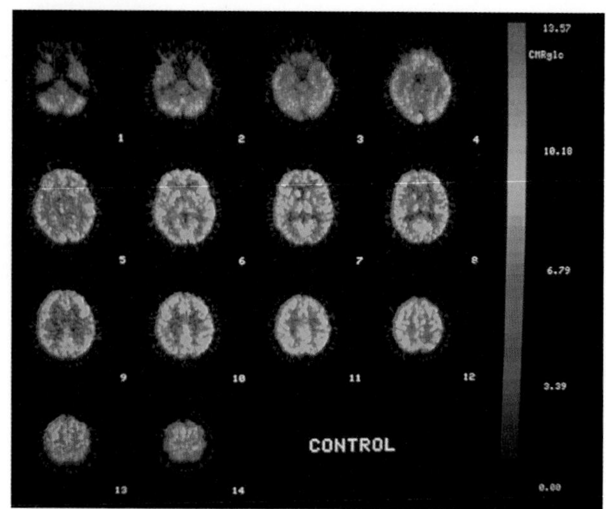

Positron Emission tomography (PET) scan control study.

A related technique is called single **photon** emission computed tomography scan (CT scan) (SPECT). SPECT is similar to PET, but the compounds used contain heavier, longer-lived radioactive atoms that emit high-energy photons, called gamma **rays**, instead of positrons. SPECT is used for many of the same applications as PET, and is less expensive than PET, but the resulting picture is usually less sharp than a PET image and reveals less information about the brain.

Risks

Some of radioactive compounds used for PET or SPECT scanning can persist for a long time in the body. Even though only a small amount is injected each time, the long half-lives of these compounds can **limit** the number of times a patient can be scanned.

Further Reading

"Brain Imaging and Psychiatry: Part 1." *Harvard Mental Health Letter,* 13 (January 1997): 1.

"Brain Imaging and Psychiatry: Part 2." *Harvard Mental Health Letter,* 13 (February 1997): 1.

Faust, Rita Baron. "Life-Saving Breakthroughs: Innovative Designs and Techniques for Treating Heart Disease." *American Health for Women,* 16 (September 1997): 65.

Kevles, Bettyann Holtzmann. *Medical Imaging in the Twentieth Century.* Rutgers University Press, 1996.

Powledge, Tabatha M. "Unlocking the Secrets of the Brain: Part 2." *BioScience,* 47 (July 17, 1997): 403.

"Studies Argue for Wider Use of PET for Cancer Patients." *Cancer Weekly Plus,* (December 15, 1997): 9.

Lisa Christenson

KEY TERMS

Electron—One of the small particles that make up an atom. An electron has the same mass and amount of charge as a positron, but the electron has a negative charge.

Gamma ray—A high-energy photon, emitted by radioactive substances.

Half-life—The time required for half of the atoms in a radioactive substance to disintegrate.

Photon—A light particle.

Positron—One of the small particles that make up an atom. A positron has the same mass and amount of charge as an electron, but the positron has a positive charge.

Postulate

A postulate is an assumption, that is, a proposition, or statement, that is assumed to be true without any **proof**. Postulates are the fundamental propositions used to prove other statements known as theorems. Once a **theorem** has been proven it is may be used in the proof of other theorems. In this way, an entire branch of **mathematics** can be built up from a few postulates. Postulate is synonymous with axiom, though sometimes axiom is taken to **mean** an assumption that applies to all branches of mathematics, in which case a postulate is taken to be an assumption specific to a given theory or branch of mathematics. Euclidean **geometry** provides a classic example. Euclid based his geometry on five postulates and five "common notions," of which the postulates are assumptions specific to geometry, and the "common notions" are completely general axioms.

The five postulates of Euclid that pertain to geometry are specific assumptions about lines, angles, and other geometric concepts. They are:

1) Any two points describe a line.

2) A line is infinitely long.

3) A **circle** is uniquely defined by its center and a point on its circumference.

4) Right angles are all equal.

5) Given a point and a line not containing the point, there is one and only one **parallel** to the line through the point.

The five "common notions" of Euclid have application in every branch of mathematics, they are:

1) Two things that are equal to a third are equal to each other.

2) Equal things having equal things added to them remain equal.

3) Equal things having equal things subtracted from them have equal remainders.

4) Any two things that can be shown to coincide with each other are equal.

5) The whole is greater than any part.

On the basis of these ten assumptions, Euclid produced the *Elements*, a 13 **volume** treatise on geometry (published c. 300 B.C.) containing some 400 theorems, now referred to collectively as Euclidean geometry.

When developing a mathematical system through logical deductive reasoning any number of postulates may be assumed. Sometimes in the course of proving theorems based on these postulates a theorem turns out to be the equivalent of one of the postulates. Thus, mathematicians usually seek the minimum number of postulates on which to base their reasoning. It is interesting to note that, for centuries following publication of the *Elements*, mathematicians believed that Euclid's fifth postulate, sometimes called the parallel postulate, could logically be deduced from the first four. Not until the nineteenth century did mathematicians recognize that the five postulates did indeed result in a logically consistent geometry, and that replacement of the fifth postulate with different assumptions led to other consistent geometries.

Postulates figure prominently in the work of the Italian mathematician Guiseppe Peano (1858-1932), formalized the language of **arithmetic** by choosing three basic concepts: **zero**; number (meaning the non-negative **integers**); and the relationship "is the successor of." In addition, Peano assumed that the three concepts obeyed the five following axioms or postulates:

1) Zero is a number.

2) If b is a number, the successor of b is a number.

3) Zero is not the successor of a number.

4) Two numbers of which the successors are equal are themselves equal.

5) If a set S of numbers contains zero and also the successor of every number in S, then every number is in S.

Based on these five postulates, Peano was able to derive the fundamental laws of arithmetic. Known as the Peano axioms, these five postulates provided not only a formal foundation for arithmetic but for many of the **constructions** upon which **algebra** depends.

Indeed, during the nineteenth century, virtually every branch of mathematics was reduced to a set of postulates and resynthesized in logical deductive fashion. The result was to change the way mathematics is viewed. Prior to the nineteenth century mathematics had been seen solely as a means of describing the physical universe. By the end of the century, however, mathematics came to be viewed more as a means of deriving the logical consequences of a collections of axioms.

In the twentieth century, a number of important discoveries in the fields of mathematics and logic showed the limitation of proof from postulates, thereby invalidating Peano's axioms. The best known of these is Gödel's theorem, formulated in the 1930s by the Austrian mathematician Kurt Gödel (1906-1978). Gödel demonstrated that if a system contained Peano's postulates, or an equivalent, the system was either inconsistent (a statement and its opposite could be proved) or incomplete (there are true statements that cannot be derived from the postulates).

See also: Logic, symbolic.

Further Reading

Boyer, Carl B. *A History of Mathematics*. 2nd ed. Revised by Uta C. Merzbach. New York: Wiley, 1991.

Paulos, John Allen. *Beyond Numeracy, Ruminations of a Numbers Man*. New York: Knopf, 1991.

Smith, Stanley A., Charles W. Nelson, Roberta K. Koss, Mervin L. Keedy, and Marvin L. Bittinger. *Addison Wesley Informal Geometry*. Reading MA: Addison Wesley, 1992.

J. R. Maddocks

Potassium see **Alkali metals**

Potassium aluminum sulfate

Potassium aluminum sulfate is chemical which conforms to the general formula $KAl(SO_4)_2$. Also known as aluminum potassium sulfate, its unique characteristics have made it an important compound to many industries.

The commercial production of potassium aluminum sulfate is typically accomplished by a method called hydrometallurgy. In this process, an aqueous solution of **sulfuric acid** is first used to extract alumina (solid Al_2O_3) from an **ore** called bauxite. This step, known as **leaching**, results in a solution which can then be reacted with potassium sulfate to form potassium aluminum sulfate. Another method of production involves converting aluminum sulfate to potassium aluminum sulfate by adding potassium sulfate. In addition to these chemical processes, potassium aluminum sulfate is also found occurring naturally in **minerals** such as alunite and kalinite. Commercially available potassium aluminum sulfate is called potassium alum, potash alum, alum flour, or alum meal.

Potassium aluminum sulfate forms a solid, white powder at room **temperature**. It is a hygroscopic material which when exposed to air, hydrates (absorbs **water**). Depending on the amount of water molecules present, these hydrates are represented by the chemical formulas $KAl(SO_4)_2 * 12H_2O$ or $K_2SO_4.Al_2(SO_4)_3 * 24H_2O$. The powder form, made up of crystals, has a melting point of 198.5degrees F (92.5°C) and can be readily dissolved in water. Additionally, this material has a property known as astringency which is an ability to constrict body tissues, and restrict the flow of **blood**.

There have been many industrial applications of potassium aluminum sulfate. It is an important part of many products created by the pharmaceutical, cosmetic, and food industries because of its astringency property. It is also used in the manufacture of **paper**, dyes, glue, and **explosives**. Additionally, it helps in the water purification process, is used to speed up the hardening of **concrete** and plaster, and acts as a catalyst in various chemical reactions.

Potassium hydrogen tartrate

Potassium hydrogen tartrate is an acid **salt** of **tartaric acid**. It is denoted by the chemical formula $KC_4H_5O_6$ and has a **molecular weight** of 188.18. It is made up of 25.53% **carbon**, 51.01% **oxygen**, 20.78% potassium and 2.68% hydrogen, and has a **density** of 1.95 g/cc. When purified, it is an odorless, white, crystalline powder that has a pleasant acidulous taste. It is used as a leavening agent in baking powders and forms naturally during wine fermentation.

Properties

Potassium hydrogen tartrate is known by a variety of names including potassium bitartrate, potassium acid tartrate, cream of tartar, and faeccula. An impure form of potassium hydrogen tartrate, called argol, is formed naturally during the **fermentation** of a variety of fruit juices. It is found as a **crystal** residue in wine casks.

One gram of potassium hydrogen tartrate dissolves in 162 ml **water**. When the water temperature is increased, so is its **solubility**. Using boiling water, one gram will dissolve in about 16 ml of water. The material is insoluble in absolute **alcohol**. The saturated aqueous solution has a **pH** of approximately 3.5. In this solution

the material dissociates into its component ions, one of which is tartaric acid. This acid was first isolated and characterized in 1769 by chemist Carl Wilhelm Scheele. He obtained it by boiling cream of tartar with chalk and then treating it with sulfuric acid.

Production

Potassium hydrogen tartrate has been known for centuries. The ancient Greeks and Romans, who found it as a **deposit** from fermented grape juice, called it tartar. Today, cream of tartar is manufactured from the waste products of the wine industry. Waste products include press cakes from unfermented or partially fermented grape juice, dried slimy sediments from wine vats, and crystalline crusts from the wine vats used in second fermentations. The crystalline material is scraped off the sides of the vats and then purified to at least 99.5%.

Uses

Cream of tartar is used for a wide variety of applications. It is one of the primary components in baking powder. Here it functions as a leavening agent. Leavening agents are compounds that are put into products like breads and rolls to generate **carbon dioxide**. The carbon dioxide is trapped in the batter creating air pockets that result in products that are lighter and crispier. In baking powder, cream of tartar specifically functions as the acidic portion that reacts with the basic component, **sodium** bicarbonate, to generate carbon dioxide gas. The limited solubility of cream of tartar in cold water helps prevent premature leavening. This is useful when mixing dough.

Beyond leavening, cream of tartar also functions as an acidulant in food products. Acidulants serve a variety of purposes in this capacity, but their major role is to make foods more palatable. Acidulants can also be used as flavoring agents because they can intensify certain tastes and mask undesirable aftertastes. They can act as buffers to control the pH during processing. They also have an antimicrobial effect and can prevent the production of spores. They are synergistic with **antioxidants** which means they help make antioxidants more effective. Acidulants are also **viscosity** modifiers. By using the appropriate **concentration** a batter can be made thicker or thinner. They are also melting modifiers and meat curing agents. The addition of cream of tartar to candy and frosting recipes results in a creamier consistency. It can also help improve the stability and **volume** of egg whites if added before beating.

Non-food applications of potassium hydrogen tartrate include its use as one of the starting materials for the production of tartaric acid. It also finds use in **metal** processing for such things as coloring and galvanic tinning of metals. In the production of wool it is used as a reducer of CrO_3 in mordants. In the pharmaceutical industry it has been used for its cathartic effect. Veterinarians use it as a laxative and diuretic. Cream of tartar is classified as a generally regarded as safe (GRAS) compound for use in food and beverage products.

KEY TERMS

Acid—A substance that produces hydrogen ions when placed in an aqueous solution.

Acidulant—A food additive that improves flavor, controls pH, acts as a preservative, and modifies the viscosity of baked goods recipes.

Antimicrobial—A material that inhibits the growth of microorganisms that cause food to spoil.

Fermentation—A process by which complex organic molecules are enzymatically broken down to simpler molecules. For example, in alcohol fermentation glucose is reduced to ethyl alcohol and carbon dioxide.

Leavening agent—A compound used in baking to produce carbon dioxide in a batter. It creates air pockets in gluten-based food products.

Solubility—The amount of a material that will dissolve in another material at a given temperature.

Further Reading

Budavari, Susan, editor.*The Merck Index.* Merck Research Laboratories, 1996.

Branen, A. Davidson, M. Salminen, S. *Food Additives.* New York: Marcel Dekker, 1990.

Perry T. Romanowski

Potassium nitrate

Potassium nitrate, also known as saltpeter or niter, is a chemical compound consisting of potassium, **nitrogen**, and **oxygen**. While it has many applications, including use as a fertilizer, its most important usage historically has been as a component of gunpowder. Over time its use as an explosive has been largely obsoleted by dynamite and TNT, but it is still used today in artillery-shell primers, hand-grenade fuses, and fireworks.

Potassium nitrate consists of 3 basic chemical elements: potassium a soft, light, silver white **metal**; nitrogen a colorless, odorless gas; and oxygen, another com-

mon gas. When these three elements are reacted in the proper proportions they form a whitish compound known as nitre, or saltpeter, which has the chemical formula KNO_3. This naturally occurring compound, which forms thin whitish glassy crusts on **rocks**, can be found in sheltered areas such as caves and particularly on soils rich in organic **matter**. Until the first World War the United States imported most of its potassium nitrate from **Europe** where it was mined from ancient seabeds. When these sources became unavailable during the war, the brines lakes in California became the principal supplier of nitre.

Since it is rich in potassium, an element which is vital for **plant** growth, large quantities of potassium nitrate are used annually as fertilizer. It also has utility as a food preservative, and although never proven, it is claimed that when ingested saltpeter has an anaphrodisiac, or sexual-desire- reducing effect. However, the most renowned use for this whitish powder was discovered over 2,200 years ago by the Chinese. When 75% potassium nitrate is mixed appropriately with 15% **carbon** (charcoal), and 10% **sulfur**, the resultant black powder has explosive properties. This mixture (which throughout history has enjoyed such colorful nicknames as "Chinese Snow" and "the Devil's Distillate") eventually became known as gunpowder. As early as A.D. 1000, it was used by its inventors in explosive grenades and bombs. By the thirteenth century, the use of gunpowder had spread throughout the western world: in 1242 the English philosopher Roger Bacon described his own preparation of this material. By the early fourteenth century, black powder and guns were being manufactured in Europe. Although the early firearms were awkward and inefficient, they were rapidly improved. Their use led to significant social changes, including the end of the European feudal system. In fact, it is arguable that exploitation of the properties of gunpowder has been responsible for many of the major social and cultural changes in history.

Originally, potassium nitrate and the other components of gunpowder were carefully hand mixed and broken into small particles using wooden stamps. Later, **water** power mechanized the stamping stage, and metal stamps replaced the wooden ones. In modern production, charcoal and sulfur are mixed by the tumbling action of **steel** balls in a rotating hollow cylinder. The potassium nitrate is pulverized separately, and the ingredients are then mixed and ground. After further crushing the gunpowder is pressed into cakes; these are then rebroken and separated into grains of specific size. Finally, the grains are tumbled in wooden cylinders to wear off rough edges. During this process graphite is introduced, a coating powder which provides a friction-reducing, moisture-resistant film.

By 1900 black powder had been virtually replaced as the standard firearms propellant. Although it had served for centuries, it had many drawbacks. It produced a large cloud of white smoke when ignited, built up a bore-obstructing residue after relatively few shots, and absorbed moisture easily. Its replacement, nitrocellulose based smokeless powders (known as guncotton), eliminated most of these disadvantages. Gunpowder had already been largely replaced as a primary blasting explosive by dynamite and TNT but it is still widely used today in artillery-shell primers, hand-grenade fuses, and fireworks.

Potassium-argon dating see **Dating techniques**

Potato

The potato is a starchy, red or brown skinned, underground stem called a **tuber**. Tubers are storage areas for nutrient reserves of plants, such as starch or sugars. A widely cultivated species, the potato **plant** has the scientific name *Solanum tuberosum* and is a member of the **nightshade** family of plants, Solanaceae. Potato plants are widely grown for their familiar edible tubers that are a mainstay of many human diets.

Potato plants are flowering plants with **flower** colors that include white, purple, violet, or **lilac** depending on the variety of plant. Natural potato plants produce a tap **root system** that is difficult to harvest. Cultivated potatoes, in contrast, have fibrous root systems that are more easily removed from **soil**, making potato harvesting less difficult. Potato tubers have indentations, called *eyes* over their outer surfaces. The eyes are places where new stems may grow outward from tubers. Also, *stolons* grow from tuber eyes. Stolons are underground root-like extensions that connect tubers to one another and link individual potato plants together vegetatively.

Potatoes are a very important food source for humans. The starchy content of potato tubers provides a good source of **energy**, and the vitamin content of potatoes is exceptional. A single medium sized potato (about 148 grams or 5.5 ounces) contains about 100 calories with no **fat**. They are easily digested since starch is quickly converted into simple sugars, which are absorbed rapidly for use by the body. Also, potatoes have a high **water** content. To illustrate their importance, it is reported that the average American consumes about 142.7 pounds of potatoes each year. According to the USDA, that includes about 48 pounds of fresh potatoes, 59 pounds of frozen potatoes (including French fries), and 16 pounds of potato chips per person per year. In the United States, Idaho grows more

Idaho potato assembly line.

potatoes than any other region and accounts for about thirty percent of all potatoes cultivated in the U.S.

A significant historical event concerning potatoes was the Great Irish Famine. In the nineteenth century, potatoes had become the major food source of the population of Ireland because of its ease in cultivation. The climate and moisture of the country was favorable for potato growth. However, in 1845, a devastating plant disease infected the potato **crops** across Ireland. The disease (which still can occur) is called the late blight, or simply the potato blight. It is caused by a fungus. The parasitic fungus, with the scientific name *Phytophthora infestans*, resulted in mass ruin of potato crops for several consecutive years, creating horrible famine. In order to escape hunger, many Irish people fled to America and Canada. In this manner, the potato famine contributed to American immigration and the growth of the Irish population in the new world.

Terry Watkins

Potato see **Nightshade family**
Potential energy see **Energy**

Pottery analysis

Man first began making pots at the end of the Stone Age (Neolithic Period), about 12,000 years ago in the Old World, and about 5,000 years ago in the New World.

By about 6500 BC, hunting and foraging had largely been abandoned in Old World Neolithic agricultural villages. The need for pottery arose during the change-over from a food-gathering to a food-producing economy. The cultivation of grain required that man be able to store cereals for future use. But pottery was also used for carrying **water**, for cooking, and for serving food.

Basketry, including clay-lined baskets, probably served adequately for food storage for awhile. It may have been the accidental burning of a clay-lined basket that led to the discovery that clay, which is malleable when wet, becomes hard and brittle when burned. Further experimentation would have revealed that the piece of burnt clay could be subjected to additional **heat** without causing the object to disintegrate, which made it suitable for cooking vessels. The manufacture and firing of pottery represented an **adaptation** of fire-based technology, which was later to evolve into furnace-based **metallurgy**.

The earliest pots were made by hand, either by being molded or by being built up. Although small pots could be molded, larger ones had to built up by placing successive rings of clay on top of each other.

With the invention of the potter's wheel, probably in the area of the Fertile Crescent, large vessels could be constructed in a few minutes, rather than several days. Until the invention of this device, women tended to be responsible for creating pottery; with its invention, pottery entered the **domain** of men.

Even the earliest pots appear to have been decorated. Decorations have ranged from simple geometric patterns to the elaborate illustrations characteristic of Chinese vases. Some early examples appear to have been made in imitation of baskets, or to have been molded inside a basket. Patterns on pots were probably created with finger nails, pointed sticks, or bird bones.

The art of pottery requires just the right material, i.e., the clay starting material must be neither too gritty nor too fine in texture. And the wet clay object must not be allowed to dry out before it is fired. Finally, the **temperature** of the firing oven must reach a critical value if the fired object is to retain its shape permanently. These discoveries may have occurred in the period of the Stone Age just preceding the Neolithic Period (that is, the Mesolithic Period), becoming universal in the Neolithic period. Pots or potsherds are frequently found in the ruins of Neolithic cultures.

Each culture evolved its own unique form of pottery. These shapes typically developed into characteristic forms that changed little over time. In addition, buried pottery does not deteriorate with time. As a result, pottery has become one of the best resources for dating an archeological site. Even if pots have become broken, the potsherds can still be pieced together into their original

form. This of course cannot be done with objects of **wood**, leather, skins, or cloth.

The presence of pots at an archeological site may reveal information about contacts that once existed between prehistoric cultures, or about trade routes in later civilizations. Pottery exported from Crete in the eighteenth century B.C., for example, has been found on the mainland of Greece, on Cyprus and on other islands in the Aegean Sea, on the coast of Syria, and in Egypt. Other discoveries have shown that by 400 B.C., Greek vases were being exported to the steppes of southern Russia, southern Germany, and northern France. The shape, size, type of clay, type of temper, surface treatment, and painting that characterize an ancient pot all provide valuable clues to the archeologist seeking to date an artifact or site.

Pottery analysis

Archeologists typically perform four types of analysis on ceramic artifacts: experimental studies, form and function analysis, stylistic analysis, and technological analysis. In experimental studies, archeologists attempt to replicate ancient methods of pottery-making in the laboratory. These studies yield valuable information about firing techniques, firing temperatures, and about the properties of coating materials. Archeologists may also study present-day pottery-making techniques in various cultures around the world to better understand how methods were used by traditional cultures.

Analyses based on form and function focus on the shapes of ceramic vessels. The underlying assumption in this approach is that the shape of the vessel was determined by the way it was used. One weakness of this approach is that it ignores other factors that may have influenced the shape the object took, such as the material properties of the clay used, the manufacturing technologies available to the potter, and any cultural factors that might have constrained the form that the vessel eventually took. When employed properly, form and function analyses can provide valuable information about ancient economic patterns, units of measure, household food production and consumption, and household sizes.

Stylistic analysis focuses on the decorative styles applied to ceramic artifacts, including painted designs, incisions, embossing, and other surface treatments. Because decorative patterns, and the information they convey, are more likely to have been determined by specific cultural elements than are form and function, stylistic analysis is the technique most frequently used to analyze ancient pottery. When the results of stylistic analyses are validated against other archeological data, it often becomes possible to trace social change in a culture through time. While there is no doubt that this type of analysis has made great contributions to archeology, there remains a need for greater rigor and consistency when applying it across different regions and time periods.

Technological analyses look at the materials from which the ceramic is made. Of chief interest are the chemical composition of the clay, the tempering materials, and the proportion of clay to temper. Technological analyses provide valuable data about variations in vessel forms, classification systems, and the origins of the materials used to construct pots. Because pots, both as objects in themselves and as vessels for other commodities such as grain, oils, wine, and **salt**, were very often trade objects, technological analyses can reveal information about ancient trade routes and trading patterns. Technological analyses may use **neutron** activation analysis, X-ray **diffraction**, or ceramic petrology to identify **trace elements** in clay or temper to gather information about the production, distribution, use and disposal of ceramic artifacts.

Technological analyses

In one type of technological analysis, the archeologist attempts to understand the physical and mechanical properties of the ceramic material. Experiments may be designed to gather information about thermal shock, tensile strength, and crack propagation in ceramic vessels. In addition, the impact of any surface treatments on a pot's function may be assessed.

In a second type of technological analysis, the types of clay and tempering materials are analyzed to determine the origins of the materials used in the pot's construction. Mineral composition may be determined by petrographic analysis or x-ray diffraction. Petrographic analysis employs a **microscope** and polarized light to identify the mineral used as temper, based on the temper's optical and morphological characteristics. In x-ray diffraction, the specimen is bombarded with electrons to obtain an x-ray diffraction pattern characteristic of the **minerals** present in the object. At an elemental level, clays can be analyzed by such techniques as optical **emission spectroscopy**, inductively coupled **plasma** spectroscopy, x-ray **fluorescence**, neutron activation, proton-induced x-ray emission, microprobe analysis, and atomic absorption spectroscopy. Each of these methods evaluates the wavelength of **energy** either emitted or absorbed when the electrons, protons, or neutrons present in the clay of the vessel are disturbed by a source of **radiation**. These indicate the chemical elements present in the **sample**.

Typological analysis and other dating techniques

Typological analysis is the systematic classification of material culture into types based on similarities in

KEY TERMS

Artifact—A manmade object that is fashioned or shaped with skill for his use.

Atomic absorption spectrometry—Method of analysis in which the specimen is placed in a flame and the light emitted is analyzed.

Ceramic petrology—Study of the origin, occurrence, structure, and history of the material used in a ceramic object.

Crack propagation—Growth of cracks in a material.

Fertile Crescent—Crescent-shaped area extending from Israel to Turkey and Iran, where domestication of plants and animals first occurred.

Firing—Treatment of a ceramic object with heat.

Inductively coupled plasma spectroscopy—An analytical technique in which plasma from the sample, heated by flame to a much higher temperature than ordinary combustion flames, is sampled either by emission spectroscopy or mass spectrometry.

Microprobe analysis—A chemical microanalysis technique based on the analysis of x-rays emitted from a very small sample area.

Morphology—Study of structure and form.

Neutron activation analysis—Method of analysis in which a specimen is bombarded with neutrons, and the resultant radio isotopes measured.

Temper—To moisten and mix clay to achieve the proper consistency for use in ceramics.

Tensile strength—The maximum stress from stretching that a material can experience without tearing.

Thermal shock—Effect of rapidly subjecting a material to a very large change in temperature.

Thermoluminescence—Light emission accompanying the heating of a material.

Typology—Classification of artifacts into groups or types.

X-ray diffraction—Scattering of x-rays by matter.

X-ray fluorescence spectrometry—A nondestructive method of analysis in which a specimen is irradiated with x-rays and the resultant spectrum is analyzed.

form, construction, style, content, and/or use. Before the advent of modern **dating techniques**, typological analysis provided the chief basis for dating material objects. The underlying premise of the technique is that, in a given region, artifacts that resemble each other were created at about the same time, and that differences can be accounted for by gradual changes in the material culture.

Ceramic objects have thus been dated relative to each other based on typological or stylistic shifts in a material culture through time (seriation). One of the earliest seriation techniques used an indexing scheme to measure the similarity between artifacts. Today, computer-based statistical methods, including multidimensional analysis, **factor** analysis, and cluster analysis, are commonly used to date objects based on stylistic similarities.

In **luminescence** dating, a ceramic object is heated to produce a thermoluminescence signal characteristic of the length of time the objects have been buried. This technique is based on the principle that objects that have been buried a long time show greater luminescence intensities than those buried a short time.

Further Reading

Fagan, Brian M., ed.*The Oxford Companion to Archeology*New York: Oxford University Press, 1996.

Maloney, Norah. *The Young Oxford Book of Archeology*New York: Oxford University Press, 1997.

Sullivan, George. *Discover Archeology: An Introduction to the Tools and Techniques of Archeological Fieldwork* Garden City, NY: Doubleday & Company, 1980.

Daniel, Glyn, ed. *The Illustrated Encyclopedia of Archeology*-New York: Thomas Y. Crowell: 1977.

Randall Frost

Pottos see **Caprimulgids**; **Lorises**

Prairie

A prairie is a natural vegetation type in which perennial herbaceous plants predominate, particularly species of **grasses**. The word "prairie" comes from the French *prérie* (later, prairie), meaning meadow. The term was first applied to the swath of mid-continental North American grassland in the 1600s by French Jesuit missionaries and explorers, because the landscape resem-

A tall grass prairie during a Montana summer.

bled, on a much vaster scale, the familiar agricultural meadows of western **Europe**. Thus, geography and nomenclature came together to distinguish the North American prairie from similar **grasslands** elsewhere in the world: the steppes of central **Asia**, the pampas of **South America**, and the veldt of southern **Africa**.

Until the settlement era, the central prairie of **North America** stretched from southern Alberta, Saskatchewan, and Manitoba south to mid-Texas, and from the foothills of the Rocky Mountains eastward into Indiana. It covered about 1.4 million sq mi (3.6 million sq km). Outlying patches occurred in Ohio, Michigan, Kentucky, and southwestern Ontario. A similar vegetation type went under the names of "plains" or "downs" in the northeastern United States.

The general trend toward increasing rainfall and increasingly rich **soil** from west to east in mid-continental North America gave rise to a descriptive classification of the prairie. Its western edge, on the high plains, became known as shortgrass prairie, because shorter grasses grew on its generally poorer and drier soils. A transitional zone running north to south along the 98th meridian, through Alberta, Saskatchewan, the Dakotas, Nebraska, Kansas, and Oklahoma, became known as mixed-grass prairie. The richest, eastern sector, which bulged eastward from the 98th meridian through Illinois and into northwestern Indiana, became known as the tallgrass or "true" prairie. This scheme gradually evolved into the one used by modern biologists to classify prairies, which takes into account soil, **bedrock**, and vegetation types and has many divisions. The tallgrass prairie is the major subject of this article.

A native prairie is sprinkled with brilliantly colored flowers of broadleafed (or dicotyledonous) plants that often exceed the height of the grasses. Some prairie grasses attain a height of 6.6 ft (2 m), and sometimes more, if soil and moisture conditions are favorable. Early settlers' descriptions of grasses taller than a person on horseback were probably exaggerated and reflected a tradition of romanticizing the landscape. Intermixed with the predominant grasses are broad-leaved plants called forbs, which lend color and diversity to the vegetation. Besides the grasses (family Poaceae), such as little and big bluestem and Indian grass, common prairie plants are species of **legumes** (Leguminosae), or flowering peas and clovers, and composites (Asteraceae), such as sunflowers, goldenrods, black-eyed susan, asters, and coneflowers.

Natural history of the prairie

Most of the prairie has developed since the most recent Ice Age, as determined from the dating of fossilized pollen grains to about 8,300 years ago. The retreating **glaciers** left a central strip of flat or slightly depressed topography overlying clay soil, or in the western states, rocky dolomite shelves. Climate, **weather**, soil, and topography then created the initial conditions for the prairie to develop. The central prairie is subject to the stresses of extreme changes in **temperature** over the course of a year, **drought**, occasional accumulation of standing **water** just below the ground surface, and drying westerly winds from the Rocky Mountains. That situation favored the growth of plants with hardy root systems and underground growing points, but whose aerial (or aboveground) parts could die back each year. Perennial grasses and low, hardy shrubs could survive in such a climate; unprotected trees could not. It is thought that the post-Ice Age climate set the stage for the development of the prairie, with soil types and frequent fires then favoring the growth of grasses and forbs.

Fire does not start a prairie, but it is a crucial **factor** in maintaining it. The pre-settlement fires were landscape-wide and moved rapidly, driven by westerly winds that traveled unimpeded across the plains. The aerial parts of prairie plants **burn**, but the roots, which in perennial grasses form a deep, thick tangle underground, do not. The fast-moving fires also consume litter, the dried stalks and **plant** remains that had died in previous **seasons** and fallen to the ground. Removal of litter gave the next season's growth greater access to air and sunlight. The burns also killed shrubs and trees, which might otherwise have invaded the prairie and displaced its species. Some prairie fires were started by lightning; others were set by Native Americans, who saw the advantage to their **horses** and to the **bison** herds they hunted of having fresh vegetation to eat.

Bison, the primary grazers on the prairie, contributed to upkeep of the **ecosystem** by consuming young shoots of trees and shrubs along with their main food of grasses and forbs. Although they were massive animals, their wide-ranging habit ensured they would not remain in one spot to churn up and destroy the roots of prairie grasses, as fenced-in cattle would later do.

Climate, bison, and fire, maintained the dynamic boundary between prairie and forest. The prairie was not devoid of trees, however. Cottonwoods, green ash, and box elder grew as a riparian community along riverbanks, and long fingers of forest extended into the prairie, often bounded on their western edges by a watercourse that served as a natural firebreak. During periods without fire, plum trees and crabapple could take hold at the edges of the prairie. Copses of trees and patches of flowers interrupted the "seas of grass" and gave an overall more mosaic appearance to the prairie.

The post-settlement prairie

For a millennia, the North American prairie (bordered on the north, east, and south by forest) existed as a complex ecosystem that supported rich life, including aboriginal human cultures. Within the span of a human lifetime, however, it was almost entirely eradicated by conversion into agricultural land-use.

The early settlers, reliant on **forests** for building materials, firewood, fencing, and hand-crafted implements, initially distrusted a land on which few or no trees grew. That changed with the discovery that the tallgrass prairie could be converted into some of the richest cropland on the **continent**. Vast acreages went under the plow; other areas were overgrazed by domestic **livestock**. The assault on the central prairie began in earnest in the 1820s and was sped up by the opening of the Erie Canal, in 1825. The development of steamship routes on the Great Lakes and the westward expansion of the railroad system, in the 1850s, also facilitated large, westward population movements. By the beginning of the Civil War, most of the tallgrass prairie had been put to the plow. The widespread availability of barbed-wire fencing by 1890 released ranchers and farmers from their greatest dependency on **wood** and marked the final domestication of the prairie.

In the pre-settlement period, almost 60% of Illinois, then nicknamed the Prairie State, was covered by tallgrass prairie. In the post-settlement era, however, only about 0.01% of the original prairie was left. Prairie originally covered 85% of Iowa; in the post-settlement period 0.02% remained. The western states, with an overall drier climate and soils less suitable for agriculture, fared somewhat better, but no state retained more than a small fraction of its original prairie.

Most prairie today represents "island" **habitat**, existing in isolated patches rather than as a continuous extent of natural vegetation. **Island** communities are more vulnerable to natural and human-caused disturbances, and experience a higher rate of species disappearance than non-island ecosystems. Typical islands of native prairie, called relics, include small cemeteries that coincidentally preserved the prairie; small preserves in arboreta and demonstration projects; and areas such as railroad embankments in cities where development was restricted or the land was considered unsuitable for building on. About 30% of the remaining prairie in Illinois exists in tiny islands of less than one acre.

KEY TERMS

Forb—A perennial, herbaceous, broad-leafed (or dicotyledonous) plant.

Grass—Any member of the family Poaceae, characterized by long narrow leaves with parallel venation and reduced flowers; usually found on seasonally dry, flat lands. The cereal grains are grasses (barley, corn, oats, rice, rye, wheat).

Island habitat—A small area of ecosystem, surrounded by a different kind of ecosystem. The species in the island habitat cannot live in or penetrate the surrounding environment.

Relic prairie—A remnant of prairie, usually small, that has never been plowed or overgrazed; virgin prairie.

The loss of the prairie was part of a broader economic movement that involved both industrialization and the development of commercial agriculture. The economic development of the former prairie states resulted in the almost total eradication of a large unit of natural vegetation. Efforts are under way to restore large tracts of reconstructed prairie that might support relatively small numbers of breeding bison. Seeding with native plants and the use of controlled burns are crucial parts of the management system being used to achieve this ecological restoration. However, the formerly extensive tallgrass prairie will never be totally recovered, because its essential land-base is needed to provide food and livelihoods for an ever-increasing population of humans.

See also Composite family (Compositaceae).

Further Reading

Coupland, Robert T., ed. *Natural Grasslands: Introduction and Western Hemisphere.* Ecosystems of the World 8A. New York: Elsevier, 1992.

Madson, John. *Tall Grass Prairie.* Helena, MT: Falcon Press, 1993.

Smith, Daryl D. "Tallgrass Prairie Settlement: Prelude to the Demise of the Tallgrass Ecosystem." In *Recapturing a Vanishing Heritage. Proceedings of the Twelfth North American Prairie Conference,* edited by Daryl D. Smith and Carol A. Jacobs. Cedar Falls: University of Northern Iowa, 1992.

Stuckey, Ronald L. "Origin and Development of the Concept of the Prairie Peninsula." In *The Prairie Peninsula—In the "Shadow" of Transeau. Proceedings of the Sixth North American Prairie Conference.* Columbus: Ohio State University, 1981.

Whitney, Gordon G. *From Coastal Wilderness to Fruited Plain: A History of Environmental Change in Temperate North America 1500 to the Present.* Cambridge, England: Cambridge University Press, 1994.

Marjorie Pannell

Prairie chicken

Prairie chickens are two North American species of **birds** in the **grouse** family (Phasianidae) in the order Galliformes, the game birds. Both the greater prairie chicken (*Tympanuchus cupido*) and the lesser prairie chicken (*T. pallidicinctus*) are brownish birds with a black band on the end of the tail. Male birds have colorful air sacs that are inflated during **courtship** and a ruff of long feathers that are erected at the same time. When wooing females, cock prairie chickens assemble in a designated arena where they engage in vigorous, ritualized combat to impress each other and the hens as they arrive. The males that are most imposing in these displays are relatively successful in mating with females from the local area. This type of communal courtship display is called a lek. The hen prairie chicken incubates the eggs and takes care of the young by herself.

The greater prairie chicken is somewhat larger than the lesser prairie chicken, with a body length of 14 in (36 cm) and orange air sacs. This species once occurred widely in many open, temperate **grasslands** and prairies, ranging from extensive dunegrass and heath communities of the Atlantic seaboard, to tall-grass and mixed-grass prairies of the middle of **North America**. The lesser prairie chicken is somewhat paler than the greater prairie chicken and has a body length of 13 in (33 cm) and reddish air sacs. This species had a much more restricted distribution than the greater prairie chicken, occurring in relatively dry shortgrass and semi-desert habitats in the south-central parts of the United States.

Both species of prairie chickens, but especially the greater, were badly overhunted throughout the nineteenth century and the first decade or so of the twentieth century. This predation by humans reduced their populations and extirpated the birds from many places. However, even more important than hunting pressures have been the long-term effects of conversion of the natural habitats of the prairie chicken into agricultural, residential, and other land uses. These conversions cause permanent losses of the **habitat** of prairie chickens and other **wildlife**, fragmenting the remaining populations, making them vulnerable to extirpation.

This display by a prairie chicken is sometimes called "booming."

In the eastern parts of its range, a subspecies of the greater prairie chicken, called the heath hen (*T. c. cupido*), was initially abundant and resident in coastal heaths and grasslands from Massachusetts to Virginia. Overhunting reduced the heath hen populations to low levels, and by the time that this bird was finally protected from hunting, most of its original natural habitat had been lost. Moreover, heath hens suffered high mortality due to introduced predators (especially domestic **cats**), and from diseases borne by introduced **pheasants**. These pressures made the few remaining populations of prairie chicken extremely vulnerable to the deleterious effects of the extreme events of winter **weather** to natural predation. The last population of heath hen lived on Cape Cod, Massachusetts, and in spite of protection from hunting for several decades, and of management to maintain its habitat in a suitable condition, the heath hen became extinct in 1932.

Attwater's greater prairie chicken (*T. c. attwateri*) is another subspecies that used to be abundant in coastal prairies of Texas and Louisiana. This bird has suffered from the combined effects of overhunting and habitat conversions to agriculture, oil and gas development, and residential development. This endangered bird now only exists in a few isolated, remnant populations, in total numbering fewer than 500 individuals. These imperilled birds are threatened by continuing habitat losses, especially to residential development. However, many of these birds live in Attwater's Prairie Chicken National Wildlife Refuge in south Texas, where the habitat is intensively managed to favor this bird. Hopefully, these efforts will prove to be successful.

Bill Freedman

Prairie dog

Prairie dogs, or barking **squirrels**, are ground-dwelling herbivores in the genus *Cynomys*, in the squirrel family Sciuridae, order Rodentia. Prairie dogs are closely related to the ground squirrels, **gophers**, and **marmots**. Prairie dogs are widespread and familiar animals of the open, arid prairies, **grasslands**, and some agricultural landscapes of the western regions of **North America**.

Biology of prairie dogs

Prairie dogs have a stout body, with a narrow, pointed head, very short ears, short legs and tail, and strong digging claws on their fingers. Their fur is short but thick, and is colored yellowish or light-brown. Although they can run quickly, prairie dogs do not wander far from the protection of their burrows.

Prairie dogs dig their burrows and grass-lined dens in well-drained soils. The surface entrance to the burrow is surrounded by a conical mound of excavated **earth**, which is designed to prevent rainwater from draining into the burrow. Nearby vegetation is kept well clipped, to provide a wide field of view for the detection of predators.

Prairie dogs are highly social animals, living in burrow complexes known as towns. Prairie dog towns can contain thousands of individuals, at a **density** as great as about 75 animals per hectare. In the past, when prairie dogs were more abundant, some of their more extensive towns may have contained millions of animals.

The social structure within prairie dog towns is determined by a dominance hierarchy, in which defended areas are controlled by mature, territory-holding males. The territory of these males is occupied by a harem of 1 to 4 breeding females, plus their pre-reproductive offspring of the previous several years. These animals join the dominant male in an integrated defence of the group's territory, in a local social subgroup called a coterie. When female prairie dogs become sexually mature at about three years of age, they may be allowed to remain in their natal coterie. However, the male animals are always driven away when they mature, and they must then engage in a high-risk wandering, searching for an opportunity to establish their own coterie.

Prairie dogs are mostly herbivorous, feeding during the day on the tissues of many species of herbaceous plants. They also eat **insects**, such as **grasshoppers**, when they are readily available. The grazing activities of prairie dogs can be intense in the vicinity of their towns, and this greatly alters the character of the vegetation.

Prairie dogs often sit upright and survey their surroundings for potential dangers. If an imminent threat is observed, these animals quickly scurry underground. If only a potential threat is perceived, the prairie dog emits a sharp **bark** to warn others of the possible danger. This action heightens the state of awareness of the entire colony, and the movements of the marauding coyote, badger, hawk, rattlesnake, or person are closely monitored. There are specific alarm calls for ground-based and aerial predators, and there is also an all-clear signal.

A black-tailed prairie dog (*Cynomys ludovicianus*) at the Sonora Desert Museum, Arizona.

Prairie dogs gain weight through the summer and autumn, and they are noticeably fat and heavy at the onset of winter. Prairie dogs are not true hibernators, entering instead into deep, long sleeps in their hay-lined dens. These intense snoozes are occasionally interrupted for feeding and toiletry. On warm, sunny days the prairie dogs may interrupt their sleepy inactivity, and emerge to the surface to feed and stretch.

Many predators hunt prairie dogs, making these animals an important element of the food web of the prairies. In addition, abandoned burrows of prairie dogs are used by many other types of animals that do not dig their own burrows, for example, burrowing **owls** (*Speotyto cunicularia*).

Prairie dogs are often perceived to be agricultural **pests**, because they can consume large quantities of forage, and thereby compete with **livestock**. Prairie dogs may also directly consume **crops**, and they are when abundant they can cause significant damage. In addition, the excavations of prairie dogs can be hazardous to unwary livestock, who can step into an access hole, or cause an underground tunnel to collapse under their weight, and perhaps break one of their legs.

For these reasons, prairie dogs have been relentlessly persecuted by humans, mostly through poisoning campaigns. Regrettably, this means that very few towns of prairie dogs continue to flourish. The great declines in the abundance of prairie dogs has had substantial, secondary consequences for the many predators that feed on these animals, including **endangered species** such as the black-footed ferret (*Mustela nigripes*) and burrowing owl.

Species of prairie dogs

The most common and widespread of the five species of prairie dog is the black-tailed prairie dog

KEY TERMS

Coterie—The local, territory-holding, social group of prairie dogs, consisting of a mature male, a harem of 1–4 breeding females, and their young offspring.

Herbivore—An animal that only eats plant foods.

(*Cynomys ludovicianus*), occuring in dry, upland prairies from southern Saskatchewan to northern Mexico. The pelage of the black-tailed prairie dog is yellowish brown, except for the dark last-third of their tail. The closely related Mexican prairie dog (*C. mexicanus*) occurs in a small area of northern Mexico, and has about one-half of its tail colored black.

The white-tailed prairie dog (*Cynomys leucurus*) occurs in prairies and grasslands of high-elevation, upland plateaus in Montana, Wyoming, Utah, and Colorado. This species is rather similar in coloration to the black-tailed prairie dog, but it utilizes different habitats, and it has a white tip to its tail. The closely related Gunnison's prairie dog (*C. gunnisoni*) of Colorado and New Mexico, and the Utah prairie dog (*C. parvidens*) of Utah have relatively restricted distributions, and they may in fact be subspecies of the white-tailed prairie dog.

See also Rodents.

Further Reading

Banfield, A.W.F. *The Mammals of Canada.* Toronto: Ont. University of Toronto Press, 1974.

Grzimek, B. (ed.). *Grzimek's Encyclopedia of Mammals.* London: McGraw Hill, 1990.

Hall, E.R. *The Mammals of North America,* 2nd ed. New York: Wiley & Sons, 1981.

Nowak, R. M. (ed.). *Walker's Mammals of the World,* 5th ed. Baltimore: Johns Hopkins University Press, 1991.

Wilson, D.E. and D. Reeder (comp.). *Mammal Species of the World,* 2nd ed. Washington, D.C.: Smithsonian Institution Press, 1993.

Bill Freedman

Prairie falcon

Falcons are very swift **birds of prey** that hunt during the day. Falcons are in the family Falconidae, of which there are 39 species, all in the genus *Falco.*

The prairie falcon (*Falco mexicanus*) is a medium-sized, light-brown falcon that breeds in wide-open, semi-arid and prairie habitats in the western United States, southwestern Canada, and northern Mexico. Prairie falcons generally breed in the vicinity of cliffs or canyons and hunt over nearby, open terrain, and sometimes on open **forests**. The prairie falcon is migratory, wintering in the southern parts of its breeding range, as far south as central Mexico.

The prairie falcon is a crow-sized bird, with a typical body length of 17 in (43 cm). It has narrow, pointed wings, a square tail, a hooked, predatory beak, and strong, raptorial feet and claws.

Like other falcons, the prairie falcon is a strong, fast flier. The usual prey of this bird is small birds and **mammals**. The prairie falcon also has spectacular nuptial displays similar to other falcons, which involve the male bird (or tiercel) making fast-flying stoops from great heights as well as other aerial acrobatics. These are all designed to impress the female with his potential prowess as a hunter.

The nest is usually located on a ledge, on a cliff, or sometimes in an abandoned tree-nest of another large bird, such as a crow or hawk. The prairie falcon lays three to six eggs, which are mostly incubated by the female, which is fed by the male as she broods. Both of the parents care for the young birds.

Prairie falcons have declined somewhat in abundance as a result of losses of **habitat** to agriculture and the effects of toxic **insecticides**. However, while they are important, their population decreases have not been as great as those of some other **raptors**, especially the **peregrine falcon (*Falco peregrinus*)**, which was much harder hit by chlorinated insecticides.

Further Reading

Ehrlich, Paul R.; David S. Dobkin, and Darryl Wheye. *The Birder's Handbook.* New York: Simon & Schuster Inc., 1988.

Peterson, Roger Tory. *North American Birds.* Houghton Miflin Interactive (CD-ROM), Somerville, MA: Houghton Miflin, 1995.

Bill Freedman
Randall Frost

Praseodymium see **Lanthanides**

Praying mantis

The praying mantis (plural praying mantids) is a carnivorous **insects** of the order Mantoidea (or Man-

A praying mantis on a pitcher plant in Bruce National Park, Ontario. The European mantis (*Mantis religiosa*) and the Chinese mantis (*Tenodera aridifolia*) are both common to northern North America and are both introduced species. The only mantids native to the continent are in the south.

todea) named for its typical stance of an upright body with the two front legs held out in a pose of prayer. The long, thick, spiny, legs and the markedly triangular head with two large compound eyes make the mantis one of the most readily identifiable of all insects. The long neck of the praying mantis is actually the prothorax which connects the head to the thorax and supports the front legs. Two other pairs of running legs attach to either side of the thorax, as do the wings, which lie folded over the slender, elongated body. The more than 1,800 species of praying mantids, range in size from 0.4-5.9 in (1-15 cm) long and are found in most tropical and temperate climates around the world.

Reproduction

Mantids' reproductive organs are located at the tip of the abdomen. Many females are flightless and attract their mates by emitting a species-specific chemical, known as a pheromone. The male is much smaller than the female and performs a brief **courtship** ritual before alighting on the female's back to mate. A popular misconception is that the female mantis attacks and eats the male after he has fertilized her. This is true in capitivity but rare in the wild; scientists are still unsure exactly why this phenomena occurs.

Female mantids **deposit** batches of between 10 and 400 fertilized eggs using their ovipositor at the tip of the abdomen. The eggs are secured to stems, leaves, or other surfaces, with each egg batch housed in an ootheca (egg case) constructed from a frothy substance produced in the abdomen. Each egg is deposited in an individual compartment inside the ootheca, and each compartment has a one-way valve permitting the young insects to hatch with minimal effort. The ootheca hardens quickly, providing protection from parasitic insects, **birds**, and the **sun**.

Some species of mantis, such as the African *Tarachodula pantherina*, construct long, narrow oothecas and guard their eggs lying over them. In about a month, wingless nymphs (young) emerge from the eggs, and look more like **ants** than mantids. This resemblance undoubtedly protects them from predatory birds which seldom attack ants. Mantis nymphs are eaten by ants, which

KEY TERMS

Crypsis—colored or shaped to blend in with a particular environment (camouflage).

Ocelli—simple eyes which detect light and dark.

Ootheca—egg case.

Ovipositor—egg laying duct at the end of the abdomen.

Prothorax—the first of three segments of the thorax.

can wipe out an entire batch of young mantis nymphs. Surviving mantis nymphs molt several times, each time becoming more like the adult, with mature wings appearing after the final molt.

Preying

Praying mantid eat live **invertebrates**, including other mantids, although larger species have been observed to eat **frogs**, small lizards, and even small species of **mice**. The combination of camouflage, extremely flexible head movements, excellent **binocular vision**, speed, dexterity, accurate judgement of direction and **distance mean** that a mantid seldom miss their **prey**. Mantids turn their heads toward an approaching meal, they fling out their front legs at lightening speed, and secure the prey on hooked spines near the tip of each leg.

The mantids first chew off the head of the prey, before gnawing its way down the body, devouring every morsel. Decapitation of larger prey is seldom possible, so these are eaten alive. One large Australian mantis (Archimantis latistylus) was observed to chew on a gecko (a small night lizard) for over 90 minutes, eating the entire **animal**, and leaving only the skull and spine. Mantids clean themselves meticulously after every meal.

Defense

Most mantids are green, brown, or grey, and sit motionless on a **leaf**, twig, or **bark**, camouflaged from predators such as birds, small animals, and other insects. The tiny South African flower-dwelling mantis, *Harpagomantis discolor,* can change color to match the **flower**. Scare tactics, which provide some defense against small predators, include raising the torso while holding the formidable forelegs high and wide, and flashing the conspicuously marked wings.

Interaction with the environment

Mantids in gardens help to control the number of pest insects but mantids cannot provide effective control for agricultural insect **pests**.

Further Reading

Preston-Mafham, Ken, *Grasshoppers and Mantids of the World.* London/Sydney: Blandford, 1990.

Marie L. Thompson

Precession of the equinoxes

The precession of the equinoxes (sometimes simply called precession), is a movement of the celestial equator, the projection of the Earth's equator into **space**, with respect to the fixed stars and the ecliptic, the path of the Sun's **motion** in space as viewed from the **Earth**. These two great circles in space are inclined to one another by an **angle** of approximately 23.5 °, called the obliquity. Their intersection defines the **equinox**. The equator moves from east to west-in the same direction as the daily motion of the Sun-at a rate of about 50.°2 per year.

Ancient Greed astronomer Hipparchus (ca. 150 B.C.) discovered precession when he compared positions of stars for his epoch with observations made 150 years earlier by Timocharis (early 3rd century B.C.). Hipparchus determined that the precession was at least 36" per year and probably in the range 45-46," close to the modern value (although the value is not the same in all parts of the sky).

Although precession was discovered in antiquity, its cause was unexplained until formulated in the seventeenth century. In his *Principia Mathematica,* Sir Issac Newton (1643-1727) demonstrated that precession results from the nonspherical shape of the Earth. Consider the motion of another nonspherical object, a spinning top. If the top were not spinning, but merely balanced on its axis, a slight push would topple it over because the gravitational pull on one side would exceed that on the other. But with the top spinning, the **force** generated by the spin prevents the top from falling, moving it in a direction **perpendicular** to the line of gravitational pull. The top's axis then precesses and traces a cone in space.

The same occurs with the Earth. The Earth is slightly flattened, with the distance from its center to the equator being 0.3% greater than the distance from its center to the poles. Both the **Sun**, moving in the ecliptic, and the **Moon**, whose **orbit** is inclined 5° to the ecliptic, generate gravitational pulls on the equatorial bulge. If the Earth were not spinning, its equator would eventually

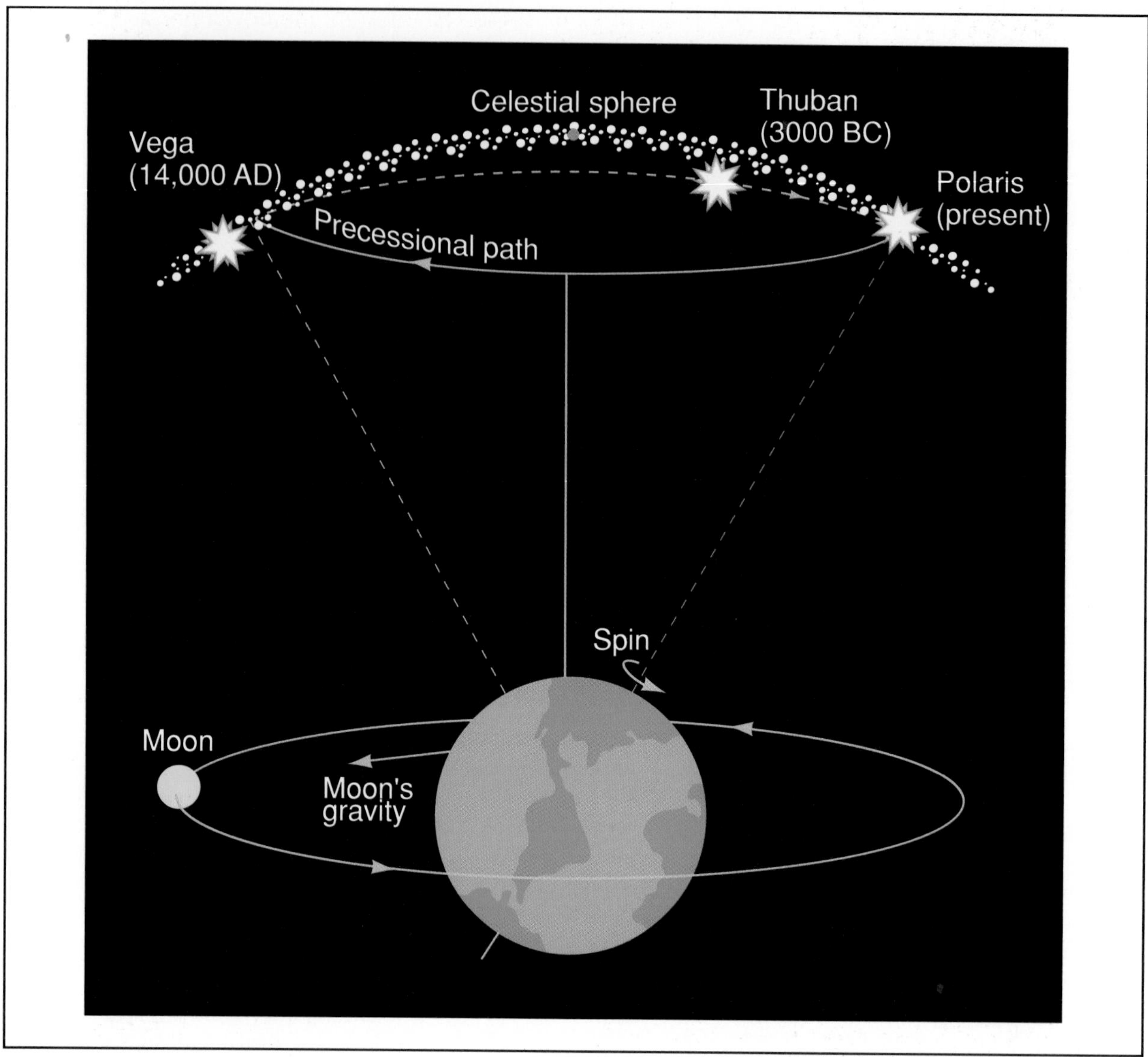

The precessional motion of the Earth.

line up near the ecliptic. But because of its daily **rotation**, the Earth, like a top, precesses; its axis of rotation traces a cone in space with a period of (360° × 60' × 60")/50. 2" per year or 25,800 years (also called a Platonic year). The precession generated by the gravitational pulls of the Sun and the Moon is called luni-solar precession and amounts to some 50.3 in per year, two-thirds of which is caused by the Moon.

But the precessional motion is actually more complicated. The Earth moves in its orbit, coinciding with the ecliptic, but it is subject to the gravitational pull of the other planets called the planetary precession. These gravitational forces cause the ecliptic, and hence the equinox, to precess at a rate of 0. 12" per year, much smaller than the luni-solar precession. The luni-solar and planetary precession together constitute the general precession. The **plane** of the Moon's orbit does not remain stationary in space; it oscillates around a **mean** value and rotates with a period of 18.6 years. These changes cause small **oscillations** in the precession, constituting an astronomical nutation, with an amplitude 9.2" and a period of 18.6 years. English astronomer James Bradley (1693-1762) announced the discovery of nutation in 1748.

Astronomical observations of the positions of celestial bodies must be corrected to account for the effects of precession and nutation. The displacement caused by precession appears negligible during the span of a human life, but the resulting movements become significant over the course of several centuries. In our time the bright **star** Polaris in the **constellation** Ursa Minor lies

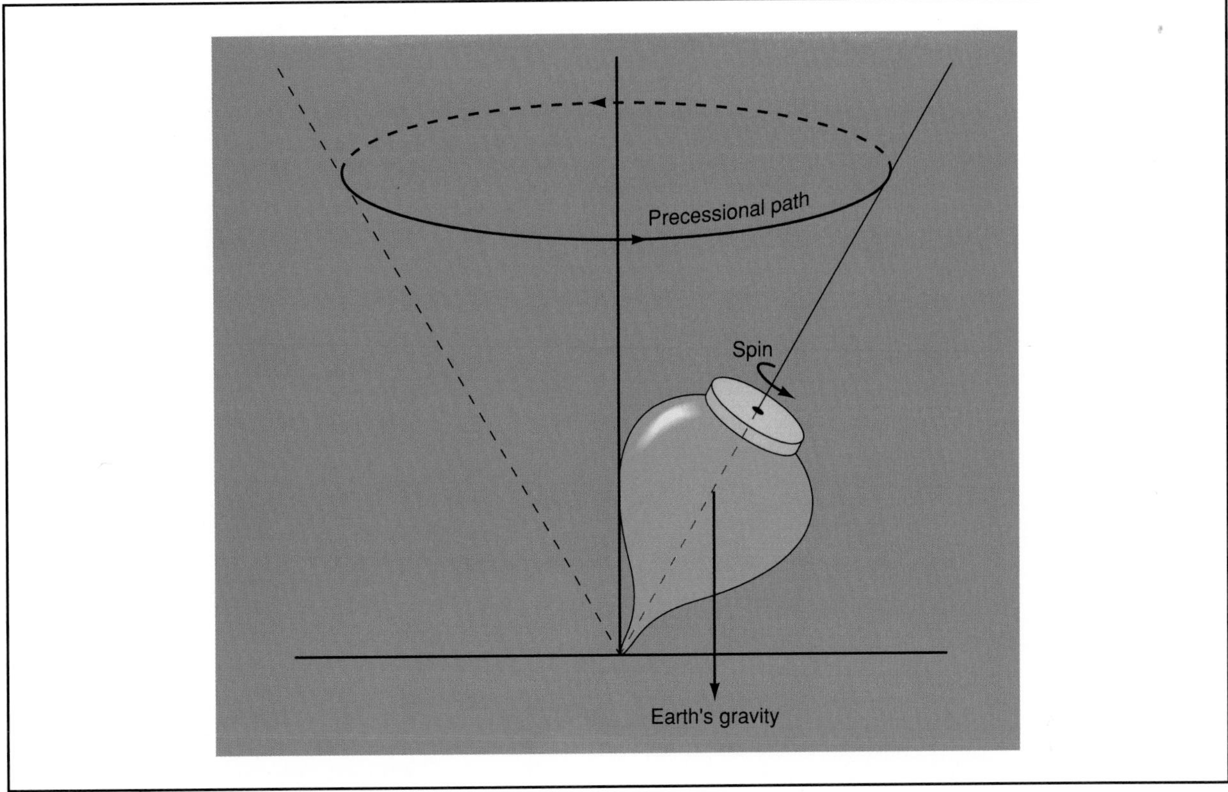

Figure 1. The precessional motion of a top.

within 1° of the north celestial pole and offers a convenient guide, as in celestial navigation, for ascertaining the northern direction. But at the time of the Egyptian Second Dynasty (ca. 2,800 B.C.) Polaris was more than 26° from the pole, whereas the star Thuban in the Draco constellation (currently 25° from the pole), was situated less than 2' from the pole. In the year 13,400 A.D. the very bright star Vega in the Lyra constellation, currently over 61° from the pole, will be located less than 5° from the pole. At that time the **seasons** in the two hemispheres will be reversed. The Northern Hemisphere will receive the most sunshine in December, and the least in June. December, January, and February will become summer months and June, July, and August winter months; the reverse will be true in the Southern Hemisphere. December, January, and February, currently summer months, will become winter months.

See also Gravity and gravitation.

Further Reading

Berry, A. *A Short History of Astronomy.* Dover, New York: 1961, Sec. 42, 213-215.

Krzeminski, Z.S." How Precession Changes the Coordinates of a Star." *Sky and Telescope.* October 1991, p. 408.

Murray, C.A. *Vectorial Astrometry.* Bristol, U.K.: Adam Hilger Ltd., 1983, Ch. 5.

Newcomb, S. *Compendium of Spherical astronomy.* Dover, New York: 1960, Ch. 9.

Richard L. Branham Jr.

Precious metals

Gold, silver, and platinum have historically been valued for their beauty and rarity. They are the precious metals. Platinum usually costs slightly more than gold, and both metals are about 80 times more costly than silver. Precious **metal** weights are given in Troy ounces (named for Troyes, France, known for its fairs during the Middle Ages) a unit approximately 10% larger than 1 oz (28.35 g).

The ancients considered gold and silver to be of noble birth compared to the more abundant metals. Chemists have retained the term noble to indicate the resistance these metals have to **corrosion**, and their natural reluctance to combine with other elements.

History

The legends of King Midas and Jason's search for the golden fleece hint at prehistoric mankind's early fas-

KEY TERMS

Celestial equator—The projection into space of the Earth's equator.

Ecliptic—Apparent path of the Sun in the sky or, alternatively, the plane of the Earth's orbit in space.

Equinox—Intersection of the celestial equator and the ecliptic.

General precession—Combined luni-solar and planetary precession.

Luni-solar precession—Precession caused by the gravitational pull of the Sun and the Moon on the Earth's equator.

Nutation—Periodic oscillation in the precession caused principally by the Moon.

Planetary precession—Precession caused by the gravitational pull of the planets on the Earth as a whole.

Obliquity—The angle formed by the intersection of the celestial equator and the ecliptic.

cination with precious metals. The proof comes in the gold and silver treasure found in ancient Egyptian tombs and even older Mesopotamian burial sites.

The course of recorded history also shows twists and turns influenced to a large degree by precious metals. It was Greek silver that gave Athens its Golden Age, Spanish gold and silver that powered the Roman empire's expansion, and the desire for gold that motivated Columbus to sail west across the Atlantic. The exploration of Latin America was driven in large part by the search for gold, and the Jamestown settlers in **North America** had barely gotten their" land legs" before they began searching for gold. Small amounts of gold found in North Carolina, Georgia, and Alabama played a role in the 1838 decision to remove the Cherokee Indians to Oklahoma. The California gold rush of 1849 made California a state in 1850, and California gold fueled northern industry and backed up union currency, two major factors in the outcome of the Civil War.

Gold

Since ancient times, gold has been associated with the **sun**. Its name is believed derived from a Sanskrit word meaning "to shine," and its chemical symbol (Au) comes from *aurum*, Latin for "glowing dawn". Pure gold has an exceedingly attractive, deep yellow color and a specific gravity of 19.3. Gold is soft enough to scratch with a fingernail, and the most malleable of metals. A block of gold about the size of a sugar cube can be beaten into a translucent film some 27 ft (8 m) on a side. Gold's purity is expressed either as fineness (parts per 1,000) or in karats (parts per 24). An **alloy** containing 50 % gold is 500 fine or 12 karat gold. Gold resists corrosion by air and most chemicals but can be dissolved in a mixture of nitric and hydrochloric acids, a solution called *aqua regia* because it dissolves the "king of metals".

Occurrence

Gold is so rare that one ton of average rock contains only about eight pennies worth of gold. Gold **ore** occurs where geologic processes have concentrated gold to at least 250 times the value found in average rock. At that **concentration** there is still one million times more rock than gold and the gold is rarely seen. Ore with visible gold is fabulously rich.

Gold most commonly occurs as a pure metal called native gold or as a natural alloy with silver called electrum. Gold and silver combined with tellurium are of local importance. Gold and silver tellurides are found, for example, in the mountains around the old **mining** boom-town of Telluride, Colorado. Gold is found in a wide variety of geologic settings, but placer gold and gold veins are the most economically important.

Placer gold

Placer gold is derived from gold-bearing rock from which the metal has been freed by **weathering**. Gravity and running **water** then combine to separate the dense grains of golds from the much lighter rock fragments. Rich concentrations of gold can develop above deeply weathered gold veins as the lighter rock is washed away. The "Welcome Stranger" from the gold fields of Victoria, **Australia**, is a spectacular 2,516 oz (71.5 kg) example of this type of occurrence.

Gold washed into **mountain** streams also forms placer deposits where the stream's **velocity** diminishes enough to **deposit** gold. Stream placers form behind boulders and other obstructions in the stream bed and where a tributary stream merges with a more slowly moving river. Placer gold is also found in gravel bars where it is deposited along with much larger rocky fragments.

The discovery of place gold set off the California gold rush of 1849 and the rush to the Klondike in 1897. The largest river placers known are in Siberia, Russia. Gold-rich sands there are removed with jets of water, a process known as hydraulic mining. An fascinating byproduct of Russia's hydraulic mining is the unearthing

Over one ton of gold bars. *Photo Researchers, Inc.*

of thousands of woolly mammoths, many with flesh intact, locked since the Ice Age in frozen **tundra** gravel.

Stream placer deposits have their giant ancient counterparts in paleoplacers, and the Witwatersrand district in South **Africa** outproduces all others combined. Gold was reported from the Witwatersrand (White Waters Ridge) as early as 1834, but it was not until 1886 that the main deposit was discovered. From that time until today, it has occupied the paramount position in gold mining history. Witwatersrand gold was deposited between 2.9 and 2.6 billion years ago in six major fields, each produced by an ancient river system.

Placer and paleoplacers are actually secondary gold deposits, their gold having been derived from older deposits in the mountains above. The California 49ers looked upstream hoping to find the mother lode, and that's exactly what they called the system of gold veins they discovered.

Gold veins

Vein gold is deposited by hot subterranean water known as a hydrothermal fluid. Hydrothermal fluids circulate through rock to leach small amounts of gold from large volumes of rock and then deposit it in fractures to form veins. Major U.S. gold vein deposits have been discovered at Lead in the Black Hills of South Dakota and at Cripple Creek on the slopes of Pike's Peak, Colorado. Important vein deposit are also found in Canada and Australia. All these important deposits where located following the discovery of placer gold in nearby streams.

Production and uses

Gold's virtual indestructibility means that almost all the gold ever mined is still in use today. It is entirely possible that some gold **atoms** that once graced the head of Cleopatra now reside in your jewelry, stereo, or teeth. Today, gold is being mined in ever increasing amounts from increasingly lower-grade deposits. It is estimated that 70% of all gold recovered has been mined in this century. Each year nearly 2,000 tons are added to the total. Nevada currently leads the nation in gold production, and the Republic of South Africa is the world's leading gold-producing nation.

Gold has traditionally been used for coinage, bullion, jewelry and other decorative uses. Gold's chemical inertness means that gold jewelry is nonallergenic and remains tarnish-free indefinitely. For much the same reasons gold has long been used in **dentistry**. Modern industry is consuming increasing quantities of gold, mostly as electrical contacts in micro circuitry.

Silver

Silver is a brilliant white metal and the best metal in terms of thermal and **electrical conductivity**. Its chemical symbol, Ag, is derived from its Latin name, *argentum*, meaning *white and shining*. Silver is not nearly as precious, dense, or noble as gold or platinum. The ease with which old silverware tarnishes is an example of its chemical reactivity. Although native silver is found in nature, it most commonly occurs as compounds with other elements, especially **sulfur**.

Hydrothermal veins constitute the most important source of silver. The Comstock Lode, a silver bonanza 15 mi (24 km) southeast of Reno, Nevada, is a well known example. Hydrothermal silver veins are formed in the same manner as gold veins, and the two metals commonly occur together. Silver, however, being more reactive than gold, can be leached from surface **rocks** and carried downward in solution. This process, called supergene enrichment, can concentrate silver into exceedingly rich deposits at depth.

Mexico has traditionally been the world's leading silver producing country, but the United States, Canada, and Peru each contribute significant amounts. Although silver has historically been considered a precious metal, industrial uses now predominate. Significant quantities are still used in jewelry, silver ware, and coinage; but even larger amounts are consumed by the photographic and **electronics** industries.

Platinum

Platinum, like silver, is a beautiful silver-white metal. Its chemical symbol is Pt and its name comes

from the Spanish world for silver (*plata*), with which it was originally confused. Its specific gravity of 21.45 exceeds that of gold, and, like gold, it is found in pure metallic chunks in stream placers. The average crustal abundance of platinum is comparable to that of gold. The melting point of platinum is 3,219°F (1,769°C), unusually high for a metal, and platinum is chemically inert even at high **temperature**. In addition, platinum is a catalyst for chemical reactions that produce a wide range of important commodities.

Platinum commonly occurs with five similar metals known as the platinum group metals. The group includes osmium, iridium, rhodium, palladium, and ruthenium. All were discovered in the residue left when platinum ore was dissolved in aqua regia. All are rare, expensive, and classified chemically as noble metals.

Platinum is found as native metal, natural alloys, and as compounds with sulfur and arsenic. Platinum ore deposits are rare, highly scattered, and one deposit dominates all others much as South Africa's Witwatersrand dominates world gold production. That platinum deposit is also in the Republic of South Africa.

Placer platinum was discovered in South Africa in 1924 and subsequently traced to a distinctively layered igneous rock known as the Bushveld Complex. Although the complex is enormous, the bulk of the platinum is found in a thin layer scarcely more than three feet thick. Nearly half of the world's historic production of platinum has come from this remarkable layer.

The Stillwater complex in the Beartooth mountains of southwestern Montana also contains a layer rich in platinum group metals. Palladium is the layer's dominant metal, but platinum is also found. The layer was discovered during the 1970s, and production commenced in 1987.

Production and uses

Platinum is used mostly in catalytic converters for vehicular **pollution** control. Low-voltage electrical contracts form the second most common use for platinum, followed closely by dental and medical applications, including dental crowns, and a variety of pins and plates used internally to secure human bones. Platinum is also used as a catalyst in the manufacture of **explosives**, fertilizer, gasoline, **insecticides**, paint, plastic, and pharmaceuticals. Platinum crucibles are used to melt high-quality optical **glass** and to grow crystals for computer chips and lasers. Hot glass fibers for insulation and nylon fibers for **textiles** are extruded through platinum sieves.

Future outlook

Because of their rarity and unique properties, the demand for gold and platinum are expected to continue to increase. Silver is more closely tied to industry, and the demand for silver is expected to rise and fall with economic conditions.

KEY TERMS

Catalyst—A substance that facilitates a chemical reaction but is not consumed in that reaction.

Electrum—A natural alloy of gold and silver.

Hydrothermal fluid—Hot water-rich fluid capable of transporting metals in solution.

Malleable—the ability of a substance to be pounded into thin sheets or otherwise worked, for example during the making of jewelry.

Placer—A mineral deposit formed by the concentration of heavy mineral grains such as gold or platinum.

Specific gravity—The ration of the weight of any volume of a substance to the weight of an equal volume of water.

Troy ounce—The Troy ounce, derived from the fourteenth-century system of weights used in the French town of Troyes, is still the basic unit of weight used for precious metals.

See also Element, chemical; Mining.

Further Reading

Boyle, Robert. *Gold History and Genesis of Deposits.* New York: Van Nostrand Reinhold, 1987.

Kesler, Stephen. *Mineral Resources, Economics and the Environment.* New York: MacMillan, 1994.

St. John, Jeffrey. *Noble Metals.* Alexandria, Va: Time-Life Books, 1984.

Eric R. Swanson

Precipitation

Precipitation is **water** in either solid or liquid form that falls from the earth's atmosphere. Major forms of precipitation include rain, snow, and hail. When air is lifted in the atmosphere, it expands and cools. Cool air cannot hold as much water in vapor form as warm air, and the condensation of vapor into droplets or ice crystals may eventually occur. If these droplets or crystals continue to grow to large sizes, they will eventually be heavy enough to fall to the earth's surface.

Types of precipitation

Precipitation in liquid form includes drizzle and raindrops. Raindrops are on the order of a millimeter (one thousandth of a meter) in radius, while drizzle drops are approximately a tenth of this size. Important solid forms of precipitation include snowflakes and hailstones. Snowflakes are formed by aggregation of solid ice crystals within a cloud, while hailstones involve supercooled water droplets and ice pellets. They are denser and more spherical than snowflakes. Other forms of solid precipitation include graupel and sleet (ice pellets). Solid precipitation may reach the earth's surface as rain if it melts as it falls. *Virga* is precipitation that evaporates before reaching the ground.

Formation of precipitation

Precipitation forms differently depending on whether it is generated by warm or cold **clouds**. Warm clouds are defined as those that do not extend to levels where temperatures are below 32°F (0°C), while cold clouds exist at least in part at temperatures below 32°F (0°C). **Temperature** decreases with height in the lower atmosphere at a moist adiabatic rate of about 6°C per 1,000 m (3.3°F per 3,281 ft), on average. High clouds, such as cirrus, are therefore colder and more likely to contain ice. As discussed below, however, temperature is not the only important **factor** in the formation of precipitation.

Precipitation formation in warm clouds

Even the cleanest air contains aerosol particles (solid or liquid particles suspended in the air). Some of these particles are called *cloud condensation nuclei*, or CCN, because they provide favorable sites on which water vapor can condense. Air is defined to be fully saturated, or have a relative humidity of 100%, when there is no net transfer of vapor molecules between the air and a **plane** (flat) surface of water at the same temperature. As air cools, its relative humidity will rise to 100% or more, and molecules of water vapor will bond together, or condense, on particles suspended in the atmosphere. Condensation will preferentially occur on particles that contain water soluble (hygroscopic) material. Types of particles that commonly act as CCN include sea-salt and particles containing sulfate or nitrate ions; they are typically about 0.0000039 in (0.0001 mm) in radius. If relative humidity remains sufficiently high, CCN will grow into cloud droplets 0.00039 in (0.01 mm) or more in size. Further growth to precipitation size in warm clouds occurs as larger cloud droplets collide and coalesce (merge) with smaller ones.

Precipitation formation in cold clouds

Although large quantities of liquid water will freeze as the temperature drops below 32°F (0°C), cloud droplets sometimes are "supercooled'; that is, they may exist in liquid form at lower temperatures down to about -40°F (-40°C). At temperatures below -40°F (-40°C), even very small droplets freeze readily, but at intermediate temperatures (between -40 and 32°F or -40 and 0°C), particles called ice nuclei initiate the freezing of droplets. An ice nucleus may already be present within a droplet, may contact the outside of a droplet and cause it to freeze, or may aid in ice formation directly from the vapor phase. Ice nuclei are considerably more rare than cloud condensation nuclei and are not as well understood.

Once initiated, ice crystals will generally grow rapidly because air that is saturated with respect to water is supersaturated with respect to ice; i.e., water vapor will condense on an ice surface more readily than on a liquid surface. The *habit*, or shape, of an ice **crystal** is hexagonal and may be plate-like, column-like, or dendritic (similar to the snowflakes cut from paper by children). Habit depends primarily on the temperature of an ice crystal's formation. If an ice crystal grows large enough to fall through air of varying temperatures, its shape can become quite intricate. Ice crystals can also grow to large sizes by aggregation (clumping) with other types of ice crystals that are falling at different speeds. Snowflakes are formed in this way.

Clouds that contain both liquid water and ice are called mixed clouds. Supercooled water will freeze when it strikes another object. If a supercooled droplet collides with an ice crystal, it will attach itself to the crystal and freeze. Supercooled water that freezes immediately will sometimes trap air, forming opaque (rime) ice. Supercooled water that freezes slowly will form a more transparent substance called clear ice. As droplets continue to collide with ice, eventually the shape of the original crystal will be obscured beneath a dense coating of ice; this is how a hailstone is formed. Hailstones may even contain some liquid water in addition to ice. Thunderstorms are dramatic examples of vigorous mixed clouds that can produce high precipitation rates. The electrical charging of precipitation particles in thunderstorms can eventually cause lightning discharges.

Measurement of precipitation

Precipitation reaching the ground is measured in terms of precipitation rate or precipitation intensity. Precipitation intensity is the depth of precipitation reaching the ground per hour, while precipitation rate may be expressed for different time periods. Typical precipitation rates for the northeastern United States are 2-3 in (50-80

mm) per month, but in Hilo, Hawaii, 49.9 in (1270 mm) of rain fell in March 1980. Average annual precipitation exceeds 80 in (2000 mm) in many locations. Because snow is less compact than rain, the **mass** of snow in a certain depth may be equivalent to the mass of rain in only about one-tenth that depth (i.e., one inch of rain contains as much water as about 10 inches of snow). Certain characteristics of precipitation are also measured by **radar** and satellites.

Hydrologic cycle

The **Earth** is unique in our **solar system** in that it contains water, which is necessary to sustain life as we know it. Water that falls to the ground as precipitation is critically important to the **hydrologic cycle**, the sequence of events that moves water from the atmosphere to the earth's surface and back again. Some precipitation falls directly into the oceans, but precipitation that falls on land can be transported to the oceans through **rivers** or underground in aquifers. Water stored in this permeable rock can take thousands of years to reach the sea. Water is also contained in reservoirs such as lakes and the **polar ice caps**, but about 97% of the earth's water is contained in the oceans. The sun's **energy** heats and evaporates water from the **ocean** surface. On average, **evaporation** exceeds precipitation over the oceans, while precipitation exceeds evaporation over land masses. Horizontal air motions can transfer evaporated water to areas where clouds and precipitation subsequently form, completing the **circle** which can then begin again.

The distribution of precipitation is not uniform across the earth's surface, and varies with time of day, season and year. The lifting and cooling that produces precipitation can be caused by solar heating of the earth's surface, or by forced lifting of air over obstacles or when two different air masses converge. For these reasons, precipitation is generally heavy in the tropics and on the upwind side of tall **mountain** ranges. Precipitation over the oceans is heaviest at about 7°N latitude (the intertropical convergence zone), where the tradewinds converge and large thunderstorms frequently occur. While summer is the" wet season" for most of **Asia** and northern **Europe**, winter is the wettest time of year for Mediterranean regions and western **North America**. Precipitation is frequently associated with large-scale low-pressure systems (cyclones) at mid-latitudes.

Human influences on precipitation

Precipitation is obviously important to humankind as a source of drinking water and for agriculture. It cleanses the air and maintains the levels of lakes, rivers, and oceans, which are sources of food and recreation. Interestingly, human activity may influence precipitation in a number of ways, some of which are intentional, and some of which are quite unintentional. These are discussed below.

Hailstones are often composed of concentric layers of clear and opaque ice. This is thought to be the result of the stone traveling up and down within the cloud during its formation. Opaque layers would be created in the upper, colder parts of the cloud, where the water droplets are small and freeze rapidly, forming ice with numerous air enclosures. In the warmer, lower parts of the cloud the water droplets would spread over the surface of the hailstone so that little air is trapped and the ice is transparent.

Cloud seeding

The irregular and frequently unpredictable nature of precipitation has led to a number of direct attempts to either stimulate or hinder the precipitation process for the benefit of humans. In warm clouds, large hygroscopic particles have been deliberately introduced into clouds in order to increase droplet size and the likelihood of collision and coalescence to form raindrops. In cold clouds, ice nuclei have been introduced in small quantities in order to stimulate precipitation by encouraging the growth of large ice crystals; conversely, large concentrations of ice nuclei have been used to try to reduce numbers of supercooled droplets and thereby inhibit precipitation formation. Silver iodide, which has a crystalline structure similar to that of ice, is frequently used as an ice nucleus in these "cloud seeding" experiments. Although certain of these experiments have shown promising results, the exact conditions and extent over which cloud seeding works and whether apparent successes are statistically significant is still a matter of debate.

Acid rain

Acid rain is a phenomenon that occurs when acidic pollutants are incorporated into precipitation. It has been

observed extensively in the eastern United States and northern Europe. **Sulfur** dioxide, a gas emitted by power plants and other industries, can be converted to acidic sulfate compounds within cloud droplets. In the atmosphere, it can also be directly converted to acidic particles, which can subsequently act as CCN or be collected by falling raindrops. About 70 Megatons of sulfur is emitted as a result of human activity each year across the **planet**. (This is comparable to the amount emitted naturally.) Also, **nitrogen** oxides are emitted by motor vehicles, converted to **nitric acid** vapor, and incorporated into clouds in the atmosphere.

Acidity is measured in terms of **pH**, the **negative** logarithm of the **hydrogen** ion **concentration**; the lower the pH, the greater the acidity. Water exposed to atmospheric **carbon** dioxide is naturally slightly acidic, with a pH of about 5.6. The pH of rainwater in remote areas may be as low as about 5.0 due to the presence of natural sulfate compounds in the atmosphere. Additional sulfur and nitrogen containing acids introduced by anthropogenic (human-induced) activity can increase rainwater acidity to levels that are damaging to aquatic life. Recent reductions in emissions of **sulfur dioxide** in the United Kingdom have resulted in partial recovery of some affected lakes.

Greenhouse effect

Recent increases in anthropogenic emissions of trace gases (for example, **carbon dioxide**, methane, and chloroflourocarbons) have resulted in concern over the so-called **greenhouse effect**. These trace gases allow energy in the form of sunlight to reach the Earth's surface, but "trap" or absorb the infrared energy (**heat**) that is emitted by the Earth. The heat absorbed by the atmosphere is partially re-radiated back to the earth's surface, resulting in warming. Trends in the concentrations of these greenhouse gases have been used in climate models (computer simulations) to predict that the global average surface temperature of the Earth will warm by 3.6–10.8°F (2–6°C) within the next century. For comparison, the difference in average surface temperature between the Ice Age 18,000 years ago and present day is about 9°F (5°C).

Greenhouse warming due to anthropogenic activity is predicted to have other associated consequences, including rising **sea level** and changes in cloud cover and precipitation patterns around the world. For example, a reduction in summertime precipitation in the Great Plains states is predicted by many models and could adversely affect crop production. Other regions may actually receive higher amounts of precipitation than they do currently. The level of uncertainty in these model simulations is fairly high, however, due to approximations that are made. This is especially true of calculations related to aerosol particles and clouds. Also, the natural variability of the atmosphere makes verification of any current or future trends extremely difficult unless actual changes are quite large.

Effects of particulate pollution on cloud microphysics

As discussed above, gas-phase pollutants such as sulfur dioxide can be converted into water-soluble particles in the atmosphere. Many of these particles can then act as nuclei of cloud droplet formation. Increasing the number of CCN in the atmosphere is expected to change the characteristics of clouds. For example, ships' emissions have been observed to cause an increase in the number of droplets in the marine stratus clouds above them. If a constant amount of liquid water is present in the cloud, the average droplet size will be smaller. Higher concentrations of smaller droplets reflect more sunlight, so if pollution-derived particles alter clouds over a large enough region, climate can be affected. Precipitation rates may also decrease, since droplets in these clouds are not likely to grow large enough to precipitate.

See also Seasons; Thunderstorm; Weather modification.

Further Reading

Mason, B.J. *Acid Rain: Its Causes and its Effects on Inland Waters.* Oxford: Clarendon Press, 1992.

KEY TERMS

Aerosol particles—Solid or liquid particles suspended in the air.

Cold cloud—A cloud that exists, at least in part, at temperatures below 32°F (0°C).

Hailstone—Precipitation that forms when supercooled droplets collide with ice and freeze.

Mixed cloud—A cloud that contains both liquid water and ice.

Supercooled—Water than exists in a liquid state at temperatures below 32°F (0°C).

Virga—Precipitation that evaporates before reaching the ground.

Warm cloud—A cloud that exists entirely at temperatures warmer than 32°F (0°C).

A cheetah and her cubs at a kill in the Kalahari, South Africa.

Rogers, R.R. and M.K. Yau. *A Short Course in Cloud Physic.s.* Oxford: Pergamon Press, 3rd Edition, 1989.

Schneider, Stephen. "The Greenhouse Effect: Science and Policy." Science 243 (1989): 771-781.

Wallace, John M. and Peter Hobbs. *Atmospheric Science: An Introductory Survey.* Orlando, Florida: Academic Press, Inc., 1977.

Cynthia Twohy Ragni

Predator

A predator is an **organism** that hunts and eats its **prey**. All predators are heterotrophs, meaning they must consume the tissues of other organisms to fuel their own growth and reproduction. The most common use of the term is to describe the many types of carnivorous animals that catch, kill, and eat other animals. There is a great diversity of such predatory animals, ranging in size from small **arthropods** such as tiny **soil mites** that eat other mites and **springtails**, to large mammalian carnivores such as lions and orcas, living in cohesive social groups and collectively hunting, killing, and feeding on prey that can weigh more than a ton.

Most **animal** predators kill their prey and then eat it. However, so-called micropredators only consume part of large prey animals, and they do not necessarily kill their quarry. Female **mosquitoes**, for example, are micropredators that seek out large prey animals for the purpose of obtaining a **blood** meal, in the process aggravating, but not killing their prey. If this sort of feeding relationship is an obligate one for the micropredator, it is referred to as parasitism.

Herbivory is another type of predation, in which animals seek out and consume a prey of **plant** tissues, sometimes killing the plant in the process. In some cases, only specific plant tissues or organs are consumed by the **herbivore**, and ecologists sometimes refer to such feeding relationships as, for example, seed predation or **leaf** predation.

Most predators are animals, but a few others are plants and **fungi**. For example, **carnivorous plants** such as pitcher plants and sundews are morphologically adapted to attracting and trapping small arthropods (see entry on carnivorous plants). The prey is then digested by en-

zymes secreted for the purpose, and some of the **nutrients** are assimilated by the predatory plant. Carnivorous plants usually grow in nutrient-poor habitats, and this is the basis in **natural selection** for the **evolution** of this unusual type of predation. A few types of fungi are also predatory, trapping small nematodes using various anatomical devices, such as sticky knobs or branches, and tiny constrictive rings that close when nematodes try to move through. Once a nematode is caught, fungal hyphae surround and penetrate their victim, and absorb its nutrients.

See also Carnivore; Heterotroph; Parasites.

Prenatal surgery

Prenatal surgery, also called fetal surgery, is medical treatment of the fetus before **birth**, while it is still in the womb. Most fetal therapies are "closed" procedures, performed without opening the womb. The rarest type of fetal surgery is known as "open surgery," in which the mother's abdomen and uterus are cut open to reveal the tiny fetus.

History of fetal surgery

The first successful fetal surgery, a **blood** transfusion, was performed by A. William Liley in 1963 in Auckland, New Zealand. He used **x rays** to see the fetus and guide his needle. Liley's success was unparalleled for years, however. Most doctors considered the pregnant womb as sacrosanct and untouchable. To treat the fetus as a patient, separate from its mother, was unthinkable. That view began to change in the early 1970s with the spread of several new diagnostic tools.

With the introduction of the ultrasound machine, a doctor could bounce sound waves into the pregnant woman's abdomen and create an image of the fetus on a TV-like screen. Amniocentesis and chorionic villi sampling procedures made it possible to remove fetal cells from the pregnant uterus for genetic testing. These tests could determine the presence of **Down Syndrome** and other genetic diseases. With these new tools of prenatal **diagnosis**, it was possible to identify abnormalities in fetuses as young as two or three months old. Yet this information often left parents with only a few limited choices. They could choose to abort a severely deformed fetus, or they could prepare for the medical treatment of their baby as soon as it was born.

A few medical researchers began imagining another option: could these fetuses be treated before birth? Beginning in the late 1970s, several young physicians began studying obstetrics, **genetics**, and pediatric surgery in their quest to perform fetal therapy. International Fetal Medicine and Surgery Society was created in order to support one another's efforts and share information. This group and another international organization known as the Fetoscopy Study Group provided a forum where new techniques in fetal medicine are presented and debated. Since then, using a variety of procedures, fetal surgeons have successfully drained a blocked bladder, removed abnormal growths from a lung, and repaired a diaphragm, the muscle that divides the abdominal and chest cavities.

Closed-womb surgery

More common than open surgery, closed-womb procedures are still rare enough to be practiced at only a few dozen specialized institutions. Sometimes these procedures are called "needle treatments." Since the first fetal blood transfusion in 1963, fetal transfusions have become one of the most accepted types of fetal therapy, although they are still uncommon. Transfusions can save the life of a fetus if the blood of the fetus and its mother are incompatible. In the case of Rh incompatibility, for instance, the antibodies in the blood of an Rh negative mother will attack the red blood cells of an Rh positive baby. Guided by ultrasound, the doctor inserts a needle through the mother's abdomen and injects compatible blood into the umbilical blood vessels. In a similar fashion, doctors use needles to deliver life-saving medications.

Sometimes twins fail to develop normally, and the poor health of one twin jeopardizes the life of the other, healthy twin. Left untreated, such pregnancies typically end with the death of both twins. In this situation, parents might permit the doctor to perform fetal surgery and terminate the abnormal twin in order to save the healthy twin. In a rare condition known as twin-twin transfusion syndrome, the blood circulation of the two twins is connected and one fetus lacks a **brain** and a **heart**. In a closed-womb procedure, surgeons have successfully used miniature instruments to tie a knot in the blood vessels linking the two twins. Although this kills the abnormal twin, the other twin is much more likely to survive.

Pregnancies that begin with triplets and quadruplets almost never result in the healthy birth of all the fetuses. Indeed, the mother risks miscarrying the entire pregnancy. In this situation, parents and surgeons may decide to reduce the pregnancy to twins in order to ensure the health of at least some of the fetuses. Unwanted fetuses are killed using a needle to inject potassium chloride into the fetal chest. This stops the heart from beating. Multiple pregnancies are becoming more widespread due to the use of fertility drugs and certain **infertility** treat-

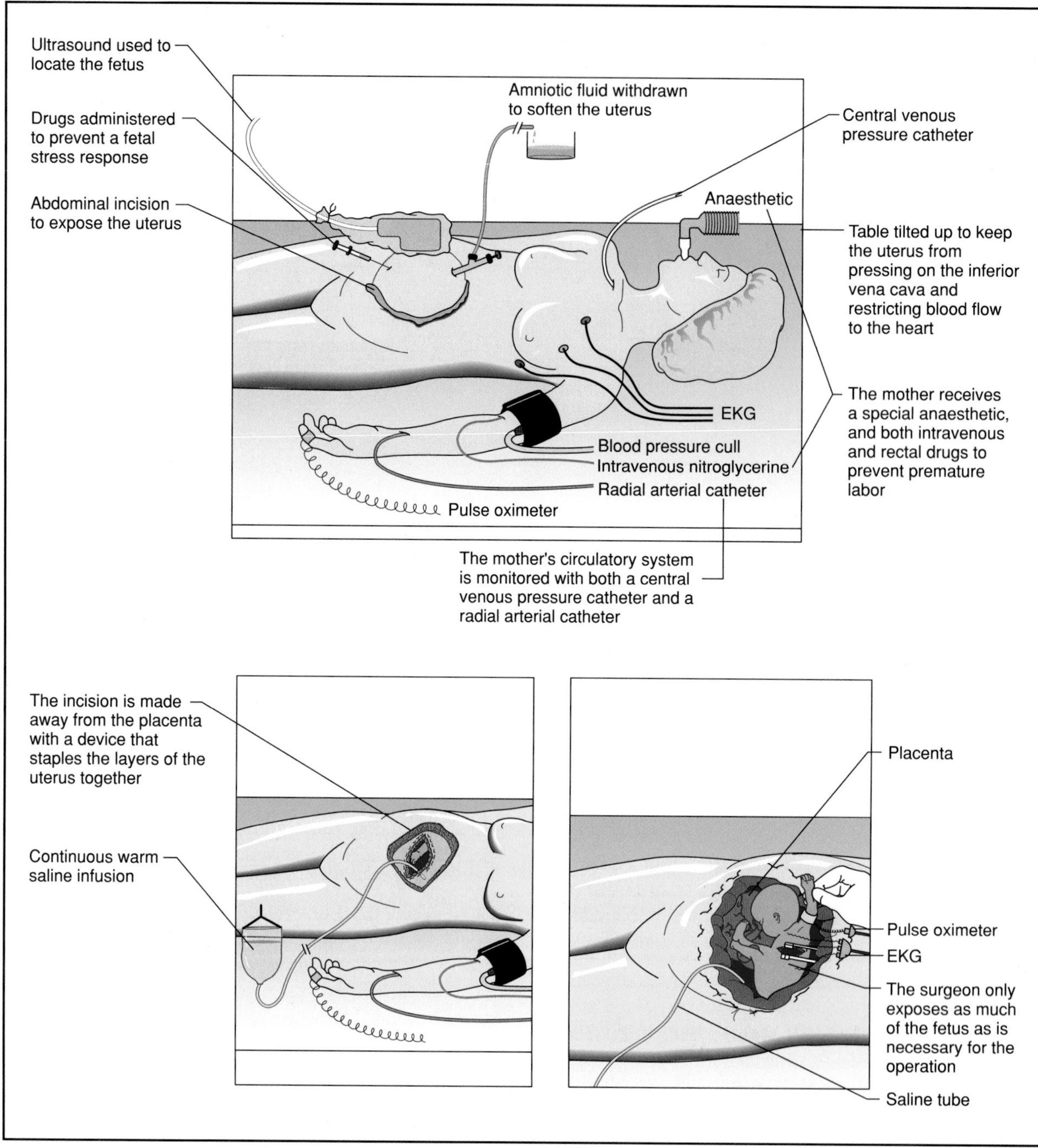

Preparation for prenatal surgery.

ments. So-called fetal reduction has therefore become a potentially more common procedure, but it remains highly controversial.

Open surgery

Open surgery is highly experimental. As of 1994, medical researchers had reported only about 55 operations in the previous 14 years. The vast majority of these were performed by pediatric surgeon Michael R. Harrison and his team at the Fetal Treatment Center at the University of California, San Francisco. Harrison's team has performed open surgery, at least once, for seven or eight different **birth defects**. Three types of open surgery have proved most promising: removing lung tumors, treating a blocked urinary tract, and re-

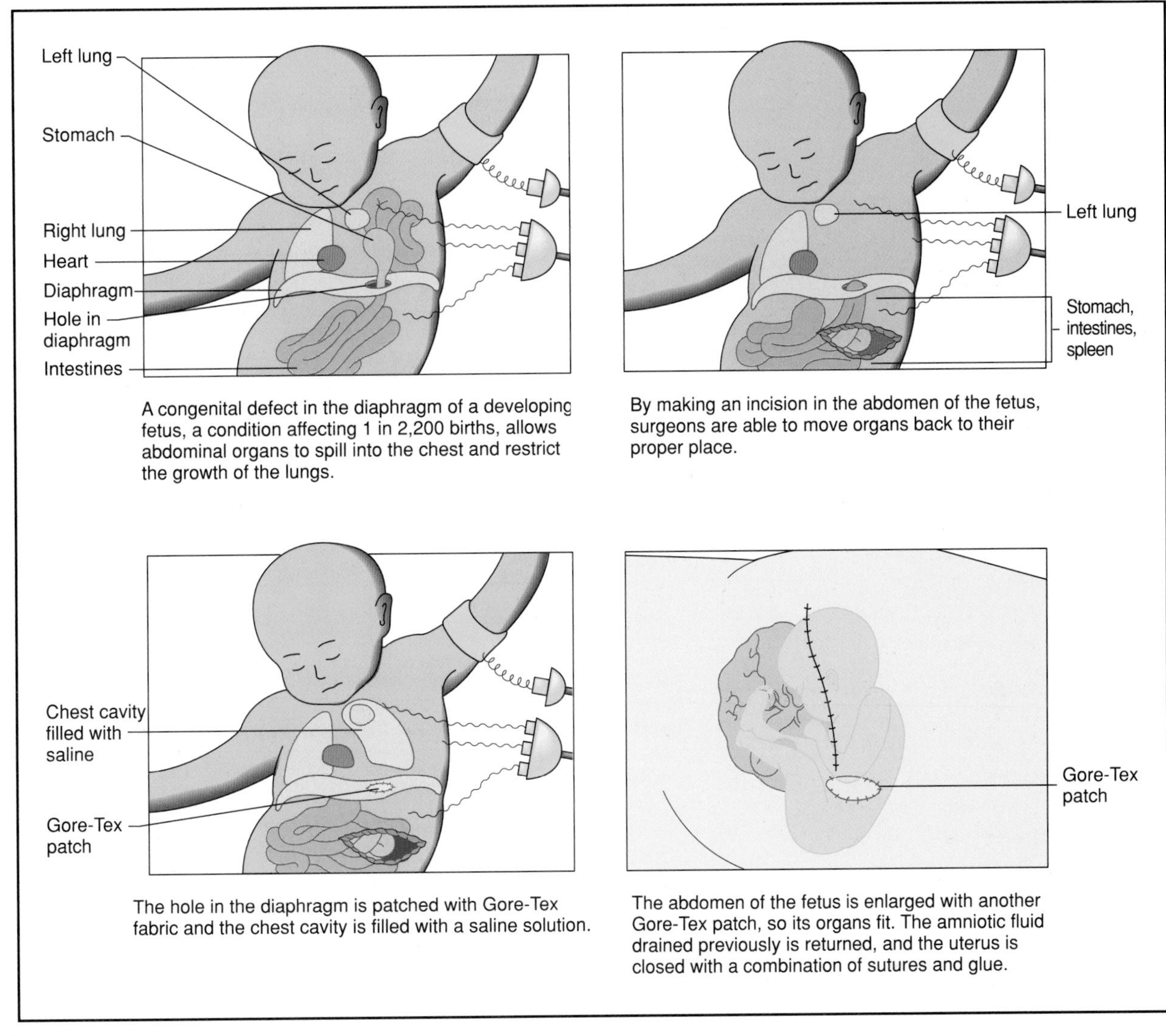
Left lung
Stomach
Right lung
Heart
Diaphragm
Hole in diaphragm
Intestines
A congenital defect in the diaphragm of a developing fetus, a condition affecting 1 in 2,200 births, allows abdominal organs to spill into the chest and restrict the growth of the lungs.
Left lung
Stomach, intestines, spleen
By making an incision in the abdomen of the fetus, surgeons are able to move organs back to their proper place.
Chest cavity filled with saline
Gore-Tex patch
The hole in the diaphragm is patched with Gore-Tex fabric and the chest cavity is filled with a saline solution.
Gore-Tex patch
The abdomen of the fetus is enlarged with another Gore-Tex patch, so its organs fit. The amniotic fluid drained previously is returned, and the uterus is closed with a combination of sutures and glue.

A specific surgical procedure to correct a defect in the diaphragm of a developing fetus.

pairing a hole in the diaphragm. Prompt treatment of these conditions early in pregnancy prevent a cascade of other problems in fetal development. A hole in the diaphragm, for instance, allows the stomach and intestines to migrate through the diaphragm and press against the lungs. This condition, known as a diaphragmatic **hernia**, halts the development of the lungs. Most babies with diaphragmatic hernias are unable to breathe at birth and die.

In open surgery, the pregnant woman is placed under **anesthesia**. The anesthetic, which crosses the placenta, puts the fetus to **sleep** as well. The surgeon then cuts through the abdomen and uterus to reach the fetus. This part of the operation is like a cesarean section. Once revealed, the tiny fetus is gently turned, so that the desired body part is exposed to the surgeon's hands. At 24 weeks, a typical age for surgery, the fetus weighs about a pound and has arms smaller than a surgeon's fingers.

When lung cysts are removed, an incision is made in the fetus's chest, and the abnormal growth is sliced off. Only solid cysts require open surgery. Other types of cysts can be treated without opening the uterus. In a closed-womb procedure, the surgeon uses a hollow needle to install a shunt that drains the cyst into the amniotic sac.

Blockages in the urinary system can also be relieved with either open or closed surgery. When blockages occur, the bladder fills with urine and balloons to immense proportions, sometimes growing larger than the fetus's head. The grotesque size and **pressure** of this **organ** disturbs the normal growth of the kidneys and lungs. In open surgery, the fetus is gently pulled, feet

first, out of the uterus until its abdomen is exposed and the blockage can be surgically corrected. In closed-womb procedures, surgeons install a shunt that permits the fetal urine to flow from the bladder into the amniotic sac.

To repair a diaphragmatic hernia, the surgeon makes two incisions into the fetus's left side: one into the chest and one into the abdomen. Next the surgeon pushes the stomach and intestines back down into their proper place. Then he or she closes the hole in the diaphragm with a patch of waterproof Gore-Tex, the fabric used in outdoor gear. Rather than close the abdominal incision, the surgeon places a Gore-Tex patch over the cut in order to allow the abdomen to expand and accommodate its newly returned organs. At birth, this patch is removed. The internal patch remains for life.

After the surgery on the fetus is finished, the mother's uterus and abdomen are closed. She can usually leave the hospital after eight days of careful monitoring. To prevent premature labor, a common problem after open surgery, the woman must stay in bed and take drugs to quell uterine contractions.

Babies who have successfully undergone surgery are born without scars, a happy and unexpected by-product of operations performed in the womb. They are usually born early, however. Thus, in addition to their original medical problem, they face the problems of any premature infant. Surgery also has a long-term effect on the mother. Since her uterus has been weakened by the incisions made during surgery, normal labor and delivery is no longer safe. To prevent uterine rupture, she must deliver this baby (and all future babies) by cesarean section, before active labor begins, to prevent uterine rupture.

The success rate of open surgery

When doctors began performing open surgery, in the early 1980s, most of the fetuses died. Some physicians were critical of the attempts. They argued that a healthy woman was put at risk in order to attempt the rescue of a fetus that would most likely die anyway. Others supported the experimental surgery and declared that this was the fetus's only chance.

Today, open surgery remains a last resort for a small number of birth defects. It is appropriate only if it can result in the normal development of the fetus. Surgery that prolongs the lives of babies suffering from incurable health problems is not acceptable. Neither is surgery that puts the mother at excessive risk. In many cases, medical treatment after the baby is born offers an equal chance of success, provided that the pregnancy is carefully supervised and that delivery is planned at a well-equipped hospital with a neonatal intensive care unit.

Ethical issues

Certain aspects of fetal surgery raise thorny ethical issues. Treating a fetus as a patient creates a situation that has never before existed. In the past, experimental treatments for the seriously ill could be justified on the grounds that the patient had everything to gain and nothing to lose. With fetal surgery, that may hold true for the fetus, of course, but the benefits and risks to the mother are far less obvious. Many mothers are willing to do whatever is necessary to give birth to a healthy baby. Yet major abdominal surgery and general anesthesia pose risks to the mother. The regimen she must follow after surgery is uncomfortable. Furthermore, the success rate for some surgeries is quite low. Most types of fetal surgery must be approved by a hospital ethics review board.

Research studies have shown that fetal surgery does not interfere with a woman's future fertility. Still, ethicists argue that a woman must always have the freedom to choose against fetal surgery. They fear that as the procedures gain acceptance and it proves more successful, women will find it increasingly difficult to say no. They also worry that a judge might order a woman to have fetal surgery against her will. Legal precedent already exists for this kind of dispute between mother and fetus. Pregnant women have been ordered to have unwanted cesarean sections after medical authorities testified that the operation was in the best interest of the unborn baby.

Fetal reduction

Fetal reduction, the systematic killing of one or more fetuses in order to save those remaining, also raises ethical issues. To a certain extent, the issues duplicate those involved in the abortion debate: when is it ethical to kill a fetus? If a woman plans to abort the whole pregnancy unless a fetal reduction is done, is it wrong to kill some fetuses so that others may live? Many fetal surgeons will not perform fetal reductions.

Future developments

Fetal surgery is no longer limited to a few techniques. With advances in knowledge and improvements in equipment, new opportunities for the treatment of more birth defects will emerge. The unexpected discovery that fetuses heal without scarring suggests that cleft palate and other facial defects might be conducive to repair in the womb. Further research is needed, however, before surgery can be justified for conditions that are not life-threatening.

Advances in fetal surgery are expected to benefit other fields of medicine as well. New strategies to prevent early labor in fetal-surgery patients, for instance,

KEY TERMS

Amniocentesis—A procedure in which amniotic fluid is removed from the pregnant uterus with a needle. Fetal cells in the fluid are studied for the presence of certain genetic defects.

Chorionic villi sampling—A procedure in which hairlike projections from the chorion, a fetal structure present early in pregnancy, are suctioned off with a catheter inserted into the uterus. These fetal cells are studied for the presence of certain genetic defects.

Closed surgery—Medical treatment performed on the fetus without opening the mother's uterus.

Diaphragmatic hernia—A serious birth defect caused by a hole in the diaphragm, the muscle that divides the abdominal and chest cavities.

Fetal reduction—Surgery performed to abort one or more fetuses in a multiple pregnancy.

Open surgery—Surgery performed directly on the fetus by opening the mother's abdomen and uterus.

Premature labor—Uterine contractions that occur before the fetus is 37 weeks old, the age it can be born safely.

Twin-twin transfusion syndrome—A condition in which abnormal blood vessels link one healthy fetus and one unhealthy fetus in a multiple pregnancy.

Ultrasound—A diagnostic technique that produces a picture of a fetus on a TV-like screen by bouncing sound waves into the pregnant uterus.

can be applied to any pregnant woman who is at risk for early labor. In a similar fashion, new tools developed for fetal surgery may find other uses in medicine. Further understanding of scarless healing may also lead to innovations in the treatment of adult surgical patients.

See also Embryo and embryonic development.

Further Reading

Begley, Sharon. "The Tiniest Patients." *Newsweek*, (June 11, 1990): 56.

Brower, Montgomery, et al. "Saving Lives Not Yet Begun." *People*, (June 18, 1990): 39-41.

Edelson, Edward. *Birth Defects*. New York: Chelsea House Publishers, 1992.

Fishman, Steve. "A View of the Womb." *Vogue*, (April 1994): 244.

Harrison, Michael R. "Fetal Surgery." In *Fetal Medicine*, special issue of *The Western Journal of Medicine*. (September 1993): 341-49.

Holloway, Marguerite. "Fetal Law." *Scientific American*, (September 1990): 46-47.

Kolata, Gina. *The Baby Doctors*. New York: Delacorte Press, 1990.

Ohlendorf-Moffat, Pat. "Surgery Before Birth." *Discover*, (February 1991): 59-65.

Sullivan, Kerry M. and N. Scott Adzick. "Fetal Surgery." *Clinical Obstetrics and Gynecology*, 37, No. 2 (June 1994): 355-69.

Liz Marshall

Prescribed burn

Prescribed fire involves the controlled burning of vegetation to achieve some desired management effect. Prescribed burns can be used to encourage a desired type of forest regeneration, to prevent the invasion of prairies by shrubs and trees, to decrease the abundance of pathogens, to prevent catastrophic wildfires by reducing the accumulation of fuel, or to create or maintain **habitat** for certain species of animals. Prescribed burns can be very useful tools in vegetation and habitat management, but it is critical that this practice be based on a sound understanding of the ecological effects the result.

Prescribed burning in forestry

Prescribed burns are an important tool in some types of management systems in **forestry**. Most commonly, fire is utilized to reduce the amount of logging debris present after clear-cutting. This practice is generally undertaken to make the site more accessible to **tree** planters. The use of prescribed burning for this purpose means that the site does not have to be prepared using more expensive physical techniques such as scarification by heavy machinery.

Sometimes prescribed fire is also useful in developing better seedbeds for planting tree seedlings. Prescribed burns can also be used to encourage natural regeneration by particular types of trees that are economically desirable such as certain species of **pines**. When using fire for this purposes, it is important to plan for the survival of an adequate number of mature seed trees. If this is not accomplished, the burned site would have to be planted with seedlings grown in a greenhouse.

Prescribed burning makes available a flush of certain **nutrients** in ash, particularly, **calcium**, **magnesium**, potassium, and **phosphorus**. However, there may be lit-

tle **biomass** of regenerating vegetation on the site immediately after a **burn**, and therefore there is little biological capability to take up soluble forms of nutrients. Hence, much of the nutrient content of the ash may be lost from the site during heavy rains. In addition, most of the organic **nitrogen** of the logging debris becomes oxidized during **combustion** to gaseous compounds such as nitric oxide, and the fixed nitrogen is therefore lost from the **ecosystem**.

The use of prescribed fire in forestry is most suitable for forest types that are naturally adapted to regeneration after **wildfire**, for example, most pine and boreal **forests**. The use of this industrial practice in other types of forests, particularly temperate rain forests, is more controversial.

Prescribed burning in vegetation management

Many natural ecosystems are maintained by wildfires. In the absence of this sort of disturbance, these ecosystems would gradually transform into another type through the process of **succession**. For example, most of the original tall-grass **prairie** of **North America** occurred in a climatic regime that was capable of supporting shrubs or oak-dominated forests. However, the extensive transformation of the prairie into these ecosystems was prevented by frequent ground fires which were lethal to woody plants but could be survived by most of the herbaceous species of the prairie. Today, tall-grass prairie has been almost entirely converted into agricultural usages, and this is one of North America's most endangered types of natural ecosystem. The few remnants of tall-grass prairie that have been protected are managed using prescribed burns to prevent the incursions of shrubs which would otherwise degrade the integrity of this ecosystem.

Tall-grass prairies are maintained by relatively frequent fires. However, some types of forests may need fires on a much longer **rotation** to prevent their conversion into another type of forest community. For example, forests in California dominated by redwoods (*Sequoia sempervirens*) need occasional fires in order to reduce the abundance of more tolerant species of trees and thereby prevent these from eventually dominating the community. Fire is also useful in the redwood ecosystem in preventing an excessive build-up of fuels that could eventually allow a devastating crown fire to occur which would kill the mature redwood trees. In some cases, prescribed burning is used to satisfy the requirement of redwood forests for low-intensity fires.

Prescribed burns can also be used to prevent catastrophic wildfires in some other types of forests. In this usage, relatively light surface fires that do not scorch the tree canopy are used to reduce the biomass of living and dead ground vegetation and shrubs and thereby reduce the amount of fuel in the forest. When this practice is carried out in some types of pine forests, there is an additional benefit through enhancement of natural regeneration of the pine species which require a mineral seedbed with little **competition** from other species of plants.

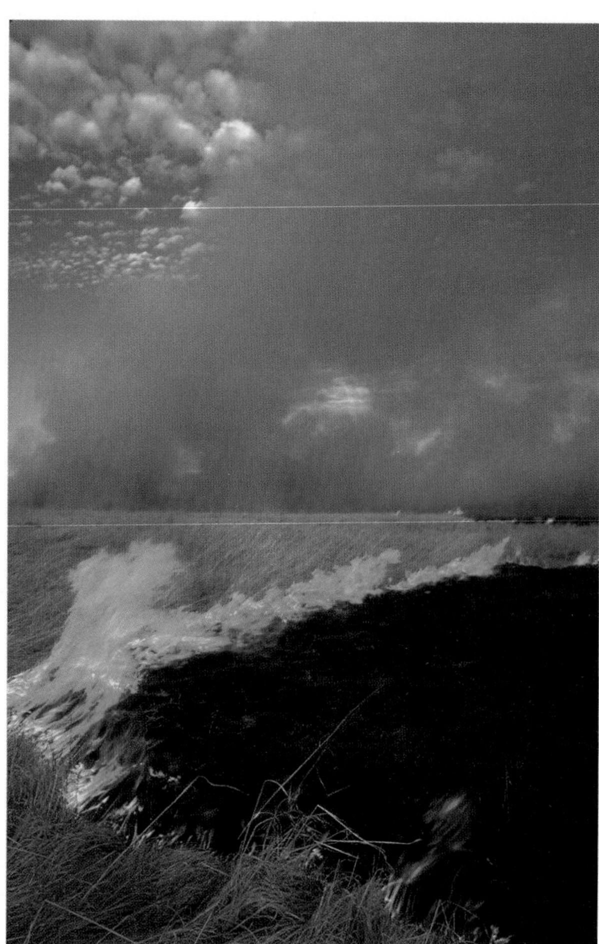

Use of controlled burning for prairie management in South Dakota.

Prescribed burning in habitat management

Prescribed fire has long been utilized to manage the habitat of certain species of animals. In North America, for example, the aboriginal nations that lived in the Great Plains often set prairie fires to improve the habitat for the large animals that they hunted as food. This was especially important to people living in regions of tall-grass prairie which could otherwise revert to shrub- and tree-dominated ecosystems that were less suitable for their most important hunted animals such as buffalo (*Bison bison*).

KEY TERMS

Prescribed burn—The controlled burning of vegetation as a management practice to achieve some ecological benefit.

Prescribed fires have also been used to enhance the habitat of some **endangered species**. For example, this practice is utilized in Michigan to develop stands of jack pine (*Pinus banksiana*) of a type required as habitat by the endangered Kirtland's warbler (*Dendroica kirtlandii*). This bird does best in even-aged stands of jack pine aged seven to 25 years old and about 6.6-19.7 ft (2-6 m) tall. **Wildlife** managers ensure a continuous availability of this kind of habitat by planting stands of jack pine and by deliberately burning older stands.

Further Reading

Freedman, B. *Environmental Ecology.* 2nd ed. San Diego: Academic Press, 1994.

Kimmins, H. *Balancing Act. Environmental Issues in Forestry.* Vancouver: University of British Columbia Press, 1992.

Bill Freedman

Pressure

Pressure is the amount of **force** applied to a given area. Acrobats and cheerleaders sometimes stand on each other's shoulders to form a human tower. Even with perfect balance, there is a **limit** to how high such a tower can be built. Ultimately, the ability of the bottom person to bear the pressure, caused by the weight of all the people stacked above, is the limiting **factor**. Pressure, then, is the amount of force applied on a given area.

In this example, increasing the number of people in the tower increases the amount of force applied to the shoulder area, which in turn causes the bottom person to be under greater pressure. But pressure can also be increased without changing the amount of applied force. If the person standing directly above were to stand on one foot, thereby shifting all the weight onto a smaller area, the bottom person would feel increased pressure on that burdened shoulder.

Turning a nail upside down and driving its large, flat head through the **wood** by hammering its point, is a more difficult task than conventional nailing. Even if you were able to hammer the point with the same force, the flat head of the nail would spread this force over a relatively large surface area. As a result, there might not be enough pressure on the surface of the wood to cause penetration.

A force exerted over a small area causes more pressure than the same force applied over a large area. This principle explains why karate experts use the side of the hand when breaking a board, instead of the full palm which has more surface and would apply less pressure to the wood.

Similarly, a force exerted over a large area causes less pressure than the same force applied over a small area. This explains why it's possible to walk on top of deep snow with large, flat snowshoes when ordinary rubber boots would cause you to sink.

The kinetic molecular theory of gases and pressure.

According to the kinetic theory, gas, like all **matter**, is composed of many small, invisible particles that are in constant **motion**. In a child's toy **balloon**, the amount of particle motion depends on the **temperature** of the gas trapped inside. The collision of the air particles with the walls of the balloon, accounts for the pressure.

Imagine a **glass** jar containing a few **steel** ball bearings. If you were to shake the jar, the steel balls would crash into the walls, and the sum of their forces would exert a pressure which might be enough to break the glass. Pressure depends on the total number of collisions and the intensity of the force with which each steel ball hits the glass. Both factors can be increased by shaking the jar more violently or in the case of the toy balloon, by increasing the temperature of the air trapped inside.

Atmospheric pressure and common measuring units for pressure

As humans living on the surface of the **earth**, we dwell at the bottom of an **ocean** of air. Each one of us supports on his or her shoulders the pressure caused by the weight of an air column that extends out to interstellar **space**.

Hold out the palm of your hand. Its area is approximately 20 squared inches and the weight of the air resting upon it is nearly 300 lbs. Yet with all this weight, your hand does not crush. This is because our bodies are used to living under such pressures. The liquids and solids inside your body grow to exert an equal pressure from the inside.

Air particles are constantly hitting every part of our bodies and the pressure they cause is known as **atmos-**

pheric pressure. At high altitudes, such as you would find in places like Mexico City or Aspen, there is less air above you and therefore less atmospheric pressure. Breathing becomes more difficult, but throwing a baseball for **distance** is easier because there is less air resistance experienced by the moving baseball.

The **barometer**, invented by Evangelista Torricelli in 1643, was the first instrument built to measure the pressure of the gases in our atmosphere. It consisted of a long glass tube closed at one end, filled with liquid mercury, and inverted into a dish of more mercury.

With this instrument, it has been observed that at **sea level**, atmospheric pressure can support the weight of about 760 mm of Hg (mercury). The exact figure depends on such things as **weather** conditions.

One standard atmosphere (1 atm) of pressure is the pressure exerted by a column of mercury that is 760 mm high at a temperature of 0degrees C. In the Universe, pressure varies from about 1 atmosphere on the Earth's surface to approximately **zero** in the **vacuum** of outer space. Much higher pressures are found at the center of stars and other massive bodies.

The pascal is the SI unit of pressure. One pascal is equal to the force of one newton applied to a surface whose area is equal to one squared meter. 1.0 Pa = 1.0 N / m^2. One atmosphere of pressure is equal to approximately 101.3 KPa.

Pressure in liquids

According to the kinetic theory, liquids are also composed of many small particles, but in contrast to gases where the particles are very far apart, liquid particles are often touching.

Liquid **water** is much more dense than air, and one litre of it contains many more particles and much more **mass** than an equivalent **volume** of air. When you dive into a **lake**, you can feel the pressure of the water above you even if you are just a few meters below the surface because your body is supporting a lot of weight. Doubling your depth below the surface causes the pressure on your body to also double.

Fill an empty juice can with water and put two holes down one side. Place one hole near the top of the can and one near the bottom. The water coming out of the bottom hole will shoot out much further than the water escaping from the hole near the top. This is because the water at the bottom of the can is supporting the weight of the water column above it and so it is under greater pressure.

Lou D'Amore

KEY TERMS

Atmospheric Pressure—The Earth's gravitational force pulls the surrounding air towards the Earth. The force created by this action causes atmospheric pressure.

Kinetic Molecular Theory— The theory that explains the behavior of matter in terms of the motion of the particles that make it up.

Newton—The SI unit of force. One newton is roughly the force exerted by the Earth on a 0.1 kg mass. This is about equal to the force exerted upward by your hand when supporting a medium sized apple.

SI units—Measurement units that are part of the metric system of measurement. This system is also called the SI system after the French name Le Systeme International d'Unites.

Prey

Prey refers to any living entities that are hunted and consumed by predators. Usually the term is used in reference to animals that are stalked, killed, and consumed by other animals, as when a **deer** is killed by a **mountain** lion. However, plants may also be considered to be the prey of herbivorous animals, and hosts may be considered the prey of their **parasites**.

Often, predators are important sources of mortality for populations of their prey. As such, predators may act as significant agents of **natural selection**, with some prey individuals being favored because they are less vulnerable to predation, while less-fit individuals of the same species suffer a disproportionate risk of mortality from this source. If differences among individuals in the vulnerability to predation have a genetic basis, then **evolution** will occur at the population level, and the prey will become more difficult to capture. This evolutionary change in the vulnerability of prey in turn exerts a selective **pressure** on the predators, so that the more capable individual hunters are favored and the population of predators becomes more effective at catching prey. This is an example of coevolution of populations of predators and prey.

There are limits, however, to how evasive prey can become, and to how effective predators can become. Eventually, extreme expression in the prey of anatomical, physiological, or behavioural characteristics that help to reduce the risks of predation may become mal-

adaptive in other respects. For example, adaptive changes in the coloration of prey may make them more cryptic, so they blend in better with the background environment and are therefore less visible to predators. However, in many species bright coloration is an important cue in terms of species recognition and mate selection, as is the case of **birds** in which the males are garishly colored and marked. In such cases, a balance must be struck among adaptations that make prey more difficult to catch, and those that are important in terms of coping with other environmental or biological factors that exert selective pressures.

Predator-prey associations of plants and herbivores also develop coevolutionary dynamics. To deter their predators, plants may evolve bad tastes, toxic chemicals, or physical defenses such as thorns and spines. At the same time, the herbivores evolve ways to overcome these defenses.

Predator satiation refers to a situation in which prey is extremely abundant during a short or unpredictable period of time, so that the capability of predators to catch and eat the prey is overwhelmed. For example, to reduce the impact of predation of their **fruits**, many species of plants **flower** and seed prolifically at unpredictable times, so herbivores cannot collect and consume all of the fruits, and many **seeds** survive. There are also many animal-prey examples of predator satiation. For example, **metamorphosis** of the larval stages of many species of **frogs** and **salamanders** is often closely synchronized, so that most individuals transform and leave the breeding pond at about the same time. This is a very risky stage of the **life history** of these animals, and although many of the individuals are predated upon, the ability of the predators to catch and process this superabundant prey is limited. Consequently, many of the recently transformed frogs and salamanders manage to survive.

Bill Freedman

Primates

Primates are an order of **mammals**. Most primates are characterized by well-developed **binocular vision**, a flattened, forward-oriented face, prehensile digits, opposable thumbs (sometimes the first and second digits on the feet are also opposable), five functional digits on the feet, nails on the tips of the digits (instead of claws), a clavicle (or collarbone), a shoulder joint allowing free movement of the arm in all directions, a tail (except for **apes**), usually only two mammae (or teats), relatively large development of the cerebral hemispheres of the **brain**, usually only one offspring born at a time, and having a strong social organization. Most species of primates are highly arboreal (that is, they live in the forest canopy), but some live mostly on the ground. Primates first evolved early in the Cenozoic Era, about 60 million years ago. The ancestral stock of the primates is thought have been small, carnivorous animals similar to modern **tree shrews** (family Tupaiidae).

There are about 12 families and 60 genera of living primates (the numbers vary depending on the particular zoological study being consulted). Most species of primates inhabit tropical and sub-tropical regions, and most occur in forested habitats. Primates are divided into two sub-orders, the Prosimii (or **prosimians**) and the Anthropoidea (**monkeys** and apes). The families and examples of component species are given below.

Prosimii (This sub-order of primates has a relatively ancient evolutionary lineage, and includes several families of **lemurs**, **lorises**, and **tarsiers**, all of which have fox-like snouts, long tails, and inhabit **forests**.

Cheirogaleidae (This is a family of five species of dwarf or mouse lemurs, which only occur on the **island** of Madagascar, off **Africa** in the Indian **Ocean**. An example is the hairy-eared dwarf lemur (*Allocebus trichotis*).

Lemuridae (This is the largest family of lemurs, consisting of about 10 species, which only occur on Madagascar and the nearby Comoro Islands. Examples are the black lemur (*Eulemur macaco*) and the ring-tailed lemur (*Lemur catta*).

Megaladapidae (This is a family of two species of sportive lemurs, which also only occur on Madagascar. An example is the grey-backed sportive lemur (*Lepilemur dorsalis*).

Indridae (This is another family of prosimians of Madagascar, including four species known as wooly lemurs. An example is the indri (*Indri indri*).

Daubentoniidae (This family has only one species, the aye-aye (*Daubentonia madagascariensis*) which live in the forests of Madagascar.

Lorisidae (This prosimian family of 12 species occurs in forests of South **Asia**, Southeast Asia, and Africa. Examples are the slender loris (*Loris tartigradus*) of India and the potto (*Perodicticus potto*) of tropical Africa.

Tarsiidae (This family includes three species of small prosimians that inhabit forests of islands of Southeast Asia. One example is the Philippine tarsier (*Tarsius syrichta*).

Anthropoidea (This sub-order includes the Old World monkeys, the **New World monkeys**, the mar-

Chimpanzees are the only primates whose genetic material closely matches that of humans.

mosets, and the apes. The various monkeys are relatively small, arboreal, and have tails, while the apes are larger, relatively intelligent, and lack a tail. Most species of anthropoid primates are arboreal and inhabit forests, but some do not.

Callitrichidae (This family includes about 33 species of small marmoset monkeys of tropical forests of **South America** and Panama. Examples include the golden-headed lion tamarin (*Leontopithecus chrysomelas*) and the pygmy marmoset (*Cebuella pygmaea*), both occurring in Brazil.

Cebidae (This family includes about 37 species of New World monkeys, distinguished by their prehensile (or grasping) tail, and nostrils separated by a relatively wide partition. Examples are the dusky titi monkey (*Cellicebus cupreus*) of northern South America and the Central American squirrel monkey (Saimiri oerstedii) of Costa Rica and Panama.

Cercopithecidae (This family includes about 60 species of Old World monkeys of Africa and Asia, characterized by non-prehensile tails, closely placed nostrils, and (usually) bare skin on the buttocks. Examples include the black colobus (*Colobus satanas*) of central Africa, the rhesus macaque (*Macaca mulatta*) of South Asia, the mandrill (*Mandrillus sphinx*) of West Africa, and the **proboscis monkey** (*Nasalis larvatus*) of Borneo.

Hylobatidae (This is a family of six species of gibbon apes, which are tail-less, highly arboreal and agile, and have loud, complex vocalizations (known as "songs"). Examples are the black gibbon (*Hylobates concolor*) of Southeast Asia and the siamang (*Symphalangus syndactylus*) of Malaysia and Sumatra.

Hominidae (This family includes five species of great apes, which are relatively large and robust, lack a tail, and are the most intelligent and socially complex species of primates. This group includes the gorilla (*Go-*

rilla gorilla) of Central Africa, the pygmy chimpanzee (*Pan paniscus*) of Congo, the chimpanzee (*Pan troglodytes*) of Central Africa, the orangutan (*Pongo pygmaeus*) of Borneo and Sumatra, and humans (*Homo sapiens*) who have worldwide distribution. All hominidae, with the exception of humans, only inhabit tropical forests.

Humans evolved about one million years ago. They are now by far the most widespread and abundant species of primate, living on all of the continents, including **Antarctica**. Humans are also the most intelligent species of primate, and probably of any species. Humans have undergone extremely complex cultural **evolution**, characterized by adaptive, progressive discoveries of social systems and technologies that are allowing this species to use the products of ecosystems in an increasingly efficient and extensive manner. **Habitat** changes associated with human activities, coupled with the harvesting of many species and ecosystems as resources, are now threatening the survival of numerous other species and natural ecosystems. This includes almost all other species of primates, whose populations have declined to the degree that the World Conservation Union (IUCN) considers them threatened by **extinction.**

Prime numbers

A prime number is any number greater than 1 that is divisible only by itself and 1. The only even prime number is 2, since all other even numbers are at least divisible by themselves, 1, and 2.

The idea of primacy dates back hundreds of years. Mathematicians began putting forth ideas concerning prime numbers as early as 400 B.C., but Greek mathematician Euclid is largely credited with publishing the first **concrete** theories involving prime numbers in his work *Elements* (est. 300 B.C.). Since then, prime numbers have proved to be elusive mysteries in the world of **mathematics**.

Finding prime numbers

Any discussion on the location process for prime numbers must begin with the statement of one fact: there is an infinite number of prime numbers. All facts in mathematics must be backed by a **proof**, and this one is no exception. Assume all prime numbers can be listed like this: p1, p2, p3, ...pN, with p1=2, p2=3, p3=5, and pN= the largest of the prime numbers (remember, we are assuming there are a finite, or limited, number of primes). Now, form the equation p1p2p3...pN + 1 = X. That means that X is equal to the product of all the primes plus 1. The number produced will not be divisible by any prime number evenly (there will always be a remainder of 1), which indicates primacy. This contradicts the original assumption, proving that there really are an infinite number of primes. Although this may seem odd, the fact remains that the supply of prime numbers is unlimited.

This fact leads to an obvious question-how can all the prime numbers be located? The answer is simple-they can't, at least not yet. Two facts contribute to the slippery quality of prime numbers, that there are so many and they don't occur in any particular order. Mathematicians may never know how to locate all the prime numbers.

Several methods to find some prime numbers do exist. The most notable of these methods is Erasthenes' Seive, which dates back to ancient Greek **arithmetic**. Named for the man who created it, it can be used to locate all the prime numbers between 2 and N, where N is any number chosen. The process begins by writing all the numbers between 2 and N. Eliminate every second number after 2. Then eliminate every third number, starting with the very next integer of 3. Start again with the next integer of 5 and eliminate every fifth number. Continue this process until the next integer is larger than the square root of N. The numbers remaining are prime. Aside from the complexity of this process, it is obviously impractical when N is a large 100 digit number.

Another question involving the location of prime numbers is determining whether or not a given number N is prime. A simple way of checking this is dividing the number N by every number between 2 and the **square root** of N. If all the divisors leave a remainder, then N is prime. This is not a difficult task if N is a small number, but once again a 100 digit number would be a monumental task.

A shortcut to this method was discovered in 1640 by a mathematician named Pierre de Fermat. He determined that if a number (X) is prime it divides evenly into b^x - b. Any number can be used in the place of b. A non-prime, or composite, used in the place of b leaves a remainder. Later it was determined that numbers exist that foil this method. Known as Carmichael numbers, they leave no remainder but are not prime. Although extremely rare, their existence draws attention to the elusive quality of prime numbers.

One final mysterious quality of prime numbers is the existence of twin primes, or prime pairs. Occasionally, two consecutive odd numbers are prime, such as 11 and 13 or 17 and 19. The problem is no theory exists to find all of them or predict when they occur.

KEY TERMS

Factors—Numbers that when multiplied equal the number to which they are factors.

Carmichael numbers—Some numbers that have qualities of primes, but are not prime.

Erasthenes' Seive—One method for locating primes.

Twin primes—Prime numbers that appear as consecutive odd integers.

Euclid—Greek scientist credited with the first theories of prime numbers.

Prime numbers in modern life

A question one might ask at this point is "How is any of this important?" Believe it or not, theories about prime numbers play an important role in big money banking around the world.

Computers use large numbers to protect money transfers between bank accounts. Cryptographers, people who specialize in creating and cracking codes, who can **factor** one of those large numbers are able to transfer money around without the consent of the bank. This results in computerized bank robbery at the international level.

Knowing how to protect these accounts relies on prime numbers, as well as other theories involving factoring. As more and more of the world uses this method of protecting its money, the value of facts concerning primes grows every day.

Further Reading

Cipra, Barry. *Science*. vol. 248. (June 31, 1990).

Peterson, I. *Science News*. vol. 142. (September 19, 1992).

Karush, William. *Dictionary of Mathematics*. Webster's New World Printing, 1989.

Newman, James R. *World of Mathematics*. vol. 1&3. Simon and Schuster, 1956.

Primroses

Primroses are perennial, herbaceous plants in the genus *Primula*, family Primulaceae. There are about 500 species of primroses. Most of these occur in arctic, boreal, and cool-temperate climates, including mountain-tops in tropical latitudes. The greatest species numbers occur in the mountains of central **Asia**, and, to a lesser degree, in northern Eurasia and **North America**. Only one species occurs in **South America**, in southern Patagonia.

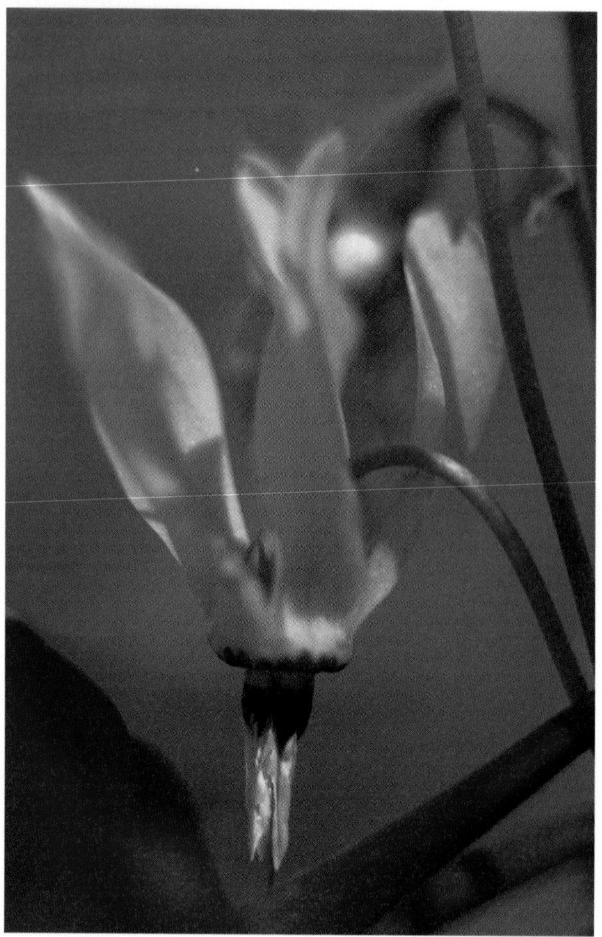

Bloom of the shooting star, a member of the primrose family.

The flowers of primroses are small but very attractive. Primrose flowers occur as solitary units, or in small groups (inflorescences). The flowers of primroses are radially symmetric, and have five partially fused petals and five sepals. Primroses have a rosette of leaves at the base of the **plant** and a taller structure that bears the flowers.

Some native primroses of North America include several species commonly known as the birds'-eye primrose. *Primula mistassinica* occurs relatively widely in boreal and cool-temperate, often stream-side habitats in the northeastern United States and much of Canada. *Primula laurentiana* occurs more locally in eastern Canada and the northeastern United States. The arctic primrose (*P. stricta*) occurs widely in moist places in the Arctic of North America and western **Europe**. Another arctic primrose (*P. borealis*) occurs in the northwestern **tundra** of Alaska and Canada as well as in eastern Siberia.

Many species and varieties of primroses are cultivated as ornamental plants. For example, the European cowslip (*Primula veris*) is commonly cultivated as a garden plant, as is *P. denticulata*. *Primula auricula* and other arctic-alpine primroses are often grown in rock gardens. *Primula obconia* is grown as a house plant.

Many horticultural hybrids of primroses have also been developed. One of the classic cases is the Kew primrose (*P. kewensis*), developed in the famous English botanical garden of that name, from a cross between a Himalayan primrose (*P. floribunda*) and an Arabian species (*P. verticillata*). In this case the original hybrids were sterile, that is, they could not reproduce sexually by the fertilizing of the pistils of one plant with pollen from another. Several of the hybrids subsequently became fertile as a consequence of a spontaneous doubling of their **chromosome** number, a characteristic that geneticists call polyploidy. This unprecedented discovery of sterile hybrids becoming fertile through polyploidy is a famous story in **botany** and **plant breeding**.

Printing

History of printing

Although a technology in which seals were first pressed into damp clay tablets is known to have been used by the Babylonians, the Chinese probably invented printing. They used carved stones for making copies by first sprinkling soot over the carving, then placing a piece of **paper** on it and rubbing until the ashes came off on the stone. The oldest known printings were produced in China 1,200 years ago. They consisted of Buddhist texts, and were made using ink blocks and small pieces of paper.

Around 800 years ago, the Chinese printer Pi Sheng first formed Chinese characters out of bits of clay. He found that by fitting the clay pieces together to spell out words, he could print entire texts. These clay pieces, which would now be called movable type, had the advantage that they could be reused. Later type was made out of **wood**.

In Korea, pieces of type were placed in a box, or form, so that they spelled out words. By pressing the form against wet sand, the individual pieces created impressions in the sand. Molten **metal** was then poured over the sand, so that it filled the letter-shaped impressions. When the metal cooled, a solid plate with raised images of the characters was formed. This metal plate was then used to print on paper. The metal plate proved easier to work with than did movable type. While a page was being printed using the metal plate, the original movable type was reassembled to make another plate. This technique is still in use, and is known as type **mold**. By 1400 A.D., Korea had the most advanced printing technology, and even commoners there were able to own copies of official publications.

In **Europe**, meanwhile, the Romans had not discovered printing, and all books were produced by hand. By about 1000 A.D. most of these handwritten books had been destroyed, and the few that survived were carried off to the East. Some of the surviving books were later returned to Europe by scholars and priests. There, scribes in monasteries made copies by hand. Each of these handwritten books required many hours of skilled labor to produce, and only the wealthy could afford to own books.

Around 1400, Europeans began to experiment with news ways to make books. They had no knowledge of Chinese printing technologies, and developed methods of printing independently of what was happening on the other side of the world. Some Europeans rediscovered the use of carved blocks, the technology the Chinese had used before they came upon the idea of movable type. But block printing was too slow and expensive to meet the rising demand for books.

The Gutenberg revolution

The first European to successfully use movable type was probably Johann Gutenberg, who was born in Germany in 1397. Gutenberg hit upon the notion of cutting each letter in the alphabet on the end of a small stick. Each letter was then pressed into a small **square** of metal, and when Gutenberg had a letter-shaped hollow for each letter of the alphabet, he could produce type.

Gutenberg fitted four pieces of wood around the letter-shaped hollow, called a matrix, to form an open box. He then poured molten metal into the box, allowing it fill up the matrix. After the metal had cooled and hardened, the sides of the box were removed, leaving a small block with the letter in relief.

Gutenberg reassembled the box to produce as many copies of each letter as he needed. The walls of the box formed a mold that could be adjusted to fit all letters. This mold made possible the development of a less expensive and faster method of printing than had previously been in use.

By trial and **error**, Gutenberg discovered that the best metal for his type was a mixture of lead, tin, and antimony. This **alloy** had the advantage that it did not shrink when cooled, so all letters resembled the original matrix, and the pieces of type could be linked in rows. Alloys of lead, tin, and antimony are still used to make type.

The first book of any note to be printed with movable type was Gutenberg's Bible, published in 1456. Copies are still in existence. Printed in Latin, its pages consist of two columns of type, each 42 lines long. It is 1282 pages long. In producing this book, the type was arranged on each page, and inked before the paper was pressed down on it. Gutenberg may have used a wine press fitted with a heavy screw to press the paper against the type. After removing the sheet of paper, the type would then have been re-inked before another sheet of paper was placed on it.

Gutenberg printed about 200 Bibles in a five-year period. Each of the printed characters in the Bible was made to resemble handwriting. Because the type in the Gutenberg Bible makes the printed page very dark, it is called black letter. Gutenberg's Bible has wide margins, and the pages are well designed.

Gutenberg died in poverty. But his invention rapidly spread to other countries in Europe. By the time that Columbus was setting off for the New World, around 14,000 separate books had been printed in Europe. As hundreds of copies of each of these books could be found, there may have been as many as 20 million books in Europe at the time.

European printers continued to experiment with Gutenberg's technology. To make printed type easier to read, the Frenchman Nicolas Jensen introduced serifs, or tiny tails, at the end of his letters. This innovation had the effect of causing the reader's **eye** to skip from one letter to the next. This type eventually became more popular than Gutenberg's black letter type, and the letters are now known as Roman-style letters, because they were designed to resemble the stone carvings in ancient Rome.

Aldus Manutius designed a narrow slanting type, now called italic in honor of Italy where Manutius lived. This enabled Manutius to place many words on a single page, and small, cheap books soon became readily available.

The early European printers arranged their type by hand, character by character in a process known as typesetting. Type was stored in cabinet drawers, called cases. Each case held a complete set of type in a particular style and size, called a font. It was the convention for printers to keep their capital letters, now referred to as upper-case letters, separate from their small, or lower-case, letters.

Letters were removed from the type case, and arranged in rows in a small metal tray. Space bars were inserted to adjust the width of the line. Filling out a line became known as justification.

When the metal tray had been filled with justified lines, the lines were transferred to a larger metal tray called a galley. The galley was inked when the printer had made sure that there were no mistakes in the set type. The printed sheet of paper that was produced became known as the galley proof.

At first, European printers traveled from town to town, taking their type and small hand-operated presses with them. They became known as journeyman printers. Later, when plenty of shops had been established where they could practice their trade, itinerant printers traveled about with only their skills.

Conventional printing methods

Conventional typesetting machines mold type from molten metal, in a process called type casting, for each new printing job. Casting type is more efficient than setting type by hand. Cast type can be melted down, and reused. Typesetting machines either cast an entire line of type at once (linotype machines) or a single letter at a time (monotype machines).

James O. Clephane and Ottmar Merganthaler developed the first commercially successful linotype machine in 1886. Their machine cast type five times faster than an individual could set type.

The linotype machine is operated by a compositor. This individual works in front of a keyboard. The keyboard consists of separate keys for each letter, number, or punctuation mark found in a case of type. The text to be set, called the copy, is placed above the keyboard. The compositor keys in the text, character by character. Each time a key is touched, a small letter matrix drops into a slot.

When the compositor has filled in the first line of type, he sends it to a mold. Molten metal is then forced into the mold to produce a metal bar with a whole line of letters in relief. This cast line is then dropped down into the galley, and the process is continued until all the copy has been set.

The advantages of monotype begin to show up with reference works and scientific publications, where complicated tables, punctuation, and figures may have to be inserted. With monotype, corrections can be made by hand without resetting the entire line.

Letterpress

Letterpress printing is an example of *relief* printing, the process in which printing ink is transferred to a printed surface from areas that are higher than the rest of the printing block. In the case of letterpress printing, each page of type is used as the mold for a papier-mache mat, which is actually a copy in reverse of that page of type. The mold in turn is used to make a metal copy of the entire page, and this metal copy is used for printing. This

was the traditional way to print newspapers. Variations of this printing technique may use plastic or rubber plates. Because several plates can be made from each original, brand new type can be introduced at regular intervals, ensuring that copies remain sharp and clear.

Large presses

In rotary presses, the plates are fastened around cylinders. These cylinders continuously turn against an endless conveyance of moving paper, printing the paper sheet as it moves past. The sheet can be printed on both sides, cut, folded, and tied up so that it comes out as stacks of finished newspaper. Fabrics are also printed on large machines in which cylinders turn against the cloth, printing colored designs on it.

In the case of cylinder presses, a flat type bed slides back and forth beneath a turning cylinder to which a paper sheet is attached. Grippers hold the sheet of paper in place against the turning cylinder before releasing it, and picking up another sheet.

Printing pictures

Images are still occasionally printed using metal plates that are engraved or etched by hand. In the case of photoengraving, a similar process makes use of a camera. First, the image is photographed to produce a negative on a sheet of transparent film. The negative is then used to print the image on a sheet of zinc that is covered with a gelatin-like substance, or **emulsion**. Chemicals in the emulsion transfer the image to the zinc sheet. The zinc sheet is then treated with chemicals that etch the metal surface except where the image appears. The image remains elevated above the etched surface, and the plate is used to print the image on paper.

Black and white photographs with many shades of gray have been traditionally handled by a process called halftone engraving. With this technique, the original picture is first photographed. Then a screen in the camera is used to break up the picture into thousands of tiny squares. The negative consists of thousands of tiny dots, one for each square. The photoengraving from this negative has many tiny dots raised in relief above the eaten-away metal surface. Portions of the plate that will appear as dark areas in the finished picture are covered with relatively large dots. The portions of the plate that will appear gray are covered with smaller dots. And the portions that will print white are covered by dots that may appear invisible to the naked eye.

Ordinary newspaper pictures are produced with screens of about 5,000 dots per square inch (or about 70 dots per linear inch). A very fine-screened engraving, such as might appear in art books and magazines, might use up to 18,000 dots per square inch (or about 135 dots per linear inch).

Color printing requires plates for each color. Most color pictures can be printed using four plates, one for black and one each for red, blue, and yellow.

Photogravure

In photogravure, ink is held in the hollows of a plate rather than on high relief. This method of printing is known as intaglio. The photogravure plate, like the halftone plate, is produced with the aid of a camera and an acid to etch away parts of the metal plate. The acid creates hollows of different depths. The deepest hollows hold the most ink and print the darkest areas in the picture. Shallow hollows hold less ink and print lighter areas.

Lithography

In **lithography**, a picture is drawn on a smooth flat stone with a special type of oily crayon. Because the printing surface is flat, lithography is an example of planographic or surface printing. Then the lithographer passes a water-soaked roller over the stone. The **water** adheres to the bare stone surface, but does not stick to the oily crayon marks. Another roller soaked with printer's ink is passed over the stone. Since the ink will not mix with water, it cannot stick to the wet stone, but does stick to the oily crayon marks. When a sheet of paper is pressed against the inked stone, the paper takes up ink only from the places where the crayon lines are. This produces a print of the original drawing on paper.

Photolithography is a variation of lithography performed by machine and using a camera. In this case, a zinc plate is used instead of the stone. The picture is placed on the plate by photographic means rather than by hand. Characters and words can also be printed on the plate. The zinc plate is then curved around the printing cylinder. As the cylinder turns, the plate first presses against a wet roller, and then against an ink roller. This has the effect of covering the blackened portions of the plate with ink. The inked plate next rolls against a rubber-blanketed cylinder so that the image is picked up. The blanketed cylinder then transfers the image to the paper. This kind of printing is known as offset printing.

Phototypesetting

Rather than using hollowed-out metal plates, phototypesetting machines use strips of photographic film to carry images of the text that will be printed. The phototypesetting machine produces images on fresh, unexposed film. Conventional phototypesetters can expose up

to 50 characters per second, but usually expose closer to 30 characters per second. Phototypesetting does not use hot metal. Instead, type is set by exposing a light-sensitive material (film or paper) to light projected through a character negative. A computer controls timing.

Another revolution?

In the early 1980s the personal computer made its first appearance in many homes and businesses. A panoply of software applications followed suit, and before long the era of desktop publishing had been ushered in. The first desktop publishing systems consisted of a personal computer and a dot-matrix or daisy wheel printer. With the introduction of the **laser** printer in 1985, desktop publishing was on its way.

Recent advances in on-line document delivery systems, many incorporating multimedia techniques, have led some to suggest that we are in the midst of a revolution in publishing that will eventually prove to be as far reaching as the revolution that Gutenberg's printing press set in progress over 500 years ago.

Desktop publishing

In desktop publishing, text is first prepared on a word processor, and illustrations are prepared using drawing software. Photographs or other art may also be captured electronically using a scanner. The electronic files are next sent to a computer running a page-layout application. Page layout software is the heart of desktop publishing. This software allows the desktop publisher to manipulate text and illustrations on a page.

Depending upon the printing quality desired, the electronic pages may either be printed on a desktop printer, or sent to a printing bureau where the electronic document is loaded onto a high-end computer. If the document is sent to a printing bureau, the scanned images may be replaced with higher-resolution electronic images before printing.

If the document is to be produced in color, the printing bureau will use color separation software to produce four electronic documents, each representing the amount of cyan, magenta, yellow, and black that go on one page. The color separation process produces four full-sized transparent negatives. When these negatives are superposed, they produce an accurate gray-scale negative of the whole page.

Flexible plates are then made from the four negatives, with one ink color per plate. Clear areas on the film end up a solid raised areas on the plate. In this case, all of the color is printed on the paper. Gray areas, which become regions of raised dots on the plate, put down limited amounts of ink on the paper. Black areas produce no raised areas, so the paper remains white. The plates are then attached to four **rollers**, one for each color. As the paper passes under each of the rollers, it gets a coat of one of the four colors.

Most desktop printers create images by drawing dots on paper. The standard printer resolution is 300 dots per inch, but higher resolutions are available. This is much higher than the computer terminal's resolution of 72 dots per inch.

Dot-matrix printers

Dot-matrix printers work by drawing dots in much the same way that typewriters produce characters. They create whole letters by striking a sheet of paper through an inked ribbon. The dot matrix printer is ideally suited for printing carbon-copy forms, but does not find much current use in desktop publishing.

Laser printers

Laser printers currently accommodate the high **volume** printing needs of many large organizations, and meet the more modest requirements of individuals and small businesses. In laser printing, electronic signals describing the document are first sent from the desktop publishing computer to the printer's logic board. Printing fonts are next loaded into the printer's **memory**. The printer's central processing unit then sends light signal instructions to a laser, which focuses a beam of light on a rotating drum in the printer. This beam is turned on where black dots will appear, and turned off where the page will remain white.

The rotating drum is coated with a negatively charged, light sensitive material that becomes positively charged wherever the light strikes it. Negatively charged toner particles are attracted to positively charged regions on the drum. This creates the image to be printed on the drum.

A sheet of paper is drawn from the printer's paper tray so that it passes between the drum and a positively charged wire. The positively charged wire draws the negatively charged toner particles from the drum to the paper. Finally, the toner is bonded to the paper as it passes through two rollers that are heated to about 160degrees C.

Ink jet printers

Ink jet printers offer low cost printing alternatives to laser printers, while retaining some of the print quality of laser printers. They operate silently, are lightweight, and make good home printers.

KEY TERMS

Case—A shallow tray divided into compartments to hold fonts of different types. The case is usually arranged in a set of two, the upper case for capital letters and the lower case for small letters.

Desktop publishing—The writing, assembling, design, and printing of publications using microcomputers. Depending upon the printing quality desired, the electronic pages may either be printed on a desktop printer, or sent to a printing bureau where the electronic document is loaded onto a highend computer.

Font—A complete set of type in a particular style and size.

Galley—A metal tray filled with lines of set type.

Galley proof—A copy of the lines of type in a galley made before the material has been set up in pages. The galley proof is usually printed as a single column of type with wide margins for marking corrections.

Intaglio printing—The process of printing in which the design or text is engraved into the surface of a plate so that when the ink is wiped off, ink remains in the grooves and is transferred to paper in printing. Photogravure is a type of intaglio printing.

Justification—Filling out a line of type with space bars to a specified length.

Linotype—Typecasting machine which casts a whole line of type at once.

Monotype—Typecasting machine which casts single letters.

Planographic printing—The process of printing from a flat surface, also known as surface printing. Lithography and photolithography are two examples of planographic printing.

Relief printing—The process of printing from letters or type in which the printing ink is transferred to the printed surface from areas that are higher than the rest of the block. Letterpress printing is an example of relief printing.

In ink jet printing, liquid ink is pumped into a set of chambers, each containing a heating element. There the ink is heated until it vaporizes. The vaporous ink is then forced through tiny nozzles, squirting dots on the paper. As each line of text is written, the paper advances slightly to accept another line.

Further Reading

Birkerts, Sven. *The Gutenberg Elegies.* Boston: Faber and Faber, 1994.

Epstein, Sam and Beryl. *The First Book of Printing.* New York: Franklin Watts, Inc., 1975.

Gaskell, Philip. *A New Introduction to Bibliography.* Oxford, 1972.

McLuhan, Marshall. *Understanding Media: The Extensions of Man.* New York: McGraw-Hill, 1965.

Rizzo, John and K. Daniel Clark. *How Macs Work.* Emeryville: Ziff-Davis Press, 1993.

Randall Frost

Prions

The term prion (derived from "proteinaceous infectious particle") refers to an infectious agent consisting of a tiny protein that lacks genes, but can proliferate inside the host, causing slowly developing neurodegenerative diseases in animals and humans. Prions are thought to cause several diseases that attack the **brain**, such as **Creutzfeldt-Jakob disease** in humans, scrapie in **sheep**, and bovine spongiform encephalopathy (mad cow disease) in cows.

The normal form of the prion, PrP^c, is a cell-membrane protein that may play a role in nerve signaling in the brain. The very existence of prions has been disputed by researchers ever since these agents were first postulated in 1981 by Stanley B. Prusiner, a neurologist at the University of California at San Francisco, and his collaborators. Since then, however, there has been increasing evidence that it is tiny, virus-like particles lacking genetic material that induce normal **proteins** to change their shape, causing neurodegenerative diseases in animals and humans. This may explain the onset of diseases previously called "slow viral infections," which are not thought to be caused by viruses.

British radiobiologist Ticvah Alper found the first indication that such an infectious agent might cause disease. In the mid-1970s, Alper found that the infectious agent that causes scrapie, a brain disease of sheep and **goats**, was extremely small and resistant to ultraviolet **radiation**, which is known to inactivate genetic material.

More evidence accumulated for the existence of prions during the 1980s: for example, the isolation of rods thought to be prion proteins (PrP) from the brains of **hamsters** infected with scrapie and humans with Creutzfeldt-Jakob disease. The term prion disease now refers to any disease in which there is an accumulation of the abnormal form of PrP, known as PrP^{Sc}. The abnormal prion protein has a different shape than the normal protein, and is resistant to enzymes that degrade proteins, such as proteases.

Aggregates of prions appear to compose the amyloid plaques ("clumps") and fibrils (tiny fibers) seen in the brains of infected humans and animals. These insoluble aggregates appear to trap other things, such as nucleic acids, the building blocks of genes. When the abnormal protein gets into the brains of animals or humans, it converts normal prion proteins into the abnormal form. The accumulation of abnormal proteins in the brain is marked by the formation of spongy holes.

In 1994, researchers at the Massachusetts Institute of Technology and the Laboratory of Persistent Viral Diseases at the Rocky Mountain Laboratories of the National Institutes of Health in Hamilton, Montana, reported that, in the test tube, the abnormal form of the prion protein found in hamsters can convert the normal form into the protease-resistant version. In 1993, researchers at the University of California at San Francisco discovered that the normal prion's shape consists of many helical turns, while the abnormal prion has a flatter shape.

Prion diseases can arise by direct **infection**, by inherited genes that produce the abnormal prion protein, or by genetic **mutation**. PrP^{c} is encoded by a single **gene** on human **chromosome** 20 (chromosome 2 in **mice**). The prion is thought to arise during translation of the PrP^{c} gene into the protein, during which time it is modified to the PrP^{Sc} form. The abnormal form of the protein appears to share the same **amino acid** sequence as the normal protein, but the modification causes differences in their biochemical properties. This permits separation of the two proteins by biochemical analytical methods. The modification is rare, occurring only about once in a million times in the general population. The onset of this disorder occurs in middle age. However, some mutations of the PrP gene can cause onset of prion disease earlier than middle age.

Of particular interest is the similarity between prion disease and **Alzheimer's disease**, a more commonly known form of **dementia**. Alzheimer's disease occurs when a **cell membrane** protein, called amyloid precursor protein (APP), is modified into a form called beta(A4). This modified form is deposited in plaques, whose presence is common in elderly people. And like the PrP gene, certain mutations in the APP gene cause this series of events to occur earlier in life, during later middle age.

In humans, prion diseases can occur in one of several forms. Creutzfeldt-Jakob disease (CJD) is a fatal brain disease lasting less than two years. The symptoms include dementia, myoclonus (muscle spasms), severe spongiform **encephalitis** (brain deterioration marked by a spongy appearance of **tissue** caused by the vacuolization of nerve cell bodies and cell processes in the gray **matter**), loss of nerves, astrocytosis (an increase in the number of astrocytes—brain cells that repair damage), and the presence of abnormal protein plaques in neurons. Gerstmann-Straussler-Scheinker **syndrome** (GSS) is similar to CJD but lasts for more than two years.

Kuru is a fatal, CJD-like form of spongiform encephalopathy lasting less than three years. The symptoms include loss of nerves, astrocytosis, dementia, and sometimes spongiform encephalopathy. Kuru has been reported in tribes people from Papua New Guinea, who had practiced cannibalism, and therefore were directly exposed to a deceased person's diseased brain tissue.

Atypical prion disease is a form of dementia diagnosed by biochemical tests and genetic criteria, but does not otherwise resemble CJD closely. Finally, fatal familial **insomnia** (FFI) is an atypical prion disease characterized by degeneration of the thalamus and hypothalamus, leading to insomnia and dysautonomia (abnormal **nervous system** functioning).

GSS and atypical prion disease (including FFI) are usually inherited. CJD may be inherited, acquired or sporadic; it is usually neither **epidemic** nor **endemic**. However, kuru and CJD that arise as a complication of medical treatment are both acquired by **contamination** of the patient with PrP^{Sc} from another infected human. Human prion disease, however, has never been traced to infection from an **animal**.

With respect to bovine spongiform encephalopathy (BSE), the issue is one of concern regarding transmission from cattle, or from cattle products, to human beings. While no cases are documented that contain conclusive evidence for cross-species contamination, fear is abound that the possibility exists and is therefore a viable threat to public health and safety.

BSE, or mad cow disease, was first identified in a laboratory in Weybridge, England in 1988. Since then, a great deal of public concern has been raised about BSE and beef products. After the initial realization of the prion nature of the infectious agent, the UK government introduced legislation that required destruction and analysis of all cattle suspected of BSE infection. Likewise, all animals to be slaughtered are to be inspected

specifically for BSE according to the new legislation. In 1997, an addendum to the laws surrounding BSE stated that specified risk material containing beef matter was to be banned from animal feed, cosmetic and pharmaceutical preparations, as well as including new rules on beef labeling and tracing procedures. While initiated in 1988, the epidemic reached a peak in 1993 with thousands of cows affected, believed to have been caused by contaminated feed. Fear from other countries, including the United States, stemmed from the belief that tainted British beef products held the possibility of causing CJD in humans. In reality, there is only a limited link between BSE and CJD in humans. Since the 1993 epidemic, however, the British Ministry of Agriculture, Fisheries, and Food (BMAFF) reports a steady and continual decline in the number of cases of mad cow disease.

CJD, GSS, and atypical prion dementia are not different diseases; rather, they are descriptions of how prion infection affects individual patients. In fact, members of the same family can have three distinct versions of a prion infection linked to the same mutation. Indeed, it was the demonstration that inherited cases of human transmissible spongiform encephalopathy were linked to PrP gene mutations that confirmed prions are central to these diseases. The concept of PrP gene mutations has subsequently been used for **diagnosis** and in genetic counseling.

Many specific mutations leading to prion disease have been reported. One example is six point mutations in codons 102, 117, 178, 198, 200, and 217 (a codon is a trio of nucleotides in a gene that codes for a specific amino acid in the protein represented by that gene). Insertional mutations consisting of extra 2, 5, 6, 7, 8, or 9 octapeptide repeats have also been associated with prion disease. The presence of PrP gene mutations does not in itself support a diagnosis of prion disease, however, since not all such mutations produce their characteristic effects in an individual possessing the mutation. Moreover, the presence of such a mutation does not protect the patient from other, much more common neurological diseases. Therefore, in the presence of a PrP **gene mutation** the patient may not have prion disease, but may have a different brain disease.

Further complicating the picture of prion diseases is the fact that, while spongiform encephalitis is found regularly and extensively in sporadic CJD, in cases of familial CJD it is found only in association with a mutation in codon 200 of the PrP gene. Spongiform encephalitis is not found to any significant extent in other prion diseases.

A particularly notable aspect of prion diseases associated with mutations at codon 198 or 217, is the common occurrence of large numbers of neurofibrillary tangles and amyloid plaques, without spongiform encephalitis. If conventional histological techniques are used, this picture appears indistinguishable from Alzheimer's disease. However, immunostaining of the plaques with antibodies to PrP establishes the diagnosis of prion disease.

One prion disease, CJD, is easily transmissible to animals, especially primates, by injecting homogenates (finely divided and mixed tissues) of brains (rather than pure prions) from cases of acquired, sporadic, or inherited spongiform encephalitis in humans into the cerebrums of animals. However, the disease, which may take 18 months to two years to develop, results from the transformation of PrP^c into PrP^{Sc}, rather than from the replication of an agent that actually causes the disease.

Moreover, there is experimental evidence for transmission of CJD to humans. The evidence suggests that patients infected by receiving prion-contaminated therapeutic doses of human growth hormone or gonadotropin might pose a threat of infection to recipients of their donated **blood**.

Critics of the prion hypothesis point out that there is no proof that prions cause neurodegenerative disease. Some researchers point out that very tiny viruses are more likely the agents of what is called prion disease, and that the prion protein serves as a receptor for the **virus**. In addition, as of 1994, no one had been able to cause disease by injecting prion proteins themselves, rather than brain homogenates.

In 1994, Prusiner received the prestigious Albert Lasker award for basic medical research for his work with prions.

Further Reading

Pennisi, E. "Prying into Prions: A Twisted Tale of an Ordinary Protein Causing Extraordinary Neurological Disorders." *Science News,* 146 (24 September 1994): 202-3.

Prusiner, S. B." Biology and Genetics of Prion Diseases." *Annual Review of Microbiology,* 48 (1994): 655-86.

Prusiner, S. B. "The Prion Diseases." *Scientific American,* 272 (January 1995): 48-51+.

Shaw, I. "Mad Cows and a Protein Poison." *New Scientist,* 140 (9 October 1993): 50-1.

Marc Kusinitz

Prism

In Euclidean **geometry**, a prism is a three dimensional figure, or solid, having five or more faces, each of which is a polygon. **Polygons**, in turn, consist of any

number of straight line segments, arranged to form a flat, closed, two-dimensional figure. Thus, triangles, rectangles, pentagons, hexagons, and so on are all polygons. In addition, a prism has at least two congruent (same size and shape) faces that are **parallel** to one another. These parallel faces are called bases of the prism, and are often associated with its top and bottom. An interesting property of prisms is that every **cross section**, taken parallel to a base, is also congruent to the base. The remaining faces of a prism, called lateral faces, meet in line segments called lateral edges. Every prism has as many lateral faces, and lateral edges, as its base has sides. Thus, a prism with an octagonal (eight sided) base has eight lateral faces, and eight lateral edges. Each lateral face meets two other lateral faces, as well as the two bases. As a consequence, each lateral face is a four sided polygon. It can also be shown that, because the bases of a prism are congruent and parallel, each lateral edge of a prism is parallel to every other lateral edge, and that all lateral edges are the same length. As a result, each lateral face of a prism is a **parallelogram** (a four-sided figure with opposite sides parallel).

There are three important special cases of the prism, they are the regular prism, the right prism, and the parallelepiped. First, a regular prism is a prism with regular polygon bases. A regular polygon is one that has all sides equal in length and all angles equal in measure. For instance, a **square** is a regular **rectangle**, an equilateral triangle is a regular triangle, and a stop sign is a regular octagon. Second, a right prism is one whose lateral faces and lateral edges are **perpendicular** (at right, or 90°, angles) to it bases. The lateral faces of a right prism are all rectangles, and the height of a right prism is equal to the length of its lateral edge. The third important special case is the parallelepiped. What makes the parallelepiped special is that, just as its lateral sides are parallelograms, so are its bases. Thus, every face of a parallelepiped has four sides. A special case of the parallelepiped is the rectangular parallelepiped, which has rectangular bases (that is, parallelograms with 90° interior angles), and is sometimes called a rectangular solid. Combining terms, of course, leads to even more restricted special cases, for instance, a right, regular prism. A right, regular prism is one with regular polygon bases, and perpendicular, rectangular, lateral sides, such as a prism with equilateral triangles for bases and three rectangular lateral faces. Another special type of prism is the right, regular parallelepiped. Its bases are regular parallelograms. Thus, they have equal length sides and equal angles. For this to be true, the bases must be squares. Because it is a right prism, the lateral faces are rectangles. Thus, a cube is a special case of a right, regular, parallelepiped (one with square lateral faces), which is a special case of a right, regular prism, which is a special case of a regular prism, which is a special case of a prism.

The surface area and **volume** of a prism are two important quantities. The surface area of a prism is equal to the sum of the areas of the two bases and the areas of the lateral sides. Various formulas for calculating the surface area exist, the simplest being associated with the right, regular prisms. The volume of a prism is the product of the area of one base times the height of the prism, where the height is the perpendicular **distance** between bases.

KEY TERMS

Base—The base of a prism is one of two congruent, parallel sides, often used to indicate the top and bottom of the prism.

Edge—An edge of a prism is the line formed by intersecting faces of the prism.

Lateral face—The lateral faces of a prism are those faces other than the bases.

Parallelepiped—A parallelepiped is a prism whose bases are parallelograms.

Regular prism—A regular prism is one with regular polygons as bases.

Right prism—A right prism is one with lateral sides perpendicular to its bases.

Surface area—The surface area of a prism is equal to the number of unit squares it takes to tile the entire surface of the prism.

Volume—The volume of a prism is equal to the number of unit cubes the prism can hold.

Further Reading

Smith, Stanley A., Charles W. Nelson, Roberta K. Koss, Mervin L. Keedy, and Marvin L Bittinger. *Addison Wesley Informal Geometry.* Reading MA: Addison Wesley, 1992.

Welchons, A. M., W. R. Krickenberger, and Helen R. Pearson. *Plane Geometry.* Boston, MA: Ginn and Company, 1965.

J. R. Maddocks

Probability theory

Probability theory is a branch of **mathematics** concerned with determining the long run **frequency** or chance that a given event will occur. This chance is de-

termined by dividing the number of selected events by the number of total events possible. For example, each of the six faces of a die has one in six probability on a single toss. Inspired by problems encountered by 17th century gamblers, probability theory has developed into one of the most respected and useful branches of mathematics with applications in many different industries. Perhaps what makes probability theory most valuable is that it can be used to determine the expected outcome in any situation from the chances that a plane will crash to the probability that a person will win the lottery.

History of probability theory

The branch of mathematics known as probability theory was inspired by gambling problems. The earliest work was performed by Girolamo Cardano (1501-1576) an Italian mathematician, physician, and gambler. In his manual *Liber de Ludo Aleae*, Cardano discusses many of the basic concepts of probability complete with a systematic analysis of gambling problems. Unfortunately, Cardano's work had little effect on the development of probability because his manual, which did not appeared in print until 1663, received little attention.

In 1654, another gambler named Chevalier de Méré created a dice proposition which he believed would make money. He would bet even money that he could roll at least one twelve in 24 rolls of two dice. However, when the Chevalier began losing money, he asked his mathematician friend Blaise Pascal (1623-1662) to analyze the proposition. Pascal determined that this proposition will lose about 51% of the time. Inspired by this proposition, Pascal began studying more of these types of problems. He discussed them with another famous mathematician, Pierre de Fermat (1601-1665) and together they laid the foundation of probability theory.

Probability theory is concerned with determining the relationship between the number of times a certain event occurs and the number of times any event occurs. For example, the number of times a head will appear when a coin is flipped 100 times. Determining probabilities can be done in two ways; theoretically and empirically. The example of a coin toss helps illustrate the difference between the two approaches. Using a theoretical approach, we reason that in every flip there are two possibilities, a head or a tail. By assuming each event is equally likely, the probability that the coin will end up heads is 1/2 or 0.5. The empirical approach does not use assumption of equal likeliness. Instead, an actual coin flipping experiment is performed and the number of heads is counted. The probability is then equal to the number of heads divided by the total number of flips.

Counting

A theoretical approach to determine probabilities requires the ability to count the number of ways certain events can occur. In some cases, counting is simple because there is only one way for an event to occur. For example, there is only one way in which a 4 will show up on a single roll of a die. In most cases, however, counting is not always an easy matter. Imagine trying to count the number of ways of being dealt a pair in 5 card poker.

The fundamental principle of counting is often used when many selections are made from the same set of objects. Suppose we want to know the number of different ways four people can line up in a carnival line. The first spot in line can be occupied by any of the four people. The second can be occupied any of the three people who are left. The third spot can be filled by either of the two remaining people, and the fourth spot is filled by the last person. So, the total number of ways four people can create a line is equal to the product $4 \times 3 \times 2 \times 1 = 24$. This product can be abbreviated as 4! (read "4 factorial"). In general, the product of the positive **integers** from 1 to n can be denoted by n! which equals $n \times (n-1) \times (n-2) \times ...2 \times 1$. It should be noted that 0! is by definition equal to 1.

The example of the carnival line given above illustrates a situation involving permutations. A permutation is any arrangement of n objects in a definite order. Generally, the number of permutations of n objects is n! Now, suppose we want to make a line using only two of the four people. In this case, any of the four people can occupy the first space and any of the three remaining people can occupy the second space. Therefore, the number of possible arrangements, or permutations, of two people from a group of four, denoted as $P_{4,2}$ is equal to $4 \times 3 = 12$. In general, the number of permutations of n objects taken r at a time is

$$P_{n,r} = n \times (n-1) \times (n-2) \times ... \times (n-r+1)$$

This can be written more compactly as $P_{n,r} = n!/(n-r)!$

Many times the order in which objects are selected from a group does not matter. For instance, we may want to know how many different 3 person clubs can be formed from a student body of 125. By using permutations, some of the clubs will have the same people, just arranged in a different order. We only want to count then number of clubs that have different people. In these cases, when order is not important, we use what is known as a combination. In general, the number of combinations denoted as $C_{n,r}$ or

$$\binom{n}{r}$$

is equal to $P_{n,r}/r!$ or $C_{n,r} = n!/r! \times (n-r)!$ For our club example, the number of different three person clubs that can be formed from a student body of 125 is $C_{125,3}$ or $125!/3! \times 122! = 317,750$.

Experiments

Probability theory is concerned with determining the likelihood that a certain event will occur during a given **random** experiment. In this sense, an experiment is any situation which involves observation or measurement. Random experiments are those which can have different outcomes regardless of the initial conditions and will be heretofore referred to simply as experiments.

The results obtained from an experiment are known as the outcomes. When a die is rolled, the outcome is the number found on the topside. For any experiment, the set of all outcomes is called thesample space. The **sample** space, S, of the die example, is denoted by S= which represents all of the possible numbers that can result from the roll of a die. We usually consider sample spaces in which all outcomes are equally likely.

The sample space of an experiment is classified as finite or infinite. When there is a **limit** to the number of outcomes in an experiment, such as choosing a single card from a deck of cards, the sample space is finite. On the other hand, an infinite sample space occurs when there is no limit to the number of outcomes, such as when a dart is thrown at a target with a continuum of points.

While a sample space describes the set of every possible outcome for an experiment, an event is any subset of the sample space. When two dice are rolled, the set of outcomes for an event such as a sum of 4 on two dice is represented by E = .

In some experiments, multiple events are evaluated and **set theory** is needed to describe the relationship between them. Events can be compounded forming unions, intersections, and complements. The union of two events A and B is an event which contains all of the outcomes contained in event A and B. It is mathematically represented as $A \cup B$. The intersection of the same two events is an event which contains only outcomes present in both A and B, and is denoted $A \cap B$. The complement of event A, represented by A', is an event which contains all of the outcomes of the sample space not found in A.

Looking back at the table we can see how set theory is used to mathematically describe the outcome of real world experiments. Suppose A represents the event in which a 4 is obtained on the first roll and B represents an event in which the total number on the dice is 5.

$A = \{(4,1),(4,2),(4,3),(4,4),(4,5),(4,6)\}$ and
$B = \{(3,2),(2,3),(1,4)\}$

The compound set $A \cup B$ includes all of the outcomes from both sets,

$\{(4,1),(4,2),(4,3),(4,4),(4,5),(4,6),(3,2),(2,3),(1,4)\}$

The compound set $A \cap B$ includes only events common to both sets,. Finally, the complement of event A would include all of the events in which a 4 was not rolled first.

Rules of probability

By assuming that every outcome in a sample space is equally likely, the probability of event A is then equal to the number of ways the event can occur, m, divided by the total number of outcomes that can occur, n. Symbolically, we denote the probability of event A as $P(A) = m/n$. An example of this is illustrated by drawing from a deck of cards. To find the probability of an event such as getting an ace when drawing a single card from a deck of cards, we must know the number of aces and the total number of cards. Each of the 4 aces represent an occupance of an event while all of the 52 cards represent the sample space. The probability of this event is then 4/52 or .08.

Using the characteristics of the sets of the sample space and an event, basic rules for probability can be created. First, since m is always equal to or less than n, the probability of any event will always be a number from 0 to 1. Second, if an event is certain to happen, its probability is 1. If it is certain not to occur, its probability is 0. Third, if two events are mutually exclusive, that is they can not occur at the same time, then the probability that either will occur is equal to the sum of their probabilities. For instance, if event A represents rolling a 6 on a die and event B represents rolling a 4, the probability that either will occur is 1/6 + 1/6 = 2/6 or. 33. Finally, the sum of the probability that an event will occur and that it will not occur is 1.

The third rule above represents a special case of adding probabilities. In many cases, two events are not mutually exclusive. Suppose we wanted to know the probability of either picking a red card or a king. These events are not mutually exclusive because we could pick a red card that is also a king. The probability of either of these events in this case is equal to the sum of the individual probabilities minus the sum of the combined probabilities. In this example, the probability of getting a king is 4/52, the probability of getting a red card is 26/52, and the probability of getting a red king is 2/52. Therefore, the chances of drawing a red card or a king is 4/52 + 26/52 - 2/52 = .54.

Often the probability of one event is dependant on the occupance of another event. If we choose a person at random, the probability that they own a yacht is low.

However, if we find out this person is rich, the probability would certainly be higher. Events such as these in which the probability of one event is dependant on another are known as conditional probabilities. Mathematically, if event A is dependant on another event B, then the conditional probability is denoted as $P(A|B)$ and equal to $P(A \cap B)/P(B)$ when $P(B) \neq 0$. Conditional probabilities are useful whenever we want to restrict our probability calculation to only those cases in which both event A and event B occur.

Events are not always dependant on each other. These independent events have the same probability regardless of whether the other event occurs. For example, probability of passing a math test is not dependent on the probability that it will rain.

Using the ideas of dependent and independent events, a rule for determining probabilities of multiple events can be developed. In general, given dependent events A and B, the probability that both events occur is $P(A \cap B) = P(B) \times P(A|B)$. If events A and B are independent, $P(A \cap B) = P(A) \times P(B)$. Suppose we ran an experiment in which we rolled a die and flipped a coin. These events are independent so the probability of getting a 6 and a tail would be $(1/6) \times 1/2 = .08$.

The theoretical approach to determining probabilities has certain advantages; probabilities can be calculated exactly, and experiments with numerous trials are not needed. However, it depends on the classical notion that all the events in a situation are equally possible, and there are many instances in which this is not true. Predicting the **weather** is an example of such a situation. On any given day, it will be sunny or cloudy. By assuming every possibility is equally likely, the probability of a sunny day would then be 1/2 and clearly, this is nonsense.

Empirical probability

The empirical approach to determining probabilities relies on data from actual experiments to determine approximate probabilities instead of the assumption of equal likeliness. Probabilities in these experiments are defined as the **ratio** of the frequency of the occupance of an event, $f(E)$, to the number of trials in the experiment, n, written symbolically as $P(E) = f(E)/n$. If our experiment involves flipping a coin, the empirical probability of heads is the number of heads divided by the total number of flips.

The relationship between these empirical probabilities and the theoretical probabilities is suggested by the Law of Large Numbers. It states that as the number of trials of an experiment increases, the empirical probability approaches the theoretical probability. This makes sense as we would expect that if we roll a die numerous times, each number would come up approximately 1/6 of the time. The study of empirical probabilities is known as **statistics**.

Using probabilities

Probability theory was originally developed to help gamblers determine the best bet to make in a given situation. Suppose a gambler had a choice between two bets; she could either wager \$4 on a coin toss in which she would make \$8 if it came up heads or she could bet \$4 on the roll of a die and make \$8 if it lands on a 6. By using the idea of mathematical expectation she could determine which is the better bet. Mathematical expectation is defined as the average outcome anticipated when

KEY TERMS

Combination—A method of counting events in which order does not matter.

Conditional probabilities—The chances of the occupance of an event given the occupance of a related second event.

Empirical approach—A method for determining probabilities based on experimentation.

Event—A set of occurrences which satisfy a desired condition.

Independent probabilities—The chances of the occupance of one event is not affected by the occupance or non occupance of another event.

Law of Large Numbers—A mathematical notion which states that as the number of trials of an empirical experiment increases, the frequency of an event divided by the total number of trials approaches the theoretical probability.

Mathematical expectation—The average outcome anticipated when an experiment, or bet, is repeated a large number of times.

Mutually exclusive—Refers to events which can not happen at the same time.

Outcomes—The result of a single experiment trial.

Permutation—Any arrangement of objects in a definite order.

Sample space—The set of all possible outcomes for any experiment.

Theoretical approach—A method of determining probabilities by mathematically calculating the number of times an event can occur.

an experiment, or bet, is repeated a large number of times. In its simplest form, it is equal to the product of the amount a player stands to win and the probability of the event. In our example, the gambler will expect to win $8 × .5 = $4 on the coin flip and $8 × .17 = $1.33 on the roll of the die. Since the expectation is higher for the coin toss, this bet is better.

When more than one winning combination is possible, the expectation is equal to the sum of the individual expectations. Consider the situation in which a person can purchase one of 500 lottery tickets where first prize is $1000 and second prize is $500. In this case, his or her expectation is $1000 × (1/500) + $500 × (1/500) = $3. This means that if the same lottery was repeated many times, one would expect to win an average of $3 on every ticket purchased.

Further Reading

Freund, John E & Richard Smith. *Statistics: a First Course.* Englewood Cliffs, NJ: Prentice Hall Inc., 1986.

McGervey, John D. *Probabilities in Everyday Life.* New York: Ivy Books, 1986.

Perry Romanowski

Proboscis monkey

The proboscis monkey (*Nasalis larvatus*) of Borneo belongs to the primate family Cercopithecidae. It is grouped with the langurs, **leaf monkeys**, and **colobus monkeys** in the subfamily Colobinae. The feature that gives this odd-looking monkey its common name is the large, tongue-shaped nose of the adult male. This nose can be as much as 4 in (10 cm) long. It sometimes hangs down over the mouth, but extends when the male makes a loud honking noise. In the female, the nose is slightly enlarged but not as pendulous as in the male; in young proboscis monkeys, the nostrils are upturned.

The color of the proboscis monkey's coat ranges from light to reddish brown, with underparts that are gray or cream. The facial skin is reddish in adults, and blue in infants. The average head and body length is 21-30 in (53-76 cm), the weight is 16-53 lbs (7-24 kg), and the tail is 21-30 in (53-76 cm). The male can be up to twice as large as the female. The preferred **habitat** of this species is mangrove or peat swamps and riverine **forests**. Proboscis monkeys move easily through the branches of trees and, because of their partially webbed hind feet, are good swimmers in or below the **water**. They feed during the day on fruit, flowers, leaves, **seeds**, and aquatic vegetation.

Groups range in size from 3-30 individuals, usually based on one adult male and a number of adult females. These groups occupy a home range of less than 1 sq mi (2 sq km). Large troops often feed together, but individuals usually **sleep** alone in a **tree** in fairly close proximity to other troop members. Mating is probably possible at any time during the year, and a single young is born after a gestation period of about 166 days.

The proboscis monkey is **endemic** to the **island** of Borneo. Because of its relatively inaccessible habitat, the species was safe for many years from human intrusion. Today, however, even mangrove swamps are being cleared and suitable monkey habitat is being reduced. As the species becomes more accessible, it is vulnerable to hunting by local people who consider its meat a delicacy. A 1986 study estimated the total population of proboscis monkeys at approximately 250,000 individuals. The current population may be considerably smaller; one researcher recently estimated the total population in all protected areas combined at less than 5,000. International **conservation** organizations consider this species to be vulnerable (IUCN; International Union for the Conservation of Nature) or endangered (U.S. Fish and Wildlife Service).

Product of reaction see **Reaction, chemical**

Projective geometry

Projective **geometry** is the study of geometric properties which are not changed by a projective transformation. A projective transformation is one that occurs when: points on one line are projected onto another line; points in a **plane** are projected onto another plane; or points in **space** are projected onto a plane, etc. Projections can be **parallel** or central.

For example, the **Sun** shining behind a person projects his or her shadow onto the ground. Since the Sun's rays are for all practical purposes parallel, it is a parallel projection.

A slide projector projects a picture onto a screen. Since the rays of light pass through the slide, through the **lens**, and onto the screen, and since the lens acts like a point through which all the rays pass, it is a central projection. The lens is the center of the projection.

Some of the things that are not changed by a projection are collinearity, intersection, and order. If three points lie on a line in the slide, they will lie on a line on the screen. If two lines intersect on the slide, they will inter-

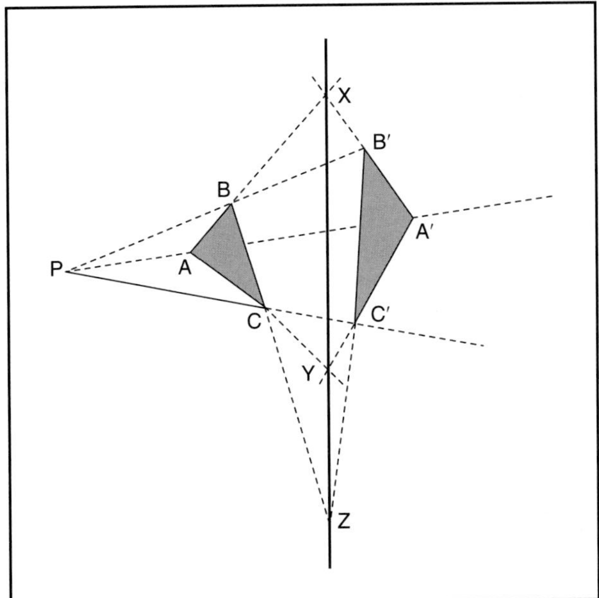

Figure 1.

sect on the screen. If one person is between two others on the slide, he or she will be between them on the screen.

Some of the things that are or can be changed by a projection are size and angles. One's shadow is short in the middle of the day but very long toward sunset. A pair of sticks which are crossed at right angles can cast shadows which are not at right angles.

Desargues' theorem

Projective geometry began with Renaissance artists who wanted to portray a scene as someone actually on the scene might see it. A painting is a central projection of the points in the scene onto a canvas or wall, with the artist's eye as the center of the projection (the fact that the rays are converging on the artist's eye instead of emanating from it doesn't change the principles involved), but the scenes, usually Biblical, existed only in the artists' imagination. The artists needed some principles of perspective to help them make their projections of these imagined scenes look real.

Among those who sought such principles was Gerard Desargues (1593-1662). One of the many things he discovered was the remarkable **theorem** which now bears his name:

If two triangles ABC and A'B'C' are perspective from a point (i.e. if the lines drawn through the corresponding vertices are concurrent at a point P), then the extensions of their corresponding sides will intersect in collinear points X, Y, and Z.

The converse of this theorem is also true: If two triangles are drawn so that the extensions of their corresponding sides intersect in three collinear points, then the lines drawn through the corresponding vertices will be concurrent.

It is not obvious what this theorem has to do with perspective drawing or with projections. If the two triangles were in separate planes, however, (in which case the theorem is not only true, it is easier to prove) one of the triangles could be a triangle on the ground and the other its projection on the artist's canvas.

If, in Figure 1, BC and B'C' were parallel, they would not intersect. If one imagines a "point at infinity," however, they would intersect and the theorem would hold true. Kepler is credited with introducing such an idea, but Desargues is credited with being the first to use it systematically. One of the characteristics of projective geometry is that two coplanar lines always intersect, but possibly at **infinity**.

Another characteristic of projective geometry is the principle of duality. It is this principle that connects Desargues' theorem with its converse, although the connection is not obvious. It is more apparent in the three postulates which Eves gives for projective geometry:

I. There is one and only one line on every two distinct points, and there is one and only one point on every two distinct lines.

II. There exist two points and two lines such that each of the points is on just one of the lines and each of the lines is on just one of the points.

III. There exist two points and two lines, the points not on the lines, such that the point on the two lines is on the line on the two points.

These postulates are not easy to read, and to really understand what they say, one should make drawings to illustrate them. Even without drawings, one can note that writing "line" in place of "point" and vice versa results in a **postulate** that says just what it said before. This is the principle of duality. One can also note that postulate I guarantees that every two lines will intersect, even lines which in Euclidean geometry would be parallel.

Coordinate projective geometry

If one starts with an ordinary Euclidean plane in which points are addressed with Cartesian coordinates, (x,y), this plane can be converted to a projective plane by adding a "line at infinity. " This is accomplished by means of homogeneous coordinates, (x_1,x_2,x_3) where $x = x_1/x_3$ and $y = x_2/x_3$. One can go back and forth between Cartesian coordinates and homogeneous coordinates quite easily. The point (7,3,5) becomes (1.4,.6) and the

point (4,1) becomes (4,1,1) or any multiple, such as (12,3,3) of (4,1,1).

One creates a point at infinity by making the third coordinate **zero**, for instance (4,1,0). One cannot convert this to Cartesian coordinates because (4/0,1/0) is meaningless. Nevertheless it is a perfectly good projective point. It just happens to be "at infinity." One can do the same thing with equations. In the Euclidean plane 3x - y + 4 = 0 is a line. Written with homogeneous coordinates $3x_1/x_3 - x_2/x_3 + 4 = 0$ it is still a line. If one multiplies through by x_3, the equation becomes $3x_1 - x_2 + 4x_3 = 0$. The point (1,7) satisfied the original equation; the point (1,7,1) satisfies the homogeneous equation. So do (0,4) and (0,4,1) and so on.

In the Euclidean plane the lines 3x - y + 4 = 0 and 3x - y + 10 = 0 are parallel and have no point in common. In homogeneous coordinates they do. In homogeneous coordinates the system $3x_1 - x_2 + 4x_3 = 0$ $3x_1 - x_2 + 10x_3 = 0$ does have a solution. It is (1,3,0) or any multiple of (1,3,0). Since the third coordinate is zero, however, this is a point at infinity. In the Euclidean plane the lines are parallel and don't intersect. In the projective plane they intersect "at infinity." The equation for the x-axis is y = 0; for the y-axis it is x = 0. The equation for the line at infinity is correspondingly $x_3 = 0$. One can use this equation to find where a **curve** crosses the line at infinity. Solving the system $3x_1 - x_2 + 4x_3 = 0$ $x_3 = 0$ yields (1,3,0) or any multiple as a solution. Therefore $3x_1 - x_2 + 4x_3 = 0$, or any line parallel to it, crosses at that point, as we saw earlier.

Conic sections can be thought of as central projections of a **circle**. The vertex of the cone is the center of the projection and the generatrices of the cone are the rays along which the circle's points are projected. One can ask where, if at all, the projection of a circle crosses the line at infinity.

A typical **ellipse** is $x^2 + 4y^2 = 1$. In homogeneous coordinates it is $x_1^2 + 4x_2^2 - x_3^2 = 0$. Solving this with $x_3 = 0$ yields $x_1^2 + 4x_2^2 = 0$, which has no solution other than (0,0,0), which is *not* a point in the projective plane.

A typical **parabola** is $x^2 - y = 0$. In homogeneous coordinates this becomes $x_1^2 - x_2x_3 = 0$. Solving this with $x_3 = 0$ yields $x_1 = 0$ and x_2 = any number. The parabola intersects the line at infinity at the single point (0,1,0). In other words it is tangent to the line at infinity.

In a similar fashion it can be shown that a **hyperbola** such as $x^2 - y^2 = 1$ crosses the line at infinity at two points, in this case (1,1,0) and (1,-1,0). These points, incidentally, are where the hyperbola's asymptotes cross the line at infinity.

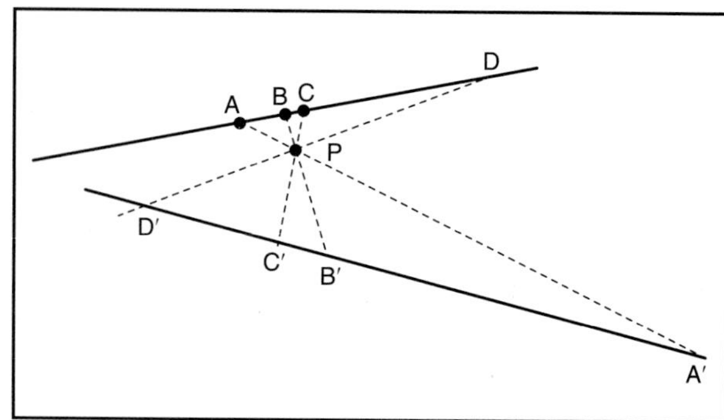

Figure 2.

Cross ratio

Projections do not keep distances constant, nor do they enlarge or shrink them in an obvious way. In Figure 2, for instance, D'C' is a little smaller than CD, but A'B' is much larger than AB. There is, however, a rather obscure constancy about a projection's effect on **distance**. It is known as the "cross ratio." If A, B, C, and D are points in order on a line and if they are projected through a point P into points A', B', C', and D' on another line, then the two expressions and are equal.

Cross rations play an important part in many of projective geometry's theorems.

J. Paul Moulton

Prokaryote

Prokaryotes are single-celled organisms such as **bacteria** that have no distinct nucleus. In addition to the lack of a nucleus, prokaryotes lack many of the other small organelles found in the larger eukaryotic cells.

A typical prokaryote is bound by a **plasma membrane** and a **cell** wall. Within this double boundary, the fluid material inside the cell (the cytoplasm) is studded with small, rounded bodies called **ribosomes**. The ribosomes are composed of nucleic acids and **proteins**, and function in protein synthesis. The chromosomes containing the hereditary material of prokaryotes are concentrated within a region called the nucleoid. Because the nucleoid is not separated from the rest of the cytoplasm by a membrane, it is not considered a true nucleus. Dissolved in the cytoplasm of prokaryotes are the various chemicals needed by the cell to function.

Prokaryotes were the first organisms to evolve on **Earth**, predating eukaryotes in the fossil record by about

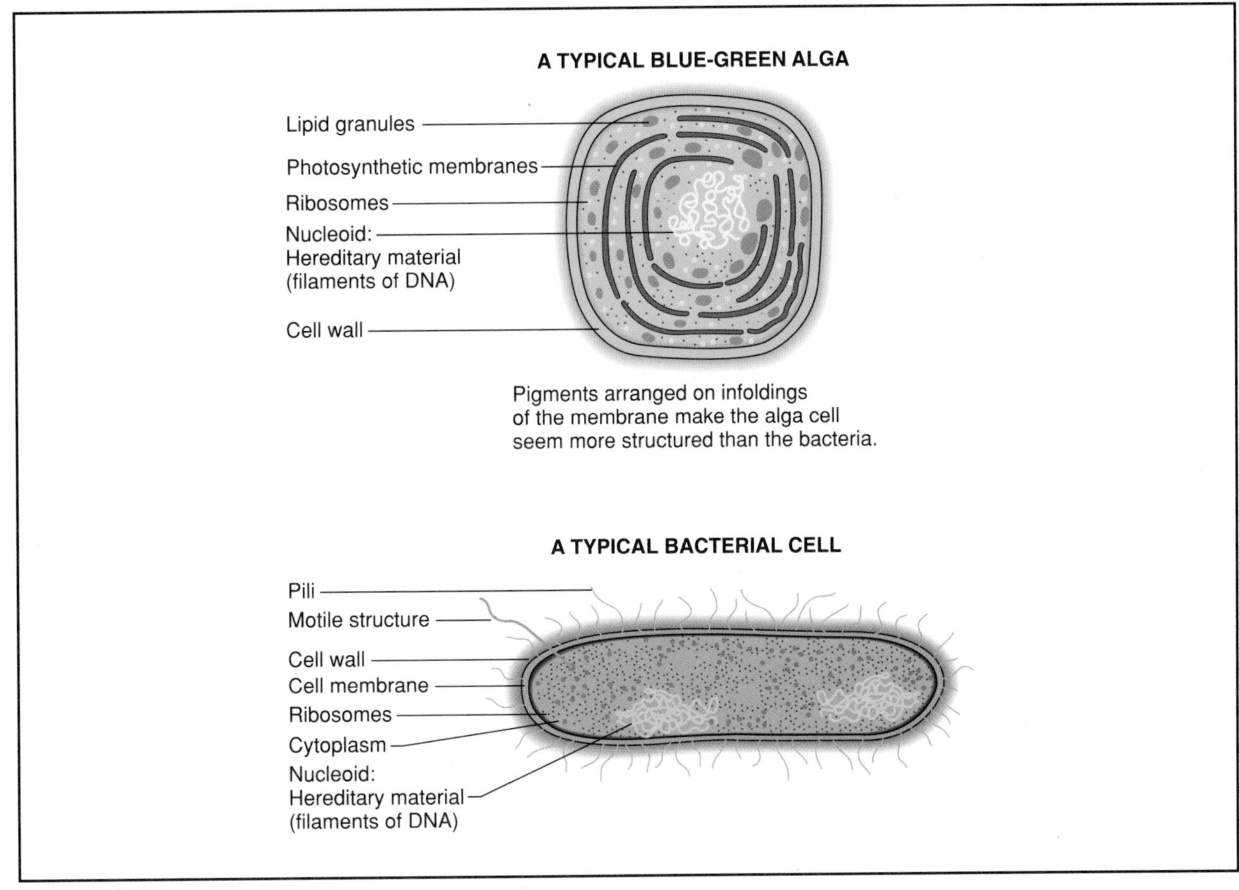

Two typical prokaryotic cells: a blue-green alga and a bacteria.

1 billion years. Appearing on Earth 3.5 billion years ago, the first prokaryotes were probably bacteria that performed **photosynthesis** (cyanobacteria), which is a process that produces carbohydrates from sunlight, **water**, and **carbon dioxide**.

Eukaryotes are thought to have evolved when cells engulfed prokaryotic cells, and incorporated them into their cytoplasm. Some of the eukaryotic organelles, particularly mitochondria (the organelle that contains energy-producing enzymes) and chloroplasts (the organelle that contains photosynthetic enzymes in photosynthetic cells) resemble individual free-living prokaryotic cells. Supporting this theory (called the endosymbiotic theory) is the fact that mitochondria and chloroplasts have their own DNA **sequences**, as if they were once separate organisms in their own right.

Prokaryotes are divided taxonomically into two large goups: the **archaebacteria** and the **eubacteria**. Archaebacteria are probably little changed from the organisms that first evolved billions of years ago. They are capable of living in extremely harsh environments, such as **salt** marshes, hot springs, or even beneath the ice. Eubacteria evolved later. Some are photosynthetic bacteria; some are chemosynthetic bacteria, making carbohydrates from other chemicals besides carbon dioxide; and some are heterotrophic bacteria, deriving **nutrients** from the environment. Heterotrophic prokaryotes include some pathogens, bacteria that cause diseases, such as **pneumonia**, **food poisoning**, and **tuberculosis**.

See also Eukaryotae.

Promethium see **Lanthanides**

Pronghorn

The pronghorn antelope (*Antilocapra americana*) is a species of ruminant that is the sole living representative of its family, the Antilocapridae. This family was much more diverse during the Pliocene and early to mid-Pleistocene periods. The Antilocapridae is an exclusively North American family, and pronghorns are not closely related to the true antelopes, which are members of the

Bovidae, a family that also includes cows, water buffalo, **sheep**, and **goats**. Pronghorns occur in the prairies and semideserts of southwestern Canada, the western United States, and northern Mexico.

Pronghorns are similar in size to the smaller **deer** of the Americas, such as the white-tailed deer (*Odocoileus virginianus*). Pronghorns stand about 3.281 ft (1 m) tall at the shoulders, and mature animals typically weigh from about 88-132 lbs (40-60 kg). Males (or bucks) are somewhat larger than females (or does). Pronghorns have and a relatively long head, with large eyes and long ears.

Pronghorns are ruminants, having a stomach divided into four chambers, each of which is concerned with a particular aspect of the digestion of the fibrous plant **biomass** that these herbivores feed upon. **Rumination** includes the rechewing of regurgitated food that has already spent some time fermenting in one of the fore pouches of the stomach. Pronghorns eat **grasses** and other herbaceous plants, as well as the tissues of woody plants.

Pronghorns have relatively small, unbranched, divergent horns, which are persistent and not shed annually as are the antlers of deer. These antlers are outgrowths of the frontal bones of the skull, and they develop in both sexes, although those of females are smaller, and are sometimes missing. Although pronghorns retain their horns throughout their life, they are the only ungulate that renew the outer sheath of the horns each year. The sheath is shed at the end of each breeding season, after the new sheath has grown upward from the skull under the old sheath. Anatomically, the horn sheath is derived from fused hairs.

Pronghorns have a polygamous breeding system. Male pronghorns fight among themselves during the summer breeding season, and they use a musky scent to mark their territory while attempting to round up as many females as possible into a harem. Most females give **birth** to twin young, known as kids. Although the kids are precocious and capable of standing and walking within a short time of their birth, their mother keeps them hidden from predators in vegetation during the day.

Pronghorns are the fastest land animals in the Americas, and are capable of running at a speed of 50 mi/h (80 km/h) over a **distance** of 1 mi (1.5 km), or at a cruising speed of about 31 mi/h (50 km/h) for longer distances. When a pronghorn senses danger, it dashes off at high speed, while alerting other animals to the threat by raising a ruff of bright white hair on the rump, which can be seen glinting in the **sun** over a great distance. However, pronghorns are very curious animals, and they can be easily attracted by a person lying on the ground and waving a red flag, or waving their arms and legs about. Unfortunately, this curiosity makes pronghorns an easy mark for hunters, because it is not difficult to lure these animals within the killing range of rifles. Interestingly, these tricks did not work well for the aboriginal plains Indians, because the pronghorns could rarely be lured close enough to be killed with a bow and arrow.

KEY TERMS

Polygamy—A breeding system in which individual males breed with numerous females.

Ruminant—Animals in the order Artiodactyla, having a four-chambered stomach, and chewing a regurgitated, pre-digested cud.

Rut—A period of sexual excitement in an animal, for example, in male pronghorns during the breeding season.

Pronghorns are migratory animals, moving extensively between their winter and summer ranges, especially in the northern parts of their range. Unfortunately, pronghorns are easily constrained by mesh or woven fences, because they will not jump vertically over a barrier. Pronghorns will, however, pass through the strands of barbed wire, as long as there is sufficient space between the strands, or between the lowest strand and the ground. If attention is given to this rather simple yet critical requirement of pronghorns, these animals can be rather easily sustained on fenced landscapes.

Prior to the settlement of the Great Plains by European farmers and ranchers, the pronghorn was an enormously abundant **animal**. It may have maintained a population of 40 million animals. At that time, only the American buffalo (*Bison bison*) was a more populous large animal in **North America**, with an estimated abundance of 60 million individuals. The ecological changes that accompanied the agricultural conversions of the prairies, coupled with rapacious market hunting during the late 19th century, caused a great diminishment in the abundance of pronghorns. By the early 19th century this species was diminished to only about 20,000 individuals in its range north of Mexico. Fortunately, thanks to strong **conservation** efforts the pronghorn now numbers more than 500,000 animals, and this species now supports a sport hunt over most of its range.

Further Reading

Banfield, A.W.F. *The Mammals of Canada*. Toronto: University of Toronto Press, 1974.

Grzimek, B. *Grzimek's Encyclopedia of Mammals*. London: McGraw Hill, 1990.

Wilson, D.E. and D. Reeder (comp.). *Mammal Species of the World.* 2nd ed. Washington, D.C.: Smithsonian Institution Press, 1993.

Bill Freedman

Proof

A proof is a logical argument demonstrating that a specific statement, proposition, or mathematical formula is true. It consists of a set of assumptions, or premises, which are combined according to logical rules, to establish a valid conclusion. This validation can be achieved by direct proof that verifies the conclusion is true, or by indirect proof that establishes that it cannot be false.

The term *proof* is derived from the Latin *probare*, meaning *to test*. The Greek philosopher and mathematician Thales is said to have introduced the first proofs into **mathematics** about 600 B.C. A more complete mathematical system of testing, or proving, the truth of statements was set forth by the Greek mathematician Euclid in his **geometry** text, *Elements*, published around 300 B.C. As proposed by Euclid, a proof is a valid argument from true premises to arrive at a conclusion. It consists of a set of assumptions (called axioms) linked by statements of deductive reasoning (known as an argument) to derive the proposition that is being proved (the conclusion). If the initial statement is agreed to be true, the final statement in the proof sequence establishes the truth of the **theorem**.

Each proof begins with one or more axioms, which are statements that are accepted as facts. Also known as postulates, these facts may be well known mathematical formulae for which proofs have already been established. They are followed by a sequence of true statements known as an argument. The argument is said to be valid if the conclusion is a logical consequence of the conjunction of its statements. If the argument does not support the conclusion, it is said to be a fallacy. These arguments may take several forms. One frequently used form can be generally stated as follows: If a statement of the form "if p then q" is assumed to be true, and if p is known to be true, then q must be true. This form follows the rule of detachment; in logic, it is called *affirming the antecedent*; and the Latin term *modus ponens* can also be used. However, just because the conclusion is known to be true does not necessarily mean the argument is valid. For example, a math student may attempt a problem, make mistakes or leave out steps, and still get the right answer. Even though the conclusion is true, the argument may not be valid.

The two fundamental types of proofs are direct and indirect. Direct proofs begin with a basic axiom and reach their conclusion through a sequence of statements (arguments) such that each statement is a logical consequence of the preceding statements. In other words, the conclusion is proved through a step by step process based on a key set of initial statements that are known or assumed to be true. For example, given the true statement that "either John eats a pizza or John gets hungry" and that "John did not get hungry," it may be proved that John ate a pizza. In this example, let p and q denote the propositions:

p: John eats a pizza.

q: John gets hungry.

Using the symbols / for "intersection" and ~ for "not," the premise can be written as follows: p / Either John eats a pizza or John gets hungry. and ~q: John did not get hungry. (Where ~q denotes the opposite of q).

One of the fundamental laws of traditional logic, the law of contradiction, tells us that a statement must be true if its opposite is false. In this case, we are given ~q: John did not get hungry. Therefore, its opposite (q: John did get hungry) must be false. But the first axiom tells us that either p or q is true; therefore, if q is false, p must be true: John did eat a pizza.

In contrast, a statement may also be proven indirectly by invalidating its negation. This method is known as indirect proof, or proof by contradiction. This type of proof aims to directly validate a statement; instead, the premise is proven by showing that it cannot be false. Thus, by proving that the statement ~p is false, we indirectly prove that p is true. For example, by invalidating the statement" cats do not meow," we indirectly prove the statement " cats meow." Proof by contradiction is also known as *reductio ad absurdum*. A famous example of *reductio ad absurdum* is the proof, attributed to Pythagoras, that the **square root** of 2 is an **irrational number**.

Other methods of formal proof include proof by exhaustion (in which the conclusion is established by testing all possible cases). For example, if experience tells us that cats meow, we will conclude that all cats meow. This is an example of inductive inference, whereby a conclusion exceeds the information presented in the premises (we have no way of studying every individual cat). Inductive reasoning is widely used in science. Deductive reasoning, which is prominent in mathematical logic, is concerned with the formal **relation** between individual statements, and not with their content. In other words, the actual content of a statement is irrelevant. If the statement" if p then q" is true, q would be true if p is true, even if p and q stood for, respectively, "The Moon is a philosopher" and "Triangles never snore."

KEY TERMS

Axiom—A premise which is taken as a self evident truth or a common notion which cannot be demonstrated in terms of simpler concepts.

Direct proof—A type of proof in which the validity of the conclusion is directly established.

Euclid—Greek mathematician who proposed the earliest form of geometry in his *Elements*, published circa 300 B.C.

Hypothesis—In mathematics, usually a statement made merely as a starting point for logical argument.

Further Reading

Dunham, William. *Journey Through Genius*. New York: Wiley, 1990.

Fawcett, Harold P. and Cummins, Kenneth B. *The Teaching of Mathematics from Counting to Calculus*. Columbus: Charles E. Merril, 1970.

Kline, Morris. *Mathematics for the Nonmathematician*. New York: Dover, 1967.

Lloyd, G. E. R. *Early Greek Science: Thales to Aristotle*. New York: W. W. Norton, 1970.

Salmon, Wesley C. *Logic*. 2nd ed. Englewood Cliffs, NJ: Prentice-Hall, 1973.

Randy Schueller

Propane see **Hydrocarbon**

Proposition see **Proof**

Propyl group

Propyl group is the name given to the portion of an organic **molecule** that is derived from propane and has the molecular structure -CH_2CH_3. A propyl group can be abbreviated -Pr. The propyl group is one of the alkyl groups defined by dropping the -ane ending from their parent compound and replacing it with -yl. The propyl group is derived from propane ($HCH_2CH_2CH_3$) by removing one of the end hydrogens. The parent compound consists of three **carbon atoms** connected by single bonds, each of which is connected to **hydrogen** atoms, resulting in each of the three carbon atoms having four bonds each. Propane is derived form the very old acid, propionic acid. Propionic acid ($CH_3CH_2CO_2H$) is the simplest organic acid which has a soapy or **fat**-like feel and was named from the Greek words *proto* for first and *pion* for fat. A very similar group to a propyl group is the isopropyl group, -$CH(CH_3)_2$, which derived by removing either of the hydrogen atoms attached to the central carbon atom of propane ($CH_3CH_2CH_3$).

Propane is a gas produced primarily from various refinery processes. It is often mixed with butane, a four carbon atomalkane, and sold as bottled gas or liquefied **petroleum** gas, LPG. The bottled gas is used as an inexpensive fuel for cooking and heating homes not located near **natural gas** lines. Since liquefied petroleum gas burns very cleanly, it is being used as an alternate fuel for cars, trucks, and buses. Many buses are using bottled gas for fuel in order to avoid polluting the air and propane gas filling stations are being established in many cities. Propane is a gaseous active ingredient used for the dispersion of various products, such as deodorants or "fix-a-flat" rubbers from aerosol cans.

Propane is a simple organic compound that is used industrially to make ethylene ($H_2C{=}CH_2$) and propylene ($CH_3CH{=}CH_2$). Ethylene and propylene are produced by heating a mixture of propane and steam to a very high **temperature**. Ethylene is used to make many compounds that contain two carbon atoms or have a two carbon atom branch attached to a chain of carbon atoms. Propylene is polymerized to make polypropylene, a plastic, which is used for car **battery** cases, toys, kitchen utensils, and containers. It can be used in chemical reactions to attach a chain of three carbon atoms to **benzene** rings and other chemicals. Propylene is used to make other chemicals that contain three carbon atoms, such as, the specialty solvent acrylonitrile and propylene oxide used in the manufacture of rubber. Isopropyl **alcohol** or rubbing alcohol is manufactured by reacting propylene with **water**. It is a good solvent and is found in many industrial and consumer products. Isopropyl alcohol is a primary ingredient of nail polish, after shave lotion, deodorant, and skin lotion. It is used to kill **microorganisms** that grow in hospitals as well as around the home with tincture of iodine and mercurophen being home medicinals which contain the active ingredient isopropyl alcohol.

When a propyl group or a chain of three carbon atoms is added to a molecule's structure, their addition gives the compound various properties that make it commercially important. The mosquito and fly repellents dipropyl isocinchomeronate and propyl N,N-diethylsuccinamate both contain the three carbon propyl chain. Valeric acid or pentanoic acid is a five carbon acid that is commercially used as a food flavor. When a propyl group is attached to the second carbon atom of this acid, 2-propylpentanoic acid or valproic acid is produced. Valproic acid is prescribed for the treatment of seizures and

KEY TERMS

Propane—Has the molecular formula, $CH_3CH_2CH_3$, and consists of three carbon atoms connected by single bonds, each of which is connected to enough hydrogen atoms to have four bonds each.

Propyl group—The portion of an organic molecule that is derived from propane and has the molecular structure —CH_2CH_3.

Isopropyl group—Has the molecular structure of —$CH(CH_3)_2$, and is derived from propane by removing either of the hydrogen atoms attached to the central carbon atom ($CH_3CH_2CH_3$).

various types of **epilepsy**. The manufacturers of **herbicides** have known for years that the presence of a isopropyl group in a molecule results in an increase in the efficiency of that compounds weed killing properties. Propham or isopropyl carbanilate has been used for this purpose since 1945.

Further Reading

McMurry, J. *Organic Chemistry.* Pacific Grove, CA: Brooks/Cole Publishing Company, 1992.

Kirk-Othmer Encyclopedia of Chemical Technology. Propylene, Volume 19, page 228, Hydrocarbons, Volume 13, page 812, and Propyl Alcohols, Volume 19, page 215, New York: John Wiley and Sons, 1991.

Andrew Poss

Prosimians

Prosimians are the most primitive of the living primates, which also include the **monkeys** and **apes**. The name prosimian means "pre-monkey." The living prosimians are placed in the suborder Prosimii, which includes four families of **lemurs**, (the Lemuridae, the Cheirogaleidae, the Indriidae, and the Daubentoniidae), the bush babies, **lorises** and pottos (family Lorisidae), and the **tarsiers** (family Tarsiidae). Some authorities also include the **tree shrews**, though others separate the treeshrews into an order of their own.

Prosimian are primarily tree-dwellers. They have a longer snout than the monkeys and apes, and the prosimian snout usually ends in a moist nose, indicating a well-developed sense of **smell**. A larger proportion of the **brain** of prosimians is devoted to the sense of smell than the sense of **vision**. Prosimians actively scent-mark their territories to warn other animals of their occupancy. The scent-marks are made with a strong-smelling fluid produced by special **glands**, or with urine or feces.

Prosimian eyes are large and are adapted for night vision, with a tapetal layer in the retina of the **eye** that reflects and reuses light. Prosimian eyes are not as well positioned for stereoscopic vision as are the eyes of other primates.

Like all primates, prosimians have hands and feet that are capable of grasping tree limbs. The second toe of the hind foot of prosimians has a long claw which they use for grooming. The other toes, on both the hands and the feet, have flattened nails instead of curved claws. Lemurs, which walk along branches on all fours, have longer hind legs than front ones. Tarsiers, which are adapted for leaping between vertical tree trunks and then clinging to them, have short legs whose bones are fused together for strength.

Prosimians have inflexible faces compared to those of monkeys and apes. Most prosimians have 36 teeth, while west simians generally have 32 teeth. The lower front teeth of prosimians lie horizontally and protrude, forming a grooming structure called a dental comb. The dental comb is used to comb fur and scrape nourishing gum from trees, after which it is cleaned with a hard structure located beneath the tongue.

Prosimians spend much less time in infancy than simians do, perhaps only about 15 percent of their lifespan as opposed to 25 to 30 percent for monkeys and apes.

The early primates were distributed throughout most of the world. Today, however, the majority of the living prosimians, the ones collectively called lemurs, live only on the large **island** of Madagascar, off **Africa**. After human beings arrived on Madagascar about 1,500 years ago, at least 14 species of lemurs have became extinct.

The smallest living Madagascar prosimian are the mouse lemurs in genus *Microcebus*, while the largest lemur is the indri (*Indri indri*). Other prosimians, often described as those that don't live in Madagascar, fall into groups-the lorises, pottos, and galagos or bushbabies of Africa, India, and Southeast **Asia**, and the tarsiers of Southeast Asia.

Further Reading

Kerrod, Robin. *Mammals: Primates, Insect-Eaters and Baleen Whales. Encyclopedia of the Animal World series.* New York: Facts on File, 1988.

Knight, Linsay. *The Sierra Club Book of Small Mammals.* San Francisco: Sierra Club Books for Children, 1993.

Napier, J.R., and Napier, P.H. *The Natural History of the Primates.* Cambridge, MA: The MIT Press, 1985.

KEY TERMS

Dental comb—A formation of lower incisor teeth that have moved close together and horizontally to make a grooming tool.

Scent-mark—To spread urine, feces, or special fluid from a body gland along a trail to let competitive animals know that the territory is taken.

Simian—Any apelike animal. Simians include monkeys and apes.

Tapetum lucidum—The special layer behind the retina of the eye of most nocturnal animals that reflects light in such a way as to amplify available light.

Napier, Prue. *Monkeys and Apes.* A Grosset All-Color guide. New York: Grosset & Dunlap, 1972.

Peterson, Dale. *The Deluge and the Ark: A Journey into Primate worlds.* Boston: Houghton Mifflin, 1989.

Preston-Mafham, Rod and Ken. *Primates of the World.* New York: facts on File, 1992.

Jean F. Blashfield

Prosthetics

Prosthetics is a branch of **surgery** that is involved in devising and fabricating a prosthesis for a missing or infirm body part. A prosthesis is an artificial part used to restore some amount of normal body function. The classic example of a prosthesis is a false leg or arm to replace one that has been amputated. A diseased **heart** valve can be removed and replaced by an artificial one.

Artificial body joints have been designed to replace diseased or impaired ones, especially those that have been damaged by osteoarthritis, the most common form of **arthritis** causing degeneration of the main body joints.

There are a wide range of prosthetic devices for different parts of the body and for internal and external use. Some prosthetic devices are used to improve a body function such as a **hearing** aid. Others, such as breast implants used after mastectomies, are mainly designed for cosmetic rather than functional purposes. Another example of a cosmetic prosthesis is a glass eye designed to replace an eye lost in surgery. Hip and knee replacements are examples of internal joint replacements with artificial parts.

Prosthodontics is a branch of **dentistry** that provides replacements of teeth and other related supportive dental structures. The two main types of replacements are either partial or complete dentures and crowns and bridges, which are placed over existing teeth.

Orthotics is a branch of medicine, allied to prosthetics, that designs devices, such as braces, to correct or control a bone deformity or other anatomical problem that interferes with the correct performance of a part of the body such as the leg, arm, or wrist.

Arthroplasty is a branch of surgical **orthopedics** in which artificial joints or parts of joints are used to replace joints in the hip, knee, finger, shoulder, and elbow.

Bionics is a field of science that combines **mathematics**, **electronics**, **biochemistry**, and **biophysics** with the study of living systems to develop innovations in both general and medical technology. It has been responsible for recent major developments in prosthetics. With the application of bionic principles, new prostheses have allowed amputees and those who are paralyzed to walk with feeling by using electronic neuromuscular stimulation. Microprocessors are able to transmit a voltage charge to muscles triggering a **reflex** response.

Artificial limbs

Artificial limbs have been used for more than 2,000 years. The earliest known artificial limb was a leg made of **metal** plates surrounding a wooden core. It was not, however, until the second world war that the major developments in artificial limbs occurred. In this period, much progress was made by surgeons and prosthetic makers to help wounded soldiers adjust to civilian life with the help of newly designed and effective prostheses.

War has been the greatest impetus for advances in prosthetic design. For centuries, **amputation** was the most common therapy for traumatic injuries to a soldier's extremities. But until the middle of the 19th century, most patients died of **infection** due to the unsanitary surgical techniques of the time, leaving little room for advances in prosthetic technology for the survivors. Amputated hands were often replaced by simple hooks, and amputated legs by wooden pegs topped with open saddle-like sockets. Since the second world war, improvements in low-weight, high-strength materials and techniques for fitting and shaping artificial limbs have made these types of prosthesis much more useful and comfortable for the patients.

Candidates for artificial limbs to replace legs, feet, arms, and hands are those who have either lost the limb as a result of surgical amputation or were born with an impaired or missing limb. The process of preparing a pa-

tient for an artificial limb begins with the amputation. The amputating surgeon considers the best design for the stump or remaining part of the limb. After the wound has healed, a prosthetist chooses an artificial limb or prosthesis that will either have to be a weight-bearing replacement, or an arm and hand prosthesis that will have to manage a number of different movements.

There are several criteria of acceptability for limb prostheses. They must be able to approximate the function of the lost limb. They should be light, comfortable to wear, and easy to put on and take off. Substitute limbs should also have a natural appearance.

Pre-constructed artificial limbs are available for ready use. Going to a prosthetist, one who specializes in constructing and fitting artificial limbs, gives better results in adjusting the prosthesis to the individual's requirements. Recent technological developments have enabled prosthetists to add to artificial joints made from plastic, **carbon** fiber, or other materials that enable the wearer to include a variety of motions to the limb prosthesis. These motions include **rotation** around the joint and counter pressures that stabilize a weight bearing joint, like the knee, or they may even be able to control the length of the stride of an artificial leg.

The prosthetist first makes a **mold** from the stump of the missing limb. This mold forms the basis for the artificial limb and holds the top of the prosthesis comfortably on the stump. The socket can be constructed from various materials, such as leather, plastic, or **wood** and is attached to the stump by a variety of means. The leg prosthesis socket in which the residual limb fits is aligned with the feet, ankles, and knees for each individual. Improvements have been made in foot design to make them more responsive and in designing comfortable and flexible sockets. Materials such as carbon graphite, **titanium**, and flexible thermoplastics have permitted great advances in leg prostheses. Applications of electronic technology allows for a wider range of sensory feedback and control of artificial knee swing and stance.

Extending from the socket is the strut, which is the artificial replacement of the thigh, lower leg, upper arm, or forearm. Different types of material can go into the making of the strut. The strut is covered by foam rubber pressed into the shape of the limb it is replacing. The outer covering for the finished prosthesis can be made from different types of materials, such as wood, leather, or metal.

The aerospace industry has provided materials and electronic technology for developing prosthetic devices that can approximate movements of the muscles. Hand and arm replacements are usually operated by voluntary muscle control from the opposite shoulder through cables that connect from the shoulder harness to the artificial hand or hook, called the terminal device. Arm prostheses may also be operated by myoelectric control. (*Myo* means muscle.) The electrochemical activity of key arm muscles is received by electrodes in the prosthesis and is then transmitted to a motor that operates the prosthesis. Although this branch of prosthetics is still in its infancy, there is great hope that electronic controls will result in much more articulate hand movement, and will eventually replace cables that can simply open or close a hook or artificial hand.

Ironically, progress in prosthetic technology has been slowed by advanced surgical techniques, which have made amputation as a result of traumatic injury much more rare. Orthopedic surgeons can now repair limbs that would have once been routinely amputated. Severed limbs can even be re-attached in many cases.

Effectiveness

Artificial legs are usually more effective than artificial arms or hands in duplicating the motions of the natural limb. The broad and straight movements of the legs are easier to duplicate than the more intricate and quicker actions of the arms and hands. To compensate for these difficulties, artificial hands and arms with advanced designs that include electronic circuitry allow for a wider range of **motion** and use. Nerve impulses reaching the stump are transformed to appropriate movements of the prosthesis. Individuals using specialized hand and arm prostheses may have several different ones for different occasions. One could be a glove for social use while another for work might be shaped like a claw or have several different power attachments.

Arthroplasty

Replacing all or part of diseased or degenerated joints through the use of prosthetic joint parts provides the basis for a form of orthopedic surgery known as arthroplasty. Hip replacements were the first arthroplasty operations. They are still being performed with a high rate of success. Other routine joint replacement operations now also include knee joint replacement, finger joint replacement, and the replacement of the shoulder and elbow.

Hip replacement

Hip replacement surgery goes back to the 1930s. By the 1960s three substantial improvements in hip surgery made this procedure both popular and successful. The materials used for the hip prostheses were made from metals and **plastics** that were strong enough to support the weight brought on the hip and were also self-lubri-

cating. Cements were developed to adhere well to the bone. Extremely antiseptic operating rooms and clothes worn by the operating personnel reduce the danger of infection that accompanies a hip replacement operation.

The hip is the joint between the pelvis and upper end of the femur (thigh bone). It is an example of a ball-and-socket-joint that is subject to several major disorders. The most common disorder is osteoarthritis. **Pain** and stiffness accompany the movements of the hip. Other types of arthritic disorders can cause similar malfunction. Fracture of the hip often occurs with the elderly, who may be prone to falls. In the case of extreme trauma there may be a dislocation of the hip, which is rare but may occur in such mishaps as an **automobile** accident.

Hip replacements are surgical procedures in which either part or all of the hip joint is replaced with artificial parts. In the operation, the hip joint is exposed from around the surrounding **fat** and muscle **tissue**. The thigh bone (femur) and pelvis is prepared to accept the two component parts for the replacement to the natural hip joint. The components consist of a metal shaft and ball as one unit replacing the shaft of the thigh bone with its natural ball and a socket that is made either from metal or plastic. The new socket receives the shaft and ball after it is cemented into the pelvis. These parts are bound into place by a special cement into the surrounding bone. After the new ball is attached to the socket, the muscles and tendons are stitched back into place and the incision is closed.

Recently, a robot has been devised that can drill a hole in the femur much more accurately than a surgeon can. The robot's precise hole can hold the prosthesis much better, thus extending the life of the hip replacement. A surgeon can be as much as thirty percent off in his drilling. When that happens, only twenty percent of the implant comes in contact with the bone, leaving wide gaps around the prosthesis. Use of the surgical robot brings ninety-six percent of the implant in contact with the bone and gaps were reduced from 0.15 in (4 mm)-0.02 in (0.05) mm. This technology is still in an early state of development.

Recovery

It takes about a week for the cement to become fixed. In that time the patient is expected not to engage in movements that would dislocate the new joint. They are given special advice on how to **sleep** (on their backs) and told not to cross their legs. Care must be exerted during this period in conducting such movements as getting in and out of a bathtub. Recent research indicates that when the candidates for hip replacement surgery perform the

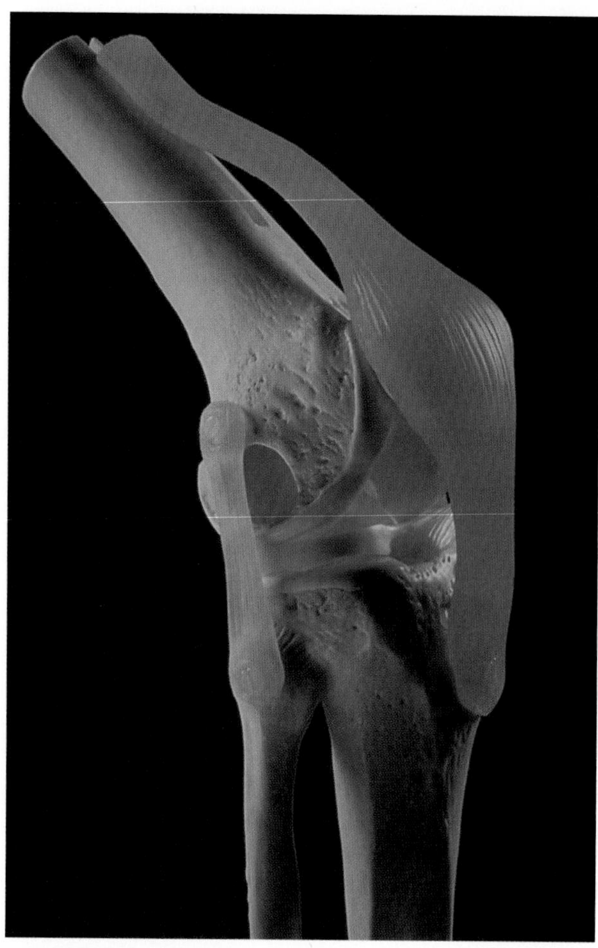

An artificial knee joint as used in replacement surgery (seen fitted to human bone samples). The replacement is made of plastic and consists of new contact surfaces, an artificial cartilage between the faces, and artificial tendons to limit flexion of the joint and prevent sideways movement.

rehabilitation exercise before the surgery the rate of recovery time is significantly reduced.

While hip joint replacements have proven to be very successful there is a problem of the cement loosening after an extended period of time. Research is being done for designs that do not rely as much on the use of cements. Hip replacements are usually not advised for those under fifty because of the unknown long-term effects, especially with the use of cement. Younger patients, however, are now considering cementless artificial hips as an alternative to the conventional procedures that do use cement. The newer technique that does not use cement takes longer, but some orthopedists believe the procedure offers better long-term results.

These newer types of hip replacements are of special interest to athletes in need of relief from hip pain.

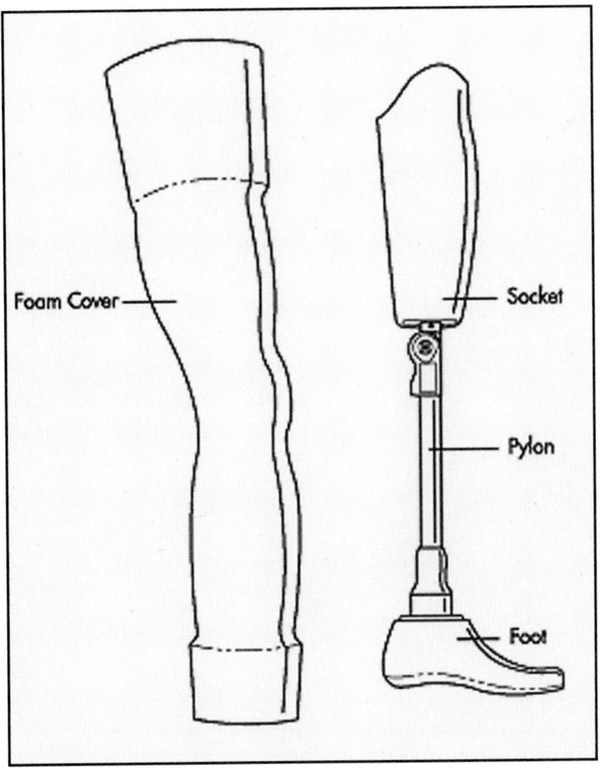

A typical above-the-knee prosthesis. The flesh-colored foam cover is worn over the working prosthesis on the right.

Athlete Bo Jackson returned to play with the Chicago White Sox after an operation that replaced his left hip.

Knee joint replacement

Large hinges were used in early examples of knee joint replacements. Operations for knee joint replacement, today, are implants within the joint using metal and plastic parts used to cover the worn parts of cartilage in the joint. The objective is to save as much of the joint as possible. This procedure is used mostly for elderly patients suffering from osteoarthritis or rheumatoid arthritis. Younger people are usually not advised to have a knee prosthesis because it reduces the range of movement for the knee and usually will not withstand the strains of vigorous use.

In the operation to install the knee prosthesis the flat undersurfaces of the knee joint are exposed. The lower end of the femur (thigh bone) is smoothed down to accept the prosthesis and then holes are drilled to fasten it. Likewise, the upper end of the tibia (leg bone) is prepared and the back part of the patella (knee cap) is prepared to accept the patellar component of the prosthesis. The parts are then cemented and tested to see if the joint movements are proper. The knee prosthesis consists of the femoral component and the tibial component along with the patella component.

The main purpose of the knee joint replacement procedure is to reduce pain and to restore some movement to the joint. The outcome of the operation lacks certainty and the duration of the prosthesis is limited. Research continues to find better cements and materials for the joints as well as designs that come closer to the actual joint.

Wrist and finger implants

The wrist is a complex joint consisting of eight bones and lies between the lower forearm and the hand. In the United States there are about 2,000 wrist implants and 7,000 hand and finger implants each year. There have been studies that indicate these implants may have damaging effects since they use silicone materials to replace damaged bone. The silicone particles may travel to nearby tissues, causing an immune response that ultimately damages surrounding bone. Many patients require additional surgery as a result. Some physicians maintain that the implants can cause more damage to the healthy bone than the harm done by the disease itself. So far the FDA has not decided to investigate these implants.

Breast implants

Due to the prevalence of breast **cancer** in women, which necessitates the removal of one or more breasts, breast reconstruction surgery is a common procedure. This involves the implantation of a sac filled with silicone gel or saline. Breast augmentation is also practiced as a purely cosmetic procedure by women who wish to enlarge their breasts.

The use of silicone in this procedure has become controversial. Silicone is a **polymer**, that is, a silicon compound united with organic compounds. While silicone rubbers have been used for many years, in 1992 the FDA asked that the use of silicone for breast implants in cosmetic surgery be suspended in order to have time to study the complaints against silicone. There have been reports of autoimmune reactions caused by implanted silicone. Some cases showed permanent sores and lumps arising after the implant. There was also a fear expressed by researchers of the possibility that silicone might migrate to the lungs, causing death. Although subsequent testing cast doubt on the actual negative side effects of silicone implants, they have been replaced in most cases by implants using saline solution.

Implanted prosthetic materials

Heart valve implants and **plastic surgery** for the face or in smoothing wrinkles employ the use of silicone

materials as well. The FDA continues to study other high-risk medical prostheses. These include inflatable penile implants, testicular implants, heart-bypass pumps, cranial stimulators, and saline-filled breast implants.

Heart transplants

Heart disease is one of the most common killers of middle-aged men and women. Artificial heart valves are now commonly transplanted into living hearts to replace malfunctioning valves. However, this procedure only treats one type of heart malfunction. Many types of artificial heart have been tested, with the hope of replacing the entire **organ** with an electro-mechanical substitute. This technique attracted a great deal of publicity in the early 1980's, when a few patients received permanent mechanical replacement hearts. Unfortunately, these patients lived only a short time after receiving the transplants. Though research continues into smaller, more reliable devices that do not trigger rejection from the body's auto-immune system, they are still considered temporary expedients that allow a patient to remain alive until a suitable human heart is available for transplantation. Even then, artificial hearts and Vascular Aid Devices (VAD) are used in only the more desperate cases, since infection and rejection can cause further damage, which would reduce the chances of a successful human heart transplant, causing the patient to be removed from the transplant list.

Bionics

The field of prosthetics has received a major impetus from the development of bionics. In bionics, engineering problems are solved by studying the properties of biological systems. For example, studying the swimming movements of **fish** and the flight of **birds** give the bionics engineer clues on how to solve problems in jet and rocket propulsion. Problems of conservation of **energy** in engineering are studied in **relation** to other biological examples.

Bionics is an outgrowth of the field of study known as **cybernetics**. The concern of cybernetics is to relate the way machines communicate, are controlled, and acquire information to similar processes in life systems. Bionics, like cybernetics, depends on the understanding of **physiology**, biochemistry, and both the physical and mechanical properties of living things. The bionic scientist must be prepared to apply mathematics, **physics**, and electronic engineering for the formulations of the interfaces between living and mechanical systems.

Bionics grew out of a concept known as the general-systems theory. Nicholas Rashevsky, a Russian-American scientist, was the first to develop a correlation between the workings of the central **nervous system** and mathematical models. After his initial studies, other physicists and engineers entered the field of bionics. They have studied the way in which visual images are established within biological visual systems. From these investigations technologically advanced cameras, **television**, and optical-recognition systems have emerged. Those who studied biological auditory systems were able to devise major improvements in **radio** transmitters and receivers.

Along with all of its other applications, bionics has been a major force in the development of prosthetics. The field of artificial organ transplantation owes its development to bionics. Artificial limbs—arms and legs—can now be electronically controlled by an electronic process that recognizes various patterns of electrical movement. Complicated movements of the prosthesis

KEY TERMS

Autoimmune reactions—The use of certain substances in prosthetic devices may trigger off the production of antibodies from the immune system causing adverse effects.

Ball and socket joint—A type of joint that allows the widest range of movement found in the hip and shoulder joint.

Bionics—A new field of science that combines engineering with biology.

FDA—The Unites States Federal Drug Administration; oversees and regulates the introduction of new drug products into the medical marketplace.

Femur—The thigh bone which is the site for the implantation of hip and knee prostheses.

Myoelectric control—The electrical stimulation of prosthetic devices from the surrounding muscle tissue.

Osteoarthritis—The most common form of arthritis which is responsible for the degeneration of the cartilage in bone joints.

Silicone—A controversial substance that has been used in breast and other types of implants. It has moved from a low-risk prosthetic material to a high-risk category by the FDA.

Socket—The part of a limb prosthesis that fits over the stump of the amputated limb.

Tibia—The leg bone.

can be brought about by microcircuits that detect the patterns of electrical impulses within the tissue of the surrounding muscle as it is expressed on the outer skin. Electronic motors then carry the prosthesis to its task.

Other prosthetic devices employing bionic principles allow some of the blind to regain a sense of sight by transmitting nerve impulses around the damaged neural pathways to ones that are still capable of transmitting signals. Hearing aids are another example of prosthetic devices that have benefitted from bionic research.

Further Reading

Council on Scientific Affairs, American Medical Association;" Silicone gel breast implants." *JAMA* 270 (1993): 2602-6.

Delisa, Joel A., et al. *Rehabilitation Medicine*. Philadelphia: Lippincott, 1993.

Jones, Stella."Making artificial organs work." *Technology Review*. v 97. Sept. 1994: 32-41.

Padula, Patricia A. and Lawrence W. Friedmann." Acquired Amputation and Prostheses Before the Sixteenth Century." *The Journal of Vascular Disease*, (February 1987).

Randall, Teri. "Silicone implants for hand and wrist." *The Journal of the American Medical Association*, v268. (1 July 1992): 13-16.

Romm, Sharon. "Arms by Design: From antiquity to the Renaissance." *Plastic and Reconstructive Surgery*, (July 1988).

Sanders, Gloria T. *Amputation Prosthetics*. F.A. Davis Company, Philadelphia, PA., 1986.

Sterling, Bruce. "The artificial body." *The Magazine of Fantasy and Science Fiction*, (Oct.-Nov. 1994): 138-147

Wilson, A. Bennet, Jr.,"History of Amputation Surgery and Prosthetics." *Atlas of Limb Prosthetics: Surgery and Prosthetic Principles*. Americal Academy of Orthopedic Surgeons, C.V. Mosby Company, St. Louis, MO., 1981

Jordan P. Richman

Protactinium see **Actinides**

Proteas

Proteas are evergreen trees and shrubs belonging to the dicotyledonous **plant** family Proteaceae and, in particular, to members of the genus *Protea*. They grow mostly in dry regions of the southern hemisphere, especially in **Australia** and South **Africa**. The family is divided into five subfamilies, 75 genera, and 1,350 species.

The Proteaceae are distinguished from closely related families by having one stamen attached to the center of each of four petals, **seeds** attached to the wall of the fruit, and flowers often aggregated into heads and enveloped by large densely hairy or showy bracts. The flowers of many species are pollinated by **birds**, **bats**, and small marsupial **mammals**.

The species of Proteaceae have two important adaptations to the dry habitats in which they grow. First, their leaves are thick and hard, a condition called sclerophylly. This prevents moisture loss and decreases damage should wilting occur. Second, their roots are clumped and very thin for efficient absorption of **water** and mineral **nutrients**. These special roots, called proteoid roots, lack the symbiotic mycorrhizal **fungi** found in the roots of most other plants.

Because the Proteaceae occur naturally only in the southern hemisphere, it is believed that the family originated on the ancient supercontinent of Gondwana. During the early Mesozoic Era, this **continent** was formed by the union of **South America**, Africa, **Antarctica**, India, and Australia-those continents where the family is found today. Until recently, these continents have been separate from the northern continents of **North America**, **Europe**, and **Asia**. For this reason, the family is not found naturally in the northern hemisphere.

The Proteaceae contain several economically important species. The Macadamia **nut** (*Macadamia integrifolia*) is considered by many people to be the most delicious nut in the world and consequently is one of the most expensive. It is native to Australia but primarily cultivated in Hawaii and southern California. The showy **flower** clusters of many species of Proteas are sold in the florist trade. The most important species (*Protea cynaroides*) comes from South Africa and has long-lasting cut flowers with heads to 8 in (20 cm) across. The silk-oak (*Grevillea robusta*), native to eastern Australia, is a commonly cultivated ornamental in California and the southern United States; it has become naturalized in waste places in Florida.

Protected area

Protected areas are parks, ecological reserves, and other tracts set aside from intense development to conserve their natural ecological values. These areas protect the **habitat** of **endangered species**, threatened ecological communities, or representative examples of widespread ecosystems, referred to as indigenous (native) **biodiversity** values. Some protected areas are intended to conserve places of scenic beauty, or sites of historical or cultural importance. Most protected areas are terrestrial, but since the late 1980s, increasing attention has been paid to marine areas as well. Human activities that do

not severely threaten the ecological values being conserved take place in some protected areas. Examples of theses activities include, research, education, **ecotourism**, spiritual activities, even hunting, fishing, and timber harvesting.

The need for protected areas

The biodiversity of **Earth** is in a fragile state. An incredible number of **plant** and **animal** species are becoming endangered, while many others have recently become extinct. These devastating ecological changes result almost entirely from human activities. The primary cause of widespread endangerment and **extinction** of biodiversity is the conversion of natural ecosystems into city, industry, and agricultural land. The harvesting of species and ecosystems as natural resources, such as **forestry**, fisheries, and hunting, is also harmful. Global environmental changes may also prove devastating to biodiversity. Increasing concentrations of greenhouse gases in the atmosphere, resulting in a gradually warming climate, is an example of this type of change.

One way of mitigating the biodiversity crisis is to establish protected areas of land and **water**. In these areas, native species and natural ecosystems are maintained without exposure to severely threatening human influences. Protected areas are essential to conserve the habitat of endangered species, and ensure the existence of rare ecosystems.

Kinds of protected areas

The International Union for the **Conservation** of Nature (IUCN) recognizes six categories of protected areas:

- Category 1 is the highest level of protection. This category includes scientific reserves and wilderness areas. They are managed to maintain native species and natural ecosystems, although use for research may be allowed. These types of highly protected areas are often relatively small, and present in most U.S. states.
- Category 2 includes national parks and equivalent reserves. These are managed primarily to protect species and ecosystems, although outdoor recreation and ecotourism is usually permitted. Two famous protected areas in the U.S. are Yellowstone and Yosemite National Parks.
- Category 3 includes national monuments and geological phenomena. Sites of aesthetic or cultural importance are also included.
- Category 4 includes habitat- and species-management areas, intended to conserve conditions required in support of productive populations of hunted species.
- Category 5 includes protected landscapes and seascapes. It is intended to sustain recreational use of such areas by humans, while also accommodating the needs of most wild species and ecosystems.
- Category 6 includes managed-resource protected areas, which are primarily managed to yield a sustainable harvest of renewable natural resources (such as timber), while also accommodating the needs of native species and ecosystems.

In 1997, there were about 10,400 protected areas covering a total of 2.1 billion acres (841 million hectares) worldwide (IUCN categories 1-5; World Resources Institute, 1998). Of this total area, about 4,500 sites, amounting to 1.2 billion acres (499 million ha), were fully conserved (IUCN categories 1-3) and could be considered true protected areas.

Systems of protected areas

Ideally, the numbers and sizes of protected areas should be designed to sustain all native species and natural ecosystems occurring within a jurisdiction (a municipality, state, or entire country). This should include terrestrial, **freshwater**, and marine species and ecosystems, and the goal should be long-term protection. To ensure there is adequate representation of all elements of indigenous biodiversity within a system of protected areas, the kinds of native species and ecosystems in the jurisdiction must be known. This knowledge makes it possible to accommodate all elements of ecological heritage within a comprehensive system plan for a network of protected areas.

The above criteria are for an ideal system of protected areas. No country has yet managed to designate a comprehensive system of protected areas, in which all native species and natural ecosystems are represented and sustained. An enormous amount of political will is required to set aside the amounts of land and water necessary to fully protect the native biodiversity of any region. Countries that have made the most progress in this regard are relatively wealthy, such as **Australia**, Canada, New Zealand, and the United States. But even in these cases, the systems of protected areas are highly incomplete.

Most of the existing protected areas are relatively small, or threatened by degrading influences occurring within their boundaries or surrounding area. It is doubtful the smaller protected areas will be able to sustain their present ecological values over the longer term, in the face of disturbances and other environmental changes. In addition, scientists are often unfamiliar with the ecological needs of endangered species and ecosystems, making proper management difficult.

Design of protected areas

The design of protected areas is an important field of research in conservation **biology**. The essential questions involve criteria for the size, shape, and positioning of protected areas to optimize their ability to protect biodiversity, while using funding as efficiently as possible. Conservation biologists recommend that protected areas be as large and numerous as possible. Other design aspects, however, are more controversial. Controversy over the design of protected areas involves the following key elements:

- Is it preferable to have one large reserve, or a number of smaller ones of the same total area? Conservation biologists identify this question with the acronym SLOSS, which stands for: single large, or several small. According to ecological theory, populations in larger protected areas should have a smaller risk of extinction, compared to those in smaller reserves. However, if there are populations in several different reserves, the redundancy might prevent extinction in the event of a catastrophic loss in one reserve.
- Reserves can also be designed to have less edge (or **ecotone**) habitat. This refers to transitions between **ecosystem** types, such as that between a forest and a field. Edge habitat is often penetrated by **invasive species** and predators, which can become important problems in some protected areas. In addition, many species require interior habitat for breeding; meaning they are intolerant of ecotones. Larger protected areas have proportionately more interior habitat, as do simple-shaped ones (a **circle** has the smallest **ratio** of edge to area).
- For many ecological functions to operate well, there must be connections among habitats. This is particularly true of the dispersal of plants and animals. This need can be accommodated if protected areas are linked by corridors of suitable habitat, or if they are clumped close together. However, corridors might also serve as conduits for invasive species and diseases.

Management of protected areas

The conservation of biodiversity in protected areas also requires the monitoring of key ecological values, such as the populations of endangered species and the health of natural ecosystems. It may also be necessary to conduct research to determine the appropriate kinds of management required, and to then implement that management. Management includes actions such as patrolling to prevent poaching of timber and animals, altering habitats to maintain their suitability for threatened species, and captive breeding and release of endangered species.

Greater protected areas

Most protected areas are connected to surrounding areas by movement of animals, the flow of water and **nutrients**, or by climatic influences. Protected areas are not isolated, rather, they are a part of a larger ecosystem. The protected area plus its immediate surrounding area, is referred to as a greater protected area, which is co-managed to sustain populations of native species and natural communities. In addition, the surrounding area may be managed to supply resources, such as timber, hunted animals, and mined **minerals**.

Further Reading

Stolton, S. and N. Dudley, eds. *Partnerships for Protection: New Strategies for Planning and Management for Protected Areas.* Earthscan Publications Ltd. 1999.

World Resources Institute. *World Resources 1998-99.* Washington, DC. 1998.

Wright, R.G. and J. Lemons, eds. *National Parks and Protected Areas: Their Role in Environmental Protection.* Blackwell Science Inc. 1996.

Bill Freedman

Proteins

Proteins are linear chains of amino acids connected by chemical bonds between the **carboxyl group** of each **amino acid** and the amine group of the one following. These bonds are called peptide bonds, and chains of only a few amino acids are referred to as polypeptides rather than proteins. Different authorities set the protein/polypeptide dividing line at anywhere from 10 to 100 amino acids, but most scientists consider the distinction too unimportant to debate.

Many proteins have components other than amino acids. For example, some may have sugar molecules chemically attached. Exactly which types of sugars are involved and where on the protein chain attachment occurs will vary with the specific protein. In a few cases, it may also vary between different people. The A, B, and O **blood** types, for example, differ in precisely which types of sugar are or are not added to a specific protein on the surface of red blood cells.

Other proteins may have fat-like (**lipid**) molecules chemically bonded to them. These sugar and lipid molecules are always added after synthesis of the protein's amino acid chain is complete. As a result, discussions of protein structure and synthesis-including this one-may virtually ignore them. Nevertheless, such molecules can significantly affect the protein's properties.

Many other types of molecules may also be associated with proteins. Some proteins, for example, have specific **metal** ions associated with them. Others carry small molecules that are essential to their activity. Still others associate with nucleic acids in chromosomal or ribosomal structures.

What proteins do

Proteins are all around us. Much of our bodies' dry weight is protein—even our bones are about one-quarter protein. The animals we eat and the microbes that attack us are likewise largely protein. The leather, wool, and silk clothing that we wear are nearly pure protein. The **insulin** that keeps diabetics alive and the "clot-busting" enzymes that may save heart attack patients are also proteins. Proteins can even be found working at industrial sites-protein enzymes produce not only the high-fructose corn syrup that sweetens most soft drinks, but also fuel-grade **ethanol** (**alcohol**) and other gasoline additives.

Within our bodies and those of other living things, proteins serve many functions. They digest foods and turn them into **energy**; they move our bodies and move molecules about within our cells; they let some substances pass through **cell** membranes while keeping others out; they turn light into chemical energy, making both **vision** and **photosynthesis** possible; they allow cells to detect and react to **hormones** and toxins in their surroundings; and, as antibodies, they protect our bodies against foreign invaders.

Many of these protein functions are addressed or referred to in other articles in this encyclopedia. Yet there are simply too many proteins—possibly more than 100,000—to even consider mentioning them all. Even trying to discuss every possible type of protein is an **exercise** in futility. Not only is the number of types enormous, but the types overlap. In producing muscle contraction, for example, the proteins actin and myosin obtain energy by breaking down **adenosine triphosphate** in an enzyme-like fashion.

Protein structure

Scientists have traditionally addressed protein structure at four levels: primary, secondary, tertiary, and quaternary. Primary structure is simply the linear sequence of amino acids in the peptide chain. Secondary and tertiary structure both refer to the three-dimensional shape into which a protein chain folds. The distinction is partly historical: secondary structure refers to certain highly regular arrangements of amino acids that scientists could detect as long ago as the 1950s, while tertiary structure refers to the complete three-dimensional shape. Determining a protein's tertiary structure can be difficult even today, although researchers have made major strides within the past decade.

The tertiary structure of many proteins shows a "string of beads" organization. The protein includes several compact regions known as domains, separated by short stretches where the protein chain assumes an extended, essentially **random** configuration. Some scientists believe that domains were originally separate proteins that, over the course of **evolution**, have come together to perform their functions more efficiently.

Quaternary structure refers to the way in which protein chains—either identical or different—associate with each other. For example, a complete **molecule** of the oxygen-carrying protein hemoglobin includes four protein chains of two slightly different types. Simple laboratory tests usually allow scientists to determine how many chains make up a complete protein molecule.

Primary structure: peptide-chain synthesis

Proteins are made (synthesized) in living things according to "directions" given by DNA and carried out by RNA and proteins. The synthesized protein's linear sequence of amino acids is ultimately determined by the linear sequence of DNA bases (base triplets known as codons) in the **gene** that codes for it. Each cell possesses elaborate machinery for producing proteins from these blueprints.

The first step is copying the DNA blueprint, essentially fixed within the cell nucleus, into a more mobile form. This form is messenger ribonucleic acid (mRNA), a single-stranded **nucleic acid** carrying essentially the same sequence of bases as the DNA gene. The mRNA is free to move into the main part of the cell, the cytoplasm, where protein synthesis takes place.

Besides mRNA, protein synthesis requires **ribosomes** and transfer ribonucleic acid (tRNA). Ribosomes are the actual "factories" where synthesis takes place, while tRNA molecules are the" trucks" that bring amino acids to the ribosome and ensure that they are incorporated at the right spot in the growing chain.

Ribosomes are extremely complex assemblages. They comprise almost 70 different proteins and at least three different types of RNA, all organized into two different-sized subunits. As protein synthesis begins, the previously separate subunits come together at the beginning of the mRNA chain; all three components are essential for the synthetic process.

Transfer RNA molecules are rather small, only about 80 nucleotides long. (Nucleotides are the fundamental building blocks of nucleic acids, as amino acids

are of proteins.) Each type of amino acid has at least one corresponding type of tRNA (sometimes more). This correspondence is enforced by the enzymes that attach amino acids to tRNA molecules, which "recognize" both the amino acid and the tRNA type and do not act unless both are correct.

Transfer RNA molecules are not only trucks but translators. As the synthetic process adds one amino acid after another, they" read" the mRNA to determine which amino acid belongs next. They then bring the proper amino acid to the spot where synthesis is taking place, and the ribosome couples it to the growing chain. The tRNA is then released and the ribosome then moves along the mRNA to the next codon-the next base triplet specifying an amino acid. The process repeats until the "stop" signal on the mRNA is reached, upon which the ribosome releases both the mRNA and the completed protein chain and its subunits separate to seek out other mRNAs.

Secondary structure

The two major types of secondary structure are the alpha helix and the beta sheet, both discovered by Linus Pauling and R. B. Corey in 1951. (Pauling received the first of his two Nobel Prizes for this discovery.) Many scientists consider a structure known as the beta turn part of secondary structure, even though the older techniques used to identify alpha helices and beta sheets cannot detect it. For completeness, some authorities also list random coil-the absence of any regular, periodic structure-as a type of secondary structure.

ALPHA HELIX

In an alpha helix, the backbone **atoms** of the peptide chain-the carboxyl **carbon** atom, the a-carbon atom (to which the side chain is attached), and the amino **nitrogen** atom-take the form of a three-dimensional **spiral**. The helix is held together by **hydrogen** bonds between each nitrogen atom and the **oxygen** atom of the carboxyl group belonging to the fourth amino acid up the chain. This arrangement requires each turn of the helix to encompass 3.6 amino acids and forces the sidechains to stick out from the central helical core like bristles on a brush.

Since amino acids at the end of an alpha helix cannot form these regular hydrogen bonds, the helix tends to become more stable as it becomes longer-that is, as the proportion of unbonded "end" amino acids becomes smaller. However, recent research suggests that most alpha helices end with specific "capping" **sequences** of amino acids. These sequences provide alternative hydrogen-bonding opportunities to replace those unavailable within the helix itself.

BETA SHEET

Beta sheets feature several peptide chains lying next to each other in the same **plane**. The stabilizing hydrogen bonds are between nitrogen atoms on one chain and carboxyl-group oxygen atoms on the adjacent chain. Since each amino acid has its amino group hydrogen-bonded to the chain on one side and its carboxyl group to the chain on the other side, sheets can grow indefinitely. Indeed, as with alpha helices, the sheet becomes more stable as it grows larger.

The backbone chains in a beta sheet can all run in the same direction (**parallel** beta sheet) or alternate chains can run in opposite directions (antiparallel beta sheet). There is no significant difference in stability between the types, and some real-world beta sheets mix the two. In each case, sidechains of alternate amino acids stick out from alternate sides of the sheet. The sidechains of adjacent backbone chains are aligned, however, creating something of an accordion-fold effect.

BETA TURN

Many antiparallel beta sheets are formed by a single peptide chain continually looping back on itself. The loop between the two hydrogen-bonded segments, known as a beta turn, consistently contains one to three (usually two) amino acids. The amino acids in a beta turn do not form hydrogen bonds, but other interactions may stabilize their positions. A further consistency is that, from a perspective where the side chain of the final hydrogen-bonded amino acid projects outward toward the viewer, the turn is always to the right.

Tertiary structure and protein folding

Within seconds to minutes of their synthesis on ribosomes, proteins fold up into an essentially compact three-dimensional shape-their tertiary structure. Ordinary chemical forces fully determine both the steps in the folding pathway and the stability of the final shape. Some of these forces are hydrogen bonds between sidechains of specific amino acids. Others involve electrical attraction between positively and negatively charged sidechains. Perhaps most important, however, are what are called hydrophobic interactions—a scientific restatement of the observation that oil and **water** do not mix.

Some amino acid sidechains are essentially oil-like (hydrophobic-literally, "water-fearing"). They accordingly stabilize tertiary structures that place them in the interior, largely surrounded by other oil-like sidechains. Conversely, some sidechains are charged or can form hydrogen bonds. These are hydrophilic, or "water-lov-

ing," sidechains. Unless they form hydrogen or electrostatic bonds with other specific sidechains, they will stabilize structures where they are on the exterior, interacting with water.

The forces that govern a protein's tertiary structure are simple. With thousands or even tens of thousands of atoms involved, however, the interactions can be extremely complex. Today's scientists are only beginning to discover ways to predict the shape a protein will assume and the folding process it will go through to reach that shape.

Recent studies show that folding proceeds through a series of intermediate steps. Some of these steps may involve substructures not preserved in the final shape. Furthermore, the folding pathway is not necessarily the same for all molecules of a given protein. Individual molecules may pass through any of several alternative intermediates, all of which ultimately collapse to the same final structure.

The stability of a three-dimensional structure is not closely related to the speed with which it forms. Indeed, speed rather than stability is the main reason that egg white can never be "uncooked." At room **temperature** or below, the most stable form of the major egg white protein is compact and soluble. At boiling-water temperatures, the most stable form is an extended chain. When the cooked egg is cooled, however, the proteins do not have time to return to their normal compact structures. Instead, they collapse into an aggregated, tangled **mass**. And although this tangled mass is inherently less stable than the protein structures in the uncooked egg white, it would take millions of years-effectively forever-for the chains to untangle themselves and return to their soluble states. In scientific terminology, the cooked egg white is said to be metastable.

Something very similar could happen in the living cell. That it rarely does so reflects eons of evolution: selection has eliminated protein sequences likely to get trapped in a metastable state. Mutations can upset this balance, however. In the laboratory, scientists have produced many mutations that disrupt a protein's tertiary structure-either rendering it unstable or allowing it to become trapped in a metastable state. In the body, some scientists suspect that **cystic fibrosis** and an inherited bone disease called osteogenesis imperfecta may be due to mutations interfering with protein folding. And some believe that **Alzheimer's disease** may also be due to improper protein folding-although not because of a **mutation**.

Scientists were recently surprised to discover that some proteins require an additional mechanism to ensure that they fold properly: association with other proteins. Since a protein's primary sequence completely determines its tertiary structure-as Christian Anfinsen and his National Institutes of Health colleagues had shown in a classic 1960 study-external mechanisms were not anticipated.

Sometimes the associated proteins become part of the final protein complex; in effect, quaternary structure forms before the final tertiary structure. In other instances, folding is assisted by a class of proteins known as chaperonins that dissociate when the process is complete. No one knows the precise role chaperonins play; it may not be the same in all cases. Scientists suspect, however, that one major chaperonin role may be to steer target proteins away from aggregation or other metastable states in which they might become trapped.

Quaternary structure, cooperativity, and hemoglobin

Some proteins have no quaternary structure. They exist in the cell as single, isolated molecules. Others exist in complexes encompassing anywhere from two to dozens of protein molecules belonging to any number of types.

Proteins may exhibit quaternary structure for a variety of reasons. Sometimes several proteins must come together to carry out a single function-or to perform it efficiently, without the substances on which they all act having to diffuse halfway across the cell. At other times the reasons are at least partially structural; for example, several proteins may come together to form an ion channel long enough to reach across the cell **membrane**. The most interesting reason, however, is that association allows changes to one molecule to affect the shape and activity of the others. Hemoglobin provides an intriguing example of this.

Hemoglobin, which makes up about a third of red blood cells' weight, is the protein that transports oxygen from the lungs to the tissues where it is used. It would be a major oversimplification, but not entirely false, to say that the protein (globin) part of hemoglobin is simply a carrier for the associated heme group.

Heme is a large "ring of rings" comprising 33 carbon, 4 nitrogen, 4 oxygen, and 30 hydrogen atoms. In the center, bonded to the four nitrogen atoms, is an **iron** atom; attraction between this iron atom and a histidine side chain on the globin is one of several forces holding the heme in place. Another histidine side chain is located slightly further from the iron atom, allowing an oxygen molecule to insert itself reversibly into the gap. In similar proteins lacking this histidine, oxygen alters the iron's **oxidation state** rather than attaching to it.

Hemoglobin consists of two copies of each of two slightly different protein molecules. All four molecules are in intimate contact with each other; thus, it is easy to see how a change in the shape of one could encourage

KEY TERMS

Alpha helix—A type of secondary structure in which a single peptide chain arranges itself in a three-dimesional spiral.

Beta sheet—A type of secondary structure in which several peptide chains arrange themselves alongside each other.

Domain—A relatively compact region of a protein, seperated from other domains by short stretches in which the protein chain is more or less extended; different domains often carry out distinct parts of the protein's overall function.

Messenger ribonucleic acid (mRNA)—A molecule of RNA that carries the genetic information for producing one or more proteins; mRNA is produced by copying one strand of DNA, but is able to move from the nucleus to the cytoplasm (where protein synthesis takes place).

Peptide bond—A chemical bond between the carboxyl group of one amino acid and the amino nitrogen atom of another.

Polypeptide—A group of amino acids joined by peptide bonds; proteins are large polypeptides, but no agreement exists regarding how large they must be to justify the name.

Primary structure—The linear sequence of amino acids making up a protein.

Quaternary structure—The number and type of protein chains normally associated with each other in the body.

Ribosome—A very large assemblage of RNA and protein that, using instructions from mRNA, synthesizes new protein molecules.

Secondary structure—Certain highly regular three-dimensional arrangements of amino acids within a protein.

Tertiary structure—A protein molecule's overall threedimensional shape.

Transfer ribonucleic acid (tRNA)—A small RNA molecule, specific for a single amino acid, that transports that amino acid to the proper spot on the ribosome for assembly into the growing protein chain.

the others to change shape as well. In fact, that is exactly what happens. When oxygen binds to one hemoglobin molecule, it forces a slight change in that molecule's shape. This change, in turn, alters the other molecules' shape so that oxygen binding is more likely. The end result is that any given hemoglobin tetramer (four-molecule complex) almost always carries either four oxygen molecules or none.

This "cooperativity," discovered by Coryell and Pauling in 1939, is extremely important for hemoglobin's function in the body. In the lungs, where there is a great deal of oxygen, binding of an oxygen molecule is quite likely. This leads almost immediate binding of three more oxygen molecules, so hemoglobin is nearly saturated with oxygen as it leaves the lungs. In the tissues, where there is less oxygen, the chance that an oxygen molecule will leave the hemoglobin tetramer becomes quite high. As a result, the other three oxygen molecules will be bound less tightly and will probably leave also. The final consequence is that most of the oxygen carried to the tissues will be released there.

Without cooperativity, hemoglobin would pick up less oxygen in the lungs and release less in the tissues. Overall oxygen transport would therefore be less efficient.

Designer proteins

Although we think of proteins as natural products, scientists are now **learning** to design proteins that will meet our needs rather than nature's. Many of today's designs involve making small changes in already existing proteins. For example, by changing two amino acids in an **enzyme** that normally breaks down proteins into short peptides, scientists have produced one that instead links peptides together. Similarly, changing three amino acids in an enzyme often used to improve detergents' cleaning power doubled the enzyme's wash-water stability.

Researchers have also designed proteins by combining different naturally occurring domains, and are actively investigating possible applications. Medical applications seem especially promising. For example, we might cure **cancer** by combining cancer-recognizing antibody domains with the cell-killing domains of **diphtheria** toxin. While native diphtheria toxin kills many types of cells in the body, scientists hope these engineered proteins will attach to, and kill, only the cancer cells against which their antibody domains are directed.

The long-term goal, however, is to design proteins from scratch. This is extremely difficult today, and will

remain so until researchers better understand the rules that govern tertiary structure. Nevertheless, scientists have already designed a few small proteins whose stability or instability helps illuminate these rules. Building on these successes, scientists hope they may someday be able to design proteins solely for our own industrial and economic needs, rather than the needs of that great protein engineering experiment known as "life."

See also Antibody and antigen; Collagen; Deoxyribonucleic acid; Metabolism; Ribonucleic acid.

Further Reading

Darby, N. J., and T. E. Creighton. *Protein Structure.* New York: Oxford University Press, 1994.

Gerbi, Susan A. *From Genes to Proteins.* Burlington, NC: Carolina Biological, 1987.

King, Jonathan. "The Unfolding Puzzle of Protein Folding." *Technology Review.* (May/June 1993): 54-61.

Lipkin, Richard. "Designer Proteins: Building Machines of Life from Scratch." *Science News.* 146 (1994): 396-397.

Yew, Nelson S. *Protein Processing Defects in Human Disease.* Austin, TX: R. G. Landes, 1994.

Zubay, Geoffrey, and Richard Palmiter. *Principles of Biochemistry, vol. 3: Nucleic Acid and Protein Metabolism.* Dubuque, IA: William C. Brown, 1994.

W. A. Thomasson

Protista

The Kingdom Protista is the most diverse of all six kingdoms. There are more than 200,000 known species of protists with many more yet to be discovered. The protists can be found in countless colors, sizes, and shapes. They inhabit just about any area where **water** is found some or all of the time. They form the base of ecosystems by making food, as is the case with photosynthetic protists, or by themselves being eaten by larger organisms. They range in size from microscopic, unicellular organisms to huge seaweeds that can grow up to 300 ft (100 m) long.

Background

The German zoologist Ernst Haeckel (1834-1919) first proposed the kingdom Protista in 1866. This early classification included any microorganism that was not a **plant** or an **animal**. Biologists did not readily accept this kingdom, and even after the American botanist Herbert F. Copeland again tried to establish its use 90 years later, there was not much support from the scientific community. Around 1960, R.Y. Stanier and C.B. Van Niel (1897-1985) proposed the division of all organisms into two groups, the prokaryotes and the eukaryotes. Eukaryotes are organisms that have membrane-bound organelles in which metabolic processes take place, while prokaryotes lack these structures. In 1969, Robert Whittaker proposed the five-kingdom system of classification. The kingdom Protista was one of the five proposed kingdoms. At this time, only unicellular eukaryotic organisms were considered protists. Since then, the kingdom has expanded to include multicellular organisms, although biologists still disagree about what exactly makes an **organism** a protist.

Classification

Protists are difficult to characterize because of the great diversity of the kingdom. These organisms vary in body form, **nutrition**, and reproduction. They may be unicellular, colonial, or multicellular. As eukaryotes, protists can have many different organelles, including a nucleus, mitochondria, contractile vacuoles, food vacuoles, eyespots, plastids, pellicles, and **flagella**. The nuclei of protists contain chromosomes, with DNA associated with **proteins**. Protists are also capable of sexual, as well as **asexual reproduction**, **meiosis**, and **mitosis**. Protists can be free-living, or they may live symbiotically with another organism. This **symbiosis** can be mutualistic, where both partners benefit, or parasitic, where the protist uses its host as a source of food or shelter while providing no advantage to the other organism. Many protists are economically important and beneficial to mankind, while others cause fatal diseases. Protists make up the majority of the **plankton** in aquatic systems, where they serve as the base of the food chain. Many protists are motile, using structures such as cilia, flagella, or pseudopodia (false feet) to move, while others are sessile. They may be autotrophs, producing their own food from sunlight, or heterotrophs, requiring an outside source of nutrition. Researchers are currently comparing the RNA (ribonucleic acid) and DNA (deoxyribonucleic acid) **sequences** of the protists with those of plants and animals, but the evidence is inconclusive. It is unknown whether protists were the precursors to plants, animals, or **fungi**. It is possible that several evolutionary lines of protists developed separately. Biologists consider the protists as a polyphyletic group, meaning they probably do not share a common ancestor. The word protist comes from the Greek word for the very first, which indicates that researchers believe protists may have been the first eukaryotes to evolve on **Earth**.

Despite the great diversity evident in this kingdom, scientists have been able to classify the protists into several groups. The protists can be classified into one of three main categories, animal-like, plant-like, and fun-

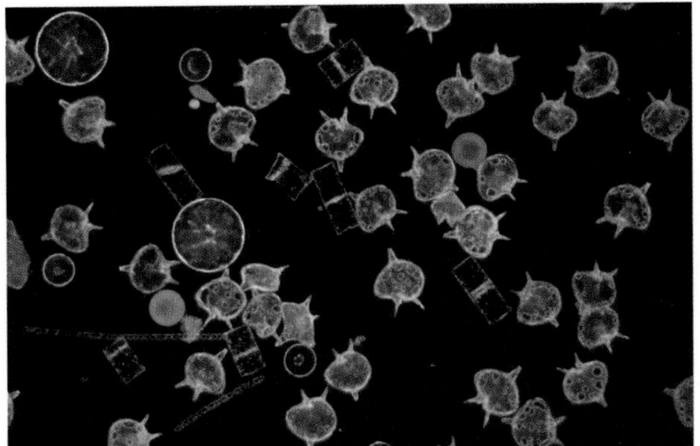

Marine plankton.

gus-like. Grouping into one of the three categories is based on an organism's mode of reproduction, method of nutrition, and motility. The animal-like protists are known as the **protozoa**, the plant-like protists are the **algae**, and the fungus-like protists are the **slime molds** and water molds.

Protozoa

The protozoa are all unicellular heterotrophs. They obtain their nutrition by ingesting other organisms or dead organic material. The word protozoa comes from the Latin word for first animals. The protozoans are grouped into various phyla based on their modes of locomotion. They may use cilia, flagella, or pseudopodia. Some protozoans are sessile, meaning they do not move. These organisms are parasitic, since they cannot actively capture food. They must live in an area of the host organism that has a constant food supply, such as the intestines or bloodstream of an animal. The protozoans that use pseudopodia to move are known as amoebas, those that use flagella are called flagellates, those that use cilia are known as the ciliates, and those that do not move are called the sporozoans.

The amoebas belong to the phylum Rhizopoda. These protists have no wall outside of their **cell membrane**. This gives the cell flexibility and allows it to change shape. The word **amoeba**, in fact, comes from the Greek word for change. Amoebas use extensions of their cell membrane, called pseudopodia, to move as well as to engulf food. When the pseudopodium traps a bit of food, the cell membrane closes around the meal. This encasement forms a food vacuole. Digestive enzymes are secreted into the food vacuole, which break down the food. The cell then absorbs the **nutrients**. Because amoebas live in water, dissolved nutrients from the environment can diffuse directly through their cell membranes. Most amoebas live in marine environments, although some **freshwater** species exist. Freshwater amoebas live in a hypotonic environment, so water is constantly moving into the cell by **osmosis**. To remedy this problem, these amoebas use contractile vacuoles to pump excess water out of the cell. Most amoebas reproduce asexually by pinching off a part of the cell membrane to form a new organism. Amoebas may form cysts when environmental conditions become unfavorable. These cysts can survive conditions such as lack of water or nutrients. Two forms of amoebas have shells, the foraminiferans and the radiolarians.

The foraminiferans have a hard shell made of **calcium carbonate**. These shells are called tests. Foraminiferans live in marine environments and are very abundant. When they die, their shells fall to the ground where they become a part of the muddy **ocean** floor. Geologists use the fossilized shells to determine the ages of **rocks** and sediments. The shells at the ocean floor are gradually converted into chalky deposits, which can be uplifted to become a land formation, such as the white cliffs of Dover in England. Radiolarians have shells made of silica instead of calcium carbonate. Both organisms have many tiny holes in their shells, through which they extend their pseudopodia. The pseudopodia act as a sticky net, trapping bits of food.

The flagellates have one or more flagella and belong to the phylum Zoomastigina. These organisms whip their flagella from side to side in order to move through their aquatic surroundings. These organisms are also known as the zooflagellates. The flagellates are mostly unicellular with a spherical or oblong shape. A few are also amoeboid. Many ingest their food through a primitive mouth, called the oral groove. While most are motile, one class of flagellates, called the Choanoflagellates, is sessile. These organisms attach to a rock or other substrate by a stalk.

The ciliates are members of the phylum Ciliophora. There are approximately 8,000 species of ciliates. These organisms move by the synchronized beating of the cilia covering their bodies. They can be found almost anywhere, in freshwater or marine environments. Probably the best-known ciliate is the organism *Paramecium*. Paramecia have many well-developed organelles. Food enters the cell through the oral groove (lined with cilia, to "sweep" the food into the cell), where it moves to the gullet, which packages the meal into a food vacuole. Enzymes released into the food vacuole break down the food, and the nutrients are absorbed into the cell. Wastes are removed from the cell through an anal pore. Contractile vacuoles pump out excess water, since paramecia live in freshwater (hypotonic) surroundings. Paramecia have two nuclei, a macronucleus and a micronucleus. The larger macronucleus controls most of the metabolic functions of the cell. The smaller micronucleus controls much of the

pathways involved in **sexual reproduction**. Thousands of cilia appear through the pellicle, a tough, protective covering surrounding the cell membrane. These cilia beat in a synchronized fashion to move the *Paramecium* in any direction. Underneath the pellicle are trichocysts, which discharge tiny spikes that help trap **prey**. Paramecia usually reproduce asexually, when the cell divides into two new organisms after all of the organelles have been duplicated. When conditions are unfavorable, however, the organism can reproduce sexually. This form of sexual reproduction is called conjugation. During conjugation, two paramecia join at the oral groove, where they exchange genetic material. They then separate and divide asexually, although this division does not necessarily occur immediately following the exchange of genetic material.

The sporozoans belong to the phylum Sporozoa. These organisms are sessile, so they cannot capture prey. Therefore, the sporozoans are all **parasites**. As their name suggests, many of these organisms produce spores, reproductive cells that can give rise to a new organism. Sporozoans typically have complex life cycles, as they usually live in more than one host in their lifetimes.

Algae

The plant-like protists, or algae, are all photosynthetic autotrophs. These organisms form the base of many food chains. Other creatures depend on these protists either directly for food or indirectly for the **oxygen** they produce. Algae are responsible for over half of the oxygen produced by photosynthesizing organisms. Many forms of algae look like plants, but they differ in many ways. Algae do not have roots, stems, or leaves. They do not have the waxy cuticle plants have to prevent water loss. As a result, algae must live in areas where water is readily available. Algae do not have multicellular gametangia as the plants do. They contain **chlorophyll**, but also contain other photosynthetic pigments. These pigments give the algae characteristic colors and are used to classify algae into various phyla. Other characteristics used to classify algae are **energy** reserve storage and cell wall composition.

Members of the phylum Euglenophyta are known as euglenoids. These organisms are both autotrophic as well as heterotrophic. There are hundreds of species of euglenoids. Euglenoids are unicellular and share properties of both plants and animals. They are plant-like in that they contain chlorophyll and are capable of **photosynthesis**. They do not have a cell wall of **cellulose**, as do plants; instead, they have a pellicle made of protein. Euglenoids are like animals in that they are motile and responsive to outside stimuli. One particular species, *Euglena*, has a structure called an eyespot. This is an area of red pigments that is sensitive to light. An *Euglena* can respond to its environment by moving towards areas of bright light, where photosynthesis best occurs. In conditions where light is not available for photosynthesis, euglenoids can be heterotrophic and ingest their food. Euglenoids store their energy as paramylon, a type of polysaccharide.

Members of the phylum Bacillariophyta are called **diatoms**. Diatoms are unicellular organisms with silica shells. They are autotrophs and can live in marine or freshwater environments. They contain chlorophyll as well as pigments called carotenoids, which give them an orange-yellow color. Their shells resemble small boxes with lids. These shells are covered with grooves and pores, giving them a decorated appearance. Diatoms can be either radially or bilaterally symmetrical. Diatoms reproduce asexually in a very unique manner. The two halves of the shell separate, each producing a new shell that fits inside the original half. Each new generation, therefore, produces offspring that are smaller than the parent. As each generation gets smaller and smaller, a lower limit is reached, approximately one quarter the original size. At this point, the diatom produces gametes that fuse with gametes from other diatoms to produce zygotes. The zygotes develop into full sized diatoms that can begin asexual reproduction once more. When diatoms die, their shells fall to the bottom of the ocean and form deposits called diatomaceous earth. These deposits can be collected and used as **abrasives**, or used as an additive to give certain paints their sparkle. Diatoms store their energy as oils or carbohydrates.

The dinoflagellates are members of the phylum Dinoflagellata. These organisms are unicellular autotrophs. Their cell walls contain cellulose, creating thick, protective plates. These plates contain two grooves at right angles to each other, each groove containing one flagellum. When the two flagella beat together, they cause the organism to spin through the water. Most dinoflagellates are marine organisms, although some have been found in freshwater environments. Dinoflagellates contain chlorophyll as well as carotenoids and red pigments. They can be free-living, or live in symbiotic relationships with **jellyfish** or corals. Some of the free-living dinoflagellates are bioluminescent. Many dinoflagellates produce strong toxins. One species in particular, *Gonyaulax catanella*, produces a lethal nerve toxin. These organisms sometimes reproduce in huge amounts in the summertime, causing a **red tide**. There are so many of these organisms present during a red tide that the ocean actually appears red. When this occurs, the toxins that are released reach such high concentrations in the ocean that many **fish** are killed. Dinoflagellates store their energy as oils or polysaccharides.

The phylum Rhodophyta consists of the red algae. All of the 4,000 species in this phylum are multicellular (with the exception of a few unicellular species) and live

in marine environments. Red algae are typically found in tropical waters and sometimes along the coasts in cooler areas. They live attached to rocks by a structure called a holdfast. Their cell walls contain thick polysaccharides. Some species incorporate calcium carbonate from the ocean into their cell walls as well. Red algae contain chlorophyll as well as phycobilins, red and blue pigments involved in photosynthesis. The red pigment is called phycoerythrin and the blue pigment is called phycocyanin. Phycobilins absorb the green, violet, and blue light waves that can penetrate deep water. These pigments allow the red algae to photosynthesize in deep water with little light available. Reproduction in these organisms is a complex alternation between sexual and asexual phases. Red algae store their energy as floridean starch.

The 1,500 species of brown algae are the members of the phylum Phaeophyta. The majority of the brown algae live in marine environments, on rocks in cool waters. They contain chlorophyll as well as a yellow-brown carotenoid called fucoxanthin. The largest of the brown algae are the kelp. The kelp use holdfasts to attach to rocks. The body of a kelp is called a thallus, which can grow as long as 180 ft (60 m). The thallus is composed of three sections, the holdfast, the stipe, and the blade. Some species of brown algae have an air bladder to keep the thallus floating at the surface of the water, where more light is available for photosynthesis. Brown algae store their energy as laminarin, a **carbohydrate**.

The phylum Chlorophyta is known as the green algae. This phylum is the most diverse of all the algae, with greater than 7,000 species. The green algae contain chlorophyll as their main pigment. Most live in fresh water, although some marine species exist. Their cell walls are composed of cellulose, which indicates the green algae may be the ancestors of modern plants. Green algae can be unicellular, colonial, or multicellular. An example of a unicellular green alga is *Chlamydomonas*. An example of a colonial algae is *Volvox*. A *Volvox* colony is a hollow **sphere** of thousands of individual cells. Each cell has a single flagellum that faces the exterior of the sphere. The individual cells beat their flagella in a coordinated fashion, allowing the colony to move. Daughter colonies form inside the sphere, growing until they reach a certain size and are released when the parent colony breaks open. *Spirogyra* and *Ulva* are both examples of multicellular green algae. Reproduction in the green algae can be both sexual and asexual. Green algae store their energy as starch.

Slime molds and water molds

The fungus-like protists resemble the fungi during some part of their life cycle. These organisms exhibit properties of both fungi and protists. The slime molds and the water molds are members of this group. They all obtain energy by decomposing organic materials, and as a result, are important for **recycling** nutrients. They can be brightly colored and live in cool, moist, dark habitats. The slime molds are classified as either plasmodial or cellular by their modes of reproduction. The plasmodial slime molds belong to the phylum Myxomycota, and the cellular slime molds belong to the phylum Acrasiomycota.

The plasmodial slime molds form a structure called a plasmodium, a **mass** of cytoplasm that contains many nuclei but has no cell walls or membranes to separate individual cells. The plasmodium is the feeding stage of the slime **mold**. It moves much like an amoeba, slowly sneaking along decaying organic material. It moves at a rate of 1 in (2.5 cm) per hour, engulfing **microorganisms**. The reproductive structure of plasmodial slime molds occurs when the plasmodium forms a stalked structure during unfavorable conditions. This structure produces spores that can be released and travel large distances. The spores land and produce a zygote that grows into a new plasmodium.

The cellular slime molds exist as individual cells during the feeding stage. These cells can move like an amoeba as well, engulfing food along the way. The feeding cells reproduce asexually through **cell division**. When conditions become unfavorable, the cells come together to form a large mass of cells resembling a plasmodium. This mass of cells can move as one organism and looks much like a garden slug. The mass eventually develops into a stalked structure capable of sexual reproduction.

The water molds and downy mildews belong to the phylum Oomycota. They grow on the surface of dead organisms or plants, decomposing the organic material and absorbing nutrients. Most live in water or in moist areas. Water molds grow as a mass of fuzzy white threads on dead material. The difference between these organisms and true fungi is the water molds form flagellated reproductive cells during their life cycles.

Disease-causing protists

Many protists can cause serious illness and disease. **Malaria**, for example, is caused by the protist *Plasmodium*. Plasmodia are sporozoans and are transferred from person to person through female *Anopheles* mosquitoes. People who suffer from malaria experience symptoms such as shivering, sweating, high fevers, and delirium. African **sleeping sickness**, also known as African trypanosomiasis, is caused by another sporozoan, *Trypanosoma*. *Trypanosoma* is transmitted through the African tsetse fly. This organism causes high fever and swollen lymph nodes. Eventually the protist makes its

KEY TERMS

Bilateral symmetry—Body plan in which the left and right halves of the animal are mirror images of each other.

Bioluminescent—A flashing of light that emanates from an organism.

Cilia—Short, hairlike projections that serve as motile structures.

Colonial—A member of a localized population of organisms.

Contractile vacuole—In some protistans, a membranous chamber that takes up excess water in the cell body, then contracts, expelling the water outside the cell through a pore.

Flagellum—Tail-like motile structure of many free-living eukaryotic cells.

Food vacuole—A membranous chamber that engulfs food and secretes digestive enzymes to break down the food into nutrients.

Gamete—A haploid cell that functions in sexual reproduction, for example, sperm and eggs.

Hypotonic—A solution with a lower salt concentration than inside a cell.

Meiosis—Two-stage nuclear division process that is the basis of gamete formation and of spore formation.

Mitochondria—An organelle that specializes in ATP formation, the "powerhouse" of the cell.

Mitosis—Type of nuclear division that maintains the parental chromosome number for daughter cells, the basis of bodily growth, and asexual reproduction.

Motile—Able to move.

Multicellular—More than one cell.

Nucleus—A membrane-bound organelle that isolates and organizes the DNA.

Organelle—An internal, membrane-bound sac or compartment that has a specific, specialized metabolic function.

Osmosis—The diffusion of water from an area of high concentration to low concentration through a membrane.

Plankton—Any community of floating organisms, mostly microscopic, living in freshwater and marine environments.

Plastid—Of many bacteria, a small, circular molecule of extra DNA that carries only a few genes and replicates independently of the bacterial chromosome.

Radial symmetry—Body plan having four or more roughly equivalent parts arranged around a central axis.

Unicellular—Single celled.

Zygote—The first cell of a new individual, formed by the fusion of a sperm nucleus with the nucleus of an egg.

way into the victim's **brain**, where it causes a feeling of uncontrollable fatigue. Giardiasis is another example of a disease caused by a protist. This illness is caused by *Giardia*, a sporozoan carried by muskrats and **beavers**. Giardiasis is characterized by fatigue, cramps, diarrhea, and weight loss. Amoebic **dysentery** occurs when a certain amoeba, *Entamoeba histolytica*, infects the large intestine of humans. It is spread through infected food and water. This organism causes bleeding, diarrhea, vomiting, and sometimes death.

Beneficial protists

Members of the kingdom Protista can also be very beneficial to life on Earth. Many species of red algae are edible and are popular foods in certain parts of the world. Red algae are rich in vitamins and **minerals**. Carageenan, a polysaccharide extracted from red algae, is used as a thickening agent in ice cream and other foods. Giant kelp **forests** are rich ecosystems, providing food and shelter for many organisms. Trichonymphs are flagellates that live in the intestines of **termites**. These protozoans break down cellulose in **wood** into carbohydrates the termites can digest.

The kingdom Protista is a diverse group of organisms. Some protists are harmful, but many more are beneficial. These organisms form the foundation for food chains, produce the oxygen we breathe, and play an important role in nutrient recycling. Many protists are economically useful as well. As many more of these unique organisms are discovered, humans will certainly enjoy the new uses and benefits protists provide.

Further Reading

Blaustein, Daniel. *Biology: The Dynamics of Life.* Westerville, OH: McGraw-Hill Companies, 1998.

Johnson, George B. *Biology: Principles and Explorations.* Orlando, FL: Holt, Rinehart and Winston, 1998.
Solomon, Eldra Pearl. *Biology.* Orlando, FL: Saunders College Publishing, 1999.
Starr, Cecie. *Biology- Concepts and Applications.* Belmont, CA: Wadsworth Publishing Company, 1997.
Tobin, Allan J. *Asking About Life.* Orlando, FL: Saunders College Publishing, 1998.

Jennifer McGrath

Proton

The proton is a positively charged subatomic particle. Protons are one of the fundamental constituents of all **atoms**. Protons, in addition to neutrons, are found in a very concentrated region of **space** within atoms referred to as the nucleus. The discovery of the proton, **neutron**, and **electron** revolutionized the way scientists viewed the atom. Recent research has shown that protons are themselves made up of even smaller particles called **quarks** and gluons.

Discovery and properties

Prior to the late nineteenth and early twentieth centuries, scientists believed that atoms were indivisible. Work by many scientists led to the nuclear model of the atom, in which protons, neutrons, and electrons make up individual atoms. Protons and neutrons are found in the nucleus, while electrons are found in a much greater **volume** around the nucleus. The nucleus represents less than 1% of the atom's total volume.

The proton's **mass** and charge have both been determined. The mass is $1.673 * 10^{-24}$ g. The charge of a proton is positive, and is assigned a value of +1. The electron has a +1 charge, and is about 2,000 times lighter than a proton. In neutral atoms, the number of protons and electrons are equal.

The number of protons (also referred to as the **atomic number**) determines the chemical identity of an atom. Each element in the **periodic table** has a unique number of protons in its nucleus. The chemical behavior of individual elements largely depends, however, on the electrons in that element. Chemical reactions involve changes in the arrangements of electrons, not in the number of protons or neutrons.

The processes involving changes in the number of protons are referred to as nuclear reactions. In essence, a nuclear reaction is the transformation of one element into another. Certain elements—both natural and artificially made—are by their nature unstable, and spontaneously break down into lighter elements, releasing **energy** in the process. This process is referred to as radioactivity. **Nuclear power** is generated by just such a process.

Inner structure

Research has shown the proton to be made up of even smaller constituent particles. A proton is found to consist of two "up" quarks, each with a +2/3 **electric charge**, and one "down" quark, with a -1/3 electric charge. The individual quarks are held together by particles called gluons. The up and down quarks are currently believed to be two of the three fundamental particles of all **matter**. Recent research has revealed the possibility of an even deeper substructure, and further work could lead to new theories which may overturn the current model of the proton's structure. There many things about protons that scientists still do not know; for example, it is not known how protons and neutrons interact in the nucleus.

See also Subatomic particles.

KEY TERMS

Atomic number—The number of protons in the nucleus of an atom.

Gluons—Subatomic particles that help to keep quarks bound together.

Quarks—Fundamental subatomic particles that are constituents of protons.

Radioactivity—Breakdown of unstable nuclei accompanied by a release of energy.

Further Reading

Baeyer, Hans Christian von. *Rainbows, Snowflakes and Quarks.* New York: Random House, 1984.
Hellemans, Alexander. "Searching for the Spin of the Proton." *Science.* 267 (March 1995): 1767.
Peterson, Ivars. "The Stuff of Protons." *Science News.* 146 (27 August 1994): 140-41.
Rothman, Tony, *Instant Physics.* New York: Fawcett Columbine, 1995.
Trefil, James. *From Atoms to Quarks.* New York: Doubleday, 1980.

Michael G. Roepel

Proton donor, acceptor see **Acids and bases**

Protozoa

Protozoa are a very varied group of single-celled organisms, with more than 50,000 different types represented. The vast majority are microscopic, many measuring less than 1/200 mm, but some, such as the **freshwater** *Spirostomun*, may reach 0.17 in (3 mm) in length, large enough to enable it to be seen with the naked **eye**. Scientists have even discovered some fossil specimens that measured 0.78 in (20 mm) in diameter. Whatever the size, however, protozoans are well-known for their diversity and the fact that they have evolved under so many different conditions. One of the basic requirements of all protozoans is the presence of **water**, but within this limitation they may live in the sea, in **rivers**, lakes or even stagnant ponds of freshwater, in the **soil** and even in some decaying matters. Many are solitary organisms, but some are colonial; some are free-living, others are sessile; and some species are even **parasites** of plants and animals—from other protozoans to humans. Many of them form complex, exquisite shapes and their beauty is often greatly overlooked on account of their diminutive size.

The **cell** body is often bounded by a thin pliable **membrane**, although some sessile forms may have a toughened outer layer formed of **cellulose**, or even distinct shells formed from a mixture of materials. All the processes of life take place within this cell wall. The inside of the membrane is filled with a fluidlike material called cytoplasm, in which a number of tiny organs float. The most important of these is the nucleus, which is essential for growth and reproduction. Also present are one or more contractile vacuoles, which resemble air bubbles, whose job it is to maintain the correct water balance of the cytoplasm and also to assist with food assimilation. Protozoans living in **salt** water do not require contractile vacuoles as the **concentration** of salts in the cytoplasm is similar to that of seawater and there is therefore no net loss or gain of fluids. Food vacuoles develop whenever food is ingested and shrink as digestion progresses. If too much water enters the cell, these vacuoles swell up, move towards the edge of the cell wall and release the water through a tiny pore in the membrane.

Some protozoans contain the green pigment **chlorophyll** more commonly associated with higher plants, and are able to manufacture their own foodstuffs in a similar manner to plants. Others feed by engulfing small particles of **plant** or animal **matter**. To assist with capturing **prey** items, many protozoans have developed an ability to move around. Some, such as *Euglena* and *Trypanosoma* are equipped with a single whiplike **flagella** which, when quickly moved back and forth, pushes the body through the surrounding water body. Other protozoans such as *Paramecium* have developed large numbers of tiny cilia around the membrane; the rhythmic beat of these hairlike structures propel the cell along and also carry food, such as **bacteria**, towards the gullet. Still others are capable of changing the shape of their cell wall. The **Amoeba**, for example, is capable of detecting chemicals given off by potential food particles such as **diatoms**, **algae**, bacteria or other protozoa. As the cell wall has no definite shape, the cytoplasm can extrude to form pseudopodia (Greek:*pseudes*, false; *pous*, foot) in various sizes and at any point of the cell surface. As the Amoeba approaches its prey, two pseudopodia extend out from the main cell and encircle and engulf the food, which is then slowly digested.

Various forms of reproduction have evolved in this group, one of the simplest involves a splitting of the cell in a process known as binary fission. In species like amoeba, this process takes place over a period of about one hour: the nucleus divides and the two sections drift apart to opposite ends of the cell. The cytoplasm also begins to divide and the cell changes shape to a dumb-bell appearance. Eventually the cell splits giving rise to two identical "daughter" cells which then resume moving and feeding. They, in turn, can divide further in this process known as **asexual reproduction**, where only one individual is involved.

Some species, which may reproduce asexually, may occasionally reproduce through sexual means, which involves the joining together, or fusion, of the nuclei from two different cells. In the case of paramecium, each individual has two nuclei: a larger macronucleus that is responsible for growth, and a much smaller micronucleus that controls reproduction. When paramecium reproduces by sexual means, two individuals join together in the region of the oral groove—a shallow groove in the cell membrane that opens to the outside. When this has taken place, the macronuclei of each begins to disintegrate, while the micronucleus divides in four. Three of these then degenerate and the remaining nucleus divides once again to produce two micronuclei that are genetically identical. The two cells then exchange one of these nuclei which, on reaching the other individual's micronucleus, fuses to form what is known as a "zygote nucleus." Shortly afterwards, the two cells separate but within each cell a number of other cellular and cytoplasmic divisions will continue to take place, eventually resulting in the production of four daughter cells from each individual.

Protozoans have evolved to live under a great range of environmental conditions. When these conditions are unfavorable, such as when food is scarce, most species are able to enter an inactive phase, where cells become non-motile and secrete a surrounding cyst that prevents desiccation and protects the cell from extreme temperatures. The cysts may also serve as a useful means of dispersal, with cells

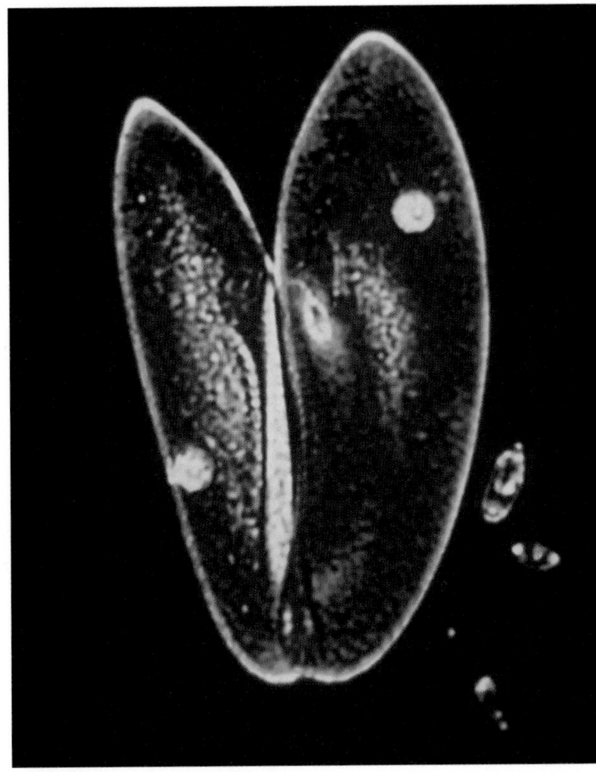

Protozoa.

being borne on the **wind** or on the feet of animals. Once the cyst reaches a more favorable situation, the outer wall breaks down and the cell resumes normal activity.

Many species are of considerable interest to scientists, not least because of the medical problems that many cause. The tiny *Plasmodium* protozoan, the cause of **malaria** in humans, is responsible for hundreds of millions of cases of illness each year, with many deaths occurring in poor countries. This parasite is transferred from a malarial patient to a healthy person by the bite of female **mosquitoes** of the genus *Anopheles.* As the mosquito feeds on a victims' **blood** the parasite passed from its salivary **glands** into the open wound. From there, they make their way to the liver where they multiply and later enter directly into red blood cells. Here they multiply even further, eventually causing the blood cell to burst and release from 6-36 infectious bodies into the blood **plasma**. A mosquito feeding on such a patients blood may absorb some of these organisms, allowing the parasite to complete its life cycle and begin the process all over again. The shock of the release of so many parasites into the human blood stream results in a series of chills and fevers—typical symptoms of malaria. Acute cases of malaria may continue for some days or even weeks, and may subside if the body is able to develop an immunity to the disease. Relapses, however, are common and malaria is still a major cause of death in the tropics. Although certain drugs have been developed to protect people from *Plasmodium* many forms of malaria have now developed, some of which are even immune to the strongest medicines.

While malaria is one of the best known diseases known to be caused by protozoans, a wide range of other equally devastating ailments are also caused by protozoan infections. Amoebic **dysentery**, for example, is caused by *Entamoeba histolytica;* African **sleeping sickness**, which is spread by the bite of the tse-tse fly, is caused by the flagellate protozoan *Trypanosoma;* a related species *T. cruzi* causes Chagas' disease in South and Central America; *Eimeria* causes coccidiosis in rabbits and poultry; and *Babesia,* spread by ticks, causes red water fever in cattle.

Not all protozoans are parasites however, although this is by far a more specialized life style than that adopted by free-living forms. Several protozoans form a unique, nondestructive, relationship with other species, such as the those found in the intestine of wood-eating **termites**. Living in the termites' intestines the protozoans are provided with free board and lodgings as they ingest the **wood** fibers for their own **nutrition**. In the process of doing so, they also release **proteins** which can be absorbed by the termite's **digestive system**, which is otherwise unable to break down the tough cellulose walls of the wood fibers. Through this mutualistic relationship, the termites benefit from a nutritional source that they could otherwise not digest, while the protozoans receive a safe home and steady supply of food.

With such a vast range of **species** in this phylum, it is not surprising that little is still known about the vast majority of species. Many protozoans serve as an essential food source for a wide range of other animals and are therefore essential for the ecological food webs of higher organisms. Many are also, of course, important for medical purposes, while others are now being used in a range of businesses that include purification of filter and sewage beds. No doubt as further research is undertaken on these minute organisms we shall learn how more of these species might be of assistance, perhaps even in combating some of the major diseases that affect civilization, including those caused by other protozoans.

Psychiatry

Psychiatry is the branch of medicine concerned with the study, **diagnosis**, and treatment of mental illnesses. The word, psychiatry, comes from two Greek words that mean mind healing. Those who practice psychiatry are called psychiatrists. In addition to their M.D.s, these

physicians have post-graduate education in the diagnosis and treatment of behaviors that are considered abnormal. They tend to view mental disorders as **diseases** and, unlike psychologists, can prescribe medicine to treat mental illness. Other medical treatments occasionally used by psychiatrists include **surgery** and electroshock therapy.

Many, but not all, psychiatrists use **psychoanalysis**, a system of talking therapy based on the theories of Sigmund Freud, in order to treat patients. Psychoanalysis often involves frequent sessions lasting over many years. According to the American Psychiatric Association, good psychiatrists use a number of types of psychotherapy in addition to psychoanalysis and prescription medication to create a treatment plan that fits a patient's needs.

The field of psychiatry is thought to have begun in the 1700s by Philippe Pinel, a Frenchman, and J. Connolly, an Englishman, who advocated humane treatment for the mentally ill. Before the work of Pinel and Connolly, most people thought that mental illness was caused by demonic possession and could be cured by exorcism. Some physicians believed a theory put forth by Hippocrates, a Greek physician who lived 400 years B.C. According to this theory, people who were mentally ill had an imbalance of the elements: **water**, **earth**, air and fire; and also of the humors: **blood** phlegm and bile.

By the late 1800s, physicians started to take a more scientific approach to the study and treatment of mental illness. E. Kraepelin had begun to make detailed written observations of how his patients' mental disturbances had came into being as well as their family histories. Freud began developing his technique of using the psychoanalytic techniques of free association and dream interpretation to trace his patients' **behavior** to repressed, or hidden drives. Others worked to classify types of abnormal behavior so that physicians could accurately diagnose patients. Today psychiatry has become more specialized with psychiatrists who focus on treating specific groups of people, such as children and adolescents, criminals, women, and the elderly.

Scientific researchers in the twentieth century have confirmed that many mental disorders have a biological basis and can be effectively treated with psychiatric drugs which fall into four categories: antipsychotics, antidepressants, mood stabilizers, and antianxiety medications.

See also Psychology.

Psychoanalysis

The term psychoanalysis has three meanings: 1) a theory of personality with an emphasis on motivation, or why we behave the way we do; 2) a method of treatment for various psychological problems; and 3) a group of techniques used to explore human nature or the mind.

History

Sigmund Freud (1856-1939) lived in an era rich with groundbreaking scientific discoveries in **physics**, **biology**, and medicine. He studied medicine with the goal of being a scientist and doing research, not of seeing patients, and as a medical student he performed laboratory research on the **nervous system**. For financial reasons Freud was forced to practice medicine and see patients, and because of his research background he began specializing in the treatment of nervous disorders or psychological problems. To improve his treatment skills he studied with the famous French psychiatrist Jean Charcot who was using hypnosis as a treatment method. But Freud felt hypnosis did not provide long term cures, and it did not get to the sources of his patients' problems. Next, Freud tried a method being used by Joseph Breuer, a Viennese physician, whereby patients' symptoms were cured by talking about them. It was through using the "talking cure" with his own modifications and revisions to it that Freud formed his theories of personality and psychoanalytic therapy.

Personality theory

Over Freud's long life his thinking evolved and he continually revised his theories. Since Freud's death, psychoanalytic theory and therapy have been modified by numerous psychoanalysts, psychologists, and psychiatrists. We will look at Freud's final version of psychoanalysis.

One of Freud's most significant contributions to **psychology** and the world at large was his view of the unconscious. To Freud the unconscious is the seat of all of our impulses, instincts, wishes, and desires, which we are usually unaware, or not conscious of. It is irrational and yet it is just this part of ourselves that controls most **behavior**.

Personality organization

Personality is composed of three interacting systems—id, ego, and superego. They are not structures or things; they are simply names for different psychological processes, and in normal circumstances they work together harmoniously.

The id, present at **birth**, is the foundation of personality containing all of the instincts and receiving its **energy** from bodily processes. Id operates according to the pleasure principle, meaning it avoids **pain** and seeks pleasure using two processes—reflex actions and primary process. Reflexes are inborn actions that reduce dis-

comfort immediately, like a sneeze. Primary process is very simply forming a wish-fulfilling image of what is desired. For example, if you were hungry you might start imagining your favorite meal. Imagining of course will not satisfy hunger, or most other needs, and the ego develops to deal with reality and satisfy the id's demands because the id cannot tell the difference between what exists in reality and what is in the mind.

The ego, on the other hand, can make that distinction and it operates according to the reality principle, mediating between the desires of the id and the realities of the outside world. Ego tries to satisfy the id's urges in the most appropriate and effective ways. For example, the id might urge the person to go to **sleep** immediately, no matter where they are. The ego would delay sleep until a convenient time and an appropriate place were found.

The superego is the third and last system of personality to develop. It represents traditional values of society as learned by the child through its parents. It is concerned with morals and tells us what is right and wrong, punishing us with guilt feelings if we do something we were taught was wrong. Both the ego and superego derive their energy from the id.

Personality development

Freud believed human behavior and thought are ruled by numerous instincts that fall into two groups—those that further life and those that further death. We know little about the death instincts, but aggression and destructiveness come from them. Life instincts further survival and reproduction. Sexual instincts are the main life instincts and they are very important in the psychoanalytic theory of development. Freud believed we pass through five stages of psychosexual development: the oral, anal, phallic, latent, and genital.

In the oral stage infants find pleasure in using their mouths to eat and suck. In the anal stage, from about age two to four, pleasure is found in the tension reducing release of waste products. During the phallic stage children become preoccupied with their genitals, and they begin to develop an attraction to their opposite sex parent, which is called the oedipus complex. How the child and his or her parents deal with the oedipus complex can have a great impact on the individual's personality. During the latency period, roughly from ages five to twelve, the sexual instincts are subdued until physiological changes in the **reproductive system** at **puberty** reawaken them. With puberty the genital stage begins, wherein the individual develops attraction to the opposite sex and becomes interested in forming a loving union with another. This is the longest of the stages, lasting from puberty until senility. It is characterized by socialization, vocational planning, and decisions about marriage and raising a family.

KEY TERMS

Ego—Mental processes that deal with reality and try to mediate between the id and the environment.

Free association—Method used in psychoanalytic therapy to bring unconscious memories to awareness. The patient tells the psychoanalyst everything he or she thinks of.

Id—Unconscious mental processes containing instincts that dominate personality.

Instincts—Mental representations of bodily needs that direct thought.

Pleasure principle—The avoidance of pain and seeking of pleasure which the id performs.

Primary process—Wish-fulfilling images formed by the id.

Psychoanalysis—A theory of personality, method of psychotherapy, and approach to studying human nature, begun by Sigmund Freud.

Psychosexual development—Five stages of development humans pass through: oral, anal, phallic, latent, genital.

Reality principle—Rational, realistic thinking the ego operates according to.

Superego—Mental processes concerned with morality as taught by parents.

Unconscious—That which we are unaware of. Ruler of behavior containing all instincts and thoughts we are unaware of.

Psychoanalytic therapy

Freud believed the foundation of personality is formed during early childhood and mental illness occurs when unpleasant childhood experiences are repressed, or kept from consciousness, because they are painful. Psychoanalytic therapy tries to uncover these repressed thoughts; in this way the patient is cured.

Freud's primary method of treatment was free association, in which the patient is instructed to say anything and everything that comes to mind. Freud found that patients would eventually start talking about dreams and painful early childhood memories. Freud found dreams especially informative about the person's unconscious wishes and desires. In fact he called dreams the "royal

road to the unconscious." The patient and analyst then try to understand what these memories, feelings, and associations mean to the patient.

Further Reading

Hall, Calvin S. and Lindzey Gardner. *Theories of Personality.* 3rd Ed. New York: John Wiley and Sons, 1978.

Hall, Calvin S. *A Primer of Freudian Psychology. Twenty-Fifth Anniversary Edition.* New York: Penguin Books, 1979.

Fancher, Raymond E. *Psychoanalytic Psychology: The Development of Freud's Thought.* New York: W.W. Norton & Company, 1973.

Greenberg, Jay R. and Stephen A. Mitchell. *Object Relations in Psychoanalytic Theory.* Cambridge, MA: Harvard University Press, 1983.

Barron, James W., Morris H. Eagle, and David L. Wolitzky, eds. *Interface of Psychoanalysis and Psychology.* Washington, D.C.: American Psychological Association, 1992.

Marie Doorey

Psychology

"Psychology" comes from the Greek words *psyche*, meaning "mind" or "soul," and *logos*, meaning *word.* It is the scientific study of human and animal **behavior** and mental processes. Behavior refers here to easily observable activities such as walking, talking, or smiling. Mental processes, such as thinking, feeling, or remembering, often cannot be directly observed and must be inferred from observable behaviors. For example, one might infer someone is feeling happy when he or she smiles, or has remembered what he or she studied when doing well on an exam. Psychology is a very broad social science with approximately 10 main fields The major unifying thread running throughout all of this diversity is use of the **scientific method** and the belief that psychological phenomena can be studied in a systematic, scientific way. Psychologists conduct research very much like scientists in other fields, developing hypotheses or possible explanations of certain facts and testing them using various research methods.

A brief history

Psychology as a separate, scientific discipline has existed for just over 100 years, but since the dawn of time people have sought to understand human and animal nature. For many years psychology was a branch of philosophy until scientific findings in the nineteenth century allowed it to become a separate field of scientific study.

In the mid-nineteenth century a number of German scientists (Johannes P. Muller, Hermann von Helmholtz, and Gustav Fechner) performed the first systematic studies of sensation and **perception** demonstrating that mental processes could be measured and studied scientifically.

In 1879 Wilhelm Wundt, a German physiologist and philosopher, established the first formal laboratory of psychology at the University of Leipzig in Germany. Wundt's work separated thought into simpler processes such as perception, sensation, emotion, and association. This approach looked at the structure of thought and came to be known as structuralism.

In 1875 William James, an American physician well-versed in philosophy, began teaching psychology as a separate subject for the first time in the United States, and he and his students began doing laboratory experiments. In contrast to structuralists, James thought consciousness flowed continuously and could not be separated into simpler elements without losing its essential nature. For instance, when we look at an apple, we see an apple, not a round, red, shiny object. James argued studying the structure of the mind was not as important as understanding how it functions in helping us adapt to our surroundings. This approach became known as functionalism.

In 1913, the American psychologist John B. Watson, argued that mental processes could not be reliably located or measured, and that only observable, measurable behavior should be the focus of psychology. This approach, known as behaviorism, held that all behavior could be explained as responses to stimuli in the environment. Behaviorists tend to focus on the environment and how it shapes behavior. For instance, a strict behaviorist trying to understand why a student studies hard might say it is because he is rewarded by his teacher for getting good grades. Behaviorists would think posessing internal motivations such as a desire to succeed or a desire to learn is unnecessary.

At about the same time behaviorism was gaining a hold in America, Gestalt psychology, founded by Max Wertheimer, Kurt Koffka, and Wolfgang Kohler, arose in Germany. Gestalt (a German word referring to wholeness) psychology focussed on perception and, like William James, argued that perception and thought cannot be broken into smaller pieces without losing their wholeness or essence. They argued that humans actively organize information and that in perception the wholeness and pattern of things dominates. For instance, when we watch movies we perceive people and things in **motion**, yet the **eye** sees what movies really are, that is, individual still pictures shown at a constant rate. The common saying "the whole is greater than the sum of its parts" illustrates this important concept.

Sigmund Freud, an Austrian physician, began his career in the 1890s and formulated **Psychoanalysis**,

which is both a theory of personality and a method of treating people with psychological difficulties. His most influential contribution to psychology was his concept of the unconscious. To Freud our behavior is largely determined by thoughts, wishes, and memories of which we are unaware. Painful childhood memories are pushed out of consciousness and become part of the unconscious from where they can greatly influence behavior. Psychoanalysis as a method of treatment strives to bring these memories to awareness and free the individual from his or her often negative influence.

The 1950s saw the development of cognitive and humanistic psychologies. Humanistic psychology was largely created by Abraham Maslow who felt psychology had focused more on human weakness than strength, mental illness over mental health, and that it neglected free will. Humanistic psychology looks at how people achieve their own unique potential or self actualization.

Cognitive psychology focuses on how people perceive, store, and interpret information, studying processes like perception, reasoning, and problem solving. Unlike behaviorists, cognitive psychologists believe it is necessary to look at internal mental processes in order to understand behavior. Cognitive psychology has been extremely influential, and much contemporary research is cognitive in nature.

Contemporary psychology

New technologies allowing visualization of the human **brain** at work and advances in knowledge of brain and nerve **cell** chemistry have influenced psychology tremendously. In one technique, called the deoxyglucose technique, a projected visual image of the brain shows where energy-producing glucose is being used by the brain at that moment. Researchers might ask subjects to solve different types of problems and look at which areas of the brain are most active. These new technologies have allowed psychologists to specify where exactly specific types of mental processes occur. This emerging field has been labelled neuropsychology or **neuroscience**.

Only behaviorism and psychoanalysis survive as separate schools of thought now. Modern psychologists tend to be eclectic, drawing upon different theories and approaches depending on what they are studying. There has been tremendous growth in the topics studied by psychologists due in part to developments in computers and data analysis. The American Psychological Association currently has 45 divisions, each representing areas of special interest to psychologists.

KEY TERMS

Behaviorism—A school of thought focusing on observable behaviors.

Cognitive psychology—The study of mental processes.

Functionalism—A school of psychology that focused on the functions or adaptive purposes of behavior.

Gestalt psychology—A school of thought that focused on perception and how the mind actively organizes sensations.

Humanistic psychology—A school of psychology emphasizing individuals' uniqueness and their capacity for growth.

Neuropsychology—The study of the brain and nervous system and their role in behavior and mental processes.

Psychoanalysis—Theory of personality and method of psychotherapy founded by Sigmund Freud.

Psychology—The study of behavior and mental processes.

Social sciences—Fields studying society and its members, e.g. history, economics, psychology.

10 main fields of psychology

* Abnormal psychology studies maladaptive behavior patterns and psychopathology.
* Clinical psychology studies and applies therapeutic methods to the treatment of individuals experiencing problems in life.
* Comparative psychology studies similarities and differences in behavior of various animal species.
* Developmental psychology studies the stability and change of characteristics, such as intelligence or social skills, over the life span.
* Educational psychology studies teaching methods to improve **learning** in the classroom.
* Industrial/Organizational psychology studies work and working environments and applies findings to improve job satisfaction and productivity.
* Personality psychologists study individual differences across a number of different personal attributes such as shyness, conscientiousness, etc.

* Physiological psychologists study biological bases of behavior, focusing on the **nervous system**.
* Social psychologists study behaviors of individuals in groups and how people affect one another's behavior.

See also Psychiatry.

Further Reading

American Psychological Association. *Careers in Psychology.* Washington, DC: American Psychological Association, 1986.

Atkinson, Rita L., Atkinson, Richard C., Smith, Edward E., Bem, Daryl J. *Introduction to Psychology.* 10th Ed. New York: Harcourt Brace Jovanovich, 1990.

Corsini, Raymond J. *Concise Encyclopedia of Psychology.* 2nd ed. New York: Wiley, 1994.

Hunt, Morton. *The Story of Psychology.* New York: Doubleday, 1993.

Marie Doorey

Psychometry

Psychometry or psychometrics is a field of **psychology** which uses tests to quantify psychological aptitudes, reactions to stimuli, types of **behavior**, etc., in an effort to devlop reliable scientific models that can be applied to larger populations.

Reliability

Reliability refers to the consistency of a test, or the degree to which the test produces approximately the same results over time under similar conditions. Ultimately, reliability can be seen as a measure of a test's precision.

A number of different methods for estimating reliability can be used, depending on the types of items on the test, the characteristic(s) a test is intended to measure, and the test user's needs. The most commonly used methods to assess reliability are the test-retest, alternate form, and split-half methods. Each of these methods attempts to isolate particular sources and types of **error**.

Error is defined as variation due to extraneous factors. Such factors may be related to the test-taker, if for instance he or she is tired or ill the day of the test and it affects the score. Error may also be due to environmental factors in the testing situation, such as an uncomfortable room **temperature** or distracting noise.

Test-retest methods look at the stability of test scores over time by giving the same test to the same people after a reasonable time **interval**. These methods try to separate out the amount of error in a score related to the passing of time. In test-retest studies, scores from the first administration of a test are compared mathematically through correlation with later score(s).

Test-retest methods have some serious limitations, one of the most important being that the first test-taking experience may affect performance on the second test administration. For instance, the individual may perform better at the second testing, having learned from the first experience. Moreover, tests rarely show perfect test-retest reliability because many factors unrelated to the tested characteristic may affect the test score. In addition, test-retest methods are only suitable to use with tests of characteristics that are assumed to be stable over time, such as intelligence. They are unsuitable for tests of unstable characteristics like emotional states such as anger or **anxiety**.

The alternate-form method of assessing reliability is very similar to test-retest reliability except that a different form of the test in question is administered the second time. Here two forms of a test are created to be as similar as possible so that individual test items should cover the same material at the same level of ease or difficulty. The tests are administered to a **sample** and the scores on the two tests are correlated to yield a **coefficient** of equivalence. A high coefficient of equivalence indicates the overall test is reliable in that most or all of the items seem to be assessing the same characteristic. Low coefficients of equivalence indicate the two test forms are not assessing the same characteristic.

Alternate form administration may be varied by the time interval between testing. Alternate form with immediate testing tries to assess error **variance** in scores due to various errors in content sampling. Alternate form with delayed administration tries to separate out error variance due to both the passage of time and to content sampling. Alternate-form reliability methods have many of the same limitations as test-retest methods.

Split-half reliability methods consist of a number of methods used to assess a test's internal consistency, or the degree to which all of the items are assessing the same characteristic. In split-half methods a test is divided into two forms and scores on the two forms are correlated with each other. This correlation coefficient is called the coefficient of reliability. The most common way to split the items is to correlate even-numbered items with odd-numbered items.

Validity

Validity refers to how well a test measures what it intends to, along with the degree to which a test validates intended inferences. Thus a test of achievement motivation should assess what the researcher defines as

achievement motivation. In addition, results from the test should, ideally, support the psychologist's insights into, for example, the individual's level of achievement in school, if that is what the test constructors intended for the test. Most psychometric research on tests focuses on their validity. Because psychologists use tests to make different types of inferences, there are a number of different types of validity. These include content validity, criterion-related validity, and construct validity.

Content validity refers to how well a test covers the characteristic(s) it is intended to measure. Thus test items are assessed to see if they are: (a) tapping into the characteristic(s) being measured; (b) comprehensive in covering all relevant aspects; and (c) balanced in their coverage of the characteristic(s) being measured. Content validity is usually assessed by careful examination of individual test items and their **relation** to the whole test by experts in the characteristic(s) being assessed.

Content validity is a particularly important issue in tests of skills. Test items should tap into all of the relevant components of a skill in a balanced manner, and the number of items for various components of the skill should be proportional to how they make up the overall ability. Thus, for example, if it is thought that **addition** makes up a larger portion of mathematical abilities than division, there should be more items assessing addition than division on a test of mathematical abilities.

Criterion-related validity deals with the extent to which test scores can predict a certain behavior referred to as the criterion. Concurrent and predictive validity are two types of criterion related validity. Predictive validity looks at how well scores on a test predict certain behaviors such as achievement, or scores on other tests. For instance, to the extent that scholastic aptitude tests predict success in future education, they will have high predictive validity. Concurrent validity is essentially the same as predictive validity except that criterion data is collected at about the same time it is collected from the predictor test. The correlation between test scores and the researcher's designated criterion **variable** indicates the degree of criterion-related validity. This correlation is called the validity coefficient.

Construct validity deals with how well a test assesses the characteristic(s) it is intended to assess. Thus, for example, with a test intended to assess an individual's sense of humor one would first ask "What are the qualities or constructs that comprise a sense of humor?" and then, "Do the test items seem to tap those qualities or constructs?" Issues of construct validity are central to any test's worth and utility, and they usually play a large part in the early stage of constructing a test and initial item construction. There is no single method for assessing a test's construct validity. It is assessed using many methods and the gradual accumulation of data from various studies. In fact, estimates of construct validity change constantly with the accumulation of additional information about how the test and its underlying construct relate to other variables and constructs.

In assessing construct validity, researchers often look at a test's discriminant validity, which refers to the degree that scores on a test do not correlate very highly with factors that theoretically they should not correlate very highly with. For example, scores on a test designed to assess artistic ability might not be expected to correlate very highly with scores on a test of athletic ability. A test's convergent validity refers to the degree that its scores do correlate with factors they theoretically would be expected to. Many different types of studies can be done to assess an instrument's construct validity.

Item analysis

In constructing various tests, researchers perform numerous item analyses for different purposes. As mentioned previously, at the initial stages of test construction, construct validity is a major concern, so that items are analyzed to see if: (a) they tap the characteristic(s) in question, and (b) taken together, the times comprehensively capture qualities of the characteristic being tested. After the items have been designed and written, they will often be administered to a small sample to see if they are understood as the researcher intended, to examine if they can be administered with ease, and to see if any unexpected problems crop up. Often the test will need to be revised.

Now the potentially revised and improved test is administered to the sample of interest, and the difficulty of the items is assessed by noting the number of incorrect and correct responses to individual items. Often the proportion of test takers correctly answering an item will be plotted in relation to their overall test scores. This provides an indication of item difficulty in relation to an individual's ability, knowledge, or particular characteristics. Item analysis procedures are also used to see if any items are biased toward or against certain groups. This is done by identifying those items certain groups of people tend to answer incorrectly.

It should be noted that in test construction, test refinement continues until validity and reliability are adequate for the test's goals. Thus item analysis, validity, or reliability data may prompt the researcher to return to earlier stages of the test design process to further revise the test.

Normative data

When the researcher is satisfied with the individual items of a test, and reliability and validity are established

KEY TERMS

Coefficient—In statistics, a number that expresses the degree of relationship between variables. It is most commonly used with a qualifying term that further specifies its meaning as in "correlation coefficient."

Correlation—A statistical measure of the degree of relationship between two variables.

Error variance—The amount of variability in a set of scores that cannot be assigned to controlled factors.

Normative data—A set of data collected to establish values representative of a group such as the mean, range, and standard deviation of their scores. It is also used to get a sense of how a skill, or characteristic is distributed in a group.

Norms—Values that are representative of a group and that may be used as a baseline against which subsequently collected data is compared.

Reliability—The consistency of a test, or the degree to which the test produces approximately the same results under similar conditions over time.

Representative sample—Any group of individuals that accurately reflects the population from which it was drawn on some characteristic(s).

Sample—Any group of people, animals, or things taken from a particular population.

Validity—How well a test measures what it intends to, as well the degree to which a test validates scientific inferences.

Variance—A measure of variability in a set of scores that may be due to many factors such as error.

at levels suitable to the intended purposes of the test, normative data is collected. Normative data is obtained by administering the test to a representative sample in order to establish norms. Norms are values that are representative of a group and that may be used as a baseline against which subsequently collected data is compared. Normative data helps get a sense of the distribution or prevalence of the characteristic being assessed in the larger population. By collecting normative data, various levels of test performance are established and raw scores from the test are translated into a common scale.

Common scales are created by transforming raw test scores into a common scale using various mathematical methods. Common scales allow comparison between different sets of scores and increase the amount of information a score communicates. For example, intelligence tests typically use a common scale in which 100 is the average score and standard deviation units are 15 or 16.

Current research/trends

Currently many new psychometric theories and statistical models are being proposed that will probably lead to changes in test construction. In addition, the use of computers to administer tests interactively is on the rise. Finally, studies of test bias and attempts to diminish it will likely increase in response to lawsuits challenging various occupational and school decisions based on test results.

Further Reading

Anastasi, A. *Psychological Testing*. New York: Macmillan, 1982.

Goldstein, G., and M. Hersen, eds. *Handbook of Psychological Assessment*. 2nd ed. New York: Pergamon Press, 1990.

Mitchell, J. *An Introduction to the Logic of Psychological Measurement*. Hillsdale, NJ: Erlbaum, 1990.

Marie Doorey

Psychosis

A psychotic state is one in which a person suffering from one of several mental illnesses loses touch with reality. People experiencing psychosis may be diagnosed as schizophrenic, manic-depressive, or delusional. Psychosis can also be induced from drug or **alcohol** abuse, reaction to medication, from exposure to some toxic substance, or from trauma to the **brain**. Psychotic episodes have a duration that may last for a brief period or may last for weeks and months at a time. Since the 1950s new medications have been developed to effectively treat psychosis and allow the person suffering from delusions or hallucinations to regain a more accurate view of reality.

There is significant evidence that the cause of psychosis lies within the limbic system, an area of the brain that lies deep within the lower, center portion of the brain and is believed to control the emotion, **behavior**, and **perception** of external and internal stimulation. The limbic system connects to all areas of the brain. It can be compared to a **telephone** network. If one line is down, communication cannot be made. Likewise, if an area within the limbic system is not functioning properly, appropriate signals cannot be sent or received, or inappropriate ones may be sent when the system is overloaded and working too hard.

Forms of psychosis

Before the careful classification of mental illnesses, anyone exhibiting psychotic behavior was thought to be schizophrenic, which is the mental illness most frequently associated with psychosis. **Schizophrenia** is a mental illness that is characterized by delusions, hallucinations, thought disorders, disorganized **speech** and behavior, and sometimes catatonic behavior. Emotions tend to flatten out and it becomes increasingly more difficult for the person to function normally in society. It is estimated that one percent of the American population is currently affected by this illness, which means there are about 1.5 million people who are ill from this disease.

In certain states of manic-depressive illness, or bipolar disorder, a patient may also suffer psychotic symptoms of delusions, hallucinations, and thought disorder. Unlike schizophrenia, those who suffer from manic-depressive illness are involved in a mood disorder, while schizophrenia is considered more of a thought disorder. In schizophrenia the mood is flat, but in manic-depression the mood can swing from great excitability to deep **depression** and feelings of hopelessness. In both phases of manic-depressive illness, many patients also experience delusions and hallucinations, which lead to misperceptions of reality.

Other psychiatric illnesses that produce psychotic episodes are delusional disorders, brief psychotic disorders that may remit within a month, substance-induced psychotic disorders, psychotic disorders due to a general medical condition, and a number of others given separate classification in the *Diagnostic and Statistical Manual of Mental Disorders (DSM-IV)*, a publication that presents guidelines for the **diagnosis** of serious mental illnesses. Diagnosis is based both on the nature of the psychosis and its duration.

Symptoms of psychosis

Hallucinations are a major symptom of psychosis and can be defined as a misperception of reality. Auditory hallucinations are the most common form. Patients hear voices that may seem to be outside his or her head or inside. The voices may be argumentative or congratulatory. Patients who exhibit visual hallucinations may have an organic problem, such as a brain lesion. Other types of hallucinations involve the sense of **smell** and touch.

There are various types of delusions that psychiatrists classify when diagnosing a patient. Erotomanic delusions involve the conviction that someone is in love with the patient. Grandiose delusions have a theme of inflated importance, power, knowledge, or a special relationship with someone important, perhaps a political leader, God, or a famous person. In a jealous type of delusion, the person feels their sexual partner is unfaithful even when there is no evidence of the fact. The main theme of a persecution delusion is that the patient is being mistreated by someone. In somatic delusions, patients feel they have a **disease** or physical defect that is also not present.

Medications for treatment

Antipsychotic medications were first used after it was noticed that a newly synthesized anesthetic had unusual ability to sedate patients who did not become unconscious from its use. Dr. Henri Laborit, a French physician, encouraged his psychiatric colleagues to try the drug on their schizophrenic patients. They were so successful with this drug, chlorpromazine, that its use spread quickly throughout the world. This was in 1952. Since then, seven different types of antipsychotic medications have been developed. Some of the brand names include Thorazine, Trilafon, and Haldol.

These medicines are administered by tablet or liquid, and under circumstances where the patient may be likely not to take the medicine, time-released injections are given. The psychiatric community approaches the prescribing of antipsychotic medicines, also called neuroleptics, somewhat on the basis of trial and **error**. They have found that when one type of antipsychotic does not work, another type very well may reduce the symptoms of psychosis. It is sometimes helpful for them if another family member is suffering from the same illness. They have found responses within families to medicines to likely be the same. This suggests that there is a genetic factor involved in mental illness that leads to psychosis.

Dosages

Antipsychotic medicines vary widely in the amount of dosage needed to stabilize patients. One patient may need only 10 or 20 mg of an antipsychotic, while another will need hundreds of milligrams. The **blood** is monitored to determine the necessary dosage. A group of patients receiving the same medication can need widely differing amounts of the same medicine to achieve the desired effect.

While medication is the foremost element of current treatment for most situations of psychosis, counseling for the patient and family is also considered an important part of treatment, both to help them understand the role of the medicine and how to deal with the illness. Before antipsychotic medication came into common use, many people suffering from psychosis had to be hospitalized.

KEY TERMS

Delusions—Incorrect beliefs about reality that may involve one's self-importance or the false belief that one is being persecuted when no such persecution is taking place.

Hallucinations—Auditory, visual, tactile, or olfactory sensations that do not exist in reality.

Manic-depressive illness—Bipolar disorder, a mental illness in which psychosis may present as a symptom and where the patient exhibits both an excited state, called mania, and a depressed state.

Neuroleptics—Medications that treat psychosis, also called antipsychotics.

Schizophrenia—A serious mental illness that is characterized by psychosis, basically a thought disorder.

Today, with a careful diagnosis and treatment therapy, many lead relatively normal and socially useful lives.

See also Antipsychotic drugs.

Further Reading

Amchin, Jess, *Psychiatric Diagnosis: A Biopsychosocial Approach Using DSM-III-R*. Washington, DC: American Psychiatric Press, 1991.

Diagnostic and Statistical Manual of Mental Disorders. Washington, DC: American Psychiatric Press, 1994.

Papolos, Demitri F. and Janice Papolos. *Overcoming Depression*. New York: Harper & Row, 1987.

Podvoll, Edward M. *The Seduction of Madness*. New York: Harper Collins, 1990.

Torrey, E. Fuller, *Surviving Schizophrenia*. New York: Harper & Row, 1988.

Vita Richman

Psychosurgery

Psychosurgery is the alteration or destruction of **brain** matter in order to alleviate severe, long-lasting, and harmful psychiatric symptoms that do not respond to psychotherapy, behavioral, physical, or drug treatments. Psychosurgery involves opening up the skull or entering the brain through natural fissures such as the **eye** sockets, and injecting various tissue-altering solutions, removing or destroying brain **tissue** using various tools, or severing certain connections between different parts of the brain. Techniques used in this controversial and now rarely performed surgical procedure have changed greatly since its beginning in the 1930s.

History

The use of psychosurgery has been traced back to approximately 2000 B.C. using archaeological evidence of skulls with relatively precise holes that seem to have been bored intentionally. It is unclear whether brain matter was directly manipulated in this process called trepanation. Its intended purpose may have been to relieve what was thought to be excess **pressure** in the skull. Some cultures seem to have performed trepanation in order to allow what they thought were bad spirits to escape.

The first report of **surgery** on the brain to relieve psychiatric symptoms has been traced to the director of a mental asylum in Switzerland, Gottlieb Burckhardt, who in 1890 removed parts of the cerebral cortex. He performed this procedure on six patients described as highly excitable. The procedure, however, did not seem to lessen the patients' degree of excitability, and in fact seemed to lead to seizures. Burckhardt's procedure met with great opposition and he was forced to stop performing the surgery.

Modern psychosurgery can be traced to the Portuguese physician Egas Moniz (1875-1955) who performed the first prefrontal leukotomy in 1935. Apparently, Moniz had been influenced by a case involving the unintentional damage of a patient's prefrontal areas of the brain in which the patient, although suffering some personality change, continued to function. Moniz also seemed to be influenced by research at Yale reporting that an agitated chimpanzee was greatly calmed after its frontal lobes had been severely damaged.

Moniz's first operation involved drilling two holes in the upper forehead area and injecting absolute **alcohol** directly into the frontal lobes of the brain. The absolute alcohol acted to destroy the brain tissue it came into contact with. In following operations, Moniz used an instrument called a leukotome, which consists of a narrow rod with a retractable wire loop at one end. Moniz would insert the instrument through the drilled holes, extend the wire loop, and rotate it to destroy brain tissue located in the frontal lobes of the brain. Moniz reported some success in removing some of the patients' more striking psychotic symptoms such as hallucinations and delusions. The **accuracy** of Moniz's findings and the degree of his success, however, are now questioned. It seems that while it lessened a patient's **anxiety** and aggression, it often produced marked personality changes and impaired intellectual performance.

The practice of psychosurgery began to receive more attention after Moniz's reports of success, and its study was taken up by a number of researchers, most notably the American physician Walter J. Freeman and neurosurgeon James W. Watts in the late 1930s. These two prominent physicians greatly publicized the prefrontal leukotomy, revised Moniz's initial procedures, and changed the procedure's name to lobotomy.

Around this time, American neurosurgeon J.G. Lyerly developed a procedure that allowed visualization of the brain during surgery. This enabled more precise surgical intervention and seemed to lead to increased use of psychosurgery. Meanwhile, Freeman and Watts continued their research, and the publication of their widely acclaimed book *Psychosurgery* in 1942 led to increases in psychosurgical procedures worldwide. During the mid-1940s, surgeons developed a number of different psychosurgical techniques intended to improve patient outcome following lobotomy, and the use of psychosurgery increased dramatically.

In the 1950s chlorpromazine and a number of antipsychotic medications were introduced and the number of lobotomies declined rapidly. These drugs not only provided relief from some patients' severe and harmful symptoms, but they were also simple and inexpensive compared to psychosurgery. Moreover, unlike psychosurgery, their effects were apparently reversible. It had become evident over time that lobotomies were not as effective as previously thought, and that, in fact, they often resulted in brain damage.

In order to understand the ease with which psychosurgical procedures were taken up by so many physicians it must be understood that most psychiatrists believed psychotic symptoms would not respond to psychotherapy, and up until the 1950s there were no effective drug treatments for serious mental disorders. Thus, psychosurgery was viewed as having the potential to treat disorders that had been seen as untreatable. Moreover, the treatment of the mentally ill at this time was largely custodial, and the number of severely disturbed individuals in mental health treatment centers was too great to be treated with psychotherapy, which was just beginning to gain acceptance in the 1940s and 1950s. In sum, psychosurgery appealed to many mental health professionals as a potentially effective and economical treatment for patients for whom there seemed to be no effective treatment.

Contemporary psychosurgery

Over time, psychosurgical procedures have been created that are more precise and restricted in terms of the amount of brain tissue affected. During the 1950s, a stereotaxic instrument was developed that held the patient's head in a stable position and allowed the more precise manipulation of brain tissue by providing a set of three-dimensional coordinates. Stereotaxic instruments generally consist of a rigid frame with an adjustable probe holder. The instrument is secured on the patient's skull, and in modern psychosurgery is used in conjunction with images of the patient's brain created with brain-imaging techniques. Brain-imaging techniques such as computed tomography and **magnetic resonance imaging** allow accurate visualization of the brain and precise location of a targeted brain area or lesion. Coordinates of the targeted visual area are then matched with points on the stereotaxic instrument's frame, which has been included in the image. Using these measurements, the attached probe holder's position is adjusted so that the probe will reach the intended area in the brain. Because of individual anatomical differences, surgeons will often electrically stimulate the targeted area observing the effect on a conscious patient in order to verify accurate placement of the probe.

Over the years, neurosurgeons have begun to use electrodes to deliver electric currents and **radio** frequency waves to specific sites in the brain rather than using various sharp instruments. Compared with the earlier lobotomies, relatively small areas of brain tissue are destroyed with these techniques. Other methods of affecting brain tissue include using cryoprobes that freeze tissue at sites surrounding the probe, radioactive elements, and ultrasonic beams. The most commonly used method today is radio frequency waves.

The more modern restricted psychosurgical procedures usually target various parts of the brain's limbic system. The limbic system is made up of a number of different brain structures that form an **arc** located in the forebrain. The limbic system seems highly involved in emotional and motivational behaviors. These techniques include destruction of small areas of the frontothalamus, orbital undercutting, cingulectomy, subcaudate tractotomy, limbic leucotomy, anterior capsulotomy, and amygdalotomy. Cingulectomy involves severing fibers in the cingulum, a prominent brain structure that is part of the limbic system. Subcaudate tractotomy was developed in 1964 in Great Britain and uses radioactive Yttrium-90 implants to interrupt the signals transmitted in the white matter of the brain. This type of psychosurgery involves a smaller lesion and decreased side effects. The limbic leucotomy was developed in 1973 and combines the subcaudate tractotomy and the cingulectomy. In this surgery, two lesions are created and brain material is destroyed using a cryoprobe or electrode. An anterior capsulotomy interrupts connections in the frontothalamus with electrodes. There seems to be marked side effects associated

with this procedure. Amygdalotomy is a type of psychosurgery in which fibers of the amygdala are severed. The amygdala is a small brain structure that is part of the temporal lobe and is classified as being a part of the limbic system. Cingulectomies are now the most common type of psychosurgery procedure used.

Psychosurgery was initially widely accepted without much evidence as to its efficacy and side effects and it has generated a great deal of controversy for many reasons. These include the fact that it involves the destruction of seemingly healthy brain tissue, it is irreversible, and, at least in its earliest procedures, frequently seemed to cause some very harmful side effects. The National Commission for the Protection of Human Subjects of Biomedical and Behavioral Research was created in the mid-1970s to examine research procedures that appeared questionable in the United States. The commission sponsored a number of studies looking at the risks and benefits of psychosurgery. Basically, the Commission concluded that psychosurgery can be highly beneficial for certain types of disorders, but that every procedure should be screened by an institutional review board before it is allowed.

In a review of psychosurgery procedures performed between 1976 and 1977, Elliot Valenstein, in a report for the Commission, concluded that approximately 60%-90% of the patients showed a marked reduction in their more severe symptoms, and a very low risk of some of the permanent negative side effects seen in earlier lobotomy procedures. Valenstein primarily looked at more restricted frontal lobe operations and cingulectomy.

Currently, psychosurgery is only performed as a last resort. Most of the psychiatric disorders that were originally treated with psychosurgery, such as **schizophrenia** and severe **depression** with psychotic symptoms, are now treated in a more satisfactory manner by drugs. Even current psychosurgical procedures appear beneficial for only a very limited number of patients. It seems that patients suffering severe major depression with physiological symptoms and obsessive tendencies along with agitation and marked tension are most likely to benefit, providing there has been a reasonably stable personality before the onset of symptoms. In rare cases, psychosurgery is performed in patients that show severe violent outbursts and who may cause harm to themselves or others. Used cautiously, these procedures can reduce some of a patient's more disturbing symptoms without producing irreversible negative effects on personality and intellectual functioning.

Patient selection

Because the positive effects of psychosurgery are limited to only a few types of psychiatric conditions, **diagnosis** and thorough evaluation of the patient is crucial. The mental health professional must first establish that the patient's condition is chronic or long-lasting, having been present continuously for a minimum of three years. In addition, the patient's symptoms must be observed to not respond to psychotherapy, behavioral, physical, or drug treatments.

Postoperative care

Most current psychosurgeries require the patient to spend only a few days in the hospital. Physical complications following the more limited psychosurgeries are relatively rare but hemorrhage may occur following surgery and **epilepsy** sometimes develops even a number of months following the surgical procedure. In general, the effects of the surgery on the patient usually take some time before they can be observed and it is essential that the patient receive thorough postoperative care and return for follow-up assessment.

In order to increase the benefit of psychosurgery, most professionals involved in psychosurgery strongly recommend intense postoperative psychiatric care. It seems that some patients benefit more from various drug, behavioral, and psychotherapy treatments following a procedure than they did prior to it.

Current status

Psychosurgery has gone through periods of widespread, relatively uncritical acceptance, and periods of great disfavor in the medical community. In the early years of its use there were no well-conducted, detailed, rigorous studies of outcome or differences in procedure. The development of various diagnostic and psychological assessment measures has enabled more rigorous follow-up studies of patients assessing the relationship between different procedures, a patient's characteristics, and their long-term outcome.

As stated previously, psychosurgical procedures have changed dramatically since their beginning. Psychosurgery is still rarely used today, despite a recent resurgence in the procedure. It is most likely to benefit patients with particular symptom patterns seen in some patients with chronic major depression or obsessive-compulsive disorder. These include compulsions, obsessions, and long-lasting, high levels of anxiety (often seen as agitation). These patients often respond well to psychosurgery. Moreover, because they are usually coherent and rational, consent can be obtained from the patient and their family. Psychosurgery has benefitted greatly from improvements in technology such as magnetic resonance imaging, probe techniques, and stereotaxic in-

KEY TERMS

Antipsychotic drugs—These drugs, also called neuroleptics, seem to block the uptake of dopamine in the brain. They help to reduce psychotic symptoms across a number of mental illnesses.

Computed tomography—A technique for visualizing a plane of the body using a number of x rays that are converted into one image by computer.

Cortex—The outer layer of the brain.

Delusions—False beliefs that seem to be beyond the bounds of possibility, they are usually absurd and bizarre, and resist invalidating evidence.

Dopamine—A neurotransmitter that acts to decrease the activity of certain nerve cells in the brain, it seems to be involved in schizophrenia.

Hallucinations—Sensory experiences for which there are no apparent physical stimuli, they can involve sight, sound, touch, taste, and smell.

Leukotomy—A rarely used psychosurgical procedure in which tissue in the frontal lobes of the brain is destroyed.

Limbic system—A part of the brain made up of a number of different structures, it forms an arc and is located in the forebrain. The limbic system seems highly involved in emotional and motivational behaviors.

Magnetic Resonance Imaging—A technique using radio frequency pulses that creates images which show various size, density and spatial qualities of the targeted body area, e.g. the brain.

Neuroimaging techniques—High technology methods that enable visualization of the brain without surgery such as computed tomography and magnetic resonance imaging.

Psychotherapy—A broad term that usually refers to interpersonal verbal treatment of disease or disorder that addresses psychological and social factors.

Stereotaxic instrument—Generally, a rigid frame with an adjustable probe holder that is secured on patient's skull for psychosurgery, it enables more accurate brain tissue manipulation.

struments. Future technological developments and increased understanding of the brain, particularly the limbic system, show potential for increasing the safety efficacy of psychosurgical techniques.

Further Reading

Jennett, B. and K.W. Lindsay. *An Introduction to Neuro-Surgery.* 5th ed. Oxford: Butterworth-Heinemann, 1994.

Valenstein, E.S. *Great and Desperate Cures: The Rise and Fall of Psychosurgery and Other Radical Treatments for Mental Illness.* New York: Basic Books, 1986.

Marie Doorey

Puberty

Puberty is the period of sexual maturity when sexual organs mature and secondary sexual characteristics develop. Puberty is also the second major growth period of life—the first being infancy. A number of **hormones** under the control of the hypothalamus, pituitary, ovaries, and testes regulate this period of sexual growth, which begins for most boys and girls between the ages of 9 and 15. The initial obvious sign of female puberty is the beginning of breast development, whereas the initial obvious sign in males is testicular enlargement. Since early signs of female puberty are more noticeable, it is sometimes assumed that female puberty precedes male puberty by quite a bit. However, males usually start puberty just a few months after females, on average. In males, puberty is marked by testicle and penile enlargement, larynx enlargement, pubic hair growth, and considerable growth in body height and weight. In females, puberty is marked by hip and breast development, uterine development, pubic hair growth, menstruation, and increases in body height and weight. Because of the extensive growth that occurs at this time, a balanced, nutritious diet with sufficient calories is important for optimal growth. Although puberty was originally used to classify the initial phase of early fertility, the term is also used to include the development and growth which culminates in fertility. In this sense, puberty usually lasts two to five years and is accompanied by the psychological and emotional characteristics called adolescence.

Physical maturity

Puberty marks the physical transition from childhood to adulthood. While the changes that accompany

this time are significant, their onset, rate, and duration vary from person to person. In general, these changes are either sexual or growth related. The pubertal growth spurt is characteristic of primates. Although other **mammals** may have increased reproductive **organ** growth, their overall size does not increase as dramatically. The major control center for human pubertal development is the hypothalamus for both sexes, but puberty is accompanied by additional growth of the adrenal **glands**, as well. The added adrenal **tissue** secretes the sex hormones, androgens or estrogens, at low levels. The adrenal sex hormones are thought to initiate the growth of pubic and axillary (under-arm) hair. This adrenal maturation is called adrenarche.

It is not known exactly what triggers puberty to begin. However, the hypothalamus sends out gonadotropin hormones responsible for sperm and egg maturation. One theory holds that normal **brain** growth towards the end of childhood includes significant hypothalamic changes. Hypothalamic receptors are thought to become more sensitive to low levels of circulating sex steroids. These changes enable the neuroendocrine system to initiate spermarche (sperm maturation) and menstruation in puberty. However, these early hormonal fluctuations begin at night and remain a nocturnal pulse for some time before they are detectable while awake. Some behavioral changes are related to pubertal hormonal changes, as well. The increase in testosterone is associated with more aggressive **behavior** in males. And libido (sex drive) increases occur for some teenagers in association with estrogen and testosterone increases. These effects are also carried out through sex hormone receptors on the hypothalamus.

Male puberty

Major pubertal hormones secreted by the hypothalamus include gonadotropin releasing hormone (GRH) and growth hormone releasing hormone (GHRH). Both target the anterior pituitary gland which, in turn, releases gonadotropins and growth hormone (also known as somatotropin). GRH is released in a pulsative fashion. This pulsation triggers release of the gonadotropins, luteinizing hormone (LH) and follicle stimulating hormone (FSH). LH stimulates testosterone release by the testes, and FSH is required for early stages of sperm maturation. GHRH is released on a daily basis throughout life, but **growth hormones** have an enhanced effect during puberty when they are combined with sex hormones.

The age of onset of puberty varies but can be between the ages of 9 and 14 in boys. However, individuals can mature as late as 20. When all of a male's organs and endocrine functions are normal but testicular development never occurs, he is said to display eunuchoidism. This name originates from China where a servile class of eunuchs were created by removing their testicles. Because of their lack of testosterone, they were less aggressive. Puberty that begins before the age of eight is called precocious. Precocious puberty can result from neurological disorders of the posterior hypothalamus or pituitary disorders such as tumors or infections.

The initial sign of male puberty is testicular enlargement. The testes secrete testosterone which stimulates many primary and secondary sexual characteristics. Testosterone causes the prostate gland and seminal vesicles to mature. The seminal vesicles begin to secrete fructose which is the primary nutrient sperm require. During puberty, primitive male germ cells begin to mature into primary spermatocytes. This early step in sperm maturation is testosterone-independent. However, the final stage of sperm maturation into spermatozoa is testosterone-dependent. Testicular size may double or quadruple at the start of puberty, but the rate of testicular growth is greatest in the middle of puberty. By the end, they will have doubled in size again. There is great variability in the final testicular size from man to man, but this difference has no affect on sexual ability.

The general progression of male genital area development is the onset of testicular enlargement, onset of penile enlargement, and the appearance of pubic hair (pubarche). The scrotal skin also becomes darker and more wrinkled. Penile enlargement usually begins about a year after testicular growth begins. The penis first becomes longer, and then becomes broader. Initial ejaculations usually occur later during **sleep**. Sperm count is low, at first.

Facial hair growth and a deepening voice are two secondary sexual characteristics which develop about two years after pubic hair appears in males. Facial hair begins on the upper lip, becomes more confluent, extends to side-burns, and then grows on the chin. Hair also begins to appear on a pubertal boy's chest and abdomen. The voice deepens by dropping in pitch due to enlargement of the vocal cords in the larynx, voice box. In addition, other body hair grows, and the areola (pigmented ring around the nipple) enlarges.

Boys grow considerably in both height and **mass** during puberty. On average, boys will grow about 3.7 in/year (9.5 cm/year) at the peak year of their growth spurt. Boys average 4 ft 7 in (1.4 m) in height prior to the onset of puberty and grow an additional 15 in (38 cm) taller during their pubertal growth spurt. At the end of puberty, the average male height is 5 ft 10 in (1.8 m). The initial growth occurs in the leg bones increasing leg length. Then the torso lengthens causing an increase in

sitting height. Between leg growth and torso growth, the arms, shoulders, and hips of boys grow considerably, as well. Muscle mass also increases-particularly in the shoulders. A temporary drop in subcutaneous **fat** occurs in the arms during this time with fat levels returning to normal at the end of puberty.

Female puberty

At the beginning of puberty, a girl's face rounds out, her hips widen, and her breasts begin to develop. Breast development can occur as early as 8 but starts between 10 and 14 for most girls. Full breast development may take 2-5 years. Pubic hair begins to grow shortly afterwards, followed by the first menstrual period, or menarche. Like male puberty, female puberty is initiated by hypothalamic hormones. GRH secreted from the hypothalamus triggers LH and FSH release from the anterior pituitary. The LH and FSH, in turn, stimulate ova maturation. GHRH is also released from the hypothalamus and stimulates growth hormone secretion from the pituitary.

Breast development is called thelarche and can be measured in stages. The initial accumulation of tissue pads the underside of the areola around the nipple. Before puberty, the areola is usually about 0.5 in (1.2 cm) in diameter. By the end of puberty, it can be about 1.5 in (3.8 cm) in diameter. The breast enlarges developing a smooth curve. Then a secondary mound of tissue grows under the areola. Usually by age 18, a girl's breasts have reabsorbed the secondary mound giving a rounded contour to the now adult shape.

Breast budding is followed by menarche between 12 and 14 for most girls. However, normal menarche may occur between 10 and 16. Menstruation occurs as part of the **menstrual cycle** which lasts about 28 days. The initial hormonal cycles associated with the menstrual period usually begin months before menarche, so for a while a girl usually has hormonal cycles without menstruation. The menstrual cycle is divided into two halves, the follicular and the luteal phases. During the follicular phase, an immature egg follicle ripens and estrogen levels rise. On around day 14, LH and FSH trigger the egg to travel into the adjacent fallopian tube. During the luteal phase, high progesterone and estrogen levels prevent another egg from beginning another cycle. After about eight days, if the egg is not fertilized, then the uterine lining is shed as menstrual **blood**. Menstruation can last one to eight days but usually lasts three to five days. The amount of blood lost varies from slight to 2.7 oz (80 ml) with the average being 1 oz (30 ml) lost for the whole period.

A number of factors affect when menstruation begins. Normal menarche is associated with good **nutrition** and health. Girls who are malnourished or ill may have later menarche. In addition, girls who are particularly athletic or involved in strenuous physical activities such as ballet often start menstruating later. Once menarche occurs, cycles are usually irregular for up to two years. Because of this irregularity, girls may be less likely to conceive during this time. However, it is possible to conceive and therefore they should use **contraception** if they are sexually active and wish to prevent pregnancy.

The pubertal growth spurt, of height and weight, in girls usually occurs a year or two before boys, on average. Increases in height and weight are followed by the increases in hip size, breast size, and body fat percentage. The peak growth **rate** during this time is 3.2 in (8 cm) per year, on average. The average female is 4 ft 3 in (1.3 m) tall at the beginning of puberty and gains 13.5 in (34 cm) total during her pubertal growth spurt. At the end of puberty, the average female height is 5 ft 4.5 in (1.6 m) tall. Girls also increase body fat at the hips, stomach, and thighs.

Related topics

Around the world, entry into adulthood is often marked ceremoniously in males and females. A rite of passage ceremony is held to honor this transition. This type of ceremony is usually held in less-industrialized countries where boys and girls are expected to assume adult roles at the end of puberty. The Arapesh of New Guinea build the young woman a menstrual hut at the home of her husband-to-be. Her girlish ornaments are removed, and the girl acquires "womanly" markings and jewelry. The ceremony marks the beginning of her fertility. Young Mano men of Liberia go through a ceremonial "death" at puberty. These young men used to be stabbed with a spear and thrown over a cliff to symbolize death and rebirth into adulthood. Actually, a protective padding kept the spear from penetrating them, and a sack of chicken blood was tied over the spot to appear as though the boy had been stuck. He was not tossed over the cliff, but a heavy object was thrown over instead to sound like he had been thrown. Pubertal Apache girls are sometimes showered with golden cattail pollen (considered holy) as part of a four-day ritual. And boys and girls in Bali, Indonesia, formally come of age when a priest files their six top teeth even so they will not appear fanged.

By comparison, industrialized countries seldom have pubertal rites of passage. In fact, puberty may not be discussed often. Instead, these teenagers are usually expected to continue their education for some time before they can settle down and have a family. The changes which accompany puberty often bring on new feelings,

KEY TERMS

Adolescence—The psychological and emotional changes which accompany puberty.

Adrenarche—Maturation of the adrenal glands to secrete low levels of sex hormones.

Androgens—Male sex hormones, particularly testosterone.

Contraceptive—Any substance or device used to prevent the fertilization of an egg by a sperm during sexual intercourse.

Fertility—The ability to impregnate or become pregnant.

Menarche—The beginning of menstruation.

Menstruation—The cyclic shedding of the endometrial lining of the uterus in fertile women who do not become pregnant.

Neuroendocrine—The interaction between the endocrine system (hormones) and the nervous system (brain) to modulate physiological events.

Sex hormones—Estrogen and testosterone.

however. Adolescents begin to contemplate independence from their parents and assume more adult roles in their family. In addition, puberty is a time when some boys and girls begin to think about their sexuality and sexual activity. Because the human body undergoes such significant and seemingly rapid changes in puberty, it can be a frightening time if a boy or girl does not understand what they are experiencing. Studies have shown that boys and girls who have been told about pubertal changes are less frightened and have fewer emotional problems related to puberty than children who have not been informed about what to expect.

With sexual maturation comes fertility. Many people do not become sexually active during puberty. But those who do have the additional adult responsibility to respect the possibility of pregnancy. For teenagers who begin having intercourse, contraceptive options exist to prevent pregnancy. Another serious consideration, however, is the possibility of contracting a sexually transmittable disease (STD). Not all STDs are curable. Some are debilitating, and others are fatal. The key is protection. Most contraceptives do not protect against both pregnancy and STD's. However, condoms (used correctly) will protect against both.

Adolescence is not a good time to play Russian roulette with a poor diet either. A diet of **potato** chips and ice cream or celery and **water** will not optimize healthy growth. They will both hinder it. Loading up on junk food or slimming down by fasting are both dangerous. During puberty, a lot of body mass is constructed, and the right nutritional building blocks are essential. **Calcium**, protein, carbohydrates, **minerals**, and vitamins are all important. And enough calories to fuel development is also needed. During puberty, adolescents need about 2,000-2,500 calories a day. Some girls become self-conscious of their developing bodies and try to minimize fatty tissue growth by fasting or making themselves throw up food they have eaten. Both of these mechanisms to stay thin are extremely dangerous, can have long-term detrimental effects on health, and should be avoided. Adolescents who can turn to a trustworthy adult with their questions or concerns about puberty may find this transition easier.

See also Adrenals; Endocrine system; Reproductive system.

Further Reading

McCoy, K., and C. Wibbelsman. *The New Teenage Body Book.* New York: The Body Press, 1992.

Lerner, R., A. Peterson, and J. Brooks-Gunn, eds. *The Encyclopedia of Adolescence.* New York: Garland, 1991.

Brierley, J. *Growth in Children.* New York: Cassell, 1993.

Louise Dickerson

Public utilities see **Municipal infrastructure**

Puffbirds

Puffbirds are 32 species of **birds** that make up the family Bucconidae. This family is in the order Piciformes, which also contains the **woodpeckers**, **toucans**, **barbets**, jacamars, and honey-guides. Puffbirds are native to lowland tropical **forests** from southern Mexico, through to Paraguay and northern Argentina in **South America**. Most species occur in Amazonia.

Puffbirds are short, squat birds, with a large head, a stout, often hooked beak, and a short tail. The puff-ball effect is further heightened by the habit these birds have of frequently raising their feathers. However, as soon as they sense an intrusion, they immediately flatten their feathers, to become less conspicuous. The plumage of puffbirds is a rather subdued grey, brown, or white.

Puffbirds sit patiently at vantage places on a **tree** branch, scanning for potential **prey**. When they spy a

An inflated blowfish.

small lizard, frog, or large insect, they sally forth and attempt to seize it. **Insects** are sometimes hawked in the air.

Puffbirds nest in cavities dug into termite nests, or in burrows excavated vertically or on a steep incline into the ground, with a chamber at the bottom. They lay two to three eggs that are incubated by both parents, which also share in the rearing of the chicks. During the day, the chicks wait to be fed near the burrow entrance, but at night they retire to the lower chamber, often camouflaging the entrance with leaves as they descend.

The white-necked puffbird (*Notharchus macrorhynchus*) is one of the more common species, occurring widely in Central and South America.

Bill Freedman

Puffer fish

Puffer **fish** or globe fish (family Tetraodontidae) are a group of tropical- and warm-temperate-dwelling **species** that are almost exclusively marine in their habits. A few **freshwater** species occur in tropical **Africa** and **Asia**. Most are typically found in shallow waters, often on coral reefs, in beds of sea grass, and in estuaries, swimming and feeding during daylight. A few species are oceanic. Their closest relatives are the similar-looking porcupine fishes (Didontidae) and the very much larger sun fishes (Molidae). Most puffer fish are recognized by their short, stout, almost bloated appearance, their small fins, and their large eyes. These fish swim by side-to-side sculling movements of the dorsal and anal fins, while the pectoral fins assist with balance and direction.

In addition to their characteristic body shape, puffer fishes can be distinguished from most other species by the fact that their bodies are virtually covered with large numbers of spines of unequal length. These are frequently more dense on the lower parts of the body. Normally these spines, which are modified scales, lie flat against the body. When the fish is threatened, however, it inflates its body by a sudden intake of a large **volume** of **water** or air, erecting its spines in the process. In this inflated stance, few larger species would be tempted to attack it and risk almost certain injury. Although puffer fish are unable to swim effectively in this position, the strategy is a deliberate antipredator action; instead of swimming, the fish drifts with the **ocean** current. In addition to this impressive defensive tactic, most puffer fish also contain a wide range of body toxins, particularly in the liver, gonads, skin, and intestine. They are widely thought of as the most poisonous of all marine animals; the various toxins attack the **nervous system** of species that eat them and may kill the **animal** unless it has the ability to detoxify the lethal products. Most puffer fish are brightly coloured—a system often employed in the animal kingdom to warn potential attackers that their flesh is at best unpalatable and at worst lethal.

Puffer fish feed on a wide range of items. Some prefer to feed almost exclusively on **plankton**, but many species also **prey** heavily on large **invertebrates** such as molluscs, crustaceans, echinoderms, **crabs**, and worms using their sharp, beak-like teeth and powerful jaws to crush and sift through the defensive body armor that these other animals use in an attempt to protect themselves from predators. The teeth of most species of puffer fish are joined to form two sharp-edged plates in each jaw.

When resting, puffer fish generally seek out a concealed part of a coral reef or similar abode and hide away in a crevice. Some bottom-dwelling species nestle into the substrate; by altering the main colours of the skin, many are able to effectively camouflage themselves from the watchful **eye** of predators.

Although puffer fishes have an impressive arsenal of defensive tactics, some species may be threatened as a result of over-fishing for resale to meet the demands of the tourist industry. On many coral reefs, puffer fish are caught and dried in their inflated position for sale to tourists. Also, despite their lethal concoction of body toxins, the flesh of puffer fish is widely sought after as a culinary delight in some countries, especially in Japan, where the dish is known as *fugu*. Needless to say, the preparation of this meal is a delicate process if one is to avoid lethal poisoning. Some restaurants have been known to retain specially trained staff to prepare such dishes.

David Stone

Pulsar

A pulsar is a celestial object that emits **radiation** pulses (bursts) of very short (one to a few milliseconds, or thousandths of a second) duration at very regular intervals from a fraction of a second to ten seconds.

The first pulsar was discovered in 1967 by Jocelyn Bell and Antony Hewish at Cambridge, England, with **radio** telescopes equipped to study the twinkling (scintillation) of radio stars. They soon discovered a radio source producing short (0.016 sec) radio pulses separated by a constant 1.3373 second **interval**. The pulses were so regular that an artificial terrestrial source was suspected for them, but careful, extended radio observations showed that their source rose and set about four minutes earlier each day, which demonstrated that the source was a celestial object (radio **star**). It received the designation CP (Cambridge Pulsar) 1919. Three more pulsars were found soon after this discovery. Their regular patterns caused some scientists to speculate that the pulsars were part of a beacon system installed by an advanced extraterrestrial civilization to aid interstellar travel.

Other scientists suggested several other more plausible hypotheses about the nature of pulsars. Among them was Thomas Gold's hypothesis that pulsars were produced by **neutron** stars. Neutron stars had never been observed, but their possible existence had been suggested by J. Robert Oppenheimer and George M. Volkoff in 1939 as a final remnant of a **supernova** explosion, where a massive star explodes and ejects most or nearly all of its **mass**. If the star's final remnant has a mass less than 1.4 solar masses, then a **white dwarf** star usually will result. However, if the remnant's mass is more than 1.4 solar masses, its gravity will cause the remnant to collapse beyond the white dwarf stage, forcing free electrons into atomic nuclei and forcing them to combine with protons to form neutrons. The collapse is finally stopped by the rigidity of nuclear **matter**; here about 1.5 solar masses is squeezed into a body with about a 6.2 mi (10 km) radius.

Support for Gold's **neutron star** model for pulsars came in 1968 when a very fast pulsar (which emits pulses every 0.33 second) was discovered in the Crab Nebula, the gaseous ejecta from a supernova observed by the Chinese in 1054. Subsequent observations showed that this pulsar emits pulses at wavelengths from gamma rays through visible light to **radio waves**. Gold's model has the neutron star rotating very fast, with its **rotation** period equal to the interval between pulses; only a neutron star could withstand such rapid rotation without disruption. Pulses are thought to be produced by radiation beamed towards the **solar system** from charged particles moving in a strongly compressed magnetic field near the pulsar.

Developments through 1995

About 1,000 pulsars are now known. Almost all are within the **Milky Way**, but several pulsars have been found in the Magellanic Clouds, the nearest external galaxies.

Additional support for the neutron star model came in 1987 at the start of the observed outburst of Supernova 1987 in the Large Megellanic Cloud, when bursts of neutrinos were detected simultaneously at two widely separated underground observatories (in Japan and Ohio, USA). The theory of supernovae predicts that most of the gravitational **energy** released during the collapse of a supernova remnant to form a neutron star will be converted to **neutrinos**. The observed supernova bursts support this theory. The search for a pulsar ar the position of Supernova 1987 continues.

Extremely fast pulsars, which emit pulses at intervals from one to several milliseconds, were discovered in the 1980s. Several of them were found to be members of **binary star** systems with very short periods of revolution.

This has **led** to speculation that millisecond pulsars are formed by the merging of a neutron star and another star in a binary system, where the transfer of mass and angular **momentum** onto the neutronstar" spins it up." The distances to most pulsars are uncertain. The nearest estimated **distance** for a pulsar, is about 280 light-years. All other pulsars seem to be considerably more distant. The Crab Nebula pulsar and the 17 pulsars that have been found in 11 globular clusters have somewhat more reliable distance estimates, but there are thousands and even tens of thousands of light-years from the solar system.

Eight of the 17 pulsars found in globular clusters are members of binary systems. Thirteen pulsars are now known to be members of binary systems. Estimates of pulsar (neutron star) masses from their orbits so far indicate masses from 1.3 to 1.6 solar masses for neutron stars. Pulsars in very close binary systems are being studied in an effort to detect relativistic effects in their strong gravitational fields, which can be used to check the predictions of the general theory of relativity. The discovery of binary pulsars has increased efforts to detect the gravitational waves predicted by this theory. Finally, the three most reliably established **extrasolar planets** have been discovered orbiting the pulsar-neutron star PSR 1257+12.

Summary

Since their discovery in 1967, pulsars have contributed greatly to fields of **astronomy** and **astrophysics** as diverse as **stellar structure** and **evolution**,

Pyramids at Giza, Egypt.

the theory of relativity, and extrasolar planets. Pulsar research continues.

See also Kepler's Laws.

Further Reading

Morrison, David and Sidney C. Wolff. *Frontiers of Astronomy.* Philadelphia: Saunders College Publishing, 1990.

Shipman, Harry L., *Black Holes, Quasars, and The Universe.* 2nd ed. Boston: Houghton Mifflin, 1980.

Frederick R. West

Pumpkin see **Gourd family**

Pyramid

A pyramid is a geometric solid of the shape made famous by the royal tombs of ancient Egypt. It is a solid whose base is a polygon and whose lateral faces are triangles with a common vertex (the vertex of the pyramid). In the case of the Egyptian pyramid of Cheops, the base is an almost perfect **square** 755 ft (230 m) on an edge, and the faces of triangles are approximately equilateral.

The base of a pyramid can be any polygon of three or more edges, and pyramids are named according to the number of edges in the base. When the base is a triangle, the pyramid is a triangular pyramid. It is also known as a **tetrahedron** since, including the base, it has four faces. When these faces are equilateral triangles, it is a square pyramid, having a square as its base.

The pyramids most commonly encountered are "regular" pyramids. These have a regular polygon for a base and isosceles triangles for lateral faces. Not all pyramids are regular, however.

The height of a pyramid can be measured in two ways, from the vertex along a line **perpendicular** to the base and from the vertex along a line perpendicular to one of the edges of the base. This latter measure is called the slant height. Unless the lateral faces are congruent triangles, however, the slant height can vary from face to face and will have little meaning for the pyramid as a whole. Unless the word slant is included, the term height (or altitude) refers to the height.

KEY TERMS

Altitude—the distance from the vertex, perpendicular to the base.

Pyramid—a solid with a polygonal base and triangular lateral faces.

Slant height—the distance form the vertex, perpendicular to the edge of the base.

If in addition to being congruent, the lateral faces are isosceles, the pyramid will be regular. In a regular pyramid, right triangles are to be found in abundance. Suppose we have a regular pyramid whose altitude is VC and slant height VD. Here the triangles VCD, VDE, VCE, and CDE are all right triangles. If in any of these triangle one knows two of the sides, one can use the **Pythagorean theorem** to figure out the third. This, in turn, can be used in other triangles to figure out still other unknown sides. For example, if a regular square pyramid has a slant height of two units and a base of two units on an edge, the lateral edges have to be $\sqrt{5}$ units and the altitude $\sqrt{3}$ units.

There are formulas for computing the lateral area and the total area of certain special pyramids, but in most instances it is easier to compute the areas of the various faces and add them up.

Volume is another matter. Figuring volume without a formula can be very difficult. Fortunately there is a rather remarkable formula dating back at least 2,300 years.

In Proposition 7 of Book XII of his *Elements,* Euclid showed that "Any **prism** which has a triangular base is divided into three pyramids equal to one another which have triangular bases." This means that each of the three pyramids into which the prism has been divided has one third the prism's volume. Since the volume of the prism is the area, B, of its base times its altitude, h: the volume of the pyramid is one third that, or Bh/3.

Pyramids whose bases are **polygons** of more than three sides can be divided into triangular pyramids and Euclid's formula applied to each. Then if B is the sum of the areas of the triangles into which the polygon has been divided, the total volume of the pyramid will again be Bh/3.

If one slices the top off a pyramid, one truncates it. If the slice is **parallel** to the base, the truncated pyramid is called a frustum. The volume of a frustum is given by the curious formula $(B + B' + \sqrt{BB'})h/3$, where B and B' are the areas of the upper and lower bases, and h is the perpendicular **distance** between them.

Further Reading

Euclid. *Elements.* New York: Dover, 1956.

Eves, Howard. *A Survey of Geometry.* Boston: Allyn and Bacon, 1963.

J. Paul Moulton

Pyrethrum see **Composite family (Compositaceae)**

Pythagorean theorem

One of the most famous theorems of **geometry**, often attributed to Pythagoras of Samos (Greece) in the sixth century B.C., states the sides a, b, and c of a right triangle satisfy the relation $c^2=a^2+b^2$ where c is the length of the hypotenuse of the triangle and a and b are the lengths of the other two sides.

This **theorem** was likely to have been known earlier to be the Babylonians, Pythagoras is said to have traveled to Babylon as a young man, where he could have learned the famous theorem. Nevertheless, Pythagoras (or some member of his school) is credited with the first **proof** of the theorem.

The converse of the Pythagorean theorem is also true. That is if a triangle with sides a, b, and c has $a^2 =b^2+c^2$, we know that the triangle is a right triangle.

A special form of the theorem was used by the Egyptians for making **square** corners when they resurveyed the land adjacent to the Nile river after the annual flood. They used a rope loop with 12 knots tied at equal intervals along the rope. Three of the knots were used as the vertices of a triangle. Since $3^2+4^2=5^2$ we know, by the converse of the Pythagorean theorem, that we have a right triangle.

Pythons

Pythons are nonvenomous constricting **snakes** in the family Boidae that are found only in the Old World. Like the **boas**, pythons retain lizard-like features such as paired lungs and the remnants of the hind limbs. Pythons are egg-laying snakes which distinguishes them from boas and sandboas which typically bear live young. Fos-

A green tree python.

sil species of pythons are known from Cretaceous period, some 200 million years ago, the separation of the old world pythons from the South American boas having taken place some 80 million years ago.

Constricting snakes do not crush their **prey** as commonly supposed, but coil tightly around the chest of the prey **animal**. When the animal exhales, the snake tightens its grip, and after two or three breaths the animal dies from suffocation or from the **pressure** on its **heart** which causes it to stop beating.

Of the 24 species of pythons, 18 are found in **Australia** and New Guinea, three in **Asia**, and three in **Africa**.

The large pythons in Australia and New Guinea include species of *Liasis* and *Morelia* which commonly exceed 10 ft (3 m) in length. The largest python in this region is the amethystine python (*Morelia amethistina*), which often exceeds 11 ft (3.5 m) but can grow up to 28 ft (8.5 m).

Australia also has the smallest pythons. Some species in the genus *Liasis* seldom exceed a yard (1 m) in length and have a slender body. The green tree python (*Chondropython viridis*) of New Guinea and northern Australia attains a length of about 7 ft (2 m), and has well-developed labial pits on the scales around the mouth which serve as **heat** receptors, allowing the snake to locate warm-blooded **birds** and **mammals** at night.

The largest known python is the Asian reticulated python (*Python reticulatus)* which has been reported to attain a length of 38 ft (11.6 m), and commonly reaches more than 25 ft (7.6 m). Reticulated pythons are longest of all snakes, while the anaconda (an aquatic boa of tropical America) is probably the heaviest.

All pythons coil around their clutch of eggs to protect them, but the female Asian rock python *(Python mdurus)* incubates its eggs on cool nights by violently contracting her muscles several times a minute thus producing body heat. The female Asian rock pythons does not eat during the entire 60-90 day incubation period, and may lose almost half her normal weight due to this activity. Most Asian rock pythons have a gentle non-aggressive nature, and are a favorite of snake-handlers.

The Malayan blood python (*Python curtus*) is an (8-ft; 2.7-m) heavy-bodied snake, so named because of the blood-red color of some individuals, not because it sucks blood. Because of its size and bright coloration, blood pythons are popular pets.

KEY TERMS

Constriction—The activity of wrapping around an object and squeezing it. Snakes that subdue their prey in this way are called "constrictors."

Genera (singular, genus)—A group of related species; the next higher level of classification above the species level.

Labial pits—Sensitive heat-receptors embedded in the scales around the mouth in boas and pythons.

Terrestrial—Living on the ground; surface dwelling.

The African rock python (*Python sebae*) grows to a length of more than 20 ft (6 m) and is able to eat animals as large as **pigs** and small antelope. Rock pythons have even been reported to (rarely) eat children. A large individual may take a food animal that weighs up to perhaps 100 lbs (50 kg). The royal or ball python (*Python regius*) and the Angola python (*Python anchietae*) rarely exceed five ft (1.5 m) in length. The ball python gets its name from its habit of curling up into a tight ball with its head in the center; in this position the python can be rolled along the ground like a ball.

Further Reading

Broadley, D.G. *Fitzsimons' Snakes of Southern Africa.* Johannesburg: Delta Books, 1983.

Cogger, H. G. *Reptiles & Amphibians of Australia.* 5th ed. Ithaca, NY: Comstock/Cornell, 1992.

Minton, S. A.. Jr., and M.R. Minton. *Giant Reptiles.* New York: Scribner's Sons, 1973.

Tweedie, M. W. F. *The Snakes of Malaya.* 3rd ed. Singapore: Singapore National Printers, 1983.

Herndon G. Dowling

Quadrant see **Sextant**

Quadrilateral

A quadrilateral is a polygon with four sides. Special cases of a quadrilateral are: (1) A trapezium—A quadrilateral with no pairs of opposite sides **parallel**. (Figure A) (2) A **trapezoid**—A quadrilateral with one pair of sides parallel. (Figure B) (3) A **parallelogram**—A quadrilateral with two pairs of sides parallel. (Figure C) (4) A **rectangle**—A parallelogram with all angles right angles. (Figure D) (5) A **square**—A rectangle having all sides of the same length. (Figure E) A complete quadrilateral is a **plane** figure in projective **geometry** consisting of lines *a,b,c,* and *d* (no two of them concurrent) and their points of intersection. (Figure F)

See also Polygons.

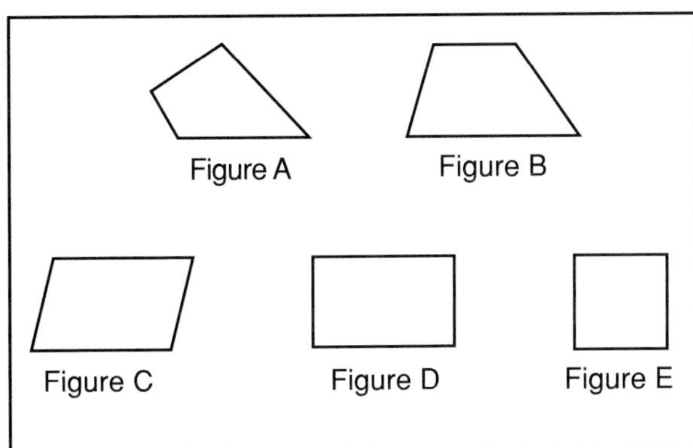

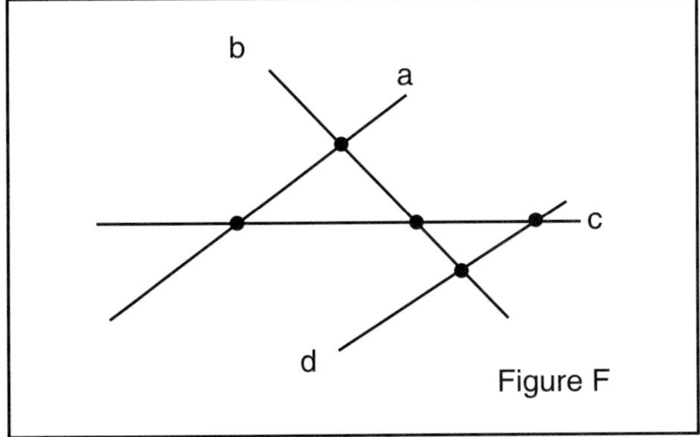

Quail

Quail are relatively small species of fowl in the family Phasianidae, which also includes **pheasants**, **partridges**, **peafowl**, **turkeys**, **guinea fowl**, and francolins.

Like other members of their family, quail have a chunky body with short, rounded wings, and a short, thick, hooked bill, in which the tip of the upper mandible hangs slightly over that of the lower. The legs and feet are stout, and are used for running as well as for scratching in the ground surface for their foods of **seeds** and **invertebrates**. Compared with other **birds** in the Phasianidae, quails are relatively small, short-necked birds, with a short tail, a serrated edge of the beak, and lacking spurs on the legs.

Quail are non-migratory, terrestrial birds, inhabiting semi-deserts, **grasslands**, open woodlands, and forest edges. Quail eat berries, seeds, buds, and leaves, as well as **insects** and other types of invertebrates that they encounter, especially as they scratch through dirt and debris on the ground. Young quail feed especially heavily on invertebrates, because they are growing rapidly and therefore need a diet rich in **proteins**.

Male quail are relatively brightly patterned and are often ornamented with unusual structures that are intended to impress the female—for example, a long plume of feathers on the head. In addition, male quail have strutting behavioral repertoires that are designed to excite potential mates.

A Gambel's quail (*Lophortyx gambelii.*) in the Arizona Sonora Desert Museum, Arizona.

KEY TERMS

Monogamy—A system in which a male and female form a pair that cooperates in breeding.

Polygyny—A breeding system in which a male will attempt to breed with as many females as possible. In birds, the female of a polygynous species usually incubates the eggs and raises the babies unaided by the male.

Sexual selection—A type of natural selection in which anatomical or behavioral traits may be favored because they confer some advantage in courtship or another aspect of breeding.

These structures and behaviors are not adaptive in the conventional sense, in fact, they likely make male quail more vulnerable to being killed by predators. These special characteristics of male quail have evolved as a result of sexual selection, a force that favors individuals that are most pleasing to the females in an aesthetic sense. Other members of the Phasianidae, such as pheasants and peafowl, have evolved even more unusual reproduction-enhancing characteristics than the quails.

Most species of quail have a monogamous breeding system, in which male and female birds pair off and cooperate in breeding. This is different from many other groups in the Phasianidae, which are polygynous. Quail nest on the ground, usually beneath a shrub or in other protective cover. In some species of quails, both the female and the male brood the eggs, and both cooperate in raising the chicks. Quail chicks are precocious and can leave the nest soon after **birth**, following their parents and feeding themselves, mostly on insects.

Species of quail

Species of quail occur in the Americas, **Africa**, Eurasia, and Australasia. Six native species of quails occur in **North America**, mostly in the west. In addition, various species of quails have been widely introduced as game birds beyond their natural range, including the common quail, bobwhite, and California quail. Other species are commonly kept in zoos and private aviaries around the world.

The bobwhite quail (*Colinus virginianus*) is the most familiar species of quail in southeastern Canada, the eastern and central United States, and south to Guatemala. This species has also been widely introduced as a gamebird. There is a relatively large, introduced population in the Pacific Northwest of the United States. This bird is named after its whistled calls of "*bob-bob-white*." The California quail (*Lophortyx californica*) occurs in open woodlands and parks of all of the Pacific states. Gambel's quail (*L. gambelii*) occurs in the southwestern states and northern Mexico. The males of both of these species have a long, black plume that stands erect on the top of their head. The plume of females is shorter.

The **mountain** quail (*Oreortyx pictus*) occurs in woodlands and chaparral at relatively high elevation in the western states. This species also has a head plume, similarly sized in both sexes.

The scaled quail (*Callipepla squamata*) and harlequin quail (*Cyrtonyx montezumae*) occur in the southwestern states and Central America.

The only species of quail in **Europe** is the common quail (*Coturnix coturnix*), which also ranges widely into **Asia** and Africa. Northern populations of this robin-sized species are migratory. Numerous attempts have been made to introduce the common quail as a game bird in North America, but none of these have established breeding populations.

Quail and people

Most species of quail are economically important as game birds and are hunted for sport or as source of wild meat. However, quail are easily over-hunted, so it is important to conserve their populations.

Quail are also kept in captivity in zoos, parks, and private aviaries, although this is somewhat less common than with pheasants and peafowl, which are larger, more colorful birds.

Unfortunately, some species of quail are becoming endangered in their native habitats. This is partly due to

excessive hunting, but more important in many cases are losses of the natural **habitat** of these birds. These ecological changes are largely due to agricultural conversions of natural habitats that quail require, and to other human influences.

Further Reading

Alderton, D. *The Atlas of Quails.* Neptune City, NJ: TFH Publications, 1992.

Harrison, C. J. O., ed. *Bird Families of the World.* New York: H.N. Abrams Pubs., 1978.

Johnsgard, P.A. *Quails, Partridges, and Francolins of the World.* Oxford: Oxford University Press, 1988.

Long, J.L. *Introduced Birds of the World.* New York: Universe Books, 1981.

Bill Freedman

Qualitative analysis

The value of a material is determined in part by the substances of which it is composed. The operations necessary to determine this composition are known as qualitative analysis. Qualitative analysis is a series of tests; responses to these tests identify the elements and compounds that make up the material.

Every substance is unique. Each has, for example, a certain **color**, texture, and appearance. These properties are, however, often insufficient to positively identify the substance although they certainly contribute to its identity. One must generally evaluate other physical and chemical characteristics to identify beyond any doubt the exact composition of a material. With 92 naturally occurring elements and an endless variety of possible combinations it is not an easy task to prove with certainty the exact composition of an unknown substance. If, upon testing, an unknown exhibits properties identical in every way to the known properties of a particular substance, then that unknown is identical to the known substance and is identified. Caution is necessary, however, for although some properties may compare within experimental **error**, all properties must correlate before the known and unknown materials can be termed identical.

Some of the more common physical properties measured for identifying an unknown substance are: melting point, color, **boiling point**, texture, density, ductility, **electrical conductivity**, malleability, thermal conductivity, refractive index, and **coefficient** of linear expansion.

Most of the properties listed exhibit measurable numerical values that can be compared to known values of elements and compounds found tabulated in various reference books. More elaborate physical testing, requiring complex scientific equipment and trained operators, deals with measurements dependent upon the internal structure of a material. Depending upon the arrangement of the particles within a substance, they interact with electromagnetic **radiation** in different ways. The result of these interactions is an **electromagnetic spectrum**, a pictorial representation of the absorption and **emission** of electromagnetic radiations of varying **energy** as they strike and pass through a substance. **x ray**, ultraviolet, visible, infrared, and other spectra when compared to similar spectra of known materials produce a match with that of the unknown if they are identical and a mismatch if they are not.

Chemical tests are widely used for qualitative analysis. If an unknown produces the same results when reacted with a certain chemical reagent as does a material of known composition, they may be identical. To be absolutely sure more then one confirmatory test is made, for although reagent A may, when added to both an known and an unknown substance, produce identical responses, reagent B when used for testing might react only with the known and not with the unknown. The analytical chemist who performs these tests must be knowledgeable both in selecting the proper test reagents and in knowing the expected results.

Various schemes for qualitative analysis exist and their study is a part of the training in many college **chemistry** programs. The most common scheme, the insoluble sulfide scheme, identifies approximately thirty of the more common metallic elements. It uses a single reagent, **hydrogen** sulfide, to separate solutions of metallic elements into groups of several substances with similar chemical properties. Other, more specific reagents, are then added to further separate within each group. Confirmatory tests are then performed, generating an insoluble colored solid, called a precipitate, or a soluble uniquely-colored product.

The nonmetallic elements, because of the greater number of reactions they can undergo, are more difficult to group. Additional confirmation tests would be necessary to identify single components within each group.

Organic materials, those based primarily on a **carbon** structure, pose a particular problem for qualitative analysis because of the presence of so many carbon **atoms**. Distinction between various organic compounds is based upon the arrangement of the carbon atoms and the other non-carbon atoms within a compound. It is possible to divide organic compounds into groups based upon these arrangements and often qualitative analysis for group identification is sufficient rather then identifying a particular compound. Some of the more

common organic functional groups, as they are called, and the arrangement of atoms characteristic of the group are listed here. The symbol R represents an underlying arrangement of carbon and hydrogen atoms. R_1 may or may not be the same as R_2: acids R-COOH; alcohols R-OH; **aldehydes** R-COH; amines R-NH_2; esters R_1-COO-R_2; ethers R_1-O-R_2; hydrocarbons R-H; ketones R_1-CO-R_2.

Organic substances with different functional groups dissolve or remain insoluble in different solvents. They also respond differently to various reagents. It is relatively easy to identify the group into which an organic compound belongs. Once separated, additional tests would be necessary to confirm the presence of a particular functional group.

Identification of a specific organic substance is difficult. Physical test are often more helpful then chemical tests. As an example, after a tentative identification has been made for an organic compound, a portion of the unknown is mixed with a portion of the pure known substance, and a melting point is measured. The tentative identification was correct if the melting point of the mixture is identical to the literature value melting point for the pure substance but incorrect if a substantially lower melting point is observed.

Spectral identification of organic substances, and this includes complex materials from living species, is probably the best means of qualitative identification. An infrared **spectrum** of an organic material exhibits numerous peaks and troughs generated by the interaction of the infrared radiation and the atoms within a **molecule** as the radiation passes through the substance or is reflected from its surface. Each functional group interacts only with infrared rays of specific energy or **frequency**. A peak observed at the frequency known to be indicative of an **alcohol** group is evidence that the substance is, indeed, an alcohol. Again, confirmatory tests, both physical and chemical, should be made for often the peak generated by one type of functional group overlaps that of another.

Other spectral procedures not related to electromagnetic radiation also evoke specific responses, spectra, from organic compounds based upon the arrangement of the atoms comprising the material. Perhaps best known of these is the technique of **nuclear magnetic resonance** (NMR) **spectroscopy**. When applied to living **tissue**, as a diagnostic tool to observe the misarrangement of molecules within a living **organism** indicating a certain disease or abnormality, this approach is known as **magnetic resonance imaging (MRI)** spectroscopy. A sample-placed within a strong magnetic field and subjected simultaneously to a strong electrical signal will, because of the magnetic properties of the protons within its atoms, respond to these outside forces. What results is a nuclear magnetic spectrum. Here, analogous to an infrared spectrum, the location of the peaks which are generated indicates how the atoms within a molecule are arranged. Nuclear magnetic spectra have an advantage over infrared spectra in one respect as they will indicate the presence and position of hydrogen atoms attached to carbon. This is very difficult to determine from an infrared spectrum.

Another spectral technique, **mass spectrometry**, measures both molecular mass of a material and information relating to how atoms are joined together. By utilizing a combination of electric and magnetic fields coupled with a subatomic bombardment of the material one breaks the substance into fragments. The mass of each fragment is recorded, a mass spectrum, and like pieces of a jigsaw puzzle, this information can be reassembled to identify the structure of the parent substance.

All of these techniques, electromagnetic spectra, nuclear magnetic spectra, and mass spectra are comparative techniques. If the spectrum observed from an unknown matches that from a known material, the two can be assumed identical.

Often substances to be analyzed are composed of complex mixtures requiring a preliminary separation before the individual components can be known. One approach to the separation and simultaneous qualitative identification of complex mixtures uses a variety of related techniques called chromatographic separations. **Chromatography** is a separation process in which the **sample** is forced to flow past a stationary adsorbent. Each component in the sample has a different degree of attraction for the stationary adsorbent, those components which are strongly attracted will adhere to the stationary material almost immediately while those with a lesser degree of attraction will be carried farther along before sticking on the stationary material. If the stationary material is an adsorbent **paper** sheet and the sample in **solution** is allowed to flow over the paper, the technique is paper chromatography. If the adsorbent is packed in a long vertical tube and the sample solution is poured into the top of the tube, the technique is column chromatography. If the adsorbent is packed into a long narrow pipe and the sample, after being placed at one end of the pipe, is pushed through with a stream of gas, the technique is gas chromatography. With all chromatographic techniques the **distance** from the starting point traveled on a flat surface by each component or the time necessary for a component to pass through a packed tube from one end to the other is characteristic of that component. Distances or times when matched with the distances or times of known

KEY TERMS

Electromagnetic radiation—Various forms of energy with both electric and magnetic components. The frequency and wavelength of their oscillations is related through the speed of light. Visible light, for example, comprises electromagnetic radiations in the wavelength range 350–750 nanometer (10–9 m).

Functional group—A particular arrangement of atoms in an organic compound that determines the dominate characteristics of that compound. An alcohol, for example, contains the grouping R-OH, where R represents a collection of carbon and hydrogen atoms and —OH identifies the compound as an alcohol.

Reagent—A chemical added to a suspect material to produce a known reaction response. If the reaction response is observed as expected the identity of the material is assumed to be known.

Spectroscopy—That branch of science in which a varying perturbing energy (electromagnetic, magnetic, etc.) is directed on a sample. The magnitude of the response as the energy varies is plotted and the resulting spectrum characteristic of the arrangement of atoms within the molecules of the sample is noted.

components indicate a qualitative match. It is wise, however, to run additional confirmatory test before a positive match is stated.

One area in which qualitative identification has become very important is the matching of human DNA tissue by law enforcement agencies to prove the presence or absence of a person at a crime scene. The details of how this is done are beyond the scope of this article but make interesting additional reading.

Further Reading

Cheronis, Nicholas D., and T.S. Ma. *Organic Functional Group Analysis.* New York: Interscience Publishers, 1964.

Schafter, James. "DNA Fingerprints on Trial." *Popular Science.* 245 (1994): 60-64, 90.

Slowinski, E.J., and W.L. Masterton. *Qualitative Analysis and the Properties of Ions in Aqueous Solution.* Philadelphia: Saunders College Publishing, 1990.

Stock, R., and C.B.F. Rice. *Chromatographic Methods.* London: Chapman and Hall, 1974.

Gordon A. Parker

Quantitative analysis

Quantitative analysis is a chemical analysis performed to find the amount of each component present in a material. It is done by either a classical or instrumental procedure.

A quantitative investigation means that the amount (quantity) or relative amount of each component present is determined. In a pure substance, the entire mass, or 100%, is composed of a single component. In materials composed of two or more substances, a quantitative investigation would determine the **mass** or relative mass present for each component within the **sample**. It is not always necessary to find quantitative values for all components that make up a substance. In most cases it is sufficient to analyze the material for one or perhaps more components of interest. The amount of active medicine within an antacid tablet, for example, is significant, whereas the fillers, binders, colorants, and flavoring agents present are of lesser importance.

$$H_2PO_4^- \longleftrightarrow H^+ + HPO_4^{2-}$$

dihydrogen phosphate; hydrogen ion; monohydrogen phosphate ion

$$H_2CO_3 \longleftrightarrow H^+ + HCO_3^-$$

carbonic acid; hydrogen ion; bicarbonate ion

$$CO_2 + H_2O \longleftrightarrow H_2CO_3$$

carbon dioxide; water; carbonic acid

A quantitative analysis involves more than simply measuring the amount of a component present in a sample.

The sample must first be prepared for measurement, usually by placing it in **solution** if it is not already in soluble form. With complex substances a preliminary separation of the desired component is often necessary to prevent other substances present from interfering with the selected analytical method.

An analyst is one who measures the components of a material quantitatively as a percent or amount present in a sample. Analysts are employed by manufacturing industries to test the reliability of their products. If an **automobile** manufacturer, for example, specifies that the **iron** content of the **steel** used in an automobile is of a certain percentage, then this value must be checked constantly by the manufacturer to see that the automobile meets specifications. This repeated checking is known as quality control and manufacturing facilities have a quality control department employing analytical chemists.

TABLE. 1 INSTRUMENTAL TECHNIQUES	
Method	***Response***
potentiometry:	Many chemical reactions produce electric energy, a battery for example. The amount of chemical to produce a measured potential is calculated.
coulometry:	The amount of electrical current and the duration over which it flows is a measure of the amount of chemical substance producing the current.
conductimetry:	The number of charged chemical components in a solution determine the resistance or conductance of a solution to the passage of electrical current.
voltammetry:	The magnitude of electric potential necessary to cause the breakdown of a chemical substance and the current resulting from that breakdown are related to the amount of chemical present.
ultraviolet, visible, infrared, and x-ray spectometry:	The extent to which these rays are absorbed by a sample depends upon the amount of sample present
thermogravimetry:	The loss in weight of a substance as it decomposes upon heating is proportional to the amount of substance initially present.
nuclear magnetic resonance:	For chemicals showing magnetic properties the strength of the magnetism is related to the amount of substance present.
nuclear activation analysis:	The amount of radioactivity produced by a substance is proportional to the amount of material emitting radiation.
mass spectrometry:	The intensity of each component fraction present as a chemical is broken apart relates to the amount initially present.

Hospitals, too, employ analytical chemists to test patients for proper amounts of medication. Athletes are subjected to quantitative testing to determine the presence and amount of possible illicit drugs in their bodies. The federal government carries out frequent quantitative measurements of environmental samples. Should, for example, a company generate greater amounts of a pollutant than is allowed by law, then the government can fine the company or force it to close until it meets government regulations. Legislators at the local, state and national level use quantitative results to formulate laws that prevent the general public from coming into contact with dangerous amounts of harmful chemicals in food, medicine, the environment, and other areas.

Various methods are employed to undertake a quantitative investigation. These methods are broadly classified as classical and instrumental methods.

Classical methods

Classical methods, employed since the beginning of modern **chemistry** in the nineteenth century, use balances and calibrated **glass** containers to directly measure the amounts of chemicals combined with an unknown substance. A classical gravimetric analysis utilizes an appropriate chemical reagent to combine with the analyte in a sample solution to form an insoluble substance, a precipitate. The precipitate is filtered, washed, dried and

weighed. From the weight of the precipitate and sample and from the known chemical composition of the precipitate, the analyst calculates the percent of analyte in the sample. A classical titrimetric, or volumetric, analysis uses *titration*, a procedure in which a solution of exactly known **concentration** reacts with the analyte in a sample solution. A chemical solution of known concentration, the titrant, is placed in a **buret**, a long calibrated tube with a valve at one end capable of dispensing variable known volumes of liquid. An indicator solution, a colored dye, is added to the unknown sample. Titrant is then delivered slowly from the buret. The indicator dye is chosen so that a color change occurs when exactly the proper amount of titrant to combine with the unknown has been added. This amount is called the equivalent point **volume**. From the strength of the titrant solution, the equivalent point volume, and the volume of unknown sample in the titration flask, the amount or percent of an analyte can be calculated.

Instrumental methods

The presence of many chemical substances can often be found by their response to some external signal. The magnitude of this response is proportional to the amount of substance present. Because electronic equipment is often necessary to generate the external signal and/or to detect the chemical response, these methods of quantitative analysis are called instrumental methods. Instrumental methods are indirect, so the detecting instrument requires **calibration** to measure the response initially from a sample with a known concentration of analyte. This is necessary to relate the response, which is often electrical, to the quantity of chemical substance. Standard solutions, containing known amounts of analyte, are first studied to calibrate the measuring instrument.

The type of instrumental method used for quantitative analysis varies with the nature of the substance being analyzed and with the amount of analyte thought to be present. While classical analytical methods are suitable for major amounts of analyte present in a sample, 1% or greater, instrumental methods are generally employed for amounts of analyte which may be less than 1% of the sample's total mass. Modern instrumental techniques are capable of analyzing the presence of a component which can comprise 0.0001% or less of its mass.

Table 1 names the more common instrumental techniques used for quantitative analysis and the type of signal they invoke from a chemical system.

A thorough understanding of chemistry is necessary in selecting the proper method for the quantitative determination of a substance. Lastly, the necessary calculations to convert the data obtained into its desired form must be carried out. Computer programs have helped considerably with this last step.

See also Nuclear magnetic resonance; Spectroscopy.

Further Reading

Harris, Daniel C. *Quantitative Chemical Analysis.* 4th ed. New York: W.H. Freeman & Company, 1995.

Skoog, Douglas A., and James J. Leary. *Principles of Instrumental Analysis.* 4th ed. Philadelphia: Saunders College Publishing, 1992.

Gordon A. Parker

KEY TERMS

Analyte—The component within a sample that is to be measured.

Classical analysis—Those procedures in which the desired component is reacted with a suitable chemical reagent, either by precipitate formation or titration.

Gravimetric analysis—A classical quantitative technique in which an added chemical forms an insoluble precipitate with the desired component. The precipitate is collected and weighed.

Instrumental analysis—A modern quantitative technique in which some property of the desired component (electrical, optical, thermal, etc.) is measured and related to the amount present.

Titrimetric analysis—A classical quantitative technique in which a solution of known concentration is reacted exactly with the desired component and a calculation preformed to find the amount present.

Quantum hall effect see **Hall effect**

Quantum mechanics

Quantum mechanics is the theory used to provide an understanding of the **behavior** of microscopic particles such as electrons and **atoms**. However, it is more than just a collection of formulae used by physicists and chemists to calculate, for example, where an **electron** might be. The quantum theory also introduced an entirely new way of thinking about very small objects that is strangely different from the way we think about macroscopic objects.

An example of a macroscopic object is a baseball. Whenever we throw a ball into the air it is a good idea to know where it will fall and how fast it will be traveling when it hits something. The most exact way to describe the ball's **motion** is by using classical mechanics which predicts the position and **velocity** of the ball at every instant during its flight. This approach fits our everyday experience since we are accustomed to seeing a ball move in a very well-defined path.

The problem comes when we try to apply the classical approach to microscopic objects. If an electron were just an exceptionally small ball, its motion would follow a path predicted by classical mechanics. However, experiments have shown that this is not the case. The best illustration of this is the "double-slit experiment," in which electrons are sent one at a time towards a wall with two small slits or holes. On the other side of the wall is a screen of some sort which detects where electrons hit, perhaps by making a spot. If one slit is covered, electrons can pass through the uncovered hole and strike the screen. The hits on the screen are directly behind the open slit, exactly what we would expect. We get the same result by opening the first slit and covering the second, only now the pattern of spots is behind the first hole.

What if both slits are open? Taking a single baseball and throwing it at the wall, we know it will either pass through one slit or the other. Of course, it might miss the holes and never make it to the screen, but that case is not particularly interesting. Our experience with macroscopic objects makes us think that the electrons will behave the same way so the screen should show electron hits only directly behind the holes. However, this is not what happens. Instead the spots are spread out over the entire screen, even in places that should be blocked by the wall as shown here. We'll see shortly that the only way for such a pattern to occur is if each electron somehow travels through both open slits! You might think that someone just made a terrible mistake when they conducted the experiment but many scientists have now verified this result (since they didn't want to believe it either after spending years **learning** classical mechanics). Apparently an entirely new way of thinking must be used for microscopic objects.

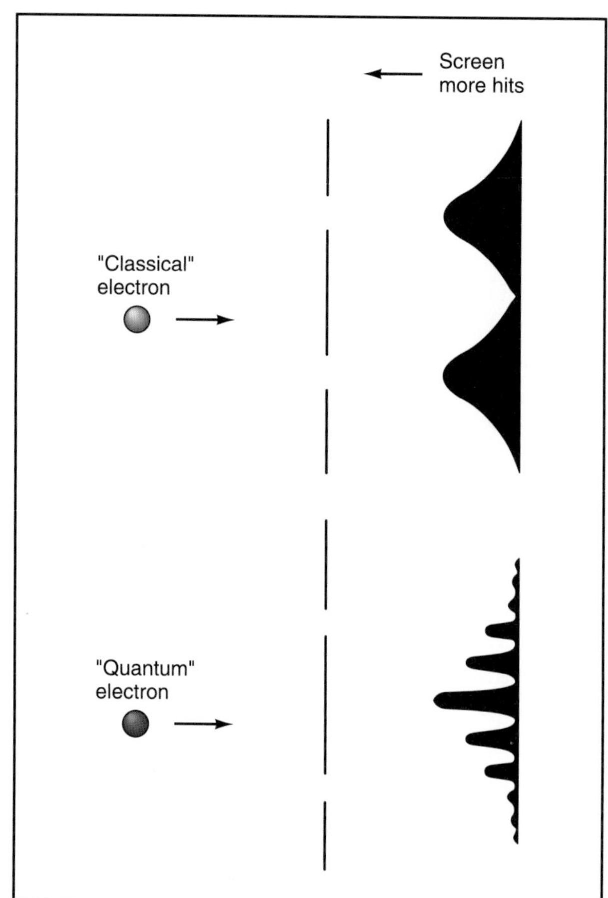

Figure 1.

The new approach

The pattern of electron hits that occurs when both slits are open appears very strange for particles. However, similar patterns are commonly produced by waves, which are disturbances in a medium that carry **energy**. Suppose you filled a bathtub with **water** and then tapped the surface with your finger after the water had become still. By disturbing the water you create a wave that will move on the surface away from your finger. The water acts as the medium through which the wave moves. If you place a piece of paper in the water, you will notice that when the wave passes through that location the paper will be disturbed. Then the paper becomes still as the wave proceeds on. This is an example of a *traveling wave* which carries the energy of your tap (in the disturbance) from place to place in the medium.

Now put a barrier in the bathtub with two openings in it. What happens if you start a wave moving toward the barrier? You would see that parts of the wave pass through the openings, splitting the original wave into two separate waves. As those new waves continue on the other side of the barrier, they recombine (or *interfere*). At some locations they reinforce and produce an even larger wave (*constructive interference*) and in others they **cancel** (*destructive interference*). You can experience the same effect by listening to the sound waves coming from two speakers producing the same musical note. If you move around (some **distance** away from the speakers), you will find places where the sound is louder. The two speakers are

producing separate but identical waves which are interfering. By marking the loudest locations on a **map**, you would draw an *interference pattern* similar to that made by the water wave after passing through the two-opening barrier. This is the same pattern that electrons make when both slits are open. The conclusion is that electrons act more like waves than they do like solid objects.

Let's try another wave experiment before talking more about electrons. Suppose instead of one wave, we produce a sequence of waves by tapping the water in a rhythm, or frequency. As the waves move through the water, the piece of paper would bob up and down at the same frequency. However, for certain rhythms the traveling waves and their **reflections** from the walls of the bathtub reinforce in an important way. The paper continues to bob up and down as before, but the disturbance in the water appears to be stationary (the wave does not travel). This is called a *standing wave*. The certain allowed frequencies that produce standing waves are determined by the dimensions of the bathtub whose walls confine the traveling waves. It is even easier to see a standing wave in the case of a guitar string. Striking the string sends many different traveling waves of different frequencies towards the ends which are held still. Standing waves occur for certain frequencies and those correspond to particular musical notes. Holding the string down at some point confines the waves more, and different standing waves appear on the string producing different notes. The energy of the wave can have any amount, depending on how hard the string was struck, and more energy translates into a louder sound (of an allowed frequency). We encounter these kinds of waves in our macroscopic world and because their motion can be understood using classical mechanics, they might be called *classical waves*.

Waves produce **interference** patterns like that of electrons in the double-slit experiment and we are accustomed to waves moving in less well-defined paths than solid objects. The new idea of quantum mechanics is to use waves to represent microscopic objects. These waves obey many of the properties of classical waves with an important conceptual difference. The "disturbance" of the new wave is not a physical motion of a medium, like the raised surface of water, it is an increased probability that the object is at a particular location. For an electron in the double-slit experiment, its traveling wave passes through both openings and interferes to produce a pattern of probability on the screen. The most probable locations (where constructive interference occurs) are the places where more electrons will hit and this is how the pattern of probabilities becomes a measurable pattern on the screen. This approach makes sense but we must give up the idea of predicting the path of objects such as electrons. Instead, in quantum mechanics we concentrate on determining the probability of obtaining a certain result when a measurement is made, for example of the position of an electron hit. This makes measurable quantities, called *observables*, particularly important.

Quantum results

Quantum mechanics requires advanced **mathematics** to give numerical predictions for the outcome of measurements. However, we can understand many significant results of the theory from the basic properties of the probability waves. An important example is the behavior of electrons within atoms. Since such electrons are confined in some manner, we expect that they must be represented by standing waves that correspond to a set of allowed frequencies. Quantum mechanics states that for this new type of wave, its frequency is proportional to the energy associated with the microscopic particle. Thus, we reach the conclusion that electrons within atoms can only exist in certain *states*, each of which corresponds to only one possible amount of energy. The energy of an electron in an atom is an example of an observable which is *quantized*, that is it comes in certain allowed amounts, called *quanta* (like quantities).

When an atom contains more than one electron, quantum mechanics predicts that two of the electrons both exist in the state with the lowest energy, called the *ground state*. The next eight electrons are in the state of the next highest energy, and so on following a specific relationship. This is the origin of the idea of electron "shells" or "orbits," although these are just convenient ways of talking about the states. The first shell is "filled" by two electrons, the second shell is filled by another eight, etc. This explains why some atoms try to combine with other atoms in chemical reactions. If an atom does not contain enough electrons to fill all of its lowest-energy shells completely, and it comes near another atom which has all its shells filled plus extra electrons, the atoms can become held together. The "bond" between the atoms comes from sharing the extra electrons. Thus quantum mechanics provides an understanding of **chemistry** by explaining why atoms combine, such as **sodium** and **chlorine** in **salt**.

This idea of electron states also explains why different atoms emit different colors of **light** when they are heated. Heating an object gives extra energy to the atoms inside it and this can transform an electron within an atom from one state to another of higher energy. The atom eventually loses the energy when the electron transforms back to the lower-energy state. Usually the extra energy is carried away in the form of light which we say was produced by the electron making a *transition*, or a change of its state. The difference in en-

ergy between the two states of the electron (before and after the transition) is the same for all atoms of the same kind. Thus, those atoms will always give off light of that energy, which corresponds to a specific **color**. Another kind of atom would have electron states with different energies (since the electron is confined differently) and so the same basic process would produce another color. Using this principle, we can determine which hot atoms are present in stars by measuring the exact colors in the emitted light.

Although quantum mechanics is relatively new, the theory has been extremely successful in explaining a wide range of phenomena. Another example would include a description of how electrons move in materials, like those that travel through the chips in a personal computer. Quantum mechanics is also used to understand superconductivity, the decay of nuclei, and how lasers work. The list could go on and on. A great number of scientists now use quantum mechanics daily in their efforts to better understand the behavior of microscopic parts of the universe. However, the basic ideas of the theory still conflict with our everyday experience and the argument about their meaning continues among the same physicists and chemists who use the quantum theory.

Development and debates

If thinking about electrons and other particles as waves seems unsettling, you're in good company. That idea has been hotly debated since the beginning of quantum mechanics by some of the greatest physicists. The search for a new theory actually began in the late 1800s when several phenomena involving light were discovered which could not be understood using classical mechanics. One of those phenomena is called "blackbody radiation," the behavior of light within a box held at a certain **temperature**. It had been known for many years that light often behaves like a wave so physicists attempted to explain **blackbody radiation** as a case of standing waves within the box. Those standing waves were treated classically, with only certain allowed frequencies but any amount of energy. The results of that approach seemed promising, but did not quite agree with the experiments.

In 1900, Max Planck published a paper that explained blackbody **radiation**, but to do so he had to assume that the energy of the standing waves was quantized. Since the frequencies already had only certain allowed values, he made the simplest assumption possible, stating that the energy was equal to the frequency multiplied by a constant. That constant was written as h and it was later named after him. Planck did not know why the energy had to be quantized; he simply had to introduce the idea of energy quanta to make the theory agree with the experiments. The quantum idea was used by other physicists including Albert Einstein to explain more phenomena involving light which had eluded the classical approach. Einstein thought of light as being a wave "packet" which became known as a *photon.*

The concepts of energy quanta and photons were not accepted immediately, since most physicists believed that light was a classical wave. However, at least the new idea was not totally foreign since Isaac Newton had attempted to treat light as particles about 200 years before. Eventually it was accepted that a light wave could behave like a particle in some circumstances. However, in 1924 Louis de Broglie suggested that the opposite might also occur; that a solid object could correspond to what he called a *matter wave.* This was a revolutionary and unsettling idea, but many physicists set about to determine where it might lead. In 1926, Erwin Schroedinger developed an equation for those waves so that the theory could be used to make numerical predictions for the behavior of many physical systems. The Schroedinger equation proved to be extremely useful in describing microscopic objects and in fact it remains the cornerstone of quantum mechanics even now. However, the real breakthrough was that energy quanta came naturally from the mathematics instead of having to be assumed as Planck had done. This was because the equation for **matter** waves was similar, but different in a subtle way from the equation for classical waves. Schroedinger called his new approach *wave mechanics* and the name quantum mechanics came later.

The usefulness of quantum mechanics can hardly be argued. However, the basic concepts were a source of debate from the very beginning. That tradition is best exemplified by the historical debates that started in the late 1920s between two giants of **physics**, Einstein and Niels Bohr. In 1927 Werner Heisenberg had recognized an important result of treating microscopic particles as waves that described their probability of being in a certain location. Heisenberg derived the *uncertainty relation* that said the uncertainty in a measurement of a particle's position multiplied by the uncertainty in its velocity must always be larger than a specific constant, which unsurprisingly includes Planck's constant. For example, if we exactly measure where a particle is at a particular time (uncertainty in position is almost **zero**), then we do not have any information about the velocity of the particle (uncertainty in velocity is extremely large). That means we have no idea were the particle is going. The uncertainty **relation** restates that we cannot think of well-defined paths for microscopic particles.

Many different interpretations arose to make sense of this and other facets of quantum mechanics, and Bohr

was the leading proponent of the *Copenhagen interpretation* (since that is where he was from). Today this is the accepted viewpoint among most, but not all physicists. The Copenhagen interpretation considers the uncertainty relation to express a fundamental **limit** to how accurately we can measure properties of microscopic particles. A way to understand this is to think how we detect a macroscopic object such as a car. We actually detect something that has bounced off the car, such as light. Suppose instead of light, we use a baseball (not really recommended) and decide whether or not a car was as at a location at a particular instant based on whether the ball bounces back to us after being thrown. The car is much larger and heavier than the baseball so we can detect where the car is without significantly disturbing the path of the **automobile**. However, what would happen if we tried to use a baseball to detect another baseball? We could find where the ball to be measured was located, but in the process it would be knocked off its original path into a new direction. If on the other hand we bounce a ping pong ball off a baseball, we have less exact information where the baseball is at a certain instant, but at least we disturb its path less. In every instance we have to interact (disturb) with an object to measure its position and the uncertainty relation simply reflects this. Why don't we notice this everyday? The answer is in the size of Planck's constant. It is so small that for macroscopic objects like a baseball the uncertainties in position and velocity are unmeasurable so the ball moves in a well-defined path. Quantum mechanics is actually around us all the time, but we just don't notice it.

Einstein had used quantum ideas, but he remained dissatisfied with quantum mechanics and particularly with Bohr's interpretation. Beginning in 1927 they began a public debate over the meaning of the new theory that raged for many years in scientific publications and often in person at conferences. Einstein felt that there must be some experiment which permitted exact measurements of position and velocity for microscopic objects. He continually challenged Bohr with suggestions of new experiments. However, in every instance Bohr was able to refute Einstein's experiments with arguments of his own that supported the Copenhagen interpretation. Einstein eventually gave up that approach but still maintained that quantum mechanics was somehow incomplete and that once the missing ideas were found, uncertainty would disappear. This search for a missing piece of the puzzle, if there is one, continues as physicists attempt to devise new experiments to more clearly understand the meaning of quantum mechanics.

KEY TERMS

Classical mechanics—A collection of theories, all derived from a few basic principles, that can be used to describe the motion of macroscopic objects.

Macroscopic—This term describes large-scale objects like those we directly interact with on an everyday basis.

Microscopic—This term describes extremely small-scale objects such as electrons and atoms with which we seldom interact on an individual basis as we do with macroscopic objects.

Observable—A physical quantity, like position, velocity or energy, which can be determined by a measurement.

Planck's constant—A constant written as h which was introduced by Max Planck in his quantum theory and which appears in every formula of quantum mechanics.

Probability—The likelihood that a certain event will occur. If something happens half of the time, its probability is 1/2 = 0.5 = 50 %.

Quantum (plural is Quanta)—An allowed amount of an observable.

Wave—Classically, a disturbance of a medium which carries energy from one place to another.

Further Reading

Albert, A. Z. *Quantum Mechanics and Experience.* Cambridge, MA: Harvard University Press, 1992.

Gregory, B. *Inventing Reality: Physics as Language.* New York: John Wiley & Sons, 1990.

Han, M. Y. *The Probable Universe.* Blue Ridge Summit, PA: TAB Books, 1993.

James J. Carroll.

Quantum number

A quantum number is a number that specifies the particular state of **motion** an atom or **molecule** is in and, usually, the **energy** of that motion.

By 1900, several phenomena were recognized that could not be explained by accepted scientific theories. One such phenomenon was the behavior of **light** itself. In 1900, however, Max Planck (1858-1947) developed a new theory that successfully described the nature of light. Part of this theory required that light having a cer-

tain **frequency** also had to have a certain specific energy. One way to state this is that the energy of a certain frequency of light was quantized. Light was considered as acting as a particle of energy, later called a **photon**.

Some of the unexplainable phenomena were related to **atoms** and molecules, and in 1925-27 Werner Heisenberg (1901-1976) and Erwin Schrödinger (1887-1961) considered that subatomic particles like electrons can act as waves (just like light waves can act as particles) and simultaneously developed **quantum mechanics**. They used different ways to describe their theories mathematically, and today most scientists use Schrödinger's way. Since Schrödinger used wave equations to describe the behavior of electrons in atoms and molecules, quantum mechanics is sometimes also referred to as wave mechanics.

Schrödinger's wave mechanics assumed that the motions of electrons, which are the basis of almost all **chemistry**, can also be described mathematically as waves, and so the idea of the wave function was established. A wave function is an equation that describes the motion of an **electron**. An electron whose motion can be described by a particular wave function is said to be in a particular state.

One of the more unusual (but useful) parts of Schrödinger's wave functions is that an electron having a particular state has a certain, specific quantity of energy. That is, wave mechanics predicts that the energy of electrons is quantized. In almost all of the wave functions, a whole number (i.e. either 1, 2, 3, or 4, ...) is part of the wave equation. This whole number is a quantum number and, for electrons in atoms, it is called the principle quantum number. The value of the energy associated with that wave function depends on the quantum number. Therefore, the quantum number ultimately predicts what value of energy an electron in a state will have. Other quantum numbers are related to other properties of an electron. In particular, the value of the angular **momentum** of an electron (that is, the momentum that the electron has as it circles about the nucleus in an atom) is also quantized, and it is related to a whole-number quantum number called the angular momentum quantum number. There is also a magnetic quantum number for electrons in atoms, which is related to how much an electron in an atom interacts with a magnetic field. The amounts of such interactions are also quantized, that is, they can have only certain values and no others.

Molecules have other types of motions that are associated with certain values of energy. For example, the atoms in molecules vibrate back and forth. Molecules in the gas phase can also rotate. For each of these kinds of motions, quantum mechanics predicts that the motions can be expressed using a wave function. Quantum mechanics further predicts that each wave function will have a certain quantized value of energy, and that this energy can be expressed by a quantum number. Hence, vibrational and rotational motions also have quantum numbers associated with them. These quantum numbers are also whole numbers.

Quantum mechanics predicts a previously- unknown property of subatomic particles that is called spin. All electrons, for example, have spin. So do protons and neutrons. However, quantum mechanics predicts that the quantum number associated with spin does not necessarily have to be a whole number; it can also be a half-integer number. For electrons, the quantum number for spin is 1/2 and, since it can spin in either one of two directions, that is, an electron can behave as if it is spinning either clockwise or counterclockwise, electrons are labeled as having spin quantum numbers of either +1/2 or -1/2. The curious thing about the spin quantum number is that it cannot have any value other than 1/2 for an electron. Other subatomic particles have their own, characteristic spin quantum numbers. Including spin, electrons in atoms can be assigned four separate quantum numbers: a principle quantum number, an angular momentum quantum number, a magnetic quantum number, and a spin quantum number. Stating the values of these four numbers expresses the complete energy state of an electron in an atom.

See also Light, theories of; Spin of subatomic particles.

KEY TERMS

Wave function—The wave equation that describes the motion of a subatomic particle.

Further Reading

Atkins, P. *Quanta: A Handbook of Concepts*. Oxford: Oxford University Press, 1991.

Han, M.Y. *The Secret Life of Quanta*. Blue Ridge Summit, PA: TAB Books, Inc., 1990.

David W. Ball

Quarks

Quarks are basic building blocks of all **matter**.

One of the greatest triumphs of modern science has been the discovery that matter—everything we see around us—is made up of smaller things. **Water** consists of molecules, and molecules are made of atoms—in

water's case, two **hydrogen atoms** and one **oxygen** atom. In turn, the atoms are made of electrons, protons, and neutrons. But what are these parts of atoms made from? Electrons are point particles, and so fundamental. The protons are neutrons are made of *quarks*.

The subatomic zoo

By the 1960s physicists had discovered a large number of new **subatomic particles** that, like the **proton** and **neutron**, attract one another through the nuclear **force** (also called the strong force). Classification of all the particles, such as those known as pions, kaons, and others only seen after the collisions of cosmic rays, was reminiscent of the chemist's classification of elements into the **periodic table**, which helped reveal their fundamental structure. Theoretical physicists set out to do something similar with all the new nuclear particles.

The American physicist Murray Gell-Mann, together with the Israeli physicist Yuval Ne'eman and, independently, the American George Zweig, introduced the idea of three basic building blocks for all particles that felt the nuclear force. Proving that physicists are not without a sense of humor, Gell-Mann called them "quarks," after a line in the James Joyce novel *Finnegans Wake*: "Three quarks for Muster Mark!" They introduced three quarks and gave them names of "up," "down," and "strange"—the names themselves are just labels, called a quark's *flavor*. They found that they were able to describe all baryons (such as the proton and the neutron) as combinations of three quarks, and mesons (such as the more rare pions, kaons, and others) with combinations of two quarks.

The quarks had to have fractional **electric charge** (of the **electron** charge) for this scheme to work, a somewhat radical idea. The up quark was proposed to have a charge of +(2/3)e (where -e is the charge on the electron), the down quark -(1/3)e, and the strange quark -(1/3)e. Then the proton could be built from two up quarks and a down, (up+up+down), and the neutron would be opposite (down+down+up). All ordinary matter that we see around us is made of up and down quarks. Quarks also have their associated antiparticles: the anti-up quark, the anti-down, and the anti-strange. The pion is an up+anti-down. Quarks also have the quantum-mechanical property of spin, equal to 1/2. ("h-bar" is proportional to Planck's constant.)

As a model this scheme could describe baryons and mesons. But did quarks actually exist? Using particle **accelerators**, Maurice Jacob and Peter Lanshoff smashed high-energy electrons into protons in 1980. They found that some electrons bounced off at large angles—a few even backwards, more than would be expected if the proton's charge was uniformly spread across its **volume**. Their results were consistent with the idea that the proton was instead composed of three hard, point-like particles. This and other experiments afterward established the physical reality of quarks.

Questions about quarks

But two questions remained for physicists to answer. The first was, if quarks had spin-1/2, and were therefore subject to the Pauli Exclusion Principle (which says that two identical spin-1/2 particles cannot be together in the same arrangement), how then could two up quarks be inside the proton at the same time? Physicists, ever inventive, solved this problem with the introduction of **color**. Each quark could also have one of three colors, which, in the whimsical ways of the quark concept, were given the names red, green, and blue. Of course, quarks do not *actually* have a color as we refer to it in every-day life—again, the colors are just labels that could just as easily been given any other names. If the two up quarks in a proton were different colors, Dr. Pauli would be happy and the quark model could go on, with the rule that all combinations of quarks had to be overall colorless: red+anti-red, for example, or red+green+blue (which, as seen through a **prism**, are what make up white light).

The second was perhaps more puzzling. Physicists found that no matter how much **energy** they used, no matter how hard they smashed things into protons or protons into things, they never found a quark all on its own. Quarks seemed to travel in well-hidden packs, only inside baryons and mesons.

This problem was solved with the introduction of a sophisticated mathematical treatment of quarks, called *quantum chromodynamics*, or QCD. This theory was borrowed from the extremely successful theory used with electric charge, quantum electrodynamics, which had been invented in the 1940s, and then enhanced. QCD gave reality to the idea of color, considering it akin to electric charge: quarks were attracted to one another through their color "charges." Whereas electrons attract and repel other electric charges by exchanging a **photon**, quarks do so by a new particle called the *gluon*, from the word "glue." But unlike photons, which have no electric charge, gluons do have a color charge, or rather, combinations of color charges. A red quark can emit a gluon and turn into a green quark. The emitted gluon will have the color combination of red+anti-green. In fact, there are eight different gluons.

Putting this all together in the QCD theory, physicists found that because gluons have color, they will attract one another. The result is that quarks do not like to be separated—they prefer to remain near one another, within the diameter of the proton (about 10^{-15} m). But try to separate them, and they emit more and more gluons until every-

thing breaks apart into new combinations of quarks, antiquarks, and gluons—that is, more particles, but no individual quarks or gluons. This strange property is called *asymptotic freedom.* Unlike the force between electric charges, which decreases with **distance**, the force between color charges *increases* with distance, and sharply.

What are the masses of the quarks? This is a difficult question, since they're never seen alone. The up and down quarks appear to have masses of about 1/3 that of the proton, and the strange quark about 1/2 that of the proton. Quantum chromodynamics and its predictions has been well-established by many different experiments, and it is the accepted theory of the nuclear force.

More particles, more quarks

As elementary particle **physics** progressed through the 1970s and 1980s, physicists found more and more exotic particles, such as the psi-meson in 1974, whose **mass** is about three times that of the proton. An accurate description of its observed properties required the addition of a fourth quark, the "charm" quark with an electric charge of +(2/3)e. In 1977 discovery of the upsilon-meson (ten times the proton mass) required the introduction of the "bottom" quark, with charge -(1/3)e. A sixth quark, the "top" quark, was found in 1994 at the Fermilab National Accelerator in Illinois, with a charge of +(2/3)e and a mass of about 180 times the proton mass, which is equivalent to that of a gold atom! All of these three heavier quarks decay very, very quickly into other particles (including the other quarks).

Scientists now believe there are only six quarks, and that quarks themselves have no internal particles—like electrons, quarks are point particles. Together with electrons and the other leptons, they accurately describe the world as it is known at the beginning of the twenty-first century. Poor Muster Mark seemed to have received only half as many quarks as he might have.

David Appell

Quartz see **Crystal**
Quartz see **Minerals**

Quasar

Quasars were first detected as celestial **radio** sources by radio telescopes in about 1950. At the time of their discovery, quasars were thought only to emit **radio waves**, as they could not be seen by optical means. As positional determinations for these sources became more accurate, scientists began to suspect that faint optical light sources might also be the sources of the radio waves that had been recorded.

Allan Sandage first reported several faint starlike objects as optical counterparts to radio sources in 1960. Maarten Schmidt in 1963 first found and identified **hydrogen emission** (bright) lines in the **spectrum** of the radio source 30273. In analyzing the data, Schmidt found that 30273 is not a **star** but is an extragalactic (outside the **Milky Way**) object traveling away from the Milky Way at about a 27,300 mi/sec (44,000 km/sec) **velocity**.

Schmidt soon found several other optical counterparts to radio sources with even stronger emissions as indicated by their spectra. These extragalactic objects were first called Quasi-Stellar Objects (QSOs); this name was soon shortened to quasar, the name now usually given to this class of objects.

In 1964, Schmidt identified the unique optical properties of quasars as listed:

1. Quasars are starlike objects identified with radio sources.
2. They have **variable** brightnesses.
3. They have large fluxes of ultraviolet **radiation**.
4. They show broad emission lines in their spectra that are identified with hydrogen and the ions of other elements.
5. Their spectra indicate rapid **motion** away from the Milky Way.

Many more quasars were discovered in the late 1960s and in the 1970s. Some of them were found at positions where no radio sources were known; these are known as radio-quiet quasars. Also, absorption (dark) spectroscopic lines were discovered in the spectra of some quasars. About 10,000 quasars have been discovered so far, and the positions, magnitudes, and spectra for 7,315 quasars have been recorded and published.

The nature of quasars

The observations described above showed that quasars are extragalactic, but many questions about their distances and nature remained unanswered. Assuming that modern astronomical theory holds true for these bodies, quasars are the most distant, and from their brightnesses, also the most luminous objects known. The most luminous ones are thousands of times more energetic than larger, luminous galaxies such as the Milky Way and Messier 31.

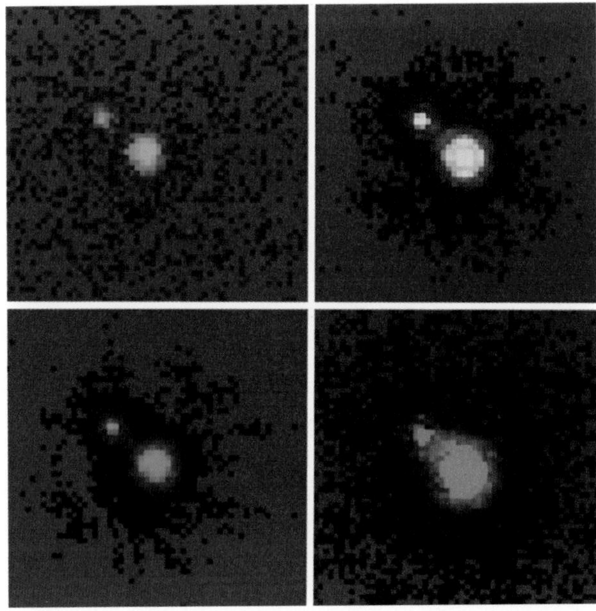

Hubble Space Telescope (HST) views of the distant quasar 120+101 indicate that its image has been split by gravitational lensing, a phenomenon by which the pull of a massive object, such as a galaxy, can bend the light of another object when the light passes near or through the massive object.

In spite of this, quasar brightnesses are quite variable, changing in times of hours and sometimes doubling their luminosities in as short a timespan as a week. This means that the main source or sources of their luminosity must be situated in a **volume** of **space** not much larger than a **solar system**, which light can cross in 12 hours. This is an enormous power source (luminosity) to fit into such a relatively small volume.

Astrophysics supplies two possible sources for such enormous **energy** from such small regions. They are:

• 1. **Matter** falling into an enormous **black hole** with a **mass** on the order of 10^{10} solar masses or more, where much of the gravitational energy released during the matter's infall towards the black hole is converted into light and other radiation in an **accretion disk** of matter surrounding the black hole.

• 2. The annihilation of ordinary matter (electrons, protons, etc.) and antimatter (positrons, etc.) as they collide at enormous rates.

The first of those is favored today by most astronomers, because there is independent evidence for the existence of such massive black holes in galaxies. The second possibility would produce enormous intensities of gamma radiation at definite energies (wavelengths); these have not been observed by the Gamma Ray Observatory (GRO) spacecraft that the NASA launched into **orbit** around the **Earth** in 1991.

These and other difficulties, which follow from the assumption that the quasars conform to Hubble's Law for the distant galaxies, led Halton Arp to suggest an alternative hypothesis. He noticed that a considerable number of quasars occur in pairs situated approximately symmetrical on opposite sides of peculiar-looking galaxies whose spectra suggest they are much closer to the Milky Way than do the spectra for the quasars. Luminous "bridges" of matter sometimes appear to join the central **galaxy** to one or both quasars. These interesting cases led Arp to suggest that quasars have been ejected by an unknown mechanism from galaxies that are much closer than the spectra observed for the quasars imply. This hypothesis makes these quasars much less luminous than they would be were they much more distant than the central galaxy.

However, Arp's hypotheses also has at least three important difficulties.

• 1. An unknown mechanism is needed to propel two large objects out of each source galaxy at velocities that are comparable with the **vacuum** velocity of light.

• 2. If quasars are ejected from peculiar galaxies in **random** directions, some of them should be ejected towards the Milky Way, and their spectra would be very different.

• 3. In some cases, closer examination has shown that the apparent bridge of gas connecting quasar and galaxy is not a bridge, but rather a streamer of gas associated with a foreground galaxy, superimposed by chance alignment with the more distant quasars.

Additional support for the "cosmological" interpretation of quasars—that they follow the Hubble law and really are as distant and luminous as that implies—comes from two very significant observations: (1) quasars have been found within clusters of normal galaxies having the same kind of spectra, thus verifying that the spectra are cosmological; and (2) most nearby quasars are embedded within detectable galaxies, which share the same kind of spectra, thereby showing not only that the type of spectra is cosmological, but also that quasars reside in the centers of galaxies. This information has persuaded most astronomers that quasars exist at very large distances, are seen as they were long ago, and are associated with an early phase in the **evolution** of galaxies.

The blazars are optically violently variable quasars and **BL Lacertae objects** that comprise a subgroup of quasars. The spectra of BL Lacertae objects make it difficult to determine the nature of these objects. BL Lacertae was found to be at the center of a giant elliptical galaxy, which Joseph Miller at Lick Observatory found in 1978.

Another interesting phenomenon discovered in the last 15 years has been the detection of double and multiple quasars that are very close together. The symmetric patterns of these multiple quasars are most readily explained by gravitational lensing of a very distant quasar's light by a galaxy that is too distant to be detected visually but is nevertheless between the quasar and the Milky Way. The lensing is caused by the bending of light in a strong gravitational field (as predicted by the General Theory of Relativity). Among the most recent examples is the Cloverleaf Quasar, where presumably an unseen galaxy between a quasar and the Milky Way has formed four images of the quasar.

The detection of galaxies associated with blazars and of multiple images of quasars presumably formed by gravitational lensing by galaxies too distant to the be detected otherwise has favored the hypothesis that the quasars are similar to distant galaxies, conform to Hubble's Law, and represent a phenomenon that was more common in earlier stages of the development of our universe than it is at present.

The most distant quasar known was discovered in November 1999 by NASA's BATSE (Burst and Transient Source Experiment) **satellite**. Known by the less than picturesque name 4C 71.07, this quasar appears to be about 11 billion light years away. The presently favored theory of the origin and evolution of our universe, the **big bang theory**, hypothesizes that our universe began to explosively expand from a singularity known as the "big bang" event some 12-15 billion years ago, and it has been expanding ever since. We therefore see quasar 4C 71.07 as it existed perhaps as little as a billion years after the big bang: a long time by human standards, but near infancy by the standards of the Universe. The big bang theory is driving the search for closer, later quasars, in order to fill in the gap in the evolution of the universe between the most distant (hence earliest) quasars now known, and the background remnant radiation from the primeval fireball of the early universe, which comes to us from the time when matter and radiation decoupled in the early evolution of the universe. Present theory estimates that this stage of the universe's evolution occurred about 700,000 years after the "big bang" singularity.

The present status

The fact is that, after over 30 years of quasar research, many difficulties still remain with the presently favored hypothesis that the quasars conform to Hubble's Law and are the most distant, fastest, and most luminous large objects known in our universe. But no other hypothesis explains them so well, and the general consensus among astronomers is that quasars are young galaxies in a very active and energetic phase. Vestigial activity at the core of the Milky Way, and the energetic sources in **active galactic nuclei**, suggest that many of today's galaxies harbor aged quasars that may once have been among the brightest in the universe. Recent observations have suggested that quasars may have formed as the result of collisions and mergers of galaxies long ago, when galaxies were young and the universe was more dense than it is today. Thus quasars, apart from their own fascinating properties, have much to tell us about the evolution of the cosmos itself.

Quetzal

The quetzal (*Pharomachrus mocinno*), also known as the resplendent quetzal or magnificent quetzal, is an astonishingly beautiful bird of tropical **forests**. It is a member of the trogon family (Trogonidae).

The quetzal has a body length of 14 in (36 cm); in addition, the male has impressive tail streamers as long as 25 in (64 cm). The mature male has a shining green body color, with a crimson belly, white under the tail, and two long, green tail-streamers. The male also has a laterally compressed, green "helmet" that extends forward over the face to the base of its bill. The female and young are a duller-green color, with a gray-green belly, a red patch and black-and-white barring under the tail. They lack the tail-streamers and crest found on the male.

The quetzal inhabits humid, montane cloud-forest, occurring in the **tree** canopy and along stand edges. It occurs over an altitudinal range of about 4,000 to 10,000 ft (1,200-3,000 m). These **birds** exist either in pairs or solitude, but may be present in small groups when feeding on a fruit-laden tree or during the non-breeding season. Quetzal feeds on **fruits**, **insects** and other **invertebrates**, small **frogs**, and lizards. It has a melodious territorial song, and several sharp call notes. The quetzal breeds from March to June, laying 2 eggs in a tree-cavity nest, and sometimes rearing two broods in a season.

The quetzal ranges widely over tropical Central America, occurring in Costa Rica, El Salvador, Guatemala, Honduras, southern Mexico, Nicaragua, and Panama. Much of its original **habitat** has been lost through **deforestation** to develop agricultural land, or damaged through timber harvesting. Quetzals are somewhat tolerant of disturbances to its habitat, as long as remnants of woodland remain, and there are sufficient fruit-bearing and cavity-containing trees for feeding and

breeding. Although not listed as an **endangered species** by the IUCN (International Union for the Conservation of Nature), the quetzal is not as abundant overall as it once was.

The quetzal held great cultural and religious significance to the Maya, Aztecs, and other indigenous peoples of Central America. It was a prominent, sacred image in artwork and legends. To harm these beautiful birds was forbidden. The quetzal is the national bird of Guatemala, and the name of Guatemalan currency.

Additional species of quetzals from **South America** include: the crested quetzal (*Pharomachrus antisianus*), the golden-headed quetzal (*P. auriceps*), the pavonine quetzal (*P. pavoninus*), and the white-tipped quetzal (*P. fulgidus*).

Bill Freedman

Quince see **Rose family**

Quinine

Quinine is an **alkaloid** obtained from the **bark** of several species of the cinchona **tree**. Until the development of synthetic drugs, quinine was used as the primary treatment of **malaria**, a **disease** that kills over 100 million people a year. The cinchona tree is native to the eastern slopes of the Andes Mountains in **South America**. Today, the tree is cultivated throughout Central and South America, Indonesia, India, and some areas in **Africa**. The cinchona tree contains more than 20 alkaloids of which quinine and quinidine are the most important. Quinidine is used to treat cardiac arrhythmias.

History

South American Indians have been using cinchona bark to treat fevers for many centuries. Spanish conquerors learned of quinine's medicinal uses in Peru, at the beginning of the 17th Century. Use of the powdered "Peruvian bark" was first recorded in religious writings by the Jesuits in 1633. The Jesuit fathers were the primary exporters and importers of quinine during this time and the bark became known as "Jesuit bark." The cinchona tree was named for the wife of the Spanish viceroy to Peru, Countess Anna del Chinchón. A popular story is that the Countess was cured of the *ague* (a name for malaria the time) in 1638. The use of quinine for fevers was included in medical literature in 1643. Quinine did not gain wide acceptance in the medical community until Charles II was cured of the *ague* by a London apothecary at the end of the 17th century. Quinine was officially recognized in an edition of the London Pharmacopoeia as "Cortex Peruanus" in 1677. Thus began the quest for quinine. In 1735, Joseph de Jussieu, a French botanist, accompanied the first non-Spanish expedition to South America and collected detailed information about the cinchona trees. Unfortunately, as Jussieu was preparing to return to France, after 30 years of research, someone stole all his work. Charles Marie de la Condamine, leader of Jussieu's expedition, tried unsuccessfully to transfer seedlings to **Europe**. Information about the cinchona tree and its medicinal bark was slow to reach Europe. Scientific studies about quinine were first published by Alexander von Humboldt and Aimé Bonpland in the first part of the 18th century. The quinine alkaloid was separated from the powdered bark and named "quinine" in 1820 by two French doctors. The name quinine comes from the Amerindian word for the cinchona tree, quinaquina, which means "bark of barks." As European countries continued extensive colonization in Africa, India and South America, the need for quinine was great, because of malaria. The Dutch and British cultivated cinchona trees in their East Indian colonies but the quinine content was very low in those species. A British collector, Charles Ledger, obtained some **seeds** of a relatively potent Bolivian species, *Cinchona ledgeriana*. England, reluctant to purchase more trees that were possibly low in quinine content, refused to buy the seeds. The Dutch bought the seeds from Ledger, planted them in Java, and came to monopolize the world's supply of quinine for close to 100 years. During World War II, the Japanese took control of Java. The Dutch took seeds out of Java but had no time to grow new trees to supply troops stationed in the tropics with quinine. The United States sent a group of botanists to Columbia to obtain enough quinine to use throughout the war. In 1944, synthetic quinine was developed by American scientists. Synthetic quinine proved to be very effective against malaria and had fewer side effects, and the need for natural quinine subsided. Over the years, the causative malarial parasite became resistant to synthetic quinine preparations. Interestingly, the **parasites** have not developed a full resistance to natural quinine.

Uses and manufacture

The chemical composition of quinine is $C_2OH_24N_2O_2{\cdot}H_2O$. Quinine is derived from cinchona bark, and mixed with lime. The bark and lime mixture is extracted with hot paraffin oil, filtered, and shaken with **sulfuric acid**. This solution is neutralized with **sodium carbonate**. As the solution cools, quinine sulfate crystallizes out. To obtain pure quinine, the quinine sulfate is

treated with **ammonia**. Crystalline quinine is a white, extremely bitter powder. The powdered bark can also be treated with solvents, such as toluene, or amyl **alcohol** to extract the quinine. Current **biotechnology** has developed a method to produce quinine by culturing **plant** cells. Grown in test tubes that contain a special medium that contains absorbent **resins**, the cells can be manipulated to release quinine, which is absorbed by the resin and then extracted. This method has high yields but is extremely expensive and fragile.

Medicinally, quinine is best known for its treatment of malaria. Quinine does not cure the disease, but treats the fever and other related symptoms. Pharmacologically, quinine is toxic to many **bacteria** and one-celled organisms, such as **yeast** and plasmodia. It also has antipyretic (fever-reducing), analgesic (pain-relieving), and local anesthetic properties. Quinine concentrates in the red **blood** cells and is thought to interfere with the protein and glucose synthesis of the malaria parasite. With treatment, the parasites disappear from the blood stream. Many malarial victims have a recurrence of the disease because quinine does not kill the parasites living outside the red blood cells. Eventually, the parasites make their way into the blood stream, and the victim has a relapse. Quinine is also used to treat myotonic dystrophy (muscle weakness, usually facial) and muscle cramps associated with early kidney failure. The toxic side effects of quinine, called Cinchonism, include dizziness, tinnitus (ringing in ears), **vision** disturbances, nausea, and vomiting. Extreme effects of excessive quinine use include blindness and deafness.

Quinine also has non-medicinal uses, such as in preparations for the treatment of sunburn. It is also used in liqueurs, bitters, and condiments. The best known nonmedicinal use is its addition to tonic **water** and soft drinks. The addition of quinine to water dates from the days of British rule in India-quinine was added to water as a prevention against malaria. About 40% of the quinine produced is used by the food and drug industry, the rest is used medicinally. In the United States, beverages made with quinine may contain not more than 83 parts per million cinchona alkaloids.

Further Reading

Cartwright, F. *Disease and History.* Crowell, 1972.

Gray, J. *Man Against Disease-Preventive Medicine.* New York: Oxford University Press, 1979.

Lewington, Anna. *Plants for People.* New York: Oxford University Press, 1990.

Christine Miner Minderovic

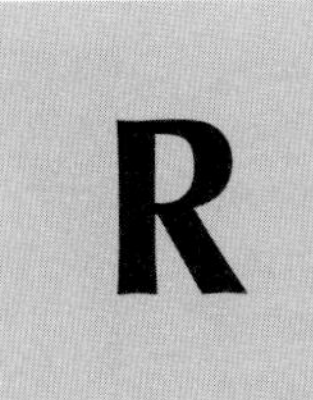

Rabbits see **Lagomorphs**

Rabies

Rabies is a viral **brain** disease that is almost always fatal if it is allowed to develop and is not prevented with prompt treatment. The disease, which typically spreads to humans from animals through a scratch or a bite, causes **inflammation** of the brain. The disease is also called hydrophobia (meaning fear of **water**) because it causes painful muscle spasms in the throat that prevent swallowing. In fact, this is what leads to fatalities in untreated cases: victims become dehydrated and die. Carriers of rabies include dogs, **cats**, **bats**, **skunks**, **raccoons,** and foxes; **rodents** are not likely to be infected. About 70% of rabies cases develop from wild **animal** bites that break the skin. Though a **vaccine** used first in 1885 is widely used, fatalities still occur due to rabies. Most fatalities take place in **Africa** and **Asia**, but some also occur in the United States. The cost of efforts to prevent rabies in the United States may be as high as $1 billion per year.

From animal to man

While many animal diseases cannot be passed from animal to man, rabies has long been known as an easy traveler from one species to the next. The disease was known among ancient people. The very name rabies, Latin for "rage" or "madness," suggests the fear with which early men and women must have viewed the disease. For centuries there was no treatment, and the disease was left to run its rapid course leading to death.

Rabies is described in medical writings dating from 300 B.C., but the method of transmission or contagion was not recognized until 1804. In 1884 the French bacteriologist Louis Pasteur developed a preventive vaccine against rabies, and modifications of Pasteur's methods are still used in rabies therapy today. The Pasteur program, or variations of it, has greatly reduced the fatalities in humans from rabies. Modern treatment, following a bite by a rabid or presumed rabid animal, consists of immediate and thorough cleansing of the bite wound and injection into the wound and elsewhere of hyperimmune antirabies serum. A 14-30 day course of daily injections of rabies vaccine is then given; booster doses are given 10 days after this course and again 20 days later.

The standard vaccine contains inactivated rabies **virus** grown in duck eggs. It is highly effective but causes neuroparalysis in about one in 30,000 persons receiving it. In the 1970s a new vaccine was developed in France and the United States that contains virus prepared from human cells grown in the laboratory. This vaccine is safer and requires a shorter course of injections. With the widespread use of vaccine, rabies cases in the U.S. declined to fewer than five per year.

The transmission of rabies is almost invariably through the bite of an infected animal. The fact that the virus is eliminated in the saliva is of great significance, and unless saliva is introduced beneath the skin, the disease is seldom transmitted. The virus has been demonstrated in the saliva of dogs 3-8 days before the onset of symptoms. However, it has also been reported that only about 50-60% of the infected dogs shed the virus in the saliva. Rare cases of rabies have been reported where only clawing and scratching occurred, or where the skin was contaminated with saliva. The virus is most concentrated in the central **nervous system** and saliva, but it has also been demonstrated in various organs of the body and milk from infected animals.

In humans, the rabies virus, in addition to entering the body by the usual route through skin broken by a bite or scratch, can enter the body through intact mucous membranes, can be inhaled as an aerosol, and can be transplanted in an infected corneal **graft**. These four cases are the only virologically documented examples of transmission of rabies from one person to another. Vertical transmission from mother to fetus and from lactating mother to suckling young has been described in nonhuman **mammals**.

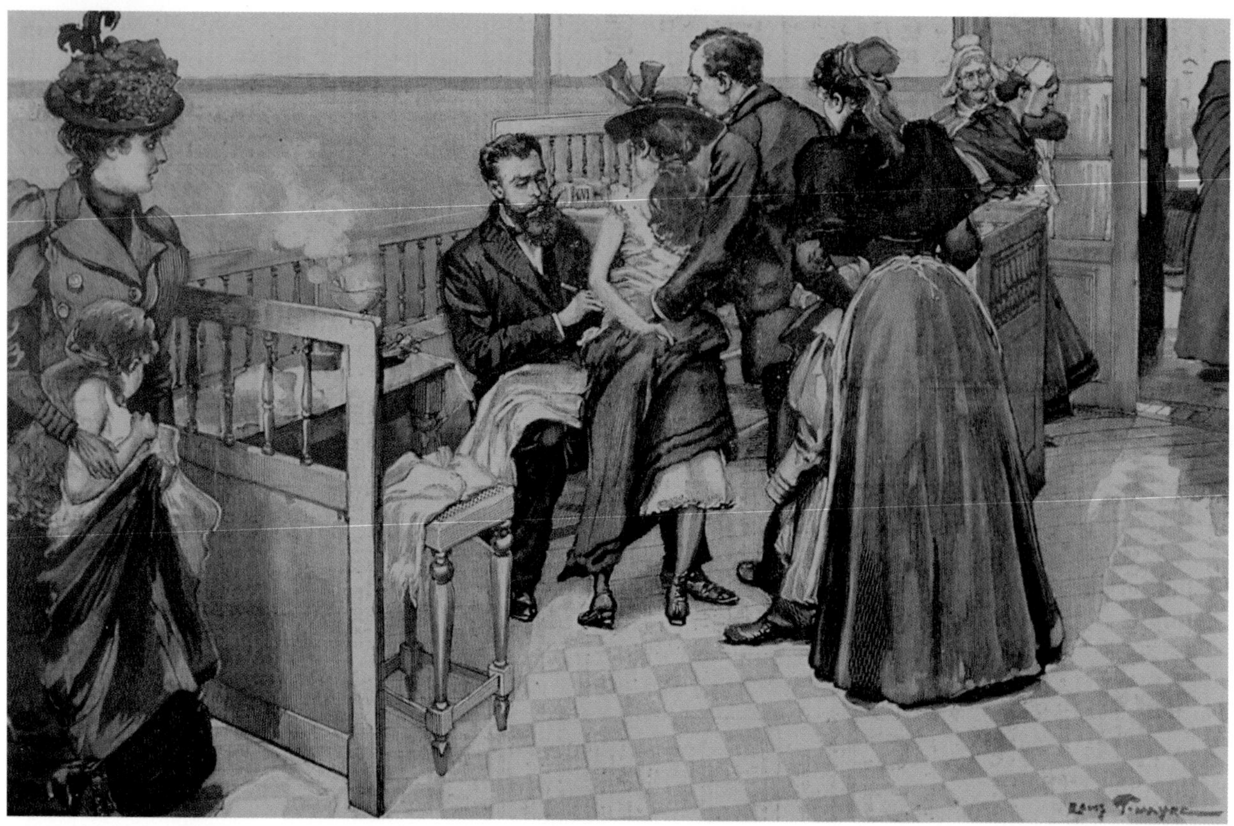

An engraving showing antirabies vaccination at the Pasteur Institute in Paris. Louis Pasteur (1822-1895) developed a rabies virus that was milder and had a shorter incubation period than the wild virus. A person bitten by a rabid animal would be inoculated with the Pasteur virus and rapidly develop immunity to the wild strain. The first human patient was successfully treated in 1885.

The incubation period in natural cases of rabies is variable. In general, the greater the quantity of virus introduced into the wound is also correlated with the length of incubation before symptoms occur. In dogs, the minimum period is ten days, the average 21-60 days, but may be as long as six months. In man, the incubation period is one to three months, with the minimum of ten days.

Rabies is caused by a number of different viruses that vary depending on geographic area and species. While the viruses are different, the disease they cause is singular in its course. The bullet-shaped virus is spread when it breaks through skin or has contact with a mucous **membrane**. The virus begins to reproduce itself initially in muscle cells near the place of first contact. At this point, within the first five days or so, treatment by vaccination has a high rate of success.

Once the rabies virus passes to the nervous system, immunization is no longer effective. The virus passes to the central nervous system, where it replicates itself in the system and moves to other tissues such as the **heart**, the lung, the liver, and the salivary **glands**. Symptoms appear when the virus reaches the spinal cord.

A bite from a rabid animal does not guarantee that one will get rabies; only about 50% of people who are bitten and do not receive treatment ever develop the disease. But it is best not to take any chances. If one is bitten by or has had any exposure to an animal that may have rabies, medical intervention should be sought immediately. Treatment virtually ensures that one will not come down with the disease. Any delay could diminish the treatment's effectiveness.

In humans and in animals, rabies may be manifest in one of two forms: the furious (agitated) type or the paralytic (dumb) type. Furious rabies in animals, especially in the dog, is characterized by altered **behavior** such as restlessness, hiding, depraved appetite, excitement, unprovoked biting, aimless wandering, excessive salivation, altered voice, pharyngeal paralysis, staggering, general paralysis, and finally death. Death usually occurs within three to four days after the onset of symptoms. The paralytic form of rabies is frequently observed in an-

imals inoculated with fixed virus, and is occasionally observed in other animals with street virus contracted under natural conditions. Animals showing this type usually show a short period of excitement followed by uncoordination, ataxia, paralysis, dehydration, and loss of weight, followed by death.

In humans, "furious" rabies patients typically show bizarre behavior, ranging from episodes of severe agitation to periods of **depression**. Confusion becomes more and more extreme as the disease progresses, and the patient can become very aggressive. Hydrophobia is always seen with this type of disease, until the patient becomes comatose while showing intermittently uncontrollable inspiratory spasms. This type of rabies is also characterized by hypersalivation, from 1-1.6 qt (1-1.5 L) of saliva in 24 hours, and excessive sweating.

The paralytic form of rabies in humans is often indistinguishable from that of most viral **encephalitis**, except for the fact that a patient suffering from rabies remains conscious during the course of the disease. Paralysis usually begins at the extremity exposed to the bite and gradually involves other extremities finally affecting the pharyngeal and respiratory muscles.

Dogs, cats, and bats

The dog is a most important animal as a disseminator of rabies virus, not only to man but also to other animals. Wild carnivora may be infected and transmit the disease. In the United States, foxes and skunks are the most commonly involved. These animals are sometimes responsible for infecting domestic farm animals.

The disease in **wildlife** (especially skunks, foxes, racoons, and bats) has become more prevalent in recent years, accounting for approximately 85% of all reported cases of animal rabies every year since 1976. Wildlife now constitutes the most important potential source of **infection** for both human and domestic animals in the United States. Rabies among animals is present throughout the United States with the exception of Hawaii, which has remained consistently rabies-free. The likelihood of different animals contracting rabies varies from one place to the next. Dogs are a good example. In areas where public health efforts to control rabies have been aggressive, dogs make up less than 5% of rabies cases in animals. These areas include the United States, most European countries, and Canada.

However, dogs are the most common source of rabies in many countries. They make up at least 90% of reported cases of rabies in most developing countries of Africa and Asia and many parts of Latin America. In these countries, public health efforts to control rabies have not been as aggressive. Other key carriers of rabies include the fox in **Europe** and Canada, the jackal in Africa, and the vampire bat in Latin America.

In the United States, 60% of all rabies cases were reported in raccoons, with 4,311 rabid raccoons reported in 1992. The high number of cases in raccoons reflects an animal **epidemic**, or, more properly, an epizootic. The epizootic began when diseased raccoons were carried from further south to Virginia and West Virginia. Since then, rabies in raccoons has spread up the eastern seaboard of the United States. Concentrations of animals with rabies include coyotes in southern Texas, skunks in California and in south and north central states, and gray foxes in southeastern Arizona. Bats throughout the United States also develop rabies. When rabies first enters a species, large numbers of animals die. When it has been around for a long time, the species adapts, and smaller numbers of animals die.

Rabies in humans

There are few deaths from rabies in the United States. Between 1980 and the middle of 1994, a total of 19 people in the United States died of rabies, far fewer than the 200 Americans killed by lightning, to give one example. Eight of these cases were acquired outside the United States. Eight of the 11 cases contracted in the United States stemmed from bat-transmitted strains of rabies.

Internationally, more than 33,000 people die annually from rabies, according to the World Health Association. A great majority of cases internationally stem from dog bites. Different countries employ different strategies in the fight against rabies. The United States depends primarily on vaccination of domestic animals and on immunization following exposure to possibly rabid animals. Great Britain, in which rabies has never been established, employs a strict quarantine for all domestic animals entering the country.

Continental Europe, which has a long history of rabies, developed an aggressive program in the 1990s of airdropping a new vaccine for wild animals. The vaccine is mixed with pellets of food for red foxes, the primary carrier there. Public health officials have announced that fox rabies may be eliminated from western Europe by the end of the decade. The World Health Organization is also planning to use the vaccine in parts of Africa.

Though the United States have been largely successful in controlling rabies in humans, the disease remains present in the animal population, a constant reminder of the serious threat rabies could become without successful prevention efforts.

KEY TERMS

Central nervous system—Part of the nervous system that includes the brain and the spinal cord.

Epizootic—The abnormally high occurrence of a specific disease in animals in a particular area, similar to a human epidemic.

Vaccine—A substance that offers prevention, treatment, or aid against infectious disease.

Virus—Infectious agent noted by its ability to replicate only when it has found a host cell.

Further Reading

Browne, Malcolm W. "Rabies, Rampant in U. S., Yields to Vaccine in Europe." *The New York Times.*(July 5, 1994): C-1.

Cantor, Scott B., Richard D. Clover, and Robert F. Thompson. "A Decision-Analytic Approach to Postexposure Rabies Prophylaxis." *American Journal of Public Health,* 84, No. 7 (July 1994): 1144-48.

Clark, Ross. "Mad Dogs and Englishmen." *The Spectator.*(August 20, 1994): 16-17.

Corey, Lawrence. "Rabies, Rhabdoviruses, and Marburg-Like Agents." In *Harrison's Principles of Internal Medicine,* vol. 1, edited by Kurt J. Isselbacher, et al. 13th ed. New York: McGraw-Hill Inc., 1994.

Fishbein, Daniel B., and Laura E. Robinson. "Rabies." *The New England Journal of Medicine,* 329, No. 22 (November 25, 1993): 1632-38.

Smith, Jane S. *Patenting the Sun.* New York: William Morrow and Company, Inc., 1990.

Patricia Braus

Raccoons

Raccoons are foxlike carnivores of North and **South America** that belong to the same family (Procyonidae) as the **coatis**, kinkajou, and the lesser **panda**. The most common species is the northern raccoon *(Procyon lotor)*, which has numerous subspecies, all with the famous black mask on their faces and rings of dark color on their tails. They are found throughout the United States, in central Canada, and south into Central America. Because of their long, warm, useful fur, they have also been introduced into other countries, notably Russia in 1936. Several other species of raccoon are found on various islands in the Caribbean.

An adult raccoon can be fairly large, with a head and body length of 2 ft (61 cm), plus a very fluffy tail up to 15 in (40 cm) long. A northern **animal** may weigh up to 30 lb (13.6 kg), while a raccoon in the Florida Keys may weigh only 6 lb (2.7 kg). Although it has a soft undercoat of uniformly tannish color, a raccoon's coarse guard hairs are striped light and dark (often brown and yellow), giving the animal a grizzled appearance. Raccoons live in just about any **habitat**, from marsh, to **prairie**, to forest, to suburb. The darkness of their coloring depends on their habitat. Animals of arid regions are lightest, those of damp **forests** are darkest. Starting in late winter, they molt all their fur, starting at the top of the head. It is autumn before the new fur coat is complete. Raccoons have fairly large, pointed ears, about 2 in (5 cm) long with white edges and a white tip.

Raccoons have "hands" rather than paws on their front feet. The five long, narrow, flexible fingers are quite sensitive and able to make delicate manipulations. The **palms** of the hands (as well as the soles of the feet) are hairless. A major part of the animal's **brain** is directed toward sensing things with its hands. The name raccoon comes from an Algonquin word meaning "he scratches with his hands." Raccoons are omnivorous, and feed primarily at night. They have acute senses of **smell** and **hearing** that direct them to food. They are drawn to **crayfish**, fruit, birds' eggs, nuts, young grass shoots, little **reptiles**, **mollusks**, poultry, **insects**, and the garbage from any can they manage to tip over. Raccoons use their sensitive hands to investigate whatever they find. This probably plays an important role in their curiosity. They enjoy manipulating whatever they come across, and that often turns them into puzzle solvers. They can easily open latches, garbage can lids, and whatever else they want to concentrate on.

The *lotor* in the raccoon's scientific name means "washer." Tradition has it that raccoons wash their food in **water** before eating. This myth arose because captive raccoons have been observed dunking their food in water. In the wild, raccoons find much of their food in the water, and scientists now think that captive raccoons are acting the same way they would in the wild by "finding" their food in the water.

In the northern part of their range, raccoons eat during the summer and then **sleep** away much of the winter. However, this dormancy, which may last four months, is not true **hibernation**. Their **metabolism** does not slow, their body **temperature** does not fall, and they will emerge from their dens during periods of relatively warm **weather**. During this winter sleep, raccoons live off **fat** reserves accumulated the previous summer and may lose as much as 50% of their body weight. In the southern parts of their range raccoons are active throughout the year. Raccoons are solitary animals, and try to

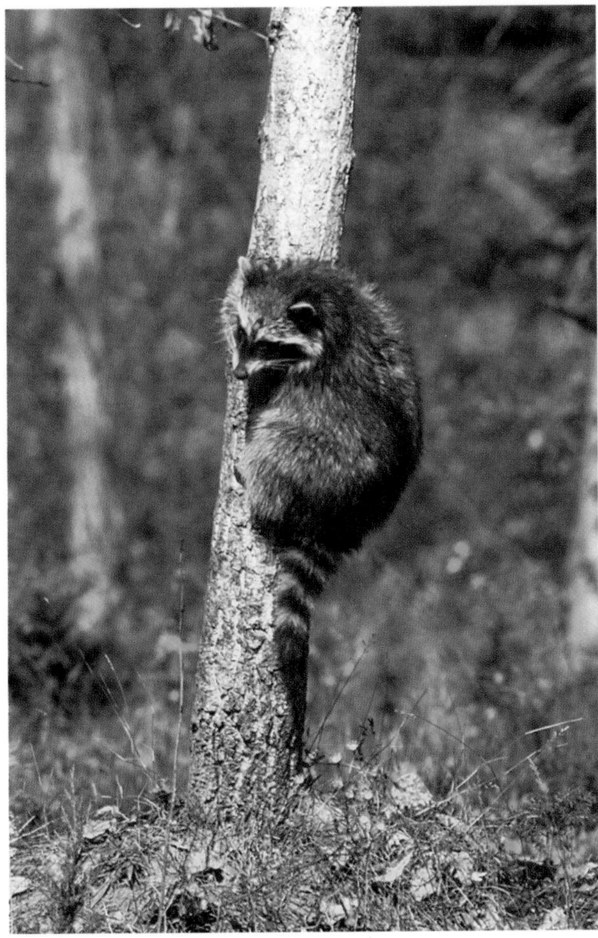

A northern raccoon (*Procyon lotor*) in Flathead National Forest in northwestern Montana.

avoid one another. In places where food is plentiful, several raccoons may feed together, but they still tend to keep their **distance** from one another.

Late in the winter, raccoons find mates. A male will mate with several females but a female will mate with only one male. After a gestation of 54-65 days, the female gives **birth** to two to seven cubs (usually three or four) in a den, often a hole in a hollow **tree**. Each cub is about 4 in (10 cm) long and weighs about 2 oz (62 g). They nurse for several weeks, as the mother gradually spends more and more time away from the den. Soon the mother moves the babies to a den on the ground, and they begin to explore their new world. Before winter, the young raccoons have dispersed to their own homes. Young females can produce their first litter when they are about a year old; males first mate when they are about two years old.

The crab-eating raccoon (*Procyon cancrivorous*) is a semi-aquatic species found in Central and northern South America. It has wiry red fur, with the familiar black mask and tail rings. It feeds on **fish** and land **crabs**, and willingly leaves the water to climb trees.

A close relative of the raccoon is the ringtail (*Bassariscus astutus*), or cacomistle, which lives in the western United States and down into central Mexico. Smaller than the raccoon, it has a white mask instead of black. Its tail is distinctly marked with bands of black and white. Before domestic **cats** were brought to the New World, cacomistles were often kept as pets.

Raccoons are intelligent and adaptable. They have been able to take most changes in their habitats in stride. However, the five **island** raccoon species are threatened, as are many island **mammals** worldwide. The Barbados raccoon *(P. gloveralleni)* may already be extinct.

In recent years, common raccoons have been hard hit with **rabies**. Because people regard them as cute and may try to **touch** them, the rabies may be spread from raccoons to people. Since 1992, an anti-rabies **vaccine** that can be distributed through food has been available for use in areas with many raccoons.

Further Reading

Holmgren, Virginia C. *Raccoons: In Folklore, History and Today's Backyards.* Capra Press, 1990.

MacClintock, Doracas. *A Natural History of Raccoons.* New York: Charles Scribner's Sons, 1981.

North, Sterling. *Raccoons Are the Brightest People.* New York: E. P. Dutton & Co., 1966.

O'Toole, Christopher, and John Stidworthy. *Mammals: The Hunters.* New York: Facts on File, 1988.

Patent, Dorothy Hinshaw. *Raccoons, Coatimundis, and Their Family.* New York: Holiday House, 1979.

Rue, Leonard Lee, III. *The World of the Raccoon.* Philadelphia: J. B. Lippincott Co., 1966.

Jean F. Blashfield

Radar

Radar (*RA*dio *D*etection *A*nd *R*anging) is an electronic detector system that measures **distance** or **velocity** by sending a signal out and receiving its return. It can pierce fog, darkness, or any atmospheric disturbance all the way to the **horizon**. Within its range, it can show an observer **clouds**, land mass, or objects such as ships, airplanes, or spacecraft. Radar can measure distance or range to a target object, and **aircraft** can use radar to determine altitude. Speed detection is another common application. Radar can be used to monitor atmospheric systems, to track storms, and to help predict the **weather**.

Military applications include weapons ranging and direction, or control of guided missiles.

To understand radar, it is necessary to understand a bit about electromagnetic waves. Unlike **water** waves, electromagnetic waves do not require a medium to travel through. They can propagate through air, **vacuum**, and certain materials. Light waves, **radio** waves, microwaves, and radar waves are all examples of electromagnetic waves. Just as light reflects off of some surfaces and travels through others, radar waves bounce off some objects and travel through others.

Basic radar operation

The simplest **mode** of radar operation is range-finding, performed by time-of-flight calculation. The unit transmits a radar signal, i.e. sends radar waves out toward the target. The waves hit the target and are reflected back in the same way that water waves are reflected from the end of a bathtub. The returning wave is received by the radar unit, and the travel time is registered. Basic **physics** tells us that distance is equal to rate of travel multiplied by the time of travel. Now all electromagnetic waves travel at the same speed in a vacuum—the speed of light, which is 3.0 × 108 m/s. This speed is reduced by some small amount when the waves are traveling in a medium such as air, but this can be calculated. If the radar system sends a pulse out toward a target and records the amount of time until the return pulse is received, the target distance can be determined by the simple equation $d = v\ t$, where d is distance, v is velocity, and t is time.

A basic radar unit consists of: a **frequency generator** and timing control unit; a transmitter with a modulator to generate a signal; an **antenna** with a parabolic reflector to transmit the signal; a duplexer to switch between transmission and reception mode; an antenna to gather the reflected signal; a receiver to detect and amplify this return; and signal processing, data processing, and data display units. If the transmitter and receiver are connected to the same antenna or to antennas in the same location, the unit is called monostatic. If the transmitter and receiver antennas are in very different locations, the unit is known as bistatic. The frequency generator/timing unit is the master coordinator of the radar unit. In a monostatic system, the unit must switch between sending out a signal and listening for the return reflected from the target; the timing unit controls the duplexer that performs the switching. The transmitter generates a radio signal that is modulated, or varied, to form either a series of pulses or a continuously varying signal. This signal is reflected from the target, gathered by the antenna, and amplified and filtered by the receiver. The signal processing unit further cleans up the signal, and the data processing unit decodes it. Finally, the data is presented to the user on the display.

Before target range can be determined, the target must be detected, an operation more complicated than it would seem. Consider radar operation again. A pulse is transmitted in the direction that the antenna is facing. When it encounters a material that is different from the surrounding medium (e.g. **fish** in water or an airplane in the air), a portion of the pulse will be reflected back toward the receiver antenna. This antenna in turn collects only part of the reflected pulse and sends it to the receiver and the processing units where the most critical operations take place. Because only a small amount of the transmitted pulse is ever detected by the receiving antenna, the signal amplitude is dramatically reduced from its initial value. At the same time, spurious **reflections** from non-target surfaces or electronic noise from the radar system itself act to clutter up the signal, making it difficult to isolate. Various filtering and amplification operations help to increase the signal-to-noise **ratio** (SNR), making it easier to lock on to the actual signal. If the noise is too high, the processing parameters incorrect, or the reflected signal amplitude too small, it is difficult for the system to determine whether a target exists or not. Real signals of very low amplitude can be swamped by **interference**, or "lost in the noise." In military applications, interference can also be generated by reflections from friendly radar systems, or from enemy electronic countermeasures that make the radar system detect high levels of noise, false targets, or clones of the legitimate target. No matter what the source, interference and signal quality are serious concerns for radar system designers and operators.

Radar tracking systems

Radar systems can send out thousands of pulses per second. Using a rapid sequence of pulses, a radar system can not only determine the range of a target, but it can also track target **motion**. Ranging can be performed with an omnidirectional antenna, but target location and tracking require a more sophisticated system with knowledge of the antenna elevation (vertical) **angle** and azimuthal (horizontal) angle with respect to some fixed coordinate system. Land-based systems generally define true north as the azimuthal reference and the local horizontal as the elevation reference. The azimuthal reference for air and sea systems is the bow of the ship, but elevation reference varies depending on the pitch and roll stabilization of the ship or plane. When you are driving a car down the street, you might characterize other cars as to your left, to your right, or behind you; you define the location of the cars in terms of your own coordinate system. Similarly, when a radar system receives the

A computer generated 3D perspective view of Death Valley, California, constructed from radar data from the Shuttle Imaging Radar-C (SIR-C) combined with a digital elevation map. The brightness range seen here is determined by the radar reflectivity of the surface. Large, bright areas on the valley floor are alluvial fans covering the smoother sand of the valley. SIR-C was carried by the space shuttle in April, 1994.

reflection from a target, it checks the orientation of the receiving antenna with respect to the coordinate axes to determine the object location. Moreover, just as you can use a roadmap to determine the absolute location of an object, so a radar system can be used to locate a target in terms of longitude and latitude. Multiple pulses are required to track the motion of a target. The pulses must be spaced far enough apart that a pulse can be sent out and return before the next pulse is sent, but this is quite feasible when you consider that a radar pulse can travel 100 mi (161 km), strike a target, and return 100 mi (161 km) in less than 1/1000 of a second.

Air Traffic Control uses radar to track and direct the courses of the many planes in civilian airspace. Civilian and military craft generally carry a beacon, or transponder, known as the Air Traffic Control Radar Beacon System (ATCRBS). An Air Traffic Control interrogator system sends a signal to the transponder that prompts it to reply with identification and altitude information. In this way, air traffic controllers can monitor the courses of planes in their region. A military version of the beacon, known as Identification, Friend or Foe (IFF) uses coded signals to identify aircraft.

Doppler radar

A specialized type of radar uses the **Doppler effect** to detect the speed of an target. You have probably observed the Doppler effect hundreds of times without realizing it. The change in pitch as a vehicle approaches, then drives past you is an example of the Doppler frequency shift. The sound waves shift to a higher frequency as the vehicle comes toward you, raising the pitch, then as the vehicle pulls away the frequency of the sound is lowered, dropping the pitch. Doppler theory tells us that

$$f_d = 2\,V_R/c$$

where f_d is the Doppler frequency shift, V_R is the radial velocity of the target (i.e. velocity along the line-of-sight), and c is the speed of propagation of the radar pulse, known for pulses traveling in air. Doppler frequency shift is the difference between the frequency of

the pulse transmitted to the target and the frequency of the return pulse. If this can be measured, then the radial speed, or speed along the line-of-can be determined. Note, however, that target velocity at right angles to the radar system line-of-sight does not cause Doppler shift. In such a case, the speed detector would register a target speed of **zero**. Similarly, if a target is moving at some angle to the direct line-of-sight, the system would only detect the radial component of its velocity. A cosine term can be added to the basic equation to account for non-radial motion. More sophisticated radar systems include this compensation, but typical law enforcement speed detectors do not, with the result that the measured velocity of the target is somewhat lower than the actual velocity.

A Doppler radar system consists of a continuously transmitting source, a mixer, and data and signal processing elements. The signal is sent out to the target continuously. When the return is received, it is "mixed" with a sample of the transmitted signal, and the frequency of the resultant output is the Doppler frequency shift caused by the radial velocity of the target. The Doppler shift is averaged over several samples and processed to yield target speed.

Effective operating range of a radar system is limited by antenna efficiency, transmitted power, the sensitivity of the detector, and the size of the target/energy it reflects. Reflection of electromagnetic waves from surfaces is fundamental to radar. All objects do not reflect radar waves equally well - the strength of the wave reflection depends on the size, shape, and composition of the object. **Metal** objects are the best reflectors, while **wood** and plastic produce weaker reflections. So-called stealth airplanes are based on this concept and are built from materials that produce a minimal reflection.

In recent years **laser** radar systems have been developed. Laser radar systems operate on essentially the same principle as conventional radar, but the significantly shorter wavelengths of visible light allow much higher resolution. Laser radar systems can be used for imaging and for measurement of reflectivity. They are used for vibration detection in automotive manufacturing and for mapping power lines. Because they are more difficult to detect than conventional radar systems, laser radar speed guns are increasingly being adopted by law enforcement agencies.

Radar has undergone considerable development since its introduction in the 1930s. It is a remarkably useful tool that touches our lives in a surprising number of ways, whether by the weather report that we listen to in the morning, or the guidance of the airplanes we ride in. It has given us a different way to see the world around us.

KEY TERMS

Bistatic—A radar system with transmitting and receiving antennas in separate locations.

Duplexer—In a monostatic system, the device that switches system operation between transmit and receive mode.

Modulation—Variation, as in modulation of an electrical signal.

Monostatic—A radar system in which a single antenna both transmits and receives; a system in which transmitting and receiving antennas are at the same location.

Transponder—A beacon. In the case of an Air Traffic Control radar beacon system, a device that is capable of transmitting certain information when queried.

Further Reading

Blake, Bernard, ed. *Jane's Radar and Electronic Warfare Systems.* Alexandria, VA: Jane's Information Group Inc., 1992.

Buchsbaum, Walter H. *Buchsbaum's Complete Handbook of Practical Electronic Reference Data.*; Englewood Cliffs, NJ: Prentice-Hall Inc., 1978.

Edde, Byron. *Radar: Principles, Technology, Applications.*; Englewood Cliffs, NJ: Prentice-Hall, 1993.

Kristin Lewotsky
Frank Lewotsky

Radar meteorology see **Atmosphere observation; Weather mapping**

Radial keratotomy

Radial keratotomy (RK) is a surgical procedure that reduces myopia (nearsightedness), or astigmatism (diminished focus) by changing the shape of the cornea—the outermost part of the eyeball. The procedure is particularly attractive to individuals who want to avoid wearing glasses or wish to be rid of the inconvenience of contact lenses. RK is a quick, relatively painless procedure that takes less than 30 minutes to perform; it is done on an outpatient basis. But while **vision** can improve immediately, the results may change, sometimes for the worse, over the following several months or years. RK

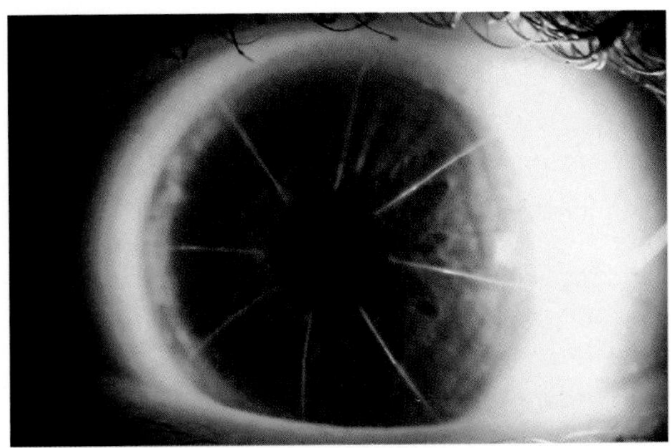

Radial keratotomy scars on the cornea of an eye.

was first attempted in Japan in 1939, then refined during the 1960s and 1970s in the Soviet Union, and first performed in the U.S. in 1978.

The cornea, the clear cover of the **eye**, and the **lens** work together to focus light **rays** entering the pupil onto the retina, the light sensitive **tissue** at the back of the eye. The cornea has a natural **curve**, and the greater the curvature, the greater its refractive power, that is, its ability to bend light so it focuses on the retina.

Normally, **pressure** inside the eyeball pushes the edges of the cornea forward slightly, flattening the central few millimeters of the cornea and reducing the amount of curvature. Candidates for RK have either excess curvature of the cornea or elongated eyeballs, both of which cause light rays to focus in front of the retina causing myopia. This makes objects at a **distance** appear blurry.

Astigmatism occurs when the surface of the cornea is not spherical in shape, but has an irregular contour. This makes it difficult to focus clearly on an object, causes a doubling or "ghosting" effect.

Keratotomy, which refers to cutting the cornea, corrects both of these problems by reducing the natural curve of the cornea and slightly flattening it. The reshaped cornea focuses light rays directly on, or very near, the retina, producing a sharper image.

System of Precise Predictable Keratorefractive Surgery

American ophthalmologists refined RK and developed newer instruments and techniques to improve results. This refined procedure, called the System of Precise Predictable Keratorefractive **Surgery**, is the standard for this type of surgery. Prospective RK patients must have healthy corneas and be deemed suitable candidates after a presurgical examination of the eye. The surgeon measures the curvature of the cornea in order to obtain a baseline from which to determine the amount of flattening that is required. Therefore, patients who wear hard contact lenses must remove them for three weeks before their preoperative eye examination, because the lenses can mold the cornea and change its natural curvature. Patients who wear soft lenses must remove them at least three days before the exam.

On the day of the examination, patients are generally given a sedative to help them relax during the operation, but the surgery itself is painless, and is not done under **anesthesia**. While on the operating table, the area around the patient's eye is cleaned, and topical anesthetic drops are administered to the eye.

The surgeon places an ultrasound probe over the eye to measure the thickness of the cornea in several spots. This measurement is critical, because each incision must penetrate to at least 75% of the depth of the cornea, which is about 0.02 in (0.5 mm) deep, in order to obtain the greatest flattening effect without penetrating the eyeball underneath.

A diamond blade secured within a slot on the handle of the cutting instrument is then adjusted to within a hundredth of a millimeter of the thinnest spot on the cornea. The surgeon then places dark lines on the cornea to guide the blade. Under high magnification with an operating **microscope**, the surgeon pushes the blade into the cornea with enough **force** to produce a slight indentation. With the blade adjusted to prevent it from being inserted too deeply, the surgeon then makes a number of incisions in the cornea which radiate from the pupil like the spokes of a wheel, leaving a central clear zone. The patient wears a patch after the operation, and recovery takes about one to two days. When RK is to be done on both eyes, they are operated on during separate visits at least several months apart.

Correcting astigmatism

Astigmatic keratotomy is similar to RK, and is performed to correct astigmatism along with nearsightedness, or when there is only astigmatism. Two incisions are made at the time of RK to flatten the astigmatic part of the cornea.

Although RK has been refined over the years, the results are not perfect in every patient. The ability of surgeons to alter the shape of the cornea is not yet as precise as the ability of lens makers to make ?a pair of glasses or contact lenses that perfectly match the requirements of the wearer.

In addition, the cornea heals slowly after RK, usually becoming flatter as it does so. Thus, some surgeons at-

tempt to compensate for this by under-correcting the cornea during the operation. Then, as the cornea flattens further during healing, the patient's eyes may approach emmetropia, or perfect vision.

Possible side effects

If the patient's vision is over-corrected during surgery, postsurgical flattening causes progressive loss of refractive power (ability to bend and focus light rays). Consequently, instead of being myopic (light rays are focused in front of the retina), the eye becomes hyperopic, or farsighted (i.e., light rays are focused in back of the retina).

As the number of RK patients increased, surgeons encountered an increasing number of potential side effects. Some patients complained of discomfort when in bright light, persistent glare, or disorienting starlike bursts of light when approaching a light at night (e.g., an oncoming vehicle's headlights). Moreover, some patients also lost their best correct visual acuity, i.e., their vision was not able to be corrected as well as before RK with properly prescribed glasses or contact lenses. Others suffered infections from **microorganisms** that infected the incisions.

A National Eye Institute study, called Prospective Evaluation of Radial Keratotomy (PERK), evaluated 693 patients 10 years after RK procedures were performed in 1982 and 1983 to reduce nearsightedness. Seventy percent did not require corrective lenses for long distance; 85% were corrected to 20/40 or better; 53% to 20/20 or better; and 43% continued to change toward farsightedness; and a significant decrease in vision, even with glasses, occurred in 3% of patients.

In the 1990s, a newer technique, called Photoreactive Keratectomy (PKR) utilized a type of **laser** called an excimer laser to decrease nearsightedness. This laser removes a very precise amount of tissue off the center of the cornea using a "cold" ultraviolet laser, changing the corneal shape to bring the focal point closer to the retina. By the late 1990s, a third correctional device, called the LASIK (LAser in SItu Keratomileusis), was being used. It combines the excimer laser and a microkeratome to also reduce nearsightedness. Although approved by the FDA independently, their combined use is not yet approved. However, in this procedure, the eye is anesthetized and a suction ring centered over the cornea to stabilize the eye. This ring also and provides "guide tracks" for the microkeratome, a very precise instrument that "shaves" a micro-thin partial flap off the center of the cornea, leaving it attached at one side like a hinge while exposing the middle portion of the cornea. The excimer laser is then used to remove tissue and reshape the center of the cornea. The flap is replaced and conforms to the flatter, reshaped cornea.

See also Vision disorders.

Marc Kusinitz

Radian see **Angle measurement**

Radiation

The word radiation comes from the Latin for "ray of light," and is used in a general sense to cover all forms of **energy** that travel through **space** from one place to another as "rays." Radiation may be in the form of a spray of **subatomic particles**, like miniature bullets from a machine gun, or in the form of electromagnetic waves, which are nothing but pure energy and which include light itself, as well as **radio** waves and several other kinds.

The word radiation is also sometimes used to describe the transfer of **heat** from a hot object to a cooler one that it is not touching; a hot object is said to radiate heat. You can "feel the heat" on your face when standing near a red-hot furnace, even if there is no movement of hot air between the furnace and you. What you are feeling is infrared radiation, a form of electromagnetic energy that makes molecules move faster, and therefore behave hotter, when it strikes them.

When many people hear the word "radiation," they think of the radiations that come from radioactive materials. These radiations, some of which are particles and some of which are electromagnetic waves, are harmful because they are of such high energy that they tear apart some **atoms** in the materials through which they pass. This is in contrast to light, for example, which has no lasting effect on, say, a pane of **glass** through which it passes.

The higher energies of radiation are called ionizing radiations because when they tear apart atoms they leave behind a trail of ions, or atoms that have had some of their electrons removed. Ionizing radiations include **x rays**, alpha particles, beta particles, and gamma rays.

Many kinds of lower-energy radiations are quite common and are harmless in reasonable amounts. They include all colors of visible light, ultraviolet and infrared light, microwaves and **radio waves**, including **radar**, TV and FM, short wave and AM. All of these radiations are electromagnetic radiations.

Electromagnetic radiation

Electromagnetic energy travels in the form of waves, moving in straight lines at a speed of 3.00×10^{10} centimeters per second, or 186,400 mi (299,918 km) per second. That speed is usually referred to as the speed of light in a **vacuum**, because light is the most familiar kind of electromagnetic radiation and because light slows down a little bit when it enters a transparent substance such as glass, **water**, or air. The speed of light in a vacuum, the **velocity** of electromagnetic waves, is a fundamental constant of nature, like π=3.14159..., for example; it cannot be changed by humans, or presumably by anything else.

Electromagnetic radiation can have a variety of energies. Because it travels in the form of waves, the energies are often expressed in terms of wavelengths. The higher the energy of a wave, the shorter its wavelength. The wavelengths of known electromagnetic radiation range from less than 10^{-10} centimeter for the highest energies up to millions of centimeters (tens of miles) for the lowest energies.

The energy of a wave can also be expressed by stating its **frequency**: the number of vibrations or cycles per second. Scientists call one cycle per second a hertz, abbreviated as Hz. Known electromagnetic radiations range in frequency from a few Hz for the lowest energies up to more than 10^{20} Hz for the highest.

Particulate radiation

Sprays or streams of invisibly small particles are often referred to as particulate radiation because they carry energy along with them as they fly through space. They may be produced deliberately in machines such as particle **accelerators**, or they may be emitted spontaneously from radioactive materials. Alpha particles and beta particles are emitted by radioactive materials, while beams of electrons, protons, mesons, neutrons, ions, and even whole atoms and molecules can be produced in accelerators, nuclear reactors, and other kinds of laboratory apparatus.

The only particulate radiations that might be encountered outside of a laboratory are the alpha and beta particles that are emitted by radioactive materials. These are charged subatomic particles: the **alpha particle** has an **electric charge** of +2 and the beta particle has a charge of +1 or -1. Because of their electric charges, these particles attract or repel electrons in the atoms of any material through which they pass, thereby ionizing those atoms. If enough of these ionized atoms happen to be parts of essential molecules in a human body, the body's **chemistry** can be altered, with unhealthful consequences.

Radiation and health

Large doses of any radiations, ionizing or not, can be dangerous. Too much sunlight, for example, can be blinding. Lasers can deliver such intense beams of light that they can **burn** through **metal**, not to mention human flesh. High levels of microwaves in ovens can cook meats and **vegetables**. On the other hand, as far as anyone has been able to determine, small amounts of any kind of radiation are harmless, including the ionizing radiations from radioactivity. That's just as well, because there are unavoidable, natural radioactive materials all around us.

Depending on the energy, intensity, and type of radiation that we are talking about, then, radiation may be harmful or quite harmless. It is all a matter of what kind and how much. Some people believe that too many TV waves, especially when tuned to certain frequencies, can turn the human **brain** into mush.

See also Electromagnetic field; Ionizing radiation; Nuclear medicine; Radioactive pollution; Radioactive waste; Radioactivity.

Robert L. Wolke

Radiation detectors

Radiation detectors are devices which sense and relay information about incoming radiation. Though the name brings to mind images of **nuclear power** plants and science fiction films, radiation detectors have found homes in such fields as medicine, **geology**, **physics**, and **biology**. The term radiation refers to energies or particles given off by radioactive **matter**. Mostly, radiation takes the form of alpha particles, beta particles, gamma rays, and **x rays**. Some of these are more easily detected than others, but all are incredibly tiny and invisible to the human **eye**. This is why scientists originally started building radiation detectors. Since people cannot sense radiation, they need assistance to observe and understand it.

It is important to note that people are always subjected to a certain amount of radiation because the **earth** contains radioactive **minerals** and cosmic rays bombard the earth from **space**. These omnipresent sources are called background radiation, and all radiation detectors have to cope with it. Some detector applications subtract off the background signals, leaving only the signals of local radioactive sources.

In general, radiation detectors do not capture radiated particles. In fact, they usually do not even witness the radiation itself. The detectors look for footprints that it

leaves behind. Each type of radiation leaves specific clues; physicists often refer to these clues as a signature. The goal in detector design is to create an environment in which the signature may be clearly written.

For example, if someone wants to study nocturnal animals, it might be wise to consider the ground covering. Looking at a layer of pine needles by day, one finds few, if any, tracks or markings. However, one can choose to study a region of soft **soil** and find many more **animal** prints. The best choice yet is fresh snow. In this case, one can clearly see the tracks of every animal that moved during the night. Moreover, the **behavior** of an animal can be documented. Where the little prints of a fox are deep and far apart, it was probably running, and where its prints are more shallow and more closely spaced, it was probably walking. Designing a radiation detector presents a similar situation. Radiation can leave its mark clearly, but only in special circumstances.

Clues are created when radiation passes too close to, (or even collides with), another object—commonly, an atom. What detectors eventually find is the atom's reaction to such an encounter. Scientists often refer to a single encounter between radiation and the detector as an event. Given a material which is sensitive to radiation, there are two main ways to tell that radiation has passed through it: optical signals, in which the material reacts in a visible way; and electrical signals, in which it reacts with a small, but measurable voltage.

Optical detectors

One type of optical detector is the film detector. This is the oldest, most simple type and one that closely resembles the analogy of tracks in snow. The film detector works much like everyday photographic film, which is sensitive to visible light. A film detector changes its appearance in spots where it encounters radiation. For instance, a film detector may be white in its pure form and subsequently turn black when hit by beta particles. Each beta particle which passes through the film will leave a black spot. Later, a person can count the spots (using a **microscope**), and the total number reveals the level of beta radiation for that environment.

Since film detectors are good at determining radiation levels, they are commonly used for radiation safety. People who work near radioactive materials can wear pieces of film appropriate for the type of radiation. By regularly examining the film, they can monitor their exposure to radiation and stay within safety guidelines. The science of determining how much radiation a person has absorbed is called dosimetry. Film detectors do have limitations. Someone studying the film cannot tell exactly when the radiation passed or how energetic it was.

An optical radiation detector more useful for experiments is a scintillation detector. These devices are all based on materials called scintillators, which give off bursts of light when bombarded by radiation. In principle, an observer can sit and watch a scintillator until it flashes. In practice, however, light bursts come in little packages called photons, and the human eye has a hard time detecting them individually. Most scintillator detectors make use of a photo multiplier, which turns visible light (i.e. optical photons) into measurable electrical signals. The signals can then be recorded by a computer. If the incoming radiation has a lot of **energy**, then the scintillator releases more light, and a larger signal is recorded. Hence, scintillation detectors can record both the energy of the radiation and the time it arrived.

Materials used in scintillation detectors include certain liquids, **plastics**, organic crystals, (such as anthracene), and inorganic crystals. Most scintillating materials show a preference for which type of radiation they will find. **Sodium** iodide is a commonly used inorganic **crystal** which is especially good at finding x rays and gamma rays. In recent years, sodium iodide has received increasing **competition** from **barium** fluoride, which is much better at determining the exact time of an event.

Electrical detectors

Electrical detectors wait for radiation to ionize part of the detector. Ionization occurs when incoming radiation separates a **molecule** or atom into a **negative** piece (one or more electrons) and a positive piece (i.e. the ion, the remaining molecule, or atom with a "plus" electrical charge). When a material has some of its **atoms** ionized, its electrical characteristics change and, with a clever design, a detecting device can sense this change.

Many radiation detectors employ an ionization chamber. Fundamentally, such a chamber is simply a container of gas which is subjected to a voltage. This voltage can be created by placing an electrically positive plate and an electrically negative plate within the chamber. When radiation encounters a molecule of gas and ionizes it, the resulting **electron** moves toward the positive plate and the positive ion moves toward the negative plate. If enough voltage has been applied to the gas, the ionized parts move very quickly. In their haste, they bump into and ionize other gas molecules. The radiation has set off a chain reaction that results in a large electrical signal, called a pulse, on the plates. This pulse can be measured and recorded as data. The principles of the ionization chamber form the basis for both the Geiger-Müller detector and the proportional detector, two of the most common and useful radiation-sensing devices.

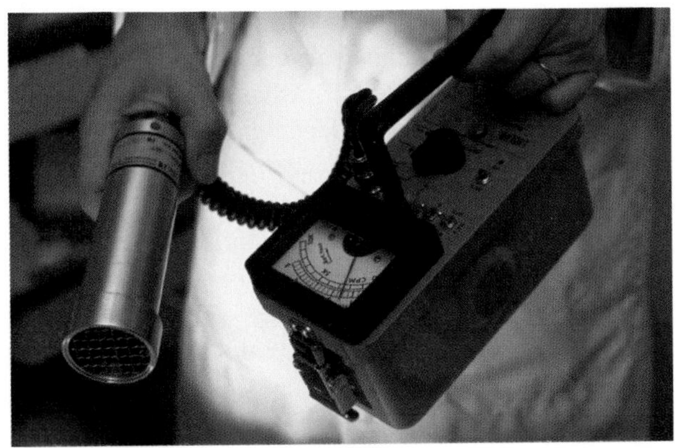

A handheld Geiger counter.

A Geiger-Müller counter in its basic form is a cylinder with a wire running through the inside from top to bottom. It is usually filled with a noble gas, like neon. The outside of the **metal** cylinder is given a negative charge, while the wire is given a positive charge. In this **geometry**, the wire and the cylinder function as the two plates of an ionization chamber. When electrons are knocked from the gas by radiation, they move to the wire, which can then relay the electrical pulse to counting equipment. The voltage applied to a Geiger-Müller detector is quite high and each ionization creates a large chain reaction. In this way, it gives the same-sized pulse regardless of the radiation's original speed or energy.

One version of the Geiger-Müller detector, the Geiger counter, channels the electrical pulses to a crude speaker which then makes a popping noise each time it detects an event. This is the most familiar of radiation detectors, particularly in films which depict radioactivity. When the detector nears a radioactive source, it finds more events and gives off a correspondingly greater number of popping sounds. Even in a more normal setting, such as the average street corner, it will pop once every few seconds because of background radiation.

A proportional detector is very similar to the Geiger-Müller detector, but a lower voltage is applied to the ionization chamber, and this allows the detector to find radiation energies. More energetic radiation ionizes more of the gas than less energetic radiation does; the proportional detector can sense the difference, and the sizes of its pulses are directly related to the radiation energies. A large pulse corresponds to highly energetic radiation, while a small pulse likewise corresponds to more lethargic events. Since it can record more information, the proportional counter is more commonly found in scientific experiments than the Geiger-Müller detector, which, like the film detector, is primarily used for radiation safety.

KEY TERMS

Background radiation—The ambient level of radiation measured in an otherwise non-radioactive setting.

Dosimetry—The science of determining the amount of radiation that an individual has encountered.

Event—A detected interaction between radiation and the detector material.

Ionization chamber—A detector in which incoming radiation reacts with the detector material, splitting individual atoms or molecules into electrically negative and positive components.

Scintillation—A burst of light given off by special materials when bombarded by radiation.

Signature—The distinctive set of characteristics that help identify an event.

Physicists who search for rare **subatomic particles** have utilized the principles of ionization chambers. They have developed many types of exotic detectors which combine ionization chambers with optical detection.

Further Reading

Delaney, C. F. G. and Finch, E. C. *Radiation Detectors: Physical Principles and Applications*. New York: Oxford University Press, 1992.

Holmes-Siedle, Andrew. *Handbook of Radiation Effects*. New York: Oxford University Press, 1993.

Horn, Delton. *Electronic Projects to Control Your Home Environment*. New York: TAB Books Inc., 1994.

Lillie, David W. *Our Radiant World*. Ames, IA: Iowa State University Press, 1986.

Mawson, Colin. *The Story of Radioactivity*. Englewood Cliffs, NJ: Prentice-Hall, 1969.

Brandon R. Brown

Radiation exposure

Radiation exposure occurs any time that **energy** in the form of electromagnetic rays or particles interacts with biological **tissue**. **Ionizing radiation** is particularly energetic; examples include: **x rays**, gamma radiation, and **subatomic particles**. Biological damages caused by exposure to ionizing range from mild tissue burns to **cancer**, genetic damage, and ultimately, death. However, there are potential benefits of controlled exposures to certain kinds

of radiation, which can be used for the detection, **diagnosis**, and treatment of certain diseases. Exposure to many types of radiation is routinely monitored using sensitive devices, such as film badges and dosimeters.

The discovery of radiation

In the mid 1880s, James Maxwell published a mathematical description of the wave **motion** of **heat** and light, the only forms of radiation known at the time. As scientists discovered other forms of radiation (such as x rays, **radio** waves, microwaves, and gamma rays) they found that their physical **behavior** could also be described by Maxwell's equations, and that they were all part of the same, continuous, **electromagnetic spectrum**.

In 1895, the French physicist Henri Becquerel began experimenting with the rare **metal**, **uranium**. He eventually discovered that uranium emitted a previously unknown form of radiation. Soon after, Pierre and Marie Curie discovered radium and polonium, which are also radioactive. These discoveries led to better understanding of the structure of the atom, and it became clear that there was another kind of radiation: ionizing radiation produced by radioactive substances. This type of radiation consists of extremely high-energy particles, which are released from the nuclei of radioactive **atoms** as they spontaneously undergo fission (i.e., break into smaller nuclei, forming different atomic elements). (Gamma rays, a form of electromagnetic radiation, are also released by some radioactive elements.) Because there are many kinds of radiation, it is subject to different classifications. Radiation can be described as electromagnetic or particulate (i.e., radioactive). These are further classified as being either ionizing or non-ionizing, depending on their energy level.

Radiation comes in many forms

The word radiation refers to two closely related things. First, it refers to forms of radiant energy, particularly that represented by subatomic particles (for example, the type of radiation released during a nuclear explosion), and by **electromagnetism** (for example, the type of radiation emitted by a light bulb, and by the **sun**). Sound is also considered a type of radiation.

The word radiation can also refer to the release and propagation through **space** of the energy itself. For example, a block of uranium releases radiation in the form of radioactive particles. Both the release of the particles, and the particles themselves, are called radiation. However, not all radiation is radioactive. The particle radiation released from uranium is radioactive, but the electromagnetic radiation emitted by a light bulb is not. Radioactivity is a form of radiation which involves the release of alpha particles, neutrons, electrons, and gamma rays, emitted by radioactive elements and substances.

Most of the radiation on the Earth's surface is electromagnetic radiation, which travels in waves of different **frequency**. (Frequency is the number of waves passing a point each second; it is the inverse of wavelength.) From the lowest to highest frequency, the **spectrum** of electromagnetic radiation is divided into the following ranges: **radio waves**, microwaves, visible light, ultraviolet light, x rays, and gamma rays. Visible light can be detected by the human **eye**, and is divided into the following color ranges: red, orange, yellow, green, blue, violet (arranged from lowest to highest frequency).

Sound, or acoustic radiation is also classified according to its frequency. In increasing order of frequency, sound radiation is classified as infrasonic, sonic, and ultrasonic.

Measuring exposure to radiation

The first commonly used unit for measuring the biological effects of x ray exposure was the roentgen. It was named after the German physicist Wilhelm Roentgen, who discovered x rays in 1895. A roentgen is the amount of radiation that produces a set number of charged ions in a certain amount of air under standard conditions. This unit is not, however, particularly useful for describing the potential effects of radiation on human or **animal** tissues. The rad unit is slightly better in this regard. It is a measure of the radiation dose absorbed by one gram of something. A rad is equal to a defined amount of energy (100 ergs) absorbed per gram.

The problem with rads as a unit of measurement for human radiation exposure is that a dose of one rad of radiation from plutonium produces a different effect on living tissue than one rad of a less harmful type of radiation. Consequently, scientists introduced the rem, which stands for "roentgen equivalent man." A rem is the dose of any radiation that produces the same biological effect, or dose equivalent, in humans as one rad of x rays.

Scientists continue to use these units, which were introduced earlier in the century, even as they become used to newer units for certain applications. The roentgen will still be the unit used to measure exposure to ionizing radiation, but the rad is being replaced with the "gray" as a measure of absorbed dose. One gray equals 100 rads. The sievert is replacing the rem as a measure of dose equivalent. One sievert equals 100 rems.

Sources of radiation

Exposure to ionizing radiation can be divided into two categories: natural and anthropogenic (i.e., associat-

ed with human activity). Background radiation is mostly due to solar radiation in the form of cosmic rays, and also radioactivity from **rocks**. Exposure to background radiation is continuous, although its intensity varies. The sun is also the main source of ultraviolet radiation. Each person in the United States receives an average radiation dose per year of about one millisievert (one-thousandth sievert; this is the same as 0.1 rem). About one-half of this exposure is due to **radon**, a natural radioactive gas released from rocks.

Radon is a breakdown product of uranium. Radon itself breaks down rapidly; its **half-life** is less than four days (this is the time for one-half of an initial quantity to decay through radioactivity). Unfortunately, radon decays into polonium-218, polonium-214, and polonium-220, which emit alpha particles. Alpha particles are heavy, charged particles that have trouble penetrating **matter** but can be dangerous if taken into the body, where they are in close contact with tissues and biochemicals (such as DNA) that are sensitive to suffering damage by ionization. Radon may be responsible for one-tenth of all deaths by lung cancer.

The actual and potential sources of anthropogenic radiation include: x rays and other types of radiation used in medicine, **radioactive waste** generated by **nuclear power** stations and scientific research centers, and **radioactive fallout** from **nuclear weapons** testing. Fallout is radioactive **contamination** of air, **water**, and land following the explosion of nuclear weapons or accidents at nuclear power stations.

Electromagnetic radiation from **television** sets and microwave ovens has been lowered to insignificant levels in recent years, thanks to federal regulations and improved designs. Some people consider high-voltage transmission lines a radiation threat, but scientific studies have not demonstrated a significant threat from this source.

Effects of radiation exposure

How energy from radiation is transferred to the body depends on the type of radiation. Visible light and infrared radiation, for example, transfer their energy to entire molecules. The absorbed energy causes greater molecular vibration, which can be measured as heat (or thermal energy).

With many forms of ionizing radiation, energy is transferred to electrons that surround atomic nuclei. Atoms affected by x rays usually absorb enough energy to lose some of their electrons, and so become ionized. (An atom is ionized when it gains or loses electrons and acquires a net electric charge.) Ultraviolet radiation causes electrons to absorb energy and jump to a higher energy **orbit** around the atomic nucleus. The sun and sunlamps emit enough ultraviolet radiation to cause sunburn, premature aging of the skin, and skin cancers. Exposure of humans and animals to ultraviolet radiation also results in the production of vitamin D, a biochemical necessary for good health.

Radiation that consists of charged particles can knock electrons out of their orbit around atoms. This also creates ions. Such radiation can also cause atoms to enter an exited state, if the electrons are bumped into higher-energy orbits. These changes result in atoms and molecules (including biochemicals) that are chemically reactive. Seeking to become stable, they interact with unaffected atoms and molecules, which may be damaged (i.e., changed) in the process, and are then unable to perform their usual metabolic functions. For example, nuclear material such as DNA molecules may be damaged to the degree that they can no longer be accurately copied. This may lead to impaired **cell** function, **cell death**, or genetic abnormalities.

Neutral particles of radiation, such as neutrons, transfer their energy to nuclei rather than to electrons. Often, neutrons strike a single **proton**, like that in a **hydrogen** nucleus, causing it to "recoil" and in the process be separated from its electrons, leaving a single, positively charged proton (this is also an ionization reaction). The **neutron** is then less energetic, and is captured by another nucleus, which releases charged particles in turn.

The specific effects of radiation on living beings depends on the type of radiation, the dose, the length of exposure, and the type of tissue exposed to the radiation. Damage caused by exposure to high levels of radiation is divided into two categories: somatic and genetic. Somatic refers to effects on the physiological functioning of the body; genetic refers to damage caused to reproductive cells, including heritable effects that can affect offspring.

Genetic damage can include mutations or broken chromosomes, the structures in cell nuclei that house DNA, and the all the genetic information of an **organism**. Many mutations, or changes in genes, are harmful. Mutations caused by radiation are fundamentally the same as mutations caused by any other influence.

Somatic damage from high doses of ionizing radiation is indicated by burns and radiation sickness, with symptoms of nausea, vomiting, and diarrhea. Long-term effects can include cancers such as leukemia. Cells are killed outright if a high dose of ionizing radiation is delivered in a short amount of time. Symptoms may appear within hours or days. The same dose delivered over a long time will not produce the same symptoms, because the body has time to repair some of the

damage caused during a long-term exposure. However, some cells may experience genetic damage that causes some forms of cancer to develop years later (this is called a latent effect).

Exposure to intense doses of high-energy electromagnetic radiation, of the kind occurring close to **radar** towers or large radio transmitters, is less common than exposure to radioactivity. However, when it does occur it can cause cataracts, **organ** damage, **hearing** loss, and other disorders to develop. The health consequences of exposure to low doses of electromagnetic radiation are the subject of much controversy. Significant health effects have so far been difficult to detect.

Future developments

The public is increasingly becoming aware of the dangers of radiation exposure. Less than a generation ago, many people considered a dark suntan to be a sign of health and vigor. Today, health experts are working hard to convince people that excessive exposure to solar ultraviolet radiation, and to similar ultraviolet emitted by lamps in tanning salons, increases the risk of skin cancers and premature aging of the skin. It is risky to expose skin to full sunlight, especially for a reason as trivial as the esthetics of a suntan. Education campaigns are also being mounted to make home owners aware of the risks posed by radon, which can accumulate in well-insulated homes with certain kinds of concrete-walled or rock-floored basements.

Technological improvements are resulting in much smaller exposures to radiation during medical diagnostic procedures. Efforts are also being made to reduce and better focus the radiation exposures used for therapeutic purposes (for example, to treat some kinds of cancers). Sophisticated developments, such as the three-dimensional x ray images produced by CAT scanners, allow health care workers to obtain more information with less exposure to radiation.

Steps are also being taken to prevent exposure resulting from anthropogenic sources of radiation in the environment. In 1986, a catastrophic accident at a **nuclear reactor** at Chernobyl in the Ukraine resulted in a huge **emission** of radioactive contaminants into the atmosphere, affecting much of **Europe**. After this disaster, networks of monitors were erected in many countries to detect future radiation leaks and warn threatened populations. The largest monitoring system is in Germany, which has installed several thousand radiation sensors. These systems will be able to detect radiation leaks coming from domestic or foreign sources shortly after nuclear accidents occur, allowing residents to seek shelter if necessary.

KEY TERMS

Cosmic rays—Ionizing radiation from the sun or other sources in outer space, consisting of atomic particles and electrons.

Electromagnetic spectrum—The type of radiation associated with photons, that includes cosmic-radiation, gamma rays, x rays, ultraviolet radiation, visible light, infrared radiation, microwaves, and radio waves.

Ionization—The production of atoms or molecules that have lost or gained electrons, and therefore have gained a net electric charge.

Nuclear reactor—A device that generates energy by controlling nuclear fission, or splitting of the atom. The heat produced is used to heat water, which drives an electrical generator. Radioactive byproducts of the fission process are used for medical, scientific, and military purposes, or are disposed as nuclear waste.

Nuclear weapon—A bomb or other explosive that derives its explosive force from the release of nuclear energy, either from fission or fusion reactions.

Radiation—Energy in the form of waves, or particles.

Radioactivity—Spontaneous release of subatomic particles or gamma rays by unstable atoms as their nuclei decay.

Uranium—A heavy element found in nature. More than 99% of natural uranium is in the isotopic form of U-238. Only the less-common U-235 readily undergoes fission.

Most nations that do not already possess nuclear weapons, have signed a pact to not develop them, and nations that already have them have agreed not to test them above ground (which leads to particularly intense emissions of radioactivity into the atmosphere). One exception is France, which continues to explode nuclear weapons in the South Pacific, thus contributing to radioactive fallout in the atmosphere.

See also Mutation; Radioactive pollution.

Further Reading

Cooper, W.J., R.D. Curry, and K. O'Shea. (eds.). *Environmental Applications of Ionizing Radiation*. John Wiley and Sons, 1998.

Eisenbud, M. and T.F. Gesell. *Environmental Radioactivity: From Natural, Industrial, and Military Sources* Academic Press, 1997.

Lillie, David W. *Our Radiant World.* Ames, Iowa: Iowa University Press, 1986.

Sherwood, Martin, and Christine Sutton. *The Physical World.* New York: Oxford University Press, 1988.

Stannard, J. Newell. *Radioactivity and Health: A History.* Columbus, Ohio: Batelle, 1990.

Dean Allen Haycock

Radical

A **radical** is an uncharged atom or **molecule** that has an unpaired, or "free," **electron**. Radicals are formed when a covalent bond in an atom or molecule is split apart and the remaining pieces retain one electron of the original shared pair. These reaction products, called free radicals, are highly reactive entities that can participate in a variety of reactions. In chemical notation, radicals are indicated by the chemical symbol of the parent compound followed by a dot ( ).

Background

Radicals are formed by the cleavage of an atom or molecule and can be grouped into three categories depending on their source. They can come from **atoms**, (e.g., H, F, Cl), inorganic molecules (e.g., such as OH, CN NO), or organic molecules (e.g., CH_3 or $C_2 H_5$). In some areas of **chemistry** the term radical is used to indicate a reaction intermediate, which exists in nature for very short periods of time. However, the term is more commonly used to describe chemical species that persist long enough to react with other molecules to form more radicals in a cascading effect. This cascade effect can create sustained reactions in chemical and biological systems.

History

Avogadro and others postulated the existence of radicals early in the nineteenth century. Unfortunately, they did not fully understand how radicals could exist in nature and therefore they incorrectly proposed structures and mechanisms of formation. Due to this lack of understanding, at the end of the century it was fairly well established that radicals could not exist. Chemists did not have real evidence of the existence of radicals until the early twentieth century when Moses Gomberg discovered the triphenyl methyl radical. He proved this radical could exist with evidence based on reaction characteristics including color changes, **molecular weight** determination, and the specie's reactivity toward iodine, **oxygen** and nitric oxide. Still, his discovery was initially met with skepticism from his peers. Additional evidence was uncovered by F. Paneth in 1929 when he found experimental **proof** that tetramethyllead ($Pb(CH_3)_4$ generates radicals as well. Eventually enough evidence was collected that convinced chemists that free radicals do exist and that they do participate in reactions.

Mode of formation

Today it is known that radicals are formed when a stable molecule is disrupted and split into two portions, each with an unpaired electrons. A variety of effects can generate this disruption including thermal **decomposition**, electric or microwave discharge, photochemical decomposition, **electrolysis**, and gamma or x-ray exposure. The free radical process involves three steps: initiation where the free radical is formed; propagation in which the radicals react with other molecules to form additional free radicals; and termination where the radicals react with each other to form non-radical products.

Chemical and biological effects

Free radical reactions are useful in certain beneficial chemical processes, such as those used in the production of rubber and **plastics**. In these processes the free radicals react quickly to form long chains of chemicals known as polymers. However, in biological systems these reactions can cause harm. For example, radicals known as superoxides are formed when oxygen molecules are split apart. While these radicals can participate in the destruction of invading organisms by white **blood** cells, they can injure or kill cells when natural **enzyme** controls fail. Unchecked they can attack lipids, **proteins**, and nucleic acids. Therefore, free radicals in the body can contribute to **cancer**, **heart** attacks, strokes, and **emphysema** and may even play a role in **arthritis** and **Alzheimer's disease**.

Detection

Free radicals were originally detected using simple analytical techniques that were based on the experiments by Paneth. Modern detection methods include a variety of spectral methods. For example, absorption **spectroscopy** is relatively simple way to detect radicals in the gas phase. A another method is based on mass spectrometry. This technique works by measuring ionization **energy** of the free radicals and can be used to quantitatively measure radical **concentration**. The best technique is considered to be electron paramagnetic **resonance** spec-

KEY TERMS

Antioxidant—An organic chemical compound capable of retarding the deterioration of other chemicals that occurs because of contact with oxygen or other oxidizing agents.

Initiation—The chemical or physical event which causes the formation of free radicals.

Quenching—The process by which antioxidant materials can absorb free radicals, thus halting potentially damaging reactions.

Superoxide—A chemical compound containing the O_2^-ion.

Termination—The final step in a free radical chain reaction. Termination occurs when two radical combine to form a non-radical product.

troscopy which can characterize radicals in liquids, solids, or gases. Furthermore, this method is very sensitive and can be used to gain information on the structure of the detected radicals.

Quenching

Free radicals can be quenched by **antioxidants**, chemicals that are capable of absorbing their extra electron. Antioxidants are free radical scavengers that can dampen the propagation reactions which create further radicals. They are important dietary supplement and find some use in topical skin care applications. Many of these radical scavengers, like vitamin E from green tea and polyphenols from red wine, are naturally occurring compounds.

Further Reading

Leffler, J., *An Introduction to Free Radicals.* 1993.

"Free radicals in liberal amounts." *Science News,* (9 July 1988): 27.

"The cellular aging process and free radicals." *Drug & Cosmetic Industry.*, February 1989, 22.

Randy Schueller

Radical

A **radical** is a symbol for the indicated root of a number, for example a square root or cube root; the term is also synonymous for the root itself.

The word radical has both Latin and Greek origins. From Latin *raidix, radicis* means "root" and in Greek *raidix* is the analog word for "branch." The concept of a radical—the root of a number—can best be understood by first tackling the idea of exponentiation, or raising a number to a given power. We indicate a number raised to the *n*th power by writing x^n. This expression indicates that we are multiplying *x* by itself *n* number of times. For example, $3^2 = 3 * 3 = 9$, and $2^4 = 2 * 2 * 2 * 2 = 16$.

Just as division is the inverse of **multiplication**, taking the root of a number is the inverse of raising a number to a power. For example, if we are seeking the **square root** of x^2, which equals $x*x$, then we are seeking the **variable** that, when multiplied by itself, is equal to x^2—namely, *x*.That is to say, $\sqrt{9} = \sqrt{32} = \sqrt{3} * 3 =$ 3.Similarly, if we are looking for the fourth root of x^4, then we are looking for the variable that multiplied by itself four times equals *x*. For example, $4\sqrt{16} = 4\sqrt{2} * 2 * 2 * 2 = 2$.

The radical $n\sqrt{}$ is the symbol that calls for the root operation; the number or variable under the radical sign is called the radicand.It is common parlance to speak of the radicand as being "under the radical." It is also common to simply use the term "radical" to indicate the root itself, as when we speak of solving algebraic equations by radicals.

The expression $n\sqrt{R} = P$ is called the radical expression, where *n* is the indicated root index, *R* is a real number and *P* is the n-th root of number *R* such that *P*n=*R*.

Types of radical operations

The most commonly encountered radicals are the square root and the cube root. We have already discussed the square root. A bare radical sign with no indicated root index shown is understood to indicate the square root.

The cube root, written $3\sqrt{R}$, is the number *P* that solves the equation *Pn*=R. For example, the cube root of 8, $3\sqrt{8}$, is 2.

The effect of *n* and *R* on *P*

Both the radicand *R* and the order of the root *R* have an effect on the root(s) *P*. For example, because a **negative** number multiplied by a negative number is a **positive number**, the even roots (*n*=2, 4, 6, 8...) of a positive number are both negative and positive: $\sqrt{9} = +/-3$, $4\sqrt{16} = +/-2$.

Because the root *P* of $n\sqrt{R}$ must be multiplied an odd number of times to generate the radicand *R*, it should be clear that the odd roots (*n*=3, 5, 7, 9...) of a

KEY TERMS

Imaginary number—A number multiplied by the imaginary unit $i.=\sqrt{-1}$.

Index—Order of the root.For example, the index of a cube root is 3.

Radicand—The number under the radical sign.

Root sign—A symbol that indicates the radical or root operation.

positive number are positive, and the odd roots of a negative number are negative. For example, $3\sqrt{8} = 2$ ($2^3 = 2 * 2 * 2 = 4 * 2 = 8$), but $3\sqrt{-8} = -2$ ($-2^3 = -2 * -2 * -2 = 4* -2 = -8$).

Taking an even root of a negative number is a trickier business altogether. As discussed above, the product of an even number of negative values is a positive number. The even root of a negative number is imaginary. That is, we define the imaginary unit $i=\sqrt{-1}$, or $i2=-1$. Then $\sqrt{-9} = \sqrt{9} * \sqrt{-1} = +/-3i$. The imaginary unit is a very useful concept in certain types of **calculus** and complex analysis.

Multiplication of radicals

The product of two radicals with same index n can be found by multiplying the radicands and placing the result under the same radical. For example, $\sqrt{9} * \sqrt{25} = \sqrt{(9*25)} = \sqrt{225} = 15$, which is equal to $3 * 5 = \sqrt{9} * \sqrt{25}$. Similarly, radicals with the same index sign can be divided by placing the quotient of the radicands under the same radical, then taking the appropriate root.

The radical of a radical can be calculated by multiplying the indexes, and placing the radicand under the appropriate radical sign. For instance, $\sqrt{3}\sqrt{64} = 6\sqrt{64} = 2$.

Kristin Lewotsky

Radio

Radio is the technology and practice that enables the transmission and reception of information carried by long-wave electromagnetic **radiation**. Radio makes it possible to establish wireless two-way communication between individual pairs of transmitter and receiver, and it is used for one-way broadcasts to many receivers. Radio signals can carry **speech**, music, **telemetry**, or digitally-encoded entertainment. Radio is used by the general public, within legal guidelines, or it it is used by private business or governmental agencies. Cordless telephones are possible because they use low-power radio transmitters to connect without wires. Cellular telephones use a network of computer-controlled low power radio transmitters to enable users to place **telephone** calls away from phone lines.

The history of radio

In the nineteenth century, in Scotland, James Clerk Maxwell described the theoretical basis for radio transmissions with a set of four equations known ever since as Maxwell's Field Equations. Maxwell was the first scientist to use mechanical analogies and powerful mathematical modeling to create a successful description of the physical basis of the **electromagnetic spectrum**. His analysis provided the first insight into the phenomena that would eventually become radio. He deduced correctly that the changing magnetic field created by accelerating charge would generate a corresponding changing electric field. The resulting changing electric field would, he predicted, regenerate a changing magnetic field in turn, and so on. Maxwell showed that these interdependent changing electric and magnetic fields would together be a part of a self-sufficient phenomenon required to travel at the speed of light.

Not long after Maxwell's remarkable revelation about electromagnetic radiation, Heinrich Hertz demonstrated the existence of **radio waves** by transmitting and receiving a microwave radio signal over a considerable **distance**. Hertz's apparatus was crude by modern standards but it was important because it provided experimental evidence in support of Maxwell's theory.

Guglielmo Marconi was awarded the Nobel Prize in **physics** in 1909 to commemorate his development of wireless telegraphy after he was able to send a long-wave radio signal across the Atlantic Ocean.

The first radio transmitters to send messages, Marconi's equipment included, used high-voltage spark discharges to produce the charge **acceleration** needed to generate powerful radio signals. Spark transmitters could not carry speech or music information. They could only send coded messages by turning the signal on and off using a telegraphy code similar to the land-line Morse code.

Spark transmitters were limited to the generation of radio signals with very-long wavelengths, much longer than those used for the present AM-broadcast band in the United States. The signals produced by a spark transmitter were very broad with each signal spread across a large share of the usable radio **spectrum**. Only a few

radio stations could operate at the same time without interfering with each other. Mechanical generators operating at a higher **frequency** than those used to produce electrical power were used in an attempt to improve on the signals developed by spark transmitters.

A technological innovation enabling the generation of cleaner, narrower signals was needed. **Electron** tubes provided that breakthrough, making it possible to generate stable radio frequency signals that could carry speech and music. Broadcast radio quickly became established as source of news and entertainment.

Continual improvements to radio transmitting and receiving equipment opened up the use of successively higher and higher radio frequencies. Short waves, as signals with wavelengths less than 200m are often called, were found to be able to reach distant continents. International broadcasting on shortwave frequencies followed, allowing listeners to hear programming from around the world.

The newer frequency-modulation system, FM, was inaugurated in the late 1930s and for more than 25 years struggled for acceptance until it eventually became the most important **mode** of domestic broadcast radio. FM offers many technical advantages over AM, including an almost complete immunity to the lightning-caused static that plagues AM broadcasts. The FM system improved the sound quality of broadcasts tremendously, far exceeding the fidelity of the AM radio stations of the time. The FM system was the creation of E. H. Armstrong, perhaps the most prolific inventor of all those who made radio possible.

In the late 1950s, stereo capabilities were added to FM broadcasts along with the ability to transmit additional programs on each station that could not be heard without a special receiver. A very high percentage of FM broadcast stations today carry these hidden programs that serve special audiences or markets. This extra program capability, called SCA for Subsidiary Communications Authorization, can be used for stock market data, pager services, or background music for stores and restaurants.

Radio and the Electromagnetic Spectrum

Radio utilizes a small part of the electromagnetic spectrum, the set of related wave-based phenomena that includes radio along with infrared light, visible light, ultraviolet light, **x rays**, and gamma rays. Picture the electromagneticspectrum as a piano keyboard: radio will be located where the piano keys produce the low frequency musical notes. Radio waves have lengths from many miles down to a fraction of a foot.

Radio waves travel at the **velocity** of electromagnetic radiation. A radio signal moves fast enough to complete a trip around the **earth** in about 1/7 second.

How Radio Signals Are Created

Jiggle a collection of electrons up and down one million times a second and a 1-MegaHertz radio signal will be created. Change the vibration frequency and the frequency of the radio signal will change.

Radio transmitters are alternating voltage generators. The constantly changing voltage from the transmitter creates a changing electric field within the **antenna**. This alternating field pushes and pulls on the conduction electrons in the wire that are free to move. The resulting charge acceleration produces the radio signal that moves away from the antenna. The radio signal causes smaller sympathetic radio frequency currents in any distant electrical conductor that can act as a receiving antenna.

Modulation

A radio signal by itself is like a mail truck without letters. A radio signal alone, without superimposed information, is called a carrier wave. An unmodulated radio signal conveys only the information that there was once a source for the signal picked up by the receiver. Adding information to a carrier signal is a process called modulation. To modulate a radio carrier means that it is changed in some way to correspond to the speech, music, or data it is to carry.

The simplest modulation method is also the first used to transmit messages. The signal is turned on and off to transmit the characters of an agreed code. Text messages can be carried by the signal modulated in this way. Unique patterns stand for letters of the alphabet, numerals, and punctuation marks.

The least complicated modulation method capable of transmitting speech or music varies the carrier signal's instantaneous power. The result is called amplitude modulation, or AM. Another common system varies the signal's instantaneous frequency at an informational rate. The result is frequency modulation, FM.

If radio is to transmit speech and music, information must be carried that mimics the pattern of changing air **pressure** the **ear** would experience **hearing** the original sound. To transmit sounds these air-pressure changes are converted into electrical signals, amplified electronically, then used to modulate the carrier.

Amplitude modulation was the first process to have the capability of transmitting speech and varied the radio signal's instantaneous power at a rate that matched the

original sound vibrations in the air. A better modulation technology followed that varied the instantaneous frequency of the radio signal but not the amplitude. Frequency modulation, or FM, has advantages compared to AM but both AM and FM are still in use.

Sound can be converted to digital data, transmitted, then used to reconstruct the original waveform in the receiver. It seems likely that a form of digital modulation will eventually supplant both FM and AM.

Demodulation

Radio receivers recover modulation information in a process called demodulation or detection. The radio carrier is discarded after it is no longer needed. The radio carrier's cargo of information is converted to sound using a loudspeaker or headphones or processed as data.

Wavelengths, Frequencies, and Antennas

Each radio signal has a characteristic wavelength just as is the case for a sound wave. The higher the frequency of the signal, the shorter will be the wavelength. Antennas for low- frequency radio signals are long. Antennas for higher frequencies are shorter, to match the length of the waves they will send or receive.

It is a characteristic of all waves, not just radio signals, that there is greater interaction between waves and objects when the length of the wave is comparable to the object's size. Just as only selected sound wavelengths fit easily into the air column inside a bugle, only chosen frequencies will be accepted by a given antenna length. Antennas, particularly transmitting antennas, function poorly unless they have a size that matches the wavelength of the signal presented to them. The radio signal must be able to fit on the antenna as a standing wave. This condition of compatibility is called **resonance**. If a transmitter is to be able to "feed" **energy** into an antenna, the antenna must be resonant or it will not "take power" from the transmitter. A receiver antenna is less critical, since inefficiency can be compensated by signal amplification in the receiver, but there is improvement in reception when receiving antennas are tuned to resonance.

If an antenna's physical length is inappropriate, capacitors or inductors may be used to make it appear electrically shorter or longer to achieve resonance.

Near 100 MHz, near the center of the FM broadcast band in most of the world, signals have a wavelength of approximately three meters. At 1 MHz, near the center of the U.S. AM broadcast band, the signal's wavelength is 327 yds (300 m), about three times the length of a football field. One wavelength is about 1 ft (0.3 m) at the ultra-high frequency used by cellular telephones.

Radio signals and energy

Energy is required to create a radio signal. Radio signals use the energy from the transmitter that accelerates **electric charge** in the transmitting antenna. A radio signal carries this energy from the transmitting antenna to the receiving antenna. Only a small fraction of the transmitter's power is normally intercepted by any one receiving antenna, but even a vanishingly-small received signal can be amplified electronically millions of times as required.

Radio signal propagation

Radio signals with very short wavelengths generally follow straight line paths much as do beams of light, traveling from transmitter to receiver as a direct wave. Radio signals with very long wavelengths follow the curvature of the earth, staying close to the surface as signals called ground waves.

Radio signals with intermediate wavelengths often reflect from layers of electrically-charged particles high above the earth's surface. These signals are known as skywaves. The layers of electrically-charged particles found between 25-200 mi (40-322 km) above the earth are collectively known as the ionosphere. The ionosphere is renewed each day when the sun's radiation ionizes **atoms** in the rarefied air at this height. At higher altitudes the distance between ions causes the ionization to persist even after the **sun** sets.

A good way to become familiar with radio propagation is to listen for distant AM-broadcast radio at various times of the day. A car radio works well for this experiment because they often have better sensitivity and selectivity than simpler personal radios.

During the daylight hours, on the standard-broadcast band, only local stations will normally be heard. It is unlikely that you will hear stations from more than 150 mi (241 km). As the sun sets you will begin to hear signals from greater distances.

AM-broadcast reception is generally limited to ground-wave radio signals when the sun is high in the sky. There is a very dense layer of the ionosphere at a height of approximately 25 miles that is continually created when the sun is high in the sky. This D layer, as it is called, absorbs medium wavelength radio signals so that skywave signals cannot reflect back to earth. The D layer dissipates quickly as the sun sets because the sun's rays are needed to refresh the ionization of this daytime-only feature of the ionosphere. After dark, when the D layer has disappeared, you will hear strong signals from far away cities.

After the D layer has disappeared, skywave signals reflect from a much higher layer of the ionosphere called

the F layer. The F layer acts as a radio mirror, bouncing skywaves back to earth far from their source. The F layer degrades in darkness as does the D layer, but since the ions are separated more widely at higher altitude, the F layer functions as a significant radio mirror until dawn. Toward morning stations at intermediate distances fade, leaving only skywave signals that reflect from the thinning ionosphere at a very shallow **angle**.

Signal absorption by the D layer is less at shorter wavelengths. Stations using higher frequencies can use skywave in the daytime. High frequencies pass through the D layer. Skywave radio circuits are usually best in the daytime for higher frequencies, just at the time that the standard-broadcast band is limited to groundwave propagation.

Forecasting long distance radio signal propagation conditions depends upon predicting conditions on the sun. It is the changing radiation from the sun that affects long distance radio circuits when the ionosphere changes as the earth rotates. On the sunlit side of the earth the ionosphere is most strongly ionized. On the night side of the earth the radio ionosphere begins to dissipate at sunset until it is almost insignificant as a radio mirror in the early morning hours. When the ionosphere is at its best as a reflector it can support communication between any locations on the earth.

When the ionosphere is more densely ionized it will reflect radio signals with a shorter wavelength than when the ionization is weaker. At any one time, between any two distant locations on the earth, there is a limiting upper frequency that can be used for radio communication. Signals higher in frequency than this maximum-usable frequency, F layer called the MUF, pass through the ionosphere without returning to earth. Slightly lower than the MUF, signals are reflected with remarkable efficiency. A radio signal using less power than a flashlight can be heard on the opposite side of the earth just below the MUF. The MUF tends to be highest when the sun is above the midpoint between two sites in radio communication.

The 11-year solar sunspot cycle has a profound effect on radio propagation. When the average number of **sunspots** is large, the sun is more effective in building the radio ionosphere. When the sun's surface is quiet the maximum-usable frequency is usually very low, peaking at less than half the MUF expected when the sun surface is covered with sunspots.

From time to time, the sun bombards the earth with charged particles that disrupt radio transmissions. When solar flares are aimed toward the earth, the **earth's magnetic field** is disturbed in a way that can cause an almost complete loss of skywave radio propagation. Microwave radio signals are not significantly disturbed by the magnetic storms since microwaves do not depend upon ionospheric reflection.

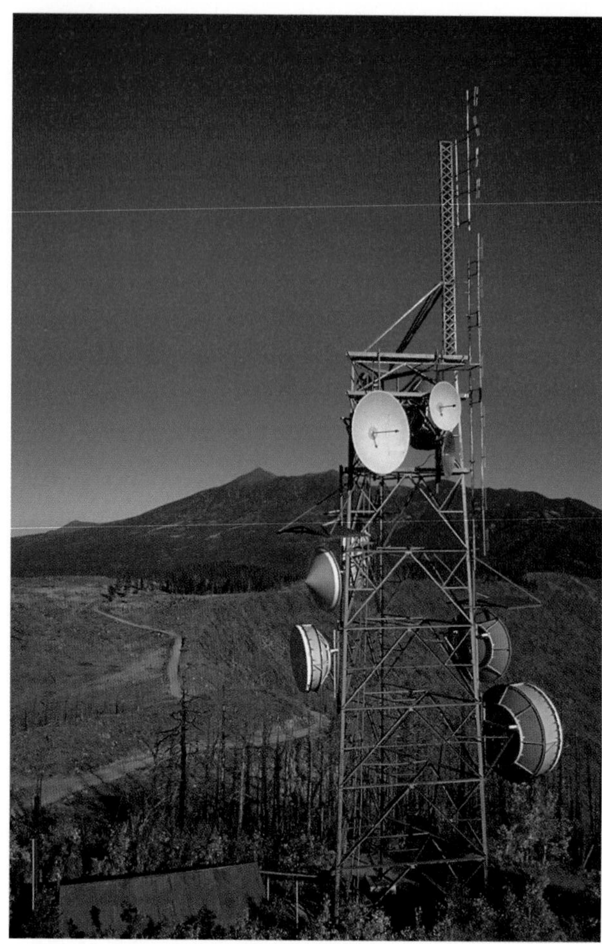

Radio towers on Elden Mountain above Flagstaff, Arizona. Each transmitting antenna has a size that matches the wavelength of the signal it transmits.

FM-broadcast signals are seldom heard reliably further than the distance to the **horizon**. This is because the frequencies assigned to these services were deliberately chosen to be too high to expect the ionosphere to reflect them back to earth. FM signals are received as direct waves, not skywaves. The limited range of FM stations is an advantage because frequency assignments can be duplicated in cities that are in fairly close proximity without encountering unacceptable **interference**. This protection is much harder to achieve where skywave propagation may permit an interfering signal to be heard at a great distance.

Shortwave radio

Shortwave radio services may change frequency often as the ionosphere's reflectivity varies. Unlike do-

KEY TERMS

Antenna—Electrical conductor optimized to radiate a radio signal

Capacitor—Electrical component that cancels magnetic property of wire.

D Layer—Arbitrary designation for the lowest layer of the ionosphere.

Electric field—Effect near electric charge explaining force between charges.

Electron tube—Active device based on control of electrons with electric fields.

F layer—Arbitrary designation for the highest layer of the ionosphere.

Gamma rays—Electromagnetic radiation with the shortest wavelengths.

Inductor—Electrical component that adds magnetic property to wire.

Infrared light—Light that cannot be seen because the wavelength is too long.

Ionized—Condition where electric charge has been stripped from atoms.

Magnetic field—Effect in space resulting from the motion of electric charge.

MegaHertz—One million cycles per second; MHz.SI abbreviation for MegaHertz.

Morse code—Dot and dash code used to send messages over telegraph wires.

Resonance—A condition favoring a selected frequency.

Selectivity—Receiver property enabling reception of only wanted signals.

Sensitivity—Receiver property enabling reception of weak signals.

Standing wave—A stationary pattern of activity resulting from interference.

Sunspots—Lessbright regions on the sun from magnetic activity.

Telemetry—Engineering and scientific measurements transmitted by radio.

X rays—Energetic radiation with longer wavelengths than gamma rays.

mestic broadcast stations that stay on a single assigned frequency, shortwave broadcast stations move frequency to take advantage of hour-to-hour and season-to-season changes in the ionosphere. As the 11-year sunspot cycle waxes and wanes, shortwave stations the world around move to shorter wavelengths when there are more sunspots and to longer wavelength bands when sunspots are minimal.

Listening to shortwave radio requires more effort than istening to local domestic radio. The best frequencies to search change from one hour to the next throughout the day. Due to the effect of the sun, shortwave signals sometimes may disappear for days at a time, then reappear with astounding strength. Many shortwave stations do not broadcast at all hours of the day. In addition, a station must be targeting your part of the world specifically; otherwise the signal will probably be weak.

Regulation of radio transmissions

The part of the electromagnetic spectrum that can be used for radio communication cannot accommodate everyone who might wish to use this resource. Access is controlled and technical standards are enforced by law. With few exceptions, radio transmissions are permitted only as authorized by licenses.

Since 1934 in the United States, licensing and equipment approval has been the responsibility of the Federal Communications Commission. Similar regulation is the rule in other countries. Technical standards are required by radio regulation. Just as traffic laws improve highway safety, laws and regulations that encourage the fair use of the limited radio spectrum help to avoid conflicts between users.

The future of radio

Radio broadcasting in the future, maybe the near future, will most probably include a newer, better digital system known as DAB, digital-audio broadcasting. Early tests indicate that a switch to digital will impart compact-disc quality to radio programming. There are two possible modes under consideration for DAB. In **Europe**, completely new stations on a different band of frequencies is favored. In the United States it seems probable that digital information will transmitted as information superimposed on the programming modulation now used. The digitized audio can be so much lower in power than the "main" programming that it will be in-

audible to listeners with analog receivers. Early program tests of this system have been successful and increases in audio quality have been significant.

Further Reading

The 1995 ARRL Handbook. The American Radio Relay League, 1995.

Now You're Talking. The American Radio Relay League, 1994.

Jacobs, George, and Cohen, Theodore J., *The Shortwave Propagation Handbook.* Cowan Publishing Corp., 1970.

Hobson, Art. *Physics: Concepts and Connections.* New York: Prentice-Hall, Inc., 1995.

Ostdiek, Vern J., and Bord, Donald J. *Inquiry Into Physics.* St. Paul: West Publishing Company, 1995.

Donald Beaty

Radio astronomy

Radio astronomy is the field of science in which information about the **solar system** and outer **space** is collected by using **radio waves** rather than visible light waves. In their broadest principles, radio astronomy and traditional optical astronomy are quite similar. Both visible **radiation** and radio waves are forms of electromagnetic radiation, the primary difference between them being the wavelength and **frequency** of the waves in each case. Visible light has wavelengths in the range between about 4,000 and 7,000 angstroms and frequencies in the range from about 10^{14} to 10^{15} cycles per second. (An angstrom is a unit of measurement equal to 10^{-8} centimeter.) In contrast, radio waves have wavelengths greater than 1 meter and frequencies of less than 10^{9} cycles per second.

Origins of radio astronomy

No one individual can be given complete credit for the development of radio astronomy. However, an important pioneer in the field was Karl Jansky, a scientist employed at the Bell Telephone Laboratories in Murray Hill, New Jersey. In the early 1930s, Jansky was working on the problem of noise sources that might interfere with the transmission of short-wave radio signals. During his research, Jansky made the surprising discovery that his instruments picked up static every day at about the same time and in about the same part of the sky. It was later discovered that the source of this static was the center of the **Milky Way Galaxy**.

Radio vs. optical astronomy

The presence of radio sources in outer space was an important breakthrough for astronomers. Prior to the 1930s, astronomers had to rely almost entirely on visible light for the information they obtained about the solar system and outer space. Sometimes that light was collected directly by the human **eye**, and others time by means of telescopes. But in either case, astronomers had at their disposal only a small fraction of all the electromagnetic radiation produced by stars, planets, and **interstellar matter**.

If an observer is restricted only to the visible region of the **electromagnetic spectrum**, she or he obtains only a small fraction of the information that is actually emitted by an astronomical object. Jansky's discovery meant that astronomers were now able to make use of another large portion of the electromagnetic spectrum—radio waves—to use in studying astronomical objects.

In some respects, radio waves are an even better tool for astronomical observation than are light waves. Light waves are blocked out by **clouds**, dust, and other materials in Earth's atmosphere. Light waves from distant objects are also invisible during daylight because light from the **Sun** is so intense that the less intense light waves from more distant objects cannot be seen. Such is not the case with radio waves, however, which can be detected as easily during the day as they can at night.

Radio telescopes

Radio telescopes and optical telescopes have some features in common. Both instruments, for example, are designed to collect, focus, and record the presence of a certain type of electromagnetic radiation—radio waves in one case and light waves in the other. However, the details of each kind of **telescope** are quite different from one other.

One reason for these differences is that the human eye cannot detect radio waves as it can light waves. So an astronomer cannot look into a radio telescope the way he or she can look into an optical telescope. Also, radio waves have insufficient **energy** to expose a photographic plate, so an astronomer cannot make a picture of a radio source in outer space as she or he can of an optical source.

The first difference between an optical telescope and a radio telescope is in the shape and construction of the collecting apparatus—the mirror in the case of the optical telescope and the "dish" in the case of the radio telescope. Because the wavelength of visible light is so small, the mirror in an optical telescope has to be shaped very precisely and smoothly. Even slight distortions in the mirror's surface can cause serious distortions of the images it produces.

In a radio telescope, however, the "mirror" does not have to be so finely honed. The wavelength of radio

waves is so long that they do not "recognize" small irregularities in the "mirror." (The word mirror is placed in quotation marks here because the collecting surface of the radio telescope looks nothing like a mirror, though it does in effect act like one.) In fact, it can be made of wire mesh, wire rods, or any other kind of material off which radio waves can be reflected.

For many years, the largest radio telescope in the world was located in a natural bowl in a **mountain** outside Arecibo, Puerto Rico. The bowl, which is 1,000 ft (305 m) wide and occupies 20 acres (8 hectares), was lined with wire mesh, off which radio waves were reflected to a wire **antenna** at the focus of the telescope. The radio waves collected along the antenna were then converted to an electrical signal which was used to operate an automatic recording device that traced the pattern of radio waves received on the wire mesh.

Increasing resolution in a radio telescope

A major drawback of the radio telescope is that it resolves images much less well than does an optical telescope. The resolving power of a telescope is its ability to separate two objects close to each other in the sky. The resolving power of early radio telescopes was often no better than about a degree of **arc** compared to a second of arc that is typical for optical telescopes.

Since the resolving power of a telescope is inversely proportional to the wavelengths of radiation it receives, the only way to increase the resolving power of a radio telescope is to increase the diameter of its dish. Fortunately, it is much easier to make a very large dish constructed of **metal** wire than to make a similar mirror made of **glass** or plastic. The Arecibo radio telescope was an example of a telescope that was made very large in order to improve its resolving power.

One could, in theory, continue to make radio telescopes larger and larger in order to improve their resolving power. However, another possibility exists. Instead of making just one telescope with a dish that is many miles in diameter, it should be possible to construct a series of telescopes whose diameters can be combined to give the same dimensions.

The radio telescope at the National Radio Astronomy Observatory near Socorro, New Mexico, is an example of such an instrument. The telescope consists of 27 separate dishes, each 85 ft (26 m) in diameter. The dishes are arranged in a Y-shaped pattern that covers an area 17 mi (27 km) in diameter at its greatest width. Each dish is mounted on a railroad car that travels along the Y-shaped track, allowing a large variety of configurations of the total observing system. The system is widely known by its more common name of the Very Large Array, or VLA.

Discoveries made in radio astronomy

The availability of radio telescopes has made possible a number of exciting discoveries about our own solar system, about galaxies, about star-like objects, and about the interstellar medium. The solar system discoveries are based on the fact that the planets and their satellites do not emit visible light themselves (they only reflect visible light), although they do emit radio waves. Thus, astronomers can collect information about the planets using radio telescopes that was unavailable to them with optical telescopes.

As an example, astronomers at the Naval Research Laboratory decided in 1955 to look for radio waves in the direction of the planet **Venus**. They discovered the presence of such waves and found them considerably more intense than had been predicted earlier. The intensity of the radio waves emitted by the planet allowed astronomers to make an estimate of its surface **temperature**, in excess of 600°F (316°C).

At about the same time as the Venus studies were being carried out, radio waves from the planet **Jupiter** were also discovered. Astronomers found that the planet emits different types of radio radiation, some consisting of short wavelengths produced continuously from the planet's surface and some consisting of longer wavelengths emitted in short bursts from the surface.

Radio studies of the Milky Way

Some of the earliest research in radio astronomy focused on the structure of our galaxy, the Milky Way Galaxy. Studying our own galaxy with light waves is extraordinarily difficult because our solar system is buried within the galaxy, and much of the light emitted by stars that make up the galaxy is blocked out by interstellar dust and gas.

Radio astronomy is better able to solve this problem because radio waves can travel through intervening dust and gas and provide images of the structures of which the galaxy is made. Of special importance in such studies is a particular line in the radio **spectrum**, the 8-inch (21-cm) line emitted by **hydrogen atoms**. When hydrogen atoms are excited, they emit energy with characteristic wavelengths in both the visual and the radio regions of the electromagnetic spectrum. The most intense of these lines in the radio region is the 8-inch (21-cm) line. Since hydrogen is by far the most abundant element in the universe, that line is widely used in the study of interstellar **matter**.

The 8-inch (21-cm) line can be used to measure the distribution of interstellar gas and dust within the galaxy. Since the galaxy is rotating around a common center, the

motion of interstellar matter with respect to our own solar system (and consequently with respect to the galactic center) can often be determined. As a result of studies such as these, astronomers have concluded that the Milky Way probably has **spiral** arms, similar to those observed for other galaxies. One major difference, however, is that the spiral arms in our galaxy appear to be narrower and more numerous than those observed in other galaxies.

Radio **emission** from molecules in the interstellar gas provides radio astronomers with another important tool for probing the structure of our galaxy. Gases such as **carbon** monoxide (CO) emit at specific radio wavelengths, and are found in dark clouds of interstellar gas and dust. Because stars form in these regions, radio astronomy yields unique information on **star** births and on young stars.

Radio galaxies

One of the earliest discoveries made in radio astronomy was the existence of unusual objects now known as radio galaxies. The first of these, a strong radio source named Cygnus A, was detected by Grote Reber in 1940 using a homemade antenna in his backyard. Cygnus A emits about a million times as much energy in the radio region of the electromagnetic spectrum as does our own galaxy in all regions of the spectrum. Powerful radio-emitting sources like Cygnus A are now known as radio galaxies.

Radio galaxies also emit optical (visible) light, but they tend to look quite different from the more familiar optical galaxies with which astronomers had long been familiar. For example, Cygnus A looks as if two galaxies are colliding with each other, an explanation that had been adopted by some astronomers before Reber's discovery. Another radio galaxy, Centaurus A, looks as if it has a dark band running almost completely through its center. Still another radio galaxy, known as M87, seems to have a large jet exploding from one side of its central body.

In most cases, the radio image of a radio galaxy is very different from the optical image. In the case of Cygnus A, for example, the radio image consists of two large lobe-shaped structures extending to very large distances on either side of the central optical image. Studies have shown that these radio-emitting segments are very much younger (about 3 million years old) compared with the central optical structures (about 10 billion years old).

Quasars and pulsars

Some of the most interesting objects in the sky have been discovered by using the techniques of radio astronomy. Included among these are the quasars and pulsars. When quasars were first discovered in 1960, they startled astronomers because they appeared to be stars that emitted both visible and radio radiation in very large amounts. Yet there was no way to explain how stars could produce radio waves in such significant amounts.

Eventually, astronomers came to the conclusion that these objects were actually star-like objects they named Quasi-Stellar Objects (QSOs), or quasars, rather than actual stars. An important breakthrough in the study of quasars occurred when astronomers measured the red-shift of the light they produced. That red-shift was very great indeed, placing some at distances of about 12 billion light-years from **Earth**. At that **distance**, quasars may well be among the oldest objects in the sky. It is possible, therefore, that they may be able to provide information about the earliest stages of the universe's history. It is now thought that quasars are the very bright centers of some distant galaxies, and so energetic probably because there is a supermassive **black hole** at the galaxy's center.

Another valuable discovery made with radio telescopes was that of pulsars. In 1967, British astronomer Jocelyn Bell noticed a twinkling-like set of radio signals that reappeared every evening in exactly the same location of the sky. Bell finally concluded that the twinkling effect was actually caused by an object in the sky that was giving off pulses of energy in the radio portion of the electromagnetic spectrum at very precise intervals, with a period of 1.3373011 seconds. She later found three more such objects with periods of 0.253065,

KEY TERMS

Frequency—The number of times per second that a wave passes a given point.

Optical astronomy—A field of astronomy that uses visible light as its source of data.

Radio galaxy—A galaxy that emits strongly in the radio region of the electromagnetic spectrum.

Radio waves—A portion of the electromagnetic spectrum with wavelengths greater than 1 meter and frequencies of less than 10^9 cycles per second.

Resolving power—The ability of a telescope to recognize two objects that are very close to each other in the sky.

Wavelength—The distance between two peaks or two troughs in a wave, such as in a ray of light.

1.187911, and 1.2737635 seconds. Those objects were soon given the name of pulsars (for *pul*sating *stars*). Evidence appears to suggest that pulsars are rotating with very precise periods, and they are now believed to be rotating **neutron** stars that emit a narrow beam of radio waves. Because the star is rotating, the beam sweeps across our sky with a precise period.

See also Galaxy; Pulsar; Quasar.

Further Reading

Editors of Time-Life Books. *Voyage through the Universe: The New Astronomy.* Alexandria, VA: Time-Life Books, 1991.

Editors of Time-Life Books. *Voyage through the Universe: The Far Planets.* Alexandria, VA: Time-Life Books, 1991.

Pasachoff, Jay M. *Contemporary Astronomy.* 4th ed. Philadelphia: Saunders College Publishing, 1989.

Verschuur, Gerrit L. *The Invisible Universe Revealed.* New York: Springer-Verlag, 1987.

David E. Newton

Radio waves

Radio waves are a form of electromagnetic **radiation** with long wavelengths and low frequencies. The radio section of the **electromagnetic spectrum** covers a fairly wide band and includes waves with frequencies ranging from about 10 kilohertz to about 60,000 megahertz (which correspond to wavelengths between 98,000 ft, or 30,000 m, and 0.2 in, or 0.5 cm). The commercial value of radio waves as a means of transmitting sounds was first appreciated by the Italian inventor Guglielmo Marconi in the 1890s. Marconi's invention led to the wireless **telegraph**, the radio, and eventually to such variations as the AM radio, FM radio, and CB (citizen's band) radio.

Propagation of radio waves

Radio waves travel by three different routes from their point of propagation to their point of detection. These three routes are through the troposphere, through the ground, and by reflection off the ionosphere. The first of these routes is the most direct. A radio wave generated and transmitted from point A may travel in a relatively straight line through the lower atmosphere to a second point, B, where its presence can be detected by a receiver. This "line of sight" propagation is similar to the transmission of a beam of light from one point to another on Earth's surface. And, as with light, this form of radio wave propagation is limited by the curvature of Earth's surface.

This description is, however, overly simplified. Radio waves are deflected in a number of ways as they move through the troposphere. For example, they may be reflected, refracted, or diffracted by air molecules through which they pass. As a consequence, radio waves can actually pass beyond Earth's optical **horizon** and, to an extent, follow Earth's curvature.

Line-of-sight transmission has taken on a new dimension with the invention of communications satellites. Today a radio wave can be aimed at an orbiting **satellite** traveling in the upper part of the atmosphere. That satellite can then retransmit the signal back to Earth's surface, where it can be picked up by a number of receiving stations. Communications satellites can be of two types. One, a passive satellite, simply provides a surface off which the radio wave can be reflected. The other type, an active satellite, picks up the signal received from Earth's surface, amplifies it, and then retransmits it to ground-based receiving stations.

Since radio waves are propagated in all directions from a transmitting **antenna**, some may reflect off the ground to the receiving antenna, where they can be detected. Such waves can also be transmitted along Earth's surface in a form known as surface waves. Radio waves whose transmission takes place in connection with Earth's surface may be modified because of changing ground conditions, such as irregularities in the surface or the amount of moisture in the ground.

Finally, radio waves can be transmitted by reflection from the ionosphere. When waves of frequencies up to about 25 megahertz (sometimes higher) are projected into the sky, they bounce off a region of the ionosphere known as the E layer. The E layer is a region of high **electron density** located about 80 kilometers (50 miles) above Earth's surface. Some reflection occurs off the F layer of the ionosphere also, located about 120 miles (200 km) above Earth's surface. Radio waves reflected by the ionosphere are also known as sky waves.

Transmission of radio waves

The radio wave that leaves a transmitting antenna originates as a sound spoken into a microphone. A microphone is a device for converting sound **energy** into electrical energy. A microphone accomplishes this transformation by any one of a number of mechanisms. In a **carbon** microphone, for example, sound waves entering the device cause a box containing carbon granules to vibrate. The vibrating carbon granules, in turn, cause a change in **electrical resistance** within the carbon box to vary, resulting in the production of an electrical current of varying strength.

A **crystal** microphone makes use of the piezoelectric effect, the production of a tiny **electric current** caused by the deformation of the crystal in the microphone. The magnitude of the current produced corresponds to the magnitude of the sound wave entering the microphone.

The electric current produced within the microphone then passes into an **amplifier** where the current strength is greatly increased. The current is then transmitted to an antenna, where the varying electrical field associated with the current initiates an electromagnetic wave in the air around the antenna. It is this radio wave that is then propagated through **space** by one of the mechanisms described above.

A radio wave can be detected by a mechanism that is essentially the reverse of the process described here. The wave is intercepted by the antenna, which converts the wave into an electrical signal that is transmitted to a radio or **television** set. Within the radio or television set, the electrical signal is converted to a sound wave that can be broadcast through speakers.

Modulating a sound wave

The simple transmission scheme outlined above cannot be used for commercial broadcasting. If a dozen stations all transmitted sounds by the mechanism described above, a receiving station would pick up a garbled combination of all transmissions. To prevent **interference** from a number of transmitting stations, all broadcast radio waves are first modulated.

Modulation is the process by which a sound wave is added to a basic radio wave known as the carrier wave. For example, an audio signal can be electronically added to a carrier signal to produce a new signal that has undergone amplitude modulation (AM). Amplitude modulation means that the amplitude (or size) of the wave of the original sound wave has been changed by adding it to the carrier wave.

Sound waves can also be modulated in such a way that their **frequency** is altered. For example, a sound wave can be added to a carrier signal to produce a signal with the same amplitude, but a different frequency. The sound wave has, in this case, undergone frequency modulation (FM).

Both AM and FM signals must be decoded at the receiving station. In either case, the carrier wave is electronically subtracted from the radio wave that is picked up by the receiving antenna. What remains after this process is the original sound wave, encoded, of course, as an electrical signal.

KEY TERMS

Antenna—A long metal wire or bar used to send out or receive radio waves.

Carrier wave—A radio wave with an assigned characteristic frequency for a given station to which is added a sound-generated electrical wave that carries a message.

Electromagnetic spectrum—The range of electromagnetic radiation that includes radio waves, x rays, visible light, ultraviolet light, infrared radiation, gamma rays, and other forms of radiation.

Frequency—The number of vibrations, cycles, or waves that pass a certain point per second.

Hertz—The unit used to measure frequency. One hertz is one cycle per second.

Modulation—The addition of a sound-generated electrical wave to a carrier wave.

Piezoelectricity—A small electrical current produced when a crystal is deformed.

Propagation—The spreading of a wave from a common origin.

Troposphere—The layer of the Earth's atmosphere nearest the Earth's surface.

Wavelength—The distance between two adjacent troughs or peaks of a wave.

All broadcasting stations are assigned characteristic carrier frequencies by the Federal Communications Commission. This system allows a number of stations to operate in the same area without overlapping. Thus, two stations a few kilometers apart could both be sending out exactly the same program, but they would sound different (and have different electric signals) because each had been overlaid on a different carrier signal.

Receiving stations can detect the difference between these two transmissions because they can tune their equipment to pick up only one or the other carrier frequency. When you turn the tuning knob on your own radio, for example, you are adjusting the receiver to pick up carrier waves from station A, station B, or some other station. Your radio then decodes the signal it has received by subtracting the carrier wave and converting the remaining electric signal to a sound wave.

The identifying characteristics by which you recognize a radio station reflect its two important transmitting features. The frequency, such as 101.5 megahertz (or simply "101.5 on your dial") identifies the carrier wave

frequency, as described above. The power rating ("operating with 50,000 watts of power") describes the power available to transmit its signal. The higher the power of the station, the greater the **distance** at which its signal can be picked up.

See also Wave motion

Further Reading

Davidovits, Peter. *Communication*. New York: Holt, Rinehart and Winston, Inc., 1972.

Dittman, Richard, and Glenn Schmieg. *Physics in Everyday Life*. New York: McGraw-Hill Book Company, 1979.

David E. Newton

Radioactive dating

In the nineteenth century, prominent scientists such as Charles Lyell, Charles Darwin, Sir William Thomson (Lord Kelvin), and Thomas Huxley, were in continual debate about the age of the **earth**. The discovery of the radioactive properties of **uranium** in 1896 by Henri Becquerel subsequently revolutionized the way scientists measured the age of artifacts and supported the theory that the earth was considerably older than what some scientists believed.

There are several methods of determining the actual or relative age of the earth's crust: examination of fossil remains of plants and animals, relating the magnetic field of ancient days to the current magnetic field of the earth, and examination of artifacts from past civilizations. However, one of the most widely used and accepted method is radioactive dating. All radioactive dating is based on the fact that a radioactive substance, through its characteristic disintegration, eventually transmutes into a stable nuclide. When the rate of decay of a radioactive substance is known, the age of a specimen can be determined from the relative proportions of the remaining radioactive material and the product of its decay.

In 1907, the American chemist Bertram Boltwood demonstrated that he could determine the age of a rock containing uranium-238 and thereby proved to the scientific community that radioactive dating was a reliable method. Uranium-238, whose **half-life** is 4.5 billion years, transmutes into lead-206, a stable end-product. Boltwood explained that by studying a rock containing uranium-238, one can determine the age of the rock by measuring the remaining amount of uranium-238 and the relative amount of lead-206. The more lead the rock contains, the older it is.

The long half-life of uranium-238 makes it possible to date only the oldest **rocks**. This method is not reliable for measuring the age of rocks less than 10 million years old because so little of the uranium will have decayed within that period of time. This method is also very limited because uranium is not found in every old rock. It is rarely found in sedimentary or metamorphic rocks, and is not found in all **igneous rocks**. Another method for dating the rocks of the earth's crust is the rubidium-87/strontium-87 method. Although the half-life of rubidium-87 is even longer than uranium-238 (49 billion years or 10 times the age of the earth), it is useful because it can be found in almost all igneous rocks. Perhaps the best method for dating rocks is the potassium-40/argon-40 method. Potassium is a very common mineral and is found in sedimentary, metamorphic, and igneous rock. Also, the half-life of potassium-40 is only 1.3 billion years, so it can be used to date rocks as young as 50,000 years old.

In 1947, a radioactive dating method for determining the age of organic materials, was developed by Willard Frank Libby, who received the Nobel Prize in **Chemistry** in 1960 for his radiocarbon research. All living plants and animals contain **carbon**, and while most of the total carbon is carbon-12, a very small amount of the total carbon is radioactive carbon-14. Libby found that the amount of carbon-14 remains constant in a living **plant** or **animal** and is in equilibrium with the environment, however once the **organism** dies, the carbon-14 within it diminishes according to its rate of decay. This is because living organisms utilize carbon from the environment for **metabolism**. Libby, and his team of researchers, measured the amount of carbon-14 in a piece of acacia **wood** from an Egyptian tomb dating 2700-2600 BC. Based on the half-life of carbon-14 (5,568 years), Libby predicted that the **concentration** of carbon-14 would be about 50% of that found in a living **tree**. His prediction was correct.

Radioactive dating is also used to study the effects of **pollution** on an environment. Scientists are able to study recent climactic events by measuring the amount of a specific radioactive nuclide that is known to have attached itself to certain particles that have been incorporated into the earth's surface. For example, during the 1960s, when many above-ground tests of **nuclear weapons** occurred, the earth was littered by cesium-137 (half-life of 30.17 years) particle fallout from the nuclear weapons. By collecting samples of sediment, scientists are able to obtain various types of kinetic information based on the concentration of cesium-137 found in the samples. Lead-210, a naturally occurring radionuclide with a half-life of 21.4 years, is also used to obtain kinetic information about the earth. Radium-226, a grandpar-

ent of lead-210, decays to radon-222, the radioactive gas that can be found in some basements. Because it is a gas, radon-222 exists in the atmosphere. Radon-222 decays to polonium-218, which attaches to particles in the atmosphere and is consequently rained out—falling into and traveling through streams, **rivers**, and lakes.

Radioactive dating has proved to be an invaluable tool and has been used in many scientific fields, including **geology**, archeology, paleoclimatology, atmospheric science, **oceanography**, **hydrology**, and biomedicine. This method of dating has also been used to study artifacts that have received a great deal of public attention, such as the Shroud of Turin, the Dead Sea Scrolls, Egyptian tombs, and Stonehenge. Since the discovery of radioactive dating, there have been several improvements in the equipment used to measure radioactive residuals in samples. For example, with the invention of accelerator mass spectometry, scientists have been able to date samples very accurately.

See also Radioactive decay.

Radioactive decay

The nucleus of each atom has a specific number of protons and neutrons and is either stable or unstable, depending on the relative number of each. The most stable **atoms** are those that have an equal number of protons and neutrons. Atoms that are unstable are radioactive. An atom that is radioactive can also be called a radionuclide. Of the known nuclides (approximately 2,000), only 264 are stable, and of the known radionuclides (approximately 1,700), only 70 occur in nature. The rest are manmade. Unstable atoms undergo a process called radioactive decay to reach a more stable state.

While a radionuclide is going through the process of decay, **energy** is released from the atom in one of three modes: alpha, beta, or gamma **radiation**. These modes may take several steps, involving only the nucleus or the entire atom. Each radionuclide has one or more characteristic modes of decay. The particular **mode** of decay determines the type of energy, or radiation, released from the atom, and consists of either **subatomic particles**, photons, or both.

Radionuclides are unstable to varying degrees. The more unstable a radionuclide is the faster it decays. The quantity of a radioactive substance is expressed as disintegrations per second, in units of Curies (Ci) named for Marie Curie, or if *Système International* is used, Becquerels (Bq) named for Henri Becquerel. The rate at which a radionuclide decays depends upon its **half-life**, the expected time required for half of the nuclei to decay to a stable state. The half-life is typically not affected by **temperature**, **pressure**, or gravitational, magnetic, or electrical fields.

When radioactivity was first discovered, it was thought that all the energy given off by the radionuclide was basically the same, with differences only in penetrating power. However, research conducted by Becquerel and Pierre Curie proved that there were three distinct modes of radioactive decay, which differed not only in their ability to penetrate, but also in their **velocity**, as well as their susceptibility to magnetic fields.

Alpha and beta radioemissions are actually particulate **matter** that is thrown out from the nucleus. An **alpha particle** is two protons and two neutrons, or in other words, it is a helium atom without the electrons. After an alpha particle is emitted, the atomic **mass** decreases by four, and the number of protons and neutrons decrease by two. Alpha decay occurs in radionuclides with an **atomic number** greater than 83 and a **mass number** greater than 209. Alpha particles interact with negatively charged electrons in the environment, which consequently use up the energy in the particle, slowing it down and greatly diminishing its penetrating power. Even a sheet of **paper** can stop an alpha particle. The direction of an alpha particle is only slightly affected by a magnetic field because the particle has a balanced change. When a radionuclide decays by alpha radiation, it does not just disappear. Instead, the radionuclide transmutes into another radionuclide or nuclide. For example, uranium-238 transmutes into several other radionuclides, including radium-226 and radon-222, before ending up as lead-206, a stable nuclide.

Beta radiation, which also involves particulate emissions, can be either be negatively charged or positively charged. Beta particles are actually created in the nucleus by either a **proton** changing into a **neutron** (positron **emission**) or a neutron changing into a proton (negatron emission). A beta particle has a higher velocity than an alpha particle, and its path is markedly deflected by a magnetic field. When a negatron is emitted from an atom, the atomic mass of the atom is unchanged, the number of protons increases by one, and the number of neutrons decreases by one. The mass remains unchanged when a positron is emitted, the number of neutrons increases by one, and the number of protons decreases by one.

An atom usually becomes excited from either of the above-mentioned decay processes and sheds excess energy in the form of a gamma ray **photon**. With gamma emissions, the atomic mass, number of protons (atomic number), or the number of neutrons, remains unchanged. The velocity of a gamma ray is almost that of light and is not affected by magnetic fields.

Radioactive fallout

Radioactive fallout is material produced by a nuclear explosion or a **nuclear reactor** accident that enters the atmosphere and eventually falls to **Earth**. This fallout consists of minute, radioactive particles of dust, **soil**, and other debris. While some fallout results from natural sources, the term is usually used in reference to radioactive particles that were released into the atmosphere by a nuclear explosion or reactor accident. Fallout refers to material that has fallen to Earth, and also to material that is still suspended in the atmosphere.

Sources of radioactive fallout

Radioactive fallout from **nuclear weapons** began in 1945 when the United States tested the first atomic bomb in New Mexico. Atomic bombs create devastating explosions by "splitting the atom," a process more properly referred to as **nuclear fission**. The powerful blast of an atomic bomb is the result of **energy** released when the nuclei of unstable heavy elements are split, such as uranium-235 and plutonium-239. Nuclear fission also generates unstable **atoms** that release **subatomic particles** and electromagnetic **radiation**, known as radioactivity. In some cases, neutrons released during fission can interact with nearby materials to create new radioactive elements.

Also in 1945, the United States exploded atomic bombs in Hiroshima and Nagasaki, Japan. There are the only nuclear weapons to have ever been used as an act of war. Since the end of World War II, the United States, the former Soviet Union, the United Kingdom, France, and China have test-exploded nuclear weapons above ground, and thereby contributed to worldwide fallout. Nuclear weapons testing was most intense between 1954 and 1961. (All of these countries have also undertaken numerous below-ground tests of nuclear weapons, as have India, Pakistan, and probably some other countries. However, below-ground testing carries little risk of causing atmospheric radioactive fallout.)

Another source of radioactive fallout is nuclear reactors. Like an atomic bomb, a nuclear reactor generates nuclear energy by splitting atoms. However, instead of releasing all of the energy in an instant, a reactor releases it slowly, in a controlled fashion. The **heat** generated by the carefully controlled nuclear reactions is used to make steam, which drives a **generator** that produces **electricity**.

After a cooling system failed at the Three Mile Island **Nuclear power** plant in Pennsylvania in 1979, a small amount of radioactive material was released into the atmosphere. Enormously larger amounts of dangerous radioactive materials were released in 1986, following a catastrophic accident at a poorly designed nuclear plant at Chernobyl in the Ukraine. After that catastrophe, significant amounts of fallout deposited over 52,000 square miles (135,000 sq km) in Belarus, Scandinavia, and elsewhere in **Europe**.

Types of fallout

Particles that make up radioactive fallout can be as small as the invisible droplets produced by an aerosol spray can, or as large as ash that falls close to a **wood** fire. The type of radioactivity in fallout depends on the nature of the nuclear reaction that emitted the particles into the atmosphere. More than 60 different types of radioactive substances may be initially present in fallout. Some of these decay into non-radioactive products in seconds, while others take centuries or longer to become non-radioactive. It takes 28 years, for example, for a **sample** of strontium-90 to lose one-half of its initial radioactivity. Strontium-90 is one of the most dangerous elements in fallout because it is treated by the **metabolism** of humans in the same manner as **calcium**, an important component of bone. If animals or humans eat food contaminated with strontium-90, it will accumulate in their bodies. Other particularly harmful products in fallout include cesium-134, cesium-137, and iodine-131.

Radiation damages and kills cells in the body. Large doses of radiation can result in burns, vomiting, and damage to the **nervous system**, **digestive system**, and bone marrow. Smaller doses can cause genetic mutations and **cancer** years after exposure.

Fallout from a nuclear explosion can be local, tropospheric, or stratospheric

Heavy objects caught in the **wind** fall to Earth before lighter objects. Under the same wind conditions, a large cinder will travel less **distance** than a small one. The same principle applies to fallout particles.

When a nuclear weapon explodes on or near the surface of the Earth, huge quantities of soil, rock, **water**, and other materials are injected into the atmosphere, creating the familiar shape of the "mushroom cloud." Depending on their size, particles in this cloud will fall to Earth relatively soon, or they may drift in the atmosphere for a long time. An underground nuclear explosion that does not break through the surface does not produce any fallout, and the radioactivity remains trapped below ground.

Local fallout deposits within about 10 miles of a typical above-ground explosion. This material resembles ash or cinders that rise through a chimney and **deposit** nearby. Emitted particles greater than about 20 micrometers in diameter usually become local fallout. This fallout can

be extremely radioactive, but only for a short time, after which its radioactivity is much less, though not **zero**.

Particles smaller than local fallout, as much as 200 times smaller, remain suspended in the lower atmosphere, or troposphere. Depending on the **weather**, these particles travel much farther than local fallout before being deposited to the surface, mostly within about one month.

Some fallout may reach the stratosphere, the high-altitude layer of atmosphere above the troposphere. To reach the stratosphere, fallout needs the **force** of the most powerful atomic explosions, caused by a **hydrogen** or thermonuclear bomb, to inject it that high. Stratospheric fallout can drift for years, and when it finally mixes with the troposphere and is deposited to the surface, it can fall-out anywhere in the world.

Recent developments affecting fallout

The former Soviet Union, the United States, and Great Britain agreed in 1963 to stop all testing of nuclear weapons in the atmosphere, under water, and in outer **space**. France and China, however, have continued such tests. The United States and Russia further agreed in 1993 to eliminate two-thirds of their nuclear warheads by 2003. This agreement, made possible by the ending of the Cold War, greatly decreases the chances of nuclear warfare and the generation of enormous quantities of fallout.

Disastrous nuclear accidents, such as those at Three Mile Island and Chernobyl, have made nuclear reactors much less popular. No nuclear reactors ordered after 1973 have been completed in the U.S., although several are under construction in Japan, Thailand, Turkey, and elsewhere.

See also Nuclear reactor; Nuclear weapons; Radioactivity.

Further Reading

Bock, G., G. Cardew, and H. Paretzhe (eds.). *Health Impacts of Large Releases of Radionucludes.* John Wiley and Sons, 1997.

Eisenbud, M. and T.F. Gesell. *Environmental Radioactivity: From Natural, Industrial, and Military Sources.* Academic Press, 1997.

Lillie, D. W. *Our Radiant World.* Ames, IA: Iowa State University Press, 1986.

Martin, A., and S. A. Herbison. *An Introduction to Radiation Protection.* London: Chapman and Hall, 1986.

Miller, Richard L. *Under the Cloud, The Decades of Nuclear Testing.* New York: The Free Press, 1986.

Nuclear Weapons Fallout Compensation. Joint Hearing before the Committee on Labor and Human Resources and the Subcommittee on the Judiciary, United States Senate, 97th Congress. Examination of the Potential Dangers of and Liability for Radioactive Emissions Resulting form The Government's Weapons Testing Program. March 12, 1982. Washington, DC: U.S. Government Printing Office, 1982.

Sternglass, Ernest J. *Secret Fallout, Low-Level Radiation from Hiroshima to Three Mile Island.* New York: McGraw-Hill Company, 1981.

Dean Allen Haycock

KEY TERMS

Isotope—One of two or more atoms having the same number of protons, but a different number of neutrons in their atomic nucleus.

Nuclear fission—A nuclear reaction in which an atomic nucleus splits into fragments, with the release of energy, including radioactivity. Also popularly known as "splitting the atom."

Nuclear reactor—A device which generates energy by controlling the rate of nuclear fission. The energy produced is used to heat water, which drives an electrical generator. By-products of the fission process may be used for medical, scientific, or military purposes, but most remain as radioactive waste materials.

Nuclear weapon—A bomb that derives its explosive force from the release of nuclear energy.

Radioactivity—Spontaneous release of subatomic particles or gamma rays by unstable atoms as their nuclei decay.

Radioisotope—A type of atom or isotope, such as strontium-90, that exhibits radioactivity.

Radioactive pollution

Certain **atoms** are radioactive, meaning they emit radioactivity during spontaneous transformation from an unstable **isotope** to a more stable one. Radioactive **pollution** results from **contamination** of the environment with such substances, which may represent a significant health risk to humans and other organisms. Radioactive pollution differs from conventional pollution in that it cannot be detoxified. Instead, radioactive materials must be isolated from the environment until their **radiation** level has decreased to a safe level, a process which requires thousands of years for some materials.

Types of radiation

Radiation is classified as being ionizing or non-ionizing. Both types can be harmful to humans and other organisms.

Non-ionizing radiation

Non-ionizing radiation is relatively long-wavelength electromagnetic radiation, such as radiowaves, microwaves, visible radiation, ultraviolet radiation, and very low-energy electromagnetic fields. Non-ionizing radiation is generally considered less dangerous than **ionizing radiation**. However, some forms of non-ionizing radiation, such as ultraviolet, can damage biological molecules and cause health problems. Scientists do not yet fully understand the longer-term health effects of some forms of non-ionizing radiation, such as that from very low-level electromagnetic fields (e.g., high-voltage power lines), although the evidence to date suggests that the risks are extremely small.

Ionizing radiation

Ionizing radiation is the short wavelength radiation or particulate radiation emitted by certain unstable isotopes during **radioactive decay**. There are about 70 radioactive isotopes, all of which emit some form of ionizing radiation as they decay from one isotope to another. A radioactive isotope typically decays through a series of other isotopes until it reaches a stable one. As indicated by its name, ionizing radiation can ionize the atoms or molecules with which it interacts. In other words, ionizing radiation can cause other atoms to release their electrons. These free electrons can damage many biochemicals, such as **proteins**, lipids, and nucleic acids (including DNA). In intense, this damage can cause severe human health problems, including cancers, and even death.

Ionizing radiation can be either short-wavelength electromagnetic radiation or particulate radiation. Gamma radiation and X-radiation are short-wavelength electromagnetic radiation. Alpha particles, beta particles, neutrons, and protons are particulate radiation. Alpha particles, beta particles, and gamma rays are the most commonly encountered forms of radioactive pollution. Alpha particles are simply ionized helium nuclei, and consist of two protons and two neutrons. Beta particles are electrons, which have a **negative** charge. Gamma radiation is high-energy electromagnetic radiation.

Scientists have devised various units for measuring radioactivity. A Curie (Ci) represents the rate of radioactive decay. One Curie is 3.7×10^{10} radioactive disintegrations per second. A rad is a unit representing the absorbed dose of radioactivity. One rad is equal to an absorbed **energy** dose of 100 ergs per gram of radiated medium. One rad = 0.01 Grays. A rem is a unit that measures the effectiveness of radioactivity in causing biological damage. One rem is equal to one rad times a biological weighting **factor**. The weighting factor is 1.0 for gamma radiation and beta particles, and it is 20 for alpha particles. One rem = 1000 millirem = 0.01 Sieverts. The radioactive **half-life** is a measure of the persistence of radioactive material. The half-life is the time required for one-half of an initial quantity of atoms of a radioactive isotope to decay to a different isotope.

Sources of radioactive pollution

In the United States, people are typically exposed to about 350 millirems of ionizing radiation per year. On average, 82% of this radiation comes from natural sources and 18% from anthropogenic sources (i.e., those associated with human activities). The major natural source of radiation is **radon** gas, which accounts for about 55% of the total radiation dose. The principal anthropogenic sources of radioactivity are medical X-rays and **nuclear medicine**. Radioactivity from the fallout of **nuclear weapons** testing and from **nuclear power** plants make up less than 0.5% of the total radiation dose, i.e., less than 2 millirems. Although the contribution to the total human radiation dose is extremely small, radioactive isotopes released during previous atmospheric testing of nuclear weapons will remain in the atmosphere for the next 100 years.

Lifestyle and radiation dose

People who live in certain regions are exposed to higher doses of radiation. For example, residents of the Rocky Mountains of Colorado receive about 30 millirems more cosmic radiation than people living at **sea level**. This is because the atmosphere is thinner at higher elevations, and therefore less effective at shielding the surface from cosmic radiation. Exposure to cosmic radiation is also high while people are flying in an airplane, so pilots and flight attendants have an enhanced, occupational exposure. In addition, residents of certain regions receive higher doses of radiation from radon-222, due to local geological anomalies. Radon-222 is a colorless and odorless gas that results from the decay of naturally occurring, radioactive isotopes of **uranium**. Radon-222 typically enters buildings from their basement, or from certain mineral-containing construction materials. Ironically, the trend toward improved home insulation has increased the amount of radon-222 which remains trapped inside houses.

Personal lifestyle also influences the amount of radioactivity to which people are exposed. For example,

miners, who spend a lot of time underground, are exposed to relatively high doses of radon-222 and consequently have relatively high rates of lung **cancer**. Cigarette smokers expose their lungs to high levels of radiation, since tobacco plants contain trace quantities of polonium-210, lead-210, and radon-222. These radioactive isotopes come from the small amount of uranium present in **fertilizers** used to promote tobacco growth. Consequently, the lungs of a cigarette smoker are exposed to thousands of additional millirems of radioactivity, although any associated hazards are much less than those of tar and **nicotine**.

Nuclear weapons testing

Nuclear weapons release enormous amounts of radioactive materials when they are exploded. Most of the radioactive pollution from nuclear weapons testing is from iodine-131, cesium-137, and strontium-90. Iodine-131 is the least dangerous of these isotopes, although it has a relatively half-life of about eight days. Iodine-131 accumulates in the thyroid gland, and large doses can cause thyroid cancer. Cesium-137 has a half-life of about 30 years. It is chemically similar to potassium, and is distributed throughout the human body. Based on the total amount of cesium already in the atmosphere, all humans will receive about 27 millirems of radiation from cesium-137 over their lifetime. Strontium-90 has a half-life of 38 years. It is chemically similar to **calcium** and is deposited in bones. Strontium-90 is expelled from the body very slowly, and the uptake of significant amounts increases the risks of developing bone cancer or leukemia.

Nuclear power plants

Many environmentalists are critical of nuclear power generation. They claim that there is an unacceptable risk of a catastrophic accident, and that nuclear power plants generate large amounts of unmanageable nuclear waste.

The U.S. Nuclear Regulatory Commission has strict requirements regarding the amount of radioactivity that can be released from a nuclear power reactor. In particular, a **nuclear reactor** can expose an individual who lives on the fence line of the power plant to no more than 10 millirems of radiation per year. Actual measurements at U.S. nuclear power plants have shown that a person who lived at the fence line would actually be exposed to much less that 10 millirems.

Thus, for a typical person who is exposed to about 350 millirems of radiation per year from all other sources, much of which is natural background, the proportion of radiation from nuclear power plants is extremely small. In fact, coal- and oil-fired power plants, which release small amounts of radioactivity contained in their fuels, are responsible for more airborne radioactive pollution in the United States than are nuclear power plants.

Although a nuclear power plant cannot explode like an atomic bomb, accidents can result in serious radioactive pollution. During the past 45 years, there have been a number of not-fully controlled or uncontrolled fission reactions at nuclear power plants in the United States and elsewhere, which have killed or injured power plant workers. These accidents occurred in Los Alamos, New Mexico; Oak Ridge, Tennessee; Richland, Washington; and Wood River Junction, Rhode Island. The most famous case was the 1979 accident at the Three Mile Island nuclear reactor in Pennsylvania, which received a great deal of attention in the press. However, nuclear scientists have estimated that people living within 50 miles (80 km) of this reactor were exposed to less than 2 millirems of radiation, most of it as iodine-131, a short-lived isotope. This exposure constituted less than one percent of the total annual radiation dose of an average person. However, these data do not mean that the accident at Three Mile Island was not a serious one; fortunately, technicians were able to re-attain control of the reactor before more devastating damage occurred, and the reactor system was well contained so that only a relatively small amount of radioactivity escaped to the ambient environment.

By far, the worst nuclear reactor accident occurred in 1986 in Chernobyl, Ukraine. An uncontrolled build-up of **heat** resulted in a meltdown of the reactor core and **combustion** of graphite moderator material in one of the several generating units at Chernobyl, releasing more than 50 million Curies of radioactivity to the ambient environment. The disaster killed 31 workers, and resulted in the hospitalization of more than 500 other people from radiation sickness. According to Ukrainian authorities, during the decade following the Chernobyl disaster an estimated 10,000 people in Belarus, Russia, and Ukraine died from cancers and other radiation-related diseases caused by the accident. In addition to these relatively local effects, the atmosphere transported radiation from Chernobyl into **Europe** and throughout the Northern Hemisphere.

More than 500,000 people in the vicinity of Chernobyl were exposed to dangerously high doses of radiation, and more than 300,000 people were permanently evacuated from the vicinity. Since radiation-related health problems may appear decades after exposure, scientists expect that many thousands of additional people will eventually suffer higher rates of thyroid cancer, bone cancer, leukemia, and other radiation-related diseases. Unfortunately, bureaucratic incompetence and a cover-up of the explosion by responsible authorities, including those in government, endangered even more

people. Many local residents did not known that they should flee the area as soon as possible, or were not provided with the medical attention they needed.

The large amount of **radioactive waste** generated by nuclear power plants is another an important problem. This waste will remain radioactive for many thousands of years, so technologists must design systems for extremely long-term storage. One obvious problem is that the long-term reliability of the storage systems cannot be fully assured, because they cannot be directly tested for the length of time they will be used (i.e., for thousands of years). Another problem with nuclear waste is that it will remain extremely dangerous for much longer than the expected lifetimes of existing governments and social institutions. Thus, we are making the societies of the following millennia, however they may be structured, responsible for the safe storage of nuclear waste that is being generated in such large quantities today.

Biological effects of radioactivity

The amount of injury caused by a radioactive isotope depends on its physical half-life, and on how quickly it is absorbed and then excreted by an **organism**. Most studies of the harmful effects of radiation have been performed on single-celled organisms. Obviously, the situation is more complex in humans and other multicellular organisms, because a single **cell** damaged by radiation may indirectly affect other cells in the individual. The most sensitive regions of the human body appear to be those which have many actively dividing cells, such as the skin, gonads, intestine, and tissues that grow **blood** cells (spleen, bone marrow, lymph organs).

Radioactivity is toxic because it forms ions when it reacts with biological molecules. These ions can form free radicals, which damage proteins, membranes, and nucleic acids. Radioactivity can damage DNA (deoxyribonucleic acid) by destroying individual bases (particularly thymine), by breaking single strands, by breaking double strands, by cross-linking different DNA strands, and by cross-linking DNA and proteins. Damage to DNA can lead to cancers, **birth** defects, and even death.

However, cells have biochemical repair systems which can reverse some of the damaging biological effects of low-level exposures to radioactivity. This allows the body to better tolerate radiation that is delivered at a low dose rate, such as over a longer period of time. In fact, all humans are exposed to radiation in extremely small doses throughout their life. The biological effects of such small doses over such a long time are almost impossible to measure, and are essentially unknown at present. There is, however, a theoretical possibility that the small amount of radioactivity released into the environment by normally operating nuclear power plants, and by previous atmospheric testing of nuclear weapons, has slightly increased the incidence of certain cancers in human populations. However, scientists have not been able to conclusively show that such an effect has actually occurred.

Currently, there is disagreement among scientists about whether there is a threshold dose for radiation damage to organisms. In other words, is there a dose of radiation below which there are no harmful biological effects? Some scientists maintain that there is no such threshold, and that radiation at any dose carries a finite risk of causing some biological damage. Furthermore, the damage caused by very low doses of radiation may be cumulative, or additive to the damage caused by other harmful agents to which humans are exposed. Other scientists maintain that there is a threshold dose for radiation damage. They believe that biological repair systems, which are presumably present in all cells, can fix the biological damage caused by extremely low doses of radiation. Thus, these scientists claim that the extremely low doses of radiation to which humans are commonly exposed are not harmful.

One of the most informative studies of the harmful effects of radiation is a long-term investigation of the survivors of the 1945 atomic blasts at Hiroshima and Nagasaki by James Neel and his colleagues. The survivors of these explosions had abnormally high rates of cancer, leukemia, and other diseases. However, there seemed to be no detectable effect on the occurrence of genetic defects in children of the survivors. The radiation dose needed to cause heritable defects in humans is higher than biologists originally expected.

Radioactive pollution is an important environmental problem. It could become much worse if extreme vigilance is not utilized in the handling and use of radioactive materials, and in the design and operation of nuclear power plants. It is also important to stop the testing of nuclear weapons, and it is crucial that they are never again used in warfare.

See also Radiation exposure; Radioactive fallout; Radioactivity; X rays.

Further Reading

Bock, G., G. Cardew, and H. Paretzhe (eds.). *Health Impacts of Large Releases of Radionucludes*. John Wiley and Sons, 1997.

Brill, A. B., et al. *Low-level Radiation Effects: A Fact Book*. New York: The Society of Nuclear Medicine, 1985.

Eisenbud, M. *Environmental Radioactivity*. New York: Norton, 1987.

Eisenbud, M. and T.F. Gesell. *Environmental Radioactivity: From Natural, Industrial, and Military Sources*. Academic Press, 1997.

KEY TERMS

Curie (Ci)—A unit representing the rate of radioactive decay. 1 Ci = 3.7×10^{10} disintegrations per second.

Ionizing radiation—Short-wavelength radiation or particulate radiation emitted by a radioactive isotope.

Isotope—A form of an atom, with a characteristic number of protons and neutrons in its nucleus, which may be radioactive.

Non-ionizing radiation—Long-wavelength electromagnetic radiation.

Rad—A unit of absorbed ionizing radiation which results in the absorption of 100 ergs of energy per gram of medium. 1 Rad = 0.01 Gray.

Radioactivity—The property of certain isotopes of some atoms which emit ionizing radiation.

Radioactive half-life—The time required for half the atoms of a radioactive isotope to decay to a more stable isotope.

Rem—A unit of the biological effectiveness of absorbed radiation, which is equal to the radiation dose in rad multiplied by a biological weighting factor, which is determined by the particular type of radiation. 1 rem = 0.01 Sievert.

Quinn, S. *Marie Curie: A Life*. New York: Simon and Schuster, 1995.

Schull, W. J., M. Otake, and J. V. Neel. "Genetic Effects of the Atomic Bombs: A Reappraisal." *Science*. 213 (1981): 1220-1227.

Peter A. Ensminger

Radioactive tracers

Radioactive tracers are substances labelled with a radioactive atom to allow easier detection and measurement. They have applications in many fields, but we will focus on their use in medicine.

Tracer Principle

The tracer principle states that radioactive isotopes have the same chemical properties as nonradioactive isotopes of the same element. Isotopes of the same element differ only in the number of neutrons in their **atoms**, which leads to nuclei with different stabilities. Unstable nuclei gain stability by **radioactive decay** which leads to different types of radioactivity. One type is gamma **radiation** which is useful in medicine because it penetrates the body without causing damage and can then be detected easily.

Tissue specificity

Radioactive tracers in medicine (also called radiopharmaceuticals) use the fact that specific tissues accumulate specific substances. Labelling one of these leads to information on the specific **tissue**. For example, the thyroid gland removes iodine from the **blood**. When ^{123}I is injected into the blood, it collects in the thyroid like any **isotope** of iodine. However, it emits gamma radiation that reveals if the gland is working at the normal rate. Many types of compounds can be radiolabelled, including salts, small organic compounds, and **proteins**, antibodies, or red blood cells.

Think about how **aircraft** have bright flashing lights on their undersides. These do not effect the aircraft's ability to fly, but make it visible in the dark night sky. The radionuclide is like a flashing light on a compound. Although we cannot see its radioactive beam with our eyes, a suitable instrument will detect it clearly against a dark nonradioactive background.

Preparation and administration of radioactive tracers

Regular chemical reactions attach the radionuclide to the rest of the tracer **molecule**. Technetium-99m (99mTc) is commonly used. This emits gamma rays of optimal **energy** for detection, with no damaging beta particles. It has a short **half-life** (six hours) which leads to fast elimination from the body by decay. It can be generated when needed from a more stable isotope, molybdenum-99.

Tracers are introduced into the body by injection, orally, or by breathing gases. Some scans are obtained immediately after administration, but others are taken hours or even days later. Scans themselves usually take 30 minutes to three hours. Patients receive about the same dose of radiation from a radioactive tracer scan as from a chest x ray.

Detection and imaging

The process of obtaining an image from a radioactive tracer is called scintigraphy. Other imaging techniques (computerized tomography, CT; **magnetic resonance imaging, MRI**) give anatomical information.

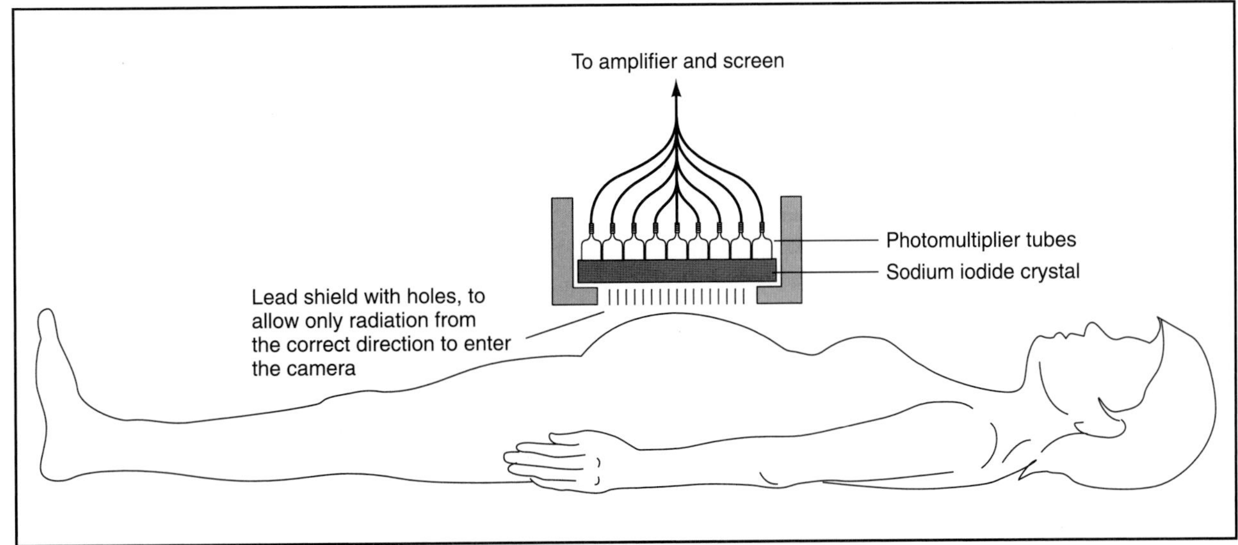

Figure 1. Schematic diagram of an Anger Scintillation Camera.

Scintigraphy gives information on the movement of compounds through tissues and vessels, and on **metabolism**. Earlier **diagnosis** is possible with scintigraphy because chemical changes often occur before structural ones. For example, a CT **brain** scan can be normal 48 hours after a **stroke**, but shows immediate changes.

Anger scintillation camera

The detector most commonly used with radioactive tracers is the Anger scintillation camera, invented by Hal Anger in the late 1950s. Gamma radiation causes crystals of **sodium** iodide to emit photons of light. This is called scintillation. This light is converted into electrical signals by photomultiplier tubes. The more photomultiplier tubes in the camera, the sharper the image. The electrical signals are electronically processed to give the final image, which is recorded permanently on a photographic plate. The Anger camera and the patient must remain stationary during imaging, which can take many minutes. To get high-quality images, the camera must be placed close to the body, which may be uncomfortable for the patient. The resulting image is planar, or two-dimensional. This is adequate for many applications, but tomography has broadened the scope of scintigraphy.

Single Photon Emission Computed Tomography (SPECT)

Tomography uses computer technology to convert numerous planar images into a three-dimensional slice through the object. This data processing is also used with CT and MRI. With radioactive tracers, it is called **emission** computed tomography, which includes single **photon** emission computed tomography (SPECT) and **positron emission tomography (PET)**. Positrons result from a different type of radioactive decay which we will not discuss here.

SPECT images are usually obtained with Anger cameras which rotate around the patient. Numerous images are obtained at different angles. Faster and bigger computers give better image quality, while improved graphics capabilities allow three-dimensional imaging. These are helpful in precisely locating areas of concern within an **organ**, but are more expensive and take longer to obtain. Hence, both planar and SPECT images will continue to be obtained.

Specific applications

Radioactive tracers are widely used to diagnose **heart** problems. Narrowing of the coronary arteries leads to coronary artery disease which often manifests itself as angina. Radiopharmaceuticals allow visualization of the **blood supply** to the heart tissue. ^{99}mTc-labels are used (e.g. sestamibi), but thallium-201 (^{201}Tl) has advantages. After reaching the heart tissue, it moves from the blood into the heart cells. Healthy cells then eliminate about 30% of the peak level of ^{201}Tl in about two hours. Damaged cells (e.g. from ischemia) will move the ^{201}Tl more slowly. Thus, ^{201}Tl gives information on both the health of the heart tissue itself and the blood flow to it.

An exciting new area of use combines radioactive tracers with monoclonal antibodies (MoAbs). Antibodies are proteins that interact with a foreign substance (antigen) in a specific way. Advances in genetic technology

KEY TERMS

Anger scintillation camera—A device used to detect gamma rays from radioactive tracers. It converts the energy from the radiation into light and then electrical signals which are eventually recorded on a photographic plate.

Isotopes—Atoms of the same element which have different numbers of neutrons. They have the same number of protons and electrons in their atoms.

Monoclonal antibody—A protein which interacts with a foreign substance (antigen) in a specific way. They are monoclonal when they are produced by a group of genetically identical cells.

Radionuclide—An isotope which gains stability through radioactive decay.

Radioactive tracer—A substance labelled with a radioactive isotope to allow easier detection and measurement.

Radiopharmaceuticals—Radioactive tracers with medical applications that are administered like other drugs.

Scintigraphy—The process of obtaining images of radioactive tracers using scintillation detectors.

Scintillation—The process by which the energy of gamma rays is converted into light energy by a suitable substance, e.g. sodium iodide.

Single photon emission computed tomography (SPECT)—The process by which gamma radiation from radionuclides which emit a single photon per decay is converted into three-dimensional images. It is a computer-based data processing method.

Tomography—A method of data processing by computers which converts numerous planar images of an object into three-dimensional images or slices through the object. It is used in many different scanning procedures.

Tracer Principle—The general principle discovered by George de Hevesy in 1912 that isotopes of the same element have the same chemical properties. They act in the same way in chemical and biological reactions.

allow biochemists to make MoAbs for many specific substances. Characteristic compounds on the surfaces of **cancer** cells can act as antigens. When radionuclide-labelled MoAbs are injected into the body, they attach to cancer cells with the corresponding antigen. The cancer cells can then be imaged, revealing their location and size. Three-dimensional imaging gives much guidance for subsequent **surgery**. Radionuclides can also be attached to emit cell-destroying radiation and thus kill cancer cells predominantly. Radiolabelled MoAbs promise to have more applications in the near future.

Further Reading

American College of Nuclear Physicians. *Nuclear Medicine T.V. Series*. Chicago: Orbis Broadcasting Group, 1995. 7 Videocassettes.

Bernier, Donald R., Paul E. Christian, and James K. Langan, Editors. *Nuclear Medicine: Technology and Techniques*. 3rd Edition. St. Louis: Mosby, 1994.

Davis, Lawrence Paul, and Darlene Fink-Bennett. "Nuclear Medicine in the Acutely Ill Patient-I." *Critical Care Clinics 10*. (April 1994): 365-381.

Reba, Richard C. "Nuclear Medicine." *Journal of the American Medical Association 270*. (July 1993): 230-232.

Zaret, Barry L. and Frans J. Wackers. "Nuclear Cardiology." *New England Journal of Medicine. 329*. (September 1993): 775-783.

Dónal P. O'Mathúna

Radioactive waste

Radioactive waste is generated during the production of **electricity** by nuclear power plants, by the eventual disposal of those facilities, and during the manufacturing and disposal of nuclear weapons and machines used in medical **diagnosis** and treatments, academic and industrial research, and certain industrial applications. Radioactive waste produces ionizing radiation, which can damage or destroy living tissues. **Ionizing radiation** transfers **energy** when it encounters biochemicals, causing them to become electrically charged, or ionized, which can damage their essential metabolic function.

Unlike conventionally toxic chemicals, the degree of danger from radioactive waste decreases over time. The **half-life** of a radioactive substance (or radioisotope) is the time required for one-half of an initial quantity to decay to other isotopes. Each radioisotope has a unique half-life, which can be only fractions of a second long, or as great as billions of years. The longer the half-life of a radioisotope, the longer is the period for which it must be safely stored or disposed until it is no longer hazardous.

Types of radioactive waste

Radioactive wastes are grouped into three categories: high-level waste, low-level waste, and transuranic

waste. High-level waste emits intense levels of ionizing **radiation** for a relatively short time, and then emits lower levels for a much longer time. Most high-level waste is used nuclear fuel rods, which must be removed from the reactor core about every 2-4 years. Large quantities of high-level wastes are also associated with the production and disposal of nuclear weapons. In 1992, about 28,000 tons (26,000 tonnes) of high-level waste were stored at commercial **nuclear power** sites in the United States, a quantity expected to double by 2002.

Low-level waste emits small amounts of ionizing radiation, usually for a long time, and it tends to be a high-volume waste. Low-level waste is produced from a variety of sources, such as filters and other cleaning material from nuclear plants, and used low-level radioisotopes from hospitals, universities, and industry. For example, in nuclear generating stations, tiny quantities of some radioactive materials may leak from the reactor. To protect the workers and the ambient environment, this radioactivity is removed with filters, which must periodically be replaced, becoming low-level waste.

Transuranic waste is produced as a by-product during controlled nuclear reactions used to generate nuclear energy (i.e., electricity). Transuranics are elements, not found in nature, that are heavier than **uranium**. Most transuranics have special properties that increase the probability of causing damage to living **tissue**. Transuranic elements are found in both high-level and low-level radioactive waste. They can be separated from low-level waste, and are then treated as high-level waste.

Storage of radioactive waste

Storage can be defined as "a method of containment with a provision for retrieval." High-level and transuranic wastes are typically stored in on-site, deep-water storage ponds with thick, stainless steel-lined **concrete** walls. After about five years, the spent fuel has lost much of its radioactivity and can be moved into dry storage facilities. These are usually on-site, above-ground facilities in which the waste is stored in thick, concrete canisters.

Low-level waste is stored in concrete cylinders in shallow burial sites at nuclear plants or at designated waste sites. Since these wastes are not as much of a concern as high-level wastes, the regulations for their storage are not as strict. Basically, the waste must be covered and stored so that contact with ambient **water** is minimal.

Transportation of radioactive waste

The regulations for transporting radioactive waste are stringent due to the possibility of a transportation accident. Various containers are used for transporting specific kinds of waste. High-level waste has the most rigorous standards, and the containers in which it is shipped must be capable of withstanding tremendous **pressure**, impact, and **heat**, and are waterproof. There have been accidents in **North America** involving trucks and trains carrying radioactive waste, but no significant amount of radioactivity has ever been released to the environment as a result.

Treatment of radioactive waste

High-level radioactive waste can be treated by fuel reprocessing, which separates still-useful fuel isotopes from the rest of the waste. The useful isotopes can then be sent to a fabrication **plant**, which produces new nuclear fuel. Some technologists view this strategy technology as an excellent alternative to long-term storage, since it is essentially a re-use practice as opposed to disposal. Fuel reprocessing plants exist in Britain, France, Japan, Germany, India, and Russia. The United States, Canada, Spain, and Sweden do not have reprocessing plants, and are planning on long-term storage of their spent fuel.

Low-level radioactive waste is commonly a high-volume material, which can often be reduced prior to storage, transport, or disposal. It can be concentrated by filtering and removing the liquid portion, so only the solid residue remains for disposal. Alternatively, the material may be solidified by fusing it into **glass** or ceramic, which are highly stable materials.

Disposal of radioactive waste

High-level and transuranic waste disposal

Radioactive waste disposal refers to the long-term removal of the waste, and is designed to have minimal contact with organisms and the ambient environment. The safe disposal of high-level and transuranic wastes from nuclear power plants and **nuclear weapons** facilities has been the center of vigorous debate for more than 50 years, and researchers and policy-makers have yet to come up with politically acceptable solutions.

The most widely supported plan involves the burial of high-level waste deep underground in a stable geological formation. Less-popular ideas include burial under a stable glacier, or dumping into a deep oceanic trench. Part of the problem with any of these ideas is that disposal requires that the site will be secure for tens of thousands of years. This probably exceeds the time for which present governmental and social institutions will persist, so far-future generations may have to deal with the high-level nuclear wastes of the present ones. Moreover, na-

ture can be a changeable, unpredictable, and powerful **force**, so there are unknown risks associated with all disposal options, and long-term, absolute guarantees cannot be given.

Low-level waste disposal

From 1940-1970, most low-level wastes were placed into **steel** drums and dumped into the **ocean** or into pits on land. However, there has been inevitable leakage from the drums, and environmentalists and the public objected to this method of disposal. Since 1970, the United States has been disposing its low-level waste at government-regulated disposal sites. In June 1990, the U. S. Nuclear Regulatory Commission (NRC) proposed that low-level radioactive waste be handled as regular garbage, due to its supposed low health risk. Epidemiologists calculated that implementing this policy might have caused 2,500 American deaths, but the NRC believed this risk was acceptable because it would save the nuclear power industry many millions of dollars every year. However, this proposal did not fully take account of recent research indicating that low-level radiation risks may be about 30 times higher than previously estimated.

Current problems in radioactive waste

The biggest technological challenge presently facing the nuclear industry is the long-term, safe disposal of high-level waste. The current preferred disposal option is to bury it deep underground. Of all technologically advanced nations, the United States is the only one that has a definite plan to develop a waste disposal site. The candidate site is in Yucca Mountain, Nevada. Huge sums of money have been spent in planning for this disposal option, but it remains controversial and is not yet built. The NRC does predict, however, that a site will be available for disposal activities in the year 2010.

Political and scientific disagreements between the state of Nevada and the federal government have delayed the process, as have arguments presented by environmental groups. The concerns largely center around the geological stability of the area, including reports from some geologists regarding possible instability of the site after construction. It has been suggested that construction activities might fracture the **bedrock**, possibly increasing water infiltration into the disposal area. Moreover, there is a relatively young **volcano** nearby, and there are 32 earthquake faults near the site. Due to the various delays, the Department of the Environment has asked Congress to allow temporary storage facilities to be built. However, some people fear that these may become permanent disposal sites for high-level waste. It seems that the only certainty is that the safe, long-term disposal of high-level radioactive wastes will continue to be an extreme challenge for technologists, and for society.

KEY TERMS

Half-life—The time required for one-half of an initial quantity of a radioactive substance to disintegrate.

High-level waste—Waste that emits intense levels of ionizing radiation for a short time, and then lower levels for a much longer time.

Ionizing radiation—Radiation that can cause tissue damage or death.

Low level waste—Waste that emits small amounts of ionizing radiation, often for a long time.

Radioisotope—A radioactive isotope. Isotopes are atoms of a particular chemical element, but they have a different atomic mass.

Transuranic waste—A special category of waste produced as a result of nuclear power generation, involving non-natural elements heavier that uranium.

See also Nuclear reactor.

Further Reading

Cohen, B. L. *The Nuclear Energy Option: An Alternative for the 90s.* New York: Plenum Press, 1990.

Miller, G. T., Jr. *Environmental Science: Sustaining the Earth.* 3rd ed. Belmont, CA: Wadsworth Publishing Company, 1991.

Nuclear Regulatory Commission. World Wide Web Homepage (electronic address-http://&.nrc.gov/nrc.html).

Price, J. *The Antinuclear Movement.* rev. ed. Boston, MA: Twayne Publishers, 1990.

Jennifer LeBlanc

Radiocarbon dating see **Dating techniques**

Radiology

Radiology is a branch of medical science that uses **x rays** and other forms of technology to image internal structures in the body. For nearly 80 years radiology was based primarily on the x ray, but since the 1970s several new imaging techniques have been developed. Some,

like computed tomography, integrates x-ray and computer technology. Others, like ultrasound and magnetic resonance imaging are nonradiologic techniques, meaning they do not use x rays or other forms of radiant **energy** to probe the human body. Although radiotherapy based on the x ray has been used to treat **cancer** since the beginning of the 20th century, most radiologists are primarily concerned with imaging the body to diagnose **disease**. However, interventional radiology is a rapidly expanding discipline in which radiologists work either alone or hand-in-hand with surgeons to treat vascular and other diseases.

The x ray: the fundamental building block of radiology

The science of radiology was born in 1895 when Wilhelm Roentgen discovered the x ray. The German scientist was studying high voltage discharges in **vacuum tubes** when he noticed that the Crookes tube he was focusing on caused a piece of screen coated with the chemical **barium** platinocyanide to fluoresce or glow. Roentgen quickly realized that he had produced a previously unknown type of invisible **radiation**. In addition, this radiant energy could pass through solids like **paper** and **wood**. He also discovered that when he placed a hand between the beam's source and the chemically coated screen, he could see the bones inside the fingers depicted on the screen. Roentgen quickly found that he could record the image with photographic paper.

Roentgen's discovery changed the course of medicine. With the ability to look inside the body without **surgery**, physicians had a new diagnostic tool that could actually locate tumors or foreign objects, like bullets, thus greatly enhancing a surgeon's ability to operate successfully. Roentgen called the new radiant energy x rays and, six years after his discovery, was awarded the Nobel Prize in **physics**.

How the x ray works

X rays are a type of radiant energy that occurs when a tungsten (a hard metallic element) target is bombarded with an **electron** beam. X rays are similar to visible **light** in that they radiate in all directions from their source. They differ, however, in that x rays are of shorter wavelength than ultraviolet light. This difference is the basis of radiology since the shorter wavelength allows x rays to penetrate many substances that are opaque to light.

An x ray of bones, organs, tumors, and other areas of the body is obtained through a cassette that holds a fluorescent screen. When activated by x rays, this screen emits light rays which produce a photochemical effect of the x rays on film. When light or x rays hit photographic film, a photochemical process takes place that results in the negative film turning black while the places not exposed to light remain clear. Images are obtained when the paper print of a negative reverses the image values. In the normal photographic process, an entire hand would be imaged because normal light cannot pass through the hand, thus creating the image on film. The desired x-ray image is obtained because x rays pass through outer **tissue** and are absorbed by bones and other structures, allowing them to be captured on film.

Over the years, radiology has fine tuned this approach to develop different x-ray devices for imaging specific areas of the body. For example, mammography is the radiological imaging of a woman's breast to determine the presence of diseases like breast cancer. Another major advance in x-ray technology was the development of radiopaque substances. When injected into the body, these substances, which do not allow x rays to pass through them, provide images of structures that would otherwise not appear on the x ray. For example, **angiography** is the imaging of **blood** vessels after injecting them with a radiopaque material. Myelography is the imaging of the spinal cord with x rays after injecting a radiopaque substance into a **membrane** covering the spine.

Ultrasound

Ultrasound was the first nonradiologic technique used to image the body. Ultrasound in radiology stems from the development of pulse-echo **radar** during World War II. First used to detect defects in **metal** structures, ultrasound, or sonography, became a useful diagnostic tool in the late 1950s and early 1970s. As its name suggests, ultrasound uses sound waves rather than electromagnetic radiation to image structures.

A common use of ultrasound is to provide images of a fetus. A sound transmitter is used to send waves into the body from various angles. As these waves bounce back off the uterus and the fetus, they are recorded both on a **television** screen and in a photograph. With the more advanced Doppler ultrasound, this technology can be used for everything from imaging atherosclerotic disease (the thickening of arteries) to evaluating the prostate and rectum.

Computers and the new era of radiology

Except for ultrasound, from the day Roentgen discovered the x ray until the early 1970s, radiology relied solely on the application of x rays through refined radiographic techniques. These applications were limited by the x ray's ability to discern only four different kinds of

matter in the body: air, **fat**, **water** (which helps make up tissue), and **minerals** (like bone). In addition, while the x ray images bone well, it cannot image what lies behind the bone unless angiography is used. For example, a standard x ray could reveal damage to the skull but would not reveal tumors or bleeding vessels in the **brain** unless they calcified or caused changes to the skull. Although the development of angiography allowed scientists to view the arteries in the brain, angiography is somewhat painful for the patient and does not reveal smaller but still serious tumors and lesions.

The high-tech era of radiology coincided with rapid advances in computer technology. By using computers to analyze and interpret vast quantities of data, scientists began to develop new and better ways to image the body. Imaging processes like computed tomography, positron emission tomography, magnetic resonance imaging, and single photo emission computed tomography all rely on the computer. With these techniques, radiologists are able to diagnose a wider range of diseases and abnormalities within the body.

Computed tomography

In 1972, radiology took a giant step forward with the development of computed tomography (CT). Although still relying on the x ray, this radiographic technique uses a computer to process the vast amount of data obtained from an electronically detected signal. Since different tissues will absorb different amounts of x rays, CT passes x-ray beams through the body at different angles on one specific **plane**, providing detailed cross sections of a specific area. This information is scanned into a digital code which the computer can transform into a video picture. These images are much superior to conventional x-ray film and can also be made into three-dimensional images, allowing the radiologist to view a structure from different angles.

As a result of this technology, physicians could view precise and small tissues in areas like the brain without causing discomfort to the patient. CT also led scientists and engineers to conduct new research into how the computer could be used to make better images of body structures.

Magnetic Resonance Imaging

Although **Magnetic Resonance Imaging (MRI)** dates back to 1946, it was used primarily to study **atoms** and molecules and to identify their properties. In 1978, the first commercial MRI scanner was available, but it was not until the 1980s that MRI became a useful tool for looking into the human body. MRI works by using a huge magnet to create a magnetic field around the patient. This field causes protons in the patient's body to "line up" in a uniform formation. A **radio** pulse is then sent through the patient, which results in the protons being knocked out of alignment. When the radio pulse is turned off, the protons create a faint but recordable pulse as they spin or **spiral** back into position. A computer is used to turn these signals into images.

This nonradiological technique has many benefits. It does not use **ionizing radiation**, which can be harmful to humans. In addition, it has superb low-contrast resolution, allowing radiologists to view and diagnose a wider range of diseases and injuries within the patient, including brain tumors and carotid artery obstructions. More recent advances in MRI technology are allowing scientists to look into how the brain actually functions.

Positron emission tomography

Positron emission tomography (PET) and single **photon** emission computed tomography (SPECT) are two more technologies that rely on computers. PET has been used primarily to study the dynamics of the human body. In other words, not just to see images, but to understand the processes that go on in certain areas of the body. For example, radioisotopes (naturally occurring or artificially developed radioactive substances) injected into a patient can be imaged through PET computerized technology, allowing scientists to watch how **metabolism** works in the brain and other parts of the body. With this technology, scientists can watch glucose metabolism, **oxygen** consumption, blood flow, and drug interactions.

SPECT uses radionuclides (radioactive atoms) to produce images similar to CT scans, but in much more precise three-dimensional images. The use of dual cameras, one above and one below the patient, enables radiologists to obtain simultaneous images that are then processed by computers to provide improved resolution of a structure in less time. In addition, small organs, like thyroid **glands**, can be better imaged for both **diagnosis** and research.

Interventional radiology

Interventional radiology is one of the more recent developments in radiology. As a subspecialty, it has evolved from a purely diagnostic application to a therapeutic specialty involving such procedures as **balloon** dilation of arteries, drainage of abscesses, removal of gallstones, and treatment of benign and malignant structures.

Interventional radiologists, who often work closely with surgeons, use a number of imaging tools to perform procedures like image-guided needle biopsy (removal of

KEY TERMS

Radiant—Anything that produces rays, such as light or heat.

Radioisotopes—An unstable isotope that emits radiation when it decays or returns to a stable state.

Radionuclides—An artificial or natural nuclide (a specific type of atom) that exhibits radioactive qualities.

Radiopaque—Anything that is opaque or impenetrable to x rays.

Radiotherapy—The use of x rays or other radioactive substances to treat disease.

tissue or fluids) and percutaneous (through the skin) needle biopsy of thoracic lesions. These procedures rely heavily on the development of imaging technologies like CT and various instruments such as **catheters** and guide wires. Advantages of interventional radiology over surgery include reduced need for **anesthesia**, shorter time to perform procedures, and improved therapeutic results.

Further Reading

Evans, Ronald G. "Radiology." *Journal of the American Medical Association.* (June 1, 1994): 1714-1715.

Hiatt, Mark. "Computers and the Revolution in Radiology." *Journal of the American Medical Association.* (April 5, 1995): 1062.

Raichle, Marcus E. "Visualizing the Mind." *Scientific American.* (April 1994): 58-62.

Selman, Joseph. *The Fundamentals of X ray and Radium Physics.* Springfield: Charles C. Thomas, 1994.

David Petechuk

Radium see **Alkaline earth metals; Radioactivity**

Radius see **Circle**

Radon

Radon is an element denoted by the atomic symbol, Rn. It has an **atomic number** of 86 and the **atomic weight** of its most stable **isotope** is 222. It is a colorless, odorless gas that emits radioactivity. It is classified as a noble gas based on its location on the **periodic table**. Radon is the heaviest element in the family of inert, or noble, gases.

The term radon refers loosely to the gas itself, which is emitted from the decay of the element radium, and to its twenty-five isotopes, all of which are also highly radioactive. Normally a colorless gas, radon can be condensed into a fluorescent liquid. Although radon's parent radium is extremely rare (it decays very rapidly), radon and its natural isotopes are also produced from **uranium** and thorium, which are much more prevalent in **minerals**, ores, and **rocks**.

Uranium miners must take special precautions to avoid radioactive poisoning by radon. The gas can also migrate upward into the **soil** and leak into buildings. Radon can seep into **groundwater** so it is not unusual to find it in public drinking supplies. The danger of this situation is caused by breathing the radon that evaporates during bathing or cooking. Eventually radon decays producing other products that can also be hazardous.

The discovery of radon is credited to Friedrich Dorn (1848-1916), a German **physics** professor. Marie Curie's experiments stimulated Dorn to begin studying the phenomenon of radioactivity. In 1900, he showed that radium emitted a radioactive gas that was called radium emanation for several years. (To this day, some scientists designate radon and its isotopes with the symbol *Em* instead of *Rn*.) Dorn's discovery represented the first clear **proof** that one element could be transmuted into another element during the **radioactive decay** process. A few years later, Sir William Ramsay, working with Robert Whytlaw-Gray (1877-1958) and other scientists, was able to map radon's characteristic **spectral lines** and determine its **density** and atomic weight.

In 1918, radon was given its modern name by scientist C. Schmidt. During the 1960s, Chinese scientists learned that radon levels in groundwater rise dramatically just before earthquakes. They have therefore predicted several quakes by monitoring radon concentrations in well **water**, and today researchers from other countries are studying this phenomenon. Radon is also used to detect leaks, measure flow rates, and inspect **metal** welds.

Until the late 1980s, the radioactive gas radon was well-known to scientists, but most people had no idea it existed. Then the threat of exposure to radioactivity from the gas brought it widespread public attention.

It was found that many lung **cancer** deaths could be directly related to radon exposure. In fact, it is estimated that radon causes 14,000 deaths annually from lung cancer. In 1988, the United States Environmental Protection Agency (EPA) estimated that ten million American homes could have harmfully high radon levels. Sales of

radon detectors boomed, and the government advised people to seal their basements and ventilate their houses if radon exceeded certain levels. Since then, some scientists have disputed the government's findings, but a few regions of the United States are still generally acknowledged to be at higher than normal risk.

In 1991, the EPA issued regulations aimed at controlling the amount of radon in drinking water. These were removed in 1997 and a new level will be reinstated in 1999 when a maximum **contamination limit** is determined.

See also Argon; Helium; Krypton; Neon; Xenon.

Ragweed see **Composite family**

Railroad see **Train and railroad**

Rails

Rails are small, shy, marshland **birds** in the family Rallidae, which includes about 129 species. This family has a worldwide distribution, occurring on all continents except **Antarctica**. Many species of rails occur only on certain remote, oceanic islands, where many of these isolated species have evolved a flightless condition because of the lack of predators. Unfortunately, this characteristic makes these birds extremely vulnerable to predators that were subsequently introduced by humans to the remote habitats of these **flightless birds**. Consequently, many of the **island** species are now extinct or endangered.

Biology of rails

Species in the rail family have a rather wide range of body and bill shapes. The true rails have a rather long, slender beak, often downward curving. The body of rails that live in marsh habitats is quite compressed laterally, a characteristic that gave rise to the saying, "skinny as a rail." Species that are commonly called rails generally live in reedy marshes, and are relatively large birds with a beak, legs, and toes that are long. Crakes are relatively small birds with stubby, chicken-like bills. Coots are duck-like, aquatic birds with lobed feet used for swimming and diving, and usually a stubby bill, although it can be massive in certain species. Gallinules or moorhens are coot-like in shape, but they have long toes that help with walking on floating aquatic vegetation.

Most species in the rail family have a subdued coloration of brown, black, and white. However, gallinules are often very colorful birds, some species being a bright, sometimes iridescent green, purple, or turquoise, usually with a red beak.

Rails eat many types of **animal** foods, including a wide range of **invertebrates**, and sometimes **fish** and **amphibians**. Most rails also eat many types of aquatic plants, and some species are exclusively **plant** eaters. Most species of rails build their nests as mounds of vegetation, in which they lay up to 12 eggs. Newly hatched rails are precocial, which means they are capable of leaving the nest almost as soon as they hatch, following their parents as they search for food.

Rails of North America

Nine species in the rail family occur regularly in **North America**, primarily in wetland habitats. The American coot (*Fulica americana*) is widespread and common in marshes and other relatively productive **wetlands**. This species has a grey body and white beak, with a vividly red frontal lobe at the top of the upper mandible, and red-colored eyes. This species chiefly feeds on aquatic vegetation, which it sometimes obtains by diving. Coots can be raucously aggressive to each other, and to other species of aquatic birds. The common gallinule or moorhen (*Gallinula chloropus*) occurs in marshes of the eastern United States, while the purple gallinule (*Porphyrula martinica*) is largely restricted to parts of Florida and Louisiana.

Some other less aquatic species of rails can also be fairly common in suitable habitats. However, these birds are very cryptic and tend to hide well in their **habitat** of tall, reedy marshes, so they are not often seen. One of these elusive species is the sora (*Porzana carolina*), the whistled calls and whinnies of which are more often heard than the birds are seen. The Virginia rail (*Rallus limicola*) is another, relatively common but evasive rail of marshes. The largest rail in North America is the king rail (*R. elegans*), with a body length of 14 in (36 cm), and occurring in marshes in the eastern United States. The clapper rail (*Rallus longirostris*) is slightly smaller at 12 in (30 cm), and is restricted to **brackish** and **salt** marshes.

Conservation of rails

Many species of rails that live on remote, oceanic islands have become flightless, because of the lack of natural predators. This is true of various **endemic** species that are specific to particular islands (that is, they do not occur anywhere else), and also of flightless populations of more wide-ranging species of rails. The benefit of flightlessness to rails living on islands is not totally clear,

but some ornithologists have speculated that this trait might have something to do with the **conservation** of **energy**, coupled with an absence of predators.

Unfortunately, flightless rails are extremely vulnerable to suffering debilitating population declines when humans introduce predators to their isolated habitats. Most commonly, these catastrophes involve accidental introductions of **rats**, or deliberate introductions of **pigs** or **cats**. At least 15 endemic species of island rails are known to have become extinct, largely as a result of introduced predators. Numerous other island rails still survive, but are endangered.

However, the real number of extinctions is undoubtedly much larger than this. Some ornithologists have speculated that each of the approximately 800 islands inhabited by Polynesians in the Pacific Ocean may have had one or several endemic species in the rail family, as well as other unique species of birds. Most of these rare and endemic species became extinct in prehistoric times, soon after the islands were discovered and colonized by prehistoric Polynesians. These extinctions occurred as a result of predation by introduced rats, over-hunting by humans, and to a lesser degree, losses of habitat.

Various species in the rail family have been hunted more recently for meat or sport. Today, however, this is a less common practice than it used to be. Some species of gallinules are sometimes considered to be **pests** of aquatic **crops**, such as **rice**, and they may be hunted to reduce that sort of agricultural damage. However, this is a relatively unusual circumstance.

Because rails are generally species of wetlands, their populations are greatly threatened by losses of that type of habitat. Wetlands are disappearing or being otherwise degraded in most parts of the world. This is occurring as a result of infilling of wetlands to develop land for urbanization, draining for agriculture, and **pollution** by **pesticides** and **fertilizers**.

See also Extinction.

Further Reading

Freedman, B. *Environmental Ecology, 2nd ed.* San Diego: Academic Press, 1994.

Harrison, C.J.O., ed. *Bird Families of the World.* New York: H.N. Abrams Pubs., 1978.

Bill Freedman

Rain see **Precipitation**

Rainbows

Water droplets and **light** form the basis of all rainbows, which are circular arcs of **color** with a common center. Because only water and light are required for rainbows, one will see them in rain, spray, or even fog.

A raindrop acts like a **prism** and separates sunlight into its individual color components through refraction, as light will do when it passes from one medium to another. When the white light of the **sun** strikes the surface of the raindrop, the light waves are bent to varying degrees depending on their wavelength. These wavelengths are reflected on the far surface of the water drop and will bend again as they exit. If the light reflects off the droplet only once, a single rainbow occurs. If the rays bounce inside and reflect twice, two rainbows will appear a primary and a secondary. The second one will appear fainter because there is less light **energy** present. It will also occur at a higher **angle**.

Not all the light that enters the raindrop will form a rainbow. Some of the light, that which hits the droplet directly at its center, will simply pass through the other side. The rays that strike the extreme lower portions of the drop will product the secondary bow, and those that enter at the top will produce the primary bow.

The formation of the **arc** was first discussed by Rene Descartes in 1637. He calculated the deviation for a ray of red light to be about 180 - 42 or 138 degrees. Although light rays may exit the drop in more than one direction, a **concentration** of rays emerge near the minimum deviation from the direction of the incoming rays. Therefore the viewer sees the highest intensity looking at the rays that have minimum deviation, which form a cone with the vertex in the observer's **eye** and with the axis passing through the Sun.

The color sequence of the rainbow is also due to refraction. It was Sir Isaac Newton, however, 30 years after Descartes, who discovered that white light was made up of different wavelengths. Red light with the longest wavelength, bends the least, while violet, being the shortest wavelength, bends the most. The vertical angle above the **horizon** will be a little less than 41° for the violet (about 40°) and a little more for the red (about 42°). The secondary rainbow has an angular radius of about 50° and its color sequence is reversed from the primary. It is universally accepted that there are seven rainbow colors, which appear in the order: red, orange, yellow, green, blue, indigo, and violet. However, the rainbow is a whole continuum of colors from red to violet and even beyond the colors that the eye can see.

Supernumerary rainbows, faintly colored rings just inside of the primary bow, occur due to **interference** effects on the light rays emerging from the water droplet after one internal reflection.

No two people will see the same rainbow. If one imagines herself or himself standing at the center of a cone cut in half lengthwise and laid on the ground flatside down, the raindrops that bend and reflect the sunlight that reach the person's eye as a rainbow are located on the surface of the cone. A viewer standing next to the first sees a rainbow generated by a different set of raindrops along the surface of a different imaging cone.

Using the concept of an imaginary cone again, a viewer could predict where a rainbow will appear by standing with his back to the sun and holding the cone to his eye so that the extension of the axis of the cone intersects the sun. The rainbow will appear along the surface of the cone as the circular arc of the rainbow is always in the direction opposite to that of the sun.

A rainbow lasts only about a half-hour because the conditions that create it rarely stay steady much longer than this. In many locations, spring is the prime rainbow- viewing month. According to David Ludlum, a **weather** historian, rainfall becomes more localized in the spring and brief showers over limited areas are a regular feature of atmospheric **behavior**. This change is a result of the higher springtime sun warming the ground more effectively than it did throughout the previous winter months. This process produces local convection. These brief, irregular periods of **precipitation** followed by sunshine are ideal rainbow conditions. Also, the sun is low enough for much of the day to allow a rainbow to appear above the horizon—the lower the sun, the higher the top of a rainbow.

The "purity" or brightness of the colors of the rainbow depends on the size of the raindrops. Large drops or those with diameters of a few millimeters, create bright rainbows with well defined colors; small droplets with diameters of about 0.01 mm produce rainbows of overlapping colors that appear nearly white.

For refraction to occur, the light must intersect the raindrops at an angle. Therefore no rainbows are seen at noon when the sun is directly overhead. Rainbows are more frequently seen in the afternoon because most showers occur in mid day rather than morning. Because the horizon blocks the other half of a rainbow, a full 360° rainbow can only be viewed from an airplane.

The sky inside the arc will appear brighter than that surrounding it because of the number of rays emerging from a raindrop at angles smaller that those that are visible. But there is essentially no light from single internal **reflections** at angles greater than those of the rainbow

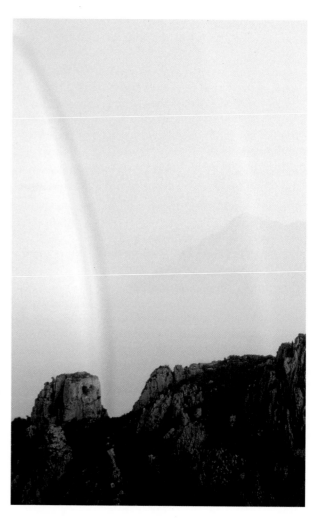

A supernumerary (double) rainbow.

rays. In addition to the fact that there is a great deal of light directed within the arc of the bow and very little beyond it, this light is white because it is a mixture of all the wavelengths that entered the raindrop. This is just the opposite in the case of a secondary rainbow, where the rainbow ray is the smallest angle and there are many rays that emerge at angles greater than this one. A dark band forms where the primary and secondary bows combine. This is known as the Alexander's Dark Band, in honor of Alexander of Aphrodisias who discovered this around 200 B.C.

If a viewer had a pair of polarizing sunglasses, he or she would see that light from the rainbow is polarized. Light vibrating horizontally at the top of the bow is much more intense than the light vibrating perpendicularly to it across the bow and it may be as much as 20 times as strong.

Although rare, a full **moon** can produce a lunar rainbow when it is bright enough to have its light refracted by raindrops just as is the case for the sun.

KEY TERMS

Lunar rainbow— A rainbow created by the white light of the moon refracted and reflected by raindrops into the atmosphere. This bow is much fainter than sunlight and will appear white to the human eye because the eye loses color sensitivity in the dark.

Polarization—The process of affecting light so that the vibrations of the wave assumes a definite form

Primary bow—The most well-known rainbow; formed when a ray of sunlight enters a raindrop, is refracted and then reflected in the inner surface of the raindrop, and emerges from the side it entered.

Reflection rainbow—One that is produced by the reflection of the source of incident light, usually the sun. The reflected rainbow may be considered a combination of two rainbows produced by sunlight coming directly from the sun and that from the reflected image of the sun.

Refraction— The bending of a wave when it enters a medium where it's speed is different.

Secondary bow—Occurs when light is reflected twice before emerging from a raindrop. The reflection causes this rainbow to be less bright than the primary rainbow. This bow is about twice as wide as the primary one, and has its colors reversed.

Vertex—The point opposite to and furthest from the base in a figure.

Further Reading

Ahrens C. Donald. *Meteorology Today.* West Publishing House. 1994.

"Chasing Rainbows," *Christian Science Monitor,* (27 July 1999).

Lutgens, Frederick, Edward Tarbuck, Dennis Tasa. *The Atmosphere: An Introduction to Meteorology.* Prentice Hall. 1997.

"The Near Sky: April Showers and Rainbows." *Sky & Telescope,* (April 1999) v. 97 i4.

Schaefer, Vincent J., John A. Day. *A Field Guide to the Atmosphere.* Houghton Mifflin. 1981.

Laurie Toupin

Rainforest

Rainforests are temperate or tropical **forests**, usually occurring as old-growth ecosystems. The world sustains many types of rainforests, which differ geographically in terms of their **species** composition and the environmental conditions in which they occur. However, the various rainforests have broad ecological similarities. A such, temperate and tropical rainforests are considered to represent biomes, or widespread kinds of natural ecosystems having broad similarities of structure and function.

Rainforests require a humid climate, with more than about 80-100 in/yr (200-250 cm/yr) of **precipitation** distributed rather equally across the **seasons**, so there is no pronounced dry period. This sort of precipitation regime does not allow any but the rarest occurrences of **wildfire**. Other catastrophic events of stand-level **tree** mortality are also rare in rainforests. As a result, this **ecosystem** usually develops into old-growth forest containing some extremely old and large trees. However, the population structure of trees in old-growth rainforest is unevenly aged because of the micro-successional dynamics associated with the deaths of individual large trees, which result in canopy gaps below which there are relatively young trees. Old-growth rainforests also have a complex physical structure, with multiple layers within the canopy, and with large, standing dead trees and decomposing logs lying on the forest floor. Although old-growth rainforests support a very large **biomass**, trees within the ecosystem are dying and decaying about as quickly as new productivity is occurring. Consequently, the net ecosystem productivity of these **old-growth forests** is very small or **zero**. Temperate rainforests are dominated by a few species of coniferous trees, while tropical rainforests are characterized by a much greater diversity of tree species, along with an enormous richness of species of other plants, animals, and **microorganisms**.

Tropical rainforests

Tropical rainforests are distributed in equatorial regions of Central and **South America** (most extensively in Amazonia), west-central equatorial **Africa**, and South and Southeast **Asia** through to New Guinea and the northeastern coast of **Australia**. Tropical rainforests are the most complex of the world's ecosystems in terms of the physical structure that they develop, and also in their tremendous **biodiversity** of species and community types. Because of these characteristics, tropical rainforests represent the acme of ecosystem development on **Earth**.

Tropical rainforests have a very complex canopy, consisting of multiple, intermeshed layers of foliage. The area of this canopy can be equivalent to 12-13 sq yds (10-11 m^2) of foliage per sq yd (m^2) of ground surface. This is among the densest foliar surfaces maintained by any of Earth's ecosystems, a characteristic that allows a relatively great efficiency of capture of solar **en-**

ergy and its conversion into **plant** biomass. Of course, the most important foliar layer of the tropical rainforest consists of the upper canopy of the largest trees, which extends to more than 330 ft (100 m) in height in some cases. However, there are also lower canopies associated with the foliage of shorter, subdominant trees, and with lianas (or vines), shrubs, and ground vegetation. These subordinate canopies are everywhere, but they are best developed where gaps in the overstory allow some sunlight to penetrate deeper into the forest.

Tropical rainforests also have a uniquely rich canopy of epiphytes, or plants that use other plants as a substrate upon which to grow. There are especially large numbers of epiphytic species in the orchid (Orchidaceae) and air-plant (Bromeliaceae) families, of **ferns** and their relatives (Pteridophytes), and of mosses, liverworts, and **lichens**. Some species of woody plants, known as strangler figs (*Ficus* spp.), begin their lives as epiphytes, but if they are successful they eventually turn into full-sized trees. The sticky, bird-dispersed **seeds** of strangler figs are adapted to finding appropriate nooks high in the canopy of a tall tree, where they germinate and live as an epiphyte, independent of the **soil** far below. However, as the seedling grows into an aerial shrub, it begins to send roots down towards the ground. If the ground is eventually reached, the strangler fig is no longer a true epiphyte, although it continues to rely on the host tree for mechanical support. Over time, the strangler fig sends more and more of these roots downwards, until their coalescing biomass eventually encircles the host tree and prevents it from growing radially, while the fig pre-empts the space occupied by its foliage. Eventually the host tree is killed, and its place in the forest canopy is assumed by the hollow-trunked strangler fig.

About 80% of the ecosystem biomass of tropical rainforests occurs as woody tissues of trees, while only about 15% of the organic **matter** occurs in soil and litter, and about 5% is foliage. (As with all forests, the biomass of animals is much less than 1% of that of the total ecosystem). In contrast, temperate forests maintain much larger fractions of their total ecosystem biomass as organic matter of the soil and forest floor. The reason for this difference is the relatively rapid rate of **decomposition** of dead biomass in the warm and humid environmental conditions of tropical rainforests. Because most of the biomass and nutrient content of tropical rainforests occurs in the biomass of living trees, and because their soils are usually highly infertile and extremely weathered, the fertility of this ecosystem is rapidly degraded after the forest is cleared. This is especially true if the site is converted to an agriculture land-use.

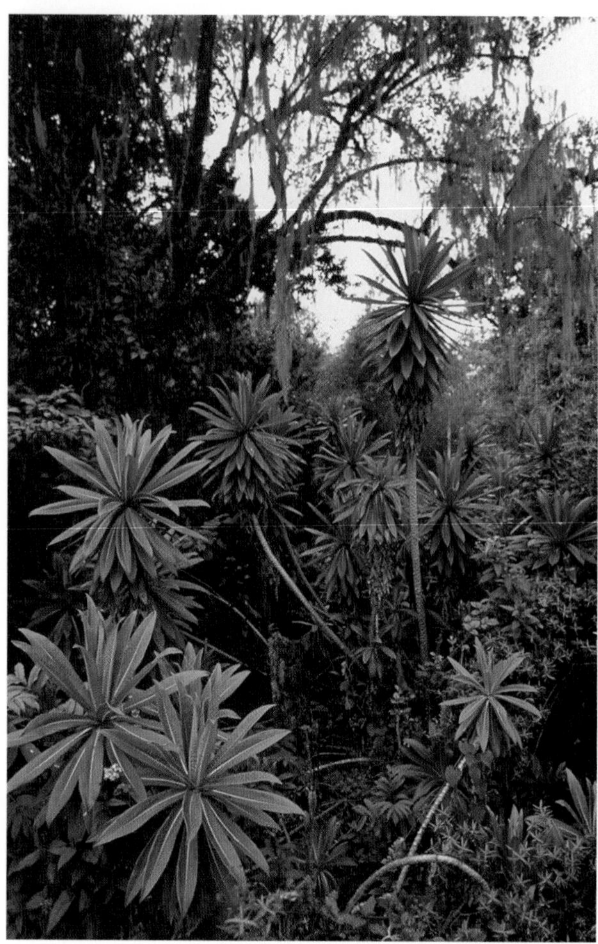

Mountain rainforest in Kenya.

An enormous number of species of plants, animals, and microorganisms occurs in tropical rainforests, and this type of ecosystem accounts for a much larger fraction of Earth's biodiversity than any other category. Of the 1.7 million species that biologists have so far identified, about 35% occur in the tropics, although less than one-half of those are from tropical rainforests. However, this is actually a gross underestimate of the importance of tropical rainforests in this regard, because relatively few of the species of this ecosystem have been identified. In fact, some biologists have estimated that as many as 30-50 million species could occur on Earth, and that about 90% of them inhabit tropical ecosystems, the great majority of those in rainforests. Most of the undiscovered species are **insects**, especially **beetles**. However, tropical rainforests also harbor immense numbers of undiscovered species of other **arthropods**, as well as many new plants and microorganisms. Even new species of **birds** and **mammals** are being discovered in tropical rainforests, further highlighting the frontier nature of the biological and ecological explorations of that biodiverse natural ecosystem.

Clearly, tropical rainforests are enormously rich in species. For example, an area of only 0.25 acre (0.1 ha) in a rainforest in Ecuador had 365 species of vascular plants, while a 7.5 acre (3 ha) plot in Borneo had more than 700 species of woody plants alone. Such rainforests typically have hundreds of species of full-sized trees. In comparison, temperate rainforests typically have no more than 10-12 species of trees, and often fewer. Tropical rainforests also typically support more than 300-400 bird species, compared with fewer than about 40 in temperate forests. If we had access to accurate knowledge of the insect species of tropical rainforests, an even more enormous difference in species richness could be demonstrated, in comparison with temperate forests. The extraordinary biodiversity of tropical rainforests is probably the most critical, defining attribute of this ecosystem, and is a natural heritage that must be preserved for all time.

Temperate rainforests

Temperate rainforests are most commonly found on the windward side of coastal **mountain** ranges. In such places warm, moisture-laden winds blowing from over the **ocean** are forced upward, where they cool, form **clouds**, and release their moisture as large quantities of rainfall. These forests have developed in high-rainfall, temperate regions along the west coasts of North and South America, New Zealand, and elsewhere.

There are many variants of temperate rainforests. In northern California, coastal rainforest can be dominated by stands of enormous redwood (*Sequoia sempervirens*) trees older than 1,000 years. More extensive old-growth rainforests elsewhere on the western coast of **North America** are dominated by other **conifer** species, especially Douglas-fir (*Pseudotsuga menziesii*) and western hemlock (*Tsuga heterophylla*), along with sitka **spruce** (*Picea sitchensis*), red cedar (*Thuja plicata*), and fir (*Abies concolor*). Rainforests also occur in wet, frost-free, oceanic environments of the Southern Hemisphere, for example, in parts of New Zealand, where this ecosystem type is dominated by southern beech (*Nothofagus* spp.) and southern **pines** (*Podocarpus* spp.).

Relatively few species have an obligate need for old-growth temperate rainforest as their **habitat**. In other words, most species that occur in old-growth temperate rainforests also occur in younger but mature forest of a similar tree-species composition. In the temperate rainforests of the Pacific coast of North America, the spotted owl (*Strix occidentalis*), marbled murrelet (*Brachyramphus marmoratus*), and some species of vascular plants, mosses, and lichens appear to require substantial areas of this ecosystem type as a major component of their habitat. However, the numbers of species dependent on temperate old-growth rainforests are very much smaller than in tropical rainforests. With respect to biodiversity issues, the importance of temperate rainforests is substantially associated with their intrinsic value as a natural type of ecosystem, and somewhat less so with the number of dependent species.

Exploitation of rainforests

Natural rainforests are an extremely valuable natural resource, mostly because they typically contain very large individual trees of commercially desirable species. These trees can be harvested and manufactured into lumber, plywood, **paper**, and other valuable **wood** products. Tropical rainforests, for example, contain large trees of commercially important species of tropical hardwoods, such as African **mahogany** (*Khaya* and *Entandrophragma* spp.), American mahogany (*Swietenia* spp.), Asian mahogany (*Shorea* spp. and *Parashorea* spp.), balsa (*Ochroma* spp.), **ebony** (*Diospyros* spp.), rosewood (*Dalbergia* spp.), rubber (*Hevea brasiliensis*), and yang (*Dipterocarpus* spp.). Temperate rainforests are also extremely valuable, because their large trees can be harvested and converted into economic products.

However, because they have little or no net production of tree biomass, it is a common practice in industrial **forestry** to clear-cut old-growth rainforests and then convert them into more productive, secondary forests. Even though another forest regenerates on the harvested site, sometimes dominated by the same tree species that occurred initially, this practice should be viewed as an ecological conversion that results in a net loss of old-growth rainforest as a natural ecosystem. All ecological conversions have attendant risks for species that require the particular habitats of the original ecosystem.

In other cases, trees may be selectively harvested from old-growth rainforests so that the physical and **ecological integrity** of the forest is left more or less intact. This is especially true of temperate rainforests, which unlike tropical rainforests, do not have interlocking webs of lianas in their overstory, so that the felling of one large tree can bring down or badly damage other trees in its vicinity. However, even selective harvesting changes the character of old-growth rainforests, so that they are no longer in their natural condition. As such, the selectively harvested ecosystem would no longer provide habitat for many of the species that depend on the habitats available in the original, old-growth rainforest. Nevertheless, selective harvesting results in a much less intensive ecological conversion than that associated with clear-cutting.

KEY TERMS

Biome—A geographically extensive ecosystem, usually characterized by its dominant life forms.

Climax—The more or less stable, plant and animal community that culminates succession under a given set of conditions of climate, site, and biota.

Community—An assemblage of populations of different species, occurring together in the same habitat.

Competition—An interaction among organisms of the same or different species, associated with their need for a common resource that is present in an insufficient supply relative to the biological demand.

Old growth—A late-successional forest, characterized by great age, an unevenly-aged population structure, domination by long-lived species, and with a complex physical structure, including multiple layers in the canopy, large trees, and many large-dimension snags and dead logs.

Selective cutting—A method of timber harvesting in which only trees of a desired species and size class are removed. This method leaves many trees standing, and although the forest is disturbed, it remains largely intact.

Species richness—the number of species occurring together in some place or area.

Because old-growth rainforests are natural ecosystems, they are considered to have great intrinsic value, which is degraded when they are harvested or otherwise disturbed. The intrinsic value of rainforests is further enhanced by the enormous richness of species of plants, animals, and microorganisms that are dependent on this specific ecosystem, particularly in the tropics. Mostly because of the intrinsic biodiversity-related value of rainforests, it is critically important that not all of the world's tracts of these natural ecosystems are converted to human uses. To prevent this terrible damage from occurring, extensive landscapes of the world's remaining rainforests, in both tropical and temperate regions, must be protected in ecological reserves and parks, where no more than traditional uses by humans are permitted.

Further Reading

Barbour, M. G., J. H. Burk, and W. D. Pitts. *Terrestrial Plant Ecology.* 2nd ed. Don Mills, Ont.: Benjamin/Cummings Pub. Co., 1987.

Begon, M., J. L. Harper, and C. R. Townsend. *Ecology. Individuals, Populations and Communities.* 2nd ed. London: Blackwell Sci. Pub., 1990.

Davis, W. *Rain Forest: Ancient Realm of the Pacific Northwest.* Chelsea Green Publishing Co., 1999.

Freedman, B. *Environmental Ecology.* 2nd ed. San Diego: Academic Press, 1994.

Maloney, B.K. (ed.). *Human Activities and the Tropical Rainforest: Past, Present, and Possible Future.* Kluwer Academic Publishers, 1998.

Bill Freedman

Random

The word "random" is used in **mathematics** much as it is in ordinary **speech**. A random number is one whose choice from a set of numbers is purely a matter of chance; a random walk is a sequence of steps whose direction after each step is a matter of chance; a random **variable** (in **statistics**) is one whose size depends on events which take place as a matter of chance.

Random numbers and other random entities play an important role in everyday life. People who frequent gambling casinos are relieved of their money by slot machines, dice games, roulette, blackjack games, and other forms of gambling in which the winner is determined by the fall of a card, by a ball landing in a wheel' s numbered slot, and so on. Part of what makes gambling attractive is the randomness of the outcomes, outcomes which are usually beyond the control of the house or the player.

Children playing tag determine who is "it" by guessing which fist conceals the rock. Who does the dishes is determined by the toss of a coin.

Medical researchers use random numbers to decide which subjects are to receive an experimental treatment and which are to receive a **placebo**. Quality control engineers test products at random as they come off the line. Demographers base conclusions about a whole population on the basis of a randomly chosen **sample**. Mathematicians use Monte Carlo methods, based on random samples, to solve problems which are too difficult to solve by ordinary means.

For absolutely unbreakable ciphers, cryptographers use pages of random numbers called one-time pads.

Because numbers are easy to handle, many randomizations are effected by means of random numbers. Video poker machines "deal" the cards by using randomly selected numbers from the set 1, 2, ..., 52, where each number stands for a particular card in the deck. Computer simulations of traffic patterns use random

numbers to mark the arrival or non-arrival of an **automobile** at an intersection.

A familiar use of random numbers is to be seen in the lotteries which many states run. In Delaware's "Play 3" lottery, for example, the winning three-digit number is determined by three randomly-selected numbered balls. The machine that selects them is designed so that the operator cannot favor one ball over another, and the balls themselves, being nearly identical in size and weight, are equally likely to be near the release mechanism when it is activated.

Random numbers can be obtained in a variety of ways. They can be generated by physical means such as tossing coins, rolling dice, spinning roulette wheels, or releasing balls from a lottery machine. Such devices must be designed, manufactured, and used with great care however. An unbalanced coin can favor one side; dice which are rolled rather than tumbled can favor the faces on which they roll; and so on. Furthermore, mathematicians have shown that many **sequences** that appear random are not.

One notorious case of faulty randomization occurred during the draft lottery of 1969. The numbers which were to indicate the order in which men would be drafted were written on slips and enclosed in capsules. These capsules were then mixed and drawn in sequence. They were not well mixed, however, and, as a consequence, the order in which men were drafted was scandalously lacking in randomness.

An interesting source of random numbers is the last three digits of the "handle" at a particular track on a particular day. The handle, which is the total amount bet that day, is likely to be a very large number, perhaps close to a million dollars. It is made up of thousands of individual bets in varying amounts. The first three digits of the handle are anything but random, but the last three digits, vary from 000 to 999 by almost pure chance. They therefore make a well-publicized, unbiased source of winning numbers for both those running and those playing illegal "numbers" games.

Cards are very poor generators of random numbers. They can be bent, trimmed, and marked. They can be dealt out of sequence. They can be poorly shuffled. Even when well shuffled, their arrangement is far from random. In fact, if a 52-card deck is given eight perfect shuffles, it will be returned to its original order.

Even a good physical means of generating random numbers has severe limitations, possibly in terms of cost, and certainly in terms of speed. A researcher who needs thousands of randomly generated numbers would find it impractical to depend on a mechanical means of generating them.

One alternative is to turn to a table of random digits which can be found in books on statistics and elsewhere. To use such tables, one starts from some randomly chosen point in the table and reads the digits as they come. If, for example, one wanted random numbers in the range 1 to 52, and found 22693 35089 ... in the table, the numbers would be 22, 69, 33, 50, 89, ... The numbers 69 and 89 are out of the desired range and would be discarded.

Another alternative is to use a **calculator** or a computer. Even an inexpensive calculator will sometimes have a key for calling up random numbers. **Computer languages** such as Pascal and BASIC include random number generators among the available functions.

The danger in using computer generated random numbers is that such numbers are not genuinely random. They are based on an **algorithm** that generates numbers in a very erratic sequence, but by computation, not chance.

For most purposes this does not matter. Slot machines, for example, succeed in making money for their owners in spite of any subtle bias or regularity they may show. There are times, however where computer-generated "random" numbers are really not random enough.

Mathematicians have devised many tests for randomness. One is to count the **frequency** with which the individual digits occur, then the frequency with which pairs, triples, and other combinations occur. If the list is long enough the "law of large numbers," says that each digit should occur with roughly the same frequency. So should each pair, each triple, each quadruple, and so on. Often, lists of numbers expected to be random fail such tests.

One interesting list of numbers tested for randomness is the digits in the decimal **approximation** for **pi**, which has been computed to more than two and a quarter billion places. The digits are not random in the sense that they occur by chance, but they are in the sense that they pass the tests of randomness. In fact, the decimal approximation for pi has been described as the "most nearly perfect random sequence of digits ever discovered." A failure to appreciate the true meaning of "random" can have significant consequences. This is particularly true for people who gamble. The gambler who plays hunches, who believes that past outcomes can influence forthcoming ones, who thinks that inanimate machines can distinguish a "lucky" person from an "unlucky" one is in danger of being quickly parted from his money. Gambling casinos win billions of dollars every year from people who have faith that the next number in a random sequence can somehow be predicted. If the sequence is truly random, it cannot.

Further Reading

Gardner, Martin. *Mathematical Circus.* New York: Alfred A. Knopf, 1979.

KEY TERMS

Chance—Occurring without human intention or predictable cause.

Random—Occurring in no predictable pattern, by chance alone.

Packel, Edward. *The Mathematics of Games and Gambling.* Washington, D.C.: The Mathematical Association of America, 1981.

Stein, S. K. "Existence out of Chaos." *Mathematical Plums.* Edited by Ross Honsberger. Washington, D. C.: The Mathematical Association of America, 1979.

J. Paul Moulton

Range of function see **Domain**

Rangeland

Rangeland is uncultivated land that is suitable for grazing and browsing animals. Rangeland is one of the major types of land in the world. (Other types are: forest, **desert**, farmland, pasture, and urban/industrial.) Rangelands are the principal source of forage for **livestock**, and they also provide **habitat** for a great variety of native plants and animals. Rangelands are also used by people for recreational purposes. Some **plant** species of rangelands are used in landscaping, and as sources of industrial chemicals, pharmaceuticals, and charcoal.

Generally, rangeland is not fertilized, seeded, irrigated, or harvested with machines. Rangelands differ in this respect from pasturelands, which require periodic cultivation to maintain introduced (non-native) species of forage plants. Pasturelands may also need **irrigation** or **fertilization**, and they are usually fenced. Rangelands were originally open, natural spaces, but much of their area has now been fenced to accommodate human uses, particularly livestock grazing. In addition, livestock grazing often utilizes **rotation** systems that require partitioning.

Rangelands were distinguished at the turn of the century by their native vegetation. Today, however, many rangelands support stands of introduced forage species that do not require cultivation.

Types of rangeland

Rangelands support plant communities that are dominated by species of perennial **grasses**, grass-like plants (or graminoids), forbs (non-graminoid, dicotyledonous plants), and shrubs. There are five basic types of rangelands worldwide: natural grassland, desert shrubland, **savanna** woodland, forest, and **tundra**. **Grasslands** do not have shrubs or trees growing on them. Desert shrublands are the most extensive and driest of the rangelands. Savanna woodlands are a transition between grasslands and **forests**, and contain herbaceous plants interspersed among scattered, low-growing shrubs and trees. Forests contain taller trees growing closer together than in savanna. Tundra areas are treeless, level plains in the Arctic or at high elevations of mountains.

North American rangelands consist of: (1) the **prairie** grasslands of the midwestern United States and extending into Canada, as well as parts of California and the northwestern states; (2) cold desert rangeland in the Great Basin of the U.S., and hot desert (Mojave, Sonoran, and Chihuahuan) of the southwestern U.S. and northern Mexico; (3) open woodlands from Washington state to Chihuahua, Mexico, and in the Rocky and Sierra-Cascade Mountains; (4) forests (western and northern coniferous, southern pine, and eastern deciduous); and (5) alpine tundra (mostly in Alaska, Colorado, and western Canada) and arctic tundra (in Alaska and northern Canada).

There are more than 283-million hectares of natural range ecosystems in the United States. However, much of the U.S. prairie grasslands have been converted to agricultural land-use. In addition, excessive grazing and fire suppression have allowed the invasion of prairie by species of woody plants, such as mesquite, in some regions.

Range management

The first principles of scientific range management were established by research in **North America** during the 1890s, and by grazing system experiments in the early 1900s. Variations of many of these practices, such as grazing rotations, had been used by pastoral herders in **Asia** and **Africa** for centuries.

Grasses of the semi-arid plains provide an excellent winter forage for livestock. Unlike their eastern counterparts, which tend to fall to the ground in winter and rot, prairie grasses cure while standing and do not have to be harvested, baled, or stored for winter use. However, if they are grazed intensively throughout the summer and autumn, prairie grasses cannot produce an adequate crop of winter forage.

Good rangeland management recognizes that perennial grasses must have sufficient time for their aboveground **biomass** to regenerate after grazing; otherwise the plants become overgrazed, and may not survive. A healthy population of native grasses helps to prevent invasion by non-native plants, some of which are unpalat-

KEY TERMS

Climax community—A community of plants and animals that persists in the presence of stable, ambient conditions, particularly climate.

Forage—Vegetation that is suitable for grazing animals.

Forb—A non-grasslike, dicotyledonous plant with broad leaves and a herbaceous stem.

Grassland—A type of rangeland that is usually free of shrubs and trees. Grasslands most commonly occur on flat, inland areas at lower elevations.

Pasture—Rangeland that is dominated by introduced species of forage plants, and that requires periodic cultivation for maintenance.

able or even poisonous to livestock. Severe overgrazing removes too many plants of all types from an area, causing a loss of **soil** moisture and fertility, and increasing **erosion**. Range managers have learned that for the long-term health of rangelands, they cannot overstock or overgraze them with cattle or other livestock. In spite of this knowledge, excessive use of rangelands remains an important problem in most parts of the world, including North America.

Further Reading

Hirschi, Ron. *Save Our Prairies and Grasslands.* New York: Delacorte Press, 1994.

Hodgson, J. and A.W. Illius. (eds.). *The Ecology and Management of Grazing Systems.* CABI Publications, 1998.

Holechek, Jerry L. "Policy Changes on Federal Rangelands: A Perspective." *Journal of Soil and Water Conservation.* (May-June 1993): 166-74.

National Research Council. *Rangeland Health: New Methods to Classify, Inventory, and Monitor Rangelands.* Washington, DC: National Academy Press, 1994.

Staub, Frank. *America's Prairies.* Minneapolis: Carolrhoda Books, 1994.

Karen Marshall

Raptors

Raptors, or **birds of prey**, are birds having the following three distinctive characteristics: strong grasping feet equipped with sharp talons, a hooked upper beak, and keen **vision**. Raptors are called birds of prey because these features allow them to be predators that hunt for their food. Many raptors are, in fact, predators. Some raptors actually hunt for and consume other birds. Other members of the group, however, eat only dead animals, called carrion. Raptors consist of two taxonomic orders of birds. The order Falconiformes is comprised of **falcons**, **hawks**, **eagles**, **vultures**, **condors**, and related birds of prey. Falconiformes birds are diurnal (daytime) predators. The order Strigiformes is composed of **owls**. Owls are also birds of prey. They are, however, nocturnal predators that are adapted to hunt primarily at night. Spectacular hunters, raptors are admired for their majestic strength. For example, eagles have often been used to symbolize dignity and magnificence on family coats of arms and national flags. The bald eagle, for example, is a national symbol for the United States, representing both strength and freedom. Despite such respect, several species of raptors have in the past been hunted to near **extinction**. Compounding their decline was the widespread use of organic **pesticides** that poisoned raptor habitats. Fortunately, **conservation** efforts have been successful in rebuilding some threatened populations.

Raptor Biology

All birds are **vertebrates** and belong to the scientific class Aves. By definition, birds possess feathers, wings, beaks, and scales on their legs and feet. Members of the class Aves are also warm-blooded, air-breathing and lay terrestrial eggs. There are two orders of raptors under the larger class of Aves: Falconiformes and Strigiformes. Birds of prey belonging to the order Falconiformes have strong bills that are hooked at the tip and sharp on the edges. This functions to cut and tear flesh from prey animals. Also, Falconiform raptors have feet with sharp, curved talons, opposable hind toes, and very sharp vision. They are generally strong flyers and carnivores.

Worldwide, there are approximately 286 **species** in the order Falconiformes. The members are distributed among five taxonomic families. The family Sagittariidae has one species, the **secretary bird** (*Sagittarius serpentarius*). Secretary birds, with lengthy limbs and short toes, resemble **cranes** but are in fact raptors. The family Pandionidae also has only one species, the osprey (*Pandion haliaetus*). Ospreys are **fish** eating raptors that have unique foot structures. An adaptive characteristic for catching fish, one front toe of the osprey can swivel backward to join the back toe. Accipitridae is the largest family containing 217 species. Bald eagles (*Haliaeetus leucocephalus*), red-tailed hawks (*Buteo jamaicensis*), **buzzards**, and some vultures belong to this family. Vultures are large black raptors with very long wings. A stereotypical **behavior** of vultures is high, circular soar-

ing in groups. Their large wingspans are adaptive for soaring, which takes advantage of thermal air currents. Their diet consists mostly of carrion, which they spot or **smell** from the air.

The family Cathartidae, the New World vultures, includes the turkey vulture (*Cathartes aura*) of **North America**. Members of this family of raptors feed primarily on carrion. Their largely unfeathered heads attached to long necks allows these birds to immerse their entire head inside of the bodies of dead animals while feeding. A characteristic that distinguishes them from Old World vultures is the presence of a perforated nostril, which creates a large hole in their beaks thought to facilitate their sense of smell.

The family Falconidae contains falcons. Falcons are a particular group of hawks belonging to the same genus. They are made distinct by their large dark eyes and notched beak. Typically, falcons have long pointed wings and tails. Unlike other hawks, however, they do not build nests from sticks. Rather, falcons carve spots on cliffs or nest in natural depressions. Falcons are famous for their acrobatic flight, and are sometimes kept by falconers as pets. Two well-known falcons of the U.S. are the American Kestrel and the Peregrine Falcon.

The phylogenetic order Strigiformes consists of owls. Owls are nocturnal predators with powerful beaks and feet, talons, large eyes capable of enhanced night vision, extremely sensitive **hearing**, and special feathers that create noiseless flight. The silent flight that owls exhibit allows them to stealthily catch prey without startling them, preventing escape. Although hawks and owls belong to separate orders, they share the common trait of being predatory and catching food with their feet. Some owls have tufts on the tops of their head, often called horns or ears, as in great honed owls. In reality, these tufts are feathers. Owl ears are located underneath feathers on the sides of their heads and are not visible. Tufts likely serve behavioral signals to other owls, or as camouflage. Like hawks, owls can be found living in the same areas year- round. There are approximately 135 owl species worldwide.

Raptors display a wide range of sizes. One of the smallest birds of prey is the pygmy falcon (*Polihierax semitorquatus*) which lives in **Africa**. This species weights only about 60 g (2.1 oz.) and has a wingspan of about 1 ft (0.3 m). The smallest North American raptor is the American kestrel. American kestrels weigh about 4 oz (120 g). and have a wingspan of about 1 ft (0.2 m). The largest diurnal bird of prey is the Andean condor, which can weigh up to 31 lbs (14 kg) and has a wingspan of up to 9 ft (3 m). The largest raptor in North America is the California condor, having an average wingspan of up to 9 ft (3 m).

Some species of raptors display sexual dimorphism. Species of animals showing sexual dimorphism have males and females that possess distinctly different physical characteristics. For example, some raptor species have females that are much larger in size than males. Others vary in coloration between males and females. Most birds of prey that are diurnal have feather color patterns that are earth tones: brown, black, gray, white. However, feather patterns themselves may be distinct, as in the bald eagle or peregrine falcon. In contrast, the skin of the heads and necks of some vultures and buzzards can be very boldly colored in red or orange. The shape of raptor wings can foretell its foraging behavior. Most hawks and eagles have wide, rounded wing margins that function in soaring upon air currents. Wide wings do not provide great speed compared to other wing shapes. Instead, hawks rely on surprise to catch prey. A few hawks, however, have short wings for bursts of speed and maneuvering in wooded areas. Falcons, in contrast, have sharp angular wings that allow these raptors to fast chase and make steep dives to catch their prey.

Raptor beaks are very strong. Beaks are composed of bone covered with plates of keratin, the tough protein found in human fingernails. Raptor beaks are sharply hooked at the tip and are sharp along their edges. Some species have beaks that reflect their feeding habits. For example, falcons have notched beaks that are used to break prey vertebrae. An equally important characteristic of raptors is their excellent vision. Vision is the most important raptor sense in hunting. When compared to many other vertebrates, raptor eyes are much larger. Their size allows for sharper images and greater sensitivity to light and color. Like humans, raptors have **binocular** vision. That is, they use both eyes to perceive images. It is estimated that raptors can see up to three times better than human beings.

Diurnal birds of prey can be found in almost any **habitat**, including such inhospitable biomes as deserts and **tundra**. Representatives of the Falconidae, Accipitridae, and Pandionidae are found on every **continent** except **Antarctica**. Other species have very localized distributions. For example, the secretary bird is restricted to sub-Saharan Africa only. New World vultures exist only in the Western Hemisphere, while Old World vultures are found exclusively in the Eastern Hemisphere.

Raptor conservation

Raptors have been greatly affected by human activity. Certain birds of prey have become threatened or endangered as the result of hunting, **pollution**, and habitat destruction. As many as 18 raptor species have been labeled as endangered or threatened in the United States.

KEY TERMS

Carrion—The decaying flesh of a dead animal that is considered food by other animals.

Diurnal—The quality of being active during the day, referring largely to foraging or hunting for food in animals.

Falconiformes—The taxonomic order of birds that includes eagles, hawks, vultures, falcons, buzzards, and condors. All members of this group are raptors.

Nocturnal—Animal foraging or hunting activity exclusively at night.

Raptor—A specific kind of bird that is predatory, has a sharp, hooked beak, talons, and excellent eyesight. Raptors are also known as birds of prey.

Sexual dimorphism—The biological characteristic of having physical attributes of one gender distinct from those of the other gender within a species.

Strigiformes—The taxonomic order of birds comprised of owls. Owls are nocturnal raptors, or birds of prey.

Talon—The extremely sharp, keratinous extensions at the end of raptor claws that function in prey capture and defense.

However, efforts to restrict hunting, create and protect preserves and **wildlife** refuges, decreased pollution, and captive breeding and **rehabilitation** efforts have helped some raptor populations to survive and regain their numbers. In the 1940s, heavy use of the pesticide DDT caused a drastic decline in bald eagle populations. By 1974, it was estimated that only 700 breeding pairs of bald eagle remained. After DDT was banned, numbers of bald eagles rose. Similarly, when the use of another potent pesticide was banned, numbers rose. During the same period, legislation was passed that prohibited poaching of bald eagles and disturbance of their nests. As a result, there are believed to be more than four thousand breeding pairs of bald eagles in the lower 48 states alone. However, given this success, several species remain endangered, one such example is the California condor. At one period, there were thousands of California condors. By 1939, however, the number of condors fell to less than 100. By 1982, fewer than 25 remained in the wild. Their decline was attributed to habitat loss, organic pesticide poisoning, and electrocution on high voltage wires. Due to their slow reproductive rate, these problems were compounded. Conservationists feared the extinction of the species and organized a huge effort to breed more California condors before they were lost. Today, because of captive breeding programs, over 100 California condors live, and some have been released back into the wild where it is hoped they will survive to reproduce on their own.

Further Reading

Arnold, Caroline.*On the Brink of Extinction: The California Condor.* San Diego: Harcourt Brace Jovanovich Publishers, 1993.

Brooke, Michael, and Tim Birkhead (eds.). *The Cambridge Encyclopedia of Ornithology.* Cambridge: Cambridge University Press, 1992.

Dewitt, Lynda. *Eagles, Hawks, and Other Birds of Prey.* New York: Franklin Watts, 1989.

Terry Watkins

Rare earth element see **Lanthanides**

Rare gases

The rare gases, also known as the noble gases, are a group of six gaseous elements found in small amounts in the atmosphere: helium (He), neon (Ne), argon (Ar), krypton (Kr), xenon (Xe), and **radon** (Rn). Collectively they make up about one percent of the earth's atmosphere. They were discovered by scientists around the turn of the century and because they were so unreactive were initially called the inert gases.

Discovery and isolation

Helium was the first of the rare gases to be discovered. In fact, its discovery is unique among the elements since it is the only element to be first identified in another part of the **solar system** before being discovered on **Earth**. In 1868 Pierre Janssen (1824-1907), a French astronomer, was observing a total solar eclipse from India. Janssen used an instrument called a **spectroscope** to analyze the sunlight. The spectroscope broke the sunlight into lines which were characteristic of the elements emitting the **light**. He saw a previously unobserved line in the solar **spectrum** which indicated the presence of a new element that Janssen named helium after the Greek word *helios,* meaning **sun**. A quarter of a century later, William Ramsay (1852-1916) studied gases emitted from radioactive **uranium** ores. With help from two British experts on **spectroscopy**, William Crooks (1832-1919) and Norman Lockyer (1836-1920), the presence of helium in earth-bound **minerals** was confirmed.

Shortly thereafter, helium was also detected as a minor component in the earth's atmosphere.

The discovery of the remaining rare gases is credited to two men, Ramsay and Lord Rayleigh (1842-1919). Beginning in 1893, Rayleigh observed discrepancies in the **density** of **nitrogen** obtained from different sources. Nitrogen obtained from the air (after removal of **oxygen**, **carbon dioxide**, and water vapor) always had a slightly higher density than when prepared from a chemical reaction (such as heating certain nitrogen-containing compounds). Ramsay eventually concluded that the nitrogen obtained from chemical reactions was pure, but nitrogen extracted from the air contained small amounts of an unknown gas which accounted for the density discrepancy. Eventually it was realized that there were several new gases in the air. The method used to isolate these new gaseous elements involved liquefying air (by subjecting it to high **pressure** and low **temperature**) and allowing the various gases to boil off at different temperatures. The names given to the new elements were derived from Greek words that reflected the difficultly in isolating them: Ne, *neos* (new); Ar, *argos* (inactive); Kr, *kryptos* (hidden); Xe, *xenon* (stranger). Radon, which is radioactive, was first detected as a gas released from radium, and subsequently identified in air. Ramsay and Rayleigh received Nobel Prizes in 1904 for their scientific contributions in discovering and characterizing the rare gases.

Properties

The rare gases form group 18 of the **periodic table** of elements. This is the vertical column of elements on the extreme right of the periodic table. As with other groups of elements, the placement of all the rare gases in the same group reflects their similar properties. The rare gases are all colorless, odorless, and tasteless. They are also monatomic gases which means that they exist as individual **atoms**.

The most noticeable feature of the rare gases is their lack of chemical reactivity. Helium, neon, and argon do not combine with any other atoms to form compounds, and it has been only in the last few decades that compounds of the other rare gases have been prepared. In 1962 Neil Bartlett (1932-), then at the University of British Columbia, succeeded in the historic preparation of the first compound of xenon. Since then, many xenon compounds containing mostly fluorine or oxygen atoms have also been prepared. Krypton and radon have also been combined with fluorine to form simple compounds. Because some rare gas compounds have powerful oxidizing properties (they can remove electrons from other substances) they have been used to synthesize other compounds.

The low reactivity of the rare gases is due to the arrangement of electrons in the rare gas atoms. The configuration of electrons in these elements makes them very stable and therefore unreactive. The reactivity of any element is due, in part, to how easily it gains or loses electrons, which is necessary for an atom to react with other atoms. The rare gases do not readily do either. Prior to Bartlett's preparation of the first xenon compound, the rare gases were widely referred to as the inert gases. Because the rare gases are so unreactive, they are harmless to living organisms. Radon, however, is hazardous because it is radioactive.

Abundance and production

Most of the rare gases have been detected in small amounts in earth minerals and in meteorites, but are found in greater abundance in the earth's atmosphere. They are thought to have been released into the atmosphere long ago as by-products of the decay of radioactive elements in the earth's crust. Of all the rare gases, argon is present in the greatest amount, about 0.9 percent by **volume**. This means there are 0.2 gal (0.9 l) of argon in every 26.4 gal (100 l) of air. By contrast, there are 78 liters of nitrogen and 21 liters of oxygen gas in every 26.4 gal (100 l) of air. The other rare gases are present in such small amounts that it is usually more convenient to express their concentrations in terms of parts per million (ppm). The concentrations of neon, helium, krypton, and xenon are, respectively, 18, 5, 1, and 0.09 ppm. For example, there are only 1.32 gal (1.5 l) of helium in every million liters of air. By contrast, helium is much more abundant in the sun and stars and consequently, next to **hydrogen**, is the most abundant element in the universe. Radon is present in the atmosphere in only trace amounts. However, higher levels of radon have been measured in homes around the United States. Radon can be released from soils containing high concentrations of uranium, and can be trapped in homes that have been weather sealed to make heating and cooling systems more efficient. Radon testing kits are commercially available for testing the radon content of household air.

Most of the rare gases are commercially obtained from liquid air. As the temperature of liquid air is raised, the rare gases boil off from the mixture at specific temperatures and can be separated and purified. Although present in air, helium is commercially obtained from **natural gas** wells where it occurs in concentrations of between one and seven percent of the naturalgas. Most of the world's helium supplies come from wells located in Texas, Oklahoma, and Kansas. Radon is isolated as a product of the **radioactive decay** of radium compounds.

KEY TERMS

Density—The mass of a substance divided by its volume. A less dense substance floats in a more dense substance; helium will rise in air.

Periodic table—A chart listing all the known elements. It is arranged so that elements with similar properties fall into one of eighteen groups. The rare gases are found in group 18. In older versions of the periodic table, this group is numbered 0, or VIII A.

Oxidation—A type of chemical reaction occurring whenever electrons are removed from a substance.

Spectroscope—A device which breaks light from hot atoms into a spectrum of individual wavelengths. Each element has its own spectrum and can therefore be identified with this instrument.

Uses

The properties of each rare gas dictate its specific commercial applications. Because they are the most abundant, and therefore the least expensive to produce, helium and argon find the most commercial applications. Helium's low density and inertness make it ideal for use in lighter-than-air craft, such as balloons and blimps. Although helium has nearly twice the density of hydrogen, it has about 98 percent of hydrogen's lifting power. A little over 324.7 gal (1,230 l) of helium lifts 2.2 lbs (one kg). Helium is also nonflammable and therefore considerably safer than hydrogen, which was once widely used in gas-filled **aircraft**. Liquid helium has the lowest **boiling point** of any known substance (about -452°F; -269°C) and therefore has many low-temperature applications in research and industry. Divers breathe an artificial oxygen-helium mixture to prevent gas bubbles forming in the **blood** as they swim to the surface from great depths. Other uses for helium have been in supersonic **wind** tunnels, as a protective gas in growing silicon and germanium crystals and, together with neon, to make gas lasers.

Neon is well known for its use in neon signs. **Glass** tubes of any shape can be filled with neon and when an electrical charge is passed through the tube, an orange-red glow is emitted. By contrast, ordinary **incandescent light** bulbs are filled with argon. Because argon is so inert, it does not react with the hot **metal** filament and prolongs the bulb's life. Argon is also used to provide an inert atmosphere in **welding** and high-temperature metallurgical processes. By surrounding hot metals with inert argon, the metals are protected from potential oxidation by oxygen in the air. Krypton and xenon also find commercial lighting applications. Krypton can be used in incandescent light bulbs and in fluorescent lamps. Both are also employed in flashing stroboscopic lights that outline commercial airport runways. Because they emit a brilliant white light when electrified, they are also used in photographic flash equipment. Due to the radioactive nature of radon, it has found medical applications in radiotherapy.

See also Elements, families of.

Further Reading

Atwood, C.H. "How much radon is too much," *Journal of Chemical Education,* vol. 69, 1992: pp 351-355.

CRC Handbook of Chemistry and Physics. 74th Edition, D.R.Lide, Ed., Boca Raton, Florida: CRC Press inc., 1991.

Emlsley, J. *The Elements.* New York: Oxford University Press, 1989.

Heiserman, D.L. *Exploring Chemical Elements and Their Compounds.* Blue Ridge Summit, PA: Tan books, 1992.

Nicholas C. Thomas

Raspberry see **Rose family**

Rate

A rate is a comparison of the change in one quantity, such as **distance**, **temperature**, weight, or time, to the change in a second quantity of this type. The comparison is often shown as a formula, a **ratio**, or a fraction, dividing the change in the first quantity by the change in the second quantity. When the changes being compared occur over a measurable period of time, their ratio determines an average rate of change. When the changes being compared both occur instantaneously, the rate is instantaneous.

One common and very important type of rate is the time rate of change. This type of rate compares the change in one quantity to a simultaneous change in time. Common examples of time rates of change are: **birth** rates, rates of speed, rates of **acceleration**, rates of pay, and interest rates. In each case, the rate is determined by dividing the change in a measured quantity (population, location, speed, and earnings, etc.) by the length of a corresponding elapsed time. For instance, distance traveled (change in location) compared to the length of time traveled (change in time) is rate of speed.

In all cases, a rate is specified by two units, one for each of the quantities being compared. For example,

speed cannot be expressed in units of distance alone, such as miles or kilometers. It is necessary to say how many units of distance are traveled in a specific period of time, such as miles per hour or kilometers per second. So the units of a rate are also a ratio—a ratio of the units used to measure the two changes being compared.

Ratio

The ratio of *a* to *b* is a way to convey the idea of relative magnitude of two amounts. Thus if the number *a* is always twice the number *b*, we can say that the ratio of *a* to *b* is "2 to 1." This ratio is sometimes written 2:1. Today, however, it is more common to write a ratio as a fraction, in this case 2/1.

At one time, ratios were in common use in solving problems and the terms "antecedent" for the numerator *a* and "consequent" for the denominator *b* were used. Today most problems concerning ratios are solved by treating ratios as fractions.

Rational number

A rational number is one that can be expressed as the **ratio** of two **integers** such as 3/4 (the ration of 3 to 4) or -5:10 (the ration of -5 to 10). Among the infinitely many rational numbers are 1.345, 1 7/8, 0, -75, $\sqrt{25}$, $\sqrt{.125}$, and 1. These numbers are rational because they can be expressed as 1345:1000, 15:8, 0:1, -75:1, 5:1, 1:2, and 1:1 respectively. The numbers π, $\sqrt{2}$, i, and $\sqrt{4}$ are not rational because none of them can be written as the ratio of two integers. Thus any integer, any common fraction, any mixed number, any finite decimal, or any repeating decimal is rational. A rational number that is the ratio of a to b is usually written as the fraction a/b.

Rational numbers are needed because there are many quantities or measures which **natural numbers** or integers alone will not adequately describe. Measurement of quantities, whether length, **mass**, or **time**, is the most common situation. Rational numbers are needed, for example, if a farmer produces and wants to sell part of a bushel of **wheat** or a workman needs part of a pound of **copper**.

The reason that rational numbers have this flexibility is that they are two-part numbers with one part available for designating the size of the increments and the other for counting them. When a rational number is written as a fraction, these two parts are clearly apparent, and are given the names "denominator" and "numerator" which specify these roles. In rational numbers such as 7 or 1.02, the second part is missing or obscure, but it is readily supplied or brought to light. As an integer, 7 needs no second part; as a rational number it does, and the second part is supplied by the obvious relationship 7 <=> 7/1. In the case of 1.02, it is the decimal point which designates the second part, in this case 100. Because the only information the decimal point has to offer is its position, the numbers it can designate are limited to powers of ten: 1, 10, 100, etc. For that reason, there are many rational numbers which decimal fractions cannot represent, 1/3 for example.

Rational numbers have two kinds of **arithmetic**, the arithmetic of decimals and the arithmetic of common fractions. The arithmetic of decimals is built with the arithmetic of integers and the rules for locating the decimal point. In multiplying 1.92 by .57, **integral** arithmetic yields 10944, and the decimal point rules convert it to 1.0944.

Common fraction arithmetic is considerably more complex and is governed by the familiar rules

$$ac/bc = a/b$$
$$a/b + c/d = (ad + bc)/bd$$
$$a/b - c/d = (ad - bc)/bd$$
$$(a/b)(c/d) = ac/bd$$
$$(a/b) \div (c/d) = (a/b)(d/c)$$
$$a/b = c/d \text{ if and only if } ad = bc$$

If one looks closely at these rules, one sees that each rule converts rational-number arithmetic into integer arithmetic. None of the rules, however, ties the value of a rational number to the value of the integers that make it up. For this the rule $(a/b)b = a, b \neq 0$ is needed. It says, for example, that two 1/2s make 1, or twenty 3/20s make 3.

The rule would also say that **zero** 5/0s make 5, if zero were not excluded as a denominator. It is to avoid such absurdities that zero denominators are ruled out.

Between any two rational numbers there is another rational number. For instance, between 1/3 and 1/2 is the number 5/12. Between 5/12 and 1/2 is the number 11/24, and so on. If one plots the rational numbers on a number line, there are no gaps; they appear to fill it up.

But they do not. In the fifth century B.C. followers of the Greek mathematician Pythagoras discovered that the diagonal of a **square** one unit on a side was irrational, that no segment, no matter how small, which measured the side would also measure the diagonal. So, no matter how many rational points are plotted on a number line, none of them will ever land on $\sqrt{2}$, or on any of the countless other irrational numbers.

Irrational numbers show up in a variety of formulas. The circumference of a **circle** is π times its diame-

ter. The longer leg of a 30°-60°-90° triangle is $\sqrt{3}$ times its shorter leg. If one needs to compute the exact length of either of these, the task is hopeless. If one uses a number which is close to π or close to $\sqrt{3}$, one can obtain a length which is also close. Such a number would have to be rational, however, because it is with rational numbers only that we have computational procedures. For π one can use 22/7, 3.14, 3.14159, or an even closer **approximation**.

More than 4,000 years ago the Babylonians coped with the need for numbers that would measure fractional or continuously **variable** quantities. They did this by extending their system for representing natural numbers, which was already in place. Theirs was a base-60 system, and the extension they made was similar to the one we currently use with our decimal system. Numbers to the left of what would be a "sexagesimal point" had place value and represented successive units, 60s, 3600s, and so on. Numbers smaller than 1 were placed to the right of the imaginary sexagesimal point and represented 60ths, 3600ths, and so on. Their system had two deficiencies which make it hard for contemporary archaeologists to interpret what they wrote (and probably made it hard for the Babylonians themselves). They had no zero to act as a place holder and they had no symbol to act as a sexagesimal point. All this had to be figured out from the context in which the number was used. Nevertheless, they had an approximation for $\sqrt{2}$ which was correct to four decimal places, and approximations for other irrational numbers as well. In fact, their system was so good that vestiges of it are to be seen today. We still break hours down sexagesimally, and the degree measure of angles as well.

The Egyptians, who lived in a later period, also found a way to represent fractional values. Theirs was not a place-value system, so the Babylonian method did not suggest itself. Instead they created unit fractions. They did not do it with a ratio, such as 1/4, however. Their symbolism was analogous to writing the unit fraction as 4^{-1} or 7^{-1}. For that reason, what we would write as 2/5 had to be written as a sum of unit fractions, typically $3^{-1} + 15^{-1}$. Clearly their system was much more awkward that of the Babylonians.

The study of rational numbers really flowered under the Greeks. Pythagoras, Eudoxus, Euclid, and many others worked extensively with ratios. Their work was limited, however, by the fact that it was almost entirely geometric. Numbers were represented by line segments, ratios by pairs of segments. The Greek astronomer Ptolemy, who lived in the second century, found it better to turn to the sexagesimal system of the Babylonians (but not their clumsy cuneiform characters) in making his extensive astronomical calculations.

KEY TERMS

Irrational number—A number which can be represented by a point on the number line but which is not rational.

Rational number—A number which can be expressed as the ratio of two integers.

Further Reading

Boyer, Carl B. *A History of Mathematics.* New York: John Wiley and Sons, 1968.

Eves, Howard. *An Introduction to the History of Mathematics.* New York: Holt, Rinehart and Winston, 1976.

Niven, Ivan. *Numbers: Rational and Irrational.* Washington, D. C.: The Mathematical Association of America, 1961.

J. Paul Moulton

Rationalization

Rationalization is a process of converting an **irrational number** into a **rational number**, which is one which can be expressed as the **ratio** of two **integers**. The numbers 1.003, -1 1/3, and 22/7 are all rational numbers. Irrational numbers are those which cannot be so expressed. The ratio **pi**, the square root of 5, and the cube root of 4 are all irrational numbers.

Rationalization is a process applied most often to the denominators of fractions, such as $5/(1 + \sqrt{+2})$. There are two reasons for this. If someone wanted to compute a rational **approximation** for such an expression, doing so would entail dividing by a many-place decimal, in this case 2.41421... With a **calculator** it would be easy to do, but if it must be done without a calculator, the process is long, tedious, and subject to errors. If the denominator were rationalized, however, the calculations would be far shorter.

The second and mathematically more important reason for rationalizing a denominator has to do with "fields," which are sets of numbers which are closed with respect to **addition**, **subtraction**, **multiplication**, and **division**. If one is working with the field of rational numbers and if one introduces a single irrational **square root** into the field, forming all possible sums, differences, products, and quotients, what happens? Are the resulting numbers made more complex in an unlimited sort of way, or does the complexity reach a particular level and stop?

The answer with respect to sums, differences, and products is simple. If the irrational square root which is introduced happens to be $\sqrt{2}$, then any possible sum, difference, or product can be put into the form p + q $\sqrt{2}$, where p and q are rational. The cube of 1 + $\sqrt{2}$, for example, can be reduced to 7 + 5 $\sqrt{2}$.

To check quotients, one can first put the numerator and denominator in the form p + q $\sqrt{2}$ (thinking of a quotient as a fraction). Then one rationalizes the denominator. This will result in a fraction whose numerator is in the form p + q $\sqrt{2}$, and whose denominator is a simple rational number. This can in turn be used with the distributive law to put the entire quotient into the form p + q $\sqrt{2}$.

How does one rationalize a denominator? The procedure relies on the algebraic identity $(x + y)(x - y) = x^2 - y^2$, which converts two linear expressions into an expression having no linear terms. If x or y happens to be a square root, the **radical** will disappear.

Using this identity can be illustrated with the example given earlier:

The procedure is not limited to expressions involving $\sqrt{2}$.

$$\frac{5}{1+\sqrt{2}} = \frac{5}{1+\sqrt{2}} \times \frac{1+\sqrt{2}}{1+\sqrt{2}}$$

$$= \frac{5-5\sqrt{2}}{1-2}$$

$$= -5+5\sqrt{2}$$

If any irrational square root, $\sqrt{7}$, $\sqrt{80}$, or $\sqrt{n}$ is introduced into the field of rational numbers, expressions involving it can be put into the form p + q $\sqrt{n}$. Then quotients involving such a form as a divisor can be computed by multiplying numerator and denominator by p - q $\sqrt{n}$, which will turn the denominator into $p^2 - nq^2$, a rational number. From there, ordinary **arithmetic** will finish the job.

Fields can be extended by introducing more than one irrational square root, or by introducing roots other than square roots, but everything becomes more complicated.

One analogous extension that is of great mathematical and practical importance is the extension of the field of **real numbers** to include $\sqrt{-1}$ or i. A process similar to the one used to rationalize denominators is used to convert a denominator from a complex number involving i into a real number.

Further Reading

Birkhoff, Garrett, and Saunders Mac Lane, *A Survey of Modern Algebra.* New York: The Macmillan Co., 1947.

Niven, Ivan, *Numbers: Rational and Irrational.* Washington, D.C.: The Mathematical Association of America, 1961.

J. Paul Moulton

Ratites see **Flightless Birds**

Rats

Rats are members of the order Rodentia, which also encompasses **beavers**, **mice**, **hamsters**, and **porcupines**. Two major families of rats and mice are recognized: the Sigmodontinae; the New World rats and mice, comprising 369 species in 73 genera, and the Murinae, the Old World rats and mice, comprising 408 species in 89 genera. The major taxonomic difference between the two subfamilies is the presence of a functional row of tubercles on the inner side of the upper molars in the Murinae.

Physical characteristics

Rats are generally small animals. A typical rat, *Rattus norvegicus* or the Norway rat, is about 9 in (23 cm) from the nose to the base of the tail when fully grown and weighs about 2 lbs (1.8 kg). One of the largest species, the southern giant slender-tailed cloud rat *Phloeomys cumingi*, has a head-body length of 19 in (48 cm) and a tail that ranges between 8-13 in (20-33 cm) long.

Rats have brown, gray, or black fur covering their body, except for their ears, tail, and feet (the familiar white lab rat is an albino form of *R. norvegicus*). Their **hearing** is excellent, and their eyes are suited for a nocturnal lifestyle. Rats typically have 16 teeth, the most prominent of which are their ever-growing incisors. The outer surface of the incisors is harder than the inner side, much like a chisel. The incisors grow throughout life from the base and are nerveless except for at the base. Rats must gnaw continually to keep the incisors down to a manageable length; if rats fail to gnaw, the teeth can grow rapidly and curl back into the roof of the mouth, or (with the lower incisors) up in front of the nose, making biting and eating difficult.

The teeth, combined with the rat's powerful jaw muscles, allow them to chew through almost anything; even **concrete** block and lead pipe have been found bearing toothmarks. The jaw muscles exert an extraordinary 24,000 lbs (12 tons) per square inch (for comparison, a great white shark bites with a **force** of 20 tons per square inch). One of the masseter muscles responsible for this tremendous biting power in the rat passes

A brown rat scavenging in a garbage can.

through the orbit, or **eye** socket, a feature unique among the **mammals**.

A rat will bite a perceived enemy, particularly if cornered or if its nest is threatened. It also often bites out of curiosity, when exploring the edibility of unfamiliar things. Unfortunately, a sleeping child or unconscious derelict may be the subject of this investigation, with potentially serious consequences. Rats do carry a variety of zoonoses (animal-borne diseases) in their saliva, on their fur, and in their external **parasites** (such as **fleas**), that can and do infect humans. Best known are rat-bite fever and **bubonic plague**, transmitted to humans by rat saliva and rat fleas, respectively. When a rat walks though garbage in which **salmonella bacteria** are present, the microbes can latch onto the rat's fur. When the rat later investigates a pile of human food, the salmonella moves from the fur to the food, and whoever eats it may develop **food poisoning**.

Behavior

Rats are social creatures, living in colonies that are housed in a complex network of underground burrows similar to the warrens dug by wild rabbits. To protect the colony from predators, the entrances to the burrows are well-hidden among **rocks**, the roots of shrubs, or under other thick vegetation. In temperate regions, most of the burrow is below the frost line, ranging from a few inches to several feet below the surface. Inside, the rats build nests of shredded vegetation, feathers, **paper**, and various other materials and huddle together for warmth.

One colony may consist of hundreds of rats of both sexes and all ages. According to observations made by zoologist S.A. Barnett, the colony is a relatively peaceful place. Due to an established social hierarchy among the males, there is little infighting for the right to mate with the females. Among rats, familiarity breeds content: seldom do rats that have grown up together in the colony fight with each other, although they may play in a rough-and-tumble fashion.

Conflict usually occurs when a new rat, especially an adult male, appears and tries to join the colony. The newcomer's status, and sometimes its fate, is determined by the first few encounters it has with the colony residents. Fights that occur are seldom intense or bloody. Dominance is quickly established, and once the newcomer adapts to its new place in the colony the issue is settled. Male newcomers that lose the fight seldom remain for long; soon after the fight they either leave the colony or die, although they are uninjured. Some zoologists hypothesize that they die of social stress.

Reproduction

The colony's size depends on two factors: the **density** of the population and the food supply. When the colony's population is low, such as at winter's end, the females will bear more young and thus the population increases steadily throughout the summer. As the population and density increase, the pregnancy rate declines accordingly.

Similarly, the greater the food supply, the larger the rat population. Female rats living near an abundant supply of food bear more young than females living further away from or without such a supply. If there is little food available, both sexes will become infertile, postponing reproduction in favor of individual survival.

The female's estrus lasts about six hours, during which she mates with several males, copulating frequently during the **heat**. After a gestation period of 22-24 days, the female gives **birth** to 6-12 blind, naked, pinkish, helpless young. By the time they are two weeks old, the young are fully furred and their eyes are open. After 22 days, they leave the nest. Males are sexually mature at three months, females slightly later.

Diet

The rat's nutritional requirements are similar to those of humans, which makes it a useful subject for scientific experimentation. They have been known to carry off beef bones left by picnickers, eating not only the remaining meat but also the bone as well, for the **calcium** and **phosphorus** it provides.

Rats will eat just about anything, including things that humans would consider far past being edible. However, they prefer grain and consume or spoil (by their

hair and droppings) millions of tons of stored food each year worldwide.

Although unimpressive to look at, rats possess remarkable physical abilities. Rats can: swim for half a mile, and tread **water** for three days; survive falling five stories and run off unharmed; fit through a hole the size of a quarter; and scale a **brick** wall. Years after the nuclear testing ceased on Engebi Island in the western Pacific Ocean, scientists found rats, "Not maimed or genetically deformed creatures, but robust **rodents** so in tune with their environment that their life spans were longer than average," one researcher observed.

Species

The most widespread species of rats are *Rattus norvegicus*, the Norway or brown rat; *Rattus rattus*, the black, ship, roof, or alexandrian rat; *R. exulans*, the Polynesian rat; and *Bandicota bengalensis*, the lesser bandicoot rat. Both *R. norvegicus* and *R. rattus* are found around the world, and these are the two commensal species found in North American cities. They are longtime residents, firmly established on this **continent** by 1775. The Norway rat is found in temperate areas worldwide, although it originated in Japan and Eastern **Asia**, where it lived in burrows along river banks and later in **rice** fields.

Rattus rattus, like *R. norvegicus*, originated in Asia. It is thought to have been brought to **Europe** during the Crusades, although some records indicate it was present in Ireland as early as the ninth century. *Rattus rattus* arrived in **North America** with the early settlers, and its presence is recorded as of 1650. Early explorers brought *R. rattus* with them to **South America** as early as 1540. The two species spread worldwide, traveling in sailing ships to new ports.

Less global but no less commensal is the Polynesian rat, found from Bangladesh to Vietnam, throughout the East Indies, and in Hawaii and on other Pacific islands. The lesser bandicoot rat has been found in its natural **habitat** of evergreen jungle and oak scrub in Sumatra, Java, Sri Lanka, Pakistan, Burma, and Penang Island off the Malay **peninsula**, but in this century it has also become common in urban areas in India (it reproduces more quickly than any other rodent; a female lesser bandicoot rat can have a litter of seven every month).

Rats and humans

These four commensal species of rat together destroy about one-fifth of the world's food harvest each year. In the United States alone, the Norway and black rat damage or destroy a billion dollars worth of property each year, not counting the accidental fires that start when they chew through electrical insulation.

These commensal rats succeed because they are generalists and opportunists. The Norway rat, for instance, adapted its natural ground-dwelling habit to take advantage of many environments: cellars, sewers, even among the bushes in front of nicely landscaped homes and apartment buildings. In some buildings, the basement is home to Norway rats while black rats inhabit the upper stories.

Rats are present in almost every major city in the world. A study of Baltimore during World War II (done in reaction to fear that the Axis would attempt rat-borne germ warfare) discovered that many blocks in "good residential areas" harbored 300 or more rats. In poor, rundown neighborhoods, the number was doubtless much higher. Some cities in North America have an estimated population of two rats for every person.

Sanitation is the major contributing factor to the number of rats that will be found in a city, but new construction in an urban area will also force rats into areas where they have not traditionally been found, as digging unearths their traditional burrows.

Most rat control efforts involve poison bait. The most common type is an anticoagulant, usually rotenone, which causes fatal internal bleeding after the rat eats it.

However, there are formidable obstacles to effective rat control. First is the rats' innate fear of anything new. Even if something as innocuous as a brick is placed near a rat colony, they will go out of their way to avoid it. So merely placing the poison does not guarantee results. In 1960, rats that were apparently unaffected by anticoagulant poisons were found on a farm in Scotland. They had evolved a genetically based resistance to the **anticoagulants**. These so-called super rats are now found in several places in Great Britain.

Rat-control experts in New York City's Central Park noticed something curious about the rats they had been poisoning: the rats abandoned their normal shy, nocturnal habits and began appearing in the park in broad daylight. Rather than killing the rats, the poisons apparently acted like a stimulant to them.

Poisons obviously have their limits. The most effective method of rat control has proved to be a general clean-up to reduce the habitat quality for the pest rodents. Members of the Inspectional Services department must supplement their poisoning efforts with the education of local residents, telling people how to store their trash in rat-proof containers and how to rat-proof buildings by plugging all entry holes with **steel** wool.

F.C. Nicholson

Rattlesnakes see **Vipers**

Rayleigh scattering

Why is the sky blue? Why are sunsets red? The answer involves Rayleigh scattering. When light strikes small particles, it bounces off in a different direction in a process called scattering. Rayleigh scattering is the scattering that occurs when the particles are smaller than the wavelength of the light. Blue light has a wavelength of about 400 nanometers, and red light has a wavelength of about 700 nanometers. Other colors of light are in between. A nanometer is a billionth of a meter. So, for Rayleigh scattering of visible light the particles must be smaller than 400 to 700 nanometers. Scattering can occur off larger particles, but it will follow a different scattering law.

The Rayleigh scattering law, derived by Lord Rayleigh in 1871, applies to particles smaller than the wavelength of the light being scattered. It states that the percentage of light that will be scattered is inversely proportional to the fourth power of the wavelength. Small particles will scatter a much higher percentage of short wavelength light than long wavelength light. Because the mathematical relationship involves the fourth power of the wavelength even a small wavelength difference can mean a large difference in scattering efficiencies. For example, applying the Rayleigh law to the wavelengths of red and blue light given above shows that small particles will scatter blue light roughly 10 times more efficiently than red light.

What does all this have to do with blue skies and sunsets? The Earth's atmosphere contains lots of particles. The dust particles scatter light but are often large enough that the Rayleigh scattering law does not apply. However the **nitrogen** and **oxygen** molecules in the Earth's atmosphere are particles small enough that Rayleigh scattering applies. They scatter blue light about 10 times as much as red light. When the **Sun** is high overhead on a clear day, some of the blue light is scattered. Much of it is scattered more than once before eventually hitting our eyes, so we see blue light coming not directly from the sun but from all over the sky. The sky is then a pretty shade of Carolina blue. In the evening, when there is less blue light coming directly from the Sun it will appear redder than it really is. What about sunsets? When the sun is low in the sky, the light must travel through much more atmosphere to reach our eyes. Even more of the blue light is scattered, and the Sun appears even redder than when it is overhead. Hence, sunsets and sunrises are red.

See also Atmosphere, compostition and structure of; Color; Electromagnetic spectrum.

Rayon see **Artificial fibers**

Rays

Rays are members of the class Chondrichthyes, the **cartilaginous fish**, that includes **sharks**, **skates**, and chimeras. The flattened shape of rays makes them unique among **fish**. Their pectoral fins are much larger than those of other fish, and are attached the length of the body, from the head to the posterior.

Rays, and their relatives the skates, comprise the order Rajiformes, which includes 318 species in 50 genera and seven families. These families inlcude the eagle rays (Myliobatidae, 20 species in three genera); the electric rays (Torpedinidae, 30 species in six genera); the mantas (Mobulidae, eight species in two genera); and the stingrays (Dasyatida, 100 species in 19 genera).

Rays are found in all of the world's oceans, in tropical, subtropical, and temperate waters. Some species, such as the great manta ray, are pelagic, spending their lives swimming; they take in **water** through the mouth, unlike bottom-dwelling species, which draw water though two holes (called spiracles) on their back. In all species of rays, the gills are on the underside of the body.

Like their relatives the sharks, rays have a well-developed lower jaw and an upper jaw which is separate from the skull. In many species of rays, the teeth have fused into strong bony plates. In Myliobatidae, these plates are strong enough to crush the shells of the clams and other **mollusks** on which the rays feed.

Many species of eaglerays have multiple rows of tooth plates, up to nine in some species of cow-nosed rays. They are generally free-swimming rays, often found in large groups. These rays are shaped like diamonds, their whip-like tails can be nearly twice the length of their bodies. Their skin is soft, and they "fly" gracefully through the water by moving their pectoral "wings" up and down.

The most remarkable feature of the electric ray is its ability to generate an electric field of considerable punch. Although an output of 75–80 volts is the norm, jolts of 200 volts have been recorded. The electric rays use this ability to stun **prey** and dissuade attackers. Most electric rays live in shallow water, spending their time on the bottom. They are generally more rounded than other

rays, and are slow swimmers. They range in size from the lesser electric ray, which grows to about 1 ft (30.5 cm) in length, to the Atlantic torpedo, which grows to over 6 ft (1.8 m) long and can weigh more than 200 lb (91 kg). Unlike other rays, electric rays lack the venomous tail spine.

The venomous tail spine gives the stingray its common name. The venom is rarely fatal to humans, but the spine is barbed and thus difficult to remove if it is inserted. More swimmers and divers are injured by stingrays annually than by all other species of fish combined. In large specimens the spine can be up to 1 ft (30.5 cm) long, and human swimmers jabbed in the chest or stomach have died. Stingrays are primarily tropical marine bottom dwellers, though two genera in **South America** have adapted to life in **freshwater**.

Like the stingray, the manta ray has a fearsome reputation among humans. For centuries it was considered a monster with the power to crush boats. Other common names for the manta ray include "devilfish" and "devil ray," derived, in part, from the hornlike projections on their heads at the sides of their mouths, which actually serve to scoop prey into the mouth. Like many of the sea's other giants, manta rays feed on **plankton**. These are the largest of the rays, growing up to 17 ft (5.2 m) long and 22 ft (6.7m) wide, and weighing up to 3,500 lbs (1,590 kg), as is the case with the Pacific manta.

Rays eat a diverse diet, ranging from plankton to mollusks and crustaceans to fish. The bottom-dwelling species are also noted scavengers, using their ability to sense electrical fields to find prey buried in the sand.

Rays produce eggs, which are either released into the environment in a protective egg case (sometimes called a mermaid's purse), or brooded inside the mother until the young rays are sufficiently developed to live on their own. Rays reproduce slowly; the manta ray, for example, produces just one offspring at a time.

Rays are edible, though they are generally considered "trash fish" by commercial fishermen, who often throw them back as bycatch (some fishermen prefer to use the flesh from the pectoral wings to bait lobster traps). A net full of schooling species, such as the cownosed ray, can outweigh the winches' ability to haul it up. Shell fishermen wage war against rays, which have a **taste** for clams and oysters. In Chesapeake Bay, fishermen drive pointed wooden stakes into the mud surrounding their shellfish beds; any ray that attempts to eat the shellfish is impaled upon the sticks. Despite these instances, rays remain quite numerous.

Reactant see **Reaction, chemical**

Giant 6 ft (1.8 m) stingrays come to divers for handouts at Stingray City, Grand Cayman.

Reaction, chemical

Chemical reactions are interactions among chemical species. They involve a rearrangement of the **atoms** in reactants to form products with new structures in such a way as to conserve atoms. They differ from physical processes or phenomena to a great extent. For instance, **hydrogen** (H_2) and **oxygen** (O_2) gases under certain conditions can react to form **water** (H_2O), which is a chemical reaction. Water then exists as solid (ice), liquid, or vapor (steam); they all have the same composition, H_2O, but exhibit a difference in how H_2O molecules are brought together due to variations in **temperature** and **pressure**. Without the existence of chemical reactions, we would have no synthetic fibers for clothing, no special alloys as structural materials, no organic compounds derived from **petroleum** for various applications, and so on.

Chemical reactions can take place in one phase alone and are termed "homogeneous." They can also

proceed in the presence of at least two phases, such as reduction of **iron ore** to iron and **steel**, which are normally described as "heterogeneous" reactions. Quite frequently the rate of chemical reaction is altered by foreign materials, so-called "catalysts", which are neither reactants nor products. Catalysts can either accelerate or hinder the reaction process. Typical examples are found in Pt as the catalyst for oxidation of **sulfur** dioxide (SO_2) and iron promoted with Al_2O_3 and K as the catalyst for **ammonia** (NH_3) synthesis. Chemical reactions can be either irreversible or reversible. In the former case, the equilibrium for the reaction highly favors formation of the products, and only a very small amount of reactants remains in the system at equilibrium. In contrast to this, a reversible reaction allows for appreciable quantities of all reactants and products co-existing at equilibrium. $H_2O + 3NO_2$ rR $2HNO_3 + NO$ is an example of a reversible reaction.

Chemical reactions may proceed as a single reaction $A \rightarrow B$, series reactions $A \rightarrow B \rightarrow C$, side-by-side **parallel** reactions $A \rightarrow B$ and $C \rightarrow D$, two competitive parallel reactions $A \rightarrow B$ and $A \rightarrow C$, or mixed parallel and series reactions $A + B \rightarrow C$ and $C + B \rightarrow D$. In order for chemical reactions to occur, reactive species have to first encounter each other so that they can exchange atoms or groups of atoms. In gas phases, this step relies on collision, whereas in liquid and solid phases, **diffusion** process (**mass** transfer) plays a key role. However, even reactive species do encounter each other, and certain **energy** inputs are required to surmount the energy barrier for the reaction. Normally, this minimum energy requirement (e.g., used to break old chemical bonds and to form new ones) is varied with temperature, pressure, the use of catalysts, etc. In other words, the rate of chemical reaction depends heavily on encounter rates or frequencies and energy availability, and it can vary from a value approaching **infinity** to essentially **zero**.

In addition to chemical change, chemical reactions are often accompanied by the absorption or **evolution** of **heat**. This of course is due to the difference in molecular structure between the products and reactants. Let us consider that a chemical reaction takes place in a vessel which can be treated as a system. If the heat flows into the vessel during reaction, the reaction is said to be "endothermic" (e.g., a **decomposition** process) and the amount of heat, say, Q, provided to the system is taken as a positive quantity. On the other hand, when the system has lost heat to the outside world, the reaction is "exothermic" (e.g., a **combustion** process) and Q is viewed as a **negative** number. Normally the heat change involved in a reaction can be measured in an adiabatic bomb calorimeter. The reaction is initiated inside a constant-volume container. The observed change in temperature and the information on the total **heat capacity** of the colorimeter are employed to calculate Q. If the heat of reaction is obtained for both the products and reactants at the same temperature after reaction and also in their standard states, it is then defined as the "standard heat of reaction", denoted by $\Delta H°$. For instance, $0.5\ N_2 + 1.5\ H_2 \rightarrow NH_3$, $\Delta H°_{29}8.$ = -11,040 cal means an exothermic reaction measured at 77°F (25°C).

Both chemical kinetics and **thermodynamics** are crucial issues in studying chemical reactions. Chemical kinetics help us search for the factors that influence the rate of reaction. It provides us with the information about how fast the chemical reaction will take place and about what the sequence of individual chemical events is to produce observed reactions. Very often, a single reaction like $A \rightarrow B$ may take several steps to complete. In other words, a chain reaction mechanism is actually involved which can include initiation, propagation, and termination stages, and their individual reaction rates may be very different. With a search for actual reaction mechanisms, the expression for overall reaction rate can be given correctly. As to determining the maximum extent to which a chemical reaction can proceed and how much heat will be absorbed or liberated, we need to estimate from thermodynamics data. Therefore, kinetic and thermodynamic information is extremely important for reactor design.

See also Catalyst; Compound, chemical.

Pang-Jen Kung

KEY TERMS

Chemical Kinetics—The study of the reaction mechanism and rate by which one chemical species is converted to another.

Equilibrium— The conditions under which a system shows no tendency for a change in its state. At equilibrium the net rate of reaction becomes zero.

Phase— A homogeneous region of matter.

Standard State— The state defined in reaction thermodynamics for calculation purposes in which the pure gas in the ideal-gas state at 1 atm and pure liquid or solid at 1 atm are taken for gas and liquid or solid, respectively.

Thermodynamics— The study of the heat of reaction and the maximum possible extent of reaction.

Real numbers

A real number is any number which can be represented by a point on a number line. The numbers 3.5, -.003, 2/3, π, and $\sqrt{2}$ are all real numbers.

The real numbers include the rational numbers, which are those which can be expressed as the **ratio** of two **integers**, and the irrational numbers, which cannot. (In the list above, all the numbers except **pi** and the **square** root of 2 are rational.)

It is thought that the first real number to be identified as irrational was discovered by the Pythagoreans in the sixth century B.C. Prior to this discovery, people believed that every number could be expressed as the ratio of two **natural numbers** (**negative** numbers had not been discovered yet). The Pythagoreans were able to show, however, that the hypotenuse of an isosceles right triangle could not be measured exactly by any scale, no matter how fine, which would exactly measure the legs.

To see what this meant, imagine a number line with an isosceles right triangle drawn upon it, as in Figure 1. Imagine that the legs are one unit long.

The Pythagoreans were able to show that no matter how finely each unit was subdivided (uniformly), point P would fall somewhere inside one of those subdivisions. Even if there were a million, a billion, a billion and one, or any other number of uniform subdivisions, point P would be missed by every one of them. It would fall inside a subdivision, not at an end. Point P represents a real number because it is a definite point on the number line, but it does not represent any **rational number** a/b.

Point P is not the only irrational point. The **square root** of any prime number is irrational. So is the cube root, or any other root. In fact, by using infinite decimals to represent the real numbers, the mathematician Cantor was able to show that the number of real numbers is uncountable. An infinite set of numbers is "countable" if there is some way of listing them that allows one to reach any particular one of them by reading far enough down the list. The set of natural numbers is **countable** because the ordinary counting process will, if it is continued long enough, bring one to any particular number in the set. In the case of the irrational numbers, however, there are so many of them that every conceivable listing of them will leave at least one of them out.

The real numbers have many familiar subsets which are countable. These include the natural numbers, the integers, the rational numbers, and the algebraic numbers (algebraic numbers are those which can be roots of polynomial equations with **integral** coefficients). The real numbers also include numbers which are "none of the above." These are the **transcendental numbers**, and they are uncountable. Pi is one.

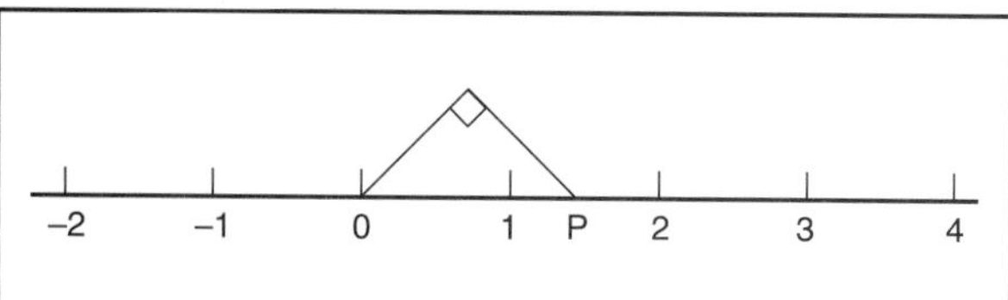

Figure 1.

Except for rare instances such as $\sqrt{2} \div \sqrt{8}$, computations can be done only with rational numbers. When one wants to use an **irrational number** such as π, $\sqrt{3}$, or e in a computation, one must replace it with a rational **approximation** such as 22/7, 1.73205, or 2.718. The result is never exact. However, one can always come as close to the exact real-number answer as one wishes. If the approximation 3.14 for π does not come close enough for the purpose, then 3.142, 3.1416, or 3.14159 can be used. Each gives a closer approximation.

Reciprocal

The reciprocal of a number is 1 divided by the number. Thus the reciprocal of 3 is 1/3; of 3/2 is 1÷(3/2)= 2/3, of a/b is b/a. If a number a is the reciprocal of the number b, then b is the reciprocal of a. The product of a number and its reciprocal is 1. Thus, 3 × 1/3 = 1, (3/2) × (2/3) = 1, and (a/b) × (b/a) = 1.

Rectangle

A rectangle is a **quadrilateral** whose angles are all right angles. The opposite sides of a rectangle are **parallel** and equal in length. Any side can be chosen as the base and the altitude is the length of a **perpendicular** line segment between the base and the opposite side (see Figure 1). A diagonal is either of the line segments joining opposite vertices.

The area of a rectangle with sides a and b is axb, the perimeter is a+b, and the length of the diagonal is

$$\sqrt{a^2 + b^2}$$

A **square** is a special case of a rectangle where all of the sides are of equal length.

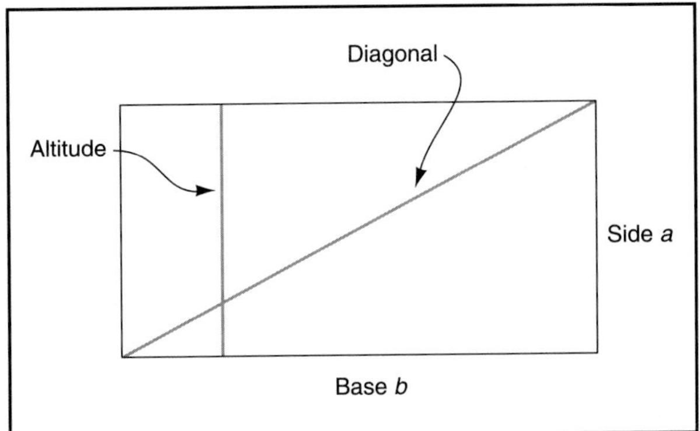

Figure 1

Recursive function see **Calculable functions**

Recycling

Recycling is a method of reusing materials that would otherwise be disposed in a **landfill** or incinerator. Discarded materials that contain **glass**, **aluminum**, **paper**, or plastic can be recycled by collecting and processing them into raw materials that are then used to manufacture new products. Recycling has many benefits: it saves money in production and **energy** costs, helps to conserve stocks of virgin resources, and decreases the amount of solid waste that must be disposed in landfills or incinerators.

The concept of recycling is not a new one. At the turn of the twentieth century, about 70% of the cities in the United States had programs to recycle certain useful materials. During World War II, 25% of the waste stream was recycled and reused. In 1960, however, only 7% of the waste stream was recycled, but since the early 1970s this has risen along with environmental consciousness, and the recycling rate was about 17% in 1990.

Process

Recycling is a four-step process. The first step is collection and separation from other trash. The second is reprocessing into a raw material, and the third is manufacturing into new products. The final step is the purchase and use of recycled products by consumers, including individuals, businesses, and government institutions.

Although this is a simple formula, recycling faces much controversy and is governed by complicated legislation. Key issues in the debate are how to make recycling more practical, and how to create favorable economics by developing markets for recycled goods. Many states are trying to encourage recycling by passing laws to favor recycling activities, such as tax credits, disposal bans, or regulations governing the recycled content of certain materials (such as newspaper). Although there is disagreement about how some of these laws and regulations should be designed and implemented, there are two issues that are more-or-less agreed upon. One is that fees for the disposal of garbage need to reflect the full costs of that service, and the other is that consumers should be charged for the amount and types of material that they discard.

The biggest problems that recycling faces are poor markets for many recyclables, and poor technology to accomplish effective recycling. There must, of course, be sufficient industrial demand for recycled materials, and also a healthy demand from consumers for products manufactured from those materials. For example, in the northwestern states, it is relatively easy to recycle newspaper, because there are paper mills in the region able to perform this function. In other areas, however, there is more difficulty in recycling newspaper because there are no local mills. These may areas suffer significant fluctuations in the price paid for used newspaper, leading to financial instability in their recycling programs.

Legislation

Legislation has a powerful role to play in encouraging or creating both a supply of recyclables and a market for recycled goods. For example, places with legislation mandating a deposit-refund system for containers (such as soda bottles) have acted to increase the supply of recyclable material. This sort of legislation requires that consumers pay a **deposit** for each container of soda, beer, or other beverage that they buy from retailers, and later obtain a refund of their deposit when they return the container for reuse or recycling.

Bans on the disposal of certain materials are another useful method for diverting waste from landfills and incinerators, and thereby increasing the availability of recyclable materials. Bans are a controversial approach, but they can be successful in prompting consumers to participate in recycling programs. Items that are commonly banned from disposal sites include lead-acid **automobile** batteries, tires, yard trimmings, and used motor oil.

Other kinds of laws can also help increase the demand for products manufactured from recycled materials. Some states require that more than a certain percentage of product be comprised of recycled material. This mandate has helped to save newspaper recycling programs, which were collapsing in the 1980s. A number of states (including Arizona, California, Connecticut, Illinois, Maryland, Missouri, North Carolina, Oregon,

Rhode **Island**, Texas, and Wisconsin, and the District of Columbia) require a minimum content of recycled fiber in newspapers printed within their jurisdiction.

Some government agencies require that labels list the environmental benefits of certain kinds of products, including their content of recycled materials. This gives consumers an opportunity to use information about environmental issues before making an informed decision to purchase particular goods.

Policies

Utilization rates and procurement polices are other methods used to promote the use of recycled material by industry. Utilization rates allow greater flexibility than minimum-content rules. The manufacturer is still required to use set amounts of recovered material in their manufacturing process, but they have more latitude in selecting how the material is used. For example, a manufacturer might use the material for its own products, or arrange to have the recovered material used elsewhere.

Procurement policies are mandates that require large government agencies, which have enormous purchasing power, to set aside some portion of their budget for the purchasing of recycled products. This helps to create more favorable economics for recycling. For example, the Environmental Protection Agency (EPA) requires that a certain proportion of its purchases, and also that of other federal agencies, involves such products as recycled paper, re-refined motor oil, and other items made from recycled materials. A disadvantage of affirmative procurement policies is that prices may be higher for recycled products, and there may be problems with the availability and quality of some goods.

Recycling collection programs

There are four commonly used methods for collecting recyclable materials: curbside collection, drop-off centers, buy-back centers, and deposit/refund programs. The fastest growing method is curbside collection. There are three major ways in which recyclable materials are collected through curbside programs: mixed wastes, mixed (or commingled) recyclables, and source-separated recyclables.

Mixed-wastes collection is essentially a modification of the conventional municipal waste-collection process. It involves the sorting of recyclables at a central facility, using a combination of automated methods (such as magnets to sort iron-containing material) and hand-sorting. An advantage of this method is that it does not disrupt the regular schedule of trash pick-up in the community.

Mixed recyclables are separated from other trash by householders and businesses, so that two streams of material are picked up at curbside: trash and recyclables. This method has a lower **contamination** level of the recyclable stream than the mixed-wastes collection system. Public education is necessary if this program is to work well, so that people know what is recyclable and what is not.

Source separation involves householders and businesses performing a higher level of sorting before pick-up. The advantage of this method is that the recyclable materials are well-sorted and can be sold at a higher price. The disadvantages are that source separation requires a high participation rate, as well as more or more-complex collection vehicles.

Drop-off centers are central places where householders or businesses can take their accumulated recyclables, rather than having them picked up at-site. This method requires public education and a high participation rate if it is to be effective. Like other collection systems, it works best if there are positive incentives to encourage participation (such as monetary redemptions), or **negative** ones to not participating (such as landfills refusing to accept recyclable materials, or charging a significant fee to take them).

Redemption or buy-back centers are similar to drop-off centers, except they purchase recyclable materials. Buy-back centers pay a unit-fee for such recyclable materials as newspapers, soda cans, glass, and plastic bottles. This system is also effective for the collection of metals, such as aluminum, **lead**, and **copper**.

After recyclables are collected and sorted by any of these methods, they are sent to a materials recovery facility (MRF), where they are prepared for re-manufacturing. A MRF can typically process 25-400 tons of material per day. Sorting is done both manually and mechanically. Newspapers are usually the major paper item, but MRFs also sort corrugated boxes, telephone books, magazines, and mixed-paper materials. MRFs also process aluminum, glass containers, plastic bottles containing polyethylene terphthalate (PET), and milk and detergent bottles containing high-density polyethylene (HDPE).

Recyclable materials

Numerous materials can be recycled or reused from the waste stream, including: aluminium cans and other materials, automobiles and **steel** appliances, clothing, construction waste, copper piping, furnishings, glass, lead-acid batteries, used motor oil, paper (cardboard, high-grade paper, newspaper, mixed paper), plastic bottles, tires, **wood** waste, and yard trimmings and other organic materials (which can be composted).

Curbside collection of recyclable household wastes in Livonia, Michigan. This municipality, and many others, mandates the recycling of glass, newsprint, steel cans, and certain kinds of plastics. Recyclable wastes are collected in bins provided by the city and placed outside for pickup.

All of the above items can be reprocessed into new products. Recycled paper, for example, can reprocessed into newsprint, writing paper, **tissue**, packaging, paperboard, and **cellulose** insulation. Plastic bottles can be reprocessed into auto parts, fiberfill, strapping, new bottles, carpet, plastic wood, and plastic bags. Some other materials can be reused directly with little or no processing, including used clothing, furniture, and lumber.

Composting

Composting is an increasingly popular method of recycling organic materials. It is an ancient practice; and low-technology farmers around the world have always composted manure and other organic materials for application to their **crops**. In fact, composting is one of the central activities in all methods of organic agriculture.

Any raw, organic materials containing vegetable or animal **matter** can be successfully composted. The composting reactions are mostly carried out by **bacteria** and **fungi**, along with other **microorganisms** and **invertebrates** of many kinds (earthworms can be highly effective in this regard). Composting proceeds best if the material is kept warm and is occasionally turned to increase the availability of **oxygen**. Composting can be done by individual householders, or in large, centralized, municipal facilities. The end-product is an amorphous, organic-rich material (or compost), which is extremely useful as an amendment to increase the organic-matter **concentration** of **soil** and enhance its tilth. Compost is also useful as an organic fertilizer. The compost can be given or sold to local horticulturists, or to farmers.

Household materials that can be readily composted include: **tree** leaves, lawn clippings, vegetable and fruit peelings and other food left-overs, seaweed, shredded cardboard, newspapers, other kinds of paper, dryer lint (if derived from **cotton** and other natural fabrics), **livestock** manure, hair, feathers, and meat. Egg-shells and wood ash can also be added to increase the nutrient content and neutralize acidity. Materials that should not be added to composters include: seed-bearing weed residues, walnut or eucalyptus leaves (these contain natural chemicals that can be toxic to cultivated plants), or dog and cat dung.

Preparing the compost

Excellent compost bins can be purchased, or they can be easily built using chicken wire and a wooden frame. The bottom of the bin should be lined with dried grass, leaves, or shredded paper. As additional organic matter is added to the pile, it can be watered if necessary and mixed to increase oxygenation. A good **temperature** for composting is about 130-140°F (54-60°C). Depending on the organic mix and time of year, a well-humified compost will develop within two to six months. Many gardeners have been composting their organic matter for years. It has only been in the past decade or so that the broader public has been encouraged to compost on a larger scale.

The "Compost Man"

Clark Gregory is a soil scientist who has been a driving force in the growing popularity of composting. When he was the composting supervisor for Fulton County, Georgia, Gregory became known as the "Compost Man." He claims that up to three-quarters of the material that is typically discarded in landfills is potentially biodegradable through composting. Gregory advocates the use of large-scale, comprehensive composting programs in all local communities, as a way or drastically reducing the amounts of solid waste that have to be landfilled. In many municipalities, just the composting of soiled paper, yard clippings, and food scraps would reduce the solid waste stream by 40%, while also helping to reduce the cost of garbage collection and disposal.

Economic benefits

Composting programs have highly favorable economics, compared with the land-filling of organic waste. For example, a composting program in Seattle is saving taxpayers about $18 per ton of organic waste, and is diverting about 554 lb (252 kg) of garbage per household out of landfills each year. Similarly, the town of Oyster Bay, Long Island, instituted a leaf-composting program that generated 11,000 tons of compost for use by local

KEY TERMS

Composting—A method of recycling organic material into humus, which is used to improve agricultural and garden soil.

Decomposers—Bacteria, fungi, and other microorganisms that break down organic material.

Humus—Organic material made up of well-decomposed, high molecular-weight compounds. Humus contributes to soil tilth, and is a kind of organic fertilizer.

Incinerator—An industrial facility that is used to burn garbage.

Landfill—An area of land that is used to dispose of solid waste and garbage.

Manure—Animal dung.

Microorganism—Bacteria, fungi, and other microscopic organisms.

Organic material—Vegetable and animal biomass.

Prefabricated—Manufactured off-site, usually referring to a construction process that eliminates or reduces assembling.

Virgin material—Material resources that have not previously been used for manufacturing or some other purpose.

gardeners, while saving $138 per ton previous spent to truck the leaves out of state for land-filling. The town of Bowling Green, Kentucky, composts more than 0.5 million cubic feet of leaves each year, producing **humus** that is sold for $5 per cubic yard, while saving $200,000 annually in disposal costs. Islip, New York, saves $5 million each year by composting grass clippings, which were once exported along with other garbage by barge to the Caribbean. If every county in the United States instituted composting programs of these kinds, the overall net savings could be $1.6 billion per year.

Zoo-Doo

Some zoos have become creative in composting and marketing the manure of their exotic animals. The Zoo-Doo Compost Company sells composted animal manure to novelty buyers and to organic gardeners. More than 160 zoo stores and 700 other retail outlets carry Zoo-Doo for sale to gag-gift buyers. In addition, gardeners buy larger quantities of the Zoo-Doo, which has a favorable nutrient **ratio** of 2:2:2 (2% each of **nitrogen**, **phosphorus**, and potassium), and is an excellent soil amendment as well as an organic fertilizer.

Researchers, environmentalists, and program administrators all agree that creativity will be one of the keys to solving many waste problems. Many landfills are nearing their **carrying capacity**, and most of the older ones will be closed by the year 2005. Recycling, composting, and reusing are all environmentally and economically beneficial ways of greatly reducing the **volume** of the solid waste stream.

See also Waste management.

Further Reading

Christopher, Tom, and Marty Asher. *Compost This Book!*. San Francisco: Sierra Club Books, 1994.

Earth Works Group. *50 Simple Things You Can Do to Save the Earth.* Berkeley: Earthworks Press, 1989.

Murphy, Pamela. *The Garbage Primer.* New York: Lyons and Burford Publishers, 1993.

Powelson, D.R. and M.A. Powelson. *The Recycler's Manual for Business, Government, and the Environmental Community.* John Wiley and Sons, 1997.

Strong, D.L. and D. Kimball. *Recycling in America: A Reference Handbook.* Abo-Clio, 1997.

Kitty Richman

Red giant star

A red giant is a **star** that has exhausted the primary supply of **hydrogen** fuel at its core and is now using another element such as helium as the fuel for its energy-producing thermonuclear fusion reactions. Hydrogen fusion continues outside the core and causes the star to expand dramatically, making it a giant. Expansion also cools the star's surface, which makes it appear red. Red giant stars are near the end of their lives, and die either in a **supernova** explosion, or more quietly as a planetary nebula. Both fates involve the expulsion of the star's outer layers, which leave behind the small, exposed core.

The onset of gianthood

Stars are self-gravitating objects, meaning that they are held together by their own gravity. A star's gravitational field tries to compress the star's **matter** toward its center, just as Earth's gravity pulls you toward its center. Since stars are gaseous, they would shrink dramatically if it were not for the thermonuclear fusion reactions occurring in their cores. These reactions, which in healthy stars involve the conversion of four hydrogen nuclei into one helium nucleus, produce **energy** that

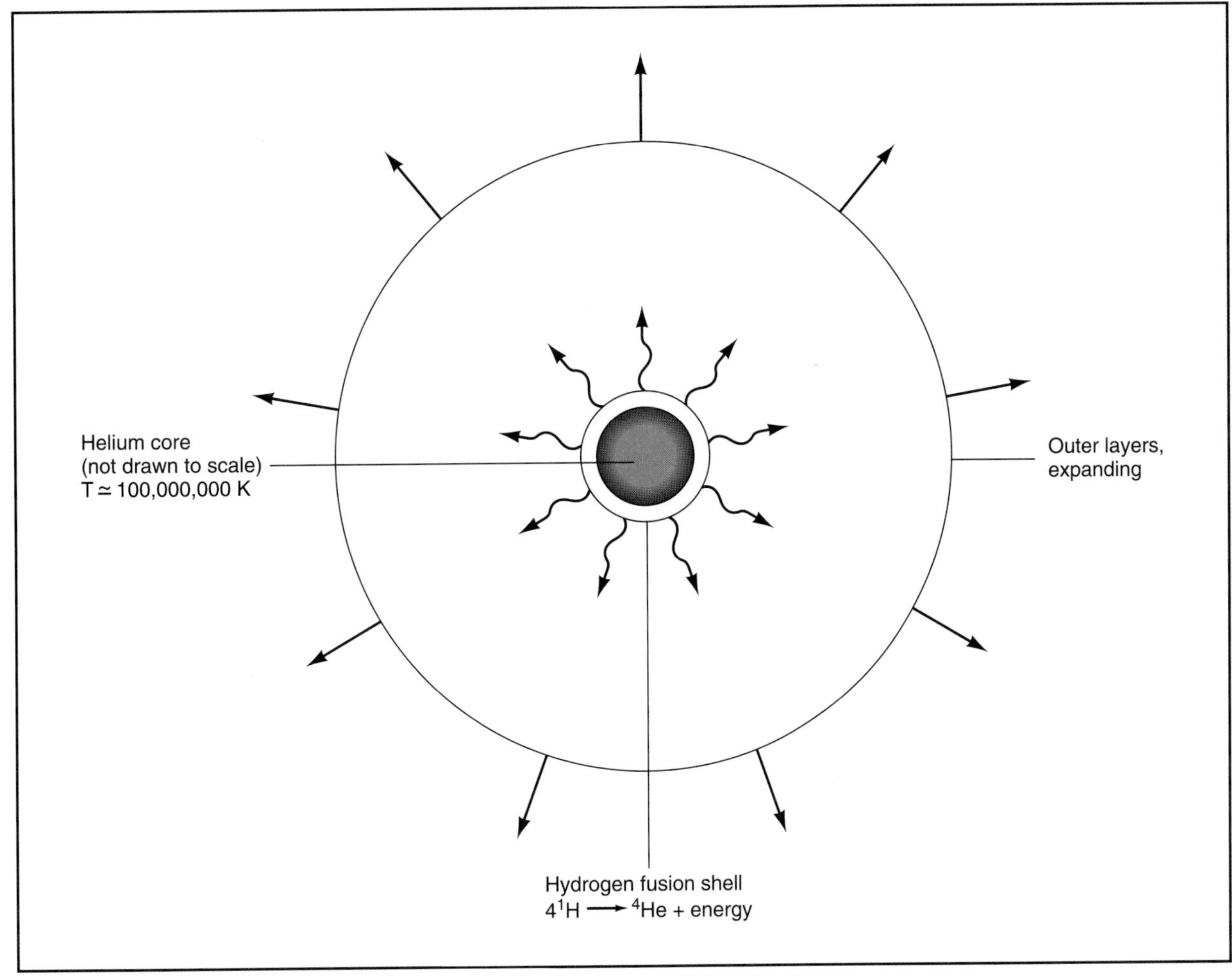

Figure 1. The main source of energy is in the core, while hydrogen continues fusing to helium in a "shell" around the core, much as a small circle of flame might creep away from a campfire. The energy produced by this shell streams outward, pushing the star's outer layers away from its center. When the star's surface expands, it also cools, because there is less energy being emitted per unit area. This causes the star to appear red. Many of the bright, red stars in the sky at night are these red giants.

heats the star's gas and enables it to resist the **force** of gravity trying to compress it.

Most stars, including the **sun**, use hydrogen as their thermonuclear fuel for two reasons: First, stars are mostly made of hydrogen, so it is abundant; second, hydrogen is the lightest, simplest element, and it will fuse at a lower **temperature** than other elements. The hydrogen-to-helium reaction, which occurs in all stars, is the "easiest" one for a star to initiate.

Although stars are huge, they eventually run out of hydrogen fuel. The time required for this to happen depends on the **mass** of the star. Stars like the sun take about 10 billion years to exhaust the hydrogen in their cores, while the most massive stars may take only a few million years. As the star begins to run out of hydrogen, the rate of fusion reactions in its core decreases. Since not as much energy is being produced, gravity begins to overcome the **pressure** of the heated gas, and the core starts to shrink. When a gas is compressed, however, it gets hotter, so as the core gets smaller, it also heats up. This is a critical point in the star's life, because if the core can **heat** up to about 100 million degrees kelvin, it will then be hot enough for helium fusion to begin. Helium, the "ashes" of the previous fusion reactions in the star's core, will become the new source of energy.

A star on the verge of helium ignition is shown here. Stars much smaller than the Sun cannot ignite their helium. Not only is their gravity too weak for their cores to achieve the necessary temperature, but their interiors are more thoroughly mixed than those of more massive stars. The helium ash in low-mass stars never gets a chance to collect at the core, where it might be used as a new fuel source.

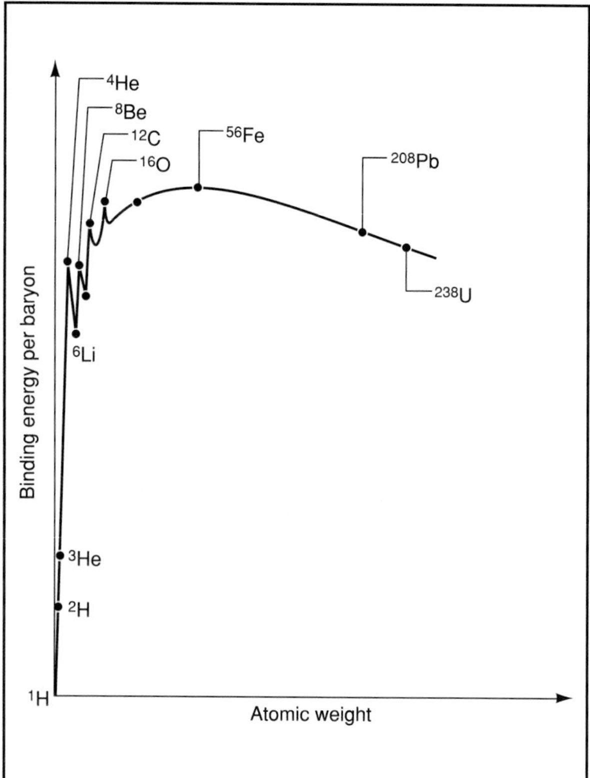

Figure 2. From hydrogen to helium there is a big change in binding energy, meaning the star gets a lot of energy out of each reaction. However, from helium to carbon, there is much less of a change. Each helium-to-carbon reaction produces less energy for the star than a hydrogen-to- helium reaction. At the same time, the high temperature of the core forces the reactions to occur quickly (this is part of the reason a giant star is so luminous). Less energy is produced per reaction, but the reactions are happening more frequently, and the helium-burning phase cannot last nearly as long as the hydrogen-burning phase.

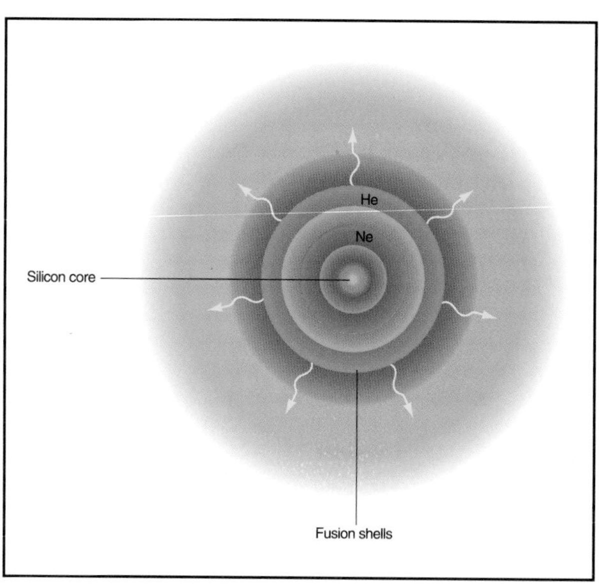

Figure 3. No element heavier than iron can be fused; however, because the binding energy curve reaches a minimum at iron (see Fig. 2). To fuse a heavier element would require an input of energy, rather than producing energy. When a star develops an iron core, it has run out of all possible fuel sources, and soon explodes as a supernova.

Stars like the sun, however, do develop a helium-rich core. When their cores get hot enough (about 100,000,000 degrees kelvin), the helium ignites, beginning to fuse into **carbon** and **oxygen**.

Events during gianthood

Helium-fusing stars have found a way to maintain themselves against their own gravity, but there is a catch. The amount of energy a star gets out of a particular fusion reaction depends on the binding energy of the elements involved.

When the helium is exhausted, the cycle just described begins anew. The core contracts and heats, and if the temperature rises to 600,000,000 degrees Kelvin, the carbon will begin reacting, producing even more energy than the helium-burning phase. This, however, will not happen in the sun. Its core will not get hot enough, and at the end of its red giant phase, the sun will shed its outer layers, which will expand into **space** as a planetary nebula. Some of these nebulae look like giant "smoke rings." All that will be left is the tiny core, made of carbon and oxygen, the ashes of the final fusion processes.

Whether destined to become a planetary nebula or a supernova, a red giant loses matter by ejecting a strong **stellar wind**. Many red giants are surrounded by **clouds** of gas and dust created by this ejected material. The loss of mass created by these winds can affect the **evolution** and final state of the star, and the ejected material has profound importance for the evolution of the **galaxy**, providing raw interstellar material for the formation of the future generations of stars.

Massive stars, however, can heat their cores enough to find several new sources of energy, such as carbon, oxygen, neon, and silicon. These stars may have several fusion shells. You can think of the whole red giant stage as an act of self-preservation. The star, in a continued effort to prevent its own gravity from crushing it, finds new sources of fuel to prolong its life for as long as it is able. The rapidly changing situation in its core may cause it to become unstable, and many red giants show marked variability. An interesting field of modern research involves creation of computer models of giant

stars that accurately reproduce the observed levels and variation of the giants' energy output.

Further Reading

Kaler, J. B., "Giants in the Sky: The Fate of the Sun," *Mercury.* March/April 1993, p. 35.
Kaufmann, W., *Discovering the Universe, 2nd ed.*, 1991.
Seeds, M. A., "Stellar Evolution," *Astronomy.* February, 1979, p. 6.

Jeffrey C. Hall

Red tide

Red **tides** are a marine phenomenon in which **water** is stained a red, brown, or yellowish color because of the temporary abundance of a particular species of pigmented dinoflagellates (these events are known as "blooms"). Also called **phytoplankton**, or planktonic **algae**, these single-celled organisms of the class Dinophyceae move using a tail-like structure called a flagellum. They also photosynthesize and it is their photosynthetic pigments that can tint the water during blooms. Dinoflagellates are common and widespread. Under appropriate environmental conditions, various species can grow very rapidly, causing red tides. Red tides occur in all marine regions with a temperate or warmer climate.

The environmental conditions that cause red tides to develop are not yet understood. However, they are likely related to some combination of nutrient availability, nutrient ratios, and water **temperature**. Red tides are ancient phenomena and were, for example, recorded in the Bible. However, it is suspected that human activities that affect nutrient concentrations in seawater may be having an important influence on the increasingly more frequent occurrences of red tides in some areas. In particular, the levels of **nitrogen**, phosphorous, and other **nutrients** in coastal waters are increasing due to runoff from **fertilizers** and **animal** waste. Complex global changes in climate also may be affecting red tides. Water used as ballast in ocean-going ships may be introducing dinoflagellates to new waters.

Sometimes the dinoflagellates involved with red tides synthesize toxic chemicals. Genera that are commonly associated with poisonous red tides are *Alexandrium*, *Dinophysis*, and *Ptychodiscus*. The algal poisons can accumulate in marine organisms that feed by filtering large volumes of water, for example, shellfish such as clams, oysters, and mussels. If these shellfish are collected while they are significantly contaminated by red-tide toxins, they can poison the human beings who eat them. Marine toxins can also affect local ecosystems by poisoning animals. Some toxins, such as that from *Ptychodiscus brevis*, the **organism** that causes Florida red tides, are airborne and can cause throat and nose irritations.

Red tides can cause ecological damage when the algal bloom collapses. Under some conditions, so much **oxygen** is consumed to support the **decomposition** of dead algal **biomass** that anoxic conditions develop. This can cause severe stress or mortality in a wide range of organisms that are intolerant of low-oxygen conditions. Some red-tide algae can also clog or irritate the gills of **fish** and can cause stress or mortality by this physical effect.

Marine toxins and their effects

Saxitoxin is a natural but potent neurotoxin that is synthesized by certain species of marine dinoflagellates. Saxitoxin causes paralytic shellfish poisoning, a toxic **syndrome** that affects humans who consume contaminated shellfish. Other biochemicals synthesized by dinoflagellates are responsible for diarrhetic shellfish poisoning, another toxic syndrome. Some red tide dinoflagellates produce reactive forms of oxygen—superoxide, **hydrogen** peroxide, and hydroxyl radical—which may be responsible for toxic effects. A few other types of marine algae also produce toxic chemicals. **Diatoms** in the genus *Nitzchia* synthesize domoic acid, a chemical responsible for amnesic shellfish poisoning in humans.

Paralytic, diarrhetic, and amnesic shellfish poisoning all have the capability of making large numbers of people ill and can cause death in cases of extreme exposure or sensitivity. Because of the risks of poisoning associated with eating marine shellfish, many countries routinely monitor the toxicity of these foods using various sorts of assays. One commonly used **bioassay** involves the injection of laboratory **mice** with an extract of shellfish. If the mice develop diagnostic symptoms of poisoning, this is an indication of **contamination** of the shellfish by a marine toxin. However, the mouse bioassay is increasingly being replaced by more accurate methods of determining the presence and **concentration** of marine toxins using analytical **biochemistry**. The analytical methods are generally more reliable and are much kinder to mice.

Marine animals can also be poisoned by toxic chemicals synthesized during blooms. For example, in 1991 a bloom in Monterey Bay, California, of the diatom *Nitzchia occidentalis* resulted in the accumulation of domoic acid in filter-feeding **zooplankton**. These small animals were eaten by small fish, which also accumulated the toxic chemical and then poisoned fish-eating **cor-**

KEY TERMS

Bloom—The occurrence of an unusually large population of one or a group of planktonic organisms, usually referring to algae.

morants and **pelicans** that died in large numbers. In addition, some humans who ate shellfish contaminated by domoic acid were made ill.

In another case, a 1988 bloom of the planktonic alga *Chrysochromulina polylepis* in the Baltic Sea caused extensive mortalities of various species of seaweeds, **invertebrates**, and fish. A bloom in 1991 of a closely related species of alga in Norwegian waters killed large numbers of **salmon** that were kept in aquaculture cages. In 1996, a red tide killed 149 endangered manatees (*Trichechus manatus latirostris*) in the coastal waters of Florida.

Even large whales can be poisoned by algal toxins. In 1985, 14 humpback whales (*Megaptera novaeangliae*) died in Cape Cod Bay, Massachusetts, during a five-week period. This unusual mortality was caused by the whales eating **mackerel** (*Scomber scombrus*) that were contaminated by saxitoxin synthesized during a dinoflagellate bloom. In one observed death, a whale was seen to be behaving in an apparently normal fashion, but only 90 minutes later it had died. The symptoms of the whale deaths were typical of the mammalian neurotoxicity that is associated with saxitoxin, and fish collected in the area had large concentrations of this very poisonous chemical in their bodies.

See also Neurotoxin; Plankton; Poisons and toxins.

Further Reading

Freedman, B. *Environmental Ecology.* 2nd ed. New York: Academic Press, 1994.

Okaichi, T., D. M. Anderson, and T. Nemoto, eds. *Red Tides: Biology, Environmental Science, and Toxicology.* New York: Elsevier, 1989.

Bill Freedman

Redshift

A redshift is caused by the **Doppler effect**, which is the change in wavelength and **frequency** of either **light** or sound as the source and observer are moving either closer together or farther apart. In **astronomy** a redshift indicates that the source is moving away, and a blueshift indicates that the source is moving closer to us. Doppler shifts have many important applications in astronomy. They help us to deduce the masses of stars and of galaxies. The redshifts for the most distant objects in the universe tell us that the universe is expanding.

Doppler effect

Listen to an ambulance or police siren as it passes. You should be able to hear a higher pitch as it is moving toward you and a lower pitch as it moves away. You are **hearing** the Doppler effect. It works for light as well as sound. The frequency (pitch for sound) and wavelength of both sound and light change if the source is moving relative to the observer. Think of the waves as either being stretched out or squeezed together. Note that either the source or the observer can be moving. When applied to light, the Doppler effect causes light from a source moving away to be shifted to a longer wavelength and light from an incoming source to be shifted to a shorter wavelength. Because red light has a longer wavelength than blue light, the shift toward a longer wavelength is a redshift.

When applied to astronomy, the Doppler effect is the only way that we can know if a celestial object is moving along our line of sight either toward or away from us. Light from an object moving toward us is blueshifted, and from an object moving away is redshifted. The amount of either blue or red shift tells us how fast the object is moving.

Astronomical applications

How do we actually measure the Doppler shift? When astronomers observe the **spectrum** of a **star** or **galaxy**, they see **spectral lines** that are produced at specific wavelengths. The wavelengths of these spectral lines are determined by the chemical composition and various physical conditions. The correct wavelengths for spectral lines produced by different elements at rest are measured in laboratories on **Earth**. To look for the Doppler shift astronomers must compare the observed wavelengths of spectral lines to the wavelengths expected from the laboratory measurements. If a spectral line is at a shorter wavelength, it is blueshifted and the star or galaxy is moving toward us. If, on the other hand, the spectral line is at a longer than expected wavelength, it is redshifted and comes from a star or galaxy that is moving away from us.

Doppler shifts of stars within our galaxy tell us about the motions of the stars within our galaxy. In turn these motions provide clues to help us understand the galaxy. The stars in our galaxy are all orbiting the center of the galaxy, but at slightly different velocities. There

are different populations of stars consisting of relatively young population I stars and older population II stars. Doppler shifts of stars belonging to these two populations tell us that the younger stars have orbital velocities fairly similar to the Sun's. The older stars, on the other hand, have orbital velocities that differ from the Sun's because they have orbits that extend above or below the **plane** of the galaxy. These **velocity** studies tell us that younger stars are distributed in a disk and older stars have a more spherical distribution. Hence the galaxy was initially spherical but has flattened into a disk.

The spectra of some stars show two sets of spectral lines that have alternating red and blue shifts. When one set of lines is redshifted the other is blueshifted. This spectral behavior indicates that the star is really a system of two stars orbiting each other so closely that they appear as one star. As each star orbits the other, it alternates between moving toward and away from us. We therefore see alternate red and blue shifts for each star. These systems are called spectroscopic binaries because the Doppler shifts in their spectra reveal their true nature as binary systems. The orbital properties of these systems are determined by the masses of the stars in the system. Hence, studying the orbits of spectroscopic binaries allows us to find the masses of the stars in the system. Binary stars are the only stars for which we can measure the **mass**, so these spectroscopic binaries are quite important. Knowing the masses of stars is important because the mass of a star is the single most important property in determining its **evolution**.

Doppler shifts also help us to find the mass of our galaxy and other galaxies. The Doppler shifts of stars and other components in our galaxy help us find the orbital velocities of these objects around the center of the galaxy. The orbital velocities of objects near the edge of the galaxy are determined by the mass of the galaxy, so we can use these velocities to derive the mass of the galaxy. For other galaxies, we can find the orbital velocities of stars near the edge of the galaxy by looking at the difference in the Doppler shift for each side of the galaxy. Again, the orbital velocities allow us to find the masses of these other galaxies.

Perhaps the most significant redshifts observed are those from distant galaxies. When Edwin Hubble first started measuring distances to galaxies, he noticed that distant galaxies all had a redshift. The more distant a galaxy is, the larger the redshift. Galaxies are moving away from us, and the more distant galaxies are moving away faster. This effect, named Hubble's Law after its discoverer, allows us to measure the **distance** to distant galaxies. More importantly, it tells us that the universe is expanding. Think of making a loaf of raisin bread. As the dough rises, the raisins move farther apart. If your pet ant named Hubble was on one of the raisins as you made the bread, it would look at the other raisins and see them moving away. If the raisins are like galaxies, and the dough like the space between galaxies, we see the same effect as the universe expands. Distant galaxies have large redshifts because they are moving away from us. Hence the universe is expanding. An apparently simple effect observed on the Earth has far-reaching implications for our understanding of the cosmos.

See also Binary stars; Electromagnetic spectrum; Stellar evolution; Stellar populations.

Further Reading

Cutnell, John D. and Kenneth W. Johnson, *Physics 3rd ed.* New York: Wiley, 1995.

Morrison, David, Sidney Wolff, and Andrew Fraknoi. *Abell's Exploration of the Universe.* 7th ed. Philadelphia: Saunders College Publishing, 1995. (Chapter 32)

Zeilik, Michael. *Astronomy: The Evolving Universe.* 7th ed. New York: Wiley, 1994.

Zeilik, Michael, Stephen Gregory, and Elske Smith. *Introductory Astronomy and Astrophysics.* Philadelphia: Saunders, 1992.

Paul A. Heckert

Reducing agent see **Oxidation-reduction reaction**

Reduction see **Oxidation-reduction reaction**

Redwood see **Swamp cypress family (Taxodiaceae)**

Reef see **Coral reef**

Reflection see **Optics**

Reflections

A reflection is one of the three kinds of transformations of **plane** figures which move the figures but do not change their shape. It is called a reflection because figures after a reflection are the mirror images of the original ones. The reflection takes place across a line called the" line of reflection." Figure 1 shows a triangle ABC and its image A'B'C'. Each individual point and its image lie on a line which is **perpendicular** to the line of reflection and are equidistant from it. An easy way to find the image of a set of points is to fold the **paper** along the line of reflection. Then, with the paper folded,

prick each point with a pin. When the paper is unfolded the pin pricks show the location of the images.

One reflection can be followed by another. The position of the final image depends upon the position of the two lines of reflection and upon which reflection takes place first.

If the lines of reflection are **parallel**, the effect is to slide the figure in a direction which is perpendicular to the two lines of reflection, and to leave the figure "right side up." This combined **motion**, which does not rotate the figure at all, is a "translation." The **distance** the figure is translated is twice the distance between the two lines of reflection and in the first-line to second-line direction.

If the lines of reflection are not parallel, the effect will be to rotate the figure around the point where the two lines of reflection cross. The **angle** of **rotation** will be twice the angle between the two lines and will be in a first-line to second-line direction. Because a figure can be moved anywhere in the plane by a combination of a translation and a rotation and can be turned over, if necessary, by a reflection, the combination of four or five reflections will place a figure anywhere on the plane that one might wish.

Someone who, instead of lifting a heavy slab of stone, moves it by turning it over and over uses this idea. In moving the stone, however, one is limited to the lines of reflection which the edges of the stone provide. Some last adjustment in the slab's position is usually required.

Reflections can also be accomplished algebraically. If a point is described by its coordinates on a **Cartesian coordinate plane**, then one can write equations which will connect a point (x,y) with its reflected image (x', y'). Such equations will depend upon which line is used as the line of reflection. By far the easiest lines to use for this purpose are the x-axis, the y-axis, the line x = y, and the line x = -y. Figures 4 and 5 show two such reflections. In Figure 4 the line of reflection is the y-axis. As the figure shows, the y-coordinates stay the same, but the x-coordinates are opposites: x' = -x and y' = y. One can use these equations in two ways. If a point such as (4,7) is given, then its image, (-4,7), can be figured out by substituting in the formulas. If a set of points is described by an equation such as 3x-2y = 5, then the equation of the image, -3x'-2y' = 5, can be found, again by substitution.

When the line of reflection is the line x = y, as in Figure 5, the equations for the reflection will be x = y,' and y = x'. These can be used the same way as before. The image of (3,1) is (1,3), and the image of the **ellipse** $x^2 + 4y^2 = 10$ is $4x^2 + y^2 = 10$ (after dropping the primes). The effect of the reflection was to change the major axis of the ellipse from horizontal to vertical.

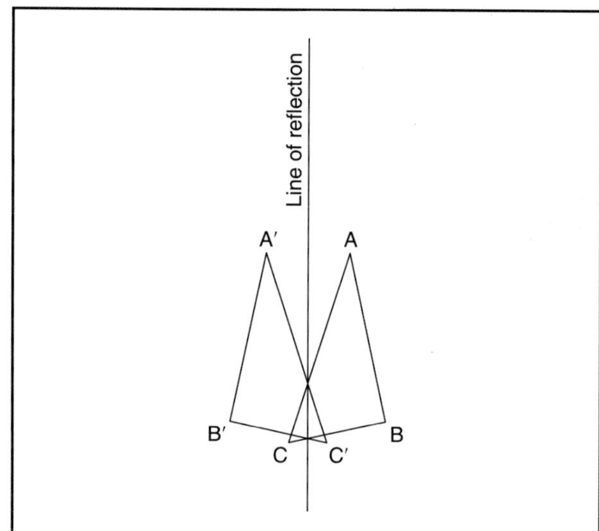

Figure 1.

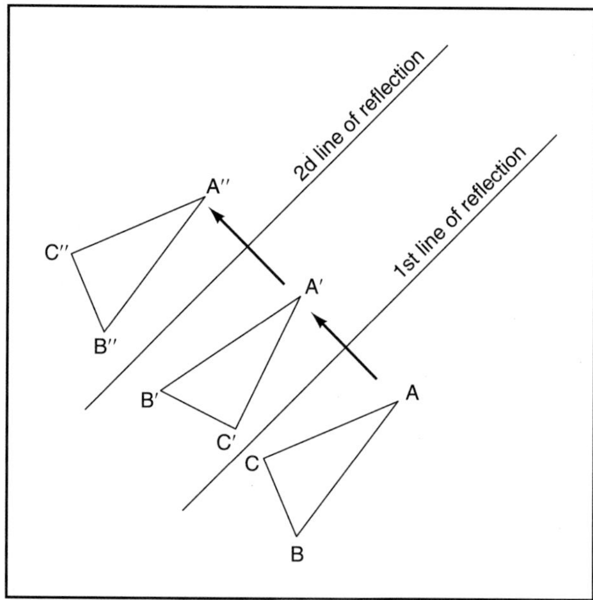

Figure 2.

When the line of reflection is the x-axis, the y-coordinates will be equal, but the x-coordinates will be opposites: x' = -x and y' = y.

When the line of reflection is the line x = -y, these equations will effect the reflection: x' = -y and y' = -x.

The idea behind a reflection can be used in many ways. One such use is to test a figure for reflective symmetry, to test whether or not there is a line of reflection, called the "axis of symmetry" which transforms the figure into itself. Letters, for example, are in some in-

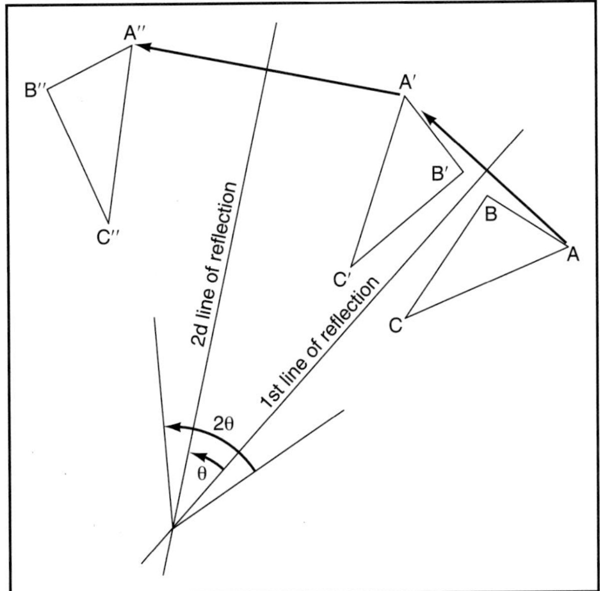

Figure 3.

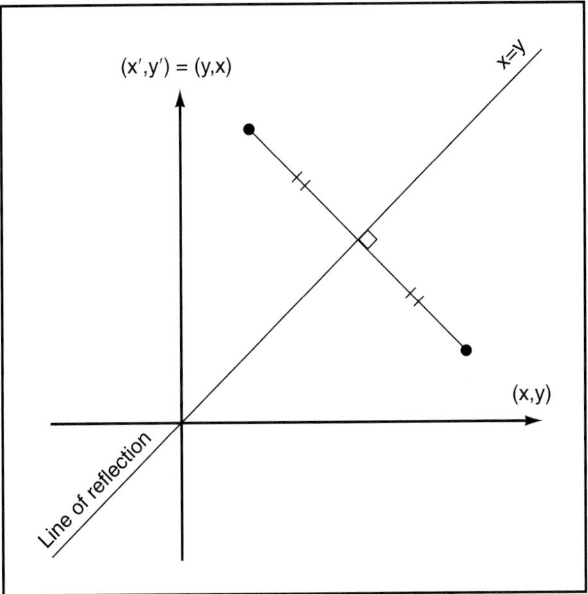

Figure 5.

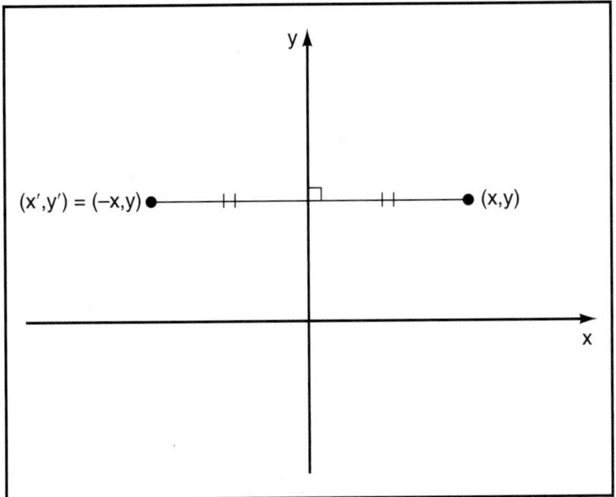

Figure 4.

stances symmetrical with respect to a line and sometimes not. The letters A, M, and W have a vertical axis of symmetry; the letters B, C, and E, a horizontal axis; and the letters H, I, and O, both. (This symmetry is highly dependent on the type face. Only the plainest styles are truly symmetrical.) If there is an axis of symmetry, a mirror held upright along the axis will reveal it.

While recognizing the reflective symmetries of letters may not be of great importance, there are situations where reflection is useful. A building whose facade has reflective symmetry has a pleasing "balance" about it. A reflecting pool enhances the scene of which it is a part.

KEY TERMS

Axis of symmetry—The line dividing a figure into parts which are mirror images.

Reflection—A transformation of figures in the plane which changes a figure to its mirror image and changes its position, but not its size or shape.

Reflective symmetry—A figure has reflective symmetry if there is a line dividing a figure into two parts which are mirror images of each other.

Or, contrarily, artists are admonished to avoid too much symmetry because too much can make a picture dull.

When tested analytically, a figure will show symmetry if its equation after the reflection is, except for the primes, the same as before. The **parabola** $y = x^2$ is symmetrical with respect to the y-axis because its transformed equation, after dropping the primes, is still $y = x^2$. It is not symmetrical with respect to the x-axis because a reflection in that axis yields $y = -x^2$. Knowing which axes of symmetry a graph has, if any, is a real aid in drawing the graph.

Further Reading

Coxester, H.S.M., and S.L. Greitzer, *Geometry Revisited.* Washington, D.C.: The Mathematical Association of America, 1967.

Kazarinoff, Nicholas D. *Geometric Inequalities.* Washington, D.C.: The Mathematical Association of America, 1961.
Pettofrezzo, Anthony. *Matrices and Transformations.* New York: Dover Publications, 1966.
Yaglom, I.M. *Geometric Transformations.* Washington, D.C.: The Mathematical Association of America, 1962.

J. Paul Moulton

Reflex

Reflexes are set motor responses to specific sensory stimuli. All reflexes share three classical characteristics: they have a sensory inflow pathway, a central relay site, and a motor outflow pathway. Together, these three elements make up the reflex **arc**. Reflexes can also be characterized according to how much neural processing is involved in eliciting a response. Some reflexes, like the short reflex in the gastrointestinal mucous membranes that secrete digestive enzymes, involve very local neural pathways. Other reflexes relay information through the spinal cord or other higher **brain** regions. However, reflexes rarely involve lengthy processing. Just as some reflexes result from neutral stimuli, others result from neuroendocrine stimuli.

The human body has numerous essential reflexes. Among them are the reflexes for swallowing, lactation (the secretion of milk), digestion, elimination of body waste, and self-preservation. Chemical sensory neurons in the stomach trigger reflexive secretion of digestive enzymes.

Reflexes can be inborn or conditioned. Although the majority of reflexes are inborn responses, some reflexes are conditioned into a person as the result of life experiences. The classical example of a conditioned reflex would be a dog's salivating in response to a dinner bell. Inborn reflexes in adults include the knee-jerk reflex and various skin reflexes to **heat** or **pressure**. Other reflexes include shivering, pupil constriction in bright light, the plantar reflex (curling up of the toes when the sole of the foot is irritated), and vomiting. Blinking can also occur reflexively as a defense mechanism; for example, as a response to air being blown on the **eye**.

Newborn reflexes are inborn primitive reflexes that are present in the first few months of life. Because they are so highly conserved in humans, these reflexes are thought to have provided some advantage to humans during **evolution**. The rooting reflex—the turning of the infant's head toward a **touch stimulus** in response to a **stroke** on the cheek—allows the infant's mouth to locate the nipple for nursing. The suckling reflex—initiated by touching the mucous membranes on the inside of the mouth with any object—also serves to facilitate nursing. The grasping reflex is seen when an infant tightly grasps an object placed firmly in its hand. The walking reflex is obvious when a young baby is held upright with feet barely touching the surface below; the infant alternately puts weight on each foot. And the Moro (or startle) reflex is evident when the baby throws out and wriggles its arms as if to hold on to something when the baby's head is left momentarily unsupported. Each of these reflexes is routinely checked by a physician during the baby's physical examinations.

Reflexes utilize or affect different types of muscle **tissue**, including smooth, cardiac, or skeletal muscle tissue. Reflexes operating in conjunction with smooth muscle tissue include those found in the urinary bladder, colon, and rectum. Typically, when an **organ** surrounded by smooth muscle expands as it is filled, stretch receptors respond to initiate reflexive movement, emptying the organ. For example, in the bladder, as urinary **volume** increases, stretch receptors in the urinary smooth muscles signal relaxation of the bladder that opens to release urine. Some reflexes, such as the urinary reflex, can be consciously regulated. For example, someone can intentionally resist urinating until a later time; however, eventually the reflex will win out.

The swallowing reflex involves both smooth and skeletal muscle responses. A **mass** of food in the throat stimulates mechanoreceptors of the pharynx which relay impulses to the medulla in the **nervous system**. The medulla, in turn, signals skeletal muscles in the upper esophagus and smooth muscles in the lower esophagus to swallow.

Some reflexes effect skeletal muscle responses. The flexor withdrawal reflex involves cutaneous (skin) receptors and skeletal muscles. A good example of this reflex is observed when someone steps on a sharp tack. **Pain** receptors in the skin send a rapid message to the dorsal (back) side of the spinal cord that sends out immediate signals from the ventral (front) side of the spinal cord to muscles in both legs causing them to cooperate simultaneously to avoid stepping on the tack. The leg that stepped on the tack must flex (close) its knee joint and raise the thigh to lift the foot off the tack. The opposite leg immediately must bear the body's full weight. Most reflexes, such as this one, are mediated by the spinal cord in **vertebrates** (backbone animals). The dorsal side of the spinal cord receives sensory input, while the ventral side sends out motor commands. As such, most reflexes are under autonomic (involuntary) control.

Some reflexes orchestrate a response to a stimulus across multiple systems. The diving response is a breathing reflex that is triggered by submergence. Although this reflex is most pronounced in infants, it has also been

KEY TERMS

Reflex arc—The path of sensory and motor transmission involved in a reflex which includes an information relay area that receives reflexive stimuli and directs a motor response.

documented in young children. This reflex prompts the subject to hold its breath when the face is submerged in **water**. The **heart** rate slows down, and **blood** flow to peripheral tissue decreases. The resulting accumulation of oxygenated blood in the central (critical) body regions helps preserve life during water submergence. Victims of prolonged submergence, however, can survive only if the water **temperature** (which decreases the metabolic rate) is exceptionally low. Reflexes are often assessed during a physical examination to determine appropriate reflex function or indicate problems with either the nervous or **muscular system**.

See also Conditioning.

Further Reading

Rhoads, R., and R. Pflanzer, eds. "The Motor System," and "Muscle." In *Physiology.* New York: Saunders College Publishing, 1992.

Ganong, W., ed. *Review of Medical Physiology.* 15th ed. Norwalk, CT: Appleton & Lange, 1991.

Louise Dickerson

Refraction see **Optics**

Refrigerated trucks and railway cars

Refrigerated trucks and railroad cars have had a great impact on the economy and eating habits of Americans. As the United States became more urbanized, the demand for fresh food shipped over long distances increased. Meat products were especially in demand.

In the mid-1800s, cattle raised in Texas were shipped by rail to Chicago, Illinois. Although it was more efficient to slaughter the cattle in Chicago and ship the carcasses to the East, rather than send live cattle east by rail, carcasses could only be shipped during the cold winter months. The first refrigerator car patent was issued in 1867 for a crude design developed by William Davis for meat-packer George Hammond. While Hammond was able to ship meat to Boston by 1872, the cars had to be reloaded with ice once a day, and the meat arrived discolored from contact with the ice.

An industrial food refrigeration unit.

The first successful refrigerator car was patented in 1877 by Joel Tiffany of Chicago. A similar design was developed the same year by meat packer Gustavus Franklin Swift (1839-1903) and his engineer, Andrew Chase. Ice stored on the car's roof dropped cold air down through the car; warm air was ventilated out through the floor. Once meat could be reliably shipped east, the Chicago slaughterhouse industry boomed, and such meat-packing companies as Swift and Armour made fortunes. Refrigeration with ice is still used in railroad cars as well as in trucks and ships, with powerful fans circulating the cooled air.

An obvious problem with iced refrigeration of transported perishable foods is that the food may spoil if the ice melts before the shipment reaches the market. In the

late 1930s, at the request of the Werner Transportation Company, Minneapolis engineer Frederick McKinley Jones (1892-1961) sought ways to build an automatic, ice-free air-cooling unit for long-distance trucking. He designed a compact, shock-proof air conditioner that could withstand the vibrations and jolting of overland travel. Jones's first air conditioning device, which was installed under the truck, failed when it was clogged with mud. A unit mounted in front of the truck, above the cab, was a success.

Jones patented his truck air conditioner in 1940. The system was later adapted for use on railroad cars and ships. Jones's invention changed the food industry. For the first time, perishable foods could be reliably transported over long distances at any time of the year. In turn, food production facilities could be located anywhere; foods could be marketed anywhere. A much greater variety of fresh and frozen foods was now available to millions of people.

Regression, marine see **Sea level**

Rehabilitation

Illness and trauma that lead to disability or functional loss can lead to an individual's need for a changed lifestyle to accommodate his reduced level of ability. A **stroke**, for example, can lead to partial paralysis; chronic **arthritis** can result in the inability to stand or to use one's hands; an **automobile** accident can cause blindness or can result in an individual's confinement to a wheelchair. To retrain someone who has experienced any of these incidents requires a rehabilitation team.

Through history disabled individuals have been ridiculed, sheltered, offered care, taught to fend for themselves, or killed. The ancient Greeks killed children born crippled. In the Middle Ages the French accorded privileges to the blind. Throughout its history the church provided a place for the disabled to live and receive care. In the 16th and 17th centuries England established hospitals and passed laws to assist the disabled. The Poor Relief Act of 1601 outlawed begging and provided the means to assist the poor and the disabled. Through these means the disabled became less dependent upon public assistance and learned self sufficiency. Almshouses were established to house and treat the infirm and this idea was brought to the new world. Pilgrims built almshouses in Boston in the 1660s.

The influx of wounded and maimed soldiers during World War I added impetus to the rehabilitation movement. In 1918, the U.S. government initiated a rehabilitation program for disabled veterans of the Great War. The aim was to enable the wounded to find jobs, so physical aspects of rehabilitation were stressed with little emphasis on psychological ramifications. The program was advanced following World War II to include the psychosocial aspects as well as the physical when veterans were trained for work and received counseling for reintegration into the community. Continued demands for such services have been brought about in this century by industrial accidents, auto accidents, sports injuries, and urban crime. Also, the life expectancy of people in developed countries has increased and with it the probability of contracting a chronic condition from stroke, **heart** attack, **cancer**, or other debilitating situation.

In 1947, the American Board of Physical Medicine and Rehabilitation recognized rehabilitation as a physician specialty. A rehabilitation specialist is called a physiatrist. In 1974, the American Nurses' Association established the Association of Rehabilitation Nurses, giving recognition to nurses in the field.

Rehabilitation of the chronically ill or injured individual does not stress cure, but focuses on training the individual to live as independently as possible with the condition, taking into consideration that the condition may change for the worse over time and the disability progress. This means that physical training must be accompanied by shoring up the individual's psychological outlook to accept the condition, accept society's lack of understanding or even rejection, and still to attain the maximum degree of autonomy.

Rehabilitation begins with the assessment of the patient's needs. An individual who was right-handed may lose the use of that arm and need to be trained to use the left hand for writing and other functions that his right arm normally accomplished. Such training consists greatly of **iteration**, the repetition of simple movements and acts to establish the nerve pathways that have not existed before. Mechanical devices requiring fine degrees of eye-hand coordination **force** fingers to maneuver in ways unaccustomed.

Patients are encouraged to take advantage of mechanical aids on the market to ease their lifestyle. Opening a jar with one hand, for example, is easily accomplished using a permanently mounted device that grasps the lid while the patient turns the jar. Doorknobs can be replaced by levers. Counter tops can be lowered and extended to provide room for the wheelchair patient to work or eat from them. Handles make getting into and out of a bathtub possible for the elderly or disabled person. Lighted magnifiers provide the means for the visually handicapped to read or carry out other tasks.

Modifications to automobile controls may enable the injured person to drive, thus divorcing him from the need for transportation to be provided. A ramp may need to be constructed to allow his wheelchair access to his home. The wheelchair-bound individual may need to relocate from a multistory living facility to one that is on one floor or one that has an **elevator**. Even carpeting must be evaluated. The person in a wheelchair may have difficulty wheeling across a deep, soft carpet. A more dense, firm floor covering can save **energy** and time.

Many injured patients can be rehabilitated by fitting a *prosthesis*, an artificial limb. Once the body has healed from **amputation** of the limb, the prosthesis can be fitted and training begun. Muscles that control the movements of the artificial limb must be trained to respond in a way that moves the prosthesis naturally. This requires seemingly endless repetitions of muscle contractions to afford effortless control of the prosthesis.

While physical training progresses, psychological counseling seeks to instill a value of self worth, to counter **depression**, to reassure the patient that he will be able to function adequately in society and in his career. The initial reaction to a debilitating injury or disease is one of anger at having been so afflicted and depression at the loss of function and freedom and fear that former friends will shun him or that family will exhibit undue sympathy. Counseling seeks to counter all these feelings and bolster the patient's confidence in himself. His changed station in life, losing function because of a stroke or being confined to a wheelchair because of an accident, will be jarring to his coworkers and friends, but usually they will accept the new person and adapt to his requirements.

Beyond the patient, his family also will require counseling to explain the patient's status, his limitations, his needs, and the family's optimal response. Coping day in and day out with a seriously handicapped family member can be grueling for the average family. Assessment of family attitudes, finances, and acceptance of the patient is crucial. The burden of caring for the patient may fall upon the shoulders of one member of the family; the wife, for example, who must care for a severely handicapped husband. Unending days of tending someone who requires close care can be physically and psychologically devastating. However, most family members can carry out their tasks and provide care if they receive some relief at intervals. Rehabilitation, therefore, also may include arrangements for a home health aide part time to provide personal time for the patient's caregiver.

Rehabilitation, therefore, far from merely providing the patient lessons on controlling a wheelchair or **learning** to walk on crutches, must take into account his environment, his mental status, his family's acceptance and willingness to help, as well as his physical needs. A replacement limb will never achieve the level of function of the original limb, but the prosthesis can serve adequately given sufficient training. The patient's psychological acceptance of his condition must be bolstered to salvage his ego and enable him to deal with the world outside his home.

KEY TERMS

Prosthesis—a man-made replacement for a lost limb or other body part. An artificial leg is a prosthesis, as is a replacement heart valve.

Prosthetist—one who designs and fits a prosthesis and helps to train the recipient in its use.

Further Reading

Pisetsky, David S. and Susan F. Trien, *The Duke University Medical Center Book of Arthritis*. New York: Fawcett Columbine, 1992.

Larry Blaser

Reindeer see **Caribou**

Reinforcement, positive and negative

Reinforcement is a term used to refer to the procedure of removing or presenting stimuli (reinforcers) to maintain or increase the **frequency** or likelihood of a response. The term is also applied to refer to an underlying process that leads to reinforcement or to the actual act of reinforcement, but many psychologists discourage such a broad application of the term. Reinforcement is usually divided into two types: positive and **negative**.

A negative reinforcer is a **stimulus** that when removed after a response, will increase the frequency or likelihood of that response. Negative reinforcers can range from uncomfortable physical sensations or interpersonal situations to actions causing severe physical distress. The sound of an alarm clock is an example of a negative reinforcer. Assuming that the sound is unpleasant, turning it off, or removing its sound, serves to reinforce getting out of bed. A positive reinforcer is a stimu-

lus which increases the frequency or likelihood of a response when its presentation is made contingent upon that response. Giving a child candy for cleaning his or her room is an example of a positive reinforcer.

Reinforcers can also be further classified as primary and conditional. Primary reinforcers naturally reinforce an **organism**. Their reinforcing properties are not learned. They are usually biological in nature, and satisfy physiological needs. Examples include air, food, and **water**. Conditioned reinforcers do not serve to reinforce responses prior to **conditioning**. They are initially neutral with respect to the response in question, but, when repeatedly paired with a primary reinforcer, they develop the power to increase or maintain a response. Conditioned reinforcers are also called secondary reinforcers.

Classical and operant conditioning

Reinforcement as a theoretical concept in **psychology** can be traced back to Russian physiologist Ivan P. Pavlovand American psychologist Edward L. Thorndike, who both studied conditioning and **learning** in animals in the early 1900s. Pavlov developed the general procedures and terminology for studying what is now called classical conditioning. This term refers to both the experimental procedure and the type of learning that occurs within that procedure. Pavlov's experiments involved giving a hungry dog dry meat powder every few minutes. The presentation of the meat powder was consistently paired with a bell tone. The meat powder made the dog salivate, and after a few experimental trials, the bell tone alone was enough to elicit salivation.

In Pavlov's terminology, the meat powder was an unconditional stimulus, because it reliably (unconditionally) led to salivation. He called the salivation an unconditional response. The bell tone was a conditioned stimulus because the dog did not salivate in response to the bell until he had been conditioned to do so through repeated pairings with the meat powder. The salivation, thus, was a conditioned response.

Thorndike's experiments involved placing **cats** inside specially designed boxes from which they could escape and get food only if they performed a specific **behavior** such as pulling on a string loop or pressing a panel. Thorndike then timed how long it took individual cats to gain release from the box over a number of trials. Thorndike found that the cats behaved aimlessly at first until they seemed to discover by chance the correct response or responses. Over repeated trials the cats began to quickly and economically execute the correct response or responses within seconds. It seemed that the initially **random** behaviors leading to release were strengthened, or reinforced, as a result of the positive consequence of escaping the box and receiving food. Thorndike also found that responses decreased and in some cases ceased altogether when the food reward was no longer given.

Thorndike's procedures were greatly modified by Burrhus F. Skinner in the 1930s and 1940s. Skinner conditioned **rats** to press down a small lever to obtain a food reward. This type of procedure and the resultant conditioning have become known as operant conditioning. The term "operant" refers to a focus on behaviors that alter, or operate on, the environment. It is also referred to as instrumental conditioning because the behaviors are instrumental in bringing about reinforcement. The food reward or any consequence that strengthens a behavior is called a "reinforcer of conditioning." The decrease in response when the food or reinforcer was taken away is known as "extinction." In operant conditioning theory, behaviors cease or are maintained by their consequences for the organism.

Reinforcement takes on slightly different meanings in the two types of conditioning. In classical conditioning, reinforcement is the unconditioned stimulus delivered either simultaneously or just after the conditioned stimulus. Here, the unconditioned stimulus reinforces the association between the conditioned and unconditioned stimulus by strengthening that association. In operant conditioning, reinforcement simply serves to strengthen the response. Furthermore, in operant conditioning the reinforcer's presentation or withdrawal is contingent upon performance of the targeted response. In classical conditioning the reinforcement or unconditional stimulus occurs whether or not the targeted response is made.

Reinforcement schedules

Reinforcement schedules are derived from the timing and patterning of reinforcement response. Reinforcement may be scheduled in numerous ways, based upon the number, or sequencing, of responses, or on certain timing intervals with respect to the response. The consequences of behaviors always operate on some sort of schedule, and the schedule can affect the behavior as much as the reinforcement itself. For this reason a significant amount of research has focused on the effects of various schedules on the development and maintenance of targeted behaviors.

In operant conditioning research, two particular types of schedules that have been studied extensively are **ratio** and **interval** schedules. In ratio schedules, reinforcers are presented based on the number of responses made. In fixed-ratio schedules, a reinforcer is presented for every fixed number of responses so that, for example, every fifth response might be reinforced. In **variable** ratio schedules, responses are reinforced using an average ratio of respons-

es, but the number of responses needed for reinforcement changes unpredictably from one reinforcement to the next. Using the interval schedule, reinforcements are presented based on the length of time between reinforcements. Thus, the first response to occur after a given time interval from the last reinforcement will be reinforced. In fixed interval schedules, the time interval remains the same between reinforcement presentation. In variable interval schedules, time intervals between reinforcements change randomly around an average time interval.

Research has shown that small differences in scheduling can create dramatic differences in behaviors. Ratio schedules usually lead to higher rates of response than interval schedules. Variable schedules, especially variable interval schedules, lead to highly stable behavior patterns. Furthermore, variably reinforced behaviors resist **extinction**, persisting long after they are no longer reinforced. This is why it is often difficult to extinguish some of our daily behaviors, since most are maintained under irregular or variable reinforcement schedules. Gambling is a clear example of this phenomenon, as only some bets are won yet gamblers continue taking their chances.

Applications

Reinforcement may be used and applied in numerous ways, not just to simple behaviors, but to complex behavior patterns as well. For example, it has been used to educate institutionalized mentally retarded children and adults using shaping or successive **approximation**. Shaping is the gradual building up of a desired behavior by systematically reinforcing smaller components of the desired behavior or similar behaviors. Much of this training has focused on self-care skills such as dressing, feeding, and grooming. In teaching a subject how to feed himself, for example, a bite of food may be made contingent on the person simply looking at a fork. The next time the food may be made contingent on the subject pointing to the fork, then touching it, and finally grasping it and bringing the food to his mouth. Shaping has also been used to decrease aggressive and self-destructive behaviors.

Another successful application of reinforcement involves using token economies, primarily in institutional settings such as jails and homes for the mentally retarded and mentally ill. Token economies are a type of behavior therapy in which actual tokens are given as conditioned reinforcers contingent on the performance of desired behaviors. The token functions like money in that it has no inherent value. Its value lies in the rewards it can be used to obtain. For example, prisoners may be given tokens for keeping their cell in order, and they may be able to use the tokens to obtain certain privileges, such as extra desserts or extra **exercise** time. Most follow-up data indicates that behaviors reinforced by tokens, or any other secondary reinforcer, are usually not maintained once the reinforcement system is discontinued. Thus, while token economies can be quite successful in regulating and teaching behaviors in certain controlled settings, they have not proven successful in creating long-term behavioral change.

Systematic desensitization is a therapeutic technique based on a learning theory that has been successfully used in psychotherapy to treat **phobias** and **anxiety** about objects or situations. Systematic desensitization consists of exposing the client to a series of progressively more tension-provoking stimuli directly related to the fear. This is done under relaxed conditions until the client is successfully desensitized to his fear. Fear of public speaking, for example, might be gradually overcome by first showing the client pictures of such situations, then movies, then taking them to an empty auditorium, then having them give a speech within the empty auditorium, etc., until his anxiety is extinguished. Systematic desensitization may be performed in numerous ways, depending on the nature of the fear and the client.

Current status/future developments

Recent trends in reinforcement research include conceptualizing the process underlying reinforcement as a physiological neural reaction. Some theorists believe the concept of reinforcement is superfluous in that some learning seems to occur without it, and simple mental associations may more adequately explain learning. The study of reinforcement is, for the most part, embedded in learning theory research.

Learning theories and the study of reinforcement achieved a central place in American experimental psychology from approximately the 1940s through the 1960s. Over time it became clear, however, that learning theories could not easily account for certain aspects of higher human learning and complex behaviors such as language and reasoning. More cognitively oriented theories focusing on internal mental processes were put forth, in part to fill that gap, and they have gained increasing support. Learning theories are no longer quite as exalted. Nonetheless, more recently, a number of psychologists have powerfully explained many apparently complex aspects of human **cognition** by applying little more than some basic principles of associative learning theory. In addition, these same principles have been persuasively used to explain certain decision-making processes, and they show potential for explaining a number of well-known yet poorly understood elements of perceptual learning. While learning theories may not be as powerful as their creators and supporters had hoped, they have added greatly to our understanding of certain aspects of

KEY TERMS

Classical conditioning—A type of conditioning or learning in which unconditioned stimuli are repeatedly paired with conditioned stimuli until the conditioned stimuli alone is able to elicit the previously unconditioned response.

Conditioned reinforcers—Also called secondary reinforcers, they do not have inherent reinforcing qualities but acquire them through repeated pairings with unconditioned reinforcers such as food or water.

Conditioning—A general term for procedures in which associative learning is the goal.

Extinction—A procedure in which reinforcement of a previously reinforced response is discontinued, it often leads to a decrease or complete stoppage of that response.

Learning theories—A number of different theories pertaining to the learning process.

Operant conditioning—Also called instrumental conditioning, it is a type of conditioning or learning in which reinforcements are contingent on a targeted response.

Reinforcement schedule—The timing and patterning of reinforcement presentation with respect to the response.

Shaping—The gradual achievement of a desired behavior by systematically reinforcing smaller components of it or similar behaviors.

Systematic desensitization—A therapeutic technique designed to decrease anxiety toward an object or situation.

Token economy—A therapeutic environment in which tokens representing rewards are used as secondary reinforcers to promote certain behaviors.

Unconditioned reinforcers—Also called primary reinforcers, they are inherently reinforcing and usually biological in nature serving to satisfy physiological needs. In classical conditioning they are also any unconditioned stimuli.

learning and of changing behavior, and they show great potential for continuing to add to our knowledge.

Further Reading

Rachlin, H. *Introduction to Behaviorism.* New York: W.H. Freeman & Co. 1990.

Schwartz, B. *Psychology of Learning and Behavior.* 3rd ed. New York: W.W. Norton & Co., Inc. 1988.

Staddon, J.E.R., and R.H. Ettinger. *Learning: An introduction to the Principles of Adaptive Behavior.* San Diego: Harcourt Brace Jovanovich. 1989.

Marie Doorey

Relation

In **mathematics**, a relation is any collection of ordered pairs. The fact that the pairs are ordered is important, and means that the ordered pair (a,b) is different from the ordered pair (b,a) unless a = b. For most useful relations, the elements of the ordered pairs are naturally associated or related in some way.

More formally, a relation is a subset (a partial collection) of the set of all possible ordered pairs (a,b) where the first element of each ordered pair is taken from one set (call it A), and the second element of each ordered pair is taken from a second set (call it B). A and B are often the same set; that is, A = B is common. The set of all such ordered pairs formed by taking the first element from the set A and the second element from the set B is called the Cartesian product of the sets A and B, and is written $A \times B$. A relation between two sets then, is a specific subset of the Cartesian product of the two sets.

Since relations are sets at ordered pairs they can be graphed on the ordinary coordinate **plane** if they have ordered pairs of **real numbers** as their elements (real numbers are all of the terminating, repeating and nonrepeating decimals); for example, the relation that consists of ordered pairs (x, y) such that x = y is a subset of the plane, specifically, those points on the line x = y. Another example of a relation between real numbers is the set of ordered pairs (x, y), such that x > y. This is also a subset of the coordinate plane, the half-plane below and to the right of the line x = y, not including the points on the line. Notice that because a relation is a subset of all possible ordered pairs (a,b), some members of the set A may not appear in any of the ordered pairs of a particular relation. Likewise, some members of the set B may not appear in any ordered pairs of the relation. The collection of all those members of the set A that appear in at least one ordered pair of a relation form a subset of A called the **domain** of the relation.

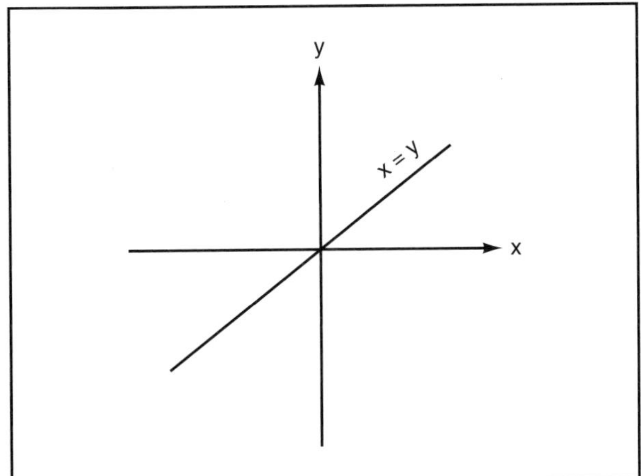

Figure 1.

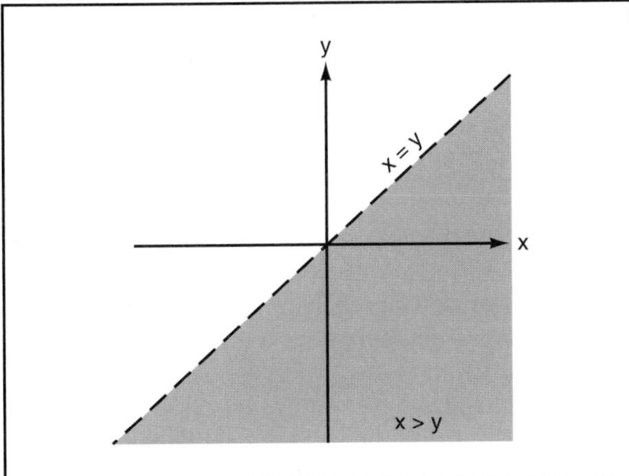

Figure 2.

The collection of members from the set B that appear in at least one ordered pair of the relation form a subset of B called the range of the relation. Elements in the range of a relation are called values of the relation. One special and useful type of relation, called a function, is very important. For every ordered pair (a,b) in a relation, if every a is associated with one and only one b, then the relation is a function. That is, a function is a relation for which no two of the ordered pairs have the same first element. Relations and functions of all sorts are important in every branch of science, because they are mathematical expressions of the physical relationships we observe in nature.

Further Reading

Kyle, James. *Mathematics Unraveled.* Blue Ridge Summit, PA: Tab Books, 1976.

McKeague, Charles P. *Intermediate Algebra, 5th edition.* Fort Worth: Saunders College Publishing, 1995.

Smith, Stanley, Randall Charles, John Dossey, Mervin Keedy, and Marvin Bittinger. *Addison-Wesley Algebra.* New York: Addison Wesley Publishing Co., 1992.

Zill, Dennis G. and Jacqueline M. Dewar. *College Algebra 2nd. ed.* New York: McGraw Hill, 1990.

J. R. Maddocks

KEY TERMS

Cartesian product—The Cartesian product of two sets A and B is the set of all possible ordered pairs (a,b) formed by taking the first element of the pair from the set A and the second element of the pair from the set B.

Domain—The set of elements appearing as first members in the ordered pairs of a relation.

Function—A function is a relation for which no two ordered pairs have the same first element.

Ordered pair—An ordered pair (a,b) is a pair of elements associated in such a way that order matters. That is, the ordered pair (a,b) is different from (b,a) unless a = b.

Range—The set of elements appearing as second members in the ordered pairs of a relation.

Set—A collection of elements or members. The elements of a set can be anything of interest, including physical as well as mathematical objects.

Subset—A subset is a set whose elements are all contained in some other set. Intuitively, a subset may be thought of as a partial collection of elements, with the exception that every set is a subset of itself.

Relative dating see **Dating techniques**

Relativity, general

Einstein's theory of relativity consists of two major portions: The special theory of relativity and the general theory of relativity. Special relativity deals with phenomena that become noticeable when traveling near the speed of light, and with reference frames that are moving at a constant **velocity** (inertial reference frames). General relativity deals with reference frames that are accelerat-

ing (noninertial reference frames), and with phenomena that occur in strong gravitational fields. General relativity also uses the curvature of **space** to explain gravity.

History

In the seventeenth century, Isaac Newton (1642-1727) completed a grand synthesis of physics that used three **laws of motion** and the law of gravity to explain motions we observe both on the **Earth** and in the heavens. These laws worked very well, but by the end of the nineteenth century, physicists began to notice experiments that did not work quite the way they should according to Newton's understanding. These anomalies led to the development of both relativity and **quantum mechanics** in the early part of the twentieth century.

One such experiment was the **Michelson-Morley experiment**, which disproved the hypothesis that propagation of light waves requires a special medium (which had been known as *ether*). Einstein took the result of this experiment as the basic assumption (namely, that the speed of light is constant) that led to the special theory of relativity.

The **orbit** of the **planet** Mercury around the **sun** has some peculiarities that cannot by explained by Newton's classical laws of **physics**. As Mercury orbits the Sun, the position where Mercury is closest to the Sun is called the perihelion. The perihelion migrates a small amount each orbit. This very small but measurable effect was reported by the astronomers Urbain Leverrier (1811-1877) and Simon Newcomb (1835-1909) in 1859 and 1895, respectively. The migration rate is 43 seconds of **arc** per century (one second of arc is 1/3,600 of a degree), so that it takes nearly 8,400 years for this **migration** to add up to one degree. This precession of Mercury's perihelion can not be easily explained by Newton's laws, but it is a natural consequence of Einstein's general theory of relativity. The effect is noticeable for Mercury but not the other planets, because Mercury is closest to the Sun, where the gravitational field is strongest. General relativity differs most from Newton's law of gravity in strong gravitational fields. The rate of this migration is what general relativity predicts and provides an important experimental confirmation to general relativity.

Preliminary concepts

To understand many concepts in relativity one needs to first understand the concept of a reference frame. A reference frame is a system for locating an object's (or event's) position in both space and time. It consists of both a set of coordinate axes and a clock. An object's position and **motion** will vary in different reference frames. If for example you are riding in a car, you are at rest in the reference frame of the car. You are, however, moving in the reference frame of the road, which is fixed to the reference frame of the Earth. The reference frames are moving relative to each other, but there is no absolute reference frame. Either reference frame is as valid as the other. A reference frame that is moving at a constant velocity is an inertial reference frame. A noninertial reference frame is accelerating or rotating. The theory of general relativity expands on the theory of special relativity by including the case of noninertial reference frames.

Special relativity combined our concepts of space and time into the unified concept of spacetime. In essence time is a fourth dimension and must be included with the three space dimensions when we talk about the location of an object or event. General relativity allows for the possibility that spacetime is curved. Gravity is a manifestation of the **geometry** of curved spacetime.

Principle of equivalence

Einstein's General Theory of Relativity, published in 1916, uses the principle of equivalence to explain the **force** of gravity. There are two logically equivalent statements of this principle. For the first statement, consider an enclosed room on the Earth. One feels a downward gravitational force. This force causes what we feel as weight, and causes falling objects to accelerate downward at a rate of 32 ft/s (9.8m/s). Now imagine the same enclosed room but in space far from any masses. There will be no gravitational forces, but if the room is accelerating at $9.8m/s^2$, then one will feel an apparent force. This apparent force will cause objects to fall at a rate of $9.8m/s^2$ and will cause one to feel normal Earth weight. We feel a similar phenomenon when we are pushed back into the seat of a rapidly accelerating car. This type of apparent force is an inertial force and is a result of an accelerating (noninertial) reference frame. The inertial force is in the opposite direction of the acceleration producing it. Is it possible to distinguish between the above two situations from within the room? No. According to the first statement of the Principle of Equivalence it is not possible without looking outside the room. Gravitational forces are indistinguishable from inertial forces caused by an accelerating reference frame.

What if the room in space is not accelerating? There will be no gravitational forces, so objects in the room will not fall, and the occupants will be weightless. The same room is now magically transported back to Earth, but by a slight **error** it ends up 100 feet above the ground rather than on the surface. The Earth's gravity will accelerate the room downward at $9.8m/s^2$. Just as when the room is accelerating in space, this acceleration will produce an inertial force that is indistinguishable from the gravitational force. But in this case the inertial force is upward, and the gravitational force is downward. Because there is no way

to distinguish between inertial and gravitational forces, and they are in the opposite direction, they **cancel** out exactly. Hence the occupants of the room are weightless. In general, objects that are in free fall will be weightless. This prediction allows us to experimentally test the Principle of Equivalence. Simply let an object fall freely and see if it is weightless. Astronauts in the **space shuttle** are weightless, not because there is no gravity, but because they are in free fall. You can show yourself that freely falling objects will be weightless. Put a small hole in the bottom of an empty plastic milk jug and fill the jug with **water**. Drop the jug. While it is falling, no water will leak out the bottom, because as a consequence of the principle of equivalence, freely falling objects will be weightless.

The second statement of the principle of equivalence involves the concept of **mass**. Mass appears in two distinct ways in Newton's Laws. In Newton's second law, the amount of force required to accelerate an object increases as its mass increases. It takes more force to accelerate a refrigerator than the can of soda that is in the refrigerator. The mass in Newton's second law is the inertial mass. In Newton's law of gravity, the gravitational force between two objects increases as the mass of the objects increases. That is why you will weigh more on a massive planet, such as **Jupiter**, than on the Earth. The mass in the law of gravity is the gravitational mass. Newton did not seriously consider the possibility that these two masses might be different. Einstein did. Are the inertial mass and the gravitational mass identically the same thing? Yes. According to the second statement of the principle of equivalence, the inertial mass and the gravitational mass are equal.

These two statements of the principle of equivalence are logically equivalent. That means that it is possible to use either statement to prove the other. This principle is the basic assumption behind the general theory of relativity.

Geometrical nature of gravity

From this principle, Einstein was able to derive his general theory of relativity, which explains the force of gravity as a result of the geometry of spacetime. To see how Einstein did this, consider the example above of the enclosed room being accelerated in space far from any masses. The person in the room throws a ball **perpendicular** to the direction of acceleration. Because the ball is not being pushed by whatever is accelerating the room, it follows a curved path as seen by the person in the room. You would see the same curved path if you threw a ball sideways in a moving car, but be careful not to hit the driver. Now replace the ball by a **light** beam shining sideways in the enclosed room. The person in the room sees the light beam follow a curved path, just as the ball does and for the same reason. Be careful, though-the deflection of the light beam is very much smaller than the ball, because the light is moving so fast it gets to the wall of the room before the room can move very far.

Now consider the same enclosed room at rest on the surface of the Earth. The ball thrown sideways will follow a downward curved path because of the Earth's gravitational field. What will the light beam do? The principle of equivalence states that it is not possible to distinguish between gravitational forces and inertial forces. Hence, any experiment will have the same result in the room at rest on the Earth as in the room accelerated in space. The light beam will therefore be deflected downward in the room on the Earth just as it would in the accelerated room in space. So, in the room on Earth, gravity deflects the light beam.

Light is deflected by a gravitational force! How? Light has no mass. According to Newton's law of gravity only objects having mass are affected by a gravitational force. What if spacetime is curved? Then we would see light and other objects follow an apparently curved path. Einstein therefore concluded that the presence of a mass curves spacetime and that gravity is a manifestation of this curvature.

Prior to Einstein, people thought of spacetime as being flat and having a Euclidean geometry. This geometry is the geometry that applies to flat surfaces and that is studied in most high school geometry classes. In general relativity however, spacetime is not always Euclidean. The presence of a mass curves or warps spacetime near the mass. The warping is similar to the curvature in a sheet of rubber that is stretched out with a weight in the center. The curvature of spacetime is harder to visualize, because it is four-dimensional spacetime rather than a two-dimensional surface. This curvature of spacetime produces the effects we see as gravity. When we travel long distances on the surface of the Earth, we must follow a curved path because the Earth is not flat. Similarly an object traveling in curved spacetime near a mass follows what we see as a curved path. For example, the Earth orbits the Sun because the spacetime near the Sun is curved. The Earth travels in a nearly circular path around the Sun as a small marble would in a circular path around a curved funnel. An object falling near the surface of the Earth is then like the marble rolling straight down the funnel.

Experimental verification

Bending of light

The first experimental confirmation of general relativity occurred in 1919, shortly after the theory was pub-

lished. Because light has no mass, Newton's law of gravity predicts that a strong gravitational field will not bend light rays. However as discussed above, general relativity predicts that a strong gravitational field will bend light rays. The curved spacetime will cause even massless light to travel in a curved path. The most convenient mass large enough to have a noticeable effect is the Sun. The apparent position of a **star** almost directly behind the Sun should be shifted a very small amount as the light rays are bent by the Sun. But, we normally can not see these stars. It is daytime. We must wait until a total solar eclipse to be able to see the stars that are almost directly behind the Sun. Shortly after Einstein published his general theory Arthur Eddington (1882-1944) mounted an expedition to observe the total eclipse of May 29, 1919. Einstein was right. The apparent positions of the stars shifted a small amount. Subsequent eclipse expeditions have further confirmed Einstein's prediction.

More recently, we see this effect with gravitational lenses. If a very distant **quasar** is almost directly behind a not-as-distant **galaxy**, the mass of the galaxy can bend the light coming from the more distant quasar. When this occurs we see a double image of the quasar with one image on each side of the nearer galaxy. A number of these gravitational lenses have been observed.

Binary pulsar

The 1993 Nobel Prize in physics was awarded to Joseph Taylor and Russell Hulse for their 1974 discovery of a binary **pulsar**. A pulsar, or rapidly rotating **neutron** star, is the final corpse for some stars that occurs when it collapses to about the size of a small city. A binary pulsar is simply two pulsars orbiting each other. Because pulsars are so collapsed they have strong enough gravitational fields that general relativity must apply. Binary pulsars can therefore provide an excellent experimental test of general relativity. About 40 binary pulsars have been discovered since Hulse and Taylor's original discovery.

Mercury's orbit shows a migration in its perihelion as it orbits the Sun. The binary pulsar displays a similar effect as the pulsars orbit each other. The effect is much greater as expected from general relativity because the pulsars have a much stronger gravitational field.

General relativity also predicts that gravity waves should exist in a way that is analogous to electromagnetic waves. Light, **radio** waves, **x rays**, infrared light, and ultraviolet light are all examples of electromagnetic waves that are **oscillations** in electric and magnetic fields. These oscillations can be caused by an oscillating **electron**. As the electron oscillates, the electron's electric field oscillates causing electromagnetic waves. Similarly as the pulsars oscillate by orbiting each other, general relativity predicts that they should cause the gravitational field to oscillate and produce gravity waves. Gravity waves have so far not been detected directly, even though several groups have been trying for over 20 years. But the binary pulsar is slowing down at a rate that suggests it is losing **energy** by emitting gravity waves. So, it could be said that the gravity waves predicted by general relativity have been detected indirectly.

Consequences of General Relativity

Karl Schwarzschild first used general relativity to predict the existence of black holes, which are stars that are so highly collapsed that not even light can escape. Because the gravitational field around a **black hole** is so strong, we must use general relativity to understand the properties of black holes. Most of what we know about black holes comes from theoretical studies based on general relativity. Ordinarily we think of black holes as having been formed from the collapse of a massive star, but Stephen Hawking has combined general relativity with quantum mechanics to predict the existence of primordial quantum black holes. These primordial black holes were formed by the extreme **turbulence** of the big bang during the formation of the universe. Hawking predicts that over sufficiently long times these quantum black holes can evaporate.

General relativity also has important implications for **cosmology**, the study of the origin of the universe. The equations of general relativity predict that the universe is expanding. Einstein noticed this result of his theory, but did not believe it. He therefore added a "cosmological constant" to his equations. This cosmological constant was basically a fudge factor that Einstein was able adjust so that his equations predicted that the universe was not expanding. Later Edwin Hubble (1889-1953), after whom the **Hubble Space Telescope** was named, discovered that the universe is expanding. Einstein visited Hubble, examined Hubble's data, and admitted that Hubble was right. Einstein later called his cosmological constant the biggest blunder of his life. Modern cosmology uses general relativity as the theoretical foundation to understand the expansion of the universe and the properties of the universe during its early history.

Albert Einstein's general theory of relativity fundamentally changed the way we understand gravity and the universe in general. So far, it has passed all experimental tests. This, however, does not mean that Newton's law of gravity is wrong. Newton's law is an approximation of general relativity. In the **approximation** of small gravitational fields, general relativity reduces to Newton's law of gravity. If at some time in the future someone does an experiment that does not agree with the theory of relativ-

KEY TERMS

General relativity—The part of Einstein's theory of relativity that deals with accelerating (noninertial) reference frames.

Principle of equivalence—The basic assumption of general relativity: gravitational forces are indistinguishable from apparent forces caused by accelerating reference frames, or alternatively, gravitational mass is identical to inertial mass.

Reference frames—A system, consisting of both a set of coordinate axes and a clock, for locating an object's (or event's) position in both space and time.

Spacetime—Space and time combined as one unified concept.

Special relativity—The part of Einstein's theory of relativity that deals only with nonaccelerating (inertial) reference frames.

ity, we will have to modify the theory just as relativity modified Newton's classical physics.

See also Gravitational lens; Light, theories of; Mercury (planet).

Further Reading

Einstein, Albert. *Relativity.* New York: Crown, 1961.

Hawking, Stephen. *A Brief History of Time.* New York: Bantam, 1988.

Pais, Abraham. *Einstein Lived Here.* Oxford: Clarendon Press 1994.

Pais, Abraham. *Subtle is the Lord.* Oxford: Clarendon Press 1982.

Will, Clifford W. *Was Einstein Right?* New York: Basic Books, 1986.

Zeilik, Michael. *Astronomy: The Evolving Universe.* 7th ed. New York: Wiley, 1994.

Paul A. Heckert

Relativity, special

Einstein's theory of relativity consists of two major portions: The special theory of relativity and the general theory of relativity. Special relativity deals with phenomena that become noticeable when traveling near the speed of **light** and reference frames that are moving at a constant **velocity**, inertial reference frames. General relativitydeals with reference frames that are accelerating, noninertial reference frames, and with phenomena that occur in strong gravitational fields. General relativity also uses the curvature of **space** to explain gravity.

History

In the 17th century, Isaac Newton completed a grand synthesis of **physics** that used three **laws of motion** and the law of gravity to explain motions we observe both on the **Earth** and in the heavens. These laws worked very well, but by the end of the 19th century, physicists began to notice experiments that did not work quite the way they should according to Newton's classical understanding. These anomalies led to the development of both relativity and **quantum mechanics** in the early part of the twentieth century.

One such experiment was the **Michelson-Morley experiment**. To understand this experiment, imagine a bored brother and sister on a long train ride. (Einstein liked thought experiments using trains.) To pass the time, they get up and start throwing a baseball up and down the aisle of the train. The boy is in the front and the girl in the back. The train is traveling at 60 mph, and they can each throw the ball at 30 mph. As seen by an observer standing on the bank outside the train, the ball appears to be traveling 30 mph (60-30) when the boy throws the ball to the girl and 90 mph (60+30) when the girl throws it back. The Michelson-Morley experiment was designed to look for similar behavior in light. The Earth orbiting the **Sun** takes the place of the train, and the measured speed of light (like the baseball's speed) should vary by the Earth's orbital speed depending on the direction the light is traveling. The experiment did not work as expected; the speed of light did not vary. Because Einstein took this result as the basic assumption that led to the special theory of relativity, the Michelson-Morley experiment is sometimes referred to as the most significant **negative** experiment in the history of science.

The **orbit** of the **planet** Mercury around the sun has some peculiarities that can not by explained by Newton's classical laws of physics. The general theory of relativity can explain these peculiarities, so they are described in the article on general relativity.

Special Relativity

To understand many concepts in relativity one first needs to understand the concept of a reference frame. A reference frame is a system for locating an object's (or event's) position in both space and time. It consists of both a set of coordinate axes and a clock. An object's position and **motion** will vary in different reference frames. Go back to the example above of the boy and girl tossing the ball back and forth in a train. The boy and girl are in

the reference frame of the train; the observer on the bank is in the reference frame of the Earth. The reference frames are moving relative to each other, but there is no absolute reference frame. Either reference frame is as valid as the other.

For his special theory of relativity, published in 1905, Einstein assumed the result of the Michelson-Morley experiment. The speed of light will be the same for any observer in any inertial reference frame, regardless of how fast the observer's reference frame is moving. Einstein also assumed that the laws of physics are the same in all reference frames. In the special theory, Einstein limited himself to the case of nonaccelerating, nonrotating reference frames (moving at a constant velocity), which are called inertial reference frames.

From these assumptions, Einstein was able to find several interesting consequences that are noticeable at speeds close to the speed of light (usually taken as greater than one tenth the speed of light). These consequences may violate our everyday common sense, which is based on the sum total of our experiences. Because we have never traveled close to the speed of light we have never experienced these effects. We can, however, accelerate atomic particles to speeds near the speed of light, and they behave as special relativity predicts.

Spacetime

Special relativity unified our concepts of space and time into the unified concept of spacetime. In essence time is a fourth dimension and must be included with the three space dimensions when we talk about the location of an object or event. As a consequence of this unification of space and time the concept of simultaneous events has no absolute meaning. Whether or not two events occur simultaneously and the order in which different events occurs depends on the reference frame of the observer.

If, for example, you want to meet a friend for lunch, you have to decide both which restaurant to eat at and when to eat lunch. If you get either the time or the restaurant wrong you are not able to have lunch with your friend. You are in essence specifying the spacetime coordinates of an event, a shared lunch. Note that both the space and time coordinates are needed, so space and time are unified into the single concept of spacetime.

Unusual effects of motion

Imagine a rocket ship traveling close to the speed of light. A number of unusual effects occur: Lorentz contraction, time dilation, and **mass** increase. These effects are as seen by an outside observer at rest. To the pilot in the reference frame of the rocket ship all appears normal. These effects will occur for objects other than rocket ships and do not depend on there being someone inside the moving object. Additionally, they are not the result of faulty measuring devices (clocks or rulers); they result from the fundamental properties of spacetime.

A rocket moving close to the speed of light will appear shorter as seen by an outside observer at rest. All will appear normal to an observer such as the pilot moving close to the speed of light inside the rocket. As the speed gets closer to the speed of light, this effect increases. If the speed of light were attainable the object would appear to have a length of **zero** to an observer at rest. The length of the rocket (or other moving object) measured by an observer at rest in the reference frame of the rocket, such as the pilot riding in the rocket, is called the proper length. This apparent contraction of a moving object as seen by an outside observer is called the Lorentz contraction.

A similar effect, time dilation, occurs for time. As seen by an outside observer at rest, a clock inside a rocket moving close to the speed of light will move more slowly. The same clock appears normal to the pilot moving along with the rocket. The clock is not defective; the rate at which time flows changes. Observers in different reference frames will measure different time intervals between events. The time **interval** between events measured both at rest in the reference frame of the events and with the events happening at the same place is called the proper time. This time dilation effect increases as the rocket gets closer to the speed of light. Traveling at the speed of light or faster is not possible according to special relativity, but if it were, time would appear to the outside observer to stop for an object moving at the speed of light and to flow backward for an object moving faster than light. The idea of time dilation is amusingly summarized in a famous limerick: "There was a young lady named Bright, Whose speed was much faster than light. She set out one day, In a relative way, And returned on the previous night." As seen by an outside observer, the mass of the rocket moving close to the speed of light increases. This effect increases as the speed increases so that if the rocket could reach the speed of light it would have an infinite mass. As for the previous two effects to an observer in the rocket, all is normal. The mass of an object measured by an observer in the reference frame in which the object is at rest is called the rest mass of the object.

These three effects are usually thought of in terms of an object, such as a rocket, moving near the speed of light with an outside observer who is at rest. But it is important to remember that according to relativity there is no preferred or absolute reference frame. Therefore the viewpoint of the pilot in the reference frame of the rocket is equally valid. To the pilot, the rocket is at rest and the outside observer is moving near the speed of light in

the opposite direction. The pilot therefore sees these effects for the outside observer. Who is right? Both are.

Speed of light limit

Think about accelerating the rocket in the above example. To accelerate the rocket (or anything else) an outside **force** must push on it. As the speed increases, the mass appears to increase as seen by outside observers including the one supplying the force (the one doing the pushing). As the mass increases, the force required to accelerate the rocket also increases. (It takes more force to accelerate a refrigerator than a feather.) As the speed approaches the speed of light the mass and hence the force required to accelerate that mass approaches **infinity**. It would take an infinite force to accelerate the object to the speed of light. Because there are no infinite forces no object can travel at the speed of light. An object can be accelerated arbitrarily close to the speed of light, but the speed of light can not be reached. Light can travel at the speed of light only because it has no mass. The speed of light is the ultimate speed **limit** in the universe.

$$E = mc^2$$

This famous equation means that **matter** and **energy** are interchangeable. Matter can be directly converted to energy, and energy can be converted to matter. The equation, $E=mc^2$, is then a formula for the amount of energy corresponding to a certain amount of matter. E represents the amount of energy, m the mass, and c the speed of light. Because the speed of light is very large a small amount of matter can be converted to a large amount of energy. This change from matter into energy takes place in nuclear reactions such as those occurring in the sun, nuclear reactors, and **nuclear weapons**. Nuclear reactions release so much energy and nuclear weapons are so devastating because only a small amout of mass produces a large amount of energy.

A pair of paradoxes

A paradox is an apparent contradiction that upon closer examination has a noncontradictory explanation. Several paradoxes arise from the special theory of relativity. The paradoxes are interesting puzzles, but more importantly, help illustrate some of the concepts of special relativity.

Perhaps the most famous is the twin paradox. Two twins are initially the same age, as is customary for twins. One of the twins becomes an astronaut and joins the first interstellar expedition, while the other twin stays home. The astronaut travels at nearly the speed of light to another **star**, stops for a visit, and returns home at nearly the speed of light. From the point of view of the twin who stayed home, the astronaut was traveling at nearly the speed of light. Because of time dilation the homebound twin sees time as moving more slowly for the astronaut, and is therefore much older than the astronaut when they meet after the trip. The exact age difference depends on the **distance** to the star and the exact speed the astronaut travels. Now think about the astronaut's reference frame. The astronaut is at rest in this frame. The Earth moved away and the star approached at nearly the speed of light. Then the Earth and star returned to their original position at nearly the speed of light. So, the astronaut expects to be old and reunite with a much younger twin after the trip. The resolution to this paradox lies in the fact that for the twins to reunite, one of them must accelerate by slowing down, turning around and speeding up. This **acceleration** violates the limitation of special relativity to inertial (nonaccelerating) reference frames. The astronaut, who is in the noninertial frame, is therefore the younger twin when they reunite after the trip. Unlike much science fiction in which star ships go into a fictional warp drive, real interstellar travel will have to deal with the realities of the twin paradox and the speed of light limit.

The garage paradox involves a very fast car and a garage with both a front and back door. When they are both at rest, the car is slightly longer than the garage, so it is not possible to park the car in the garage with both doors closed. Now imagine a reckless driver and a doorman who can open and close both garage doors as fast as he wants but wants only one door open at a time. The driver drives up the driveway at nearly the speed of light. The doorman sees the car as shorter than the garage, opens the front door, allows the car to drive in, closes the front door, opens the back door, allows the car to drive out without crashing, and closes the back door. The driver on the other hand, sees the garage as moving and the car as at rest. Hence, to the driver the garage is shorter than the car. How was it possible, in the driver's reference frame, to drive through the garage without a crash? The driver sees the same events but in a different order. The front door opens, the car drives in, the back door opens, the car drives through, the front door closes, and finally the back door closes. The key lies in the fact that the order in which events appear to occur depends on the reference frame of the observer. (See the section on spacetime.)

Experimental verification

Like any scientific theory, the theory of relativity must be confirmed by experiment. So far, relativity has passed all its experimental tests. The special theory predicts unusual behavior for objects traveling near the speed of light. So far no human has traveled near the speed of light. Physicists do, however, regularly accelerate **subatomic particles** with large particle **accelerators** like the recently canceled Superconducting Super Collider (SSC). Physicists also observe

cosmic rays which are particles traveling near the speed of light coming from space. When these physicists try to predict the behavior of rapidly moving particles using classical Newtonian physics, the predictions are wrong. When they use the corrections for Lorentz contraction, time dilation, and mass increase required by special relativity, it works. For example, muons are very short lived subatomic particles with an average lifetime of about 2 millionths of a second. However when they are traveling near the speed of light physicists observe much longer apparent lifetimes for muons. Time dilation is occurring for the muons. As seen by the observer in the lab time moves more slowly for the muons traveling near the speed of light.

Time dilation and other relativistic effects are normally too small to measure at ordinary velocities. But what if we had sufficiently accurate clocks? In 1971 two physicists, J. C. Hafele and R. E. Keating used atomic clocks accurate to about one billionth of a second (1 nanosecond) to measure the small time dilation that occurs while flying in a jet plane. They flew atomic clocks in a jet for 45 hours then compared the clock readings to a clock at rest in the laboratory. To within the **accuracy** of the clocks they used time dilation occurred for the clocks in the jet as predicted by relativity. Relativistic effects occur at ordinary velocities, but they are too small to measure without very precise instruments.

The formula $E=mc^2$ predicts that matter can be converted directly to energy. Nuclear reactions that occur in the sun, in nuclear reactors, and in nuclear weapons confirm this prediction experimentally.

Albert Einstein's Special theory of relativity fundamentally changed the way we understand time and space. So far it has passed all experimental tests. It does not however mean that Newton's law of physics is wrong. Newton's laws are an **approximation** of relativity. In the approximation of small velocities, special relativity reduces to Newton's laws. If at some time in the future someone does an experiment that does not agree with the theory of relativity, we will have to modify the theory just as relativity modified Newton's classical physics.

Further Reading

Cutnell, John D. and Kenneth W. Johnson. *Physics 3rd ed.* New York: Wiley, 1995.

Einstein, Albert. *Relativity.* New York: Crown, 1961.

Hawking, Stephen. *Black Holes and Baby Universes and Other Essays.* New York: Bantam, 1993.

Pais, Abraham. *Einstein Lived Here.* Oxford: Clarendon Press, 1994.

MMM. *Subtle is the Lord.* Oxford: Clarendon Press, 1982.

Will, Clifford W. *Was Einstein Right?* New York: Basic Books, 1986.

Paul A. Heckert

KEY TERMS

General relativity—The part of Einstein's theory of relativity that deals with accelerating (noninertial) reference frames.

Lorentz contraction—An effect that occurs in special relativity; to an outside observer the length appears shorter for an object traveling near the speed of light.

Reference frames—A system, consisting of both a set of coordinate axes and a clock, for locating an object's (or event's) position in both space and time.

Spacetime—Space and time combined as one unified concept.

Special relativity—The part of Einstein's theory of relativity that deals only with nonaccelerating (inertial) reference frames.

Time dilation—An effect that occurs in special relativity; to an outside observer time appears to slow down for an object traveling near the speed of light.

Reproductive system

The reproductive system is the structural and physiological network whose purpose is the creation of a new life to continue the species. It is the only body system which is not concerned with supporting the life of its host. Human reproduction is sexual-meaning that both a male and a female are required to produce a life. Gender is determined at conception by the sex **chromosome** in the sperm that fertilizes an egg. The developing male or female has a reproductive system characteristic of its sex. However, boys and girls can not reproduce until sexual maturation occurs at **puberty**. The male reproductive system is designed specifically to produce and deliver sperm to the egg in the female. The female reproductive system is designed to develop ova (eggs) and prepare for egg **fertilization** by a sperm. The male and female systems are both anatomically and biochemically designed to join and make a new life. However, the reproductive system is unique among body systems in that a person may choose not to use it to its full capacity-to procreate. Individuals can decide not to reproduce.

The male reproductive system

The main tasks of the male reproductive system are to provide sex **hormones**, to produce sperm, and to

transport sperm from the male to a female. The first two tasks are performed by the testes; while the third job is carried out by a series of ejaculatory ducts and the penis. The two testes are contained within the scrotum which hangs below the body between the legs. Each testis is attached at its top to an epididymis which contains numerous sperm ducts. The epidiymides (plural) send sperm through the vas deferens to the penis. However, the seminal vesicles, prostate, and bulbo-urethral **glands** each contribute to the seminal fluid which carries the sperm to the penis. The epididymides and part of the vas deferens are within the scrotum, but the glands creating the seminal fluid are in the abdomen.

Testes

Each of the testes is divided into lobes, or septae, containing coiled seminiferous tubules lined with spermatozoa-producing cells. Between the tubules are hormone-producing cells called interstitial cells, or cells of Leydig. Testosterone is produced by the interstitial cells. Since the testes-containing scrotum hangs below the body, it has a **temperature** around 89°F (32°C) which is ideal for sperm production which requires a low temperature. When the scrotum is held too close to the body by restrictive clothing, sterility can result.

The seminiferous tubules are the site of sperm maturation from original germ cells (spermatogonia) to mature sperm (spermatoza). This process begins in puberty and is called spermatogenesis. If a small section of a tubule was removed for observation, the wall would appear thick with a hole, or lumen, in the middle. The outer-most layer of this life saver-shaped cut-out is called the basal lamina. Primitive spermatogonia line the basal lamina and move through the inner layers of the tubule towards the lumen as they mature. Sertoli cells surround the maturing sperm and form tight junctions with one another to closely regulate what **nutrients** enter the developing sperm. Sertoli cells supply the spermatogenic cells with important ions such as potassium. They also form a blood-testes barrier which prevents some harmful substances from entering the tubule and spermatogenic cells and entering the man's **blood**. The unique genetic composition of individual sperm cells would cause an **immune system** attack on the circulating sperm. Sperm genetic diversity is created in the seminiferous tubule during spermatogenesis.

Spermatogenesis processes spermatogonia to spermatozoa in stages. Spermatogonia undergo mitotic divisions to yield primary spermatocytes which have 46 chromosomes identical to other cells in the male's body. Primary spermatocytes then go through two more divisions—this time meiotic—to form secondary spermatocytes and spermatids. Each final spermatid contains 23 randomly-assorted chromosomes that contain all necessary genetic information.

The final phase of spermatogenesis involves structural change. The sperm **cell** elongates, forming the long flagellum, or tail, which propels it toward an egg. Chromosomes are tightly packed into the sperm head, and an acrosomal tip appears on top of the head which contains enzymes that help the sperm burrow into an egg. In addition, mitochondria are wound around the flagellum's base to fuel the sperm's journey through the female reproductive tract. This shape change completes maturation of spermatids into spermatozoa, or sperm. However, they are still immotile. Sperm enter the lumen of the seminferous tubules and travel in a very concentrated form to the epididymis. The sperm become mobile after about two weeks in the epididymis and are sent to the vas deferens for storage.

The full maturation of a single sperm takes about 70-80 days. Hence, substances a male is exposed to during that period of time may effect the health of his sperm at the end of that time period. Sperm are always available in healthy males after puberty, because spermatogenesis is an ongoing process with cells in all stages of development existing in different layers of the seminiferous tubules. As many as several hundred million sperm can be produced each day. And one man has approximately a quarter mile of coiled seminiferous tubules which produce all these sperm.

Late spermatogenic stages are dependent on testosterone secreted by the interstitial cells of the testes. At puberty, male levels of luteinizing hormone (LH) are elevated due to increased secretion by the anterior pituitary (AP) gland. LH has also been called interstitial-cell-stimulating hormone (ICSH) in men, because it stimulates Leydig cells to secrete testosterone. Follicle-stimulating hormone (FSH) is also secreted by the AP and directs early stages of spermatogenesis. Testosterone from the testes is also necessary for secondary sexual characteristics such as facial and body hair growth, voice deepening, and pubertal genital growth.

The spermatic ducts and glands

The vas deferens carries concentrated sperm from the scrotum into the abdominal cavity to the ejaculatory duct. Sperm that remain in the ejaculatory duct longer than a couple of weeks degenerate and are disposed of. The prostate surrounds the ejaculatory duct and contains a sphincter that closes off the bladder during ejaculation. Seminal fluid from the seminal vesicles, the prostate, and the bulbo-urethral glands (or Cowper's glands) is added to the sperm. The seminal fluid plus the sperm is called semen.

Seminal fluid is designed to carry and nourish sperm. Seminal vesicles are located on either side of the bladder and contribute about 60% of the fluid. Seminal vesicle fluid is rich in essential sperm nutrients such as fructose which sustains sperm for up to 72 hours after ejaculation. Seminal vesicle fluid also supplies prostaglandins which cause uterine contractions in the female reproductive tract to facilitate sperm movement to an egg. The prostate gland provides an alkaline mixture of **calcium**, enzymes, and other components that make up about 30% of the seminal fluid. The alkaline fluid functions to neutralize the acidic vaginal environment which can kill sperm. Additional fluid is provided by the Cowper's glands (below the prostate) which secrete a pre-ejaculatory urethral lubricant that may contain some sperm. For this reason, withdrawal is not a full-proof contraceptive method. At ejaculation, additional Cowper secretions combine with the remaining seminal fluid and sperm. This semen is sent through the urethra in the penis.

The penis

The penis provides the route for transmitting sperm to an egg for reproduction. However, in its relaxed state, it can not effectively deliver sperm. In order for the sperm to have the best chance of fertilizing an egg, the penis must become erect and ejaculate semen close to an egg in the female reproductive tract.

The penis is part of the male's external reproductive system which becomes longer, thicker, and stiff during erection. It is comprised of a shaft region which is the cylindrical body of the penis and the glans, or head region. The glans and the shaft are separated at the coronal ridge which is a rim of **tissue** that is very sensitive to **touch**. The skin covering the penis is loose and allows for expansion during erection. Some males have a prepuce or foreskin, which is a movable skin that covers the penile glans. Circumcised males have had this foreskin removed. Uncircumcised males must carefully clean the foreskin daily to prevent **bacteria** and foul-smelling secretions (called smegma) from accumulating.

Three cylinders of spongy erectile tissue make up the internal portion of the penis. Two cylinders run along the inner roof of the penis and are called the corpora cavernosa. The third cylinder runs along the lower side of the penis; it contains the urethra and is called the corpus spongiosum, or spongy body. The spongy body includes the penile tip and is more sensitive to touch than the rest of the penis. Several nerves and blood vessels run through the spongy body. An erection occurs when blood flow to the spongy tissue vessels increases. An average erect penis is 6.25 in (15.9 cm) long and 1.5 in (3.8 cm) wide at its base.

Sexual arousal

Sexual intercourse does not necessarily lead to reproduction, but the **physiology** of reproductive versus non-reproductive sexual arousal is indistinguishable. Sexual arousal has been divided into four stages by Masters and Johnson. These stages are the same whether the arousal results from physical stimulation (such as touch) or mental stimulation (such as reading an arousing book). Hence, arousal can be influenced by personal beliefs, desires, or values. The stages of arousal are: excitement, plateau, orgasm, and resolution.

The male stage of sexual excitement is marked by increased blood flow to the pelvic area and penis. Increased parasympathetic nerve activity causes the blood vessels in the penis to dilate, allowing for vasocongestion which leads to an erection. This may happen in a matter of seconds. Testes size also increases, and nipples become erect in some men.

The amount of time spent in the plateau phase varies considerably. In this stage, the head of the penis enlarges and darkens from blood pooling. Testes darken, enlarge from vasocongestion, and are lifted back away from the penis. At this point, pre-ejaculatory secretion from the bulbo-urethral gland occurs, and **respiration**, **heart** rate, and blood **pressure** increase.

Male orgasm results from both emission and ejaculation. Emission is the release of the ejaculatory fluid into the urethra. Emission is caused by increased sympathetic nerve stimulation in the ejaculatory ducts and glands which leads to rhythmic contractions that force the fluid out. For ejaculation, rhythmic contractions of the urethra expel the semen (usually 3-5 ml) while the prostate gland closes off the bladder.

In the resolution phase, blood exits the penis and testes, and the penis relaxes. Respiration, blood pressure, and heart rate return to normal, and sexual arousal enters a refractory period. During the refractory period, erection can not occur. The length of refractory period varies from a couple of minutes to several hours and increases with fatigue and age.

The female reproductive system

The main tasks of the female reproductive system are to produce hormones, develop ova, receive sperm, and promote fertilization and the growth of a newly conceived life. These events occur internally. Ova mature in the ovaries. Sperm are received in the vagina and cervix. Fertilization takes place usually in the fallopian tubes and less often in the uterus, with the newly formed life developing in the endometrial lining of the uterus. The female reproductive tract can be pictured as a capital Y

with the upper arms forming the fallopian tubes. The ovaries would be at the end of these arms. The uterus would be the upper half of the supporting stalk, and the vagina would be the lower half. External female genitals are involved in female sexual arousal.

The ovaries

The ovaries are oval-shaped and about 1-1.5 in (2.5-3.8 cm) long. They are connected to the body of the uterus by an ovarian ligament which tethers the ovaries in place. The ovaries parallel the testes in that they release sex hormones and develop gametes (ova or sperm). However, the job of the ovaries differs from that of the testes: while sperm are created daily through a man's life after puberty, all of a female fetus's eggs have been created by the sixth gestational month. Several million primordial follicles capable of forming ova are formed. About 1 million primordial follicles mature into primary follicles that still exist at **birth**. (The rest have degenerated.) When puberty begins, about 400,000 follicles remain. Mature eggs leave alternating ovaries monthly beginning in puberty in a process called ovulation. Unfertilized eggs are lost through menstruation, when the uterine lining is shed. Women typically menstruate for 30-40 years losing 360-480 eggs in a lifetime. Ovulation is hormonally suppressed during pregnancy and shortly after childbirth.

The formation of mature ova in the ovaries is called oogenesis. The anterior pituitary (AP) hormones LH and FSH, which regulate spermatogenesis, also orchestrate oogenesis. However, unlike spermatogenesis which occurs daily, oogenesis is on an average 28 day (or monthly) cycle. During embryonic development, primordial follicles are formed, each of which contains an oocyte surrounded by a layer of spindle-shaped cells. These spindle cells multiple during the mid-fetal stage of development and become granulosa cells which surround the egg. Granulosa cells function much like the Sertoli cells in men: they prevent destructive drugs from getting to the egg while also providing essential nutrients for its development. Granulosa cells also secrete a rich substance that forms a follicular coating called the zona pellucida. Before birth, the cellular layers surrounding the follicle differentiate into a layer of cells called the theca interna. At birth, a baby girl's ova are suspended at the first meiotic division inside the primary follicles. After the onset of puberty, a new follicle enters the next phase of follicular growth monthly.

The first two weeks of the **menstrual cycle** are called the follicular phase because of the follicular development that occurs during that time. High FSH levels trigger this development. Although more than one follicle begins to mature each month, one follicle outgrows the others, and slow-growing follicles stay in the ovary to degenerate by a process called atresia. The granulosa cells of the dominant follicle secrete estrogens into the fluid bathing the oocyte inside the follicle. The highly vascular theca interna layer which is outside the granulosa cells releases estrogens which enter the female circulation. A build up of circulating estrogen will signal release of additional FSH and LH which initiate the second half of the menstrual cycle. Around day 14 of the cycle, LH and FSH surge to initiate ovulation. Ovulation entails the release of the mature oocyte from the ovarian follicle as it ruptures from the surface of the ovary into the abdominal cavity. Once released, the ovum is caught by the fimbria, which are finger-like projections off the ends of the fallopian tubes. The follicle which housed the growing egg remains in the ovary and is transformed into the corpus luteum. The corpus luteum secretes high levels of progesterone and some estrogen. The corpus luteum secures a position near the ovarian blood vessels to supply these hormones which prevent another follicle from beginning maturation. If the ovum is fertilized, then these hormone levels continue into pregnancy to prevent another cycle from beginning. However, if fertilization does not occur, then the corpus luteum degenerates allowing the next cycle to start. The second 14 days of the menstrual cycle are called the luteal phase because of the corpus luteum's hormonal control over this half of the cycle.

The fallopian tubes

The optimal time for an oocyte to be fertilized is when it enters a fallopian tube. The fallopian tubes are fluid-filled, cilia-lined channels about 4-6 in (10-15 cm) long that carry the oocyte to the uterus. At ovulation, the primary oocyte completes its suspended **meiosis** and divides in two. A secondary oocyte and a small polar body result. If the secondary oocyte is fertilized, then it will go through another division which forms another polar body.

As the ripening egg travels along the fallopian tube, it is washed along by cilia which knock away residual nutrient cells on the outside of the egg. This array of cells leaving the cell forms a radiant cluster called the corona radiata. If sperm have made their way to the fallopian tube, then they have already been capacitated. Capacitation is the modification of a sperm's acrosomal tip which enables it to burrow into the egg. Fertilization blocks the ability of additional sperm to enter the egg. Once the nuclei of the egg and sperm cells have fused, the new cell is called a zygote. The zygote contains all the genetic information required to become a complete human being. This new life signifies the beginning of successful reproduction. As the zygotic cell divides into more cells, it travels from the fallopian tube to the uterus.

The uterus

The uterus, or womb, is a muscular, inverted pear-shaped **organ** in the female pelvis which is specifically designed to protect and nurture a growing baby. It averages 3 in (7.6 cm) long by 2 in (5 cm) wide. Although, during pregnancy, it expands with the growing embryo and fetus. Embryo is a term used to describe a human in the first eight weeks of development. After that, the human is called a fetus.

During the follicular phase of the menstrual cycle, the lining (or endometrium) of the uterus becomes thick and filled with many blood vessels in preparation for supporting an embryo. If fertilization does not occur within about eight days of ovulation, then this lining is shed in menstrual blood through the cervix. This cycle continues until **menopause**, when menstruation becomes less frequent and eventually stops altogether.

The cervix is the base of the uterus which extends into the vagina. The narrow passageway of the cervix is just large enough to allow sperm to enter and menstrual blood to exit. During childbirth, it becomes dilated (open) to allow the baby to move into the vagina, or birth **canal**. However, for most of the pregnancy, the cervix becomes plugged with thick mucous to isolate the developing baby from vaginal events. For this reason, non-reproductive, sexual intercourse is usually safe during pregnancy.

The uterus is required for reproduction. With all the male and female aspects contributing to reproduction, a number of diseases, **genetic disorders**, and other variables can cause **infertility**, which afflicts 10-15% of couples trying to conceive. Technologies such as **in vitro fertilization** exist for some couples with infertility due to ovarian, fallopian tube, or sperm problems. However, without a uterus, a human baby can not grow. The uterus plays an integral hormonal and physical role in housing and nourishing the baby.

The vagina

The vagina is a muscular tube about 5 in (12.7 cm) long. A thin layer of tissue called the hymen may cover the vaginal opening, but is usually gone in physically or sexually active females. A mucous **membrane** lines and moistens the vagina. During sexual intercourse, the vagina is lubricated further and functions to direct the penis toward the cervix to optimize fertilization. During childbirth, the vagina stretches to accommodate the passage of the baby. Both the uterus and the vagina contract to relatively original sizes some time after delivery.

Some contraceptive devices act as a barrier between semen and the vagina or semen and the cervix. A condom placed correctly on a man's penis can prevent sperm from entering the vagina. A diaphragm is a rubber, cup-shaped contraceptive inserted into the vagina prior to intercourse that acts as a physical barrier between semen and the cervix; it is usually used along with a spermicidal jelly to chemically kill sperm. Other contraceptives, such as the birth control pill and depo-provera usually inhibit the function of progesterone to prevent the uterine lining from shedding.

External genitals and sexual arousal

External female genitals include the mons veneris, labia majora, labia minora, clitoris, and vestibule. They differ in size and color from female to female, but their location and function are consistent. The mons is a pad of fatty tissue filled with many nerve endings which becomes covered with pubic hair in puberty. The labia majora are two folds of skin which protect the opening to the urethra and internal genitals. Pubic hair grows on their outer surface in puberty. These **fat** padded folds of skin contain sweat glands, nerve endings, and numerous blood vessels. Inside these outer skin folds are the labia minora which are hairless. The labia minora form a spongy covering for the vaginal entrance. These smaller skin folds meet at the top of the genitals to form the clitoral hood. The hood houses the clitoris, a very sensitive organ which has a spongy shaft and a nerve-rich glans (tip). Between the labia minora and the vagina is the area called the vestibule. Within the vestibule are the two Bartholin's glands which lubricate the vagina.

Sexual arousal in females parallels the arousal stages in males. Female sexual arousal is not required to reproduce, but it does facilitate reproduction. In the excitement phase, blood flow to the vagina increases which, in turn, pushes fluid into the vaginal canal. This lubricating process is called transudation and allows for comfortable penile insertion. During this phase, blood infiltrates the spongy clitoris and labia, and the cervix and uterus are lifted up away from the vagina. Nipples often become erect, and respiration, heart rate, and blood pressure increase.

During the plateau stage, the vagina expands, forming a pocket near the cervix which is an ideal **deposit** site for sperm; this is called "tenting." The increased sensitivity of the clitoris causes it to retract in the clitoral hood, and breasts sometimes become flushed. In the orgasmic phase, the vaginal opening contracts rhythmically for about 15 seconds. Unlike the lengthy refractory period which males experience in the resolution stage, females are more likely to be multi-orgasmic and capable of more closely spaced orgasms. In the resolution stage, genital blood flow returns to normal. Respiration, heart rate, and blood pressure also return to normal. Within 72 hours of sexual intercourse reproduction will either have successfully begun or not succeeded.

KEY TERMS

Androgen—Male sex hormones including testosterone and androstenedione.

Meiosis—In meiosis, a cell's 46 chromosomes duplicate and go through two successive cellular divisions to create germ cells (sperm and eggs) each containing 23 chromosomes.

Mitosis—In mitosis, the 46 human chromosomes double and divide into two daughter cells each containing 46 chromosomes.

Oogenesis—The formation of mature eggs in the female ovaries after the onset of puberty.

Seminiferous Tubules—Tubes lining the testes which produce sperm.

Spermatogenesis—The formation of mature sperm in the male testes after the onset of puberty.

Spermatozoa—Mature sperm capable of fertilizing an egg.

See also Contraception; Hormones; Sexual reproduction; Sexually transmitted diseases.

Further Reading

Avraham, R. *The Reproductive System.* New York: Chelsea House Publishers, 1991.

Rhoads, R., and R. Pflanzer, eds. *Human Physiology.* 2nd ed. New York: Saunders College Publishing, 1992.

Louise Dickerson

Reproductive toxicant

Reproductive toxicants are substances which adversely affect fertility or a developing embryo or fetus. Toxicants, strictly speaking, are poisons. However, reproductive toxicants loosely include any infectious, physical, chemical, or environmental agent which has a damaging effect on fertility or embryonic development. Some substances which have a beneficial effect on one occasion (such as a dental x ray or aspirin) could be detrimental reproductively. The best defense against these toxicants is knowing what to avoid when.

Roughly 10-15% of couples trying to have a baby experience **infertility**. Infertility in men is usually due to low or abnormal sperm production or blockage in the male reproductive tract. Excessive **alcohol**, illegal drugs (like **cocaine**), **radiation** treatment, or infectious gonorrhea can all lead to sperm population problems. Female infertility is usually due to hormonal imbalance or Pelvic Inflammatory Disease (PID). PID can be caused by **sexually transmitted diseases** (including gonorrhea) and can scar fallopian tubes, blocking egg travel and implantation. In addition, women whose mothers received the synthetic hormone **diethylstilbestrol (DES)** during pregnancy have higher infertility rates.

Infertility has additional causes. **Copper** or hormone deficiencies can cause infertility. Excessive iodine intake can cause infertility. And the **cancer** treatments radiation and chemotherapy can both be reproductively toxic. Cancer patients can freeze-store their sperm, eggs, or both for later implantation.

Toxicants which reach the developing baby by maternal exposure are called **teratogens**. Known teratogens include: excessive alcohol, tobacco smoke, certain medications, cocaine, **x rays**, some infectious agents, mercury, and lead. Most pose less threat to a mature adult than they do to a developing baby.

Alcohol is a devastating toxicant. Not only can alcohol increase abnormal sperm production in men, but it can also cause **Fetal Alcohol Syndrome** (FAS) in developing infants. FAS is characterized by mental impairment, malformed facial features, poor coordination, **heart** defects, and other problems. Pregnant women who drink risk FAS in their unborn children.

Women who smoke during pregnancy have more miscarriages, still-births, and low birth-weight babies than non-smokers. And they have twice as many cases of cervical cancer as non-smokers. Cervical cancer can complicate conception or lead to infertility. Some evidence indicates that pregnant women who smoke also have more children with poor mental **concentration**.

Some drugs are teratogens. Aspirin and ergotamine (headache treatments) can cause abnormalities and miscarriages, respectively. The antibiotic tetracycline disfigures developing teeth. And certain diuretics, particularly Lasix, decrease levels of potassium (an essential **electrolyte**) in the fetus. **Thalidomide**, a sleeping drug never FDA-approved, causes limb deformities. Prescribers should always know if their patient is pregnant.

Other hazards pregnant women should avoid are **x rays** and certain infectious agents. Dental x rays in the first 12 weeks of pregnancy can double the risk of childhood cancers. And pregnant women should guard against contracting toxoplasmosis, rubella, and chicken pox. Toxoplasmosis is caused by a parasite in cat fur or feces which can cause infant blindness or death. Pregnant women should have someone else handle their **cats**.

Rubella and chicken pox, if contracted during pregnancy, can also cause **birth defects.**

Reptiles

The class Reptilia includes over 6,000 species grouped into four orders: the **turtles** (Chelonia), the **snakes** and lizards (Squamata), the **crocodiles** and alligators (Crocodilia), and the tuataras (Sphenodonta). Other, now extinct, reptilian orders included Earth's largest terrestrial animals, and some enormous marine creatures. The fishlike ichthyosaurs were large marine reptiles, as were the long-necked plesiosaurs. The pterosaurs were large flying or gliding reptiles. The most famous of the extinct reptilian orders were the dinosaurs, which included immense, ferocious predators such as *Tyrannosaurus rex*, and enormously large herbivores such as *Apatosaurus*.

The first reptiles known in the fossil record occurred about 340 million years ago, during the Carboniferous period. The last representatives of the dinosaurs became extinct about 65 million years ago, after being the dominant large animals of the **earth** for more than 250 million years. Some paleontologists believe that the dinosaurs are not actually extinct, and that they survive today as **birds**, with which dinosaurs are known to have shared many anatomical, physiological, and behavioral traits.

Reptiles are extremely diverse in their form and function. They characteristically have four legs (although some groups have secondarily become legless), a tail, and a body covered by protective scales or plates developed from the epidermis. Reptiles have internal **fertilization**, and their eggs have a series of membranes around the embryo that allow the exchange of respiratory gases and metabolic waste (known as amniotic eggs). Amniotic eggs were an important evolutionary **adaptation** for conserving moisture and allowed the adoption of a terrestrial way of life. Reptiles have direct development, meaning they lack a larval stage, and their eggs produce miniature replicas of adult animals. Most reptiles are **oviparous**, laying eggs in a warm place that incubates the eggs until they hatch. Some species are **ovoviviparous**, with the female retaining the eggs inside her reproductive tract throughout their development, so that live young reptiles are born.

Some species of reptiles are dangerous to humans and to agricultural and domestic animals. Crocodiles and alligators can be predators of humans and other large animals, while some species of snakes are venomous and may bite people or **livestock** when threatened. Many species of reptiles are economically important, and are hunted as food, for their eggs, or for their skin which can be manufactured into an attractive leather. Many species of reptiles are kept as interesting pets or in zoos.

Unfortunately, some people have an inordinate fear of reptiles, and this has commonly led to the persecution of these animals. Many species of reptiles are endangered, having suffered the loss of their natural **habitat**, which has been used for agriculture, **forestry**, or residential development.

See also Blind snakes; Boas; Elapid snakes; Geckos; Gila monster; Iguanas; Monitor lizards; Pythons; Tuatara lizard; Vipers.

Resins

Historically, the term resin has been applied to a group of substances obtained as gums from trees or manufactured synthetically. Strictly speaking, however, resins are complex mixtures, whereas gums are compounds that can be represented by a chemical formula.

The word gum was originally applied to any soft sticky product derived from trees; for example, the latex obtained from Hevea trees, which is the source of natural or gum rubber. Natural rubber, i.e, chemically unsaturated polyisoprene, is a polymeric material that can also be produced synthetically. (A **polymer** is a macromolecular compound made up of a large number of repeating units, called mers.) Thus, although the term resin when applied to polymers actually antedates the understanding of the **chemistry** of polymers and originally referred to the resemblance of polymer liquids to the pitch on trees, it has by association also come to refer to synthetic polymers.

Natural resins

The term natural resins usually refers to **plant** products consisting of amorphous mixtures of **carboxylic acids**, essential oils, and isoprene-based hydrocarbons; these materials occur as tacky residues on the **bark** of many varieties of trees and shrubs. In addition, natural resins have also come to describe shellac, which is a natural, alcohol-soluble, flammable material made from deposits on **tree** twigs left by the lac insect in India; amber, which is a fossilized polymeric material derived from a coniferous tree; and natural liquid substances such as linseed and similar drying oils.

Vegetable-derived natural resins generally fall in one of four categories:

TABLE 1. THERMOSETTING SYNTHETIC RESINS

Synthetic Resin	*1994 U.S. Sales (in million of pounds)*	*Major Applications*
phenolics	3222	electrical products such as ovens and toasters, wiring devices, switch gears, pulleys, pot and cutlery handles
unsaturated polyesters	1496	construction and transportation industries
polyurethanes	1102	building insulation, refrigeration
amino resins	2185	wiring devices, molded products, electrical parts, adhesives and bonding agents
epoxy resins	602	coatings, reinforcement, electrical and electronic applications, adhesives, flooring, and construction

TABLE 2. GUM RESINS

Resin	*Source*	*Applications*
galbanum	gum resin from perennial herb of western Asia	medicinal uses
myrrh	gum resin from small trees of India, Arabia, and northeast Africa	incense and perfumes; medicinal tonics, stimulants, antiseptics
asafetida	gum resin from perennial herb	Asian food flavoring; used for medicines and perfumes in the United States.
creosote bush resin	amber-colored, soft, and sticky gum resin from the leaves of the greasewood bush or creosote bush of the desert regions of Mexico and the southwestern United States	adhesives, insecticides, core binders, insulating compounds, pharmaceuticals
okra gum	gum resin from the pods of a plant native to Africa but now grown in many countries	foodstuffs, pharmaceuticals; used for its antioxidizing and chemically stabilizing properties, and as a gelation agent
ammoniac resin	gum resin from the stems of a desert perennial plant of Persia and India	adhesives, perfumes, medicinal stimulants

TABLE 3. THERMOPLASTIC SYNTHETIC RESINS		
Synthetic resin	***1994 U.S. Sales (in million of pounds)***	***Major applications***
polyethylene	25,683	packaging and non-packaging films
polypropylene	9752	fibers and filaments
polystyrene	5877	molded products such as cassettes, audio equipment cabinets; packaging film; food-stock trays
acrylonitrile/butadiene/styrene (ABS)	1489	injection-molded automotive components
polyethylene terephthalate (PET)	—	food packaging
polyvinyl chloride	11,123	flooring; pipes and conduits; siding
polycarbonate	695	compact discs and optical memory discs
nylon	921	transportation industry products
thermoplastic elastomers	867	automotive, wire and cable, adhesive, footwear, and mechanical goods industries
liquid crystal polymers	—	chemical pumps, electronic components, medical components, automotive components
acetals	214	transportation industry products
polyurethane	1790	flexible foams in the transportation industry
thermoplastic polyester	3441	engineering plastics

1.) Rosins, which are resinous products obtained from the pitch of pine trees. Rosins are used in varnishes, adhesives, and various compounds.

2.) Oleoresins, which are natural resins containing essential oils of plants.

3.) Gum resins, which are natural mixtures of true gums and resins including natural rubber, **gutta percha**, gamboge, myrrh, and olibanum.

4.) Fossil resins, which are natural resins from ancient trees that have been chemically altered by long exposure. Examples of fossil resins include amber and copal.

Synthetic resins

Synthetic resins are polymeric materials, which are better known as **plastics**. The term plastic better describes polymeric material to which additives have been added. There are two important classes of synthetic resins: thermosetting resins and thermoplastic resins.

Thermosetting resins

Thermosetting resins form a highly diverse, versatile, and useful class of polymeric materials. They are used in such applications as moldings, lamination, foams, textile finishing, coatings, sealants, and adhesives.

A thermosetting resin cures to an infusible and insoluble **mass** with either the application of **heat** or a catalyst. The thermosetting resins are dominated by phenolics, polyesters, polyurethanes, and amino resins. Together, these account for about 70% of the commercially important thermosets.

Thermoplastic resins

Thermoplastic resins are polymeric materials that can be softened and resoftened indefinitely by the application of heat and **pressure**, provided that the heat that is applied does not chemically decompose the resin. Table 3 lists some commercially important synthetic thermoplastic resins, their uses, and their levels of consumption.

Further Reading

Brady, G. S., and H. R. Clause. *Materials Handbook.* New York: McGraw Hill, Inc. 1991.

Engineered Materials Handbook. Metals Park, OH: ASM International, 1988.

Randall Frost

KEY TERMS

Gum—A viscous secretion of some trees and shrubs that hardens upon drying.

Synthetic—Referring to a substance that either reproduces a natural product or that is a unique material not found in nature, and which is produced by means of chemical reactions.

Thermoplastic—A high molecular weight polymer that softens when heated and that returns to its original condition when cooled to ordinary temperatures.

Thermoset—A high molecular weight polymer that solidifies irreversibly when heated.

Resistance, electrical see **Electrical resistance**

Resolving power see **Telescope**

Resonance

There are many instances in which we want to add **energy** to the **motion** of an object which is oscillating. In order for this transfer to be efficient, the oscillation and the source of new energy have to be "matched" in a very specific way. When this match occurs, we say that the oscillation and source are in resonance.

A simple example of an oscillation that we have all seen is that of a child on a playground swing. The motion starts when someone pulls the swing to a position away from the point of stable equilibrium and lets go. The child then moves back and forth, but gradually slows down as the energy of the motion is lost due to **friction** in the joint where the rope or chain of the swing attaches to its support. Of course, the child wants to continue moving, usually higher and faster, and this requires the addition of more energy. It is easy to accomplish this by pushing the swing, but we all know from experience that the timing is critical. Even a small push can add energy efficiently if it occurs just at the instant when the swing has moved to its highest position and begins to move back to the point of stable equilibrium. If the push occurs a little too late, not all of the energy of the push is added (inefficient). Even worse, if the push occurs too soon, the result will be to slow down the swing (removing energy instead of adding it). Also, it obviously does no good to push at other times when the swing has moved away (it looks strange and anyway, there is **zero** efficiency since no energy is transferred into the motion). The trick is to push at the "right" instant during every repetition of the swinging motion. When this occurs, the adult's push (the energy source in this case) and the oscillation are in resonance.

The feature of the motion that must be matched in resonance is the **frequency**. For any oscillation, the motion takes a specific amount of time to repeat itself (its period for one cycle). Therefore, a certain number of cycles occurs during each second (the frequency). The frequency tells us how often the object returns to its position of maximum displacement and as we know for the swing, that is the best location at which to add energy. Resonance occurs when the rhythm of the energy source matches the natural, characteristic frequency of the oscillation. For this reason, the latter is often called the resonant frequency. It is common to say that the source of energy provides a driving **force**, as in the case where a push is needed to add energy to the motion of a swing.

In a way, resonance is just a new name for a familiar situation. However, resonance is also important in other instances which are less obvious, like lasers and electronic circuits. A particularly interesting example is the microwave oven, which cooks food without external

heat. Even if an object like a book (or a steak) appears to be stationary, it is composed of microscopic **atoms** which are oscillating around positions of stable equilibrium. Those motions are too small to see, but we can feel them since the **temperature** of an object is related to their amplitudes-the larger the amplitudes, the hotter the object. This is very similar to the motion of the child on the swing in which a larger amplitude means more energy. If we can add energy to the motion of a swing by a driving force in resonance, then we should be able to add energy (heat) to a steak very efficiently. Conventional ovens cook food from the outside, for example by heating air molecules which bump into atoms at the surface of the food. However, the microwave oven uses resonance to cook from the inside.

The **water molecule** is made of one **oxygen** atom and two **hydrogen** atoms which are held together, not in a straight line, but in a "V" shape. The oxygen atom is located at the bottom of the "V" and the hydrogen atoms are at ends of the arms. It should not be too surprising to learn that water molecules and even the oxygen and hydrogen atoms within them can oscillate. However, experiments discovered a specific oscillation (really a **rotation** of the entire molecule) that is particularly important. The characteristic frequency of that oscillation falls within the same range as the microwave type of electromagnetic **radiation**. Microwaves are commonly used in **radar**, so a large amount of work had already been done to develop dependable, relatively compact devices to produce them. The breakthrough was in realizing that a good steak (even a bad one) contains a large amount of water. If we place a steak within a microwave oven and turn it on, microwaves are produced within the interior of the oven at the resonant frequency of the water molecule. The microwaves act as the driving force to add energy by making the molecules oscillate with greater amplitude. This heats the steak, cooking it from within.

There are many other situations when resonance is important. For example, a rock guitarist must be careful when playing in front of a powerful speaker. When a string vibrates (oscillates) after being struck, an electromagnetic pick-up converts that motion into an electrical pulse which is then sent to an **amplifier** and on to the speaker. If the sound vibration from the speaker (same frequency as that of the string oscillation) happens to match a resonant frequency of the guitar body, feedback can occur. Actually, this is an example of positive feedback. The sound adds energy to the guitar body, which also vibrates; this adds energy to the string to produce a larger electrical signal, and even more sound. This pattern can repeat until the **volume** at this resonant frequency grows to drown out other notes, and the rest of the band. Similarly, resonance can have destructive consequences. A famous case is that of the Tacoma Narrows Bridge in Washington State, where winds managed to act as a driving force to make the bridge sway wildly until it collapsed by adding energy to an oscillation at the resonant frequency.

KEY TERMS

Cycle— One repetition of an oscillation as an object travels from any point (in a certain direction) back to the same point and begins to move again in the original direction.

Frequency— The number of cycles of an oscillating motion which occur per second. One cycle per second is called a Hertz, abbreviated as Hz.

Resonant Frequency— A particular frequency that is characteristic of an oscillation. A driving force can efficiently add energy to an oscillation when tuned to the resonant frequency.

Positive Feedback— This occurs when an oscillation "feeds back" to continually increase its amplitude. The added energy comes from some external source, like a guitar amplifier, which produces a driving force at the same frequency as that of the original oscillation.

See also Oscillations.

Further Reading

Clark, J. *Matter and Energy: Physics in Action.* New York: Oxford University Press, 1994.

Epstein, L.C. *Thinking Physics: Practical Lessons in Critical Thinking.* Second Edition, San Francisco: Insight Press, 1994.

Ehrlich, R. *Turning the World Inside Out, and 174 Other Simple Physics Demonstrations.* Princeton, NJ: Princeton University Press, 1990.

James J. Carroll

Resources, natural

Natural resources, unlike man-made resources, exist independently of human labor. Natural resources can be viewed as an endowment or a gift to humankind. These resources are, however, not unlimited and must be used with care. Some natural resources are called "fund resources" because they can be exhausted through use, like the burning of **fossil fuels**. Other fund resources such as metals can be dissipated or wasted if they are discarded instead of being reused or recycled. Some natural re-

sources can be used up like fund resources, but they can renew themselves if they're not completely destroyed. Examples of the latter would include the **soil**, **forests**, and fisheries.

Because of population growth and a rising standard of living, the demand for natural resources is steadily increasing. For example, the rising demand for **minerals**, if continued, will deplete the known and expected reserves within the coming decades.

The world's industrialized nations are consuming nonrenewable resources at an accelerating pace, with the United States ranking first on a per capita basis. With only 5% of the global population, Americans consumes 30% of the world's resources. Because of their tremendous demand for goods, Americans have also created more waste than is generated by any other country. The environment in the United States has been degraded with an ever-increasing **volume** and variety of contaminants. In particular, a complex of synthetic chemicals with a vast potential for harmful effects on human health has been created. The long-term effects of a low dosage of many of these chemicals in our environment will not be known for decades. The three most important causes for global environmental problems today are population growth, excessive resource consumption, and high levels of **pollution**. All of these threaten the natural resource base.

Respiration

Respiration is the physiological process by which organisms supply **oxygen** to their cells and the cells use that oxygen to produce high **energy** molecules. Respiration occurs in all types of organisms, including **bacteria**, protists, **fungi**, plants, and animals. In higher animals, respiration is often separated into three separate components: (a) external respiration, the exchange of oxygen and **carbon** dioxide between the environment and the **organism**; (b) internal respiration, the exchange of oxygen and **carbon dioxide** between the internal body fluids, such as **blood**, and individual cells; and (c) **cellular respiration**, the biochemical oxidation of glucose and consequent synthesis of ATP (**adenosine triphosphate**).

External respiration

External respiration, commonly known as breathing, is the exchange of oxygen and carbon dioxide between an **animal** and its environment. Most animals use specialized organs or **organ** systems, such as lungs, trachea, or gills, for external respiration.

In all cases, exchange of gases between the environment and an animal occurs by **diffusion** through a wet surface on the animal which is permeable to oxygen and carbon dioxide. Diffusion is the **random** movement of molecules and causes a net movement of molecules from a region of high **concentration** to a region of low concentration. Thus, oxygen moves into an organism because its concentration is lower inside than in the environment (air or **water**); carbondioxide moves out of an organism because its concentration is higher inside than in the environment.

Different organisms have different mechanisms for extracting oxygen from their environments. Below, we classify animal-gas exchange mechanisms into five categories.

1. Direct Diffusion. **Sponges**, **jellyfish**, and terrestrial **flatworms** use this primitive method. In direct diffusion, oxygen diffuses from the environment through cells on the animal's surface and then diffuses to individual cells inside. The primitive animals which use this method do not have respiratory organs. Obviously, an animal with small surface areas and large **volume** cannot rely on direct diffusion, since little oxygen would reach the interior of the body. Microbes, fungi, and plants all obtain the oxygen they use for cellular respiration by direct diffusion through their surfaces.

2. Diffusion into Blood. Annelids (**segmented worms**) and **amphibians** use this method. In this method, oxygen diffuses through a moist layer of epidermal cells on the body surface and from there through capillary walls and into the blood stream. Once oxygen is in the blood, it moves throughout the body to different tissues and cells. While this method does not rely upon respiratory organs and is thus quite primitive, it is somewhat more advanced than direct diffusion.

3. Tracheae. **Insects** and terrestrial **arthropods** use this method. In tracheal respiration, air moves through openings in the body surface called spiracles and then into special tubes called tracheae (singular, trachea) which extend into the body. The tracheae divide into many small branches which contact the muscles and organs. In small insects, air moves into the tracheae passively, whereas in large insects, body movements facilitate tracheal air movement. An advantage of tracheal respiration is that it provides oxygen directly to the muscles. Muscle cells use this oxygen, together with the carbohydrates and other energetic molecules in the hemolymph (insect blood), to generate the energy needed for flight.

4. Gills. **Fish** and other aquatic animals use this method. Gills are specialized tissues with many infoldings, each covered by a thin layer of cells and impregnated with blood capillaries. They take up oxygen dissolved

in water and expel carbon dioxide dissolved in blood. Gills work by a mechanism called countercurrent exchange, in which blood and water flow in discrete pathways and opposite directions. This allows gills to more efficiently extract oxygen from water and expel carbon-dioxide into the water. Certain details of gill **anatomy** differ among different species.

5. Lungs. Terrestrial **vertebrates** use this method. Lungs are special organs in the body cavity which are composed of many small chambers impregnated with blood capillaries. After air enters the lungs, oxygen diffuses into the blood stream through the walls of these capillaries. It then moves from the lung capillaries to the different muscles and organs of the body. Humans and other **mammals** have lungs in which air moves in and out through the same pathway. In contrast, **birds** have more specialized lungs which use a mechanism called crosscurrent exchange. Like the countercurrent exchange mechanism of gills, air flows through the crosscurrent exchange system of bird lungs in one direction only, making for more efficient oxygen exchange.

Internal respiration

Internal respiration is the exchange of oxygen and carbon dioxide between blood and cells in different tissues of an animal's body. Internal respiration occurs in animals with a circulation system (categories 2, 4, and 5 above). Animals with gills or lungs take up oxygen and transport oxygen-rich blood throughout the body; they transport carbon dioxide-rich blood from the body back into the respiratory organs where it is expelled. The oxygen-rich blood and carbon dioxide-rich blood do not mix, making for an efficient internal respiration system. Mammals and birds have a double circulation system for blood, in which separate pumps in the left and right chambers of the **heart** move the oxygen-rich blood in the arteries and carbon dioxide-rich blood in the veins.

The blood of vertebrates and some **invertebrates** contains a protein (such as hemoglobin, hemocyanin, or chlorocruorin), which binds oxygen and transports it from the respiratory organs throughout the body. These oxygen-binding **proteins** greatly improve the oxygen carrying ability of blood. For example, human hemoglobin contains about 98% of the oxygen in a human's blood.

Hemoglobin is a red protein which binds oxygen and occurs in the red blood cells of vertebrates. Each **molecule** of hemoglobin contains an **iron** atom and can bind up to four molecules of oxygen. In muscles, hemoglobin passes its oxygen to myoglobin. Myoglobin is an oxygen-binding protein which makes muscles red and transports oxygen to the cells of the muscle. In turn, muscle cells use the oxygen from myoglobin to power muscle movement by cellular respiration.

Some segmented worms (annelids) have a green blood protein, called chlorocruorin, which binds iron and serves as an oxygen carrier. Some invertebrates have a blue blood protein, called hemocyanin, which binds **copper** and serves as an oxygen carrier.

Cellular respiration

Cellular respiration is an intracellular process in which glucose ($C_6H_{12}O_6$) is oxidized and the energy is used to make ATP (adenosine triphosphate). ATP is a high energy molecule which organisms use to drive energy-requiring processes such as biosynthesis, transport, growth, and movement. The general features of cellular respiration are the same in most organisms.

Cellular respiration consists of many separate enzymatic reactions. The entire process can be summarized in the chemical equation:

$$C_6H_{12}O_6 + 36ADP + 36Pi + 36H+ + 6O_2 \rightarrow 6CO_2 + 36ATP + 42H_2O \ (1)$$

Cellular respiration is divided into three sequential series of reactions: **glycolysis**, the **citric acid** cycle, and the **electron** transport chain. In higher organisms (eukaryotes), glycolysis occurs in the cytosol of the **cell**, the aqueous region outside the nucleus; the citric acid cycle and electron transport chain occur in the mitochondria, cellular organelles (intracellular organ-like structures) which have characteristic double membranes and are specialized for ATP production.

Glycolysis

Glycolysis can be defined simply as the lysis, or splitting, of sugar. More particularly, it is the controlled breakdown of glucose, a 6-carbon **carbohydrate**, into pyruvate, a 3-carbon carbohydrate. Organisms frequently store complex carbohydrates, such as glycogen or starch, and break these down into glucose units which can then enter into glycolysis.

Two features of glycolysis suggest that it has an ancient evolutionary origin. First, the same series of reactions occur in virtually all cells, including bacteria, plants, fungi, and animals. Second, glycolysis does not require oxygen, making it appropriate for primeval cells which had to live in a world with very little atmospheric oxygen.

Glycolysis has several important features:

(1) It breaks down one molecule of glucose, a 6-carbon molecule, into two molecules of pyruvate, a 3-carbon molecule, in a controlled manner by 10 or more enzymatic reactions. The oxidation of glucose is controlled

so that the energy in this molecule can be used to manufacture other high energy compounds (see 2 and 3 below).

(2) It makes a small amount of ATP, a process known as substrate-level phosphorylation. For each glucose molecule that is broken down by glycolysis, there is a net gain of two molecules of ATP.

(3) It makes NADH (reduced nicotinamide adenine dinucleotide), a high energy molecule which can be used to make ATP in the electron transfer chain (see below). For each glucose molecule that is broken down by glycolysis, there is a net gain of two molecules of NADH.

(4) It makes compounds which can be used to synthesize **fatty acids**. In particular, some of the carbohydrate intermediates of glycolysis are used by other enzymatic reactions to synthesize fatty acids, the major constituents of lipids, important energy storage molecules.

Cirtric acid cycle

After pyruvate (a 3-carbon molecule) is synthesized by glycolysis, it moves into the mitochondria and is oxidized to form carbon dioxide (a 1-carbon molecule) and acetyl CoA (a two carbon molecule). Cells can also make acetyl CoA from fats and amino acids and this is how cells often derive energy, in the form of ATP, from molecules other than glucose or complex carbohydrates.

After acetyl CoA forms, it enters into a series of nine sequential enzymatic reactions, known as the citric acid cycle. These reactions are so named because the first reaction makes one molecule of citric acid (a 6-carbon molecule) from one molecule of acetyl CoA (a 2-carbon molecule) and one molecule of oxaloacetic acid (a 4-carbon molecule). A complete round of the citric acid cycle expels two molecules of carbon dioxide and regenerates one molecule of oxaloacetic acid, hence the cyclic nature of these reactions. The citric acid cycle is sometimes called the **Krebs cycle**, in honor of Hans Krebs, the English biochemist who first proposed that pyruvate is broken down by a cycle of biochemical reactions.

The citric acid cycle has several important features:

(1) It makes NADH (reduced nicotinamide adenine dinucleotide) and $FADH_2$ (reduced flavin adenine dinucleotide), high energy molecules which are used to make ATP in the electron transfer chain (see below). For each glucose molecule which initially enters glycolysis, the citric acid cycle makes 6 molecules of NADH and 2 molecules of $FADH_2$.

(2) It makes GTP (guanosine triphosphate) by a process known as substrate-level phosphorylation. GTP is a high energy molecule which cells can easily use to make ATP by a separate mitochondrial reaction. For each molecule of glucose which initially enters glycolysis, the citric acid cycle makes two molecules of ATP.

(3) Some of the intermediates of the citric acid cycle reactions are used to make other important compounds. In particular, certain intermediates are used to synthesize amino acids, the building blocks of proteins, nucleotides, the building blocks of DNA, and other important molecules.

Electron transfer chain

The electron transfer chain is the final series of biochemical reactions in cellular respiration. It consists of a series of organic electron carriers associated with the inner **membrane** of the mitochondria. Cytochromes are among the most important of these electron carriers. Like hemoglobin, cytochromes are colored proteins which contain iron in a nitrogen-containing heme group. The final electron acceptor of the electron transfer chain is oxygen, which produces water as a final product of cellular respiration (see equation 1).

The main function of the electron transfer chain is the synthesis of 32 molecules of ATP from the controlled oxidation of the eight molecules of NADH and two molecules of $FADH_2$, made by the oxidation of one molecule of glucose in glycolysis and the citric acid cycle. This oxygen-requiring process is known as oxidative phosphorylation.

The electron transfer chain slowly extracts the energy from NADH and $FADH_2$ by passing electrons from these high energy molecules from one electron carrier to another, as if along a chain. As this occurs, protons (H^+s) are pumped across the inner membrane of mitochondria, creating a **proton** gradient which is subsequently used to make ATP by a process known as chemiosmosis.

Anaerobic respiration

The above reactions of cellular respiration are often referred to as **aerobic** respiration because the final series of reactions, the electron transfer chain, require oxygen as an electron acceptor. When oxygen is absent or in short supply, cells may rely upon glycolysis alone for their supply of ATP. Glycolysis presumably originated in primitive cells early in the Earth's history when very little oxygen was present in the atmosphere.

In an **anaerobic** environment, pyruvate is typically broken down into lactate or into acetaldehyde and then **ethanol**, instead of being degraded to acetyl CoA and then introduced to the citric acid cycle. The NADH which is made during glycolysis (see above) is required for synthesis of ethanol or lactate. Obviously, exclusive reliance upon glycolysis for the manufacture of ATP is very inefficient, since only two molecules of ATP are

made from each glucose molecule, whereas aerobic respiration makes 36 molecules of ATP from each glucose molecule (see equation 1).

Needless to say, synthesis of ethanol is essential in the making of wine and beer. In this case, the sugars present in the must (sweet juice of the crushed **grapes**) or wort (sweet liquid from the malted **barley**) are broken down to pyruvate and from there into ethanol. Interestingly, when humans drink ethanol, our livers metabolize it in the reverse direction, into acetaldehyde and other carbohydrates. Accumulation of acetaldehyde has been implicated in causing hangovers as well as in fetal **alcohol syndrome**, a suite of developmental abnormalities in an infant caused by exposure to alcohol as a fetus.

Efficiency of cellular respiration

One can easily determine the **energy efficiency** of cellular respiration by calculating the standard free energy change, a thermodynamic quantity, between the reactants and products of equation 1. On this basis, biochemists often quote the overall efficiency of cellular respiration as about 40%, with the additional 60% of the energy given off as **heat**.

However, many cells regulate the different enzymes of respiration so that they are in nonequilibrium states, leading to a higher overall efficiency. Calculations of the free energy change, a different thermodynamic quantity, account for these regulatory effects and show that cellular respiration often has an efficiency of 60% or more.

Interestingly, some plants have two separate electron transfer chains in their mitochondria. The alternate electron transfer chain only operates occasionally, but when it does, it gives off most of its energy as heat, rather than ATP. This seemingly wasteful generation of heat is so great in some species that it volatilizes chemicals in their flowers which attract insect pollinators.

See also Respiratory system.

Further Reading

Galston, A. W. *Life Processes of Plants: Mechanisms for Survival.* New York: W. H. Freeman, 1993.

Hall, D. L. *Why Do Animals Breathe*? Ayer Press, Inc., 1981.

Nicholls, P. *The Biology of Oxygen.* Carolina Biological, Inc., 1982.

Randall, D. J., et al. *The Evolution of Air Breathing in Vertebrates.* Cambridge: Cambridge University Press, 1981.

Salisbury, F.B. and C.W. Ross. *Plant Physiology.* Wadsworth Inc., 1992.

Storer, T.I., R.L. Usinger, R.C. Stebbins, J.W. Nybakken. *General Zoology.* McGraw-Hill, Inc., 1979.

Stryer, L. *Biochemistry.* W.H. Freeman and Company, 1981.

Peter A. Ensminger

KEY TERMS

ATP (adenosine triphosphate)—High energy molecule which cells use to drive energy-requiring processes such as biosynthesis, transport, growth, and movement.

Chemiosmosis—Process in which a difference in H^+ concentration on different sides of the inner mitochondrial membrane drives ATP synthesis.

Diffusion—Random movement of molecules which leads to a net movement of molecules from a region of high concentration to a region of low concentration.

Eukaryote— Cell whose DNA occurs within a nucleus.

Fetal Alcohol Syndrome—Suite of developmental abnormalities of an infant, caused by exposure to alcohol as a fetus.

Hemoglobin—Blood protein which has an iron-containing heme group and can bind four molecules ofoxygen.

Mitochondrion (plural, Mitochondria)—Cellular organelle of eukaryotes which produces ATP.

Respirator

A respirator is a means to provide needed **oxygen** to a patient, to infuse medication directly into the lungs, or to provide the power to breathe to someone who is unable to do so on his own. A respirator may be needed following a serious trauma that interferes with the individual's breathing or for a person who has contracted a disease such as **poliomyelitis** that has affected the nerves that control **respiration**. Also, a respirator often breathes for an individual who has had **surgery** because the **muscle relaxants** that are given for the procedure may render the respiratory muscles inactive.

Respirators come in many forms. A simple tube that discharges oxygen into the nose is the simplest. This device does not breathe for the patient, but enriches his air intake with oxygen.

Other respirators are mechanical ventilators that force air into the patient's lungs or expand his chest to allow air to move into the lungs. The primary indications that an individual needs artificial ventilation are inadequate breathing on the part of the patient; that is, apnea (no breathing) or hypoventilation (lowered rate of breathing), either of which results in lowered **blood** oxygen

(hypoxemia) levels, the second indication. These patients will have inadequate lung expansion so too little air is moved in and out, respiratory muscle fatigue, unstable respiratory drive, or they work excessively at breathing. A patient with a closed head injury may need respiratory assistance to raise the **Ph** of the blood to an alkaline level, which helps to prevent the **brain** from swelling.

Persons who have chronic obstructive pulmonary disease or **emphysema**, either of which will become worse over time, eventually will require mechanical ventilation. Because theirs is a chronic disease process that is incurable, however, physicians hold off the assisted ventilation as long as possible. Once on the assistance device the patient will need to use it for the rest of his life.

Thus, mechanical ventilation is applied to adjust alveolar ventilation to a level that is as normal as possible for each patient, to improve oxygenation, to reduce the work of breathing, and to provide prophylactic ventilation to patients who have had surgery.

Respirators may be either positive **pressure** or **negative** pressure types. Positive pressure ventilators force air into the lungs, negative pressure machines expand the chest to suck air into the lungs.

Positive pressure ventilators

Positive pressure ventilators are attached to a tube leading directly into the trachea or windpipe. These machines then force air into the lungs at sufficient force to expand the chest and lungs. The most sophisticated positive pressure respirators have an alarm system to sound if the device fails, gas blenders to infuse more than one gas into the lungs, pop-off valves to relieve pressure if the machine begins to build gas pressures to undesirable levels, humidifiers to moisturize the gas or nebulizers to infuse a medication into the gas stream, gas sampling ports, and thermometers.

Positive pressure respirators are pressure cycled or pressure limited, time cycled, **volume** cycled, or a combination of these.

Pressure cycled or pressure limited respirators force gas into the patient's lungs until a preset pressure is reached. A valve in the machine closes off the gas stream and the patient exhales. These machines now are used only in cases of drug overdose or with comatose patients whose lungs are easy to ventilate. With this type of respirator the preset pressure is not always delivered. Changes in airway resistance can influence the pressure detected by the machine so the gas may be cut off at what the machine detects as the set pressure when in fact the gas entering the lungs is far below the desired level. The postoperative patient who may have improved lung mechanics because of muscle relaxants given for surgery may become overventilated because resistance to the infusion is lower and the preset pressure is not attained until more than the desired level of gas has been delivered. Bronchial spasms also may influence the amount of gas reaching the lungs. The spasmodic bronchi will reduce in diameter and increase the resistance to the pump, so the preset pressure is detected at too low a level.

Volume cycled machines deliver a preset volume of gas into the lungs without regard for pressure. These machines are capable of delivering gas at high pressure, so they can overcome **respiratory system** resistance such as stiff lungs to administer the needed oxygen. They are used often in critical care situations.

Time cycled machines, as the name implies, deliver gas for a set time, shut off to allow the patient to exhale, then deliver again for the set time. Pressure and flow of the gas may vary over the time, depending upon patient characteristics, but these factors are not considered with time cycled machines.

Any of these positive pressure machines now can be controlled by computer and the volume, time, or pressure reset from breath to breath, according to need.

A unique type of positive pressure apparatus is designed to deliver very rapid, shallow breaths over a short time. Some are designed to deliver 60-100 breaths per minute, others 100-400 breaths, and a very high **frequency** oscillator is available to deliver very small tidal volumes of gas at the rate of 900-3,000 breaths a minute. These small volumes provide oxygenation at lower positive pressures. This may be important in that it reduces cardiac depression and does not interfere with blood return to the **heart**. Also, the patient requires less sedation.

Negative pressure ventilators

Negative pressure ventilators do not pump air into the lungs. Instead they expand the chest to suck air into the lungs. These respirators come in three types: the tank, the cuirass, and body wrap.

The tank negative pressure respirator is commonly called the **iron** lung. Familiar during the poliomyelitis **epidemic** of the 1950s, the tank is a cylindrical container into which the patient is placed with his head protruding from an opening at one end. Air in the tank is sucked out periodically, which expands the patient's chest to force him to inhale. Then the pressure in the tank is normalized and the patient exhales. Of course, the patient in an iron lung is immobile. One side effect of long-term iron lung occupancy is the possibility of so-called tank shock, the pooling of blood in the patient's abdomen, which reduces venous return to the right atrium of the heart.

A more convenient form of negative pressure respirator is called the cuirass, or chest shell. It is a molded, plas-

KEY TERMS

Alveolar—Reference to the alveoli, the tiny air sacs of the lungs that exchange oxygen for carbon dioxide in the blood.

Bronchiolar—Reference to the bronchioles, the small air tubes that supply air to the alveoli in the lungs.

tic dome that fits closely to the patient's body over the chest. As in the iron lung, the air is pumped out of the cuirass which forces the chest to expand and air to be pulled into the lungs. When the pressure is normalized the chest relaxes and the patient exhales. The primary problem with the cuirass is that a poorly fitted one can cause pressure sores at the points where the seal is not adequate.

The pulmowrap is an impervious wrapping placed around the patient and connected to a pump. Here again air is removed from the wrap to expand the lungs.

See also Respiratory diseases.

Further Reading

Larson, David E., ed. *Mayo Clinic Family Healthbook.* New York, William Morrow & Co. Inc., 1990.

Larry Blaser

Respiratory diseases

There are many different types of respiratory diseases that interfere with the vital process of breathing. Respiratory obstructions arising from diseases can occur in the nasal area, the regions of the throat and windpipe (upper **respiratory system**), or in the bronchial tubes and lungs (lower respiratory system). The common cold and allergic reactions to airborne pollens block the nasal passages by creating nasal **inflammation** (rhinitis). Viral and bacterial infections of the upper respiratory tract inflame various parts of the airways. These infections lead to fever, irritation, coughing, and phlegm, which is mixture of mucus and pus. Inflammations may occur in the throat (pharynx), tonsils, larynx, and bronchial tubes. Damage to these parts of the respiratory system and to the lungs can also result from the inhalation of tobacco smoke, **air pollution** caused by **smog**, and industrial waste products.

With the mid-twentieth-century discovery and use of **antibiotics**, the two major respiratory killers of the past, **tuberculosis** and **pneumonia**, were brought under control. In place of those diseases, lung **cancer** began to emerge in the 1940s as an **epidemic** disease among those who are heavy smokers of cigarettes and those who are exposed to some forms of hazardous environmental **pollution**. Worksite populations exposed to such materials as **asbestos**, chromium, and radioactive substances were also found to have a higher incidence of lung cancer.

Colds, flu, and allergies

Colds, like flu and allergies, challenge the breathing process. There are no cures for these conditions, but they are usually not life threatening, unlike many other respiratory diseases. Prescription medicines and over-the-counter medications may provide temporary relief of the discomforts associated with colds, flu, and allergies, while **asthma**, tuberculosis, and other respiratory diseases require long-range medical attention and supervision.

Colds

The entire tubular system for bringing air into the lungs is coated by a moist mucous **membrane** that helps to clean the air and fight **infection**. In the case of a cold, the mucous membrane is fighting any one of over 200 viruses. If the **immune system** is unsuccessful in warding off such a **virus**, the nasal passages and other parts of the upper respiratory tract become inflamed, swollen, and congested, thus interfering with the breathing process. The body uses the **reflex** actions of sneezing and coughing to expel mucus, a thick sticky substance that comes from the mucous membranes and other secretions. These secretions come up from the infected areas as phlegm.

Coughing is a reflex action that helps to expel infected mucus or phlegm from the airways of the lungs by causing the diaphragm to contract spasmodically. It is characterized by loud explosive sounds that can often indicate the nature of the discomfort. While coughing is irritating and uncomfortable, losing the ability to cough can be fatal in an illness such as pneumonia, where coughing is essential to break up the mucous and other infected secretions produced by the body in its battle against the disease.

Antibiotics kill **bacteria** but not viruses; hence they are not effective against cold viruses. The body has to build up its own defense against them. Since there are so many different types of viruses that can cause a cold, no **vaccine** to protect against the cold has as yet been developed. Though the common cold by itself is not a serious condition, it poses a threat because of the complications that may arise from it, especially for children, who are much more prone to colds than older people. Colds are usually contracted in the winter months, but there are other seasonal conditions that make individuals receptive to colds.

Influenza

Other viruses cause different types of **influenza**, such as swine flu, Asian flu, Hong Kong flu, and Victoria flu. Some of the symptoms of influenza resemble the common cold, but influenza is a more serious condition than a cold. It is a disease of the lungs and is highly contagious. Its symptoms include fever, chills, weakness, and aches. It can be especially dangerous to the elderly, children, and the chronically ill. After World War I, a flu epidemic killed 20 million people throughout the world. Fortunately, there has so far not been a repetition of such a severe strain of flu. Flu vaccines provide only seasonal immunity, and each year new serums have to be developed for the particular strain that appears to be current in that period of time.

Allergic rhinitis

Every season throughout the world, ragweed and pollens from **grasses**, plants, and trees produce the reactions of sneezing, runny nose, swollen nasal **tissue**, headaches, blocked sinuses, fever, and watery, irritated eyes in those who are sensitive to these substances. These are the symptoms of hay fever, which is one of the common allergies. The term hay fever is really a misnomer because the condition is not caused by hay and does not cause fever. Allergic respiratory disturbances may also be provoked by dust particles. Usually, the allergic response is due more to the feces of the dust mite that inhabits the dust particle. The dust mite's feces are small enough to be inhaled and to create an allergic respiratory response.

Colds and allergic rhinitis both cause the nasal passages and sinuses to become stuffed and clogged with excess mucous. In the case of a cold, a viral infection is responsible for the production of excess mucus. Inhaling steam with an aromatic oil is recommended for the cold. Decongestants are recommended to avoid infection from the excess mucous of the common cold. In seasonal allergic rhinitis, the symptoms result from an exaggerated immune response to what, in principle, is a harmless substance. Histamines released by the mast cells play a major role in an allergic immune response, and it is these chemicals, for the most part, that are responsible for the **allergy** symptoms.

Treatments

Antihistamines are used to block the body's production of histamines that cause allergy symptoms. Cold medicines usually contain antihistamines, decongestants, and non-narcotic analgesics like aspirin. Though the antihistamines are not effective against the cold viruses, they do cause drowsiness, and that may help to alleviate the sleeplessness that often accompanies a cold. The analgesics help against the fever and headaches that accompany a cold, while the decongestant temporarily relieves a stuffy nose.

While decongestants can be taken orally, the two most effective ways of taking decongestants are nose drops and nasal sprays. Caution should be taken to prevent what is known as the rebound congestion effect. The decongestant medicine is applied right to the site of the swollen tissues, where it relieves the congestion in minutes by constricting the **blood** vessels. When decongestants are discontinued after prolonged use, the body may fail to marshal its own constrictive response. The congestion can then become worse than before the medicine was taken. Therefore, it is advisable to use decongestants for only a short period of time.

Bronchial diseases

Asthma, chronic **bronchitis**, and **emphysema** are complex illnesses for which there is no simple treatment. Treatments depend on the severity of the conditions. All three conditions are characterized by an involuntary smooth muscle constriction in the walls of the bronchial tubes. When nerve signals from the autonomic **nervous system** contract the bronchial muscles, the openings of the tubes close to the extent of creating a serious impediment to the patient's breathing.

Acute bronchitis is a short-term illness that occurs as a result of a viral infection of the bronchi. It is treated with antibiotics and may require attention in a hospital. Chronic bronchitis is a long-term illness that can be caused by such environmental factors as air pollution, tobacco smoke, and other irritants. There is a persistent cough and congestion of the airways.

In emphysema, the air spaces spread out beyond the bronchial tubes. Both chronic bronchitis and emphysema restrict air flow and there is a wheezing sound to the breathing. Unlike asthma, however, these two illnesses are not easily reversible. Airway constriction in the case of bronchitis and emphysema is less severe than in the case of an asthma attack, however.

Asthma is a disorder of the autonomic nervous system. While the cause for the condition is unknown, there is a connection between allergies and asthma in that an allergic reaction can trigger an asthma attack. Nerve messages cause muscle spasms in the lungs that either narrow or close the airway passages. These airways consist of narrow tube-like structures that branch off from the main bronchi and are called bronchioles. It is the extreme contraction of the muscle walls of the bronchioles that is responsible for the asthma attack. These attacks come and go in irregular patterns, and they vary in degree of severity.

Bronchodilators

Bronchodilators are used in the treatment of asthma, chronic bronchitis, and emphysema. A bronchodilator is a medicine used to relax the muscles of the bronchial tubes. It is usually administered as a mist through an inhaler. Some are given orally as a tablet. Administered with an inhaler, they go straight to the lungs for fast action. Since they do not enter the bloodstream, they have few side effects.

Anticholinergic bronchodilators are also taken by inhalation. They take more time to work than the sympathomimetic medicines, but they remain effective for a longer period of time. Their job is more prevention than immediate relief. They work by countering signals from the parasympathetic nervous system to constrict the bronchioles. These signals send their messages to the cholinergic receptors on the muscle wall of the bronchioles. The anticholinergic medicine blocks the receptor. Atropine is an example of an anticholinergic bronchodilator.

Xanthines date back to the ancient world. They have been used as medicines for a number of conditions. **Caffeine** is a type of xanthine. Theophylline is the active ingredient of the xanthines. They relax smooth muscle and stimulate the **heart**. They are particularly effective in relaxing the muscle walls of the bronchioles. Taken orally, they act directly on the muscle tissue. It is not certain how the xanthines work, but they seem to prevent mast cells from releasing histamines while inhibiting other enzymatic actions.

Tuberculosis

Tuberculosis is an infectious disease of the lungs caused by bacteria called tubercle bacilli. It was one of the major causes of death until the introduction of antibiotics in the 1940s. The bacillus is transmitted by the coughing of an individual who has an advanced case of the disease and infects the lungs of uninfected people who inhale the infected droplets. The disease is also spread through unpasteurized milk, since animals can be infected with the bacteria. The disease is dormant in different parts of the body until it becomes active and attacks the lungs, leading to a chronic infection with such symptoms as fatigue, loss of weight, night fevers and chills, and persistent coughing that brings up sputum-streaked blood. The virulent form of the infection can then spread to other parts of the body. Without treatment the condition is usually fatal.

In the past, well-to-do tubercular patients were often sent to rest homes called sanitoriums, preferably located in a **mountain** area or **desert** retreat, so they could enjoy the benefits of clean air. Today, tuberculosis is treated with antituberculous drugs, such as streptomycin, which are taken over a long period of time.

Populations most at risk of contracting TB are people who have certain types of medical conditions or use drugs for medical conditions that weaken the immune system; people in low-income groups; people from poorer countries with high TB rates; people who work in or are residents of long-term care facilities (nursing homes, prisons, hospitals); and people who are very underweight, as well as alcoholics and intravenous drug users.

Pneumonia

Pneumonia, another life threatening disease, is an infection or inflammation of the lungs caused by bacteria, viruses, mycoplasma (**microorganisms** that show similarities to both viruses and bacteria), and **fungi**, as well as such inorganic agents as inhaled dusts or gases. The irritation to the lung tissues from these sources destroys the alveoli (air sacs) of the lung. Blood cells from lung capillaries then fill the alveolar spaces. The affected part of the lung loses its **elasticity** and can no longer fulfill its vital tasks of supplying the rest of the body with **oxygen** and eliminating **carbon dioxide** gas. Symptoms of this disease include pleurisy (chest **pain**), high fever, chills, severe coughing that brings up small amounts of mucus, sweating, blood in the sputum (pus and mucus), and labored breathing.

Pneumonia infections are divided into two classes: in lobar pneumonia one lobe of the lung is affected, whereas bronchial pneumonia shows up as patches of infection that spread to both lungs. Pneumococcus bacteria are responsible for most bacterial pneumonia. The lobes of the lung become filled with fluid, and the bacterial infection spreads to other parts of the body. There is a vaccine for this type of pneumonia. Viruses cause about half of all the pneumonias. Influenza viruses may invade the lungs, which in this case, do not become filled with fluid. The symptoms of viral pneumonia, which are not as serious as those of bacterial pneumonia and last for shorter periods of time, are similar to those of influenza.

Mycoplasma pneumonia is not as severe as bacterial pneumonia, either. Even if untreated, this type of pneumonia is associated with a low death rate. A more recent type of pneumonia that made its appearance with the **AIDS** epidemic is pneumocystis carinii pneumonia (PCP). It is caused by a fungus and is often the first sign of illness a person with AIDS experiences. Other less common pneumonias are beginning to appear more frequently and require preventive measures (if possible, early detection and effective treatment). In 1936 pneumonia was the main cause of death in the United States. Since then it has been controlled by antibiotics, but as resistant strains of bacteria have developed, the number of cases has increased. In 1979 pneumonia and influenza

KEY TERMS

Antibiotics—Drugs used to kill disease-causing bacteria, but are ineffective against viruses.

Bronchioles—The smallest tubes of the bronchi that lead to the air sacs (alveoli).

Bonchodilators—Drugs used to dilate the bronchioles.

Carcinoma of the lung—The most common form of lung cancer.

Histamines—Chemicals in the body that play a major role in allergic responses.

Pneumoconioses—The class of respiratory diseases caused by the inhalation of inorganic chemicals.

Pneumocystis carinii pneumonia—A type of pneumonia occurring in AIDS, which is caused by fungi.

Pulmonary fibrosis—Scarring of the lung tissue from disease or drugs.

Rhinitis—The common condition of upper respiratory tract inflammation occurring in both colds and allergy.

TB skin test—The use of tuberculin, a protein produced by the tuberculosis bacillus, to test for TB.

combined formed the sixth major cause of death in the United States.

Cancer

As a respiratory disease, lung cancer has now become the leading cause of death from cancer in men. It accounts for the second largest number of cancer deaths in women. Cigarette smoking and air pollution are considered to be the two main causes of lung cancer. The three types of lung cancer are carcinomas, lymphomas, and sarcomas. The survival rate after five years for carcinomas, which can originate in the trachea, bronchi, or alveoli, is low. Lymphomas originate in the lymph nodes, while sarcomas develop either in the lungs or in other body tissues. Treatment includes the use of chemotherapy, **radiation**, and **surgery**, that is, the removal of the affected parts of the lung.

Miscellaneous disorders

Noncancerous (benign) tumors may occur throughout the respiratory system. Although benign tumors are less serious than malignant ones, they can still cause serious obstructions of the airways and other complications. They may later become malignant.

Different types of drugs like heroin can cause **edema** (lung fluid). Anticancer drugs can cause pulmonary fibrosis (scar tissue), which will interfere with breathing. There are also children's diseases like cystic fibrosis, which affects secretion by the **glands** and results in pulmonary disorders along with other complications. **Whooping cough** (pertussis), which may lead to pneumonia and respiratory distress **syndrome** in newborns, especially premature ones, is another example of a children's disease.

Structural disorders may occur after changes in the shape of respiratory organs take place, following diseases such as pneumonia or tuberculosis or from hereditary causes. There are also a number of diseases caused by the inhalation of dust products from **coal mining** (black lung disease), sandblasting (silicosis), and manufacturing (asbestosis and berylliosis). These diseases are classified as pneumoconioses. The respiratory tract can also be affected by many diseases in other organs or systems of the body such as the heart, kidneys, and immune system.

Further Reading

Baum, Gerald L. and Emanuel Wolinsky. *Textbook of Pulmonary Diseases*. Boston: Little, Brown, 1994.

Levitzky, Michael G. *Introduction to Respiratory Care*. Philadelphia: Saunders, 1990.

Silverstein, Alvin. *Human Anatomy and Physiology*. New York: John Wiley, 1983.

Wilkins, Robert L. *Clinical Assessment in Respiratory Care*. St. Louis: Mosby, 1990.

Respiratory system

Aerobic organisms take in **oxygen** from the external environment and release **carbon dioxide** in a process known as **respiration**. At the most basic level, this exchange of gases takes place in cells and involves the release of **energy** from food materials by oxidation. Carbon dioxide is produced as a waste product of these oxidation reactions. The gas exchange in cells is called **cellular respiration**. In single-celled organisms, the oxygen and carbon dioxide simply diffuse through the **cell membrane**. Respiration in multicellular organisms, however, is a much more complex process involving a specialized respiratory system that plays an intermediary role between the cells and the external environment. While the respiratory organs of some complex organisms such as **insects** communicate directly with internal tissues, respiration in **vertebrates** also involves the **circulatory system**, which carries gases between cells and respiratory organs.

The respiratory system must meet two important criteria. First, the respiratory surface must be large enough to take in oxygen in sufficient quantities to meet the organism's needs and release all waste gas quickly. Some animals, such as the earthworm, use the entire body surface as a respiratory **organ**. The internal respiratory organs of vertebrates generally have many lobes to enlarge the surface area. Second, the respiratory membrane must be moist, since gases require **water** to diffuse across membranes. The watery environment keeps the respiratory surface moist for aquatic animals. A problem exists for land animals, whose respiratory surfaces can dry out in open air. As a result, animals such as the earthworm must live in damp places. Internal respiratory organs provide an environment that is easier to keep moist.

Respiration in the earthworm

The earthworm uses its moist outer skin as a respiratory organ. Oxygen diffuses across the body surface and enters **blood** in the dense capillary mesh that lies just below the skin. Blood carries the oxygen to the body cells. There, it picks up carbon dioxide and transports it to the skin capillaries where it diffuses out of the body. The skin is effective as an organ of respiration in small wormlike animals where there is a high **ratio** of surface to **volume**.

Respiration in insects

Tiny air tubes called tracheae branch throughout the insect's body. Air enters the tracheae through holes in the body wall called spiracles, which are opened and closed by valves. In larger insects, air moves through the tracheae when the body muscles contract. The tracheae are invaginated-folded into the body, that is-and thereby kept moist. Thickened rings in the walls of the tracheae help support them. These vessels branch into smaller vessels called tracheoles, which lack the supportive rings. The tracheoles carry air directly to the surface of individual cells, where they branch further to deliver oxygen and pick up carbon dioxide. A fluid in the endings of tracheoles regulates how much air contacts the cells. If a cell needs oxygen, the fluid pulls back and exposes the cell membrane to the air.

Respiratory system of fish

Gills mediate the gas exchange in **fish**. These organs, located on the sides of the head, are made up of gill filaments, feathery structures that provide a large surface for gas exchange. The filaments are arranged in rows in the gill arches, and each filament has lamellae, discs that contain capillaries. Blood enters and leaves the gills through these small blood vessels. Although gills are restricted to a small section of the body, the immense respiratory surface created by the gill filaments provides the whole **animal** with an efficient gas exchange. The surrounding water keeps the gills wet.

A flap, the operculum, covers and protects the gills of **bony fish**. Water containing dissolved oxygen enters the fish's mouth, and the animal moves its jaws and operculum in such a way as to pump the incoming water through the gills. As water passes over the gill filaments, blood inside the capillaries picks up the dissolved oxygen. Since the blood in the capillaries flows in a direction opposite to the flow of water around the gill filaments, there is a good opportunity for absorption. The circulatory system then transports the oxygen to all body tissues and picks up carbon dioxide, which is removed from the body through the gills. After the water flows through the gills, it exits the body behind the fish's operculum.

Respiration in terrestrial vertebrates

Lungs are the internal respiratory organs of **amphibians**, **reptiles**, **birds**, and **mammals**. The lungs, paired invaginations located in one area of the body, provide a large, thin, moist surface for gas exchange. Lungs work with the circulatory system, which transports oxygen from inhaled air to all tissues of the body. The circulatory system also transports carbon dioxide from body cells to the lungs to be exhaled. The process of inhaling and exhaling is called pulmonary ventilation.

Besides these similarities, there is a great variety in the respiratory systems of terrestrial vertebrates. **Frogs**, for instance, have balloon-like lungs that do not have a very large surface area. **Diffusion** across the frog's moist skin supplements the gas exchange through the lungs. Birds have about eight thin-walled air sacs attached to their lungs. The air sacs take up **space** in the entire body cavity and in some of the bones. When birds inhale, air passes through a tube called the bronchus and enters the air sacs located in the posterior (rear) of the animal. At the same time, air in the lungs moves forward to air sacs located in the anterior (front). When birds exhale, the air from the anterior air sacs moves to the outside, while air from the posterior sacs moves into the lungs. This efficient system moves air forward through the lungs both when the bird inhales and exhales. Blood in the capillaries of the lungs flows against the air current, which again increases respiratory efficiency. Birds are capable of flying at high altitudes, where the air has a low oxygen content, because of these adaptations of the respiratory system.

Human respiratory system

The human respiratory system, working in conjunction with the circulatory system, supplies oxygen and re-

moves carbon dioxide. The respiratory system conducts air to the respiratory surfaces of lung units. There, the blood in the lung capillaries readily absorbs oxygen, and gives off carbon dioxide gathered from the body cells. The circulatory system transports oxygen-laden blood to the body cells and picks up carbon dioxide. The term respiration describes the exchange of gases across cell membranes both in the lungs (external respiration) and in the body tissues (internal respiration). Pulmonary ventilation, or breathing, exchanges volumes of air with the external environment.

The respiratory tract

The human respiratory system consists of the respiratory tract and the lungs. The respiratory tract can again be divided into an upper and a lower part. The upper part consists of the nose, nasal cavity, pharynx (throat) and larynx (voicebox). The lower part consists of the trachea (windpipe), bronchi, and bronchial tree. The respiratory tract cleans, warms, and moistens air during its trip to the lungs. The nose has openings to the outside that allow air to enter. Hairs inside the nose trap dirt and keep it out of the respiratory tract. The external nose leads to a large cavity within the skull. This cavity and the space inside the nose make up the nasal cavity. A nasal septum, supported by cartilage and bone, divides the nasal cavity into a right and left side. Epithelium, a layer of cells that secrete mucus and cells equipped with cilia, lines the nasal passage. Mucus moistens the incoming air and traps dust. The cilia move pieces of the mucus with its trapped particles to the throat, where it is spit out or swallowed. Stomach acids destroy **bacteria** in swallowed mucus. Sinuses, epithelium-lined cavities in bone, surround the nasal cavity. Blood vessels in the nose and nasal cavity release **heat** and warm the entering air.

Air leaves the nasal cavity and enters the throat or pharynx. From there it passes into the larynx, which is located between the pharynx and the trachea or windpipe. A framework of cartilage pieces supports the larynx, which is covered by the epiglottis, a flap of elastic cartilage that moves up and down like a trap door. When we breathe, the epiglottis stays open, but when we swallow, it closes. This valve mechanism keeps solid particles and liquids out of the trachea. If we breathe in something other than air, we automatically cough and expel it. Should these protective mechanisms fail, allowing solid food to lodge in and block the trachea, the victim is in imminent danger of asphyxiation.

Air enters the trachea in the neck. Epithelium lines the trachea as well as all the other parts of the respiratory tract. C-shaped cartilage rings reinforce the wall of the trachea and all the passageways in the lower respiratory tract. Elastic fibers in the trachea walls allow the airways to expand and contract when we inhale and exhale, while the cartilage rings prevent them from collapsing. The trachea divides behind the sternum to form a left and right bronchus, each entering a lung. Inside the lungs, the bronchi subdivide repeatedly into smaller airways. Eventually they form tiny branches called terminal bronchioles. Terminal bronchioles have a diameter of about 0.02 in (0.5 mm). The branching air-conducting network within the lungs is called the bronchial tree.

The respiratory tract is not dedicated to respiration alone but plays a major role in many other bodily functions as well. The pharynx in particular is a multipurpose organ. It is a passageway for food as well as air, since the mouth cavity also leads to it. The back of the pharynx leads into the esophagus (food tube) of the **digestive system**. The front leads into the larynx and the rest of the respiratory system. Small amounts of air pass between holes in the pharynx and the Eustachian tubes of the **ear** to equalize the gas **pressure** inside the ears, nose, and throat. The pharynx also contains lymph **glands** called tonsils and adenoids, which play a role in the **immune system**. Finally, the pharynx, which doubles as a resonating chamber, also plays a role in the production of sound, to which many other parts of the respiratory tract also contribute.

The vocal cords, a pair of horizontal folds inside the larynx, vibrate to produce sound from exhaled air. When we speak, muscles change the size of the vocal cords and the space between them, known as the glottis. The shape and size of the vocal cords determine the pitch of the sound produced. The glottis widens for deep tones and narrows for high-pitched ones. Longer, thicker vocal cords, which vibrate more slowly, produce a deeper sound. The **force** with which air is expelled through the larynx determines the volume of the sound produced. Voice quality also depends on several other factors, including the shape of the nasal cavities, sinuses, pharynx, and mouth, which all function as resonating chambers.

The lungs

The lungs are two cone-shaped organs located in the thoracic cavity, or chest, and are separated by the **heart**. The right lung is somewhat larger than the left. The pleural membrane surrounds and protects the lungs. One layer of the pleural membrane attaches to the wall of the thoracic cavity, and the other layer encloses the lungs. A fluid between the two membrane layers reduces **friction** and allows smooth movement of the lungs during breathing. The lungs are divided into lobes, each one of which receives its own bronchial branch. The bronchial branch subdivides and eventually leads to the terminal bronchi. These tiny airways lead into structures called respiratory bronchioles.

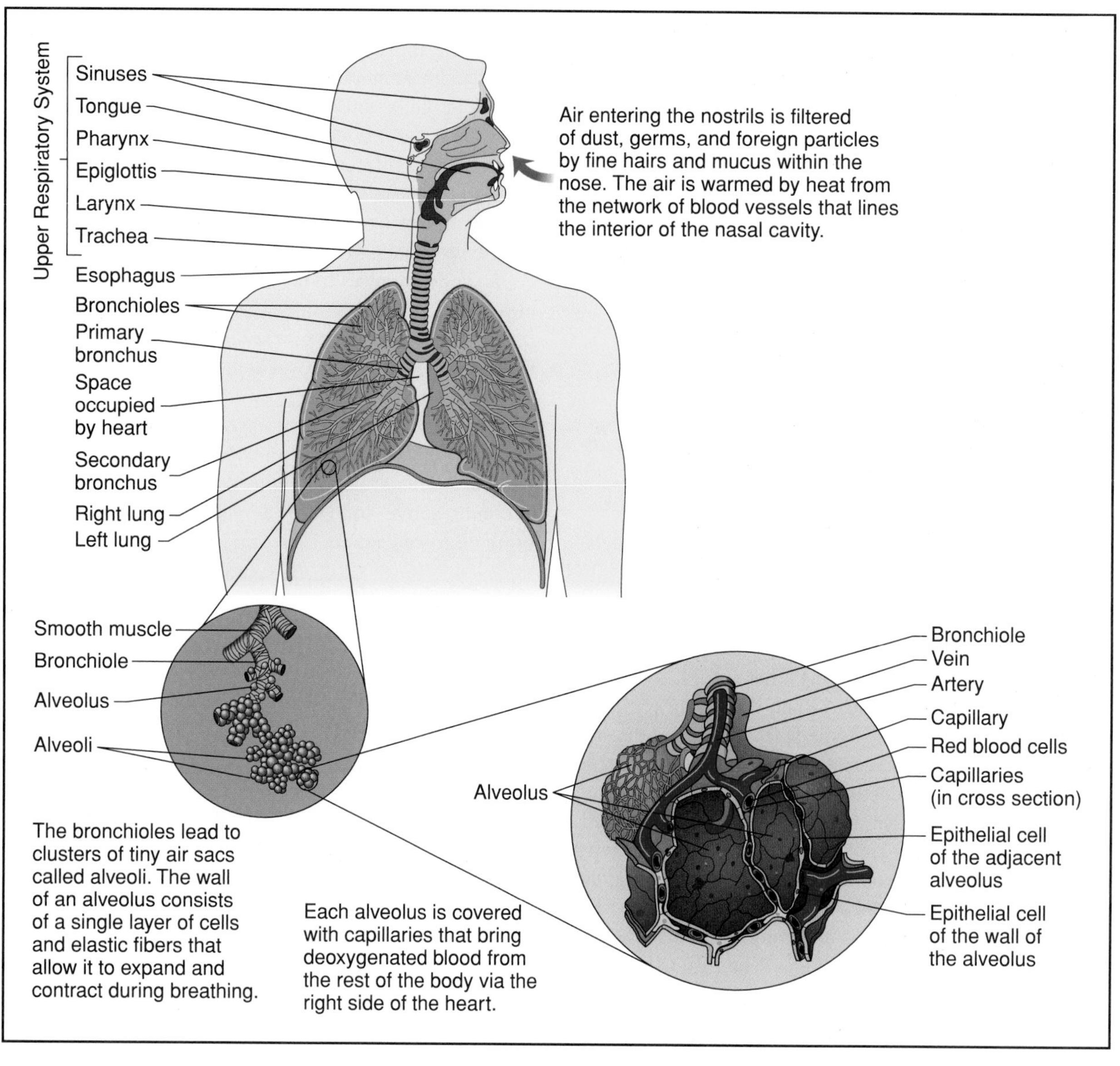
Upper Respiratory System
Sinuses
Tongue
Pharynx
Epiglottis
Larynx
Trachea
Esophagus
Bronchioles
Primary bronchus
Space occupied by heart
Secondary bronchus
Right lung
Left lung
Air entering the nostrils is filtered of dust, germs, and foreign particles by fine hairs and mucus within the nose. The air is warmed by heat from the network of blood vessels that lines the interior of the nasal cavity.
Smooth muscle
Bronchiole
Alveolus
Alveoli
The bronchioles lead to clusters of tiny air sacs called alveoli. The wall of an alveolus consists of a single layer of cells and elastic fibers that allow it to expand and contract during breathing.
Alveolus
Each alveolus is covered with capillaries that bring deoxygenated blood from the rest of the body via the right side of the heart.
Bronchiole
Vein
Artery
Capillary
Red blood cells
Capillaries (in cross section)
Epithelial cell of the adjacent alveolus
Epithelial cell of the wall of the alveolus

The human respiratory system.

The respiratory bronchioles branch into alveolar ducts that lead into outpocketings called alveolar sacs. *Alveoli*, tiny expansions of the wall of the sacs, form clusters that resemble bunches of grapes. The average person has a total of about 300 million gas-filled alveoli in the lungs. These provide an enormous surface area for gas exchange. Spread flat, the average adult male's respiratory surface would be about 750 sq ft (70 m^2), approximately the size of a handball court. Arterioles and venules make up a capillary network that surrounds the alveoli. Gas diffusion occurs rapidly across the walls of the alveoli and nearby capillaries. The alveolar-capillary membrane together is extremely thin, about 0.5 in (6-37m) thick.

The rate of external respiration in the lungs depends on several factors. One is the difference in **concentration** (partial pressure) of the respiratory gases in the alveolus and in the blood. Oxygen diffuses out of the alveolus into the blood because its partial pressure is greater in the alveolus than in the capillary. In the capillary, oxygen binds reversibly to hemoglobin in red blood cells and is transported to body tissues. Carbon dioxide diffuses out of the capillary and into the alveolus because its partial pressure is greater in the capillary than in the alveolus. In addition, the rate of gas exchange is higher as the surface area is larger and the membrane thinner. Finally, the diffusion rate depends on airflow. Rapid breathing brings in more air and speeds up the gas exchange.

The result of external respiration is that blood leaves the lungs laden with oxygen and cleared of carbon dioxide. When this blood reaches the cells of the body, internal respiration takes place. Under a higher partial pressure in the capillaries, oxygen breaks away from hemoglobin, diffuses into the **tissue** fluid, and then into the cells. Conversely, concentrated carbon dioxide under higher partial pressure in the cells diffuses into the tissue fluid and then into the capillaries. The deoxygenated blood carrying carbon dioxide then returns to the lungs for another cycle.

Pulmonary ventilation

Pulmonary ventilation, or breathing, exchanges gases between the outside air and the alveoli of the lungs. Ventilation, which is mechanical in nature, depends on a difference between the atmospheric air pressure and the pressure in the alveoli. When we expand the lungs to inhale, we increase internal volume and reduce internal pressure. Lung expansion is brought about by two important muscles, the diaphragm and the intercostal muscles. The diaphragm is a dome-shaped sheet of muscle located below the lungs that separates the thoracic and abdominal cavities. When the diaphragm contracts, it moves down. The dome is flattened, and the size of the chest cavity is increased, lowering pressure on the lungs. When the intercostal muscles, which are located between the ribs, contract, the ribs move up and outward. Their action also increases the size of the chest cavity and lowers the pressure on the lungs. By contracting, the diaphragm and intercostal muscles reduce the internal pressure relative to the **atmospheric pressure**. As a consequence, air rushes into the lungs. When we exhale, the reverse occurs. The diaphragm relaxes, and its dome curves up into the chest cavity, while the intercostal muscles relax and bring the ribs down and inward. The diminished size of the chest cavity increases the pressure in the lungs, thereby forcing out the air.

Physicians use an instrument called a **spirometer** to measure the tidal volume, that is, the amount of air we exchange during a ventilation cycle. Under normal circumstances, we inhale and exhale about 500 ml, or about a pint, of air in each cycle. Only about 350 ml of the tidal volume reaches the alveoli. The rest of the air remains in the respiratory tract. With a deep breath, we can take in an additional 3,000 ml (3 liters or a little more than 6 pints) of air. The total lung capacity is about 6 liters on average. The largest volume of air that can be ventilated is referred to as the vital capacity. Trained athletes have a high vital capacity. Regardless of the volume of air ventilated, the lung always retains about 1200 ml (3 pints) of air. This residual volume of air keeps the alveoli and bronchioles partially filled at all times.

A healthy adult ventilates about 12 times per minute, but this rate changes with **exercise** and other factors. The basic breathing rate is controlled by breathing centers in the medulla and the pons in the **brain**. Nerves from the breathing centers conduct impulses to the diaphragm and intercostal muscles, stimulating them to contract or relax. There is an inspiratory center for inhaling and an expiratory center for exhaling in the medulla. Before we inhale, the inspiratory center becomes activated. It sends impulses to the breathing muscles. The muscles contract and we inhale. Impulses from a breathing center in the pons turn off the inspiratory center before the lungs get too full. A second breathing center in the pons stimulates the inspiratory center to prolong inhaling when needed. During normal quiet breathing, we exhale passively as the lungs recoil and the muscles relax. For rapid and deep breathing, however, the expiratory center becomes active and sends impulses to the muscles to bring on forced exhalations.

The normal breathing rate changes to match the body's needs. We can consciously control how fast and deeply we breathe. We can even stop breathing for a short while. This occurs because the cerebral cortex has connections to the breathing centers and can override their control. Voluntary control of breathing allows us to avoid breathing in water or harmful chemicals for brief periods of time. We cannot, however, consciously stop breathing for a prolonged period. A buildup of carbon dioxide and **hydrogen** ions in the bloodstream stimulates the breathing centers to become active no matter what we want to do. For this reason, people cannot kill themselves by holding their breath.

We are not in conscious control of all the factors that affect our breathing rate. For example, tension on the vessels of the bronchial tree affects the breathing rate. Specialized stretch receptors in the bronchi and bronchioles detect excessive stretching caused by too much air in the lungs. They transmit the information on nerves to the breathing centers, which in turn inhibit breathing. Certain chemical substances in the blood also help control the rate of breathing. Hydrogen ions, carbon dioxide, and oxygen are detected by specialized chemoreceptors. Inside cells, carbon dioxide (CO_2) combines with water (H_2O) to form carbonic acid (H_2CO_3). The carbonic acid breaks down rapidly into hydrogen ions and bicarbonate ions. Therefore, an increase in carbon dioxide results in an increase in hydrogen ions, while a decrease in carbon dioxide brings about a decrease in hydrogen ions. These substances diffuse into the blood. When we exercise, our cells use up oxygen and produce carbon dioxide at a higher than average rate. As a result, chemoreceptors in the medulla and in parts of the peripheral **nervous system** detect a raised level of carbon dioxide and hydrogen

ions. They signal the inspiratory center, which in turn sends impulses to the breathing muscles to breathe faster and deeper. A lack of oxygen also stimulates increased breathing, but it is not as strong a **stimulus** as the carbon dioxide and hydrogen ion surpluses. A large decrease in oxygen stimulates the peripheral chemoreceptors to signal the inspiratory center to increase breathing rate.

In addition to chemoreceptors, there are receptors in the body that detect changes in movement and pressure. Receptors in joints detect movement and signal the inspiratory center to increase breathing rate. When receptors in the circulatory system detect a rise in blood pressure, they stimulate slower breathing. Lowered blood pressure stimulates more rapid breathing. Increased body **temperature** and prolonged **pain** also elevate the rate of pulmonary ventilation.

Respiratory disorders

The respiratory system is open to airborne microbes and to outside **pollution**. It is not surprising that **respiratory diseases** occur, in spite of the body's defenses. Some respiratory disorders are relatively mild and, unfortunately, very familiar. We all experience the excess mucus, coughing, and sneezing of the common cold from time to time. The common cold is an example of rhinitis, an **inflammation** of the epithelium lining the nose and nasal cavity. Viruses, bacteria, and allergens are among the causes of rhinitis.

Since the respiratory lining is continuous, nasal cavity infections often spread. **Laryngitis**, an inflammation of the vocal cords, results in hoarseness and loss of voice. Swelling of the inflamed vocal cords interferes with or prevents normal vibration. Pathogens, irritating chemicals in the air, and overuse of the voice are causes of laryngitis.

Pneumonia, inflammation of the alveoli, is most commonly caused by bacteria and viruses. During a bout of pneumonia, the inflamed alveoli fill up with fluid and dead bacteria, and the external respiration rate drops. Patients come down with fever, chills, and pain, coughing up phlegm and sometimes blood. Sufferers of **bronchitis**, an inflammation of the bronchi, also cough up thick phlegm. There are two types of bronchitis, acute and chronic. Acute bronchitis can be a complication of a cold or flu. Bacteria, smoking, and **air pollution** can also cause acute bronchitis. This type of bronchitis clears up in a short time.

Chronic bronchitis and **emphysema** are termed chronic obstructive pulmonary disease (COPD), in which the airways are obstructed and the respiratory surface is diminished. COPD patients do not improve without treatment. Air pollution and cigarette smoking are the main causes of COPD. Nonsmokers who inhale the smoke of others—passive smokers, that is—are also at risk. Smoking stimulates the lining cells in the bronchi to produce mucus. This causes the epithelium lining the bronchi and its branches to thicken and thereby narrow. Patients cough up phlegm and experience breathlessness as well as strain on the heart. In emphysema, also caused by smoking, the alveolar walls disintegrate and the alveoli blend together. They form large air pockets from which the air does not escape. This cuts down the surface area for gas exchange. It becomes difficult for the patient to exhale. The extra work of exhaling over several years can cause the chest to enlarge and become barrel-shaped. The body is unable to repair the damage to the lungs brought on by COPD, and the disease can lead to respiratory failure. During respiratory failure, the respiratory system does not supply sufficient oxygen to sustain the **organism**.

In addition to COPD, lung **cancer** also destroys lung tissue. The most common type of cancer in the United States, lung cancer is the leading cause of cancer death in men. It is the second leading cause of cancer death, after breast cancer, in women. Cigarette smoking is the main cause of lung cancer. Passive smokers are also at risk. Air pollution, radioactive **minerals**, and **asbestos** also cause lung cancer. The symptoms of the disease include a chronic cough from bronchitis, coughing up blood, shortness of breath, and chest pain. Lung cancer can spread in the lung area. Unchecked, it can metastasize (spread) to other parts of the body. Physicians use

KEY TERMS

Alveolus—Microscopic cavity in the lung that functions in gas exchange between the lungs and the bloodstream.

Breathing centers—Specialized areas in the medulla and pons that regulate the basic rate of breathing.

Bronchial tree—Branching, airconducting subdivisions of the bronchi in the lungs.

COPD—Chronic obstructive pulmonary disease, in which the air passages of the lungs become narrower and obstructed. Includes chronic bronchitis and emphysema.

Gill filaments—Finely divided surface of a gill of a fish or other aquatic animal where gas exchange takes place.

Tracheae—Tubes in land arthropods that conduct air from opening in body walls to body tissues.

surgery, anticancer drugs, and **radiation** therapy to destroy the cancer cells and contain the disease.

See also Cigarette smoke.

Further Reading

Campbell, Neil. *Biology.* Redwood City, CA: The Benjamin Cummings Publishing Co., 1993.

Crapo, Robert O. "Pulmonary Function Testing." *New England Journal of Medicine.* (July 7, 1994).

Essenfeld, Bernice, Carol R. Gontang, and Randy Moore. *Biology.* Menlo Park, CA: Addison-Wesley Publishing Co., 1996.

The Human Voice. VHS. Princeton, N.J.: Films for the Humanities and Sciences, 1995.

Marieb, Elaine N. *Human Anatomy and Physiology.* Redwood City, CA: The Benjamin Cummings Publishing Co., 1992.

Respiration. VHS. Princeton, N.J.: Films for the Humanities and Sciences, 1995.

Bernice Essenfeld

Restoration ecology

Restoration **ecology** refers to activities that are undertaken to increase populations of an **endangered species** or to manage or reconstruct a threatened **ecosystem**. Ecological restoration is an extremely difficult and expensive endeavor, and is only undertaken when the population of an endangered species is considered too small to be self-maintaining or the area of a threatened ecosystem is not large enough to allow its persistence over the longer term.

Restoration ecology can have various goals. A common focus is on endangered species and their **habitat**. In such a case, a species might be preserved in its remaining natural habitat, conserved by strictly controlling its exploitation, enhanced by a captive breeding and release program, and/or have its habitat managed to ensure its continued suitability.

If a complement of species is being managed in some region, for example in a national park, the goal might focus on ensuring that all of the known native species are present and capable of sustaining their populations. If some species have been extirpated, there may be an effort to introduce new breeding populations. Habitat management might also be a component of this sort of multi-species goal.

If an endangered natural community is the focus, a project in restoration ecology might attempt to repair degraded remnants that still remain, or try to reconstruct a facsimile of the natural community. These might be accomplished by introducing native species that are missing from the ecosystem, and by managing the environment to ensure the survival of all components of the community in an appropriate balance of abundances. The goal of community-level projects is to restore ecological communities that are as similar as possible to original ones and are also self-maintaining. Of course, this aspiration is never exactly attainable, although it can be approached to a significant degree.

Difficulties of ecological restoration

For a number of scientific reasons, it is difficult to undertake management actions in restoration ecology. There are additional constraints associated with a lack of funding, which are not discussed here.

One important problem is that there is usually an imperfect understanding of the nature of the original ecological communities that used to occur in a place or region. In large part, this problem is associated with ecology being a relatively recent science. Therefore, there is little information about the extent of natural ecosystems before they became degraded by human activities, and of their composition and relative abundance of species. Often, small fragments of natural ecosystems continue to persist in ecologically degraded landscapes, but it is not known if they are representative of what used to occur more widely, or whether the remnants are themselves degraded in some important respects.

For example, tall-grass **prairie** was once a very extensive natural ecosystem in parts of central **North America**. Unfortunately, this ecosystem is now critically endangered because almost all of its original area has been converted to intensively managed agricultural ecosystems. A few small remnants of tall-grass prairie have managed to survive. However, ecologists do not know the degree to which these are typical of the original tall-grass prairie, and what fraction of the original complement of species is now missing.

Another difficulty of restoration ecology is that some natural ecosystems require a great length of time to develop their mature character. As a result, it can take decades and even centuries for some types of natural ecosystems to be restored. Therefore, it is impossible for individual ecologists, and difficult for society, to commit to the restoration of certain types of endangered ecosystems. For example, some types of old-growth **forests** do not reach their dynamic equilibrium of species composition, **biomass**, and functional character until at least 3-5 centuries have passed since the most recent, stand-replacing disturbance. Clearly, any initiative to reconstruct these kinds of **old-growth forests** on degraded land must

be prepared to design with these conditions in mind, and to follow through over the longer term.

Another dilemma facing restoration ecologists is their incomplete understanding of the ecology of the species they are working with, of the relationships among those species, and of the influence of non-living environmental factors. This lack of ecological knowledge is an important challenge to restoration ecologists.

A problem that must be dealt with in many situations is the fact that environmental conditions may have changed significantly, perhaps permanently, from those occurring originally. Under an altered environmental regime, it may not be feasible to restore original ecosystem types. Some alternative end-goals may have to be developed and pursued by restoration ecologists.

These various problems of restoration ecology are important, and the difficulties they engender should not be underestimated. However, the problems should be regarded as challenges, and not as reasons to refuse projects in restoration ecology. Enormous benefits can potentially be attained by successful restoration of the populations of endangered species or of threatened ecological communities. These gains involve the preservation of indigenous **biodiversity** values, the **conservation** of **ecological integrity**, and perhaps the protection of future resource opportunities for use by humans.

Programs of restoration ecology require an integrated application of ecological knowledge. Most activities in applied ecology focus on the exploitation and management of species and ecosystems for the direct benefit for humans, as occurs in agriculture, **forestry**, and fisheries management. In restoration ecology, however, the **exercise** in applied ecology is undertaken to achieve some natural benefit in terms of the preservation or conservation of biodiversity and environmental quality.

Restoration ecology is a severe test of our knowledge of ecological principles and of environmental influences on species and their communities. It takes an extraordinarily deep understanding of ecology to successfully convert degraded environments and ecosystems into self-maintaining populations and analogs of original natural communities.

Restoration, rehabilitation, and replacement

At the species level, the goal of restoration ecology is to develop sustainable populations of target species. At the community level, the goal is to rehabilitate or reconstruct an entire ecosystem, making it as similar as possible to an original natural ecosystem that has become endangered. Regrettably, for the reasons suggested previously, these desirable goals may not be achievable in some situations, and less lofty aspirations may have to be identified and pursued by restoration ecologists.

If the environment has been permanently degraded, for example, by the massive **erosion** of **soil** or the accumulation of persistent pollutants, the only achievable goal for restoration ecology might be to rehabilitate the site to some acceptable ecological condition. This could occur through the development of a community that is reasonably similar to an original type, even though not all native species can be accommodated and there are other important differences in the structure and function of the new ecosystem.

In even more degraded environments, the only attainable goal might be replacement, or the development of some acceptable new ecosystem on the managed site. The criteria for replacement might only be to achieve a stable, self-maintaining ecosystem on the site, using native species wherever possible. This is done to restore some degree of ecological integrity, natural aesthetics, recreational opportunity, and perhaps economically useful productivity such as forest or agricultural products.

Some successful examples of restoration ecology

The simplest applications of restoration ecology focus on the protection of populations of endangered species. In some cases, these efforts can succeed by only controlling the killing of the species by hunters. For example, on the west coast of North America, populations of the sea otter (*Enhydra lutris*) were badly overhunted during the fur trade of the 19th century, to the degree that the species was thought to be extinct. However, during the 1930s small populations of sea **otters** were discovered in the Aleutian Islands and off northern California. These animals were strictly protected, and their surplus production dispersed naturally to colonize other suitable habitat, a process that was aided by some longer-distance introductions by humans. The sea otter is no longer endangered.

Some other previously endangered species of North America whose populations were successfully enhanced mostly by controlling human-caused mortality include the **pronghorn** antelope (*Antilocapra americana*), American elk (*Cervus canadensis*), American beaver (*Castor canadensis*), Guadalupe fur seal (*Arctocephalus townsendi*), northern fur seal (*Callorhinus ursinus*), gray seal (*Halichoerus gryptus*), northern elephant seal (*Mirounga angustirostris*), and humpback whale (*Megaptera novaeangliae*). All of these species had been excessively exploited for their meat or fur, but then rebounded in abundance after hunting was stopped or strictly regulated.

Some other depleted species have been restored by controlling their mortality through hunting, while also protecting or enhancing their **critical habitat**. The **wood** duck (*Aix sponsa*), for example, was endangered by over-hunting for its meat and beautiful feathers, and by degradation of its habitat by the drainage of **wetlands** and timber harvesting. The species has now recovered substantially because of limits on hunting, the protection of some remaining swamps, and because of programs in which nest boxes are provided for this cavity-nesting species. These nest boxes have also benefited another rare duck, the hooded merganser (*Lophodytes cucullatus*). An unrelated nest-box program has been crucial in allowing some recovery of abundance of eastern and western **bluebirds** (*Siala sialis* and *S. mexicana*).

Other endangered species have benefited from programs of habitat management, coupled with their captive breeding and release to enhance wild populations or to reintroduce the species to suitable habitat from which it had been extirpated. The endangered whooping **crane** (*Grus americana*) has been managed in this way, and this has allowed its abundance to be increased from only 15 individuals in 1941 to 250 **birds** in 1993 (145 of those individuals were in captivity). Other examples of endangered species that have been enhanced in part by captive breeding and release programs include the eastern population of the peregrine falcon (*Falco peregrinus anatum*), trumpeter swan (*Olor buccinator*), wild turkey (*Meleagris gallopavo*), and pine marten (*Martes americana*).

Some other endangered species require active management of their habitat, which has become too fragmented and small in area to support the species, or has degraded for other reasons. A North American example of this type of management concerns the endangered Kirtland's warbler (*Dendroica kirtlandii*), which only breeds in even-aged stands of jack pine (*Pinus banksiana*) in Michigan. The availability of appropriate habitat for this bird is maintained by planting jack pine, and by the use of prescribed burning to develop the middle-aged stands that are optimal for the warbler. In addition, Kirtland's warbler has suffered badly from the depredations of a nest parasite, the brown-headed cowbird (*Molothrus ater*). Intense efforts must be made to reduce the population of the parasite within the breeding range of Kirtland's warbler, and to remove its eggs that may be laid in nests of the endangered species. These intensive efforts have allowed the small breeding population of Kirtland's warbler to be maintained. However, the species remains endangered, possibly because of habitat limitations on its wintering range, which appears to be in mountainous areas of Cuba.

In a few cases, restoration ecologists have focused not on particular endangered species, but on entire ecosystems. In such cases, restoration efforts initially involve the protection of remnant areas of endangered natural areas. This must be coupled with active management of the protected areas if this is required to avoid degradation of their ecological integrity. For example, tall-grass prairie is an endangered ecosystem which now exists in much less than 1% of its original extent in North America, almost all of the rest having been converted to agricultural land-use. Ecological reserves are being established to protect many of the last remnants of tall-grass prairie, but these must be managed properly if they are to remain in a healthy condition. In large part, the requirement for management is due to the fact that the environment of the tall-grass prairie is also capable of supporting shrubs or oak-dominated forest, and will do so unless successional processes are interrupted by occasional light fires. The burns are lethal to woody plants but are survived by the perennial, herbaceous species of the prairie. Historically, prairie fires would have been ignited naturally by lightning or by aboriginal hunters who were trying to maintain extensive habitat for the large **mammals** that they hunted. Today, the small remnants of tall-grass prairie that are protected in ecological reserves must be managed using prescribed burns.

The ultimate application of restoration ecology is in the reconstruction of reasonable facsimiles of natural ecosystems, beginning with some degraded condition of land or **water**. Because of its inherent difficulty, expense, and the need for a commitment over a long period of time, this approach has rarely been used. However, such reconstruction is necessary if highly endangered natural ecosystems and their dependent species are to be restored to a sustainable extent and abundance.

The best example of this intensive, bottom-up practice of restoration ecology is the reestablishment of prairie communities on land that has been used for agriculture for many decades. In such cases, it is assumed that the existing environment is still more-or-less suitable for the occurrence of prairie vegetation, and all that is needed is to reintroduce the component species and to manage their habitat until they can develop a self-maintaining ecosystem. One famous example of this practice is the restoration of prairie on agricultural land in Madison by botanists from the University of Wisconsin, beginning in 1934. The planting and management of these restored prairies has been difficult and time consuming, and great diligence was required to achieve success. Initially, the vigor and persistence of some of the introduced agricultural species, especially several blue-grasses (*Poa pratensis* and *P. compressa*), proved to be very troublesome. However, this management problem was overcome by the discovery that these **grasses** could not survive prescribed burns, while well-established prairie species could.

The successful reconstruction of fairly extensive, semi-natural prairie by dedicated and determined botanists

from the University of Wisconsin is a demonstration of the great ecological benefits that can be achieved through restoration ecology. However, this is also an illustration of the great difficulties that must be overcome to achieve these successes of restoring indigenous biodiversity. Although much can be accomplished by restoration ecologists, it is expensive and difficult for them to attain their goals, and successful rescues of endangered species and threatened ecosystems are not always possible.

Wherever feasible, it is much more preferable to preserve species and natural communities in large, self-organizing protected areas, which are capable of accommodating natural ecological dynamics and therefore do not require management by humans to maintain their integrity. This is by far the best pathway to the preservation of Earth's biodiversity.

See also Captive breeding and reintroduction; Sustainable development.

Further Reading

Begon, M., J. L. Harper, and C. R. Townsend. *Ecology. Individuals, Populations and Communities.* 2nd ed. London: Blackwell Sci. Pub., 1990.

Freedman, B. *Environmental Ecology.* 2nd. ed. San Diego: Academic Press, 1994.

Harris, J.A., P. Birch, and J. Palmer. *Land Restoration and Reclamation: Principles and Practice.* Addison-Wesley Publishing Co., 1997.

Urbanska, K.M., N.R. Webb, P.J. Edwards, and P.H. Enckell. (eds.) *Restoration Ecology and Sustainable Development.* Cambridge University Press, 1998.

Bill Freedman

Retrograde motion

Retrograde **motion** means "moving backward," and describes the loop or Z-shaped path that planets farther from the **Sun** than **Earth** appear to trace in the sky over the course of a few months. All the visible planets farther from the Sun than Earth (**Mars**, **Jupiter**, **Saturn**, and, for the eagle-eyed, **Uranus**) show retrograde motion. Planets appear to move from west to east relative to the stars, but if you carefully chart an outer planet's motion for several months you will notice it appear to stop, reverse direction for a few weeks, then stop again and resume its former west-to-east motion.

This is an optical illusion produced as the Earth, which orbits the Sun faster than any of the outer planets, catches up and passes them in its **orbit**. The changing line of sight from Earth to the **planet** makes it appear that the planet has stopped and begun to move back-

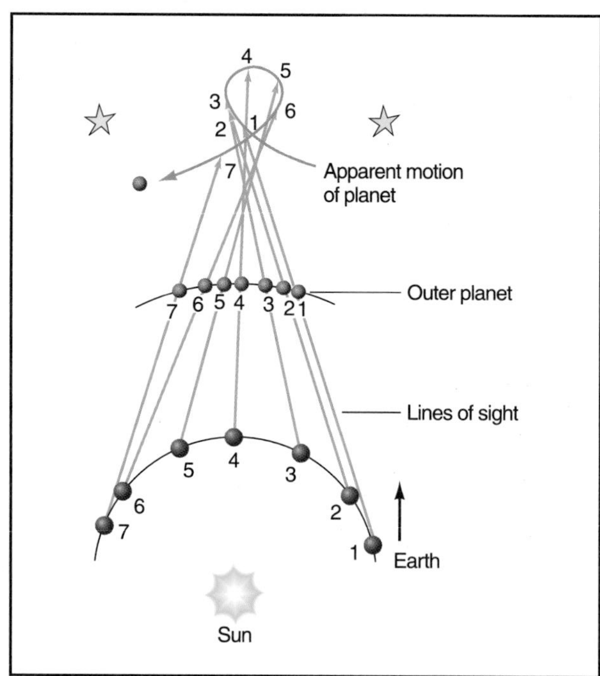

Figure 1.

wards, though it is still moving in its original direction. Retrograde motion of the planets confounded early astronomers such as Ptolemy (*ca.* 2nd century AD), who believed that Earth was at the center of the Universe. For such a system the planet indeed had to be going backwards, because the Earth was stationary. This changed when Nikolaus Copernicus (1473-1543) argued that Earth orbits the Sun like all the other planets, providing a more natural explanation for retrograde motion. Inner planets exhibit retrograde motion as well, as they catch up with and pass Earth, moving between it and the Sun.

You can see retrograde motion for yourself if you do this experiment. Have a friend stand 50 yards away and begin jogging in the direction shown. After 10 seconds, start running faster than your friend in the same direction. Watch your friend relative to some distant trees. As you catch up, your friend will appear to stop relative to the trees, move backwards, and then move forward again. Just like the planets, your friend is always going in the same direction, but relative to the trees the situation looks quite different! Because the effect described above is an optical illusion, it is sometimes called *apparent retrograde motion*. This distinguishes it from *true retrograde motion*, which is the revolution or **rotation** of an object in the **solar system** in a clockwise direction as seen from the north pole (i.e., looking "down" on the solar system). All the planets orbit the Sun in a counterclockwise direction as seen from the north pole, and this motion is called *prograde*. However, some of the satellites of the planets (such

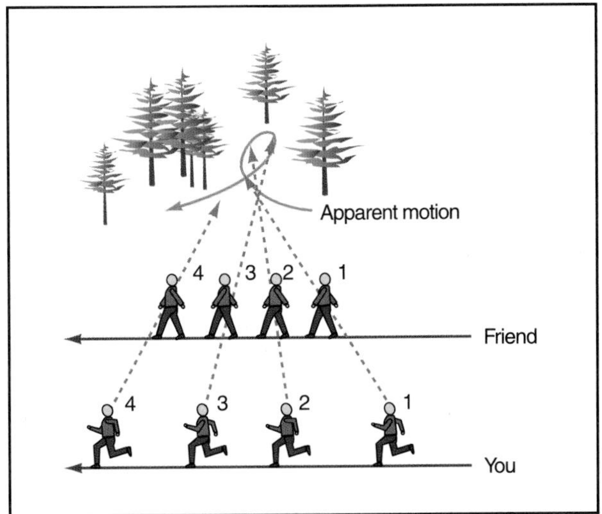

Figure 2.

as Phoebe, a **satellite** of Saturn, and Triton, the largest satellite of **Neptune**) orbit in a retrograde direction. And while Earth rotates about its axis in a prograde sense, **Venus**, Uranus, and **Pluto** exhibit retrograde rotation.

Retrovirus

Retroviruses are viruses in which the genetic material consists of **ribonucleic acid (RNA)** instead of the usual **deoxyribonucleic acid (DNA)**. So far, researchers have discovered only a handful of retroviruses that infect humans. Human immunodeficiency **virus** (HIV), the virus that causes acquired immune deficiency **syndrome (AIDS)**, is a retrovirus. Another human retrovirus, human T-cell leukemia virus (HTLV), was discovered three years prior to the discovery of HIV. Both HTLV and HIV attack human immune cells called **T cells**. T cells are the linchpin of the human immune response. When T cells are infected by these retroviruses, the **immune system** is disabled and several serious illnesses result. HTLV causes a fatal form of **cancer** called adult T-cell leukemia. HTLV **infection** of T cells changes the way the T cells work in the body, causing cancer. HIV infection of T cells, however, eventually kills T cells, rendering the immune system powerless to stave off infections from **microorganisms**.

How retroviruses infect cells

Retroviruses are sphere-shaped viruses that contain a single strand or a couple of strands of RNA. The sphere-shaped capsule of the virus consists of various **proteins**. The capsule is studded on the outside with proteins called receptor proteins. In HIV, these receptor proteins bind to special proteins on T cells called CD4 receptors. CD4 stands for "cluster of differentiation," and CD type 4 is found on specific T cells called helper cells. The human retroviruses discovered so far bind only to CD4 receptors, which makes their affinity for T helper cells highly specific.

The retrovirus receptor docks with a CD4 receptor on a T **cell**, and enters the T cell through the T cell **membrane**. Once inside, the retrovirus begins to replicate. But because the retrovirus's genetic material consists of RNA, not DNA, replication is more complicated in a retrovirus than it is for a virus that contains DNA.

In all living things, DNA is the template by which RNA is transcribed. DNA is a double-stranded **molecule** that is located within the nucleus of cells. Within the nucleus, DNA transcribes RNA, a single-stranded **nucleic acid**. The RNA leaves the nucleus through tiny pores and enters the cytoplasm, where it directs the synthesis of proteins. This process has been called the "central dogma" of genetic transcription. No life form has been found that violates this central dogma—except retroviruses. In retroviruses, the RNA is used to transcribe DNA, which is exactly opposite to the way genetic material is transcribed in all other living things. This reversal is why they are named retrograde, or backwards, viruses.

In addition to RNA, retroviruses contain an **enzyme** called reverse transcriptase. This is the enzyme that allows the retrovirus to make a DNA copy from RNA. Once this DNA copy is made, the DNA inserts itself into the T cell's DNA. The inserted DNA then begins to produce large numbers of viral RNA that are identical to the infecting virus's RNA. This "new" RNA is then transcribed into the proteins that make up the infecting retrovirus. In effect, the T cell is turned into a factory that produces more retroviruses. Because reverse transcriptase enzyme is unique to retroviruses, drugs that inhibit the action of this enzyme are used to treat retroviral infection, such as HIV. Reverse transcriptase is vital for retrovirus replication, but not for human cell replication. Therefore, modern reverse transcriptase inhibitor drugs are specific for retroviruses. Often, reverse transcriptase inhibitors are used in combination with other drugs to treat HIV infection.

Retroviruses are especially lethal to humans because they cause a permanent change in the T cell's DNA. Other viruses merely commandeer their host cell's cytoplasm and chemical resources to make more viruses; unlike retroviruses, they do not insert their DNA into the host cell's DNA. Nor do most viruses attack the body's T

cells. Therefore, most people's cells can recover from an attack from a virus: eventually, the body's immune system discovers the infection and neutralizes the viruses that have been produced. Any cells that contain viruses are not permanently changed by the viral infection. But because retroviruses affect a permanent change within important cells of the immune system, recovery from a retrovirus infection does not occur. All human retrovirus infections are lethal.

HTLV: a cancer-causing virus

In 1980, researchers headed by Robert Gallo at the National Cancer Institute discovered the first human retrovirus. They found the virus within leukemic T cells of patients with an aggressive form of T cell cancer. These patients were from the southern United States, Japan, and the Caribbean. Almost all patients with this form of cancer were found to have antibodies (immune system proteins made in response to an infection) to HTLV.

The cancer that afflicted these people is called adult T cell leukemia (ATL). ATL is characterized by skin lesions; enlargement of the liver, spleen, and lymph nodes; and disturbances of the central **nervous system**, lungs, and gastrointestinal tract. People with ATL may also develop a neurodegenerative disorder called tropical spastic paraparesis (TSP) (also called HTLV-associated myelopathy, HAM) in which the legs become progressively weak. Paralysis may result from this condition.

ATL is a fatal **disease**. The average length of survival, from the time of initial **diagnosis** to death, is only about 11 months. At this time, no treatment, except for symptomatic relief, is available.

HTLV infection is **endemic** in parts of **Asia**, **Africa**, **Europe**, and the western hemisphere. It is not particularly common in the United States. In the Japanese population, infection rates vary between 0% and 12% of the population. Furthermore, the rate of seropositivity (an indication of whether a person's **blood** tests positive for antibodies against the virus) in people without ATL rises from about 2% of the population of children aged 10, to 30% of the adult population aged 60. Transmission of HTLV may be the same as for HIV: sexual transmission; from mother to child in utero or through breast feeding; through blood transfusions; and through IV drug use. HTLV has been found in mother's milk and in semen. Given the mode of transmission, it's likely that one-third to one-half of people who live in endemic areas acquire the virus at some point during their lifetime. But unlike HIV infection, which virtually guarantees that a person will develop AIDS, infection with HTLV does not automatically lead to ATL.

HIV

HIV is perhaps the most famous retrovirus. Discovered independently by several researchers in 1983-1984, HIV is now known to be the causative agent of AIDS. People with AIDS test positive for HIV antibodies, and the virus itself has been isolated from people with the disease.

In the United States, AIDS was first recognized in 1981 in male homosexuals. In other countries, notably Africa, AIDS was noted in the 1970s and was (and is) primarily a disease transmitted through heterosexual intercourse. HIV antibody tests performed on stored blood samples taken from people in Uganda, Tanzania, Kenya, and the Ivory Coast revealed that 1-3% of the samples were positive for HIV. HIV is also transmitted through blood transfusions, IV drug use, in utero, and through breast feeding. About one million people in the Unites States are currently infected with HIV, and about 250,000 people have died from AIDS. The incidence of AIDS stemming from HIV infection is almost 100%.

HIV attacks T cells by docking with the CD4 receptor on its surface. Once inside the cell, HIV begins to transcribe its RNA into DNA, and the DNA is inserted into the T cell's DNA. However, new HIV is not released from the T cell right away. Instead, the virus stays latent within the cell, sometimes for 10 years or more. For reasons that are not yet clear, at some point the virus again becomes active within the T cell, and HIV particles are made within the cell. The new HIV particles bud out from the cell membrane and attack other T cells. Soon, all of the T cells of the body are infected and die. This infection cycle explains why very few virus particles are found in people with the HIV infection (those who do not yet have AIDS); many particles are found in people who have full-blown AIDS.

When a person is first infected with HIV, he or she may experience flu-like symptoms, such as a fever and lack of appetite. The lymph nodes may also swell. It takes about three months for antibodies against HIV to be detected in an HIV-antibody blood test. Most people with HIV infection experience no symptoms at all for several years. Then, some people develop AIDS-related complex, a series of symptoms that include swollen lymph nodes, fever, fatigue, malaise, lack of appetite, and diarrhea. At about 10 years after infection, AIDS develops.

AIDS is a syndrome, a constellation of diseases that is caused by one infectious agent. The diseases typical of AIDS are called opportunistic infections and reflect the disabling of the immune system that occurs with HIV infection of T cells. A normal, healthy immune system can stave off many infections, and a person does not even realize his or her immune system is under attack. In a person with AIDS, the immune system succumbs to a vari-

ety of infections, such as *Pneumocystis carinii* **pneumonia**, cytomegalovirus infection, and toxoplasmosis (a parasitic disease carried by **cats**).

No cure has yet been found for AIDS. Researchers are still unsure about many aspects of HIV infection, and research into the immune system is still a relatively new science. Several anti-retroviral drugs, such as AZT, ddI, and ddC, have been administered to people with AIDS. These drugs do not cure HIV infection; they merely postpone the development of AIDS. AIDS is invariably fatal.

Other retroviruses

Simian immunodeficiency virus (SIV) is the primate version of HIV. In fact, **monkeys** infected with SIV are used to test AIDS drugs for humans. Rous sarcoma virus (RSV) causes cancer in chickens and was the first retrovirus identified. Feline leukemia virus (FELV) causes feline leukemia in cats and is characterized by symptoms similar to AIDS. Feline leukemia is a serious disease that, like AIDS, is fatal. Unlike AIDS, a **vaccine** has been developed to prevent this disease.

Prevention

No cure exists for HTLV-related ATL or AIDS. Researchers are testing several vaccines against HIV, but so far, none have conveyed adequate protection. Prevention is the only way to avoid these diseases. Since both may be transmitted during sexual contact, using condoms and avoiding unsafe sexual practices in which blood, semen, or vaginal fluids are exchanged has been shown to be highly effective in preventing retrovirus transmission. Avoiding IV drug use or the sharing of needles is another way to prevent transmission. Blood transfusions in the United States and most developed countries are now safe from **contamination** with HIV, since all blood is tested for the presence of the virus. HTLV is not as large a threat in the United States as it is in areas endemic for the virus; it has been estimated that HTLV-infected blood donors constitute about 0.025% of all U.S. blood donors. Currently, the United States does not test its **blood supply** for HTLV.

KEY TERMS

Acquired immune deficiency syndrome (AIDS)—A set of life threatening, opportunistic infections that strike people who are infected with the retrovirus HIV.

Adult T cell leukemia (ATL)—A form of cancer caused by the retrovirus HTLV.

Antibody—Immune proteins made by the immune system in response to infection; tests can be developed that search for antibodies specific for a particular virus in the blood.

Deoxyribonucleic acid (DNA)—The basic genetic material of all cells; in the nucleus, DNA provides the template for the transcription of RNA.

Human immunodeficiency virus (HIV)—Retrovirus that causes AIDS.

Human T- cell leukemia virus (HTLV)—Retrovirus that causes ATL.

Ribonucleic acid (RNA)—Nucleic acid that is transcribed from DNA in the nucleus of cells; RNA functions in the synthesis of proteins in cells; also the genetic material of retroviruses.

Reverse transcriptase—The enzyme that allows a retrovirus to transcribe DNA from RNA.

Seropositive—Describes the condition in which one's blood tests "positive" for an antibody against a specific microorganism.

T cell—The linchpin of the human immune system; alerts the immune system that a microorganism has invaded the body; is the primary kind of cell infected by the retroviruses HIV and HTLV.

Transcription—The process in which a strand of RNA is made from strands of DNA; in retrovirus infection of T cells, transcription proceeds in the opposite direction, from RNA to DNA.

Further Reading

Boyles, Salynn, ed. "Evolutionary Link is Suggested for HIV-1." *AIDS Weekly* (13 Dec 1999).

Cullen, Bryan R., ed. *Human Retroviruses.* Oxford, NY: IRL Press at Oxford University Press, 1993.

Gallo, Robert. "The First Human Retrovirus." *Scientific American,* 255. (December 1986): 88.

Gallo, Robert. *Virus Hunting: AIDS, Cancer, and the Human Retrovirus: A Story of Scientific Discovery.* New York: Basic Books, 1991.

Gallo, Robert and Jay Gilbert, eds. *The Human Retroviruses.* San Diego: Academic Press, 1991.

Montagna, Richard. "HTLV: A New AIDS-like Threat." *Saturday Evening Post,* 261 (5) (July-August 1989): 82.

Volderbing, Paul A. "HIV, HTLV-1, and CD4+ Lymphocytes: Troubles in the Relationship." *Journal of the American Medical Association,* 271 (5) (2 February 1994): 392.

Zhang, Z., et. al. "Sexual Transmission and Propagation of SIV and HIV in Resting and Activated [CD4.sup.+] T Cells." *Science,* 286. (5443). (12 Nov 1999): 1353.

Kathleen Scogna

KEY TERMS

Cerebral edema—A condition in which fluid presses on the brain, causing severe pressure and compression.

Encephalopathy—A condition in which the brain swells.

pain relievers, such as acetaminophen, are recommended for children and teenagers. Although children represent the majority of Reye's syndrome patients, adults can also develop Reye's syndrome. Therefore, pain relief for cold and flu symptoms, as well as for other viral infections such as chicken pox and mumps, should be restricted to nonaspirin medications in both children and adults.

See also Acetylsalicylic acid.

Kathleen Scogna

Reye's syndrome

Reye's **syndrome** is a serious medical condition associated with viral **infection** and aspirin intake. It usually strikes children under age 18, most commonly those between the ages of five and 12. Symptoms of Reye's syndrome develop after the patient appears to have recovered from the initial viral infection. Symptoms include fatigue, irritability, and severe vomiting. Eventually, neurological symptoms such as delirium and **coma** may appear. One third of all Reye's syndrome patients die, usually from **heart** failure, gastrointestinal bleeding, kidney failure, or cerebral **edema** (a condition in which fluid presses on the **brain**, causing severe **pressure** and compression).

Reye's syndrome is a particularly serious **disease** because it causes severe liver damage and swelling of the brain, a condition called encephalopathy. Recovery from the illness is possible if it is diagnosed early. Even with early **diagnosis**, some patients who survive Reye's syndrome may have permanent neurological damage, although this damage can be subtle.

Reye's syndrome was discovered in 1963 by Dr. Ralph D. Reye. However, the connection between aspirin and viral infection was not made until the 1980s. In a study conducted by the Centers for Disease Control, 25 out of 27 children who developed Reye's syndrome after a bout with chicken pox had taken aspirin during their illness. In 140 of the children with chicken pox who had not taken aspirin, only 53 developed Reye's syndrome. Researchers are still unsure about the exact mechanism that causes aspirin to damage the liver and brain during viral infections. Some researchers suspect that aspirin inhibits key enzymes in the liver, leading to liver malfunction. However, why the combination of aspirin intake and viral infection may lead to Rye's syndrome has never been fully explained.

Since the early 1980s, public health officials and physicians have warned parents about giving children aspirin to reduce **pain** during viral infections. As a result of these warnings, the numbers of cases of Reye's syndrome have dropped significantly: in 1977, 500 cases were reported; in 1989, only 25 cases were reported. Nonaspirin

Rh factor

Rh **factor** is a **blood** protein that plays a critical role in some pregnancies. People without Rh factor are known as Rh negative, while people with the Rh factor are Rh positive. If a woman who is Rh negative is pregnant with a fetus who is Rh positive, her body will make antibodies against the fetus's blood. This can cause Rh disease, also known as hemolytic disease of the newborn, in the baby. In severe cases, Rh disease leads to **brain** damage and even death. Since 1968, a **vaccine** has existed to prevent the mother's body from making antibodies against the fetus's blood.

Importance of the Rh factor

Rh factor is an antigen found on the red blood cells of most people. Rh factor, like the blood types A, B, and O, is inherited from one's parents. A simple blood test can determine blood type, including the presence of the Rh factor. About 85% of white Americans and 95% of African Americans are Rh positive. A person's own health is not affected by the presence or absence of Rh factor.

Rh factor is important only during a pregnancy in which an Rh negative woman is carrying a fetus who might be Rh positive. This can occur when an Rh negative woman conceives a baby with an Rh positive man. The **gene** for Rh positive blood is dominant over the gene for Rh negative blood, so their baby will be Rh positive. If the Rh positive father also carries the gene for Rh negative blood, his babies have a 50% chance of inheriting Rh negative blood and a 50% chance of inheriting Rh positive blood. If both parents are Rh negative, their babies will always be Rh negative. In order to protect their future babies from Rh disease, all women of childbearing age should know their Rh status before becoming pregnant.

Rh factor in pregnancy

The danger of Rh disease begins when the mother's Rh negative blood is exposed to the baby's Rh positive

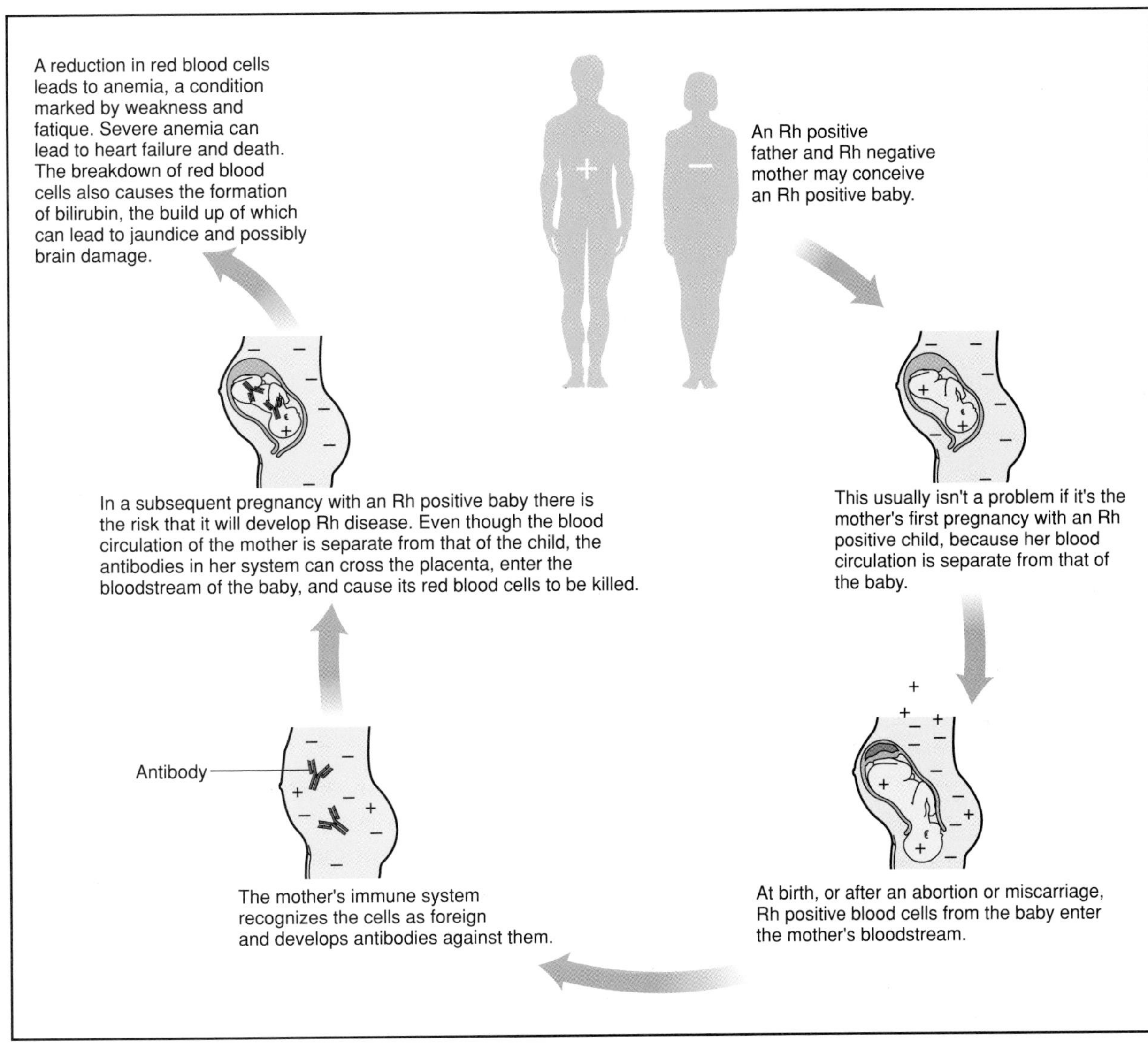
A reduction in red blood cells leads to anemia, a condition marked by weakness and fatique. Severe anemia can lead to heart failure and death. The breakdown of red blood cells also causes the formation of bilirubin, the build up of which can lead to jaundice and possibly brain damage.
An Rh positive father and Rh negative mother may conceive an Rh positive baby.
In a subsequent pregnancy with an Rh positive baby there is the risk that it will develop Rh disease. Even though the blood circulation of the mother is separate from that of the child, the antibodies in her system can cross the placenta, enter the bloodstream of the baby, and cause its red blood cells to be killed.
This usually isn't a problem if it's the mother's first pregnancy with an Rh positive child, because her blood circulation is separate from that of the baby.
Antibody
The mother's immune system recognizes the cells as foreign and develops antibodies against them.
At birth, or after an abortion or miscarriage, Rh positive blood cells from the baby enter the mother's bloodstream.

Rh disease.

blood. This mixing of blood occurs at the time of **birth**, and after an abortion or miscarriage. It is also apt to happen during prenatal tests like amniocentesis and **chorionic villus sampling**. More rarely, blood from the mother and fetus may mingle during pregnancy, before birth. When this contact between the two blood types occurs, the mother's body responds by building antibodies to fight the foreign Rh blood protein. The mother's blood is now said to be "sensitized" against Rh factor blood.

Once a mother's blood has become sensitized, her antibodies will attack the blood of any Rh positive fetus that she carries. The antibodies will destroy the fetus's red blood cells. If this happens, the infant will suffer from several serious conditions. It will become anemic, a condition caused by a reduction in red blood cells and marked by weakness and fatigue. Severe **anemia** can lead to **heart** failure and death. The breakdown of red blood cells will also cause the formation of a reddish-yellow substance known as bilirubin. An infant with high levels of bilirubin will look yellowish. This is known as **jaundice**. Brain damage can occur if the bilirubin level gets high enough. The disease caused by Rh incompatibility is called Rh disease, also known as hemolytic disease of the newborn or erythroblastosis fetalis.

Rh disease is usually not a problem during a first pregnancy. This is because the Rh negative mother probably will not become sensitized until her blood mixes with the baby's blood during birth. Her baby will be born before her blood can produce antibodies against the baby's Rh positive blood. Once a mother is sensitized, however, any future babies with Rh positive blood will be at risk for Rh disease.

Since 1968, a vaccine has existed to prevent sensitization from ever occurring. This is the best way to eliminate Rh disease. Available as an injection, the vaccine is called Rh immune globulin (brand name RhoGAM). It blocks the action of the antibodies and prevents the mother's blood from attacking the baby's blood. To be effective, the vaccine must be given any time fetal blood mixes with maternal blood: after birth, abortion, miscarriage, or prenatal tests like amniocentesis and chorionic villus sampling. The vaccine is typically given within 72 hours of any of these events. Since mixing of the blood may occur during the last three months of pregnancy, some health care providers recommend receiving the vaccine at 28 weeks of pregnancy.

Treatment for Rh disease

If a woman has become sensitized during a previous pregnancy, she can still take steps to prevent future babies who are Rh positive from developing Rh disease. Unfortunately, once a woman has the harmful antibodies in her blood, there is no way to remove them.

A pregnant woman who has already been sensitized from a previous pregnancy will want her doctor to carefully monitor the level of antibodies in her blood throughout her pregnancy. As long as the antibody levels remain relatively low, no problem exists. But if those levels rise, the fetus will need special attention. High antibody levels mean that the fetus's red blood cells are being attacked and destroyed.

A fetus whose red blood cells are being destroyed will need a blood transfusion while it is still in the uterus. Two or three transfusions may be necessary before the baby is born. If the fetus shows signs of illness close to its anticipated birth, the physician may elect to deliver the baby early, either through an induced birth or with a cesarean section. The baby will then receive a transfusion after birth.

Eliminating Rh disease

Until the introduction of the Rh immune globulin vaccine, Rh disease could not be prevented. About 45 babies per 10,000 births developed the disease each year before widespread use of the vaccine in the early 1970s. The number of newborns with Rh disease has dropped dramatically since the introduction of the vaccine, to about 10 per 10,000 in the early 1990s. The prevention of Rh disease is one of the triumphs of modern medicine.

Nevertheless, the number of newborns born in the United States each year with Rh disease is still relatively high. The disease is not completely eradicated. Further steps must be taken, since this is a preventable disease.

KEY TERMS

Bilirubin—Reddish-yellow substance formed by the breakdown of red blood cells.

Prenatal test—Procedure done to determine the presence of disease or defect in a fetus.

Sensitization—Occurs when a mother's blood produces antibodies against the blood of her Rh positive fetus.

The majority of cases of Rh disease are the result of women not receiving the vaccine at the appropriate time. Poor women without health insurance, who are likely to lack adequate prenatal care, are especially vulnerable to this oversight. Older women may have become sensitized before the vaccine was available. Foreign-born women may not have had access to the vaccine. With further diligence, health care providers hope to eradicate Rh disease.

See also Antibody and antigen.

Further Reading

Heins, Henry C. "Should You Worry About Rh Disease?" *American Baby.* (April 1992): 24.

March of Dimes Public Health Education Information Sheet *Planning for Pregnancy, Birth, and Beyond.* Washington, D.C.: American College of Obstetricians and Gynecologists, 1990.

Reuben, Carolyn. *The Health Baby Book.* New York: Jeremy P. Tarcher/Perigee Books, 1992.

Rich, Laurie A. *When Pregnancy Isn't Perfect.* New York: Dutton, 1991.

Liz Marshall

Rheas see **Ratites**

Rhenium see **Element, chemical**

Rhesus monkeys

Rhesus **monkeys** (*Macaca mulatta*) are **macaques** belonging to the primate family Cercopithecidae. These medium-sized monkeys are colored from golden-brown to gray-brown. Rhesus monkeys spend most their time on the ground, although they take to trees readily, and have great agility in climbing and leaping. Typical body weights range from 11-26.5 lb (5-12 kg) for adult male

rhesus monkeys, and from 9 to 24 lb (4-11 kg) for adult females. The facial skin of rhesus monkeys is light tan, while the skin of the rump becomes pink to reddish in adult females during estrus, when mating takes place.

Rhesus monkeys have the widest geographic distribution of any species of non-human primate, occurring naturally in Afghanistan, Pakistan, India, Nepal, Bhutan, Myanmar, Laos, Thailand, Vietnam, and China. In India, rhesus monkeys live in **desert** habitats of Rajasthan, the agricultural plains of the Gangetic **Basin**, the tropical **forests** of southeastern **Asia**, the temperate pine forests of the Himalaya mountains, and the rugged mountains of north central China. Rhesus monkeys are the most adaptable of all non-human primates, with the broadest range of **habitat**, and the most cosmopolitan food habits. These monkeys are generally herbivorous, eating a wide variety of natural and cultivated plants, but they also forage occasionally for **insects**. In agricultural areas, rhesus monkeys frequently raid both field **crops** such as **rice**, **wheat**, pulses (a leguminous, bean-like **plant**), and sugar cane, and garden **vegetables** and **fruits**, such as bananas, papayas, mangos, tomatoes, squash, and melons. In forest areas, rhesus monkeys feed on more than 100 different species of trees, vines and shrubs, on fruits, buds, young leaves, and even **bark** and roots, of species such as sheesham, ficus, and neem.

Rhesus monkeys are intensely social animals, living in groups of 10–60 individuals or more. An average group of 30 monkeys would have 4–5 adult males, 8–10 adult females, 6–8 infants (less than one year of age), and 8–10 juveniles (one to three or four years of age).

Both male and female rhesus monkeys have social hierarchies of dominance, established by aggressive **behavior** and social tradition. Once established, dominance is usually maintained by social gestures and communication. Young adult males often leave the groups in which they were born, wander independently, and attempt to enter other social groups. Females usually stay in their natal groups, forming consistent lineages and social traditions within the group.

Mating occurs throughout the year, but is most prevalent from September to December, and most young are born from March to June, after a gestation period averaging 164 days. Young monkeys are cared for intently by the mother for a year. Typically 60-80% of the adult females in a social group give **birth** to one young every year. Infants are weaned by about one year of age, and enter the juvenile period, in which they still retain an association with their mother, but also spend more time independently and with other juveniles. At this time, they are delightfully rambunctious in play with games of running, climbing, chasing, jumping, wrestling, and swimming.

A mother Rhesus monkey with her infant.

Sexual maturity is normally reached at about three and a half to four years of age for females, and between four and five years of age for males. Rhesus monkeys live up to 25 years, some even reach 30 years.

Forty years ago, the rhesus monkey population in India alone was about 2 million. Rhesus monkeys are used extensively in biomedical research, pharmaceutical testing, and **vaccine** production. Rhesus monkey populations declined drastically to under 200,000 in India, according to a three-year field census by the Zoological Survey of India, completed in the mid-1970s. In 1978, the government of India banned the export of rhesus monkeys, increased **conservation** programs, and improved food production in India. The rhesus monkey population in India has now increased to between 800,000 and 1 million.

Rhesus monkeys have been a mainstay of biomedical research in many areas of human **physiology**, **immunology**, and health, and they have also been used widely in psychological studies, especially of behavioral development, **learning**, and social adjustments. The

human **blood factor**, Rh, is named for the rhesus monkey, because our understanding of blood antigens was most clearly demonstrated in studies of these monkeys. Rhesus monkeys were used for the discovery, development, and testing of the polio vaccine. The use of rhesus monkeys in laboratory programs is opposed by some **animal** rights groups, but many scientists feel that the use of these animals is essential and justified given their uniquely valuable contributions for medical knowledge, so long as that use is humane. Virtually all rhesus monkeys used in biomedical or behavioral research in the United States are bred in colonies under close veterinary supervision, excellent conditions, and humane care.

In India, Nepal, and China, rhesus monkeys enjoy a deep cultural and religious affection, especially by people of Hindu and Buddhist faiths. Rhesus monkeys feature prominently in the Hindu epic story the *Ramayana*, in which rhesus monkeys enabled Rama (the incarnation of the god Vishnu, the embodiment of good) to defeat Ravana (the Devil King). Ravana had abducted Sita, Rama's wife, and taken her away to the **island** of Ceylon (Sri Lanka). Hanuman, the monkey god, and his troop of monkeys enabled Rama to find Sita and rescue her from the evil Ravana. Hanuman and his troop were actually langur monkeys, but rhesus monkeys also enjoy a sacred status in traditional Hinduism.

Rhesus monkeys have had a significant impact on human societies, particularly in the areas of science, culture, and **ecology**. The conservation and wise management of these valuable animals, and of all primates, should be a major priority throughout the world.

Further Reading

Hearn, J. P. "Conservation of Primate Species Studied in Biomedical Research." *American Journal of Primatology.* 34, No. 1 (1994): 1-108.

Lindburg, D. G. "The Rhesus Monkey in North India: An Ecological and Behavioral Study." In *Primate Behavior: Developments in Field and Laboratory Research.* L. A. Rosenblum. New York: Academic Press, 1971.

Southwick, C. H., and M. F. Siddiqi. "Population Status of Primates in Asia, with Emphasis on Rhesus Macaques in India." *American Journal of Primatology.* 34 (1994): 51-59.

Charles H. Southwick

Rheumatic fever

Rheumatic fever is a rare complication that occurs after an **infection** with *Streptococcus pyogenes* bacteria. The most common type of *S. pyogenes* infection is "strep throat," in which the tissues that line the pharynx become infected with the **bacteria**. Rheumatic fever does not occur if the initial strep infection is treated with **antibiotics**. Major symptoms of rheumatic fever include infection of the protective layers of the **heart**; **arthritis** (an **inflammation** of the joints), skin rashes, and chorea (a condition characterized by abrupt, purposeless movements of the face, hands, and feet). Rheumatic fever is treated with antibiotics, but recurrences are common. To prevent recurrences, preventive antibiotic therapy is administered for at least three years after an initial occurrence.

Rheumatic fever occurs most frequently among the poor in large cities, perhaps because this segment of the population does not have access to health care and is not treated promptly for strep infections. Rheumatic fever is also common in developing countries without access to antibiotics.

Cause of rheumatic fever

Rheumatic fever occurs as a result of a primary infection with *Streptococcus pyogenes*. If the infection is not treated, the body's **immune system** starts to overreact to the presence of the bacteria in the body. Illnesses caused by such overreactions of the immune system are called hypersensitive reactions. Some of the symptoms of rheumatic fever, particularly the involvement of the heart, are thought to be caused by the hypersensitive reactions. Other symptoms may be caused by the release of toxins from the *S. pyogenes* bacteria that are spread to other parts of the body through the bloodstream.

Not all strains of *S. pyogenes* cause rheumatic fever; only certain strains of *S. pyogenes*, called the M strains, have been implicated in cases of rheumatic fever. In addition, not everyone infected with these strains of *S. pyogenes* will progress to rheumatic fever. Individuals with a specific type of antigen (an immune protein) on their immune cells, called the human leukocyte antigen (HLA), are predisposed to develop rheumatic fever following an untreated strep infection. The specific type of HLA antigen that predisposes a person to develop rheumatic fever is called the class II HLA. These individuals develop their susceptibility during early childhood. Children under two years of age rarely contract rheumatic fever; the incidence of the disease increases during childhood from ages five to 15 and then decreases again in early adulthood. Researchers are not sure about the exact mechanism that leads to susceptibility or the role that the class II antigen plays in susceptibility to rheumatic fever.

Signs and symptoms of rheumatic fever

Rheumatic fever can be difficult to diagnose because the signs and symptoms are diverse. In order to simplify **diagnosis**, rheumatic fever is indicated if a person has

two major manifestations of rheumatic fever, or one major manifestation and two minor manifestations. In both cases, evidence of strep infection is also necessary.

Major signs of rheumatic fever

The most common sign of rheumatic fever is arthritis, or inflammation of the joints. Arthritis occurs in 75% of rheumatic fever patients. The arthritis is extremely painful and involves the larger joints of the body, such as the knee, elbow, wrist, and ankle. Symptoms include tenderness, warmth, severe **pain**, and redness. The inflammation resolves by itself in two to three weeks with no lasting effects.

Another common sign of rheumatic fever is carditis, or infection of the linings of the heart. Carditis occurs in 40-50% of patients. Often, the aortic (the valve that connects the left ventricle of the heart to the aorta) and mitral (the valve that connects the left atrium and left ventricle) valves become scarred, leading to a condition called stenosis. In stenosis, the delicate leaflets that make up the valve weld together. The valve is essentially "frozen" shut, obstructing the flow of **blood** through the heart. Carditis and stenosis cause few symptoms but are serious manifestations of rheumatic fever. If the carditis is severe, it may lead to heart failure. Congestive heart failure, in which the heart gradually loses its ability to pump blood, occurs in 5-10% of patients with rheumatic fever.

The third most common sign of rheumatic fever occurring in 15% of patients is chorea, in which the face, hands, and feet move in a rapid, non-purposeful way. Patients with chorea may also laugh or cry at unexpected moments. Chorea disappears within a few weeks or months, but is a particularly distressing sign of rheumatic fever.

The least common sign of rheumatic fever occurring in less than 10% of patients is the appearance of subcutaneous (under the skin) nodules. These nodules are painless and localize over the bones and joints. Nodules may last about a month before they disappear. A skin rash called erythema marginatum is also a sign of rheumatic fever. The rash is ring-shaped and painless, and may persist for hours or days and then recur.

Minor signs of rheumatic fever

Typical minor signs of rheumatic fever include fever, joint pain, prior history of rheumatic fever, and laboratory evidence of a hypersensitive immune response to strep bacteria.

Treatment and prevention

Rheumatic fever is treated primarily with antibiotics. In severe cases of carditis, corticosteroids may be used to reduce inflammation. Because rheumatic fever tends to recur, patients must continue antibiotic therapy in order to prevent subsequent strep infections. Typically, this preventive antibiotic therapy should last for three to five years after the initial infection. Some researchers recommend that preventive antibiotics be administered until early adulthood.

Aspirin is useful in treating arthritis caused by rheumatic fever. In fact, if arthritic symptoms respond particularly well to aspirin, the diagnosis of rheumatic fever is strengthened.

Rheumatic fever can be prevented entirely if strep infections are diagnosed correctly and antibiotic treatment is initiated within 10 days of onset. A severe sore throat that is red and swollen, accompanied by fever and general fatigue, should be examined by a physician and tested for the presence of strep bacteria. Patients diagnosed with strep throat must be sure to take their full course of antibiotics, as incompletely healed infections may also lead to rheumatic fever.

KEY TERMS

Antibiotic—A drug that targets and kills bacteria.

Antigen—Immune proteins that identify cells; for instance, a bacterium has a typical set of antigens that identify it as a bacterium.

Aortic stenosis—The welding of the leaflets of the valve that connects the left ventricle to the aorta.

Arthritis—Inflammation of the joints.

Carditis—Infection of the protective layers of the heart.

Chorea—Rapid, random movements of the face, hands, and feet.

Human leukocyte antigen—A type of antigen present on white blood cells; divided into several distinct classes; each individual has one of these distinct classes present on their white blood cells.

Hypersensitive reaction—An immune reaction in which the body's immune system overreacts to the presence of antigens in the body; may lead to disease.

Mitral stenosis—The welding of the leaflets that make up the mitral valve of the heart.

Further Reading

Dinsmoor, Robert. "Watch your Strep." *Current Health 2*.20 (7): 14, March 1994.

Fischetti, Vincent A. "Streptococcal M Protein." *Scientific American.* 244 (6): 58, June 1991.

"Guidelines for the Diagnosis of Rheumatic Fever: Jones Criteria," 1992 update. *Journal of the American Medical Association.* 268 (15): 2069, October 21, 1992.

Guthrie, Robert. "Streptococcal Pharyngitis." *American Family Physician.* 42 (6): 1558, December 1990.

Harrington, John T. "My Three Valves." *New England Journal of Medicine.* 328 (18): 1345, May 6, 1993.

Kathleen Scogna

Rhinoceros

Rhinos are heavily built, thick-skinned, herbivorous **mammals** with one or two horns, and three toes on each foot. The family Rhinocerotidae includes five species found in **Asia** or **Africa**, all of which are threatened by **extinction**.

The two-ton, one-horned Great Indian rhinoceroses (*Rhinoceros unicornis*) is a shy and inoffensive **animal** that seldom acts aggressively. This rhino was once abundant in Pakistan, northern India, Nepal, Bangladesh, and Bhutan. Today there are about 2,000 Great Indian rhinos left in two reserves, located in Assam, India, and in southern Nepal.

The smaller, one-horned Javan rhinoceros (*Rhinoceros sondaicus*) is the only species in which the females are hornless. Javan rhinos once ranged throughout southeast Asia, but are now on the edge of extinction, with only about 65 individuals remaining in reserves in Java and Vietnam.

The Sumatran rhinoceros (*Didermocerus sumatrensis*) is the smallest species of rhino. It has two horns and a hairy hide. There are two subspecies: *D. s. sumatrensis* of Sumatra and Borneo, and *D. s. lasiotis* of Thailand, Malaysia, and Burma. Sumatran rhinos are found in hilly jungle and once coexisted in southeast Asia with Javan rhinos. Only about 700 Sumatran rhinos still exist.

The two-horned white, or square-lipped, rhinoceros (*Ceratotherium simum*) of the African **savanna** is the second-largest land mammal (after the African **elephant**). It stands 7 ft (2 m) at the shoulder, and weighs more than 3 tons (2,700 kg). White rhinos have a wide upper lip, useful for grazing. There are two subspecies: the northern white rhino (*C. s. cottoni*) and the southern white rhino (*C. s. simum*). Once common in Sudan, Uganda, and Zaire, northern white rhinos are now extremely rare, with only 40 individuals left (28 in Zaire, the rest in zoos). Southern white rhinos are doing somewhat better, with 4,800 individuals left in the wild, and are the world's most abundant rhino.

A white rhinoceros. There are two subspecies of white rhinoceros in Africa. The northern white rhinoceros is found only in Zaire and is a critically endangered subspecies. The southern subspecies is found in South Africa, Botswana, Zimbabwe, Namibia, Swaziland, Kenya, Mozambique, and Zambia.

The smaller, two-horned black rhinoceros (*Diceros bicornis*) has a pointed upper lip for browsing on leaves and twigs. Black rhinos (which are actually dark brown) can be aggressive but their poor eyesight makes for blundering charges. Black rhinos were once common throughout sub-Saharan Africa, but now are found only in Kenya, Zimbabwe, Namibia, and South Africa. In the late 1990s there were fewer than 1,000 black rhinos left in the wild, compared to 100,000 only 35 years previously.

Widespread poaching has caused crashes in the populations of all species of rhinos. These animals are slaughtered for their horn, which is made of hardened, compressed, hair-like fibers. The horn sells for extremely high prices. In Asia, rhino horn is prized for its supposed medicinal properties, and powdered horn can fetch $12,700 per lb ($28,000 per kg). Rhino horn is also valuable for sale in Yemen, where it is used to make traditional dagger-handles. Because their horns are so valuable, rhinos have been over-hunted throughout their range. They now survive only where there is strict protection from poachers.

Captive-breeding programs for endangered rhinos are hindered by the general lack of breeding success for these animals in zoos, and a slow reproduction rate of only one calf every 3-5 years. The present world rhino population of less than 10,000 is much smaller than half the estimated "safe" long-term survival number of 22,500.

Further Reading

Cunningham, C. and J. Berger. *Horn of Darkness: Rhinos on the Edge.* Oxford University Press, 1997

Watt, E.M. *Black Rhinoceros.* Raintree/Steck Vaughan, 1998.

Rhizome

A rhizome is a root-like, underground stem, growing horizontally on or just under the surface of the ground, and capable of producing shoots and roots from its nodes. Rhizomes are most commonly produced by perennial, herbaceous species of plants, that die back to the ground at the end of the growing season, and must grow a new shoot at the beginning of the next season. Rhizomes are capable of storing **energy**, usually as starch, which is used to fuel the regeneration of new shoots. Rhizomes are also sometimes called rootstocks.

Plant species that have well developed rhizomes often rely on these organs as a means of propagation. However, the regeneration of plants through the spreading of rhizomes and development of new shoots is a type of non-sexual, vegetative propagation, because the progeny are genetically identical to the parent. Horticulturalists take advantage of the ease of propagation of certain plants with rhizomes by using bud-containing segments of these organs to grow new plants. This is the major method by which many ornamental species, such as iris (*Iris* spp.), are propagated. Some agricultural plants are also propagated in this way, such as **sugarcane** (*Saccharum officinarum*), **arrowroot** (*Canna edulis*), **ginger** (*Zingiber officinale*), and **potato** (*Solanum tuberosa*). In the case of some agricultural species, the rhizome is also the harvested part of the plant. The potato, for example, has discrete, modified sections of its rhizomes, called tubers, that are modified to store starch. Potato tubers are, of course, an important agricultural product.

Some species of **tree** can regenerate extensively by issuing new vegetative shoots from their underground rhizomes, after damages caused by disturbance by fire or harvesting. In **North America**, trembling aspen (*Populus tremuloides*) can regenerate very effectively in this way, and stands dominated by genetically identical "trees" of this species can sometimes occupy an area of several to many hectares (up to 40 ha). These stands may represent the world's largest "individual" organisms, in terms of **biomass**.

See also Asexual reproduction; Corm; Root system.

Rhodium see **Element, chemical**
Rhododendron see **Heath family**

Rhubarb

Rhubarbs are several species of large-leaved, perennial, herbaceous plants in the **buckwheat** family (Polygonaceae). Rhubarbs originated in eastern **Asia** and were not cultivated in **Europe** until the nineteenth century. Rhubarbs have been used as medicinal plants, as food, and as garden ornamentals.

The initial uses of rhubarb were medicinal, for which both the medicinal rhubarb (*Rheum officinale*) and, to a lesser degree, the edible rhubarb (*R. rhaponticum*) are used. In China, the roots of rhubarb are dried and pulverized, and are used to treat various ailments. Rhubarb is commonly used as a laxative, to treat indigestion, and as a tonic. These were also the first uses of rhubarb in Europe, but later on it was discovered that the petioles, or leafstalks, of the **plant** are edible and tasty when properly prepared.

The edible part of the rhubarb is the petiole of the **leaf**, which is usually a bright-red color due to the presence of pigments known as anthocyanins. The actual leaf blade has concentrations of **oxalic acid** great enough to be considered poisonous, and is not eaten. Large doses of rhubarb leaf can cause convulsions and **coma**. Rhubarb petioles are extremely bitter because of their large content of organic acids, including oxalic and malic acids. The tartness of these acids can be neutralized by cooking rhubarb with a pinch of baking soda (**sodium** bicarbonate), and rhubarb is also usually sweetened with sugar or fruit before being eaten. Rhubarb is usually steamed or stewed to prepare it for eating, and it is often baked into pies or used as a component of jam and sauces.

Rhubarbs are commonly planted as an attractive, reddish-colored foliage plant in gardens. Various species are used for this purpose, including the Indian or China rhubarb (*R. palmatum*).

Ribbon worms

Ribbon worms, also called bootlace worms or proboscis worms, derive their common names from their threadlike or ribbonlike form, and from the characteristic reversible proboscis which they use in **prey** capture or in burrowing. The phylum Nemertea (or Rhynchocoela) includes approximately 900 described species of these worms. Most of them are marine, living in sand or mud, or under shells and **rocks**; a few are known from **freshwater** and terrestrial habitats. Many are brightly colored, especially red, orange, and yellow.

The body is either cylindrical or flat, unsegmented, and varies in length from a few centimeters to over 98 ft (30 m). Moreover, it is highly extensible, and can be stretched to many times its normal length. The proboscis

is located in a fluid-filled cavity. Increase in **pressure** of the fluid causes the proboscis to be inverted through an opening situated just above the mouth. Proboscis retraction is effected by means of a retractor muscle. In some species the proboscis is armed with a stylet. A ribbon worm's food consists of **segmented worms** and small crustaceans which are encountered and captured by trial and **error**. Whenever the worm is successful in this endeavor, the proboscis coils around the prey **organism**, and then is retracted to bring the food to the mouth. The digestive tube is straight and non-muscular, and movement of food in it occurs mainly by ciliary action. An anus is present at the posterior end.

In ribbon worms there is no cavity between the body wall and the gut; instead, the space is filled by a spongy **tissue** called parenchyma. (This "acoelomate" condition is found also in the flatworms.) Sexes are separate. An individual worm has multiple testes or ovaries, each with a separate opening to the outside. **Fertilization** is external. In most species, the zygote develops into a ciliated, helmet-shaped larval form called pilidium. Most nemerteans also possess remarkable powers of regeneration, which can be an important means of **asexual reproduction**. Representative genera of ribbon worms include *Cerebratulus*, *Lineus*, and *Tubulanus*.

Ribonuclease

Ribonuclease (RNase) is the name of a group of enzymes that change **ribonucleic acid (RNA)** by digesting (cutting) phosphorus-**oxygen** bonds. The RNases are the subject of wide investigation in the laboratory, though scientists are still **learning** the many ways they work in living cells.

The best-studied RNase is from the pancreas of cattle. Its main portion, called ribonuclease A, was the first **enzyme** whose entire sequence of amino acids was determined. It was also the first protein to be totally synthesized from **amino acid**.

Pancreatic ribonuclease was first described in 1920 by the American biochemist Walter Jones (1865-1935), who showed that it could digest **yeast** RNA. It was partially purified in 1938 by the American microbiologist René Jules Dubos (1901-1982) and isolated in crystalline form late two years later by M. Kunitz. RNase's sequence and three-dimensional structure were determined in 1962 by the American biochemists Christian Anfinsen (1916-), Stanford Moore (1913-1982), and William H. Stein (1911-1980), who received the 1972 Nobel Prize in **chemistry** for the accomplishment.

Anfinsen was born in Monessen, Pennsylvania, received his Ph.D. in **biochemistry** from Harvard University in 1943, and joined the staff of the National Institutes of Health. He wanted to learn how the peptide (protein) chain was instructed to fold into its three-dimensional shape. By discovering the amino acid sequence in parts of the **molecule**, he showed that the sequence itself was all the information needed for folding.

Stein and Moore performed their sequencing work at Rockefeller University. Stein, from New York City, received a Ph.D. from Columbia University in 1938. Moore was born in Chicago, grew up in Nashville, Tennessee, and earned a Ph.D. in organic chemistry from the University of Wisconsin in 1938. The two scientists wanted to learn how ribonuclease's structure was related to its activity. An active site is the portion of the enzyme that binds to the reacting substance (the substrate). First Stein and Moore discovered that the amino acids at the active site—were much more active in the molecule than in free form. They discovered how to chemically identify the active amino acids within the chain, and finally, determined the entire amino acid sequence.

In 1968, ribonuclease was synthesized by two different methods. Ralph Hirschmann (1922-) at Merck Sharp and Dohme Inc. Research Laboratories synthesized individual **proteins** and then chained them together. Bruce Merrifield (1921-), at Rockefeller University, automated the synthesis process by attaching the amino acids one by one to a solid plastic **matrix**, which eliminated intermediate steps. For developing this process, Merrifield received the 1984 Nobel Prize in chemistry.

In the living **cell**, RNases may break down RNA that has served its purpose, so that the components can be used again. Or RNases may play a part in forming an RNA molecule for a specific purpose, such as messenger RNA and ribosomal RNA. The roles of other RNases are still unknown.

Some RNases act only on specific groups, such as pyrimidine bases. Some RNases work only on specific RNA structures. Exoribonucleases act only the free ends of RNA molecules; endoribonucleases work elsewhere in the molecule. Some RNases work on RNA from the 5' to 3' direction, others from 3' to 5' (3' and 5' are locations where nucleotide bases attach to phosphates and sugars).

Ribonuclease P requires an RNA component in order to be active. Its discovery in the late 1970s by the American biophysicist Sidney Altman (1939-) earned him part of the 1989 Nobel prize in chemistry. RNase H functions by breaking down a copy of the RNA molecule when it is no longer needed for viral reproduction. It is a

component of reverse transcriptase, made by retroviruses (viruses with RNA genetic material).

Mammals' cells also produce RNase inhibitors, which keep RNases from breaking down RNA molecules.

Ribonucleic acid (RNA)

Ribonucleic acid, generally abbreviated RNA, is an organic chemical substance in living cells that plays several essential roles in the transfer of genetic information from one generation to the next. The hereditary information itself is contained in a similar organic substance known as **deoxyribonucleic acid** (DNA). RNA is what enables this genetic information to be copied from the parent's DNA and inherited by the offspring.

Both RNA and DNA are nucleic acids, so called because they are found in **cell** nuclei. (RNA is also found in other parts of the cell.) Nucleic acids are the storehouse and delivery system of our genetic traits. The actual biological processes that they prescribe are carried out mostly by our proteins-our enzymes, **hormones**, and muscles. In other words, nucleic acids are the instruction manual for life's protein-built operating equipment.

Nucleic acids consist of high-molecular-weight **polymer** molecules or macromolecules (macro- means long or large), which are made up of hundreds or thousands of smaller **monomer** molecules called nucleotides, all bound together. Each nucleotide monomer **molecule** consists of a sugar part, a phosphate part, and an amine part. The main difference between RNA and DNA is that in RNA the sugar is ribose ($C_5H_{10}O_5$), while in DNA it is deoxyribose ($C_5H_{10}O_4$). The prefix "deoxy-" tells us that one **oxygen** atom is "missing" from the ribose.

Like other nucleic acids, RNA is built up from the nucleotides in much the same way that **proteins** are built up from amino acids; they even coil up into long spirals, as some protein molecules do. In a long **nucleic acid** polymerspiral, the backbone consists of alternating sugar and phosphate parts, with the amine parts sticking out like branches from the backbone.

In the figure, the coiled backbone has been stretched out into a zigzag line, like an overstretched slinky. In the figure, S stands for a sugar part and P stands for a phosphate part. As to the amine parts (which are also referred to as bases), there are only four that are important in RNA: adenine, cytosine, guanine, and uracil. Scientists symbolize them as A, C, G, and U. DNA contains thymine instead of uracil: T instead of U.

The story of RNA

Our knowledge of the **chemistry** of the living cell's nucleus began in 1869, when Friedrich Miescher (1844-95) separated nuclei from the other parts of the cells and isolated from the nuclei some phosphorus-containing substances that we now call nucleic acids. It was later found that there were two kinds of nucleic acids, according to the amines, or bases, that they can be broken down into. One kind, obtained from **animal glands** and now called DNA, could be broken down into adenine, cytosine, guanine, and thymine, while the other kind, obtained from **yeast** cells and now called RNA, produced adenine, cytosine, guanine, and uracil. It was not until the 1940s that biochemists realized that both DNA and RNA are present in all living cells, whether **plant** or animal. Although DNA is present only in the nuclei, RNA is found also in the cytoplasm-the protoplasm outside the nuclei.

From then on, our knowledge of the role of RNA in living cells depended on advances in our understanding of DNA. In 1953, James D. Watson (1928-) and Francis H. C. Crick (1916-) put together the results of their own experiments and those of many other researchers, and concluded that the molecular structure of DNA must be a **double helix**: two long molecular threads or strands, twisted around each other. Based on that structure, they suggested a copying mechanism for the genetic information that the DNA contains. RNA appeared to be the prime candidate for the job of reading and translating the genetic information that the DNA contains. At first, it was thought that there was only one kind of RNA, but dozens of kinds with specialized functions are now known.

How RNA works

In DNA, all the information about inherited characteristics exists in the form of genes-arrangements of the four amines in a specific order on a DNA molecule-just as the words in a sentence must be arranged in a specific order if they are to convey real information instead of nonsense. These **sequences** of amine "words" constitute a set of instructions for exactly which proteins must be manufactured in order to create a specific trait-either brown eyes or green eyes in a human, or a muscle cell for a lizard's tail or a **brain** cell for an **elephant**. RNA is what translates these instructions into action.

In order for the genetic instructions to be carried out, at least three things must happen: someone or something must read off the amine sequences in the DNA molecule and write them down; then someone or something must deliver these instructions to the protein factory; and final-

Molecular structure of RNA.

ly, someone or something must collect all the right **amino acid** parts that are to be assembled into the finished proteins. Different kinds of RNA provide these services.

One kind of RNA "writes down" or transcribes the DNA's amine sequence onto its own molecule, like writing crib notes on the back of your hand. Then, a *messenger RNA* takes these instructions out of the nucleus and delivers them to the *ribosomes*—the cells' protein factories. Finally, *transfer RNA* collects the necessary amino acids and transfers them to the **ribosomes** for assembly into proteins. All of these processes are made possible by specific *enzymes*—chemicals that speed up vital chemical reactions in living things, making them go millions of times faster than they would otherwise.

It may sound as if the RNA molecules are thinking, but of course they are not. They do all of these jobs through highly specific match-ups between the shapes and atomic groupings of various nucleic acid molecules. When a certain job needs to be done, an appropriate service molecule is handy that exactly matches a part of the needy molecule, and so it reacts with it.

In the first step of the gene-transmitting process, the DNA's double helix unwinds to produce two separated strands with their amines sticking out from the backbones. These strands of DNA then serve as an exposed pattern for the production of matching strands of RNA. That is, each protruding amine on the DNA strand picks up a partner amine to bond to according to its highly selective preference: cytosine and guanine (C and G) will always bond together, while adenine and thymine (A and T) will always bond together. In this way, a strand of RNA is built up (with Us instead of Ts) that is exactly *complementary* to the amine sequence on the DNA: it has Gs where the Cs were and *vice versa*, and it has As where the Ts were and Us where the As were. Similarly, if you hold a book up to a mirror, the image in the mirror will be complementary to the actual writing on the page. All of the information is still there, but it has been *transcribed*, or re-written, into a complementary or matching form. This first step of the process is therefore called *transcription*.

In the next step of the gene-transmitting process, the information in the RNA strand is edited or streamlined to produce a strand of *messenger RNA* (mRNA) that is capable of escaping from the nucleus and carrying the essential genetic information to the ribosomes, which are out in the cell's cytoplasm.

In the cytoplasm are several kinds of smaller RNA molecules called *transfer RNA* (tRNA), which are swimming around in the pool of amino acids and other chemicals that surround the ribosomes. In the pool, each of these tRNA molecules carries around—is attached to—one particular kind of amino acid molecule, waiting to fill an order from the mRNA. The tRNA molecules read the instructions on the mRNA, and wherever the mRNA needs a particular amino acid, the corresponding tRNA molecule drags its attached amino acid into the protein factory. Thus the desired proteins are built up from the proper amino acids.

By these miraculous but purely chemical processes, each new generation inherits the exact kinds of proteins that are needed to make all the specific enzymes, hormones and cells in all the organs of all the plants and animals on **Earth**, from microbe to man.

KEY TERMS

Cytoplasm—All the protoplasm in a living cell that is located outside of the nucleus, as distinguished from *nucleoplasm*, which is the protoplasm in the nucleus.

Gene—A specific sequence of amines, or bases, on a DNA molecule. The sequence is a code for the production of a specific kind of protein or RNA molecule, and therefore for a specific inherited characteristic.

Nucleus—The part of a living cell that is enclosed within a membrane and that contains all the genetic information in the form of DNA.

Protoplasm—The thick, semi-fluid, semi-transparent substance that is the basic living matter in all plant and animal cells.

Further Reading

Amend, John R., Bradford P. Mundy, and Melvin T. Arnold, *General, Organic and Biological Chemistry.* Philadelphia: Saunders, 1990.

Berg, Paul, and Maxine Singer, *Dealing with Genes—the Language of Heredity.* Mill Valley, CA: University Science Press, 1992.

Darnell, James E., "RNA." *Scientific American.* Oct. 1985.

Robert L. Wolke

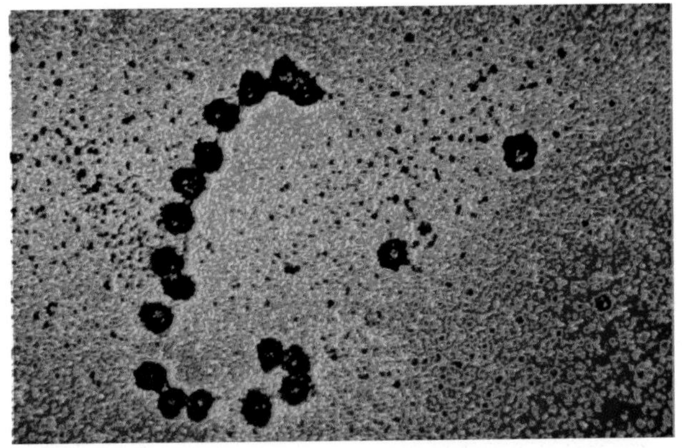

Ribosomes translating MRNA strand to produce proteins.

ribosomal RNA (rRNA). During translation, the two separate subunits of a ribosome clasp around a single mRNA **molecule**. As the ribosome reads the information, it slides along the length of the mRNA molecule until it reaches the end and drops off, leaving the finished protein product. Messenger RNA molecules that have many ribosomes attached to them simultaneously, called polysomes, are formed when multiple protein products are produced from the same mRNA molecule. Ribosomes are found existing free within the cytosol, or as attached structures of the rough endoplasmic reticulum, the organelle which modifies and refines non-functional proteins into functional ones.

Terry Watkins

Ribosomes

Ribosomes are protein manufacturers within cells. Huge molecules of DNA, or deoxyribonucleic acid, coiled within the chromosomes of every living **organism** use a universal language called the genetic code. Employed by all cells in the same fashion, the information encoded in DNA acts as a set of instructions for the synthesis of vital protein molecules. Cells assemble thousands of different kinds of **proteins** using the information within DNA. To construct an analogy, if a single **cell** were a kitchen, DNA would be a master cookbook and protein molecules would be the meals prepared using the cookbook. In this cellular kitchen, then, ribosomes are the molecular chefs.

The protein molecules made are not directly constructed from DNA. They are synthesized by ribosomes, which use messenger ribonucleic acid (mRNA) molecules as guides. Constructed by copying portions of DNA in chromosomes, mRNA molecules are able to leave the nucleus of the cell and go to the site of protein synthesis in the cytosol (or cytoplasm). Once in the cytosol, the process of interpreting the recipe of DNA into protein involves two phases. The first is called transcription. Transcription creates the mRNA copy of a **gene** to be expressed. The process is like creating many photocopies of a portion of DNA that can then be sent elsewhere in the cell.

The second process, called translation, directly involves ribosomes, which interpret the "photocopied" information of mRNA molecules. Like barcode scanners in grocery store check-out registers that interpret the black and white UPC code bars of products, ribosomes "read" nucleotide **sequences** of mRNA and construct protein molecules from amino acids using the encoded information.

Ribosomes are composed of two parts, a large subunit and a small subunit. Additionally, ribosomes contain a distinct kind of RNA found only in ribosomes, called

Rice

Rice is a **species** of grass (family Poaceae) that is an extremely important cereal crop. Two species of rice are grown as food: *Oryza sativa* and *O. glaberrima*. The natural range of both these rice species is tropical **Asia**, although rice can also be cultivated in warm-temperate regions. Of the two species, *O. sativa* is much more widely grown. In addition, there are seven major varieties of *O. sativa* (and also a much larger number of minor varieties), variously cultivated on four continents, and each with slightly different characteristics. Rice varieties vary in height from less than 3 ft (1m) to over 15 ft (5 m) tall, and they also vary in other important respects.

Rice is usually cultivated as a semi-aquatic **plant** that is harvested once a year. Less commonly, there may be several **crops** per year, or the rice may be cultivated as an upland crop (that is, not in **water**). Flooded fields used for rice cultivation are sometimes known as "paddies." The portion of the rice plant that is eaten is the seed, called a grain (or caryopsis).

Rice feeds more people in the world than any other crop. The global production of rice was 656 billion tons (596 million metric tonnes) in 1999, cultivated over an area of 383 million acres (155 million ha). In the United States, 10.5 million-tons (9.6 million tonnes) were grown on 3.6 million acres (1.44 million ha).

Rice has been an extremely important plant in the development of many human cultures, being intimately intermingled in their economy, food resource, and society. For instance, rice plays an important role in Japanese culture. It is viewed as a symbol of health and abundance, is prominent in religious rituals and folklore, and even has deities associated with it. In fact, the emperor of Japan, ac-

cording to Shinto belief, is the mortal form of the god of the rice plant. Similar cultural aspects showing the importance of rice are seen in societies of India and other Asian nations. In western culture, including the United States, a familiar use for rice that reveals its prominence among grains is its use at weddings—the traditional throwing of rice grains at newlyweds after their matrimonial ceremony is a symbol of fertility, prosperity, and good luck.

Terry Watkins

Richter magnitude scale see **Earthquakes**

Rickettsia

Rickettsia are a group of **bacteria** that cause a number of serious human diseases, including the spotted fevers and **typhus**. Rod- or sphere-shaped, rickettsia lack both **flagella** (whip-like organs that allow bacteria to move) and pili (short, flagella-like projections that help bacteria adhere to host cells). Specific species of rickettsia include *Rickettsia rickettsii*, which causes the dangerous Rocky **Mountain** spotted fever; *R. akari*, which causes the relatively mild rickettsial pox; *R. prowazekii*, which causes the serious disease **epidemic** typhus; *R. typhi*, the cause of the more benign **endemic** or rat typhus; and *R. tsutsugamushi*, the cause of scrub typhus.

Rickettsial disease transmission

Rickettsia are transmitted to humans by **insects** such as ticks, **mites**, and chiggers. Usually the insect has acquired the bacteria from larger animals which they parasitize, such as **rats**, **mice**, and even humans. When an insect infected with rickettsia bites a human, the bacteria enter the bloodstream. From there, unlike most other bacteria which cause **infection** by adhering to cells, rickettsia enter specific human cells, where they reproduce. Eventually these host cells lyse (burst open), releasing more rickettsia into the bloodstream. Most rickettsial diseases are characterized by fever and a rash. Although all can be effectively cured with **antibiotics**, some of the rickettsial diseases, such as epidemic typhus and Rocky Mountain spotted fever, can be fatal if not treated promptly.

The spotted fevers

Rocky Mountain spotted fever is one of the most severe rickettsial diseases. First recognized in the Rocky Mountains, it has since been found to occur throughout the United States. The Centers for Disease Control report about 600-1,000 cases occurring annually, but this number may be underestimated due to underreporting. *Rickettsia rickettsii* are carried and transmitted by four species of the hard-shelled tick, all of which feed on humans, wild and domestic animals, and small **rodents**. When a tick feeds on an infected **animal**, the bacteria are transmitted to the tick, which can in turn infect other animals with its bite. Human-to-human transmission of *R. rickettsii* does not occur. Once inside the human bloodstream, the bacteria invade cells that line the small **blood** vessels.

The symptoms of Rocky Mountain spotted fever reflect the presence of bacteria inside blood vessel cells. Within two to 12 days of being bitten by an infected tick, the infected person experiences a severe headache, fever, and malaise. After about two to four days, a rash develops, first on the extremities, then the trunk. A characteristic sign of this disease is that the rash involves the soles of the feet and palms of the hands. If the disease is not treated with antibiotics, the infected blood vessel cells lyse, causing internal hemorrhage, blockage of the blood vessels, and eventual death of the cells. Shock, kidney failure, **heart** failure, and **stroke** may then occur. Rocky Mountain spotted fever is fatal if not treated.

A similar but milder disease is rickettsial pox, caused by *R. akari*. These bacteria are transmitted by mites which live preferentially on the common house mouse, only occasionally biting humans. Rickettsial pox is characterized by a rash that does not affect the palms or soles of the feet. The rash includes a lesion called an eschar-a sore that marks the spot of the infected mite bite. The mild course of this disease and the presence of the rash has sometimes led to its misdiagnosis as chicken pox, but the eschar clearly distinguishes rickettsial pox from chicken pox.

Outside of the United States, spotted fevers such as North Asian tick typhus, Queensland tick typhus, and boutonneuse fever are caused by other rickettsia species. As their names suggest, these diseases are found in **Asia**, Mongolia, and the Siberian region of Russia; in **Australia**; and in the Mediterranean region, **Africa**, and India, respectively. Symptoms of these spotted fevers resemble those of rickettsial pox. Although these spotted fevers share some of the symptoms of Rocky Mountain spotted fever, they are milder diseases and are usually not fatal.

Rickettsial typhus diseases

Three forms of typhus are also caused by rickettsia. Epidemic typhus is caused by *R. prowazekii*, a bacterium that is transmitted by the human body louse. Consequently, episodes of this disease occur when humans are brought into close contact with each other under unsanitary conditions. Endemic typhus and scrub typhus are

caused by *R. typhi* and *R. tsutsugamushi*, respectively. Transmitted by rat **fleas**, endemic typhus is a mild disease of fever, headache, and rash. Scrub typhus, named for its predilection for scrub habitats (although it has since been found to occur in **rain forests**, savannas, beaches, and deserts as well) is transmitted by chiggers. Unlike endemic typhus, scrub typhus is a serious disease that is fatal if not treated.

Nonpathogenic rickettsia

Not all rickettsia cause disease. Some species, such as *R. parkeri* and *R. montana,* normally live inside certain species of ticks and are harmless to the insect. These rickettsia are nonpathogenic (they do not cause disease) to humans as well.

Prevention

With the exception of epidemic typhus, no **vaccine** exists to prevent rickettsial infection. Prevention of these diseases should focus on the elimination of insect carriers with **insecticides** and wearing heavy clothing when going into areas in which rickettsial carriers dwell. For instance, appropriate clothing for a forest expedition should include boots, long-sleeved shirts, and long pants. Treating the skin with insect repellents is also recommended to prevent insect bites.

It is important to know how to remove a tick if one is found on the skin. It takes several hours from the time a rickettsia-infected tick attaches to the skin for the rickettsia to be transmitted to the human bloodstream, so removing a tick promptly is crucial. When removing a tick, be careful not to crush it, as crushing may release rickettsia that can contaminate the hands and fingers. Use tweezers to grasp the tick as close to the skin as possible, and then pull slowly away from the skin. Make sure the mouthparts are removed from the skin (sometimes the body of a tick will separate from the head as it is being pulled). Do not try to remove a tick with gasoline or try to **burn** a tick off the skin with a match. After the tick is removed, wash your hands immediately. If you cannot remove the tick yourself, seek medical help.

KEY TERMS

Pathogenic—Able to cause disease.

Rocky Mountain spotted fever—A disease caused by *Rickettsia ricketsii* transmitted by the hard-shelled tick. The disease is characterized by a fever and a rash that starts on the extremities, including the soles of the feet and palms of the hands.

Typhus—A disease caused by various species of *Rickettsia,* characterized by a fever, rash, and delirium. Typhus is transmitted by insects such as lice and chiggers. Two forms of typhus, epidemic disease and scrub typhus, are fatal if untreated.

Further Reading

Harden, Victoria Angela. *Rocky Mountain Spotted Fever: History of a Twentieth-Century Disease.* Baltimore: Johns Hopkins University Press, 1990.

Joklik, Wolfgang, et al. *Zinsser Microbiology.* 20th edition. Norwalk, CT: Appleton and Lange, 1992.

Miksanek, Tony. "An Independent Diagnosis." *Discover.* 14 (February 1993): 26.

National Institute of Allergy and Infectious Diseases. *Rocky Mountain Spotted Fever.* Bethesda, MD: U.S. Department of Health, Education, and Welfare, Public Health Service, National Institute of Health, National Institute of Allergy and Infectious Diseases, Office of Reporting and Public Response, 1975.

Petri, William Jr. "Tick-borne Diseases." *American Family Physician.* 37 (June 1988): 95-105.

Salgo, Miklos P., et al. "A Focus of Rocky Mountain Spotted Fever within New York City." *The New England Journal of Medicine.* 318 (26 May 1988): 1345-48.

Kathleen Scogna

Right angle see **Angle**

Rivers

A river is a natural stream of **freshwater** with significant **volume** when compared to the volume of its smaller tributaries. Conveying surface **water** run-off on land, rivers are normally the main channels or largest tributaries of drainage systems. Typical rivers begin with a flow from headwater areas made up of small tributaries, such as springs. They then travel in meandering paths at various speeds; finally, they discharge into **desert** basins, into major lakes, or most likely, into oceans.

Sixteen of the world's largest rivers account for close to half of the world's river flow. By far, the largest river is the Amazon River, running 3,900 mi (6,275 km) long. Discharging an average of four million cubic feet (112,000 cu m) of water each second, the Amazon River alone accounts for 20% of the water discharged each year by the Earth's rivers.

Formation of rivers

Precipitation, such as rainwater or snow, is the source of the water flowing in rivers. Rainwater can ei-

ther return to the oceans as run-off, it can be evaporated directly from the surface from which it falls, or it can be passed into the **soil** and mantle rock. Water can reappear in three ways: (l) by **evaporation** from the Earth's surface; (2) by **transpiration** from vegetation; (3) by exudation out of the **Earth**, thereby forming a stream. The third way, by exudation, is of primary importance to the formation of rivers.

When a heavy rain falls on ground that is steeply sloped or is already saturated with water, waterrun-off trickles down the Earth's surface, rather than being absorbed. Initially, the water runs in an evenly distributed, paper-thin sheet, called surface run-off. After it travels a short **distance**, the water begins to run in **parallel** rills and, at the same time, gathers **turbulence**. As these rills pass over fine soil or silt, they begin to dig shallow channels, called runnels. This is the first stage of **erosion**.

These parallel rills do not last very long, perhaps only a few yards. Fairly soon, the rills unite with one another, until enough of them merge to form a stream. After a number of rills converge, the resulting stream is a significant, continuously flowing body of water, called a brook. The brook now flows through what is termed a valley. As a brook gains sufficient volume from **groundwater** supplies, the volume of water it carries becomes more constant. Once the volume of water carried reaches a certain level, the brook becomes a river.

River systems

Rivers can have different origins and, as they travel, often merge with other bodies of water. Thus, the complete river system consists of not only the river itself but also of all the converging tributaries. Every river has a point of origin. Because gravity plays a key role in the direction that rivers take, rivers almost always follow a down hill gradient. Thus, the point of origin for rivers tends to be the highest point in the watercourse. Some rivers start from springs, which are the most common type of river source in humid climates. Springs occur as groundwater rises to the earth's surface and flows away. Other rivers are initiated by run-off from melting **glaciers** located high in the mountains. Often, rivers having their origins in huge glaciers are quite large by the time they emerge from openings in the ice.

Lakes and marshes are the sources for other rivers. As river sources, lakes can be classified in three ways. They can be true sources for rivers; they can be an accumulation of water from small feeder streams; or they can hide a spring that is actually the true source of the river. The Great Lakes are prime examples of source lakes. Although there are a few springs that feed them, the majority of the water coming into the lakes arises from precipitation falling onto their surfaces. Therefore, they, not their tributaries, are the source of surrounding rivers.

As rivers make the trip from their source to their eventual destination, the larger ones tend to meet and merge with other rivers. Resembling the trunk and branches of a **tree**, the water flowing in the main stream often meets the water from its tributaries at sharp angles, combining to form the river system. As long as there are no major areas of seepage and as long as the evaporation level remains reasonable, the volume of water carried by rivers increases from its source to its mouth with every tributary.

When two bodies of water converge, it is clearly evident as their shorelines merge. However, the water from the two bodies often continues to flow separately, like two streams flowing in a common river bed. This occurrence is especially clear when two rivers meet that contain different amounts and types of suspended sediment. For example, when the Ohio and the Mississippi rivers meet, a clear difference in the color of water in the Mississippi river can be seen. Specifically, there is a strip of clear water one quarter of a mile wide on the river's eastern side that runs for miles. To the west of this strip, however,the water color is a cloudy yellow.

Along its path, a single river obtains water from surface run-off from different sections of land. The area from which a particular section of a river obtains its water is defined as a catchment area (sometimes called a drainage area). The lines that divide different catchment areas are called watersheds. A **watershed** is usually the line that joins the highest point around a particular river **basin**. Therefore, at every point along the line of a watershed, there is a downward slope going into the middle of the catchment area.

Climactic influences

Rivers are highly influenced by the prevailing climate conditions. The climate determines the amount of precipitation, its seasonality, and its form as rainwater or as ice. Because of the climate and subsequent rainfall patterns, three general types of rivers exist. The first are the perennial or permanent rivers. Normally, these rivers are located in more humid climates where rainfall exceeds evaporation rates. Thus, although these rivers may experience seasonal fluctuations in their levels of water, they have constant streamflow throughout the year. With few exceptions, streamflow in these rivers increases downstream, and these rivers empty into larger bodies of water, such as oceans. In fact, 68% of rivers drain into oceans. All of the world's major rivers are perennial rivers.

The second type of river is the periodic river. These rivers are characterized with predictably intermittent streamflow. Usually appearing in arid climates where

evaporation is greater than precipitation, these rivers run dry on occasion, but there are regular intervals of streamflow. Typically, these rivers have a decrease in streamflow as they travel due largely to high levels of evaporation. Often, they do not reach the sea, but instead run into an inland drainage basin.

The third type of river is the episodic river. These rivers are actually the run-off channels of very dry regions. In these regions of the world, there are only slight amounts of rainfall and it evaporates quickly. This type of streamflow occurs rarely.

Interestingly, some rivers span two types of climactic regions. These rivers, known as exotic rivers, begin in humid or polar regions and flow into dry areas. The largest of these rivers have enough water at their sources to enable them to reach the sea. The Nile River, for example, gets sufficient water at its humid source to travel over the Nubian and Arabian deserts. While it receives a substantial amount of water from the Blue Nile at Kartoum, it then must travel 1,676 mi (2,700 km) before it reaches the Mediterranean Sea.

Hydrological cycle

The **hydrologic cycle** is very important to the existence of rivers, indeed, to all life on Earth. Without it, every stream and watercourse would dry up. The hydrological cycle is the continuous alternation between evaporation of surface water, precipitation, and streamflow. It is a cycle in which water evaporates from the oceans into the atmosphere and then falls as rain or snow on land. The water, then, is absorbed by the land and, after some period of time, makes its way back to the oceans to begin the cycle again. Scientists have found that the total amount of water on the earth has not changed in three billion years. Therefore, this cycle is said to be constant throughout time.

The water content of the atmosphere is estimated to be no greater than 0.001% of the total volume of water on the **planet**. Despite its seemingly insignificant amount, atmospheric water is essential in the hydrological cycle. As water falls as rain, three things can happen. First, usually some of the rain falls directly into rivers. Second, some of it is soaked up by ground, where it is either stored as moisture for the soil or where it seeps into ground water aquifers. Third, rainfall can freeze and become either ice or snow. Interestingly, water is sometimes stored outside the hydrological cycle for years in cavities as fossil ground water in continental glaciers. The next event, evaporation, is the most critical link in the cycle of water circulation. If rain water evaporates too rapidly, rivers cannot form. For example, in hot deserts, heavy downpours sometimes occur, but the water evaporates completely in a short period of time. However, as long as the evaporation is slower than the typical amount of rainfall, viable rivers can exist.

Rivers, like precipitation and evaporation, are a vital part of the hydrological cycle. Somewhat surprisingly, of all of the forms of water in nature, watercourses-rivers and streams-make up the smallest total amount of water on Earth, about 0.0001% of the total volume. However, when combined with the precipitation falling on the **ocean** and the run-off from melting ice in **Antarctica** and Greenland, rivers replace about the same amount of water as is evaporated by the oceans. In addition to this, because they carry water away from saturated soil, they prevent marshes and bogs from forming in many low-lying areas.

Although the hydrologic cycle is a constant phenomenon, it is not always evident in the same place, year after year. If it occurred consistently in all locations, floods and droughts would not exist. Thus, each year some places on Earth experience more than average rainfall, while other places endure droughts. It is not surprising, then, that people living near rivers often endure floods at some time or other.

River floods

River levels have a direct influence on the activities and well-being of human beings. While low flowing rivers interfere with transport, trade, and navigation, high water threatens human life and property. Basically, floods are a result of a river's discharge behavior and the climate within which it is located. The most common cause of **flooding** is when it rains extremely hard or for an unusually long period of time. Additionally, areas that experience a great deal of snow in the wintertime are prone to springtime flooding when the snow and ice melt, especially if the thaw is relatively sudden. Furthermore, rainfall and snowmelt can sometimes combine to cause floods, such as when rain falls on an area covered with melting snow.

Under normal conditions, rivers move fairly slowly as they transport silt and other debris produced by rain and snow. During floods, however, this transport is achieved much more rapidly, sometimes with beneficial side effects and sometimes with disastrous ones. One example of beneficial flooding is where the high water transports new top soil to local **crops**. Furthermore, floods can provide local crops badly needed moisture. The negative aspects of flooding are fairly obvious; often people drown and their property is destroyed.

Rivers in more humid regions are less likely to experience significant flooding than those located in more

The Parana River in Brazil.

arid climates. In fact, floods in humid areas occur an average of about one time per year. Although on rare occasions these rivers experience larger floods, the water is normally no more than twice the size of a normal flood. While rivers in arid regions experience small flooding on an annual basis as well, when they experience rare, large floods, it can be devastating.

Human control of rivers

For centuries, rivers have been very important to human society. Aside from soil, no other feature on Earth is as closely bound to the advancement of human civilization. Trying to control river flow has been a key part of civil engineering. This is especially true because of the need to avoid natural flooding and the desire to take advantage of the benefits that flood plains offer agriculture. Furthermore, managing rivers can also satisfy human needs to store water for times of **drought**. Thus, civil engineers have a number of goals. They try to conserve water flow for release at times when human need is greatest. They try to keep water quality above acceptable levels. And they try to confine flood flows to designated channels or to planned flood storage areas.

While the techniques of river management are fairly well understood, true river management is not commonly put into practice because of the expense and the size of the projects involved. In fact, none of the major rivers in the world is controlled or even managed in a way that modern engineering and biological techniques would allow. So far, only medium-sized streams have been successfully managed. For example, the San Joaquin in California has been completely developed to take advantage of the **irrigation** opportunities that the stream offers.

KEY TERMS

Brook—A significant, continuously flowing body of water formed by the convergence of a number of rills.

Catchment area—The area from which a particular section of a river obtains its water; also known as a drainage area.

Erosion—To gradually wear away an area by abrasion; relates especially to runnels and river beds.

Exudation—The process of water oozing out of the ground.

Hydrological cycle—The continuous alternation between evaporation of surface water, precipitation, and stream flow.

Perennial rivers—Located in more humid climates where rainfall exceeds evaporation rates. Although these rivers may experience seasonal fluctuations in their levels of water, they have constant stream flow throughout the year.

Periodic rivers—Characterized with predictably intermittent streamflow. Usually appearing in arid climates where evaporation is greater than precipitation, these rivers run dry on occasion, but there are regular intervals of streamflow.

Rill—A small channel of water that forms from surface run-off; a small brook.

Runnels—Eroded channels in the ground in which rills of water pass over fine soil.

Transpiration—The process of water being emitted into the atmosphere through vegetation.

Tributary—A stream or other body of water that flows into a larger one.

Valley—The area in which a brook flows.

Watershed—A ridge of high land that demarks different catchment areas draining into different river systems.

See also Dams; Lake; Water conservation.

Further Reading

Crickmay, C. H., *The Work of the River.* New York: American Elsevier Publishing Company, Inc., 1974.

Czaya, Eberhard. *Rivers of the World.* New York: Van Nostrand Reinhold Company, 1981.

Parker, Sybil P., and Robert A. Corbitt, eds. *McGraw-Hill Encyclopedia of Environmental Science and Engineering.* 3rd ed. New York: McGraw-Hill, Inc., 1992.

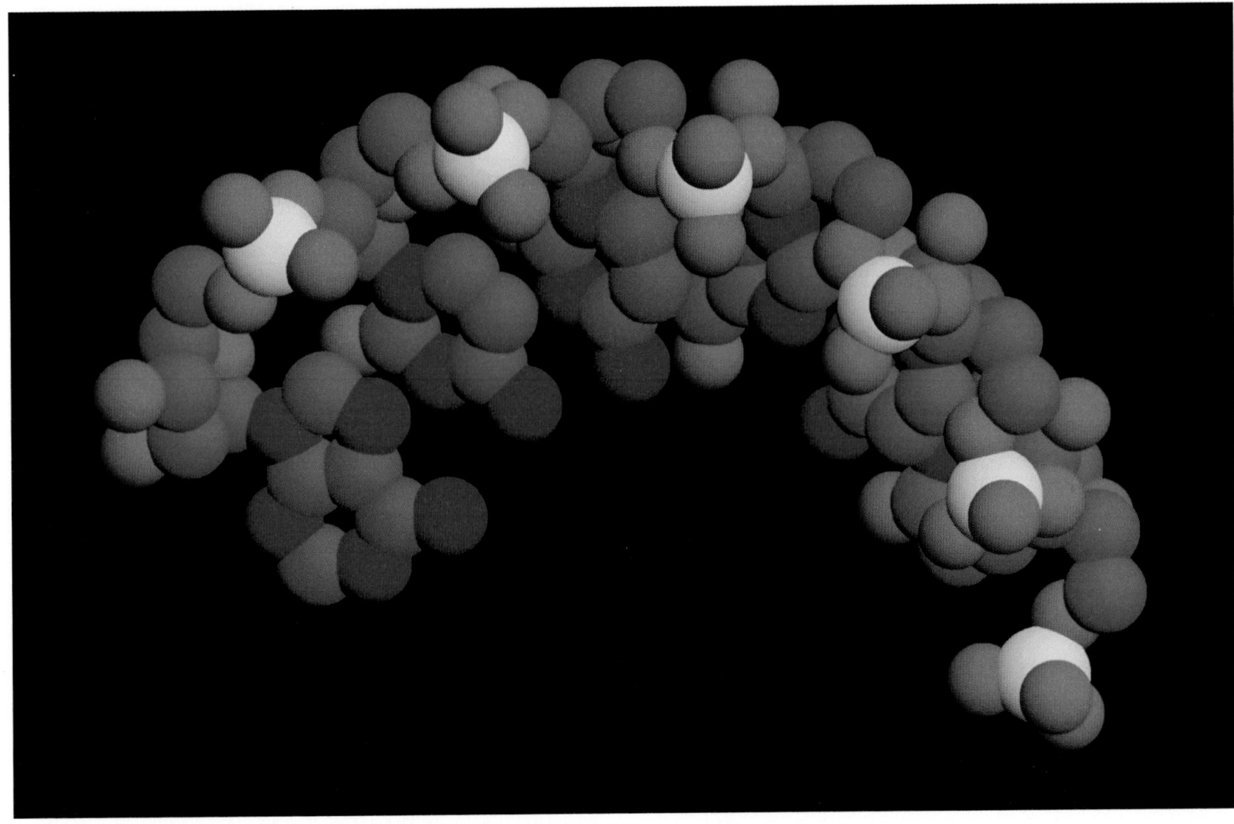

A computer-generated model of ribonucleic acid (RNA).

Parker, Sybil P., ed. *McGraw-Hill Encyclopedia of Oceans, and Atmospheric Sciences.* New York: McGraw-Hill, Inc., 1980.

Kathryn D. Snavely

RNA see **Ribonucleic acid (RNA)**

RNA function

RNA is a **nucleic acid** that has a variety of functions in a **cell**. Depending on the type of RNA it can function as a carrier for genetic information, a catalyst for biochemical reactions, an adapter **molecule** in protein synthesis, and a structural molecule in cell organelles.

Since the discovery of DNA in the early 1950s, scientists have studied the function and structure of nucleic acids. The various types and functions of RNA have been investigated by numerous researchers. Perhaps most famous is Severo Ochoa who received a Nobel Prize for his work on RNA in 1959.

There are five major types of RNA that are found in the cells of eukaryotes. These include heterogeneous nuclear RNA, messenger RNA (mRNA), transfer RNA tRNA), ribosomal RNA (rRNA), and small nuclear RNA. Each has a different role in various cellular processes. In addition to these forms, RNA is a key component of certain viruses.

One of the primary functions of RNA is to facilitate the translation of DNA into a useful protein. This process begins in the nucleus of the cell with a series of enzymatic reactions that copy DNA, producing heterogeneous nuclear RNA. Since hnRNA is a direct copy of DNA, it contains exons and introns which are coding and noncoding regions of nucleotides. It undergoes **RNA splicing** which removes the introns and converts it to mRNA. mRNA is transported out of the nucleus into the cytoplasm of the cell. In this way, it functions as a carrier for information from the cells DNA to the protein synthesizing organelles; the **ribosomes**.

The ribosomes interact with the mRNA and construct a protein based on the nucleotide sequence. Part of this process involves another type of RNA that is located in the ribosome called transfer RNA. tRNA is an adapter

molecule which functions as a bridge between the codons on the mRNA and the amino acids that are used to construct the protein. During protein synthesis, one end of the tRNA interacts with three nucleotides on the mRNA. The other end of the tRNA carries an **amino acid**. This amino acid is then transferred and chemically bonded to a series of amino acids to produce a protein. Another type of RNA that is involved in protein synthesis is ribosomal RNA. rRNA has two functions in a ribosome. First, it provides the structure and shape for the catalytic areas of the ribosome. Second, it helps speed up, or catalyze, the action of the tRNA.

While DNA and RNA are very similar in their composition, RNA has a much more versatile role. This is because it can not only carrier genetic information, it can also catalyze reactions. RNA molecules that catalyze reactions are known as ribozymes. As previously mentioned, rRNA functions as a ribozyme during protein synthesis. Another form of RNA that acts as a ribozyme is small nuclear RNA (snRNA). During the process of RNA splicing snRNA catalyzes reactions in the spliceosome, a group of biomolecules that splice hnRNA. snRNA also plays a structural role in this process.

In addition to these beneficial cellular roles, RNA can also have a **negative** impact. Certain viruses contain RNA as their primary genetic material. These viruses are made up of a protein coat and a strand of RNA. They inject their RNA into a cell where it either gets translated by cellular enzymes or gets incorporated into the cell's genome. When conditions are right, the **virus** genes are expressed causing the cell to malfunction. Other types of viruses known as viroids are composed entirely of circular RNA.

RNA splicing

RNA Splicing is a biological reaction in which introns are removed from a transcribed RNA to create mRNA. This process occurs in conjunction with the transcription of DNA to mRNA.

The theory that RNA splicing occurs was only suggested recently. Before 1977, scientists were not aware that eukaryote genes were dramatically different than prokaryotes. However, it was known that eukaryotes had significantly more DNA than prokaryotes. This difference, called the C-value paradox, led to the discovery that eukaryotes had interrupted genes. These are genes containing exons and introns; nucleotide **sequences** that are both coding and non-coding. Evidence for RNA splicing was obtained when nuclear RNA was compared to mRNA. It was found that nuclear RNA was much longer than mRNA suggesting mRNA was further processed before being transported to the cytoplasm.

RNA splicing is one step in the overall process in which the genetic code is transcribed into mRNA and then translated into **proteins**. It is known to occur in the nucleus of the **cell** where DNA transcription takes place. During the process of transcription, each nucleotide from the specific **gene** is translated into RNA. This results in an RNA **molecule** that contains sequence of both the exons and the introns. Since the introns do not code for proteins, they are removed by RNA splicing.

There are several types of known splicing systems. One system involves a spliceosome which is an array of proteins that function together. The human spliceosome has been found to contain 44 different components. Another type of system involves excision of introns by the RNA itself. Still another type involves the removal of introns by tRNA.

The spliceosome system has been one of the most thoroughly studied splicing system. It is responsible for removing an intron that is located between two exons. The process begins with a set of enzymes that recognize and bind to the splice sites. These sites are located at the exon-intron boundaries and are made up of four nucleotides, two at each end of the intron. The bond between the left exon and intron is cut by enzymes in the spliceosome. This is a transesterification chemical reaction. Next, the intron is folded over on itself to the right, forming a molecular lariat structure. Another set of enzymes cuts the right end of the intron and finally joins the two exons.

The existence of a processing system for changing nuclear RNA to mRNA was surprising to scientists at first. It seems strange that a cell would waste the **energy** required to maintain an amount of genetic material that does not directly aid in the production of proteins. To explain this phenomena, researchers have attempted to find a function for introns. Current theories suggested that introns play a regulatory role in gene expression. Also, they may help cells produce multiple proteins from a single gene.

Road building see **Freeway**

Roadrunners see **Cuckoos and coucals**

Robins

Robins are songbirds in the family Musicicapidae, in the thrush subfamily, Turdinae, which contains more than 300 species, including various **thrushes**, chats, solitaires, redstarts, nightingale, wheatear, and others. The

members of this family, known as robins, tend to have dark backs and reddish breasts. Except for this superficial resemblance, these robins are not particularly closely related, other than being members of the same avian family. Like other thrushes, robins are highly musical, with rich and loud songs. Because some species of robins are relatively familiar **birds** that live in close proximity to humans, their songs are well known and highly appreciated by many people.

The European robin (*Erithacus rubecula*) is the archetypal "robin red-breast" of Christmas card scenes. Robins elsewhere were given their common name, robin, because of their superficial likeness to the European robin, which to many English-speaking colonists was a common and much-loved songbird of gardens and rural places. During the era of European exploration and conquest of distant lands, these settlers longed for familiar surroundings and contexts in their newly colonized, but foreign countries. Consequently, they often introduced European species to achieve that effect, and named native species after familiar European ones with which there was a outward resemblance. As a result of this socio-cultural process, many species in the thrush family were variously named "robin" in far-flung places that were settled by the British, including **Australia**, **Asia**, and **North America**. The Australian robin belongs to the super family Corvoidea, in the family Eopsaltriidae.

The European robin has a body length of 5.5 in (14 cm), an olive-brown back, a white belly, and a orange-rust breast and face. This species is common and widespread in **Europe** and western Russia, where it breeds in **forests**, shrubby habitats, hedgerows, and urban and suburban parks and gardens. The European robin is a migratory species, wintering in North **Africa**. The closely related Japanese robin (*E. akahinge*) has a more reddish brown coloration of the face and breast, and breeds on many of the islands of Japan and on nearby Sakhalin and the Kurils of far-eastern Russia.

The American robin is probably the most familiar native species of bird to North Americans. American robins live up to 10 years, breed when one year old and lay four to six eggs. They suffer high mortality with up to 50% of the population dying annually. The American robin is considerably larger than the European robin, weighing up to 2.8 oz (80 g) with a body length of 8.7 in (22 cm), a slate-grey back, a white throat, and a brick-red breast. Young birds have a spotted breast, with reddish tinges on the flanks. The American robin is very widespread in North America, breeding from just south of the high-arctic **tundra** at the **limit** of trees and taller shrubs, to southern Mexico. The American robin utilizes most natural habitats, minimally requiring only a few shrubs for nesting, and its food of abundant **invertebrates** during the breeding season. The American robin also widely occurs in suburban and urban parks and gardens. Most American robins are migratory, wintering in the southern parts of their breeding range and as far south as Guatemala. However, some birds winter relatively far north in southern Canada and the northern states, where they subsist primarily on berries during the cold months.

The American robin is an accomplished and pleasing singer. Because the species is so widespread, virtually all North Americans hear, and are warmed by, the lovely melody of the robin during the spring and summer, although many people do not recognize its song as such. Those who do, however, widely regard the early migrating American robin to be a longed-for harbinger of springtime and warmer **weather**, because this bird often arrives at the northern parts of its range and sings while there is still snow on the ground.

Status of North American Robins

- American Robin (*Turdus migratorius*). On rare occasions the cowbird may lay eggs in the robin's nest. The American Robin was once hunted or food. It has expanded into the Great Plains and dry western lowlands with the planting of trees, the erection of structures, and the introduction of **irrigation** systems, all of which have increased the availability of nesting sites and moist land for foraging. Today, this bird is abundant and widespread, and the population shows no signs of changing.
- Clay-colored Robin (*Turdus grayi*). Southwestern stray. A native of eastern Mexico and northern Columbia, this bird is now a frequent visitor to southernmost Texas where it has been known to nest.
- Rufous-backed Robin (*Turdus rufopalliatus*). Southwestern stray. A native of Mexico, this bird has been making winter appearances in the United States since 1960. Strays have been in Arizona, Texas, New Mexico, and California.
- Siberian Blue Robin (*Luscinia cyane*). Alaskan stray. A native of eastern Asia, this bird is an accidental visitor to the outer Aleutians.
- White-throated Robin (*Turdus assimilis*). Southwestern stray. A native of the **mountain** tropics, this bird has been an occasional winter stray to southern Texas.

Further Reading

Ehrlich, Paul R. David S. Dobkin, and Darryl Wheye. *The Birder's Handbook.* New York: Simon & Schuster Inc., 1988.

Peterson, Roger Tory. *North American Birds.* Houghton Miflin Interactive (CD-ROM), Somerville, MA: Houghton Miflin, 1995.

Bill Freedman
Randall Frost

Robotics

Robotics is the science of designing and building machines that can be programmed to perform more than one function traditionally performed by humans. The word robot comes from a play written in 1920 by the Czech author Karel Capek. Capek's *R.U.R.* (for Rossum's Universal Robots) is the story of an inventor who creates humanlike machines designed to take over many forms of human work.

Historical background

The idea of a machine that looks and behaves like a human being goes back at least 2,000 years. According to Greek mythology, Hephaestus, the god of fire, constructed artificial women out of gold. These women were able to walk, talk, and even to think.

By the 18th century, scientists and inventors had created an impressive array of mechanical figures that looked and acted like humans and other animals. The French Jacquet-Droz brothers, Pierre and Henri-Louis, for example, constructed a doll that was able to play the piano, swaying in time with the music, and a young scribe who could write messages of up to 40 characters.

Many of these early accomplishments had little practical value. They were built in order to impress or charm viewers, or to demonstrate the inventor's creative and technological skills. That line of research continues today. Many modern robots have little function beyond demonstrating what can be done in building machines that more and more closely resemble the appearance and function of humans.

One function for such robots is in advertising. They are used to publicize some particular product or to inform the general public about the robots themselves. Robots of this kind are most commonly found at conventions, conferences, or other large meetings. As one example, a robot named Argon was used in April 1983 to walk a dog through a veterinary congress in London, promoting the "Pets Are Good People" program.

Robots at work: the present day

Robots have come to play a widespread and crucial role in many industrial operations today. These robots are almost always of the Jacquard type—with few human features—rather than the Jacquet-Droz, doll-like style. The work that robots do can be classified into three major categories: in the assembly and finishing of products; in the movement of materials and objects; and in the performance of work in environmentally difficult or hazardous situations.

The most common single application of robots is in **welding**. About a quarter of all robots used by industry have this function. In a typical operation, two pieces of **metal** will be moved within the welding robot's field and the robot will apply the **heat** needed to create the weld. Welding robots can have a variety of appearances, but they tend to consist of one large arm that can rotate in various directions. At the end of the arm is a welding gun that actually performs the weld.

Closely related types of work now done by robots include cutting, grinding, polishing, drilling, sanding, painting, spraying, and otherwise treating the surface of a product. As with welding, activities of this kind are usually performed by one-armed robots that hang from the ceiling, project outward from a platform, or reach into a product from some other **angle**.

There are some obvious advantages for using a robot to perform tasks such as these. They are often boring, difficult, and sometimes dangerous tasks that have to be repeated over and over again in exactly the same way. Why should a human be employed to do such repetitive work, robotics engineers ask, when a machine can do the same task just as efficiently?

That argument can be used for many of the other industrial operations in which robots have replaced humans. Another example of such operations is the assembly of individual parts into some final product, as in the assembly of **automobile** parts in the manufacture of a car. At one time, this kind of assembly could have been done only by a crew of humans, each of whom had his or her own specific responsibility: moving a body section into position, welding it into place, installing and tightening bolts, turning the body for the next operation, and so forth. In many assembly plants today, the **assembly line** of humans has been replaced by an assembly line of robots that does the same job, but more safely and more efficiently than was the case with the human team.

Movement of materials

Many industrial operations involve the lifting and moving of large, heavy objects over and over again. For example, a particular process may require the transfer of **steel** ingots onto a conveyor belt and then, at some later point, the removal of shaped pieces of steel made from those ingots. One way to perform these operations is with heavy machinery operated by human workers. But another method that is more efficient and safer is to substitute robots for the human and his or her machine.

Another type of heavy-duty robot is an exoskeleton, that is, a metallic contraption that surrounds a human worker. The human can step inside the exoskeleton, placing his or her arms and legs into the corresponding limbs

of the exoskeleton. By operating the exoskeleton's controls, the human can magnify his or her strength many times, picking up and handling objects that would otherwise be much too heavy for the operator's own capacity.

Mobile robots are used for many heavy-duty operations. The robots operate on a system of wheels or legs, on a track, or with some other system of locomotion. They pick up a material or an object in one location and move it to a different location. The robots need not be designed to handle very large loads only. As an example, some office buildings contain tracks along which mobile robots can travel delivering mail to various locations within the building.

Hazardous or remote duty robots

A common application of robots is for use in places that humans can go only at risk to their own health or safety or that humans can not go at all. Industries where nuclear materials are used often make use of robots so that human workers are not exposed to the dangerous effects of radioactive materials. In one type of machine, a worker sits in a chair and places his or her hands and arms into a pair of sleeves. The controls within the sleeves are connected to a robot arm that can reach into a **protected area** where radioactive materials are kept. The worker can operate the robot arm and hand to perform many delicate operations that would otherwise have to be carried out by a human worker.

Robots have also been useful in **space** research. In 1975, for example, two space probes code-named Viking 1 and Viking 2 landed on the planet **Mars**. These probes were two of the most complex and sophisticated robots ever built. Their job was to analyze the planet's surface. In order to accomplish this task, the probes were equipped with a long arm that was able to operate across a 120-degree radius, digging into the ground and taking out samples of Martian **soil**. The samples were then transported to one of three chemical laboratories within the robot, where they underwent automated chemical analysis. The results of these analyses were then transmitted by automatic **telemetry** to receiving stations on **Earth**.

How robots work

In order for a robot to imitate the actions of a human being, it has to be able to perform three fundamental tasks. First, it must be conscious of the world around it, just as humans obtain information about the world from our five senses. Second, the robot must somehow "know" what to do. One way for it to get that knowledge is to have a human prepare a set of instructions that are then implanted into the robot's "brain." Alternatively, it must be able to analyze and interpret data it has received from its senses and then make a decision based on that data as to how it should react. Third, the robot must be able to act on the instructions or data it has received.

Not all robots have all of these functions. For example, some of the earliest "for fun" robots like the Jacquet-Droz doll and scribe" knew" what to do because of the instructions that had been programmed into them by their inventors. The inventors also gave their toys the mechanical means with which to carry out their instructions: arms, fingers, torsos, eyes, and other body parts that were able to move in specific ways.

Mechanical systems

The humanlike movements that a robot makes as it works can be accomplished with a relatively small number of mechanical systems. One of those systems is known as the rectangular or cartesian coordinate system. This system consists of a set of components that can move in any one of three directions, all at right angles to each other.

Think of a three-dimensional system in which an x-axis and a y-axis define a flat **plane**. **Perpendicular** to that plane is a third axis, the z-axis. A rule can be made to travel along the x-axis, along the y-axis, or along the z-axis. Overall, the ruler has the ability to move in three different directions, back and forth along the x- and y-axes and up and down along the z-axis. A system of this type is said to have three degrees of freedom because it has the ability to move in three distinct directions.

Another type of mechanical system is the cylindrical coordinate system. This system consists of a cylinder with a solid column through the middle of it. The cylinder can move up and down on the column (one degree of freedom), and an arm attached to the outside of the cylinder can rotate around the central column (a second degree of freedom). Finally, the arm can be constructed so that it will slide in and out of its housing attached to the cylinder (a third degree of freedom).

A third type of mechanical system is the spherical coordinate system. To understand this system, imagine a rectangular box-shaped component attached to a base. The box can rotate on its own axis (one degree of freedom) or tilt up or down on its axis (a second degree of freedom). An arm attached to the box may also be able to extend or retract, giving it a third degree of freedom.

Many robots have more than three degrees of freedom because they consist of two or more simple systems combined with each other. For example, a typical industrial robot might have one large arm constructed on a cartesian coordinate system. At the end of the arm there might then be a wrist-type component with the same or a different mechanical system. Attached to the wrist might then be a hand with fingers, each with a mechanical sys-

A police robot handling a live bomb by remote control.

tem of its own. Combinations of mechanical systems like this one make it possible for an industrial robot to perform a variety of complex maneuvers not entirely different from those of a human arm, wrist, hand, and finger.

Sensory systems

The component of modern robots that was most commonly missing from their early predecessors was the ability to collect data from the outside world. Humans accomplish this task, of course, by means of our hands, eyes, ears, noses, and tongues. With some important exceptions, robots usually do not need to have the ability to hear, **smell**, or **taste** things in the world around them, but they are often required to be able to "see" an object or to "feel" it.

The simplest optical system used in robots is a photoelectric **cell**. A **photoelectric cell** converts light **energy** into electrical energy. It allows a robot to determine "yes/no" situations in its field of **vision**, such as whether a particular piece of equipment is present or not. Suppose, for example, that a robot looks at a place on the table in front of it where a tool is supposed to be. If the tool is present, light will be reflected off it and sent to the robot's photoelectric cell. There, the light waves will be converted to an electrical current that is transmitted to the robot's computer-brain.

More complex robot video systems make use of **television** cameras. The images collected by the cameras are sent to the robot's "brain," where they are processed for understanding. One means of processing is to compare the image received by the television camera with other images stored in the robot's computer-brain.

The human sense of **touch** can be replicated in a robot by means of tactile sensors. One kind of tactile sensor is nothing more than a simple switch that goes from one position to another when the robot's fingers come into contact with a solid object. When a finger comes into contact with an object, the switch may close, allowing an electrical current to flow to the **brain**. A more sophisticated sense of touch can be provided by combining a group of tactile sensors at various positions on the robot's hand. This arrangement allows the robot to estimate the shape, size, and contours of an object being examined.

Are robots human?

Probably the most important development in the history of robotics has been the **evolution** of the microcom-

KEY TERMS

Degrees of freedom—The number of geometric positions through which a robot can move.

Exoskeleton—An external bodily framework; in the field of robotics, an exoskeleton is a metallic frame within which a human can stand or sit in order to manipulate the frame itself.

Tactile sensor—A device that converts mechanical pressure into an electrical current.

puter. The microcomputer makes it possible to store enormous amounts of information as well as huge processing programs into the brain of a robot. With the aid of a microcomputer, a robot can not only be provided with far more basic programming than had been possible before, but it can also be provided with the programming needed to help the robot teach itself, that is, to learn. For example, some computers designed to carry out repetitious tasks have developed the ability to learn from previous mistakes and, therefore, to work more efficiently in the future.

As robots become increasingly sophisticated, the question has arisen as to what the differences are between a robot and a human. That question is obviously very complex philosophically, and cannot be answered to the satisfaction of scientists.

See also Artificial intelligence; Automation.

Further Reading

Aleksander, Igor, and Piers Burnett. *Reinventing Man: The Robot Becomes Reality.* New York: Holt, Rinehart and Winston, 1983.

Asimov, Isaac, and Karen A. Frenkel. *Robots: Machines in Man's Image.* New York: Harmony Books, 1985.

D'Ignazio, Fred. *Working Robots.* New York: Elsevier/Nelson Books, 1982.

Malone, Robert. *The Robot Book.* New York: Harvest/HBJ Book, 1978.

Metos, Thomas. *Robots A to Z.* New York: Julian Messner, 1980.

Reichardt, Jasia. *Robots: Fact, Fiction, and Prediction.* New York: Penguin Books, 1978.

David E. Newton

Rockets and missiles

The term rocket refers both to a non-air-breathing **jet engine** and to any vehicle it propels. Rocket fuels may be either solid or liquid. In the former case, the rocket is commonly known as a rocket engine, while in the latter case, it is usually called a rocket motor.

A missile is an unmanned vehicle propelled through **space**, usually carrying some type of explosive intended to do harm to an enemy. A missile, like a rocket, usually carries its own means of propulsion. It may also carry its own guidance system or, alternatively, it may be guided by a ground-based command center.

Rockets have two primary functions. First, they are used to carry out research on the Earth's atmosphere, other parts of the **solar system**, and outer space. Rockets designed to carry instruments no farther than the upper levels of the atmosphere are known as sounding rockets. Those designed to lift spacecraft into **orbit** or into outer space are known as boosters or as carrier vehicles.

The second function of rockets is as components of missiles. A large fraction of the research and development on modern rocketry systems has been carried out by and/or under the supervision of the military services.

History

The first rocket was almost certainly constructed in China, but the date of that invention is not known. There is evidence that the Chinese knew about black gunpowder at least two centuries before the **birth** of Christ, but the explosive was probably used exclusively for ceremonial purposes. The concept of using gunpowder to propel an object through space probably did not arise for more than a thousand years, perhaps during the 13th century. Records of the time indicate that gunpowder was attached to sticks for use as offensive weapons during battle. The birth of rocketry was, therefore, intimately associated with their first use as missiles.

For a short period of time, rockets were a reasonably effective weapon in warfare. For example, French troops under Joan of Arc apparently used simple rockets to defend the city of Orleans in 1429. Military strategists of the time devised imaginative and sometimes bizarre variations on the rocket for use in battles, but such concepts were apparently seldom put into practice. The development of more efficient weapons of war, in any case, soon relegated the use of rockets to recreational occasions, such as those still popular in the United States at Fourth of July celebrations.

Scientific basis of rocketry

The scientific principle on which rocket propulsion is based was first enunciated in 1687 by Sir Isaac Newton. In his monumental work on **force** and **motion**, *Philosophiae Naturalis Principia Mathematica* (*Mathematical Principles of Natural Philosophy*), Newton laid

out three **laws of motion**. The third of these stated that for every action, there is an equal and opposite reaction. For example, if you push your finger into a **balloon** filled with **water**, the water-filled balloon pushes back with an equal force.

The application of Newton's Third Law to propulsion is illustrated in a variety of marine animals that use the principle as a means of movement. The body of the **squid**, for example, contains a sac that holds a dark, watery fluid. When the squid finds it necessary to move, it contracts the sac and expels some of the fluid from an opening in the back of its body. In this case, the expulsion of the watery fluid in a backward direction can be thought of as an "action." The equal and opposite reaction that occurs to balance that action is the movement of the squid's body in a forward direction.

Rocket propulsion

A rocket is propelled in a forward direction when, like the squid, a fluid is expelled from the back of its body. In the most common type of rocket, the expelled fluid is a **mass** of hot gases produced by a chemical reaction inside the body of the rocket. In other types of rockets, the expelled fluid may be a stream of charged particles or **plasma** produced by an electrical, nuclear, or solar process.

Chemical rockets are of two primary types, those that use liquid fuels and those that use solid fuels. The most familiar type of liquid rocket is one in which liquid **oxygen** is used to oxidize liquid **hydrogen**. In this reaction, water vapor at very high temperatures (about 4,935°F (2,725°C) is produced. The water vapor is expelled from the rear of the rocket, pushing the rocket itself forward.

The liquid oxygen/liquid hydrogen rocket requires an external source of **energy**, such as an electrical spark, in order for a chemical reaction to occur. Some combinations of fuel and oxidizer, however, will ignite as soon as they are brought into contact. Such combinations are known as hypergolic systems. An example of a hypergolic system is the liquid combination of **nitrogen** tetroxide and monomethylhydrazine. These two compounds react spontaneously with each other when brought into contact to produce a **temperature** of the order of 5,200°F (2,871°C).

The use of liquid fuels in rockets requires a number of special precautions. For example, with a liquid oxygen/liquid hydrogen system, both liquids must be kept at very low temperatures. Oxygen gas does not become a liquid until it is cooled below -297°F(-183°C) and hydrogen gas, not until it is cooled below -421°F (-252°C). The two liquids must, therefore, first be cooled to very low temperatures and then kept in heavily insulated containers until they are actually brought into combination in the rocket engine.

Hypergolic systems also require special care. Since the two liquids that make up the system react with each other spontaneously, they must be kept isolated from each other until **combustion** is actually needed.

A third type of liquid propellant is known as a monopropellant. As the name suggests, a monopropellant consists of only a single compound. An example is **hydrogen peroxide**. When the proper catalyst is added to hydrogen peroxide, the compound decomposes, forming oxygen and water vapor, and producing **heat** sufficient to raise the temperature of the product gases to 1,370°F (743°C). The expulsion of these hot gases provides the thrust needed in a rocket.

Liquid fuel rockets have a number of advantages. For example, they can be turned on and off rather simply (at least in concept) by opening and closing the valves that feed the two components to each other. In general, they tend to provide more power than do solid rockets. Also, when problems develop in a liquid fuel rocket, they tend to be less serious than those in a solid-fuel rocket.

However, liquid-fuel rockets also have a number of serious disadvantages. One has been pointed out above, namely that the liquid components often require very special care. Also, liquid fuels must be added to a rocket just before its actual ignition since the components can not be stored in the rocket body for long periods of time. Finally, the mechanical demands needed for the proper operation of a liquid-fuel operation can be very complex and, therefore, subject to a number of possible failures.

Solid fuel rockets

Like liquid-fuel rockets, solid-fuel rockets have both advantages and disadvantages. The rocket can be fueled a long time in advance of a launch without too much danger of the fuel's deteriorating or damaging the rocket body. The construction of the rocket body needed to accommodate the solid fuel is also much simpler than that which is needed for a liquid-fuel rocket. Finally, the fuels themselves in a solid-fuel rocket tend to be safer and easier to work with than those in a liquid fuel rocket.

Still, solid-fuel rockets have their own drawbacks. Once the fuel in a solid-fuel rocket begins to **burn**, there is no way to slow it down or turn it off. That means that some of the most serious accidents that can occur with a rocket are those that involve solid-fuel combustion that gets out of control.

The solid fuels used in rockets tend to have a claylike texture. The material, called the grain, contains the oxidizer, the fuel, a binder, and other components all mixed with each other. Ignition occurs when a spark sets

First flight of the Ariane 4 rocket.

off a chemical reaction between the oxidizer and the fuel. The chemical reaction that results produces large volumes of hot gases that escape from the rear of the rocket engine.

Many combinations of materials have been used for the grain in a solid-fuel rocket. One common mixture consists of powdered **aluminum metal** as the fuel and ammonium perchlorate or ammonium nitrate as the oxidizer. The flame produced by the reaction between these two substances has a temperature of at least 5,400°F (2,982°C). Nitroglycerine in combination with easily oxidizable organic compounds is also widely used. Such combinations have flame temperatures of about 4,100°F (2,260°C).

The shape into which the grain is formed is especially important in the operation of the solid-fuel rocket. The larger the surface area of grain exposed, the more rapidly the fuel will burn. One could construct a solid-fuel rocket by simply packing the rocket body with the fuel. However, simply boring a hole through the center of the fuel will change the rate at which the fuel will burn. One of the most common patterns now used is a **star** shape. In this pattern, the solid fuel is actually put together in a machine that has a somewhat complex cookie-cutter shape in its interior. When the fuel has been cured and removed from the machine, it looks like a cylinder of cookie dough with its center cut out in the shape of a seven-pointed star.

In some cases, a rocket engineer might want to slow down the rate at which a solid fuel burns. In that case, the surface area of fuel can be decreased or a slow-burning chemical can be added to the fuel, reducing the fuel's tendency to undergo combustion. A grain that has been treated with an inhibitor of this kind is known as a restricted-burning grain.

Specific impulse

The effectiveness of a fuel in propelling a rocket can be measured in a number of ways. For example, the thrust of a rocket is the mass that can be lifted by a particular rocket fuel. The thrust of most rocket propulsion systems is in the range from 500,000 to 14,700,000 newtons (10,000 to 3,300,000 pounds).

The **velocity** of exhaust gases is also an indication of how effectively the rocket can lift its payload, the cargo being carried by the rocket. One of the most useful measures of a rocket's efficiency, however, is specific impulse. Specific impulse (I_{sp}) is a measure of the mass that can be lifted by a given fuel system for each pound of fuel consumer per second of time. The unit in which Isp is measured is seconds.

For example, suppose that a rocket burns up one pound of fuel for every 400 lbs (182 kg) of weight that it lifts from the ground per second. Then its specific impulse is said to be 400 seconds. A typical range of specific impulse values for rocket engines would be between 200 to 400 seconds. Solid rockets tend to have lower specific impulse values than do liquid rockets.

Multistage rockets

In some cases, rocket engineers combine solid and liquid rockets in the same vehicle in order to take advantage of the unique advantages each has to offer. A classical example is the National Aeronautics and Space Administration's Space Shuttles. The shuttles make use of 67 individual rockets in order to lift the vehicle off the Earth's surface, maneuver it through space, and control its re-entry to the Earth's surface. Forty-nine of those rockets are liquid engines and the other 18, solid motors.

The three largest of these rockets are liquid oxygen/ liquid hydrogen engines that provide part of the thrust needed to lift the shuttle off the pad. Two more liquid rockets, powered by a nitrogen tetroxide/ monomethylhydrazine mixture, are used to place the shuttle into

orbit and to carry out a number of orbital maneuvers. Another 44 nitrogen tetroxide/monomethylhydrazine rockets are used for fine tuning the shuttle's orientation in orbit.

Of the solid fuel rockets, two, the solid rocket booster motors, provide nearly 15,000 newtons (3,300,000 pounds) of thrust at take-off. The remaining 16 rockets, composed of ammonium perchlorate, aluminum, and polybutadiene, are used to separate the solid rocket booster capsules from the main shuttle body for re-use.

Non-chemical rockets

Rockets that operate with solid and liquid chemicals are currently the only kinds of vehicles capable of lifting off the Earth's surface for scientific research or military applications. But both types of chemical rockets suffer from one serious drawback for use in vehicles traveling through outer space. The fuels they use are much too heavy for long **distance** travel above the Earth's atmosphere. In other words, their specific impulse is too small to be of value in outer space travel.

Rocket engineers have long recognized that other types of rockets would be more useful in travel outside the Earth's atmosphere. These rockets would operate with power systems that are very light in comparison to chemical rockets. As early as 1944, for example, engineers were exploring the possibility of using nuclear reactors to power rockets. The rocket would carry a small **nuclear reactor**, the heat from which would be used to vaporize hydrogen gas. The hydrogen gas would then be expelled from the rear of the rocket, providing its propulsive force. Calculations indicate that a nuclear rocket of this type would have a specific impulse of about 1,000 seconds, more than twice that of the traditional chemical rocket.

Other types of so-called low-thrust rockets have also been suggested. In some cases, the propulsive force comes from **atoms** and molecules that have been ionized within the rocket body and then accelerated by being placed within a magnetic or electrical field. In other cases, a gas such as hydrogen is first turned into a plasma, and then ionized and accelerated. As attractive as some of these ideas sound in theory, they have thus far found relatively few practical applications in the construction of rocket engines.

Missiles

The modern age of missile science can probably be said to have begun toward the end of World War II. During this period, German rocket scientists had developed the ability to produce vehicles that could deliver warheads to targets hundreds or thousands of miles from their launch point. For a period of time, it appeared that the German V-2 rocket-missile might very well turn the tide of the war and bring victory to Germany.

The Cold War that followed the end of World War II provided a powerful incentive for the United States, the then Soviet Union, and a few other nations to spend huge amounts of money on the development of newer and more sophisticated missile systems. Missiles have the great advantage of being able to deliver a large destructive force at great distance from the launch site. The enemy can be damaged or destroyed with essentially no damage to the party launching the missile.

As the Cold War developed, however, it became obvious that the missile-development campaign was a never-ending battle. Each new development by one side was soon made obsolete by improvements in anti-missile defense mechanisms by the other side. As a result, there is now a staggering variety of missile types with many different functions and capabilities.

Missile classification

Missiles can be classified in a number of different ways. Some are said to be unguided because, once they are launched, there is no further control over their flight. The German V-2 rockets were unguided missiles. Such missiles can be directed at the launch site in the general vicinity of a target, but once they are on their way, there is no further way that their path can be adjusted or corrected.

The vast majority of missiles, however, are guided missiles. This term refers to the fact that the missile's pathway can be monitored and changed either by instruments within the missile itself or by a guidance station.

Missiles can also be classified as aerodynamic or ballistic missiles. An aerodynamic missile is one equipped with wings, fins, or other structures that allow it to maneuver as it travels to its target. Aerodynamic missiles are also known as cruise missiles. Ballistic missiles are missiles that follow a free-fall path once they have reached a given altitude. In essence, a ballistic missile is fired into the air, the way a baseball player makes a throw from the outfield, and the missile (the ball) travels along a path determined by its own velocity and the Earth's gravitational attraction.

Finally, missiles can be classified according to the place from which they are launched and the location of their final target. V-2 rockets were surface-to-surface missiles since they were launched from a station on the ground in Germany and were designed to strike targets on the ground in Great Britain.

An air-to-air missile is one fired from the air (usually from an **aircraft**) with the objective of destroying another aircraft. One of the best known air-to-air missiles is the United States' Sidewinder missile, first put into operation in 1956. The first Sidewinders were 9.31 ft (2.84

m) long and 5.00 in (12.7 cm) in diameter, with a weight of 165 lbs (5 kg) and a range of 0.68 mi (1.1 km).

A surface-to-air missile is one fired from a ground station with the goal of destroying aircraft. The first surface-to-air missile used by the United States military was the Nike Ajax, a rocket with a weight of 2,295 lbs (1,042 kg), a length of 34.8 ft (10.6 m), a diameter of 12.0 in (30.5 cm),and a range of 30 mi (48 km).

Some other types of missiles of importance to the military are anti-ship and anti-submarine missiles, both of which can be launched from ground stations, from aircraft, or from other ships. Military leaders were at one time also very enthusiastic about another type of missile, the anti-ballistic missile (ABM). The ABM program was conceived of as a large number of solid rockets that could be aimed at incoming missiles. U.S. engineers developed two forms of the ABM: the Spartan, designed for long-distance defensive uses, and the Spring, designed for short-range interception. The Soviet Union, in the meanwhile, placed its reliance on an ABM given the code name of Galosh. The ABM program came to a halt in the mid-1970s when the cost of implementing a truly effective defensive system became apparent.

Structure of the missile

Any missile consists essentially of four parts: a body, known as the airframe; the propulsive system; the weapon; and the guidance system. Specifications for the airframes of some typical rockets were given above. The propulsive systems used in missiles are essentially the same as those described for rockets above. That is, they consist of one or more liquid rockets, one or more solid rockets, or some combination of these.

In theory, missiles can carry almost any kind of chemical, biological, or nuclear weapon. Anti-tank missiles, as an example, carry very high powered chemical **explosives** that allow them to penetrate a 24 in (60 cm) thick piece of metal. **Nuclear weapons** have, however, become especially popular for use in missiles. One reason, of course, is the destructiveness of such weapons. But another reason is that anti-missile jamming programs are often good enough today to make it difficult for even the most sophisticated guided missile to reach its target without **interference**. Nuclear weapons cause destruction over such a wide area, however, that defensive jamming is less important than it is with more conventional explosive warheads.

Guidance systems

At one time, the methods used to guide a missile to its target were relatively simple. One of the most primitive of these systems was the use of a conducting wire trailed behind the missile and attached to a ground monitoring station. The person controlling the missile's flight could make adjustments in its path simply by sending electrical signals along the trailing wire. This system could be used, of course, only at a distance equal to the length of wire that could be carried by the missile, a distance of about 984 ft (300 m).

The next step up from the trailing wire guidance system is one in which a signal is sent by radio from the guidance center to the missile. Although this system is effective at much longer ranges than the trailing wire system, it is also much more susceptible to interference (jamming) by enemy observers. Much of the essence of the missile battles that took place on **paper** during the Cold War was between finding new and more secure ways to send messages to a missile, and new and more sophisticated ways to interrupt and "jam" those signals.

Some missile systems carry their own guidance systems within their bodies. One approach is for the missile to send out **radio waves** aimed at its target and then to monitor and analyze the waves that are reflected back to it from the target. With this system, the missile can constantly make adjustments that keep it on its path to the target. As with ground-directed controls, however, a system such as this one is also subject to jamming by enemy signals.

Another guidance system makes use of a TV camera mounted in the nose of the missile. The camera is preprogrammed to lock in on the missile's target. Electronic and computer systems on board the missile can then keep the rocket on its correct path.

KEY TERMS

Ballistic missile—A missile that travels at a velocity less than that needed to place it in orbit and which, therefore, follows a trajectory back to the Earth's surface.

Grain—The fuel in a solid propellant.

Hypergolic system—A propellant system in which the components ignite spontaneously upon coming into contact.

Monopropellant—A system in which fuel and oxidizer are combined into a single component.

Specific impulse—The thrust provided to a rocket by a fuel as measured in pounds of payload lifted per pound of fuel per second.

Further Reading

Collinson, Charles, "Missile," in *McGraw-Hill Encyclopedia of Science & Technology.* 7th edition, vol. 11. New York: McGraw-Hill Book Company, 1992.

"Missile" and "Rocket," in *The Illustrated Science and Invention Encyclopedia*. vols. 12 and 15. Westport, CT: H. S. Stuttman, Inc., Publishers, 1982.

Sutton, George P., "Rocket Propulsion," in *McGraw-Hill Encyclopedia of Science & Technology*. 7th edition, vol. 15. New York: McGraw-Hill Book Company, 1992.

David E. Newton

Rocks

Geologists define rocks as aggregates of **minerals**. Minerals are naturally-occurring, inorganic substances with specific chemical compositions and structures. A rock can consist of many crystals of one mineral, or combinations of many minerals. Several exceptions, such as **coal** and obsidian, are not composed of minerals but are considered to be rocks. Common uses for rocks include building materials, roofs, sculpture, jewelry, tombstones, chalk, and coal for **heat**. Many metals are derived from rocks known as ores. Oil and **natural gas** are also found in rocks.

Prehistoric humans used rocks as early as 2,000,000 B.C. Flint and other hard rocks were important raw materials for crafting arrowheads and other tools. By 500,000 B.C., rock caves and structures made from stones had become important forms of shelter for early man. During that time, early man had learned to use fire, a development that allowed humans to cook food and greatly expand their geographical range. Eventually, probably no later than 5000 B.C., humans realized that metals such as gold and **copper** could be derived from rocks. Many ancient monuments were crafted from stone, including the pyramids of Egypt, built from limestone around 2500 B.C., and the buildings of Chichen Itza in Mexico, also of limestone, built around 450 A.D.

Since at least the 1500s, scientists have studied minerals and **mining**, fundamental aspects of the study of rocks. Georgius Agricola (the Latin name for Georg Bauer) published *De Re Metallica* (*Concerning Metallic Things*) in 1556. By 1785, the British geologist James Hutton published *Theory of the Earth*, in which he discussed his observations of rocks in Great Britain and his conclusion that the **Earth** is much older than previous scientists had estimated.

Types of rocks

Geologists, scientists who study the Earth and rocks, distinguish three main groups of rocks: **igneous rocks**, sedimentary rocks, and metamorphic rocks. These distinctions are made on the basis of the types of minerals in the rock, the shapes of individual mineral grains, and the overall texture of the rock, all of which indicate the environment, **pressure**, and **temperature** in which the rock formed.

Igneous rocks

Igneous rocks form when molten rock, known as **magma** (if below the surface of the Earth) or lava (at the surface of the Earth), crystallizes. The minerals in the rock crystallize or grow together so that the individual crystals **lock** together. Igneous rocks and magma make up much of the oceanic and continental crust, as well as most of the rock deeper in the Earth.

Igneous rocks can be identified by the interlocking appearance of the crystals in them. Typical igneous rocks do not have a layered texture, but exceptions exist. For example, in large bodies of igneous rock, relatively dense crystals that form early can sink to the bottom of the magma, and less dense layers of crystals that form later can accumulate on top. Igneous rocks can form deep within the Earth or at the surface of the Earth in volcanoes. In general, igneous rocks that form deep within the Earth have large crystals that indicate a longer period of time during which the magma cools. Igneous rocks that form at or near the surface of the Earth, such as volcanic igneous rocks, cool quickly and contain smaller crystals that are difficult to see without magnification. Obsidian, sometimes called volcanic **glass**, cools so quickly that no crystals form. Nevertheless, obsidian is considered to be an igneous rock.

Igneous rocks are classified on the basis of their mineral content and the size of the crystals in the rock. Extrusive igneous rocks have small crystals and crystallize at or near the Earth's surface. Intrusive igneous rocks cool slowly below the Earth's surface and have larger crystals. Rocks made up of dense, dark-colored minerals such as olivine, pyroxene, amphibole, and plagioclase are called mafic igneous rocks. Lighter-colored, less dense minerals, including quartz, mica, and feldspar, make up felsic igneous rocks.

Common igneous rocks include the felsic igneous rocksgranite and rhyolite, and the mafic igneous rocks gabbro and basalt. Granite is an intrusive igneous rocks that includes large crystals of the minerals quartz, feldspar, mica, and amphibole that form deep within the Earth. Rhyolite includes the same minerals, but forms as extrusive igneous rock near the surface of the Earth or in volcanoes and cools quickly from magma or lava, so its crystals are difficult to observe with the naked **eye**. Similarly, gabbro is more coarse-grained than basalt and forms deeper in the Earth, but both rocks include the minerals pyroxene, feldspar, and olivine.

Fabulous exposures of igneous rocks occur in the volcanoes of Hawaii, volcanic rocks of Yellowstone National Park (located in Wyoming, Idaho, and Montana), and in Lassen Volcanic National Park and Yosemite National Park (both in California).

Sedimentary rocks

Sedimentary rocks are those made of grains of pre-existing rocks or organic material that, in most cases, have been eroded, deposited, compacted, and cemented together. They typically form at the surface of the Earth as sediment moves as a result of the action of **wind**, **water**, ice, gravity, or a combination of these. Sedimentary rocks also form as chemicals precipitate from seawater, or through accumulation of organic material such as **plant** debris or **animal** shells. Common sedimentary rocks include shale, sandstone, limestone, and conglomerate. Sedimentary rocks typically have a layered appearance because most sediments are deposited in horizontal layers and are buried beneath later deposits of sediments over long periods of time. Sediments deposited rapidly, however, tend to be poorly layered if layers are present at all.

Sedimentary rocks form in many different environments at the surface of the Earth. Eolian, or wind blown, sediments can accumulate in deserts. **Rivers** carry sediments and **deposit** them along their banks or into lakes or oceans. **Glaciers** form unusual deposits of a wide variety of sediments that they pick up as the glacier expands and moves; glacial deposits are well-exposed in the northern United States. Sediments can travel in currents below **sea level** to the deepest parts of the **ocean** floor. Secretion of **calcium** carbonate shells by reef-building organisms produce large quantities of limestone. **Evaporation** of seawater has resulted in the formation of widespread layers of **salt** and gypsum. Swamps rich in plants can produce coal if organic material accumulates and is buried before **aerobic bacteria** can destroy the dead plants.

Sedimentary rocks are classified on the basis of the sizes of the particles in the rock and the composition of the rock. Clastic sedimentary rocks comprise fragments of preexisting rocks and organic **matter**. Non-clastic sedimentary rocks include rocks that precipitate from sea water, such as salts, and rocks formed from organic matter or organic activity, such as coal and limestone made by reef-building organisms like coral. Grain sizes in sedimentary rocks range from fine clay and silt to sand to boulders.

The sediment in a **sedimentary rock** reflects its environment of deposition. For example, wind-blown sand grains commonly display evidence of abrasion of their surfaces as a result of colliding with other grains. Sediments transported long distances tend to decrease in size and are more rounded than sediment deposited near their precursor rocks because of wearing against other sediments or rocks. Large or heavy sediments tend to settle out of water or wind if the **energy** of the water or wind is insufficient to carry the sediments. Sediments deposited rapidly as a result of slides or slumps tend to include a larger range of sediment sizes, from large boulders to pebbles to sand grains and flakes of clay. Such rocks are called conglomerate. Along beaches, the rhythmic activity of waves moving sediment back and forth produces sandstones in which the grains are well-rounded and of similar size. Glaciers pick up and carry a wide variety of sediments and often scratch or scrape the rocks over which they travel.

Sedimentary rocks are the only rocks in which fossils can be preserved because at the elevated temperatures and pressures in which igneous and metamorphic rocks form, fossils and organic remnants are destroyed. The presence of fossils and the types of fossilorganisms in a rock provide clues about the environment and age of sedimentary rocks. For example, fossils of human beings are not present in rocks older than approximately 2,000,000 years because humans did not exist before then. Similarly, **dinosaur** fossils do not occur in rocks younger than about 65,000,000 years because dinosaurs became extinct at that time. **Fish** fossils in sedimentary rock indicate that the sediments that make up the rock were deposited in a **lake**, river, or marine environment. By establishing the environment of the fossils in a rock, scientists learn more about the conditions under which the rock formed.

Spectacular exposures of sedimentary rocks include the Grand Canyon (Arizona), the eolian sandstones of Zion National Park (Utah), the limestones of Carlsbad National Park (New Mexico), and glacial features of Voyagers National Park (Minnesota).

Metamorphic rocks

Metamorphic rocks are named for the process of **metamorphism**, or change, that affects rocks. The changes that form metamorphic rocks usually include increases in the temperature (generally to at least 392°F (200°C) and the pressure of a precursor rock, which can be igneous, sedimentary, or metamorphic, to a degree that the minerals in the rock are no longer stable. The rock might change in mineral content or appearance, or both. Clues to identifying metamorphic rocks include the presence of minerals such as mica, amphibole, staurolite, and garnet, and layers in which minerals are aligned as a result of pressure applied to the rock. Common metamorphic rocks include slate, schist, and gneiss. Metamorphic rocks commonly occur in mountains, such as the Appalachian Mountains, parts of California, and the ancient, eroded metamorphic rocks in the Llano **Uplift** of central Texas.

Metamorphic rocks are classified according to their constituent minerals and texture. Foliated metamorphic rocks are those that have a layered texture. In foliated metamorphic rocks, elongate or platy minerals such as mica and amphibole become aligned as a result of pressure on the rock. Foliation can range from alternating layers of light and dark minerals typical of gneiss to the seemingly perfect alignment of platy minerals in slate. Some meta-

KEY TERMS

Cementation—Process through which minerals are glued together, usually as a result of precipitation of solids from solutions in sediments. Calcite, quartz, and clay minerals such as chlorite are common cement-forming minerals in sedimentary rocks.

Compaction—Reduction of volume of material. Sediments typically compact following burial beneath newer sediments.

Igneous rock—Rock formed by crystallization of molten minerals.

Lava—Molten rock that occurs at the surface of the Earth, usually through volcanic eruptions. Lava crystallizes into igneous rock when it cools.

Magma—Molten rock found below the surface of the Earth. It can crystallize, or solidify, to form igneous rock.

Metamorphic rock—Rock formed by alteration of preexisting rock through changes in temperature, pressure, or activity of fluids.

Mineral—A naturally-occurring, inorganic substance with a definite chemical composition and structure.

Rock—An aggregate of minerals.

Rock cycle—The processes through which rocks change from one type to another, typically through melting, metamorphism, uplift, weathering, burial, or other processes.

Sedimentary rock—Rock formed by deposition, compaction, and cementation of weathered rock, or by chemical precipitation. Salt and gypsum form from evaporation and precipitation processes.

Uplift—Movement of rock bodies to shallower positions in or on the Earth.

Weathering—The process through which rocks become separated from each other, breaking apart into sediments.

morphic rocks are unfoliated and have a massive texture devoid of layers. **Mineralogy** of metamorphic rocks reflects the minerals content of the precursor rock and the pressure and temperature at which metamorphism occurs.

As sediments undergo metamorphism, the layers of sediment can be folded or become more pronounced as pressure on the rock increases. Elongate or platy minerals in the rock tend to become aligned in the same direction. For example, when shale metamorphoses to slate, it becomes easier to split the well-aligned layers of the slate into thin, flat sheets. This property of slate makes it an attractive roofing material. Marble-metamorphosed limestone-typically does not have the pronounced layers of slate, but is used for flooring and sculptures.

Metamorphism of igneous rocks can cause the different minerals in the rocks to separate into layers. When granite metamorphoses into gneiss, layers of light-colored minerals and dark-colored minerals form. As with sedimentary rocks, elongate or platy minerals become well-aligned as pressure on the rock increases.

It is possible for metamorphic rocks to metamorphose into other metamorphic rocks. In some regions, especially areas where mountain-building is taking place, it is not unusual for several episodes of metamorphism to affect rocks. It can be difficult to unravel the effects of each episode of metamorphism.

The rock cycle

The rock cycle is a depiction of how the three main rock types can change from one type to another. As rocks exposed at the surface **weather**, they form sediments that can be deposited to form sedimentary rocks. As sedimentary rocks are buried beneath more sediment, they are subjected to increases in both pressure and temperature, which can result in metamorphism and the formation of **metamorphic rock**. If the temperature of metamorphism is extremely high, the rock might melt completely and later recrystallize as an igneous rock. Igneous, sedimentary, and metamorphic rocks can erode and later form sedimentary rock. Rocks can move through the rock cycle along other paths, but uplift or burial, **weathering**, and changes in temperature and pressure are the primary causes of changes in rocks from one type to another.

Current research

Scientists who study rocks attempt to answer a wide variety of questions: What do rocks and the ratios of stable to unstable isotopes within rocks tell us about the age of the Earth, the times at which the Earth's tectonic plates collided to produce mountains, and **global warming**? At what times were glaciers present on different continents? Where might we expect to have earthquakes and volcanic eruptions? What types of fossils occur in rocks and how do the fossils differ among rocks from all

over the world? In which rocks might we find safe supplies of water, hydrocarbons, and mineral resources such as copper, diamonds, graphite, and **aluminum**? Although these problems are not often easy to solve, rocks supply important information about them.

Scientists examine rocks in various settings. Some scientists go out to places where rocks are exposed at the surface of the Earth in order to map occurrences and to collect samples of rocks for further study in the laboratory. Others work exclusively in the laboratory examining thin slices of rock under microscopes, determining the structure and chemical composition of individual crystals within a rock, determining the ratios of different isotopes of **atoms** within a **crystal** or rock, or examining the fossils in rocks. Scientists who work in different areas of the Earth try to compare the rocks and fossils they find in order to determine how the Earth has changed through time. For example, the eastern coast of **South America** and the western coast of **Africa** share many common rocks and fossils, suggesting that these areas might have been closer in the past.

Scientists also pay close attention to several significant ongoing phenomena: large, destructive earthquakes in California and Japan; a surge in the Bering Glacier of Alaska, the largest glacier in **North America**; and volcanic activity in Chile, Indonesia, Papua New Guinea, and Zaire. In addition, studies of how and where rocks form continue.

See also Metal; Ore.

Rodents

A rodent is any mammal that belongs to the order Rodentia, which includes most **mammals** equipped with continuously growing incisor teeth that are remarkably efficient for gnawing on tough **plant** matter. The name rodent comes from the Latin word *rodere* meaning "to gnaw." Rodents live in virtually every **habitat**, often in close association with humans. This close association between rodents and humans is frequently detrimental to human interests, since rodents (especially **rats** and **mice**) eat huge quantities of stored food and spread serious, often fatal, diseases. There are far more members in the order Rodentia than in any other order of mammals. Nearly 40% of all mammal species belong to this order.

Some rodents such as **beavers** have been economically important. Others, such as **guinea pigs**, **hamsters**, and **gerbils**, are fun pets. However, most of the about 1,600 species (the exact number changes frequently as various groups of rodents are studied closely) play little role in human lives. Instead, they carry on their own lives in virtually every environment, rarely noticed by the humans around them.

KEY TERMS

Canines—Pointed teeth of most mammals, used for stabbing food. Rodents lack canine teeth.

Cheek-teeth—Molars and premolars, the grinding teeth located on the side of the mouth in rodents and many other mammals.

Incisors—The front cutting teeth of a mammal. In rodents, they grow continuously.

Rodents are distinguished from other mammals primarily by their 16 teeth. **Lagomorphs** (rabbits and hares) also have continuously growing incisors, and they were, for many years, included among the rodents. But they have an additional pair of tiny incisors that grows just behind the big front teeth, so they are now classified in a separate order.

The two pairs of rodent incisors work together, like scissors. They grow continuously from **birth** and must regularly be used for gnawing to keep them worn down and sharp. They have a heavy coating of enamel on the front surface but none on the back. Because the enamel wears away more slowly than the rest of the tooth, a sharp, chisel-like edge is maintained on the gnawing teeth. If a rodent breaks one of its incisors, the **animal** usually soon dies because it cannot eat properly.

Unlike many mammals, rodents have no canine teeth. Instead, there's an empty space between the incisors and flat-topped cheek-teeth, or molars, at the side of the mouth. This space lets rodents suck in their cheeks or lips to shield their mouths and throats from chips flying from whatever material they are gnawing. When using their cheek-teeth to grind up the plant matter they have gnawed, rodents have special jaw muscles that keep their incisors out of the way.

Rodents are divided into three groups according to the way their jaw muscles and associated skull structures are arranged. This is very important because these muscles control gnawing.

The squirrel-like rodents (Sciuromorpha) have a very simple jaw muscle that extends onto the snout in front of the **eye**. This group includes the **squirrels** as well as such unsquirrel-like animals as beavers and pocket **gophers**. They are mostly found in the northern hemisphere.

The mouse-like or rat-like rodents (Myomorpha) have jaw muscles that anchor on the side of the nose. Be-

A mole rat, *Cryptomys hottentotus,* from southern Africa.

cause their jaw muscles are the most efficient, this group contains the most species and is found all over the world. It includes the mice, rats, **voles**, **lemmings**, and even the riverbank-dwelling **muskrat**. Two-thirds of all rodents belong to only one family in this group, the mice.

The cavy-like rodents (Caviomorpha) have very large cheekbones and muscles that anchor to the side of the face. This group includes the **porcupines**, as well as primarily South American mammals such as the cavy. Some fossil mammals in this group were as large as **bears**. The Old World members of this group are sometimes placed in a separate group called the porcupine-like rodents (Hystricomorpha).

Most rodents are very small, averaging less than 5 oz (150 g). However, the capybara, a large South American rodent, may weigh as much as 145 lb (66 kg). Rodents usually breed easily and quickly, producing large litters. This fact played a major role in their worldwide distribution. Genetic changes can develop into new species quite rapidly when animals breed so quickly. Such changes allowed rodents to take over many habitats that might not otherwise have been suitable. Rodents swim, glide, burrow, climb, and survive different uncomfortable climates.

Rodents are known to carry disease-causing agents of at least 20 important human diseases including **bubonic plague**. About 500 years ago, at least 25 million people died in **Europe** from the "black death," as the plague was called. The plague-causing **bacteria** (*Yersinia pestis*) were carried by **fleas** that were spread from rodents to people.

See also Agouti; Capybaras; Chinchilla; Chipmunks; Coypu; Deer mouse; Dormouse; Groundhogs; Jerboas; Kangaroo rats; Mole-rats; Prairie dog.

Further Reading

Hanney, Peter W. *Rodents: Their Lives and Habits.* New York: Taplinger Publishing Co., 1975.

Knight, Linsay. *The Sierra Club Book of Small Mammals.* San Francisco: Sierra Club Books, 1993.

Jean F. Blashfield

Rollers

Rollers are 16 species of terrestrial **birds** in the family Coraciidae. Rollers occur in **Africa**, Eurasia, and

Australia. Most species are tropical, but some occur in temperate climates.

Rollers are stout-bodied birds, ranging in body length from 9.5 to 13 inches (24 to 33 cm). Most species have rounded wings, and a **square** or forked tail, although a few have elongated, decorative tail feathers. Rollers have a short neck and short legs with strong feet. Their beak is stout, broad, slightly downward curving, and hooked at the tip.

Rollers are generally attractive, brightly colored birds, with patches of brown, yellow, blue, purple, green, black, or white. The sexes do not differ in coloration. Rollers received their common name from the habit of many species performing aerial rolls and tumbles during their prenuptial display flights.

Many species of rollers feed by hunting from a conspicuous **perch** and making quick sallies to predate on **insects**, lizards, small **mammals**, or other suitable **prey** that they detect visually. Flying prey may be pursued aerially, or the rollers may seize their prey on the ground.

Rollers defend a territory by conspicuous visual displays, and not by song. Rollers nest in cavities in trees, earthen banks, or rock piles. The three to six eggs are incubated by both parents, who also rear the young together.

The most diverse genus is *Coracias*, nine species of which breed in Africa alone. The racquet-tailed roller (*C. spatulata*) is an especially attractive African species, having a pale-blue body, with violet and brown wings, and two elongated, outer tail feathers. The European roller (*Coracias garrulus*) is a migratory species of **Europe**, wintering in the tropics of Africa.

The dollarbird or broad-billed roller (*Eurystomus orientalis*) is a blue-bodied bird with white wing-patches. The dollarbird ranges widely from India and China, through Indonesia and New Guinea, to Australia and the Solomon Islands. Various subspecies of the dollarbird have evolved in some parts of its range.

Bill Freedman

Root see **Radical**

Root of equation see **Solution of equation**

Root system

In most plants, the root system is a below-ground structure that serves primarily to anchor the **plant** in the **soil** and take up **water** and **minerals**. Roots may be less familiar than the more visible flowers, stems, and leaves, but they are no less important to the plant.

Roots have four regions: a root cap; a zone of division; a zone of elongation; and a zone of maturation. The root cap is a cup-shaped group of cells at the tip of the root which protects the delicate cells behind the cap as it pushes through the soil. The root cap secretes mucigel, a substance that acts as a lubricant to aid in its movement. The root cap also plays a role in a plant's response to gravity. If a flower pot is placed on its side, the stem would grow upward toward the light, and the root cap would direct the roots to grow downward. Above the root cap is the zone of division, and above that is the zone of elongation. The zone of division contains growing and dividing meristematic cells. After each **cell division**, one daughter cell retains the properties of the meristem cell, while the other daughter cell (in the zone of elongation) elongates sometimes up to as much as 150 times. As a result, the root tip is literally pushed through the soil.

In the zone of maturation, cells differentiate and serve such functions as protection, storage, and conductance. Seen in **cross section**, the zone of maturation of many roots has an outer layer (the epidermis), a deeper level (the cortex), and a central region that includes the conducting vascular **tissue**.

The epidermis is usually a single layer of cells at the outer edge of the root, which absorbs water and dissolved minerals, a function greatly facilitated by the presence of root hairs. Root hairs form from the outward growth of epidermal cells and are restricted to a small area near the root tip. A single four-month-old rye plant was estimated to have approximately 14 billion root hairs.

The cortex occupies most of the **volume** of young roots, and is important for storing substances such as starch.

At the root's center is the region of vascular tissue which functions in the transport of water up the root and into the stem (in xylem tissue), and in the transport of carbohydrates and other substances from the stem down into the root (in phloem tissue). Cells in the xylem and phloem either attach to each other end-to-end or are tapered, with overlapping walls, facilitating the movement of substances from cell to cell. In many plants, a single cluster of xylem and phloem cells occupies a relatively small area of the root cross section. In other plants, a cylinder of vascular tissue forms a ring around a center of relatively undifferentiated cells, called the pith.

Roots often form symbiotic associations with soil **fungi** called mycorrhizae. In this association, the plant benefits from **phosphorus** that is taken up and supplied by the fungus, and the fungus benefits from carbohydrates produced by the plant. Plants grown in the ab-

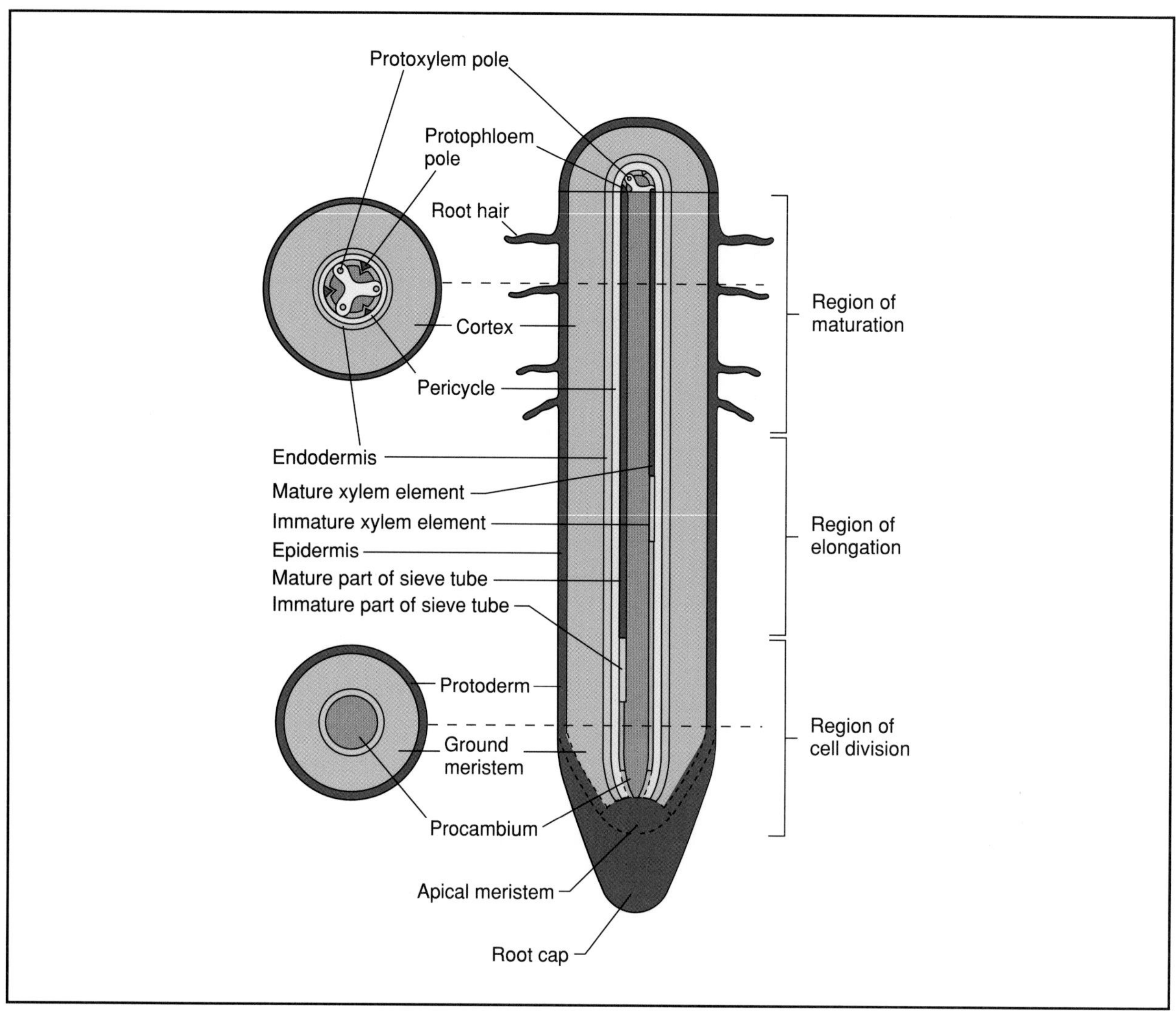

Figure 1. Early stages in the development of a root tip, illustrating its four regions.

sence of soil mycorrhizae generally do less well than when mycorrhizae are present.

Another symbiotic root association is between plants such as peas and beans (family Leguminosae) and *Rhizobium* bacteria. The **bacteria** penetrate the root cells, multiply, and in doing so form nodules where the bacteria have access to carbohydrates synthesized by the plant. In return, the bacteria "fix" **nitrogen**, converting nitrogen gas from the atmosphere into nitrogen-containing compounds that can be used by plants.

Types of roots

In most trees and wildflowers, one root, the taproot, is more prominent than the other fibrous roots. The taproot is usually relatively large in diameter and extends more deeply than the plant's other roots, and often has additional lateral roots.

Other plants, particularly **grasses**, have fibrous root systems formed from many roots of more or less equal size. In general, taproots extend more deeply than fibrous roots, with fibrous roots occupying a greater proportion of the upper soil layers.

Plants may also form other types of roots, such as buttress roots, which form large above-ground support structures such as the lower trunks of plants like the bald cypress and some fig trees. Buttress roots are especially useful in supporting these trees in moist soil. Prop roots arise either from the lower stem (as in corn) or from lower branches (as in red mangrove, banyan, and certain **palms**), and provide extra stability for these shallow-rooted plants. Climbing plants (such as ivy) produce roots that aid in attaching the plant to other plants, buildings, and walls. Other air roots, such as those found in mangroves, grow up out of the oxygen-deprived mud in which these plants

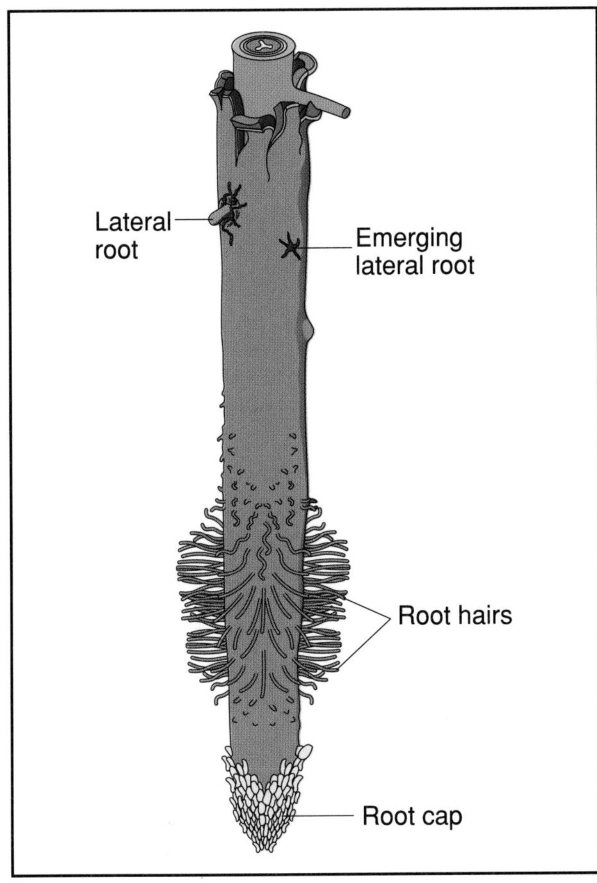

Figure 2. The root cap shown in relation to root hairs and emerging lateral roots.

typically grow and aid in the uptake of **oxygen**. This growth is unusual for roots, for these roots grow away from the **force** of gravity, rather than toward it. Perhaps the most unusual root system is that of the flower-pot plant, whose roots grow into a hollow structure formed from the plant's own modified leaves. This hollow structure collects rainwater, which the roots then absorb.

Importance of roots

Carrots, sugar beets, turnips, and cassava are all roots specialized for the storage of carbohydrates. These compounds are stored over winter by the plant for use in the following growing season.

Onions, garlic, potatoes, and **ginger** grow underground but are not roots; Rather, they are stem tissue modified to serve a storage function. A root is defined by its structure, rather than its function.

Roots penetrate, bind, and stabilize the soil, so helping to prevent soil **erosion**. Roots also stimulate the growth of soil micro- and macroorganisms, compact the soil, alter soil **chemistry** through their secretions, and add organic material upon their death.

See also Mycorrhiza; Nitrogen fixation.

KEY TERMS

Cortex—Tissue located between the epidermis and the central vascular tissue. Functions primarily in storage and in movement of water into the vascular cylinder.

Epidermis—The outermost and usually single layer of cells in the root. Gives rise to root hairs.

Fibrous root system—A root system comprised of many roots of approximately equal size. Fibrous roots are found primarily in the upper horizons of the soil.

Meristem—A group of cells whose primary function is cell division. Divisions result in one daughter cell that continues to function as a meristem cell and one daughter cell that differentiates into a different cell type.

Mucigel—A polysaccharide produced by roots that aids root penetration, inhibits desiccation, and increases absorption.

Taproot—The dominant root formed by most plants, and from which additional lateral roots arise.

Further Reading

Capon, B. *Botany for Gardeners.* Portland: Timber Press, 1990.

Mauseth, J. D. *Botany: An Introduction to Plant Biology.* Philadelphia: Saunders College Publishing, 1991.

Moore, R., and W. D. Clark. *Botany: Plant Form and Function.* Dubuque, IA: Wm. C. Brown, 1995.

Raven, P. H., R. F. Evert, and S. E. Eichhorn. *Biology of Plants.* 4th ed. New York: Worth, 1986.

Steven B. Carroll

Rose family

The rose family (Rosaceae), in the order Rosales, is a large **plant** family containing more than 100 genera and 2,000 species of trees, shrubs, and herbs. This family is represented on all continents except **Antarctica**, but the majority of species are found in **Europe**, **Asia**, and **North America**. Fossil evidence from Colorado, reliably identified as belonging to the genus *Rosa*, suggests that this family has been in existence for at least 35 million years.

Most species in the Rosaceae have leaves with serrated margins and a pair of stipules where the **leaf** joins the stem. The majority of tree-sized arborescent species have leaves that are simple except for species of **mountain** ash (*Sorbus* spp.), which have compound leaves divided into five to seven leaflets. Conversely, most woody shrubs and herbs have compound leaves which are composed of three to 11 leaflets. Branch spines and prickles are common on trees and shrubs in the rose family. However, there is variability in the appearance of these structures even among species which occur in very similar habitats. For example, blackbrush, (*Coleogyne ramosissima*), a species found in pinion-juniper woodlands in the American Southwest, has long spines on which it bears flowers, while Apache plume (*Fallugia paradoxa*, is found in the same region and **habitat** but has no spines. On a much larger scale, trees of the genus *Crataegus*, which are collectively called thornapples or hawthorns, have prominent branch spines while most species of *Malus* and *Prunus* are without spines. Herbaceous species typically lack spines or prickles.

Flowers in this family are typically radially symmetrical flat discs (actinomorphic) and contain both male and female floral structures in a single **flower**. Flower ovaries may be positioned below the sepals and petals (inferior) or above them (superior). In flowers having an inferior ovary, the carpels are surrounded by a hollow receptacle. Flowers typically have five sepals, five petals, numerous stamens, and one to 50 carpels. Carpels in this family tend to remain free instead of becoming fused into a many chambered, single carpel. Anthers have two chambers, called locules, which split lengthwise to release thousands of pollen grains. Another distinguishing feature of flowers in this family is the presence of a structure called the epicalyx. The epicalyx is composed of five sepal-like structures which occur below and alternate with the true calyx.

Most species have large white, pink, or red petals which are designed to attract pollinating **insects**. Many white and pale pink flowers also produce volatile esters, chemicals which we perceive as pleasant odors, but are produced to attract insects. The chief pollinators of rose flowers are **bees** ranging in size from tiny, metallic green flower bees of the genus *Augochlora*, through honey bees (*Apis*), to large bumble bees (*Bombus*). These pollinators are unspecialized and also pollinate many other species which have actinomorphic flowers and offer copious pollen as a reward for flower visitation.

Insect **pollination** is the most common type in the Rosaceae, but some species have evolved to be pollinated by **wind**. Flowers adapted for wind pollination are found in species of *Acaena*, which are native to windswept mountain areas of New Zealand, **Australia**, and the Andes Mountains of **South America**. Wind pollination also occurs in species of the genus *Poterium* which are native to high elevations in Europe, western Asia and northern **Africa**. Both of these genera inhabit habitats where the combination of frequent low temperatures and windy periods make wind more reliable than insects as a mechanism to achieve pollination. Also, unlike the usual bisexual condition found in insect pollinated flowers, species of *Acaena* and *Poterium* have distinct male and female flowers.

Woody shrubs and herbs in the Rosaceae also propagate through asexual means. Shrubs in the genera *Chaenomeles* (flowering quince), *Rosa* (Rose) and *Rubus* (blackberry and raspberry) produce **suckers** from their rootstock or spread by rhizomes. Species of *Rubus* may also spread by stems that produce roots when they bend and the tip touches the ground. Some herbaceous species of the genera *Fragaria* (strawberry), *Duchesnea* (Indian strawberry), and *Potentilla* (cinquefoil) produce plantlets at the end of stolons which take root and eventually live as independent, but genetically identical plants.

There are many different types of **fruits** in the rose family, ranging from single-seeded, soft, fleshy, fruits known as drupes to harder, fleshy pseudocarps such as a pome or hip. In the genera *Malus* (apples and crabapples), *Chaenomeles*, and *Rosa,* the true fruit is engulfed in a fleshy structure called the hypanthium, which is composed of the swollen bases of petals and sepals. In the mature pseudocarp (pome or hip), the true fruit is centrally located and contains five distinct carpels which may contain one or more **seeds** each. The fleshy **tissue** which surrounds the fruit is the hypanthium. This type of fruit is called a pome or hip.

In the genus *Prunus* (cherry, peach, and plum), fruits contain a single seed enclosed in a hard structure that is not part of the seed coat called the endocarp. The mesocarp and ectocarp are fleshy. This type of fruit is called a drupe.

Other members of the rose family have a small drupe called a drupelet, as in the genus *Rubus*. In these plants, several distinct pistils are attached to the receptacle, each of which becomes a drupelet. Because there are as many as 30 drupelets on each receptacle, the fruit of a blackberry is referred to as a aggregate fruit. The commercial raspberry is the result of crosses among the dominant parent plant, *Rubus ideas*, and other *Rubus* species. Similarly, in the genus *Fragaria* (strawberry), there are as many as 50 distinct, single-ovule pistils in each individual flower. Here, however, the matured carpel becomes a small, dry, hard, and single-seed containing fruit called an achene. The bright red structure on which all these achenes rest is developed from the floral receptacle and is the part of the flower which we eat. The commer-

A dwarf apple tree.

cial strawberry is a cultivated version of the sand strawberry, *Fragaria chiloensis*, which is native to dunes on the western coast of North America.

Most members of the Rosaceae have fruits that are fleshy and conspicuously red, purple or yellow in color. These fruits serve as important sources of **nutrition** for many species of wild animals. From the evolutionary perspective of the plant, the function of these edible fruits is not primarily to serve as food. Instead, these pomes, drupes, and aggregate fruits are designed to entice an **animal** into eating the fruit, so the enclosed seeds are then either discarded or ingested. In this way, the plant offers food to the animal, and the animal acts as an agent of seed dispersal for the plant. The hard endocarp of drupes and drupelets enables the enclosed seed to pass safely through the digestive tract of a bird and to be excreted intact.

Certain species in the Rosaceae are also of importance because of their value as ecological indicators of habitat conditions. In open habitats where **soil** is acidic, species such as the cinquefoils, *Potentilla canadensis* and *P. simplex*, can become common understory herbs. Also in this type of habitat, Indian strawberry (*Duchesnea indica*) may become quite common. *Duchesnea indica* is interesting because it has a similar appearance and growth habit to strawberries (*Fragaria*). However, where true strawberries have flowers with white petals, *D. indica* has yellow petals. Also, leaflets of *Fragaria* species have smaller serrations on the margins, and are more generally round in shape than are leaflets of *D. indica*. The rose family has both specialized and unspecialized insect herbivores. Unspecialized herbivores such as the rose chafer, (*Macrodactylus subspinosis*), and the Japanese beetle, (*Popillia japonica*), eat the flowers of roses and other plants. More specialized herbivores include the rose curculio, (*Rhynictes bicolor*), a bright-red weevil that eats parts of flowers in the rose genus *(Rosa)* and is rarely found on flowers of other genera in the Rosaceae, or on species of other plant families. One of the most specialized herbivores is the rose leafhopper, (*Typhlocyba rosae*), which has adjusted to the secondary chemistry of rose plants and does not attack flowers, but instead feeds on sap from stems.

Most of the tree-sized species of the Rosaceae which provide us with edible fruit, such as apricot (*Prunus armeniaca*), domestic apple (*Malus pumila)*, peach (*Prunus persica*), pear (*Pyrus communis* and *P. pyrifolia*), and plum (*Prunus domestica*), are native to Europe and Asia and have been in cultivation for hundreds of years. Today, there are relatively few cultivars of apple, peach, and plum available for sale. However, 100 years ago there were many different cultivated versions of each of these species. One of the most popular cherry trees in cultivation, sour cherry (*Prunus cerasus*), is also probably native to Europe or Asia, although its true origin is unknown.

In addition, many species of *Malus* and *Prunus* are native to North America. Beach plum (*Prunus maritima*) and black cherry (*P. serotina*) are common members of barrier **island** maritime forest and mainland **forests** of southeastern North America. Choke cherry (*Prunus virginiana*) and sweet cherry (*Prunus avium*) are common components of recently disturbed areas within inland forests in eastern North America. Sweet cherry is also a popular cultivated species.

Climbing species of *Rosa* are far less common than those with a shrub growth habit. Species such as dog rose (*R. canina*) of Europe and *R. virginiana* of eastern North America are noted for their prodigious growth, in which stems may attain lengths of several meters. This is possible because these climbing species do not devote as much growth to structural support, as do shrub roses, and instead use surrounding vegetation for support. With this growth form, climbing roses may obscure and kill supporting vegetation and can cover a substantial surface area with an impenetrable thicket. European folk tales feature the vigorous growth of climbing rose plants which was said to have engulfed even the largest man-made structures. In fact, the stems of the dog rose may reach 9.8 ft (3 m) in length. This may have been enough engulf an abandoned cottage. This probably suggests the extent to which species such as *R. canina*, also called English briar, have been associated with human culture since ancient times.

The genus *Rosa* is of major importance in the floriculture industry, and today there are well over 300 kinds of **hybrid** roses in cultivation. Rose hybrids are divided into "new" and "old" types. Old hybrid roses such as "Rosa Mundi" and "Frau Karl Drushki" result from simple crosses between European species and moderate selection for double-petalled flowers. Some of the older hybrid roses retain functional anthers and may form hips.

The modern hybrids, such as "Peace," differ from old hybrids in that hybridization has been more intensive

Ornamental rose.

and selection has led to exclusively sterile polypetalous cultivars. Because selection has focused on obtaining forms with large flowers and many petals, modern hybrid roses are commonly not very resistant to pathogens, and are susceptible to bacterial and fungal infections. Also, where wild roses suffer few major infestations from insect herbivores, modern rose hybrids are susceptible to attack from many generalist herbivores including species of **aphids** and **earwigs**.

In addition to the genus *Rosa,* many other members of the rose family are also valued as ornamentals. Plants of the genera *Chaenomeles, Filipendula, Geum, Kerria, Potentilla*, and *Spirea,* are commonly used in landscaping and in flower gardens as ornamentals. Some species of *Potentilla* and *Geum* native to Europe and Asia have also been extensively hybridized to yield double petalled, sterile cultivars. One species of *Geum* native to North America, *G. rivale*, or Indian chocolate, was once a dietary item in the cultures of Native American groups in eastern North America.

Trees in the genera *Crataegus, Cotoneaster*, and *Sorbus* are valued not only for their flowers but also for their interesting leaves and fruit clusters. Another popular cultivated member of the rosaceae is the climbing, woody plant *Pyracantha coccinea*. This plant produces many clusters of white flowers in spring and orange-red fruits in fall which are eaten by migrating **birds**.

In addition to important contributions to our food and **horticulture**, the Rosaceae has been important in human culture. The best-known flower in the family is that of the genus after which the family is named, *Rosa.* This genus is well represented in Europe and the Mediterranean region, where it has been used for ornamental purposes for several thousand years. The earliest known, man-made image of a rose is in a fresco found in the city of Knossos on Crete. This image dates back to the sixteenth century B.C. On the nearby island of Rhodes, 6,000-year-old coins had the image of a rose flower. The island's name, Rhodes, may in fact be derived from the word rose.

In many cultures of Europe and Asia a white rose flower symbolizes purity, while a red rose flower symbolizes strength. In ancient Greece and Rome, rose petals were strewn along the path where important people walked, and in Sybaris, an ancient city in Italy, mattresses were filled with rose petals. This may be where we get the phrase, "a bed of roses." The Romans may have also constructed special houses for the cultivation of rose plants during the winter. These houses were heated by hot **water** running through pipes. This system

would have made rose petals available for use during winter festivities. Also, during certain festivals, when a rose flower was placed on the ceiling of a room, anything said *sub rosa,* (that is, "under the rose"), could not be repeated to anyone else.

Rose flowers have also been important in British heraldry. For example, rose flowers were traditional symbols used by royal families in England. White and red roses were the symbols of the two competing royal lines of England that fought the War of the Roses. Another famous member of the rose family, the rowan **tree** (*Sorbus aucuparia*), was sacred to the Celtic peoples.

In more modern times, rose petals have been used to add color to wine, and scent to **soap**. Also, rose hips are a natural, herbal source of vitamin C for people.

The genus *Rosa* is widespread and indigenous to many areas of North America, Asia, and Europe. The majority of *Rosa* species grow in a shrub habit, and can be difficult to tell apart at first glance. Several other species native to Europe and North America grow as climbing vines or brambles. European and Asian shrub species such as Turkestan rose, (*R. rugosa*), damask rose, *(R. damascena)*, and tea rose, *(R. odorata)*, have been grown near human habitations for centuries, and have been extensively hybridized in horticulture. In North America, similar appearing shrub roses can be found in a wide range of habitats. Species such as swamp rose (*Rosa palustris*) can be found in low and marshy ground in the east, while **prairie** rose *(R. arkansana)* grows in dry upland areas of the tallgrass prairie in the midwest. In the arid southwest, Fendler rose (*R. fendleri*) can be found growing on dry mountain slopes, while Arizona rose (*R. arizonica*) can be found growing along streams and forest edges. While most of these shrub rose species may attain mature heights of 3.3-6.6 ft (1-2 m), their root systems may be far more substantial. For example, the **root system** of *Rosa arkansana* may extend to a depth of 19.7-23 ft (6-7 m) into the soil.

Because Atlantic coastal **barrier islands** are located along migratory bird routes and because few wind-dispersed plant seeds may reach these remote islands, the maritime forest plant communities are composed of many bird dispersed species, many of which belong to the rose family. For example, *Prunus maritima* and *P. serotina* are commonly found on barrier islands from Massachusetts to Florida. Birds eat fruits from established plants on some islands and defecate seeds onto different islands, thereby spreading these plants across most of the chain of barrier islands. This relationship, between species of *Prunus* and birds, is exemplified by the species named *Prunus avium*, also called bird cherry and by one of the common names for *P. serotina*, wild bird cherry. This relationship between many fruits produced by members of the rose family and birds is common, and is also the reason why certain species such as blackberry and hawthorn can often be found growing in suburban lawns when no parent plants are established in the immediate area. While most fruits of the rose family are eaten by birds, fruits of the prostrate growing strawberries may be eaten by a wider variety of **wildlife** such as **mammals** and **reptiles**. For instance, the aggregate fruits of wild strawberry (*Fragaria virginiana*) are a favorite food of box **turtles** (*Terrapene ornata* and *T. caroliniana*).

Many members of the rose family, particularly species of the intermountain west, are important forage plants for cattle. Species such as bitter cherry (*Prunus emarginata*), cliffrose (*Cowania mexicana* var. *stansburiana*), **desert** peach *(Prunus andersonii*), and fern bush, *(Chamaebataria millefolium*) are eaten by **sheep** and cattle and are browsed on by **deer**. Perhaps the most important species to cattle ranchers is bitterbrush *(Purshia tridentata*). Bitterbrush is similar in appearance to sagebrush *(Artemisia tridentata*; family Asteraceae), and grows in the same ecological conditions. However, while sagebrush is not edible, bitterbrush is edible, nutritious, and abundant.

Further Reading

Goody, J. *The Culture of Flowers*. New York: Cambridge University Press, 1993.

Heywood, V. H., ed. *Flowering Plants of the World*. Englewood Cliffs, NJ: Prentice Hall, 1985.

Jones, S. B., and A. E. Luchsinger. *Plant Systemmatics*. New York: McGraw-Hill, 1986.

Medsger, O. P. *Edible Wild Plants*. New York: Collier Books, 1966.

Morley, B. D., and B. Everard. *Wild Flowers of the World*. New York: Exeter Books, 1983.

Mozingo, H. *Shrubs of the Great Basin*. Reno: University of Nevada Press, 1987.

Perry, F., and L. Greenwood. *Flowers of the World*. New York: Bonanza Books, 1972.

Smith, J. P. *Vascular Plant Families*. Eureka, CA: Mad River Press, 1977.

Stephen R. Johnson

Rotation

A rotation is one of three rigid motions that move a figure in a **plane** without changing its size or shape. As its name implies, a rotation moves a figure by rotating it around a center somewhere on a plane. This center can be somewhere inside or on the figure, or outside the figure completely. The two other rigid motions are **reflections** and **translations**.

Figure 1 illustrates a rotation of 30° around a point C. This rotation is counterclockwise, which is consid-

KEY TERMS

Endocarp—The innermost layer of tissue in a fruit. Fruits of all flowering plants have three distinct layers of tissue called ectocarp, mesocarp, and endocarp, respectively.

Hip—A false fruit typical of the genus *Rosa*. It is composed of a hollow, cup-shaped receptacle that differs from a pome in texture and color of tissues.

Prickle—A short, woody, pointed growth which originates in the epidermis of a plant. Prickles are common plant adaptations to discourage herbivores and in some climbing species. Prickles may also provide a means of attachment to a supporting structure.

Receptacle—The enlarged tip of a peduncle where the parts of a flower are attached. Four distinct whorls of modified leaves, the sepals, petals, stamens, and carpels make up the parts of the flower. Each carpel is composed of a stigma, style, and ovary.

Spine—A modified leaf or part of a leaf that is formed into a sharp point.

Stipule—Single or paired leaflike structures occurring at the base of a leaf or sometimes along a petiole. Stipules may serve as protective structures for developing leaves.

ered positive. Clockwise rotations are **negative**. The "product" of two rotations, that is, following one rotation with another, is also a rotation. This assumes that the center of rotation is the same for both. When one moves a heavy box across the room by rotating it first on one corner then on the other, that "product" is not a rotation.

Rotations are so commonplace that it is easy to forget how important they are. A person orients a **map** by rotating it. A clock shows time by the rotation of its hands. A person fits a key in a **lock** by rotating the key until its grooves match the pattern on the keyhole. Rotating an M 180° changes it into a W; 6s and 9s are alike except for a rotation.

Rotary motions are one of the two basic motions of parts in a machine. An **automobile** wheel converts rotary **motion** into translational motion, and propels the car. A drill bores a hole by cutting away material as it turns. The **earth** rotates on its axis. The earth and the **moon** rotate around their centers of gravity, and so on.

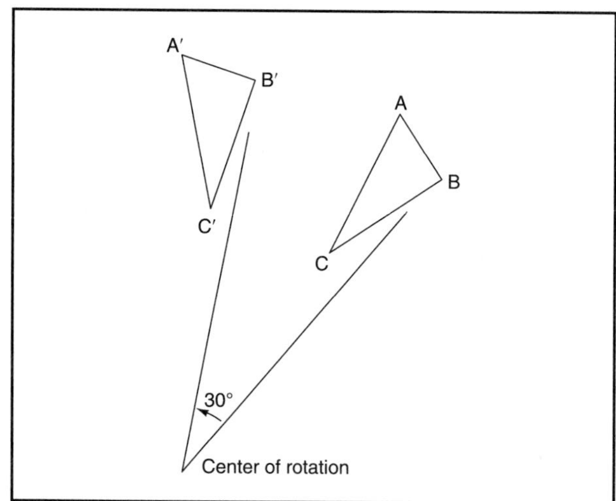

Figure 1.

Astronomy prior to Copernicus was greatly complicated by trying to use the earth as the center of the rotation of the planets. When Kepler and Copernicus made the **sun** the gravitational center, the motions of the planets became far easier to predict and explain (but even with the sun as the center, planetary motion is not strictly rotational).

When points are represented by coordinates, a rotation can be effected algebraically. How hard this is to do depends upon the location of the center of rotation and on the kind of coordinate system which is used. In the two most commonly employed systems, the rectangular Cartesian coordinate system and the polar coordinate system, the center of choice is the origin or pole.

In either of these systems a rotation can be thought of as moving the points and leaving the axes fixed, or vice versa. The mathematical connection between these alternatives is a simple one: rotating a set of points clockwise is equivalent to rotating the axes, particularly with reflections, it is usually preferable to leave the axes in place and move the points.

When a point or a set of points is represented with **polar coordinates**, the equations that connect a point (r,θ) with the rotated image (r',θ') are particularly simple. If θ_1 is the **angle** of rotation:

$$r' = r$$

$$\theta' = \theta + \theta_1$$

Thus, if the points are rotated 30° counterclockwise, (7,80°) is the image of 7,50°). If the set of points described by the equation $r = \theta/2$ is rotated π units clockwise, its image is described by $r = (\theta - \pi)/2$. Rectangular coordinates are related to polar coordinates by the equations $x = r \cos \theta$ and $y = r \sin \theta$.

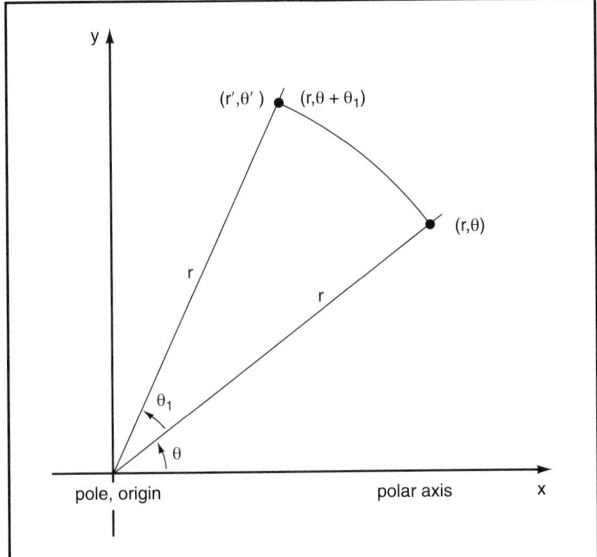

Figure 2.

Therefore the equations which connect a point (x, y) with its rotated image (x', y') are

$$x' = r \cos(\theta + \theta_1) \text{ and } y' = r \sin(\theta + \theta_1).$$

Using the trigonometric identities for $\cos(\theta + \theta_1)$ and $\sin(\theta + \theta_1)$, these can be written $x' = x \cos \theta_1 - y \sin \theta_1$ and $y' = x \sin \theta_1 + y \cos \theta_1$ or, after solving for x and y: $x = x' \cos \theta_1 + y \sin \theta_1$ and $y = -x' \sin \theta_1 + y \cos \theta_1$.

To use these equations one must resort to a table of sines and cosines, or use a **calculator** with SIN and COS keys.

One can use the equations for a rotation many ways. One use is to simplify an equation such as $x^2 - xy + y^2 = 5$. For any second-degree polynomialequation in x and y there is a rotation which will eliminate the xy term. In this case the rotation is 45°, and the resulting equation, after dropping the primes, is $3x^2 + y^2 = 10$.

Another area in which rotations play an important part is in rotational symmetry. A figure has rotational symmetry if there is a rotation such that the original figure and its image coincide. A **square**, for example, has rotational symmetry because any rotation about the square's center which is a multiple of 90° will result in a square that coincides with the original. An ordinary gear has rotational symmetry. So do the numerous objects such as vases and bowls which are decorated repetitively around the edges. Actual objects can be checked for rotational symmetry by looking at them. Geometric figures described analytically can be tested using the equations for rotations. For example, the **spiral** r = 28 has two-fold rotational symmetry. When the spiral is rotated 180°, the image coincides with the original spiral.

KEY TERMS

Rotation—A motion of a figure in the plane which rotates the figure without changing its size or shape.

Rotational symmetry—A property of a figure that allows it to coincide with its image after a suitable rotation.

Further Reading

Alperin, Jonathan. "Groups and Symmetry." In *Mathematics Today.* edited by Lynn Arthur Steen. New York: Springer-Verlag, 1978.

Coxeter, H.S.M., and S. L. Greitzer. *Geometry Revisited.* Washington, D.C.: The Mathematical Association of America, 1967.

Hilbert, D. and S. Cohn-Vossen. *Geometry and the Imagination.* New York: Chelsea Publishing Co., 1952

Pettofrezzo, Anthony. *Matrices and Transformations.* New York: Dover Publications, 1966.

Weyl, Hermann. "Symmetry." In *The World of Mathematics.* edited by James Newman. New York: Simon and Schuster, 1956.

Yaglom, I.M. *Geometric Transformations.* Washington, D.C.: The Mathematical Association of America, 1962.

J. Paul Moulton

Roundworms

With more than 10,000 species described, roundworms (phylum Nematoda) are among the most numerous and widespread animals. They occur in all habitats, including **freshwater**, marine, and terrestrial ecosystems, from the tropics to the polar regions. They often occur in staggering numbers: 10.8 sq ft (1 sq m) of mud has been found to contain more than four million nematodes. Because of their distribution and ability to adapt to different situations, it is not surprising to find that nematodes have adapted to a wide range of living conditions. Many are free-living, but others are parasitic on both plants and animals.

All nematodes are characterised by their slender, elongate body, in which the two ends are slightly tapered to form a head and anal region. Many species measure less than 0.04 in (1 mm) in length; most are microscopic. The body is enclosed in a thin layer of **collagen** which represents the body wall, and is also supplied with a layer of muscle, enabling the worm to move in a sideways manner by contracting and expanding these muscles.

Among the free-living species, many roundworms are carnivorous, feeding on a wide range of protozoans as well as other nematodes; aquatic species feed largely

on **bacteria**, **algae**, and microscopic **diatoms**. Some terrestrial species attack the roots of plants, extracting **nutrients** and essential fluids.

Most nematodes are dioecious (either male or female), with males commonly being smaller than females. When ready to breed, females of some species are thought to give off a pheromone that serves to attract potential suitors. During copulation, the male inserts its sperm into the female and **fertilization** takes place. The egg then develops a toughened outer coating and may either be held within the body for a short period or released to the outside. In **hermaphrodite** species, the sperm develop ahead of the eggs and are stored in special chambers until the eggs are ready for fertilization to take place. The young larvae that emerge progress through a series of body moults until they develop adult characteristics.

Many species of parasitic nematodes are unable to complete their life cycle without the presence of another **animal**. Commonly eggs are deposited on plants, which are then ingested or absorbed into the body in some other manner. Once within the host animal, the eggs hatch and burrow their way into the flesh (often the intestine or lungs), where they attach firmly to the lining of the chamber and begin to mature. From there the nematodes absorb nutrients from the host animal and release additional eggs, which pass out of the body in the feces.

Although some nematodes are beneficial in the manner in which they break down dead or decaying **matter**, many are of considerable economic importance: a great number are **pests** of animals and **plant crops**, while others are the cause of serious illnesses in humans. The tiny hookworms, for example, are believed to affect millions of people worldwide, causing serious bleeding and **tissue** damage. Larvae of the guinea worm (*Dracunculus medinensis*), which lives in freshwater streams in parts of **Africa** and **Asia**, seek an open wound in the body through which they pass and become installed in the **connective tissue**. Females of this species may develop to a length exceeding 3.3 ft (1 m), causing considerable discomfort.

See also Parasites.

David Stone

Rubber plant see **Spurge family**
Rubidium see **Alkali metals**

Rumination

Rumination is a specialized digestion process found in most hoofed **mammals** with an even number of toes-such as cattle, **sheep**, **goats**, **deer**, antelope, **camels**, buffalo, giraffes, and chevrotains. All of these plant-eating animals lack the **enzyme** cellulase, which is capable of breaking down the tough **cellulose** in **plant cell** walls. The stomach of these grazing herbivores consists of four chambers—the rumen, the reticulum, the omasum, and the abomasum—each playing different roles in the digestion process. The ruminant **animal** swallows its food rapidly without chewing, and later regurgitates it (brings it back up into the mouth), then masticates it (chews), and finally re-swallows it.

When grazing, ruminants swallow their food rapidly, sending large amounts into the largest chamber of the stomach, the rumen, where it is stored and partly digested before regurgitation and chewing when the animal is resting. Rumination is an adaption by which herbivores can spend as little time as possible feeding (when they are most vulnerable to predation) and then later digest their food in safer surroundings. Muscular contractions of the stomach move food back and forth between the rumen and the second stomach chamber, the reticulum, which is often called the honeycomb due to the complex appearance of its inner lining. **Bacteria** and **microorganisms** in the rumen (which can digest cellulose) begin the digestion of the plant fibers. Fine fibers are broken down, so providing protein, vitamins, and organic acids which are then absorbed into the bloodstream of the animal. Coarser plant fibers are passed from the rumen to the reticulum, where further bacterial **fermentation** takes place, and the food is formed into soft chunks called the cud. The cud is regurgitated and ground thoroughly between the molars with an almost circular **motion** of the lower jaw.

During the chewing process, called chewing the cud, copious quantities of highly alkaline saliva aid in breaking down the fibers, and the food is re-swallowed, this time bypassing the rumen and entering the smallest chamber, the omasum, or third stomach. Here, **water** and essential acids are reabsorbed. It is the third stomach of a bullock which is eaten as tripe. Muscular contraction by the walls of the omasum mashes and compacts the food still further, passing it directly into the fourth stomach, the abomasum, where gastric secretions further digest the food before it moves into the intestine.

Large amounts of two gases, **carbon dioxide** and methane, form during bacterial fermentation in the first two chambers-the reticulorumen. Here, frothing occurs as part of the digestive process. Often, however, excessive frothing caused by certain foods traps gas normally eliminated by belching, and bloating occurs. Certain cows are particularly susceptible to this, and farmers often lose animals unless these gases are released. Anti-foaming medications sometimes help, as does an invasive procedure which punctures the stomach wall and allows gases to es-

cape. The methane produced by the digestive systems of the billions of domestic ruminants in the world is considered by some to be a major **factor** in the destruction of the **ozone** layer in the upper atmosphere.

See also Antelopes and gazelles; Cattle family; Giraffes and Okapi; Herbivore.

Rushes

Rushes are monocotyledonous plants in the genus *Juncus*. Rushes make up most of the species in the family Juncaceae. There are about 400 species in the rush family, distributed among eight or nine genera. The most species-rich groups are the rushes (*Juncus* spp.) with 225 species, and the wood-rushes (*Luzula* spp.) with 80 species.

Species in the rush family occur worldwide, but they are particularly abundant in moist and wet habitats of cool-temperate, boreal, arctic, and alpine zones, especially in the Northern Hemisphere.

Biology of rushes

Rushes are grass- and sedge-like in their superficial morphology, but they differ from plants in these families (Poaceae and Cyperaceae, respectively) in important respects.

Most species of rushes are herbaceous perennial plants, although a few have an annual life cycle. Many species of rushes typically grow erect, but a few grow close to the ground surface. The stems of rushes are usually hollow, cylindrical, or somewhat flattened, and often with occasional cross-sections or nodes. The leaves of rushes are commonly arranged around the base of the flowering stems, but in some species the leaves are reduced to small sheaths around the flower-bearing shoots. The roots of rushes are generally fibrous, and some species have well developed systems of rhizomes.

Rushes have small, inconspicuous florets with many reduced floral parts. The florets are typically aggregated into inflorescences or groups of various types and are wind-pollinated. Each floret typically contains both staminate and pistillate parts and is therefore bisexual. The fruit is a small capsule that contains large numbers of tiny **seeds**.

Rushes in North America

Many species of rushes are native to **North America**, but some of these are also found on other continents. The Baltic rush (*Juncus balticus*) is a very widespread species and is common along moist lakeshores in Eurasia and in North and **South America**. The soft rush (*J. effusus*) and path rush (*J. tenuis*) are similarly cosmopolitan species. Unlike the previous species, which are perennial, the toad rush (*J. bufonius*) is an annual species of moist soils, and it also has a very wide distribution, occurring on most continents.

Some species of rushes can grow as aquatic plants that root in the sediment of shallow **water** but grow into the atmosphere where they develop their flowers. Examples of these relatively tall rushes include *Juncus articulatus* and *J. militaris* which can grow as tall as 3.3 ft (1 m).

Rushes in ecosystems

The usual **habitat** of rushes is **wetlands** of many types, including marshes, fens, wet meadows, and the shallow-water edges of streams, ponds, and lakes. Rushes can be quite abundant and productive in some of these habitats, but they rarely dominate the vegetation over an extensive area.

Rushes are an important component of the habitat of many species of animals, especially in wetlands. For example, some of the best habitats for waterfowl will have an abundant component of rushes. Some species of **birds** eat the seeds of rushes, while other species graze on the leaves and shoots.

Economically important rushes

Rushes are not of much direct economic benefit to humans. The Japanese mat rush or soft rush (*Juncus effusus*) and the wicker rush (*J. squarrosus*) are used for weaving and making wicker chair-bottoms. Rushes are rarely cultivated for these purposes. The raw materials are usually collected from habitats that are being managed for other purposes or from natural wetlands.

Rushes are sometimes abundant in pastures, but they are not a preferred forage species because their stems are not very palatable or nutritious for domestic **livestock**.

Rushes also provide useful ecological functions in some of the habitats in which they are abundant. For example, on sloping ground with moist **soil** rushes may be important in binding the surface soil and thereby helping to prevent some **erosion**.

A few species of rushes have naturally spread or been introduced by humans beyond their native habitats and are considered to be weeds in some parts of their new range. In North America, the soft rush and path rush (*J. tenuis*) are minor weeds of pastures, lawns, and some other habitats.

See also Grasses.

Spike rushes.

KEY TERMS

Cosmopolitan—In biogeography, this refers to species that are widely distributed, occurring on many of the continents, as are the cases of some species of rushes.

Floret—This is a small flower, often with some reduced or missing parts. Florets are generally arranged within a dense cluster.

Inflorescence—This is a grouping or arrangement of florets or flowers into a composite structure.

Rhizome—This is a modified stem that grows horizontally in soil or sediment. Roots and upward-growing shoots develop at the stem nodes.

Further Reading

Woodland, D. W. *Contemporary Plant Systematics.* Englewood Cliffs, NJ: Prentice-Hall, 1991.

Bill Freedman

Rusts and smuts

Rusts and smuts are **fungi** belonging to the orders Urediniales (rusts) and Ustilaginales (smuts) which are basidiomycete fungi. The rusts have complicated life cycles which involve the **infection** of two different **plant** species. The most well-known members of these groups are **wheat** rust (*Puccinia graminis tritici)* and corn smut (*Ustilago myadis).* Rust fungi attack plants such as **ferns**, gymnosperms, and flowering plants. When a wheat plant is infested by *Puccinia graminis tritici,* the infestation may become obvious during the summer growing season when rust colored growth appears on the stems of infected plants. Fungal hyphae are composed of groups of **spore** generating structures (sporangia) called *uredinia* that rupture the stem and become visible. It is the spores released from the uredinia (called *urediniospores*) that infect new wheat plants and spread the disease. In the fall, *Puccinia* produces black sporangia (called telia) and the infected wheat plants have distinct black patches on their stems. Spores from the telia (called teliospores) do not attack other wheat plants but instead infect **barberry** plants. Teliospores which land on barberry leaves germinate and form small cup-shaped structures called spermagonia. Each spermagonium produces long filaments called receptive hyphae which extend above the spermagonium and spermatia, which are sexual gametes. The spermagonium also produces a nectar-like substance which is attractive to **flies**. Spermatia are mixed with this **nectar** and flies transfer the spermatia from adjacent spermagonia as they feed. New fungal mycelia, resulting from the union of the spermatia with the receptive hyphae of spermagonia of different genetic strains, grow on the underside of the barberry **leaf**. There, the mycelium produces a larger bell-shaped sporangium called an aecium, which generates aeciospores which in turn infect new wheat plants.

Smut fungi differ from rust fungi in several ways. While rust fungi require two different hosts to complete their life cycle, smut fungi may complete their life cycle on only one host, which is always a flowering plant. Another difference between rust and smut fungi is seen in the way that they infect their host plants. Infections from rust fungi are localized to that part of the plant close to where a germinated urediniospore, aeciospore, or teliospore becomes established. Smut fungi spread to infest the entire plant from a single initial infection site, often targeting specific organs. This is exemplified by the smut fungus *Ustilago violacea* which attacks plants of the genus *Silene. Ustilago violacea* infests the entire plant but its presence within the

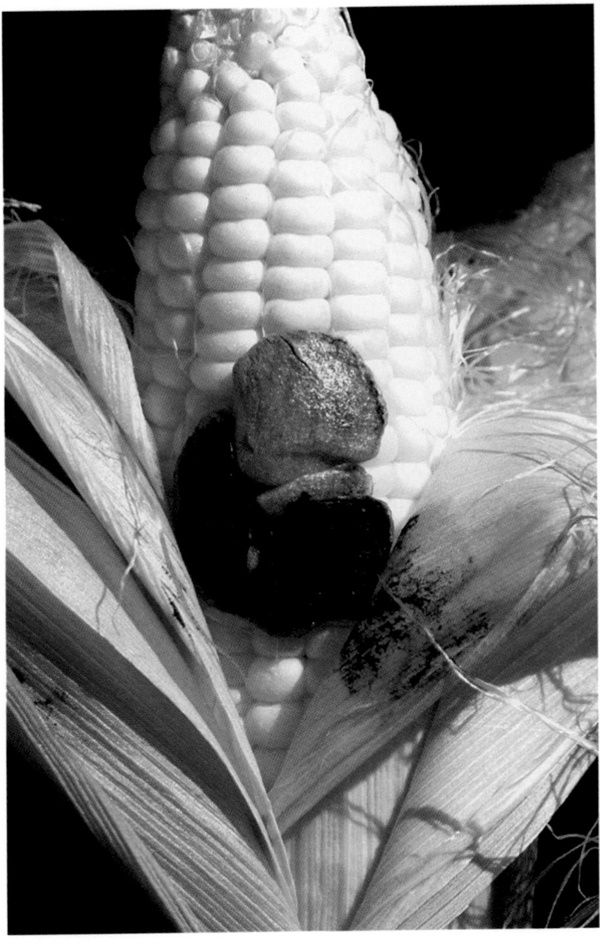

Smut on corn.

plant is only apparent where mycelia grow within the anthers of the plant. There, hyphae divide to become teliospores and these take the place of pollen grains. Pollinating **insects** then carry the teliospores from infected *Silene* plants to uninfected ones. Teliospores mature along with the *Silene* flower and fall to the ground along with **seeds** of the host *Silene* plant. When the seeds germinate, the smut fungus teliospores germinate along with them and immediately infect the *Silene* seedlings. *Ustilago myadis,* is a well-known smut fungus that infects corn, where its immature teliospores are enclosed in sacs which replace the kernels of corn. When these sacs burst, *U. myadis* spores are released and cling to normal corn kernels. When these kernels are planted, teliospores are planted along with them, infecting new corn plants when they germinate.

Rust and smut fungi are both of great economic importance due to their destruction of cash **crops**. An effort to eliminate *Puccinia graminis tritici* by the eradication of barberry was not successful. This rust fungus is now controlled by selection for genetically resistant wheat plants, but rust fungi frequently mutate and override wheat resistance, so an ongoing genetic selection program for wheat is necessary. Another economically important rust fungus is *Gymnosporangium juniperus-virginiae,* which has as its two plant hosts the common **juniper** (*Juniperus virginianus*) and the domestic apple, and other species of the **rose family**. This fungus produces large orange colored spore-generating structures on juniper trees, which then infect apple trees, causing the **tree** to produce deformed and unmarketable apples. The best way to avoid ruined apples is to keep apple trees away from juniper trees and to remove all infected juniper trees in the area.

One way that humans have reduced infection of corn by smut has been to wash away any clinging fungal spores from the kernels of corn. In the southwestern United States and in Mexico immature corn smut sacs are fried and eaten as a delicacy.

See also Fungicide.

KEY TERMS

Aecium (pl. Aecia)—Ulcer-like sporangium produced by mycelium in the spring stage of a rust fungus.

Hypha (pl. Hyphae)—A single strand of a fungus. Many strands (hyphae) together are called mycelium.

Spermagonium (pl. Spermagonia)—Small pustules formed by mycelium in the early spring stage of a rust fungus.

Telium (pl. Telia)—Sporangium produced by mycelium in the fall or early spring stage of rust or smut fungi.

Uredinium (pl. Uredinia)—Sporangium produced by mycelium in the summer stage of a rust fungus.

Further Reading

Bold, H. C., C. J. Alexopoulos, and T. Delevoryas. *Morphology of Plants and Fungi.* New York: Harper & Row, 1980.

Kendrick, B. *The Fifth Kingdom.* Waterloo, Ontario: Mycologue Publications, 1985.

Simpson, B. B., and M. C. Ogrorzaly. *Economic Botany: Plants in Our World.* New York: McGraw-Hill, 1986.

Stephen R. Johnson

Ruthenium see **Element, chemical**

Rutherfordium see **Element, transuranium**

Rye see **Grasses**

S

Saiga antelope

The saiga antelope (*Saiga tatarica*) is a relatively northern, Eurasian antelope in the family Bovidae. Historically, the range of the saiga antelope extended from Poland in the west, to the Caucasus Mountains of northwestern Turkey, Georgia, and Azerbaijan, the vicinity of the Caspian Sea in Kazakhstan, and as far east as Mongolia. However, mostly because of overhunting, this species now only occurs in a relatively small part of its former range, mostly in Kazakhstan.

The **habitat** of the saiga antelope is treeless **grasslands**, known as steppe, in eastern Eurasia. Much of this natural habitat has been converted to agricultural use, an ecological change that has contributed to the decline in saiga populations.

Saiga are large animals, with a body length of 4-5.6 ft (1.2-1.7 m), and a weight of 79-152 lbs (36-69 kg). Their pelage is cinnamon-brown during the summer, and thicker and whitish during the winter. Male saiga antelopes have horns.

A male saiga antelope (*Saiga tatarica*).

The saiga has downward-pointing nostrils, and an inflated nasal cavity that has a convoluted development of the internal, bony structures. The nasal tracts are also lined with fine hairs, and mucous **glands**. These structures may be useful in warming and moistening inhaled air, or they may somehow be related to the keen sense of **smell** of the saiga antelope.

Saiga aggregate into large herds during the winter. The herds typically migrate to the south, to spend that difficult season in relatively warm valleys. Males move north first in the spring, followed later by females. The young saiga antelopes are born in the early springtime. Saiga forage on a wide range of **grasses** and forbs.

Remarkably, it appears that the saiga occurred in **North America** at the end of the most recent Ice Age. Along with other large **mammals** of eastern Eurasia, the saiga likely colonized western North America by traversing a land bridge from Siberia, which was exposed because **sea level** was relatively low as a result of so much **water** being tied up in continental ice sheets. About 11,000 years ago, at a time roughly coincident with the colonization of North America by humans migrating from Siberia, the saiga and many other species of large animals became extinct in North America. This wave of extinctions affected more than 75 species of mammals, including ten species of **horses**, several species of **bison**, four species of elephants (including the mastodon and several types of mammoths), the saber-tooth tiger, the American lion, and the saiga antelope. A widely held theory is that these extinctions were caused directly or indirectly by primitive, colonizing humans that acted as effective predators and overhunted these animals.

Up until about the 1920s and 1930s, the populations of saiga in Eurasia were rather small and endangered. The most important reasons for the decline of saiga were loss-

es of habitat and, most importantly, overhunting of these animals for sport, and for the horns of the male animals. The horns are sought for use in traditional Chinese medicine, because of their presumed pharmaceutical qualities. During the 1920s, the government of the then-Soviet Union instituted a strict program of protection of the saiga, and its populations are now relatively large, probably more than one million individuals. Nevertheless, the saiga is classified as a vulnerable species by the IUCN (International Union for the **Conservation** of Nature).

See also Endangered species.

Bill Freedman

Salamanders

Salamanders and **newts** are aquatic or amphibious animals in the order Caudata (sometimes known as the Urodela). There are about 350 species of salamanders, included in 54 genera. Salamanders have an ancient fossil lineage, extending back to the Upper Jurassic period, more than 140 million years ago.

Like other **amphibians**, salamanders have a complex life cycle, the stages of which are egg, larva, and adult. The morphology, **physiology**, and **ecology** of salamanders in their different stages are very different, and the transitional process involves a complex **metamorphosis**.

Salamanders are most abundant in the temperate regions of the northern hemisphere, with fewer species occurring elsewhere. The greatest number of species of salamanders occurs in the eastern United States, and to a lesser degree in eastern China.

Biology of salamanders

Species of salamanders display a wide range of body plans and life histories. The smallest salamander is an unnamed species of *Thorius* from Mexico, mature males of which have a total body length of only 1 in (2.5 cm). The world's largest living salamanders can be as long as 5.5 ft (1.7 m). These are the giant Asiatic salamanders, *Andrias davidianus* and *A. japonicus*, which can achieve body weights of 88 lb (40 kg) or more. One individual giant Japanese salamander (*A. japonicus*) lived for an extraordinary 55 years in captivity.

Adult salamanders have four relatively small, similar-sized walking legs, and a long tail. The skeletal structure of living salamanders is relatively little modified from their geologically ancient relatives, and among the tetrapod **vertebrates** is considered to be relatively primitive.

Some species of salamanders have lost key elements of the skeleton during their **evolution**. For example, species within the salamander family Sirenidae have lost their limbs, and are eel-like in appearance. Remarkably, the numbers and shapes of limb bones are not necessarily the same within some salamander species, as is the case of the red-backed salamander (*Plethodon cinereus*) of **North America**. Within the same population, individuals of this species can have varying numbers of limb bones, and these structures can vary significantly in size, shape, and degree of calcification.

Salamanders have a protrusile tongue, used for feeding and sensory purposes. Many species are very brightly colored, usually to warn predators of the poisonous nature of the skin of these animals. Some salamanders secrete a chemical known as tetrodotoxin from their skin **glands**. This is one of the most poisonous substances known, and it can easily kill predators that are intolerant of the chemical, as most are.

Salamanders vary greatly in their reproductive **biology**. Salamanders typically have internal **fertilization**, meaning the ova are fertilized by male sperm within the reproductive tract of the female. During the breeding season, male salamanders of many species **deposit** packets of sperm, known as spermatophores, on the surface of aquatic sediment or debris. The male salamander then manipulates a female to pass over the spermatophores, which are picked up by the slightly prehensile lips of her cloaca, and stored in a special, internal structure known as a spermatheca. The sperm then fertilize the ova as they are laid by the female, producing fertile zygotes. These are then laid as single eggs encased in a protective jelly, or sometimes as a larger egg **mass** that can contain several or many eggs within a jelly **matrix**.

Hatched larvae of typical salamanders look rather similar to the adults, but they are fully aquatic animals, with gill slits and external gills, a large head, teeth, a flattened tail used for swimming, and initially they lack legs. The metamorphosis to the adult form involves the loss of the external gills, the growth of legs, and the development of internal lungs, which, together with the moist skin of the body, act in the exchange of respiratory gases. Adult salamanders also have eyelids that can close.

Salamanders in the family Plethodontidae show direct development. For example, the aquatic larval state of the fully terrestrial red-backed salamander occurs within the egg. What hatches from the egg is a miniature replica of the adult salamander. The red-backed salamander lacks lungs, so that all gas exchange occurs across the moist skin of the body and mouth.

The female of the European salamander, *Salamandra atra*, retains the eggs within her body. There they de-

A salamander (*Tylototriton verrucosus*).

velop through the larval stage, so that the young are born as miniature adults.

Some salamanders do not have a terrestrial adult stage, and become sexually mature even though they still retain many characteristics of the larval stage. This phenomenon is known as neoteny, and occurs in species such as the mudpuppy (*Necturus maculosus*) of central and eastern North America. Neoteny also occurs in the axolotyl (*Ambystoma mexicanum*), a rare species found in Mexico, in which the breeding adults have external gills, a large head, a flattened tail, and other typically larval traits. The axolotyl is a common species in laboratories where developmental biology is studied, and sometimes individuals of this species will undergo metamorphosis and develop more typical, adult characteristics. Often, particular populations of other species in the genus *Ambystoma* will display neoteny, for example the tiger salamander (*A. tigrinum*), common in small lakes and ponds over much of North America.

The red-spotted newt (*Notophthalmus viridescens*) of North America has two distinct, adult stages. The stage that follows from transformation of the aquatic larva is known as the red eft. This is a bright-red colored, adult form that wanders widely for several years in **forests**, especially on moist nights. The red eft eventually returns to an aquatic **habitat**, adopts a yellowish color, and becomes a breeding adult.

Salamanders with a terrestrial adult stage generally have a keen ability to home back to the vicinity of their natal or home pond. One study done in California found that red-bellied newts (*Taricha rivularis*) were capable of returning to their native stream over a **distance** of 5 mi (8 km), within only one year.

Salamanders in North America

Most of the 112 species of North America salamanders occur in the Appalachian region. In terms of species

richness of salamanders, no other part of the **earth** compares with Appalachia. However, salamanders also occur over most of the rest of North America, in moist habitats ranging from boreal to subtropical.

The mudpuppies and waterdogs are five species of aquatic, neotenous salamanders in the family Necturidae, occurring in eastern North America. The most widespread and abundant species is the mudpuppy (*Necturus maculosus*).

The hellbender (*Cryptobranchus alleganiensis*) is the only North American representative of the Cryptobranchidae, the family of giant salamanders. The hellbender is an impressively large **animal**, which can reach a body length of 2.5 ft (74 cm). Hellbenders live in streams and **rivers**. The hellbender is one of the relatively few salamanders that does not have internal fertilization of its eggs. The male hellbender deposits sperm over the ova after they are laid, so that external fertilization takes place.

Amphiumas (family Amphiumidae) are long, eel-like, aquatic creatures with tiny legs, that live in streams, swamps, and other wet places in the extreme southeastern United States. Amphiumas are vicious animals when disturbed, and can inflict a painful bite. The most widespread of the three North American species is the two-toed amphiuma (*Amphiuma means*) of Florida and parts of coastal Georgia and the Carolinas. The three-toed amphiuma (*Amphiuma tridactylum*) can achieve a body length of about 3 ft (1 m), and is the longest amphibian in North America.

Sirens (family Sirenidae) are also long and slender, aquatic salamanders. Sirens have diminutive forelimbs, and they lack hind limbs. These animals are aquatic, and they retain gills and other larval characters as adults. Mating of sirens has not been observed, but it is believed that they have external fertilization. There are three species of sirens in North America, the most widespread of which is the lesser siren (*Siren intermedia*), occurring in the drainage of the Mississippi River and in the southeastern states. The greater siren (*S. lacertina*) of the southeastern coastal plain can be as long as 3 ft (95 cm).

The mole salamanders (family Ambystomidae) are terrestrial as adults, commonly burrowing into moist ground or rotting **wood**. The largest of the 17 North American species is the tiger salamander (*Ambystoma tigrinum*), measuring up to 12 in (30 cm) in length. This is a widespread species, occurring over most of the United States, parts of southern Canada, and into northern Mexico. The Pacific giant salamander (*Dicamptodon ensatus*) of the temperate rainforests of the west coast is another large species, with a length of up to 12 in (30 cm). Other relatively widespread mole salamanders are the spotted salamander (*A. maculatum*) of the eastern United States and southeastern Canada, the marbled salamander (*A. opacum*) of the southeastern states, and the blue-spotted salamander (*A. laterale*) of northeastern North America.

There are at least 77 species of lungless salamanders (family Plethodontidae) in North America. The red-backed salamander (*Plethodon cinereus*) is a common and widespread species in the northeastern U.S. and southeastern Canada. The ensatina salamander (*Ensatina eschscholtzi*) occurs in subalpine **conifer** forests of the humid west coast.

There are six species of newts (family Salamandridae) in North America. The eastern newt (*Notophthalmus viridescens*) is widespread in the east. Initially transformed adults usually leave their natal pond to wander in moist forests for several years as the red-eft stage. The eft eventually returns to an aquatic habitat where it transforms into a sexually mature adult, and it spends the rest of its life in this stage. Some races of eastern newts do not have the red eft stage. The most widespread of the western newts is the rough-skinned newt (*Taricha granulosa*), occurring in or near various types of still-water aquatic habitats of the humid west coast.

Salamanders and humans

Other than a few species that are sometimes kept as unusual pets, salamanders have little direct economic value. However, salamanders are ecologically important in some natural communities, in part because they are productive animals that may be fed upon by a wide range of other animals. In addition, salamanders are interesting creatures, with great intrinsic value.

Considering these direct and indirect values of salamanders, it is very unfortunate that so many species are threatened by population declines, and even **extinction**. The most important threat to salamanders is the conversion of their natural habitats, such as mature forests, into other types of ecosystems, such as agricultural fields, residential developments, and clear-cuts and other types of harvested forests. These converted ecosystems do not provide adequate habitat for many species of salamanders, and sometimes for none at all. It is critically important that a sufficient area of natural forest and other native habitat types be provided to sustain populations of species of salamanders, and other native wild life.

On January 31, 2000, the U.S. Fish And Wildlife Service, Division Of Endangered Species, listed the following 11 species of North American salamanders as being endangered.

- Barton Springs Salamander (*Eurycea sosorum*). First listed: April 30, 1997. Historic range: Texas

KEY TERMS

Complex life cycle—A life marked by several radical transformations in anatomy, physiology, and ecology.

Neoteny—The retardation of typical development processes, so that sexual maturity occurs in animals that retain many juvenile characteristics.

- Cheat Mountain Salamander (*Plethodon nettingi*). First listed: August 18, 1989. Historic range: West Virginia
- California Tiger Salamander [*Ambystoma californiense* (*A. tigrinum c.*)]. First listed: January 19, 2000. Historic range: California
- Desert Slender Salamander (*Batrachoseps aridus*). First listed: June 4, 1973. Historic range: California
- Flatwoods Salamander (*Ambystoma cingulatum*). First listed: April 1, 1999. Historic range: Alabama, Florida, Georgia, South Carolina
- Red Hills Salamander (*Phaeognathus hubrichti*). First listed: December 3, 1976. Historic range: Alabama
- San Marcos Salamander (*Eurycea nana*). First listed: July 14, 1980. Historic range: Texas
- Santa Cruz Long-toed Salamander (*Ambystoma macrodactylum croceum*). First listed: March 11, 1967. Historic range: California
- Shenandoah Salamander (*Plethodon shenandoah*). First listed: August 18, 1989. Historic range: Virginia
- Sonoran Tiger Salamander (*Ambystoma tigrinum stebbinsi*). First listed: January 6, 1997. Historic range: Arizona, Mexico
- Texas Blind Salamander (*Typhlomolge rathbuni*). First listed: March 11, 1967. Historic range: Texas

Further Reading

Bishop, S. C. *Handbook of Salamanders.* New York: Cornell University Press, 1994.

Carroll, R. L. *Vertebrate Paleontology and Evolution.* New York: Freeman, 1988.

Duellman, W. E., and L. Trueb. *Biology of Amphibians.* New York: McGraw-Hill, 1986.

Harris, C. L. *Concepts in Zoology.* New York: HarperCollins, 1992.

Smith, H. M. *Amphibians of North America.* New York: Golden Press, 1978.

Bill Freedman
Randall Frost

Salmon

Salmon are various species of medium-sized, fusiform (a vertically compressed, torpedo shape) **fish** with small scales. Their fins are arranged like those of most **freshwater** fish. On the underside are two pectoral fins, a pair of pelvic fins, an anal fin, and a caudal (or tail) fin. On the back are a dorsal fin and a smaller adipose fin located in front of the tail. The mouth is wide and has numerous strong teeth. The coloring ranges from silvery, to green, brown, gold, or red, and changes with environmental conditions and stage of life. At sea, the muscle of most salmon becomes pink-colored as they accumulate **fat**; in freshwater, most species become somewhat paler-green. Salmon are native to the Northern Hemisphere, but some species have been introduced to the Southern Hemisphere. The lifestyles of the various species are broadly similar; they lay their eggs in freshwater, are born and spend their early juvenile life there, then migrate to **ocean** to feed, and return as adults to their natal river to spawn.

Salmon belong to the family (Salmonidae), in the suborder Salmonoidei of the order Salmoniformes. The salmon family is broken down into three subfamilies, containing species of salmon, whitefish, and grayling. Within the subfamily of salmon, there are five genera: *Salmo* (Salmon, also containing trout), *Oncorhynchus* (Pacific Salmon), *Hucho, Salvelinus* (Charrs), and *Brachymystax.*

Atlantic salmon (*Salmo salar*)

Atlantic salmon live in the north Atlantic Ocean, from Cape Cod to Greenland, and from the Arctic coast of western Russia south to northern Spain. This is perhaps the best known species in the family Salmonidae. It has a rounded body and a slightly forked caudal fin. Their scales are round and show annual growth rings, and their position can be interpreted to reveal aspects of an individual's life history, such as the number of times it has spawned. The lower jaw of males develops a pronounced upward hook, similar to an underbite.

Life cycle of Atlantic Salmon

The life-cycle of the Atlantic salmon is typical of other species. While some populations live their entire lives in inland waters, most leave the river where they were born, going out to sea to feed and grow. At sea, Atlantic salmon feed voraciously on smaller species of fish. When they become sexually mature they return to their natal freshwater **habitat** to spawn. Individuals may enter the **rivers** at different times of the year, but spawning always takes place in the wintertime, from about October to January.

Sockeye salmon (*Oncorhynchus nerka*).

When preparing to spawn, the female digs a shallow nest, called a redd, by pushing pebbles on the river floor out of the way with her tail. The redd is generally 6-12 in (15-30 cm) deep, and a few stones are usually present on the bottom. In a crouching position, the female then lays her eggs; at the same time, the male, also crouching, fertilizes them with his milt. While this is occurring, young males who have never been to sea may dart in and out of the nest, spreading their own sperm. This **behavior** ensures that most of the eggs will be fertilized.

The female repeats this nesting procedure several times in separate locations, moving upstream each time. She covers her older nests with the pebbles from the newer ones, thus protecting her eggs. Overall, spawning lasts about two weeks, during which time the salmon lose about 35% of their body weight. In this depleted condition, they are known as kelts. They return downstream, and in their weakened physical state, many of them die of disease or are taken by predators. Unlike Pacific salmon, Atlantic salmon are capable of spawning more than once during their life. Typically, about 5-10% of the kelts return to spawn the following year.

The eggs stay in the nest all winter and hatch in the springtime. During their incubation, it is important that they have a steady supply of clean freshwater and **oxygen**. When they hatch, they are said to be in the alevin stage, and they feed on the remainder of their yolk sac. When the yolk runs out of **nutrients**, the young, now called fry, come out of the gravel and feed on aquatic **invertebrates**. As they grow, they become parrs, and are camouflaged by dark splotches on their body. The young salmon spend 1-6 years in their natal river. When they grow to 4-7.5 in (10-19 cm) long, they lose their splotches, becoming completely silver, and migrate out to sea. At this point they are called smolts.

The smolts remain at sea for one to five years, feeding on fish and growing and building up a large store of fat. Then they return to freshwater to breed, usually to the river where they were born. They swim energetically up streams and rivers, going through rapids, and even leaping up small waterfalls. They do not feed during this **migration**. They may travel hundreds of miles inland during this trip. During their journey, they change color and physical appearance. Originally silver, they turn brown or green, and males develop a hooked lower jaw, called a kype. Males use their kypes for fighting other males while defending their breeding territory.

KEY TERMS

Adipose fin—A small, extra dorsal fin located well back on the fish's spine in front of the tail.

Alevin stage—The time in a salmon's life right after it hatches when it feeds on its yolk sac.

Anal fin—Located on the belly just before the tail fin.

Caudal fin—Tail fin.

Dorsal fin—Front-most fin located on a fish's back.

Fry—Follows the alevin stage, when the young fry leaves the gravel and feeds on invertebrates.

Kelts—Atlantic salmon that have lived through their spawning, and try to return to sea. They may spawn again the following year.

Kype—The hooked lower jaw of a male Atlantic salmon, grown when spawning to fight other males.

Parrs—The name for salmon when they have grown around an inch or so long and become camouflaged by dark splotches on their body.

Pectoral fins—The first two fins on the fish's lower sides, almost to its belly.

Pelvic fin—Located on the fish's belly, slightly to the rear of the dorsal fin and in front of the anal fin.

Redd—A shallow nest dug by the female prior to spawning.

Smolts—When the salmon grows 4–7.5 in (10–18 cm) long, it loses its splotches, becomes silver colored, and migrates to sea.

Pacific salmon (*Oncorhynchus* species)

Pacific salmon have an elongated, compressed body, and their head comes to a point at their mouth, which contains well-developed teeth. When they feed at sea, their coloring is metallic blue with a few brown spots, and their flesh is pale pink and contains 9-11% fat. When spawning in freshwater their external coloring turns greenish yellow with pinkish red streaks on the sides.

Pacific salmon live off the coast of areas in the northern Pacific Ocean, from California to Japan to Russia. Some species extend to the southern Arctic Ocean. There are seven species of Pacific salmon, five of which are native to North American waters. The largest species is the king salmon, also called the chinook or quinnat salmon. One large king salmon was caught that weighed 125 lb (57 kg), but a more common maximum weight is around 55 lb (25 kg). Other species of Pacific salmon weigh 3-18 lb (1.5-8 kg).

Spawning activities are similar to those of the Atlantic salmon. The majority of species spawn in the winter, and the activity occurs over three to five days. The eggs are about 7 mm in diameter. However, both males and females die soon after spawning.

Water pollution, fishing, and fish-farming

Because of their migratory habits and abundance, salmon have a long history of being a valuable source of food for people. In fact, before **water pollution** became a major problem, these fish were cheap and easy to get. However, with the onset of the **industrial revolution**, many rivers became polluted or were blocked by **dams**, and salmon populations declined or disappeared. Furthermore, decreases in salmon populations were intensified by increased fishing in salmon feeding habitat at sea. Fishery biologists are attempting to stem the salmon declines by enhancing wild stocks, for example, by releasing large numbers of captive-reared, young fish. This so-called "stock enhancement" can help, but it is also necessary to stop or repair the damage to aquatic habitat, and control the rate of fishing.

As a result of their decline, salmon became a high priced luxury item. Subsequently, the industry of fish farming arose, introducing the practice of rearing salmon in cages in embayments or at sea, or in ponds on land. The most popular species of salmon being farmed are Atlantic salmon, rainbow trout, Coho salmon, pink salmon, and American brook trout. Fish farming has helped to offset some of the decreases in salmon populations. However, other important problems have developed, because of chemicals used to prevent diseases in captive salmon and the build-up of organic sludge beneath fish-cages. Until measures are taken to control **water pollution** and to stop overfishing, salmon populations will not be able to return to their once abundant numbers.

Further Reading

Drummond, Stephen Sedwick. *The Salmon Handbook.* London: Robert Hartnoll, 1982.

Grzimek, H.C. Bernard, ed. *Grzimek's Animal Life Encyclopedia.* New York: Van Nostrand Reinhold,1975.

Nelson, Joseph S. *Fishes of the World*. 3rd ed. New York: Wiley, 1994.

Kathryn Snavely

Salmonella

Salmonella is the common name given to a type of **food poisoning** caused by the **bacteria** called *Salmonella enteritidis* (other types of illnesses are caused by other species of *Salmonella* bacteria, including **typhoid fever**). When people eat food contaminated by *S. enteritidis*, they suffer from **inflammation** of hte stomach and intestines, with diarrhea and vomiting resulting. This illness is called gastroenteritis.

Salmonella food poisoning is most often caused by improperly handled or cooked poultry or eggs. Because chickens carrying the bacteria do not appear at all ill, infected chickens go on to lay eggs or to be used as meat.

Early in the study of Salmonella food poisoning, it was thought that *Salmonella* bacteria were only found in eggs which had cracks in them. It was thought that the bacteria existed on the outside of the eggshell, and could only find their way in through such cracks. Stringent guidelines were put into place to ensure that cracked eggs do not make it to the marketplace, and to make sure that the outside of eggshells are all carefully disinfected. However, outbreaks of Salmonella poisoning continued. Research then ultimately revealed that, because the egg shell has tiny pores, even uncracked eggs which have been left for a time on a surface (such as a chicken's roost) contaminated with *Salmonella* could become contaminated. Subsequently, further research has demonstrated that the bacteria can also be passed from the infected female chicken directly into the substance of the egg prior to the shell forming around it.

Currently, the majority of Salmonella food poisoning occurs due to unbroken, disinfected grade A eggs, which have become infected through bacteria which reside in the hen's ovaries. In the United States, the highest number of cases of Salmonella food poisoning occur in the Northeast, where it is believed that about one out of 10,000 eggs is infected with *Salmonella* .

The only way to avoid Salmonella poisoning is to properly cook all food which could potentially harbor the bacteria. Neither drying nor freezing are reliable ways to kill *Salmonella*; only sufficient **heat** can be trusted to kill *Salmonella*. While the most common source for human **infection** with *Salmonella* bacteria is poultry products, other carriers include pets such as **turtles**, chicks, ducklings, and **iguanas**. Products which contain **animal** tissues may also be contaminated with *Salmonella*.

While anyone may contract Salmonella food poisoning from contaminated foods, the disease proves most threatening in infants, the elderly, and individuals with weakened immune systems. People who have had part or all of their stomach or their spleen removed, as well as individuals with sickle **cell anemia**, **cirrhosis** of the liver, leukemia, lymphoma, **malaria**, louse-borne relapsing fever, or Acquired Immunodeficiency **syndrome** (**AIDS**) are particularly susceptible to Salmonella food poisoning. In the United States, about 15% of all cases of food poisoning are caused by *Salmonella*.

Causes & symptoms

Salmonella food poisoning occurs most commonly when people eat undercooked chicken or eggs, or sauces, salad dressings, or desserts containing raw eggs. The bacteria can also be spread if raw chicken, for example, contaminates a cutting board or a cook's hands, and is then spread to some other food which isn't cooked. Cases of Salmonella infections in children have been traced to the children handling a pet (such as a turtle or an iguana) and then eating without first washing their hands. An individual who has had Salmonella food poisoning will continue to pass the bacteria into their feces for several weeks after the initial illness. Poor handwashing can allow others to become infected.

Symptoms of Salmonella food poisoning generally occur about 12-72 hours after the bacteria is acquired. Half of all patients experience fever; other symptoms include nausea, vomiting, diarrhea, and abdominal cramping and **pain**. The stools are usually quite liquid, but rarely contain mucus or **blood**. Diarrhea usually lasts about four days. The entire illness usually resolves itself within about a week.

While serious complications of Salmonella food poisoning are rare, individuals with other medical illnesses are at higher risk. Complications occur when the *Salmonella* bacteria make their way into the bloodstream. Once in the bloodstream, the bacteria can invade any **organ** system, causing disease. Infections which can be caused by *Salmonella* include:

- bone infections (osteomyelitis)
- joint infections (**arthritis**)
- infections of the sac containing the **heart** (pericarditis)
- infections of the tissues which cover the **brain** and spinal cord (**meningitis**)
- liver infections (**hepatitis**)
- lung infections (**pneumonia**)

- infections of aneurysms (aneurysms are abnormal outpouchings which occur in weakened areas of blood vessel walls
- infections in the center of already-existing tumors or cysts

Diagnosis

Salmonella food poisoning is diagnosed by examining a stool **sample**. Under appropriate laboratory conditions, the bacteria in the stool can be encouraged to grow, and then processed and viewed under a **microscope** for identification.

Treatment

Simple cases of Salmonella food poisoning are usually treated by encouraging good fluid intake, to avoid dehydration. Although the illness is caused by a bacteria, studies have shown that using **antibiotics** doesn't really shorten the course of the illness. Instead, antibiotics have the adverse effect of lengthening the amount of time the bacteria appear in the feces, thus potentially increasing others' risk of exposure to *Salmonella.*

Antibiotics are used when *Salmonella* causes more severe types of infection. In these cases, ampicillin, chloramphenicol, or quinolones can be taken by mouth, or given through a needle inserted in a vein (intravenously).

Prevention

Efforts to prevent Salmonella food poisoning have been greatly improved now that it is understood that eggs can be contimaminated during their development inside the hen. Flocks are carefully tested, and eggs from infected chickens can be pasteurized to kill the bacteria. Efforts have been made to carefully educate the public about safe handling and cooking practices for both poultry and eggs. People who own pets that can carry *Salmonella* are also being more educated about more careful handwashing practices. It is unlikely that a human immunization will be developed, because there are so many different types of *Salmonella enteritidis*. However, researchers are close to producing an oral **vaccine** for poultry, which will prevent the *Salmonella* bacteria from infecting meat or eggs.

Further Reading

Keusch, Gerald T. "Diseases Caused by Gram-Negative Bacteria" *Harrison's Principles of Internal Medicine.* New York: McGraw-Hill, 1998.

Stix, Gary. "Egg Savers: A Poultry Vaccine May Help Remove the Stigma from Breakfast," *Scientific American.* November 3, 1997.

"Salmonellosis: Frequently Asked Questions." Center for Disease Control, http://www.cdc.gov/ncidod/diseases/foodborn/salmon.htm.

"*Salmonella enteritidis* Infection." National Center for Infectious Disease, Division of Bacterial and Mycotic Diseases, http://www.cdc.gov/ncidod/index.htm.

"*Salmonella spp.*" Foodborne Pathogenic Microorganisms and Natural Toxins Handbook of the United States Food and Drug Administration, http://www.fda.gov/.

Rosalyn Carson-DeWitt

Salt

Salt, the most commmonly known of which is **sodium chloride**, or table salt, is a compound formed by the chemical reaction of an acid with a base. During this reaction, the acid and base are neutralized producing salt, **water** and **heat**. Sodium chloride, is distributed throughout nature as deposits on land created by the **evaporation** of ancient seas and is also dissolved in the oceans. Salt is an important compound with many uses including **food preservation**, **soap** production, and de-icing roads and walkways. It is also the primary source of **chlorine** and sodium for industrial chemicals.

Generally speaking, a salt can be any compound formed by the reaction of an acid with a base. **Energy**, in the form of heat, is given off during this **neutralization** reaction so it is said to be exothermic. The most common salt, sodium chloride (NaCl), is a product of the reaction between hydrochloric acid (HCl) and the base **sodium hydroxide** (NaOH). In this reaction, positively charged **hydrogen** ions (H+) from the acid are attracted to negatively charged hydroxyl ions (OH-) from the base. These ions combine and form water. After the water forms, the sodium and chlorine ions remain dissolved and the acid and base are said to be neutralized. Solid salt is formed when the water evaporates and the negatively charged chlorine ions combine with the positively charged sodium ions.

Solid sodium chloride exists in the form of tiny, cube-shaped particles called crystals. These crystals are colorless, have a **density** of 2.165 g/cm^3 and melt at 1,472°F (800.8°C). They also dissolve in water, separating into the component sodium and chlorine ions. This process known as ionization is important to many industrial chemical reactions.

Common salt (sodium chloride) is found throughout nature. It is dissolved in the oceans with an average **concentration** of 2.68%. On land, thick salt deposits, formed by the evaporation of prehistoric oceans, are widely distributed. These deposits are true sedimentary **rocks** and are referred to as rock salt or halite.

People obtain salt from the environment in many different ways. Solid salt deposits are mined directly as rock salt and purified. Salt from sea water is isolated by solar evaporation. Underground salt deposits are solution-mined. This type of **mining** involves pumping water underground to dissolve the salt **deposit**, recovering the water with salt dissolved in it, and evaporating the water to isolate the salt.

Beyond being essential to the survival of most plants and animals, salt is also used extensively in many industries. In the food industry it is used to preserve meats and **fish** because it can slow down the growth of unhealthy **microorganisms**. It is also used to improve the flavor of many foods. In the cosmetic industry it is used to make soaps and shampoos. In other chemical industries it is the primary source of sodium and chlorine which are both raw materials used for various chemical reactions. Salt is used when manufacturing **paper**, rubber, and **ceramics**. And it is commonly used for de-icing roads during the winter.

See also Acids and bases.

Salt, table see **Sodium chloride**

Saltpeter see **Potassium nitrate**

Saltwater

Saltwater, or **salt water**, is a geological term that refers to naturally occurring solutions containing large concentrations of dissolved, inorganic ions. In addition, this term is often used as an adjective in **biology**, usually to refer to marine organisms, as in saltwater **fish**.

Saltwater most commonly refers to oceanic waters, in which the total **concentration** of ionic solutes is typically about 35 grams per litre (also expressed as 3.5%, or 35 parts per thousand). As a result of these large concentrations of dissolved ions, the **density** of saltwater (1.028 g/L at 4° C) is slightly greater than that of **freshwater** (1.00 g/L). Therefore, freshwater floats above saltwater in poorly mixed situations where the two types meet, as in estuaries and some underground reservoirs.

The ions with the largest concentrations in marine waters are **sodium**, chloride, sulfate, **magnesium**, **calcium**, potassium, and carbonate. In oceanic waters, sodium and chloride are the most important ions, having concentrations of 10.8 g/L and 19.4 g/L, respectively. Other important ions are sulfate (2.7 g/L), magnesium (1.3 g/L), and calcium and potassium (both 0.4 g/L). However, in inland saline waters, the concentrations and relative proportions of these and other ions can vary widely.

Other natural waters can also be salty, sometimes containing much larger concentrations of salt than the oceans. Some lakes and ponds, known as salt or brine surface waters, can have very large concentrations of dissolved, ionic solutes. These water bodies typically occur in a closed **basin**, with inflows of water but no outflow except by **evaporation**, which leaves salts behind. Consequently, the salt concentration of their contained water increases progressively over time. For example, the Great Salt Lake of Utah and the Dead Sea in Israel have salt concentrations exceeding 20%, as do smaller, saline ponds in Westphalia, Germany, and elsewhere in the world.

Underground waters can also be extremely salty. Underground saltwaters are commonly encountered in **petroleum** and gas well-fields, especially after the **hydrocarbon** resource has been exhausted by **mining**.

Both surface and underground saltwaters are sometimes "mined" for their contents of economically useful **minerals**.

Saltwater intrusions can be an important environmental problem, which can degrade water supplies required for drinking or **irrigation**. Saltwater intrusions are caused in places near the **ocean** where there are excessive withdrawals of underground supplies of fresh waters. This allows underground saltwaters to migrate inland, and spoil the quality of the aquifer for most uses. Saltwater intrusions are usually caused by excessive usages of ground water for irrigation in agriculture, or to supply drinking water to large cities.

Samarium see **Lanthanides**

Sample

A sample is a subset of actual observations taken from any larger set of possible observations. The larger set of observations is known as a *population*. For example, suppose that a researcher would like to know how many hours the average 11th grade student in the United States spends studying English literature every night. One way to answer that question would be to interview a select number (say 50, 500, or 5,000) of 11th grade students and ask them how many hours they spend on English literature each evening. The researcher could then draw some conclusions about the time spent studying English literature by all 11th grade students based on what he or she learned from the sample that was studied.

Samples and populations

Sampling is a crucial technique in the science of statistical analysis. It represents a compromise between a researcher collecting all possible information on some topic and the amount of information that he or she can realistically collect. For example, in the example used above, the ideal situation might be for a researcher to collect data from every single 11th grade student in the United States. But the cost, time, and effort required to do this kind of study would be enormous. No one could possibly do such a study.

The alternative is to select a smaller subset of 11th grade students and collect data from them. If the sample that is chosen is typical of all 11th grade students throughout the United States, the data obtained could also be considered to be typical. That is, if the average 11th grade student in the sample studies English literature two hours every evening, then the researcher might be justified in saying that the average 11th grade student in the United States also studies English literature two hours a night.

Random samples

The key to using samples in statistical analysis is to be sure that they are **random**. A random sample is one in which every member of the population has an equal chance of being selected for the sample. For example, a researcher could not choose 11th grade students for a sample if they all came from the same city, from the same school, were of the same sex, or had the same last name. In such cases, the sample chosen for study would not be representative of the total population.

Many systems have been developed for selecting random samples. One approach is simply to put the name of every member of the population on a piece of **paper**, put the pieces of paper into a large fishbowl, mix them up, and then draw names at random for the sample. Although this idea sounds reasonable, it has a number of drawbacks. One is that complete mixing of pieces of paper is very difficult. Pieces may stick to each other, they may be of different sizes or weight, or they may differ from each other in some other respect. Still, this method is often used for statistical studies in which precision is not crucial.

Today, researchers use computer programs to obtain random samples for their studies. When the United States government collects **statistics** on the number of hours people work, the kinds of jobs they do, the wages they earn, and so on, they ask a computer to sift through the names of every citizen for whom they have records and choose every hundredth name, every five-hundredth name, or to make selections at some other **interval**. Only the individuals actually chosen by the computer are used for the sample. From the results of that sample, extrapolations are made for the total population of all working Americans.

KEY TERMS

Extrapolation—The process of using some limited set of data to make predictions about a broader set of data on the same subject.

Population—Any set of observations that could potentially be made.

Random sample—A sample in which every member of the population has an equal chance of being selected for the sample.

Sample size and accuracy

The choice a researcher always has to make is how large a sample to choose. It stands to reason that the larger the sample, the more accurate will be the results of the study. The smaller the sample, the less accurate the results. Statisticians have developed mathematical formulas that allow them to estimate how accurate their results are for any given sample size. The sample size used depends on how much money they have to spend, how accurate the final results need to be, how much variability among data are they willing to accept, and so on.

Interestingly enough, the sample size needed to produce accurate results in a study is often surprisingly small. For example, the Gallup Poll regularly chooses samples of people of whom they ask a wide variety of questions. The organization is perhaps best known for its predictions of presidential and other elections. For its presidential election polls, the Gallup organization interviews no more than a few thousand people out of the tens of millions who actually vote. Yet, their results are often accurate within a percentage point or so of the actual votes cast in an election. The secret of success for Gallup-and for other successful polling organizations - is to be sure that the sample they select is truly random, that is, that the people interviewed are completely typical of everyone who belongs to the general population.

Further Reading

McCarthy, Philip J. *Introduction to Statistical Reasoning*. New York: McGraw-Hill, 1957.

McCollough, Celeste, and Loche Van Atta. *Statistical Concepts: A Program for Self-Instruction.* New York: McGraw Hill, 1963.

White, Robert S. *Statistics.* 3rd ed. New York: Holt, Rinehart and Winston, 1989.

David E. Newton

Sampling techniques see **Archaeology**

Sand see **Sediment and sedimentation**

Sand dollars

Sand dollars or sea biscuits (phylum Echinodermata, class Echinoidea) are closely related to heart urchins and **sea urchins**, although they lack the visible long, protective spines of the latter. The body is flattened and almost circular in appearance—an **adaptation** for burrowing in soft sediment. It is protected by a toughened exterior known as the test, and is covered with short spines. The most striking feature of a sand dollar, however, is the distinctive five-arm body pattern on the upper surface. The mouth is located at the center of this pattern. Unlike sea urchins and most other echinoderms, sand dollars are bilaterally symmetrical. Ranging in colors from black to purple, these animals live below the low tide mark in all oceans of the world.

Sand dollars are active burrowing animals and do so with assistance from their moveable spines, which clear a path through the sediment. They are only capable of movement in a forward direction. Some species cover themselves with sediment while others leave their posterior end exposed. When submerged, the **animal** raises its hind end into the **water** column, its posterior end remaining buried in the sediment. By aligning itself at right angles to the water current, it is guaranteed a constant source of food.

Sand dollars feed on tiny food particles that are obtained from the sediment while burrowing or from the water current. In contrast to the majority of other burrowing **invertebrates**, sand dollars do not ingest vast quantities of sediment and sift through the materials. Instead, as the materials pass over the animal's body, particles are sorted between the spines; fine food items fall to the body where they are trapped in a layer of mucus secreted by the spines. Tiny cilia between the spines move this mucus to and along a series of special grooves on the animal's body towards the mouth. Some species, such as *Dendraster exocentricus*, feed on **diatoms** and other suspended matter.

Adult sand dollars are either male or female. During the breeding season, large quantities of eggs and sperm are released into the sea, where **fertilization** takes place. The resulting larvae are free-living and, after some time in the water column, settle to the sea bed and undergo a process known as **metamorphosis**, which results in a minute replica of the adult sand dollar.

Sandfish

A sandfish is a sand-dwelling lizard of the family Scincidae (a skink) found in **desert** regions of North **Africa** and southwestern **Asia**. It receives the name "sandfish" because it literally "swims" through the loose sand of its preferred **habitat**.

Six or seven species of the genus *Scincus* are called sandfish. They range from Algeria, in northwestern Africa, to the Sind desert region of Pakistan. The best known of these, the medicinal skink (*Scincus scincus*) was used in potions for "the most diverse complaints" in olden times.

These lizards are especially modified for living in sandy regions. They are six or seven inches long (about 20 cm), with a moderately stout body and a relatively short tail. The head is conical with a shovel-shaped snout, and the lower jaws are countersunk behind the snout and upper jaws—a common **adaptation** in desert animals that prevents sand from getting into the mouth. The eyes are rather small and have a transparent "window" formed by several large scales in the lower lid. The body scales are smooth. The ears are completely covered by scales and hidden from view. The limbs are well-formed and the toes are flattened and have a series of elongated scales along their sides. This presumably aids them in walking over the surface of the sand at night, but they spend most of their time below the surface and move by folding their legs back and swimming with sinuous lateral movements. As expected in such a habitat, the upper part of the body is light tan (sand-colored), with some scattered, vertically elongated brown blotches on the sides. The lower surface is white.

The habits and **life history** of these lizards are little known. They presumably feed on **insects** and other desert-dwelling **arthropods**.

See also Skinks.

Sandpipers

Sandpipers are a varied group of **shore birds** in the family Scolopacidae, order Charadriiformes. The 85

species in this family include the sandpipers, **curlews**, snipes, woodcocks, godwits, dowitchers, turnstones, and phalaropes. This family occurs worldwide, except in **Antarctica**. Thirty-seven species in the sandpiper family breed regularly in **North America**. The smaller species of sandpipers and the closely related **plovers** (family Charadriidae) are commonly known as "peeps" to bird watchers, because of their high pitched vocalizations.

It is difficult to describe a "typical" sandpiper. Members of this family vary greatly in body size and shape, for example, ranging from 5-24 in (13-61 cm) in body length, with either short or long legs, a beak that is straight, curves upward, or curves downward, and a neck that is either long or short. There are also great variations in color and **behavior** within this group of **birds**. Because of the enormous variations between species, the sandpiper family is extremely interesting, but difficult to concisely define.

Most sandpipers feed actively, by walking and running in search of small **invertebrates**. Most sandpipers typically feed by poking their bill into soft mud or **soil**, probing for invertebrates, or the birds pick invertebrates from the surface of the substrate or from debris. However, the two species of turnstone, including the ruddy turnstone (*Arenaria interpres*) of North America and Eurasia, feed uniquely by turning over small stones and beach debris, searching for crustaceans hiding beneath. Curlews, such as the whimbrel (*Numenius phaeopus*), often eat berries in addition to invertebrates.

Most sandpipers nest on the ground, usually making an open scrape that is well camouflaged by its surroundings and difficult to locate. When predators or humans are close to the nest, many sandpipers will exhibit a distraction display, calling vociferously, running nearby on the ground, and sometimes feigning a broken wing, all the while attempting to lure the intruder safely away from the nest. Sandpiper chicks are precocial. That is, they can leave their nest within hours of hatching, and they roam and feed under the close attention of their parents.

Many species of sandpipers, especially the larger ones, breed monogamously as solitary pairs, which often aggressively defend their territory against intruders of the same species. However, some species of sandpiper have a polyandrous breeding system, in which a female mates with one or several males, leaving them with eggs to incubate and care for, while she lays another clutch to incubate and care for by herself. In phalaropes, such as the red-necked phalarope (*Phalaropus lobatus*) of North America and Eurasia, it is the female that is relatively brightly colored, and who courts the plainer-colored male, who then incubates the eggs and rears the young. This represents a reversal of the usual roles of the sexes.

A red-backed sandpiper (*Calidris alpina*) at the Ottawa National Wildlife Refuge, Ohio. This bird feeds by probing or rapidly "stitching" with its bill (like the needle of a sewing machine), leaving a line of tiny holes in the mud.

The ruff (*Philomachus pugnax*) of Eurasia has an unusual, promiscuous **courtship** and breeding system called lekking, in which the male birds (called ruffs) exhibit a remarkable array of "ear" and "collar" feathers of differing shapes and colors. These are displayed erect to each other and to females (called reeves) during a frenzied, communal courtship at a designated arena.

Depending on the species, the appropriate **habitat** of members in the sandpiper family may be shorelines, mudflats, **wetlands**, prairies, **tundra**, or fields. However, most species in this family breed at relatively high latitudes of the Northern Hemisphere, with some species occurring to the very limits of land on northern Greenland and Ellesmere Island. Sandpipers that breed at high latitudes undertake long-distance migrations between their breeding and wintering ranges. The most accomplished migrant is the surfbird (*Aphriza virgata*), which breeds in **mountain** tundra in central Alaska, and winters on the Pacific Coast as far south as Tierra del Fuego at the southern tip of **South America**. Other extreme cases are the red knot (*Calidris canutus*) and the sanderling (*Calidris alba*), which breed in the High Arctic of North America (and Eurasia) but winter on the coasts of northern South America and Central America.

Other species are more temperate in at least part of their breeding range, such as the American woodcock (*Philohela minor*) of the eastern United States and southeastern Canada, and the spotted sandpiper (*Actitis macularia*) of temperate and boreal North America. Only a few species breed in the tropics. For example, the East Indian woodcock (*Scolopax saturata*), closely related to the Eurasian woodcock (*S. rusticolla*), ranges from South **Asia** to New Guinea. Only a few species of sandpipers are exclusively of the Southern Hemisphere.

These include the New Zealand snipe (*Coenocorypha aucklandica*), breeding on a few islands in the vicinity of New Zealand, and the Tuamotu sandpiper (*Aechmorhynchus cancellatus*) of the Tuamotu Archipelago of the South Pacific Ocean.

Some species of sandpiper are rare and endangered. In North America, the Eskimo curlew (*Numenius borealis*) is perilously endangered because of overhunting. The last observed nest of this species was in 1866, but there have been a number of sightings of Eskimo curlews in recent decades, so it appears that the species is not extinct, although it is critically endangered. Another North American species, Cooper's sandpiper (*Pisobia cooperi*), apparently became extinct in 1833 because of overhunting. Other than its size and taste, virtually nothing was learned about this species before it disappeared.

During their migrations, certain species of sandpipers are highly social, sometimes occurring in huge flocks of their own species, often mixed with similar sized sandpipers and plovers. For example, semipalmated sandpipers (*Calidris pusilla*) aggregate in individual flocks of hundreds of thousands of individuals when they stage in the Bay of Fundy of eastern Canada during their southward **migration**. This is a **critical habitat** for these and other shore birds, because they must "fatten up" on the large populations of amphipods in tidal mudflats of the Bay of Fundy, in preparation for the arduous, usually non-stop flight to the wintering habitats of the coasts of Central America, the Caribbean, and northern South America.

Most species of sandpipers occur predictably in large flocks in particular places and **seasons**, especially in their staging habitats during migration and on the wintering grounds. Sandpipers and associated shore birds are highly vulnerable at these times and places to both excessive hunting and habitat loss. These sorts of habitats are absolutely critical to the survival of these species, and they must be preserved in their natural condition if sandpipers and associated **wildlife** are to survive.

Further Reading

Harrison, C. J. O., ed. *Bird Families of the World.* New York: H.N. Abrams, 1978.

Hayman, P., J. Marchant, and T. Prater. *Shore Birds. An Identification Guide to the Waders of the World.* London: Croom Helm, 1986.

Richards, A. *Birds of the Tideline. Shore Birds of the Northern Hemisphere.* Surrey, England: Dragon's World, 1988.

Bill Freedman

Sap see **Tree**

Sapodilla tree

The sapodilla, *Achra zapota,* or plum **tree** is a large evergreen tree native to Central and **South America**. Sapodilla trees can often grow to 100 ft (30 m) tall with a girth of some 7 ft (2 m). The flowers are white to cream and usually open at night. The **seeds** of these trees are dispersed by **bats**, which excrete them after consuming the fruit.

The durable **wood** of the sapodilla tree is used in building construction as well as for making furniture and ornaments. It is also desired for its soft, sweet-tasting fruit, the sapodilla plum or chiku. However, humans have primarily cultivated this species for its whitish latex, which is used to produce chicle, the elastic component of early forms of chewing gum.

Sardines

Sardines are silvery, laterally-flattened **fish**. They are members of the order Clupeiformes, commonly known as the herring order, and the suborder Clupeoidei. These fish usually live in warm marine waters, are found around the shores of every **continent**, and are an extremely valuable food fish.

There are four families in the order Clupeiformes. Two of the families contain only a single species; one is the denticle herring and the other is the wolf herring. The third family contains various species of anchovies. The fourth family, the family Clupeidae, is the largest family in the order, containing sardines, true **herrings**, shads, and menhadens. The sardines are classified in three genera: *Sardina, Sardinops,* and *Sardinella.* These genera contain approximately 22 species.

General characteristics and habits

Sardines have a flat body which is covered with large, reflective, silvery scales. In the middle of their belly, they have a set of specialized scales, known as scutes, which are jagged and point backwards. Having very small teeth or no teeth at all, sardines eat **plankton**, which they filter from the **water** through their gills. While numerous species of sardines live off the coasts of India, China, Indonesia, and Japan, single sardine species dominate in areas like the English Channel and the California coast. Sardines are basically a warm-water fish, but occur as far north as Norway.

Schools, or shoals, of sardines swim near the water surface and are primarily marine, although some live in **freshwater**. Most species are migratory; in the Northern

Hemisphere, for example, they migrate northward in the summer and southward in the winter. During spring and summer, they spawn. After doing this, the young commonly move closer to the shore to feed. The young sardines eat plant plankton (or **phytoplankton**), while adults eat animal plankton (**zooplankton**). All sardine species are important **prey** for larger fish.

Details about the three genera

The genus of true sardines, *Sardina*, contains only one species, *Sardina pilchardus*. Also referred to as pilchards, these sardines live off of the European coast in the Atlantic Ocean and in the Mediterranean and Black Seas. Their **habitat** is limited to areas where the **temperature** measures at or above 68°F (20°C). During the past 50 years, they have been found further and further northward, probably as a result of increases in global and seawater temperatures.

True sardines grow to about 10-12 in (25-30 cm) in body length. Their spawning period is rather long because of their wide distribution; in fact, depending on their location, fish of this species spawn almost continuously somewhere in their habitat. In the Atlantic Ocean, these sardines migrate northward in the summer and southward in the fall to take advantage of better feeding opportunities.

The largest of the sardine genera, *Sardinella*, contains about 16 species, and fish from this genus are known by a variety of common names. For example, in the eastern United States, people refer to them as anchovies and Spanish sardines. In the southern Pacific, they are called oil or Indian sardines. These sardines inhabit the tropical parts of the Atlantic and Indian Oceans as well as the western portion of the Pacific Ocean. *Sardinella aurita*, the largest of all sardine species, is found in the Mediterranean and Black Seas and along the African coast. The majority of fish in this genus grow no longer than 4-8 in (10-20 cm) long and have only limited commercial value as a food source.

The third genus, *Sardinops*, contains five species, all with fairly similar characteristics. These species are: the Pacific sardine, the South American sardine, the Japanese sardine, the South African sardine, and the Australian sardine. They can grow to about 12 in (30 cm) long and, with the exception of the Australian sardine, are very important commercially.

One well known species within the genus *Sardinops* is the Pacific sardine (*Sardinops sagax*), which lives along the coasts of eastern **Asia** and western **North America**. In North America, they are found from Baja California to British Columbia. Although this species spawns from January until June, most spawning occurs in March and April; and spawning occurs as far as 300 nautical miles away from shore.

Three or four days after spawning, the larvae hatch and make their way toward the coast; they measure about 3-5 in (7-12 cm). At this point, they are caught in large quantities by humans and used for bait to catch **tuna**. When they grow to about 7 in (17 cm), they leave the coast and meet the adults in the open sea. At two or three years old, they measure between 7-10 in (17-25 cm) and attain sexual maturity. These fish can live as long as 13 years. The population of this species is declining, probably because of overfishing.

Sardines are a very important source of food for many human populations. In fact, their importance is equal to that of the herring. People consume sardines in a variety of ways: dried, salted, smoked, or canned. People also use sardines for their oil and for meal.

See also Anchovy

Further Reading

Lythgoe, John, and Gillian Lythogoe. *Fishes of the Sea*. Cambridge, MA: Blandford Press, 1991.

Nelson, Joseph S. *Fishes of the World*. 3rd ed. New York: Wiley, 1994.

Nikolskii, G.V. *Special Ichthyology*. Jerusalem: Israel Program for Scientific Translations, 1961.

Webb, J.E. *Guide to Living Fishes*. London: Macmillan, 1991.

Kathryn D. Snavely

Satellite

While the word "satellite" simply means some object or person that is attendant to another more important object or person, in **astronomy** it has taken on a much more specific meaning. Here the term refers to any object that is orbiting another larger more massive object under the influence of their mutual gravitational **force**. Thus any planetary **moon** is most properly called a satellite of that **planet**. Since the word is used to describe a single object, it is not used to designate rings of material orbiting a planet even though such rings might be described as being made up of millions of satellites. In those rare instances where the **mass** of the satellite approaches that of the object around which it orbits, the system is sometimes referred to as a binary. This is the reason that some people refer to **Pluto** and its moon Charon as a binary planet. This description is even more appropriate for some recently discovered asteroids which are composed of two similar sized objects orbiting each other.

In this century we have launched from the **Earth** objects that **orbit** the Earth and other planets. A tradition

***Intelsat VI* floating over the Earth. Within hours of this shot, astronauts grabbed the satellite, attached a perigee stage, and released it back into space.**

has developed to refer to these objects as man-made satellites to distinguish them from the naturally occurring kind. Surveillance satellites orbiting the Earth have been used to measure everything from aspects of the planet's **weather** to movements of ships. Communications satellites revolve about the earth in geostationary orbits 25,000 mi (40,225 km) above the surface and a recent generation of navigation satellites enables one's location on the surface of the earth to be determined with errors measured in centimeters.

Surveillance satellites have been placed in orbit about the Moon, **Mars**, and **Venus** to provide detailed maps of their surfaces and measure properties of their surrounding environment. This program will soon be extended to **Jupiter** and **Saturn**.

Spacecraft missions to other planets in the **solar system** have revealed the existence of numerous previously unknown natural satellites. In addition, the nature of many of the planetary satellites has become far clearer as a result of these voyages. It is said that more information concerning the four major Galilean Satellites of Jupiter was gained from the first flyby by *Pioneer 10* then had been gained since the time of Galileo. The knowledge gained from the satellites in our solar system have revealed considerable insights into their formation and **evolution**. As we continue to probe the solar system, there can be little doubt that our knowledge of the satellites of the planets will continue to broaden our understanding of planetary moons and the nature of the solar system as a whole.

See also Gravity and gravitation; Space probe.

Satellite meteorology see **Atmosphere observation**; **Weather mapping**

Saturated fat see **Fat**

Saturated hydrocarbons see **Hydrocarbon**

Saturated solution see **Solution**

Saturn

Saturn is the most remote of the planets that were known to the ancient astronomers. It is the sixth **planet** from the **Sun**. Nine and a half times larger than **Earth**,

TABLE 1. SATURIAN SATELLITES LARGER THAN 200 KM IN DIAMETER[2]

Name	*Diameter (km)*	*Density (kg/m³)*	*Albedo*	*Mean distance (10000 km)*	*Orbital period (day)*
Phoebe	220	—	0.05	12,960	550.46
Hyperion	255	—	0.3	1481	21.276
Mimas	390	1200	0.8	187	0.942
Enceladus	500	1100	1.0	238	1.370
Tethys	1060	1200	0.8	295	1.888
Dione	1120	1400	0.6	378	2.737
Iapetus	1460	1200	0.08 - 0.4	3561	79.331
Rhea	1530	1300	0.6	526	4.517
Titan	5550	1880	0.2	1221	15.945

[2] Distances are given in units of 1000 km. The albedo is a measure of the amount of sunlight reflected by the satellite. An albedo of zero corresponds to no reflection, while an albedo of unity corresponds to complete reflection.

the giant gas planet is circled by a series of intricate rings consisting of many small, ice-covered particles. In addition, Saturn is host to several large, ice-covered moons and the unusual **satellite**, Titan. Titan is the only satellite in the **solar system** to maintain a permanent and extensive nitrogen atmosphere.

Basic properties

Saturn orbits the Sun at a **mean** distance of 9.539 Astronomical Units (AU). Its slightly eccentric (non-circular) **orbit**, however, allows the planet to be far as 10.069 AU from the Sun, and as close as 9.008 AU. While the time required for Saturn to repeat relative alignments with the Sun and Earth (its synodic period) is 378.1 days, it takes Saturn a full 29.46 years to complete one circuit about the Sun.

Saturn can be a prominent night-sky object. In comparison to the stars, Saturn may, under ideal conditions, and when it is at its closest to the Earth, be the third brightest object in the night sky. At its most brilliant, the only stars that can outshine Saturn are Sirius (Canis Majoris), in the Northern Hemisphere, and Canopus (Carina) in the Southern Hemisphere.

From the Earth, Saturn subtends a maximum angular diameter of about six one-thousands of a degree. This translates to an equatorial diameter of 74,855 mi (120,540 km), making Saturn 9.45 times larger than the Earth, and the second largest planet, behind **Jupiter**, in the solar system. In spite of its great apparent size, Saturn spins on its axis some 2.25 times more rapidly than the Earth. The **rotation** period measured at Saturn's equator is 10 hours 14 minutes. Saturn's high rotation rate causes the polar regions of its atmosphere to become squashed, giving the planet a slightly non-spherical appearance. Measurements of the equatorial and polar diameters reveal that Saturn is about 8,073 mi (13,000 km) wider across its equator than it is from pole to pole.

Since Saturn has many natural satellites, Kepler's third law can be used to determine the planet's **mass**. If the Earth is taken as the unit of measure, then Saturn has a mass equivalent to 95.17 Earth masses. Saturn is the

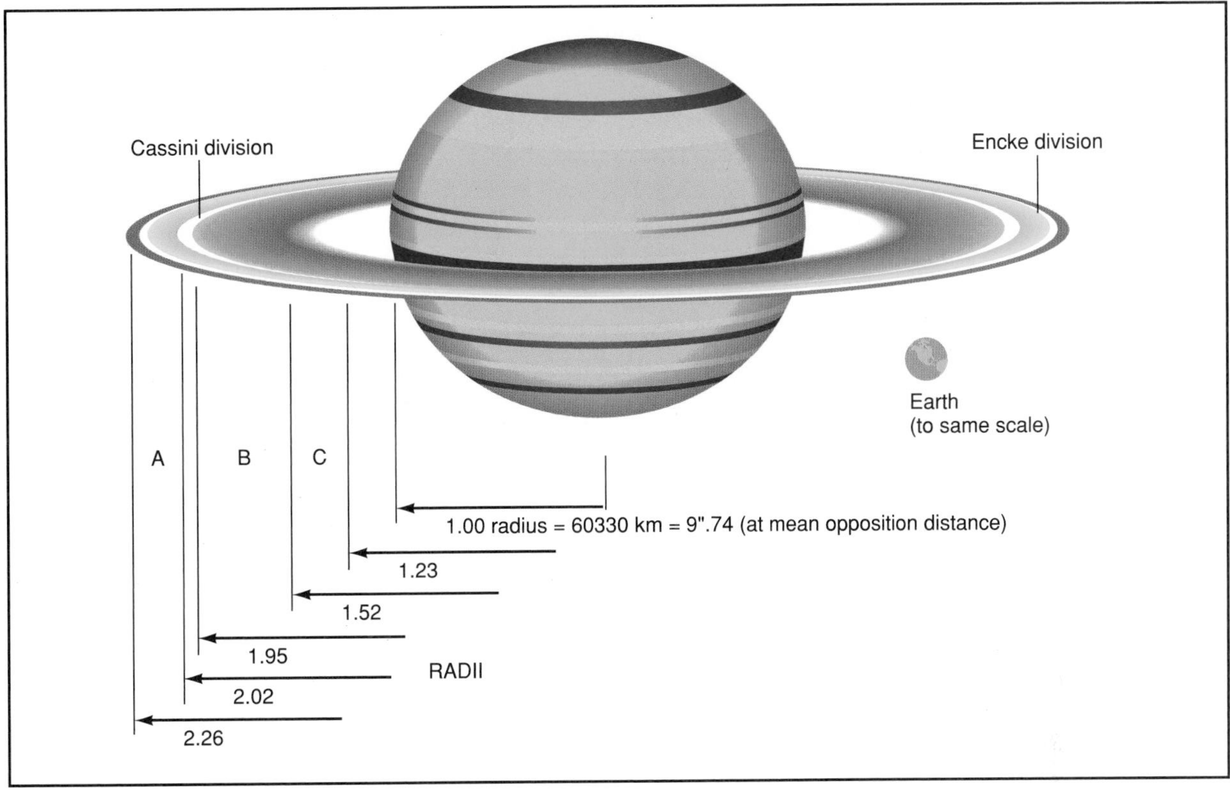

Figure 1. Main ring features visible from Earth.

second most massive planet in the solar system (Jupiter is the most massive), weighing in at 1/3500 the mass of the Sun, or 95 times the mass of the Earth.

Saturn has a bulk **density** of 0.69 g/cm^3, the lowest of all the planets in the solar system. The low bulk density of the planet indicates that it must be composed of mainly **hydrogen** and helium. It is believed that Saturn has an internal structure similar to that of Jupiter, and theoretical models of the planet's interior suggest that it has a rocky inner core that accounts for about 26% of its mass. The central core is surrounded by a large mantle of liquid metallic hydrogen, and the mantle itself is surrounded by a liquid and gaseous molecular hydrogen atmosphere.

When the *Voyager* spacecraft flew past Saturn in 1980 and 1981, it was confirmed that the planet supports a magnetic field. It is believed that the magnetic field is produced in the planet's large metallic hydrogen mantle, just like the magnetic field that is produced on Jupiter. The magnetic field at Saturn's cloud tops, however, is about ten times weaker than that observed on Jupiter. When compared at their equators, Saturn's magnetic field is only about two-thirds as strong as the **Earth's magnetic field**. The rotation rate of Saturn's inner mantle can be deduced from variations in the planet's magnetic field, and measurements indicate that the interior rotates once every 10 hours 40 minutes.

Careful measurements of Saturn's **energy** budget (energy in versus energy out) have found that the planet radiates about 2.5 times more energy into **space** than it receives from the Sun. This excess of radiated energy indicates that the planet must have an internal **heat** source. It is believed that Saturn draws its extra energy from the "raining-out" of atmospheric helium. Just as water can condense in terrestrial **clouds**, to produce rain, so the conditions in Saturn's atmosphere allow helium droplets to form. As the condensed helium droplets fall through Saturn's atmosphere they carry kinetic energy of **motion** into the planet's lower atmospheric layers. Ultimately the energy of the falling droplets is absorbed into the sub-surface layers and the temperature in those regions increases. It is the gradual release of the thermal energy stored in the sub-surface layers that causes the heat excess in Saturn's energy budget. Strong support for the helium condensation model was obtained during the *Voyager* encounters, when it was found that the abundance of helium in Saturn's atmosphere was much lower than that observed in Jupiter's. The condensation and subsequent surface depletion of helium has not occurred on Jupiter because its atmosphere is warmer than Saturn's.

Saturn's atmosphere

The intensity of sunlight at Saturn's orbit is about one one-hundredth of that at the orbit of the Earth, and about a quarter of that at the orbit of Jupiter. Consequently, and in spite of its internal heat source, Saturn is a cold world. When compared at the same **pressure**, Saturn's atmosphere is some 270°F (150°C) cooler than that of the Earth's, and about 90°F (50°C) cooler than that of Jupiter's.

Saturn does not have a distinctive banded structure like that observed on Jupiter. Rather, the planet has a more uniform appearance and coloration. The outermost regions of Saturn's atmosphere support **ammonia**, ammonium hydrosulfide, and **water** clouds, along with the hydrogen and helium. While faint atmospheric bands can be observed on Saturn's disk, it appears that the chemical process responsible for the distinctive colorations observed in Jupiter's bands do not operate in Saturn's atmosphere.

The few cloud features that are distinguishable on Saturn's disk are probably due to rising columns of warm gas. Such columns produce regions of local high-pressure and establish circulation patterns just like those observed around storms in the Earth's atmosphere. The Saturnian **storm** features are not as pronounced, or as long-lived as those observed on Jupiter, and Saturn has no long-lived feature similar to Jupiter's Great Red Spot.

Saturn rotates at almost the same rate as Jupiter and, like Jupiter, the planet's atmospheric rotation rate varies with latitude. The higher latitude regions of Saturn's atmosphere rotate at about the same rate as the planet's interior (10 hours 40 minutes). The 26 minute difference between the equatorial and higher latitude rotation rates indicates that the equatorial gas must be moving eastward at a **velocity** some 500 m/sec faster than that of the gas at higher latitudes.

Saturnian storms

Isolated spots and cloud features are only occasionally distinguishable on Saturn's disk from Earth. The noted astronomer William Herschel (1738-1822), for example, reported seeing small spots on Saturn's disk in 1780. Since that time, however, very few other features have been reported. The most dramatic recurring feature to be observed on Saturn, however, is its Great White Spot. This feature was first observed by the American astronomer Asaph Hall (1829-1907) on 7 December 1876, and six subsequent displays have been recorded. The last apparition of a large Saturnian spot was observed by the **Hubble Space Telescope** (HST) during September of 1990. A smaller white spot was also observed by the HST in September of 1994.

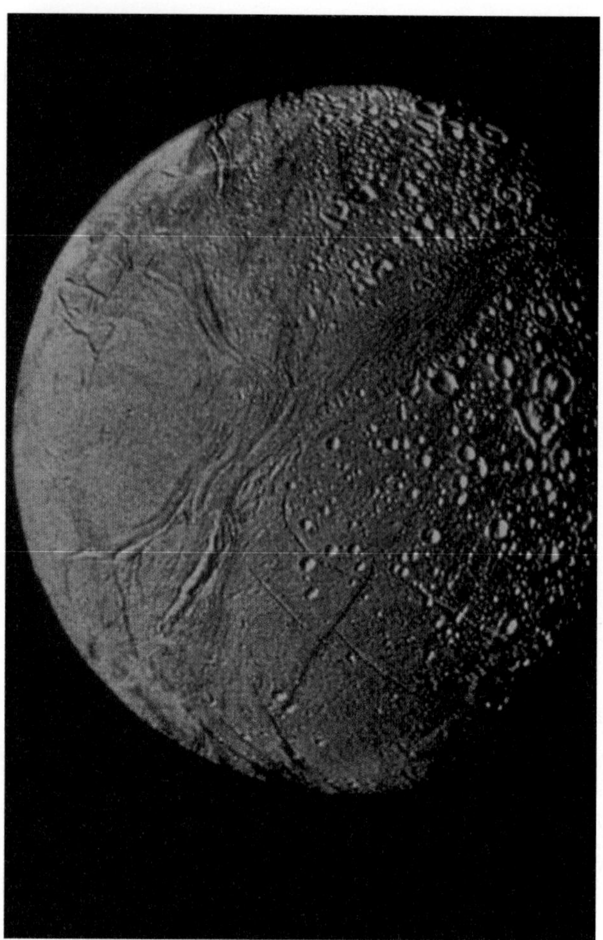

Enceladus, one of Saturn's seven intermediate moons, is the most reflective body in the solar system, largely because its surface is a thin crust of always new ice. It is thought that the crust is continually being fractured and recoated from the interior.

The white spots observed on Saturn's disk are thought to be giant storm systems. When they first appear, the Great White Spots are circular in form and some 12,420 mi (20,000 km) in diameter. Atmospheric winds gradually stretch and distort the spots into wispy bands, which can often be seen for several months. All of the Great White Spots have been observed in Saturn's northern hemisphere, with a recurrence **interval** equal to one Saturnian year (29.51 years). That the storms repeat every Saturnian year suggests we are seeing a seasonal effect, with the storms being produced whenever Saturn's northern hemisphere is tilted by its maximum amount toward the Sun. It is likely that storms also occur in Saturn's southern hemisphere, when it is tilted toward the Sun, but the viewing **angle** for seeing such events from the Earth is not favorable.

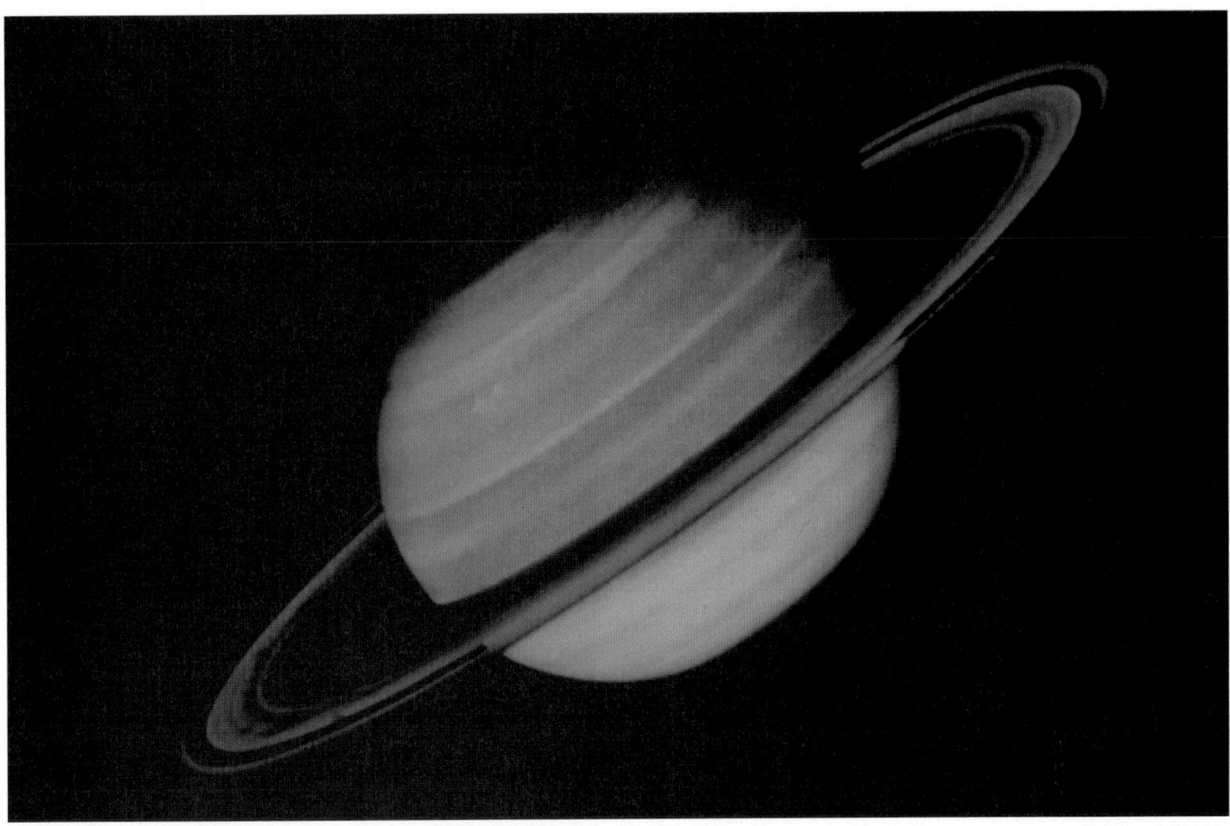

Saturn, the second largest planet in the solar system, and its system of rings.

It is believed that the Great White Spots are produced by an up-welling of warm gas. Indeed, they have been likened to atmospheric "burps." In this manner the spots are similar to the cumulonimbus thunderheads observed in terrestrial storm systems. The prominent white color of the Saturnian storms is due to the freezing-out of ammonia ice crystals. The crystals form as the warm gas pushes outward into the frigid outer layers of the planet's atmosphere.

Saturn's rings

When Galileo Galilei first pointed his **telescope** towards Saturn in 1610, he saw two features protruding from the planet's disk. These puzzling side-lobes were in reality Saturn's ring feature. Galileo's telescope was in fact too small to resolve the shape and extent of the rings. When these side-lobes started vanishing, as the rings began gradually assuming a position edgewise to the Earth, Galileo was not able to explain the nature of his observations. The Dutch astronomer Christiaan Huygens (1629-1695) was the first scientist to suggest, in 1659, on the basis of earlier observations, that Saturn was surrounded by a flattened ring.

Soon after Huygens had suggested that a ring existed around Saturn, the Italian-born French astronomer Jean-Dominique Cassini (1625-1712) discovered, in 1675, that there were in fact several rings about the planet. Several divisions in Saturn's rings are now recognized, and the dark band between the so called A- and B-rings is known as the Cassini Division. The A-ring is further sub-divided by a dark band, called the Encke Division after the German astronomer Johann F. Encke (1791-1865), who first observed the feature in 1838.

Saturn's rings are best seen when the planet is near opposition. At this time the planet is at its closest approach to the Earth, and the rings are seen at their greatest viewing angle. The rings are aligned with Saturn's equator, and consequently they are tilted at an angle of 26.7 degrees to the **plane** of the planet's orbit about the Sun. During the course of one Saturnian year the rings, as seen from Earth, are alternatively viewed from above and then below. Twice each Saturnian year, i.e., once every 15 years, the rings are seen edge-on, an event called a ring plane crossing. That the rings nearly disappear from view when seen edge-on indicates that they must be very thin. Recent measurements suggest that the rings are no more than 1.24 mi (2 km) thick.

That the rings of Saturn cannot be solid was first proved theoretically by the Scottish physicist James Clerk Maxwell (1831-1879) in 1857. Maxwell showed that a solid planetary disk would literally tear itself apart, and so he concluded that the rings must be composed of many small "moonlets." Subsequent observations have confirmed Maxwell's deductions, and it is now known that the rings are made of chunks of ice and ice-coated rock.

Images obtained by the *Voyager* and *Pioneer* space probes have shown that the rings are really composed of numerous ringlets. The apparently empty regions between ringlets are thought to be caused by either resonances with Saturnian moons, or by a mechanism called shepherding. Just as divisions have been produced in the asteroid belt (Kirkwood gaps) through gravitational resonances with Jupiter, so gaps have been formed in Saturn's rings due to resonances with its major satellites. The Cassini Division, for example, is the result of a 2-to-1 **resonance** with the **moon** Mimas. Some of the narrow rings are believed to be maintained by shepherding satellites. By being in close orbit on either side of a ring, the shepherding satellites prevent the ring particles from dispersing into higher or lower orbits. The faint, 62 mi (100 km) wide F-ring that surrounds the prominent A-ring, for example, is maintained by two small satellites, Prometheus (62 mi/100 km in diameter) and Pandora (56 mi/90 km in diameter). Indeed, the F-ring, which was discovered by the *Pioneer 11* **space probe** in 1979, shows some remarkably complex structures, with the ring being made of several interlaced and braided particle strands.

In 1995 and 1996, ring plane crossings occurred three times with respect to Earth, as well as once with respect to the Sun. This provided a unique opportunity for observing the rings and satellites of Saturn, since glare from the rings is greatly reduced during ring plane crossing, enabling astronomers to observe faint objects. On the ring plane crossing of May 22, 1995, the Hubble Space Telescope (HST) discovered as many as four new Saturn moons, including a third shepherd satellite which may account for the braiding of the F-ring. The HST also discovered that the orbit of Prometheus had shifted, perhaps due to a collision with the F ring.

During the August 10, 1995 ring plane crossing, the HST detected clouds of debris near the outer edge of the ring system. These may be the remains of small satellites, shattered in collisions, perhaps with a comet. These clouds may be the source of material for Saturn's rings.

Saturn's icy moons

Saturn is parent to many satellites. The known Saturnian moons range in size from a few tens of kilometers up to several thousand kilometers in diameter. In all, 18 of Saturn's moons have received officially sanctioned names from the International Astronomical Union. Titan, the largest and first of Saturn's moons to be discovered, was first observed by Huygens in 1655. The satellites discovered by Cassini were Iapetus (1671), Rhea (1672), Dione (1684), and Thetys (1684). Herschel discovered Mimas and Enceladus in 1789. The latest of Saturn's moons to be named was the 12.4 mi (20 km)-sized Pan, discovered by M. Showalter in 1990.

The densities derived for the larger Saturian moons are all about 1 g/cm^3, and consequently their interiors must be composed of mainly water and ice. All of the larger Saturnian satellites, except Phoebe, were photographed during the *Voyager* fly-bys, and while the images obtained showed, as expected, extensive impact cratering, they also revealed many unexpected features indicating that several of the satellites had undergone extensive surface modification.

The *Voyager* images showed that Rhea and Mimas have old, heavily cratered surfaces, just as one would expect for small, geologically inactive bodies. Interestingly, however, images of Mimas revealed a remarkably large impact crater, subsequently named Herschel, that was nearly one third the size of the satellite itself. If the body that struck Mimas to produce Herschel had been slightly larger it probably would have shattered the moon.

In contrast to Rhea and Mimas, the surfaces of Dione and Tethys, while still heavily cratered, show evidence for substantial resurfacing and internal activity. Both moons were found to support smooth, planar regions suggesting that icy material has oozed from the interior to the surface. The Saturnian moon that shows the greatest evidence for resurfacing and internal activity is Enceladus. The surface of this moon is covered by a patchwork of smooth, icy surfaces, which are so shiny that they reflect nearly 100% of the light that strikes them. Plains, and even the most heavily cratered regions show fewer craters than the other Saturnian satellites. Enceladus also shows many surface cracks and ridges. Planetary geologists believe that the smooth regions on the surface of Enceladus may be no older than 100 million years. Since bodies as small as Enceladus, which is some 310 mi (500 km) in diameter, should have cooled off very rapidly after their formation, it is presently unclear how such recent resurfacing could have taken place. It has been speculated that the interior of Enceladus is liquid even to this day.

Voyager images of Iapetus revealed a remarkable brightness difference between the moon's leading and trailing hemispheres. Iapetus, just like the other Saturnian moons, circles Saturn in a synchronous fashion, that is, it keeps the same hemisphere directed toward Saturn

at all times (just like our Moon, as seen from Earth). The images recorded by the *Voyager* spacecraft showed that the leading hemisphere, the one that points in the direction in which Iapetus is moving about Saturn, is much darker than the trailing hemisphere. Indeed, while the trailing hemisphere reflects about 40% of the light that falls on it, the leading hemisphere reflects around 8%. The leading hemisphere is so dark, in fact, that no impact craters are visible. The most probable explanation for the dark coloration on Iapetus is that the moon has accumulated a thick frontal layer of dark, dusty material swept-up as it orbits around Saturn.

Perhaps Titan is the most remarkable of all of Saturn's moons. With a diameter in excess of 3,100 mi (5,000 km), Titan is larger than the planet Mercury. The suggestion that Titan might have an atmosphere appears to have been first made by the Spanish astronomer Jose Comas Sola (1868-1937), who noted, in 1903, that the central regions of the moon's disk were brighter than its limb. Convincing spectroscopic evidence for the existence of a Titanian atmosphere was obtained in 1944 by American astronomer Gerard P. Kuiper (1905-1973).

The initial Earth-based observations revealed that Titan had an atmosphere containing methane and ethane. The *Voyager 1* space probe, however, showed that Titan's atmosphere is mostly **nitrogen**, with additional **trace elements** of propane, acetylene and ethylene. The **atmospheric pressure** at the moon's surface is nearly twice the atmospheric pressure experienced at sea-level on Earth.

Titan's hazy, aerosol atmosphere is estimated to be about 250 mi (400 km) thick, with the main body of the satellite being about 3,200 mi (5,150 km) in diameter. The escape velocity from Titan is a mere 1.5 mi/sec (2.5 km/sec), and consequently the most likely reason that Titan has been able to maintain its atmosphere for so long is the fact that the Saturnian system itself originally formed at a low **temperature**. Titan's present-day surface temperature is about 201°F (94°C). The world's largest telescope, the Keck telescope on Mauna Kea in Hawaii, detected dark areas on Titan in 1996 that scientists believe are frozen seas of hydrocarbons.

Titan's atmosphere is a distinctive orange color in appearance, and it is believed that this coloration is caused by complex chemical reactions. Telescopic measurements made at optical wavelengths have not been able to probe the surface of Titan; the atmospheric haze that surrounds the moon is just too thick. Recently, however, observations made at infrared wavelengths have been able to observe surface features, and Mark Lemmon and co-workers at the University of Arizona reported in early 1995 that Titan, as might well be expected, is in synchronous rotation about Saturn.

KEY TERMS

Albedo—The fraction of sunlight that a body reflects. An albedo of zero indicates complete absorption, while an albedo of unity indicates total reflection.

Oblateness—A measure of polar to equatorial flattening. A sphere has zero oblateness.

Shepherding satellite—A satellite that restricts the motion of ringlet particles, preventing them from dispersing.

One of the many interesting features revealed by the *Voyager* space probes was that Titan's atmosphere exhibits a distinct hemispherical asymmetry at visual wavelengths. The asymmetry observed on Titan is different from that seen on Iapetus, in the sense that the division on Titan is between the north and south hemispheres, rather than the leading and trailing hemispheres. When the *Voyager* probes imaged Titan, the northern hemisphere was slightly darker than the southern hemisphere. Follow-up observations of Titan made with the Hubble Space Telescope found that the hemispherical color asymmetry had switched during the ten years since the *Voyager* encounters, with the southern hemisphere being the darker one in 1990. It is believed that the color variation and hemisphere switching is a seasonal heating effect driven by periodic changes in Saturn's distance from the Sun. The Cassini spacecraft, launched in 1997, will reach Saturn in 2004, orbiting the planet and sending a probe to Titan.

See also Kepler's laws; Planetary ring systems.

Further Reading

Moore, Patrick. *The Guinness Book of Astronomy.* Enfield, England: Guinness Books, 1988.

Nicholson, Philip, D. "Saturn's Rings Turn Edge On." *Sky and Telescope,* (May 1995).

Rothery, David. "Icy Moons of the Solar System." *New Scientist,* (28 March 1992).

Sanchez-Lavega, Agustin. "Saturn's Great White Spots." *Sky and Telescope,* (August 1989).

Martin Beech

Savanna

A savanna is a **plant** community characterized by a continuous grassy layer, often with scattered trees or

Zebras on the savanna in Masai Mara, Kenya.

shrubs, that is subject to regular, severe **drought** and occasional bush fires. A savanna is also the flat, open landscape in which such plant communities thrive. The word savanna comes from the Taino word *zabana,* which was used to describe a grassy, treeless plain. (Taino was the language of a now extinct Native American group that lived in the Greater Antilles and Bahamas.) The word entered the English, French, and Spanish languages almost simultaneously, between 1529 and 1555, as a result of Spanish exploration of the Caribbean.

Savannas occur in a broad band around the globe, occupying much of the land in the tropics and semitropics that is not a rain forest or a **desert**. Savanna **grasslands** occur predominantly in **South America**, **Africa**, Madagascar, the Indian subcontinent, and northern **Australia**. Over time, the original meaning of savanna as a treeless, grassy plain has been lost, and the scientific definition has becoming increasingly broad. Thus, the term now encompasses the treeless grasslands of Florida; the grasslands with palm trees in the Orinoco **basin** in Venezuela; the open *pampas*, semi-enclosed *cerrados*, and thorny, brushy *caatingas* of Brazil; the woodlands (*miombo*) and park like grasslands (*veldt*) of southern Africa; and various grasslands in **Asia** that resulted from cutting of **forests** over the centuries. Overall, savanna accounts for 20% of the land cover on **Earth**, and some savanna is to be found on every **continent**.

Savannas still defy adequate classification, although several complex schemes have been developed that take into account **soil** types, **distance** between plants, average height of the woody layer in relation to the herbaceous (grassy) layer, and similar quantifiable factors. A useful four-part descriptive classification divides savannas according to the increasing proportion of trees and shrubs: grassy savannas, open savannas, closed savannas, and woodland. Even in the most heavily wooded savannas, however, where trees may reach 40% of the cover, the primary flow of **energy** and **nutrients** is still through the grassy layer.

The water economy

Water—its availability, its timing, its distribution—is the primary **factor** shaping the dynamics of the savanna **ecosystem**. The savanna experiences recurrent episodes of drought lasting 4-8 months out of the year. During the xeropause, or "dry spell," plant activities—growing, dying, decomposing—continue, but at vastly

reduced rates. Studies have shown that resistance to drought is more important to savanna vegetation than resistance to fire. The plants that thrive in the savannas employ many strategies to exploit available **water** and to survive the xeropause. The mechanisms of survival endow the savanna with its characteristic appearance.

The common savanna **grasses** grow in tussock form; from protected underground growing points, the seasonal grasses grow in a bunch 12 in (30 cm) high or higher. A dense **root system** allows the individual plant to survive the annual drought, when the aerial (aboveground) grasses die. Typical savanna grasses are the **sedges** (Latin family name, Cyperaceae), the true grasses (Gramineae), and the bunch grasses (for example, the genera *Andropogon* and *Stipa*). The grasses are chiefly of the C4 group; that is, they follow the C4 pathway of **photosynthesis**, which benefits from high light intensity (such as is found in the tropics), high temperatures, and high **evaporation** rates. The dominance of C4 grasses is a useful way to demarcate savannas from temperate grasslands, where the grasses are predominantly of the C3 group.

The primary water recruitment strategy of savanna **tree** species is to maintain an extensive root system. The root system may extend deep underground, sometimes reaching the water table, or it may be a shallow, lateral system designed to harvest water over a broad area. The leaves of the trees are often tough and fibrous; they may be leathery, sandpapery, or hairy—all features that enable them to husband water. Most leaves are lost during the dry period. Thorns, which may represent leaves that have been reduced through **evolution** to save water, are common on African savanna tree and shrub species. Many savanna tree types are unfamiliar to North Americans. The more familiar ones are *Eucalyptus*, *Acacia*, and *Adansonia*, the last of which includes the storied baobab tree. **Seeds** grow within thick casings that allow them to survive until the first rainfall before germinating. And in the midst of this thorny, corky, leathery protection, delicate, showy flowers bloom briefly on grasses and shrubs.

Having survived the dry season, savanna plants next must survive the rainy season, which is not simply a respite from drought but a completely different life episode. For many savanna grasses, the entire reproductive cycle must be accomplished during the rainy season. As the new leaves, which serve photosynthesis, and new flowers are borne in close succession, the energy needs of the grasses zoom upward. These energy-consuming activities must then be reined in and shut down to a semidormant state in preparation for the next dry period. This general pattern has shown some partitioning, with precocious species blooming even before the start of the rainy season, early and intermediate bloomers blooming serially during the rainy season, and late bloomers blooming at the end of the rainy season or after the start of the dry season. The temporal niching strategies of similar species may take advantage of different nutrient availability, or may be driven by some other, unknown factor. For each species, however, the cycle of growth and dormancy is driven by water availability, not by **genetics**.

In contrast to the grasses, savanna trees may conduct the entirety of their reproductive cycle during the dry season. Such a strategy would maximize the amount of foliage available for photosynthesis during the rainy season.

Besides water, other primary factors that affect the savanna ecosystem are fire and soil type. Fire triggers the growth of seeds, protected in seed beds underground during the dry season. Fire also limits the growth of trees, maintaining the distinction between savanna and forest. In particular, juvenile trees that have not reached a certain height are susceptible to fire; the lack of young trees contributes to the open appearance of a savanna. Some fires result from lightning strikes, but the majority are set by humans as part of hunting or agricultural pursuits. Fire improves soil by adding the nutrients **calcium**, **magnesium**, and potassium, which occur in the ashes, to the soil. The timing of fire—early or late in the dry season—is critical, however, and the ideal time seems to differ for different plant associations.

Soil determines whether the deep roots will grow to their potential length. Different soils have different moisture-holding and drainage capacities. The soils underlying savannas cover a wide range of types, and it is thought that at least some of these soils are inhospitable to tree growth, thereby maintaining the characteristic physiognomy of the savanna. Soil type and bedrock **geology** have a major controlling influence over the plant communities that will grow in them. Depending on their structure, degree of porosity, and so forth, the major soil types may determine whether a savanna is classified as moist or arid, independent of the amount of rainfall. There is usually a noticeable disconformity in soil type at the boundary between forest and savanna, and again at the boundary between savanna and desert.

The faunas of the savannas

The wild animals most commonly associated with savannas are herbivores, browsers of grass, palatable shrubs, and tree leaves, and the carnivores that prey on them. The greatest species richness occurs on the African savannas, where climatic changes over geological time have favored the evolution and branching of many different **animal** species. Indeed, it is probable that the first bipedal humans walked upright on African savannas.

KEY TERMS

Primary consumer—An organism that consumes primary producers as food; the latter are organisms—chiefly green plants—that convert simple organic substances to more complex ones that can be used as food.

Xeropause—A period of low biological activity in plants as a consequence of insufficient water.

The best-known species of African herbivores include the **elephant**, **rhinoceros**, zebra, 78 species of antelopes and buffalo, hippopotamus, pig, **oryx**, gemsbock, impala, **waterbuck**, kudu, **eland**, and hartebeest. On the Serengeti plains in Tanzania and elsewhere in Africa the proximity of different types of savanna vegetation, affording browse at different times of the year, has led to the great annual migrations of wild game.

In savanna ecosystems the herbivores are the primary consumers; they browse available producers such as grass. The African savannas also support large populations of secondary consumers—those that eat other animals. Among them are the lion, **hyena**, wild dog, anteater, and bat. **Reptiles**, **birds**, and **insects** are also well represented on African savannas.

The savannas on other continents show highly impoverished or restricted faunas, in comparison to those of the African savannas. Some highly restricted species are the capybara, a large rodent that lives on the Brazilian *campos*, and the **kangaroos and wallabies** of Australia. The prehistoric American savannas once included **mammals** such as camelids, mastodons, giant ground **sloths**, and **deer**. Climatic changes in the Pleistocene that reduced available browse are believed to have contributed to the demise of these species.

Today, domestic herds, especially **sheep**, cattle, and **goats**, graze the savannas side by side with the wild herbivores. If not too numerous, they are absorbed by the savanna ecosystem, with no change to the ecosystem. In India and West Africa, however, large domestic herds that exceed the **carrying capacity** of the land have devastated the savannas. Areas around waterholes and population centers are especially vulnerable to overgrazing. Because most of the world's savannas occur in developing countries, where the local economy relies on exploitation of natural resources, the careful husbandry of the savannas and the methods by which savanna grasslands are converted to farming or grazing use are likely to prove critical to the future survival of these large units of vegetation.

Further Reading

Bourlière, François. "Mammals as Secondary Consumers in Savanna Ecosystems." In *Tropical Savannas. Ecosystems of the World.* edited by David W. Goodall. Amsterdam: Elsevier, 1983.

Bourlière, François, and Hadley, M. "Present-Day Savannas: An Overview." In *Tropical Savannas. Ecosystems of the World.* edited by David W. Goodall. Amsterdam: Elsevier, 1983.

Cole, Monica M. *The Savannas: Biogeography and Geobotany.* London: Academic Press, 1986.

Sarmiento, Guillermo. *The Ecology of Neotropical Savannas.* Cambridge: Harvard University Press, 1984.

Walker, Brian H., ed. *Determinants of Tropical Savannas.* Oxford: IRL Press, 1987.

Marjorie Panel

Savant

Savants are people with extremely outstanding abilities, often in music, **mathematics**, **memory**, or art. Their talents stand in marked contrast to their intelligence in other areas, which is well below normal. For example, a savant who, given any date in the past hundred years, could say what day of the week it fell on, might not be able to perform simple tasks like tying his shoes or catching a bus. The cause of this condition, commonly labeled savant **syndrome**, has yet to be fully determined.

Savant syndrome was first formally described in 1877 by British physician J. Langdon Down, who lectured the Royal Society of London about mentally retarded individuals he had seen performing amazing mental feats at Earlswood Asylum. Down called these people idiot savants because of their low level of intelligence. At that time the word "idiot" was the scientific classification for people who functioned at a two-year-old level, having IQs no higher than 25. Researchers today believe that the term idiot savant is misleading, because most savants, although developmentally disabled, function at higher levels of intelligence than this; all savants reported in medical and psychological literature have had IQs of at least 40.

Today, some people with savant syndrome are called autistic savants. This is because many savants suffer from infantile **autism**, a developmental disorder involving some degree of retardation that first shows itself during infancy. Disturbed social interactions are a key part of autism. Autistic children dislike being held or touched, avoid eye contact, have poorly developed communication skills, and often perform unusual repetitive behaviors such as head banging or rocking back and forth. The cause of autism is unknown.

In the hundred years that have passed since Down brought savants to the attention of the scientific community, hundreds of cases have been reported. Despite the level of interest it has generated, savant syndrome is a rare condition. Only an estimated one out of every 2,000 mentally retarded people living in institutions can be called a savant. It is known that the rate of savant syndrome is as much as six times higher among males than among females. Some researchers believe that this is because more males are autistic than females. According to one study, about one in ten autistic children have special abilities that could classify them as savants.

Talents of savants

The kinds of talents displayed by savants throughout the last century are remarkably similar. Music and memory appear to be the most common skills displayed in savant syndrome. Often these two skills are tied together.

Most savants with musical skills express their talents by playing the piano, singing, or humming. One savant, an African American slave named Blind Tom who was born in 1849, reportedly could play a different piece of music on the piano with each hand while singing a third.

The memory capacity displayed by many savants is truly astounding. Some savants have memorized entire telephone directories; others have memorized sporting **statistics** or everyone they have met during their adult lives. They might memorize entire books, or population figures for all the cities in the country in which they live.

Mathematical calculation talents reported in savants have ranged from being able to figure and report the cube roots of six digit numbers within seconds to calculating complex word problems which would take a normal person hours to solve. Calendar calculation—the ability to provide the day of the week on which a certain date fell or will fall—is a talent of some savants that requires not only memorization of large quantities of material, but mathematical abilities as well. One set of twin savants reportedly can do this for a time span of 8,000 years.

The artistic talents of savants have been noted over the years. One three-year-old mentally retarded girl could make accurate drawings of any **animal** that she saw. Some visually artistic savants seem to specialize in certain subjects. Other skills that some savants exhibit are the ability to memorize maps, an extremely sensitive sense of **touch** and **smell**, and the ability to measure the passage of time without a clock. Model building and memorization in languages the savant does not understand have also been recorded.

Savant or genius

The skills displayed by savants, whether they are memorizing and reciting entire books or instantly calculating the **square root** of any number, are unlike the high levels of individual skills sometimes displayed by people of normal intelligence. Savant skills often appear in an individual very suddenly, rather than developing over time; the abilities are fully formed, and don't increase as the savant grows older. One musical savant could hum complicated opera arias when she was six months old. Another, at the age of four, could flawlessly play the works of Mozart at the piano. In some cases, savant skills disappear just as suddenly as they appeared.

The skills of savants appear to be almost robotlike in nature. For example, a musical savant may be able to reproduce a complex musical piece after **hearing** it once, but if the original rendition contains a mistake, the savant will repeat that mistake. An artistic savant may be able to produce an impressive copy of a specific artist's work, but most cannot evolve a recognizable style of his or her own.

Neither do savants seem able to make connections between their talents and the rest of their lives or the world around them. Further, they do not appear to be able to reason about what they are doing. For instance, a savant who can read and perfectly memorize a book containing the complete works of Shakespeare, even to the point of being able to recite a specific page of text when given a page number, probably cannot explain what those plays and poems mean. Furthermore, he or she might be unable to recall the same text if given some other cue, such as the title of a specific work. A musical savant will more than likely be unable to read music. A savant who can make complex mathematical calculations might be unable to make change for a dollar.

Savants' skills do not seem to require their total attention. Many can play a piece of music, draw a picture, or make complex mathematical calculations while their mind appears to be elsewhere. They seem to exercise their talents without conscious effort, as if some part of their **brain**, unconnected to the rest, operates automatically.

Causes of savant syndrome

Researchers remain uncertain about what causes some mentally retarded or autistic people to become savants. Some believe that certain savants have eidetic (intensely visual) memories. Their skills are based entirely on their ability to memorize. While this theory can account for some savant skills, it fails to explain others.

Some experts believe that intelligence is not a single quality, but rather that mental ability is separated into

KEY TERMS

Abstract thinking—The ability to understand abstract concepts such as love, justice, truth and friendship.

Autism—A developmental disorder that involves some degree of retardation along with disturbed social interactions.

Developmental disability—The failure to pass through the normal stages of mental and emotional growth as one matures.

Intelligence—The ability to solve problems and cope successfully with one's surroundings.

IQ—A number calculated by dividing mental age as measured on an intelligence test by a child's chronological age.

multiple intelligences which may be unrelated to one another. If this is true, it could explain how mental retardation or autism and savant skills can coexist in one person. Some experts suspect that mentally retarded savants have inherited two separate genes, one for mental retardation and one for the special ability; however, only some savants have family histories that contain special skills.

Some researchers have speculated that autistic or mentally retarded persons may receive only a limited amount of sensory stimulation. This low level of stimulation might be due to biological causes, or could be due to the fact that such people are sometimes ignored by others and live in relative isolation. According to this theory, the resulting boredom could lead to the development of super-intense concentration levels that normal people are unable to achieve. Again, this theory can account for some but not all savants.

Another theory holds that since savants cannot think abstractly, they come to rely entirely on concrete thinking, channeling all of their mental energy into one form of expression, be it art or calendar calculating. Finally, some researchers think that savants may have some brain injury or abnormality on the left side of the brain, the side which controls language, or to other areas of the brain which control abstract thinking. While this may be true for some savants, others show normal electrical activity in the brain when they are tested.

See also Down's syndrome.

Further Reading

Dalphonse, Sherri. "The Mysterious Powers of Peter Guthrie." *Reader's Digest.* 142 (February 1993): 859.

Howe, Michael. *Fragments of Genius: The Strange Feats of Idiots Savants.* New York: Routledge, 1989.

Sacks, Oliver. "A Neurologists Notebook: Prodigies." *The New Yorker.* (9 January 1995): 44-65.

Kay Marie Porterfield

Sawfish

Sawfish are marine shark-like **cartilaginous fish** in the family Pristidae in order Rajiformes. Sawfish are characterized by their long snout nose which has sharp teeth on each side. Like other **rays**, sawfish lurk to attack schools of **prey** fish with its long snout, and devour the injured **fish**. The long snout also serves as a defensive weapon, inflicting serious injury on any enemy attacking it. Sawfish have gill slits on the undersurface of the body on both sides, posterior to the mouth, as in other rays.

Sawfish are generally found in shallow waters in tropical seas, with some species occurring in **brackish** or fresh **water**. A population of sawfish lives in Lake Nicaragua, completely separated from the sea. Sawfish can grow to large sizes. The small tooth sawfish, *Pristits pectinata* averages 15 ft (5 m) in length, and specimens have been found up to 20 ft (6 m) long and weighing 800 lb (360 kg). This species lives in the warm waters of the Atlantic from the Mediterranean to **Africa** and across the Atlantic Ocean to the coast of Brazil. Another Atlantic species is the large-tooth sawfish, *P. perotteti.*

Sawfish in the Indo-Pacific Ocean grow to large sizes. Specimens of marine sawfish, *P. microdon* and *P. cuspidatus*, have been observed in the **rivers** of Thailand. *Pristis pristis* is found far up major rivers in African while *P. leichhardit* prefers fresh water.

Saxifrage family

The saxifrages, currants, and gooseberries are about 40 genera and about 850 species of plants that make up the family Saxifragaceae. These plants occur in all parts of the world, but are most diverse and prominent in arctic, boreal, and montane habitats of **North America** and Eurasia. The largest genera in the family are the saxifrages (*Saxifraga* spp.), of which there are about 300 species, most of which occur in the tundras of alpine and arctic environments, and the currants and gooseberries (*Ribes*), with about 150 species in boreal and temperate habitats.

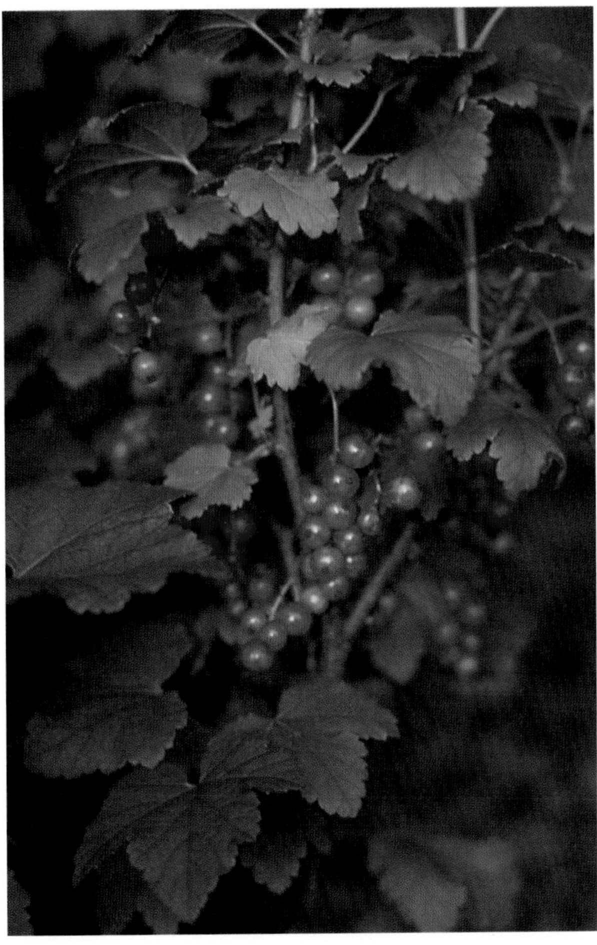

Red currant.

Most species in the saxifrage family are perennial herbs, while others are woody shrubs or small trees. Their leaves are usually simple, small, with a toothed margin or tip, and can be arranged alternately or oppositely on the stem. The flowers are perfect (that is, bisexual), containing both female and male reproductive structures. There are usually five sepals and five petals, and usually twice as many stamens as petals. The pistil usually has two (but as many as four) carpels, each with its own stigma and style, producing a distinctive, split unit with outward-curving stigmatic tips. The fruit is a dry capsule, containing many small **seeds**, or in the case of *Ribes*, a many-seeded berry. The stems of the shrub-sized currants and gooseberries (*Ribes* spp.) are often armed with spines and prickles.

Species in North America

Species of the saxifrage family are prominent in certain habitats in North America. The genera are described below, with particular reference to species occurring in North America.

The most diverse group is the saxifrages. The swamp saxifrage (*Saxifraga pensylvanica*) occurs in wet meadows, bogs, and moist woods over much of eastern North America, while the early saxifrage (*S. virginiensis*) occurs in dry **forests** and rocky habitats. Most species, however, are alpine or arctic in their distribution. Relatively widespread species that occur in both alpine and arctic tundras include the purple mountain saxifrage (*S. oppositifolia*), golden saxifrage (*S. aizodes*), spider-plant (*S. flagellaris*), prickly saxifrage (*S. tricuspidata*), snow saxifrage (*S. nivalis*), and bulblet saxifrage (*S. cernua*).

The lace flowers or foam-flowers occur in moist woods and include *Tiarella cordifolia* of eastern North America and *T. trifoliata* and *T. unifoliata* of western North America.

Miterworts occur in moist woods and bogs. *Mitella diphylla* and *M. nuda* occur in the east, while *M. pentandra* is in western North America.

Several species of grass-of-parnassus occur in cool, open, wet places, including the widespread northern grass-of-parnassus (*Parnassia palustris*).

Currants and gooseberries are shrubs that occur extensively in boreal and temperate habitats. The bristly black currant (*Ribes lacustre*), northern black currant (*R. hudsonianum*), skunk currant (*R. glandulosum*), and northern red currant (*R. triste*) all occur widely in boreal and montane habitats. More temperate species include wild black currant (*R. americanum*), gooseberry (*Ribes hirtellum*), swamp currant (*R. lacustre*), and golden currant (*R. odoratum*).

The hydrangea (*Hydrangea arborescens*) is another native shrub in the saxifrage family that occurs in southeastern North America.

Ecological and economic importance

Species in the saxifrage family are important components of certain natural habitats, especially in alpine and arctic tundras, where as many as 7-10 species of *Saxifraga* can occur in the same local **habitat**.

Many species in the saxifrage family are grown as ornamentals in **horticulture**. Various species of native and Eurasian *Saxifraga* are commonly grown in rock gardens. Some other species native to temperate North America are also sometimes grown in horticulture, including bishop's cap (*Mitella* spp.), coral bells or alum root (*Heuchera* spp.), and lace flower or foam-flower (*Tiarella* spp.). Currants and gooseberries that flower prominently are also grown as ornamental shrubs in gardens, including *Ribes alpinum*, *R. americanum*, *R. speciosum*, and other species. Hydrangeas are also cultivat-

KEY TERMS

Alternate host—Many pathogens and parasites must infect two or more different species in order to complete their reproductive cycle. If one of those alternate hosts can be eliminated from the ecosystem, then disease transmission can be interrupted, and the other host can be productive and healthy.

Boreal—This refers to the conifer-dominated forest that occurs in the sub-Arctic, and gives way to tundra at more northern latitudes.

Montane—This refers to the conifer-dominated forest that occurs below the alpine tundra on mountains.

Perfect—In the botanical sense, this refers to flowers that are bisexual, containing both male and female reproductive parts.

Raceme—An elongate inflorescence, consisting of individual flowers arranged along a linear axis, with the oldest ones being closest to the bottom.

Tundra—This is a treeless ecosystem that occurs at high latitude in the Arctic and Antarctic, and at high altitude on mountains.

ed as flowering shrubs, including the Eurasian species, *Hydrangea paniculata* and *H. macrophylla.*

The **fruits** of currants and gooseberries are important agricultural **crops** in some areas, particularly in **Europe** and **Asia**. Currants and gooseberries are not, however, widely grown in North America, because they are an alternate host for white pine blister rust (*Cronartium ribicola*), an important, introduced fungal pathogen of white pine (*Pinus strobus*) and other five-needled **pines**, which are economically important species of trees.

The most common species of currants and gooseberries in cultivation are the red-fruited currant (*Ribes rubrum*; there is also a white-fruited variety of this species) of Europe, the black-fruited currant (*R. nigrum*) of Eurasia, and the gooseberry (*R. grossularia*) of Eurasia, which can have red, yellow, green, or white fruits, depending on the variety. Native North American species with abundant, edible fruits include the wild black currant (*Ribes americanum*) and wild gooseberry (*Ribes hirtellum*). The species of *Ribes* that are known as currants have smooth fruits and stems, and their flowers and fruits occur in elongate inflorescences known as racemes. The gooseberries have prickly or spiny stems and fruits, and their flowers and fruits occur in a solitary fashion. Most currants and gooseberries are dried as a means of preservation, or are used to make jams, jellies, pies, and wine.

Further Reading

Klein, R.M. *The Green World. An Introduction to Plants and People.* New York: Harper and Row, 1987.

Woodland, D.W. *Contemporary Plant Systematics.* Englewood Cliffs, NJ: Prentice-Hall, 1991.

Bill Freedman

Scalar

A scalar is a number or measure, usually representing a physical quantity, that is not dependent upon direction. For example, **distance** is a scalar quantity since it may be expressed completely as a pure number without reference to spacial coordinates. Other examples of scalar quantities include **mass**, **temperature**, and time.

The term scalar originally referred to any quantity which is measurable on a scale. Take, for example, the numbers on a **thermometer** scale which measure temperature. These values require a positive or **negative** sign to indicate whether they are greater or less than **zero**, but they do not require an indication of direction because they have no component which describes their location in **space**. Such physical quantities which can be described completely by a pure number and which do not require a directional component are referred to as scalar quantities, or scalars. On the other hand, there are other physical measurements which have not only a magnitude (scalar) component but a directional component as well. For example, although we do not normally think of it as such, **velocity** is described not only by speed, but by the direction of movement too. Similarly, other physical quantities such as **force**, spin, and **magnetism** also involve spacial orientation. The mathematical expression used to describe such a combination of magnitude and direction is *vector* from the Latin word for "carrier." In its simplest form a vector can be described as a directed line segment. For example, if A and B are two distinct points, and AB is the line segment runs from A to B, then AB can also be called vector, v. Scalars are components of vectors which describe its magnitude, they provide information about the size of vectors. For example, for a vector representing velocity, the scalar which describes the magnitude of the movement is called speed. The direction of movement is described by an **angle**, usually designated as q (theta).

KEY TERMS

Dot product—Another term for scalar multiplication.

Scalar multiplication—The multiplication of a scalar and a vector which yields another vector of different magnitude.

Scalar product—The result of multiplication of two vectors, the value must be a real or complex number.

Vector multiplication—The multiplication of two vectors to yield a scalar product.

The ability to separate scalar components from their corresponding vectors is important because it allows mathematical manipulation of the vectors. Two common mathematical manipulations involving scalars and vectors are scalar **multiplication** and vector multiplication. Scalar multiplication is achieved by multiplying a scalar and a vector together to give another vector with different magnitude. This is similar to multiplying a number by a scale **factor** to increase or decrease its value in proportion to its original value. In the example above, if the velocity is described by vector v and if c is a **positive number**, then cv is a different vector whose direction is that of v and whose length is |c||v|. It should be noted that a negative value for c will result in a vector with the opposite direction of v. When a vector is multiplied by a scalar it can be made larger or smaller, or its direction can be reversed, but the angle of its direction relative to another vector will not change. Scalar multiplication is also employed in **matrix** algebra, where vectors are expressed in rectangular arrays known as matrices.

While scalar multiplication results in another vector, vector multiplication (in which two vectors are multiplied together) results in a scalar product. For example, if u and v are two different vectors with an angle between them of q, then multiplying the two gives the following: u • v = |u||v|cosq. In this operation the value of the cos q cancels out and the result is simply the scalar value, uv. The scalar product is sometimes called the dot product since a dot is used to symbolize the operation.

Further Reading

Dunham, William. *Journey Through Genius.* New York: John Wiley, 1990.

Fawcett, Harold P., and Kenneth B. Cummins. *The Teaching of Mathematics from Counting to Calculus.* Columbus, OH: Charles E. Merrill, 1970.

Lloyd, G.E.R. *Early Greek Science: Thales to Aristotle.* New York: W.W. Norton, 1970.

Randy Schueller

Scale insects

Scale **insects**, mealybugs, or coccids are a diverse group of species of insects in the superfamily Coccoidea, order Homoptera. The females of scale insects are wingless, and are also often legless and virtually immobile. For protection, female scale insects are covered by a scale-like, waxy material. Like other homopterans, scale insects are herbivores with piercing mouth parts that are used to suck juices from **plant** tissues. Male scale insects generally have a pair of wings and can fly, although some species are wingless. Male scale insects only have vestigial mouth parts and do not feed, dying soon after mating.

Like other homopterans, scale insects have an incomplete **metamorphosis** with three stages: egg, nymph, and adult. The first nymphal stage is known as a "crawler," because it has legs and actively moves about. After the next molt, however, the legs are lost in most species, and the scale insect becomes sessile, secreting a scale-like, waxy covering for protection.

Some species of scale insects are economically important as agricultural **pests**, because of the severe damage that they cause to some crop plants. This injury is usually associated with mechanical damage to foliage caused by piercing by the feeding apparatus of the scale insect. Damage is also caused by the withdrawal of large quantities of carbohydrates and other **nutrients** with the sap.

The cottony cushion scale (*Icerya purchasi*) is an important pest of citrus **crops** in the southern United States, where it has been introduced from its native **Australia**. This species is much less of a pest than it used to be, because it has been relatively well controlled by several predators that were later discovered in their native **habitat** and subsequently introduced to the United States, namely, the vedalia lady beetle (*Vedalia cardinalis*) and a parasitic fly (*Cryptochetum iceryae*). This case is commonly cited as one of the great successes of non-pesticidal, biological control of a serious insect pest.

The California red scale (*Aonidiella aurantii*) is another important agricultural pest of western **citrus trees**. The San Jose scale (*Quadraspidiotus perniciosus*) was introduced to **North America** from **Asia** in the 1880s, and is a serious pest of many species of orchard and ornamental trees and shrubs. Various species of mealybugs are also important pests, for example, the citrus mealy-

bug (*Planococcus citri*), and the greenhouse mealybug (*Pseudococcus longispinus*).

Females of the Indian lac insect (*Laccifer lacca*) of southern and southeastern Asia produce large quantities of a waxy substance that is collected, refined, and used to prepare a varnish and shellac. Males of the Chinese wax scale (*Ericerus pela*) secrete relatively large amounts of a white wax, which can be collected for use in making candles. The Indian wax scale (*Ceroplastes ceriferus*) produces a wax that is collected for use in traditional medicine.

The tamarisk manna scale (*Trabutina mannipara*) occurs in the Middle East, where it feeds on tamarisk trees (*Tamarix* spp.). The females of this insect excrete large quantities of honeydew, which in arid regions can accumulate abundantly on foliage, drying into a sweet, sugar-rich material known as manna. Manna is featured in the Old Testament of the Bible, in which it is portrayed as a miraculous food delivered from the heavens, sustaining the Israelites as they wandered in the wilderness after their exodus from Egypt (Exodus 16: 14-36).

Bill Freedman

Scandium see **Element, chemical**

Scanners, digital

As computers become more important for publishing and producing graphics, so does a method of translating photographs and other images into a language computers can understand and work with. Just as compact discs take the continuous spectrum of sound produced by a voice or a guitar and translate it into the 1s and 0s of digital code, so a digital scanner takes the continuous tones in a photograph, and turns them into digital code. Digital code is the language understood by computers. All words, numbers, images, and instructions to the computer ultimately consist of series of ones and zeroes.

There are two principal types of digital scanners: expensive, highest-quality models using lasers, and less expensive, desktop scanners using more conventional light sources. This entry will concentrate more on the desktop scanners because they are more commonly used.

A basic scan is like a digital photocopy

The first stage in the operation of a typical desktop scanner is much like making a photocopy. An image is placed on a transparent plate, and illuminated by an incandescent or **fluorescent light**. The light reflects off the image and goes through a **lens**. In a photocopier the lens focuses the light onto a plate that creates an **electric charge** that attracts toner particles. In a scanner, the lens instead focuses the reflected light onto a dense row of electronic light sensors.

Some manufacturers have used larger arrays of light sensors to read an entire image at once, but most scanners read images one line of pixels at a time. Each light sensor puts out an **electric current** proportionate to the intensity of light striking it. This output is translated into digital code by an analog-to-digital converter chip. The signal, which now represents the tonal values of the original image in digital form, is ready to be read by a computer.

After being scanned by a digital scanner, a photograph consists of a grid of points called pixels. A pixel is the smallest unit of information in a digital image. Each pixel has data attached that tells the computer what color to assign the pixel. For black-and-white-images, that data is usually a level of gray from 0, which is black, to 255, which is white. It sometimes may have more or fewer levels, depending on the sensitivity of the scanner.

Black-and-white **photography** uses particles of silver so small they cannot be seen. In essence, each pixel from a digital scanner is like a silver particle; the more pixels a scan contains per square inch, the more like a 'real' photograph it will look. The number of pixels a digital scan contains per square-inch is called its resolution.

Color scanning

Color scans work along principals similar to those of black-and-white scans. Color film consists of three transparent layers—one red, one blue and one green—that together create a full color image. Similarly, a digital color image really consists of three gray-scale images (often called layers). One layer defines which areas will be green in the final color image, while the others do the same for red and blue. To create these layers, the scanner must be able to 'see' which parts of the color image being scanned are blue, red or green.

The simplest way of creating these three images, is to shine the scanner's light through a red, green or blue **color** filter before it strikes the photograph being scanned. An image is scanned three times, once with each filter, to create the three layers. This method is relatively time-consuming because each image must be scanned three times, and problems can arise if the three scans are not aligned precisely. If they are misaligned by

even a fraction of a pixel, discolorations and other problems may occur in the final image.

Some scanners use three different light sources to create red, green and blue light. The lights turn on and off sequentially for each line of pixels scanned. The three images are aligned correctly because the scan takes place in a single pass. Another method uses a single white light, but uses filters to break it into its red, green and blue components after the light reflects from the image being scanned. Each color of light is then focused onto its own row of light sensors, so they can be read simultaneously.

Digital scanners for publishing

High-end digital scanners, typically used for magazine publishing, often use lasers to read original images. The image is placed in a transparent drum which rotates past the **laser**, scanning them one pixel at a time. After computer processing to ensure the image will print correctly, the images are printed onto film in a process that again uses a laser.

A primary reason that digital scanners became popular beginning in the 1980s was that they created better published results more cheaply. Photographs reproduced in magazines and newspapers are converted into patterns of dots, called halftones, for publication. Before digital scanners, halftones were produced using cameras. With scanners, halftones in most cases could be made more cheaply and easily. Using digital scanners also allowed for adjusting the size, sharpness and type of halftone screen to a degree not possible with cameras.

Scanners that can read

Scanning artwork and photographs for reproduction is only one reason to use a digital scanner. Another important use is to enable computers to read printed documents, a process called optical character recognition. In this process, a black-and-white digital scan is first made of a document. Using various software programs, a computer is able to recognize this image as various letters and words. The text can then be edited in a word-processing program, just like text typed in by a person at a keyboard.

Because converting **paper** documents to digital format is very important to many businesses, some scanners have been made for this specific purpose. The primary technology is the same as for desktop scanners, but these special scanners use a mechanism that feeds pieces of paper one-by-one onto the scanning plate.

See also Computer, digital; Photocopying

KEY TERMS

Digital code—Binary code, the series of ones and zeroes that make up all information used by a computer.

Halftone screen—Pattern of minute dots that defines a color or a black-and-white tone on a printed page.

Light sensor—Device that translates light into an electric current, the stronger the light the stronger the current.

Optical character recognition—Process in which a typewritten document is scanned as an image, and translated into words using computer software.

Pixel—The smallest unit of color or tonality in a digital image; a single point.

Resolution—The number of pixels a scanner can read per square inch.

Further Reading

Alford, Roger C. "How Scanners Work." *Byte.* (June 1992).

Roth, Steve. "Scanners in View." *MacWorld.* (October 1991).

Smith, Mark. "The Sharper Image: A Scanner Update." *American Printer.* (February 1988).

Scott M. Lewis

Scanning tunneling microscope see **Microscopy**

Scarlet fever

Scarlet fever (sometimes called scarlatina), is a bacterial **disease**, so named because of its characteristic bright red rash. Before the twentieth century, and the age of **antibiotics**, scarlet fever (at one time called "the fever") was a dreaded disease and a leading cause of death in children. The disease is caused by group A beta-hemolytic streptococcus **bacteria** (genus *Streptococcus pyogenes*), the same bacteria that cause **tonsillitis** and streptococcal pharyngitis ("strep throat"). Scarlet fever occurs when group A streptococcal pharyngitis is caused by a lysogenic strain of the streptococcus bacteria that produce a pyrogenic exotoxin (erythrogenic toxin), which causes the rash.

Current research suggests that the erythrogenic toxin produced by the bacteria is actually one of three

exotoxins, called streptococcal pyrogenic exotoxins A, B, and C. Some people possess a neutralizing antibody to the toxin and are protected from the disease. So, if a person has "strep throat," scarlet fever can develop only if the infecting bacteria is an erythrogenic toxin producer, and if the person lacks immunity to the disease.

The first stage of scarlet fever is essentially "strep throat" (sore throat, fever, headache, sometimes nausea and vomiting). The second stage, which defines, or provides, the **diagnosis** for scarlet fever, is a red rash appearing two to three days after the first symptoms. Areas covered by the rash are bright red with darker, elevated red points, resembling red "goose pimples" and having a texture like sandpaper. The tongue has a white coating with bright red papillae showing through, later becoming a glistening "beefy" red (strawberry or raspberry tongue). The rash, which blanches (fades) with **pressure**, appears first on the neck and then spreads to the chest, back, trunk, and then extremities. The extent of the rash depends on the severity of the disease. The rash does not appear on the palms or soles of hands and feet, nor on the face, which is brightly flushed with a pale area circling the mouth (circumoral pallor). The rash usually lasts four to five days and then fades away. The red color of the rash is due to toxic injury to the tiny **blood** vessels in the skin, causing them to dilate and weaken. Another characteristic of scarlet fever is the peeling of skin (desquamation) after the rash fades away. The peeling occurs between the 5th-25th day, starting with a fine scaling of the face and body, and then extensive peeling of the palms and soles. The outer layer of skin, damaged as a result of the erythrogenic toxin, is replaced by new skin growth at the intermediate level of the epidermis (skin).

The disease is usually spread from person to person by direct, close contact or by droplets of saliva from sneezing or coughing. Therefore, scarlet fever can be "caught" from someone who has only streptococcal pharyngitis. Scarlet fever is most common among children, although any age is susceptible. Scarlet fever can also develop because of a group A streptococcal **infection** in a wound, or from food contaminated by the same bacteria. Today, scarlet fever is not a common occurrence, most likely due to early treatment of "strep throat" and possibly because antibiotics have made their way into the food chain. Complications and treatment of scarlet fever are the same as with streptococcal pharyngitis, but have also become uncommon due to the widespread use of antibiotics.

Penicillin is the drug of choice unless the infected person is allergic to it. After 24 hours of treatment with penicillin, the infected person is no longer contagious, but the patient should take the antibiotic for 10 days to ensure total eradication of the bacteria. If left untreated, suppurative (pus-forming) complications such as sinusitis, otitis media (middle **ear** infection), or mastoiditis (infection of the mastoid bone, just behind the ear), can occur. Treatment of scarlet fever is especially important to prevent nonsuppurative complications such as acute **rheumatic fever** or acute glomerulonephritis (**inflammation** of the kidneys).

KEY TERMS

Beta-hemolytic—One of three types of hemolytic reactions on a blood agar medium. Beta-hemolytic produces a clear zone around a colony of bacteria.

Erythrogenic—Producing erythema, a redness of the skin, produced by the congestion of the capillaries.

Group A streptococcus—A serotype of the streptococcus bacteria, based on the antigen contained in the cell wall.

Lysogenic—Producing lysins or causing lysis (dissolution).

Pyogenic—Pus producing.

Pyrogenic—Fever producing.

Streptococcus—A genus of microorganism. The bacteria are gram-positive spheres that grow in a chain. Classification depends on antigenic composition, pattern of hemolysis observed on a blood agar growth plate, growth characteristics, and biochemical reactions.

Further Reading

Mandell, Gerald L., ed. *Principles and Practice of Infectious Diseases.* 4th ed. New York: Churchill Livingstone, 1994.

Simpson, Howard. *Invisible Armies-The Impact of Disease of American History.* New York: Bobbs-Merrill, 1980.

Textbook of Medicine. 19th ed. Philadelphia: W.B. Saunders, 1994.

Christine Miner Minderovic

Scavenger

A scavenger is an **animal** that seeks out and feeds upon dead and/or decaying organic **matter**. Some scavengers specialize on feeding upon dead animals, or carrion, while others feed more generally on dead plants and animals.

Vultures feeding on a giraffe in Kenya.

Scavengers are part of the detrital food web of ecosystems. Scavengers provide a very important ecological service, because they help to rapidly reduce dead animals and plants to simpler constituents, and thereby prevent an excessive accumulation of dead **biomass**. Large quantities of dead animal biomass can represent a indirect health hazard to living animals, by enhancing the survival of pathogens. A similar effect can be caused to living plants by dead **plant** biomass. Excessive accumulations of dead plants can also bind up much of the nutrient capital of ecosystems, so that not enough is recycled for use by living plants, and **ecosystem** productivity becomes constrained by nutrient limitations. The valuable ecological service of **recycling** of dead biomass is not just performed by scavengers—other detritivores such as **bacteria**, and **fungi** are also important, and in fact are largely responsible for the final stages of the **decomposition** and humification process. However, scavengers are important in the initial stages of biomass decomposition and recycling.

There are many examples of scavengers. **Invertebrates** are the most abundant scavengers in terrestrial ecosystems, especially earthworms and **insects** such as **beetles**, **flies**, and **ants**. Many marine crustaceans are important scavengers, including most species of **crabs** and gammarids. Some **birds** are specialized as scavengers, most notably the New World **vultures** (family Cathartidae) and Old World vultures (family Accipitridae). The turkey vulture (*Cathartes aura*) of the Americas is one of the only bird species that has a sense of **smell**, which is utilized to find carrion. Some **mammals** are opportunistic scavengers, eating dead animals when they can find them. Examples of such species in **North America** are black bear (*Ursus americanus*), grizzly bear (*Ursus arctos*), and **wolverine** (*Gulo gulo*).

See also Food chain/web.

Schizophrenia

Schizophrenia is a psychotic disorder (or a group of disorders) marked by severely impaired thinking, emotions, and behaviors. The term schizophrenia comes from two Greek words that mean "split mind." It was coined around 1908, by a Swiss doctor named Eugen Bleuler, to describe the splitting apart of mental functions that he regarded as the central characteristic of

schizophrenia. (Note that the splitting apart of mental functions in schizophrenia differs from the "split personality" of people with multiple personality disorder.) Schizophrenic patients are typically unable to filter sensory stimuli and may have enhanced perceptions of sounds, colors, and other features of their environment. Most schizophrenics, if untreated, gradually withdraw from interactions with other people, and lose their ability to take care of personal needs and grooming.

Although schizophrenia was described by doctors as far back as Hippocrates (500 B.C.), it is difficult to classify in any satisfactory way. Many writers prefer the plural terms schizophrenias or schizophrenic disorders to the singular schizophrenia because of the lack of agreement in classification, as well as the possibility that different subtypes may eventually be shown to have different causes.

The schizophrenic disorders are a major social tragedy because of the large number of persons affected and because of the severity of their impairment. It is estimated that people who suffer from schizophrenia fill 50% of the hospital beds in psychiatric units and 25% of all hospital beds. A number of studies indicate that about 1% of the world's population is affected by schizophrenia, without regard to race, social class, level of education, or cultural influences. (However, outcome may vary from culture to culture, depending on the familial support of the patient.) Most patients are diagnosed in their late teens or early twenties, but the symptoms of schizophrenia can emerge at any point in the life cycle. The male/female **ratio** in adults is about 1.2:1. Male patients typically have their first acute episode in their early twenties, while female patients are usually closer to 30 when they are diagnosed.

Schizophrenia is rarely diagnosed in preadolescent children, although patients as young as five or six have been reported. Childhood schizophrenia is at the upper end of the spectrum of severity and shows a greater gender disparity. It affects one or two children in every 10,000; the male/female ratio is 2:1.

The course of schizophrenia in adults can be divided into three phases or stages. In the acute phase, the patient has an overt loss of contact with reality (psychotic episode) that requires intervention and treatment. In the second or stabilization phase, the initial psychotic symptoms have been brought under control but the patient is at risk for relapse if treatment is interrupted. In the third or maintenance phase, the patient is relatively stable and can be kept indefinitely on antipsychotic medications. Even in the maintenance phase, however, relapses are not unusual and patients do not always return to full functioning.

Recently, some psychiatrists have begun to use a classification of schizophrenia based on two main types. People with Type I, or positive schizophrenia, have a rapid (acute) onset of symptoms and tend to respond well to drugs. They also tend to suffer more from the "positive" symptoms, such as delusions and hallucinations. People with Type II, or **negative** schizophrenia, are usually described as poorly adjusted before their schizophrenia slowly overtakes them. They have predominantly "negative" symptoms, such as withdrawal from others and a slowing of mental and physical reactions (psychomotor retardation).

The fourth (1994) edition of the *Diagnostic and Statistical Manual of Mental Disorders* (*DSM-IV*) specifies five subtypes of schizophrenia:

Paranoid

The key feature of this subtype of schizophrenia is the combination of false beliefs (delusions) and hearing voices (auditory hallucinations), with more nearly normal emotions and cognitive functioning. (Cognitive functions include reasoning, judgment, and memory.) The delusions of paranoid schizophrenics usually involve thoughts of being persecuted or harmed by others or exaggerated opinions of their own importance, but may also reflect feelings of jealousy or excessive religiosity. The delusions are typically organized into a coherent framework. Paranoid schizophrenics function at a higher level than other subtypes, but are at risk for suicidal or violent **behavior** under the influence of their delusions.

Disorganized

Disorganized schizophrenia (formerly called hebephrenic schizophrenia) is marked by disorganized **speech**, thinking, and behavior on the patient's part, coupled with flat or inappropriate emotional responses to a situation (affect). The patient may act silly or withdraw socially to an extreme extent. Most patients in this category have weak personality structures prior to their initial acute psychotic episode.

Catatonic

Catatonic schizophrenia is characterized by disturbances of movement that may include rigidity, stupor, agitation, bizarre posturing, and repetitive imitations of the movements or speech of other people. These patients are at risk for **malnutrition**, exhaustion, or self-injury. This subtype is presently uncommon in **Europe** and the United States. Catatonia as a symptom is most commonly associated with mood disorders.

Undifferentiated

Patients in this category have the characteristic positive and negative symptoms of schizophrenia but do not meet the specific criteria for the paranoid, disorganized, or catatonic subtypes.

Residual

This category is used for patients who have had at least one acute schizophrenic episode but do not presently have strong positive psychotic symptoms, such as delusions and hallucinations. They may have negative symptoms, such as withdrawal from others, or mild forms of positive symptoms, which indicate that the disorder has not completely resolved.

Theories of causality

One of the reasons for the ongoing difficulty in classifying schizophrenic disorders is incomplete understanding of their causes. As of 1998, it is thought that these disorders are the end result of a combination of genetic, neurobiological, and environmental causes. A leading neurobiological hypothesis looks at the connection between the disease and excessive levels of dopamine, a chemical that transmits signals in the **brain** (**neurotransmitter**). The genetic factor in schizophrenia has been underscored by recent findings that first-degree biological relatives of schizophrenics are 10 times as likely to develop the disorder as are members of the general population.

Prior to recent findings of abnormalities in the brain structure of schizophrenic patients, several generations of psychiatrists advanced a number of psychoanalytic and sociological theories about the origins of schizophrenia. These theories ranged from hypotheses about the patient's problems with **anxiety** or aggression to theories about **stress** reactions or interactions with disturbed parents. Psychosocial factors are now thought to influence the expression or severity of schizophrenia, rather than cause it directly.

Another hypothesis suggests that schizophrenia may be caused by a **virus** that attacks the hippocampus, a part of the brain that processes sense perceptions. Damage to the hippocampus would account for schizophrenic patients' vulnerability to sensory overload. As of mid-1998, researchers were preparing to test antiviral medications on schizophrenics.

Symptoms of schizophrenia

Patients with a possible **diagnosis** of schizophrenia are evaluated on the basis of a set or constellation of symptoms; there is no single symptom that is unique to schizophrenia. In 1959, the German psychiatrist Kurt Schneider proposed a list of so-called first-rank symptoms, which he regarded as diagnostic of the disorder.

These symptoms include:

- Delusions
- Somatic
- Hallucinations
- Hearing voices commenting on the patient's behavior
- Thought insertion or thought withdrawal.

Somatic hallucinations refer to sensations or perceptions concerning body organs that have no known medical cause or reason, such as the notion that one's brain is radioactive. Thought insertion and/or withdrawal refer to delusions that an outside force (for example, the FBI, the CIA, Martians, etc.) has the power to put thoughts into one's mind or remove them.

Positive symptoms

The positive symptoms of schizophrenia are those that represent an excessive or distorted version of normal functions. Positive symptoms include Schneider's first-rank symptoms as well as disorganized thought processes (reflected mainly in speech) and disorganized or catatonic behavior. Disorganized thought processes are marked by such characteristics as looseness of associations, in which the patient rambles from topic to topic in a disconnected way; tangentiality, which means that the patient gives unrelated answers to questions; and "word salad," in which the patient's speech is so incoherent that it makes no grammatical or linguistic sense. Disorganized behavior means that the patient has difficulty with any type of purposeful or goal-oriented behavior, including personal self-care or preparing meals. Other forms of disorganized behavior may include dressing in odd or inappropriate ways, sexual self-stimulation in public, or agitated shouting or cursing.

Negative symptoms

The *DSM-IV* definition of schizophrenia includes three so-called negative symptoms. They are called negative because they represent the lack or absence of behaviors. The negative symptoms that are considered diagnostic of schizophrenia are a lack of emotional response (affective flattening), poverty of speech, and absence of volition or will. In general, the negative symptoms are more difficult for doctors to evaluate than the positive symptoms.

Diagnosis

A doctor must make a diagnosis of schizophrenia on the basis of a standardized list of outwardly observable

symptoms, not on the basis of internal psychological processes. There are no specific laboratory tests that can be used to diagnose schizophrenia. Researchers have, however, discovered that patients with schizophrenia have certain abnormalities in the structure and functioning of the brain compared to normal test subjects. These discoveries have been made with the help of imaging techniques such as computed tomography scans (CT scans).

When a psychiatrist assesses a patient for schizophrenia, he or she will begin by excluding physical conditions that can cause abnormal thinking and some other behaviors associated with schizophrenia. These conditions include organic brain disorders (including traumatic injuries of the brain) temporal lobe **epilepsy**, Wilson's disease, Huntington's chorea, and **encephalitis**. The doctor will also need to rule out substance abuse disorders, especially amphetamine use.

After ruling out organic disorders, the doctor will consider other psychiatric conditions that may include psychotic symptoms or symptoms resembling **psychosis**. These disorders include mood disorders with psychotic features; delusional disorder; dissociative disorder not otherwise specified (DDNOS) or **multiple personality disorder**; schizotypal, schizoid, or paranoid personality disorders; and atypical reactive disorders. In the past, many individuals were incorrectly diagnosed as schizophrenic. Some patients who were diagnosed prior to the changes in categorization introduced by *DSM-IV* should have their diagnoses, and treatment, reevaluated. In children, the doctor must distinguish between psychotic symptoms and a vivid fantasy life, and also identify **learning** problems or disorders. After other conditions have been ruled out, the patient must meet a set of criteria specified by *DSM-IV*:

- *Characteristic symptoms.* The patient must have two (or more) of the following symptoms during a one-month period: delusions; hallucinations; disorganized speech; disorganized or catatonic behavior; negative symptoms.
- Decline in social, interpersonal, or occupational functioning, including self-care.
- *Duration.* The disturbed behavior must last for at least six months.
- *Diagnostic exclusions.* Mood disorders, substance abuse disorders, medical conditions, and developmental disorders have been ruled out.

Treatment

The treatment of schizophrenia depends in part on the patient's stage or phase. Patients in the acute phase are hospitalized in most cases, to prevent harm to the patient or others and to begin treatment with antipsychotic medications. A patient having a first psychotic episode should be given a CT or MRI (**magnetic resonance imaging**) scan to rule out structural brain disease.

Antipsychotic medications

The primary form of treatment of schizophrenia is antipsychotic medication. Antipsychotic drugs help to control almost all the positive symptoms of the disorder. They have minimal effects on disorganized behavior and negative symptoms. Between 60-70% of schizophrenics will respond to antipsychotics. In the acute phase of the illness, patients are usually given medications by mouth or by intramuscular injection. After the patient has been stabilized, the antipsychotic drug may be given in a long-acting form called a depot dose. Depot medications last for two to four weeks; they have the advantage of protecting the patient against the consequences of forgetting or skipping daily doses. In addition, some patients who do not respond to oral neuroleptics have better results with depot form. Patients whose long-term treatment includes depot medications are introduced to the depot form gradually during their stabilization period. Most people with schizophrenia are kept indefinitely on antipsychotic medications during the maintenance phase of their disorder to minimize the possibility of relapse.

As of 1998, the most frequently used antipsychotics fall into two classes: the older dopamine receptor antagonists, or DAs, and the newer serotonin **dopamine** antagonists, or SDAs. (Antagonists block the action of some other substance; for example, dopamine antagonists counteract the action of dopamine.) The exact mechanisms of action of these medications are not known, but it is thought that they lower the patient's sensitivity to sensory stimuli and so indirectly improve the patient's ability to interact with others.

Dopamine receptor antagonist

The dopamine antagonists include the older antipsychotic (also called neuroleptic) drugs, such as haloperidol (Haldol), chlorpromazine (Thorazine), and fluphenazine (Prolixin). These drugs have two major drawbacks: it is often difficult to find the best dosage level for the individual patient, and a dosage level high enough to control psychotic symptoms frequently produces extrapyramidal side effects, or EPS. EPSs include parkinsonism, in which the patient cannot walk normally and usually develops a tremor; dystonia, or painful muscle spasms of the head, tongue, or neck; and akathisia, or restlessness. A type of long-term EPS is called tardive dyskinesia, which features slow, rhythmic, automatic movements. Schizophrenics with **AIDS** are especially vulnerable to developing EPS.

KEY TERMS

Affective flattening—A loss or lack of emotional expressiveness. It is sometimes called blunted or restricted affect.

Akathisia—Agitated or restless movement, usually affecting the legs and accompanied by a sense of discomfort. It is a common side effect of neuroleptic medications.

Catatonic behavior—Behavior characterized by muscular tightness or rigidity and lack of response to the environment. In some patients rigidity alternates with excited or hyperactive behavior.

Delusion—A fixed, false belief that is resistant to reason or factual disproof.

Depot dosage—A form of medication that can be stored in the patient's body tissues for several days or weeks, thus minimizing the risks of the patient's forgetting daily doses. Haloperidol and fluphenazine can be given in depot form.

Dopamine receptor antagonists (DAs)—The older class of antipsychotic medications, also called neuroleptics. These primarily block the site on nerve cells that normally receives the brain chemical dopamine.

Dystonia—Painful involuntary muscle cramps or spasms. Dystonia is one of the extrapyramidal side effects associated with antipsychotic medications.

Extrapyramidal symptoms (EPS)—A group of side effects associated with antipsychotic medications. EPS include parkinsonism, akathisia, dystonia, and tardive dyskinesia.

First-rank symptoms—A set of symptoms designated by Kurt Schneider in 1959 as the most important diagnostic indicators of schizophrenia. These symptoms include delusions, hallucinations, thought insertion or removal, and thought broadcasting. First-rank symptoms are sometimes referred to as Schneiderian symptoms.

Hallucination—A sensory experience of something that does not exist outside the mind. A person can experience a hallucination in any of the five senses. Auditory hallucinations are a common symptom of schizophrenia.

Huntington's chorea—A hereditary disease that typically appears in midlife, marked by gradual loss of brain function and voluntary movement. Some of its symptoms resemble those of schizophrenia.

Negative symptoms—Symptoms of schizophrenia that are characterized by the absence or elimination of certain behaviors. DSM-IV specifies three negative symptoms: affective flattening, poverty of speech, and loss of will or initiative.

Neuroleptic—Another name for the older type of antipsychotic medications given to schizophrenic patients.

Parkinsonism—A set of symptoms originally associated with Parkinson's disease that can occur as side effects of neuroleptic medications. The symptoms include trembling of the fingers or hands, a shuffling gait, and tight or rigid muscles.

Positive symptoms—Symptoms of schizophrenia that are characterized by the production or presence of behaviors that are grossly abnormal or excessive, including hallucinations and thought-process disorder. DSM-IV subdivides positive symptoms into psychotic and disorganized.

Poverty of speech—A negative symptom of schizophrenia, characterized by brief and empty replies to questions. It should not be confused with shyness or reluctance to talk.

Psychotic disorder—A mental disorder characterized by delusions, hallucinations, or other symptoms of lack of contact with reality. The schizophrenias are psychotic disorders.

Serotonin dopamine antagonists (SDAs)—The newer second-generation antipsychotic drugs, also called atypical antipsychotics. SDAs include clozapine (Clozaril), risperidone (Risperdal), and olanzapine (Zyprexa).

Wilson's disease—A rare hereditary disease marked by high levels of copper deposits in the brain and liver. It can cause psychiatric symptoms resembling schizophrenia.

Word salad—Speech that is so disorganized that it makes no linguistic or grammatical sense.

SERATONIN DOPAMINE ANTAGONISTS

The serotonin dopamine antagonists, also called atypical antipsychotics, are newer medications that include clozapine (Clozaril), risperidone (Risperdal), and olanzapine (Zyprexa). The SDAs have a better effect on the negative symptoms of schizophrenia than do the older drugs and are less likely to produce EPS than the older compounds. The newer drugs are significantly more expensive in the short term, although the SDAs may reduce long-term costs by reducing the need for hospitalization. They are also presently unavailable in injectable forms. The SDAs are commonly used to treat patients who respond poorly to the DAs. However, many psychiatrists now regard the use of these atypical antipsychotics as the treatment of first choice.

Psychotherapy

Most schizophrenics can benefit from psychotherapy once their acute symptoms have been brought under control by antipsychotic medication. Psychoanalytic approaches are not recommended. Behavior therapy, however, is often helpful in assisting patients to acquire skills for daily living and social interaction. It can be combined with occupational therapy to prepare the patient for eventual employment.

Family therapy

Family therapy is often recommended for the families of schizophrenic patients, to relieve the feelings of guilt that they often have as well as to help them understand the patient's disorder. The family's attitude and behaviors toward the patient are key factors in minimizing relapses (for example, by reducing stress in the patient's life), and family therapy can often strengthen the family's ability to cope with the stresses caused by the schizophrenic's illness. Family therapy focused on communication skills and problem-solving strategies is particularly helpful. In addition to formal treatment, many families benefit from support groups and similar mutual help organizations for relatives of schizophrenics.

Prognosis

One important prognostic sign is the patient's age at onset of psychotic symptoms. Patients with early onset of schizophrenia are more often male, have a lower level of functioning prior to onset, a higher rate of brain abnormalities, more noticeable negative symptoms, and worse outcomes. Patients with later onset are more likely to be female, with fewer brain abnormalities and thought impairment, and more hopeful prognoses.

The average course and outcome for schizophrenics are less favorable than those for most other mental disorders, although as many as 30% of patients diagnosed with schizophrenia recover completely and the majority experience some improvement. Two factors that influence outcomes are stressful life events and a hostile or emotionally intense family environment. Schizophrenics with a high number of stressful changes in their lives, or who have frequent contacts with critical or emotionally overinvolved family members, are more likely to relapse. Overall, the most important component of long-term care of schizophrenic patients is complying with their regimen of antipsychotic medications.

Further Reading

Campbell, Robert Jean. *Psychiatric Dictionary,* New York and Oxford, UK: Oxford University Press, 1989.

Clark, R. Barkley. "Psychosocial Aspects of Pediatrics & Psychiatric Disorders." In *Current Pediatric Diagnosis & Treatment,* edited by William W. Hay Jr., et al. Stamford, CT: Appleton & Lange, 1997.

Day, Max, and Elvin V. Semrad. "Schizophrenia: Comprehensive Psychotherapy." In *The Encyclopedia of Psychiatry, Psychology, and Psychoanalysis*, edited by Benjamin B. Wolman. New York: Henry Holt and Company, 1996.

Eisendrath, Stuart J. "Psychiatric Disorders." In *Current Medical Diagnosis & Treatment 1998*, edited by Lawrence M. Tierney Jr., et al. Stamford, CT: Appleton & Lange, 1997.

Marder, Stephen R. "Schizophrenia." In *Conn's Current Therapy*, edited by Robert E. Rakel. Philadelphia: W. B. Saunders Company, 1998.

"Psychiatric Disorders: Schizophrenic Disorders." In *The Merck Manual of Diagnosis and Therapy*, Vol. I, edited by Robert Berkow, et al. Rahway, NJ: Merck Research Laboratories, 1992.

"Schizophrenia and Other Psychotic Disorders." In *Diagnostic and Statistical Manual of Mental Disorders,* 4th ed. Washington, DC: The American Psychiatric Association, 1994.

Schultz, Clarence G. "Schizophrenia: Psychoanalytic Views." In *The Encyclopedia of Psychiatry, Psychology, and Psychoanalysis*, edited by Benjamin B. Wolman. New York: Henry Holt and Company, 1996.

Tsuang, Ming T., et al. "Schizophrenic Disorders." In *The New Harvard Guide to Psychiatry*, edited by Armand M. Nicholi, Jr. Cambridge, MA, and London, UK: The Belknap Press of Harvard University Press, 1988.

Wilson, Billie Ann, et al. *Nurses Drug Guide 1995*. Norwalk, CT: Appleton & Lange, 1995.

Winerip, Michael. "Schizophrenia's Most Zealous Foe." *The New York Times Magazine,* (February 22, 1998): 26-29.

Rebecca J. Frey

Scientific method

Scientific thought aims to make correct predictions about events in nature. Although the predictive nature of

scientific thought may not at first always be apparent, a little reflection usually reveals the predictive nature of any scientific activity. Just as the engineer who designs a bridge ensures that it will withstand the forces of nature, so the scientist considers the ability of any new scientific model to hold up under scientific scrutiny as new scientific data become available.

It is often said that the scientist attempts to understand nature. But ultimately, understanding something means being able to predict its behavior. Scientists therefore usually agree that events are not understandable unless they are predictable. Although the word science describes many activities, the notion of prediction or predictability is always implied when the word science is used.

Until the seventeenth century, scientific prediction simply amounted to observing the changing events of the world, noting any irregularities, and making predictions based upon those regularities. The Irish philosopher and bishop George Berkeley (1685-1753) was the first to rethink this notion of predictability.

Berkeley noted that each person experiences directly only the signals of his or her five senses. An individual can infer that a natural world exists as the source of his sensations, but he or she can never know the natural world directly. One can only know it through one's senses. In everyday life people tend to forget that their knowledge of the external world comes to them through their five senses.

The physicists of the nineteenth century described the atom as though they could see it directly. Their descriptions changed constantly as new data arrived, and these physicists had to remind themselves that they were only working with a mental picture built with fragmentary information.

Scientific models

In 1913, Niels Bohr used the term *model* for his published description of the **hydrogen** atom. This term is now used to characterize theories developed long before Bohr's time. Essentially, a model implies some correspondence between the model itself and its object. A single correspondence is often enough to provide a very useful model, but it should never be forgotten that the intent of creating the model is to make predictions.

There are many types of models. A conceptual model refers to a mental picture of a model that is introspectively present when one thinks about it. A geometrical model refers to diagrams or drawings that are used to describe a model. A mathematical model refers to equations or other relationships that provide quantitative predictions.

It is an interesting fact that if a mathematical model predicts the future accurately, there may be no need for interpretation or visualization of the process described by the mathematical equations. Many mathematical models have more than one interpretation. But the interpretations and visualization of the mathematical model should facilitate the creation of new models.

New models are not constructed from observations of facts and previous models; they are postulated. That is to say that the statements that describe a model are assumed and predictions are made from them. The predictions are checked against the measurements or observations of actual events in nature. If the predictions prove accurate, the model is said to be validated. If the predictions fail, the model is discarded or adjusted until it can make accurate predictions.

The formulation of the scientific model is subject to no limitations in technique; the scientist is at liberty to use any method he can come up with, conscious or unconscious, to develop a model. Validation of the model, however, follows a single, recurrent pattern. Note that this pattern does not constitute a method for making new discoveries in science; rather it provides a way of validating new models after they have been postulated. This method is called the scientific method.

The scientific method 1) postulates a model consistent with existing experimental observations; 2) checks the predictions of this model against further observations or measurements; 3) adjusts or discards the model to agree with new observations or measurements.

The third step leads back to the second, so, in principle, the process continues without end. (Such a process is said to be recursive.) No assumptions are made about the reality of the model. The model that ultimately prevails may be the simplest, most convenient, or most satisfying model; but it will certainly be the one that best explains those problems that scientists have come to regard as most acute.

Paradigms are models that are sufficiently unprecedented to attract an enduring group of adherents away from competing scientific models. A paradigm must be sufficiently open-ended to leave many problems for its adherents to solve. The paradigm is thus a theory from which springs a coherent tradition of scientific research. Examples of such traditions include Ptolemaic **astronomy**, Copernican astronomy, Aristotelian dynamics, Newtonian dynamics, etc.

To be accepted as a paradigm, a model must be better than its competitors, but it need not and cannot explain all the facts with which it is confronted. Paradigms acquire status because they are more successful than their competitors in solving a few problems that scientists have come to regard as acute. Normal science con-

sists of extending the knowledge of those facts that are key to understanding the paradigm, and in further articulating the paradigm itself.

Scientific thought should in principle be cumulative; a new model should be capable of explaining everything the old model did. In some sense the old model may appear to be a special case of the new model. In fact, whether this is so seems to be open to debate.

The descriptive phase of normal science involves the acquisition of experimental data. Much of science involves classification of these facts. Classification systems constitute abstract models, and it is often the case that examples are found that do not precisely fit in classification schemes. Whether these anomalies warrant reconstruction of the classification system depends on the consensus of the scientists involved.

Predictions that do not include numbers are called qualitative predictions. Only qualitative predictions can be made from qualitative observations. Predictions that include numbers are called quantitative predictions. Quantitative predictions are often expressed in terms of probabilities, and may contain estimates of the **accuracy** of the prediction.

Historical evolution of the scientific method

The Greeks constructed a model in which the stars were lights fastened to the inside of a large, hollow **sphere** (the sky), and the sphere rotated about the **Earth** as a center. This model predicts that all of the stars will remain fixed in position relative to each other. But certain bright stars were found to wander about the sky. These stars were called planets (from the Greek word for wanderer). The model had to be modified to account for **motion** of the planets. In Ptolemy's (90-168 A.D.) model of the **solar system**, each **planet** moves in a small circular **orbit**, and the center of the small **circle** moves in a large circle around the Earth as center.

Copernicus (1473-1543) assumed the **Sun** was near the center of a system of circular orbits in which the Earth and planets moved with fair regularity. Like many new scientific ideas, Copernicus' idea was initially greeted as nonsense, but over time it eventually took hold. One of the factors that led astronomers to accept Copernicus' model was that Ptolemaic astronomy could not explain a number of astronomical discoveries.

In the case of Copernicus, the problems of calendar design and astrology evoked questions among contemporary scientists. In fact, Copernicus's theory did not lead directly to any improvement in the calendar. Copernicus's theory suggested that the planets should be like the earth, that **Venus** should show phases, and that the universe should be vastly larger than previously supposed. Sixty years after Copernicus's death, when the **telescope** suddenly displayed mountains on the **moon**, the phases of Venus, and an immense number of previously unsuspected stars, the new theory received a great many converts, particularly from non-astronomers.

The change from the Ptolemaic model to Copernicus's model is a particularly famous case of a paradigm change. As the Ptolemaic system evolved between 200 B.C. and 200 A.D., it eventually became highly successful in predicting changing positions of the stars and planets. No other ancient system had performed as well. In fact the Ptolemaic astronomy is still used today as an engineering **approximation**. Ptolemy's predictions for the planets were as good as Copernicus's. But with respect to planetary position and **precession of the equinoxes**, the predictions made with Ptolemy's model were not quite consistent with the best available observations. Given a particular inconsistency, astronomers for many centuries were satisfied to make minor adjustments in the Ptolemaic model to account for it. But eventually, it became apparent that the web of complexity resulting from the minor adjustments was increasing more rapidly than the accuracy, and a discrepancy corrected in one place was likely to show up in another place.

Tycho Brahe (1546-1601) made a lifelong study of the planets. In the course of doing so he acquired the data needed to demonstrate certain shortcomings in Copernicus's model. But it was left to Johannes Kepler (1571-1630), using Brahe's data after the latter's death, to come up with a set of laws consistent with the data. It is worth noting that the quantitative superiority of Kepler's astronomical tables to those computed from the Ptolemaic theory was a major factor in the conversion of many astronomers to Copernicanism.

In fact, simple quantitative telescopic observations indicate that the planets do not quite obey **Kepler's laws**, and Isaac Newton (1642-1727) proposed a theory that shows why they should not. To redefine Kepler's laws, Newton had to neglect all gravitational attraction except that between individual planets and the sun. Since planets also attract each other, only approximate agreement between Kepler's laws and telescopic observation could be expected.

Newton thus generalized Kepler's laws in the sense that they could now describe the motion of any object moving in any sort of path. It is now known that objects moving almost as fast as the speed of light require a modification of Newton's laws, but such objects were unknown in Newton's day.

Newton's first law says that a body at rest remains at rest unless acted upon by an external **force**. His second

KEY TERMS

Inference—The action of drawing a conclusion from data or premises. Compare with deduction, an inference from the general to the particular.

Normal science—Scientific activity involving the extension of knowledge of facts key to understanding a paradigm, and in further articulating the paradigm itself. Most scientific activity falls under the category of normal science.

Paradigm—A model that is sufficiently unprecedented to attract an enduring group of adherents away from competing scientific models. A paradigm must be sufficiently open-ended to leave many problems for its adherents to solve.The paradigm is thus a theory from which springs a coherent tradition of scientific research. Examples of such traditions include Ptolemaic astronomy, Copernican astronomy, Aristotelian dynamics, Newtonian dynamics, etc.

Postulate—Something assumed as a basis of reasoning.

Qualitative prediction—A prediction that does not include numbers. Only qualitative predictions can be made from qualitative observations.

Quantitative prediction—A prediction that includes numbers. Quantitative predictions are often expressed in terms of probabilities, and may contain estimates of the accuracy of the prediction.

law states quantitatively what happens when a force is applied to an object. The third law states that if a body A exerts a force F on body B, then body B exerts on body A a force that is equal in magnitude but opposite in direction to force F. Newton's fourth law is his law of gravitational attraction.

Newton's success in predicting quantitative astronomical observations was probably the single most important factor leading to acceptance of his theory over more reasonable but uniformly qualitative competitors.

It is often pointed out that Newton's model includes Kepler's laws as a special case. This permits scientists to say they understand Kepler's model as a special case of Newton's model. But when one considers the case of Newton's laws and relativistic theory, the special case argument does not hold up. Newton's laws can only be derived from Albert Einstein's (1876-1955) relativistic theory if the laws are reinterpreted in a way that would have only been possible after Einstein's work.

The variables and parameters that in Einstein's theory represent spatial position, time, **mass**, etc. appear in Newton's theory, and there still represent **space**, time, and mass. But the physical natures of the Einsteinian concepts differ from those of the Newtonian model. In Newtonian theory, mass is conserved; in Einstein's theory, mass is convertible with **energy**. The two ideas converge only at low velocities, but even then they are not exactly the same.

Scientific theories are often felt to be better than their predecessors because they are better instruments for solving puzzles and problems, but also for their superior abilities to represent what nature is really like. In this sense, it is often felt that successive theories come ever closer to representing truth, or what is "really there." Thomas Kuhn, the historian of science whose writings include the seminal book *The Structure of Scientific Revolution* (1962), found this idea implausible. He pointed out that although Newton's mechanics improve on Ptolemy's mechanics, and Einstein's mechanics improve on Newton's as instruments for puzzle-solving, there does not appear to be any coherent direction of development. In some important respects, Professor Kuhn has argued, Einstein's general theory of relativity is closer to early Greek ideas than relativistic or ancient Greek ideas are to Newton's.

See also Geocentric theory; Heliocentric theory; Laws of motion; Relativity, general; Relativity, special.

Randall Frost

Scorpion flies

The scorpion fly, despite its name, is neither a scorpion nor a fly. The name is a suggestion of the general appearance of the insect. They have four membranous wings that are the same size and shape. The head is rather elongated and points down in a beak-like fashion with the chewing mouthparts located at the tip of the beak. The genital segment of the male scorpion fly has an enlarged, rounded appearance. In addition, it curves up over the back of the insect, resembling a scorpion's tail. However, the tail is not an offensive weapon; it is used for grasping the female during copulation.

Scorpion flies are so unique they have been given their own taxonomic order: Mecoptera. They undergo complete **metamorphosis** and most are 0.4-0.8 in (9-22 mm) in length. The majority of the Mecopterans that are encountered in the wild constitute two of the five fami-

lies: Panorpidae (common or "true" scorpion flies) and Bittacidae (hanging scorpion flies). The three remaining families, Panorpodidae, Meropeidae, and Boreidae, have a combined total of 14 North American species and are not very common.

The Panorpidae are, for the most part, scavengers. The larvae and the adults feed on dead animals, including **insects** with the occasional diet supplement of mosses, pollen, fruit, and **nectar**. The eggs are laid in the **soil** in small clusters, eventually hatching into larvae that have a catapillar-like appearance. If the larvae are not on the surface feeding, they are in shallow burrows that have been dug in the soil. Pupation takes place in an elongated **cell** just under ground by the fourth instar larvae.

The Bittacidae are similar in appearance to the Panorpidae but lack the scorpion-like tail. In addition, the Bittacids are hunters. The second and third pair of legs are extremely long and raptorial (modified for grasping), thus preventing the insect from standing in a normal fashion. By hanging from the front pair of legs, the Bittacids reach for passing **prey** with the hind legs, hence the nickname "hanging scorpion fly." Prey often includes spiders, **moths**, **flies**, and other small, soft-bodies insects.

Scorpionfish

Scorpionfish are ray-finned bony marine **fish** belonging to the family Scorpaenidae. Most of the 300 species of scorpionfish live in the seas around **North America**. A major anatomical characteristic of scorpionfish is a bony structure extending from the **eye** to the operculum or gill cover. The common name of scorpionfish refers to the spiny condition of the members of this family which includes extremely venomous fishes, many of which are colored red.

The plumed scorpionfish, *Scorpaena grandicornis*, of the Atlantic derives its name from the spines and fleshy outgrowths around its head that superficially resemble the shaggy mane of a lion. The first dorsal fin bears a series of heavy sharp spines of which the most anterior ones are hollow and contain poison **glands** at their base.

The plumed scorpionfish is relatively small, ranging from 6-12 in (15-30.5 cm) and is found in the subtropical seas from Florida to the Caribbean.

The western representative of this group is the California scorpionfish, *S. guttata,* which is found off the coast of California. They can reach 1.5 ft (0.5 m) in length, and are a red color dorsally, grading gradually to

A lionfish (*Pterois volitans*) in the Coral Sea.

pink below. California scorpionfish are a favorite of sport fishermen but dangerous to catch because of 12 pointed spines on the dorsal fin.

The deadliest species of scorpionfish are found in the Indo-Pacific region. The stonefish (genus *Syanceja*) may lurk on coral reefs or on rocky bottoms in shallow **water**. Venom injected from the hollow spine (like a hypodermic needle) may result in extreme **pain** which may persist for a long time, frequently resulting in death.

Scorpions see **Arachnids**

Screamers

Screamers are three species of large **birds** in the family Anhimidae. This family is in the order Anseriformes, which also includes the **ducks**, **geese**, and **swans**, although screamers bear little superficial resemblance to these waterfowl. Screamers are non-migratory birds that inhabit a wide range of aquatic habitats in the tropics of **South America**, especially marshy places.

Screamers are large birds, with a body length of 28-36 in (71-91 cm), and a heavy body, weighing as much as 10 lb (4.5 kg). The wings are large and rounded, and have two pairs of prominent, sharp spurs at the bend (which is anatomically analogous to the wrist). The spurs are used to attack other screamers intruding on a defended territory, or in defense against predators. The legs and feet are long and strong, and the toes are slightly webbed. The head has a crest at the back, and the beak is small, downward curved, and fowl-like in appearance. Almost all of the bones of screamers are hollow, and their body has numerous air-sacs. Both of these features serve to lighten the weight of these large-bodied birds. The coloration of

screamers is typically grey, with some black markings. The sexes are alike in size and coloration.

Screamers are strong but slow fliers, and they often soar. Screamers are semi-aquatic animals, spending much of their time walking about in the vicinity of aquatic habitats, and often on mats of floating vegetation, but not usually in the **water** itself. They feed on aquatic plants, and sometimes on **insects**.

True to their name, screamers have very loud, shrill cries that they use to proclaim their breeding territory. Screamers build their nest on the ground, and lay 1-6 unspotted eggs. The eggs are incubated by both parents, who also raise the young together. The babies are precocious, and can leave the nest soon after they are born, following their parents and mostly feeding themselves. Screamers are monogamous, and pair for life.

The horned screamer (*Anhima cornuta*) has a 6 in (15 cm) long, forward-hanging, horny projection on its forehead, probably important in species recognition, or in courting displays. This species ranges through much of the South American tropics.

The black-necked or northern screamer (*Chauna chaviaria*) occurs in Colombia and northern Venezuela. The crested or southern screamer (*C. torquata*) occurs in Brazil, Bolivia, northern Argentina, and Paraguay.

Screwpines

Screwpines are shrubs, trees, or vines belonging to the family Pandanaceae in order Pandanales, and the class Arecidae, which also includes the **palms**. Screwpines are native to the tropics of South and Southeast **Asia**, northern **Australia**, and west **Africa**. Despite their common name, screwpine are not related to the true **pines**, which are gymnosperms of the phylum Coniferophyta.

Screwpines are common elements of wet riverside and coastal **forests**. Screwpines typically grow with many stilt-like, prop roots arising from the stem of the **plant**, much like red mangroves. These prop roots provide additional support for the plants, which grow in soft, wet substrates.

Screwpines are much used by local peoples. In India, male flowers of breadfruit pardanus or pardong (*Pandanus odoratissimus*) are soaked in **water** to extract a perfume. In Malaysia, leaves of the thatch screwpine (*Pandanus tectorius*), are used for roof thatching and for flavoring certain kinds of bread. On Madagascar, leaves of the common screwpine (*P. utilis*) are used to make woven baskets and mats.

The **fruits** of many screwpines are large and greatly resemble pineapples. Fruits of *P. odoratissimus* serve as a source of **nutrition** in much of the Old World tropics. Breadfruit was the major cargo being carried by the mutinous British merchant ship, *Bounty*. Many other species of *Pandanus* produce large and nutritious fruits that are eaten by local people.

Screwpines are also fairly commonly used in the florist's trade. Several species are used, but *Pandanus vetchii* is the most popular. There is even a florist's cultivar of *P. vetchii* on the market called *compacta*.

See also Gymnosperm; Mangrove tree; Wetlands.

Sculpins

The sculpins are about 300 species of small, rather grotesquely shaped **fish** that make up the family Cottidae. Most species of sculpins occur in cold or cool-temperate marine waters of the Northern Hemisphere, but a few species occur in fresh waters of northern **Asia**, **Europe**, and **North America**.

Sculpins are short, stout-bodied fishes, with a large and broad head, large eyes, a large mouth, and broad, coarsely veined fins. Sculpins are bottom-dwelling fishes, feeding voraciously on diverse types of aquatic **invertebrates** and **plant** matter. Sculpins do not have typical scales covering their body, but are coated by a slimy mucus, with numerous tubercles or prickles that give these fish a rough feel when handled.

Most species of sculpin occur in northern marine waters. The sea raven (*Hemitripterus americanus*) occurs on continental-shelf waters of the northeastern Atlantic Ocean, from New England to Labrador. This is a relatively large species of sculpin, attaining a weight as much as 6.5 lb (3 kg). When they are captured, sea ravens will quickly swallow **water** and air to distend their body, presumably hoping to make it more difficult to be swallowed whole by a **predator**.

The grubby (*Myoxocephalus aenaeus*) is a smaller species of the northeastern Atlantic, sometimes considered a nuisance by human fishers because when this fish is abundant it takes baited hooks set for other species.

Several species of sculpins occur in fresh waters in North America. The slimy sculpin (*Cottus cognatus*) is a 5-8-cm-long species that is very widespread in boreal and temperate regions of the **continent**. The similar-sized, mottled sculpin (*Cottus bairdi*) is widespread in northeastern regions. The deepwater sculpin (*Myoxocephalus quadricornis*) is a relatively large species, attaining a

length of up to 8.4 in (21 cm), and occurring in deeper waters of the Great Lakes and some other large lakes.

Sea anemones

Sea anemones are invertebrate animals belonging to the phylum Coelenterata, a term that means hollow gut. Sea anemones are found in all major oceans from the polar regions to the equator. All are exclusively marine-dwelling with a strong tendency for shallow, warm waters. More than 1,000 species have been described so far. These vary considerably in size, with a body diameter that ranges from just 0.15 in (4 mm) to more than 3.3 ft (1 m), and a height of 0.6 in (1.5 cm) to 2 in (5 cm). Many are strikingly colored with vivid hues of blue, yellow, green, or red or a combination of these, but others may blend into the background through an association with symbiotic **algae** that live within the body wall of the anemone.

Related to corals and more distantly to **jellyfish**, sea anemones have a very simple structure, comprising an outer layer of cells which surround the body, an inner layer lining the gut cavity, and a separating layer of jelly-like material that forms the bulk of the **animal**. The central gut serves as stomach, intestine, **circulatory system**, and other purposes. The single mouth, through which all materials enter and leave the gut, is typically surrounded by a ring of tentacles that vary in size, appearance, and arrangement according to the species. Many of these tentacles are armed with special barbed stinging cells (nematocysts). These are used both in defense and in capturing **prey**. Whenever the tentacles come into contact with a foreign object, special capsules in the **cell** walls are triggered to unleash a number of nematocysts, some of which may carry toxic materials that serve to sting or paralyze the intruding object. Some tentacles produce a sticky mucus substance which serves a similar purpose, repelling potential predators and adhering to any small passing animals.

Unlike their coralline relatives, sea anemones are solitary animals that live firmly attached by a pedal disk to some object, either a branching coral, submerged **rocks**, or shells. A few species even bury themselves partly in soft sediments. All are free-living species that feed on a wide range of **invertebrates**; some of the larger species even feed on small **fish** that are captured and paralyzed by the nematocysts. In general, however, most of the smaller food items are captured by the regular beating movements of the tentacles, which draw small food particles down towards the mouth region. As food such as **plankton** is trapped on the surface of the tentacles, the latter bend down towards the mouth and **deposit** the food.

A mottled sculpin.

Sea anemones can reproduce by sexual or asexual means. Some species are either male or female, while others may be hermaphroditic. In the latter, eggs and sperm are produced at different times and released to the sea where external **fertilization** may take place. Another means of reproduction is by fission, with the adult anemone splitting off new daughter cells that, in time, develop to full size.

Some species of anemones have developed specialized living relationships with other species of animals. A number of **crabs** encourage sea anemones to attach themselves to their shells. Some species, such as the soft-bodied hermit crabs which live inside discarded mollusc shells, even go to the extreme of transferring the sea anemone to another shell when they move into another larger shell. Other crabs have been observed to attach sea anemones to their claws—an **adaptation** that may help in further deterring would-be predators. While the crabs clearly benefit for additional camouflage and greater security, the anemone is guaranteed of being in a place of clear open **water** for feeding; it may also benefit from some morsels of food captured by the crab.

An even greater level of cooperation is evident in the relationship that has developed between some species of sea anemones and single species of fishes. Clownfish, for example, are never found in nature without an anemone. For these fish, the anemone, which is capable of killing fish of a greater size, is its permanent home. Depending on its size, each anemone may host one or two fish of the same species, as well as their offspring. When threatened by a **predator**, the fish dive within the ring of tentacles, where they are protected by the anemone's **battery** of stinging cells. Taking further advantage of this safe place, clownfish also lay their eggs directly on the anemone. No direct harm comes to the

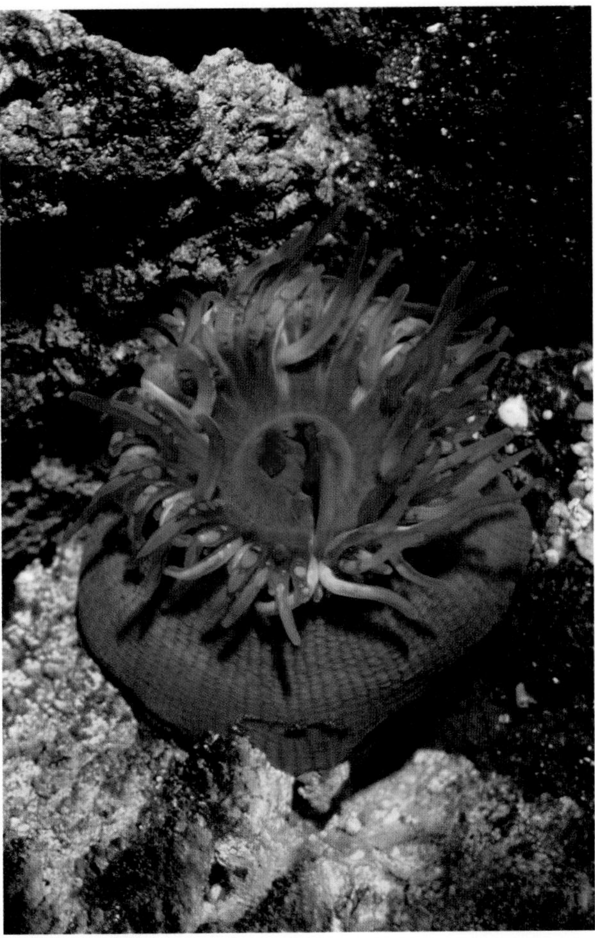

A sea anemone.

anemone through this association. In return for this protection, the fish help repel other fish from attacking the anemone and also serve to keep their host clear of **parasites** and other materials that may become entangled in their tentacles which could interrupt their feeding behaviour. No one is quite sure how these fishes avoid the lethal stinging actions of the anemone's tentacles. Some fish are known to have a thicker skin and to produce a mucus covering that may help protect them from being stung. Other species have been seen to nibble tiny parts of the tentacles and, in this way, may be able to develop some degree of immunity to the toxins carried in the nematocysts. Both of these reactions are, however, host specific: an anemone fish placed on a different species of anemone will almost certainly be killed, as it is not recognized by the anemone.

David Stone

Sea cow see **Manatee**

Sea cucumbers

Sea cucumbers are echinoderms, belonging to the class Holothuroidea of the order Echinodermata. About 1,000 species have been described, which vary in size from only 1.2 in (3 cm) to more than 3.3 ft (1 m) in length. Sea cucumbers occur in all of the oceans, being found in waters up to 655 ft (200 m) in depth, and perhaps deeper. In appearance, these animals range from an almost spherical to long and worm-like in shape. Most are colored black, brown, or olive-green, although tropical species may be reddish, orange, or violet.

Sea cucumbers are slow-moving, bottom-dwelling, marine **invertebrates** that are usually partially or completely immersed in the soft substrate. Some species have numerous small, foot-like structures (pseudopods) that enable them to move slowly along the bottom, but the majority move by contracting the muscular wall of the body in a similar manner to that of earthworms. Their elongate form facilitates a burrowing lifestyle.

The body of sea cucumbers is a tube-like arrangement. The outer body has a tough, leathery texture, although a few species have hardened calcareous patches for additional protection from predators. The head region is adorned with a cluster of tentacles (usually 10 to 30) surrounding a simple mouth. Sea cucumbers are deposit- or suspension-feeders, particularly on small invertebrates, **algae**, **bacteria**, and organic detritus. They feed by brushing their tentacles across the substrate to find food, or by extending the tentacles into the **water** column and trapping food directly. If they find food, the tentacles are bent inwards to reach the gullet, where the particles are removed for ingestion. At the same time, the tentacles are re-covered in a sticky mucus emitted from special **glands** that line the pharynx, preparing them once again for catching **prey**. Burrowing species ingest large amounts of sediment and absorb organic **nutrition** from that **matrix**.

Most sea cucumbers are either male or female, although a few species are hermaphroditic (i.e., each individual contains organs of both sexes). In most species the process of **fertilization** takes place outside of the body. The fertilized eggs develop into free-living larvae that are dispersed with water currents. A few species of cold-water sea cucumbers brood their larvae in special pouches on their body.

Being soft-bodied animals, sea cucumbers are prone to predation by a wide range of species, including **crabs**, **lobsters**, **starfish**, and **fish**. Remaining partly concealed in sediment provides the **animal** with some degree of security. In addition, when disturbed or threatened sea cucumbers are capable of emitting large quantities of

sticky filaments from their anus, which may engulf the potential **predator** and incapacitate it long enough for the sea cucumber to escape, or on occasion, may even kill the predator.

In some parts of the world, particularly Southeast **Asia** and China, sea cucumbers are considered a delicacy and are widely harvested as food. Often preserved dried, this *trepang* or *bêche de mer* is an ingredient of some kinds of oriental cuisine. Recent increases in market demand have had a significant impact on local populations of sea cucumbers, and overharvesting has resulted in the virtual disappearance of these animals from wide areas.

Further Reading

Lambert, P. *Sea Cucumbers of British Columbia, Southeast Alaska, and Puget Sound.* University of British Columbia Press, 1997.

Sea floor spreading see **Plate tectonics**

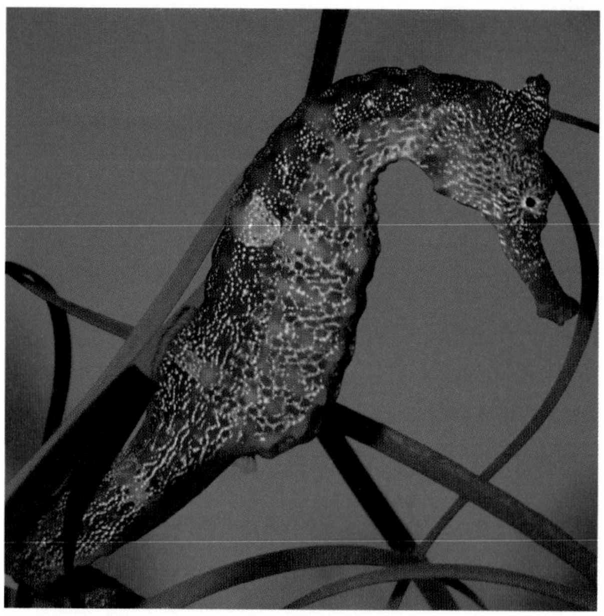

A common seahorse (*Hippocampus ingens*).

Sea horses

Sea horses are **bony fish** (or teleosts) in the family Syngnathidae, which includes about 230 species in 55 genera, most of which are pipefishes. The "true" sea horses comprise some 25 species in the genera *Hippocampus* and *Phyllopteryx*, which make up the subfamily Hippocampinae.

Species of sea horses occur in warm-temperate and tropical waters of all of the world's oceans. The usual **habitat** is near the shore in shallow-water places with seagrass, **algae**, or corals that provide numerous hiding places for these small, slow-moving **fish**. Sea horses may also occur in open-water situations, hiding in drifting mats of the floating alga known as sargasso-weed or *Sargassum*. The lined sea horse (*Hippocampus erectus*) is one of the more familiar species, occurring on the Atlantic coast of the Americas.

Biology of sea horses

Sea horses have an extremely unusual and distinctive morphology. Their body is long, narrow, segmented, and encased in a series of ring-like, bony plates. Sea horses have a long, tubular snout, tipped by a small, toothless mouth. They have relatively large eyes, and small, circular openings to the gill chamber. The head of sea horses is held at a right **angle** to the body, and it has a superficial resemblance to that of a horse; hence the common name of these small fish.

Sea horses swim in an erect stance, buoyed in this position by their swim bladder. Sea horses lack pectoral and dorsal fins, but use their anal fin to move in a slow and deliberate manner. Sea horses have a prehensile tail, which is used to anchor the **animal** to a solid structure to prevent it from drifting about.

Because they are so slow-moving, sea horses are highly vulnerable to predators. To help them deal with this danger, Sea horses are cryptically marked and colored to match their surroundings, and they spend much of their time hiding in quiet places. Sea horses mostly feed on **zooplankton** and other small creatures, such as fish larvae. The size range of the **prey** of sea horses is restricted by the small mouth of these animals.

Sea horses take close care of their progeny. The female sea horse has a specialized, penis-like structure that is used to deposit her several hundred eggs into a brood-pouch located on the belly of the male, known as a marsupium. The male secretes sperm into his marsupium, achieving external **fertilization** of the eggs. The male sea horse then broods the eggs within his pouch until they hatch. Soon afterwards, swimming, independent young are released to live in the external environment.

Because sea horses are such unusual creatures, they are often kept as pets in **saltwater** aquaria. They are also sometimes dried and sold as souvenirs to tourists. Sea horses for these purposes are captured in the wild. Sea horses are also prized in eastern Asian **herbal medicine**. Millions of sea horses are caught for these uses each year,

particularly the medicinal uses. Unfortunately, the exploitation is much too intense, and is causing the populations of most species to decline precipitously. Consequently, all species of seahorses are considered to be vulnerable to becoming extinct. Regrettably, although their perilous situation is well known, seahorses are not yet being well protected from the over-exploitation. If they do not soon receive effective protection, some of their species will become extinct, and all others will be endangered.

Further Reading

Nelson, J.S. *Fishes of the World.* 2nd ed. New York: Wiley, 1984.

Scott, W.B., and M.G. Scott. *Atlantic Fishes of Canada.* Toronto: University of Toronto Press, 1988.

Bill Freedman

Sea level

To most people sea level is the point at which the surface of the land and sea meet. Officially known as the sea level datum **plane**, it is a reference point used in measuring land elevation and **water** depths. It refers to the vertical **distance** from the surface of the **ocean** to some fixed point on land, or a reference point defined by people. Sea level became a standardized measure in 1929. **Mean** sea level is the average of the changes in the level of the ocean over time, and it is to this measure that we refer when we use the term sea level.

Constant **motion** of water in the oceans causes sea levels to vary. Sea level in Maine is about 10 in (25 cm) higher than it is in Florida. Pacific coasts sea level is approximately 20 in (50 cm) higher than the Atlantic.

Rotation of the **Earth** causes all fluids to be deflected when they are in motion. This deflection (or curvature of path) is known as the **Coriolis effect**. Ocean water and atmospheric winds are both influenced in the same way by the Coriolis effect. It creates a clockwise deflection in the northern hemisphere and a counterclockwise deflection in the southern.

Mean sea level can also be influenced by air **pressure**. If the air pressure is high in one area of the ocean and low in another, water will flow to the low pressure area. Higher pressure exerts more **force** against the water, causing the surface level to be lower than it is under low pressure. That is why a **storm** surge (sea level rise) occurs when a hurricane reaches land. Air pressure is unusually low in the eye of a hurricane, and so water is forced towards the eye, creating coastal **flooding**.

These wave-cut marine terraces in Iran are evidence of a historic lowering of the sea level.

Increases in **temperature** can cause sea level to rise. Warmer air will increase the water temperature, which causes water molecules to expand and increase the **volume** of the water. The increase in volume causes the water level to become higher.

Mean sea level has risen about 4 in (10 cm) during the last hundred years. Several studies indicate this is due to an average increase of 1.8°F (1°C) in world-wide surface temperatures. Some scientists believe rising sea levels will create environmental, social, and economic problems, including the submerging of coastal lands, higher water tables, **salt** water invasion of fresh water supplies, and increased rates of coastal **erosion**.

Sea level can be raised or lowered by tectonic processes, which are movements of the Earth's crustal plates. Major changes in sea level can occur over **geologic time** due to land movements, ice loading from **glaciers**, or increase and decrease in the volume of water trapped in ice caps.

About 30,000 years ago, sea level was nearly the same as it is today. During the ice age 15,000 years ago, it dropped and has been rising ever since.

Sea lily

Resembling a **plant** more than an **animal**, sea lilies are some of the most attractive but least-known animals of the deep oceans. Sea lilies are members of the class Crinoidea (phylum Echinodermata), a class that also includes the **feather stars**. Sea lilies are also related to more familiar echinoderms such as **sea urchins**, **starfish**, and **sea cucumbers**. Unlike these small, squat forms, however, the main body of a sea lily is composed of an extended, slender stalk that is usually anchored by a sim-

ple rootlike arrangement of arms. The main body, which has a jointed appearance, may reach up to 27.5 in (70 cm) in length, but most living species are much smaller. (Some fossil species have been discovered with a stalk exceeding 82 ft, or 25 m, in length.) Some sea lilies have a branched structure, while others are simple and straight in design. Sea lilies vary considerably in color, but most are delicate shades of yellow, pink, or red.

The main part of the body, the calyx, is carried at the top of the stalk, rather like a crown. This contains the main body organs and is further developed with a series of 5-10 featherlike arms. The number of arms appears to vary with **water temperature**: some of the larger, tropical species may have up to 200 arms. Each arm is further adorned with a large number of delicate pinnules which, when extended, increase the area available for trapping food. When the animal is not feeding, or if the arms are in danger of being eaten by a predatory **fish** or crustacean, the arms may be folded and the entire crown withdrawn. The mouth is located in the central disk at the base of these arms. The arms and pinnules together trap fine particles of food from the swirling water currents. Tiny grooves on the surface of each pinnule lead into larger grooves on the main arm, like streams joining a river, and continue across the surface of the calyx to the mouth.

Rather than being composed of living **tissue**, much of the body is made up of **calcium** carbonate, which provides a rigid framework that supports the head of the animal. Within this protective armour, the actual movements of the sea lily are restricted to simple bending, unlike the movements of feather stars, which are mobile and may move from safe resting places to an exposed site for feeding purposes.

Until recently, most sea lilies were only known from fossil remains. These species appear to have been quite abundant at certain times in the geological history of **Earth**. Today, some 80 species are known to exist. Despite this, little is known about these animals, largely because the vast majority tend to live in deep **ocean** trenches, often at depths of 3,935-4,265 ft (1,200-1,300 m) and occasionally as deep as 29,530 ft (9,000 m). Virtually no light penetrates the water at these depths, and living organisms are few and widely scattered. Most species living at such depths need to conserve their **energy**, and sea lilies, by virtue of their few living organs and tissues, probably have a very low rate of **metabolism**. Most of the food they receive comes in the form of "fecal rain" from the upper water levels: as animals and plants die, parts of their bodies fall through the water column where it is scavenged by other organisms. Although scavenging animals are widespread and numerous in the oceans, some of these materials do eventually reach the deepest regions and, in so doing, ensure a steady if limited supply of foodstuffs to specialized species such as sea lilies.

David Stone

Sea lions

Sea lions are large marine **mammals** in the family Otariidae, sub-order Pinnipedia, order Carnivora, found now along the Pacific and South Atlantic coasts and on many islands of the southern hemisphere. Sea lions may have appeared first on the Pacific shores during the Lower Miocene. They are less fully adapted to aquatic life than are the true **seals** (family Phocidae of the same sub-order Pinnipedia) and are believed to be evolutionarily more primitive than the seals.

Large male sea lions are about 8.2 ft (2.5 m) long, weigh about 1,144 lb (520 kg), and have a mane on the neck reaching the shoulders. Females are usually less than 6.6 ft (2 m) long and lack a mane. Adults are darker than the young, especially after the third year of life, although some are known to be gray, even pale gold or dull yellow. Newborn sea lions, on the other hand, are brown or dark brown. The fur of sea lions consists of one layer of coarse hair, with little undercoat fur, although a few underhairs may be present. For this reason the pelts of sea lions are valued for leather, not for fur.

Sea lions are often mistaken for seals when seen in zoos or in circuses. Sea lions have small external ears (which are absent in seals) and a short tail (which seals lack). The hind limbs of sea lions can be turned forward to aid with locomotion on land (which seals cannot do). In the **water**, sea lions use the front flippers for low-speed swimming and the hind flippers to swim faster.

Sea lions have a total of 34-38 teeth. The first and second upper incisors are small and divided by a deep groove into two cusps, and the third, outer, upper incisor is canine-like. The canine teeth are large, conical, pointed, and recurved. The premolars and molars are similar, with one main cup. The number of upper molars varies within and among the different genera of the otarids. The skull is somewhat elongated and rounded, but quite bear-like.

Sea lion eyes are protected from blowing sand by the third eyelid (nictitating **membrane**). Sea lions lack tear ducts, and their tears may be seen running down their face. The whiskers of sea lions are particularly sensitive.

The best known species of sea lion include *Zalophus californianus,* of which there are three isolated populations along the coast of California and in Japan. *Otaria byronia* is a species found in **South America**; *Neophoca*

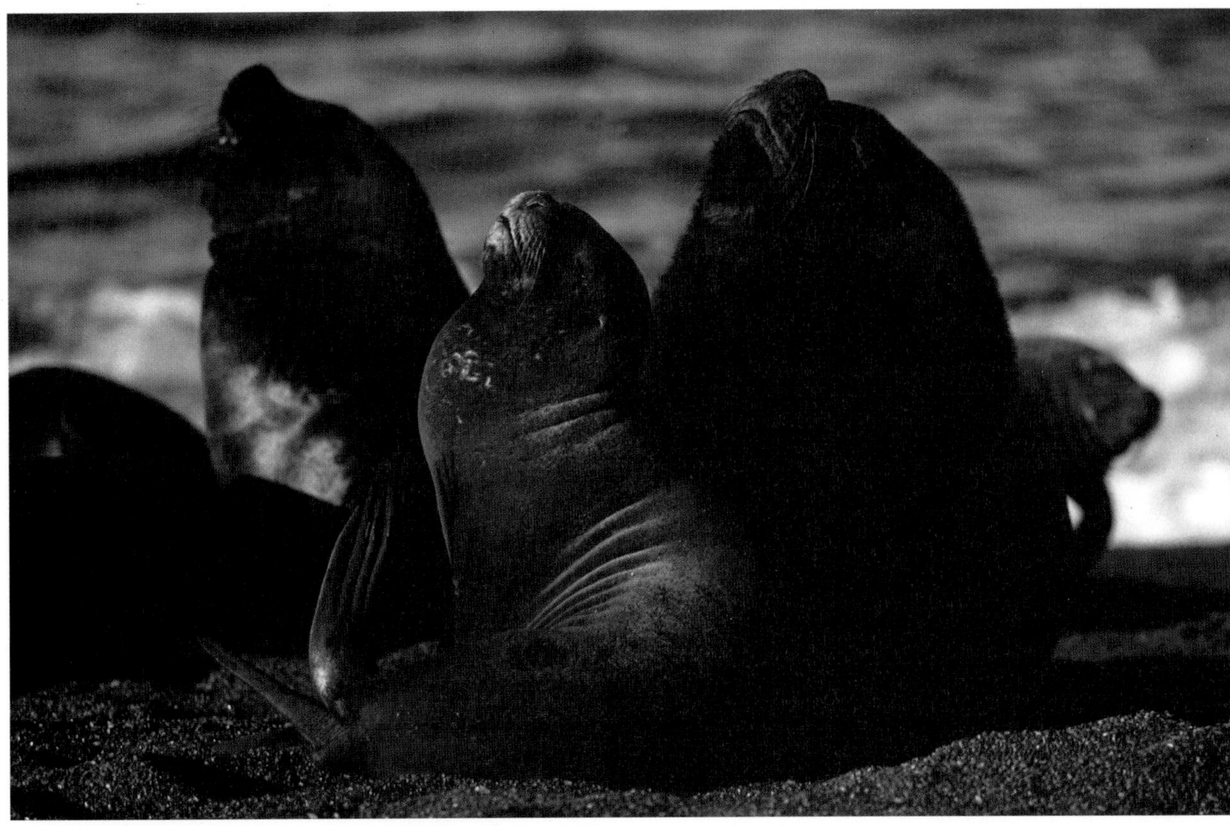

South American sea lions on the edge of the beach.

cinerea is a species of Australian sea lion confined to the waters west of Adelaide, while *N. hookeri* is found around the coast of New Zealand. *Eumetopias jubatus* is the northern or Steller sea lion found from northern California to Alaska.

The diet of sea lions has been studied by observing feeding directly by examining the stomach contents, regurgitated food, and feces. California sea lions feed mostly on **fish** such as hake or herring as well as on **squid** and **octopus**. The less common Steller sea lion on the coast of northern California and Oregon eats **flatfish** and rockfish, but in Alaskan waters it also eats sculpin and occasionally **salmon**. Fragments of **crabs** from the Pribilof Islands were found in stomachs of sea lions from that area, together with **shrimp** and common bivalve **mollusks**. Sea lions are known to accumulate as much as 35 lb (16 kg) of food in their stomach. The New Zealand sea lion *(Neophoca hookeri)* was reported to feed on **penguins**. Harem bulls (except perhaps those of the genus *Neophoca)* do not feed at all during the breeding season.

California sea lions are the trained animals of circuses and old time vaudeville. The feeding of sea lions have a great fascination for zoo visitors, but many sea lions fall victim to objects dropped into their pools, which they tend to swallow. A documented sea lion death was attributed to swallowing many stones weighing a total of 60 lb (27.3 kg). Other deaths were due to swallowing fallen leaves, which the **animal** could not digest. Although a few stones in a sea lion's stomach are not abnormal, animals kept within narrow confines may experience serious problems. A California sea lion born in a zoo was unable to feed itself at the age of 10 months and it had to be captured each day to be fed. As a consequence it suffered a torn diaphragm and a fatal pleuroperitoneal hemorrhage. In recent years great progress has been made in the management of zoological parks and public aquariums which permits sea lions and other marine mammals to live for many years.

Outside of the breeding season, sea lions live in large apparently unorganized herds, but with the approach of summer they separate into breeding and nonbreeding herds. The breeding herd consists of harem bulls, sexually mature cows, and newborn pups. Cows usually mature sexually about the end of the fourth year. The average harem consists of one bull with nine females. Bulls identify themselves by barking, advertise their location, declaring social status, or warning potential intruders.

The non-breeding sites where sea lions come out of the water are called hauling grounds. California sea lions gather in breeding sites, called rookeries, in May and August. Adult females stay most of the year at the breeding sites.

Copulation occurs predominantly on land. Gestation takes about 330 days and the females breed soon after the young (usually one, rarely two) are born. California and Stellar sea lion pups may suckle beyond their first year. Only the mother cares for the young which usually cannot swim for about two weeks.

The pups at **birth** are 30 in (76.9 cm) long and weigh 12.5 lb (5.7 kg). At six months they weigh 60 lb (27.3 kg). California sea lion milk has 35% **fat** and 13% protein, compared with cow's milk which has 3.45% fat and 3.3% protein. When the pup is born the mother makes loud trumpteting barks, and the pup answers with tiny bleats. They repeat and learn each other's sounds. After four days the mother goes to sea to find food and when she returns she calls and finds her own pup: they **touch**, sniff, rub noses, and recognize each other by their odor. Newborn sea lions have temporary teeth, which are replaced at four months. The teeth of sea lions are not used to chew food, which is swallowed whole. Estimates of the age of sea lions in the wild are based on the condition and size of their teeth. It is believed that in their natural **habitat** sea lions live about 15 years, while in captivity they may live up to 30 years. Food needs are relatively high: a one-year-old eats 5.1-9.9 lb (2.3-4.5 kg) of food daily, and an adult female consumes from 25-60 lb (11.4-27.2 kg).

Research on the social **behavior** of sea lions has been carried out both in their natural habitat and under laboratory conditions. California and Steller sea lions, especially the younger ones, display social interactions characterized by playful activities which take up about one third of their time. Otherwise they rest, often in contact with four or five larger animals. Young California sea lions exhibit manipulative play, tossing and retrieving small **rocks** or bits of debris. In the process they produce a variety of sounds, including barks, clicks, bangs, buzzes, and growls. All these sounds appear to have a social function. Sometimes they relate to a dominant-subordinate **relation** with a larger male who may be chasing, intimidating, and restricting the movement of a smaller male, especially when there is an incentive such as food, resting position, swimming pool space, or females. Aerial barking is typical of larger males to achieve dominance over the younger ones. Dominant or alpha animals occur in a sea lion group, and dominant and agonistic behavior has been extensively studied. Sea lions were also the first animals studied to determine the characteristics by which zoo animals recognize their keepers; this research was done in the early 1930s.

The diving performance of sea lions has been studied extensively. Diving **vertebrates** are known to exhibit bradycardia (a distinct slowing of the **heart** rate) during rapid submersion. At the moment of diving the nostrils are shut, and bradycardia can be produced even on land, without diving, by closing the nostrils. California sea lions have been trained to retrieve underwater rings placed at different depths and attached to a buoy in such a way as to determine that the animal reached the target. They were also trained to push signal arrays, and have returned in answer to the signal of a small waterproof strobe light. With appropriate training, taking only a few months, any **lake**, river, and even open sea are suitable test sites.

California sea lions may swim at speeds of 11-24 mph (17.7-38.7 kph) and dive to the depth of 1,300 ft (396.2 m). They may stay submerged for 10-15 minutes at a time. When they dive their heart beat may slow from 85 beats per minute on land to only 10 beats per minute. At such time the **blood** flow is reduced to all parts of the body, except to the **brain**. These are very important and valuable adaptations. In addition, thick body fat, called blubber, keeps sea lions warm in the cold seas. On land sea lions keep cool in hot **weather** by lying on wet sand.

Since 1972 the Marine Mammal Protection Act has protected sea lions along the cost of the United States in their breeding sites. There are about 100,000 sea lions in California. In the oceans the chief predators of sea lions are **sharks** and killer whales. Steller sea lions in the Arctic are also hunted by polar **bears**. In the United States, sea lions that are injured or ill are taken to Marine Mammal Centers to recover from injury, illness, or **malnutrition**. When ready to return to their natural habitat, a tag of the National Marine Fisheries Service is attached to one of back flippers. These tags help identify sea lions when rescued again, and to monitor their movements and activities.

See also Walruses.

Further Reading

Evans, Phyllis R. *The Sea World Book of Seals and Sea Lions.* New York: Harcourt Brace, 1986.

Ridgway, S. H., and R. Harrison, eds. *Handbook of Marine Mammals.* Vol. 1. The Walrus, Sea Lions, Fur Seals, and Sea Otter. London: Academic Press, 1981.

Riedman, Marianne. *The Pinnipeds: Seals, Sea Lions, and Walruses.* Berkeley: University of California Press, 1990.

Seals and Sea Lions of the World. New York: Facts on File, 1994.

Sophie Jakowska

Sea moths

Sea **moths** are small **fish** of the family Pegasidae, order Pegasiformes, subclass Actinopterygii, class Oste-

ichthyes. They are characterized by very large wing-like pectoral fins, which make them look like moths. They are found only in tropical Indian and West Pacific Oceans where they live mainly on sandy bottoms. There are about six species, of which *Pegasus volitans* is typical and reaches about 6 in (15 cm) in length. The body of sea moths is oddly shaped, broad and flat in front, tapering towards the tail. They seem encased in rings of bony plates like in an armor. The snout is pronounced and at times resembles a duck bill. They are also called dragonfish.

Sea snakes see **Elapid snakes**

Sea spiders

Sea spiders (phylum Arthropoda, class Pycnogonida) are a group of **arthropods** that take their common name from their superficial resemblance to the true spiders. Although rarely seen, these are widespread animals occurring in every **ocean**, with a preference for cooler waters. Sea spiders occupy a wide range of habitats: some species have been recorded from a depth of 19,685 ft (6,000 m), but the majority live in shallow coastal waters. Some 600 species have so far been identified. Most sea spiders are small animals, measuring from 0.04-0.4 in (1-10 mm) in length, but some deep sea species may reach a length of almost 2.4 in (6 cm). The body itself is usually quite small, the main **mass** of the spider being accounted for by its extremely long legs. The legs are attached to the anterior portion of the body (the prosoma) and are usually eight in number, although some species may have 10 or even 12 pairs. The body is segmented with the head bearing a proboscis for feeding, a pair of pincherlike claws known as chelicera, and a pair of segmented palps that are sensory and probably assist with detecting **prey**. Most sea spiders are either a white color or the color of their background; there is no evidence that they can change their body coloration to match different backgrounds. Many deep sea species are a reddish-orange color.

The majority of sea spiders crawl along the substrate in search of food and mates. They are often found attached to **sea anemones**, bryozoans, or **hydra**, on which they feed. They are all carnivorous species and feed by either grasping small prey with the chelicera, tearing off tiny polyps from corals or **sponges**, or by directly sucking up body fluids through the mouth, which is positioned at the extreme tip of the proboscis.

An unusual behavioral feature displayed by sea spiders is the male's habit of looking after the eggs once they have been laid by the female. As the female lays her eggs, they are fertilized by the male who then transfers them to his own body. Here they are grouped onto a special pair of legs known as ovigerous legs (which are greatly enlarged in males). Large masses of eggs may be collected—often as many as 1,000 on each leg. The male carries these egg clusters for several weeks until they hatch into tiny larvae that are known as a protonymphon. Even at this stage, some species continue to care for their offspring until they have further developed-a strategy designed to protect the vulnerable offspring from the wide range of potential predators that exist in these waters.

Sea squirts and salps

Classified within the same phylum (Chordata), sea squirts and salps belong to separate classes, the Ascidiacea and Thaliacea, respectively. Both groups are also known as tunicates, a group of primitive **chordates** which have a primitive feature known as the notochord-the earliest and simplest equivalent to the vertebrae of more developed animals. In appearance adult sea squirts and salps are barrel-shaped animals, resembling a small open bag with a tough surrounding "tunic" that has two openings through which **water** passes. Water enters the body through one of these openings through the buccal siphon, passing into a large and highly perforated sac where it is strained for food particles before passing out through a second opening, the atrial or cloacal siphon. Food particles such as **plankton** that have been retained in the sac pass directly into the stomach where they are digested. When the **animal** is not feeding, the buccal siphon is closed, thereby stopping the water flow. All adult sea squirts are sessile, being attached to **rocks**, shells, piers, **wood** pilings, ships, and even the sea bed where this provides a firm base.

One of the most obvious differences between sea squirts and salps is that the latter group have their openings at opposite ends of the body, whereas these are both arranged on the upper part of a sea squirt's body. The flow of water directly through a salp's body may therefore also be exploited as a simple means of moving from one place to another, although most salps rely on the larval phase of development for dispersal and long-distance movement.

The notochord, which distinguishes these animals from other soft-bodied marine organisms, is not visible in adult sea squirts or salps. Instead it makes an appearance in the larval stage, which resembles a tadpole. The larvae are free-living, and when they settle, they undergo a state of change known as **metamorphosis** in which the

notochord and nerve cord are lost and a simplified adult structure develops.

Sea squirts and salps are among the most successful colonizing marine animals and are commonly found on most seashores, with their range extending down to moderate depths. Sea squirts are often solitary, but some species may form colonies with the individuals united at the base, while others may form a gelatinous encrustation on the surface of rocks or on weeds. In colonial species, each individual has its own mouth opening but the second, or atrial opening, is common to the group.

Sea urchins

Sea urchins (phylum Echinodermata) are small marine species that have a worldwide distribution. All are free-living and solitary in nature; some 800 species have been identified to date. The body is characterized by its rounded or oval shape and, in most species, by the presence of large numbers of sharp spines of varying lengths. The underside is usually flattened in contrast to the convex upper surface. The term Echinodermata is taken from the Greek words *echinos* (spiny) and *derma* (skin) and is used to describe a wide range of animals, including **starfish** (Asteroidea), brittle stars (Ophiuroidea), sea lilies (Crinoidea), **sea cucumbers** (Holothuroidea), and the closely related **sand dollars** in the same taxonomic class, Echinoidea. In appearance, sea urchins may be black, brown, green, white, red, purple, or a combination of these colors. Most species measure from 2.4-4.7 in (6-12 cm), but some tropical species may reach a diameter of 13.8 in (35 cm). The entire body is contained within a toughened skeleton, or test. This consists of a number of closely fitting plates arranged in rows. The spines are usually circular and taper to a fine point; some may bear poisonous tips. The spines are attached to muscles in the body wall and, through a special ball and socket type arrangement, can be moved in any direction. The entire test, spines, and other external appendages are covered in a thin layer of **tissue**.

Adult sea urchins are radially symmetrical with unsegmented bodies. The body is made up of five equal and similar parts. They possess a spacious body cavity, which houses the digestive and reproductive organs as well as the large feeding parts and other organs. All echinoderms have a unique **organ** called a **water** vascular system which serves as a filtering mechanism and fluid circulating system.

Sea urchins are highly mobile and move by means of hundreds of tiny tube feet, called podia, which arise from pores in the test. When moving, these are extended in one direction and then shortened, pulling the body along in the process. The spines may also assist with movement. Most often sea urchins are found on rocky shorelines, rock pools, and sheltered depressions of coral reefs. Many remain attached to seaweed fronds. Some species that live in exposed habitats—for example, where wave action is strong—can burrow into soft **rocks** by continuously rubbing the spines against the rock substrate. In this way species such as *Paracentrotus lividus* and *Strongylocentrotus purpuratus* are able to obtain shelter. The tube feet, which may also function as tiny suction cups, enable sea urchins to climb wet rocks and steep cliffs with ease.

Sea urchins feed on a wide range of species, with an apparent preference for **algae** and sessile animals such as corals. Some species are carnivorous, while many deep sea species are thought to be detritus feeders. All sea urchins have an elaborate feeding mechanism known as Aristotle's lantern, after the Greek philosopher who first described this apparatus. This is made up of five large calcareous plates, each of which is sharply edged and forward pointing. Supported by a framework of rods and bars, the plates are capable of moving in all directions and provide the urchin with an effective rasping and chewing tool.

In between the spines are large numbers of tiny organs known as pedicellariae. These are small pincer-like structures that are used to remove debris from the surface of the body, but are also used to capture **prey** and pass food particles towards the mouth, which is located on the underside of the body.

All sea urchins are dioecious-either male or female. When mature, the gonads release large quantities of sperm and eggs into the sea. **Fertilization** is external in most sea urchins, although a few cold water species may retain their eggs near the mouth opening where they are protected by spines. The resulting larvae, known as an echinopluteus, are free-swimming and join the myriad of other tiny organisms that make up the **plankton** of the sea. As the echinopluteus matures, it begins to develop a hard outer covering. When this happens, it settles on the sea bed and undergoes a complex process of **metamorphosis**, the resulting **organism** being a minute (usually measuring less than 0.04 in or 1 mm) replica of the adult.

Despite their apparently formidable suit of armor, sea urchins are frequently eaten by seabirds, many of which drop the urchins from a height to break the hard outer test. Sea urchins are also preyed upon by **crabs** and a wide range of **fish**, such as parrot fishes, which are specialized at chewing hard materials such as corals. One specialist feeder on sea urchins is the sea otter. When the otter dives to find sea urchins, it also retrieves a small

rock from the sea bed; when it surfaces, it lies on its back, places the stone on its abdomen, and smashes the urchins against the stone, breaking through the test and reaching the flesh. Some of the larger tropical species such as *Tripneustes ventricocus* are also collected as a source of protein by **island** dwellers in the West Indies. Many other sea urchins are also collected and dried for sale to tourists. Overharvesting of ertain species has led to laws limiting their collection in some areas.

David Stone

Seaborgium see **Element, transuranium**

Seals

Seals are large carni vorous marine **mammals** in the order Pinnipedia that feed on **fish**, **squid**, and shell-fish; some even feed on **penguins**. They are aquatic animals that spend time on shores and ice floes. Seals have streamlined bodies and webbed digits, with the forelimbs acting as flippers, while the hind limbs are backwardly directed in swimming and act as a propulsive tail. A small tail is also present. There are three families of pinnipeds: the Otariidae (**sea lions**), the Odobenidae (the walrus), and the Phocidae (the true seals). The "earless" seals of the Phocidae, such as the monk seal and the ringed seal, lack external **ear** flaps, while the seals with external ears include the walrus, sea lions, and fur seals.

Seals are mammals

Seals are air-breathing mammals, with fur, placental development, and lactation of the newborns. Moreover, seals are endotherms, maintaining a constant internal **temperature** of about 97.7–99.5°F (36.5–37.5°C) regardless of the outside temperature.

General characteristics of seals

All seals are carnivores, eating fish, crustaceans, and krill (shrimp-like animals). Seals are related to terrestrial carnivores such as dogs and **cats**; they breed and rest on land, but are equally comfortable on land or in **water**. The thick layer of fatty blubber underneath the skin of seals serves to insulate the **animal**, to assist with buoyancy, and as an **energy** reserve when food is scarce.

The body

The body of a typical seal is long and streamlined. Each seal has four flippers, two in front and two in back. The hair covering the seal's entire body is of two types: soft underfur which insulates the seal against cold when on land, and coarser guard hairs above the underfur, which form the first line of protection against cold air temperatures. Whiskers, located on either side of the mouth, over the eyes, and around the nose, serve as tactile organs that help seals locate food and alert the seal to predators.

Temperature regulation

Seals regulate their body temperature in several ways. In cold temperatures, the peripheral **blood** vessels constrict, conserving **heat** by keeping the warm blood away from the external environment, while insulating blubber reduces heat loss. The hind flippers have numerous superficial blood vessels close to the skin and only a few deep blood vessels. When cold, seals press the hind flippers together, in effect "pooling" the heat contained in the numerous superficial vessels. The superficial vessels then conduct this heat to the deeper vessels, which keeps the internal organs warm and functioning properly.

A few species of seals are found in warmer climates. When seals get too hot, they lie in the surf, seek shade, or remain inactive. When the heat becomes extreme, they enter the water to cool off. Sea lions and fur seals are particularly sensitive to heat. When the outside temperature reaches 86°F (30°C), they are unable to maintain a stable internal temperature; in this condition, they stay immobile, or seek water if the temperature rises. The inability to dissipate heat makes these seals vulnerable to heat-related illness.

Internal organs

The small intestine of a seal is extremely long—an unusual feature for carnivores, which generally have short intestines. Long intestines are usually found in plant-eating animals, which need a long intestine to process the tough woody stems and fibers in their diet. Several theories have been proposed to explain the unusually long seal intestine. One theory holds that the high metabolic rate of seals makes a long intestine necessary. Another theory suggests that the heavy infestations of parasitic worms found in seals compromise normal intestinal function, and the greater length compensates for low-functioning areas of the intestine.

Another unusual feature of the seal's digestive tract is the stomach, which contains stones, some of them quite large. Small stones are probably swallowed accidentally, but some of the large stones might be deliberately swallowed. It is thought that these stones help seals to eject fish bones from the stomach, and may assist in

breaking up big chunks of food, since seals do not chew their food but swallow all items in one piece. Another interesting theory is that the stones might act as ballance, stabilizing the seal body and preventing the seal from tipping or rolling in the water.

Nervous system

The **nervous system** of a seal consists of the **brain** and spinal cord, along with a branching **tree** of nerves. Seal brains are relatively large in **relation** to their body weight: the brain accounts for about 35% of total body weight. This percentage is considerable when compared to the percentage of brain weight to total body weight in most terrestrial mammals. The spinal cord is quite short in seals, compared to other mammals.

Seal senses include **touch**, **smell**, **taste**, sight, **hearing**, and perhaps **echolocation**. Hearing in seals is especially keen, while smell is not well developed. Seal **vision** is remarkable in that vision underwater is about the same as a cat' s vision on land. Seal researchers have observed evidence of echolocation, in which an animal navigates by sensing the echo of sounds it emits that then bounce off of objects. Underwater, seals do indeed make clicks and similar sounds that suggest echolocation, but so far no definitive evidence has emerged that establishes the presence of this sense in seals.

Diving and reproduction

Half of a seal's life is spent on land, the other half in water. Seals are diving mammals, and have evolved the ability to stay underwater for long periods of time. The reproductive **behavior** of seals also demonstrates the "double life" of seals. Some seals migrate to long distances across the oceans to breed or feed.

Diving

Seals are accomplished divers, and have evolved a number of adaptations that allow them to survive underwater. Some seals, such as the Weddell seal, can stay underwater for over an hour. In order for an air-breathing animal such as a seal to remain submerged for such a long period of time, it must have a means of conserving **oxygen**. Another crucial diving **adaptation** is adjustment to the high **pressure** of the water at great depths. Pressure increases by 1 atmosphere for every 33 ft (10 m) of water, and at great depths, there is a danger that the weight of the water will crush an animal. Some seals, however, can dive to great depths and remain unaffected by the extremely high water pressure. Similarly, seals that dive to these depths have evolved a way to deal with decompression sickness. When a human comes to the surface rapidly after a deep dive, the swift change in pressure forces **nitrogen** out of the blood. The nitrogen bubbles that form in the blood vessels cause decompression sickness—the painful condition known as "the bends," named for the fact that people in this condition typically bend over in **pain**. If the nitrogen bubbles are numerous, they can block blood vessels, and if this happens in the brain it leads to a **stroke** and possibly death. Humans can prevent the bends by rising to the surface slowly. Seals, on the other hand, have evolved a way to avoid decompression altogether.

Northern elephant seals (*Mirounga angustirostris*) at the Ano Nueva Reserve, California. This species takes its name from its great size and overhanging snout: bulls weigh several tons and may be up to 20 ft (6.1 m) in length.

Oxygen-conserving adaptations

A diving seal uses oxygen with great efficiency. Seals have about twice as much blood per unit of **volume** as humans (in seals, blood takes up 12% of the total body weight; in humans, it takes up 7%). Blood carries oxygen from the lungs to other body tissues, so the high volume of blood in a seal makes it an efficient transporter of oxygen. In addition, the red blood cells of a seal contain a lot of hemoglobin. Hemoglobin transports oxygen in red blood cells, binding oxygen in the lungs and then releasing it into the body tissues. The high amount of hemoglobin in a seal's blood allows a high amount of oxygen to be ferried to the seal's tissues. The muscles of a seal also contain oxygen stores, bound to myoglobin, a protein similar in structure to hemoglobin.

Before a seal dives, it usually exhales. Only a small amount of oxygen is left behind in the body, and what little oxygen is left is used to its best advantage due to the oxygen-conserving adaptations. If a seal dives for an extraordinarily long period of time—such as an hour or more—body functions that don't actually require oxygen

Northern fur seal with his harem of female cows.

to work start to function anaerobically (without oxygen). The **heart** rate also slows, further conserving oxygen.

Avoiding decompression and dealing with water pressure

Decompression sickness occurs because nitrogen leaks out from the blood as water pressure changes. Since seals don't have a lot of gaseous air within their bodies at the start of a dive, the problem of decompression is avoided—there's not as much air for nitrogen to leak out of. Exhaling most of its oxygen at the start of a dive also helps the seal withstand water pressure. Human divers without a breathing apparatus are affected by high water pressures because they need air to supply oxygen underwater, and this air in the lungs is compressed underwater. Seals, which don't have this pool of compressible air, are unaffected by water pressure. Seals close their outside orifices before a dive, making then water-tight and incompressible and allowing dives to depths of 200 ft (60 m) or more.

Reproduction

Seal pups are born on land in the spring and summer. To take advantage of warmer seasonal environments and plentiful food, some seal species are migratory, feeding in one spot in the summer and early autumn, and then traveling to a warmer spot in the autumn and winter to give **birth** and mate shortly afterwards. Seals can give birth in large groups, in which a crowd of seals have returned to a particular spot to breed, or they can give birth alone. Migratory seals usually give birth in groups, after which they mate with males and conceive another pup.

Another way to ensure that a pup is born at an optimal time is to delay implantation of the embryo inside the uterus. In seals, **fertilization** (the meeting of

egg and sperm) may take place in April, but the embryo might not implant in the mother's uterus until October. This phenomenon of delayed implantation also occurs in roe **deer**, **armadillos**, and **badgers**. The total gestation period (the time it takes for the pup to develop inside its mother) is 9-15 months, depending on the species. The average active gestation period (the time from implantation to birth) is probably about 3-5 months.

Diversity

There are 19 species of earless seals, 9 species of sea lions, 5 species of fur seals, and 1 species of walrus.

Of the earless seals, some of the more familiar are the harbor seals that are found in the North Atlantic and Pacific Oceans. These seals position themselves on **rocks** or sandbars uncovered by low **tides**, swimming only when the high tide reaches them and threatens their **perch**. The seals that both entertain and annoy residents of San Francisco Bay with their loud barks and enormous appetites are harbor seals.

Another earless seal is the **elephant** seal, which can weigh up to 4 tons. The largest of all pinnipeds, the male elephant seal has a characteristic inflatable proboscis (nose) reminiscent of an elephant's trunk.

The harp seal was at one time one of the most endangered of the earless seals, since the pure white coat of the harp seal pup was prized by the fur industry. Harp seals are migratory animals and are found in the Arctic Atlantic.

Among the eared seals, the long-tusked walrus is one of the most familiar. **Walruses** use their tusks to lever themselves out of the water; at one time it was thought that they also used them to dig up food. Walruses can weigh up to 2 tons, feeding on **mollusks**, which they delicately suck out of the shell before spitting it out. Like all eared seals, walruses have front flippers that can be rotated forward, allowing them to walk and run on land, walk backward, and rest upright on their front flippers.

Sea lions are eared seals, commonly seen performing tricks in zoological parks. They lack the thick underfur seen in the earless seals, and so have not been hunted heavily for their pelts. In contrast, the fur seals are eared seals that have almost vanished completely due to intense hunting but are now protected: in 1972, the United States passed the Marine Mammal Protection Act, which outlaws the killing of seals for their fur and other products and restricts the selling of these products within the United States. As a result, fur seals and other seal species should remain relatively undisturbed by humans.

Further Reading

Allen, Sarah G., et al. "Red-Pelaged Harbor Seals of the San Francisco Bay Region." *Journal of Mammology* 74 (August 1993): 588-93

Campagna, Claudio. "Super Seals." *Wildlife Conservation* 95 (July-August 1992): 22-27

Golden, Frederic. "Hot-Blooded Divers." *Sea Frontiers* 38 (October 1992): 92-99

King, Judith. *Seals of the World.* Ithaca, N.Y.: Cornell University Press, 1983

Kooyman, Gerald L. *Weddell Seal: Consummate Diver.* Cambridge: Cambridge University Press, 1981

Monastersky, Richard. "The Cold Facts of Life: Tracking the Species That Thrive in the Harsh Antarctic." *Science News* 143 (24 April 1993): 269-71

Shafer, Kevin. "The Harps of St. Lawrence." *Wildlife Conservation* 96 (January-February 1993): 20-25

Zimmer, Carl. "Portrait in Blubber." *Discover* 13 (March 1992): 86-89

Kathleen Scogna

Seamounts

Seamounts are **submarine** mountains, often volcanic cones, that project 150-3,000 ft (50-1,000 m) or more above the **ocean** floor. They are formed primarily by rapid undersea buildups of basalt, a dark, fine-grained rock that is the main component of the ocean's crust.

Seamounts form by submarine volcanism. After repeated eruptions, the **volcano** builds upwards into shallower **water**. If a seamount eventually breaches the water's surface, it becomes an **island**. Wave action can then erode the exposed rock, and the peak may be flattened or leveled off. Flat-topped, submerged seamounts, called guyots or tablemounts, are seamounts that once breached the ocean's surface, but later subsided.

Sometimes seamounts occur as matching pairs located on opposite sides of an oceanic ridge. Speculation on the origins of these features led to the idea that such pairs were once part of a single volcanic complex that had split and separated. This helped support the concept that there are spreading centers along the ocean ridges where slabs or plates of the earth's **lithosphere** are moving away from each other. Volcanic eruptions form new seafloor and seamounts in the gap, or rift, that develops. This spreading, an **integral** part of the theory of **plate tectonics** (which explains the **motion** of the earth's plates) has been measured to occur at a rate of between 0.8-4.0 in (2-10 cm) per year.

Seamounts are more numerous than terrestrial volcanoes and reach greater heights. They may form in

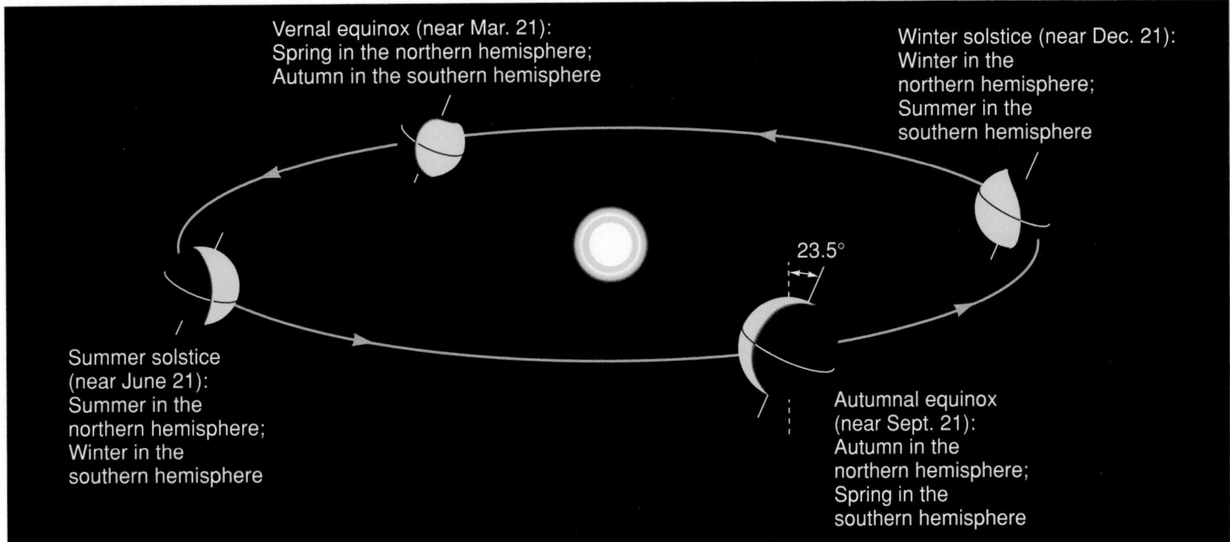

The seasons.

groups or clusters, or can be found aligned in submarine volcanic **mountain** chains known as oceanic ridges. As seamounts slowly move away from the oceanic ridge due to seafloor spreading, their tremendous **mass** causes them to subside. At the same time, sediment "rains" down from above, slowly burying them over millions of years. As a result, especially tall seamounts may occur as isolated features rising from the **abyssal plain**. This is the deep, flat section of the ocean floor far removed from an oceanic ridge, where sediments are often thousands of feet thick. Somewhat closer to an **oceanic ridge**, where sediments are not so thick, the tops of partially buried seamounts form what are called abyssal hills.

Some seamounts are very tall, broad volcanic features with gentle slopes, known as shield volcanoes. Mauna Kea on the island of Hawaii is a good example. It rises over 32,810 ft (10,000 m) above the ocean floor, making Mauna Kea—not Mt. Everest in the Himalayas—the world's highest mountain. These massive volcanic structures form when isolated hot plumes of molten rock rise from the Earth's mantle, forming what is called a **hot spot**. Iceland is another example of an island formed by hot spot activity.

Seasons

Seasons on the **Earth** are found only in the *temperate zones*. These zones extend from 23.5° north (and south) latitude to 66.5° north (and south) latitude. In these regions of the Earth nature exhibits four seasons; spring, summer, autumn (or fall) and winter. Each season is characterized by differences in **temperature**, amounts of **precipitation**, and the length of daylight. Spring comes from an Old English word meaning to rise. Summer originated as a Sanskrit word meaning half year or season. Autumn comes originally from a Etruscan word for maturing. Winter comes from an Old English word meaning wet or water. The equatorial regions or torrid zones have no appreciable seasonal changes and here one generally finds only a wet season and a dry season. In the polar regions we have only a light season and a dark season.

In the Northern Hemisphere, astronomers assign an arbitrary starting date for each season. Spring begins around March 21 and summer begins around June 21. Autumn begins around September 23 and Winter around December 21. Because every fourth year is a leap year and February then has 29 days, the dates of these seasonal starting points change slightly. In the Southern Hemisphere the seasons are reversed with spring beginning in September, summer in December, fall in March, and winter in June. Seasons in the Southern Hemisphere are generally milder due to the moderating presence of larger amounts of **ocean** surface as compared to the Northern Hemisphere.

Changes in the seasons are caused by the Earth's movement around the **Sun**. Because the Earth orbits the Sun at varying distances, many people think that the seasons result from the changes in the Earth-Sun **distance**. This belief is incorrect. In fact, the Earth is actually closer to the Sun in January compared to June by approximately three million miles.

The Earth makes one complete revolution about the Sun each year. The reason for the seasons is that the axis of the **Earth's rotation** is tilted with respect to the **plane** of its **orbit**. This tilt, called the obliquity of the Earth's axis, is 23.5degrees from a line drawn **perpendicular** to the plane of the Earth's orbit. As the Earth orbits the Sun, there are times of the year when the North Pole is alternately tilted toward the Sun (during northern hemispheric summer) or tilted away from the Sun (during northern hemispheric winter). At other times the axis is generally **parallel** to the incoming Sun's rays. During summer, two effects contribute to produce warmer **weather**. First, the Sun's rays fall more directly on the Earth's surface and this results in a stronger heating effect. The second reason for the seasonal temperature differences results from the differences in the amount of daylight hours versus nighttime hours. The Sun's rays warm the Earth during daylight hours and the Earth cools at night by re-radiating **heat** back into **space**. This is the major reason for the warmer days of summer and cooler days of winter. The orientation of the Earth's axis during summer results in longer periods of daylight and shorter periods of darkness at this time of year. At the mid-northerly latitudes summer days have about 16 hours of warming daylight and only eight hours of cooling nights. During mid-winter the pattern is reversed and we have longer nights and shorter days. To demonstrate that it is the daylight versus darkness **ratio** that produces climates that make growing seasons possible, one should note that even in regions only 30° from the poles one finds plants such as **wheat**, corn, and potatoes growing. In these regions the Sun is never very high in the sky but because of the orientation of the Earth's axis, the Sun remains above the **horizon** for periods for over 20 hours a day from late spring to late summer.

Astronomers have assigned names to the dates at which the official seasons begin. When the axis of the Earth is perfectly parallel to the incoming Sun's rays in spring the Sun stands directly over the equator at noon. As a result, daylight hours equal night time hours everywhere on the Earth. This gives rise to the name given to this date, the vernal **equinox**. Vernal refers to spring and the word equinox means *equal night*. On the first day of fall, the autumnal equinox also produces 12 hours of daylight and 12 hours of darkness everywhere on the Earth.

The name given for the first day of summer results from the observation that as the days get longer during the spring, the Sun's height over its noon horizon increases until it reaches June 21. Then on successive days it dips lower in the sky as the Earth moves toward the autumn and winter seasons. This gives rise to the name for that date, the Summer **Solstice**, because it is as though the Sun "stands still" in its noon height above the horizon. The Winter Solstice is likewise named because on December 21 the sun reaches the lowest noon time height and appears to "stand still" on that date as well.

In the past, early humans celebrated the changes in the seasons on some of these cardinal dates. The vernal equinox was a day of celebration for the early Celtic tribes in ancient Britain, France, and Ireland. Other northern European tribes also marked the return of warmer weather on this date. Even the winter solstice was a time to celebrate, as it marked the lengthening days that would lead to spring. The ancient Romans celebrated the Feast of Saturnalia on the winter solstice. And even though there are no historical records to support the choice of a late December date for the **birth** of Christ, Christians in the fourth century A.D. chose to celebrate his birth on the winter solstice. In the Julian calender system in use at that time this date fell on December 25.

See also Global climate.

Further Reading

Abell, George, David Morrison, and Sydney Wolff. *Exploration of the Universe*. 6th ed. Philadelphia: Saunders, 1993.

Hartman, William. *The Cosmic Voyage*. Belmont, CA: Wadsworth, 1992.

KEY TERMS

Autumnal equinox—The date in the fall of the year when the Earth experiences 12 hours of daylight and 12 hours of darkness, usually about September 23rd.

Obliquity—The amount of tilt of the Earth's axis. This tilt is equal to 23.5 degrees drawn from a line perpendicular to the orbit of the Earth.

Summer solstice—The date on which the Sun is highest in the sky at noon, usually about June 21st.

Temperate zones—The two regions on the Earth bounded by the 23.5 degree latitude and the 66.5 degree latitude.

Torrid zone—A zone on the Earth bounded by 23.5 degrees North and South Latitude.

Vernal equinox—The date in the spring of the year when the Earth experiences 12 hours of daylight and 12 hours of darkness, usually on March 21st.

Winter solstice—The date on which the Sun's noontime height is at its lowest, usually on December 21st.

Pasachoff, Jay. *Astronomy: From the Earth to the Universe, 4th ed.* Philadelphia: Saunders, 1991.

Zeilik, Michael. *Astronomy: The Evolving Universe.* 4th ed. New York: Wiley, 1991.

Darrel B. Hoff

Seaweed see **Algae**

Secondary pollutants

Secondary pollutants are not emitted directly to the air, **water**, or **soil**. Secondary pollutants are synthesized in the environment by chemical reactions involving primary, or emitted chemicals.

The best known of the secondary pollutants are certain gases that are synthesized by photochemical reactions in the lower atmosphere. The primary emitted chemicals in these reactions are hydrocarbons and gaseous oxides of **nitrogen** such as nitric oxide and nitrogen dioxide. These emitted chemicals participate in a complex of ultraviolet-driven photochemical reactions on sunny days to synthesize some important secondary pollutants, most notably **ozone**, peroxy acetyl nitrate, **hydrogen** peroxide, and **aldehydes**. These secondary compounds, especially ozone, are the harmful ingredients of oxidizing or photochemical smogs that cause damages to people and vegetation exposed to this type of **pollution**.

Most ozone is found in the upper atmosphere, where it acts to screen out much of the harmful **radiation** from the **sun**. Upper-level ozone is an important part of the earth's life support sytem. Lower-level ozone is created when sunlight hits hydrocarbons and nitrogen oxides released into the lower atmosphere by industrial and natural processes. Ozone is well known as an irritant to human respiratory systems, as a strong oxidant that causes materials to age rapidly and degrade in strength, and as a toxic chemical to plants. In terms of causing damage to agricultural and wild plants, ozone is the most damaging air pollutant in **North America**. Low-level ozone also acts as a greenhouse gas, restricting the escape of **heat** from the earth's surface and thus contributing to the **global warming** process.

Scientists estimate that the amount of low-level ozone currently in the earth's atmosphere is 100-200 times higher than it was only 100 years ago. The formation of low-level ozone can be slowed by reducing emissions of human-created hydrocarbons and nitrogen oxides into the atmosphere. Reducing **hydrocarbon** emissions by using catalytic converters on vehicles and generally reducing **automobile** travel time helps, as does the use of filtering devices to scrub industrial air emissions. However, many filters and converters fail to remove nitrogen oxides from emissions, and human-produced nitrogen oxides can combine with naturally produced hydrocarbons just as easily as with human-produced hydrocarbons. Planting tress and plants doesn't help, but the development and installation of converters and filters for removing both hydrocarbons and nitrogen oxides can.

Secondary pollutants can also be formed in other ways. For example, when soils and surface waters become acidified through atmospheric depositions or other processes, naturally occurring **aluminum** in soil or sediment **minerals** becomes more soluble and therefore, becomes more available for uptake by organisms. The soluble, ionic forms of aluminum are the most important toxic **factor** to plants growing in acidic soils and to **fish** in acidic waters. In this context, aluminum can be considered to be a secondary pollutant because it is made biologically available as a consequence of acidification.

A few **pesticides** generate toxic chemicals when they are chemically transformed in the environment, and this phenomenon can also be considered to represent a type of secondary pollution. For example, dithiocarbamate is a **fungicide** used in the cultivation of potatoes. Ethylene thiourea is an important metabolite of this chemical, formed when the original fungicide is broken down by **microorganisms** in soil. Ethylene thiourea is relatively stable in soils and also somewhat mobile so that it can leach into ground water. Ethylene thiourea has been demonstrated to be carcinogenic in **mammals**, and it therefore represents an important type of toxicity that was not characteristic of the original fungicide.

See also Smog.

Secretary bird

The secretary bird (*Sagittarius serpentarius*) is the only member of the family Sagittariidae. This family is part of the Accipitriformes, which includes other hawk-like **raptors** such as **hawks**, **eagles**, **vultures**, kites, **falcons**, and the osprey.

The secretary bird is native to sub-Saharan **Africa**, and occurs in open **grasslands** and savannas. The species is wide-ranging, and some populations are nomadic, wandering extensively in search of locations with large populations of small **mammals** or **insects**, their principal foods.

Secretary **birds** are large birds, standing as tall as 4 ft (1.2 m), and weighing about 9 lb (4 kg). Their wings are long and pointed, and the neck is long. Secretary

birds have a strong, hooked, raptorial beak, and a prominent crest on the back of their heads. The legs are very long, and the strong feet have sharp, curved claws.

The basic coloration of secretary birds is gray, with black feathers on the upper legs, on the trailing half of the wings, and on the base of the tail. Two long, central, black-tipped feathers extend from the base of the tail. There are bare, orange-colored patches of skin around the eyes. The sexes are similarly colored, but male secretary birds are slightly larger.

Secretary birds are believed to have received their common name after the feathers of their backward-pointing crest, which are thought to vaguely resemble quill-pens stuck into the woolly wig of a human scribe of the nineteenth century. Their erect posture and grey-and-black plumage is also thought to suggest the formal attire and demeanor of a human secretary.

Secretary birds hunt during the day, mostly by walking deliberately about to find **prey**, which when discovered are run down and captured. Secretary birds occasionally stamp the ground with their feet, to cause prey to stir and reveal its presence. The food of secretary birds consists of small mammals, birds, **reptiles**, and large insects, such as **grasshoppers** and **beetles**. They are known to kill and eat **snakes**, including deadly poisonous ones, which like other larger prey items are dexterously battered to death with the feet. Because of their occasional snake-killing propensities, secretary birds are highly regarded by some people.

Secretary birds can fly well, and sometimes soar, but they do not do so very often. They prefer to run while hunting, and to escape from their own dangers. They roost in trees at night, commonly in pairs.

Secretary birds are territorial. They build a bulky, flat nest of twigs in a thorny **tree**, which may be used for several years. Secretary birds lay 2-3 eggs. These are incubated by both sexes, which also share the duties of caring for the young. The babies are downy and feeble at **birth**. The young are initially fed directly with nutritious, regurgitated fluids, and later on with solid foods that are regurgitated onto the nest, for the young to feed themselves with. Young secretary birds do not fight with each other, unlike the young of many other species of raptors. Consequently, several offspring may be raised from the same brood. They typically fledge after about two months.

Secretary birds are commonly considered to be a beneficial species, because they eat large numbers of potentially injurious small mammals, insects, and to a lesser degree, snakes. Secretary birds are sometimes kept as pets, partly because they will kill large numbers of small mammals and snakes around the home. Unfortunately, the populations of these birds are declining in many areas, due largely to **habitat** changes, but also to excessive collecting of the eggs and young.

A secretary bird. Standing nearly 4 ft (1.2 m) high, the bird can kill the most venemous of snakes by striking them repeatedly with its taloned feet. In South Africa it has sometimes been tamed and kept around homes to aid in rodent and snake control.

Sedges

Sedges are monocotyledonous plants in the genus *Carex* that make up most of the species in the family Cyperaceae. This family consists of about 4,000 species distributed among about 90 genera, occurring world-wide in moist habitats in all of the major climatic zones. The sedges are the largest group in the family with about 1,100 species, followed by the papyrus or nut-sedges (*Cyperus* spp.; 600 species), bulrushes (*Scirpus* spp.; 250 species), and beak-rushes (*Rhynchospora* spp.; 250 species).

The major importance of sedges and other members of this family is their prominent role in many types of ecological communities and the fact that they are an important source of food for many species of grazing animals. A few species are also of minor economic importance as food for humans.

Biology of sedges

Sedges are superficially grass-like in their morphology, but they differ from the **grasses** (family Poaceae) in some important respects.

Most species of sedges are perennial plants, with only a few having an annual life cycle. Sedges are herba-

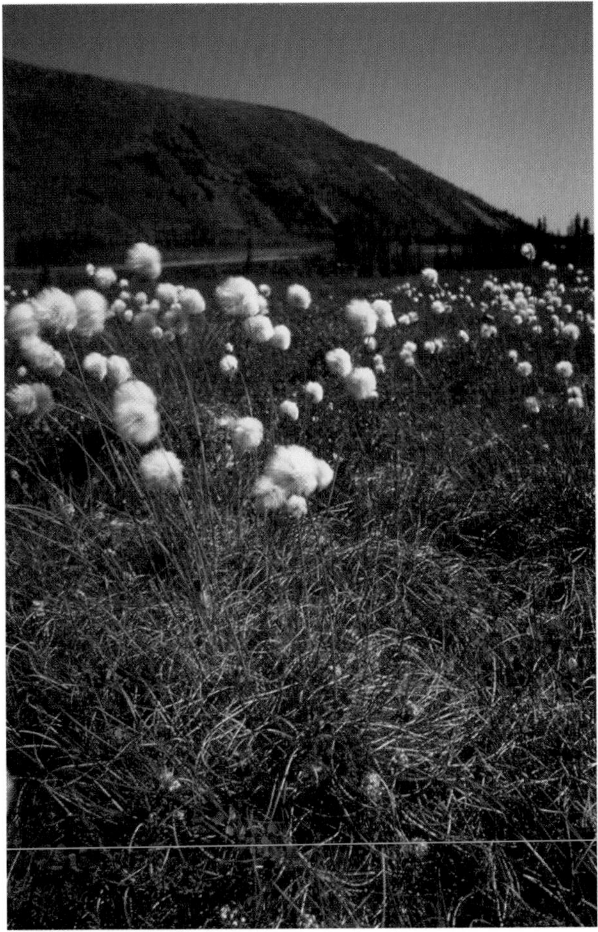

Cottongrass in the Yukon.

ceous, dying back to the ground surface at the end of the growing season but then re-growing the next season by sprouting from underground rhizomes or roots. One distinguishing characteristic of the sedge is its three-angled or triangular cross-section of the stem.

The flowers of sedges are small and have some reduced or missing parts. Referred to as florets, they are either male (staminate) or female (pistillate), although both sexes can be present in the same cluster of florets, or inflorescence. Usually, the staminate florets occur in a discrete zone at the top of the inflorescence, with the pistillate florets beneath. Sedges achieve **pollination** by shedding their pollen to the **wind**, which then carries these grains to the stigmatic surfaces of female florets. The **fruits** of sedges are dry, one-seeded achenes, sometimes enclosed within an inflated structure called a perigynium.

Wetlands are usually the **habitat** for various types of sedges. Sedges may occur as terrestrial plants rooted in moist ground or as emergent aquatic plants, often rooted in the sediment of shallow **water** at the edge of a pond or **lake**, but with the flowering stalk and some of their leaves emergent into the atmosphere. Some species of sedge can occur in habitats that are rather dry, as in the case of some arctic and alpine sedges.

Sedges in ecosystems

Sedges are an important component of the **plant** communities of many types of natural habitats, particularly in marshes, swamps, and the shallow-water habitats along the edges of streams, ponds, and lakes. Because sedges are a relatively nutritious food for grazing animals, places rich in these plants are an important type of habitat for many types of herbivorous animals. These can range from the multitudinous species of **insects** and other **invertebrates** that feed on sedges, to much larger grazing animals such as elk (*Cervus canadensis*), white-tailed **deer** (*Odocoileus virginianus*) and other herbivores. Even grizzly **bears** (*Ursus arctos*) will feed intensively on sedges at certain times of the year when other sources of **nutrition** are not abundant, for example, in the springtime after the bear has emerged from its winter **hibernation**.

Sedges and their relatives can sometimes dominate extensive tracts of vegetation, especially in places where shallow-water wetlands have developed on relatively flat terrain. For example, the extensive marshes and wet prairies of the Everglades of south Florida are dominated by the sawgrass (*Cladium jamaicensis*), a member of the sedge family.

Economically important sedges

No species of true sedges (that is, species of *Carex*) are of direct economic importance to humans. However, a few species in other genera of the sedge family are worth mentioning in this respect. The papyrus or **paper** rush (*Cyperus papyrus*) grows abundantly in marshes in parts of northern **Africa** and elsewhere, where it has been used for millennia to make paper, to construct reed-boats, to make thatched roofs, to strengthen dried mud-bricks, and for other purposes. There are numerous biblical references to the great abundance of papyrus that used to occur in wetlands in northern Egypt, but these marshy habitats have now been drained, and the species is considered to be rare in that region.

The stems of papyrus and other species of *Cyperus* and the related bulrushes (*Scirpus* spp.) have also been used for weaving into mats and baskets. A species that should be mentioned in this regard is the Chinese mat grass (*Cyperus tegetiformis*), which is commonly used for matting in eastern **Asia**.

KEY TERMS

Achene—A dry, one-seeded fruit, such as those of members of the sedge family.

Floret—A small flower, often with some reduced or missing parts. Florets are often arranged within dense clusters, such as the inflorescences of species in the sedge family.

Inflorescence—A grouping or arrangement of florets or flowers into a composite structure.

Perigynium—A sac-like bract that surrounds the ovary or seed in many members of the sedge family.

The bulbous tubers of the edible nut-sedge (*Cyperus esculentus*) and the water **chestnut** (*Eleocharis tuberosa*) are harvested and eaten as a starchy food. The water chestnut probably originated in China and the edible nut-sedge in Egypt.

A few species of sedges and related plants are considered to be significant weeds in some places. In **North America**, for example, the edible nut-sedge has escaped from cultivation and has become a weed of wetlands in some regions.

Further Reading

Woodland, D.W. *Contemporary Plant Systematics.* Englewood Cliffs, NJ: Prentice-Hall, 1991.

Bill Freedman

Sediment and sedimentation

Sediments are loose **Earth** materials such as sand that accumulate on the land surface, in river and **lake** beds, and on the **ocean** floor. Sediments form by **weathering** of rock. They then erode from the site of weathering and are transported by **wind**, **water**, ice, and **mass** wasting, all operating under the influence of gravity. Eventually sediment settles out and accumulates after transport; this process is known as deposition. Sedimentation is a general term for the processes of **erosion**, transport, and deposition. Sedimentology is the study of sediments and sedimentation.

There are three basic types of sediment: rock fragments, or clastic sediments; mineral deposits, or chemical sediments; and rock fragments and organic **matter**, or organic sediments. Dissolved **minerals** form by weathering **rocks** exposed at the Earth's surface. Organic matter is derived from the decaying remains of plants and animals.

Weathering

Clastic and chemical sediments form during weathering of **bedrock** or pre-existing sediment by both physical and chemical processes. Organic sediments are also produced by a combination of physical and chemical weathering. Physical (or mechanical) weathering-the disintegration of Earth materials-is generally caused by abrasion or fracturing, such as the striking of one pebble against another in a river or stream bed, or the cracking of a rock by expanding ice. Physical weathering produces clastic and organic sediment.

Chemical weathering, or the decay and dissolution of Earth materials, is caused by a variety of processes. However, it results primarily from various interactions between water and rock material. Chemical weathering may alter the mineral content of a rock by either adding or removing certain chemical components. Some mineral by-products of chemical weathering are dissolved by water and transported below ground or to an ocean or lake in solution. Later, these dissolved minerals may precipitate out, forming deposits on the roof of a **cave** (as stalactites), or the ocean floor. Chemical weathering produces clastic, chemical, and organic sediments.

Erosion and transport

Erosion and transport of sediments from the site of weathering are caused by one or more of the following agents: gravity, wind, water, or ice. When gravity acts alone to move a body of sediment or rock, this is known as **mass wasting**. When the forces of wind, water, or ice act to erode sediment, they always do so under the influence of gravity.

Agents of erosion and transport

Gravity

Large volumes of sediment, ranging in size from mud to boulders, can move downslope due to gravity, a process called mass wasting. Rock falls, landslides, and mudflows are common types of mass wasting. If you have ever seen large boulders on a roadway you have seen the results of a rock fall. Rock falls occur when rocks in a cliff face are loosened by weathering, break loose, and roll and bounce downslope. Landslides consist of rapid downslope movement of a mass of rock or **soil**, and require that little or no water be present. Mud

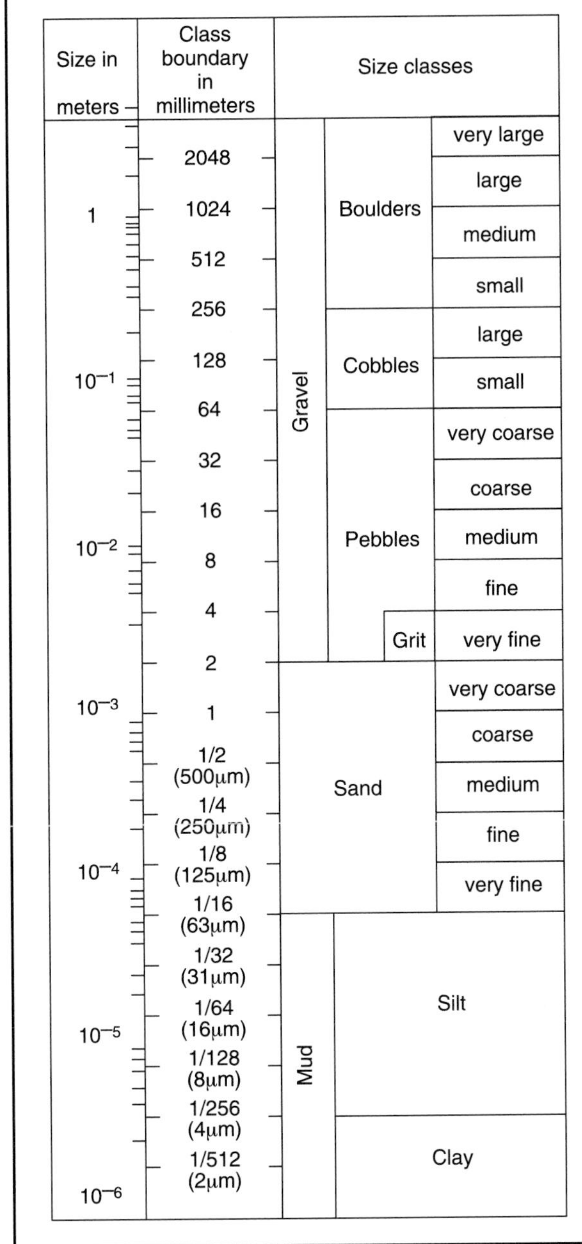

Size in meters
Class boundary in millimeters
Size classes
1
10⁻¹
10⁻²
10⁻³
10⁻⁴
10⁻⁵
10⁻⁶
2048
1024
512
256
128
64
32
16
8
4
2
1
1/2 (500μm)
1/4 (250μm)
1/8 (125μm)
1/16 (63μm)
1/32 (31μm)
1/64 (16μm)
1/128 (8μm)
1/256 (4μm)
1/512 (2μm)
Gravel
Boulders
very large
large
medium
small
Cobbles
large
small
Pebbles
very coarse
coarse
medium
fine
Grit
very fine
Sand
very coarse
coarse
medium
fine
very fine
Mud
Silt
Clay

Figure 1. Table of names for sedimentary particles based on grain size.

flows occur when a hillside composed of fine grained material becomes nearly saturated by heavy rainfall. The water helps lubricate the sediment, and a lobe of mud quickly moves downslope. Other types of mass wasting include slump, creep, and **subsidence**.

Water

Water is the most effective agent of transport, even in the **desert**. When you think of water erosion, you probably think of erosion mainly by stream water, which is channelized. However, water also erodes when it flows over a lawn or down the street, in what is known as sheet flow. Even when water simply falls from the sky and hits the ground in droplets, it erodes the surface. The less vegetation that is present, the more water erodes - as droplets, in sheets, or as channelized flow.

Wind

You may think of wind as a very important agent of erosion, but it is really only significant where little or no vegetation is present. For this reason, deserts are well known for their wind erosion. However, as mentioned above, even in the desert, infrequent, but powerful rain storms are still the most important agent of erosion. This is because relatively few areas of the world have strong prevailing winds with little vegetation, and because wind can rarely move particles larger than sand or small pebbles.

Glacial ice

Ice in **glaciers** is very effective at eroding and transporting material of all sizes. Glaciers can move boulders as large as a house hundreds of miles.

If you look around, glaciers are not a very common sight these days. However, at times in the geologic past, continent-sized glaciers covered vast areas of the Earth at middle to high latitudes. Today, continental glaciers occur only on **Antarctica** and Greenland. In addition, many smaller glaciers exist at high altitudes on some mountains. These are called alpine glaciers.

Sediment erosion

Generally, erosive agents remove sediments from the site of weathering in one of three ways: impact of the agent, abrasion (both types of mechanical erosion, or corrasion), or corrosion (chemical erosion). The mere impact of wind, water, and ice erodes sediments; for example, flowing water exerts a **force** on sediments causing them to be swept away. The eroded sediments may already be loose, or they may be torn away from the rock surface by the force of the water. If the flow is strong enough, clay, silt, sand, and even gravel, can be eroded in this way.

Abrasion is the second mechanism of sediment erosion. Abrasion is simply the removal of one Earth material by the impact of another. Rock hounds smooth stones by "tumbling" them in a container with very hard sand or silt particles known as **abrasives**. When you use sand paper to smooth a **wood** surface, you are using the abrasive qualities of the sand embedded in the paper to erode the wood. In nature, when water (or wind or ice) flows over a rocky surface (for example, a stream bed), sedi-

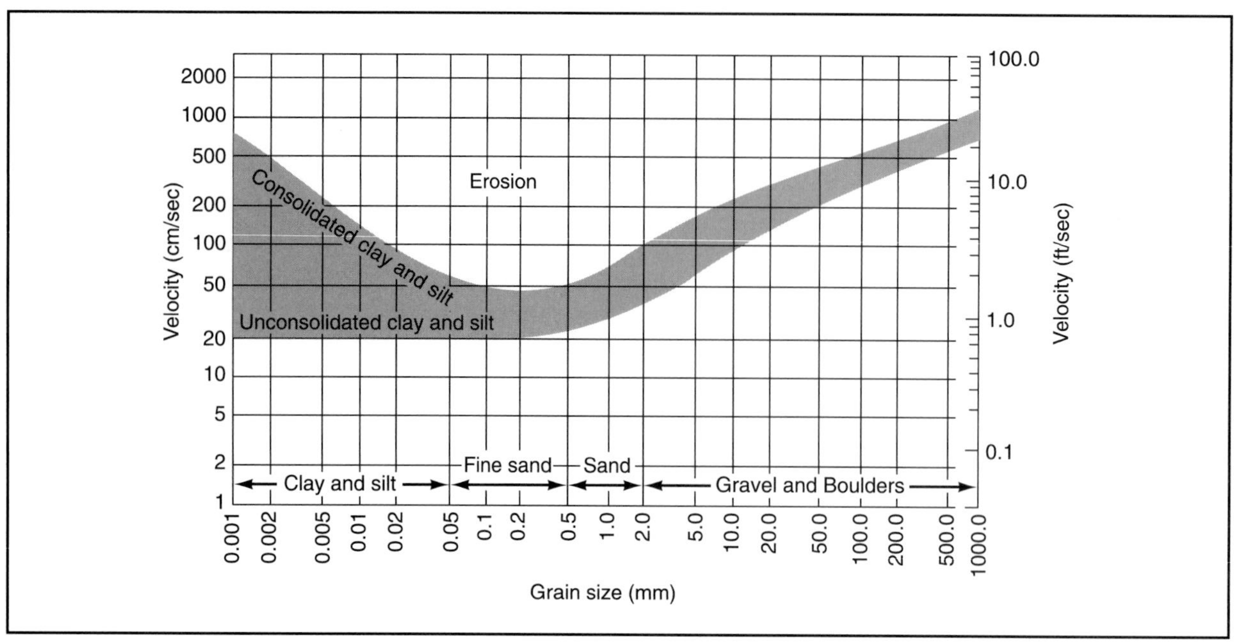

Figure 2. This graph illustrates that consolidated, fine-grained clay deposits subjected to stream erosion can be nearly as difficult to erode as gravel and boulders.

mentary particles that are being transported by the flow strike the surface, and occasionally knock particles loose. Keep in mind that while the bedrock surface is abraded and pieces are knocked loose, the particles in transport are also abraded, becoming rounder and smoother with time.

Corrosion, or chemical erosion, the third erosional mechanism, is the dissolution of rock or sediment by the agent of transport. Wind is not capable of corrosion, and corrosion by ice is a much slower process than by liquid water. Corrosion in streams slowly dissolves the bedrock or sediments, producing mineral solutions (minerals dissolved in water) and aiding in the production of clastic sediments by weakening rock **matrix**.

Sediment size

Sediments come in all shapes and sizes. Sediment sizes are classified by separating them into a number of groups, based on metric measurements, and naming them using common terms and size modifiers. The terms, in order of decreasing size, are boulder (> 256 mm), cobble (256 - 64 mm), pebble (64 - 2 mm), sand (2 - 1/16 mm), silt (1/16 - 1/256 mm), and clay (< 256 mm). The modifiers in decreasing size order, are very coarse, coarse, medium, fine, and very fine. For example, sand is sediment that ranges in size from 2 millimeters to 1/16 mm. Very coarse sand ranges from 2 mm to 1 mm; coarse from 1 mm to 1/2 mm; medium from 1/2 mm to 1/4 mm; fine from 1/4 mm to 1/8 mm; and very fine from 1/8 mm to 1/16 mm. Unfortunately, the entire classification is not as consistent as the terminology for sand—not every group includes size modifiers.

Sediment load

When particles are eroded and transported by wind, water, or ice, they become part of the transport medium's sediment load. There are three categories of load that may be transported by an erosional agent: dissolved load, suspended load, and bedload. Wind is not capable of dissolving minerals, and so it does not transport any dissolved load. The dissolved load in water and ice is not visible; to be deposited, it must be chemically precipitated.

Sediment can be suspended in wind, water, or ice. Suspended sediment is what makes stream water look dirty after a rainstorm and what makes a wind **storm** dusty. Suspended sediment is sediment that is not continuously in contact with the underlying surface (a stream bed or the desert floor) and so is suspended within the medium of transport. Generally, the smallest particles of sediment are likely to be suspended; occasionally sand is suspended by powerful winds and pebbles are suspended by flood waters. However, because ice is a solid, virtually any size sediment can be part of the suspended sediment load of a glacier.

Bedload consists of the larger sediment that is only sporadically transported. Bedload remains in almost con-

tinuous contact with the bottom, and moves by rolling, skipping, or sliding along the bottom. Pebbles on a river bed or beach are examples of bedload. Wind, water, and ice can all transport bedload, however, the size of sediment in the bedload varies greatly among these three transport agents.

Because of the low **density** of air, wind only rarely moves bedload coarser than fine sand. Some streams transport pebbles and coarser sediment only during floods, while other streams may transport, on a daily basis, all but boulders with ease.

Flood water greatly increase the power of streams. For example, many streams can move boulders during **flooding**. Flooding also may cause large sections of a river bank to be washed into the water and become part of its load. Bank erosion during flood events by a combination of abrasion, hydraulic impact, and mass wasting is often a significant source of a stream's load. Ice in glaciers, because it is a solid, can transport virtually any size material, if the ice is sufficiently thick, and the slope is steep.

For a particular agent of transport, its ability to move coarse sediments as either bedload or suspended load is dependant on its **velocity**. The higher the velocity, the coarser the load.

Rounding and sorting of sediment

Transport of sediments causes them to become rounder as their irregular edges are removed both by abrasion and corrosion. Beach sand becomes highly rounded due to its endless rolling and bouncing in the surf. Of the agents of transport, wind is most effective at mechanically rounding (abrading) clastic sediments, or clasts. Its low density does not provide much of a "cushion" between the grains as they strike one another.

Sorting, or separation of clasts into similar sizes, also happens during sediment transport. Sorting occurs because the size of grains that a medium of transport can move is limited by the medium's velocity and density. For example, in a stream on a particular day, water flow may only be strong enough to transport grains that are finer than medium-grained sand. So all clasts on the surface of the stream bed that are equal to or larger than medium sand will be left behind. The sediment, therefore, becomes sorted. The easiest place to recognize this phenomenon is at the beach. Beach sand is very well sorted because coarser grains are only rarely transported up the beach face by the approaching waves, and finer material is suspended and carried away by the surf.

Ice is the poorest sorter of sediment. Glaciers can transport almost any size sediment easily, and when ice flow slows down or stops, the sediment is not deposited, due to the density of the ice. As a result, sediments deposited directly by ice when it melts are usually very poorly sorted. Significant sorting only occurs in glacial sediments that are subsequently transported by meltwater from the glacier. Wind, on the other hand, is the best sorter of sediment, because it can usually only transport sediment that ranges in size from sand to clay. Occasional variation in wind speed during transport serves to further sort out these sediment sizes.

Deposition

Mechanical deposition

When the velocity (force) of the transport medium is insufficient to move a clastic (or organic) sediment particle it is deposited. As you might expect, when velocity decreases in wind or water, larger sediments are deposited first. Sediments that were part of the suspended load will drop out and become part of the bed load. If velocity continues to drop, nearly all bedload movement will cease, and only clay and the finest silt will be left suspended. In still water, even the clay will be deposited, over the next day or so, based on size- from largest clay particles to the smallest.

During its trip from **outcrop** to ocean, a typical sediment grain may be deposited, temporarily, thousands of times. However, when the transport medium's velocity increases again, these deposits will again be eroded and transported. Surprisingly, when compacted fine-grained clay deposits are subjected to stream erosion, they are nearly as difficult to erode as pebbles and boulders. Because the tiny clay particles are electrostatically attracted to one another, they resist erosion as well as much coarser grains. This is significant, for example, when comparing the erodibility of stream bank materials - clay soils in a river bank are fairly resistant to erosion, whereas sandy soils are not.

Eventually the sediment will reach a final resting place where it remains long enough to be buried by other sediments. This is known as the sediment's depositional environment.

Chemical deposition

Unlike clastic and organic sediment, chemical sediment can not simply be deposited by a decrease in water velocity. Chemical sediment must crystallize from the solution, that is, it must be precipitated. A common way for **precipitation** to occur is by **evaporation**. As water evaporates from the surface, if it is not replaced by water from another source (rainfall or a stream) any dissolved minerals in the water will become more concentrated

until they begin to precipitate out of the water and accumulate on the bottom. This often occurs in the desert in what are known as salt pans or lakes. It may also occur along the sea coast in a **salt** marsh.

Another mechanism that triggers mineral precipitation is a change in water temperature. When ocean waters with different temperatures mix, the end result may be sea water in which the concentration of dissolved minerals is higher than can be held in solution at that water temperature, and minerals will precipitate. For most minerals, their tendency to precipitate increases with decreasing water **temperature**. However, for some minerals, calcite (calcium carbonate) for example, the reverse is true.

Minerals may also be forced to precipitate by the biological activity of certain organisms. For example, when **algae** remove **carbon dioxide** from water, this decreases the acidity of the water, promoting the precipitation of calcite. Some marine organisms use this reaction, or similar chemical reactions, to promote mineral precipitation and use the minerals to form their skeletons. Clams, **snails**, hard corals, **sea urchins**, and a large variety of other marine organisms form their exoskeletons by manipulating water **chemistry** in this way.

Depositional environments

Landscapes form and constantly change due to weathering and sedimentation. The area where a sediment accumulates and is later buried by other sediments is known as its depositional environment. There are many large-scale, or regional, environments of deposition, as well as hundreds of smaller subenvironments within these regions. For example, **rivers** are regional depositional environments. Some span distances of hundreds of miles and contain a large number of subenvironments, such as channels, backswamps, floodplains, abandoned channels, and sand bars. These depositional subenvironments can also be thought of as depositional landforms, that is, landforms produced by deposition rather than erosion.

Depositional environments are often separated into three general types, or settings: terrestrial (on land), marginal marine (coastal), and marine (open ocean). Examples of each of these three regional depositional settings are as follows: terrestrial-alluvial fans, glacial valleys, lakes; marginal marin-beaches, deltas, estuaries, tidal mud and sand flats; marine-coral reefs, abyssal plains, continental slope.

Sedimentary structures

During deposition of sediments physical structures form that are indicative of the conditions that created

Sorted sediment in a gravel pit south of West Bend, Wisconsin.

them. These are known as sedimentary structures. They may provide information about water depth, current speed, environmental setting (for example, marine versus fresh water) or a variety of other factors. Among the more common of these are: bedding planes, beds, channels, cross-beds, ripples, and mud cracks.

Bedding planes are the surfaces separating layers of sediment, or beds, in an outcrop of sediment or rock. The beds represent episodes of sedimentation, while the bedding planes usually represent interruptions in sedimentation, either erosion or simply a lack of deposition. Beds and bedding planes are the most common sedimentary structures.

As you know, rivers flow in elongated depressions called channels. When river deposits are preserved in the sediment record (for example as part of a **delta** system), channels also are preserved. These channels appear in rock outcrops as narrow to broad, v- or u-shaped, "bellies" or depressions at the base of otherwise flat beds. Preserved channels are sometimes called cut-outs, because they "cut-out" part of the underlying bed.

Submerged bars along a coast or in a river form when water currents or waves transport large volumes of sand or gravel along the bottom. Similarly, wind currents form dunes from sand on a beach or a desert. While these depositional surface features, or bedforms, build up in size, they also migrate in the direction of water or wind flow. This is known as bar or **dune** migration. Suspended load or bedload material moves up the shallowly inclined, upwind or upcurrent (stoss) side and falls over the crest of the bedform to the steep, downwind or downcurrent (lee) side. If you cut through the bedform **perpendicular** to its long axis (from the stoss to the lee side) what you would observe are inclined beds of sediment, called cross-beds, that are the preserved leeward faces of the bedform. In an outcrop, these cross-beds can

often be seen stacked one atop another; some may be oriented in opposing directions, indicating a change in current or wind direction.

When a current or wave passes over sand or silt in shallow water, it forms ripples on the bottom. Ripples are actually just smaller scale versions of dunes or bars. Rows of ripples form perpendicular to the flow direction of the water. When formed by a current, these ripples are asymmetrical in cross-section and move downstream by erosion of sediment from the stoss side of the ripple, and deposition on the lee side. Wave-formed ripples on the ocean floor have a more symmetrical profile, because waves move sediments back and forth, not just in one direction. In an outcrop, ripples appear as very small cross-beds, known as cross-laminations, or simply as undulating bedding planes.

When water is trapped in a muddy pool that slowly dries up, the slow sedimentation of the clay particles forms a mud layer on the bottom of the pool. As the last of the water evaporates, the moist clay begins to dry up and crack, producing mud cracks as well as variably shaped mud chips known as mud crack **polygons**. Interpreting the character of any of the sedimentary structures discussed above (for example, ripples) would primarily provide information concerning the nature of the medium of transport. Mud cracks, preserved on the surface of a bed, give some idea of the nature of the depositional environment, specifically that it experienced alternating periods of wet and dry.

The fate of sediments

All clastic and organic sediments suffer one of two fates. Either they accumulate in a depositional environment, then get buried and lithified (turned to rock by compaction and cementation) to produce **sedimentary rock**, or they are re-exposed by erosion after burial, but before lithification, and go through one or more new cycles of weathering-erosion-transport-deposition-burial.

Chemical sediments, while still in solution, can instead follow a number of different paths, known as geochemical cycles. These pathways include ending up as: chemical sedimentary rocks, cement in clastic rocks, parts of living organisms, gases in the atmosphere, ice at the poles, or water in underground reservoirs. Dissolved minerals may remain in these settings for millions of years or quickly move on to another stage in the cycle.

Whether clastic, chemical, or organic, all sediments are part of what is called the rock cycle, an endless series of interrelated processes and products that includes all Earth materials.

Environmental impacts of sedimentation

Erosion, weathering, and sedimentation constantly work together to reshape the Earth's surface. These are natural processes that sometimes require us to adapt and adjust to changes in our environment. However, too many people and too much disturbance of the land surface can drastically increase sedimentation rates, leading to significant increases in the **frequency** and severity of certain natural disasters. For example, disturbance by construction and related land development is sometimes a contributing factor in the mudflows and landslides that occur in certain areas of California. The resulting damage can be costly both in terms of money and lives.

According to The Earth Report, the world's rivers carry as much as 24 million tons of sediment to the ocean each year. About two-thirds of this may be directly related to human activity, which greatly accelerates the natural rate of erosion. This causes rapid loss of fertile topsoil, which leads to decreased crop productivity.

Increased sedimentation also causes increased size and frequency of flooding. As stream channels are filled in, the capacity of the channel decreases. As a result, streams flood more rapidly during a rainstorm, as well as more often, and they drain less quickly after flooding. Likewise, sedimentation can become a major problem on dammed rivers. Sediment accumulates in the lake created by the dam rather than moving farther downstream and accumulating in a delta. Over time, trapped sediment reduces the size of the lake and the useful life of the dam. In areas that are forested, lakes formed by **dams** are not as susceptible to this problem. Sedimentation is not as great due to interception of rainfall by the trees and underbrush.

Vegetative cover also prevents soil from washing into streams by holding the soil in place. Without vegetation, erosion rates can increase significantly. Human activity that disturbs the natural landscape and increases sediment loads to streams also disturbs aquatic ecosystems.

Many state and local governments are now developing regulations concerning erosion and sedimentation resulting from private and commercial development. Only by implementing such measures can we hope to curb these and other destructive side effects, thereby preserving the environment as well as our quality of life.

See also Deposit.

Further Reading

Dixon, Dougal, and Raymond Bernor. *The Practical Geologist.* New York: Simon and Schuster, 1992.

Leopold, Luna. *A View of the River.* Cambridge: Harvard University Press, 1994.

KEY TERMS

Bedload—Sediment that is capable of being moved by an agent of transport (wind, water, or ice) but which remains in almost constant contact with the substrate (for example, a stream bed) as it moves.

Bedrock—The unweathered or partially weathered solid rock layer, which is exposed at the Earth's surface or covered by a thin mantle of soil or sediment.

Clay—The finest of sediment particles, less than 1/256 of a millimeter in diameter.

Delta—A landform that develops where a stream deposits sediment at the edge of a standing body of water (lake or sea).

Floodplain—The flat, low-lying area adjacent to a stream that becomes covered with water during flooding; flood waters deposit sand, silt and clay on this surface.

Geochemical cycle—A number of interrelated environments or settings through which a chemical can move as a result of changes in state or incorporation into different compounds.

Grain size—The size of a particle of sediment, ranging from clay to boulders; smaller size sediment is called fine grained, larger sediment is coarse grained.

Mass wasting—Movement of large masses of sediment primarily in response to the force of gravity.

Outcrop—A natural exposure of rock at the Earth's surface.

Pebbles—Coarse particles of sediment larger than sand (2 mm) and smaller than boulders (256 mm).

Sand—Sediment particles smaller than pebbles and larger than silt, ranging in size from 1/16 of a millimeter to 2 millimeters.

Sediment—Fragments of Earth materials that have weathered loose from rock exposed at the Earth's surface.

Sedimentation—The process by which sediment is removed from one place, and transported to another, where it accumulates.

Silt—Sediment larger than clay, but smaller than sand, ranging in size from 1/16 millimeter to 1/256 millimeter.

Siever, Raymond. *Sand.* Scientific American Library Series. New York: W.H.: Freeman, 1988.

Westbroek, Peter. *Life as a Geological Force: Dynamics of the Earth.* New York: W. W. Norton, 1991.

Clay Harris

Sedimentary environment

A sedimentary, or depositional, environment is an area on the Earth's surface, such as a **lake** or stream, where large volumes of sediment accumulate. All environments of deposition belong to one of three settings: terrestrial, coastal (or marginal marine), and marine. Subenvironments, each with their own characteristic environmental factors and sedimentary deposits, make up a sedimentary environment. For instance, streams consist of channel, sand bar, levee and floodplain subenvironments, among others.

Sedimentary environments display great complexity and almost infinite variety. Variations in environmental factors such as climate, latitude, surface topography, subsurface **geology**, and sediment supply help determine the characteristics of a particular sedimentary environment, and the resulting sedimentary deposits. This entry deals only with typical examples of common environments, with greatly simplified descriptions.

Terrestrial environments

Water, **wind**, and ice erode, transport, and **deposit** terrigenous sediments on land. Geologists recognize five common terrestrial sedimentary environments: stream, lake, **desert**, glacial and volcanic.

Streams are the most widespread terrestrial sedimentary environment. In fact, because they dominate landscapes in both humid and arid climates, stream valleys are the most common **landform** on **Earth**. Streams naturally meander and coarse-grained sediments accumulate along the inside of meanders where water **velocity** decreases, forming sand and gravel bars. When flood waters overflow a stream's banks, fine-grained sediment accumulates on the land surface, or floodplain, adjacent to the channel. Coarser sediment collects on the channel banks during floods, forming a narrow deposit called a

levee. Sorting, rounding, and sediment load generally increase downstream.

Where a stream rapidly changes from a high to low slope on land, for example at the base of a **mountain**, gravel, sand, silt and clay form a sediment pile called an alluvial fan. Where a stream flows into standing water its sediments produce a deposit called a **delta**. Deltas are usually finer grained than alluvial fans. In both alluvial fans and deltas, grain size rapidly decreases downslope.

Most lakes form from water contributed by one or more streams as well as **precipitation** directly into the lake. As it arrives at a lake, stream velocity drops very rapidly, depositing the coarsest sediment at the lakeshore and forming a delta. Farther from shore, as the water continues to lose velocity, finer and finer grained sediment falls to the lake bottom. Only in the deepest part of the lake is water movement slow enough to permit the finest grained sediment to accumulate. This produces thin layers of clay. Hence, grain size generally decreases from the lakeshore to its center.

Deserts develop where rainfall is too sparse to support abundant plants. Contrary to popular belief, deserts are not typically vast seas of sand. Instead, they consist mostly of a mixture of gravel and sand. However, the sand may be eroded away, or deflated, by the wind leaving behind a layer of gravel called a desert pavement, or reg. The deflated sand is later heaped into piles downwind, producing dunes. In spite of the prevalence of regs and dunes in deserts, water is nonetheless the most important agent of **erosion**. Alluvial fans are common at the base of mountains. Dry lake beds, or playas, and **salt** deposits, or sabkhas, resulting from lake **evaporation**, commonly occupy the adjacent valley floor.

Where snowfall exceeds snowmelt, ice accumulation eventually forms a glacier. Alpine **glaciers** occur throughout the world on mountains at high elevations. Modern continental glaciers now cover **Antarctica** and Greenland. From around two million years ago to about ten thousand years ago—the Pleistocene Epoch, or "Ice Age"—glaciers deposited sediments over large areas at mid-to high-latitudes. These glacial ice deposits, called till, are characterized by very poor sediment sorting. They generally are thick, widespread sheets or narrow, sinuous ridges. Ice meltwater forms thick, widespread layers of sediment, called stratified drift, with good sorting.

Though volcanism involves igneous processes, volcanic sediments compose much of terrestrial volcanic deposits. These volcaniclastic, or pyroclastic, sediments form when ash, cinders, and larger volcanic materials fall to the ground during eruptions. Running water often modifies volcaniclastic sediments after deposition. They also may move downhill as a mudflow, or lahar, when saturated with water. Generally, volcaniclastic sediments form thin lobe-shaped deposits and widespread sheets, which thicken toward the volcanic source.

Coastal environments

Where the land meets the sea, interplay between terrestrial and marine processes causes sedimentary environments to be very complex. In areas where wave **energy** is low and the tidal range (the difference between high tide and low tide) is also low, terrestrial processes usually dominate. For example, sediments flowing into the sea from a river will form a well-developed delta. If wave energy is high and tidal range low, the river's sediments will be reworked into a beach or barrier island. However, if tidal range is high, tidal currents flood the river mouth daily, forming a drowned river mouth, or estuary, with scattered sand bars.

In coastal areas remote from **rivers**, the nature of the coast changes rapidly. The balance between tidal and wave processes influences coastal character. The higher the tidal range, the more important tidal processes become. In wave-dominated areas, currents flowing **parallel** to the shoreline move sand along the coast, producing **barrier islands** and beaches for long stretches. If a barrier island protects the coast, channels, or tidal inlets, pass between the islands and allow tidal currents to flow from the open **ocean** into the bay behind the island. Landward from the bay, a tidal marsh will occur. When high tide approaches and tidal currents flow landward, the marsh will be flooded. As the water level drops toward low tide, tidal currents flow seaward, exposing the marsh to the elements. If no barrier island is present, coasts are rather simple with only occasional river mouths and coastal marshes to break the monotony of long stretches of beach.

Where tidal range is high, strong tidal currents dominate coastal processes. Tidal sand flats occur below low tide level. These are generally covered with large ripples to small sand dunes. Between the low tide and high tide marks, ripples are abundant on a mixed sand and mud flat. A mud flat, backed by a tidal marsh, forms above the high tide mark. Landward of the low tide level, tidal creeks cut through the deposits as well.

Marine environments

Sediments may accumulate and be preserved virtually anywhere in the oceans. Consequently, marine sedimentary environments are numerous and widespread. They also range tremendously in water depth; therefore, depth plays a major role in shaping these environments. For simplicity, marine environments can be divided into two broad

groups: shelf and deep oceanic. Shelf environments range in depth from low tide level to depths of 425 ft (130 m), typical for the outer edge of the **continental shelf**.

Continental shelf environments

The average continental shelf is about 45 mi (75 km) wide. Shelf sediments generally decrease in grain size with increasing **distance** from shore. This occurs for two reasons: (1) greater distance from sediment sources and (2) decreasing sediment movement (transport) with increasing water depth.

Shelf sediments vary significantly with latitude. At high latitudes, glacial ice flowing into coastal water generates **icebergs**, which transport large sediment loads of various sizes out onto the shelf. As icebergs melt, they drop their load. These glaciomarine sediments are generally less sorted and coarser grained than lower latitude deposits. In fact, boulders known as dropstones occur on the sea floor in deep water, hundreds of miles from shore.

Rivers deliver most of the sediments to mid-latitude shelves. Therefore, grain size routinely decreases with distance from shore; sediment sorting also tends to be rather good. Shallow water, nearshore sediments form thick sand blankets with abundant ripple marks. As depth increases and water movement decreases, average grain size decreases, and sand, silt, and clay occur interbedded. In water depths greater than 150-200 ft (45-60 m), even **storm** waves do not stir the bottom; consequently, silts and clays predominate. Scattered sand deposits are also located on outer shelf margins. During periods of lower **sea level**, rivers flowing across what is now the inner shelf deposited these so-called relict sediments.

At low latitudes, bottom-dwelling plants and animals secrete large volumes of **calcium carbonate**, producing thick blankets of carbonate sediment. Perhaps the best known carbonate environment is the coral reef. Corals produce a rigid framework of carbonate rock (limestone), which is also a major source of sediment of various grain sizes. Where stream input is great, terrigenous sediments discourage habitation by carbonate-producing organisms and dilute any carbonate sediment that is produced.

Deep oceanic environments

Seaward of the continental shelves, continental slopes incline more steeply, so relict and modern sediments form deposits called deep-sea fans. These are similar to alluvial fans, but generally consist of sand- to clay-sized particles with little or no gravel. Deep-sea fans form the continental rise, a continuous apron of sediment at the base of the continental slope.

Even farther from land, the monotonous abyssal plains begin. Here mostly clay-sized sediment forms sheets up to 0.6 mi (1 km) thick. These deposits, composed of sediments that settle through the water column from shallow depths, thin to a feather edge at the oceanic ridges where new sea floor forms. Abyssal sediments are generally a mixture of three grain types: carbonate muds and siliceous muds of biogenic (organic) origin, and red clays of terrigenous origin. Carbonate-rich muds generally accumulate in water depths of less than 2-2.5 mi (3-4 km); at deeper depths, colder water and higher pressures combine to dissolve the carbonate. Siliceous muds occur where abundant **nutrients** in surface waters support high rates of biogenic silica (SiO_2) production. Red clays, transported from the land by winds and stream flow, predominate where quantities of carbonate and siliceous muds are insufficient to dilute these fine-grained terrigenous deposits.

Interpreting the sedimentary record

Geologists associate subenvironments with specific sediment features by observing modern sedimentary environments and the resulting sediments. These features include sediment composition, sediment texture (size, shape and sorting), vertical changes in grain size, and various sedimentary structures such as wave and current ripples, desiccation cracks in mud, **plant** and **animal** remains, and bedding thickness. The assortment of sediment features that is typical of a particular subenvironment is called a sedimentary facies.

Geologists compile characteristic facies from each sedimentary environment and produce what is called a facies model. A facies model may be a complex diagram, a table of information, or simply a detailed verbal description. It indicates which sedimentary features characterize a particular environment, and the lateral and vertical distribution of facies within sedimentary deposits.

Geologists use facies models for paleoenvironmental reconstruction—deducing the environment where sediments or sedimentary **rocks** originate. This is useful for predicting the distribution of economically important earth materials, such as gold, tin, **coal**, oil, or gas, in a sedimentary deposit. When doing paleoenvironmental reconstructions, geologists look for sources of variation in environmental conditions. For example, rising sea level or a decreasing sediment supply influence the sediment deposit formed, so facies models are altered accordingly. Geologists constantly work on refining facies models to improve the **accuracy** of paleoenvironmental reconstructions.

Further Reading

Emiliani, Cesare. *Planet Earth: Cosmology, Geology, and the Evolution of Life and Environment.* England: Cambridge University Press.1996.

KEY TERMS

Biogenic sediment—Sediment produced by, or from the skeletal remains of, an organism.

Grain size—The size of a sediment particle; for example, gravel (greater than 2mm), sand (2mm-1/16 mm), silt (1/16 mm-1/256 mm) and clay (less than 1/256 mm).

Sediment load—The amount of sediment transported by wind, water, or ice.

Sorting—The range of grain sizes present in a sediment deposit; a sediment with a narrow range of grain sizes is said to be well sorted.

Terrigenous sediment—Sediment eroded from a terrestrial source.

Fox, William. *At the Sea's Edge: An Introduction to Coastal Oceanography for the Amateur Naturalist.* New York: Prentice Hall. 1983.

Leeder, Mike. *Sedimentology and Sedimentary Basins: From Turbulence to Tectonics.* London: Blackwell Science. 1999.

Trefil, James. *A Scientist at the Seashore.* New York: Charles Scribner's Sons. 1984.

Clay Harris

Sedimentary rock

Sedimentary **rocks** form at or near the Earth's surface from the weathered remains of pre-existing rocks or organic debris. The term sedimentary rock applies both to consolidated, or lithified sediments (bound together, or cemented) and unconsolidated sediments (loose, like sand). Although there is some overlap, most sedimentary rocks belong to one of the following groups-clastic, chemical, or organic.

Mechanical **weathering** breaks up rocks, while chemical weathering dissolves and decomposes rocks. Weathering of igneous, metamorphic, and sedimentary rocks produces rock fragments, or clastic sediments, and mineral-rich **water**, or mineral solutions. After transport and laying down, or deposition, of sediments by **wind**, water, or ice, compaction occurs due to the weight of overlying sediments that accumulate later. Finally, **minerals** from mineral-rich solutions may crystallize, or precipitate, between the grains and act as cement. If so, cementation of the unconsolidated sediments forms a consolidated rock. Clastic rocks are classified based on their

A sample of limestone.

grain size. The most common clastic sedimentary rocks are shale (grains less than 1/256 mm in diameter), siltstone (1/256 mm-1/16 mm), sandstone (1/16 mm-2 mm), and conglomerate (greater than 2 mm).

Chemical or crystalline sedimentary rocks form from mineral solutions. Under the right conditions, minerals precipitate out of mineral-rich water to form layers of one or more minerals, or chemical sediments. For example, suppose **ocean** water is evaporating from an enclosed area, such as a bay, faster than water is flowing in from the open ocean. **Salt** deposits will form on the bottom of the bay as the **concentration** of dissolved minerals in the bay water increases. This is similar to putting salt water into a **glass** and letting the water evaporate; a layer of interlocking salt crystals will precipitate on the bottom of the glass. Due to their interlocking crystals, chemical sediments always form consolidated sedimentary rocks. Chemical rocks are classified based on their mineral composition. Rock salt (composed of the mineral halite, or table salt), rock gypsum (composed of gypsum), and crystalline limestone (composed of calcite) are common chemical sedimentary rocks.

Organic sedimentary rocks form from organically derived sediments. These organic sediments come from either animals or plants and usually consist of body

parts. For example, many limestones are composed of abundant marine fossils so these limestones are of organic rather than chemical origin. **Coal** is an organic rock composed of the remains of plants deposited in coastal swamps. The sediments in some organic rocks (for example, fossiliferous limestone) undergo cementation; other sediments may only be compacted together (for example, coal). Geologists classify organic rocks by their composition.

Every rock has a story to tell, and sedimentary rocks are like a good mystery novel-they reveal an intriguing story but only to readers who recognize and correctly interpret the available clues. The origin (clastic, chemical, or organic) and composition of a sedimentary rock provide geologists with many insights into the environment where it was deposited. Geologists use this information to interpret the geologic history of an area, and to search for economically important rocks and minerals.

See also Deposit; Sediment and sedimentation.

Sedimentary structures see **Sediment and sedimentation**; **Sedimentary rock**

Seed ferns

The seed **ferns** are an extinct group of plants known technically as the Pteridospermales. As indicated by their name, the seed ferns had leaves which were fernlike in appearance, and they reproduced by making **seeds**. Some seed ferns resembled **tree** ferns (family Cyatheaceae), a still-living group of tropical plants which are treelike in appearance but which reproduce by making spores. The seed ferns, however, were more prostrate in stature.

The seed ferns originated during the middle Devonian period, about 380 million years ago. They were dominant plants from the late Devonian to the Permian period, about 300 million years ago, but became extinct shortly thereafter.

Although seed ferns resembled the true ferns (order Polypodiates), there are two major differences between them. First, seed ferns reproduced by making seeds, whereas ferns reproduce by making spores. Second, the stem of seed ferns increased in girth through the life of the **plant**, due to **cell** division in a specialized outer cell layer in the stem known as the cambium. The cambium of seed ferns produced secondary xylem and phloem—cells specialized for **water** and food transport—much as the cambium of vascular seed plants do today.

Many botanists believe that seed ferns or a close relative were the first plants to reproduce by making seeds. The development of reproduction by seeds was an important evolutionary advance, because it meant that plants no longer had to rely on water as a dispersal agent for their sperm cells. Therefore, seed production enabled the seed ferns and their descendants to colonize relatively drier kinds of terrestrial habitats. The modern seed-producing plants are the evolutionary descendants of the seed ferns, and are the dominant plants in nearly all terrestrial ecosystems today.

The seed ferns did not have flowers, so they could be considered primitive gymnosperms. However, the seeds of seed ferns developed on fertile leaves, which were very similar to their sterile leaves, which lacked seeds. In this respect, the seed ferns were very different from modern gymnosperms, such as conifers and **cycads**, which bear their seeds in cones, which are highly specialized reproductive structures.

The stems and vascular systems of seed ferns had certain ultrastructural features similar to those of cycads, a small group of gymnosperms currently found in tropical and subtropical regions. In addition, the ultrastructure of the seed of seed ferns was similar to that of cycads. Thus, many botanists believe that the cycads are direct descendants of the seed ferns.

See also Plant breeding.

Peter A. Ensminger

Seeds

Seeds are the products of the **sexual reproduction** of plants, and for this reason the genetic information of seeds is influenced by both of the parents. Sexual reproduction is important for two reasons. The first involves the prevention of the loss of potentially important genetic information, a process that occurs when non-sexual means of propagation are prevalent. The other benefit of sexual reproduction is associated with the provision of new genetic combinations upon which **natural selection** acts, so that species continue to evolve populations that are favorably adapted to a dynamically changing environment.

Plants have evolved various mechanisms for the dissemination of their seeds, so that new plants can be established at some **distance** from their parent. The dispersal of seeds is important in expanding the range of **plant** species, especially if species are to take advantage of **habitat** opportunities that may be created by disturbances and other ecological processes.

The seeds of some plant species are important to humans, as sources of food, while other seeds are important as raw materials for the manufacture of industrial chemicals, and other products.

Biology of seeds

Seeds develop from the fertilized ovules of female (pistillate) floral parts, following **fertilization** by pollen released from the male (staminate) floral parts. If ovules and pollen come from different individual plants, then the genetic makeup of the seed represents a mixture of the two parent plants, and sexual reproduction is said to have occurred.

In some plant species (known as monoecious plants), pollen from a plant may fertilize its own ovules, a phenomenon that is known as self-pollination. This can occur when flowers contain both pistillate and staminate organs (these are known as "perfect" flowers). Self-fertilization can also occur when the same flowers on the same plant are either male or female. Although self-pollination results in genetic mixing, the degree of mixing is much less than in true, sexual reproduction. If self-fertilization occurs frequently, the eventual result is a loss of genetic variation through inbreeding, which may have deleterious consequences on the evolutionary fitness of the plant.

Most plant species avoid self-pollination, and encourage cross-pollination among genetically different individuals of the species. One such **adaptation** involves individual plants that produce only male flowers or only female flowers (these are known as dioecious plants). In addition, many plant species have **pollination** systems that encourage out-crossing, such as pollination by the **wind**. Other plants are pollinated by **insects** or **birds** that carry the pollen to the receptive stigmatic surfaces of other plants of the same species. The benefit of out-crossing is to reap the evolutionary benefits of sexual reproduction by producing genetically diverse seeds.

A seed is more than just a fertilized ovule; it also contains the embryonic tissues of the adult plant, including a rudimentary root, shoot, and leaves. These structures are surrounded by tissues containing starch and/or oil that are intended to provide nourishment for **germination** and the early growth of the seedling. The walls of the ovule develop into a hard seed coat, intended to provide protection for the tender, internal tissues.

The above description gives an idea of the basic, anatomical structure of seeds. However, the actual proportion of the various tissues in the seed varies according to species. Orchids (family Orchidaceae), for example, have tiny, dust-like seeds that consist of little more than core embryonic tissues, with very little in the way of **energy** reserves. In contrast, the gigantic seeds of the Seychelles Islands coconut (*Lodoicea maldivica*) can weigh more than 11.5 lb (25 kg), most of which is nutritional reserve surrounded by fibrous, protective husk.

The seeds of many plant species are dispersed as individual units throughout the environment, while those of other species are encased as groups of seeds inside of **fruits** of various sorts. These fruits are usually intended for ingestion by animals, which then disperse the seeds widely (see below).

Dissemination of seeds

A plant seed is a unique genetic entity, a biological individual. However, a seed is in a diapause state, an essentially dormant condition, awaiting the ecological conditions that will allow it to grow into an adult plant, and produce its own seeds. Seeds must therefore germinate in a safe place, and then establish themselves as a young seedling, develop into a juvenile plant, and finally become a sexually mature adult that can pass its genetic material on to the next generation. The chances of a seed developing are generally enhanced if there is a mechanism for dispersing to an appropriate habitat some distance from the parent plant.

The reason for dispersal is that closely related organisms have similar ecological requirements. Consequently, the competitive stress that related organisms exert on each other is relatively intense. In most cases, the immediate proximity of a well-established, mature individual of the same species presents difficult environment for the germination, establishment, and growth to maturity of a seed. Obviously, **competition** with the parent plant will be greatly reduced if its seeds have a mechanism to disperse some distance away.

However, there are some important exceptions to this general rule. For example, the adults of annual species of plants die at the end of their breeding season, and in such cases the parent plants do not compete with their seeds. Nevertheless, many annuals have seeds that are dispensed widely. Annual plants do well in very recently disturbed, but fertile habitats, and many have seeds with great dispersal powers. Annual species of plants are generally very poor competitors with the longer-lived plant species that come to dominate the site through the ecological process of **succession**. As a result, the annuals are quickly eliminated from the new sites, and for this reason the annual species must have seeds with great dispersal capabilities, so that recently disturbed sites elsewhere can be discovered and colonized, and regional populations of the species can be perpetuated.

Plants have evolved various mechanisms that disperse their seeds effectively. Many species of plants have seeds with anatomical structures that make them very buoyant, so they can be dispersed over great distances by the winds. Several well-known examples of this sort are the fluffy seeds of the familiar dandelion (*Taraxacum officinale*) and fireweed (*Epilobium augustifolium*). The dandelion is a weed species, and it continuously colonizes recently disturbed habitats, before the mature plants are eliminated from their rapidly-maturing habitats. Favorable disturbances for weed species such as dandelions are often associated with human activities, such as the demolition of old buildings, the development of new lawns, or the abandonment of farmland. In the case of the fireweed, it is recently burned **forests** or clear-cuts that are colonized by aerially-dispersed seeds. The adult plants of the dandelion and fireweed produce enormous numbers of seeds during their lifetime, but this is necessary to ensure to that a few of these seeds will manage to find a suitable habitat during the extremely risky, dispersal phase of the life cycles of these and other aerially dispersed species.

The seeds of maple trees (*Acer* spp.) are aerially dispersed, and have a one-sided wing that causes them to swirl propeller-like after they detach from the parent **tree**. This allows even light breezes to carry the maple seeds some distance from their parent before they hit the ground.

Some plants have developed an interesting method of dispersal, known as "tumbleweeding." These plants are generally annual species, and they grow into a roughly spherical shape. After the seeds are ripe, the mature plant detaches from the ground surface, and is then blown about by the wind, shedding its seeds widely as it tumbles along.

The seeds of many other species of plants are dispersed by animals. Some seeds have structures that allow them to attach to the fur or feathers of passing animals, who then carry the seeds some distance away from the parent plant before they are deposited to the ground. Familiar examples of this sticking sort of seed are those of the beggar-ticks (*Bidens frondose*) and the burdock (*Arctium minus*). The spherical fruits of the burdock have numerous hairs with tiny hooked tips that stick to fur (and to clothing, and were the botanical model from which the inspiration for velcro, a fastening material, was derived.

Another mechanism by which seeds are dispersed by animals involves their encasement in a fleshy, edible fruit. Such fruits are often brightly colored, have pleasant odors, and are nutritious and attractive to herbivorous animals. These animals eat the fruit, seeds and all. After some time, the **animal** defecates, and the seeds are effectively dispersed some distance from the parent plant. The seeds of many plants with this sort of animal-dispersal strategy actually require passage through the gut of an animal before they will germinate, a characteristic that is referred to as scarification. Some familiar examples of species that develop animal-dispersed fruits include the cherries (*Prunus* spp.), tomato (*Lycopersicon esculentum*), and watermelon (*Citrullus vulgaris*).

A close-up of grass seed on grass.

After seeds have been dispersed into the environment, they may remain in a dormant state for some time, until appropriate cues are sensed for germination and seedling establishment. Especially in forests, there can be a large reservoir of viable but dormant seeds, known as a "seed bank," within the surface organic layer of the **soil**. The most prominent species in the seed bank are often particularly abundant as adult plants during the earlier stages of forest succession, that is, following disturbance of the stand by a **wildfire**, windstorm, or clear-cut. These early-successional species cannot survive as adult plants during the earlier stages of forest succession, that is, following disturbance of the stand by a wildfire, windstorm, or clear-cut. These early-successional species cannot survive as adult plants beneath a mature forest canopy, but in many cases they can continue to exist in the forest as living but dormant seeds in the surface organic layer, often in great abundance. Species that commonly exhibit this strategy of a persistent seed bank include the cherries (*Prunus* spp.), blackberries, and raspberries (*Rubus* spp.).

Uses of seeds

The seeds of some species of plants are extremely important for human welfare. In some cases, this is because the seeds (or the fruits that contain them) are used as a source of food, but there are some other important uses of seeds as well.

KEY TERMS

Dioecious—Referring to cases where individual plants have either all staminate (that is, male) or all pistillate (female) florets.

Dispersal—Here, this referring to the spreading of propagules outward from their point of origin, as when seeds disperse away from their parent plant, using wind or an animal vector.

Germination—The beginning of growth of a seed.

Monoecious—Referring to cases in which individual plants are bisexual, having both staminate and pistillate floral parts.

Perfect flowers—Referring to cases in which individual flowers are bisexual, having both staminate and pistillate organs.

Pollination—The transfer of pollen from its point of origin (that is, the anther of the stamen) to the receptive surface of the pistil (i.e., the stigma) of the same species.

Scarification—The mechanical or chemical abrasion of a hard seedcoat in order to stimulate or allow germination to occur.

Seed bank—The population of viable seeds that occurs in the surface organic layer and soil of an ecosystem, especially in forests.

Succession—A process of ecological change, involving the progressive replacement of earlier communities with others over time, and generally beginning with the disturbance of a previous type of ecosystem.

Seeds as food

There are numerous examples of the use of seeds as food for humans. The seeds may be eaten directly, or used to manufacture flour, starch, oil, **alcohol**, or some other edible products. The seeds of certain agricultural **grasses** are especially important foodstuffs, for example, those of **wheat** (*Triticum aestivum*), **rice** (*Oyza sativa*) maize (*Zea mays*), **sorghum** (*Sorghum bicolor*), and **barley** (*Hordeum vulgare*). Other edible seeds include those of the **legumes**, the second-most important family of plants after the grasses, in terms of providing foods for human consumption. Examples of legumes whose seeds are eaten by people include the peanut (*Arachis hypogaea*), **soybean** (*Glycine max*), lentil (*Lens esculenta*), common pea (*Pisum sativum*), and common bean (*P. vulgaris*). Other edible seeds include those of the coconut (*Cocos nucifera*), walnut (*Juglans regia*), pecan (*Carya illinoensis*), and sunflower (*Helianthus annua*).

Many other seeds are eaten with their fruits, although it is generally the encasing fruit walls that are the sought-after source of **nutrition**. A few examples of edible fruits include those of the pumpkin or squash (*Cucurbita pepo*), bell **pepper** (*Capsicum anuum*), apple (*Malus pumila*), sweet cherry (*Prunus avium*), strawberry (*Fragaria vesca*), raspberry (*Rubus idaeus*), and sweet orange (*Citrus sinensis*).

Other uses of seeds

The seeds of some plants have other uses, including serving as resources for the manufacturing of industrial chemicals, such as grain alcohol (**ethanol**), derived from a **fermentation** of the seeds of corn, wheat, or some other plants. The seeds of some plants are used as attractive decorations, as is the case of the Job's tears (*Coix lachryma-jobi*), a grass that produces large, white, shiny seeds that are used to make attractive necklaces and other decorations, often dyed in various attractive colors.

Further Reading

Klein, R. M. *The Green World: An Introduction to Plants and People*. New York: Harper & Row, 1987.

Woodland, D. W. *Contemporary Plant Systematics*. Upper Engelwood Cliffs, NJ: Prentice-Hall, 1991.

Bill Freedman

Segmented worms

Segmented worms (phylum Annelida) are so named because of their elongated, more or less cylindrical bodies divided by grooves into a series of ringlike segments. Typically, the external grooves correspond to internal partitions called septa, which divide the internal body space into a series of compartments. Perhaps the most familiar examples of segmented worms are the common earthworms or night crawlers, and the **freshwater** leeches. Actually, the more numerous and typical members of the phylum are marine, crawling or hiding under **rocks**, or living in burrows, or in tubes, or in the sediment.There are approximately 15,000 living species of annelids, placed in three major classes: the Polychaeta (mostly marine), the Oligochaeta (mostly terrestrial), and the Hirudinea (mostly freshwater).

Polychaetes are either "errant"—moving and feeding actively, or "sedentary"—with a passive lifestyle.

The basic body plan of an errant form is illustrated by the sandworm *Nereis*. The anterior end of *Nereis* is specialized to form a "head," possessing two pairs of eyes and several pairs of sensory appendages. The remainder of the body consists of a large number (100 or more) of similar segments, each with a pair of distinct lateral appendages called parapodia. The parapodium is muscular, highly mobile, and divided into two lobes, an upper, or dorsal, "notopodium," and a lower, or ventral "neuropodium." Each lobe bears a bundle of bristles, or setae. The setae, made of a substance called chitin, are used in crawling or in swimming. *Nereis* is a **carnivore**. Its food consists of small live organisms, or fragments of dead organisms, which it grasps by means of a pair of powerful jaws located at the tip of an eversible muscular pharynx. The food is ground up and digested as it passes through successive parts of the straight, tubular gut. The undigested residue is discarded through the anus located at the posterior end. Most other body systems are arranged on a "segmental plan," which means that structures performing a particular body function are repeated in each segment. Thus, for excretion each segment contains a pair of coiled, ciliated tubes called nephridia. At one end the nephridial tube opens into the spacious cavity (called coelom) between the body wall and the gut; at the other end it opens to the outside. There is a well developed **circulatory system**. The **blood**, which is red in color due to the presence of hemoglobin, circulates in blood vessels. Gas exchange occurs between blood and sea **water** across the thin, leaflike lobes of the parapodia. Each body segment also has a pair of nerve ganglia and three or four pairs of nerves for receiving sensory input and coordinating muscular activity. Ganglia in successive segments are connected by means of a pair of longitudinal nerve cords, so that nerve impulses can be transmitted back and forth between each segment and the "cerebral ganglion" or "brain" located in the head. Sexes are separate, although no external characteristics distinguish males from females. There are no permanent testes or ovaries; rather, sperm and eggs develop from the lining of the body cavity during the breeding season (early spring), and fill the coelomic space. They are released into the surrounding water by rupture of the body wall. **Fertilization** is external. Many errant polychaetes, including *Nereis*, congregate in **ocean** waters in enormous numbers in order to spawn. The fertilized egg (zygote) develops into a ciliated, planktonic larva called the trochophore, which gradually transforms into a segmented juvenile. The worm grows in length by adding new segments at the posterior end. Even after attaining the adult stage, many polychaetes are able to regenerate body segments, especially toward the posterior end, if segments are lost because of attacks by predators, or if they break off to release gametes. Polychaetes vary in length from a few cm to over 1.6 ft (0.5 m). Most are between 5.9 to 9.9 in (15 and 25 cm) long.

Sedentary polychaetes live in burrows which they excavate in sand or mud; or in tubes which they construct from body secretions, or sand grains, or mud, or a combination of these. *Arenicola* (lugworm), *Chaetopterus* (parchment worm), *Clymenella* (bamboo worm), and *Sabella* (fanworm) are among the well known examples of sedentary forms. Sedentary worms lack eyes and sensory appendages, although some of them have respiratory appendages and feeding tentacles. Their parapodia and setae are either greatly reduced or highly specialized. Sedentary polychaetes feed passively; in passive feeding, food particles are drawn toward the mouth by ciliated tentacles, or are trapped in mucus which is then conveyed to the mouth.

Oligochaetes, for example the earthworm *Lumbricus*, commonly live in burrows in the **soil**, although a few genera (for example *Tubifex, Stylaria, Aeolosoma*) occur in freshwater. Earthworms and other oligochaetes differ from the typical polychaete in lacking sensory appendages and parapodia; in possessing fewer setae; in being hermaphroditic, having permanent gonads, and requiring internal fertilization; in depositing eggs in small capsules called cocoons; and in not having a larval stage. The material forming the cocoon is secreted from a specialized area of the body called the clitellum. Like polychaetes, oligochaetes have well developed powers of regeneration. Freshwater oligochaetes are typically microscopic in size; earthworms commonly attain a length of 11.8 in (30 cm) or more. The giant earthworm of **Australia** (genus *Megascolides*) measures more than 9.8 ft (3 m).

The class Hirudinea comprises leeches, which are mostly blood sucking **parasites** of aquatic **vertebrates**; some leeches are predators.The vast majority of leeches live in freshwater habitats such as ponds and lakes, while a few are semi-terrestrial and some are marine. A leech has a relatively small and fixed number (30-35) of body segments, although its body has a large number of superficial groovelike markings giving it the appearance of more extensive segmentation. With the exception of one small group, setae are absent. Eyes are usually present, but there are no sensory appendages or parapodia. The mouth is located in the middle of an anterior sucker. A posterior sucker is present at the opposite end. The **suckers** are used for attachment to the substrate during the characteristic looping movements, and for attachment to the host during feeding. Blood-sucking leeches secrete saliva containing an anti-coagulant. The stomach of the blood-sucking leech has many paired, sac-like extensions for storing the blood. Digestion of the blood proceeds very slowly. A bloodsucking leech needs to feed only occasionally, and can go for long periods between

KEY TERMS

Chitin—A type of polysaccharide containing nitrogen.

Ganglion (pl. ganglia)—A collection of nerve cell bodies forming a discrete unit.

Plankton—A collective term for organisms that live suspended in the water column in large bodies of water.

Seta—A stiff bristle made of chitin, projecting from the skin, in annelids and some other invertebrates.

Trochophore—Topshaped, microscopic, ciliated larva found in annelids and some other invertebrate groups.

meals. Predatory leeches feed on aquatic **invertebrates** such as **snails**, worms, and insect larvae. Like oligochaetes, leeches are hermaphroditic, and have permanent gonads, internal fertilization, and a clitellum. The smallest leeches are only about 0.2 in (5 mm) long; the largest reach 17.7 in (45 cm) when fully extended. Among the common North American genera of freshwater leeches are *Glossiphonia, Haemopis, Macrobdella,* and *Placobdella*. The medicinal leech, *Hirudo medicinalis,* is native to **Europe**.

Annelids are of great ecological significance in marine and terrestrial habitats. Polychaetes, and especially their larvae, constitute important links in food chains in the ocean. Earthworms play an important role in natural turning over of soil. Medicinal leeches have been used for bloodletting for centuries, and even now they are in demand as a source of the anticoagulant hirudin. Leeches are also important in scientific research, especially in trying to understand the complexities of the **nervous system**.

Further Reading

Brusca, Richard C. and Gary J. Brusca. *Invertebrates*. Sunderland, MA: Sinauer Associates, 1990.

Meincoth, N. A. *The Audubon Society Field Guide to North American Seashore Creatures*. New York: Knopf, 1981.

Pearse, Vicki, John Pearse, Mildred Buchsbaum, and Ralph Buchsbaum. *Living Invertebrates*. Pacific Grove, CA: Boxwood, 1987.

Pennak, Robert W. *Fresh-water Invertebrates of the United States*. 3rd ed. New York: Wiley, 1989.

Ruppert, Edward E. and Robert D. Barnes. *Invertebrate Zoology*. 6th ed. Fort Worth: Saunders College Publishing, 1994.

R. A. Virkar

Seismic reflection see **Subsurface detection**

Seismic refraction see **Subsurface detection**

Seismograph

A seismograph is an instrument for detecting and recording **motion** in the Earth's surface as a result of earthquakes. Such devices have a very long history that can be dated to the second century A.D. when the Chinese astronomer and mathematician Chang Heng invented a simple seismoscope. The term seismoscope is reserved for instruments that detect **earth** movements, but do not record such movements. In Chang's device, a **metal** pendulum was suspended inside a jar that held metal balls on its outer rim. When an earth movement occurred, the pendulum swayed back and forth causing the release of one or more balls into the mouths of bronze **toads** resting at the base of the jar. The number of balls released and the direction in which they fell told the magnitude and location of the earth movement.

The modern seismograph

Seismographs today consist of three essential parts. One is a seismometer, a device (like the seismoscope) that detects earth movements. A second component is a device for keeping time so that each earth movement can be correlated with a specific hour, minute, and second. The third component is some device for recording the earth movement and the time at which it occurred. The written record produced by a seismograph is called a seismogram.

Type of seismometers

A number of possible arrangements have been designed for detecting the motion of the Earth's surface in comparison to some immoveable standard. Early seismometers, for example, extended Chang's invention by measuring the amount by which a pendulum attached to a fixed support moved. Today, however, most seismometers can be classified as inertial or strain devices.

In an inertial seismometer, a heavy mass is suspended by a spring from a heavy support that is attached to the ground. When the ground begins to move, that motion is taken up by the spring and the mass remains motionless with reference to the frame from which it is suspended. The relative motion of the frame with regard to the mass can then be detected and recorded.

A strain seismometer is also known as a linear extensometer. It consists of two heavy objects sunk into the

ground. When earth movement occurs, the two objects change their position relative to each other, a change that can be detected and recorded. Many variations in the extent design of this system have been designed. For example, a beam of light can be aimed between the two objects, and any movement in the ground can be detected by slight changes in the beam's path.

A common variation of the strain seismometer is known as a tiltmeter. As the name suggests, the tiltmeter measures any variation in the horizontal orientation of the measuring device. Tiltmeters often make use of two liquid surfaces as the measuring instrument. When an earth movement occurs, the two surfaces will be displaced from each other by some amount. The amount of displacement, then, is an indication of the magnitude of the earth movement.

Recording systems

One of the simplest approaches to the recording of earth movements is simply to attach a pen to the moving element in a seismometer. The pen is then suspended over a rotating drum to which is attached a continuous sheet of graph **paper**. As the drum rotates at a constant speed, the pen draws a line on the graph paper. If no earth movement occurs, the line is nearly straight. Earth movements that do occur are traced as sharp upward and downward markings on the graph. Since the rate at which the drum rotates is known, the exact timing of earth movements can be known.

In some kinds of recording devices, the moving pen is replaced by a beam of light. Earth movements can then be recorded photographically as the beam of light travels over a moving photographic film. This type of device has the advantage that **friction** between pen and rotating graph paper is eliminated.

Practical considerations

Seismographs must be designed so as to take into consideration the fact that small-scale earth movements are constantly taking place. The seismogram produced by a simple seismograph sitting on a laboratory table, for example, would show not a straight line but a fairly constant wiggly line resulting from these regular microearthquakes.

Two methods are commonly used to eliminate this background noise in the detection of earthquakes. The first is to sink the supports for the seismograph as deeply into **bedrock** as possible. When this is done, movements in the more unstable parts of the Earth's upper layers can be eliminated. A second approach is to lay out a network of seismographs. The data obtained from this network can then be averaged out so as to reduce or eliminate the minor fluctuations detected by any one instrument.

KEY TERMS

Inertia—The tendency of an object to retain the state it is in.

Pendulum—A device consisting of a weight hung from a support system so that the weight can swing back and forth as a result of the Earth's gravitational field.

Seismoscope—A primitive type of seismograph that was capable of detecting movements in the Earth's surface, but that did not record those movements.

Seismometer—A component of a seismograph that detects earth movements.

The Richter scale

A variety of methods have been devised for expressing the magnitude, or intensity, of earth movements. For many years, the most popular of these has been the Richter scale, named after seismologist Charles F. Richter, who developed the scale in 1935. The Richter scale is logarithmic. That is, each increase of one unit on the scale represents an increase of ten in the intensity of the earth movement measured. An **earthquake** that measures 6.0 on the Richter scale, as an example, is ten times as intense as one that measures 5.0 and one hundred times as intense as one that measures 4.0.

See also Earth's interior.

Further Reading

Richter, C. F. *Elementary Seismology.* San Francisco: W. H. Freeman, 1958.

Scholz, C. H. *The Mechanics of Earthquakes and Faulting.* New York: Cambridge University Press, 1990.

David E. Newton

Selenium see **Element, chemical**

Sensory system see **Nervous system**

Sequences

A sequence is an ordered list of numbers. It can be thought of as a **function**, f(n), where the argument, n, takes on the natural-number values 1, 2, 3, 4, ... (or occasionally 0, 1, 2, 3, 4, ...). A sequence can follow a regular

pattern or an arbitrary one. It may be possible to compute the value of f(n) with a formula, or it may not.

The terms of a sequence are often represented by letters with subscripts, a_n, for example. In such a representation, the subscript n is the argument and tells where in the sequence the term a_n falls. When the individual terms are represented in this fashion, the entire sequence can be thought of as the set, or the set where n is a natural number. This set can have a finite number of elements, or an infinite number of elements, depending on the wishes of the person who is using it.

One particularly interesting and widely studied sequence is the **Fibonacci sequence**: 1, 1, 2, 3, 5, 8, ... It is usually defined recursively: $a_n = a_n\text{-}2 + a_n\text{-}1$. In a recursive definition, each term in the sequence is defined in terms of one or more of its predecessors (recursive definitions can also be called "iterative"). For example, a_6 in this sequence is the sum of 3 and 5, which are the values of a_4 and a_5, respectively.

Another very common sequence is 1, 4, 9, 16, 25,. .., the sequence of square numbers. This sequence can be defined with the simple formula $a_n = n^2$, or it can be defined recursively: $a_n = a_{n-1} + 2n - 1$.

Another sequence is the sequence of **prime numbers**: 2, 3, 5, 7, 11, 13, ... Mathematicians have searched for centuries for a formula which would generate this sequence, but no such formula has ever been found.

One mistake that is made frequently in working with sequences is to assume that a pattern that is apparent in the first few terms must continue in subsequent terms. For example, one might think from seeing the five terms 1, 3, 5, 7, 9 that the next term must be 11. It can, in fact, be any number whatsoever. The sequence can have been generated by some **random** process such as reading from a table of random digits, or it can have been generated by some obscure or complicated formula. For this reason a sequence is not really pinned down unless the generating principle is stated explicitly. (Psychologists who measure a subject's intelligence by asking him or her to figure out the next term in a sequence are really testing the subject's ability to read the psychologist's mind.) Sequences are used in a variety of ways. One example is to be seen in the divide-and-average method for computing square roots. In this method one finds the **square root** of N by computing a sequence of approximations with the formula $a_n = (a_{n-1} + N/a_{n-1})/2$. One can start the sequence using any value for a_1 except **zero** (a **negative** value will find the negative root). For example, when N = 4 and $a_1 = 1$

$$a_1 = 1.0$$
$$a_2 = 2.5$$
$$a_3 = 2.05$$
$$a_4 = 2.0006$$
$$a_5 = 2.0000$$

This example illustrates several features that are often encountered in using sequences. For one, it often only the last term in the sequence that matters. Second, the terms can converge to a single number. Third, the iterative process is one that is particularly suitable for a computer program. In fact, if one were programming a computer in BASIC, the recursive formula above would translate into a statement such as R = (R + N/R)/2.

Not all sequences converge in this way. In fact, this one does not when a negative value of N is used. Whether a convergent sequence is needed or not depends on the use to which it is put. If one is using a sequence defined recursively to compute a value of a particular number only a convergent sequence will do. For other uses a divergent sequence may be suitable.

Mortgage companies often provide their customers with a computer print-out showing the balance due after each regular payment. These balances are computed recursively with a formula such as $A_n = (A_{n-1})(1.0075) - P$, where A_n stands for the balance due after the n-th payment. In the formula $(A_{n-1})(1.0075)$ computes the amount on a 9% mortgage after one month's interest has been added, and $(A_{n-1})(1.0075) - P$ the amount after the payment P has been credited. The sequence would start with A_0, which would be the initial amount of the loan. On a 30-year mortgage the size of P would be chosen to bring A_{360} down to zero. As anyone who has bought a house knows, this sequence converges, but *very* slowly for the first few years.

Tables, such as tables of **logarithms**, square roots, trigonometric functions, and the like are essentially paired sequences. In a table of square roots, for instance

1.0	1.00000
1.1	1.04881
1.2	1.09545

the column on the left is a sequence and the column on the right the sequence where each b_n equals the square root of a_n. By juxtaposing these two sequences, one creates a handy way of finding square roots.

Sequences are closely allied with (and sometimes confused with) series. A sequence is a list of numbers; a series is a sum. For instance 1/1, 1/2, 1/3, 1/4, ... is a harmonic sequence; while 1/1 + 1/2 + 1/3 + 1/4 + ... is a harmonic series.

Further Reading

Finney, Ross L., et al. *Calculus: Graphical, Numerical, Algebraic. of a Single Variable.* Reading, MA: Addison Wesley, 1994.

KEY TERMS

Convergent—A sequence is convergent if, as one goes further and further down the list, the terms from some point on get arbitrarily close to a particular number.

Divergent—A sequence which is not convergent is divergent.

Sequence—A list of numbers arranged in a particular order.

Gardner, Martin. *Mathematical Circus.* New York: Knopf, 1979.

Stewart, Ian. "Mathematical Recreations." *Scientific American.* (May 1995).

J. Paul Moulton

Sequoia

Sequoias are species of coniferous trees in the genus *Sequoia*, family Taxodiaceae. Sequoias can reach enormous height and girth and can attain an age exceeding 1,000 years. These giant, venerable trees are commonly regarded as botanical wonders.

About 40 species of sequoias are known from the fossil record, which extends to the Cretaceous, about 60 million years ago. At that time, extensive **forests** dominated by sequoias and related conifers flourished in a warm and wet climatic regime throughout the Northern Hemisphere. Ancient fossil stands of sequoias and other conifers have even been found in the high Arctic of Ellesmere Island and Spitzbergen. This indicates a relatively mild climatic regime in the Arctic in the distant past, compared with the intensely cold and dry conditions that occur there today. Similarly, the famous Petrified Forest located in a **desert** region of Arizona is dominated by fossilized sequoia trees and their relatives that lived in that area many millions of years ago. Clearly, compared with their present highly restricted distribution, redwoods were abundant and widespread in ancient times.

Only two species of sequoias still survive. Both of these species occur in relatively restricted ranges in northern and central California and southern Oregon. The specific reasons why these species have survived only in these places and not elsewhere are not known. Presumably, the local site conditions and disturbance regime have continued to favor redwoods in these areas and allowed these trees to survive the ecological onslaught of more recently evolved species of conifers and **angiosperm** trees.

The ancient **biomass** of ancient species of the redwood family are responsible for some of the deposits of **fossil fuels** that humans are so quickly using today as a source of **energy** and for the manufacturing of **plastics**.

Biology and ecology of sequoias

The two living species of sequoias are the redwood or coast redwood (*Sequoia sempervirens*) and the giant sequoia, big **tree**, or Sierra redwood (*S. gigantea*, sometimes placed in another genus, *Sequoiadendron*). Both of these species can be giants, reaching an enormous height and girth. However, the tallest individuals are redwoods, while the widest ones are giant sequoias.

The redwood occurs in foggy **rainforest** of the Coast Range from **sea level** to about 3,300 ft (1,000 m) in elevation. The range of the redwood extends from just south of San Francisco, through northern California, to southern Oregon. This tree has evergreen, flattened, needle-like foliage that superficially resembles that of yews (*Taxus* spp., family Taxodiaceae) and has two whitish stripes underneath. The seed-bearing female cones are as long as 1 in (2.5 cm) and have 15-20 scales. The **seeds** tend not to germinate prolifically. If cut down, redwoods will regenerate well by vegetative sprouts from the stump and roots, an unusual characteristic among the conifers. Redwoods have a thick, reddish, fibrous **bark** as much as 10 in (25 cm) deep. Redwood trees commonly achieve a height of 200-280 ft (60-85 m). Exceptional trees are as tall as 360 ft (110 m), can have a basal diameter of 22 ft (6.7 m), and can be older than 1,400 years. No other living trees have achieved such lofty heights.

The giant redwood has a somewhat more inland distribution in northern California. This species occurs in groves on the western side of the Sierra Nevada Mountains, at elevations of 4,000-8,000 ft (1,200-2,400 m) with fairly abundant **precipitation** and **soil** moisture. The giant redwood has scale-like, awl-shaped foliage, very different in form from that of the redwood. The female cones are rounder and larger than those of the redwood, up to 3.5 in (9 cm) long and containing 24-40 wedge-shaped scales. The bark is fibrous and thick and can be as much as 24 in (60 cm) thick at the base of large trees. One of the largest known individuals is known as the General Sherman Tree, which is 274 ft (83 m) tall, has a basal diameter of 31 ft (9.4 m), and is estimated to be a venerable 3,800 years old. In terms of known longevity of any **organism**, the giant redwood is marginally second only to individuals of the bristlecone pine (*Pinus aristata*) of subalpine **habitat** of the southwestern United States.

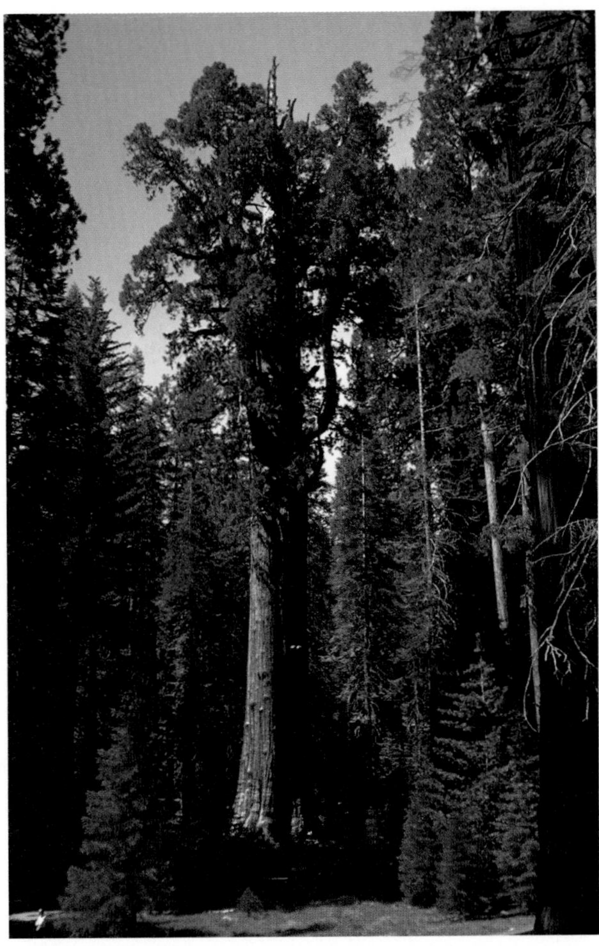

The General Sherman tree in Sequoia National Park, California.

Other living relatives of sequoias are the bald cypress (*Taxodium distichum*) of the southeastern United States and the Montezuma bald cypress (*T. mucronatum*) of parts of Mexico. Asian relatives, sometimes cultivated as unusual ornamentals in **North America**, include the metasequoia or dawn redwood (*Metasequoia glyptostroboides*) and the Japanese cedar or sugi (*Cryptomeria japonica*). The dawn redwood of central China was described in the fossil record prior to being observed as living plants by astonished western botanists in the 1940s. For this reason, the dawn redwood is sometimes referred to as a "living fossil."

Wildfire is important in the **ecology** of redwood forests, but especially in groves of giant redwood. Young seedlings and trees of giant redwood are vulnerable to fire, but older, larger trees are resistant to ground-level fires because of their thick bark. In addition, older redwoods tend to have lengthy expanses of clear trunk between the ground and their first live branches so that devastating crown fires are not easily ignited. Some of the competitor trees of the giant redwood are not so tolerant of fire, so this disturbance helps to maintain the redwood groves.

The development of lower- and mid-height canopies of other species of **conifer** trees in an old-growth stand of giant redwoods could potentially provide a "ladder" of flammable biomass that could allow a devastating crown fire to develop, which might kill the large redwood trees. Because giant redwoods do not sprout from their stump after their above-ground biomass is killed, they could end up being replaced by other species after a grove is badly damaged by a crown fire. This could result in the loss of a precious natural stand of giant redwoods, representing a tragic loss of the special **biodiversity** values of this type of rare natural **ecosystem**.

To prevent the development of a vigorous understory of other species of trees in old-growth groves of giant redwoods, these stands are sometimes managed using prescribed burns. Fire allows open stands of redwoods to occur, while preventing the development of a potentially threatening, vigorous population of other species of trees, such as white fir (*Abies concolor*) and Douglas-fir (*Pseudotsuga menziesii*). Fire may also be important in the preparation of a seedbed suitable for the occasional establishment of seedlings of giant redwood.

Economic importance

The coast redwood has an extremely durable **wood**, and it is highly resistant to decay caused by **fungi**. The heartwood is an attractive reddish color, while the outer sapwood is paler. The grain of redwood lumber is long and straight, and the wood is strong, although rather soft. Redwood trees are harvested and used to make durable posts, poles, and pilings, and are manufactured into value-added products such as structural lumber, outdoor siding, indoor finishing, furniture and cabinets, and sometimes into shakes, a type of roofing shingle made by splitting rather than sawing blocks of wood.

Because of its great usefulness and value, the coast redwood has been harvested rather intensively. If the logged site and regeneration are appropriately managed after the harvesting of redwoods, it will regenerate rather well to this species. Consequently, there is little risk of the commercial **extinction** of this valuable natural resource. However, few natural stands of the coast redwood have survived the onslaught of commercial exploitation, so its distinctive old-growth ecosystem is at great risk of ecological extinction. Natural, self-organizing, old-growth redwood forests can only be preserved, and this must be done in rather large ecological reserves, such as parks, if this ecosystem is to be sustained over the longer term.

KEY TERMS

Commercial extinction—A situation in which it is no longer economically profitable to continue to exploit a depleted natural resource. The resource could be a particular species or an entire ecosystem, such as a type of old-growth forest.

Ecological (or biological) extinction—A representative of a distinct ecosystem or living individuals of a particular species (or another biological taxon) that no longer occurs anywhere on Earth.

Prescribed burn—The controlled burning of vegetation as a management practice to achieve some ecological benefit.

Sprout—Non-sexual, vegetative propagation or regeneration of a tree. Sprouts may issue from a stump, roots, or a stem.

Compared with the coast redwood, the giant redwood is of much less commercial importance and is relatively little used. Most of the best surviving old-growth groves of this species are protected from exploitation in National Parks and other types of ecological reserves. However, there is increasing interest in developing commercial stands of the giant redwood elsewhere within its natural range, while continuing to protect the surviving old-growth stands.

Both species of sequoias are sometimes grown as ornamental trees in warm, moist, temperate climates outside of their natural range. Sequoias have been especially popular in **horticulture** in parts of England.

See also Fossil and Fossilization.

Further Reading

Weatherspoon, C. P., Y. R. Iwamoto, and D. D. Douglas. eds. *Management of Giant Sequoia.* Berkeley, CA: Pacific Southwest Forest and Range Experiment Station, 1985.

Bill Freedman

Seriation see **Dating techniques**

Servomechanisms

The name servomechanism means, quite literally, slave machine. A servomechanism is a physical device that responds to an input control-signal by forcing an output actuator to perform a desired function. Servomechanisms are often the connection between computers, **electronics**, and mechanical actions. If computers are the brains, servomechanisms are the muscles and the hands that do physical work. Servomechanisms use electronic, hydraulic, or mechanical devices to control power. Servomechanisms enable a control operator to perform dangerous tasks at a **distance** and they are often employed to control massive objects using fingertip control.

The power-steering assistance accessory on almost all automobiles is a familiar example of a servomechanism. Automotive power steering uses hydraulic fluid under great **pressure** to power an actuator that redirects the wheels of a car as needed. The driver gently turns the steering wheel and the power-assist servomechanism provides much of the necessary **energy** needed to position the wheels.

The new Boeing 777 is the first heavy jet plane engineered to fly with all major flight-control functions managed by servomechanisms. The design of this revolutionary plane is based on the so-called "fly-by-wire" system. In normal flight a digital signal communicates the pilot's instructions electrically to control servomechanisms that position the plane's control surfaces as needed.

High-performance airplanes need special servomechanisms called flight-control systems to compensate for performance instabilities that would otherwise compromise their safety. The aerodynamic designs that optimize a plane's performance sometimes cause instabilities that are difficult for a pilot to manage.

A plane may have a tendency to pitch up and down uncontrollably, or yaw back and forth under certain conditions. These two instabilities may combine with a third problem where the plane tends to roll unpredictably. Sensors called accelerometers pick up these **oscillations** before the pilot is aware of them and servomechanisms introduce just the right amount of correction needed to stop the unwanted activity. The servos that perform this magic are called pitch dampers, yaw dampers, and roll dampers. Their effect is to smooth out the performance of a plane so that it does only what it should. Without servomechanism technology flight-control systems would be impossible and the large safe **aircraft** we take for granted would be impractical.

Open-loop servomechanisms

Servomechanisms are classified on the basis of whether they depend upon information sampled at the output of the system for comparison with the input instructions. The simplest servomechanisms are called

open-loop servomechanisms and do not feed back the results of their output. Open-loop servomechanisms do not verify that input instructions have been satisfied and they do not automatically correct errors.

An example of an open-loop servomechanism is a simple motor used to rotate a television-antenna. The motor used to rotate the **antenna** in an open-loop configuration is energized for a measured time in the expectation that antenna will be repositioned correctly. There is no automatic check to verify that the desired action has been accomplished. An open-loop servomechanism design is very unsatisfactory as a basis for an antenna rotator, just as it is usually not the best choice for other applications.

When **error** feedback is included in the design the result is called a closed-loop servomechanism. The servo's output result is sampled continuously and this information is continuously compared with the input instructions. Any important difference between the feedback and the input signal is interpreted as an error that must corrected automatically. Closed-loop servo systems automatically null, or **cancel**, disagreements between input instructions and output results.

The key to understanding a closed-loop servomechanism is to recognize that it is designed to minimize disagreements between the input instructions and the output results by forcing an action that reduces the error.

A more sophisticated antenna rotator system, compared to the open-loop version described earlier, will use the principles of the closed-loop servomechanism. When it is decided that the antenna is to be turned to a new direction the operator will introduce input information that creates a deliberate error in the servomechanism's feedback loop. The servo's electronic controller senses this purposely-introduced change and energizes the rotator's motor. The antenna rotates in the direction that tends to null the error. When the error has been effectively canceled, the motor is turned off automatically leaving the antenna pointing in the desired direction. If a strong **wind** causes the antenna turn more slowly than usual the motor will continue to be energized until the error is canceled. If a strong wind repositions the antenna improperly the resulting error will cause the motor to be energized once again, bringing the antenna back into alignment.

Another example of a simple closed-loop servomechanism is a thermostatically-controlled gas furnace. A sensor called a **thermostat** determines that **heat** is required, closing a switch that actuates an **electric circuit** that turns on the furnace. When the building's **temperature** reaches the set point the electric circuit is de-energized, turning off the fuel that supplies the flame. The feedback loop is completed when warmed air of the desired temperature is sensed by the thermostat.

Overshoot and hunting

A gas-furnace controller example above illustrates a potential problem with servomechanisms that must be solved when they are designed. If not properly engineered, closed-loop servomechanisms tend to be unstable. They must not overcontrol. The controller must be intelligent enough to shut down the actuator just before satisfaction is accomplished. Just as a car driver must slow down gradually before stopping at an intersection, a servomechanism must anticipate the effects of inertial **mass**. The inertia may be mechanical or it may be thermal, as in the case of the gas furnace. If the furnace flame were to continue to **burn** until the air temperature reaches the exact set point on the temperature selector, the residual heat in the furnace firebox would continue to heat the house, raising the temperature excessively. The room temperature will overshoot the desired value, perhaps uncomfortably. Most space-heating furnace control thermostats include a heat-anticipation provision designed to minimize thermal overshoot. A properly-adjusted anticipation control turns off the furnace's flame before the room temperature reaches the desired set point, allowing the temperature to coast up to the desired value as the furnace cools.

Mechanical inertia and servomechanisms

There is a similar overshoot problem that requires compensation by mechanical servomechanisms. If a servo is used to manipulate a massive object such as a **radar** antenna weighing 1,000 lb (454 kg) or more, the actuator must anticipate the antenna's approach to a newly-selected position. The inertial mass of the antenna will otherwise cause it to overshoot the desired alignment. When the feedback signal is compared with the input and the control electronics discovers the overshoot, the antenna will reverse direction in an attempt to correct the new error. If the antenna overshoots again this may lead to a continuing oscillation called hunting where the antenna continually seeks a null but always turns too far before shutting down, requiring a continuing series of corrections. The resulting oscillation is very undesirable.

Servomechanisms must use very sophisticated electronic circuits that act as electronic anticipators of the load's position and speed to minimize instability while simultaneously maintaining a fast response to new instructions. Better servomechanism designs adjust the timing of error signals to provide just the right amount of

KEY TERMS

Digital—Information processed as encoded on or off data bits.

Electronic—Devices using active components to control power.

Error—A signal proportional to the servomechanism correction.

Feedback—Comparing output and input to determine correction.

Hunting—Repetitious failure of a servomechanism's response.

Hydraulic—Power transfer using fluid under great pressure.

Inertia—Tendency to continue a present activity.

Null—Minimum, a zeroed condition.

Phase shift—Change in timing relative to standard reference.

Pitch Instability—Cyclic up and down oscillation.

Roll Instability—A cylinder's tendency to oscillate about its long axis.

Thermostat—A device used to sense temperature.

Yaw Instability—Tendency to develop side-to-side rotational motions.

anticipation under varying circumstances. The electrical phase-shift network needed to produce a stable servomechanism must be designed with great care.

Enabling servomechanisms

Various servomechanisms provide the enabling connection between data and mechanical actions. If all servomechanisms were to disappear from technology overnight, our world would be much less comfortable, much less safe, and certainly less convenient.

See also Computer, digital.

Further Reading

Albus, James S., and John M. Evans, Jr.. "Robot Systems." *Scientific American.* (1976).

Asimov, Isaac. *Understanding Physics.* New York: Dorset, 1988.

Faillot, J. L., ed. *Vibration Control of Flexible Servo Mechanisms.* New York: Springer-Verlaag, 1994.

Johnson, Eric R. *Servomechanisms.* Prentice-Hall, Inc.

Tustin, Arnold. "Feedback." *Scientific American.* September, 1952.

Donald Beaty

Sesame

Sesame are plants in the genus *Sesamum,* family Pedaliaceae, which are grown for their edible **seeds** and oil. Sesame is native to **Africa** and **Asia**, and was brought to **North America** from Africa during the slave trade. There are about 15 species of sesame, but only two, *S. indicum and* S. orientale, are cultivated for commercial purposes. Evidence has shown that sesame has been used for thousands of years as the **plant** was mentioned in the Ebers Papyrus (from about 3,800 years ago).

The sesame plant is an annual and grows best on sandy loam. The stems are round and shiny, and reach an average of 3-4 ft (90-120 cm) tall. Leaves growing near the bottom of the stem are fleshy, lance-shaped, and are arranged opposite from one another. Leaves toward the top are alternate, oblong, and more slender than the bottom leaves. The flowers are purple or white, about 1 in (2.5-3 cm) long, and trumpet shaped. The flowers are followed by seed pods filled with small, flat, yellowish white seeds (*S. indicum*), or brownish-black seeds (*S. orientale*). The seeds are harvested, usually after four months. The stems are cut and allowed to dry, and then the seed pods split open, and the seeds can be shaken out.

The seeds are crushed and pressed to extract the oil. Sesame oil is used for cooking, especially in China, India, and Egypt. Some margarines contain sesame oil. The oil has been used as a laxative, in the manufacture of fine soaps, and is a popular massage oil. The seed oil from *S. orientale* is suitable for industrial purposes. The seeds are used for baking, often sprinkled on bread. *Tahini* is a paste made from the seeds, and is an important ingredient in many Middle Eastern dishes.

Set theory

Set theory is concerned with understanding those properties of sets that are independent of the particular elements that make up the sets. Thus the axioms and theorems of set theory apply to all sets in general, whether they are composed of numbers or physical objects. The foundations of set theory were largely developed by the German mathematician George Cantor in the latter part of the nineteenth century. The generality of set theory leads to few direct practical applications. Instead, precisely because of its generality, portions of the theory are used in developing the **algebra** of groups, rings, and fields, as well as, in developing a logical basis for **calculus**, **geometry**, and **topology**. These branches of **mathe-**

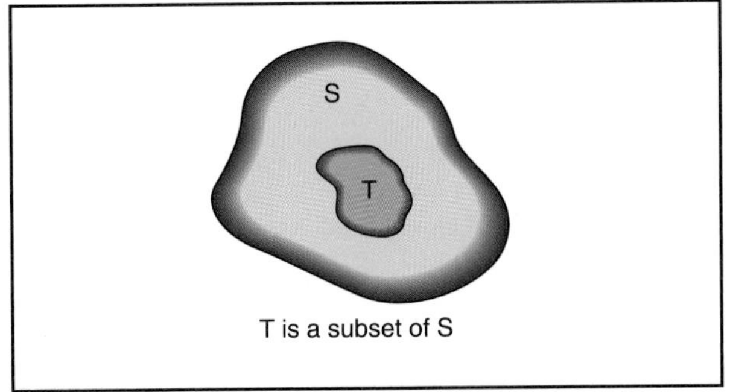

Figure 1a.

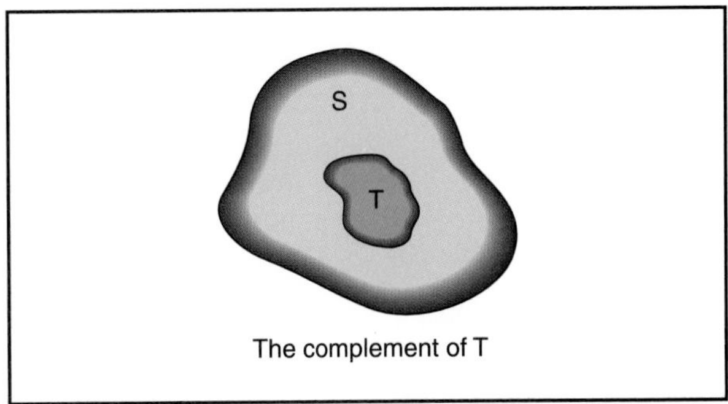

Figure 1a.

matics are all applied extensively in the fields of **physics**, **chemistry**, **biology**, and electrical and computer engineering.

Definitions

A set is a collection. As with any collection, a set is composed of objects, called members or elements. The elements of a set may be physical objects or mathematical objects. A set may be composed of baseball cards, salt shakers, tropical fish, numbers, geometric shapes, or abstract mathematical constructs such as functions. Even ideas may be elements of a set. In fact, the elements of a set are not required to have anything in common except that they belong to the same set. The collection of all the junk at a rummage sale is a perfectly good set, but one in which few of the elements have anything in common, except that someone has gathered them up and put them in a rummage sale.

In order to specify a set and its elements as completely and unambiguously as possible, standard forms of notation (sometimes called *set-builder notation*) have been adopted by mathematicians. For brevity a set is usually named using an uppercase Roman letter, such a S. When defining the set S, curly brackets are used to enclose the contents, and the elements are specified, inside the brackets. When convenient, the elements are listed individually. For instance, suppose there are 5 items at a rummage sale. Then the set of items at the rummage sale might be specified by R=. If the list of elements is long, the set may be specified by defining the condition that an object must satisfy in order to be considered an element of the set. For example, if the rummage sale has hundreds of items, then the set R may be specified by R =. This is the set of all x such that x is a real number, and 0 is less than x, and x is less than 1. The special symbol ø is given to the set with no elements, called the empty set or null set. Finally, it means that x is an element of the set A, and means that x is not an element of the set A.

Properties

Two sets S and T are equal, if every element of the set S is also an element of the set T, and if every element of the set T is also an element of the set S. This means that two sets are equal only if they both have exactly the same elements. A set T is called a proper subset of S if every element of T is contained in S, but not every element of S is in T. That is, the set T is a partial collection of the elements in S.

In set notation this is written $T \subset S$ and read "T is contained in S." S is sometimes referred to as the parent or universal set. Also, S is a subset of itself, called an improper subset. The complement of a subset T is that part of S that is not contained in T, and is written T'. Note that if T' is the empty set, then S and T are equal.

Sets are classified by size, according to the number of elements they contain. A set may be finite or infinite. A finite set has a whole number of elements, called the *cardinal number* of the set. Two sets with the same number of elements have the same **cardinal number**. To determine whether two sets, S and T, have the same number of elements, a **one-to-one correspondence** must exist between the elements of S and the elements of T. In order to associate a cardinal number with an infinite set, the transfinite numbers were developed. The first transfinite number $\aleph_0$, is the cardinal number of the set of **integers**, and of any set that can be placed in one-to-one correspondence with the integers. For example, it can be shown that a one-to-one correspondence exists between the set of rational numbers and the set of integers. Any set with cardinal number $\aleph_0$ is said to be a **countable** set. The second transfinite number $\aleph_1$ is the cardinal number of the **real numbers**. Any set in one-to-one correspondence with the real numbers has a cardinal number of $\aleph_1$, and is referred to as uncountable. The irrational numbers have cardinal number $\aleph_1$. Some interesting differences exist between subsets of finite sets and subsets of infinite sets. In particular, every proper subset of a finite set has a smaller cardinal number than its par-

ent set. For example, the set S = has a cardinal number of 10, but every proper subset of S (such as) has fewer elements than S and so has a smaller cardinality. In the case of infinite sets, however, this is not true. For instance, the set of all odd integers is a proper subset of the set of all integers, but it can be shown that a one-to-one correspondence exists between these two sets, so that they each have the same cardinality.

A set is said to be ordered if a **relation** (symbolized by <) between its elements can be defined, such that for any two elements of the set:

1) either b < c or c < b for any two elements

2) b < b has no meaning

3) if b < c and c < d then b < d.

In other words, an ordering relation is a rule by which the members of a set can be sorted. Examples of ordered sets are: the set of positive integers, where the symbol (<) is taken to mean less than; or the set of entries in an encyclopedia, where the symbol (<) means alphabetical ordering; or the set of U.S. World Cup soccer players, where the symbol (<) is taken to mean shorter than. In this last example the symbol (<) could also mean faster than, or scored more goals than, so that for some sets more than one ordering relation can be defined.

Operations

In addition to the general properties of sets, there are three important set operations, they are union, intersection, and difference. The union of two sets S and T, written S∪T, is defined as the collection of those elements that belong to either S or T or both. The union of two sets corresponds to their sum.

The intersection of the sets S and T is defined as the collection of elements that belong to both S and T, and is written S∩T. The intersection of two sets corresponds to the set of elements they have in common, or in some sense to their product.

The difference between two sets, written S-T, is the set of elements that are contained in S but not contained in T.

If S is a subset of T, then S-T = Ø, and if the intersection of S and T (S∩T) is the null set, then S-T = S.

Applications of set theory

Because of its very general or abstract nature, set theory has many applications in other branches of mathematics. In the branch called analysis, of which differential and **integral** calculus are important parts, an understanding of **limit** points and what is meant by the **continuity** of a function are based on set theory. The algebraic treatment of set operations leads to **Boolean Algebra**, in which the operations of intersection, union, and difference are interpreted as corresponding to the logical operations "and," "or," and "not," respectively. Boolean Algebra in turn is used extensively in the design of digital electronic circuitry, such as that found in calculators and personal computers. Set theory provides the basis of topology, the study of sets together with the properties of various collections of subsets.

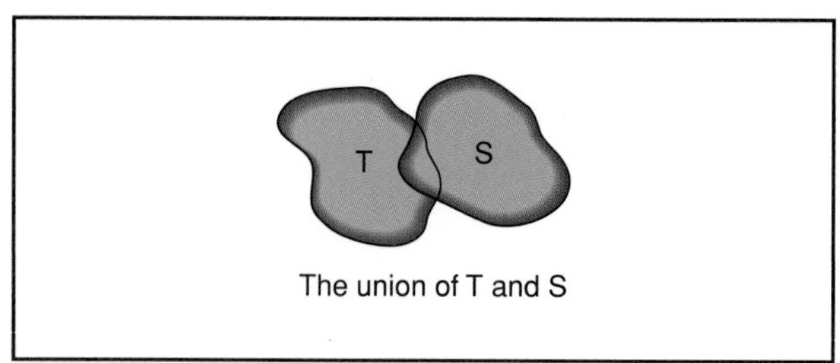

Figure 2a.

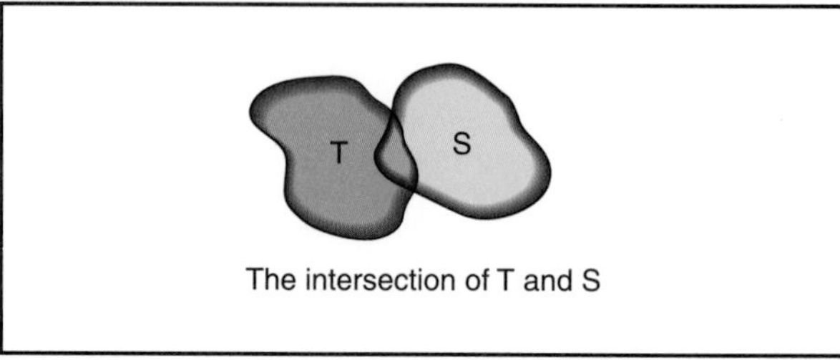

Figure 2b.

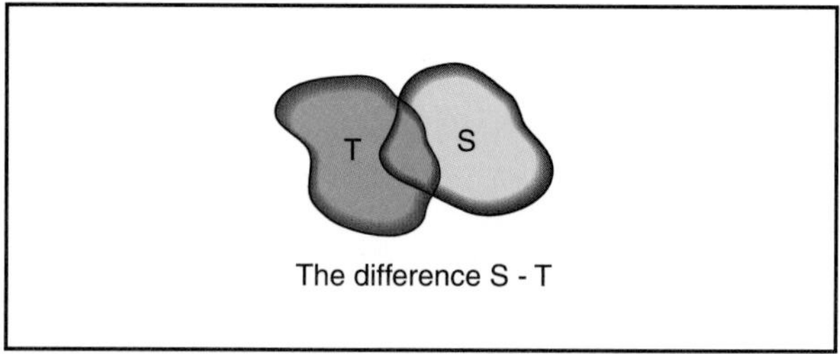

Figure 2c.

Further Reading

Buxton, Laurie. *Mathematics for Everyone.* New York: Schocken Books, 1985.

Christian, Robert R. *Introduction to Logic and Sets.* Waltham, MA: Blaisdell, 1965.

Dauben, Joseph Warren. *Georg Cantor: His Mathematics and Philosophy of the Infinite.* Cambridge: Harvard University Press, 1979.

KEY TERMS

Complement—That part of a set S which is not contained in a particular subset T. Written T′, the union of T and T′ equal S.

Difference—The difference between two sets S and T, written ST is that part of S which is not in T.

Dimension—A measure of the spatial extent of a set.

Element—Any member of a set. An object in a set.

Intersection—The intersection of two sets is itself a set comprised of all the elements common to both sets.

Set—A collection of objects, physical or abstract.

Subset—A set T is called a subset of another set S if every member of T is also a member of S.

Union—The union of two sets is the set that contains all the elements found in either of both of the two sets.

Kyle, James. *Mathematics Unraveled.* Blue Ridge Summit, PA: Tab Book, 1976.

Mandlebrot, Benoit B. *The Fractal Geometry of Nature.* New York: W. H. Freeman, 1983.

Moore, A. W. "A Brief History of Infinity." *Scientific American.* 272, No. 4 (1995): 112-16.

J. R. Maddocks

Sewage treatment

Sewerage and sewage must be defined at the outset because they are often used incorrectly. Sewerage is a system of pipes used to collect and carry sewage, which is the wastewater discharged from domestic premises. Domestic sewage consists of human wastes, **paper**, and vegetable **matter**. This type of waste is organic because it consists of compounds containing **carbon** and can be broken down by **microorganisms** into simpler compounds, which are stable and not liable to cause a nuisance. Sewage can consist of 99.9% **water** and 0.1% solids.

Raw sewage is a health and environmental concern. It carries a host of **bacteria** and viruses, causing diseases such as typhoid, **cholera**, and **dysentery**. Decaying organic waste is broken down by microorganisms that require substantial amounts of **oxygen**. If raw sewage is released directly into **rivers**, lakes, and oceans, it will significantly, and often catastrophically, reduce the oxygen levels in the water, killing **fish**, native microorganisms, and **plant** life.

In natural sewage decay, organic waste is consumed by microorganisms such as bacteria and **fungi**. Initially, this decay is **aerobic** (requiring oxygen). If the quantity of material is too large, however, the oxygen is depleted and the decay mechanism becomes **anaerobic** (carried out in the absence of oxygen). Anaerobic decay is slower than aerobic decay, and produces toxic reduction compounds like methane and **hydrogen** sulfide. The natural process is acceptable for very limited amounts of sewage but impractical for the quantities produced by municipalities. As a result, bulk treatment methods have been developed.

In general, municipal sewage treatment is an iterative process. The process begins by screening out large solids, such as trash, with bars or large mesh screens. Next, grit is settled out in preliminary settling tanks. The sewage then proceeds to further separation by moving through a series of holding tanks where the heavy matter (sludge) falls to the bottom, where it is later removed, and the floating matter rises to the top where it can be skimmed off. Once filtered, sewage is sent to tanks where it is processed biologically, using aerobic organisms. In addition, sewage can be chemically treated to bring **pH** to an acceptable region, and to remove **hazardous wastes**.

These are methods of sewage treatment, but not all of them are employed at every sewage treatment plant. The specific methods of treatment is dependant upon both the location of final release and the nature of the sewage being treated.

Separation of liquid and biosolids

After trash and bulk **contamination** are removed from waste water by screening, the next step is the removal of suspended matter. This can be accomplished by several methods, the simplest of which is gravity sedimentation. Wastewater is held in a tank or vessel until heavier particles have sunk to the bottom and light materials have floated to the top. The top of the tank can be skimmed to remove the floating material and the clarified liquid can be drained off. In batch mode sedimentation, several tanks of sewage will go through the settling process before the accumulated sludge is removed from the bottom of the tank.

The settling process can be hastened by use of chemical precipitants such as **aluminum** sulfate. Gentle stirring with rods, another method, encourages the aggregation of a number of fine, suspended materials. As the clots of material grow larger and heavier, they sink. Sus-

pended matter can be encouraged to float by exposing it to fine bubbles, a method known as dissolved-air floatation. The bubbles adhere to the matter and cause it to float to the surface, where it can be removed by skimming.

Another method of **filtration**, generally used after gravity sedimentation, is deep bed filtration. Partially processed liquid from the sedimentation tanks, called effluent, flows over a bed of graded sand and crushed **coal**. This material not only strains the larger particles from the effluent, but further clarifies it by removing fine particles via adhesion. The filtering material attracts these small particles of sewage by electrostatic charge, pulling them out of the main flow and resulting in significantly clearer liquid. Alternately, effluent can be filtered by a fine mesh screen or cloth, in a method known as surface filtration, or solid material can be pulled out by **centrifuge**.

At this point the original raw sewage has been essentially separated into two parts: sludge, or biosolids; and clarified effluent. Both parts still contain disease carrying, oxygen consuming pathogens, and need further processing. Earlier, we discussed the biological decay of raw sewage. Theoretically, both biosolids and effluent can be processed using biological treatment methods, but at this point cost considerations come into play. Biological treatment of dense sludge is time-consuming, requiring large tanks to allow complete processing, whereas that of effluent is fairly efficient. Thus, biosolids are generally processed by different methods than effluent.

After settling out, biosolids can be removed from the bottom of the sedimentation tank. These tanks may have a conical shape to allow the sludge to be removed through a valve at the tip, or they may be flat bottomed. The sludge can be dried and incinerated at temperatures between 1,500–3,000°F (816–1,649°C), and the resulting ashes, if non-toxic, can be buried in a **landfill**. **Composting** is another method of sludge disposal. The biosolids can be mixed with **wood** chips to provide roughage and aeration during the decay process. The resulting material can be used as fertilizer in agriculture. Properly diluted, sludge can also be disposed of through land application. Purely municipal sludge, without chemicals or heavy metals, makes a great spray-on fertilizer for non-food plants. It is used in **forestry**, and on such commercial **crops** as **cotton** and tobacco. It must be monitored carefully, though, so that it does not contaminate ground water.

Biomanagement of effluent

Though the biological treatment methods described here can be applied to any raw sewage, for the reasons described earlier, they are generally only used to process effluent that has already had the bulk of the solid material removed. As such, it is mostly water, though still containing unacceptable levels of pathogens and oxygen-consuming organisms.

An early method of biological treatment used natural **soil**. Sewage was allowed to percolate down through the soil where it was processed by aerobic organisms. Such treatment methods were not practical for the large volumes of sewage produced by towns of any appreciable size. If a significant amount of solids accumulated, the reaction would become anaerobic, with the attendant disadvantages of odor and slow decay.

Contact gravel beds are an improved form of the natural soil method. This type of processing is usually performed in batch mode. Gravel beds several feet deep enclosed in tanks are charged with effluent. Voids in the gravel guarantee aeration, and the aerobic decay process proceeds more rapidly than the natural soil method. After a batch is processed, the beds can be left empty so that the gravel can re-aerate.

A more efficient version of contact gravel beds are percolating or trickling filters, still in common use. Effluent is trickled over gravel beds continuously, and the voids between the gravel provide aeration. The beds rapidly become "charged" with a slime layer containing complex **ecosystem** made up of bacteria, viruses, **protozoa**, fungi, **algae**, nematodes, and **insects**. The various life forms in this biological mat maintain a balance, some feeding on the effluent, some feeding on one another, keeping the filter from becoming clogged. The new grown solid material can be flushed out with the purified water, then removed in settling tanks called **humus** tanks.

Scientists studying biological treatment methods at the turn of the century discovered that if sewage is left in a tank and aerated, with the liquid periodically removed and replaced with fresh sewage, the sludge that settles in the tank will develop into a potent "microorganism stew." This material, known as activated sludge, can oxidize organic sewage far more rapidly than the organisms in trickling filters or contact gravel beds.

In activated sludge processing systems, the effluent is introduced at one end of a large tank containing activated sludge and is processed as it travels down to the outflow pipe at the far end. The mixture is agitated to keep the sludge in suspension and ensure adequate aeration. Air can be bubbled through the tank to introduce additional oxygen if necessary. After outflow, the processed liquid is held in sedimentation tanks until the sludge settles out. The now purified water is then released to a river or other body of water and the settled sludge is removed and returned to the main processing tank. Over time, the activated sludge accumulates, and

must be treated in the same way as the biosolids discussed earlier.

Algal ponds are a variation on the activated sludge method. Algae on the surface of a pond of effluent aerate the liquid by **photosynthesis**. The bulk of the processing is still performed by bacteria.

Some wastes contain too high a level of toxic materials to be processed using biological methods. Even small amounts of toxic chemicals can kill off activated sludge or other biological systems, causing the municipality to restart the culture while the sewage waits to be processed. If wastes are too wet to incinerate, wet air oxidation can be used in which oxygen and hot effluent are mixed in a reactor. Another process for dealing with toxic waste is vitrification, in which the material is essentially melted into **glass** by a pair of electrodes. The material is inert and immobilized, and can be buried with a higher degree of safety than in its previous state.

Urban stormwater runoff

Stormwater is another issue in sewage treatment. During rainstorms, the water washing down the buildings, streets, and sidewalks is collected into the sewers. A portion of the stormwater can be processed by the sewage treatment plant, but once the plant reaches overflow, the water is often released directly into the environment. Most systems are not designed to process more than a small percentage of the overflow from major storms.

Stormwater overflow is a major source of **pollution** for urban rivers and streams. It has a high percentage of heavy metals (cadmium, lead, nickel, zinc) and toxic organic pollutants, all of which constitute a health and environmental hazard. It can also contain grease, oil, and other automotive product pollution from street runoff, as well as trash, **salt**, sand, and dirt. Large amounts of runoff can flush so-called dry **weather** deposition from sewer systems, causing overflow to contain the same types of pathogens as raw sewage. The runoff is oxygen-demanding, meaning that if routed directly into rivers, streams, and oceans, it will rob the water of the oxygen needed to support life.

Historically, stormwater runoff has not been considered part of the sewage treatment plan. Most municipal sewage treatment facilities have only minimal space for storing runoff, after which it is routed directly into receiving waterways. Government and engineers are studying various ways of lessening the problem, including construction of catchbasins to hold runoff, flushing sewers regularly to reduce dry-weather deposition of sewage, implementing sewer flow control systems, and a number of strategies to reduce deposition of litter and chemicals on city streets. Economical methods of creating storage tanks and performing preliminary and secondary treatment of the runoff water are being developed. According to some estimates, it could cost the U.S. as much as $300 billion for combined sewer overflow and urban stormwater runoff control. It is left to be seen how much more the environmental effects of uncontrolled runoff will cost.

Septic tanks

Not all homes and businesses are connected to municipal sewage systems. Some are too remote, or in towns too small for sewage systems and treatment plants. In such cases, septic systems must be used.

A septic system consists of a septic tank, a drain field or leach field, and associated piping. Gray water from washing and black water from household toilets runs through water-tight sewage pipe to the septic tank. Anaerobic decay takes place in the septic tank, primarily in a layer of floating scum on top of the sewage. An outlet pipe leads to the drain field. The sewage undergoes final processing in the drain field, including filtration and aerobic decay.

When sewage reaches the septic tank, solids settle out of it. Anaerobic bacteria, **yeast**, fungi, and actinomycetes break down the biosolids, producing methane and hydrogen sulfide. Fine solids, grease and oils form a layer of scum on the surface of the liquid, insulating the anaerobic community from any air in the tank.

There are numerous septic tank designs. The primary requirements are that the tank be watertight, that it have inspection/cleaning ports, and that it be large enough to contain three to five days worth of sewage from the household. This ensures that the anaerobic creatures are able to process the sewage prior to its release to the drain field, and that the tank does not fill up and/or overflow; a rather revolting prospect. This outflow pipe is normally at a lower level than the inflow pipe and at the far end of the tank from the inflow pipe, to ensure that only processed sewage is released. Many septic tank designs include baffles or multiple chambers to force the black water through maximum processing prior to release to drain field.

Aerobic decay of the sewage takes place in the drain field. The outflow from the septic tank, called effluent, still contains pathogens. Effluent travels through a network of pipes set in gravel several feet below ground. The sections of pipe are slightly separated at the joints, allowing the liquid to seep out. The soil and gravel of the drain field filter the effluent and expose it aerobic bacteria, fungi, and protozoa that feed on the organic material, converting it to soluble **nutrients**. The liquid eventually

either percolates down to the water table or returns to the surface via **evaporation** or **transpiration** by plants.

Roughly 4 ft (1.2 m) of soil are needed to process effluent, although authorities differ on the exact number, which varies with the makeup of the drain field soil. In other words, effluent passed through a couple yards of soil is pure enough to drink. To ensure a significant margin of safety, a drain field must be from 50-400 ft (15.2-121.9 m) from the nearest water supply, depending on the soil and the number of people served by the aquifer.

Some areas use **incineration** for the disposal of sludge. Earlier incinerators proved very expensive to operate and for this reason many of the plants were abandoned. Many grass-roots organizations also disapprove of incinerators because of health reasons. Incinerators release carcinogenic (cancer-causing) and toxic chemicals from their smoke stacks, including heavy metals (such as arsenic, lead, cadmium, mercury, chromium and beryllium); acid gases, including hydrogen fluoride; partially-burned organic material such as polyvinyl chloride (PVC), herbicide residues and wood preservatives; other organic chemicals, including **polycyclic aromatic hydrocarbons** (PAHs); and dioxins and furans. One recent analysis identified 192 volatile organic compounds being emitted by a solid waste incinerator. In more recent years, a new form of incinerator has been developed based on the use of a fluidized bed which is proving more successful.

Under the Clean Water Act (CWA), sewage treatment plants and factories must obtain pollution permits, or legally binding agreements, that limit the volumes and types of pollution discharged into the nation's lakes and rivers. These permits form the basis of virtually all water-pollution tracking and reduction, as well as enforcement of **water pollution** laws. They must be renewed at least every five years, and with each new permit the amount of polluted discharge allowed is to be lowered toward the eventual goal of **zero** pollution. At the beginning of 2000, The Friends of the **Earth** (FOE) and Environmental Working Group conducted a review of the publicly available water-pollution records from the 50 states and the District of Columbia. The FOE rated states on a pass-fail basis. The grade assigned to each state was based on the percentage of expired permits as of the start of this year. States with more than 10% of their permits expired were failed based on a 10% maximum permit backlog set by the United States Environmental Protection Agency (EPA). They found that 44 states and the District of Columbia failed their criterion.

The average person produces roughly 60 gal (227 l) of sewage daily, including both black and grey water. Municipal treatment plants and septic systems use mechanical and biological treatment methods to process out most of the pathogens and oxygen-consuming organisms. Toxic wastes are more difficult to remove, and are present in significant volumes in largely untreated stormwater runoff. In particular, industrial effluent presents environmental and health risks. It falls to us as citizens to be responsible in our use and disposal of these substances, which eventually find their way back into the environment.

KEY TERMS

Active sludge—Sewage that has been aerated in a tank and has developed powerful organic oxidation capabilities.

Aerobic—Carried out in the presence of oxygen.

Algal ponds—A variation on the active sludge method in which aeration is performed by algae photosynthesis.

Anaerobic—Carried out without the presence of oxygen.

Biosolids—Feces.

Black water—Sewage that contains biosolids, e.g. water from the toilet.

Drain field—Underground layer of soil and gravel where aerobic decay of septic tank effluent takes place.

Effluent—Liquid that flows from a septic tank or sedimentation tank; pathogens—bacteria and viruses capable of causing disease.

Grey water—Sewage that does not contain biosolids, e.g. water from the kitchen sink or the shower.

Leach field—Drain field.

Percolating filters—A sewage treatment system in which effluent is trickled over gravel beds and efficiently purified by bacteria.

Septic tank—Tank in which anaerobic decay of sewage takes place.

Sewerage—Piping and collection system for sewage.

See also Poisons and toxins; Waste management.

Further Reading

Alth, M. and C. Alth. *Constructing and Maintaining Your Well and Septic System.* Blue Ridge Summit, PA: Tab Books, 1984.

Cheremisinoff, P. *Biomanagement of Wastewater and Waste.* Englewood Cliffs, NJ: Prentice-Hall, 1994.

Escritt, L. *Sewerage and Sewage Treatment.* New York: Wiley, 1984.

Kristin Lewotsky

Sewing machine

A sewing machine is a mechanical device equipped with a needle (or needles) threaded at the point-end, which puncture the fabric periodically as it moves under the needle; each stitch is created as the thread loops onto itself (chain stitch) or locks around a second strand of thread (lock stitch), sewing the fabrics together. Sewing machines are used in both the home and industry, but are designed differently for each setting. Those for the home tend to be more versatile in terms of the number and kinds of stitches they can perform, but they operate more slowly than industrial machines, and have a shorter life span. Industrial machines are heavier, have a much longer life span, are capable of thousands of stitches per inch, and may be designed for very specialized tasks.

History

Near the end of the eighteenth century, a London cabinetmaker patented the design of a primitive machine for chain-stitch sewing that used a forked needle, which passed through a hole made by the sewer using an awl. Over the next several decades, inventors in **Europe** and the United Stated advanced the sewing machine concept. Early machine-sewers operated their machines by turning a hand wheel that moved the needle up and down, and in and out of the fabric. By the early 1830s, with the introduction of New Yorker Walter Hunt's lock stitch machine, and with the addition of the feed mechanism that moved the fabric automatically beneath the needle, the mechanics of the sewing machine as we know it today had been worked out. But it wasn't until Isaac Singer—the first manufacturer to make sewing machines widely available—that sewing machines became a fixture in the average household. Singer introduced a lock-stitch machine in 1851, the first powered by a foot treadle, a pump or lever device that turned a flywheel and belt drive.

As clothing manufacture moved into factories at the turn of the century, sewing machine design branched out as well. Sewing machines designed for home use have remained versatile, capable of performing different kinds of stitching for a variety of tasks such as making buttonholes, or sewing stretchy fabrics using the zig-zag stitch, in which the needle moves back and forth horizontally. More recently, manufacturers of home machines are have incorporated computerized controls that can be programmed to create a multitude of decorative stitches as well as the basics.

Sewing machines intended for industrial use evolved along a different track. In the factory setting, where time and efficiency are at a premium, machines have to be very fast, capable of producing thousands stitches per second. Clothing manufacturers also realized that sewing machines designed to do just one task, such as making a collar, attaching buttons, making buttonholes, setting in pockets, and attaching belt loops, could perform these tasks much more quickly than a less specialized machines.

Types of sewing machines

Sewing machines are designed to create one of two basic types of stitches. The chainstitch is created as a single thread loops through itself on the underside or edge of the fabric, and is used for such purposes as button holes and edgings. The lock stitch is created as two separate threads—one below the fabric in a bobbin, the other above on a spool, lock together from the top and the bottom of the fabric at each stitch. The lock stitch is used most widely in both industrial and home sewing, and is stronger than the chain stitch, but because it puts more tension on the thread, cannot be created as quickly. (Industrial lockstitch machines can sew up to 6,000 stitches per minute, while the fastest chainstitch machines can sew 10,000 stitches per minute.) In the early 1970s, manufacturers of industrial machines began to incorporate computerized technology into their products. Because these machines could be programmed to perform a number of the steps previously done by the operator, the new technology halved the number of steps (from 16-8) in a labor-intensive task such as stitching together the various parts of a collar (top ply [outer collar], interlining, lower ply, two-piece collarband, and collarband interlining).

Innovations in the 1970s led to the design of three types of machines. Dedicated machines incorporate microprocessors capable of controlling the assembly of apparel parts such as collars, and the operator simply loads the pre-cut clothing parts into these machines. Programmable convertible machines can be converted to perform a number of different tasks, and in this case, too, the operator just loads the pre-cut fabrics. Operator-programmable machines can be taught new sewing procedures as the operator performs the task with the machine in "teach" mode, and the machine "learns" the various parts of a task. The machine can then perform most of the functions except placing the material.

KEY TERMS

Chainstitch—Stitch usually created with a single thread that loops through itself on the underside of the fabric, which is used for such purposes as button holes and edging.

Lockstitch—A stitch created as two separate threadsone below the fabric in a bobbin, the other above, lock together from the top and the bottom of the fabric at each stitch. The lock stitch is stronger but cannot be created as quickly as the chain stitch, because it puts more tension on the thread.

Future developments

In both industrial and domestic machines, computer technology is the driving force for change. In the industrial setting, this change has three goals: to speed up operation of the sewing machines; to make the operator's job easier as materials move through their station more quickly; and to make the assembly of small parts of a garment easier with the design of more specialized sewing machines. In the industrial setting, where the **pressure** toward innovation is highest, machines are likely to move toward higher levels of **automation**.

See also Textiles.

Further Reading

Hoffman and Rush. *Microelectronics and Clothing: The Impact of Technical Change on a Global Industry.* New York: Praeger, 1988.

Beth Hanson

Sex change

Sex change, also called transsexuality, is a procedure by which an individual of one sex is hormonally and surgically altered to attain the characteristics of the other sex. A male is changed into a female or a female into a male, complete with altered genitalia and other secondary sex characteristics.

It has been estimated that one male in every 20,000-30,000 wants to become female. The number of females who desire a sex change is not known, but it is estimated that for every female wishing a sex change there may be four males.

Transsexuals usually see themselves as being of the wrong sex early in life. They feel that they are trapped in the wrong body. Though they have sexual desires for persons of the same sex, it is not as a homosexual. A homosexual, one who desires a sexual relationship with someone of his or her own sex, is comfortable with his sex and does not desire to change. The transsexual views himself as a female (or herself as a male) and visualizes his female persona as being mated to a male. As children, transsexuals often will play with the toys of the opposite sex and sometimes will cross dress in clothing of the opposite sex. They also may be more comfortable socializing with members of the opposite sex inasmuch as they view themselves as having similar likes, dislikes, and desires.

Attempts to understand the underlying reasons for a person desiring a sex change have not been successful. Hormone studies have found them to have normal hormonal patterns for their sex. Examination of their childhood and home environment has shown that some transsexuals are from broken homes, others from homes with weak or ineffectual fathers and strong mothers, and still others from homes of loving and sharing parents. Genetic investigations also have found nothing. At least one investigator blames an abnormal prenatal neuroendocrine pattern, so the individual is born with the underlying transsexualism already imprinted. Such a hormonal upset might be caused by trauma to the mother, stress, use of drugs, or other reason while the developing infant was early in growth in the womb. This theory also remains to be proved.

The sex-change procedure

Many potential transsexuals will do nothing about their seeming need to be of the opposite sex. They will marry, have a family, and attempt to fit in with society's expectations for a person of their sex. Secretly they may cross dress in clothing of the opposite sex's in private. Usually their families know nothing of this practice. A person who wears the clothing of the opposite sex is called a transvestite. A true transvestite enjoys cross dressing but has no inclination to undergo a sex change.

Other persons, however, have feelings too strong to subdue and they will eventually seek professional help in their conversion to the opposite sex. The first documented case of a complete conversion of a male to a female was that of Christine Jorgenson. Born a male, he underwent sex-change hormonal therapy and **surgery** to become a female in 1952. She later married. A number of medical facilities have since been established around the world and specialize in the complex process of transsexualism.

The first steps in the sex change process involve long sessions of counseling to ascertain that the individ-

ual is dedicated to changing sex, has thought it through thoroughly, and will be comfortable with his decision. Assuming the counseling provides the physician with information pointing to the resolute determination for a sex change, the patient will move on to the next level.

Hormone therapy, that is replacement of one's natural **hormones** with those of the opposite sex, is the beginning of the transsexual process. Women will receive androgens, male hormones, and males will be given estrogen and progesterone, the female hormones that are responsible for the secondary sex characteristics.

Male secondary sex characteristics include facial hair growth, larger muscle development, deep voice, and a heavier skeleton. Female characteristics include the development of breasts, a smoother, more rounded body as a result of a layer of **fat** that men do not have, a voice higher in pitch because of a smaller larynx and shorter vocal cords, lack of facial hair, and certain anatomic characteristics in the skeleton to facilitate childbirth.

Males will be given large doses of female hormones to override the effects of the androgens. Females will receive testosterone, the male hormone. Changes will become evident very soon after hormone therapy begins. The male will no longer grow whiskers and he may lose the characteristic hair growing on his chest. A woman receiving androgens will experience facial hair growth as well as changes in the pattern of fat deposits in her body. Voices in both sexes will change only minimally because the size of the larynx and the vocal cords are unchanged by hormones. The female who becomes male will have a voice uncharacteristically high for a male, and the male who becomes a female will have an unusually low-pitched voice for a woman. All of these observations are based on averages for males and females. Some small males or large females may seem more completely to change because they have the characteristics of the opposite sex to begin with.

The transsexual process is enhanced by surgical removal of the individual's genitalia and construction of genitals of the assumed sex. This is a difficult procedure in either sex, but more so in the female inasmuch as her genitalia are internal.

The surgical procedure on the male involves removal of the penis and the scrotum with the testes. A pseudo-vagina can be constructed from the skin of the penis. This is everted and sewn into a tube that is inserted into the man's body and sewn to the skin. Steps must be taken during the first few weeks following surgery to keep this makeshift vagina open. Construction of female breasts can be accomplished by using fat from the individual's body under the skin over the pectoral muscles. The woman also may wear strategically placed padding to simulate breast growth.

KEY TERMS

Genitalia—The sex organs; in the male, the penis and in the female the vagina.

Larynx—The voice box or Adam's apple. It is connected at the bottom to the trachea, the tube leading to the lungs. The vocal cords lie under the epiglottis, the flap at the top.

Secondary sex characteristics—Those unique traits that mark an individual as a male or female. Facial hair is a male characteristic and breast development is a female one, for example.

Uterus—The organ in which a growing fetus develops until birth.

Removal of the scrotum and testes also removes the source of the male hormones, so the therapy with female hormones can assume dominance. The secondary sex characteristics of the male will be blunted. Facial hair will stop growing and body contours may change over time to more closely resemble those of the female. The newly created woman will be required to take female hormones for the remainder of her life. Her reconstructed vagina will enable her to have vaginal sex with a male, though of course she is not able to bear children.

Surgery on the female transsexual is more complex. The female reproductive organs are internal, so an incision is required to remove the ovaries, uterus, and vagina. A penis can be constructed and attached, but from that time on the new male must be careful to maintain strict hygiene to prevent bladder **infection**. Usually the woman's breasts also are removed, leaving a small scar. Male hormone therapy now will be dominant and the new male will begin to grow facial hair and perhaps hair on his chest. He will still be of slight build compared to the average male and will be unable to father children. An implanted penile prosthesis will enable him to attain an erection, and a scrotum containing prosthetic testes will complete the reconstruction and yield an anatomically correct male.

Now, instead of being trapped in a body of the wrong sex, the new man or woman is comfortable in his or her new identity and will go on to live a normal life for one of the chosen sex.

See also Reproductive system.

Larry Blaser

Sextant

The optical instruments called sextants have been used as navigation aids for centuries, especially by seafarers. In its simplest form, a sextant consists of an eyepiece and an angular scale called the "**arc**," fitted with an arm to mark degrees. By manipulating the parts, a user can measure the angular **distance** between two celestial bodies, usually the **Earth** and either the **Sun** or **Moon**. The observer can thereby calculate his or her position of latitude by using a trigonometric operation known as triangulation. The word sextant derives from a Latin term for one sixth of a **circle**, or 60 degrees. This term is applied generally to a variety of instruments today regardless of the spans of their arcs.

One of the earliest precursors to the sextant was referred to as a latitude hook. This invention of the Polynesians could only be used to travel from one place at a particular latitude to another at the same latitude. The hook end of the device served as a frame for the North Star, a fixed celestial body also known as Polaris. By sighting the star through the hook at one tip of the wire, you could discover you were off-course if the **horizon** line did not exactly intersect the straight tip at the opposite end.

Christopher Columbus used a quadrant during his maiden voyage. The measuring was done by a plumb bob, a little weight hung by a string that was easily disturbed by the pitching or **acceleration** of a ship. The biggest drawback to such intermediate versions of the sextant was the persistent requirement to look at both the horizon and the chosen celestial body at once. This always introduced a reading **error**, caused by ocular **parallax**, which could set a navigator up to 90 mi (145 m) off-course. Inventions such as the cross-staff, backstaff, sea-ring and nocturnal could not ease the tendency towards such errors.

Although Isaac Newton discovered the principle which guides modern sextants, and even designed a prototype in 1700, John Hadley in England and Thomas Godfrey in America simultaneously constructed working models of the double-reflecting sextant 30 years later. These machines depended upon two **mirrors** placed **parallel** to each other, as in a periscope. Just the way a transversing line cuts two parallel lines at matching angles, a ray of light bounces on and off first one, then the other mirror. You displace the mirrors by adjusting the measuring arm along the arc, in order to bring a celestial object into view. The number of degrees of this displacement is always half the angular altitude of the body, in relation to the horizon.

Although it has been largely replaced by **radar** and **laser** surveillance technology, the sextant is still used by navigators of small craft, and applied to simple **physics** experiments. Marine sextants depend upon the visible horizon of the sea's surface as a base line. Air sextants were equipped with a liquid, a flat pane of **glass**, and a pendulum or **gyroscope** to provide an artificial horizon.

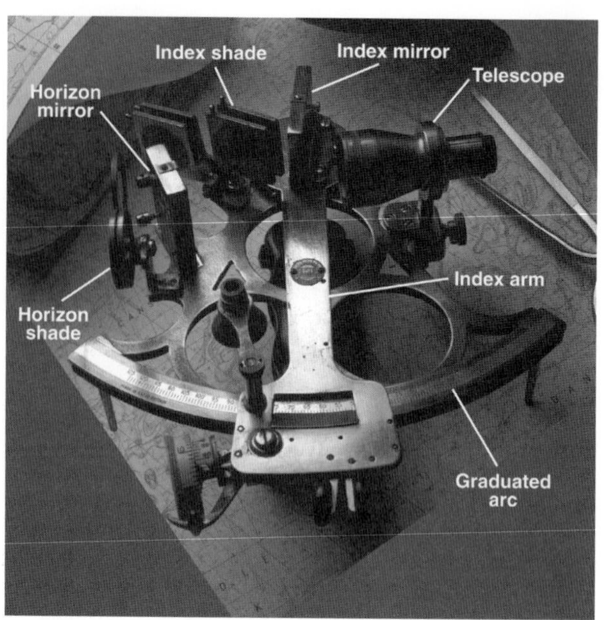

A sextant.

Sexual behavior see **Courtship**

Sexual reproduction

Sexual reproduction is the process through which two parents produce offspring which are genetically different from themselves and have new combinations of their characteristics. This contrasts with **asexual reproduction**, where one parent produces offspring genetically identical to itself. During sexual reproduction, each parent contributes one haploid **gamete** (a sex **cell** with half the normal number of chromosomes). The two sex cells fuse during **fertilization** and form a diploid zygote (which has the normal number of chromosomes). Recombination, which is the production of variations in **gene** combinations, occurs at fertilization, so bringing together new combinations of alleles. Crossing-over, the exchange of pieces of chromosomes by two homologous chromosomes, also brings about genetic variation during sexual reproduction. Sexual reproduction is advantageous because it generates variations in characters that can adapt a species over time and improve its chances of survival.

Sexual reproduction occurs in practically all forms of life. Even **bacteria**, which are always haploid, exchange genetic material. Eukaryotes, organisms possessing a nuclear **membrane**, generally produce haploid gametes (or sex cells). A gamete, such as an egg or a sperm, possesses half the normal number of chromosomes, and is produced by **meiosis**, which is reduction **cell division**, which reduces the number of chromosomes from diploid in the parent cell to haploid in the gametes. When the gametes fuse at fertilization, they restore the normal number of chromosomes. Conjugation, alternation of generations, and **animal** reproduction illustrate various modes of sexual reproduction.

Conjugation

Conjugation is a process of genetic recombination that occurs between two organisms (such as bacteria) in addition to asexual reproduction. Conjugation only occurs between cells of different mating types. In bacteria, cells designated F+ and F- lie close together, and a narrow bridge of cytoplasm forms between them. F+ cells contain a plasmid or reproductive **factor** that is made of DNA, which replicates within the bacterial cell. A copy is transferred from a donor F+ cell to a recipient F-. *Spirogyra*, a **freshwater** filamentous alga, also exhibits conjugation, where two nearby filaments develop extensions that contact each other. The walls between the connecting channels disintegrate, and one cell moves through the conjugation tube into the other. The cells fuse to form a diploid zygote, the only diploid stage in the life of *Spirogyra*. The black bread **mold**, *Rhizopus*, reproduces asexually by spores and sexually by conjugation. During conjugation, the tips of short hyphae act as gametes, and fuse. The resulting zygote develops a protective wall and becomes dormant. Finally, meiosis occurs, and a haploid bread mold germinates and grows spore-producing sporangia.

Alternation of generations

In plants, sexual and asexual reproduction unite in a single cycle called alternation of generations. During alternation of generations, a gametophyte, (a haploid gamete-producing **plant**), alternates with a sporophyte (a diploid spore-producing plant). In *Ectocarpus*, a brown aquatic alga, the two generations are equally prominent, whereas in mosses, the gametophyte generation dominates. In **ferns** and seed plants, the sporophyte dominate, because the sporophyte generation is better adapted to survive on land.

Mosses are small plants that lack vascular **tissue** and do not produce **seeds**, and depend on a moist environment to survive. The green leafy ground cover of mosses that we are familiar with is the haploid gametophyte. The gametophyte develops sex organs, a male antheridium and a female archegonium on the same or different plants. The antheridium produces flagellated sperm cells that swim to the egg cells in the archegonium. After fertilization, the zygote grows into a diploid sporophyte. The sporophyte consists of a foot, stalk, and capsule. It remains attached to the gametophyte. Cells in the capsule undergo meiosis and develop into haploid spores. When released, spores grow into gametophytes with rootlike, leaflike and stemlike parts.

Ferns, in the form of the familiar green leafy plants, represent the diploid sporophyte generation. Ferns have a vascular system and true roots, stems, and leaves, but they do not produce seeds. Sporangia, or **spore** cases, develop on the leaves of ferns, and produce haploid spores by means of meiosis. The spores germinate into haploid green gametophytes. The fern gametophyte is a tiny heart-shaped structure that bears antheridia and archegonia. Flagellated sperm swim to the eggs in a layer of ground **water**. Although the sporophyte is adapted to land life, this need for water limits the gametophyte. After fertilization, the diploid zygote develops into the sporophyte.

In flowering plants, the diploid sporophytes are plants with roots, leaves, stems, flowers and seeds. Anthers within the **flower** contain four sporangia. Cells in the sporangia undergo meiosis and produce haploid microspores. The wall of each microspore thickens, and the haploid nucleus of the microspore divides by **mitosis** into a generative nucleus and a tube nucleus. These microspores are now called pollen, and each pollen grain is an immature male gametophyte. **Pollination** occurs when pollen escapes from the anthers and lands on the stigma of a flower, either of the same plant or a different plant. There, a pollen tube begins to grow down the style toward the ovary of the pistil, and the two nuclei move into the pollen tube. The generative nucleus divides to form two haploid sperm cells. The germinated pollen grain is now a mature male gametophyte. Finally, the pollen tube penetrates the ovary and the sperm enter. The ovary contains sporangia called ovules. Meiosis occurs within each ovule forming four haploid megaspores. Three disintegrate, and the remaining megaspore undergoes repeated mitosis to form the female gametophyte. The female gametophyte is a haploid seven-celled structure. One of the seven cells is an egg cell. Another of the seven cells contains two nuclei called polar nuclei. When the two sperm cells enter, double fertilization occurs. One sperm fertilizes the egg, forming a zygote that develops into a diploid embryo sporophyte. The two polar nuclei fuse and their product unites with the second sperm forming a triploid endosperm. The endosperm serves as stored food for

the embryo sporophyte. After fertilization, the ovule matures into a seed, consisting of embryo, stored food, and seed coat. In angiosperms, the ovary usually enlarges to become a fruit. Upon **germination**, the seed develops into a mature diploid sporophyte plant. Internal fertilization and seeds help adapt flowering plants to life on land.

Animal reproduction

During sexual reproduction in animals, a haploid sperm and unites with a haploid egg cell to form a diploid zygote. The zygote divides mitotically and differentiates into an embryo. The embryo grows and matures. After **birth** or hatching, the animal develops into a mature adult capable of reproduction. Some **invertebrates** reproduce by self-fertilization, in which an animal's sperm fertilizes its own eggs. Self- fertilization is common in tapeworms and other internal **parasites**, which lack the opportunity to find a mate. Most animals, however, use cross fertilization, in which different individuals donate the egg and the sperm. Even hermaphrodites animals (such as the earthworms) that produce both types of gametes use cross-fertilization.

Animals exhibit two patterns for bringing sperm and eggs together. One is external fertilization, whereby animals shed eggs and sperm into the surrounding water. The flagellated sperm need an aquatic environment to swim to the eggs, the eggs require water to prevent drying out. Most aquatic invertebrates, most **fish**, and some **amphibians** use external fertilization. These animals release large numbers of sperm and eggs, thereby overcoming large losses of gametes in the water. In addition, courting **behavior** in some species brings about the simultaneous release of the gametes, which helps insure that sperm and egg meet.

The other pattern of sexual reproduction is internal fertilization, whereby the male introduces sperm inside the females reproductive tract where the eggs are fertilized. Internal fertilization is an adaption for life on land, for it reduces the loss of gametes that occurs during external fertilization. Sperms are provided with a fluid (semen) that provides an aquatic medium for the sperm to swim when inside the male's body. Mating behavior and reproductive readiness are coordinated and controlled by **hormones** so that sperm and egg are brought together at the appropriate time.

After internal fertilization, most **reptiles** and all **birds** lay eggs that are surrounded by a tough membrane or a shell. Their eggs have four membranes, the amnion, the allantois, the yolk sac and the chorion. The amnion contains the fluid surrounding the embryo; the allantois stores the embryo's urinary wastes and contains **blood** vessels that bring the embryo **oxygen** and take away **carbon dioxide**. The yolk sac holds stored food, and the chorion surrounds the embryo and the other membranes. After the mother lays her eggs, the young hatch.

Mammals employ internal fertilization, but except for the Australian montremes such as the duckbill **platypus** and the echidna, mammals do not lay eggs. The fertilized eggs of mammals implant in the uterus which develops into the placenta, where the growth and differentiation of the embryo occur. Embryonic **nutrition** and **respiration** occur by **diffusion** from the maternal bloodstream through the placenta. When development is complete, the birth process takes place.

See also Chromosome; Deoxyribonucleic acid.

KEY TERMS

Ovule—Sporangium in a seed plant that gives rise to the female gametophyte and after fertilization becomes the seed.

Plasmid—Circular piece of DNA in the cytoplasm of bacteria that replicates independently of the cell's chromosome.

Recombination—A new arrangement of alleles that results from sexual reproduction and crossing-over.

Further Reading

Campbell, Neil A. *Biology.* Redwood City, CA: Benjamin/Cummings, 1993.

Essenfeld, Bernice, Carol R. Gontang, and Randy Moore. *Biology* Menlo Park: Addison Wesley, 1996.

Films for the Humanities and Sciences. *The Chemistry of Fertilization.* Princeton, 1994.

Kerr, Richard A. "Timing Evolution's Early Bursts." *Science.* (6 January 1995).

Richardson, Sarah. "Guinness Book Gametes." *Discover.* (March 1995).

Sikkel, Paul C. "Honey, I Ate the Kids." *Natural History.* (December 1994).

Taylor, Martha. *Campbell's Biology Student Study Guide.* Redwood City, CA: Benjamin/Cummings, 1990.

Bernice Essenfeld

Sexually transmitted diseases

Long known as venereal disease, after **Venus**, the Roman goddess of love, sexually transmitted diseases

are increasingly common. The more than 20 known sexually transmitted diseases range from old to new, from the life-threatening to painful and unsightly. The life-threatening sexually transmitted diseases are syphilis, which has been known for centuries, and Acquired Immune Deficiency Syndrome (AIDS), which was first identified in 1981.

Most sexually transmitted diseases can be treated successfully, although untreated sexually transmitted diseases remain a huge public health problem. Untreated sexually transmitted diseases can cause everything from blindness to **infertility**. While AIDS is the most widely publicized sexually transmitted disease, others are more common. More than 13 million Americans of all backgrounds and economic levels develop sexually transmitted diseases every year. Prevention efforts focus on teaching the physical signs of sexually transmitted diseases, instructing individuals on how to avoid exposure, and emphasizing the need for regular check-ups.

The great imitator

The history of sexually transmitted disease is controversial. Some historians believe that syphilis emerged as a new disease in the fifteenth century. Others cite Biblical and other ancient texts as proof that syphilis and perhaps gonorrhea were ancient as well as contemporary burdens. The dispute can best be understood with some knowledge of the elusive nature of gonorrhea and syphilis, called "the great imitator" by the eminent physician William Osler (1849-1919).

No laboratory tests existed to diagnose gonorrhea and syphilis until the late nineteenth and early twentieth centuries. This means that early clinicians based their **diagnosis** exclusively on symptoms, all of which could be present in other illnesses. Symptoms of syphilis during the first two of its three stages include chancre sores, skin rash, fever, fatigue, headache, sore throat, and swollen **glands**. Likewise, many other diseases have the potential to cause the dire consequences of late-stage syphilis. These range from blindness to mental illness to **heart** disease to death. Diagnosis of syphilis before laboratory tests were developed was complicated by the fact that most symptoms disappear during the third stage of the disease.

Symptoms of gonorrhea may also be elusive, particularly in women. Men have the most obvious symptoms, with **inflammation** and discharge from the penis from two to ten days after **infection**. Symptoms in women include a painful sensation while urinating or abdominal **pain**. However, women may be infected for months without showing any symptoms. Untreated gonorrhea can cause infertility in women and blindness in infants born to women with the disease.

The nonspecific nature of many symptoms linked to syphilis and gonorrhea means that historical references to sexually transmitted disease are open to different interpretations. Historians who believe that sexually transmitted disease was present in ancient times often refer to the Bible, which is rich with possible allusions to sexually transmitted disease.

One possible reference is found in Deuteronomy 28, which gives Moses' words concerning the price of disobeying religious law. "The Lord will smite thee with the botch of Egypt.... The Lord will smite thee with madness, and blindness, and astonishment of heart." Biblical scholars observe that a "botch" is a boil, possibly a reference to chancre sores. Mental illness, blindness, and heart disease are all symptoms of untreated syphilis, and it is possible that the divine punishment to be meted out is in fact the disease in question.

There is also evidence that sexually transmitted disease was present in ancient China, according to Frederic Buret, a nineteenth-century scholar cited by Theodor Rosebury. Buret argued that the ancient Chinese had used mercury as treatment for sexually transmitted disease. Mercury was also used widely to treat sexually transmitted disease in **Europe** and the United States until the modern era.

During the Renaissance, syphilis became a common and deadly disease in Europe. It is unclear whether new, more dangerous strains of syphilis were introduced or whether the syphilis which emerged at that time was, indeed, a new illness. Historians have proposed many theories to explain the dramatic increase in syphilis during the era. One theory suggests that Columbus and other explorers of the New World carried syphilis back to Europe. In 1539, the Spanish physician Rodrigo Ruiz Diaz de Isla treated members of the crew of Columbus for a peculiar disease marked by eruptions on the skin. Other contemporary accounts tell of epidemics of syphilis across Europe in 1495. Another theory suggests that syphilis developed as a consequence of mixing the germ pools of European and African people in the New World.

The abundance of syphilis during the Renaissance made the disease a central element of the dynamic culture of the period. The poet John Donne (1572-1631) was one of many thinkers of that era who saw sexually transmitted disease as a consequence of man's weakness. Shakespeare (1564-1616) also wrote about syphilis, using it as a curse in some plays and referring to the "tub of infamy," a nickname for a common medical treatment for syphilis. The treatment involved placing syphilitic in-

dividuals in a tub where they received mercury rubs. Mercury, which is now known to be a toxic chemical, did not cure syphilis, but is thought to have helped relieve some symptoms. Other treatments for syphilis included the induction of fever and the use of purgatives to flush the system.

The sculptor Benvenuto Cellini (1500-1571) is one of many individuals who wrote about their own syphilis during the era: "The French disease, for it was that, remained in me more than four months dormant before it showed itself." Cellini's reference to syphilis as the "French disease" was typical of Italians at the time and reflects a worldwide eagerness to place the origin of syphilis far away from one's own home. The French, for their part, called it the "Neapolitan disease," and the Japanese called it the "Portuguese disease." The name syphilis was bestowed on the disease by the Italian Girolamo Fracastoro (1478-1553), a poet, physician, and scientist. Fracastoro created an allegorical story about syphilis in 1530 entitled "Syphilis, or the French Disease." The story proposed that syphilis developed on **Earth** after a shepherd named Syphilis foolishly cursed at the **Sun**. The angry Sun retaliated with a disease that took its name from the foolish shepherd, who was the first individual to get sick.

For years, medical experts used syphilis as a catch-all diagnosis for sexually transmitted disease. Physicians assumed that syphilis and gonorrhea were the same thing until 1837, when Philippe Ricord (1800-89) reported that syphilis and gonorrhea were separate illnesses. The late nineteenth and early twentieth centuries saw major breakthroughs in the understanding of syphilis and gonorrhea. In 1879, Albert Neisser (1855-1916) discovered that gonorrhea was caused by a bacillus, which has since been named *Neisseria gonorrhoeae.* Fritz Richard Schaudinn (1871-1906) and Paul Erich Hoffmann (1868-1959) identified a special type of spirochete **bacteria**, now known as *Treponema pallidum,* as the cause of syphilis in 1905.

Effective treatment developed

Further advances occurred quickly. August von Wassermann (1866-1925) developed a **blood** test for syphilis in 1906, making testing for syphilis a simple procedure for the first time. Just four years later in 1910, the first effective therapy for syphilis was introduced in the form of Salvarsan, an organic arsenical compound. The compound was one of many effective compounds introduced by the German physician Paul Ehrlich (1854-1915), whose conviction that specific drugs could be effective against **microorganisms** has proven correct. The drug is effective against syphilis, but it is toxic and even fatal to some patients.

The development of Salvarsan offered hope for individuals with syphilis, but there was little public understanding about how syphilis was transmitted in the early twentieth century. In the United States this stemmed in part from government enforcement of laws prohibiting public discussion of certain types of sexual information. One popular account of syphilis from 1915 warned that one could develop syphilis after contact with whistles, pens, pencils, toilets, and toothbrushes.

The U.S. government exploited the ignorance of the disease among the general public as late as the mid-twentieth century in order to study the ravages of untreated syphilis. The Tuskegee Syphilis Study was launched in 1932 by the U.S. Public Health Service. The almost 400 black men who participated in the study were promised free medical care and burial money. Although effective treatments had been available for decades, researchers withheld treatment, even when penicillin became available in 1943, and carefully observed the unchecked progress of symptoms. Many of the participants fathered children with **congenital** syphilis, and many died. The study was finally exposed in the media in the early 1970s, and thus ended one of the more egregious instances of racist public health policy in the United States. When the activities of the study were revealed, a series of new regulations governing human experimentation were passed by the government.

A more public discussion of sexually transmitted disease was conducted by the military during World Wars I and II. During both wars, the military conducted aggressive public information campaigns to limit sexually transmitted disease among the armed forces. One poster from World War II showed a grinning skull on a woman dressed in an evening gown striding along with Adolf Hitler and Emperor Hirohito. The poster's caption reads "V.D. Worst of the Three," suggesting that venereal disease could destroy American troops faster than either of America's declared enemies.

Concern about the human cost of sexually transmitted disease helped make the production of the new drug penicillin a wartime priority. Arthur Fleming (1881-1955), who is credited with the discovery of penicillin, first observed in 1928 that the penicillium **mold** was capable of killing bacteria in the laboratory; however, the mold was unstable and difficult to produce. Penicillin was not ready for general use or general clinical testing until after Howard Florey (1898-1968) and Ernst Boris Chain (1906-1979) developed ways to purify and produce a consistent substance.

The introduction of penicillin for widespread use in 1943 completed the transformation of syphilis from a life-threatening disease to one that could be treated easi-

ly and quickly. U.S. rates of cure were 90-97% for syphilis by 1944, one year after penicillin was first distributed in the country. Death rates dropped dramatically. In 1940, 10.7 out of every 100,000 people died of syphilis. By 1970, it was 0.2 per 100,000.

Such progress infused the medical community with optimism. A 1951 article in the *American Journal of Syphilis* asked, "Are Venereal Diseases Disappearing?" By 1958, the number of cases of syphilis had dropped to 113,884 from 575,593 in 1943, the year penicillin was introduced.

Continuing challenge

Venereal disease was not eliminated, and sexually transmitted diseases continue to ravage Americans and others in the 1990s. Though penicillin has lived up to its early promise as an effective treatment for syphilis, the number of cases of syphilis has increased since 1956. In addition, millions of Americans suffer from other sexually transmitted diseases, many of which were not known a century or more ago, such as Acquired Immune Deficiency Syndrome (AIDS). By the 1990s, sexually transmitted diseases were among the most common infectious diseases in the United States.

Some sexually transmitted diseases are seen as growing at **epidemic** rates. For example, syphilis, gonorrhea, and chancroid, which are uncommon in Europe, Japan and **Australia**, have increased at epidemic rates among certain urban minority populations. A 1980 study found the rate of syphilis was five times higher among blacks than among whites. The Public Health Service reports that as many as 30 million Americans have been affected by genital herpes. Experts have also noted that sexually transmitted disease appears to increase in areas where AIDS is common.

Shifting sexual and marital habits are two factors behind the growth in sexually transmitted disease. Americans are more likely to have sex at an earlier age than they did in years past. They also marry later in life than Americans did two to three decades ago, and their marriages are more likely to end in divorce. These factors make Americans more likely to have many sexual partners over the course of their lives, placing them at greater risk of sexually transmitted disease.

Public health officials report that fear and embarrassment continue to limit the number of people willing to report signs of sexually transmitted disease. Literature from the Public Health Service reminds readers that sexually transmitted diseases "affect men and women of all backgrounds and economic levels." Sexually transmitted disease has been seen as "a symbol of **pollution** and contamination" and as a sign of a decaying society since the nineteenth century in the United States. Some commentators still suggests that sexually transmitted disease represents a type of divine punishment for amoral **behavior**. This attitude could be seen vividly in 1983, when Nixon speech writer Patrick Buchanan said that AIDS was nature's retribution for homosexuals, who "have declared war on Nature." Such comments perpetuate the shame linked to sexually transmitted disease.

From Chlamydia to AIDS

All sexually transmitted diseases have certain elements in common. They are most prevalent among teenagers and young adults, with nearly 66% occurring in people under 25. In addition, most can be transmitted in ways other than through sexual relations. For example, AIDS and **Hepatitis** B can be transmitted through contact with tainted blood, but they are primarily transmitted sexually. In general, sexual contact should be avoided if there are visible sores, warts, or other signs of disease in the genital area. The risk of developing most sexually transmitted diseases is reduced by using condoms and limiting sexual contact.

Sexually transmitted diseases vary in their susceptibility to treatment, their signs and symptoms, and the consequences if they are left untreated. Some are caused by bacteria. These usually can be treated and cured. Others are caused by viruses and can typically be treated but not cured.

Bacterial sexually transmitted diseases include syphilis, gonorrhea, chlamydia, and chancroid. Syphilis is less common than many other sexually transmitted diseases in the United States, with 134,000 cases in 1990. The disease is thought to be more difficult to transmit than many other sexually transmitted diseases. Sexual partners of an individual with syphilis have about a 10% chance of developing syphilis after one sexual contact, but the disease has come under increasing scrutiny as researchers have realized how easily the HIV **virus** which causes AIDS can be spread through open syphilitic chancre sores.

Gonorrhea is far more common than syphilis, with 750,000 cases of gonorrhea reported annually in the U.S. The gonococcus bacterium is considered highly contagious. Public health officials suggest that all individuals with more than one sexual partner should be tested regularly for gonorrhea. Penicillin is no longer the treatment of choice for gonorrhea, because of the numerous strains of gonorrhea that are resistant to penicillin. Newer strains of **antibiotics** have proven to be more effective. Gonorrhea infection overall has diminished in the U.S., but the incidence of gonorrhea among black Americans has increased.

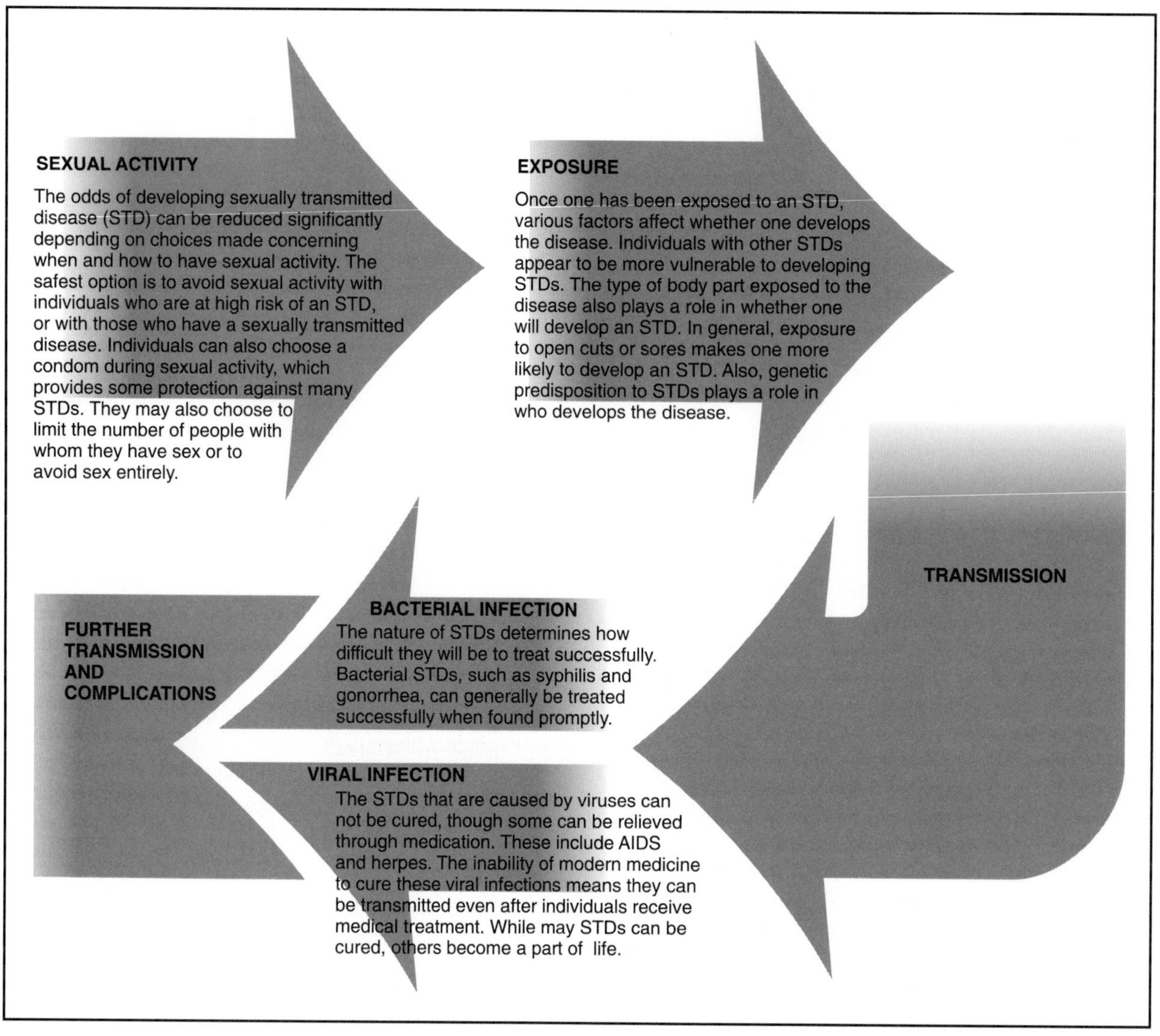

SEXUAL ACTIVITY
The odds of developing sexually transmitted disease (STD) can be reduced significantly depending on choices made concerning when and how to have sexual activity. The safest option is to avoid sexual activity with individuals who are at high risk of an STD, or with those who have a sexually transmitted disease. Individuals can also choose a condom during sexual activity, which provides some protection against many STDs. They may also choose to limit the number of people with whom they have sex or to avoid sex entirely.
EXPOSURE
Once one has been exposed to an STD, various factors affect whether one develops the disease. Individuals with other STDs appear to be more vulnerable to developing STDs. The type of body part exposed to the disease also plays a role in whether one will develop an STD. In general, exposure to open cuts or sores makes one more likely to develop an STD. Also, genetic predisposition to STDs plays a role in who develops the disease.
TRANSMISSION
FURTHER TRANSMISSION AND COMPLICATIONS
BACTERIAL INFECTION
The nature of STDs determines how difficult they will be to treat successfully. Bacterial STDs, such as syphilis and gonorrhea, can generally be treated successfully when found promptly.
VIRAL INFECTION
The STDs that are caused by viruses can not be cured, though some can be relieved through medication. These include AIDS and herpes. The inability of modern medicine to cure these viral infections means they can be transmitted even after individuals receive medical treatment. While may STDs can be cured, others become a part of life.

The progression of a sexually transmitted disease (STD).

Chlamydia infection is considered the most common sexually transmitted disease in the United States. About four million new cases of chlamydia infection are reported every year. The infection is caused by the bacterium *Chlamydia trachomatis*. Symptoms of chlamydia are similar to symptoms of gonorrhea, and the disease often occurs at the same time as gonorrhea. Men and women may have pain during urination or notice an unusual genital discharge one to three weeks after exposure. However, many individuals, particularly women, have no symptoms until complications develop.

Complications resulting from untreated chlamydia occur when the bacteria has a chance to travel in the body. Chlamydia can result in pelvic inflammatory disease in women, a condition which occurs when the infection travels up the uterus and fallopian tubes. This condition can lead to infertility. In men, the infection can lead to epididymitis, inflammation of the epididymis, a structure on the testes where spermatozoa are stored. This too can lead to infertility. Untreated chlamydia infection can cause **eye** infection or **pneumonia** in babies of mothers with the infection. Antibiotics are successful against chlamydia.

The progression of chancroid in the United States is a modern-day indicator of the **migration** of sexually transmitted disease. Chancroid, a bacterial infection caused by *Haemophilus ducreyi,* was common in **Africa** and rare in the United States until the 1980s. Beginning in the mid-1980s, there were outbreaks of chancroid in a number of large cities and migrant-labor communities in the United States. The number of chancroid cases increased dramatically, from 665 in 1984 to 4,714 in 1989.

In men, who are most likely to develop chancroid, the disease is characterized by painful open sores and swollen lymph nodes in the groin. The sores are generally softer than the harder chancre seen in syphilis. Women may also develop painful sores. They may feel pain urinating and may have bleeding or discharge in the rectal and vaginal areas. Chancroid can be treated effectively with antibiotics.

Viruses more difficult to treat

There are no cures for the sexually transmitted diseases caused by viruses: AIDS, genital herpes, viral hepatitis, and genital warts. Treatment is available for most of these diseases, but the virus cannot be eliminated from the body.

AIDS is the most life-threatening sexually transmitted disease, a disease which is usually fatal and for which there is no cure. The disease is caused by the human immunodeficiency virus (HIV), a virus which disables the **immune system**, making the body susceptible to injury or death from infection and certain cancers. HIV is a **retrovirus** which translates the RNA contained in the virus into DNA, the genetic information code contained in the human body. This DNA becomes a part of the human host **cell**. The fact that viruses become part of the human body makes them difficult to treat or eliminate without harming the patient.

AIDS can remain dormant for years within the human body. More than 200,000 cases of AIDS have been reported in the United States since the disease was first identified in 1981, and at least one million other Americans are believed to be infected with the HIV virus. Initial symptoms of AIDS include fever, headache, or enlarged lymph nodes. Later symptoms include **energy** loss, frequent fever, weight loss, or frequent **yeast** infections. HIV is transmitted most commonly through sexual contact or through use of contaminated needles or blood products. The disease is not spread through casual contact, such as the sharing of towels, bedding, swimming pools, or toilet seats.

Genital herpes is a widespread, recurrent, and incurable viral infection. About 500,000 new cases are reported in the United States annually. The prevalence of herpes infection reflects the highly contagious nature of the virus. About 75% of the sexual partners of individuals with the infection develop genital herpes.

The herpes virus is common. Most individuals who are exposed to one of the two types of herpes simplex virus never develop any symptoms. In these cases, the herpes virus remains in certain nerve cells of the body, but does not cause any problems. Herpes simplex virus type 1 most frequently causes cold sores on the lips or mouth, but can also cause genital infections. Herpes simplex virus type 2 most commonly causes genital sores, though mouth sores can also occur due to this type of virus.

In genital herpes, the virus enters the skin or mucous **membrane**, travels to a group of nerves at the end of the spinal cord, and initiates a host of painful symptoms within about one week of exposure. These symptoms may include vaginal discharge, pain in the legs, and an itching or burning feeling. A few days later, sores appear at the infected area. Beginning as small red bumps, they can become open sores which eventually become crusted. These sores are typically painful and last an average of two weeks.

Following the initial outbreak, the virus waits in the nerve cells in an inactive state. A recurrence is created when the virus moves through the **nervous system** to the skin. There may be new sores or simply a shedding of virus which can infect a sexual partner. The number of times herpes recurs varies from individual to individual, ranging from several times a year to only once or twice in a lifetime. Occurrences of genital herpes may be shortened through use of an antiviral drug which limits the herpes virus's ability to reproduce itself.

Genital herpes is most dangerous to newborns born to pregnant women experiencing their first episode of the disease. Direct newborn contact with the virus increases the risk of neurological damage or death. To avoid exposure, physicians usually deliver babies using cesarean section if herpes lesions are present.

Hepatitis, an inflammation of the liver, is a complicated illness with many types. Millions of Americans develop hepatitis annually. The hepatitis A virus, one of four types of viral hepatitis, is most often spread by **contamination** of food or **water**. The hepatitis B virus is most often spread through sexual contact, through the sharing of intravenous drug needles, and from mother to child. Hospital workers who are exposed to blood and blood products are also at risk. Hepatitis C and Hepatitis D (less commonly) may also be spread through sexual contact.

A yellowing of the skin, or **jaundice**, is the best known symptom of hepatitis. Other symptoms include dark and foamy urine and abdominal pain. There is no cure for hepatitis, although prolonged rest usually enables individuals with the disease to recover completely.

Many people who develop hepatitis B become carriers of the virus for life. This means they can infect others and face a high risk of developing liver disease. There are as many as 300 million carriers worldwide, and about 1.5 million in the United States. A vaccination is available against hepatitis B.

The link between human papillomavirus, genital warts, and certain types of **cancer** has drawn attention to

the potential risk of genital warts. There are more than 60 types of human papillomavirus. Many of these types can cause genital warts. In the U.S., about 1 million new cases of genital warts are diagnosed every year.

Genital warts are very contagious, and about two-thirds of the individuals who have sexual contact with someone with genital warts develop the disease. There is also an association between human papillomavirus and cancer of the cervix, anus, penis, and vulva. This means that people who develop genital warts appear to be at a higher risk for these cancers and should have their health carefully watched. Contact with genital warts can also damage infants born to mothers with the problem.

Genital warts usually appear within three months of sexual contact. The warts can be removed in various ways, but the virus remains in the body. Once the warts are removed the chances of transmitting the disease are reduced.

Many questions persist concerning the control of sexually transmitted diseases. Experts have struggled for years with efforts to inform people about transmission and treatment of sexually transmitted disease. Frustration over the continuing increase in sexually transmitted disease is one factor which has fueled interest in potential vaccines against certain sexually transmitted diseases.

Vaccines in the making

A worldwide research effort to develop a **vaccine** against AIDS has resulted in a series of vaccinations now in clinical trials. Efforts have focused in two areas, finding a vaccine to protect individuals against the HIV virus and finding a vaccine to prevent the progression of HIV to AIDS in individuals who already have been exposed to the virus. One of many challenges facing researchers has been the ability of the HIV virus to change, making efforts to develop a single vaccine against the virus futile.

Researchers also are searching for vaccines against syphilis and gonorrhea. Experiments conducted on prisoners more than 40 years ago proved that some individuals could develop immunity to syphilis after inoculation with live *Treponema pallidum,* but researchers have still not been able to develop a vaccine against syphilis which is safe and effective. In part this stems from the unusual nature of the syphilis bacteria, which remain potentially infectious even when its cells are killed. An effective gonorrhea vaccine has also eluded researchers.

Immunizations are available against Hepatitis A and Hepatitis B (Hepatitis D is prevented by the Hepatitis B vaccine). The virus which causes Hepatitic C, however, is able to change its form (mutate) quite rapidly, thereby hampering efforts to develop a vaccine against it.

KEY TERMS

Bacteria—Microscopic organisms whose activities range from the development of disease to fermentation. Bacteria range in shape from spherical to rod-shaped to spiral. Different types of bacteria cause many sexually transmitted diseases, including syphilis, gonnorrhea and chlamydia. Bacteria also cause diseases ranging from typhoid to dysentery to tetanus.

Chancre—A lesion which occurs in the first stage of syphilis, at the place where the infection entered the body. The lesion is usually red and crusted initially.

Epididymis—A cordlike structure located on the testes in which spermatozoa are stored.

Spirochete—A bacterium shaped like a spiral.

Treponema—A subgroup in the spirochaetacae family of bacteria featuring microorganisms shaped like a spiral that move with a snapping and bending motion. One member of the subgroup, *Treponema pallidum,* causes syphilis.

Virus—Agent of infection which does not have its own metabolism and reproduces only in the living cells of other hosts. Viruses can live on bacteria, animals or plants, and range in appearance from rod-shaped to tadpole-shaped, among other forms. Diseases caused by viruses include Acquired Immune Deficiency Syndrome (AIDS), genital herpes, and influenza.

Without vaccinations for most of the sexually transmitted diseases, health officials depend on public information campaigns to limit the growth of the diseases. Graphic posters, public advertisements for condoms, informational brochures at college campuses, and other techniques have been attempted to make information about sexually transmitted diseases easily available.

Some critics have claimed that the increasing incidence of sexually transmitted diseases suggest that current techniques are failing. In other countries, however, the incidence of sexually transmitted disease has fallen during the same period it has risen in the United States. For example, in Sweden the gonorrhea rate fell by more than 95% from 1970 to 1989 after vigorous government efforts to control sexually transmitted disease in Sweden.

Yet the role of government funding for community health clinics, **birth** control, and public information

campaigns on sexually transmitted disease has long been controversial. Public officials continue to debate the wisdom of funding public distribution of condoms and other services that could affect the transmission of sexually transmitted disease. Although science has made great strides in understanding the causes and cures of many sexually transmitted diseases, society has yet to reach agreement on how best to attack them.

See also Reproductive system; Sexual reproduction.

Further Reading

Aral, Sevgi O., and King K. Holmes. "Sexually Transmitted Diseases in the AIDS Era." *Scientific American.* (February 1991): 62-9.

Brandt, Allan M. *No Magic Bullet: A Social History of Venereal Disease in the United States Since 1880.* New York: Oxford University Press, 1987.

Droegemueller, William. "Infections of the Lower Genital Tract." In *Comprehensive Gynecology,* edited by Arthur L. Herbst, Daniel R. Mishell, Morton A. Stenchever, and William Droegemueller. St. Louis: Mosby Year Book, 1992, pp. 633-90.

"Facts About STDS." National Institute of Allergy and Infectious Diseases, National Institutes of Health, Bethesda, Md., June 1992.

Henderson, Charles. "Vaccines for STDS: Possibility or Pipe Dream." *AIDS Weekly.* (2 May 1994): 8.

Magner, Lois N. "Syphilis, the Scourge of the Renaissance." In *A History of Medicine.* New York: Marcel Dekker, 1992.

Rosebury, Theodor. *Microbes and Morals. The Strange Story of Venereal Disease.* New York: Viking, 1971.

Thomas, Stephen B., and Sandra Crouse Quinn. "The Tuskegee Syphilis Study, 1932-1972: Implications for HIV Education and AIDS Risk Education Programs in the Black Community." *The American Journal of Public Health.* (November 1991): 1498.

Patricia Braus

Sharks

The sharks are a group of about 350 related species of **cartilaginous fish**, members of which are found in every **ocean** in the world. Far from their reputation as primitive monsters, the sharks are, in fact, some of the most fascinating, well-adapted marine organisms. Their many structural and functional adaptations, such as their advanced reproductive systems and complex sensory abilities, combine to make them very well suited to their environment.

Evolution and classification

Sharks are often described as "primitive" animals, and little changed in millions of years of **evolution**. It is true that the first sharks evolved in the oceans more than 300 million years ago, in the Devonian era. However, the earliest species of sharks are all extinct. The species living in the oceans today evolved only 70-100 million years ago. The fact that the general body plan of the earliest sharks was so similar to that of living ones is a testimony to the suitability of their **adaptation** to the environment in which sharks still live.

Sharks and other modern **fish** are descended from primitive fish, called Placoderms, that were covered with bony, armor-like plates. The descendants of the Placoderms lost the armor, but retained an internal skeleton. Most types of modern fish, such as trout, **minnows**, and **tuna**, have a bony skeleton. Sharks and their relatives, the **skates** and **rays**, are distinguished from other types of fish in that they have cartilage rather than bone as their skeletal material (cartilage is a translucent, flexible, but strong material that also makes up the ears and nose of **mammals**, including humans). Thus, the sharks are called the "cartilaginous fishes" (class Chondrichthyes).

Overview of shark groups

There are eight orders of living sharks.

The Angelshark Order includes the angelsharks and sand devils. These sharks are flattened like rays and tend to live on the ocean bottom in **water** depths to 4,200 ft (1,300 m). They are found in most oceans, except the central Pacific and Indian Oceans and the polar areas. There are thirteen species, most of which are less than 60 in (1.5 m) long.

The Dogfish Order includes the dogfish sharks, bramble sharks, and roughsharks. This is a group of 82 species, 73 of which are dogfish sharks. Dogfish sharks generally have a cylindrical body and elongated snout. They are found in all oceans, usually in deep water. Their size ranges from the 10-in (25 cm) pygmy sharks to the 23-ft (7 m) sleeper sharks.

The Sawshark Order consists of five species of sawsharks, with a long, flattened, saw-like snout. They are bottom-dwelling in temperate to tropical oceans, to depths of 3,000 ft (900 m). Adults are 3-5 ft (1-1.6 m) long.

The Frilled shark Order consists of the frilled, cow, six-gill, and seven-gill sharks. There are five species, which are found in all oceans, mostly on continental shelves from 300-6,150 ft (90-1,875 m). The body length ranges from 77 in (195 cm) for frilled sharks to 16.5 ft (5 m) for a species of six-gill shark.

The Bullhead shark Order consists of eight species of bullhead sharks. They have a wide head, short snout, and flattened teeth for crushing hard **prey**. They are

A sand tiger shark (*Odontaspis taurus.*).

found in warm continental waters of the Indian and Pacific Oceans, to depths of 900 ft (275 m).

The Carpetshark Order includes zebra sharks, nurse sharks, and whale sharks. This is a diverse group of 33 species, all found in warm water, mostly in the Indian Ocean and western Pacific. They may forage on the surface or at the bottom, mostly near shore to depths of about 330 ft (100 m). These sharks have two small projections called barbels under their snout, and most have a shortened, rounded nose and slender, elongated tail fins. Most species are 3-8 ft (1-3 m) long, but whale sharks may reach over 40 ft (12 m). Whale sharks are the largest fish in the world.

The **Mackerel** shark Order includes the sand tigers, basking sharks, megamouth sharks, mako sharks, and white sharks. There are sixteen species, which are found in all but polar waters. The megamouth sharks were only discovered in 1982. The species in this order are found near shore or far from land, in shallow water and to depths of 3,900 ft (1,200 m). Most have a powerful, cylindrical body and elongated snout. Their length ranges from 3-19 ft (1-6 m), with basking sharks reaching over 33 ft (10 m).

The Groundshark Order includes the catsharks, hammerhead sharks, and requiem sharks. The latter subgroup contains the blue, tiger, and bull sharks. The groundshark group consists of 197 species found in all ocean habitats. It includes most of the species considered dangerous to humans.

Structural and functional adaptations

Sharks are generally fusiform in body shape, with a narrow snout, wider body, and a tapering tail. Sharks have one or two fins on their dorsal surface (back), a pair of pectoral fins, a pair of pelvic fins, usually a sin-

gle anal fin on the ventral surface (belly), and a caudal (tail) fin. Usually the upper lobe of the caudal fin is larger than the lower lobe. The pelvic fins of male sharks have a projection called a clasper, which is used in **sexual reproduction**.

Locomotion and buoyancy

Sharks swim by moving their caudal fin from side to side in a sweeping **motion**, which propels them forward through the water. The large upper lobe of the caudal fin of most sharks provides most of the forward thrust. Sharks, like makos, which sometimes need to swim at high speed, also have a well-developed lower caudal fin lobe for greater thrust. As a shark moves through the water, it angles the pectoral fins to change direction.

Sharks are slightly heavier than water, so they naturally tend to sink. Buoyancy or lift is provided in two ways. First, sharks store large quantities of oil in their liver. Because oil is less dense than water, storing this oil decreases the overall **density** of the shark, and increases its buoyancy. Second, as a shark swims, its pectoral fins provide lift, in much the same way the wings of an airplane does. If a shark stops swimming it will sink, but its stored oil and relatively light skeleton help it to float and decreases the amount of **energy** that must be expended on swimming.

Temperature regulation

Sharks are "cold-blooded" (or poikilothermic) animals, meaning their body **temperature** is the same as that of the water in which they live. The term cold-blooded is misleading, however, because sharks living in warm water are "warm-blooded" in actual temperature.

Some fast-swimming sharks in the Mackerel shark Order (for example the mako and white sharks) can actually raise their core body temperature somewhat above that of their surroundings. In these sharks, **heat** generated as they swim is conserved by a special vascular network surrounding the muscles. This network helps to conserve heat in the body core, rather than allowing it to dissipate into the cooler water. Just as chemical reactions in a laboratory proceed faster when heat is applied, so too do metabolic reactions at higher temperatures. With their higher core body temperature, these species are able to be more active and efficient predators than most other sharks and **bony fish**.

Respiration

Sharks use their gills to absorb **oxygen** from the water. Most sharks have five gill slits on each side of their body, behind the mouth and above the pectoral fins. Water enters the mouth of the shark, enters a canal between the mouth and the gills (the orobranchial cavity), and then passes back to the outside through the gill openings. As the water passes over the gills, oxygen is absorbed into the **blood** across the thin skin of the gill surface, and **carbon dioxide** moves into the water.

Water can flow across the gills by two mechanisms. First, as the shark is swimming it may hold its mouth open, allowing water to flow in and then out through the gill slits as the fish moves forward. Some sharks, however, can get enough oxygen when they are not swimming by gulping water into their mouth, then forcing the water out through the gills with muscular contractions of the orobranchial cavity. It is not true that all sharks must always keep swimming to breathe.

Water and salt balance

Fish living in the ocean are in danger of dehydrating because water moves out of their body into their salty environment through the process of **osmosis**. Basically, this occurs because the salt **concentration** in the ocean is much higher than that in the blood of fish. In part, sharks solve their dehydration problem by having a relatively high internal concentration of salts and other molecules. In addition to the salts naturally present, sharks have additional solutes (i.e., dissolved substances) in their blood, so the total osmotic activity of dissolved substances is similar to that in seawater. They maintain their blood at this concentration by excreting the excess salt they ingest in their diet. A special gland near the end of the intestine, called the rectal gland, absorbs extra salt from the blood and passes it into the intestine to be excreted. These two adaptations function together to ensure that sharks do not dehydrate.

Sensory systems

Sharks have the same five senses of sight, **hearing**, **smell**, **taste**, and **touch** that humans have. Moreover, some of these senses are more acute in sharks. Sharks also have an additional sense; they can detect weak electric fields in the water.

Sharks are known to possess a complex visual system, and can even see color. A problem for sharks is that, if they are in deep or murky water, the light level is very low. Several features of the shark **eye** make it well-suited to **vision** in dim light. Unlike most fish, sharks have a pupil that can adjust to the amount of light in the environment. Also, shark eyes have high numbers of the structures that actually detect light (the rods), so that even in low light an image is formed. Finally, sharks have a special reflective **membrane** (the tapetum lu-

cidum) at the back of the eye, which enhances their vision in low light even further. **Cats** have a similar membrane in their eyes, which is why their eyes seem to reflect light in the dark. The membrane, for both cats and sharks, helps them see in dim light.

Two tiny pores on the top of the sharks head lead to their inner ears. The inner **ear** contains organs for detecting sound waves in the water, as well as three special canals that help the **animal** orient in the water. The sound receptors are very sensitive, especially to irregular and low-frequency (20-300 Hz) sounds. These are the types of noises a wounded prey animal would be likely to make. The **distance** at which a shark can hear a sound depends on the intensity of the sound at its source: a vigorous disturbance or a loud underwater noise will produce sound waves that travel further in the water than those produced by a smaller disturbance.

A shark's nostrils are two pores on the front of its snout. As the shark swims forward, water passes through the nostrils and chemicals in the water are detected as odors. The nose is used only for detecting odors, not for breathing. Some sharks can detect as little as five drops of fish extract in a swimming pool of water. Sharks can easily use their sense of smell to detect and home in on prey, by swimming in the direction of the increasing scent.

Evidence suggests that sharks can taste their food, and that they have preferred prey. Small taste buds line the mouth and throat of sharks, and they seem to reject foods based on their taste. Some scientists believe that the reason most shark attacks on humans involve only one bite is that the animal realizes, after biting, that the person does not taste like prey should.

Sharks have two types of touch sense. One is the ability to sense when an object touches their body. The second is the ability to detect an object by the movements of the water it causes. This is similar to how you might detect where a fan is located in a room, because you can feel the movement of the air on your skin. Sharks and other fish have a specialized, very sensitive receptor system for detecting these types of water movements. This sensory system involves a series of tiny, shallow canals and pits running beneath the surface of the skin, known as the lateral line and the pit organs. The movement of water against the canals and pits is detected in receptor organs, and this information is used to "visualize" the presence of nearby organisms and objects.

All organisms in sea water generate a weak electric field around them, like an invisible halo. Small pits in the skin of sharks end in receptors that can detect extremely low-voltage electric fields in the water. Sharks use this sense to locate their prey at close range. Some sharks can even find their prey under sand and mud.

Feeding and diet

All sharks are carnivorous, meaning that they only eat other animals. The range of prey eaten by sharks is extremely broad, from **snails** to **sea urchins**, **crabs**, fish, rays, other sharks, **seals**, and **birds**. Some sharks eat carrion (animals that are already dead), but most only eat live prey. Sharks eat relatively little for their size, compared to mammals, because they do not use energy to maintain a high body temperature. Sharks eat the equivalent of 1-10% of their body weight per week, usually in one or two meals. Between meals they digest their food, and they do not eat again until they have finished digesting their previous meal.

Sharks that eat prey with hard shells, such as bullhead sharks, have flat crushing teeth. Bullheads eat a variety of prey, including **barnacles**, crabs, sea stars, and snails, which they crush with their rear teeth. The two largest sharks, whale sharks and basking sharks, eat nothing larger than 1-2 in (2-5 cm) long. These whales filter their tiny prey (called krill) from the water using their gills as giant strainers. The whales swim through the water with their mouth open, and small crustaceans in the water get caught in mesh-like extensions of the gills. Once caught, the krill are funneled back to the whale's throat and swallowed.

Species such as white sharks, makos, tiger sharks, and hammerheads attack and eat large fish, other sharks, and marine mammals such as seals. The feeding **biology** of the white shark has been well studied. This shark often approaches its prey from below and behind, so it is less visible to its victim. It approaches slowly to within a few meters, then rushes the final distance. If the prey is too large to be taken in one bite, the shark will bite hard once, and then retreat as the prey bleeds. When the prey is weakened, the shark again approaches for the kill.

Reproduction and growth

Sharks have fascinating reproductive systems, with some advanced features for such an ancient group of organisms. Unlike bony fish, sharks have internal **fertilization**. The male shark uses projections from his pectoral fins, called claspers, to anchor himself to the female. He then transfers packets of sperm into the female's urogenital opening, using pulses of water. The sperm fertilize the eggs inside the female, but what happens next to the developing embryo depends on the species.

Some species of sharks lay eggs with the developing embryo covered by a tough, protective case. This is known as **oviparous** reproduction. The embryos of these sharks are well supplied with nutritious yolk, unlike the tiny eggs of most bony fish. After some time, the egg

hatches and a young shark emerges. Bullhead sharks, whale sharks, and zebra sharks are examples of oviparous species.

Female sharks of most species are **ovoviviparous** live-bearers, which means they retain their eggs inside the body until the young hatch, which are then born "alive." This method provides the young with protection from predators during their earliest developmental stages. Examples of ovoviviparous sharks are dogfish sharks, angelsharks, and tiger sharks. Some species of sharks have a modification of this type of reproduction. In the white and mako sharks, the embryos hatch inside the mother at age three months, but then stay in the mother for some additional time, obtaining nourishment by eating nutrient-rich, unfertilized eggs the mother produces for them. A further bizarre twist occurs in the sand tiger shark, in which the earliest embryo to hatch in each uterus eats its siblings, so only two offspring are born (one from each uterus).

The most advanced form of shark reproduction occurs in the hammerheads and requiem sharks (except the tiger shark). In these sharks, early in embryonic development a connection (placenta) is created between the embryo and the mother. The embryo obtains **nutrients** through the placenta for the remainder of its growth, before being born alive. This type of development is called **viviparity**, and it is similar to the development process of mammals.

Compared to most bony fish, sharks reproduce and grow relatively slowly. Bony fish tend to lay thousands or more tiny eggs, most of which are scattered into the environment and die. Sharks have relatively few (**zero** to around 100) offspring each year, and the mother invests much energy in each to increase the chance that it will survive. Some female sharks put so much energy into a litter that they must take two years to recover their strength before breeding again. Although young sharks are born relatively large and able to take care of themselves, they grow slowly, sometimes only a few centimeters a year. It may take 15-20 years for an individual to reach sexual maturity. Such low reproductive rates and slow growth combine to make sharks highly vulnerable to overfishing.

Conservation

Historically, sharks have been fished for their meat and for liver oil, which was the best source of vitamin A until the 1940s. Shark fin soup is a traditional Asian delicacy and shark meat has recently gained popularity; these are greatly increasing the killing of sharks in marine fisheries. In addition to their food value, many sharks are caught and killed for sport by individuals and in specific shark-catching competitions. Often, sharks are unintentionally caught in nets and lines set for other species. Modern methods used by many commercial fishing fleets involve either baited long-lines stretching for miles, or long drift-nets that entangle and kill anything in their path. Sharks caught by these methods are often either dumped, or are finned (the fins are removed for shark fin soup) and thrown back to die. In the 1980s, 50% of sharks caught recreationally and 90% of sharks caught commercially were discarded back to the ocean dead.

Since the mid-1960s, scientists studying sharks have warned that indiscriminate and wholesale slaughter of these animals was driving their populations to a dangerously low level. Many people, with visions of sharks as monsters, had little interest in saving them. Some sharks do attack humans. However, the risks are very small: a person's chance of being killed by lightning is 30 times greater than that of dying in a shark attack. Each year, humans kill more than one million sharks for every human bitten by a shark.

It is now quite clear that the fishing mortality described above is having a severely negative effect on shark populations. Sharks have relatively low reproductive and growth rates, and they are being fished much faster than they can replace themselves. Scientists have determined the maximum number of sharks that can be caught each year to maintain the population. In the 1980s, the actual amount of sharks killed in areas of the North Atlantic Ocean exceeded that number by 35-70%. Without rapid changes in this wasteful overfishing, many shark species will become endangered.

There are numerous reasons to conserve shark populations, in addition to the fact that they are beautiful animals about which there remains much to learn. Perhaps most importantly, sharks are important predators in marine habitats. Removing them will affect the populations of their prey, which would have impacts on all other species living in the **ecosystem**. On a different note, scientists have recently discovered a chemical in shark blood called squalamine, which functions as an antibiotic. Further tests on this chemical and others from sharks may produce chemicals toxic to **cancer** cells. If sharks become endangered, it will not be possible to harvest these medically useful chemicals.

The United States Department of Commerce has established guidelines for and restrictions on shark fishing based on the acceptable maximum catch estimated by researchers. The guidelines **limit** the recreational and commercial catch of sharks, prohibit finning, and reduce the numbers of shark fishing tournaments. In **Australia**, species such as the great white shark have been declared endangered, and are now protected from indiscriminate killing. With wider enforcement, guidelines such as these may mean that sharks live to enjoy another 350 million years roaming the world's oceans.

KEY TERMS

Cartilage—A translucent, flexible material that composes the skeleton in sharks and their relative.

Continental shelf—A relatively shallow submarine area at the edges of continents and large islands.

Fusiform—Having a shape that tapers towards each end.

Pectoral fins—The most forward pair of fins on the underside of fish.

Pelvic fins—The rear-most pair of fins on the underside of fish.

Placenta—A connection between a mother and a developing embryo, through which the latter receives nutrients.

Temperate—Having a moderate climate, or temperatures between polar and tropical.

Further Reading

Gruber, Samuel H., ed. *Discovering Sharks: A Volume Honoring the Work of Stewart Springer.* Highlands, NJ: American Littoral Society, 1991.

Manire, Charles A. and Samuel H. Gruber. "Many Sharks May Be Headed Toward Extinction." *Conservation Biology.* 4 (1990): 10-11.

Stevens, John D., ed. *Sharks.* London: Merehurst Press, 1987.

Amy Kenyon-Campbell

Sheep

Sheep are ruminant members of the Bovidae family. They belong to the genus *Ovis*, which contains three species, *Ovis musimon*, *Ovis orientalis*, and *Ovis aries*.

Sheep evolved about 2,500,000 years ago. They were the first animals to become domesticated, approximately 9,000 to 10,000 B.C. *Ovis musimon*, the European moufflon, is still found wild in Sardinia and Corsica and *0. orientalis,* the Asiatic moufflon, also roams freely in **Asia** Minor and the Caucasus. There are specimens of these wild species in many zoos. The European moufflon is horned, with a massive circular rack and its wool coat hidden under the long guard hairs. The rams will weigh up to 600 lb (270 kg), as heavy as some of the smaller cattle breeds. The Asiatic moufflon is similar in appearance to the European moufflon, but weighs one-third less. Over the years, the domesticated sheep has undergone so many changes through controlled breeding that it is now its own species, *Ovis aries*.

Sheep domestication and the harvesting of wool is an ancient practice. Wool fabrics have been found in prehistoric ruins 10,000 years old. The beginnings of sheep domestication seem to center in Iran, Iraq, and Turkey around 6,000 B.C.; then the practice was spread by the Phoenicians to **Africa** and Spain. By 4,000 B.C. domesticated sheep had appeared in China and the British Isles. On an uninhabited isle near St. Kilda in the Scottish Hebrides is a flock of primitive sheep called Soay sheep, which are survivors of the Bronze Age. They exhibit the characteristics halfway between the moufflon and modern breeds, including brown coloring, massive curved horns and kempy wool. The neighboring sheep farmers pay an annual visit to this isle, where they round up the sheep, shear and cull the flock, then depart for another year, leaving the flock to fend for themselves.

Spanish farmers developed the Merino breed of sheep in the sixteenth and seventeenth centuries, and the fineness of its wool is unsurpassed even today. In the seventeenth century Robert Bakewell, in England, using his newly discovered breeding methods developed the Southdown and the Leicester, led the way to improvements in other breeds. Because most sheep breeders in England were small farmers, they created several distinctive breeds to meet requirements of the their locals and to satisfy the local wool markets. So some of the breeds were developed for the quality of their meat, some for their fine wool, some for their coarse wool (for carpets, etc.), some for their ability to produce milk, and others for their hardiness.

The Merino was so outstanding that Spain refused to export the breed in an attempt to keep its monopoly. Louis XVI of France asked for and received a flock of 366 and used them to build his own breed of fine wools, the Rambouillet. Both the Merino and Rambouillet have since been the basis for upgrading the qualities of wool for other breeds.

The Finnish Landrace breed is noted for its tendency to have a litter of young rather than a single lamb. The Russian Romanov also has multiple births, and breeders are now importing these into the United States, hoping to incorporate this trait into the established types. The Merino, prized for its wool, does not reproduce as successfully as other breeds, so a program to interbreed the Merino with the Landrace or Romanov would benefit both breeds.

In the United States, sheep are not commonly thought of as milk producers, but there are many cultures that commonly use the milk for drinking, cheese making, and butter. Worldwide, sheep milk production was esti-

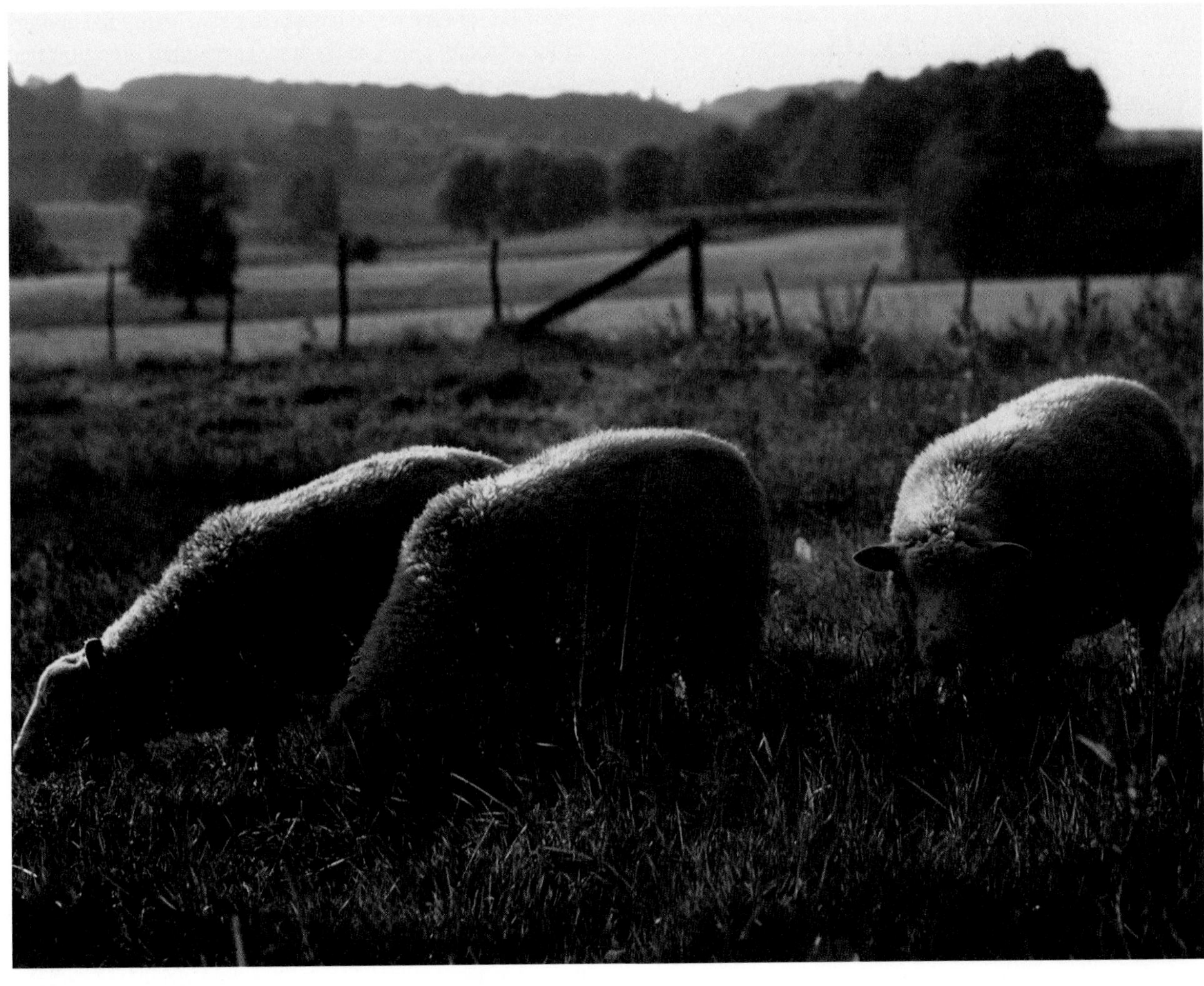

Sheep grazing in a field.

mated at 9.04 million tons in 1988. Sheep milk is much richer than cow's milk, though; cow's milk contains 3-6% butterfat, and ewe's milk contains 6-9%. A single ewe produces an average of one pint of milk per day.

French Roquefort cheese is made from ewe's milk. In the United States, a similar cheese is made from cow's milk and is called blue cheese. The blue streaks are caused by bacterium *Penicillium roqueforti*. Feta, originally from Greece, is also made from sheep's milk and is produced in several countries around the Mediterranean. The very popular Akawi comes from the area of Acre in Israel. Numerous local brands of white cheese are also found in the Balkans.

Sheep skins were the source of parchment from around 600 B.C. through the Middle Ages. The invention of printing, though, spurred the need for and manufacture of **paper** substitutes. Sheep parchment was one of the materials onto which the Dead Sea Scrolls were lettered, as well as most of the illuminated manuscripts of the monasteries. It is still used on occasions for degrees or meritorious citations, though true parchment is most often replaced by a paper product that resembles it.

Next to meat and wool, probably the most noted of sheep products is the Scottish haggis, the main course for festive times. It is a mixture of diced **heart**, liver, and lungs with turnips and oatmeal, all stuffed into a sheep's stomach and baked. When ready to serve a bagpiper precedes it into the dining hall. The sheep's **blood**, gathered during the slaughter, is the main ingredient in black pudding or a beverage. **Soap** and tallow come from the hard white **fat**, and some bones became shuttle bobbins in the weaving process. The intestines are the source of catgut.

Christopher Columbus brought over sheep, **horses**, and cattle on his second, third, and fourth voyages to the New World, as did many explorers who followed him. These animals served as the basic breeding stock for the

KEY TERMS

Clip—The fleece shorn from a single sheep or a whole flock.

Grade—The fineness or coarseness of the fleece. Can also refer to flocks or individuals, a grade animal denotes lower quality.

Kempy wool—Guard hairs mixed into the wool, an undesirable trait.

Ram—Male sheep.

missions that Spain was setting up in the New World. A century after, sheep numbered in the hundreds of thousands in Mexico and the Southwest, and their numbers continued to increase in spite of predators, Indians, and other setbacks.

The Bighorn sheep is native to **North America**, but had no part in the development of the domesticated sheep business. In fact, the sheep which were imported from **Europe** carried and spread diseases that decimated their wild cousins. Predators such as the coyote, the eagle, and **mountain** lion also that take their toll on wild sheep populations. Recently, it was discovered that the presence of llamas, **donkeys**, and cattle in the flock will help prevent predation. Certain breeds of dogs that are raised with the flock also protect the sheep by attacking predators.

Most of the sheep flocks on the western United States ranges carry Rambouillet and Merino blood, as they are often bred for their wool. It is the custom to castrate the ram lambs in these flocks and to use purebred rams from outside the flock to upgrade the wool. These males are retained for three to five years for shearing, and when the quality or quantity of their coat begins to decrease, they are sent to market and sold for meat.

Ewes are kept longer than the rams, up to seven or eight years, as they also produce a lamb every year in addition to their wool. A single lamb is the norm, but through selective breeding the farmer can sometimes achieve a larger lamb crop. Lambs bred for meat come from smaller farm flocks in the eastern and midwestern areas of the country.

Wool production in the United States has steadily declined since World War II, in spite of government subsidies, and now about 75% of the country's wool is imported. **Australia** produces about 25% of the world's wool. The development of cheaply-made synthetic fibers has greatly reduced the demand of the **natural fibers** such as wool.

The Merino and the improved British breeds constitute the majority of the modern breeds. Nearly all have a white fleece, as brown or black wool will not dye as readily. Wool is graded depending on the quality and length of the fibers. The blood system, most commonly used, grades the fleece as Fine, 1/2, 3/8 1/4, Low, and Braid.

See also Livestock.

J. Gordon Miller

Shell midden analysis

In **archaeology**, the term shell midden analysis refers to the study of marine shell valves that were once used as food by prehistoric peoples. In the United States, North American Indian tribes who lived near coastal areas often collected clams, oysters, mussel, and other species of shellfish to supplement their diets. Once the meat was extracted, the remaining shells were sometimes used to make ornaments such as beads or carved into fishhooks. However, most of the shell was simply thrown away as waste. It was not uncommon for prehistoric peoples to discard unwanted refuse at centralized trash sites. Over many hundreds of years, shell refuse and **soil** would build up at these trash sites, resulting in the formation of mounds on what was once level ground. Along the coast of California, for example, shell middens are one of the most distinctive types of archaeological sites. Some of the largest of these middens are over 30 ft (9 m) in depth and may extend more than one-quarter mile (400 m) across.

Once a shell midden has been excavated by archaeologists, the first step in the analysis is to catalog the finds. Typically, the process of cataloguing involves counting the actual number of shell valve specimens that have been recovered. This process includes speciation, determining what species of shells are represented in the collection. Shells are visually inspected, separated according to genera or family, and then subclassified into species. Because certain shellfish species are known to live in specific marine habitats, such as mud flats or open surf, the information gathered from this preliminary study can reveal where and how far prehistoric peoples traveled to gather shells.

Marine shell valves, such as clams, are also studied for their growth rings, which are similar to the growth rings of a **tree**. These rings or ridges on the outer surface of the shell can yield information regarding the relative age of the **animal** before it was harvested. Additionally,

growth rings can reveal the approximate season of the year when the shellfish was collected. This information is extremely useful to the overall archaeological study, and can be used as evidence in determining whether the campsite associated with the shell midden was inhabited only on a seasonal basis or all year long.

Perhaps the most important analysis conducted on marine shell is radiocarbon or C-14 dating. Often, village and campsites do not produce sufficient quantities of organic material to conduct radiocarbon analyses. However, archaeological sites that have associated shell middens nearby can usually produce more than enough material for extensive radiocarbon studies.

Under controlled scientific excavations and laboratory analysis, shell middens can supply information on marine shell harvesting techniques, trade, subsistence, settlement patterns, and prehistoric environmental conditions. Coupling this data with information from other studies adds to our understanding of the culture and lifestyles of ancient peoples.

Shingles

Shingles, also known as herpes zoster, are small, painful skin lesions caused by the same **virus** that causes chicken pox, the varicella zoster virus (VZV). Shingles usually occur in older individuals and in people who have weakened immune systems, such as **organ** transplant patients taking drugs to suppress their immune systems or people with Acquired Immune Deficiency Syndrome (AIDS). Shingles occur when the varicella zoster virus migrates along the sensory nerves to the skin surface. Along the way, the virus causes **inflammation** of these sensory nerves, causing severe **pain**. Shingles may persist for one to three weeks, and in some cases, may leave scars after they heal. Shingles usually heal without treatment, but pain medication is helpful. In some people, particularly older individuals, the pain may persist for months and even years after the shingles themselves have disappeared. This lingering pain probably stems from nerve damage.

The most common sites for shingles to erupt are the face and back; shingles are rarely found on the arms and legs. The eyes are sometimes affected by shingles. In some cases of shingles, the virus affects nerves in the face, a condition called Ramsey-Hunt syndrome. This **syndrome** is characterized by facial paralysis (Bell's palsy) and deafness, and may sometimes lead to encephalities, an **infection** of the **brain**. Other complications of shingles include bladder and bowel disturbances if the shingles affect the nerves that control these areas, and serious **eye** complications if the shingles affect the nerves that lead to the eyes.

Although the connection still is not clear, scientists theorize that some people who have been infected with varicella zoster virus continue to harbor the virus in their nervous systems. During times of stress or when the **immune system** is weakened, the latent virus reactivates, and then migrates down the sensory nerves to cause shingles lesions on the skin. This tenuous connection between chicken pox and shingles has raised concerns about the experimental chicken pox **vaccine** that is currently undergoing safety tests, since the varicella zoster virus used in the vaccine could theoretically lead to shingles later in life. However, no data is available that links an increased risk of shingles and the chicken pox vaccine.

Shingles are not life-threatening, but the severe pain associated with the lesions and their tendency to recur make shingles a serious health concern. No preventative measures can be taken. Antiviral drugs, such as acyclovir, may lessen the duration of the lesions. Steroids may also be helpful against pain that persists after the lesions heal.

Shore birds

Shore birds, sometimes called waders, include representatives from a number of families in the order Charadriiformes, including **plovers** (Charadriidae), **oystercatchers** (Haematopodidae), avocets and stilts (Recurvirostridae), **jacanas** (Jacanidae), and **sandpipers**, snipe, phalaropes, and their close relatives (Scolopacidae).

Despite their classification in the same order, shore birds are not closely related to each other. Their affinity is ecological, and involves a tendency to live near **water**. Collectively, species in the families listed above comprise a highly varied and widespread group of birds that utilize a great range of habitats, even deserts. However, most of these shore birds are commonly found in and around the shores, beaches, and mudflats of marine and fresh waters.

Many species of shore birds are hunted as game birds. In **North America**, hunted species of shore birds include relatively inland species such as snipes (*Capella gallinago*) and woodcocks (*Philohela minor*), and species more typical of marine habitats such as black-bellied plovers (*Squatarola squatarola*), whimbrels (*Numenius americanus*), and willets (*Catoptrophorus semipalmatus*). In recent decades, hunting of these species has been relatively limited. However, during the nine-

teenth century and first decade or so of the twentieth century shore birds (and most other hunted species of **wildlife**) were relentlessly hunted during their migrations and on their wintering grounds. As a direct result of this overhunting, and to some degree because of losses of natural **habitat**, the populations of most species of shore birds declined drastically in North America and elsewhere. One initially uncommon species, the Cooper's sandpiper (*Pisobia cooperi*), became extinct by 1833 because of excessive hunting. A larger species, the eskimo curlew (*Numenius borealis*), was reduced to extremely small numbers, and, as the population has not recovered, this shore bird remains on the list of **endangered species**.

Many species of shore birds predictably congregate in large numbers at particular times of year, generally during the spring or autumn migrations, or during winter. For some smaller species, those massed populations can be extraordinarily large. For example, during the fall **migration** more than one million semipalmated sandpipers (*Calidris pusilla*) congregate to feed on invertebrate-rich mudflats in the Bay of Fundy of eastern Canada, appearing in flocks that can exceed hundreds of thousands of individuals. Clearly, these mudflats represent habitat that is critical to the survival of semipalmated sandpipers. It is imperative that critical habitats like this be preserved, as must a sufficient number of places used by smaller numbers of shore birds, if these animals are to sustain viable populations over a long period.

See also Stilts and avocets.

Shoreline protection

Shoreline protection is the engineering effort designed to lessen or eliminate coastal **erosion**. Because **sea level** is rising and we have chosen to develop coastal areas, shoreline erosion has become a common and urgent problem for many communities. In essence, shoreline protection consists of engineered structures or other solutions meant to slow erosion by rising sea levels and **storm** wave action.

The shoreline is the area located between the low tide mark and the highest point on land that storm waves impact. They are dynamic features in that they move landward or seaward depending on rise or fall of sea level and the amount of **uplift** or **subsidence** (sinking) of the area. Currently sea level is rising—in the past century it has risen more than 4.5 in (12 cm) globally. Two-thirds of the world's people currently live near shorelines. New York, Los Angeles, Tokyo, London, and Rio de Janeiro are just a few of the major cities built near the sea.

In the past, shoreline protection was considered a local project. A single landowner or community designed a site-specific defense against erosion. While this effort might solve their erosion situation, the problem with this approach is that it often results in erosion on adjacent or nearby stretches of coast. Then the adjacent or nearby communities must also take defensive action. Unfortunately many coastal dwellers still tend to defend shorelines in this manner. However, other residents are finally beginning to grasp the concept that the shoreline environment is a system in its entirety, with many processes at work within it. If you make changes to any part of the system, a natural response, however unexpected, is likely to occur.

Types of Shorelines

Not every shoreline is identical. Those located where **mountain** building processes, such as uplift and folding and faulting are active, consist of rough, steep cliffs and rocky stretches reaching out into the sea, as well as beaches. These coastlines tend to be irregular, jutting in and out along their length. Shorelines found where these processes are not active tend to have long, wide beaches and often are characterized by islands located seaward of the shoreline, known as **barrier islands**. Both of these shoreline environments face unique erosion problems.

Crashing waves exert tremendous erosional power on rocky cliffs and so present serious problems to communities and homeowners that build roads and other structures upon these cliffs. Lateral erosion rates from constant wave action are as much as 6 ft (2 m) per year in some areas of the world. To slow the undercutting of cliffs, **concrete** structures or large boulders are often placed at the water's edge to absorb the **force** of breaking waves. However, minimizing the effect of urbanization on the cliffs is at least as important to slowing the rate of erosion. Constructing roads, homes, and other structures on sea cliffs increases the load on a cliff face and tends to weaken it, increasing the likelihood of slumping or landsliding. Storm **water** runoff from urban areas can also quickly weaken or erode cliffs. Taking measures to restrict these practices is a practical and effective approach to slowing coastal erosion.

Beaches, whether they are nestled in bays between rocky protrusions or stretch for hundreds of miles uninterrupted, are also subjected to powerful erosional forces. **Rivers** are the main source of sediment for many of our beaches. Once the sediment is deposited on the beach, currents transport it along the shoreline, in a

process known as longshore drift. Eventually some of the sediment is lost in deep trenches or canyons, often called sinks, on the sea floor. The system made up of these combined processes is called a littoral cell.

Our shorelines consist of numerous littoral cells providing beaches with their allotment or "budget" of sediment. Each beach has a unique sediment budget. If more sediment is brought in than is lost, the budget is positive and the beach grows, but if the opposite occurs, beach erosion takes place. The **dams** we construct upriver can **limit** the amount of sediment initially reaching the beach. The hard structures placed along our coasts for shoreline protection further rob beaches of sediment by keeping it from being transported downcurrent. In addition, waves, their height, how fast they follow one another, and their direction, directly affect the amount of sediment on shore. Storm waves are particularly damaging to sandy beaches. Human activity also plays a substantial part in causing erosion of our beaches. Structures designed to stabilize or add sediment on one beach often deplete sediment on beaches downcurrent. Perhaps the most significant threat to beaches, however, is rising sea level along coasts where buildings are at risk from beach erosion.

Types of Shoreline Protection

Historically, the structures developed for shoreline protection were constructed of durable materials such as rock and reinforced concrete. They were designed to withstand the force of wave action. Such "hard" stabilization methods are still in use today and include seawalls, revetments, breakwaters, impermeable groins, and jetties.

Seawalls are structures built at the water's edge of concrete or large stone (riprap). Their purpose is to bear the full brunt of the wave action, thereby protecting the cliff face. However, they also encourage the beach in front of them to narrow. In addition, they are considered an eyesore to many people.

Revetments of broken concrete or riprap are powerful devices for reducing the **energy** from wave action, and they are repaired inexpensively. Their irregular surface offers protection from wave runup, or the movement of breaking waves up the shore. Revetments often limit access to the beach and, as with seawalls, they can be rather unsightly.

Groins are sediment traps. They jut out at right angles from the shore and catch sediment carried by longshore drift on their upcurrent side. However, this sediment never reaches the downcurrent side of the groin, so the beach narrows. For this reason multiple groins are usually constructed in an area.

Breakwaters may be connected to the shoreline at one end or completely separate from it. Their purpose is to bear the brunt of the waves, producing calmer water shoreward of the structure. Jetties are used to keep a channel open and are placed one on each side of the channel's outlet. Both of these structures impact littoral longshore transport causing beach buildup on their updrift sides and erosion downdrift. Dredging is often required to keep them functioning.

While "hard" structures continue to be used for shoreline defense, "soft" stabilization methods are becoming more prevalent in coastal areas, either as the sole method of protection or in conjunction with "hard" stabilization practices. The most utilized form of "soft" shoreline protection is **beach nourishment**, or the replenishing of sands on an eroding or retreating beach. Its greatest advantage is that nourishment extends the time until erosion undermines the structures behind the beach. Beach nourishment also allows for a wider, more usable beach, which provides better recreational areas and economic revenue for those living near it. But it also has disadvantages. It is extremely costly, and nourishment must be performed every few years to keep beaches from retreating after storms. In addition, impacts to the beach **ecosystem** often occur during, or as a result of, the nourishment. If excessively muddy sands are used, organisms may be smothered, and building beaches steeper than their original profile may limit their use by various forms of marine life.

Recently new types of "soft" stabilization have been introduced. Wave screens, submerged breakwaters, active submerged breakwaters and floating breakwaters do not disturb or change current flow, but rather allow water and **fish** to pass through their partially transparent structure. Improved physical structures that aid in shoreline protection are not the only ideas under consideration for the future. Enhancement of the environment through vegetation of the shores and an understanding of how each inhabitant of the shore environment contributes to the health and well being of the coast must play an active part in coastal planning.

For example, recent research has shown the eggs of the Loggerhead turtle provide much-needed **nutrients** to beach areas where they nest. These nutrients ensure healthy stands of coastal vegetation, which help keep the beach in place. In an effort to protect the threatened **turtles**, their nests are often relocated, depriving the original nesting sites of these nutrients. Taking into account such nuances when considering the type of shoreline protection to use will allow for a more complete and natural form of shoreline protection.

Past trends in shoreline protection have involved fighting the sea with expensive engineered defenses. The realization that shorelines are dynamic and erosion is a natural and inevitable process has more recently led to

KEY TERMS

Barrier island—An island separated from the mainland by a lagoon. They are formed from deposition of sediment during shoreline processes.

Beach nourishment—Bringing in sediment from an outside source to rebuild an eroding beach.

Longshore drift—Transport of sediments by currents flowing parallel to the beach.

Littoral cell—The system of sediment movement that delivers sediment to the shoreline, transports it along the shoreline, and may eventually result in its loss in deeper water away from the shore.

some revolutionary and certainly controversial ideas in the fight against shoreline erosion. Sea levels are expected to continue their current rate of rise or to accelerate. Should they increase dramatically, expensive engineered structures and replenished beaches will be no match for the sea. Some communities have considered the idea of relocating buildings. Along very densely populated coastlines this is not really a feasible alternative, but the idea of restricting coastal development is gaining supporters. North Carolina has strict regulations governing the types and sizes of structures that can be built on its shoreline. Many believe we must establish wise shoreline **land use** and development guidelines, and that if we choose to build near the shore it is only with the understanding that structures constructed there are not considered permanent and will be given up to the sea should shorelines move landward.

Further Reading

Abrahamson, D.E., ed. *The Challenge of Global Warmin.* Washington, D.C., Island Press, 1989.

Bird, E.C.F. and M.L. Schwartz. *The World's Coastline.* New York, NY: Van Nostrand Reinhold Co., 1985.

Flanagan, R.*"Beaches on the brink," Earth 2*, no. 6: 24-33.

National Research Council. *Beach Nourishment and Protection.* Washington, DC., National Academy of Sciences, 1995.

Williams, S.J., et al.*"Coasts in crisis." U.S. Geological Survey Circular* 1075.

Monica Anderson

Shrews

Shrews are small, mouse-like **mammals** of the family Soricidae, class Insectivora. They have large cutting, or incisor teeth, similar to those of a mouse. But unlike a mouse (which is a rodent and thus has teeth that continually grow), the teeth of shrews must last a lifetime. Also, their snout is narrower and more pointed than that of a mouse.

There are more than 260 species of shrews. They vary upward in size from the pygmy white-toothed, or Etruscan shrew (*Suncus etruscus*), weighing only 0.07 ounce (2 g) and 1.3 inch (3.5 cm) long, and probably the smallest mammal in the world. The largest species are the rat-sized musk shrew (*Sorex murinus*) and the African forest shrew (*Crocidura odorata*), which may reach a weight of more than 3.7 ounces (106 g). There are some genera of shrews that have been examined so rarely by biologists that little is known about them.

Shrews live everywhere but the southern half of **South America**, **Australia**, and **Antarctica**. Some of them even live in Arctic regions. The tiny pygmy shrew (*Microsorex hoyi*), for example, has a range that extends from the **tundra** of northern Alaska and Canada southward to New England. It is just a millimeter longer than the Etruscan shrew. The pygmy shrew is so small that it has been known to use burrows created by **beetles**.

One characteristic indicating that shrews are more primitive (i.e., with an older evolutionary lineage) than most mammals is the presence of a cloaca in many species. This is an external opening into which both the genital and urinary tracts empty. **Reptiles**, from which mammals evolved, also have a cloaca.

Shrews digest their food very rapidly, so quickly, in fact, that much of it is not fully digested. Consequently, some shrews re-eat their feces, to capture the undigested **nutrients**. Having a large surface: volume **ratio**, and a very high metabolic rate, shrews must eat almost continuously to get enough food **energy** to support themselves. This is particularly the case of the smallest species.

The shrew family is divided into two subfamilies, the red-toothed shrews, which get their name from the fact that the tips of their teeth are colored, usually reddish, and the white-toothed shrews, which do not have that coloration. All shrews have a long snout, which gives their head a triangular shape when seen from above. Their snout is mobile and continually moves so that their vibrissae (long, sensory hairs) can do their job. The snout ends in a moist pad. Most shrews have dark-brown fur, though some tend toward yellow, reddish, or gray.

The eyes and ears of shrews are clearly visible on their head (as opposed to the related **moles**, which have these organs covered with fur). Shrews do not see very well, relying more on **smell**, **touch**, and **hearing**, especially to avoid their primary enemies. The latter are mostly **birds of prey** and small predatory mammals, such as **weasels**.

A common, or masked shrew.

Sound is very important in the life of shrews. Squeaks, squeals, and high-pitched clicks are made on various occasions. Female shrews looking for a mate make a small peeping sound. For the most part, though, shrews of the same species avoid each other, except at mating time. Their territories rarely overlap, and if they meet, they chitter loudly at each other until one gives way. Some shrews can apparently use their high-pitches squeaks as a kind of **sonar**; the noises echo back from objects, helping the shrews to define their local environment. Many shrew sounds are so high pitched that they cannot be detected by humans.

Shrews prefer moist, well-vegetated habitats. They prey on various **invertebrates**, such as earthworms and insect larvae, though some shrews will also eat **seeds** and nuts. A group called the **water** shrews feeds on aquatic life in ponds, lakes, and streams. Unlike moles, shrews do not burrow much, tending to spend their time on the surface or just under loose cover of plants and litter. They will, however, take up residence in burrows abandoned by other digging animals. Shrew territories are marked by a musky odor. A few species of shrews will climb shrubs and trees in search of prey.

Several genera of water shrews dig burrows in the banks of **rivers** and lakes, with the entrances underwater. They feed on aquatic worms, **snails**, and insect larvae. Their long, narrow toes have an edging of stiff hairs that works as a substitute for webbed toes. Only one species, *Nectogale elegans*, has webbed feet.

Some shrews, such as the American short-tailed shrew (*Blarina brevicauda*), have poison in their salivary **glands** that allows them to prey on animals much larger than themselves. Some water shrews with poisonous bites can kill large **fish**. The poison, which acts on the prey's **nervous system**, has been known to cause **pain** in bitten humans for several days.

KEY TERMS

Cloaca—A chamber into which both the digestive system waste and the reproductive system empty before exiting the body.

Birth and death

Within a colony of shrews, the breeding season may last seven or eight months. The female weaves an enclosed, dome-shaped nest of **grasses** and **moss**, often hidden beneath a log or in a burrow. After a gestation period of 25-30 days, she produces 5-11 blind and hairless young. The young make loud squeals that sound almost like barks. By the time the female stops nursing the young, they are almost as large as she is. Some mother shrews take their young on exploration adventures in which each one links to the sibling before by grasping its fur in the mouth, making a living chain of shrews. They reach sexual maturity at less than a year and begin to breed in late spring.

The common shrew (*Sorex araneus*) of **Europe** averages about 2.3 in (6 cm) long plus a tail about half that length, and weighs about 0.35 oz (10 g). It often lives near human dwellings, liking compost heaps and hedgerows. It has the ability to become pregnant with a new litter immediately after giving **birth** to the previous litter. Thus a female may be nursing and gestating at the same time. Both events last only about two weeks.

Most shrews die before a new winter sets in, giving them a life span of little more than a year. Only the most recent generation survives the winter. They also molt twice a year, growing summer fur in the springtime, and winter fur in autumn. Because shrews are extremely nervous little mammals with a high metabolic rate, they can die of starvation after just a few hours without food. They can also die of fright.

See also Tree shrews.

Further Reading

Bailey, Jill. *Discovering Shrews, Moles & Voles.* New York: The Bookwright Press, 1989.

Caras, Roger A. *North American Mammals: Fur-Bearing Animals of the United States and Canada.* New York: Meredith Press, 1967.

Kerrod, Robin. *Mammals: Primates, Insect-Eaters and Baleen Whales.* Encyclopedia of the Animal World Series. New York: Facts on File, 1988.

A Northern shrike perched on a branch.

Nicoll, Martin E. and Galen Rathbun. *African Insectivora and Elephant-Shrews: An Action Plan for Their Conservation.* Island Press, 1991.

Jean F. Blashfield

Shrikes

Shrikes are 72 species of perching **birds** that make up the family Laniidae, in the order Passeriformes. The diversity of shrikes is greatest in **Africa**, with species also occurring in **Europe**, **Asia**, and Southeast Asia as far south as New Guinea. Two species occur in **North America**. Shrikes occur in a wide range of habitats, including forest edges, open forest, savanna, grassland, and some types of shrubby cultivated land.

Shrikes are medium-sized birds with body lengths ranging from 6-14 in (15-36 cm). They have a relatively large head, and a stout beak, with a notch on each side and a pronounced hook at the tip of the upper mandible. The wings are pointed, the legs are strong, and the feet have sharp claws. Most species are gray or brown on the back and wings, with black markings, and whiter below. Some species, however, can have a rather colorful plumage.

Shrikes are aggressive predators. They typically hunt from a perch that gives them a wide vantage of their surroundings. When **prey** is detected, the shrike swoops at it, and kills it with a sharp blow with the beak. Shrikes feed on large **insects**, **reptiles**, small **mammals**, and small birds. Shrikes carry their prey in their beak, and many species commonly impale their food on a thorn or barbed wire. This is done either to store for later consumption, or to hold the body still while it is torn apart during eating. Shrikes are some-

times called butcher-birds, because of their habit of lardering (or storing) their meat.

Shrikes build a bulky, cup-shaped nest in a shrub or **tree**. They lay 2-6 eggs, which are incubated by the female. The male assists with the rearing of the young birds.

The northern or great grey shrike (*Lanius excubitor*) ranges from Canada to northern Mexico, and is also widespread in Europe, Asia, and North Africa. The loggerhead shrike (*L. ludovicianus*) is a smaller species with a more southern distribution, and it only breeds in North America. Populations of both of these species, but particularly those of the loggerhead shrike, appear to have declined substantially. The causes of the declines of these predatory birds are not well known, but are thought to be largely due to **pesticides** in their food web, and **habitat** changes, especially those associated with the intensification of agriculture.

See also Vireos.

Shrimp

Shrimps are common, small **invertebrates** that occur in all marine ecosystems; in addition, some species have adapted to living in **freshwater**. All members of this group (class **Crustacea**, order Decapoda) are adapted for swimming. Most species, however, are bottom-dwelling animals that swim only occasionally.

The body of most species of shrimps is compressed side-ways, or it may be more cylindrical in cross-section. The body consists of a well-developed thorax and abdomen enclosed in a tough carapace made of chitin, which often extends to the base of the legs, protecting the delicate gills. The first three pairs of thoracic limbs (or maxillipeds) are modified for use in feeding, specifically for grasping food. The other five pairs of thoracic legs, the first of which is usually larger than the others, have pinching claws that serve in handling **prey** as well for defensive purposes. These legs are also used for walking. The head is well developed and bears stalked eyes, a pair of mandibles, a pair of antennae, and smaller antennules. The antennae may be considerably longer than the body. Both the antennules and antennae play an important sensory role, detecting prey as well as changes in salinity and **water temperature**. At the end of the abdomen there is often a swimming fin formed by structures called the uropods and telson.

Unlike **crabs** and **lobsters**, their decapod relatives, shrimps can be highly gregarious and may swim and feed in large schools. Many species of shrimp are nocturnal, remaining concealed amid seaweed or hidden in the crevices of coral reefs during the day. Some species bury themselves in the sand, the only tell-tale sign of their presence being their long tentacles. At night they emerge to feed on smaller crustaceans, small **fish**, worms, and the eggs and larvae of a wide range of species.

One group of shrimps has developed an unusual means of capturing prey. The pistol or snapping shrimps (Alphaeidae) live in burrows that they excavate in sand on the seabed. One of their front claws is greatly enlarged, typically measuring more than half of the body length. The tip of this claw is modified as a broad base-plate, to which is attached a hinged joint; this is reminiscent of old-time muskets that had a powder pan which was ignited when a hammer hit it. The purpose of this device in the snapping shrimps is not primarily to grasp passing prey, but to stun them. When the shrimp feels threatened or detects potential prey nearby, the "hammer" is pulled back so that it is at a right **angle** to the base of the claw. When the hammer is released it produces a loud snapping noise, the shock wave of which can be sufficient to stun or even kill a small prey individual. The prey is then dragged into the shrimp's burrow and consumed. Pistol shrimps are also highly territorial, and use their snapping mechanism to deter other shrimps, and other invertebrates, from invading their territory and tunnels.

A number of shrimp species have developed elaborate social relationships with other marine animals. Certain species of shrimps live among the spines of **sea urchins** and the tentacles of **sea anemones**, feeding on **plankton** and small crustaceans. They also feed on the detritus produced as the urchin or anemone eats. The precise benefit to the host is not clear, but the shrimps may help deter small grazing fishes, or they may keep the tentacles or spines of the host free of debris and **algae**. A much refined association involves the cleaner shrimps, such as species of *Periclimenes* and *Stenopus*, which perform an essential service to many large fish by removing **parasites** from their body and cleaning injured tissues. To do so, the cleaner shrimps may have to enter the mouth of the host, a potentially lethal undertaking in view of the fact that most of the fish are large enough to make a meal out of the shrimp. However, the sanitary service is of such great importance to the fish that it never consumes its hygienist. Many fishes signal their desire to be cleaned by changing their body color, or by opening their mouth and extending their gill covers. In return for this service, the shrimps obtain much, if not all of their daily food requirements by eating the parasites or diseased flesh they find while cleaning. The cleaner shrimps are brightly colored and advertise their services to fish by perching in an exposed place and waving their long tentacles.

During the breeding season, many species of shrimp forsake their usual **habitat** in shallow water and migrate to deeper places where they mate and lay their eggs. Females lay huge numbers of eggs, often greater than half a million, which are released directly to the water and not retained on the body for hatching (crabs and lobsters do the latter). The microscopic eggs hatch into tiny larvae, known as nauplii, which drift with the current for several weeks before changing to the adult form. As the larvae grow, they undergo a number of molts until they acquire adult characters and eventually migrate toward shallower near-shore habitat where they live until the next breeding season.

Shrimps are an important part of the marine food web. They are eaten by a wide range of fishes, and even by marine **mammals** such as **seals** and whales. Larger species of shrimps are also sought out by commercial fisheries, which harvest huge amounts of these crustaceans for human consumption. Some species of shrimps are also cultivated in aquaculture in tropical countries.

See also Zooplankton.

David Stone

Sickle cell anemia

Sickle cell anemia is an inherited **blood** disorder that arises from a single **amino acid** substitution in one of the component **proteins** of hemoglobin. The component protein, or globin, that contains the substitution is defective. Hemoglobin molecules constructed with such proteins have a tendency to stick to one another, forming strands of hemoglobin within the red blood cells. The cells that contain these strands become stiff and elongated—that is, sickle shaped.

Sickle-shaped cells—also called sickle cells—die much more rapidly than normal red blood cells, and the body cannot create replacements fast enough. Anemia develops due to the chronic shortage of red blood cells. Further complications arise because sickle cells do not fit well through small blood vessels, and can become trapped. The trapped sickle cells form blockages that prevent oxygenated blood from reaching associated tissues and organs. Considerable **pain** results in addition to damage to the tissues and organs. This damage can lead to serious complications, including **stroke** and an impaired **immune system**. Sickle cell anemia primarily affects people with African, Mediterranean, Middle Eastern, and Indian ancestry. In the United States, African Americans are particularly affected.

A peppermint shrimp.

Hemoglobin structure

Normal hemoglobin is composed of a heme **molecule** and two pairs of proteins called globins. Humans have the genes to create six different types of globins—alpha, beta, gamma, delta, epsilon, and zeta—but do not use all of them at once. Which genes are expressed depends on the stage of development: embryonic, fetal, or adult. Virtually all of the hemoglobin produced in humans from ages 2-3 months onward contains a pair of alpha-globin and beta-globin molecules.

Sickle cell hemoglobin

A change, or **mutation**, in a **gene** can alter the formation or function of its product. In the case of sickle cell hemoglobin, the gene that carries the blueprint for beta-globin has a minute alteration that makes it different from the normal gene. This mutation affects a single **nucleic acid** along the entire DNA strand that makes up the beta-globin gene. (Nucleic acids are the chemicals that make up deoxyribonucleic acid, known more familiarly as DNA.) Specifically, the nucleic acid, adenine, is replaced by a different nucleic acid called thymine.

Because of this seemingly slight mutation, called a point mutation, the finished beta-globin molecule has an amino acid substitution: valine occupies the spot normally taken by glutamic acid. (Amino acids are the building blocks of all proteins.) This substitution creates a beta-globin molecule—and eventually a hemoglobin molecule—that does not function normally.

Normal hemoglobin, referred to as hemoglobin A, transports **oxygen** from the lungs to tissues throughout the body. In the smallest blood vessels, the hemoglobin exchanges the oxygen for **carbon dioxide**, which it carries back to the lungs for removal from the body. The defective hemoglobin, designated hemoglobin S, can also

transport oxygen. However, once the oxygen is released, hemoglobin S molecules have an abnormal tendency to clump together. Aggregated hemoglobin molecules form strands within red blood cells, which then lose their usual shape and flexibility.

The rate at which hemoglobin S aggregation and cell sickling occur depends on many factors, such as the blood flow rate and the **concentration** of hemoglobin in the blood cells. If the blood flows at a normal rate, hemoglobin S is reoxygenated in the lungs before it has a chance to aggregate. The concentration of hemoglobin within red blood cells is influenced by an individual's hydration level—that is the amount **water** contained in the cells. If a person becomes dehydrated, hemoglobin becomes more concentrated in the red blood cells. In this situation, hemoglobin S has a greater tendency to clump together and induce sickle cell formation.

Sickle cell anemia

Genes are inherited in pairs, one copy from each parent. Therefore, each person has two copies of the gene that makes beta-globin. As long as a person inherits one normal beta-globin gene, the body can produce sufficient quantities of normal beta-globin. A person who inherits a copy each of the normal and abnormal beta-globin genes is referred to as a carrier of the sickle cell trait. Generally, carriers do not have symptoms, but their red blood cells contain some hemoglobin S.

A child who inherits the sickle cell trait from both parents—a 25% possibility if both parents are carriers—will develop sickle cell anemia. Sickle cell anemia is characterized by the formation of stiff and elongated red blood cells, called sickle cells. These cells have a decreased life span in comparison to normal red blood cells. Normal red blood cells survive for approximately 120 days in the bloodstream; sickle cells last only 10-12 days. As a result, the bloodstream is chronically short of red blood cells and the affected individual develops anemia.

The sickle cells can create other complications. Due to their shape, they do not fit well through small blood vessels. As an aggravating **factor**, the outside surfaces of sickle cells may have altered chemical properties that increase the cell's "stickiness." These sticky sickle cells are more likely to adhere to the inside surfaces of small blood vessels, as well as to other blood cells. As a result of the sickle cells' shape and stickiness, blockages occasionally form in small blood vessels. Such blockages prevent oxygenated blood from reaching areas where it is needed, causing extreme pain, as well as **organ** and **tissue** damage.

However, the severity of the symptoms cannot be predicted based solely on the genetic inheritance. Some individuals with sickle cell anemia develop health- or life-threatening problems in infancy, but others may have only mild symptoms throughout their lives. For example, genetic factors, such as the continued production of fetal hemoglobin after **birth**, can modify the course of the disease. Fetal hemoglobin contains gamma-globin in place of beta-globin; if enough of it is produced, the potential interactions between hemoglobin S molecules are reduced.

Affected populations

Worldwide, millions of people carry the sickle cell trait. Individuals whose ancestors lived in sub-Saharan **Africa**, the Middle East, India, or the Mediterranean region are the most likely to have the trait. The areas of the world associated with the sickle cell trait are also strongly affected by **malaria**, a disease caused by blood-borne **parasites** transmitted through mosquito bites. According to a widely accepted theory, the genetic mutation associated with the sickle cell trait occurred thousands of years ago. Coincidentally, this mutation increased the likelihood that carriers would survive malaria outbreaks. Survivors then passed the mutation on to their offspring, and the trait became established throughout areas where malaria was common.

Although modern medicine offers drug therapies for malaria, the sickle cell trait endures. Approximately 2 million Americans are carriers of the sickle cell trait. Individuals who have African ancestry are particularly affected; one in 12 African Americans are carriers. An additional 72,000 Americans have sickle cell anemia, meaning they have inherited the trait from both parents. Among African Americans, approximately one in every 500 babies is diagnosed with sickle cell anemia. Hispanic Americans are also heavily affected; sickle cell anemia occurs in one of every 1,000-1,400 births. Worldwide, it has been estimated that 250,000 children are born each year with sickle cell anemia.

Causes & symptoms

Sickle cell anemia results from an inheritance of the sickle cell trait—that is, a defective beta-globin gene—from each parent. Due to this inheritance, hemoglobin S is produced. This hemoglobin has a tendency to aggregate and form strands, thereby deforming the red blood cells in which it is contained. The deformed, short-lived red blood cells cause effects throughout the body.

Symptoms typically appear during the first year or two of life, if the **diagnosis** has not been made at or before birth. However, some individuals do not develop symptoms until adulthood and may not be aware that they have the genetic inheritance for sickle cell anemia.

Anemia

Sickle cells have a high turnover rate, and there is a deficit of red blood cells in the bloodstream. Common symptoms of anemia include fatigue, paleness, and a shortness of breath. A particularly severe form of anemia—aplastic anemia—occurs following **infection** with parvovirus. Parvovirus causes extensive destruction of the bone marrow, bringing production of new red blood cells to a halt. Bone marrow production resumes after 7-10 days; however, given the short lives of sickle cells, even a brief shut-down in red blood cell production can cause a precipitous decline in hemoglobin concentrations. This is called "aplastic crisis."

Painful crises

Painful crises, also known as vaso-occlusive crises, are a primary symptom of sickle cell anemia in children and adults. The pain may be caused by small blood vessel blockages that prevent oxygen from reaching tissues. An alternate explanation, particularly with regard to bone pain, is that blood is shunted away from the bone marrow but through some other mechanism than blockage by sickle cells.

These crises are unpredictable, and can affect any area of the body, although the chest, abdomen, and bones are frequently affected sites. There is some evidence that cold temperatures or infection can trigger a painful crisis, but most crises occur for unknown reasons. The **frequency** and duration of the pain can vary tremendously. Crises may be separated by more than a year or possibly only by weeks, and they can last from hours to weeks.

The hand-foot **syndrome** is a particular type of painful crisis, and is often the first sign of sickle cell anemia in an infant. Common symptoms include pain and swelling in the hands and feet, possibly accompanied by a fever. Hand-foot syndrome typically occurs only during the first four years of life, with the greatest incidence at one year.

Enlarged spleen and infections

Sickle cells can impede blood flow through the spleen and cause organ damage. In infants and young children, the spleen is usually enlarged. After repeated incidence of blood vessel blockage, the spleen usually atrophies by late childhood. Damage to the spleen can have a negative impact on the immune system, leaving individuals with sickle cell anemia more vulnerable to infections. Infants and young children are particularly prone to life-threatening infections.

Anemia can also impair the immune system, because stem cells—the precursors of all blood cells—are earmarked for red blood cell production rather than white blood cell production. White blood cells form the cornerstone of the immune system within the bloodstream.

Delayed growth

The **energy** demands of the bone marrow for red blood cell production compete with the demands of a growing body. Children with sickle cell anemia have delayed growth and reach **puberty** at a later age than normal. By early adulthood, they catch up on growth and attain normal height; however, weight typically remains below average.

Stroke

Blockage of blood vessels in the **brain** can have particularly harsh consequences and can be fatal. When areas of the brain are deprived of oxygen, control of the associated functions may be lost. Sometimes this loss is permanent. Common stroke symptoms include weakness or numbness that affects one side of the body, sudden loss of **vision**, confusion, loss of **speech** or the ability to understand spoken words, and dizziness. Children between the ages of 1-15 are at the highest risk of suffering a stroke. Approximately two-thirds of the children who have a stroke will have at least one more.

Acute chest syndrome

Acute chest syndrome can occur at any age, and is caused by sickle cells blocking the small blood vessels of the lungs. This blockage is complicated by accompanying problems such as infection and pooling of blood in the lungs. Affected persons experience fever, cough, chest pain, and shortness of breath. Recurrent attacks can lead to permanent lung damage.

Other problems

Males with sickle cell anemia may experience a condition called priapism. (Priapism is characterized by a persistent and painful erection of the penis.) Due to blood vessel blockage by sickle cells, blood is trapped in the tissue of the penis. Damage to this tissue can result in permanent impotence in adults.

Both genders may experience kidney damage. The environment in the kidney is particularly conducive for sickle cell formation; even otherwise asymptomatic carriers may experience some level of kidney damage. Kid-

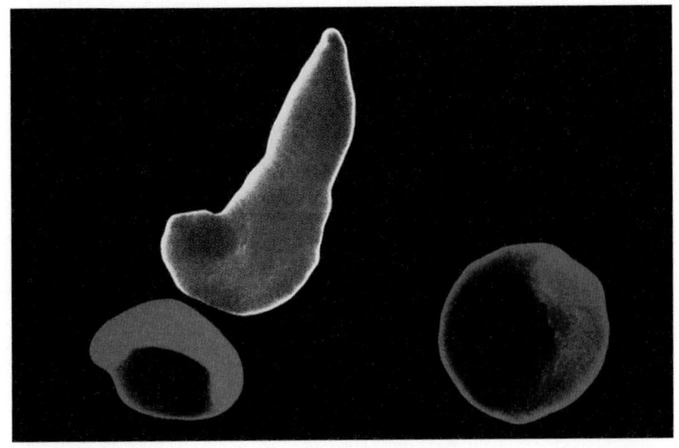

A scanning electron microscopy (SEM) scan of red blood cells taken from a person with sickle cell anemia. The blood cells at the bottom are normal; the diseased, sickle-shaped cell appears at the top.

ney damage is indicated by blood in the urine, incontinence, and enlarged kidneys.

Jaundice and an enlarged liver are also commonly associated with sickle cell anemia. Jaundice, indicated by a yellow tone in the skin and eyes, may occur if bilirubin levels increase. Bilirubin is the final product of hemoglobin degradation, and is typically removed from the bloodstream by the liver. Bilirubin levels often increase with high levels of red blood cell destruction, but jaundice can also be a sign of a poorly functioning liver.

Some individuals with sickle cell anemia may experience vision problems. The blood vessels that feed into the retina—the tissue at the back of the eyeball—may be blocked by sickle cells. New blood vessel can form around the blockages, but these vessels are typically weak or otherwise defective. Bleeding, scarring, and retinal detachment may eventually lead to blindness.

Diagnosis

Sickle cell anemia is suspected based on an individual's ethnic or racial background, and on the symptoms of anemia. A blood count reveals the anemia, and a sickle cell test reveals the presence of the sickle cell trait.

The sickle cell test involves mixing equal amounts of blood and a two percent solution of **sodium** bisulfite. Under these circumstances, hemoglobin exists in its deoxygenated state. If hemoglobin S is present, the red blood cells are transformed into the characteristic sickle shape. This transformation is observed with a **microscope**, and quantified by expressing the number of sickle cells per 1,000 cells as a percentage. The sickle cell test confirms that an individual has the sickle cell trait, but it does not provide a definitive diagnosis for sickle cell anemia.

To confirm a diagnosis of the sickle cell trait or sickle cell anemia, another laboratory test called gel **electrophoresis** is performed. This test uses an electric field applied across a slab of gel-like material to separate protein molecules based on their size, shape, or electrical charge. Although hemoglobin S (sickle) and hemoglobin A (normal) differ by only one amino acid, they can be clearly separated using gel electrophoresis. If both types of hemoglobin are identified, the individual is a carrier of the sickle cell trait; if only hemoglobin S is present, the person most likely has sickle cell anemia.

The gel electrophoresis test is also used as a screening method for identifying the sickle cell trait in newborns. More than 40 states screen newborns in order to identify carriers and individuals who have inherited the trait from both parents.

Treatment

Early identification of sickle cell anemia can prevent many problems. The highest death rates occur during the first year of life due to infection, aplastic anemia, and acute chest syndrome. If anticipated, steps can be taken to avert these crises. With regard to long-term treatment, prevention of complications remains a main goal. Sickle cell anemia cannot be cured—other than through a risky bone marrow transplant—but treatments are available for symptoms.

Pain management

Pain is one of the primary symptoms of sickle cell anemia, and controlling it is an important concern. The methods necessary for pain control are based on individual factors. Some people can gain adequate pain control through over-the-counter oral painkillers (analgesics), local application of **heat**, and rest. Others need stronger methods, which can include administration of narcotics.

Blood transfusions

Blood transfusions are usually not given on a regular basis but are used to treat painful crises, severe anemia, and other emergencies. In some cases, such as treating spleen enlargement or preventing stroke from recurring, blood transfusions are given as a preventative measure. Regular blood transfusions have the potential to decrease formation of hemoglobin S, and reduce associated symptoms. However, regular blood transfusions introduce a set of complications, primarily **iron** loading, risk of infection, and sensitization to proteins in the transfused blood.

KEY TERMS

Amino acid—A type of molecule used as a building block for protein construction.

Anemia—A condition in which the level of hemoglobin falls below normal values due to a shortage of mature red blood cells. Common symptoms include pallor, fatigue, and shortness of breath.

Bilirubin—A yellow pigment that is the end result of hemoglobin degradation. Bilirubin is cleared from the blood by action of liver enzymes and excreted from the body.

Bone marrow—A spongy tissue located in the hollow centers of certain bones, such as the skull and hip bones. Bone marrow is the site of blood cell generation.

Bone marrow transplantation—A medical procedure in which normal bone marrow is transferred from a healthy donor to an ailing recipient. An illness that prevents production of normal blood cells—such as sickle cell anemia—may be treated with a bone marrow transplant.

Gel electrophoresis—A laboratory test that separates molecules based on their size, shape, or electrical charge.

Globin—One of the component protein molecules found in hemoglobin. Normal adult hemoglobin has a pair each of alpha-globin and beta-globin molecules.

Heme—The iron-containing molecule in hemoglobin that serves as the site for oxygen binding.

Hemoglobin—The red pigment found within red blood cells that enables them to transport oxygen throughout the body. Hemoglobin is a large molecule composed of five component molecules: a heme molecule and two pairs of globin molecules.

Hemoglobin A—Normal adult hemoglobin which contains a heme molecule, two alpha-globin molecules, and two beta-globin molecules.

Hemoglobin S—Hemoglobin that is produced in association with the sickle cell trait; the beta-globin molecules of hemoglobin S are defective.

Hydroxyurea—A drug that has been shown to induce production of fetal hemoglobin. Fetal hemoglobin has a pair of gamma-globin molecules in place of the typical beta-globins of adult hemoglobin. Higher-than-normal levels of fetal hemoglobin can prevent sickling from occurring.

Iron loading—A side effect of frequent transfusions in which the body accumulates abnormally high levels of iron. Iron deposits can form in organs, particularly the heart, and cause life-threatening damage.

Jaundice—A condition characterized by higher-than-normal levels of bilirubin in the bloodstream and an accompanying yellowing of the skin and eyes.

Mutation—A change in a gene's DNA. Whether a mutation is harmful is determined by the effect on the product for which the gene codes.

Nucleic acid—A type of chemical that is used as a component for building DNA. The nucleic acids found in DNA are adenine, thymine, guanine, and cytosine.

Red blood cell—Hemoglobin-containing blood cells that transport oxygen from the lungs to tissues. In the tissues, the red blood cells exchange their oxygen for carbon dioxide, which is brought back to the lungs to be exhaled.

Screening—Process through which carriers of a trait may be identified within a population.

Sickle cell—A red blood cell that has assumed a elongated shape due to the presence of hemoglobin S.

Sickle cell test—A blood test that identifies and quantifies sickle cells in the bloodstream.

Drugs

Infants are typically started on a course of penicillin that extends from infancy to age six. This treatment is meant to ward off potentially fatal infections. Infections at any age are treated aggressively with **antibiotics**. Vaccines for common infections, such as pneumococcal **pneumonia**, are administered when possible.

Emphasis is being placed on developing drugs that treat sickle cell anemia directly. The most promising of these drugs in the late 1990s is hydroxyurea, a drug that was originally designed for anticancer treatment. Hy-

droxyurea has been shown to reduce the frequency of painful crises and acute chest syndrome in adults, and to lessen the need for blood transfusions. Hydroxyurea seems to work by inducing a higher production of fetal hemoglobin. The major side effects of the drug include decreased production of platelets, red blood cells, and certain white blood cells. The effects of long-term hydroxyurea treatment are unknown.

Bone marrow transplantation

Bone marrow transplantation has been shown to cure sickle cell anemia in severely affected children. Indications for a bone marrow transplant are stroke, recurrent acute chest syndrome, and chronic unrelieved pain. Bone marrow transplants tend to be the most successful in children; adults have a higher rate of transplant rejection and other complications.

The procedure requires a healthy donor whose marrow proteins match those of the recipient. Typically, siblings have the greatest likelihood of having matched marrow. Given this restriction, fewer than 20% of sickle cell anemia individuals may be candidates. The percentage is reduced when factors such as general health and acceptable risk are considered. The procedure is risky for the recipient. There is approximately a 10% fatality rate associated with bone marrow transplants done for sickle cell anemia treatment. Survivors face potential long-term complications, such as chronic **graft** versus host disease (an immune-mediated attack by the donor marrow against the recipient's tissues), **infertility**, and development of some forms of **cancer**.

Alternative treatment

In general, treatment of sickle cell anemia relies on conventional medicine. However, alternative therapies may be useful in pain control. Relaxation, application of local warmth, and adequate hydration may supplement the conventional therapy. Further, maintaining good health through adequate **nutrition**, avoiding stresses and infection, and getting proper rest help prevent some complications.

Prognosis

Several factors aside from genetic inheritance determine the prognosis for affected individuals. Therefore, predicting the course of the disorder based solely on genes is not possible. In general, given proper medical care, individuals with sickle cell anemia are in fairly good health most of the time. The life expectancy for these individuals has increased over the last 30 years, and many survive well into their 40s or beyond. In the United States, the average life expectancy for men with sickle cell anemia is 42 years; for women, it is 48 years.

Prevention

The sickle cell trait is a genetically linked, inherited condition. Inheritance cannot be prevented, but it may be predicted. Screening is recommended for individuals in high-risk populations; in the United States, African Americans and Hispanic Americans have the highest risk of being carriers.

Screening at birth offers the opportunity for early intervention; more than 40 states include sickle cell screening as part of the usual battery of blood tests done for newborns. Pregnant women and couples planning to have children may also wish to be screened to determine their carrier status. Carriers have a 50% chance of passing the trait to their offspring. Children born to two carriers have a 25% chance of inheriting the trait from both parents and having sickle cell anemia. Carriers may consider genetic counseling to assess any risks to their offspring. The sickle cell trait can also be identified through prenatal testing; specifically through use of amniotic fluid testing or **chorionic villus sampling**.

Further Reading

Beutler, Ernest. "The Sickle Cell Diseases and Related Disorders." In *Williams Hematology,* edited by Ernest Beutler, et al. 5th ed. New York: McGraw-Hill, 1995.

Bloom, Miriam. *Understanding Sickle Cell Disease.* Jackson, MS: University Press of Mississippi, 1995.

Embury, Stephen H., et al., eds. *Sickle Cell Disease: Basic Principles and Clinical Practice.* New York: Raven Press, 1994.

Davies, Sally C. "Management of Patients with Sickle Cell Disease." *British Medical Journal,* 315. (September 13, 1997): 656.

Reed, W., and E.P. Vichinsky. "New Considerations in the Treatment of Sickle Cell Disease." *Annual Review of Medicine,* 49 (1998): 461.

Serjeant, Graham R. "Sickle-Cell Disease." *The Lancet,* 350 (September 6, 1997): 725.

Sickle Cell Disease Association of America. http://sicklecelldisease.org/.

Julia Barrett

Sieve of Eratosthenes

Sieve of Eratosthenes is an almost mechanical procedure for separating out composite numbers and leaving the primes. It was invented by the Greek scientist and mathematician Eratosthenes who lived approximately 2,300 years ago.

The **natural numbers** 1, 2, 3, 4, ... can be classified into three groups: the **prime numbers**, which have no proper divisors other than 1; the composite numbers, which have two or more proper divisors; and 1 itself, which is neither prime nor composite. Thus 2, 3, and 5 are primes, while 4, 6, and 8 are composite. (A proper divisor of a given number is a whole number which is smaller than the given number and divides it without a remainder.) If one writes the natural numbers in order, 1, 2, 3, 4, 5, 6, 7, 8, 9, 10, 11, 12, 13, 14, ..., every second number will be a multiple of 2; every third number, a multiple of 3; every fourth number, a multiple of 4; and so on. Eratosthenes' sieve makes use of this fact.

First, one writes the natural numbers in order, omitting the 1. Then one circles the 3 and crosses out every third number, including 6 and 12, which are already crossed out. The numbers that are left have neither 2 nor 3 as divisors.

One continues this process for as long as one likes. The circled numbers, 2, 3, 5, 7, 11, 13, ...are primes; the crossed-out numbers, 4, 6, 8, 9, 10, 12, 14, ... are composite.

Although the sieve can be a tedious process for discovering large primes, it is still very useful. For one thing, it involves no **arithmetic** other than counting. For another, if one uses it for the first n natural numbers, it will pick out all the primes in that range. Furthermore, it is a procedure that can be effectively turned over to a computer, using a language such as Fortran, BASIC, or Pascal. According to **Ore**, every table of primes has been constructed with the method described by Eratosthenes. This includes tables of all the primes up to one hundred million.

What it will not do is provide a simple test of a given number. In order to decide by means of the sieve whether a number such as 9577 is prime, one would have to find all the primes up to 9577. One cannot use the sieve to test the number directly.

Actually doing this, although tedious, is not quite as bad as it sounds. If 9577 is going to be crossed out, it will have been crossed out by the time one circles 97 and crosses out every ninety-seventh number beyond. The reason for this is that for 9577 to be composite, it must be the product of two factors, say p and q. That is, 9577 = pq. The larger of these factors must be equal to or greater than the **square root** of 9577; and the smaller, less than or equal to it. Since the **square root** of 9577 is approximately 97.86, one of its supposed factors has to be 97 or less. Of course, that's still a lot of work. There are twenty-four primes less than 97, with circling and crossing out to be done for each one of them.

As this example shows, the crossing out process is more efficient than it first appears to be. In general, if one crosses out all the multiples of primes up to, and including a number n, then all the composite numbers up to and including the square of n will have been crossed out. When one crosses out all the multiples of 2 and 3, all the composite numbers up to 9 have been crossed out, and this can be verified by the example above. Crossing out the multiples of 2, 3, and 5 crosses out all the composite numbers up to and including 25. The examples above don't extend far enough to show this, but the reader can check it for himself or herself.

There is a variation on the sieve that allows one to do more than sort the natural numbers into two classes. In this procedure one writes the natural numbers in the following array. In the second row one starts under the 2 and skips one space between each of the natural numbers. In the third row one starts under the 3 and skips two spaces, and so on.

This procedure lists all of a number's proper divisors directly below it. Thus 7 has only 1 as a proper divisors directly below it, while 12 has 6, 4, 3, 2, and 1. Seven is therefore a prime number, and 12 is composite.

J. Paul Moulton

KEY TERMS

Proper divisor—A natural number which divides a given natural number without a remainder, and is smaller than the given number.

Sifakas see **Lemurs**

Silica see **Silicon**

Silicate see **Silicon**

Silicon chip see **Integrated circuit**

Silicone see **Silicon**

Silk cotton family (Bombacaceae)

The silk cotton family (Bombacaceae) is a group of about 200 species of tropical trees, some of which are of commercial importance as sources of lumber, fibrous material, or food. Species in the silk cotton family occur

Baobab trees in western Australia.

KEY TERMS

Buttress—Many species of tropical-forest trees are shallow-rooted, and they grow buttresses at the base of their stem as stabilizing structures against the swaying forces of the wind. Buttresses can occur as a greatly broadened base of the trunk, or as large, vertical footings that project from the base.

Kapok—A fluffy, white material derived from the fruits of several species in the silk cotton family, and commonly used as a stuffing for pillows, mattresses, and similar items.

in all regions of tropical forest, but they are most diverse in Central and **South America**.

Biology of silk cotton trees

Silk cotton trees often attain a very large size, and can be taller than 98 ft (30 m). Their trunks are commonly of a peculiar, bottom-heavy, bottle shape, and their **wood** is usually soft and light in **density**. Many species in this family have buttresses at the base of their stem. The leaves of silk cotton trees are arranged alternately along the stem, have a toothless margin, may be simple or compound, and are typically shed during the dry season.

The flowers of trees in the silk cotton family are large and attractive, and develop during the leafless season. The fruit is a capsule, and the **seeds** commonly have long, silken hairs attached.

Economic importance

Various species of trees in the silk cotton family are economically important. Some species are harvested for their wood, which is rather soft and can be easily carved into dugout canoes and other useful products. Balsa wood is an extremely light yet strong wood that is obtained from the fast-growing balsa **tree** (*Ochroma pyramidale*). This species is native to tropical **forests** of Central and northern South America, but most balsa wood is now harvested from plantations. Balsa wood is widely used to make architectural and other models, and to manufacture airplanes, flotation devices, and bottle corks.

Balsa wood was also used to construct the *Kon Tiki*, a simply-built raft used by Thor Heyerdahl, an anthropologist and adventurer. Heyerdahl crossed the Pacific Ocean from east to west in 1947 to test his theory about the movements of pre-historic peoples. In part, Heyerdahl's ideas were based on the observation that the sweet **potato** (*Ipomoea batatas*) had been cultivated by pre-historic peoples in tropical America, Oceania, and southeast **Asia**. Heyerdahl hypothesized that there had been exchanges of goods and information among these far-flung peoples, and they may have used simple balsa rafts or other vessels as a means of trans-oceanic transportation.

Kapok is a very fluffy material made from the abundant silken hairs that are attached to the ripe seeds of several species in the silk cotton family. Most important in this respect is the silk cotton or kapok tree (*Ceiba pentandra*), originally from the tropical Americas but now widely planted in **Africa** and Asia. Less prominent as a source of kapok is the silk tree (*Bombax ceiba*) of southern Asia. The kapok is derived from long, fine hairs that develop from the inner wall of the 4-6 in (10-15 cm) long seedpods of these trees. The silken hairs are not attached to the seeds, as they are in cotton (*Gossypium hirsutum*), an unrelated fibre-producing **plant**. A mature kapok tree can be as tall as 98 ft (30 m), and can yield up to 11 lb (5 kg) of fluffy fibres each year. Kapok is commonly used for stuffing cushions, mattresses, and furniture, and for other purposes that require a soft, voluminous filling. Kapok is **water** repellant and extremely light, but it tangles easily, is somewhat brittle, and tends to eventually disintegrate. In recent decades, kapok has been increasingly replaced by synthetic foams for many of its previous uses as stuffing.

The baobab trees (*Adansonia* spp.) of Africa and India are of religious importance to some indigenous peoples, who consider this species to be a tree-of-life. One West African belief holds that the first human was born from the trunk of a baobab tree, whose grossly swollen stems somewhat resemble the profile of a pregnant woman. It was further believed that after **birth**, that first human was nurtured by the vaguely breast-shaped **fruits** of the baobab. This interesting species is pollinated by

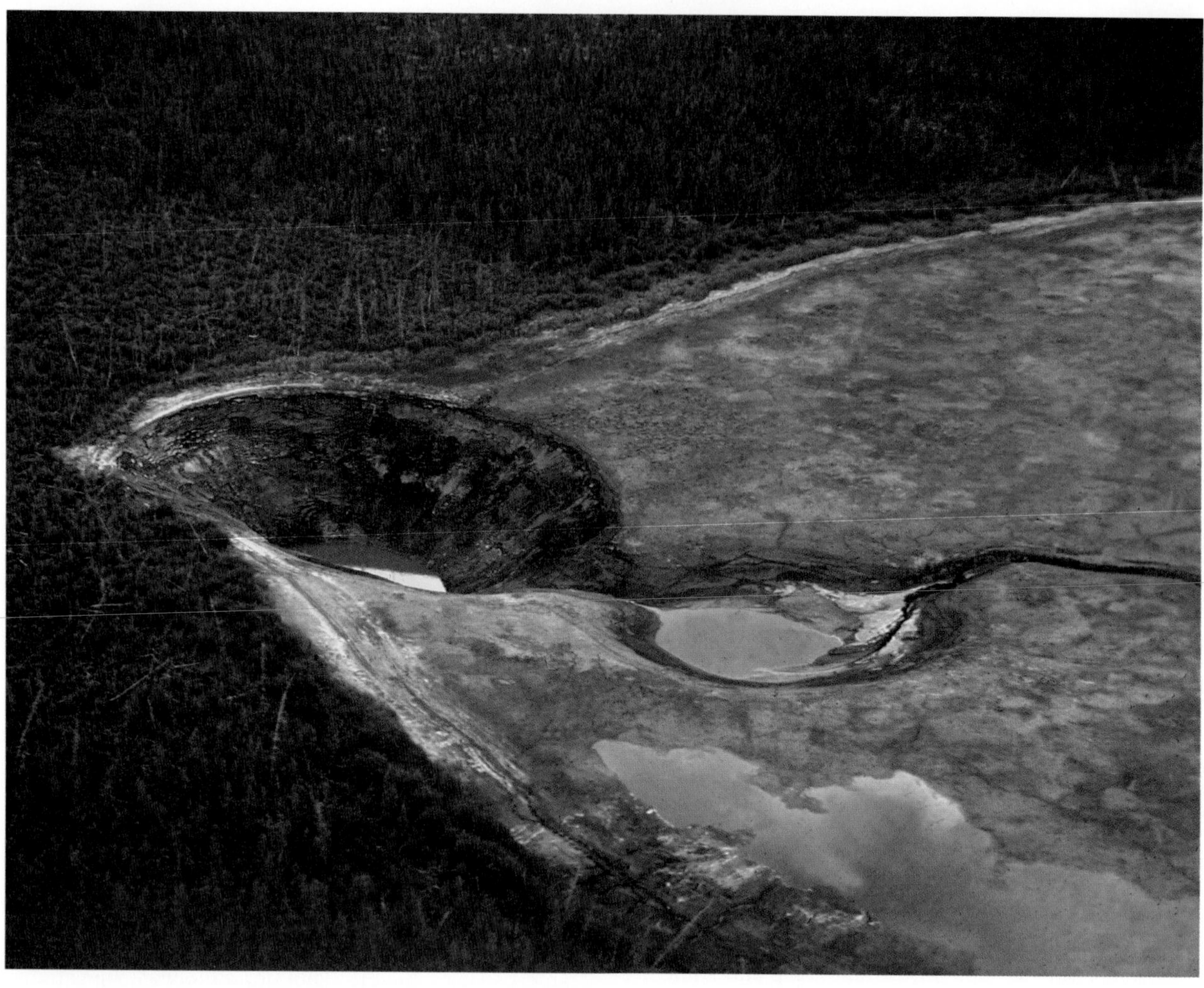

Vanishing Lake, a large sinkhole.

plants, which live in small cavities that are associated with spines on the twigs and branches of the baobab tree.

Durians are among the world's most interesting edible fruits, and are gathered from the durian tree (*Durio zibethinus*). Durian fruits can be as large as 8 in (20 cm) in size, and have a greenish, spiny exterior, and a whitish, custard-like interior. Durian fruits have a foul, sulphurous **smell**, but if their rather disgusting aroma can be ignored, these fruits are delicious to eat. Durians are especially popular in Southeast Asia. Because of the foul smell of durian fruits, many hotels in that region have signs posted that ask their guests to not eat this food in their rooms.

See also Natural fibers.

Further Reading

Hartmann, H.T., A.M. Kofranek, V.E. Rubatzky, and W.J. Flocker. *Plant Science. Growth, Development, and Utilization of Cultivated Plants.* Englewood Cliffs, NJ: Prentice-Hall, 1988.

Woodland, D.W. *Contemporary Plant Systematics.* Englewood Cliffs, NJ: Prentice-Hall, 1991.

Bill Freedman

Silt see **Sediment and sedimentation**

Silver see **Element, chemical**; **Precious metals**

Sinkholes

Sinkholes are cavities that form when **water** erodes easily dissolved, or soluble, rock located beneath the ground surface. Water moves along joints, or fractures,

enlarging them to form a channel that drains sediment and water into the subsurface. As the rock erodes, materials above subside into the openings. At the surface, sinkholes often appear as bowl-shaped depressions. If the drain becomes clogged with rock and **soil**, the sinkhole may fill with water. Many ponds and small lakes form this way.

Abundant sinkholes as well as caves, disappearing streams, and springs, characterize a type of landscape known as **karst topography**. Karst topography forms where **groundwater** erodes subsurface carbonate rock, such as limestone and dolomite, or evaporite rock, such as gypsum and **salt**. **Carbon dioxide** (CO_2), when combined with the water in air and soil, acidifies the water. The slight acidity intensifies the corrosive ability of the water percolating into the soil and moving through fractured rock.

Geologists classify sinkholes mainly by their means of development. Collapse sinkholes are often funnel shaped. They form when soil or rock material collapses into a **cave**. Collapse may be sudden and damage is often significant; cars and homes may be swallowed by these sinkholes.

Solution sinkholes form in rock with multiple vertical joints. Water passing along these joints expands them allowing cover material to move into the openings. Solution sinkholes usually form slowly and minor damage occurs, such as cracking of building foundations.

Alluvial sinkholes are previously exposed sinkholes that, over time, partly or completely filled with **earth** material. They can be hard to recognize and some are relatively stable.

Rejuvenated sinkholes are alluvial sinkholes in which the cover material once again begins to subside, producing a growing depression.

Uvalas are large sinkholes formed by the joining of several smaller sinkholes. Cockpits are extremely large sinkholes formed in thick limestone; some are more than a kilometer in diameter.

Sinkholes occur naturally, but are also induced by human activities. Pumping water from a well can trigger sinkhole collapse by lowering the water table and removing support for a cave's roof. Construction over sinkholes can also cause collapse. Sinkhole development may damage buildings, pipelines and roadways. Damage from the Winter Park sinkhole in Florida is estimated at greater than $2 million. Sinkholes may also serve as routes for the spread of **contamination** to groundwater when people use them as refuse dumps.

In areas where evaporite rock is common, human activities play an especially significant role in the formation of sinkholes. Evaporites dissolve in water much easier than do carbonate **rocks**. Salt **mining** and drilling into evaporite deposits allows water that is not already saturated with salt to easily dissolve the rock. These activities have caused the formation of several large sinkholes.

Sinkholes occur worldwide, and in the United States are common in southern Indiana, southwestern Illinois, Missouri, Kentucky, Tennessee, and Florida. In areas with known karst topography, subsurface drilling or geophysical remote sensing may be used to pinpoint the location of sinkholes.

Monica Anderson

Siphillis see **Sexually transmitted diseases**
Sisal see **Amaryllis family**

Skates

Skates are members of the class Chondrichthyes, the **cartilaginous fish**, the same class that contains **sharks**, **rays**, and chimeras. Skates, and their relatives the rays, comprise the order Rajiformes, which contains 318 species in 50 genera and 7 families. The skate family (Rajidae) is the largest family, encompassing about 120 species in 10 genera.

The many species of skate vary greatly in size. The largest species, the big skate (*Raja binoculata*), is found off the Pacific coast of **North America**, and can grow to 8 ft (2.4 m) in length and weigh more than 200 lbs (90 kg) The smallest species, the little skate (*R. erinacea*), grows to about 20 in (51 cm) and weighs less than 1 lb (0.4 kg). Also called the hedgehog skate, it is the most common skate off the Atlantic coast of North America.

Skates and rays are unusual among **fish** because of their flattened shape. The pectoral fins of skates are much larger than those of other fish, and are attached the length of the body, from the head to the posterior. These fins are particularly large in the skates, creating a shelf-like effect because they encompass the head. Skates also have an elongated snout.

Skates are common in both tropical and temperate oceans, where they are found at depths ranging from 100-7,000 ft (30-2,135 m) with young animals usually found in shallower **water**. Curiously, skates are not found in the waters around Hawaii, Polynesia, Micronesia, and northeastern **South America**.

Skates are primarily bottom dwellers, often burying themselves in bottom sand or mud to deceive potential

prey and to avoid predators. In order to breathe while lying on the bottom, skates have two openings on their back called spiracles, immediately behind their eyes. Skates draw water in through the spiracles, which then passes out though the gill slits on their undersides. When skates swim, they undulate their pectoral "wings," setting up a ripple effect that drives them forward through the water in a graceful manner.

The tail of a skate is shorter than that of its relatives the rays, and is studded with strong, sharp spines. These spines are effective in defense. Spines are also found on the back, and they can create a painful injury if stepped on by an unwary wader. Some species also have an electrical **organ** in their tail, which is not nearly as powerful as that found in the electric rays. These four-volt organs are thought to play a part in **courtship**.

Like their relatives the sharks, skates have well-developed lower jaws; the upper jaw is separate from the skull. In many species, the teeth have fused into bony plates that are strong enough to crush the shells of the clams and other shelled **mollusks** on which the skates feed. Skates also eat fish, **octopus**, crab, and lobster.

Studies have shown that skates have an excellent electromagnetic sense. They pick up weak electrical signals by means of the ampullae of Lorenzini, delicate organs in the snout. Researchers have noted transient slowdowns in the **heart** rate when skates have detected voltages as low as 0.01 microvolt—this is the highest electrical sensitivity known among any animals. A small fish, such as a flounder, naturally produces an electrical field greater than 0.01 microvolt, so no matter how well a flounder may be hidden by burial in sand, a skate can detect it.

Skates lay eggs, which are released into the environment in a protective egg case. The rectangular case is leathery and has a long tendril streaming from each corner; the tendrils anchor the case to seaweed or **rocks**. Sometimes called a mermaid's purse, the egg case protects the young skates during the six to nine months it takes for them to hatch. Empty cases often wash up on beaches.

Skates are edible, although they are generally considered "trash fish" by American commercial fishers, who usually throw them back. Some fishers prefer to use the flesh from the pectoral wings as bait for lobster traps.

The European, or gray skate (*Raja batis*) is an important food species in **Europe**. Many tons of this 100-lb (45.5-kg) skate are taken each year. Most of the "meat" is cut from the fleshy pectoral fins. The barndoor skate (*Raja laevis*) of the northwest Atlantic has become endangered through excessive by-catch in commercial fisheries directed to other species, such as cod and haddock.

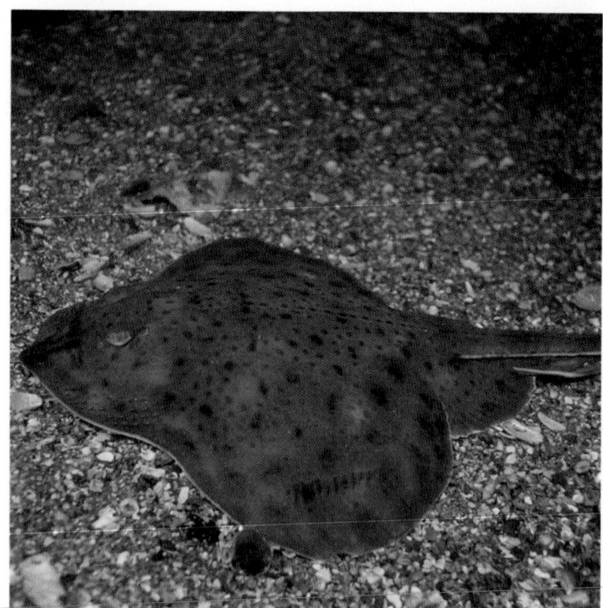

A winter skate.

Further Reading

Michael, Scott W. *Reef Sharks and Rays of the World: A Guide to Their Identification, Behavior, and Ecology.* Monterey, CA: Sea Challengers, 1993.

F. C. Nicholson

Skeletal system

Inside every person is a skeleton, a sturdy framework of about 206 bones that protects the body's organs, supports the body, provides attachment points for muscles to enable body movement, functions as a storage site for **minerals** such as **calcium** and **phosphorus**, and produces **blood** cells.

The skeletal system is a living, dynamic system, with networks of infiltrating blood vessels. Living mature bone is about 60% calcium compounds and about 40% **collagen**. Hence, bone is strong, hard and slightly elastic. All humans were born with over 300 bones but some bones, such as those in the skull and lower spine, fuse during growth, thereby reducing the number. Although mature bones consist largely of calcium, most bones in the skeleton of **vertebrates**, including humans, began as cartilage. Some animals, such as **sharks** and sting **rays**, retain their cartilaginous skeleton in adulthood. Cartilage is a type of **connective tissue**, and contains collagen and elastin fibers.

Individual bones meet at areas called joints and are held in place by connective **tissue**. Most joints, such as the elbow, are called synovial joints, for the synovial **membrane** which envelopes the joint and secretes a lubricating fluid. Cartilage lines the surface of many joints and helps reduce **friction** between bones. The connective tissues linking the skeleton together at the joints are tendons and ligaments. Ligaments and tendons are both made up of collagen, but serve different functions. Ligaments link bones together and help prevent dislocated joints. Tendons link bone to muscle.

Because the bones making up the human skeleton are inside the body, the skeleton is called an endoskeleton. Some animals, such as the crab, have an external skeleton called an exoskeleton.

Structure

The human skeletal system is divided into two main groups: the axial skeleton and the appendicular skeleton. The axial skeleton includes bones associated with the body's main axis, the spine. This includes the spine and the skull and rib cage, which are connected to the spine. The appendicular skeleton is attached to the axial skeleton and consists of the bones associated with the body's appendages—the arms and legs. This includes the bones of the pectoral girdle, or shoulder area, bones of the pelvic girdle, or hip area, and arm and leg bones.

Axial skeleton

There are 28 bones in the skull. Of these, 8 bones comprise the cranium and provide protection for the **brain**. In adults, these bones are flat and interlocking at their joints, making the cranium immobile. Fibrous joints, or sutures occur where the bony plates of the cranium meet and interlock. Cartilage-filled spaces between the cranial bones of infants, known as soft spots or fontanelles, allow their skull bones to move slightly during **birth**. This makes birth easier and helps prevent skull fractures, but may leave the infant with an odd-shaped head temporarily while the skull regains its shape. Eventually, the fontanelles in an infant's head are replaced by bone and fibrous joints develop. In addition to protecting the brain, skull bones also support and protect the sensory organs responsible for sight, **hearing**, **smell** and **taste**.

The eight bones of the cranium are: frontal, parietal (2), temporal (2), ethmoid, sphenoid and occipital. The frontal bone forms the forehead and eyebrows. Behind the frontal bone are the two parietal bones. Parietal bones form the roof of the cranium and **curve** down to form the sides of the cranium. Also forming the sides of the cranium are the two temporal bones, located behind the eyes. Each temporal bone encloses the cochlea and labyrinth of the inner **ear**, and the ossicles, three tiny bones of the middle ear which are not part of the cranium. The ossicles are the malleus (hammer), incus (anvil), and stapes (stirrups). The temporal bones also attach to the lower jaw, and this is the only moveable joint in the skull. Between the temporal bones is the irregular shaped sphenoid bone, which provides protection for the pituitary gland. The small ethmoid bone forms part of the **eye** socket next to the nose. Olfactory nerves, or sense of smell nerves, pass through the ethmoid bone on their way to the brain. Forming the base and rear of the cranium is the occipital bone. The occipital bone has a hole, called the foramen magnum, through which the spinal cord passes and connects to the brain.

Fourteen bones shape the cheeks, eyes, nose and mouth. These include the nasal (2), zygomatic (2), maxillae (2), and the mandible. The upper, bony bridge of the nose is formed by the nasal bones and provides an attachment site for the cartilage making up the softer part of the nose. The zygomatic bones form the cheeks and part of the eye sockets. Two bones fuse to form the maxillae, the upper jaw of the mouth. These bones also form hard palate of the mouth. Failure of the maxillary bones to completely fuse in the fetus results in the condition known as cleft palate. The mandible forms the lower jaw of the mouth and is moveable, enabling chewing of food and **speech**. The mandible is the bone which connects to the temporal bones. The joint between these bones, the temporomandibular joint, is the source of the painful condition known as temporomandibular joint dysfunction, or TMJ dysfunction. Sufferers of TMJ dysfunction experience a variety of symptoms including headaches, a sore jaw and a snapping sensation when moving the jaw. There a several causes of the dysfunction. The cartilage disk between the bones may shift, or the connective tissue between the bones may be situated in a manner that causes misalignment of the jaw. Sometimes braces on the teeth can aggravate TMJ dysfunction. The condition may be corrected with **exercise**, or in severe cases, **surgery**.

Located behind these facial bones are other bones which shape the interior portions of the eyes, nose and mouth. These are the lacrimal (2), palatine (2), conchae (2), and vomer bones. In addition to these 28 skull bones is the hyoid bone, located at the base of the tongue. Technically, the hyoid bone is not part of the skull but it is often included with the skull bones. It provides an attachment site for the tongue and some neck muscles.

Several of the facial and cranial bones contain sinuses, or cavities, that connect to the nasal cavity and drain into it. These are the frontal, ethmoid, sphenoid and maxillae bones, all located near the nose. Painful sinus

headaches result from the build up of **pressure** in these cavities. Membranes that line these cavities may secrete mucous or become infected, causing additional aggravation for humans.

The skull rests atop of the spine, which encases and protects the spinal cord. The spine, also called the vertebral column or backbone, consists of 33 stacked vertebrae, the lower ones fused. Vertebra are flat with two main features. The main oval shaped, bony **mass** of the vertebra is called the centrum. From the centrum arises a bony ring called the neural arch which forms the neural canal (also called a vertebral foramen), a hole for the spinal cord to pass through. Short, bony projections (neural spines) arise from the neural arch and provide attachment points for muscles. Some of these projections (called transverse processes) also provide attachment points for the ribs. There are also small openings in the neural arch for the spinal nerves, which extend from the spinal cord throughout the body. Injury to the column of vertebrae may cause serious damage to the spinal cord and the spinal nerves, and could result in paralysis if the spinal cord or nerves are severed.

There are seven cervical, or neck, vertebrae. The first one, the atlas, supports the skull and allows the head to nod up and down. The atlas forms a condylar joint (a type of synovial joint) with the occipital bone of the skull. The second vertebra, the axis, allows the head to rotate from side to side. This rotating synovial joint is called a pivot joint. Together, these two vertebrae make possible a wide range of head motions.

Below the cervical vertebrae are the 12 thoracic, or upper back, vertebrae. The ribs are attached to these vertebrae. Thoracic vertebrae are followed by five lumbar, or lower back, vertebrae. Last is the sacrum, composed of five fused vertebrae, and the coccyx, or tail bone, composed of four fused bones.

The vertebral column helps to support the weight of the body and protects the spinal cord. Cartilaginous joints rather than synovial joints occur in the spine. Disks of cartilage lie between the bony vertebrae of the back and provide cushioning, like shock absorbers. The vertebrae of the spine are capable of only limited movement, such bending and some twisting.

A pair of ribs extends forward from each of the 12 thoracic vertebrae, for a total of 24 ribs. Occasionally, a person is born with an extra set of ribs. The joint between the ribs and vertebrae is a gliding (or plane) joint, a type of synovial joint, as ribs do move, expanding and contracting with breathing. Most of the ribs (the first seven pair) attach in the front of the body via cartilage to the long, flat breastbone, or sternum. These ribs are called true ribs. The next three pair of ribs are false ribs.

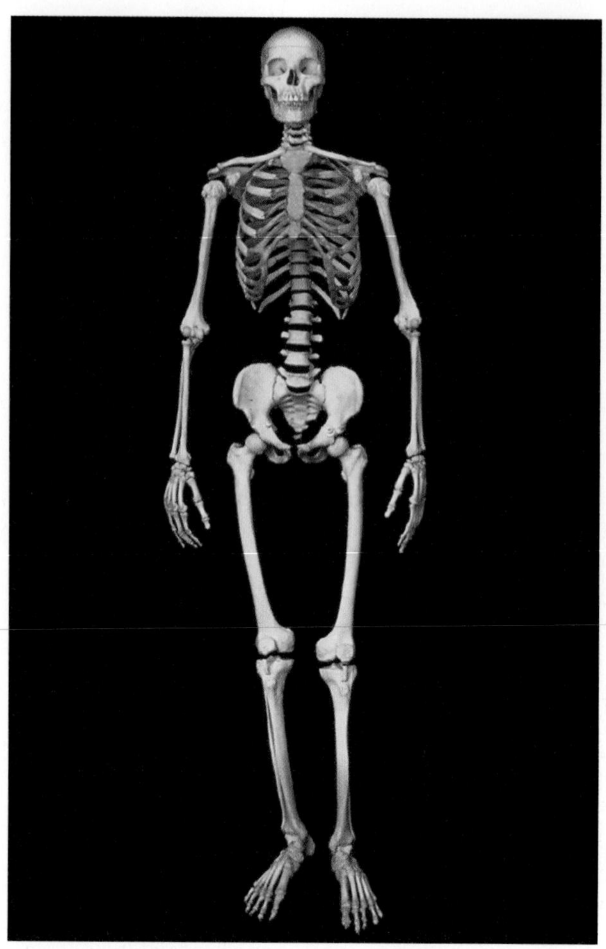

A frontal view of the human skeleton.

False ribs attach to another rib in front instead of the sternum, and are connected by cartilage. The lower two pair of ribs which do not attach anteriorly are called floating ribs. Ribs give shape to the chest and support and protect the body's major organs, such as the **heart** and lungs. The rib cage also provides attachment points for connective tissue, to help hold organs in place. In adult humans, the sternum also produces red blood cells as well as providing an attachment site for ribs.

Appendicular skeleton

The appendicular skeleton joins with the axial skeleton at the shoulders and hips. Forming a loose attachment with the sternum is the pectoral girdle, or shoulder. Two bones, the clavicle (collar bone) and scapula (shoulder blade) form one shoulder. The scapula rest on top of the ribs in the back of the body. It connects to the clavicle, the bone which attaches the entire shoulder structure to the skeleton at the sternum. The clavicle is a slender bone that is easily broken. Because the scapula is so

loosely attached, it is easily dislocated from the clavicle, hence the dislocated shoulder injuries commonly suffered by persons playing sports. The major advantage to the loose attachment of the pectoral girdle is that it allows for a wide range of shoulder motions and greater overall freedom of movement.

Unlike the pectoral girdle, the pelvic girdle, or hips, is strong and dense. Each hip, left and right, consists of three fused bones, the ilium, ischium and pubic. Collectively, these three bones are known as the innominate bone. The innominates fuse with the sacrum to form the pelvic girdle. Specifically, the iliums shape the hips and the two ischial bones support the body when a person sits. The two pubic bones meet anteriorly at a cartilaginous joint. The pelvic girdle is bowl-shaped, with an opening at the bottom. In a pregnant woman, this bony opening is a passageway through which her baby must pass during birth. To facilitate the baby's passage, the body secretes a hormone called relaxin which loosens the joint between the pubic bones. In addition, the pelvic girdle of women is generally wider than that of men. This also helps to facilitate birth, but is a slight impediment for walking and running. Hence, men, with their narrower hips, are better adapted for such activities. The pelvic girdle protects the lower abdominal organs, such as the intestines, and helps supports the weight of the body above it.

The arms and legs, appendages of the body, are very similar in form. Each attaches to the girdle, pectoral or pelvic, via a ball and socket joint, a special type of synovial joint. In the shoulder, the socket, called the glenoid cavity, is shallow. The shallowness of the glenoid cavity allows for great freedom of movement. The hip socket, or acetabulum, is larger and deeper. This deep socket, combined with the rigid and massive structure of the hips, give the legs much less mobility and flexibility than the arms.

The humerus, or upper arm bone, is the long bone between the elbow and the shoulder. It connects the arm to the pectoral girdle. In the leg the femur, or thigh bone, is the long bone between the knee and hip which connects the leg to the pelvic girdle. The humerus and femur are sturdy bones, especially the femur, which is a weight bearing bone. Since the arms and legs are jointed, the humerus and femur are connected to other bones at the end opposite the ball and socket joint. In the elbow, this second joint is a type of synovial joint called a hinge joint. Two types of synovial joints occur in the knee region, a condylar joint (like the condylar joint in the first vertebra) which connects the leg bones, and a plane, or gliding joint, between the patella (knee cap) and femur.

At the elbow the humerus attaches to a set of **parallel** bones, the ulna and radius, bones of the forearm. The radius is the bone below the thumb that rotates when the hand is turned over and back. The ulna and radius then attach to the carpel bones of the wrist. Eight small carpel bones make up the wrist and connect to the hand. The hand is made up of five long, slender metacarpal bones (the palms) and 14 phalanges of the hand (fingers and thumb). Some phalanges form joints with each other, giving the human hand great dexterity.

Similarly, in the leg, the femur forms a joint with the patella and with the fibula and tibia bones of the lower leg. The tibia, or shin bone, is larger than the fibula and forms the joint behind the patella with the femur. Like the femur, the tibia is also a weight bearing bone. At the ankle joint, the fibula and tibia connect to the tarsals of the upper foot. There are seven tarsals of the upper foot, forming the ankle and the heel. The tarsals in turn connect to five long, slender metatarsals of the lower foot. The metatarsals form the foot's arch and sole and connect to the phalanges of the feet (toes). The 14 foot phalanges are shorter and less agile than the hand phalanges. Several types of synovial joints occur in the hands and feet, including plane, ellipsoid and saddle. Plane joints occur between toe bones, allowing limited movement. Ellipsoid joints between the finger and palm bones give the fingers circular mobility, unlike the toes. The saddle joint at the base of the thumb helps make the hands the most important part of the body in terms of dexterity and manipulation. A saddle joint also occurs at the ankles.

Types of bone

Bones may be classified according to their various traits, such as shape, origin, and texture. Four types are recognized based on shape. These are long bones, short bones, flat bones and irregular bones. Long bones have a long central shaft, called the diaphysis, and two knobby ends, called the epiphysis. In growing long bones, the diaphysis and epiphysis are separated by a thin sheet of cartilage. Examples of long bones include bones of the arms and legs, the metacarpals of the hand, metatarsals of the foot, and the clavicle. Short bones are about as long as wide. The patella, carpels of the wrist and tarsals of the ankle are short bones. Flat bones take several shapes, but are characterized by being relatively thin and flat. Examples include the sternum, ribs, hip bones, scapula and cranial bones. Irregular bones are the odd-shaped bones of the skull, such as the sphenoid, the sacrum and the vertebrae. The common characteristic of irregular bones is not that they are similar to each other in appearance, but that they can't be placed in any of the other bone categories.

Bones may also be classified based on their origin. All bone (as well as muscles and connective tissue) originates from an embryonic connective tissue called mes-

enchyme, which makes mesoderm, also an embryonic tissue. Some mesoderm forms the cartilaginous skeleton of the fetus, the precursor for the bony skeleton. However, some bones, such as the clavicle and some of the facial and cranial bones of the skull, develop directly from mesenchyme, thereby bypassing the cartilaginous stage. These types of bone are called membrane bone (or dermal bone). Bone which originates from cartilage is called endochondral bone.

Finally, bones are classified based on texture. Smooth, hard bone called compact bone forms the outer layer of bones. Inside the outer compact bone is cancellous bone, sometimes called the bone marrow. Cancellous bone appears open and spongy, but is actually very strong, like compact bone. Together, the two types of bone produce a light, but strong, skeleton.

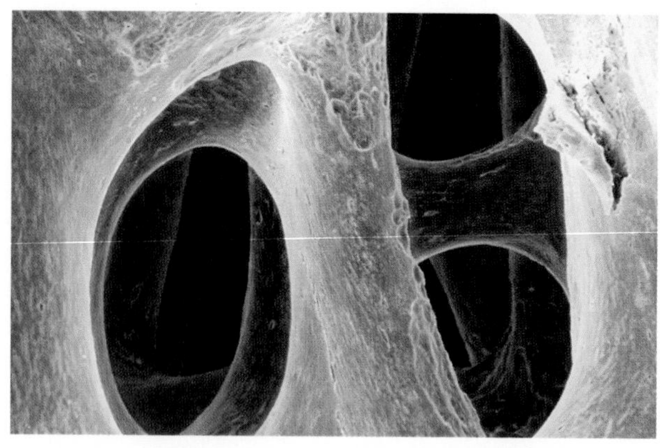

A scanning electron micrograph (SEM) of normal human cancellous (spongy) bone. The shafts of long bones such as the femur are comprised of two types of bone of differing densities: compact bone forms the outer region, and cancellous bone forms the core. In living cancellous bone, the cavities of the open structure contain bone marrow.

Bone development and growth

Since most bone begins as cartilage, it must be converted to bone through a process called **ossification**. The key players in bone development are cartilage cells (chondrocytes), bone precursor cells (osteoprogenitor cells), bone deposition cells (osteoblasts), bone resorption cells (osteoclasts) and mature bone cells (osteocytes).

During ossification, blood vessels invade the cartilage and transport osteoprogenitor cells to a region called the center of ossification. At this site, the cartilage cells die, leaving behind small cavities. Osteoblast cells form from the progenitor cells and begin depositing bone tissue, spreading out from the center. Through this process, both the spongy textured cancellous bone and the smooth outer compact bone forms. Two types of bone marrow, red and yellow, occupy the spaces in cancellous bone. Red marrow produces red blood cells while yellow marrow stores **fat** in addition to producing blood cells. Eventually, in compact bone, osteoblast cells become trapped in their bony cavities, called lacunae, and become osteocytes. Neighboring osteocytes form connections with each other and thus are able to transfer materials between cells. The osteocytes are part of a larger system called the Haversian system. These systems are like long tubes, squeezed tightly together in compact bone. Blood vessel, lymph vessels and nerves run through the center of the tube, called the Haversian canal, and are surrounded by layers of bone, called lamellae, which house the osteocytes. Blood vessels are connected to each other by lateral canals called Volkmann's canals. Blood vessels are also found in spongy bone, without the Haversian system. A protective membrane called the periosteum surrounds all bones.

Bone development is a complex process, but it is only half the story. Bones must grow, and they do so via a process called remodeling. Remodeling involves resorption of existing bone inside the bone (enlarging the marrow cavities) and deposition of new bone on the exterior. The resorptive cells are the osteoclasts and osteoblast cells lay down the new bone material. As remodeling progresses in long bones, a new center of ossification develops, this one at the swollen ends of the bone, called the epiphysis. A thin layer of cartilage called the epiphyseal plate separates the epiphysis from the shaft and is the site of bone deposition. When growth is complete, this cartilage plate disappears, so that the only cartilage remaining is that which lines the joints, called hyaline cartilage. Remodeling does not end when growth ends. Osteocytes, responding to the body's need for calcium, resorb bone in adults to maintain a calcium balance. This process can sometimes have detrimental affects on the skeleton, especially in pregnant women and women who bear many children.

Bones and medicine

Even though bones are very strong, they may be broken, but fortunately, most fractures do heal. The healing process may be stymied if bones are not reset properly or if the injured person is the victim of **malnutrition**. Osteoprogenitor cells migrate to the site of the fracture and begin the process of making new bone (osteoblasts) and reabsorbing the injured bone (osteoclasts). With proper care, the fracture will fully heal, and in children, often without a trace.

Bones are affected by poor diet and are also subject to a number of diseases and disorders. Some examples in-

KEY TERMS

Bone—Composed primarily of a non-living matrix of calcium salts and a living matrix of collagen fibers, bone is the major component that makes up the human skeleton. Bone produces blood cells and functions as a storage site for elements such as calcium and phosphorus.

Calcium—A naturally occurring element which combines primarily with phosphate to form the nonliving matrix of bones.

Cartilage—A type of connective tissue that takes three forms: elastic cartilage, fibrocartilage and hyaline cartilage. Hyaline cartilage forms the embryonic skeleton and lines the joints of bones.

Haversian system—Tubular systems in compact bone with a central Haversian canal which houses blood and lymph vessels surrounded by circular layers of calcium salts and collagen, called lamellae, in which reside osteocytes.

Marrow—A type of connective tissue which fills the spaces of most cancellous bone and which functions to produce blood cells and store fat.

Ossification—The process of replacing connective tissue such as cartilage and mesenchyme with bone.

Osteoblast—The bone cell which deposits calcium salts and collagen during bone growth, bone remodeling and bone repair.

Osteoclast—The bone cell responsible for reabsorbing bone tissue in bone remodeling and repair.

Osteocyte—Mature bone cell which functions mainly to regulate the levels of calcium and phosphate in the body.

Skeleton—Consists of bones and cartilage which are linked together by ligaments. The skeleton protects vital organs of the body and enables body movement.

Synovial joint—One of three types of joints in the skeleton and by far the most common. Synovial joints are lined with a membrane which secretes a lubricating fluid. Includes ball and socket, pivot, plane, hinge, saddle, condylar and ellipsoid joints.

Vertebrates—Includes all animals with a vertebral column protecting the spinal cord such as humans, dogs, birds, lizards and fish.

clude scurvy, rickets, **osteoporosis**, **arthritis** and bone tumors. Scurvy results from the lack of vitamin C. In infants, scurvy causes poor bone development. It also causes membranes surrounding the bone to bleed, forming clots which are eventually ossified, and thin bones which break easy. In addition, adults are affected by bleeding gums and loss of teeth. Before modern times, sailors were often the victims of scurvy, as they were at sea for long periods of time with limited food. Hence, they tried to keep a good supply of citrus **fruits**, such as oranges and limes, on board, as these fruits supply vitamin C.

Rickets is a children's disease resulting from a deficiency of vitamin D. This vitamin enables the body to absorb calcium and phosphorus, and without it, bones become soft and weak and actually bend, or bow out, under the body's weight. Vitamin D is found in milk, eggs and liver, and may also be produced by exposing the skin to sunlight. Pregnant women can also suffer from a vitamin D deficiency, osteomalacia, resulting in soft bones. The elderly, especially women who had several children in a row, sometimes suffer from osteoporosis, a condition in which a significant amount of calcium from bones is dissolved into the blood to maintain the body's calcium balance. Weak, brittle bones dotted with pits and pores are the result.

Another condition commonly afflicting the elderly is arthritis, an often painful **inflammation** of the joints. Arthritis is not, however, restricted to the elderly, as even young people may suffer from this condition. There are several types of arthritis, such as rheumatoid, rheumatic and degenerative. Arthritis basically involves the inflammation and deterioration of cartilage and bone at the joint surface. In some cases, bony protuberances around the rim of the joint may develop. Unfortunately, most people will probably develop arthritis if they live long enough. Degenerative arthritis is the type that commonly occurs with age. The knee, hip, shoulder and elbow are the major targets of degenerative arthritis. A number of different types of tumors, some harmless and others more serious, may also affect bones.

See also Orthopedics.

Further Reading

Bower, B. "Fossils Put a New Face on Lucy's Species." *Science News.* 145 (2 April 1994): 212.

Fischman, J. "Putting a New Spin on the Birth of Human Birth." *Science*. 264:1082-1083, 1994.

Miller, A. "Collagen: The Organic Matrix of Bone." *Phil. Trans. Roy.* Soc. Lond. ser. B 304:455-477, 1984.

Shipman, P., A. Walker, and D. Bichell. *The Human Skeleton*. Cambridge: Harvard University Press, 1985.

Snow, C. C., B. P. Gatliff, and K. R. McWilliams. "Reconstruction of Facial Features from the Skull: An Evaluation of its Usefulness in Forensic Anthropology." *American Journal of Physical Anthropology*. (1970).

Steele, D.G., and C.A. Bramblett. *The Anatomy and Biology of the Human Skeleton*. College Station: A&M; University Press, 1988.

Stevenson, J. "The Strong-boned Weavers of Spitalfields." *Discover.* (August, 1993).

Elaine L. Martin

Skinks

Skinks are smooth, shiny-scaled lizards in the family Scincidae, most of which occur in tropical and subtropical climates, although a few occur in the temperate zones. Most species of skinks occur in **Africa**, South and Southeast **Asia**, and **Australia**, with relatively few others occurring in **Europe** and North and **South America**.

Their body is roughly cylindrical with distinctive overlapping scales on their belly, and a head that ends in a pointed snout. Most skinks have well-developed legs and feet with five toes, but some species are legless slitherers, which can be distinguished from **snakes** by their shiny, uniform scales, their ear-holes, and the structure of their eyelids.

Skinks are quick, active animals, and most species are difficult to catch. They are also very squirmy and difficult to hold, commonly attempting to bite, and their tail often breaks off easily when they are handled. The broken tail will regenerate from the stump, but not to the original length and coloration.

About one-third of the more than 800 species of skinks are **ovoviviparous**, meaning the female retains the eggs inside of her body until they hatch, so that "live" young are born. The other species of skinks are viviparous-that is, they lay eggs.

Skinks are terrestrial animals, hunting during the day for **insects** and other small **arthropods**, while the larger species also hunt and eat small **mammals** and **birds**. During the night skinks typically hide under **rocks** or logs, in crevices of various kinds, or in a burrow that the **animal** digs in soft substrates. Most species occur in habitats that are reasonably moist and skinks are not found in arid environments.

North American species of skinks

Most species of skinks in **North America** are in the genus *Eumeces*. The five-lined skink (*Eumeces fasciatus*) is widespread in the eastern United States and southern Ontario in open **forests**, cutovers, and other exposed habitats having an abundance of damp ground debris. This species has a distinctive pattern of five lines running down its back.

The broad-headed skink (*E. laticeps*) also occurs in the eastern United States. During the breeding season, the males of both of these species develop a bright red head. Other males react aggressively to this color, through ritualized displays, and sometimes by fighting. The females skinks, however, do not have red heads and are not treated this way.

The great plains skink (*E. obsoletus*) occurs in prairies of the west, while the four-lined skink (*E. tetragrammus*) occurs in Texas and Mexico.

The females of most species of *Eumeces*skinks brood their eggs and recently hatched young. One female great plains skink was observed curled around her clutch of 19 eggs under loose tree **bark**. The mother skink cleaned and moistened her eggs by licking them, turned them frequently to facilitate even incubation and proper development, helped the young to hatch when they were ready to do so, and brooded the young and licked them clean. This degree of parental care is unusual among **reptiles**.

The ground skink (*Leiolopisma laterale*) occurs throughout the southeastern United States, hiding in **plant** litter on the forest floor, and sometimes in suburban gardens. The sand skink (*Neoseps reynoldsi*) is a rare species that only occurs in two isolated areas in Florida.

Other species of skinks

One of the most unusual species of skinks is the Australian stump-tailed skink (*Tiliqua rugosa*), one of very few species that does not have a long, pointed tail. The stubby tail of this species looks remarkably like the head, and the animal may have to be examined closely to tell which way it is pointing. This species is sometimes called the pine-cone lizard, because of its unusually large body scales. Unlike most skinks, this lizard is mainly herbivorous.

The giant skink (*Corucia zebrata*) of the Solomons and nearby islands in the Pacific Ocean is another unusual species of skink. This tropical forest lizard spends much of its time climbing in trees. It has a prehensile tail and strong, clawed feet to aid with its clamberings. The giant skink can attain a body length of 26 in (65 cm), and is the largest species in its family.

A juvenile 5-lined skink (*Eumeces fasciatus*).

The snake skinks are various species in the genus *Ophiomorus*, which either have greatly reduced limbs, or are completely legless. Species of snake skinks occur in southwestern Asia and the Middle East.

The recently extinct skink, *Didosaurus mauritianus*, was the world's largest species of skink, occurring on Mauritius and nearby islands in the Indian Ocean. This skink was rendered extinct by mammalian predators that humans introduced to its **island** habitats, particularly **rats**, **mongooses**, and **pigs**. Mauritius was also the home of the world's most famous extinct animal, the turkey-sized flightless bird known as the dodo (*Raphus cucullatus*).

Further Reading

Grzimek, B., ed. *Grzimek's Encyclopedia of Animals*. London: McGraw Hill, 1990.

Bill Freedman

Skuas

Skuas comprise five species of sea **birds** in the family Stercorariidae, order Charadriiformes. These birds breed on the coastal **tundra** and barrens of the Arctic and Antarctic, and winter at sea and in coastal waters.

Skuas are gull-like in many respects, with long, pointed wings, short legs, and webbed feet. However, skuas have a strongly hooked beak, elongated central tail feathers, and a generally dark coloration, although some birds are of a lighter-colored phase. Skuas also display a very different **behavior** from **gulls**. Skuas are swift, strong, and maneuverable fliers. They are predators of small **mammals**, eggs and the young of birds and **fish**, and they also eat carrion when available. Skuas are *kleptoparasites*—piratical feeders that rob other birds of their **prey**. For example, skuas may aerially harass gulls until they drop or disgorge fish that they have caught, which is then nimbly retrieved and eaten by the skua.

Although not necessarily common, all five species of skua are widespread in northern regions of both **North America** and Eurasia. The great skua (*Catharacta skua*) is a large, brown sea bird that breeds on various islands of the North Atlantic, on **Antarctica**, and in subantarctic regions. The south polar skua (*C. maccormicki*) is similar in size and shape to the great skua. This species only breeds on Antarctica and on a few subantarctic islands such as the South Shetlands, although it wanders widely in the oceans of the Northern Hemisphere during its non-breeding season.

The other three species of skuas are usually called jaegers in North America. All three species have Holarctic distributions, meaning that they breed in northern regions of both Eurasia and North America. The pomarine jaeger (*Stercorarius pomarinus*) is the most robust of the jaegers, while the parasitic jaeger (*S. parasiticus*) is somewhat smaller and more widespread. The long-tailed jaeger (*S. longicaudus*) is the smallest and least uncommon species, breeding as far north as the **limit** of land on Ellesmere Island and Greenland.

Bill Freedman

Skunk cabbage see **Arum family**

Skunks

Skunks are small North American **mammals** that share the **carnivore** family Mustelidae with **weasels**, **otters**, **badgers**, and the honey badger. They are distinguished from those other animals by their striking black and white color and their long-haired, fluffy tails. They are about the size of domestic **cats**.

While many animals have anal **glands** that give off sharp odors, the skunks are the best known for this trait. They have two sets of glands located by the rectum, into which the glands discharge an evil-smelling yellow fluid. Whether or not the contents are released is completely under the control of the **animal**. In the skunks normal activity, heavy musk-scented fluid is released with solid waste so that other animals can identify it.

When the animal is frightened, it can explosively release the musk, which, along with stamping its feet and

turning its back, tells a **predator** to back off. If it lets go, it has quite accurate aim—preferably into the enemy's face—for a **distance** of more than 6 ft (2 m). Foxes will usually be driven away by the spray, but some large **owls** are able to just ignore the odor and will attack the skunk anyway. The skunk is forced to spray using up one of its reportedly one to eight shots of musk. When they are gone, the animal no longer has a defense. It is vulnerable until its body has time to produce more musk.

The spotted skunks (two species in genus *Spilogale* covering most of the United States) have one more defense warning in their arsenal. After waving its fluffy tail, a spotted skunk does a handstand from its front feet, arches over, and then sprays backward.

The common spotted skunk *(S. putorius,* its species name means "stinker") has just a small white patch on the forehead, and the lengthwise white stripes are broken up into numerous spots of white. The end of the very large tail is white. These skunks are smaller than the others, with the pygmy spotted skunk *(S. pygmaea)* perhaps no more than 8 in (20 cm), including the tail.

Skunks eat primarily small **rodents**, **insects**, eggs, and fruit. They dig out their food with fairly long claws on their front feet. They usually live near farms and even in suburban areas because they are so good at hunting rodents. However, they are likely to go after poultry, too.

They make dens either in other animals' burrows, under **rocks**, or in hollow logs. During a cold winter, they spend a great deal of time lazing in their dens, but they don't truly hibernate. During the rest of the year, they **sleep** in their dens during the day and forage at night.

A single dominant male skunk will have a territory that includes the smaller territories of several solitary females. Most unusually, the female skunk does not ovulate, or produce eggs, unless she is being vigorously copulated with. The mating act goes on for an hour or more, giving her body time to produce the egg that is fertilized. In some skunks, but not all, the egg may float freely in the uterus, waiting until outside conditions are just right before it implants and begins to develop. Actual gestation takes about a month. Usually three to six babies are born. The male plays no role whatsoever in raising the young. A young skunk has the ability to spray by the time it is one month old. Born in late spring, the babies are usually out on their own by fall. If a skunk can survive **rabies** and automobiles, it may live to be seven or eight years old.

In the United States, the chief problem with skunks is not their odor but the fact that they are the main carrier of the very serious disease called rabies. A rabid skunk does not give the warnings that other skunks do. They just attack with their teeth whenever they get within range of something moving.

KEY TERMS

Anal gland—A pouched organ located by the anus that produces a bad-smelling fluid.

Musk—A fluid with a heavy scent; a skunk's musk—chemically called butylmercaptanis—the strongest in the animal kingdom.

Rabies—A fatal disease of the nervous system that can be passed on to humans by the bite of a wild animal.

Rectum—A chamber just before the anus, at the end of the digestive system.

The most common species is the striped skunk *(Mephitis mephitis,* meaning "terrible smell") of southern Canada south into Mexico. It has two white strips from the crown of its head, down the length of its back. A narrow white strip runs down its face from its forehead to its snout. The hooded skunk *(M. macroura)* lives in Arizona, Texas, and south into Central America. Its broad white stripe continues into a completely white tail.

Five species of hog-nosed skunks *(Conepatus)* live from Colorado down into Argentina. They lack the white strip that goes down the nose of all other skunks, and their hairless noses are narrow and project forward into a piglike snout. They use this snout to root into **soil** for the insects and other **invertebrates** that they eat. Hog-nosed skunks have much coarser fur than the other skunks, which have often been hunted for their soft fur.

Further Reading

Green, Carl R. and William R. Sanford. *The Striped Skunk.* Wildlife Habits and Habitats series. New York: Crestwood House, 1985.

Knight, Linsay. *The Sierra Club Book of Small Mammals.* San Francisco, CA: Sierra Club Books for Children, 1993.

Skunks and Their Relatives. Zoobooks series. San Diego, CA: Wildlife Education, Ltd., 1988.

Jean F. Blashfield

Slash-and-burn agriculture

Slash-and-burn is an agricultural system used in tropical countries, in which a forest is cut, the debris is burned, and the land is then used to grow **crops**. Slash-and-burn conversions are relatively stable and long-term in nature, and they are the leading cause of tropical **deforestation**.

Slash-and-burn agriculture in Peru.

Usually, some type of slash-and-burn system is used when extensive areas of tropical forest are converted into large scale, industrial agriculture, usually intended to supply commodities for an export market, rather than for local use. The slash-and-burn system is also widely used by individual, poor farmers when they develop agricultural land for subsistence farming and to supply cash goods to a local market. The poor farmers operate on a smaller scale, but there are many such people, so that huge areas are ultimately affected.

Slash-and-burn agriculture often follows soon after the natural tropical forest has been commercially logged, mostly because the network of logging roads that is constructed allows access to the otherwise almost impenetrable forest interior. Slash-and-burn agriculture may also be facilitated by government agencies, through the construction of roads that are specifically intended to help poor, landless people convert the forest into agricultural land. In other cases, slash-and-burn occurs in the absence of logging and planned roads, as a rapidly creeping deforestation that advances as poor people migrate to the forest frontier in search of land on which to grow food.

Shifting cultivation

The slash-and-burn method differs from a much more ancient system known as shifting cultivation. Shifting cultivation has long been used by humans for subsistence agriculture in tropical **forests** worldwide, and variants of this system are known as *swidden* in **Africa**, as *caingin* in the Philippines, as *milpa* in Central America, and by other local names elsewhere. The major difference between the slash-and-burn system and shifting cultivation is in the length of time for which the land is used for agriculture. In the slash-and-burn system, the conversion is long-term, often permanent. Shifting cultivation is a more ephemeral use of the land for cultivation.

Shifting cultivation begins when a small area of tropical forest, typically less than one to several acres, is cleared of trees and shrubs by an individual farmer. The **biomass** is burned, and the site is then used to grow a mixture of agricultural crops for a few years. After this time, vigorous developments of weeds and declining fertility due to nutrient losses require that the land be abandoned for a fallow period of 15-30 years or more. Meanwhile new tracts of forest are successively cleared and cultivated for several years. Clearly, the shifting cultiva-

tion system is only sustainable if the population **density** is small, and if the major goal of agriculture is subsistence, rather than market farming.

Because the slash-and-burn system is a longer-term, often permanent conversion of the tropical forest into agriculture, without an extended fallow period, its associated environmental problems tend to be more severe than those that are normally caused by the smaller scale, shifting cultivation systems. However, severe environmental problems can also be caused if too many people practice shifting cultivation in a small area of forest.

Problems of tropical deforestation

In spite of the fact that many mature tropical forests sustain an enormous biomass of many species of trees, the **soil** of many forested sites is actually quite infertile. The intrinsically poor fertility of many tropical soils is due to (1) their great age, (2) the often large rates of **precipitation**, which encourage nutrient losses through **leaching**, and (3) the moist, warm climate, which encourages microbial **decomposition** and causes tropical forest soils to contain relatively little organic **matter**, so there is little ability to retain organic forms of **nutrients** in soil. The natural tropical-forest **ecosystem** and its species are well adapted to this soil **infertility**, being efficient at absorbing nutrients occurring in small concentrations in soil, and at recycling nutrients from dead biomass. As a result, much of the total nutrient capital of tropical forests is typically present in the living vegetation, particularly in trees. When these trees are felled and burned, there is a pulse of increased nutrient availability associated with ash. However, this is a short-term phenomenon, and much of the nutrient is rapidly leached or washed away under the influence of the wet climate. The overall effect of slash-and-burn forest conversions, and to a lesser degree shifting cultivation, is a rapid decline in fertility of the land.

In addition, some tropical soils are subject to a degrading process known as laterization, in which mineral silicates are dissolved by rainwater and carried downward, leaving behind insoluble oxides of **iron** and **aluminum**. Lateritic soils are very infertile, and in extreme cases can become rocklike in consistency. Once this stage of degradation is reached, it can be impossible to cultivate the land because it is too hard to plow, and **plant** roots cannot penetrate into the substrate. The rate of laterization is greatly increased by clearing the tropical forest, and in cases of extreme damage by this process, the productive capability of the land can remain degraded for centuries.

Tropical deforestation also carries other important environmental risks. Tropical forests store huge quantities of **carbon** in their living biomass, especially in trees. When tropical forests are converted into agriculture, much less carbon is stored on the land, and the difference is made up by a large **emission** of **carbon dioxide** to the atmosphere. During the past several decades, tropical deforestation and the use of **fossil fuels** have been the major causes of the increasing atmospheric concentrations of carbon dioxide, which may have important implications for global climatic warming. In addition, old-growth tropical forests are the most highly developed and biodiverse ecosystems on **Earth**. Tropical deforestation, mostly caused by slash-and-burn agriculture, is the major cause of the great wave of extinctions that is presently afflicting Earth's **biodiversity**.

Further Reading

Freedman, B. *Environmental Ecology.* 2nd ed. San Diego: Academic Press, 1994.

Miller, K., and L. Tangley. *Trees of Life. Saving Tropical Forests and Their Biological Wealth.* Boston, MA: Beacon Press, 1991.

Bill Freedman

Sleep

Sleep is a state of physical inactivity and mental rest in which conscious awareness, thought, and voluntary movement cease and intermittent dreaming takes place. This natural and regular phenomenon essential to all living creatures normally happens with the eyes closed and is divided into two basic types: REM (rapid **eye** movement) and NREM (non-rapid eye movement) sleep. As passive as sleep appears, it is actually a very active and deliberate process in which the brain busily turns off wakeful functions while turning on sleep mechanisms. No one knows exactly why we must sleep or how it happens, but the quality, quantity, and type of sleep impacts the quality, quantity, and effectiveness of our wakeful mental and physical activities. These, in turn, influence the quality, quantity, and timing of sleep.

Beliefs, theories, and scientific observations of sleep

At one time, it was believed that the mind simply turned off during sleep, or that the soul left the body during sleep. Aristotle thought that the digestion of food created vapors which naturally rose upward, causing the **brain** to become drowsy. Dreams—the only part of sleep the sleeper actually experiences—were often interpreted as prophetic revelations. Today, dream interpretation is

used in some psychoanalytic and self-awareness activities for personal insight and revelation.

Despite the fact that most people spend more time sleeping than in any other single activity, scientists still lack much knowledge about why we need sleep or what triggers it. Serious scientific studies only began about 50 years ago, and several different theories have been developed, none of which have been proven. It is known, however, that the higher the organism on the evolutionary chain (humans being the highest) the more important sleep becomes.

According to the restorative theory of sleep, body tissues heal and regenerate during non-REM sleep and brain **tissue** heals during REM sleep. This theory seems generally accepted for brain tissue restoration, particularly in the cerebral cortex, which cannot rest during the waking state. However, some researchers question its validity regarding body tissue restoration, believing that sleep simply acts as an immobilizer, forcing the body to rest, with rest and nourishment being the actual restorative factors. The release during sleep of **growth hormones**, testosterone, and other anabolic (constructive) **hormones** leads some experts to support the restorative theory, while others believe this release is coincidental to, and not caused by, sleep.

The **energy conservation** theory of sleep notes that animals which **burn** energy quickly and produce their own body **heat**, such as humans do, sleep more than those with slow metabolisms (energy consumption) or that do not produce body heat (**snakes**, for instance). This theory is based upon the observation that metabolic rates decrease during slow-wave sleep—the last two stages of the four-stage, NREM sleep cycle and which some researchers believe is the most important stage.

According to the adaptive theory of sleep, sleep encourages adaption to the environment for increased chances of survival. Animals such as **cats** that spend little time searching for food and have few natural enemies may sleep 15 hours a day for long periods. Grazing animals like buffalos and **horses** which spend many hours foraging and which are at risk from natural predators sleep only two to four hours a day in short spurts. Proponents of the adaptive theory believe early humans slept in caves to protect themselves from night-stalking animals .

Because **instinct** plays an important role in the survival of any species, including humans, the instinct theory presumes sleep, like mating or hunger, is a survival instinct.

Studies show that new information is best retained when introduced just before sleep begins and retained less well after waking or if REM sleep is interrupted. These observations lead to the **memory** consolidation theory of sleep. REM sleep seems to play an important role in storing information.

Why we sleep and how it is triggered

Enforced sleep-deprivation experiments

In the attempt to understand our need for sleep, experiments in sleep deprivation play an important role. Total sleep deprivation longer than 40 hours proves impossible, however, due to brief, totally unpreventable periods of "microsleep" which will happen even during physical activity. These microsleeps barely last a few seconds, but they may explain performance lapses in waking activities. They demonstrate the body's obvious need for sleep and may even have some restorative function.

While sleep deprivation can eventually cause death, sleep deprivation lasting up to 10 days shows no serious, prolonged consequences and does not cause severe psychological problems or mental illness as once thought. In 1965, for example, 17-year-old Randy Gardner decided to attempt a new world record for total sleep deprivation as his high school science fair project. He succeeded in staying awake for an incredible 264 hours. When researchers and psychiatrists from Stanford University heard of Gardner's experiment, they rushed to the scene and monitored his progress. On the last night, one researcher took Randy to an arcade to keep him awake. Randy won every game, indicating that prolonged sleep deprivation did not seriously impair his physical or psychomotor functioning. After his extraordinary vigil, Randy slept just 14 hours and 40 minutes, awoke naturally around 10:00 p.m., stayed awake 24 hours, and slept a normal eight hours. Follow-up over the years has shown that Gardner suffered no adverse effects from his experience.

Losing more than one night's sleep does produce a noticeable increase in irritability, lethargy, disinterest, and even paranoia. While not seriously impaired, psychomotor performance and **concentration** are adversely affected. While autonomic (involuntary) **nervous system** activity increases during sleep deprivation to keep **heart** rate, **blood pressure**, breathing, and body temperature normal, physical fitness cannot be maintained and immunological functions seem to suffer.

Biological determinants of sleep

Another question which remains only partially answered is how sleep onset is determined and why. The factors involved include circadian rhythms (biological

time clocks); the degree of stimulation in the wakeful state; the degree of personal sleepiness; the decrease in core body temperature; a quiet and comfortable sleep environment; **conditioning** arising from "bedroom cues"; and **homeostasis**, the automatic attempt by the body to maintain balance and equilibrium (for example, the air **temperature** may fall to 50°F [10°C], but our body burns calories to maintain its normal temperature of 98.6°F [37°C]).

The fact that sleep deprivation increases the desire for sleep firmly points to a homeostatic element in sleep. This is intricately linked to highly influential circadian rhythms controlled by centers probably located in the hypothalamus, part of the brain primarily involved in autonomic nervous system functions. Circadian rhythms determine our approximate 24- to 25-hour sleep-wake pattern and a similar cycle in the rise and fall of core body temperature and other physiological functions.

It is not yet known whether two separate biological clocks influence sleep-wake cycles and temperature levels and, if so, if a single "control clock" regulates them both. However, body temperature drops slightly in the evening as sleep draws near, reaches its lowest point around 2:00-4:00 A.M., rises slightly before awakening, and increases to maximum as the day progresses. This pattern is not a result of being asleep or awake, for body temperature does not drop during daytime naps nor does it rise at night after a sudden change in sleep schedule, such as shift work. It takes about two weeks for circadian rhythms controlling temperature levels to get back into sync with sleep-wake states.

Studies done on human circadian rhythms in situations totally devoid of time cues (such as sunrise, sunset, clocks, etc.) show that these rhythms are controlled completely internally and usually run on a cycle of almost 25 rather than 24 hours. In normal situations, factors called "zeitgebers" (from the German *zeit* for time and *geber* for giver) such as daylight, environmental noises, clocks, and work schedules virtually force us to maintain a 24-hour cycle. Therefore, our circadian rhythms must "phase advance" from their normal, approximate 25-hour cycle to an imposed 24-hour cycle.

The body has difficulty adapting to much more than an hour of phase-advance in one day. Drastic time changes-like those caused by rapid long-distance travel such as flying-require either phase-advancement or phase-delay. This is why travelers experience "jet lag." Recovery from east-west travel requiring phase-delay adjustments is usually quicker than in phase-advancement resulting from west-east travel. Some people seem simply unable to phase-advance their biological clocks, which often results in **sleep disorders**.

The structure of sleep

Measurement of electrical impulses in the sleeping brain

The greatest contribution to sleep study was the development of the EEG, or electroencephalogram, by German psychiatrist Hans Berger in 1929. This electrode, attached to the scalp with glue, records electrical impulses in the brain called brain waves. The discovery triggered investigations into sleep in major centers around the world. Specific brain wave patterns became evident and sleep was generally classified into distinct stages.

In 1953, Professor Nathanial Kleitman and his graduate student Eugene Aserinsky reported their close observations of a sleep stage they called REM-rapid eye movement. An electro-oculogram, or EOG, taped close to the eyelids, recorded both vertical and horizontal eye movement, which became rapid and sporadic during REM sleep. The electromyogram, or EMG, recorded chin and neck muscle movement which, for as yet undetermined reasons, completely relaxed during REM sleep. Kleitman and Aserinsky found that when subjects were awakened from REM sleep they almost always reported a dream, which was seldom the case when awakened from non-REM sleep.

Following the initial REM discoveries, sleep research greatly increased. One important discovery arising from this research was the high prevalence of sleep disorders, some of which now explain problems previously blamed on obscure physical or psychological disorders but which could not be effectively treated by medicine or **psychiatry**.

Combined, the EEG, EOG, and EMG produce a fascinating picture of sleep's structure. These monitoring devices transfer electronic **stimulus** to magnetic tapes, or on to **paper** via mechanical pens. The number of complete brain wave cycles per second are measured in "hertz" (Hz) by the EEG. The difference between the highest and lowest point of each wave (the peak and trough) is measured in" amplitude," (millionths of a volt, or microvolts-uV). As sleep approaches and deepens, hertz decrease and amplitude increases.

Stages of sleep

Very specific rhythms occur in different stages of the sleep-wake cycle. Beta rhythms are fast, low voltage waves (usually above 15 Hz and below 10 uV) which appear in alert, wakeful states. In the quiet, restful wakeful state prior to sleep onset, or in relaxed meditative state with the eyes closed, the brain displays alpha rhythms of about 8-11 Hz and 50 uV. Fairly high chin muscle activity and slow, rolling eye movements are recorded. Alpha

waves disappear with visual imagery or opening the eyes, which causes alpha blocking.

Non-REM sleep is generally believed to occur in four stages and is characterized by lack of dreaming. As the sleeper enters the drowsy, light sleep of stage 1, theta rhythms, ranging between 3.5-7.5 Hz with a lower voltage, appear. The sleeper is generally nonresponsive during this stage, which takes up about 5% of the sleep cycle, but is easily awakened. Once again, high chin muscle activity occurs and there is occasional slow, rolling eye movement.

Within a few minutes, the sleeper enters stage 2 sleep. Brain waves slow even further and spindles (short bursts of electrical impulses at about 12-14 Hz which increase and decrease in amplitude) appear, along with K-complexes (sharp, high voltage wave groups, often followed by spindles). These phenomenon may be initiated by internal or external stimuli or by some as yet unknown source deep within the brain. A few delta waves may appear here. This portion of sleep occupies about 45% of the sleep cycle.

Normally, stage 3 sleep, comprised of 20-50% low frequency/high voltage delta waves, follows stage 2 as a short (about 7% of total sleep) transition to stage 4 sleep, which shows slower **frequency** higher voltage delta wave activity above 50%. There is virtually no eye movement during stages 2, 3, and 4.

In stage 4 sleep, some sleep spindles may occur, but are difficult to record. This stage occupies about 13% of the sleep cycle, seems to be affected more than any other stage by the length of prior wakefulness, and reflects the most cerebral "shutdown." Accordingly, some researchers believe this stage to be the most necessary for brain tissue restoration. Usually grouped together, stages 3 and 4 are called delta, or slow wave sleep (SWS), and is normally followed by REM sleep.

The sleep cycle from stage 1 through REM occurs three to five times a night in a normal young adult. Stages 3 and 4 decrease with each cycle, while stage 2 and REM sleep occupy most of the last half of the night's sleep. Time spent in each stage varies with age, and age particularly influences the amount time spent in SWS. From infancy to young adult, SWS occupies about 20-25% of total sleep time and perhaps as little as 5% by the age of 60. This loss of time is made up in stage 1 sleep and wakeful periods.

The period comprised of the four stages between sleep onset and REM is known as REM latency. REM onset is indicated by a drop in amplitude and rise in frequency of brain waves. The subject's eyes flicker quickly under the eyelids, dream activity is high, and the body seems to become paralyzed because of the decrease in skeletal muscle tone. After REM, the subject usually returns to stage 2 sleep, sometimes after waking slightly. REM sleep occurs regularly during the night. The larger the brain, the longer the period between REM episodes-about 90 minutes for humans and 12 minutes in **rats**.

REM sleep is triggered by neural functions deep within the brain, which releases one type of **neurotransmitter** (chemical agent) to turn REM sleep on and another to turn it off. Whereas autonomic activity (such as breathing and heart rate) slows and becomes more regular during non-REM sleep, it becomes highly irregular during REM sleep. Changes in blood pressure, heart rate, and breathing regularity take place, there is virtually no regulation of body temperature, and clitoral and penile erections are often reported. Most deaths, particularly of ill or aged individuals, happen early in the morning when body temperature is at its lowest and the likelihood of REM sleep is highest.

REM activity is seen in the fetus as early as six months after conception. By the time of birth, the fetus will spend 90% of its sleep time in REM but only about half that after **birth**. REM constitutes about 20-30% of a normal young adult's sleep, decreasing with age. These

KEY TERMS

Alpha/beta/delta/theta rhythms—Brain wave activity occurring in different stages of wakefulness or sleep identified by amplitude and frequency.

Amplitude—Difference between the highest and lowest point of a wave.

Autonomic nervous system—The part of the nervous system that regulates automatic bodily functions, such as heart rate and body temperature.

Circadian rhythms—Internally controlled patterns which run on a cycle of approximately 25 hours and govern sleep-wake states, core body temperature, and other biological functions.

Homeostasis—The body's automatic attempt to maintain balance and stability of certain internal functions, such as body temperature, influenced by the external environment.

Metabolism—Chemical changes in body tissue which convert nutrients into energy for use by all vital bodily functions.

Phase advance/phase delay—Adjustment of circadian rhythms from their internal, biologically controlled cycle of approximately 25 hours to the 24-hour-a-day cycle imposed by the Sun.

observations support one of several theories about our need for REM sleep which suggests that, to function properly, the central nervous system requires considerable stimulation, particularly during development. Because it receives no environmental stimulation during the long hours of sleep, it is possible that the high amount of brain wave activity in REM sleep provides the necessary stimulation.

See also Biological rhythms.

Further Reading

Anch, A. Michael et al. *Sleep: A Scientific Perspective.* Englewood Cliffs, N.J.: Prentice Hall, 1988.

Ellman, Steven J., and John S. Antrobus, eds. *The Mind in Sleep: Psychology and Psychophysiology.* New York: John Wiley & Sons, 1991.

Horne, James. *Why We Sleep: The Functions of Sleep in Humans and Other Mammals.* Oxford: Oxford University Press, 1988.

Montplaisir, Jacques, and Roger Godbout, eds. *Sleep and Biological Rhythms: Basic Mechanisms and Applications to Psychiatry.* New York: Oxford University Press, 1990.

Moorcroft, William H., and Luther College. *Sleep, Dreaming, and Sleep Disorders: An Introduction.* Lanham: University Press of America, 1989.

Reite, Martin, Kim Nagel, and John Rudd. *Concise Guide to Evaluation and Management of Sleep Disorders.* Washington, DC: American Psychiatric Press, 1990.

Stampi, Claudio, ed. *Why We Nap: Evolution, Chronobiology, and Functions of Polyphasic and Ultrashort Sleep.* Boston: Birkhauser, 1992.

Marie L. Thompson

Sleep disorders

Sleep disorders are chronic **sleep** irregularities, which drastically interfere with normal nighttime sleep or daytime functioning. Sleep-related problems are the most common complaint heard by doctors and psychiatrists, the two most common being **insomnia** (inability to go to sleep or stay asleep), and hypersomnia (excessive daytime sleepiness). While most people experience both problems at some time, it is only when they cause serious intrusions into daily living that they warrant investigation as disorders.

Sleep disorders research is a relatively new field of medicine stimulated by the discovery in 1953 of REM (Rapid Eye Movement) sleep and the more recent discovery in the 1980s that certain irregular breathing patterns during sleep can cause serious illness and sometimes death. While medical knowledge of sleep disorders is expanding rapidly, clinical educational programs still barely touch on the subject, about which many physicians, psychiatrists and neurologists remain seriously undereducated.

Insomnias and hypersomnias

Insomnias include problems with sleep onset (taking longer than 30 minutes falling asleep), sleep maintenance (waking five or more times during the night or for a total of 30 minutes or more), early arousal (less than 6.5 hours of sleep over a typical night), light sleep, and **conditioning** (**learning** not to sleep by associating certain bedtime cues with the inability to sleep). Insomnias may be transient (lasting no longer than three weeks) or persistent. Most people experience transient insomnias, perhaps due to stress, excitement, illness, or even a sudden change to high altitude. These are treatable by short-term prescription drugs and, sometimes, relaxation techniques. When insomnia becomes persistent, it is usually classed as a disorder. Persistent insomnias may result from medical and/or psychiatric disorders, prescription drug use, and substance abuse, and often result in chronic fatigue, impaired daytime functioning, and hypersomnia.

Hypersomnias manifest as excessive daytime sleepiness, uncontrollable sleep attacks, and, in the extreme, causes people to fall asleep at highly inappropriate times, such as driving a car or when holding a conversation. Most hypersomnias, like narcolepsy and those associated with apnea (breathing cessation), are caused by some other disorder and are therefore symptomatic. Some, however, like Idiopathic Central **Nervous System** (CNS) Hypersomnia and Kleine-Levin Syndrome, are termed "idiopathic" for their unknown origin. CNS Hypersomnia causes a continuous state of sleepiness from which long naps and nighttime sleep provides no relief. This is usually a life-long disorder and treatment is still somewhat experimental and relatively ineffective. Kleine-Levin Syndrome is a rare disorder seen three times as often in males as females, beginning in the late teens or twenties. Symptoms are periods of excessive sleepiness, excessive overeating, abnormal **behavior**, irritability, loss of sexual inhibition, and sometimes hallucinations. These periods may last days or weeks, occur one or more times a year, and disappear about the age of 40. Behavior between attacks is normal, and the sufferer often has little recall of the attack. Stimulant drugs may reduce sleepiness for brief periods, and **lithium** meets with some success in preventing recurrence.

Observation and classification of sleep disorders

Sleep abnormalities intrigued even the earliest medical writers who detailed difficulties that people experi-

enced with falling asleep, staying asleep, or staying awake during the day. By 1885, Henry Lyman, a professor of neurology in Chicago, classified insomnias into two groups: those resulting from either abnormal internal or physical functions; or from external, environmental influences. In 1912, Sir James Sawyer reclassified the causes as either medical; or psychic, toxic, or senile. Insomnias were divided into three categories in 1927: inability to fall asleep, recurrent waking episodes, and waking earlier in the morning than appropriate. Another reclassification, also into three categories, was made in 1930: insomnia/hypersomnia, unusual sleep-wake patterns, and parasomnias (interruption of sleep by abnormal physical occurrences). One change to that grouping was made in 1930 when hypersomnias and insomnias became separate categories.

Intense escalation of sleep study in the 1970s saw medical centers begin establishing sleep disorder clinics where researchers increasingly uncovered abnormalities in sleep patterns and events. It was during this decade that sleep disorders became an independent field of medical research and the increasing number of sleep disorders being identified necessitated formal classification.

Dyssomnias

This group includes both insomnias and hypersomnias, and is divided into three categories: Intrinsic, Extrinsic, and Circadian Rhythm Sleep Disorders. Intrinsic Sleep Disorders originate within the body and include narcolepsy, sleep apnea, and periodic limb movements.

Narcolepsy is associated with REM sleep and the central nervous system. It causes frequent sleep disturbances and thus excessive daytime drowsiness. Subjects may fall asleep without warning, experience cataplexy—muscle weakness associated with sudden emotional responses like anger, which may cause collapse—and temporarily be unable to move right before falling asleep or just after waking up. While narcolepsy is manageable clinically and brief naps of 10-20 minutes may be somewhat refreshing, there is no cure.

Apnea is the brief cessation of breathing. Obstructive Sleep Apnea is caused by the collapse of the upper airway passages that prevent air intake, while Central Apnea occurs when the diaphragm and chest muscles cease functioning momentarily. Both apneas result in a suffocating sensation, which goes unnoticed but causes enough arousal to enable breathing to begin again. Bed partners report excessive snoring and repeated brief pauses in breathing. Apneas may disrupt sleep as many as several hundred times a night, naturally resulting in excessive daytime sleepiness. Severe episodes can actually cause death, usually from **heart** failure. Treatment for obstructive apnea includes pumping air through a nasal mask to keep air passages open, while some success in treating central apnea can be obtained with drugs and mechanical breathing aids.

Periodic Limb Movement (PLM) and Restless Leg Syndrome (RLS) result in sleep disruptions and therefore hypersomnia. PLM occurs during sleep and subjects experience involuntary leg jerks (sometimes arms also). The subject is unaware of these movements but bed partners complain of being kicked and hit. In RLS, "crawling" or "prickling" sensations seriously interfere with sleep onset. Although their causes are yet unknown, certain drugs, stretching, **exercise**, and avoiding stress and excessive tiredness seem to provide some relief.

Extrinsic Sleep Disorders are caused by external influences such as drugs and **alcohol**, poor sleep hygiene, high altitude, and lack of regular sleep limit-setting for children.

Drug and Alcohol Related Sleep Disorders result from stimulant, sedative, and alcohol use, all of which can affect, and severely disrupt, the sleep-wake schedule. Stimulants, including **amphetamines**, **caffeine**, and some weight loss agents, can cause sleep disturbances and may eventually result in a "crash" and the need for excessively long periods of sleep. Prolonged use of sedatives, including sleeping pills, often result in severe " rebound insomnia" and daytime sleepiness. Sudden withdrawal also produces these effects. Alcohol, while increasing total sleep time, also increases arousals, snoring, and the incidence and severity of sleep apnea. Prolonged abuse severely reduces REM and delta (slow-wave) sleep, and sudden withdrawal results in severe sleep-onset difficulties, significantly reduced delta sleep, and "REM rebound," causing intense nightmares and **anxiety** dreams for prolonged periods.

Circadian Rhythm Sleep Disorders either affect or are affected by circadian rhythms, which determine our approximate 25-hour biological sleep-wake pattern and other biological functions. Disorders may be transient or permanent.

Jet-Lag and Shift Work-Related Circadian Rhythm Disorders are transient. Because our biological clock runs slightly slower than the 24-hour **Sun** clock, it must adjust to external time cues like alarm clocks and school or work schedules. Circadian rhythms must therefore "phase-advance" to fit the imposed 24-hour day. The body has difficulty phase-advancing more than one hour each day, therefore people undergoing drastic time changes after long-distance air travel suffer from "jet lag." Hypersomnia, insomnia, and a decrease in alertness and performance are not uncommon and may last up to 10 days, particularly after eastward trips longer than six

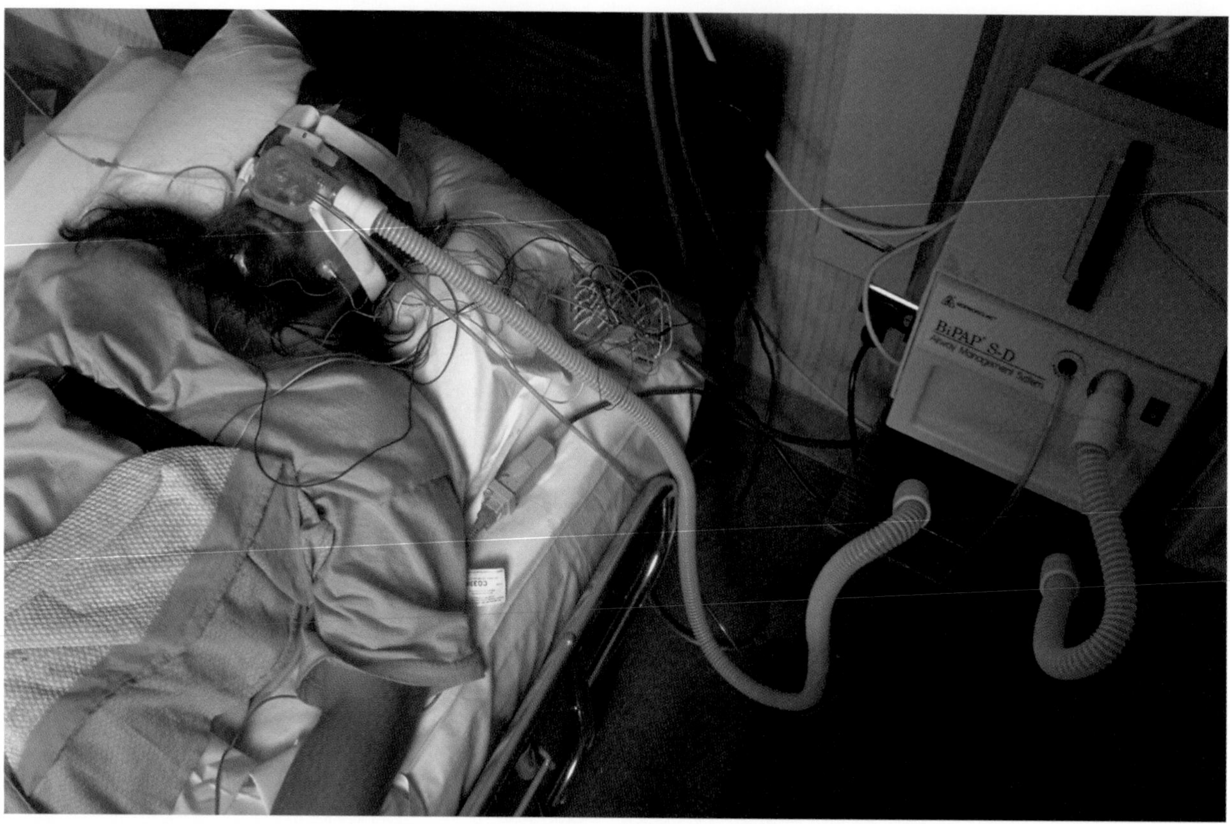

A patient with acute sleep apnea is hooked up for a night's sleep at a Stanford University Lab.

hours. Night-shift workers, whether permanent or alternating between day and night shifts, experience similar symptoms, which may become chronic because circadian rhythms induce maximum sleepiness during the Sun-clock's night and alertness during the Sun-clock's day, regardless of how long a person works nights.

Delayed Sleep Phase Syndrome is a chronic condition in which waking to meet normal daily schedules is extremely difficult. Such people are often referred to as "night people" because they feel alert late in the day and at night while experiencing fatigue and sleepiness in the mornings and early afternoons. This is because their biological morning is the middle of the actual night. Phase-delaying the sleep-wake schedule by going to bed three hours later and sleeping three hours longer until the required morning arousal time is reached, can often synchronize the two. Exposure to artificial, high-intensity, full **spectrum** light from about 7-9 a.m. often proves helpful.

Advanced Sleep Phase Syndrome is much less prevalent and shows the reverse pathology to phase-delayed syndrome. Phase-advancing the sleep-wake schedule and light therapy during evening hours may prove helpful.

Parasomnias

Parasomnias are events caused by physical intrusions into sleep which are thought to be triggered by the central nervous system. These dysfunctions do not interfere with actual sleep processes and do not cause insomnia or hypersomnia. They appear more frequently in children than adults.

Arousal Disorders appear to be associated with neurological arousal mechanisms. They usually occur early in the night during slow-wave rather than REM sleep and are therefore not the "acting out" of a dream.

Sleepwalking occurs during sleep. The subject may seem wide awake but displays a blank expression, seldom responds when spoken to, is difficult to awaken, moves clumsily, and sometimes bumps into objects, although they will often maneuver effectively around them. Some sleepwalkers perform dangerous activities, like driving a car. Although rarely the case with children, serious injuries can occur. Subjects displaying dangerous tendencies should take precautions like locking windows and doors. Episodes average about 10 minutes, seldom occur more than once in any given night, and are seldom remembered.

Night or Sleep Terrors are sudden partial awakenings during non-REM sleep. Traditionally, a sufferer sits bolt upright in bed in a state of extreme panic, screams loudly, sweats heavily, and displays a rapid heart beat and dilated pupils. The patient will sometimes talk, and might even flee from bed in terror, often running into objects and causing injury. Episodes last about 15 minutes, after which sleep returns easily. There is seldom any recollection of the event. If woken, the subject may display violence and confusion and should, instead, be gently guided back to bed.

Rapid Eye Movement (REM) Sleep Parasomnias take place during sleep and include nightmares and the recently discovered REM sleep behavior disorder. This potentially injurious disorder is seen mostly in elderly men and results in aggressive behavior while sound asleep such as punching, kicking, fighting, and leaping from bed in an attempt to act out a dream. Subjects report their dreams, usually of being attacked or chased, become more violent and vivid over the years. Some sufferers even tie themselves into bed to avoid injury. Unfortunately, this disorder was seriously misdiagnosed until recently. It is now readily diagnosable and easily treated.

Sleep-Wake Transition Disorders usually occur during transition from one sleep stage to another, or while falling asleep or waking up. Manifestations include sleeptalking, leg cramps, headbanging, hypnic jerks (sleep starts), and teeth-grinding.

Other Parasomnias include excessive snoring, abnormal swallowing, bedwetting, sleep paralysis, and sudden unexplained death during sleep.

Diagnosis of sleep disorders

Identifying each specific sleep disorder is imperative for effective treatment, as treatment for one may adversely effect another. While sleeping pills may help in some instances, in others they exacerbate the problem. The most important step in **diagnosis** is the sleep history, a highly detailed diary of symptoms and sleep-wake patterns. The patient records events such as daily schedule; family history of sleep complaints; prescription or nonprescription drug use; and symptoms—when they occur, how long they last, their intensity, whether they are seasonal, what improves or worsens them, and effects of stress, family or environmental factors. Important contributors are family members or friends; for example, a bed partner or parent may be the only observer of unusual occurrences during the patient's sleep.

The sleeping brain—the new frontier

Many undiscovered secrets lie hidden behind the doors of sleep and its related disorders. However, the future looks bright for sufferers of sleep disorders. Intense interest from researchers, satisfaction of an increasing number of accurately diagnosed and treated patients, advances in technology, and the recent formation of a National Institute of Health Commission on Sleep by the United States Congress, suggest that research, training, education, and recognition in this area of medicine will continue to flourish.

See also Sleeping sickness.

KEY TERMS

Apnea—Cessation of breathing.

Delta sleep—Slow-wave, stage 4 sleep that normally occurs before the onset of REM sleep.

Extrinsic—Caused by something on the outside.

Hypersomnia—Excessive daytime sleepiness.

Idiopathic—Disease of unknown origin.

Insomnia—Inability to go to sleep or stay asleep.

Intrinsic—Not dependent on external circumstances.

Parasomnia—Interruption of sleep by abnormal physical occurrences.

Polysomnography—Electronic monitoring equipment measuring brain waves, eye and muscle movement, heart rate, and other physiological functions.

REM sleep—The period of sleep during which eyes move rapidly behind closed eyelids and when dreams most commonly occur.

Further Reading

"Insomnia and Related Sleep Disorders." *Psychiatric Clinics of North America,* 16 (December 1993).

Moorcroft, William H. *Sleep, Dreaming and Sleep Disorders.* Lanham/London: University Press of America, Inc., 1989.

Reite, Martin, Kim Nagel, and John Ruddy. *Concise Guide to Evaluation and Management of Sleep Disorders.* Washington, DC: American Psychiatric Press, Inc., 1990.

Thorpy, Michael J., ed. *International Classification of Sleep Disorders: Diagnostic and Coding Manual.* Lawrence: Allen Press, 1990.

Thorpy, Michael J., ed. *Handbook of Sleep Disorders.* New York/Basel: Marcel Dekker, 1990.

Yager, Jan, and Michael J. Thorpy. *The Encyclopedia of Sleep and Sleep Disorders.* New York: Facts on File, 1991.

Marie L. Thompson

Sleeping sickness

Sleeping sickness is a protozoan **infection** passed to humans through the bite of the tsetse fly. It progresses to death within months or years if left untreated.

Causes of sleeping sickness, and geographical distribution of the disease

Protozoa are single-celled organisms considered to be the simplest **animal** life form. The protozoa responsible for sleeping sickness are a flagellated variety (**flagella** are hair-like projections from the **cell** which aid in mobility) which exist only in **Africa**. The type of protozoa causing sleeping sickness in humans is referred to as the *Trypanosoma brucei* complex. It is divided further into Rhodesian (Central and East Africa) and Gambian (Central and West Africa) subspecies.

The Rhodesian variety live within antelopes in **savanna** and woodland areas, causing no disruption to the antelope's health. (While the protozoa cause no illness in antelopes they are lethal to cattle who may become infected.) The protozoa are acquired by tsetse **flies** who bite and suck the **blood** of an infected antelope or cow.

Within the tsetse fly, the protozoa cycle through several different life forms, ultimately migrating to the salivary **glands** of the tsetse fly. Once the protozoa are harbored in the salivary glands they can be deposited into the bloodstream of the fly's next blood meal.

Humans most likely to become infected by Rhodesian trypanosomes are game wardens or visitors to game parks in East Africa. The Rhodesian variety of sleeping sickness causes a much more severe illness with a greater likelihood of eventual death.

The Gambian variety of *Trypanosoma* thrives in tropical **rain forests** throughout Central and West Africa, does not infect game or cattle, and is primarily a threat to people dwelling in such areas. It rarely infects visitors.

Symptoms and progression of sleeping sickness

The first sign of sleeping sickness may be a sore appearing at the tsetse fly bite site about two to three days after having been bitten. Redness, **pain**, and swelling occur.

Two to three weeks later Stage I disease develops as a result of the protozoa being carried through the blood and lymphatic circulations. This systemic (meaning that symptoms affect the whole body) phase of the illness is characterized by a high fever that falls to normal then re-spikes. A rash with intense itching may be present, and headache and mental confusion may occur. The Gambian form includes extreme swelling of lymph **tissue**, enlargement of the spleen and liver, and greatly swollen lymph nodes. Winterbottom's sign is classic of Gambian sleeping sickness; it consists of a visibly swollen area of lymph nodes located behind the **ear** and just above the base of the neck. During this stage the **heart** may be affected by a severe inflammatory reaction particularly when the infection is caused by the Rhodesian form.

Many of the symptoms of sleeping sickness are actually the result of attempts by the patient's **immune system** to get rid of the invading **organism**. The overly exuberant cells of the immune system damage the patient's organs, **anemia**, and leaky blood vessels. These leaky blood vessels help to spread the protozoa throughout the patient's body.

One reason for the immune system's intense reaction to the Trypanosomes is also the reason why the Trypanosomes survive so effectively. The protozoa are able to change rapidly specific markers on their outer coats. These kinds of markers usually stimulate the host's immune system to produce immune cells specifically to target the markers and allow quick destruction of these invading cells. Trypanosomes are able to express new markers at such a high rate of change that the host's immune system cannot catch up.

Stage II sleeping sickness involves the **nervous system**. The Gambian strain has a clearly delineated phase in which the predominant symptomatology involves the **brain**. The patient's **speech** becomes slurred, mental processes slow, and he or she sits and stares or sleeps for long periods of time. Other symptoms resemble **Parkinson's disease**: imbalance when walking, slow and shuffling gait, trembling of the limbs, involuntary movement, muscle tightness, and increasing mental confusion. These symptoms culminate in **coma**, then death.

Diagnosis

Diagnosis of sleeping sickness can be made by microscopic examination of fluid from the site of the tsetse fly bite or swollen lymph nodes for examination. A method to diagnose Rhodesian trypanosome involves culturing blood, bone marrow, or spinal fluid. These cultures are injected into **rats** to promote the development of blood-borne protozoan infection. This infection can be detected in blood smears within one to two weeks.

Treatment

Medications effective against the *Trypanosoma brucei* complex protozoa have significant potential for side

KEY TERMS

Immune system—That network of tissues and cells throughout the body which is responsible for ridding the body of invaders such as viruses, bacteria, protozoa, etc.

Protozoa—Single-celled organisms considered to be the simplest life form in the animal kingdom.

effects. Suramin, eflornithine, pentamidine, and several drugs which contain arsenic (a chemical which is potentially poisonous) are effective anti-trypanosomal agents. Each of these drugs requires careful monitoring to ensure that they do not cause serious complications such as a fatal hypersensitivity reaction, kidney or liver damage, or **inflammation** of the brain.

Prevention

Prevention of sleeping sickness requires avoiding contact with the tsetse fly; insect repellents and clothing which covers the limbs to the wrists and ankles are mainstays. There are currently no immunizations available to prevent sleeping sickness.

Further Reading

Andreoli, Thomas E. et al. *Cecil Essentials of Medicine.* Philadelphia: W.B. Saunders Company, 1993.

Berkow, Robert and Andrew J. Fletcher. *The Merck Manual of Diagnosis and Therapy.* Rahway: Merck Research Laboratories, 1992.

Isselbacher, Kurt J. et al. *Harrison's Principles of Internal Medicine.* New York: McGraw Hill, 1994.

Mandell, Douglas et al. *Principles and Practice of Infectious Diseases.* New York: Churchill Livingstone Inc., 1995.

Sherris, John et al. *Medical Microbiology.* Norwalk: Appleton & Lange, 1994.

Rosalyn Carson-DeWitt

Sleet see **Precipitation**

Slime molds

Slime molds are organisms in two taxonomic groups, the cellular slime molds (Phylum Acrasiomycota) and the plasmodial slime molds (Phylum Myxomycota). Organisms in both groups are eukaryotic (meaning that their cells have nuclei) and are fungus-like in appearance during part of their life cycle. For this reason, they were traditionally included in mycology textbooks. However, modern biologists consider both groups to be only distantly related to the **fungi**. The two groups of slime molds are considered separately below.

Cellular slime molds

Species in this group are microscopic during most stages of their life cycle, when they exist as haploid (having one copy of each **chromosome** in the nucleus), single-celled amoebas. The amoebas typically feed on **bacteria** by engulfing them, in a process known as phagocytosis, and they reproduce by **mitosis** and fission. **Sexual reproduction** occurs but is uncommon. Most of what we know about this group is from study of the species *Dictyostelium discoideum.* When there is a shortage of food, the individual haploid amoebas of a cellular slime **mold** aggregate into a mass of cells called a pseudoplasmodium. A pseudoplasmodium typically contains many thousands of individual cells. In contrast to the plasmodial slime molds, the individual cells in a pseudoplasmodium maintain their own **plasma** membranes during aggregation. The migrating amoebas often form beautiful aggregation patterns, which change form over time.

After a pseudoplasmodium has formed, the amoebas continue to aggregate until they form a mound on the ground surface. Then, the mound elongates into a "slug." The slug is typically less than 0.04 in (1 mm) in length and migrates in response to **heat**, **light**, and other environmental stimuli.

The slug then develops into a sporocarp, a fruiting body with cells specialized for different functions. A sporocarp typically contains about 100,000 cells. The sporocarp of *Dictyostelium* is about 0.08 in (2 mm) tall and has cells in a base, stalk, and ball-like cap. The cells in the cap develop into asexual reproductive spores which germinate to form new amoebas. The different species of cellular slime molds are distinguished by sporocarp morphology.

Dictyostelium discoideum

Dictyostelium discoideum has been favored by many biologists as a model **organism** for studies of development, **biochemistry**, and **genetics**. Aspects of its development are analogous to that of higher organisms, in that a mass of undifferentiated cells develops into a multicellular organism, with different cells specialized for different functions. The development of *Dictyostelium* is much easier to study in the laboratory than is the development of higher organisms.

A food shortage induces aggregation in *Dictyostelium*. In aggregation, individual amoebas near the center of a group of amoebas secrete pulses of cAMP (cyclic adenosine-3'5'-monophosphate). The cAMP binds to special receptors on the plasma membranes of nearby amoebas, causing the cells to move toward the cAMP source for about a minute. Then, these amoebas stop moving and in turn secrete cAMP, to induce other more distant amoebas to move toward the developing aggregation. This process continues until a large, undifferentiated mass of cells, the pseudoplasmodium, is formed.

Interestingly, cAMP is also found in higher organisms, including humans. In *Dictyostelium* and these higher organisms, cAMP activates various biochemical pathways and is synthesized in response to **hormones**, neurotransmitters, and other stimuli.

Plasmodial slime molds

The plasmodial slime molds are relatively common in temperate regions and can be found living on decaying plant **matter**. There are about 400 different species. Depending on the species, the color of the amorphous **cell** mass, the plasmodium, can be red, yellow, brown, orange, green, or other colors. The color of the plasmodium and the morphology of the reproductive body, the sporocarp, are used to identify the different species.

The plasmodial slime molds are superficially similar to the cellular slime molds. Both have a haploid **amoeba** phase in when cells feed by phagocytosis, followed by a phase with a large amorphous cell mass, and then a reproductive phase with a stalked fruiting body.

However, the plasmodial slime molds are distinguished from the cellular slime molds by several unique features of their life cycle. First, the germinating spores produce flagellated as well as unflagellated cells. Second, two separate haploid cells fuse to produce a zygote with a diploid nucleus. Third, the zygote develops into a plasmodium which typically contains many thousands of diploid nuclei, all surrounded by a continuous plasma **membrane**.

The cytoplasm of the plasmodium moves about within the cell, a process known as cytoplasmic streaming. This is readily visible with a **microscope**. The function of cytoplasmic streaming is presumably to move **nutrients** about within the giant cell.

Notable species

In nature, plasmodial slime molds grow well in wet and humid environments, and under such conditions the plasmodium of some species can be quite large. After a particularly wet spring in Texas in 1973, several residents of a Dallas suburb reported a large, moving, slimy mass, which they termed "the Blob." The Blob apparently terrified numerous residents. Reporters in the local press speculated that the Blob was a mutant bacterium. Others speculated that it came from another **planet** and would soon take over the **Earth**! Fortunately, a local mycologist soberly identified the Blob as *Fuligo septica,* a species of plasmodial slime mold.

Another plasmodial slime mold, *Physarum polycephalum,* is easily grown in the laboratory and is often used by biologists as a model organism for studies of cytoplasmic streaming, biochemistry, and **cytology**. The plasmodium of this species moves in response to various stimuli, including ultraviolet and blue light. The **proteins** actin and myosin are involved in this movement. Interestingly, actin and myosin also control the movement of muscles in higher organisms, including humans.

KEY TERMS

Cytoplasmic streaming—Intracellular movement of cytoplasm thought to be a mechanism for moving nutrients about within the cell.

Diploid—Nucleus or cell containing two copies of each chromosome, generated by fusion of two haploid nuclei.

Haploid—Nucleus or cell containing one copy of each chromosome.

Phagocytosis—A type of cellular ingestion in which cell protrusions surround and then engulf a food particle.

Pseudoplasmodium—An aggregate mass of cellularslime mold amoebas formed in response to a food shortage.

Sporocarp—The fruiting body of a slime mold; it produces spores to generate new amoebas.

Zygote—A diploid cell which results from the fusion of two haploid cells.

Further Reading

Julich, W. *Color Atlas of Micromycetes.* VCH Publishers, 1993.

Katsaros, P. *Illustrated Guide to Common Slime Molds.* Eureka, CA: Mad River Press, 1989.

Kessin, R. H., and M. M. van Lookeren Campagne. "The Development of a Social Amoeba." *American Scientist.* 80 (1992): 556-65.

Margulis, L., and K. V. Schwartz. *Five Kingdoms.* San Francisco, W. H. Freeman, 1988.

Peter A. Ensminger

A three-toed sloth.

Sloths

Sloths are **mammals** of the Central and South American jungle that spend their lives in trees, eating leaves in a very slow, or "slothful," manner. They belong to order Edentata, which means "without teeth." However, sloths are not actually without teeth. They have molars, or chewing teeth, that have no roots and continue to grow throughout their lives. **Anteaters**, for which this order was named, actually have no teeth.

The two kinds of sloths belong to two different families of edentates. The three-toed sloths makes up family Bradypodidae. Three-toed sloths make a sound that has been described as "ai-ai," which has given them the name of ai. The two-toed sloths are family Megalonychidae. Actually, though, these animals should be called "two- and three-fingered" sloths because all five species have three toes on each of their hind feet.

The three **species** of three-toed sloths are smaller than the two-toed. Their head-body length ranges from about 18-24 in (50-60 cm), with a weight of only about 9 lb (4 kg). The two-toed species are larger, with a head-body length up to 28 in (70 cm) and weighing up to 17 lb (8 kg). The famed extinct ground sloth, *Mylodon listai,* which was about the size of an **elephant**, belonged to the two-toed family.

Sloths have quite flat faces on very round heads, with round eyes, a round snout, and round nostrils. Even their tiny round ears are hidden in their coarse, dense fur. The hair of the fur, which is usually light brown or gray, is grooved. Within these grooves grow **algae**, encouraged to grow by the high humidity of the **rain forest**, so the **animal** more often looks green than brown. This coloration keeps the animal camouflaged against predators. The coarse hair of the two-toed sloths is much longer than that of the three-toed, about 6 in (15 cm), compared to 2-3 in (5-7 cm). Both of them have a soft undercoat of denser fur. Because they spend most of their lives upside down, their fur parts on their bellies instead of along their backs.

There is a good reason why the word "sloth" means laziness and slowness. These animals do everything slowly. They live strictly by browsing on leaves in trees. Their entire bodies are adapted for this activity. Their limbs are geared for clinging to **tree** branches-upside down. Their claws are 3- 4 in (8-10 cm) long and **curve** tightly around branches.

Their stomachs are equipped with several chambers in order to digest **plant** material that would poison other animals. The chambers also contain **bacteria** that help digest the tough material in leaves. Their digestive systems work just as slowly as the animals' reputation. It can take a month or more for the huge quantity of leaves they eat to make their way through the system. Then the waste remains in the body except for their very occasional—and painfully slow—trips to the ground, when they defecate at the base of the tree in which they live, perhaps once a week.

In addition, their body metabolisms are geared toward **conservation** of **energy**. Instead of depending on their **metabolism** to keep them warm, as most mammals do, they warm up in the **sun** and cool down in the shade of the high canopies where they live. Their system of blood-carrying arteries and veins is arranged so that the **heat** carried by the **blood** continues to circulate in the body instead of being lost out the fingers and toes. This arrangement is of real benefit to an animal that becomes uncomfortable if the **temperature** drops below 80°F (26.6°C).

They do not even waste energy getting into position for **sleep**. They just fall asleep as they are, generally upside down, with the head falling forward onto the chest. They spend at least 20 hours a day sleeping. During those remaining four hours, they eat. They move very slowly, just a gentle hand-over-hand motion, no leaping, no quick turns. They do make progress, however. They go after the leaves on different branches. They even change trees frequently. However, when they reach the ground, all they can do is pull themselves along with their strong front arms. Their muscles will not support their weight.

Female sloths don't change their habits just because they have babies. The young are born after varying gestation periods (almost a year in Hoffman's two-toed

KEY TERMS

Defecate—To eliminate solid waste from the body.

Metabolism—The total energy use of the body necessary for maintaining life.

sloth, *Choloepus hoffmanni*, of Nicaragua to Central Brazil). The single baby is born up in the tree, where the mother turns into the infant's nest. She stays upside down and the baby snuggles down to nurse. It continues to nurse for a month, gradually taking in more and more nearby leaves. The mother carries the baby until it is at least six months old. About three months after that, it must head off on its own.

In some parts of Central America, members of the two different families share the same area. When this occurs, there are usually more of the smaller three-toed sloths than the bigger two-toed. The two species are active at different times of the day or night. They also have different tastes in trees, so they don't compete.

Edentates are regarded as the remains of a large group of South American animals that spread throughout that **continent** many millions of years ago, probably from **North America**. There were once many more sloths. The ground sloths were known and killed by early natives before becoming extinct. Today, the maned sloth (*B. torquatus*) of Brazil, is classified by the World Conservation Monitoring Center as endangered. Remaining sloths are isolated to the Atlantic coastal **forests** of eastern Brazil, with some pockets of individuals surviving elsewhere. The maned sloth is endangered because its coastal **habitat** has almost entirely been taken over by resort and urban development. Less than 3% now remains. Also, sloths are hunted for food and traditional medicinal purposes, adding to the threat of their **extinction**.

Further Reading

Hartman, Jane E. *Armadillos, Anteaters, and Sloths: How They Live.* New York: Holiday House, 1980.

Hoke, John. *Discovering the World of the Three-Toed Sloth.* New York: Franklin Watts, 1976.

Jean F. Blashfield

Slugs

Slug is a common name for a group of terrestrial **snails** like molluscs with little or no external shell. Examples of common slugs are *Limax maximus*, the large garden slug, and *Limax agrestis*, which eats grain seedlings and is regarded as a farm pest in **Europe**. Other urban species are *Arion circumscriptus* and *Limax flavus*.

Slugs are classified in the gastropod subclass Pulmonata. The pulmonates are those animals of land and fresh **water** that lack the gills of most snails, but generally have a "lung" formed from a portion of the mantle. Slugs use the whole body integument for exchange of respiratory gases. They tend to occupy places that minimize water loss and **temperature** extremes, often hidden in the daytime and active at night. Evidence of their nocturnal activity are the slime trails often found on sidewalks in the morning.

Sea slugs are also shell-less snails, but they are much more colorful and varied, and they are classified as class Opisthobranchia, order Nudibranchia. The nudibranchs have a snail-like body, with tentacles on the head, an elongated foot, and pointed tail end. The dorsal surface has projections called cerata, or papillae or branchial plumes, which may look showy or bizarre to us, but not at all unusual to other nudibranchs. These presumably function in the place of gills to increase respiratory surface, but also sometimes serve as camouflage. Most nudibranchs are 1 in (2.5 cm) or less in length, but some Pacific coast species are larger.

Smallpox

Smallpox is an **infection** caused by the variola **virus**, a member of the poxvirus family. Throughout history, smallpox has caused huge epidemics resulting in great suffering and enormous death tolls worldwide. In 1980, the World Health Organization (WHO) announced that a massive program of vaccination against the disease had resulted in the complete eradication of the virus (with the exception of stored virus in two laboratories).

Symptoms and progression of the disease

Smallpox was an extraordinarily contagious disease. The virus spread from contact with victims, as well as from contaminated air droplets and even from objects used by other smallpox victims (books, blankets, etc.).

After acquisition of the virus, there was a 12-14 day incubation period, during which the virus multiplied, but no symptoms appeared. The onset of symptoms occurred suddenly and included fever and chills, muscle aches, and a flat, reddish-purple rash on the chest, abdomen, and back.

Smallpox on the arm of a man in India.

These symptoms lasted about three days, after which the rash faded and the fever dropped. A day or two later, the fever would return, along with a bumpy rash starting on the feet, hands, and face. This rash progressed from the feet along the legs, from the hands along the arms, and from the face down the neck, ultimately reaching and including the chest, abdomen and back. The individual bumps, or papules, filled with clear fluid, and, over the course of 10-12 days, became pus-filled. The pox would eventually scab over, and when the scab fell off, left behind was a pock or pit which remained as a permanent scar.

Death from smallpox usually followed complications such as bacterial infection of the open skin lesions, **pneumonia**, or bone infections. A very severe and quickly fatal form of smallpox was called "sledgehammer smallpox," and resulted in hemorrhage from the skin lesions, as well as from the mouth, nose, and other areas of the body.

No treatment was ever discovered to treat the symptoms of smallpox, or to shorten the course of the **disease.**

Diagnosis

Diagnosis, up until the eradication of smallpox, consisted of using an **electron microscope** to identify the virus in fluid from the papules, in the patient's urine, or in the **blood** prior to the appearance of the papular rash.

The discovery of the vaccine

Fascinating accounts have been written describing ways in which different peoples tried to vaccinate themselves against smallpox. In China, India, and the Americas, from about the tenth century, it was noted that individuals who had had even a mild case of smallpox could not be infected again. Material from people ill with smallpox (fluid or pus from the papules, the scabs) was scratched into the skin of people who had never had the illness, in an attempt to produce a mild reaction and its accompanying protective effect. These efforts often resulted in full-fledged smallpox, and probably served only to help effectively spread the infection throughout the community. In fact, such crude vaccinations against smallpox were against the law in Colonial America.

In 1798, Edward Jenner published a paper in which he discussed his important observation that milkmaids who contracted a mild infection of the hands (called cowpox, and caused by a relative of variola) appeared to be immune to smallpox. He created an immunization against smallpox that used the pussy material found in the lesions of cowpox infection. Jenner's paper led to much work in the area of vaccinations and ultimately resulted in the creation of a very effective **vaccine**, which utilizes the vaccinia virus-another close relative of variola.

Global eradication of smallpox virus

Smallpox is dangerous only to human beings. Animals and **insects** can neither be infected by smallpox, nor carry the virus in any form. Humans cannot carry the virus, unless they are symptomatic. These important facts entered into the 1967 decision by the WHO to attempt worldwide eradication of the smallpox virus.

The methods used in WHO's eradication program were simple: 1) careful surveillance for all smallpox infections worldwide to allow for quick diagnosis and immediate quarantine of patients; 2) immediate vaccination of all contacts of any patient diagnosed with smallpox infection to interrupt the virus' usual pattern of contagion.

The WHO's program was extremely successful, and the virus was declared eradicated worldwide in May of 1980. Two laboratories (in Atlanta, Georgia and in Moscow, Russia) retain samples of the smallpox virus,

KEY TERMS

Epidemic—A situation in which a particular infection is experienced by a very large percentage of the people in a given community within a given time frame.

Eradicate—To completely do away with something, ending its existence.

Hemorrhage—Massive, uncontrollable bleeding.

Lesion—The tissue disruption or the loss of function caused by a particular disease process.

Papules—Firm bumps on the skin.

because some level of concern exists that another poxvirus could mutate (undergo genetic changes) and cause human infection. Other areas of concern include the possibility of smallpox virus being utilized in a situation of **biological warfare**, or the remote chance that smallpox virus could somehow escape from the laboratories which are storing it. For these reasons, large quantities of vaccine are stored in different countries around the world, so that response to any future threat by the smallpox virus can be prompt.

Further Reading

Isselbacher, Kurt J., et al. *Harrison's Principles of Internal Medicine.* New York: McGraw Hill, 1994.

Lyons, Albert S. and R. Joseph Petrucelli, II. *Medicine: An Illustrated History.* New York: Harry N. Abrams, Inc., 1987.

Mandell, Douglas, et al. *Principles and Practice of Infectious Diseases.* New York: Churchill Livingstone, 1995.

Sherris, John C., et al. *Medical Microbiology.* Norwalk, CT: Appleton & Lange, 1994.

Rosalyn Carson-DeWitt

Smell

Smell is the ability of an **organism** to sense and identify a substance by detecting trace amounts of the substance that evaporate. Researchers have noted similarities in the sense of smell between widely differing species that reveal some of the details of how the chemical signal of an odor is detected and processed.

A controversial history

The sense of smell has been a topic of debate from humankind's earliest days. The Greek philosopher Democritus of Abdera (460-360 B.C.) speculated that we smell "atoms" of different size and shape that come from objects. His countryman Aristotle (384-322 B.C.), on the other hand, guessed that odors are detected when the "cold" sense of smell meets "hot" smoke or steam from the object being smelled. It was not until the late 18th century that most scientists and philosophers reached agreement that Democritus was basically right: the smell of an object is due to volatile, or easily evaporated, molecules that emanate from it.

In 1821 the French anatomist Hippolyte Cloquet (1787-1840) rightly noted the importance of smell for **animal** survival and reproduction; but his theorizing about the role of smell in human sex, as well as mental disorders, proved controversial. Many theories of the nineteenth century seem irrational or even malignant today. Many European scientists of that period fell into the trap of an essentially circular argument, which held that non-Europeans were more primitive, and therefore had a more developed sense of smell, and therefore were more primitive. However, other thinkers—Cloquet for one—noted that an unhealthy fixation on the sense of smell seemed much more common in "civilized" Europeans than to "primitives." The first half of the twentieth century saw real progress in making the study of smell more rational. The great Spanish neuroanatomist Santiago Ramón y Cajal (1852-1934) traced the architecture of the nerves leading from the nose to and through the **brain**. Other scientists carried out the first methodical investigations of how the nose detects scent molecules, the sensitivity of the human nose, and the differences between human and animal olfaction. But much real progress on the workings of this remarkable sense has had to wait upon the recent application of molecular science to the odor-sensitive cells of the nasal cavity.

A direct sense

Smell is the most important sense for most organisms. A wide variety of species use their sense of smell to locate **prey**, navigate, recognize and perhaps communicate with kin, and mark territory. Perhaps because the task of *olfaction* is so similar between species, in a broad sense the workings of smell in animals as different as **mammals**, **reptiles**, **fish**, and even **insects** are remarkably similar.

The sense of smell differs from most other senses in its directness: we actually smell microscopic bits of a substance that have evaporated and made their way to the olfactory epithelium, a section of the mucus **membrane** in the roof of the olfactory cavity. The olfactory epithelium contains the smell-sensitive endings of the olfactory nerve cells, also known as the olfactory ep-

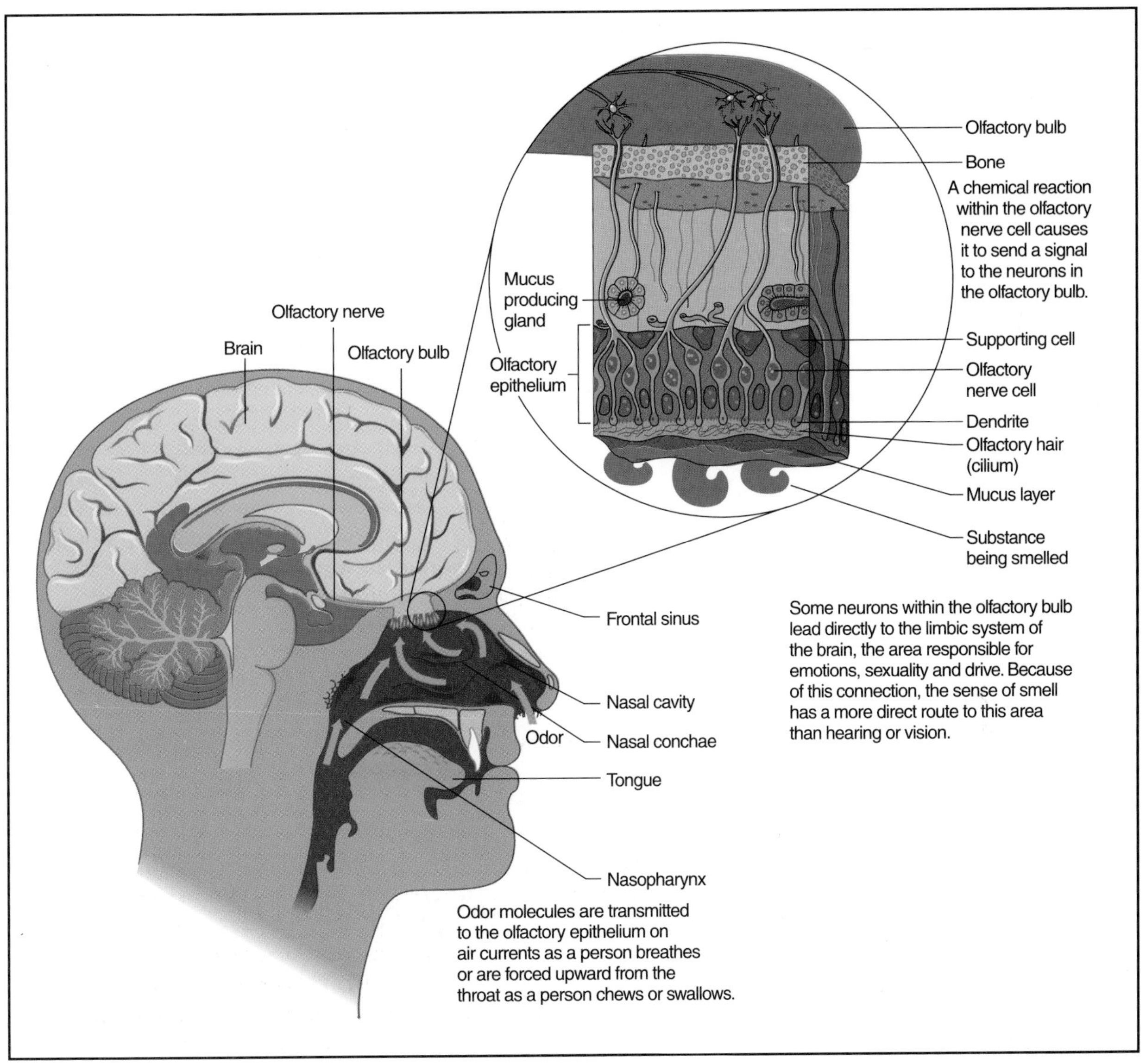
Olfactory bulb
Bone
A chemical reaction within the olfactory nerve cell causes it to send a signal to the neurons in the olfactory bulb.
Mucus producing gland
Olfactory epithelium
Supporting cell
Olfactory nerve cell
Dendrite
Olfactory hair (cilium)
Mucus layer
Substance being smelled
Olfactory nerve
Brain
Olfactory bulb
Frontal sinus
Some neurons within the olfactory bulb lead directly to the limbic system of the brain, the area responsible for emotions, sexuality and drive. Because of this connection, the sense of smell has a more direct route to this area than hearing or vision.
Nasal cavity
Odor
Nasal conchae
Tongue
Nasopharynx
Odor molecules are transmitted to the olfactory epithelium on air currents as a person breathes or are forced upward from the throat as a person chews or swallows.

The process by which olfactory information is transmitted to the brain.

ithelial cells. These cells detect odors through receptor **proteins** on the **cell** surface that bind to odor-carrying molecules. A specific odorant docks with an olfactory receptor protein in much the same way as a key fits in a lock; this in turn excites the nerve cell, causing it to send a signal to the brain. This is known as the stereospecific theory of smell.

In the past few years molecular scientists have cloned the genes for the human olfactory receptor proteins. Although there are perhaps tens of thousands (or more) of odor-carrying molecules in the world, there are only hundreds, or at most about 1,000 kinds of specific receptors in any species of animal. Because of this, scientists do not believe that each receptor recognizes a unique odorant; rather, similar odorants can all bind to the same receptor. In other words, a few loose-fitting odorant "keys" of broadly similar shape can turn the same receptor "lock." Researchers do not know how many specific receptor proteins each olfactory nerve cell carries, but recent work suggests that the cells specialize just as the receptors do, and any one olfactory nerve cell has only one or a few receptors rather than many.

It is the combined pattern of receptors that are tweaked by an odorant that allow the brain to identify it, much as yellow and red light together are intepreted by the brain as orange. (In fact, just as people can be color-blind to red or green, they can be "odor-blind" to certain simple molecules because they lack the receptor for that mole-

cule.) In addition, real objects that we smell produce multiple odor-carrying molecules, so that the brain must analyze a complex mixture of odorants to recognize a smell.

Just as the sense of smell is direct in detecting fragments of the objects, it is also direct in the way the signal is transmitted to the brain. In most senses, such as **vision**, this task is accomplished in several steps: a receptor cell detects light and passes the signal to a nerve cell, which passes it on to another nerve cell in the central **nervous system**, which then relays it to the visual center of the brain. But in olfaction, all these jobs are performed by the olfactory nerve cell: in a very real sense, the olfactory epithelium is a direct outgrowth of the brain.

The olfactory nerve cell takes the scent message directly to the nerve cells of the olfactory bulb of the brain (or, in insects and other **invertebrates** that lack true brains, the olfactory ganglia), where multiple signals from different olfactory cells with different odor sensitivities are organized and processed. In higher species the signal then goes to the brain's olfactory cortex, where higher functions such as **memory** and emotion are coordinated with the sense of smell.

KEY TERMS

Olfactory bulb—The primitive part of the brain that first processes olfactory information; in insects, its function is served by nerve-cell bundles called olfactory ganglia

Olfactory cortex—The parts of the cerebral cortex that make use of information from the olfactory bulb.

Olfactory epithelium—The patch of mucus membrane at the top of the nasal cavity that is sensitive to odor.

Olfactory nerve cell—The cell in the olfactory epithelium that detects odor and transmits the information to the olfactory bulb of the brain.

Pheromones—Scent molecules made by the body that attract a mate and help initiate mating behaviors.

Receptor protein—A protein in a cell that sticks to a specific odorant or other signal molecule.

Stereospecific theory—The theory that the nose recognizes odorants when they bind to receptor proteins that recognize the odorants' molecular shape.

Volatile—Easily evaporated.

Vomeronasal organ—A pit on the roof of the mouth in most vertebrates that serves to detect odor molecules that are not as volatile as those detected by the nose.

Human vs. animal smell

There is no doubt that many animals have a sense of smell far superior than humans. This is why, even today, humans use dogs to find lost persons, hidden drugs, and **explosives**, although research on "artificial noses" that can detect scent even more reliably than dogs continues. Humans are called microsmatic, rather than macrosmatic, because of their humble abilities of olfaction.

Still, the human nose is capable of detecting over 10,000 different odors, some in the range of parts per trillion of air; and many researchers are beginning to wonder whether smell does not play a greater role in human **behavior** and **biology** than has been thought. For instance, research has shown that human mothers can smell the difference between a vest worn by their baby and one worn by another baby only days after the child's **birth**.

Yet some olfactory abilities of animals are probably beyond humans. Most **vertebrates** have many more olfactory nerve cells in a proportionately larger olfactory epithelium than humans, which probably gives them much more sensitivity to odors. The olfactory bulb in these animals takes up a much larger proportion of the brain than humans, giving them more ability to process and analyze olfactory information.

In addition, most land vertebrates have a specialized scent **organ** in the roof of their mouth called the vomeronasal organ (also known as the *Jacobson's organ* or the *accessory olfactory organ*). This organ, believed to be vestigial in humans, is a pit lined by a layer of cells with a similar structure to the olfactory epithelium, which feeds into its own processing part of the brain, called the accessory olfactory bulb (an area of the brain absent in humans).

The vomeronasal sense appears to be sensitive to odor molecules with a less volatile, possibly more complex molecular structure than the odorants to which humans are sensitive. This sense is important in reproduction, allowing many animals to sense sexual attractant odors, or *pheromones*, thus governing mating behavior. It is also used by reptilian and mammalian predators in tracking prey.

Unknown territory

Researchers have learned a lot about how the olfactory nerve cells detect odorants. However, they have not

yet learned how this information is coded by the olfactory cell. Other topics of future research will be how olfactory cell signals are processed in the olfactory bulb, and how this information relates to higher brain functions and our awareness of smell.

Scientists are only beginning to understand the role that smell plays in animal, and human,behavior. The vomeronasal sense of animals is still largely not understood. Some researchers have even suggested that the human vomeronasal organ might retain some function, and that humans may have pheromones that play a role in sexual attraction and mating - although this hypothesis is very controversial.

In addition, detailed study of the biology of the olfactory system might yield gains in other fields. For instance, olfactory nerve cells are the only nerve cells that are derived from the central nervous system that can regenerate, possibly because the stress of their exposure to the outside world gives them a limited lifespan. Some researchers hope that studying regeneration in olfactory nerve cells or even transplanting them elsewhere in the body can lead to treatments for as yet irreversible damage to the spine and brain.

Further Reading

Dajer, Tony. "How the nose knows." *Discover.* January 1992.

Farbman, Albert I. "The cellular basis of olfaction." *Endeavour.* vol. 18 no. 1, 1994.

Getchel, T. V. *et al.*, eds. *Smell and taste in health and disease.* New York: Raven Press, 1991.

"A nose by any other name." *The Economist.* September 1991.

Pennisi, Elizabeth. "Nose nerve cells show transplant potential." *Science News.* April 1993.

Whitfield, Philip, and D. M. Stoddart. *Hearing, taste and smell: pathways of perception.* Tarrytown, NY: Torstar Books, 1984.

Kenneth B. Chiacchia

Smog

Smog refers to an atmospheric condition of atmospheric instability, poor visibility, and large concentrations of gaseous and particulate air pollutants. The word "smog" is an amalgam of the words "smoke" and "fog." There are two types of smog: reducing smog characterized by **sulfur dioxide** and particulates, and photochemical smog characterized by **ozone** and other oxidants.

Reducing Smog

Reducing smog refers to **air pollution** episodes characterized by high concentrations of sulfur dioxide and smoke (or particulate **aerosols**). Reducing smog is also sometimes called London-type smog, because of famous incidents that occurred in that city during the 1950s.

Reducing smogs first became common when industrialization and the associated burning of **coal** caused severe air pollution by sulfur dioxide and soot in European cities. This air-pollution problem first became intense in the nineteenth century, when it was first observed to damage human health, buildings, and vegetation.

There have been a number of incidents of substantial increases in human illness and mortality caused by reducing smog, especially among higher-risk people with chronic respiratory or **heart diseases**. These toxic pollution events usually occurred during prolonged episodes of calm atmospheric conditions, which prevented the dispersion of emitted gases and particulates. These circumstances resulted in the accumulation of large atmospheric concentrations of sulfur dioxide and particulates, sometimes accompanied by a natural fog, which became blackened by soot. The term smog was originally coined as a label for these coincident occurrences of atmospheric pollution by sulfur dioxide and particulates.

Coal smoke, in particular, has been recognized as a pollution problem in England and elsewhere in **Europe** for centuries, since at least 1500. Dirty, pollution-laden fogs occurred especially often in London, where they were called "pea-soupers." The first convincing linkage of a substantial increase in human mortality and an event of air pollution was in Glasgow in 1909, when about 1,000 deaths were attributed to a noxious smog during an episode of atmospheric stagnation. A North American example occurred in 1948 in Donora, Pennsylvania, an industrial town located in a valley near Pittsburgh. In that case, a persistent fog and stagnant air during a four-day period coupled with large emissions of sulfur dioxide and particulates from heavy industries to cause severe air pollution. A large increase in the rate of human mortality was associated with this smog; 20 deaths were caused in a population of only 14,100. An additional 43% of the population was made ill in Donora, 10% severely so.

The most famous episode of reducing smog was the so-called "killer smog" that afflicted London in the early winter of 1952. In this case, an extensive atmospheric stability was accompanied by a natural, white fog. In London, these conditions transformed into a noxious "black fog" with almost **zero** visibility, as the concentrations of sulfur dioxide and particulates progressively built up. The most important sources of emissions of these pollutants were the use of coal for the generation of **electricity**, for other industrial purposes, and to **heat** homes because of the cold temperatures. In total, this

smog caused 18 days of greater-than-usual mortality, and 3,900 deaths were attributed to the deadly episode, mostly of elderly or very young persons, and those with pre-existing respiratory or coronary diseases.

Smogs like the above were common in industrialized cities of Europe and **North America**, and they were mostly caused by the uncontrolled burning of coal. More recently, the implementation of clean-air policies in many countries has resulted in large improvements of air quality in cities, so that severe reducing smogs no longer occur there. Once the severe effects of reducing smogs on people, buildings, vegetation, and other resources and values became recognized, mitigative actions were developed and implemented.

However, there are still substantial problems with reducing smogs in rapidly industrializing regions of eastern Europe, the former Soviet Union, China, India, and elsewhere. In these places, the social priority is to achieve rapid economic growth, even if environmental quality is compromised. As a result, control of the emissions of pollutants is not very stringent, and reducing smogs are still a common problem.

Oxidizing Smog

To a large degree, oxidizing or Los Angeles-type smogs have supplanted reducing smog in importance in most industrialized countries. Oxidizing smogs are common in sunny places where there are large emissions to the atmosphere of nitric oxide and hydrocarbons, and where the atmospheric conditions are frequently stable. Oxidizing smogs form when those emitted (or primary) pollutants are transformed through photochemical reactions into **secondary pollutants**, the most important of which are the strong oxidant gases, ozone and peroxyacetyl nitrate. These secondary gases are the major components of oxidizing smog that are harmful to people and vegetation.

Typically, the concentrations of these various chemicals vary predictably during the day, depending on their rates of **emission**, the intensity of sunlight, and atmospheric stability. In the vicinity of Los Angeles, for example, ozone concentrations are largest in the early-to-mid afternoon, after which these gases are diluted by fresh air blowing inland from the Pacific Ocean. These winds blow the polluted smog further inland, where pine **forests** are affected on the windward slopes of nearby mountains. The photochemical reactions also cease at night, because sunlight is not available then. This sort of daily cycle is typical of places that experience oxidizing smog.

Humans are sensitive to ozone, which causes irritation and damage to membranes of the **respiratory system** and eyes, and induces **asthma**. People vary greatly in their sensitivity to ozone, but hypersensitive individuals can suffer considerable discomfort from exposure to oxidizing smog. However, in contrast to some of the events of reducing smog, ozone and oxidizing smog more generally do not appear to cause the death of many large people. Ozone is also by far the most important gaseous pollutant in North America, in terms of causing damage to agricultural and wild plants.

Further Reading

Freedman, B. *Environmental Ecology.* 2nd ed. San Diego: Academic Press, 1994.

Harrison, R.M., and R.E. Hester. (eds.). *Air Pollution and Health.* Royal Society of Chemistry, 1998.

Hemond, H. F., and E. J. Fechner. *Chemical Fate and Transport in the Environment.* San Diego: Academic Press, 1994.

Warner, C.F., W.T. Davis, and K. Wark. *Air Pollution: Its Origin and Control.* Addison-Wesley Pub., 1997

Bill Freedman

Snails

Snails are **mollusks** typically with a coiled, more or less helical, shell as their most conspicuous external feature. When active, snails creep on a broad muscular foot, and display a head with eyes and sensory tentacles. Inside the shell is an asymmetrical visceral **mass** and one or more gills or lungs used for **respiration**. Beneath the head is a mouth equipped with a radula, a spiky, long, rasping tongue-like **organ** used to scrape **algae** off **rocks** or to bore holes in the shells of other mollusks. The shell of snails is secreted by an enveloping layer of **tissue** called the mantle. Some snails, such as the tiny caecums of **salt** marshes, may be only 0.08 in (2 mm) in height, while other species, such as the horse conch of southern Florida, may grow to 23.6 in (60 cm).

The degree of coiling of the shells is highly variable from one species to another. **Limpets** exhibit very little coiling, and abalones have a shell that is broad and flat, with scarcely two-and-a-half turns or whorls. In terebrids, there may be as many as 25 coils with a spire so sharp that it is difficult to count the smaller whorls. In a peculiar snail called *Vermicularia,* the turns lose contact as the shell grows, and a process of uncoiling occurs, resulting in a shell that looks like certain calcareous worm tubes. The coiling of the shells of snails may be right-handed or left-handed. Among the oldest fossils the types were of roughly equal **frequency**, but most living species are right-handed. If one holds a snail shell with

A land snail.

the central axis vertical and the spire on top, the opening, from which emerge the head and foot, is usually on the right. In the whelk *Busycon perversum,* the aperture is on the left. Many snails have a partly mineralized, leathery operculum that closes the door on predators when the soft parts are withdrawn inside the shell.

Snails, **slugs**, and nudibranchs are classified in the class Gastropoda (meaning stomach-foot) in the phylum Molluska. There are more species of gastropods than species of the other five classes of mollusks combined. The exact number is uncertain, because new species are found whenever a biologist enters an area rarely visited by collectors, and gastropod taxonomists are constantly adding and subtracting species from the list of those already named and described. Estimates range from a total of 55,000 to 100,000 species of mollusks.

Snails are assigned to subclasses according to the position of the gills: for example, the Prosobranchia have gills in front of the **heart** and other viscera, while the Opisthobranchia have gills behind. Associated with this anatomical difference, the prosobranchs have the auricle of the heart anterior to the ventricle and the visceral nerve cord in a figure eight, while opisthobranchs have auricle posterior to ventricle, and an oval nerve loop. The Prosobranchia, which are entirely marine, are further divided into order Archaeogastropoda, with paired gills and numerous teeth in the radula, and the order Caenogastropoda, with a single set of gills and few teeth. The prefixes mean ancient and recent, respectively, suggesting that the first set of traits evolved earlier. The Nudibranchia (sea slugs) lack a shell and have atypical gills as adults, although the young look very much like other snails. The third subclass, the Pulmonata, contains all snails with a lung rather than gills, and includes most of the terrestrial snails and many of the **freshwater** snails.

The common names whelk and conch refer to large snails. Whelk, derived from an old English word, is reserved for members of a single family (the Buccinidae), containing animals up to 6 in (15.2 cm) in height, which are predators and scavengers of the northern Atlantic littoral zone. Their empty shells are often inhabited by hermit **crabs**.

Conch comes from the Latin and Spanish *concha,* meaning shell. Conchs are the largest snails, with enough meat in the foot to make them popular in stews and salads. The species names of conchs indicate their size. *Strombus gigas,* the queen conch (family Strom-

bidae), has a massive shell with a pink lining, up to 11.8 in (30 cm) high. *Pleuroploca gigantea,* the Florida horse conch (family Fasciolaridae), has an even larger but somewhat thinner shell up to 23.6 in (60 cm) high. The area around Key West, Florida, has been called the Conch Republic, and people there are known as "conchs." Both **bivalves** and gastropods are found as fossils in early Cambrian rocks, which contain the first abundant **animal** fossils. In geological terms, many forms appeared abruptly, giving rise to the expression "Cambrian explosion" to signify the metazoan **radiation** of 550 million years ago. The Burgess Shale, an exceptionally well-preserved record of animal life of the mid-Cambrian, contains slit-shells, snails similar to modern species of *Pleurotomaria.* The slit-shells are assigned to the order Archaeogastropoda, having two long gill plumes, regarded as a primitive feature. The right gill is absent in the Caenogastropoda.

The consensus among zoologists is that the mollusks evolved from a worm-like ancestor, because patterns of early development, very conservative traits, are similar to those of living worms. Most frequently mentioned are sipunculids, but polychaetes, and echiurid worms are also good candidates for the living worms most resembling the presumed ancestor of mollusks. These groups share spiral cleavage and determinate development. When the fertilized egg begins to divide into 2, 4, 8, 16, etc. cells, division is not at right angles to the previous **plane** of cleavage but in an oblique direction, so that the new cells from a spiral pattern, quite unlike the orthoradial cleavage pattern seen in echinoderms, for example. Determinate development means that each part of the surface of the egg leads to a definite structure of the embryo, such as gut, head, limbs, and so on. In other words, the fates of the cells produced in early divisions are fixed. This is a feature of development in **arthropods**, annelids, and mollusks, taken to indicate that the phyla are related. With the fossil evidence so ambiguous and DNA data relatively sparse, relations among the phyla have had to depend heavily on features of early development Spiral cleavage, in a way, foreshadows not only the later coiling of the shell but another type of twisting that occurs during development, known as torsion. As the young snail grows, the whole visceral sac rotates about a longitudinal axis 180° or half a turn to the right. With respect to the head and foot, the midgut and anus are at first situated ventro-posteriorly, and after torsion they are displaced dorsad and to the right. This puts the end of the gut in the mantle cavity, above the head. The gonad and digestive gland lie in the hind end of the animal, which is quite isolated from the outside, inside the spire in coni-spiral forms. The result of torsion is an embryo that looks symmetrical externally, but is twisted inside. Gastropod torsion is a morphogenic event that enables the veliger larva to retract head and foot completely and seal the opening of the shell with the operculum. The condition persists in most juvenile and adult snails, although some opisthobranchs undergo de-torsion. It seems reasonable, but the evidence fails to support the hypothesis that torsion was the result of selective pressure to improve defense against predation. This idea was tested experimentally: planktonic predators devoured pre- and post-torsion veligers with equal frequency.

It seems probable that prosobranchs with shells coiled in one plane were first in **evolution**, and that the piling up of whorls to make sharply pointed shells occurred in several lines. Opisthobranchs show loss of gill on one side and loss of shell in family Aplysidae and order Nudibranchia, indicating a more recent origin. Finally, the pulmonates probably derived from opisthobranchs by development of a lung from the mantle cavity when the snails invaded the land in the Mesozoic Era.

Regarding the **biology** of reproduction, snails are generally of two sexes. They mate, the female receives sperm from the male, and lays fertilized eggs, which develop into swimming larvae. The pulmonates, a large group that includes terrestrial snails and many that live in lakes and ponds, have a different method. They are hermaphroditic, each individual is both male and female, and when they mate each snail fertilizes the eggs of the other. Then each animal deposits a jelly-coated mass of developing eggs in a place selected to avoid drying out or predation. A number of gastropods, such as limpets, are sequential hermaphrodites, the same individual is male at first maturity, and later becomes female. Female snails are usually larger than males.

Snails have occupied practically every type of **habitat** that supports animal life. Dehydration appears to be the greatest danger for terrestrial snails, while predation is the greatest danger for marine snails. Bieler has estimated that 53% of all snail species are prosobranchs, largely marine, 4% opisthobranchs, entirely marine, and the remaining 43% pulmonates, terrestrial and freshwater. In intertidal zones, numbers of prosobranchs such as the common periwinkle *Littorina littorea* seem as uncountable as stars in the sky. According to Abbott, *Littorina* probably reached **North America** from **Europe** on driftwood "before the time of the Vikings" (about 1000 A.D.) and gradually extended its range from Newfoundland to Ocean City, Maryland. In exchange, about 100 years ago we gave northern Europe the common slipper shell *Crepidula fornicata,* which has proliferated to the point of being a pest of English oyster beds.

Shell collecting has been a popular hobby for about 200 years, and the most attractive and valuable

shells are those of snails. Visitors to the beaches of southwest Florida can hardly avoid becoming collectors, the shells are so varied and abundant. Malacologists have mixed feelings about shell collecting. No matter how rare or how beautiful, a shell that lacks a label specifying date, place, conditions, and name of collector is scientifically worthless.

A number of snails are of culinary interest, especially in France and in French restaurants worldwide. Escargots are usually the large land snails *Helix pomatia* or *Helix aspersa,* both often the subjects of biochemical studies. *Helix aspersa*, from the Mediterranean, has escaped and multiplied in Charleston, South Carolina and other southern towns. Called the speckled garden snail, these animals can be prevented from destroying garden plants by using them as a table delicacy. In Burgundy, France, snails are served with garlic butter and much discussion of the proper wine to accompany them.

Marine snails are edible also, although not as popular as marine bivalves such as scallops and oysters. Abalones are also called ormers, and furnish a kind of seafood steak in coastal regions. After eliminating the visceral mass, the meat is tenderized with a wooden hammer ("pas d'ormeau sans marteau"), and is best fried or en blanquette, a white stew. The foot of the whelk *Buccinum undatum* is cooked and served either cold or warm in a white wine sauce.

Further Reading

Abbott, R. T. *Seashells of North America.* Golden Press: New York, 1968.

Bieler, R. "Gastropod Phylogeny and Systematics." *Annual Review of Ecological Systematics.* 23 (1992): 311-338.

Emerson, W. K., and M. K. Jacobson. *The American Museum of Natural History Guide to Shells.* New York: Knopf, 1976.

Ruppert, E., and R. Fox. *Seashore Animals of the Southeast.* Columbia: University of South Carolina Press, 1988.

Simon, Hilda. *Snails of Land and Sea.* New York: Vanguard, 1976.

Vermeij, G. J. *A Natural History of Shells.* Princeton, NJ: Princeton University Press, 1993.

Carl S. Hammen

Snakeflies

Snakeflies are **insects** in the family Raphidiidae, in the order Neuroptera, which also contains the closely related alderflies (Sialidae) and **dobsonflies** (Corydalidae). There are not many **species** of snakeflies. The approximately 20 species that occur in **North America** are all western in their distributions.

Snakeflies have a complete **metamorphosis**, with four stages in their **life history**: egg, larva, pupa, and adult. The larvae of snakeflies are terrestrial, usually occurring under loose **bark** of trees, or sometimes in litter on the forestfloor. Snakefly larvae are predators, especially of **aphids**, caterpillars, and the larvae of wood-boring **beetles**.

The adult stage of snakeflies is a weakly flying **animal**. Adult snakeflies are also predators of other insects, although they are rather short-lived, and their biological purpose is focused on breeding. Their eggs are usually laid in crevices in the bark of trees.

Like other insects in the order Neuroptera, adult snakeflies have long, transparent wings, with a fine venation network. The common name of the snakeflies derives from the superficially snaky appearance that is suggested by the unusually long, necklike appearance of the front of their thorax (that is, the prothorax), and their rather long, tapering head.

Agulla unicolor is a relatively widespread, dark-brown species of snakefly that occurs in montane **forests** of western North America. *Raphidia bicolor* is another western species, which occurs in apple orchards and can be a valuable **predator** of the codling moth (*Carpocapsa pomonella*), an important pest.

Bill Freedman

Snakes

Snakes are limbless **reptiles** with an elongated, cylindrical body, scaly skin, lidless eyes, and a forked tongue. Most **species** are non-venomous, some are mildly venomous, and others produce a deadly venom. All snakes are carnivores (or meat-eaters). They are also cold blooded (or ectotherms), meaning their body **temperature** is determined by the environment, rather than being internally regulated (however, snakes will bask in the **sun** to warm up, and hide in shade to cool down). Because they are ectotherms, snakes are found mainly in tropical and temperate regions throughout the world, and are rare or absent in cold climatic zones.

The 2,700 species of snakes fall into three superfamilies. The Scolecophidia (or Typhlopoidea) comprised the **blindsnakes**. The Boidea includes relatively primitive (i.e., evolutionarily more ancient) snakes, and includes the family Boidae, consisting of the **boas** and **pythons**. The Colubroidea includes the advanced (i.e.,

more recent) snakes, and includes the family Colubridae (harmless king snakes), the Elapidae (venomous cobras and their relatives), and the Viperidae (adders and pit **vipers**, which are also venomous).

The family Colubridae is huge, with over 300 genera and 1,400 species, and includes the majority of living species. Most colubrids are harmless (e.g., king snakes). However, the rear-fanged snakes (which lack hollow fangs) have a poison that they inject by chewing on the **prey**, rather than by a strike. The family Elapidae includes most of the poisonous snakes (cobras, coral snakes, mambas, and kraits), which have fixed, grooved or hollow fangs in the front of the mouth. The base of the fangs is connected to a venom gland, and poison is injected when the victim is bitten. The family Viperidae includes the vipers and pit vipers, which are the most specialized venom injectors. These snakes have long, hollow fangs that fold back when the mouth is closed, and swing forward and down when the mouth is open in the strike position. The pit vipers include some of the most dangerous snakes in the Americas, such as the rattlesnakes, **water** moccasin, copperhead, bushmaster, and fer-de-lance. In the United States, the venomous snakes include the rattlesnakes, cottonmouth, coral snake, and copperhead. Many other venomous snakes are found in **Australia**, **Africa**, **Asia**, and **South America**.

The thread snake (4.5 in long; 11.5 cm) is the shortest snake, while the longest is the South American anaconda, measuring up to 37 ft (11 m). Snakes are among the most feared and misunderstood of any animals, and are even blamed for the downfall of humankind in the biblical story of Adam and Eve.

Evolution

Along with lizards, snakes are classified in the order Squamata, one of the four living orders of reptiles. The other three are the Crocodilia (**crocodiles** and alligators), Testudinae (tortoises and **turtles**), and Rhynchocephalia (the tuatara). Snakes are the most recently evolved of the modern reptiles, first appearing in the fossil record about 120 million years ago. It is thought that snakes evolved from lizard-like creatures that gradually lost their legs, external ears, eyelids, frills, and spines, presumably to facilitate unencumbered burrowing and movement through thick underbrush when foraging for food or fleeing from predators.

Appearance and behavior

Scales

Snakes are covered in dry, glistening scales. Many species have a body pattern of various colors, sometimes quite bright. The dorsal (or back) scales protect the body from **friction** and dehydration, and the ventral (or belly) scales aid in movement by gripping the surface while powerful muscles propel the body forward, usually with a side-to-side, waving **motion**. This method of locomotion means that snakes cannot move backward.

Instead of eyelids, the eyes of snakes are covered and protected by a single, clear scale. Several times a year, at intervals determined by the growth rate, age, and rate of **metabolism**, snakes molt their epidermal skin, shedding it in one complete piece. They do this by rubbing their head against a stick or another rough surface, which starts the shedding at the mouth. Once the first bit of molted skin catches on something, the snake literally crawls out of the rest, which is discarded inside-out.

Hunting and defense

The coloring and patterning of many snakes provides an excellent camouflage from predators and prey. **Tree** snakes may be green colored as camouflage amongst leaves; ground snakes may be brown or dusty gray to blend with litter and **rocks**; and sea snakes are dark above and light beneath (this is known as counter-shading, and is also commonly seen in **fish**). Some snakes are brightly colored with vivid patterns, such as the highly venomous coral snake with its red (or orange), black, and yellow (or white) rings. Often, poisonous snakes are highly colorful as a way of warning potential predators to leave them alone.

Snakes attack prey only when hungry, and will try to bite a human only if they feel seriously threatened. If possible, a frightened snake will almost always try to flee. However, if there is no time for flight, or if a snake feels cornered, it may try to strike in defense. Venomous snakes have two fangs in the upper jaw that can penetrate the flesh of their prey, while poison **glands** pump poison through grooves inside or outside of the fangs. When hunting, some poisonous snakes inject their prey with toxin and wait until the **animal** is no longer struggling before eating it. In this use, snake venom is a feeding aid, serving to both subdue the prey and to aid in its digestion. Snake venoms are cocktails of complex enzyme-like chemicals, and they act on the prey in several different ways. Some venoms are neurotoxins, paralyzing parts of the **nervous system**. Others prevent the **blood** from clotting, while yet others cause blood to clot. Some destroy red and white blood cells, and others destroy **tissue** more generally.

Non-venomous constrictors (such as boas, pythons, and anacondas) simultaneously snatch their prey in their jaws, and rapidly coil their body around the animal, squeezing it to prevent breathing. The prey dies by suf-

focation; its bones are usually not broken during the constriction.

Feeding

The teeth of snakes cannot chew and break up a carcass, so they swallow their prey whole. With the aid of elasticized ligaments on their specially hinged lower jaw, the mouth can open to an incredible 150-degree **angle**, permitting the consumption of animals several times larger than the snake's head. The largest recorded feast was a 130-pound antelope swallowed by an African rock python.

Snakes' teeth curve inward and help prevent their prey from escaping. The strong jaw and throat muscles work the food down the esophagus and into the stomach, where digestion begins. Digestion time varies according to temperature. In one study, a captive python at a temperature of 87°F (30°C) digested a rabbit in four days; at a cooler temperature (64°F; 18°C) digestion took more than two weeks.

The interval between meals also varies, and some snakes may go weeks or even months without food. In temperate climates, snakes fast during the winter **hibernation**, which may last six months. Pregnant females may hibernate and fast for seven months, and both sexes fast briefly before shedding.

Snakes have extremely poor eyesight and **hearing**. They detect their prey through vibrations and **heat** and chemical perceptions, all of which are highly developed and efficient senses in snakes. Pit vipers (such as rattlesnakes) have tiny hollows (or "pits") on the side or top of their snout, which have sensors that can detect the body heat of a bird or mammal at a considerable **distance**. The flicking, forked tongue of a snake acts as a chemical collector, drawing chemical "smells" into the mouth to be analyzed by sensors (Jacobson's organs) on the palate. This mechanism also allows male snakes to detect the **hormones** of females in reproductive condition.

Mating and reproduction

Insemination takes place through the vent (or cloaca) of the female, an opening located beneath and near the end of the body, just before the tail. Male snakes lack a true penis, and instead have paired structures called hemipenes, which emerge from their vent during mating. Sperm runs in a groove along each hemipenis. Female snakes may mate with several different males. Gestation time varies widely, from only 30 days in some species to as much as 300 days in others. Most species lay eggs, with the young forcing their way out of the pliable, porous shell when their incubation is over. Other snakes give **birth** to fully formed young—the eggs are retained in the body of the female until they hatch, so that "live" young are born (this is known as ovoviviparay). Some species of pythons incubate their eggs—the female coils around her eggs and shivers to generate heat, keeping them warm until they hatch. In general, however, snake eggs and young receive little or no parental care.

KEY TERMS

Carnivore—A flesh-eating animal.

Ectotherm—A cold-blooded animal, whose internal body temperature is similar to that of their environment. Ectotherms produce little body heat, and are dependent on external sources (such as the sun) to keep their body temperature high enough to function efficiently.

Jacobson's organs—Chemical sensors located on the palate of a snake, and used to detect chemical "smells."

Molt—To shed a outer layer of skin (epidermis) at regular intervals.

Snakes and humans

Snakes have fascinated and frightened people for millennia. Some cultures worship snakes, seeing them as creators and protectors, while others fear snakes as devils and symbols of death.

While some people keep snakes as interesting pets, most people harbor an irrational fear of these reptiles. Unfortunately, this attitude leads to the deaths of many harmless snakes. Certainly, a few deadly species of snakes can kill a human, and no snake should be handled unless positively identified as harmless. However, the estimated risk of a person suffering a bite from a venomous snake in the United States is 20 times less than being struck by lightning—this is an extremely small risk. Snakes are useful predators, helping to reduce populations of pest **rats** and **mice**. A well-educated, healthy respect for snakes is a benefit to both snakes and humans.

See also Elapid snakes.

Further Reading

Angeletti, L. R., et al. "Healing Rituals and Sacred Serpents." *The Lancet*. 340 (25 July 1992): 223-25.

Diamond, Jared. "Dining with Snakes." *Discover.* (April 1994): 48-59.

Forsyth, Adrian. "Snakes Maximize Their Success with Minimal Equipment." *The Smithsonian.* (February 1988): 158-65.

Indian paintbrush (*Castilleja* sp.).

Mattison, Christopher. *Snakes of the World*. New York: Facts on File, 1986.

Morris, Ramona, and Desmond Morris. *Man and Snakes*. New York: McGraw-Hill, 1965.

Pinney, Roy. *The Snake Book*. New York: Doubleday, 1981.

Roberts, Mervin F. *A Complete Introduction to Snakes*. Neptune City, N.J.: T. F. H. Publications, 1987.

Seigel, Richard A., and Joseph T. Collins. *Snakes: Ecology and Behavior*. New York: McGraw-Hill, 1993.

Schwenk, Kurt. "Why Snakes Have Forked Tongues." *Science*. 263 (18 March 1994): 1573-77.

Marie L. Thompson

Snapdragon family

The snapdragon or figwort family (Scrophulariaceae), class Dicotyledon, is composed of about 3-4,000 species and 200 genera of vascular plants. Species in this family occur on all continents except **Antarctica**, but are most diverse in temperate and **mountain** ecosystems.

Most species in the snapdragon family are perennial herbs, growing new above-ground shoots each year from a long-lived rootstock or **rhizome** system. Some species are partially parasitic, obtaining some of their **nutrition** by tapping the roots of other species of plants. The flowers of these plants are bilaterally symmetric (each half is a mirror image of the other), and are usually pollinated by **insects**. Like other flowers that must attract animals to achieve **pollination**, those of most species in the snapdragon family are showy and attractive.

Some species are of economic importance. An **alkaloid** chemical variously known as **digitalis**, digitalin, or digitoxin is obtained from the foxglove (*Digitalis purpurea*), and is a valuable cardiac glycoside, used in stimulating the **heart**. In larger doses, however, this chemical can be poisonous.

Various species in the snapdragon family are grown as attractive ornamentals in gardens and greenhouses. Some of the more commonly cultivated groups include the snapdragons (*Antirrhinum* spp.), slipper **flower** (*Calceolaria*), foxglove, monkey flower (*Mimulus* spp.), speedwell (*Veronica* spp.), and beard-tongue (*Penstemon* spp.).

Many species in the snapdragon family are native to various habitats in **North America**. Some of the most attractive wild species are the paintbrushes, such as the

spectacular, scarlet painted-cup (*Castilleja coccinea*). Other attractive native species include the turtlehead (*Chelone glabra*), the various species of eyebright (*Euphrasia* spp.), and the louseworts and **wood** betonies (*Pedicularis* spp.). The latter group includes the Furbish's lousewort (*P. furbishiae*), a rare and **endangered species** that only occurs in the valley of the Saint John River in Maine and New Brunswick. The Furbish's lousewort became highly controversial because of the risks posed to its survival by the construction of a hydroelectric reservoir that would have flooded most of its known **habitat**.

Some species in the snapdragon family have been introduced to North America, where they have become weeds. Examples of these invasive plants include the mullein (*Verbascum thapsis*), displaying yellow flowers and developing a flowering stalk 6.6 ft (2 m) or more tall, and the smaller **plant** known as butter-and-eggs (*Linaria vulgaris*).

See also Parasites.

Bill Freedman

Snow see **Precipitation**
Snowdrop see **Amaryllis family**

Soap

Soap is a cleansing agent created by the chemical reaction of a fatty acid with an alkali **metal** hydroxide. Chemically speaking, it is a **salt** composed of an alkalimetal, such as **sodium** or potassium, and a mixture of "fatty" **carboxylic acids**. The cleansing action of soap comes from its unique ability to surround oil particles, causing them to be dispersed in **water** and easily rinsed away. Soap has been used for centuries and continues to be widely used as a cleansing agent, mild antiseptic and ingestible antidote to some forms of poisoning.

The history of soap

It is unknown exactly when soap was discovered. Data suggest it was known to the Phoenicians as early as around 600 B.C., and was used to some extent by the ancient Romans. During these times, soap was made by boiling tallow (**animal fat**) or vegetable oils with alkali containing **wood** ashes. This costly method of production coupled with negative social attitudes toward cleanliness made soap a luxury item affordable only to the rich until the late eighteenth century.

Methods of soapmaking improved when two scientific discoveries were made in the late eighteenth and early nineteenth centuries. In 1790, the French chemist Nicholas Leblanc (1742-1806) invented a process for creating caustic soda (**sodium hydroxide**) from common table salt (**sodium chloride**). His invention made inexpensive soap manufacture possible by enabling chemists to develop a procedure whereby natural fats and oils can react with caustic soda. The method was further refined when another French chemist, Michel Eugène Chevreul (1786-1889), discovered the nature of fats and oils in 1823. As soap production became less expensive and attitudes toward cleanliness changed, soapmaking became an important industry.

What is soap?

Soap is a salt of an alkali metal, such as sodium or potassium, with a mixture of "fatty" carboxylic acids. It is the result of a chemical reaction, called saponification, between triglycerides and a base such as sodium hydroxide. During this reaction, the triglycerides are broken down into their component **fatty acids**, and neutralized into salts by the base. In addition to soap, this chemical reaction produces glycerin.

Soap has the general chemical formula RCOOX. The X represents an alkali metal, an element in the first column on the **periodic table** of elements. The R represents a **hydrocarbon** chain composed of a line of anywhere from 8-22 **carbon atoms** bonded together and surrounded by **hydrogen** atoms. An example of a soap **molecule** is sodium palmitate (C16).

How is soap made?

Before the end of World War II, soap was manufactured by a "full-boiled" process. This process required mixing fats and oils in large, open kettles, with caustic soda (NaOH) in the presence of steam. With the addition of tons of salt, the soap was made to precipitate out and float to the top. Here, it was skimmed off and made into flakes or bars. This process required large amounts of **energy** and over six days to complete one batch.

After World War II, a continuous process of soap manufacture became popular. In the continuous process of soap manufacture, fats and oils react directly with caustic soda. The saponification reaction is accelerated by being run at high temperatures (248°F; 120°C) and pressures (2 atm). Glycerin is washed out of the system and soap is obtained after centrifugation and **neutralization**. This process has several advantages over the "full-boiled" process. It is more energy efficient, time efficient, allows greater control of soap composition and

concentration, and the important by-product, glycerin, is readily recovered.

Both manufacturing methods yield pure soap. Certain chemicals can be added to this pure soap to improve its physical characteristics. The foam in soap is enhanced by additives such as fatty acids. Glycerin is added to reduce the harshness of soap on the skin. Other additives include fragrances and dyes.

How does soap work?

Because soap is a salt, it partially separates into its component ions in water. The active ion of the soap molecule is the $RCOO^-$. The two ends of this ion behave in different fashions. The carboxylate end ($-COO^-$) is hydrophilic (water-loving), and is said to be the "head" of the ion. The hydrocarbon portion is lipophilic (oil-loving) and is called the "tail" of the molecule. This unusual molecular structure is responsible for the unique surface and **solubility** characteristics of soaps and other surfactants (agents affecting the surface of a material).

In a mixture of soap and water, soap molecules are uniformly dispersed. This system is not a true solution, however, because the hydrocarbon portions of the soap's ions are attracted to each other and form spherical aggregates known as micelles. The molecules tails that are incompatible with water are in the interior of these micelles, while the hydrophilic heads remain on the outside to interact with water. When oil is added to this system, it is taken into these micelles as tiny particles. Then it can be rinsed away.

Characteristics and uses of soap

Soaps are excellent cleansing agents and have good biodegradability. A serious drawback which reduces their general use, is the tendency for the carboxylate ion to react with $Ca+$ and $Mg+$ ions in **hard water**. The result is a water insoluble salt which can be deposited on clothes and other surfaces. These hard water plaques whiten fabric colors and also create rings found in sinks and bath tubs. Another problem with using soaps is their ineffectiveness under acidic conditions. In these cases, soap salts do not dissociate into their component ions, and this renders them ineffective as cleansing agents.

Although primarily used for their cleansing ability, soaps are also effective as mild antiseptics and ingestible antidotes for mineral acid or heavy metal poisoning. Special metallic soaps, made from soap and heavier metals, are used as additives in polishes, inks, paints, and lubricating oils.

See also Emulsion.

KEY TERMS

Carboxylic acid—A compound containing a carbon atom chemically bonded to two oxygen atoms.

Continuous process—A method of manufacturing soap which involves removing glycerin during the reaction between fats and oils and caustic soda.

Emulsifier—Chemical which has both water soluble and oil soluble portions and is capable of forming nearly homogenous mixtures of typically incompatible materials such as oil and water.

Fatty Acid—A carboxylic acid which is attached to a chain of at least 8 carbon atoms.

Full-boiled process—A method of manufacturing soap which involves boiling fats and oils with caustic soda.

Micelle—Particle formed when the molecules of an emulsifier surround oil droplets allowing them to be dispersed in water.

Saponification—A chemical reaction involving the breakdown of triglycerides to component fatty acids, and the conversion of these acids to soap.

Triglycerides—A molecule containing three fatty acids chemically bonded to a glycol molecule.

Further Reading

Boys, C. V. *Soap Bubbles: Their Colors and Forces Which Mold Them.* New York: Dover: 1959.

Fishbein, Morris, ed. *Medical Uses of Soap.* Philadelphia: J.B. Lippincott, 1945.

Garrett, H. E. *Surface Active Chemicals.* New York: Pergamon Press, 1972.

Levitt, Benjamin. *Oil, Fat and Soap.* New York: Chemical Publishing Co., 1951.

"Soap: Great American Clean." *Mademoiselle.* 97 (March 1991): 196-69.

Perry Romanowski
Randy Schueller

Sociobiology

Sociobiology, also called behavioral **ecology**, is the study of the **evolution** of social **behavior** in all organisms, including human beings. The highly complex behaviors of individual animals become even more intri-

cate when interactions among groups of animals are considered. **Animal** behavior within groups is known as *social* behavior. Sociobiology asks about the evolutionary advantages contributed by social behavior and describes a *biological* basis for such behavior. It is theory that uses **biology** and **genetics** to explain why people (and animals) behave the way they do.

Sociobiology is a relatively new science. In the 1970s, Edward O. Wilson, now a distinguished professor of biology at Harvard University, pioneered the subject. In his ground-breaking and controversial book, *Sociobiology: The New Synthesis*, Dr. Wilson introduced for the first time the idea that behavior is likely the product of an interaction between an individual's genetic makeup and the environment (or culture in the case of human beings). Wilson's new ideas rekindled the debate of "Nature vs. Nurture," wherein nature refers to genes and nurture refers to environment.

Sociobiology is often subdivided into three categories: narrow, broad, and pop sociobiology. Narrow sociobiology studies the function of specific behaviors, primarily in non-human animals. Broad sociobiology examines the biological basis and evolution of general social behavior. Pop sociobiology is concerned specifically with the evolution of human social behavior.

Sociobiologists focus on reproductive behaviors because reproduction is the mechanism by which genes are passed on to future generations. It is believed that behavior, physically grounded in an individual's genome (or genes), can be acted upon by **natural selection**. Natural selection exerts its influence based upon the fitness of an **organism**. Individuals that are *fit* are better suited (genetically) to their environment and therefore reproduce more successfully. An organism that is fit has more offspring than an individual that is unfit. Also, fitness requires that the resulting offspring must survive long enough to themselves reproduce. Because sociobiologists believe that social behavior is genetically based, they also believe that behavior is heritable and can therefore contribute to (or detract from) an individual's fitness. Examples of the kinds of reproductive interactions in which sociobiologists are interested include **courtship**, mating systems like monogamy (staying with one mate), polygamy (maintaining more than one female mate), and polyandry (maintaining more than one male mate), and the ability to attract a mate (called *sexual selection.*)

Sociobiology also examines behavior that indirectly contributes to reproduction. An example is the theory of optimal foraging which explains how animals use the least amount of **energy** to get the maximum amount of food. Another example is altruistic behavior (**altruism** means selfless). Dominance hierarchies, **territoriality**, ritualistic (or symbolic) behavior, communication (transmitting information to others through displays), and **instinct** versus **learning** are also topics interpreted by sociobiology.

Sociobiology applied to human behavior involves the idea that the human **brain** evolved to encourage social behaviors that increase reproductive fitness. For example, the capacity for learning in human beings is a powerful characteristic. It allows people to teach their relatives (or others) important life skills that are passed-down from generation to generation. However, the ability to learn is also a **variable** trait. That is, not every person learns as quickly or as well as every other person. A sociobiologist would explain that individuals who learn faster and more easily have increased fitness. Another example is smiling. The act of smiling in response to pleasurable experiences is a universal social behavior among people. Smiling is observed in every culture. Furthermore, smiling is an example of an instinct that is modified by experience. Therefore, because the behavior is instinctual, it has a genetic and inheritable basis. Because it is altered by experience, the behavior is socially relevant. Sociobiologists might speculate, then, that since smiling is a visual cue to other individuals that you are pleased, people who tend to smile more easily are more likely to attract a suitable mate, and are therefore more fit.

The discipline of sociobiology is an important set of ideas because nearly every animal species spends at least part of its life cycle in close association with other animals. However, it is also riddled with debate, principally because it attempts to not only explain the behavior of animals but also of human beings. More dangerously, it tries to describe "human nature." The idea that human behavior is subject to genetic control has been used in the past to justify racism, sexism, and class injustices. In this respect, sociobiology is similar to Social Darwinism. For this reason, sociobiology remains a controversial discipline. Further criticisms include the observation that sociobiology contains an inappropriate amount of anthropomorphism (giving human characteristics to animals) and it excessively generalizes from individuals to whole groups of organisms. Despite criticism, however, sociobiology is an enlightening new aspect of biology which, taken in context, can bridge the gap between life science and the humanities.

See also Evolutionary theory.

Sodium

The chemical element of **atomic number** 11. Symbol Na, **atomic weight** 22.9898, specific gravity 0.97, melting point 208°F (97.8°C), **boiling point** 1,621.4°F (883°C).

Sodium is the second element in group 1 of the **periodic table**. Its chemical symbol reflects its Latin name of natrium. The element was first isolated by the English chemist Sir Humphry Davy in 1807. Only one stable **isotope** of sodium exists in nature, sodium-23. However, at least six radioactive isotopes have been prepared synthetically. They include sodium-20, sodium-21, sodium-22, sodium-24, sodium-25, and sodium-26.

General properties

Sodium is a soft **metal** that can be cut easily with a table knife. Its **density** is so low that it will float when placed into **water**. At the same time, the metal is so active that it reacts violently with the water, producing **sodium hydroxide** and **hydrogen** gas as products. Sufficient **heat** is produced in the reaction to cause the metal to heat and to ignite the hydrogen produced in the reaction.

Freshly cut sodium metal has a bright, shiny surface that quickly becomes a dull gray as it reacts with **oxygen** in the air around it. Over time, the metal becomes covered with a white crust of sodium oxide that prevents further reaction of the metal and oxygen.

Sodium forms a very large number of compounds in nature, and an even larger number have been prepared synthetically. These compounds include binary compounds of sodium with metals, non-metals, and metalloids, as well as ternary, and more complex compounds. Included among these are such well-known substances as **sodium chloride** (table **salt**), **sodium bicarbonate** (baking soda), sodium borate (borax), **sodium carbonate** (soda ash), **monosodium glutamate (MSG)**, sodium hydroxide (caustic soda or lye), sodium nitrate (Chilean saltpeter), sodium silicate (water **glass**), and sodium tartrate (sal tartar).

Where it comes from

Sodium is the sixth most common element in the Earth's crust with an estimated abundance of 2.83%. It is the second most abundant element in sea water after **chlorine**. One point of interest is that, although the abundance of sodium and potassium is approximately equal in crustal **rocks**, the former is 30 times more abundant in sea water than is the latter. The explanation for this difference lies in the greater **solubility** of sodium compounds than of potassium compounds.

Sodium never occurs free in nature because it is so active. For all practical purposes, the only compound from which it is prepared commercially is sodium chloride. That compound is so abundant and so inexpensive that there is no economic motivation for selecting another sodium compound for its commercial production.

By far the largest producer of sodium chloride in the world is the United States, where about a quarter of the world's supply is obtained. China, Germany, the United Kingdom, France, India, and members of the former Soviet Union are other major producers of salt. The greatest portion of salt obtained in the United States comes from brine, a term used for any naturally occurring solution of sodium chloride in water. The term includes, but is not restricted to, sea water, subterranean wells, and **desert** lakes such as the Great Salt Lake and the Dead Sea. The second largest source of sodium chloride in the United States is rock salt. Rock salt is generally obtained from underground mines created by the **evaporation** and then the burying of ancient seas.

How the metal is obtained

The isolation of sodium from its compounds long presented a problem for chemists because of the element's reactivity. **Electrolysis** of a sodium chloride solution will not produce the element, for example, because any sodium produced in the reaction will immediately react with water .

The method finally developed by Sir Humphry Davy in the early nineteenth century has become the model on which modern methods for the production of sodium are based. In this method, a compound of sodium (usually sodium chloride) is first fused (melted) and then electrolyzed. In this process, liquid sodium metal collects at the **cathode** of the electrolytic cell and gaseous chlorine is released at the **anode**.

The apparatus most commonly used today for the preparation of sodium is the Downs cell, named for its inventor, J. Cloyd Downs. The Downs cell consists of a large **steel** tank lined with a refractory material containing an **iron** cathode near the bottom of the tank and a graphite anode near the top. A molten mixture of sodium chloride and **calcium** chloride is added to the tank. The presence of calcium chloride to the extent of about 60% lowers the melting point of the sodium chloride from 1,472°F (800°C) to about 1,076°F (580°C).

When an electrical current is passed through the mixture in the cell, sodium ions migrate to the cathode, where they pick up electrons and become sodium **atoms**. Chlorine ions migrate to the anode, where they lose electrons and become chlorine atoms. Since the molten sodium metal is less dense than the sodium chloride/calcium chloride mixture, it rises to the top of the cell and is drawn off. The chlorine gas escapes through a vent attached to the anode at the top of the cell. Sodium metal produced by this method is about 99.8% pure. The Downs cell is such an efficient and satisfactory method

for preparing sodium that the vast majority of the metal's production is accomplished by this means.

How we use it

Sodium metal has relatively few commercial uses. The most important is as a heat exchange medium in fast breeder nuclear reactors. A heat exchange medium is a material that transports heat from one place to another. In the case of a **nuclear reactor**, the heat exchange medium absorbs heat produced in the reactor core and transfers that heat to a cooling unit. In the cooling unit, the heat is released to the atmosphere, is used to boil water to power an electrical generating unit, or is transferred to a system containing circulating water for release to the environment.

Liquid sodium is a highly effective heat exchange medium for a number of reasons. First, it has a high **heat capacity** (that is, it can absorb a lot of heat per gram of metal) and a low **neutron** absorption cross-section (that is, it does not take up neutrons from the reactor core). At the same time, the metal has a low melting point and a low **viscosity**, allowing it to flow through the system with relatively little resistance.

For many years, the most important commercial application of sodium metal was in the manufacture of anti-knock additives such as tetraethyl and tetramethyl **lead**. An **alloy** of sodium and lead was used to react with alkyl chlorides (such as ethyl chloride) to produce these compounds. In 1959, about 70% of all the sodium produced in the United States was used for this purpose. As compounds of lead such as tetraethyl and tetramethyl lead have been phased out of use for environmental reasons, however, this use of sodium has declined dramatically.

Another important use of sodium metal is in the manufacture of other metals, such as **zirconium** and **titanium**. Originally, **magnesium** metal was the reducing agent of choice in these reactions, but sodium has recently become increasingly popular in the preparation of both metals. When sodium is heated with a chloride of one of these metals, it replaces (reduces) the metal to yield the pure metal and sodium chloride.

About 10% of all sodium produced is used to make specialized compounds such as sodium hydride (NaH), sodium peroxide (Na_2O_2), and sodium alkoxides (NaOR). Small amounts of the metal are used as a catalyst in the manufacture of synthetic elastomers.

Compounds of sodium

Sodium chloride is the most widely used sodium compound. Due to its availability and minimal amount of preparation, there is no need for it to be manufactured commercially. A large fraction of the sodium chloride used commercially goes to the production of other sodium compounds, such as sodium hydroxide, sodium carbonate, sodium sulfate, and sodium metal itself.

For many centuries, sodium chloride has also been used in the food industry, primarily as a preservative and to enhance the flavors of foods. In fact, many seemingly distinct methods of **food preservation**, such as curing, pickling, corning, and salting differ only in the way in which salt is used to preserve the food. Scientists are uncertain as to the mechanism by which salting preserves foods, but they believe that some combination of dehydration and high salinity create conditions unfavorable to the survival of pathogens.

Sodium hydroxide and sodium carbonate traditionally rank among the top 25 chemicals in terms of **volume** produced in the United States. In 1988, for example, the first of these was the seventh most widely produced chemical, with a production of 24.0 billion lb (10.9 billion kg), and the latter ranked number eleven, with a production of 19.1 billion lb (8.65 billion kg).

The number one use of sodium hydroxide is in the manufacture of a large number of other chemical products, the most important of which are **cellulose** products (including cellulose film) and rayon. **Soap** manufacture, **petroleum** refining, and pulp and **paper** production account for about one tenth of all sodium hydroxide use.

Two industries account for about one third each of all the sodium carbonate use in the United States. One of these is glass-making and the other is the production of soap, detergents, and other cleansing agents. Paper and pulp production, the manufacture of **textiles**, and petroleum production are other important users of sodium carbonate.

Ranking number 45 on the list of the top 50 chemicals produced in the United States in 1988 was sodium sulfate. For many years, the largest fraction of sodium sulfate (also known as salt cake) was used in the production of kraft paper and paperboard. In recent years, an increasing amount of the chemical has gone to the manufacture of glass and detergents.

Just behind sodium sulfate on the list of top 50 chemicals in 1988 was sodium silicate, also known as water glass. Water glass is used as a catalyst, in the production of soaps and detergents, in the manufacture of adhesives, in the treatment of water, and in the bleaching and sizing of textiles.

Chemical properties

As described above, sodium reacts violently with water and with oxygen to form sodium hydroxide and

KEY TERMS

Alkene—An organic compound whose molecules contain a carbon-carbon double bond.

Diene—An organic compound whose molecules contain two carbon-carbon double bonds.

Electrolysis—The process by which an electrical current is used to break down a compound into its component elements.

Heat exchange medium—A material that transports heat from one place to another.

Metalloid—An element with properties intermediary between those of a metal and a nonmetal.

Ternary compound—A compound that contains three elements.

Viscosity—The resistance to flow exhibited by a substance.

sodium oxide, respectively. The element also reacts vigorously with fluorine and chlorine, at room **temperature**, but with bromine and iodine only in the vapor phase. At temperatures above 392°F (200°C), sodium combines with hydrogen to form sodium hydride, NaH, a compound that then decomposes, but does not melt, at about 752°F (400°C).

Sodium reacts with **ammonia** in two different ways, depending upon the conditions under which the reaction takes place. In liquid ammonia with a catalyst of iron, cobalt or nickel, sodium reacts to form sodium amide ($NaNH_2$) and hydrogen gas. In the presence of hot coke (pure **carbon**), sodium reacts with ammonia to form sodium cyanide (NaCN) and hydrogen gas.

Sodium also reacts with a number of organic compounds. For example, when added to an **alcohol**, it reacts as it does with water, replacing a single hydrogen atom to form a compound known as an alkoxide. Sodium also reacts with alkenes and dienes to form addition products, one of which formed the basis of an early synthetic rubber known as buna (for *bu*tadiene and *Na* [for sodium]) rubber. In the presence of organic halides, sodium may replace the halogen to form an organic sodium derivative.

See also Sodium benzoate; Sodium hypochlorite.

Further Reading

Greenwood, N. N., and A. Earnshaw. *Chemistry of the Elements*. Oxford: Pergamon Press, 1990.

Hawley, Gessner G. *The Condensed Chemical Dictionary* .9th edition. New York: Van Nostrand Reinhold Company, 1977.

Joesten, Melvin O., David O. Johnson, John T. Netterville, and James L. Wood. *World of Chemistry*. Philadelphia: Saunders College Publishing, 1991.

Lemke, Charles H. *Kirk-Othmer Encyclopedia of Chemical Technology*. New York: John Wiley, 1981.

McGraw-Hill Encyclopedia of Science & Technology. 6th edition. New York: McGraw-Hill Book Company, 1987.

Newton, David E. *The Chemical Elements*. New York: Franklin Watts, 1994.

David E. Newton

Sodium benzoate

Sodium benzoate is the sodium **salt** of **benzoic acid**. It is an aromatic compound denoted by the chemical formula $C_7H_5NaO_2$ with a **molecular weight** of 144.11. In its refined form, sodium benzoate is a white, odorless compound that has a sweet, astringent **taste,** and is soluble in **water**. Sodium benzoate has antimicrobial characteristics, and is typically used as a preservative in food products.

Chemical & physical properties

Sodium benzoate is supplied as a white powder or flake. During use it is mixed dry in bulk liquids where it promptly dissolves. Approximately 1.75 oz (50 g) will readily dissolve in 3 fl oz (100 ml) of water. In contrast, benzoic acid has a significantly lower water **solubility** profile. When placed in water, sodium benzoate dissociates to form sodium ions and benzoic acid ions. Benzoic acid is a weak organic acid that contains a **carboxyl group** and occurs naturally in some foods; including cranberries, prunes, cinnamon and cloves. It is also formed by most **vertebrates** during **metabolism**.

Sodium benzoate is an antimicrobial active against most **yeast** and bacterial strains. It works by dissociating in the system and producing benzoic acid. Benzoic acid is highly toxic to microbes, however, it is less effective against molds. Overall, it is more effective as the **pH** of a system is reduced with the optimal functional range between pH 2.5-4.0. The antimicrobial effect is also enhanced by the presence of **sodium chloride**.

Production

There are three methods for the commercial preparation of sodium benzoate. In one method, naphthalene is oxidized with vanadium pentoxide to give phthalic an-

hydride. This is decarboxylated to yield benzoic acid. In a second method, toluene is mixed with **nitric acid** and oxidized to produce benzoic acid. In a third method, benzotrichloride is hydrolyzed and then treated with a mineral acid to give benzoic acid. Benzotrichloride is formed by the reaction of **chlorine** and toluene. In all cases, the benzoic acid is further refined to produce sodium benzoate. One way this is done is by dissolving the acid in a **sodium hydroxide** solution. The resulting chemical reaction produces sodium benzoate and water. The crystals are isolated by evaporating off the water.

Safety

Some toxicity testing has shown sodium benzoate to be poisonous at certain concentrations. However, research conducted by the U.S. Department of Agriculture (USDA) has found that in small doses and mixed with food, sodium benzoate is not deleterious to health. Similar conclusions were drawn about larger doses taken with food, although certain physiological changes were noted. Based on this research and subsequent years of safety data, the United States government has determined sodium benzoate to be generally recognized as safe (GRAS). It is allowed to be used in food products at all levels below 0.1%. Other countries allow higher levels, up to 1.25%.

Studies investigating the accumulation of sodium benzoate in the body have also been done. This led to the discovery of a natural metabolic process that combines sodium benzoate with glycine to produce hippuric acid, a material that is then excreted. This excretion mechanism accounts for nearly 95% of all the ingested sodium benzoate. The remainder is thought to be detoxified by conjugation with glycuronic acid.

Uses

Sodium benzoate has been used in a wide variety of products because of its antimicrobial and flavor characteristics. It is the most widely used food preservative in the world, being incorporated into both food and soft drink products. It is used in margarines, salsas, maple syrups, pickles, preserves, jams and jellies. Almost every diet soft drink contains sodium benzoate, as do some wine coolers and fruit juices. It is also used in personal care products like toothpaste, dentifrice cleaners, and mouthwashes. As a preservative, sodium benzoate has the advantage of low cost. A drawback is its astringent taste that can be avoided by using lower levels with another preservative like potassium sorbate.

In addition to its use in food, it is used as an intermediate during the manufacture of dyes. It is an antiseptic medicine and a rust and **mildew** inhibitor. It is also used in tobacco and pharmaceutical preparations. In the free-acid form, it is used as a **fungicide**. A relatively recent use for sodium benzoate is as a **corrosion** inhibitor in engine coolant systems. Sodium benzoate has recently been incorporated into **plastics**, like polypropylene, where it has been found to improve clarity and strength.

KEY TERMS

Acid—A substance that produces hydrogen ions when placed in an aqueous solution.

Antimicrobial—A material that inhibits the growth of microorganisms that cause food to spoil.

Oxidation—A process by which a compound loses electrons.

Preservative—A compound added to food products to ensure they do not spoil.

Solubility—The amount of a substance that will dissolve in a solution at a given temperature.

Branen, A., Davidson, M., Salminen, S. *Food Additives.* New York: Marcel Dekker, 1990.

Budavari, Susan editor. *The Merck Index.* Merck Research Laboratories, 1996.

Institute of Food Technologists. 221 N. LaSalle St., Suite 300 Chicago, IL 60601-1291. (312)782-8424. http://www.ift.org.

Luck, Erich & Martin Jager. *Antimicrobial Food Additives: Characteristics, Uses, Effects.* Springer Verlag, 1997.

National Food Processors Association. 1350 I Street, NW, Suite 300, Washington, D.C. 20005-3305. (202)639-5900. http://www.nfpa-food.org.

The Food Processors Institute. 1350 I Street, NW, Suite 300, Washington, D.C. 20005. (202)639-5944. http://www.fpi-food.org.

Sodium bicarbonate

Sodium bicarbonate ($NaHCO_3$), also known as baking soda or sodium **hydrogen** carbonate, is a white powder that readily dissolves in **water** to produce sodium (Na^+) ions and bicarbonate (HCO_3^-) ions. In the presence of acids, these ions create **carbon dioxide** gas (CO_2) and water. Baking soda, a weak base, is used in antacids, fire extinguishers, and baking powder. In almost all of its common uses, sodium bicarbonate is employed to produce carbon dioxide gas.

Use in antacids

Many commercial preparations of antacids contain sodium bicarbonate. Alka-Seltzer antacid contains sodium bicarbonate in addition to **citric acid** ($C_6H_8O_7$), which is used to dissolve the sodium bicarbonate. Pure baking soda will also relieve heartburn, but the citric acid in commercial antacids improves the **taste** and accelerates the disintegration of the tablet. When sodium bicarbonate is dissolved in water, the compound separates into ions, or charged particles, of sodium (Na^+) and bicarbonate (HCO_3^-). The bicarbonate ions then react with acids as shown below. The symbol (aq), meaning aqueous, shows that the substance is dissolved in water; the symbol (g) refers to a gas, and (l) means a liquid. The hydrogen ions (H^+) are from acids.

$$H^+ (aq) + HCO_3^- (aq) \rightarrow H_2O + CO_2 (g)$$

As shown above, one hydrogen ion and one bicarbonate ion react to produce a **molecule** of water and a molecule of carbon dioxide gas. This can be demonstrated at home by filling a reclosable plastic bag with one ounce (30 ml) of vinegar. The vinegar represents stomach acid. A teaspoon (5 ml) of baking soda (or an Alka-Seltzer tablet) is then dropped in the bag and the bag is quickly reclosed. The fizzing is caused by the production of carbon dioxide gas. The bag will quickly fill up with gas, demonstrating why many people burp after taking an antacid. This belching helps relieve the **pressure** that builds up in the stomach. In spite of its widespread use, sodium bicarbonate can be harmful in large doses by disrupting the levels of sodium ions in the bloodstream. In a few rare cases, some people have consumed such large amounts of sodium bicarbonate that their stomachs were damaged by the internal pressure that built up from the carbon dioxide gas.

Use in fighting fires

When sodium bicarbonate is heated above 518°F (270°C) it decomposes and produces carbon dioxide. Since carbon dioxide gas is more dense than air, it tends to sink; thus carbon dioxide can smother a fire by obstructing the flow of **oxygen** to the fuel, which needs oxygen to continue burning. Sodium bicarbonate is employed in fire extinguishers and is widely used on electrical fires.

Use in baking

Baking powder consists of sodium bicarbonate mixed with a weak acid. In much the same manner as citric acid produces carbon dioxide gas in some antacids, the weak acid in baking powder-often **potassium hydrogen tartrate** ($KHC_4H_4O_6$)-provides a source of hydrogen ions; the ions react with the sodium bicarbonate to produce carbon dioxide gas, which makes dough and batter rise. Baking powder is often used as a source of carbon dioxide in baking instead of **yeast**, since yeast produces a distinct taste that is not desirable in all foods, such as cakes.

See also Acids and bases.

KEY TERMS

Antacid—A basic (alkaline) chemical that relieves the effects of excess stomach acids.

Aqueous—A solution dissolved in water; salt water could be called aqueous salt.

Ion—An atom or a group of atoms with a charge, either positive or negative.

Further Reading

Campbell, Hannah. "The Baker's Friend: How America's Best Brand of Baking Soda Was Born." *Country Living.* vol. 12, March 1989.

Lewis, Richard L. *Food Additives Handbook.* New York: Van Nostrand Reinhold, 1989.

Norton, Clark. "Facts on Fizz; Bubbly or Creamy, Calcium or Aluminum? Here's How to Choose a Heartburn Remedy." *Health.* vol. 5, July/August 1991.

"Stomach Acid-An Old Remedy." *Consumer Reports.* vol. 59, February 1994.

Louis Gotlib

Sodium carbonate

Sodium carbonate is a chemical compound which conforms to the general formula Na_2CO_3.

It is commonly referred to as soda ash because it was originally obtained from the ashes of burnt seaweeds. Now, soda ash is primarily manufactured by a method known as the Solvay process. Currently, it is one of the top industrial chemicals, in terms of **volume**, produced in the United States. It is mostly used in the manufacture of **glass**, but is also used in the manufacture of other products and is an important precursor to many of the sodium compounds used throughout industry.

Manufacture of sodium carbonate

The process for obtaining sodium carbonate has changed significantly over time. It was originally pro-

duced by burning seaweeds that were rich in sodium. When the weeds were burned, sodium would be left in the ashes in the form of sodium carbonate. Although this process was effective, it could not be used to produce large volumes.

The first process that allowed production of significant amounts of sodium carbonate was a synthetic process known as the LeBlanc process, developed by the French chemist Nicolas LeBlanc (1742-1806). In this process, **salt** was reacted with **sulfuric acid** to produce sodium sulfate and hydrochloric acid. The sodium sulfate was heated in the presence of limestone and **coal** and the resulting mixture contained **calcium** sulfate and sodium carbonate, which was then extracted out.

Two significant problems with the LeBlanc process, high expense and significant **pollution**, inspired a Belgian chemical engineer named Ernest Solvay (1838-1922) to develop a better process for creating sodium carbonate. In the Solvay process, **ammonia** and **carbon dioxide** are used to produce sodium carbonate from salt and limestone. Initially, the ammonia and carbon dioxide are reacted with **water** to form the weak electrolytes, ammonium hydroxide and carbonic acid. These ions react further and form **sodium bicarbonate**. Since the bicarbonate barely dissolves in water, it separates out from the solution. At this point, the sodium bicarbonate is filtered and converted into sodium carbonate by heating.

Synthetic production is not the only method of obtaining sodium carbonate. A significant amount is mined directly from naturally occurring sources. The largest natural sources for sodium carbonate in the United States are found around Green River, Wyoming, and in the dried-up **desert** Lake Searles in California.

Properties of sodium carbonate

At room **temperature**, sodium carbonate (Na_2CO_3) is an odorless, grayish white powder which is hygroscopic. This means when it is exposed to air, it can spontaneously absorb water molecules. Another familiar compound that has this hygroscopic quality is sugar. Sodium carbonate has a melting point of 1,564°F (851°C), a **density** of 2.53 g/cm^3, and is soluble in water. A water solution of soda ash has a basic **pH** and a strong alkaline **taste**. When it is placed in a slightly acidic solution, it decomposes and forms bubbles. This effect, called effervescence, is found in many commercial antacid products which use sodium carbonate as an active ingredient.

Anhydrous (without water) sodium carbonate can absorb various amounts of water and form hydrates which have slightly different characteristics. When one water **molecule** per molecule of sodium carbonate is absorbed, the resulting substance, sodium carbonate monohydrate, is represented by the chemical formula $Na_2CO_3 \cdot HOH$. This compound has a slightly lower density than the anhydrous version. Another common hydrate is formed by the absorption of ten water molecules per molecule of sodium carbonate. This compound, $Na_2CO_3 \cdot 10HOH$, known as sodium carbonate decahydrate, exists as transparent crystals which readily effervesce when exposed to air.

KEY TERMS

Anhydrous—A compound which does not contain any absorbed water.

Hydrate—A compound which contains a certain amount of absorbed water.

Hygroscopic—A compound which has a tendency to absorb water molecules.

LeBlanc process—A method of sodium carbonate production using salt, limestone, and coal.

Soda ash—A name for sodium carbonate which reflects its original source, the ashes of burnt seaweed.

Solvay process—The current synthetic method of sodium carbonate production from ammonia, carbon dioxide, salt, and limestone.

Uses of sodium carbonate

Sodium carbonate is utilized by many industries during the manufacture of different products. The most significant user is the glass industry which uses sodium carbonate to decompose silicates for glass making. The cosmetic industry uses it for manufacturing **soap**. The chemical industry uses it as a precursor to numerous sodium containing reagents. It is also important in **photography**, the textile industry, and water treatment. In addition to these industrial applications, sodium carbonate is used in medicine as an antacid.

See also Glass; Sodium

Further Reading

Budavari, Susan, ed. *The Merck Index*. Rahway: Merck & Co., Inc., 1989.

Faith, W.L., Donald Keyes & Ronald Clark. *Industrial Chemicals*. New York: John Wiley & Sons, 1966.

Zumdahl, Steven S. *Chemistry*. Lexington: D.C. Heath and Company, 1986.

Perry Romanowski

Sodium chloride

Sodium chloride (chemical formula NaCl), known as table **salt**, rock salt, sea salt and the mineral halite, is an ionic compound consisting of cube-shaped crystals composed of the elements **sodium** and **chlorine**. This salt has been of importance since ancient times and has a large and diverse range of uses. It can be prepared chemically and is obtained by **mining** and evaporating **water** from seawater and brines.

Properties

Sodium chloride is colorless in its pure form. It is somewhat hygroscopic, or absorbs water from the atmosphere. The salt easily dissolves in water. Its dissolution in water is **endothermic,** which means it takes some **heat energy** away from the water. Sodium chloride melts at 1,474°F (801°C), and it conducts **electricity** when dissolved or in the molten state.

Bonds

An ionic compound such as sodium chloride, is held together by an ionic bond. This type of bond is formed when oppositely charged ions attract. This attraction is similar to that of two opposite poles of a magnet. An ion or charged atom is formed when the atom gains or loses one or more electrons. It is called a **cation** if a positive charge exists and an **anion** if a **negative** charge exists.

Sodium (chemical symbol Na) is an alkali **metal** and tends to lose an **electron** to form the positive sodium ion (Na^+). Chlorine (chemical symbol Cl) is a **nonmetal** and tends to gain an electron to form the negative chloride ion (Cl^-).

The oppositely charged ions Na^+ and Cl^- attract to form an ionic bond. Many sodium and chloride ions are held together this way, resulting in a salt with a distinctive **crystal** shape. The three-dimensional arrangement or crystal lattice of ions in sodium chloride is such that each Na^+ is surrounded by 6 anions (Cl^-) and each Cl^- is surrounded by 6 cations (Na^+). Thus the ionic compound has a balance of oppositely charged ions and the total positive and negative charges are equal.

Location and processing

Sodium chloride, found abundantly in nature, occurs in seawater, other saline waters or brines and in dry rock salt deposits. It can be obtained by mining and evaporating water from brines, and seawater. This salt can also be prepared chemically by reacting hydrochloric acid (chemical formula HCl) with **sodium hydroxide** (chemical formula NaOH) to form sodium chloride and water. Countries leading in the production of salt include the United States, China, Mexico and Canada.

Mining

Two ways of removing salt from the ground are room and pillar mining and solution mining. In the room and pillar method, shafts are sunk into the ground and miners use techniques such as drilling and blasting to break up the rock salt. The salt is then removed in such a way that empty rooms remain that are supported by pillars of salt.

In solution mining, water is added to the salt **deposit** to form brine. Brine is a solution of sodium chloride and water that may or may not contain other salts. In one technique, a well is drilled in the ground and two pipes (a smaller pipe placed inside a larger one) are placed in it. Fresh water is pumped through the inner pipe to the salt. The dissolved salt forms brine which is pumped through the outer pipe to the surface and removed.

Evaporation

A common way to produce salt from brine is by evaporating the water using **vacuum** pans. In this method brine is boiled and agitated in huge tanks called vacuum pans. High quality salt cubes form and settle to the bottom of the pans. The cubes are then collected, dried and processed.

Solar **evaporation** of seawater to obtain salt is an old method that is widely used today. It uses the **Sun** as a source of energy. This method is successful in places that have abundant sources of salt water, land for evaporating ponds, and hot, dry climates to enhance evaporation. Seawater is passed through a series of evaporating ponds. **Minerals** contained in the seawater precipitate, or drop out of solution at different rates. Most of them precipitate before sodium chloride and therefore are left behind as the seawater is moved from one evaporating pond to another.

Uses

Since ancient times, the salt sodium chloride has been of importance. It has been used in numerous ways including the flavoring and preserving of food and even as a form of money. This salt improves the flavor of food items such as breads and cheeses, and it is an important preservative in meat, dairy products, margarine and other items, because it retards the growth of **microorganisms**. Salt promotes the natural development of color in ham and hot dogs and enhances the tender-

KEY TERMS

Brine—A solution of sodium chloride and water that may or may not contain other salts.

Ion—A charged atom that results when the atom gains or loses one or more electrons.

Ionic bond—A bond that forms when oppositely charged ions attract each other.

Ionic compound—A compound or substance that is held together by ionic bonds.

Solar evaporation—A method of water evaporation that uses the sun as a source of energy.

ness of cured meats like ham by causing them to absorb water. In the form of iodized salt, it is a carrier of iodine. (Iodine is necessary for the synthesis of our thyroid **hormones** which influence growth, development and metabolic rates).

The chemical industry uses large amounts of sodium chloride salt to produce other chemicals. Chlorine and sodium hydroxide are electrolytically produced from brine. Chlorine products are used in metal cleaners, **paper bleach**, **plastics** and water treatment. The chemical soda ash, which contains sodium, is used to manufacture **glass**, soaps, paper, and water softeners. Chemicals produced as a result of sodium chloride reactions are used in ceramic glazes, **metallurgy**, curing of hides, and **photography**.

Sodium chloride has a large and diverse range of uses. It is spread over roads to melt ice by lowering the melting point of the ice. The salt has an important role in the regulation of body fluids. It is used in medicines and **livestock** feed. In addition, salt caverns are used to store chemicals such as **petroleum** and **natural gas**.

See also Food preservation; Ionization; Saltwater.

Further Reading

Emsley, John. *The Consumer's Good Chemical Guide*. New York: W.H. Freeman & Spektrum, 1994.

Hazen, Robert and Trefil, James. *Science Matters*. New York: Doubleday, 1991.

Lide, David, ed. *Handbook of Chemistry and Physics*. 74th edition. Boca Raton: CRC Press, 1993.

Tocci, Salvatore and Viehland, Claudia. *Chemistry Visualizing Matter.* New York: Holt, Rinehart and Winston.

Tzimopoulos, Nicholas, Metcalfe, H. Clark, Williams, John and Castaka, Joseph. *Modern Chemistry*. New York: Holt, Rinehart and Winston, 1990.

Dana M. Barry

Sodium hydroxide

Sodium hydroxide, NaOH, also known as lye or caustic soda, is an extremely caustic (corrosive and damaging to human **tissue**) white solid that readily dissolves in **water**. Sodium hydroxide is used in the manufacture of soaps, rayon, and **paper**, in **petroleum** refining, and in homes as drain cleaners and oven cleaners. Sodium hydroxide is one of the strongest bases commonly used in industry. Solutions of sodium hydroxide in water are at the upper limit (most basic) of the **pH** scale. Sodium hydroxide is made by the **electrolysis** (passing an **electric current** through a solution) of solutions of **sodium chloride** (table **salt**) to produce sodium hydroxide and **chlorine** gas.

Sodium hydroxide in household products

Two of the more common household products containing sodium hydroxide are drain cleaners such as Drano, and oven cleaners such as Easy-Off. When most pipes are clogged it is with a combination of fats and grease. Cleaners that contain sodium hydroxide (either as a solid or already dissolved in water) convert the fats to **soap**, which dissolves in water. In addition, when sodium hydroxide dissolves in water a great deal of **heat** is given off. This heat helps to melt the clog. Sodium hydroxide is very damaging to human tissue (especially eyes). If a large amount of solid drain cleaner is added to a clogged drain, the heat produced can actually boil the water, leading to a splash in the eyes of a solution caustic enough to cause blindness. Some drain cleaners also contain small pieces of **aluminum metal**. Aluminum reacts with sodium hydroxide in water to produce **hydrogen** gas. The bubbles of hydrogen gas help to agitate the mixture, helping to dislodge the clog.

Oven cleaners work by converting built up grease (fats and oils) into soap, which can then be dissolved and wiped off with a wet sponge.

Industrial uses of sodium hydroxide

Sodium hydroxide is used to neutralize acids and as a source of sodium ions for reactions that produce other sodium compounds. In petroleum refining it is used to neutralize and remove acids. The reaction of **cellulose** with sodium hydroxide is a key step in the manufacturing of rayon and cellophane.

See also Sodium.

Further Reading

"Corticosteroids Can't Counter Caustics," *Science News*. Vol. 138, p. 174, Sept. 15, 1990.

KEY TERMS

Base—A solution with a pH greater than seven, having a greater concentration of hydroxide ions (OH) than hydrogen ions (H^+)

Caustic—Damaging to human tissue.

pH scale—A scale used to measure the acidity or alkalinity (basicity) of a substance. It ranges from 0 to 14, with pH's below seven being acidic and greater than 7 being basic (or alkaline). A pH of 7 is neutral. pH's less than 2 or greater than 12 can be caustic to human tissue.

Soluble—Capable of being dissolved. Sugar is soluble in water.

"How Lye is Made and Some Uses," *Countryside and Small Stock Journal.* Vol. 78, p. 37, March-April 1994.

Louis Gotlib

Sodium hypochlorite

Sodium hypochlorite (NaOCl) is a chemical compound consisting of **sodium**, **oxygen**, and **chlorine** that has been used for centuries for bleaching and disinfecting. Today, sodium hypochlorite (commonly called chorine **bleach**) is **mass** produced by the **chlorination** of soda ash and is employed in many household products, including laundry bleaches, hard surface cleaners, **mold** and **mildew** removers, and drain cleaners.

Sodium hypochlorite is the **salt** formed by a negatively charged hypochlorite ion (OCl^-) and a positively charged sodium ion (Na^+). Pure hypochlorite is highly reactive and unstable; therefore, it is usually supplied as a dilute aqueous solution. In solution, hypochlorite eventually decomposes to yield a variety of by-products including oxygen, chlorine gas, and salt. One of these by products, hypochlorous acid, is a powerful oxidizing agent (meaning it can accept electrons from other materials) that lends hypochlorite excellent bleaching and disinfecting abilities. The term "available chlorine" is often used to describe the **concentration** of hypochlorous acid in solution (which provides a measure of the solution's oxidative ability).

Due to its reactive nature, hypochlorite is particularly sensitive to the presence of trace metals such as **copper**, nickel, **iron**, chromium, cobalt and manganese that catalyze its **decomposition**. In fact, it is so reactive that it will aggressively attack many materials, including rubber, most types of fabrics, and certain **plastics**. Therefore, care must be taken in handling and storing hypochlorite solutions; all vessels should be **glass**, PVC plastic, porcelain, or glazed earthenware.

Hypochlorite was first produced in 1789 in Javelle, France, by passing chlorine gas through a solution of **sodium carbonate**. The resulting liquid, known as "Eau de Javelle" or "Javelle water" was a weak solution of sodium hypochlorite. However, this process was not very efficient and alternate production methods were sought. One such method involved the extraction of chlorinated lime (known as bleaching powder) with sodium carbonate to yield low levels of available chlorine. This method was commonly used to produce hypochlorite solutions for use as a hospital antiseptic which was sold under the trade names "Eusol" and "Dakin's solution." Near the end of the nineteenth century, E. S. Smith patented a method of hypochlorite production involving **hydrolysis** of brine to produce caustic soda and chlorine gas which then mix to form hypochlorite. Both electric power and brine solution were in cheap supply at this time and various enterprising marketers took advantage of this situation to satisfy the market's demand for hypochlorite. Bottled solutions of hypochlorite were sold under numerous trade names; one such early brand produced by this method was called Parozone. Today, an improved version of this method, known as the Hooker process, is the only large scale industrial method of sodium hypochlorite production.

Over the last few hundred years, one of the primary uses for sodium hypochlorite has been for the bleaching of fabrics, particularly **cotton**. Virgin cotton fibers are not pure white and must be processed to remove their natural coloration. Cotton bleaching has been practiced since the time of ancient the Egyptians who exposed fabric to sunlight to cause whitening. Even as late as the end of the eighteenth century, the British textile industry would bleach linen fabric by soaking it in sour milk for at least 48 hours, then exposing it to sunlight by laying out miles of treated fabrics on specially designated **grasslands**. In the 1800s, C. Berthellot attempted to take advantage of chlorine's bleaching ability, but, because it is a gas in its natural state, the chlorine was difficult to control. Subsequently, a process was developed to deliver chlorine as a dry powder by treating **calcium carbonate** with chlorine gas. However, this method of bleaching was far from ideal since it resulted in damage to the fabric wherever the concentrated hypochlorite powder came into contact with the fibers. Industrial fabric bleaching was vastly improved with the development of commercial bottled solutions of hypochlorite (also called chlorine bleach). Sodi-

KEY TERMS

Available chlorine—A measure of the oxidative potential of a chlorine containing solution.

Bleaching powder—A dry bleach made by treating calcium carbonate with chlorine gas.

Chlorine—A chemical element whose strong oxidizing abilities make it useful as a disinfectant and deodorizer.

Dakin's solution—An aqueous solution of hypochlorite (approximately 0.5%) in water used as a hospital antiseptic.

Javelle water—The first known production of hypochlorite which was made by passing chlorine gas through a solution of sodium carbonate.

Sodium hypochlorite—A chemical compound consisting of sodium, oxygen and chlorine (NaOCL) which has been used for centuries for its bleaching and disinfectant properties.

um hypochlorite gained widespread use not only as for industrial fabric treatment but also as a home laundry bleach. It is still sold today as a 5% solution in **water**.

Another important use for hypochlorite is as a sanitizer or disinfectant. Both of these uses rely on the hypochlorite's ability to destroy **microorganisms**. The same oxidative mechanism responsible for hypochlorite's bleaching ability also makes it an effective germicide. Although this mechanism was not understood at the time, hypochlorite (in the form of bleaching powder) was used as early as 1800 to counteract bad odors associated with disease. In fact, it has been said that no single element has played so important a role in combating disease over the last century as chlorine in its various forms. It should also be noted that hypochlorite is corrosive at high concentrations and was only used on the skin at very dilute levels. Its disinfectant properties have also been utilized for the sanitization of food processing equipment, particularly milking utensils used in the dairy industry. One marked advantage of hypochlorite for these applications is the fact that it, in addition to working quickly, rapidly breaks down to innocuous compounds. For this reason it is also useful in chlorination of sewage effluents and swimming pool water. Today, its primary uses are in lavatory bowl deodorizers and sanitizers.

New and improved ways to use hypochlorite are still being developed. In recent years, a number of improved bleach-containing products have been brought to market as chemists have learned to combine sodium hypochlorite with cleaning agents, thickeners and fragrance compounds to create efficacious products with improved aesthetic properties. For example, hypochlorite-based hard surface cleaners for kitchen counter tops, mold and mildew removers for showers and baths, and drain cleaners for kitchen and bathroom sinks are now commercially available.

See also Antisepsis.

Further Reading

Chalmers, Louis. *Household and Industrial Chemical Specialities*. Vol. 1. Chemical Publishing Co. Inc., 1978.

Schwarcz, Leonard. *Sanitary Chemicals*. New York: Mac Nair-Dorland Co., 1953.

Randy Schueller

Software see **Computer software**

Soil

Soil is a complex mixture of pulverized rock and decaying organic **matter**, which covers most of the terrestrial surface of the **Earth**. Soil not only supports a huge number of organisms below its surface—bacteria, **fungi**, worms, **insects** and small **mammals**, which all play a role in soil formation—but it is essential to all life on Earth. Soil provides a medium in which plants can grow, supporting their roots and providing them with **nutrients** for growth. Soil filters the sky's **precipitation** through its many layers, recharging the aquifers and **groundwater** reserves from which we drink. Slowing the movement of rainfall by absorption, soil prevents damaging floods. By holding air in its pores, soil provides **oxygen** to **plant** roots and to the billions of other organisms inhabiting soil. Soil receives and thrives on organic matter as it dies, assuring that it returns to a form useful to subsequent living organisms. Soil has built up over eons on top of **bedrock**, the solid rock layer that makes up the crust of the Earth, as exposed **rocks** have weathered and eroded and organic matter, including plant and **animal** life, have decomposed and become part of the soil. The word soil comes from the Latin word for floor, *solum*.

Soil formation

Soils began to form billions of years ago as rain washed **minerals** out of the once molten rocks that were cooling on the planet's surface. The rains leached potassium, **calcium**, and magnesium—minerals essential for plant growth from the rock, creating the conditions in

which very simple plants could evolve. Plant life eventually spread and flourished, and as each plant died and decomposed, it added nutrients and **energy** to the mineral mixture, making the soil more fertile for new plants.

Soil now covers the Earth in depths from a few inches to several feet, and these soils are constantly forming and changing. Soils are created from "parent" material, loose earthy matter scattered over the Earth by **wind**, **water**, or glacial ice, or weathered in place from rocks.

Parent material is turned into soil as other reactions take place on exposed rock surfaces. Water-borne acids react with elements in the rock and slowly change them into soil components. Minerals that break down relatively easily—feldspars and micas—become clay, the smallest soil particles with diameters less than 0.0002 mm, while harder minerals like quartz turn into sand (0.05-2.0 mm) and silt (0.0002-0.05 mm).

As the parent material weathers, the nutrients necessary for plant growth are released, and plants begin to establish themselves. As they die, they leave behind organic residues on which animals, **bacteria**, and fungi feed. Their consumption breaks down the organic matter further, enriching the parent material for plant growth. Over time, more and more organic matter mixes with the parent material.

Wherever soil is found, its development is controlled by five important factors: climate, parent material, living organisms, topography, and time.

A region's climate determines the range and fluctuation of **temperature** and the amount of precipitation that falls to the earth, which in turn controls the chemical and physical processes responsible for the **weathering** of parent materials. Weathering, in turn, controls the rate at which plant nutrients are released. Nutrient flow, along with temperature and precipitation, determines the types of plants a region can support.

A soil's parent material plays an important role in determining the **chemistry** and texture of soil (the size and shape of soil particles). The rate at which water moves through soil is controlled in part by the texture of the soil. Soils from some parent materials **weather** more or less quickly than others. Soils derived from quartz minerals, for example, weather more slowly than those derived from silicate materials.

The numbers and kinds of living organisms in a given region help determine the chemical composition of soil. Grassland soils are chemically different from those that develop beneath **forests**, and even within these broad categories of vegetative cover, soil profiles can differ; for example, different soils develop under conifers than under deciduous trees.

The layers of soil are called horizons. Together they make up the soil profile.

Topography, the configuration of the Earth's surface, affects soil development because it determines the rate at which precipitation washes over soil and how soils erode. Smooth, flat lands hold water longer than hilly regions, where water moves more quickly down slopes. Swamps, marshes, and bogs are formed as low-lying areas hold water over time. Soil erodes, or wears away, more quickly on sloping land than flat.

Time plays an important role in soil development: soils are categorized as young, mature, or old, depending on how the above factors are combined, and the rate at which they work.

Soil profiles and horizons

Below the surface of the earth lie layers of soil that are exposed when people dig into the earth, or by natural forces like earthquakes. These cross-sections of soil, called soil profiles, are composed of horizontal layers or *horizons* of soil of varying thickness and color, each representing a distinct soil that has built up over a long time period. Soil horizons contain soils of different ages and composition, and soil scientists can tell a lot about a region's climate, geography, and even agricultural history by reading the story of the region's soils through these layers.

A soil **horizon** is a horizontal layer of soil with physical or chemical characteristics that separate it from layers above and below. More simply, each horizon contains chemicals, such as rust-like **iron** oxides, or soil particles that differ from adjacent layers. Soil scientists generally name these horizons (from top to bottom) O, A, B, C, and R, and often subdivide them to reflect more specific characteristics within each layer. Considered together, these horizons constitute a soil profile.

Horizons usually form in residual soils: soils not transported to their present location by water, wind, or

glaciers, but formed "in place" by the weathering of the bedrock beneath them. It takes many thousand to a million years to achieve a mature soil with fully developed horizons.

The O horizon (sometimes known as the A_0) consists of freshly dead and decaying organic matter—mostly plants but also small (especially microscopic) animals or the occasional rigid cow. A gardener would call this organic matter (minus the cow) compost or **humus**. Below the O lies the A horizon, or topsoil, composed of organic material mixed with soil particles of sand, silt, and clay. Frolicking earthworms, small animals, and water mix the soil in the A horizon. Water forced down through the A by gravity carries clay particles and dissolved minerals (such as iron oxides) into the B horizon in a process called **leaching**; therefore, the A is known as the Zone of Leaching. These tiny clay particles zig-zag downward through the spaces (pores) between larger particles like balls in a Japanese pachinko game. Sometimes the lower half of the A horizon is called the E (Eluvial) horizon, meaning it is depleted of clay and dissolved minerals, leaving coarser grains.

The leached material ends up in the B horizon, the Zone of Accumulation. The B horizon, stained red by iron oxides, tends to be quite clay-like. If the upper horizons erode, plant roots have a tough time penetrating this clay; and rain which falls on the exposed clay can pool on the surface and possibly drown plants or flood basements.

Sometimes the top of the B horizon develops a dense layer called a fragipan—a claypan (compacted by vehicles) or a hardpan (cemented by minerals). In arid climates, intense **evaporation** sucks water and its dissolved minerals upward. This accumulation creates a hardpan impenetrable to any rain percolating (sinking) downward, resulting in easily evaporated pools or rapid runoff. If the hardpan is composed of the calcium-rich mineral calcite, it is called *caliche*. If composed of iron oxides, it is called an "ironpan." Fragipans are extremely difficult for crop roots and water to penetrate. The A and B horizons together make up the solum, or true soil.

Partially weathered bedrock composes the C horizon. Variously sized chunks of the rock below are surrounded by smaller bits of rock and clay weathered from those chunks. Some of the original rock is intact, but other parts have been chemically changed into new minerals.

The R layer (D horizon) is the bedrock, or sometimes, the sediment from which the other horizons develop. Originally, this rock lay exposed at the surface where it weathered rapidly into soil. The depth from the surface to the R layer depends on the interrelationships between the climate, the age of the soil, the slope, and the number of organisms. Most people do not consider the R layer as soil, but include it in the profile anyway, since the weathering of this bedrock usually produces the soil above it.

In a perfect world, all soils demonstrate these horizons, making the lives of soil scientists and soil students blissful. In reality, however, some soils, like transported soils (moved to their present locations by water, wind, or glaciers), lack horizons because of mixing while moving or because of youth. In other soils, the A and B rest on bedrock, or **erosion** strips an A, or other complicated variations. Around the world, scientists classify soils by these horizonal variations.

Aging soils

Like all living things, soils age. Exposure to wind, rain, sun, and fluctuating temperatures combine to push soils through four stages of development: parent material, immature soil, mature soil, and old-age soil.

As noted above, parent materials are loose materials weathered from rocks. As plants establish themselves in parent material, organics accumulate, and the upper soil layer becomes richer and darker, and evolves into an A horizon. At this point, the soil has only A and C horizons and is in the immature stage, which it usually reaches in less than 100 years.

Through continued weathering and plant growth, the soil gathers more nutrients, and can support more demanding species. Soils break down into smaller particles such as clay, and as water moves down through the matrix, it carries these fine soil particles with it. As they accumulate in the underlying layer, these particles form a B horizon. Soils that have A, B, and C layers are described as mature.

Gradually, as weathering continues, plant growth and water percolation remove nearly all of the mineral nutrients from soil, and acidic by-products begin to develop. When a soil lacks the nutrients or contains enough acids that plant growth is slowed, the soil has reached old age.

Soil categories

Soil scientists have developed a number of systems for identifying and classifying soils. Some broad systems of soil classification are used worldwide, and one of the most widely applied is that developed by the U.S. Department of Agriculture. It includes 11 major soil orders: alfisols, andisols, aridisols, entisols, histosols, inceptisols, mollisols, oxisols, spodisols, ultisols, and vertisols. Each major order is subdivided into suborders, groups, subgroups, families, and series.

Soils are also classified at an extremely specific level: soils are named after a local landmark such as a

town, school, church, or stream near where the soil is first identified. There are soils named Amarillo and Fargo, for example, identifying their origins in northwestern Texas and North Dakota, respectively. Soils that share characteristics that fall within defined limits share the same name, and these soils form a soil series. (Local names for soil series are usually used within countries but not across boundaries, even though soils on different continents share the same characteristics.)

Soil groups and agriculture

Plants have adapted to the globe's variety of soils and can grow in almost every soil and under all variations of weather, yet plants grow better in some places than others, especially in places where nutrients are most readily available from the soil.

The tropical belt around the Earth's equator contains the globe's "oldest" soils. Under heavy rainfalls and high temperatures, most nutrients have leached out of these soils. They generally contain high levels of iron oxides, which is why most tropical and subtropical (lateritic) soils are red in color. Yet many tropical soils are able to support rich, dense forests because organic matter is readily available on the surface of the soil as tropical vegetation falls to the ground and decays quickly. When tropical forests are cleared, the hot sun and heavy rains destroy the exposed organics, leaving very hard, dry soil that is poor for cultivation.

Soils in **desert** regions are usually formed from sandstone and shale parent rocks. Like tropical soils, desert soils contain little organic matter, in this case because the sparse rainfall in arid regions limits plant growth. Desert soils are generally light in color and shallow. Desert subsoils may also contain high levels of salts, which discourage plant growth, and rise to the surface under rains and **irrigation**, forming a white crust as the water evaporates.

Tundra (a Finnish word meaning "barren land") soils, dark mucky soils, cover treeless plains in arctic and subarctic regions. Below the A horizon lie darker subsoils, and below that, in arctic regions, lies permafrost. While these soils are difficult to farm because of their high water content and because permafrost prevents plant roots from penetrating very deeply, tundras naturally support a dense growth of flowering plants.

Below the great flat plains of the midwestern United States and the grassy plains of South **Africa**, Russia, and Canada lie deep layers of black soil atop a limestone-like layer, which has leached out of the soil into the subsoil. These soils are termed *chernozem* soils, a term that comes from the Russian word for "black earth." These soils are highly productive.

The most productive soils for agriculture are alluvial soils, which are found alongside **rivers** and at their mouths, where floods bring sediments containing sand, silt, and clay up onto the surrounding lands. These are young soils high in mineral content, which act as nutrients to plants.

Life in the soil

Soils teem with life. In fact, more creatures live below the surface of the Earth than live above. Among these soil dwellers are bacteria, fungi, and **algae**, which feed on plant and animal remains breaking them down into humus, the organic component of soil, in the process. The numbers of these microscopic soil organisms is vast—a gram of soil, which would fit into a peanut shell, can contain from several hundred million to a few billion **microorganisms**. The importance of their actions to the health of the soil is equally large.

Bacteria are the most abundant life form in most soils and are responsible for the decay of the residue from **crops**. Certain bacteria convert **ammonia** in soils into **nitrogen**, a fundamental plant nutrient. Some algae perform the same function (assuring a nitrogen supply) in **rice** paddy soils. Algae are numerous on the surfaces of moist soil. Fungi teem in soils, and range from several celled fungi to the large wild **mushrooms** that grow on moist soil. Fungi are capable of decomposing a greater variety of organic compounds than bacteria.

Nematodes are also abundant in most soils, and these eel-shaped, colorless worms are slightly larger than bacteria, algae, and fungi. An acre of soil may hold as many as 1 million nematodes. Most nematodes feed on dead plants, but some are **parasites**, and eat the roots of crops such as citrus, **cotton**, alfalfa, and corn.

Ants abound in soils. They create mazes of tunnels and construct mounds, mixing soils and bringing up subsurface soils in the process. They also gather vegetation into their mounds, which, as a result, become rich in organic matter. By burrowing and recolonizing, ants can eventually rework and fertilize the soil covering an entire **prairie**.

Earthworms burrow through soils, mixing organics with minerals as they go, and aerating the soil. Some earthworms pull leaves from the forest floor into their burrows, called middens, enriching the soil. The burrowing of the 4,000 or so worms that can inhabit an acre of soil turns and aerates soil, bringing 7-18 tons of soil to the surface annually.

Larger animals inhabit soils, including **moles**, which tunnel just below the surface eating earthworms, grubs, and plant roots, loosening the soil and making it more

KEY TERMS

Alluvial soils—Soils containing sand, silt, and clay, which are brought by flooding onto lands along rivers; these young soils are high in mineral content, and are the most productive soils for agriculture.

Bedrock—The solid rock that surrounds the core of the earth, lying beneath the A, B, and C horizons of soil.

Clay—The portion of soil comprising the smallest soil particles, those with diameters less than 0.002 mm, which is composed mainly of hydrous aluminum silicates and other minerals.

Horizons—Layers of soil that have built up over time and lie parallel to the surface of the Earth; these are composed of soils of varying thickness, color, and composition.

Nutrients—The portion of the soil necessary to plants for growth, including nitrogen, potassium, and other minerals.

Organic matter—The carbonaceous portion of the soil that derives from once living matter, including, for the most part, plants.

Parent material—Loose mineral matter scattered over the Earth by wind, water, or glacial ice, or weathered in place from rocks.

Percolation—The movement of water down through soil layers, through which minerals and nutrients are moved through soil.

Sand—The granular portion of soil composed of the largest soil particles (0.05-2.0 mm) and derived mainly from quartz.

Silt—Soil particles derived mainly from sedimentary materials that range between 0.0002-0.05 mm in size.

Soil series—Soils that share a defined set of characteristics and share the same name.

Topsoil—Soil lying on the Earth that contains high levels of organic matter, and which is the soil necessary for agriculture.

porous. **Mice** also burrow, as do ground **squirrels**, **marmots**, and prairie dogs; all bringing tons of subsoil material to the surface. These animals all prefer dry areas, so the soils they unearth are often sandy and gravelly.

See also Land use; Soil conservation.

Further Reading

Adams, John A. *Dirt*. College Station, TX: Texas A&M; University Press, 1986.

Brady, Nyle C. *The Nature and Properties of Soils*. New York: Macmillan, 1989.

Foth, Henry D. *Fundamentals of Soil Science*. New York: John Wiley & Sons, 1990.

Harpstead, M.I., F.D. Hole, and W.F. Bennet. *Soil Science Simplified*. Ames, IA: Iowa State University Press, 1988.

Hillel, Daniel. *Out of the Earth*. New York: The Free Press, 1991.

Beth Hanson

Soil conservation

Soil conservation refers to maintaining the productivity of agricultural land by control of the **erosion** of **soil** by **wind** or **water**. Soil conservation practices use the land according to its needs and capabilities.

Erosion is any process by which soil is transported from one place to another. At naturally occurring rates, land typically loses about one inch (2.5 cm) of topsoil in 100-250 years. A tolerable rate of soil erosion is considered to be 48-80 lb of soil per acre (55-91 kg per hectare) each year. Natural **weathering** processes that produce soil from rock can replace soil at about this rate. However, cultivation, construction, and other human activities have greatly increased the rate of soil erosion in most regions. Some areas of **North America** are losing as much as 18 tons of soil per acre (40 tonnes per hectare) per year.

Soil erosion not only results in the loss of soil particles, but also organic **matter** and **nutrients**. The first 7-8 inches (18-20 cm) of soil is the surface layer (topsoil) that provides most of the nutrients needed by plants. Because most erosion occurs from the surface of the soil, this vital layer is the most susceptible to being lost. The **fertilizers** and **pesticides** in some eroded soils may also pollute **rivers** and lakes. Eroded soil damages **dams** and culverts, fisheries, and reservoirs when it accumulates in those structures as sediment (this is known as sedimentation).

History

Human activities have caused increases of soil erosion since the beginning of agriculture more than 5,000 years ago. Plentiful land and a scarcity of labor in some countries encouraged farmers to "wear out" a piece of land, abandon it, and then move on to more fertile ground. This practice is still common in some developing countries, in the form of shifting cultivation or "slash and burn." This involves farmers cutting down an area of forest, burning the downed vegetation, and planting their **crops** among the ashes. After several years, the farmer moves to another area of forest and repeats the process. Although shifting cultivation is commonly considered to be a major cause of soil erosion, if sufficient time is allowed between clearings, soil fertility can maintain itself over the longer term.

Practices to protect the land from erosion have existed for several thousand years, particularly in the tropics and subtropics. For example, Chinese artifacts dating from about 4,500 years ago (2,500 BCE) depict terraces used to control erosion on cultivated slopes. Similarly, terraces have been used to grow **rice** in the Philippines for more than 1,000 years.

In the United States, abusive agricultural practices in combination with **drought** caused the great duststorms of 1934 and 1935, which carried huge quantities of soil from the Great Plains to the Atlantic Ocean. Soil conservation became a practice of national importance as a result of those storms. President Franklin Roosevelt signed bills in 1935 that established the Soil Conservation Service, an agency responsible for implementing practices to control soil erosion. Individual states also passed laws establishing nearly 3,000 local soil conservation districts.

For the next several decades, U.S. farmers produced consistent surpluses of agricultural commodities. They had little incentive to push the land for higher yields. However, in the 1970s grain exports increased, especially to the Soviet Union. Farmers were encouraged to cultivate marginal lands to fill the export quotas. Those areas, amounting to almost two million acres (800,000 hectares), included land on slopes and wetter areas that are relatively vulnerable to erosion.

The concern of the environmental movement about water quality in the 1970s helped to return attention to the problem of soil erosion. Excessive amounts of **phosphorus** and **nitrogen** occurred in streams and lakes as result of agricultural **fertilization** practices, and this added to public criticism of soil conservation programs. Congress passed the Soil and Water Resource Conservation Act to evaluate and conserve soil, water, and related resources on non-federal land.

The 1985 Food Security Act encouraged land management practices that were intended to reduce soil erosion. The Act removed up to 45 million acres (18 million hectares) of highly erosion-prone land from intensive cultivation. It also prevented the conversion of rangelands into cultivated fields through its "sodbuster" provision. The Act withdrew some commodity (feed grain, **wheat**, rice, upland **cotton**, etc.) acreage from production, through multiyear acreage set-asides and conservation easements. It also required farmers to develop plans and apply management practices that would keep soil erosion on highly erodible lands within acceptable limits.

How soil erodes

Soil erosion is caused mainly by the actions of water and wind. There are several different types of water-caused erosion: sheet, rill, gully, and stream channel. In sheet erosion, the flow of water over the surface of the soil detaches and transports particles in thin layers. Concentrated flows of water form small channels or grooves (rills), and eventually develop larger gullies that carry away large amounts of soil. Sometimes, underground tunnels are formed by erosion of the subsoil. Eventually, the tunnel roof falls in to form deeper gullies. Stream channels erode when soil is removed from the fringing banks, or from within the channel of the stream itself.

Soil erosion is influenced by several variables, especially climate, soil type, **density** and types of plants and animals, and topography. Climatic factors include **precipitation**, **evaporation**, **temperature**, wind, humidity, and solar **radiation**. Frequent and extreme changes in these conditions, such as freezes and thaws and severe rainstorms, often increase the rate of erosion.

Soil conditions that affect erosion include detachability and transportability. Detachability is the tendency of soil particles to separate from each other. Detachability increases as the size of soil particles increases. Transportability is the ease with which soil is carried from one location to another. Transportability increases as the size of soil particles decreases.

Vegetation helps to reduce erosion by intercepting rainfall, decreasing the surface **velocity** of runoff, physically restraining soil movement, improving the porosity of the soil so that percolation is rapid, and by decreasing the amount of runoff, by evaporating water to the atmosphere through **plant transpiration**.

Soil topography features that influence soil erosion include the degree, shape, and length of the slope, and the size and shape of the **watershed**. Erosion increases rapidly with increasing steepness and length of slope.

Soil conservation methods

Comprehensive soil conservation is more than just the control of erosion. It also includes the maintenance of organic matter and nutrients in soil. Soil conservation practices also prevent the buildup of toxic substances in the soil, such as salts and excessive amounts of pesticides. Soil conservation maintains or improves soil fertility, as well as its tilth, or structure. These all increase the capacity of the land to support the growth of plants on a sustainable basis.

There are two basic approaches to soil erosion control: barrier and cover. The barrier approach uses banks or walls such as earthen structures, grass strips, or hedgerows to check runoff, wind velocity, and soil movement. Barrier techniques are commonly used all over the world.

The cover approach maintains a soil cover of living and dead plant material. This cover lessens the impact and runoff of rain water, and decreases the amount of soil carried with it. This may be done through the use of cover crops, mulch, minimum tillage, or agroforestry.

Barrier approaches

Terracing is the construction of earthen embankments that look like long stair-steps running across the slope of rolling land. A terrace consists of a channel with a ridge at its outer edge. The channel intercepts and diverts downhill runoff. Terraces help to prevent soil erosion by increasing the length of the slope, thereby reducing the speed of overland water flow to allow for greater infiltration. The channels redirect excess runoff to a controlled outlet. Terraces help prevent the formation of gullies and retain runoff water to allow sediment to settle.

Extensive systems of irrigated terraces have long been used in numerous countries, including Yemen, the central Andes, the southwestern United States, Ethiopia, Zimbabwe, and northern Cameroon. Soil terraces occur widely in Southeast and South **Asia**, New Guinea, East **Africa**, and Nigeria.

The construction of reservoirs, usually ponds, is another barrier method for intercepting the surface runoff of water and sediment. Reservoirs increase soil moisture, thereby improving the resistance of soil to erosion. Water stored in reservoirs is also available for use in **irrigation**.

Contouring is plowing, planting, cultivating, or harvesting across the slope of the land, instead of up and down the hillside. Contouring reduces the velocity of surface runoff by impounding water in small depressions.

Cover approaches

Strip or alley cropping grows alternate strips of different crops in the same field. For example, rows of annual cultivated crops such as corn or potatoes, which have the most potential to cause erosion because of frequent plowing, are rotated with small grains such as oats that allow less erosion, and also with dense perennial **grasses** and **legumes** such as lespedeza and clover, which provide the best erosion control because the soil is not disturbed very often.

A combination of contouring and strip cropping provides relatively efficient erosion control and **water conservation**. Both contour and strip crops can be planted with shrubs and trees, known as windbreaks or shelterbelts, that form perennial, physical barriers to control wind erosion. In addition, shrubs and trees produce litter that increases soil cover, while helping to accumulate soil upslope to eventually develop terraces, and stabilizing the soil with their root systems.

Protective cover cropping and conservation tillage are systems of reduced or no-tillage that leave crop debris covering at least 30% of the soil surface. Crop residues on the surface decompose more slowly than those that are plowed into the soil, and they release nitrogen more uniformly and allow plants to use it more efficiently. Crop residues also reduce wind velocity at the surface, trap eroding soil, and slow down surface and subsurface runoff of water. Residues also attract earthworms to the surface, whose burrows act as drains for the percolation of runoff water during heavy rains. Crop residues also provide insulation that lowers spring and summer soil temperatures, and increases soil moisture by reducing evaporation. In areas that are more productive under irrigation, conservation tillage reduces water requirements by one-third to one-half, compared with conventionally tilled areas.

Degrees of conservation tillage range from no-till, in which the soil is not plowed and **seeds** are planted by a drilling technique, to varying degrees of tillage. However, during tillage the soil is not completely turned, as it would be if a moldboard plow was used. Weeds and pest **insects** are controlled using **herbicides** and **insecticides**, respectively. Conservation tillage eliminates the need to let fields lie fallow (unplanted) for a year to "rest." Fallow acreage is somewhat prone to soil erosion and to becoming dominated by intruding vegetation.

Another cover approach can provide temporary erosion control, such as that needed at construction sites. When certain chemical substances known as polymers are added to the soil, they form aggregates with the soil particles. These additives have no toxic effect, but stabilize the soil to provide temporary erosion control until a longer-lived plant cover can be established.

See also Contour plowing; Slash-and-burn agriculture.

KEY TERMS

Contouring—Plowing along a slope, rather than up and down it, to create furrows that catch soil and water runoff.

Fertility—The capacity of the soil to support plant productivity.

Minimum tillage—A farming method in which one or more planting operations is eliminated so as to reduce the exposure of the soil to erosion by wind and water.

Strip cropping—A farming method in which alternating bands of soil are planted in crops that are prone to soil erosion and others that prevent it.

Terracing—Converting a slope into a series of steps consisting of horizontal ledges and vertical walls.

Topsoil—The uppermost layer of soil, to a depth of approximately 18-20 cm, which is the primary feeding zone for agricultural plants.

Further Reading

Hallsworth, E. G. *Anatomy, Physiology and Psychology of Erosion.* New York: John Wiley & Sons, 1987.

Lake, Edwin B. and Aly M. Shady. "Erosion Reaches Crisis Proportions." *Agricultural Engineering.* (November 1993): 8-13.

Michaelson, E.L., J. Carlson, and R.L. Papendick. *Conservation Farming in the United States.* CRC Press, 1998 .

Schwab, Glenn O., et al. *Soil and Water Conservation Engineering.* 4th ed. New York: John Wiley & Sons, 1993.

Troeh, Frederick R., J. Arthur Hobbs, and Roy L. Donahue. *Soil and Water Conservation.* 2nd ed. Englewood Cliffs, NJ: Prentice-Hall, 1991.

Young, Anthony. *Agroforestry for Soil Conservation.* Wallingford, UK: C.A.B. International, 1989.

Karen Marshall

Solar activity cycle

The solar activity cycle is the periodic, typically 11-year-long variation in the number of active features (for example, **sunspots**) visible on the Sun's apparent surface or in its atmosphere. Over a period of 11 years, the number of sunspots gradually rises from a low level, reaches a maximum near the midpoint of the cycle, and then declines to a minimum. Solar activity is governed by the sun's magnetic field, and one of the unsolved problems in **astronomy** is the origin of the regular changes in the magnetic field that drive the activity cycle.

Discovery of the activity cycle

The most easily observed solar active features are sunspots, which are relatively cool regions on the sun's surface that appear as dark areas to viewers on **Earth**. Galileo Galilei (1564-1642) made some of the first telescopic observations of sunspots in 1610, but it was not until 1843 that the amateur astronomer Heinrich Schwabe noticed that the number of sunspots rose and fell in a cyclic fashion. One of the chief ways that scientists today track solar activity is by monitoring sunspots.

The overall sunspot record appears in Figure 1. The horizontal axes of these graphs show time, beginning in 1610 and continuing to 1980, and the vertical axes show the sunspot number. From one minimum to the next is usually about 11 years, but this is not always the case. From 1645 to 1715, the cycle disappeared. This period is called the "Maunder Minimum" after the British solar astronomer E. Walter Maunder. (In the early 1800s, the cycles were very long-nearly 14 years rather than 11.)

Between 1645 and 1715, when no sunspots were observed, the Northern Hemisphere experienced a mini Ice Age. Indirect evidence suggests that the **Sun** was also inactive around 1300—the same time that there is evidence for severe **drought** in western **North America** and long, cold winters in **Europe**. Although other minima are believed to have occurred in the past, no sunspot records exist prior to 1610. There has also been speculation that a "Maunder Maximum" might someday occur. Solar maximums are accompanied by many sunspots, solar flares, and coronal **mass** ejections, all with the potential of disrupting communications and **weather** on Earth.

Accompanying the variations in sunspot number are corresponding changes in other types of solar activity. Prominences appear as large regions of glowing gas suspended in magnetic field loops arching far above the solar surface. Sometimes there are violent flares, which are eruptions in the solar atmosphere that almost always occur near sunspots. **Matter** ejected from the Sun by flares sometimes streams into the Earth's atmosphere, where it can interfere with **radio** communications and cause aurorae (the so-called "northern lights" or" southern lights"). The **radiation** accompanying solar flares has on occasion subjected airline passengers to doses of X-rays comparable to what they might expect to get in a doctor's office.

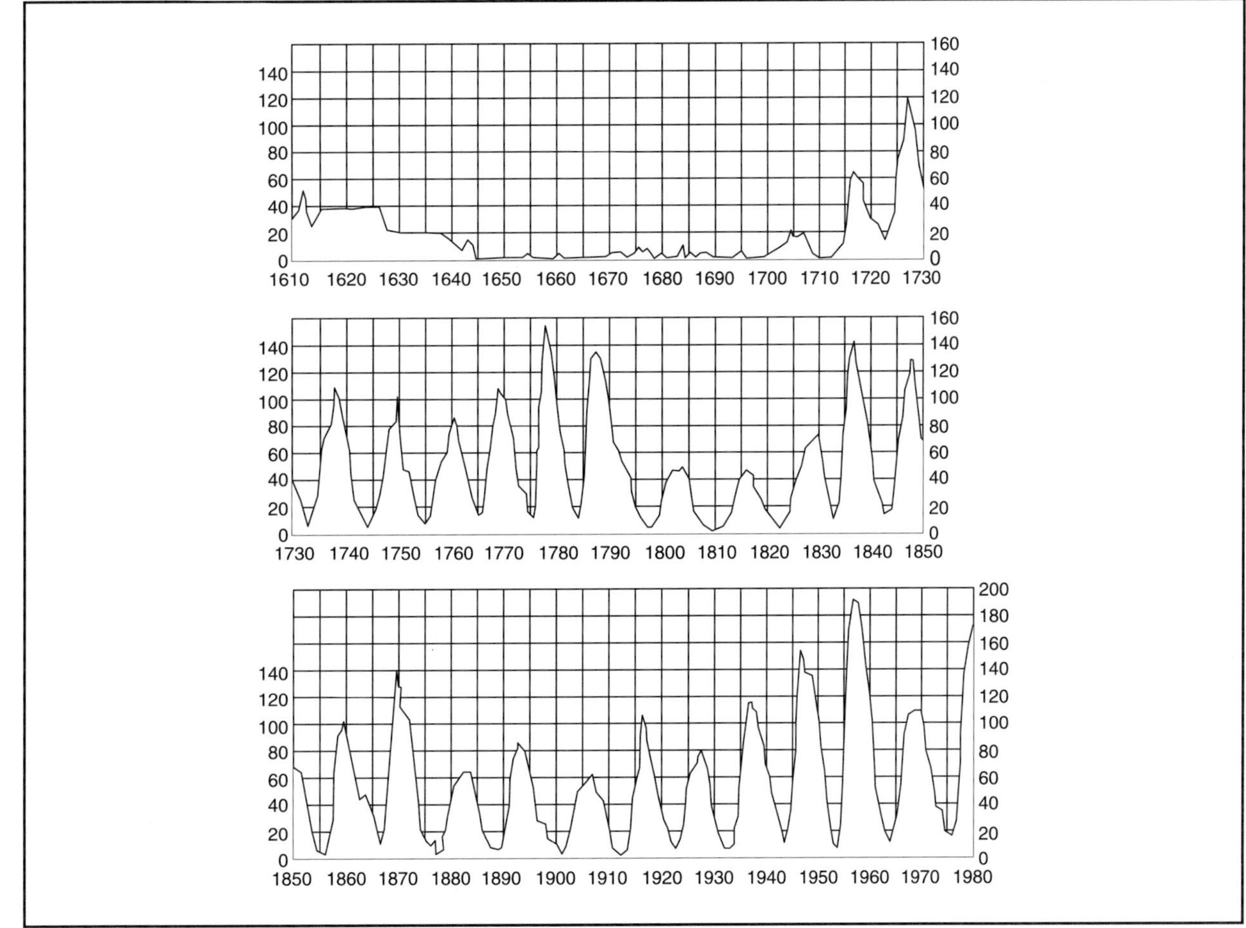

Figure 1. Annual mean sunspot numbers from 1610-1980.

Cause of the activity cycle

No one has yet fully explained the origin of the solar activity cycle. Astronomers have developed several possible scenarios, or models, that reproduce the general characteristics of the cycle, but the details remain elusive. One of the most well-known of these models was developed in the early 1960s by Horace Babcock.

Unlike the Earth, the Sun is made of gas, and this makes a big difference in how these two bodies rotate. To see how Earth rotates, look at a spinning **compact disc**. Every part of the disc completes one **rotation** in the same amount of time. To see how the Sun rotates, study the surface of a freshly made cup of instant coffee. The foam on the surface rotates at different speeds: the inner parts rotate faster, so that **spiral** patterns form on the surface of the coffee. This is called differential rotation, and it is how any liquid or gaseous body rotates. Therefore the Sun, being gaseous, rotates differentially: the equator completes one rotation every 26 days, while regions near the poles rotate once every 36 days.

This is important because the Sun's magnetic field, like **Earth's magnetic field**, gets carried along with the rotating material. When the magnetic field at the sun's equator has been carried through one complete rotation, the more slowly rotating field at higher latitudes has fallen behind. Over the course of many rotations, the field gets more and more twisted and tangled. And now the punch line: solar active features, like sunspots, are associated with regions of strong and complex magnetic fields. So the more twisted the magnetic field gets, the more activity there is. Finally, when the magnetic field gets tangled to a critical level, it rearranges itself into a simpler configuration, just as when you twist a rubber band too many times, it snaps. As the magnetic field's complexity decreases, so does the activity, and soon the cycle is complete. None of this happens on Earth, because Miami, Florida, and Fairbanks, Alaska, both rotate once every 24 hours. There is no differential rotation on Earth to tangle its magnetic field.

Coronal mass ejections (CMEs) are solar bursts that are as powerful as billions of nuclear explosions. These

ejections are the largest explosions in the **solar system**, typically hurling up to 11 billion tons of ionized gas into **space**. CMEs produce geomagnetic storms that reach the earth in about four days. These storms can damage satellites, disrupt communication networks, and cause power outages. The 1989 power blackout in the northeast portion of the United States and Canada was triggered by a geomagnetic **storm** that overloaded part of the power grid and caused a blackout to propagate through the system. Satellites have been disrupted, and on occasion destroyed, by the radiation accompanying CMEs. For these reasons, operators of satellites, power systems, pipelines, and other sensitive systems follow solar-terrestrial activities by monitoring data from ground and orbiting solar telescopes, magnetometers, and other instruments.

In 1999, scientists reported a strong correlation between an S-shaped pattern that is sometimes observed on the sun's surface and the probability that a coronal mass ejection will occur from that region within several days. These S-shaped regions are believed to be produced by the twisted solar magnetic fields. If the correlation holds up under closer examination, it may be possible to predict CMEs as routinely as meteorolgists predict weather patterns.

The poles of the sun's magnetic field change places each 11-year activity cycle. The north pole becomes the south magnetic pole, and vice versa. Thus the 11-year cycle of sunspot **frequency** is actually half of a 22-year solar cycle in which the magnetic field reverses itself repeatedly. Actually, the length of the activity cycle isn't exactly 11 years; that's just an average value. Year 2000 saw the start of Cycle 23, i.e., the 23rd cycle since reliable data first became available.

In the course of each 11-year cycle, an increasing number of sunspots appear at high latitudes and then drift towards the equator. As already noted, sunspots are actually regions of intense magnetic activity where the solar atmosphere is slightly cooler than the surroundings. This is the reason sunspot regions appear black when viewed through viewing filters. Sunspots are formed when the magnetic field lines just below the sun's surface become twisted, and poke though the solar photosphere, i.e., the region of the Sun's surface that can be seen by viewers on Earth. The twisted magnetic field above sunspots are frequently found in the same places that solar flares appear.

Sunspots pump x rays, high-energy protons, and electrified gases into space. That is the reason sunspots can affect satellites and power and communications systems on Earth.

In 1998, scientists reported finding giant convective cells (red and blue blotches) on the face of the sun. Although evidence of the existence of these structures had been sought for more than 30 years, they had not been seen before because their movements were buried in the more violent, small-scale activities on the Sun. These blue and red shifts are believed to correspond to the rising and falling of gases and their spreading out across the solar surface.

The flow of solar gases is more powerful than the solar magnetic fields, so the gases can carry magnetic structures with them. The eruption of these magnetic structures from the surface and their looping into space and back coincides closely with the appearance of sunspots.

See also Global climate; Solar flare; Total solar irradiance.

KEY TERMS

Differential rotation—Describes how a nonsolid object, like the Sun, rotates. Different parts of the object rotate at different rates; the Sun's equator, for example, completes one rotation faster (26 days) than its poles (36 days).

Maunder minimum—The period of time from 1645-1715 when the solar activity cycle disappeared entirely. This period also corresponds to a time of unusually severe winters in Europe, suggesting that the solar cycle may be somehow connected to dramatic variations in Earth's climate.

Sunspot number—An international estimate of the total level of sunspot activity on the side of the Sun facing the Earth, tabulated at the Zurich Observatory. Observations from around the world are sent to Zurich, where they are converted into an official sunspot number. Since the Sun rotates, the sunspot number changes daily.

Further Reading

Eddy, J. A. *The Ancient Sun*. ed. R. O. Pepin, J. A. Eddy, & R. B. Merrill. New York: Pergamon, 1980.

Mitton, Simon. *Daytime Star: The Story of Our Sun*. New York: Chas. Scribner's Sons, 1981.

Voyage through the Universe: The Sun. New York: Time-Life Books, 1990.

Jeffrey C. Hall
Randall Frost

Solar energy see **Alternative energy sources**

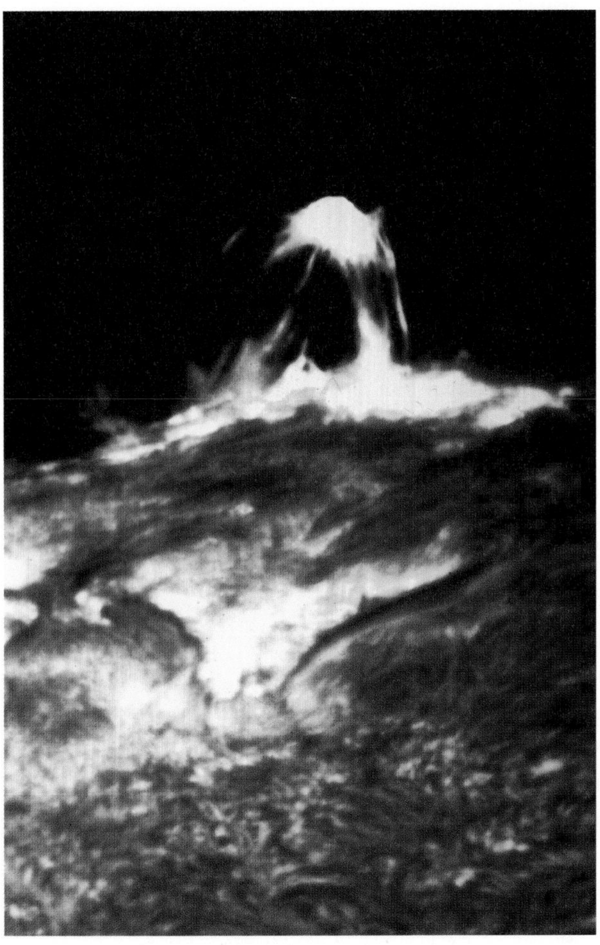

A solar flare erupting from the chromosphere of the Sun.

Solar flare

A solar flare is a sudden, localized release of **energy** in the Sun's outer atmosphere. This energy, in the form of **radiation**, is distributed throughout the **electromagnetic spectrum**, allowing flares to be seen at many different wavelengths, from the x ray to the **radio** regions.

The first recorded observation of a solar flare was in 1859 by Richard Carrington, who saw a sudden brightening in white light while observing **sunspots**. Most flares, however, are detectable only with a filter which passes wavelengths of **light** corresponding to certain **spectral lines**. The most common filter used is hydrogen-alpha (Ha), the first line of the **hydrogen** Balmer series, at 6,563 Å. Flares are also detected at x ray, ultraviolet, and radio wavelengths. X ray and ultraviolet observations are done from above the Earth's atmosphere, using sounding rockets and satellites.

Flares are believed to be caused when magnetic reconnection occurs in a solar active region. The flares are associated with the magnetic fields accompanying sunspots in the sun's photosphere. Since flares are correlated with sunspots, their occurrence follows the eleven-year solar cycle. The sun's magnetic field lines connect the north and south magnetic poles, but are filled with kinks, causing them to emerge through the solar surface at the locations of sunspots. Bundles of field lines, called magnetic flux tubes, occasionally become twisted, trapping excess magnetic energy. These twists may suddenly straighten out, returning the magnetic field lines to a more orderly form, and releasing enormous quantities of energy in the process. When this happens, huge quantities of charged particles are ejected into **space**, and radiation is emitted, particularly at x-ray wavelengths. Typical flares only cover a tiny fraction of the **Sun**, and last for only a few minutes.

Because the largest solar flares can produce substantial amounts of radiation and particles, their effects can be seen on the **Earth**. Solar flares whose charged particles travel towards and collide with the Earth (called a solar **storm**) affect radio transmissions, produce beautiful auroras (or the northern and southern lights), and can cause disruption of power transmission. Flares can also be a danger to spacecraft **electronics**, which must be shielded or radiation hardened to protect them, and astronauts, who could be exposed to lethal doses of radiation if not protected. Because of these effects, scientists hope to be able to predict when flares will occur, but they are not able to do so at this time. However, they do know that large solar flares are more likely near the peak of the Sun's 11-year cycle. The next peak will occur between 1999 and 2004.

Solar prominence

Solar prominences are large, glowing **clouds** of gas suspended in magnetic field loops above the Sun's photosphere. Although impossible to see in white light (the brilliance of the photosphere blots them out), they are easily visible in **hydrogen** alpha images (pictures taken in light emitted by hydrogen **atoms**, the principal constituent of the **Sun**). Prominences have been observed during **eclipses** for hundreds of years, but it was not until the twentieth century that they were observed in detail.

Prominences arise as products of the **solar activity cycle**. The hot gas that comprises the Sun is magnetized, and as the Sun rotates and the **heat** of its interior churns

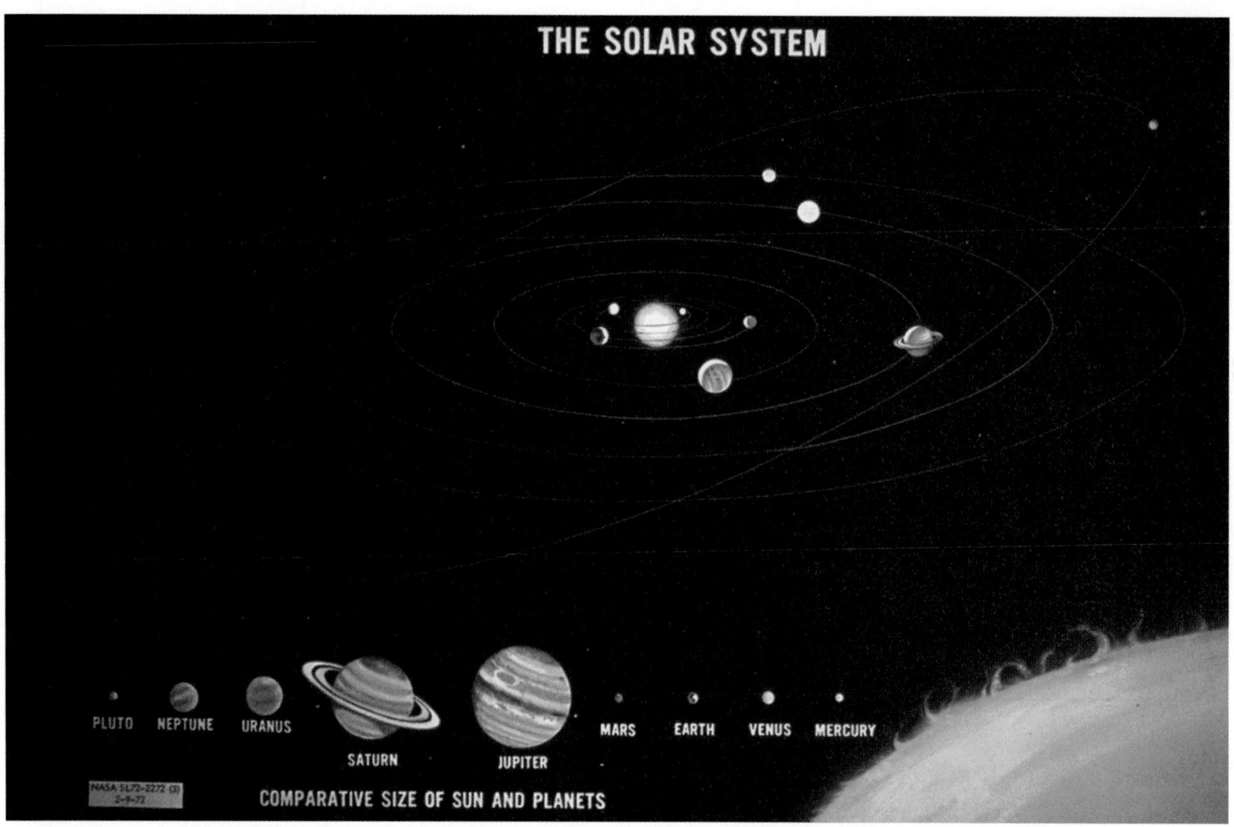

An illustration showing the orbits of the planets in the Solar system (top) and their comparative sizes (bottom).

its subsurface layer in great convective bubbles, the magnetic field becomes increasingly tangled. Large magnetic loops burst through the Sun's photosphere and into its atmosphere. At the focal points of these loops one often finds **sunspots**, while trapped in the upper part of the loop is hot (about 10,000 k), glowing hydrogen gas. These glowing loops are prominences, and not surprisingly, they are most common at the height of the solar activity cycle, and decrease in number as the complex magnetic field rearranges itself into simpler configurations and the activity cycle declines. Because the magnetic loops are not static, prominences evolve on time scales of days. As a magnetic loop expands, the **pressure** of the material inside it may become sufficient to break through the field, and the prominence will then dissipate. The gas inside a prominence flows from one part of the loop to the other as well, making prominences dynamic objects for study from Earth-based and **satellite** telescopes.

Prominences are typically huge; several Earths could fit inside a typical prominence loop. Graceful quiescent prominences last for up to several days, while their more violent cousins, the eruptive prominences, only last for a matter of hours. Prominences do not appear to be confined to the Sun; evidence exists for gigantic, prominence-like structures on other stars. Some stellar prominences have been suggested to extend as far as an entire stellar radius from the surface of their parent **star**. Such a structure would dwarf even the largest solar prominences.

Jeffrey Hall

Solar radiation see **Sun**

Solar system

The solar system is comprised of the **Sun**, nine major planets, some 100,0000 asteroids larger than 0.6 mi (1 km) in diameter, and perhaps 1 trillion cometary nuclei. While the major planets lie within 40 Astronomical Units (AU) of the Sun, the outermost boundary of the solar system stretches to 1 million AU, one third the way to the nearest **star**. It is believed that the solar system was formed through the collapse of a spinning cloud of interstellar gas and dust.

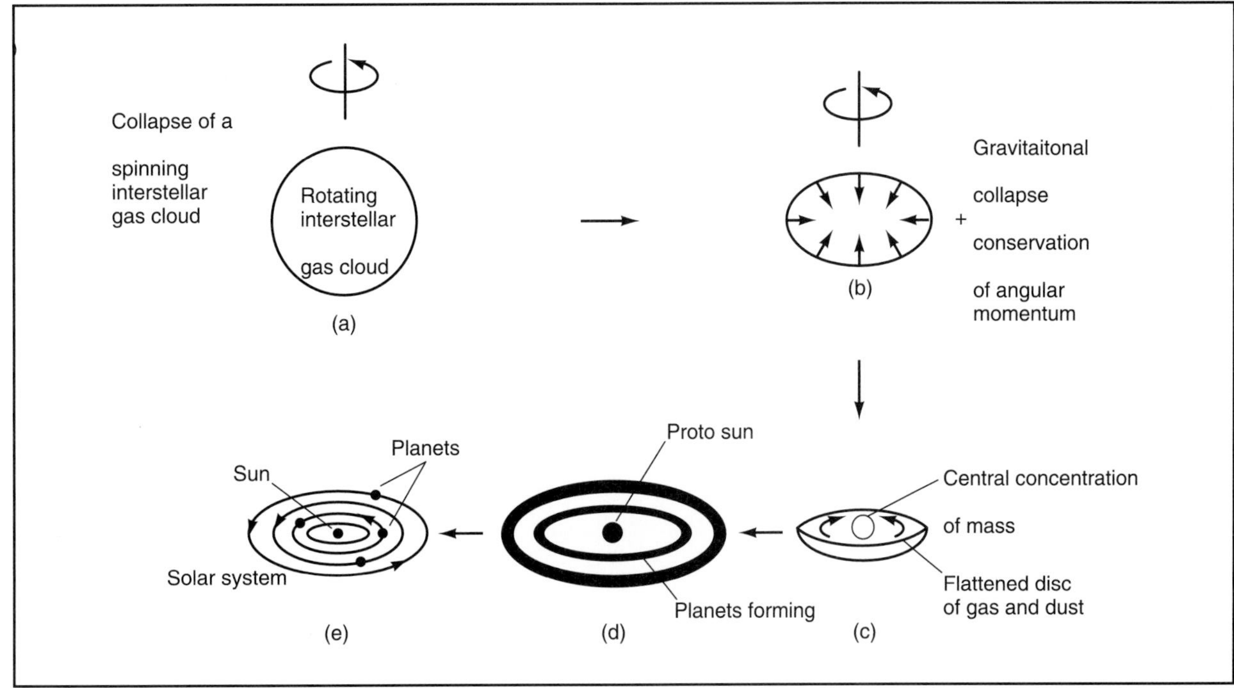

Figure 1.

What and where is the solar system?

The central, and most important object in our solar system is the Sun. It is the largest and most massive object in the solar system—its diameter is 109 times that of **Earth**, and it is 333,000 times more massive. The extent of the solar system is determined by the gravitational attraction of the Sun. Indeed, the boundary of the solar system is defined as the surface within which the gravitational pull of the Sun dominates over that of the **galaxy**. Under this definition, the solar system extends outwards from the Sun to a **distance** of about 100,000 AU. The solar system is much larger, therefore, than the distance to the remotest known **planet**, **Pluto**, which orbits the Sun at a **mean** distance of 39.44 AU.

The Sun and the solar system are situated some 26,000 light years from the center of our galaxy. Traveling at a **velocity** of 220 km/, the sun takes about 240 million years to complete one **orbit** about the galactic center, and since its formation, the Sun has completed about 19 such trips. As it orbits the center of the galaxy the Sun also moves in an oscillatory fashion above and below the galactic **plane** (the Sun's **motion** is similar to that of a carousel fair-ground ride) with a period of about 30 million years. During their periodic sojourns above and below the plane of the galaxy, the Sun and solar system suffer gravitational encounters with other stars and giant molecular **clouds**. These close encounters result in the loss of objects (essentially dormant cometary nuclei located in the outer Oort cloud) that are on, or near, the boundary of the solar system. These encounters also nudge some cometary nuclei toward the inner solar system, where they may be observed as long-period **comets**.

Solar system inventory

One of the central and age-old questions concerning the solar system is, "How did it form?" From the very outset, we know that such a question has no simple answer, and rather than attempting to explain specific observations about our solar system, scientists have tried to build-up a general picture of how stars and planets might form. Therefore, scientists do not try to explain why there are nine major planets within our solar system, or why the second planet is 17.8 times less massive than the seventh one. Rather, they seek to explain, for example, the compositional differences that exist between the planets. Indeed, it has long been realized that it is the chemical and dynamical properties of the planets that place the most important constraints on any theory that attempts to explain the origin of our solar system.

The objects within our solar system demonstrate several essential dynamical characteristics. When viewed from above the Sun's north pole, all of the planets orbit the Sun along near-circular orbits in a counterclockwise manner. The Sun also rotates in a counterclockwise direction. With respect to the Sun, therefore, the planets have prograde orbits. The major planets, asteroids and short-

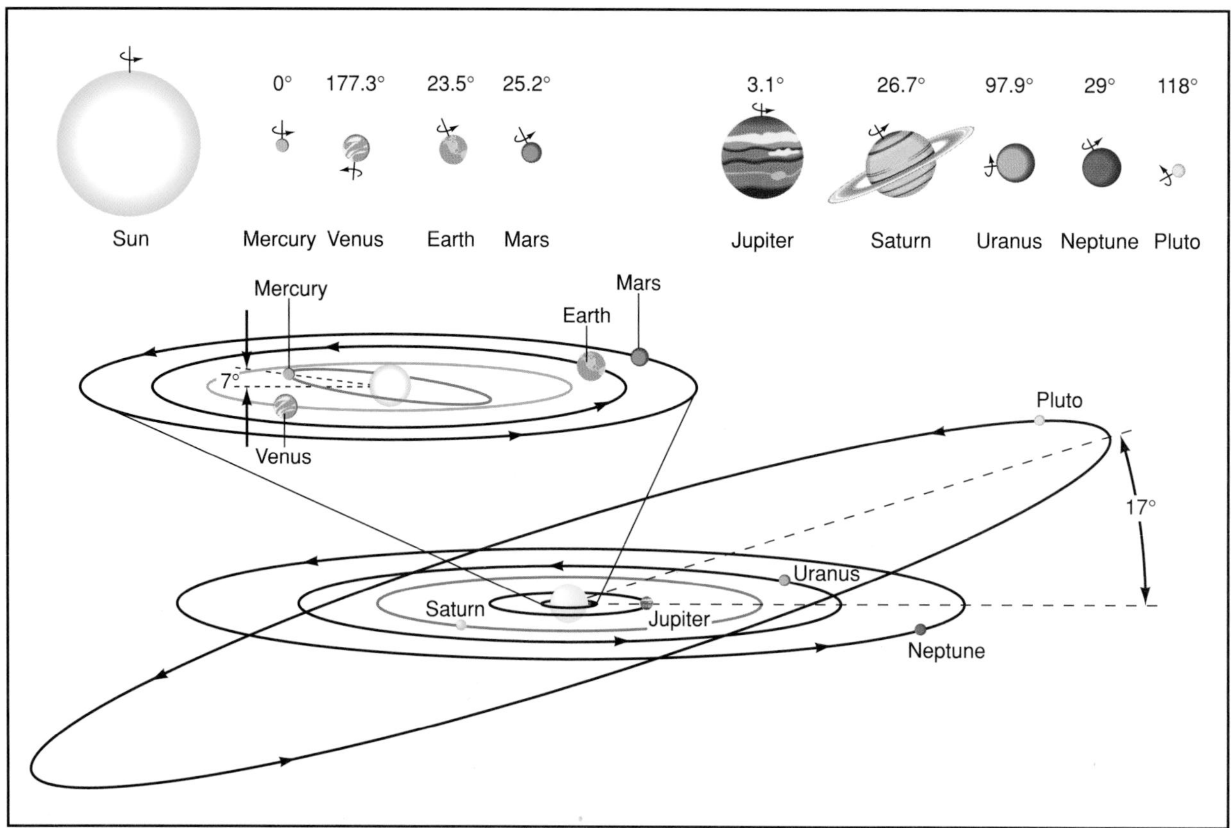

Figure 2. Schematic of present-day solar system.

period comets all move along orbits only slightly inclined to one another. This is why, for example, that when viewed from Earth, the asteroids and planets all appear to move in the narrow zodiacal band of constellations. All of the major planets, with three exceptions, spin on their central axes in the same direction that they orbit the Sun. That is, the planets mostly spin in a prograde motion. The planets **Venus**, **Uranus**, and Pluto are the three exceptions, having retrograde (backwards) spins.

The distances at which the planets orbit the Sun increase geometrically, and it appears that each planet is roughly 64% further from the Sun than its nearest inner neighbor. This observation is reflected in the so-called Titius-Bode rule which is a mathematical **relation** for planetary distances. The formula for the rule is $d(AU) = (4 + 3 \times 2^n) / 10$, where n = 0, 1, 2, 3,...,etc. represents the number of each planet, and d is the distance from the Sun, expressed in astronomical units. The formula gives the approximate distance to Mercury when n = 0, and the other planetary distances follow in sequence. It should be pointed out here that there is no known physical explanation for the Titius-Bode rule, and it may well be just a numerical coincidence. Certainly, the rule predicts woefully inaccurate distances for the planets **Neptune** and Pluto.

One final point on planetary distances is that the separation between successive planets increases dramatically beyond the orbit of **Mars**. While the inner, or terrestrial planets are typically separated by distances of about four-tenths of an AU, the outer, or Jovian planets are typically separated by 5-10 AU. This observation alone suggests that the planetary formation process was "different" somewhere beyond the orbit of Mars.

While the asteroids and short-period comets satisfy, in a general sense, the same dynamical constraints as the major planets, we have to remember that such objects have undergone significant orbital **evolution** since the solar system formed. The asteroids, for example, have undergone many mutual collisions and fragmentation events, and the cometary nuclei have suffered from numerous gravitational perturbations from the planets. Long-period comets in particular have suffered considerable dynamical evolution, first to become members of the Oort cloud, and second to become comets visible in the inner solar system.

The compositional make-up of the various solar system bodies offers several important clues about the conditions under which they formed. The four interior planets—**Mercury**, Venus, Earth, and Mars—are classified as ter-

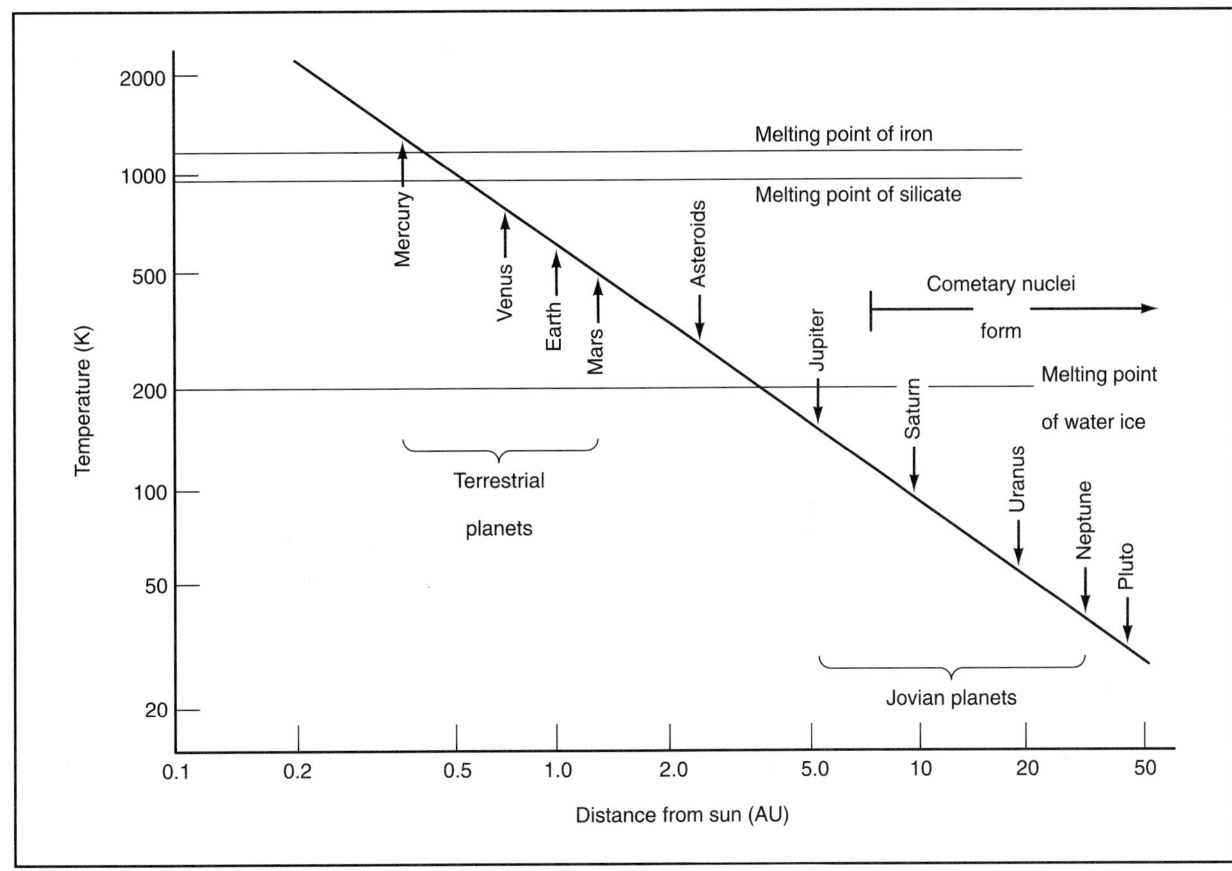

Figure 3. Condensation sequence and temperature versus distance relation in the young solar nebula.

restrial and are composed of rocky material surrounding an iron-nickel metallic core. On the other hand, **Jupiter**, **Saturn**, Neptune, and Uranus are classified as the "gas giants" and are large masses of **hydrogen** in gaseous, liquid, and solid form surrounding Earth-size rock and **metal** cores. Pluto fits neither of these categories, having an icy surface of frozen methane. Pluto more greatly resembles the satellites of the gas giants, which contain large fractions of icy material. This observation suggests that the initial conditions under which ices might have formed only prevailed beyond the orbit of Jupiter.

In summary, any proposed theory for the formation of the solar system must explain both the dynamical and chemical properties of the objects in the solar system. It must also be sufficient flexibility to allow for distinctive features such as retrograde spin, and the chaotic **migration** of cometary orbits.

The solar nebula hypothesis

Astronomers almost universally believe that the best descriptive model for the formation of the solar system is the solar nebula hypothesis. The essential idea behind the solar nebula model is that the Sun and planets formed through the collapse of a rotating cloud of interstellar gas and dust. In this way, planet formation is thought to be a natural consequence of **star formation**.

The solar nebula hypothesis is not a new scientific proposal. Indeed, the German philosopher Immanuel Kant first discussed the idea in 1755. Later, the French mathematician Pierre-Simon Marquis de Laplace developed the model in his text, *The System of the World,* published in 1796. The model is still under development today.

The key idea behind the solar nebula hypothesis is that once a rotating interstellar gas cloud has commenced gravitational collapse, then the **conservation** of angular **momentum** will force the cloud to develop a massive, central condensation that is surrounded by a less massive flattened ring, or disk of material. The nebula hypothesis asserts that the Sun forms from the central condensation, and that the planets accumulate from the material in the disk. The solar nebula model naturally explains why the Sun is the most massive object in the solar system, and why the planets rotate about the Sun in the same sense, along nearly circular orbits and in essentially the same plane.

During the gravitational collapse of an interstellar cloud, the central regions become heated through the release of gravitational **energy**. This means that the young solar nebular is hot, and that the gas and (vaporized) dust in the central regions is well-mixed. By constructing models to follow the gradual cooling of the solar nebula, scientists have been able to establish a chemical condensation sequence. Near to the central proto-sun, the nebular **temperature** will be very high, and consequently no solid **matter** can exist. Everything is in a gaseous form. As one moves further away from the central proto-sun, however, the temperature of the nebula falls off. At distances beyond 0.2 AU from the proto-sun, the temperature drops below 2,000K (3,100°F; 1,700°C). At this temperature metals and oxides can begin to form. Still further out (at about 0.5 AU), the temperature will drop below 1,000K (1,300°F; 730°C), and silicate **rocks** can begin to form. Beyond about 5 AU from the proto-sun, the temperature of the nebula will be below 200K (-100°F; -73°C), and ices can start to condense. The temperature and distance controlled sequence of chemical condensation in the solar nebula correctly predicts the basic chemical make-up of the planets.

The angular momentum problem

Perhaps the most important issue to be resolved in future versions of the solar nebula model is that of the distribution of angular momentum. The problem for the solar nebula theory is that it predicts that most of the **mass** and angular momentum should be in the Sun. In other words, the Sun should spin much more rapidly than it does. A mechanism is therefore required to transport angular momentum away from the central proto-sun and redistribute it in the outer planetary disk. One proposed transport mechanism invokes the presence of magnetic field in the nebula, while another mechanism proposed the existence of viscous stresses produced by **turbulence** in the nebular gas.

Building the planets

Precise dating of meteorites and lunar rock samples indicate that the solar system is 4.6 billion years old. The meteorites also indicate an age spread of about 20 million years, during which time the planets themselves formed.

The standard solar nebula model suggests that the planets were created through a multi-step process. The first important step is the coagulation and sedimentation of rock and ice grains in the mid-plain of the nebula. These grains and aggregates, 0.4 in (1 cm) to 3 ft (1 m) in size, continue to accumulate in the mid-plain of the nebula to produce a swarm of some 10 trillion larger bodies, called planetesimals, that are some 0.6 mi (1 km), or so in size. Finally, the planetesimals themselves accumulate into larger, self-gravitating bodies called proto-planets. The proto-planets were probably a few hundred kilometers in size. Finally, growth of proto-planet-sized objects results in the planets.

The final stages of planetary formation were decidedly violent—it is believed that a collision with a Mars-sized proto-planet produced the earth's **Moon**. Likewise, it is thought that the retrograde rotations of Venus and Uranus may have been caused by glancing proto-planetary impacts. The rocky and icy planetesimals not incorporated into the proto-planets now orbit the Sun as asteroids and cometary nuclei. The cometary nuclei that formed in the outer solar nebula were mostly ejected from the nebula by gravitational encounters with the large Jovian planets and now reside in the Oort cloud.

One problem that has still to be worked-out under the solar nebula paradigm concerns the formation of Jupiter. The estimated accumulation time for Jupiter is about 100 million years, but it is now known that the solar nebula itself probably only survived for between 100,000 to 10 million years. In other words, the accumulation process in the standard nebula model is too slow by a least a **factor** of 10 and maybe 100. Indeed, much has yet to be learned of how our solar system formed.

Active study of our solar system has been taking place throughout the 1990s and beyond. Several probes and robots—such as the Galileo spacecraft, the Cassini mission, and the **Mars Pathfinder** mission—have been launched towards other planets and their moons, sending back information about their composition that may further explain the evolution of our solar system. The NEAR spacecraft flew by the asteroid Mathilde and found it to have a surprisingly low **density**.

Of great importance to the study of solar systems was the discovery in 1999 of an entire solar system around a star that is not our Sun. Forty-four light-years from Earth, three large planets were found circling the star Upsilon Andromedae. Astronomers suspect the planets are similar to Jupiter and Saturn—huge spheres of gas without a solid surface. The discovery of at least one other solar system in our galaxy could yield important insight into the formation of evolution of solar systems in general.

Further Reading

Hughes, David. "Where Planets Boldly Grow." *New Scientist.* (12 December 1992): 29-33.

Murray, Carl. "Is the Solar System Stable?" *New Scientist* .(25 November 1989): 60-63.

KEY TERMS

Accretion—The process by which the mass of a body increases by the gravitational attraction of smaller objects.

Angular momentum—The product of orbital distance, orbital speed, and mass. In a closed system, angular momentum is a conserved quantity—it can be transferred from one place to another, but it cannot be created or destroyed.

Oort Cloud—A vast, spherical cloud of some one trillion cometary nuclei that orbit the Sun. The cloud, named after Dutch astronomer Jan Oort who first suggested its existence, extends to a distance of 105 AU from the Sun.

Planetesimal—Small, 0.6 mi (1 km) sized objects made of rock and/or ice that accrete to form proto-planets.

Prograde rotation—Rotational spin in the same sense as the orbital motion. For solar system objects, the orbital motion is counterclockwise, and prograde spin results in the object revolving from east to west.

Retrograde rotation—Rotational spin in the opposite sense to the orbital motion. For solar system objects the orbital motion is counterclockwise, and retrograde spin results in the object revolving from west to east.

Woolfson, M. M. "The Solar System-Its Origin and Evolution." *The Quarterly Journal of the Royal Astronomical Society.* 34 (1993): 1-20.

Wyrun-Williams, Gareth. *The Fullness of Space.* Cambridge: Cambridge University Press, 1992.

Martin Beech

Solar wind

The *solar wind* is a continuous stream of particles that flows outward from the **Sun** through the **solar system**. The particles escape from the Sun because its outer atmosphere is very hot, and the **atoms** there move too rapidly for the sun's gravity to hold onto them. The solar **wind**, which is made mainly of ionized **hydrogen** (free protons and electrons), flows away from the Sun at a **velocity** of several hundred kilometers per second. The solar wind continues past the outermost **planet**, **Pluto**, to the point where it becomes indistinguishable from the interstellar gases; this marks the end of the sun's **domain** and is called the heliopause. Little of the solar wind reaches Earth's atmosphere, because the charged particles are deflected by our planet's magnetic field.

Origin and nature of the solar wind

One of the mysteries of the Sun is that its atmosphere becomes hotter at larger heights from its visible surface, or photosphere. While the photosphere has a **temperature** of 9,981°F (5,527°C), the chromosphere, only a few thousand kilometers higher, is more than twice as hot. Further out is the corona, with gas heated to one or two million degrees Kelvin.

Although the reasons for this temperature rise are not well understood, the effects on the particles comprising the gas are known. The hotter a gas is, the faster its particles move. In the corona, the free protons and electrons move so rapidly that the sun's gravity cannot hold them, and they escape entirely, flowing into the solar system. This stream of particles is called the solar wind.

The solar wind is made mainly of free protons and electrons. These particles are much lighter than the atoms (such as **iron**) in the solar corona, so the Sun has a weaker hold on them than on their heavier counterparts. When the solar wind reaches **Earth**, the protons and electrons are flowing along at speeds up to 621 mi/s (1,000 km/s). By comparison, a commercial jet might fly 621 mi/hr (1,000 km/hr), and only if it has a good tailwind pushing it along. The solar wind could flow from New York to Los Angeles in less than ten seconds.

There is, therefore, gas from the Sun literally filling the solar system. We cannot see it, however, because there is not much of it—only a few protons and electrons per cubic centimeter. The solar wind therefore represents an insignificant source of **mass** loss for the Sun, not nearly enough to have any impact on its structure or **evolution**. (Some very massive stars do have strong winds that affect how they evolve.)

The solar wind and Earth

Beautiful aurorae are caused when charged particles, like protons and electrons, stream into the earth's atmosphere and excite the **nitrogen** and **oxygen** atoms in the upper atmosphere. When these atoms return to their normal, nonexcited state, they emit the shimmering, green or red curtains of light so familiar to Canadians or Americans living in the northern states.

If the solar wind is continuous, why don't we see aurorae all the time? Earth is surrounded by a magnetic

field, generated by its **rotation** and the presence of molten, conducting iron deep in its interior. This magnetic field extends far into **space** and deflects most particles that encounter it. Most of the solar wind therefore streams around the Earth before continuing on its way into space. Some particles get through, however, and they eventually find their way into two great rings of charged particles that surround the entire Earth. These are called the *Van Allen belts*, and they lie well outside the atmosphere, several thousand kilometers up.

Besides the gentle, continuous generation of the solar wind, however, the Sun also periodically injects large quantities of protons and electrons into the solar wind. This happens after a flare, a violent eruption in the Sun's atmosphere. When the burst of particles reaches the earth, the magnetic field is not sufficient to deflect all the particles, and the **Van Allen belts** are not sufficient to trap them all above the atmosphere. Like **water** overflowing a bucket, the excess particles stream along **Earth's magnetic field** lines and flow into the upper atmosphere near the poles. This is why aurorae typically appear in extreme northern or southern latitudes, though after particularly intense solar flares, aurorae may be seen in middle latitudes as well.

The solar wind and the heliopause

Six billion kilometers from the Sun is the planet Pluto. At this **distance**, the Sun is only a brilliant point of light, and gives no warmth to **heat** the dead and icy surface of its most distant planet.

The solar wind still flows by, however. As it gets farther from the Sun, it becomes increasingly diffuse, until it finally merges with the interstellar medium, the gas between the stars that permeates the **Galaxy**. This is the heliopause, the distance at which the Sun's neighborhood formally ends. Scientists believe the heliopause lies between two and three times as far from the Sun as Pluto. Determining exact location is the final mission of the *Pioneer* and *Voyager* spacecraft, now out past Pluto, their flybys of the planets complete. Someday, perhaps in twenty years, perhaps not for fifty, they will reach the heliopause. They will fly right through it: there is no wall there, nothing to reveal the subtle end of the Sun's domain. And at that point, these little machines of man will have become machines of the stars.

Further Reading

Beatty, J., and Chaikin, A., *The New Solar System.* Cambridge: Cambridge, University Press, 1990.

Kaufmann, W., *Discovering the Universe.* 2nd ed. San Francisco: Freeman, 1991.

Jeffrey C. Hall

Solder and soldering iron

Soldering is the process by which two pieces of **metal** are joined to each other by means of an **alloy**. The tool used to make this kind of joint is called a soldering iron, and the alloy from which the connection is made is called a solder. Soldering can be used for making either a mechanical or an electrical connection. An example of the former case is the situation in which a plumber uses plumber's solder to connect two pieces of pipe with each other. An example of the latter case is the situation in which a worker connects an electrical wire to a printed board.

The technique of soldering has been known to human artisans for many centuries. Some metal work recovered from the remains of ancient Egypt and Mesopotamia, for example, contains evidence of primitive forms of soldering. As workers became more familiar with the properties of metals in the late Middle Ages, soldering became a routine technique in metal work of various kinds.

Solders

The vast majority of solders are alloys that contain tin, **lead**, and, sometimes, one or more other metals. For example, the well-known general solder known as plumbers' solder consists of 50% lead and 50% tin. A solder used to join surfaces that contain silver is made of 62% tin, 36% lead, and 2% silver. And a solder that melts at unusually low temperatures can be made from 13% tin, 27% lead, 10% cadmium, and 50% bismuth. The most widely used solders for making electrical connections consist of 60-63% tin and 37-40% lead.

Solder alloys are available in many forms, such as wire, bar, foil, rings, spheres, and paste. The specific kind of solder selected depends on the kind of junction to be formed. Foil solder, for example, may be called when the junction to be formed has a particular shape that can be stamped or cut out prior to the actual soldering process.

The soldering principle

The solder alloy used to join two pieces of metal, the "parent" metals, has a melting point less than that of either parent metal. When it is placed between the two parents, it slowly changes from a liquid to a solid. The soldering iron is used to melt the solder and it is then allowed to cool.

While the process of solidification is taking place, the solder alloy begins to form a new alloy with each of the parent metals. When the solder finally cools, there-

fore, the joint consists of five segments: parent metal #1; a new alloy of parent metal #1 and the solder alloy; the solder alloy itself; a new alloy of parent metal #2 and the sold alloy; and parent metal #2.

The primary function to the soldered junction, of course, is to provide a connection between the two parent metals. However, the junction is not a permanent one. In fact, an important characteristic of the soldered connection is that it can be broken apart with relative ease.

The soldering technique

The first step in making a soldered connection is to **heat** the solder alloy until it melts. In the most primitive form of soldering irons, this can be accomplished simply by heating a metal cylinder and using it to melt the alloy and attach it to the parent metals. However, most soldering irons are now heated by an electrical current that is designed to apply exactly the right amount of solder in precisely the correct position between the two parent metals.

The joining of two parent metals is usually more difficult than might be suggested by the foregoing description because most metal oxidize when exposed to air. That means that the faces (that is, the metals oxides that cover their surfaces) of the two parent metals must be cleaned before soldering can begin. In addition, care must be taken that the surfaces do not re-oxidize at the high **temperature** used in making the solder. The most common way of accomplishing this goal is to use an acidic flux in addition to the solder itself. An acidic flux is a material that can be mixed with the solder, but that melts at a temperature less than the solder's melting point. As soldering begins, therefore, the flux insures that any new oxide formed on the parent metals will be removed.

Brazing and welding

Brazing and **welding** have sometimes been described as specialized forms of soldering. These two techniques also involve the joining of two metals with each other, but each differs from soldering in some important ways. Probably the single most important difference is the temperature range at which each takes place. While most forms of soldering occur at temperatures in the range from 356°F (180°C) to 590°F (310°C), brazing usually takes place in the range from 1,022°F (550°C) to 2,012°F (1,100°C), and welding in the range from 1,832°F (1,000°C) to 6,332°F (3,500°C).

The first step in both brazing and welding is to clean the two surfaces to be joined. In brazing, a filler is then inserted into the gap between the two surfaces and heat is added, either at the same time or immediately after the filler has been put into place. The filler then fuses to form a strong bond between each of the two surfaces. The filler used in brazing is similar to solder and performs the same function, but it melts at a higher temperature than does solder.

During the welding process, a thin stick of filler is added to the gap between the two surfaces to be joined. At the same time, a hot flame is applied to the gap. The filler melts, as do the surfaces of both metals being joined to each other. In this case, the two metal surfaces are actually joined together and not just to the filler itself, as is the case with soldering and brazing.

Most alloys used for brazing contain **copper** and zinc, often with one or more other metals. The term brazing itself, in fact, derives from the fact that copper and zinc are also the major components of the alloy known as brass.

See also Metal production.

KEY TERMS

Acidic—Having the qualities of an acid, one of which is that it will react with and neutralize metallic oxides.

Alloy—A mixture of two or more metals that has properties especially useful for one or more purposes.

Flux—A low melting point material used in soldering and other processes that helps keep surfaces clean and aids in their joining with each other.

Parent metal—One of the two metals that is joined to each other during soldering, brazing, or welding.

Further Reading

Cieslak, M. J., et al., eds. *The Metal Science of Joining.* Warrendale, PA: Minerals, Metals, and Materials Society, 1992.

Lieberman, Eli. *Modern Soldering and Brazing Techniques.* Troy, MI: Business News, 1988.

Pecht, Michael G. *Soldering Processes and Equipment.* New York: John Wiley & Sons, 1993.

Rahn, Armin. *The Basics of Soldering.* New York: John Wiley & Sons, 1993.

Sistare, George, and Frederick Disque. "Solders and Brazing Alloys." *Kirk-Othmer Encyclopedia of Chemical Technology.* 3rd edition. New York: John Wiley & Sons, 1983. vol. 21,: 342 - 355.

The Illustrated Encyclopedia of Science and Technology. vol. 16. Westport, CT: H. S. Stuttman, 1982.

Solders and Soldering: Materials, Design, Production and Analysis for Reliable Bonding. 3rd edition. New York: McGraw-Hill, 1987.

David E. Newton

Sole see **Flatfish**
Solid see **Phases of matter**
Solid see **States of matter**
Solid state physics see **Physics**
Soliton see **Tsunami**

Solstice

The term solstice refers to the two dates of the year on which the **Sun** reaches its northernmost and southernmost declinations (*declination* is the celestial equivalent of latitude).

During the spring we frequently hear someone remark that "the days are getting longer," or during the fall that they are getting shorter. This phenomenon occurs because Earth's rotational axis is tilted with respect to the **plane** of its **orbit** around the Sun. As **Earth** revolves around the Sun, the latitude that is directly facing the Sun (which defines the Sun's declination) changes. At one point in Earth's orbit, the northern hemisphere is tilted toward the Sun, and the Sun appears higher in the sky for northern latitudes; six months later, when Earth has moved around to the other side of its orbit, the northern hemisphere is tilted away from the Sun, and the Sun appears higher for southern latitudes. The solstices refer to the days on which the Sun's apparent northward or southward **motion** reverses direction. The word solstice itself is derived from two Latin words meaning "Sun stands."

There are two solstices every year. One occurs on or around June 22, and it is the time of year when the days are long and hot in the United States; Americans call this the summer solstice. It is just the opposite for Australians, however. If the northern hemisphere is tilted toward the Sun, the southern hemisphere must be tilted away; and indeed, June and July are the coolest months of the year in Sydney. Conversely, on or about December 22, the northern hemisphere reaches the winter solstice, when the Sun appears to trace its lowest path across the sky. At the same time, it is high summer in **Australia**. For this reason, the 2000 Summer Olympics, in Sydney, Australia, were scheduled for September rather than July as they were for the 1996 Atlanta, Georgia, games; most of the world's countries are in the northern hemisphere, and it would hardly have been proper to ask the cyclists and marathoners to be completing their preparations in January!

Jeffrey Hall

Solubility

Solubility in the general sense refers to the property of being soluble-being able to dissolve, usually in a liquid. Chemists, however, use the word solubility to also mean the maximum amount of a chemical substance that dissolves in a given amount of solvent at a specific **temperature**.

How much sugar could you dissolve in a cup of hot coffee? Certainly one teaspoonful would mix into the liquid and disappear quite easily. But after trying to dissolve several more teaspoonfuls, there will come a point where the extra sugar you add will simply not dissolve. No amount of stirring will make the sugar disappear and the crystals just settle down to the bottom of the cup. At this point the coffee is said to be saturated -it cannot dissolve any more sugar. The amount of sugar that the coffee now holds is "the solubility of sugar in coffee" at that temperature.

A sponge gets saturated when you are using it to wipe up spilled milk from a kitchen counter. At first, a dry sponge soaks up milk very quickly. But with further use, the sponge can only push milk along the counter-its absorbing action is lost. This sponge is now holding its maximum amount of milk. Similarly, a saturated solution is one that is holding its maximum amount of a given dissolved material.

The sugar you add to a cup of coffee is known as the solute. When this solute is added to the liquid, which is termed the solvent, the dissolving process begins. The sugar molecules separate and diffuse or spread evenly throughout the solvent particles, creating a homogeneous mixture called a **solution**. Unsaturated solutions are able to dissolve more solute, but eventually the solution becomes saturated.

Common measuring units

Solubility is often expressed in grams of solute per 0.2 lb (100 g) of solvent, usually **water**. At 122°F (50°C), the solubility of sugar in water is approximately 130 g/sugar in 100 g water. If you were to add 0.26 lb (130 g) of sugar to 0.2 lb (100 g) of water at 122°F (50°C), the resulting solution would be saturated. Adding 0.26 lb (131 g) would mean that even with con-

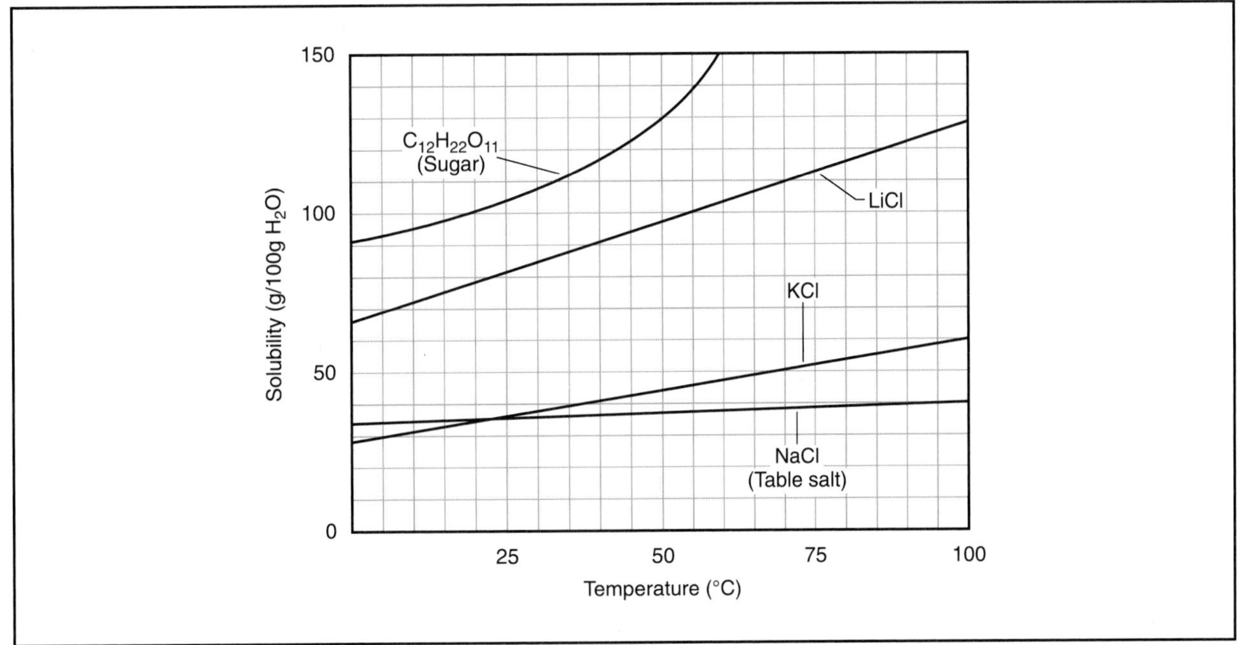

Figure 1. Solubility curve for various solutes in water.

tinuous stirring, 0.002 lb (1 g) of sugar would remain at the bottom of your container.

Sometimes, solubility is expressed as grams of solute per 0.2 lb (100 g) of solution. In this case the value of the solubility of sugar in 0.2 lb (100 g) of solution at 122°F (50°C) would be less than 0.26 lb (130 g), because unlike the previous example where the weight of the solvent was fixed, the weight of a solution changes as solute is added.

Other commonly used units include g/L, (grams of solute per liter of solution) and m/L, (moles of solute per liter of solution). Solubility units always express the maximum amount of solute that will dissolve in either a given amount of solvent, or a given amount of solution, at a specific temperature.

Effect of temperature on solubility

For most solutes, the higher the temperature of the solvent, the faster its rate of dissolving and the greater its solubility.

When making iced tea in summertime, it's best to dissolve the sugar in the hot tea before adding the ice cubes and refrigerating. Trying to dissolve sugar in a mixture of tea and ice is a much slower process and will often result in a build up of sugar at the bottom of your glass.

Figure 1 shows that the solubility of sugar and the three other compounds listed increases with rising temperature. Most solid compounds show the same **behavior**. One theory to explain this observation suggests that hot solvent particles, which move faster than cold ones, are on average more spread out. This creates larger spaces and increases the amount of solute that can fit into the solvent.

Bases, however, are less soluble in hot water than in cold. The solubility of **carbon dioxide** gas in soda pop actually decreases as temperature is increased. An open bottle of pop taken from a refrigerator soon loses its fizz if stored in a warm environment. As the pop warms, up the carbon dioxide gas dissolved in it becomes less soluble.

You may have noticed the same thing happening when heating a pot of water on a kitchen stove. Tap water contains dissolved air and when heated, small bubbles form, rise to the surface and leave. This reduced solubility of air is one cause of thermal **pollution**. Industries often use **lake** water as a coolant for their machinery. Before the hot water can be returned to the lake it must be allowed to cool down; otherwise it can be harmful to some **fish** because warm water holds less dissolved air and therefore less **oxygen**.

Effect of chemical bonding on solubility

Not all substances are equally soluble at the same temperature. At 41°F (5°C), the solubility of table sugar is more than three times greater than that of table **salt**, as shown in Figure 1.

KEY TERMS

Homogeneous—Having one phase, one uniform color and texture.

Saturated—Full. Containing a maximum amount.

Solute—Usually a solid. It is the least abundant component of a solution.

Solvent—Usually a liquid. It is the most abundant component of a solution.

Solution—A transparent, homogeneous mixture.

Thermal pollution—A type of water pollution where a rise in temperature results in the reduced solubility of air and oxygen.

Even substances such as ordinary glass, which appear not to dissolve, actually do so, but their solubility values are extremely small.

The types of bonds or forces that hold sugar particles together are different from those found in glass. The interaction between the attractive forces holding these particles together and the attractive forces to the molecules of solvents accounts for the different solubilities.

Lou D'Amore

Solute see **Solution**

Solution

A solution is a homogenous (uniform throughout) mixture, on a molecular level, of two or more substances. It is formed when one or more substances are dissolved in one or more other substances. The scientific nature of solutions is a relatively recent discovery, though solutions in one form or another have been used by people throughout history.

The substances (solids, liquids, or gasses) in a solution make up two phases, the solvent and the solute. The solvent is the substance which typically determines the physical state of the solution (solid, liquid or gas). The solute is the substance which is dissolved by the solvent. For example, in a solution of **salt** and **water**, water is the solvent and salt is the solute.

Solutions are formed because the molecules of the solute are attracted to the molecules of the solvent. When the attractive forces of the solvent are greater than the molecular forces holding the solute together, the solute dissolves. There are no rules which will determine whether substances will dissolve however, the cardinal rule of **solubility** is "like dissolves like." Oil and water don't mix, but oil in oil does.

The substances which make up a solution can be either solids, liquids, gasses, or a combination of any of these. Brass is a solution of solid **copper** and zinc. Gasoline is a complex solution of liquids. Air is a solution of gasses. Soda pop is a solution of solid sugar, liquid water and **carbon dioxide** gas. The properties of solutions are best understood by studying solutions with liquid solvents.

When water is the solvent, the solutions are called aqueous solutions. In aqueous solutions, dissolved material often separates into charged components called ions. For example, salt (NaCl) ionizes into Na^+ ions and Cl^- ions in water. The ionic nature of liquid solutions was first identified by Svante Arrhenius (1859-1927) who, in the early 1880s, studied the way **electricity** passed through a solution. His ionic theory states that charged particles in a solution will conduct electricity. At the time, his theory was controversial and scorned by the majority of scientists. In the late 1890s, however, when scientists discovered that **atoms** contained charges, the ionic theory was accepted. He was awarded the Nobel prize in 1903 for his work in understanding the nature of solutions.

Because of molecular interaction, the physical properties of a solution are often different from the properties of the pure substances of which they are composed. For example, water freezes at 32°F (0°C), but a solution of water and salt freezes below 32°F (0°C). This is why salt melts ice.

Unlike pure substances, solutions do not have a definite composition. Their composition is dependent on the amount of solute dissolved in the solvent. Concentrated solutions have relatively high amounts of solute dissolved in the solvent while dilute solutions have relatively low amounts. The **concentration** of a solution is typically expressed in terms of grams of solute per liter of solvent. The concentration of a solution of 0.2 oz (5 g) of sugar dissolved in 3.5 oz (100 g) of water is .05 or 5%.

Every solute has a certain degree of solubility in a solvent. Solubility is a number which indicates the normal concentration, at a certain **temperature**, in which no more dissolving will take place. For example, if a teaspoon of sugar is added to a glass of water, it dissolves, and an unsaturated solution is created. However, if more and more sugar is added, it eventually forms a pile of undissolved sugar on the bottom of the glass. At this point, the normal maximum concentration is exceeded and a saturated solution is created.

The solubility of a solute in a solvent is affected by various factors. Molecular structure, **pressure**, and temperature all affect the solubility of a system. Heating a solution can increase or decrease solubility. Increasing pressure has a similar effect.

A solution is an important form of **matter** and is the basis of many of the products we use everyday. From glues to shampoos, soda pops to medicines, solutions will undoubtedly be used by people forever.

See also Mixture, chemical; Solubility

Solution of equation

The solution of an equation is the set of all values which, when substituted for unknowns, make an equation true. For equations having one unknown, raised to a single power, two fundamental rules of **algebra**, including the additive property and the multiplicative property, are used to determine its solutions. Solutions for equations with multiple unknown variables are found by using the principles for a system of equations. Equations with terms raised to a power greater than one can be solved by factoring and, in some specific cases, by the quadratic equation.

The idea of a solution of equations has existed since the time of the Egyptians and Babylonians. During these times, they used simple algebraic methods to determine solutions for practical problems related to their everyday life. The methods used by the ancients were preserved in a treatise written by the Arabian mathematician Al-Kowarizmi (825 A.D.). In this work, he includes methods for solving linear equations as well as second degree equations. Solutions for some higher degree equations were worked out during the sixteenth century by an Italian mathematician named Gerolamo Cardano (1501-1576).

Methods for solving simple equations

An equation is an algebraic expression which typically relates unknown variables to other variables or constants. For example, $x + 2 = 15$ is an equation, as is $y^2 = 4$. The solution, or root, of an equation is any value or set of values which can be substituted into the equation to make it a true statement. For our first example, the solution for x is 13. The second example has two values which will make the statement true, namely 2 and -2. These values make up the solution set of the equation.

Using the two fundamental rules of algebra, solutions to many simple equations can be obtained. The first rule states that the same quantity can be added to both sides of an equation without changing the solution to the equation. For example, the equation $x + 4 = 7$ has a solution of $x = 3$. According to the first rule, we can add any number to both sides of the equation and still get the same solution. By adding 4 to both sides, the equation becomes $x + 8 = 11$ but the solution remains $x = 3$. This rule is known as the additive property of equality. To use this property to find the solution to an equation, all that is required is choosing the right number to add. The solution to our previous example $x + 4 = 7$ can be found by adding -4 to both sides of the equation. If this is done, the equation simplifies to $x + 4 - 4 = 7 - 4$ or $x = 3$ and the equation is solved.

The second fundamental rule, known as the multiplicative property of equality, states that every term on both sides of an equation can be multiplied or divided by the same number without changing the solution to the equation. For instance, the solution for the equation $y - 2 = 10$ is $y = 12$. Using the multiplicative rule, we can obtain an equivalent equation, one with the same solution set, by multiplying both sides by any number, such as 2. Thus the equation becomes $2y - 4 = 20$, but the solution remains $y = 12$. This property can also be used to solve algebraic equations. In the case of the equation $2x = 14$, the solution is obtained by dividing both sides by 2. When this is done $2x/2 = 14/2$ the equation simplifies to $x = 7$.

Often, both of these rules must be employed to solve a single equation, such as the equation $4x + 7 = 23$. In this equation, -7 is added to both sides of the equation and it simplifies to $4x = 16$. Both sides of this equation are then divided by 4 and it simplifies to the solution, $x = 4$.

Solving more complex equations

Most equations are given in a more complicated form which can be simplified. Consider the equation $4x - x - 5 = 2x + 7$. The first step in solving this equation is to combine like terms on each side of the equation. On the right side there are no like terms, but the 4x and -x on the left side are like terms. This equation, when simplified, becomes $3x - 5 = 2x + 7$. The next step is to eliminate the unknown from one side of the equation. For this example, this is accomplished by adding -2x to both sides of the equation, which gives $x - 5 = 7$. Using the additive property, the solution is obtained by adding 5 to both sides of the equation, so $x = 12$.

The whole process for solving single **variable** algebraic equations can be summarized by the following steps. First, eliminate any parentheses by multiplying out factors. Second, add the like terms in each side. Third, eliminate the unknown from one side of the equation using the multiplicative or additive properties. Fourth, eliminate the constant term from the side with

the unknown using the additive property. Finally, eliminate any **coefficient** on the unknown by using the multiplicative property.

Solving multivariable equations

Many algebraic equations contain more than one variable, so the complete solution set can not be found using the methods described thus far. Equations with two unknowns are called linear equations and can be represented by the general formula $ax + by = c$; where a, b, and c are constants and x and y are variables. The solution of this type of equation would be the ordered pair of x and y which makes the equation true. For example, the solution set for the equation $x + y = 7$ would contain all the pairs of values for x and y which satisfy the equation, such as (2,5), (3,4), (4,3) etc. In general, to determine the solution to a linear equation with two variables, the equation is rewritten and solved in terms of one variable. The solution for the equation $x + y = 7$, then becomes any pair of values which makes $x = 7 - y$ true.

Often multiple linear equations exist which relate two variables in the same system. All of the equations related to the variables are known as a system of equations and their solution is an ordered pair which makes every equation true. These equations are solved by methods of graphing, substitution, and elimination.

Solving second degree and higher equations

Equations which involve unknowns raised to a power of one are known as first degree equations. Second degree equations also exist which involve at least one variable that is squared, or raised to a power of two. Equations can also be third degree, fourth degree, and so on. The most famous second degree equation is the quadratic equation, which has the general form $ax^2 + bx + c = 0$; where a, b, and c are constants and a is not equal to 0. The solution for this type of equation can often be found by a method known as factoring.

Since the quadratic equation is the product of two first degree equations, it can be factored into these equations. For example, the product of the two expressions $(x + 2)(x - 3)$ provides us with the quadratic expression $x^2 - x - 6$. The two expressions $(x + 2)$ and $(x - 3)$ are called factors of the quadratic expression $x^2 - x - 6$. By setting each **factor** of a quadratic equation equal to **zero**, solutions can be obtained. In this quadratic equation, the solutions are $x = -2$ and $x = 3$.

Finding the factors of a quadratic equation is not always easy. To solve this problem, the quadratic formula was invented so that any quadratic equation can be solved. The quadratic equation is stated as follows for the general equation $ax^2 + bx + c = 0$

$$x = \frac{-b \pm (b^2 - 4ac)^{1/2}}{2a}$$

To use the quadratic formula, numbers for a, b, and c are substituted into the equation, and the solutions for x are determined.

See also Algebra; Equation; Systems of equations

Further Reading

Carrie, Dennis. *Precalculus.* Boston: Houghton Mifflin Company, 1990.

Marcucci, Robert & Harold Schoen. *Beginning Algebra.* Boston: Houghton Mifflin Company, 1990.

Saxon, John. *Algebra I: An Incremental Development.* Norman: Grassdale Publishers Inc, 1981.

Perry Romanowski

KEY TERMS

Additive property—The property of an equation which states that a number can be added to both sides of an equation without effecting its solution.

Factoring—A method of reducing a higher degree equation to the product of lower degree equations.

First degree equation—An algebraic expression which contains an unknown raised to the first power.

Multiplicative property—The property of an equation which state that all the terms in an equation can be multiplied by the same number without effecting the final solution.

Second degree equation—An algebraic expression which contains an unknown raised to the second power.

Solvent see **Solution**

Sonar

Sonar, an acronym for SOund Navigation And Ranging, is a technique based on **echolocation** used for the detection of objects underwater. It was originally developed to detect **icebergs** after the sinking of the *Titanic*

in 1912. World War I stimulated further sonar development for **submarine** detection. Sonar uses acoustic, or sound, waves that are actually mechanical vibrations that travel quite efficiently in **water**. The more well-known **radar** (for **RAdio** Detection And Ranging, invented later), employs **radio waves** and is used in the atmosphere. Radio waves lose too much **energy** when they travel, or propagate, through the water. Likewise, the propagation of acoustic waves in air is inefficient.

Sonar equipment is used on most ships for measuring the depth of the water. This is accomplished by sending an acoustic pulse and measuring the time for the echo, or return from the bottom. By knowing the speed of sound in the water, the depth is computed by multiplying the speed by one half of the time travelled (for a one-way trip). Sonar is also used to detect large underwater objects and to search for large **fish** concentrations. More sophisticated sonar systems for detection and tracking are found aboard naval vessels and submarines. In nature, **bats** are well known for making use of echolocation, as are porpoises and some species of whales. Sonar should not be confused with ultrasound, which is simply sound at frequencies higher than the threshold of human **hearing** - greater than 15,000-20,000 cycles per second, or hertz (Hz). Ultrasound is used on a very small scale, at high power, to break up material and for cleaning purposes. Lower power ultrasound is used therapeutically, for treatment of muscle and **tissue** injuries.

Sonar is very directional, so the signals are sent in narrow beams in various directions to search the water. Sonar usually operates at frequencies in the 10,000-50,000 Hz range. Though higher frequencies provide more accurate location data, propagation losses also increase with **frequency**. Lower frequencies are therefore used for longer range detection (up to 10 mi [17,600 yds]) at the cost of location **accuracy**.

Acoustic waves are detected using hydrophones that are essentially underwater microphones. Hydrophones are often deployed in large groups, called arrays, forming a sonar net. Sonar arrays also give valuable directional information on moving sources. **Electronics** and signal processing play a large role in hydrophone and general sonar system performance.

The propagation of sound in water is quite complex and depends very much on the **temperature**, **pressure**, and depth of the water. Salinity, the quantity of **salt** in water, also changes sound propagation speed. In general, the temperature of the **ocean** is warmest at the surface and decreases with depth. Water pressure, however, increases with depth, due to the water **mass**. Temperature and pressure, therefore, change what is called the refractive index of the water. Just as light is refracted, or bent by a **prism**, acoustic waves are continuously refracted up or down and reflected off the surface or the bottom. A sonar beam propagating along the water in this way resembles a car traveling along regularly spaced hills and valleys. As it is possible for an object to be hidden between these hills, the water conditions must be known in order to properly assess sonar performance.

In location and tracking operations, two types of sonar modes exist, active and passive. Echolocation is an active technique in which a pulse is sent and then detected after it bounces off an object. Passive sonar is a more sensitive, listening-only sonar that sends no pulses. Most moving objects underwater make some kind of noise. This means that they can be detected just by listening for the noise. Examples of underwater noise are marine life, cavitation (small collapsing air pockets caused by propellers), hull popping of submarines changing depth, and engine vibration. Some military passive sonars are so sensitive they can detect people talking inside another submarine. Another advantage of

KEY TERMS

Acoustics—The study of the creation and propagation of mechanical vibration causing sound.

Active sonar—Mode of echo location by sending a signal and detecting the returning echo.

Array—A large group of hydrophones, usually regularly spaced, forming a sonar net.

Hertz (Hz)—Unit of frequency; 1 Hz equals one cycle per second.

Hydrophone—An underwater microphone sensitive to acoustic disturbances.

Passive sonar—A sensitive listening-only mode to detect presence of objects making noise.

Propagation—Traveling or penetration of waves through a medium.

Radar—RAdio Detection And Ranging.

Refractive index—(characteristic of a medium) Degree to which a wave is refracted, or bent.

Sonar—SOund Navigation And Ranging.

Ultrasound—Acoustic vibrations with frequencies higher than the human threshold of hearing.

Wave—The unit of a periodic disturbance characterized by a frequency and maximum amplitude.

passive sonar is that it can also be used to detect an acoustic signature. Each type of submarine emits certain acoustic frequencies and every vessel's composite acoustic pattern is different, just like a fingerprint or signature. Passive sonar is predominantly a military tool used for submarine hunting. An important element of hunting is not to divulge one's own position. However, if the passive sonar hears nothing, one is obliged to turn to active **mode** but in doing so, risks alerting the other of his presence. The use of sonar in this case has become a sophisticated tactical exercise.

Other, non-military, applications of sonar, apart from fish finding, include searching for shipwrecks, probing harbors where visibility is poor, **oceanography** studies, searching for underwater geological faults and mapping the ocean floor.

Further Reading

Clancy, Tom. *The Hunt for Red October.* 1985.

Griffen, D.R. *Listening in the Dark: The Acoustic Orientation of Bats and Men.* 1958.

Kellogg, W.N. *Porpoises and Sonar.* 1961.

Tucker. D.G. and B.K. Gazey. *Underwater Observation Using Sonar.* 1966.

Urick, R.J. *Principles of Underwater Sound for Engineers.* 1967.

David Lunney

Song birds

Song birds are any **bird**s that sing musically, almost all of which are in the suborder Oscines of the order Passeriformes, or perching birds. Passeriform birds have feet adapted for gripping branches, **plant** stems, and similar perches, and they comprise about one-third of living bird families, and one-half of the species.

A major function of singing in birds is to proclaim the location and limits of a breeding territory, that is, an area of **habitat** that is defended against other birds of the same species, and sometimes against other species as well. Usually, only the male of the species sings. By singing loudly and in a manner that is specific to the species, individual song birds advertise their presence, and their ownership of the local habitat. Usually, a vigorous song by a resident bird is sufficient to deter would-be competitors, but sometimes it is not. In such cases, the conflict can intensify into visual displays at close range, and sometimes into out-and-out fighting, until a winner emerges.

The **frequency** and intensity of the songs is usually greatest at the beginning of the breeding season, while territories are actively being established. Once a territory is well ensconced, the frequency and loudness of the song often decrease, because all that is required at that stage is occasional reminders to neighbours that the territory remains occupied by the same individual. However, another important function of singing is to attract a mate, and if a territorial male bird has not been successful in achieving this goal, he will continue to sing often and loudly well into the breeding season, until a female finds and chooses him, or he gives up.

With a bit of effort and **concentration**, it is not too difficult to learn to identify bird species on the basis of their song. In fact, this is the basis of the most common method by which song birds are censused in **forests**, where it can be very difficult to see these small, cryptic animals because of dense foliage. During surveys of song birds, observations are made on different dates of the places at which singing by various species occurs in the forest. Clusters of observations of singing by a particular species at about the same place but on different dates are ascribed to a particular male bird, and are used to designate his territory.

There are great differences in the songs of various bird species, which can range from the faint, high-pitched twitterings of the cedar waxwing (*Bombycilla cedrorum*), to the loud and raucous jays of the blue jay (*Cyanocitta cristata*); the enormously varied and twice-repeated phrases of the brown thrasher (*Toxostoma rufum*); the whistled deea-deee of the black-capped chickadee (*Parus atricapillus*); the aerial twinklings of the horned lark (*Eremophila alpestris*); the witchety wichy of the common yellowthroat (*Geothlypis trichas*), a species of warbler; and the euphonious flutings and trills of the **wood** thrush (*Hylocichla mustelina*).

Bill Freedman

Sonoluminescence

Sonoluminescence is the **emission** of **light** from bubbles of air trapped in **water** which contains intense sound waves. Hypothesized in 1933 by Reinhardt Mecke of the University of Heidelberg, from the observation that intense sound from military **sonar** systems could catalyze chemical reactions in water, it was first observed in 1934 by H. Frenzel and H. Schultes at the University of Cologne. Modern experiments show it to be a result of heating in a bubble when the surrounding sound waves compress its **volume** by approximately a million-fold.

The precise details of light generation within an air bubble are not presently known. Certain general features of the process are well understood, however. Owing to water's high degree of incompressibility, sound travels through it in the form of high speed, high **pressure** waves. Sound waves in air have smaller pressure, since air is highly compressible. The transmitted power in a wave is proportional to the product of its pressure and the amplitude of its vibrational **motion**. This means that the **wave motion** is strongly amplified when a sound wave travels from water to air.

Since the speed of sound is much greater in water than in air, a small bubble within water carrying sound waves will be subjected to essentially the same pressure at every point on its surface. Thus, the sound waves within the bubble will be nearly spherical.

Spherical symmetry, along with the large amplitude of displacement of the surface of the bubble, results in extreme compression of the air at the center of the bubble. This compression takes place *adiabatically*, that is, with little loss of **heat**, until the air is at a high enough **temperature** to emit light. Temperatures within a sonoluminescing bubble range between 10,000–100,000K (17,540–179,541°F; 9,727–99,727°C).

Theorists are working on models of sonoluminescing bubbles in which the inward-traveling wave becomes a shock wave near the center of the bubble; this is thought to account for the extremely high temperatures there. Although the maximum temperatures within a sonoluminescing bubble are not known with any certainty, some researchers are investigating the possibility of using these imploding shock waves to obtain the million-degree temperatures needed for controlled **nuclear fusion**.

Sorghum

Sorghum (genus *Sorghum*) refers to various species of **grasses** (family Poaceae) that are cultivated as food **crops**. Because the relationships among the various species and their hybrids are highly complex and not well understood, the cultivated grain sorghums are usually named as *Sorghum bicolor*.

Sorghum is a tropical grass, well adapted to high productivity in a hot and dry climatic regime, and **water** efficient (water transpired per unit of atmospheric **carbon dioxide** fixed during **photosynthesis**). The wild progenitors of domesticated sorghum are thought to have inhabited the savannah of northern and central **Africa**, and perhaps India. Wild sorghum still occurs in these regions and their grains are gathered for food by local people. Sorghum was domesticated as a grain-crop approximately 5,000 years ago. Modern varieties grow 3-15 ft tall (1-5 m). The grains are born in a dense cluster (known as a panicle) at the top of the **plant**.

Sorghum is one of the world's major cultivated crops, ranking fourth among the cereals. In 1999, about 113 million acres (45.9 million ha) of sorghum were grown worldwide, and total production was 74.9 million tons of grain (68.1 million tonnes). Most of the world's sorghum crop is grown in Africa, where it is a leading cereal (although surpassed during the twentieth century by maize [*Zea mays*] in many countries).

There are four main cultivated groups of sorghum:

- The grain sorghums are ground into flour for baking bread and cakes, boiled as a gruel, fermented into beer, or fed to **livestock**. Sorghum grain is highly nutritious, containing about 12% protein. Grain sorghums are by far the most important sorghum crop.
- The sweet sorghum contains a high **concentration** of sucrose in its stems and is used to make table sugar in the same way as sugar cane (*Saccharum officinarum*). However, the sorghum sugar is not usually crystallized, but is boiled down into a dark-brown syrup similar to molasses.
- The forage sorghums are used directly as **animal** feed or they are chopped and fermented to manufacture silage.
- The broom-corn sorghums are cultivated for their thin, wiry, brushy stalks that are bound into"corn" brooms. This is no longer a common use, as natural-fiber brooms have been replaced by synthetic ones.

Bill Freedman

Sound see **Acoustics**

South America

The South American **continent** stretches from about 10° above the equator to almost 60° below it, encompassing an area of about 7 million sq mi (18 million sq km). It is divided into 10 countries. The continent can be divided into three main regions with distinct environmental and geological qualities: the highlands and plateaus of the east, which are the oldest geological feature in the continent; the Andes Mountains, which line the west coast and were created by the subduction of the

Nazca plate beneath the continent; and the riverplain, between the highlands, which contains the Amazon River. The South American climate varies greatly based on the **distance** from the equator and the altitude of the area, but the range of temperatures seldom reaches 36°F (2°C), except in small areas.

The continent

The continent of South America extends over 68° of latitude, and encompasses an area of 6,880,706 sq. mi (17,821,028 sq. km). This is almost 12% of the surface area of the Earth. It is about 3,180 mi (5,100 km) wide at its widest point.

The highlands and plateaus

The Eastern highlands and plateaus are the oldest geological region of South America, and are believed to have bordered on the African continent at one time, before the **motion** of the Earth's crust and **continental drift** separated the continents. They can be divided into three main sections. The Guiana Highlands are in the northeast, in the Guianan states, south Venezuela and northeastern Brazil. Their highest peak, Roraima, reaches a height of 9,220 ft (2,810 m). This is a moist region with many waterfalls; and it is in this range, in Venezuela, that the highest waterfall in the world is found. It is called Angel Falls, and falls freely for 2,630 ft (802 m).

The Brazilian Highlands make up more than one half of the area of Brazil, and range in altitude between 1,000-5,000 ft (305-1524 m). The highest **mountain** range of this region is called Serra da Mantiqueira, and its highest peak, Pico da Bandeira, is 9,396 ft (2,864 m) above sea level.

The Patagonian Highlands are in the south, in Argentina. The highest peak attains an altitude of 9,462 ft (2,884 m), and is called Sierra de Cordoba.

The Andes

The great mountain range of South America is the Andes Mountains, which extends more than 5,500 mi (8,900 km) all the way down the western coast of the continent. The highest peak of the Andes, called Mount Aconcagua, is on the western side of central Argentina, and is 22,828 ft (6,958 m) high.

The Andes were formed by the motion of the Earth's crust, which is cut up into different tectonic plates. Some of them are continental plates, which are at a greater altitude than the other type of plate, the oceanic plates. All of these plates are in motion relative to each other, and the places where they border each other are regions of instability where various geological structures are formed, and where earthquakes and volcanic activity is frequent. The west coast of South America is a subduction zone, which means that the oceanic plate, called the Nazca plate, is being forced beneath the adjacent continental plate. The Andes mountains were thrust upwards by this motion, and can still be considered "under construction" by the Earth's crust. In addition to the Nazca plate, the South American and Antarctic plates converge on the west coast in an area called the Chile Triple Junction, at about 46°S latitude. The complexity of plate tectonics in this region makes it a locality of interest for geologists.

The geological instability of the region makes earthquakes common all along the western region of the continent, particularly along the southern half of Peru.

The Andes are dotted with volcanoes; some of the highest peaks in the mountain range are volcanic in origin, many of which rise above 20,000 ft (6,100 m). There are 3 major areas in which volcanoes are concentrated. The first of these appears between latitude 6°N and 2°S, and straddles Colombia and Ecuador. The second, and largest region, lies between latitudes 15° and 27°S; it is about 1,240 mi (2,000 km) long and 62-124 mi (100-200 km) wide, and borders Peru, Bolivia, Chile, and Argentina. This is the largest **concentration** of volcanos in the world, and the highest volcanoes in the world are found here; but it is an area of low volcanic activity, and it is generally geysers which erupt here. The third region of volcanic concentration is also the most active. It lies in the central valley of Chile, mostly between 33° and 44°S.

The climate in the Andes varies greatly, depending on both altitude and latitude, from hot regions to Alpine meadow regions to the **glaciers** of the South. The snowline is highest in southern Peru and northern Chile, at latitude 15-20°S, where it seldom descends below 19,000 ft (5,800 m). This is much higher than at the equator, where the snowline descends to 15,000 ft (4,600 m). This vagary is attributed to the extremely dry climate of the lower latitude. In the far south of the continent, in the region known as Tierra del Fuego, the snowline reaches as low as 2,000 ft (600 m) above **sea level**.

The Andes are a rich source of mineral deposits, particularly **copper**, silver, and gold. In Venezuela, they are mined for copper, **lead**, **petroleum**, phosphates, and **salt**; diamonds are found along the Rio Caroni. Columbia has the richest deposits of **coal**, and is the largest producer of gold and platinum in South America. It is also wealthy in emeralds, containing the largest deposits in the world, with the exception of Russia. In Chile, the Andes are mined largely for their great copper stores, in addition to lead, zinc, and silver. Bolivia has enormous

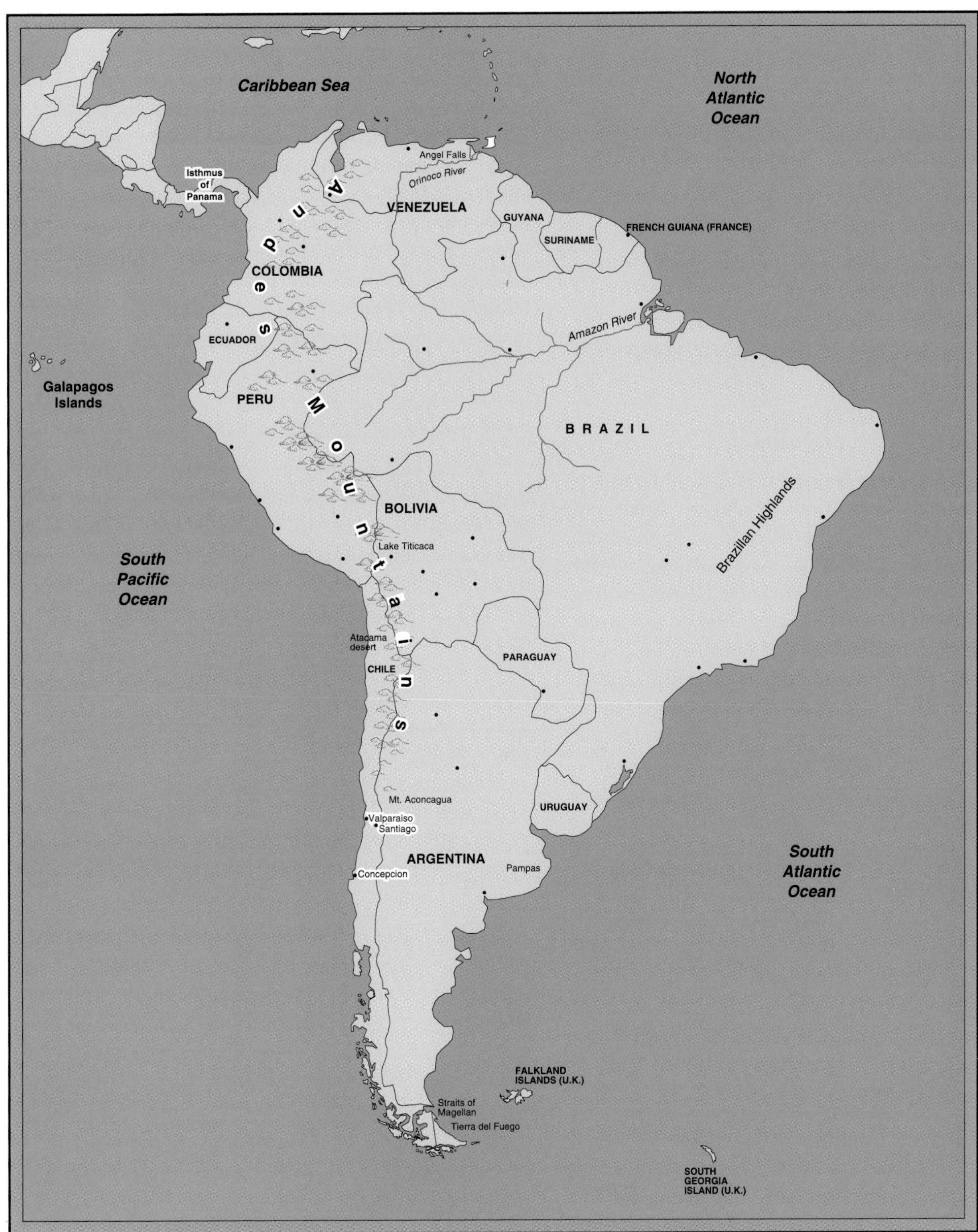

South America.

tin mines. The Andes are also a source of tungsten, antimony, nickel, chromium, cobalt, and **sulfur**.

The Amazon basin

The Amazon **basin** is the largest river basin found in the world, covering an area of about 2.73 million sq. mi (7 million sq. km). The second largest river basin, which is the basin of the River Zaire in the African Congo, is not even half as large. The **water** resources of the area are spectacular; the **volume** of water which flows from the basin into the sea is about 11% of all the water drained from the continents of the **earth**. The greatest flow occurs in July, and the least is in November. While there are

many **rivers** flowing through the basin, the most important and well-known of these is the Amazon. The width of the Amazon ranges from about 1 mi (1.6 km) to as wide as 8-10 km (5-6 mi), and although it is usually only about 20-40 ft (6-12 m) deep, there are narrow channels where it can reach a depth of 300 ft (100 m).

The Amazon basin was once an enormous bay, before the Andes were pushed up along the coasts. As the mountain range grew, they held back the **ocean** and eventually the bay became an inland sea. This sea was finally filled by the **erosion** of the higher land surrounding it, and finally a huge plain, criss-crossed by countless waterways, was created. Most of this region is still at sea level, and is covered by lush jungle and extensive **wetlands**. This jungle region has the largest extent of any rain forest in the world, and is thought to have upwards of 100 different species per **square** kilometer. Despite the profusion of life that abounds here, the **soil** is not very rich; the fertile regions are those which receive a fresh layer of river silt when the Amazon floods, which occurs almost every year.

The climate

The climate of South America varies widely over a large range of altitudes and latitudes, but only in isolated regions is the **temperature** range greater than about 20°C (36°F). The coldest part of the continent is in the extreme southern tip, in the area called Tierra del Fuego; in the coldest month of the year, which is July, it is as cold as 0°C (32°F) there. The highest temperature of the continent is reached in a small area of northern Argentina, and is about 42°C (108°F). However, less than 15 days a year are this warm, and the average temperature in the same area for the hottest month of the year, which is January, is about 29°C (84°F).

The countries

Colombia

Colombia borders on Venezuela, Brazil, Ecuador, and Peru, and encompasses an area of 440,831 sq. mi (1,141,748 sq. km). It is found where Panama of Central America meets the South American continent, and its location gives it the interesting feature of having coastal regions bordering on both the Atlantic and the Pacific oceans. It is a country of diverse environments, including coastal, mountain, jungle, and **island** regions, but in general can be considered to consist of two major areas based on altitude: the Andes mountains, and the lowlands.

The Andes in Colombia can be divided into three distinct ranges, which run approximately from north to south in **parallel** ridges. The Cordillera Occidental, or westernmost range, attains a maximum altitude of about 10,000 ft (3,000 m). The Cordillera Oriental, which is the eastern range, is much higher, and many of its peaks are covered with snow all year round. Its highest peak is about 18,000 ft (5,490 m) high, and it has many beautiful waterfalls, such as the Rio Bogota which falls 400 ft (120 m). The Cordillera Central, as its name implies, runs between the Occidental and Oriental Cordilleras. It contains many active volcanoes as well as the highest peak in Colombia, Pico Cristobal Colon, which is 19,000 ft (5,775 m) high.

The lowlands of the east cover two thirds of Colombia's land area. It is part of the Orinoco and Amazon basins, and thus is well-watered and fertile. Part of this region is covered with rich equatorial rain forest. The northern lowlands of the coastal region also contain several rivers, and the main river of Colombia, the Magdalena, begins there.

Venezuela

Venezuela covers an area of 352,144 sq. mi (912,0250 sq. km). It is the most northern country of South America, and can be divided up into four major regions. The Guiana Highlands in the southeast make up almost half of Venezuela's land area, and are bordered by Brazil and Guyana. It is here that the famous Angel Falls, the highest waterfall in the world, is found. The Northern Highlands, which are a part of the Andes mountains, contain the highest peak in Venezuela - Pico Bolivar, which reaches a height of 16,427 ft (5,007 m). This range borders on much of the coastal region of Venezuela, and despite its proximity to both the Carribean and the equator, it has many peaks which are snow-covered year-round. The Maracaibo basin, one-third of which is covered by **Lake** Maracaibo, is found in the northwest. It is connected to the Carribean sea, and although it contains fresh water at one end of the lake, as it nears the ocean it becomes more saline. Not surprisingly, most of the basin consists of wetlands. The Llanos de Orinoco, which borders on Colombia in the southwestern part of Venezuela, is watered by the Orinoco River and its tributaries. The Orinoco has a yearly discharge almost twice as large as that of the Mississippi, and from June to October, during the rainy season, many parts of the Llanos are inaccessible due to **flooding**.

Ecuador

Ecuador received its name from the fact that it straddles the equator. Its area is 103,930 sq. mi (269,178 sq. km), making it the smallest of the Andean countries. Its eastern and western lowlands regions are divided by the Andes Mountains, which run through the center of the

country. This part of the Andes contains an extremely active **volcano** region; the world's highest active volcano, Cotopaxi, which reaches an altitude of 19,347 ft (5,897 m), is found here. The western lowlands on the coast contain a tropical rain forest in the north, but become extremely dry in the south. The eastern lowlands are part of the Amazon basin, and are largely covered by tropical **rainforest**. The rivers Putumayo, Napo, and Pastaza flow through this area.

Ecuador also owns the famous Galapagos Islands, which lie about 650 mi (1,040 km) off the coast. These 12 islands are all volcanic in origin, and several of the volcanoes are still active. The islands are the home of many species unique to the world, including perhaps the most well-known of their numbers, the Galapagos tortoise.

Peru

Peru covers an area of 496,225 sq. mi (1,285,216 sq. km), making it the largest of the Andean countries. Like Ecuador, it is split by the Andes mountain into two distinct sections. The eastern coastal region is mostly covered with mountains, and in many places the ocean borders on steep cliffs. In the northern part, however, there is a relatively flat region which is suitable for agriculture. In the east, the lowlands are mostly covered by the thick tropical rain forest of the Amazon basin. The southern part of the Andes in Peru contain many volcanoes, some of which are still active, and Lake Titicaca, which is shared by Bolivia. Lake Titicaca is famous among archaeologists for its ancient Incan and pre-Incan ruins. It is extraordinary that the many fortresses, palaces, and temples found there were built of stone, for no stone is found anywhere close by, and some of the blocks weigh more than 20 tons (18 tonnes). However, Lake Titicaca is also remarkable for itself, for of the large lakes with no ocean outlet, it is the highest in the world. It is 125 mi (200 km) at its largest length and 69 mi (110 km) at its largest breadth, which is not quite half as large as Lake Ontario; but it lies at an altitude of 12, 507 ft (3,812 m) above sea level.

Bolivia

Bolivia has an area of 424,164 sq. mi (1,098,581 sq. km), and is the only landlocked country in South America besides Paraguay. The western part of the country, which borders on Ecuador and Chile, is covered by the Andes mountains, and like most of this part of the Andes, it contains many active volcanoes. In the southern part of the range, the land becomes more arid, and in many places salt marshes are found. Among these is Lake Poopo, which lies 12,120 ft (3,690 m) above sea level. This saline lake is only 10 ft (3 m) deep. In the northern part of the range, the land becomes more habitable, and it is here that Lake Titicaca, which is shared with Peru, is found.

The eastern lowlands of Bolivia are divided into two distinct regions. In the north, the fertile Llanos de Mamore is well-watered and is thickly covered with vegetation. The southeastern section, called the Gran Chaco, is a semiarid **savanna** region.

Chile

Chile is the longest, narrowest country in the world; although it is 2,650 mi (4,270 km) long, it is only about 250 mi (400 km) wide at its greatest width. It encompasses an area of 284,520 sq. mi (736,905 sq. km). The Andes divides into two branches along the eastern and western edges of the country. The eastern branch contains the highest of the Andean peaks, Aconcagua, which is 20,000 ft (6,960 m), and the highest point on the continent. The Andes in Chile has the greatest concentration of volcanoes on the continent, containing over 2,000 active and dormant volcanoes, and the area is plagued by earthquakes.

In the western coastal region of north and central Chile, the land meets the ocean in a long line of cliffs which reach about 8,800 ft (2,700 m) in altitude. The southern section of this coastal mountain range moves offshore, forming a group of about 3,000 islands extending in a line all the way to Cape Horn, which is the southernmost point on the continent. The coast in this area is quite remarkable in appearance, having numerous fjords. There are many volcanic islands off the coast of Chile, including the famous Easter Island, which contains some extremely unusual archeological remains.

The southern part of the coastal region of Chile is a pleasant, temperate area, but in the north it contains the Atacama **Desert**, which is the longest and driest desert in the world. Iquique, Chile, which lies in this region, is reported to have at one time suffered 14 years without any rain at all. The dryness of the area is believed to be due to a sudden temperature inversion as clouds move from the cold waters off the shore and encounter the warmth of the continent; this prevents water from precipitating from the **clouds** when they reach the shoreline. It has been suggested also that the sudden rise of the Andes Mountains on the coast contributes to this effect.

Argentina

Argentina, the second-largest of the South American countries, covers an area of 1,073,399 sq. mi (2,780,092 sq. km). The Andes Mountains divide western Argentina from Chile, and in the south, known as Tierra de Fuego, this range is still partly covered with glaciers.

A large part of Argentina is a region of lowlands and plains. The northern part of the lowlands, called the Chaco, is the hottest region in Argentina. A little further south, between the rivers Parana and Uruguay, there is an area called Mesopotamia. For most of the year the area is marshland, due to flooding of the rivers during the rainy season. In the northwestern part of Argentina near the Paraguay and Brazilian borders, are found the remarkable Iguassa Falls. They are 2.5 mi (4 km) wide and 269 ft (82 m) high. As a comparison, Niagara Falls is only 5,249 ft (1,599 m) wide and 150-164 ft (46-50 m) high. The greatest part of the lowland plains are called the Pampa, which is humid in the east and semi-arid in the west.

The southern highlands of Patagonia, which begins below the Colorado River, is a dry and mostly uninhabited region of plateaus. In the area known as Tierra del Fuego, the southernmost extension of the Andes is found. They are mostly glaciated, and many beautiful glacial lakes are found here. Where the mountains descend into the sea, the glaciers have shaped them so that the coast has a fjord-like appearance.

The Falkland Islands lie off the eastern coast of Argentina. They are a group of about 200 islands which mostly consist of rolling hills and peat valleys, although there are a few low mountains north of the main islands. The sea around the Falkland Islands is quite shallow, and for this reason they are believed to lie on an extension of the **continental shelf**.

Paraguay

Paraguay, which has an area of 157,048 sq. mi (406,752 sq. km), is completely landlocked. About half of the country is part of the Gran Chaco, a large plain west of the Paraguay River, which also extends into Bolivia and Argentina. The Gran Chaco is swampy in places, but for the most part consists of scrub land with a few isolated patches of forest. East of the Paraguay river, there is another plain which is covered by forest and seasonal marshes. This region becomes a country of flat plateaus in the easternmost part of Paraguay, most of which are covered with evergreen and deciduous **forests**.

Uruguay

Uruguay, which is 68,037 sq. mi (176,215 sq. km) in area, is a country bounded by water. To the east, it is bordered by the Atlantic Ocean, and there are many lagoons and great expanses of dunes found along the coast. In the west, Uruguay is bordered by the river Uruguay, and in the south, by the La Plata estuary. Most of the country consists of low hills with some forested areas.

Brazil

With an area of 3,286,487 sq. mi (8,511,965 sq. km), Brazil is by far the largest country in South America, taking up almost half of the land area of the continent. It can be divided into two major geographical regions: the highlands, which include the Guiana Highlands in the far north and the Brazilian Highlands in the center and southeast, and the Amazon basin.

The highlands mostly have the appearance of flat tablelands which are cut here and there by deep rifts and clefts which drain them; these steep river valleys are often inaccessible. In some places the highlands have been shaped by erosion so that their surfaces are rounded and hill-like, or even give the appearance of mountain peaks. Along the coast the plateaus plummet steeply to the ocean to form great cliffs, which can be as high as 7,000-8,000 ft (2,100-2,400 m). Except for the far north of Brazil, there are no coastal plains.

The lowlands of Brazil are in the vast Amazon basin, which is mostly covered with dense tropical rain forest - the most enormous tract of unbroken rainforest in the world. The many rivers and tributaries which water the region create large marshes in places. The Amazon is home to many indigenous peoples and as yet uncounted species of animals and plants found no where else in the world. The Amazon rainforest is one of the world's greatest resources; both as a natural wonder and as a source of medicinal and edible plants and exotic woods.

Brazil also has many island territories, most of which, however, are quite small; the largest, called Fernando de Noronha, has an area of 10 sq. mi (26 sq. km). The majority of the remaining islands are only seasonally inhabited.

French Guiana

French Guiana encompasses and area of 35,900 sq. mi. (93,000 sq. km), and is found north of Brazil. The area furthest inland is a region of flat plateaus which becomes rolling hills in the central region of the country, while the eastern coastal area is a broad plain consisting mostly of poorly drained marshland. Most of the country is covered with dense tropical rain forest, and the coast is lined with mangrove swamps. French Guiana possesses a few island territories as well, and the most famous of these, Devil's Island, the former site of a French penal colony.

Suriname

North of French Guiana lies Suriname, another tiny coastal country which has an area of 63,251 sq. mi. (163,820 sq. km). The southern part of the country is part of the Guiana Highlands, and consists of very flat

KEY TERMS

Continental drift—The movement of continents which is due to the motion of the Earth's crust.

Continental shelf—Part of the Earth's crust which lies above the ocean crust.

Deciduous—Plants which shed their foliage seasonally.

Fjords—Areas along the coast where the sea runs in a long channel between steep cliffs.

Geysers—Underground springs which periodically explode upwards, forming tall fountains of hot water.

Lithosphere—The Earth's crust, along with the upper part of the mantle.

Oceanic crust—The part of the Earth's crust that lies beneath the oceans, which is further down than the continental crust.

Savanna—A treeless plain of high grasses found in tropical climates.

Scrub land—Region covered with low, stunted trees.

Subduction—The motion of a tectonic plate which forces it beneath a neighboring plate.

Tectonic—Of or pertaining to a planet's crust.

plateaus cut across by great rifts and steep gullies. These are covered with thick tropical rain forest. North of the highlands is an area of rolling hills and deep valleys formed by rivers and covered with forest. The extreme north of Suriname lies along the coast and is a flat swamp. Several miles of mangrove swamps lie between this region and the coast.

Guyana

East of Suriname is the country of Guyana, with a land area of 83,000 sq. mi. (215,00 sq. km). In the western and southern parts of Guyana are the Guiana Highlands. As with Suriname and French Guyana, these are cut up deeply by steep and sudden rivervalleys, and covered with dense rain forest. The western part of the Guiana Highlands are called the Pakaraima Mountains, and are much higher than the other plateaus in Guyana, reaching an altitude of as much as 9,220 ft (2,810 m). The highlands become a vast area of rolling hills in the central part of Guyana due to the effects of erosion; this sort of terrain takes up more than two thirds of the country. In the north along the coast is a swampy region as in Suriname and French Guiana, with many lagoons and mangrove swamps.

Further Reading

Brawer, Moshe. *Atlas of South America.* New York: Simon & Schuster, 1991.

Carlson, Fred. *Geography of Latin America.* Englewood Cliffs, NJ: Prentice Hall, Inc., 1952

Zeil, Werner. *The Andes: A Geological Review.* Berlin: Gebruder Borntraeger, 1979.

Sarah A. de Forest

Soybean

The soybean (*Glycine max*) is a domesticated species in the pea family (Fabaceae). Like other cultivated species in this family, soybean has symbiotic *Rhizobium* **bacteria** growing in nodules on its roots. These bacteria fix atmospheric **nitrogen** gas into **ammonia** and allow the crop to grow with relatively little additional **fertilization** of this key nutrient. Soybean is an annual, dicotyledonous **plant**. It has compound leaves, a bush-like growth form, and whitish or purple, bilaterally symmetric flowers. The bean-like, 2-3 in (5-7 cm) long **fruits** contain 2-4 hard, round **seeds**. Depending on the variety, the seeds can be colored black, brown, green, white, or yellow.

Soybean was domesticated in China around 5,000 years ago. Although it has been cultivated in east **Asia** for thousands of years, it was not commonly grown in **Europe** or **North America** until the twentieth century. It is now cultivated worldwide, where conditions permit, and is one of the most useful and most important food **crops**. In 1999, about 178 million acres (71.9 million ha) of soybean were grown worldwide, and total production was 176 million tons of grain (160 million tonnes).

Soybeans contain as much as 45% protein and 30% **carbohydrate**. They are used to prepare a wide variety of highly nutritious foods. The beans can be boiled, baked, or eaten as tender sprouts. Soybeans can also be used to manufacture tofu (a soft, cheesy curd), tempe (a soya cake impregnated with a fungus), soy milk (a white liquid preparation), and soy sauce (a black, salty liquid used to flavor). Soybeans are also processed as ingredients for cooking oil, margarine, vegetable shortening, mayonnaise, food supplements (such as **lecithin**), pharmaceutical preparations, and even paints and **plastics**. In addition to these many useful products for humans, large amounts of soybeans are fed to **livestock**.

Bill Freedman

Space

Space is the three-dimensional extension in which all things exist and move. We intuitively feel that we live in an unchanging space. In this space, the height of a **tree** or the length of a table is exactly the same for everybody. Einstein's *special theory of relativity* tells us that this intuitive feeling is really an illusion. Neither space nor **time** is the same for two people moving relative to each other. Only a combination of space and time, called *space-time*, is unchanged for everyone. Einstein's *general theory of relativity* tells us that the **force** of gravity is a result of a warping of this space-time by heavy objects, such as planets. According to the *big bang theory* of the origin of the universe, the expansion of the universe began from infinitely curved space-time. We still do not know whether this expansion will continue indefinitely or whether the universe will collapse again in a big crunch. Meanwhile, astronomers are **learning** more and more about outer space from terrestrial and orbiting telescopes, *space probes* sent to other planets in the **solar system**, and other scientific observations. This is just the beginning of the exploration of the unimaginably vast void, beyond the Earth's outer atmosphere, in which a journey to the nearest **star** would take 3,000 years at a million miles an hour.

The difference in the **perception** of space and time, predicted by the special theory of relativity, can be observed only at very high velocities close to that of light. A man driving past at 50 mph (80 kph) will appear only a hundred million millionth of an inch thinner as you stand watching on the sidewalk. By themselves, three-dimensional space and one-dimensional time are different for different people. Taken together, however, they form a four-dimensional space-time in which distances are same for all observers. We can understand this idea by using a two-dimensional analogy. Let us suppose your definition of south and east is not the same as mine. I travel from city A to city B by going 10 miles along my south and then 5 miles along my east. You travel from A to B by going 2 miles along your south and 11 miles along your east. Both of us, however, move exactly the same **distance** of 11.2 miles southeast from city A to B. In the same way, if we think of space as south and time as east, space-time is something like south-east.

The general theory of relativity tells us that gravity is the result of the curving of this four-dimensional space-time by objects with large **mass**. A flat stretched rubber **membrane** will sag if a heavy **iron** ball is placed on it. If you now place another ball on the membrane, the second ball will roll towards the first. This can be interpreted in two ways; as a consequence of the curvature of the membrane, or as the result of an attractive force exerted by the first ball on the second one. Similarly, the curvature of space-time is another way of interpreting the attraction of gravity. An extremely massive object can **curve** space-time around so much that not even light can escape from its attractive force. Such objects, called *black holes*, could very well exist in the universe. Astronomers believe that the disk found in 1994 by the Hubble **telescope**, at the center of the elliptical **galaxy** M87 near the center of the Virgo cluster, is material falling into a supermassive **black hole** estimated to have a mass three billion times the mass of the **Sun**.

The relativity of space and time and the curvature of space-time do not affect our daily lives. The high velocities and huge concentrations of **matter**, needed to manifest the effects of relativity, are found only in outer space on the scale of planets, stars, and galaxies. Our own **Milky Way** galaxy is a mere speck, 100,000 light years across, in a universe that spans ten billion light years. Though astronomers have studied this outer space with telescopes for hundreds of years, the modern space age began only in 1957 when the Soviet Union put the first artificial **satellite**, *Sputnik 1*, into **orbit** around the **Earth**. At present, there are hundreds of satellites in orbit gathering information from distant stars, free of the distorting effect of the Earth's atmosphere. Even though no manned spacecraft has landed on other worlds since the Apollo **moon** landings, several space probes, such as the *Voyager 2* and the *Magellan*, have sent back photographs and information from the moon and from other planets in the solar system. There are many questions to be answered and much to be achieved in the exploration of space. The Hubble telescope, repaired in space in 1993, has sent back data that has raised new questions about the age, origin, and nature of the universe. The launch of an United States astronaut to the Russian *Mir* space station in March 1995, the planned docking of the United States space shuttle *Atlantis* with *Mir*, and the proposed international space station, have opened up exciting possibilities for space exploration.

See also Big bang theory; Cosmology; Relativity, general; Relativity, special.

Further Reading

Bruning, David. "A Galaxy of News." *Astronomy.* (June 1995): 40.

Burrows, William E. *Exploring Space.* New York: Random House, 1990.

Krauss, Lawrence M. *Fear of Physics.* New York: BasicBooks, 1993.

KEY TERMS

Big bang theory—The currently accepted theory that the universe began in an explosion.

Black hole—An object, formed by a very massive star collapsing on itself, which exerts such a strong gravitational attraction that nothing can escape from it.

General theory of relativity—Albert Einstein's theory of physics, according to which gravity is the result of the curvature of space-time.

Light year—The distance traveled by light in one year at the speed of 186,000 miles per second.

Space probe—An unmanned spacecraft that orbits or lands on the Moon or another planet to gather information that is relayed back to Earth.

Space station—A manned artificial satellite in orbit about the Earth, intended as a base for space observation and exploration.

Space-time—A three-dimensional space and a one-dimensional time combined to form a four-dimensional location in which any event can be placed.

Special theory of relativity—Albert Einstein's theory of physics (in the absence of gravity) according to which the speed of light is constant, but space and time may be different for different observers.

Thorne, Kip S. *Black Holes and Time Warps*. New York: W. W. Norton & Company, 1994.

Sreela Datta

Space probe

A space probe is any unmanned instrumented spacecraft designed to carry out physical studies of **space** environment. As distinguished from satellites orbiting the **Earth** under the influence of gravitational attraction, a space probe is rocketed into space with sufficient speed to escape the earth's gravity and to reach a trajectory aimed at a pre-selected target.

The first recorded mention of a possibility of an unmanned probe dates back to 1919, when American physicist R. H. Goddard suggested that a flash of an explosion produced by a rocket on the Moon's surface could be monitored from Earth with a **telescope**. Vague scientific value of such an experiment, along with the absence of an appropriate technological base for its realization, made the idea look still-born. However, it took only 33 years for the concept of space experiment to reappear. In 1952, the term "space probe" was introduced by E. Burgess and C. A. Cross in a short paper presented to the British Interplanetary Society. Five years later, the hardware projects, like the Pioneer probes, began to materialize.

The space probe is used mostly for the acquisition of scientific data enriching our general knowledge on properties of outer space and spacial bodies. Each probe (sometimes a series of several identical craft) is constructed to meet very specific goals of a particular mission, and thus represents a unique and sophisticated creation of contemporary engineering art. Nevertheless, there are some common basic problems underlying any space mission-whether it is an Earth **satellite**, a crewed flight, or an automated probe: how to get to the destination point, how to collect the information required, and finally, how to transfer the information back to Earth. Successful resolution of these principal issues is impossible without a developed net of high-tech Earth-based facilities, used for assembling and testing the spacecraft-rocket system, for launching the probe into the desired trajectory, and for providing necessary control of probe-equipment operation, as well as for receiving the information transmitted back to Earth.

In general, a space probe may be considered as a combination of mutually adjusted systems of the on-ground facilities, the launch vehicle, and the spacecraft itself interacting with each other through numerous spatial, mechanical, electromagnetic, biological and other links (interfaces). Each system, in turn, splits into an amount of subsystems with interfaces of their own. Thus, the notion of a space probe is the fusion of frontier science achievements with the most advanced technologies. **Celestial mechanics**, rocketry, precision instrumentation, as well as telecommunications, are only a few of the fundamentals involved.

As compared to crewed flights, automated space missions cost essentially less. Yet, they still are a serious financial burden. For 30 years, the United States and the Soviet Union were the only powers with permanent programs of space exploration in their quest for technological and political superiority. Since scientific value of space-probe missions cannot be quantified and expressed as direct commercial profits, the vanishing of political reasons for enormous financial sacrifices resulted in drastic slowing and even shutting down the numerous space projects. In absence of the global political **competition**, only joint international efforts of many interested nations can keep systematic and diverse space research

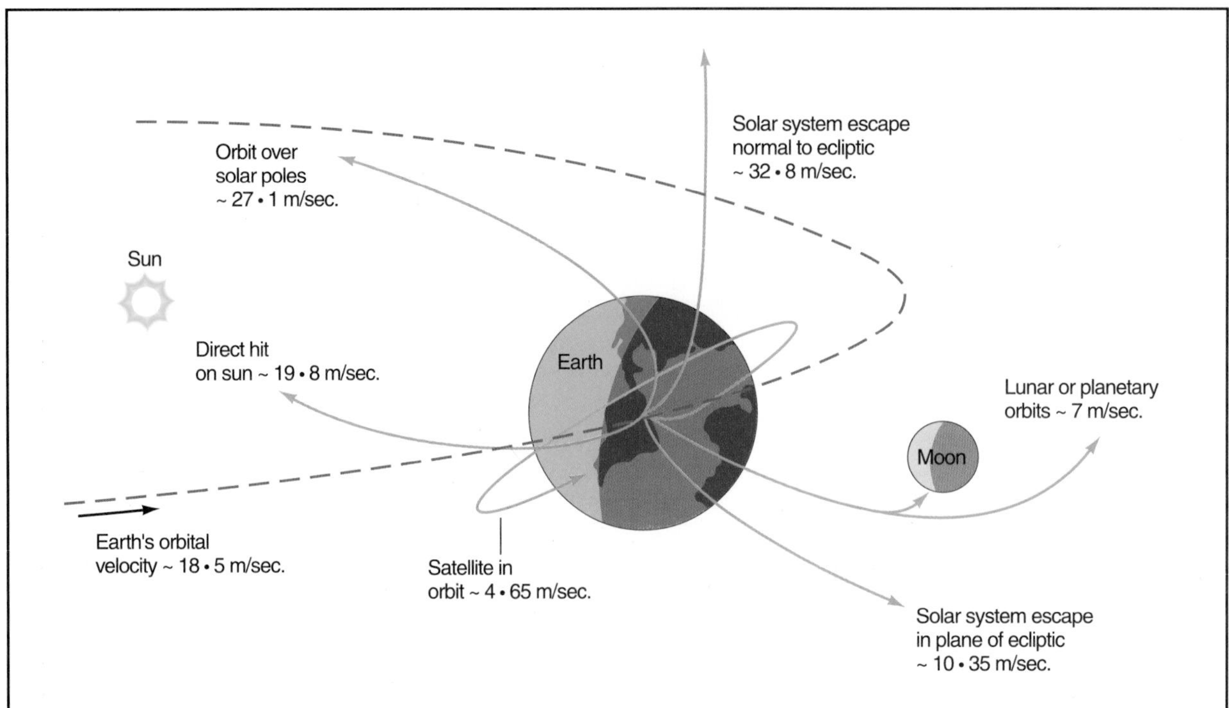

Figure 1.

alive, with the emphasis on small unmanned remote-controlled space probes capable of performing experiments reliably and relatively inexpensively.

Probe flight and supporting facilities

A probe's journey into far space can be divided into several stages. First, the probe has to overcome the Earth's gravity. Escape velocities vary for different types of trajectories.

During the second stage, the probe continues to move under the influence of the **Sun** alone. The third (approach) stage starts when the probe falls under the gravitational attraction of a nearby space body. The calculation of the entire trajectory from Earth to the point of destination is a complicated task because it should take into consideration numerous mutually conflicting demands: to maximize the payload but to minimize the cost, to shorten mission duration but to avoid such hazards as solar flares or meteoroid swarms, to remain within the range of the communication system but to avoid the unfavorable influence of big spatial bodies, etc.

Sometimes, strong gravitational fields of planets can be utilized to increase the probe's **velocity** and to change its direction considerably without firing the engines and using fuel. For instance, if used properly, Jupiter's massive gravitational pull can accelerate a probe enough to leave the **solar system** in any direction. The " gravitational assistance" or "swing-by" effect was successfully used in the American missions to Mercury via **Venus**, to the far planets of the solar system, and in the present voyage of the *Galileo* craft to **Jupiter**. Figure 2 illustrates how the gravitational influence of a **planet** accelerates the probe while changing its original trajectory.

Projecting of payloads into designated trajectories is achieved by means of expendable launch vehicles (ELVs). A wide variety of ELVs possessed by the United States use the same basic technology-two or more rocket-powered stages which are discarded when their engine burns are completed. Similar to the operation of a jet **aircraft**, the **motion** of a rocket is caused by a continuous ejection of a stream of hot gases in the opposite direction. The rocket's role as a prime mover makes it very important for the system's overall performance and cost. Out of 52 space-probe missions launched in the United States during the period from 1958 to 1988, 13 went wrong because of launch vehicle's failures and only five because of probe equipment's malfunctions.

All supporting Earth-based facilities can be divided into three major categories: test grounds, where the spacecraft and its components are exposed to different extreme conditions to make sure that they are able to withstand tough stresses of outer space; check-out and launch ranges, where the lift-off procedure is preceded by a thorough examination of all spacecraft-rocket interfaces; and

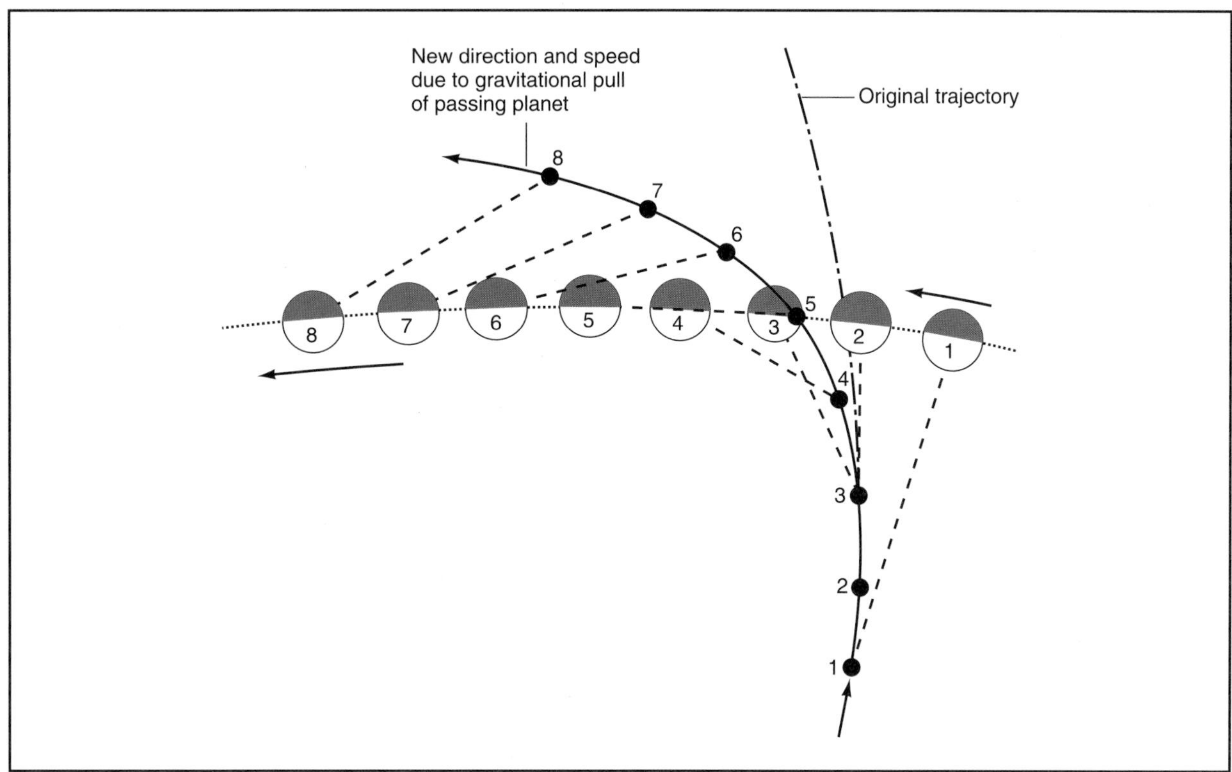

Figure 2.

post-launch facilities, which are used to track, communicate with, and process the data received from the probe.

As a matter of fact, hundreds of people and billions of dollars worth of facilities are involved in following the flight of each probe and in intercepting the data it transmits toward Earth. Already-developed facilities always have to be adopted in accordance with the specific spacecraft design. Today, the United States possesses two major launch ranges, several world-wide tracking networks, and dozens of publicly and privately owned test facilities.

Space-probe general design and classification

Any space probe is a self-contained piece of machinery designed to perform a variety of prescribed complex operations for a long time, sometimes for decades. There are ten major constituents of the spacecraft's entity that are responsible for its vital functions: (1) power supply, (2) propulsion, (3) altitude control, (4) environmental control, (5) computer subsystem, (6) communications, (7) engineering, (8) scientific instrumentation, (9) guidance control, and (10) entire structural platform.

(1) The power supply provides well-regulated electrical power to keep the spacecraft active. Usually the solar-cell arrays transforming the sun's illumination into **electricity** are used. Far from the Sun, where solar **energy** becomes too feeble, electricity may be generated by **nuclear power** devices. (2) The propulsion subsystem enables the spacecraft to maneuver when necessary, either in space or in a planet's atmosphere, and has a specific configuration depending upon the mission's goals. (3) The altitude-control subsystem allows to orient the spacecraft for a specific purpose, such as to aim solar panels at the Sun, antennas at Earth and sensors at scientific targets. It also aligns engines in the proper direction during the maneuver. (4) The environmental-control subsystem maintains the **temperature**, **pressure**, **radiation** and magnetic field inside the craft within the acceptable levels to secure proper functioning of equipment. (5) The computer subsystem performs data processing, coding, and storage along with routines for internal checking and maintenance. It times and initiates the pre-programmed actions independently of Earth. (6) The communication subsystem transmits data and receives commands from Earth. It also transmits identifying signals that allow ground crews to track the probe. (7) The engineering-instrumentation subsystem continuously monitors the "health" of the spacecraft's "organism" and submits status reports to Earth. (8) The scientific-instrumentation subsystem is designed to carry out the experiments se-

lected for a particular mission, for example, to explore planetary geography, **geology**, atmospheric **physics** or electromagnetic environment. (9) The guidance-and-control subsystem is supposed to detect deviations from proper performance, determine corrections and to dispatch appropriate commands. In many respects, this subsystem resembles a human **brain**, since it makes active decisions, having analyzed all available information on the spacecraft's status. (10) The structural subsystem is a skeleton of the spacecraft; it supports, unites and protects all other subsystems.

Depending upon mission's target, the probes may be classed as lunar, solar, planetary (Mercurian, Venusian, Martian, Jovian) or interplanetary probes. Another classification is based upon the mission type: flyby, orbiter, or soft-lander.

Famous space-probe missions of the past

Thousands of probes launched since 1959 are grouped into families, which usually encompass craft similar by design, mission, or both. In the United States there were a series of interplanetary probes (Pioneer, Voyager), of lunar probes (Ranger, Surveyor, and Lunar Orbiter), of planetary probes (Mariner, Viking, Pioneer Venus). In the Soviet Union the names of the probe families were Luna (Russian for **Moon**), **Mars**, and Venera (Russian for Venus).

The next generation of unmanned space probes

A new program recently initiated by NASA and named Discovery has an objective to find cheaper ways to explore the solar system. The program is supposed to supplement larger, more expensive and scarce missions. It will increase flight rate-a new mission every 12 to 18 months- and provide for a more continuous accumulation of diverse scientific information on asteroids, planets and the Sun itself. In the frame of the Discovery program, the Mars Environmental Survey (MESUR) Pathfinder, and the Near-Earth Asteroid Rendezvous (NEAR) are planned for launch in 1996. The MESUR Pathfinder mission includes landing low-power, low-mass instruments, and a small six-wheeled rover to analyze **soil** and rock samples from the Martian surface. NEAR will journey through the main asteroid belt, flying by the asteroid Iliya in 1996. After a gravity boost from Earth, NEAR will encounter a near-Earth object 433 Eros in December 1998 and will spend up to a year station-keeping with this irregularly shaped body approximately 22 mi (35 km) across.

In general, the solar system exploration will follow the trends outlined by the past missions. These trends include the investigation of the inner planets (Mercury, Venus, Moon and Mars), of the outer planets (Jupiter, **Saturn**, **Uranus**, **Neptune** and **Pluto**), of interplanetary medium and small bodies (asteroids, **comets**), and, probably, of other planetary systems.

In the near term, Japan plans to launch a spacecraft called "Planet B" toward Venus in March, 1996. The missions of comet explorer CRAF (Comet Rendezvous and Asteroid Flyby) and of Saturn orbiter/ Titan probe "Cassini/Huygens" are planned by NASA for 1996 and 1997. CRAF's objective is a detailed study of gas and dust emissions of the short-period comet Temple 2. The probe will travel 14,904 mi (24,000 km) down the comet's **plasma** tail and will attempt to approach the nucleus after the comet's activity slows down. CRAF will also study the 68 mi (110 km)-wide dark asteroid 739 Mandeville during the close flyby. Cassini will explore the Saturnian system and deliver the descent robotic laboratory to Titan- one of Saturn's moons- to measure properties of its atmosphere all the way through to the surface. The orbiter will make a radarmapping of the Titan's surface.

Other major planetary missions are the Mars Surveyor Program and the Pluto Fast Flyby and Comet Nucleus Sample Return (CNSR). Mars Surveyor is a decade long program involving orbiters and landers for systematic intense global investigation of Mars beginning 1996. Pluto Fast Flyby will use two lightweight spacecraft launched separately to reach the Pluto-Sharon system in 6-8 years and to **map** the surface composition of both bodies. It has a planned launch date of about 2000. CNSR is projected to start its way to the Comet Finlay in November 2000 and to reach it in January 2007. After taking a sample of the comet's nucleus, it will return to Earth in September 2008.

Other probable missions include Mercury orbiter, Venus environmental satellite, comet life history investigation, and NEARS (Near-Earth Asteroid Returned Samples), which, as compared to NEAR, will be equipped with a special "shooter" for firing up sample tubes into the asteroid's surface. After collecting up to 21 oz (600 g) of sample, the probe Huygens, with a well-equipped probe, will return to Earth.

See also Rockets and missles; Spacecraft, manned.

Further Reading

Burnham D., "Return to the Moon?" *Spaceflight*. Vol. 31 Nov., 1991.

The Cambridge Encyclopedia of Space. Cambridge University Press, 1990.

Curtis A.R. *Space Almanac*. Arcsoft Publishers, 1990.

KEY TERMS

Gravitation—The force whereby any two particles of matter attract each other throughout the universe.

Interface—A common boundary between two parts of a system, whether material or nonmaterial.

Trajectory—The path described by any body moving through space.

Griffin M.D., *Space Vehicle Design*. American Institute of Aeronautics and Astronautics, 1991.

Kerr R.A., "Scaling Down Planetary Science." *Science*. Vol. 264 (May 27. 1994).

Palocz S. "Mars Observer Mission and Systems Overview." *Journal of Spacecrafts and Rockets*. Vol. 28 (Sept./Oct. 1991).

Voyage to the Planets. Today Home Entertainment, 1988. Videocassette.

Wertz J.R., *Space Mission Analysis and Design*. Kluwer Academic, 1991.

Zubrin R., S. Price, B. Clark. "A New MAP for Mars." *Aerospace America*. Vol. 31 (Sept. 1994.)

Elena V. Ryzhov

Space shuttle

The space shuttle is a reusable spacecraft that takes off like a rocket, travels around the **Earth** like a spacecraft, and then lands once again like a glider. The first space shuttle was the *Columbia*, whose maiden voyage took place in April 1981. Four additional shuttles were later added to the fleet: *Discovery*, *Challenger*, *Atlantis*, and *Enterprise*. The first shuttle launched by the Soviet Union (now Russia) was *Buran*, which made its debut in November 1988.

Mission of the space shuttle

At one time, both the United States and the Soviet Union envisioned complex space programs that included two parts: (1) space stations orbiting around the Earth and/or other planets, and (2) shuttle spacecraft that would transport humans, equipment, raw materials, and finished products to and from the space station. For economic reasons, each nation eventually ended up concentrating on only one aspect of the complete program. The Soviets built and for many years have operated advanced space stations (*Salyut* and *Mir*), while Americans have focused their attention on the shuttle system.

The shuttle system has been given the name Space Transportation System (STS), of which the shuttles have been the key element. Lacking a space station with which to interact, the American shuttles have operated with two major goals: (1) the conduct of scientific experiments in a zero-gravity environment, and (2) the launch, capture, repair, and release of satellites.

Now an international program, STS depends heavily on the contributions of other nations in the completion of its basic missions. For example, its Spacelab modules - the areas in which astronauts carry out most of their experiments - are designed and built by the European Space Agency, and the extendable arm used to capture and release satellites - the remote manipulator system or Canadarm - is constructed in Canada.

Structure of the shuttle

The space shuttle has four main parts: (1) the orbiter itself; (2) the three main engines attached to the orbiter; (3) two solid rocket engines; and (4) an external fuel tank. Although the Russian *Buran* differs in some details from the U.S. space shuttle fleet, the main features of all shuttles are very similar.

The orbiter

The orbiter is approximately the size of a commercial DC-9 airplane with a length of 121 ft (37 m) and a wing span of 78 ft (23 m). Its net weight is about 161,000 lb (73,200 kg). It is sub-divided into two main parts, the crew cabin and the cargo bay. The upper level of the crew cabin is the flight deck from which astronauts control the spacecraft's flight in **orbit** and during descent. Below the flight deck is the crew's personal quarters, containing personal lockers, sleeping, eating, and toilet facilities, and other necessary living units. The crew cabin is physically isolated from the cargo bay and is provided with **temperature** and **pressure** conditions similar to those on the Earth's surface. The cabin's atmosphere is maintained with a composition equivalent to that of near-Earth atmosphere, 80% **nitrogen** and 20% **oxygen**.

The cargo bay is a large space 15 ft (4.5 m) by 60 ft (18 m) in which the shuttle's payloads are stored. The cargo bay can hold up to about 65,000 lb (30,000 kg) during ascent, although it is limited to about half that amount during descent.

In 1973, an agreement was reached between NASA and the European Space Agency (ESA) for the construction by ESA of a pressurized work space that could be loaded into the shuttle's cargo bay. The work space, des-

The space shuttle *Discovery* being moved by crawler to the top of pad 39B at the Kennedy Space Center.

ignated as Spacelab, was designed for use as a science laboratory in which a wide array of experiments could be conducted. Each of these Spacelab modules is 8.9 ft (2.7 m) long and 13 ft (3.9 m) in diameter. The equipment needed to carry out experiments is arranged in racks along the walls of the Spacelab, and the whole module is then loaded into the cargo bay of the shuttle prior to take-off. When necessary, two Spacelab modules can be joined to form a single larger work space.

Shuttle power systems

The power needed to lift a space shuttle into orbit comes from two solid-fuel rockets, each 149 ft (45.5 m) in length and 12 ft (4 m) in diameter, and the shuttle's own liquid-fuel engines. The fuel used in the solid rockets is composed of finely-divided **aluminum**, ammonium perchlorate, and a special **polymer** designed to form a rubbery mixture. The mixture is molded in such a way as to produce an 11-point starred figure. This shape exposes the maximum possible surface area of fuel during ignition, making **combustion** as efficient as possible within the engine.

The two solid-fuel rockets carry 1.1 million lb (500,000 kg) of fuel each, and **burn** out completely only 125 seconds after the shuttle leaves the launch pad. At solid-engine burnout, the shuttle is at an altitude of 161,000 ft (47,000 m) and 244 nautical miles (452 km) down range from launch site. At that point, explosive charges holding the solid rockets to the main shuttle go off and detach the rockets from the shuttle. The rockets are then returned to Earth by means of a system of parachutes that drops them into the Atlantic Ocean at a speed of 55 mi (90 km) per hour. The rockets can then be collected by ships, returned to land, refilled, and re-used in a later shuttle launch.

The three liquid-fueled shuttle engines have been described as the most efficient engines ever built by hu-

mans. At maximum capacity, they achieve 99% efficiency during combustion. They are supplied by fuel (liquid **hydrogen**) and oxidizer (liquid oxygen) stored in the 154 ft (46.2 m) external fuel tank. The fuel tank itself is sub-divided into two parts, one of which holds the liquid oxygen and the other, the liquid hydrogen. The fuel tank is maintained at the very low temperature (less than -454°F [-270°C]) to keep hydrogen and oxygen in their liquid state. The two liquids are pumped into the shuttle's three engines through 17 in (43 cm)-diameter lines that carry 1,035 gal (3,900 l) of fuel per second. Upon ignition, each of the liquid-fueled engines develops 75,000 horsepower of thrust.

The three main engines burn out after 522 seconds, when the shuttle has reached an altitude of 57 nautical miles (105 km) and is down range 770 nautical miles (1,426 km) from the launch site. At this point, the external fuel tank is also jettisoned. Its return to the Earth's surface is not controlled, however, and it is not recoverable for future use.

Final orbit is achieved by means of two small engines, the Orbital Maneuvering System (OMS) Engines located on external pods at the rear of the orbiter's body. The OMS engines are fired first to insert the orbiter into an elliptical orbit with an apogee of 160 nautical miles (296 km) and a perigee of 53 nautical miles (98 km) and then again to accomplish its final circular orbit with a radius of 160 nautical miles (296 km).

Orbital maneuvers

Humans and machinery work together to control the movement of the shuttle in orbit and during its descent. For making fine adjustments, the spacecraft depends on six small vernier jets, two in the nose and four in the OMS pods of the spacecraft. These jets allow human or computer to make modest adjustments in the shuttle's flight path in three directions.

The computer system used aboard the shuttle is an example of the redundancy built into the spacecraft. Five discrete computers are used, four networked with each other using one computer program, and one operating independently using a different program. The four linked computers constantly communicate with each other, testing each other's decisions and deciding when one (or two or three) is not performing properly and eliminating that computer (or those computers) from the decision-making process. In case all four of the interlinked computers malfunction, decision-making is turned over automatically to the fifth computer.

This kind of redundancy is built into every essential feature of the shuttle's operation. For example, three independent hydraulic systems are available, all operating with independent power systems. The failure of one or even two of the systems does not, therefore, place the shuttle in a critical failure mode.

Orbital activities

The space shuttles have performed a myriad of scientific and technical tasks in their nearly two decades of operation. Many of these have been military missions about which we have relatively little information. The launching of military spy satellites is an example of these.

Some examples of the kinds of activities carried out during shuttle flights include the following:

- After the launch of the *Challenger* shuttle (STS-41B) on February 3, 1984, astronauts Bruce McCandless II and Robert L. Stewart conducted the first ever untethered space walks using Manned Maneuvering Unit backpacks that allowed them to propel themselves through space near the shuttle. The shuttle also released into orbit two communication satellites, the Indonesian *Palapa* and the American *Westar* satellites. Both satellites failed soon after release but were recovered and returned to Earth by the *Discovery* during its flight that began on November 8, 1984.
- During the flight of *Challenger* (STS-51B) that began on April 29, 1985, crew members carried out a number of experiments in Spacelab 3 determining the effects of **zero** gravity on living organisms and on the processing of materials. They grew crystals of mercury (II) oxide over a period of more than four days, observed the **behavior** of two **monkeys** and 24 **rats** in a zero-gravity environment, and studied the behavior of liquid droplets held in suspension by sound waves.
- The mission of STS-51I (*Discovery*) was to **deposit** three communications satellites in orbit. On the same flight, astronauts William F. Fisher and James D. Van Hoften left the shuttle to make repairs on a Syncom **satellite** that had been placed in orbit during flight STS-51D but that had then malfunctioned.

Descent maneuvers

Some of the most difficult design problems faced by shuttle engineers were those created during the re-entry process. When the spacecraft has completed its mission in space and is ready to leave orbit, its OMS fires just long enough to slow the shuttle by 200 mi (320 km) per hour. This modest change in speed is enough to cause the shuttle to drop out of its orbit and begin its ascent to Earth.

The re-entry problems occur when the shuttle reaches the outermost regions of the upper atmosphere, where significant amounts of atmospheric gases are first encountered. **Friction** between the shuttle - now traveling at

17,500 mi (28,000 km) per hour - and air molecules causes the spacecraft's outer surface to begin to **heat** up. Eventually, it reaches a temperature of 3,000°F (1,650°C).

Most materials normally used in **aircraft** construction would melt and vaporize at these temperatures. It was necessary, therefore, to find a way of protecting astronauts inside the shuttle cabin from this searing heat. The solution invented was to use a variety of insulating materials on the shuttle's outer skin. Parts less severely heated during re-entry are covered with 2,300 flexible quilts of a silica-glass composite. The more sensitive belly of the shuttle is covered with 25,000 insulating tiles, each 6 in (15 cm) **square** and 5 in (12 cm) thick, made of a silica-borosilicate **glass** composite.

The portions of the shuttle most severely stressed by heat - the nose and the leading edges of the wings - are coated with an even more resistant material known as carbon-carbon. Carbon-carbon is made by attaching a carbon-fiber cloth to the body of the shuttle and then baking it to convert it to a pure **carbon** substance. The carbon-carbon is then coated to prevent oxidation of the material during descent.

Landing

Once the shuttle reaches the Earth's atmosphere, it ceases to operate as a rocket ship and begins to function as a glider. Its movements are controlled by aerodynamic controls, such as the tail rudder, a large flap beneath the main engines, and elevons, small flaps on its wings. These devices allow the shuttle to descend to the Earth traveling at speeds of 8,000 mi (13,000 km) per hour, while dropping vertically at the rate of 140 mi (225 km) per hour. When the aircraft finally touches down, it is traveling at a speed of about 190 knots (100 m per second), and requires about 1.5 mi (2.5 km) to come to a stop.

The *Challenger* disaster

Terrible disasters have been associated with every aspect of both the Soviet and American space programs. Unfortunately, the Space Transportation System has been no different in this respect. Mission STS-51L was scheduled to take off on January 28, 1986 using the shuttle *Challenger*. Only 72 seconds into the flight, the shuttle's external tank exploded, and all seven astronauts on board were killed.

The *Challenger* disaster prompted one of the most comprehensive studies of a major accident ever conducted. On June 6, 1986, the Presidential Commission appointed to analyze the disaster published its report. The reason for the disaster, according to the commission, was the failure of an O-ring at a joint connecting two sections of one of the solid rocket engines. Flames escaping from the failed joint reached the external fuel tank, set it on fire, and then caused an explosion of the whole spacecraft.

As a result of the *Challenger* disaster, a number of design changes were made in the shuttle. Most of these (254 modifications in all) were made in the orbiter. Another 30 changes were made in the solid rocket booster, 13 in the external tank, and 24 in the shuttle's main engine. In addition, an escape system was developed that would allow crew members to abandon a shuttle in case of emergencies, and NASA reexamined and redesigned its launch-abort procedures. Also, NASA was instructed to reassess its ability to carry out the ambitious program of shuttle launches that it had been planning.

The U.S. Space Transportation System was essentially shut down for a period of 975 days while NASA carried out necessary changes and tested new systems. Then, on September 29, 1988, the first post- *Challenger* mission was launched, STS-26. On that flight, *Discovery* carried NASA's TDRS-C communications satellite into orbit, putting the American STS program back on schedule once more.

See also Rockets and missiles; Spacecraft, manned; Space probe.

Further Reading

Barrett, Norman S. *Space Shuttle.* New York: Franklin Watts, 1985.

KEY TERMS

Booster—A rocket engine used to help get a large spacecraft such as the space shuttle into orbit.

Orbiter—The portion of the space shuttle that contains the crew cabin and the cargo bay, where astronauts live and work while in space.

Payload—The amount of something that can be lifted into space by a rocket or system of rockets.

Redundancy—A system in which more than one copy of any given instrument or device is included so that, in the case of any one of those copies, others may take over and duplicate its function.

Spacelab—A working module constructed by the European Space Agency for use in the space shuttle as the working space in which many different kinds of experiments can be carried out.

Zero-gravity—Any region in which gravitational force—such as that of the Earth—is so small as to be undetectable. Astronauts traveling aboard a space shuttle in orbit around the Earth are in a zero-gravity situation.

Curtis, Anthony R. *Space Almanac*. Woodsboro, MD: Arcsoft Publishers, 1990.

Dotto, Lydia, Stephen Hart, Gina Maranto, and Peter Pocock. *How Things Work in Space*. Alexandria, VA: Time-Life Books, 1991.

Dwiggins, Don. *Flying the Space Shuttles*. New York: Dodd, Mead, 1985.

McGraw-Hill Encyclopedia of Science & Technology. 7th edition. New York: McGraw-Hill Book Company, 1992.

Seltzer, Richard J. "Faulty joint behind space shuttle disaster," *Chemical & Engineering News*. (23 June 1986): 9- 15.

David E. Newton

Spacecraft, manned

Manned spacecraft are vehicles with the capability of maintaining life outside of the Earth's atmosphere. Partially in recognition of the fact that women as well as men are active participants in **space** travel programs, manned spacecraft are now frequently referred to as crewed spacecraft.

In its earliest stages, crewed space flight was largely an **exercise** in basic research. Scientists were interested in collecting fundamental information about the **Moon**, the other planets in our **solar system**, and outer space. Today, crewed space flight is also designed to study a number of practical problems, such as the **behavior** of living organisms and inorganic materials in **zero** gravity conditions.

Crewed vs. uncrewed flight

Since the dawn of the modern space age in the 1950s, considerable debate has focused on the relative merits of crewed versus uncrewed space travel. Some experts have argued that scientists can learn almost all they want to know about the solar system and outer space by using uncrewed, mechanized space probes. Such probes can be designed to carry out most of the operations normally performed by humans at much less cost and little or no risk to human life. The enormous complexity of crewed space flight is, they say, not justified by the modest additional benefits obtained by including human beings in a space vehicle. Other authorities insist that there is no substitute in space exploration for the intelligent presence of human beings. Only humans can make the instantaneous decisions and take the unexpected actions that may be necessary during space exploration.

To this debate has been added a number of non-scientific, usually political elements. One is the purely emotional appeal of placing human beings on the Moon and other planets, a long-time goal of science fiction writers. A second is the national glory that comes from being the first nation on **Earth** to achieve the conquest of space. Whatever the technical arguments have been about crewed versus uncrewed space flight, political factors were crucial in tipping the scales toward the former early on in the space programs of both the Soviet Union and the United States.

In the 1990s, however, some of the magic of space exploration appears to have diminished. Facing budgetary contraints and a weaker world economy, the world's space powers have begun to reassess the relative position of crewed versus uncrewed travel in some of their space programs.

Overview

For the first three decades of the modern space era, two nations, the United States and Russia (formerly, the Soviet Union), have dominated crewed space travel. In 1987, the European Space Agency committed itself to participation in future crewed space programs, some operated independently and some in cooperation with the United States and Russia. Japan and Canada later made similar commitments.

The history of crewed space programs in both Russia and the United States consisted of a number of steps that led to the possibility of placing humans on the Moon or another **planet**, or in **orbit** around the Earth or one of our neighbors in the solar system. These steps have been necessary in order to solve the many complex problems involved with keeping humans alive in outer space and bringing them back to Earth unharmed.

One-person crewed spacecraft

The first and simplest crewed spacecraft were designed to carry a single passenger. In the Soviet Union, these vehicles were designated by the code-name Vostok ("East") and in the United States they were known as Mercury spacecraft. The first Vostok flight was piloted by Yuri A. Gargarin and was launched from the Tyuratam Kosmodrom on 12 April 1961. In all, a total of six Vostok flights were completed over a period of just over two years. The last of these carried the first woman to fly in outer space, Valentina Tereshkova. Tereshkova spent three days in *Vostok 6* between 16 and 19 June 1963.

The Vostok spacecraft was essentially a spherical cabin with a single seat and all of the equipment necessary to support life and communicate with Earth stations. It also held an ejection seat, necessary because the Soviets planned for re-entries to be terminated on the ground. The ejection seat activated at an altitude of about 23,000

ft (7,000 m), allowing the pilot to experience a soft landing separately from his or her spacecraft.

The U.S. Mercury program followed a pattern very similar to that of the Vostok series. In the first Mercury flight, American astronaut Alan B. Shephard traveled for 15 minutes in a suborbital flight only three weeks after Yuri Gargarin's first space trip. Nine months after Shephard's flight, John Glenn became the first American to orbit the Earth in a spacecraft designated as *Mercury 6*. The Mercury spacecraft was a double-walled bell-shaped cabin made of **titanium** and nickel **alloy** with an insulating ceramic outer coat.

Two- and three-person spacecraft

The Mercury program came to a conclusion just a month before the end of the Vostok program and was followed by the U.S. two-person spacecraft, the Gemini. The Gemini cabin was, of course, larger than that of the Mercury, but it was also much more complex and sophisticated. The purpose of the Gemini program was to learn more about humans' ability to maneuver a spacecraft, to carry out extravehicular activities ("EVA" or "space walks"), to rendezvous and dock with other spacecraft, and to perform other operations that would be necessary in the later Apollo program.

A total of ten successful Gemini missions were completed during 1965 and 1966. During one of these, *Gemini 4*, astronaut Edward White performed the first extravehicular activity (EVA), a "space walk," by an American. White remained in space for a period of 21 minutes at the end of a 25 foot (7.5 m) umbilical cord connecting him to the main spacecraft.

The Soviets decided to bypass two-person spacecrafts entirely, and went directly to the development of a three-person vehicle. That program was code-named the Voskhod ("Rising") series. The Voskhod spacecraft lacked the ejection seat that had been standard in Vostok vehicles. The space previously used for that seat was replaced with seating for two more persons as well as an air-lock that allowed EVA during the second Voskhod flight. That EVA, performed by cosmonaut A. A. Leonov on 18 March 1965, marked the first time any human had traveled outside a spacecraft during space flight.

The Soyuz and Apollo programs

Both Voskhod and Gemini programs lasted for about two years, to be replaced, in turn, by spacecraft designed to carry humans to the Moon. These programs were known as Soyuz ("Union") in the Soviet Union and Apollo in the United States. At an early stage, the Soviets appear to have abandoned the goal of placing humans

The liftoff of *Apollo 11* from pad 39A at Kennedy Space Center on July 16, 1969 at 9:32 A.M. Crewmen Neil A. Armstrong, Michael Collins, and Edwin E. Aldrin Jr. achieved the first successful manned lunar landing on the *Apollo 11* mission.

on the Moon, and redesigned the Soyuz instead as an orbiting space station. The Soyuz spacecraft consists of three primary components: the re-entry vehicle, the orbital module, and the service module.

The re-entry vehicle is designed to hold crew members during take-off, orbital flight, descent, and landing. It has an approximately bell-shaped appearance and contains the controls needed to maneuver the spacecraft. The orbital module contains the living and working quarters used by cosmonauts while the spacecraft is in orbit. A docking system is provided at the front end of the orbital module. The service module contains the fuel and engines needed for maneuvering the spacecraft while it is in orbit.

The first test of the Soyuz spacecraft took place in April 1967, ending in disaster when cosmonaut V. M. Komarov was killed when his parachute landing system

failed. A second Soyuz accident occurred on June 30, 1971, when a **pressure** valve in the vehicle apparently failed to close properly during descent, air leaked out of the spacecraft, and all three Soviet cosmonauts suffocated to death before their ship reached ground. Blame for this accident was later placed on the eagerness of Soviet politicians to put a three-man team into space before a vehicle suitable for such a flight was available. Because of crowded conditions in the Soyuz cabin, the three cosmonauts were unable to wear space suits that would have prevented their deaths. In all subsequent Soyuz flights, the spacecraft was redesigned to permit the wearing of space suits. The space needed for this modification meant, however, that the vehicle could carry only two passengers.

The Apollo spacecraft consisted of three main parts: the command module, the service module and the lunar module. The complete vehicle was designed with the objective of carrying three persons to the Moon, allowing one or more to walk on the Moon's surface and carry out scientific experiments, and then returning the crew to the Earth's surface.

The Apollo command module was a conical space in which the crew lived, worked, and operated the spacecraft. It was about 10 ft (3 m) high and nearly 13 ft (4 m) wide with a total **volume** of about 210 cubic ft (6 cubic m). The service module had a cylindrical shape with the same diameter as the command module and roughly twice its length. The service module held the propulsion systems needed for maneuvering in orbit, the electrical systems, and other sub-systems needed to operate the spacecraft in space.

The lunar module was used for carrying two astronauts from the Apollo spacecraft itself to the Moon's surface. One part of the lunar module, the descent stage, contained the equipment necessary to carry astronauts to the Moon's surface. It was left there after lunar research had been completed. The ascent stage of the lunar module rested on top of the descent stage and was used to carry astronauts back to the mother ship at the completion of their moonwalk.

The Apollo series included a total of 11 crewed flights conducted over a period of four years between 1968 and 1972. The climax of the series occurred on July 20, 1969, when American astronauts Neil A. Armstrong and Edwin E. Aldrin, Jr., walked on the Moon's surface and collected samples of lunar **soil**. Five more landings on the Moon's surface were completed before the Apollo program was ended. During the last three landings on the Moon's surface, astronauts were able to use a lunar roving vehicle (LRV) for their movement on the Moon's surface. The LRV was about 10 ft (3 m) long and 6 ft (1.8 m) wide with an Earth weight of 460 lbs (209 kg). It was carried to the moon inside the lunar module in a folded position and then unfolded for travel when the lunar module landed on the moon's surface.

As with the Soviet Union space program, the American space effort has experienced its own share of accidents and disasters. The most serious of these occurred on January 27, 1967, during tests for the first Apollo flight, designated as *Apollo 204*. Fire broke out in the command module of the Apollo spacecraft and three astronauts, Roger Chaffee, Virgil Grissom, and Edward White, lost their lives. This disaster caused a delay of 18 months in the Apollo program while engineers restudied and redesigned the Apollo spacecraft to improve its safety.

Space stations

Since the early 1970s, space programs in both the Soviet Union and the United States have focused on the development of an orbiting space station. The emphasis in these two nations has been, however, somewhat different.

The development of a successful space station requires two major accomplishments: the construction of a **habitat** in space in which humans can live and work for long periods of time (months or years), and the development of a ferry system by which men, women, and materials are transported from Earth to the space station and back. The Soviets have focused on the first of these two features and the Americans on the second.

Salyut and Mir space stations

The first series of space stations developed by the Soviets was given the code name Salyut. Salyut space stations were 65 ft (19.8 m) long and 13 ft (4 m) wide with a total weight of about 19 tons. *Salyut 1* was launched on April 19, 1971, to be followed by six more vehicles of the same design. Each station was occupied by one or more "host" crews, each of whom spent many weeks or months in the spacecraft, and a number of "visiting" crews, who stayed in the spacecraft for no more than a few days. The visiting crews always contained cosmonauts from nations friendly to the Soviet Union, such as Bulgaria, Cuba, Czechoslovakia, East Germany, Hungary, Poland, and Vietnam. Between February 8, 1984, and October 2, 1985, Soviet cosmonauts in *Salyut 7* set an endurance record of 237 days.

The first in a more advanced Soviet space station, code-named Mir ("Peace"), was launched on February 19, 1986. The Mir spacecraft is considerably more complex than its Salyut predecessor with a central core 43 ft (13 m) long and 13.6 ft (4.1 m) wide. Six docking ports on this central core permit the attachment of four research laboratories, as well as the docking of two shuttle

spacecraft bringing new cosmonauts and additional materials and supplies. During 1988, cosmonauts Musa Manrov and Vladimir Titov set records for the longest period of time in space for humans of 366 days.

Skylab and the space shuttle

The only space station comparable to Salyut and Mir developed by the United States was the *Skylab* vehicle launched on May 14, 1973. The *Skylab* program consisted of two phases. First, the unoccupied orbital workshop itself was put into orbit. Then, three separate crews of three astronauts each visited and worked in the space station. The three crews spent a total of 28, 59, and 84 days in the summer and winter of 1973 and 1974. During their stays in *Skylab*, astronauts carried out a wide variety of experiments in the fields of solar and stellar **astronomy**, zero-gravity technology, **geophysics** and space **physics**, Earth observation, and biomedical studies.

Interest among U.S. space scientists has focused less on the construction of a space station itself and more on the development of spacecraft that will carry humans and materials to and from space stations. This program has been designated as the Space Transportation System (STS), known more popularly as the **space shuttle** series. Space shuttles are very large spacecraft designed to carry a crew of seven and payloads of up to 65,000 lb (30,000 kg). The spacecraft itself looks very much like a jet airplane with a length of 122 ft (37 m) and wingspan of 78 ft (24 m). Space shuttles are lifted into orbit on top of a huge external tank carrying liquid fuel and oxidizer and solid rocket boosters.

The first space shuttle, *Columbia*, was launched on April 12, 1981, and remained in orbit for three days. Later, three more shuttles, *Challenger*, *Discovery*, and *Atlantis* were added to the STS fleet.

Challenger was later lost in the worst space disaster in human history. On January 28, 1986, 73 seconds after takeoff, *Challenger* exploded, killing all seven astronauts aboard. Research later showed that a failed O-ring gasket had allowed hot gases to escape from one of the shuttle's solid fuel boosters, setting fire to the spacecraft itself. The *Challenger* disaster caused NASA to reconsider its ambitious program of 24 shuttle flights every year. Its current plans aim, instead, for an average of 14 flights per year using four shuttle spacecraft. In order to complete this program of launches, the agency placed an order for a replacement for *Challenger*, named *Endeavour*, in July 1987.

The Soviet space shuttle program comparable to the American STS effort has been code-named Buran ("Blizzard"). The first Buran vehicle was launched on November 15, 1988. It resembles the U.S. shuttle vehicles, but lacks its own propulsion system. It is, thus, less an **aircraft** than a space glider. The function of the Buran vehicles is to act as supply ferries for the *Mir* and, later, Russian space stations.

Soviet-U.S. cooperation in space

For the first decade, Soviet and American space programs worked independently of each other, in fairly intense **competition** most of the time. However, space scientists on both sides of that competition recognized early on the importance of eventually developing joint programs. This recognition led to the creation of the Apollo-Soyuz Test Project (ASTP). The purpose of this project was to make possible the docking of two crewed spacecraft, an Apollo and Soyuz vehicle, in orbit.

The goal of ASTP was accomplished between July 15 and 24, 1975, when the last Apollo flight docked with a Soyuz spacecraft for a total of 47 hours and 17 minutes. During that time, two Soviet cosmonauts and three American astronauts visited each others' spacecrafts and conducted a series of scientific and technical experiments.

In spite of the success of the ASTP, it was nearly two decades before another such accomplishment was recorded. Early in 1995, the American space shuttle *Discovery* docked with the Russian space station *Mir*. U.S. astronauts then entered the Russian vehicle and exchanged gifts with their Russian counterparts.

The future of crewed space flight

The ultimate goal of space programs in both the Soviet Union and the United States has been the construction of an Earth-orbiting space station. Today, the most-likely realization of that goal would appear to be the proposed space station *Freedom.*

Planning for *Freedom* was initiated in 1984 as the result of a directive by then-President Ronald Reagan. According to original plans, construction of the space station was to have begun in 1995 and to have been completed four years later. However, government budget problems in the United States and recessions in much of the rest of the world raised questions about the expenditure of funds for the project. The space station became much smaller when in 1993 President Bill Clinton called for it to be redesigned. The redesigned plan considerably reduced the size of the space station, and took international partners in order to further reduce U.S. costs.

In December 1993 the countries involved in the space station project invited Russia to join them. The Russians agreed, and the station's name changed from *Freedom* to *Alpha* .

With Russian participation, the space station project underwent some major changes. Russia's experience of over 20 years of operating space stations paved the way for the space station to take on a new appearance. The project name was changed again, to the *International Space Station,* with the first phase being the Shuttle-Mir missions. There were nine docking missions between 1995 and 1998, determining the technologies needed to build the space station, examining the space environment, and conducting experiments. From 1998, the second phase, construction and operation of the station—finally got under way.

The *International Space Station* (ISS) project is NASA's biggest project since the Apollo Project. Since the mid-1990s, NASA has been faced with with harsh budget cuts, and Russia, too, has struggled economically. To avoid delays and keep reductions in the scale of the space station project to a minimum, international cooperation has become more important than ever, with 16 countries participating. In January 1998, Russian President Boris Yeltsin agreed to allocate more funds to the International Space Station project, easing fears among other project partner countries that Russia was losing enthusiasm for the project.

Construction of ISS began in November 1998 with the launch of the Zarya cargo block from Russia. As of 1999, a total of 44 launches will be needed to complete the facility in 2004. When complete, the ISS will have an end-to-end length of 356 feet (longer than a football field), 290 feet wide, and 143 feet tall. It will have a **mass** of nearly one million pounds (450,000 kg), have a pressurized living and working space of 46,000 cubic feet (1,300 cubic meters), enough for up to seven astronauts and scientists, traveling in low Earth orbit. It will cost about $30 billion.

Technical requirements of crewed spacecraft

A very large number of complex technical problems must be solved in the construction of spacecraft that can carry humans into space. Most of these problems can be classified in one of three major categories: communication, environmental and support, and re-entry.

Communication refers to the necessity of maintaining contact with members of a space mission as well as monitoring their health and biological functions and the condition of the spacecraft in which they are traveling. Direct communication between astronauts and cosmonauts can be accomplished by means of **radio** and **television** messages transmitted between a spacecraft and ground stations. To facilitate these communications, receiving stations at various locations around Earth have been established. Messages are received and transmitted to and from a space vehicle by means of large antennas located at these stations.

Many different kinds of instruments are needed within the spacecraft to monitor cabin **temperature**, pressure, humidity, and other conditions as well as biological functions such as **heart** rate, body temperature, **blood** pressure, and other vital functions. Constant monitoring of spacecraft hardware is also necessary. Data obtained from these monitoring functions is converted to radio signals that are transmitted to Earth stations, allowing ground-based observers to maintain a constant check on the status of both the spacecraft and its human passengers.

Environmental controls

The fundamental requirement of a crewed spacecraft is, of course, to provide an atmosphere in which humans can survive and carry out the jobs required of them. This means, first of all, providing the spacecraft with an Earth-like atmosphere in which humans can breathe. Traditionally, the Soviet Union has used a mixture of **nitrogen** and **oxygen** gases somewhat like that found in the Earth's atmosphere. American spacecraft, however, have employed pure oxygen atmospheres at pressures of about 5 lb per **square** inch, roughly one-third that of normal air pressure on the Earth's surface.

The level of **carbon dioxide** within a spacecraft must also be maintained at a healthy level. The most direct way of dealing with this problem is to provide the craft with a base, usually **lithium** hydroxide, which will absorb carbon dioxide exhaled by astronauts and cosmonauts. Humidity, temperature, odors, toxic gases, and sound levels are other factors that must be controlled at a level congenial to human existence.

Food and **water** provisions present additional problems. The space needed for the storage of conventional foodstuffs is prohibitive for spacecraft. Thus, one of the early challenges for space scientists was the development of dehydrated foods or foods prepared in other ways so that they would occupy as little space as possible. Space scientists have long recognized that food and water supplies present one of the most challenging problems of long-term space travel, as would be the case in a space station. Suggestions have been made, for example, for the purification and **recycling** of urine as drinking water and for the use of exhaled carbon dioxide in the growth of plants for foods in spacecraft that remain in orbit for long periods of time.

Power sources

An important aspect of spacecraft design is the provision for power sources needed to operate communica-

tion, environmental, and other instruments and devices within the vehicle. The earliest crewed spacecrafts had fairly simple power systems. The Mercury series of vehicles, for example, were powered by six conventional batteries. As spacecraft increased in size and complexity, however, so did their power needs. The Gemini spacecrafts required an additional conventional **battery** and two **fuel cells**, while the Apollo vehicles were provided with five batteries and three fuel cells.

Physiological effects

One of the most serious on-going concerns of space scientists about crewed flights has been their potential effects on the human body. An important goal of nearly every space flight has been to determine how the human body reacts to a zero-gravity environment.

At this point, scientists have some answers to that question. For example, we know that one of the most serious dangers posed by extended space travel is the loss of **calcium** from bones. Also, the absence of gravitational forces results in a space traveller's blood collecting in the upper part of his or her body, especially in the left atrium. This knowledge has led to the development of special devices that modify the loss of gravitational effects during space travel.

Redundancy of systems

One of the challenges posed by crewed space flight is the need for redundancy in systems. Redundancy means that there must be two or three of every instrument, device, or spacecraft part that is needed for human survival. This level of redundancy is not necessary with uncrewed spacecraft where failure of a system may result in the loss of a **space probe**, but not the loss of a human life. It is crucial, however, when humans travel aboard a spacecraft.

An example of the role of redundancy was provided during the *Apollo 13* mission. That mission's plan of landing on the moon had to be aborted when one of the fuel cells in the service module exploded, eliminating a large part of the spacecraft's power supply. A back-up fuel **cell** in the lunar module was brought on line, however, allowing the spacecraft to return to the Earth without loss of life.

Space suits

Space suits are designed to be worn by astronauts and cosmonauts during take-off and landing and during extravehicular activities (EVA). They are, in a sense, a space passenger's own private space vehicle and present, in miniature, most of the same environmental problems as does the construction of the spacecraft itself. For example, a space suit must be able to protect the space traveller from marked changes in temperature, pressure, and humidity, and from exposure to **radiation**, unacceptable solar glare, and micrometeorites. In addition, the space suit must allow the space traveller to move about with relative ease and to provide a means of communicating with fellow travellers in a spacecraft or with controllers on the Earth's surface. The removal and storage of human wastes is also a problem that must be solved for humans wearing a space suit.

The *Salyut 7* space station photographed in orbit. Attached to the space station at the bottom, with the separate solar panels, is the *Soyuz T14* ferry spacecraft. *Soyuz T14* was launched on September 17, 1985 and carried cosmonauts Vladimir Vasyutin, Alexander Volkov, and Georgi Grechko to *Salyut 7.* Their mission was terminated when Vasytin became seriously ill, and they returned to Earth on November 22, 1985.

Re-entry problems and solutions

Ensuring that astronauts and cosmonauts are able to survive in space is only one of the problems facing space

scientists. A spacecraft must also be able to return its human passengers safely to the Earth's surface. In the earliest crewed spacecrafts, this problem was solved simply by allowing the vehicle to travel along a ballistic path back to the Earth's atmosphere and then to settle on land or sea by means of one or more large parachutes. Later spacecraft were modified to allow pilots some control over their re-entry path. The space shuttles, for example, can be piloted back to Earth in the last stages of re-entry in much the same way that a normal airplane is flown.

Perhaps the most serious single problem encountered during re-entry is the **heat** that develops as the spacecraft returns to the Earth's atmosphere. **Friction** between vehicle and air produces temperatures that approach 3,092°F (1,700°C). Most metals and alloys would melt or fail at these temperatures. To deal with this problem, spacecraft designers have developed a class of materials known as ablators that absorb and then radiate large amounts of heat in brief periods of time. Ablators have been made out of a variety of materials, including phenolic **resins**, epoxy compounds, and silicone rubbers.

Some are beginning to look beyond space shuttle flights, which are becoming almost commonplace, and the International Space Station. While NASA's main emphasis for some time will be unmanned probes and robots, the most tempting target for a manned spacecraft will surely be **Mars**. Besides issues of long-term life support, any such mission will have to deal with long-term exposure to space radiation. Without sufficient protection, galactic cosmic **rays** would penetrate spacecraft and astronaut's bodies, damaging their DNA and perhaps disrupting nerve cells in their brains over the long-term. (Manned flights to the Moon were protected from cosmic rays by the Earth's magnetosphere.) Shielding would be necessary, but it is always a trade-off between human protection and spacecraft weight. Moreover, estimates show it could add billions of dollars to the cost of any such flight.

With the routineness of manned space flights has come the dawn of the age of space tourism. Rocket pioneer Werhner von Braun was one of the first to support such an idea, and many have thought about it since. In the first decade of the twentieth-first century, several companies may offer suborbital space flights to anyone who can afford a ticket (probably around $100,000). Tourists will be able to see space from above earth's atmosphere and experience weightlessness. Someday, perhaps, they will dock at orbiting hotels and eat dinner by the light of the Earth.

See also Space probe.

Further Reading

Compton, W. David, and Charles D. Benson. *Living and Working in Space.* Washington, D.C.: NASA, 1983.

Dotto, Lydia, Stephen Hart, Gina Maranto, and Peter Pocock. *How Things Work in Space.* Alexandria, VA: Time-Life Books, 1991.

Johnson, N. L. *Soviet Year in Space.* Colorado Springs, CO: Teledyne Brown Engineering, published annually.

McGraw-Hill Encyclopedia of Science & Technology. 7th edition. New York: McGraw-Hill Book Company, 1992.

Newton, David E. *U.S. and Soviet Space Programs.* New York: Franklin Watts, 1988.

Oberg, James E. *The New Race for Space.* Harrisburg, PA: Stackpole Books, 1984.

David E. Newton

KEY TERMS

Crewed spacecraft—A vehicle designed to travel outside the Earth's atmosphere carrying one or more humans.

Docking—The process by which two spacecraft join to each other while traveling in orbit.

EVA—Extravehicular activity, a term describing the movement of a human being outside an orbiting spacecraft.

LRV—Lunar roving vehicle, a car-like form of transportation used by astronauts in moving about on the moon's surface.

Module—A cabin-like space in a spacecraft, usually part of a larger system.

Orbital flight—The movement of a spacecraft around some astronomical body such as the Earth or moon.

Redundancy—The process by which two or more identical items are included in a spacecraft to increase the safety of its human passengers.

Space shuttle—A crewed spacecraft used to carry humans and materials from the Earth's surface into space.

Space station—An orbiting space vehicle designed to stay in space for long periods of time and to accommodate the work of humans in and around the vehicle.

Spanish moss see **Bromeliad family**

Sparrows and buntings

The typical sparrows, buntings, and their allies are 281 species of **birds** that comprise the subfamily Ember-

izinae, family Emberizidae. The emberizid sparrows and buntings occur in a great variety of habitats, and are widely distributed, occurring on all of the habitable continents except for Southeast **Asia** and **Australia**. The greatest diversity of species, however, occurs in the Americas.

The phylogenetic relationships within the family Emberizidae are complex and incompletely understood, and its systematics have been subject to recent revisions. The Emberizidae is now considered by most ornithologists to contain the following subfamilies: (1) the Emberizinae, containing typical sparrows and buntings; (2) the Parulinae, or American wood-warblers; (3) the Thraupinae, or **tanagers**; (4) the Cardinalinae, or cardinals and typical grosbeaks, (5) the Icterinae, or American **blackbirds**, meadowlarks, **orioles**, bobolink, and cowbirds, and (6) the Coerebinae, or bananaquits.

However, this taxonomic arrangement remains controversial, and some ornithologists and many textbooks and field guides continue to rank each of these groups as full families. Nevertheless, these are all distinctive groups of birds, regardless of our understanding of their evolutionary relationships, and whether we call them subfamilies or families.

A further point of discussion concerns the use of the words "sparrow" and "bunting," both of which are taxonomically ambiguous terms. In the general sense, sparrows can be various species of conical-billed, seed-eating birds. These can include species in the family of the weaver **finches**, Ploceidae, such as the house sparrow (*Passer domesticus*). However, the "typical" sparrows are species of the Americas in the subfamily Emberizinae, and these are the birds that are described in this entry.

Similarly, buntings can be certain species in the subfamily Cardinalinae, such as the indigo bunting (*Passerina cyanea*). Buntings can also be species in the Emberizinae, mostly of the Old World genus *Emberiza*, plus several other genera that occur in **North America**. It is the emberizid buntings that are the "typical" buntings.

Biology of sparrows and buntings

The emberizid sparrows and buntings are all smallish birds with a short, stout, conical-shaped bill, well-adapted for picking and crushing **seeds** as food.

The various species of emberizids are rather similarly colored in shades of streaky grays and browns. However, the particular species can usually be identified on the basis of diagnostic, albeit sometimes subtle differences in the patterns and colorations of their plumage. In addition, species can always be separated on the basis of their preferred breeding **habitat**, and on their distinctive songs and call-notes. Most species of emberizids have streaked patterns on their back and breast, and some have bold markings of black, white, or **chestnut** around the head. Many species have a sexually dimorphic plumage, in which the females have a relatively subdued, cryptic coloration, while the plumage of males is brighter and more boldly patterned and colored.

Emberizids mostly forage on or near the ground, commonly scratching and kicking with their feet in the surface dirt and litter, searching for food items. The usual food of most species of emberizids is seeds. However, during the nesting season, **insects** and other **invertebrates** are a relatively important food item, especially for feeding to fast-growing babies, which require a diet rich in protein.

Emberizids are highly territorial during their breeding season, proclaiming their territory by singing, which in many species is quite loud, rich, and musical. Some species of open habitats, such as prairies and **tundra**, deliver their song while engaged in a slowly descending flight.

The emberizids occur in a great variety of habitats, although most species are partial to places that are relatively open, interspersed with shrubs or trees, or more densely shrubby. Few species occur in mature, densely stocked, closed **forests**.

Species that breed in relatively northern habitats with severe winters are all migratory. These birds take advantage of the often great availability of foods during the growing season in northern latitudes, but spend their non-breeding season farther to the south, where food is more available during winter, and general living conditions are more benign. During the non-breeding season, most migratory species of emberizids occur in flocks. Species that forage in open habitats, such as fields and prairies, generally form especially large flocks.

Sparrows and buntings in North America

There are about 50 species of emberizid sparrows and their allies that breed regularly in North America. Some of the more widespread of these are briefly described below.

The song sparrow (*Melospiza melodia*) is one of the most widespread of the sparrows, breeding over much of Canada and the United States, and as far south as Mexico. The usual habitat of this abundant bird is shrubby, commonly beside lakes, **rivers**, or streams, along forest edges, in regenerating burns or cut-overs, and in parks and gardens. This species has a dark-brown plumage, with a dark spot in the middle of its streaky breast.

Lincoln's sparrow (*Melospiza lincolnii*) is a similar-looking, close relative of the song sparrow, but is much-

less familiar to most people because of its habit of skulking unseen within dense vegetation. This species breeds extensively in Canada and the western mountains of the United States. The swamp sparrow (*M. georgiana*) is similar to the previous two species, but breeds in shrubby **wetlands** beside lakes, rivers, and streams, and in more-extensive marshes. This species breeds widely in eastern Canada and the northeastern states, and winters in the eastern United States.

The fox sparrow (*Passerella iliaca*) is a relatively large, heavily streaked bird that breeds in thickets, regenerating burns and cutovers, and open forests. The fox sparrow occurs in the boreal and montane zones, and ranges as far south as central Utah, Colorado, and Nevada.

The savannah sparrow (*Passerculus sandwichensis*) is a very widespread species, breeding in suitably open, grassy habitats over all of Canada and much of the United States. This species mostly winters in the southern United States and parts of Central America. The savannah sparrow is a heavily streaked, brownish bird with distinctive, light-yellow patches over the eyes. The Ipswich sparrow (*P. sandwichensis princeps*) is a large, light-colored subspecies that breeds only in dune-grass habitats on Sable Island in the western Atlantic Ocean, and winters along the Atlantic Coast of the United States. The Ipswich sparrow is sometimes treated as a distinct species (*P. princeps*).

The white-throated sparrow (*Zonotrichia albicollis*) breeds over much of temperate and boreal Canada and New England. The usual habitat of this species is brushy, and includes open forests, forest edges, regenerating burns and cutovers, and abandoned farmland. The territorial song of this abundant species consists of a series of loud, clear whistles, and is one of the most familiar sounds of the springtime in woodlands within its range. Birdwatchers in the United States learn the very distinctive song of the white-throated sparrow as : " *old Sam Peabody, Peabody, Peabody*," but Canadians memorize it as:" *I-love Canada, Canada, Canada*." The head of the white-throated sparrow is prominently marked with light-shaded stripes, which can be colored either bright-white or tan. Individuals with white stripes are relatively aggressive in the defense of their territory, and in their general interactions with others of their species. Consequently, a hyperaggressive male "white-stripe" can mate successfully with a relatively submissive female "tan-stripe," but not with a female white-stripe, because the two would fight too much.

The white-crowned sparrow (*Zonotrichia leucophrys*) breeds widely in boreal and montane coniferous forests across Canada and the western United States, and winters in the southern States. The golden-crowned sparrow (*Z. atricapilla*) is a closely related species, breeding in coastal, coniferous rainforests of western Alaska and British Columbia, and wintering in the coastal, western United States.

The chipping sparrow (*Spizella passerina*) breeds in open, treed habitats from the boreal region through to Nicaragua in Central America, and winters in the southern United States and further south. This common species has a rufous cap, a bright-white line through the **eye**, and a whitish, unstreaked breast. The American **tree** sparrow (*S. arborea*) breeds in shrubby habitats and open forests throughout most of the northern boreal forest. Tree sparrows winter in large flocks in fields and brushy habitats throughout central North America. The clay-colored sparrow (*S. pallida*) breeds in shrubby meadows, riparian habitats, and forest edges of the **prairie** region of North America, and winters in Texas and Mexico.

The vesper sparrow (*Pooecetes gramineus*) breeds in natural prairies, and in weedy fields and pastures throughout north-temperate regions of North America.

The larksparrow (*Chondestes grammacus*) breeds in open, dry habitats with scattered trees, including native prairies and abandoned agricultural lands. Lark sparrows occur over most of the central and western United States. These birds have bright, chestnut-and-white patterns on their head.

The black-throated or **desert** sparrow (*Amphispiza bilineata*) occurs in arid habitats in the southwestern United States and northern Mexico. This species has a grey back, a black breast, and black-and-white stripes on the face. The closely related sage sparrow (*A. belli*) breeds in dry, shrubby habitats of the western states.

The grasshoppersparrow (*Ammodramus savannarum*) breeds in drier prairies, hayfields, and old-fields in central regions of the **continent**. LeConte's sparrow (*A. leconteii*) breeds in tall, moist, grassy and sedge meadows in the prairies, and winters in the southeastern states. The sharp-tailed sparrow (*A. caudacuta*) breeds in **salt** marshes along the Atlantic and Hudson Bay seacoasts, and in **brackish** wet meadows in the prairies.

The dark-eyed junco (*Junco hyemalis*) breeds in recently disturbed coniferous forests throughout Canada and much of the western United States. This species winters in weedy fields and brushy habitats throughout the United States. The dark-eyed junco has a grey head and breast, and depending on the subspecies, either a grey or a brownish back and wings.

The lark bunting (*Calamospiza melanocorys*) breeds in shortgrass prairies and semi-deserts from southern Alberta to northern Texas. Males have a black body with

large, white wing-patches, while females look like more-typical sparrows, with a streaky brown plumage.

The towhees are relatively large, long-tailed, ground-feeding species of shrubby habitats. The rufous-sided towhee (*Piplio erythrophthalmus*) breeds in thick, brushy habitats through southern Canada and the United States, and as far south as Guatemala in Central America. Males have a black back, rufous sides, and a white belly, while females have a brown back - both sexes usually have brilliant-red eyes. The rufous-sided towhee is named after one of its call notes, which sounds like "*tow-whee*," and this bird also has a loud, easily recognizable song that sounds like: " *drink-your-teeeea*." The green-tailed towhee (*P. chlorurus*) breeds in brushy habitats in the western United States, while the brown towhee (*P. fuscus*) occurs in shrubby habitats in the southwest, including suburban gardens and parks.

The Lapland longspur (*Calcarius lapponicus*) breeds throughout the northern tundra of North America, and also in northern **Europe** and Asia, where it is known as the Lapland bunting. This species winters in native prairies and agricultural landscapes to the south of its breeding range. The very attractive, breeding plumage of the males includes a jet-black face and bib, and a bright-chestnut back of the head, but the non-breeding plumage is much more subdued. The McCown's longspur (*C. mccownii*) breeds in the short-grass prairies of North America, and winters to the south in Texas and Mexico. The chestnut-collared longspur (*C. ornatus*) has a similar distribution.

The snow bunting, snowflake, or snowbird (*Plectrophenax nivalis*) breeds throughout the arctic tundra of North America, and also in arctic regions of Europe and Asia. The snow bunting winters widely in temperate regions of North America, sometimes occurring in large flocks in snow-covered agricultural areas and coastal dunes. The male snow bunting has an attractive, highly contrasting, black-and-white plumage, with the head and breast being a bright white, and the wings and back a jet black. Females have a more subdued, light-brownish coloration. Because it tends to appear just as the snow starts to fly, the snow bunting is a familiar harbinger of winter for people in its southern, non-breeding range. However, for people living in small communities in the tundra of northern Canada, returning snow buntings are a welcome herald of the coming springtime, following a long, hard winter. The closely related McKay's bunting (*P. hyperboreus*) breeds on several islands in the Bering Sea, and winters in coastal, western Alaska.

Sparrows and buntings elsewhere

Species of buntings of the genus *Emberiza* do not breed in North America, but are relatively diverse in

A song sparrow (*Melospiza melodia*) at Isle Royale National Park, Michigan.

Eurasia and **Africa**. In fact, of the 40 species of enberizids breeding in the Old World, 37 are in the genus *Emberiza*. One widespread species is the yellow-hammer (*Emberiza citrinella*), a familiar, yellow-bellied bird of forest edges and shrubby habitats. The reed bunting (*E. schoeniclus*) is a black-headed, brown-backed species of marshy habitats and wet meadows.

Sparrows and humans

Species of sparrows are among the more common species of birds that visit seed-bearing feeders. This is particularly true during the wintertime, when natural seeds can be difficult to find because of the snowpack. Bird-feeding has a significant economic impact, with millions of dollars being spent each year in North America to purchase and provision backyard feeders.

Some species of sparrows are fairly easy to keep in captivity, and they are kept as pet cagebirds. Especially commonly kept are species of *Emberiza* buntings, particularly in Europe.

Some sparrows have become rare and endangered because of changes in their habitat caused by humans. In the United States, certain subspecies of the seaside sparrow (*Ammodramus maritimus*) have been affected in this way. The dusky seaside sparrow (*A. m. nigrescens*) was a locally distributed bird of salt marshes on the east coast of Florida, and was once considered to be a distinct species (as *Ammospiza nigrescens*), but recent taxonomists have lumped with related birds within a seaside sparrow "superspecies." Unfortunately, the dusky seaside sparrow became extinct in 1987, when the last known individual, a male bird, died in captivity. This bird became extinct as a result of losses of habitat through drainage and construction activities, and perhaps toxicity due to the spraying of **insecticides** to control **mosquitoes** in its

KEY TERMS

Extinct—A situation in which no representative of a species or other taxon occur anywhere on Earth.

Extirpation—A situation in a species or other taxon no longer occurs in some part of its former range, although it still occurs elsewhere.

Sexual dimorphism—The occurrence of different coloration or shape between the sexes. In many species of emberizids, the males are colored brightly and in bold patterns, while the plumage of the females is more drab and cryptic.

Superspecies—A complex of closely related groups of organisms that are geographically, ecologically, and morphologically distinct, but are nevertheless considered to be the same species. The seasise sparrows are a superspecies, in which many of the various subspecies were formerly believed to be separate species.

salt-marsh habitat, which was close to places used for tourism and residential land-uses. The closely related Cape Sable seaside sparrow (*A. m. mirabilis*) of southern Florida has similarly become endangered, and several of its former populations have been extirpated.

The San Clemente sage sparrow (*Amphispiza belli clementeae*) is an endangered subspecies of the sage sparrow that is resident to the island of San Clemente off the coast of southern California. This species has suffered because of habitat degradations caused by introduced populations of **goats** and **pigs**. The Zapata sparrow (*Terreornis inexpectata*) is a rare and **endangered species** that only occurs in two small areas on the island of Cuba.

See also Weaver finches.

Further Reading

Byers, C., U. Olsson, and J. Curson. *Buntings and Sparrows.* Golden, CO.: Pica Press, 1995.

Ehrlich, P., D. Dobkin, and D. Wheye. *The Birders Handbook.* New York: Simon and Schuster, 1989.

Farrand, J. (ed.). *The Audubon Society Master Guide to Birding.* New York: A.A. Knopf, 1983.

Harrison, C.J.O. (ed.). *Bird Families of the World.* New York: H.N. Abrams Pubs., 1978.

Trollope, J. *The Care and Breeding of Seed-eating Birds.* Dorset, United Kingdom: Blandford Press, 1983.

Bill Freedman

Spatial perception see **Depth perception**

Species

The most widely accepted definition of a species is the biological species concept proposed by Ernst Mayr in the 1940s. A species is a population of individual organisms that can interbreed in nature, mating and producing fertile offspring in a natural setting. Species are organisms that share the same **gene** pool, and therefore genetic and morphological similarities.

Species determination

All organisms are given two names (a binomial name); the first is the genus name and the second is the species name, for example *Homo sapiens*, the name for humans. The Linnaean classification system places all organisms into a hierarchy of ranked groups. The genus includes one or more related species, while a group of similar genera are placed in the same family. Similar families are grouped into the same order, similar orders in the same class, and similar classes in the same phylum.

Organisms are assigned to the higher ranks of the Linnaean classification scheme largely on the basis of shared similarities (syna pomorphisus). Species are identified on the basis of an organism's ability to interbreed, in addition to its morphological, behavioral, and biochemical characters. Although species are defined as interbreeding populations, taxonomists rarely have information on an organism's breeding **behavior** and therefore often infer interbreeding groups on the basis of **reproductive system** morphology, and other shared characters.

In the last 20 years, modern molecular techniques such as DNA hybridization have allowed biologists to gain extensive information on the genetic **distance** between organisms, which they use to construct hypotheses about the relatedness of organisms. From this information researchers hypothesize as to whether or not the populations are genetically close enough to interbreed.

While the biological species concept has historically been the most widely used definition of a species, more recently the phylogenetic and ecological species concepts have taken the forefront as a more inclusive and useful definition. Whereas the biological species concept defines a species as a group of organisms that are reproductively isolated (able to successfully breed only within the group), the phylogenetic species concept considers tangible (and measurable) differences in characteristics. This idea, also called the cladistic species concept, examines the degree of genetic similarity between groups of related individuals (called clades) as well as their similarities in physical characteristics. For instance, the biological species concept might group

Two lesser earless lizards, *Holbrookia maculata*. They are genetically the same species, but the upper one is from White Sands.

coyotes and wolves together as one species because they can successfully breed with one another. In contrast, the phylogenetic concept would definitively split coyotes and wolves into two species based upon the degree of divergence in genetic characters and larger observable traits (like coat color, for instance). In contrast to these, the ecological species concept might classify wolves and coyotes as different species by comparing the differing environmental resources that they exploit, called adaptive zones. Currently, the precise definition of a species is a topic under constant scientific debate and likely will never fully be resolved. Rather, the definition may change with the perspectives and needs of each sub-discipline within **biology** (**ecology** versus zoology, for example). A pluralist approach combines some or all of these species concepts to arrive at a more inclusive definition.

Speciation

Speciation is the process whereby a single species develops over time into two distinct reproductively isolated species. Speciation events are of two types—either allopatric or sympatric. Allopatric speciation results from the division of a population of organisms by a geographical barrier. The isolation of each of the two populations slowly results in differences in the gene pools until the two populations are unable to interbreed either because of changes in mating behavior or because of incompatibility of the DNA from the two populations. The early stages of allopatric speciation are often evident when one examines the same species of **fish** from different ponds. Fish from the two ponds may not appear to be morphologically different, but there may be slight differences in the gene pools of each population. If the two fish populations remain separated for enough generations, they may eventually become two separate reproductively isolated species.

Sympatric speciation is less frequent than allopatric speciation and occurs when a group of individuals becomes reproductively isolated from the larger population occupying the same range. This type of speciation may result from genetic changes (or mutations) occurring within individuals that inhibits them from interbreeding with others, except those in which the same **mutation** has occurred. Polyploid **plant** species, that is, species with more than two copies of each **chromosome**, are thought to have arisen by sympatric speciation.

KEY TERMS

Allopatric speciation—Speciation resulting from a population being geographically divided.

Lenin system—Classification scheme used by taxonomists which places organisms into a hierarchy of groups.

Morphology—The physical properties possessed by an organism.

Polyploid—An organism with more than two copies of each chromosome.

Sympatric speciation—Speciation that occurs when a subpopulation becomes reproductively isolated from a larger population occupying the same range.

More than 1.5 million species have been described and it is estimated that there are between 10-50 million species currently inhabiting **Earth**.

See also Genetics; Mutation; Taxonomy.

Further Reading

Cockburn, Andrew. *An Introduction to Evolutionary Ecology.* Boston: Blackwell Scientific Publications, 1991.

Mayr, Ernst, and Peter Ashlock. *Principles of Systematic Zoology.* 2nd ed. New York: McGraw-Hill, 1991.

Purves, William, Gordon Orians, and H. Heller. *Life: The Science of Biology.* 3rd ed. Sunderland, Massachusetts: Sinaur Associates, Inc., 1992.

Wilson, Edward. *The Diversity of Life.* Cambridge, Massachusetts: Belknap Press, 1992.

Steven MacKenzie

Spectral classification of stars

Although the composition of most stars is very similar, there are systematic variations in stellar spectra based on their temperatures. A typical **star** has a **spectrum** consisting of a continuous range of colors overlaid with dark lines. The positions, strengths, and shapes of these lines are determined by the **temperature**, **density**, gravitational fields, **velocity**, and other properties of the star. In order to be able to study stars systematically, it is useful to classify stars with others that have similar properties. This is the basis for the classification scheme used by astronomers. Stars are classified according to the patterns and relative strengths of their dark **spectral lines**, which are indicators of both their temperature and their intrinsic luminosity, or brightness. Although roughly 10% of stars do not fit into the classification scheme, it provides a convenient way to understand the systematics of stellar formation and **evolution**.

Background

When the light from a star is divided into its component colors using a spectrograph, it appears as a continuous band of colors, broken up by dark, narrow lines. These lines are created by **atoms** and ions (atoms missing one or more electrons) in the outer layers of a star's atmosphere. These layers absorb light at specific wavelengths, which are unique for each type of atom or ion. Atomic **physics** predicts the positions and intensities of these lines, called absorption lines, based on the temperature and composition of the star. Thus, the number, strengths, and positions of these lines vary from star to star.

The first stellar spectra were observed in 1814, long before the atomic physics that creates them was understood. In an attempt to understand the processes which formed the spectra, similar stars with similar spectra were grouped together in the hopes that stars which were alike would produce similar spectra. In 1863, Father Angelo Secchi made one of the first attempts at trying to classify stars, when he divided stars into two groups based on their spectral lines. He eventually extended this categorization, dividing more than 4,000 stars into four classes.

The basis of our current system of classification of spectral types began in the late 1800s at the Harvard College Observatory, under the direction of Professor Edward C. Pickering. Williamina P. Fleming initially classified 10,000 stars using the letters of the alphabet to denote the strength of their **hydrogen** absorption lines, with A being the strongest, followed by B, C, etc. At the time, she did not know that these lines were due to hydrogen, but since they were visible in almost all stellar spectra, they provided a convenient means by which to organize her data.

Several years later, the classifications were reordered to be in what we now know to be the order of decreasing temperature: O, B, A, F, G, K, M, in order to have a smooth transition between the class boundaries. This reordering was done primarily by Annie Jump Cannon, also at the Harvard Observatory, in preparing the Henry Draper catalog of 225,000 stars. She also further subdivided each class into as many as ten subclasses, by adding the numbers 0 through 9 after the letter, to account for changes within a class. This spectral classification scheme was formally adopted by the International Astronomical Union in 1922, and is still used today.

It was not until 1925 that the theoretical basis behind the ordering was discovered. At first, scientists believed that the strength of the lines directly determined the amount of each element found in the star, but the situation proved more complex than that. Most stars have very similar compositions, so the strength of hydrogen (and other) lines in the spectrum is not a measure of the makeup of the star. Instead, it is a measure of temperature, as a result of the atomic physics processes occurring in the star. At relatively low temperatures, the gas in a stellar atmosphere contains many atoms, (and even some molecules), and these produce the strongest absorption lines. At higher temperatures, molecules are destroyed and atoms begin losing electrons, and absorption lines of ions begin to appear. More and more ionization occurs as the temperature increases, further altering the pattern of absorption lines. Thus, the smooth sequence of line patterns is actually a temperature sequence.

Another of the early classification workers at Harvard, Antonia Maury, noted that certain dark lines (absorption lines) in stellar spectra varied in width. She attempted a classification based partially on line widths, but this was not adopted by Annie Cannon in her classification, and was not used in the Henry Draper catalog. But Maury's work laid the foundation for the subsequent discovery that the line widths were related to stellar size: very large stars, now called giants or supergiants, have thin lines due to their low **atmospheric pressure**. These stars are very luminous because they have large surface areas, and so line width was eventually recognized as an indicator of stellar luminosity.

In 1938, W. W. Morgan at the Yerkes Observatory added a second dimension to the classification scheme, by using the luminosity of the star as an additional classifying feature. He used roman numerals to represent the various types of stars. In 1943, the MKK Atlas of Stellar Spectra (after Morgan, P. C. Keenan, and E. Kellman) was published, formalizing this system. Approximately 90% of stars can be classified using the MKK system.

Description of the spectral classes

The temperature range of each class, along with the most prominent spectral lines which form the basis of the spectral identification, are described below. A common mnemonic for remembering the order of the spectral classes is Oh Be A Fine Girl (or guy) Kiss Me. In the original scheme there were a few additional classes (S, R, C, N) which turned out to represent stars that actually do have abnormal compositions. Today, these stars are usually in transient evolutionary phases, and are not included in the standard spectral classifications.

KEY TERMS

Absorption spectrum—A continuous spectrum, with gaps at discrete wavelengths. The positions of the gaps depends on the component atoms.

Ionized—Missing one or more electrons, resulting in a charged atom.

Spectrograph—A device for measuring the spectrum of light.

Spectrum—A display of the intensity of radiation vs. wavelength. The plural form is spectra.

O (30,000 - 60,000 K, blue-white)-At such high temperatures, most of the hydrogen is ionized, and thus the hydrogen lines are less prominent than in the B and A classes (ionized hydrogen with no remaining **electron** has no spectral lines). Much of the helium is also ionized. Lines from ionized **carbon**, **nitrogen**, **oxygen** and silicon are also seen.

B (10,000 - 30,000 K, blue white)-In stars in this spectral class, the hydrogen lines are stronger than in O stars, while the lines of ionized helium are weaker. Ionized carbon, oxygen, and silicon are seen.

A (7500 - 10,000 K, blue white)-A stars have the strongest hydrogen lines (recall the ordering of the original Harvard classification). Other prominent lines are due to singly ionized **magnesium**, silicon and **calcium**.

F (6000 - 7500 K, yellow-white)-Lines from ionized calcium are prominent features in F stars.

G (5000 - 6000 K, yellow)-The ionized calcium lines are strongest in G stars. The **sun** is a G2 star.

K (3500 - 5000 K, orange)-The spectra of K stars contain many lines from neutral elements.

M (less than 3500 K, red)-Molecular lines seen in the spectra of M stars mean that the temperature is low enough that molecules have not been broken up into their constituent atoms. **Titanium** oxide (TiO) is particularly prominent.

The MKK luminosity classes are: I-Supergiants; II-Bright Giants; III-Normal Giants; IV-Subgiants; V-Main Sequence.

See also Spectroscopy.

Further Reading

Hearnshaw, J.B., *The Analysis of Starlight: One Hundred and Fifty Years of Astronomical Spectroscopy.* Cambridge: Cambridge University Press, 1986.

Pasachoff, Jay M., *Contemporary Astronomy.* fourth edition. Philadelphia: Saunders College Publishing, 1989.

Unsöld, Albrecht and Baschek, Bodo, *The New Cosmos.* Berlin: Springer-Verlag, 1991.

David Sahnow

Spectral lines

A spectral line is **light** of a single **frequency**, or wavelength, which is emitted by an atom when an **electron** changes its **energy** level. Because the energy levels of the electron vary from element to element, scientists can determine the chemical composition of an object from a distance by examining its **spectrum**. In addition, the shift of a spectral line from its predicted position can show the speed at which an astronomical object is moving away from **Earth**. The measurement of spectral lines is the basis of much of modern **astronomy**.

History

Isaac Newton was the first to discover that light from the **sun** was composed of multiple frequencies. In 1666, by using a **prism** to break sunlight into its component colors, and then recombining them with a second prism, he showed that the light coming from the sun consisted of a continuous array of colors. Until then, some believed that the colors shown by a prism were generated by the prism itself, and were not intrinsic to the sunlight.

Later experiments showed that some light sources, such as gas discharges, emit at only certain well-defined frequencies rather than over a continuous distribution of colors; the resultant image is called an **emission** spectrum. (plural, spectra). Still other sources were found to produce nearly continuous spectra (i.e., smooth **rainbows** of color) with distinct gaps at particular locations; these are known as absorption spectra. By making observations of a variety of objects, Gustav Kirchhoff was able to formulate three laws to describe spectra. Kirchhoff's laws can be put into modern form as follows: (1) an opaque object emits a continuous spectrum; (2) a glowing gas has an emission line spectrum; and (3) a source with a continuous spectrum which has a cooler gas in front of it gives an absorption spectrum.

The observation of spectra was used to discover new elements in the 1800s. For example, the element helium, although it exists on Earth, was first discovered in the Sun by observing its spectrum during an eclipse.

Observations of particular elements showed that each had a characteristic spectrum. In 1885, Johann Balmer developed a simple formula which described the progression of lines seen in the spectrum of **hydrogen**. His formula showed that the wavelengths of the lines were related to the **integers** via a simple equation. Others later discovered additional series of lines in the hydrogen spectrum, which could be explained in a similar manner.

Niels Bohr was the first to explain the mechanism by which spectral lines occur at their characteristic wavelengths. He postulated that the electrons in an atom can be found only at a series of unique energy levels, and that light of a particular wavelength was emitted when the electron made a transition from one of these levels to another. The relationship between the wavelength of emitted light and the change in energy was given by Planck's law, which states that energy is inversely proportional to wavelength (and hence directly proportional to frequency). Thus, for a given atom, light could only be emitted at certain discrete wavelengths, corresponding to the energy difference between electron energy levels. Similarly, only wavelengths corresponding to the difference between energy levels could be absorbed by an atom. This picture of the hydrogen atom, known as the Bohr atom, has since been found to be too simplified a model to describe **atoms** in detail, but it remains the best physical model for understanding atomic spectra.

Spectrographs

Astronomers use a device called a spectrograph to disperse light into its constituent wavelengths in the same way that Newton's prism divided sunlight into its component colors. Spectrographs may have a prism or a **diffraction** grating (an optical element consisting of a ruled surface which disperses light due to diffraction) as their dispersive element. The resultant spectrum may be recorded on film, electronically in a computer, or simply viewed with the **eye**. Because each element has a unique spectral signature, scientists can determine which elements make up a distant object by examining the often complicated pattern of spectral lines seen in that object. By recalling Kirchhoff's laws, they can also determine the **physics** of the object being observed. For example, stars show an absorption spectrum, and they can be thought of as a hot object surrounded by a cooler gas.

Spectra can also be used to determine the relative abundances of the elements in a **star**, by noting the relative strength of the lines. Knowing the physics of the atoms involved allows a prediction of the relative strengths of different lines. In addition, because ions (atoms which have lost some of their electrons and become charged) have different characteristic wavelengths, and the ionization states are a measure of **temperature**, the temperature of a star can be determined from the measured spectra.

The minimum width of a spectral line is governed by the tenets of **quantum mechanics**, but physical processes can increase this width. Collisions between atoms, **pressure**, and temperature all can increase the observed width of a line. In addition, the width of the spectrograph entrance slit, or properties of the **diffraction grating,** provides a minimum width for the lines. The observed line widths can therefore be used to determine the processes occurring in the object being observed.

Spectrographs are characterized by their wavelength coverage and their resolution. A spectrograph normally consists of an entrance slit or aperture, a number of transmissive elements such as lenses, prisms, transmission gratings and windows, or reflective surfaces such as **mirrors** and reflection gratings. The configuration and types of materials used depend on the wavelength range being investigated, since different materials have different reflective and transmissive properties; typically, reflective systems are used in the ultraviolet region of the spectrum, where few materials transmit well. The resultant spectrum is an image of the entrance slit at different wavelengths.

The resolution of a spectrograph describes its ability to separate two nearby spectral lines. In a complex spectrum, there may be hundreds of spectral lines from many different elements, and it is important to be able to separate lines which may be adjacent.

Spectroscopy is also used in the laboratory. Applications include determining the composition of plasmas, and identifying chemical compounds.

Doppler shift

Another way that spectral lines are used in astronomy is to determine the **velocity** of an object. An object which is moving away from Earth will have its spectral lines shifted to longer wavelengths due to the Doppler shift acting on the emitted photons. Similarly, objects moving towards Earth will be shifted to shorter wavelengths. By measuring the shift of a spectrum, the velocity with which the object is moving with respect to the earth can be determined. A shift to longer wavelengths is called a red shift, since red light appears on the long wavelength side of the visible spectrum, while a shift to shorter wavelengths is called a blue shift.

Doppler shift measurements of spectral lines have been used to measure the velocities of winds in stars, the speeds of outflowing gases from stars and other objects; the rotational **motion** of material in the center of galaxies, and the recession of galaxies due to the expansion of the universe. The latter measurements are particularly important, since they allow astronomers to probe the structure of the Universe.

KEY TERMS

Absorption spectrum—A continuous spectrum with gaps at discrete wavelengths, corresponding to the photon energies of the component atoms.

Bohr atom—A model of the atom, proposed by Niels Bohr, that describes the electrons in well-defined energy levels.

Doppler shift—The shift in frequency (and hence wavelength) caused by the motion of an object while it emits electromagnetic radiation.

Emission spectrum—A spectrum containing narrow spectral lines at frequencies corresponding to the photon energies of the atoms making up the object being observed.

Energy level—An allowed energy state of an electron in the Bohr model of the atom.

Photon—A single quantum of light.

Planck's law—A relationship describing the proportionality between the frequency of light and the energy of a photon.

Resolution—The ability of a spectrograph to separate two adjacent spectral lines.

Spectrograph—A device for measuring the spectrum of light.

Spectrum—A display of the intensity of radiation vs. wavelength. The plural form is spectra.

See also Doppler effect; Galaxy; Redshift; Spectral classification of stars; Spectrum.

Further Reading

Aller, Lawrence H. *Atoms, Stars, and Nebulae.* New York: Cambridge University Press, 1991.

Kaufmann, William J. III. *Universe.* New York: W. H. Freeman and Company, 1991.

David Sahnow

Spectrometry see **Spectroscopy**

Spectroscope

A spectroscope is an instrument used to observe the atomic spectrum of a given material. Because **atoms** can absorb or emit **radiation** only at certain specific wave-

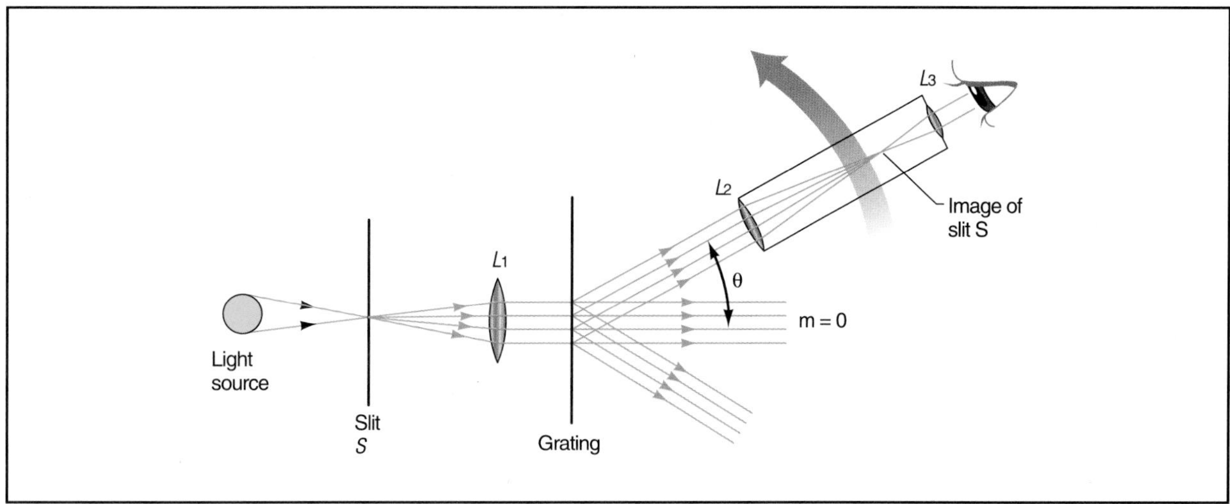

Figure 1. A simple grating spectroscope.

lengths defined by **electron** transitions, the **spectrum** of each type of atom is directly related to its structure. There are two classifications of atomic spectra: absorption and **emission**.

An absorption spectrum is produced when light passes through a cool gas. From **quantum mechanics** we know that the **energy** of light is directly proportional to its wavelength. For a given type of atom, a **photon** of light at some specific wavelength can transfer its energy to an electron, moving that electron into a higher energy level. The atom is then in an "excited state." The electron absorbs the energy of the photon during this process. Thus, a white light spectrum will show a dark line where light of that energy/wavelength has been absorbed as it passed through the gas. This is called an absorption spectrum.

The **energy transfer** is reversible. Consider the excited state photon in the example above. When that electron relaxes into its normal state, a photon of the same wavelength of light will be emitted. If a gas is heated, rather than bombarded with light, the electrons can be pushed into an excited state and emit photons in much the same way. A spectrum of this emission will show bright lines at specific wavelengths. This is known as an emission spectrum.

Instruments for viewing spectra

Light entering a spectroscope is carrying spectral information. The information is decoded by splitting light into its spectral components. In its simplest form, a spectroscope is a viewing instrument consisting of a slit, a collimator, a dispersing element, and a focusing objective (see Figure 1). Light passes through the slit and enters the collimator. A collimator is a special type of **lens** that "straightens out" light coming in at various angles so that all of the light is travelling the same direction. The wavefront is converted into a planar wavefront; if you wish to think of light as rays, all the light rays are made to travel in **parallel**.

Next, light enters the dispersing element. A dispersing element spreads light of multiple wavelengths into discrete colors. A **prism** is an example of a dispersing element. White light entering the prism is separated out into the colors of the spectrum. Another type of dispersing element is a **diffraction grating**. A diffraction grating redirects light at a slightly different **angle** depending on the wavelength of the light. Diffraction gratings can be either reflection gratings or transmission gratings. A grating is made of a series of fine, closely spaced lines. Light incident on the grating is reflected at an angle that varies as wavelength. Thus, white light will be divided into the spectral colors, and each color will appear at a discretely spaced position. A transmission grating works similar to a reflection grating, except that light travels through it and is refracted or bent at different angles depending on wavelength. The focusing objective is just a lens system, such as that on a **telescope**, that magnifies the spectrum and focuses it for viewing by **eye**.

A spectroscope gives useful information, but it is only temporary. To capture spectroscopic data permanently, the spectrograph was developed. A spectrograph operates on the same principles as a spectroscope, but it contains some means to permanently capture an image of the spectrum. Early spectrographs contained photographic cameras that captured the images on film. Modern spectrographs contain sophisticated charge coupled device (CCD) cameras that convert an optical signal into

an electrical signal; they capture the image and transfer it to video or computer for further analysis.

A spectroscopic instrument in great demand today is the spectrometer. A spectrometer can provide information about the amount of radiation that a source emits at a certain wavelength. It is similar to the spectroscope described above, except that it has the additional capability to determine the quantity of light detected at a given wavelength.

There are three basic types of spectrometers: monochromators, scanning monochromators, and polychromators. A monochromator selects only one wavelength from the source light, whereas a scanning monochromator is a motorized monochromator that scans an entire wavelength region. A polychromator selects multiple wavelengths from the source.

A spectrophotometer is an instrument for recording absorption spectra. It contains a radiant light source, a **sample** holder, a dispersive element, and a detector. A sample can be put into the holder in front of the source, and the resulting light is dispersed and captured by a photographic camera, a CCD array, or some other detector.

An important class of spectrometer is called an imaging spectrometer. These are remote sensing instruments capable of acquiring images of the Earth's surface from an **aircraft** or from a **satellite** in **orbit**. Quantitative data about the radiant intensity or reflectivity of the scene can be calculated, yielding important diagnostic information about that region. For example, a number of important rock-forming **minerals** have absorption features in the infrared spectral region. When sunlight hits these **rocks** and is reflected back, characteristic wavelengths of the light are absorbed for each type of rock. An imaging spectrometer takes a picture of a small region of rocks, splits the light from the image into different wavelengths, and measures how much reflected light is detected at each wavelength. By determining which quantities and wavelengths of light are absorbed by the region being imaged, scientists can determine the composition of the rocks. With similar techniques, imaging spectrometers can be used to **map** vegetation, track **acid rain** damage in **forests**, and track pollutants and effluent in coastal waters.

Another class of spectrometer highly useful to the **laser** industry is the spectrum analyzer. Although lasers are nominally monochromatic sources, there are actually slight variations in the wavelengths of light emitted. Spectrum analyzers provide detailed information about the wavelength and quality of the laser output, critical information for many scientific applications.

See also Diffraction; Electromagnetic spectrum; Spectroscopy.

KEY TERMS

Absorption spectrum—The colors of light absorbed by a cool gas.

CCD camera/array—A charge coupled device that converts and optical signal (light) into an electrical signal for transfer to video display or computer.

Collimator—An optical element that aligns incoming light rays so that they are parallel.

Diffraction grating—A dispersive element consisting of a surface scribed with very fine, closely spaced grooves that cause different wavelengths of light to reflect or refract (bend) different amounts.

Emission spectrum—The colors of light emitted by a heated gas. An emission spectrum is usually viewed through a slit, and the viewing optics generate an image of the slit in whatever colors of light are emitted. The emission spectrum appears as a row of colored lines, and thus are commonly termed spectral lines.

Imaging spectrometer—An imaging instrument capable of determining radiant intensity of spectral components of the surface being imaged.

Monochromator—A device that selects out discrete wavelengths of light; it often includes a diffraction grating.

Spectrograph—An instrument for recording atomic spectra.

Spectrometer—An instrument for determining radiant intensity of atomic spectra.

Further Reading

Parker, Sybil, ed. *The Spectroscopy Sourcebook.* New York: McGraw-Hill, 1987.

Spex, Jobin Yvon. *Guide for Spectroscopy.* Edison, NJ: Instruments S.A.

Kristin Lewotsky

Spectroscopy

The absorption, **emission**, or scattering of electromagnetic **radiation** by **atoms** or molecules is referred to as spectroscopy. A transition from a lower **energy** level to a higher level with transfer of electromagnetic energy

to the atom or **molecule** is called absorption; a transition from a higher energy level to a lower level is called emission (if energy is transferred to the **electromagnetic field**); and the redirection of light as a result of its interaction with **matter** is called scattering.

When atoms or molecules absorb electromagnetic energy, the incoming energy transfers the quantized atomic or molecular system to a higher energy level. Electrons are promoted to higher orbitals by ultraviolet or visible light; vibrations are excited by infrared light, and rotations are excited by microwaves. Atomic-absorption spectroscopy measures the **concentration** of an element in a **sample**, whereas atomic-emission spectroscopy aims at measuring the concentration of elements in samples. UV-VIS absorption spectroscopy is used to obtain qualitative information from the electronic absorption **spectrum**, or to measure the concentration of an analyte molecule in solution. Molecular **fluorescence** spectroscopy is a technique for obtaining qualitative information from the electronic fluorescence spectrum, or, again, for measuring the concentration of an analyte in solution.

Infrared spectroscopy has been widely used in the study of surfaces. The most frequently used portion of the infrared spectrum is the region where molecular vibrational frequencies occur. This technique was first applied around the turn of the twentieth century in an attempt to distinguish **water** of crystallization from water of constitution in solids. Forty years later, the technique was being used to study surface hydroxyl groups on oxides and interactions between adsorbed molecules and hydroxyl groups.

Ultraviolet spectroscopy takes advantage of the selective absorbency of ultraviolet radiation by various substances. The technique is especially useful in investigating biologically active substances, such as compounds in body fluids, and drugs and narcotics either in the living body (in vivo) or outside it (in vitro). Ultraviolet instruments have also been used to monitor air and water **pollution**, to analyze dyestuffs, to study carcinogens, to identify food additives, to analyze **petroleum** fractions, and to analyze pesticide residues. Ultraviolet photoelectron spectroscopy, a technique that is analogous to x-ray photoelectron spectroscopy, has been used to study **valence** electrons in gases.

Microwave spectroscopy, or molecular rotational **resonance** spectroscopy, addresses the microwave region and the absorption of energy by molecules as they undergo transitions between rotational energy levels. From these spectra it is possible to obtain information about molecular structure, including bond distances and bond angles. One example of the application of this technique is in the distinction of trans and gauche rotational isomers. It is also possible to determine **dipole** moments and molecular collision rates from these spectra.

In **nuclear magnetic resonance** (NMR), resonant energy is transferred between a radio-frequency alternating magnetic field and a nucleus placed in a field sufficiently strong to decouple the nuclear spin from the influence of atomic electrons. Transitions induced between substates correspond to different quantized orientations of the nuclear spin relative to the direction of the magnetic field. Nuclear magnetic resonance spectroscopy has two subfields: broadline NMR and high resolution NMR. High resolution NMR has been used in inorganic and organic **chemistry** to measure subtle electronic effects, to determine structure, to study chemical reactions, and to follow the **motion** of molecules or groups of atoms within molecules.

Electron paramagnetic resonance is a spectroscopic technique similar to nuclear magnetic resonance except that microwave radiation is employed instead of **radio** frequencies. Electron paramagnetic resonance has been used extensively to study paramagnetic species present on various solid surfaces. These species may be **metal** ions, surface defects, or adsorbed molecules or ions with one or more unpaired electrons. This technique also provides a basis for determining the bonding characteristics and orientation of a surface complex. Because the technique can be used with low concentrations of active sites, it has proven valuable in studies of oxidation states.

Atoms or molecules that have been excited to high energy levels can decay to lower levels by emitting radiation. For atoms excited by light energy, the emission is referred to as atomic fluorescence; for atoms excited by higher energies, the emission is called atomic or optical emission. In the case of molecules, the emission is called fluorescence if the transition occurs between states of the same spin, and phosphorescence if the transition takes place between states of different spin.

In x-ray fluorescence, the term refers to the characteristic **x rays** emitted as a result of absorption of x rays of higher **frequency**. In electron fluorescence, the emission of electromagnetic radiation occurs as a consequence of the absorption of energy from radiation (either electromagnetic or particulate), provided the emission continues only as long as the **stimulus** producing it is maintained.

The effects governing x-ray photoelectron spectroscopy were first explained by Albert Einstein in 1905, who showed that the energy of an electron ejected in photoemission was equal to the difference between the **photon** and the binding energy of the electron in the target. In the 1950s, researchers began measuring binding energies of core electrons by x-ray photoemission. The discovery

that these binding energies could vary as much as 6 eV, depending on the chemical state of the atom, led to rapid development of x-ray photoelectron spectroscopy, also known as Electron Spectroscopy for Chemical Analysis (ESCA). This technique has provided valuable information about chemical effects at surfaces. Unlike other spectroscopies in which the absorption, emission, or scattering of radiation is interpreted as a function of energy, photoelectron spectroscopy measures the kinetic energy of the electrons(s) ejected by x-ray radiation.

Mössbauer spectroscopy was invented in the late 1950s by Rudolf Mössbauer, who discovered that when solids emit and absorb gamma rays, the nuclear energy levels can be separated to one part in 10^{14}, which is sufficient to reflect the weak interaction of the nucleus with surrounding electrons. The **Mössbauer effect** probes the binding, charge distribution and symmetry, and magnetic ordering around an atom in a solid **matrix**. An example of the Mössbsauer effect involves the Fe-57 nuclei (the absorber) in a sample to be studied. From the ground state, the Fe-57 nuclei can be promoted to their first excited state by absorbing a 14.4-keV gamma-ray photon produced by a radioactive parent, in this case Co-57. The excited Fe-57 nucleus then decays to the ground state via electron or gamma-ray emission. Classically, one would expect the Fe-57 nuclei to undergo recoil when emitting or absorbing a gamma-ray photon (somewhat like what a person leaping from a boat to a dock observes when his boat recoils into the **lake**); but according to **quantum mechanics**, there is also a reasonable possibility that there will be no recoil (as if the boat were embedded in ice when the leap occurred).

When electromagnetic radiation passes through matter, most of the radiation continues along its original path, but a tiny amount is scattered in other directions. Light that is scattered without a change in energy is called **Rayleigh scattering**; light that is scattered in transparent solids with a transfer of energy to the solid is called Brillouin scattering. Light scattering accompanied by vibrations in molecules or in the optical region in solids is called Raman scattering.

In vibrational spectroscopy, also known as Raman spectroscopy, the light scattered from a gas, liquid, or solid is accompanied by a shift in wavelength from that of the incident radiation. The effect was discovered by the Indian physicist C. V. Raman in 1928. The Raman effect arises from the inelastic scattering of radiation in the visible region by molecules. Raman spectroscopy is similar to infrared spectroscopy in its ability to provide detailed information about molecular structures. Before the 1940s, Raman spectroscopy was the method of choice in molecular structure determinations, but since that time, infrared measurements have largely supplemented it. Infrared absorption requires that a vibration change the dipole moment of a molecule, but Raman spectroscopy is associated with the change in polarizability that accompanies a vibration. As a consequence, Raman spectroscopy provides information about molecular vibrations that is particularly well suited to the structural analysis of covalently bonded molecules, and to a lesser extent, of ionic crystals. Raman spectroscopy is also particularly useful in studying the structure of polyatomic molecules. By comparing spectra of a large number of compounds, chemists have been able to identify characteristic frequencies of molecular groups, e.g., methyl, carbonyl, and hydroxyl groups.

See also Quantum chemistry; Fluorescence and phosphorescence; Chemical compound; Magnetism.

Spectrum

Certain properties of objects or physical processes, such as the **frequency** of **light** or sound, the masses of the component parts of a **molecule**, or even the ideals of a political party, may have a wide variety of values. The distribution of these values, arranged in increasing or decreasing order, is the *spectrum* of that property. For example, sunlight is made up of many different colors of light, the full spectrum of which are revealed when sunlight is dispersed, as it is in a rainbow. Similarly, the distribution of sounds over a range of frequencies, such as a musical scale, is a sound spectrum. The masses of fragments from an ionized molecule, separated according to their mass-to-charge **ratio**, constitute a **mass** spectrum. Opposing political parties are often said to be on opposite ends of the (political) spectrum. The term spectrum is also used to describe the graphical illustration of a spectrum of values. The plural of spectrum is spectra.

The spectrum of light

The spectrum of colors contained in sunlight was discovered by Sir Isaac Newton in 1666. In fact, the word "spectrum" was coined by Newton to describe the phenomenon he observed. In a report of his discovery published in 1672, Newton described his experiment as follows:

"I procured me a triangular glass **prism**, ... having darkened my chamber and made a small hole in my window shuts, to let in a convenient quantity of the sun's light, I placed my prism at this entrance, that it might be thereby refracted to the opposite wall. It was at first a pleasing divertissement to view the vivid and intense colours produced thereby." A diagram of Newton's ex-

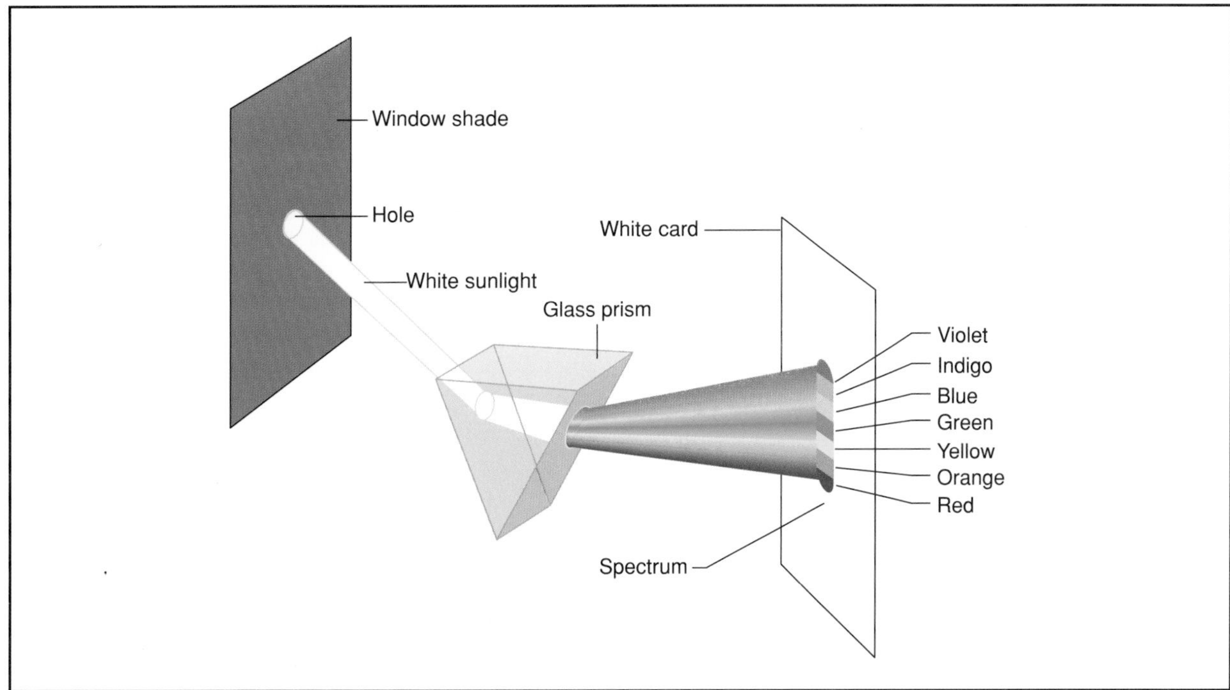

Figure 1. A diagram of Newton's 1666 spectrum experiment.

periment is illustrated here. Newton divided the spectrum of colors he observed into the familiar sequence of seven fundamental colors: red, orange, yellow, green, blue, indigo, violet (ROYGBIV). He chose to divide the spectrum into seven colors in analogy with the seven fundamental notes of the musical scale. However, both divisions are completely arbitrary as the sound and light-spectrum each contain a continuous distribution (and therefore an infinite number) of "colors" and "notes."

The wave nature of Light

Light can be pictured as traveling in the form of a wave. A wave is a series of regularly spaced peaks and troughs. The **distance** between adjacent peaks (or troughs) is the *wavelength*, symbolized by the Greek letter lambda (λ). For a light wave traveling at a speed, c, the number of peaks (or troughs) which pass a stationary point each second is the *frequency* of the wave, symbolized by the Greek letter nu (ν). The units of frequency are number per second, termed Hertz (Hz). The frequency of a wave is related to the wavelength and the speed of the wave by the simple **relation**: $\nu = c/\lambda$. The speed of light depends on the medium through which it is passing, but, as light travels primarily only through air or **space**, its speed may be considered to be constant, with a value of 3.0×10^8 meters/sec. Therefore, since c is a constant, light waves may be described by either their frequency or their wavelength, which can be interconverted through the relation $\nu = c/\lambda$.

Interestingly, Newton did not think light traveled as a wave, but rather he believed light to be a stream of particles, which he termed corpuscles, emitted by the light source and seen when they physically entered the **eye**. It was Newton's contemporary, the Dutch astronomer Christiaan Huygens (1629-1695), who first theorized that light traveled from the source as a series of waves. In the quantum mechanical description of light, the basic tenets of which were developed in the early 1900s by Max Plank and Albert Einstein, light is considered to possess both particle and wave characteristics. A "particle" of light is called a **photon**, and can be thought of as a bundle of **energy** emitted by the light source. The energy carried by a photon of light, E, is equal to the frequency of the light, ν, multiplied by a constant: $E = h\nu$, where h is Plank's constant, ($h = 6.626 \times 10^{-34}$ Joules-seconds), named in honor of Max Plank. Thus, according to the quantum mechanical theory of light, light traveling through air or space may be described by any one of *three* inter-related quantities: frequency, wavelength, or energy. A spectrum of light may therefore be represented as a distribution of intensity as a function of any (or all) of these measurable quantities.

The electromagnetic spectrum

Light is a form of electromagnetic **radiation**. Electromagnetic waves travel at the speed of light and can have almost any frequency or wavelength. The distribution of electromagnetic radiation according to its frequen-

cy or wavelength (or energy) is the *electromagnetic spectrum*. The **electromagnetic spectrum** is the continuous distribution of *frequencies* of electromagnetic radiation ranging from approximately 10^5 Hz (**radio waves**) up to greater than 10^{20} Hz (x-rays and gamma rays). Equivalently, it is the distribution of *wavelengths* of electromagnetic radiation ranging from very long ($\lambda = 10^6$ meters, radio waves) to the very short wavelengths of x-rays and gamma rays ($\lambda = 10^{-15}$ meters). Note that the higher frequencies correspond to lower wavelengths and vice versa ($\nu = c/\lambda$). Finally, the electromagnetic spectrum can also be separated according to the *photon energy* of the radiation, ranging from 10^{-29} Joules (radio waves) up to 10^{-14} Joules (x-rays and gamma rays). Note that photon energy increases with increasing frequency ($E=h\nu$).

The electromagnetic spectrum can be divided into regions which exhibit similar properties, each of which itself constitutes a spectrum: the x-ray spectrum, the ultraviolet spectrum, the visible spectrum (which we commonly refer to as "light"), the infrared spectrum and the radio-frequency spectrum. However, these divisions are arbitrary and do not imply a sharp change in the character of the radiation. The visible light spectrum, while comprising only a small portion of the entire electromagneticspectrum, can be further divided into the colors of the rainbow as was demonstrated by Newton. The other regions of the electromagnetic spectrum, although invisible to our eyes, are familiar to us through other means: **x rays** expose x-ray sensitive film, ultraviolet light causes sunburn, microwaves **heat** food, and radio frequency waves carry radio and **television** signals.

The interaction of electromagnetic radiation with **matter** is studied in the field of **spectroscopy**. In this field, spectra are used as a means to graphically illustrate which frequencies, wavelengths, or photon energies of electromagnetic radiation interact the strongest with the material under investigation. These spectra are usually named according to the spectroscopic method used in their generation: **nuclear magnetic resonance** (NMR) spectroscopy generates NMR spectra, microwave spectroscopy generates microwave spectra, and so forth. In addition, these spectra may also be named according to the origin or final fate of the radiation (**emission** spectrum, absorption spectrum), the nature of the material under study (atomic spectrum, molecular spectrum) and the width of the electromagnetic spectrum which undergoes the interaction (discrete, line, continuous, or band spectrum).

Emission spectra

The spectrum of electromagnetic radiation *emitted* by a source is an *emission spectrum*. One way of producing electromagnetic radiation is by heating a material

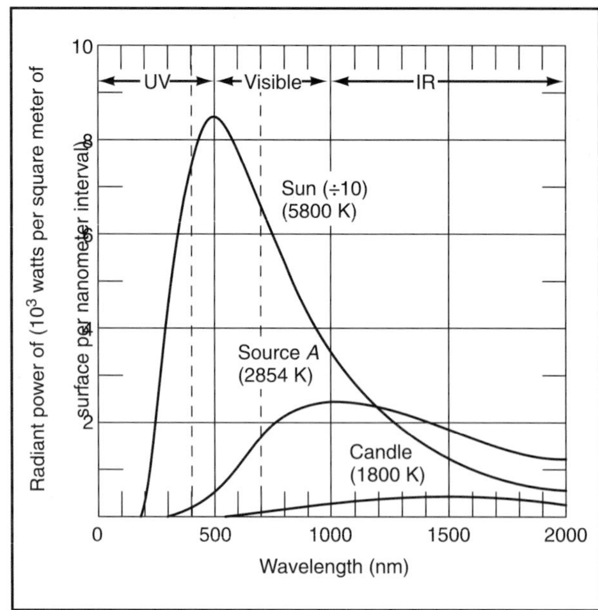

Figure 2. Black body emission spectra for sources at three different temperatures, corresponding to the Sun, a 500-watt incandescent light bulb and a candle.

until it glows, or emits light. For example, a piece of **iron** heated in a blacksmith's furnace will emit visible light as well as infrared radiation (heat). Similarly, a light bulb uses electrical current to heat a tungsten filament encased in an evacuated glass bulb. The **Sun** is a source of radiation in the infrared, visible and ultraviolet regions of the electromagnetic spectrum. Radiation produced by a thermal source is called black body, or incandescent radiation. Spectra such as these, in which the intensity varies smoothly over the distribution range, are called *continuous spectra*.

Atoms that have been heated (typically by a high-energy source such as an electric spark or a flame), will also emit electromagnetic radiation. However, if there are only a few atoms present so that they do not collide with one another, such as in a low-pressure gas, the excited atoms will emit radiation at only a few specific wavelengths. For example, a vapor of neon atoms in a glass tube excited by an electrical discharge produces the familiar red color of neon lights by emitting light of only red wavelength. In contrast to a continuous spectrum, atomic emission spectra generally exhibit high intensity at only a few wavelengths and very low intensity at all others; such discontinuous spectra are called *discrete spectra*.

Absorption spectra

Atomic and molecular materials can also absorb electromagnetic radiation. The set of wavelengths or fre-

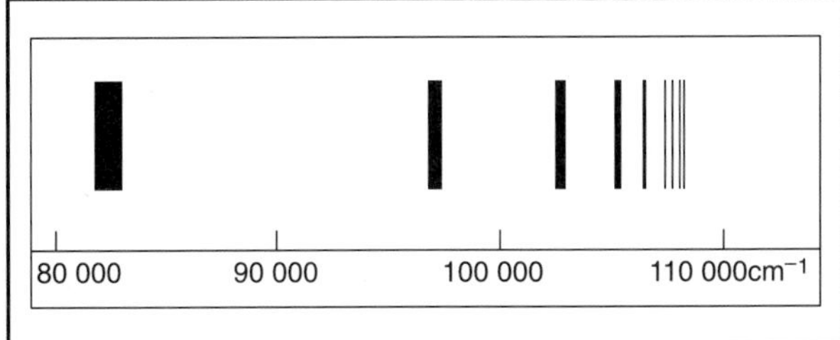

Figure 3. Schematic of the absorption spectrum of atomic hydrogen recorded on a photographic plate.

quencies of electromagnetic radiation absorbed by any single, pure material is unique to that material, and can be used as a "fingerprint" to identify the material. The record of the absorbed wavelengths or frequencies is an *absorption spectrum.*

The instrument used to measure the absorption spectrum of a material is called a spectrometer. Newton's experiment, illustrated in Figure 1, has all but one of the components of a simple absorption spectrometer: a **sample** placed between the light source and the prism. With a sample in place, some of the wavelengths of sunlight (consisting of all visible wavelengths) will be absorbed by the sample. Light not absorbed by the sample will, as before, be separated (dispersed) into its component wavelengths (colors) by the prism. The appearance of the spectrum will resemble that obtained without the sample in place, with the exception that those wavelengths which have been absorbed are missing, and will appear as dark lines within the spectrum of colors. If a piece of the photographic film is used instead of the card, the absorption spectrum can be recorded.

The absorption spectrum of gaseous **hydrogen** atoms recorded on a photographic plate is presented here. Atomic spectra recorded on photographic plates were among the earliest to be studied, and the appearance of these spectra led to the use of the term *"line spectrum"* to describe atomic spectra (either emission or absorption). The term is still commonly used even if the spectra are not recorded photographically.

Molecules also absorb electromagnetic radiation, but in contrast to atoms, molecules will absorb broader regions, or bands, of the electromagnetic spectrum. Molecular spectra are therefore often referred to as *band spectra.*

See also Blackbody radiation; Spectral lines.

KEY TERMS

Absorption spectrum—The record of wavelengths (or frequencies) of electromagnetic radiation absorbed by a substance; the absorption spectrum of each pure substance is unique.

Band spectrum—A spectrum in which the distribution of values of the measured property occurs in distinct groups. In an absorption spectrum, the absorbed wavelengths (or frequencies) occur in broad, but distinct, groups. Band spectra are usually associated with molecular absorbers.

Continuous spectrum—A spectrum in which there are no breaks in the distribution of values associated with the measured property.

Electromagnetic spectrum—The continuous distribution of all electromagnetic radiation with wavelengths ranging from approximately 10^{15} to 10^{6} meters which includes: gamma rays, x rays, ultraviolet, visible light, infrared, microwaves, and radio waves.

Emission spectrum—The record of wavelengths (or frequencies) of electromagnetic radiation emitted by a substance which has previously absorbed energy, typically from a spark or a flame. The emission spectrum of each pure substance is unique.

Frequency—For a traveling wave, the number of wavelengths that pass a stationary point per unit of time, usually expressed in #/sec, or Hertz (Hz), and symbolized by ν.

Line spectrum—A spectrum, usually associated with isolated atomic absorbers or emitters, in which only a few discrete values of the measured property occur. Line spectra are also called discrete spectra.

Wavelength—The distance between adjacent peaks or troughs on a repeating wave, symbolized by λ.

Further Reading

Crooks, J. E. *The Spectrum in Chemistry.* London: Academic Press, 1978.

Nassau, K. *The Physics and Chemistry of Color.* New York: John Wiley and Sons, 1983.

Pavia, D. L. *Introduction to Spectroscopy: A Guide for Students of Organic Chemistry.* Philadelphia: W.B. Saunders Co., 1979.

Walker, J. "The Amature Scientist: The Spectra of Streetlights Illuminate Basic Principles of Quantum Mechanics" *Scientific American.* 138-42, 250 (January 1984): 138-42.

Karen Trentelman